HAVE YOU THOUGHT ABOUT
Customizing THIS BOOK?

THE PRENTICE HALL JUST-IN-TIME PROGRAM IN DECISION SCIENCE

You can combine chapters from this book with chapters from any of the Prentice Hall titles listed on the following page to create a text tailored to your specific course needs. You can add your own material or cases from our extensive case collection. By taking a few minutes to look at what is sitting on your bookshelf and the content available on our Web site, you can create your ideal textbook.

The Just-In-Time program offers:

➡ **Quality of Material to Choose From**—In addition to the books listed, you also have the option to include any of the cases from Prentice Hall Case Series and/or the Portfolio Custom Case Series which gives you access to cases (and teaching notes where available) from Darden, Harvard, Ivey, NACRA, and Thunderbird. Most cases can be viewed online at our Web site.

➡ **Flexibility**—Choose only that material you want, either from one title or several titles (plus cases) and sequence it in whatever way you wish.

➡ **Instructional Support**—You have access to all instructor's materials that accompany the traditional textbook and desk copies of your JIT book.

➡ **Outside Materials**—There is also the option to include up to 20% of the text from materials outside of Prentice Hall Custom Business Resources.

➡ **Cost Savings**—Students pay only for material you choose. The base price is $5.00, plus $2.00 for case material, plus $.08 per page. The text can be shrink-wrapped with other Pearson textbooks for a 10% discount. Outside material is priced at $.10 per page plus permission fees.

➡ **Quality of Finished Product**—Custom cover and title page—including your name, school, department, course title, and section number. Paperback, perfect bound, black-and-white printed text. Customized table of contents and index. Sequential pagination throughout the text. CD-ROMs can be included with the custom book if applicable.

Visit our Web site at http://www.prenhall.com/custombusiness

and download order forms online.

THE PRENTICE HALL
Just-In-Time program

BUSINESS STATISTICS

- Berenson/Levine/Krehbiel/Stephan, BASIC BUSINESS STATISTICS, 8/e
- Groebner/Shannon/Fry/Smith, BUSINESS STATISTICS, 5/e
- Levine/Berenson/ Krehbiel/ Stephan, STATISTICS FOR MANAGERS USING MICROSOFT EXCEL 3/e
- Levine/Krehbiel/Berenson, BUSINESS STATISTICS: A FIRST COURSE 3/e
- Newbold/Carlson/Thorne, STATISTICS FOR BUSINESS AND ECONOMICS, 5/e
- Shannon/Groebner/Fry/Smith, A COURSE IN BUSINESS STATISTICS, 3/e

PRODUCTION/OPERATIONS MANAGEMENT

- Anupindi/Chopra/Deshmukh/Van Mieghem/Zemel, MANAGING BUSINESS PROCESS FLOWS
- Chopra/Meindl, SUPPLY CHAIN MANAGEMENT
- Foster, MANAGING QUALITY
- Handfield/Nichols, Jr., SUPPLY CHAIN MANAGEMENT
- Haksever/Render/Russell/Murdick, SERVICE MANAGEMENT AND OPERATIONS, 2/e
- Hanna/Newman, INTEGRATED OPERATIONS MANAGEMENT
- Heineke/Meile, GAMES AND EXERCISES IN OPERATIONS MANAGEMENT
- Heizer/Render, OPERATIONS MANAGEMENT, 6/e
- Heizer/Render, PRINCIPLES OF OPERATIONS MANAGEMENT, 4/e
- Krajewski/Ritzman, OPERATIONS MANAGEMENT, 6/e
- Latona/Nathan, CASES AND READINGS IN POM
- Russell/Taylor, OPERATIONS MANAGEMENT, 4/e
- Schmenner, PLANT AND SERVICE TOURS IN OPERATIONS MANAGEMENT, 5/e
- Nicholas, PROJECT MANAGEMENT, 2/e

MANAGEMENT SCIENCE/OPERATIONS RESEARCH

- Eppen/Gould, INTRODUCTORY MANAGEMENT SCIENCE, 5/e
- Moore/Weatherford, DECISION MODELING WITH MICROSOFT EXCEL, 6/e
- Render/Stair/Hanna, QUANTITATIVE ANALYSIS FOR MANAGEMENT, 8/e
- Render/Stair/Balakrishnan, MANAGERIAL DECISION MODELING WITH SPREADSHEETS
- Render/Stair, CASES AND READINGS IN MANAGEMENT SCIENCE
- Taylor, INTRODUCTION TO MANAGEMENT SCIENCE, 7/e

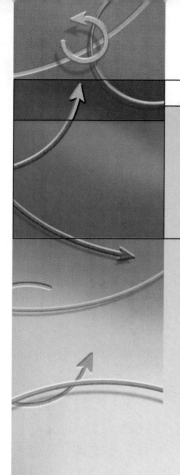

FOUNDATIONS OF OPERATIONS MANAGEMENT

LARRY P. RITZMAN
Boston College

LEE J. KRAJEWSKI
University of Notre Dame

Prentice Hall
Upper Saddle River, NJ 07458

Library of Congress Cataloging-in-Publication Data

Ritzman, Larry P.
    Foundations of operations management / Larry P. Ritzman, Lee J. Krajewski.
        p. cm.
    Includes bibliographical references and index.
    ISBN: 0-01-300852-19
        1. Production management.   I. Krajewski, Lee J. II. Title.

TS155 .K7875 2003
658.5—dc21   2002070928

Exective Editor: Tom Tucker
Editor-in-Chief: P.J. Boardman
Assistant Editor: Erika Rusnak
Editorial Assistant: Jisun Lee
Senior Media Project Manager: Nancy Welcher
Executive Marketing Manager: Debbie Clare
Marketing Assistant: Amanda Fischer
Managing Editor (Production): Cynthia Regan
Production Assistant: Dianne Falcone
Permissions Coordinator: Suzanne Grappi
Associate Director, Manufacturing: Vincent Scelta
Production Manager: Arnold Vila
Designer: Blair Brown
Cover Design/Cover Illustration: Blair Brown
Interior Design/Illustration (Interior): Proof Positive
Manager, Print Production: Christy Mahon
Composition: Progressive Information Technologies
Full-Service Project Management: Progressive Publishing Alternatives
Printer/Binder: Von Hoffmann Press

Credits and acknowledgments borrowed from other sources and reproduced, with permission, in this textbook appear on appropriate page within text and on page 473.

Microsoft Excel, Solver, and Windows are registered trademarks of Microsoft Corportion in the U.S.A. and other countries. Screen shots and icons reprinted with permission from the Microsoft Corporation. This book is not sponsored or endorsed by or affiliated with Microsoft Corporation.

10 9 8 7 6
ISBN 0-13-008521-9

Dedicated with love
to our Families

Barbara Ritzman
Karen and Matt; Kristin and Alayna
Lisa and Todd; Cody, Cole, and Taylor
Kathryn and Paul
Mildred and Ray

Judie Krajewski
Gary
Lori and Dan; Aubrey and Madeline
Carrie and Jon; Jordanne
Selena and Jeff
Virginia and Jerry
Virginia and Larry

LARRY P. RITZMAN is the Thomas J. Galligan, Jr. Professor in Operations and Strategic Management at Boston College. He previously served at The Ohio State University for twenty-three years, where he acted as department chairperson and received several awards for both teaching and research. He received his doctorate at Michigan State University, having had prior industrial experience at the Babcock and Wilcox Company. Over the years, he has been privileged to teach and learn more about operations management with numerous students at all levels—undergraduate, MBA, executive MBA, and doctorate.

Particularly active in the Decision Sciences Institute, Larry has served as Council Coordinator, Publications Committee Chair, Track Chair, Vice President, Board Member, Executive Committee Member, Doctoral Consortium Coordinator, and President. He was elected a Fellow of the Institute in 1987 and earned the Distinguished Service Award in 1996. He has received three best-paper awards. He is a frequent reviewer, discussant, and session chair for several other professional organizations.

Larry's areas of particular expertise are operations strategy, production and inventory systems, forecasting, multistage manufacturing, disaggregation, scheduling, and layout. An active researcher, Larry's publications have appeared in such journals as *Decision Sciences, Journal of Operations Management, Production and Operations Management, Harvard Business Review,* and *Management Science.* He has served in various editorial capacities for several journals.

LEE J. KRAJEWSKI is the William R. and F. Cassie Daley Professor of Manufacturing Strategy at the University of Notre Dame. Prior to joining Notre Dame, Lee was a faculty member at The Ohio State University, where he received the University Alumni Distinguished Teaching Award and the College of Business Outstanding Faculty Research Award. He initiated the Center for Excellence in Manufacturing Management and served as its director for four years. In addition, he received the National President's Award and the National Award of Merit of the American Production and Inventory Control Society. He served as President Elect of the Decision Sciences Institute and was elected a Fellow of the Institute in 1988.

Lee's career spans more than thirty-two years of research and education in the field of operations management. He has designed and taught courses at both graduate and undergraduate levels on topics such as manufacturing strategy, introduction to operations management, operations design, and manufacturing planning and control systems.

Lee served as the editor of *Decision Sciences,* was the founding editor of the *Journal of Operations Management* (1980–1983), and has served on several editorial boards. Widely published himself, Lee has contributed numerous articles to such journals as *Decision Sciences,* the *Journal of Operations Management, Management Science, Harvard Business Review,* and *Interfaces,* to name just a few. He has received five bestpaper awards. Lee's areas of specialization include manufacturing strategy, manufacturing planning and control systems, supply-chain management, and master production scheduling.

Brief Contents

Contents

PREFACE

We wrote this book to address the growing demand in operations management for a brief book that still retains the rich set of pedagogical features. Most students who take this course, either at the undergraduate or graduate level, major in functional areas other than operations. Instructors are looking for a briefer book that conveys the essential ideas and techniques without the encyclopedic amount of information found in standard textbooks. The book is suitable for the MBA market because of its managerial perspective and strong coverage of process management. MBA students need to understand the interrelated processes of a firm, which connects operations with all other functional areas of an organization. They need to understand how each part of an organization, not just the operations function, must design and manage processes and deal with quality, technology, and staffing issues. The book is also suitable for undergraduates because it provides the pedagogical structure (clear explanations, step-by-step examples of quantitative techniques, numerous solved problems and homework problems, and the like) that undergraduates need.

Foundations of Operations Management provides a brief version of the up-to-date material in the 6th edition of our full-length textbook, *Operations Management,* and yet keeps much of the essential content. This streamlined version was created in part by transferring some content to the Student CD-ROM and to our Interactive Web site. We also did considerable pruning on a paragraph-by-paragraph basis to weed out material not needed for a streamlined "foundations" book. Chapters are consolidated as appropriate to create a smaller number of learning units. In so doing, we create opportunities in and out of the classroom for various forms of active learning: experiential exercises, cases, virtual tours, discussion questions, OM Explorer activities, video discussions, and Internet activities.

There are three main learning goals for this edition. Our first goal is to help students become effective managers in today's competitive, global environment. They discover the challenge of both managing activities throughout the organization, and how the operations function fits into the organization. Second, we seek to help students discover the excitement of the dynamic field of operations management (OM). We engage them by offering interesting examples at numerous firms that bring operations alive, presenting new technologies for enhancing decision-making and data gathering, and including realistic cases that encourage open debate of important issues. Third, to put the subject in appropriate context, we want students to understand what managers do about processes, to realize that operations management involves many cross-functional links, and to learn more about the tools that managers can use to make better operating decisions.

ORGANIZATION

We have organized the text so that it moves from strategic choices to tactical decisions.

Chapter 1, "Competing with Operations," merges Chapters 1 and 2 from *Operations Management,* 6th ed., and sets the tone of the text. We view organizations as composed of many processes, and show that operations principles and techniques are most suited for their management and analysis. This approach, which carries forward throughout the text, appeals to students regardless of their academic major. This chapter also establishes the basic principles of operations strategy.

Chapter 2, "Process Management," provides more insight on the management of processes and on how key process choices should be made. It provides a systematic approach to improving processes, including taking advantage of several software packages. The material on service process management is reinforced. To streamline the chapter, we deleted the sections on job design considerations and the Extend simulation case, and shifted the Big Picture of King Soopers Bakery to the Student CD-ROM.

Chapter 3, "Managing Project Processes," has substantial managerial material regarding project management. The material follows the introduction to project processes in Chapter 2 and it provides some quantitative material earlier in the course. Understanding project management is needed by students regardless of their functional major. Slimming down this chapter included moving the Big Picture on the Coors Field Baseball Stadium Project to the Student CD-ROM.

Chapter 4, "Managing Technology," though considerably streamlined, still describes important developments on e-commerce (both B2B and B2C), the Internet, and enterprise resource planning (ERP). More advanced topics, such as the R&D stages, are eliminated from this brief book. Together, a chapter, case, and video on technology management explores the challenges of choosing and implementing new technology.

Chapter 5, "Quality," merges two chapters from *Operations Management,* 6th ed. It brings together TQM concepts with statistical process control techniques. As with other chapters, the discussion questions, experiential exercises, and cases are moved to the Student CD-ROM.

Chapter 6, "Capacity," examines another dimension of designing processes. It covers the Theory of Constraints, economies and diseconomies of scale, capacity strategies, and a systematic approach to capacity planning. We describe useful quantitative techniques, such as decision trees and simulation, and explain techniques in OM Explorer. Supplement 6S, provided at the end of the chapter, bolsters the discussion on waiting lines.

Chapter 7, "Location and Layout," merges two chapters from the 6th edition. It continues the focus on decisions that require long-term commitments about the process. Managers must help determine where to locate new facilities (including global operations), and how to organize the layout of the processes within a facility. Discussion of these decisions completes our coverage of how to design processes for service providers and manufacturers. Examples of streamlining include dropping the discussion of global hot spots, the advanced location and layout techniques, and the line-balancing heuristic rules.

Chapter 8, "Supply-Chain Management," begins the second half of the book. The focus moves to executing the plans and operating the process once designed. It brings out many of the newer developments occurring with supply chains, such as e-purchasing (including catalog hubs, exchanges, and auctions), postponement, channel assembly, and green purchasing. It addresses order entry and order fulfillment processes, the impact of the Internet, and new measures of supply-chain performance.

Chapter 9, "Forecasting," spans the full range of forecasting approaches. It begins with qualitative techniques and concludes with time series models. Three solvers and four tutors in OM Explorer provide computer power to understand and implement these models. The chapter has the latest information on combination forecasts and focus forecasting. The opening vignette demonstrates how important forecasts are throughout the organization and supply chain.

Chapter 10, "Inventory Management," remains much the same as in the 6th edition. Streamlining began by moving the discussion questions, experiential exercise, and case to the Student CD-ROM. Some examples were also cut, in favor of support by the OM Explorer tutors.

Chapter 11, "Aggregate Planning and Scheduling," brings together Chapters 14 and the second half of Chapter 17 from the 6th edition. The first part of Chapter 17 on operations scheduling becomes a new supplement on the Student CD-ROM. This approach allows the student to understand the whole continuum of planning levels of output and workforce levels over time, as illustrated by the *Service Scheduling at Air New Zealand* video.

Chapter 12, "Resource Planning," covers manufacturing and also has a section on services. This latter section addresses resources such as financial assets, human resources, equipment, and inventories.

Chapter 13, "Lean Systems," concludes the book. It is much like the 6th edition, except that some examples are deleted and some end-of-chapter materials are moved to the Student CD-ROM. As with the other chapters, the CD-ROM and Interactive Web site resources are summarized at the end of the chapter.

SPECIAL FEATURES OF BOOK

Following are highlights of our coverage of the ever-changing field of operations management. These changes are based on extensive feedback from professors and students. All of these changes support the overall text philosophy.

- **Streamlined.** We trimmed the textbook to just 13 chapters and one supplement (Waiting lines). CD-ROM Resources support the basic text with 11 other supplements, experiential exercises, cases, and the like. A complete set of support materials is provided.

- **Pedagogical Structure.** Retains all of the colorful and instructive formatting of *Operations Management,* 6th ed.—not only in the textbook itself, but also in the Student CD-ROM and Interactive Web site. The book includes full-color art, clear explanations, step-by-step examples of quantitative techniques, solved problems, and numerous homework exercises. Students learn a framework for solving problems and experience the use of powerful decision-making tools.

- **Active Learning.** Motivating students to learn and apply OM concepts to processes is an important ingredient to a successful course. We have retained several popular and time-tested features that give students a deeper understanding of realistic business issues and enable them to become active participants in and out of the classroom. For example, OM Explorer tutors, end-of-chapter cases, and experiential exercises involve the students in actually applying the concepts and theories explained in the text. The multiple activities available at the textbook's Interactive Web site expand learning beyond the textbook and the classroom.

- **Across the Organization.** Each chapter begins and ends with a discussion of how the topic of the chapter is important to professionals throughout the organization. In every chapter, cross-functional connections link operations management to accounting, finance, human resources, marketing, and management information systems.

- **Central Role of Processes.** We focus on processes—the fundamental unit of work in all organizations. It is all about processes! This unifying theme builds bridges between chapters and opens up the topics in operations to all students, regardless of their majors or career paths. It creates a better "buy-in" for a course in operations management, because students understand that processes underlie activities throughout the organization, not just in one functional area.

- **A Balanced Perspective.** We believe that OM texts should address both the "big picture" strategic issues and also the analytic tools that facilitate decision making. It is not just about "concepts" or just about "numbers," but recognizes both dimensions. We continue to provide a balanced treatment of manufacturing and services throughout the text, and give special recognition to service provider processes with an *S* icon in the margin.

- **CD-ROM Resources.** This Student CD-ROM is packaged free with each new copy of the text. Resources include OM Explorer, textbook supplements, and other important supplements.

  - *OM Explorer*—A complete software decision support package designed *specifically for this text*. It has the look and feel of an Excel worksheet environment. One distinguishing feature is the inclusion of 66 tutors that provide coaching for all of the difficult analytical methods presented in the text. The package also contains 40 solvers, powerful routines to solve problems often encountered in practice.

  - *Tutor Exercises*—A variety of exercises on using the tutors in OM Explorer.

  - *Textbook Supplements*—Eleven self-contained supplements: Decision Making, Financial Analysis, Measuring Output Rates, Learning Curve Analysis, Computer-Integrated Manufacturing, Acceptance Sampling Plans, Simulation, Special Inventory Models, Linear Programming, Operations Scheduling, and Master Production Scheduling.

  - *Other Resources*—Equation summaries, discussion questions, cases, experiential exercises, the Big Pictures, and two written tours—all provided on a chapter-by-chapter basis.

- **Internet Resources.** This element appears at the end of each chapter and describes the many tools and activities at the Interactive Web site that are designed specifically for each chapter. Resources include Internet activities, Internet tours, and tutor exercises. The Internet has become a critical tool for success in business. Students can get online to build research skills and reinforce their understanding of operations management concepts.

  - *Study Guide Tests*—A compendium of true and false, multiple-choice, and essay questions that allows online testing, or gives students feedback on how well they have mastered the concepts and techniques in each chapter.

  - *In the News*—Current articles that apply to each chapter.

  - *Simulations*—Modeling processes with a simulation capability.

  - *Internet Activities*—How different companies handle decision areas covered in each chapter.

  - *Experiential Learning Exercises.* There are seven experiential learning modules: *Min-Yo Garment Company* (Chapter 1), *SPC with a Coin Catapult* (Chapter 5), *The Pizza Connection* case (Chapter 7), *Sonic Distributors* (Chapter 8), *Yankee Fork and Hoe Company* case (Chapter 9), *Swift Electronic Supply* (Chapter 10), and *Memorial Hospital* (Chapter 11). Each of these experiences is an in-class exercise that actively involves the students. Each has been thoroughly tested in class and proven to be a valuable learning tool. The *Swift Electronic Supply* exercise has been created especially for this new text.

  - *Cross-Functional Cases*—Two new cross-functional cases have been developed for this book. These unique learning experiences demonstrate how all function areas must be coordinated for a winning formula. The *Brunswick Distributing Co.* shows how various operating decisions relate to popular business performance measures through an Excel spreadsheet. It could be used in Chapter 1 to introduce the impact of operations decisions on business performance, or in Chapter 8 to support the importance of distribution and supply chain issues. The second case is *R. U. Reddie for Location,* which links the operations considerations in a location decision with the financial considerations of cash flows and internal rate of return.

- *Virtual Tours*—Tours to actual sites at different companies, and applied to content and managerial issues of specific chapters.

- **Flexibility.** For those who want the flexibility to expand or enrich their course the Student CD-ROM includes OM Explorer, cases, quantitative supplements, experiential exercises, and more. The book's flexibility allows instructors to design courses that match the unique needs of the student body.

- **Cases.** All chapters have at least one case (on the Student CD-ROM) that can either serve as a basis for classroom instruction or provide an important capstone problem to the chapter, challenging students to grapple with the issues of the chapter in a less structured and more comprehensive way. Many of the cases can be used as in-class exercises without prior student preparation.

- **Chapter Opening Vignettes.** Each chapter opens with an example of how a company actually dealt with the specific process issues addressed in the chapter. See Chapter 5, "Quality," which also illustrates how the video series is linked to the text.

- **Managerial Practices.** Boxed inserts show operations management in action at various firms. Balanced between service and manufacturing organizations, these updated inserts present current examples of how companies—successfully or unsuccessfully—deal with certain process issues facing them.

- **Examples.** Numerous examples throughout each chapter are a popular feature and are designed to help students understand the quantitative material presented. Each one concludes with the "Decision Point," which focuses on the decision implications for managers. Whenever a new technique is presented, an example is immediately provided to walk the student through the solution. Often, a Tutor in the OM Explorer package reinforces the example.

- **Solved Problems.** At the end of each chapter, detailed solutions demonstrate how to solve problems with the techniques presented in each chapter. These solved problems reinforce basic concepts and serve as models for students to refer to when doing the problems that follow.

- **The Big Picture.** Four full-color, two-page spreads in the Student CD-ROM present the layouts of the Lower Florida Keys Hospital (Chapter 1), Chaparral Steel (Chapter 1), King Soopers Bakery (Chapter 2), and Coors Field baseball stadium (Chapter 3).

- **Screen Captures.** The streamlined book still includes many screen captures demonstrating the use of OM Explorer, Microsoft Project, and SmartDraw. The text integrates these packages into the analysis of meaningful problems. See Chapter 2 for SmartDraw, Chapter 3 for MicroSoft Project, and Chapter 11 for OM Explorer.

- **Company URLs.** The URLs are provided for all companies featured in the Opening Vignettes and Managerial Practices, allowing students to explore them more fully beyond what is said in the text.

- **Margin Items.** A number of margin items are continued even in this brief book:
  - *Questions from Managers*—These voices from the real world highlight key concepts being presented.
  - *Definitions*—Short definitions of boldfaced terms are provided for easy reference.

- *Service Icon*—The icon indicates coverage of a service application.
- *Tutor Icons*—This icon will indicate where an OM Explorer tutor can be applied to better understand an example.

ENHANCED INSTRUCTIONAL SUPPORT SYSTEM

- **Instructor's Solutions Manual.** The *Instructor's Solutions Manual,* created by the authors, so as to keep it current and eliminate any errors, provides complete solutions to all discussion questions, problems, and notes for each case, experiential exercise, and cross-functional case. Selected computer screenshots are included to illustrate the different software capabilities available. Each case note includes a brief synopsis of the case, a description of the purposes for using the case, recommendations for analysis and goals for student learning from the case, and detailed teaching suggestions for assigning and discussing the case with students. The Solutions Manual is intended for instructors who may in turn choose to share parts of it with students, possibly through an online course. An electronic version of the whole manual is available on the Instructor's Resource CD-ROM and is also available for download at the text's accompanying Companion Web site.

- **Instructor's Resource Manual.** The *Instructor's Resource Manual,* by Tom Wood of James Madison University, includes sample course outlines, a summary of the various ancillaries that go with the text, Annotated Chapter Outlines for each chapter and supplement, and in-class exercises called "Applications." Solutions to the in-class Applications are supplied as transparency masters. Due to the numerical aspects of the Applications, many instructors prefer to use overhead transparencies to show the solutions to Applications after students have had time to develop their own answers. An electronic version of the Instructor's Resource Manual is available on the Instructor's Resource CD-ROM and is also available for download at the text's accompanying Companion Web site.

- **Test Item File.** *The Test Item File,* by Ross Fink of Bradley University, contains true/false, multiple choice, fill-in-the-blank, short answer, and problem questions for each chapter and supplement. An electronic version of the Test Item File is available on the Instructor's Resource CD-ROM.

- **TestGEN-EQ.** The print test item file is designed for use with the TestGen-EQ test-generating software. This computerized package allows instructors to custom design, save, and generate classroom tests. The test program permits instructors to edit, add, or delete questions from the test banks; edit existing graphics and create new graphics; analyze test results; and organize a database of tests and student results. This new software allows for greater flexibility and ease of use. It provides many options for organizing and displaying tests, along with a search and sort feature. This software is available on the Instructor's Resource CD-ROM.

- **PowerPoint Presentations.** An extensive set of PowerPoint slides have been created by Jeff Heyl of Lincoln University in New Zealand. This impressive set of slides illuminates and builds upon key concepts in the text. The PowerPoint slides are available to adopters in electronic form on the Instructor's Resource CD-ROM and can also be downloaded at the text's accompanying Companion Web site.

- **Video Package.** The video package contains the following videos: *TQM at Christchurch Parkroyal, Process Choice at the King Soopers Bakery, Waiting Lines at First Bank Villa Italia, Inventory and Textbooks, Service Scheduling at Air New Zealand, Project Management at Nantucket Nectars,* and *Managing Information Technology at Prentice Hall.* The videos provide pedagogical value in that they incorporate summary "bullet point" screens and interviews with managers regarding significant issues.

- **Instructor's Resource CD-ROM.** The Instructor's Resource CD-ROM includes electronic files for the complete *Instructor's Solutions Manual,* the *Test Item File,* the computerized *Test Item File, PowerPoint presentations,* and *Instructor's Resource Manual.* Providing these materials as MS Word and PowerPoint files, rather than pdf files, allows the instructor to customize portions of the material and provide them to students as appropriate.

  Companion Web site (www.prenhall.com/ritzman):

  This content-rich, interactive Web site is a great starting point for operations management resources and features a range of student and instructor resources including: *In the News articles, Tutor Exercises, Internet Activities, Virtual Tours, additional Faculty Tours links, PowerPoint presentations,* and an *Interactive Study Guide* featuring true/false, multiple choice, and essay questions. In the faculty resources section instructors can download the *Instructor's Resource Manual, Instructor's Solutions Manual,* and answers to all of the *In the News* articles and Internet Exercises.

- **WebCT, Blackboard, CourseCompass.** Prentice Hall now makes its class-tested online course content available in WebCT, Blackboard, and CourseCompass. Instructors receive easy-to-use design templates, communication, testing, and course management tools. To learn more, contact your local Prentice Hall representative or go to http://www.prenhall.com/demo for a quick preview of our online solutions.

ACKNOWLEDGMENTS

We wish to thank various people at Prentice Hall who made up the publishing team. Those most closely involved with the project and for whom we hold the greatest admiration include Tom Tucker, Executive Editor, who conceived the idea of the brief book and then supervised the overall project; Jisun Lee, who kept us moving forward on our manuscript revisions; Erika Rusnak, who coordinated the various print ancillaries to create excellent resource support; Nancy Welcher, Senior Media Project Manager, who artfully created the Interactive Web site and produced all Internet and CD-ROM materials; Cindy Regan, Managing Editor, who managed to assemble an excellent product on time from a seemingly endless array of components; Donna Mulder, Copy Editor, who knows how to turn our prose into much better materials; and Debbie Clare, Marketing Manager, whose marketing insights and promotional efforts make all the work of the publishing team worthwhile. We are especially appreciative of the refinements done by KMT to the OM Explorer software, particularly by Richard Cranford and Jim Kinlan. Thanks also go to Howard Weiss, in whose capable hands OM Explorer now rests.

We also thank our colleagues who provided extremely useful guidance for this First Edition of our brief book. They include the following:

Joel D. Goldhar,
Illinois Institute of Technology

Timothy D. Fry,
University of South Carolina

Constantin A. Vaitsos,
University of Southern California

David G. Hollingworth,
Rensselaer Polytechnic Institute

Anne Davey,
Northeastern State University

Terry Munson,
Montana State University—Northern

Donald R. Millage, Jr.,
Marion College of Fond du Lac

William J. Tallon,
Northern Illinois University

Vaidy Jayaraman,
University of Miami

Kudos go to Larry Meile of Boston College, who creatively pulled together the various materials that went into the OM Explorer and Internet Activities sections. Brooke Saladin's cases continue to make it easy for instructors to add interest and excitement to their classes. Three graduate students at Boston College also provided valued inputs. Vidya Ganapathy and Lynette Kelley provided valuable insights on what materials and resources are most valued by students, and Carolina Charrie showed a special ability to spot any possible glitches in OM Explorer. We also gratefully acknowledge two graduate students at the University of Notre Dame. Carl Liu and David Ngata were instrumental in developing the Swift Electronics Supply and the Brunswick Distributors cases. In addition, Cheryl Pauley and Deborah Robinson made sure everything was in order before shipping materials to the publisher at the last moment.

Larry P. Ritzman
Boston College

Lee J. Krajewski
University of Notre Dame

Competing with Operations

Across the Organization

Competitive operations is important to . . .

- ❏ **accounting,** which prepares financial and cost accounting information that aids operations managers in designing and operating production systems.
- ❏ **finance,** which manages the cash flows and capital investment requirements that are created by the operations function.
- ❏ **human resources,** which hires and trains employees to match process needs, location decisions, and planned production levels.
- ❏ **management information systems,** which develop information systems and decision support systems for operations managers.
- ❏ **marketing,** which helps create the demand that operations must satisfy, link customer demand with staffing and production plans, and keep the operations function focused on satisfying customers' needs.
- ❏ **operations,** which designs and operates processes to give the firm a sustainable competitive advantage.

Learning Goals

After reading this chapter, you will be able to . . .

1. describe operations in terms of inputs, processes, outputs, information flows, suppliers, and customers.
2. describe operations as a function alongside finance, accounting, marketing, and human resources.
3. explain how operations management is fundamental to both manufacturers and service providers.
4. describe the role of operations strategy as a source of competitive strength in a global marketplace.
5. explain how to link marketing strategy to operations strategy through the use of competitive priorities.
6. explain how operations strategy is a pattern of decisions directed at processes, systems, and procedures in order to achieve certain competitive priorities.
7. discuss the need for operations management to develop and maintain both intraorganizational and interorganizational relationships.

FedEx (www.fedex.com) is a $17 billion-a-year delivery service company that thrives on speed and reliability. FedEx delivers 4.5 million packages a day—25 percent of the world's package delivery business. Because 70 percent of the packages that FedEx delivers go by plane, it can charge premium prices for the service. For the past 25 years, companies have used FedEx delivery services when they suddenly realized that they were short of critical parts or that they were low on goods demanded by customers. Companies have traditionally chosen FedEx because of its technological superiority in tracking packages. The Internet, however, has changed the way business is conducted. Many businesses are now using complex Web-based systems designed to eliminate much of the unpredictability in their operations by communicating directly with customers and suppliers. E-mail reliably delivers documents instantaneously, and low-cost truck lines, discount air carriers, and even ocean vessels can now track shipments via the Internet.

While these technological advances have been an advantage to some firms, they have cut into the demand for FedEx's traditional services. The growth potential now is in ground transportation services,

An employee of FedEx Home Delivery division drops off a delivery at a residence. Emphasizing low-cost operations and dependable deliveries, FedEx changed its operations strategy to reflect technological changes.

presently dominated by United Parcel Service. This demand is fueled by Internet companies such as Amazon.com that rely heavily on ground transportation services to deliver packages directly to the customer's door and by the vast business-to-business supply networks energized by Web-based purchasing systems. To remain competitive in this changing environment, FedEx is changing its operations strategy. In particular, it is creating two new divisions: FedEx Ground and FedEx Home Delivery. FedEx Ground focuses on business-to-business deliveries via a recently procured trucking company; FedEx Home Delivery specializes in deliveries to residences. Both divisions will strive for low-cost operations and dependable deliveries—a change from the goals of present operations, which stress speed. In addition, FedEx will rely on its core competency in technology. It is investing $100 million in processes that will coordinate the flow of goods from a company such as Cisco with shipments from suppliers of major components, all to be delivered to a customer within a short window of time for assembly of the final product. FedEx is relying on its operations to compete successfully in a dynamic environment being reshaped by the Internet.

OPERATIONS MANAGEMENT DEALS WITH processes that produce goods and services that people use every day. *Processes* are the fundamental activities that organizations use to do work and achieve their goals. The changes at FedEx provide one example of designing processes for competitive operations. Major processes must be created for the new ground delivery businesses that satisfy the needs of customers. The new delivery system will involve the coordination of processes from all functional areas of the firm.

What processes have you been involved with?

By selecting appropriate techniques and developing sound operations strategies, managers can design and operate processes to give companies a competitive edge. Helping you understand how to make operations a competitive weapon begins with this chapter and continues throughout the book.

WHAT IS A PROCESS?

process Any activity or group of activities that takes one or more inputs, transforms and adds value to them, and provides one or more outputs for its customers.

external customers Customers who are either end users or intermediaries (such as manufacturers, wholesalers, or retailers) buying the firm's finished products and services.

internal customers One or more other employees who rely on inputs from earlier processes in order to perform processes in the next office, shop, or department.

A **process** is any activity or group of activities that takes one or more inputs, transforms and adds value to them, and provides one or more outputs for its customers. The type of processes may vary. For example, at a factory a primary process would be a physical or chemical change of raw materials into products. But there also are many nonmanufacturing processes at a factory, such as order fulfillment, making due-date promises to customers, and inventory control. At an airline, a primary process would be the movement of passengers and their luggage from one location to another, but there are also processes for making reservations, checking in passengers, and scheduling crews.

As Figure 1.1 illustrates, processes have inputs and customer outputs. Inputs include human resources (workers and managers), capital (equipment and facilities), purchased materials and services, land, and energy. The numbered circles represent operations through which services, products, or customers pass and where processes are performed. The arrows represent flows and can cross because one job or customer can have different requirements (and thus, a different flow pattern) than the next job or customer. Processes provide outputs—often services (which can take the form of information)—to their "customers." Both manufacturing and service organizations now realize that every process and every person in an organization has customers. Some are **external customers,** who may be either end users or intermediaries (such as manufacturers, wholesalers, or retailers) buying the firm's finished products and services. Others are **internal customers** who may be one or more other employees who rely on inputs from earlier processes in order to perform processes in the next office, shop, or department. Either way, processes must be managed with the customer in mind.

Figure 1.1 can represent a whole firm, a department or small group, or even a single individual. Each one has inputs and uses processes at various operations to provide outputs. The dashed lines represent two special types of input: participation by customers and information on performance from both internal and external sources. Participation by customers occurs not only when they receive outputs but also when

FIGURE 1.1

Processes and Operations

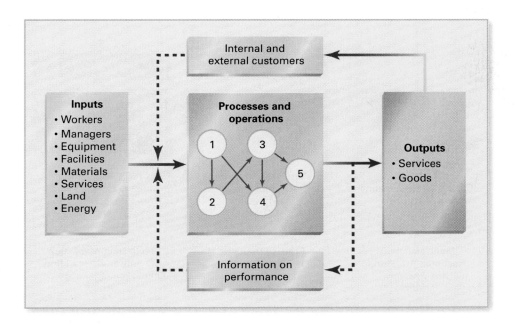

they take an active part in the processes, such as when students participate in a class discussion. Information on performance includes internal reports on customer service or inventory levels and external information from market research, government reports, or telephone calls from suppliers. Managers need all types of information to manage processes most effectively.

NESTED PROCESSES. Processes can be broken down into subprocesses, which can in turn be broken down into still more subprocesses. We refer to this concept of a process within a process as a "**nested process.**" One part of a process can be separated from another for several reasons. One person or one department may be unable to do all parts of the process, or different segments in the process may require different skills. Some parts of the process may be standardized for all customers, making high-volume operations possible. Other parts of the process may be customized, requiring processes best suited to flexible, low-volume operations.

nested process The concept of a process within a process.

As Figure 1.2 illustrates, a large bank has thousands of nested processes. *Retail* processes represent one of several parts of its business. The others include operations (such as cash management, loan operations, and trading operations), products (such as auto finance, cards, and mortgages), and wholesale (such as trading, loan administration, and leasing). In turn, there are four basic groupings of processes within retail processes—distribution, compliance, finance, and human resources. Distribution, for example, can be broken down into 15 nested processes, including processing teller line transactions, tracking and managing branch sales activity, and providing an ATM hotline. Processing teller line transactions then breaks down into 15 distinct processes, including processing deposits, cashing checks, and providing access to safe-deposit boxes. Nested within processing deposits are still other steps. Nested processes sometimes are performed sequentially. Often they can be performed independently of each other, although all of the activities nested within a process must be performed to provide the full set of services.

FIGURE 1.2

Nested Processes at a Large Bank

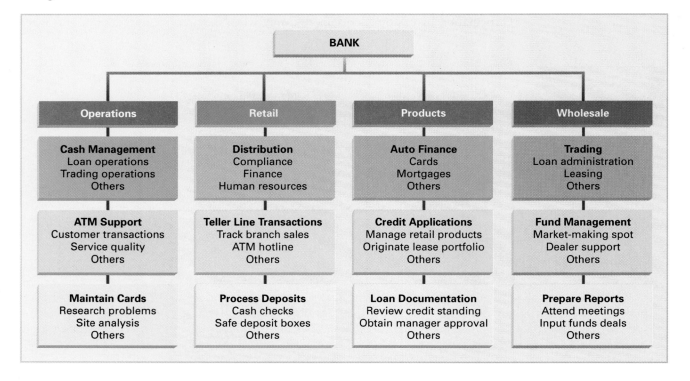

WHAT IS OPERATIONS MANAGEMENT?

operations management
The direction and control of the processes that transform inputs into products and services.

The term **operations management** refers to the direction and control of the processes that transform inputs into products and services. Broadly interpreted, operations management underlies all functional areas, because processes are found in all business activities. Narrowly interpreted, operations refers to a particular department (or more likely several departments). The operations area manages the processes that produce the primary services or products for the external customers but is closely involved with the other areas of a firm.

With either the broad or narrow view, managing operations is crucial to each area of an organization because only through successful management of people, capital, information, and materials can it meet its goals. As tomorrow's manager, you must understand the fundamentals of operations, regardless of your skill area, current major, or future career path. As you study operations management, keep two principles in mind:

1. Each part of an organization, not just the operations function, must design and operate processes and deal with quality, technology, and staffing issues.
2. Each part of an organization has its own identity and yet is connected with operations.

OPERATIONS MANAGEMENT AS A SET OF DECISIONS

What types of decisions are involved in managing operations?

Here, we preview the types of decisions that operations managers make. These decisions define both the scope and content of operations management (OM) and the organization of this book. Some decisions are strategic in nature; others are tactical. Strategic plans are developed further into the future than tactical plans. Thus, strategic decisions are less structured and have long-term consequences, whereas tactical decisions are more structured, routine, and repetitive and have short-term consequences. Strategic choices also tend to focus on the entire organization, cutting across departmental lines; tactical decisions tend to focus on departments, teams, and tasks. The decisions may be divided into five categories: strategic choices; process; quality; capacity, location, and layout; and operating decisions. This text follows that flow of decisions. See Supplement A, "Decision Making" on the Student CD-ROM for traditional tools that are useful in operations management.

OPERATIONS MANAGEMENT AS A FUNCTION

How does operations differ from other functions?

As a firm grows in size, different departments must be created that assume responsibility for certain clusters of processes. Often these departments are organized around *functions* (sometimes called *functional areas*). Figure 1.3 shows that operations is one of several functions within an organization. Each function is specialized, having its own knowledge and skill areas, primary responsibilities, processes, and decision domains. Regardless of how lines are drawn, departments and functions remain interrelated. Many processes are enterprisewide and cut across departmental boundaries. Thus, coordination and effective communication are essential to achieving organizational goals.

In large organizations, the *operations* (or *production*) *department* is usually responsible for the actual transformation of inputs into finished products or services. *Accounting* collects, summarizes, and interprets financial information. *Distribution* deals with the movement, storage, and handling of inputs and outputs. *Engineering* develops product and service designs and production methods. *Finance* secures and invests the company's capital assets. *Human resources* (or *personnel*) hires and trains employees. *Marketing* generates demand for the company's output.

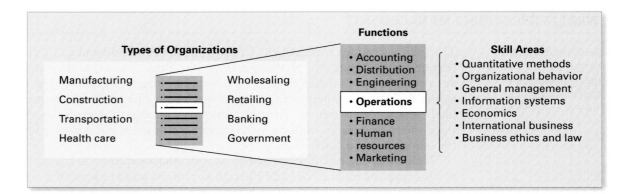

FIGURE 1.3

*Operations
Management as
a Function*

Some organizations never need to perform certain functions. Other organizations may save money by contracting for a function, such as legal services or engineering, when they need it, rather than maintain an in-house department. In small businesses, the owners might manage one or more functions, such as marketing or operations.

As you can see from Figure 1.3, operations managers draw on many skill areas: quantitative analysis to solve problems; knowledge of information systems to manage vast quantities of data; concepts of organizational behavior to aid in designing jobs and managing the workforce; and an understanding of international business methods to gain useful ideas about facility location, technology, and inventory management.

TRENDS IN OPERATIONS MANAGEMENT

Several business trends are currently having a great impact on operations management: the growth of the service sector; productivity changes; global competitiveness; environmental, ethical, and diversity issues; and technological change. (See Chapter 4, "Managing Technology".) In this section, we look at these trends and their implications for operations managers.

SERVICE SECTOR GROWTH

What are the implications of recent employment and productivity trends in the service sector?

The service sector of the economy is significant. As Figure 1.4 shows, services may be divided into three main groups:

1. government (local, state, and federal)
2. wholesale and retail sales
3. other services (transportation, public utilities, communication, health, financial services, real estate, insurance, repair services, business services, and personal services)

Between 1955 and 1999, the number of U.S. jobs in service-producing industries rose from 60 to 80 percent of total nonfarm jobs. Manufacturing and other goods-producing industries currently account for the remaining 20 percent. Thus, although the absolute number of manufacturing jobs has increased (from 20.5 to 25.2 million), the percentage of manufacturing jobs in the total economy has declined. Similar increases in the percentage of the workforce in service jobs are taking place in the other industrial countries. For example, the share of the workforce in service jobs is well above 60 percent in Britain, Canada, France, and Japan.

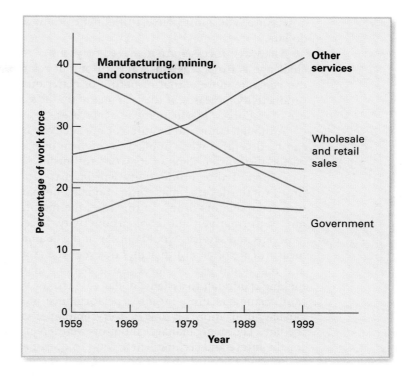

FIGURE 1.4

Percentage of Jobs in the U.S. Service Sector

Source: Economic Report of the President, 2000.

Nonetheless, manufacturing remains a significant part of the U.S. economy. Moreover, the service and manufacturing sectors of the economy are complementary. For example, the output of many firms is purchased by other firms as inputs. More than 25 percent of these intermediate outputs, such as express mail and consulting services, are classified as services while going to companies in the nonservice sector.

PRODUCTIVITY CHANGES

productivity The value of outputs (goods and services) produced divided by the values of input resources (wages, costs of equipment, and the like).

Productivity is the value of outputs (goods and services) produced divided by the values of input resources (wages, cost of equipment, and the like) used:

$$\text{Productivity} = \frac{\text{Output}}{\text{Input}}$$

Many measures of productivity are possible, and all are rough approximations. For example, value of output can be measured by what the customer pays or simply by the number of units produced or customers served. The value of inputs can be judged by their cost or simply by the number of hours worked.

Managers usually pick several reasonable measures and monitor trends to spot areas needing improvement. For example, a manager at an insurance firm might measure office productivity as the number of insurance policies processed per employee each week. A manager at a carpet company might measure the productivity of installers as the number of square yards of carpet installed per hour. Both of these measures reflect *labor productivity,* which is an index of the output per person or hour worked. Similar measures may be used for *machine productivity,* where the denominator is the number of machines. Accounting for several inputs simultaneously is also possible. *Multifactor productivity* is an index of the output provided by more than one of the resources used in production. For example, it may be the value of the output divided by the sum of labor, materials, and overhead costs. When developing such

TUTOR 1.1

a measure, you must convert the quantities to a common unit of measure, typically dollars.

The way processes are managed plays a key role in productivity improvement. The challenge is to increase the value of output relative to the cost of input. If processes can generate more output or output of better quality using the same amount of input, productivity increases. If they can maintain the same level of output while reducing the use of resources, productivity also increases.

Although labor and multifactor productivity measures can be informative, they also can be deceptive when applied to the firm or process levels. For example, a firm can decide to transfer some of its work to outside suppliers and lay off some of its own workforce. Labor productivity will increase considerably, because the value of the firm's total sales (the numerator) remains unchanged while the number of employees (the denominator) drops. In this case, the multifactor productivity measure would be more informative than labor productivity, because the increased cost of purchased materials and services would appear in the denominator of the ratio. Both productivity measures are often insufficient, however, when tracking performance at the department and individual process level. Customers of many processes are internal customers, making it difficult to assign a dollar value to the value of process output. Just as important, managers must monitor performance measures on quality, inventory levels, capacity utilization, on-time delivery, employee satisfaction, customer satisfaction, and the like. The smart manager monitors *multiple* measures of performance, setting goals for the future and seeking better ways to design and operate processes.

Is productivity increasing faster in manufacturing or in services?

It is interesting and even surprising to break out productivity improvements between the manufacturing and services sectors. Although employment in the U.S. service sector has grown rapidly, productivity gains have been much lower. The sector's lagging productivity slows overall growth. Major trading partners such as Japan and Germany have experienced the same problem. There are signs of improvement. The surge of investment across national boundaries can stimulate productivity gains by exposing service firms to greater competition and providing the motivation to increase productivity. Perhaps the investment in information technology also will begin to pay off for service providers, as workers and managers begin to use new technologies for competitive advantage. However, productivity improvement is a particular concern in services. If productivity growth stagnates, so does the overall standard of living.

GLOBAL COMPETITION

Today, businesses accept the fact that, to prosper, they must view customers, suppliers, facility locations, and competitors in global terms. Most products today are global composites of materials and services from throughout the world. Your Gap polo shirt is sewn in Honduras from cloth cut in the United States. Sitting in the theater, you munch a Nestlé's Crunch bar (Swiss) while watching a Columbia Pictures movie (Japanese) at a Cineplex theater (Canadian).

Strong global competition affects industries everywhere. For example, U.S. manufacturers have experienced declining shares of the domestic and international markets in steel, appliances and household durable goods, machinery, and chemicals. Even so, in globally competitive manufacturing industries, the United States attracts 37 percent of sales, Japan 32 percent, and Europe 31 percent. In fact, the United States garners 48 percent of corporate profits in these industries, particularly in energy equipment, aerospace, data processing and software, electronic components, beverages and tobacco, and health and personal care products.

With the value of world trade in services now at more than $1.5 trillion per year, banking, law, data processing, airlines, and consulting services operations are beginning to face many of the same international pressures as U.S. manufacturers. And regional trading blocs such as the European Union (EU) and North American Free Trade Agreement (NAFTA) further change the competitive landscape in both services and manufacturing.

ETHICAL, WORKFORCE DIVERSITY, AND ENVIRONMENTAL ISSUES

How do ethics and the environment affect operations?

Businesses face more ethical quandaries than ever before, intensified by an increasing global presence and rapid technological change. Companies are locating new operations, and have more suppliers and customers, in other countries. Potential ethical dilemmas arise when business can be conducted by different rules. Some countries are more sensitive than others about lavish entertainment, conflicts of interest, bribery, discrimination against minorities and women, poverty, minimum-wage levels, unsafe workplaces, and workers' rights. Managers must decide in such cases whether or not to design and operate processes that do more than just meet local standards that are lower than those back home. In addition, technological change brings debates about data protection and customer privacy, such as on the Internet. In an electronic world, businesses are geographically far from their customers, and a reputation of trust may become even more important.

One expert suggests a more ethical approach to business in which firms

❏ have responsibilities that go beyond producing goods and services at a profit
❏ help solve important social problems
❏ respond to a broader constituency than shareholders alone
❏ have impacts beyond simple marketplace transactions
❏ serve a range of human values that go beyond the merely economic

Environmental issues such as toxic wastes, poisoned drinking water, poverty, air quality, and global warming are getting more emphasis. In the past, many people viewed environmental problems as quality-of-life issues; in the 2000s, many people see them as survival issues. Interest in a clean, healthy environment is increasing. Industrial nations have a particular burden because their combined populations, representing only 25 percent of the total global population, consume 70 percent of all resources.

Leading companies have found that workforce diversity can provide a forum for unique perspectives and solutions.

Just seven nations, including the United States and Japan, produce almost half of all greenhouse gases. The United States and some European nations now spend 2 percent of their gross domestic products on environmental protection, a level that environmentalists believe should be increased.

The message is clear: Consideration of ethics, workforce diversity, and the environment is becoming part of every manager's job. When designing and operating processes, they should consider integrity, respect for the individual, and respecting the customer along with more conventional performance measures such as productivity, quality, cost, and profit.

CORPORATE STRATEGY

competitive priorities
Operating advantages that a firm's processes must possess to outperform its competitors.

The trends in operations management present a dynamic environment within which firms must find their competitive niche. Operations can be used as a competitive weapon; however, the firm must have a sound operations strategy that focuses on customers. Developing a customer-driven operations strategy begins with *corporate strategy,* which coordinates the firm's overall goals with its core competencies. It determines which customers the firm will serve, which new products or services it will produce, which responses it will take to changes in its business and socioeconomic environment, and which strategy it will employ in international markets. Based on the corporate strategy, a *market analysis* categorizes the firm's customers, identifies their needs, and assesses competitor's strengths. This information is used to develop **competitive priorities,** which are the operating advantages that the firm's processes must possess to outperform its competitors. The competitive priorities and the directives from corporate strategy provide input for the *functional strategies,* or the goals and long-term plans of each functional area. Through its strategic planning process, each functional area is responsible for identifying ways to develop the capabilities it will need to carry out functional strategies and achieve corporate goals. This input, along with the current status and capability of each area, is fed back into the corporate strategic planning process to indicate whether corporate strategy should be modified. Figure 1.5 shows how corporate strategy, market analysis, competitive priorities, and functional strategies are linked.

Corporate strategy specifies the business(es) that the company will pursue, isolates new opportunities and threats in the environment, and identifies the growth objectives that it should achieve. Also addressed is business strategy or how a firm can differentiate itself from the competition. Choices could include producing standardized products versus customized products or competing on the basis of cost advantage versus responsive delivery. Corporate strategy provides an overall direction that serves as the framework for carrying out all the organization's functions.

STRATEGIC CONSIDERATIONS
Developing a corporate strategy involves three considerations: responding to pressures for flexibility, monitoring and adjusting to changes in the business environment, and identifying and developing the firm's core competencies.

FLEXIBILITY. E-commerce companies as well as traditional Rust Belt companies have found that they must frequently revise corporate strategies to remain competitive, even on a weekly or quarterly basis. Low economic barriers to entry in such businesses as retailing or finance have caused tremendous competition and the need to reevaluate strategies on a short-term basis. In addition, the Internet has put companies in close

FIGURE 1.5

Competitive Priorities: Link Between Corporate Strategy and Functional Area Strategies

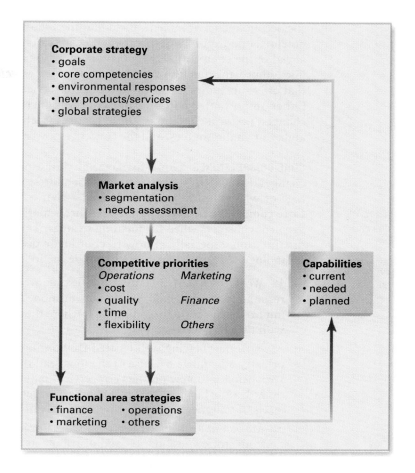

touch with their customers, both through direct sales and by soliciting feedback. Customers tell companies what they want, and companies must respond or lose out. Such conditions call for flexibility in the strategic planning process. There are five ways companies can respond to the need for flexibility:

- ❑ *Scenario Building.* Strategists plan several different outcomes for each initiative, thus permitting quick responses to competitive threats.
- ❑ *Reality Checks.* Key decision makers meet regularly at short intervals to assess ways that rivals might make inroads in the marketplace.
- ❑ *Communication.* To get everyone thinking of the effects of the change on their operations, executives announce strategy shifts to employees within hours of a decision.
- ❑ *Hires.* Employers fill jobs with people who thrive on change and ambiguity.
- ❑ *Shortening the Budget Cycle.* To ensure that individual and departmental goals are properly revised, managers link the budget review to strategy review.

From a strategic perspective, the message is clear: Develop a capability for change.

How can management identify and deal with environmental change when formulating corporate strategy?

ENVIRONMENT. The external business environment in which a firm competes changes continually, and an organization needs to adapt to those changes. Adaptation begins with *environmental scanning,* the process by which managers monitor trends in the socioeconomic environment, including the industry, the marketplace, and society, for potential opportunities or threats. A crucial reason for environmental scanning is to stay ahead of the competition. Competitors may be gaining an edge by broadening product lines, improving quality, or lowering costs. New entrants into the market or competitors that offer substitutes for a firm's product or service may threaten continued profitability. Other important environmental concerns include economic trends, technological changes, political conditions, social changes (such as attitudes toward work), the availability of vital resources, and the collective power of customers or suppliers.

CORE COMPETENCIES. Good managerial skill alone cannot overcome environmental changes. Rather, corporate strategy must address them. Firms succeed by taking advantage of what they do particularly well—that is, the organization's unique strengths. **Core competencies** are the unique resources and strengths that an organization's management considers when formulating strategy. They reflect the collective learning of the organization, especially in how to coordinate diverse processes and integrate multiple technologies. These competencies include the following.

> **core competencies** The unique resources and strengths that an organization's management considers when formulating strategy.

1. *Workforce.* A well-trained and flexible workforce allows organizations to respond to market needs in a timely fashion. This competency is particularly important in service organizations, where the customer comes in direct contact with the employees.

2. *Facilities.* Having well-located facilities—offices, stores, and plants—is a primary advantage because of the long lead time needed to build new ones. Expansion into new products or services may be accomplished quickly. In addition, flexible facilities that can handle a variety of products or services at different levels of volume provide a competitive advantage.

3. *Market and Financial Know-How.* An organization that can easily attract capital from stock sales, market and distribute its products, or differentiate its products from similar products on the market has a competitive edge.

4. *Systems and Technology.* Organizations with expertise in information systems will have an edge in industries that are data—and information—intensive, such as banking. Particularly advantageous is expertise in Internet technologies and applications, such as business-to-consumer and business-to-business systems. Having the patents on a new technology is also a big advantage.

The flexibility of the Internet emphasizes the need for companies to evaluate carefully what their core competencies really are. In the process, some companies have actually redefined themselves. Hewlett-Packard, for example, is hoping to use the Internet to remake one of its divisions from a manufacturer of large computers to an e-services company that will provide computing power over the Internet. It has always been true that competitors will eventually overtake a company that stops innovating and upgrading. The Internet, however, has shortened the grace period that companies once enjoyed.

GLOBAL STRATEGIES

> What role does operations play in entering international markets?

Identifying opportunities and threats today requires a global perspective. A global strategy may include buying foreign parts or services, combating threats from foreign competitors, or planning ways to enter markets beyond traditional national boundaries. Although warding off threats from global competitors is necessary, firms should also actively seek to penetrate foreign markets. Two effective global strategies are strategic alliances and locating abroad.

STRATEGIC ALLIANCES. One way for a firm to open foreign markets is to create a *strategic alliance*. A strategic alliance is an agreement with another firm that may take one of three forms. A *collaborative effort* often arises when one firm has core competencies that another needs but is unwilling or unable to duplicate. Such relationships are common in buyer–supplier relationships. Another form of strategic alliance is the *joint venture* in which two firms agree to produce a product or service jointly. This approach often is used by firms to gain access to foreign markets. Finally, *technology licensing* is an agreement in which one company licenses its production or service methods to another.

LOCATING ABROAD. Another way to enter global markets is to locate operations in a foreign country. However, managers must recognize that what works well in their home country might not work well elsewhere. The economic and political environment or customers' needs may be very different. For example, McDonald's is known for the consistency of its products—a Big Mac tastes the same anywhere in the world. However, a family-owned chain, Jollibee Foods Corporation, has become the dominant fast-food chain in the Philippines. Jollibee caters to a local preference for sweet-and-spicy flavors, which it incorporates into its fried chicken, spaghetti, and burgers. Jollibee's strength is its understanding of local tastes and claims that its burger is similar to the one a Filipino would cook at home. McDonald's responded by introducing its own Filipino-style spicy burger, but competition is stiff. McDonald's experience demonstrates that, to be successful, corporate strategies must recognize customs, preferences, and economic conditions in other countries.

MARKET ANALYSIS

One key to success in formulating a customer-driven operations strategy for both manufacturing and service firms is understanding what the customer wants and how to provide it better than the competition does. *Market analysis* first divides the firm's customers into market segments and then identifies the needs of each segment. In this section, we define and discuss the concepts of market segmentation and needs assessment.

MARKET SEGMENTATION

Market segmentation is the process of identifying groups of customers with enough in common to warrant the design and provision of products or services that the larger group wants and needs. In general, to identify market segments, the analyst must determine the characteristics that clearly differentiate each segment. A sound marketing program can then be devised and an effective operating strategy developed to support it.

Once the firm has identified a market segment, it can incorporate the needs of customers into the design of the product or service and the processes for its production. The following characteristics are among those that can be used to determine market segments.

1. *Demographic Factors.* Age, income, educational level, occupation, and location can differentiate markets.

2. *Psychological Factors.* Factors such as pleasure, fear, innovativeness, and boredom can serve to segment markets.

3. *Industry Factors.* Customers may utilize specific technologies (e.g., electronics, robotics, or microwave telecommunications), use certain materials (e.g., rubber,

oil, or wood), or participate in a particular industry (e.g., banking, health care, or automotive). These factors are used for market segmentation when the firm's customers use its goods or services to produce other goods or services.

At one time, managers thought of customers as a homogeneous mass market. Managers now realize that two customers may use the same product for very different reasons. Identifying the key factors in each market segment is the starting point in devising a customer-driven operations strategy.

NEEDS ASSESSMENT

The second step in market analysis is to make a *needs assessment*, which identifies the needs of each segment and assesses how well competitors are addressing those needs. Once it has made this assessment, the firm can differentiate itself from its competitors. The needs assessment should include both the tangible and the intangible product attributes and features that a customer desires. These attributes and features, known as the *customer benefit package* (Collier, 1994), consist of a core product or service and a set of peripheral products or services. The customer views the customer benefit package as a whole. For example, when you purchase an automobile, the core product is the car itself—its features and qualities. However, the peripheral services offered by the dealer play a key role in whether you will buy the car. They include the manner in which you are treated by the salesperson, the availability of financing, and the quality of postsale service at the dealership. Thus, the customer benefit package is the automobile plus the services provided by the dealership. Customers won't be completely satisfied unless they receive the entire customer benefit package.

Understanding the customer benefit package for a market segment enables management to identify ways to gain competitive advantage. Each market segment has market needs that can be related to product/service, process, or demand attributes. Market needs may be grouped as follows:

❒ *Product* or *Service Needs.* Attributes of the product or service, such as price, quality, and degree of customization desired.

❒ *Delivery System Needs.* Attributes of the processes and the supporting systems and resources needed to deliver the customer benefit package, such as availability, convenience, courtesy, safety, accuracy, reliability, delivery speed, and delivery dependability.

❒ *Volume Needs.* Attributes of the demand for the product or service, such as high or low volume, degree of variability in volume, and degree of predictability in volume.

❒ *Other Needs.* Other attributes, such as reputation and number of years in business, after-sale technical support, ability to invest in international financial markets, competent legal services, and product or service design capability.

COMPETITIVE PRIORITIES AND OPERATIONS STRATEGY

What are the key capabilities that operations must develop to compete successfully in a market segment?

A customer-driven **operations strategy** reflects a clear understanding of the firm's long-term goals as embodied in its corporate strategy. It also requires a cross-functional effort by marketing and operations to understand the needs of each market segment and to specify the operating advantages that the firm needs to outperform competitors. Operating advantages must be related to each of the firm's processes. We call these operating advantages *competitive priorities*. In this text, we focus on competitive priorities for processes that relate to the product or service itself, to its delivery system, and to related volume factors. There are eight possible competitive priorities for processes, which fall into four groups:

Cost	1.	Low-cost operations
Quality	2.	High-performance design
	3.	Consistent quality
Time	4.	Fast delivery time
	5.	On-time delivery
	6.	Development speed
Flexibility	7.	Customization
	8.	Volume flexibility

A firm is composed of many processes that must be coordinated to provide the overall desirable outcome for the customer. Most customers view a business as an aggregate process that accepts orders for products or services and finally delivers them in a fashion that satisfies their needs. However, as we have already discussed, a business consists of many *nested* processes, each one performing operations needed to serve the firm's customers. In addition, many of a firm's processes may even serve more than one market segment. The challenge for management is to assign the appropriate competitive priorities to each process so as to support the needs of the firm's customers.

COST

Lowering prices can increase demand for products or services, but it also reduces profit margins if the product or service cannot be produced at lower cost. To compete based on cost, operations managers must address labor, materials, scrap, overhead, and other costs to design a system that lowers the cost per unit of the product or service. Often, lowering costs requires additional investment in automated facilities and equipment. The Managerial Practice feature shows how Costco uses operations strategy to lower costs and increase margins.

QUALITY

Quality is a dimension of a product or service that is defined by the customer. Today, more than ever, quality has important market implications. As for operations, two competitive priorities deal with quality: high-performance design and consistent quality.

HIGH-PERFORMANCE DESIGN. The first priority, **high-performance design,** may include superior features, close tolerances, and greater durability; helpfulness, courteousness, and availability of service employees; convenience of access to service locations; and safety of products or services. High-performance design determines the level of operations performance required in making a product or performing a service.

CONSISTENT QUALITY. The second quality priority, **consistent quality,** measures the frequency with which the product or service meets design specifications. Customers want products or services that consistently meet the specifications they contracted for, have come to expect, or saw advertised. To compete on the basis of consistent quality, managers need to design and monitor operations to reduce errors. Although consistent quality is as important now as it has ever been, it is increasingly expected by customers. A firm that does not have consistent quality does not last long in a competitive global marketplace.

MANAGERIAL PRACTICE
Using Operations for Profit at Costco

Looking for bargains on items ranging from watermelons to symphonic baby grand pianos? One company addressing those needs is Costco (www.costco.com), a wholesale club with 347 stores that generate $31 billion in annual revenue and $542 million in annual profits. Its closest competitor is Wal-Mart's Sam's Club, whose 200 more stores generate $1 billion less in annual revenue. Individual and business customers pay Costco from $45 to $100 a year for a membership and the privilege of buying staple items in bulk quantities and other select items at big discounts.

What makes Costco so successful? It has linked the needs of its customers to its operations by developing a customer-driven operations strategy that supports its retailing concept. Costco's competitive priorities are low-cost operations, quality, and flexibility. A visit to one of Costco's stores will show how these competitive priorities manifest themselves.

Low-Cost Operations

Customers come to Costco because of low prices, which are possible because processes are designed for efficiency. The store is actually a warehouse where products are stacked on pallets with little signage. New products can replace old products efficiently. In addition, Costco managers are tough price negotiators with suppliers because they buy in high volumes. Suppliers are expected to change factory runs to produce specially built packages that are bigger but cheaper per unit. Costco's profit margins are low, but annual profits are high because of the volume.

Quality

Customers are not looking for high levels of customer service, but they are looking for high value. In addition to low prices, Costco backs everything it sells with a return-anything-at-any-time guarantee. Customers trust Costco, which has generated an 86 percent membership renewal rate—the highest in the indus-

Shoppers checking out the bargains that they found at one of Costco's wholesale clubs. Costco operates member-centered discount warehouse outlets in North America and Asia.

try. To support the need for high value, operations must ensure that products are of high quality and undamaged when placed in the store.

Flexibility

One of the key aspects of Costco's operations is the fact that it carries only 4,000 carefully selected items in a typical store, while a Wal-Mart Superstore carries 125,000 items. However, items change frequently to provide return customers with a "surprise" aspect to the shopping experience. Processes must be flexible to accommodate a dynamic store layout. In addition, the supply chain must be carefully managed because the products are constantly changing.

Source: "Inside the Cult of Costco." *Fortune* (September 6, 1999), pp. 184–190.

TIME

As the saying goes, "time is money." Some companies do business at "Internet speed," while others thrive on consistently meeting delivery promises. Three competitive priorities deal with time: fast delivery time, on-time delivery, and development speed.

fast delivery time The elapsed time between receiving a customer's order and filling it.

lead time The way industrial buyers often refer to fast delivery time.

FAST DELIVERY TIME. The first time priority, **fast delivery time,** is the elapsed time between receiving a customer's order and filling it. Industrial buyers often call it **lead time.** An acceptable delivery time can be a year for a complex, customized machine, several weeks for scheduling elective surgery, and minutes for an ambulance. Manufacturers can shorten delivery times by storing inventory; manufacturers and service providers can do so by having excess capacity.

on-time delivery
Measurement of the frequency with which delivery-time promises are met.

development speed
Measurement of how quickly a new product or service is introduced, covering the elapsed time from idea generation through final design and production.

time-based competition
The process by which managers define the steps and time needed to deliver a product or service, and then critically analyze each step to determine whether they can save time without hurting quality.

concurrent engineering
A process during which design engineers, manufacturing specialists, marketers, buyers, and quality specialists work jointly to design a product or service and select the production process.

customization The ability to satisfy the unique needs of each customer by changing product or service designs.

volume flexibility The ability to accelerate or decelerate the rate of production quickly to handle large fluctuations in demand.

ON-TIME DELIVERY. The second time priority, **on-time delivery**, measures the frequency with which delivery-time promises are met. Manufacturers measure on-time delivery as the percentage of customer orders shipped when promised, with 95 percent often considered the goal. A service provider, such as a supermarket, might measure on-time delivery as the percentage of customers who wait in the checkout line for less than three minutes.

DEVELOPMENT SPEED. The third time priority, **development speed**, measures how quickly a new product or service is introduced, covering the elapsed time from idea generation through final design and production. Getting the new product or service to market first gives the firm an edge on the competition that is difficult to overcome in a rapidly changing business environment. Development speed is especially important in the fashion apparel industry.

TIME-BASED COMPETITION. Many companies focus on the competitive priorities of development speed and fast delivery time. With **time-based competition**, managers carefully define the steps and time needed to deliver a product or service and then critically analyze each step to determine whether they can save time without hurting quality. In a process called **concurrent engineering**, design engineers, manufacturing specialists, marketers, buyers, and quality specialists work jointly to design a product or service and select the production process. Ford Motor Company, for example, gives full responsibility for each new product to a program manager who forms a product team representing every revelant part of the organization. In such a system, each department can raise concerns or anticipate problems while there is still time to alter the product. Changes are much simpler and less costly at this step than after the product or service has been introduced to the market.

FLEXIBILITY

Flexibility is a characteristic of a firm's operations that enables it to react to customer needs quickly and efficiently. Some firms give top priority to two types of flexibility: customization and volume flexibility.

CUSTOMIZATION. **Customization** is the ability to satisfy the unique needs of each customer by changing product or service designs. Customization typically implies that the operating system must be flexible to handle specific customer needs and changes in designs.

VOLUME FLEXIBILITY. **Volume flexibility** is the ability to accelerate or decelerate the rate of production quickly to handle large fluctuations in demand. Volume flexibility is an important operating capability that often supports the achievement of other competitive priorities (e.g., development speed or fast delivery times). The time between peaks may be years, as with cycles in the home-building industry or political campaigns. It may be months, as with ski resorts or the manufacture of lawn fertilizers. It may even be hours, as with the systematic swings in demand at a large postal facility where mail is received, sorted, and dispatched.

SELECTING COMPETITIVE PRIORITIES

You might wonder why firms have to choose among competitive priorities. Why not compete in all areas at once and dramatically improve your competitive position? In certain situations, firms *can* improve on all competitive priorities simultaneously. For example, in a manufacturing firm, scrap from mistakes in operations and the need to rework defective parts and products sometimes account for 20 to 30 percent of a product's cost. By reducing defects and improving quality, the firm can reduce costs, improve productivity, and cut delivery time—all at the same time.

At some point, though, further improvements in one area may require a trade-off with one or more of the others. A survey of manufacturers indicated that raising the degree of customization or producing high-performance design products may lead to both higher costs and higher prices.[1] Therefore, firms must choose a select set of competitive priorities to emphasize.

Sometimes trade-offs are not possible because a competitive priority has become a requirement for doing business in a particular market segment.[2] Such a requirement is called an *order qualifier*. In such situations, customers will not place orders for products or services unless a certain level of performance can be demonstrated. Fulfilling the order qualifier will not ensure competitive success in a market; it will only position the firm to compete. For example, in the market for TV sets, one measure of quality is product reliability. Customers expect to purchase a set that will not require repairs for many years. Products that do not live up to that level of quality do not last long in the market. In the electronics industry in general, product reliability is rapidly becoming an order qualifier.

SERVICE STRATEGIES

Competitive priorities provide a basis for the design of processes. Standardized services, assemble-to-order, and customized-services strategies are used for processes devoted to the delivery of services.

standardized-services strategy The service strategy utilized by processes that provide services with little variety in high volumes.

STANDARDIZED-SERVICES STRATEGY

Processes that provide services with little variety in high volumes tend to use the **standardized-services strategy.** Typical competitive priorities are consistent quality, on-time delivery, and low cost. Because of the high volume, processes providing the primary service can be organized so that the flow of customers follows a linear pattern in the facility. For example, the U.S. Postal Service uses standardized-service strategies for the letter mail process and the parcel process. The millions of letters and parcels that arrive daily for processing are sorted by destination and loaded into trucks according to customers' priorities. Parcel processing is separate from letter processing because of the different market segments and because of the nature of the automated sorting equipment required for each type of item. The tasks required of the employees and equipment are repetitive and routine, ideal for the standardized-services strategy. FedEx and UPS use a standardized-services strategy for the same reasons.

assemble-to-order services strategy The service strategy that designs operations to include processes that produce a set of standardized services and processes that are devoted to assembling standardized offerings for a specific customer's needs.

ASSEMBLE-TO-ORDER SERVICES STRATEGY

The **assemble-to-order services strategy** amounts to designing operations to include processes that produce a set of standardized services and processes that are devoted to assembling standardized offerings for a specific customer's needs. The assembly processes must be flexible so that the correct package can be assembled for the customer. Typical competitive priorities are customization and fast delivery time. For example, long-distance telephone service providers offer customized service packages to retain customers in a highly competitive industry. Internet access, cellular phone

[1]Safizadeh, H. M., L. P. Ritzman, D. Sharma, and C. Wood. "An Empirical Analysis of the Product–Process Matrix," *Management Science,* vol. 42, no. 11 (1996), pp. 1576–1591.
[2]Hill, Terry. *Manufacturing Strategy: Text and Cases,* 3d ed. Homewood, IL.: Irwin, 2000.

FIGURE 1.6

Health Clinic Process

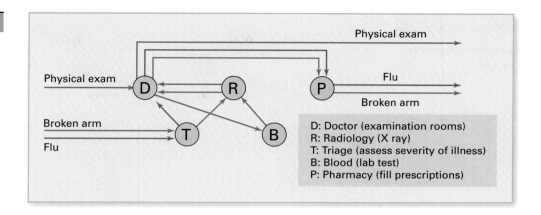

Physical exam

Physical exam

Flu

Broken arm

Broken arm

Flu

D: Doctor (examination rooms)
R: Radiology (X ray)
T: Triage (assess severity of illness)
B: Blood (lab test)
P: Pharmacy (fill prescriptions)

service, credit cards, satellite broadcast service, personal 800 numbers, and cable TV are among the list of options. The assembly process could be automated, as on a Web page, or personalized through telemarketing. Companies such as AT&T, MCI, and Sprint work with the customer to assemble the appropriate mix of services and provide a billing service that combines all charges on one itemized bill.

CUSTOMIZED-SERVICES STRATEGY

customized-services strategy A service strategy designed to provide individualized services.

Processes designed to provide individualized services tend to use a **customized-services strategy.** Typical competitive priorities include high-performance design and customization. Volume, in terms of service requirements per customer, is low. Nested processes tend to be grouped by the function they perform, and customers are routed from process to process until the service is completed. This strategy enables the production of a high variety of customized services while providing reasonable utilization of the processes. For example, Figure 1.6 shows the flow pattern of patients through a health clinic process. Although there are five processes providing services, any one customer may not need all of them. The customers may have to compete for the resources: Note that all patients must see the doctor. Many different routing patterns may exist in a facility employing a customized-services strategy.

MANUFACTURING STRATEGIES

Manufacturing strategies differ from those in services because of the ability to use inventories. Make-to-stock, assemble-to-order, and make-to-order strategies address the competitive priorities of processes devoted to manufacturing.

MAKE-TO-STOCK STRATEGY

make-to-stock strategy A manufacturing strategy that involves holding items in stock for immediate delivery, thereby minimizing customer delivery times.

Manufacturing firms that hold items in stock for immediate delivery, thereby minimizing customer delivery times, use a **make-to-stock strategy.** This strategy is feasible for standardized products with high volumes and reasonably accurate forecasts. For example, in Figure 1.7, which depicts a final automobile assembly process, both the midsize 6-cylinder and the compact 4-cylinder models are assembled on the same line. Collectively, the volume of the two models is sufficient to warrant a make-to-stock strategy for the facility. The routing pattern for the two products is straightforward, with four processes devoted to the two products. This strategy is also applicable to situations in which the firm is producing a unique product for a specific customer if the volumes are high enough.

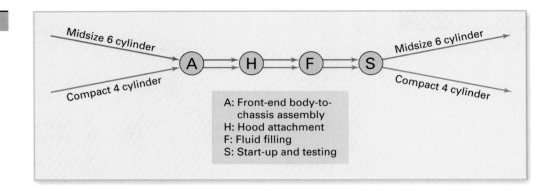

Automobile Assembly Process

mass production The approach used by firms that employ a make-to-stock strategy.

The term **mass production** is often used to define firms using a make-to-stock strategy. Because their environment is stable and predictable, mass-production firms typically have a bureaucratic organization, and workers repeat narrowly defined tasks. The competitive priorities for these companies typically are consistent quality and low costs.

ASSEMBLE-TO-ORDER MANUFACTURING STRATEGY

assemble-to-order manufacturing strategy An approach to producing customized products from relatively few assemblies and components after customer orders are received.

The **assemble-to-order manufacturing strategy** is an approach to producing customized products from relatively few assemblies and components after customer orders are received. Typical competitive priorities are customization and fast delivery time. The assemble-to-order strategy involves assembly processes and fabrication processes. Because they are devoted to manufacturing standardized components and assemblies in high volumes, the fabrication processes focus on creating appropriate amounts of inventories for the assembly processes. Stocking finished products would be economically prohibitive because the numerous possible options make forecasting relatively inaccurate. For example, a manufacturer of upscale upholstered furniture can produce hundreds of a particular style of sofa, no two alike, to meet customers' selections of fabric and wood. Once the specific order from the customer is received, the assembly processes create the product from the standardized components and assemblies produced by the fabrication processes. The fabrication processes should be efficient to keep costs low, while the assembly processes should be flexible to produce the varied products demanded by the customers.

MAKE-TO-ORDER STRATEGY

make-to-order strategy A strategy used by manufacturers that make products to customer specifications in low volumes.

Manufacturers that make products to customer specifications in low volumes tend to use a **make-to-order strategy.** With this strategy, a firm is viewed as a set of processes that can be used in many different ways to satisfy the unique needs of customers. This strategy provides a high degree of customization, which is a major competitive priority for these manufacturers. Because most products, components, and assemblies are custom-made, the manufacturing process must be flexible to accommodate the variety. Specialized medical equipment, castings, and expensive homes are suited to the make-to-order strategy.

MASS CUSTOMIZATION

At one extreme of the assemble-to-order strategy is **mass customization**, whereby a firm's flexible processes generate customized products or services in high volumes at reasonably low costs. Mass customizers attempt to provide the variety inherent in an assemble-to-order strategy but often focus on relatively high-volume markets. A key to

mass customization
An example of the assemble-to-order strategy, whereby a firm's flexible processes generate customized products or services in high volumes at reasonably low costs.

being a successful mass customizer is postponing the task of differentiating a product or service for a specific customer until the latest possible moment. Doing so allows the greatest application of standard modules of the product or service before specific customization. Hewlett-Packard (HP) provides a good example of mass customization. HP postpones assembly of the printer with the country-specific power supply and packaging of the appropriate manuals until the last link in the process—the distributor in the region where the printer is being delivered. Being a successful mass customizer such as HP may require redesign of products or services and processes. We will have more to say about postponement in Chapter 8, "Supply-Chain Management."

PRODUCT OR SERVICE IMPLICATIONS

A product or service should be designed so that it consists of independent modules that can be assembled into different forms easily and inexpensively. For example, the Ritz-Carlton, an upscale chain of hotels, records the preferences expressed by customers during their stay and uses them to tailor the services that customers receive on their next visit. Requests for items such as hypoallergenic pillows, additional towels, or even chocolate chip cookies are recorded for future use so that personalized goods and services can be added to a standard Ritz-Carlton room for repeat customers.

What are the operations implications of being a mass customizer?

PROCESS IMPLICATIONS

Processes should be designed so that they can be used to meet a wide variety of needs. We discuss process management in more detail in Chapter 2; however, one key to supporting mass customization is to design processes as independent modules that can be arranged to provide customization at the latest possible moment, as HP did with its printers. Benetton did a similar thing in its sweater manufacturing process. Rather than dyeing the yarn before manufacturing the sweater, Benetton reversed the dyeing and knitting processes so that sweaters were dyed after the customer had placed an order or the color preferences of consumers for the upcoming season had been determined. By rearranging the processes, Benetton saved millions of dollars in write-offs for obsolete inventory.

INTERNET IMPLICATIONS

The Internet has been a valuable technology for mass-customization strategies. Web pages can be designed to attract customers and allow them to configure their own products or

A couple checking in at the Ritz-Carlton, where services are customized to individual preferences.

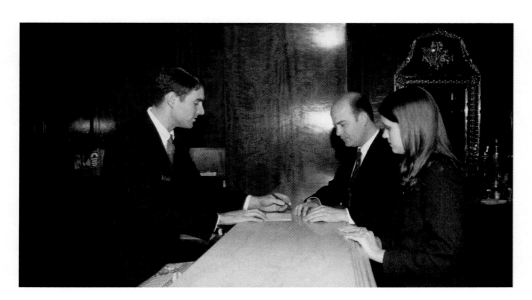

services easily and quickly. Customers to Amazon.com fill baskets of goods from a vast array of possibilities, each one different from the next customer's. Dell sells computers through a Web page that allows consumers to configure their own computers from a large variety of options. Fleet Corporation, a large bank, offers investment services along with its banking services for its Internet customers. Ford and GM are building systems to permit customers to configure their own automobiles over the Internet. Each of these ventures provides customers an enormous amount of choice in the products or services they buy, but they also put a lot of pressure on the processes that must produce them. Flexibility and short response times are prized qualities for mass-customization processes.

OPERATIONS STRATEGY AS A PATTERN OF DECISIONS

Operations strategy translates service or product plans and competitive priorities for each market segment into decisions affecting the processes that support those market segments. Figure 1.8 shows how corporate strategy provides the umbrella for key operations management decisions. The operations manager must select a service or manufacturing strategy for each process. This strategy determines how the firm's processes are organized to handle the volume and variety of products or services for each specific market segment. This initial choice sets in motion a series of other decisions that governs the design of the processes, systems, and procedures that support the operations strategy. These decisions are not static; they must be constantly reevaluated according to the

FIGURE 1.8

Connection Between Corporate Strategy and Key Operations Management Decisions

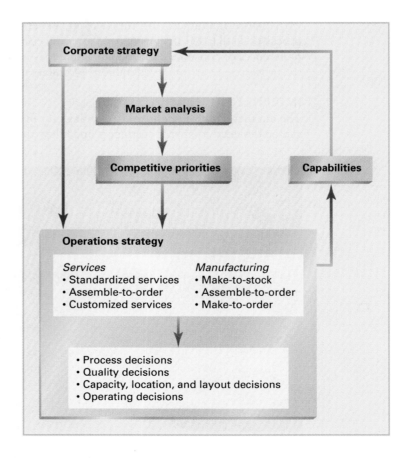

dynamics of the marketplace. We cover these decisions in detail throughout this text. Nonetheless, from a strategic perspective, operations managers are responsible for making the decisions that ensure the firm has the capability to address the competitive priorities of new and existing market segments as they evolve. Furthermore, the pattern of decisions for one organization may be different from that of another, even if they are both in the same industry, because of differences in core competencies, market segments served, and degree of Web integration. Each process must be analyzed from the perspective of the customers it serves, be they external or internal.

OPERATIONS MANAGEMENT ACROSS THE ORGANIZATION

We have described operations management as designing and operating processes in both manufacturing and services, as a set of decisions, and as one of several functional areas within an organization. In this final section, we describe operations management as an interfunctional imperative and a competitive weapon for organizations.

OPERATIONS MANAGEMENT AS AN INTERFUNCTIONAL IMPERATIVE

Operations managers need to build and maintain solid relationships both interorganizationally and intraorganizationally. We discuss interorganizational relationships, such as those with suppliers, later in the book (see Chapter 8, "Supply-Chain Management"). Here, our focus is on intraorganizational relationships, which call for cross-functional coordination.

Too often managers allow artificial barriers to be erected between functional areas and departments. In these situations, jobs or tasks move sequentially from marketing to engineering to operations. The result is often slow or poor decision making because each department bases its decisions solely on its own limited perspective, not the organization's overall perspective. A new approach being tried by many organizations is to replace sequential decision making with more cross-functional coordination and flatter organizational structures. For example, Hallmark Cards formed cross-functional teams and cut its product development time by 50 percent.

CROSS-FUNCTIONAL COORDINATION. Cross-functional coordination is essential to effective operations management. For example, consider how other functional areas interact with operations. Perhaps the strongest connection is with the marketing function, which determines the need for new products and services and the demand for existing ones. Operations managers must bring together human and capital resources to handle demand effectively. The operations manager must consider facility locations and relocations to serve new markets, and the design of layouts for service organizations must match the image that marketing seeks to convey to the customer. Marketing and sales make delivery promises to customers, which must be related to current operations capabilities. Marketing demand forecasts guide the operations manager in planning output rates and capacities.

The operations manager also needs feedback from the accounting function to understand current performance. Financial measures help the operations manager assess labor costs, the long-term benefits of new technologies, and quality improvements. Accounting can help the operations manager monitor the production system's vital signs by developing multiple tracking methods. The operations manager can then identify problems and prescribe remedies. Accounting also has an impact on the operations function because of the order-fulfillment cycle, which begins when the customer places an order and is completed when operations hands it off to accounting for billing.

In securing and investing the company's capital assets, finance influences operations' decisions about investments in new technology, layout redesign, capacity expansion, and even inventory levels. Similarly, human resources interacts with operations to hire and train workers and aids in changeovers related to new process and job designs. Human resources can help make promotions and transfers into and out of operations easier, thereby encouraging cross-functional understanding. Engineering can also have a big impact on operations. In designing new products, engineering needs to consider technical trade-offs. It must ensure that product designs do not create costly specifications or exceed operations capabilities.

ACHIEVING CROSS-FUNCTIONAL COORDINATION. Several approaches may be used to achieve cross-functional coordination. Each organization should select some blend of them to get everyone pulling in the same direction.

How can coordination be achieved with other functional areas?

❏ A unified strategy should be developed by management as a starting point, giving each department a vision of what it must do to help fulfill the overall organizational strategy.

❏ The organizational structure and management hierarchy can be redesigned to promote cross-functional coordination. Drawing departmental lines around areas of specialization may work against integration by creating insular views and "turf battles." Another option is to organize around major product lines or processes.

❏ The goal-setting process and reward systems can encourage cross-functional coordination. So can bringing people together from different functional areas—through task forces or committees—to make decisions and solve problems.

❏ Improvements to information systems also can boost coordination. Information must in part be tailored to the needs of each functional manager. However, sharing information helps harmonize the efforts of managers from different parts of the organization and enables them to make decisions consistent with organizational goals.

❏ Informal social systems are another device that can be used to encourage better understanding across functional lines. Joint cafeteria facilities, exercise rooms, and social events can help build a sense of camaraderie, as can corporate training and development programs.

❏ Employee selection and promotion also can help foster more cross-functional coordination by encouraging broad perspectives and common goals. Of course, employees must first be competent in their own skill areas.

The best mix of approaches depends on the organization. Some organizations need more coordination than others. The need is greatest when functions are dispersed (owing to organizational structure or geographical distance), organizations are large, and many products or services are customized. The need is also crucial in service organizations that have high customer contact and provide services directly to the customer.

OPERATIONS MANAGEMENT AS A COMPETITIVE WEAPON

In the global era, business and government leaders are increasingly recognizing the importance of involving the whole organization in making strategic decisions. Because the organization usually commits the bulk of its human and financial assets to operations, operations is an important function in meeting global competition. More than 30 years ago, Wickham Skinner suggested that operations could be either a competitive weapon or a millstone (see Skinner, 1969). He concluded that, all too often, operations policies covering inventory levels, schedules, and capacity reflect incorrect assumptions about corporate strategy and may work against a firm's strategic goals. This lack of understanding can waste a firm's resources for years.

Largely because of foreign competition and the explosion of new technologies, recognition is growing that a firm competes not only by offering new products and services, creative marketing, and skillful finance but also with unique competencies in operations. The organization that can offer superior products and services at lower prices is a formidable competitor.

EQUATION SUMMARY

1. Productivity is the ratio of output to input, or

$$\text{Productivity} = \frac{\text{Output}}{\text{Input}}$$

CHAPTER HIGHLIGHTS

❐ Every organization must manage processes and the operations by which these processes are performed. Processes are the fundamental activity that organizations use to do work and achieve their goals. Value is added for the customer by transforming inputs into outputs for customers. Inputs include human resources (workers and managers), capital resources (equipment and facilities), purchased materials and services, land, and energy. Outputs are goods and services.

❐ The concept of processes applies not just to an entire organization but also to the work of each department and individual. Each has work processes and customers (whether internal or external).

❐ A process can be broken down into subprocesses, which in turn can be broken down still further. A process within a process is known as a *nested process.*

❐ Types of decisions with which operations managers are involved include *strategic choices* (operations strategy); *process* (process management, project processes, managing technology); *quality* (total quality management and statistical process control); *capacity, location,* and *layout;* and *operating decisions* (supply-chain management, forecasting, inventory management, aggregate planning, resource planning, lean systems, and scheduling).

❐ Decisions within operations should be linked. For example, quality, process, capacity, and inventory decisions affect one another and should not be made independently. Strategy (long-range plans) and tactical analysis (for short-range decision making) should complement each other.

❐ Operations requires utilization of a variety of skills and technologies. It plays a key role in determining productivity, which is the prime determinant of profitability and, in the aggregate, a nation's standard of living.

❐ Smart managers use multiple performance measures to monitor and improve performance.

❐ Several trends are at work in operations management: Service sector employment is growing; productivity is a concern, particularly in the service sector; and global competition is intensifying. The pursuit of better quality, competition based on time, and rapid technological change are also important trends. Awareness in business education of environmental, ethical, and workforce diversity concerns is increasing.

❐ Operations managers must deal with both intra-organizational and interorganizational relationships. For operations to be used successfully as a competitive weapon, it must address interfunctional concerns. Tomorrow's managers in every functional area must understand operations.

❐ Corporate strategy involves monitoring and adjusting to changes in the external environment and exploiting core competencies. The Internet has caused firms to reevaluate their strategic planning process. Firms taking a global view may form strategic alliances through collaborative efforts, joint ventures, or licensing of technology.

❐ Market analysis is key to formulating a customer-driven operations strategy. Market segmentation and needs assessment are methods of pinpointing elements of a product or service that satisfy customers.

❑ Customer-driven operations strategy requires translating market needs into desirable capabilities for the operations function, called competitive priorities. There are eight priorities: low-cost operations, high-performance design, consistent quality, fast delivery time, on-time delivery, development speed, customization, and volume flexibility. Trade-offs among them are sometimes necessary. Management must decide on which dimensions the firm's processes should excel.

❑ With time-based competition, managers seek to save time on the various steps taken to deliver a product or service.

❑ Concurrent engineering during product and service planning involves operations and other functions early in the development and testing of a new product or service.

❑ Processes devoted to producing services choose one of the following three operations strategies: standardized services, which facilitate low-cost operations, consistent quality, and on-time delivery; assemble-to-order services, which facilitate customization and fast delivery time; and customized services, which facilitate high-performance design and customization.

❑ Processes devoted to manufacturing choose one of the following three operations strategies: make-to-stock, which facilitates low costs, consistent quality, and fast delivery time; manufacturing assemble-to-order, which facilitates fast delivery time and customization; and make-to-order, which facilitates customization and low volumes.

❑ Mass customization is a form of the assemble-to-order strategy, whereby a firm uses both flexible and standard processes to produce customized products or services in high volumes at reasonable costs.

❑ Operations strategy is a pattern of decisions, starting with a choice of service or manufacturing strategy and addressing the many processes that support it.

CD-ROM RESOURCES

The Student CD-ROM that accompanies this text contains the following resources, which allow you to further practice and apply the concepts presented in this chapter.

❑ **OM Explorer Tutor:** OM Explorer contains a tutor program that will help you learn more about productivity measures. See the Chapter 1 folder in OM Explorer. See also the exercise requiring the use of the tutor program.

❑ **Equation Summary:** All the equations for this chapter can be found in one convenient location.

❑ **Discussion Questions:** Seventeen questions will challenge your understanding of the role of operations management and operations strategy.

❑ **Cases:**

• Chad's Creative Concepts: Traditionally a custom manufacturer, how should Chad Thomas cope with the new move into standard products sold by retail outlets?

• BSB, Inc.: The Pizza Wars Come to Campus: How should Renee Kershaw react to product proliferation?

❑ **Tours :** See how the Lower Florida Key Health System community hospital uses a customized services strategy and how Chaparral Steel designed its processes for competitive operations.

❑ **Experiential Exercise:** Min-Yo Garment Company. Experience the challenges of matching markets with the capability of your manufacturing process in this exciting in-class simulation.

❑ **Supplement A:** Decision Making. This supplement provides the background to use break-even analysis, preference matrices, decision theory, and decision trees.

INTERACTIVE RESOURCES

The Interactive Web site associated with this text (www.prenhall.com/ritzman) contains many tools and activities specifically designed for this chapter. The following items are recommended to enhance your understanding of the material in this chapter.

❐ **Internet Activities:** Try out 11 different links to explore operations strategy topics including global competition, environmental leadership, competitive priorities, core competencies, high-performance design, product variety, expansion strategies, and starting a new business.

❐ **Internet Tours:** Compare the operations strategy of Baja Spas to that of Hershey Foods and the manufacturing processes of Thompson-Shore Book Bindery to those of the ski producer, K2 Corporation.

SELECTED REFERENCES

Berry, W. L., C. Bozarth, T. Hill, and J. E. Klompmaker. "Factory Focus: Segmenting Markets from an Operations Perspective." *Journal of Operations Management,* vol. 10, no. 3 (1991), pp. 363–387.

Blackburn, Joseph. *Time-Based Competition: The Next Battleground in American Manufacturing.* Homewood, IL.: Business One–Irwin, 1991.

Bowen, David E., Richard B. Chase, Thomas G. Cummings, and Associates. *Service Management Effectiveness.* San Francisco: Jossey-Bass, 1990.

Buchholz, Rogene A. "Corporate Responsibility and the Good Society: From Economics to Ecology." *Business Horizons* (July–August 1991), pp. 19–31.

Collier, David A. *The Service Quality Solution.* Milwaukee: ASQC Quality Press, and Burr Ridge, IL.: Irwin Professional Publishing, 1994.

Feitzinger, Edward, and Hau L. Lee. "Mass Customization at Hewlett-Packard: The Power of Postponement." *Harvard Business Review,* vol. 75, no. 1 (1997), pp. 116–121.

Fitzsimmons, James A., and Mona Fitzsimmons. *Service Management for Competitive Advantage.* New York: McGraw-Hill, 1994.

Gilmore, James H., and B. Joseph Pine II. "The Four Faces of Mass Customization." *Harvard Business Review,* vol. 75, no. 1 (1997), pp. 91–101.

Hammer, Michael, and Steven Stanton. "How Process Enterprises Really Work." *Harvard Business Review* (November–December 1999), pp. 108–120.

Hayes, Robert H., and Gary P. Pisano. "Beyond World-Class: The New Manufacturing Strategy." *Harvard Business Review* (January–February 1994), pp. 77–86.

Heskett, James L., and Leonard A. Schlesenger. "The Service-Driven Service Company." *Harvard Business Review* (September–October 1991), pp. 71–81.

Hill, Terry. *Manufacturing Strategy: Text and Cases,* 3d ed. Homewood, IL.: Irwin/McGraw-Hill, 2000.

"The Horizontal Corporation." *Business Week* (December 20, 1993), pp. 76–81.

Kaplan, Robert S., and David P. Norton. *Balanced Scoreboard.* Boston, MA: Harvard Business School Press, 1997.

O'Reilly, Brian. "They've Got Mail!" *Fortune* (February 7, 2000), pp. 101–112.

Pine, B. Joseph II, Bart Victor, and Andrew C. Boynton. "Making Mass Customization Work." *Harvard Business Review* (September–October 1993), pp. 108–119.

Post, James E. "Managing as If the Earth Mattered." *Business Horizons* (July–August 1991), pp. 32–38.

Prahalad, C. K., and Venkatram Ramaswamy. "Co-opting Customer Competence." *Harvard Business Review* (January–February 2000), pp. 79–87.

Roach, Stephen S. "Services Under Siege — The Restructuring Imperative." *Harvard Business Review* (September–October 1991), pp. 82–91.

Roth, Aleda V., and Marjolijn van der Velde. "Operations as Marketing: A Competitive Service Strategy." *Journal of Operations Management,* vol. 10, no. 3 (1993), pp. 303–328.

Safizadeh, H. M., L. P. Ritzman, D. Sharma, and C. Wood. "An Empirical Analysis of the Product–Process Matrix." *Management Science,* vol. 42, no. 11 (1996), pp. 1576–1591.

Schmenner, Roger W. *Service Operations Management.* Englewood Cliffs, NJ: Prentice-Hall, 1995.

"Service Exports and the U.S. Economy." *International Trade Association*. U.S. Government. www.ita.doc.gov/industry/osi/se.html.

Skinner, Wickham. "Manufacturing—Missing Link in Corporate Strategy." *Harvard Business Review* (May–June 1969), pp. 136–145.

Skinner, Wickham. "Manufacturing Strategy on the 'S' Curve." *Production and Operations Management,* vol. 5, no. 1 (1996), pp. 3–14.

Stalk, George, Jr., P. Evans, and P. E. Schulman. "Competing on Capabilities: The New Rules of Corporate Strategy," *Harvard Business Review* (March–April 1992), pp. 57–69.

"Time for a Reality Check in Asia." *Business Week* (December 2, 1996), pp. 58–66.

van Biema, Michael, and Bruce Greenwald, "Managing Our Way to Higher Service-Sector Productivity." *Harvard Business Review* (July–August 1997), pp. 87–95.

Ward, Peter T., Deborah J. Bickford, and G. Keong Leong. "Configurations of Manufacturing Strategy, Business Strategy, Environment and Structure." *Journal of Management,* vol. 22, no. 4 (1996), pp. 597–626.

Wheelwright, Steven C., and H. Kent Bowen. "The Challenge of Manufacturing Advantage." *Production and Operations Management,* vol. 5, no. 1 (1996), pp. 59–77.

Womack, James P., Daniel T. Jones, and Daniel Roos. *The Machine That Changed the World.* New York: HarperPerennial, 1991.

Process Management

Across the Organization

Process management is important to . . .

- ❑ **accounting,** which seeks better ways to perform its work processes and provides cost analyses of process improvement proposals.
- ❑ **finance,** which seeks better processes to perform its work, does financial analyses of new process proposals, and looks for ways to raise funds to finance automation.
- ❑ **human resources,** which melds process and job design decisions into an effective whole.
- ❑ **management information systems,** which identifies how information technologies can support the exchange of information.
- ❑ **marketing,** which seeks better processes to perform its work and explores opportunities to expand market share by encouraging ongoing customer dialogue.
- ❑ **operations,** which designs and manages production processes in order to maximize customer value and enhance a firm's core competencies.

Learning Goals

After reading this chapter, you will be able to . . .

1. describe each of the main process decisions and how they must relate to volume.
2. explain when less vertical integration and more outsourcing are appropriate and how resource flexibility supports competitive priorities.
3. describe the different ways that customer contact can affect a process.
4. explain the meaning of automation and economies of scope.
5. discuss how service strategy, capital intensity, and customer involvement influence processes of service providers.
6. explain the concept of focused factories and how it applies to service providers.
7. explain how to analyze a process, using such supporting tools as flow diagrams, process charts, and simulation.
8. describe the key elements of process reengineering and analyze a process for improvements, using flow diagrams, process charts, and a questioning attitude.

Duke Power (www.duke-energy.com) is a true pioneer of the enterprise process. The electric utility arm of Duke Energy, Duke Power serves nearly 2 million customers in North and South Carolina. In 1995, with deregulation looming, the company realized that its processes had to do a much better job of customer service. But the existing organizational structure of Customer Operations, the business unit responsible for delivering electricity to customers, was getting in the way of process improvements. The unit was divided into four regional profit centers, and regional vice presidents had little time for wrestling with process improvements for customer service. And even if they had, there was no way to coordinate their efforts across regions.

The new structure at Duke Power requires collaboration between process managers and the regional vice presidents. Teamwork is essential in the design and operation of processes.

To resolve the problem, Duke Power identified the five core processes that together encompassed the essential work of Customer Operations: developing market strategies, maintaining customers, providing reliability and integrity, delivering products and services, and calculating and collecting revenues. Each process was assigned an owner, and the five process owners, like the four existing regional vice presidents, now report directly to the head of Customer Operations. Process owners are senior managers with end-to-end responsibility for enterprise processes, and they embody the company's commitment to better process management.

With the new structure, regional vice presidents continue to manage their own workforces—the process owners have only small staffs—but process owners have been given vast authority over the design and operation of the processes. They decide how work will proceed at every step. Then they establish performance targets and set budgets among regions. In other words, while regions have authority over people, they are evaluated on how well they meet goals set by process owners. This structure requires a new collaborative style of management, in which the process managers and regional vice presidents act as partners rather than rivals. Teams are composed of individuals with broad process knowledge and they are measured on performance. They take over most of the managerial responsibilities usually held by supervisors. Supervisors, in turn, become more like coaches. Because the same employees are often involved in several processes, sometimes simultaneously, processes overlap. Process owners promote process improvements and continually seek to add value to the customer.

Source: Stanton, Steven. "How Process Enterprises Really Work," *Harvard Business Review* (November–December 1999), pp. 108–117.

ONE ESSENTIAL ISSUE IN the design of processes is deciding how to make products or provide services. Deciding on processes involves many different choices in selecting human resources, equipment, and materials. Processes are involved in how marketing prepares a market analysis, how accounting bills customers, how a retail store provides services on the sales floor, and how a manufacturing plant performs its assembly operations. Process decisions can affect an organization's ability to compete over the long run.

Process decisions are also strategic in nature. As we saw in Chapter 1, they should further a company's long-term competitive goals. In making process decisions, managers focus on controlling such competitive priorities as quality, flexibility, time, and cost. For example, firms can improve their ability to compete on the basis of time by examining each step of their processes and finding ways to respond more quickly to their customers. Productivity (and, therefore, cost) is affected by choices made when processes are designed. Process management is an ongoing activity, with the same principles applying to both first-time and redesign choices. Thus, the processes at Duke Power are in constant change.

We begin by defining five basic process decisions: process choice, vertical integration, resource flexibility, customer involvement, and capital intensity. We discuss these decisions for both manufacturing and service processes, and methods of focusing operations. We pay particular attention both to ways in which services strategy, capital intensity, and customer involvement affect service operations and to methods for focusing operations. We then present a systematic approach to designing processes, using flow diagrams, process charts, and simulation. We conclude with two basic philosophies of analyzing and modifying processes—reengineering and process improvement.

WHAT IS PROCESS MANAGEMENT?

process management
The selection of the inputs, operations, work flows, and methods that transform inputs into outputs.

A process involves the use of an organization's resources to provide something of value. No product can be made and no service provided without a process, and no process can exist without a product or service.

Process management is the selection of the inputs, operations, work flows, and methods that transform inputs into outputs. Input selection begins by deciding which processes are to be done in-house and which processes are to be done outside and purchased as materials and services. Process decisions also deal with the proper mix of human skills and equipment and which parts of the processes are to be performed by each. Decisions about processes must be consistent with competitive priorities (see Chapter 1, "Competing with Operations") and the organization's ability to obtain the resources necessary to support them.

Process decisions must be made when

- ❑ a new or substantially modified product or service is being offered
- ❑ quality must be improved
- ❑ competitive priorities have changed
- ❑ demand for a product or service is changing
- ❑ current performance is inadequate
- ❑ the cost or availability of inputs has changed
- ❑ competitors are gaining by using a new process
- ❑ new technologies are available

Not all such situations lead to changes in current processes. Process decisions must also take into account other choices, such as quality, capacity, layout, and inventory. Moreover, managers must consider advances in technology and changing competitor capabilities. The impact on the environment is another consideration. A good example is McDonald's. It made subtle changes in the processes used to package food, reducing waste by more than 30 percent since 1990 and becoming one of the country's leading buyers of recycled materials. The greening of McDonald's entailed replacing "clamshell" boxes with special light-weight paper, introducing shorter napkins, and relying less on plastics in straws, dining trays, and playground equipment.

McDonald's is now looking at a plan to turn waste into fertilizer, so that eating out could generate less waste than eating at many homes.

There are two principles concerning process management that are particularly important.

1. Processes underlie all work activity and are found in all organizations and in all functions of an organization. Accounting uses certain processes to do payroll, ledger control, and revenue accounting. Finance uses other processes to evaluate investment alternatives and project financial performance. Human resources uses various processes to administer benefits, recruit new employees, and conduct training programs. Marketing uses its own processes to do market research and communicate with external customers.

2. Processes are nested within other processes along an organization's supply chain. A firm's **supply chain** (sometimes called the *value chain*) is an interconnected set of linkages among suppliers of materials and services that spans the transformation processes that convert ideas and raw materials into finished goods and services. One key decision, which we cover here, is selecting the parts of the chain to provide internally and how best to perform these processes. An essential task is to coordinate process linkages. Whether processes are internal or external, management must pay particular attention to the interfaces between processes. Having to deal with these interfaces underscores the need for cross-functional coordination (see Chapter 1, "Competing with Operations") and coordination with suppliers and customers (see Chapter 8, "Supply-Chain Management").

supply chain An inter-connected set of linkages among suppliers of materials and services that spans the transformation processes that convert ideas and raw materials into finished goods and services; also referred to as the value chain.

MAJOR PROCESS DECISIONS

Process decisions directly affect the process itself and indirectly the products and services that it provides. Whether dealing with processes for offices, service providers, or manufacturers, operations managers must consider five common process decisions: process choice, vertical integration, resource flexibility, customer involvement, and capital intensity. Process decisions act as building blocks that are used in different ways to implement operations strategy.

PROCESS CHOICE

How can operations strategy best be implemented?

process choice A process decision that determines whether resources are organized around products or processes.

One of the first decisions a manager makes in designing a well-functioning process is **process choice**, which determines whether resources are organized around products or processes. The choice is strongly influenced by the competitive priorities (see Chapter 1, "Competing with Operations") given to the process. However, what is emphasized for the overall facility or product line is not necessarily what should be emphasized for each of the processes or subprocesses that provide the product or service. The manager has five process types, which form a continuum, to choose from:

1. project
2. job
3. batch
4. line
5. continuous

Figure 2.1 shows that these types of processes are found in manufacturing and services organizations alike. In fact, some manufacturers' processes provide a service and do not involve manufacturing, as Figure 2.1a demonstrates with the project process examples. The fundamental message in Figure 2.1 is that the best choice for a process depends on the volume and degree of customization required of the process. A process choice might apply to an entire process or just one subprocess within it. For example, one of a service facility's processes might best be characterized as a job process and another process as a line process. Because our definition of a process in Chapter 1 provides a basic understanding of processes in general, we now concentrate on the differences among the five process choices.

PROJECT PROCESS. Examples of a project process are building a shopping center, forming a project team to do a task (such as a student team doing a course project), planning a major event, running a political campaign, putting together a comprehensive training program, doing management consulting work, or developing a new technology or

FIGURE 2.1a

The Influence of Customization and Volume on Process Choice

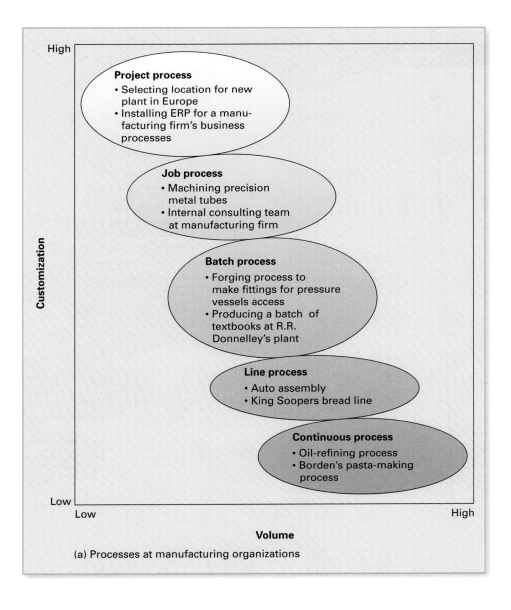

project process A process characterized by a high degree of job customization, the large scope of each project, and the release of substantial resources once a project is completed.

product. A **project process** is characterized by a high degree of job customization, the large scope of each project, and the release of substantial resources once a project is completed. A project process lies at the high-customization, low-volume end of the process-choice continuum. The sequence of operations and the process involved in each are unique to the project, creating one-of-a-kind products or services made specifically to customer order. Although some projects may look similar, each is unique. Project processes are valued on the basis of their capabilities to do certain kinds of work rather than their ability to produce specific products or services. Projects tend to be complex, take a long time, and be large. Many interrelated tasks must be completed, requiring close coordination (see Chapter 3, "Managing Project Processes"). Resources needed for a project are assembled and then released for further use after the project is finished. Projects typically make heavy use of certain skills and resources at particular stages and then have little use for them the rest of the time. With a project process, work flows are redefined with each new project.

FIGURE 2.1b

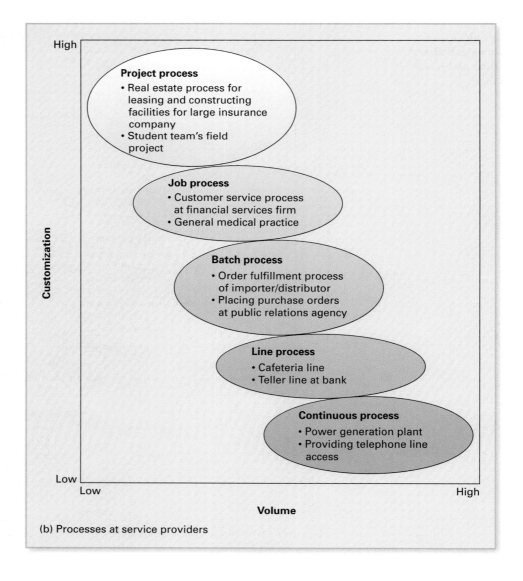

(b) Processes at service providers

JOB PROCESS. Next in the continuum of process choices is the job process. Examples are machining a metal casting for a customized order, providing emergency room care, handling special-delivery mail, and making customized cabinets. A **job process** creates the flexibility needed to produce a variety of products or services in significant quantities. Customization is relatively high and volume for any one product or service is low. However, volumes are not as low as for a project process, which by definition does not produce in quantity. The workforce and equipment are flexible and handle various tasks.

As with a project process, companies choosing a job process often bid for work. Typically, they make products to order and do not produce them ahead of time. The specific needs of the next customer are unknown, and the timing of repeat orders from the same customer is unpredictable. Each new order is handled as a single unit—as a job.

A job process primarily organizes all like resources around itself (rather than allocating them out to specific products and services); equipment and workers capable of certain types of work are located together. These resources process all jobs requiring that type of work. Because customization is high and most jobs have a different sequence of processing steps, this process choice creates *jumbled flows* through the operations rather than a line flow. A **line flow** means that materials, information, or customers move linearly from one operation to the next according to a fixed sequence. While there is considerable variability in the flows through a job process, there can be some line flows within it. Some subprocesses nested within the process can be identical for all jobs or customers. For example, the auto finance process at a bank is a job process, but subprocesses (such as handling retail loan payments) are batch or line processes. Also, some customers of a job process place repeat orders from time to time. These conditions create higher volumes, some line flows, and more make-to-stock and standardized-service possibilities than are found with a project process.

BATCH PROCESS. Examples of a batch process are scheduling air travel for a group, making components that feed an assembly line, processing mortgage loans, and manufacturing capital equipment. A **batch process** differs from the job process with respect to volume, variety, and quantity. The primary difference is that volumes are higher because the same or similar products or services are provided repeatedly. Another difference is that a narrower range of products and services is provided. Variety is achieved more through an assemble-to-order strategy than the job process's make-to-order or customized-services strategies (see Chapter 1, "Competing with Operations"). Some of the components going into the final product or service may be processed in advance.

A third difference is that production lots or customer groups are handled in larger quantities (or *batches*) than they are with job processes. A batch of one product or customer grouping is processed, and then production is switched to the next one. Eventually, the first product or service is produced again. A batch process has average or moderate volumes, but variety is still too great to warrant dedicating a separate process for each product or service. The flow pattern is jumbled, with no standard sequence of operations throughout the facility. However, more dominant paths emerge than at a job process, and some segments of the process have a line flow.

LINE PROCESS. Products created by a line process include automobiles, appliances, and toys. Services based on a line process are fast-food restaurants and cafeterias. A **line process** lies between the batch and continuous processes on the continuum, volumes are high, and products or services are standardized, which allows resources to be organized around a product or service. There are line flows, with little inventory held between operations. Each operation performs the same process over and over, with little variability in the products or services provided.

job process A process with the flexibility needed to produce a variety of products or services in significant qualities.

line flow The linear movement of materials, information, or customers from one operation to the next according to a fixed sequence.

batch process A process that differs from the job process with respect to volume, variety, and quality.

line process A process that lies between the batch and continuous processes on the continuum, volumes are high, and products or services are standardized, which allows resources to be organized around a product or service.

Production orders are not directly linked to customer orders, as is the case with project and job processes. Service providers with a line process follow a standardized-services strategy. Manufacturers with line processes often follow a make-to-stock strategy, with standard products held in inventory so that they are ready when a customer places an order. This use of a line process is sometimes called *mass production*, which is what the popular press commonly refers to as a manufacturing process. However, the assemble-to-order strategy and *mass customization* (see Chapter 1, "Competing with Operations") are other possibilities with line processes. Product variety is possible by careful control of the addition of standard options to the main product or service.

CONTINUOUS PROCESS. Examples are petroleum refineries, chemical plants, and plants making beer, steel, and food (such as Borden's huge pasta-making plant). Firms with such facilities are also referred to as the *process industry*. An electric generation plant represents one of the few continuous processes found in the service sector. A **continuous process** is the extreme end of high-volume, standardized production with rigid line flows. Its name derives from the way materials move through the process. Usually, one primary material, such as a liquid, gas, or powder, moves without stopping through the facility. The processes seem more like separate entities than a series of connected operations. The process is often capital-intensive and operated round the clock to maximize utilization and to avoid expensive shutdowns and start-ups.

VERTICAL INTEGRATION

All businesses buy at least some inputs to their processes, such as professional services, raw materials, or manufactured parts, from other producers. **Vertical integration** is the degree to which a firm's own production system or service facility handles the entire supply chain. The more that the processes are performed in-house rather than by suppliers or customers, the greater is the degree of vertical integration. Management decides the level of vertical integration by looking at all the processes performed between the acquisition of raw materials or outside services and the delivery of finished products or services. If it doesn't perform some processes itself, it must rely on **outsourcing,** or paying suppliers and distributors to perform those processes and provide needed services and materials. When managers opt for more vertical integration, there is by definition less outsourcing. These decisions are sometimes called **make-or-buy decisions,** with a *make* decision meaning more integration and a *buy* decision meaning more outsourcing. After deciding what to outsource and what to do in-house, management must find ways to coordinate and integrate the various processes and suppliers involved (see Chapter 8, "Supply-Chain Management").

BACKWARD AND FORWARD INTEGRATION. Vertical integration can be in two directions. **Backward integration** represents movement upstream toward the sources of raw materials and parts, such as a major grocery chain having its own plants to produce house brands of ice cream, frozen pizza dough, and peanut butter. **Forward integration** means that the firm acquires more channels of distribution, such as its own distribution centers (warehouses) and retail stores. It can also mean that the firm goes even further by acquiring its business customers.

ADVANTAGES OF VERTICAL INTEGRATION AND OUTSOURCING. The advantages of more vertical integration are the disadvantages of more outsourcing. Similarly, the advantages of more outsourcing are disadvantages of more vertical integration. Managers must study the options carefully before making choices. Break-even analysis and financial analysis (see Supplement A, "Decision Making" and Supplement B, "Financial Analysis" on the

---

continuous process The extreme end of high-volume, standardized production with rigid line flows.

Which services and products should be created in-house?

vertical integration The degree to which a firm's own production system or service facility handles the entire supply chain.

outsourcing Allotting payment to suppliers and distributors to provide needed services and materials and to perform those processes that the organization does not perform itself.

make-or-buy decisions Decisions that either involve more integration (a *make* decision) or more outsourcing (a *buy* decision).

backward integration A firm's movement upstream toward the sources of raw materials and parts.

forward integration A firm's movement downstream by acquiring more channels of distribution, such as its own distribution centers (warehouses) and retail sources.

Student CD-ROM) are good starting points. However, the need for strategic fit is fundamental to all choices and must reflect qualitative as well as quantitative factors if analyses are to be complete.

Advantages of Vertical Integration. More vertical integration can sometimes improve market share and allow a firm to enter foreign markets more easily than it could otherwise. A firm can also achieve savings if it has the skills, volume, and resources to perform processes at lower cost and produce higher-quality goods and services than outsiders can. Doing the work in-house may mean better quality and more timely delivery—and taking better advantage of the firm's human resources, equipment, and space. Extensive vertical integration is generally attractive when input volumes are high because high volumes allow task specialization and greater efficiency. It is also attractive if the firm has the relevant skills and views the processes that it is integrating as particularly important to its future success.

Management must identify, cultivate, and exploit its core competencies to prevail in global competition. Recall that core competencies are the collective learning of the firm, especially its ability for coordinating diverse processes and integrating multiple technologies (see Chapter 1, "Competing with Operations"). They define the firm and provide its reason for existence. Management must look upstream toward its suppliers and downstream toward its customers and bring in-house those processes that give it the right core competencies—those that allow the firm to organize work and deliver value better than its competitors. Management should also realize that if the firm outsources a critical process, it may lose control over that area of its business—and perhaps the ability to bring the work in-house later.

Advantages of Outsourcing. Outsourcing offers several advantages to firms. It is particularly attractive to those that have low volumes. Outsourcing can also provide better quality and cost savings. For example, foreign locations sometimes offer lower wages and yield higher productivity. Firms are doing more outsourcing than ever before.

Two factors contributing to this trend are global competition and information technology. Globalization creates more supplier options, and advances in information technology make coordination with suppliers easier. IKEA, the largest retailer of home furnishings, has 30 buying offices around the world to seek out suppliers. Its Vienna-based business service department runs a computer database that helps suppliers locate raw materials and new business partners. Cash registers at its stores around the world relay sales data to the nearest warehouse and its operational headquarters in Älmhult, Sweden, where its information systems provide the data needed to control its shipping patterns worldwide.

virtual corporation
A situation in which competitors enter into short-term partnerships to respond to market opportunities.

network companies
Companies that contract with other firms for most of their production and for many of their other functions.

The Virtual Corporation. Information technology allows suppliers to come together as a virtual corporation. In a **virtual corporation,** competitors actually enter into short-term partnerships to respond to market opportunities. Teams in different organizations and at different locations collaborate on design, production, and marketing, with information going electronically from place to place. They disband when the project is completed. Virtual corporations allow firms to change their positions flexibly in response to quickly changing market demands.

An extreme case of outsourcing is **network companies,** which contract with other firms for most of their production—and for many of their other functions. Li & Fung, which we discussed in the Managerial Practice, is a good example. The name comes from their employees spending most of their time on the telephone or at the computer, coordinating suppliers. If demand for the network company's products or services

MANAGERIAL PRACTICE

Choosing the Right Amount of Vertical Integration

More Integration (Less Outsourcing)

The Citgo Petroleum Corporation's (www.citgo.com) triangular emblem is more visible at U.S. gas stations thanks to its addition of 14,000 new U.S. outlets, surpassing the number bearing the rival Texaco star. The red, white, and blue emblem is a symbol of a massive push into the United States by parent Petroleos de Venezuela (PDVSA), the $22 billion Venezuelan state oil company. It also signals a drive by key producers in OPEC to lock up shares in global markets by investing heavily in "downstream" refining and retailing as the cartel loses its hold on crude supplies and prices. "We believe that the fundamentals of the oil business indicate that you should be as integrated as possible," says the PDVSA president.

Tulsa-based Citgo, PDVSA's $10 billion U.S. refining and marketing subsidiary, has been growing at double-digit rates. To add to its six refineries in the United States, it is discussing ventures with Phillips Petroleum Company, Mobil Corporation, and others that could add retailing strength. In Europe, it has a joint refining venture with Germany's Veba. PDVSA's strategy of increased vertical integration is being embraced by other big OPEC members. Saudi Arabia and Kuwait, for example, are buying into refineries in markets such as the Philippines and India.

Less Integration (More Outsourcing)

Li & Fung (www.lifung.com), Hong Kong's largest export trading company, has a predominantly American and European customer base. This multinational firm outsources most of its manufacturing, using what is called "dispersed manufacturing" or "borderless manufacturing." It still performs the higher-value-added processes in Hong Kong but outsources lower-value-added processes to the best possible locations around the world. Thus, it retains processes for designing products, buying and inspecting raw materials, managing factories and developing production schedules, and controlling quality. But it does not manage the workers, and it does not own the factories.

Li & Fung's approach goes beyond outsourcing to suppliers and letting them worry about contracting for raw materials. Any single factory is small and does not have the buying power to demand fast deliveries and good prices. Li & Fung may know, for instance, that The Limited is going to order 100,000 garments but does not yet know the style or colors. The firm reserves undyed yarn from its yarn supplier and locks up capacity at supplier mills for weaving. Because this approach is more complicated, Li & Fung was forced to get smart about logistics and dissecting the value chain. It is an innovator in supply-chain management techniques, using a host of information-intensive service processes for product development, sourcing, shipping, handling, and logistics. For its enterprise process of executing and tracking orders, it has its own standardized, fully computerized operating system, and everybody in the company uses it. Essentially, therefore, Li & Fung manages information and the relationships among 350 customers and 7,500 suppliers and does so with a lot of phone calls, faxes, and on-site visits. In time, the firm will need a sophisticated information system with an open architecture that can handle work in Hong Kong and New York, as well as in places like Bangladesh, where you cannot always count on a good phone line.

The competitive priorities of customization and fast delivery usually do not match up well together, but Li & Fung achieves both by organizing around small, customer-focused units. One unit might be a theme-store division that serves a handful of customers such as Warner Brothers stores and Rainforest Café. Its retailing customers are in consumer-driven, fast-moving markets and face the problem of obsolete inventory with a vengeance. If a retailer shortens its buying cycle from three months to five weeks, it gains eight weeks to develop a better sense of where the market is heading. Forecasting accuracy improves, and there is less need for markdowns of obsolete inventory at the end of the selling season. Such payoffs to Li & Fung's customers make it a valued supplier. During the last decade, the focus was on supplier partnerships to improve cost and quality. In today's faster-paced markets, the focus has shifted to innovation, flexibility, and speed.

Sources: "Stepping on the Gas with Citgo," *Business Week* (March 11, 1996); "Fast, Global, and Entrepreneurial: Supply Chain Management, Hong Kong Style: An Interview with Victor Fung," *Harvard Business Review* (September–October 1998), pp. 103–115.

changes, its employees simply pass this message along to suppliers, who change their output levels. Network companies can move in and out of markets, riding the waves of fashion and technology. However, network companies are vulnerable to new competition because the investment barriers to enter their businesses are low and because they lose business if their suppliers integrate forward or their customers integrate backward.

RESOURCE FLEXIBILITY

resource flexibility The ease with which employees and equipment can handle a wide variety of products, output levels, duties, and functions.

flexible workforce A workforce whose members are capable of doing many tasks, either at their own workstations or as they move from one workstation to another.

The choices that management makes concerning competitive priorities determine the degree of flexibility required of a company's resources—its employees, facilities, and equipment. **Resource flexibility** is the ease with which employees and equipment can handle a wide variety of products, output levels, duties, and functions. For example, when a process handles products and services with short life cycles or high customization, employees need to perform a broad range of duties and equipment must be general purpose. Otherwise, resource utilization will be too low for economical operation.

WORKFORCE. Operations managers must decide whether to have a flexible workforce. Members of a **flexible workforce** are capable of doing many tasks, either at their own workstations or as they move from one workstation to another. However, such flexibility often comes at a cost, requiring greater skills and, thus, more training and education. Nevertheless, benefits can be large: Worker flexibility can be one of the best ways to achieve reliable customer service and alleviate capacity bottlenecks. Resource flexibility helps to absorb the feast-or-famine workloads in individual operations that are caused by low-volume production, jumbled routings, and fluid scheduling.

The type of workforce required also depends on the need for volume flexibility. When conditions allow for a smooth, steady rate of output, the likely choice is a permanent workforce that expects regular full-time employment. If the process is subject to hourly, daily, or seasonal peaks and valleys in demand, the use of part-time or temporary employees to supplement a smaller core of full-time employees may be the best solution. However, this approach may not be practical if knowledge and skill requirements are too high for a temporary worker to grasp quickly. Controversy is growing over the practice of replacing full-time workers with temporary or part-time workers.

EQUIPMENT. When products or services have a short life cycle and a high degree of customization, low volumes mean that process managers should select flexible, general-purpose equipment. Figure 2.2 illustrates this relationship by showing the total cost lines for two different types of equipment that can be chosen for a process. Each line represents the total annual cost of the process at different volume levels. It is the sum of fixed costs and variable costs (see Supplement A, "Decision Making" on the Student CD-ROM). When volumes are low (because customization is high), process 1 is the better choice. It calls for inexpensive general-purpose equipment, which keeps investment in equipment low and makes fixed costs (F_1) small. Its variable unit cost is high, which

Relationship Between Process Costs and Product Volume

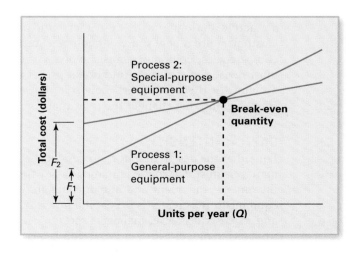

gives its total cost line a relatively steep slope. Process 1 does the job but not at peak efficiency. However, volumes are not high enough for total variable costs to overcome the benefit of low fixed costs.

Conversely, process 2 is the better choice when volumes are high and customization is low. Its advantage is low variable unit cost, as reflected in the flatter total cost line. This efficiency is possible when customization is low because the equipment can be designed for a narrow range of products or tasks. Its disadvantage is high equipment investment and, thus, high fixed costs (F_2). When annual volume produced is high enough, spreading these fixed costs over more units produced, the advantage of low variable costs more than compensates for the high fixed costs.

TUTOR 2.1

CUSTOMER INVOLVEMENT

The fourth significant process decision deals with **customer involvement**, the ways in which customers become part of the process and the extent of their participation. The amount of customer involvement may range from self-service to customization of product to deciding the time and place that the service is to be provided.

How much should customers be involved in processes?

customer involvement The ways in which customers become part of the process and the extent of their participation.

SELF-SERVICE. Self-service is the process decision of many retailers, particularly when price is a competitive priority. To save money, some customers prefer to do part of the process formerly performed by the manufacturer or dealer. Manufacturers of goods such as toys, bicycles, and furniture may also prefer to let the customer perform the final assembly because production, shipping, and inventory costs frequently are lower, as are losses from damage. The firms pass the savings on to customers as lower prices.

PRODUCT SELECTION. A business that competes on customization frequently allows customers to come up with their own product specifications or even become involved in designing the product. A good example of customer involvement is in custom-designed and custom-built homes: The customer is heavily involved in the design process and inspects the work in process at various times.

TIME AND LOCATION. When services cannot be provided in the customer's absence, customers may determine the time and location that the service is to be provided. If the service is delivered to the customer, client, or patient by appointment, decisions involving the location become part of process design. Will the customer be served only on the supplier's premises, will the supplier's employees go to the customer's premises, or will the service be provided at a third location?

In a market where customers are technology enabled, companies can now engage in an active dialogue with customers and make them partners in creating value. Customers are a new source of competence for an organization. To harness customer competencies, companies must involve customers in an ongoing dialogue. They also must revise some of their traditional processes, such as pricing and billing systems, to account for their customers' new role. For example, in business-to-business relationships, the Internet changes the roles that companies play with other businesses.

How much should a firm depend on machinery and automated processes?

capital intensity The mix of equipment and human skill in a process.

CAPITAL INTENSITY

For either the design of a new process or the redesign of an existing one, an operations manager must determine the amount of capital intensity required. **Capital intensity** is the mix of equipment and human skills in the process; the greater the relative cost of equipment, the greater is the capital intensity. As the capabilities of technology increase and its costs decrease, managers face an ever-widening range of choices, from operations utilizing very little automation to those requiring task-specific equipment and

automation A system, process, or piece of equipment that is self-acting and self-regulating.

very little human intervention. **Automation** is a system, process, or piece of equipment that is self-acting and self-regulating. Although automation is often thought to be necessary to gain competitive advantage, it has both advantages and disadvantages. Thus, the automation decision requires careful examination.

One advantage of automation is that adding capital intensity can significantly increase productivity and improve quality. One big disadvantage of capital intensity can be the prohibitive investment cost for low-volume operations. Look again at Figure 2.2. Process 1, which uses general-purpose equipment, is not capital-intensive and, therefore, has small fixed costs, F_1. Although its variable cost per unit produced is high, as indicated by the slope of the total cost line, process 1 is well below the break-even quantity if volumes are low. Generally, capital-intensive operations must have high utilization to be justifiable. Also, automation does not always align with a company's competitive priorities. If a firm offers a unique product or high-quality service, competitive priorities may indicate the need for skilled servers, hand labor, and individual attention rather than new technology.

fixed automation A manufacturing process that produces one type of part or product in a fixed sequence of simple operations.

FIXED AUTOMATION. Manufacturers use two types of automation: fixed and flexible (or programmable). Particularly appropriate for line and continuous process choices, **fixed automation** produces one type of part or product in a fixed sequence of simple operations. Until the mid-1980s, most U.S. automobile plants were dominated by fixed automation—and some still are. Chemical processing plants and oil refineries also utilize this type of automation.

Operations managers favor fixed automation when demand volumes are high, product designs are stable, and product life cycles are long. These conditions compensate for the process's two primary drawbacks: large initial investment cost and relative inflexibility. The investment cost is particularly high when a single, complex machine (called a *transfer machine*) must be capable of handling many operations. Because fixed automation is designed around a particular product, changing equipment to accommodate new products is difficult and costly. However, fixed automation maximizes efficiency and yields the lowest variable cost per unit if volumes are high.

flexible (or programmable) automation A manufacturing process that can be changed easily to handle various products.

FLEXIBLE AUTOMATION. **Flexible (or programmable) automation** can be changed easily to handle various products. The ability to reprogram machines is useful for both low-customization and high-customization processes. In the case of high customization, a machine that makes a variety of products in small batches can be programmed to alternate between products. When a machine has been dedicated to a particular product or family of products, as in the case of low customization and a line flow, and the product is at the end of its life cycle, the machine can simply be reprogrammed with a new sequence of operations for a new product.

Cummins Engine Company, a manufacturer of diesel engines based in Columbus, Indiana, utilizes such flexibility to handle frequent design modifications. For example, in the first 18 months after introducing new compression brakes for its engines, Cummins's engineers made 14 design changes to the brakes. If the brakes had been made on less-flexible machines, these improvements probably would have taken several years and millions of dollars to implement—and, in fact, might not have been made.

RELATIONSHIPS BETWEEN DECISIONS

How should decisions be coordinated with processes?

The process manager should understand how these five process decisions usually tie together, so as to spot ways of improving poorly designed processes. The common denominator in this relationship is volume, which in turn comes from the operations strategy (see Chapter 1, "Competing with Operations").

Figure 2.3 summarizes the relationship between volume and process decisions for service operations. They also apply to manufacturing operations, although with services particular attention must be given to the following two major process decisions:

1. customer involvement
2. capital intensity and automation

High volumes at a service process typically mean all of the following:

1. *A Line Process.* Line flows are preferred, with jobs or customers moving through a series of standardized steps. Each customer gets the same basic service, and service specifications are tightly controlled. Standardized services increase volumes and process repeatability. One example is the front-end process of a cafeteria line, where the customer moves from one station to the next, making food selections and then paying at the end of the line. Other examples include processes in public transportation; movie theaters; backroom processes in

Volume and the Major Process Decisions

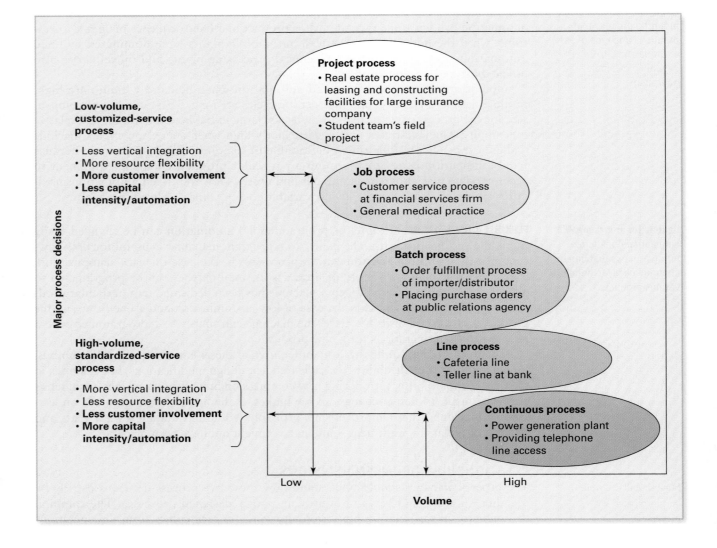

banking, insurance, and postal service; airport baggage handling; spectator sports; and large lecture halls.

2. *More Vertical Integration.* High volumes make it more likely that the service provider will keep the process in-house rather than outsourcing.

3. *Less Resource Flexibility.* High process volumes and repetition create less need for resource flexibility, which can be more expensive. Resources can be dedicated to each standardized service. Skill levels are not high, and jobs are more specialized.

4. *Less Customer Involvement.* Often the customer is not present when the process is performed, as in the backroom operations of financial services institutions. The little contact that occurs between employees and customers is for standardized services. If the customer is involved in the process, it is in performing self-service activities to get lower prices or in selecting from standard service options rather than getting customized treatment.

5. *More Capital Intensity and Automation.* Because the customer is not involved with the process, automation possibilities increase. High process volumes and repetition also allow for more automation. Capital intensity is high, making labor intensity low. Of course, there can be exceptions to always automating high-volume standardized services. Examples are wholesalers, full-service retailers, and large university lecture halls. In such cases, capital intensity is low because the nature of the work being done makes it difficult to achieve automation for these processes.

Low volumes typically mean all of the following:

1. *A Project or Job Process.* Processes must be defined for each new project or job and change considerably from one to the next. Customized treatment means a low-volume process, and each customer requires different changes in the process itself. Examples are processes for management consultants, lawyers, physicians, gourmet restaurants, and corporate bankers. Each customer has individual needs that must be understood and accounted for in the process. Considerable attention is given to a customer's unique requirements and preferences.

2. *Less Vertical Integration.* Low volumes make it more likely that the service provider will seek to outsource many processes rather than keeping them in-house.

3. *More Resource Flexibility.* Employees and equipment must be able to handle new or unique services on demand. Thus, they must be versatile and flexible and able to handle a wide array of customer requests. Skill levels are high and jobs enlarged.

4. *More Customer Involvement.* Employees interact frequently with customers, often on a one-to-one basis, to understand and diagnose each customer's individual needs. They must be able to relate well to their customers, not merely possess technical skills. Exercising judgment as they provide new or unique services and solutions is commonplace.

5. *Less Capital Intensity and Automation.* Because of the infinite variability of problems confronted, the mental and physical requirements of these services are difficult to automate. Capital intensity is low, which means high labor intensity; the high skill levels required are very expensive. Employees have a great deal of operating discretion and relatively loose superior–subordinate relationships. Exceptions do occur, such as certain processes at medical facilities in a smaller community. Some low-volume processes are capital-intensive, because certain expensive equipment is needed to perform services regardless of the volume.

Of course, these are general tendencies rather than rigid prescriptions. Exceptions can be found, but these relationships provide a way of understanding how process decisions can be linked coherently.

ECONOMIES OF SCOPE

Should more economies of scope be sought?

Note that capital intensity and resource flexibility vary inversely in Figure 2.3. If capital intensity is high, resource flexibility is low. In certain types of manufacturing operations, such as machining and assembly, programmable automation breaks this inverse relationship between resource flexibility and capital intensity (see Supplement E, "Computer-Integrated Manufacturing" on the Student CD-ROM). It makes possible both high capital intensity and high resource flexibility, creating economies of scope. **Economies of scope** reflect the ability to produce multiple products more cheaply in combination than separately. In such situations, two conflicting competitive priorities—customization and low price—become more compatible. However, taking advantage of economies of scope requires that a family of parts or products have enough collective volume to utilize equipment fully. Adding a product to the family results in one-time programming (and sometimes fixture) costs. (*Fixtures* are reusable devices that maintain exact tolerances by holding the product firmly in position while it is processed.)

economies of scope Economies that reflect the ability to produce multiple products more cheaply in combination than separately.

Economies of scope also apply to service processes. Consider, for example, Disney's approach to the Internet. When the company's managers entered the volatile Internet world, their businesses were only weakly tied together. They wanted plenty of freedom to evolve in and even shape emerging markets. They wanted flexibility and agility, not control, in these fast-moving markets. Disney's Infoseek business, in fact, was not even fully owned. However, once its Internet markets became more crystallized, managers at Disney moved to reap the benefits of economies of scope. They aggressively linked their Internet processes with one another and with other parts of Disney. They bought the rest of the Infoseek business and then combined it with Internet businesses such as Disney Travel Online into a single business (Go.com). They made their content Web sites accessible from a single portal (Go Network) and created new links to established businesses like ESPN. A flexible technology that handles many services together can be less expensive than handling each one separately, particularly when the markets are not too volatile.

GAINING FOCUS

How can operations be focused?

Before 1970, many firms were willing to endure the additional complexity that went with size. New products or services were added to a facility in the name of better utilizing fixed costs and keeping everything under the same roof. The result was a jumble of competitive priorities, process choices, and technologies. In the effort to do everything, nothing was done well.

FOCUSED FACTORIES. Hewlett-Packard, S. C. Johnson and Sons, Japan's Ricoh and Mitsubishi, and Britain's Imperial Chemical Industries PLC are some of the firms that have created **focused factories**, splitting large plants that produced all the company's products into several specialized smaller plants. The theory is that narrowing the range of demands on a facility will lead to better performance because management can concentrate on fewer tasks and lead a workforce toward a single goal. In some situations, a plant that used to produce all the components of a product and assemble them may split into one that produces the components and one that assembles them so that each can focus on its own individual process technology.

focused factories The result of a firm's splitting large plants that produced all the company's products into several specialized smaller plants.

FOCUS BY PROCESS SEGMENTS. A facility's process often can neither be characterized nor actually designed for one set of competitive priorities and one process choice. At a services facility, some parts of the process might seem like a job process and other parts like a line process. Such arrangements can be effective, provided that sufficient focus is given to each process. **Plants within plants (PWPs)** are different operations within a facility with individualized competitive priorities, processes, and workforces under the same roof. Boundaries for PWPs may be established by physically separating subunits or simply by revising organizational relationships. At each PWP, customization, capital intensity, volume, and other relationships are crucial and must be complementary. The advantages of PWPs are fewer layers of management, greater ability to rely on team problem solving, and shorter lines of communication between departments.

Another way of gaining focus is with the use of cells. A **cell** is a group of two or more dissimilar workstations located close to each other that process a limited number of parts or models with similar process requirements. A cell has line flows, even though the operations around it may have flexible flows (see Chapter 7, "Location and Layout"). The small size of focused factories, PWPs, and cells offers a flexible, agile system that competes better on the basis of short lead times.

FOCUSED SERVICE OPERATIONS. Service industries also have implemented the concepts of focus, PWPs, and cells. Specialty retailers, such as Gap and The Limited, opened stores that have smaller, more accessible spaces. These focused facilities have generally chipped away at the business of large department stores. Using the same philosophy, some department stores are focusing on specific customers or products. Remodeled stores create the effect of many small boutiques under one roof.

plants within plants (PWPs) Different operations within a facility with individual competitive priorities, processes, and workforces under the same roof.

cell A group of two or more dissimilar workstations located close to each other that process a limited number of parts or models with similar process requirements.

DESIGNING PROCESSES

The five main process decisions represent broad, strategic issues. The next issue in process management is determining exactly how each process will be performed. We begin with a systematic approach to analyzing a process, spotting areas for improvement, developing ways to improve them, and implementing the desired changes. Three supporting techniques—flow diagrams, process charts, and simulation—can give good insights into both the current process and proposed changes. We conclude with two different but complementary philosophies for designing processes: process reengineering and process improvement. Both approaches are actually projects, which we discuss in the next chapter.

A SYSTEMATIC APPROACH

Managers or teams might use process reengineering or process improvement, but process analysis should follow a systematic procedure. Here is a six-step procedure that can pay off with improvements.

1. *Describe the more strategic dimensions of the process.* What are the competitive priorities, operations strategy, process choice, and other major process decisions that apply? If it is an ongoing process, look for unexpected departures from the norms shown in Figure 2.3. If there are unexpected relationships, are they justified or are they symptoms that the process needs to be changed?

2. *Identify the inputs, outputs, and customers of the process.* Make a comprehensive list so that the value-added capability of the process can be evaluated. Consider both internal and external customers.

3. *Identify the important performance measures, sometimes called "metrics," of the process.* Possible performance measures could be multiple measures of quality, customer satisfaction, throughput time, cost, errors, safety, environmental measures, on-time delivery, flexibility, and the like.

4. *Document the process.* Use "as is" for an ongoing process and "as proposed" for a process being designed for the first time. Be particularly alert for one or more of the following characteristics.

❏ Customers are dissatisfied with the value of the product or service that they receive from the process.

❏ The process introduces too many quality problems or errors.

❏ The process is slow in responding to customers.

❏ The process is costly.

❏ The process is often a bottleneck (see Chapter 6, "Capacity"), with work piling up waiting to go through it.

❏ The process creates disagreeable work, pollution, waste, or little value added.

Collect information on each part of the process and for each of the performance measures selected in step 3. Whenever possible, benchmark against similar processes within or external to the firm to expose areas of substandard performance.

5. *Redesign or refine the process to achieve better performance.* In order to do so, the manager or team should ask six questions.

a. *What* is being done?

b. *When* is it being done?

c. *Who* is doing it?

d. *Where* is it being done?

e. *How* is it being done?

f. *How well* does it do on the various performance measures?

Answers to these questions are challenged by asking still another series of questions. *Why* is the process even being done? *Why* is it being done where it is being done? *Why* is it being done when it is being done? Such questioning often leads to creative answers and breakthroughs in process design. Once again, benchmarking against processes elsewhere, either inside or outside the organization, can pay off with new ideas and substantial improvements.

Xerox has invested in excess of 400 million pounds to create 4,100 jobs in two new facilities in Ireland by 2003. Benchmarking has helped Xerox create state-of-the-art facilities. Here teams of technicians explore ways to improve products at the Electronics facility at the Xerox Technology Park in Dundalk.

6. *Evaluate the changes and implement those that appear to give the best payoffs on the various performance measures selected in step 3.* Later on, after the process has been changed, check to see if the changes worked. Go back to step 1 as needed.

THREE TECHNIQUES

Three techniques are effective for documenting and evaluating processes: flow diagrams, process charts, and simulation. We fully describe the first two techniques, leaving a fuller treatment of simulation for Supplement G, "Simulation" on the Student CD-ROM. Later on, we also introduce more techniques for analyzing processes that focus on quality improvement (see Chapter 5, "Quality"). These techniques involve the systematic observation and recording of process details to allow better assessment. They also lend themselves to brainstorming the process for improvements, which is step 5. Finally, they are useful for performing step 6 because they should be reapplied to the newly proposed process, along with information on how performance measures are affected. Thus, they provide a "before" and "after" look at the process. Important inputs to these three techniques are time estimates of how long it takes to do various tasks. There are several ways to make these estimates, ranging from reasoned guesses to the more formal methods discussed in Supplement D, "Learning Curve Analysis" and Supplement C, "Measuring Output Rates" on the Student CD-ROM.

FLOW DIAGRAMS. A **flow diagram** traces the flow of information, customers, employees, equipment, or materials through a process. There is no precise format, and the diagram can be drawn simply with boxes, lines, and arrows. Figure 2.4 is a diagram

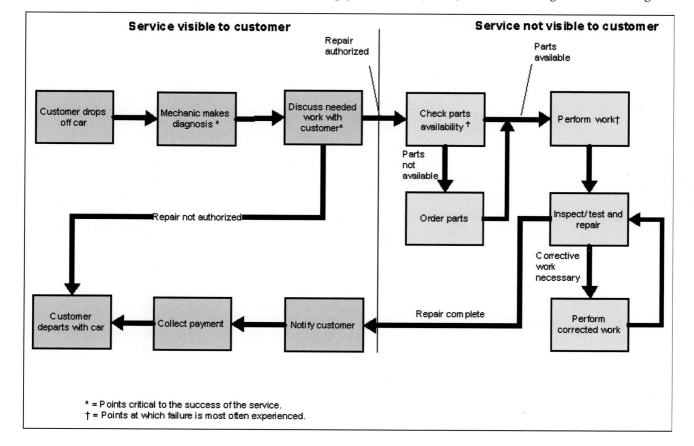

flow diagram A diagram that traces the flow of information, customers, employees, equipment, or materials through a process.

of an automobile repair process, beginning with the customer's call for an appointment and ending with the customer's pickup of the car and departure. Various software packages are available to draw flow diagrams; this one was created using SmartDraw (see the link to its download at the Interactive Web site). In this figure, the dotted *line of visibility* divides activities that are directly visible to the customers from those that are invisible. Such information is particularly valuable for service operations involving considerable customer contact. Operations that are essential to success and where failure occurs most often are identified. Other formats are just as acceptable, and it is often helpful to show beside each box

1. total elapsed time
2. quality losses
3. error frequency
4. capacity
5. cost

Sometimes flow diagrams are overlaid on a facility's layout. To make this special kind of flow diagram, the analyst first does a rough sketch of the area in which the process is performed. On a grid the analyst plots the path followed by the person, material, or equipment, using arrows to indicate the direction of movement or flow.

process chart An organized way of recording all the activities performed by a person, by a machine, at a workstation, with a customer, or on materials.

PROCESS CHARTS. A **process chart** is an organized way of recording all the activities performed by a person, by a machine, at a workstation, with a customer, or on materials. For our purposes we group these activities into five categories.

❑ *Operation.* Changes, creates, or adds something. Drilling a hole and serving a customer are examples of operations.

❑ *Transportation.* Moves the study's subject from one place to another (sometimes called *materials handling*). The subject can be a person, a material, a tool, or a piece of equipment. A customer walking from one end of a counter to the other, a crane hoisting a steel beam to a location, and a conveyor carrying a partially completed product from one workstation to the next are examples of transportation.

❑ *Inspection.* Checks or verifies something but does not change it. Checking for blemishes on a surface, weighing a product, and taking a temperature reading are examples of inspections.

❑ *Delay.* Occurs when the subject is held up awaiting further action. Time spent waiting for materials or equipment, cleanup time, and time that workers, machines, or workstations are idle because there is nothing for them to do are examples of delays.

❑ *Storage.* Occurs when something is put away until a later time. Supplies unloaded and placed in a storeroom as inventory, equipment put away after use, and papers put in a file cabinet are examples of storage.

Depending on the situation, other categories can be used. For example, subcontracting for outside services might be a category, or temporary storage and permanent storage might be two separate categories. Choosing the right category for each activity requires taking the perspective of the subject charted. A delay for the equipment could be inspection or transportation for the operator.

To complete a chart for a new process, the analyst must identify each step performed. If the process is an existing one, the analyst can actually observe the steps, categorizing each step according to the subject being studied. The analyst then

FIGURE 2.5

Process Chart for Emergency Room Admission (Created with OM Explorer)

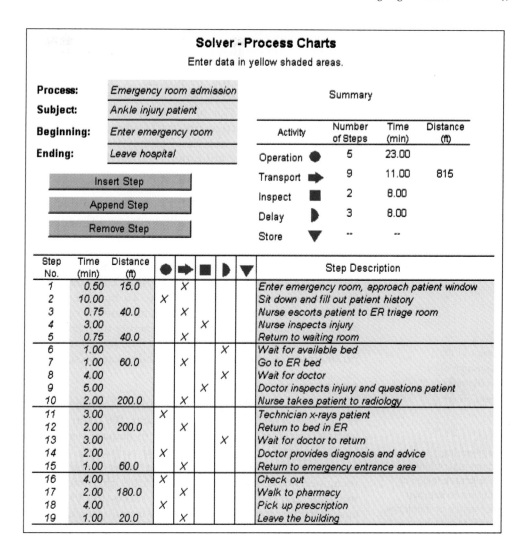

Solver - Process Charts

Enter data in yellow shaded areas.

Process:	Emergency room admission
Subject:	Ankle injury patient
Beginning:	Enter emergency room
Ending:	Leave hospital

Insert Step

Append Step

Remove Step

Summary

Activity		Number of Steps	Time (min)	Distance (ft)
Operation	●	5	23.00	
Transport	➡	9	11.00	815
Inspect	■	2	8.00	
Delay	▶	3	8.00	
Store	▼	--	--	

Step No.	Time (min)	Distance (ft)	●	➡	■	▶	▼	Step Description
1	0.50	15.0		X				Enter emergency room, approach patient window
2	10.00		X					Sit down and fill out patient history
3	0.75	40.0		X				Nurse escorts patient to ER triage room
4	3.00				X			Nurse inspects injury
5	0.75	40.0		X				Return to waiting room
6	1.00					X		Wait for available bed
7	1.00	60.0		X				Go to ER bed
8	4.00					X		Wait for doctor
9	5.00				X			Doctor inspects injury and questions patient
10	2.00	200.0		X				Nurse takes patient to radiology
11	3.00		X					Technician x-rays patient
12	2.00	200.0		X				Return to bed in ER
13	3.00					X		Wait for doctor to return
14	2.00		X					Doctor provides diagnosis and advice
15	1.00	60.0		X				Return to emergency entrance area
16	4.00		X					Check out
17	2.00	180.0		X				Walk to pharmacy
18	4.00		X					Pick up prescription
19	1.00	20.0		X				Leave the building

records the distance traveled and the time taken to perform each step. After recording all the activities and steps, the analyst summarizes the number of steps, times, and distances data. Figure 2.5 shows a process chart prepared using OM Explorer's *Process Chart* solver. It is for a patient with a twisted ankle being treated at a hospital. The process begins at the entrance and ends with the patient exiting after picking up the prescription.

After a process is charted, the analyst sometimes estimates the annual cost of the entire process. It becomes a benchmark against which other methods for performing the process can be evaluated. Annual labor cost can be estimated by finding the product of (1) time in hours to perform the process each time, (2) variable costs per hour, and (3) number of times the process is performed each year, or

TUTOR 2.2

$$\begin{array}{c} \text{Annual} \\ \text{labor cost} \end{array} = \left(\begin{array}{c} \text{Time to perform} \\ \text{the process} \end{array} \right) \left(\begin{array}{c} \text{Variable costs} \\ \text{per hour} \end{array} \right) \left(\begin{array}{c} \text{Number of times process} \\ \text{performed per year} \end{array} \right)$$

In the case of the patient in Figure 2.5, this conversion wouldn't be necessary, with total patient time being sufficient. What is being tracked is the patient's time, not the time and costs of the service providers.

SIMULATION MODELS. A flow diagram is a simple but powerful tool for understanding each of the activities that make up a process and how they tie together. A process chart provides information similar to a table rather than a diagram but also provides time and cost information for the process. A simulation model goes one step further by showing how the process performs dynamically over time. **Simulation** is an act of reproducing the behavior of a process using a model that describes each step of the process. Once the current process is modeled, the analyst can make changes in the process to measure the impact on certain performance measures, such as response time, waiting lines, resource utilization, and the like. To learn more about how simulation works, see Supplement G, "Simulation" on the Student CD-ROM.

simulation The act of reproducing the behavior of a process using a model that describes each step of the process.

THE GOAL: PROCESS IMPROVEMENT. Flow diagrams, process charts, and simulation models are means to an end—continually improving the process. After a chart has been prepared, either for a new or for an existing process, it becomes the basis for brainstorming the process for improvement ideas. During this creative part of process analysis, the analyst asks the what, when, who, where, how long, and how questions, challenging each of the steps of the process charted. The summary of the process chart indicates which activities take the most time. To make a process more efficient, the analyst should question each delay and then analyze the operation, transportation, inspection, and storage activities to determine whether they can be combined, rearranged, or eliminated. There is always a better way, but someone must think of it. Improvements in productivity, quality, time, and flexibility can be significant.

Do some of the organization's key processes need reengineering?

PROCESS REENGINEERING

Processes can be designed or redesigned using two different approaches: process reengineering and process improvement. We begin with process reengineering, which is getting considerable attention today in management circles.

Reengineering is the fundamental rethinking and radical redesign of processes to improve performance dramatically in terms of cost, quality, service, and speed. Process reengineering is about reinvention rather than incremental improvement. It is strong medicine and not always needed or successful. Pain, in the form of layoffs and large cash outflows for investments in information technology, almost always accompanies massive change. However, reengineering processes can have big payoffs. For example, Bell Atlantic reengineered its telephone business. After five years of effort, it cut the time to connect new customers from 16 days to just hours. The changes caused VeriZon to lay off 20,000 employees, but the company is decidedly more competitive.

reengineering The fundamental rethinking and radical redesign of processes to improve performance dramatically in terms of cost, quality, service, and speed.

A process selected for reengineering should be a core process, such as a firm's order-fulfillment activities. Reengineering then requires focusing on that process, often using cross-functional teams, information technology, leadership, and process analysis. Let us examine each element of the overall approach.

CRITICAL PROCESSES. The emphasis of reengineering should be on core business processes rather than on functional departments such as purchasing or marketing. By focusing on processes, managers may spot opportunities to eliminate unnecessary work and supervisory activities rather than worry about defending turf. Because of the time and energy involved, reengineering should be reserved for essential processes, such as new-product development or customer service. Normal process-improvement activities can be continued with the other processes.

STRONG LEADERSHIP. Senior executives must provide strong leadership for reengineering to be successful. Otherwise, cynicism, resistance ("we tried that before"), and boundaries between functional areas can block radical changes. Managers can help overcome resistance by providing the clout necessary to ensure that the project proceeds within a strategic context. Executives should set and monitor key performance objectives for the process. Top management should also create a sense of urgency, making a case for change that is compelling and constantly refreshed.

CROSS-FUNCTIONAL TEAMS. A team, consisting of members from each functional area affected by the process change, is charged with carrying out a reengineering project. For instance, in reengineering the process of handling an insurance claim, three departments should be represented: customer service, adjusting, and accounting. Reengineering works best at high-involvement workplaces, where self-managing teams and employee empowerment are the rule rather than the exception. Top-down and bottom-up initiatives can be combined—top-down for performance targets and bottom-up for deciding how to achieve them.

INFORMATION TECHNOLOGY. Information technology is a primary enabler of process engineering (see Chapter 4, "Managing Technology"). Most reengineering projects design processes around information flows such as customer order fulfillment. The process owners who will actually be responding to events in the marketplace need information networks and computer technology to do their jobs better. The reengineering team must determine who needs the information, when they need it, and where.

CLEAN-SLATE PHILOSOPHY. Reengineering requires a "clean-slate" philosophy—that is, starting with the way the customer wants to deal with the company. To ensure a customer orientation, teams begin with internal and external customer objectives for the process. Often teams first establish a price target for the product or service, deduct profits desired, and then find a process that provides what the customer wants at the price the customer will pay. Reengineers start from the future and work backward, unconstrained by current approaches.

PROCESS ANALYSIS. Despite the clean-slate philosophy, a reengineering team must understand things about the current process: what it does, how well it performs, and what factors affect it. Such understanding can reveal areas in which new thinking will provide the biggest payoff. The team must look at every procedure involved in the process throughout the organization, recording each step, questioning why it is done, and then eliminating everything that is not really necessary. Information on standing relative to the competition, process by process, is also valuable.

Like many new techniques and concepts in operations management, reengineering was highly touted in the early 1990s, almost as a recipe for instant competitive advantage. It has led to many successes and will continue to do so. However, actual experience gives a better picture of the method. It is not simple or easily done, nor is it appropriate for all processes or all organizations. Many firms can't invest the time and resources to implement a radical, clean-slate approach. Moderate gains that better fit corporate strategy and culture might give greater cumulative results than the pursuit of breakthrough. Significant process improvements that have nothing to do with information technology can be realized. A firm must not only improve cross-functional processes but also the processes within each functional area. Finally, the best understanding of a process, and how to improve it, often lies with the people who perform the work each day, not cross-functional teams or top management.

PROCESS IMPROVEMENT

Process improvement is the systematic study of the activities and flows of each process to improve it. Its purpose is to "learn the numbers," understand the process, and dig

Can flow diagrams and process charts be used to study and improve operations?

process improvement The systematic study of the activities and flows of each process to improve it.

out the details. Once a process is really understood, it can be improved. The relentless pressure to provide better quality at a lower price means that companies must continually review all aspects of their operations. Process improvement goes on, whether or not a process is reengineered.

Each aspect of the process is examined. An individual or a whole team examines the process, using flow diagrams and process charts as primary tools. Once the process is understood, they brainstorm different aspects of it, listing as many solutions as possible. They are guided by the principle that the process *can* be improved—that there is *always* a better way. One must look for ways to streamline tasks, eliminate whole processes entirely, cut expensive materials or services, improve the environment, or make jobs safer. One must find the ways to trim costs and delays and improve customer satisfaction.

PROCESS MANAGEMENT ACROSS THE ORGANIZATION

Processes are everywhere and are the basic unit of work. They are found in accounting, finance, human resources, management information systems, marketing, and operations. Managers in all departments must make sure that their processes are adding as much customer value as possible. They must be open to change in their processes, whether coming from a major reengineering effort or simply from an ongoing effort at process improvement. Managers must also understand that enterprise processes cut across organizational lines, regardless of whether the firm is organized along functional, product, regional, or process lines.

Duke Power, our chapter opener, shows processes at work. Its customer operations unit had five core processes that cut across boundaries between its four regions. The calculate and collect revenues process is most closely aligned with accounting, the deliver products and services process with operations, the develop market strategies process and maintain customers process with marketing, and the provide reliability and integrity process with quality assurance (see Chapter 5, "Quality"). Cross-functional coordination paid off in better performance. This payoff came in part by reorganizing to create process owners but also by creating a new collaborative style of management. The process owners and regional vice presidents acted as partners rather than rivals.

CHAPTER HIGHLIGHTS

❏ Process management deals with *how* to make a product or service. Many choices must be made concerning the best mix of human resources, equipment, and materials.

❏ Process management is of strategic importance and is closely linked to a firm's long-term success. It involves the selection of inputs, operations, work flows, and methods used to produce goods and services.

❏ Process decisions are made in the following circumstances: a new product is to be offered or an existing product modified, quality improvements are necessary, competitive priorities are changed, demand levels change, current performance is inadequate, competitor capabilities change, new technology is available, or cost or availability of inputs changes.

❏ The five major process decisions are process choice, degree of capital intensity, resource flexibility, vertical integration, and customer involvement. Basic *process choices* are project, job, batch, line, and continuous. *Capital intensity* is the mix of capital equipment and human skills in a process. *Resource flexibility* is the degree to which equipment is general purpose and individuals can handle a wide variety of work. *Vertical integration* involves decisions about whether to outsource certain processes. *Customer involvement* is the extent to which customers are allowed to interact with the process. Self-service, product selection, and the timing and location of the interaction must all be considered.

❏ Fixed automation maximizes efficiency for high-volume products with long life cycles, but flexible (programmable) automation provides economies of scope. Flexibility is gained and setups are minimized because the machines can be reprogrammed to follow new instructions.

❑ The variable underlying the relationships among the five major process decisions is volume, which in turn is shaped by operations strategy. For example, high volume is associated with a line or continuous process, vertical integration, little resource flexibility, little customer involvement, and capital intensity.

❑ Service operations follow the same pattern and are best understood through the lens of service strategy, customer involvement, and automation.

❑ Focusing operations avoids confusion among competitive priorities, process choices, and technologies. Focused facilities, plants within plants, and cells are ways to achieve focus in both manufacturing and service operations.

❑ Three basic techniques for analyzing process activities and flows are flow diagrams, process charts, and simulation. They are ways to organize the detailed study of process components.

❑ Process reengineering uses cross-functional teams to rethink the design of critical processes. Process improvement is a systematic analysis of activities and flows that occurs continuously.

SOLVED PROBLEM 1

An automobile service is having difficulty providing oil changes in the 29 minutes or less mentioned in its advertising. You are to analyze the process of changing automobile engine oil. The subject of the study is the service mechanic. The process begins when the mechanic directs the customer's arrival and ends when the customer pays for the services.

SOLUTION

Figure 2.6 shows the completed process chart. The process is broken into 21 steps. A summary of the times and distances traveled is shown in the upper right-hand corner of the process chart. The times add up to 28 minutes, which does not allow much room for error if the 29-minute guarantee is to be met and the mechanic travels a total of 420 feet.

SOLVED PROBLEM 2

What improvement can you make in the process shown in Figure 2.6?

SOLUTION

Your analysis should verify the following three ideas for improvement. You may also be able to come up with others.

1. *Move Step 17 to Step 21.* Customers shouldn't have to wait while the mechanic cleans the work area.

2. *Store Small Inventories of Frequently Used Filters in the Pit.* Steps 7 and 10 involve travel to the storeroom. If the filters are moved to the pit, a copy of the reference material must also be placed in the pit. The pit will have to be organized and well lighted.

3. *Use Two Mechanics.* Steps 10, 12, 15, and 17 involve running up and down the steps to the pit. Much of this travel could be eliminated. The service time could be shortened by having one mechanic in the pit working simultaneously with another working under the hood.

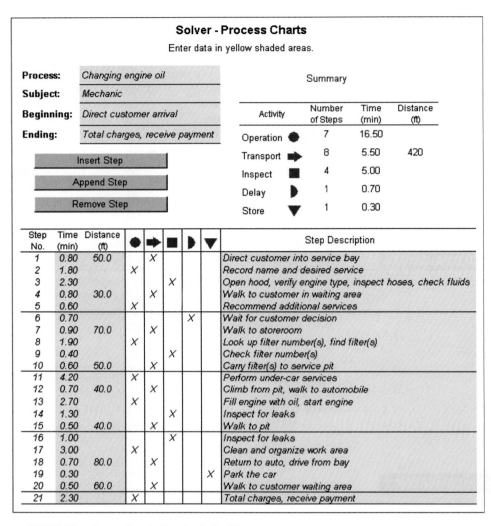

Solver - Process Charts

Enter data in yellow shaded areas.

Process: Changing engine oil

Subject: Mechanic

Beginning: Direct customer arrival

Ending: Total charges, receive payment

Insert Step

Append Step

Remove Step

Summary

Activity	Number of Steps	Time (min)	Distance (ft)
Operation ●	7	16.50	
Transport ➡	8	5.50	420
Inspect ■	4	5.00	
Delay ▶	1	0.70	
Store ▼	1	0.30	

Step No.	Time (min)	Distance (ft)	●	➡	■	▶	▼	Step Description
1	0.80	50.0		X				Direct customer into service bay
2	1.80		X					Record name and desired service
3	2.30				X			Open hood, verify engine type, inspect hoses, check fluids
4	0.80	30.0		X				Walk to customer in waiting area
5	0.60		X					Recommend additional services
6	0.70						X	Wait for customer decision
7	0.90	70.0		X				Walk to storeroom
8	1.90		X					Look up filter number(s), find filter(s)
9	0.40				X			Check filter number(s)
10	0.60	50.0		X				Carry filter(s) to service pit
11	4.20		X					Perform under-car services
12	0.70	40.0		X				Climb from pit, walk to automobile
13	2.70		X					Fill engine with oil, start engine
14	1.30				X			Inspect for leaks
15	0.50	40.0		X				Walk to pit
16	1.00				X			Inspect for leaks
17	3.00		X					Clean and organize work area
18	0.70	80.0		X				Return to auto, drive from bay
19	0.30						X	Park the car
20	0.50	60.0		X				Walk to customer waiting area
21	2.30		X					Total charges, receive payment

FIGURE 2.6 • Process Chart for Changing Engine Oil

CD-ROM RESOURCES

The Student CD-ROM that accompanies this text contains the following resources, which allow you to further practice and apply the concepts presented in this chapter.

❐ **OM Explorer Tutors:** OM Explorer contains two tutor programs that will help you learn about process charts and break-even analysis applied to equipment selection. See the folder for Chapter 2 in OM Explorer. See also the two Tutor Exercises on break-even analysis for equipment selection and on process charts.

❐ **OM Explorer Solvers:** OM Explorer has one program that will help with the general use of process charts. See the folder for Process Management in OM Explorer for this routine.

❐ **Discussion Questions:** Three questions will expand your thinking on the ethical, environmental, and political dimensions of designing processes.

❐ **Case:** Custom Molds Inc. How should the Millers design their processes, given the changing environment?

❐ **The Big Picture:** Process Choice at King Soopers Bakery. See how three different process choices are used under the same roof, depending on volume and the degree of product customization.

❐ **Supplement A:** Decision Making. Learn about break-even analysis applied to processes and outsourcing decisions.

❐ **Supplement B:** Financial Analysis. Learn about several tools evaluating revised processes that involve large capital investments.

❐ **Supplement C:** Measuring Output Rates. Learn about several tools for estimating the time it takes for each step in a process.

❐ **Supplement D:** Learning Curve Analysis. Learn about how to account for learning effects when estimating time requirements for new or revised processes.

❐ **Supplement E:** Computer-Integrated Manufacturing. Read about how complex computer systems can give manufacturers more resource flexibility.

❐ **Supplement G:** Simulation. Learn how to simulate a process and understand how it performs dynamically over time.

INTERACTIVE RESOURCES

The Interactive Web site associated with this text (www.prenhall.com/ritzman) contains many tools and activities specifically designed for this chapter. The following items are recommended to enhance your understanding of the material in this chapter.

❐ **Internet Activities:** Try out the links covering outsourcing at Ryder and process improvement at Freightliner.

❐ **Internet Tours:** Check out three different process choices at the Kokomo Opalescent Glass Factory, Buck Knives, and a sugar processing facility.

❐ **SmartDraw:** Use the link to experience a software package that is used in practice to prepare flow diagrams of processes.

PROBLEMS

An icon next to a problem identifies the software that can be helpful but is not mandatory. Problems 5 and 6 apply break-even analysis (discussed in Supplement A, "Decision Making" on the Student CD-ROM) to process decisions.

1. 💿 **OM Explorer** Your class has volunteered to work for Referendum #13 on the November ballot, which calls for free tuition and books for all college courses except operations management. Support for the referendum includes assembling 10,000 yard signs (preprinted water-resistant paper signs to be glued and stapled to a wooden stake) on a fall Saturday. Construct a flow diagram and a process chart for yard sign assembly. What inputs in terms of materials, human effort, and equipment are involved? Estimate the amount of volunteers, staples, glue, equipment, lawn and garage space, and pizza required.

2. 💿 **SmartDraw** Prepare a flow diagram for a process of your choice.

3. Diagrams of two self-service gasoline stations, both located on corners, are shown in Figures 2.7(a) and (b). Both have two rows of four pumps and a booth at which an attendant receives payment for the gasoline. At neither station is it necessary for the customer to pay in advance. The exits and entrances are marked on the diagrams. Analyze the flows of cars and people through each station.

   a. Which station has the more efficient flows from the standpoint of the customer?

   b. Which station is likely to lose more potential customers who cannot gain access to the pumps because another car is headed in the other direction?

   c. At which station can a customer pay without getting out of the car?

4. 💿 **OM Explorer** The management of the Just Like Home restaurant has asked you to analyze some of its processes. One of these processes is making a single-scoop ice cream cone. Cones can be ordered by a server (for table service) or by a customer (for takeout). Figure 2.8 illustrates the process chart for this operation.

   • The ice cream counter server earns $10 per hour (including variable fringe benefits).
   • The process is performed 10 times per hour (on average).
   • The restaurant is open 363 days a year, 10 hours a day.

   a. Complete the summary (top-right) portion of the chart.

   b. What is the total labor cost associated with the process?

   c. How can this operation be made more efficient? Draw a process chart of the improved process. What are the annual labor savings if this new process is implemented?

5. 💿 **OM Explorer** Dr. Gulakowicz is an orthodontist. She estimates that adding two new chairs will increase fixed costs by $150,000, including the annual equivalent cost of the capital investment and the salary of one more technician. Each new patient is expected to bring in $3,000 per year in additional revenue, with variable costs estimated at $1,000 per patient. The two new chairs will allow her to expand her practice by as many as 200 patients annually. How many patients would have to be added for the new process to break even?

6. 💿 **OM Explorer** Two different manufacturing processes are being considered for making a new product. The first process is less capital-intensive, with fixed costs of only

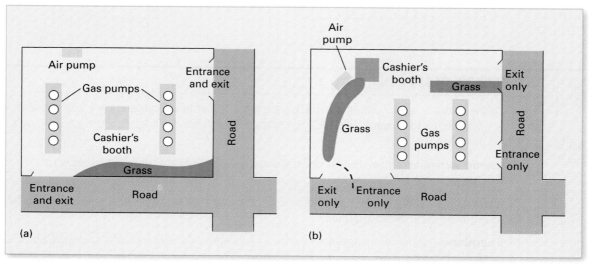

FIGURE 2.7

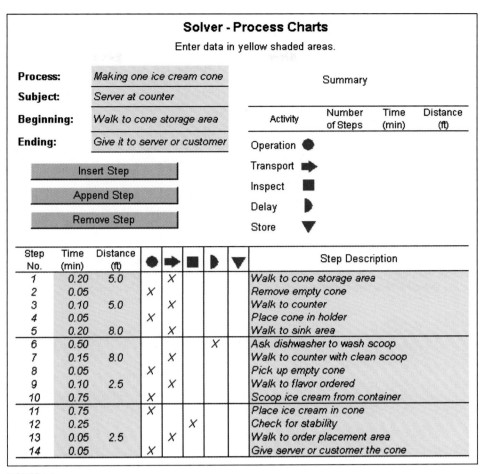

Solver - Process Charts

Enter data in yellow shaded areas.

Process:	Making one ice cream cone
Subject:	Server at counter
Beginning:	Walk to cone storage area
Ending:	Give it to server or customer

Insert Step

Append Step

Remove Step

Summary

Activity	Number of Steps	Time (min)	Distance (ft)
Operation ●			
Transport ➡			
Inspect ■			
Delay ▶			
Store ▼			

Step No.	Time (min)	Distance (ft)	●	➡	■	▶	▼	Step Description
1	0.20	5.0			X			Walk to cone storage area
2	0.05		X					Remove empty cone
3	0.10	5.0			X			Walk to counter
4	0.05		X					Place cone in holder
5	0.20	8.0			X			Walk to sink area
6	0.50						X	Ask dishwasher to wash scoop
7	0.15	8.0			X			Walk to counter with clean scoop
8	0.05		X					Pick up empty cone
9	0.10	2.5			X			Walk to flavor ordered
10	0.75		X					Scoop ice cream from container
11	0.75		X					Place ice cream in cone
12	0.25					X		Check for stability
13	0.05	2.5			X			Walk to order placement area
14	0.05		X					Give server or customer the cone

FIGURE 2.8

$50,000 per year and variable costs of $700 per unit. The second process has fixed costs of $400,000 but variable costs of only $200 per unit.

a. What is the break-even quantity, beyond which the second process becomes more attractive than the first?

b. If the expected annual sales for the product is 800 units, which process would you choose?

Advanced Problem

7. This problem should be solved as a team exercise. Shaving is a process that most men perform each morning. Assume that the process begins at the bathroom sink with the shaver walking (say, 5 feet) to the cabinet (where his shaving supplies are stored) to pick up bowl, soap, brush, and razor. He walks back to the sink, runs the water until it gets warm, lathers his face, shaves, and inspects the results. Then he rinses the razor, dries his face, walks over to the cabinet to return the bowl, soap, brush, and razor, and comes back to the sink to clean it up and complete the process.

a. ● **OM Explorer** Develop a process chart for shaving. (Assume suitable values for the time required for the various activities involved in the process.)

b. Brainstorm to generate ideas for improving the shaving process. (Do not try to evaluate the ideas until the group has compiled as complete a list as possible. Otherwise judgment will block creativity.)

SELECTED REFERENCES

Brown, Donna. "Outsourcing: How Corporations Take Their Business Elsewhere." *Management Review* (February 1992), pp. 16–19.

Byrne, John A. "The Virtual Corporation." *Business Week* (February 8, 1993), pp. 98–102.

Dixon, J. Robb, Peter Arnold, Janelle Heineke, Jay S. Kim, and Paul Mulligan. "Business Process Reengineering: Improving in New Strategic Directions." *California Management Review* (Summer 1994), pp. 1–17.

Goldhar, J. D., and Mariann Jelinek. "Plan for Economies of Scope." *Harvard Business Review* (November–December 1983), pp. 141–148.

Grover, Varun, and Manoj K. Malhotra, P. S. "Business Process Reengineering: A Tutorial on the Concept, Evolution, Method, Technology and Application." *Journal of Operations Management,* vol. 15, no. 3 (1997), pp. 194–213.

Hall, Gene, Jim Rosenthal, and Judy Wade. "How to Make Reengineering Really Work." *Harvard Business Review* (November–December 1993), pp. 119–131.

Hammer, M. *Beyond Reengineering.* New York: HarperBusiness, 1996.

Hammer, Michael, and James Champy. *Reengineering the Corporation: A Manifesto for Business Revolution.* New York: HarperBusiness, 1993.

Harrigan, K. R. *Strategies for Vertical Integration.* Lexington, MA: D. C. Heath, 1983.

Malhotra, Manoj K., and Larry P. Ritzman. "Resource Flexibility Issues in Multistage Manufacturing." *Decision Sciences,* vol. 21, no. 4 (1990), pp. 673–690.

Normann, Richard, and Rafael Ramirez. "From Value Chain to Value Constellation: Designing Interactive Strategy." *Harvard Business Review* (July–August 1993), pp. 65–77.

Port, Otis. "The Responsive Factory." *Business Week,* Enterprise 1993, pp. 48–51.

"Process, Process, Process." *Planning Review* (special issue), vol. 22, no. 3 (1993), pp. 1–56.

"Reengineering: The Hot New Managing Tool." *Fortune* (August 23, 1994), pp. 41–48.

Safizadeh, M. Hossen, Larry P. Ritzman, and Debasish Mallick, "Revisiting Alternative Theoretical Paradigms in Manufacturing." *Production and Operations Management,* vol. 9, no. 2 (2000), pp. 111–127.

Tonkin, Lea A. P. "Outsourcing: A Tool, Not a Solution." *Target,* vol. 15, no. 2 (1999), pp. 44–45.

Managing Project Processes

Across the Organization

Managing project processes is important to . . .

- ❏ **finance,** which uses project processes for financing new business acquisitions.
- ❏ **human resources,** which uses project processes for initiating new training and development programs.
- ❏ **management information systems,** which uses project processes for designing new information systems to support reengineered processes.
- ❏ **marketing,** which uses project processes to design and execute new product advertising campaigns.
- ❏ **operations,** which uses project processes to manage the introduction of new technologies for the production of goods and services.

Learning Goals

After reading this chapter, you will be able to . . .

1. identify the three major activities associated with successful project processes.
2. diagram the network of interrelated activities in a project.
3. identify the sequence of critical activities that determines the duration of a project.
4. compute the probability of completing a project on time.
5. understand how to monitor and control projects.

Bechtel Group, Inc. (www.bechtel.com), is a 102-year-old, $12.6 billion-a-year construction contractor that specializes in large projects. The venerable company built Hoover Dam early in the twentieth century and has built scores of rail systems, refineries, airports, and power plants since then. Bechtel led the rebuilding of Kuwait after Desert Storm and became the first U.S. company to be granted a construction license in China. Bechtel's traditional bricks-and-mortar customers chose the company because of its ability to deliver projects on time. However, Bechtel's new customers include fleet-footed Internet companies that thrive on speed. They have chosen Bechtel because of another of its capabilities—the ability to deliver projects quickly. For example, Webvan Group, Inc., wanted to build 26 distribution centers in two years, each with 330,000 square feet of space. Equinix, Inc., contracted for 30 high-security data centers worldwide in four years, each filled with security gadgetry such as doors that open only when a handprint is verified by computer. iMotors.com, a company that sells refurbished autos online, wanted Bechtel to build 30 plants over a two-year period. Web-based companies such as these typically want to set up facilities nationwide or around the world with short lead times and do not have the time to deal with a multitude of local contractors. Bechtel satisfies their needs.

Bechtel must set up a project process for each major project it undertakes with on-time delivery and short delivery lead times in mind. Because of the complexity of many ongoing projects with diverse needs, processes must also be flexible enough to respond to changes in schedules or requirements. Communication is a major issue; it takes an average of five days to get a piece of paper from Bechtel's Singapore office to a project in Thailand. Paperwork ranging from routine requests for information to detailed architectural drawings can suffer unnecessary delays when it must be copied and faxed or sent by mail, thereby delaying decisions and lengthening a project. Bechtel has, thus, initiated a Web-based communications system that provides access to project information electronically. Members of the project team can access schedules, progress reports, drawings, and messages at one Web site without having to rely on faxes. Decisions on various issues can be made quickly, thereby reinforcing Bechtel's competitive priorities.

Bechtel Group was the construction contractor for the Hoover Dam, the highest dam in the Western Hemisphere. On the Colorado River, it has a power capacity of 1,345 megawatts.

COMPANIES SUCH AS BECHTEL are experts at managing projects. They have mastered the ability to schedule activities and monitor progress within strict time, cost, and performance guidelines. A **project** is an interrelated set of activities that has definite starting and ending points and that results in a unique outcome for a specific allocation of resources. Typical competitive priorities for such processes include on-time delivery and customization (see Chapter 2, "Process Management"). A project process is the mechanism for completing a project.

Project processes can be complex and challenging to manage. Projects often cut across organizational lines because they need the skills of multiple professions and organizations. Furthermore, each project is unique, even if it is routine, requiring new combinations of skills and resources in the project process. Uncertainties, such as the advent of new technologies or the activities of competitors, can change the character of

project An interrelated set of activities that has definite starting and ending points and that results in a unique outcome for a specific allocation of resources.

projects and require responsive countermeasures. Finally, project processes themselves are temporary because personnel, materials, and facilities are organized to complete a project within a specified time frame and then disbanded. In this chapter, we discuss three major activities associated with managing project processes: defining and organizing projects, planning projects, and monitoring and controlling projects.

DEFINING AND ORGANIZING PROJECTS

Successful projects begin with a clear definition of scope, objectives, and tasks. However, a successful project *process* begins with a clear understanding of its organization and how personnel are going to work together to complete the project. In this section, we will address two important activities in this initial phase of managing projects: selecting the project manager and team and defining scope and objectives.

SELECTING THE PROJECT MANAGER AND TEAM

Project managers should be good motivators, teachers, and communicators. They should be able to organize a set of disparate activities and work with personnel from a variety of disciplines. These qualities are important because project managers have the responsibility to see that their projects are completed successfully. The project manager is responsible for establishing the project goals and providing the means to achieve them. The project manager must also specify how the work will be done and ensure that any necessary training is conducted. Finally, the project manager evaluates progress and takes appropriate action when schedules are in jeopardy.

The project team is a group of people led by the project manager. Members of the project team may represent entities internal to the firm, such as marketing, finance, accounting, or operations, or entities external to the firm, such as customers or suppliers. A clear definition of who is on the team is essential, as is a clear understanding of their specific roles and responsibilities, such as helping to create the project plan, performing specific tasks, and reporting progress and problems. Everyone performing work for the project should be a part of the project team. Consequently, the size and makeup of the team may fluctuate during the life of the project.

DEFINING THE SCOPE AND OBJECTIVES

A thorough statement of project scope, time frame, and allocated resources is essential to managing the project process. The scope provides a succinct statement of project objectives and captures the essence of the desired project outcomes in the form of major deliverables, which are concrete outcomes of the project process. These deliverables become the focus of management attention during the life of the project. Each of the deliverables requires activities to achieve it; therefore, it is important to avoid many changes to the scope of the project once it is underway. Changes to the scope of a project inevitably increase costs and delay completion. Collectively, changes to scope are called *scope creep* and, in sufficient quantity, are primary causes of failed projects.

The time frame for a project should be as specific as possible. For example, "by the first quarter, 2005" is too vague for most purposes. Some people could interpret it as the beginning and others the end. Even though it should be considered only as a target at this early stage of the project plan, the time frame should be much more specific, as in "the billing process reengineering project should be completed by January 1, 2005."

Although specifying an allocation of resources to a project may be difficult at the early stages of planning, it is important for managing the project process. The allocation could be expressed as a dollar figure or as full-time equivalents of personnel time.

For example, the allocated resources in a project might be $250,000. Avoid statements such as "with available resources" because they are too vague and imply that there are sufficient resources to complete the project when there may not be. A specific statement of allocated resources makes it possible to make adjustments to the scope of the project as it proceeds.

PLANNING PROJECTS

Once the project has been defined and the project process organized, the team must formulate a plan that identifies the specific tasks to be accomplished and a schedule for their completion. Planning projects involves five steps:

1. defining the work breakdown structure
2. diagramming the network
3. developing the schedule
4. analyzing cost–time trade-offs
5. assessing risks

DEFINING THE WORK BREAKDOWN STRUCTURE

The **work breakdown structure (WBS)** is a statement of all work that has to be completed. Perhaps the single most important contributor to delay is the omission of work that is germane to the successful completion of the project. The project manager must work closely with the team to identify all work tasks. Typically, in the process of accumulating work tasks, the team generates a hierarchy to the work breakdown. Major work components are broken down to smaller tasks by the project team. Care must be taken to include all important tasks in the WBS, otherwise project delays are possible. For example, a project for improving the delivery of groceries directly to consumers might have as a major activity "build a warehouse," which might be further refined to a host of construction-related tasks including "pour a foundation" and "wire for electrical service." Easily overlooked, however, are tasks such as "getting final approval for the warehouse" or "preparing final reports," which can take considerable time and can affect the completion date of the project.

An **activity** is the smallest unit of work effort consuming both time and resources that the project manager can schedule and control. Each activity in the work breakdown structure must have an "owner" who is responsible for doing the work. *Task ownership* avoids confusion in the execution of activities and assigns responsibility for timely completion. The team should have a defined procedure for assigning tasks to team members, which can be democratic (consensus of the team) or autocratic (project manager).

DIAGRAMMING THE NETWORK

Network planning methods can help managers monitor and control projects. These methods treat a project as a set of interrelated activities that can be visually displayed in a **network diagram,** which consists of nodes (circles) and arcs (arrows) that depict the relationships between activities. Two network planning methods were developed in the 1950s. The **program evaluation and review technique (PERT)** was created for the U.S. Navy's Polaris missile project, which involved 3,000 separate contractors and suppliers. The **critical path method (CPM)** was developed as a means of scheduling maintenance shutdowns at chemical-processing plants. Although early versions of PERT and CPM differed in their treatment of activity–time estimates, today the differences

work breakdown structure (WBS) A statement of all work that has to be completed.

activity The smallest unit of work effort consuming both time and resources that the project manager can schedule and control.

What tools are available for scheduling and controlling projects?

network diagram A network planning method, designed to depict the relationships between activities, which consists of nodes (circles) and arcs (arrows).

program evaluation and review technique (PERT) A network planning method created for the U.S. Navy's Polaris missile project in the 1950s, which involved 3,000 separate contractors and suppliers.

critical path method (CPM) A network planning method developed in the 1950s by J. F. Kelly of Remington-Rand and M. R. Walker of Du Pont as a means of scheduling maintenance shutdowns at chemical-processing plants.

between PERT and CPM are minor. For purposes of our discussion, we refer to them collectively as PERT/CPM. These methods offer several benefits to project managers, including the following.

1. Considering projects as networks forces project teams to identify and organize the data required and to identify the interrelationships between activities. This process also provides a forum for managers of different functional areas to discuss the nature of the various activities and their resource requirements.

2. Networks enable project managers to estimate the completion time of projects, an advantage that can be useful in planning other events and in conducting contractual negotiations with customers and suppliers.

3. Reports highlight the activities that are crucial to completing projects on schedule. They also highlight the activities that may be delayed without affecting completion dates, thereby freeing up resources for more critical activities.

4. Network methods enable project managers to analyze the time and cost implications of resource trade-offs.

precedence relationship
A relationship that determines a sequence for undertaking activities; it specifies that one activity cannot start until a preceding activity has been completed.

ESTABLISHING PRECEDENCE RELATIONSHIPS. Diagramming the project as a network requires establishing the precedence relationships between activities. A **precedence relationship** determines a sequence for undertaking activities; it specifies that one activity cannot start until a preceding activity has been completed. For example, brochures announcing a conference for executives must first be designed by the program committee (activity A) before they can be printed (activity B). In other words, activity A must *precede* activity B. For large projects, this task is essential because incorrect or omitted precedence relationships will result in costly delays. The precedence relationships are represented by a network diagram.

activity-on-node (AON) network An approach used to create a network diagram, in which nodes represent activities and arcs represent the precedence relationships between them.

ACTIVITY-ON-NODE (AON) NETWORKS. A networking approach useful for creating a network diagram is the **activity-on-node (AON) network,** in which nodes represent activities and arcs represent the precedence relationships between them. This approach is *activity oriented*. Here, precedence relationships require that an activity not begin until all preceding activities have been completed. Arrows represent the precedence relationships, and the direction of an arrow represents the sequence of activities. In AON networks, when there are multiple activities with no predecessors, it is usual to show them emanating from a common node called Start. When there are multiple activities with no successors, it is usual to show them connected to a node called Finish. We will use AON networks later to describe assembly lines (see Chapter 7, "Location and Layout").

EXAMPLE 3.1   *Diagramming a Hospital Project*

In the interest of better serving the public in Benjamin County, St. Adolf's Hospital has decided to relocate from Christofer to Northville, a large suburb that at present has no primary medical facility. The move to Northville will involve constructing a new hospital and making it operational. Judy Kramer, executive director of the board of St. Adolf's, must prepare for a hearing, scheduled for next week, before the Central Ohio Hospital Board (COHB) on the proposed project. The hearing will address the specifics of the total project, including time and cost estimates for its completion.

With the help of her team, Kramer has developed a work breakdown structure consisting of 11 major project activities. The team also has specified the immediate predecessors (those activities that must be completed before a particular activity can begin) for each activity, as shown in the following table. Draw the network diagram.

ACTIVITY	DESCRIPTION	IMMEDIATE PREDECESSOR(S)
A	Select administrative and medical staff.	—
B	Select site and do site survey.	—
C	Select equipment.	A
D	Prepare final construction plans and layout.	B
E	Bring utilities to the site.	B
F	Interview applicants and fill positions in nursing, support staff, maintenance, and security.	A
G	Purchase and take delivery of equipment.	C
H	Construct the hospital.	D
I	Develop an information system.	A
J	Install the equipment.	E, G, H
K	Train nurses and support staff.	F, I, J

SOLUTION

The AON network for the hospital project, based on Kramer's 11 activities and their precedence relationships, is shown in Figure 3.1. It depicts activities as circles, with arrows indicating the sequence in which they are to be performed. The numbers represent estimated times in weeks for each activity. Activities A and B emanate from a *start* node because they have no immediate predecessors. The arrows connecting activity A to activities C, F, and I indicate that all three require completion of activity A before they can begin. Similarly, activity B must be completed before activities D and E can begin, and so on. Activity K connects to a *finish* node because no activities follow it. The start and finish nodes do not actually represent activities. They merely provide beginning and ending points for the network.

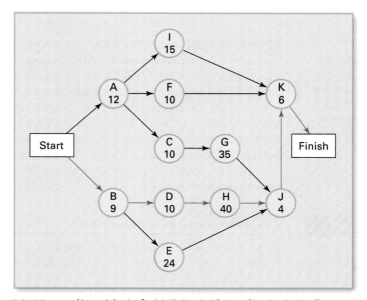

FIGURE 3.1 • Network for the St. Adolf's Hospital Project, Showing Activity Times

Modeling a large project as a network forces the project team to identify the necessary activities and recognize the precedence relationships. If this preplanning is skipped, unexpected delays often occur.

DEVELOPING THE SCHEDULE

Which activities determine the duration of an entire project?

Next, the project team must make time estimates for activities. When the same type of activity has been done many times before, time estimates are apt to have a relatively high degree of certainty. There are several ways to get time estimates in such an environment. First, statistical methods can be used if the project team has access to data on actual activity times experienced in the past (see Supplement C, "Measuring Output Rates" in the Student CD-ROM). Second, if activity times improve with the number of replications, the times can be estimated using learning curve models (see Supplement D, "Learning Curve Analysis" in the Student CD-ROM). Finally, the times for first-time activities are often estimated using managerial opinions based on similar prior experiences (see Chapter 9, "Forecasting"). If there is a high degree of uncertainty in the estimates, probability distributions for activity times can be used. We discuss two approaches for incorporating uncertainty in project networks when we address risk assessment later. For now, we assume that the activity times are known with certainty. We will use the estimated time for each activity in Figure 3.1.

A crucial aspect of project management is estimating the time of completion. If each activity in relocating the hospital were done in sequence, with work proceeding on only one activity at a time, the time of completion would equal the sum of the times for all the activities, or 175 weeks. However, Figure 3.1 indicates that some activities can be carried on simultaneously given adequate resources. We call each sequence of activities between the project's start and finish a **path**. The network describing the hospital relocation project has five paths: A–I–K, A–F–K, A–C–G–J–K, B–D–H–J–K, and B–E–J–K. The **critical path** is the sequence of activities between a project's start and finish that takes the longest time to complete. Thus, the activities along the critical path determine the completion time of the project; that is, if one of the activities on the critical path is delayed, the entire project will be delayed. The estimated times for the paths in the hospital project network are

path The sequence of activities between a project's start and finish.

critical path The sequence of activities between a project's start and finish that takes the longest time to complete.

Path	Estimated Time (wk)
A–F–K	28
A–I–K	33
A–C–G–J–K	67
B–D–H–J–K	69
B–E–J–K	43

The activity string B–D–H–J–K is estimated to take 69 weeks to complete. As the longest, it constitutes the critical path and is shown in red in Figure 3.1.

Because the critical path defines the completion time of the project, Judy Kramer and the project team should focus on these activities. However, projects can have more than one critical path. If activity A, C, or G were to fall behind by two weeks, the string A–C–G–J–K would become a second critical path. Consequently, the team should be aware that delays in activities not on the critical path could cause delays in the entire project.

Manually finding the critical path in this way is easy for small projects; however, computers must be used for large projects. Computers calculate activity slack and prepare periodic reports, enabling managers to monitor progress. **Activity slack** is the maximum length of time that an activity can be delayed without delaying the entire project. Activities on the critical path have zero slack. Constantly monitoring the progress of activities with little or no slack enables managers to identify activities that need to be expedited to keep the project on schedule. Activity slack is calculated from

activity slack The maximum length of time that an activity can be delayed without delaying the entire project.

four times for each activity: earliest start time, earliest finish time, latest start time, and latest finish time.

EARLIEST START AND EARLIEST FINISH TIMES. The earliest start and earliest finish times are obtained as follows.

earliest finish time (EF) An activity's earliest start time plus its estimated duration, t, or EF = ES + t.

earliest start time (ES) The earliest finish time of the immediately preceding activity.

- The **earliest finish time (EF)** of an activity equals its earliest start time plus its estimated duration, t, or EF = ES + t.
- The **earliest start time (ES)** for an activity is the earliest finish time of the immediately preceding activity. For activities with more than one preceding activity, ES is the latest of the earliest finish times of the preceding activities.

To calculate the duration of the entire project, we determine the EF for the last activity on the critical path.

LATEST START AND LATEST FINISH TIMES. To obtain the latest start and latest finish times, we must work backward from the finish node. We start by setting the latest finish time of the project equal to the earliest finish time of the last activity on the critical path.

latest finish time (LF) The latest start time of the activity immediately following.

latest start time (LS) The latest finish time of an activity minus its estimated duration, t, or LS = LF − t.

- The **latest finish time (LF)** for an activity is the latest start time of the activity immediately following it. For activities with more than one activity immediately following, LF is the earliest of the latest start times of those activities.
- The **latest start time (LS)** for an activity equals its latest finish time minus its estimated duration, t, or LS = LF − t.

EXAMPLE 3.2   *Calculating Start and Finish Times for the Activities*

Calculate the ES, EF, LS, and LF times for each activity. Which activity in the hospital project should Kramer start immediately?

SOLUTION

To compute the early start and early finish times, we begin at the start node at time zero. Because activities A and B have no predecessors, the earliest start times for these activities are also zero. The earliest finish times for these activities are

$$EF_A = 0 + 12 = 12 \quad \text{and} \quad EF_B = 0 + 9 = 9$$

Because the earliest start time for activities I, F, and C is the earliest finish time of activity A,

$$ES_I = 12, \quad ES_F = 12, \quad \text{and} \quad ES_C = 12$$

Similarly,

$$ES_D = 9 \quad \text{and} \quad ES_E = 9$$

After placing these ES values on the network diagram as shown in Figure 3.2, we determine the EF times for activities I, F, C, D, and E:

$$EF_I = 12 + 15 = 27, \quad EF_F = 12 + 10 = 22, \quad EF_C = 12 + 10 = 22$$
$$EF_D = 9 + 10 = 19, \quad \text{and} \quad EF_E = 9 + 24 = 33$$

The earliest start time for activity G is the latest EF time of all immediately preceding activities. Thus,

$$ES_G = EF_C \qquad ES_H = EF_D$$
$$= 22 \qquad\qquad = 19$$

$$EF_G = ES_G + t \qquad EF_H = ES_H + t$$
$$= 22 + 35 \qquad\quad = 19 + 40$$
$$= 57 \qquad\qquad = 59$$

Because activity J has several predecessors, the earliest time that activity J can begin is the latest of the EF times of any of its preceding activities: EF_G, EF_H, EF_E. Thus, $EF_J = 59 + 4 = 63$. Similarly, $ES_K = 63$ and $EF_K = 63 + 6 = 69$. Because activity K is the last activity on the critical path, the earliest the project can be completed is week 69. The earliest start and finish times for all activities are shown in Figure 3.2.

To compute the latest start and latest finish times, we begin by setting the latest finish activity time of activity K at week 69, its earliest finish time. Thus, the latest start time for activity K is

$$LS_K = LF_K - t = 69 - 6 = 63$$

If activity K is to start no later than week 63, all its predecessors must finish no later than that time. Consequently,

$$LF_I = 63, \qquad LE_F = 63, \qquad \text{and} \qquad LF_J = 63$$

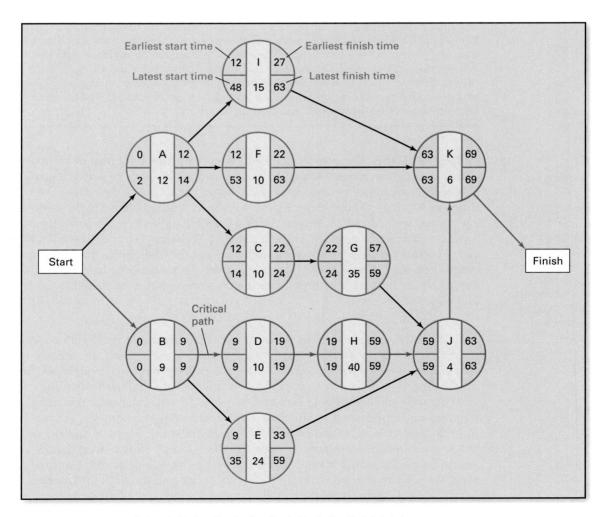

FIGURE 3.2 • Network for the Hospital Project, Showing Data Needed for Activity Slack Calculation

The latest start times for these activities are shown in Figure 3.2 as

$$LS_I = 63 - 15 = 48, \qquad LS_F = 63 - 10 = 53, \qquad \text{and} \qquad LS_J = 63 - 4 = 59$$

After obtaining LS_J, we can calculate the latest start times for the immediate predecessors of activity J:

$$LS_G = 59 - 35 = 24, \qquad LS_H = 59 - 40 = 19, \qquad \text{and} \qquad LS_E = 59 - 24 = 35$$

Similarly, we can now calculate latest start times for activities C and D:

$$LS_C = 24 - 10 = 14 \qquad \text{and} \qquad LS_D = 19 - 10 = 9$$

Activity A has more than one immediately following activity: I, F, and C. The earliest of the latest start times is 14 for activity C. Thus,

$$LS_A = 14 - 12 = 2$$

Similarly, activity B has two immediate followers, D and E. Because the earliest of the latest start times of these activities is 9,

$$LS_B = 9 - 9 = 0$$

Decision Point The earliest or latest start dates can be used for developing a project schedule. For example, Kramer should start activity B immediately because the latest start date is 0; otherwise, the project will not be completed by week 69. When the LS is greater than the ES for an activity, that activity could be scheduled for any date between ES and LS. Such is the case for activity E, which could be scheduled to start anytime between week 9 and week 35, depending on the availability of resources. The earliest start and earliest finish times and the latest start and latest finish times for all activities are shown in Figure 3.2. ⌐

Gantt chart A project schedule, usually created by the project manager using computer software, that superimposes project activities, with their precedence relationships and estimated duration times, on a time line.

PROJECT SCHEDULE. The project manager, often with the assistance of computer software, creates the project schedule by superimposing project activities, with their precedence relationships and estimated duration times, on a time line. The resulting diagram is called a **Gantt chart.** Figure 3.3 shows a Gantt chart for the hospital project created with Microsoft Project 2000, a popular software package for project management that can be accessed at the Interactive Web site. The critical path is shown in red. The chart clearly shows which activities can be undertaken simultaneously and when they should be started. In this example, the schedule calls for all activities to begin at their earliest start times. Gantt charts are popular because they are intuitive and easy to construct.

ACTIVITY SLACK. Information on slack can be useful because it highlights activities that need close attention. In this regard, activity slack is the amount of schedule slippage that can be tolerated for an activity before the entire project will be delayed. Activities on the critical path have zero slack. Slack at an activity is reduced when the estimated time duration of an activity is exceeded or when the scheduled start time for the activity must be delayed because of resource considerations. For example, activity G in the hospital project is estimated to have two weeks of slack. Suppose that the orders for the new equipment are placed in week 22, the activity's earliest start date. If the supplier informs the project team that it will have a two-week delay in the normal delivery time, the activity time becomes 37 weeks, consuming all the slack and making activity G critical. Management must carefully monitor the delivery of the equipment to avoid delaying the entire project.

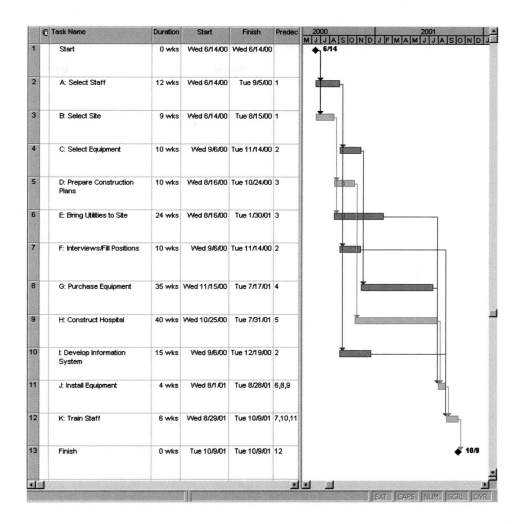

FIGURE 3.3

MS Project Gantt Chart for the Hospital Project Schedule

Sometimes managers can manipulate slack to overcome scheduling problems. Slack information helps the project team make decisions regarding the reallocation of resources. When resources can be used on several different activities in a project, they can be taken from activities with slack and given to activities that are behind schedule until the slack is used up.

There are two types of activity slack. **Total slack** for an activity is a function of the performance of activities leading to it. It can be calculated in one of two ways for any activity:

$$S = LS - ES \qquad or \qquad S = LF - EF$$

total slack Slack shared by other activities; calculated as LS − ES or LF − EF.

Free slack is the amount of time that an activity's earliest finish time can be delayed without delaying the earliest start time of any activity immediately following it. The distinction between the two types of slack is important for making resource-allocation decisions. If an activity has total slack but no free slack, any slippage in its start date will affect the slack of other activities. However, the start date for an activity with free slack can be delayed without affecting the schedules of other activities.

free slack The amount of time that an activity's earliest finish time can be delayed without delaying the earliest start time of any activity immediately following it.

EXAMPLE 3.3

Calculating Activity Slack

Calculate the slack for the activities in the hospital project. Use the data in Figure 3.2.

SOLUTION

The following table from Microsoft Project 2000 shows the total slack and free slack for each activity. Figure 3.4 shows activities B, D, H, J and K are on the critical path because they have zero slack.

Decision Point   The total slack at an activity depends on the performance of activities leading to it. If the project team decides to schedule activity A to begin in week 2 instead of immediately, the total slack for activities C and G would be zero. Thus, total slack is shared among all activities on a particular path. The table also shows that several activities have free slack. For example, activity G has two weeks of free slack. If the schedule goes as planned to week 22 when activity G is scheduled to start, and the supplier for the equipment asks for a two-week extension on the delivery date, the project team knows that the delay will not affect the schedule for the other activities. Nonetheless, activity G would be on the critical path.

	Task Name	Start	Finish	Late Start	Late Finish	Free Slack	Total Slack
1	Start	Wed 6/14/00	Wed 6/14/00	Wed 6/14/00	Wed 6/14/00	0 wks	0 wks
2	A: Select Staff	Wed 6/14/00	Tue 9/5/00	Wed 6/28/00	Tue 9/19/00	0 wks	2 wks
3	B: Select Site	Wed 6/14/00	Tue 8/15/00	Wed 6/14/00	Tue 8/15/00	0 wks	0 wks
4	C: Select Equipment	Wed 9/6/00	Tue 11/14/00	Wed 9/20/00	Tue 11/28/00	0 wks	2 wks
5	D: Prepare Constructi	Wed 8/16/00	Tue 10/24/00	Wed 8/16/00	Tue 10/24/00	0 wks	0 wks
6	E: Bring Utilities to Site	Wed 8/16/00	Tue 1/30/01	Wed 2/14/01	Tue 7/31/01	26 wks	26 wks
7	F: Interviews/Fill Posit	Wed 9/6/00	Tue 11/14/00	Wed 6/20/01	Tue 8/28/01	41 wks	41 wks
8	G: Purchase Equipme	Wed 11/15/00	Tue 7/17/01	Wed 11/29/00	Tue 7/31/01	2 wks	2 wks
9	H: Construct Hospital	Wed 10/25/00	Tue 7/31/01	Wed 10/25/00	Tue 7/31/01	0 wks	0 wks
10	I: Develop Information	Wed 9/6/00	Tue 12/19/00	Wed 5/16/01	Tue 8/28/01	36 wks	36 wks
11	J: Install Equipment	Wed 8/1/01	Tue 8/28/01	Wed 8/1/01	Tue 8/28/01	0 wks	0 wks
12	K: Train Staff	Wed 8/29/01	Tue 10/9/01	Wed 8/29/01	Tue 10/9/01	0 wks	0 wks
13	Finish	Tue 10/9/01	Tue 10/9/01	Tue 10/9/01	Tue 10/9/01	0 wks	0 wks

FIGURE 3.4 • Schedule Table Showing Activity Slacks for the Hospital Project

ANALYZING COST–TIME TRADE-OFFS

How do project planning methods increase the potential to control costs and provide better customer service?

Keeping costs at acceptable levels is almost always as important as meeting schedule dates. The reality of project management is that there are always time–cost trade-offs. For example, a project can often be completed earlier than scheduled by hiring more workers or running extra shifts. Such actions could be advantageous if savings or additional revenues accrue from completing the project early. *Total project costs* are the sum of direct costs, indirect costs, and penalty costs. These costs are dependent either on activity times or on project completion time. *Direct costs* include labor, materials, and any other costs directly related to project activities. Managers can shorten individual activity times by using additional direct resources such as overtime, personnel, or equipment. *Indirect costs* include administration, depreciation, financial, and other variable overhead costs that can be avoided by reducing total project time: The shorter the duration of the project, the lower the indirect costs will be. Finally, a project may incur penalty costs if it extends beyond some specific date, whereas a bonus may be provided for early completion. Thus, a project manager may consider *crashing,* or expediting, some activities to reduce overall project completion time and total project costs. The Managerial Practice feature shows how substantial project penalty costs can be.

MANAGERIAL PRACTICE
Project Delays Are Costly for Amtrak and Its Suppliers

Amtrak (www.amtrak.com), also known as the National Railroad Passenger Corporation, is a $1.84 billion-a-year federally funded corporation whose mandate is to provide passenger rail service to major cities. Competition in the transportation industry is fierce; passengers can use airplanes, busses, cars, and trains to get to their destinations. To gain a larger share of transportation services in the Northeast, Amtrak initiated the Acela Regional project in 1996, with a goal of providing high-speed electric rail service between Boston and Washington, DC, by December, 1999. The project included enhancements to existing rail infrastructure, particularly the 156-mile stretch between New Haven and Boston. Amtrak and its contractors erected 12,200 catenary poles, strung 1,550 miles of electrical wire across three states, and built 25 power stations. In addition, Amtrak installed 115 miles of continuous welded rail, laid 455,000 concrete ties, and poured 500,000 tons of ballast to allow for the faster acceleration and higher top speeds than could be achieved with existing diesel technology.

A key deliverable in the project was the Acela Express train, which is capable of 150 mile-per-hour speeds and includes such amenities as modem jacks at every seat and microbrews on tap. Each train has two locomotives, a business-class car, six coach-class cars, and a café car. In September 1999, Amtrak, though on schedule with the electrification part of the project, discovered that the delivery of 20 locomotives was going to be delayed. The development of the locomotives, which were designed and manufactured by a consortium of two companies, began in 1996 and was on schedule until it was discovered during testing that the wheels underwent excessive wear. Additional design and testing would add several months to the promised delivery date. Without the locomotives, Amtrak could not test the rails and electrification improvements on schedule. The

The Acela Express, North America's first high-speed passenger train, leaves New York on November 16, 2000, enroute to Boston on its inaugural run. The train, which started its trip in Washington, DC, reached New York in two hours and twenty-six minutes. Regular passenger service began in December 2000.

inaugural of the new service would have to be delayed, causing Amtrak to lose some needed revenue.

The contract between Amtrak and the consortium specified penalties for late delivery of the locomotives. The fines started at $1,000 per day per train and went as high as $13,500 per day per train as delays continued. The fines were over and above compensation for certain other damages to Amtrak caused by nonperformance of the consortium.

Sources: "Fast Train to Nowhere?" *Business Week* (September 27, 1999), p. 56.

ASSESSING RISKS

Risk is a measure of the probability and consequence of not reaching a defined project goal. Risk involves the notion of uncertainty as it relates to project timing and costs. Often project teams must deal with uncertainty caused by labor shortages, weather, supply delays, or the outcomes of critical tests. A major responsibility of the project manager at the start of a project is to develop a *risk-management plan*. Team members should have an opportunity to describe the key risks to the project's success and prescribe ways to circumvent them, either by redefining key activities or by developing contingency plans in the event problems occur. A good risk-management plan will quantify the risks and predict their impact on the project. For each risk, the outcome is either acceptable or unacceptable, depending on the project manager's tolerance level for risk.

How can uncertainty
in time estimates be
incorporated into project
planning?

PERT/CPM networks can be used to quantify risks associated with project timing. Often the uncertainty associated with an activity can be reflected in the activity's time duration. For example, an activity in a new-product development project might be developing the enabling technology to manufacture it, an activity that may take from eight months to a year. To incorporate uncertainty into the network model, probability distributions of activity times can be used. There are two approaches: computer simulation and statistical analysis. With simulation, the time for each activity is randomly chosen from its probability distribution (see the Simulation supplement). The critical path of the network is determined and the completion date of the project computed. The procedure is repeated many times, which results in a probability distribution for the completion date.

The statistical analysis approach requires that activity times be stated in terms of three reasonable time estimates:

optimistic time The shortest time in which an activity can be completed, if all goes exceptionally well.

1. The **optimistic time** (*a*) is the shortest time in which the activity can be completed, if all goes exceptionally well.
2. The **most likely time** (*m*) is the probable time required to perform the activity.
3. The **pessimistic time** (*b*) is the longest estimated time required to perform the activity.

most likely time The probable time required to perform an activity.

In the remainder of this section, we will discuss how to calculate activity statistics using these three time estimates and how to analyze project risk using probabilities.

pessimistic time The longest estimated time required to perform an activity.

CALCULATING TIME STATISTICS. With three time estimates—the optimistic, most likely, and pessimistic—the project manager has enough information to estimate the probability that an activity will be completed on schedule. To do so, the project manager must first calculate the mean and variance of a probability distribution for each activity. In PERT/CPM, each activity time is treated as though it were a random variable derived from a beta probability distribution. This distribution can have various shapes, allowing the most likely time estimate (*m*) to fall anywhere between the pessimistic (*b*) and optimistic (*a*) time estimates. The most likely time estimate is the *mode* of the beta distribution, or the time with the highest probability of occurrence. This condition is not possible with the normal distribution, which is symmetrical, because the normal distribution requires the mode to be equidistant from the end points of the distribution.

Two other key assumptions are required. First, we assume that *a*, *m*, and *b* can be estimated accurately. The estimates might best be considered values that define a reasonable time range for the activity duration negotiated between the project manager and the team members responsible for the activities. Second, we assume that the standard deviation σ of the activity time is one-sixth the range $b - a$. Thus, the chance that actual activity times will fall between *a* and *b* is high. Why does this assumption make sense? If the activity time followed the normal distribution, six standard deviations would span approximately 99.74 percent of the normal distribution.

Even with these assumptions, derivation of the mean and variance of each activity's probability distribution is complex. These derivations show that the mean of the beta distribution can be estimated by using the following weighted average of the three time estimates:

$$t_e = \frac{a + 4m + b}{6}$$

The variance of the beta distribution for each activity is

$$\sigma^2 = \left(\frac{b - a}{6} \right)^2$$

The variance, which is the standard deviation squared, increases as the difference between *b* and *a* increases. This result implies that the less certain a person is in estimating the actual time for an activity, the greater will be the variance.

ANALYZING PROBABILITIES. Because time estimates for activities involve uncertainty, project managers are interested in determining the probability of meeting project completion deadlines. To develop the probability distribution for project completion time, we assume that the duration time of one activity does not depend on that of any other activity. This assumption enables us to estimate the mean and variance of the probability distribution of the time duration of the entire project by summing the duration times and variances of the activities along the critical path. However, if one work crew is assigned two activities that can be done at the same time, the activity times will be interdependent. In addition, if other paths in the network have small amounts of slack, one of them might become the critical path before the project is completed. In such a case, we should calculate a probability distribution for those paths.

Because of the assumption that the activity duration times are independent random variables, we can make use of the central limit theorem, which states that the sum of a group of independent, identically distributed random variables approaches a normal distribution as the number of random variables increases. The mean of the normal distribution is the sum of the expected activity times on the path. In the case of the critical path, it is the earliest expected finish time for the project:

$$T_E = \Sigma \text{ (Activity times on the critical path)} = \text{Mean of normal distribution}$$

Similarly, because of the assumption of activity time independence, we use the sum of the variances of the activities along the path as the variance of the time distribution for that path. That is,

$$\sigma^2 = \Sigma \text{ (Variances of activities on the critical path)}$$

To analyze probabilities of completing a project by a certain date using the normal distribution, we use the *z*-transformation formula:

$$z = \frac{T - T_E}{\sqrt{\sigma^2}}$$

where

$$T = \text{due date for the project}$$

$$T_E = \text{earliest expected completion date for the project}$$

The procedure for assessing the probability of completing any activity in a project by a specific date is similar to the one just discussed. However, instead of the critical path, we would use the longest time path of activities from the start node to the activity node in question. See the Solved Problem for this chapter for an example of calculating the probability of completing a project on time.

MONITORING AND CONTROLLING PROJECTS

Once project planning is over, the challenge becomes keeping the project on schedule within the budget of allocated resources. In this section, we discuss how to monitor project status and resource usage. In addition, we identify the features of project management software useful for monitoring and controlling projects.

MONITORING PROJECT STATUS

A good tracking system will help the project team accomplish its project goals. Often the very task of monitoring project progress motivates the team as it sees the benefits of its planning efforts come to fruition. It also focuses attention on the decisions that must be made as the project unfolds. Effective tracking systems collect information on three topics: open issues, risks, and schedule status.

OPEN ISSUES AND RISKS. One of the duties of the project manager is to make sure that issues that have been raised during the project actually get resolved in a timely fashion. The tracking system should remind the project manager of due dates for open issues and who was responsible for seeing that they are resolved. Likewise, it should provide the status of each risk to project delays specified in the risk-management plan so that the team can review them at each meeting. The project manager should also enter new issues or risks into the system as they arise. To be effective, the tracking system requires team members periodically to update information regarding their respective responsibilities. Although the tracking system can be computerized, it can also be as simple as using e-mail, voice mail, or meetings to convey the necessary information.

SCHEDULE STATUS. Even the best laid project plans can go awry. Monitoring slack time in the project schedule can help the project manager control activities along the critical path. Suppose in the hospital project that activity A is completed in 16 weeks rather than the anticipated 12 weeks and that activity B takes 10 weeks instead of the expected 9 weeks. Table 3.1 shows how these delays affect slack times as of the sixteenth week of the project. Activities A and B are not shown because they have already been completed.

Negative slack occurs when the assumptions used to compute planned slack are invalid. Activities C, G, J, and K, which depend on the timely completion of activities A and B, show negative slack because they have been pushed beyond their planned latest start dates. The activities at the top of Table 3.1 are more critical than those at the bottom because they are the furthest behind schedule and affect the completion time of the entire project. To meet the original completion target of week 69, the project manager must try to make up two weeks of time somewhere along path C–G–J–K. Moreover, one week will have to be made up along path D–H. If that time is made up, there will be two critical paths: C–G–J–K and D–H–J–K. Many project managers work with computer scheduling programs that generate slack reports like the one shown in Table 3.1.

MONITORING PROJECT RESOURCES

The resources allocated to a project are consumed at an uneven rate that is a function of the timing of the schedules for the project's activities. Projects have a *life cycle* that

TABLE 3.1				
Slack Calculations After Activities A and B Have Been Completed				

Activity	Duration	Earliest Start	Latest Start	Slack
C	10	16	14	−2
G	35	26	24	−2
J	4	61	59	−2
K	6	65	63	−2
D	10	10	9	−1
H	40	20	19	−1
E	24	10	35	25
I	15	16	48	32
F	10	16	53	37

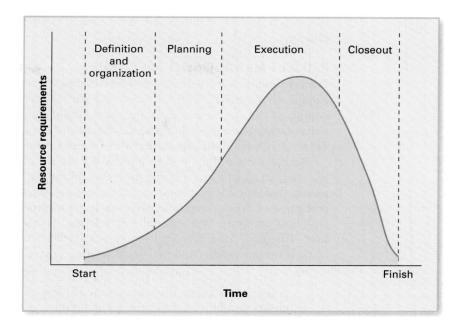

FIGURE 3.5

Project Life Cycle

consists of four major phases: definition and organization, planning, execution, and closeout. Figure 3.5 shows that each of the four phases requires different resource commitments.

We have already discussed the activities associated with the project definition and organization and project planning phases. The phase that takes the most resources is the *execution phase,* during which managers focus on activities pertaining to deliverables. The project schedule becomes very important because it shows when each resource devoted to a given activity will be required. Monitoring the progress of activities throughout the project is important in order to avoid potential overloading of resources. Problems arise when a specific resource, such as a construction crew or staff specialist, is required on several activities with overlapping schedules. Project managers have several options to alleviate resource problems, including:

❑ *Resource leveling,* which is an attempt to reduce the peaks and valleys in resource needs by shifting the schedules of conflicting activities within their earliest and latest start dates. If an activity must be delayed beyond its latest start date, the completion date of the total project will be delayed unless activities on the critical path can be reduced to compensate.

❑ *Resource allocation,* which is an attempt to shift resources from activities with slack to those on the critical path where resources are overloaded. A slack report such as the one in Table 3.1 identifies potential candidates for resource shifting. However, efficiency can be compromised if shifted employees do not have all the skills required for their new assignments.

❑ *Resource acquisition,* which simply adds more of an overloaded resource to maintain the schedule of an activity.

The project *closeout* is an activity that many project managers forget to include in their consideration of resource usage. The purpose of this final phase in the project life cycle is to write final reports and complete remaining deliverables. A very important aspect of this phase, however, is compiling the team's recommendations for improving the project process of which they were a part. Many team members will be assigned to other projects where they can apply what they learned.

PROJECT MANAGEMENT SOFTWARE

Project management software is accessible to most organizations and is being used extensively in government, services, and manufacturing. Ford Motor Company used computerized network planning for retooling assembly lines, and Chrysler Corporation used it for building a new assembly plant. Other users include the San Francisco Opera Association, the Walt Disney Company, and Procter & Gamble.

Bechtel Group, Inc., had to purchase a sophisticated software package because of the complexity of its scheduling problems. However, with the advent of personal computers, "off-the-shelf" project management software has become accessible to many companies. Large as well as small projects are routinely managed with the assistance of standard computerized scheduling packages. Software costs have come down, and user–computer interfaces are friendly. Standard software programs may differ in terms of their output reports and may include one or more of the following capabilities:

❑ *Gantt Charts and PERT/CPM Diagrams.*   The graphics capabilities of software packages allow for visual displays of project progress on Gantt charts and PERT/CPM network diagrams. Most packages allow the user to display portions of the network on the video monitor to analyze specific problems.

❑ *Project Status and Summary Reports.*   These reports include budget variance reports that compare planned to actual expenses at any stage in the project, resource histograms that graphically display the usage of a particular resource over time, status reports for each worker by task performed, and summary reports that indicate project progress to top management.

❑ *Tracking Reports.*   These reports identify areas of concern such as the percentage of activity completion with respect to time, budget, or labor resources. Most software packages allow multiple projects to be tracked at the same time. This feature is important when resources must be shared jointly by several projects.

❑ *Project Calendar.*   This feature allows the project manager to lay out calendars based on actual workdays, weekends, and vacations and enables the software to present all schedules and reports in terms of the project calendar.

❑ *What-If Analysis.*   Some packages allow the project manager to enter proposed changes to activity times, precedence relationships, or start dates in order to see what effect the changes might have on the project completion date.

Today there are more than 200 software packages, most of which are user friendly and available for the PC.

MANAGING PROJECT PROCESSES ACROSS THE ORGANIZATION

Projects are big and small. They are contained within a single department or cut across several departments. Many organizations have several projects going on at any one time, addressing issues of concern to finance, marketing, accounting, human resources, information systems, or operations. Regardless of the scope, projects are completed with the use of a project process. The size of the project team may be small and the need for project management software marginal, but successful projects will use the principles we discussed in this chapter regardless of the discipline the project addresses.

The applicability of project processes is pervasive across all types of organizations and disciplines. Managers often find themselves working with counterparts from other departments. For example, consider a project to develop a corporate database at a bank. Because no department knows exactly what services a customer is receiving from the other departments, the project will consolidate information about corporate customers from many areas of the bank into one corporate database. From this information corporate banking services could be designed not only to better serve the corporate customers but to provide a basis for evaluating the prices that the bank charges. Marketing is interested in knowing all the services a customer is receiving so that it can package and sell other services that the customer may not be aware of. Finance is interested in how "profitable" a customer is to the bank and whether provided services are appropriately priced. The project team should consist of representatives from marketing, the finance departments with a direct interest in corporate clients, and management information systems. Projects such as this one are becoming more common as companies take advantage of the Internet to provide services and products directly to the customer.

EQUATION SUMMARY

1. Start and finish times:

   ES = max [EF times of all activities immediately preceding activity]

   EF = ES + t

   LS = LF − t

   LF = min [LS times of all activities immediately following activity]

2. Activity slack:

   $$S = \text{LS} - \text{ES} \qquad \text{or} \qquad S = \text{LF} - \text{EF}$$

3. Activity time statistics:

   $$t_e = \frac{a + 4m + b}{6} \qquad \text{(expected activity time)}$$

   $$\sigma^2 = \left(\frac{b - a}{6}\right)^2 \qquad \text{(variance)}$$

4. *z*-transformation formula:

   $$z = \frac{T - T_E}{\sqrt{\sigma^2}}$$

   where

   T = due date for the project

   T_E = Σ (expected activity times on the critical path)

   = mean of normal distribution

   σ^2 = Σ (variances of activities on the critical path)

CHAPTER HIGHLIGHTS

- ❐ A project is an interrelated set of activities that often transcends functional boundaries. A project process is the organization and management of the resources dedicated to completing a project. Managing project processes involves defining and organizing, planning, and monitoring and controlling the project.

- ❐ Project planning involves defining the work breakdown structure, diagramming the network, developing a schedule, analyzing cost–time trade-offs, and assessing risks.

- ❐ Project planning and scheduling focus on the critical path: the sequence of activities requiring the greatest cumulative amount of time for completion. Delay in critical activities will delay the entire project.

- ❐ Risks associated with the completion of activities on schedule can be incorporated in project networks by recognizing three time estimates for each activity and then calculating expected activity times and variances. The probability of completing the schedule by a certain date can be computed with this information.

- ❐ Monitoring and controlling the project involves the use of activity-time slack reports and reports on actual resource usage. Overloads on certain resources can be rectified by resource leveling, allocation, or acquisition.

SOLVED PROBLEM

An advertising project manager has developed the network diagrams shown in Figure 3.6 for a new advertising campaign. In addition, the manager has gathered the time information for each activity, as shown in the accompanying table.

	TIME ESTIMATES (wk)			
ACTIVITY	Optimistic	Most Likely	Pessimistic	IMMEDIATE PREDECESSOR(S)
A	1	4	7	—
B	2	6	7	—
C	3	3	6	B
D	6	13	14	A
E	3	6	12	A, C
F	6	8	16	B
G	1	5	6	E, F

a. Calculate the expected time and variance for each activity.

b. Calculate the activity slacks and determine the critical path using the expected activity times.

c. What is the probability of completing the project within 23 weeks?

SOLUTION

a. The expected time for each activity is calculated as follows:

$$t_e = \frac{a + 4m + b}{6}$$

ACTIVITY	EXPECTED TIME (wk)	VARIANCE
A	4.0	1.00
B	5.5	0.69
C	3.5	0.25
D	12.0	1.78
E	6.5	2.25
F	9.0	2.78
G	4.5	0.69

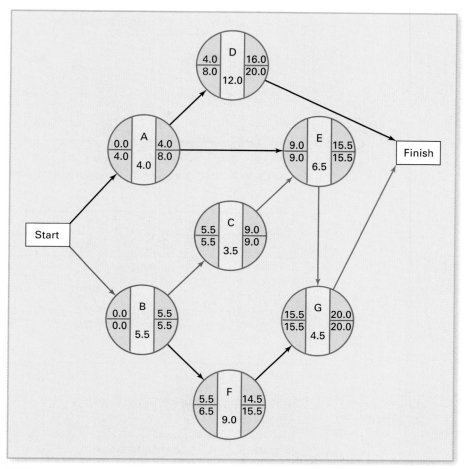

FIGURE 3.6 • AON Network with All Time Estimates Needed to Calculate Slack

b. We need to calculate the earliest start, latest start, earliest finish, and latest finish times for each activity. Starting with activities A and B, we proceed from the beginning of the network and move to the end, calculating the earliest start and finish times:

ACTIVITY	EARLIEST START (wk)	EARLIEST FINISH (wk)
A	0	0 + 4.0 = 4.0
B	0	0 + 5.5 = 5.5
C	5.5	5.5 + 3.5 = 9.0
D	4.0	4.0 + 12.0 = 16.0
E	9.0	9.0 + 6.5 = 15.5
F	5.5	5.5 + 9.0 = 14.5
G	15.5	15.5 + 4.5 = 20.0

Based on expected times, the earliest finish for the project is week 20, when activity G has been completed. Using that as a target date, we can work backward through the network, calculating the latest start and finish times (shown graphically in Figure 3.6):

ACTIVITY	LATEST START (wk)	LATEST FINISH (wk)
G	15.5	20.0
F	6.5	15.5
E	9.0	15.5
D	8.0	20.0
C	5.5	9.0
B	0.0	5.5
A	8.0	12.0

We now calculate the activity slacks and determine which activities are on the critical path:

ACTIVITY	START		FINISH		ACTIVITY SLACK	CRITICAL PATH
	Earliest	Latest	Earliest	Latest		
A	0.0	4.0	4.0	8.0	4.0	No
B	0.0	0.0	5.5	5.5	0.0	Yes
C	5.5	5.5	9.0	9.0	0.0	Yes
D	4.0	8.0	16.0	20.0	4.0	No
E	9.0	9.0	15.5	15.5	0.0	Yes
F	5.5	6.5	14.5	15.5	1.0	No
G	15.5	15.5	20.0	20.0	0.0	Yes

The paths and their total expected times and variances are

PATH	TOTAL EXPECTED TIME (wk)	TOTAL VARIANCE
A–D	4 + 12 = 16	1.00 + 1.78 = 2.78
A–E–G	4 + 6.5 + 4.5 = 15	1.00 + 2.25 + 0.69 = 3.94
B–C–E–G	5.5 + 3.5 + 6.5 + 4.5 = 20	0.69 + 0.25 + 2.25 + 0.69 = 3.88
B–F–G	5.5 + 9 + 4.5 = 19	0.69 + 2.78 + 0.69 = 4.16

The critical path is B–C–E–G, with a total expected time of 20 weeks. However, path B–F–G is 19 weeks and has a large variance.

c. We first calculate the *z*-value:

$$z = \frac{T - T_E}{\sqrt{\sigma^2}} = \frac{23 - 20}{\sqrt{3.88}} = 1.52$$

Using the Normal Distribution appendix, we find that the probability of completing the project in 23 weeks or less is 0.9357. Because the length of path B–F–G is very close to that of the critical path and has a large variance, it might well become the critical path during the project.

CD-ROM RESOURCES

The Student CD-ROM that accompanies this text contains the following resources, which allow you to further practice and apply the concepts presented in this chapter.

- ❏ **OM Explorer Tutors:** OM Explorer contains five tutor programs to enhance your understanding of learning curves, time study sample sizes, normal times for an activity, standard times for an activity, and the work sampling approach. See the Supplement C and Supplement D folders in OM Explorer.

- ❏ **OM Explorer Solvers:** OM Explorer contains three programs designed to solve general problems involving time study, work sampling, and learning curves. See the Measuring Output Rates and Learning Curves folders in OM Explorer.

- ❏ **Equation Summary:** All the equations for this chapter can be found in one convenient location.

- ❏ **Discussion Questions:** Three questions will challenge your understanding of the role of project management by asking you to reflect on your experiences.

- ❏ **Case:** The Pert Studebaker. Will Vikky Roberts complete the project on time and within budget?

- ❏ **Big Picture:** Coors Field Baseball Stadium. See how a major league baseball stadium is constructed and how project leader John Lehigh and his team coped with the many unforeseen events.

- ❏ **Supplement C:** Measuring Output Rates. This supplement presents several tools for estimating the time to perform a repetitive task after all learning effects have worn off.

- ❏ **Supplement D:** Learning Curve Analysis. This supplement provides the background to estimate the time or resources required to perform an activity consisting of the production of a given number of identical units.

INTERACTIVE RESOURCES

The Interactive Web site associated with this text (www.prenhall.com/ritzman) contains many tools and activities specifically designed for this chapter. The following items are recommended to enhance your understanding of the material in this chapter.

- ❏ **Internet Activities:** Try out three different links to project management topics including scheduling at the Olympics and managing construction projects.

- ❏ **Internet Tour:** Explore the management of a project process at the Rieger Orgelbau Pipe Organ Factory.

- ❏ **MS Project:** Use the link on the Interactive Web site to download a trial version of the popular MS Project software.

PROBLEMS

An icon next to a problem identifies the software that can be helpful but is not mandatory.

1. ● **MS Project** Consider the following data for a project.

ACTIVITY	ACTIVITY TIME (DAYS)	IMMEDIATE PREDECESSOR(S)
A	2	—
B	4	A
C	5	A
D	2	B
E	1	B
F	8	B, C
G	3	D, E
H	5	F
I	4	F
J	7	G, H, I

    a. Draw the network diagram.

    b. Calculate the critical path for this project.

    c. How much total slack is in activities G, H, and I?

2. ● **MS Project** A project has the following precedence relationships and activity times.

ACTIVITY	ACTIVITY TIME (wks)	IMMEDIATE PREDECESSOR(S)
A	4	—
B	10	—
C	5	A
D	15	B, C
E	12	B
F	4	D
G	8	E
H	7	F, G

    a. Draw the network diagram.

    b. Calculate the total slack for each activity. Which activities are on the critical path?

3. ● **MS Project** Consider the following project information.

ACTIVITY	ACTIVITY TIME (wk)	IMMEDIATE PREDECESSOR(S)
A	4	—
B	3	—
C	5	—
D	3	A, B
E	6	B
F	4	D, C
G	8	E, C
H	12	F, G

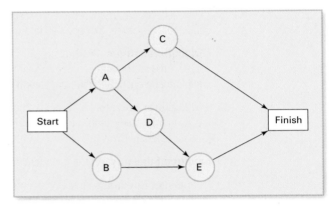

FIGURE 3.7 • Project Diagram

    a. Draw the network diagram for this project.

    b. Specify the critical path.

    c. Calculate the total slack for activities A and D.

    d. What happens to the slack for D if A takes five weeks?

4. ● **MS Project** Recently, you were assigned to manage a project for your company. You have constructed a network diagram depicting the various activities in the project (Fig. 3.7). In addition, you have asked your team to estimate the amount of time that they would expect each of the activities to take. Their responses are shown in the following table.

	TIME ESTIMATES (DAYS)		
ACTIVITY	Optimistic	Most Likely	Pessimistic
A	5	8	11
B	4	8	11
C	5	6	7
D	2	4	6
E	4	7	10

    a. What is the expected completion time of the project?

    b. What is the probability of completing the project in 21 days?

    c. What is the probability of completing the project in 17 days?

5. ● **MS Project** The director of continuing education at Bluebird University has just approved the planning for a sales-training seminar. Her administrative assistant has identified the various activities that must be done and their relationships to each other, as shown in Table 3.2.

    Because of the uncertainty in planning the new course, the assistant also has supplied the following time estimates for each activity.

TABLE 3.2 *Activities for the Sales-Training Seminar*

ACTIVITY	DESCRIPTION	IMMEDIATE PREDECESSOR(S)
A	Design brochure and course announcement.	—
B	Identify prospective teachers.	—
C	Prepare detailed outline of course.	—
D	Send brochure and student applications.	A
E	Send teacher applications.	B
F	Select teacher for course.	C, E
G	Accept students.	D
H	Select text for course.	F
I	Order and receive texts.	G, H
J	Prepare room for class.	G

ACTIVITY	TIME ESTIMATES (DAYS)		
	Optimistic	Most Likely	Pessimistic
A	5	7	8
B	6	8	12
C	3	4	5
D	11	17	25
E	8	10	12
F	3	4	5
G	4	8	9
H	5	7	9
I	8	11	17
J	4	4	4

The director wants to conduct the seminar 47 working days from now. What is the probability that everything will be ready in time?

6. Jason Ritz, district manager for Gumfull Foods, Inc., is in charge of opening a new fast-food outlet in the college town of Clarity. His major concern is the hiring of a manager and a cadre of hamburger cooks, assemblers, and dispensers. He also has to coordinate the renovation of a building that was previously owned by a pet-supplies retailer. He has gathered the data shown in Table 3.3.

Top management has told Ritz that the new outlet is to be opened as soon as possible. Every week that the project can be shortened will save the firm $1,200 in lease costs. Ritz thought about how to save time during the project and came up with two possibilities. One was to employ Arctic, Inc., a local employment agency, to locate some good prospects for the manager's job. This approach would save three weeks in activity A and cost Gumfull Foods $2,500. The other was to add a few workers to shorten the time for activity B by two weeks at an additional cost of $2,700.

Help Jason Ritz by answering the following questions.

a. How long is the project expected to take?

b. Suppose that Ritz has a personal goal of completing the project in 14 weeks. What is the probability that this will happen?

c. What additional expenditures should be made to reduce the project's duration? Use the expected time for each activity as though it were certain.

7. **MS Project** Reliable Garage is completing production of the J2000 kit car. The following data are available for the project.

ACTIVITY	ACTIVITY TIME (wks)	IMMEDIATE PREDECESSOR(S)
A	2	—
B	6	A
C	4	B
D	5	C
E	7	C
F	5	C
G	5	F
H	3	D, E, G

TABLE 3.3 *Data for the Fast-Food Outlet Project*

ACTIVITY	DESCRIPTION	IMMEDIATE PREDECESSOR(S)	TIME (wk)		
			a	m	b
A	Interview at college for new manager.	—	2	4	6
B	Renovate building.	—	5	8	11
C	Place ad for employees and interview applicants.	—	7	9	17
D	Have new-manager prospects visit.	A	1	2	3
E	Purchase equipment for new outlet and install.	B	2	4	12
F	Check employee applicant references and make final selection.	C	4	4	4
G	Check references for new manager and make final selection.	D	1	1	1
H	Hold orientation meetings and do payroll paperwork.	E, F, G	2	2	2

a. Draw the network diagram for the project.

b. Determine the project's critical path and duration.

c. What is the total slack for each activity?

8. 💿 **MS Project** The following information concerns a new project your company is undertaking.

ACTIVITY	ACTIVITY TIME (wks)	IMMEDIATE PREDECESSOR(S)
A	10	—
B	11	—
C	9	A, B
D	5	A, B
E	8	A, B
F	13	C, E
G	5	C, D
H	10	G
I	6	F, G
J	9	E, H
K	11	I, J

a. Draw the network diagram for this project.

b. Determine the critical path and project completion time.

9. The project manager of Good Public Relations has gathered the data shown in Table 3.4 for a new advertising campaign.

a. How long is the project likely to take?

TABLE 3.4 *Activity Data for Advertising Project*

ACTIVITY	TIME ESTIMATES (DAYS)			IMMEDIATE PREDECESSOR(S)
	Optimistic	Most Likely	Pessimistic	
A	8	10	12	—
B	5	8	17	—
C	7	8	9	—
D	1	2	3	B
E	8	10	12	A, C
F	5	6	7	D, E
G	1	3	5	D, E
H	2	5	8	F, G
I	2	4	6	G
J	4	5	8	H
K	2	2	2	H

b. What is the probability that the project will take more than 38 weeks?

c. Consider the path A–E–G–H–J. What is the probability that this path will exceed the expected project duration?

10. 🌐 **MS Project** Fronc is a wedding coordinator. Beatrice Wright and William Bach have asked Fronc to help them organize their wedding. Create a network showing the precedence relationships for the activities listed in Table 3.5.

TABLE 3.5 *Will & Bea Wright-Bach Wedding Activities*

ACTIVITY	DESCRIPTION	ACTIVITY	DESCRIPTION
Start	Accept proposal	O	Order cake, mints, cashews
A	Select and print announcements	P	Photographer
B	Blood tests	Q	Reserve reception hall
C	Color theme selection	R	Rings
D1	Wedding dress	S	Bachelor party
D2	Bridesmaids' dresses	T	Tuxedo rental
D3	Bride's mother's dress	U	Ushers
D4	Groom's mother's dress	V	Reserve church
E	Establish budget and net worth of parents	W	Wedding ceremony
F	Flowers	X	Select groomsmen, ring bearer
G	Gifts for wedding party	Y	Select bridesmaids, flower girls
H	Honeymoon planning	Z	Rehearsal and prenuptial dinner
I	Mailed invitations	AA	Prenuptial agreement
J	Guest list	BB	Groom's nervous breakdown
K	Caterer	CC	Register for china, flatware, gifts
L	Marriage license	DD	Dance band
M	Menu for reception	EE	Thank-you notes
N	Newspaper picture, society page announcement	FF	Finish

SELECTED REFERENCES

Branston, Lisa. "Construction Firms View the Web as a Way to Get Out From Under a Mountain of Paper." *The Wall Street Journal* (November 15, 1999).

Celand, D. I. *Project Management: Strategic Design and Implementation.* New York: McGraw-Hill, 1994.

Day, P. J. *Microsoft Project 4.0 for Windows and the Macintosh: Setting Project Management Standards.* New York: Van Nostrand Reinhold, 1995.

IPS Associates. *Project Management Manual.* Boston: Harvard Business School Publishing, 1996.

Kerzner, Harold. *Applied Project Management: Best Practices on Implementation.* New York: John Wiley & Sons, 2000.

Kerzner, Harold. *Project Management: A Systems Approach to Planning, Scheduling and Controlling,* 6th ed. New York: John Wiley & Sons, 1998.

Meredith, Jack R., and Samuel J. Mantel. *Project Management: A Managerial Approach,* 4th ed. New York: John Wiley & Sons, 2000.

"Project Management Software Buyer's Guide." *Industrial Engineering* (March 1995), pp. 36–37.

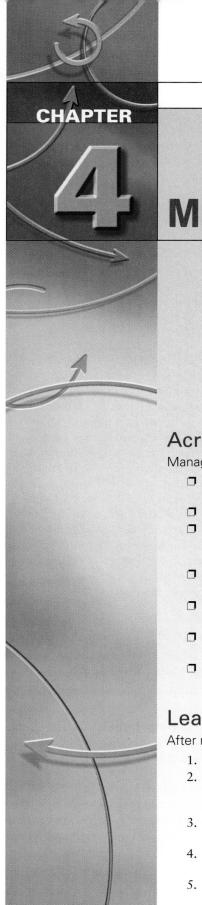

Managing Technology

Across the Organization

Management of technology is important to . . .

- ❐ **accounting,** which can use new technologies to perform its work better and provide important information on new product and process proposals.
- ❐ **engineering,** which designs products and processes that use new technologies.
- ❐ **finance,** which seeks better ways to perform its work, provides input to top management on the financial advisability of new products and process changes, and looks for ways to finance technological change.
- ❐ **human resources,** which needs to anticipate and manage the impact that technological change has on the workforce.
- ❐ **management information systems,** which help identify new information technologies and implements them when approved.
- ❐ **marketing,** which seeks better technologies for its processes and how new product and service possibilities can better meet customer needs.
- ❐ **operations,** which needs new technologies to produce products and services more effectively and provide better value to customers.

Learning Goals

After reading this chapter, you will be able to . . .

1. define the meaning of technology and describe how best to manage it.
2. demonstrate the importance of technology to the firm's supply chain and within each functional area and discuss real examples of its impact in manufacturing and service industries.
3. describe the fundamental role of the computer and information technology in reshaping an organization's processes.
4. describe how the Internet, electronic commerce, and enterprise resource planning are changing business processes.
5. identify the factors that managers must consider when making technological choices.

Technology needs to be managed, like any other aspect of processes. Such is the case at Seven-Eleven Japan (www.sej.co.jp), which has invested aggressively in information technology (IT) over the years. Since Seven-Eleven Japan began in the early 1970s, founder Toshifumi Suzuki has sought to upgrade processes that better satisfy customers' demand for convenience, quality, and service. Achieving these competitive priorities has led to the continual application of information technology. The company's information system rivals any in the West for just-in-time logistics excellence and deep knowledge of customers. It allows stores to be very responsive to consumers' shifting tastes. If a particular type of *bento* (take-out lunch box) sells out by midday, extra stock can be in the stores by early afternoon. If it's raining and *bentos* will not be in high demand, deliveries are reduced. However, the information system reminds operators to put umbrellas on sale next to the cash register.

Several lessons can be learned from Seven-Eleven Japan on the task of managing technology. Its managers see IT as just one competitive lever among many and, as such, a way to improve processes. They choose technology, whether old or new, that helps them achieve process performance goals. Investments are chosen to add customer value to processes and to help managers learn how to understand their customers better. IT

projects are not assessed primarily by financial metrics and "value for money" thinking. Instead, performance-improvement goals drive investments. Rather than seeking "technology solutions" and "technology for technology's sake," Seven-Eleven Japan executives prefer "appropriate technology" to "first-mover" advantages. They identify the tasks to be done and desired performance levels. Then they pick a technology that suits the people doing the work. This approach avoids new IT that is difficult to use, counterintuitive, and annoying—a problem that plagues many firms.

The company is also expanding its e-commerce initiatives, both in the United States and Japan. The process is envisioned somewhat differently in Japan, where there is a widespread preference for cash payments and money transfers instead of credit cards. The shopper in Tokyo would browse on the Web and place the order electronically, just as in the United States. The difference is that, a few days later, the shopper will traipse to his or her local Seven-Eleven, fork over some yen to the clerk, and receive his or her purchases.

Seven-Eleven Japan uses technology to expand its services to customers. Here a customer picks up a book she purchased from an online bookseller. The book has been delivered to the Seven-Eleven for pickup.

Sources: Earl, Michael, and M. M. Bensaou. "The Right Mind-Set for Managing Information Technology." *Harvard Business Review* (September–October 1998), pp. 119–129; "E-Commerce Japanese Style." *Wired* (June 1999), www.wired.com/news/business/0,1367,20061,00.html.

TECHNOLOGICAL CHANGE IS A major factor in gaining competitive advantage. It can create whole new industries and dramatically alter the landscape in existing industries. The development and innovative use of technology can give a firm a distinctive competence that is difficult to match, as with Seven-Eleven Japan. Competitive advantage comes not just from creating new technology but also by applying and integrating existing technologies. Advances in technology spawn new products and services and reshape processes. Thus, technology takes many forms, beginning with ideas, knowledge, and experience, and then uses them to create new and better ways of doing things.

In this chapter, we explore how technology can create a competitive advantage. We begin with a general definition of technology and then apply it specifically to products, processes, and information. We single out for more discussion two high-growth information technologies: e-commerce and enterprise resource planning. Finally, we examine the management of technology strategy, offering guidelines on choosing new technologies.

THE MEANING AND ROLE OF TECHNOLOGY

What are the key aspects of technology and its management?

technology The know-how, physical equipment, and procedures used to produce products and services.

support network A network comprised of the physical, informational, and organizational relationships that make a technology complete and allow it to function as intended.

We define **technology** as the know-how, physical equipment, and procedures used to produce products and services. Know-how is the knowledge and judgment of how, when, and why to employ equipment and procedures. Craftsmanship and experience are embodied in this knowledge and often cannot be written into manuals or routines. Equipment consists of such tools as computers, scanners, ATMs, or robots. Procedures are the rules and techniques for operating equipment and performing the work. All three components work together, as illustrated by air-travel technology. Knowledge is reflected in scheduling, routing, and pricing decisions. The airplane is the equipment, consisting of many components and assemblies. The procedures are rules and manuals on aircraft maintenance and how to operate the airplane under many different conditions. Technologies do not occur in a vacuum but are embedded in support networks. A **support network** comprises the physical, informational, and organizational relationships that make a technology complete and allow it to function as intended. Thus, the support network for air-travel technology includes the infrastructure of airports, baggage-handling facilities, travel agencies, air traffic control operations, and the communication systems connecting them.

THREE PRIMARY AREAS OF TECHNOLOGY

Within an organization, technologies reflect what people are working on and what they are using to do that work. The most widespread view of technology is that of *product technology*, which a firm's engineering and research groups develop when creating new products and services. Another view is that of *process technology*, which a firm's employees use to do their work. A third area, which is becoming increasingly important, is *information technology*, which a firm's employees use to acquire, process, and communicate information. The way in which a specific technology is classified depends on its application. A product technology to one firm may be part of the process technology of another.

Operations managers are interested in all three aspects of technology. Product technology is important because a firm's processes must be designed to produce products and services spawned by technological advances. Process technology is important because it can improve methods currently used in the production system. Information technology is important because it can improve the way information is used to operate the firm's processes.

product technology Ideas that are developed within the organization and translated into new products and services.

PRODUCT TECHNOLOGY. Developed within the organization, **product technology** translates ideas into new products and services. Product technology is developed primarily by engineers and researchers. They develop new knowledge and ways of doing things, merge them with and extend conventional capabilities, and translate them into specific products and services with features that customers value. Developing new product technologies requires close cooperation with marketing to find out what customers really want and with operations to determine how goods or services can be produced effectively.

What process technologies
are used in a supply chain?

process technology The
methods by which an
organization does things.

PROCESS TECHNOLOGY. The methods by which an organization does things rely on the application of **process technology.** Some of the large number of process technologies used by an organization are unique to a functional area; others are used more universally. Of interest are the many technologies used in a firm's supply chain (see Chapter 2, "Process Management" and Chapter 8, "Supply-Chain Management").

Figure 4.1 shows how technologies support the processes in the supply chain for both service providers and manufacturers. Each technology can be broken further into still more technologies.

Supplement E, "Computer-Integrated Manufacturing" on the Student CD-ROM describes a new family of manufacturing technologies and will give you a sense of the widening array of possibilities. All functional areas, not just those areas directly involved with the supply chain, rely on process technologies. Figure 4.2 identifies the process technologies commonly used in these other functional areas.

Developments in process technology for each area can be dramatic. Consider sales processes that use vending machines to distribute products. This process technology is shedding its low-tech image. New electronic vending machines are loaded with circuit boards and microprocessors rather than gears and chains. They determine how much product is left, audit coin boxes, and make sure that the mechanisms work properly. These capabilities simplify product ordering and inventory control processes.

With more sophisticated versions, vending machine communication may even allow companies at distant locations to change product prices, reset thermostats, and verify credit cards. Handheld computers have also caught on, and some drivers tending vending machines use them to "read" the status of certain machines in just sec-

FIGURE 4.1

*Process Technologies
Along the Supply Chain*

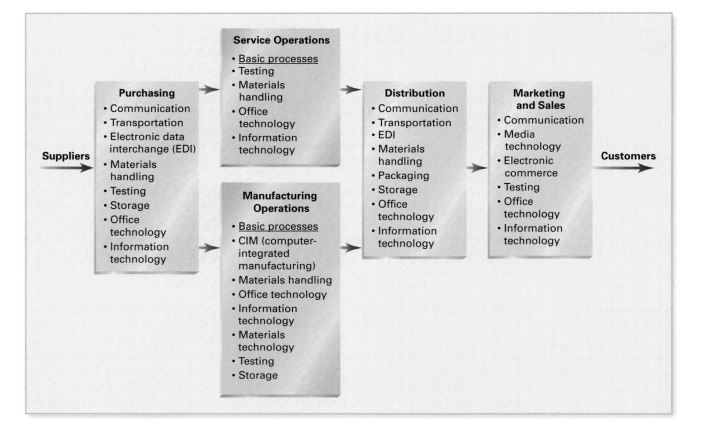

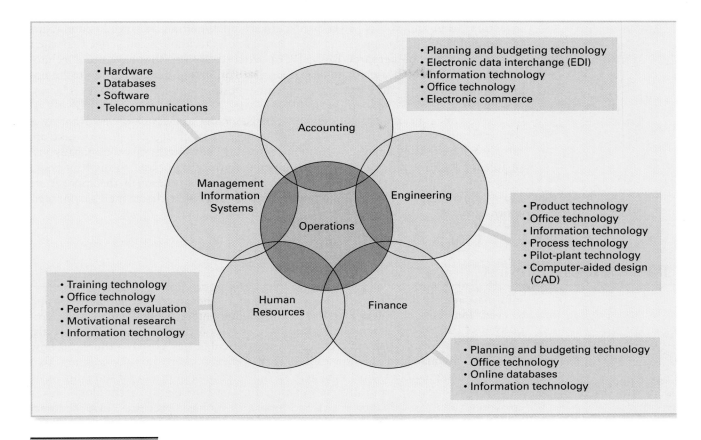

- Planning and budgeting technology
- Electronic data interchange (EDI)
- Information technology
- Office technology
- Electronic commerce

- Hardware
- Databases
- Software
- Telecommunications

- Product technology
- Office technology
- Information technology
- Process technology
- Pilot-plant technology
- Computer-aided design (CAD)

- Training technology
- Office technology
- Performance evaluation
- Motivational research
- Information technology

- Planning and budgeting technology
- Office technology
- Online databases
- Information technology

Accounting

Management Information Systems

Engineering

Operations

Human Resources

Finance

FIGURE 4.2

Technologies for Other Functional Areas

onds. When the data are processed, the computers prepare restocking lists for route drivers. Now that replenishments can be made more quickly and accurately, some customers are reporting inventory reductions of 20 percent with no loss in service—a reduction that amounts to a significant savings in addition to the time savings for the drivers.

information technology
Technology used to acquire, process, and transmit information with which to make more effective decisions.

INFORMATION TECHNOLOGY. Managers use **information technology** to acquire, process, and transmit information with which to make more effective decisions. Information technology pervades every functional area in the workplace (see Figs. 4.1 and 4.2). Nowhere is it more revolutionary than in offices, whether main offices, branch offices, back offices, front offices, sales offices, or functional area offices. Office information technologies include various types of telecommunication systems, word processing, computer spreadsheets, computer graphics, e-mail, online databases, the Internet, and intranets.

TECHNOLOGY'S ROLE IN IMPROVING BUSINESS PERFORMANCE

Why is technology so important to operations managers?

Technology is probably the most important force driving the increase in global competition. As various studies show, companies that invest in and apply new technologies tend to have stronger financial positions than those that do not. One study of more than 1,300 manufacturers in Europe, Japan, and North America focused more on process technologies and revealed a strong link between financial performance and technological innovation. Companies with stellar performance in annual sales, inventory turns, and profits had more experience with multiple advanced manufacturing technologies and demonstrated more leadership in technological change than their underperforming counterparts (Roth, 1996). Even small firms that have more technological know-how and use computer-based information and manufacturing technologies more intensively enjoy stronger competitive positions (Lefebvre, Langley, Harvey, and Lefebvre, 1992).

At the same time, the relationship between technology and competitive advantage is often misunderstood. High technology and technological change for its own sake are not always best. They might not create a competitive advantage, be economically justifiable, fit with the desired profile of competitive priorities, or add to the firm's core competencies. In other words, being a high-tech firm is not necessarily the appropriate use of technology. For many jobs, a simple handsaw is a better choice than a computer-controlled laser.

INFORMATION TECHNOLOGY

Information technology is crucial to operations everywhere along the supply chain and to every functional area (see Figs. 4.1 and 4.2). Computers are spawning a huge proportion of current technological changes and innovations, either directly or indirectly. Computer-based information technology, in particular, has greatly influenced how operations are managed and how offices work. Office workers can now do things that were not even possible a short time ago, such as accessing information simultaneously from several locations and diverse functional areas. Information technology makes cross-functional coordination easier and links a firm's basic processes. In a manufacturing plant, information technologies can link people with the work centers, databases, and computers.

Let us first examine the four basic building blocks of information technology. Then we can show how they are being used in two of the fastest-growing areas of information technology: e-commerce and enterprise resource planning.

COMPONENTS OF INFORMATION TECHNOLOGY

What are the components of information technology?

Information technology is made up of four subtechnologies:

1. hardware
2. software
3. databases
4. telecommunications

HARDWARE. A computer and the devices connected to it, which can include (among other things) an Intel semiconductor or a PixelVision flat-panel monitor, are called **hardware.** Improved hardware memory, processing capability, and speed have, in large part, driven recent technological change. Scientists and engineers at computer and telecommunications companies and academics are the primary sources of these advances.

hardware A computer and the devices connected to it.

software The computer programs that make hardware work and carry out different application tasks.

SOFTWARE. The computer programs that make hardware work and carry out different application tasks are called **software.** It has become such an important technology that people often get the mistaken impression that software is the sum total of information systems. Application software, such as that provided by Microsoft, Sun, and others, is what computer users work with. It allows information to be recorded, manipulated, and presented as output that is invaluable in performing work and managing operations. Information systems specialists, both inside and outside a firm, work with the managers who ultimately must decide what the firm's systems should do, who should have access to them, and how the information should be used.

Software is available for use with almost all the decision tools described in this book, including flow diagramming, statistical process control techniques, learning curves, simulation, queuing models, location and layout techniques, forecasting models, linear programming, production and inventory control systems, and scheduling techniques. Software is essential to many manufacturing capabilities, such as computer-aided design and manufacturing, robots, automated materials handling, computerized numerically controlled machines, automated guided vehicles, and flexible manufacturing systems (see Supplement E, "Computer-Integrated Manufacturing" on the Student CD-ROM). Software also provides various executive support systems, including management information systems and decision support systems. These software tools allow managers to evaluate business issues quickly and effectively.

database A collection of interrelated data or information stored on a data storage device such as a computer hard drive, a floppy disk, or tape.

DATABASES. A **database** is a collection of interrelated data or information stored on a data storage device such as a computer hard drive, a floppy disk, or tape. A database can be a firm's inventory records, time standards for different kinds of processes, cost data, or customer demand information. For example, a database helps the New York Police Department target its assault on neighborhood drug trafficking by keeping track of drug-selling locations and activity. Thousands of online databases are also available commercially. Some are organized according to numbers: economic indicators, stock market prices, and the like. Others are built on collections of key subjects or words: weather data, ski conditions, and full texts of major newspapers and journals around the world, to name a few.

American Express uses its database of some 30 million cardholders to offer an innovative marketing program called CustomExtras. Marketing information contains customers' purchase records and other information. Using proprietary software with this database allows American Express to add personalized offers and messages to the invoices of selected customers. The database tracks customer reactions to these offers and eligibility for reward programs and redemptions. This one-to-one marketing process is based on the notion that different customers should be treated differently and that the best customers should get the most attention. This approach has relevance for airlines, mutual fund companies, mass-customization manufacturers, and many other types of business.

telecommunications The final component of information technology that makes electronic networks possible.

TELECOMMUNICATIONS. The final component of information technology, which many believe might be the most important, is **telecommunications**. Fiber optics, telephones, modems, fax machines, and their related components make electronic networks possible. Such networks, and the use of compatible software, allow computer users at one location to communicate directly with computer users at another location and can pay big dividends. Sun Microsystems, Inc., used to need almost a month to close its financial books after each quarter ended. Now, all transactions are made on one network of Sun computers, permitting the quarterly accounting process to be completed in only 24 hours. Sun also has cut in half the time it required to receive payment after an order is delivered. General Electric has set up a new corporate **intranet**—an internal Internet network, surrounded by a firewall for security purposes—that connects the organization's various electronic systems. An employee at GE's motors business division in Indiana, for example, can use the intranet to find out how buyers in other divisions

intranet An internal Internet network surrounded by a firewall for security purposes.

rate a potential supplier. To help draw employees into using the system, the company's home page displays a particularly popular piece of data: GE's current stock price.

Connecting different organizations by computer has also paid dividends. Wal-Mart Stores, Inc., revolutionized retailing during the past decade by linking its computers with those of its suppliers. Its pioneering use of computer networks to conduct business electronically squeezed cost and time from its supply chains (see Chapter 8, "Supply-Chain Management"). Such private networks are now about to move to the wide-open Internet as components of the information superhighway.

E-COMMERCE

electronic commerce (e-commerce) The application of information and communication technology anywhere along the entire supply chain of business processes.

Global access to the Internet gives organizations unprecedented market and process information. The Web has a huge impact on how firms interact with their suppliers, customers, employees, and investors. **Electronic commerce (e-commerce)** is the application of information and communication technology anywhere along the entire supply chain of business processes. Both whole processes and subprocesses nested within them can be conducted as e-commerce. E-commerce encompasses business-to-business as well as business-to-consumer and consumer-to-business transactions. It is the sharing of business information, maintaining business relationships, and conducting business transactions by means of telecommunications networks. It is, however, more than simply buying and selling goods electronically and includes the use of network communications technology to perform processes up and down the supply chain, both within and outside the organization. E-commerce—the paperless exchange of business information—allows firms to improve their processes that give competitive advantage by cutting costs, improving quality, and increasing the speed of service delivery.

THE INTERNET

What is the Internet?

Internet A network of networks; a medium to exchange all forms of digital data, including text, graphics, audio, video, programs, and faxes.

E-commerce is not limited to the Internet and Web-based systems to perform transactions, because it includes proprietary services such as EDI (see Chapter 8, "Supply-Chain Management"). However, the Internet is the fundamental enabling technology for e-commerce, and so we begin our discussion with it. The **Internet** is a network of networks—thousands of interconnected communications networks and millions of users. It is a medium to exchange all forms of digital data, including text, graphics, audio, video, programs, and faxes. It is also an infrastructure for providing various services, such as e-mail, electronic data interchange (EDI), file transfer protocol (FTP), UserNet News, and the World Wide Web. It works because Internet software is designed according to a common set of protocols (TCP/IP) for routing and transporting data. This protocol suite sets standards by which computers communicate with each other.

WORLD WIDE WEB

World Wide Web An Internet service that consists of software called Web servers running on thousands of independently owned computers and computer networks that work together.

One of the most popular Internet services is the World Wide Web, which emerged in 1993. The **World Wide Web** consists of software called *Web servers* running on thousands of independently owned computers and computer networks that work together as part of this Internet service. All information on the Web originates within computers dedicated to the role of serving every imaginable type of data and information. Users request information from the Web using software called Web browsers. **Web browsers,** such as Microsoft's Internet Explorer and Netscape's Navigator, are software that allow users to view documents at Web sites. The Web is user friendly because the user has several tools from which to select Web sites. *Search engines* are navigational services

Web browsers Software that allows users to view documents at Web sites.

that allow users to search the Web. Most search engines have developed into *portals*—Web sites that provide a variety of services in addition to search, including chat, free e-mail, bulletin boards, news, stock quotes, and games. Yahoo! (www.yahoo.com) is a good example of a widely used portal, with 50 million visitors to its site each month. Each visitor is counted only once, regardless of how many times he or she visits the site. The open protocols of the Net allow anyone with an Internet connection to share data with other users, regardless of the type of access device employed. Of course, some sites might prohibit unauthorized access or transmission.

HOW E-COMMERCE AFFECTS PROCESSES

How does electronic commerce affect business processes?

It is no secret that e-commerce is growing and changing at breathtaking speed. For example, it took Sam Walton 12 years to reach $150 million in sales at Wal-Mart, but Amazon.com did it in 3. GE was the first firm to do $1 billion of business on the Internet, and Intel sold its first billion in goods online in less than a week. Relative to the size of the whole economy, the dollar value of e-commerce transactions is still small, but both the new Internet-based companies (the so-called dot-coms) and the traditional producers of goods and services are increasingly turning to the Web. E-commerce cuts costs because it links companies to their customers and suppliers, improves inventory management, automates fax-and-phone procurement processes, and provides inexpensive sales, marketing, and customer support channels. The Managerial Practice describes a major e-commerce initiative in the financial services industry.

BUSINESS-TO-CONSUMERS (B2C) COMMERCE

Many of the advantages of e-commerce were first exploited by retail "e-businesses," such as Amazon.com, E*Trade, and Auto-by-tel. These three companies created Internet versions of traditional bookstores, brokerage firms, and auto dealerships. Business-to-consumer e-commerce, sometimes called "B2C e-commerce," offers individual consumers a new buying alternative. The Internet is changing operations, processes, and cost structures for many retailers, and the overall growth in usage has been dramatic. Online business sales to individual customers reached over $30 billion in 2000, more than double the total for the previous year.

However, the mix of companies using B2C e-commerce is shifting. It is no longer limited to the original dot-com retailers, because their emergence forced their "brick-and-mortar" competitors to reconsider their own e-commerce options. Now many of these more established companies are operating their own online stores and putting pressure on dot-com retailers. A shakeout is occurring for those online retailers that face slim profit margins, too little product differentiation, and not enough size to control their own order-fulfillment processes and guarantee customer satisfaction. Anyone with an Internet connection can open a store in cyberspace, but delivering the goods to consumers has proven to be a much more complicated task.

B2C e-commerce offers a new distribution channel, and consumers can avoid shopping at crowded department stores, with their checkout lines and parking-space shortages. A business can publish information using hypertext markup language (HTML) not only on the World Wide Web but also on major online services. Many leading retailers and catalog companies have opened Web "stores" where consumers can browse thousands of virtual aisles and millions of items. Such methods allow customers to do much more shopping in an hour than they could possibly do in person at a traditional retail outlet. Browsers can find intriguing products at exotic sites, such as an authentic turn-of-the-century rocking horse from a London antique broker, a gift pack of 7-ounce portions of beef Wellington, and a personalized Louisville Slugger baseball bat. The most popular online purchases are books, travel arrangements, CDs,

MANAGERIAL **PRACTICE**
Web-Based Financial Services with Clicks and Mortar

Boston-based Fleet, the eighth-largest U.S. bank (www.fleet.com), earlier spent $40 million on a computerized *data warehouse* that collects and sorts details about customers. More recently, it applied that same tailored marketing strategy, known as *data mining*, to online customers. The idea is to pitch products so that middle-aged customers will not be offered student loans and college students will not be bombarded with home-equity refinancing plans.

Fleet's latest leap into cyberspace is what it calls its biggest technology bet ever. Fleet will spend up to $100 million over the next two years to launch a comprehensive Web-based financial service that will place banking, stock trading, mutual funds, credit cards, mortgages, financial news, bill payment, and incentives all on one Web site for 8 million household customers in the northeastern United States. Among the planned cyber offerings: real-time account data, mortgage application-taking, portfolio calculators, corporate research, investment advice from high-end financial publishers, and even reduced monthly fees from Microsoft Network, the Internet service provider. The project will be rolled out in stages and would be the newest entrant in the fast-shifting world of Web finance. It has already linked its basic Web bank services with Quick & Reilly, its discount stockbrokerage, so customers can now bank and trade stocks in one place. Fleet sees Quick & Reilly, a national franchise that it acquired in 1997, as its secret weapon. Fleet believes that the best financial product on the Web is the brokerage product. High-yield certificates of deposit and checking accounts that are the staple offerings of Internet-only banks do not give Fleet a competitive advantage.

Fleet's bet is about more than technology. It is a bet that the future of online banking is inseparable from the future of online investing, a trend that has taken off in recent years. Still, Fleet's move is a leap into uncertainty, and some executives decline to say how much the online business could add to Fleet's bottom line. The payoffs from the project are not yet clear. "We're not at this point thinking of going national with a broad Internet product," says Charles Gifford, Fleet president and former BankBoston head. "I'm not sure how you make money on it." While many banks have Web outputs and a few, like Fleet, own brokerages, Fleet will be one of a tiny group to offer bank products and stock trading in one place. Fleet's efforts reflect a dilemma faced by banks now grappling with an investing revolution that has lured legions online and left banks in the dust. To date, most institutions have experienced the Internet as a money-losing proposition, but everybody still wants to be out there with an Internet presence. Given these uncertainties, Fleet is hedging its bet. Its basic strategy is to stick with old-fashioned bricks-and-mortar branches and automated teller machines while developing a major virtual presence—an idea known as "clicks and mortar."

Source: "Fleet Poised to Place Bet on Net Finance." *The Boston Globe* (October 27, 1999).

---

computer software, health and beauty products, and clothing. Banking and financial services are further down the line but are growing (as the example of Fleet Bank demonstrates). E-commerce is particularly attractive for products that the consumer does not have to look at carefully or touch. The Internet has an advantage with higher-value branded convenience goods over the in-store experience.

The Internet also has potential in "greening" the environment. There is less need for building retail space, warehouse space, and commercial office space. Energy saved means less pollution from power plants, which release greenhouse gases into the atmosphere. Furthermore, fewer trips to malls and stores would mean savings on gasoline. Less reliance on catalogs would save millions of tons of paper.

The question of security, primarily involving credit card numbers, continues to make many people reluctant to buy over the Internet. However, a card number follows a prescribed path and is encrypted the moment it leaves the computer. **Encryption** is the process of coding customer information and sending it over the Internet in "scrambled" form. Although no credit card transaction is entirely secure, the risk of fraud on the Internet is no higher than giving a credit card number over the phone or handing a credit card to a salesclerk.

encryption The process of coding customer information and sending it over the Internet in "scrambled" form.

BUSINESS-TO-BUSINESS (B2B) COMMERCE

Many of the same advantages that arise from B2C e-commerce hold for business-to-business (B2B) e-commerce. E-commerce helps businesses enhance the services they offer to customers. Business-to-business transactions continue to outpace business-to-consumer transactions in e-commerce. Because trade between businesses makes up more than 70 percent of the regular economy, it is no surprise that B2B e-commerce also dwarfs the B2C variety. In 2000, B2B e-commerce was $335 billion and represented only 3 percent of the total U.S. nonservice market. But growth is expected to be very rapid, reaching $6 trillion, or 45 percent of the total market, by 2005. That is 10 times the amount expected for B2C trade.

Consider Fruit of the Loom, Inc., an apparel maker that depends on its wholesalers to ship products to various retailer customers. It put its wholesalers on the Web and gave each one a complete computer system that displays colorful catalogs, processes electronic orders round the clock, and manages inventories. If one of its distributors is out of stock, the company's central warehouse is notified to ship replacement stock directly to the customer. Building such an integrated e-commerce system took only a few months, using software from Connect, Inc., called OneServer, and a catalog program from Snickleways Interactive to get online. The firm's retailer customers need only an Internet connection and some Web-browsing software.

Electronic commerce can transform almost all B2B processes, not just their sales processes. Even more impressive is how the Web is streamlining the supply-chain process. It can dramatically reduce a firm's purchasing costs, as transactions move away from the numbing pace of paper to the lightning speed of electronics. By eliminating paper forms, firms spend less time and money rekeying information into different computers and correcting the inevitable errors. Electronic commerce previously operated primarily on private links. However, software and security measures now allow the Web to become the global infrastructure for e-commerce. Moving from private networks to the Internet allows a company to reach thousands of new businesses around the world.

Currently, e-commerce is dominated by the model of one seller to many buyers, as is the case with Fruit of the Loom. However, e-commerce is beginning to take place in *virtual marketplaces*. These trading posts allow buyers and sellers who may not know each other to meet electronically and trade products and services without the aid or cost of traditional agents and brokers. Web marketplaces are growing for B2B trade. Analogies in the B2C world include eBay and Priceline.com, although the B2B customers are companies. For example, Ford, GM, and DaimlerChrysler are putting together a marketplace to procure parts from suppliers. Similar marketplaces are forming around the buying and selling of paper, plastic, steel, bandwidth, chemicals, and the like.

ENTERPRISE RESOURCE PLANNING

What is ERP?

enterprise resource planning (ERP) A large, integrated information system that supports many enterprise processes and data storage needs.

Enterprise resource planning (ERP) refers to a large, integrated information system that supports many enterprise processes and data storage needs. An **enterprise process** is a companywide process that cuts across functional areas, business units, geographic regions, and product lines. Also known as an *enterprise system*, ERP is essentially a collection of compatible software modules, possibly interfacing to existing (sometimes called "legacy") information systems, that allow a company to have one comprehensive, fully integrated information system.

We cover different aspects of ERP in several places throughout this book. For example, we describe the process decisions about how work is to be performed in

enterprise process A companywide process that cuts across functional areas, business units, geographic regions, and product lines.

Chapter 2, "Process Management." Designing an ERP system requires that a company carefully define its major processes so that appropriate decisions about the coordination of legacy systems and new software modules can be made. Processes to be used by ERP applications must also be fully specified. In many cases, a company's processes must be reengineered before the company can enjoy the benefits of an integrated information system. In Chapter 8, "Supply-Chain Management," we describe how ERP systems help coordinate relations among customers, internal operations, and suppliers. Finally, in Chapter 12, "Resource Planning," we examine ERP from the perspective of what it has to offer by way of resource planning, both in manufacturing and service organizations.

WHAT ERP DOES

By integrating functional areas, ERP systems allow a firm to concentrate on enterprise processes rather than functional boundaries. For example, suppose that a U.S. manufacturer of telecommunication products has an ERP system and that an Athens-based sales representative wants to prepare a customer quote. When the salesperson enters information about the customer's needs into a laptop computer, the ERP system automatically generates a formal contract, in Greek, giving the product's specifications, delivery date, and price. After the customer accepts it, the salesperson makes an entry, whereupon ERP verifies the customer's credit limit and records the order. The next application takes over to schedule shipment using the best routing. Backing up from the delivery date, it reserves the necessary materials from inventory and determines when to release production orders to its factories and purchase orders to its suppliers. Another application updates the sales and production forecasts, while still another credits the sales representative's payroll account the appropriate commission in drachma. The accounting application calculates the actual product cost and profitability, in U.S. dollars, and reflects the transaction in the accounts payable and accounts receivable ledgers. Divisional and corporate balance sheets are updated, as are cash levels. In short, the system supports all of the enterprise processes that are activated as a result of the sale.

ERP APPLICATIONS

ERP revolves around a single comprehensive database that can be made available across the entire organization (or enterprise). Of course, security locks are possible and highly recommended in order to protect sensitive data from accidental or malicious damage. It provides visibility to relevant data enterprisewide, for all products, at all locations, and at all times. The database collects data from and feeds it into the various modular applications (or "suites") of the software system. As new information is entered as a *transaction* in one application, related information is automatically updated in the other applications, including (but not limited to) financial and accounting information, human resources and payroll information, supply-chain information, and customer information. ERP streamlines data flows throughout the organization and allows management direct access to a wealth of real-time operating information. It seamlessly connects information among different enterprise processes and can eliminate many of the cross-functional coordination problems that existed under prior poorly integrated and noninterfaced legacy systems. Figure 4.3 shows some of the typical applications, with a few subprocesses nested within each one. Some of the applications are for back-office operations such as manufacturing and payroll, while others are for front-office operations such as customer service and employee self-service.

ERP is used by both service providers and manufacturers. Amazon.com is a value-added reseller that uses ERP. The supply-chain application is of particular importance

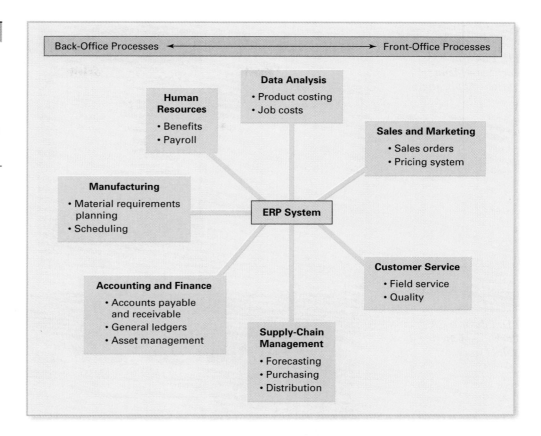

FIGURE 4.3

ERP Application Modules

Source: Scalle, Cedric X., and Mark J. Cotteleer. *Enterprise Resource Planning (ERP)*. Boston, MA: Harvard Business School Publishing, No. 9-699-020, 1999.

because it allows Amazon.com to link customer orders to warehouse shipments and, ultimately, to supplier-replenishment orders. Universities put particular emphasis on the human resources and accounting and finance applications, and manufacturers have an interest in almost every application suite. Not all applications in Figure 4.3 need be integrated into an ERP system, but those left out will not share their information in the corporate database.

HOW TO USE ERP

Most ERP systems today use a graphical user interface, although the older keyboard-driven, text-based systems are still very popular because of their dependability and technical simplicity. Users navigate through various screens and menus. When they are trained, such as during ERP implementation, the focus is on these screens and how to use them to get their jobs done. The biggest supplier of these off-the-shelf commercial ERP packages is Germany's SAP AG (www.sap.com), followed by Oracle (www.oracle.com), PeopleSoft (www.peoplesoft.com), J.D. Edwards (www.jdedwards.com), and Baan (www.baan.com). Figure 4.4 shows screen shots of the J.D. Edwards ERP software, called OneWorld. Part (a) shows the menu for the various applications. Within the Distribution suite, for example, a user may select the Sales Order Entry process. Part (b) shows the screen for entering a sales order.

INTEROPERABILITY. ERP has changed a good deal over the last five years. One important direction is **interoperability**—the ability of one piece of software to interact with others. Electronic data interchange, a system that allows data interchange between companies on a batch basis (see Chapter 8, "Supply-Chain Management"), has been a

interoperability The ability of one piece of software to interact with others.

FIGURE 4.4A

J.D. Edwards ERP Package—Menu for Various Applications

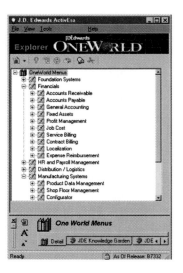

FIGURE 4.4B

J.D. Edwards ERP Package—Entering a Sales Order

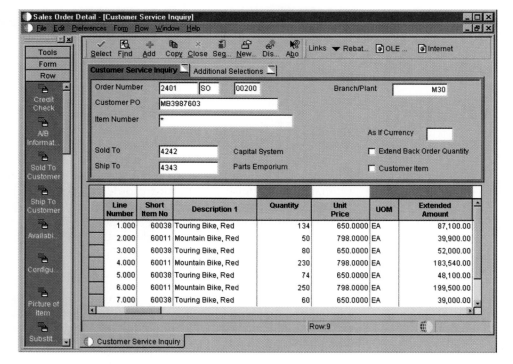

major workhorse over the years. However, there is increasing interest in moving to the "new economy" of e-commerce. Thus, considerable attention is now being given to XML (eXtensible Markup Language), IBM's Message Queue (MQ Series), and Microsoft's MSMQ as vehicles for this new approach. XML, for example, lets companies structure and exchange information without rewriting existing systems or adding large amounts of heavyweight middleware. These enablers of collaborative commerce are shaping the ways in which previously disparate and possibly competing pieces of software are working together to add value and reduce costs. The goal of all such methods is to automate, in almost real time, the sharing of information across enterprise boundaries.

A team of three employees at ATOFINA Chemicals, Inc. keep things under control using various computer technologies after implementing ERP. Previously it took many more people, more handoffs between people, and more time delays to get an order processed.

TECHNOLOGY STRATEGY

Which technologies should be pursued and when?

Because technology is changing so rapidly and because of the many technologies available, operations managers must more than ever make intelligent, informed decisions about new product and process technologies. The stakes are high because such choices affect the human as well as the technical aspects of operations. Here we examine how technologies should be chosen and how these choices link with strategy to create a competitive advantage. An appropriate technology is one that fits corporate and operations strategies and gives the firm a sustainable advantage. Several tests of a potential technological change should be made. If the change being considered fails these tests, it shouldn't be pursued even if it represents an impressive technological accomplishment. Tests leading to *technological choice* are valid for both manufacturers and service providers.

Technology strategy deals with more than just technological choice. It also determines whether an organization should be a leader or follower in technological change and aids in evaluating radically new technologies when conventional financial analyses won't do the job.

TECHNOLOGY AS A COMPETITIVE ADVANTAGE

A new technology should create some kind of competitive advantage. *Competitive advantage* is created by increasing the value of a product to a customer or reducing the costs of bringing the product to market. The potential for increasing value and reducing costs from a new technology is vast. The most obvious cost-reduction strategy is that of reducing the *direct costs* of labor and materials. Labor savings are still used to justify most automation projects, but labor is a shrinking component—only 10 to 15 percent—of total costs. Therefore, to understand a new technology's true value, a manager should assess factors other than cost savings.

For example, *sales* can increase, as MCI Communications found when it spent $300 million to update its computer systems and offer innovative residential calling services. *Quality* can improve, as illustrated by the new magnetic resonance imaging (MRI) machines that can diagnose heart and liver diseases without using X rays and radioactive materials. With MRIs, scanning times are reduced from about 45 to 20 minutes, thus increasing the number of patients who can be served, reducing costs per patient, and increasing patient comfort. In manufacturing, Giddings & Lewis makes groups of machine tools by using automated materials handling equipment and computer control. These systems reduce human error and, thus, improve product quality. In addition, they yield *quicker delivery times* by reducing processing times. These reductions in turn allow for *smaller inventories,* with less inventory held on the shop floor. Finally the *environment* can even improve, such as with a noise reduction system or with the reduction in air emissions or waste.

Of course, new technology also can have its downside. Investment in new technology can be forbidding, particularly for complex and expensive projects that require new facilities or extensive facility overhaul. The investment also can be risky because of uncertainties in demand and in per-unit benefits. Finally, technology may have hidden costs, requiring different employee knowledge and skills to maintain and operate the new equipment. Such requirements may generate employee resistance and lower morale and increase turnover. Thus, the operations manager must sort out the many benefits and costs of different technological choices.

FIT WITH COMPETITIVE PRIORITIES

Another important test is how technological change will help a firm achieve the competitive priorities of cost, quality, time, and flexibility. Such a change should have a positive impact on one or more of these priorities, particularly on those that are emphasized for the product or service in question and on determining whether this advantage can be protected from imitation. For example, FedEx promises fast delivery time (overnight delivery) and that parcels will be "absolutely, positively" delivered on time. FedEx chose bar code technology to give it an early ability to track packages throughout the handling cycle—a capability possessed by none of its competitors at the time. Combining this technology with its own fleet of airplanes allowed its operations to support its strategic orientation and gave FedEx a large market share. Its competitors could not easily match FedEx's differentiation strategy on the basis of time.

FIRST-MOVER CONSIDERATIONS

Should the firm be a technology leader or follower?

This strategic consideration deals with *when* to adopt a new technology rather than which technology to choose. Being the first to market with a new technology offers a firm numerous advantages that can outweigh the financial investment needed. Technological leaders lay down the competitive rules that others will follow with regard to a new product or process. A "first-mover" may be able to gain an early large market share that creates an entry barrier for other firms. Even if competitors are able to match the new technology, the first-mover's initial advantage in the market can endure. Being first can give a firm the reputation that emulators will find difficult to overcome.

Of course, a company that pursues a first-mover strategy faces risks that can jeopardize its financial and market position. First, pioneering costs can be high, with R&D costs exceeding the firm's financial capabilities. Second, market demand for a new technology is speculative, and estimates of future financial gains may be overstated. Third, a new product or process technology may well become outdated quickly because of new technological breakthroughs. Thus, managers must carefully analyze these risks and benefits before deciding which technologies to pursue.

ECONOMIC JUSTIFICATION

Managers should make every effort to translate considerations of sources of competitive advantages, fit with competitive priorities, existence of core competencies, and first-mover strategy into a financial analysis to estimate whether investment in a new technology is economically justified. Operations managers should state precisely what they expect from a new technology and then quantify costs and performance goals. They should determine whether the expected after-tax cash flows resulting from the investment are likely to outweigh the costs, after accounting for the time value of money. Traditional techniques such as the net present value method, internal rate of return method, and the payback method can be used to estimate financial impact (see Supplement B, "Financial Analysis" on the Student CD-ROM).

However, uncertainties and intangibles must also be considered, even though they cannot be easily measured. For example, there may be uncertainty about whether a new technology can be successfully developed. If it is a known technology, uncertainty may exist about how well it can be adapted to current processes or vice versa. Certain downstream benefits may be hard to quantify. For example, flexible automation might be of value for products that will be introduced well into the future, long after the life of the product for which it was first implemented. For these reasons, financial analyses should be augmented by qualitative judgments.

Operations managers must look beyond the direct costs of a new technology to its impact on customer service, delivery times, inventories, and resource flexibility. These are often the most important considerations. Quantifying such intangible goals as the ability to move quickly into a new market may be difficult. However, a firm that fails to make technological changes along with its competitors can quickly lose its competitive advantage and face declining revenues and layoffs. Justification should begin with financial analyses recognizing all quantifiable factors that can be translated into dollar values. The resulting financial measures should then be merged with an evaluation of the qualitative factors and intangibles involved. The manager can then estimate the risks associated with uncertain cost and revenue estimates. Decision-making tools such as the preference matrix approach, decision theory, and decision trees can help the manager make a final decision (see Supplement A, "Decision Making" on the Student CD-ROM).

DISRUPTIVE TECHNOLOGIES

What is a disruptive technology and how can it be dealt with?

Many companies have invested aggressively and successfully in technologies to retain current customers and to improve current processes. They have done all the right things in terms of seeking a competitive advantage and funding the technology projects that should lead to the highest profit margins and largest market share, relative to their *current* customers. They have pursued new process technologies that address the next-generation performance requirements of their customers. And yet, paradoxically, what seems like good business practice may be devastating and prevent many firms from investing in the technologies that *future* customers will want and need.

This paradox is likely to occur because of disruptive technologies, which occur infrequently and are nearly impossible to justify on the basis of rational, analytical investment techniques. A **disruptive technology** is one that

disruptive technology A technology that has performance attributes that are not valued yet by *existing* customers or for current products, or performs much worse on some performance attributes that existing or future customers value but will quickly surpass existing technologies on such attributes when it is refined.

1. has performance attributes that are not valued yet by *existing* customers or for current products, or
2. performs much worse on some performance attributes that existing or future customers value but will quickly surpass existing technologies on such attributes when it is refined.

COUNTERING DISRUPTIVE TECHNOLOGIES. How can a company deal with the paradox of disruptive technology? The first step is to recognize that it is a disruptive rather than a sustaining technology. One indicator could be internal disagreement over the advisability of producing the new technology. Marketing and financial managers will rarely support a disruptive technology, but technical personnel may argue forcibly that a new technology market can be achieved. A second indicator is to compare the likely slope of performance improvement of the technology with market demand. If its performance trajectory, as judged by knowledgeable analysts, is much faster than market expectations, it might be a disruptive technology that could become strategically crucial. It might best meet future market needs even though it is currently an inferior product.

Managers must be willing to undertake major and rapid change with disruptive technologies that are strategically crucial, even if doing so means initially serving emerging markets and realizing low profit margins. When both technology and customers change rapidly, as at many high-tech firms, one of two conflicting methods can be used to manage disruptive technologies. One method is to develop these technologies in a different part of the organization, with one part of the firm pursuing innovation and the other parts pursuing efficiency and continual improvement of technologies for existing customer bases. A team, sometimes referred to as a *skunk works*, can be formed to develop the new technology without disrupting normal operations. Such teams often work in close quarters, without many amenities, but band together in almost missionary zeal.

The other method is to use different methods of management at different times in the course of technological development. Firms can alternate periods of consolidation and continuity with sharp reorientation, interspersing periods of action and change with periods of evaluation and efficiency. With either method, the operations manager must seek ways to improve continually the existing technologies driving the production system, while being alert for radical innovations and discontinuities that can make technologies obsolete.

MANAGING TECHNOLOGY ACROSS THE ORGANIZATION

Technologies are embedded in processes throughout an organization (see Fig. 4.2). In each of their functional areas and business units, both service providers and manufacturers use many technologies. For example, Seven-Eleven Japan uses point-of-sale technology to assess customers' needs (*marketing*) and to control inventory in its supply chain (*operations*). Technology also creates special needs for training and supporting employees (*human resources*). The New York Stock Exchange uses computer equipment and software (*management information systems*) to streamline trading processes (*finance*). *Engineering* is heavily involved in R&D, creating new products and services and applying them to the organization's processes. Fleet Bank's new Web services show how B2B e-commerce has an increasingly important role in the marketing of financial services. The very essence of enterprise resource planning illustrates many of the ways in which this chapter's topic, management of technology, is important to all business areas. ERP makes connections among applications in sales and marketing, customer service, supply-chain management, accounting and finance, manufacturing, and human resources.

CHAPTER HIGHLIGHTS

☐ Technology consists of physical equipment, procedures, know-how, and the support network used at operations to produce products and services. Managers must make informed decisions about which technological possibilities to pursue and how best to implement those chosen.

☐ Innovation and technological change are primary sources of productivity improvement and drivers of global competition.

Organizations more experienced at adapting to changing technologies tend to enjoy stronger competitive positions worldwide.

☐ Technologies are involved in all the processes along a firm's supply chain and in each of the firm's functional areas. Office and information technologies are pervasive. Managers need to invest the time to learn about the technologies that are used or could be used at their organizations.

- Information technology deals with how managers use and communicate information to make decisions effectively. Hardware, software, databases, and telecommunications are the main components that make up information technology.

- The Internet is a network of networks, allowing the exchange of text, graphics, video, programs, and faxes. It is connected to almost 200 countries and will soon have half a billion users around the globe.

- Electronic commerce, both B2C and B2B, is creating totally new ways for a firm to relate to customers, suppliers, employees, and investors.

- Enterprise resource planning is a large, integrated information system. Its applications cut across many processes, functional areas, business units, regions, and products.

- High-tech options are not necessarily appropriate solutions to operations problems. Tests of the advisability of technological change include competitive advantages measured in terms of costs, sales, quality, delivery times, inventory, and the environment; financial analyses; first-mover or follower considerations; identifying disruptive technologies; fit with competitive priorities; and core competencies.

CD-ROM RESOURCES

The Student CD-ROM that accompanies this text contains the following resources, which allow you to further practice and apply the concepts presented in this chapter.

- **Discussion Questions:** Five questions expand your thinking on evaluating new technologies, including their potential payoffs and costs.

- **Case: Bill's Hardware:** Should Bill Murton adopt the POS system, and how should he vote?

- **Supplement A:** Decision Making. Learn about the preference matrix approach, decision theory, and decision trees for evaluating new technologies for possible adoption.

- **Supplement E:** Computer-Integrated Manufacturing. See how to integrate product design and engineering, process planning, and manufacturing by means of complex computer systems.

INTERACTIVE RESOURCES

The Interactive Web site associated with this text (www.prenhall.com/ritzman) contains many tools and activities specifically designed for this chapter. The following items are recommended to enhance your understanding of the material in this chapter.

- **Internet Activities:** Try out the links on managing technology at ZDNet, CDNOW, Wal-Mart, Internet Ventures, Hewitt Associates, and Cables & Wireless Networks.

- **Internet Tours:** Check out the Martex Circuits on the application of process technology and the New York Stock Exchange on two ways it uses technology.

- **SmartDraw:** Use the link to experience a software package that is used in practice to prepare decision trees.

PROBLEMS

An icon next to a problem identifies the software that can be helpful but is not mandatory. Problems 1–3 require reading Supplement A, "Decision Making" and problem 4 requires reading Supplement B, "Financial Analysis" on the Student CD-ROM. Problem 5 should be solved as a team exercise.

1. **OM Explorer** You have been asked to analyze four new advanced manufacturing technologies and recommend the best one for adoption by your company. Management has rated these technologies with respect to seven criteria, using a 0–100 scale (0 = worst; 100 = best). Management has given the performance criteria different weights. Table 4.1 summarizes the relevant information. Which technology would you recommend?

TABLE 4.1 *Analysis of New Technologies*

| CRITERION | WEIGHT | TECHNOLOGY RATING | | | |
		A	B	C	D
Financial measures	25	60	70	10	100
Volume flexibility	15	90	25	60	80
Quality of output	20	70	90	75	90
Required facility space	5	60	20	40	50
Market share	10	60	70	90	90
Product mix flexibility	20	90	80	30	90
Required labor skills	5	80	40	20	10

2. **OM Explorer** Hitech Manufacturing Company must select a process technology for one of its new products from among three different alternatives. The following cost data have been obtained for the three process technologies.

COST	PROCESS A	PROCESS B	PROCESS C
Fixed costs per year	$20,000	$40,000	$100,000
Variable costs per unit	$15	$10	$6

a. Find the range for the annual production volume in which each process will be preferred.

b. If the expected annual production volume is 12,000 units, which process should be selected?

3. **SmartDraw** Super Innovators, Inc., is faced with the decision of switching its production facilities to new (promising but not yet completely tried) processing technology. The technology may be implemented in one or two steps, with the option to stop after the initial step. Because the benefits from the new technology (cost savings and productivity improvements) are subject to uncertainty, the firm is considering two options. The first option is to make the full switchover in one step to take advantage of economies of scale in investment and opportunities to gain a larger market share. For this choice the investment cost is $5 million. The expected present value of the cash flows is $20 million if the new processing technology works as well as expected and $6 million if it does not work as well as expected. The second option is to implement part of the system as a first step and then extend the system to full capability. If the technology does not work as well as expected and the firm had decided to go for the full switchover, the total investment cost could be higher (because of diseconomies of scale) and the payoff could be lower. The investment cost for the initial step is $2 million, and the present value of the combined investment in two steps will be $6 million. If both steps are implemented, the expected present value of the cash flows is $15 million if the new processing technology works as well as expected and $8 million otherwise. If only the first step is implemented, the expected present value of the cash flows is $4 million if the new processing technology works as well as expected and $2 million otherwise. The firm estimates that there is a 40 percent chance that the new technology will work as well as expected.

a. Draw a decision tree to solve this problem.

b. What should the firm do to achieve the highest expected payoff?

4. **OM Explorer** First State Bank is considering installing a new automatic teller machine (ATM) at either of two new locations: inside a supermarket or inside the bank itself. An initial investment of $60,000 is required for the ATM regardless of location. The operating costs of the ATM at the supermarket would be $15,000 per year and of the ATM inside the bank $10,000 per year. The higher costs of the supermarket ATM reflect the additional cost of leasing supermarket space and transportation. Revenue generated from new accounts because of the installation of each ATM should also differ, with the supermarket ATM generating $55,000 per year and the bank ATM $52,000 per year. Assume a tax rate of 30 percent and a desired rate of return of 18 percent on investment. The ATMs have an expected life of eight years, with no salvage value at the end of that time. Use MACRS depreciation allowances, noting that the ATMs may be considered as assets in the five-year class.

a. Calculate the net present value for each alternative.

b. Based on your analysis, which location do you recommend?

5. Imagine that you are a member of the operations management team in a firm that manufactures flashlights. Your firm is faced with the problem of choosing the equipment and

process technology for manufacturing the casings for the flashlights. After an evaluation of several alternative technologies, the choice has been narrowed to two technologies: (i) deep drawing of metal bars on a press using a die, and (ii) injection molding of a variety of plastic materials. Compare the two technologies in terms of how each one will influence various elements of the operating system.

a. First, make a list of the various elements (e.g., equipment, raw materials, building, operators, safety, etc.) and then indicate how the two technologies influence each element.

b. For which of these elements is the contrast between the influences of the two technologies most striking?

SELECTED REFERENCES

Alsop, Stewart. "Sun's Java: What's Hype and What's Real." *Fortune* (July 7, 1997); pp. 191–192.

Bower, Joseph L., and Clayton M. Christensen. "Disruptive Technologies: Catching the Wave." *Harvard Business Review* (January–February 1995), pp. 43–53.

Burgelman, Robert A., Modesto A. Maidique, and Steven C. Wheelwright. *Strategic Management of Technology and Innovation*. Chicago: Irwin, 1996.

Cohen, Morris A., and Uday M. Apte. *Manufacturing Automation*. Chicago: Irwin, 1997.

Collier, David A. *Service Management: The Automation of Services*. Reston, VA: Reston, 1985.

Davenport, Thomas H. "Putting the Enterprise into the Enterprise System." *Harvard Business Review* (July–August 1998), pp. 121–131.

Earl, Michael, and M. M. Bensaou. "The Right Mind-Set for Managing Information Technology." *Harvard Business Review* (September–October 1998), pp. 119–129.

Iansiti, Marco, and Jonathan West. "Technology Integration: Turning Great Research into Great Products." *Harvard Business Review* (May–June 1997), pp. 69–79.

Jacobs, F. Robert, and D. Clay Whybark. *Why ERP?* New York: Irwin McGraw-Hill, 2000.

Lefebvre, Louis A., Ann Langley, Jean Harvey, and Elisabeth Lefebvre. "Exploring the Strategy–Technology Connection in Small Manufacturing Firms." *Production and Operations Management*, vol. 1, no. 3 (1992), pp. 269–285.

Noori, Hamid. *Managing the Dynamics of New Technology*. Englewood Cliffs, NJ: Prentice-Hall, 1990.

Pisano, Gary P., and Steven C. Wheelwright. "High-Tech R&D." *Harvard Business Review* (September–October 1995), pp. 93–105.

Quinn, James B., and Penny C. Paquette. "Technology in Services: Creating Organizational Revolutions." *Sloan Management Review* (Winter 1990), pp. 67–78.

Roth, Aleda V. "Neo-Operations Strategy: Linking Capabilities-Based Competition to Technology." In *Handbook of Technology Management*, G. H. Gaynor (ed.). New York: McGraw-Hill, 1996, pp. 38.1–38.44.

Scalle, Cedric X., and Mark J. Cotteleer. *Enterprise Resource Planning (ERP)*. Boston, MA: Harvard Business School Publishing, No. 9–699–020, 1999.

Skinner, Wickham. "Operations Technology: Blind Spot in Strategic Management." *Interfaces*, vol. 14 (January–February 1984), pp. 116–125.

Quality

Across the Organization

Quality is important to . . .

- ❏ **accounting,** which must measure and estimate the costs of poor quality and provide error-free data to its internal customers.
- ❏ **finance,** which must assess the cash flow implications of TQM programs and provide defect-free financial reports to its internal customers.
- ❏ **human resources,** which recruits employees who value quality work and motivates and trains them.
- ❏ **management information systems,** which designs the systems for tracking productivity and quality performance.
- ❏ **marketing,** which uses quality and performance data for promotional purposes.
- ❏ **operations,** which designs and implements TQM programs.

Learning Goals

After reading this chapter, you should be able to . . .

1. define *quality* from the customer's perspective.
2. describe the principles of a TQM program and how the elements fit together to make improvements in quality and productivity.
3. discuss how TQM programs improve quality through benchmarking, product and service design, quality function deployment, and quality-conscious purchasing.
4. distinguish among the various tools for improving quality and explain how each should be used.
5. discuss how control charts are developed and used.
6. construct $\bar{x}$, R, p, and c charts and use them to determine whether a process is out of statistical control.
7. determine whether a process is capable of producing a product or service to specifications.

The Parkroyal Christchurch, a luxury hotel in Christchurch, New Zealand, has 297 guest rooms, three restaurants, three lounges, and 338 employees to serve 2,250 guests each week who purchase an average of 2,450 meals. Even though the operation is complex, service quality gets top priority at the Parkroyal because customers demand it. Customers have many opportunities to evaluate the quality of service they are receiving. For example, prior to the guest's arrival, the reservation staff has gathered a considerable amount of information about the guest's particular likes and dislikes. This information (e.g., preference for firm pillows or extra towels) is distributed to housekeeping and other hotel operations and is used to customize the service that each guest receives. Upon arrival, a guest is greeted by a porter who opens the car door and unloads the luggage. Then the guest is escorted to the receptionist who registers the guest and assigns the room. Finally, when the guest goes to dinner, servers and cooks must also live up to the high standard of quality that distinguishes the Parkroyal from its competitors.

The Parkroyal Christchurch offers the utmost in quality for its guests. The Café offers a wide variety of dishes that must live up to the reputation of the hotel.

How can such a level of quality be sustained? The Parkroyal has empowered employees to take preventive and, if necessary, corrective action without management approval. Also, management and employees use line charts, histograms, and other graphs to track performance and identify areas needing improvement. In the restaurants, photos of finished dishes remind employees of presentation and content. Finally, in this service business with high customer contact, employee recruiting, training, and motivation are essential for achieving and sustaining high levels of service quality.

Source: Operations Management in Action video.

total quality management (TQM) A philosophy that stresses three principles: customer satisfaction, employee involvement, and continuous improvements in quality.

THE CHALLENGE FOR BUSINESS today is to produce quality products or services efficiently. The Parkroyal Christchurch is but one example of a company that has met the challenge and is using quality as a competitive weapon. This chapter explores the competitive implications of quality, focusing on the philosophy and tools of total quality management, which many firms have embraced. **Total quality management (TQM)** stresses three principles: customer satisfaction, employee involvement, and continuous improvements in quality. As Figure 5.1 indicates, TQM also involves benchmarking, product and service design, process design, purchasing, and problem-solving tools. We also address statistical process control, which consists of techniques useful for appraising and monitoring quality in operating systems.

QUALITY: A MANAGEMENT PHILOSOPHY

We've previously identified two competitive priorities that deal with quality: high-performance design and consistent quality (see Chapter 1, "Competing with Operations"). These priorities characterize an organization's competitive thrust. Strategic plans that recognize quality as an essential competitive priority must be

FIGURE 5.1

TQM Wheel

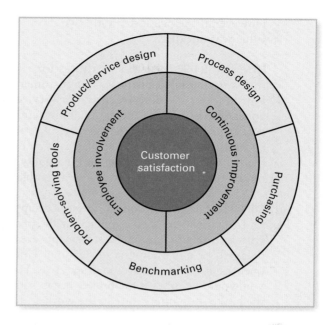

based on some operational definition of quality. In this section, we discuss various definitions of quality and emphasize the importance of bridging the gap between consumer expectations of quality and operating capabilities.

CUSTOMER-DRIVEN DEFINITIONS OF QUALITY

How do customers perceive the quality of services?

quality The ability of a firm to meet or exceed the expectations of the customer.

Customers define **quality** in various ways. In a general sense, quality may be defined as meeting or exceeding the expectations of the customer. For practical purposes, it is necessary to be more specific. Quality has multiple dimensions in the mind of the customer, and one or more of the following definitions may apply at any one time.

CONFORMANCE TO SPECIFICATIONS. Customers expect the products or services they buy to meet or exceed certain advertised levels of performance. For example, Seagate, a disk drive manufacturer, advertises that its high-performance Cheetah disk drives have a "mean time between failures" of 1.2 million hours. All the components of the disk drive must conform to their individual specifications to achieve the desired performance of the complete product. Customers will measure quality by the performance of the complete product and the length of time between failures.

In service systems conformance to specifications is also important, even though tangible outputs are not produced. Specifications for a service operation may relate to on-time delivery or response time. Bell Canada measures the performance of its operators in Ontario by the length of time to process a call (called "handle time"). If the group average time exceeds the standard of 23 seconds, managers work with the operators to reduce it.

VALUE. Another way customers define quality is through value, or how well the product or service serves its intended purpose at a price customers are willing to pay. How much value a product or service has in the mind of the customer depends on the customer's expectations before purchasing it. For example, if you spent $2.00 for a plastic ballpoint pen and it served you well for six months, you might feel that the purchase was worth the price. Your expectations for the product were met or exceeded.

However, if the pen lasted only two days, you might be disappointed and feel that the value was not there.

FITNESS FOR USE. In assessing fitness for use, or how well the product or service performs its intended purpose, the customer may consider the mechanical features of a product or the convenience of a service. Other aspects of fitness for use include appearance, style, durability, reliability, craftsmanship, and serviceability. For example, you may judge your dentist's quality of service on the basis of the age of her equipment because new dental technology greatly reduces the discomfort associated with visits to the dentist. Or you may define the quality of the entertainment center you purchased on the basis of how easy it was to assemble and how well it housed your equipment.

SUPPORT. Often the product or service support provided by the company is as important to customers as the quality of the product or service itself. Customers get upset with a company if financial statements are incorrect, responses to warranty claims are delayed, or advertising is misleading. Good product support can reduce the consequences of quality failures in other areas. For example, if you just had a brake job done, you would be upset if the brakes began squealing again a week later. If the manager of the brake shop offers to redo the work at no additional charge, the company's intent to satisfy the customer is clear.

PSYCHOLOGICAL IMPRESSIONS. People often evaluate the quality of a product or service on the basis of psychological impressions: atmosphere, image, or aesthetics. In the provision of services, where the customer is in close contact with the provider, the appearance and actions of the provider are very important. Nicely dressed, courteous, friendly, and sympathetic employees can affect the customer's perception of service quality. For example, rumpled, discourteous, or grumpy waiters can undermine a restaurant's best efforts to provide high-quality service. In manufacturing, product quality often is judged on the basis of the knowledge and personality of salespeople, as well as the product image presented in advertisements.

 These consumer-driven definitions of quality are applicable to traditional bricks-and-mortar businesses as well as Internet businesses, which use business-to-consumer (B2C) systems to sell merchandise ranging from textbooks to groceries directly to consumers (see Chapter 4, "Managing Technology," and Chapter 8, "Supply-Chain Management"). How does the customer in such situations define quality service? The following factors influence a customer's perception of service on the Internet:

❏ *Web Page.*   A good Web site is easy to navigate and convenient to use and place orders (*fitness for use; psychological impressions*). It also provides ample information about the product or service that the customer wants to purchase and information about other similar or related items the customer may be interested in (*value*). Billing is accurate (*support*).

❏ *Product Availability.*   Having a wide variety of selections and having the specific product the customer wants to purchase ready to ship are keys to good service marks (*value*).

❏ *Delivery Performance.*   Often delivery is promised within a certain time frame (*conformance to specifications*) and the faster, the better (*value*). Deliveries are made at a time and location convenient to the customer, such as a home residence between the hours of 4 and 6 P.M. (*fitness for use; value; conformance to specifications*).

❏ *Personal Contact.*   The opportunity to talk to a live person is often comforting to a customer who is doubtful of the right choice (*psychological impressions*).

With nearly an estimated $4 billion in online revenues lost annually because of poor service quality, it is clear that factors such as these are very important for the success of Internet companies.

QUALITY AS A COMPETITIVE WEAPON

Attaining quality in all areas of a business is a difficult task. To make things even more difficult, consumers change their perceptions of quality. In general, a business's success depends on the accuracy of its perceptions of consumer expectations and its ability to bridge the gap between those expectations and operating capabilities. Good quality pays off in higher profits. High-quality products and services can be priced higher than comparable lower-quality ones and yield a greater return for the same sales dollar. Poor quality erodes the firm's ability to compete in the marketplace and increases the costs of producing its product or service. For example, by improving conformance to specifications, a firm can increase its market share *and* reduce the cost of its products or services, which in turn increase profits. Management is better able to compete on both price and quality. Consumers are much more quality-minded now than in the past.

THE COSTS OF POOR QUALITY

What are the costs of poor quality?

Most experts on the costs of poor quality estimate losses in the range of 20 to 30 percent of gross sales for defective or unsatisfactory products. Four major categories of costs are associated with quality management: prevention, appraisal, internal failure, and external failure.

PREVENTION COSTS

prevention costs Costs associated with preventing defects before they happen.

Prevention costs are associated with preventing defects before they happen. They include the costs of redesigning the process to remove the causes of poor quality, redesigning the product to make it simpler to produce, training employees in the methods of continuous improvement, and working with suppliers to increase the quality of purchased items or contracted services. In order to improve quality, firms have to invest additional time, effort, and money. We explore these costs further later in this chapter.

APPRAISAL COSTS

appraisal costs Costs incurred in assessing the level of quality attained by the operating system.

Appraisal costs are incurred in assessing the level of quality attained by the operating system. Appraisal helps management identify quality problems. As preventive measures improve quality, appraisal costs decrease, because fewer resources are needed for quality inspections and the subsequent search for causes of any problems that are detected.

INTERNAL FAILURE COSTS

internal failure costs Costs resulting from defects that are discovered during the production of a product or service.

Internal failure costs result from defects that are discovered during the production of a product or service. They fall into two major cost categories: *yield losses,* which are incurred if a defective item must be scrapped, and *rework costs,* which are incurred if the item is rerouted to some previous operation(s) to correct the defect or if the service must be performed again. For example, if the final inspector at an automobile paint shop discovers that the paint on a car has a poor finish, the car may have to be completely resanded and repainted. The additional time spent correcting such a mistake results in lower productivity for the sanding and painting departments. In addition, the car may not be finished by the date on which the customer is expecting it. Such activities are great candidates for continuous improvement projects.

EXTERNAL FAILURE COSTS

external failure costs
Costs that arise when a defect is discovered after the customer has received the product or service.

External failure costs arise when a defect is discovered after the customer has received the product or service. For instance, suppose that you have the oil changed in your car and that the oil filter is improperly installed, causing the oil to drain onto your garage floor. You might insist that the company pay for the car to be towed and restore the oil and filter immediately. External failure costs to the company include the towing and additional oil and filter costs, as well as the loss of future revenue because you decide never to take your car back there for service. Dissatisfied customers talk about bad service or products to their friends, who in turn tell others. If the problem is bad enough, consumer protection groups alert the media. The potential impact on future profits is difficult to assess, but without doubt external failure costs erode market share and profits. Encountering defects and correcting them after the product is in the customer's hands is costly.

warranty A written guarantee that the producer will replace or repair defective parts or perform the service to the customer's satisfaction.

External failure costs also include warranty service and litigation costs. A **warranty** is a written guarantee that the producer will replace or repair defective parts or perform the service to the customer's satisfaction. Usually, a warranty is given for some specified period. For example, television repairs are usually guaranteed for 90 days and new automobiles for five years or 50,000 miles, whichever comes first. Warranty costs must be considered in the design of new products or services, particularly as they relate to reliability (discussed later in this chapter).

EMPLOYEE INVOLVEMENT

One of the important elements of TQM is employee involvement as shown in Figure 5.1. A program in employee involvement includes changing organizational culture and encouraging teamwork.

CULTURAL CHANGE

How can employees be included in the quality improvement process?

The challenge of quality management is to instill an awareness of the importance of quality in all employees and to motivate them to improve product quality. With TQM, everyone is expected to contribute to the overall improvement of quality—from the administrator who finds cost-saving measures to the salesperson who learns of a new customer need to the engineer who designs a product with fewer parts to the manager who communicates clearly with other department heads. In other words, TQM involves all the functions that relate to a product or service.

One of the main challenges in developing the proper culture for TQM is to define *customer* for each employee. In general, customers are internal or external (see Chapter 1, "Competing with Operations"). External customers are the people or firms who buy the product or service. In this sense, the entire firm is a single unit that must do its best to satisfy external customers. However, communicating customers' concerns to everyone in the organization is difficult. Some employees, especially those having little contact with external customers, may have difficulty seeing how their jobs contribute to the whole effort. However, each employee also has one or more internal customers—employees in the firm who rely on the output of other employees. For example, a machinist who drills holes in a component and passes it on to a welder has the welder as her customer. Even though the welder is not an external customer, he will have many of the same definitions of quality as an external customer, except that they will relate to the component instead of a complete product. All employees must do a good job of serving their internal customers if external customers ultimately are to be satisfied. The concept of internal customers works if each

internal customer demands only value-added activities of their internal suppliers: that is, activities that the external customer will recognize and pay for. The notion of internal customers applies to all parts of a firm and enhances cross-functional coordination. For example, accounting must prepare accurate and timely reports for management, and purchasing must provide high-quality materials on time for operations.

In TQM, everyone in the organization must share the view that quality control is an end in itself. Errors or defects should be caught and corrected at the source, not passed along to an internal customer. This philosophy is called *quality at the source*. In addition, firms should avoid trying to "inspect quality into the product" by using inspectors to weed out defective products or unsatisfactory services after all operations have been performed. In some manufacturing firms, workers have the authority to stop a production line if they spot quality problems.

TEAMS

How can a company develop teams?

teams Small groups of people who have a common purpose, set their own performance goals and approaches, and hold themselves accountable for success.

Employee involvement is a key tactic for improving competitiveness. One way to achieve employee involvement is by the use of **teams,** which are small groups of people who have a common purpose, set their own performance goals and approaches, and hold themselves accountable for success. Teams differ from the more typical "working group" because

- ❏ the members have a common commitment to an overarching purpose that all believe in and that transcends individual priorities;
- ❏ the leadership roles are shared rather than held by a single, strong leader;
- ❏ performance is judged not only by individual contributions but also by collective "work products" that reflect the joint efforts of all the members;
- ❏ open-ended discussion, rather than a managerially defined agenda, is prized at meetings; and
- ❏ the members of the team do real work together, rather than delegating to subordinates.

Management plays an important role in determining whether teams are successful. Survey results suggest that the following approaches lead to more successful teams (Katzenbach and Smith, 1993):

1. The team's project should be meaningful, with well-defined performance standards and direction.

2. Particular attention should be paid to creating a positive environment at the first few meetings.

3. Team members should create clear rules regarding attendance, openness, constructive confrontation, and commitment to the team.

4. To foster a sense of accomplishment, the team should set a few immediate performance-oriented tasks and goals that will allow it to achieve some early successes.

5. People outside the team should be consulted for fresh ideas and information.

6. If possible, team members should spend lots of time together to foster creative insights and personal bonding.

7. Managers should look for ways beyond direct compensation to give the team positive reinforcement.

The three approaches to teamwork most often used are problem-solving teams, special-purpose teams, and self-managing teams. All three use some amount of **employee empowerment,** which moves responsibility for decisions farther down the organizational chart—to the level of the employee actually doing the job.

PROBLEM-SOLVING TEAMS. First introduced in the 1920s, problem-solving teams, also called **quality circles,** became more popular in the late 1970s after the Japanese had used them successfully. Problem-solving teams are small groups of supervisors and employees who meet to identify, analyze, and solve production and quality problems. The philosophy behind this approach is that the people who are directly responsible for making the product or providing the service will be best able to consider ways to solve a problem. Also, employees take more pride and interest in their work if they are allowed to help shape it. The teams typically consist of 5 to 12 volunteers, drawn from different areas of a department or from a group of employees assigned to a particular task, such as automobile assembly or credit application processing. The teams meet several hours a week to work on quality and productivity problems and make suggestions to management. Such teams are used extensively by Japanese-managed firms in the United States. The Japanese philosophy is to encourage employee inputs while maintaining close control over their job activities. Although problem-solving teams can successfully reduce costs and improve quality, they die if management fails to implement many of the suggestions generated.

SPECIAL-PURPOSE TEAMS. An outgrowth of the problem-solving teams, **special-purpose teams** address issues of paramount concern to management, labor, or both. For example, management may form a special-purpose team to design and introduce new work policies or new technologies or to address customer service problems. Essentially, this approach gives workers a voice in high-level decisions. Special-purpose teams, which first appeared in the United States in the early 1980s, are becoming more popular.

SELF-MANAGING TEAMS. The **self-managing team** approach takes worker participation to its highest level: A small group of employees work together to produce a major portion, or sometimes all, of a product or service. Members learn all the tasks involved in the

employee empowerment An approach to teamwork that moves responsibility for decisions farther down the organizational chart—to the level of the employee actually doing the job.

quality circles Another name for problem-solving teams; small groups of supervisors and employees who meet to identify, analyze, and solve production and quality problems.

special-purpose teams Groups that address issues of paramount concern to management, labor, or both.

self-managing team A
small group of employees
who work together to
produce a major portion,
or sometimes all, of a
product or service.

operation, rotate from job to job, and take over managerial duties such as work and
vacation scheduling, ordering supplies, and hiring. In some cases, team members design
the process and have a high degree of latitude as to how it takes shape. Self-managing
teams essentially change the way work is organized because employees have control
over their jobs. Only recently have self-managing teams begun to catch on in the United
States, but some have increased productivity by 30 percent or more in their firms.

CONTINUOUS IMPROVEMENT

continuous improvement
The philosophy of
continually seeking ways
to improve operations,
based on a Japanese
concept called *kaizen.*

Continuous improvement, based on a Japanese concept called *kaizen,* is the philosophy
of continually seeking ways to improve operations. In this regard, it is not unique to
quality but applies also to process improvement. Continuous improvement involves
identifying benchmarks of excellent practice and instilling a sense of employee ownership in the process. The focus can be on reducing the length of time required to process
requests for loans at a bank, the amount of scrap generated at a milling machine, or the
number of employee injuries at a construction site. Continuous improvement also can
focus on problems with customers or suppliers, such as customers who request frequent changes in shipping quantities and suppliers who fail to maintain high quality.
The bases of the continuous improvement philosophy are the beliefs that virtually any
aspect of an operation can be improved and that the people most closely associated
with an operation are in the best position to identify the changes that should be made.
The idea is not to wait until a massive problem occurs before acting.

GETTING STARTED WITH CONTINUOUS IMPROVEMENT
Instilling a philosophy of continuous improvement in an organization may be a lengthy
process, and several steps are essential to its eventual success.

1. Train employees in the methods of statistical process control (SPC) and other
   tools for improving quality and performance.
2. Make SPC methods a normal aspect of daily operations.
3. Build work teams and employee involvement.
4. Utilize problem-solving tools within the work teams.
5. Develop a sense of operator ownership in the process.

Note that employee involvement is central to the philosophy of continuous improvement. However, the last two steps are crucial if the philosophy is to become part of
everyday operations. Problem solving addresses the aspects of operations that need
improvement and evaluates alternatives for achieving improvements. A sense of operator ownership emerges when employees feel as though they own the processes and
methods they use and take pride in the quality of the product or service they produce. It
comes from participation on work teams and in problem-solving activities, which instill
in employees a feeling that they have some control over their workplace and tasks.

PROBLEM-SOLVING PROCESS

plan–do–check–act cycle
A cycle, also called the
Deming Wheel, used by
firms actively engaged in
continuous improvement
to train their work teams
in problem solving.

Most firms actively engaged in continuous improvement train their work teams to use
the **plan–do–check–act cycle** for problem solving. Another name for this approach is
the Deming Wheel. Figure 5.2 shows this cycle, which lies at the heart of the continuous improvement philosophy. The cycle comprises the following steps.

1. *Plan.* The team selects a process (e.g., activity, method, machine, or policy)
   that needs improvement. The team then documents the selected process, usually
   by analyzing data (using the tools we discuss later in the chapter); sets qualitative

FIGURE 5.2

Plan–Do–Check–Act Cycle

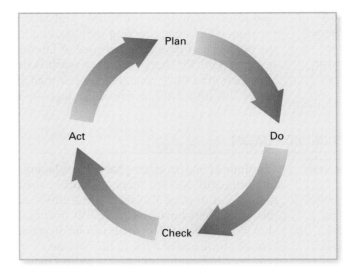

goals for improvement; and discusses various ways to achieve the goals. After assessing the benefits and costs of the alternatives, the team develops a plan with quantifiable measures for improvement.

2. *Do*. The team implements the plan and monitors progress. Data are collected continuously to measure the improvements in the process. Any changes in the process are documented, and further revisions are made as needed.

3. *Check*. The team analyzes the data collected during the *do* step to find out how closely the results correspond to the goals set in the *plan* step. If major short-comings exist, the team may have to reevaluate the plan or stop the project.

4. *Act*. If the results are successful, the team documents the revised process so that it becomes the standard procedure for all who may use it. The team may then instruct other employees in the use of the revised process.

Problem-solving projects often focus on those aspects of operations that do not add value to the product or service. Value is added during operations such as machining a part or serving a customer on a Web page. No value is added in activities such as inspecting parts for quality defects or routing requests for loan approvals to several different departments. The idea of continuous improvement is to reduce or elimi-nate activities that do not add value and, thus, are wasteful. For example, suppose that a firm has identified three non-value-added activities in the manufacture of its products: inspection of each part, repair of defects, and handling of materials between operations. The time that parts spend in each activity is not adding value to the prod-uct and, hence, is not generating revenue for the firm. Continuous improvement projects might focus on reducing materials handling time by rearranging machine loca-tions to minimize the distances traveled by materials or improving the methods for producing the parts to reduce the need for inspection and rework.

IMPROVING QUALITY THROUGH TQM

What factors in the operations system are causing major quality problems?

Programs of employee involvement and continuous improvement are aimed at improving quality in a general sense. However, TQM often focuses on processes such as purchasing, product and service design, and process design, and utilizes tools such as quality func-tion deployment, benchmarking, and data analysis.

PURCHASING CONSIDERATIONS

Most businesses depend on outside suppliers for some of the materials, services, or equipment used in producing their products and services. Large companies have hundreds and even thousands of suppliers, some of which supply the same types of parts. The quality of these inputs can affect the quality of the firm's work, and purchased parts of poor quality can have a devastating effect.

Both the buyer's approach and specification management are keys to controlling supplier quality. The firm's buyer must emphasize not only the cost and speed of delivery to the supplier but also the quality of the product. A competent buyer will identify suppliers that offer high-quality products or services at a reasonable cost. After identifying these suppliers, the buyer should work with them to obtain essentially defect-free parts. To do so may require examining and evaluating trade-offs between receiving off-specification materials and seeking corrective action.

The specifications for purchased parts and materials must be clear and *realistic*. As a check on specifications, buyers in some companies initiate *process capability studies* for important products, a topic we address later in this chapter. These studies amount to trial runs of small product samples to ensure that all components, including the raw materials and purchased parts, work together to form a product that has the desired quality level at a reasonable cost. Analysis of study results may identify unrealistic specifications and the need for changes.

PRODUCT AND SERVICE DESIGN

Because design changes often require changes in methods, materials, or specifications, they can increase defect rates. Change invariably increases the risk of making mistakes, so stable product and service designs can help reduce internal quality problems. However, stable designs may not be possible when a product or service is sold in markets globally. Although changed designs have the potential to increase market share, management must be aware of possible quality problems resulting from the changes. If a firm needs to make design changes to remain competitive, it should carefully test new designs and redesign the product or service and the process with a focus on the market. Implementing both strategies involves a trade-off: Higher quality and increased competitiveness are exchanged for added time and cost.

reliability The probability that a product will be functional when used.

Another dimension of quality related to product design is **reliability,** which refers to the probability that the product will be functional when used. Products often consist of a number of components that all must be operative for the product to perform as intended. Sometimes products can be designed with extra components (or subsystems) so that if one component fails another can be activated.

Suppose that a product has n subsystems, each with its own reliability measure (the probability that it will operate when called upon). The reliability of each subsystem contributes to the quality of the total system; that is, the reliability of the complete product equals the product of all the reliabilities of the subsystems, or

$$r_s = (r_1)(r_2) \cdots (r_n)$$

where

$$r_s = \text{reliability of the complete product}$$
$$n = \text{number of subsystems}$$
$$r_n = \text{reliability of the subsystem or component } n$$

This measure of reliability is based on the assumption that the reliability of each component or subsystem is independent of the others.

**TUTOR
5.1**

Suppose that a small portable radio designed for joggers has three components: a motherboard with a reliability of 0.99, a housing assembly with a reliability of 0.90, and a headphone set with a reliability of 0.85. The reliabilities are the probabilities that each subsystem will still be operating two years from now. The reliability of the portable radio is

$$r_s = (0.99)(0.90)(0.85) = 0.76$$

The poor headsets and housings hurt the reliability of this product. Suppose that new designs resulted in a reliability of 0.95 for the housing and 0.90 for the headsets. Product reliability would improve to

$$r_s = (0.99)(0.95)(0.90) = 0.85$$

Manufacturers must be concerned about the quality of every component, because the product fails when any one of them fails.

PROCESS DESIGN

The design of the process used to produce a product or service greatly affects its quality. Managers at the First National Bank of Chicago noticed that customers' requests for a letter of credit took four days to go through dozens of steps involving nine employees before a letter of credit would be issued. To improve the process and shorten the waiting time for customers, the bank trained letter-of-credit issuers to do all the required tasks so that the customer could deal with just one person. In addition, customers were given the same employee each time they requested a letter. First National Bank of Chicago now issues letters of credit in less than a day.

The purchase of new machinery can help prevent or overcome quality problems. Suppose that the design specification for the distance between two holes in a metal plate is 3.000 ± 0.0005 in. Suppose also that too many plates are defective; that is, the space between holes falls outside the design specification. One way to reduce the percentage of defective parts produced by the process would be to purchase new machinery with the capability of producing metal plates with holes 3.000 ± 0.0003 in. apart. The cost of the new machinery is the trade-off for reducing the percentage of defective parts and their cost.

One of the keys to obtaining high quality is concurrent engineering (see Chapter 1, "Competing with Operations" and Chapter 2, "Process Management"), in which operations managers and designers work closely together in the initial phases of product or service design to ensure that production requirements and process capabilities are synchronized. The result is much better quality and shorter development time. NCR, an Atlanta company that makes terminals for checkout counters, used concurrent engineering to develop a new model in 22 months, or half the usual time. The terminal had 85 percent fewer parts and could be assembled in only two minutes. Quality rejects and engineering changes dropped significantly. The National Institute of Standards and Technology estimates that manufacturing firms using concurrent engineering need 30 to 70 percent less development time, require 20 to 90 percent less time to market, and produce 200 to 600 percent better-quality products. The Managerial Practice feature tells how Teradyne implemented concurrent engineering.

QUALITY FUNCTION DEPLOYMENT

quality function deployment (QFD) A means of translating customer requirements into the appropriate technical requirements for each stage of product or service development and production.

A key to improving quality through TQM is linking the design of products or services to the processes that produce them. **Quality function deployment (QFD)** is a means of translating customer requirements into the appropriate technical requirements for each stage of product or service development and production. In 1978, Yoji Akao and

MANAGERIAL **PRACTICE**
TQM and Concurrent Engineering at Teradyne

Teradyne (www.teradyne.com), a $1.5-billion-a-year company with assembly plants in California, Massachusetts, New Hampshire, Illinois, Ireland, and Japan, produces testing systems for newly made chips, printed circuit boards and modules, computerized phone systems, and even software. Its newest product, called the Catalyst, has 250,000 parts and costs between $1.5 and $2 million. Teradyne produces the Catalyst in a plant with only 69 assemblers and 51 test workers, mostly in teams of 14 divided into shifts that work around the clock to put together a single machine in as little as two weeks. Catalyst has become the leading product in its field, and Teradyne has become a favorite of Wall Street because it has not had a losing quarter since 1991, while its major competitors have had a much rockier road.

Teradyne management attributes much of its success to the installation of TQM. Key aspects of the implementation of TQM were total involvement of management and employees and concurrent engineering. Although the company had already tried quality programs in the past, Alexander d'Arbelof, cofounder and CEO, decided to get personally involved by studying TQM and leading the implementation effort. He used three quality improvement teams to address three goals: increase market share, reduce costs, and reduce cycle time. The teams, composed of managers who were scientists and engineers, used their background and training to analyze the issues needing attention. Their common sense along with the TQM problem-solving approach generated solutions that improved operations. For example, Teradyne had been purchasing circuit boards from suppliers based on their capacities, rather than on who could do the job best. Changing their approach resulted in savings of $6 million a year, with an increase in quality. To maintain top management involvement, a top executive serves as a companywide TQM director on a rotating basis, and each division has its own TQM chief. Finally, employees were rewarded for company success through new profit sharing, stock option, and stock purchase plans.

A second key aspect of the implementation was the realization of design engineers and manufacturing assemblers that they

Concurrent engineering, a key to the successful implementation of TQM, has contributed to the success of Teradyne through improved process and product designs. To ensure the best in quality, great care goes into assembling the Catalyst's test head, which contains 700 cable connections.

would be much better off working together—using concurrent engineering. Before TQM, engineers would literally send prototypes down elevators from their upstairs laboratories to assemblers who had to figure out how to deal with design problems or send the prototype back with complaints. For example, assemblers would wonder why they must use 20 different types of screws and six different tools to fasten them. After TQM, assemblers had an equal voice with design engineers and, for the first time, the design engineers were required to work on the factory floor as a team with the assemblers to iron out design problems on the prototype models. As a result, the prototypes were built in 2.5 as opposed to 4 weeks, and with far fewer types of screws.

Source: Gene Bylinsky. "America's Elite Factories." *Fortune* (August 16, 1999), pp. 136P–136T.

Shigeru Mizuno published the first work on QFD, showing how design considerations could be "deployed" to every element of competition. Since then, more than 200 U.S. companies have used the approach, including Digital Equipment, Texas Instruments, Hewlett-Packard, AT&T, ITT, Ford, Chrysler, General Motors, Procter & Gamble, Polaroid, and Deere & Company.

This approach seeks answers to the following six questions.

1. *Voice of the Customer.* What do our customers need and want?
2. *Competitive Analysis.* In terms of our customers, how well are we doing relative to our competitors?
3. *Voice of the Engineer.* What technical measures relate to our customers' needs?
4. *Correlations.* What are the relationships between the voice of the customer and the voice of the engineer?
5. *Technical Comparison.* How does our product or service performance compare to that of our competition?
6. *Trade-Offs.* What are the potential technical trade-offs?

The competitive analysis provides a place to start looking for ways to gain a competitive advantage. Then the relationships between customer needs and engineering attributes need to be specified. Finally, the fact that improving one performance measure may detract from another must be recognized.

The QFD approach provides a way to set targets and debate their effects on product quality. Engineering uses the data to focus on significant product design features. Marketing uses this input for determining marketing strategies. Operations uses the information to identify the processes that are crucial to improving product quality as perceived by the customer. As a result, QFD encourages interfunctional communication for the purpose of improving the quality of products and services.

BENCHMARKING

How good is the company's quality relative to that of competitors?

benchmarking A continuous, systematic procedure that measures a firm's products, services, and processes against those of industry leaders.

Benchmarking is a continuous, systematic procedure that measures a firm's products, services, and processes against those of industry leaders. Companies use benchmarking to understand better how outstanding companies do things so that they can improve their own operations. Typical measures used in benchmarking include cost per unit, service upsets (breakdowns) per customer, processing time per unit, customer retention rates, revenue per unit, return on investment, and customer satisfaction levels. Those involved in continuous improvement efforts rely on benchmarking to formulate goals and targets for performance. Benchmarking consists of four basic steps.

1. *Planning.* Identify the product, service, or process to be benchmarked and the firm(s) to be used for comparison, determine the measures of performance for analysis, and collect the data.
2. *Analysis.* Determine the gap between the firm's current performance and that of the benchmark firm(s) and identify the causes of significant gaps.
3. *Integration.* Establish goals and obtain the support of managers who must provide the resources for accomplishing the goals.
4. *Action.* Develop cross-functional teams of those most affected by the changes, develop action plans and team assignments, implement the plans, monitor progress, and recalibrate benchmarks as improvements are made.

The benchmarking process is similar to the plan–do–check–act cycle in continuous improvement, but benchmarking focuses on setting quantitative goals for continuous improvement. *Competitive* benchmarking is based on comparisons with a direct industry competitor. *Functional* benchmarking compares areas such as administration, customer service, and sales operations with those of outstanding firms in any industry. For instance, Xerox benchmarked its distribution function against L.L. Bean's because Bean is renowned as a leading retailer in distribution efficiency and customer service.

Internal benchmarking involves using an organizational unit with superior performance as the benchmark for other units. This form of benchmarking can be advantageous for firms that have several business units or divisions. All forms of benchmarking are best applied in situations in which a long-term program of continuous improvement is needed.

DATA ANALYSIS TOOLS

The first step in improving the quality of an operation is data collection. Data can help uncover operations requiring improvement and the extent of remedial action needed. There are nine tools for organizing and presenting data to identify areas for quality and performance improvement: flow diagrams, process charts, checklists, histograms and bar charts, Pareto charts, scatter diagrams, cause-and-effect diagrams, graphs, and control charts. We have already discussed flow diagrams and process charts in Chapter 2, "Process Management," and we discuss control charts in depth later when we address statistical process control. In this section we demonstrate the use of the other six methods to emphasize the breadth of applications possible.

CHECKLISTS. Data collection through the use of a checklist is often the first step in the analysis of quality problems. A **checklist** is a form used to record the frequency of occurrence of certain product or service characteristics related to quality. The characteristics may be measurable on a continuous scale (e.g., weight, diameter, time, or length) or on a yes-or-no basis (e.g., paint discoloration, odors, rude servers, or too much grease).

HISTOGRAMS AND BAR CHARTS. The data from a checklist often can be presented succinctly and clearly with histograms or bar charts. A **histogram** summarizes data measured on a continuous scale, showing the frequency distribution of some quality characteristic (in statistical terms, the central tendency and dispersion of the data). Often the mean of the data is indicated on the histogram. A **bar chart** is a series of bars representing the frequency of occurrence of data characteristics measured on a yes-or-no basis. The bar height indicates the number of times a particular quality characteristic was observed.

PARETO CHARTS. When managers discover several quality problems that need to be addressed, they have to decide which should be attacked first. Vilfredo Pareto, a nineteenth-century Italian scientist whose statistical work focused on inequalities in data, proposed that most of an "activity" is caused by relatively few of its factors. In a restaurant quality problem, the activity could be customer complaints and the factor could be "discourteous waiter." For a manufacturer, the activity could be product defects and a factor could be "missing part." Pareto's concept, called the 80–20 rule, is that 80 percent of the activity is caused by 20 percent of the factors. By concentrating on the 20 percent of the factors (the "vital few"), managers can attack 80 percent of the quality problems.

The few vital factors can be identified with a **Pareto chart,** a bar chart on which the factors are plotted in decreasing order of frequency along the horizontal axis. The chart has two vertical axes, the one on the left showing frequency (as in a histogram) and the one on the right showing the cumulative percentage of frequency. The cumulative frequency curve identifies the few vital factors that warrant immediate managerial attention.

SCATTER DIAGRAMS. Sometimes managers suspect but are not sure that a certain factor is causing a particular quality problem. A **scatter diagram,** which is a plot of two variables showing whether they are related, can be used to verify or negate the suspicion. Each

---

How can areas for quality improvement be identified?

checklist A form used to record the frequency of occurrence of certain product or service characteristics related to quality.

histogram A summarization of data measured on a continuous scale, showing the frequency distribution of some quality characteristic (in statistical terms, the central tendency and dispersion of the data).

bar chart A series of bars representing the frequency of occurrence of data characteristics measured on a yes-or-no basis.

Pareto chart A bar chart on which the factors are plotted in decreasing order of frequency along the horizontal axis.

TUTOR 5.2

scatter diagram A plot of two variables showing whether they are related.

point on the scatter diagram represents one data observation. For example, the manager of a castings shop may suspect that casting defects are a function of the diameter of the casting. A scatter diagram could be constructed by plotting the number of defective castings found for each diameter of casting produced. After the diagram is completed, any relationship between diameter and number of defects could be observed.

CAUSE-AND-EFFECT DIAGRAMS. An important aspect of TQM is linking each aspect of quality prized by the customer to the inputs, methods, and process steps that build a particular attribute into the product. One way to identify a design problem that needs to be corrected is to develop a **cause-and-effect diagram** that relates a key quality problem to its potential causes. First developed by Kaoru Ishikawa, the diagram helps management trace customer complaints directly to the operations involved. Operations that have no bearing on a particular defect aren't shown on the diagram for that defect.

cause-and-effect diagram A diagram that relates a key quality problem to its potential causes.

The cause-and-effect diagram sometimes is called a *fishbone diagram*. The main quality problem is labeled as the fish's "head," the major categories of potential causes as structural "bones," and the likely specific causes as "ribs." When constructing and using a cause-and-effect diagram, an analyst identifies all the major categories of potential causes for the quality problem. For example, these might be personnel, machines, materials, and processes. For each major category, the analyst lists all the likely causes of the quality problem. For example, under personnel might be listed "lack of training," "poor communication," and "absenteeism." Brainstorming helps the analyst identify and properly classify all suspected causes. The analyst then systematically investigates the causes listed on the diagram for each major category, updating the chart as new causes become apparent. The process of constructing a cause-and-effect diagram calls management and worker attention to the primary factors affecting product or service quality.

graphs Representations of data in a variety of pictorial forms, such as line graphs and pie charts.

GRAPHS. Graphs represent data in a variety of pictorial formats, such as line graphs and pie charts. *Line graphs* represent data sequentially with data points connected by line segments to highlight trends in the data. Line graphs are used in control charts and forecasting (see Chapter 9, "Forecasting"). Pie charts represent quality factors as slices of a pie; the size of each slice is in proportion to the number of occurrences of the factor. Pie charts are useful for showing data from a group of factors that can be represented as percentages totaling 100 percent.

Each of the tools for improving quality that we have just discussed may be used independently, but their power is greatest when they are used together. In solving a quality problem, managers often must act as detectives, sifting data to clarify the issues involved and deducing the causes. We call this process *data snooping*. Example 5.1 demonstrates how four of the tools for improving quality can be used for data snooping.

| EXAMPLE 5.1 | *Identifying Causes of Poor Headliner Quality* |

The Wellington Fiber Board Company produces headliners, the fiberglass components that form the inner roof of passenger cars. Management wanted to identify which defects were most prevalent and to find the cause.

SOLUTION

Figure 5.3 shows the sequential application of several tools for improving quality.

Step 1. A checklist of different types of defects was constructed from last month's production records.

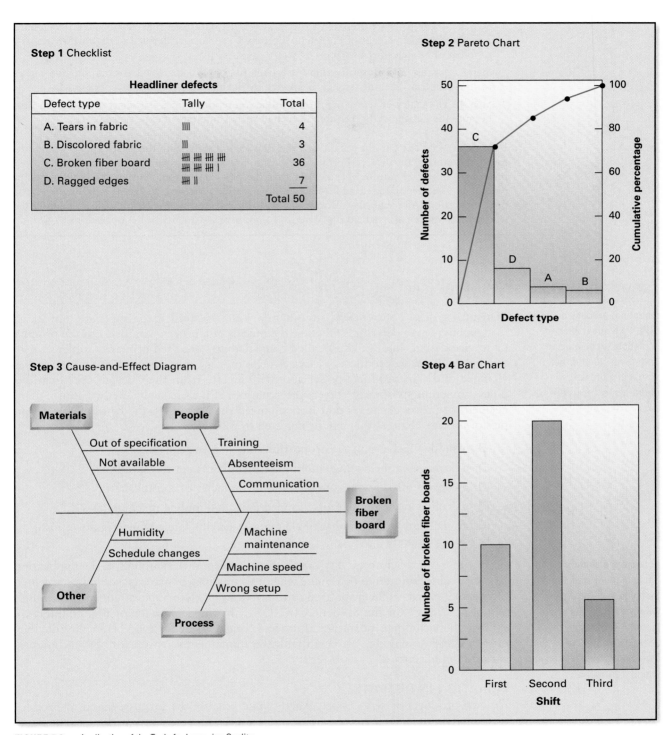

Step 1 Checklist

Headliner defects

Defect type	Tally	Total
A. Tears in fabric	IIII	4
B. Discolored fabric	III	3
C. Broken fiber board	### ### ### ### ### ### ### I	36
D. Ragged edges	### II	7
	Total	50

Step 2 Pareto Chart

Step 3 Cause-and-Effect Diagram

Step 4 Bar Chart

FIGURE 5.3 • Application of the Tools for Improving Quality

Step 2. A Pareto chart prepared from the checklist data indicated that broken fiber board accounted for 72 percent of the quality defects. The manager decided to dig further into the problem of broken fiber board.

Step 3. A cause-and-effect diagram for broken fiber board identified several potential causes for the problem. The one strongly suspected by the manager was employee training.

Step 4. The manager reorganized the production reports into a bar chart according to shift because the personnel on the three shifts had varied amounts of experience.

Decision Point The bar chart indicated that the second shift, with the least experienced workforce, had most of the defects. Further investigation revealed that workers were not using proper procedures for stacking the fiber boards after the press operation, causing cracking and chipping. The manager initiated additional training sessions focused on board handling after the press operation. Although the second shift was not responsible for all the defects, finding the source of many defects enabled the manager to improve the quality of her operations. ❐

STATISTICAL PROCESS CONTROL (SPC)

statistical process control (SPC) The application of statistical techniques to determine whether the output of a process conforms to the product or service design.

Statistical process control (SPC), another data analysis tool, is the application of statistical techniques to determine whether the output of a process conforms to the product or service design. In SPC, tools called control charts are used primarily to detect production of defective products or services or to indicate that the production process has changed and that products or services will deviate from their design specifications unless something is done to correct the situation. SPC can also be used to inform management of process changes that have changed the output for the better. Some examples of process changes that can be detected by SPC are

- ❐ a sudden increase in the proportion of defective gear boxes
- ❐ a decrease in the average number of complaints per day at a hotel
- ❐ a consistently low measurement in the diameter of a crankshaft
- ❐ a decline in the number of scrapped units at a milling machine
- ❐ an increase in the number of claimants receiving late payment from an insurance company

acceptance sampling The application of statistical techniques to determine whether a quantity of material should be accepted or rejected based on the inspection or test of a sample.

Another approach to quality management, **acceptance sampling,** is the application of statistical techniques to determine whether a quantity of material should be accepted or rejected, based on the inspection or test of a sample (see Supplement F, "Acceptance Sampling Plans" on the Student CD-ROM). In the remainder of this chapter, we explore the techniques of statistical process control to understand better the role they play in decision making. We begin with the fundamental reason for SPC techniques: variation in outputs.

VARIATION IN OUTPUTS

No two products or services are exactly alike because the processes used to produce them contain many sources of variation, even if the processes are working as intended. For example, the diameters of two crankshafts may vary because of differences in tool wear, material hardness, operator skill, or temperature during the period in which they were produced. Similarly, the time required to process a credit card application varies because of the load on the credit department, the financial background of the applicant, and the skills and attitudes of the employees. Nothing can be done to eliminate variation in process output completely, but management can investigate the *causes* of variation to minimize it. There are two basic categories of variation in output: common causes and assignable causes.

common causes of variation The purely random, unidentifiable sources of variation that are unavoidable with the current process.

COMMON CAUSES. **Common causes of variation** are the purely random, unidentifiable sources of variation that are unavoidable with the current process. For example, a machine that fills cereal boxes will not put exactly the same amount of cereal in each box. If you weighed a large number of boxes filled by the machine and plotted the results in a scatter diagram, the data would tend to form a pattern that can be described as a *distribution*. Such a distribution may be characterized by its mean, spread, and shape. Equations for the sample mean and standard deviation can be found in the Equation Summary at the end of this chapter.

1. The *mean* is the sum of the observations divided by the total number of observations.
2. The *spread* is a measure of the dispersion of observations about the mean. Two measures commonly used in practice are the range and the standard deviation. The *range* is the difference between the largest observation in a sample and the smallest. The *standard deviation* is the square root of the variance of a distribution. Relatively small values for the range or the standard deviation imply that the observations are clustered near the mean.
3. Two common *shapes* of process distributions are symmetric and skewed. A *symmetric* distribution has the same number of observations above and below the mean. A *skewed* distribution has a preponderance of observations either above or below the mean.

If process variability comes solely from common causes of variation, a typical assumption is that the distribution is symmetric, with most observations near the center.

assignable causes of variation Any variation-causing factors that can be identified and eliminated.

What trade-offs are involved in using attribute measurements instead of variable measurements of quality?

ASSIGNABLE CAUSES. The second category of variation, **assignable causes of variation,** also known as *special causes,* includes any variation-causing factors that can be identified and eliminated. Assignable causes of variation include an employee needing training or a machine needing repair. Assignable causes can change the distribution of the output of a process by causing the mean to shift, the variation to change, or the preponderance of observations to reside above or below the mean. A process is said to be in statistical control when the location, spread, or shape of its distribution does not change over time. After the process is in statistical control, managers use SPC procedures to detect the onset of assignable causes so that they can be eliminated.

variables Product or service characteristics, such as weight, length, volume, or time, that can be measured.

attributes Product or service characteristics that can be quickly counted for acceptable quality.

QUALITY MEASUREMENTS. To detect abnormal variations in output, employees or their equipment must be able to measure quality characteristics. Quality can be evaluated in two ways. One way is to measure **variables**—that is, product or service characteristics, such as weight, length, volume, or time, that can be *measured*. The advantage of measuring a quality characteristic is that if a product or service misses its quality specifications, the employee knows by how much. The disadvantage is that such measurements typically involve special equipment, employee skills, exacting procedures, and time and effort.

Another way to evaluate quality is to measure **attributes**—that is, product or service characteristics that can be quickly *counted* for acceptable quality. The method allows employees to make a simple yes–no decision about whether a product or service meets the specifications. Attributes often are used when quality specifications are complex and measuring by variables is difficult or costly. Some examples of attributes that can be counted are the number of insurance forms containing errors that cause underpayments or overpayments and the proportion of washing machines failing final inspection. The advantage of attribute counts is that less effort and fewer resources are needed than for measuring variables. The disadvantage is that, even though attribute counts can reveal that quality of performance has changed, they may not be of much use in indicating by how much.

SAMPLING. The most thorough approach to inspection is to inspect each product or service at each stage of the process for quality. This method, called *complete inspection,* is used when the costs of passing defects to the next workstation or external customer outweigh the inspection costs. Firms often use automated inspection equipment that can record, summarize, and display data. Many companies have found that automated inspection equipment can pay for itself in a reasonably short time.

sampling plan A plan that specifies a sample size, the time between successive samples, and decision rules that determine when action should be taken.

A well-conceived **sampling plan** can approach the same degree of protection as complete inspection. A sampling plan specifies a **sample size**, which is a quantity of randomly selected observations of process outputs; the time between successive samples; and decision rules that determine when action should be taken. Sampling is appropriate when inspection costs are high because of the special knowledge, skills, procedures, or expensive equipment required to perform the inspections or when testing is destructive.

sample size A quantity of randomly selected observations of process outputs.

SAMPLING DISTRIBUTIONS. The purpose of sampling is to calculate a variable or attribute measure for some quality characteristic of the sample. That measure is then used to assess the performance of the process itself. For example, an important quality dimension is the weight of the product in a box of cereal. Suppose that management wants the box-filling machine to produce boxes so that the average weight is 425 grams. That is, it wants the process distribution to have a mean of 425 grams. An inspector periodically taking a sample of five boxes filled by the machine and calculating the sample mean (a variable measure) could use it to determine how well the machine is doing.

Plotting a large number of these means would show that they have their own distribution, with a mean centered on 425 grams, as did the process distribution, but with much less variability. The reason is that means offset the highs and lows of the individual box weights. Figure 5.4 shows the relationship between the sampling distribution and the process distribution with common causes of variation for the box weights.

Some sampling distributions (e.g., for means with sample sizes of 4 or more and proportions with sample sizes of 20 or more) can be approximated by the *normal* distribution, allowing the use of the normal tables. We can determine the probability that any particular sample result will fall outside certain limits. For example, there is a

FIGURE 5.4

Relationship Between the Distribution of Sample Means and the Process Distribution

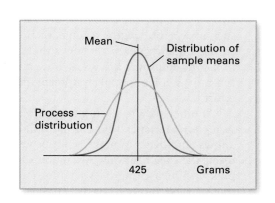

2.28 percent chance, or (100 − 95.44)/2, that a sample mean will be more than 2 standard deviations *greater* than the mean. The ability to assign probabilities to sample results is important for the construction and use of control charts.

CONTROL CHARTS

control chart A time-ordered diagram that is used to determine whether observed variations are abnormal.

To determine whether observed variations are abnormal, we can measure and plot the quality characteristic taken from the sample on a time-ordered diagram called a **control chart.** A control chart has a nominal value, or central line, which typically is a target that managers would like the process to achieve, and two control limits based on the sampling distribution of the quality measure. The control limits are used to judge whether action is required. The larger value represents the *upper control limit* (UCL), and the smaller value represents the *lower control limit* (LCL). Figure 5.5 shows how the control limits relate to the sampling distribution. A sample statistic that falls between the UCL and the LCL indicates that the process is exhibiting common causes of variation; a statistic that falls outside the control limits indicates that the process is exhibiting assignable causes of variation.

Observations falling outside the control limits do not always mean poor quality. For example, in Figure 5.5 the assignable cause may be a new billing process introduced to reduce the number of incorrect bills sent to customers. If the proportion of incorrect bills, the quality statistic from a sample of bills, falls *below* the LCL of the control chart, the new procedure has likely changed the billing process for the better and a new control chart should be constructed.

Managers or employees responsible for monitoring a process can use control charts in the following ways:

1. Take a random sample from the process, measure the quality characteristic, and calculate a variable or attribute measure.
2. If the statistic falls outside the chart's control limits, look for an assignable cause.
3. Eliminate the cause if it degrades quality; incorporate the cause if it improves quality. Reconstruct the control chart with new data.
4. Repeat the procedure periodically.

FIGURE 5.5

Relationship of Control Limits to Sampling Distribution and Observations from Three Samples

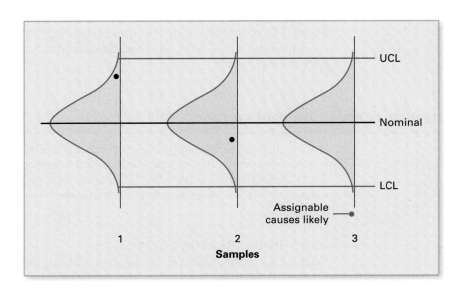

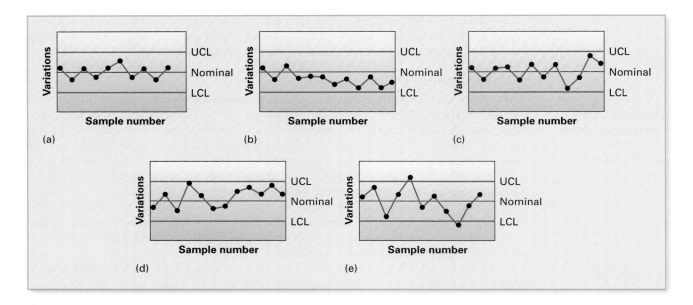

FIGURE 5.6

*Control Chart
Examples*

Sometimes problems with a process can be detected even though the control limits have not been exceeded. Figure 5.6 contains five examples of control charts. Chart (a) shows a process that is in statistical control. No action is needed. However, chart (b) shows a pattern called a *run,* or a sequence of observations with a certain characteristic. A typical rule is to take remedial action when there is a trend of five or more observations, even if the points have not yet exceeded the control limits.

Chart (c) shows that the process has taken a sudden change from its normal pattern. The last four observations are unusual: three rising toward the UCL and the fourth remaining above the nominal value. A manager should be concerned with such sudden changes even though the control limits have not been exceeded. Chart (d) demonstrates another situation in which action is needed even though the limits haven't been exceeded. Whenever a run of five or more observations above or below the nominal value occurs, the operator should look for a cause. The probability is very low that such a result could take place by chance. Finally, chart (e) indicates that the process went out of control twice because two sample results fell outside the control limits. The probability that the process distribution has changed is high. We discuss more implications of being out of statistical control when we discuss process capability later in this chapter.

STATISTICAL PROCESS CONTROL METHODS

Statistical process control (SPC) methods are useful for both measuring the current quality of products or services and detecting whether the process itself has changed in a way that will affect quality. In this section, we first discuss mean and range charts for variable measures of quality and then consider control charts for product or service attributes.

CONTROL CHARTS FOR VARIABLES

Control charts for variables are used to monitor the mean and the variability of the process distribution.

R-chart A chart used to monitor process variability.

R-CHARTS. A range chart, or **R-chart**, is used to monitor process variability. To calculate the range of a set of sample data, the analyst subtracts the smallest from the largest measurement in each sample. If any of the data fall outside the control limits, the process variability is not in control.

The control limits for the R-chart are

$$\text{UCL}_R = D_4\overline{R} \qquad \text{and} \qquad \text{LCL}_R = D_3\overline{R}$$

where

$\overline{R}$ = average of several past R values and the central line of the control chart

D_3, D_4 = constants that provide 3 standard deviation (three-sigma) limits for a given sample size

Values for D_3 and D_4 are contained in Table 5.1 and change as a function of the sample size. Note that the spread between the control limits narrows as the sample size increases. This change is a consequence of having more information on which to base an estimate for the process range.

x̄-chart A chart used to measure the mean.

x̄-CHARTS. An $\overline{x}$-chart (read "x-bar chart") is used to measure the mean. When the assignable causes of process variability have been identified and the process variability is in statistical control, the analyst can construct an $\overline{x}$-chart to control the process average. The control limits for the $\overline{x}$-chart are

$$\text{UCL}_{\overline{x}} = \overline{\overline{x}} + A_2\overline{R} \qquad \text{and} \qquad \text{LCL}_{\overline{x}} = \overline{\overline{x}} - A_2\overline{R}$$

where

$\overline{\overline{x}}$ = central line of the chart and either the average of past sample means or a target value set for the process

A_2 = constant to provide three-sigma limits for the sample mean

The values for A_2 are contained in Table 5.1. Note that the control limits use the value of $\overline{R}$; therefore, the $\overline{x}$-chart must be constructed *after* the process variability is in control.

Analysts can develop and use $\overline{x}$- and R-charts in the following way:

Step 1. Collect data on the variable quality measurement (such as weight, diameter, or time) and organize the data by sample number. Preferably, at least 20 samples should be taken for use in constructing a control chart.

TABLE 5.1

Factors for Calculating Three-Sigma Limits for the x̄-Chart and R-Chart

Source: 1950 ASTM Manual on Quality Control of Materials, copyright © American Society for Testing Materials. Reprinted with permission.

Size of Sample (n)	Factor for UCL and LCL for x̄-Charts (A₂)	Factor for LCL for R-Charts (D₃)	Factor for UCL for R-Charts (D₄)
2	1.880	0	3.267
3	1.023	0	2.575
4	0.729	0	2.282
5	0.577	0	2.115
6	0.483	0	2.004
7	0.419	0.076	1.924
8	0.373	0.136	1.864
9	0.337	0.184	1.816
10	0.308	0.223	1.777

Step 2. Compute the range for each sample and the average range, $\overline{R}$, for the set of samples.

Step 3. Use Table 5.1 to determine the upper and lower control limits of the R-chart.

Step 4. Plot the sample ranges. If all are in control, proceed to step 5. Otherwise, find the assignable causes, correct them, and return to step 1.

Step 5. Calculate $\overline{x}$ for each sample and the central line of the chart, $\overline{\overline{x}}$.

Step 6. Use Table 5.1 to determine the parameters for $\text{UCL}_{\overline{x}}$ and $\text{LCL}_{\overline{x}}$ and construct the $\overline{x}$-chart.

Step 7. Plot the sample means. If all are in control, the process is in statistical control in terms of the process average and process variability. Continue to take samples and monitor the process. If any are out of control, find the assignable causes, correct them, and return to step 1. If no assignable causes are found after a diligent search, assume that the out-of-control points represent common causes of variation and continue to monitor the process.

EXAMPLE 5.2

Using $\overline{x}$- and R-Charts to Monitor a Process

The management of West Allis Industries is concerned about the production of a special metal screw used by several of the company's largest customers. The diameter of the screw is critical. Data from five samples are shown in the accompanying table. The sample size is 4. Is the process in control?

TUTOR 5.3

SOLUTION

Step 1. For simplicity we have taken only five samples. In practice, more than 20 samples would be desirable. The data are shown in the following table.

Data for the $\overline{x}$- and R-Charts: Observations of Screw Diameter (in.)

SAMPLE NUMBER	OBSERVATION				R	$\overline{x}$
	1	2	3	4		
1	0.5014	0.5022	0.5009	0.5027	0.0018	0.5018
2	0.5021	0.5041	0.5024	0.5020	0.0021	0.5027
3	0.5018	0.5026	0.5035	0.5023	0.0017	0.5026
4	0.5008	0.5034	0.5024	0.5015	0.0026	0.5020
5	0.5041	0.5056	0.5034	0.5047	0.0022	0.5045
				Average	0.0021	0.5027

Step 2. Compute the range for each sample by subtracting the lowest value from the highest value. For example, in sample 1 the range is $0.5027 - 0.5009 = 0.0018$ in. Similarly, the ranges for samples 2, 3, 4, and 5 are 0.0021, 0.0017, 0.0026, and 0.0022 in., respectively. As shown in the table, $\overline{R} = 0.0021$.

Step 3. To construct the R-chart, select the appropriate constants from Table 5.1 for a sample size of 4. The control limits are

$$\text{UCL}_R = D_4\overline{R} = 2.282(0.0021) = 0.00479 \text{ in.}$$

$$\text{LCL}_R = D_3\overline{R} = 0(0.0021) = 0 \text{ in.}$$

Step 4. Plot the ranges on the R-chart, as shown in Figure 5.7. None of the sample ranges falls outside the control limits. Consequently, the process variability is in statistical control. If any of the sample ranges had fallen outside of the limits, or an unusual pattern had appeared (see

Figure 5.6), we would have had to search for the causes of the excessive variability, correct them, and repeat step 1.

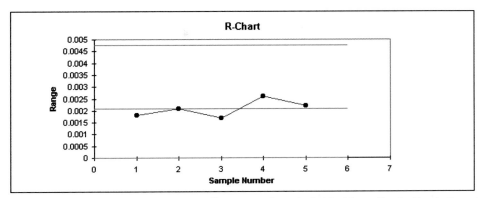

FIGURE 5.7 • Range Chart from the OM Explorer $\bar{x}$- and R-Chart Solver for the Metal Screw, Showing That the Process Variability Is in Control

Step 5. Compute the mean for each sample. For example, the mean for sample 1 is

$$\frac{0.5014 + 0.5022 + 0.5009 + 0.5027}{4} = 0.5018 \text{ in.}$$

Similarly, the means of samples 2, 3, 4, and 5 are 0.5027, 0.5026, 0.5020, and 0.5045 in., respectively. As shown in the table, $\bar{\bar{x}} = 0.5027$.

Step 6. Now construct the $\bar{x}$-chart for the process average. The average screw diameter is 0.5027 in. and the average range is 0.0021 in., so use $\bar{\bar{x}} = 0.5027$, $\bar{R} = 0.0021$, and A_2 from Table 5.1 for a sample size of 4 to construct the control limits:

$$\text{UCL}_{\bar{x}} = \bar{\bar{x}} + A_2\bar{R} = 0.5027 + 0.729(0.0021) = 0.5042 \text{ in.}$$
$$\text{LCL}_{\bar{x}} = \bar{\bar{x}} - A_2\bar{R} = 0.5027 - 0.729(0.0021) = 0.5012 \text{ in.}$$

Step 7. Plot the sample means on the control chart, as shown in Figure 5.8.

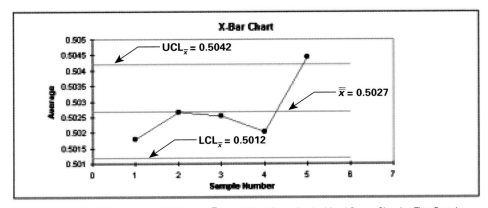

FIGURE 5.8 • The $\bar{x}$-Chart from the OM Explorer $\bar{x}$- and R-Chart Solver for the Metal Screw, Showing That Sample 5 Is Out of Control

The mean of sample 5 falls above the upper control limit, indicating that the process average is out of control and that assignable causes must be explored, perhaps using a cause-and-effect diagram.

Decision Point A new employee operated the lathe machine that makes the screw on the day the sample was taken. Management initiated a training session for the employee. Subsequent samples showed that the process was back in statistical control. ❐

If the standard deviation of the process distribution is known, another form of the $\bar{x}$-chart may be used:

$$\text{UCL}_{\bar{x}} = \bar{\bar{x}} + z\sigma_{\bar{x}} \qquad \text{and} \qquad \text{LCL}_{\bar{x}} = \bar{\bar{x}} - z\sigma_{\bar{x}}$$

where

$\sigma_{\bar{x}} = \sigma/\sqrt{n} =$ standard deviation of sample means

$\sigma =$ standard deviation of the process distribution

$n =$ sample size

$\bar{\bar{x}} =$ average of sample means or a target value set for the process

$z =$ normal deviate

The analyst can use an R-chart to be sure that the process variability is in control before constructing the $\bar{x}$-chart. The advantage of using this form of the $\bar{x}$-chart is that the analyst can adjust the spread of the control limits by changing the value of z. See Solved Problem 5 for a detailed example of this approach.

CONTROL CHARTS FOR ATTRIBUTES

Of the alternative attribute process charts available, which one can best be used in a given situation?

Two charts commonly used for quality measures based on product or service attributes are the *p*- and *c*-charts. The *p*-chart is used for controlling the proportion of defective products or services generated by the process. The *c*-chart is used for controlling the number of defects when more than one defect can be present in a product or service.

p-chart A chart used for controlling the proportion of defective products or services generated by the process.

p-CHARTS. The *p*-chart is a commonly used control chart for attributes. The quality characteristic is counted rather than measured, and the entire item or service can be declared good or defective. For example, in the banking industry, the attributes counted might be the number of nonendorsed deposits or the number of incorrect financial statements sent. The method involves selecting a random sample, inspecting each item in it, and calculating the sample proportion defective, *p*, which is the number of defective units divided by the sample size.

Sampling for a *p*-chart involves a yes–no decision: The item or service either is or is not defective. The underlying statistical distribution is based on the binomial distribution. However, for large sample sizes, the normal distribution provides a good approximation to it. The standard deviation of the distribution of proportion defective, σ_p, is

$$\sigma_p = \sqrt{\bar{p}(1 - \bar{p})/n}$$

where

$n =$ sample size

$\bar{p} =$ historical average population proportion defective or target value and central line on the chart

The central line on the *p*-chart may be the average of past sample proportion defective or a target that management has set for the process. We can use σ_p to arrive at the upper and lower control limits for a *p*-chart:

$$\mathrm{UCL}_p = \bar{p} + z\sigma_p \qquad \text{and} \qquad \mathrm{LCL}_p = \bar{p} - z\sigma_p$$

where

z = normal deviate (number of standard deviations from the average)

The chart is used in the following way. Periodically, a random sample of size n is taken, and the number of defective products or services is counted. The number of defectives is divided by the sample size to get a sample proportion defective, p, which is plotted on the chart. When a sample proportion defective falls outside the control limits, the analyst assumes that the proportion defective generated by the process has changed and searches for the assignable cause. Observations falling below the LCL_p indicate that the process may actually have improved. The analyst may find no assignable cause because there is always a small chance that an "out-of-control" proportion will have occurred randomly. However, if the analyst discovers assignable causes, those sample data should not be used to calculate the control limits for the chart. See Solved Problem 3 for a detailed solution to a problem requiring the use of the p-chart.

**TUTOR
5.4**

***c*-CHARTS.** Sometimes products have more than one defect per unit. For example, a roll of carpeting may have several defects, such as tufted or discolored fibers or stains from the production process. Other situations in which more than one defect may occur include defects in a television picture tube face panel, accidents at a particular intersection, and complaints at a hotel. When management is interested in reducing the number of defects per unit, another type of control chart, the ***c*-chart,** is useful.

***c*-chart** A chart used for controlling the number of defects when more than one defect can be present in a product or service.

The underlying sampling distribution for a c-chart is the Poisson distribution. It is based on the assumption that defects occur over a continuous region and that the probability of two or more defects at any one location is negligible. The mean of the distribution is $\bar{c}$ and the standard deviation is $\sqrt{\bar{c}}$. A useful tactic is to use the normal approximation to the Poisson so that the central line of the chart is $\bar{c}$ and the control limits are

$$\mathrm{UCL}_c = \bar{c} + z\sqrt{\bar{c}} \qquad \text{and} \qquad \mathrm{LCL}_c = \bar{c} - z\sqrt{\bar{c}}$$

**TUTOR
5.5**

See Solved Problem 4 for a detailed example of the use of a c-chart.

PROCESS CAPABILITY

What determines whether a process is capable of producing the products or services that customers demand?

process capability The ability of the process to meet the design specifications for a product or service.

Statistical process control techniques help managers achieve and maintain a process distribution that does not change in terms of its mean and variance. The control limits on the control charts signal when the mean or variability of the process changes. However, a process that is in statistical control may not be producing products or services according to their design specifications because the control limits are based on the mean and variability of the *sampling distribution*, not the design specifications. **Process capability** refers to the ability of the process to meet the design specifications for a product or service. Design specifications often are expressed as a **nominal value,** or target, and a **tolerance,** or allowance above or below the nominal value. For example, design specifications for the useful life of a lightbulb might have a nominal value of 1,000 hours and a tolerance of ± 200 hours. This tolerance gives an *upper specification* of 1,200 hours and a *lower specification* of 800 hours. The process producing the bulbs must be capable of doing so within these design specifications; otherwise, it will produce a certain proportion of defective bulbs. Management also is interested in

nominal value A target for design specifications.

tolerance An allowance above or below the nominal value.

detecting occurrences of lightbulb life exceeding 1,200 hours because something might be learned that can be built into the process in the future.

DEFINING PROCESS CAPABILITY

Figure 5.9 shows the relationship between a process distribution and the upper and lower specifications for the process producing lightbulbs under two conditions. In Figure 5.9(a), the process is capable because the extremes of the process distribution fall within the upper and lower specifications. In Figure 5.9(b) the process is not capable because it produces too many bulbs with short lives.

Figure 5.9 shows clearly why managers are so concerned with reducing process variability. The less variability—represented by lower standard deviations—the less frequently bad output is produced. Figure 5.10 shows what reducing variability means for a process distribution that is a normal probability distribution. The firm with two-sigma quality (the tolerance limits equal the process distribution mean ±2 standard deviations) produces 4.56 percent defective parts, or 45,600 defective parts per million. The firm with four-sigma quality produces only 0.0063 percent defectives, or 63 defective parts per million. Finally, the firm with six-sigma quality produces only 0.0000002 percent defectives, or 0.002 defective parts per million.

How can a manager determine quantitatively whether a process is capable? Two measures commonly are used in practice to assess the capability of a process: process capability ratio and process capability index.

PROCESS CAPABILITY RATIO. A process is *capable* if it has a process distribution whose extreme values fall within the upper and lower specifications for a product or service. As a general rule, most values of any process distribution fall within ±3 standard deviations of the mean. For example, if the process distribution is normal, 99.74 precent of the values fall within ±3 standard deviations. In other words, the range of values of the quality measure generated by a process is approximately 6 standard deviations of the process distribution. Hence, if a process is capable, the difference between the upper

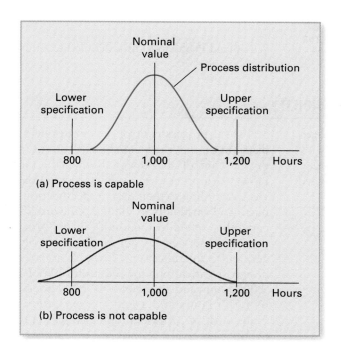

(a) Process is capable

(b) Process is not capable

FIGURE 5.10

Effects of Reducing Variability on Process Capability

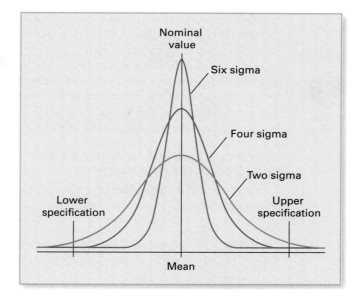

and lower specification, called the *tolerance width*, must be greater than 6 standard deviations. The **process capability ratio, C_p**, is defined as

$$C_p = \frac{\text{Upper specification} - \text{Lower specification}}{6\sigma}$$

where

$$\sigma = \text{standard deviation of the process distribution}$$

process capability ratio, C_p The tolerance width divided by 6 standard deviations (process variability).

A C_p value of 1.0 implies that the firm is producing three-sigma quality (0.26 percent defects) and that the process is consistently producing outputs within specifications even though some defects are generated. C_p values greater than 1.0 imply higher levels of quality achievement. Firms striving to achieve greater than three-sigma quality use a critical value for the ratio that is greater than 1.0. For example, a firm targeting six-sigma quality will use 2.0, a firm targeting five-sigma quality will use 1.67, and a firm striving for four-sigma quality will use 1.33. Processes producing products or services with less than three-sigma quality will have C_p values less than 1.0.

PROCESS CAPABILITY INDEX. The process is capable only when the capability ratio is greater than the critical value and the process distribution is centered on the nominal value of the design specifications. For example, the bulb-producing process may have a process capability ratio greater than 1.33. However, if the mean of the distribution of process output, $\bar{\bar{x}}$, is closer to the lower specification, defective bulbs may still be generated. Likewise, if $\bar{\bar{x}}$ is closer to the upper specification, very good bulbs may be generated. Thus, we need to compute a capability index that measures the potential for the process to generate outputs relative to either upper or lower specifications.

process capability index, C_{pk} An index that measures the potential for a process to generate defective outputs relative to either upper or lower specifications.

The **process capability index, C_{pk}**, is defined as

$$C_{pk} = \text{Minimum of} \left[\frac{\bar{\bar{x}} - \text{Lower specification}}{3\sigma}, \frac{\text{Upper specification} - \bar{\bar{x}}}{3\sigma} \right]$$

We take the minimum of the two ratios because it gives the *worst-case* situation. If C_{pk} is greater than the critical value (say, 1.33 for four-sigma quality) and the process capability ratio is also greater than the critical value, we can finally say the process is capable. If C_{pk} is less than 1.0, the process average is close to one of the tolerance limits and is generating defective output.

The capability index will always be less than or equal to the capability ratio. When C_{pk} equals C_p, the process is centered between the upper and lower specifications and, hence, the mean of the process distribution is centered on the nominal value of the design specifications. See Solved Problem 5 for a detailed example of the process capability ratio and the process capability index.

**TUTOR
5.6**

USING CONTINUOUS IMPROVEMENT TO DETERMINE THE CAPABILITY OF A PROCESS

To determine the capability of a process to produce within the tolerances, use the following steps.

Step 1. Collect data on the process output, and calculate the mean and the standard deviation of the process output distribution.

Step 2. Use the data from the process distribution to compute process control charts, such as an $\bar{x}$- or an R-chart.

Step 3. Take a series of random samples from the process and plot the results on the control charts. If at least 20 consecutive samples are within the control limits of the charts, the process is in statistical control. If the process is not in statistical control, look for assignable causes and eliminate them. Recalculate the mean and standard deviation of the process distribution and the control limits for the charts. Continue until the process is in statistical control.

Step 4. Calculate the process capability ratio and the process capability index. If the results are acceptable, document any changes made to the process and continue to monitor the output by using the control charts. If the results are unacceptable, further explore assignable causes for reducing the variance in the output or centering the process distribution on the nominal value. As changes are made, recalculate the mean and standard deviation of the process distribution and the control limits for the charts and repeat step 3.

QUALITY ENGINEERING

quality engineering An approach originated by Genichi Taguchi that involves combining engineering and statistical methods to reduce costs and improve quality by optimizing product design and manufacturing processes.

How can quality engineering help improve the quality of products and services?

quality loss function The rationale that a product or service that barely conforms to the specifications is more like a defective product or service than a perfect one.

Originated by Genichi Taguchi, **quality engineering** is an approach that involves combining engineering and statistical methods to reduce costs and improve quality by optimizing product design and manufacturing processes. Taguchi believes that unwelcome costs are associated with *any* deviation from a quality characteristic's target value. Taguchi's view is that there is a **quality loss function** of zero when the quality characteristic of the product or service is exactly on the target value and that the value rises exponentially as the quality characteristic gets closer to the tolerance limits. The rationale is that a product or service that barely conforms to the specifications is more like a defective product or service than a perfect one. Taguchi concluded that managers should continually search for ways to reduce *all* variability from the target value in the production process and not be content with merely adhering to specification limits.

INTERNATIONAL QUALITY DOCUMENTATION STANDARDS

Once a company has gone through the effort of making its processes capable, it must document its level of quality so as to better market its products or services. This is especially important in international trade. However, if each country had its own set of

From a quality perspective, how can an organization prepare to do business in foreign markets?

standards, companies selling in international markets would have difficulty complying with quality documentation standards in the countries where they did business. To overcome this problem, the International Organization for Standardization devised a set of standards called ISO 9000 for companies doing business in the European Union. Subsequently, a new set of documentation standards, ISO 14000, was devised for environmental management systems.

THE ISO 9000 DOCUMENTATION STANDARDS

ISO 9000 A set of standards governing documentation of a quality program.

ISO 9000 is a set of standards governing documentation of a quality program. Companies become certified by proving to a qualified external examiner that they have complied with all the requirements. Once certified, companies are listed in a directory so that potential customers can see which companies have been certified and to what level. Compliance with ISO 9000 standards says *nothing* about the actual quality of a product. Rather, it indicates to customers that companies can provide documentation to support whatever claims they make about quality.

ISO 9000 actually consists of five documents: ISO 9000–9004. ISO 9000 is an overview document, which provides guidelines for selection and use of the other standards. ISO 9001 is a standard that focuses on 20 aspects of a quality program for companies that design, produce, install, and service products. These aspects include management responsibility, quality system documentation, purchasing, product design, inspection, training, and corrective action. It is the most comprehensive and difficult standard to attain. ISO 9002 covers the same areas as ISO 9001 for companies that produce to the customer's designs or have their design and service activities at another location. ISO 9003 is the most limited in scope and addresses only the production process. ISO 9004 contains guidelines for interpreting the other standards.

ISO 14000—AN ENVIRONMENTAL MANAGEMENT SYSTEM

ISO 14000 Documentation standards that require participating companies to keep track of their raw materials use and their generation, treatment, and disposal of hazardous waste.

The ISO 14000 documentation standards require participating companies to keep track of their raw materials use and their generation, treatment, and disposal of hazardous wastes. Although not specifying what each company is allowed to emit, the standards require companies to prepare a plan for ongoing improvement in their environmental performance. ISO 14000 is a series of five standards that cover a number of areas, including the following:

- ❐ *Environmental Management System.* Requires a plan to improve performance in resource use and pollutant output.
- ❐ *Environmental Performance Evaluation.* Specifies guidelines for the certification of companies.
- ❐ *Environmental Labeling.* Defines terms such as *recyclable, energy efficient,* and *safe for the ozone layer.*
- ❐ *Life-Cycle Assessment.* Evaluates the lifetime environmental impact from the manufacture, use, and disposal of a product.

To maintain their certification, companies must be inspected by outside, private auditors on a regular basis.

BENEFITS OF ISO CERTIFICATION

Completing the certification process can take as long as 18 months and involve many hours of management and employee time. The cost of certification can exceed $1 million for large companies. Despite the expense and commitment involved in ISO certification, it bestows significant external and internal benefits. The external benefits come from the potential sales advantage that companies in compliance have. Companies looking for a supplier will more likely select a company that has demonstrated compliance with ISO documentation standards, all other factors being equal. Registered companies report an average of 48 percent increased profitability and 76 percent improvement in marketing. Consequently, more and more firms are seeking certification to gain a competitive advantage. Hundreds of thousands of manufacturing sites worldwide are ISO 9000 certified.

Internal benefits relate directly to the firm's TQM program. The British Standards Institute, a leading third-party auditor, estimates that most ISO 9000–registered companies experience a 10 percent reduction in the cost of producing a product because of the quality improvements they make while striving to meet the documentation requirements. Certification in ISO 9000 requires a company to analyze and document its procedures, which is necessary in any event for implementing continuous improvement, employee involvement, and similar programs. The internal benefits can be significant. The guidelines and requirements of the ISO documentation standards provide companies with a jump start in pursuing TQM programs.

MALCOLM BALDRIGE NATIONAL QUALITY AWARD

Malcolm Baldrige National Quality Award
An award named for the late secretary of commerce, who was a strong proponent of enhancing quality as a means of reducing the trade deficit; the award promotes, recognizes, and publicizes quality strategies and achievements.

Regardless of where a company does business, it is clear that all organizations have to produce high-quality products and services if they are to be competitive. To emphasize that point, in August 1987, Congress signed into law the Malcolm Baldrige National Quality Improvement Act, creating the **Malcolm Baldrige National Quality Award** (www.quality.nist.gov). Named for the late secretary of commerce, who was a strong proponent of enhancing quality as a means of reducing the trade deficit, the award promotes, recognizes, and publicizes quality strategies and achievements.

The application and four-stage review process for the Baldrige award is rigorous, but often the process helps companies define what quality means for them. The seven major criteria for the award are

1. *Leadership.*   Leadership system, values, expectations, and public responsibilities.
2. *Strategic Planning.*   The effectiveness of strategic and business planning and deployment of plans, focusing on performance requirements.
3. *Customer and Market Focus.*   How the company determines customer and market requirements and achieves customer satisfaction.
4. *Information Analysis.*   The effectiveness of information systems to support customer-driven performance excellence and marketplace success.
5. *Human Resource Focus.*   The success of efforts to realize the full potential of the workforce to create a high-performance organization.
6. *Process Management.*   The effectiveness of systems and processes for assuring the quality of products and services.
7. *Business Results.*   Performance results and competitive benchmarking in customer satisfaction, financials, human resources, suppliers, and operations.

Customer satisfaction underpins these seven criteria. Criterion 7, business results, is given the most weight in selecting winners.

TQM ACROSS THE ORGANIZATION

Total quality management is a philosophy that must permeate the entire organization if it is to be successful. The payoffs can be great; however, everyone must be involved. TQM has value for manufacturing as well as service companies. For example, Merrill Lynch Credit Corporation (MLCC), a winner of the Malcolm Baldrige National Quality Award, found out that focusing on quality management and performance excellence throughout the organization has significant rewards. MLCC, which originates over $4 billion in loans a year and manages a portfolio of nearly $10 billion, has 8 core and 10 support processes, involving 830 employees, that need to be coordinated. Communication from top to bottom in the organization is critical. Each year senior managers translate the company's strategic imperatives into a few critical objectives, which are accompanied by specific targets and measures. These objectives become the basis for determining employee performance plans, which in turn facilitate the communication loop between top management and the employees. Employees are empowered to take initiative and responsibility, especially in being flexible in responding rapidly to customer needs and in individual development. Employees receive an average of 74 hours of training a year, emphasizing the need to keep abreast of changes in technology to better serve customers.

A key element of MLCC's quality initiative is the "voice of the client" process, which identifies customer satisfaction drivers for each market segment and credit category. These priority customer requirements provide the basis for key performance measures for the eight core processes. In addition, data snooping is used to analyze customer satisfaction data to detect trends. Negative trends and recurring problems trigger process improvement teams to develop countermeasures and to prevent recurrences. Clients receive feedback on the resolution of the problem within five working days. MLCC's complete organizational commitment is exemplary of the pervasiveness of TQM, and it has paid off. In the two years after the initiation of the TQM philosophy, net income rose 100 percent, return on equity increased 74 percent, and return on assets improved 36 percent.

CD-ROM RESOURCES

The Student CD-ROM that accompanies this text contains the following resources, which allow you to further practice and apply the concepts presented in this chapter.

- ❏ **OM Explorer Tutors:** OM Explorer contains eight tutor programs to enhance your understanding of reliability, Pareto charts, $\bar{x}$- and R-charts, p-charts, c-charts, process capability, constructing and operating characteristic (OC) curves, and calculating the average outgoing quality level (AOQL). See the Chapter 5 folder in OM Explorer. See also the exercises requiring the use of these tutor programs.

- ❏ **OM Explorer Solvers:** OM Explorer contains seven programs designed to solve general problems involving reliability, TQM charts, $\bar{x}$- and R-charts, p-charts, c-charts, process capability, and single-sampling plans. See the Quality and Acceptance Sampling folders in OM Explorer.

- ❏ **Equation Summary:** All the equations for this chapter can be found in one convenient location.

- ❏ **Discussion Questions:** Five questions will challenge your understanding of the importance of quality for competitive operations.

continued

continued

❐ **Cases:**

❐ **Cranston Nissan.** Analyze the many instances of service quality breakdown that one of the authors of this text experienced.

❐ **Jose's Authentic Mexican Restaurant.** How can quality be improved at this restaurant?

❐ **Tours:** See how the management of Lower Florida Keys Health System designs its processes to achieve high-performance design quality as a competitive priority and how Chaparral Steel builds quality into its products at each step of manufacturing.

❐ **Experiential Exercise:** Statistical Process Control with a Coin Catapult. Experience the gathering of data and the development of control charts for variable or attribute measures in this entertaining in-class exercise.

❐ **Supplement F:** Acceptance Sampling Plans. Use this supplement to learn how to design single-sampling plans and estimate the average outgoing quality of your plan.

INTERACTIVE RESOURCES

The Interactive Web site associated with this text (www.prenhall.com/ritzman) contains many tools and activities specifically designed for this chapter. The following items are recommended to enhance your understanding of the material in this chapter.

❐ **Internet Activities:** Try out 13 different links to explore quality topics including global and industry quality awards, international documentation standards, definitions of quality in services and manufacturing, product safety, the role of the Internet in quality, using quality as a competitive weapon, and using SPC in practice.

❐ **Internet Tours:** Compare the processes used to achieve high quality at Steinway Pianos and Verne Q. Powell Flutes, and discover the quality measures used at Stickley Furniture.

EQUATION SUMMARY

1. The reliability of a product: $r_s = (r_1)(r_2) \cdots (r_n)$

2. Mean: $\bar{x} = \dfrac{\sum\limits_{i=1}^{n} x_i}{n}$

3. Standard deviation of a sample: $\sigma = \sqrt{\dfrac{\sum(x_i - \bar{x})^2}{n-1}}$ or $\sigma = \sqrt{\dfrac{\sum x^2 - \dfrac{(\sum x_i)^2}{n}}{n-1}}$

4. Control limits for variable process control charts

   a. *R*-chart, range of sample:

   Upper control limit = $\text{UCL}_R = D_4 \bar{R}$

   Lower control limit = $\text{LCL}_R = D_3 \bar{R}$

b. $\bar{x}$-chart, sample mean:

Upper control limit $= \text{UCL}_{\bar{x}} = \bar{\bar{x}} + A_2\bar{R}$

Lower control limit $= \text{LCL}_{\bar{x}} = \bar{\bar{x}} - A_2\bar{R}$

c. When the standard deviation of the process distribution, σ, is known:

Upper control limit $= \text{UCL}_x = \bar{\bar{x}} + z\sigma_x$

Lower control limit $= \text{LCL}_x = \bar{\bar{x}} - z\sigma_x$

where

$$\sigma_{\bar{x}} = \frac{\sigma}{\sqrt{n}}$$

5. Control limits for attribute process control charts

a. *p*-chart, proportion defective:

Upper control limit $= \text{UCL}_p = \bar{p} + z\sigma_p$

Lower control limit $= \text{LCL}_p = \bar{p} - z\sigma_p$

where

$$\sigma_p = \sqrt{\bar{p}(1 - \bar{p})/n}$$

b. *c*-chart, number of defects:

Upper control limit $= \text{UCL}_c = \bar{c} + z\sqrt{\bar{c}}$

Lower control limit $= \text{LCL}_c = \bar{c} - z\sqrt{\bar{c}}$

6. Process capability ratio: $C_p = \dfrac{\text{Upper specification} - \text{Lower specification}}{6\sigma}$

7. Process capability index:

$$C_{pk} = \text{Minimum of} \left[\frac{\bar{\bar{x}} - \text{Lower specification}}{3\sigma}, \frac{\text{Upper specification} - \bar{\bar{x}}}{3\sigma} \right]$$

CHAPTER HIGHLIGHTS

❏ Total quality management stresses three principles: a customer-driven focus, employee involvement, and continuous improvements in quality.

❏ The consumer's view of quality may be defined in a variety of ways. The customer may make a quantitative judgment about whether a product or service meets specified design characteristics. In other situations, qualitative judgments about value, fitness for the customer's intended use, product or service support, and aesthetics may take on greater importance. One TQM responsibility of marketing is to listen to customers and report their changing perceptions of quality.

❏ Quality can be used as a competitive weapon. High-performance design and consistent quality are competitive priorities associated with quality. World-class competition requires businesses to produce quality products or services efficiently.

❏ Responsibility for quality is shared by all employees in the organization. Employee involvement programs include leadership in changing organizational culture, individual development, awards and incentives, and teamwork.

❏ Continuous improvement involves identifying benchmarks of excellent practice and instilling a sense of ownership in employees so that they will continually identify product, services, and process improvements that should be made.

❏ Quality management is important because of its impact on market share, price, and profits and because of the costs of poor quality. The four main categories of costs associated with quality management are prevention, appraisal, internal failure, and external failure. If quality is to be improved, prevention costs must increase. Appraisal, internal failure, and external failure costs all decline as quality is improved through preventive measures.

❑ Benchmarking is a comparative measure. It is used to establish goals for continuous improvement. Forms of benchmarking include competitive, functional, and internal.

❑ Concurrent engineering improves the match between product design and production process capabilities. The higher quality and shorter product-development times associated with concurrent engineering are competitive advantages.

❑ Quality improvement requires close cooperation among functions (design, operations, marketing, purchasing, and others). Quality function deployment (QFD) encourages interfunctional planning and communication.

❑ Keys to controlling supplier quality are the buyer's approach and specification management. The buyer must consider quality, delivery, and cost. Specifications must be clear and realistic. Improved communication between purchasing and other departments is needed.

❑ Approaches to organizing and presenting quality improvement data include checklists, histograms and bar charts, Pareto charts, scatter diagrams, cause-and-effect diagrams, graphs, and control charts.

❑ A key to meeting design specifications in a product or service is to reduce output variability. When a process is in a state of statistical control, outputs subject to common causes of variation follow a stable probability distribution. When assignable causes of variation are present, the process is out of statistical control. Statistical process control (SPC) methods are used to detect the presence of assignable causes of variation.

❑ Statistical process control charts are useful for measuring the current quality generated by the process and for detecting whether the process has changed to the detriment of quality. Thus, R-charts are used to monitor process variability, $\bar{x}$- and p-charts identify abnormal variations in the process average, and c-charts are used for controlling the number of defects when a product or service process could result in multiple defects per unit of output. The presence of abnormal variation triggers a search for assignable causes.

❑ Process variability should be in control before process average control charts are constructed. The reason is that the average range is used in the calculation of control limits for process average control charts. Crucial decisions in the design of control charts are sample size and control limits.

❑ The central line of a control chart can be the average of past averages of the quality measurement or a management target related to product or service specifications. The spread in control limits affects the chances of detecting a shift in the process average or range, as well as the chances of searching for assignable causes when none exist.

❑ A process can be in statistical control but still not be capable of producing all of its output within design specifications. The process capability ratio and the process capability index are quantitative measures used to assess the capability of a process.

❑ The Malcolm Baldrige National Quality Award promotes, recognizes, and publicizes the quality strategies and achievements of outstanding American manufacturers, service providers, and small businesses.

❑ ISO 9000 is a set of standards governing the documentation of quality programs. ISO 14000 standards require participating companies to keep track of their raw materials use and their generation, treatment, and disposal of hazardous wastes.

SOLVED PROBLEM 1

Vera Johnson and Merris Williams manufacture vanishing cream. The following are the operations and reliabilities of their packaging operation. The reliabilities are the probabilities that each operation will be performed to the desired specifications.

OPERATION	RELIABILITY
Mix	0.99
Fill	0.98
Cap	0.99
Label	0.97

Johnson and Williams ask their spouses to keep track of and analyze reported defects. They find the following.

DEFECT	FREQUENCY
Lumps of unmixed product	7
Over- or underfilled jars	18
Jar lids did not seal	6
Labels rumpled or missing	29
Total	60

a. What is the reliability of the packaging operation?

b. Draw a Pareto chart to identify the vital defects.

SOLUTION

a. The formula is

$$r_s = (r_1)(r_2) \cdots (r_n)$$

Substituting $r_1 = 0.99$, $r_2 = 0.98$, ..., gives

$$r_s = (0.99)(0.98)(0.99)(0.97)$$
$$= 0.9317, \text{ or about 93\% reliability}$$

b. Defective labels account for 48.33% of the total number of defects:

$$\frac{29}{60} \times 100\% = 48.33\%$$

Improperly filled jars account for 30% of the total number of defects:

$$\frac{18}{60} \times 100\% = 30.00\%$$

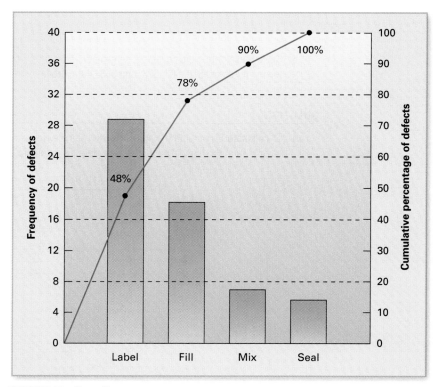

FIGURE 5.11 • Pareto Chart

The cumulative percentage for the two most frequent defects is

$$48.33\% + 30.00\% = 78.33\%$$

Lumps represent $\dfrac{7}{60} \times 100\% = 11.67\%$ of defects; the cumulative percentage is

$$78.33\% + 11.67\% = 90.00\%$$

Defective seals represent $\dfrac{6}{60} \times 100\% = 10\%$ of defects; the cumulative percentage is

$$10\% + 90\% = 100.00\%$$

The Pareto chart is shown in Figure 5.11.

SOLVED PROBLEM 2

The Watson Electric Company produces incandescent lightbulbs. The following data on the number of lumens for 40-watt lightbulbs were collected when the process was in control.

	OBSERVATION			
SAMPLE	1	2	3	4
1	604	612	588	600
2	597	601	607	603
3	581	570	585	592
4	620	605	595	588
5	590	614	608	604

a. Calculate control limits for an *R*-chart and an $\bar{x}$-chart.

b. Since these data were collected, some new employees were hired. A new sample obtained the following readings: 570, 603, 623, and 583. Is the process still in control?

SOLUTION

a. To calculate $\bar{x}$, compute the mean for each sample. To calculate *R*, subtract the lowest value in the sample from the highest value in the sample. For example, for sample 1,

$$\bar{x} = \frac{604 + 612 + 588 + 600}{4} = 601$$

$$R = 612 - 588 = 24$$

SAMPLE	$\bar{x}$	R
1	601	24
2	602	10
3	582	22
4	602	32
5	604	24
Total	2,991	112
Average	$\bar{\bar{x}} = 598.2$	$\bar{R} = 22.4$

The R-chart control limits are

$$UCL_R = D_4\bar{R} = 2.282(22.4) = 51.12$$
$$LCL_R = D_3\bar{R} = 0(22.4) = 0$$

The $\bar{x}$-chart control limits are

$$UCL_x = \bar{\bar{x}} + A_2\bar{R} = 598.2 + 0.729(22.4) = 614.53$$
$$LCL_x = \bar{\bar{x}} - A_2\bar{R} = 598.2 - 0.729(22.4) = 581.87$$

b. First check to see whether the variability is still in control based on the new data. The range is 53 (or 623−570), which is outside the upper control limit for the R-chart. Even though the sample mean, 594.75, is within the control limits for the process average, process variability is not in control. A search for assignable causes must be conducted.

SOLVED PROBLEM 3

The data processing department of the Arizona Bank has five data entry clerks. Each day their supervisor verifies the accuracy of a random sample of 250 records. A record containing one or more errors is considered defective and must be redone. The results of the last 30 samples are shown in the table. All were checked to make sure that none were out of control.

SAMPLE	NUMBER OF DEFECTIVE RECORDS	SAMPLE	NUMBER OF DEFECTIVE RECORDS	SAMPLE	NUMBER OF DEFECTIVE RECORDS
1	7	11	18	21	17
2	5	12	5	22	12
3	19	13	16	23	6
4	10	14	4	24	7
5	11	15	11	25	13
6	8	16	8	26	10
7	12	17	12	27	14
8	9	18	4	28	6
9	6	19	6	29	11
10	13	20	11	30	9
				Total	300

a. Based on these historical data, set up a p-chart using $z = 3$.
b. Samples for the next four days showed the following:

SAMPLE	NUMBER OF DEFECTIVE RECORDS
31	17
32	15
33	22
34	21

What is the supervisor's assessment of the data-entry process likely to be?

SOLUTION

a. From the table, the supervisor knows that the total number of defective records is 300 out of a total sample of 7,500 [or 30(250)]. Therefore, the central line of the chart is

$$\bar{p} = \frac{300}{7,500} = 0.04$$

The control limits are

$$UCL_p = \bar{p} + z\sqrt{\frac{\bar{p}(1-\bar{p})}{n}} = 0.04 + 3\sqrt{\frac{0.04(0.96)}{250}} = 0.077$$

$$LCL_p = \bar{p} - z\sqrt{\frac{\bar{p}(1-\bar{p})}{n}} = 0.04 - 3\sqrt{\frac{0.04(0.96)}{250}} = 0.003$$

b. Samples for the next four days showed the following:

SAMPLE	NUMBER OF DEFECTIVE RECORDS	PROPORTION
31	17	0.068
32	15	0.060
33	22	0.088
34	21	0.084

Samples 33 and 34 are out of control. The supervisor should look for the problem and, upon identifying it, take corrective action.

SOLVED PROBLEM 4

The Minnow County Highway Safety Department monitors accidents at the intersection of Routes 123 and 14. Accidents at the intersection have averaged three per month.

a. Which type of control chart should be used? Construct a control chart with three-sigma control limits.

b. Last month seven accidents occurred at the intersection. Is this sufficient evidence to justify a claim that something has changed at the intersection?

SOLUTION

a. The safety department cannot determine the number of accidents that did *not* occur, so it has no way to compute a proportion defective at the intersection. Therefore, the administrators must use a *c*-chart for which

$$UCL_c = \bar{c} + z\sqrt{\bar{c}} = 3 + 3\sqrt{3} = 8.20$$
$$LCL_c = \bar{c} - z\sqrt{\bar{c}} = 3 - 3\sqrt{3} = -2.196$$

There cannot be a negative number of accidents, so the lower control limit in this case is adjusted to zero.

b. The number of accidents last month falls within the upper and lower control limits of the chart. We conclude that no assignable causes are present and that the increase in accidents was due to chance.

SOLVED PROBLEM 5

Pioneer Chicken advertises "lite" chicken with 30 percent fewer calories. (The pieces are 33 percent smaller.) The process average distribution for "lite" chicken breasts is 420 calories, with a standard deviation of the population of 25 calories. Pioneer randomly takes samples of six chicken breasts to measure calorie content.

a. Design an $\bar{x}$-chart, using the process standard deviation.

b. The product design calls for the average chicken breast to contain 400 ± 100 calories. Calculate the process capability ratio (target = 1.33) and the process capability index. Interpret the results.

SOLUTION

a. For the process standard deviation of 25 calories, the standard deviation of the sample mean is

$$\sigma_{\bar{x}} = \frac{\sigma}{\sqrt{n}} = \frac{25}{\sqrt{6}} = 10.2 \text{ calories}$$

$$\text{UCL}_{\bar{x}} = \bar{\bar{x}} + z\sigma_{\bar{x}} = 420 + 3(10.2) = 450.6 \text{ calories}$$

$$\text{LCL}_{\bar{x}} = \bar{\bar{x}} - z\sigma_{\bar{x}} = 420 - 3(10.2) = 389.4 \text{ calories}$$

b. The process capability ratio is

$$C_p = \frac{\text{Upper specification} - \text{Lower specification}}{6\sigma} = \frac{500 \text{ calories} - 300 \text{ calories}}{6(25)} = 1.333$$

The process capability index is

$$C_{pk} = \text{Minimum of} \left[\frac{\bar{\bar{x}} - \text{Lower specification}}{3\sigma}, \frac{\text{Upper specification} - \bar{\bar{x}}}{3\sigma} \right]$$

$$= \text{Minimum of} \left[\frac{420 - 300}{3(25)} = 1.60, \frac{500 - 420}{3(25)} = 1.07 \right] = 1.07$$

Because the process capability ratio is greater than 1.33, the process should be able to produce the product reliably with four-sigma quality. However, the process capability index is 1.07, so the current process is not centered properly for four-sigma quality. The mean of the process distribution is too close to the upper specification.

PROBLEMS

An icon next to a problem identifies the software that can be helpful but is not mandatory.

1. **OM Explorer** Contented Airlines (CA) is reluctant to begin service at the new Delayed Indefinitely Airport (DIA) until the automated baggage-handling system can transport luggage to the correct location with at least 99 percent reliability for any given flight. Lower reliability will result in damage to CA's reputation for quality service. The baggage system will not deliver to the right location if any of its subsystems fail. The subsystems and their reliability for satis-

factory performance during operation for any given flight are shown in the following table.

SUBSYSTEM	RELIABILITY
Power supply	70.0% surge free
Scanner reading	99.8% accurate
Computer software	98.2% glitch free
Mechanical systems	97.5% jam free
Operators	96.0% error free

a. What is the reliability of the luggage system for any given flight?

b. When the passenger shuttle system operates, power surges trip the motors on the baggage system. Each of the luggage system motors must then be manually reset. Installing surge protectors increases power supply reliability to 99.9 percent. What is the reliability of the luggage system?

c. What could be done to improve the reliability of the luggage system?

2. 💿 **OM Explorer** Smith, Schroeder, and Torn (SST) is a short-haul household furniture moving company. SST's labor force, selected from the local community college football team, is temporary and part-time. SST is concerned with recent complaints, as tabulated on the following tally sheet.

COMPLAINT	TALLY
Broken glass	///// ///// ///
Delivered to wrong address	///// ////
Furniture rubbed together while on truck	///// ///// ///// /////
Late delivery	/////
Late arrival for pickup	///// ///// ///// ///
Missing items	///// ///// ///// ///// ///// /
Nicks and scratches from rough handling	///// /////
Soiled upholstery	///// ///

a. Draw a bar chart and a Pareto chart to identify the most serious moving problems.

b. Use a cause-and-effect diagram to identify potential causes of complaints.

3. Oregon Fiber Board makes roof liners for the automotive industry. The manufacturing manager is concerned about product quality. She suspects that one particular defect, tears in the fabric, is related to production-run size. An assistant gathers the following data from production records.

RUN	SIZE	DEFECTS (%)	RUN	SIZE	DEFECTS (%)
1	1,000	3.5	11	6,500	1.5
2	4,100	3.8	12	1,000	5.5
3	2,000	5.5	13	7,000	1.0
4	6,000	1.9	14	3,000	4.5
5	6,800	2.0	15	2,200	4.2
6	3,000	3.2	16	1,800	6.0
7	2,000	3.8	17	5,400	2.0
8	1,200	4.2	18	5,800	2.0
9	5,000	3.8	19	1,000	6.2
10	3,800	3.0	20	1,500	7.0

a. Draw a scatter diagram for these data.

b. Does there appear to be a relationship between run size and percent defects? What implications does this have for Oregon Fiber Board's business?

4. 💿 **SmartDraw** The operations manager for Superfast Airlines at Port Columbus International Airport noticed an increase in the number of delayed flight departures. She brainstormed possible causes with her staff:

- Aircraft late to gate
- Acceptance of late passengers
- Passengers arrive late at gate
- Passenger processing delays at gate
- Late baggage to aircraft
- Other late personnel or unavailable items
- Mechanical failures

Draw a cause-and-effect diagram to organize the possible causes of delayed flight departures into the following major categories: equipment, personnel, material, procedures, and "other factors" beyond managerial control. Provide a detailed set of causes for each major cause identified by the operations manager and incorporate them in your cause-and-effect diagram.

5. 💿 **OM Explorer** At Conner Company, a custom manufacturer of printed circuit boards, the finished boards are subjected to a final inspection prior to shipment to its customers. As Conner's quality assurance manager, you are responsible for making a presentation to management on quality problems at the beginning of each month. Your assistant has analyzed the reject memos for all the circuit boards that were rejected during the past month. He has given you a summary statement listing the reference number of the circuit board and the reason for rejection from one of the following categories:

A = Poor electrolyte coverage

B = Improper lamination

C = Low copper plating

D = Plating separation

E = Improper etching

For 50 circuit boards that had been rejected last month, the summary statement showed the following:

C B C C D E C C B A D A C C C B C A C D C A C C B
A C A C B C C A C A A C C D A C C C E C C A B A C

a. Prepare a tally sheet (or checklist) of the different reasons for rejection.

b. Develop a Pareto chart to identify the more significant types of rejection.

c. Examine the causes of the most significant type of defect, using a cause-and-effect diagram.

6. **OM Explorer** The Marlin Company produces plastic bottles to customer order. The quality inspector randomly selects four bottles from the bottle machine and measures the outside diameter of the bottle neck, a critical quality dimension that determines whether the bottle cap will fit properly. The dimensions (in.) from the last six samples are

	BOTTLE			
SAMPLE	1	2	3	4
1	0.604	0.612	0.588	0.600
2	0.597	0.601	0.607	0.603
3	0.581	0.570	0.585	0.592
4	0.620	0.605	0.595	0.588
5	0.590	0.614	0.608	0.604
6	0.585	0.583	0.617	0.579

a. Assume that only these six samples are sufficient and use the data to determine control limits for an R- and an $\bar{x}$-chart.

b. Suppose that the specification for the bottle neck diameter is 0.600 ± 0.050 in. If the population standard deviation is 0.012 in, and if management has targeted three-sigma quality, is the process capable of producing the bottle?

7. **OM Explorer** A textile manufacturer wants to set up a control chart for irregularities (e.g., oil stains, shop soil, loose threads, and tears) per 100 square yards of carpet. The following data were collected from a sample of twenty 100-square-yard pieces of carpet.

Sample	1	2	3	4	5	6	7	8	9	10
Irregularities	11	8	9	12	4	16	5	8	17	10
Sample	11	12	13	14	15	16	17	18	19	20
Irregularities	11	5	7	12	13	8	19	11	9	10

a. Using these data, set up a c-chart with $z = 3$.

b. Suppose that the next five samples had 15, 18, 12, 22, and 21 irregularities. What do you conclude?

8. **OM Explorer** The production manager at Sunny Soda, Inc., is interested in tracking the quality of the company's 12-ounce bottle filling line. The bottles must be filled within the tolerances set for this product because the dietary information on the label shows 12 ounces as the serving size. The design standard for the product calls for a fill level of 12.00 ± 0.10 ounces. The manager collected the following sample data (in fluid ounces per bottle) on the production process:

	OBSERVATION			
SAMPLE	1	2	3	4
1	12.00	11.97	12.10	12.08
2	11.91	11.94	12.10	11.96
3	11.89	12.02	11.97	11.99
4	12.10	12.09	12.05	11.95
5	12.08	11.92	12.12	12.05
6	11.94	11.98	12.06	12.08
7	12.09	12.00	12.00	12.03
8	12.01	12.04	11.99	11.95
9	12.00	11.96	11.97	12.03
10	11.92	11.94	12.09	12.00
11	11.91	11.99	12.05	12.10
12	12.01	12.00	12.06	11.97
13	11.98	11.99	12.06	12.03
14	12.02	12.00	12.05	11.95
15	12.00	12.05	12.01	11.97

a. Are the process average and range in statistical control?

b. If management wants three-sigma quality, is the process capable of meeting the design standard? Explain.

9. **OM Explorer** Management at Webster chemical company is concerned as to whether caulking tubes are being properly capped. If a significant proportion of the tubes are not being sealed, Webster is placing its customers in a messy situation. Tubes are packaged in large boxes of 144. Several boxes are inspected, and the following numbers of leaking tubes are found:

SAMPLE	TUBES	SAMPLE	TUBES	SAMPLE	TUBES
1	3	8	6	15	5
2	5	9	4	16	0
3	3	10	9	17	2
4	4	11	2	18	6
5	2	12	6	19	2
6	4	13	5	20	1
7	2	14	1	Total	72

Calculate p-chart three-sigma control limits to assess whether the capping process is in statistical control.

10. **OM Explorer** The Precision Machining Company makes handheld tools on an assembly line that produces one product every minute. On one of the products, the critical quality dimension is the diameter (measured in thousandths of an inch) of a hole bored in one of the assemblies. Management wants to detect any shift in the process average diameter from 0.015 in. Management considers the variance in the process to be in control. Historically, the average range has been 0.002 in., regardless of the process

TABLE 5.2   *Sample Data for Precision Machining Company*

MINUTES	DIAMETER										
1–12	15	16	18	14	16	17	15	14	14	13	16	17
13–24	15	16	17	16	14	14	13	14	15	16	15	17
25–36	14	13	15	17	18	15	16	15	14	15	16	17
37–48	18	16	15	16	16	14	17	18	19	15	16	15
49–60	12	17	16	14	15	17	14	16	15	17	18	14
61–72	15	16	17	18	13	15	14	14	16	15	17	18
73–80	16	16	17	18	16	15	14	17				

average. Design an $\bar{x}$-chart to control this process, with a center line at 0.015 in. and the control limits set at three sigmas from the center line.

Management has provided the results of 80 minutes of output from the production line, as shown in Table 5.2. During this 80 minutes, the process average changed once. All measurements are in thousandths of an inch.

a. Set up an $\bar{x}$-chart with $n = 4$. The frequency should be sample four, then skip four. Thus, your first sample would be for minutes 1–4, the second would be for minutes 9–12, and so on. When would you stop the process to check for a change in the process average?

b. Set up an $\bar{x}$-chart with $n = 8$. The frequency should be sample eight, then skip four. When would you stop the process now? What can you say about the desirability of large samples on a frequent sampling interval?

11. ● **OM Explorer** The plant manager at Northern Pines Brewery decided to gather data on the number of defective bottles generated on the line. Every day a random sample of 250 bottles was inspected for fill level, cracked bottles, bad labels, and poor seals. Any bottle failing to meet the stan-

dard for any of these criteria was counted as a reject. The study lasted 30 days and yielded the data in Table 5.3. Based on the data, what can you tell the manager about the quality of the bottling line? Do you see any nonrandom behavior in the bottling process? If so, what might cause this behavior?

12. ● **OM Explorer** Red Baron Airlines serves hundreds of cities each day, but competition is increasing from smaller companies affiliated with major carriers. One of the key competitive priorities is on-time arrivals and departures. Red Baron defines *on time* as any arrival or departure that takes place within 15 minutes of the scheduled time. To stay on top of the market, management has set the high standard of 98 percent on-time performance. The operations department was put in charge of monitoring the performance of the airline. Each week, a random sample of 300 flight arrivals and departures was checked for schedule performance. Table 5.4 contains the numbers of arrivals and departures over the last 30 weeks that did not meet Red Baron's definition of on-time service. What can you tell management about the quality of service? Can you identify any nonrandom behavior in the process? If so, what might cause the behavior?

TABLE 5.3   *Sample Data for Northern Pines Brewery*

SAMPLES	NUMBER OF REJECTED BOTTLES IN SAMPLE OF 250									
1–10	4	9	6	12	8	2	13	10	1	9
11–20	4	6	8	10	12	4	3	10	14	5
21–30	13	11	7	3	2	8	11	6	9	5

TABLE 5.4   *Sample Data for Red Baron Airlines*

SAMPLES	NUMBER OF LATE PLANES IN SAMPLE OF 300 ARRIVALS AND DEPARTURES									
1–10	3	8	5	11	7	2	12	9	1	8
11–20	3	5	7	9	12	5	4	9	13	4
21–30	12	10	6	2	1	8	4	5	8	2

SELECTED REFERENCES

Barnard, William, and Thomas F. Wallace. *The Innovation Edge*. Essex Junction, VT: Oliver Wight Publications, Inc., 1994.

Besterfield, Dale. *Quality Control*, 6th ed. Upper Saddle River, NJ: Prentice-Hall, 2001.

Brown, Ed. "The Best Business Hotels." *Fortune* (March 17, 1997), pp. 204–205.

Collier, David A., *The Service Quality Solution*. New York: Irwin Professional Publishing; Milwaukee: ASQC Quality Press, 1994.

Crosby, Philip B. *Quality Is Free: The Art of Making Quality Certain*. New York: McGraw-Hill, 1979.

Deming, W. Edwards. *Out of the Crisis*. Cambridge, MA: Massachusetts Institute of Technology Center for Advanced Engineering Study, 1986.

Denton, D. Keith. "Lessons on Competitiveness: Motorola's Approach." *Production and Inventory Management Journal* (Third Quarter 1991), pp. 22–25.

Duncan, Acheson J. *Quality Control and Industrial Statistics*, 5th ed. Homewood, IL.: Irwin, 1986.

Feigenbaum, A. V. *Total Quality Control: Engineering and Management*, 3d ed. New York: McGraw-Hill, 1983.

Hauser, John R., and Don Clausing. "The House of Quality." *Harvard Business Review* (May–June 1988), pp. 63–73.

Juran, J. M., and Frank Gryna, Jr. *Quality Planning and Analysis*, 2d ed. New York: McGraw-Hill, 1980.

Kalinosky, Ian S., "The Total Quality System—Going Beyond ISO 9000." *Quality Progress* (June 1990), pp. 50–53.

Katzenbach, Jon R., and Douglas K. Smith. "The Discipline of Teams." *Harvard Business Review* (March–April 1993), pp. 111–120.

Miller, Bill. "ISO 9000 and the Small Company: Can I Afford It?" *APICS—The Performance Advantage* (September 1994), pp. 45–46.

Mitra, Amitava. *Fundamentals of Quality Control and Improvement*, 2nd ed. Upper Saddle River, NJ: Prentice-Hall, 1998.

Nakhai, Benham, and Joao S. Neves. "The Deming, Baldrige, and European Quality Awards." *Quality Progress* (April 1994), pp. 33–37.

Neves, Joao S., and Benham Nakhai. "The Evolution of the Baldrige Award." *Quality Progress* (June 1994), pp. 65–70.

Prahalad, C. K., and M. S. Krishnan. "The New Meaning of Quality in the Information Age." *Harvard Business Review* (September–October 1999), pp. 109–118.

Rabbitt, John T., and Peter A. Bergh. *The ISO 9000 Book*. White Plains, NY: Quality Resources, 1993.

Roth, Daniel. "Motorola Lives!" *Fortune* (September 27, 1999), pp. 305–306.

Rust, Roland T., Timothy Keiningham, Stephen Clemens, and Anthony Zahorik. "Return on Quality at Chase Manhattan Bank," *Interfaces*, vol. 29, no. 2 (March–April 1999), pp. 62–72.

Sanders, Lisa. "Going Green with Less Red Tape." *Business Week* (September 23, 1996), pp. 75–76.

Sullivan, Lawrence P. "The Power of Taguchi Methods." *Quality Progress*, vol. 20, no. 6 (1987), pp. 76–79.

"Want EC Business? You Have Two Choices." *Business Week* (October 19, 1992), pp. 58–59.

"Why Online Browsers Don't Become Buyers." *Computerworld* (November 29, 1999), p. 14.

Capacity

Across the Organization

Capacity is important to . . .

- ☐ **accounting,** which prepares the cost accounting information needed to evaluate capacity expansion decisions.
- ☐ **finance,** which performs the financial analysis of proposed capacity expansion investments and raises funds to support them.
- ☐ **human resources,** which must hire and train employees to support capacity plans.
- ☐ **management information systems,** which designs databases used in determining work standards that help in calculating capacity gaps.
- ☐ **marketing,** which provides demand forecasts needed to identify capacity gaps.
- ☐ **operations,** which must select capacity strategies that provide the capacity levels to meet future demand most effectively.
- ☐ **purchasing,** which obtains outside capacity that is outsourced.

Learning Goals

After reading this chapter, you will be able to . . .

1. describe different ways to measure capacity, establish maximum capacity, and calculate capacity utilization.
2. discuss long- and short-term strategies to ease bottlenecks and the concept of the theory-of-constraints approach.
3. explain the reasons for economies and diseconomies of scale.
4. discuss strategic issues such as capacity cushions, timing and sizing options, and linkages with other decisions.
5. calculate capacity gaps and then evaluate plans for filling them.
6. describe how waiting-line models, simulation, and decision trees can assist capacity decisions.

In 1995, the Chemical Banking Corporation and the venerable Chase Manhattan Corporation, the bank of the Rockefellers, merged. With combined assets of $297 billion, the new Chase (www.chase.com) dwarfed even Citicorp, the largest U.S. bank until this merger. Combining two operations that competed directly in two markets, the new Chase Bank had more than $163 billion in overall deposits and some 4 million consumer accounts. One primary motivation for increasing its capacity was cost savings. Chase expected to cut 12,000 employees and $1.5 billion in annual expenses by the first quarter of 1999. Back in 1991, Chemical itself had merged with Manufacturers Hanover Corporation, which cut 6,200 jobs and $750 million in annual costs. By late 1999, Chase expanded its capacity again when Chase Global Investor Services acquired Morgan Stanley's Trust Company. By January 2001, it had acquired J.P. Morgan and considerable expertise in investment banking, becoming J.P. Morgan Chase & Co. (www.jpmorganchase.com). The Morgan Stanley acquisition, for example, gave $400 billion of assets in trust to Chase to manage. In addition to economies-of-scale benefits, the acquisition added almost 330 highly trained professional staff to its firm. In the investment banking industry where it is often said that "the assets go home at night," management estimates that it costs about $250,000 per person to recruit, train, and retain such professionals.

A doubling of capacity is by no means unique, as the banking industry is in the biggest wave of consolidation in its history. In part, consolidation is a sensible response to excess capacity. Banking is also becoming a technology-driven business. More than ever, financial products and services, from loans to credit cards, are marketed through computers and telephones instead of through bank branches. Banks able to make large investments in technology gain an unparalleled ability to reach customers nationwide. Unprecedented capital investments create the need to spread costs over a broader customer base. The electronic revolution also undermines a bank's traditional role of intermediary between borrowers and savers, making it easier for both kinds of customers to get together directly. Lower profit margins in retail banking encourage moves into wholesale business, such as investment banking, where size and large capacity can, to some extent, be equated with strength. The trend toward megabanks has been obvious in North America but now has gripped France, Germany, and even Japan—though banks there are moving toward union at a typically sedate pace. Dealing with a product—money—that moves across borders electronically, banks are quick to feel the forces of globalization and technological change.

Although these reasons for large size can be impressive, there can also be qualms about capacity getting too big. When that happens, customers may withdraw their accounts and turn to smaller banks that meet a variety of personal and business banking needs. To protect revenue, large banks must offer the same exceptional service that small banks offer. Small banks almost have it easier than big banks because they're accustomed to giving a high degree of personalized service. A large bank must try to provide the same level and type of service that customers want.

The headquarters of Chase Manhattan Bank in New York, just before the merger with J.P. Morgan. Consolidation of operations not only can lead to cost savings but provides economies-of-scale benefits in an increasingly technology-driven industry.

Source: "The Bank-Merger Splurge," *The Economist* (August 28, 1999).

capacity The maximum rate of output for a process.

AFTER DECIDING WHAT PRODUCTS or services should be offered and how they should be made, management must plan the capacity of its processes. The new J.P. Morgan Chase's experience demonstrates how important capacity plans are to an organization's future. **Capacity** is the maximum rate of output for a process. The operations manager must provide the capacity to meet current and future demand; otherwise, the organization will miss opportunities for growth and profits.

Capacity plans are made at two levels. Long-term capacity plans, which we describe in this chapter, deal with investments in new facilities and equipment. These plans cover at least two years into the future, but construction lead times alone can force much longer time horizons. Currently, U.S. firms invest more than $600 billion annually in *new* plant and equipment. Service industries account for more than 68 percent of the total. Such sizable investments require top-management participation and approval because they are not easily reversed. Short-term capacity plans focus on workforce size, overtime budgets, inventories, and other types of decisions that we explore in later chapters.

CAPACITY PLANNING

Capacity planning is central to the long-term success of an organization. Too much capacity can be as agonizing as too little, as the Managerial Practice demonstrates. When choosing a capacity strategy, managers have to consider questions such as the following: How much of a cushion is needed to handle variable, uncertain demand? Should we expand capacity before the demand is there or wait until demand is more certain? A systematic approach is needed to answer these and similar questions and to develop a capacity strategy appropriate for each situation.

MEASURES OF CAPACITY

How should the maximum rate of output be measured?

No single capacity measure is applicable to all types of situations. A retailer measures capacity as annual sales dollars generated per square foot; an airline measures capacity as available seat-miles (ASMs) per month; a theater measures capacity as number of seats; and a job shop measures capacity as number of machine hours. In general, capacity can be expressed in one of two ways: output measures or input measures.

Output measures are the usual choice for high-volume processes that produce only one type of product. However, many organizations produce more than one product or service. For example, a restaurant may be able to handle 100 take-out customers *or 50* sit-down customers per hour. It might also handle 50 take-out *and* 25 sit-down customers or many other combinations of the two types of customers. As the amount of customization and variety in the product mix becomes excessive, output-based capacity measures become less useful. Output measures are best utilized when the firm provides a relatively small number of standardized products and services, or when applied to individual processes within the overall firm. For example, a bank would have one capacity measure for processes that serve customers with B2C e-commerce and another measure for customers served with traditional "brick-and-mortar" facilities (see Chapter 4, "Managing Technology").

Input measures are the usual choice for low-volume, flexible processes. For example, in a photocopy shop, capacity can be measured in machine hours or number of machines. Just as product mix can complicate output capacity measures, so too can demand complicate input measures. Demand, which invariably is expressed as an output rate, must be converted to an input measure. Only after making the conversion can a manager compare demand requirements and capacity on an equivalent basis. For

MANAGERIAL PRACTICE

The Agony of Too Much—and Too Little—Capacity

Carnival Cruise Line (www.carnivalcorp.com) has a fleet of cruise ships that ply the waters off Florida. The capacity of these ships is huge. The *Destiny* is its largest, which displaces 100,000 tons and can carry over 3,100 passengers. But Carnival has been sailing in choppy seas during the last year, plagued by three onboard fires and technical problems. The most pressing problem, however, is the glut of new ships being added throughout the industry. Carnival alone is bringing in a cadre of 15 new amenity-filled ships, boosting its fleet to 61. With other cruise lines also adding to their fleets, the number of available beds jumped by 12 percent in 2000. But historically passenger volume has grown at only about 8 percent annually. Carnival argues that with the baby boomers now approaching their peak cruise-vacation years, the industry has lots of room to grow beyond the 6.5 million people who will book a cruise this year. "What is important to us is that we're building over the next five years $6.5 billion worth of new ships," says COO Frank. "We're going to continue to grow our business, and we're going to grow it profitably." Not everyone is convinced. Some experts worry about the overcapacity issue and Carnival's decreasing return on investment. During 2000, the company's share prices plunged by more than 50 percent. For now, Carnival is filling its berths by slashing prices. After years of rising prices in this industry, the capacity glut is causing the steep discounts. For a seven-day cruise, the cheapest fare has dropped from $599 to $549, and discounted tickets have gone as low as $359. Carnival is also adding a variety of shorter and cheaper voyages as a way to expand the market, because high utilization is a key to success when its resources are so capital-intensive.

The aircraft industry experienced the opposite problem in the late 1980s—not enough capacity. The world's airlines reequipped their fleets to carry more passengers on existing planes and vied to buy a record number of new commercial passenger jets. Orders received by Boeing (www.boeing.com), Airbus (www.airbus.com),

Passengers on the sundeck of a cruise liner enjoying the sun. Such ships have a huge capacity and investment costs are steep, making high utilization a key factor for success.

and McDonnell Douglas surged to more than 2,600 planes. McDonnell Douglas alone had a backlog of some $18 billion in firm orders for its MD-80 and new MD-11 widebody—enough to keep its plant fully utilized for more than three years. Despite the number of orders, Douglas's commercial aircraft division announced a startling loss, Airbus struggled to make money, and even mighty Boeing fought to improve subpar margins. Capacity shortage caused many problems for McDonnell Douglas: Its suppliers were unable to keep pace, its doubled workforce was inexperienced and less productive, and considerable work had to be subcontracted to other plants. The result was that costs skyrocketed and profits plummeted. In 1997, Boeing acquired McDonnell Douglas.

Sources: "Carnival Isn't Shipshape These Days," *Business Week* (April 24, 2000); "Floating Fantasy," *The Economist* (January 10, 1998).

example, the manager of a copy center must convert its annual demand for copies from different clients to the number of machines required.

UTILIZATION. Capacity planning requires a knowledge of the current capacity of a process and its utilization. **Utilization,** or the degree to which equipment, space, or labor is currently being used, is expressed as a percent:

utilization The degree to which equipment, space, or labor is currently being used.

$$\text{Utilization} = \frac{\text{Average output rate}}{\text{Maximum capacity}} \times 100\%$$

**TUTOR
6.1**

The average output rate and the capacity must be measured in the same terms—that is, time, customers, units, or dollars. The utilization rate indicates the need for adding extra capacity or eliminating unneeded capacity. The greatest difficulty in calculating utilization lies in defining *maximum capacity,* the denominator in the ratio. Two definitions of maximum capacity are useful: peak capacity and effective capacity. See Tutor 6.1 on the Student CD-ROM for how to calculate utilization using these two capacity measures.

PEAK CAPACITY. The maximum output that a process or facility can achieve under ideal conditions is called **peak capacity.** When capacity is measured relative to equipment alone, the appropriate measure is **rated capacity:** an engineering assessment of maximum annual output, assuming continuous operation except for an allowance for normal maintenance and repair downtime. Peak capacity can be sustained for only a short time, such as a few hours in a day or a few days in a month. A process reaches it by using marginal methods of production, such as excessive overtime, extra shifts, temporarily reduced maintenance activities, overstaffing, and subcontracting. Although they can help with temporary peaks, these options cannot be sustained for long. Employees do not want to work excessive overtime for extended periods, overtime and night-shift premiums drive up costs, and quality drops.

peak capacity The maximum output that a process or facility can achieve under ideal conditions.

rated capacity An engineering assessment of maximum annual output, assuming continuous operation except for an allowance for normal maintenance and repair downtime.

effective capacity The maximum output that a process or firm can economically sustain under normal conditions.

EFFECTIVE CAPACITY. The maximum output that a process or firm can economically sustain under normal conditions is its **effective capacity.** In some organizations, effective capacity implies a one-shift operation; in others, it implies a three-shift operation. For this reason, Census Bureau surveys define *capacity* as the greatest level of output the firm can *reasonably sustain* by using realistic employee work schedules and the equipment currently in place.

When operating close to peak capacity, a firm can make minimal profits or even lose money despite high sales levels. Cummins Engine Company reacted a few years ago to an unexpected demand surge caused by the weakened dollar by working at peak capacity: The plant operated three shifts, often seven days a week. Overtime soared and exhausted workers dragged down productivity. Productivity also suffered when Cummins called back less-skilled workers, laid off during an earlier slump. These factors together caused Cummins to report a quarterly loss of $6.2 million, even as sales jumped.

bottleneck An operation that has the lowest effective capacity of any operation in the process and, thus, limits the system's output.

INCREASING MAXIMUM CAPACITY. Most processes involve multiple operations, and often their effective capacities are not identical. A **bottleneck** is an operation that has the lowest effective capacity of any operation in the process and, thus, limits the system's output. Figure 6.1(a) shows a process where operation 2 is a bottleneck that limits the output to 50 units per hour. In effect, the process can produce only as fast as the slowest operation. Figure 6.1(b) shows the process when the capacities are perfectly balanced, making every operation a bottleneck. True expansion of a process's capacity occurs only when bottleneck capacity is increased. In Figure 6.1(a), initially adding capacity at operation 2 (and not operation 1 or 3) will increase system capacity. However, when operation 2's capacity reaches 200 units per hour, as in Figure 6.1(b), all three operations must be expanded simultaneously to increase capacity further.

A project or job process does not enjoy the simple line flows shown in Figure 6.1. Its operations may process many different items, and the demands on any one operation could vary considerably from one day to the next. Bottlenecks can still be identified by computing the average utilization of each operation. However, the variability in

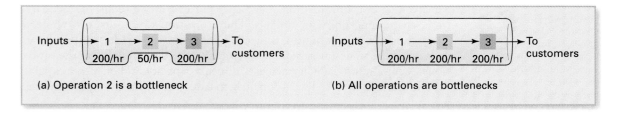

(a) Operation 2 is a bottleneck   (b) All operations are bottlenecks

FIGURE 6.1

*Capacity Bottlenecks at
a Three-Operation
Facility*

workload also creates *floating bottlenecks*. One week the mix of work may make operation 1 a bottleneck, and the next week it may make operation 3 the constraint. This type of variability increases the complexity of day-to-day scheduling. In this situation, management prefers lower utilization rates, which allow greater slack to absorb unexpected surges in demand.

The long-term capacity of bottleneck operations can be expanded in various ways. Investments can be made in new equipment and in brick-and-mortar facility expansions. The bottleneck's capacity also can be expanded by operating it more hours per week, such as going from a one-shift operation to multiple shifts, or going from five workdays per week to six or seven workdays per week. Managers also might relieve the bottleneck by redesigning the process, either through process reengineering or process improvement (see Chapter 2, "Process Management").

THEORY OF CONSTRAINTS

Long-term capacity expansions are not the only way to ease bottlenecks. Overtime, temporary or part-time employees, and temporarily outsourcing during peak periods are short-term options. Managers should also explore ways to increase the effective capacity utilization at bottlenecks, without experiencing the higher costs and poor customer service usually associated with maintaining output rates at peak capacity. The key is to carefully monitor short-term schedules (see Chapter 11, "Aggregate Planning and Scheduling"), keeping bottleneck resources as busy as practical. They should minimize the idle time lost at bottlenecks because jobs or customers are delayed at upstream operations in the process or because the necessary materials or tools are temporarily unavailable. They should also minimize the time spent unproductively for setups, which is changing over from one product or service to another. When a changeover is made at a bottleneck operation, the number of units or customers processed before the next changeover should be large compared to the number processed at less critical operations. Maximizing the number processed per setup means that there will be fewer setups per year and, thus, less total time lost to setups.

Developing schedules that focus on bottlenecks has great potential for improving a firm's financial performance. The **theory of constraints (TOC)**, sometimes referred to as the **drum–buffer–rope method,** is an approach to management that focuses on whatever impedes progress toward the goal of maximizing the flow of total value-added funds or sales less sales discounts and variable costs. The impediments, or bottlenecks, might be overloaded processes such as order entry, new product development, or a manufacturing operation. The fundamental idea is to focus on the bottlenecks to increase their throughput, thereby increasing the flow of total value-added funds. In terms of TOC, the key to the performance of the overall system lies in how the bottlenecks are scheduled.

With TOC, the bottlenecks are scheduled to maximize their throughput of products or services while adhering to promised completion dates. For example, manufacturing garden rakes involves the attachment of a bow to the head. Rake heads must be

**theory of constraints
(TOC)** An approach to
management that focuses
on whatever impedes
progress toward the goal
of maximizing the flow of
total value-added funds or
sales less discounts and
variable costs. **Also
referred to as
drum–buffer–rope
method.**

drum–buffer–rope method
See Theory of constraints.

processed on the blanking press, welded to the bow, cleaned, and attached to the handle to make the rake, which is packaged and finally shipped to Sears, Kmart or Wal-Mart according to a specific delivery schedule. Suppose that the delivery commitments for all styles of rakes for the next month indicate that the welder is loaded at 105 percent of its capacity but that the other processes will be used at only 75 percent of their capacities. According to TOC, the welder is a bottleneck resource, whereas the blanking, cleaning, handle attaching, packaging, and shipping processes are nonbottleneck resources. Any idle time on the welder is a lost opportunity to generate total value-added funds. To maximize throughput of the rake manufacturing system, managers should focus on the welder schedule.

Application of TOC involves the following steps.

1. *Identify the System Bottleneck(s).*   For the rake example, the bottleneck is the welder because it is restricting the firm's ability to meet the shipping schedule and, hence, total value-added funds.

2. *Exploit the Bottleneck(s).*   Create schedules that maximize the throughput of the bottleneck(s). For the rake example, schedule the welder to maximize its utilization while meeting the shipping commitments to the extent possible.

3. *Subordinate All Other Decisions to Step 2.*   Nonbottleneck resources should be scheduled to support the schedule of the bottleneck and not produce more than it can handle. That is, the blanking press should not produce more than the welder can handle, and the activities of the cleaning and subsequent operations should be based on the output rate of the welder.

4. *Elevate the Bottleneck(s).*   After the scheduling improvements in steps 1–3 have been exhausted and the bottleneck is still a constraint to throughput, management should consider increasing the capacity of the bottleneck. For example, if welding is still a constraint after exhausting schedule improvements, consider increasing its capacity by adding another shift or another welding machine.

5. *Do Not Let Inertia Set In.*   Actions taken in steps 3 and 4 will improve the welder throughput and may alter the loads on other processes. Consequently, the system constraint(s) may have shifted.

Details on the scheduling method used in TOC can be found in Simons and Simpson III (1997).

Large corporations have applied the principles of the theory of constraints. These corporations include Delta Airlines, National Semiconductor, ITT, Dresser Industries, Allied-Signal, Bethlehem Steel, United Airlines, Johnson Controls, and Rockwell Automotive. Smaller companies can also use TOC.

ECONOMIES OF SCALE

What is the maximum reasonable size for a facility?

economies of scale
A concept that states that the average unit cost of a good or service can be reduced by increasing its output rate.

A concept known as **economies of scale** states that the average unit cost of a good or service can be reduced by increasing its output rate. There are four principal reasons why economies of scale can drive costs down when output increases: Fixed costs are spread over more units, construction costs are reduced, costs of purchased materials are cut, and process advantages are found.

SPREADING FIXED COSTS. In the short term, certain costs do not vary with changes in the output rate. These fixed costs include heating costs, debt service, and management salaries. Depreciation of plant and equipment already owned is also a fixed cost in the accounting sense. When the output rate—and, therefore, the facility's utilization rate—increase, the average unit cost drops because fixed costs are spread over more units.

REDUCING CONSTRUCTION COSTS. Certain activities and expenses are required in building small and large facilities alike: building permits, architects' fees, rental of building equipment, and the like. Doubling the size of the facility usually does not double construction costs. The construction cost of equipment or a facility often increases relative to its surface area, whereas its capacity increases in proportion to its cubic volume.

CUTTING COSTS OF PURCHASED MATERIALS. Higher volumes can reduce the costs of purchased materials and services. They give the purchaser a better bargaining position and the opportunity to take advantage of quantity discounts. Retailers such as Wal-Mart Stores and Toys " Я " Us reap significant economies of scale because their national and international stores sell huge volumes of each item. Producers that rely on a vast network of suppliers (e.g., Toyota) and food processors (e.g., Kraft General Foods) also can buy inputs for less because of the quantity they order.

FINDING PROCESS ADVANTAGES. High-volume production provides many opportunities for cost reduction. At a higher output rate, the process shifts toward a line process, with resources dedicated to individual products. Firms may be able to justify the expense of more efficient technology or more specialized equipment. The benefits from dedicating resources to individual products or services may include speeding up the learning effect, lowering inventory, improving process and job designs, and reducing the number of changeovers.

DISECONOMIES OF SCALE

diseconomies of scale
When the average cost per unit increases as the facility's size increases.

At some point a facility can become so large that **diseconomies of scale** set in; that is, the average cost per unit increases as the facility's size increases. The reason is that excessive size can bring complexity, loss of focus, and inefficiencies that raise the average unit cost of a product or service. There may be too many layers of employees and bureaucracy, and management loses touch with employees and customers. The organization is less agile and loses the flexibility needed to respond to changing demand. Many large companies become so involved in analysis and planning that they innovate less and avoid risks. The result is that small companies outperform corporate giants in numerous industries.

Figure 6.2 illustrates the transition from economies of scale to diseconomies of scale. The 500-bed hospital shows economies of scale because the average unit cost at its *best operating level,* represented by the blue dot, is less than that of the 250-bed hospital. However, further expansion to a 750-bed hospital leads to higher average unit costs and diseconomies of scale. One reason the 500-bed hospital enjoys greater economies of scale than the 250-bed hospital is that the cost of building and equipping

FIGURE 6.2

*Economies and
Diseconomies of Scale*

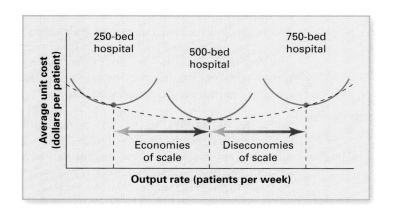

it is less than twice the cost for the smaller hospital. The 750-bed facility would enjoy similar savings. Its higher average unit costs can be explained only by diseconomies of scale, which outweigh the savings realized in construction costs.

Figure 6.2 does not mean that the optimal size for all hospitals is 500 beds. Optimal size depends on the number of patients per week to be served. On the one hand, a hospital serving a small community would have lower costs by choosing a 250-bed capacity rather than the 500-bed capacity. On the other hand, assuming the same cost structure, a large community will be served more efficiently by two 500-bed hospitals than by one 1,000-bed facility.

An example of going too far with one huge facility is the Incredible Universe superstores of Tandy Corporation. This Fort Worth–based electronics retailer opened its first superstore in 1992. The average store packed some 85,000 products into 185,000 square feet, or more than four times the average at rival Circuit City Stores. The superstores never were profitable. Tandy opted to sell all 17 Incredible Universe stores at bargain-basement prices and focus on Radio Shack. The lack of focus and huge size of the superstores made it impossible to generate enough sales per square foot to make the stores profitable.

CAPACITY STRATEGIES

Operations managers must examine three dimensions of capacity strategy before making capacity decisions: sizing capacity cushions, timing and sizing expansion, and linking capacity and other operating decisions.

SIZING CAPACITY CUSHIONS. Average utilization rates should not get too close to 100 percent. When they do, that usually is a signal to increase capacity or decrease order acceptance so as to avoid declining productivity. The **capacity cushion** is the amount of reserve capacity that a firm maintains to handle sudden increases in demand or temporary losses of production capacity; it measures the amount by which the average utilization (in terms of *effective* capacity) falls below 100 percent. Specifically,

$$\text{Capacity cushion} = 100\% - \text{Utilization rate (\%)}$$

Historically, U.S. manufacturers have maintained an average cushion of 18 percent. The appropriate size of the cushion varies by industry. In the capital-intensive paper industry, where machines can cost hundreds of millions of dollars each, cushions well under 10 percent are preferred. The less capital-intensive hotel industry breaks even with a 60 to 70 percent utilization (40 to 30 percent cushion) and begins to suffer customer-service problems when the cushion drops to 20 percent.

Businesses find large cushions appropriate when demand varies. In certain service industries (e.g., groceries), demand on some days of the week is predictably higher than on other days, and there are even hour-to-hour patterns. Long customer waiting times are not acceptable because customers grow impatient if they have to wait in a supermarket checkout line for more than a few minutes. Prompt customer service requires supermarkets to maintain a capacity cushion large enough to handle peak demand.

Large cushions also are necessary when future demand is uncertain, particularly if resource flexibility is low. Waiting-line analysis (see Supplement 6S, "Waiting Lines") and simulation (see Supplement G, "Simulation" on the Student CD-ROM) can help managers anticipate better the relationship between capacity cushion and customer service.

Another type of demand uncertainty occurs with a changing product mix. Though total demand might remain stable, the load can shift unpredictably from one work center to another as the mix changes.

How much capacity cushion is best for various processes?

capacity cushion The amount of reserve capacity that a firm maintains to handle sudden increases in demand or temporary losses of production capacity; it measures the amount by which the average utilization (in terms of *effective* capacity) falls below 100 percent.

Supply uncertainty also favors large capacity cushions. Capacity often comes in large increments, so expanding even by the minimum amount possible may create a large cushion. Firms also need to build in excess capacity to allow for employee absenteeism, vacations, holidays, and any other delays. Penalty costs for overtime and subcontracting can create the need for further increases in capacity cushions.

The argument in favor of small cushions is simple: Unused capacity costs money. For capital-intensive firms, minimizing the capacity cushion is vital. Studies indicate that businesses with high capital intensity achieve a low return on investment when the capacity cushion is high. This strong correlation does not exist for labor-intensive firms, however. Their return on investment is about the same because the lower investment in equipment makes high utilization less critical. Small cushions have other advantages; they reveal inefficiencies that may be masked by capacity excesses—problems with absenteeism, for example, or unreliable suppliers. Once managers and workers have identified such problems, they often can find ways to correct them.

Should an expanionist or a wait-and-see strategy be followed?

TIMING AND SIZING EXPANSION. The second issue of capacity strategy is when to expand and by how much. Figure 6.3 illustrates two extreme strategies: the *expansionist strategy,* which involves large, infrequent jumps in capacity, and the *wait-and-see strategy,* which involves smaller, more frequent jumps.

The timing and sizing of expansion are related; that is, if demand is increasing and the time between increments increases, the size of the increments must also increase. The expansionist strategy, which stays ahead of demand, minimizes the chance of sales lost to insufficient capacity. The wait-and-see strategy lags behind demand, relying on short-term options such as use of overtime, temporary workers, subcontractors, stockouts, and postponement of preventive maintenance to meet any shortfalls.

Several factors favor the expansionist strategy. Expansion may result in economies of scale and a faster rate of learning, thus helping a firm reduce its costs and compete on price. This strategy might increase the firm's market share or act as a form of preemptive marketing. By making a large capacity expansion or announcing that one is imminent, the firm uses capacity to preempt expansion by other firms. These other firms must sacrifice some of their market share or risk burdening the industry with overcapacity. To be successful, however, the preempting firm must have the credibility to convince the competition that it will carry out its plans—and must signal its plans before the competition can act.

The conservative wait-and-see strategy is to expand in smaller increments, such as by renovating existing facilities rather than building new ones. Because the wait-and-see strategy follows demand, it reduces the risks of overexpansion based on overly

FIGURE 6.3

Two Capacity Strategies

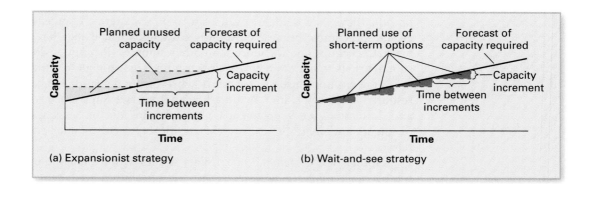

(a) Expansionist strategy

(b) Wait-and-see strategy

optimistic demand forecasts, obsolete technology, or inaccurate assumptions regarding the competition.

However, this strategy has its own risks, such as being preempted by a competitor or being unable to respond if demand is unexpectedly high. The wait-and-see strategy has been criticized as a short-term strategy typical of some U.S. management styles. Managers on the fast track to corporate advancement tend to take fewer risks. They earn promotions by avoiding the big mistake and maximizing short-term profits and return on investment. The wait-and-see strategy fits this short-term outlook but can erode market share over the long run.

Management may choose one of these two strategies or one of the many between these extremes. With strategies in the more moderate middle, firms may expand more frequently (on a smaller scale) than with the expansionist strategy but do not always lag behind demand as with the wait-and-see strategy. An intermediate strategy could be to *follow the leader,* expanding when others do. If others are right, so are you, and nobody gains a competitive advantage. If they make a mistake and overexpand, so have you, but everyone shares in the agony of overcapacity.

How should capacity and competitive priorities be linked? Capacity and other types of decisions?

LINKING CAPACITY AND OTHER DECISIONS. Capacity decisions should be closely linked to strategies and processes throughout the organization. When managers make decisions about location, resource flexibility, and inventory, they must consider the impact on capacity cushions. Capacity cushions buffer the organization against uncertainty, as do resource flexibility, inventory, and longer customer lead times. If a system is well balanced and a change is made in some other decision area, then the capacity cushion may need change to compensate.

For example, capacity cushions at a process can be lowered if less emphasis is placed on fast deliveries (*competitive priorities*), yield losses (*quality*) drop, investment in capital-intensive equipment increases (*managing technology*), worker flexibility increases (*process management*), and if inventory is used more to smooth the output rate (*aggregate planning and scheduling*).

A SYSTEMATIC APPROACH TO CAPACITY DECISIONS

How can capacity plans be systematically developed?

Although each situation is somewhat different, a four-step procedure generally can help managers make sound capacity decisions. In describing this procedure, we assume that management has already performed the preliminary step of determining existing capacity.

1. Estimate future capacity requirements.
2. Identify gaps by comparing requirements with available capacity.
3. Develop alternative plans for filling the gaps.
4. Evaluate each alternative, both qualitatively and quantitatively, and make a final choice.

STEP 1: ESTIMATE CAPACITY REQUIREMENTS

The foundation for estimating long-term capacity needs is forecasts of demand, productivity, competition, and technological changes that extend well into the future. Unfortunately, the farther ahead you look, the more chance you have of making an inaccurate forecast (see Chapter 9, "Forecasting").

The demand forecast has to be converted to a number that can be compared directly with the capacity measure being used. Suppose that capacity is expressed as the number of available machines at an operation. When just one product (service) is being processed, the number of machines required, M, is

$$\text{Number of machines required} = \frac{\text{Processing hours required for year's demand}}{\substack{\text{Hours available from one machine per year,} \\ \text{after deducting desired cushion}}}$$

$$M = \frac{Dp}{N[1 - (C/100)]}$$

where

D = number of units (customers) forecast per year

p = processing time (in hours per unit or customer)

N = total number of hours per year during which the process operates

C = desired capacity cushion

The processing time, p, in the numerator depends on the process and methods selected to do the work (see Chapter 2, "Process Management"). Estimates of p come from established work standards (see Supplement C, "Measuring Output Rates" on the Student CD-ROM). The denominator is the total number of hours, N, available for the year, multiplied by a proportion that accounts for the desired capacity cushion, C. The proportion is simply $1.0 - C$, where C is converted from a percent to a proportion by dividing by 100.

If multiple products or services are involved, extra time is needed to change over from one product or service to the next. **Setup time** is the time required to change a machine from making one product or service to making another. Setup time is derived from process decisions, as is processing time (see Chapter 2, "Process Management"). The total setup time is found by dividing the number of units forecast per year, D, by the number of units made in each lot, which gives the number of setups per year, and then multiplying by the time per setup. For example, if the annual demand is 1,200 units and the average lot size is 100, there are $1,200/100 = 12$ setups per year. Accounting for both processing and setup time when there are multiple products (services), we get

setup time The time required to change a machine from making one product or service to making another.

$$\text{Number of machines required} = \frac{\substack{\text{Processing } and \text{ setup hours required for} \\ \text{year's demand, summed over all products}}}{\substack{\text{Hours available from one machine per year,} \\ \text{after deducting desired cushion}}}$$

$$M = \frac{[Dp + (D/Q)s]_{\text{product 1}} + [Dp + (D/Q)s]_{\text{product 2}} + \cdots + [Dp + (D/Q)s]_{\text{product } n}}{N[1 - (C/100)]}$$

where

Q = number of units in each lot

s = setup time (in hours) per lot

Always round up the fractional part unless it is cost efficient to use short-term options such as overtime or stockouts to cover any shortfalls.

EXAMPLE 6.1	*Estimating Requirements*

**TUTOR
6.2**

A copy center in an office building prepares bound reports for two clients. The center makes multiple copies (the lot size) of each report. The processing time to run, collate, and bind each copy depends on, among other factors, the number of pages. The center operates 250 days per year, with one eight-hour shift. Management believes that a capacity cushion of 15 percent (beyond the allowance built into time standards) is best. It currently has three copy machines.

Based on the following table of information, determine how many machines are needed at the copy center.

ITEM	CLIENT X	CLIENT Y
Annual demand forecast (copies)	2,000	6,000
Standard processing time (hour/copy)	0.5	0.7
Average lot size (copies per report)	20	30
Standard setup time (hours)	0.25	0.40

SOLUTION

$$M = \frac{[Dp + (D/Q)s]_{\text{product 1}} + [Dp + (D/Q)s]_{\text{product 2}} + \cdots + [Dp + (D/Q)s]_{\text{product } n}}{N[1 - (C/100)]}$$

$$= \frac{[2{,}000(0.5) + (2{,}000/20)(0.25)]_{\text{client X}} + [6{,}000(0.7) + (6{,}000/30)(0.40)]_{\text{client Y}}}{[(250 \text{ days/year})(1 \text{ shift/day})(8 \text{ hours/shift})](1.0 - 15/100)}$$

$$= \frac{5{,}305}{1{,}700} = 3.12$$

Rounding up to the next integer gives a requirement of four machines.

Decision Point The copy center's capacity is being stretched and no longer has the desired 15 percent capacity cushion. Not wanting customer service to suffer, management decided to use overtime as a short-term solution to handle past-due orders. If demand continues at the current level or grows, it will acquire a fourth machine. □

STEP 2: IDENTIFY GAPS

capacity gap Any difference (positive or negative) between projected demand and current capacity.

A **capacity gap** is any difference (positive or negative) between projected demand and current capacity. Identifying gaps requires use of the correct capacity measure. Complications arise when multiple operations and several resource inputs are involved. Expanding the capacity of some operations may increase overall capacity. However, if one operation is a bottleneck, capacity can be expanded only if the capacity of the bottleneck operation is expanded.

STEP 3: DEVELOP ALTERNATIVES

base case The act of doing nothing and losing orders from any demand that exceeds current capacity.

The next step is to develop alternative plans to cope with projected gaps. One alternative, called the **base case,** is to do nothing and simply lose orders from any demand that exceeds current capacity. Other alternatives are various timing and sizing options for adding new capacity, including the expansionist and wait-and-see strategies illustrated in Figure 6.3. Additional possibilities include expanding at a different location and using short-term options such as overtime, temporary workers, and subcontracting.

STEP 4: EVALUATE THE ALTERNATIVES

In this final step, the manager evaluates each alternative, both quantitatively and qualitatively.

QUALITATIVE CONCERNS. Qualitatively, the manager has to look at how each alternative fits the overall capacity strategy and other aspects of the business not covered by the financial analysis. Of particular concern might be uncertainties about demand, competitive reaction, technological change, and cost estimates. Some of these factors cannot be quantified and have to be assessed on the basis of judgment and experience. Others can be quantified, and the manager can analyze each alternative by using different assumptions about the future. One set of assumptions could represent a worst case, in which demand is less, competition is greater, and construction costs are higher than expected. Another set of assumptions could represent the most optimistic view of the future. This type of "what-if" analysis allows the manager to get an idea of each alternative's implications before making a final choice.

QUANTITATIVE CONCERNS. Quantitatively, the manager estimates the change in cash flows for each alternative over the forecast time horizon compared to the base case. **Cash flow** is the difference between the flows of funds into and out of an organization over a period of time, including revenues, costs, and changes in assets and liabilities. The manager is concerned here only with calculating the cash flows attributable to the project.

cash flow The difference between the flows of funds into and out of an organization over a period of time, including revenues, costs, and changes in assets and liabilities.

A good example of capacity's impact on revenues is a steakhouse restaurant in Lexington, Kentucky. Customers liked the neon signs that dotted the wall, the blaring jukebox, and the way they could throw peanut shells on the floor. However, they had to wait as long as two hours to be seated, and the choice of items on the menu was limited. The restaurant expanded capacity by adding more seats and enlarging the kitchen to handle larger volumes and offer more choices. Within months, the restaurant started to bring in $80,000 a week, a 60 percent increase. This facility became the prototype for Logan's Roadhouse, Inc., the Nashville-based dining chain that was one of the fastest-growing companies in 1996. Logan's has since opened 10 restaurants in Indiana, Kentucky, and Tennessee. Each one costs $2.2 million to build, but high volume yields a sales average of some $3.8 million a year.

| EXAMPLE 6.2 | *Evaluating the Alternatives* |

TUTOR 6.3

Grandmother's Chicken Restaurant is experiencing a boom in business. The owner expects to serve a total of 80,000 meals this year. Although the kitchen is operating at 100 percent capacity, the dining room can handle a total of 105,000 diners per year. Forecasted demand for the next five years is 90,000 meals for the next year, followed by a 10,000-meal increase in each of the succeeding years.

One alternative is to expand both the kitchen and the dining room now, bringing their capacities up to 130,000 meals per year. The initial investment would be $200,000, made at the end of this year (year 0). The average meal is priced at $10, and the before-tax profit margin is 20 percent. The 20 percent figure was arrived at by determining that, for each $10 meal, $6 covers variable costs and $2 goes toward fixed costs (other than depreciation). The remaining $2 goes to pretax profit.

What are the pretax cash flows from this project for the next five years compared to those of the base case of doing nothing?

SOLUTION

Recall that the base case of doing nothing results in losing all potential sales beyond 80,000 meals. With the new capacity, the cash flow would equal the extra meals served by having a 130,000-meal capacity, multiplied by a profit of $2 per meal. In year 0, the only cash flow is −$200,000 for the initial investment. In year 1, the 90,000-meal demand will be completely satisfied by the expanded capacity, so the incremental cash flow is $(90,000 − 80,000)(2) = \$20,000$. For subsequent years, the figures are as follows:

Year 2:   Demand = 100,000; Cash flow = (100,000 − 80,000)2 = $40,000

Year 3:   Demand = 110,000; Cash flow = (110,000 − 80,000)2 = $60,000

Year 4:   Demand = 120,000; Cash flow = (120,000 − 80,000)2 = $80,000

Year 5:   Demand = 130,000; Cash flow = (130,000 − 80,000)2 = $100,000

If the new capacity were smaller than the expected demand in any year, we would subtract the base case capacity from the new capacity (rather than the demand).

Decision Point Before deciding on this capacity alternative, the owner should account for the time value of money, applying such techniques as the present value or internal rate of return methods (see Supplement B, "Financial Analysis" on the Student CD-ROM). The owner should also examine the qualitative concerns. For example, the homey atmosphere that the restaurant has projected may be lost with expansion. Furthermore, other alternatives should be considered, (see Solved Problem 2). ☐

TOOLS FOR CAPACITY PLANNING

What tools can help in planning capacities?

Long-term capacity planning requires demand forecasts for an extended period of time. Unfortunately, forecast accuracy declines as the forecasting horizon lengthens. In addition, anticipating what competitors will do increases the uncertainty of demand forecasts. Finally, demand during any period of time is not evenly distributed; peaks and valleys of demand may (and often do) occur within the time period. These realities necessitate the use of capacity cushions. In this section, we introduce three tools that deal more formally with demand uncertainty and variability: waiting-line models, simulation, and decision trees. Waiting-line models and simulation account for the random, independent behavior of many customers, in terms of both their time of arrival and their processing needs. Decision trees allow anticipation of events such as competitors' actions.

WAITING-LINE MODELS

Waiting-line models often are useful in capacity planning. Waiting lines tend to develop in front of a work center, such as an airport ticket counter, a machine center, or a central computer. The reason is that the arrival time between jobs or customers varies and the processing time may vary from one customer to the next. Waiting-line models use probability distributions to provide estimates of average customer delay time, average length of waiting lines, and utilization of the work center. Managers can use this information to choose the most cost-effective capacity, balancing customer service and the cost of adding capacity.

Supplement 6S, "Waiting Lines," follows this chapter and provides a fuller treatment of these models. It introduces formulas for estimating important characteristics of a waiting line, such as average customer waiting time and average facility utilization, for different facility designs. For example, a facility might be designed to have one or multiple lines at each operation and to route customers through one or multiple operations. Given the estimating capability of these formulas and cost estimates for waiting and idle time, managers can select cost-effective designs and capacity levels that also provide the desired level of customer service.

Figure 6.4 shows output from OM Explorer's Solver for Waiting Lines. The process modeled, a professor meeting students during office hours, has an arrival rate of three students per hour and a service rate of six students per hour. The output shows that the capacity cushion is 50 percent (1 – average server utilization of 0.50). This result is expected because the processing rate is double the arrival rate. What might not be expected is that a typical student spends 0.33 hour either in line or talking with the professor, and the probability of having two or more students at the office is 0.125. These numbers are surprisingly high, given such a large capacity cushion.

SIMULATION

More complex waiting-line problems must be analyzed with simulation (see Supplement G, "Simulation" on the Student CD-ROM). It can identify the process's bottlenecks

Solver - Waiting Lines

Enter data in yellow shaded areas.

◉ Single-server model   ○ Multiple-server model   ○ Finite-source model

Servers	1	(Number of servers is assumed to be 1 in single-server model.)
Arrival Rate (λ)	3	
Service Rate (μ)	6	

Probability of zero customers in the system (P_0)	0.5000
Probability of [at most ▼] 2 customers in the system (P_n)	0.8750
Average utilization of the server (ρ)	0.5000
Average number of customers in the system (L)	1.0000
Average number of customers in line (L_q)	0.5000
Average waiting/service time in the system (W)	0.3333
Average waiting time in line (W_q)	0.1667

FIGURE 6.4

Solver Output for Waiting Line During Office Hours

and appropriate capacity cushions, even for complex processes with random demand patterns with predictable surges in demand during a typical day.

For example, the Extend simulation package (www.imaginethatinc.com) allows you to build dynamic models and systems. Figure 6.5(a) graphs the waiting lines at three operations (review, violations, and payments) that exist in a driver's license renewal process. Figure 6.5(b) focuses on the violations operation, giving the kind of statistics provided by waiting-line models. The operation's utilization is 0.91 (a 9 percent cushion) and the lines are very long, with an average of over 17 customers waiting in line during the day. Most would agree that this level of service is unacceptable and that capacity is insufficient.

DECISION TREES

A decision tree can be particularly valuable for evaluating different capacity expansion alternatives when demand is uncertain and sequential decisions are involved (see Supplement A, "Decision Making" on the Student CD-ROM). For example, the owner of Grandmother's Chicken Restaurant (see Example 6.2) may expand the restaurant now only to discover in year 4 that demand growth is much higher than forecasted. In that case, she needs to decide whether to expand further. In terms of construction costs and downtime, expanding twice is likely to be much more expensive than building a large facility from the outset. However, making a large expansion now when demand growth is low means poor facility utilization. Much depends on the demand.

Figure 6.6 shows a decision tree for this view of the problem with new information provided. Demand growth can be either low or high, with probabilities of 0.4 and 0.6, respectively. The initial expansion in year 1 (square node 1) can either be small or large. The second decision node (square node 2), whether to expand at a later date, is reached only if the initial expansion is small and demand turns out to be high. If demand is high and if the initial expansion was small, a decision must be made about a second expansion in year 4. Payoffs for each branch of the tree are estimated. For example, if the initial expansion is large, the financial benefit is either $40,000 or $220,000, depending on whether demand is low or high. Weighting these payoffs by the probabilities yields an expected value of $148,000. This expected payoff is higher than the $109,000 payoff for the small initial expansion, so the better choice is to make a large expansion in year 1.

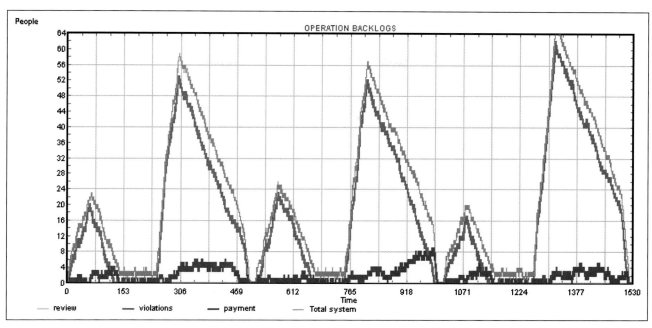

(a) Waiting lines for three simulated days

FIGURE 6.5

Extend Model for Driver's License Renewals

(b) Utilization at violations subprocess

FIGURE 6.6

A Decision Tree for Capacity Expansion (Payoffs in Thousands of Dollars)

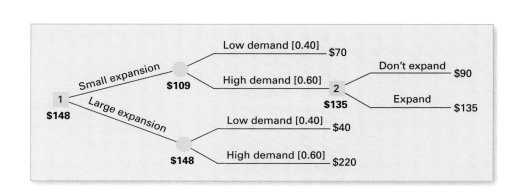

MANAGING CAPACITY ACROSS THE ORGANIZATION

Managers make capacity choices at the organization level, as illustrated by J.P. Morgan Chase & Co. in our chapter opener. They also must make capacity decisions at the individual-process level in accounting, finance, human resources, information technology, marketing, and operations. Capacity issues can cut across departmental lines, because relieving a bottleneck in one part of an organization does not have the desirable effect unless a bottleneck in another part of the organization is also addressed. Managers everywhere must understand capacity measures, economies and diseconomies of scale, capacity cushions, timing-and-sizing strategies, capacity cushions, and trade-offs between customer service and capacity utilization. They also must understand how such capacity decisions link with other decisions that have to be made about their processes.

EQUATION SUMMARY

1. Utilization, expressed as a percent:

$$\text{Utilization} = \frac{\text{Average output rate}}{\text{Maximum capacity}} \times 100\%$$

2. Capacity cushion, C, expressed as a percent:

$$C = 100\% - \text{Utilization (\%)}$$

3. a. Capacity requirement for one product:

$$M = \frac{Dp}{N[1 - (C/100)]}$$

b. Capacity requirement for multiple products:

$$M = \frac{[Dp + (D/Q)s]_{\text{product 1}} + [Dp + (D/Q)s]_{\text{product 2}} + \cdots + [Dp + (D/Q)s]_{\text{product } n}}{N[1 - (C/100)]}$$

CHAPTER HIGHLIGHTS

❏ Operations managers plan for timely acquisition, use, and disposition of capacity.

❏ Long-term capacity planning is crucial to an organization's success because it often involves large investments in facilities and equipment and because such decisions are not easily reversed.

❏ Capacity can be stated in terms of either input or output measures. Output measures giving the number of products or services completed in a time period are useful when a firm provides *standardized* products or services. However, a statement of the number of *customized* products or services completed in a time period is meaningless because the work content per unit varies. Demand for customized products and services must be translated into input measures, such as labor hours, machine hours, and material requirements.

❏ Operating at peak capacity calls for extraordinary effort, using marginal production methods, that usually is not sustainable. Maximum output under normal conditions is called effective capacity. The operation having the lowest effective capacity is called a bottleneck and limits the capacity of the entire system. Variable workloads and changing product mix complicate measuring capacity and can cause different operations to become bottlenecks under varying circumstances. Such floating bottlenecks make determining a firm's effective capacity difficult.

❏ Focusing capacity and scheduling decisions on bottleneck resources with an approach called the theory of constraints (TOC) can help maximize the flow of total value-added funds.

❏ Economies of scale derive from spreading fixed costs, reducing construction costs, reducing purchased materials costs, and obtaining process advantages. Diseconomies of scale cause some firms to focus their operations and move to smaller, rather than larger, facilities.

❏ The desirable amount of capacity cushion varies, depending on competitive priorities, cost of unused capacity, resource flexibility, supply uncertainties, shelf life, variability and uncertainty of demand, and other factors.

❏ Three capacity strategies are expansionist, wait and see, and follow the leader. The expansionist strategy is attractive when there are economies of scale, learning effects, and a chance for preemptive marketing. The wait-and-see strategy minimizes risk by relying more on short-term options. The follow-the-leader strategy maintains the current balance between competitors.

❏ Capacity choices must be linked to other operations management decisions.

❏ The four steps in capacity planning are (1) estimate capacity requirements, (2) identify gaps, (3) develop alternatives, and (4) evaluate the alternatives.

❏ Waiting-line models help the manager choose the capacity level that best balances customer service and the cost of adding more capacity. As waiting-line problems involve more servers, mathematical models quickly become very complex. Simulation is used to analyze most multiple-server waiting-line situations. Decision trees are schematic models that can be helpful in evaluating different capacity-expansion alternatives when demand is uncertain and sequential decisions are involved.

SOLVED PROBLEM 1

You have been asked to put together a capacity plan for a critical bottleneck operation at the Surefoot Sandal Company. Your capacity measure is number of machines. Three products (men's, women's, and children's sandals) are manufactured. The time standards (processing and setup), lot sizes, and demand forecasts are given in the following table. The firm operates two 8-hour shifts, 5 days per week, 50 weeks per year. Experience shows that a capacity cushion of 5 percent is sufficient.

	TIME STANDARDS			
PRODUCT	Processing (hr/pair)	Setup (hr/lot)	LOT SIZE (pairs/lot)	DEMAND FORECAST (pairs/yr)
Men's sandals	0.05	0.5	240	80,000
Women's sandals	0.10	2.2	180	60,000
Children's sandals	0.02	3.8	360	120,000

a. How many machines are needed?

b. If the operation currently has two machines, what is the capacity gap?

SOLUTION

a. The number of hours of operation per year, N, is

$$N = (2 \text{ shifts/day}) (8 \text{ hours/shift}) (250 \text{ days/machine-year})$$

$$= 4,000 \text{ hours/machine-year}$$

The number of machines required, M, is the sum of machine-hour requirements for all three products divided by the number of productive hours available for one machine:

$$M = \frac{[Dp + (D/Q)s]_{men} + [Dp + (D/Q)s]_{women} + [Dp + (D/Q)s]_{children}}{N[1 - (C/100)]}$$

$$= \frac{\begin{array}{c}[80,000(0.05) + (80,000/240)0.5] + [60,000(0.10) + (60,000/180)2.2] \\ + [120,000(0.02) + (120,000/360)3.8]\end{array}}{4,000[1 - (5/100)]}$$

$$= \frac{14,567 \text{ hours/year}}{3,800 \text{ hours/machine-year}} = 3.83 \quad \text{or} \quad 4 \text{ machines}$$

Solver Capacity Requirements

Enter data in yellow-shaded areas.

Shifts/Day	2	Components	3
Hours/Shift	8		
Days/Week	5	↑	More Components
Weeks/Year	50	↓	Fewer Components
Cushion (as %)	5%		
Current capacity	2		

Components	Processing (hr/unit)	Setup (hr/lot)	Lot Size (units/lot)	Demand Forecasts Pessimistic	Expected	Optimistic
Men's sandals	0.05	0.5	240		80,000	
Women's sandals	0.10	2.2	180		60,000	
Children's sandals	0.02	3.8	360		120,000	

Productive hours from one capacity unit for a year 3,800

	Pessimistic Process	Setup	Expected Process	Setup	Optimistic Process	Setup
Men's sandals	0	0.0	4,000	166.7	0	0.0
Women's sandals	0	0.0	6,000	733.3	0	0.0
Children's sandals	0	0.0	2,400	1,266.7	0	0.0
	0	0.0	12,400	2,166.7	0	0.0
Total hours required		0.0		14,566.7		0.0
Total capacity requirements (M)		0.00		3.83		0.00
Rounded		0		4		0

Scenarios that can be met with current systems/capacity: **Pessimistic, Optimistic**

If capacity increased by	0%
Expanded current capacity	3,800

	Pessimistic	Expected	Optimistic
Total capacity requirements (M)	0.00	3.83	0.00
Rounded	0	4	0

Scenarios that can be met with expanded current capacity: **Pessimistic, Optimistic**

FIGURE 6.7 • Using the *Capacity Requirements Solver* for Solved Problem 1

b. The capacity gap is 1.83 machines (3.83 − 2). Two more machines should be purchased, unless management decides to use short-term options to fill the gap.

The *Capacity Requirements Solver* in OM Explorer confirms these calculations, as Figure 6.7 shows, using only the "Expected" scenario for the demand forecasts.

SOLVED PROBLEM 2

The base case for Grandmother's Chicken Restaurant (see Example 6.2) is to do nothing. The capacity of the kitchen in the base case is 80,000 meals per year. A capacity alternative for Grandmother's Chicken Restaurant is a two-stage expansion. This alternative expands the kitchen at the end of year 0, raising its capacity from 80,000 meals per year to that of the dining area (105,000 meals per year). If sales in year 1 and 2 live up to expectations, the capacities of both the kitchen and the dining room will be expanded at the *end* of year 3 to 130,000 meals per year. The initial investment would be $80,000 at the end of year 0 and an additional investment of $170,000 at the end of year 3. The pretax profit is $2 per meal. What are the pretax cash flows for this alternative through year 5, compared with the base case?

SOLUTION

Table 6.1 shows the cash inflows and outflows. The year 3 cash flow is unusual in two respects. First, the cash inflow from sales is $50,000 rather than $60,000. The increase in sales over the base is 25,000 meals (105,000 − 80,000) instead of 30,000 meals (110,000 − 80,000) because the restaurant's capacity falls somewhat short of demand. Second, a cash outflow of $170,000 occurs at the end of year 3, when the second-stage expansion occurs. The net cash flow for year 3 is $50,000 − $170,000 = −$120,000.

TABLE 6.1 *Cash Flows for Two-Stage Expansion at Grandmother's Chicken Restaurant*

YEAR	PROJECTED DEMAND (meals/yr)	PROJECTED CAPACITY (meals/yr)	CALCULATION OF INCREMENTAL CASH FLOW COMPARED TO BASE CASE (80,000 meals/yr)	CASH INFLOW (Outflow)
0	80,000	80,000	Increase kitchen capacity to 105,000 meals =	($80,000)
1	90,000	105,000	90,000 − 80,000 = (10,000 meals)($2/meal) =	$20,000
2	100,000	105,000	100,000 − 80,000 = (20,000 meals)($2/meal) =	$40,000
3	110,000	105,000	105,000 − 80,000 = (25,000 meals)($2/meal) =	$50,000
			Increase total capacity to 130,000 meals =	($170,000)
				($120,000)
4	120,000	130,000	120,000 − 80,000 = (40,000 meals)($2/meal) =	$80,000
5	130,000	130,000	130,000 − 80,000 = (50,000 meals)($2/meal) =	$100,000

SOLVED PROBLEM 3

Penelope and Peter Legume own a small accounting service and one personal computer. If their customers keep organized records, either of the owners can use the computer to prepare one tax return per hour, on average. During the first two weeks of April, both Legumes work seven 12-hour shifts. This allows them to use their computer around the clock.

a. What is the peak capacity, measured in tax returns per week?

b. The Legumes normally operate from 9 A.M. to 7 P.M., five days per week. What is their effective capacity, measured in tax returns per week?

c. During the third week of January, the Legumes processed 40 tax returns. What is their utilization, as a percentage of effective capacity?

SOLUTION

a.   Peak capacity = (12 hours/shift) (2 shifts/day) (7 days/week) (1 return/hour)

           = 168 returns/week

b. Although both Legumes may be present in the shop, the capacity is limited by the number of hours their one computer is available:

      Effective capacity = (10 hours/day) (5 days/week) (1 return/hour)

           = 50 returns/week

c. Utilization is the ratio of output to effective capacity:

$$\text{Utilization} = \frac{40 \text{ returns/week}}{50 \text{ returns/week}} \times 100\%$$

$$= 80\%$$

CD-ROM RESOURCES

The Student CD-ROM that accompanies this text contains the following resources, which allow you to further practice and apply the concepts presented in this chapter.

- ❒ **OM Explorer Tutors:** OM Explorer contains three tutor programs that will help you learn about capacity (capacity utilization, capacity requirements, and projecting cash flows) and three programs about waiting lines (single-server, multiple-server, and finite-source models). See the folders for Chapter 6 and Supplement 6S in OM Explorer. See also the two Tutor Exercises on capacity utilization and capacity requirements.

- ❒ **OM Explorer Solvers:** OM Explorer has one program to help with general capacity planning problems on capacity requirements and one on analyzing waiting lines. See the folders for Capacity and Waiting Lines in OM Explorer for these routines.

- ❒ **Equation Summary:** All the equations for this chapter can be found in one convenient location.

- ❒ **Discussion Questions:** Four questions expand your thinking on economies of scale, safety issues, and capacity cushions.

- ❒ **Case:** Fitness Plus, Part A: How should Fitness Plus measure its capacity, and what capacity strategy is best?

- ❒ **Supplement A:** Decision Making. See how to construct decision trees for uncertain, sequential capacity decisions.

- ❒ **Supplement C:** Measuring Output Rates. See how processing times can be estimated as inputs to capacity planning.

- ❒ **Supplement G:** Simulation. Read about how simulation can give important insights on the performance of processes and can help make the right capacity decisions.

INTERACTIVE RESOURCES

The Interactive Web site associated with this text (www.prenhall.com/ritzman) contains many tools and activities specifically designed for this chapter. The following items are recommended to enhance your understanding of the material in this chapter.

- ❒ **Internet Activities:** Try out two links covering capacity utilization at AOL and capacity expansion at Texaco. Also see the link about waiting lines on the Web.

- ❒ **Internet Tours:** Check out capacity issues at the Camarillo, California, Sanitary District and waiting lines at Paris Companies Cleaners.

- ❒ **SmartDraw:** Use the link to experience a software package that is used in practice to prepare decision trees.

PROBLEMS

An icon next to a problem identifies the software that can be helpful but is not mandatory.

1. **OM Explorer** Bob Greer operates Bob's Garage and Manhole Cover Recycling Center at the corner of Lookout Highway and Ruff Road. Bob's Garage has one bay dedi- cated to wheel alignments. Although the recycling center is open at night, the garage normally is open only on weekdays from 7 A.M. to 7 P.M. and on Saturdays from 8 A.M. to noon. An alignment takes an average of 60 minutes to complete, although Bob charges customers for two hours according to

a nationally published mechanic's labor-standard manual. During March, the height of pothole season, Bob's Garage is open from 6 A.M. to 10 P.M. on weekdays and from 6 A.M. to 6 P.M. on Saturdays.

a. What are the garage's peak and effective capacities in alignments per week?

b. During the second week in March, Bob's Garage completed 90 alignments. What is the utilization as a percentage of effective capacity? As a percentage of peak capacity?

2. **OM Explorer** Sterling Motors is a telephone or mail-order dealer in British auto parts. Sterling has six telephones for receiving orders. Order takers answer the telephones, check inventory availability, and prepare picking tickets for the warehouse stockpickers. One order may consist of several lines, with a different part or multiple of a part ordered on each line. Each order taker can prepare picking tickets at a rate of one line every three minutes. The telephones are normally answered weekdays from 6 A.M. to 4 P.M., Pacific Time. Stockpickers can fill and package parts at a rate of one line every five minutes. Sterling employs eight stockpickers, who normally work weekdays from 8 A.M. to 5 P.M. (except for lunch hours).

a. What is the effective capacity of order taking in lines per week? Stockpicking?

b. For three weeks after the spring catalog is mailed in May, the eight warehouse employees work 10 hours per day between 7 A.M. and 6 P.M., six days per week. What is the peak capacity of the system in lines per week?

c. During the second week of May, Sterling filled 5,000 order lines. What is the utilization as a percentage of effective capacity? As a percentage of peak capacity?

3. **OM Explorer** The Clip Joint operates four barber's chairs in the student center. During the week before semester break and the week before graduation, The Clip Joint experiences peak demands. Military-style haircuts take 5 minutes each, and other styles require 20 minutes each. Operating from 9 A.M. to 6 P.M. on the six days before semester break, The Clip Joint completes 500 military-style haircuts and 400 other haircuts. During a comparable six-day week before graduation, The Clip Joint completes 700 military-style haircuts and 300 other haircuts. In which week is utilization higher?

4. **OM Explorer** Up, Up, and Away is a producer of kites and wind socks. Relevant data on a bottleneck operation in the shop for the upcoming fiscal year are given in the following table:

ITEM	KITES	WIND SOCKS
Demand forecast	30,000 units/year	12,000 units/year
Lot size	20 units	70 units
Standard processing time	0.3 hour/unit	1.0 hour/unit
Standard setup time	3.0 hours/lot	4.0 hours/lot

The shop works two shifts per day, eight hours per shift, 200 days per year. There currently are four machines, and a 25 percent capacity cushion is desired. How many machines should be purchased to meet the upcoming year's demand without resorting to any short-term capacity solutions?

5. **OM Explorer** Tuff-Rider, Inc., manufactures touring bikes and mountain bikes in a variety of frame sizes, colors, and component combinations. Identical bicycles are produced in lots of 100. The projected demand, lot size, and time standards are shown in the following table:

ITEM	TOURING	MOUNTAIN
Demand forecast	5,000 units/year	10,000 units/year
Lot size	100 units	100 units
Standard processing time	1/4 hour/unit	1/2 hour/unit
Standard setup time	2 hours/lot	3 hours/lot

The shop currently works eight hours a day, five days a week, 50 weeks a year. It has five workstations, each producing one bicycle in the time shown in the table. The shop maintains a 15 percent capacity cushion. How many workstations will be required next year to meet expected demand without using overtime and without decreasing the firm's current capacity cushion?

6. **OM Explorer** Worcester Athletic Club is considering expanding its facility to include two adjacent suites. The owner will remodel the suites in consideration of a seven-year lease. Expenditures for rent, insurance, utilities, and exercise equipment leasing would increase by $45,000 per year. This expansion would increase Worcester's lunchtime rush hour capacity from the present 150 members to 225 members. A maximum of 30 percent of the total membership attends the Athletic Club during any one lunch hour. Therefore, Worcester's facility can presently serve a total membership of 500. Membership fees are $40 per month. Based on the following membership forecasts, determine what before-tax cash flows the expansion will produce for the next several years:

YEAR	1	2	3	4	5	6	7
MEMBERSHIP	450	480	510	515	530	550	600

7. The Astro World amusement park has the opportunity to expand its size now (the end of year 0) by purchasing adjacent property for $250,000 and adding attractions at a cost of $550,000. This expansion is expected to increase attendance by 30 percent over projected attendance without expansion. The price of admission is $30, with a $5 increase planned for the beginning of year 3. Additional operating costs are expected to be $100,000 per year. Estimated attendance for the next five years, *without expansion*, follows:

YEAR	1	2	3	4	5
ATTENDANCE	30,000	34,000	36,250	38,500	41,000

  a. What are the pretax combined cash flows for years 0 through 5 that are attributable to the park's expansion?
  b. Ignoring tax, depreciation, and the time value of money, determine how long it will take to recover (pay back) the investment.

8. Kim Epson operates a full-service car wash, which operates from 8 A.M. to 8 P.M., seven days a week. The car wash has two stations: an automatic washing and drying station and a manual interior cleaning station. The automatic washing and drying station can handle 30 cars per hour. The interior cleaning station can handle 200 cars per day. Based on a recent year-end review of operations, Kim estimates that future demand for the interior cleaning station for the seven days of the week, expressed in average number of cars per day, would be as follows:

DAY	Mon.	Tues.	Wed.	Thurs.	Fri.	Sat.	Sun.
CARS	160	180	150	140	280	300	250

  By installing additional equipment (at a cost of $50,000) Kim can increase the capacity of the interior cleaning station to 300 cars per day. Each car wash generates a pretax contribution of $4.00. Should Kim install the additional equipment if she expects a pretax payback period of three years or less?

Advanced Problems

Problems 9, 10 and 11 require reading of Supplement A, "Decision Making." Problem 11 requires reading of Supplement B, "Financial Analysis" on the Student CD-ROM.

9. **SmartDraw** A manager is trying to decide whether to buy one machine or two. If only one machine is purchased and demand proves to be excessive, the second machine can be purchased later. Some sales would be lost, however, because the lead time for delivery of this type of machine is six months. In addition, the cost per machine will be lower if both machines are purchased at the same time. The probability of low demand is estimated to be 0.30 and that of high demand to be 0.70. The after-tax net present value of the benefits (NPV) from purchasing two machines together is $90,000 if demand is low and $170,000 if demand is high.

  If one machine is purchased and demand is low, the NPV is $120,000. If demand is high, the manager has three options. Doing nothing, which has an NPV of $120,000; subcontracting, with an NPV of $140,000; and buying the second machine, with an NPV of $130,000.

  a. Draw a decision tree for this problem.
  b. What is the best decision and what is its expected payoff?

10. **SmartDraw** Acme Steel Fabricators has experienced booming business for the past five years. The company fabricates a wide range of steel products, such as railings, ladders, and light structural steel framing. The current manual method of materials handling is causing excessive inventories and congestion. Acme is considering the purchase of an overhead rail-mounted hoist system or a forklift truck to increase capacity and improve manufacturing efficiency.

  The annual pretax payoff from the system depends on future demand. If demand stays at the current level, the probability of which is 0.50, annual savings from the overhead hoist will be $10,000. If demand rises, the hoist will save $25,000 annually because of operating efficiencies in addition to new sales. Finally, if demand falls, the hoist will result in an estimated annual loss of $65,000. The probability is estimated to be 0.30 for higher demand and 0.20 for lower demand.

  If the forklift is purchased, annual payoffs will be $5,000 if demand is unchanged, $10,000 if demand rises, and −$25,000 if demand falls.

  a. Draw a decision tree for this problem and compute the expected value of the payoff for each alternative.
  b. Which is the best alternative, based on the expected values?

11. **SmartDraw** The vice president of operations at Dintell Corporation, a major supplier of passenger-side automotive air bags, is considering a $50 million expansion at the firm's Fort Worth production complex. The most recent economic projections indicate a 0.60 probability that the overall market will be $400 million per year over the next five years and a 0.40 probability that the market will be only $200 million per year during the same period. The marketing department estimates that Dintell has a 0.50 probability of capturing 40 percent of the market and an equal probability of obtaining only 30 percent of the market. The cost of goods sold is estimated to be 70 percent of sales. For planning purposes, the company currently uses a 12 percent discount rate, a 40 percent tax rate, and the MACRS depreciation schedule

(see Supplement B, "Financial Analysis" on the Student CD-ROM). The criteria for investment decisions at Dintell are (1) the net expected present value must be greater than zero; (2) there must be at least a 70 percent chance that the net present value will be positive; and (3) there must be no more than a 10 percent chance that the firm will lose more than 20 percent of the initial value.

a. Based on the stated criteria, determine whether Dintell should fund the project.

b. What effect will a probability of 0.70 of capturing 40 percent of the market have on the decision?

c. What effect will an increase in the discount rate of 15 percent have on the decision? A decrease of 10 percent?

d. What effect will the need for another $10 million in the third year have on the decision?

SELECTED REFERENCES

Bakke, Nils Arne, and Ronald Hellberg. "The Challenges of Capacity Planning." *International Journal of Production Economics,* 31–30 (1993), pp. 243–264.

Goldratt, E. Y., and J. Cox. *The Goal.* New York: North River, 1984.

Hammesfahr, R. D., Jack, James A. Pope, and Alireza Ardalan. "Strategic Planning for Production Capacity." *International Journal of Operations and Production Management,* vol. 13, no. 5 (1993), pp. 41–53.

"How Goliaths Can Act Like Davids." *Business Week/Enterprise* (1993), pp. 192–200.

Ritzman, Larry P., and M. Hossein Safizadeh. "Linking Process Choice with Plant-Level Decisions about Capital and Human Resources." *Production and Operations Management*, vol. 8, no. 4 (1999), pp. 374–392.

Simons, Jacob, Jr., and Wendell P. Simpson III. "An Exposition of Multiple Constraint Scheduling as Implemented in the Goal System (Formerly Disaster™)." *Production and Operations Management,* vol. 6, no. 1 (Spring 1997), pp. 3–22.

6S

Waiting Lines

Learning Goals

After reading this supplement, you will be able to . . .

1. recognize the elements of a waiting-line problem in a real situation.
2. use waiting-line models to estimate the operating characteristics of a system.
3. know when to use the single-server, multiple-server, and finite-source models.
4. describe how waiting-line models can be used to make managerial decisions.

ANYONE WHO HAS HAD to wait at a stoplight, at McDonald's, or at the registrar's office has experienced the dynamics of waiting lines. Perhaps one of the best examples of effective management of waiting lines is that of Walt Disney World. One day there may be only 25,000 customers, but on another day there may be 90,000. Careful analysis of process flows, technology for people-mover (materials handling) equipment, capacity, and layout keeps the waiting times for attractions to acceptable levels.

The analysis of waiting lines is of concern to managers because it affects design, capacity planning, layout planning, inventory management, and scheduling. In this supplement we discuss why waiting lines form, the uses of waiting-line models in operations management, and the structure of waiting-line models. We also discuss the decisions managers address with the models. Waiting lines can also be analyzed using computer simulation. Software such as SimQuick, an optional simulation package, can be used to analyze the problems in this supplement (see Supplement G, "Simulation" for more details).

WHY WAITING LINES FORM

waiting line One or more "customers" waiting for service.

A **waiting line** is one or more "customers" waiting for service. The customers can be people or inanimate objects such as machines requiring maintenance, sales orders waiting for shipping, or inventory items waiting to be used. A waiting line forms because of a temporary imbalance between the demand for service and the capacity of the system to provide the service. In most real-life waiting-line problems, the demand rate varies; that is, customers arrive at unpredictable intervals. Most often, the rate of producing the service also varies, depending on customer needs. Suppose that bank customers arrive at an average rate of 15 per hour throughout the day and that the bank can process an average of 20 customers per hour. Why would a waiting line ever develop? The answers are that the customer arrival rate varies throughout the day and the time required to process a customer can vary. During the noon hour, 30 customers may arrive at the bank. Some of them may have complicated transactions, requiring above-average process times. The waiting line may grow to 15 customers for a period of time before it eventually disappears. Even though the bank manager provided for more than enough capacity on average, waiting lines can still develop.

Waiting lines can develop even if the time to process a customer is constant. For example, a subway train is computer controlled to arrive at stations along its route. Each train is programmed to arrive at a station, say, every 15 minutes. Even with the constant service time, waiting lines develop while riders wait for the next train or cannot get on a train because of the size of the crowd at a busy time of the day. Consequently, variability in the rate of demand determines the sizes of the waiting lines in this case. In general, if there is no variability in the demand and service rates and enough capacity has been provided, no waiting lines form.

USES OF WAITING-LINE THEORY

Waiting-line theory applies to service as well as manufacturing firms, relating customer arrival and service-system processing characteristics to service-system output characteristics. In our discussion, we use the term *service* broadly—the act of doing work for a customer. The service system might be hair cutting at a hair salon, satisfying customer complaints, or processing a production order of parts on a certain machine. Other examples of customers and services include lines of theatergoers waiting to purchase tickets, trucks waiting to be unloaded at a warehouse, machines waiting to be repaired by a maintenance crew, and patients waiting to be examined by a physician. Regardless of the situation, waiting-line problems have several common elements.

STRUCTURE OF WAITING-LINE PROBLEMS

customer population An input that generates potential customers.

service facility A person (or crew), a machine (or group of machines), or both necessary to perform the service for the customer.

Analyzing waiting-line problems begins with a description of the situation's basic elements. Each specific situation will have different characteristics, but four elements are common to all situations:

1. an input, or **customer population**, that generates potential customers
2. a waiting line of customers
3. the **service facility,** consisting of a person (or crew), a machine (or group of machines), or both necessary to perform the service for the customer
4. a **priority rule,** which selects the next customer to be served by the service facility

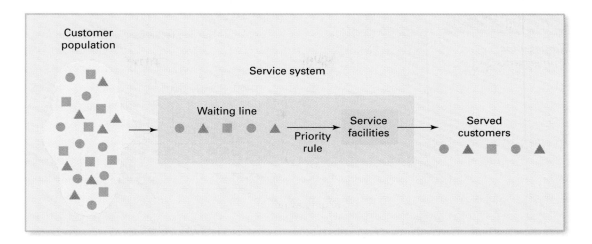

FIGURE 6S.1

*Basic Elements of
Waiting-Line Models*

priority rule A rule that
selects the next customer
to be served at the service
facility.

service system The
number of lines and the
arrangement of the
facilities.

Figure 6S.1 shows these basic elements. The **service system** describes the number of lines and the arrangement of the facilities. After the service has been performed, the served customers leave the system.

CUSTOMER POPULATION

A customer population is the source of input to the service system. If the potential number of new customers for the service system is appreciably affected by the number of customers already in the system, the input source is said to be *finite*. For example, suppose that a maintenance crew is assigned responsibility for the repair of 10 machines. The customer population for the maintenance crew is 10 machines in working order. The population generates customers for the maintenance crew as a function of the failure rates for the machines. As more machines fail and enter the service system, either waiting for service or being repaired, the customer population becomes smaller and the rate at which it can generate another customer falls. Consequently, the customer population is said to be finite.

Alternatively, an *infinite* customer population is one in which the number of customers in the system does not affect the rate at which the population generates new customers. For example, consider a mail-order operation for which the customer population consists of shoppers who have received a catalog of products sold by the company. Because the customer population is so large and only a small fraction of the shoppers place orders at any one time, the number of new orders it generates is not appreciably affected by the number of orders waiting for service or being processed by the service system. In this case, the customer population is said to be infinite.

Customers in waiting lines may be *patient* or *impatient*, which has nothing to do with the colorful language a customer may use while waiting in line for a long time on a hot day. In the context of waiting-line problems, a patient customer is one who enters the system and remains there until being served; an impatient customer is one who either decides not to enter the system (balks) or leaves the system before being served (reneges). For the methods used in this supplement, we make the simplifying assumption that all customers are patient.

THE SERVICE SYSTEM

The service system may be described by the number of lines and the arrangement of facilities.

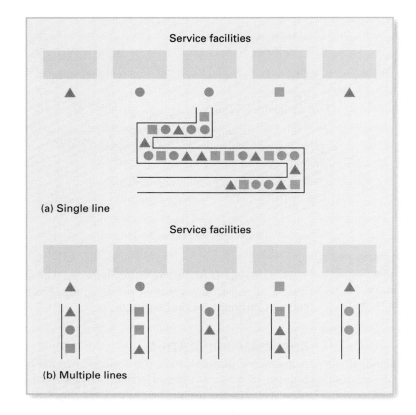

NUMBER OF LINES. Waiting lines may be designed to be a *single line* or *multiple lines*. Figure 6S.2 shows an example of each arrangement. Generally, single lines are utilized at airline counters, inside banks, and at some fast-food restaurants, whereas multiple lines are utilized in grocery stores, at drive-in bank operations, and in discount stores. When multiple servers are available and each one can handle general transactions, the single-line arrangement keeps servers uniformly busy and gives customers a sense of fairness. Customers believe that they are being served on the basis of when they arrived, not how well they guessed their waiting time when selecting a particular line. The multiple-line design is best when some of the servers provide a limited set of services. In this arrangement, customers select the services they need and wait in the line where that service is provided, such as at a grocery store where there are special lines for customers paying with cash or having fewer than 10 items.

Sometimes queues are not organized neatly into "lines." Machines that need repair on the production floor of a factory may be left in place, and the maintenance crew comes to them. Nonetheless, we can think of such machines as forming a single line or multiple lines, depending on the number of repair crews and their specialties. Likewise, passengers who telephone for a taxi also form a line even though they may wait at different locations.

ARRANGEMENT OF SERVICE FACILITIES. Service facilities consist of the personnel and equipment necessary to perform the service for the customer. Figure 6S.3 shows examples of the five basic types of service facility arrangements. Managers should choose an arrangement based on customer volume and the nature of services performed. Some services require a single step, also called a **phase**, whereas others require a sequence of steps.

phase A single step in providing a service.

Weary tourists wait to check in at a hotel registration desk.

In the *single-channel, single-phase* system, all services demanded by a customer can be performed by a single-server facility. Customers form a single line and go through the service facility one at a time. Examples are a drive-through car wash and a machine that must process several batches of parts.

The *single-channel, multiple-phase* arrangement is used when the services are best performed in sequence by more than one facility, yet customer volume or other constraints limit the design to one channel. Customers form a single line and proceed sequentially from one service facility to the next. An example of this arrangement is a McDonald's drive-through, where the first facility takes the order, the second takes the money, and the third provides the food.

FIGURE 6S.3

Examples of Service Facility Arrangements

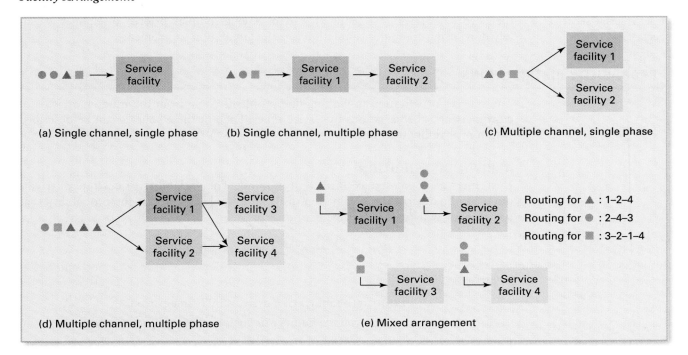

The *multiple-channel, single-phase* arrangement is used when demand is large enough to warrant providing the same service at more than one facility or when the services offered by the facilities are different. Customers form one or more lines, depending on the design. In the single-line design, customers are served by the first available server, as in the lobby of a bank. If each channel has its own waiting line, customers wait until the server for their line can serve them, as at a bank's drive-through facilities.

The *multiple-channel, multiple-phase* arrangement occurs when customers can be served by one of the first-phase facilities but then require service from a second-phase facility, and so on. In some cases, customers cannot switch channels after service has begun; in others they can. An example of this arrangement is a laundromat. Washing machines are the first-phase facilities, and dryers are the second-phase facilities. Some of the washing machines and dryers may be designed for extra-large loads, thereby providing the customer a choice of channels.

The most complex waiting-line problem involves customers who have unique sequences of required services; consequently, service cannot be described neatly in phases. A *mixed* arrangement is used in such a case. In the mixed arrangement, waiting lines can develop in front of each facility, as in a job shop, where each customized job may require the use of various machines and different routings.

PRIORITY RULE

The priority rule determines which customer to serve next. Most service systems that you encounter use the first-come, first-served (FCFS) rule. The customer at the head of the waiting line has the highest priority, and the customer who arrived last has the lowest priority. Other priority disciplines might take the customer with the earliest promised due date (EDD) or the customer with the shortest expected processing time (SPT). We focus on FCFS in this supplement and discuss EDD and SPT elsewhere (see Chapter 11, "Aggregate Planning and Scheduling").

preemptive discipline A rule that allows a customer of higher priority to interrupt the service of another customer.

A **preemptive discipline** is a rule that allows a customer of higher priority to interrupt the service of another customer. For example, in a hospital emergency room, patients with the most life-threatening injuries receive treatment first, regardless of their order of arrival. Modeling of systems having complex priority disciplines is usually done using computer simulation (see the Simulation supplement).

PROBABILITY DISTRIBUTIONS

The sources of variation in waiting-line problems come from the random arrivals of customers and the variations in service times. Each of these sources can be described with a probability distribution.

ARRIVAL DISTRIBUTION

Customers arrive at service facilities randomly. The variability of customer arrivals often can be described by a Poisson distribution, which specifies the probability that *n* customers will arrive in T time periods:

$$P(n) = \frac{(\lambda T)^n}{n!}\, e^{-\lambda T} \qquad \text{for } n = 0, 1, 2, \ldots$$

where

$P(n)$ = probability of n arrivals in T time periods

λ = average number of customer arrivals per period

$e = 2.7183$

The mean of the Poisson distribution is λT, and the variance also is λT. The Poisson distribution is a discrete distribution; that is, the probabilities are for a specific number of arrivals per unit of time.

EXAMPLE 6S.1

Calculating the Probability of Customer Arrivals

Management is redesigning the customer service process in a large department store. Accommodating four customers is important. Customers arrive at the desk at the rate of two customers per hour. What is the probability that four customers will arrive during any hour?

SOLUTION

In this case $\lambda = 2$ customers per hour, $T = 1$ hour, and $n = 4$ customers. The probability that four customers will arrive in any hour is

$$P(4) = \frac{[2(1)]^4}{4!} \, e^{-2(1)} = \frac{16}{24} \, e^{-2} = 0.090$$

Decision Point The manager of the customer service desk can use this information to determine the space requirements for the desk and waiting area. There is a relatively small probability that four customers will arrive in any hour. Consequently, seating capacity for two or three customers should be more than adequate unless the time to service each customer is lengthy. Further analysis on service times is warranted. ❐

interarrival times The time between customer arrivals.

Another way to specify the arrival distribution is to do it in terms of customer **interarrival times**—that is, the time between customer arrivals. If the customer population generates customers according to a Poisson distribution, the *exponential distribution* describes the probability that the next customer will arrive in the next T time periods. As the exponential distribution also describes service times, we discuss the details of this distribution in the next section.

SERVICE TIME DISTRIBUTION

The exponential distribution describes the probability that the service time of the customer at a particular facility will be no more than T time periods. The probability can be calculated by using the formula

$$P(t \leq T) = 1 - e^{-\mu T}$$

where

μ = mean number of customers completing service per period

t = service time of the customer

T = target service time

The mean of the service time distribution is $1/\mu$, and the variance is $(1/\mu)^2$. As T increases, the probability that the customer's service time will be less than T approaches 1.0.

For simplicity, let us look at a single-channel, single-phase arrangement.

EXAMPLE 6S.2

Calculating the Service Time Probability

The management of the large department store in Example 6S.1 must determine if more training is needed for the customer service clerk. The clerk at the customer service desk can serve an average of three customers per hour. What is the probability that a customer will require less than 10 minutes of service?

SOLUTION

We must have all the data in the same time units. Because $\mu = 3$ customers per *hour*, we convert minutes of time to hours, or $T = 10$ minutes $= 10/60$ hour $= 0.167$ hour. Then

$$P(t \leq T) = 1 - e^{-\mu T}$$
$$P(t \leq 0.167 \text{ hour}) = 1 - e^{-3(0.167)} = 1 - 0.61 = 0.39$$

Decision Point The probability that the clerk will require only 10 minutes or less is not very high, which leaves the possibility that customers may experience lengthy delays. Management should consider additional training for the clerk so as to reduce the time it takes to process a customer request. ⌐

Some characteristics of the exponential distribution do not always conform to an actual situation. The exponential distribution model is based on the assumption that each service time is independent of those that preceded it. In real life, however, productivity may improve as human servers learn about the work. Another assumption underlying the model is that very small, as well as very large, service times are possible. However, real-life situations often require a fixed-length start-up time, some cutoff on total service time, or nearly constant service time.

USING WAITING-LINE MODELS TO ANALYZE OPERATIONS

Operations managers can use waiting-line models to balance the gains that might be made by increasing the efficiency of the service system against the costs of doing so. In addition, managers should consider the costs of *not* making improvements to the system: Long waiting lines or long waiting times may cause customers to balk or renege. Managers should therefore be concerned about the following operating characteristics of the system.

1. *Line Length.* The number of customers in the waiting line reflects one of two conditions. Short queues could mean either good customer service or too much capacity. Similarly, long queues could indicate either low server efficiency or the need to increase capacity.

2. *Number of Customers in System.* The number of customers in queue and being served also relates to service efficiency and capacity. A large number of customers in the system causes congestion and may result in customer dissatisfaction, unless more capacity is added.

3. *Waiting Time in Line.* Long lines do not always mean long waiting times. If the service rate is fast, a long line can be served efficiently. However, when waiting time seems long, customers perceive the quality of service to be poor. Managers may try to change the arrival rate of customers or design the system to make long wait times seem shorter than they really are. For example, at Walt Disney World customers in line for an attraction are entertained by videos and also are informed about expected waiting times, which seems to help them endure the wait.

4. *Total Time in System.* The total elapsed time from entry into the system until exit from the system may indicate problems with customers, server efficiency, or capacity. If some customers are spending too much time in the service system, there may be a need to change the priority discipline, increase productivity, or adjust capacity in some way.

5. *Service Facility Utilization.* The collective utilization of service facilities reflects the percentage of time that they are busy. Management's goal is to

maintain high utilization and profitability without adversely affecting the other operating characteristics.

The best method for analyzing a waiting-line problem is to relate the five operating characteristics and their alternatives to dollars. However, placing a dollar figure on certain characteristics (such as the waiting time of a shopper in a grocery store) is difficult. In such cases, an analyst must weigh the cost of implementing the alternative under consideration against a subjective assessment of the cost of *not* making the change.

We now present three models and some examples showing how waiting-line models can help operations managers make decisions. We analyze problems requiring the single-server, multiple-server, and finite-source models, all of which are single phase. References to more advanced models are cited at the end of this supplement.

SINGLE-SERVER MODEL

The simplest waiting-line model involves a single server and a single line of customers. To further specify the model, we make the following assumptions:

1. The customer population is infinite and all customers are patient.
2. The customers arrive according to a Poisson distribution with a mean arrival rate of λ.
3. The service distribution is exponential with a mean service rate of μ.
4. Customers are served on a first-come, first-served basis.
5. The length of the waiting line is unlimited.

With these assumptions we can apply various formulas to describe the operating characteristics of the system:

$$\rho = \text{average utilization of the system}$$
$$= \frac{\lambda}{\mu}$$

$$P_n = \text{probability that } n \text{ customers are in the system}$$
$$= (1 - \rho)\rho^n$$

$$L = \text{average number of customers in the service system}$$
$$= \frac{\lambda}{\mu - \lambda}$$

$$L_q = \text{average number of customers in the waiting line}$$
$$= \rho L$$

$$W = \text{average time spent in the system, including service}$$
$$= \frac{1}{\mu - \lambda}$$

$$W_q = \text{average waiting time in line}$$
$$= \rho W$$

EXAMPLE 6S.3	*Calculating the Operating Characteristics of a Single-Channel, Single-Phase System*

The manager of a grocery store in the retirement community of Sunnyville is interested in providing good service to the senior citizens who shop in his store. Presently, the store has a separate checkout counter for senior citizens. On average, 30 senior citizens per hour arrive at the counter, according to a Poisson distribution, and are served at an average rate of 35 customers per hour, with exponential service times. Find the following operating characteristics:

  a. Probability of zero customers in the system
  b. Utilization of the checkout clerk
  c. Number of customers in the system
  d. Number of customers in line
  e. Time spent in the system
  f. Waiting time in line

SOLUTION

The checkout counter can be modeled as a single-channel, single-phase system. Figure 6S.4 shows the results from the *Waiting-Lines* Solver from OM Explorer. Manual calculations of the equations for the *single-server model* are demonstrated in Solved Problem 1 at the end of the supplement.

Solver - Waiting Lines

Enter data in yellow - shaded areas.

◉ Single-server model   ○ Multiple-server model   ○ Finite-source model

Servers		(Number of servers is assumed to be 1 in single-server model.)
Arrival Rate (λ)	30	
Service Rate (μ)	35	

Probability of zero customers in the system (P_0)		0.1429
Probability of exactly ▾ 0 customers in the system		0.1429
Average utilization of the server (ρ)		0.8571
Average number of customers in the system (L)		6.0000
Average number of customers in line (L_q)		5.1429
Average waiting/service time in the system (W)		0.2000
Average waiting time in line (W_q)		0.1714

FIGURE 6S.4

Both the average waiting time in the system (W) and the average time spent waiting in line (W_q) are expressed in hours. To convert the results to minutes, simply multiply by 60 minutes/hour. For example, $W = 0.20(60) = 12.00$ minutes, and $W_q = 0.1714(60) = 10.28$ minutes. ❐

EXAMPLE 6S.4	*Analyzing Service Rates with the Single-Server Model*

The manager of the Sunnyville grocery in Example 6S.3 wants answers to the following questions:

  a. What service rate would be required to have customers average only eight minutes in the system?
  b. For that service rate, what is the probability of having more than four customers in the system?
  c. What service rate would be required to have only a 10 percent chance of exceeding four customers in the system?

TUTOR 6S.1

SOLUTION

The *Waiting-Lines* Solver from OM Explorer could be used iteratively to answer the questions. Here we show how to solve the problem manually.

a. We use the equation for the average time in the system and solve for μ.

$$W = \frac{1}{\mu - \lambda}$$

$$8 \text{ minutes} = 0.133 \text{ hour} = \frac{1}{\mu - 30}$$

$$0.133\mu - 0.133(30) = 1$$

$$\mu = 37.52 \text{ customers/hour}$$

b. The probability that there will be more than four customers in the system equals 1 minus the probability that there are four or fewer customers in the system.

$$P = 1 - \sum_{n=0}^{4} P_n$$

$$= 1 - \sum_{n=0}^{4} (1 - \rho)\rho^n$$

and

$$\rho = \frac{30}{37.52} = 0.80$$

Then

$$P = 1 - 0.2(1 + 0.8 + 0.8^2 + 0.8^3 + 0.8^4)$$

$$= 1 - 0.672 = 0.328$$

Therefore, there is a nearly 33 percent chance that more than four customers will be in the system.

c. We use the same logic as in part (b), except that μ is now a decision variable. The easiest way to proceed is to find the correct average utilization first and then solve for the service rate.

$$P = 1 - (1 - \rho)(1 + \rho + \rho^2 + \rho^3 + \rho^4)$$

$$= 1 - (1 + \rho + \rho^2 + \rho^3 + \rho^4) + \rho(1 + \rho + \rho^2 + \rho^3 + \rho^4)$$

$$= 1 - 1 - \rho - \rho^2 - \rho^3 - \rho^4 + \rho + \rho^2 + \rho^3 + \rho^4 + \rho^5$$

$$= \rho^5$$

or

$$\rho = P^{1/5}$$

If $P = 0.10$,

$$\rho = (0.10)^{1/5} = 0.63$$

Therefore, for a utilization rate of 63 percent, the probability of more than four customers in the system is 10 percent. For $\lambda = 30$, the mean service rate must be

$$\frac{30}{\mu} = 0.63$$

$$\mu = 47.62 \text{ customers/hour}$$

Decision Point The service rate would only have to modestly increase to achieve the eight-minute target. However, the probability of having more than four customers in the system is too high. The manager must now find a way to increase the service rate from 35 per hour to approximately 48 per hour. She can increase the service rate in several different ways, ranging from employing a high school student to help bag the groceries to installing electronic point-of-sale equipment that reads the prices from bar-coded information on each item. ⊐

MULTIPLE-SERVER MODEL

With the multiple-server model, customers form a single line and choose one of s servers when one is available. The service system has only one phase. We make the following assumption in addition to those for the single-server model: There are s identical servers, and the service distribution for each server is exponential, with a mean service time of $1/\mu$.

With these assumptions, we can apply several formulas to describe the operating characteristics of the service system:

$$\rho = \text{average utilization of the system}$$

$$= \frac{\lambda}{s\mu}$$

$$P_0 = \text{probability that zero customers are in the system}$$

$$= \left[\sum_{n=0}^{s-1} \frac{(\lambda/\mu)^n}{n!} + \frac{(\lambda/\mu)^s}{s!} \left(\frac{1}{1-\rho} \right) \right]^{-1}$$

$$P_n = \text{probability that } n \text{ customers are in the system}$$

$$= \begin{cases} \dfrac{(\lambda/\mu)^n}{n!} P_0, & 0 < n < s \\[2mm] \dfrac{(\lambda/\mu)^n}{s!s^{n-s}} P_0, & n \geq s \end{cases}$$

$$L_q = \text{average number of customers in line}$$

$$= \frac{P_0(\lambda/\mu)^s \rho}{s!(1-\rho)^2}$$

$$W_q = \text{average waiting time of customers in line}$$

$$= \frac{L_q}{\lambda}$$

$$W = \text{average time spent in the system, including service}$$

$$= W_q + \frac{1}{\mu}$$

$$L = \text{average number of customers in the service system}$$

$$= \lambda W$$

A U.S. Postal Service
worker loads a
delivery van.

EXAMPLE 6S.5

Estimating Idle Time and Hourly Operating Costs with the Multiple-Server Model

The management of the American Parcel Service terminal in Verona, Wisconsin, is concerned about the amount of time the company's trucks are idle, waiting to be unloaded. The terminal operates with four unloading bays. Each bay requires a crew of two employees, and each crew costs $30 per hour. The estimated cost of an idle truck is $50 per hour. Trucks arrive at an average rate of three per hour, according to a Poisson distribution. On average, a crew can unload a semitrailer rig in one hour, with exponential service times. What is the total hourly cost of operating the system?

**TUTOR
6S.2**

SOLUTION

The *multiple-server model* is appropriate. To find the total cost of labor and idle trucks, we must calculate the average number of trucks in the system.

Figure 6S.5 shows the results for the American Parcel Service problem using the *Waiting-Lines* Solver from OM Explorer. Manual calculations using the equations for the *multiple-server model* are demonstrated in Solved Problem 2 at the end of this supplement. The results show that the four-bay design will be utilized 75 percent of the time and that the average number of trucks either being serviced or waiting in line is 4.53 trucks. We can now calculate the hourly costs of labor and idle trucks:

Labor cost:	$30(s) = $30(4)$	$= $120.00
Idle truck cost:	$50(L) = $50(4.53)$	$= \underline{226.50}$
	Total hourly cost	$= $346.50

Decision Point Management must now assess whether $346.50 per day for this operation is acceptable. Attempting to reduce costs by eliminating crews will only increase the waiting time

Solver - Waiting Lines

Enter data in yellow-shaded areas.

○ Single-server model   ◉ Multiple-server model   ○ Finite-source model

Servers	4
Arrival Rate (λ)	3
Service Rate (μ)	1

Probability of zero customers in the system (P_0)	0.0377
Probability of [exactly ▼] 0 customers in the system	0.0377
Average utilization of the server (ρ)	0.7500
Average number of customers in the system (L)	4.5283
Average number of customers in line (L_q)	1.5283
Average waiting/service time in the system (W)	1.5094
Average waiting time in line (W_q)	0.5094

FIGURE 6S.5

of the trucks, which is more expensive per hour than the crews. However, if the service rate can be increased through better work methods, for example, L can be reduced and daily operating costs will be less. ❐

FINITE-SOURCE MODEL

We now consider a situation in which all but one of the assumptions of the single-server model are appropriate. In this case, the customer population is finite, having only N potential customers. If N is greater than 30 customers, the single-server model with the assumption of an infinite customer population is adequate. Otherwise, the finite-source model is the one to use. The formulas used to calculate the operating characteristics of this service system are

P_0 = probability that zero customers are in the system

$$= \left[\sum_{n=0}^{N} \frac{N!}{(N-n)!} \left(\frac{\lambda}{\mu} \right)^n \right]^{-1}$$

ρ = average utilization of the server

$$= 1 - P_0$$

L_q = average number of customers in line

$$= N - \frac{\lambda + \mu}{\lambda} (1 - P_0)$$

L = average number of customers in the system

$$= N - \frac{\mu}{\lambda} (1 - P_0)$$

W_q = average waiting time in line

$$= L_q[(N - L)\lambda]^{-1}$$

$$W = \text{average time in the system}$$

$$= L[(N - L)\lambda]^{-1}$$

| EXAMPLE 6S.6 | *Analyzing Maintenance Costs with the Finite-Source Model* |

**TUTOR
6S.3**

The Worthington Gear Company installed a bank of 10 robots about three years ago. The robots greatly increased the firm's labor productivity, but recently attention has focused on maintenance. The firm does no preventive maintenance on the robots because of the variability in the breakdown distribution. Each machine has an exponential breakdown (or interarrival) distribution with an average time between failures of 200 hours. Each machine hour lost to downtime costs $30, which means that the firm has to react quickly to machine failure. The firm employs one maintenance person, who needs 10 hours on average to fix a robot. Actual maintenance times are exponentially distributed. The wage rate is $10 per hour for the maintenance person, who can be put to work productively elsewhere when not fixing robots. Determine the daily cost of labor and robot downtime.

SOLUTION

The *finite-source model* is appropriate for this analysis because there are only 10 machines in the customer population and the other assumptions are satisfied. Here, $\lambda = 1/200$, or 0.005 breakdown per hour, and $\mu = 1/10 = 0.10$ robot per hour. To calculate the cost of labor and robot downtime, we need to estimate the average utilization of the maintenance person and L, the average number of robots in the maintenance system. Figure 6S.6 shows the results for the Worthington Gear Problem using the *Waiting-Lines* Solver from OM Explorer. Manual computations using the equations for the *finite-source model* are demonstrated in Solved Problem 3 at the end of this supplement. The results show that the maintenance person is utilized only 46.2 percent of the time and the average number of robots waiting in line or being repaired is 0.76 robot. However, a failed robot will spend an average of 16.43 hours in the repair system, of which 6.43 hours of that time is spent waiting for service.

The daily cost of labor and robot downtime is

Labor cost:	($10/hour)(8 hours/day)(0.462 utilization) = $ 36.96
Idle robot cost:	(0.76 robot)($30/robot hour)(8 hours/day) = 182.40
	Total daily cost = $219.36

Inputs

Solver - Waiting Lines

Enter data in yellow-shaded areas.

○ Single-server model   ○ Multiple-server model   ◉ Finite-source model

Customers	10
Arrival Rate (λ)	0.005
Service Rate (μ)	0.1

Probability of zero customers in the system (P_0)	0.5380
Probability of [fewer than ▼] 0 customers in the system	#N/A
Average utilization of the server (ρ)	0.4620
Average number of customers in the system (L)	0.7593
Average number of customers in line (L_q)	0.2972
Average waiting/service time in the system (W)	16.4330
Average waiting time in line (W_q)	6.4330

FIGURE 6S.6

Decision Point   The labor cost for robot repair is only 20 percent of the idle cost of the robots. Management might consider having a second repair person on call in the event two or more robots are waiting for repair at the same time. ❐

DECISION AREAS FOR MANAGEMENT

After analyzing a waiting-line problem, management can improve the service system by making changes in one or more of the following areas.

1. *Arrival Rates.*   Management often can affect the rate of customer arrivals, λ, through advertising, special promotions, or differential pricing. For example, a telephone company uses differential pricing to shift residential long-distance calls from daytime hours to evening hours.

2. *Number of Service Facilities.*   By increasing the number of service facilities, such as tool cribs, toll booths, or bank tellers, or by dedicating some facilities in a phase to a unique set of services, management can increase system capacity.

3. *Number of Phases.*   Managers can decide to allocate service tasks to sequential phases if they determine that two sequential service facilities may be more efficient than one. For instance, in the assembly-line problem discussed in Chapter 7, "Location and Layout," the decision concerns the number of phases needed along the assembly line. Determining the number of workers needed on the line also involves assigning a certain set of work elements to each one. Changing the facility arrangement can increase the service rate, μ, of each facility and the capacity of the system.

4. *Number of Servers per Facility.*   Managers can influence the service rate by assigning more than one person to a service facility.

5. *Server Efficiency.*   By adjusting the capital-to-labor ratio, devising improved work methods, or instituting incentive programs, management can increase the efficiency of servers assigned to a service facility. Such changes are reflected in μ.

6. *Priority Rule.*   Managers set the priority rule to be used, decide whether to have a different priority rule for each service facility, and decide whether to allow preemption (and, if so, under what conditions). Such decisions affect the waiting times of the customers and the utilization of the servers.

7. *Line Arrangement.*   Managers can influence customer waiting times and server utilization by deciding whether to have a single line or a line for each facility in a given phase of service.

Obviously, these factors are interrelated. An adjustment in the customer arrival rate, λ, might have to be accompanied by an increase in the service rate, μ, in some way. Decisions about the number of facilities, the number of phases, and waiting-line arrangements also are related.

For each of the problems we analyzed with the waiting-line models, the arrivals had a Poisson distribution (or exponential interarrival times), the service times had an exponential distribution, the service facilities had a simple arrangement, and the priority discipline was first come, first served. Waiting-line theory has been used to develop other models in which these criteria are not met, but these models are very complex. Many times the nature of the customer population, the constraints on the line, the priority rule, the service-time distribution, and the arrangement of the facilities are such that waiting-line theory is no longer useful. In these cases, simulation often is used (see Supplement G, "Simulation").

EQUATION SUMMARY

1. Customer arrival Poisson distribution: $P_n = \dfrac{(\lambda T)^n}{n!} e^{-\lambda T}$

2. Service-time exponential distribution: $P(t \le T) = 1 - e^{-\mu T}$

	SINGLE-SERVER MODEL	MULTIPLE-SERVER MODEL	FINITE-SOURCE MODEL
Average utilization of the system	$\rho = \dfrac{\lambda}{\mu}$	$\rho = \dfrac{\lambda}{s\mu}$	$\rho = 1 - P_0$
Probability that n customers are in the system	$P_n = (1 - \rho)\rho^n$	$P_n = \begin{cases} \dfrac{(\lambda/\mu)^n}{n!} P_0, & 0 < n < s \\ \dfrac{(\lambda/\mu)^n}{s! \, s^{n-s}} P_0, & n \ge s \end{cases}$	
Probability that zero customers are in the system	$P_0 = 1 - \rho$	$P_0 = \left[\displaystyle\sum_{n=0}^{s-1} \dfrac{(\lambda/\mu)^n}{n!} + \dfrac{(\lambda/\mu)^s}{s!} \left(\dfrac{1}{1 - \rho} \right) \right]^{-1}$	$P_0 = \left[\displaystyle\sum_{n=0}^{N} \dfrac{N!}{(N-n)!} \left(\dfrac{\lambda}{\mu} \right)^n \right]^{-1}$
Average number of customers in the service system	$L = \dfrac{\lambda}{\mu - \lambda}$	$L = \lambda W$	$L = N - \dfrac{\mu}{\lambda}(1 - P_0)$
Average number of customers in the waiting line	$L_q = \rho L$	$L_q = \dfrac{P_0(\lambda/\mu)^s \rho}{s!(1 - \rho)^2}$	$L_q = N - \dfrac{\lambda + \mu}{\lambda}(1 - P_0)$
Average time spent in the system, including service	$W = \dfrac{1}{\mu - \lambda}$	$W = W_q + \dfrac{1}{\mu}$	$W = L[(N - L)\lambda]^{-1}$
Average waiting time in line	$W_q = \rho W$	$W_q = \dfrac{L_q}{\lambda}$	$W_q = L_q[(N - L)\lambda]^{-1}$

SUPPLEMENT HIGHLIGHTS

❐ Waiting lines form when customers arrive at a faster rate than they are being served. Because customer arrival rates vary, long waiting lines may occur even when the system's designed service rate is substantially higher than the average customer arrival rate.

❐ Four elements are common to all waiting-line problems: a customer population, a waiting line, a service system, and a priority rule for determining which customer is to be served next.

❐ Waiting-line models have been developed for use in analyzing service systems. If the assumptions made in creating a waiting-line model are consistent with an actual situation, the model's formulas can be solved to predict the performance of the system with respect to server utilization, average customer waiting time, and the average number of customers in the system.

SOLVED PROBLEM 1

A photographer at the post office takes passport pictures at an average rate of 20 pictures per hour. The photographer must wait until the customer blinks or scowls, so the time to take a picture is exponentially distributed. Customers arrive at a Poisson-distributed average rate of 19 customers per hour.

a. What is the utilization of the photographer?

b. How much time will the average customer spend at the photograph step of the passport issuing process?

SOLUTION

a. The assumptions in the problem statement are consistent with a single-server model. Utilization is

$$\rho = \frac{\lambda}{\mu} = \frac{19}{20} = 0.95$$

b. The average customer time spent at the photographer's station is

$$W = \frac{1}{\mu - \lambda} = \frac{1}{20 - 19} = 1 \text{ hour}$$

SOLVED PROBLEM 2

The Mega Multiplex Movie Theater has three concession clerks serving customers on a first-come, first-served basis. The service time per customer is exponentially distributed with an average of 2 minutes per customer. Concession customers wait in a single line in a large lobby, and arrivals are Poisson distributed with an average of 81 customers per hour. Previews run for 10 minutes before the start of each show. If the average time in the concession area exceeds 10 minutes, customers become dissatisfied.

a. What is the average utilization of the concession clerks?

b. What is the average time spent in the concession area?

SOLUTION

a. The problem statement is consistent with the multiple-server model, and the average utilization rate is

$$\rho = \frac{\lambda}{s\mu} = \frac{81 \text{ customers/hour}}{(3 \text{ servers}) \left(\dfrac{60 \text{ minutes/server hour}}{2 \text{ minutes/customer}} \right)} = 0.90$$

The concession clerks are busy 90 percent of the time.

b. The average time spent in the system, W, is

$$W = W_q + \frac{1}{\mu}$$

Here

$$W_q = \frac{L_q}{\lambda}, \qquad L_q = \frac{P_0(\lambda/\mu)^s \rho}{s!(1 - \rho)^2}, \qquad \text{and} \qquad P_0 = \left[\sum_{n=0}^{s-1} \frac{(\lambda/\mu)^n}{n!} + \frac{(\lambda/\mu)^s}{s!} \left(\frac{1}{1 - \rho} \right) \right]^{-1}$$

We must solve for P_0, L_q, and W_q, in that order, before we can solve for W:

$$P_0 = \left[\sum_{n=0}^{s-1} \frac{(\lambda/\mu)^n}{n!} + \frac{(\lambda/\mu)^s}{s!} \left(\frac{1}{1 - \rho} \right) \right]^{-1}$$

$$= \frac{1}{1 + \frac{(81/30)}{1} + \frac{(2.7)^2}{2} + \left[\frac{(2.7)^3}{6} \left(\frac{1}{1 - 0.9} \right) \right]}$$

$$= \frac{1}{1 + 2.7 + 3.645 + 32.805} = \frac{1}{40.15} = 0.0249$$

$$L_q = \frac{P_0(\lambda/\mu)^s \rho}{s!(1 - \rho)^2} = \frac{0.0249 \, (81/30)^3 (0.9)}{3!(1 - 0.9)^2} = \frac{0.4411}{6(0.01)} = 7.352 \text{ customers}$$

$$W_q = \frac{L_q}{\lambda} = \frac{7.352 \text{ customers}}{81 \text{ customers/hour}} = 0.0908 \text{ hour}$$

$$W = W_q + \frac{1}{\mu} = 0.0908 \text{ hour} + \frac{1}{30} \text{ hour} = (0.1241 \text{ hour}) \left(\frac{60 \text{ minutes}}{\text{hour}} \right)$$

$$= 7.45 \text{ minutes}$$

With three concession clerks, customers will spend an average of 7.45 minutes in the concession area.

SOLVED PROBLEM 3

The Severance Coal Mine serves six trains having exponentially distributed interarrival times averaging 30 hours. The time required to fill a train with coal varies with the number of cars, weather-related delays, and equipment breakdowns. The time to fill a train can be approximated by a negative exponential distribution with a mean of 6 hours 40 minutes. The railroad requires the coal mine to pay very large demurrage charges in the event that a train spends more than 24 hours at the mine. What is the average time a train will spend at the mine?

SOLUTION

The problem statement describes a finite-source model, with $N = 6$. The average time spent at the mine is $W = L [(N - L)\lambda]^{-1}$, with $1/\lambda = 30$ hours/train, $\lambda = 0.8$ train/day, and $\mu = 3.6$ trains/day. In this case,

$$P_0 = \left[\sum_{n=0}^{N} \frac{N!}{(N - n)!} \left(\frac{\lambda}{\mu} \right)^n \right]^{-1} = \frac{1}{\sum_{n=0}^{6} \frac{6!}{(6 - n)!} \left(\frac{0.8}{3.6} \right)^n}$$

$$= \frac{1}{\left[\frac{6!}{6!} \left(\frac{0.8}{3.6} \right)^0 \right] + \left[\frac{6!}{5!} \left(\frac{0.8}{3.6} \right)^1 \right] + \left[\frac{6!}{4!} \left(\frac{0.8}{3.6} \right)^2 \right] + \left[\frac{6!}{3!} \left(\frac{0.8}{3.6} \right)^3 \right] + \left[\frac{6!}{2!} \left(\frac{0.8}{3.6} \right)^4 \right] + \left[\frac{6!}{1!} \left(\frac{0.8}{3.6} \right)^5 \right] + \left[\frac{6!}{0!} \left(\frac{0.8}{3.6} \right)^6 \right]}$$

$$= \frac{1}{1 + 1.33 + 1.48 + 1.32 + 0.88 + 0.39 + 0.09} = \frac{1}{6.49} = 0.1541$$

$$L = N - \frac{\mu}{\lambda}(1 - P_0) = 6 - \left[\frac{3.6}{0.8}(1 - 0.1541)\right] = 2.193 \text{ trains}$$

$$W = L[(N - L)\lambda]^{-1} = \frac{2.193}{(3.807)0.8} = 0.72 \text{ day}$$

Arriving trains will spend an average of 0.72 day at the coal mine.

CD-ROM RESOURCES

The Student CD-ROM that accompanies this text contains the following resources, which allow you to further practice and apply the concepts presented in this supplement.

❐ **OM Explorer Tutors:** OM Explorer contains three tutor programs that will help you learn how to use the single-server, multiple-server, and finite-population models. See the Supplement 6S folder in OM Explorer.

❐ **OM Explorer Solvers:** OM Explorer has a program that can be used to solve general problems involving waiting lines. See the Waiting Lines folder in OM Explorer for this routine.

❐ **Equation Summary:** All the equations for this supplement can be found in one convenient location.

INTERACTIVE RESOURCES

The Interactive Web site associated with this text (www.prenhall.com/ritzman) contains many tools and activities specifically designed for this supplement. The following items are recommended to enhance your understanding of the material in this chapter.

❐ **Internet Activities:** Try out an Internet activity that addresses the issue of long waiting times for a Web page to load.

❐ **Internet Tours:** Learn about the waiting lines that develop at the Paris Companies Cleaners, a large industrial fabric cleaner.

PROBLEMS

An icon next to a problem identifies the software that can be helpful but is not mandatory.

1. 💿 **OM Explorer** The Solomon, Smith, and Samson law firm produces many legal documents that must be typed for clients and the firm. Requests average 8 pages of documents per hour, and they arrive according to a Poisson distribution. The secretary can type 10 pages per hour on average according to an exponential distribution.

   a. What is the average utilization rate of the secretary?

   b. What is the probability that more than 4 pages are waiting or being typed?

   c. What is the average number of pages waiting to be typed?

2. 💿 **OM Explorer** Benny's Arcade has six video game machines. The average time between machine failures is 50 hours. Jimmy, the maintenance engineer, can repair a machine in 15 hours on the average. The machines have an exponential failure distribution, and Jimmy has an exponential service-time distribution.

a. What is Jimmy's utilization?

b. What is the average number of machines out of service, that is, waiting to be repaired or being repaired?

c. What is the average time a machine is out of service?

3. ● **OM Explorer** Moore, Aiken, and Payne is a dental clinic serving the needs of the general public on a first-come, first-served basis. The clinic has three dental chairs, each staffed by a dentist. Patients arrive at the rate of five per hour, according to a Poisson distribution, and do not balk or renege. The average time required for a dental checkup is 30 minutes, according to an exponential distribution.

a. What is the probability that no patients are in the clinic?

b. What is the probability that six or more patients are in the clinic?

c. What is the average number of patients waiting?

d. What is the average total time that a patient spends in the clinic?

4. ● **OM Explorer** Fantastic Styling Salon is run by two stylists, Jenny Perez and Jill Sloan, each capable of serving five customers per hour, on average. Eight customers, on average, arrive at the salon each hour.

a. If all arriving customers wait in a common line for the next available stylist, how long would a customer wait in line, on average, before being served?

b. Suppose that 50 percent of the arriving customers want to be served only by Perez and that the other 50 percent want only Sloan. How long would a customer wait in line, on average, before being served by Perez? By Sloan? What is the average customer waiting time in the line?

c. Do you observe a difference in the answers to parts (a) and (b)? If so, why? Explain.

5. ● **OM Explorer** You are the manager of a local bank where three tellers provide services to customers. On average, each teller takes three minutes to serve a customer. Customers arrive, on average, at a rate of 50 per hour. Having recently received complaints from some customers that they have had to wait for a long time before being served, your boss asks you to evaluate the service system. Specifically, you must provide answers to the following questions:

a. What is the average utilization of the three-teller service system?

b. What is the probability that no customers are being served by a teller or are waiting in line?

c. What is the average number of customers waiting in line?

d. On average, how long does a customer wait in line before being served?

e. On average, how many customers would be at a teller's station and in line?

6. ● **OM Explorer** Jake Tweet hosts a psychology talk show on WTPG radio. Jake's advice averages 8 minutes per caller but varies according to an exponential distribution. The average time between calls is 20 minutes, exponentially distributed. Generating calls in this local market is difficult, so Jake doesn't want to lose any calls to busy signals. The radio station has only three telephone lines. What is the probability that a caller receives a busy signal?

7. ● **OM Explorer** The supervisor at the Precision Machine Shop wants to determine the staffing policy that minimizes total operating costs. The average arrival rate at the tool crib, where tools are dispensed to the workers, is eight machinists per hour. Each machinist's pay is $20 per hour. The supervisor can staff the crib either with a junior attendant who is paid $5 per hour and can process 10 arrivals per hour or with a senior attendant who is paid $12 per hour and can process 16 arrivals per hour. Which attendant should be selected, and what would be the total estimated hourly cost?

8. ● **OM Explorer** The daughter of the owner of a local hamburger restaurant is preparing to open a new fast-food restaurant called Hasty Burgers. Based on the arrival rates at her father's outlets, she expects customers to arrive at the drive-in window according to a Poisson distribution, with a mean of 20 customers per hour. The service rate is flexible; however, the service times are expected to follow an exponential distribution. The drive-in window is a single-server operation.

a. What service rate is needed to keep the average number of customers in the service system (waiting line and being served) to four?

b. For the service rate in part (a), what is the probability that more than four customers are in line and being served?

c. For the service rate in part (a), what is the average waiting time in line for each customer? Does this average seem satisfactory for a fast-food business?

9. ● **OM Explorer** Three employees in the maintenance department are responsible for repairing the video games at Pinball Wizard, a video arcade. A maintenance worker can fix one video game machine every eight hours on average, with an exponential distribution. An average of one video game machine fails every three hours, according to a Poisson distribution. Each down machine costs the Wizard $10 per hour in lost income. A new maintenance worker would cost $8 per hour.

Should the manager hire any new personnel? If so, how many? What would you recommend to the manager, based on your analysis?

10.   **OM Explorer** The College of Business and Public Administration at Benton University has a copy machine on each floor for faculty use. Heavy use of the five copy machines causes frequent failures. Maintenance records show that a machine fails every 2.5 days (or $\lambda = 0.40$ failure/day). The college has a maintenance contract with the authorized dealer of the copy machines. Because the copy machines fail so frequently, the dealer has assigned one person to the college to repair them. This person can repair an average of 2.5 machines per day. Using the finite-source model, answer the following questions:

   a.   What is the average utilization of the maintenance person?

   b.   On average, how many copy machines are being repaired or waiting to be repaired?

   c.   What is the average time spent by a copy machine in the repair system (waiting and being repaired)?

11.   **OM Explorer** You are in charge of a quarry that supplies sand and stone aggregates to your company's construction sites. Empty trucks from construction sites arrive at the quarry's huge piles of sand and stone aggregates and wait in line to enter the station, which can load either sand or aggregate. At the station, they are filled with material, weighed, checked out, and proceed to a construction site. Currently, nine empty trucks arrive per hour, on average. Once a truck has entered a loading station, it takes six minutes for it to be filled, weighed, and checked out. Concerned that trucks are spending too much time waiting and being filled, you are evaluating two alternatives to reduce the average time the trucks spend in the system. The first alternative is to add side boards to the trucks (so that more material could be loaded) and to add a helper at the loading station (so that filling time could be reduced) at a total cost of $50,000. The arrival rate of trucks would change to six per hour, and the filling time would be reduced to four minutes. The second alternative is to add another loading station at a cost of $80,000. The trucks would wait in a common line and the truck at the front of the line would move to the next available station.

   Which alternative would you recommend if you want to reduce the current average waiting time in the system?

SELECTED REFERENCES

Cooper, Robert B. *Introduction to Queuing Theory,* 2d ed. New York: Elsevier–North Holland, 1980.

Hillier, F. S., and G. S. Lieberman. *Introduction to Operations Research,* 2d ed. San Francisco: Holden-Day, 1975.

Moore, P. M. *Queues, Inventories and Maintenance.* New York: John Wiley & Sons, 1958.

Saaty, T. L. *Elements of Queuing Theory with Applications.* New York: McGraw-Hill, 1961.

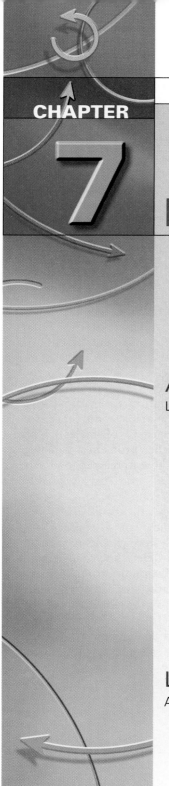

Location and Layout

Across the Organization

Location and layout are important to . . .

- ☐ **accounting,** which prepares cost estimates for changing layouts and operating at new locations.
- ☐ **distribution,** which seeks warehouse layouts that make materials handling easier and make customer response times shorter.
- ☐ **engineering,** which considers the impact of product design choices on layout.
- ☐ **finance,** which performs the financial analysis for investments in new layouts or in facilities at new locations.
- ☐ **human resources,** which hires and trains employees to support new or relocated operations.
- ☐ **management information systems,** which provides information technologies that link operations at different locations.
- ☐ **marketing,** which assesses how new locations and revised layouts will appeal to customers.
- ☐ **operations,** which seeks facility locations and layouts that best balance multiple performance criteria.

Learning Goals

After reading this chapter, you will be able to . . .

1. discuss the managerial challenges in global operations.
2. describe the factors affecting location choices, both in manufacturing and services.
3. apply the load–distance method and break-even analysis to single-site location problems and the transportation method to locating a facility within a network of facilities.
4. describe the four basic layout types and when each is best used.
5. identify the types of performance criteria that are important in evaluating layouts.
6. explain how cells can help create hybrid layouts.
7. recommend how to design process layouts and product layouts.

A 35-year-old mother does not know it, but the Internet has made her trips to the mall a little easier. In 2000, RiverTown Crossings (www.rivertowncrossings.com) located a new facility in Grandville, Michigan. Since then she rarely ventures beyond just one section of the mall—the one with Abercrombie Kids, Gap Kids, Gymboree, and other kids' clothing stores. She can shop in that wing and find almost everything she needs. In an effort to compete with the allure of online shopping, the mall owner, General Growth Properties, Inc. (www.generalgrowth.com), selected a layout that runs counter to decades of retailing wisdom: It clustered competing stores together. Shoppers were asking for such clusters long before Web retailing took off, and General Growth began experimenting with the idea three years ago. Now, all of its new malls will have clusters. 🅂

Worried about a future when shoppers point and click instead of park and walk and wait in line, developers are finally trying to make it more convenient to shop in malls. Some owners are revising their existing layouts by removing large fixtures, such as planters and fountains, to clear sightlines to storefronts. Others are adding directories that are easier to understand than current mall maps. A few malls in the design stages are opting to put anchor department stores closer together—a layout that cuts down on walking. A few malls are trying to offer shoppers elements of the Web using high-tech directories. At the Dayton Mall, in Ohio, sleek electronic kiosks give shoppers e-mail access and

let them search for names of stores carrying types of merchandise, such as "sweaters." The kiosks also have printers that can spit out a map with a store's location highlighted.

Beneath the new layout designs is an old retailing secret: The traditional mall was designed to be difficult. This planned inconvenience made customers who wanted to comparison-shop walk from one end of the mall to the other, so that they had every chance to make impulse purchases in between. Many developers left little to chance in directing the traffic flow to their advantage, using plants, carpeting, and other fixtures to set winding routes past stores.

Revising the layout of existing malls to make them more convenient is costly. Most of them are jungles of escalators, fountains, and play areas—and those are the easy obstacles. The tougher problem is figuring out how to rearrange similar stores that are probably operating on long leases. After all, a mall developer cannot simply order four shoe store tenants to pick up and move. And many retailers still prefer to keep their distance from competitors. RiverTown's Hallmark Gold Crown store is located on the first level on the north end of the mall, while an American Greetings store is on the second level on the south end. Hallmark Cards' location strategy calls for space between its stores and competitors.

The Internet has revolutionized the way traditional businesses design their processes, even to the point of layout design. RiverTown Crossings Mall has clustered company stores to improve comparison shopping, a convenience that Web retailing already offers online customers.

Source: "Making Malls (Gasp!) Convenient." *Wall Street Journal* (February 8, 2000).

I N A TYPICAL YEAR in the United States, manufacturers build more than 3,000 new plants and expand 7,500 others. Service providers build and remodel innumerable stores, office buildings, warehouses, and other facilities. Choosing where to locate new manufacturing facilities, service outlets, or branch offices, and how to lay them out, are strategic decisions. The location and layout of a business's facilities have significant impacts on the company's operating costs, the prices it charges for goods and services, and its ability to compete in the marketplace.

Analyzing location patterns to discover a firm's underlying strategy is fascinating. For example, why does White Castle often locate restaurants near manufacturing plants? Why do competing new-car sales showrooms cluster near one another? White Castle's strategy is to cater to blue-collar workers. As a result, it tends to locate near the target population and away from competitors such as Wendy's and McDonald's. In contrast, managers of new-car showrooms deliberately locate near one another because customers prefer to do their comparison shopping in one area. In each case, management's location decision reflects a particular strategy.

Recognizing the strategic impact of location decisions, we first examine the most important trend in location patterns: the globalization of operations. We then consider qualitative factors that influence location choices. Next we present some analytic techniques for making single- or multiple-facility location decisions. Finally, we turn to facility layout, beginning with strategic issues and then describing ways to design effective layouts.

THE GLOBALIZATION AND GEOGRAPHIC DISPERSION OF OPERATIONS

Should facilities be opened overseas?

globalization The description of a businesses' deployment of facilities and operations around the world.

The term **globalization** describes businesses' deployment of facilities and operations around the world. Worldwide exports now account for more than 30 percent of worldwide gross national product, up from 12 percent in 1962. Globalization results in more exports to and imports from other countries, often called *offshore* sales and imports. Offshore sales and purchases by U.S. manufacturers have increased to 14 percent of total sales and 10 percent of total purchases. The volume of corporate voice, data, and teleconferencing traffic between countries is growing at an annual rate of 15 to 20 percent—about double the corporate domestic rate—indicating how businesses are increasingly bridging national boundaries.

Globalization of services is also widespread. The value of world trade in services is roughly 20 percent of total world trade. Banking, law, information services, airlines, education, consulting, and restaurant services are particularly active globally. For example, McDonald's opened a record 220 restaurants in foreign countries in just one year. Wal-Mart Stores, the world's largest retailer, paid $10.8 billion in 1999 for the United Kingdom's Asda Group PLC, whose large stores and selection of goods closely mirror its own. The purchase is part of Wal-Mart's push to expand across Europe. Small companies also are beginning to export their services. The Tokyo city government awarded a $50 million contract to a New York architect to design and build a $1 billion International Forum complex in downtown Tokyo. India's Steel Authority hired a Silver Spring, Maryland, consulting firm to design and implement quality systems for its five major steel plants.

DISADVANTAGES TO GLOBALIZATION

Of course, operations in other countries can have disadvantages. A firm may have to relinquish proprietary technology if it turns over some of its component manufacturing to offshore suppliers or if suppliers need the firm's technology to achieve desired quality and cost goals.

There may be political risks. Each nation can exercise its sovereignty over the people and property within its borders. The extreme case is nationalization, in which a government may take over a firm's assets without paying compensation. Also, a firm may alienate customers back home if jobs are lost to offshore operations.

Employee skills may be lower in foreign countries, requiring additional training time. Korean firms moved much of their sports shoe production to low-wage Indonesia and China, but they still manufacture hiking shoes and in-line roller skates in Korea because of the greater skills required.

When a firm's operations are scattered, customer response times can be longer. Effective cross-functional connections also may be more difficult if face-to-face discussions are needed.

MANAGING GLOBAL OPERATIONS

How should global operations be managed, and what are their biggest challenges?

All the concepts and techniques described in this book apply to operations throughout the world. However, location decisions involve added complexities when a firm sets up facilities abroad. One study (see Klassen and Whybark, 1994) revealed that the most important barrier to effective global manufacturing operations is that many firms do not take a global view of their market opportunities and competitors. Global markets impose new standards on quality and time. Managers should not think about domestic markets first and then global markets later, if at all. Also, they must have a good understanding of their competitors, which requires greater appraisal capabilities when the competitors are global rather than domestic. Other important challenges of managing multinational operations include other languages and customs, different management styles, unfamiliar laws and regulations, and different costs.

OTHER LANGUAGES. The ability to communicate effectively is important to all organizations. Most U.S. managers are fluent only in English and, thus, are at a disadvantage when dealing with managers in Europe or Asia who are fluent in several languages. For example, despite the vast potential for trade with Russia, few U.S. students and managers are studying Russian.

DIFFERENT NORMS AND CUSTOMS. Several U.S. franchisers, such as Century 21 Real Estate, Levi Strauss, and Quality Inns International, found that even when the same language is spoken, different countries have unique norms and customs that shape their business values. The goals, attitudes toward work, customer expectations, desire for risk taking, and other business values can vary dramatically from one part of the world to another. For example, a survey showed that more than two-thirds of Japanese managers believed that business should take an active role in environmental protection, whereas only 25 percent of Mexican managers agreed.

WORKFORCE MANAGEMENT. Employees in different countries prefer different management styles. Managers moving to operations in another country often must reevaluate their on-the-job behaviors (e.g., superior–subordinate relationships), assumptions about workers' attitudes, and hiring and promotion practices. Practices that work well in one country may be ineffective in another.

UNFAMILIAR LAWS AND REGULATIONS. Managers in charge of overseas plants must deal with unfamiliar labor laws, tax laws, and regulatory requirements. The after-tax consequences of an automation project, for instance, can be quite different from country to country because of different tax laws. Legal systems also differ. Some policies and practices that are illegal in one country might be acceptable or even mandated elsewhere in the world.

UNEXPECTED COST MIX. Firms may shift some of their operations to another country because of lower inventory, labor, materials, and real estate costs. However, these same differences may mean that policies that worked well in one economic environment—such as automating a process—might be a mistake in the new environment.

Radisson Hotels International's decision to open the upscale Radisson Slavjanskaya, the first American-managed hotel in Moscow, led to the range of challenges that can be encountered in managing global operations.

In dealing with global operations, managers must decide how much of the firm's operations to shift overseas and how much control the home office should retain. At one extreme, firms can rely on their home offices for strategic direction and are highly centralized. At the other extreme, firms can have a worldwide vision but allow each subsidiary to operate independently. Here the manager must be able to manage highly decentralized organizations that have a complex mix of product strategies, cultures, and consumer needs.

FACTORS AFFECTING LOCATION DECISIONS

Which factors are dominant in picking a new location? Which are secondary?

facility location The process of determining a geographic site for a firm's operations.

Facility location is the process of determining a geographic site for a firm's operations. Managers of both service and manufacturing organizations must weigh many factors when assessing the desirability of a particular site, including proximity to customers and suppliers, labor costs, and transportation costs. Managers generally can disregard factors that fail to meet at least one of the following two conditions.

1. The factor must be sensitive to location. That is, managers shouldn't consider a factor that is not affected by the location decision. For example, if community attitudes are uniformly good at all the locations under consideration, community attitudes shouldn't be considered as a factor.

2. The factor must have a high impact on the company's ability to meet its goals. For example, although different locations will be at different distances from suppliers, if shipments and communication can take place by overnight delivery, faxing, and other means, distance to suppliers shouldn't be considered as a factor.

Managers can divide location factors into dominant and secondary factors. Dominant factors are those derived from competitive priorities (cost, quality, time, and flexibility) and have a particularly strong impact on sales or costs. For example, a favorable labor climate and monetary incentives are dominant factors when locating call centers in Texas. Secondary factors also are important, but management may downplay or even ignore some of them if other factors are more important. Thus, for

GM's Saturn plant, which makes many parts on site, inbound transportation costs were considered to be a secondary factor.

DOMINANT FACTORS IN MANUFACTURING

Six groups of factors dominate location decisions for new manufacturing plants. Listed in order of importance, they are

1. favorable labor climate
2. proximity to markets
3. quality of life
4. proximity to suppliers and resources
5. proximity to the parent company's facilities
6. utilities, taxes, and real estate costs

FAVORABLE LABOR CLIMATE. A favorable labor climate may be the most important factor in location decisions for labor-intensive firms in industries such as textiles, furniture, and consumer electronics. Labor climate is a function of wage rates, training requirements, attitudes toward work, worker productivity, and union strength. Many executives perceive weak unions or a low probability of union organizing efforts as a distinct advantage.

Having a favorable climate applies not just to the workforce already on site but in the case of relocation decisions to the employees that a firm hopes will transfer or will be attracted there. A good example is MCI Communications Corporations's decision to relocate its Systems Engineering division from its Washington, D.C., headquarters to Colorado Springs. This 4,000-employee division was MCI's brain trust that had created numerous breakthrough products. Management reasoned that this location would inspire the workers and that the mountains, low crime rate, healthy climate, and rock-bottom real estate prices would surely attract the best and brightest computer software engineers. The results were quite different than expected. Numerous executives and engineers and hundreds of the division's 51 percent minority population said "no" to the transfer or fled MCI soon after relocating. Colorado Springs' isolated and politically conservative setting repelled many employees who were used to living in larger, ethnically diverse urban areas. The relocated engineers also felt isolated from both top management and the marketing staff. That prevented the daily, informal contact that had spawned many successful innovations. Whereas Colorado Springs seemed destined to become a major center for MCI, it ended up being just a branch.

PROXIMITY TO MARKETS. After determining where the demand for goods and services is greatest, management must select a location for the facility that will supply that demand. Locating near markets is particularly important when the final goods are bulky or heavy and *outbound* transportation rates are high. For example, manufacturers of products such as plastic pipe and heavy metals all emphasize proximity to their markets.

quality of life A factor that can sometimes make the difference in location decisions; good schools, recreational facilities, cultural events, and an attractive lifestyle are all taken into consideration when determining quality of life.

QUALITY OF LIFE. Good schools, recreational facilities, cultural events, and an attractive lifestyle contribute to **quality of life**. This factor is relatively unimportant on its own, but it can make the difference in location decisions. In the United States during the past two decades, more than 50 percent of new industrial jobs went to nonurban regions. A similar shift is taking place in Japan and Europe. Reasons for this movement include high costs of living, high crime rates, and general decline in the quality of life in many large cities.

PROXIMITY TO SUPPLIERS AND RESOURCES. Firms dependent on inputs of bulky, perishable, or heavy raw materials emphasize proximity to suppliers and resources. In such cases, *inbound* transportation costs become a dominant factor, encouraging such firms to locate facilities near suppliers. For example, locating paper mills near forests and food processing facilities near farms is practical. Another advantage of locating near suppliers is the ability to maintain lower inventories.

PROXIMITY TO THE PARENT COMPANY'S FACILITIES. In many companies, plants supply parts to other facilities or rely on other facilities for management and staff support. These ties require frequent coordination and communication, which can become more difficult as distance increases.

UTILITIES, TAXES, AND REAL ESTATE COSTS. Other important factors that may emerge include utility costs (telephone, energy, and water), local and state taxes, financing incentives offered by local or state governments, relocation costs, and land costs. For example, MCI was attracted by being able to buy an abandoned 220,000 square foot IBM factory for its new Colorado Springs facility for just $13.5 million, a bargain by Washington standards. It was also able to wrangle $3.5 million in incentives from local governments. These strong attractions were much less important, in retrospect, than finding a favorable labor climate for its employees.

OTHER FACTORS. Still other factors may need to be considered, including room for expansion, construction costs, accessibility to multiple modes of transportation, the cost of shuffling people and materials between plants, insurance costs, competition from other firms for the workforce, local ordinances (such as pollution or noise control regulations), community attitudes, and many others. For global operations, firms are emphasizing local employee skills and education and the local infrastructure. Many firms are concluding that large, centralized manufacturing facilities in low-cost countries with poorly trained workers are not sustainable. Smaller, flexible facilities serving multiple markets allow the firm to deal with nontariff barriers such as sales-volume limitations, regional trading blocs, political risks, and exchange rates.

DOMINANT FACTORS IN SERVICES

The factors mentioned for manufacturers also apply to service providers with one important addition: the impact that the location might have on sales and customer satisfaction. Customers usually care about how close a service facility is, particularly if the process requires considerable customer contact.

How does the location decision for service facilities differ from that for manufacturing facilities?

PROXIMITY TO CUSTOMERS. Location is a key factor in determining how conveniently customers can carry on business with a firm. For example, few people will patronize a remotely located dry cleaner or supermarket if another is more convenient. Thus, the influence of location on revenues tends to be the dominant factor. The key is proximity to customers who will patronize the facility and seek its services.

TRANSPORTATION COSTS AND PROXIMITY TO MARKETS. For warehousing and distribution operations, transportation costs and proximity to markets are extremely important. With a warehouse nearby, many firms can hold inventory closer to the customer, thus reducing delivery time and promoting sales. For example, Invacare Corporation of Elyria, Ohio, gained a competitive edge in the distribution of home health care products by decentralizing inventory into 32 warehouses across the country. With

Invacare's new distribution network, the dealers get daily deliveries of products from one source. Invacare's location strategy shows how timely delivery can be a competitive advantage.

Should a firm be a leader or a follower in picking locations for new retail outlets?

LOCATION OF COMPETITORS. One complication in estimating the sales potential at different locations is the impact of competitors. Management must not only consider the current location of competitors but also try to anticipate their reaction to the firm's new location. Avoiding areas where competitors are already well established often pays. However, in some industries, such as new-car sales showrooms and fast-food chains, locating near competitors is actually advantageous. The strategy is to create a **critical mass,** whereby several competing firms clustered in one location attract more customers than the total number who would shop at the same stores at scattered locations. Recognizing this effect, some firms use a follow-the-leader strategy when selecting new sites.

critical mass A situation whereby several competing firms clustered in one location attract more customers than the total number who would shop at the same stores at scattered locations.

SITE-SPECIFIC FACTORS. Retailers also must consider the level of retail activity, residential density, traffic flow, and site visibility. Retail activity in the area is important, as shoppers often decide on impulse to go shopping or to eat in a restaurant. Traffic flows and visibility are important because businesses' customers arrive in cars. Management considers possible traffic tie-ups, traffic volume and direction by time of day, traffic signals, intersections, and the position of traffic medians. Visibility involves distance from the street and size of nearby buildings and signs. High residential density ensures nighttime and weekend business when the population in the area fits the firm's competitive priorities and target market segment.

LOCATING A SINGLE FACILITY

Having examined trends and important factors in location, we now consider more specifically how a firm can make location decisions. In this section, we consider the case of locating only one new facility. When the facility is part of a firm's larger network of facilities, we assume that there is no interdependence; that is, a decision to open a restaurant in Tampa, Florida, is independent of whether the chain has a restaurant in Austin, Texas. Let's begin by considering how to decide whether a new location is needed and then examine a systematic selection process aided by the load–distance method to deal with proximity.

SELECTING ON-SITE EXPANSION, NEW LOCATION, OR RELOCATION

Should a firm expand on site, add a new facility, or relocate the existing facility?

Management must first decide whether to expand on site, build another facility, or relocate to another site. A survey of Fortune 500 firms showed that 45 percent of expansions were on site, 43 percent were in new plants at new locations, and only 12 percent were relocations of all facilities. On-site expansion has the advantage of keeping management together, reducing construction time and costs, and avoiding splitting up operations. However, a firm may overexpand a facility, at which point diseconomies of scale set in (see Chapter 6, "Capacity"). Poor materials handling, increasingly complex production control, and simple lack of space all are reasons for building a new plant or relocating the existing one.

The advantages of building a new plant or moving to a new retail or office space are that the firm does not have to rely on production from a single plant, can hire new and possibly more productive labor, can modernize with new technology, and can reduce transportation costs. Most firms that choose to relocate are small (less than 10 employees). They tend to be single-location companies cramped for space and needing to redesign their production processes and layouts. More than 80 percent of all relocations are within 20 miles of the first location, which enables the firm to retain its current workforce.

COMPARING SEVERAL SITES

A systematic selection process begins after there is a perception or evidence that opening a retail outlet, warehouse, office, or plant in a new location will increase profits. A team may be responsible for the selection decision in a large corporation, or an individual may make the decision in a small company. The process of selecting a new facility location involves a series of steps.

1. Identify the important location factors and categorize them as dominant or secondary.

2. Consider alternative regions; then narrow the choices to alternative communities and finally to specific sites.

3. Collect data on the alternatives from location consultants, state development agencies, city and county planning departments, chambers of commerce, land developers, electric power companies, banks, and on-site visits. Governmental data provide a statistical mother lode. For example, the U.S. Census Bureau has a minutely detailed computerized map of the entire United States—the so-called Tiger file. Its formal name is the Topologically Integrated Geographic Encoding and Reference file (tiger.census.gov). It lists in digital form every highway, street, bridge, and tunnel in the 50 states. When combined with a database, such as the results of the 2000 census or a company's own customer files, Tiger gives desktop computer users the ability to ask various "what-if" questions about different location alternatives. The Internet also has Web sites (see maps.yahoo.com, www.mapquest.com, and maps.expedia.com) that provide maps, distances and travel time, and routes between any two locations, such as between Toronto, Ontario, and San Diego, California.

4. Analyze the data collected, beginning with the *quantitative* factors—factors that can be measured in dollars, such as annual transportation costs or taxes. These dollar values may be broken into separate cost categories (e.g., inbound and outbound transportation, labor, construction, and utilities) and separate revenue sources (e.g., sales, stock or bond issues, and interest income). These financial factors can then be converted to a single measure of financial merit and used to compare two or more sites.

5. Bring the qualitative factors pertaining to each site into the evaluation. A *qualitative* factor is one that cannot be evaluated in dollar terms, such as community attitudes or quality of life. To merge quantitative and qualitative factors, some managers review the expected performance of each factor, while others assign each factor a weight of relative importance and calculate a weighted score for each site, using a preference matrix. What is important in one situation may be unimportant or less important in another. The site with the highest weighted score is best.

After thoroughly evaluating between 5 and 15 sites, those making the study prepare a final report containing site recommendations, along with a summary of the data and analyses on which they are based. An audiovisual presentation of the key findings usually is delivered to top management in large firms.

**TUTOR
7.1**

| EXAMPLE 7.1 | *Calculating Weighted Scores in a Preference Matrix* |

A new medical facility, Health-Watch, is to be located in Erie, Pennsylvania. The following table shows the location factors, weights, and scores (1 = poor, 5 = excellent) for one potential site. The weights in this case add up to 100 percent. A weighted score will be calculated for each site. What is the weighted score for this site?

LOCATION FACTOR	WEIGHT	SCORE
Total patient miles per month	25	4
Facility utilization	20	3
Average time per emergency trip	20	3
Expressway accessibility	15	4
Land and construction costs	10	1
Employee preferences	10	5

SOLUTION

The weighted score (*WS*) for this particular site is calculated by multiplying each factor's weight by its score and adding the results:

$$WS = (25 \times 4) + (20 \times 3) + (20 \times 3) + (15 \times 4) + (10 \times 1) + (10 \times 5)$$
$$= 100 + 60 + 60 + 60 + 10 + 50$$
$$= 340$$

The total weighted score of 340 can be compared with the total weighted scores for other sites being evaluated. ⊐

Should a firm locate near its suppliers, workforce, or customers?

load–distance method
A mathematical model used to evaluate locations based on proximity factors.

Euclidean distance The straight-line distance, or shortest possible path, between two points.

APPLYING THE LOAD–DISTANCE METHOD

In the systematic selection process, the analyst must identify attractive candidate locations and compare them on the basis of quantitative factors. The load–distance method can facilitate this step. Several location factors relate directly to distance: proximity to markets, average distance to target customers, proximity to suppliers and resources, and proximity to other company facilities. The **load–distance method** is a mathematical model used to evaluate locations based on proximity factors. The objective is to select a location that minimizes the total weighted loads moving into and out of the facility. The distance between two points is expressed by assigning the points to grid coordinates on a map. An alternative approach is to use time rather than distance.

DISTANCE MEASURES. For a rough calculation, which is all that is needed for the load–distance method, either a Euclidean or rectilinear distance measure may be used. **Euclidean distance** is the straight-line distance, or shortest possible path, between two points. To calculate this distance, we create a graph. The distance between two points, say points *A* and *B*, is:

$$d_{AB} = \sqrt{(x_A - x_B)^2 + (y_A - y_B)^2}$$

where

d_{AB} = distance between points *A* and *B*

x_A = *x*-coordinate of point *A*

y_A = *y*-coordinate of point *A*

x_B = *x*-coordinate of point *B*

y_B = *y*-coordinate of point *B*

rectilinear distance The distance between two points with a series of 90-degree turns, as along city blocks.

TUTOR 7.2

Rectilinear distance measures distance between two points with a series of 90° turns, as along city blocks. The distance traveled in the *x*-direction is the absolute value of the difference in *x*-coordinates. Adding this result to the absolute value of the difference in the *y*-coordinates gives

$$d_{AB} = |x_A - x_B| + |y_A - y_B|$$

For assistance in calculating distances using either measure, see Tutor 7.2 in OM Explorer.

CALCULATING A LOAD–DISTANCE SCORE. Suppose that a firm planning a new location wants to select a site that minimizes the distances that loads, particularly the larger ones, must travel to and from the site. Depending on the industry, a *load* may be shipments from suppliers, between plants, or to customers, or it may be customers or employees traveling to or from the facility. The firm seeks to minimize its load–distance, or *ld*, score, generally by choosing a location so that large loads go short distances.

To calculate a load–distance, *ld*, score for any potential location, we use either of the distance measures and simply multiply the loads flowing to and from the facility by the distances traveled. These loads may be expressed as tons or number of trips per week. The score is the sum of these load–distance products.

The goal is to find one acceptable facility location that minimizes the score, where the location is defined by its *x*-coordinate and *y*-coordinate. Practical considerations rarely allow managers to select the exact location with the lowest possible score. For example, land may not be available there at a reasonable price, or other location factors may make the site undesirable.

CENTER OF GRAVITY. Testing different locations with the load–distance model is relatively simple if some systematic search process is followed. A good starting point is the **center of gravity** of the target area. The center of gravity's *x*-coordinate, denoted x^*, is found by multiplying each point's *x*-coordinate (x_i) by its load (l_i), summing these products ($\Sigma\, l_i x_i$), and then dividing by the sum of the loads ($\Sigma\, l_i$). The *y*-coordinate, denoted y^*, is found the same way, with the *y*-coordinates used in the numerator. The formulas are

center of gravity A good starting point in evaluating locations is with the load–distance model; the center of gravity's *x*-coordinate is found by multiplying each point's *x*-coordinate by its load (*l*), summing these products, and then dividing by the sum of the loads.

$$x^* = \frac{\sum_i l_i x_i}{\sum_i l_i} \quad \text{and} \quad y^* = \frac{\sum_i l_i y_i}{\sum_i l_i}$$

This location usually is not the optimal one for the Euclidean or rectilinear distance measures, but it still is an excellent starting point. Calculate the load–distance scores for locations in its vicinity until you're satisfied that your solution is near optimal.

EXAMPLE 7.2

TUTOR 7.3

Finding the Center of Gravity

The new Health-Watch facility is targeted to serve seven census tracts in Erie, Pennsylvania. Customers will travel from the seven census tract centers to the new facility when they need health care. What is the target areas center of gravity for the Health-Watch medical facility?

SOLUTION

To calculate the center of gravity, we begin with the information in the following table in which population is given in thousands:

CENSUS TRACT	POPULATION			
	(*x, y*)	(*l*)	*lx*	*ly*
A	(2.5, 4.5)	2	5	9
B	(2.5, 2.5)	5	12.5	12.5
C	(5.5, 4.5)	10	55	45
D	(5, 2)	7	35	14
E	(8, 5)	10	80	50
F	(7, 2)	20	140	40
G	(9, 2.5)	14	126	35
	Totals	68	453.5	205.5

Next we solve for x^* and y^*.

$$x^* = \frac{453.5}{68} = 6.67$$

$$y^* = \frac{205.5}{68} = 3.02$$

Decision Point The center of gravity is (6.67, 3.02), which is not necessarily optimal. Using the center of gravity as a starting point, managers can now search in its vicinity for the optimal location. ◻

USING BREAK-EVEN ANALYSIS

How does the expected output level of the facility affect location choice?

Break-even analysis (see Supplement A, "Decision Making" on the Student CD-ROM) can help a manager compare location alternatives on the basis of quantitative factors that can be expressed in terms of total cost. It is particularly useful when the manager wants to define the ranges over which each alternative is best. The basic steps for graphic and algebraic solutions are as follows.

1. Determine the variable costs and fixed costs for each site. Recall that *variable* costs are the portion of the total cost that varies directly with the volume of output. Recall that fixed costs are the portion of the total cost that remains constant regardless of output levels.

2. Plot the total cost lines—the sum of variable and fixed costs—for all the sites on a single graph (for assistance, see Tutors A.1 and A.2 in OM Explorer.

3. Identify the approximate ranges for which each location has the lowest cost.

4. Solve algebraically for the break-even points over the relevant ranges.

EXAMPLE 7.3

Break-Even Analysis for Location

TUTOR 7.4

An operations manager has narrowed the search for a new facility location to four communities. The annual fixed costs (land, property taxes, insurance, equipment, and buildings) and the variable costs (labor, materials, transportation, and variable overhead) are

COMMUNITY	FIXED COSTS PER YEAR	VARIABLE COSTS PER UNIT
A	$150,000	$62
B	$300,000	$38
C	$500,000	$24
D	$600,000	$30

a. Plot the total cost curves for all the communities on a single graph. Identify on the graph the approximate range over which each community provides the lowest cost.

b. Using break-even analysis, calculate the break-even quantities over the relevant ranges.

c. If the expected demand is 15,000 units per year, what is the best location?

SOLUTION

a. To plot a community's total cost line, let us first compute the total cost for two output levels: $Q = 0$ and $Q = 20,000$ units per year. For the $Q = 0$ level, the total cost is simply the fixed costs. For the $Q = 20,000$ level, the total cost (fixed plus variable costs) is

COMMUNITY	FIXED COSTS	VARIABLE COSTS (COST PER UNIT)(NO. OF UNITS)	TOTAL COST (FIXED + VARIABLE)
A	$150,000	$62(20,000) = $1,240,000	$1,390,000
B	$300,000	$38(20,000) = $ 760,000	$1,060,000
C	$500,000	$24(20,000) = $ 480,000	$ 980,000
D	$600,000	$30(20,000) = $ 600,000	$1,200,000

Figure 7.1 shows the graph of the total cost lines. The line for community A goes from (0, 150) to (20, 1,390). The graph indicates that community A is best for low volumes, B for intermediate volumes, and C for high volumes. We should no longer consider community D, as both its fixed *and* its variable costs are higher than community C's.

b. The break-even quantity between A and B lies at the end of the first range, where A is best, and the beginning of the second range, where B is best. We find it by setting their total cost equations equal to each other and solving:

$$\begin{array}{cc} (A) & (B) \end{array}$$

$$\$150,000 + \$62Q = \$300,000 + \$38Q$$

$$Q = 6,250 \text{ units}$$

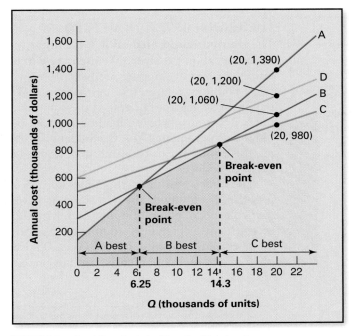

FIGURE 7.1 • Break-Even Analysis of Four Candidate Locations

The break-even quantity between B and C lies at the end of the range over which B is best and the beginning of the final range where C is best. It is

$$
\begin{matrix} \text{(B)} & & \text{(C)} \end{matrix}
$$

$$
\$300{,}000 + \$38Q = \$500{,}000 + \$24Q
$$

$$
Q = 14{,}286 \text{ units}
$$

No other break-even quantities are needed. The break-even point between A and C does not mark either the start or the end of one of the three relevant ranges.

Decision Point Management located the new facility at Community C, because the 15,000 units-per-year demand forecast lies in the high-volume range. ❑

LOCATING A FACILITY WITHIN A NETWORK OF FACILITIES

When a firm with a network of existing facilities plans a new facility, one of two conditions exists: Either the facilities operate independently (e.g., a chain of restaurants, health clinics, banks, or retail establishments) or the facilities interact (e.g., component manufacturing plants, assembly plants, and warehouses). Independently operating units can be located by treating each as a separate single facility, as described in the preceding section. Locating interacting facilities introduces new issues, such as how to allocate work between the facilities and how to determine the best capacity for each. Changing work allocations in turn affects the size (or capacity utilization) of the facilities. Thus, the multiple-facility location problem has three dimensions—location, allocation, and capacity—that must be solved simultaneously. In many cases, the analyst can identify a workable solution merely by looking for patterns in the cost, demand, and capacity data and using trial-and-error calculations. In other cases, more formal approaches are needed.

THE TRANSPORTATION METHOD

What is the best way to partition work among various facilities?

transportation method
A quantitative approach that can help solve multiple-facility location problems.

The **transportation method** is a quantitative approach that can help solve multiple-facility location problems. We use it here to determine the allocation pattern that minimizes the cost of shipping products from two or more plants, or *sources of supply*, to two or more warehouses, or *destinations*.[1] We focus on the setup and interpretation of the problem, leaving the rest of the solution process to a software package on a computer. The transportation method is based on linear programming (see Supplement I, "Linear Programming" on the Student CD-ROM). More efficient algorithms for solving this problem can be found in textbooks covering quantitative methods and management science.

The transportation method does not solve *all* facets of the multiple-facility location problem. It only finds the *best* shipping pattern between plants and warehouses for a particular set of plant locations, each with a given capacity. The analyst must try a variety of location–capacity combinations and use the transportation method to find the optimal distribution for each one. Distribution costs (variable shipping and possibly variable production costs) are but one important input in evaluating a particular

---

[1] It can also be used to determine an optimal production plan (see Chapter 11, "Aggregate Planning and Scheduling") or an optimal allocation of service accounts to service centers.

location–allocation combination. Investment costs and other fixed costs also must be considered, along with various qualitative factors. This complete analysis must be made for each reasonable location–capacity combination. Because of the importance of making a good decision, this extra effort is well worth its cost.

SETTING UP THE INITIAL TABLEAU. The first step in solving a transportation problem is to format it in a standard matrix, sometimes called a *tableau*. The basic steps in setting up an initial tableau are as follows:

1. Create a row for each plant (existing or new) being considered and a column for each warehouse.
2. Add a column for plant capacities and a row for warehouse demands and then insert their specific numerical values.
3. Each cell not in the requirements row or capacity column represents a shipping route from a plant to a warehouse. Insert the unit costs in the upper right-hand corner of each of these cells.

The Sunbelt Pool Company is considering building a new 500-unit plant, because business is booming. One possible location is Atlanta. Figure 7.2 shows a tableau with its plant capacity, warehouse requirements, and shipping costs. The tableau shows, for example, that shipping one unit from the existing Phoenix plant to warehouse 1 costs $5.00. Costs are assumed to increase linearly with the size of the shipment; that is, the cost is the same *per unit* regardless of the size of the total shipment.

In the transportation method, the sum of the shipments in a row must equal the corresponding plant's capacity. For example, in Figure 7.2, the total shipments from the Atlanta plant to warehouses 1, 2, and 3 must add up to 500. Similarly, the sum of shipments to a column must equal the corresponding warehouse's demand requirements. Thus, shipments to warehouse 1 from Phoenix and Atlanta must total 200 units.

DUMMY PLANTS OR WAREHOUSES. The transportation method also requires that the sum of capacities equal the sum of demands, which happens to be the case at 900 units (see Figure 7.2). In many real problems, total capacity may exceed requirements, or vice versa. If capacity exceeds requirements by *r* units, we add an extra column (a *dummy warehouse*) with a demand of *r* units and make the shipping costs in the newly created cells $0. Shipments are not actually made, so they represent unused plant capacity.

FIGURE 7.2

Initial Tableau

Plant	Warehouse			Capacity
	1	2	3	
Phoenix	5.0	6.0	5.4	400
Atlanta	7.0	4.6	6.6	500
Requirements	200	400	300	900 / 900

Similarly, if requirements exceed capacity by *r* units, we add an extra row (a *dummy plant*) with a capacity of *r* units. We assign shipping costs equal to the stockout costs of the new cells. If stockout costs are unknown or are the same for all warehouses, we simply assign shipping costs of $0 per unit to each cell in the dummy row. The optimal solution will not be affected because the shortage of *r* units is required in all cases. Adding a dummy warehouse or dummy plant ensures that the sum of capacities equals the sum of demands. Some software packages automatically add them when we make the data inputs.

FINDING A SOLUTION. After the initial tableau has been set up, the goal is to find the least-cost allocation pattern that satisfies all demands and exhausts all capacities. This pattern can be found by using the transportation method, which guarantees the optimal solution. The initial tableau is filled in with a feasible solution that satisfies all warehouse demands and exhausts all plant capacities. Then a new tableau is created, defining a new solution that has a lower total cost. This iterative process continues until no improvements can be made in the current solution, signaling that the optimal solution has been found. When using a computer package, all that you have to input is the information for the initial tableau.

Another procedure is the simplex method (see Supplement I, "Linear Programming" on the Student CD-ROM), although more inputs are required. The transportation problem is actually a special case of linear programming, which can be modeled with a decision variable for each cell in the tableau, a constraint for each row in the tableau (requiring that each plant's capacity be fully utilized), and a constraint for each column in the tableau (requiring that each warehouse's demand be satisfied).

Whichever method is used, the number of nonzero shipments in the optimal solution will never exceed the sum of the numbers of plants and warehouses minus 1. The Sunbelt Pool Company has two plants and three warehouses, so there need not be more than four (or 3 + 2 − 1) shipments in the optimal solution.

| EXAMPLE 7.4 | *Interpreting the Optimal Solution* |

The printout in Figure 7.3 from OM Explorer is for the Sunbelt Pool Company. Tutor 7.5 is set up to handle up to three sources and four destinations (for larger problems, use the *Transportation Method* Solver). With only two sources, we make the third row a dummy with a capacity of 0, and the fourth warehouse a dummy with a demand of 0. The bold numbers show

TUTOR 7.5

Enter data in yellow shaded areas.

Solve

Sources	Destinations				Capacity
	Warehouse 1	Warehouse 2	Warehouse 3	Dummy	
Phoenix	5 **200**	6	5.4 **200**	0	400
Atlanta	7	4.6 **400**	6.6 **100**	0	500
Dummy	0	0	0	0	0
					900
Requirements	200	400	300	0	900

| Costs | $1,000 | $1,840 | $1,740 | $0 | |
| Total Cost | | | | | $4,580 |

FIGURE 7.3 · Optimal Tableau for Sunbelt Pool Company Using Tutor 7.5

the optimal shipments. Verify that each plant's capacity is exhausted and that each warehouse's demand is filled. Also confirm that the total transportation cost of the solution is $4,580.

SOLUTION

Phoenix ships 200 units to warehouse 1 and 200 units to warehouse 3, exhausting its 400-unit capacity. Atlanta ships 400 units of its 500-unit capacity to warehouse 2 and the remaining 100 units to warehouse 3. All warehouse demand is satisfied: Warehouse 1 is fully supplied by Phoenix and warehouse 2 by Atlanta. Warehouse 3 receives 200 units from Phoenix and 100 units from Atlanta, satisfying its 300-unit demand. The total transportation cost is 200($5.00) + 200($5.40) + 400($4.60) + 100($6.60) = $4,580.

Decision Point Management must evaluate other plant locations before deciding on the best one. The optimal solution does not necessarily mean that the best choice is to open an Atlanta plant. It just means that the best allocation pattern for the current choices on the other two dimensions of this multiple-facility location problem (i.e., a capacity of 400 units at Phoenix and the new plant's location at Atlanta) results in total *transportation* costs of $4,580. ❐

THE LARGER SOLUTION PROCESS. Other costs and various qualitative factors also must be considered as additional parts of a complete evaluation. For example, the annual profits earned from the expansion must be balanced against the land and construction costs of a new plant in Atlanta. Thus, management might use the preference matrix approach (see Example 7.1) to account for the full set of location factors.

The analyst should also evaluate other capacity and location combinations. For example, one possibility is to expand at Phoenix and build a smaller plant at Atlanta. Alternatively, a new plant could be built at another location, or several new plants could be built. The analyst must repeat the analysis for each such likely location strategy.

WHAT IS LAYOUT PLANNING?

What are some key layout questions that need to be addressed?

layout planning Planning that involves decisions about the physical arrangement of economic activity centers within a facility.

economic activity center Anything that consumes space; for example, a person or a group of people, a teller window, a machine, a workbench or workstation, a department, a stairway or an aisle, a timecard rack, a cafeteria or a storage room.

Layout planning involves decisions about the physical arrangement of economic activity centers within a facility. An **economic activity center** can be anything that consumes space: a person or group of people, a teller window, a machine, a workbench or workstation, a department, a stairway or an aisle, a timecard rack, a cafeteria or storage room, and so on. Layout planning translates the broader decisions about a firm's competitive priorities, process, and capacity into actual physical arrangements of people, equipment, and space. The goal is to allow workers and equipment to operate most effectively. Before a manager can make decisions regarding physical arrangement, four questions must be addressed.

1. *What Centers Should the Layout Include?* Centers should reflect process decisions and maximize productivity. For example, a central storage area for tools is most efficient for certain processes, but keeping tools at individual workstations makes more sense for other processes.

2. *How Much Space and Capacity Does Each Center Need?* Inadequate space can reduce productivity, deprive employees of privacy, and even create health and safety hazards. However, excessive space is wasteful, can reduce productivity, and can isolate employees unnecessarily.

3. *How Should Each Center's Space Be Configured?* The amount of space, its shape, and the elements in a center are interrelated. For example, placement of a desk and chair relative to the other furniture is determined by the size and shape

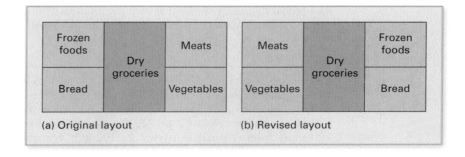

of the office, as well as the activities performed there. Providing a pleasing atmosphere also should be considered as part of the layout configuration decisions, especially in retail outlets and offices.

4. *Where Should Each Center Be Located?*   Location can significantly affect productivity. For example, employees who must frequently interact with one another face-to-face should be placed in a central location rather than in separate, remote locations to reduce time lost traveling back and forth.

The location of a center has two dimensions: (1) *relative location,* or the placement of a center relative to other centers, and (2) *absolute location,* or the particular space that the center occupies within the facility. Both affect a center's performance. Look at the grocery store layout in Figure 7.4(a). It shows the location of five departments, with the dry groceries department allocated twice the space of each of the others. The location of frozen foods relative to bread is the same as the location of meats relative to vegetables, so the distance between the first pair of departments equals the distance between the second pair of departments. Relative location is normally the crucial issue when travel time, materials handling cost, and communication effectiveness are important.

Now look at the plan in Figure 7.4(b). Although the relative locations are the same, the absolute locations have changed. This modified layout might prove unworkable. For example, the cost of moving the meats to the northwest corner could be excessive. Or customers might react negatively to the placement of vegetables in the southwest corner, preferring them to be near the entrance.

STRATEGIC ISSUES

How should layout reflect competitive priorities?

Layout choices can help immensely in communicating an organization's product plans and competitive priorities. If a retailer plans to upgrade the quality of its merchandise, the store layout should convey more exclusiveness and luxury. The photo of a Limited Too store shows a much different atmosphere, because its target market is clothing for girls between 7 and 14 years old.

Layout has many practical and strategic implications. Altering a layout can affect an organization and how well it meets its competitive priorities by

- ❐ facilitating the flow of materials and information
- ❐ increasing the efficient utilization of labor and equipment
- ❐ increasing customer convenience and sales at a retail store
- ❐ reducing hazards to workers
- ❐ improving employee morale
- ❐ improving communication

The type of operation determines layout requirements. For example, in warehouses, materials flows and stockpicking costs are dominant considerations. In retail stores, customer convenience and sales may dominate, whereas communication effectiveness and team building may be crucial in an office.

Among the several fundamental layout choices available to managers are whether to plan for current or future (and less predictable) needs, whether to select a single-story or multistory design, whether to open the planning process to employee suggestions, what type of layout to choose, and what performance criteria to emphasize. Because of their strategic importance, we focus on the last two choices.

LAYOUT TYPES

Should a layout be process, product, hybrid, or fixed position?

The choice of layout type depends largely on process choice. There are four basic types of layout: process, product, hybrid, and fixed position.

PROCESS LAYOUT. With a job process, which is best for low-volume, high-variety production, the operations manager must organize resources (employees and equipment) around the process. A **process layout,** which groups workstations or departments according to function, accomplishes this purpose. For example, in the metal-working job shop shown in Figure 7.5(a), all drills are located in one area of the machine shop and all milling machines are located in another. The process layout is most common when the same operation must intermittently produce many different products or serve many different customers. Demand levels are too low or unpredictable for management to set aside human and capital resources exclusively for a particular product line or type of customer. Advantages of a process layout over a product layout [illustrated by Figure 7.5(b), where centers are arranged in a linear path] include general-purpose and less capital-intensive resources, more flexibility to handle changes in product mix, more specialized employee supervision when job content requires a good deal of technical knowledge, and higher equipment utilization. When volumes are low, dedicating resources to each product or service (as done with a product layout) would require more equipment than pooling the requirements for all products does.[2] a major challenge in designing a process layout is to locate centers so that they bring some order to the apparent chaos of the flexible flow operation.

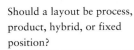

process layout A layout that groups workstations or departments according to function.

PRODUCT LAYOUT. With line or continuous processes, which are best for repetitive or continuous production, the operations manager dedicates resources to individual products or

---

[2]However, management won't allow utilization to get too high. A larger capacity cushion with process layouts absorbs the more unpredictable demands of customized products and services.

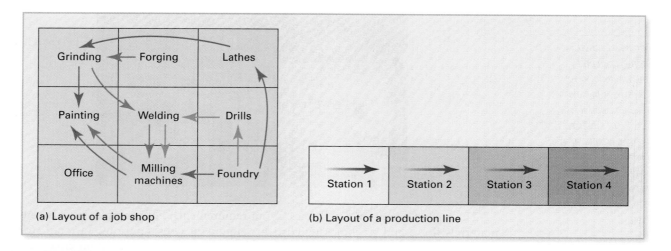

(a) Layout of a job shop

(b) Layout of a production line

FIGURE 7.5

Two Layout Types

product layout A layout in which workstations or departments are arranged in a linear path.

tasks. This strategy is achieved by a **product layout,** illustrated by Figure 7.5(b), in which workstations or departments are arranged in a linear path. As in an automated car wash, the product or customer moves along in a smooth, continuous flow. Resources are arranged around the product's route rather than shared across many products. Product layouts are common in high-volume types of operations. Although product layouts often follow a straight line, a straight line is not always best, and layouts may take an L, O, S, or U shape. A product layout often is called a *production line* or an *assembly line.* The difference between the two is that an assembly line is limited to assembly processes, whereas a production line can be used to perform other processes such as machining.

Product layouts often rely heavily on specialized, capital-intensive resources. When volumes are high, the advantages of product layouts over process layouts include faster processing rates, lower inventories, and less unproductive time lost to changeovers and materials handling. There is less need to decouple one operation from the next, allowing management to cut inventories. The Japanese refer to a line process as *overlapped operations,* whereby materials move directly from one operation to the next without waiting in queues.

For product layouts, deciding where to locate centers is easy because operations must occur in a prescribed order. Centers can simply be placed to follow the product's routing, ensuring that all interacting pairs of centers are as close together as possible or have a common boundary. The challenge of product layout is to group activities into workstations and achieve the desired output rate with the least resources. The composition and number of workstations are crucial decisions, which we explore later in the chapter.

hybrid layout A layout in which some portions of the facility are arranged in a process layout and others are arranged in a product layout.

HYBRID LAYOUT. A **hybrid layout** uses an intermediate strategy, in which some portions of the facility are arranged in a process layout and others are arranged in a product layout. Hybrid layouts are used in facilities having both fabrication and assembly operations, as would be the case if both types of layout shown in Figure 7.5 were in the same building. Fabrication operations—in which components are made from raw materials—have a jumbled flow, whereas assembly operations—in which components are assembled into finished products—have a line flow. Operations managers also create hybrid layouts when introducing cells and flexible automation, such as a flexible manufacturing system (see Supplement E, "Computer-Integrated Manufacturing" on the Student CD-ROM). A *cell* is two or more dissimilar workstations located close together through which a limited number of parts or models are processed with line flows (see Chapter 2, "Process Management").

FIXED-POSITION LAYOUT. The fourth basic type of layout is the **fixed-position layout.** In this arrangement, the product is fixed in place; workers, along with their tools and equipment, come to the product to work on it. Many project processes have this arrangement. This type of layout makes sense when the product is particularly massive or difficult to move, as in shipbuilding, assembling locomotives, making huge pressure vessels, building dams, or repairing home furnaces. A fixed-position layout minimizes the number of times that the product must be moved and often is the only feasible solution.

PERFORMANCE CRITERIA

Other fundamental choices facing the layout planner concern *performance criteria,* which may include one or more of the following factors:

- ❏ level of capital investment
- ❏ requirements for materials handling
- ❏ ease of stockpicking
- ❏ work environment and "atmosphere"
- ❏ ease of equipment maintenance
- ❏ employee attitudes
- ❏ amount of flexibility needed
- ❏ customer convenience and level of sales

Managers must decide early in the process which factors to emphasize in order to come up with a good layout solution. In most cases, multiple criteria are used. For example, a warehouse manager may emphasize ease in stockpicking, flexibility, and amount of space needed (capital investment), whereas a retail store manager may emphasize flexibility, atmosphere, customer convenience, and sales. Sales are particularly important to retailers, which place items with high profitability per cubic foot of shelf space in the most prominent display areas and impulse-buy items near the entrance or checkout counter.

CAPITAL INVESTMENT. Floor space, equipment needs, and inventory levels are assets that the firm buys or leases. These expenditures are an important criterion in all settings. If an office layout is to have partitions to increase privacy, the cost rises. Even increasing space for filing cabinets can add up. A four-drawer lateral file occupies about nine square feet, including the space needed to open it. At $25 per square foot, that translates into a floor space "rental" of $225 a year.

MATERIALS HANDLING. Relative locations of centers should restrict large flows to short distances. Centers between which frequent trips or interactions are required should be placed close to one another. In a manufacturing plant, this approach minimizes materials handling costs. In a warehouse, as the Managerial Practice demonstrates, stockpicking costs can be reduced with a good layout design. In a retail store, customer convenience improves if items are grouped predictably to minimize customer search and travel time. In an office, communication and cooperation often improve when people or departments that must interact frequently are located near one another, because telephone calls and memos can be poor substitutes for face-to-face communication. Spatial separation is one big reason why cross-functional coordination between departments can be challenging.

fixed-position layout An arrangement in which the product is fixed in place; workers, along with their tools and equipment, come to the product to work on it.

What performance criteria should be emphasized?

MANAGERIAL PRACTICE
Warehouse Layouts and E-Commerce

There is a sprawling warehouse ringed by soybean and dairy farms in St. Cloud, Minnesota, that is one of the nerve centers of the Web-retailing revolution. Hundreds of employees whiz through the warehouse aisles on forklifts and cargo haulers, filling orders for the Web sites of Wal-Mart (www.walmartstores.com), Fingerhut (www.fingerhut.com), and other online retailers. The workers snatch goods off thousands of shelves and deliver them to an army of packers, who box the orders and drop them on conveyer belts. Every item has a special code to speed up the packing. A 27-in. television takes an X1, indicating the item is heavy and must be shipped by itself. Lighter-weight valuable items, like VCRs, take a 200 code. That means it requires an additional layer of wrapping paper to help disguise it on a customer's doorstep. Red lights scan each package as it zips by on the conveyer belt. If the weight of the box does not match the specifications on the label, the package is automatically shunted aside so a human inspector can make sure items weren't incorrectly added or omitted. The result is a high-tech process that has become one of the Internet's biggest and most admired distribution centers. The crew can process as many as 30,000 items an hour, and as many as 100 trailer loads of goods arrive each day at the warehouse.

Fingerhut has learned a lot on warehousing processes and layouts. One floor manager, for instance, noticed that employees who pick goods off the shelf would be more efficient if they did not have to travel from one end of the warehouse to the other to fill an order.

Fingerhut wrote a computer program to group customer orders for similar products, so that whenever possible, one employee could fill a bundle of orders without leaving a particular aisle. Each item's location in the warehouse layout is precisely charted. Green-and-white checkered pillow shams, for instance, recently occupied bin YH959 on the second shelf of aisle 52 in building 23A. Computers scan each customer's order, checking the dimensions of every item on the list to calculate the smallest possible box that can be used for shipping. Packages that pass inspection are then routed to one of 38 bays at the shipping dock, where trucks await to haul the goods away for mailing points all over the United States. A dedicated fleet of trucks departs daily to local post offices in points as far away as Seattle or Jacksonville, Florida. By paying local postage fees, Fingerhut saves a bundle on shipping costs.

At the Fingerhut warehouse in St. Cloud, Minnesota, a computer program is used to route the order pickers efficiently. Multiple orders of similar products can be filled without having to travel long distance.

Fingerhut's warehouse illustrates a fact of life on the Internet: While anyone with a computer and an Internet connection can open up a "store" in cyberspace, delivering the goods to consumers has proven to be a much more complicated task. Major retailers, from traditional brick-and-mortar chains such as Macy's (www.federated-fds.com/divisions/mae_1_3.asp) to Web powerhouse Amazon.com Inc., learned that lesson the hard way during the Christmas of 1998, when an unexpected surge of online orders left thousands of irritated customers who did not get their gifts in time for the holidays. Since that time, Fingerhut's expertise has helped it score some of the biggest coups. It now ships all the online orders for mammoth Wal-Mart Stores, Inc., along with Fingerhut's own vast mail-order and online operations. Federated Department Stores, Inc. (www.federated-fds.com), gave it an even bigger vote of confidence in 1999 by spending $1.7 billion to buy Fingerhut, which now is handling orders for Macy's, Bloomingdale's, and Federated's other chains.

Source: "Retailing: Behind Doors of a Warehouse: Heavy Lifting of E-Commerce." *Wall Street Journal* (September 3, 1999).

FLEXIBILITY. A flexible layout allows a firm to adapt quickly to changing customer needs and preferences and is best for many situations. **Layout flexibility** means either that the facility remains desirable after significant changes occur or that it can be easily and inexpensively adapted in response to changes. The changes can be in the mix of customers served by a store, goods made at a plant, space requirements in a warehouse, or organizational structure in an office. Using modular furniture and partitions, rather than permanent load-bearing walls, is one way to minimize the cost of office layout changes. So can having wide bays (fewer columns), heavy-duty floors, and extra electrical connections in a plant.

OTHER CRITERIA. Other criteria that may be important include labor productivity, machine maintenance, work environment, and organizational structure. For example, labor productivity can be affected if certain workstations can be operated by common personnel in some layouts but not in others. Downtime spent waiting for materials can be caused by materials handling difficulties resulting from poor layout.

layout flexibility The property of a facility to be desirable after significant changes occur, or to be easily and inexpensively adapted in response to changes.

CREATING HYBRID LAYOUTS

Can some miniature product layouts be created in a facility?

When volumes are not high enough to justify dedicating a single line of multiple workers to a single product, managers still may be able to derive the benefits of product layout—line flows, simpler materials handling, low setups, and reduced labor costs—by creating product layouts in some portions of the facility. Two techniques for creating hybrid layouts are one-worker, multiple-machines (OWMM) cells and group technology (GT) cells. They are special types of cells, which we described earlier as a way to focus operations (see Chapter 2, "Process Management").

ONE WORKER, MULTIPLE MACHINES

If volumes are not sufficient to keep several workers busy on one production line, the manager might set up a line small enough to keep one worker busy. A one-person cell is the theory behind the **one-worker, multiple-machines (OWMM) cell**, in which a worker operates several different machines simultaneously to achieve a line flow. Having one worker operate several identical machines is not unusual. However, with an OWMM cell, several different machines are in the line.

one-worker, multiple-machines (OWMM) cell A one-person cell in which a worker operates several different machines simultaneously to achieve a line flow.

An OWMM arrangement reduces both inventory and labor requirements. Inventory is cut because, rather than piling up in queues, materials move directly into the next operation. Labor is cut because more work is automated. The addition of several low-cost automated devices can maximize the number of machines included in an OWMM arrangement: automatic tool changers, loaders and unloaders, start and stop devices, and fail-safe devices that detect defective parts or products. Japanese manufacturers are applying the OWMM concept widely because of their desire to achieve low inventories.

GROUP TECHNOLOGY

A second option for achieving product layouts with low-volume processes is **group technology (GT)**. This manufacturing technique creates cells not limited to just one worker and has a unique way of selecting work to be done by the cell. The GT method groups parts or products with similar characteristics into *families* and sets aside groups of machines for their production. Families may be based on size, shape, manufacturing or routing requirements, or demand. The goal is to identify a set of products with similar processing requirements and minimize machine changeover or setup. For example,

group technology (GT) An option for achieving product layouts with low-volume processes; creates cells not limited to just one worker and has a unique way of selecting work to be done by the cell.

all bolts might be assigned to the same family because they all require the same basic processing steps regardless of size or shape.

Once parts have been grouped into families, the next step is to organize the machine tools needed to perform the basic processes on these parts into separate cells. The machines in each cell require only minor adjustments to accommodate product changeovers from one part to the next in the same family. By simplifying product routings, GT cells reduce the time a job is in the shop. Queues of materials waiting to be worked on are shortened or eliminated. Frequently, materials handling is automated so that, after loading raw materials into the cell, a worker does not handle machined parts until the job has been completed.

Figure 7.6 compares process flows before and after creation of GT cells. Figure 7.6(a) shows a shop floor where machines are grouped according to function: lathing, milling, drilling, grinding, and assembly. After lathing, a part is moved to one of the milling machines, where it waits in line until it has a higher priority than any other job

FIGURE 7.6

Process Flows Before and After the Use of GT Cells

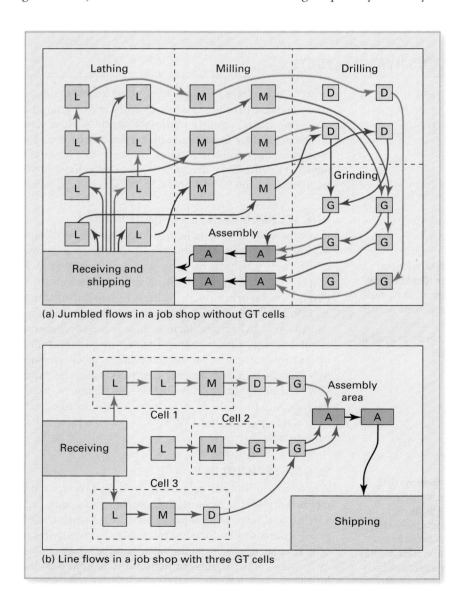

(a) Jumbled flows in a job shop without GT cells

(b) Line flows in a job shop with three GT cells

competing for the machine's capacity. When the milling operation on the part has been finished, the part is moved to a drilling machine, and so on. The queues can be long, creating significant time delays. Flows of materials are very jumbled because the parts being processed in any one area of the shop have so many different routings.

By contrast, the manager of the shop shown in Figure 7.6(b) has identified three product families that account for a majority of the firm's production. One family always requires two lathing operations followed by one operation at the milling machines. The second family always requires a milling operation followed by a grinding operation. The third family requires the use of a lathe, milling machine, and drill press. For simplicity, only the flows of parts assigned to these three families are shown. The remaining parts are produced at machines outside the cells and still have jumbled routings. Some equipment might have to be duplicated, as when a machine is required for one or more cells and for operations outside the cells. However, by creating three GT cells, the manager has definitely created more line flows and simplified routings.

DESIGNING PROCESS LAYOUTS

How can a better process layout be found for a facility?

The approach to designing a layout depends on whether a process layout or a product layout has been chosen. A fixed-position format basically eliminates the layout problem, whereas the design of the hybrid layout partially uses process-layout principles and partially uses product layout principles.

Process layout involves three basic steps, whether the design is for a new layout or for revising an existing one: (1) gather information, (2) develop a block plan, and (3) design a detailed layout.

STEP 1: GATHER INFORMATION

Longhorn Machine is a machine shop that produces a variety of small metal parts on general-purpose equipment. A full shift of 26 workers and a second shift of 6 workers operate its 32 machines. Three types of information are needed to begin designing a revised layout for Longhorn Machine: space requirements by center, available space, and closeness factors.

SPACE REQUIREMENTS BY CENTER. Longhorn has grouped its processes into six different departments: burr and grind, NC equipment, shipping and receiving, lathes and drills, tool crib, and inspection. The exact space requirements of each department, in square feet, are as follows:

Department	Area Needed (ft^2)
1. Burr and grind	1,000
2. NC equipment	950
3. Shipping and receiving	750
4. Lathes and drills	1,200
5. Tool crib	800
6. Inspection	700
Total	5,400

The layout designer must tie space requirements to capacity plans, calculate the specific equipment and space needs for each center, and allow circulation space such as aisles and the like.

Current Block Plan for Longhorn Machine

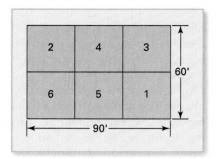

block plan A plan that allocates space and indicates placement of each department.

AVAILABLE SPACE. A **block plan** allocates space and indicates placement of each department. To describe a new facility layout, the plan need only provide the facility's dimensions and space allocations. When an existing facility layout is being modified, the current block plan also is needed. Longhorn's available space is 90 feet by 60 feet, or 5,400 square feet. The designer could begin the design by dividing the total amount of space into six equal blocks (900 square feet each), even though inspection needs only 700 square feet and lathes and drills needs 1,200 square feet. The equal-space approximation shown in Figure 7.7 is sufficient until the detailed layout stage, when larger departments (such as lathes and drills) are assigned more block spaces than smaller departments.

CLOSENESS FACTORS. The layout designer must also know which centers need to be located close to one another. Location is based on the number of trips between centers and qualitative factors.

trip matrix A matrix that gives the number of trips (or some other measure of materials movement) between each pair of departments per day.

The following table shows Longhorn's **trip matrix,** which gives the number of trips (or some other measure of materials movement) between each pair of departments per day. The designer estimates the number of trips between centers by using routings and ordering frequencies for typical items made at the plant, by carrying out statistical sampling, or by polling supervisors and materials handlers. Only the right-hand portion of the matrix, which shows the number of trips in *both* directions, is used. For example, there are 75 trips per day between departments 2 (NC equipment) and 5 (tool crib). Showing the merged flow totals eliminates the need to add the flow in one direction to the flow in the other direction. The totals give clues as to which departments should be located close together. For example, the largest number of trips is between departments 3 and 6 (at 90 trips), with 1 and 6 close behind (at 80 trips). Thus, the designer should locate department 6 near both 1 and 3, which is not the arrangement in the current layout.

Trip Matrix

Department	\multicolumn{6}{c}{Trips Between Departments}					
	1	2	3	4	5	6
1. Burr and grind	—	20		20		80
2. NC equipment		—	10		75	
3. Shipping and receiving			—	15		90
4. Lathes and drills				—	70	
5. Tool crib					—	
6. Inspection						—

REL Chart

Department	Closeness Rating Between Departments						Closeness Ratings	
	1	**2**	**3**	**4**	**5**	**6**	**Rating**	**Definition**
1. Burr and grind	—	E (3, 1)	U	I (2, 1)	U	A (1)	A	Absolutely necessary
							E	Especially important
2. NC equipment		—	O (1)	U	E (1)	I (6)	I	Important
							O	Ordinary closeness
3. Shipping and receiving			—	O (1)	U	A (1)	U	Unimportant
							X	Undesirable
4. Lathes and drills				—	E (1)	X (5)	**Explanation Codes**	
							Code	**Meaning**
5. Tool crib					—	U	1	Materials handling
							2	Shared personnel
6. Inspection						—	3	Ease of supervision
							4	Space utilization
							5	Noise
							6	Employee attitudes

REL chart A chart that reflects the qualitative judgments of managers and employees and that can be used in place of a trip matrix.

A **REL chart** (REL is short for *relationships*), which reflects the qualitative judgments of managers and employees, can be used in place of a trip matrix. In the accompanying REL chart for Longhorn Machine, an A rating represents the judgment that locating two particular departments close to each other is absolutely necessary; E is for especially important, I for important, O for ordinary closeness, U for unimportant, and X for undesirable. The A rating is higher than the E, but as the assessment is qualitative, the designer does not know by how much. One advantage of a REL chart is that the manager can account for multiple performance criteria when selecting closeness ratings, whereas a trip matrix focuses solely on materials handling or stockpicking costs. For example, the desired closeness between departments 1 and 2 is rated E because of two considerations: ease of supervision and materials handling.

OTHER CONSIDERATIONS. Finally, the information gathered for Longhorn includes performance criteria that depend on the *absolute* location of a department. Longhorn has two criteria based on absolute location:

1. Shipping and receiving (department 3) should remain where it is because it is next to the dock.
2. Lathes and drills (department 4) should remain where it is because relocation costs would be prohibitive.

Noise levels and management preference are other potential sources of performance criteria that depend on absolute location. A REL chart or trip matrix cannot reflect these criteria, because it reflects only *relative* location considerations. The layout designer must list them separately.

STEP 2: DEVELOP A BLOCK PLAN
The second step in layout design is to develop a block plan that best satisfies performance criteria and area requirements. The most elementary way to do so is by trial and error. Because success depends on the designer's ability to spot patterns in the data, this approach does not guarantee the selection of the best or even a nearly best solution. When supplemented by the use of a computer to evaluate solutions, however, such an approach often compares quite favorably with more sophisticated computerized techniques.

| EXAMPLE 7.5 | *Developing a Block Plan* |

Develop an acceptable block plan for Longhorn, using trial and error. The goal is to minimize materials handling costs.

SOLUTION

A good place to start is with the largest closeness ratings in the trip matrix (say, 70 and above). Beginning with the largest number of trips and working down the list, you might plan to locate departments as follows:

Departments 3 and 6 close together   Departments 2 and 5 close together

Departments 1 and 6 close together   Departments 4 and 5 close together

Departments 3 and 4 should remain at their current locations because of the "other considerations."

If after several attempts you cannot meet all five requirements, drop one or more and try again. If you can meet all five easily, add more (such as for interactions below 70).

The block plan in Figure 7.8 shows a trial-and-error solution that satisfies all five requirements. We started by keeping departments 3 and 4 in their original locations. As the first requirement is to locate departments 3 and 6 close to each other, we put 6 in the southeast corner of the layout. The second requirement is to have departments 1 and 6 close together, so we placed 1 in the space just to the left of 6, and so on.

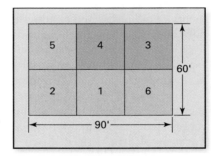

FIGURE 7.8 • Proposed Block Plan

Decision Point This solution fell into place easily for this particular problem, but it might not be the best layout. Management wants to consider several alternative layouts before making a final choice and needs some measure of effectiveness with which to compare them. ❐

When *relative* locations are a primary concern, such as for effective materials handling, stockpicking, and communication, the load–distance method can be used to compare alternative block plans. Just as with facility location decisions, we can use the total load–distance, or *ld*, score by multiplying each load by the distance traveled and then summing over all of the loads. Here the loads are just the numbers in the trip matrix. Each load goes between two centers (each represented by a row and a column in the matrix). The distance (actual, Euclidean, or rectilinear) between them is calculated from the block plan being evaluated. Of course, the loads need not be trips; any numerical closeness measure related to distance will do.

| EXAMPLE 7.6 | *Calculating the Total Desirability Score* |

How much better, in terms of the *ld* score, is the proposed block plan? Use the rectilinear distance measure.

SOLUTION

The accompanying table lists each pair of departments that has a nonzero closeness factor in the trip matrix. For the third column, calculate the rectilinear distances between the departments in the current layout. For example, in Figure 7.7, departments 1 and 2 are in the southeast and northwest blocks of the plant, respectively. The distance between the centers of these blocks is 3 units (two horizontally and one vertically). For the fourth column, we multiply the loads by the distances and then add the results for a total *ld* score of 785 for the current plan. Similar calculations for the proposed plan in Figure 7.8 produce an *ld* score of only 400. For example, between departments 1 and 2 is just 1 unit of distance (one horizontally and none vertically).

DEPARTMENT PAIR	CLOSENESS FACTOR, *I*	CURRENT PLAN		PROPOSED PLAN	
		Distance *d*	Load–Distance Score, *ld*	Distance *d*	Load–Distance Score, *ld*
1, 2	20	3	60	1	20
1, 4	20	2	40	1	20
1, 6	80	2	160	1	80
2, 3	10	2	20	3	30
2, 5	75	2	150	1	75
3, 4	15	1	15	1	15
3, 6	90	3	270	1	90
4, 5	70	1	70	1	70
			ld = 785		*ld* = 400

To be exact, we could multiply the two *ld* total scores by 30 because each unit of distance represents 30 feet. However, the relative difference between the two totals remains unchanged.

Decision Point Although the *ld* score for the proposed layout represents an almost 50 percent improvement, management is not sure the improvement outweighs the cost of relocating four of the six departments (all but 3 and 4). ◻

Although the *ld* score in Example 7.6 for the proposed layout represents an almost 50 percent improvement, the designer may be able to do better. However, the designer must first determine whether the revised layout is worth the cost of relocating four of the six departments (all but 3 and 4). If relocation costs are too high, a less-expensive proposal must be found.

STEP 3: DESIGN A DETAILED LAYOUT

After finding a satisfactory block plan, the layout designer translates it into a detailed representation, showing the exact size and shape of each center, the arrangement of elements (e.g., desks, machines, and storage areas), and the location of aisles, stairways, and other service space. These visual representations can be two-dimensional drawings, three-dimensional models, or computer-aided graphics. This step helps decision makers discuss the proposal and problems that might otherwise be overlooked.

DESIGNING PRODUCT LAYOUTS

How can a better product layout for a facility be determined?

Product layouts raise management issues entirely different from those of process layouts. Often called a production or assembly line, a product layout arranges workstations in sequence. The product moves from one station to the next until its completion at the end of the line. Typically, one worker operates each station, performing repetitive tasks. Little inventory is built up between stations, so stations cannot operate

line balancing The
assignment of work to
stations in a line so as
to achieve the desired
output rate with the
smallest number of
workstations.

work elements The
smallest units of work that
can be performed
independently.

immediate predecessors
Work elements that must
be done before the next
element can begin.

precedence diagram
A diagram that allows one
to visualize immediate
predecessors better; work
elements are denoted by
circles, with the time
required to perform the
work shown below each
circle.

independently. Thus, the line is only as fast as its slowest workstation. In other words, if the slowest station takes 45 seconds per unit, the line's fastest possible output is one product every 45 seconds.

LINE BALANCING

Line balancing is the assignment of work to stations in a line so as to achieve the desired output rate with the smallest number of workstations. Normally, one worker is assigned to a station. Thus, the line that produces at the desired pace with the fewest workers is the most efficient one. Line balancing must be performed when a line is set up initially, when a line is rebalanced to change its hourly output rate, or when product or process changes. The goal is to obtain workstations with well-balanced workloads (e.g., every station takes roughly 45 seconds per unit produced).

The analyst begins by separating the work into **work elements,** the smallest units of work that can be performed independently. The analyst then obtains the labor standard (see Supplement C, "Measuring Output Rates" on the Student CD-ROM) for each element and identifies the work elements, called **immediate predecessors,** that must be done before the next can begin.

PRECEDENCE DIAGRAM. Most lines must satisfy some technological precedence requirements—that is, certain work elements must be done before the next can begin. However, most lines also allow for some latitude and more than one sequence of operations. To help you visualize immediate predecessors better, let us run through the construction of a **precedence diagram.**[3] We denote the work elements by circles, with the time required to perform the work shown below each circle. Arrows lead from immediate predecessors to the next work element.

EXAMPLE 7.7	*Constructing a Precedence Diagram*

Green Grass, Inc., a manufacturer of lawn and garden equipment, is designing an assembly line to produce a new fertilizer spreader, the Big Broadcaster. Using the following information on the production process, construct a precedence diagram for the Big Broadcaster.

WORK ELEMENT	DESCRIPTION	TIME (sec)	IMMEDIATE PREDECESSOR(S)
A	Bolt leg frame to hopper	40	None
B	Insert impeller shaft	30	A
C	Attach axle	50	A
D	Attach agitator	40	B
E	Attach drive wheel	6	B
F	Attach free wheel	25	C
G	Mount lower post	15	C
H	Attach controls	20	D, E
I	Mount nameplate	18	F, G
		Total 244	

SOLUTION

Figure 7.9 shows the complete diagram. We begin with work element A, which has no immediate predecessors. Next, we add elements B and C, for which element A is the only immediate predecessor. After entering labor standards and arrows showing precedence, we add elements D and E,

---

[3] Precedence relationships and precedence diagrams are important in the entirely different context of project scheduling (see Chapter 3, "Managing Project Processes").

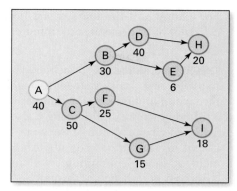

FIGURE 7.9 • Precedence Diagram for Assembling the Big Broadcaster

and so on. The diagram simplifies interpretation. Work element F, for example, can be done anywhere on the line after element C is completed. However, element I must await completion of elements F and G.

Decision Point Management now has enough information to develop a layout that clusters work elements to form workstations, with a goal being to balance the workloads, and in the process minimize the number of workstations required. ⊐

What should be a line's output rate?

DESIRED OUTPUT RATE. The goal of line balancing is to match the output rate to the production plan. For example, if the production plan calls for 4,000 units per week and the line operates 80 hours per week, the desired output rate ideally would be 50 units (4,000/80) per hour. Matching output to demand ensures on-time delivery and prevents buildup of unwanted inventory. However, managers should avoid rebalancing a line too frequently, because each time a line is rebalanced, many workers' jobs on the line must be redesigned, temporarily hurting productivity and sometimes even requiring a new detailed layout for some stations.

Some automobile plants avoid frequent changes by eliminating a shift entirely when demand falls and inventory becomes excessive, rather than gradually scaling back the output rate. Managers can also add shifts to increase equipment utilization, which is crucial for capital-intensive facilities. However, higher pay rates or low demand may make multiple shifts undesirable or unnecessary.

cycle time The maximum time allowed for work on a unit at each station.

CYCLE TIME. After determining the desired output rate for a line, the analyst can calculate the line's cycle time. A line's **cycle time** is the maximum time allowed for work on a unit at each station.[4] If the time required for work elements at a station exceeds the line's cycle time, the station will be a bottleneck, preventing the line from reaching its desired output rate. The target cycle time is the reciprocal of the desired hourly output rate:

$$c = \frac{1}{r}$$

where

c = cycle time in hours per unit

r = desired output rate in units per hour

---

[4] Except in the context of line balancing, *cycle time* has a different meaning. It is the elapsed time between starting and completing a job. Some researchers and practitioners prefer the term *lead time*.

For example, if the line's desired output rate is 60 units per hour, the cycle time is $c = 1/60$ hour per unit, or 1 minute.

THEORETICAL MINIMUM. To achieve the desired output rate, managers use line balancing to assign every work element to a station, making sure to satisfy all precedence requirements and to minimize the number of stations, *n,* formed. If each station is operated by a different worker, minimizing *n* also maximizes worker productivity. Perfect balance is achieved when the sum of the work-element times at each station equals the cycle time, *c,* and no station has any idle time. For example, if the sum of each station's work-element times is 1 minute, which is also the cycle time, there is perfect balance. Although perfect balance usually is unachievable in practice, owing to the unevenness of work-element times and the inflexibility of precedence requirements, it sets a benchmark, or goal, for the smallest number of stations possible. The **theoretical minimum (TM)** for the number of stations is

theoretical minimum (TM) A benchmark or goal for the smallest number of stations possible, where the total time required to assemble each unit (the sum of all work-element standard times) is divided by the cycle time.

$$TM = \frac{\Sigma t}{c}$$

where

> Σt = total time required to assemble each unit (the sum of all work-element standard times)
> c = cycle time

For example, if the sum of the work-element times is 15 minutes and the cycle time is 1 minute, TM = 15/1, or 15 stations. Any fractional values obtained for TM are rounded up because fractional stations are impossible.

IDLE TIME, EFFICIENCY, AND BALANCE DELAY. Minimizing *n* automatically ensures (1) minimal idle time, (2) maximal efficiency, and (3) minimal balance delay. Idle time is the total unproductive time for all stations in the assembly of each unit:

$$\text{Idle time} = nc - \Sigma t$$

where

> n = number of stations
> c = cycle time
> Σt = total standard time required to assemble each unit

Efficiency is the ratio of productive time to total time, expressed as a percent:

$$\text{Efficiency(percent)} = \frac{\Sigma t}{nc} (100)$$

balance delay The amount by which efficiency falls short of 100 percent.

Balance delay is the amount by which efficiency falls short of 100 percent:

$$\text{Balance delay(percent)} = 100 - \text{Efficiency}$$

As long as *c* is fixed, we can optimize all three goals by minimizing *n.*

| EXAMPLE 7.8 | *Calculating the Cycle Time, Theoretical Minimum, and Efficiency* |

**TUTOR
7.6**

Green Grass's plant manager has just received marketing's latest forecasts of Big Broadcaster sales for the next year. She wants its production line to be designed to make 2,400 spreaders per week for at least the next three months. The plant will operate 40 hours per week.

   a. What should be the line's cycle time?

   b. What is the smallest number of workstations that she could hope for in designing the line for this cycle time?

   c. Suppose that she finds a solution that requires only five stations. What would be the line's efficiency?

SOLUTION

a. First convert the desired output rate (2,400 units per week) to an hourly rate by dividing the weekly output rate by 40 hours per week to get $r = 60$ units per hour. Then the cycle time is

$$c = \frac{1}{r} = \frac{1}{60} \text{ hour/unit} = 1 \text{ minute/unit}$$

b. Now calculate the theoretical minimum for the number of stations by dividing the total time, Σt, by the cycle time, $c = 1$ minute $= 60$ seconds. Assuming perfect balance, we have

$$\text{TM} = \frac{\Sigma t}{c} = \frac{244 \text{ seconds}}{60 \text{ seconds}} = 4.067, \quad \text{or} \quad 5 \text{ stations}$$

c. Now calculate the efficiency of a five-station solution, assuming for now that one can be found:

$$\text{Efficiency(percent)} = \frac{\Sigma t}{nc}(100) = \frac{244}{5(60)}(100) = 81.3\%$$

Decision Point Thus, if the manager finds a solution with five stations, that is the minimum number of stations possible. However, the efficiency (sometimes called the *theoretical maximum efficiency*) will be only 81.3 percent. Perhaps the line should be operated less than 40 hours per week and the employees transferred to other kinds of work when the line does not operate. ❏

FINDING A SOLUTION. Often, many assembly-line solutions are possible, even for such simple problems as Green Grass's. The goal is to cluster the work elements into workstations so that (1) the number of workstations required is minimized, and (2) the precedence and cycle-time requirements are not violated. Here we use the trial-and-error method to find a solution, although commercial software packages are also available. Figure 7.10 shows a good solution that creates just five workstations. We know that is the minimum number possible, because five is the theoretical minimum (see Example 7.8). All of the precedence and cycle-time requirements are also satisfied. For example, workstation S5 consists of work elements E, H, and I, which one worker will perform on each unit that comes along the assembly line. The total processing time per unit is 44 seconds (or 6 + 20 + 18), which does not exceed the cycle time of 60 seconds (see Example 7.8). Furthermore, the immediate predecessors of these three work elements are assigned to this workstation or upstream workstations, so their precedence requirements are satisfied. For example, the worker at workstation S5 can do element I at any time but will not start element H until element E is finished.

OTHER CONSIDERATIONS

In addition to balancing a line for a given cycle time, managers must also consider four other options: pacing, behavioral factors, number of models produced, and cycle times.

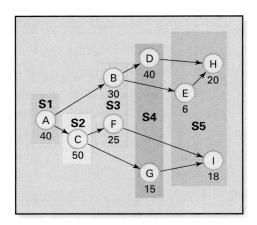

FIGURE 7.10 • Big Broadcaster Precedence Diagram Solution

PACING. The movement of product from one station to the next as soon as the cycle time has elapsed is called **pacing**. Pacing allows materials handling to be automated and requires less inventory storage area. However, it is less flexible in handling unexpected delays that require either slowing down the entire line or pulling unfinished work off line to be completed later.

BEHAVIORAL FACTORS. The most controversial aspect of product layouts is behavioral response. Studies have shown that installing production lines increases absenteeism, turnover, and grievances. Paced production and high specialization (say, cycle times of less than two minutes) lower job satisfaction. Workers generally favor inventory buffers as a means of avoiding mechanical pacing. One study even showed that productivity increased on unpaced lines.

NUMBER OF MODELS PRODUCED. A **mixed-model line** produces several items belonging to the same family. In contrast, a single-model line produces one model with no variations. Mixed-model production enables a plant to achieve both high-volume production *and* product variety. However, it complicates scheduling and increases the need for good communication about the specific parts to be produced at each station.

CYCLE TIMES. A line's cycle time depends on the desired output rate (or sometimes on the maximum number of workstations allowed). In turn, the maximum line efficiency varies considerably with the cycle time selected. Thus, exploring a range of cycle times makes sense. A manager might go with a particularly efficient solution even if it does not match the output rate. The manager can compensate for the mismatch by varying the number of hours the line operates through overtime, extending shifts, or adding shifts. Multiple lines might even be the answer.

pacing The movement of product from one station to the next after the cycle time has elapsed.

What can be done to humanize product layouts?

Should a mixed-model line be considered?

mixed-model line A product line that produces several items belonging to the same family.

LOCATION AND LAYOUT PLANNING ACROSS THE ORGANIZATION

Location decisions affect processes and departments throughout the organization. When locating new retail facilities, marketing must carefully assess how the location will appeal to customers. Relocating whole or part of an organization can significantly affect workforce attitudes and the ability to operate effectively across department lines.

Operations also has an important stake in location decisions. The choices can significantly affect supply-chain effectiveness, workforce productivity, and the ability to provide quality products and services.

Similarly, layouts have a big impact throughout a business because every facility has a layout. Good layouts can improve coordination across departmental lines and functional area boundaries. Each process in a facility has a layout that should be carefully designed. The layouts of retail operations, such as the RiverTown Crossings mall, can affect customer attitudes and, therefore, sales. How a manufacturing or warehousing process is laid out affects materials handling costs, throughput times, and worker productivity. Redesigning layouts can require significant capital investments, which need to be analyzed from an accounting and financial perspective. Layouts also affect employee attitudes, whether on a production line or in an office.

EQUATION SUMMARY

1. Euclidean distance: $d_{AB} = \sqrt{(x_A - x_B)^2 + (y_A - y_B)^2}$

2. Rectilinear distance: $d_{AB} = |x_A - x_B| + |y_A - y_B|$

3. Load–distance score: $ld = \sum_i l_i d_i$

4. Center of gravity: $x^* = \dfrac{\sum_i l_i x_i}{\sum_i l_i}$ and $y^* = \dfrac{\sum_i l_i y_i}{\sum_i l_i}$

5. Cycle time (in seconds): $c = \dfrac{1}{r}$ (3,600 seconds/hour)

6. Theoretical minimum number of workstations: $TM = \dfrac{\sum t}{c}$

7. Idle time (in seconds): $nc - \sum t$

8. Efficiency (percent): $\dfrac{\sum t}{nc} = (100)$

9. Balance delay (percent): $100 - $ Efficiency

CHAPTER HIGHLIGHTS

❏ The globalization of operations affects both manufacturing and service industries. More facilities are being located in other countries, and offshore sales (and imports) are increasing. Offsetting the advantages of global operations are differences in language, regulations, and culture that create new management problems.

❏ Location decisions depend on many factors. For any situation some factors may be disregarded entirely; the remainder may be divided into dominant and secondary factors.

❏ Favorable labor climate, proximity to markets, quality of life, proximity to suppliers and resources, and proximity to other company facilities are important factors in most manufacturing plant location decisions. Proximity to markets, clients, or customers usually is the most important factor in service industry location decisions. Competition is a complicating factor in estimating the sales potential of a location. Having competitors' facilities nearby may be an asset or a liability, depending on the type of business.

❏ One way of evaluating qualitative factors is to calculate a weighted score for each alternative location by using the preference matrix approach. The load–distance method brings together concerns of proximity (to markets, suppliers, resources, and other company facilities) during the early stages of location analysis. By making a full grid or patterned search of an area, an analyst identifies locations resulting in lower *ld* scores. The center of gravity of an area is a good starting point for making a patterned search. Break-even analysis can help compare location alternatives when location factors can be expressed in terms of variable and fixed costs.

❏ Multiple-facility problems have three dimensions: location, allocation, and capacity. The transportation method is a basic tool for finding the best allocation pattern for a particular combination of location–capacity choices. Transportation costs are recalculated for each location–capacity combination under consideration. The transportation method's single criterion for determining the best shipping pattern is minimum transportation costs. To complete the location study, the analysis must be expanded to account for the full set of location factors.

❏ Location analysis can become complex for multiple facilities. A variety of computerized heuristic, simulation, and optimization models have been developed over the last two decades to help analysts deal with this complexity.

❏ Layout decisions go beyond placement of economic activity centers. Equally important are which centers to include, how much space they need, and how to configure their space.

❏ There are four layout types: process, product, hybrid, and fixed position. Management's choice should reflect process choice. Flexible flows call for a process layout, whereas line flows call for a product layout. Hybrid layouts include OWMM, GT cells, and FMS.

❏ Capital investment, materials handling cost, and flexibility are important criteria in judging most layouts. Entirely different criteria, such as encouraging sales or communication, might be emphasized for stores or offices.

❏ If product volumes are too low to justify dedicating a production line to a single product, obtaining overlapped operations may still be possible. In such cases, the one-worker, multiple-machines (OWMM) concept or group technology (GT) cells, where machines are arranged to produce families of parts, may be feasible.

❏ Designing a process layout involves gathering the necessary information, developing an acceptable block plan, and translating the block plan into a detailed layout. Information needed for process layouts includes space requirements by center, available space, the block plan for existing layouts, closeness ratings, and performance criteria relating to absolute location concerns. Closeness ratings can be tabulated on either a trip matrix or a REL chart. A manual approach to finding a block plan begins with listing key requirements, which may be based on high closeness ratings or on other considerations. Trial and error is then used to find a block plan that satisfies most of the requirements. A load–distance score is helpful in evaluating the plan for relative location concerns.

❏ In product layouts, workstations are arranged in a somewhat naturally occurring, commonsense sequence as required for high-volume production of only one product or a family of products. Because the physical arrangement is determined by the product's design, management concerns become line balance, pacing, behavior, number of models, and cycle times.

❏ In line balancing, tasks are assigned to stations so as to satisfy all precedence and cycle-time constraints while minimizing the number of stations required. Balancing minimizes idle time, maximizes efficiency, and minimizes delay. The desired output rate from a line depends not only on demand forecasts but also on frequency of rebalancing, capacity utilization, and job specialization.

SOLVED PROBLEM 1

An electronics manufacturer must expand by building a second facility. The search has been narrowed to four locations, all acceptable to management in terms of dominant factors. Assessment of these sites in terms of seven location factors is shown in Table 7.1. For example, location A has a factor score of 5 (excellent) for labor climate; the weight for this factor (20) is the highest of any.

TABLE 7.1   *Factor Information for Electronics Manufacturer*

LOCATION FACTOR	FACTOR WEIGHT	FACTOR SCORE FOR EACH LOCATION			
		A	B	C	D
1. Labor climate	20	5	4	4	5
2. Quality of life	16	2	3	4	1
3. Transportation system	16	3	4	3	2
4. Proximity to markets	14	5	3	4	4
5. Proximity to materials	12	2	3	3	4
6. Taxes	12	2	5	5	4
7. Utilities	10	5	4	3	3

Calculate the weighted score for each location. Which location should be recommended?

SOLUTION

Based on the weighted scores in Table 7.2, location C is the preferred site, although location B is a close second.

TABLE 7.2   *Calculating Weighted Scores for Electronics Manufacturer*

LOCATION FACTOR	FACTOR WEIGHT	WEIGHTED SCORE FOR EACH LOCATION			
		A	B	C	D
1. Labor climate	20	100	80	80	100
2. Quality of life	16	32	48	64	16
3. Transportation system	16	48	64	48	32
4. Proximity to markets	14	70	42	56	56
5. Proximity to materials	12	24	36	36	48
6. Taxes	12	24	60	60	48
7. Utilities	10	50	40	30	30
Totals	100	348	370	374	330

SOLVED PROBLEM 2

The operations manager for Mile-High Beer has narrowed the search for a new facility location to seven communities. Annual fixed costs (land, property taxes, insurance, equipment, and buildings) and variable costs (labor, materials, transportation, and variable overhead) are shown in Table 7.3.

TABLE 7.3   *Fixed and Variable Costs for Mile-High Beer*

COMMUNITY	FIXED COSTS PER YEAR	VARIABLE COSTS PER BARREL
Aurora	$1,600,000	$17.00
Boulder	$2,000,000	$12.00
Colorado Springs	$1,500,000	$16.00
Denver	$3,000,000	$10.00
Englewood	$1,800,000	$15.00
Fort Collins	$1,200,000	$15.00
Golden	$1,700,000	$14.00

a. Which of the communities can be eliminated from further consideration because they are dominated (both variable and fixed costs are higher) by another community?

b. Plot the total cost curves for all remaining communities on a single graph. Identify on the graph the approximate range over which each community provides the lowest cost.

c. Using break-even analysis (see Supplement A, "Decision Making" on the Student CD-ROM), calculate the break-even quantities to determine the range over which each community provides the lowest cost.

SOLUTION

a. Aurora and Colorado Springs are dominated by Fort Collins, as both fixed and variable costs are higher for those communities than for Fort Collins. Englewood is dominated by Golden.

b. Figure 7.11 shows that Fort Collins is best for low volumes, Boulder for intermediate volumes, and Denver for high volumes. Although Golden is not dominated by any community, it is the second or third choice over the entire range. Golden does not become the lowest cost choice at any volume.

c. The break-even point between Fort Collins and Boulder is

$$\$1,200,000 + \$15Q = \$2,000,000 + \$12Q$$
$$Q = 266,667 \text{ barrels per year}$$

The break-even point between Denver and Boulder is

$$\$3,000,000 + \$10Q = \$2,000,000 + \$12Q$$
$$Q = 500,000 \text{ barrels per year}$$

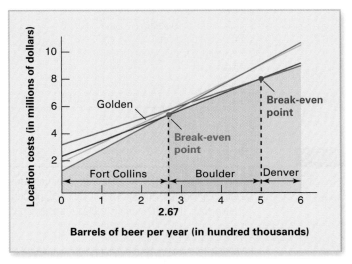

FIGURE 7.11

SOLVED PROBLEM 3

A supplier to the electric utility industry has a heavy product, and transportation costs are high. One market area includes the lower part of the Great Lakes region and the upper portion of the southeastern region. More than 600,000 tons are to be shipped to eight major customer locations, as shown in Table 7.4.

TABLE 7.4 *Markets for Electric Utilities Supplier*

CUSTOMER LOCATION	TONS SHIPPED	XY-COORDINATES
Three Rivers, MI	5,000	(7, 13)
Fort Wayne, IN	92,000	(8, 12)
Columbus, OH	70,000	(11, 10)
Ashland, KY	35,000	(11, 7)
Kingsport, TN	9,000	(12, 4)
Akron, OH	227,000	(13, 11)
Wheeling, WV	16,000	(14, 10)
Roanoke, VA	153,000	(15, 5)

a. Calculate the center of gravity, rounding distance to the nearest tenth.

b. Calculate the load–distance score for this location, using rectilinear distance.

SOLUTION

a. The center of gravity is (12.4, 9.2).

$$\sum_i l_i = 5 + 92 + 70 + 35 + 9 + 227 + 16 + 153 = 607$$

$$\sum_i l_i x_i = 5(7) + 92(8) + 70(11) + 35(11) + 9(12) + 227(13) + 16(14) + 153(15)$$
$$= 7,504$$

$$x^* = \frac{\sum_i l_i y_i}{\sum_i l_i} = \frac{7,504}{607} = 12.4$$

$$\sum_i l_i y_i = 5(13) + 92(12) + 70(10) + 35(7) + 9(4) + 227(11) + 16(10) + 153(5) = 5,572$$

$$y^* = \frac{\sum_i l_i y_i}{\sum_i l_i} = \frac{5,572}{607} = 9.2$$

b. The load–distance score is

$$ld = \sum_i l_i d_i = 5(5.4 + 3.8) + 92(4.4 + 2.8) + 70(1.4 + 0.8) + 35(1.4 + 2.2)$$
$$+ 9(0.4 + 5.2) + 227(0.6 + 1.8) + 16(1.6 + 0.8) + 153(2.6 + 4.2)$$
$$= 2,662.4$$

where $d_i = |x_i - x^*| + |y_i - y^*|$

SOLVED PROBLEM 4

The Arid Company makes canoe paddles to serve distribution centers in Worchester, Rochester, and Dorchester from existing plants in Battle Creek and Cherry Creek. Annual demand is expected to increase as projected in the bottom row of the tableau shown in Figure 7.12. Arid is considering locating a plant near the headwaters of Dee Creek. Annual capacity for each plant is shown in the right-hand column of the tableau. Transportation costs per paddle are shown in the tableau in the small boxes. For example, the cost to ship one paddle from Battle Creek to Worchester is $4.37. The optimal allocations are also shown. For example, Battle Creek ships 12,000 units to Rochester. What are the estimated transportation costs associated with this allocation pattern?

Source	Destination			Capacity
	Worchester	Rochester	Dorchester	
Battle Creek	$4.37	$4.25 **12,000**	$4.89	12,000
Cherry Creek	$4.00 **6,000**	$5.00 **4,000**	$5.27	10,000
Dee Creek	$4.13	$4.50 **6,000**	$3.75 **12,000**	18,000
Demand	6,000	22,000	12,000	40,000

FIGURE 7.12

SOLUTION

The total cost is $167,000.

Ship 12,000 units from Battle Creek to Rochester @ $4.25.	Cost = $51,000
Ship 6,000 units from Cherry Creek to Worchester @ $4.00.	Cost = $24,000
Ship 4,000 units from Cherry Creek to Rochester @ $5.00.	Cost = $20,000
Ship 6,000 units from Dee Creek to Rochester @ $4.50.	Cost = $27,000
Ship 12,000 units from Dee Creek to Dorchester @ $3.75.	Cost = $45,000
	Total $167,000

SOLVED PROBLEM 5

A defense contractor is evaluating its machine shop's current process layout. Figure 7.13 shows the current layout, and the table shows the trip matrix for the facility. Safety and health regulations require departments E and F to remain at their current locations.

	TRIPS BETWEEN DEPARTMENTS					
DEPARTMENT	A	B	C	D	E	F
A	—	8	3		9	5
B		—		3		
C			—		8	9
D				—		3
E					—	3
F						—

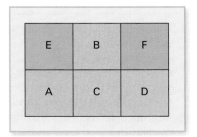

FIGURE 7.13 • Current Layout

a. Use trial and error to find a better layout.

b. How much better is your layout than the current one, in terms of the *ld* score? Use rectilinear distance.

SOLUTION

a. In addition to keeping departments E and F at their current locations, a good plan would locate the following department pairs close to each other: A and E, C and F, A and B, and C and E. Figure 7.14 was worked out by trial and error and satisfies all these requirements. Start by placing E and F at their current locations. Then, because C must be as close as possible to both E and F, put C between them. Place A directly south of E, and B next to A. All of the heavy traffic concerns have now been accommodated. Department D is located in the remaining space.

		CURRENT PLAN		PROPOSED PLAN	
DEPARTMENT PAIR	NUMBER OF TRIPS (1)	DISTANCE (2)	LOAD × DISTANCE (1) × (2)	DISTANCE (3)	LOAD × DISTANCE (1) × (3)
A, B	8	2	16	1	8
A, C	3	1	3	2	6
A, E	9	1	9	1	9
A, F	5	3	15	3	15
B, D	3	2	6	1	3
C, E	8	2	16	1	8
C, F	9	2	18	1	9
D, F	3	1	3	1	3
E, F	3	2	6	2	6
			$ld = \overline{92}$		$ld = \overline{67}$

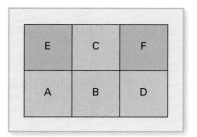

FIGURE 7.14 • Proposed Layout

b. The table reveals that the *ld* score drops from 92 for the current plan to 67 for the revised plan, a 27 percent reduction.

SOLVED PROBLEM 6

A company is setting up an assembly line to produce 192 units per eight-hour shift. The following table identifies the work elements, times, and immediate predecessors.

WORK ELEMENT	TIME (sec)	IMMEDIATE PREDECESSOR(S)
A	40	None
B	80	A
C	30	D, E, F
D	25	B
E	20	B
F	15	B
G	120	A
H	145	G
I	130	H
J	115	C, I
Total	720	

a. What is the desired cycle time?

b. What is the theoretical minimum number of stations?

c. Use trial and error to work out a solution, and show your solution on a precedence diagram.

d. What are the efficiency and balance delay of the solution found?

SOLUTION

a. Substituting in the cycle-time formula, we get

$$c = \frac{1}{r} = \frac{8 \text{ hours}}{192 \text{ units}} (3{,}600 \text{ seconds/hour}) = 150 \text{ seconds/unit}$$

b. The sum of the work-element times is 720 seconds, so

$$TM = \frac{\Sigma t}{c} = \frac{720 \text{ seconds/unit}}{150 \text{ seconds/unit-station}} = 4.8, \quad or \quad 5 \text{ stations}$$

which may not be achievable.

c. The precedence diagram is shown in Figure 7.15. Each row in the following table shows work elements assigned to each of the five workstations in the proposed solution.

STATION	WORK ELEMENT	WORK-ELEMENT TIME (sec)	CUMULATIVE TIME TIME (sec)	IDLE TIME (C = 150 sec)
S1	A	40	40	110
	B	80	120	30
	D	25	145	5
S2	G	120	120	30
	E	20	140	10
S3	H	145	145	5
S4	I	130	130	20
	F	15	145	5
S5	C	30	30	120
	J	115	145	5

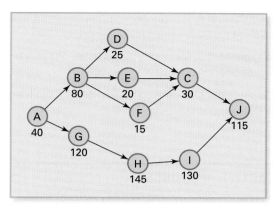

FIGURE 7.15

d. Calculating the efficiency, we get

$$\text{Efficiency} = \frac{\Sigma t}{nc}(100) = \frac{720 \text{ seconds/unit}}{5(150 \text{ seconds/unit})}(100)$$

$$= 96\%$$

Thus, the balance delay is only 4 percent (100 − 96).

CD-ROM RESOURCES

The Student CD-ROM that accompanies this text contains the following resources, which allow you to further practice and apply the concepts presented in this chapter.

- ❏ **OM Explorer Tutors:** OM Explorer contains six tutor programs that will help you learn how to use the preference matrix, distance measures, center of gravity, break-even analysis, transportation method, and line balancing. See the Chapter 7 folder in OM Explorer. See also the four Tutor Exercises on making location decisions.

- ❏ **OM Explorer Solvers:** OM Explorer has three programs that can be used to solve general problems involving the center of gravity, transportation method, and process layouts. See the Location and Layout folders in OM Explorer for these routines.

- ❏ **Equation Summary:** All the equations for this chapter can be found in one convenient location.

- ❏ **Discussion Questions:** Six questions will challenge your understanding of location factors, ethical obligations in location, layout criteria, office layout, and layout differences between a health system and a steel factory.

- ❏ **Cases:**

  - ❏ Imaginative Toys: What are the dominant and secondary factors in this location decision?

  - ❏ Hightec, Inc.: What block plan do you propose, and why is it effective?

  - ❏ The Pizza Connection: Prepare a revised layout and explain why it addresses the issues that Dave Collier identified.

  - ❏ R. U. Reddie for Location: To maximize the net present value of the investment in a new plant, should Rhonda Reddie build the plant in Denver or St.Louis?

- ❏ **Experiential Exercise:** Use *The Pizza Connection* case as an in-class team experience.

❐ **Supplement A:** Decision Making. See how to do break-even analysis that can be applied to location analysis.

❐ **Supplement C:** Measuring Output Rates. See how to obtain the labor standards needed for the task times in line balancing.

❐ **Supplement I:** Linear Programming. Learn about linear programming, an important tool in solving multiple-facility location problems.

INTERACTIVE RESOURCES

The Interactive Web site associated with this text (www.prenhall.com/ritzman) contains many tools and activities specifically designed for this chapter. The following items are recommended to enhance your understanding of the material in this chapter.

❐ **Internet Activities:** Try out 10 links for four different Internet activities on location and layout, including location partnering by McDonald's, map site capabilities, *Newport News* fixed-position layouts, and the layouts of a cookie factory.

❐ **Internet Tours:** Learn about the location factors at a cheese factory and the Jack Daniels Distillery and about the plant layout of a furniture manufacturer.

PROBLEMS

An icon next to a problem identifies the software that can be helpful but is not mandatory. The software is available on the Student CD-ROM.

1. **OM Explorer** Calculate the weighted score for each location (A, B, C, and D) shown in Table 7.5. Which location would you recommend?

2. **OM Explorer** John and Jane Darling are newlyweds trying to decide among several available rentals. Alternatives were scored on a scale of 1 to 5 (5 = best) against weighted performance criteria, as shown in Table 7.6. The criteria included rent, proximity to work and

recreational opportunities, security, and other neighborhood characteristics associated with the couple's values and lifestyle. Alternative A is an apartment, B is a bungalow, C is a condo, and D is a downstairs apartment in Jane's parents' home.

TABLE 7.6   *Factors for Newlyweds*

LOCATION FACTOR	FACTOR WEIGHT	FACTOR SCORE FOR EACH LOCATION			
		A	B	C	D
1. Rent	25	3	1	2	5
2. Quality of life	20	2	5	5	4
3. Schools	5	3	5	3	1
4. Proximity to work	10	5	3	4	3
5. Proximity to recreation	15	4	4	5	2
6. Neighborhood security	15	2	4	4	4
7. Utilities	10	4	2	3	5
Total	100				

Which location is indicated by the preference matrix? What qualitative factors might cause this preference to change?

3. **OM Explorer** Two alternative locations are under consideration for a new plant: Jackson, Mississippi, and Dayton, Ohio. The Jackson location is superior in terms of costs. However, management believes that sales volume would decline if this location were chosen because it is

TABLE 7.5   *Factors for Locations A–D*

LOCATION FACTOR	FACTOR WEIGHT	FACTOR SCORE FOR EACH LOCATION			
		A	B	C	D
1. Labor climate	5	5	4	3	5
2. Quality of life	30	2	3	5	1
3. Transportation system	5	3	4	3	5
4. Proximity to markets	25	5	3	4	4
5. Proximity to materials	5	3	2	3	5
6. Taxes	15	2	5	5	4
7. Utilities	15	5	4	2	1
Total	100				

farther from the market, and the firm's customers prefer local suppliers. The selling price of the product is $250 per unit in either case. Use the following information to determine which location yields the higher total profit contribution per year.

LOCATION	ANNUAL FIXED COST	VARIABLE COST PER UNIT	FORECAST DEMAND PER YEAR
Jackson	$1,500,000	$50	30,000 units
Dayton	$2,800,000	$85	40,000 units

4. 💿 **OM Explorer** Fall-Line, Inc., is a Great Falls, Montana, manufacturer of a variety of downhill skis. Fall-Line is considering four locations for a new plant: Aspen, Colorado; Medicine Lodge, Kansas; Broken Bow, Nebraska; and Wounded Knee, South Dakota. Annual fixed costs and variable costs per pair of skis are shown in the following table:

LOCATION	ANNUAL FIXED COSTS	VARIABLE COSTS PER PAIR
Aspen	$8,000,000	$250
Medicine Lodge	$2,400,000	$130
Broken Bow	$3,400,000	$ 90
Wounded Knee	$4,500,000	$ 65

a. Plot the total cost curves for all the communities on a single graph (see Solved Problem 2). Identify on the graph the range in volume over which each location would be best.

b. What break-even quantity defines each range?

Although Aspen's fixed and variable costs are dominated by those of the other communities, Fall-Line believes that both the demand and the price would be higher for skis made in Aspen than for skis made in the other locations. The following table shows those projections:

LOCATION	PRICE PER PAIR	FORECAST DEMAND PER YEAR
Aspen	$500	60,000 pairs
Medicine Lodge	$350	45,000 pairs
Broken Bow	$350	43,000 pairs
Wounded Knee	$350	40,000 pairs

c. Determine which location yields the highest total profit contribution per year.

d. Is this location decision sensitive to forecast accuracy? At what minimum sales volume does Aspen become the location of choice?

5. The operations manager for Hot House Roses has narrowed the search for a new facility location to seven communities. Annual fixed costs (land, property taxes, insurance, equip-

ment, and buildings) and variable costs (labor, materials, transportation, and variable overhead) are shown in the following table:

COMMUNITY	FIXED COSTS PER YEAR	VARIABLE COSTS PER DOZEN
Aurora, CO	$210,000	$7.20
Flora, IL	$200,000	$7.00
Garden City, KS	$150,000	$9.00
Greensboro, NC	$280,000	$6.20
Roseland, LA	$260,000	$6.00
Sunnyvale, CA	$420,000	$5.00
Watertown, MA	$370,000	$8.00

a. Which of the communities can be eliminated from further consideration because they are dominated (both variable and fixed costs are higher) by another community?

b. Plot the total cost curves for the remaining communities on a single graph. Identify on the graph the approximate range over which each community provides the lowest cost.

c. Using break-even analysis (see Supplement A, "Decision Making" on the Student CD-ROM), calculate the break-even quantities to determine the range over which each community provides the lowest cost.

6. 💿 **OM Explorer** The following three points are the locations of important facilities in a transportation network: (20, 20), (30, 50), and (60, 0). The coordinates are in miles.

a. Calculate the Euclidean distances (in miles) between each of the three pairs of facilities.

b. Calculate these distances using rectilinear distances.

7. 💿 **OM Explorer** Centura High School is to be located at the population center of gravity of three communities: Boelus, population 228; Cairo, population 737; and Dannebrog, population 356. The coordinates (on a grid of square miles) for the communities are provided in Figure 7.16. Where should

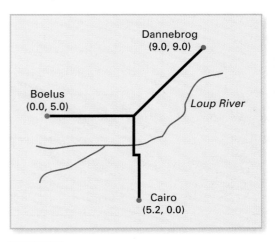

FIGURE 7.16

Centura High School be located? (Round to 0.1 mile.) What factors may result in locating at the site indicated by this technique?

8. **OM Explorer** A larger and more modern main post office is to be constructed at a new location in Davis, California. Growing suburbs have shifted the population density from where it was 40 years ago, when the current facility was built. Annette Werk, the postmaster, asked her assistants to draw a grid map of the seven points where mail is picked up and delivered in bulk. The coordinates and trips per day to and from the seven mail source points and the current main post office, M, are shown in the following table. M will continue to act as a mail source point after relocation.

MAIL SOURCE POINT	ROUND TRIPS PER DAY (*l*)	*xy*-COORDINATES (MILES)
1	6	(2, 8)
2	3	(6, 1)
3	3	(8, 5)
4	3	(13, 3)
5	2	(15, 10)
6	7	(6, 14)
7	5	(18, 1)
M	3	(10, 3)

a. Calculate the center of gravity as a possible location for the new facility (round to the nearest whole number).

b. Compare the load–distance scores for the location in part (a) and the current location, using rectilinear distance.

9. **OM Explorer** Paramount Manufacturing is investigating which location would best position its new plant relative to two suppliers (located in cities A and B) and one market

area (represented by city C). Management has limited the search for this plant to those three locations. The following information has been collected:

LOCATION	*xy*-COORDINATES (MILES)	TONS PER YEAR	FREIGHT RATE ($/TON-MILE)
A	(100, 200)	4,000	3
B	(400, 100)	3,000	1
C	(100, 100)	4,000	3

a. Which of the three locations gives the lowest total cost, based on Euclidean distances? [*Hint:* The annual cost of inbound shipments from supplier A to the new plant is $12,000 per mile (4,000 tons per year × $3 per ton-mile)].

b. Which location is best, based on rectilinear distances?

c. What are the coordinates of the center of gravity?

10. **OM Explorer** Fire Brand makes picante sauce in El Paso and New York City. Distribution centers are located in Atlanta, Omaha, and Seattle. For the capacities, locations, and shipment costs per case shown in Figure 7.17, determine the shipping pattern that will minimize transportation costs. What are the estimated transportation costs associated with this optimal allocation pattern?

11. **OM Explorer** The Pelican Company has four distribution centers (A, B, C, and D) that require 40,000, 60,000, 30,000, and 50,000 gallons of diesel fuel, respectively, per month for their long-haul trucks. Three fuel wholesalers (1, 2, and 3) have indicated their willingness to supply as many as 50,000, 70,000, and 60,000 gallons of fuel, respectively. The total cost (shipping plus price) of delivering 1,000 gallons of fuel from each wholesaler to each distribution center is shown in the table on the left side of the next page:

Source	Destination			Capacity
	Atlanta	Omaha	Seattle	
El Paso	$4	$5	$6	12,000
New York City	$3	$7	$9	10,000
Demand	8,000	10,000	4,000	22,000

FIGURE 7.17

| Factory | Shipping Cost per Case to Warehouse | | | | | Capacity |
	W1	W2	W3	W4	W5	
F1	$1 **60,000**	$3 **20,000**	$4	$5	$6	80,000
F2	$2	$2	$1 **50,000**	$4 **10,000**	$5	60,000
F3	$1	$5	$1	$3 **20,000**	$1 **40,000**	60,000
F4	$5	$2 **50,000**	$4	$5	$4	50,000
Demand	60,000	70,000	50,000	30,000	40,000	250,000

FIGURE 7.18

| | DISTRIBUTION CENTER | | | |
WHOLESALER	A	B	C	D
1	1.30	1.40	1.80	1.60
2	1.30	1.50	1.80	1.60
3	1.60	1.40	1.70	1.50

a. Determine the optimal solution. Show that all capacities have been exhausted and that all demands can be met with this solution.

b. What is the total cost of the solution?

12. ● **OM Explorer** The Acme Company has four factories that ship products to five warehouses. The shipping costs, requirements, capacities, and optimal allocations are shown in Figure 7.18. What is the total cost of the optimal solution?

13. ● **OM Explorer** Baker Machine Company is a job shop specializing in precision parts for firms in the aerospace industry. Figure 7.19 shows the current block plan for the key

manufacturing centers of the 75,000-square-foot facility. Referring to the trip matrix below the figure, use rectilinear distance (the current distance from inspection to shipping and receiving is 3 units) to calculate the change in the load–distance, ld, score if Baker exchanges the locations of the tool crib and inspection.

Trip Matrix

| | TRIPS BETWEEN DEPARTMENTS | | | | | |
DEPARTMENT	1	2	3	4	5	6
1. Burr and grind	—	8	3		9	5
2. NC equipment		—		3		
3. Shipping and receiving			—		8	9
4. Lathes and drills				—		3
5. Tool crib					—	3
6. Inspection						—

14. ● **OM Explorer** Use trial and error to find a particularly good block plan for Baker Machine (see Problem 13). Because of excessive relocation costs, shipping and receiving (department 3) must remain at its current location. Compare ld scores to evaluate your new layout, again assuming rectilinear distance.

15. ● **OM Explorer** Richard Garber is the head designer for Matthews and Novak Design Company. Garber has been called in to design the layout for a newly constructed office building. From statistical samplings over the past three months, Garber developed the trip matrix shown for daily trips between the department's offices.

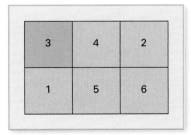

FIGURE 7.19

Trip Matrix

DEPARTMENT	TRIPS BETWEEN DEPARTMENTS					
	A	B	C	D	E	F
A	—	25	90			165
B		—			105	
C			—		125	125
D				—	25	
E					—	105
F						—

a. If other factors are equal, which two offices should be located closest together?

b. Figure 7.20 shows an alternative layout for the department. What is the total load–distance score for this plan, based on rectilinear distance and assuming that offices A and B are 3 units of distance apart?

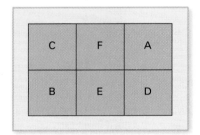

FIGURE 7.20

c. Switching which two departments will most improve the total load–distance score?

16. 💿 **OM Explorer** A firm with four departments has the following trip matrix and the current block plan shown in Figure 7.21.

a. What is the load–distance score for the current layout (assuming rectilinear distance)?

Trip Matrix

DEPARTMENT	TRIPS BETWEEN DEPARTMENTS			
	A	B	C	D
A	—	12	10	8
B		—	20	6
C			—	0
D				—

b. Develop a better layout. What is its total load–distance score?

17. As director of the Office of Budget Management for New Mexico's state government, Mike Rogers manages a department of 120 employees assigned to eight different sections.

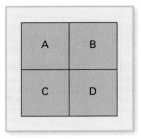

FIGURE 7.21 • Current Block Plan

Because of budget cuts, 30 employees from another department have been transferred and must be placed somewhere within the existing space. While changing the layout, Rogers wants to improve communication and create a good work environment. One special consideration is that the state controlling board (section 2) should occupy the northeast location. The trip matrix shown in Table 7.7 was developed from questionnaires sent to each of the 120 current employees. It contains section names, area requirements, and closeness ratings.

a. Develop a square block plan (4 rows and 4 columns) for Rogers.

b. What behavioral issues does Rogers need to address when revising the layout?

18. 💿 **OM Explorer** Use trial and error to balance the assembly line described in the following table and Figure 7.22 so that it will produce 40 units per hour.

a. What is the cycle time?

b. What is the theoretical minimum number of workstations?

c. Which work elements are assigned to each workstation?

d. What are the resulting efficiency and balance delay percentages?

WORK ELEMENT	TIME (sec)	IMMEDIATE PREDECESSOR(S)
A	40	None
B	80	A
C	30	A
D	25	B
E	20	C
F	15	B
G	60	B
H	45	D
I	10	E, G
J	75	F
K	15	H, I, J
Total	415	

TABLE 7.7 *Trip Matrix*

| | TRIPS BETWEEN SECTIONS | | | | | | | | AREA NEEDED |
SECTION	1	2	3	4	5	6	7	8	(blocks)
1. Administration	—	3	2	10		2	2		1
2. State controlling board		—		3		2	2		5
3. Program clearinghouse			—			2	2	6	1
4. Social services				—		5	3	2	2
5. Institutions					—	8			3
6. Accounting						—			2
7. Education							—		1
8. Internal audit								—	1

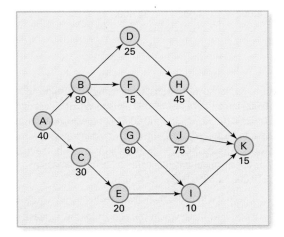

FIGURE 7.22

19. 💿 **OM Explorer** Johnson Cogs wants to set up a line to produce 60 units per hour. The work elements and their precedence relationships are shown in the following table.

   a. What is the theoretical minimum number of stations?

   b. How many stations are required using trial and error to find a solution?

   c. Suppose that a solution requiring five stations is obtained. What is its efficiency?

WORK ELEMENT	TIME (sec)	IMMEDIATE PREDECESSOR(S)
A	40	None
B	30	A
C	50	A
D	40	B
E	6	B
F	25	C
G	15	C
H	20	D, E
I	18	F, G
J	30	H, I
Total	274	

20. 💿 **OM Explorer; SmartDraw** The *trim line* at PW is a small subassembly line that, along with other such lines, feeds into the final chassis line. The entire assembly line, which consists of more than 900 workstations, is to make PW's new E cars. The trim line itself involves only 13 work elements and must handle 20 cars per hour. In addition to the usual precedence constraints, there are two *zoning constraints*. First, work elements 11 and 12 should be assigned to the same station; both use a common component, and assigning them to the same station conserves storage space. Second, work elements 8 and 10 cannot be performed at the same station. Work-element data are as follows:

WORK ELEMENT	TIME (sec)	IMMEDIATE PREDECESSOR(S)
A	1.8	None
B	0.4	None
C	1.6	None
D	1.5	A
E	0.7	A
F	0.5	E
G	0.8	B
H	1.4	C
I	1.4	D
J	1.4	F, G
K	0.5	H
L	1.0	J
M	0.8	I, K, L

   a. Draw a precedence diagram.

   b. What cycle time (in minutes) results in the desired output rate?

   c. What is the theoretical minimum number of stations?

   d. Using trial and error, balance the line as best you can.

   e. What is the efficiency of your solution?

21. 💿 **OM Explorer** Pucchi, Inc., makes designer dog collars in Chihuahua, Mexico; Saint Bernard, Ohio; and Yorkshire, New York. Distribution centers are located in Baustin, Vegas, Nawlns, and New Yawk. The shipping costs, require-

Factory	Shipping Cost per Collar to Distribution Centers					Capacity
	Baustin	Vegas	NawIns	New Yawk	Dummy	
Chihuahua	$8	$5	$4	$9	$0	12,000
Saint Bernard	$4	$6	$3	$3	$0	7,000
Yorkshire	$2	$8	$6	$1	$0	4,000
Demand	4,000	6,000	3,000	8,000	2,000	23,000

FIGURE 7.23

ments, and capacities are shown in Figure 7.23. Use the transportation method to find the shipping schedule that minimizes shipping cost.

22. 💿 **OM Explorer** The Ajax International Company has four factories that ship products to five warehouses. The shipping costs, requirements, and capacities are shown in Figure 7.24. Use the transportation method to find the shipping schedule that minimizes shipping cost.

23. 💿 **OM Explorer** Consider further the Ajax International Company situation described in Problem 22. Ajax has decided to close F3 because of high operating costs. In addition, the company has decided to add 50,000 units of capacity to F4. The logistics manager is worried about the effect of this move on transportation costs. Presently, F3 is shipping 30,000 units to W4 and 50,000 units to W5 at a cost of $140,000 [or 30,000(3) + 50,000(1)]. If these warehouses were to be served by F4, the cost would increase to $350,000 [or 30,000(5) + 50,000(4)]. As a result, the Ajax logistics manager has requested a budget increase of $210,000 (or $350,000 − $140,000).

a. Should the logistics manager get the budget increase?

b. If not, how much would you budget for the increase in shipping costs?

24. 💿 **OM Explorer** The Chambers Corporation produces and markets an automotive theft-deterrent product, which it stocks in various warehouses throughout the country.

Factory	Shipping Cost per Case to Warehouse						Capacity
	W1	W2	W3	W4	W5	Dummy	
F1	$1	$3	$3	$5	$6	$0	50,000
F2	$2	$2	$1	$4	$5	$0	80,000
F3	$1	$5	$1	$3	$1	$0	80,000
F4	$5	$2	$4	$5	$4	$0	40,000
Demand	45,000	30,000	30,000	35,000	50,000	60,000	250,000

FIGURE 7.24

Recently, its market research group compiled a forecast indicating that a significant increase in demand will occur in the near future, after which demand will level off for the foreseeable future. The company has decided to satisfy this demand by constructing new plant capacity. Chambers already has plants in Baltimore and Milwaukee and has no desire to relocate those facilities. Each plant is capable of producing 600,000 units per year.

After a thorough search, the company developed three site and capacity alternatives. *Alternative 1* is to build a 600,000-unit plant in Portland. *Alternative 2* is to build a 600,000-unit plant in San Antonio. *Alternative 3* is to build a 300,000-unit plant in Portland and a 300,000-unit plant in San Antonio. The company has four warehouses that distribute the product to retailers. The market research study provided the following data:

WAREHOUSE	EXPECTED ANNUAL DEMAND
Atlanta (AT)	500,000
Columbus (CO)	300,000
Los Angeles (LA)	600,000
Seattle (SE)	400,000

The logistics department compiled the following cost table that specified the cost per unit to ship the product from each plant to each warehouse in the most economical manner, subject to the reliability of the various carriers involved:

PLANT	WAREHOUSE			
	AT	CO	LA	SE
Baltimore	$0.35	$0.20	$0.85	$0.75
Milwaukee	$0.55	$0.15	$0.70	$0.65
Portland	$0.85	$0.60	$0.30	$0.10
San Antonio	$0.55	$0.40	$0.40	$0.55

As one part of the location decision, management wants an estimate of the total distribution cost for each alternative. Use the transportation method to calculate these estimates.

25. **OM Explorer** CCI Electronics makes various products for the communications industry. One of its manufacturing plants makes a device for sensing when telephone calls are placed. A from–to matrix is shown in Table 7.8; the current layout appears in Figure 7.25. Management is reasonably satisfied with the current layout, although it has heard some complaints about the placement of departments D, G, K, and L. Use information in the from–to matrix to create a trip matrix, and then find a revised block plan for moving only the four departments about which complaints have been made. Show that the load–distance score is improved. Assume rectilinear distance.

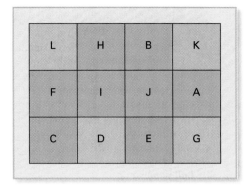

FIGURE 7.25 • Current Block Plan

26. A paced assembly line has been devised to manufacture calculators, as the following data show:

STATION	WORK ELEMENT ASSIGNED	WORK ELEMENT TIME (min)
S1	A	2.7
S2	D, E	0.6, 0.9
S3	C	3.0
S4	B, F, G	0.7, 0.7, 0.9
S5	H, I, J	0.7, 0.3, 1.2
S6	K	2.4

a. What is the maximum hourly output rate from this line? (*Hint*: The line can go only as fast as its slowest workstation.)

b. What cycle time corresponds to this maximum output rate?

c. If a worker is at each station and the line operates at this maximum output rate, how much idle time is lost during each 10-hour shift?

d. What is the line's efficiency?

27. The associate administrator at Getwell Hospital wants to evaluate the layout of the outpatient clinic. Table 7.9 shows the interdepartmental flows (patients/day) between departments; Figure 7.26 shows the current layout.

a. Determine the effectiveness of the current layout, as measured by the total *ld* score, using rectilinear distances.

b. Try to find the best possible layout based on the same effectiveness measure.

c. What is the impact on your new solution if it must be revised to keep department 1 at its present location?

d. How should the layout developed in part (c) be revised if the interdepartmental flow between the examining room and the X-ray department is increased by 50 percent? Decreased by 50 percent?

TABLE 7.8 *From–To Matrix*

DEPARTMENT	A	B	C	D	E	F	G	H	I	J	K	L
A. Network lead forming	—											80
B. Wire forming and subassembly		—							50	70		
C. Final assembly			—		120							
D. Inventory storage				—	40							
E. Presoldering			80		—					90		
F. Final testing						—	120					
G. Inventory storage		30					—	40	50			
H. Coil winding								—	80			
I. Coil assembly			70		40				—		60	
J. Network preparation	90									—		
K. Soldering			80								—	
L. Network insertion			60									—

TRIPS BETWEEN DEPARTMENTS

TABLE 7.9 *Trip Matrix*

TRIPS BETWEEN DEPARTMENTS

DEPARTMENT	1	2	3	4	5	6	7	8
1. Reception	—	25	35	5	10	15		20
2. Business office		—	5	10	15			15
3. Examining room			—	20	30	20		10
4. X-ray				—	25	15		25
5. Laboratory					—	20		25
6. Surgery						—	40	
7. Postsurgery							—	15
8. Doctor's office								—

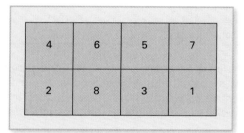

FIGURE 7.26 • Current Layout

SELECTED REFERENCES

Andel, T. "Site Selection Tools Dig Data." *Transportation & Distribution,* vol. 37, no. 6 (1996), pp. 77–81.

Bartness, A. D. "The Plant Location Puzzle." *Harvard Business Review* (March–April, 1994), pp. 20–30.

Bitner, Mary Jo. "Servicescapes: The Impact of Physical Surroundings on Customers and Employees." *Journal of Marketing,* vol. 56 (April 1992), pp. 57–71.

"The Boom Belt." *Business Week* (September 27, 1993), pp. 98–104.

Bozer, Y. A., and R. D. Meller. "A Reexamination of the Distance-Based Layout Problem." *IIE Transactions,* vol. 29, no. 7 (1997), pp. 549–560.

Cook, Thomas M., and Robert A. Russell. *Introduction to Management Sciences.* Englewood Cliffs, NJ: Prentice-Hall, 1993.

"Cool Offices." *Fortune* (December 9, 1996), pp. 204–210.

"Cummins Engine Flexes Its Factory." *Harvard Business Review* (March–April 1990), pp. 120–127.

DeForest, M. E. "Thinking of a Plant in Mexico?" *The Academy of Management Executive,* vol. 8, no. 1 (1994), pp. 33–40.

Drezner, Z. *Facility Location: A Survey of Applications and Methods.* Secaucus, NJ: Springer-Verlag, 1995.

Ferdows, Kasra. "Making the Most of Foreign Factories." *Fortune* (March–April 1997), pp. 73–88.

Frazier, G. V., and M. T. Spriggs, "Achieving Competitive Advantage Through Group Technology," *Business Horizons,* vol. 39, no. 3 (1996), pp. 83–90.

Heragu, Sunderesh. *Facilities Design.* Boston, MA: PWS Publishing Company, 1997.

Hyer, N. L., and K. H. Brown. "The Discipline of Real Cells." *Journal of Operations Management,* vol. 17, no. 5 (1999), pp. 557–574.

Kanter, Rosabeth Moss. "Transcending Business Boundaries: 12,000 World Managers View Change." *Harvard Business Review* (May–June 1991), pp. 151–164.

Klassen, Robert D., and D. Clay Whybark. "Barriers to the Management of International Operations." *Journal of Operations Management,* vol. 11, no. 4 (1994), pp. 385–396.

"Long Distance: Innovative MCI Unit Finds Culture Shock in Colorado Springs." *Wall Street Journal* (June 25, 1996).

MacCormack, Alan D., Lawrence James Newman III, and David B. Rosenfield. "The New Dynamics of Global Manufacturing Site Location." *Sloan Management Review* (Summer 1994), pp. 69–77.

"Making Malls (Gasp!) Convenient." *Wall Street Journal* (February 8, 2000).

"Mexico: A Rough Road Back." *Business Week* (November 13, 1995), pp. 104–107.

"Retailing: Confronting the Challenges that Face Bricks-and-Mortar Stores." *Harvard Business Review* (July–August 1999), p. 159.

Sugiura, Hideo. "How Honda Localizes Its Global Strategy." *Sloan Management Review* (Fall 1990), pp. 77–82.

Sule, D. R. *Manufacturing Facilities: Location, Planning, and Design.* Boston, MA: PWS Publishing Company, 1994.

Suresh, N. C., and J. M. Kay, eds. *Group Technology and Cellular Manufacturing: A State-of-the-Art Synthesis of Research and Practice.* Boston, MA: Kluwer Academic Publishers, 1997.

"Tools of the Remote Trade," *Business Week* (March 27, 2000), p. F20.

Vargos, G. A., and T. W. Johnson. "An Analysis of Operational Experience in the U.S./Mexico Production Sharing (Maquiladora) Program." *Journal of Operations Management,* vol. 11, no. 1 (1993), pp. 17–34.

"Will This Open Space Work?" *Harvard Business Review* (May–June 1999), p. 28.

Supply-Chain Management

Across the Organization

Supply-chain management is important to . . .

- ❐ **distribution,** which determines the best placement of finished goods inventories and selects the appropriate modes of transportation for serving the external supply chain.
- ❐ **finance** and **accounting,** which must understand how the performance of the supply chain affects key financial measures and how information flows into the billing process.
- ❐ **information systems,** which designs the information flows that are essential to effective supply-chain performance.
- ❐ **marketing,** which involves contact with the firm's customers and needs a supply chain that ensures responsive customer service.
- ❐ **operations,** which is responsible for managing effective supply chains.
- ❐ **purchasing,** which selects the suppliers for the supply chain.

Learning Goals

After reading this chapter, you will be able to . . .

1. define the nature of supply-chain management for both manufacturers and service providers.
2. describe the strategic importance of supply-chain management and give real examples of its application in manufacturing and service industries.
3. explain how the Internet has changed the ways companies are managing the customer and supplier interfaces.
4. discuss how critical operating measures of supply-chain performance are linked to key financial measures.
5. distinguish between efficient supply chains and responsive supply chains, and discuss the environments best suited for each one.
6. describe the causes of supply-chain dynamics and their effects.

The Dell Computer Corporation (www.dell.com), a mass customizer of personal computers, is experiencing phenomenal growth and profitability in an industry that traditionally has low profit margins. In 1996, Dell was selling laptops, desktops, and servers at the rate of $1 million a day. Today, Dell's Web site sells more than $30 million in products a day. This success has catapulted Dell into the number 1 position among PC makers, ahead of Compaq, Apple Computer, and IBM. What is Dell's secret? In a single word— speed. A customer's order for a customized computer can be on a delivery truck in 36 hours. This capability allows Dell to keep parts costs and inventories low—16 days of sales—thereby enabling it to sell at prices 10 to 15 percent below those of competitors.

Employees at Dell's Austin, Texas, plant assemble, test, and package servers to customer order.

A primary factor in filling customers' orders is Dell's manufacturing operations and the performance of its suppliers. Dell's manufacturing process is flexible enough to postpone the ordering of components and the assembly of computers until an order is booked. In addition, Dell's warehousing plan calls for the bulk of its components to be warehoused within 15 minutes of its Austin (Texas), Limerick (Ireland), and Penang (Malaysia) plants. Dell's top 33 suppliers, which supply 90 percent of its goods, use a Web site for data on how they measure up to Dell's standards, what orders they've shipped, and the best way to ship. Dell plans to link the supplier Web site to its order placement Web site so that as customers place orders, the suppliers will know when to ship components such as motherboards or liquid-crystal displays. Dell's focus is on how fast the inventory moves, not on how much is there. At Austin, Dell does not actually have to order the components because the suppliers restock the warehouse and manage their own inventories. Dell uses the components as needed and is not billed for them until they leave the warehouse. This system of suppliers and manufacturing operations has proven to be a great advantage over competitors. For example, if Compaq suddenly needed a supply of components from its warehouse, 12 to 18 hours would be required to get them; at IBM or Gateway, two days would be needed. For Dell, only minutes are required.

Dell's efficient operations carry over to service providers, who also are used to lower costs and reduce lead time. For example, Dell might send an e-mail message to UPS requesting that a computer monitor from Sony be sent to a certain customer as part of a purchased computer system. UPS pulls a monitor from the monitor supplier's stocks and schedules it to arrive with the PC, saving Dell shipping and inventory costs.

Such careful management of the materials and services from the suppliers through production to the customer lets Dell operate more efficiently than any other computer company.

Sources: "The Power of Virtual Integration: An Interview with Dell Computer's Michael Dell." *Harvard Business Review* (March–April 1998), pp. 72–85; Roth, Daniel. "Dell's Big New Act." *Fortune* (December 6, 1999), pp. 152–156.

supply-chain management
The synchronization of a firm's processes and those of its suppliers to match the flow of materials, services, and information with customer demand.

SUPPLY-CHAIN MANAGEMENT SEEKS TO synchronize a firm's processes and those of its suppliers to match the flow of materials, services, and information with customer demand. Supply-chain management has strategic implications because the supply system can be used to achieve important competitive priorities, as with Dell Computer Corporation. It also involves the coordination of key processes in the firm such as order placement, order fulfillment, and purchasing, which are supported by marketing, finance, engineering, information systems, operations, and logistics. We begin by taking a bird's-eye view of supply-chain management, focusing on its implications for manufacturers and service providers. We then describe how companies manage their customer and supplier interfaces. Next, we discuss the important operating and financial measures of supply-chain performance, followed by a comparison of two supply-chain designs and their strategic implications. We conclude with discussions of the dynamics of supply chains and supply-chain software.

OVERVIEW OF SUPPLY-CHAIN MANAGEMENT

How is inventory created?

inventory A stock of materials used to satisfy customer demand or support the production of goods and services.

raw materials (RM) The inventories that are needed for the production of goods and services.

work-in-process (WIP) Items such as components or assemblies needed for a final product in manufacturing.

finished goods (FG) The items in manufacturing plants, warehouses, and retail outlets that are sold to the firm's customers.

A basic purpose of supply-chain management is to control inventory by managing the flows of materials. **Inventory** is a stock of materials used to satisfy customer demand or support the production of goods or services.

Inventory exists in three aggregate categories, which are useful for accounting purposes. **Raw materials (RM)** are inventories needed for the production of goods or services. They are considered to be inputs to the transformation processes of the firm, whether they produce a product or a service. **Work-in-process (WIP)** consists of items such as components or assemblies needed for a final product in manufacturing. WIP is also present in some service operations, such as repair shops, restaurants, check processing centers, and package delivery services. **Finished goods (FG)** in manufacturing plants, warehouses, and retail outlets are the items sold to the firm's customers. The finished goods of one firm may actually be the raw materials for another.

Figure 8.1 shows how inventory can be held in different forms and at various stocking points. In this example, raw materials—the finished goods of the supplier—are held both by the supplier and the manufacturer. Raw materials at the plant pass through one or more processes, which transform them into various levels of WIP inventory. Final processing of this inventory yields finished goods inventory. Finished goods can be held at the plant, the distribution center (which may be a warehouse owned by the manufacturer or the retailer), and retail locations.

Managing the flow of material is common to organizations in every segment of the economy: churches, governments, manufacturers, wholesalers, retailers, and universities. Manufacturers make products from materials and services they purchase from outside suppliers. Service providers use materials in the form of physical items purchased from suppliers. For example, churches buy envelopes, brochures, audiotapes, file folders, audio equipment, hymnals, and devotional readings. The typical U.S. manufacturer spends more than 60 percent of its total income from sales on purchased materials and services. A typical service provider might spend 30 to 40 percent of total

FIGURE 8.1

Inventory at Successive Stocking Points

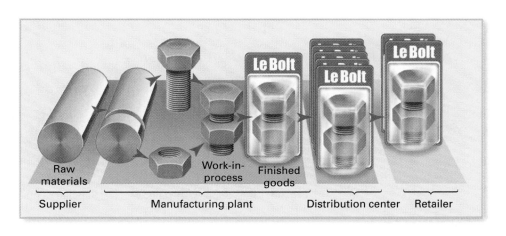

revenues on purchased materials and services. Companies today are relying more than ever on suppliers from around the world. Because materials comprise such a large component of the sales dollar, companies can reap large profits with a small percentage reduction in the cost of materials. That is one reason why supply-chain management is a key competitive weapon.

SUPPLY CHAINS

Recall that the interconnected set of linkages between suppliers of materials and services that spans the transformation of raw materials into products and services and delivers them to a firm's customers is known as the supply chain (see Chapter 2, "Process Management"). An important part of this process is provision of the information needed for planning and managing the supply chain. This information comes from internal and external sources and is disseminated to decision makers through ERP systems, which often contain supply-chain management modules.

The supply chain for a firm can be very complicated, as Figure 8.2 illustrates. However, the supply chain depicted is an oversimplification because many companies have hundreds, if not thousands, of suppliers. In this case, the firm owns its own distribution and transportation services. However, companies that engineer products to customer specifications normally do not have distribution centers as part of their supply chains. Such companies often ship products directly to their customers. Suppliers are often identified by their position in the supply chain. Here, tier 1 suppli-

FIGURE 8.2

Supply Chain for a Manufacturing Firm

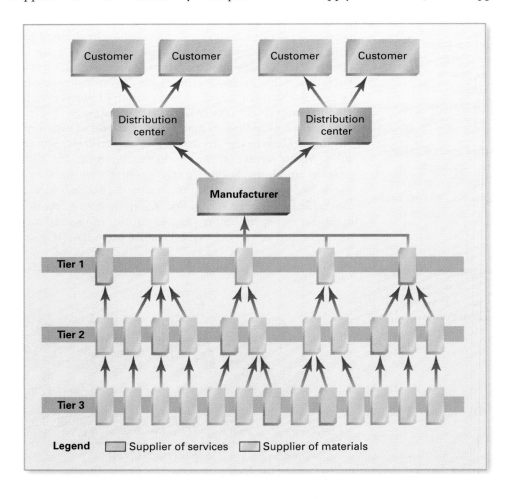

ers provide materials or services that are used directly by the firm, tier 2 suppliers supply tier 1 suppliers, and so on.

What is the best way to control suppliers in a complex supply chain?

The value of supply-chain management becomes apparent when the complexity of the supply chain is recognized. As we showed earlier, the flow of materials determines inventory levels. The performance of numerous suppliers determines the inward flow of materials. The performance of the firm's marketing, production, and distribution processes determines the outward flow of products.

Imagine the chaos if all the firm's suppliers acted independently and never adjusted to changes in the firm's schedules. Hence, management of the flow of materials is crucial, but how much control does a firm have over its suppliers? One way to gain control is to buy controlling interest in the firm's major suppliers, which is called *backward integration* (see Chapter 2, "Process Management"). The firm can then ensure its priority with the supplier and more forcefully lead efforts to improve efficiency and productivity. However, purchasing other companies takes a lot of capital, which reduces a firm's flexibility. Moreover, if demand drops, the firm cannot simply reduce the amount of materials purchased from the supplier to reduce costs because the supplier's fixed costs remain.

Another approach is to write agreements with the first-tier suppliers that hold them accountable for the performance of their own suppliers. For example, customers can provide a uniform set of guidelines to be followed throughout the supply chain. Companies such as Ford and Chrysler in the automotive industry have guidelines for quality, delivery, and reporting procedures to be followed by any company producing an item that ultimately becomes part of an automobile. First-tier suppliers then incorporate these guidelines in agreements with their own suppliers. This approach allows each first-tier supplier to manage its own suppliers without its customers having to do it for them.

SUPPLY CHAINS FOR SERVICE PROVIDERS

Supply-chain management is just as important for service providers as it is for manufacturers. Service providers must purchase the equipment, supplies, and services they need to produce their own services. An airline's supply chain provides soft drinks, peanuts, in-flight meals, and airsickness bags as well as maintenance and repair items such as engine parts and motor lubricants. Generally, a service provider's supply chain must be designed so that the right resources and tools are available to perform a service. In this regard, the service supply chain focuses on providing the appropriate supporting inventories, acquiring and scheduling the human and capital resources, and fulfilling the customer orders to satisfaction. For example, Figure 8.3 is a simplified diagram of a supply chain for an electric utility company that shows several types of first-tier suppliers. Utilities need to replace failed equipment in the field and may spend as much as one-half of their purchase expenditures for support services such as facilities maintenance, janitorial services, and computer programming.

Supply-chain management offers service providers the opportunity to increase their competitiveness. The Managerial Practice feature shows how the Arizona Public Service company reduced costs and lowered prices with the help of an electronic purchasing system developed in conjunction with its suppliers.

purchasing The management of the acquisition process, which includes deciding which suppliers to use, negotiating contracts, and deciding whether to buy locally.

What is the best approach for developing an integrated supply chain?

DEVELOPING INTEGRATED SUPPLY CHAINS

Successful supply-chain management requires a high degree of functional and organizational integration. Such integration does not happen overnight. Traditionally, organizations have divided the responsibility for managing the flow of materials and services among three departments: purchasing, production, and distribution. **Purchasing** is the management of the acquisition process, which includes deciding which suppliers to

MANAGERIAL PRACTICE

Supply-Chain Management at Arizona Public Service

Arizona Public Service (APS), (www.apsc.com) is the largest utility company in Arizona, serving 705,000 customers and generating $1.7 billion in revenues annually. The company has three diverse business units: Generation (fossil fuel and nuclear power), Transmission, and Cooperative Services, each with very different supply-chain requirements. Even though APS is a very successful utility company, it faces new challenges. The deregulation of the generation and cooperative services segments of the industry by Congress and the states has made the $200 billion industry fully competitive. Companies such as APS are preparing for added competition by driving down operating costs and improving customer services. For example, at APS, expenditures related to the procurement of equipment and services amounted to more than 33 percent of revenues. Because of the diversity of its business units, 20 percent of the items listed in the company's inventory catalog were duplicates. The costs of duplicate orders directly affected the profitability of the utility company.

Two Arizona Public Service employees are high above to repair some telephone lines in Flagstaff, Arizona.

APS decided to scrutinize its supply chain for ways to increase efficiency and invest in new technology to support the management of materials and provision of services. But first it had to overcome some old practices. For example, expensive line transformers were held in inventory in case a replacement was needed in the field. In addition, the company considered large inventories of replacement parts and other items needed to support the transmission of electric power and daily office operations to be a value-added aspect of doing business. Presumably, management believed that fast replacement of failed items was desirable and that stocking allowed buyers to get the best prices. Now management views these practices as expensive and time-consuming.

APS's solution was to develop an electronic system in accordance with prearranged price, quality, and delivery agreements with its suppliers. The system enables both buyers and other company personnel to buy products and services through the streamlined processes of three online software modules.

Materials Catalog. This module lists items kept on hand at various warehouse locations. Personnel needing materials from this catalog merely enter the items from their PC workstations. The system keeps track of the inventories and informs buyers when replenishment orders are required.

Description Buy. For items not listed in the materials catalog, users can determine whether the items have already been ordered by other users. If so, another order may not be needed. Once a user has selected the needed items, a point-and-click action submits the online material and service request form, which is automatically routed to a company buyer.

Express Buy. For certain low-cost, high-volume items, APS maintains a list of approved suppliers that have entered into preestablished purchase agreements involving prices, payment terms, and delivery lead times. The module is linked to the suppliers' catalogs electronically and enables company personnel to order directly from the suppliers without involving a buyer.

The electronic system handles 50,000 to 80,000 transactions *daily*, or roughly one-half of the company's purchase orders. The time involved in obtaining materials and services has been drastically reduced to a few hours for items from the warehouse, 4 days (previously 22 days) for items ordered through the Description Buy module, and less than 48 hours for Express Buy items. The time spent on improving supply-chain performance was worthwhile. APS trimmed inventory by 20 percent, reduced materials management personnel by 25 percent, and reduced purchasing costs by 5 percent. In turn, APS reduced consumer electric rates by 5 percent.

Sources: Ettinger, Al. "Reinventing the Supply Chain: Bringing Materials Management to Light." *APICS—The Performance Advantage* (February 1997), pp. 42–45; Turdrick, James. "Supply-Chain Management: Not Just for Manufacturing Anymore." *APICS—The Performance Advantage* (December 1999), pp. 39–42.

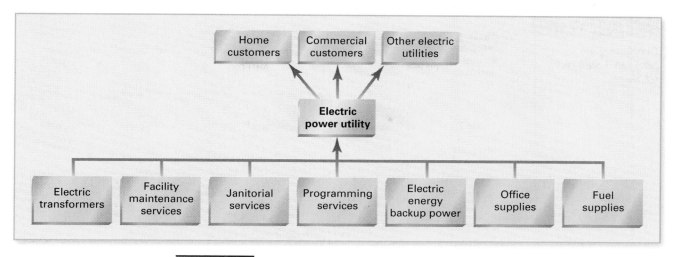

FIGURE 8.3 *Supply Chain for an Electric Power Utility, Showing Tier 1 Suppliers Only*

production The management of the transformation process devoted to producing the product or service.

distribution The management of the flow of materials from manufacturers to customers and from warehouses to retailers, involving the storage and transportation of products.

materials management The decisions that are made by a firm concerning the purchase of materials and services, inventories, production levels, staffing patterns, schedules, and distribution.

use, negotiating contracts, and deciding whether to buy locally. Purchasing is usually responsible for working with suppliers to ensure the desired flow of materials and services for both short and long terms. Purchasing may also be responsible for the levels of raw materials and maintenance and repair inventories. **Production** is the management of the transformation processes devoted to producing the product or service. It is responsible for determining production quantities and scheduling the machines and employees directly responsible for the production of the good or service. **Distribution** is the management of the flow of materials from manufacturers to customers and from warehouses to retailers, involving the storage and transportation of products. It may also be responsible for finished goods inventories and the selection of transportation service providers. Typically, firms willing to undergo the rigors of developing integrated supply chains progress through a series of phases, as Figure 8.4 shows. In phase 1, a starting point for most firms, external suppliers and customers are considered to be independent of the firm. Relations with these entities are formal, and there is little sharing of operating information and costs. Internally, purchasing, production, and distribution act independently, each optimizing its own activities without considering the other entities. Each external and internal entity in the supply chain controls its own inventories and often utilizes control systems and procedures that are incompatible with those of other entities. Because of organizational and functional boundaries, large amounts of inventory exist in the supply chain and the overall flow of materials and services is ineffective.

In phase 2, the firm initiates internal integration by creating a materials management department. **Materials management** is concerned with decisions about purchasing materials and services, inventories, production levels, staffing patterns, schedules, and distribution. The focus is on the integration of those aspects of the supply chain directly under the firm's control to create an *internal supply chain.* Firms in this phase utilize a seamless information and materials control system from distribution to purchasing, integrating marketing, finance, accounting, and operations. Efficiency and electronic linkages to customers and suppliers are emphasized. Nonetheless, the firm still considers its suppliers and customers to be independent entities and focuses on tactical, rather than strategic, issues.

Internal integration must precede phase 3, supply-chain integration. The internal supply chain is extended to embrace suppliers and customers, thereby linking it to the

FIGURE 8.4

*Developing an
Integrated Supply
Chain*

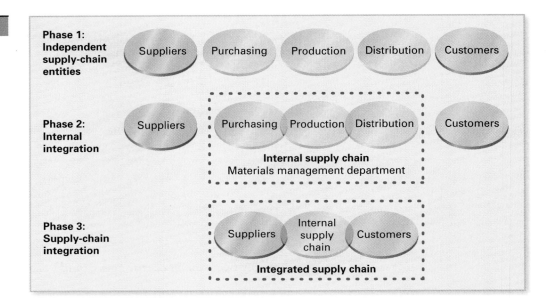

external supply chain, which is not under the direct control of the firm. The firm must change its focus from a product or service orientation to a customer orientation. This new focus means that the firm must identify the appropriate competitive priorities for each of its market segments. For its industrial customers, the firm must develop a better understanding of their products, culture, markets, and organization. Rather than merely react to customer demand, the firm strives to work with its customers so that both benefit from improved flows of materials and services. Similarly, the firm must develop better understanding of its suppliers' organizations, capacities, and strengths and weaknesses—and include its suppliers earlier in the design process for new products or services. Phase 3 embodies what we call supply-chain management and seeks to integrate the internal and external supply chains.

The integrated supply chain provides a framework for the operating decisions in a firm. Managing the internal supply chain involves issues of forecasting, inventory management, aggregate planning and scheduling, and resource planning, all topics in the remaining chapters of this text. In this chapter, we focus on the interfaces shown in Figure 8.4 between the internal supply chain and the customers and suppliers.

MANAGING THE CUSTOMER INTERFACE

The Internet has dramatically changed the way companies serve their customers. Traditional supply chains involve factories, warehouses, distributors, and retailers. Some companies, however, have been able to use the Internet to eliminate certain elements of their supply chains by substituting information for inventories. Other firms have used it to reduce the transaction costs in their supply chains. We use the term *customer* to refer to an entity the firm is trying to serve, which could be a consumer or a business. The popular literature has termed Internet systems dealing with consumers as *business-to-consumer systems,* or B2C. Systems dealing with businesses are called *business-to-business systems,* or B2B. (See Chapter 4, "Managing Technology" for a discussion of B2C and B2B systems.) Regardless of who the customer may be, in this section we explore the impact of the Internet on the order-placement and the order-fulfillment processes.

ORDER-PLACEMENT PROCESS

order-placement process
The activities required to register the need for a product or service and to confirm the acceptance of the order.

The **order-placement process** involves the activities required to register the need for a product or service and to confirm the acceptance of the order. These activities are initiated by the customer but consummated by the firm producing the product or service. Since it is the order-placement process that generates demand for the supply chain, it is to the firm's advantage to make it simple and fast. The Internet has enabled firms to reengineer their order-placement process to benefit both the customer and the firm. The Internet provides the following advantages for a firm's order-placement process.

COST REDUCTION. Using the Internet can reduce the costs of processing orders because it allows for greater participation by the customer (see Chapter 2, "Process Management"). Customers can select the products or services they want and place an order with the firm without actually talking to anyone. This approach reduces the need for call centers, which are labor intensive and often take longer to place orders.

REVENUE FLOW INCREASE. A firm's Web page can allow customers to enter credit card information or purchase-order numbers as part of the order-placement process. This approach reduces the time lags often associated with billing the customer or waiting for checks sent in the mail.

GLOBAL ACCESS. Another advantage the Internet has provided firms is the opportunity to accept orders 24 hours a day. Traditional bricks-and-mortar firms take standard orders during their normal business hours. Firms with Internet access can reduce the time it takes to satisfy a customer, thereby gaining a competitive advantage over bricks-and-mortar firms.

PRICING FLEXIBILITY. Firms with their products and services posted on the Web can easily change prices as the need arises, thereby avoiding the cost and delay of publishing new catalogs. Customers placing orders have current prices to consider when making their choices. From the perspective of supply chains, Dell Computer Corporation uses this capability to control for component shortages. Because of its direct-sales approach and promotional pricing, Dell can steer customers to certain configurations of computers for which ample supplies exist.

ORDER-FULFILLMENT PROCESS

order-fulfillment process
The activities required to deliver a product or service to a customer.

The **order-fulfillment process** involves the activities required to deliver a product or service to a customer. This process might be called upon to address any of the competitive priorities falling under the categories of cost, quality, time, or flexibility. We have separated the order-placement process from the order-fulfillment process in our discussion; however, in many instances, they occur simultaneously. For example, a customer at a Barnes and Noble store has in effect ordered a book, performing the work to actually find it in the inventory, and the store has delivered it when she checks out at the service desk. However, Barnes and Noble also has a Web page, where the order-placement and the order-fulfillment processes are separated. Customers doing business on its Web page must accept a delay in receiving their books, a delay Barnes and Noble seeks to minimize in its supply chain. Designing the order-fulfillment process can have competitive implications.

As we mentioned earlier, many activities of the order-fulfillment process associated with the internal supply chain are covered in the chapters to follow. In this section, we will focus on information sharing, the placement of inventories, and postponement.

INFORMATION SHARING. The Internet provides a quick and efficient means to share information along the supply chain. Within a firm, ERP systems facilitate the flow of information across functional areas, business units, geographic regions, and product lines. For a manufacturing firm, accurate information about its customer's operations, such as current inventory positions, future demands and production schedules, or expected orders for the firm's products, enables the firm's order-fulfillment process to better anticipate the future needs of its customers. The supply chain can better match supply with demand, thereby reducing inventory costs and decreasing the time to fulfill orders. For a service provider, accurate forecasts of its customers' demand enables the firm to derive its own forecasts of demand for its services. For example, UPS can better plan its delivery services when it has information about the demands faced by its major corporate customers. While electronic sharing of information can improve supply-chain operations, those firms that have successfully integrated the internal and external supply chains can only enjoy the advantage. Going online may require a significant investment in information systems and support.

INVENTORY PLACEMENT. A fundamental supply-chain decision is where to locate an inventory of finished goods. Placing inventories can have strategic implications, as in the case of international companies locating *distribution centers* (DC) in foreign countries to preempt local competition by reducing delivery times to its customers. However, the issue for any firm producing standardized products is where to position the inventory in the supply chain. At one extreme, the firm could keep all the finished-goods inventory at the manufacturing plant and ship directly to each of its customers. The advantage would come from what is referred to as **inventory pooling,** which is a reduction in inventory and safety stock because of the merging of variable demands from the customers. A higher-than-expected demand from one customer can be offset by a lower-than-expected demand from another. We discuss the methods for determining the amount of safety stock in Chapter 10, "Inventory Management." A disadvantage of placing inventory at the plant, however, is the added cost of shipping smaller, uneconomical quantities directly to the customers, typically over long distances.

Another approach is to use **forward placement,** which means locating stock closer to customers at a warehouse, DC, wholesaler, or retailer. Forward placement can have two advantages for the order-fulfillment process—faster delivery times and reduced transportation costs—that can stimulate sales. As inventory is placed closer to the customer, such as at a DC, the pooling effect of the inventories is reduced, but the time to get the product to the customer is also reduced. Consequently, service to the customer is quicker, and the firm can take advantage of larger, less costly shipments to the DCs. The extreme application of forward placement is to locate the inventories at the customer. This tactic is referred to as **vendor-managed inventories (VMI).** Some manufacturers, such as Dell Computer, have inventories of materials on consignment from their suppliers. Dell pays for the materials only when they are used. In deciding where to place inventories, firms must balance the inventory and transportation costs against the need to reduce the time to fulfill orders. One form of the VMI method is **continuous replenishment** in which the supplier monitors inventory levels at the customer and replenishes the stock as needed to avoid shortages. Manufacturing firms using a make-to-stock strategy, and traditional retailers using a standardized services strategy, often use forward placement.

POSTPONEMENT. Assemble-to-order and mass customization firms use a tactic called **postponement,** which refers to delaying the customizing of a product or service until the last possible moment. Mass-customized products are assembled from a variety of standard components according to the specifications from a customer. When the order-placement process is separated from the order-fulfillment process, manufactur-

---

Should distribution centers be added to position inventory closer to the customer?

inventory pooling A reduction in inventory and safety stock because of the merging of variable demands from customers.

forward placement Locating stock closer to customers at a ware-house, DC, wholesaler, or retailer.

vendor-managed inventories (VMI) An extreme application of the forward placement tactic, which involves locating the inventories at the customer.

continuous replenishment A VMI method in which the supplier monitors inventory levels at the customer and replenishes the stock as needed to avoid shortages.

postponement A tactic used by assemble-to-order and mass-customization firms that refers to delaying the customizing of a product or service until the last possible moment.

ing and order fulfillment can take place after the customer has placed the order. The manufacturing process must be flexible to quickly respond to the customer's order. By forcing customization to the last possible moment, the manufacturing process spends more of its time on standardized components and assemblies, which are less costly to produce.

Postponement can be extended to the distribution channel. **Channel assembly** is the process of using members of the distribution channel as if they were assembly stations in the factory. Distributors might perform the final, customized assembly of a product for delivery to a particular customer. A special case of channel assembly is the organization and shipment of many disparate items for assembly at the customer's site. As we mentioned in the opener to Chapter 1, "Competing with Operations," FedEx is devising a system for Cisco that will transport as many as 100 different boxes destined for one of Cisco's customers from factories around the world and deliver them at the customer's door within hours of each other for final assembly. Such a system bypasses warehouses in the supply chain and reduces the cost and time required to fulfill an order.

channel assembly The process of using members of the distribution channel as if they were assembly stations in the factory.

MANAGING THE SUPPLIER INTERFACE

The application of ERP has forced firms to reengineer their enterprise processes to take advantage of large, integrated information systems. The Internet, however, has not only enabled firms to improve their processes for interfacing with customers, it has also changed the way firms deal with their suppliers. In this section, we will discuss electronic purchasing (e-purchasing), the considerations firms make when selecting suppliers or outsourcing internal processes, the implications for centralized buying, and the reasons why value analysis is important.

E-PURCHASING

The emergence of virtual marketplaces, enabled by Internet technologies, has provided firms with many opportunities to improve their purchasing processes. Not all e-purchasing opportunities, however, involve the Internet. In this section, we will discuss four approaches to e-purchasing: electronic data interchange, catalog hubs, exchanges, and auctions.

electronic data interchange (EDI) A technology that enables the transmission of routine business documents having a standard format from computer to computer over telephone or direct leased lines.

ELECTRONIC DATA INTERCHANGE. The most used form of e-purchasing today is **electronic data interchange (EDI)**, a technology that enables the transmission of routine business documents having a standard format from computer to computer over telephone or direct leased lines. Special communications software translates documents into and out of a generic form, allowing organizations to exchange information even if they have different hardware and software components. Invoices, purchase orders, and payments are some of the routine documents that EDI can handle—it replaces the phone call or mailed document. An electronic purchasing system with EDI might work as follows. Buyers browse an electronic catalog and click on items to purchase from a supplier. A computer sends the order directly to the supplier. The supplier's computer checks the buyer's credit and determines that the items are available. The supplier's warehouse and shipping departments are notified electronically, and the items are readied for shipment. Finally, the supplier's accounting department bills the buyer electronically. EDI saves the cost of opening mail, directing it to the right department, checking the document for accuracy, and reentering the information in a computer system. It also improves accuracy, shortens response times, and can even reduce inventory. Savings (ranging from $5 to $125 per document) are considerable in light of the hundreds to thousands of documents many firms typically handle daily.

catalog hubs An approach to e-purchasing that is used to reduce the costs of placing orders to suppliers as well as the costs of the goods or services themselves.

CATALOG HUBS. **Catalog hubs** can be used to reduce the costs of placing orders to suppliers as well as the costs of the goods or services themselves. Suppliers post their catalog of items on the hub, and buyers select what they need and purchase them electronically. However, a buying firm can negotiate prices with specific suppliers for items such as office supplies, technical equipment, specialized items, services, or furniture. The catalog that the buying firm's employees see consists only of the approved items and their negotiated prices. Employees use their PCs to select the items they need, and the system generates the purchase orders, which are electronically dispatched to the suppliers. The hub connects the firm to potentially hundreds of suppliers through the Internet, saving the costs of EDI, which requires one-to-one connections to individual suppliers.

exchange An electronic marketplace where buying firms and selling firms come together to do business.

EXCHANGES. An **exchange** is an electronic marketplace where buying and selling firms come together to do business. The exchange maintains relationships with buyers and sellers, making it easy to do business without the aspect of contract negotiations or other sorts of long-term conditions. Exchanges are often used for "spot" purchases, which are needed to satisfy an immediate need at the lowest possible cost. Commodity items such as oil, steel, or energy fit this category. However, exchanges can also be used for almost any item. For example, Marriott International and Hyatt Corporation are forming an exchange for hotels. Hotels traditionally have bought supplies from thousands of firms, each focusing on selected items such as soap, food, and equipment, using faxes, telephones, and forms that were made in quadruplicate. Placing orders was expensive, and there was little opportunity to do comparison shopping. The new exchange will have one-stop shopping for hotels using the service.

auction An extension of the exchange in which firms place competitive bids to buy something.

AUCTIONS. An extension of the exchange is the **auction**, where firms place competitive bids to buy something. For example, a site may be formed for a particular industry at which firms with excess capacity or materials can offer them for sale to the highest bidder. Bids can either be closed or open to the competition. Industries where auctions have value include steel, chemicals, and the home mortgage industry, where financial institutions can bid for mortgages.

An approach that has received considerable attention is the so-called *reverse auction,* in which suppliers bid for contracts with buyers. One such site is FreeMarkets, an electronic marketplace where Fortune 500 companies offer supply contracts for open bidding. Each bid is posted, so suppliers can see how much lower their next bid must be to remain in the running for the contract. Each contract has an electronic prospectus that provides all the specifications, conditions, and other requirements that are nonnegotiable. The only thing left to determine is the cost to the buyer. Savings can be dramatic.

Our discussion of these electronic approaches in purchasing should not leave the impression that cost is the only consideration in selecting a supplier. Exchanges and auctions are more useful for commodities, near-commodities, or infrequently needed items that require only short-term relationships with suppliers. The past two decades have taught us the lesson that suppliers should be thought of as partners when the needed supply is significant and steady over extended periods of time. Supplier involvement in product or service design and supply-chain performance improvement requires long-term relationships not found by competitive pricing on the Internet. We now turn to the considerations firms give to establishing long-term relationships with suppliers.

SUPPLIER SELECTION AND CERTIFICATION

Purchasing is the eyes and ears of the organization in the supplier marketplace, continuously seeking better buys and new materials from suppliers. Consequently, purchasing is in a good position to select suppliers for the supply chain and to conduct certification programs.

SUPPLIER SELECTION. Three criteria most often considered by firms selecting new suppliers are price, quality, and delivery. Because firms spend a large percentage of their total income on purchased items, finding suppliers that charge low *prices* is a key objective. However, the *quality* of a supplier's materials also is important. The hidden costs of poor quality can be high, particularly if defects are not detected until after considerable value has been added by subsequent operations (see Chapter 5, "Quality"). For a retailer, poor merchandise quality can mean loss of customer goodwill and future sales. Finally, shorter lead times and on-time *delivery* help the buying firm maintain acceptable customer service with less inventory.

A fourth criterion is becoming very important in the selection of suppliers—environmental impact. Many firms are engaging in **green purchasing,** which involves identifying, assessing, and managing the flow of environmental waste and finding ways to reduce it and minimize its impact on the environment. Suppliers are being asked to be environmentally conscious when designing and manufacturing their products, and claims such as *green, biodegradable, natural,* and *recycled* must be substantiated when bidding on a contract. In the not-too-distant future, this criterion could be one of the most important in the selection of suppliers.

SUPPLIER CERTIFICATION. Supplier certification programs verify that potential suppliers have the capability to provide the materials or services the buying firm requires. Certification typically involves site visits by a cross-functional team from the buying firm who do an in-depth evaluation of the supplier's capability to meet cost, quality, delivery, and flexibility targets from process and information system perspectives. The team may consist of members from operations, purchasing, engineering, information systems, and accounting. Every aspect of producing the materials or services is explored through observation of the processes in action and review of documentation for completeness and accuracy. Once certified, the supplier can be used by purchasing without its having to make background checks. Performance is monitored and performance records are kept. After a certain period of time, or if performance declines, the supplier may have to be recertified.

SUPPLIER RELATIONS

The nature of relations maintained with suppliers can affect the quality, timeliness, and price of a firm's products and services.

COMPETITIVE ORIENTATION. The **competitive orientation** to supplier relations views negotiations between buyer and seller as a zero-sum game: Whatever one side loses, the other side gains. Short-term advantages are prized over long-term commitments. The buyer may try to beat the supplier's price down to the lowest survival level or to push demand to high levels during boom times and order almost nothing during recessions. In contrast, the supplier presses for higher prices for specific levels of quality, customer service, and volume flexibility. Which party wins depends largely on who has the most clout.

Purchasing power determines the clout that a firm has. A firm has purchasing power when its purchasing volume represents a significant share of the supplier's sales or the purchased item or service is standardized and many substitutes are available. For

What criteria should be used to select suppliers and how should suppliers be certified?

green purchasing The process of identifying, assessing, and managing the flow of environmental waste and finding ways to reduce it and minimize its impact on the environment.

competitive orientation A supplier relation that views negotiations between buyer and seller as a zero-sum game: Whatever one side loses, the other side gains; short-term advantages are prized over long-term commitments.

How can purchasing power be used effectively in a supply chain?

example, Staples merged with Office Depot to create a chain of 1,100 office supply stores in the United States and Canada. The buying power of the new company is enormous. Clout is also used in the health care industry. Premier, Inc., a cooperative with 1,759 member hospitals, spends $10 billion a year on materials and services for its members. Suppliers are uneasy because they have to give Premier prices far lower than they do their other customers to keep its business, reflecting Premier's purchasing power. For example, Premier got a 30 percent savings in dye used in medical imaging and a 25 percent savings in the film for that process. Premier will buy from the lowest bidder without much loyalty to any supplier. Analysts estimate that Premier has helped reduce the cost of health care by $2 billion a year because of its efforts.

cooperative orientation
A supplier relation in which the buyer and seller are partners, each helping the other as much as possible.

COOPERATIVE ORIENTATION. With the **cooperative orientation** to supplier relations, the buyer and seller are partners, each helping the other as much as possible. A cooperative orientation means long-term commitment, joint work on quality, and support by the buyer of the supplier's managerial, technological, and capacity development. A cooperative orientation favors few suppliers of a particular item or service, with just one or two suppliers being the ideal number. As order volumes increase, the supplier gains repeatability, which helps movement toward high-volume operations at a low cost. When contracts are large and a long-term relationship is ensured, the supplier might even build a new facility and hire a new workforce, perhaps relocating close to the buyer's plant. Reducing the number of suppliers also can help the buyer, as suppliers become almost an extension of the buyer.

A cooperative orientation means that the buyer shares more information with the supplier on its future buying intentions. This forward visibility allows suppliers to make better, more reliable forecasts of future demand. The buyer visits suppliers' plants and cultivates cooperative attitudes. The buyer may even suggest ways to improve the suppliers' operations. This close cooperation with suppliers could even mean that the buyer does not need to inspect incoming materials. It also could mean giving the supplier more latitude in specifications, involving the supplier more in designing parts, implementing cost-reduction ideas, and sharing in savings.

A cooperative orientation has opened the door for innovative arrangements with suppliers. One extreme example of such an arrangement is the Volkswagen (VW) factory in Brazil. There seven major suppliers make components on their own equipment. Then their own workers actually assemble the components into finished trucks and buses. Of 1,000 workers at the plant, only 200 are VW employees. This arrangement has several advantages. First, VW's capital investment is less: VW provides the building and the assembly-line conveyors, but suppliers install their own tools and fixtures. Second, if sales of trucks and buses go below the projected 30,000 annual capacity, all the partners take a hit, not just VW. Third, parts will arrive just before they are needed, so everyone's inventory costs will be low. Finally, improvements by suppliers in the assembly process will benefit all parties.

One advantage of reducing the number of suppliers in the supply chain is a reduction in the complexity of managing them. However, reducing the number of suppliers for an item or service may have the disadvantage of increased risk of an interruption in supply. Also, there is less opportunity to drive a good bargain in prices unless the buyer has a lot of clout. **Sole sourcing**, which is the awarding of a contract for an item or service to only one supplier, can amplify any problems with the supplier that may crop up.

sole sourcing The awarding of a contract for an item or service to only one supplier.

Both the competitive and cooperative orientations have their advantages and disadvantages. The key is to use the approach that serves the firm's competitive priorities best. Some companies utilize a mixed strategy. A company can pursue a competitive orientation by seeking price reductions from its suppliers of common supplies and infrequently purchased items on an electronic marketplace, and also use a cooperative orientation with suppliers of higher volume, more continually used materials and services and negotiating long-term contracts with them. However, a cooperative orientation does not preclude the obligation to reduce costs. For example, automakers make long-term commitments to selected suppliers but require continuous improvement programs to gain annual price reductions from them (see Chapter 5, "Quality"). Such commitments can give suppliers enough volume to invest in cost-saving equipment and new capacity.

OUTSOURCING

What are the implications for supply-chain management of outsourcing an activity?

A special case of the cooperative orientation is *outsourcing* (see Chapter 2, "Process Management"). The decision to outsource an activity, sometimes referred to as the *make-or-buy decision,* has implications for supply-chain management because it affects the number of activities under the direct control of the firm in its *internal supply chain*. This decision is not trivial because a firm must first have a clear understanding of its core competencies (see Chapter 1, "Competing with Operations") and retain them. Outsourcing has direct relevance for supply-chain management because of its implications for control and flexibility.

DEGREE OF SOURCING CONTROL. Sourcing control amounts to choosing the appropriate contract relationship with the supplier. These relationships range from full ownership, strategic alliances (see Chapter 1, "Competing with Operations"), and long-term contracts, which provide high degrees of control, to short-term contracts, which provide low degrees of control. The more important the activity is for the achievement of the firm's competitive priorities, the greater the degree of control the firm will want.

FLEXIBILITY TO CHANGE THE SUPPLY CHAIN. A firm has a more flexible arrangement with a supplier if it has a short-term agreement with it. The firm can choose to renegotiate the terms of the contract or change suppliers frequently. These options are not available if the firm enters into long-term arrangements with a supplier. If market needs change, or the supplier experiences business difficulties, the firm will have a more difficult time changing suppliers if it has a long-term commitment.

Consequently, supply-chain managers must balance the advantages of high degrees of control with those of flexibility to change. Long-term arrangements should be used only when the firm is confident that the supplier will fit into its long-term strategic plans.

DaimlerChrysler outsources major subassemblies to improve efficiency. This "rolling chassis" is built by the Dana Corporation in Curitiba, Brazil, and then shipped to the nearby DaimlerChrysler plant where the Dakota pickup truck is assembled. It is the largest module built to date by auto industry suppliers.

CENTRALIZED VERSUS LOCALIZED BUYING

When an organization has several facilities (e.g., stores, hospitals, or plants), management must decide whether to buy locally or centrally. This decision has implications for the control of supply-chain flows.

Centralized buying has the advantage of increasing purchasing clout. Savings can be significant, often on the order of 10 percent or more. Increased buying power can mean getting better service, ensuring long-term supply availability, or developing new supplier capability. Companies with overseas suppliers favor centralization because of the specialized skills (e.g., understanding of foreign languages and cultures) needed to buy from foreign sources. Buyers also need to understand international commercial and contract law regarding the transfer of goods and services. Another trend that favors centralization is the growth of computer-based information systems and the Internet, which give specialists at headquarters access to data previously available only at the local level.

Probably the biggest disadvantage of centralized buying is loss of control at the local level. When plants or divisions are evaluated as profit or cost centers, centralized buying is undesirable for items unique to a particular facility. These items should be purchased locally whenever possible. The same holds for purchases that must be closely meshed with production schedules. Further, localized buying is an advantage when the firm has major facilities in foreign countries because the managers there, often foreign nationals, have a much better understanding of the culture than a staff would at the home office. Also, centralized purchasing often means longer lead times and another level in the firm's hierarchy. Perhaps the best solution is a compromise strategy, whereby both local autonomy and centralized buying are possible. For example, the corporate purchasing group at IBM negotiates contracts on a centralized basis only at the request of local plants. Then management at one of the facilities monitors the contract for all the participating plants.

VALUE ANALYSIS

A systematic effort to reduce the cost or improve the performance of products or services, either purchased or produced, is referred to as **value analysis.** It is an intensive examination of the materials, processes, information systems, and flows of material involved in the production of an item. Benefits include reduced production, materials, and distribution costs; improved profit margins; and increased customer satisfaction. Because teams involving purchasing, production, and engineering personnel from both the firm and its major suppliers play a key role in value analysis, another potential benefit is increased employee morale.

Value analysis encourages employees of the firm and its suppliers to address questions such as the following: What is the function of the item? Is the function necessary? Can a lower-cost standard part that serves the purpose be identified? Can the item be simplified, or its specifications relaxed, to achieve a lower price? Can the item be designed so that it can be produced more efficiently or more quickly? Can features that the customer values highly be added to the item? Value analysis should be part of a continual effort to improve the performance of the supply chain and increase the value of the item to the customer.

Value analysis can focus solely on the *internal* supply chain with some success, but its true potential lies in applying it to the *external* supply chain as well. An approach that many firms are using is called **early supplier involvement,** which is a program that includes suppliers in the design phase of a product or service. Suppliers provide suggestions for design changes and materials choices that will result in more efficient operations and higher quality. In the automotive industry, an even higher level of early supplier involvement is known as **presourcing,** whereby suppliers are

---

value analysis A systematic effort to reduce the cost or improve the performace of products or services, either purchased or produced.

How can suppliers get involved in value analysis to benefit the supply chain?

early supplier involvement A program that includes suppliers in the design phase of a product or service.

presourcing In the automotive industry, a level of supplier involvement in which suppliers are selected early in a vehicle's concept development stage and are given significant, if not total, responsibility for the design of certain components or systems.

selected early in a vehicle's concept development stage and are given significant, if not total, responsibility for the design of certain components or systems. Presourced suppliers also take responsibility for the cost, quality, and on-time delivery of the items they produce.

MEASURES OF SUPPLY-CHAIN PERFORMANCE

As we have shown, supply-chain management involves managing the flow of materials that create inventories in the supply chain. For this reason, managers closely monitor inventories to keep them at acceptable levels. The flow of materials also affects various financial measures of concern to the firm. In this section, we first define the typical inventory measures used to monitor supply-chain performance. We then present some process measures. Finally, we relate some commonly used supply-chain performance measures to several important financial measures.

INVENTORY MEASURES

All methods of measuring inventory begin with a physical count of units, volume, or weight. However, measures of inventories are reported in three basic ways: average aggregate inventory value, weeks of supply, and inventory turnover.

The **average aggregate inventory value** is the total value of all items held in inventory for a firm. We express all the dollar values in this inventory measure at cost because we can then sum the values of individual items in raw materials, work-in-process, and finished goods: Final sales dollars have meaning only for final products or services and cannot be used for all inventory items. It is an average because it usually represents the inventory investment over some period of time. Suppose that item A is a raw material that is transformed into a finished product, item B. One unit of item A may be worth only a few dollars, whereas one unit of item B may be valued in the hundreds of dollars because of the labor, technology, and other value-added operations performed in manufacturing the product. This measure for an inventory consisting of only items A and B is

$$
\begin{aligned}
\text{Average aggregate} \atop \text{inventory value} = &\left(\begin{array}{c}\text{Number of units of item A}\\\text{typically on hand}\end{array}\right)\left(\begin{array}{c}\text{Value of each}\\\text{unit of item A}\end{array}\right) \\
&+ \left(\begin{array}{c}\text{Number of units of item B}\\\text{typically on hand}\end{array}\right)\left(\begin{array}{c}\text{Value of each}\\\text{unit of item B}\end{array}\right)
\end{aligned}
$$

Summed over all items in an inventory, this total value tells managers how much of a firm's assets are tied up in inventory. Manufacturing firms typically have about 25 percent of their total assets in inventory, whereas wholesalers and retailers average about 75 percent.

To some extent, managers can decide whether the aggregate inventory value is too low or too high by historical or industry comparison or by managerial judgment. However, a better performance measure would take demand into account. **Weeks of supply** is an inventory measure obtained by dividing the average aggregate inventory value by sales per week at cost. (In some low-inventory operations, days or even hours are a better unit of time for measuring inventory.) The formula (expressed in weeks) is

$$
\text{Weeks of supply} = \frac{\text{Average aggregate inventory value}}{\text{Weekly sales (at cost)}}
$$

Although the numerator includes the value of all items (raw materials, WIP, and finished goods), the denominator represents only the finished goods sold—at cost rather

---

Margin notes:

What measures of inventory are important to supply-chain management?

average aggregate inventory value The total value of all items held in inventory for a firm.

weeks of supply An inventory measure obtained by dividing the average aggregate inventory value by sales per week at cost.

inventory turnover An
inventory measure
obtained by dividing
annual sales at cost by the
average aggregate
inventory value
maintained during
the year.

**TUTOR
8.1**

than the sale price after markups or discounts. This cost is referred to as the *cost of goods sold*.

Inventory turnover (or *turns*) is an inventory measure obtained by dividing annual sales at cost by the average aggregate inventory value maintained during the year, or

$$\text{Inventory turnover} = \frac{\text{Annual sales (at cost)}}{\text{Average aggregate inventory value}}$$

The "best" inventory level, even when expressed as turnover, cannot be determined easily. Although six or seven turns per year is typical, the average high-tech firm settles for only about three turns. At the other extreme, some automobile firms report 40 turns per year for selected products. See the Solved Problem at the end of this chapter for a detailed example of the three inventory measures.

PROCESS MEASURES

We have discussed three major processes related to supply-chain management: order placement, order fulfillment, and purchasing. Supply-chain managers monitor performance by measuring costs, time, and quality. Table 8.1 contains examples of operating measures for the three processes.

Managers periodically collect data on measures such as these and track them to note changes in level or direction. Statistical process control charts can be used to determine if the changes are statistically significant, thereby prompting management's attention (see Chapter 5, "Quality"). The impact of improvements to the three processes can be monitored using control charts.

How are operating
measures of supply-chain
performance related to a
firm's typical financial
measures?

LINKS TO FINANCIAL MEASURES

Effective management of the supply chain has fundamental impact on the financial status of a firm. Inventory should be considered an investment because it is created for future use. However, it ties up funds that might be used more profitably in other operations. Managing the supply chain so as to reduce the aggregate inventory investment will reduce the *total assets* portion of the firm's balance sheet. An important financial measure is *return on assets* (ROA), which is net income divided by total assets. Consequently, reducing aggregate inventory investment will increase ROA. Nonetheless, the objective should be to have the *proper* amount of inventory, not the least amount of inventory.

Weeks of inventory and inventory turns are reflected in another financial measure, *working capital*, which is money used to finance ongoing operations. Increases in

TABLE 8.1	**Order Placement**	**Order Fulfillment**	**Purchasing**
Supply-Chain Process Measures	❑ Percentage of orders taken accurately ❑ Time to complete the order-placement process ❑ Customer satisfaction with the order-placement process	❑ Percentage of incomplete orders shipped ❑ Percentage of orders shipped on time ❑ Time to fulfill the order ❑ Percentage of returned items or botched services ❑ Cost to produce the item or service ❑ Customer satisfaction with the order-fulfillment process	❑ Percentage of suppliers' deliveries on time ❑ Suppliers' lead times ❑ Percentage of defects in purchased materials and services ❑ Cost of purchased materials and services

inventory investment require increased payments to suppliers, for example. Decreasing weeks of supply or increasing inventory turns reduces the pressure on working capital by reducing inventories. Increasing inventory turns can be accomplished by improving the order-placement, order-fulfillment, or purchasing processes. For example, reducing supplier lead times has the effect of reducing weeks of supply and increasing inventory turns: Matching the input and output flows of materials is easier because shorter-range, more reliable forecasts of demand can be used. Similarly, improvements in the other measures in Table 8.1 can be traced to improvements in working capital.

Managers can also reduce production and material costs through effective supply-chain management. Costs of materials are determined through the financial arrangements with suppliers, and production costs are a result of the design and execution of the internal supply chain. In addition, the percent of defects, experienced in the external as well as internal supply chains, also affects the costs of operation. Improvements in these measures are reflected in the *cost of goods sold* and ultimately in the *net income* of the firm. They also have an effect on *contribution margin,* which is the difference between price and variable costs to produce a good or service. Reducing production and material costs, and quality defect costs, increases the contribution margin, allowing for greater profits. Contribution margins are often used as inputs to decisions regarding the portfolio of products or services the firm offers.

Supply-chain performance measures related to time also have financial implications. Many manufacturers and service providers measure the percent of on-time deliveries of their product or services to their customers as well as materials and services from their suppliers. Increasing the percent of on-time deliveries to customers will increase *total revenue* because satisfied customers will buy more products and services from the firm. Increasing the percent of on-time deliveries from suppliers has the effect of reducing the costs of production and raw materials inventories, which has implications for the cost of goods sold and contribution margins.

The Internet has brought another financial measure related to time to the forefront: *cash-to-cash,* which is the time lag between paying for the materials and services needed to produce a product or service and receiving payment for it. The shorter the time lag, the better the *cash flow* position of the firm. There is less need for working capital; therefore, the firm can use the freed-up funds for projects or investments. Reengineering the order-placement process so that payment for the product or service is made at the time the order is placed can reduce the time lag. Billing the customer after the order is shipped or the service performed increases the need for working capital. The ultimate is to have a negative cash-to-cash situation, which is possible when the customer pays for the product before the firm has to pay for the materials needed to make it. In such a case, the firm must be using an assemble-to-order strategy and have supplier inventories on consignment, which allows the firm to pay for materials as it uses them. Dell Computer, in the chapter opener, is a prime example of a negative cash-to-cash situation.

SUPPLY-CHAIN LINKS TO OPERATIONS STRATEGY

What is the appropriate supply-chain design for a particular competitive environment?

Operations strategy seeks to link the design and use of a firm's infrastructure and processes to the competitive priorities of each of its products or services so as to maximize its potential in the marketplace. A supply chain is a network of firms. Thus, each firm in the chain should build its own supply chain to support the competitive priorities of its products or services. In this section, we discuss two distinct supply-chain designs and demonstrate how they can support the operations strategies of firms.

EFFICIENT VERSUS RESPONSIVE SUPPLY CHAINS

Even though extensive technologies such as EDI, the Internet, computer-assisted design, flexible manufacturing, and automated warehousing have been applied to all stages of the supply chain, the performance of many supply chains has been dismal. A recent study of the U.S. food industry estimated that poor coordination among supply-chain partners was wasting $30 billion annually. One possible cause for failures is that managers do not understand the nature of the demand for their products or services and therefore can't devise a supply chain that would best satisfy that demand. Two distinct designs used to competitive advantage are *efficient supply chains* and *responsive supply chains* (Fisher, 1997). The purpose of efficient supply chains is to coordinate the flow of materials and services so as to minimize inventories and maximize the efficiency of the manufacturers and service providers in the chain. Responsive supply chains are designed to react quickly to market demands by positioning inventories and capacities in order to hedge against uncertainties in demand. Table 8.2 shows the environments that best suit each design.

The nature of demand for the firm's products or services is a key factor in the best choice of supply-chain design. Efficient supply chains work best in environments where demand is highly predictable, such as demand for staple items purchased at grocery stores or demand for a package delivery service. The focus of the supply chain is on the efficient flows of materials and services, that is, keeping inventories to a minimum. Because of the markets the firms serve, product or service designs last a long time, new introductions are infrequent, and variety is small. Such firms typically produce for markets in which price is crucial to winning an order; therefore, contribution margins are low and efficiency is important. Consequently, the firm's competitive priorities are low-cost operations, consistent quality, and on-time delivery.

Responsive supply chains work best when firms offer a great variety of products or services and demand predictability is low. The firms may not know what products or services they need to provide until customers place orders. In addition, demand may be short-lived, as in the case of fashion goods. The focus of responsive supply chains is reaction time so as to avoid keeping costly inventories that ultimately must be sold at deep discounts. Such is the operating environment of mass customizers or firms utilizing the assemble-to-order operations strategy (see Chapter 1, "Competing with Operations"). To be competitive, such firms must frequently introduce new products or services. Nonetheless, because of the innovativeness of their products or services, these firms enjoy high contribution margins. Typical competitive priorities are development speed, fast delivery times, customization, volume flexibility, and high-performance design quality.

A firm may need to utilize both types of supply chain, especially when it focuses its operations on specific market segments (see Chapter 2, "Process Management") or when it uses postponement. For example, the supply chain for a standard product such as an oil tanker has different requirements than that for a customized product such as

TABLE 8.2		
Environments Best Suited for Efficient and Responsive Supply Chains		

Factor	Efficient Supply Chains	Responsive Supply Chains
Demand	Predictable; low forecast errors	Unpredictable; high forecast errors
Competitive priorities	Low cost; consistent quality; on-time delivery	Development speed; fast delivery times; customization; volume flexibility; high-performance design quality
New-product introduction	Infrequent	Frequent
Contribution margins	Low	High
Product variety	Low	High

a luxury liner, even though both are ocean-going vessels and both may be manufactured by the same company. You might also see both types used in the same supply chain. For example, Gillette uses an efficient supply chain to manufacture its products so that it can utilize a capital-intensive manufacturing process and then postpones the packaging of the products until the very last moment to be responsive to the needs at the retail level. The packaging operation involves customization in the form of printing in different languages. Just as processes can be broken into parts, with different process choices for each (see Chapter 2, "Process Management"), so can supply-chain processes be segmented to achieve optimal performance.

THE DESIGN OF EFFICIENT AND RESPONSIVE SUPPLY CHAINS

Table 8.3 contains the basic design features for efficient and responsive supply chains. The higher in an efficient supply chain that a firm is, the more likely it is to have a line flow strategy that supports high volumes of standardized products or services. Consequently, suppliers in efficient supply chains should have low capacity cushions because high utilization keeps the cost per unit low. High inventory turns are desired because inventory investment must be kept low to achieve low costs. Firms should work with their suppliers to shorten lead times, but care must be taken to use tactics that do not appreciably increase costs. For example, lead times for a supplier could be shortened by switching from rail to air transportation; however, the added cost may offset the savings obtained from the shorter lead times. Suppliers should be selected with emphasis on low prices, consistent quality, and on-time delivery. Because of low capacity cushions, disruptions in an efficient supply chain can be costly and must be avoided.

Because of the need for quick reactions and the high levels of product or service variety, firms in a responsive supply chain should have a flexible, or intermediate, flow strategy. Consequently, suppliers should have high capacity cushions. Inventories should be positioned in the chain to support delivery speed, but inventories of expensive finished goods should be avoided. Firms should aggressively work with their suppliers to shorten lead times because that allows firms to wait longer before committing to customer orders. Firms should select suppliers to support the competitive priorities of the products or services provided, which in this case would include the ability to provide quick deliveries, customize parts or components, adjust volumes quickly to match demand cycles in the market, and provide high-performance quality. Our discussion of the Dell Computer Company at the beginning of this chapter is an example of the use of a responsive supply chain for competitive advantage.

Poor supply-chain performance often is the result of using the wrong supply-chain design for the products or services provided. A common mistake is to use an efficient

TABLE 8.3	

Design Features for Efficient and Responsive Supply Chains

Factor	Efficient Supply Chains	Responsive Supply Chains
Operations strategy	Make-to-stock or standardized services; emphasize high-volume, standardized products, or services	Assemble-to-order, make-to-order, or customized services emphasize product or service variety
Capacity cushion	Low	High
Inventory investment	Low; enable high inventory turns	As needed to enable fast delivery time
Lead time	Shorten, but do not increase costs	Shorten aggressively
Supplier selection	Emphasize low prices; consistent quality; on-time delivery	Emphasize fast delivery time; customization; volume flexibility; high-performance design quality

supply chain in an environment that calls for a responsive supply chain. Over time, a firm may add options to its basic product, or introduce variations of that product, so that the variety of products and options increases dramatically and demand predictability drops. Yet, the firm continues to measure the performance of its supply chain as it always has, emphasizing efficiency, even when contribution margins would allow a responsive supply-chain design. Clearly, effective alignment of supply-chain operations to its competitive priorities has strategic implications for a firm.

SUPPLY-CHAIN DYNAMICS

What causes the fluctuations in supply chains and what are the consequences?

Supply chains often involve linkages among many firms. Each firm depends on other firms for materials, services, and information needed to supply its immediate customer in the chain. Because firms typically are owned and managed independently, the actions of downstream members (toward the ultimate user of the product or service) of the supply chain can adversely affect the operations of upstream members (toward the lowest tier in the supply chain). Figure 8.5(a) shows a segment of a supply chain involving three firms. Firm A has two customers and is directly served by firm B, which is served by firm C. Information flows from A to B and from B to C, often with a considerable lag. A recent study by the Automotive Industry Action Group (AIAG) found that it takes four to six weeks for materials release information to filter down to the last tier in the automotive supply chain. Further, the information from firm A that does reach the bottom of the chain is often distorted by the ordering policies of firm B that are reflected in its materials purchases from firm C. As a result, firm C has to develop volume flexibility even when it is part of an efficient supply chain. Figure 8.5(b) shows that a relatively short-term increase in firm A's demand can lead to significant materials requirement swings for firm C. If firm B mistakenly thinks that the increase in requirements from firm A is long term and orders a large quantity of material from firm C, it will reduce its order quantity next time because its inventory levels are too high, causing the swings for firm C. These dynamics are often referred to as the *bullwhip effect*.

What causes supply-chain dynamics? The causes are both external and internal.

FIGURE 8.5

Supply-Chain Dynamics

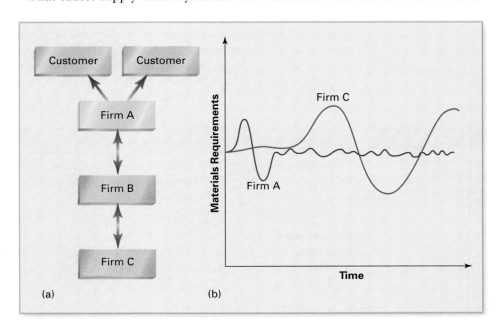

(a)

(b)

EXTERNAL SUPPLY-CHAIN CAUSES

A firm has the least amount of control over the external supply chain. Consequently, it must design its operations with the understanding that it may have to respond to disruptions caused by suppliers or customers. Typical disruptions include the following.

❑ *Volume Changes.*   Customers may change the quantity of the product or service they had ordered for a specific date or unexpectedly demand more of a standard product or service. If the market demands short lead times, the firm needs quick reactions from its suppliers. For example, an electric utility experiencing an unusually warm day may require immediate power backup from another utility to avoid a brownout in its region.

❑ *Product and Service Mix Changes.*   Customers may change the mix of items in an order and cause a ripple effect throughout the supply chain. For example, a major-appliance store chain may change the mix of washing machines in its orders from 60 percent Whirlpool brand and 40 percent Kitchen Aid brand to 40 percent Whirlpool and 60 percent Kitchen Aid. This decision changes the production schedule of the Whirlpool plant that makes both brands, causing imbalances in its inventories. Further, the company that makes the face plates for the washing machines must change its schedules, thereby affecting its suppliers.

❑ *Late Deliveries.*   Late deliveries of materials or delays in essential services can force a firm to switch its schedule from production of one product model to another. Firms that supply model-specific items may have their schedules disrupted. For example, the Whirlpool plant may find that a component supplier for its Model A washing machine could not supply the part on time. To avoid shutting down the assembly line, an expensive action, Whirlpool may decide to switch to Model B production. Suddenly there is a big demand on the suppliers for Model B–specific parts.

❑ *Underfilled Shipments.*   Suppliers that send partial shipments do so because of disruptions at their own plants. The effects of underfilled shipments are similar to those of late shipments unless there is enough to allow the firm to operate until the next shipment.

INTERNAL SUPPLY-CHAIN CAUSES

A famous line from a Pogo cartoon is "We have seen the enemy, and it is us!" Unfortunately, this statement is true for many firms when it comes to disruptions in the supply chain. A firm's own operations can be the culprit in what becomes the source of constant dynamics in the supply chain. Typical internal supply-chain disruptions include the following.

❑ *Internally Generated Shortages.*   There may be a shortage of parts manufactured by a firm because of machine breakdowns or inexperienced workers. This shortage may cause a change in the firm's production schedule that will affect suppliers. Labor shortages, owing to strikes or high turnover, have a similar effect. A strike at a manufacturing plant will reduce the need for trucking services, for example.

❑ *Engineering Changes.*   Changes to the design of products or services can have a direct impact on suppliers. For example, changing cable TV feed lines to fiber-optic technology increases the benefits to the cable company's customers but affects demand for cable. Similarly, reducing the complexity of a dashboard assembly may not be noticeable (functionally) to the buyers of an automobile, but it will change demand for the outsourced parts that go into the dashboard.

❑ *New Product or Service Introductions.*   New products or services always affect the supply chain. A firm decides how many introductions there will be, as well as their timing, and hence introduces a dynamic in the supply chain. New products or services may even require a new supply chain or addition of new members to an existing supply chain. For example, introduction of a new refrigerated trucking service will have an impact on the suppliers of refrigerated trucks and the maintenance items for the new service.

❑ *Product or Service Promotions.*   A common practice of firms producing standardized products or services is to use price discounts to promote sales. This practice has the effect of creating a spike in demand that is felt throughout the supply chain. That is what the Campbell Soup Company found out when its annual deep-discount pricing program caused customers to buy large quantities of chicken soup, which had the effect of causing overtime production at its plants.

❑ *Information Errors.*   Demand forecast errors can cause a firm to order too many, or too few, materials and services. Also, forecast errors may cause expedited orders that force suppliers to react more quickly to avoid shortages in the supply chain. In addition, errors in the physical count of items in stock can cause shortages (panic purchases) or too much inventory (slowdown in purchases). Finally, communication links between buyers and suppliers can be faulty. For example, inaccurate order quantities and delays in information flows will affect supply-chain dynamics.

External and internal disruptions such as these impair the performance of any supply chain. However, they are particularly costly in an *efficient supply chain* because suppliers are less able to react to changes in schedules. Many disruptions are caused by ineffective coordination between external and internal supply chains or poorly executed internal supply-chain operations. Because supply chains involve so many firms and separate operations, it is unrealistic to think that all disruptions can be eliminated. Nonetheless, the challenge for supply-chain managers is to remove as many disruptions as possible and design a supply chain that minimizes the impact of those that they cannot eliminate.

SUPPLY-CHAIN SOFTWARE

Supply-chain software provides the capability to share information with suppliers and customers and make decisions affecting the internal and external supply chains. Supply-chain applications are often a part of enterprise resource planning (ERP) systems (see Chapter 4, "Managing Technology") or can be purchased independently from a variety of vendors. For example, Pepperidge Farm purchased a supply-chain management system to improve customer service, reduce costs in finished goods inventory, and gain efficiencies in materials purchasing. Pepperidge Farm produces fresh breads made-to-order as well as a number of other products that are made-to-stock. The system has the following modules:

❑ *Order Commitment.*   Accepts customer orders, allocates resources to ensure that delivery is possible, and commits the firm to a specified delivery date.

❑ *Transportation Management.*   Schedules freight movements, provides routing capability, allocates resources, and tracks shipments worldwide.

❑ *Purchasing Management.*   Links to suppliers to share information and manage procurement contracts.

❑ *Demand Management.*   Provides multiple forecasting algorithms and causal modeling to assist in estimating demands, allowing for management overrides to incorporate real-time customer information (see Chapter 9, "Forecasting").

❐ *Vendor-Managed Inventory.* Coordinates the replenishment of inventories stored at the customer's site.

❐ *Replenishment Planning.* Facilitates the order-fulfillment process by orchestrating the flow of inventory through the various stocking points in the distribution channel and allocates inventories among customers when shortages exist.

❐ *Configuration.* Enables the assemble-to-order strategy by checking for the availability of all components before accepting an order and facilitates the substitution of components or features based on availability.

❐ *Material Planning.* Determines the replenishment of components and assemblies to support the master schedule of finished products (see Chapter 12, "Resource Planning").

❐ *Scheduling.* Provides multisite schedules with the capability to reschedule as needed (see Supplement J, "Operations Scheduling" on the Student CD-ROM).

❐ *Master Planning.* Offers optimization tools to allocate and coordinate limited resources across the distribution network based upon user strategies.

❐ *Strategic Planning.* Provides tools for designing global supply chains, which assist in deciding inventory levels and the appropriate product mix across the distribution network and the best production and storage locations subject to customer and resource constraints.

The Pepperidge Farm system is representative of the software packages available from a number of vendors. The supply-chain software business is booming—a recent survey by AMR Research Inc. indicated that software purchases of industrial enterprise applications, which includes ERP and supply-chain management systems, will increase at an annual compounded rate of 36 percent for the next several years. Most companies will purchase the software rather than create their own.

SUPPLY-CHAIN MANAGEMENT ACROSS THE ORGANIZATION

Supply chains permeate the entire organization. It is hard to envision a process in a firm that is not in some way affected by a supply chain. Supply chains must be managed to coordinate the inputs with the outputs in a firm so as to achieve the appropriate competitive priorities of the firm's enterprise processes. The Internet has offered firms an alternative to traditional methods for managing the supply chain. However, the firm must be committed to reengineering its information flows throughout the organization. The supply-chain processes most affected are the order-placement, order-fulfillment (including the internal supply chain), and purchasing processes. These processes intersect all of the traditional functional areas of the firm.

Supply-chain management is essential for manufacturing as well as service firms. In fact, service providers are beginning to realize the potential for organizational benefits through the reengineering of supply-chain processes. For example, hospitals have notoriously held to old-fashioned approaches for purchasing and materials management. Even with the advent of group purchasing organizations and centralized buying groups such as Premier, Inc., the materials management department in a typical hospital collects orders from throughout the hospital for medical supplies and equipment ranging from latex gloves to operating tables from a stack of often-outdated catalogs. Prices must be checked and the orders sent by phone or fax to literally thousands of distributors and suppliers. Can this process be improved? Columbia/HCA Healthcare Corporation and Tenet Healthcare Corporation think so. They are funding separate ventures that will create an electronic marketplace for placing orders online. The systems will include catalog hubs, which will contain several hundred-thousand medical and surgical supplies. Of course, to take full advantage of the marketplace, the hospitals will have to reengineer their processes to enable electronic ordering. The potential benefits to the health care industry for improved supply-chain practices are enormous. It is estimated that of the $83 billion hospitals spend annually on supplies, $11 billion could be eliminated by improved supply-chain management.

EQUATION SUMMARY

1. Weeks of supply $= \dfrac{\text{Average aggregate inventory value}}{\text{Weekly sales (at cost)}}$

2. Inventory turnover $= \dfrac{\text{Annual sales (at cost)}}{\text{Average aggregate inventory value}}$

CHAPTER HIGHLIGHTS

❐ A basic purpose of supply-chain management is to control inventory by managing the flows of materials that create it. Three aggregate categories of inventories are raw materials, work-in-process, and finished goods. An important aspect of supply-chain management is materials management, which coordinates the firm's purchasing, production control, and distribution functions.

❐ A supply chain is a set of linkages among suppliers of materials and services that spans the transformation of raw materials into products and services and delivers them to a firm's customers. Supply chains can be very complicated, involving thousands of firms at various tiers in the chain. Both service providers and manufacturers have supply chains to manage.

❐ Firms that develop an integrated supply chain first link purchasing, production, and distribution to create an internal supply chain that is the responsibility of a materials management department. Then they link suppliers and customers, an external supply chain, to the internal supply chain to form an integrated supply chain.

❐ The Internet has dramatically changed the way companies can manage their supply chains. The order-placement process can be reengineered to allow for more customer involvement and less employee involvement, to remain open for business 24 hours a day, and to enable the firm to use pricing as a means to control for material or product shortages. Designing the order-fulfillment process involves decisions regarding the postponement of customization until the last possible moment, forward placement of inventories, and final assembly of orders in the distribution channel.

❐ Electronic purchasing is changing the way that many firms are handling the purchasing function. Electronic data inter-change (EDI) has been used since the 1970s. It is now more accessible through the Internet and will enable firms to include more suppliers in their supply chains. Catalog hubs, exchanges, and auctions are among the latest innovations brought on by the Internet.

❐ Buyers can take two approaches in dealing with their suppliers. The competitive orientation pits supplier against supplier in an effort to get the buyer's business. Price concessions are a major bargaining point, and the amount of clout that a buyer or supplier may have often determines the outcome of the negotiations. The cooperative orientation seeks to make long-term commitments to a small number of suppliers with advantages accruing to both parties. The ultimate form of a cooperative orientation is sole sourcing, whereby only one supplier is responsible for providing an item or service. The orientation utilized should be chosen so as to achieve the firm's competitive priorities.

❐ It is becoming more and more popular to award the supply of an item or service previously produced by the firm to another firm under a long-term arrangement. It is important for supply-chain management because it shifts an activity from direct control in an internal supply chain to less control in an external supply chain.

❐ Value analysis is used to reduce the cost or improve the performance of products or services either purchased or produced. It is an intensive examination of the materials, process, and information flows involved in the production of an item. Programs such as early supplier involvement and presourcing involve suppliers in the value analysis.

❐ Supply-chain performance is tracked with inventory measures such as aggregate inventory level, weeks of supply, and inventory turnover. Supply-chain process measures include production and materials costs, percent defects, percent on-time delivery, and supplier lead times. These measures are related to financial measures such as total assets, ROA, working capital, contribution margin, total revenue, and cash-to-cash.

❑ Efficient supply chains are designed to coordinate the flows of materials and services so as to minimize inventories and maximize the efficiency of the firms in the supply chain. Responsive supply chains are designed to react quickly to market demand through judicious use of inventories and

capacities. A common error that firms make is to use an efficient supply-chain design when product variety is high and product demand is unpredictable.

❑ Because supply chains consist of many independent firms linked to other firms, disruptions at the top end can spread through the entire supply chain, causing firms lower in the supply chain to experience significant swings in demand. Such disruptions are caused by the dynamics of both external and internal supply chains.

SOLVED PROBLEM

A firm's cost of goods sold last year was $3,410,000, and the firm operates 52 weeks per year. It carries seven items in inventory: three raw materials, two work-in-process items, and two finished goods. The following table contains last year's average inventory level for each item, along with its value.

a. What is the average aggregate inventory value?

b. What weeks of supply does the firm maintain?

c. What was the inventory turnover last year?

CATEGORY	PART NUMBER	AVERAGE LEVEL	UNIT VALUE
Raw materials	1	15,000	$ 3.00
	2	2,500	5.00
	3	3,000	1.00
Work-in-process	4	5,000	14.00
	5	4,000	18.00
Finished goods	6	2,000	48.00
	7	1,000	62.00

SOLUTION

a.

PART NUMBER	AVERAGE LEVEL	UNIT VALUE	TOTAL VALUE
1	15,000 ×	$ 3.00 =	$ 45,000
2	2,500 ×	$ 5.00 =	$ 12,500
3	3,000 ×	$ 1.00 =	$ 3,000
4	5,000 ×	$ 14.00 =	$ 70,000
5	4,000 ×	$ 18.00 =	$ 72,000
6	2,000 ×	$ 48.00 =	$ 96,000
7	1,000 ×	$ 62.00 =	$ 62,000
	Average aggregate inventory value	=	$360,500

b. Average weekly sales at cost = $3,410,000/52 weeks = $65,577/week

$$\text{Weeks of supply} = \frac{\text{Average aggregate inventory value}}{\text{Weekly sales (at cost)}} = \frac{\$360,500}{\$65,577} = 5.5 \text{ weeks}$$

c. $$\text{Inventory turnover} = \frac{\text{Annual sales (at cost)}}{\text{Average aggregate inventory value}} = \frac{\$3,410,000}{\$360,500} = 9.5 \text{ turns}$$

CD-ROM RESOURCES

The Student CD-ROM that accompanies this text contains the following resources, which allow you to further practice and apply the concepts presented in this chapter.

- ❏ **OM Explorer Tutor:** OM Explorer contains a tutor program that will help you learn how to calculate inventory measures. See the Chapter 8 folder in OM Explorer. See also the exercise requiring the use of this tutor program.

- ❏ **OM Explorer Solver:** The Inventory Estimator in OM Explorer can be used to solve general problems involving the common inventory measures. See the Supply-Chain Management folder in OM Explorer.

- ❏ **Equation Summary:** All the equations for this chapter can be found in one convenient location.

- ❏ **Discussion Questions:** Four questions will challenge your understanding of supply-chain management and how to work with suppliers.

- ❏ **Cases:**

  - ❏ **Wolf Motors:** How should John Wolf restructure the purchasing process at his newly acquired automotive dealership?

  - ❏ **Brunswick Distribution, Inc.:** Use the DuPont Analysis spreadsheet to determine the effects of purchasing additional warehouse facilities or investing in an improved distribution system on key business measures.

- ❏ **Experiential Exercise: Sonic Distributors.** You will experience the challenges of managing a distribution chain in this exciting in-class simulation.

INTERACTIVE RESOURCES

The Interactive Web site associated with this text (www.prenhall.com/ritzman) contains many tools and activities specifically designed for this chapter. The following items are recommended to enhance your understanding of the material in this chapter.

- ❏ **Internet Activities:** Try out four different links to supply-chain topics including continuous replenishment, supplier requirements, and supply-chain strategies.

- ❏ **Internet Tour:** Explore the link between operations and supply-chain design at the Peavey Drum Factory.

PROBLEMS

1. **OM Explorer** Buzzrite company ended the current year with annual sales (at cost) of $48 million. During the year, the inventory turned over six times. For the next year, Buzzrite plans to increase annual sales (at cost) by 25 percent.

   a. What is the increase in the average aggregate inventory value required if Buzzrite maintains the same inventory turnover during the next year?

   b. What change in inventory turns must Buzzrite achieve if, through better supply-chain management, it wants to support next year's sales with no increase in the average aggregate inventory value?

2. **OM Explorer** Jack Jones, the materials manager at Precision Enterprises, is beginning to look for ways to reduce inventories. A recent accounting statement shows the following inventory investment by category: raw materials $3,129,500; work-in-process $6,237,000; and finished goods $2,686,500. This year's cost of goods sold will be about $32.5 million. Assuming 52 business weeks per year, express total inventory as

   a. weeks of supply.

   b. inventory turns.

3. 🔘 **OM Explorer** Beagle Company uses a weighted score for the evaluation and selection of its suppliers. Each supplier is rated on a 10-point scale (10 = highest) for four different criteria: price, quality, delivery, and flexibility (to accommodate changes in quantity and timing). Because of the volatility of the business in which Jennings operates, flexibility is given twice the weight of each of the other three criteria, which are equally weighted. Table 8.4 shows the scores for three potential suppliers for the four performance criteria. Based on the highest weighted score, which supplier should be selected?

TABLE 8.4 *Supplier Performance Scores*

CRITERIA	SUPPLIER A	SUPPLIER B	SUPPLIER C
Price	8	6	6
Quality	9	7	7
Delivery	7	9	6
Flexibility	5	8	9

4. 🔘 **OM Explorer** Sterling, Inc., operates 52 weeks per year, and its cost of goods sold last year was $6,500,000.

The firm carries eight items in inventory: four raw materials, two work-in-process items, and two finished goods. Table 8.5 shows last year's average inventory levels for these items, along with their unit values.

a. What is the average aggregate inventory value?

b. How many weeks of supply does the firm have?

c. What was the inventory turnover last year?

TABLE 8.5 *Inventory Items*

CATEGORY	PART NUMBER	AVERAGE INVENTORY UNITS	VALUE PER UNIT
Raw materials	RM-1	20,000	$ 1
	RM-2	5,000	5
	RM-3	3,000	6
	RM-4	1,000	8
Work-in-process	WIP-1	6,000	10
	WIP-2	8,000	12
Finished goods	FG-1	1,000	65
	FG-2	500	88

SELECTED REFERENCES

Bowersox, D. J., and D. J. Closs. *Logistical Management: The Integrated Supply Chain Process.* New York: McGraw-Hill, 1996.

Bridleman, Dan, and Jeff Herrmann. "Supply-Chain Management in a Make-to-Order World." *APICS—The Performance Advantage* (March 1997), pp. 32–38.

Dyer, Jeffrey H. "How Chrysler Created an American Keiretsu." *Harvard Business Review* (July–August 1996), pp. 42–56.

Fisher, Marshall L. "What Is the Right Supply Chain for Your Product?" *Harvard Business Review* (March–April 1997), pp. 105–116.

Gurusami, Senthil A. "Ford's Wrenching Decision." *OR/MS Today* (December 1998), pp. 36–39.

Harwick, Tom. "Optimal Decision Making for the Supply Chain." *APICS—The Performance Advantage* (January 1997), pp. 42–44.

Kaplan, Steven, and Mohanbir Sawhney. "E-Hubs: The New B2B Marketplaces." *Harvard Business Review* (May–June 2000), pp. 97–103.

Latamore, G. Benton. "Supply Chain Optimization at Internet Speed." *APICS—The Performance Advantage* (May, 2000), pp. 37–40.

Lee, Hau L., and Corey Billington. "Managing Supply Chain Inventory: Pitfalls and Opportunities." *Sloan Management Review* (Spring 1992), pp. 65–73.

Maloni, M., and W. C. Benton. "Power Influences in the Supply Chain." *Journal of Business Logistics*, vol. 21 (2000), pp. 49–73.

Melnyk, Steven A., and Robert Handfield. "Green Speak." *Purchasing Today*, vol. 7, no. 7 (1996), pp. 32–36.

Tully, Shawn. "The B2B Tool That Really Is Changing the World." *Fortune* (March 20, 2000), pp. 132–145.

Forecasting

Across the Organization

Forecasting is important to . . .

- ❏ **finance,** which uses long-term forecasts to project needs for capital.
- ❏ **human resources,** which uses forecasts to estimate the need for workers.
- ❏ **management information systems,** which design and implement forecasting systems.
- ❏ **marketing,** which develops sales forecasts that are used for medium and long-range plans.
- ❏ **operations,** which develops and uses forecasts for decisions such as scheduling workers, short-term inventory replenishment, and long-term planning for capacity.

Learning Goals

After reading this chapter, you will be able to . . .

1. identify the five basic demand patterns that combine to produce a demand time series.
2. choose the appropriate forecasting technique for a given decision problem.
3. describe the different types of judgmental forecasting approaches and when to apply them.
4. use the computer to produce a linear regression forecasting model.
5. compute forecasts, using the most common approaches for time-series analysis.
6. explain the various measures of forecast errors and how to use them in monitoring and controlling forecast performance.

One of the critical drivers of supply-chain success is effective customer demand planning, which begins with accurate forecasts. Lucent Technologies (www.lucent.com), formed in 1995 when AT&T divided into three major businesses, is a leading supplier of data networking systems. To improve its forecasting and planning, Lucent established a group called Customer Demand Planning (CDP), which is also a core business process. The CDP process is a business planning process enabling sales teams (and customers) to develop demand forecasts as input to inventory and production planning, revenue planning, and service planning processes. *Forecasting* is seen at Lucent as the process of developing the most probable view of what future demand will be, given a set of assumptions about technology, competitors, pricing, marketing expenditures, and sales efforts. *Planning,* on the other hand, is the process of making management decisions on how to deploy resources to best respond to the demand forecasts.

CDP is critical to the business because of the large number of "internal customers" that need accurate, credible forecasts. By 1999, there were over 2,000 different individuals from 33 countries using CDP forecasts. It generates over 16,000 monthly forecasts for over 2,000 product lines, using a single global schedule, data repository, and set of procedures. The CDP forecasting system forecasts in units, which can then be converted to revenue forecasts using historical average price data. Those who provide input to the CDP system have the ability to enter forecasts using a number of different forecast hierarchy levels, ranging from product families to individual products broken down by customer, project, or total application (a predefined combination of several different products). The normal time horizon for the CDP forecasting process is a rolling 12-month horizon. The CDP system is designed to be "user friendly" for those people in Lucent's sales organization who input information into the forecast. The user interface is designed to provide a "point-and-click" environment. In order to provide salespeople making inputs into the forecast with the most recent information, three years of global customer demand history, plus year-to-date customer demand, is provided by the system. This history is updated weekly. In addition, known future demand, which takes the form of long-term contract business for which there are not yet specific orders, is detailed for 12 months into the future. Also, order-level information is available for the previous three months and for all future-committed orders. The system also provides the capability for sales teams to enter subjective information, including the forecast risk and the significant upside or downside variables.

A knowledge core group converts such information into initial forecasts, using statistical tools such as time-series forecasts and regression. These initial forecasts are then distributed to managers who make their judgmental adjustments.

This CDP forecasting process worked very well until demand nose-dived in 2001 throughout the computer and information technology industry. Initially, Lucent managers could not believe that the downturn would continue, and so their adjustments of the initial forecasts were overly optimistic. Production schedules and purchases from suppliers called for excessively high volumes, and inventories piled up. Once it became clear that the decline was real, the cutbacks in workforce and production levels had to be even more severe than if they had been made earlier.

Source: Moon, Mark A., John T. Mentzer, and Dwight E. Thomas, Jr. "Customer Demand Planning at Lucent Technologies; A Case Study in Continuous Improvement Through Sales Forecast Auditing." *Industrial Marketing Management*, vol. 29, no. 1 (2000).

Why is forecasting important?

forecast A prediction of future events used for planning purposes.

A forecast is a prediction of future events used for planning purposes. Changing business conditions resulting from global competition, rapid technological change, and increasing environmental concerns exert pressure on a firm's capability to generate accurate forecasts. Forecasts are needed to aid in determining what resources are needed, scheduling existing resources, and acquiring additional resources. Accurate forecasts allow schedulers to use capacity efficiently, reduce customer response times, and cut inventories.

Forecasting methods may be based on mathematical models using historical data available, qualitative methods drawing on managerial experience, or a combination of both. Variations of these methods are valuable in estimating future processing times and learning-curve effects (see Supplement C, "Measuring Output Rates" and Supplement D, "Learning Curve Analysis" on the Student CD-ROM). In this chapter, our focus is on demand forecasts. We will explore several forecasting methods commonly used today and their advantages and limitations. We also identify the decisions that managers should make in designing a forecasting system.

DEMAND CHARACTERISTICS

At the root of most business decisions is the challenge of forecasting customer demand. It is a difficult task because the demand for goods and services can vary greatly. For example, demand for lawn fertilizer predictably increases in the spring and summer months; however, the particular weekends when demand is heaviest may depend on uncontrollable factors such as the weather. Sometimes patterns are more predictable. Thus, weekly demand for haircuts at a local barbershop may be quite stable from week to week, with daily demand being heaviest on Saturday mornings and lightest on Mondays and Tuesdays. Forecasting demand in such situations requires uncovering the underlying patterns from available information. In this section, we first discuss the basic patterns of demand.

time series The repeated observations of demand for a product or service in their order of occurrence.

The repeated observations of demand for a product or service in their order of occurrence form a pattern known as a **time series**. The five basic patterns of most demand time series are

1. *horizontal* or the fluctuation of data around a constant mean
2. *trend,* or systematic increase or decrease in the mean of the series over time
3. *seasonal,* or a repeatable pattern of increases or decreases in demand, depending on the time of day, week, month, or season
4. *cyclical,* or less predictable gradual increases or decreases in demand over longer periods of time (years or decades)
5. *random,* or unforecastable, variation in demand

Cyclical patterns arise from two influences. The first is the business cycle, which includes factors that cause the economy to go from recession to expansion over a number of years. The other influence is the product or service life cycle, which reflects the stages of demand from development through decline. Business cycle movement is difficult to predict because it is affected by national or international events, such as presidential elections or political turmoil in other countries. Predicting the rate of demand buildup or decline in the life cycle also is difficult. Sometimes firms estimate demand for a new product by starting with the demand history for the product it is replacing.

Four of the patterns of demand—horizontal, trend, seasonal, and cyclical—combine in varying degrees to define the underlying time pattern of demand for a product or service. The fifth pattern, random variation, results from chance causes and, thus, cannot be predicted. Random variation is an aspect of demand that makes every forecast wrong. Figure 9.1 shows the first four patterns of a demand time series, all of which contain random variation. A time series may comprise any combination of these patterns.

Patterns of Demand

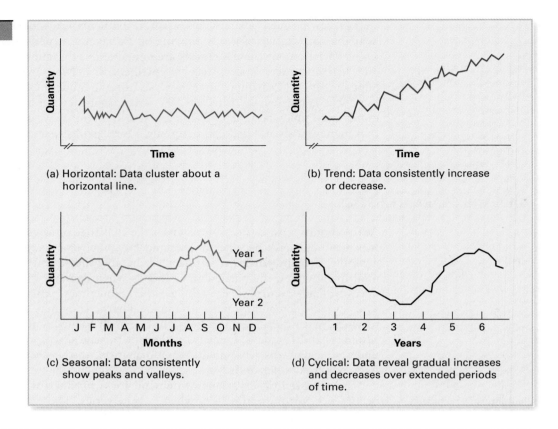

(a) Horizontal: Data cluster about a horizontal line.

(b) Trend: Data consistently increase or decrease.

(c) Seasonal: Data consistently show peaks and valleys.

(d) Cyclical: Data reveal gradual increases and decreases over extended periods of time.

DESIGNING THE FORECASTING SYSTEM

Before using forecasting techniques to analyze operations management problems, a manager must make three decisions: (1) what to forecast, (2) what type of forecasting technique to use, and (3) what type of computer hardware or software (or both) to use. We discuss each of these decisions before examining specific forecasting techniques.

DECIDING WHAT TO FORECAST

What makes a forecasting system best for any particular situation?

Although some sort of demand estimate is needed for the individual goods or services produced by a company, forecasting total demand for groups or clusters and then deriving individual product or service forecasts may be easiest. Also, selecting the correct unit of measurement (e.g., product or service units or machine-hours) for forecasting may be as important as choosing the best method.

LEVEL OF AGGREGATION. Few companies err by more than 5 percent when forecasting total demand for all their products. However, errors in forecasts for individual items may be much higher. By clustering several similar products or services in a process called **aggregation,** companies can obtain more accurate forecasts. Many companies utilize a two-tier forecasting system, first making forecasts for families of goods or services that have similar demand requirements and common processing, labor, and materials requirements and then deriving forecasts for individual items. This approach maintains consistency between planning for the final stages of manufacturing (which requires the unit forecasts) and longer-term planning for sales, profit, and capacity (which requires the product family forecasts). We return to this point later (see Chapter 11, "Aggregate Planning and Scheduling").

aggregation The act of clustering several similar products or services so that companies can obtain more accurate forecasts.

When are time-series
methods best and when
are causal or judgment
methods best?

judgment method A qualitative method that
translates the opinions of
managers, expert
opinions, consumer
surveys, and sales-force
estimates into quantitative
estimates.

causal method A quantitative method that uses
historical data on
independent variables,
such as promotional
campaigns, economic
conditions, and
competitors' actions, to
predict demand.

time-series analysis
A statistical approach that
relies heavily on historical
demand data to project
the future size of demand
and recognizes trends and
seasonal patterns.

UNITS OF MEASUREMENT. The most useful forecasts for planning and analyzing operations problems are those based on product or service units, such as customers needing maintenance service or repairs for their cars, rather than dollars. Forecasts of sales revenue are not very helpful because prices often fluctuate. Forecasting the number of units of demand—and then translating these estimates to sales revenue estimates by multiplying them by the price—often is the better method. If accurately forecasting the number of units of demand for a product or service is not possible, forecasting the standard labor or machine *hours* required of each of the critical resources, based on historical patterns, often is better. For companies producing goods or services to customer order, estimates of labor or machine-hours are important to scheduling and capacity planning.

CHOOSING THE TYPE OF FORECASTING TECHNIQUE

The forecaster's objective is to develop a useful forecast from the information at hand with the technique appropriate for the different characteristics of demand. This choice sometimes involves a trade-off between forecast accuracy and costs, such as software purchases, the time required to develop a forecast, and personnel training. Two general types of forecasting techniques are used for demand forecasting: qualitative methods and quantitative methods. Qualitative methods include **judgment methods,** which translate the opinions of managers, expert opinions, consumer surveys, and sales-force estimates into quantitative estimates. Quantitative methods include causal methods and time-series analysis. **Causal methods** use historical data on independent variables, such as promotional campaigns, economic conditions, and competitors' actions, to predict demand. **Time-series analysis** is a statistical approach that relies heavily on historical demand data to project the future size of demand and recognizes trends and seasonal patterns.

A key factor in choosing the proper forecasting approach is the time horizon for the decision requiring forecasts. Forecasts can be made for the short term, medium term, and long term. Table 9.1 contains examples of demand forecast applications and the typical planning horizon for each.

TABLE 9.1	
Demand Forecast Applications	

	Time Horizon		
Application	**Short Term (0–3 months)**	**Medium Term (3 months– 2 years)**	**Long Term (more than 2 years)**
Forecast quantity	Individual products or services	Total sales Groups or families of products or services	Total sales
Decision area	Inventory management Final assembly scheduling Workforce scheduling Master production scheduling	Staff planning Production planning Master production scheduling Purchasing Distribution	Facility location Capacity planning Process management
Forecasting technique	Time series Causal Judgment	Causal Judgment	Causal Judgment

MANAGERIAL PRACTICE
Wal-Mart Uses the Internet to Improve Forecast Performance

Wal-Mart has long been known for its careful analysis of cash register receipts and working with suppliers to reduce inventories. However, like many other major retailers, it does not share its forecasts with its suppliers. The result is forecast errors as much as 60 percent of actual demand. Retailers order more than they need in order to avoid product shortages and lost sales, and suppliers produce more than they can sell. This behavior contributes to the costly effects of materials flow dynamics in supply chains (see Chapter 8, "Supply-Chain Management").

To combat the ill effects of forecast errors on inventories, Benchmarking Partners, Inc., with funding from Wal-Mart, IBM, SAP, and Manugistics, has developed a software package called CFAR (pronounced "see far"), which stands for "collaborative forecasting and replenishment." A key benefit of the package is the capability of providing more reliable medium-term forecasts. The system allows manufacturers and merchants to work together on forecasts by using the Internet rather than fax or phone, which would be a heavy burden with the thousands of items stocked at each store requiring weekly forecasts.

The system works in the following way. A retailer and a manufacturer independently calculate the demand they expect for a product six months into the future, taking into consideration factors such as past sales trends and promotion plans. They then exchange their forecasts over the Internet. If the forecasts differ by more than a predetermined percent (such as 10 percent), the retailer and the manufacturer use the Internet to exchange written comments and supporting data. The parties go through as many cycles as it takes to converge on an acceptable forecast. This iterative process may take additional effort, but the potential payoff in working capital savings is great. For example, in the U.S. economy alone, such coordination could save as much as $179 billion in inventory investment.

Wal-Mart has initiated CFAR with Warner-Lambert, the manufacturer of Listerine. Procter & Gamble and some 20 other large companies will also use the system. Although CFAR is in its infancy and is still unproven, it warrants careful consideration because it represents an approach that will likely become more prevalent in the future.

Source: "Clearing the Cobwebs from the Stockroom." *Business Week* (October 21, 1996), p. 140.

FORECASTING WITH COMPUTERS

In many short-term forecasting applications, computers are a necessity. Often companies must prepare forecasts for hundreds or even thousands of products or services repeatedly. For example, a large network of health care facilities must calculate demand forecasts for each of its services for every department. This undertaking involves voluminous data that must be manipulated frequently. Analysts must examine the time series for each product or service and arrive at a forecast. However, as the Managerial Practice feature demonstrates, new software can ease the burden of coordinating forecasts between retailers and suppliers.

JUDGMENT METHODS

When adequate historical data are lacking, as when a new product is introduced or technology is expected to change, firms rely on managerial judgment and experience to generate forecasts. Judgment methods can also be used to modify forecasts generated by quantitative methods. In this section, we discuss four of the more successful methods currently in use: sales-force estimates, executive opinion, market research, and the Delphi method.

SALES-FORCE ESTIMATES

How can reasonable forecasts be obtained when no historical information is available?

Sometimes the best information about future demand comes from the people closest to the customer. **Sales-force estimates** are forecasts compiled from estimates of future demands made periodically by members of a company's sales force. This approach has several advantages.

sales-force estimates
The forecasts that are compiled from estimates of future demands made periodically by members of a company's sales force.

❑ The sales force is the group most likely to know which products or services customers will be buying in the near future and in what quantities.

❑ Sales territories often are divided by district or region. Information broken down in this manner can be useful for inventory management, distribution, and sales-force staffing purposes.

❑ The forecasts of individual sales-force members can be combined easily to get regional or national sales.

But it also has several disadvantages.

❑ Individual biases of the salespeople may taint the forecast; moreover, some people are naturally optimistic, whereas others are more cautious.

❑ Salespeople may not always be able to detect the difference between what a customer "wants" (a wish list) and what a customer "needs" (a necessary purchase).

❑ If the firm uses individual sales as a performance measure, salespeople may underestimate their forecasts so that their performance will look good when they exceed their projections or may work hard only until they reach their required minimum sales.

EXECUTIVE OPINION

executive opinion A forecasting method in which the opinions, experience, and technical knowledge of one or more managers are summarized to arrive at a single forecast.

When a new product or service is contemplated, the sales force may not be able to make accurate demand estimates. **Executive opinion** is a forecasting method in which the opinions, experience, and technical knowledge of one or more managers are summarized to arrive at a single forecast. As we discuss later, executive opinion can be used to modify an existing sales forecast to account for unusual circumstances, such as a new sales promotion or unexpected international events. Executive opinion can also be used for **technological forecasting**. The quick pace of technological change makes keeping abreast of the latest advances difficult (see Chapter 4, "Managing Technology").

technological forecasting
An application of executive opinion in light of the difficulties in keeping abreast of the latest advances in technology.

This method of forecasting has several disadvantages. Executive opinion can be costly because it takes valuable executive time. Although that may be warranted under certain circumstances, it sometimes gets out of control. In addition, if executives are allowed to modify a forecast without collectively agreeing to the changes, the resulting forecast will not be useful. The key to effective use of executive opinion is to ensure that the forecast reflects not a series of independent modifications but consensus among executives on a single forecast.

MARKET RESEARCH

market research A systematic approach to determine consumer interest in a product or service by creating and testing hypotheses through data-gathering surveys.

Market research is a systematic approach to determine consumer interest in a product or service by creating and testing hypotheses through data-gathering surveys. Conducting a market research study includes

1. designing a questionnaire that requests economic and demographic information from each person interviewed and asks whether the interviewee would be interested in the product or service

2. deciding how to administer the survey, whether by telephone polling, mailings, or personal interviews

3. selecting a representative sample of households to survey, which should include a random selection within the market area of the proposed product or service

4. analyzing the information using judgment and statistical tools to interpret the responses, determine their adequacy, make allowance for economic or competitive factors not included in the questionnaire, and analyze whether the survey represents a random sample of the potential market

Market research may be used to forecast demand for the short, medium, and long term. Accuracy is excellent for the short term, good for the medium term, and only fair for the long term. Although market research yields important information, one shortcoming is the numerous qualifications and hedges typically included in the findings. Another is that the typical response rate for mailed questionnaires is poor (30 percent is often considered high). Yet another shortcoming is the possibility that the survey results do not reflect the opinions of the market. Finally, the survey might produce imitative, rather than innovative, ideas because the customer's reference point is often limited.

DELPHI METHOD

Delphi method A process of gaining consensus from a group of experts while maintaining their anonymity.

The **Delphi method** is a process of gaining consensus from a group of experts while maintaining their anonymity. This form of forecasting is useful when there are no historical data from which to develop statistical models and when managers inside the firm have no experience on which to base informed projections. A coordinator sends questions to each member of the group of outside experts, who may not even know who else is participating. Anonymity is important when some members of the group tend to dominate discussion or command a high degree of respect in their fields. In an anonymous group, the members tend to respond to the questions and support their responses freely. The coordinator prepares a statistical summary of the responses along with a summary of arguments for particular responses. The report is sent to the same group for another round, and the participants may choose to modify their previous responses. These rounds continue until consensus is obtained.

The Delphi method can be used to develop long-range forecasts of product demand and new-product sales projections. It can also be used for technological forecasting. The Delphi method can be used to obtain a consensus from a panel of experts who can devote their attention to following scientific advances, changes in society, governmental regulations, and the competitive environment. The results can provide direction for a firm's research and development staff.

GUIDELINES FOR USING JUDGMENT FORECASTS

Judgment forecasting is clearly needed when no quantitative data are available to use quantitative forecasting approaches. However, judgment approaches can be used in concert with quantitative approaches to improve forecast quality. Among the guidelines for the use of judgment to adjust the results of quantitative forecasts are the following:

❏ *Adjust quantitative forecasts when their track record is poor and the decision maker has important contextual knowledge.*   Contextual knowledge is knowledge that practitioners gain through experience, such as cause-and-effect relationships, environmental cues, and organizational information, that may have an effect on the variable being forecast. Often these factors cannot be incorporated into quantitative forecasting approaches. The quality of forecasts generated by quantitative approaches also deteriorates as the variability of the data increases, particularly for time series. The more variable the data, the more likely it is that judgment forecasting will improve the forecasts. Consequently, the decision maker can bring valuable contextual information to the forecasting process when the quantitative approaches alone are inadequate.

❐ *Make adjustments to quantitative forecasts to compensate for specific events.* Specific events such as advertising campaigns, the actions of competitors, or international developments often are not recognized in quantitative forecasting and should be acknowledged when a final forecast is being made.

In the remainder of this chapter, we focus on the commonly used quantitative forecasting approaches.

CAUSAL METHODS: LINEAR REGRESSION

linear regression A causal method in which one variable (the dependent variable) is related to one or more independent variables by a linear equation.

dependent variable The variable that one wants to forecast.

Causal methods are used when historical data are available and the relationship between the factor to be forecasted and other external or internal factors (e.g., government actions or advertising promotions) can be identified. These relationships are expressed in mathematical terms and can be very complex. Causal methods provide the most sophisticated forecasting tools and are very good for predicting turning points in demand and preparing long-range forecasts. Although many causal methods are available, we focus here on linear regression, one of the best-known and most commonly used causal methods.

In **linear regression,** one variable, called a **dependent variable,** is related to one or more **independent variables** by a linear equation. The dependent variable, such as demand for doorknobs, is the one the manager wants to forecast. The independent variables, such as advertising expenditures and new housing starts, are assumed to affect the dependent variable and thereby "cause" the results observed in the past. Figure 9.2 shows how a linear regression line relates to the data. In technical terms, the regression line minimizes the squared deviations from the actual data.

In the simplest linear regression models, the dependent variable is a function of only one independent variable and, therefore, the theoretical relationship is a straight line:

$$Y = a + bX$$

FIGURE 9.2

Linear Regression Line Relative to Actual Data

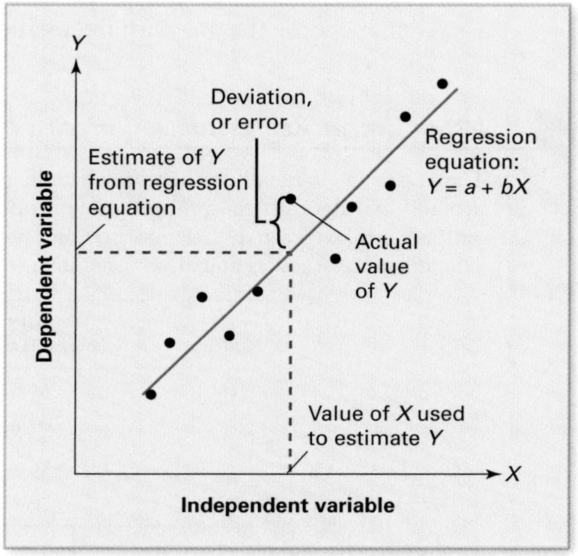

independent variables
Variables that are
assumed to affect the
dependent variable and
thereby "cause" the
results observed in the
past.

where

$$Y = \text{dependent variable}$$
$$X = \text{independent variable}$$
$$a = Y\text{-intercept of the line}$$
$$b = \text{slope of the line}$$

The objective of linear regression analysis is to find values of a and b that minimize the sum of the squared deviations of the actual data points from the graphed line. Computer programs are used for this purpose. For any set of matched observations for Y and X, the program computes the values of a and b and provides measures of forecast accuracy. Three measures commonly reported are the sample correlation coefficient, the sample coefficient of determination, and the standard error of the estimate.

The *sample correlation coefficient, r,* measures the direction and strength of the relationship between the independent variable and the dependent variable. The value of r can range from -1.00 to $+1.00$. A correlation coefficient of $+1.00$ implies that period-by-period changes in direction (increases or decreases) of the independent variable are always accompanied by changes in the same direction by the dependent variable. An r of -1.00 means that decreases in the independent variable are always accompanied by increases in the dependent variable, and vice versa. A zero value of r means that there is no relationship between the variables. The closer the value of r is to ± 1.00, the better the regression line fits the points.

The *sample coefficient of determination* measures the amount of variation in the dependent variable about its mean that is explained by the regression line. The coefficient of determination is the square of the correlation coefficient, or r^2. The value of r^2 ranges from 0.00 to 1.00. Regression equations with a value of r^2 close to 1.00 are desirable because the variations in the dependent variable and the forecast generated by the regression equation are closely related.

The *standard error of the estimate, s_{yx},* measures how closely the data on the dependent variable cluster around the regression line. Although it is similar to the sample standard deviation, it measures the error from the dependent variable, Y, to the regression line, rather than to the mean. Thus, it is the standard deviation of the difference between the actual demand and the estimate provided by the regression equation. When determining which independent variable to include in the regression equation, you should choose the one with the smallest standard error of the estimate.

EXAMPLE 9.1	*Using Linear Regression to Forecast Product Demand*

The person in charge of production scheduling for a company must prepare forecasts of product demand in order to plan for appropriate production quantities. During a luncheon meeting, the marketing manager gives her information about the advertising budget for a brass door hinge. The following are sales and advertising data for the past five months:

MONTH	SALES (thousands of units)	ADVERTISING (thousands of $)
1	264	2.5
2	116	1.3
3	165	1.4
4	101	1.0
5	209	2.0

The marketing manager says that next month the company will spend $1,750 on advertising for the product. Use linear regression to develop an equation and a forecast for this product.

SOLUTION

We assume that sales are linearly related to advertising expenditures. In other words, sales are the dependent variable, Y, and advertising expenditures are the independent variable, X. Using the paired monthly observations of sales and advertising expenditures supplied by the marketing manager, we use the Regression Solver (see OM Explorer on the Student CD-ROM) to determine the best values of a, b, the correlation coefficient, the coefficient of determination, and the standard error of the estimate.

$$a = -8.137$$
$$b = 109.230X$$
$$r = 0.980$$
$$r^2 = 0.960$$
$$s_{yx} = 15.603$$

The regression equation is

$$Y = -8.137 + 109.230X$$

and the regression line is shown in Figure 9.3.

Are advertising expenditures a good choice to use in forecasting sales? Note that the sample correlation coefficient, r, is 0.98. Because the value of r is very close to 1.00, we conclude that there is a strong positive relationship between sales and advertising expenditures and that the choice was a good one.

Next, we examine the sample coefficient of determination, r^2, or 0.96. This value of r^2 implies that 96 percent of the variation in sales is explained by advertising expenditures. Most relationships between advertising and sales in practice are not this strong because other

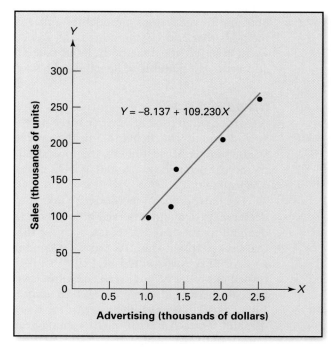

FIGURE 9.3 • Linear Regression Line for the Sales Data

variables such as general economic conditions and the strategies of competitors often combine to affect sales.

As the advertising expenditure will be $1,750, the forecast for month 6 is

$$Y = -8.137 + 109.230(1.75)$$
$$= 183.016 \quad \text{or} \quad 183,016 \text{ units}$$

Decision Point The production scheduler can use this forecast to determine the quantity of brass door hinges needed for month 6. Suppose that she has 62,500 units in stock. The requirement to be filled from production is $183,015 - 62,500 = 120,015$ units, assuming that she does not want to lose any sales. ◻

Often several independent variables may affect the dependent variable. For example, advertising expenditures, new corporation start-ups, and residential building contracts may be important for estimating the demand for door hinges. In such cases, *multiple regression analysis* is helpful in determining a forecasting equation for the dependent variable as a function of several independent variables. Such models can be analyzed with OM Explorer and can be quite useful for predicting turning points and solving many planning problems.

TIME-SERIES METHODS

Rather than using independent variables for the forecast as regression models do, time-series methods use historical information regarding only the dependent variable. These methods are based on the assumption that the dependent variable's past pattern will continue in the future. Time-series analysis identifies the underlying patterns of demand that combine to produce an observed historical pattern of the dependent variable and then develops a model to replicate it. In this section, we focus on time-series methods that address the horizontal, trend, and seasonal patterns of demand. Before we discuss statistical methods, let us take a look at the simplest time-series method for addressing all patterns of demand—the naive forecast.

NAIVE FORECAST

naive forecast A time-series method whereby the forecast for the next period equals the demand for the current period.

A method often used in practice is the **naive forecast,** whereby the forecast for the next period equals the demand for the current period. So, if the actual demand for Wednesday is 35 customers, the forecasted demand for Thursday is 35 customers. If the actual demand on Thursday is 42 customers, the forecasted demand for Friday is 42 customers.

The naive-forecast method may take into account a demand trend. The increase (or decrease) in demand observed between the last two periods is used to adjust the current demand to arrive at a forecast. Suppose that last week the demand was 120 units and the week before it was 108 units. Demand increased 12 units in one week, so the forecast for next week would be $120 + 12 = 132$ units. If the actual demand next week turned out to be 127 units, the next forecast would be $127 + 7 = 134$ units. The naive-forecast method also may be used to account for seasonal patterns. If the demand last July was 50,000 units, the forecast for this July is 50,000 units. Similarly, forecasts of demand for each month of the coming year may simply reflect actual demand in the same month last year.

The advantages of the naive-forecast method are its simplicity and low cost. The method works best when the horizontal, trend, or seasonal patterns are stable and random variation is small. If random variation is large, using last period's demand to estimate next period's demand can result in highly variable forecasts that are not useful for planning purposes. Nonetheless, if its level of accuracy is acceptable, the naive forecast is an attractive approach for time-series forecasting.

ESTIMATING THE AVERAGE

Every demand time series has at least two of the five patterns of demand: horizontal and random. It *may* have trend, seasonal, or cyclical patterns. We begin our discussion of statistical methods of time-series forecasting with demand that has no trend, seasonal, or cyclical patterns. The horizontal pattern in a time series is based on the mean of the demands, so we focus on forecasting methods that estimate the average of a time series of data. Consequently, for all the methods of forecasting we discuss in this section, the forecast of demand for *any* period in the future is the average of the time series computed in the current period. For example, if the average of past demand calculated on Tuesday is 65 customers, the forecasts for Wednesday, Thursday, and Friday are 65 customers each day.

Consider Figure 9.4, which shows patient arrivals at a medical clinic over the past 28 weeks. Assume that the demand pattern for patient arrivals has no trend, seasonal, or cyclical pattern. The time series has only a horizontal and random pattern. As no one can predict random error, we focus on estimating the average. The statistical techniques useful for forecasting such a time series are (1) simple moving averages, (2) weighted moving averages, and (3) exponential smoothing.

simple moving average method A time-series method used to estimate the average of a demand time series by averaging the demand for the *n* most recent time periods.

SIMPLE MOVING AVERAGES. The **simple moving average method** is used to estimate the average of a demand time series and thereby remove the effects of random fluctuation. It is most useful when demand has no pronounced trend or seasonal influences. Applying a moving average model simply involves calculating the average demand for the *n* most recent time periods and using it as the forecast for the next time period. For the next period, after the demand is known, the oldest demand from the previous average is replaced with the most recent demand and the average is recalculated. In this way, the *n* most recent demands are used, and the average "moves" from period to period.

Specifically, the forecast for period $t + 1$, can be calculated as

$$F_{t+1} = \frac{\text{Sum of last } n \text{ demands}}{n} = \frac{D_t + D_{t-1} + D_{t-2} + \cdots + D_{t-n+1}}{n}$$

FIGURE 9.4

Weekly Patient Arrivals at a Medical Clinic

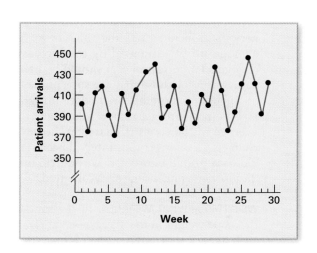

where

$$D_t = \text{actual demand in period } t$$

$$n = \text{total number of periods in the average}$$

$$F_{t+1} = \text{forecast for period } t + 1$$

With the moving average method, the forecast of next period's demand equals the average calculated at the end of this period.

| EXAMPLE 9.2 | *Using the Moving Average Method to Estimate Average Demand* |

**TUTOR
9.1**

a. Compute a *three-week* moving average forecast for the arrival of medical clinic patients in week 4. The numbers of arrivals for the past three weeks were

WEEK	PATIENT ARRIVALS
1	400
2	380
3	411

b. If the actual number of patient arrivals in week 4 is 415, what is the forecast for week 5?

SOLUTION

a. The moving average forecast at the end of week 3 is

$$F_4 = \frac{411 + 380 + 400}{3} = 397.0$$

b. The forecast for week 5 requires the actual arrivals from weeks 2–4, the three most recent weeks of data.

$$F_5 = \frac{415 + 411 + 380}{3} = 402.0$$

Decision Point Thus, the forecast at the end of week 3 would have been 397 patients for week 4. The forecast for week 5, made at the end of week 4, would have been 402 patients. In addition, at the end of week 4 the forecast for week 6 and beyond is also 402 patients. ⌐

The moving average method may involve the use of as many periods of past demand as desired. The stability of the demand series generally determines how many periods to include (i.e., the value of n). Stable demand series are those for which the average (to be estimated by the forecasting method) only infrequently experiences changes. Large values of n should be used for demand series that are stable and small values of n for those that are susceptible to changes in the underlying average.

Including more historical data in the average by increasing the number of periods results in a forecast that is less susceptible to random variations. If the underlying average in the series is changing, however, the forecasts will tend to lag behind the changes for a longer time interval because of the additional time required to remove the old data from the forecast. We address other considerations in the choice of n when we discuss choosing a time-series method.

weighted moving average method A time-series method in which each historical demand in the average can have its own weight; the sum of the weights is equal to 1.0.

WEIGHTED MOVING AVERAGES. In the simple moving average method, each demand has the same weight in the average—namely, $1/n$. In the **weighted moving average method**, each historical demand in the average can have its own weight. The sum of the weights

**TUTOR
9.2**

equals 1.0. For example, in a *three-period* weighted moving average model, the most recent period might be assigned a weight of 0.50, the second most recent might be weighted 0.30, and the third most recent might be weighted 0.20. The average is obtained by multiplying the weight of each period by the value for that period and adding the products together:

$$F_{t+1} = 0.50D_t + 0.30D_{t-1} + 0.20D_{t-2}$$

For a numerical example of using the weighted moving average method to estimate average demand, see Tutor 9.2 in OM Explorer. The advantage of a weighted moving average method is that it allows you to emphasize recent demand over earlier demand. The forecast will be more responsive than the simple moving average forecast to changes in the underlying average of the demand series. Nonetheless, the weighted moving average forecast will still lag behind demand because it merely averages *past* demands. This lag is especially noticeable with a trend because the average of the time series is systematically increasing or decreasing.

The weighted moving average method has the same shortcomings as the simple moving average method: Data must be retained for *n* periods of demand to allow calculation of the average for each period. Keeping this amount of data is not a great burden in simple situations, such as the preceding three- and six-week examples. For a company that has to forecast many different demands, however, data storage and update costs may be high. Managers must balance the cost of keeping such detailed records against the usefulness of the forecasts.

exponential smoothing method A weighted moving average method that calculates the average of a time series by giving recent demands more weight than earlier demands.

EXPONENTIAL SMOOTHING. The **exponential smoothing method** is a sophisticated weighted moving average method that calculates the average of a time series by giving recent demands more weight than earlier demands. It is the most frequently used formal forecasting method because of its simplicity and the small amount of data needed to support it. Unlike the weighted moving average method, which requires *n* periods of past demand and *n* weights, exponential smoothing requires only three items of data: the last period's forecast; the demand for this period; and a smoothing parameter, alpha (α), which has a value between 0 and 1.0. To obtain an exponentially smoothed forecast we simply calculate a weighted average of the most recent demand and the forecast calculated last period. The equation for the forecast is

$$F_{t+1} = \alpha(\text{Demand this period}) + (1 - \alpha)(\text{Forecast calculated last period})$$
$$= \alpha D_t + (1 - \alpha)F_t$$

An equivalent equation is

$$F_{t+1} = F_t + \alpha(D_t - F_t)$$

This form of the equation shows that the forecast for the next period equals the forecast for the current period plus a proportion of the forecast error for the current period.

The emphasis given to the most recent demand levels can be adjusted by changing the smoothing parameter. Larger α values emphasize recent levels of demand and result in forecasts more responsive to changes in the underlying average. Smaller α values treat past demand more uniformly and result in more stable forecasts. This approach is analogous to adjusting the value of *n* in the moving average methods, except there smaller values of *n* emphasize recent demand and larger values give greater weight to past demand. In practice, various values of α are tried and the one producing the best forecasts is chosen.

Exponential smoothing requires an initial forecast to get started. There are two ways to get this initial forecast: Either use last period's demand or, if some historical data are available, calculate the average of several recent periods of demand. The effect of the initial estimate of the average on successive estimates of the average diminishes over time because, with exponential smoothing, the weights given to successive historical demands used to calculate the average decay exponentially. We can illustrate this effect with an example. If we let $\alpha = 0.20$, the forecast for period $t + 1$ is

$$F_{t+1} = 0.20D_t + 0.80F_t$$

Using the equation for F_t, we expand the equation for F_{t+1}:

$$F_{t+1} = 0.20D_t + 0.80(0.20D_{t-1} + 0.80F_{t-1}) = 0.20D_t + 0.16D_{t-1} + 0.64F_{t-1}$$

Continuing to expand, we get

$$F_{t+1} = 0.20D_t + 0.16D_{t-1} + 0.128D_{t-2} + 0.1024D_{t-3} + \cdots$$

Eventually, the weights of demands many periods ago approach zero. As with the weighted moving average method, the sum of the weights must equal 1.0, which is implicit in the exponential smoothing equation.

| EXAMPLE 9.3 | *Using Exponential Smoothing to Estimate Average Demand* |

Again consider the patient arrival data in Example 9.2. It is now the end of week 3. Using $\alpha = 0.10$, calculate the exponential smoothing forecast for week 4.

SOLUTION

TUTOR 9.3

The exponential smoothing method requires an initial forecast. Suppose that we take the demand data for the past two weeks and average them, obtaining $(400 + 380)/2 = 390$ as an initial forecast. To obtain the forecast for week 4, using exponential smoothing with $\alpha = 0.10$, we calculate the average at the end of week 3 as

$$F_4 = 0.10(411) + 0.90(390) = 392.1$$

Thus, the forecast for week 4 would be 392 patients. If the actual demand for week 4 proved to be 415, the new forecast for week 5 would be

$$F_5 = 0.10(415) + 0.90(392.1) = 394.4$$

or 394 patients. Note that we used F_4, not the integer-value forecast for week 4, in the computation for F_5. In general, we round off (when it is appropriate) only the final result to maintain as much accuracy as possible in the calculations.

Decision Point Using this exponential smoothing model, the analyst's forecasts would have been 392 patients for week 4 and then 394 patients for week 5 and beyond. As soon as the actual demand for week 5 is known, then the forecast for week 6 will be updated. ▢

Exponential smoothing has the advantages of simplicity and minimal data requirements. It is inexpensive to use and, therefore, very attractive to firms that make thousands of forecasts for each time period. However, its simplicity also is a disadvantage when the underlying average is changing, as in the case of a demand series with a trend. Like any method geared solely to the assumption of a stable average, exponential smoothing results will lag behind changes in the underlying average of demand. Higher α values may help reduce forecast errors when there is a change in the average of the time series; however, the lags will still be there if the average is changing systematically. Typically, if large α values (e.g., >0.50) are required for an exponential smoothing application, chances are good that a more sophisticated model is needed because of a significant trend or seasonal influence in the demand series.

INCLUDING A TREND

Let's now consider a demand time series that has a trend. A trend in a time series is a systematic increase or decrease in the average of the series over time. Where a trend is present, exponential smoothing approaches must be modified; otherwise, the forecasts always will be below or above the actual demand.

To improve the forecast we need to calculate an estimate of the trend. We start by calculating the *current* estimate of the trend, which is the difference between the average of the series computed in the current period and the average computed last period. To obtain an estimate of the long-term trend, you can average the current estimates. The method for estimating a trend is similar to that used for estimating the demand average with exponential smoothing.

The method for incorporating a trend in an exponentially smoothed forecast is called the **trend-adjusted exponential smoothing method.** With this approach the estimates for both the average and the trend are smoothed, requiring two smoothing constants. For each period, we calculate the average and the trend:

trend-adjusted exponential smoothing method The method for incorporating a trend in an exponentially smoothed forecast.

$$A_t = \alpha(\text{Demand this period}) + (1 - \alpha)(\text{Average} + \text{Trend estimate last period})$$
$$= \alpha D_t + (1 - \alpha)(A_{t-1} + T_{t-1})$$
$$T_t = \beta(\text{Average this period} - \text{Average last period})$$
$$+ (1 - \beta)(\text{Trend estimate last period})$$
$$= \beta(A_t - A_{t-1}) + (1 - \beta)T_{t-1}$$
$$F_{t+1} = A_t + T_t$$

where

A_t = exponentially smoothed average of the series in period t

T_t = exponentially smoothed average of the trend in period t

α = smoothing parameter for the average, with a value between 0 and 1

β = smoothing parameter for the trend, with a value between 0 and 1

F_{t+1} = forecast for period $t + 1$

To make forecasts for periods beyond the next period, we multiply the trend estimate (T_t) by the number of additional periods that we want in the forecast and add the results to the current average (A_t).

Estimates for last period's average and trend needed for the first forecast can be derived from past data or based on an educated guess if no historical data exist. To find values for α and β, often an analyst systematically adjusts α and β until the forecast errors are lowest. This process can be carried out in an experimental setting with the model used to forecast historical demands.

For numerical examples of the trend-adjusted exponential smoothing method, see Solved Problem 4 at the end of this chapter and Tutor 9.4 in OM Explorer.

TUTOR 9.4

SEASONAL PATTERNS

Many organizations experience seasonal demand for their goods or services. Seasonal patterns are regularly repeating upward or downward movements in demand measured in periods of less than one year (hours, days, weeks, months, or quarters). In this context, the time periods are called *seasons*. For example, customer arrivals at a fast-food shop on any day may peak between 11 A.M. and 1 P.M. and again from 5 to 7 P.M.

Here the seasonal pattern lasts a day, and each hour of the day is a season. Similarly, the demand for haircuts may peak on Saturday, week to week. In this case, the seasonal pattern lasts a week, and the seasons are the days of the week. Seasonal patterns may last a month, as in the weekly applications for driver's license renewals, or a year, as in the monthly volumes of mail processed and the monthly demand for automobile tires.

An easy way to account for seasonal effects is to use one of the techniques already described but to limit the data in the time series to those time periods in the same season. For example, if there is day-of-the-week seasonal effect, then one time series would be for Mondays, one for Tuesdays, and so on. If the naive forecast is used, then the forecast for this Tuesday is the actual demand seven days ago (last Tuesday), rather than the actual demand one day ago (Monday). This method accounts for seasonal effects but has the disadvantage of discarding considerable information on past demand.

Other methods are available that analyze all past data, using one model to forecast demand for all of the seasons. We describe only the **multiplicative seasonal method,** whereby seasonal factors are multiplied by an estimate of average demand to arrive at a seasonal forecast. The four-step procedure presented here involves the use of simple averages of past demand, although more sophisticated methods for calculating averages, such as a moving average or exponential smoothing approach, could be used. The following description is based on a seasonal pattern lasting one year and seasons of one month, although the procedure can be used for any seasonal pattern and season of any length.

1. For each year, calculate the average demand per season by dividing annual demand by the number of seasons per year. For example, if the total demand for a year is 6,000 units and each month is a season, the average demand per season is 6,000/12 = 500 units.

2. For each year, divide the actual demand for a season by the average demand per season. The result is a *seasonal index* for each season in the year, which indicates the level of demand relative to the average demand. For example, suppose that the demand for March was 400 units. The seasonal index for March then is 400/500 = 0.80, which indicates that March's demand is 20 percent below the

multiplicative seasonal method A method whereby seasonal factors are multiplied by an estimate of average demand to arrive at a seasonal forecast.

Greeting cards have a strong seasonal demand pattern. Here the manager of a Hallmark card shop discusses inventory needs with her employees.

average demand per month. Similarly, a seasonal index of 1.14 for April implies that April's demand is 14 percent greater than the average demand per month.

3. Calculate the average seasonal index for each season, using the results from step 2. Add the seasonal indices for a season and divide by the number of years of data. For example, suppose that we have calculated three seasonal indices for April: 1.14, 1.18, and 1.04. The average seasonal index for April is (1.14 + 1.18 + 1.04)/3 = 1.12. This is the index we will use for forecasting April's demand.

4. Calculate each season's forecast for next year. Begin by estimating the average demand per season for next year. Use the naive method, moving averages, exponential smoothing, trend-adjusted exponential smoothing, or linear regression to forecast annual demand. Divide annual demand by the number of seasons per year. Then obtain the seasonal forecast by multiplying the seasonal index by the average demand per season.

At the end of each year, the average seasonal factor for each quarter can be updated. We calculate the average of all historical factors for the quarter or, if we want some control over the relevance of past demand patterns, we calculate a moving average or single exponential smoothed average.

For numerical examples of the multiplicative seasonal method, see Solved Problem 5 at the end of this chapter or experiment with the Seasonal Forecasting solver in OM Explorer on the Student CD-ROM.

CHOOSING A TIME-SERIES METHOD

We now turn to factors that managers must consider in selecting a method for time-series forecasting. One important consideration is forecast performance, as determined by forecast errors. Managers need to know how to measure forecast errors and how to detect when something is going wrong with the forecasting system. After examining forecast errors and their detection, we discuss criteria that managers can use to choose an appropriate time-series forecasting method.

FORECAST ERROR

Forecasts almost always contain errors. Forecast errors can be classified as either *bias errors* or *random errors*. Bias errors are the result of consistent mistakes—the forecast is always too high or too low. These errors often are the result of neglecting or not accurately estimating patterns of demand, such as a trend, seasonal, or cyclical pattern.

The other type of forecast error, random error, results from unpredictable factors that cause the forecast to deviate from the actual demand. Forecasting analysts try to minimize the effects of bias and random errors by selecting appropriate forecasting models, but eliminating all forms of errors is impossible.

MEASURES OF FORECAST ERROR. Before they can think about minimizing forecast error, managers must have some way to measure it. **Forecast error** is simply the difference between the forecast and actual demand for a given period, or

$$E_t = D_t - F_t$$

forecast error The difference found by subtracting the forecast from actual demand for a given period.

where

$$E_t = \text{forecast error for period } t$$
$$D_t = \text{actual demand for period } t$$
$$F_t = \text{forecast for period } t$$

However, managers usually are more interested in measuring forecast error over a relatively long period of time.

cumulative sum of forecast errors (CFE)
A measurement of the total forecast error that assesses the bias in a forecast.

The **cumulative sum of forecast errors (CFE)** measures the total forecast error:

$$\text{CFE} = \Sigma E_t$$

Large positive errors tend to be offset by large negative errors in the CFE measure. Nonetheless, CFE is useful in assessing bias in a forecast. For example, if a forecast is always lower than actual demand, the value of CFE will gradually get larger and larger. This increasingly large error indicates some systematic deficiency in the forecasting approach. Perhaps the analyst omitted a trend element or a cyclical pattern, or perhaps seasonal influences changed from their historical pattern. Note that the average forecast error is simply

$$\overline{E} = \frac{\text{CFE}}{n}$$

mean squared error (MSE)
A measurement of the dispersion of forecast errors.

standard deviation (σ)
A measurement of the dispersion of forecast errors.

mean absolute deviation (MAD) A measurement of the dispersion of forecast errors.

The **mean squared error (MSE), standard deviation (σ),** and **mean absolute deviation (MAD)** measure the dispersion of forecast errors:

$$\text{MSE} = \frac{\Sigma E_t^2}{n}$$

$$\sigma = \sqrt{\frac{\Sigma(E_t - \overline{E})^2}{n - 1}}$$

$$\text{MAD} = \frac{\Sigma |E_t|}{n}$$

The mathematical symbol | | is used to indicate the absolute value—that is, it tells you to disregard positive or negative signs. If MSE, σ, or MAD is small, the forecast is typically close to actual demand; a large value indicates the possibility of large forecast errors. The measures differ in the way they emphasize errors. Large errors get far more weight in MSE and σ because the errors are squared. MAD is a widely used measure of forecast error because managers can easily understand it; it is merely the mean of the forecast errors over a series of time periods, without regard to whether the error was an overestimate or an underestimate. MAD also is used in tracking signals and inventory control. Later, we discuss how MAD or σ can be used to determine safety stocks for inventory items (see Chapter 10, "Inventory Management").

mean absolute percent error (MAPE) A measurement that relates the forecast error to the level of demand and is useful for putting forecast performance in the proper perspective.

The **mean absolute percent error (MAPE)** relates the forecast error to the level of demand and is useful for putting forecast performance in the proper perspective:

$$\text{MAPE} = \frac{[\Sigma \, |E_t|/D_t]100}{n} \quad \text{(expressed as a percent)}$$

For example, an absolute forecast error of 100 results in a larger percentage error when the demand is 200 units than when the demand is 10,000 units.

| EXAMPLE 9.4 | *Calculating Forecast Error Measures* |

The following table shows the actual sales of upholstered chairs for a furniture manufacturer and the forecasts made for each of the last eight months. Calculate CFE, MSE, σ, MAD, and MAPE for this product.

MONTH, t	DEMAND, D_t	FORECAST, F_t	ERROR, E_t	ERROR SQUARED, E_t^2	ABSOLUTE ERROR, $\lvert E_t \rvert$	ABSOLUTE PERCENT ERROR, $(\lvert E_t \rvert / D_t)(100)$
1	200	225	−25	625	25	12.5%
2	240	220	20	400	20	8.3
3	300	285	15	225	15	5.0
4	270	290	−20	400	20	7.4
5	230	250	−20	400	20	8.7
6	260	240	20	400	20	7.7
7	210	250	−40	1,600	40	19.0
8	275	240	35	1,225	35	12.7
		Total	−15	5,275	195	81.3%

SOLUTION

Using the formulas for the measures, we get

Cumulative forecast error: $\quad \text{CFE} = -15$

Average forecast error: $\quad \overline{E} = \dfrac{\text{CFE}}{8} = -1.875$

Mean squared error: $\quad \text{MSE} = \dfrac{\Sigma\, E_t^2}{n} = \dfrac{5{,}275}{8} = 659.4$

Standard deviation: $\quad \sigma = \sqrt{\dfrac{\Sigma\,[E_t - (-1.875)]^2}{7}} = 27.4$

Mean absolute deviation: $\quad \text{MAD} = \dfrac{\Sigma\,\lvert E_t \rvert}{n} = \dfrac{195}{8} = 24.4$

Mean absolute percent error: $\quad \text{MAPE} = \dfrac{[\Sigma\,\lvert E_t \rvert / D_t]\,100}{n} = \dfrac{81.3\%}{8} = 10.2\%$

A CFE of −15 indicates that the forecast has a tendency to overestimate demand. The MSE, σ, and MAD statistics provide measures of forecast error variability. A MAD of 24.4 means that the average forecast error was 24.4 units in absolute value. The value of σ, 27.4, indicates that the sample distribution of forecast errors has a standard deviation of 27.4 units. A MAPE of 10.2 percent implies that, on average, the forecast error was about 10 percent of actual demand. These measures become more reliable as the number of periods of data increases.

Decision Point Although reasonably satisfied with these forecast performance results, the analyst decided to test out a few more forecasting methods before reaching a final forecasting method to use for the future. ❑

tracking signal A measure that indicates whether a method of forecasting is accurately predicting actual changes in demand.

TRACKING SIGNALS. A **tracking signal** is a measure that indicates whether a method of forecasting is accurately predicting actual changes in demand. The tracking signal measures the number of MADs represented by the cumulative sum of forecast errors, the CFE. The CFE tends to be 0 when a correct forecasting system is being used. At any time, however, random errors can cause the CFE to be a nonzero number. The tracking signal formula is

$$\text{Tracking signal} = \dfrac{\text{CFE}}{\text{MAD}}$$

What types of controls are
needed for the forecasting
system?

Each period, the CFE and MAD are updated to reflect current error, and the tracking signal is compared to some predetermined limits. The MAD can be calculated in one of two ways: (1) as the simple average of all absolute errors (as demonstrated in Example 9.4) or (2) as a weighted average determined by the exponential smoothing method:

$$\text{MAD}_t = \alpha |E_t| + (1 - \alpha)\text{MAD}_{t-1}$$

If forecast errors are normally distributed with a mean of 0, there is a simple relationship between σ and MAD:

$$\sigma = (\sqrt{\pi/2})(\text{MAD}) \cong 1.25(\text{MAD})$$
$$\text{MAD} = 0.7978\sigma \cong 0.8\sigma$$

where

$$\pi = 3.1416$$

This relationship allows use of the normal probability tables to specify limits for the tracking signal. If the tracking signal falls outside those limits, the forecasting model no longer is tracking demand adequately. A tracking system is useful when forecasting systems are computerized because it alerts analysts when forecasts are getting far from desirable limits. Table 9.2 shows the area of the normal probability distribution within the control limits of 1 to 4 MAD.

Figure 9.5 shows tracking signal results for 23 periods plotted in a *control chart*. The control chart is useful for determining whether any action needs to be taken to improve the forecasting model. In the example, the first 20 points cluster around 0, as we would expect if the forecasts are not biased. The CFE will tend toward 0. When the underlying characteristics of demand change but the forecasting model does not, the tracking signal eventually goes out of control. The steady increase after the 20th point in Figure 9.5 indicates that the process is going out of control. The 21st and 22nd points are acceptable, but the 23rd point is not.

FORECAST ERROR RANGES. Calculating MAD can also provide additional information. Forecasts that are stated as a single value, such as 1,200 units or 26 customers, can be less useful because they do not indicate the range of likely errors that the forecast typically generates. A better approach can be to provide the manager with a forecasted value and an error range. For example, suppose that the forecasted value for a product is 1,000 units, with a MAD of 20 units. Table 9.2 shows that there is about a 95 percent chance that actual demand will fall within ±2.5 MAD of the forecast; that is, for

TABLE 9.2	Control Limit Spread (number of MAD)	Equivalent Number of σ*	Percent of Area Within Control Limits[†]
Percent of the Area of the Normal Probability Distribution Within the Control Limits of the Tracking Signal	±1.0	±0.80	57.62
	±1.5	±1.20	76.98
	±2.0	±1.60	89.04
	±2.5	±2.00	95.44
	±3.0	±2.40	98.36
	±3.5	±2.80	99.48
	±4.0	±3.20	99.86

*The equivalent number of standard deviations is found by using the approximation of MAD $\cong 0.8\sigma$.

[†]The area of the normal curve included within the control limits is found in the Appendix. For example, the cumulative area from $-\infty$ to 0.80σ is 0.7881. The area between 0 and $+0.80\sigma$ is $0.7881 - 0.5000 = 0.2881$. Since the normal curve is symmetric, the area between -0.80σ and 0 is also 0.2881. Therefore, the area between $\pm 0.80\sigma$ is $0.2881 + 0.2881 = 0.5762$.

Tracking Signal

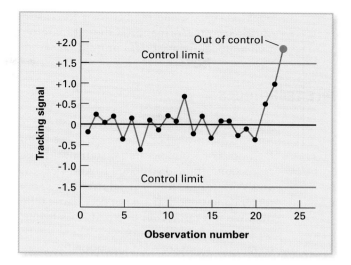

a forecast of 1,000 units, we can say with a 95 percent confidence level that actual demand will fall in the range of 950 to 1,050 units.

CRITERIA FOR SELECTING TIME-SERIES METHODS

> What is involved in choosing the best time-series forecasting method?

Forecast error measures provide important information for choosing the best forecasting method for a product or service. They also guide managers in selecting the best values for the parameters needed for the method: n for the moving average method, the weights for the weighted moving average method, and α for the exponential smoothing method. The criteria to use in making forecast method and parameter choices include (1) minimizing bias, (2) minimizing MAD or MSE, (3) meeting managerial expectations of changes in the components of demand, and (4) minimizing the forecast error last period. The first two criteria relate to statistical measures based on historical performance, the third reflects expectations of the future that may not be rooted in the past, and the fourth is a way to use whatever method seems to be working best at the time a forecast must be made.

USING STATISTICAL CRITERIA. Statistical performance measures can be used in the selection of a forecasting method. Two guidelines that help when searching for the best time-series models are:

1. For projections of more stable demand patterns, use lower α and β values or larger n values to emphasize historical experience.
2. For projections of more dynamic demand patterns, using the models covered in this chapter, try higher α and β values or smaller n values. When historical demand patterns are changing, recent history should be emphasized.

Often the forecaster must make trade-offs between bias (CFE) and the measures of forecast error dispersion (MAD, MSE, and MAPE). Managers also must recognize that the best technique in explaining the past data is not necessarily the best to predict the future. For this reason, some analysts prefer to use a **holdout set** as a final test. To do so, they set aside some of the more recent periods from the time series, and use only the earlier time periods to develop and test different models. Once the final models have been selected in the first phase, then they are tested again with the holdout set. Whether this idea is used or not, managers should monitor future forecast errors, perhaps with

holdout set Actual demands from the more recent time periods in the time series, which are set aside to test different models developed from the earlier time periods.

tracking signals, and modify their forecasting approaches as needed. Maintaining data on forecast performance is the ultimate test of forecasting power—rather than how well a model fits past data or holdout samples.

USING MULTIPLE TECHNIQUES

We have described several individual forecasting methods and shown how to assess their forecast performance. However, there is no need to rely on only a single forecasting method. For example, initial statistical forecasts using several time-series methods and regression can be distributed to knowledgeable individuals, such as marketing directors and sales teams, for their adjustments. They can account for current market and customer conditions that are not necessarily reflected in past data. Furthermore, there can be multiple forecasts from different sales teams, and some teams may have a better record on forecast errors than others. There are two approaches to using several forecasting techniques in unison—combination forecasts and focus forecasting.

COMBINATION FORECASTS

combination forecasts Forecasts that are produced by averaging independent forecasts based on different methods or different data, or both.

Research during the last two decades suggest that combining forecasts from multiple sources often produces more accurate forecasts. **Combination forecasts** are forecasts that are produced by averaging independent forecasts, based on different methods or different data or both. It is intriguing that combination forecasts often perform better over time than do even the *best* single forecasting procedure. For example, suppose that the forecast for next period is 100 units from technique #1 and 120 units from technique #2, and that technique #1 has provided more accurate forecasts to date. The combination forecast for next period, giving equal weight to each technique, is 110 units (or $0.5 \times 100 + 0.5 \times 120$). When this averaging technique is used consistently into the future, its combination forecasts often will be much more accurate than those of any single best forecasting technique (in this example, technique #1). Combining is most effective when the individual forecasts bring different kinds of information into the forecasting process. Forecasters have achieved excellent results by weighting forecasts equally, and this is a good starting point. However, unequal weights may provide better results under some conditions.

FOCUS FORECASTING

Is the most sophisticated forecasting system always the best one to use?

focus forecasting A method of forecasting that selects the best forecast from a group of forecasts generated by simple techniques.

Another way to take advantage of multiple techniques is **focus forecasting**, which selects the best forecast from a group of forecasts generated by individual techniques. Every period all techniques are used to make forecasts for each item. The forecasts are made on the computer, because there can be 100,000 different items at a company such as American Hardware Supply. Using historical data as the starting point for each method, the computer generates forecasts for the current period. The forecasts are compared to actual demand, and the method that produces the forecast with the least error is used to make the forecast for the next period. The method used for each item may change from period to period.

FORECASTING ACROSS THE ORGANIZATION

The organizationwide forecasting process cuts across functional areas. Forecasting overall demand typically originates with marketing, but internal customers throughout the organization depend on forecasts to formulate and execute their plans. Forecasts are critical inputs to business plans, annual plans, and budgets. Finance needs forecasts to project cash flows and capital requirements. Human resources needs forecasts to anticipate hiring and training needs. Marketing is a primary source for sales forecast information, because they are closest to external customers. Operations needs forecasts to plan output levels, purchases of materials and services, workforce and output schedules, inventories, and long-term capacities.

Managers throughout the organization make forecasts on many variables other than future demand, such as competitor strategies, regulatory changes, technological change, processing times, supplier lead times, and quality losses. Tools for making these forecasts are basically the same ones covered here for demand: judgment, opinions of knowledgeable people, averages of past experience, regression, and time-series techniques. Using them, forecasting performance can be improved, but forecasts are rarely perfect. As Mark Twain said in *Following the Equator,* "prophesy is a good line of business, but it is full of risks." Smart managers recognize this reality and find ways to update their plans when the inevitable forecast error or unexpected event occurs.

EQUATION SUMMARY

1. Naive forecasting: Forecast $= D_t$

2. Simple moving average: $F_{t+1} = \dfrac{D_t + D_{t-1} + D_{t-2} + \cdots + D_{t-n+1}}{n}$

3. Weighted moving average:

$$F_{t+1} = \text{Weight}_1(D_t) + \text{Weight}_2(D_{t-1}) + \text{Weight}_3(D_{t-2}) + \cdots + \text{Weight}_n(D_{t-n+1})$$

4. Exponential smoothing: $F_{t+1} = \alpha D_t + (1 - \alpha)F_t$

5. Trend-adjusted exponential smoothing:

$$A_t = \alpha D_t + (1 - \alpha)(A_{t-1} + T_{t-1})$$
$$T_t = \beta(A_t - A_{t-1}) + (1 - \beta)T_{t-1}$$
$$F_{t+1} = A_t + T_t$$

6. Forecast error:

$$E_t = D_t - F_t$$
$$\text{CFE} = \Sigma E_t$$
$$\text{MSE} = \frac{\Sigma E_t^2}{n}$$
$$\bar{E} = \text{CFE}/n$$
$$\sigma = \sqrt{\frac{\Sigma(E_t - \bar{E})^2}{n - 1}}$$
$$\text{MAD} = \frac{\Sigma |E_t|}{n}$$
$$\text{MAPE} = \frac{[\Sigma |E_t|/D_t]100}{n}$$

7. Exponentially smoothed error: $\text{MAD}_t = \alpha|E_t| + (1 - \alpha)\text{MAD}_{t-1}$

8. Tracking signal: $\dfrac{\text{CFE}}{\text{MAD}},$ or $\dfrac{\text{CFE}}{\text{MAD}_t}$

CHAPTER HIGHLIGHTS

❑ The five basic patterns of demand are the horizontal, trend, seasonal, cyclical, and random variation.

❑ Designing a forecasting system involves determining what to forecast, which forecasting technique to use, and how computerized forecasting systems can assist managerial decision making.

❑ Level of data aggregation and units of measure are important considerations in managerial decisions about what to forecast. Two general types of demand forecasting are used: qualitative methods and quantitative methods. Qualitative methods include judgment methods, and quantitative methods include causal methods and time-series analysis.

❑ Judgment methods of forecasting are useful in situations where relevant historical data are lacking. Sales-force estimates, executive opinion, market research, and the Delphi method are judgment methods. Judgment methods require the most human interaction and so are the most costly of these methods. Facility location and capacity planning are examples of long-term decisions that justify the expense of generating a judgment forecast.

❑ Causal forecasting methods hypothesize a functional relationship between the factor to be forecasted and other internal or external factors. Causal methods identify turning points in demand patterns but require more extensive analysis to determine the appropriate relationships between the item to be forecast and the external and internal factors. Causal methods tend to be used in medium-term production

planning for product families. Linear regression is one of the more popular causal forecasting methods.

❑ Time-series analysis is often used with computer systems to generate quickly the large number of short-term forecasts required for scheduling products or services. Simple moving averages, weighted moving averages, and exponential smoothing are used to estimate the average of a time series. The exponential smoothing technique has the advantage of requiring that only a minimal amount of data be kept for use in updating the forecast. Trend-adjusted exponential smoothing is a method for including a trend estimate in exponentially smoothed forecasts. Estimates for the series average and the trend are smoothed to provide the forecast.

❑ Although many techniques allow for seasonal influences, a simple approach is the multiplicative seasonal method, which is based on the assumption that the seasonal influence is proportional to the level of average demand.

❑ The cumulative sum of forecast errors (CFE), mean squared error (MSE), standard deviation of forecast errors (σ), mean absolute deviation (MAD), and mean absolute percent error (MAPE) are all measures of forecast error used in practice. The CFE and MAD are used to develop a tracking signal that determines when a forecasting method no longer is yielding acceptable forecasts. Forecast error measures also are used to select the best forecast methods from available alternatives.

❑ Combination forecasts produced by averaging two or more independent forecasts often provide more accurate forecasts.

SOLVED PROBLEM 1

Chicken Palace periodically offers carryout five-piece chicken dinners at special prices. Let Y be the number of dinners sold and X be the price. Based on the historical observations and calculations in the following table, determine the regression equation, correlation coefficient, and coefficient of determination. How many dinners can Chicken Palace expect to sell at $3.00 each?

OBSERVATION	PRICE, X	DINNERS SOLD, Y
1	$ 2.70	760
2	$ 3.50	510
3	$ 2.00	980
4	$ 4.20	250
5	$ 3.10	320
6	$ 4.05	480
Total	$19.55	3,300
Average	$ 3.258	550

SOLUTION

We use the computer to calculate the best values of *a, b*, the correlation coefficient, and the coefficient of determination.

$$a = 1,450.12$$
$$b = -276.28$$
$$r = -0.84$$
$$r^2 = 0.71$$

The regression line is

$$Y = a + bX = 1,450.12 - 276.28X$$

The correlation coefficient ($r = -0.84$) shows a negative correlation between the variables. The coefficient of determination ($r^2 = 0.71$) indicates that other variables (in addition to price) appreciably affect sales.

If the regression equation is satisfactory to the manager, estimated sales at a price of $3.00 per dinner may be calculated as follows:

$$Y = a + bX = 1,450.12 - 276.28(3.00)$$
$$= 621.28, \quad \text{or} \quad 621 \text{ dinners}$$

SOLVED PROBLEM 2

The Polish General's Pizza Parlor is a small restaurant catering to patrons with a taste for European pizza. One of its specialties is Polish Prize pizza. The manager must forecast weekly demand for these special pizzas so that he can order pizza shells weekly. Recently demand has been as follows:

WEEK OF	PIZZAS	WEEK OF	PIZZAS
June 2	50	June 23	56
June 9	65	June 30	55
June 16	52	July 7	60

a. Forecast the demand for pizza for June 23 to July 14 by using the simple moving average method with $n = 3$. Then repeat the forecast by using the weighted moving average method with $n = 3$ and weights of 0.50, 0.30, and 0.20, with 0.50 applying to the most recent demand.

b. Calculate the MAD for each method.

SOLUTION

a. The simple moving average method and the weighted moving average method give the following results.

CURRENT WEEK	SIMPLE MOVING AVERAGE FORECAST FOR NEXT WEEK	WEIGHTED MOVING AVERAGE FORECAST FOR NEXT WEEK
June 16	$\dfrac{52 + 65 + 50}{3} = 55.7$, or 56	$[(0.5 \times 52) + (0.3 \times 65) + (0.2 \times 50)] = 55.5$, or 56
June 23	$\dfrac{56 + 52 + 65}{3} = 57.7$, or 58	$[(0.5 \times 56) + (0.3 \times 52) + (0.2 \times 65)] = 56.6$, or 57
June 30	$\dfrac{55 + 56 + 52}{3} = 54.3$, or 54	$[(0.5 \times 55) + (0.3 \times 56) + (0.2 \times 52)] = 54.7$, or 55
July 7	$\dfrac{60 + 55 + 56}{3} = 57$	$[(0.5 \times 60) + (0.3 \times 55) + (0.2 \times 56)] = 57.7$, or 58

b. The mean absolute deviation is calculated as follows:

		SIMPLE MOVING AVERAGE		WEIGHTED MOVING AVERAGE	
WEEK	ACTUAL DEMAND	Forecast	Absolute Errors, $\|E_t\|$	Forecast	Absolute Errors, $\|E_t\|$
June 23	56	56	$\|56 - 56\| = 0$	56	$\|56 - 56\| = 0$
June 30	55	58	$\|55 - 58\| = 3$	57	$\|55 - 57\| = 2$
July 7	60	54	$\|60 - 54\| = 6$	55	$\|60 - 55\| = 5$
		MAD =	$\dfrac{0 + 3 + 6}{3} = 3$	MAD =	$\dfrac{0 + 2 + 5}{3} = 2.3$

For this limited set of data, the weighted moving average method resulted in a slightly lower mean absolute deviation. However, final conclusions can be made only after analyzing much more data.

SOLVED PROBLEM 3

The monthly demand for units manufactured by the Acme Rocket Company has been as follows:

MONTH	UNITS	MONTH	UNITS
May	100	September	105
June	80	October	110
July	110	November	125
August	115	December	120

a. Use the exponential smoothing method to forecast the number of units for June to January. The initial forecast for May was 105 units; $\alpha = 0.2$.

b. Calculate the absolute percentage error for each month from June through December and the MAD and MAPE of forecast error as of the end of December.

c. Calculate the tracking signal as of the end of December. What can you say about the performance of your forecasting method?

SOLUTION

a.

CURRENT MONTH, t	$F_{t+1} = \alpha D_t + (1 - \alpha)F_t$	FORECAST, MONTH $t + 1$
May	$0.2(100) + 0.8(105) = 104.0$, or 104	June
June	$0.2(80) + 0.8(104.0) = 99.2$, or 99	July
July	$0.2(110) + 0.8(99.2) = 101.4$, or 101	August
August	$0.2(115) + 0.8(101.4) = 104.1$, or 104	September
September	$0.2(105) + 0.8(104.1) = 104.3$, or 104	October
October	$0.2(110) + 0.8(104.3) = 105.4$, or 105	November
November	$0.2(125) + 0.8(105.4) = 109.3$, or 109	December
December	$0.2(120) + 0.8(109.3) = 111.4$, or 111	January

b.

MONTH, t	ACTUAL DEMAND, D_t	FORECAST, F_t	ERROR, $E_t = D_t - F_t$	ABSOLUTE ERROR, $\|E_t\|$	ABSOLUTE PERCENTAGE ERROR, $(\|E_t\|/D_t)\,(100\%)$
June	80	104	−24	24	30.0%
July	110	99	11	11	10.0
August	115	101	14	14	12.2
September	105	104	1	1	0.9
October	110	104	6	6	5.4
November	125	105	20	20	16.0
December	120	109	11	11	9.2
Total	765		39	87	83.7%

$$\text{MAD} = \frac{\Sigma \,|E_t|}{n} = \frac{87}{7} = 12.4 \quad \text{and} \quad \text{MAPE} = \frac{\Sigma \,[|E_t|(100)]/D_t}{n} = \frac{83.7\%}{7} = 11.9$$

c. As of the end of December, the cumulative sum of forecast errors (CFE) is 39. Using the mean absolute deviation calculated in part (b), we calculate the tracking signal:

$$\text{Tracking signal} = \frac{\text{CFE}}{\text{MAD}} = \frac{39}{12.4} = 3.14$$

The probability that a tracking signal value of 3.14 could be generated completely by chance is very small. Consequently, we should revise our approach. The long string of forecasts lower than actual demand suggests use of a trend method.

SOLVED PROBLEM 4

The demand for Krispee Crunchies, a favorite breakfast cereal of people born in the 1940s, is experiencing a decline. The company wants to monitor demand for this product closely as it nears the end of its life cycle. The trend-adjusted exponential smoothing method is used with $\alpha = 0.1$ and $\beta = 0.2$. At the end of December, the January estimate for the average number of cases sold per month, A_t, was 900,000 and the trend, T_t, was −50,000 per month. The following table shows the actual sales history for January, February, and March. Generate forecasts for February, March, and April.

MONTH	SALES
January	890,000
February	800,000
March	825,000

SOLUTION

We know the initial condition at the end of December and actual demand for January, February, and March. We must now update the forecast method and prepare a forecast for April. All data are expressed in thousands of cases. Our equations for use with trend-adjusted exponential smoothing are

$$A_t = \alpha D_t + (1 - \alpha)(A_{t-1} + T_{t-1})$$
$$T_t = \beta(A_t - A_{t-1}) + (1 - \beta)T_{t-1}$$
$$F_{t+1} = A_t + T_t$$

For January, we have

$$A_{Jan} = 0.1(890,000) + 0.9(900,000 - 50,000)$$
$$= 854,000 \text{ cases}$$
$$T_{Jan} = 0.2(854,000 - 900,000) + 0.8(-50,000)$$
$$= -49,200 \text{ cases}$$
$$F_{Feb} = A_{Jan} + T_{Jan} = 854,000 - 49,200 = 804,800 \text{ cases}$$

For February, we have

$$A_{Feb} = 0.1(800,000) + 0.9(854,000 - 49,200)$$
$$= 804,320 \text{ cases}$$
$$T_{Feb} = 0.2(804,320 - 854,000) + 0.8(-49,200)$$
$$= -49,296 \text{ cases}$$
$$F_{Mar} = A_{Feb} + T_{Feb} = 804,320 - 49,296 = 755,024 \text{ cases}$$

For March, we have

$$A_{Mar} = 0.1(825,000) + 0.9(804,320 - 49,296)$$
$$= 762,021.6, \quad \text{or} \quad 762,022 \text{ cases}$$
$$T_{Mar} = 0.2(762,022 - 804,320) + 0.8(-49,296)$$
$$= -47,896.4, \quad \text{or} \quad -47,897 \text{ cases}$$
$$F_{Apr} = A_{Mar} + T_{Mar} = 762,022 - 47,897 = 714,125 \text{ cases}$$

SOLVED PROBLEM 5

The Northville Post Office experiences a seasonal pattern of daily mail volume every week. The following data for two representative weeks are expressed in thousands of pieces of mail:

DAY	WEEK 1	WEEK 2
Sunday	5	8
Monday	20	15
Tuesday	30	32
Wednesday	35	30
Thursday	49	45
Friday	70	70
Saturday	15	10
Total	224	210

a. Calculate a seasonal factor for each day of the week.

b. If the postmaster estimates that there will be 230,000 pieces of mail to sort next week, forecast the volume for each day of the week.

SOLUTION

a. Calculate the average daily mail volume for each week. Then for each day of the week divide the mail volume by the week's average to get the seasonal factor. Finally, for each day, add the two seasonal factors and divide by 2 to obtain the average seasonal factor to use in the forecast (see part (b)).

	WEEK 1		WEEK 2		AVERAGE SEASONAL FACTOR [(1) + (2)]/2
DAY	**Mail Volume**	**Seasonal Factor (1)**	**Mail Volume**	**Seasonal Factor (2)**	
Sunday	5	5/32 = 0.15625	8	8/30 = 0.26667	0.21146
Monday	20	20/32 = 0.62500	15	15/30 = 0.50000	0.56250
Tuesday	30	30/32 = 0.93750	32	32/30 = 1.06667	1.00209
Wednesday	35	35/32 = 1.09375	30	30/30 = 1.00000	1.04688
Thursday	49	49/32 = 1.53125	45	45/30 = 1.50000	1.51563
Friday	70	70/32 = 2.18750	70	70/30 = 2.33333	2.26042
Saturday	15	15/32 = 0.46875	10	10/30 = 0.33333	0.40104
Total	224		210		
Average	224/7 = 32		210/7 = 30		

b. The average daily mail volume is expected to be 230,000/7 = 32,857 pieces of mail. Using the average seasonal factors calculated in part (a), we obtain the following forecasts:

DAY	CALCULATION	FORECAST
Sunday	0.21146(32,857) =	6,948
Monday	0.56250(32,857) =	18,482
Tuesday	1.00209(32,857) =	32,926
Wednesday	1.04688(32,857) =	34,397
Thursday	1.51563(32,857) =	49,799
Friday	2.26042(32,857) =	74,271
Saturday	0.40104(32,857) =	13,177
	Total	230,000

CD-ROM RESOURCES

The Student CD-ROM that accompanies this text contains the following resources, which allow you to further practice and apply the concepts presented in this chapter.

❑ **OM Explorer Tutors:** OM Explorer contains four tutor programs that will help you learn how to use the moving average, weighted moving average, exponential smoothing, and trend-adjusting exponential smoothing techniques. See the Chapter 9 folder in OM Explorer. See also the Student CD-ROM for a Tutor Exercise that uses three tutors to forecast newspaper subscriptions.

❑ **OM Explorer Solvers:** OM Explorer has three programs that can be used to solve general problems involving regression analysis, seasonal forecasting, and time-series models. See the Forecasting folder in OM Explorer for these routines.

❑ **Equation Summary:** All the equations for this chapter can be found in one convenient location.

❑ **Discussion Questions:** Two questions will challenge your understanding of forecasting, applied to air visibility data subscriptions for a biweekly newspaper.

❑ **Case:** Yankee Fork and Hoe Company: What are your forecasts for bow rakes in year 5?

❑ **Experiential Exercise:** Use the Yankee Fork and Hoe Company case as an in-class team experience.

❑ **Supplement C:** Measuring Output Rates. See how variations of forecasting techniques are used to estimate future processing times.

❑ **Supplement D:** Learning Curve Analysis. See how variations of forecasting techniques are used to analyze learning curves.

INTERACTIVE RESOURCES

The Interactive Web site associated with this text (www.prenhall.com/ritzman) contains many tools and activities specifically designed for this chapter. The following items are recommended to enhance your understanding of the material in this chapter.

❒ **Internet Activities:** Try out four different links to forecasting topics, including global warming, governmental data, and a forecasting pool.

❒ **Internet Tours:** Check out the manufacturing process at Ferrara Pan Candy Company and the forecasting issues involved.

PROBLEMS

An icon next to a problem identifies the software that can be helpful but is not mandatory. The software is available on OM Explorer.

1. 💿 **OM Explorer** Sales for the past 12 months at Dalworth Company are given here.

MONTH	SALES ($ Millions)	MONTH	SALES ($ Millions)
January	20	July	53
February	24	August	62
March	27	September	54
April	31	October	36
May	37	November	32
June	47	December	29

a. Use a three-month moving average to forecast the sales for the months April through December.

b. Use a four-month moving average to forecast the sales for the months May through December.

c. Compare the performance of the two methods by using the mean absolute deviation as the performance criterion. Which method would you recommend?

d. Compare the performance of the two methods by using the mean absolute percent error as the performance criterion. Which method would you recommend?

e. Compare the performance of the two methods by using the mean squared error as the performance criterion. Which method would you recommend?

2. 💿 **OM Explorer** Karl's Copiers sells and repairs photocopy machines. The manager needs weekly forecasts of service calls so that he can schedule service personnel. The forecast for the week of July 3 was 24 calls. The manager uses exponential smoothing with $\alpha = 0.20$. Forecast the number of calls for the week of August 7, which is next week.

WEEK OF	ACTUAL SERVICE CALLS
July 3	24
July 10	32
July 17	36
July 24	23
July 31	25

3. 💿 **OM Explorer** Consider the sales data for Dalworth Company given in Problem 1.

a. Use a three-month weighted moving average to forecast the sales for the months April through December. Use weights of (3/6), (2/6), and (1/6), giving more weight to more recent data.

b. Use exponential smoothing with $\alpha = 0.6$ to forecast the sales for the months April through December. Assume that the initial forecast for January was $22 million.

c. Compare the performance of the two methods by using the mean absolute deviation as the performance criterion. Which method would you recommend?

d. Compare the performance of the two methods by using the mean absolute percent error as the performance criterion. Which method would you recommend?

e. Compare the performance of the two methods by using the mean squared error as the performance criterion. Which method would you recommend?

4. A convenience store recently started to carry a new brand of soft drink in its territory. Management is interested in estimating future sales volume to determine whether it should continue to carry the new brand or replace it with another brand. At the end of April, the average monthly sales volume of the new soft drink was 700 cans and the trend was +50 cans per month. The actual sales volume figures for May, June, and July are 760, 800, and 820, respectively. Use trend-adjusted exponential smoothing with $\alpha = 0.2$ and $\beta = 0.1$ to forecast usage for June, July, and August.

5. The following data are for calculator sales in units at an electronics store over the past five weeks:

WEEK	SALES
1	46
2	49
3	43
4	50
5	53

Use trend-adjusted exponential smoothing with $\alpha = 0.2$ and $\beta = 0.2$ to forecast sales for weeks 3–6. Assume that the average of the time series was 45 units and that the average trend was +2 units per week just before week 1.

6. 🌐 **OM Explorer** The manager of Snyder's Garden Center must make her annual purchasing plans for rakes, gloves, and other gardening items. One of the items she stocks is Fast-Grow, a liquid fertilizer. The sales of this item are seasonal, with peaks in the spring, summer, and fall months. Quarterly demand (in cases) for the past two years follows:

QUARTER	YEAR 1	YEAR 2
1	40	60
2	350	440
3	290	320
4	210	280
Total	890	1,100

If the expected sales for Fast-Grow are 1,150 cases for year 3, use the multiplicative seasonal method to prepare a forecast for each quarter of the year.

7. 🌐 **OM Explorer** The manager of a utility company in the Texas panhandle wants to develop quarterly forecasts of power loads for the next year. The power loads are seasonal, and the data on the quarterly loads in megawatts (MW) for the last four years are as follows:

YEAR	QUARTER 1	QUARTER 2	QUARTER 3	QUARTER 4
1	103.5	94.7	118.6	109.3
2	126.1	116.0	141.2	131.6
3	144.5	137.1	159.0	149.5
4	166.1	152.5	178.2	169.0

The manager has estimated the total demand for the next year at 780 MW. Use the multiplicative seasonal method to develop the forecast for each quarter.

8. 🌐 **OM Explorer** Demand for oil changes at Garcia's Garage has been as follows:

MONTH	NUMBER OF OIL CHANGES
January	41
February	46
March	57
April	52
May	59
June	51
July	60
August	62

a. Use simple linear regression analysis to develop a forecasting model for monthly demand. In this application, the dependent variable, Y, is monthly demand and the independent variable, X, is the month. For January, let $X = 1$; for February, let $X = 2$; and so on.

b. Use the model to forecast demand for September, October, and November. Here, $X = 9$, 10, and 11, respectively.

9. 🌐 **OM Explorer** At a hydrocarbon processing factory, process control involves periodic analysis of samples for a certain process quality parameter. The analytic procedure currently used is costly and time consuming. A faster and more economical alternative procedure has been proposed. However, the numbers for the quality parameter given by the alternative procedure are somewhat different from those given by the current procedure, not because of any inherent errors but because of changes in the nature of the chemical analysis. Management believes that, if the numbers from the new procedure can be used to forecast reliably the corresponding numbers from the current procedure, switching to the new procedure would be reasonable and cost effective. The following data were obtained for the quality parameter by analyzing samples using both procedures:

CURRENT, Y	PROPOSED, X	CURRENT, Y	PROPOSED, X
3.0	3.1	3.1	3.1
3.1	3.9	2.7	2.9
3.0	3.4	3.3	3.6
3.6	4.0	3.2	4.1
3.8	3.6	2.1	2.6
2.7	3.6	3.0	3.1
2.7	3.6	2.6	2.8

a. Use linear regression to find a relation to forecast Y, the quality parameter from the current procedure, using the values from the proposed procedure, X.

b. Is there a strong relationship between Y and X? Explain.

10. ⊙ **OM Explorer** The director of a large public library must schedule employees to reshelve books and periodicals checked out of the library. The number of items checked out will determine the labor requirements. The following data reflect the numbers of items checked out of the library for the past three years:

MONTH	YEAR 1	YEAR 2	YEAR 3
January	1,847	2,045	1,986
February	2,669	2,321	2,564
March	2,467	2,419	2,635
April	2,432	2,088	2,150
May	2,464	2,667	2,201
June	2,378	2,122	2,663
July	2,217	2,206	2,055
August	2,445	1,869	1,678
September	1,894	2,441	1,845
October	1,922	2,291	2,065
November	2,431	2,364	2,147
December	2,274	2,189	2,451

The director needs a time-series method for forecasting the number of items to be checked out during the next month. Find the best simple moving average forecast you can. Decide what is meant by "best" and justify your decision.

11. ⊙ **OM Explorer** Using the data in Problem 10, find the best exponential smoothing solution you can. Justify your choice.

12. ⊙ **OM Explorer** Using the data in Problem 10, find the best trend-adjusted exponential smoothing solution you can. Compare the performance of this method with those of the best moving average method and the exponential smoothing method. Which of the three would you choose?

13. ⊙ **OM Explorer** Cannister, Inc., specializes in the manufacture of plastic containers. The data on the monthly sales of 10-ounce shampoo bottles for the last five years are as follows:

YEAR	1	2	3	4	5
January	742	741	896	951	1,030
February	697	700	793	861	1,032
March	776	774	885	938	1,126
April	898	932	1,055	1,109	1,285
May	1,030	1,099	1,204	1,274	1,468
June	1,107	1,223	1,326	1,422	1,637
July	1,165	1,290	1,303	1,486	1,611
August	1,216	1,349	1,436	1,555	1,608
September	1,208	1,341	1,473	1,604	1,528
October	1,131	1,296	1,453	1,600	1,420
November	971	1,066	1,170	1,403	1,119
December	783	901	1,023	1,209	1,013

a. Using the multiplicative seasonal method, calculate the monthly seasonal indices.

b. Develop a simple linear regression equation to forecast annual sales. For this regression, the dependent variable, Y, is the demand in each year and the independent variable, X, is the index for the year (i.e., $X = 1$ for year 1, $X = 2$ for year 2, and so on until $X = 5$ for year 5).

c. Forecast the annual sales for year 6 by using the regression model you developed in part (b).

d. Prepare the seasonal forecast for each month by using the monthly seasonal indices calculated in part (a).

14. ⊙ **OM Explorer** A certain food item at P&Q Supermarkets has the demand pattern shown in the following table. Find the "best" forecast you can for month 25 and justify your methodology. You may use some of the data to find the best parameter value(s) for your method and the rest to test the forecast model. Your justification should include both quantitative and qualitative considerations.

MONTH	DEMAND	MONTH	DEMAND
1	33	13	37
2	37	14	43
3	31	15	56
4	39	16	41
5	54	17	36
6	38	18	39
7	42	19	41
8	40	20	58
9	41	21	42
10	54	22	45
11	43	23	41
12	39	24	38

15. ⊙ **OM Explorer** A manufacturing firm has developed a skills test, the scores from which can be used to predict workers' production rating factors. Data on the test scores of various workers and their subsequent production ratings are shown.

WORKER	TEST SCORE	PRODUCTION RATING	WORKER	TEST SCORE	PRODUCTION RATING
A	53	45	K	54	59
B	36	43	L	73	77
C	88	89	M	65	56
D	84	79	N	29	28
E	86	84	O	52	51
F	64	66	P	22	27
G	45	49	Q	76	76
H	48	48	R	32	34
I	39	43	S	51	60
J	67	76	T	37	32

a. Using linear regression, develop a relationship to forecast production ratings from test scores.

b. If a worker's test score was 80, what would be your forecast of the worker's production rating?

c. Comment on the strength of the relationship between the test scores and production ratings.

SELECTED REFERENCES

Armstrong, J. S. *Long-range Forecasting: From Crystal Ball to Computer.* New York: John Wiley & Sons, 1995.

Bowerman, Bruce L., and Richard T. O'Connell. *Forecasting and Time Series: An Applied Approach,* 3 d ed., Belmont, CA: Duxbury Press, 1993.

Clemen, R. T. "Combining Forecasts: A Review and Annotated Bibliography." *International Journal of Forecasting,* vol. 5 (1989), pp. 559–583.

Hudson, William J. *Executive Economics: Forecasting and Planning for the Real World of Business.* New York: John Wiley & Sons, 1993.

Li, X. "An Intelligent Business Forecaster for Strategic Business Planning." *Journal of Forecasting,* vol. 18, no. 3 (1999), pp. 181–205.

Lim, J. S., and M. O'Connor. "Judgmental Forecasting with Time Series and Causal Information." *International Journal of Forecasting,* vol. 12 (1996), pp. 139–153.

Melnyk, Steven. "1997 Forecasting Software Product Listing." *APICS—The Performance Advantage* (April 1997), pp. 62–65.

Principles of Forecasting: A Handbook for Researchers and Practitioners, J. Scott Armstrong (ed.). Norwell, MA: Kluwer Academic Publishers, 2001. Also visit (www-marketing.wharton.upenn.edu/ forecast) for valuable information on forecasting, including frequently asked questions, forecasting methodology tree, and dictionary.

Sanders, Nada R., and L. P. Ritzman. "Bringing Judgment into Combination Forecasts." *Journal of Operations Management,* vol. 13 (1995), pp. 311–321.

Sanders, Nada R., and K. B. Manrodt. "Forecasting Practices in U.S. Corporations: Survey Results." *Interfaces,* vol. 24 (1994), pp. 91–100.

Sanders, Nada R., and Larry P. Ritzman. "The Need for Contextual and Technical Knowledge in Judgmental Forecasting." *Journal of Behavioral Decision Making,* vol. 5, no. 1 (1992), pp. 39–52.

Smith, Bernard. *Focus Forecasting: Computer Techniques for Inventory Control.* Boston: CBI Publishing, 1984.

Yurkiewicz, Jack. "Forecasting 2000." *OR/MS Today,* vol. 27, no. 1 (2000), pp. 58–65.

Inventory Management

Across the Organization

Inventory management is important to . . .

- ☐ **accounting,** which provides the cost estimates used in inventory control, pays suppliers, and bills customers.
- ☐ **finance,** which deals with the implications of interest or investment opportunity costs on inventory management and anticipates how best to finance inventory and the cash flows related to inventory.
- ☐ **management information systems,** which develops and maintains the systems for managing inventories.
- ☐ **marketing and sales,** which create the need for inventory systems and rely on inventories to satisfy customers.
- ☐ **operations,** which has the responsibility to control the firm's inventories.

Learning Goals

After reading this chapter, you will be able to . . .

1. describe the cost and service trade-offs involved in inventory decisions.
2. distinguish between the different types of inventory and know how to manage their quantities.
3. compute the economic order quantity and apply it in various situations.
4. develop policies for both continuous review and periodic review inventory control systems.
5. identify ways to maintain accurate inventory records.

The Internet has opened a realm of business opportunities not even dreamed about 10 years ago. Many Internet companies, however, were formed under the assumption that customers, retailers, manufacturers, distributors, and service providers can be linked electronically in a seamless network thereby eliminating the need for costly warehouses and retail stores. They thought that inventory management and distribution can be outsourced to someone else. If that assumption is true, then why have some major Internet companies gone against that conventional Internet wisdom? For example, Amazon.com (www.amazon.com) invested $300 million for 3 million square feet of warehouse space.

The answer is that Internet companies are learning the lessons learned earlier by their bricks-and-mortar cousins—excellent customer service requires control over inventories. The Christmas of 1999 was a disaster for many "e-tailers." Etoys (www.etoys.com), while achieving on-time delivery for 96 percent of its orders, still got a black eye for shipping thousands of orders late. Now, Etoys must restore investor confidence by increasing total revenues and profitability. Its stock fell 90 percent in one year, placing its very existence in jeopardy.

Inventory management has become an important activity for many Internet companies. Customer delivery must be fast and contain exactly what the customer ordered. Here an employee packages an Amazon.com order for shipment.

Toysrus.com (www.toysrus.com) was unable to ship many orders on time, which prompted the Federal Trade Commission to impose a fine for not informing its customers of the delayed shipments.

Low revenues from Internet operations caused Toysrus.com to seek an alliance with Amazon, whereby Amazon would manage the customer service, warehousing, and shipping and Toysrus.com would buy and manage the inventory of toys. The alliance builds on Toysrus' competence for managing toy inventories through traditional bricks-and-mortar operations that support its retail stores and Amazon's competence for customer service management. Even Amazon, however, had a difficult time. Most of its customers were happy, but it bought far too much inventory—including such things as a 50-week supply of Kermit the Frog telephones—leading to a major charge against earnings for unsold goods. Consequently, it is clear that inventory management is just as important now as it has ever been.

Source: Bannon, Lisa, and Joseph, Pereira. "Two Big Online Toy Sellers Fight over Delivery Speed and Exclusive Rights," *Wall Street Journal* (September 25, 2000), p. B1; Hof, Robert D. "What's with All the Warehouses?" *Business Week* (November 1, 1999), p. EB 88.

INVENTORY MANAGEMENT IS AN important concern for managers in all types of businesses. For companies that operate on relatively low profit margins, poor inventory management can seriously undermine the business. The challenge is not to pare inventories to the bone to reduce costs or to have plenty around to satisfy all demands but to have the right amount to achieve the competitive priorities for the business most efficiently. In this chapter, we first introduce the basic concepts of inventory management for all types of businesses and then discuss inventory control systems appropriate for retail and distribution inventories. Later in the book, we focus on systems primarily used for manufacturing inventories (see Chapter 12, "Resource Planning" and Chapter 13, "Lean Systems").

INVENTORY CONCEPTS

Inventory is created when the receipt of materials, parts, or finished goods exceeds their disbursement; it is depleted when their disbursement exceeds their receipt (see Chapter 8, "Supply-Chain Management"). In this section, we identify the pressures for high and low inventories, define the different types of inventory, discuss tactics that can be used to reduce inventories when appropriate, identify the trade-offs involved in making manufacturing inventory placement decisions, and discuss how to identify the inventory items needing the most attention.

PRESSURES FOR LOW INVENTORIES

What are the costs for holding inventories?

inventory holding cost
The variable cost of keeping items on hand, including interest, storage and handling, taxes, insurance, and shrinkage.

An inventory manager's job is to balance the conflicting costs and pressures that argue for both low and high inventories and determine appropriate inventory levels. The primary reason for keeping inventories low is that inventory represents a temporary monetary investment in goods on which a firm must pay (rather than receive) interest. **Inventory holding** (or carrying) **cost** is the variable cost of keeping items on hand, including interest, storage and handling, taxes, insurance, and shrinkage. When these components change with inventory levels, so does the holding cost. Companies usually state an item's holding cost per period of time as a percent of its value. The annual cost to maintain one unit in inventory typically ranges from 20 to 40 percent of its value. Suppose that a firm's holding cost is 30 percent. If the average value of total inventory is 20 percent of sales, the average annual cost to hold inventory is 6 percent [0.30(0.20)] of total sales. This cost is sizable in terms of gross profit margins, which often are less than 10 percent. Thus, the components of holding cost create pressures for low inventories.

INTEREST OR OPPORTUNITY COST. To finance inventory, a company may obtain a loan or forgo the opportunity of an investment promising an attractive return. Interest or opportunity cost, whichever is greater, usually is the largest component of holding cost, often as high as 15 percent.

STORAGE AND HANDLING COSTS. Inventory takes up space and must be moved into and out of storage. Storage and handling costs may be incurred when a firm rents space on either a long- or short-term basis. There also is an opportunity cost for storage when a firm could use storage space productively in some other way.

TAXES, INSURANCE, AND SHRINKAGE. More taxes are paid if end-of-year inventories are high, and insurance on assets increases when there is more to insure. Shrinkage takes three forms. Pilferage, or theft of inventory by customers or employees, is a significant percentage of sales for some businesses. Obsolescence occurs when inventory cannot be used or sold at full value, owing to model changes, engineering modifications, or unexpectedly low demand. Obsolescence is a big expense in retail clothing, where drastic discounts on seasonal clothing are offered at the end of a season. Deterioration through physical spoilage or damage results in lost value. Food and beverages, for example, lose value and might even have to be discarded when their shelf life is reached. When the rate of deterioration is high, building large inventories may be unwise.

PRESSURES FOR HIGH INVENTORIES

Why are inventories necessary?

The fact that inventory held in the U.S. economy exceeds the $1.3 trillion mark suggests that there are pressures for large inventories, despite the expense. Let us look briefly at each type of pressure.

CUSTOMER SERVICE. Creating inventory can speed delivery and improve on-time delivery. Inventory reduces the potential for stockouts and backorders, which are key concerns of wholesalers and retailers. A **stockout** occurs when an item that is typically stocked is not available to satisfy a demand the moment it occurs, resulting in loss of the sale. A **backorder** is a customer order that cannot be filled when promised or demanded but is filled later. Customers may be willing to wait for a backorder but next time may take their business elsewhere. Sometimes customers are given discounts for the inconvenience of waiting.

ORDERING COST. Each time a firm places a new order, it incurs an **ordering cost**, or the cost of preparing a purchase order for a supplier or a production order for the shop. For the same item, the ordering cost is the same, regardless of the order size: The purchasing agent must take the time to decide how much to order and, perhaps, select a supplier and negotiate terms. Time also is spent on paperwork, follow-up, and receiving. In the case of a production order for a manufactured item, a blueprint and routing instructions often must accompany the shop order. The Internet (see Chapter 4, "Managing Technology" and Chapter 8, "Supply-Chain Management") can help streamline the order process and reduce the costs of placing orders.

SETUP COST. The cost involved in changing over a machine to produce a different component or item is the **setup cost**. It includes labor and time to make the changeover, cleaning, and new tools or fixtures. Scrap or rework costs can be substantially higher at the start of the run. Setup cost also is independent of order size, so there is pressure to order a large supply of the component and hold it in inventory.

LABOR AND EQUIPMENT UTILIZATION. By creating more inventory, management can increase workforce productivity and facility utilization in three ways. First, placing larger, less frequent production orders reduces the number of unproductive setups, which add no value to a product or service. Second, holding inventory reduces the chance of costly rescheduling of production orders because the components needed to make the product are not in inventory. Third, building inventories improves resource utilization by stabilizing the output rate for industries when demand is cyclical or seasonal. The firm uses inventory built during slack periods to handle extra demand in peak seasons and minimizes the need for extra shifts, hiring, layoffs, overtime, and additional equipment.

TRANSPORTATION COST. Sometimes outbound transportation cost can be reduced by increasing inventory levels. Having inventory on hand allows more carload shipments and minimizes the need to expedite shipments by more expensive modes of transportation. Forward placement of inventory can also reduce outbound transportation cost, even though the pooling effect is lessened and more inventory is necessary (see Chapter 8, "Supply-Chain Management"). Inbound transportation cost also may be reduced by creating more inventory. Sometimes several items are ordered from the same supplier. Combining these orders and placing them at the same time may lead to rate discounts, thereby decreasing the costs of transportation and raw materials.

PAYMENTS TO SUPPLIERS. A firm often can reduce total payments to suppliers if it can tolerate higher inventory levels. Suppose that a firm learns that a key supplier is about to increase prices. It might be cheaper for the firm to order a larger quantity than usual—in effect delaying the price increase—even though inventory will increase temporarily. Similarly, a firm can take advantage of quantity discounts. A **quantity discount**, whereby the price per unit drops when the order is sufficiently large, is an incentive to order larger quantities.

---

stockout The situation that occurs when an item that is typically stocked is not available to satisfy a demand the moment it occurs, resulting in loss of the sale.

backorder A customer order that cannot be filled when promised or demanded but is filled later.

ordering cost The cost of preparing a purchase order for a supplier or a production order for the shop.

setup cost The cost involved in changing over a machine to produce a different component or item.

quantity discount A drop in the price per unit when the order is sufficiently large.

TYPES OF INVENTORY

What types of inventory does a business own?

Another perspective on inventory is to classify it by how it is created. In this context, there are four types of inventory for an item: cycle, safety, anticipation, and pipeline. They cannot be identified physically; that is, an inventory manager can't look at a pile of widgets and identify which ones are cycle inventory and which ones are pipeline inventory. However, conceptually, each of the four types comes into being in an entirely different way. Once you understand these differences, you can prescribe different ways to reduce inventory, which we discuss in the next section.

cycle inventory The portion of total inventory that varies directly with lot size.

CYCLE INVENTORY. The portion of total inventory that varies directly with lot size is called **cycle inventory**. Determining how frequently to order, and in what quantity, is called **lot sizing**. Two principles apply.

lot sizing The determination of how frequently and in what quantity to order inventory.

1. The lot size, Q, varies directly with the elapsed time (or cycle) between orders. If a lot is ordered every five weeks, the average lot size must equal five weeks' demand.

2. The longer the time between orders for a given item, the greater the cycle inventory must be.

At the beginning of the interval, the cycle inventory is at its maximum, or Q. At the end of the interval, just before a new lot arrives, cycle inventory drops to its minimum, or 0. The average cycle inventory is the average of these two extremes:

$$\text{Average cycle inventory} = \frac{Q + 0}{2} = \frac{Q}{2}$$

This formula is exact only when the demand rate is constant and uniform. However, it does provide a reasonably good estimate even when demand rates are not constant. Factors other than the demand rate (e.g., scrap losses) also may cause estimating errors when this simple formula is used.

safety stock inventory Surplus inventory that a company holds to protect against uncertainties in demand, lead time, and supply.

SAFETY STOCK INVENTORY. To avoid customer service problems and the hidden costs of unavailable components, companies hold safety stock. **Safety stock inventory** protects against uncertainties in demand, lead time, and supply. Safety stocks are desirable when suppliers fail to deliver the desired quantity on the specified date with acceptable quality or when manufactured items have significant amounts of scrap or rework. Safety stock inventory ensures that operations are not disrupted when such problems occur, allowing subsequent operations to continue.

To create safety stock, a firm places an order for delivery earlier than when the item is typically needed.[1] The replenishment order, therefore, arrives ahead of time, giving a cushion against uncertainty. For example, suppose that the average lead time from a supplier is three weeks but a firm orders five weeks in advance just to be safe. This policy creates a safety stock equal to a two weeks' supply (5 − 3).

anticipation inventory Inventory used to absorb uneven rates of demand or supply.

ANTICIPATION INVENTORY. Inventory used to absorb uneven rates of demand or supply, which businesses often face, is referred to as **anticipation inventory**. Predictable, seasonal demand patterns lend themselves to the use of anticipation inventory. Manufacturers of air conditioners, for example, can experience 90 percent of their annual demand during just three months of a year. Such uneven demand may lead a manufacturer to stockpile anticipation inventory during periods of low demand so that

---

[1] When orders are placed at fixed intervals, there is a second way. Each new order placed is larger than the quantity typically needed through the next delivery date.

output levels do not have to be increased much when demand peaks. Smoothing output rates with inventory can increase productivity because varying output rates and workforce size can be costly. Anticipation inventory also can help when supply, rather than demand, is uneven. A company may stock up on a certain purchased item if its suppliers are threatened with a strike or have severe capacity limitations.

pipeline inventory
Inventory moving from point to point in the materials flow system.

PIPELINE INVENTORY. Inventory moving from point to point in the materials flow system is called **pipeline inventory**. Materials move from suppliers to a plant, from one operation to the next in the plant, from the plant to a distribution center or customer, and from the distribution center to a retailer. Pipeline inventory consists of orders that have been placed but not yet received. For example, NUMMI, the joint venture between General Motors and Toyota in California, uses parts produced in the Midwest. Shipments arrive daily at the plant, but the transportation lead time requires a pipeline inventory of parts in rail cars enroute from the Midwest at all times. Pipeline inventory between two points, for either transportation or production, can be measured as the average demand during lead time, $\overline{D}_L$, which is the average demand for the item per period (d) times the number of periods in the item's lead time (L) to move between the two points, or

$$\text{Pipeline inventory} = \overline{D}_L = dL$$

Note that the lot size does not directly affect the average level of the pipeline inventory. Increasing Q inflates the size of each order, so if an order has been placed but not received, there is more pipeline inventory for that lead time. But that increase is canceled by a proportionate decrease in the number of orders placed per year. The lot size can *indirectly* affect pipeline inventory, however, if increasing Q causes the lead time to increase. Here $\overline{D}_L$ and, therefore, pipeline inventory will increase. See Solved Problem 1 for a detailed example of how to estimate the various types of inventory.

**TUTOR
10.1**

INVENTORY REDUCTION TACTICS

Managers always are eager to find cost-effective ways to reduce inventory. Later in this chapter, we examine various ways for finding optimal lot sizes (see also Supplement H, "Special Inventory Models" on the Student CD-ROM). Here we discuss something more fundamental—the basic tactics (which we call *levers*) for reducing inventory. A primary lever is one that must be activated if inventory is to be reduced. A secondary lever reduces the penalty cost of applying the primary lever and the need for having inventory in the first place.

What are the options for reducing inventory prudently?

CYCLE INVENTORY. The primary lever is simply to reduce the lot size. Methods of just-in-time production (see Chapter 13, "Lean Systems") use extremely small lots, compared to traditional lot sizes equaling several weeks' (or even months') supply. However, making such reductions in Q without making any other changes can be devastating. For example, setup costs can skyrocket, which leads to use of the two secondary levers.

1. Streamline methods for placing orders and making setups, which reduces ordering and setup costs and allows Q to be reduced.

2. Increase repeatability to eliminate the need for changeovers. **Repeatability** is the degree to which the same work can be done again. It can be increased through high product demand; use of specialization; devoting resources exclusively to a product; using the same part in many different products; flexible automation; the one-worker, multiple-machines concept; or group technology (see Chapter 2, "Process Management" and Chapter 7, "Location and Layout"). Increased

repeatability The degree to which the same work can be done again.

repeatability may justify new setup methods, reduce transportation costs, and allow quantity discounts from suppliers.

SAFETY STOCK INVENTORY. The primary lever for reducing safety stock inventory is to place orders closer to the time when they must be received. However, this approach can lead to unacceptable customer service—unless demand, supply, and delivery uncertainties can be minimized. Four secondary levers can be used.

1. Improve demand forecasts so that there are fewer surprises from customers. Perhaps customers can even be encouraged to order items before they need them.

2. Cut lead times of purchased or produced items to reduce demand uncertainty during lead time. For example, local suppliers with short lead times could be selected whenever possible.

3. Reduce supply uncertainties. Suppliers may be more reliable if production plans are shared with them, permitting them to make more realistic forecasts. Surprises from unexpected scrap or rework can be reduced by improving manufacturing processes. Preventive maintenance can minimize unexpected downtime caused by equipment failure.

4. Rely more on equipment and labor buffers, such as capacity cushions and cross-trained workers. These are the only buffers available to businesses in the service sector because they can't inventory their services.

ANTICIPATION INVENTORY. The primary lever for reducing anticipation inventory is simply to match demand rate with production rate. Secondary levers are used to level customer demand in one of the following ways:

1. Add new products with different demand cycles so that a peak in the demand for one product compensates for the seasonal low for another.

2. Provide off-season promotional campaigns.

3. Offer seasonal pricing plans.

PIPELINE INVENTORY. An operations manager has direct control over lead time but not demand rate. Because pipeline inventory is a function of demand during lead time, the primary lever is to reduce the lead time. Two secondary levers can help managers cut lead times.

1. Find more responsive suppliers and select new carriers for shipments between stocking locations or improve materials handling within the plant. Introducing a computer system could overcome information delays between a distribution center and retailer.

2. Decrease Q, at least in those cases in which lead time depends on lot size. Smaller jobs generally require less time to complete.

PLACEMENT OF MANUFACTURING INVENTORIES

Should most inventory be held at the raw materials, work-in-process, or finished goods level? Which items should be standards?

special An item made to order; if purchased, it is bought to order.

standard An item that is made to stock and normally is available when needed.

Just as distribution managers decide where to place finished goods inventory (see Chapter 8, "Supply-Chain Management"), manufacturing managers make similar decisions for raw materials and work-in-process within the plant. In general, managers make inventory placement decisions by designating an item as either a special or a standard. A **special** is an item made to order, or if purchased, it is bought to order. Just enough are ordered to cover the latest customer request. A **standard** is an item that is made to stock and normally is available when needed. When a company makes more of its items as standards, particularly at the finished goods level, it places inventory closer to the customer.

Inventory held toward the finished goods level means short delivery times—but a higher dollar investment in inventory. Alternatively, holding inventory at the raw materials level would reduce the cost of carrying inventory—but at the expense of the quick customer response time.

IDENTIFYING CRITICAL INVENTORY ITEMS WITH ABC ANALYSIS

Which items demand the closest attention and control?

ABC analysis The process of dividing items into three classes according to their dollar useage so that managers can focus on items that have the highest dollar value.

**TUTOR
10.2**

Thousands of items are held in inventory by a typical organization, but only a small percentage of them deserves management's closest attention and tightest control. **ABC analysis** is the process of dividing items into three classes according to their dollar usage so that managers can focus on items that have the highest dollar value. This method is the equivalent of creating a Pareto chart (see Chapter 5, "Quality") except that it is applied to inventory rather than quality. As Figure 10.1 shows, class A items typically represent only about 20 percent of the items but account for 80 percent of the dollar usage. Class B items account for another 30 percent of the items but only 15 percent of the dollar usage. Finally, 50 percent of the items fall in class C, representing a mere 5 percent of the dollar usage.

The goal of ABC analysis is to identify the inventory levels of class A items and enable management to control them tightly by using the levers just discussed. The analyst begins by multiplying the annual demand rate for one item by the dollar value (cost) of one unit to determine its dollar usage. After ranking the items on the basis of dollar usage and creating the Pareto chart, the analyst looks for "natural" changes in slope. The dividing lines in Figure 10.1 between classes are inexact. Class A items could be somewhat higher or lower than 20 percent of all items, but normally account for the bulk of the dollar usage.

A manager can direct that class A items be reviewed frequently to reduce the average lot size and keep inventory records current. Class B items are candidates for systems where purchase or replenishment decisions can be programmed. Finally, a stockout of a class C item can be as crucial as for a class A or B item, but the inventory holding cost of class C items tends to be low. These features suggest that higher inventory levels can be tolerated and that more safety stock, larger lot sizes, and perhaps even a visual system, which we discuss later, may suffice for class C items. See Solved Problem 2 for a detailed example of ABC analysis.

FIGURE 10.1

Typical Chart from ABC Analysis

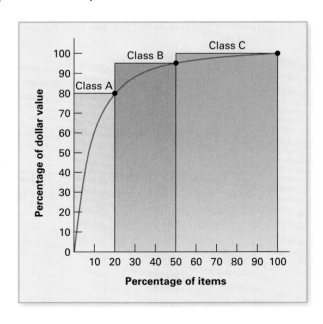

ECONOMIC ORDER QUANTITY

economic order quantity (EOQ) The lot size that minimizes total annual inventory holding and ordering costs.

Recall that managers face conflicting pressures to keep inventories low enough to avoid excess inventory holding costs but high enough to reduce the frequency of orders and setups. A good starting point for balancing these conflicting pressures and determining the best cycle-inventory level for an item is finding the **economic order quantity (EOQ)**, which is the lot size that minimizes total annual inventory holding and ordering costs. The approach to determining the EOQ is based on the following assumptions:

1. The demand rate for the item is constant (e.g., always 10 units per day) and known with certainty.

2. There are no constraints (e.g., truck capacity or materials handling limitations) on the size of each lot.

3. The only two relevant costs are the inventory holding cost and the fixed cost per lot for ordering or setup.

4. Decisions for one item can be made independently of decisions for other items (i.e., no advantage is gained in combining several orders going to the same supplier).

5. There is no uncertainty in lead time or supply. The lead time is constant (e.g., always 14 days) and known with certainty. The amount received is exactly what was ordered and it arrives all at once rather than piecemeal.

The economic order quantity will be optimal when the five assumptions are satisfied. In reality, few situations are so simple and well behaved. In fact, different lot-sizing approaches are needed to reflect quantity discounts, uneven demand rates, or interactions between items (see Supplement H, "Special Inventory Models" on the Student CD-ROM). However, the EOQ often is a reasonable first approximation of average lot sizes, even when one or more of the assumptions do not quite apply.

CALCULATING THE EOQ

How much should be ordered?

We begin by formulating the total cost for any lot size Q. Next, we derive the EOQ, which is the Q that minimizes total cost. Finally, we describe how to convert the EOQ into a companion measure, the elapsed time between orders.

When the EOQ assumptions are satisfied, cycle inventory behaves as shown in Figure 10.2. A cycle begins with Q units held in inventory, which happens when a new order is received. During the cycle, on-hand inventory is used at a constant rate and,

FIGURE 10.2

Cycle-Inventory Levels

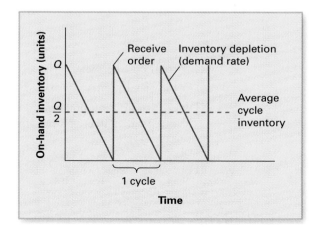

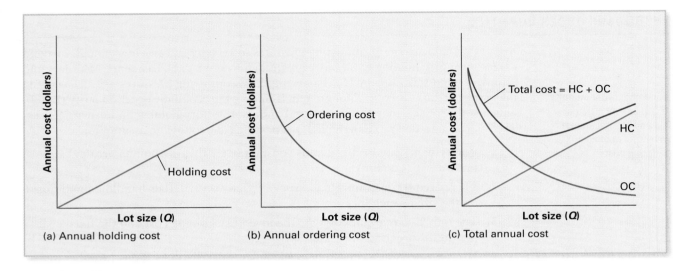

(a) Annual holding cost   (b) Annual ordering cost   (c) Total annual cost

Graphs of Annual Holding, Ordering, and Total Costs

because demand is known with certainty and the lead time is a constant, a new lot can be ordered so that inventory falls to 0 precisely when the new lot is received. Because inventory varies uniformly between Q and 0, the average cycle inventory equals half the lot size, Q.

The annual holding cost for this amount of inventory, which increases linearly with Q, as Figure 10.3(a) shows, is

Annual holding cost = (Average cycle inventory)(Unit holding cost)

The annual ordering cost is

Annual ordering cost = (Number of orders/year)(Ordering or setup cost)

The average number of orders per year equals annual demand divided by Q. For example, if 1,200 units must be ordered each year and the average lot size is 100 units, then 12 orders will be placed during the year. The annual ordering or setup cost decreases nonlinearly as Q increases, as shown in Figure 10.3(b), because fewer orders are placed.

The total annual cost,[2] as graphed in Figure 10.3(c), is the sum of the two cost components:

Total cost = Annual holding cost + Annual ordering or setup cost[3]

$$C = \frac{Q}{2}(H) + \frac{D}{Q}(S)$$

where

C = total cost per year

Q = lot size, in units

H = cost of holding one unit in inventory for a year, often calculated as a proportion of the item's value

---

[2] Expressing the total cost on an annual basis usually is convenient (though not necessary). Any time horizon can be selected, as long as D and H cover the same time period. If the total cost is calculated on a monthly basis, D must be monthly demand and H must be the cost of holding a unit for one month.

[3] The number of orders actually placed in any year is always a whole number, although the formula allows the use of fractional values. However, rounding is not needed because what is being calculated is an average for multiple years. Such averages often are nonintegers.

D = annual demand, in units per year

S = cost of ordering or setting up one lot, in dollars per lot

Consider the following example. A museum of natural history opened a gift shop two years ago. Managing inventories has become a problem. Low inventory turnover is squeezing profit margins and causing cash-flow problems. One of the top-selling items in the container group at the museum's gift shop is a birdfeeder. Sales are 18 units per week, and the supplier charges $60 per unit. The cost of placing an order with the supplier is $45. Annual holding cost is 25 percent of a feeder's value, and the museum operates 52 weeks per year. Management chose a 390-unit lot size so that new orders could be placed less frequently. Figure 10.4 displays the impact of using several Q values for the birdfeeder. Eight different lot sizes were evaluated in addition to the current one. Both holding and ordering costs were plotted, but their sum—the total cost curve—is the important feature. The graph shows that the best lot size, or EOQ, is the lowest point on the total cost curve, or between 50 and 100 units. Obviously, reducing the current lot-size policy ($Q = 390$) can result in significant savings.

A more efficient approach is to use the EOQ formula:

$$\text{EOQ} = \sqrt{\frac{2DS}{H}}$$

We use calculus to obtain the EOQ formula from the total cost formula. We take the first derivative of the total cost function with respect to Q, set it equal to 0, and solve for Q. As Figure 10.4 indicates, the EOQ is the order quantity for which annual holding cost equals annual ordering cost. Using this insight, we can also obtain the EOQ formula by equating the formulas for annual ordering cost and annual holding cost and solving for Q. The graph in Figure 10.4 also reveals that, when the annual holding cost for any Q exceeds the annual ordering cost, as with the 390-unit order, we can immediately conclude that Q is too big. A smaller Q reduces holding cost and increases ordering cost, bringing them into balance. Similarly, if the annual ordering cost exceeds the annual holding cost, Q should be increased.

FIGURE 10.4

Total Inventory Cost Function for Birdfeeder

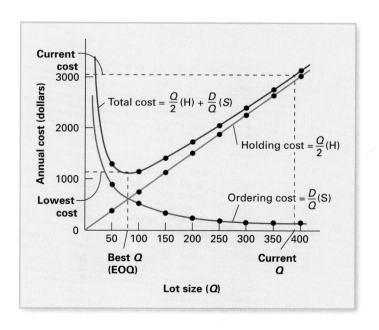

time between orders (TBO) The average elapsed time between receiving (or placing) replenishment orders of *Q* units for a particular lot size.

Sometimes inventory policies are based on the time between replenishment orders, rather than the number of units in the lot size. The **time between orders** (TBO) for a particular lot size is the average elapsed time between receiving (or placing) replenishment orders of *Q* units. Expressed as a fraction of a year, the TBO is simply *Q* divided by annual demand. When we use the EOQ and express time in terms of months, the TBO is

$$\text{TBO}_{\text{EOQ}} = \frac{\text{EOQ}}{D} \text{ (12 months/year)}$$

In Example 10.1, we show how to calculate TBO for years, months, weeks, and days.

EXAMPLE 10.1

TUTOR 10.3

Finding the EOQ, Total Cost, and TBO

For the birdfeeder example, calculate the EOQ and its total cost. How frequently will orders be placed if the EOQ is used?

SOLUTION

Using the formulas for EOQ and annual cost, we get

$$\text{EOQ} = \sqrt{\frac{2DS}{H}} = \sqrt{\frac{2(936)(45)}{15}} = 74.94, \quad \text{or} \quad 75 \text{ units}$$

Figure 10.5 shows that the total annual cost is much less than the $3,033 cost of the current policy of placing 390-unit orders.

When the EOQ is used, the time between orders (TBO) can be expressed in various ways for the same time period.

$$\text{TBO}_{\text{EOQ}} = \frac{\text{EOQ}}{D} = \frac{75}{936} = 0.080 \text{ year}$$

$$\text{TBO}_{\text{EOQ}} = \frac{\text{EOQ}}{D} \text{ (12 months/year)} = \frac{75}{936}(12) = 0.96 \text{ month}$$

$$\text{TBO}_{\text{EOQ}} = \frac{\text{EOQ}}{D} \text{ (52 weeks/year)} = \frac{75}{936}(52) = 4.17 \text{ weeks}$$

$$\text{TBO}_{\text{EOQ}} = \frac{\text{EOQ}}{D} \text{ (365 days/year)} = \frac{75}{936}(365) = 29.25 \text{ days}$$

Decision Point Using the EOQ, about 12 orders per year will be required. Using the current policy of 390 units per order, an average of 2.4 orders will be needed each year (every five months). The current policy saves on ordering costs but incurs a much larger cost for carrying the cycle inventory. While it is easy to see which option is best on the basis of total ordering and holding costs, other factors may affect the final decision. For example, if the supplier would

---

Parameters			
Current Lot Size (Q)	390	Economic Order Quantity	75
Demand (D)	936		
Order Cost (S)	$45		
Unit Holding Cost (H)	$15		
Annual Costs		**Annual Costs based on EOQ**	
Orders per Year	2.4	Orders per Year	12.48
Annual Ordering Cost	$108.00	Annual Ordering Cost	$561.60
Annual Holding Cost	$2,925.00	Annual Holding Cost	$562.50
Annual Inventory Cost	$3,033.00	Annual Inventory Cost	$1,124.10

FIGURE 10.5

reduce the price per unit for large orders, it may be better to order the larger quantity (see Supplement H, "Special Inventory Models" on the Student CD-ROM). ❏

UNDERSTANDING THE EFFECT OF CHANGES

How often should demand estimates, cost estimates, and lot sizes be updated?

Subjecting the EOQ formula to sensitivity analysis can yield valuable insights into the management of inventories. Sensitivity analysis is a technique for systematically changing crucial parameters to determine the effects of change (see Supplement A, "Decision Making" on the Student CD-ROM). Let us consider the effects on the EOQ when we substitute different values into the numerator or denominator of the formula.

A CHANGE IN THE DEMAND RATE. Because D is in the numerator, the EOQ (and, therefore, the best cycle-inventory level) increases in proportion to the square root of the annual demand. Therefore, when demand rises, the lot size also should rise but more slowly than actual demand.

A CHANGE IN THE SETUP COSTS. Because S is in the numerator, increasing S increases the EOQ and, consequently, the average cycle inventory. Conversely, reducing S reduces the EOQ, allowing smaller lot sizes to be produced economically. This relationship explains why manufacturers are so concerned about cutting setup time and costs. When weeks of supply decline, inventory turns increase. When setup cost and setup time become trivial, a major impediment to small-lot production is removed.

A CHANGE IN THE HOLDING COSTS. Because H is in the denominator, the EOQ declines when H increases. Conversely, when H declines, the EOQ increases. Larger lot sizes are justified by lower holding costs.

ERRORS IN ESTIMATING *D, H,* AND *S*. Total cost is fairly insensitive to errors, even when the estimates are wrong by a large margin. The reasons are that errors tend to cancel each other out and that the square root reduces the effect of the error. Suppose that we incorrectly estimate the holding cost to be double its true value—that is, we calculate EOQ using $2H$, instead of H. For Example 10.1, this 100 percent error increases total cost by only 6 percent, from \$1,124 to \$1,192. Thus, the EOQ lies in a fairly large zone of acceptable lot sizes, allowing managers to deviate somewhat from the EOQ to accommodate supplier contracts or storage constraints. See Solved Problems 3 and 4 for two examples demonstrating the sensitivity of order quantity decisions and total annual costs in the face of parameter estimation errors.

INVENTORY CONTROL SYSTEMS

independent demand items Items for which demand is influenced by market conditions and is not related to the inventory decisions for any other item held in stock.

The EOQ and other lot-sizing methods (see Supplement H, "Special Inventory Models" on the Student CD-ROM) answer the important question: How much should we order? Another important question that needs an answer is: When should we place the order? An inventory control system responds to both questions. In selecting an inventory control system for a particular application, the nature of the demands imposed on the inventory items is crucial. An important distinction between types of inventory is whether an item is subject to dependent or independent demand. Retailers and distributors must manage **independent demand items**—that is, items for which demand is influenced by market conditions and is not related to the inventory decisions for any other item held in stock. Independent demand inventory includes

1. wholesale and retail merchandise

2. service industry inventory, such as stamps and mailing labels for post offices, office supplies for law firms, and laboratory supplies for research universities

3. end-item and replacement-part distribution inventories

4. maintenance, repair, and operating (MRO) supplies—that is, items that don't become part of the final product or service, such as employee uniforms, fuel, paint, and machine repair parts

How can inventory be controlled if fixing the lot-size quantity is advantageous?

Managing independent demand inventory can be tricky because demand is influenced by external factors. For example, the owner of a bookstore may not be sure how many copies of the latest best-seller customers will purchase during the coming month. As a result, she may decide to stock extra copies as a safeguard. Independent demand such as the demand for various book titles must be forecasted (see Chapter 9, "Forecasting").

In this chapter, we focus on inventory control systems for independent demand items, which is the type of demand the bookstore owner, other retailers, and distributors face. Even though demand from any one customer is difficult to predict, low demand from some customers often is offset by high demand from others. Thus, total demand for any independent demand item may follow a relatively smooth pattern, with some random fluctuations. *Dependent demand items* are those required as components or inputs to a product or service. Dependent demand exhibits a pattern very different from that of independent demand and must be managed with different techniques (see Chapter 12, "Resource Planning").

In this section, we discuss and compare two inventory control systems: the continuous review system, called a Q system, and the periodic review system, called a P system. We close with a look at hybrid systems, which incorporate features of both the P and Q systems.

CONTINUOUS REVIEW (Q) SYSTEM

continuous review (Q) system A system designed to track the remaining inventory of an item each time a withdrawal is made to determine whether it is time to replenish.

reorder point (ROP) system See **Continuous review (Q) system.**

inventory position (IP) The measurement of an item's ability to satisfy future demand.

scheduled receipts (SR) Orders that have been placed but not yet received.

open orders See **Scheduled receipts (SR).**

reorder point (R) The predetermined minimum level that an inventory position must reach before a fixed quantity Q of the item is ordered.

A **continuous review (Q) system,** sometimes called a **reorder point (ROP) system** or fixed order-quantity system, tracks the remaining inventory of an item each time a withdrawal is made to determine whether it is time to reorder. In practice, these reviews are done frequently (e.g., daily) and often continuously (after each withdrawal). The advent of computers and electronic cash registers linked to inventory records has made continuous reviews easy. At each review a decision is made about an item's inventory position. If it is judged to be too low, the system triggers a new order. The **inventory position** (IP) measures the item's ability to satisfy future demand. It includes **scheduled receipts (SR),** which are orders that have been placed but not yet received, plus on-hand inventory (OH) minus backorders (BO). Sometimes scheduled receipts are called **open orders.** More specifically,

$$\text{Inventory position} = \text{On-hand inventory} + \text{Scheduled receipts} - \text{Backorders}$$
$$\text{IP} = \text{OH} + \text{SR} - \text{BO}$$

When the inventory position reaches a predetermined minimum level, called the **reorder point (R),** a fixed quantity Q of the item is ordered. In a continuous review system, although the order quantity Q is fixed, the time between orders can vary. Hence, Q can be based on the EOQ, a price break quantity (the minimum lot size that qualifies for a quantity discount), a container size (such as a truckload), or some other quantity selected by management.

SELECTING THE REORDER POINT WHEN DEMAND IS CERTAIN. To demonstrate the concept of a reorder point, suppose that the demand for feeders at the museum gift shop in

FIGURE 10.6

Q System When Demand and Lead Time Are Constant and Certain

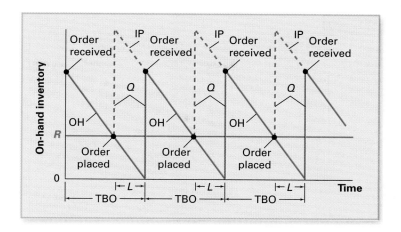

Example 10.1 is always 18 per week, the lead time is a constant two weeks, and the supplier always ships on time the exact amount ordered. With both demand and lead time certain, the museum's buyer can wait until the inventory position drops to 36 units, or (18 units/week)(2 weeks), to place a new order. Thus, in this case, the reorder point, R, equals the *demand during lead time*, with no added allowance for safety stock.

Figure 10.6 shows how the system operates when demand and lead time are constant. The downward-sloping line represents the on-hand inventory, which is being depleted at a constant rate. When it reaches reorder point R (the horizontal line), a new order for Q units is placed. The on-hand inventory continues to drop throughout lead time L until the order is received. At that time, which marks the end of the lead time, on-hand inventory jumps by Q units. A new order arrives just when inventory drops to 0. The time between orders (TBO) is the same for each cycle.

The inventory position, IP, shown in Figure 10.6 corresponds to the on-hand inventory, except during the lead time. Just after a new order is placed, at the start of the lead time, IP increases by Q, as shown by the dashed line. The IP exceeds OH by this same margin throughout the lead time.[4] At the end of the lead time, when the scheduled receipts convert to on-hand inventory, IP = OH once again. The key point here is to compare IP, not OH, with R in deciding whether to reorder. A common error is to ignore scheduled receipts or backorders.

SELECTING THE REORDER POINT WHEN DEMAND IS UNCERTAIN. In reality, demand and lead times are not always predictable. For instance, the museum's buyer knows that *average* demand is 18 feeders per week and that the *average* lead time is two weeks. That is, a variable number of feeders may be purchased during the lead time, with an average demand during lead time of 36 feeders (assuming that each week's demand is identically distributed). This situation gives rise to the need for safety stocks. Suppose that she sets R at 46 units, thereby placing orders before they typically are needed. This approach will create a safety stock, or stock held in excess of expected demand, of 10 units (46 − 36) to buffer against uncertain demand. In general,

$$\text{Reorder point} = \text{Average demand during lead time} + \text{Safety stock}$$

Figure 10.7 shows how the Q system operates when demand is variable and uncertain. We assume that the variability in lead times is negligible and, therefore, can be

---

[4] A possible exception is the unlikely situation when more than one scheduled receipt is open at the same time because of long lead times.

FIGURE 10.7

*Q System When
Demand Is Uncertain*

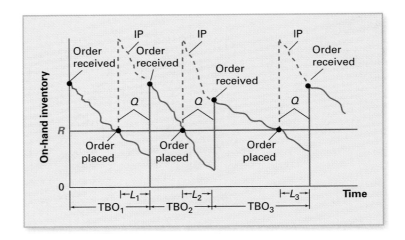

FIGURE 10.7

*Q System When
Demand Is Uncertain*

treated as a constant, as we did in the development of the EOQ model. The wavy downward-sloping line indicates that demand varies from day to day. Its slope is steeper in the second cycle, which means that the demand rate is higher during this time period. The changing demand rate means that the time between orders changes, so $TBO_1 \neq TBO_2 \neq TBO_3$. Because of uncertain demand, sales during lead time are unpredictable, and safety stock is added to hedge against lost sales. This addition is why R is higher in Figure 10.7 than in Figure 10.6. It also explains why the on-hand inventory usually doesn't drop to 0 by the time a replenishment order arrives. The greater the safety stock and, thus, the higher reorder point R, the less likely a stockout.

Because the average demand during lead time is variable and uncertain, the real decision to be made when selecting R concerns the safety stock level. Deciding on a small or large safety stock is a trade-off between customer service and inventory holding costs. Cost minimization models can be used to find the best safety stock, but they require estimates of stockout and backorder costs, which are usually difficult to make with any precision. The usual approach for determining R is for management—based on judgment—to set a reasonable service-level policy for the inventory and then determine the safety stock level that satisfies this policy.

CHOOSING AN APPROPRIATE SERVICE-LEVEL POLICY. Managers must weigh the benefits of holding safety stock against the cost of holding it. One way to determine the safety stock is to set a **service level**, or **cycle-service level**—the desired probability of not running out of stock in any one ordering cycle, which begins at the time an order is placed and ends when it arrives in stock. In a bookstore, the manager may select a 90 percent cycle-service level for a book. In other words, the probability is 90 percent that demand will not exceed the supply *during the lead time*. The probability of running short during the lead time, creating a stockout or backorder, is only 10 percent $(100 - 90)$. This stockout risk, which occurs only during the lead time in the Q system, is greater than the overall risk of stockout because the risk is nonexistent outside the ordering cycle.

To translate this policy into a specific safety stock level, we must know how demand during the lead time is distributed. If demand varies little around its average, safety stock can be small. Conversely, if demand during lead time varies greatly from one order cycle to the next, the safety stock must be large. Variability is measured with probability distributions, which are specified by a mean and a variance.

FINDING THE SAFETY STOCK. When selecting the safety stock, the inventory planner often assumes that demand during lead time is normally distributed, as shown in

service level The desired probability of not running out of stock in any one ordering cycle, which begins at the time an order is placed and ends when it arrives in stock.

cycle-service level See Service level.

*Finding Safety Stock
with a Normal
Probability Distribution
for an 85 Percent
Cycle-Service Level*

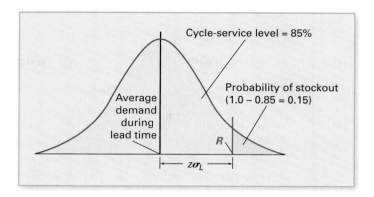

Figure 10.8. The average demand during the lead time is the centerline of the graph, with 50 percent of the area under the curve to the left and 50 percent to the right. Thus, if a cycle-service level of 50 percent were chosen, reorder point R would be the quantity represented by this centerline. As R equals demand during the lead time plus the safety stock, the safety stock is 0 when R equals this average demand. Demand is less than average 50 percent of the time and, thus, having no safety stock will be sufficient only 50 percent of the time.

To provide a service level above 50 percent, the reorder point must be greater than average demand during the lead time. In Figure 10.8, that requires moving the reorder point to the right of the centerline so that more than 50 percent of the area under the curve is to the left of R. An 85 percent cycle-service level is achieved in Figure 10.8, with 85 percent of the area under the curve to the left of R (in blue) and only 15 percent to the right (in pink). We compute the safety stock by multiplying the number of standard deviations from the mean needed to implement the cycle-service level, z, by the standard deviation of demand during lead time probability distribution[5], σ_L:

$$\text{Safety stock} = z\sigma_L$$

The higher the value of z, the higher the safety stock and the cycle-service level should be. If $z = 0$, there is no safety stock, and stockouts will occur during 50 percent of the order cycles.

Finding the Safety Stock and R

**TUTOR
10.4**

Records show that the demand for dishwasher detergent during the lead time is normally distributed, with an average of 250 boxes and $\sigma_L = 22$. What safety stock should be carried for a 99 percent cycle-service level? What is R?

SOLUTION

The first step is to find z, the number of standard deviations to the right of average demand during the lead time that places 99 percent of the area under the curve to the left of that point (0.9900 in the body of the table in the Normal Distribution appendix). The closest number in the table is 0.9901, which corresponds to 2.3 in the row heading and 0.03 in the column heading.

---

[5] Some inventory planners using manual systems prefer to work with the mean absolute deviation (MAD) rather than the standard deviation because it is easier to calculate. To approximate the standard deviation you simply multiply the MAD by 1.25. Then proceed to calculate the safety stock.

Adding these values gives a z of 2.33. With this information, you can calculate the safety stock and reorder point:

$$\text{Safety stock} = z\sigma_L = 2.33(22) = 51.3, \quad \text{or} \quad 51 \text{ boxes}$$

$$\text{Reorder point} = \text{Average demand during lead time} + \text{Safety stock}$$

$$= 250 + 51 = 301 \text{ boxes}$$

We rounded the safety stock to the nearest whole number. In this case, the theoretical cycle-service level will be less than 99 percent. Raising the safety stock to 52 boxes will yield a cycle-service level greater than 99 percent.

Decision Point Management can control the quantity of safety stock by choosing a service level. Another approach to reducing safety stock is to reduce the standard deviation of demand during the lead time, which can be accomplished by closer coordination with major customers through information technology. ⌐

Finding the appropriate reorder point and safety stock in practice requires estimating the demand distribution for the lead time. Sometimes average demand during the lead time and the standard deviation of demand during the lead time, σ_L, are not directly available and must be calculated by combining information on the demand rate with information on the lead time. There are two reasons for this additional calculation.

1. Developing estimates first for demand and then for the lead time may be easier. Demand information comes from the customer, whereas lead times come from the supplier.

2. Records are not likely to be collected for a time interval that is exactly the same as the lead time. The same inventory control system may be used to manage thousands of different items, each with a different lead time. For example, if demand is reported *weekly*, records can be used directly to compute the average and the standard deviation of demand during the lead time if the lead time is exactly one week. However, the average and standard deviation of demand during the lead time for a lead time of three weeks are more difficult to determine.

We can get at the more difficult case by making some reasonable assumptions. Suppose that the average demand, d, is known along with the standard deviation of demand, σ_t, over some time interval t (say, days or weeks), where t does not equal the lead time. Also, suppose that the probability distributions of demand for each time interval t are identical and independent of each other. For example, if the time interval is a week, the probability distributions of demand are the same each week (identical d and σ_t), and the total demand in one week does not affect the total demand in another week. Let L be the constant lead time, expressed as a multiple (or fraction) of t. If t represents a week and the lead time is three weeks, $L = 3$. Under these assumptions, average demand during the lead time will be the sum of the averages for each of the L identical and independent distributions of demand, or $d + d + d + \cdots = dL$. In addition, the variance of the demand distribution for the lead time will be the sum of the variances of the L identical and independent distributions of demand, or $\sigma_t^2 + \sigma_t^2 + \sigma_t^2 + \cdots = \sigma_t^2 L$. Finally, the standard deviation of the sum of two or more identically distributed independent random variables is the square root of the sum of their variances, or

$$\sigma_L = \sqrt{\sigma_t^2 L} = \sigma_t \sqrt{L}$$

Figure 10.9 shows how the demand distribution for the lead time is developed from the individual distributions of weekly demands, where $d = 75$, $\sigma_t = 15$, and $L = 3$ weeks. In this case, average demand during the lead time is $(75)(3) = 225$ units and

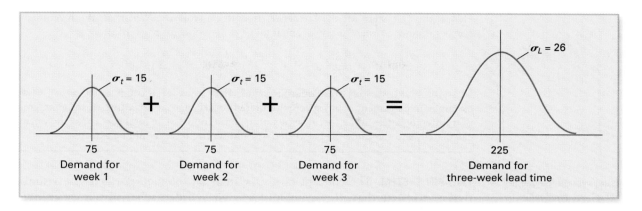

FIGURE 10.9

*Development of
Demand Distribution
for the Lead Time*

$\sigma_L = 15\sqrt{3} = 25.98$, or 26. More complex formulas or simulation must be used when both demand and the lead time are variable or when the supply is uncertain. In such cases, the safety stock must be larger than otherwise.

CALCULATING TOTAL Q SYSTEM COSTS. Total costs for the continuous review (Q) system is the sum of three cost components:

Total Q system cost = Annual cycle inventory holding cost + Annual ordering cost + Annual safety stock holding cost

$$C = \frac{Q}{2}(H) + \frac{D}{Q}(S) + Hz\,\sigma_L$$

The annual cycle inventory holding cost and annual ordering costs are the same equations we used for computing the annual cost for the EOQ. The annual cost of holding the safety stock is computed under the assumption that the safety stock is on hand all the time. Referring to Figure 10.7, in each order cycle, sometimes, we will have experienced a demand greater than the average demand during lead time, and sometimes we will have experienced less. On average over the year, we can assume the safety stock will be on hand.

EXAMPLE 10.3

Finding the Safety Stock and R When the Demand Distribution for the Lead Time Must Be Developed

Let's return to the birdfeeder example. Suppose that the average demand is 18 units per week with a standard deviation of 5 units. The lead time is constant at two weeks. Determine the safety stock and reorder point if management wants a 90 percent cycle-service level. What is the total cost of the Q system?

SOLUTION

In this case, $t = 1$ week, $d = 18$, and $L = 2$, so

$$\sigma_L = \sigma_t\sqrt{L} = 5\sqrt{2} = 7.1$$

Consult the body of the normal table for 0.9000, which corresponds to a 90 percent cycle-service level. The closest number is 0.8997, which corresponds to a z value of 1.28. With this information, we calculate the safety stock and reorder point as follows:

Safety stock = $z\sigma_L = 1.28(7.1) = 9.1$,   or   9 units

Reorder point = dL + Safety stock
$$= 2(18) + 9 = 45 \text{ units}$$

Hence, the Q system for the birdfeeder operates as follows: Whenever the inventory position reaches 45 units, order 75 units. The total Q system cost for the birdfeeder is

$$C = \frac{75}{2}(\$15) + \frac{936}{75}(\$45) + 9(\$15) = \$562.50 + \$561.60 + \$135 = \$1{,}259.10$$

Decision Point Various order quantities and safety stock levels can be used in the Q system. For example, management could specify a different order quantity (because of shipping constraints) or a different safety stock (because of storage limitations). The total costs of such systems can be calculated, and the trade-off between costs and service levels could be assessed. ⊐

visual system A system that allows employees to place orders when inventory visibly reaches a certain marker.

TWO-BIN SYSTEM. The concept of a Q system can be incorporated in a **visual system,** that is, a system that allows employees to place orders when inventory visibly reaches a certain marker. Visual systems are easy to administer because records are not kept on the current inventory position. The historical usage rate can simply be reconstructed from past purchase orders. Visual systems are intended for use with low-value items that have a steady demand, such as nuts and bolts or office supplies. Overstocking is common, but the extra inventory holding cost is minimal because the items have relatively little value.

two-bin system A visual system version of the *Q* system, in which an item's inventory is stored at two different locations.

A visual system version of the Q system is the **two-bin system** in which an item's inventory is stored at two different locations. Inventory is first withdrawn from one bin. If the first bin is empty, the second bin provides backup to cover demand until a replenishment order arrives. An empty first bin signals the need to place a new order. Premade order forms placed near the bins let workers send one to purchasing or even directly to the supplier. When the new order arrives, the second bin is restored to its normal level and the rest is put in the first bin. The two-bin system operates like a Q system, with the normal level in the second bin being the reorder point R. The system also may be implemented with just one bin by marking the bin at the reorder point level.

PERIODIC REVIEW (*P*) SYSTEM

How can inventories be controlled if the time between replenishment orders should be fixed?

An alternative inventory control system is the **periodic review (*P*) system,** sometimes called a *fixed interval reorder system* or *periodic reorder system,* in which an item's inventory position is reviewed periodically rather than continuously. Such a system can simplify delivery scheduling because it establishes a routine. A new order is always placed at the end of each review, and the time between orders (TBO) is fixed at P. Demand is a random variable, so total demand between reviews varies. In a P system, the lot size, Q, may change from one order to the next, but the time between orders is fixed. An example of a periodic review system is that of a soft-drink supplier making weekly rounds of grocery stores. Each week the supplier reviews the store's inventory of soft drinks and restocks the store with enough items to meet demand and safety stock requirements until the next week.

periodic review (*P*) system A system in which an item's inventory position is reviewed periodically rather than continuously.

Four of the original EOQ assumptions are maintained: that there are no constraints on the size of the lot, that the relevant costs are holding and ordering costs, that decisions for one item are independent of decisions for other items, and that there is no uncertainty in lead times or supply. However, demand uncertainty is again allowed for. Figure 10.10 shows the periodic review system under these assumptions. The downward-sloping line again represents on-hand inventory. When the predetermined time, P, has elapsed since the last review, an order is placed to bring the inventory position, represented by the dashed line, up to the target inventory level, T. The lot size for the first review is Q_1, or the difference between inventory position IP_1 and T. As with the continuous review system, IP and OH differ only during the lead time. When the order arrives, at the end of the lead time, OH and IP again are identical. Figure 10.10 shows that lot sizes vary from one

FIGURE 10.10

*P System When
Demand Is Uncertain*

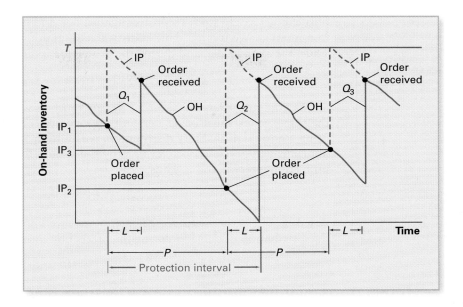

order cycle to the next. Because the inventory position is lower at the second review, a greater quantity is needed to achieve an inventory level of T.

SELECTING THE TIME BETWEEN REVIEWS. To run a P system, managers must make two decisions: the length of time between reviews, P, and the target inventory level, T. Let us first consider the time between reviews, P. It can be any convenient interval, such as each Friday or every other Friday. Another option is to base P on the cost trade-offs of the EOQ. In other words, P can be set equal to the average time between orders for the economic order quantity, or TBO_{EOQ}. Because demand is variable, some orders will be larger than the EOQ and some will be smaller. However, over an extended period of time, the average lot size should equal the EOQ. If other models are used to determine the lot size (e.g., those described in Supplement H, "Special Inventory Models" on the Student CD-ROM), we divide the lot size chosen by the annual demand, D, and use this ratio as P. It will be expressed as the fraction of a year between orders, which can be converted into months, weeks, or days as needed.

protection interval The
time interval for which
inventory must be planned
when each new order is
placed.

SELECTING THE TARGET INVENTORY LEVEL. Now let us consider how to calculate the target inventory level, T. Figure 10.10 reveals that an order must be large enough to make the inventory position, IP, last beyond the next review, which is P time periods away. At that time a new order is placed, but it does not arrive until after the lead time, L. Therefore, as Figure 10.10 shows, a **protection interval** of $P + L$ periods is needed, or the time interval for which inventory must be planned when each new order is placed. A fundamental difference between the Q and P systems is the length of time needed for stockout protection. A Q system needs stockout protection only during the lead time because orders can be placed as soon as they are needed and will be received L periods later. A P system, however, needs stockout protection for the longer $P + L$ protection interval because orders are placed only at fixed intervals and the inventory isn't checked until the next designated review time.

As with the Q system, we need to develop the appropriate distribution of demand during the protection interval to specify the system fully. In a P system, we must develop the distribution of demand for $P + L$ time periods. The target inventory level T must equal the expected demand during the protection interval of $P + L$ periods, plus enough safety stock to protect against demand uncertainty over this same protection interval. We use the same statistical assumptions that we made for the Q system. Thus, the average demand during the protection interval is $d(P + L)$, or

$$T = d(P + L) + (\text{Safety stock for protection interval})$$

We compute safety stock for a P system much as we did for the Q system. However, the safety stock must cover demand uncertainty for a longer period of time. When using a normal probability distribution, we multiply the desired standard deviations to implement the cycle-service level, z, by the standard deviation of demand during the protection interval, σ_{P+L}. Thus,

$$\text{Safety stock} = z\sigma_{P+L}$$

Based on our earlier logic for calculating σ_L, we know that the standard deviation of the distribution of demand during the protection interval is

$$\sigma_{P+L} = \sigma_t \sqrt{P + L}$$

Because a P system requires safety stock to cover demand uncertainty over a longer time period than a Q system, a P system requires more safety stock; that is, σ_{P+L} exceeds σ_L. Hence, to gain the convenience of a P system requires that overall inventory levels be somewhat higher than those for a Q system.

CALCULATING TOTAL *P* SYSTEM COSTS. The total costs for the P system are the sum of the same three cost elements as for the Q system. The differences are in the calculation of the order quantity and the safety stock. Referring to Figure 10.10, the average order quantity will be the average consumption of inventory during the P periods between orders. Consequently, $Q = dP$. Total costs for the P system are

$$C = \frac{dp}{2}\,(H) + \frac{D}{dp}\,(S) + Hz\sigma_{P+L}$$

The Managerial Practice feature shows how Hewlett-Packard implemented a periodic review system for many of its business units.

EXAMPLE 10.4   *Calculating P and T*

**TUTOR
10.5**

Again let us return to the birdfeeder example. Recall that demand for the birdfeeder is normally distributed with a mean of 18 units per week and a standard deviation in weekly demand of 5 units. The lead time is 2 weeks, and the business operates 52 weeks per year. The Q system developed in Example 10.3 called for an EOQ of 75 units and a safety stock of 9 units for a cycle-service level of 90 percent. What is the equivalent P system? What is the total cost? Answers are to be rounded to the nearest integer.

SOLUTION

We first define D and then P. Here P is the time between reviews, expressed as a multiple (or fraction) of time interval t ($t = 1$ week because the data are expressed as demand *per week*):

$$D = (18 \text{ units/week})(52 \text{ weeks/year}) = 936 \text{ units}$$

$$P = \frac{EOQ}{D}\,(52) = \frac{75}{936}\,(52) = 4.2, \quad \text{or} \quad 4 \text{ weeks}$$

MANAGERIAL PRACTICE
Implementing a Periodic Review Inventory System at Hewlett-Packard

Hewlett-Packard (www.hp.com) manufactures computers, accessories, and a wide variety of instrumentation devices in more than 100 separate businesses, each responsible for its own product designing, marketing, and manufacturing processes as well as the required inventories to service its customers. At most HP businesses, inventory-driven costs (which include currency devaluation, obsolescence, price protection, and financing) are now the biggest control lever that the manufacturing organization has on business performance, measured in terms of return on assets or economic value added. Inventory is a major cost driver and the most variable element on the balance sheet.

Most of HP's business units were inefficient, carrying more inventory than needed in order to achieve a desired level of product delivery performance. They often used simplified approaches such as ABC analysis to determine their safety stocks for independent demand items, ignoring supply or demand uncertainty, part commonality, desired part availability, or cost. The solution was to develop a periodic review system that used part availability targets and included as many uncertainties as possible. The system, although in principle similar to the *P* system discussed in this chapter, uses complex equations to determine the review interval and target inventory parameters. The complexity arises from considering uncertainties in supply as well as demand in the determination of the safety stocks.

Even though the system could be shown to reduce inventories and improve customer service, no benefits would be realized until the planning and procurement staff actually used it. Since each business unit had some unique characteristics, the results had to be easily understandable and credible, and the system had to be easily configurable to each situation. Consequently, HP developed a software wizard that allows the user to enter product data and costs in a friendly environment, develops the equations for the periodic review system, and then translates the results to the user's format requirements. The wizard is programmed in Excel, which allows users access to all of Excel's functionality for conducting their own analyses.

The periodic review system and the software wizard have been very successful. At HP's Integrated Circuit Manufacturing Division, for example, planners cut inventories by $1.6 million while simultaneously improving on-time delivery performance from 93 percent to 97 percent. Other benefits included less expediting, fewer disagreements about operating policy, and more control of the production system. The system is used across a wide variety of product lines and geographies worldwide. HP believes that, without exception, the product lines now have more efficient operations.

Source: Cargille, Brian, Steve Kakouros, and Robert Hall. "Part Tool, Part Process: Inventory Optimization at Hewlett-Packard Co." *OR/MS TODAY* (October 1999), pp. 18–24.

With $d = 18$ units per week, we can also calculate P by dividing the EOQ by d to get $75/18 = 4.2$, or 4 weeks. Hence, we would review the birdfeeder inventory every 4 weeks. We now find the standard deviation of demand over the protection interval ($P + L = 6$):

$$\sigma_{P+L} = \sigma_t\sqrt{P + L} = 5\sqrt{6} = 12 \text{ units}$$

Before calculating T, we also need a z value. For a 90 percent cycle-service level, $z = 1.28$ (see the Normal Distribution appendix). We now solve for T:

$$\text{T = Average demand during the protection interval + Safety stock}$$
$$= d(P + L) + z\sigma_{P+L}$$
$$= (18 \text{ units/week})(6 \text{ weeks}) + 1.28(12 \text{ units}) = 123 \text{ units}$$

Every 4 weeks we would order the number of units needed to bring inventory position IP (counting the new order) up to the target inventory level of 123 units. The safety stock for this P system is $1.28(12) = 15$ units.

The total *P* system cost for the birdfeeder is

$$C = \frac{4(18)}{2}\,(\$15) + \frac{936}{4(18)}\,(\$45) + 15(\$15) = \$540 + \$585 + \$225 = \$1,350$$

Decision Point The *P* system requires 15 units in safety stock, while the *Q* system only needs 9 units. If cost were the only criterion, the *Q* system would be the choice for the birdfeeder. As we discuss in the next section, there are other factors that may sway the decision in favor of the *P* system. ◻

SINGLE-BIN SYSTEM. The concept of a *P* system can be translated into a simple visual system of inventory control. In the **single-bin system**, a maximum level is marked on the storage shelf or bin on a measuring rod, and the inventory is brought up to the mark periodically—say, once a week. The single bin may be, for example, a gasoline storage tank at a service station or a storage bin for small parts at a manufacturing plant.

COMPARATIVE ADVANTAGES OF THE *Q* AND *P* SYSTEMS
Neither the *Q* nor *P* system is best for all situations. Three *P*-system advantages must be balanced against three *Q*-system advantages. The advantages of one system are implicitly disadvantages of the other one. The primary advantages of *P* systems are the following:

1. Administration of the system is convenient because replenishments are made at fixed intervals. Employees can regularly set aside a day or part of a day to concentrate on this particular task. Fixed replenishment intervals also allow for standardized pickup and delivery times.
2. Orders for multiple items from the same supplier may be combined into a single purchase order. This approach reduces ordering and transportation costs and may result in a price break from the supplier.
3. The inventory position, IP, needs to be known only when a review is made (not continuously, as in a *Q* system). However, this advantage is moot for firms using computerized record-keeping systems, in which a transaction is reported upon each receipt or withdrawal. When inventory records are always current, the system is called a **perpetual inventory system**.

The primary advantages of *Q* systems are the following:

1. The review frequency of each item may be individualized. Tailoring the review frequency to the item can reduce total ordering and holding costs.
2. Fixed lot sizes, if large enough, may result in quantity discounts. Physical limitations such as truckload capacities, materials handling methods, and furnace capacities also may require a fixed lot size.
3. Lower safety stocks result in savings.

In conclusion, the choice between *Q* and *P* systems is not clear-cut. Which one is better depends on the relative importance of its advantages in various situations. Management must weigh each alternative carefully in selecting the best system.

HYBRID SYSTEMS

Various hybrid inventory control systems merge some but not all the features of the *P* and *Q* systems. We briefly examine two such systems: optional replenishment and base stock.

OPTIONAL REPLENISHMENT SYSTEM. Sometimes called the optional review, min–max, or (s, S) system, the **optional replenishment system** is much like the P system. It is used to review the inventory position at fixed time intervals and, if the position has dropped to (or below) a predetermined level, to place a variable-sized order to cover expected needs. The new order is large enough to bring the inventory position up to a target inventory, similar to T for the P system. However, orders are not placed after a review unless the inventory position has dropped to the predetermined minimum level. The minimum level acts as reorder point R does in a Q system. If the target is 100 and the minimum level is 60, the minimum order size is 40 (or 100 − 60). The optional review system avoids continuous reviews and so is particularly attractive when both review and ordering costs are significant.

BASE-STOCK SYSTEM. In its simplest form, the **base-stock system** issues a replenishment order, Q, each time a withdrawal is made, for the same amount as the withdrawal. This one-for-one replacement policy maintains the inventory position at a base-stock level equal to expected demand during the lead time plus safety stock. The base-stock level, therefore, is equivalent to the reorder point in a Q system. However, order quantities now vary to keep the inventory position at R at all times. Because this position is the lowest IP possible that will maintain a specified service level, the base-stock system may be used to minimize cycle inventory. More orders are placed but each is smaller. This system is appropriate for very expensive items, such as replacement engines for jet airplanes. No more inventory is held than the maximum demand expected until a replacement order can be received. The base-stock system is used in just-in-time systems (see Chapter 13, "Lean Systems").

INVENTORY RECORD ACCURACY

Regardless of the inventory system in use, record accuracy is crucial to its success. One method of achieving and maintaining accuracy is to assign responsibility to specific employees for issuing and receiving materials and accurately reporting each transaction. A second method is to secure inventory behind locked doors or gates to prevent unauthorized or unreported withdrawals. This method also guards against storing new receipts in the wrong locations, where they can be lost for months. **Cycle counting** is a third method, whereby storeroom personnel physically count a small percentage of the total number of items each day, correcting errors that they find. Class A items are counted most frequently. A final method for computerized systems is to make logic error checks on each transaction reported and fully investigate any discrepancies. Discrepancies may include (1) actual receipts when there is no record of scheduled receipts, (2) disbursements that exceed the current on-hand balance, and (3) receipts with an inaccurate (nonexistent) part number.

These four methods can keep inventory record accuracy within acceptable bounds. Accuracy pays off mainly through better customer service, although some inventory reductions can be achieved by improving accuracy. A side benefit is that auditors may not require end-of-year counts if records prove to be sufficiently accurate.

INVENTORY MANAGEMENT ACROSS THE ORGANIZATION

Inventories are important to all types of organizations and their employees. Inventories affect everyday operations because they must be counted, paid for, used in operations, used to satisfy customers, and managed. Inventories require an investment of funds, as does the purchase of a new machine. Monies invested in inventory are not available for investment in other things; thus, they represent a drain on the cash flows of an organization. Carrying that notion to its extreme, one may conclude that inventories should be eliminated. Not only is that idea impossible but also it is hazardous to the financial health of an organization.

We have focused on independent demand inventories in this chapter. These inventories are often found in retail and distribution operations. Consequently, independent demand inventories are often the last stocking point before the consumer. Companies concerned with customer service know that availability of products is a key selling point in many markets. Earlier we discussed Internet retail companies that have discovered a competitive advantage by controlling their own inventories rather than outsourcing that function to someone else. The consequences in Internet markets for lack of supply are dire—plummeting stock prices, financial restructuring, outsider acquisition, or bankruptcy.

Is inventory a boon or a bane? Certainly, profitability is reduced if there is too much inventory, and customer confidence is damaged if there is too little inventory. The goal should not be to minimize inventory or to maximize customer service but rather to have the right amount to support the competitive priorities of the company. The Internet has provided many alternatives for a successful business model. To date we have seen pure Internet companies, combinations of Internet and bricks and mortar, and totally bricks and mortar. Each of these models provides a different set of capabilities and opportunities to exploit different competitive priorities. Regardless of the model, inventory management will play a major role.

EQUATION SUMMARY

1. Cycle inventory $= \dfrac{Q}{2}$

2. Pipeline inventory $= dL$

3. Total annual cost $=$ Annual holding cost $+$ Annual ordering or setup cost

$$C = \frac{Q}{2}\,(H) + \frac{D}{Q}\,(S)$$

4. Economic order quantity: $EOQ = \sqrt{\dfrac{2DS}{H}}$

5. Time between orders, expressed in weeks: $TBO_{EOQ} = \dfrac{EOQ}{D}\,(52 \text{ weeks/year})$

6. Inventory position $=$ On-hand inventory $+$ Scheduled receipts $-$ Backorders

$$IP = OH + SR - BO$$

7. Continuous review system:

    Reorder point (R) $=$ Average demand during the protection interval $+$ Safety stock

$$= dL + z\sigma_L$$

    Protection interval $=$ Lead time (L)

    Standard deviation of demand during the lead time $= \sigma_L = \sigma_t\sqrt{L}$

Order quantity $=$ EOQ

Replenishment rule: Order EOQ units when IP $\leq R$

Total Q system cost: $C = \dfrac{Q}{2}(H) + \dfrac{D}{Q}(S) + Hz\sigma_L$

8. Periodic review system:

Target inventory level $(T) =$ Average demand during the protection interval $+$ Safety stock

$$= d(P + L) + z\sigma_{P+L}$$

Protection interval $=$ Time between orders $+$ Lead time $= P + L$

Review interval $=$ Time between orders $= P$

Standard deviation of demand during the protection interval $= \sigma_{P+L} = \sigma_t\sqrt{P + L}$

Order quantity $=$ Target inventory level $-$ Inventory position $= T - $ IP

Replenishment rule: Every P time periods order $T - $ IP units

Total P system cost: $C = \dfrac{dP}{2}(H) + \dfrac{D}{dP}(S) + Hz\sigma_{P+L}$

CHAPTER HIGHLIGHTS

❏ Inventory investment decisions involve trade-offs among the conflicting objectives of low inventory investment, good customer service, and high resource utilization. Benefits of good customer service and high resource utilization may be outweighed by the cost of carrying large inventories, including interest or opportunity costs, storage and handling costs, taxes, insurance, shrinkage, and obsolescence. Order quantity decisions are guided by a trade-off between the cost of holding inventories and the combined costs of ordering, setup, transportation, and purchased materials.

❏ Cycle, safety stock, anticipation, and pipeline inventories vary in size with order quantity, uncertainty, production rate flexibility, and lead time, respectively.

❏ Inventory placement at the plant level depends on whether an item is a standard or a special and on the trade-off between short customer response time and low inventory costs.

❏ ABC analysis helps managers focus on the few significant items that account for the bulk of investment in inventory. Class A items deserve the most attention, with less attention justified for class B and class C items.

❏ Independent demand inventory management methods are appropriate for wholesale and retail merchandise, service industry supplies, finished goods and service parts replenishment, and maintenance, repair, and operating supplies.

❏ A basic inventory management question is whether to order large quantities infrequently or to order small quantities frequently. The EOQ provides guidance for this choice by indicating the lot size that minimizes (subject to several assumptions) the sum of holding and ordering costs over some period of time, such as a year.

❏ In the continuous review (Q) system, the buyer places orders of a fixed lot size Q when the inventory position drops to the reorder point. In the periodic review (P) system, every P fixed time interval the buyer places an order to replenish the quantity consumed since the last order.

❏ The base-stock system minimizes cycle inventory by maintaining the inventory position at the base-stock level. Visual systems, such as single-bin and two-bin systems, are adaptations of the P and Q systems that eliminate the need for records.

SOLVED PROBLEM 1

353A distribution center (DC) experiences an average weekly demand of 50 units for one of its items. The product is valued at $650 per unit. Average inbound shipments from the factory warehouse average 350 units. Average lead time (including ordering delays and transit time) is 2 weeks. The DC operates

52 weeks per year; it carries a 1-week supply of inventory as safety stock and no anticipation inventory. What is the average aggregate inventory being held by the DC?

SOLUTION

TYPE OF INVENTORY	CALCULATION OF AVERAGE INVENTORY QUANTITY	
Cycle	$\dfrac{Q}{2} = \dfrac{320}{2} =$	175 units
Safety stock	1-week supply =	50 units
Anticipation	None	
Pipeline	$dL =$ (50 units/week)(2 weeks) =	100 units
	Average aggregate inventory =	325 units

SOLVED PROBLEM 2

Booker's Book Bindery divides inventory items into three classes according to their dollar usage. Calculate the usage values of the following inventory items and determine which is most likely to be classified as an A item.

PART NUMBER	DESCRIPTION	QUANTITY USED PER YEAR	UNIT VALUE ($)
1	Boxes	500	3.00
2	Cardboard (square feet)	18,000	0.02
3	Cover stock	10,000	0.75
4	Glue (gallons)	75	40.00
5	Inside covers	20,000	0.05
6	Reinforcing tape (meters)	3,000	0.15
7	Signatures	150,000	0.45

SOLUTION

PART NUMBER	DESCRIPTION	QUANTITY USED PER YEAR		UNIT VALUE ($)		ANNUAL DOLLAR USAGE ($)
1	Boxes	500	×	3.00	=	1,500
2	Cardboard (square feet)	18,000	×	0.02	=	360
3	Cover stock	10,000	×	0.75	=	7,500
4	Glue (gallons)	75	×	40.00	=	3,000
5	Inside covers	20,000	×	0.05	=	1,000
6	Reinforcing tape (meters)	3,000	×	0.15	=	450
7	Signatures	150,000	×	0.45	=	67,500
					Total	81,310

The annual dollar usage for each item is determined by multiplying the annual usage quantity by the value per unit as shown in Figure 10.11. The items are sorted by annual dollar usage, in declining order. Finally, A–B and B–C class lines are drawn roughly according to the guidelines presented in the text. Here, class A includes only one item (signatures), which represents only 1/7, or 14 percent, of the items but accounts for 83 percent of annual dollar usage. Class B includes the next two items, which taken together represent 28 percent of the items and account for 13 percent of annual dollar usage. The final four, class C, items represent over half the number of items but only 4 percent of total annual dollar usage.

Part #	Description	Qty Used/Year	Value	Dollar Usage	Pct of Total	Cumulative % of Dollar Value	Cumulative % of Items	Class
7	Signatures	150,000	$0.45	$67,500	83.0%	83.0%	14.3%	A
3	Cover stock	10,000	$0.75	$7,500	9.2%	92.2%	28.6%	B
4	Glue	75	$40.00	$3,000	3.7%	95.9%	42.9%	B
1	Boxes	500	$3.00	$1,500	1.8%	97.8%	57.1%	C
5	Inside covers	20,000	$0.05	$1,000	1.2%	99.0%	71.4%	C
6	Reinforcing tape	3,000	$0.15	$450	0.6%	99.6%	85.7%	C
2	Cardboard	18,000	$0.02	$360	0.4%	100.0%	100.0%	C
Total				$81,310				

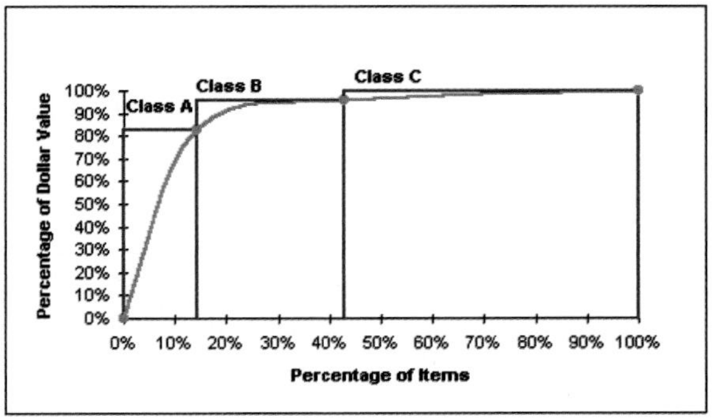

FIGURE 10.11

SOLVED PROBLEM 3

In Example 10.1, the economic order quantity, EOQ, is 75 units when annual demand, D, is 936 units/year, setup cost, S, is $45, and holding cost, H, is $15/unit/year. Suppose that we mistakenly estimate inventory holding cost to be $30/unit/year.

a. What is the new order quantity, Q, if $D = 936$ units/year, $S = 45, and $H = $30/unit/year?

b. What is the change in order quantity, expressed as a percentage of the economic order quantity (75 units)?

SOLUTION

a. The new order quantity is

$$EOQ = \sqrt{\frac{2DS}{H}} = \sqrt{\frac{2(936)($45)}{$30}} = \sqrt{2,808} = 52.99, \quad \text{or} \quad 53 \text{ units}$$

b. The percentage change is

$$\left(\frac{53 - 75}{75}\right)(100) = -29.33\%$$

The new order quantity (53) is about 29 percent smaller than the correct order quantity (75).

SOLVED PROBLEM 4

In Example 10.1, the total cost, C, is $1,124/year.

a. What is the annual total cost when $D = 936$ units/year, $S = 45, $H = $15/unit/year, and Q is the result from Solved Problem 3(a)?

b. What is the change in total cost, expressed as a percentage of the total cost ($1,124)?

SOLUTION

a. With 53 as the order quantity, the annual cost is

$$C = \frac{Q}{2}(H) + \frac{D}{Q}(S) = \frac{53}{2}(\$15) + \frac{936}{53}(\$45) = \$397.50 + \$794.72$$

$$= \$1{,}192.22, \quad \text{or} \quad \text{about } \$1{,}192$$

b. The percentage change is

$$\left(\frac{\$1{,}192 - \$1{,}124}{\$1{,}124}\right)(100) = 6.05\%, \quad \text{or} \quad \text{about } 6\%$$

A 100 percent error in estimating the holding cost caused the order quantity to be 29 percent too small, and that in turn increased annual costs by about 6 percent.

SOLVED PROBLEM 5

A regional warehouse purchases hand tools from various suppliers and then distributes them on demand to retailers in the region. The warehouse operates five days per week, 52 weeks per year. Only when it is open can orders be received. The following data are estimated for 3/8-inch hand drills with double insulation and variable speeds:

Average daily demand = 100 drills
Standard deviation of daily demand (σ_t) = 30 drills
Lead time (L) = 3 days
Holding cost (H) = \$9.40/unit/year
Ordering cost (S) = \$35/order
Cycle-service level = 92%

The warehouse uses a continuous review (Q) system.

a. What order quantity, Q, and reorder point, R, should be used?

b. If on-hand inventory is 40 units, there is one open order for 440 drills, and there are no backorders, should a new order be placed?

SOLUTION

a. Annual demand is

$$D = (5 \text{ days/week})(52 \text{ weeks/year})(100 \text{ drills/day}) = 26{,}000 \text{ drills/year}$$

The order quantity is

$$EOQ = \sqrt{\frac{2DS}{H}} = \sqrt{\frac{2(26{,}000)(\$35)}{\$9.40}} = \sqrt{193{,}167} = 440.02, \quad \text{or} \quad 440 \text{ drills}$$

and the standard deviation is

$$\sigma_L = \sigma_t\sqrt{L} = (30 \text{ drills})\sqrt{3} = 51.96, \quad \text{or} \quad 52 \text{ drills}$$

A 92 percent cycle-service level corresponds to $z = 1.41$ (see the Normal Distribution appendix). Therefore,

Safety stock = $z\sigma_L$ = 1.41(52 drills) = 73.38,   or   73 drills

Average demand during the lead time = 100(3) = 300 drills

Reorder point = Average demand during the lead time + Safety stock

$$= 300 \text{ drills} + 73 \text{ drills} = 373 \text{ drills}$$

With a continuous review system, $Q = 440$ and $R = 373$.

b. Inventory position = On-hand inventory + Scheduled receipts − Backorders

$$IP = OH + SR - BO = 40 + 440 - 0 = 480 \text{ drills}$$

Even though IP(480) exceeds R(373), do not place a new order.

SOLVED PROBLEM 6

Suppose that a periodic review (P) system is used at the warehouse, but otherwise the data are the same as in Solved Problem 5.

a. Calculate the P (in workdays, rounded to the nearest day) that gives approximately the same number of orders per year as the EOQ.

b. What is the value of the target inventory level, T? Compare the P system to the Q system in Solved Problem 6.

c. It is time to review the item. On-hand inventory is 40 drills; there is a scheduled receipt of 440 drills and no backorders. How much should be reordered?

SOLUTION

a. The time between orders is

$$P = \frac{EOQ}{D}(260 \text{ days/years}) = \frac{440}{26,000}(260) = 4.4, \quad \text{or} \quad 4 \text{ days}$$

b. Figure 10.12 shows that $T = 812$. The corresponding Q system for the hand drill requires less safety stock.

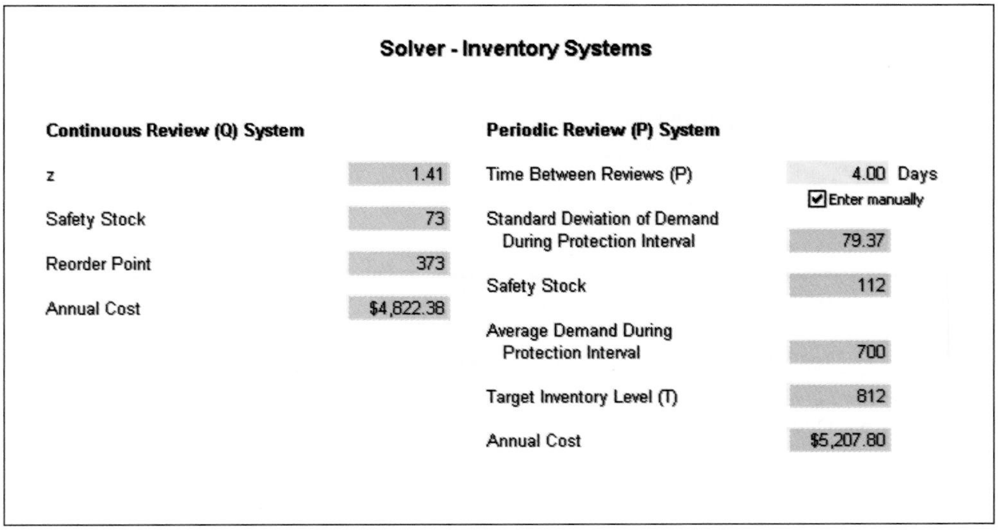

Solver - Inventory Systems

Continuous Review (Q) System

z	1.41
Safety Stock	73
Reorder Point	373
Annual Cost	$4,822.38

Periodic Review (P) System

Time Between Reviews (P)	4.00 Days ☑Enter manually
Standard Deviation of Demand During Protection Interval	79.37
Safety Stock	112
Average Demand During Protection Interval	700
Target Inventory Level (T)	812
Annual Cost	$5,207.80

FIGURE 10.12

c. Inventory position is the amount on hand plus scheduled receipts minus backorders, or

$$IP = OH + SR - BO = 40 + 440 - 0 = 480 \text{ drills}$$

The order quantity is the target inventory level minus the inventory position, or

$$Q = T - IP = 812 \text{ drills} - 480 \text{ drills} = 332 \text{ drills}$$

In a periodic review system, the order quantity for this review period is 332 drills.

CD-ROM RESOURCES

The Student CD-ROM that accompanies this text contains the following resources, which allow you to further practice and apply the concepts presented in this chapter.

❑ **OM Explorer Tutors:** OM Explorer contains five tutor programs that will help you learn how to estimate inventory levels, calculate EOQs and total costs, determine the safety stock and reorder point for Q systems, calculate the review period and target inventory level for P systems, and perform ABC analysis. See the Chapter 10 folder in OM Explorer. See also the exercises requiring the use of these tutor programs.

❑ **OM Explorer Solver:** OM Explorer has five programs that can be used to solve general problems involving inventory level estimation, Q or P system development, economic production lot size calculation, quantity discount analysis, and one-period inventory decisions. See the Inventory folder in OM Explorer.

❑ **Equation Summary:** All the equations for this chapter can be found in one convenient location.

❑ **Discussion Questions:** Three questions will challenge your understanding of practical inventory management.

❑ **Case:** Parts Emporium. Analyze the situation for two parts, develop the appropriate inventory system for each one, and estimate the savings relative to current practice.

❑ **Experiential Exercise:** Swift Electronic Supply. Design an inventory system and test it under actual conditions in this interactive simulation.

❑ **Supplement A:** Decision Making. Use this supplement to get background information on how to do sensitivity analysis.

❑ **Supplement G:** Simulation. Learn how to conduct simulations and keep track of the results.

❑ **Supplement H:** Special Inventory Models. See how to apply additional inventory tools including the economic production lot size model, the analysis of quantity discounts, and the one-period inventory model.

INTERACTIVE RESOURCES

The Interactive Web site associated with this text (www.prenhall.com/ritzman) contains many tools and activities specifically designed for this chapter. The following items are recommended to enhance your understanding of the material in this chapter.

❑ **Internet Activities:** Try out six different links to inventory topics including field service inventories, supplier relationships, software support, and safety stocks.

❑ **Internet Tour:** Explore inventory issues for a high-volume batch process at the Stickley Furniture Factory.

PROBLEMS

1. **OM Explorer** A part is produced in lots of 1,000 units. It is assembled from two components worth $50 total. The value added in production (for labor and variable overhead) is $60 per unit, bringing total costs per completed unit to $110. The average lead time for the part is six weeks and annual demand is 3,800 units. There are 50 business weeks per year.

   a. How many units of the part are held, on average, in cycle inventory? What is the dollar value of this inventory?

   b. How many units of the part are held, on average, in pipeline inventory? What is the dollar value of this inventory? *Hint:* Assume that the typical part in pipeline inventory is 50 percent completed. Thus, half the labor and variable overhead costs has been added, bringing the unit cost to $80, or $50 + $60/2.

2. **OM Explorer** Lockwood Industries is considering the use of ABC analysis to focus on the most critical items in its inventory. For a random sample of 8 items, the following table shows the annual dollar usage. Rank the items and assign them to the A, B, or C class.

ITEM	DOLLAR VALUE	ANNUAL USAGE
1	$0.01	1,200
2	$0.03	120,000
3	$0.45	100
4	$1.00	44,000
5	$4.50	900
6	$0.90	350
7	$0.30	70,000
8	$1.50	200

3. **OM Explorer** Yellow Press, Inc., buys slick paper in 1,500-pound rolls for textbook printing. Annual demand is 2,500 rolls. The cost per roll is $800, and the annual holding cost is 15 percent of the cost. Each order costs $50.

   a. How many rolls should Yellow Press order at a time?

   b. What is the time between orders?

4. **OM Explorer** At Dot Com, a large retailer of popular books, demand is constant at 32,000 books per year. The cost of placing an order to replenish stock is $10, and the annual cost of holding is $4 per book. Stock is received 5 working days after an order has been placed. No back-ordering is allowed. Assume 300 working days a year.

   a. What is Dot Com's optimal ordering quantity?

   b. What is the optimal number of orders per year?

   c. What is the optimal interval (in working days) between orders?

   d. What is demand during the lead time?

   e. What is the reorder point?

   f. What is the inventory position immediately after an order has been placed?

5. **OM Explorer** Sam's Cat Hotel operates 52 weeks per year, 6 days per week, and uses a continuous review inventory system. It purchases kitty litter for $11.70 per bag. The following information is available about these bags.

   Demand = 90 bags/week
   Order cost = $54/order
   Annual holding cost = 27% of cost
   Desired cycle-service level = 80%
   Lead time = 3 weeks (18 working days)
   Standard deviation of weekly demand = 15 bags

   Current on-hand inventory is 320 bags, with no open orders or backorders.

   a. What is the EOQ? What would be the average time between orders (in weeks)?

   b. What should R be?

   c. An inventory withdrawal of 10 bags was just made. Is it time to reorder?

   d. The store currently uses a lot size of 500 bags (i.e., $Q = 500$). What is the annual holding cost of this policy? Annual ordering cost? Without calculating the EOQ, how can you conclude from these two calculations that the current lot size is too large?

   e. What would be the annual cost saved by shifting from the 500-bag lot size to the EOQ?

6. **OM Explorer** Consider again the kitty litter ordering policy for Sam's Cat Hotel in Problem 5.

   a. Suppose that the weekly demand forecast of 90 bags is incorrect and actual demand averages only 60 bags per week. How much higher will total costs be, owing to the distorted EOQ caused by this forecast error?

   b. Suppose that actual demand is 60 bags but that ordering costs are cut to only $6 by using the Internet to automate order placing. However, the buyer does not tell anyone, and the EOQ isn't adjusted to reflect this reduction in S. How much higher will total costs be, compared to what they could be if the EOQ were adjusted?

7. **OM Explorer** Petromax Enterprises uses a continuous review inventory control system for one of its inventory items. The following information is available on the item. The firm operates 50 weeks in a year.

   Demand = 50,000 units per year
   Ordering cost = $35 per order
   Holding cost = $2 per unit per year
   Average lead time = 3 weeks
   Standard deviation of weekly demand = 125 units.

a. What is the economic order quantity for this item?

b. If Petromax wants to provide a 90 percent cycle-service level, what should be the safety stock and the reorder point?

8. **OM Explorer** Suppose that Sam's Cat Hotel in Problem 5 uses a *P* system instead of a *Q* system. The average daily demand is 15 bags (90/6), and the standard deviation of *daily* demand is 6.124 bags ($15/\sqrt{6}$).

a. What *P* (in working days) and *T* should be used to approximate the cost trade-offs of the EOQ?

b. How much more safety stock is needed than with a *Q* system?

c. It's time for the periodic review. How much should be ordered?

9. **OM Explorer** Your firm uses a continuous review system and operates 52 weeks per year. One of the items handled has the following characteristics.

Demand (D) = 20,000 units/year
Ordering cost (S) = $40/order
Holding cost (H) = $2/unit/year
Lead time (L) = 2 weeks
Cycle-service level = 95%
Demand is normally distributed, with a standard deviation of *weekly* demand of 100 units.
Current on-hand inventory is 1,040 units, with no scheduled receipts and no backorders.

a. Calculate the item's EOQ. What is the average time, in weeks, between orders?

b. Find the safety stock and reorder point that provide a 95 percent cycle-service level.

c. For these policies, what are the annual costs of (i) holding the cycle inventory and (ii) placing orders?

d. A withdrawal of 15 units just occurred. Is it time to reorder? If so, how much should be ordered?

10. **OM Explorer** Suppose that your firm uses a periodic review system, but otherwise the data are the same as in Problem 9.

a. Calculate the *P* that gives approximately the same number of orders per year as the EOQ. Round your answer to the nearest week.

b. Find the safety stock and the target inventory level that provide a 95 percent cycle-service level.

c. How much larger is the safety stock than with a *Q* system?

11. **OM Explorer** A company begins a review of ordering policies for its continuous review system by checking the current policies for a sample of items. Following are the characteristics of one item.

Demand (D) = 64 units/week (Assume 52 weeks per year.)
Ordering and setup cost (S) = $50/order
Holding cost (H) = $13/unit/year
Lead time (L) = 2 weeks
Standard deviation of *weekly* demand = 12 units
Cycle-service level = 88%

a. What is the EOQ for this item?

b. What is the desired safety stock?

c. What is the reorder point?

d. What are the cost implications if the current policy for this item is $Q = 200$ and $R = 180$?

12. **OM Explorer** Using the same information as in Problem 11, develop the best policies for a periodic review system.

a. What value of *P* gives the same approximate number of orders per year as the EOQ? Round to the nearest week.

b. What safety stock and target inventory level provide an 88 percent cycle-service level?

13. **OM Explorer** Wood County Hospital consumes 1,000 boxes of bandages per week. The price of bandages is $35 per box, and the hospital operates 52 weeks per year. The cost of processing an order is $15, and the cost of holding one box for a year is 15 percent of the value of the material.

a. The hospital orders bandages in lot sizes of 900 boxes. What *extra cost* does the hospital incur, which it could save by using the EOQ method?

b. Demand is normally distributed, with a standard deviation of weekly demand of 100 boxes. The lead time is 2 weeks. What safety stock is necessary if the hospital uses a continuous review system and a 97 percent cycle-service level is desired? What should be the reorder point?

c. If the hospital uses a periodic review system, with $P = 2$ weeks, what should be the target inventory level, T?

14. The Georgia Lighting Center stocks more than 3,000 lighting fixtures, including chandeliers, swags, wall lamps, and track lights. The store sells at retail, operates 6 days per week, and advertises itself as the "brightest spot in town." One expensive fixture is selling at an average rate of 5 units per day. The reorder policy is $Q = 40$ and $R = 15$. A new order is placed on the day the reorder point is reached. The lead time is 3 business days. For example, an order placed on Monday will be delivered on Thursday. Simulate the performance of this *Q* system for the next 3 weeks (18 workdays). Any stockouts result in lost sales (rather than backorders). The beginning inventory is 19 units, and there are no scheduled receipts. Table 10.1 simulates the first week of operation. Extend Table 10.1 to simulate operations for the next 2 weeks if demand for the next 12 business days is 7, 4, 2, 7,

	BEGINNING	ORDERS	DAILY	ENDING	INVENTORY	ORDER
WORKDAY	INVENTORY	RECEIVED	DEMAND	INVENORY	POSITION	QUANTITY
1. Monday	19	—	5	14	14	40
2. Tuesday	14	—	3	11	51	—
3. Wednesday	11	—	4	7	47	—
4. Thursday	7	40	1	46	46	—
5. Friday	46	—	10	36	36	—
6. Saturday	36	—	9	27	27	—

TABLE 10.1 *First Week of Operation*

3, 6, 10, 0, 5, 10, 4, and 7. See Supplement G, "Simulation" on the Student CD-ROM.

a. What is the average daily ending inventory over the 18 days?

b. How many stockouts occurred?

15. Simulate Problem 14 again, but this time use a P system with $P = 8$ and $T = 55$. Let the first review occur on the first Monday. As before, the beginning inventory is 19 units, and there are no scheduled receipts. See Supplement G, "Simulation" on the Student CD-ROM.

a. What is the average daily ending inventory over the 18 days?

b. How many stockouts occurred?

SELECTED REFERENCES

Berlin, Bob. "Solving the OEM Puzzle at Valleylab." *APICS—The Performance Advantage* (March 1997), pp. 58–63.

Chikan, A., A. Milne, and L. G. Sprague. "Reflections on Firm and National Inventories." Budapest: International Society for Inventory Research, 1996.

"Factors That Make or Break Season Sales." *Wall Street Journal* (December 9, 1991).

Greene, James H. *Production and Inventory Control Handbook*, 3d ed. New York: McGraw-Hill, 1997.

Inventory Management Reprints. Falls Church, VA.: American Production and Inventory Control Society, 1993.

Krupp, James A. G. "Are ABC Codes an Obsolete Technology?" *APICS—The Performance Advantage* (April 1994), pp. 34–35.

Silver, Edward A. "Changing the Givens in Modeling Inventory Problems: The Example of Just-In-Time Systems." *International Journal of Production Economics*, vol. 26 (1996) pp. 347–351.

Silver, Edward A., D. F. Pyke, and Rein Peterson. *Inventory Management, Production Planning and Scheduling*, 3d ed. New York: John Wiley & Sons, 1998.

Tersine, Richard J. *Principles of Inventory and Materials Management*, 4th ed. Upper Saddle River, NJ: Prentice-Hall, 1994.

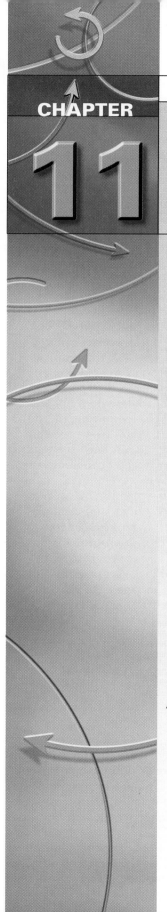

Aggregate Planning and Scheduling

Across the Organization

Aggregate planning is important to . . .

- ❑ **accounting,** which prepares cost accounting information needed to evaluate aggregate plans and which administers the billing process that is driven by schedules.
- ❑ **distribution,** which coordinates the outbound flow of materials in the supply chain with the aggregate plan and schedules.
- ❑ **finance,** which knows the financial condition of the firm, seeks ways to contain expensive inventory accumulations, and develops plans to finance the cash flows created by the aggregate plan and schedules.
- ❑ **human resources,** which is aware of how labor market conditions and training capacities constrain aggregate plans and schedules.
- ❑ **management information systems,** which develops information systems and decision support systems for developing aggregate plans and schedules.
- ❑ **marketing,** which provides demand forecasts and information on competition and customer preferences.
- ❑ **operations,** which develops plans and schedules that are the best compromise among cost, customer service, inventory investment, stable workforce levels, and facility utilization.
- ❑ **purchasing,** which provides information on supplier capabilities and coordinates the inbound flow of materials and services in the supply chain with the aggregate plan and schedules.

Learning Goals

After reading this chapter, you will be able to . . .

1. identify the dimensions on which aggregation is done and explain why aggregation helps in the planning process.
2. list the different types of reactive and aggressive alternatives and discuss the advantages and limitations of each.
3. use a spreadsheet approach to evaluate different level, chase, and mixed strategies for both service providers and manufacturers.
4. describe how the transportation method can be applied to aggregate planning problems.
5. distinguish between the ways that service managers schedule customers to provide timely service and utilize fixed capacity.
6. schedule a workforce to allow each employee to have two consecutive days off.

How important is scheduling to an airline company? Certainly, customer satisfaction regarding on-time schedule performance is critical in a highly competitive industry such as air transportation. In addition, airlines lose a lot of money when expensive equipment such as an aircraft is idle. Flight and crew scheduling, however, is a very complex process. For example, Air New Zealand (www.airnz.com) has 8,000 employees and operates 85 domestic and 50 international flights daily. Scheduling begins with a five-year market plan that identifies the new and existing flight segments that are needed to remain competitive in the industry. This general plan is further refined to a three-year plan and then put into an annual plan where the flight segments have specific departure and arrival times.

Next, crew availability must be matched to the flight schedules. There are two types of crews—pilots and attendants—each with their own set of constraints. Pilots, for example, cannot be scheduled for more than 35 hours in a seven-day week and no more than 100 hours in a 28-day cycle and must have a 36-hour break every seven days and 30 days off in an 84-day cycle. Sophisticated optimization models are used to design generic minimum-cost tours of duty that cover every flight and recognize all the constraints. Each tour of duty begins and ends at a crew base and consists of an alternating sequence of duty periods and rest periods with duty periods including one or more flights. The tours of duty are posted and crew members bid on them within a specified period of time. Actual crew rosters are constructed from the bids received. The roster must ensure that each flight has a qualified crew complement and that each crew member has a feasible line of work over the roster period.

From the crew's point of view, it is also important to satisfy as many crew requests and preferences as possible.

Scheduling does not end with the definition of the flights and crew rosters. Daily disruptions such as severe weather conditions or mechanical failures can cause schedule changes to crews, pilots, and even aircraft. Customers expect a fast resolution of the problem, and the company needs to find the least-cost solution. In the airline industry, the aggregate planning and scheduling process can determine a company's long-term competitive strength.

Pilot training in the B747 simulator at New Zealand Airlines. Refresher training "duties" occur at specific frequencies and have to be built into flight crew rosters. Good flight and crew schedules are vital to on-time performance. Sophisticated scheduling techniques are used to handle the complexities of these scheduling problems.

Sources: Ryan, David M. "Optimization Earns Its Wings." *OR/MS Today* (April 2000), pp. 26–30; "Service Scheduling at Air New Zealand." *Operations Management In Action Video Series.* Upper Saddle River, NJ: Prentice-Hall, 2000.

AIR NEW ZEALAND develops schedules through a series of steps starting with long-term plans and ending with detailed schedules for its crews. Although not all companies plan their resource requirements for five years ahead, almost all have some sort of annual plan. They then break down the annual plan into detailed, short-term schedules for specific jobs, customers, and employees. In this chapter, we examine both ends of this planning continuum.

The starting point usually is a financial assessment of the organization's near future—that is, for one or two years ahead. It is called either a business plan (in for-profit firms) or an annual plan (in nonprofit services). A **business plan** is a projected

business plan A projected statement of income, costs, and profits.

statement of income, costs, and profits. It usually is accompanied by budgets, a projected (pro forma) balance sheet, and a projected cash-flow statement, showing sources and allocations of funds. The business plan unifies the plans and expectations of a firm's operations, finance, sales, and marketing managers. In particular, it reflects plans for market penetration, new product introduction, and capital investment. Manufacturing firms and for-profit service organizations, such as a retail store, firm of attorneys, or hospital, prepare such plans. A nonprofit service organization, such as the United Way or a municipal government, prepares a different type of plan, called an **annual plan** or **financial plan.**

Given the business or annual plan, a company develops an **aggregate plan** for its processes, which is a statement of its production rates, workforce levels, and inventory holdings based on estimates of customer requirements and capacity limitations. This statement is time-phased, meaning that the plan is projected for several time periods (such as months) into the future.

A manufacturing firm's aggregate plan, called a **production plan,** generally focuses on production rates and inventory holdings, whereas a service firm's aggregate plan, called a **staffing plan,** centers on staffing and other labor-related factors. For both types of company, the plan must balance conflicting objectives involving customer service, workforce stability, cost, and profit.

From aggregate plans, managers and analysts prepare detailed operating plans. For manufacturing companies, they translate production plans into schedules for individual products and the components that go into them. For service firms, they translate the staffing plan into detailed workforce schedules. The staffing plan presents the number and types of employees needed, whereas the **workforce schedule** details the specific work schedule for each category of employee. For example, a staffing plan might allocate 10 police officers for the day shift in a particular district; the workforce schedule might assign five of them to work Monday through Friday and the other five to work Wednesday through Sunday to meet the varying daily needs for police protection in that district.

An analogy for the different planning levels is a student's calendar. Basing the choice of a school on career goals—a plan covering four or five years—corresponds to the highest planning level. Basing the choice of classes on that school's requirements— a plan for the next school year—corresponds to the middle planning level (or aggregate plan). Finally, scheduling group meetings and study times around work requirements in current classes—a plan for the next few weeks—corresponds to the most detailed planning level.

Aggregate plans and schedules are the focus of this chapter, but we discuss other aspects of the overall planning process in Chapter 12, "Resource Planning," and Chapter 13, "Lean Systems," as well as in the Master Production Scheduling and Operations Scheduling supplements on the Student CD-ROM.

annual plan or financial plan A plan for financial assessment used by a nonprofit service organization.

aggregate plan A statement of a company's production rates, workforce levels, and inventory holdings based on estimates of customer requirements and capacity limitations.

production plan A manufacturing firm's aggregate plan, which generally focuses on production rates and inventory holdings.

staffing plan A service firm's aggregate plan, which centers on staffing and other labor-related factors.

workforce schedule A schedule that details the specific work schedule for each category of employee.

THE PURPOSE OF AGGREGATE PLANS

What items should be aggregated?

In this section, we explain why companies need aggregate plans and how they use them to take a macro, or big-picture, view of their business. The aggregate plan is useful because it focuses on a general course of action, consistent with the company's strategic goals and objectives, without getting bogged down in details. For this reason, production and staffing plans are prepared by grouping, or aggregating, similar products, services, units of labor, or units of time. For instance, a manufacturer of bicycles that produces 12 different models of bikes might divide them into two groups, mountain bikes and road bikes, for the purpose of preparing the aggregate plan. It might also consider its workforce needs in terms of units of labor needed per month. In general, companies aggregate products or services, labor, and time.

PRODUCT FAMILIES

Recall that a group of products or services that have similar demand requirements and common processing, labor, and materials requirements is called a product family (see Chapter 9, "Forecasting"). Sometimes product families relate to market groupings or, in the case of production plans, to specific manufacturing processes. A firm can aggregate its products or services into a set of relatively broad families, avoiding too much detail at this stage of the planning process. Common and relevant measurements, such as units, dollars, standard hours, gallons, or pounds, should be used. For example, consider the bicycle manufacturer that has aggregated all products into two families: mountain bikes and road bikes.

LABOR

A company can aggregate labor in various ways, depending on workforce flexibility. For example, if workers at the bicycle manufacturer are trained to work on either mountain bikes or road bikes, for planning purposes management can consider its workforce to be a single aggregate group, even though the skills of individual workers may differ.

Alternatively, management can aggregate labor along product family lines by splitting the workforce into subgroups and assigning a different group to the production of each product family. In service operations, such as a city government, workers are aggregated by the type of service they provide: fire fighters, police officers, sanitation workers, and administrators.

TIME

planning horizon The length of time covered by an aggregate plan.

A **planning horizon** is the length of time covered by an aggregate plan. Typically, the planning horizon is one year, although it can differ in various situations. To avoid the expense and disruptive effect of frequent changes in output rates and the workforce, adjustments usually are made monthly or quarterly. In other words, the company looks at time in the aggregate—months, quarters, or seasons, rather than days or hours. In practice, planning periods reflect a balance between the needs for (1) a limited number of decision points to reduce planning complexity and (2) flexibility to adjust output rates and workforce levels when demand forecasts exhibit seasonal variations.

MANAGERIAL IMPORTANCE OF AGGREGATE PLANS

In this section, we concentrate on the managerial inputs, objectives, alternatives, and strategies associated with aggregate plans.

MANAGERIAL INPUTS

What kind of cross-functional coordination is needed?

Figure 11.1 shows the types of information that managers from various functional areas supply to aggregate plans. One way of ensuring the necessary cross-functional coordination and supply of information is to create a committee of functional-area representatives. Chaired by a general manager, the committee has the overall responsibility to make sure that company policies are followed, conflicts are resolved, and a final plan is approved. Coordinating the firm's functions, either in this way or less formally, helps synchronize the flow of materials, services, and information through the supply chain and best meet customer demand.

Managerial Inputs from Functional Areas to Aggregate Plans

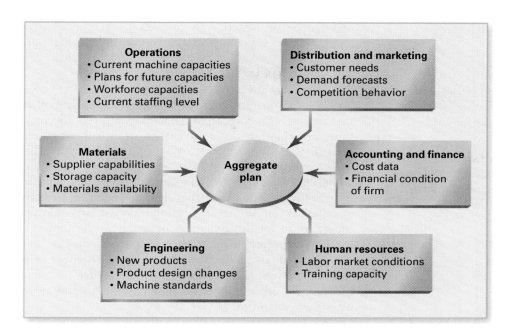

TYPICAL OBJECTIVES

The many functional areas in an organization that give input to the aggregate plan typically have conflicting objectives for the use of the organization's resources. Six objectives usually are considered during development of a production or staffing plan, and conflicts among them may have to be resolved:

1. *Minimize Costs/Maximize Profits.* If customer demand is not affected by the plan, minimizing costs will also maximize profits.

2. *Maximize Customer Service.* Improving delivery time and on-time delivery may require additional workforce, machine capacity, or inventory resources.

3. *Minimize Inventory Investment.* Inventory accumulations are expensive because the money could be used for more productive investments.

4. *Minimize Changes in Production Rates.* Frequent changes in production rates can cause difficulties in coordinating the supplying of materials and require production line rebalancing.

5. *Minimize Changes in Workforce Levels.* Fluctuating workforce levels may cause lower productivity because new employees typically need time to become fully productive.

6. *Maximize Utilization of Plant and Equipment.* Line processes require uniformly high utilization of plant and equipment.

The weight given to each one in the plan involves cost trade-offs and consideration of nonquantifiable factors. For example, maximizing customer service with fast, on-time delivery can be improved by increasing—not minimizing—the stock of finished goods in a production plan. Or, for example, a staffing plan that minimizes costs may not minimize changes in workforce levels or maximize customer service.

Balancing these various objectives to arrive at an acceptable aggregate plan involves consideration of various alternatives. The two basic types of alternatives are reactive and aggressive. Reactive alternatives are actions that respond to given demand patterns, whereas aggressive alternatives are actions that adjust demand patterns.

REACTIVE ALTERNATIVES

What options should be considered in responding to uneven demand?

reactive alternatives
Actions that can be taken to cope with demand requirements.

Reactive alternatives are actions that can be taken to cope with demand requirements. Typically, an operations manager controls reactive alternatives. That is, the operations manager accepts forecasted demand as a given and modifies workforce levels, overtime, vacation schedules, inventory levels, subcontracting, and planned backlogs to meet that demand.

WORKFORCE ADJUSTMENT.   Management can adjust workforce levels by hiring or laying off employees. The use of this alternative can be attractive if the workforce is largely unskilled or semiskilled and the labor pool is large. However, for a particular company, the size of the qualified labor pool may limit the number of new employees that can be hired at any one time. Also, new employees must be trained, and the capacity of the training facilities themselves might limit the number of new hires at any one time. In some industries, laying off employees is difficult or unusual for contractual reasons (unions); in other industries, such as tourism and agriculture, seasonal layoffs and hirings are the norm.

ANTICIPATION INVENTORY.   A plant facing seasonal demand can stock *anticipation inventory* (see Chapter 10, "Inventory Management") during light demand periods and use it during heavy demand periods. Although this approach stabilizes output rates and workforce levels, it can be costly because the value of the product is greatest in its finished state. Stocking components and subassemblies that can be assembled quickly when customer orders come in might be preferable to stocking finished goods.

Service providers generally cannot use anticipation inventory because services can't be stocked. In some instances, however, services can be performed prior to actual need. For example, telephone company workers usually lay cables for service to a new subdivision before housing construction begins. They can do this work during a period when the workload for scheduled services is low.

WORKFORCE UTILIZATION.   An alternative to workforce adjustment is workforce utilization involving overtime and undertime. **Overtime** means that employees work longer than the regular workday or workweek and receive additional pay for the extra hours. It can be used to satisfy output requirements that cannot be completed on regular time. However, overtime is expensive (typically 150 percent of the regular-time pay rate). Moreover, workers often do not want to work a lot of overtime for an extended period of time, and excessive overtime may result in declining quality and productivity.

overtime The time that employees work that is longer than the regular workday or workweek, for which they receive additional pay for the extra hours.

undertime The situation that occurs when employees do not work *productively* for the regular-time workday or workweek.

Undertime means that employees do not work *productively* for the regular-time workday or workweek. For example, they do not work productively for eight hours per day or for five days per week. Undertime occurs when labor capacity exceeds a period's demand requirements (net of anticipation inventory) and this excess capacity cannot or should not be used productively to build up inventory or to satisfy customer orders earlier than the delivery dates already promised. When products or services are customized, anticipation inventory isn't usually an option. A product cannot be produced to inventory if its specifications are unknown or if customers are unlikely to want what has been produced in advance because it doesn't meet their exact requirements.

Undertime can either be paid or unpaid. An example of *unpaid undertime* is when part-time employees are paid only for the hours or days worked. Perhaps they only work during the peak times of the day or peak days of the week. Sometimes part-time arrangements provide predictable work schedules, such as the same hours each day for five consecutive days each week. At other times, such as with stockpickers at some warehouse operations, worker schedules are unpredictable and depend on customer shipments expected for the next day. If the workload is light, some workers are not called in to work. Such arrangements are more common in low-skill positions or when the supply of workers seeking such an arrangement is sufficient. Although unpaid undertime may minimize costs, the firm must balance cost considerations against the ethical issues of being a good employer.

An example of *paid undertime* is when employees are kept on the payroll rather than being laid off. In this scenario, employees work a full day and receive their full salary but are not as productive because of the light workload. Some companies use paid undertime (though they do not call it that) during slack periods, particularly with highly skilled, hard-to-replace employees or when there are obstacles to laying off workers. The disadvantages of paid undertime include the cost of paying for work not performed and lowered productivity.

VACATION SCHEDULES.   A firm can shut down during an annual lull in sales, leaving a skeleton crew to cover operations and perform maintenance. Employees might be required to take all or part of their allowed vacation time during this period. Use of this alternative depends on whether the employer can mandate the vacation schedules of its employees. In any case, employees may be strongly discouraged from taking vacations during peak periods or encouraged to take vacations during periods when replacement part-time labor is most abundant.

SUBCONTRACTORS.   Subcontractors can be used to overcome short-term capacity shortages, such as during peaks of the season or business cycle. Subcontractors can supply services, make components and subassemblies, or even assemble an entire product. If the subcontractor can supply components or subassemblies of equal or better quality less expensively than the company can produce them itself, these arrangements may become permanent.

BACKLOGS, BACKORDERS, AND STOCKOUTS.   Firms that maintain a backlog of orders as a normal business practice can allow the backlog to grow during periods of high demand and then reduce it during periods of low demand. A **backlog** is an accumulation of customer orders that have been promised for delivery at some future date. Firms that use backlogs do not promise instantaneous delivery, as do wholesalers or retailers farther forward in the supply chain. Instead, they impose a lead time between when the order is placed and when it is delivered. Firms that are most likely to use backlogs—and increase the size of them during periods of heavy demand—make customized products and provide customized services. They tend to have a make-to-order or customized services strategy and include job shops, TV repair shops, automobile repair shops, and dental offices. Backlogs reduce the uncertainty of future production requirements and also can be used to level these requirements. However, they become a competitive disadvantage if they get too big. Fast delivery time often is an important competitive priority (see Chapter 1, "Competing with Operations"), but large backlogs mean long delivery times.

Manufacturers with a make-to-stock strategy, and service providers with a standardized services strategy (see Chapter 1, "Competing with Operations"), are expected to provide immediate delivery. For them, poor customer service during peak demand periods takes the form of backorders and stockouts rather than large backlogs. A **backorder** is an order that the customer expected to be filled immediately but reluctantly

backlog An accumulation of customer orders that have been promised for delivery at some future date.

backorder An order that the customer expected to be filled immediately but reluctantly asks that it be delivered as soon as possible.

stockout An order that is lost and causes the customer to go elsewhere.

asks that it be delivered as soon as possible. Although the customer isn't pleased with the delay, the customer order is not lost and is filled at a later date. A **stockout** is much the same, except that the order is lost and the customer goes elsewhere. A backorder adds to the next period's requirement, whereas a stockout doesn't increase future requirements. Backorders and stockouts can lead dissatisfied customers to do their future business with another firm. Generally, backorders and stockouts are to be avoided. Planned stockouts may be used, but only when the expected loss in sales and customer goodwill is less than the cost of using other reactive alternatives or aggressive alternatives or adding the capacity needed to satisfy demand.

In conclusion, decisions about the use of each alternative for each period of the planning horizon specify the output rate for each period. In other words, the output rate is a function of the choices among these alternatives.

AGGRESSIVE ALTERNATIVES

How can demand be leveled to reduce operating costs?

aggressive alternatives Actions that attempt to modify demand and, consequently, resource requirements.

Coping with seasonal or volatile demand by using reactive alternatives can be costly. Another approach is to attempt to change demand patterns to achieve efficiency and reduce costs. **Aggressive alternatives** are actions that attempt to modify demand and, consequently, resource requirements. Typically, marketing managers are responsible for specifying these actions in the marketing plan.

complementary products Products or services having similar resource requirements but different demand cycles.

COMPLEMENTARY PRODUCTS.   One way a company can even out the load on resources is to produce **complementary products** or services having similar resource requirements but different demand cycles. For example, in the service sector, city parks and recreation departments can counterbalance seasonal staffing requirements for summer activities by offering ice skating, tobogganing, or indoor activities during the winter months. The key is to find products and services that can be produced with existing resources and can level off the need for resources over the year.

CREATIVE PRICING.   Promotional campaigns are designed to increase sales with creative pricing. Examples include automobile rebate programs, price reductions for winter clothing in the late summer months, reduced prices on airline tickets for travel during off-peak periods, and "two for the price of one" automobile tire sales.

PLANNING STRATEGIES

Managers often combine reactive and aggressive alternatives in various ways to arrive at an acceptable aggregate plan. For the remainder of this chapter, let us assume that the expected results of the aggressive alternatives have already been incorporated into the demand forecasts of product families or services. This assumption allows us to focus on the reactive alternatives that define output rates and workforce levels. Countless aggregate plans are possible even when just a few reactive alternatives are allowed. Four very different strategies, two chase strategies and two level strategies, are useful starting points in searching for the best plan. These strategies can be implemented with a limited or expanded set of reactive alternatives, as shown in the table on the next page. The specific reactive alternatives allowed, and how they are mixed together, must be stated before a chase or level strategy can be translated into a unique aggregate plan.

chase strategy A strategy that matches demand during the planning horizon by varying either the workforce level or the output rate.

CHASE STRATEGIES. A **chase strategy** *matches* demand during the planning horizon by varying either (1) the workforce level or (2) the output rate. When a chase strategy uses the first method, varying the *workforce level* to match demand, it relies on just one reactive alternative—workforce variation. Sometimes called the *capacity strategy*, it uses hiring and layoffs to keep the workforce's regular-time capacity equal to demand. This chase strategy has the advantages of no inventory investment, overtime, or under-time. However, it has some drawbacks, including the expense of continually adjusting

Strategy	Possible Alternatives During Slack Season	Possible Alternatives During Peak Season
1. **Chase #1:** vary *workforce level* to match demand	Layoffs	Hiring
2. **Chase #2:** vary *output rate* to match demand	Layoffs, undertime, vacations	Hiring, overtime, subcontracting
3. **Level #1:** constant *workforce level*	No layoffs, building anticipation inventory, undertime, vacations	No hiring, depleting anticipation inventory, overtime, subcontracting, backorders, stockouts
4. **Level #2:** constant *output rate*	Layoffs, building anticipation inventory, undertime, vacations	Hiring, depleting anticipation inventory, overtime, subcontracting, backorders, stockouts

workforce levels, the potential alienation of the workforce, and the loss of productivity and quality because of constant changes in the workforce.

The second chase strategy, varying the *output rate* to match demand, opens up additional reactive alternatives beyond changing the workforce level. Sometimes called the *utilization strategy,* the extent and timing of the workforce's utilization are changed through overtime, undertime, and when vacations are taken. Subcontracting, including temporary help during the peak season, is another way of matching demand.

LEVEL STRATEGIES. A **level strategy** maintains a (1) constant workforce level or (2) constant output rate during the planning horizon. These two strategies differ from chase strategies not only because either the workforce or output rate is held constant but also because anticipation inventory, backorders, and stockouts are added to the list of possible reactive alternatives. For this reason, they are sometimes called *inventory strategies.*

When a level strategy uses the first method, maintaining a constant *workforce level,* it might consist of not hiring or laying off workers (except at the beginning of the planning horizon), building up anticipation inventories to absorb seasonal demand fluctuations, using undertime in slack periods and overtime up to contracted limits for peak periods, using subcontractors for additional needs as necessary, and scheduling vacation timing to match slack periods.

Even though a constant workforce must be maintained with this first level strategy, many aggregate plans are possible. The constant workforce can be sized many ways. It can be so large as to minimize the planned use of overtime and subcontractors (which creates considerable undertime) or so small as to rely heavily on overtime and subcontractors during the peak seasons (which places a strain on the workforce and endangers quality). Thus, the advantages of a stable workforce must be weighed against the disadvantages of the other alternatives allowed, such as increased undertime, overtime, and inventory.

When a level strategy uses the second method, maintaining a constant *output rate,* it allows hiring and layoffs in addition to the other alternatives of the first level strategy. The output rate can be level even if the workforce fluctuates, depending on the set of alternatives that is used in the strategy. The key to identifying a level strategy is whether the workforce or output rate is constant.

MIXED STRATEGIES. Used alone, chase and level strategies are unlikely to produce the best acceptable aggregate plan. Improvements are likely by considering plans that are neither pure level nor chase strategies. The workforce (or output rate) is not exactly level and yet

level strategy A strategy that maintains a constant workforce level or constant output rate during the planning horizon.

mixed strategy A strategy that considers and implements a fuller range of reactive alternatives and goes beyond a "pure" chase or level strategy.

does not exactly match demand. Instead, the best strategy for a process is a **mixed strategy** that considers and implements a fuller range of reactive alternatives and goes beyond a "pure" chase or level strategy. Whether management chooses a pure strategy or some mix, the strategy should reflect the organization's environment and planning objectives. For example, for the municipal street repair department, which faces seasonal demand shifts and needs an ample supply of unskilled labor, possible strategies include varying the workforce level, reducing overtime, and eliminating subcontracting.

THE PLANNING PROCESS

Figure 11.2 shows the process for preparing aggregate plans. It is dynamic and continuing, as aspects of the plan are updated periodically when new information becomes available and new opportunities emerge.

DETERMINING DEMAND REQUIREMENTS

The first step in the planning process is to determine the demand requirements for each period of the planning horizon using one of the many methods that we have already discussed. For staffing plans, the planner bases forecasts of staff requirements for each workforce group on historical levels of demand, managerial judgment, and existing backlogs for services. For example, a director of nursing in a hospital can develop a direct-care index for a nursing staff and translate a projection of the month-to-month patient census into an equivalent total amount of nursing care time—and, thus, the number of nurses—required for each month of the year.

For production plans, however, the requirements represent the demand for finished goods and the external demand for replacement parts. The planner can derive future requirements for finished goods from backlogs (for make-to-order operations) or from forecasts for product families made to stock (for make-to-stock operations). Sometimes distributors or dealers indicate their requirements for finished goods in advance of actual orders, providing a reliable forecast of requirements from those sources.

IDENTIFYING ALTERNATIVES, CONSTRAINTS, AND COSTS

The second step is to identify the alternatives, constraints, and costs for the plan. We presented the reactive alternatives used in aggregate plans earlier, so we now focus on constraints and costs.

Constraints represent physical limitations or managerial policies associated with the aggregate plan. Examples of physical constraints might include training facilities capa-

FIGURE 11.2

The Process for Preparing Aggregate Plans

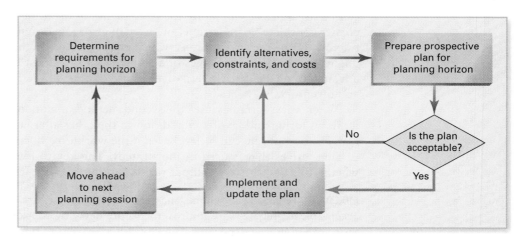

ble of handling only so many new hires at a time, machine capacities that limit maximum output, or inadequate inventory storage space. Policy constraints might include limitations on the amount of backordering or the use of subcontracting or overtime, as well as the minimum inventory levels needed to achieve desired safety stocks.

Typically, many plans can satisfy a specific set of constraints. The planner usually considers several types of costs when preparing aggregate plans:

1. *Regular-Time Costs.* These costs include regular-time wages paid to employees plus contributions to such benefits as health insurance, dental care, Social Security, and retirement funds and pay for vacations, holidays, and certain other types of absence.

2. *Overtime Costs.* Overtime wages typically are 150 percent of regular-time wages, exclusive of fringe benefits. Some companies offer a 200 percent rate for working overtime on Sundays and holidays.

3. *Hiring and Layoff Costs.* Hiring costs include the costs of advertising jobs, interviews, training programs for new employees, scrap caused by the inexperience of new employees, loss of productivity, and initial paperwork. Layoff costs include the costs of exit interviews, severance pay, retraining remaining workers and managers, and lost productivity.

4. *Inventory Holding Costs.* Inventory holding costs include costs that vary with the *level* of inventory investment: the costs of capital tied up in inventory, variable storage and warehousing costs, pilferage and obsolescence costs, insurance costs, and taxes.

5. *Backorder and Stockout Costs.* As discussed earlier, the use of backorders and stockouts involves costs of expediting past-due orders, costs of lost sales, and the potential cost of losing the customer's sales to competitors in the future (sometimes called loss of goodwill).

PREPARING AN ACCEPTABLE PLAN

The third step is to prepare the aggregate plan. Developing an acceptable plan is an iterative process; that is, plans may need to go through several revisions and adjustments (see Figure 11.2). A prospective, or tentative, plan is developed to start. A production plan with monthly periods, for example, must specify monthly production rates, inventory and backorder accumulations, subcontracted production, and monthly workforce levels (including hires, layoffs, and overtime). The plan must then be checked against constraints and evaluated in terms of strategic objectives. If the prospective plan is not acceptable for either of those reasons, a new prospective plan must be developed.

IMPLEMENTING AND UPDATING THE PLAN

The final step is implementing and updating the aggregate plan. Implementation requires the commitment of managers in all functional areas. The planning committee may recommend changes in the plan during implementation or updating to balance conflicting objectives better. Acceptance of the plan does not necessarily mean that everyone is in total agreement, but it does imply that everyone will work to achieve it.

AGGREGATE PLANNING WITH SPREADSHEETS

Here we use a *spreadsheet* approach of stating a strategy, developing a plan, comparing the developed plan to other plans, and finally modifying the plan or strategy as necessary, until we are satisfied with the results. We demonstrate this approach by developing two staffing plans, the first based on a level strategy and the second on a chase

Should a level workforce strategy or some variable workforce strategy be used in providing services?

strategy. We then consider a mixed strategy for a manufacturer facing a different demand pattern and cost structure.

After a plan has been formulated, it is evaluated by use of a spreadsheet. One part of the spreadsheet shows the *input values* that give the demand requirements and the reactive alternative choices period by period. Another part shows the *derived values* that must follow from the input values. The final part of the spreadsheet shows the *calculated costs* of the plan. Along with qualitative considerations, the calculated cost of each plan determines whether the plan is satisfactory or whether a revised plan should be considered. When seeking clues about how to improve a plan already evaluated, we identify its highest cost elements. Revisions that would reduce these specific costs might produce a new plan with lower overall costs. Spreadsheet programs make analyzing these plans easy for developing sound aggregate plans.

LEVEL STRATEGY WITH OVERTIME AND UNDERTIME

One possible level strategy, which uses a constant number of employees that will satisfy demand during the planning horizon, is determined by using the maximum amount of overtime in the peak period. Undertime is used in slack periods. The workforce level does not change, except possibly for hiring or layoffs at the beginning of the first period if the current and desired constant workforce levels do not match. The level strategy can lead to considerable undertime, which is the amount of time by which capacity exceeds demand requirements, summed over all periods for the time horizon. The cost of this unused capacity depends on whether undertime is paid or unpaid.

EXAMPLE 11.1 | *A Level Strategy with Overtime and Undertime*

**TUTOR
11.1**

The manager of a large distribution center must determine how many part-time stockpickers to maintain on the payroll. She wants to develop a staffing plan with a level workforce, implemented with overtime and undertime. Her objective is to keep the part-time workforce stable and to minimize undertime usage. She will achieve this goal by using the maximum amount of overtime possible in the peak period.

The manager divides the next year into 6 time periods, each one 2 months long. Each part-time employee can work a maximum of 20 hours per week on regular time, but the actual number can be less. The distribution center shortens each worker's day during slack periods rather than pay undertime. Once on the payroll, each worker is used each day but may work only a few hours. Overtime can be used during peak periods to avoid excessive undertime.

Workforce requirements are shown as the number of part-time employees required for each time period at the maximum regular time of 20 hours per week. For example, in period 3, an estimated 18 part-time employees working 20 hours per week on regular time will be needed.

			TIME PERIOD				
	1	2	3	4	5	6	TOTAL
Requirement*	6	12	18	15	13	14	78

*Number of part-time employees

Currently, 10 part-time clerks are employed. They haven't been subtracted from the requirements shown. Constraints on employment and cost information are as follows:

1. The size of training facilities limits the number of new hires in any period to no more than 10.

2. No backorders are permitted; demand must be met each period.

3. Overtime cannot exceed 20 percent of the regular-time capacity (i.e., 4 hours) in any period. Therefore, the most that any part-time employee can work is 1.20 (20) = 24 hours per week.

4. The following costs can be assigned:

Regular-time wage rate	$2,000 per time period at 20 hours per week
Overtime wages	150 percent of the regular-time rate
Hiring	$1,000 per person
Layoffs	$500 per person

SOLUTION

For this particular level strategy, the manager begins by finding the number of part-time employees at 24 hours per week (20×1.20) needed to meet the peak requirement. The most overtime that she can use is 20 percent of the regular-time capacity, w, so

$$1.20w = 18 \text{ employees required in peak period (period 3)}$$

$$w = \frac{18}{1.20} = 15 \text{ employees}$$

A 15-employee staff size minimizes the amount of undertime for this level strategy. As there already are 10 part-time employees, the manager should immediately hire 5 more. The complete plan is shown in Figure 11.3.

The input values are the requirement, a 15-person workforce level, undertime, and overtime for each period. The first row of derived values is called *productive time*, which is that portion of the workforce's regular time that is paid for and used productively. In any period, the productive time equals the workforce level minus undertime. The hires and layoffs rows can be derived from the workforce levels. In this example, the workforce is increased for period 1 from its initial size of 10 employees to 15, which means that 5 employees are hired. Because the workforce size remains constant throughout the planning horizon, there are no other hirings or layoffs.

For this particular example, overtime and undertime can be derived directly from the first two rows of input values. When a period's workforce level exceeds the requirement, overtime is zero and undertime equals the difference. When a period's workforce level is less than the requirements, undertime is zero and overtime equals the difference. For the general case when other alternatives (such as vacations, inventory, and backorders) are possible, however, the overtime and undertime cannot be derived just from information on requirements and workforce levels. Thus, undertime and overtime are shown as input values (rather than derived values) in the spreadsheet, and the user must be careful to specify consistent input values.

Another decision to be made is how to apportion undertime and overtime to employees. Except for periods 3 and 4, the employees will have some undertime or work less than the maximum 20 hours per week, because the requirement for those periods is less than 15 employees. In

	1	2	3	4	5	6	Total
Requirement	6	12	18	15	13	14	78
Workforce level	15	15	15	15	15	15	90
Undertime	9	3	0	0	2	1	15
Overtime	0	0	3	0	0	0	3
Productive time	6	12	15	15	13	14	75
Hires	5	0	0	0	0	0	5
Layoffs	0	0	0	0	0	0	0
Costs	1	2	3	4	5	6	Totals
Productive time	$12,000	24,000	30,000	30,000	26,000	28,000	$150,000
Undertime	$0	0	0	0	0	0	$0
Overtime	$0	0	9,000	0	0	0	$9,000
Hires	$5,000	0	0	0	0	0	$5,000
Layoffs	$0	0	0	0	0	0	$0
Total cost	$17,000	24,000	39,000	30,000	26,000	28,000	$164,000

FIGURE 11.3

period 1, for example, 15 employees are on the payroll, but only 120 hours, or 6(20), per week are needed. Consequently, each employee might work only 8 hours per week. Alternatively, the manager could assign 5 employees to 4 hours per week and 10 employees to 10 hours per week. A similar approach can be applied to overtime.

The calculated costs for this plan are $164,000, which seems reasonable because the minimum conceivable cost is only $156,000 (78 periods × $2,000/period). This cost could be achieved only if the manager found a way to cover the requirement for all 78 periods with regular time. This plan seems reasonable primarily because it involves the use of large amounts of undertime (15 periods), which in this example are unpaid. The only ways to reduce costs are somehow to reduce the premium for 3 overtime periods (3 periods × $1,000/period) or to reduce the hiring cost of 5 employees (5 hires × $1,000/person). Nonetheless, better solutions may be possible. For example, undertime can be reduced by delaying the hiring until period 2 because the current workforce is sufficient until then. This delay would decrease the amount of unpaid undertime, which is a qualitative improvement. However, this modification creates mixed strategy rather than a level strategy with a constant workforce out to the horizon, which is the one illustrated here.

Decision Point   The manager, now having a point of reference with which to compare other plans, decided to evaluate some other plans before making a final choice, beginning with the chase strategy. ⬚

CHASE STRATEGY WITH HIRING AND LAYOFFS

Consider the chase strategy that adjusts workforce levels as needed to achieve requirements without using overtime, undertime, or subcontractors. This chase strategy can result in a large number of hirings and layoffs. However, many employees, such as college students, prefer part-time work. As the photo shows, FedEx also prefers the flexibility offered by part-time employees. With this chase strategy, the workforce level row is identical to the requirement row, with no overtime in any period.

EXAMPLE 11.2	*A Chase Strategy with Hiring and Layoffs*

The manager now wants to determine the staffing plan for the distribution center using the chase strategy so as to avoid all overtime and undertime.

SOLUTION

This strategy simply involves adjusting the workforce as needed to meet demand, as shown in Figure 11.4.

The manager should plan to lay off 4 part-time employees immediately because the current staff is 10 and the staff level required in period 1 is only 6. The workforce then should steadily build to 18 by period 3. After that, the manager can reduce the workforce except for the secondary peak in period 6, when she should hire 1 more employee.

TUTOR
11.2

	1	2	3	4	5	6	Total
Requirement	6	12	18	15	13	14	78
Workforce level	6	12	18	15	13	14	78
Undertime	0	0	0	0	0	0	0
Overtime	0	0	0	0	0	0	0
Productive time	6	12	18	15	13	14	78
Hires	0	6	6	0	0	1	13
Layoffs	4	0	0	3	2	0	9
Costs	1	2	3	4	5	6	Totals
Productive time	$12,000	24,000	36,000	30,000	26,000	28,000	$156,000
Undertime	$0	0	0	0	0	0	$0
Overtime	$0	0	0	0	0	0	$0
Hires	$0	6,000	6,000	0	0	1,000	$13,000
Layoffs	$2,000	0	0	1,500	1,000	0	$4,500
Total cost	$14,000	30,000	42,000	31,500	27,000	29,000	$173,500

FIGURE 11.4

The $173,500 cost of this plan is considerably higher than for the level strategy. The spreadsheet shows that most of the cost increase comes from frequent hiring and layoffs, which add $17,500 to the cost of productive regular-time costs. Clearly, a low-cost solution must avoid frequent workforce adjustments by using more overtime and undertime, particularly because part-time employees offer flexible work hours and because undertime is not a payroll cost.

Decision Point Having found this chase strategy worse than the level strategy, the manager decided to formulate some mixed strategies that keep more of the elements of a level strategy. ❐

MIXED STRATEGIES

The manager of the distribution center in Example 11.1 might find even better solutions with a mixed strategy, which varies the workforce level or output rate somewhat but not to the extreme of a chase strategy. She might also consider a fuller range of reactive alternatives, such as vacations, subcontracting, and even customer service reductions (increased backlogs, backorders, or stockouts).

Manufacturers often have still another alternative, building up anticipation inventory to help smooth the output rate. When inventory is introduced, however, care must be taken to recognize differences in how requirements and reactive alternatives are measured. The workforce level might be expressed as the number of employees, but the requirements and inventory are expressed as units of the product. Relationships between the requirements and reactive alternatives must account for these differences. The OM Explorer spreadsheets require a common unit of measure, so we must translate some of the data prior to entering the input values. Perhaps the easiest approach is to express the requirements and reactive alternatives as *employee-period equivalents*. If demand requirements are given as units of product, we can convert them to employee-period equivalents by *dividing* them by the productivity of a worker. For example, if the demand is for 1,500 units of product and the average employee produces 100 units in one period, the demand requirement is 15 employee-period equivalents.

This translation from product units to employee-period equivalents also applies to the initial inventory or backorders at the beginning of period 1, if they are given as product units. To convert the spreadsheet results back to product units, we simply *multiply* employee-period equivalents by the productivity rate. For example, an ending inventory of 20 employee-period equivalents would translate back to 2,000 units of product, or 20 × 100.

	1	2	3	4	5	6	Total
Requirement	24	142	220	180	136	168	870
Workforce level	120	152	158	158	158	158	904
Undertime	0	0	0	0	4	0	4
Overtime	0	0	0	4	0	6	10
Vacation time	20	6	0	0	4	10	40
Subcontracting time	0	0	0	0	0	0	0
Backorders	0	0	0	0	0	0	0
Productive time	100	146	158	158	150	148	860
Inventory	76	80	18	0	14	0	188
Hires	0	32	6	0	0	0	38
Layoffs	0	0	0	0	0	0	0

Costs	1	2	3	4	5	6	Totals
Productive time	$400,000	584,000	632,000	632,000	600,000	592,000	$3,440,000
Undertime	$0	0	0	0	16,000	0	$16,000
Overtime	$0	0	0	24,000	0	36,000	$60,000
Vacation time	$80,000	24,000	0	0	16,000	40,000	$160,000
Inventory	$3,040	3,200	720	0	560	0	$7,520
Backorders	$0	0	0	0	0	0	$0
Hires	$0	76,800	14,400	0	0	0	$91,200
Layoffs	$0	0	0	0	0	0	$0
Subcontracting	$0	0	0	0	0	0	$0
Total cost	$483,040	688,000	647,120	656,000	632,560	668,000	$3,774,720

Figure 11.5 demonstrates a mixed strategy for a manufacturer using the Aggregate Planning with Spreadsheets Solver of OM Explorer. It demonstrates the full range of reactive alternatives. The plan calls for expanding the workforce in periods 2 and 3, varying the anticipation inventory level, scheduling vacations during slack periods, and planning no backorders or subcontracting. We know it is a mixed strategy because (1) neither the workforce nor output rate matches the requirements as with a chase strategy (note that inventory varies from one period to the next) and (2) neither the workforce nor output rate is constant as with a level strategy.

TRANSPORTATION METHOD OF PRODUCTION PLANNING

Should subcontracting be used to achieve short-term capacity increases or should some combination of inventory accumulation and overtime be used?

transportation method of production planning The use of the transportation method to solve production planning problems, assuming that a demand forecast is available for each period, along with a workforce level plan for regular time.

The major advantage of the spreadsheet approach is its simplicity; however, the planner still must make many choices for each period of the planning horizon. The large costs involved with aggregate plans are a motivation to seek the best possible plan.

Here we present and demonstrate the **transportation method of production planning.** Earlier we applied it to locating a facility within a network of facilities (see Chapter 7, "Location and Layout"). The transportation method, when applied to aggregate planning, is particularly helpful in determining anticipation inventories. Thus, it relates more to manufacturers' production plans than to service providers' staffing plans. In fact, the workforce levels for each period are inputs to the transportation method rather than outputs from it. Different workforce adjustment plans, ranging from the chase strategy to the level strategy, must be tried. Thus, several transportation method solutions may be obtained before a final plan is selected.

Use of the transportation method for production planning is based on the assumption that a demand forecast is available for each period, along with a workforce level plan for regular time. Capacity limits on overtime and subcontractor production also are needed for each period. Another assumption is that all costs are linearly related to the amount of goods produced—that is, that a change in the amount of goods produced creates a proportionate change in costs.

FIGURE 11.6

Transportation Method of Production Planning

Alternatives		Time Period				Unused Capacity	Total Capacity
		1	2	3	4		
Period	Beginning inventory	0	h	2h	3h	4h	I_0
1	Regular time	r	r + h	r + 2h	r + 3h	u	R_1
1	Overtime	c	c + h	c + 2h	c + 3h	0	O_1
1	Subcontract	s	s + h	s + 2h	s + 3h	0	S_1
2	Regular time	r + b	r	r + h	r + 2h	u	R_2
2	Overtime	c + b	c	c + h	c + 2h	0	O_2
2	Subcontract	s + b	s	s + h	s + 2h	0	S_2
3	Regular time	r + 2b	r + b	r	r + h	u	R_3
3	Overtime	c + 2b	c + b	c	c + h	0	O_3
3	Subcontract	s + 2b	s + b	s	s + h	0	S_3
4	Regular time	r + 3b	r + 2b	r + b	r	u	R_4
4	Overtime	c + 3b	c + 2b	c + b	c	0	O_4
4	Subcontract	s + 3b	s + 2b	s + b	s	0	S_4
Requirements		D_1	D_2	D_3	$D_4 + I_4$	U	

With these assumptions, the transportation method yields the optimal mixed-strategy production plan for the planning horizon.

PRODUCTION PLANNING WITHOUT BACKORDERS. We start with a table—called a *tableau*—of the workforce levels, capacity limits, demand forecast quantities, beginning inventory level, and costs for each period of the planning horizon. Figure 11.6 shows such a tableau for a four-period production plan, where

h = holding cost per unit per period

r = cost per unit to produce on regular time

c = cost per unit to produce on overtime

s = cost per unit to subcontract

u = undertime cost per unit

b = backorder cost per unit per period

I_0 = beginning inventory level

I_4 = desired inventory level at the end of period 4

R_t = regular-time capacity in period t

O_t = overtime capacity in period t

S_t = subcontracting capacity in period t

D_t = forecasted demand for period t

U = total unused capacities

Note that each row in the tableau represents an alternative for supplying output. For example, the first row shows the beginning inventory (the amount currently on hand) for the present time (period 0), which can be used to satisfy demand in any of the four periods. The second row is for regular-time production in period 1, which can also be used to satisfy demand in any of the four periods the plan will cover. The third and fourth rows are for two other production alternatives (overtime and subcontracting) in period 1 for meeting demand in any of the four periods.

The columns represent the periods that the plan must cover, plus the unused and total capacities available. The box in the upper right-hand corner of each cell shows the cost of producing a unit in one period and, in some cases, carrying the unit in inventory for sale in a future period. For example, in period 1 the regular-time cost to produce one unit is r (column 1). To produce the unit in period 1 for sale in period 2, the cost is $r + h$ (column 2) because we must hold the unit in inventory for one period. Satisfying a unit of demand in period 3 by producing in period 1 on regular time and carrying the unit for two periods costs $r + 2h$ (column 3), and so on. The cells in color at the bottom left of the tableau imply backorders (or producing in a period to satisfy in a past period). We can disallow backorders by making the backorder cost an arbitrarily large number. If backorder costs are so large, the transportation method will try to avoid backorders because it seeks a solution that minimizes total cost. If that is not possible, we increase the staffing plan and the overtime and subcontracting capacities.

The least expensive alternatives are those in which the output is produced and sold in the same period. However, we may not always be able to use those alternatives exclusively because of capacity restrictions. Finally, the per-unit holding cost for the beginning inventory in period 1 is 0 because it is a function of previous production planning decisions. Similarly, the target inventory at the end of the planning horizon is added to the forecasted demand for the last period. No holding cost is charged because we have already decided to have a specified ending inventory; in this regard, it is a sunk cost.[1]

Use the following procedure to develop an acceptable aggregate plan.

Step 1. Select a workforce adjustment plan (or R_t values), using a chase strategy, level strategy, or a mixed strategy. Identify the capacity constraints on overtime (O_t values) and on subcontracting (S_t values). Usually, a period's overtime capacity is a percentage of its regular-time capacity. Also identify the on-hand anticipation

---

[1]If we were analyzing the implications of different ending inventory levels, the holding cost of the ending inventory would have to be added to the costs because ending inventory level would be a decision variable.

inventory (I_0 values) currently available before the start of period 1. Input these values to the computer routine, which in turn inserts these values in the last column of the transportation tableau.

Step 2. Input the cost parameters (h, r, c, s, u, and b) for the different reactive alternatives. The computer software uses them to compute the values in the box of the upper right-hand corner of each cell.

Step 3. Forecast the demand for each future period, and insert the forecasts as the values in the tableau's last row. The last period's requirement should be increased to account for any desired inventory at the end of the planning horizon. The unused capacity cell in the last row equals the total demand requirements in the last row, minus the total capacity in the tableau's last column.

Step 4. Solve the transportation problem just formulated with a computer routine to find the optimal solution (based on the workforce adjustment plan). The sum of all entries in a row equals the total capacity for that row, and the sum of all entries in a column must equal the requirements for that column.

Step 5. Return to step 1 and try other staffing plans until you find the solution that best balances cost and qualitative considerations.

EXAMPLE 11.3

**TUTOR
11.3**

Preparing a Production Plan with the Transportation Method

The Tru-Rainbow Company produces a variety of paint products for both commercial and private use. The demand for paint is highly seasonal, peaking in the third quarter. Current inventory is 250,000 gallons, and ending inventory should be 300,000 gallons.

Tru-Rainbow's manufacturing manager wants to determine the best production plan using the following demand requirements and capacity plan. Demands and capacities here are expressed in thousands of gallons (rather than employee-period equivalents). The manager knows that the regular-time cost is $1.00 per unit, overtime cost is $1.50 per unit, subcontracting cost is $1.90 per unit, and inventory holding cost is $0.30 per gallon per quarter.

	QUARTER				
	1	**2**	**3**	**4**	**TOTAL**
Demand	300	850	1,500	350	3,000
Capacities					
Regular time	450	450	750	450	2,100
Overtime	90	90	150	90	420
Subcontracting	200	200	200	200	800

The following constraints apply:

1. Maximum allowable overtime in any quarter is 20 percent of the regular-time capacity in that quarter.

2. The subcontractor can supply a maximum of 200,000 gallons in any quarter. Production can be subcontracted in one period and the excess held in inventory for a future period to avoid a stockout.

3. No backorders or stockouts are permitted.

SOLUTION

Figure 11.7 shows the tableau solution to the problem that OM Explorer produces. The *Results Worksheet* of Tutor 11.3 summarizes the costs of this prospective production plan, as shown in the two rows below the tableau. These numbers can be confirmed as the sum of the products calculated by multiplying the allocation in each cell by the cost per unit in that

Solve

	Period	Quarter 1	2	3	4	Unused Capacity	Total Capacity
	Beginning Inventory	0 / **250**	$0.30	$0.60	$0.90	0	250
1	Regular Time	$1.00 / **30**	$1.30 / **420**	$1.60 / -	$1.90 / -	-	450
	Overtime	$1.50 / -	$1.80 / **90**	$2.10 / -	$2.40 / -	-	90
	Subcontract	$1.90 / **20**	$2.20 / -	$2.50 / -	$2.80 / -	180	200
2	Regular Time	999	$1.00 / **340**	$1.30 / **110**	$1.60 / -	-	450
	Overtime	999	$1.50 / -	$1.80 / **90**	$2.10 / -	-	90
	Subcontract	999	$1.90 / -	$2.20 / **200**	$2.50 / -	-	200
3	Regular Time	999	999	$1.00 / **750**	$1.30 / -	-	750
	Overtime	999	999	$1.50 / **150**	$1.80 / -	-	150
	Subcontract	999	999	$1.90 / **200**	$2.20 / -	-	200
4	Regular Time	999	999	999	$1.00 / **450**	-	450
	Overtime	999	999	999	$1.50 / **90**	-	90
	Subcontract	999	999	999	$1.90 / **110**	90	200
	Requirements	300	850	1500	650	270	3570

	Q1	Q2	Q3	Q4
Costs	68	1,048	2,100	794
Total Cost				4,010

FIGURE 11.7

cell. Computing the cost column by column, as done by Tutor 11.3, yields a total cost of $4,010,000, or $4,014 × 1,000.

Quarter 1:	250($0) + 30($1.00) + 20($1.90)	= $ 68
Quarter 2:	420($1.30) + 90($1.80) + 340($1.00)	= 1,048
Quarter 3:	110($1.30) + 90($1.80) + 200($2.20) + 750($1.00) + 150($1.50) + 200($1.90)	= 2,100
Quarter 4:	450($1.00) + 90($1.50) + 110($1.90)	= 794
	Total	= $4,010

To interpret the solution, we can convert the tableau solution into the following table. For example, the total regular-time production in quarter 1 is 450,000 gallons (30,000 gallons to meet demand in quarter 1 and 420,000 gallons to help satisfy demand in quarter 2).

QUARTER	REGULAR-TIME PRODUCTION	OVERTIME PRODUCTION	SUB-CONTRACTING	TOTAL PRODUCTION	ANTICIPATION INVENTORY
1	450	90	20	560	250 + 560 − 300 = 510
2	450	90	200	740	510 + 740 − 850 = 400
3	750	150	200	1,100	400 + 1,100 − 1,500 = 0
4	450	90	110	650	0 + 650 − 350 = 300
Totals	2,100	420	530	3,050	

Note: Anticipation inventory is the amount at the end of each quarter, where Beginning inventory + Total production − Demand = Ending inventory.

The anticipation inventory held at the end of each quarter is obtained in the last column. For any quarter, it is the quarter's beginning inventory plus total production (regular-time and over-time production, plus subcontracting) minus demand. For example, for quarter 1 the beginning inventory (250,000) plus the total from production and subcontracting (560,000) minus quarter 1 demand (300,000) results in an ending inventory of 510,000, which also is the beginning inventory for quarter 2.

Decision Point This plan requires too much overtime and subcontracting. The manager decided to search for a better capacity plan—with increases in the workforce to boost regular-time production capacity—that could lower production costs, perhaps even low enough to offset the added capacity costs. ⊐

ADDITIONAL CAPACITY PLANS. A series of capacity plans can be tried and compared to find the best plan. Even though this process in itself involves trial and error, the trans-portation method yields the best mix of regular time, overtime, and subcontracting for each capacity plan.

MANAGERIAL CONSIDERATIONS

Other mathematical techniques are available. For example, the Linear Programming supplement on the Student CD-ROM shows how to formulate different aggregate planning and scheduling problems as linear programming models—and how to solve them once modeled.

Although such techniques can be useful in developing sound aggregate plans, they are only aids to the planning process. As you have seen, the planning process is dynamic and often complicated by conflicting objectives. Analytic techniques can help managers evaluate plans and resolve conflicting objectives, but managers—not techniques—make the decisions.

After arriving at an acceptable aggregate plan, management must implement it. However, the aggregate plan is stated in aggregate terms. The first step in implementa-tion, therefore, is to disaggregate the plan—that is, break it down into specific prod-ucts, workstations, and dates (see Chapter 12, "Resource Planning" and Chapter 13, "Lean Systems," and the Master Production Scheduling and Operations Scheduling supplements on the Student CD-ROM). The final step is to develop detailed schedules. **Scheduling** allocates resources over time to accomplish specific tasks.

To conclude this chapter, we discuss scheduling in both manufacturing and service organizations and some useful techniques for generating schedules. Two basic types of scheduling are used: **workforce scheduling,** which determines when employees work, and **operations scheduling,** which assigns jobs to machines or workers to jobs. At Air New Zealand, managers work with crew members to develop their workforce schedules. In manufacturing, operations scheduling is crucial because many performance measures, such as on-time delivery, inventory levels, the manufacturing cycle time, cost, and quality, relate directly to the scheduling of each production lot. Workforce scheduling is equally crucial because measures of performance such as customer waiting time, waiting-line length, utilization, cost, and quality are related to the availability of the servers.

scheduling The allocation of resources over time to accomplish specific tasks.

workforce scheduling A type of scheduling that determines when employees work.

operations scheduling A type of scheduling that assigns jobs to machines or workers to jobs.

SCHEDULING IN MANUFACTURING

Operations schedules are short-term plans designed to implement the master produc-tion schedule. Operations scheduling focuses on how best to use existing capacity, tak-ing into account technical production constraints. Often several jobs (e.g., open orders for components) must be processed at one or more workstations. Typically, a variety of tasks can be performed at each workstation. If schedules are not carefully planned to

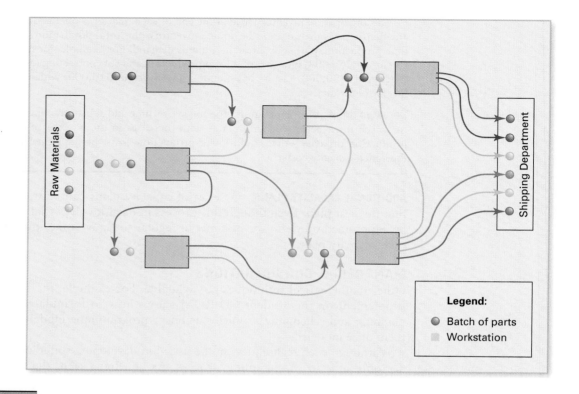

FIGURE 11.8

*Diagram of a
Manufacturing Process*

avoid bottlenecks, waiting lines may develop. For example, Figure 11.8 depicts the complexity of scheduling a manufacturing process. When a job order is received for a part, the raw materials are collected and the batch is moved to its first operation. The colored arrows show that jobs follow different routes through the manufacturing process, depending on the product being made. At each workstation someone must determine which job to process next because the rate at which jobs arrive at a workstation often differs from the rate at which the workstation can process them, thereby creating a waiting line. In addition, new jobs can enter the manufacturing process at any time, thereby creating a dynamic environment. Such complexity puts pressure on managers to develop scheduling procedures that will handle efficiently the production stream.

Here we introduce the problem of scheduling by presenting a traditional manual tool for scheduling called the Gantt chart. (For more on the performance measures and specific scheduling approaches used in manufacturing, see the Operations Scheduling supplement on the Student CD-ROM.) There are two basic manufacturing environments: job shops and flow shops. A **job shop** is a firm that specializes in low- to medium-volume production utilizing job or batch processes (see Chapter 2, "Process Management"). Tasks in this type of flexible flow environment are difficult to schedule because of the variability in job routings and the continual introduction of new jobs to be processed. A **flow shop** specializes in medium- to high-volume production and utilizes line or continuous processes. Tasks are easier to schedule because in a line flow facility the jobs have a common flow pattern through the system. Nonetheless, scheduling mistakes can be costly in either situation.

job shop A firm that specializes in low- to medium-volume production utilizing job or batch processes.

flow shop A firm that specializes in medium- to high-volume production and utilizes line or continuous processes.

GANTT CHARTS

The Gantt chart, which we introduced in Chapter 3, "Managing Project Processes," can be used as a tool for sequencing work on machines and monitoring its progress.

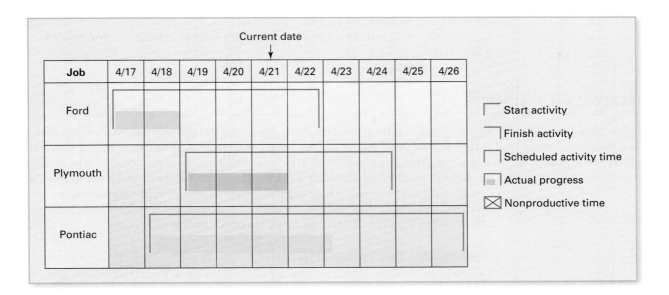

FIGURE 11.9

Gantt Chart of Job Progress for an Auto Parts Company

The chart takes two basic forms: the job or activity progress chart and the machine chart. Both types of Gantt charts present the ideal and the actual use of resources over time. The *progress chart* graphically displays the current status of each job relative to its scheduled completion date. For example, suppose that an automobile parts manufacturer has three jobs under way, one each for Ford, Plymouth, and Pontiac. The actual status of these orders is shown by the colored bars in Figure 11.9, the red lines indicate the desired schedule for the start and finish of each job. For the current date, April 21, this Gantt chart shows that the Ford order is behind schedule because operations has completed only the work scheduled through April 18. The Plymouth order is exactly on schedule, and the Pontiac order is ahead of schedule.

Figure 11.10 shows a *machine chart* for the automobile parts manufacturer. This chart depicts the sequence of future work at the two machines and also can be used to monitor progress. Using the same notation as in Figure 11.9, the chart shows that for the current date of April 21, the Plymouth job is on schedule at the grinder because the actual progress coincides with the current date. The Pontiac order has finished at the lathe, which is now idle. The plant manager can easily see from the Gantt machine

FIGURE 11.10

Gantt Chart for Machines at an Auto Parts Company

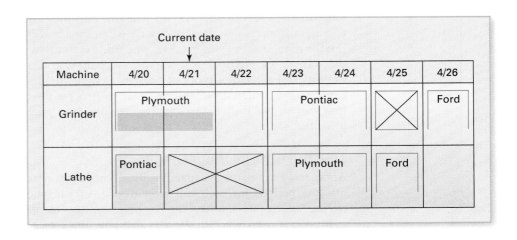

chart the consequence of juggling the schedules. The usual approach is to juggle the schedules by trial and error until a satisfactory level of selected performance measures is achieved.

SCHEDULING IN SERVICES

What scheduling methods can be used to manage the capacity of a service system?

One important distinction between manufacturing and services that affects scheduling is that service operations cannot create inventories to buffer demand uncertainties. A second distinction is that in service operations demand often is less predictable. Customers may decide on the spur of the moment that they need a hamburger, a haircut, or a plumbing repair. Thus, capacity, often in the form of employees, is crucial for service providers. In this section, we discuss various ways in which scheduling systems can facilitate the capacity management of service providers.

SCHEDULING CUSTOMER DEMAND

One way to manage capacity is to schedule customers for arrival times and definite periods of service time. With this approach, capacity remains fixed and demand is leveled to provide timely service and utilize capacity. Three methods are commonly used: appointments, reservations, and backlogs.

APPOINTMENTS.   An appointment system assigns specific times for service to customers. The advantages of this method are timely customer service and high utilization of servers. Doctors, dentists, lawyers, and automobile repair shops are examples of service providers that use appointment systems. Doctors can use the system to schedule parts of their day to visit hospital patients, and lawyers can set aside time to prepare cases. If timely service is to be provided, however, care must be taken to tailor the length of appointments to individual customer needs rather than merely scheduling customers at equal time intervals.

RESERVATIONS.   Reservation systems, although quite similar to appointment systems, are used when the customer actually occupies or uses facilities associated with the service. For example, customers reserve hotel rooms, automobiles, airline seats, and concert seats. The major advantage of reservation systems is the lead time they give service managers to plan the efficient use of facilities. Often reservations require some form of down payment to reduce the problem of no-shows.

BACKLOGS.   A less precise way to schedule customers is to allow backlogs to develop; that is, customers never know exactly when service will commence. They present their service request to an order taker, who adds it to the waiting line of orders already in the system. TV repair shops, restaurants, banks, grocery stores, and barber shops are examples of the many types of businesses that use this system. Various priority rules can be used to determine which order to process next. The usual rule is first come, first served, but if the order involves rework on a previous order, it may get a higher priority.

SCHEDULING THE WORKFORCE

Another way to manage capacity with a scheduling system is to specify the on-duty and off-duty periods for each employee over a certain time period, as in assigning postal clerks, nurses, pilots, attendants, or police officers to specific workdays and shifts. This approach is used when customers demand quick response and total demand can be forecasted with reasonable accuracy. In these instances, capacity is adjusted to meet the expected loads on the service system.

Recall that workforce schedules translate the staffing plan into specific schedules of work for each employee. Determining the workdays for each employee in itself does not make the staffing plan operational. Daily workforce requirements, stated in aggregate terms in the staffing plan, must be satisfied. The workforce capacity available each day must meet or exceed daily workforce requirements. If it does not, the scheduler must try to rearrange days off until the requirements are met. If no such schedule can be found, management might have to change the staffing plan and authorize more employees, overtime hours, or larger backlogs.

CONSTRAINTS. The technical constraints imposed on the workforce schedule are the resources provided by the staffing plan and the requirements placed on the operating system. However, other constraints, including legal and behavioral considerations, also can be imposed. For example, Air New Zealand is required to have at least a minimum number of flight attendants on duty at all times. Similarly, a minimum number of fire and safety personnel must be on duty at a fire station at all times. Such constraints limit management's flexibility in developing workforce schedules.

The constraints imposed by the psychological needs of workers complicate scheduling even more. Some of these constraints are written into labor agreements. For example, an employer may agree to give employees a certain number of consecutive days off per week or to limit employees' consecutive workdays to a certain maximum. Other provisions might govern the allocation of vacation, days off for holidays, or rotating shift assignments. In addition, preferences of the employees themselves need to be considered.

One way that managers deal with certain undesirable aspects of scheduling is to use a **rotating schedule,** which rotates employees through a series of workdays or hours. Thus, over a period of time, each person has the same opportunity to have weekends and holidays off and to work days, as well as evenings and nights. A rotating schedule gives each employee the next employee's schedule the following week. In contrast, a **fixed schedule** calls for each employee to work the same days and hours each week.

DEVELOPING A WORKFORCE SCHEDULE. Suppose that we are interested in developing an employee schedule for a company that operates seven days a week and provides each employee two consecutive days off. In this section, we demonstrate a method that recognizes this constraint.[2] The objective is to identify the two consecutive days off for each employee that will minimize the amount of total slack capacity. The work schedule for each employee, then, is the five days that remain after the two days off have been determined. The procedure involves the following steps.

Step 1. From the schedule of net requirements for the week, find all the pairs of consecutive days that exclude the maximum daily requirements. Select the unique pair that has the lowest total requirements for the two days. In some unusual situations, all pairs may contain a day with the maximum requirements. If so, select the pair with the lowest total requirements. Suppose that the numbers of employees required are

Monday:	8	Friday:	7
Tuesday:	9	Saturday:	4
Wednesday:	2	Sunday:	2
Thursday:	12		

rotating schedule
A schedule that rotates employees through a series of workdays or hours.

fixed schedule
A schedule that calls for each employee to work the same days and hours each week.

How can an effective workforce schedule be developed for a service system?

---

[2]See Tibrewala, Philippe, and Brown (1972) for an optimizing approach.

The maximum capacity requirement is 12 employees on Thursday. The pair having the lowest total requirements is Saturday–Sunday, with $4 + 2 = 6$.

Step 2.   If a tie occurs, choose one of the tied pairs, consistent with provisions written into the labor agreement, if any. Alternatively, the tie could be broken by asking the employee being scheduled to make the choice. As a last resort, the tie could be broken arbitrarily. For example, preference could be given to Saturday–Sunday pairs.

Step 3.   Assign the employee the selected pair of days off. Subtract the requirements satisfied by the employee from the net requirements for each day the employee is to work. In this case, the employee is assigned Saturday and Sunday off. After requirements are subtracted, Monday's requirement is 7, Tuesday's is 8, Wednesday's is 1, Thursday's is 11, and Friday's is 6. Saturday's and Sunday's requirements do not change because no employee is yet scheduled to work those days.

Step 4.   Repeat steps 1–3 until all requirements have been satisfied or a certain number of employees have been scheduled.

This method reduces the amount of slack capacity assigned to days having low requirements and forces the days having high requirements to be scheduled first. It also recognizes some of the behavioral and contractual aspects of workforce scheduling in the tie-breaking rules. However, the schedules produced might *not* minimize total slack capacity. Different rules for finding the days-off pair and breaking ties are needed to ensure minimal total slack capacity.

EXAMPLE 11.4   *Developing a Workforce Schedule*

**TUTOR
11.5**

The Amalgamated Parcel Service is open seven days a week. The schedule of requirements is

Day	M	T	W	Th	F	S	Su
Number of employees	6	4	8	9	10*	3	2

The manager needs a workforce schedule that provides two consecutive days off and minimizes the amount of total slack capacity. To break ties in the selection of off days, the scheduler gives preference to Saturday–Sunday if it is one of the tied pairs. If not, she selects one of the tied pairs arbitrarily.

SOLUTION

Friday contains the maximum requirements (designated by an *), and the pair S–Su has the lowest total requirements. Therefore, employee 1 is scheduled to work Monday–Friday. The revised set of requirements, after scheduling employee 1, is

Day	M	T	W	Th	F	S	Su
Number of employees	5	3	7	8	9*	3	2

Note that Friday still has the maximum requirements and that the requirements for S–Su are carried forward because these are employee 1's days off. These updated requirements are the ones the scheduler uses for the next employee.

The unique minimum again is on S–Su, so the scheduler assigns employee 2 to a M–F schedule. She then reduces the requirements for M–F to reflect the assignment of employee 2.

The day-off assignments for the remaining employees are shown in Table 11.1. In this example, Friday always has the maximum requirements and should be avoided as a day off. The schedule for the employees is shown in Table 11.2.

TABLE 11.1 *Scheduling Days Off*

M	T	W	Th	F	S	Su	EMPLOYEE	COMMENTS
4	2	6	7	8*	3	2	3	S–Su has the lowest total requirements. Reduce the requirements to reflect a M–F schedule for employee 3.
3	1	5	6	7*	3	2	4	M–T has the lowest total requirements. Assign employee 4 to a W–Su schedule and update the requirements.
3	1	4	5	6*	2	1	5	S–Su has the lowest total requirements. Assign employee 5 to a M–F schedule and update the requirements.
2	0	3	4	5*	2	1	6	M–T has the lowest total requirements. Assign employee 6 to a W–Su schedule and update the requirements.
2	0	2	3	4*	1	0	7	S–Su has the lowest total requirements. Assign employee 7 to a M–F schedule and update the requirements.
1	0	1	2	3*	1	0	8	Three pairs have the minimum requirement and the lowest total: S–Su, M–T, and T–W. Choose S–Su according to the tie-breaking rule. Assign employee 8 a M–F schedule and update the requirements.
0	0	0	1	2*	1	0	9	Arbitrarily choose Su–M to break ties because S–Su does not have the lowest total requirements. Assign employee 9 to a T–S schedule.
0	0	0	0	1*	0	0	10	Choose S–Su according to the tie-breaking rule. Assign employee 10 a M–F schedule.

TABLE 11.2 *Final Schedule*

EMPLOYEE	M	T	W	Th	F	S	Su	TOTAL
1	X	X	X	X	X	off	off	
2	X	X	X	X	X	off	off	
3	X	X	X	X	X	off	off	
4	off	off	X	X	X	X	X	
5	X	X	X	X	X	off	off	
6	off	off	X	X	X	X	X	
7	X	X	X	X	X	off	off	
8	X	X	X	X	X	off	off	
9	off	X	X	X	X	X	off	
10	X	X	X	X	X	off	off	
Capacity, C	7	7	10	10	10	3	2	50
Requirements, R	6	4	8	9	10	3	2	42
Slack, $C - R$	1	3	2	1	0	0	1	8

Decision Point With its substantial amount of slack capacity, the schedule is not unique. Employee 9, for example, could have Su–M, M–T, or T–W off without causing a capacity shortage. Indeed, the company might be able to get by with one fewer employee because of the total of eight slack days of capacity. However, all 10 employees are needed on Fridays. If the manager were willing to get by with only nine employees on Fridays or if someone could work one day of overtime on a rotating basis, he would not need employee 10. As indicated in the table, the net requirement left for employee 10 to satisfy amounts to only one day, Friday. Thus, employee 10 can be used to fill in for vacationing or sick employees. ◗

MANAGERIAL **PRACTICE**
Course Scheduling at the University of California, Los Angeles

Manually scheduling undergraduate, MBA, and doctoral courses at the Anderson Graduate School of Management at the University of California, Los Angeles (www.agsm.ucr.edu), used to take two people as many as three days each quarter. The complexity comes from myriad faculty preferences and facility and administrative constraints. For example, teachers may prefer to teach their assigned courses back-to-back, on the same days, and in the afternoon. In addition, there are only eight time slots in a day to start core MBA classes and limits to the number of rooms that can handle case discussion, large lectures, or computer access. Courses taught by the same instructor must not overlap, and courses must be scheduled at times so that students can take all required courses offered each quarter. Scheduling the 25 core MBA courses and 120 noncore courses to maximize faculty preferences, meet student needs, and satisfy all the constraints obviously is difficult.

Scheduling of the courses is now done with computer assistance. Core courses are scheduled first because they have limited starting times and all MBA students must enroll in them. Data on the number of sections of the core courses to be offered, facility and administrative constraints, and the teaching preferences of the faculty who will teach the core courses are entered into a com-

puter model that assigns faculty to courses and courses to time slots that maximizes teaching preferences and meets all constraints. Not all teaching preferences can be satisfied. If the teacher's time preferences can be changed, however, the model can be used again to produce a completely new schedule in seconds.

Another model was developed to assign noncore courses to times and teachers to courses so that faculty preferences are maximized. Inputs to the model include the teaching assignments of the core courses, as a teacher can teach both a core and noncore course, the schedule of the core courses, classroom availability, and faculty preferences.

The system has been implemented and is running smoothly. The scheduling system improves the quality of the final course schedule and saves time. The entire schedule of courses can now be produced in only three hours, which includes time needed to resolve conflicts with faculty preferences.

Source: Stallaert, Jan. "Automated Timetabling Improves Course Scheduling at UCLA." *Interfaces*, vol. 27, no. 4 (July–August 1997), pp. 67–81.

COMPUTERIZED WORKFORCE SCHEDULING SYSTEMS. Workforce scheduling often entails myriad constraints and concerns. In some types of firms, such as telephone companies, mail-order catalog houses, or emergency hotline agencies, employees must be on duty 24 hours a day, seven days a week. Sometimes a portion of the staff is part-time, allowing management a great deal of flexibility in developing schedules but adding considerable complexity to the requirements. The flexibility comes from the opportunity to match anticipated loads closely by using overlapping shifts or odd shift lengths; the complexity comes from having to evaluate the numerous possible alternatives. Management also must consider the timing of lunch breaks and rest periods, the number and starting times of shift schedules, and the days off for each employee. An additional typical concern is that the number of employees on duty at any particular time be sufficient to answer calls within a reasonable amount of time.

Computerized scheduling systems are available to cope with the complexity of workforce scheduling. For example, L.L.Bean's telephone service center must be staffed with telephone operators seven days a week, 24 hours a day. The company uses 350 permanent and temporary employees. The permanent workers are guaranteed a minimum weekly workload apportioned over a seven-day week on a rotating schedule. The temporary staff works a variety of schedules, ranging from a full six-day week to a guaranteed weekly minimum of 20 hours. The company uses a computer program to forecast the hourly load for the telephone service center, translate the workload into capacity requirements, and then generate week-long staffing schedules for the permanent and temporary telephone operators to meet these demand requirements. The program selects the schedule that minimizes the sum of expected costs of over- and understaffing. The Managerial Practice describes the computerized scheduling system used by the Anderson Graduate School of Management at UCLA.

AGGREGATE PLANNING AND SCHEDULING ACROSS THE ORGANIZATION

Aggregate planning is meaningful throughout the organization. First, the aggregate planning process requires managerial inputs from all of a firm's functions and must reconcile sometimes conflicting needs and objectives. Marketing provides inputs on demand and customer requirements, and accounting provides important cost data and the firm's financial condition. One of finance's objectives might be to cut inventory, whereas operations might argue for a more stable workforce and for less reliance on overtime. Second, each function is affected by the plan. An aggregate plan puts into effect decisions on expanding or reducing the size of the workforce, which has a direct impact on the hiring and training requirements for the human resources function. As an aggregate plan is implemented, it creates revenue and cost streams that finance must deal with as it manages the firm's cash flows. Third, each department and group in a firm has its own workforce. Managers of its processes must make choices on hiring, overtime, and vacations. Aggregate planning is an activity for the whole organization.

Schedules are also a part of everyday life, whether the business is an airline, computer manufacturer, or university. Schedules involve an enormous amount of detail and affect every process in the firm. For example, product, service, and employee schedules determine specific cash flow requirements, trigger the billing process into action, and initiate requirements for the employee training process. The order-fulfillment process depends on good performance in terms of due dates for promised products or services, which is the result of a good scheduling process. In addition, when customers place orders using a Web-based order-entry process, the scheduling process determines when they can expect to receive the product or service. Certainly, regardless of the discipline, schedules affect everyone in a firm.

CHAPTER HIGHLIGHTS

❏ Aggregate plans (production plans or staffing plans) are statements of strategy that specify time-phased production or service rates, workforce levels, and (in manufacturing) inventory investment. These plans show how the organization will work toward longer-term objectives while considering the demand and capacity that are likely to exist during a planning horizon of only a year or two. In manufacturing organizations, the plan linking strategic goals to the master production schedule is called the production plan. In service organizations, the staffing plan links strategic goals to the workforce schedule.

❏ To reduce the level of detail required in the planning process, products or services are aggregated into families, and labor is aggregated along product family lines or according to the general skills or services provided. Time is aggregated into periods of months or quarters.

❏ Managerial inputs are required from the various functional areas in the organization. This approach typically raises conflicting objectives, such as high customer service, a stable workforce, and low inventory investment. Creativity and cross-functional compromise are required to reconcile these conflicts.

❏ The two basic types of alternatives are reactive and aggressive. Reactive alternatives take customer demand as a given. Aggressive alternatives attempt to change the timing or quantity of customer demand to stabilize production or service rates and reduce inventory requirements.

□ Four pure, but generally high-cost planning strategies are the two level strategies, which maintain a constant workforce size or production rate, and the two chase strategies, which vary workforce level or production rate to match fluctuations in demand.

□ Developing aggregate plans is an iterative process of determining demand requirements; identifying relevant constraints, alternatives, and costs; preparing and approving a plan; and implementing and updating the plan.

□ Although spreadsheets, the transportation method, and linear programming can help analyze complicated alternatives, aggregate planning is primarily an exercise in conflict resolution and compromise. Ultimately, decisions are made by managers, not by quantitative methods.

□ Scheduling is the allocation of resources over a period of time to accomplish a specific set of tasks. Two basic types of scheduling are workforce scheduling and operations scheduling. Scheduling applications are becoming more common in ERP systems.

□ Gantt charts are useful for depicting the sequence of work at a particular workstation and for monitoring the progress of jobs in the system.

□ Capacity considerations are important for scheduling services. If the capacity of the operating system is fixed, loads can be leveled by using approaches such as appointments, reservations, and backlogs. If service is determined by labor availability, workforce scheduling may be appropriate.

□ A workforce schedule translates a staffing plan into a specific work schedule for each employee. Typical workforce scheduling considerations include capacity limits, service targets, consecutive days off, maximum number of workdays in a row, type of schedule (fixed or rotating), and vacation and holiday time.

SOLVED PROBLEM 1

**TUTOR
11.4**

The Cranston Telephone Company employs workers who lay telephone cables and perform various other construction tasks. The company prides itself on good service and strives to complete all service orders within the planning period in which they are received.

Each worker puts in 600 hours of regular time per planning period and can work as much as an additional 100 hours overtime. The operations department has estimated the following workforce requirements for such services over the next four planning periods:

Planning Period	1	2	3	4
Demand (hours)	21,000	18,000	30,000	12,000

Cranston pays regular-time wages of $6,000 per employee per period for any time worked up to 600 hours (including undertime). The overtime pay rate is $15 per hour over 600 hours. Hiring, training, and outfitting a new employee cost $8,000. Layoff costs are $2,000 per employee. Currently, 40 employees work for Cranston in this capacity. No delays in service or backorders are allowed. Use the spreadsheet approach to answer the following questions:

a. Develop a level workforce plan that uses only the overtime and undertime alternatives. Maximize the use of overtime during the peak period so as to minimize the workforce level and amount of undertime.

b. Prepare a chase strategy using only the workforce adjustment alternative of hiring and layoffs. What are the total numbers of employees hired and laid off?

c. Propose an effective mixed-strategy plan.

d. Compare the total costs of the three plans.

SOLUTION

a. The peak demand is 30,000 hours in period 3. As each employee can work 700 hours per period (600 on regular time and 100 on overtime), the level workforce that minimizes undertime is 30,000/700 = 42.86, or 43, employees. The level strategy calls for three employees to be hired in the first quarter and for none to be laid off. To convert the demand requirements into employee-period equivalents, divide the demand in hours by 600. For example, the demand of 21,000 hours in period 1 translates into 35 employee-period equivalents (21,000/600) and demand in the third period translates into 50

Starting workforce	40		Regular-time hrs per worker	600
Regular-time wages	$6,000		Max overtime hrs per worker	100
(per worker per quarter)			Overtime rate ($/hour)	$15
☑ Employees paid for undertime			Cost to hire one worker	$8,000
Level Strategy ▼			Cost to lay off one worker	$2,000
Required staff level	43			

| | Quarter | | | | |
	1	2	3	4	Total
Requirement (hrs)	21,000	18,000	30,000	12,000	81000
Workforce level (workers)	43	43	43	43	172
Undertime (hours)	4,800	7,800	0	13,800	26400
Overtime (hours)	0	0	4,200	0	4200
Productive time (hours)	21,000	18,000	25,800	12,000	76800
Hires (workers)	3	0	0	0	3
Layoffs (workers)	0	0	0	0	0
Costs					
Productive time	$210,000	$180,000	$258,000	$120,000	$768,000
Undertime	48,000	78,000	0	138,000	264,000
Overtime	0	0	63,000	0	63,000
Hires	24,000	0	0	0	24,000
Layoffs	0	0	0	0	0
Total Cost					$1,119,000

FIGURE 11.11

employee-period equivalents (30,000/600). Figure 11.11 shows one solution using the "level strategy" option of Tutor 11.4.

b. The chase strategy workforce is calculated by dividing the demand for each period by 600 hours, or the amount of regular-time work for one employee during one period. This strategy calls for a total of 20 workers to be hired and 40 to be laid off during the four period plan. Figure 11.12 shows the "chase strategy" solution that Tutor 11.4 produces.

Starting workforce	40		Regular-time hrs per worker	600
Regular-time wages	$6,000		Max overtime hrs per worker	100
(per worker per quarter)			Overtime rate ($/hour)	$15
☑ Employees paid for undertime			Cost to hire one worker	$8,000
Chase Strategy ▼			Cost to lay off one worker	$2,000
Required staff level	---			

| | Quarter | | | | |
	1	2	3	4	Total
Requirement (hrs)	21,000	18,000	30,000	12,000	81,000
Workforce level (workers)	35	30	50	20	135
Undertime (hours)	0	0	0	0	0
Overtime (hours)	0	0	0	0	0
Productive time (hours)	21,000	18,000	30,000	12,000	81,000
Hires (workers)	0	0	20	0	20
Layoffs (workers)	5	5	0	30	40
Costs					
Productive time	$210,000	$180,000	$300,000	$120,000	$810,000
Undertime	0	0	0	0	0
Overtime	0	0	0	0	0
Hires	0	0	160,000	0	160,000
Layoffs	10,000	10,000	0	60,000	80,000
Total Cost					$1,050,000

FIGURE 11.12

Solver - Aggregate Planning with Spreadsheets

Enter data in yellow-shaded areas.

☑ Employees Paid for Undertime

	1	2	3	4	Total
Requirement	35	30	50	20	135
Workforce level	35	35	43	30	143
Undertime	0	5	0	10	15
Overtime	0	0	7	0	7
Productive time	35	30	43	20	128
Hires	0	0	8	0	8
Layoffs	5	0	0	13	18

Costs	1	2	3	4	Totals
Productive time	$210,000	180,000	258,000	120,000	$768,000
Undertime	$0	30,000	0	60,000	$90,000
Overtime	$0	0	63,000	0	$63,000
Hires	$0	0	64,000	0	$64,000
Layoffs	$10,000	0	0	26,000	$36,000
Total cost	$220,000	210,000	385,000	206,000	$1,021,000

FIGURE 11.13

c. The mixed strategy plan that we propose uses a combination of hires, layoffs, and overtime to reduce total costs. The workforce is reduced by 5 at the beginning of the first period, increased by 8 in the third period, and reduced by 13 in the fourth period. Switching to the general-purpose *Aggregate Planning with Spreadsheets Solver* for this mixed strategy, and hiding any unneeded columns and rows, we get the results shown in Figure 11.13. The Solver can evaluate any aggregate plan that is proposed. Its format is much the same as that for Tutor 11.4, except that the data in the top half of the spreadsheet (above the cost data) are expressed as employee-period equivalents rather than as hours.

d. The total cost of the level strategy is $1,119,000. The chase strategy results in a total cost of $1,050,000. The mixed-strategy plan was developed by trial and error and results in a total cost of $1,021,000. Further improvements to the mixed strategy are possible.

SOLVED PROBLEM 2

The Arctic Air Company produces residential air conditioners. The manufacturing manager wants to develop a production plan for the next year based on the following demand and capacity data (in hundreds of product units):

	PERIOD					
	Jan–Feb (1)	Mar–Apr (2)	May–Jun (3)	Jul–Aug (4)	Sep–Oct (5)	Nov–Dec (6)
Demand	50	60	90	120	70	40
Capacities						
Regular time	65	65	65	80	80	65
Overtime	13	13	13	16	16	13
Subcontractor	10	10	10	10	10	10

Undertime is unpaid, and no cost is associated with unused overtime or subcontractor capacity. Producing one air-conditioning unit on regular time costs $1,000, including $300 for labor. Producing a unit on overtime costs $1,150. A subcontractor can produce a unit to Arctic Air specifications for $1,250. Holding an air conditioner in stock costs $60 for each two-month period, and 200 air conditioners are currently in stock. The plan calls for 400 units to be in stock at the end of period 6. No backorders are allowed. Use the transportation method to develop the aggregate plan that minimizes costs.

SOLUTION

The following table identifies the optimal production and inventory plans and concludes with a cost summary. Figure 11.14 shows the tableau that corresponds to this solution. An arbitrarily large cost ($99,999 per period) was used for backorders, which effectively ruled them out. Again, all production quantities are in hundreds of units. Note that demand in period 6 is 4,400. That amount is the period 6 demand plus the desired ending inventory of 400. The anticipation inventory is measured as the amount at the end of each period. Cost calculations are based on the assumption that workers are not paid for undertime or are productively put to work elsewhere in the organization whenever they are not needed for this work. The total cost of this plan is $44,287,000.

Production Plan

PERIOD	REGULAR-TIME PRODUCTION	OVERTIME PRODUCTION	SUBCONTRACTING	TOTAL
1	6,500	—	—	6,500
2	6,500	400	—	6,900
3	6,500	1,300	—	7,800
4	8,000	1,600	1,000	10,600
5	7,000	—	—	7,000
6	4,400	—	—	4,400

Anticipation Inventory

PERIOD	BEGINNING INVENTORY PLUS TOTAL PRODUCTION MINUS DEMAND	ANTICIPATION (ENDING) INVENTORY
1	200 + 6,500 − 5,000	1,700
2	1,700 + 6,900 − 6,000	2,600
3	2,600 + 7,800 − 9,000	1,400
4	1,400 + 10,600 − 12,000	0
5	0 + 7,000 − 7,000	0
6	0 + 4,400 − 4,000	400

Alternatives		Time Period						Unused Capacity	Total Capacity
		1	2	3	4	5	6		
Period	I_0	0	60	120	180	240	300		
		2						0	2
1	R_1	1,000	1,060	1,120	1,180	1,240	1,300		
		48		17				0	65
	R_1	1,150	1,210	1,270	1,330	1,390	1,450		
								13	13
	S_1	1,250	1,310	1,370	1,430	1,490	1,550		
								10	10
2	R_2	99,999	1,000	1,060	1,120	1,180	1,240		
			60	5				0	65
	O_2	99,999	1,150	1,210	1,270	1,330	1,390		
					4			9	13
	S_2	99,999	1,250	1,310	1,370	1,430	1,490		
								10	10
3	R_3	99,999	99,999	1,000	1,060	1,120	1,180		
				65				0	65
	O_3	99,999	99,999	1,150	1,210	1,270	1,330		
				3	10			0	13
	S_3	99,999	99,999	1,250	1,310	1,370	1,430		
								10	10
4	R_4	99,999	99,999	99,999	1,000	1,060	1,120		
					80			0	80
	R_4	99,999	99,999	99,999	1,150	1,210	1,270		
					16			0	16
	S_4	99,999	99,999	99,999	1,250	1,310	1,370		
					10			0	10
5	R_5	99,999	99,999	99,999	99,999	1,000	1,060		
						70		10	80
	O_5	99,999	99,999	99,999	99,999	1,150	1,210		
								16	16
	S_5	99,999	99,999	99,999	99,999	1,250	1,310		
								10	10
6	R_6	99,999	99,999	99,999	99,999	99,999	1,000		
							44	21	65
	O_6	99,999	99,999	99,999	99,999	99,999	1,150		
								13	13
	S_6	99,999	99,999	99,999	99,999	99,999	1,250		
								10	10
D		50	60	90	120	70	44	132	566

FIGURE 11.14

SOLVED PROBLEM 3

The Food Bin grocery store operates 24 hours per day, seven days per week. Fred Bulger, the store manager, has been analyzing the efficiency and productivity of store operations recently. Bulger decided to observe the need for checkout clerks on the first shift for a one-month period. At the end of the month, he calculated the average number of checkout registers that should be open during the first shift each day. His results showed peak needs on Saturdays and Sundays.

Day	M	T	W	Th	F	S	Su
Number of employees	3	4	5	5	4	7	8

Bulger now has to come up with a workforce schedule that guarantees each checkout clerk two consecutive days off but still covers all requirements.

a. Develop a workforce schedule that covers all requirements while giving two consecutive days off to each clerk. How many clerks are needed? Assume that the clerks have no preference regarding which days they have off.

b. Plans can be made to use the clerks for other duties if slack or idle time resulting from this schedule can be determined. How much idle time will result from this schedule and on what days?

SOLUTION

a. We use the method demonstrated in Example 11.4 to determine the number of clerks needed.

	DAY						
	M	**T**	**W**	**Th**	**F**	**S**	**Su**
Requirements	3	4	5	5	4	7	8*
Clerk 1	off	off	X	X	X	X	X
Requirements	3	4	4	4	3	6	7*
Clerk 2	off	off	X	X	X	X	X
Requirements	3	4	3	3	2	5	6*
Clerk 3	X	X	X	off	off	X	X
Requirements	2	3	2	3	2	4	5*
Clerk 4	X	X	X	off	off	X	X
Requirements	1	2	1	3	2	3	4*
Clerk 5	X	off	off	X	X	X	X
Requirements	0	2	1	2	1	2	3*
Clerk 6	off	off	X	X	X	X	X
Requirements	0	2*	0	1	0	1	2*
Clerk 7	X	X	off	off	X	X	X
Requirements	0	1*	0	1*	0	0	1*
Clerk 8	X	X	X	X	off	off	X
Requirements	0	0	0	0	0	0	0

*Maximum requirements.

The minimum number of clerks is eight.

b. Based on the results in part (a) the number of clerks on duty minus the requirements is the number of idle clerks available for other duties:

	DAY						
	M	**T**	**W**	**Th**	**F**	**S**	**Su**
Number on duty	5	4	6	5	5	7	8
Requirements	3	4	5	5	4	7	8
Idle clerks	2	0	1	0	1	0	0

The slack in this schedule would indicate to Bulger the number of employees he might ask to work part-time (fewer than five days per week). For example, clerk 7 might work Tuesday, Saturday, and Sunday, and clerk 8 might work Tuesday, Thursday, and Sunday to eliminate slack from the schedule.

CD-ROM RESOURCES

The Student CD-ROM that accompanies this text contains the following resources, which allow you to further practice and apply the concepts presented in this chapter.

- ❑ **OM Explorer Tutors:** OM Explorer contains five tutor programs that will help you learn how to implement a level strategy, chase strategy, transportation method, various staffing strategies, and workforce scheduling. See the Chapter 11 folder in OM Explorer. See also the Tutor Exercises on developing a level strategy and creating a workforce schedule.

- ❑ **OM Explorer Solvers:** OM Explorer has four programs that can be used to solve general aggregate planning problems with spreadsheets, production planning with the transportation method, and workforce scheduling. See the Aggregate Planning and Scheduling folders in OM Explorer for these routines.

- ❑ **Discussion Questions:** Three questions raise important considerations in layoff costs, workforce variability, and a company's responsibilities to a community.

- ❑ **Cases:**

    - ❑ **Memorial Hospital:** What nurse staffing plan do you propose?

    - ❑ **Food King:** What schedule do you propose for stockers and baggers?

- ❑ **Experiential Exercise:** Use the Memorial Hospital case as an in-class team experience.

- ❑ **Supplement I: Linear Programming.** See how linear programming problems can be solved and how both aggregate planning and scheduling problems can be modeled.

- ❑ **Supplement J: Operations Scheduling.** Read about various scheduling approaches in job shop and flow shop environments.

- ❑ **Supplement K: Master Production Scheduling.** See how the production plan gets broken down into plans for individual products.

INTERACTIVE RESOURCES

The Interactive Web site associated with this text (www.prenhall.com/ritzman) contains many tools and activities specifically designed for this chapter. The following items are recommended to enhance your understanding of the material in this chapter.

- ❑ **Internet Activities:** Try out eight different links to aggregate planning and scheduling topics, including job opportunities, handling seasonal demands at H&R Block, NUMMI's scheduling system, and scheduling assistance offered by United Airlines.

- ❑ **Internet Tours:** Check out the aggregate planning strategies at Statton Furniture Comapny and the scheduling issues at d'Elegant Van Conversion.

PROBLEMS

An icon next to a problem identifies the software that can be helpful but is not mandatory. The software is available on the Student CD-ROM.

1. 🌐 **OM Explorer** The Barberton Municipal Division of Road Maintenance is charged with road repair in the city of Barberton and surrounding area. Cindy Kramer, road mainte-

nance director, must submit a staffing plan for the next year based on a set schedule for repairs and on the city budget. Kramer estimates that the labor hours required for the next four quarters are 6,000, 12,000, 19,000, and 9,000, respectively. Each of the 11 workers on the workforce can contribute 500 hours per quarter. Payroll costs are $6,000 in wages per worker for regular time worked up to 500 hours, with an overtime pay rate of $18 for each overtime hour. Overtime is limited to 20 percent of the regular-time capacity in any quarter. Although unused overtime capacity has no cost, unused regular time is paid at $12 per hour. The cost of hiring a worker is $3,000, and the cost of laying off a worker is $2,000. Subcontracting is not permitted.

a. Find a level workforce plan that allows no delay in road repair and minimizes undertime. Overtime can be used to its limits in any quarter. What is the total cost of the plan and how many undertime hours does it call for?

b. Use a chase strategy that varies the workforce level without using overtime or undertime. What is the total cost of this plan?

c. Propose a plan of your own. Compare your plan with those in parts (a) and (b) and discuss its comparative merits.

2. **OM Explorer** Bob Carlton's golf camp estimates the following workforce requirements for its services over the next two years.

Quarter	1	2	3	4
Demand (*hours*)	4,200	6,400	3,000	4,800

Quarter	5	6	7	8
Demand (*hours*)	4,400	6,240	3,600	4,800

Each certified instructor puts in 480 hours per quarter regular time and can work an additional 120 hours overtime. Regular-time wages and benefits cost Carlton $7,200 per employee per quarter for regular time worked up to 480 hours, with an overtime cost of $20 per hour. Unused regular time for certified instructors is paid at $15 per hour. There is no cost for unused overtime capacity. The cost of hiring, training, and certifying a new employee is $10,000. Layoff costs are $4,000 per employee. Currently, eight employees work in this capacity.

a. Find a level workforce plan that allows for no delay in service and minimizes undertime. What is the total cost of this plan?

b. Use a chase strategy that varies the workforce level without using overtime or undertime. What is the total cost of this plan?

c. Propose a low-cost, mixed-strategy plan and calculate its total cost.

If total demand is the same, what level of production rate is needed now?

3. **OM Explorer** Management at the Davis Corporation has determined the following demand schedule (in units).

Month	1	2	3	4
Demand	500	800	1,000	1,400

Month	5	6	7	8
Demand	2,000	1,600	1,400	1,200

Month	9	10	11	12
Demand	1,000	2,400	3,000	1,000

An employee can produce an average of 10 units per month. Each worker on the payroll costs $2,000 in regular-time wages per month. Undertime is paid at the same rate as regular time. In accordance with the labor contract in force, Davis Corporation does not work overtime or use subcontracting. Davis can hire and train a new employee for $2,000 and lay one off for $500. Inventory costs $32 per unit on hand at the end of each month. At present, 140 employees are on the payroll.

a. Prepare a production plan with a level workforce strategy. The plan may call for a one-time adjustment of the workforce before month 1.

b. Prepare a production plan with a chase strategy that varies the workforce without undertime, overtime, and subcontracting.

c. Compare and contrast the two pure-strategy plans on the basis of annual costs and other factors that you believe to be important.

d. Propose a mixed-strategy plan that is better than the two pure-strategy plans. Explain why you believe that your plan is better.

4. **OM Explorer** The Flying Frisbee Company has forecasted the following staffing requirements for full-time employees. Demand is seasonal, and management wants three alternative staffing plans to be developed.

Month	1	2	3	4
Requirement	2	2	4	6

Month	5	6	7	8
Requirement	18	20	12	18

Month	9	10	11	12
Requirement	7	3	2	1

The company currently has 10 employees. No more than 10 new hires can be accommodated in any month because of limited training facilities. No backorders are allowed, and overtime cannot exceed 25 percent of regular-time capacity in any month. There is no cost for unused overtime capacity. Regular-time wages are $1,500 per month, and overtime wages are 150 percent of regular-time wages. Undertime is paid at the same rate as regular time. The hiring cost is $2,500 per person, and the layoff cost is $2,000 per person.

a. Prepare a staffing plan utilizing a level workforce strategy. The plan may call for a one-time adjustment of the workforce before month 1.

b. Using a chase strategy, prepare a plan that is consistent with the constraint on hiring and minimizes use of overtime.

c. Prepare a low-cost, mixed-strategy plan.

d. Which strategy is most cost-effective? What are the advantages and disadvantages of each plan?

5. 💿 **OM Explorer** The Twilight Clothing Company makes jeans for children. Management has just prepared a forecast of sales (in pairs of jeans) for next year and now must prepare a production plan. The company has traditionally maintained a level workforce strategy. Currently, there are eight workers, who have been with the company for a number of years. Each employee can produce 2,000 pairs of jeans during a two-month planning period. Every year management authorizes overtime in periods 1, 5, and 6, up to a maximum of 20 percent of regular-time capacity. Management wants to avoid stockouts and backorders and will not accept any plan that calls for such shortages. At present, there are 12,000 pairs of jeans in finished goods inventory. The demand forecast is as follows:

Period	1	2	3
Sales	25,000	6,500	15,000

Period	4	5	6
Sales	19,000	32,000	29,000

a. Is the level workforce strategy feasible with the current workforce, assuming that overtime is used only in periods 1, 5, and 6? Explain.

b. Find two alternative plans that would satisfy management's concern over stockouts and backorders, disregarding costs. What trade-offs between these two plans must be considered?

6. 💿 **OM Explorer** Gerald Glynn manages the Michaels Distribution Center. After careful examination of his database information, he has determined the daily requirements for part-time loading dock personnel. The distribution center operates seven days a week, and the daily part-time staffing requirements are

Day	M	T	W	Th	F	S	Su
Requirements	6	3	5	3	7	2	3

Find the minimum number of workers Glynn must hire. Prepare a workforce schedule for these individuals so that each will have two consecutive days off per week and all staffing requirements will be satisfied. Give preference to the pair S–Su in case of a tie.

7. Cara Ryder manages a ski school in a large resort and is trying to develop a schedule for instructors. The instructors receive little salary and work just enough to earn room and board. They do receive free skiing, spending most of their free time tackling the resort's notorious double black diamond slopes. Hence, the instructors work only four days a week. One of the lesson packages offered at the resort is a four-day beginner package. Ryder likes to keep the same instructor with a group over the four-day period, so she schedules the instructors for four consecutive days and then three days off. Ryder uses years of experience with demand forecasts provided by management to formulate her instructor requirements for the upcoming month.

Day	M	T	W	Th	F	S	Su
Requirements	7	5	4	5	6	9	8

a. Determine how many instructors Ryder needs to employ. Give preference to Saturday and Sunday off. (*Hint*: Look for the group of three days with lowest requirements.)

b. Specify the work schedule for each employee. How much slack does your schedule generate for each day?

8. 💿 **OM Explorer** The mayor of Massilon, Ohio, wanting to be environmentally progressive, has decided to implement a recycling plan. All residents of the city will receive a special three-part bin to separate their glass, plastic, and aluminum, and the city will be responsible for picking up the materials. A young city and regional planning graduate, Michael Duffy, has been hired to manage the recycling program. After carefully studying the city's population density, Duffy decides that the following numbers of recycling collectors will be needed.

Day	M	T	W	Th	F	S	Su
Requirements	12	7	9	9	5	3	6

The requirements are based on the populations of the various housing developments and subdivisions in the city and surrounding communities. To motivate residents of some areas to have their pickups scheduled on weekends, a special tax break will be given.

a. Find the minimum number of recycling collectors required if each employee works five days a week and has two consecutive days off. Give preference to S–Su when that pair is involved in a tie.

b. Specify the work schedule for each employee. How much slack does your schedule generate for each day?

c. Suppose that Duffy can smooth the requirements further through greater tax incentives. The requirements then will be 8 on Monday and 7 on the other days of the week. How many employees will be needed now? Find the optimal solution in terms of minimal total slack capacity. Does smoothing of requirements have capital investment implications? If so, what are they?

Additional applications of production-planning problems may be found in the Linear Programming supplement on the Student CD-ROM.

9. **OM Explorer** The Bull Grin Company makes a supplement for the animal feed produced by a number of companies. Sales are seasonal, but Bull Grin's customers refuse to stockpile the supplement during slack sales periods. In other words, the customers want to minimize their inventory investments, insist on shipments according to their schedules, and will not accept backorders.

Bull Grin employs manual, unskilled laborers, who require little or no training. Producing 1,000 pounds of supplement costs $830 on regular time and $910 on overtime. There is no cost for unused regular-time, overtime, or subcontractor capacity. These figures include materials, which account for 80 percent of the cost. Overtime is limited to production of a total of 20,000 pounds per quarter. In addition, subcontractors can be hired at $1,000 per thousand pounds, but only 30,000 pounds per quarter can be produced this way.

The current level of inventory is 40,000 pounds, and management wants to end the year at that level. Holding 1,000 pounds of feed supplement in inventory per quarter costs $100. The latest annual forecast is shown in Table 11.3.

Use the transportation method of production planning to find the optimal production plan and calculate its cost, or use the spreadsheet approach to find a good production plan and calculate its cost.

10. **OM Explorer** The Cut Rite Company is a major producer of industrial lawn mowers. The cost to Cut Rite for hiring a semiskilled worker for its assembly plant is $3,000 and for laying one off is $2,000. The plant averages an output of 36,000 mowers per quarter with its current workforce of 720 employees. Regular-time capacity is directly proportional to the number of employees. Overtime is limited to a maximum of 3,000 mowers per quarter, and subcontracting is limited to 1,000 mowers per quarter. The costs to produce one mower are $2,430 on regular time (including materials), $2,700 on overtime, and $3,300 via subcontracting. Unused regular-time capacity costs $270 per mower. There is no cost for unused overtime or subcontractor capacity. The current level of inventory is 4,000 mowers, and management wants to end the year at that level. Customers do not tolerate backorders, and holding a mower in inventory per quarter costs $300. The demand for mowers this coming year is

Quarter	1	2	3	4
Demand	10,000	41,000	77,000	44,000

Two workforce plans have been proposed, and management is uncertain as to which one to use. The table shows the number of employees per quarter under each plan.

Quarter	1	2	3	4
Plan 1	720	780	920	720
Plan 2	860	860	860	860

a. Which plan would you recommend to management? Explain, supporting your recommendation with an analysis using the transportation method of production planning.

b. If management used creative pricing to get customers to buy mowers in nontraditional time periods, the following demand schedule would result:

Quarter	1	2	3	4
Demand	20,000	54,000	54,000	44,000

Which workforce plan would you recommend now?

TABLE 11.3 *Forecasts and Capacities*

| | PERIOD | | | | |
	Quarter 1	Quarter 2	Quarter 3	Quarter 4	TOTAL
Demand (pounds)	130,000	400,000	800,000	470,000	1,800,000
Capacities (pounds)					
Regular time	390,000	400,000	460,000	380,000	1,630,000
Overtime	20,000	20,000	20,000	20,000	80,000
Subcontract		30,000	30,000	30,000	30,000

11. **⬤ OM Explorer** The Holloway Calendar Company produces a variety of printed calendars for both commercial and private use. The demand for calendars is highly seasonal, peaking in the third quarter. Current inventory is 165,000 calendars, and ending inventory should be 200,000 calendars.

Ann Ritter, Holloway's manufacturing manager, wants to determine the best production plan for the demand requirements and capacity plan shown in the following table. (Here, demand and capacities are expressed in thousands of calendars rather than employee-period equivalents.) Ritter knows that the regular-time cost is $0.50 per unit, overtime cost is $0.75 per unit, subcontracting cost is $0.90 per unit, and inventory holding cost is $0.10 per calendar per quarter.

	QUARTER				
	1	**2**	**3**	**4**	**TOTAL**
Demand	250	515	1,200	325	2,290
Capacities					
Regular time	300	300	600	300	1,500
Overtime	75	75	150	75	375
Subcontracting	150	150	150	150	600

a. Recommend a production plan to Ritter, using the transportation method of production planning. (Do not allow any stockouts or backorders to occur.)

b. Interpret and explain your recommendation.

c. Calculate the total cost of your recommended production plan.

12. **⬤ OM Explorer** Little 6, Inc., an accounting firm, forecasts the following weekly workload during the tax season:

	DAY						
	M	**T**	**W**	**Th**	**F**	**S**	**Su**
Personal tax returns	24	14	18	18	10	28	16
Corporate tax returns	18	10	12	15	24	12	4

Corporate tax returns each require 4 hours of an accountant's time, and personal returns each require 90 minutes. During tax season, each accountant can work up to 10 hours per day. However, error rates increase to unacceptable levels when accountants work more than five consecutive days per week.

a. Create an effective and efficient work schedule.

b. Assume that Little 6 has three part-time employees available to work three days per week. How could these employees be effectively utilized?

SELECTED REFERENCES

Andrews, B. H., and H. L. Parsons. "L. L. Bean Chooses a Telephone Agent Scheduling System." *Interfaces* (November–December 1989), pp. 1–9.

Armacost, R. L., R. L. Penlesky, and S. C. Ross. "Avoiding Problems Inherent in Spreadsheet-Based Simulation Models—An Aggregate Planning Application." *Production and Inventory Management,* vol. 31 (1990), pp. 62–68.

Ashton, James E., and Frank X. Cook, Jr. "Time to Reform Job Shop Manufacturing." *Harvard Business Review* (March–April 1989), pp. 106–111.

Browne, J. J., and J. Prop. "Supplement to Scheduling Routine Work Hours." *Industrial Engineering* (July 1989), p. 12.

Buxey, G. "Production Planning and Scheduling for Seasonal Demand." *International Journal of Operations and Production Management,* vol. 13, no. 7 (1993), pp. 4–21.

Dillon, Jeffrey E., and Spyros Kontogiorgis. "US Airways Optimizes the Scheduling of Reserve Flight Crews." *Interfaces* (September–October 1999), pp. 123–131.

Fisher, M. L., J. H. Hammond, W. R. Obermeyer, and A. Raman. "Making Supply Meet Demand in an Uncertain World." *Harvard Business Review,* vol. 72, no. 3 (1994), pp. 83–93.

Heskett, J., W. E. Sasser, and C. Hart. *Service Breakthroughs: Changing the Rules of the Game.* New York: The Free Press, 1990.

Lesaint, David, Christos Voudouris, and Nader Azarmi. "Dynamic Workforce Scheduling for British Telecommunications plc." *Interfaces* (January–February 2000), pp. 45–56.

Port, Otis. "Customers Move Into the Driver's Seat." *Business Week* (October 4, 1999), pp. 103–106.

Ryan, D. M. "Optimization Earns Its Wings." *OR/MS Today,* vol. 27, no. 2 (2000), pp. 26–30.

Sipper, D., and R. Bulfin. *Production: Planning, Control, and Integration.* New York: McGraw-Hill, 1997.

Tibrewala, R. K., D. Philippe, and J. J. Browne. "Optimal Scheduling of Two Consecutive Idle Periods." *Management Science,* vol. 19, no. 1 (1972), pp. 71–75.

Voet, M., and P. Dewilde. "Choosing a Scheduling Package." *APICS— The Performance Advantage* (November 1994), pp. 28–31.

Vollmann, Thomas E., William Berry, and D. Clay Whybark. *Manufacturing Planning and Control Systems,* 4th ed. Homewood, Ill.: Irwin Professional Publication, 1997.

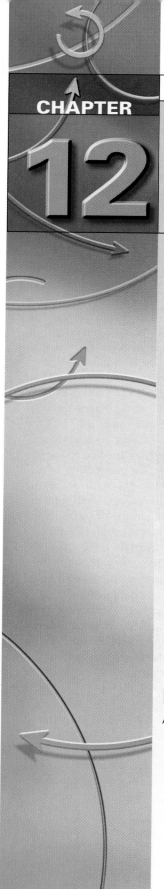

Resource Planning

Across the Organization

Resource planning is important to . . .

- ❒ **accounting,** which coordinates the payments to suppliers and billings to customers with the resource plan.
- ❒ **finance,** which plans for adequate working capital to support the schedules generated in the resource plan.
- ❒ **human resources,** which determines the implications of the resource plan on personnel requirements.
- ❒ **management information systems,** which must identify the information requirements of managers and the information that can be generated from the resource plan.
- ❒ **marketing,** which makes reliable delivery commitments to customers.
- ❒ **operations,** which is responsible for inventories and the utilization of the resources required by the firm's processes to meet customer demand.

Learning Goals

After reading this chapter, you will be able to . . .

1. distinguish between independent and dependent demand and their differences when planning for the replenishment of materials.
2. explain the logic of material requirements planning, how it can be used to plan distribution inventories, and how to schedule the receipt of materials to meet promised delivery dates.
3. identify the key outputs from the resource planning process and how they are used.
4. provide examples of the effective use of manufacturing resource planning and its benefits to various functional areas of the firm.
5. discuss resource planning for service providers and how it can be accomplished.

What do Wrangler or Lee jeans, Timber Creek khakis, Vanity Fair underwear, Healthtex clothes for kids, Jantzen bathing suits, and JanSport backpacks have in common, other than that you can find them in diverse retail outlets such as Wal-Mart, Target, and Macy's? One-hundred-year-old VF Corp. (www.vfc.com), a $5.5 billion-a-year company in Greensboro, North Carolina, and the world's largest apparel producer, manufactures all of these products and many more. While VF's stock has been a steady performer, its sales were flat and management realized that the corporation needed shaking up. VF's 14 divisions were operated as independent entities, each with its own purchasing, production, marketing, and computer systems. Management initiated a drive to focus its key business processes on identifying and fulfilling customer needs. The restructuring resulted in five "coalitions": Jeanswear, Intimates, Playwear, Knitwear, and International Operations and Marketing. Each coalition will phase into the integrated system over time.

Data on quality are important inputs for VF's ERP system. Here an employee inspects jeans to assure they conform to VF's quality standards and meet customer expectations.

The coalitions need to work together to take advantage of common resources. However, resource planning across such a complex environment poses major challenges. To establish the critical information links between the coalitions, VF decided to install a modified version of the R/3 ERP system from SAP AG specifically designed for apparel and footwear manufacturers as the core integrating system (www.sap.com). However, VF also decided to use the *best of breed* implementation strategy, which allowed VF to choose the best applications modules from any vendor or retain some of its own legacy systems. For example, the heart of the system has only four R/3 modules: order management, production planning, materials management, and finance. However, each coalition has its favorite applications from other vendors that have to be included. Intimates uses WebPDM from Gerber to cut product design costs and Rhythm from i2 to optimize materials utilization and assembly-line space. Information from Rhythm is fed back to the R/3 production planning module. Jeanswear is using software from Logility to make customer forecasts, which are fed back to the production planning and financial modules in R/3. VF's own customized software tracks production in the plants, using information from the R/3 production planning, order management, and materials management modules and then reports back to R/3 for the fine-tuning of production plans. VF also has developed a "micromarketing" system that forecasts the need for a specific size and color of Wrangler jeans (say), for the beginning of summer, at a particular Wal-Mart store.

Key modules in the new system for resource planning are material requirements planning and capacity planning. The material requirements planning system is contained in the production planning module and uses forecasts from the Logility sales and demand planning module to determine the purchase quantities and delivery dates for supplies and materials such as leather, fabric, or linings; the production of finished goods such as jeans, backpacks, or shirts; and the manufacture of assemblies such as shoe soles or bootlegs. The output from material requirements planning is useful for planning production as well as financial resources. For example, the timing of planned-purchase quantities can be translated into the need for funds to pay for them. The output can also be used by the capacity planning module, which facilitates the planning for critical resources such as skilled employees or specialized equipment to support the production plan.

VF has a great start but has a long way to go. Jeanswear was the first to completely implement the common systems platform, and Intimates is the next to go online. VF has spent more than $100 million on the new system, which is not unusual for complex environments such as this one.

Sources: Brown, Eryn. "VF Corp. Changes Its Underware." *Fortune* (December 7, 1998), pp. 115–118; "SAP Consumer Products for Apparel & Footwear" (July 2000); VFC Press Release. "VF Corporation Launches First Large Scale Apparel Industry-Specific SAP Solution." (May 31, 2000).

The VF Corporation demonstrates that companies can gain a competitive edge by integrating processes through an effective operations information system. Maintaining an efficient flow of materials and services from suppliers and managing internal activities relating to materials and other resources are essential to a profitable operation. Operations management ensures that all resources needed to produce finished products or services are available at the right time. For a manufacturer, this task may mean keeping track of thousands of subassemblies, components, and raw materials. For a service provider, this task may mean keeping track of various materials and supplies and time requirements for many different categories of employees and equipment.

We begin this chapter with a discussion of material requirements planning (MRP), which is a key element of manufacturing resource planning systems. We discuss the important concept of dependent demand and all the information inputs to MRP that are used to generate the reports needed for managing manufacturing and distribution inventories as well as other resources. We also devote an entire section to resource planning for service providers and demonstrate how the concept of dependent demands can be used to manage supplies, human resources, equipment, and financial resources. Resource planning techniques are important elements of ERP systems for manufacturers as well as service providers (see Chapter 5, "Managing Technology").

OVERVIEW OF MATERIAL REQUIREMENTS PLANNING

material requirements planning (MRP) A computerized information system developed specifically to aid in managing dependent demand inventory and scheduling replenishment orders.

Material requirements planning (MRP)—a computerized information system—was developed specifically to aid companies manage dependent demand inventory and schedule replenishment orders. MRP systems have proven to be beneficial to many companies. In this section, we discuss the nature of dependent demands and identify some of the benefits firms have experienced with these systems.

DEPENDENT DEMAND

To illustrate the concept of dependent demand, let us consider a Huffy bicycle produced for retail outlets. The bicycle, one of many different types held in inventory at Huffy's plant, has a high-volume demand rate over time. Demand for a final product such as a bicycle is called *independent demand* because it is influenced only by market conditions and not by demand for any other type of bicycle held in inventory (see Chapter 10, "Inventory Management"). Huffy must *forecast* that demand (see Chapter 9, "Forecasting"). However, Huffy also keeps many other items in inventory, including handlebars, pedals, frames, and wheel rims, used to make completed bicycles. Each of these items has a **dependent demand** because the quantity required is a function of the demand for other items held in inventory. For example, the demand for frames, pedals, and rims is *dependent* on the production of completed bicycles. Operations can *calculate* the demand for dependent demand items once the bicycle production levels are announced. For example, every bicycle needs two wheel rims, so 1,000 completed bicycles need $1,000(2) = 2,000$ rims. Statistical forecasting techniques aren't needed for these items.

dependent demand A demand that occurs because the quantity required is a function of the demand for other items held in inventory.

parent Any item manufactured from one or more components.

component An item that may go through one or more operations to be transformed into or become part of one or more parents.

The bicycle, or any other good manufactured from one or more components, is called a **parent**. The wheel rim is an example of a **component**—an item that may go through one or more operations to be transformed into or become part of one or more parents. The rim may have several different parents because it might be used for more than one style of bicycle. The parent–component relationship can cause erratic dependent demand patterns for components. Suppose that every time inventory falls to 500 units (a reorder point), an order for 1,000 more bicycles is placed, as shown in Figure 12.1(a). The assembly supervisor then authorizes the withdrawal of 2,000 rims from inventory, along with other components for the finished product; demand for the

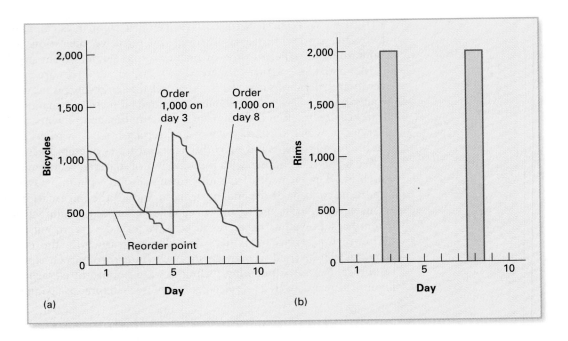

FIGURE 12.1

Lumpy Dependent Demand Resulting from Continuous Independent Demand

rim is shown in Figure 12.1(b). So, even though customer demand for the finished bicycle is continuous and uniform, the production demand for wheel rims is "lumpy"; that is, it occurs sporadically, usually in relatively large quantities. Thus, the *production* decisions for the assembly of bicycles, which account for the costs of assembling the bicycles and the projected assembly capacities at the time the decisions are made, determine the demand for rims.

Managing dependent demand inventories is complicated because some components may be subject to both dependent and independent demand. For example, operations needs 2,000 wheel rims for the new bicycles, but the company also sells replacement rims for old bicycles directly to retail outlets. This practice places an independent demand on the inventory of rims. Material requirements planning can be used in complex situations involving components that may have independent demand as well as dependent demand inventories.

BENEFITS OF MATERIAL REQUIREMENTS PLANNING

Why should companies invest in an MRP system?

For years, many companies tried to manage production and delivery of dependent demand inventories with independent demand systems, but the outcome was seldom satisfactory. However, because it recognizes dependent demands, the MRP system enables businesses to reduce inventory levels, utilize labor and facilities better, and improve customer service. These successes are due to three advantages of material requirements planning.

1. Statistical forecasting for components with lumpy demand results in large forecasting errors. Compensating for such errors by increasing safety stock is costly, with no guarantee that stockouts can be avoided. MRP calculates the dependent demand of components from the production schedules of their parents, thereby providing a better forecast of component requirements.

2. MRP systems provide managers with information useful for planning capacities and estimating financial requirements. Production schedules and materials purchases can be translated into capacity requirements and dollar amounts and can be

projected in the time periods when they will appear. Planners can use the information on parent item schedules to identify times when needed components may be unavailable because of capacity shortages, supplier delivery delays, and the like.

3. MRP systems automatically update the dependent demand and inventory replenishment schedules of components when the production schedules of parent items change. The MRP system alerts the planners whenever action is needed on any component.

INPUTS TO MATERIAL REQUIREMENTS PLANNING

MRP explosion A process that converts the requirements of various final products into a material requirements plan that specifies the replenishment schedules of all the subassemblies, components, and raw materials needed by the final products.

bill of materials (BOM) A record of all the components of an item, the parent–component relationships, and usage quantities derived from engineering and process designs.

The key inputs of an MRP system are a bill of materials database, master production schedules, and an inventory record database, as shown in Figure 12.2. Using this information, the MRP system identifies actions that operations must take to stay on schedule, such as releasing new production orders, adjusting order quantities, and expediting late orders.

An MRP system translates the master production schedule and other sources of demand, such as independent demand for replacement parts and maintenance items, into the requirements for all subassemblies, components, and raw materials needed to produce the required parent items. This process is called an **MRP explosion** because it converts the requirements of various final products into a *material requirements plan* that specifies the replenishment schedules of all the subassemblies, components, and raw materials needed by the final products.

BILL OF MATERIALS

The replenishment schedule for a component is determined from the production schedules of its parents. Hence, the system needs accurate information on parent–component relationships. A **bill of materials (BOM)** is a record of all the components of an item, the parent–component relationships, and usage quantities derived from engineering and process designs. In Figure 12.3, the BOM of a simple ladder-back chair shows that the chair is made from a ladder-back subassembly, a seat subassembly, legs, and leg supports. In turn, the ladder-back subassembly is made from legs and back slats, and the seat subassembly is made from a seat frame and a cushion. Finally, the seat frame is

FIGURE 12.2

Material Requirements Plan Inputs

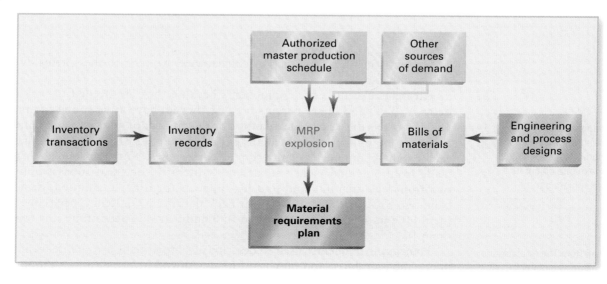

FIGURE 12.3

Bill of Materials for a Ladder-Back Chair

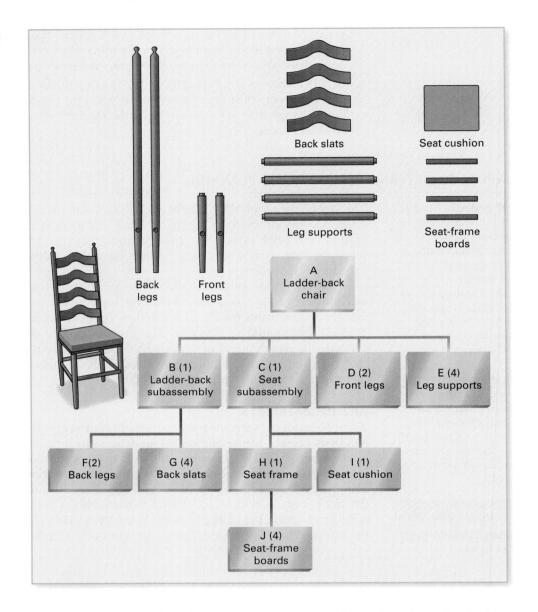

made from seat-frame boards. For convenience, we refer to these items by the letters shown in Figure 12.3.

All items except A are components because they are needed to make a parent. Items A, B, C, and H are parents because they all have at least one component. The BOM also specifies the **usage quantity,** or the number of units of a component needed to make one unit of its immediate parent. Figure 12.3 shows usage quantities for each parent–component relationship in parentheses. Note that one chair (item A) is made from one ladder-back subassembly (item B), one seat subassembly (item C), two front legs (item D), and four leg supports (item E). In addition, item B is made from two back legs (item F) and four back slats (item G). Item C needs one seat frame (item H) and one seat cushion (item I). Finally, item H needs four seat-frame boards (item J).

Four terms frequently used to describe inventory items are end items, intermediate items, subassemblies, and purchased items. An **end item** typically is the final product

usage quantity The number of units of a component needed to make one unit of its immediate parent.

end item The final product sold to a customer.

sold to the customer; it is a parent but not a component. Item A in Figure 12.3, the completed ladder-back chair, is an end item. Accounting statements classify inventory of end items as either work-in-process (WIP), if work remains to be done, or finished goods. An **intermediate item** is one such as B, C, or H that has at least one parent and at least one component. Some products have several levels of intermediate items; the parent of one intermediate item also is an intermediate item. Inventory of intermediate items—whether completed or still on the shop floor—is classified as WIP. A **subassembly** is an intermediate item that is *assembled* (as opposed to being transformed by other means) from *more* than one component. Items B and C are subassemblies. A **purchased item** has no components because it comes from a supplier, but it has one or more parents. Examples are items D, E, F, G, I, and J in Figure 12.3. Inventory of purchased items is treated as raw materials in accounting statements.

A component may have more than one parent. **Part commonality,** sometimes called *standardization of parts* or *modularity,* is the degree to which a component has more than one immediate parent. As a result of commonality, the same item may appear in several places in the bill of materials for a product, or it may appear in the bills of materials for several different products. For example, the seat assembly in Figure 12.3 is a component of the ladder-back chair and of a kitchen chair that is part of the same family of products. The usage quantity specified in the bill of materials relates to a specific parent–component relationship. The usage quantity for any component can change, depending on the parent item. Part commonality increases volume and repeatability for some items—which has several advantages for process design (see Chapter 2, "Process Management")—and helps minimize inventory costs. Today, with the need for greater efficiency in all firms, part commonality is used extensively.

intermediate item An item that has at least one parent and at least one component.

subassembly An intermediate item that is *assembled* (as opposed to being transformed by other means) from *more* than one component.

purchased item An item that has one or more parents, but no components because it comes from a supplier.

part commonality The degree to which a component has more than one immediate parent.

MASTER PRODUCTION SCHEDULE

The second input into a material requirements plan is the **master production schedule (MPS),** which details how many end items will be produced within specified periods of time. It breaks the aggregate production plan (see Chapter 11, "Aggregate Planning and Scheduling") into specific product schedules. Figure 12.4 shows how an aggregate plan for a family of chairs breaks down into the weekly master production schedule for each specific chair type (the time period can be hours, days, weeks, or months). Here the scheduled quantities are shown in the week they must be released to the shop to start final assembly so as to meet customer delivery promises. We use the MPS "start"

Why is the master production schedule important to the material requirements plan?

FIGURE 12.4

Master Production Schedule for a Family of Chairs

	April				May			
	1	2	3	4	5	6	7	8
Ladder-back chair	150					150		
Kitchen chair				120			120	
Desk chair		200	200		200			200
Aggregate production plan for chair family	670				670			

master production schedule (MPS) A part of the material requirements plan that details how many end items will be produced within specified periods of time.

quantities throughout this chapter. The chair example demonstrates the following aspects of master scheduling:

1. The sums of the quantities in the MPS must equal those in the aggregate production plan. This consistency between the plans is desirable because of the economic analysis done to arrive at the aggregate plan.

2. The aggregate production quantities must be allocated efficiently over time. The specific mix of chair types—the amount of each type as a percentage of the total aggregate quantity—is based on historic demand and marketing and promotional considerations. The planner must select lot sizes for each chair type, taking into consideration economic factors such as production setup costs and inventory carrying costs.

3. Capacity limitations, such as machine or labor capacity, storage space, or working capital, may determine the timing and size of MPS quantities. The planner must acknowledge these limitations by recognizing that some chair styles require more resources than others and setting the timing and size of the production quantities accordingly.

The MPS start quantities are used in the MRP system to determine the components needed to support the schedule. Details of how to develop the MPS are contained in Supplement K, "Master Production Scheduling" on the Student CD-ROM.

INVENTORY RECORD

Inventory records are the final input to MRP, and the basic building blocks of up-to-date records are inventory transactions (see Figure 12.2). Transactions include releasing new orders, receiving scheduled receipts, adjusting due dates for scheduled receipts, withdrawing inventory, canceling orders, correcting inventory errors, rejecting shipments, and verifying scrap losses and stock returns. Recording such transactions is essential for maintaining the accurate records of on-hand inventory balances and scheduled receipts necessary for an effective MRP system.

inventory record A record that shows an item's lot-size policy, lead time, and various time-phased data.

The **inventory record** divides the future into time periods called *time buckets*. In our discussion, we use weekly time buckets for consistency with our MPS example, although other time periods could as easily be used. The inventory record shows an item's lot-size policy, lead time, and various time-phased data. The purpose of the inventory record is to keep track of inventory levels and component replenishment needs. The time-phased information contained in the inventory record consists of

1. gross requirements
2. scheduled receipts
3. projected on-hand inventory
4. planned receipts
5. planned order releases

We illustrate the discussion of inventory records with the seat subassembly, item C, shown in Figure 12.3. It is used in two products: a ladder-back chair and a kitchen chair.

gross requirements The total demand derived from *all* parent production plans.

GROSS REQUIREMENTS. The **gross requirements** are the total demand derived from *all* parent production plans. They also include demand not otherwise accounted for, such as demand for replacement parts for units already sold. Figure 12.5 shows an inventory record for item C, the seat subassembly. Item C is produced in lots of 230 units and has a lead time of two weeks. The inventory record also shows item C's gross requirements for the next eight weeks, which come from the master production schedules for the

FIGURE 12.5

Material Requirements Planning Record for the Seat Subassembly

Item: C Description: Seat subassembly							Lot Size: 230 units Lead Time: 2 weeks	
	Week							
	1	2	3	4	5	6	7	8
Gross requirements	150	0	0	120	0	150	120	0
Scheduled receipts	230	0	0	0	0	0	0	0
Projected on-hand inventory 37	117	117	117	–3	–3	–153	–273	–273
Planned receipts								
Planned order releases								

Explanation:
Gross requirements are the total demand for the two chairs. Projected on-hand inventory in week 1 is 37 + 230 – 150 = 117 units.

ladder-back and kitchen chairs (see Figure 12.4). The MPS start quantities for each parent are added to arrive at each week's gross requirements. The seat subassembly's gross requirements exhibit lumpy demand: Operations will withdraw seat subassemblies from inventory in only four of the eight weeks.

The MRP system works with release dates to schedule production and delivery for components and subassemblies. Its program logic anticipates the removal of all materials required by a parent's production order from inventory at the *beginning* of the parent item's lead time—when the scheduler first releases the order to the shop.

SCHEDULED RECEIPTS. Recall that *scheduled receipts* (sometimes called *open orders*) are orders that have been placed but not yet completed. For a purchased item, the scheduled receipt could be in one of several stages: being processed by a supplier, being transported to the purchaser, or being inspected by the purchaser's receiving department. If production is making the item in-house, the order could be one the shop floor being processed, waiting for components, waiting in queue, or waiting to be moved to its next operation. According to Figure 12.5, one 230-unit order of item C is due in week 1. Given the two-week lead time, the inventory planner released the order two weeks ago.

projected on-hand inventory An estimate of the amount of inventory available each week after gross requirements have been satisfied.

PROJECTED ON-HAND INVENTORY. The **projected on-hand inventory** is an estimate of the amount of inventory available each week after gross requirements have been satisfied.

The beginning inventory, shown as the first entry (37) in Figure 12.5, indicates on-hand inventory available at the time the record was computed. As with scheduled receipts, entries are made for each actual withdrawal and receipt to update the MRP database. Then, when the MRP system produces the revised record, the correct inventory will appear.

Other entries in the row show inventory expected in future weeks. Projected on-hand inventory is calculated as

$$\begin{pmatrix} \text{Projected on-hand} \\ \text{inventory balance} \\ \text{at end of week } t \end{pmatrix} = \begin{pmatrix} \text{Inventory on} \\ \text{hand at end of} \\ \text{week } t - 1 \end{pmatrix} + \begin{pmatrix} \text{Scheduled} \\ \text{or planned} \\ \text{receipts in} \\ \text{week } t \end{pmatrix} - \begin{pmatrix} \text{Gross} \\ \text{requirements} \\ \text{in week } t \end{pmatrix}$$

planned receipts Orders that are not yet released to the shop or the supplier.

The projected on-hand calculation includes the consideration of **planned receipts,** which are orders not yet released to the shop or the supplier. In any week, there will never be both a scheduled receipt and a planned receipt. In Figure 12.5, the planned receipts are all zero. The on-hand inventory calculations for each week are

$$
\begin{array}{lrcrcrcr}
\text{Week 1:} & 37 & + & 230 & - & 150 & = & 117 \\
\text{Weeks 2 and 3:} & 117 & + & 0 & - & 0 & = & 117 \\
\text{Week 4:} & 117 & + & 0 & - & 120 & = & -3 \\
\text{Week 5:} & -3 & + & 0 & - & 0 & = & -3 \\
\text{Week 6:} & -3 & + & 0 & - & 150 & = & -153 \\
\text{Week 7:} & -153 & + & 0 & - & 120 & = & -273 \\
\text{Week 8:} & -273 & + & 0 & - & 0 & = & -273 \\
\end{array}
$$

In week 4, the balance drops to -3 units, which indicates that a shortage of 3 units will occur unless more seat subassemblies are built. This condition signals the need for a planned receipt to arrive in week 4. In addition, unless more stock is received, the shortage will grow to 273 units in weeks 7 and 8.

PLANNED RECEIPTS. Planning for receipt of new orders will keep the projected on-hand balance from dropping below zero. The planned receipt row is developed as follows:

1. Weekly on-hand inventory is projected until a shortage appears. Completion of the initial planned receipt is scheduled for the week when the shortage is projected. The addition of the newly planned receipt should raise the projected on-hand balance so that it equals or exceeds zero. It will exceed zero when the lot size exceeds requirements in the week it is planned to arrive.

2. Projection of on-hand inventory continues until the next shortage occurs. This shortage signals the need for the second planned receipt.

This process is repeated until the end of the planning horizon by proceeding column by column through the MRP record—filling in planned receipts as needed and completing the projected on-hand inventory row. Figure 12.6 shows the planned receipts for the seat subassembly. In week 4, the projected on-hand inventory will drop below zero, so a planned receipt of 230 units is scheduled for week 4. The updated inventory on-hand balance is 117 (inventory at end of week 3) + 230 (planned receipts) − 120 (gross requirements) = 227 units. The projected on-hand inventory remains at 227 for week 5 because there are no scheduled receipts or gross requirements. In week 6, the projected on-hand inventory is 227 (inventory at end of week 5) − 150 (gross requirements) = 77 units. This quantity is greater than zero, so no new planned receipt is needed. In week 7,

FIGURE 12.6

Completed Inventory Record for the Seat Subassembly

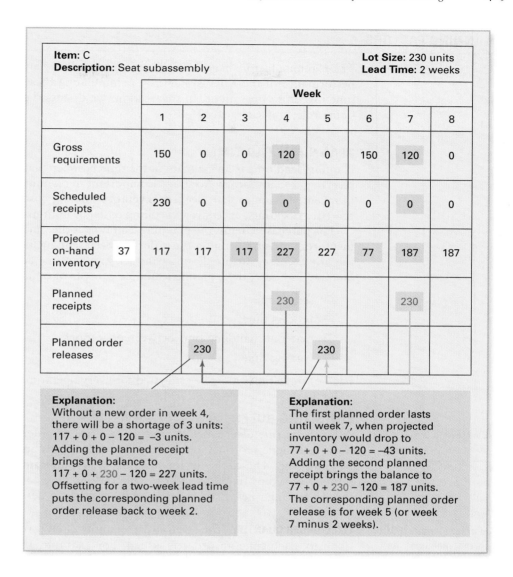

Item: C
Description: Seat subassembly

Lot Size: 230 units
Lead Time: 2 weeks

		Week						
	1	2	3	4	5	6	7	8
Gross requirements	150	0	0	120	0	150	120	0
Scheduled receipts	230	0	0	0	0	0	0	0
Projected on-hand inventory	37 117	117	117	227	227	77	187	187
Planned receipts				230			230	
Planned order releases		230			230			

Explanation:
Without a new order in week 4, there will be a shortage of 3 units: $117 + 0 + 0 - 120 = -3$ units. Adding the planned receipt brings the balance to $117 + 0 + 230 - 120 = 227$ units. Offsetting for a two-week lead time puts the corresponding planned order release back to week 2.

Explanation:
The first planned order lasts until week 7, when projected inventory would drop to $77 + 0 + 0 - 120 = -43$ units. Adding the second planned receipt brings the balance to $77 + 0 + 230 - 120 = 187$ units. The corresponding planned order release is for week 5 (or week 7 minus 2 weeks).

however, a shortage will occur unless more seat subassemblies are received. With a planned receipt in week 7, the updated inventory balance is 77 (inventory at end of week 6) + 230 (planned receipts) − 120 (gross requirements) = 187 units.

planned order release An indication of when an order for a specified quantity of an item is to be issued.

PLANNED ORDER RELEASES. A planned order release indicates when an order for a specified quantity of an item is to be issued. We must place the planned order release quantity in the proper time bucket. To do so, we must assume that all inventory flows—scheduled receipts, planned receipts, and gross requirements—occur at the same point of time in a time period. Some firms assume that all flows occur at the beginning of a time period; others assume that they occur at the end of a time period or at the middle of the time period. Regardless of when the flows are assumed to occur, we find the release date by subtracting the lead time from the receipt date. For example, the release date for the first planned order release in Figure 12.6 is 4 (planned receipt date) − 2 (lead time) = 2 (planned order release date). Figure 12.6 shows the planned order releases for the seat subassembly.

PLANNING FACTORS

The planning factors in an MRP inventory record play an important role in the overall performance of the MRP system. By manipulating these factors, managers can fine-tune inventory operations. In this section, we discuss the planning lead time, the lot-sizing rule, and safety stock.

PLANNING LEAD TIME

Planning lead time is an estimate of the time between placing an order for an item and receiving it in inventory. Accuracy is important in planning lead time. If an item arrives in inventory sooner than needed, inventory holding costs increase. If an item arrives too late, stockouts, excessive expediting costs, or both may occur.

For purchased items, the planning lead time is the time allowed for receiving a shipment from the supplier after the order has been sent, including the normal time to place the order. Often, the purchasing contract stipulates the delivery date. For items manufactured in-house, the planning lead time consists of estimates for

- ❑ setup time
- ❑ process time
- ❑ materials handling time between operations
- ❑ waiting time

Each of these times must be estimated for every operation along the item's route.

LOT-SIZING RULES

How important is the choice of lot-sizing rules?

A lot-sizing rule determines the timing and size of order quantities. A lot-sizing rule must be assigned to each item before planned receipts and planned order releases can be computed. The choice of lot-sizing rules is important because they determine the number of setups required and the inventory holding costs for each item. We present three lot-sizing rules: fixed order quantity, periodic order quantity, and lot for lot.

fixed order quantity (FOQ) A rule that maintains the same order quantity each time an order is issued.

TUTOR 12.1

FIXED ORDER QUANTITY. The **fixed order quantity (FOQ)** rule maintains the same order quantity each time an order is issued. For example, the lot size might be the size dictated by equipment capacity limits, as when a full lot must be loaded into a furnace at one time. For purchased items, the FOQ could be determined by the quantity discount level, truckload capacity, or minimum purchase quantity. Alternatively, the lot size could be determined by the economic order quantity (EOQ) formula (see Chapter 10, "Inventory Management"). Figure 12.6 illustrates the FOQ rule. However, if an item's gross requirement within a week is particularly large, the FOQ might be insufficient to avoid a shortage. In such unusual cases, the inventory planner must increase the lot size beyond the FOQ, typically to a size large enough to avoid a shortage. Another option is to make the order quantity an integer multiple of the FOQ. This option is appropriate when capacity constraints limit production to FOQ sizes (at most) and setup costs are high.

periodic order quantity (POQ) A rule that allows a different order quantity for each order issued but tends to issue the order at predetermined time intervals.

PERIODIC ORDER QUANTITY. The **periodic order quantity (POQ)** rule allows a different order quantity for each order issued but tends to issue the order at predetermined time intervals, such as every two weeks. The order quantity equals the amount of the item needed during the predetermined time between orders and must be large enough to prevent shortages. Specifically, the POQ is

**TUTOR
12.1**

$$\begin{pmatrix} \text{POQ lot size} \\ \text{to arrive in} \\ \text{week } t \end{pmatrix} = \begin{pmatrix} \text{Total gross requirements} \\ \text{for } P \text{ weeks, including} \\ \text{week } t \end{pmatrix} - \begin{pmatrix} \text{Projected on-hand} \\ \text{inventory balance at} \\ \text{end of week } t-1 \end{pmatrix}$$

This amount exactly covers P weeks' worth of gross requirements. That is, the projected on-hand inventory should equal zero at the end of the Pth week. The POQ rule does *not* mean that operations must issue a new order every P weeks. Rather, when an order *is* planned, its lot size must be enough to cover P successive weeks. One way to select a P value is to divide the average lot size desired, such as the EOQ (see Chapter 10, "Inventory Management"), or some other applicable lot size, by the average weekly demand. That is, express the target lot size as a desired weeks of supply (P) and round to the nearest integer. See Solved Problem 2 for a detailed example of the POQ rule.

lot-for-lot (L4L) A rule under which the lot size ordered covers the gross requirements of a single week.

LOT FOR LOT. A special case of the POQ rule is the **lot-for-lot (L4L)** rule, under which the lot size ordered covers the gross requirements of a single week. Thus, $P = 1$, and the goal is to minimize inventory levels. This rule ensures that the planned order is just large enough to prevent a shortage in the single week it covers. The L4L lot size is

**TUTOR
12.2**

$$\begin{pmatrix} \text{L4L lot size} \\ \text{to arrive in} \\ \text{week } t \end{pmatrix} = \begin{pmatrix} \text{Gross requirements} \\ \text{for week } t \end{pmatrix} - \begin{pmatrix} \text{Projected on-hand} \\ \text{inventory balance at} \\ \text{the end of week } t-1 \end{pmatrix}$$

The projected on-hand inventory combined with the new order will equal zero at the end of week t. Following the first planned order, an additional planned order will be used to match each subsequent gross requirement. See Solved Problem 2 for a detailed example of the L4L rule.

COMPARISON OF LOT-SIZING RULES. Choosing a lot-sizing rule can have important implications for inventory management. Lot-sizing rules affect inventory costs and setup or ordering costs. The FOQ, POQ, and L4L rules differ from one another in one or both respects. We can make the following three generalizations.

1. The FOQ rule generates a high level of average inventory because it creates inventory *remnants*. A remnant is inventory carried into a week but is too small to prevent a shortage. Remnants occur because the FOQ does not match requirements exactly. For example, according to Figure 12.6, the stockroom must receive a planned order in week 7, even though 77 units are on hand at the beginning of that week. The remnant is the 77 units that the stockroom will carry for three weeks, beginning with receipt of the first planned order in week 4. Although they increase average inventory levels, inventory remnants introduce stability into the production process by buffering unexpected scrap losses, capacity bottlenecks, inaccurate inventory records, or unstable gross requirements.

2. The POQ rule reduces the amount of average on-hand inventory because it does a better job of matching order quantity to requirements. It adjusts lot sizes as requirements increase or decrease.

3. The L4L rule minimizes inventory investment, but it also maximizes the number of orders placed. This rule is most applicable to expensive items or items with small ordering or setup costs. It is the only rule that can be used for a low-volume item made to order.

FIGURE 12.7

*Inventory Record for
the Seat Subassembly
Showing the Application
of a Safety Stock*

Tutor: FOQ, POQ, and L4L Rules

FOQ Rule								Lot Size	230
								Lead Time	2
								Safety Stock	80
		1	2	3	4	5	6	7	8
Gross Requirements		150	0	0	120	0	150	120	0
Scheduled Receipts		230	0	0	0	0	0	0	0
Projected On-Hand Inventory	37	117	117	117	227	227	307	187	187
Planned Receipts		0	0	0	230	0	230	0	0
Planned Order Releases		0	230	0	230	0	0	0	0

By avoiding remnants, both the POQ and the L4L rule may actually *introduce* instability by tying the lot-sizing decision so closely to requirements. If any requirement changes, so must the lot size, which can disrupt component schedules. Last-minute increases in parent orders may be hindered by missing components.

SAFETY STOCK

An important managerial issue is the quantity of safety stock to require. It is more complex for dependent demand items than for independent demand items. Safety stock for dependent demand items with lumpy demand (gross requirements) is valuable only when future gross requirements, the timing or size of scheduled receipts, and the amount of scrap are uncertain. Safety stock should be reduced and ultimately removed as the causes of the uncertainty are eliminated. The usual policy is to use safety stock for end items and purchased items to protect against fluctuating customer orders and unreliable suppliers of components and to avoid using it as much as possible for intermediate items. Safety stocks can be incorporated in the MRP logic by scheduling a planned receipt whenever the projected on-hand inventory balance drops below the desired safety stock level (rather than zero as before). The objective is to keep a minimum level of planned inventories equal to the safety stock quantity. Figure 12.7 shows what happens when there is a requirement for 80 units of safety stock for the seat assembly using a FOQ of 230 units. Compare these results to Figure 12.6. The net effect is to move the second planned order release from week 5 to week 4 to avoid going below 80 units in week 6.

OUTPUTS FROM MATERIAL REQUIREMENTS PLANNING

Material requirements planning systems provide many reports, schedules, and notices to help managers control dependent demand inventories, as indicated in Figure 12.8. In this section, we discuss the MRP explosion process, action notices that alert managers to items needing attention, and capacity reports that project the capacity requirements implied by the material requirements plan.

MATERIAL REQUIREMENTS PLANNING EXPLOSION

What information is available from MRP systems that will provide help in managing materials better?

MRP translates, or *explodes*, the master production schedule and other sources of demand into the requirements for all subassemblies, components, and raw materials needed to produce parent items. This process generates the material requirements plan for each component item.

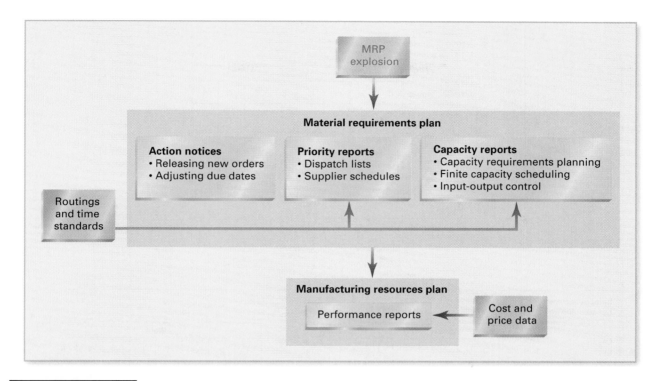

Material Requirements Planning Outputs

An item's gross requirements are derived from three sources:

1. the MPS for immediate parents that are end items
2. the planned order releases for parents below the MPS level
3. any other requirements not originating in the MPS, such as the demand for replacement parts

Consider the seat subassembly (Item C) for which we have developed the inventory record shown in Figure 12.6. The seat subassembly requires a seat cushion and a seat frame, which in turn needs four seat-frame boards. Its BOM is shown in Figure 12.3. How many seat cushions should we order from the supplier? How many seat frames should we produce to support the seat subassembly schedule? How many seat-frame boards do we need to make? The answers to these questions depend on the inventories we already have of these items and the replenishment orders already in progress. MRP can help answer these questions through the explosion process.

Figure 12.9 shows the MRP records for the seat subassembly and its components. We have already shown how to develop the MRP record for the seat subassembly. We now concentrate on the MRP records of its components. The lot-size rules are an FOQ of 300 units for the seat frame, L4L for the seat cushion, and an FOQ of 1,500 for the seat-frame boards. All three components have a one-week lead time. The key to the explosion process is to determine the proper timing and size of the gross requirements for each component. When we have done that, we can derive the planned order release schedule for each component by using the logic we have already demonstrated.

In our example, the components have no independent demand for replacement parts. Consequently, in Figure 12.9, the gross requirements of a component come from the planned order releases of its parents. The seat frame and the seat cushion get their gross requirements from the planned order release schedule of the seat subassembly. Both components have gross requirements of 230 units in weeks 2 and 5, the same

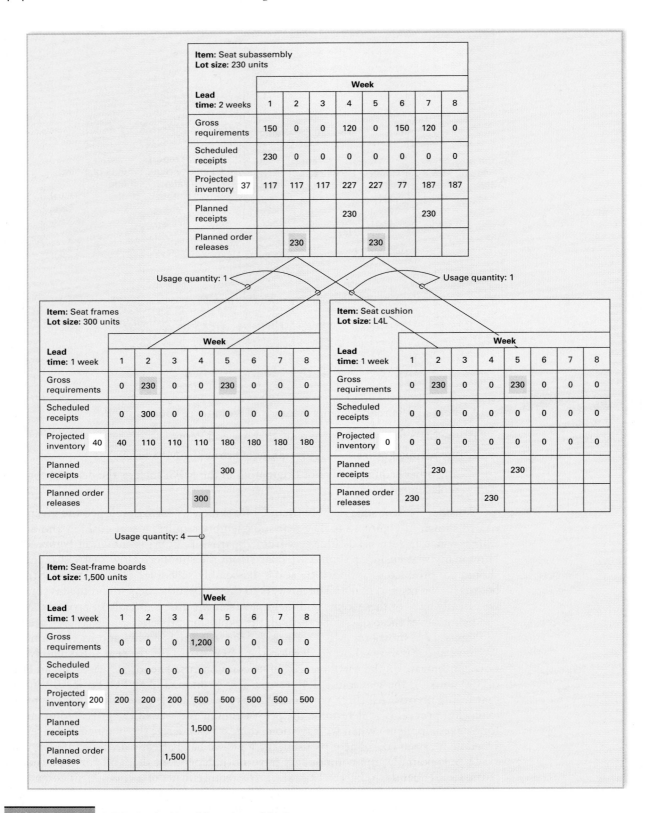

FIGURE 12.9 *MRP Explosion of Seat Assembly Components*

weeks in which we will be releasing orders to make more seat subassemblies. In week 2, for example, the materials handler for the assembly department will withdraw 230 seat frames and 230 seat cushions from inventory so that the assembly department can produce the seat subassemblies in time to avoid a stockout in week 4. The materials plans for the seat frame and the seat cushion must allow for that.

Using the gross requirements in weeks 2 and 5, we can develop the MRP records for the seat frame and the seat cushion, as shown in Figure 12.9. For a scheduled receipt of 300 in week 2, an on-hand quantity of 40 units, and a lead time of one week, we need to release an order of 300 seat frames in week 4 to cover the assembly schedule for the seat subassembly. The seat cushion has no scheduled receipts and no inventory on hand; consequently, we must place orders for 230 units in weeks 1 and 4, using the L4L logic with a lead time of one week.

Once we have determined the replenishment schedule for the seat frame, we can calculate the gross requirements for the seat-frame boards. We plan to begin producing 300 seat frames in week 4. Each frame requires 4 boards, so we need to have $300(4) = 1,200$ boards available in week 4. Consequently, the gross requirement for seat-frame boards is 1,200 in week 4. Given no scheduled receipts, 200 boards in stock, a lead time of one week, and an FOQ of 1,500 units, we need a planned order release of 1,500 in week 3.

The questions we posed earlier can now be answered. The following orders must be released: 300 seat frames in week 4, 230 seat cushions in each of weeks 1 and 4, and 1,500 seat-frame boards in week 3.

ACTION NOTICES

action notice A computer-generated memo used by inventory planners to make decisions about releasing new orders and adjusting the due dates of scheduled receipts.

Once computed, inventory records for any item appearing in the bills of materials can be printed in hard copy or displayed on a computer video screen. Inventory planners use a computer-generated memo called an **action notice** to make decisions about releasing new orders and adjusting the due dates of scheduled receipts. These notices are generated every time the system is updated. The action notice alerts planners to only the items that need their attention such as those items that have a planned order release in the current period or those that need their due dates adjusted because of changes to parent item schedules or the availability of raw materials and components. They can then view the full records for those items and take the necessary actions. An action notice can simply be a list of part numbers for items needing attention. Or it can be the full record for such items, with a note at the bottom identifying the action needed.

CAPACITY REPORTS

How can capacity constraints be recognized in the material requirements plan?

capacity requirements planning (CRP) A technique used for projecting time-phased capacity requirements for workstations; its purpose is to match the material requirements plan with the plant's production capacity.

By itself, the MRP system does not recognize capacity limitations when computing planned orders. That is, it may call for a planned order release that exceeds the amount that can be physically produced. An essential role of managers is to monitor the capacity requirements of material requirements plans, adjusting a plan when it cannot be met. In this section, we discuss three sources of information for short-term decisions that materials managers continually make: capacity requirements planning reports, finite capacity scheduling reports, and input–output reports.

CAPACITY REQUIREMENTS PLANNING. One technique for projecting time-phased capacity requirements for workstations is **capacity requirements planning (CRP)**. Its purpose is to match the material requirements plan with the plant's production capacity. The technique is used to calculate workload according to work required to complete the scheduled receipts already in the shop and to complete the planned order releases not yet released. This task involves the use of the inventory records, which supply the planned order releases and the status of the scheduled receipts; the item's routing, which specifies the workstations that must process the item; average lead times between each workstation; and the average processing and setup times at each workstation. Using the MRP dates for arrival of replenishment orders for an item to avoid shortages, CRP traces back through the item's routing to estimate when the scheduled receipt or planned order will reach each workstation. The system uses the processing and setup times to estimate the load that the item will impose on each station for each planned order and scheduled receipt of the item. The workloads for each workstation are obtained by adding the time that each item needs at a particular workstation. Critical workstations are those at which the projected loads exceed station capacities.

Figure 12.10 shows a capacity requirements report for a lathe station that turns wooden table legs. Each of four lathes is scheduled for two shifts per day. The lathe station has a maximum capacity of 320 hours per week. The *planned* hours represent labor requirements for all planned orders for items that need to be routed through the lathe station. The *actual* hours represent the backlog of work visible on the shop floor (i.e., scheduled receipts). Combining requirements from both sources gives *total* hours. Comparing total hours to actual capacity constraints gives advance warning of any potential problems. The planner must manually resolve any capacity problems uncovered.

For example, the CRP report shown in Figure 12.10 would alert the planner to the need for scheduling adjustments. Unless something is done, the current capacity of 320 hours per week will be exceeded in week 34 and again in week 36. Requirements for all other time periods are well below the capacity limit. Perhaps the best choice is to release some orders earlier than planned so that they will arrive at the lathe station in weeks 32, 33, and 35 rather than weeks 34 and 36. This adjustment will help smooth capacity and alleviate bottlenecks. Other options might be to change the lot sizes of

FIGURE 12.10

Capacity Requirements Report

Date:					Week: 32	
Plant 01 Dept. 03: Lathe Station						
Capacity: 320 hours per week						

	Week					
	32	33	34	35	36	37
Planned hours	90	156	349	210	360	280
Actual hours	210	104	41	0	0	0
Total hours	300	260	390	210	360	280

Explanation:
Projected capacity requirements exceed weekly hours of capacity.

some items, use overtime, subcontract, off-load to another workstation, or simply let the bottlenecks occur.

FINITE CAPACITY SCHEDULING. In large production facilities thousands of orders may be in progress at any one time. Manually adjusting the timing of these orders with the use of spreadsheets or wall-mounted magnetic schedule boards is virtually impossible. The best solutions—those that meet the MRP schedule due dates and do not violate any constraints—may never be identified because of the time needed to explore the alternatives. A useful tool for these situations is a **finite capacity scheduling (FCS)** system, which is an algorithm designed to schedule a group of orders appropriately across an entire shop. The system utilizes routings for the items manufactured, resource constraints, available capacity, shift patterns, and a scheduling rule to be used at each workstation to determine the priorities for orders (see Supplement J, "Operations Scheduling" on the Student CD-ROM).

To be effective, the FCS system needs to be integrated with MRP. The MRP system can download the orders that need to be scheduled, but the FCS system needs much more than that. An FCS system operates at a finer level of detail than MRP and needs to know the status of each machine and when the current order will finish processing, the maintenance schedule, the routings, the setup times, machine speeds and capabilities, and resource capacities, for example. The FCS system uses that information to determine actual, realistic start and end times of jobs and uploads the results to MRP for subsequent replanning. The FCS system provides a more accurate picture than MRP of when the orders will be completed because MRP uses estimates for job waiting times in job lead times, does not recognize capacities when making the materials plans, and often uses aggregated time buckets (e.g., weeks). If these realistic completion times conflict with the MRP schedule, it may have to be revised and the FCS system rerun. Many companies are using advanced planning and scheduling (APS) systems that link their FCS and MRP systems to their ERP and supply-chain management systems (see Chapter 11, "Aggregate Planning and Scheduling").

LINKS TO FUNCTIONAL AREAS

The basic MRP system has its roots in the batch manufacturing of discrete parts involving assemblies that must be stocked to support future manufacturing needs. The focus is on producing schedules that meet the materials needs identified in the master production schedule. When managers realized that the information in an MRP system would be useful to functional areas other than operations, MRP evolved into **manufacturing resource planning (MRP II)**, a system that ties the basic MRP system to the company's financial system. Figure 12.11 shows an overview of an MRP II system. The focus of MRP II is to aid the management of a firm's resources by providing information based on the production plan to all functional areas. MRP II enables managers to test "what-if" scenarios by using simulation. For example, managers can see the effect of changing the MPS on the purchasing requirements for certain critical suppliers or the workload on bottleneck work centers without actually authorizing the schedule. In addition, management can project the dollar value of shipments, product costs, overhead allocations, inventories, backlogs, and profits by using the MRP plan along with prices and product and activity costs from the accounting system. Also, information from the MPS, scheduled receipts, and planned orders can be converted into cash flow projections, broken down by product families. For example, the projected on-hand quantities in MRP inventory records allow the computation of future levels of inventory investment. These levels are obtained simply by multiplying the quantities by the per-unit value of each item and adding these amounts for all items belonging to the

---

finite capacity scheduling (FCS) An algorithm designed to schedule a group of orders appropriately across an entire shop.

manufacturing resource planning (MRP II) A system that ties the basic MRP system to the company's financial system.

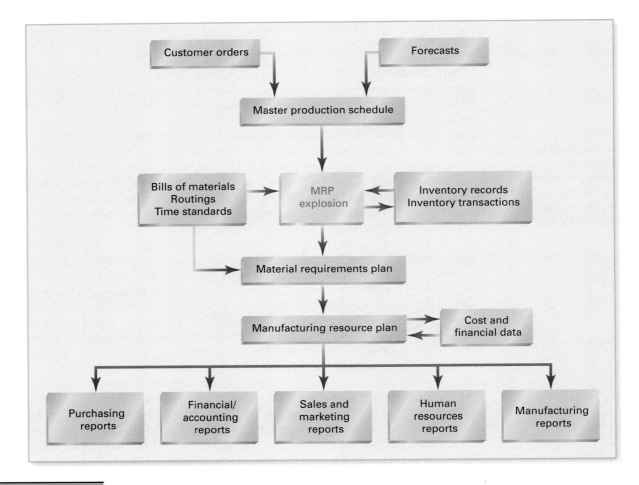

FIGURE 12.11

*Overview of a
Manufacturing
Resource Planning
System*

same product family. Similar computations are possible for other performance measures of interest to management.

Information from MRP II is used by managers in manufacturing, purchasing, marketing, finance, accounting, and engineering. MRP II reports help these managers develop and monitor the overall business plan and recognize sales objectives, manufacturing capabilities, and cash flow constraints. MRP II is used extensively and provides benefits beyond that of MRP alone. The Managerial Practice feature shows how MRP II can support a firm's strategy in the computer industry.

MRP AND THE ENVIRONMENT

Consumer and governmental concern about deterioration of the natural environment has driven manufacturers to reengineer their processes to become more environmentally friendly. Recycling of base materials is becoming more commonplace and products are being designed for ease of remanufacturing after their useful lives. Nonetheless, manufacturing processes often produce a number of wastes that need to be properly disposed of. Wastes come in many forms, including

❑ effluents such as carbon monoxide, sulfur dioxide, and hazardous chemicals that are associated with the processes used to manufacture the product

❑ materials such as metal shavings, oils, and chemicals that are associated with specific operations

MANAGERIAL PRACTICE
IBM's Rochester Plant Uses MRP to Execute Its Fast Turn-Around Strategy

IBM's Rochester, Minnesota, plant (www.research.ibm.com) is responsible for the final assembly of IBM's AS/400 midrange computers. The complex includes a printed circuit board assembly and testing facility that provides subassemblies to the final assembly lines. Each AS/400 computer is assembled to customer order, which the plant does more than 50,000 times per year. There are more than 10,000 different configurations. The plant must manage over 57,000 parts and assemblies no matter where they might be in the 3.6 million square feet of space the facility occupies, a daunting task without the help of modern systems. To remain competitive in this industry, IBM must promise delivery of complete computers within 96 hours of receiving the order. In addition, because of the short lead times, the plant must procure materials before firm customer orders are received, which requires careful management of inventory levels and shortages.

A core element of the plant's fast turn-around strategy is a MAPICS MRP II system (www.mapics.com), which took 18 months to install. In addition, IBM developed an application called Production Resource Manager (PRM), which interfaces with a firm's MRP II or ERP systems. In addition to typical inputs to an MRP II system, PRM requires *bills of capacity*, production, suppliers and inventory constraints, and optimization objectives such as maximizing profits, minimizing costs, or minimizing inventories. The bills of capacity are analogous to bills of material except they contain the amounts of specific capacities that are needed by a particular configuration of the final product and when they are needed. PRM takes the MRP II plan for component and purchased material replenishment orders and modifies it as needed to account for supply and component availability, capacity constraints, and objectives. The many outputs include a master production schedule, an optimal component production schedule, a revised shipment schedule, and a critical parts list.

IBM's Rochester, Minnesota, plant produces AS/400 computers in more than 10,000 configurations. Management uses an MRP II system to coordinate the production of 50,000 computers a year.

The system has enabled the Rochester plant to improve its inventory accuracy to 99 percent and reduce safety stocks by 15 to 25 percent. The system also includes a cost accounting module, which makes costing information that used to take more than a week to obtain immediately available. In addition, planners can simulate "what-if" scenarios quickly to see the impacts of various events on the production schedule. MRP II and the PRM application have enabled IBM's Rochester plant to execute its fast turn-around strategy.

Sources: "Success Stories: IBM Rochester Minnesota, USA." MAPICS, Inc. (2000), Weaver, Russ. "PRM in Action at Rochester, MN" IBM Corporation (1996), Weaver, Russ. "Production Resource Manager." IBM Corporation (1996).

❏ packaging materials such as unusable cardboard and plastics associated with certain products or purchased items

❏ scrap associated with unusable product or component defects generated by the manufacturing process

Companies can modify their MRP systems to assist them in tracking these wastes and planning for their disposition. The type and amount of waste associated with each item can be entered into its bill of materials by treating the waste much like you would a component of the item. When the master production schedule is developed for a product, reports can be generated that project the amount of waste that is expected and when it will occur. Although this approach requires substantial modification of a firm's bills of materials, the benefits are also substantial. Firms can identify their waste problems in advance and consequently plan for the proper disposal of them. The firms also have a means to generate any formal documentation required by the government to verify compliance with environmental laws and policies.

DISTRIBUTION REQUIREMENTS PLANNING

The principles of MRP can also be applied to distribution inventories, or stocks of items held at retailers and distribution centers. Consider the distribution system in Figure 12.12. The top level represents retail stores at various locations throughout the country. At the middle level are regional distribution centers (DCs) that replenish retail store inventories on request. The bottom level consists of one or more plants that supply the DCs. In the past, plants tended to schedule production to meet the forecasted demand patterns of the DCs. The DCs, in turn, replenished their inventories based on past demand patterns of the retail stores, reordering stocks from the factory whenever the inventory position reached a predetermined reorder point. The retailers followed a similar procedure, ordering stock from the distributor.

To illustrate the shortcomings of this approach, let us suppose that customer demand for a product suddenly increases by 10 percent. What will happen? Because the retailers carry some inventory, there will be some delay before the DCs feel the impact of the full 10 percent increase. Still more time passes before the plants feel the effect of the full increase, reflected as higher demand from the DCs. Thus, for months the plants could continue underproducing at their normal rate. When the deficiency finally becomes apparent, the plants must increase their output by much more than 10 percent to replenish inventory levels.

Distribution requirements planning (DRP) is an inventory control and scheduling technique that applies MRP principles to distribution inventories. It helps avoid self-induced swings in demand. An inventory record is maintained for each item at each location. The planned order releases projected at the retail level are used to derive the gross requirements for each item at the DC level from standard MRP logic and bills of materials. Next, planned order releases at the DC level are computed, from which the gross requirements for the plant level can be derived. This information provides the basis for updating the master production schedule at the plant.

Use of DRP requires an integrated information system. If the manufacturer operates its own DCs and retail stores, called *forward integration*, gathering demand information and relaying it back to the plants is easy. If the manufacturer does not own the DCs and retail stores, all three levels must agree to convey planned order releases from

distribution requirements planning (DRP) An inventory control and scheduling technique that applies MRP principles to distribution inventories.

Can MRP be used for distribution inventories?

FIGURE 12.12

Distribution System, Showing Supply Links from Plants to Distribution Centers and Retail Stores

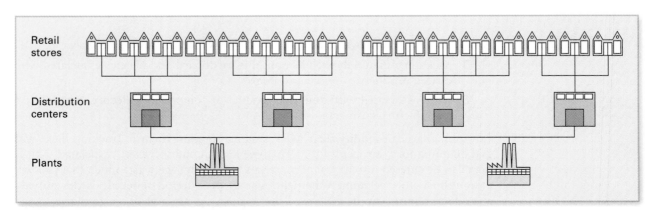

Retail stores

Distribution centers

Plants

one level to the next. Open communication can be extended from manufacturers to their suppliers, giving suppliers a better idea of future demand. Reducing demand uncertainty can pay off in lower inventories, better service, or both.

SERVICE RESOURCE PLANNING

Service providers must plan for resources just as manufacturers do. A major difference, however, is that the need for resources in a service company is capacity driven, as opposed to material driven. We have seen how manufacturing companies can disaggregate a master production schedule of finished products into the plans for assemblies, components, and purchased materials, which in turn can be translated into the needs for resources such as staff, equipment, supporting materials, and financial assets. Service providers must plan for the same resources; however, the focus is on maintaining the capacity to serve as opposed to producing a product to stock. Utilization of resources is important because materials are only a fraction of a typical service provider's investment in capital and people. In this section, we will discuss the concept of dependent demands for service providers and the use of a bill of resources.

DEPENDENT DEMAND

How can the concept of dependent demand be useful to service providers?

When we discussed MRP earlier in this chapter, we introduced the concept of *dependent demand,* which is demand for an item that is a function of the demand for some other item the company produces. For service resource planning, it is useful to define the concept of dependent demand to include demands for resources that are driven by forecasts of customer requests for services or by plans for various activities in support of the services the company provides. For example, a resource every service provider manages closely is cash. Forecasts of customer requests for services drive the need to purchase supporting materials and outside services. Staffing levels, a function of the forecasts, and employee schedules, a function of the forecasts and the staffing plan, drive the payroll (see Chapter 11, "Aggregate Planning and Scheduling"). These actions increase the firm's accounts payable. As services are actually completed the accounts receivable increase. Both the accounts receivable and the accounts payable help predict the amount and timing of cash flows for the firm. Here are some other examples of dependent demands for service providers.

RESTAURANTS. Every time you order from the menu at a restaurant, you initiate the need for supporting materials (uncooked food items, plates, and napkins), staff (chef, servers, and dishwashers), and equipment (stoves, ovens, and cooking utensils). Using a forecast of the demand for each type of meal, the manager of the restaurant can estimate the need for resources. Many restaurants have "specials" on certain days, such as fish frys on Fridays or prime ribs on Saturdays. Specials improve the accuracy of the forecast for meal types and typically signal the need for above-average levels of staff help.

AIRLINES. Whenever an airline schedules a flight, there are requirements for supporting materials (meals, beverages, and fuel), staff (pilots, flight attendants, and airport services), and equipment (plane and airport gate). Forecasts of customer patronage of each flight help determine the amount of supporting materials and the type of plane needed. A master schedule of flights based on the forecasts can be exploded to determine the resources needed to support the schedule.

A couple enjoys eating at a fine restaurant. Each meal initiates the need to buy supporting supplies, staff, and equipment.

HOSPITALS. With the exception of the emergency room, appointments, a form of master schedule for specific services, generally drive the short-term need for health care resources in hospitals. Forecasts of requests for various services provided by the hospital drive the long-term needs. When you schedule a surgical procedure, you generate a need for supporting materials (medicines, surgical gowns, and linens), staff (surgeon, nurses, and anesthesiologist), and equipment (operating room, surgical tools, and recovery bed). Hospitals must take care so that certain equipment or personnel do not become overcommitted. That is why an appointment for a hernia operation is put off until the surgeon is available, even though the appropriate operating room, nurses, and other resources are available.

HOTELS. The major fixed assets at a hotel are the rooms where guests stay. Given the high capital costs involved, hotels try to maintain as high a utilization rate as possible by offering group rates or special promotions at certain times of the year. Reservations, supplemented by forecasts of "walk-in" customers, provide a master schedule of needs for the hotel's services. When a traveler makes a reservation at a hotel, a need is generated for supporting materials (soap and towels), staff (front desk, housekeeping, and concierge), and equipment (fax, television, and exercise bicycle).

BILL OF RESOURCES

bill of resources (BOR)
A record of all the required materials, equipment time, staff, and other resources needed to provide a service, the parent–component relationships, and the usage quantities.

The service analogy to the BOM in a manufacturing company is the **bill of resources (BOR)**, which is a record of all the required materials, equipment time, staff, and other resources needed to provide a service, the parent–component relationships, and the usage quantities. Given a master schedule of services, the bills of resources can be used to derive the time-phased requirements for the firm's critical resources, as we did for the inventory records in MRP. A BOR for a service provider can be as complex as a BOM for a manufacturer. Consider a hospital that has just scheduled treatment of a patient with an aneurysm. As shown in Figure 12.13, the BOR for treatment of an aneurysm has seven levels, starting at the top (end item): (1) discharge; (2) intermediate care; (3) postoperative care—step down; (4) postoperative care—intensive; (5) surgery; (6) preoperative care—angiogram; and (7) preoperative care—testing. Each level of the BOR has a set of material and resource requirements and a lead time. For example, at

FIGURE 12.13

Bill of Resources for Treating an Aneurysm

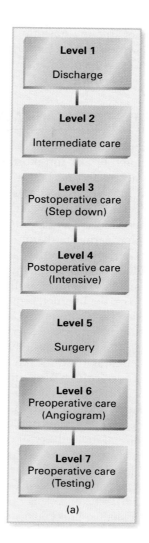

Level 1

Discharge

Level 2

Intermediate care

Level 3
Postoperative care
(Step down)

Level 4
Postoperative care
(Intensive)

Level 5

Surgery

Level 6
Preoperative care
(Angiogram)

Level 7
Preoperative care
(Testing)

(a)

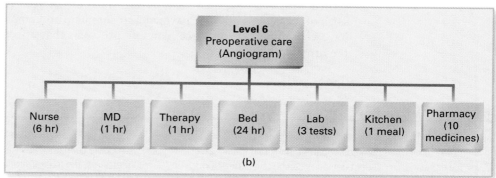

Level 6
Preoperative care
(Angiogram)

| Nurse (6 hr) | MD (1 hr) | Therapy (1 hr) | Bed (24 hr) | Lab (3 tests) | Kitchen (1 meal) | Pharmacy (10 medicines) |

(b)

level 6 shown in Figure 12.13(b), the patient needs 6 hours of nurses' time, 1 hour of the primary MD's time, 1 hour of the respiratory therapist's time, 24 hours of bed time, 3 different lab tests, 1 dietary meal, and 10 different medicines from the pharmacy. The lead time for this level is 1 day. The lead time for the entire stay for treatment of the aneurysm is 12.2 days. A master schedule of patient admissions and the BORs for each illness enable the hospital to manage their critical resources. Reports analogous to those we discussed for MRP II can be generated for the managers of the major processes in the hospital.

RESOURCE PLANNING ACROSS THE ORGANIZATION

Resource planning lies at the heart of any organization. We have seen examples of how traditional bricks-and-mortar organizations such as manufacturers, restaurants, airlines, hospitals, and hotels organize their resource planning efforts by utilizing integrated information systems that connect the organization's enterprise processes and functional areas. But what about the so-called dot-coms, which rely extensively on Internet connectivity to customers and suppliers? They too have resource planning concerns that permeate the organization. For example, consider online grocers, which do not have the retail outlets and checkout counters their bricks-and-mortar competitors do. What resource planning must online grocers do? To be competitive in a very competitive industry where profit margins are low, they must make it easy for the customer to shop on the Internet, provide a wide variety of goods, and make sure the deliveries of groceries are on time and cost efficient. Their Web pages must be designed to keep track of customers' preferences so that weekly shopping is easier and shoppers are apprised of specials and promotions that sometimes are keyed to the availability of goods in stock. The demands for goods at their warehouses are derived from the orders placed by customers at their Web sites. They must manage their resources at the warehouses to ensure a wide variety of grocery options for customers, enough stock to minimize stockouts, and adequate personnel to fill orders. Online grocers must do the order picking, packing, and handling that customers normally do at traditional supermarkets. In addition, the delivery of customer orders is derived from the delivery time requested by the customers as well as the completion of the packing process. The delivery of groceries is complicated by the fact that they cannot be left at the door if the customer is not home, and rural deliveries are usually far apart from each other and difficult to efficiently schedule. This operation needs a specialized delivery fleet, capable of moving perishable, bulky items over short distances. Effective management of the delivery service is critical to an online grocery's success. Finally, online grocers are also concerned with planning their cash flows, which are derived from the timing between its sales of groceries and their payments to suppliers and employees. Dot-com companies have very important resource planning problems that affect all the major processes of the firm.

CHAPTER HIGHLIGHTS

❏ Dependent demand for component items can be calculated from production schedules of parent items in a manufacturing company. Dependent demands can be calculated from forecasts and other resource plans in a service company.

❏ Material requirements planning (MRP) is a computerized scheduling and information system that offers benefits in managing dependent demand inventories because it (1) recognizes the relationship between production schedules and the demand for component items, (2) provides forward visibility for planning and problem solving, and (3) provides a

way to change materials plans in concert with production schedule changes. MRP has three basic inputs: bills of materials, the master production schedule, and inventory records.

❏ A bill of materials is a diagram or structured list of all components of an item, the parent–component relationships, and usage quantities.

❏ A master production schedule (MPS) states the number of end items to be produced during specific time periods within an intermediate planning horizon. The MPS is developed within the overall guidelines of the production plan.

❏ The MRP is prepared from the most recent inventory records for all items. The basic elements in each record are gross requirements, scheduled receipts, projected on-hand inventory, planned receipts, and planned order releases. Several quantities must be determined for each inventory record, including lot size, lead time, and safety stock.

❏ The MRP explosion procedure determines the production schedules of the components that are needed to support the master production schedule. The planned order releases of a parent, modified by usage quantities shown in the bill of materials, become the gross requirements of its components.

❏ MRP systems provide outputs such as the material requirements plan, action notices, capacity reports, and performance reports. Action notices bring to a planner's attention new orders that need to be released or items that have open orders with misaligned due dates.

❏ Capacity requirements planning (CRP) is a technique for estimating the workload required by a master schedule. CRP uses routing information to identify the workstations involved and MRP information about existing inventory, lead-time offset, and replacement part requirements to calculate accurate workload projections. Finite capacity scheduling (FCS) determines a schedule for production orders that recognizes resource constraints.

❏ Manufacturing resource planning (MRP II) ties the basic MRP system to the financial and accounting systems. Advanced systems integrate management decision support for all business functions.

❏ Service providers can take advantage of MRP principles by developing bills of resources that include requirements for materials, labor, and equipment.

SOLVED PROBLEM 1

Refer to the bill of materials for item A shown in Figure 12.14.

If there is no existing inventory, how many units of G, E, and D must be purchased to produce five units of end item A?

SOLUTION

Five units of G, 30 units of E, and 20 units of D must be purchased to make 5 units of A. The usage quantities shown in Figure 12.14 indicate that 2 units of E are needed to make 1 unit of B and that 3 units of B are needed to make 1 unit of A; therefore, 5 units of A require 30 units of E ($2 \times 3 \times 5 = 30$). One unit of D is consumed to make 1 unit of B, and 3 units of B per unit of A result in 15 units of D ($1 \times 3 \times 5 = 15$);

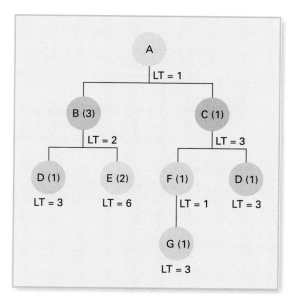

FIGURE 12.14

plus 1 unit of D in each unit of C and 1 unit of C per unit of A result in another 5 units of D
$(1 \times 1 \times 5 = 5)$. The total requirements to make 5 units of A are 20 units of D $(15 + 5)$. The calculation
of requirements for G is simply $1 \times 1 \times 1 \times 5 = 5$ units.

SOLVED PROBLEM 2

The MPS for product A calls for the assembly department to begin final assembly according to the following schedule: 100 units in week 2; 200 units in week 4; 120 units in week 6; 180 units in week 7;
and 60 units in week 8. Develop a material requirements plan for the next eight weeks for items B, C,
and D. The BOM for A is shown in Figure 12.15, and data from the inventory records are shown in
Table 12.1.

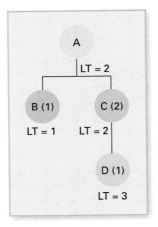

FIGURE 12.15

TABLE 12.1 *Inventory Record Data*

	ITEM		
DATA CATEGORY	B	C	D
Lot-sizing rule	POQ $(P = 3)$	L4L	FOQ $= 500$ units
Lead time	1 week	2 weeks	3 weeks
Scheduled receipts	None	200 (week 1)	None
Beginning (on-hand) inventory	20	0	425

SOLUTION

We begin with items B and C and develop their inventory records, as shown in Figure 12.16. The MPS
for item A must be multiplied by 2 to derive the gross requirements for item C because of the usage
quantity. Once the planned order releases for item C are found, the gross requirements for item D can
be calculated.

Notice that an action notice would call for delaying the scheduled receipt for item C from week 1 to
week 2. Other action notices would notify planners that items B and D have a planned order release in
the current week.

Item: B
Description:

Lot Size: POQ (*P* = 3)
Lead Time: 1 week

		Week									
		1	2	3	4	5	6	7	8	9	10
Gross requirements			100		200		120	180	60		
Scheduled receipts											
Projected on-hand inventory	20	20	200	200	0	0	240	60	0	0	0
Planned receipts			280				360				
Planned order releases		280				360					

Item: C
Description:

Lot Size: L4L
Lead Time: 2 weeks

		Week									
		1	2	3	4	5	6	7	8	9	10
Gross requirements			200		400		240	360	120		
Scheduled receipts		200 →									
Projected on-hand inventory	0	200	0	0	0	0	0	0	0	0	0
Planned receipts					400		240	360	120		
Planned order releases			400		240	360	120				

FIGURE 12.16

Item: D Description:								Lot Size: FOQ = 500 units Lead Time: 3 weeks		
		Week									
		1	2	3	4	5	6	7	8	9	10
Gross requirements			400		240	360	120				
Scheduled receipts											
Projected on-hand inventory	425	425	25	25	285	425	305	305	305	305	305
Planned receipts					500	500					
Planned order releases		500	500								

FIGURE 12.16 (*continued*)

CD-ROM RESOURCES

The Student CD-ROM that accompanies this text contains the following resources, which allow you to further practice and apply the concepts presented in this chapter.

- ❏ **OM Explorer Tutor:** OM Explorer contains a tutor program that will help you learn how to use the FOQ, POQ, and L4L decision rules for inventory lot-sizing decisions. See the Chapter 12 folder in OM Explorer. See also the exercise requiring the use of this tutor program.

- ❏ **OM Explorer Solver:** OM Explorer has three programs that can be used to solve general problems involving single-item MRP inventory records, MRP records for multiple-level bills of material, and master production schedules. See the Resource Planning folder in OM Explorer.

- ❏ **Discussion Questions:** Three questions will challenge your understanding of the usefulness of MRP to all functional areas of a business and how the principles of resource planning can be applied to service firms.

- ❏ **Case:** Flashy Flashers, Inc. Determine the requirements for materials and components in a practical setting and assess the implications for MRP implementation at an automotive electric component manufacturer.

- ❏ **Supplement J:** Operations Scheduling. Use this supplement to see how resource planning systems link to advanced planning systems in practice.

- ❏ **Supplement K:** Master Production Scheduling. Learn how to develop master production schedules and how customer due-date promises are linked to production schedules.

INTERACTIVE RESOURCES

The Interactive Web site associated with this text (www.prenhall.com/ritzman) contains many tools and activities specifically designed for this chapter. The following items are recommended to enhance your understanding of the material in this chapter.

❏ **Internet Activities:** Try out three different links to resource planning topics including commonality, MRP II, and service resource management.

❏ **Internet Tour:** Explore materials, equipment, and labor resource management at American Acoustech Guitars.

PROBLEMS

1. Consider the bill of materials in Figure 12.17.
   a. How many immediate parents (one level above) does item I have? How many immediate parents does item E have?
   b. How many unique components does item A have at all levels?
   c. Which of the components are purchased items?
   d. How many intermediate items does item A have at all levels?
   e. Given the lead times noted on Figure 12.17, how far in advance of shipment is the earliest purchase commitment required?

2. Item A is made from components B, C, and D. Item B is a subassembly that requires 2 units of C and 1 unit of E.

Item D also is an intermediate item, made from F. All other usage quantities are 2. Draw the bill of materials for item A.

3. A milling machine workstation makes small gears used in a transmission gear box. As of week 22, the capacity requirements planning (CRP) report for the workstation revealed the following information. The planned hours for weeks 22, 23, 24, 25, 26, and 27 were 40, 60, 100, 120, 175, and 160, respectively. The actual hours for the same weeks were 90, 75, 80, 0, 0, and 0. Each of two machines at the workstation is scheduled for two shifts per day. The workstation has a maximum capacity of 160 hours per week. Does the CRP report reveal any problems at the workstation? If so, what are they and what should be done to correct them?

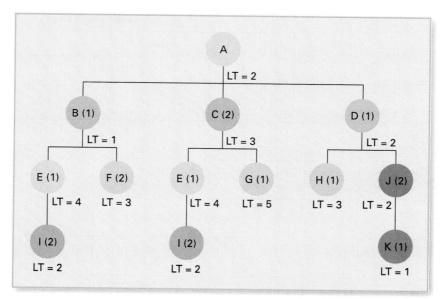

FIGURE 12.17

Item: M405—X Description: Table top assembly								Lot Size: Lead Time: 2 weeks			
	Week										
	1	2	3	4	5	6	7	8	9	10
Gross requirements	90		85		80		45	90		
Scheduled receipts	110									
Projected on-hand inventory 40										
Planned receipts										
Planned order releases										

FIGURE 12.18

4. The partially completed inventory record in Figure 12.18 shows gross requirements, scheduled receipts, lead time, and current on-hand inventory.

    a. Complete the last three rows of the record for an FOQ of 110 units.

    b. Complete the last three rows of the record by using the L4L lot-sizing rule.

    c. Complete the last three rows of the record by using the POQ lot-sizing rule, with $P = 2$.

Item: Driveshaft								Lot Size: Lead Time: 3 weeks
	Week							
	1	2	3	4	5	6	7	8
Gross requirements	35	25	15	20	40	40	50	50
Scheduled receipts	80							
Projected on-hand inventory 10								
Planned receipts								
Planned order releases								

FIGURE 12.19

5. ● **OM Explorer** The partially completed inventory record in Figure 12.19 shows gross requirements, scheduled receipts, lead time, and current on-hand inventory.

   a. Complete the last three rows of the inventory record for an FOQ of 50 units.

   b. Complete the last three rows of the record by using the L4L lot-sizing rule.

   c. Complete the last three rows of the record by using the POQ lot-sizing rule, with $P = 4$.

6. ● **OM Explorer** The BOM for product A is shown in Figure 12.20, and data from the inventory records are shown in Table 12.2. In the master production schedule for product A, the MPS start row has 500 units in week 6. The lead time

for production of A is two weeks. Develop the material requirements plan for the next six weeks for items B, C, and D. (*Hint*: You cannot derive an item's gross requirements unless you know the planned order releases of all its parents.)

TABLE 12.2 *Inventory Record Data*

	ITEM		
DATA CATEGORY	**B**	**C**	**D**
Lot-sizing rule	L4L	L4L	FOQ = 2,000
Lead time	3 weeks	1 week	1 week
Scheduled receipts	None	None	2,000 (week 1)
Beginning inventory	0	0	200

7. ● **OM Explorer** The BOMs for products A and B are shown in Figure 12.21. Data from inventory records are shown in Table 12.3. The MPS calls for 85 units of product A to be started in week 3 and 100 units in week 6. The MPS for product B calls for 180 units to be started in week 5. Develop the material requirements plan for the next six weeks for items C, D, E, and F. Identify any action notices.

TABLE 12.3 *Inventory Record Data*

	ITEM			
DATA CATEGORY	**C**	**D**	**E**	**F**
Lot-sizing rule	FOQ = 220	L4L	FOQ = 300	POQ ($P = 2$)
Lead time	3 weeks	2 weeks	3 weeks	2 weeks
Scheduled receipts	280 (week 1)	None	300 (week 3)	None
Beginning inventory	25	0	150	600

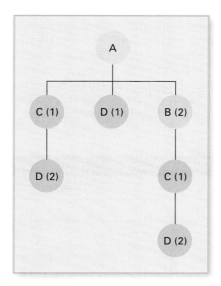

FIGURE 12.20

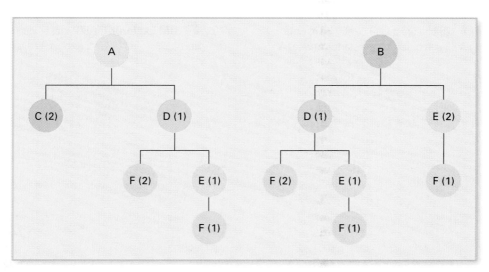

FIGURE 12.21

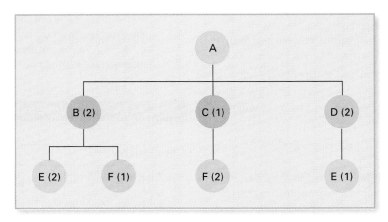

FIGURE 12.22

8. **⊕ OM Explorer** Figure 12.22 illustrates the BOM of product A. The MPS start row in the master production schedule for product A calls for 50 units in week 2, 65 units in week 5, and 80 units in week 8. Item C is produced to make A and to meet the forecasted demand for replacement parts. Past replacement part demand has been 20 units per week (add 20 units to C's gross requirements). The lead times for items F and C are one week, and for the other items the lead time is two weeks. No safety stock is required for items B, C, D, E, and F. The L4L lot-sizing rule is used for items B and F; the POQ lot-sizing rule ($P = 3$) is used for C. Item E has an FOQ of 600 units, and D has an FOQ of 250 units. On-hand inventories are 50 units of B, 50 units of C, 120 units of D, 70 units of E, and 250 units of F. Item B has a scheduled receipt of 50 units in week 2.

Develop a material requirements plan for the next eight weeks for items B, C, D, E, and F.

9. The following information is available for three MPS items.

Item A	An 80-unit order is to be started in week 3.
	A 55-unit order is to be started in week 6.
Item B	A 125-unit order is to be started in week 5.
Item C	A 60-unit order is to be started in week 4.

Develop the material requirements plan for the next six weeks for items D, E, and F, identifying any action notices that would be provided. The BOMs are shown in Figure 12.23, and data from the inventory records are shown in Table 12.4. (*Warning*: There is a safety stock requirement for item F. Be sure to plan a receipt for any week in which the projected on-hand inventory becomes less than the safety stock.)

TABLE 12.4 *Inventory Record Data*

DATA CATEGORY	ITEM		
	D	E	F
Lot-sizing rule	FOQ = 150	L4L	POQ ($P = 2$)
Lead time	3 weeks	1 week	2 weeks
Safety stock	0	0	30
Scheduled receipts	150 (week 3)	120 (week 2)	None
Beginning inventory	150	0	100

10. **⊕ OM Explorer** The BOM for product A is shown in Figure 12.24. The MPS for product A calls for 120 units to be

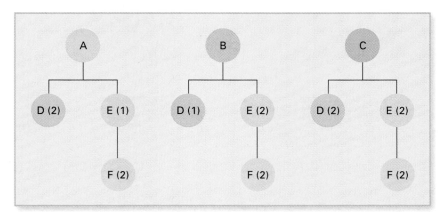

FIGURE 12.23

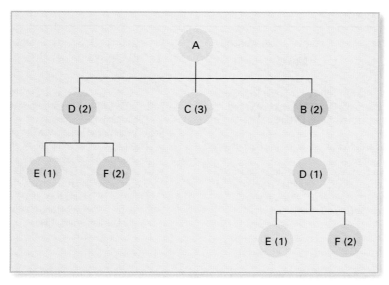

FIGURE 12.24

TABLE 12.5 *Inventory Record Data*

DATA CATEGORY	ITEM				
	B	C	D	E	F
Lot-sizing rule	L4L	FOQ = 700	FOQ = 700	L4L	L4L
Lead time	3 weeks	3 weeks	4 weeks	2 weeks	1 week
Safety stock	0	0	0	50	0
Scheduled receipts	150 (week 2)	450 (week 2)	700 (week 1)	None	1,400 (week 1)
Beginning inventory	125	0	235	750	0

started in weeks 2, 4, 5, and 8. Table 12.5 shows data from the inventory records. Develop the material requirements plan for the next eight weeks for each item. (*Warning*: Note that item E has a safety stock requirement.)

11. ⊙ **OM Explorer** Develop the material requirements plan for all components and intermediate items associated with

end item A for the next ten weeks. Refer to Solved Problem 1 (Table 12.6) for the bill of materials and Table 12.6 for component inventory record information. The MPS for product A calls for 50 units to be started in weeks 2, 6, 8, and 9. (*Warning*: Note that items B and C have safety stock requirements.)

TABLE 12.6 *Inventory Record Data*

DATA CATEGORY	ITEM					
	B	C	D	E	F	G
Lot-sizing rule	L4L	L4L	POQ (P = 2)	L4L	L4L	FOQ = 100
Lead time	2 weeks	3 weeks	3 weeks	6 weeks	1 week	3 weeks
Safety stock	30	10	0	0	0	0
Scheduled receipts	150 (week 2)	50 (week 2)	None	400 (week 6)	40 (week 3)	None
Beginning inventory	30	20	60	400	0	0

SELECTED REFERENCES

Blackstone, J. H. *Capacity Management.* Cincinnati: South-Western, 1989.

Conway, Richard W. "Linking MRP II and FCS." *APICS—The Performance Advantage* (June 1996), pp. 40–44.

Haddock, Jorge, and Donald E. Hubicki. "Which Lot-Sizing Techniques Are Used in Material Requirements Planning?" *Production and Inventory Management Journal,* vol. 30, no. 3 (1989), pp. 53–56.

Hoy, Paul A. "The Changing Role of MRP II." *APICS—The Performance Advantage* (June 1996), pp. 50–53.

Melnyk, Steven A., Robert Stroufe, Frank Montabon, Roger Calantone, R. Lal Tummala, and Timothy J. Hinds. "Integrating Environmental Issues into Material Planning: 'Green' MRP." *Production and Inventory Management Journal* (Third Quarter 1999), pp. 36–45.

Ormsby, Joseph G., Susan Y. Ormsby, and Carl R. Ruthstrom. "MRP II Implementation: A Case Study." *Production and Inventory Management,* vol. 31, no. 4 (1990), pp. 77–82.

Prouty, Dave. "Shiva Finite Capacity Scheduling System." *APICS—The Performance Advantage* (April 1997), pp. 58–61.

Ptak, Carol. *MRP and Beyond.* Homewood, IL: Irwin Professional Publication, 1996.

Roth, Aleda V., and Roland Van Dierdonck. "Hospital Resource Planning: Concepts, Feasibility, and Framework." *Production and Operations Management,* vol. 4, no. 1 (1995), pp. 2–29.

Vollmann, T. E., W. L. Berry, and D. C. Whybark. *Manufacturing Planning and Control Systems,* 4th ed. Homewood, IL: Irwin Professional Publications, 1997.

Wallace, Tom. *MRP II: Making It Happen.* Essex Junction, VT: Oliver Wight Ltd. Publishers, 1994.

Lean Systems

Across the Organization

Lean systems are important to . . .

- ❐ **accounting,** which often must adjust its billing and cost accounting practices to take advantage of lean systems.
- ❐ **engineering,** which must design products that use more common parts so that fewer setups are required and focused factories and group technology can be used.
- ❐ **finance,** which must secure the working capital needed for a lean system.
- ❐ **human resources,** which must recruit, train, and evaluate the employees needed to successfully operate a lean system.
- ❐ **management information systems,** which must integrate the lean system with other information systems in the firm.
- ❐ **marketing,** which relies on lean systems to deliver high-quality products or services on time, at reasonable prices.
- ❐ **operations,** which is responsible for using the lean system in the production of goods or services.

Learning Goals

After reading this chapter, you will be able to . . .

1. identify the characteristics of lean systems that enable the realization of the lean system philosophy.
2. describe how lean systems can facilitate the continuous improvement of operations.
3. calculate the number of containers of a specific part required for a system.
4. explain how the principles of the lean system philosophy can be applied by service providers.
5. discuss the strategic advantages of lean systems and the implementation issues associated with the application of these systems.

f you were to select one company that is exemplary of excellence in automobile manufacturing, it would probably be Toyota (www.toyota.com). Worldwide in its presence, it has a total investment of $12 billion in 10 manufacturing plants that employ 30,500 associates in North America alone. Toyota was at the forefront of firms developing lean systems for manufacturing, and today the Toyota Production System (TPS) is one of the most admired lean manufacturing systems in existence. Replicating the system, however, is fraught with difficulties. What makes the system tick, and why could Toyota employ the system in so many different plants when others have difficulty?

Most outsiders see the Toyota Production System as a set of tools and procedures that are readily visible during a plant tour. While they are important for the success of the TPS, they are not the keys to the heart of the system. What most people overlook is that Toyota has built a learning organization over the course of 50 years. Lean systems require constant improvements to increase efficiency and reduce waste. Toyota has created a system that stimulates employees to experiment with their environment by seeking better ways whenever things go wrong. Toyota sets up all operations as experiments and teaches employees at all levels how to use the scientific method of problem solving.

There are four underlying principles of the Toyota Production System. First, all work must be completely specified as to content, sequence, timing, and outcome. Detail is important, otherwise there is no foundation for improvements. Second, every customer–supplier connection must be direct, unambiguously specifying the people involved, the form and quantity of the goods or services to be provided, the way the requests are made by each customer, and the expected time in which the requests will be met. Customer–supplier connections can be internal—employee to employee—or external—company to company.

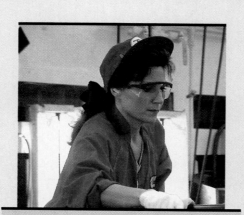

A team member is preparing a vehicle for an application of paint at the Toyota manufacturing facility at Georgetown, Kentucky. Painting is one of the most detailed processes at the plant, using both water-borne and solvent-based paints. The metal of the vehicles is carefully checked for any imperfections before the first coat of paint is ever applied. Note the clothing and gloves that the employee wears, designed to keep the vehicles from being accidentally marred in the painting process.

Third, the pathway for every product and service must be simple and direct. That is, goods and services do not flow to the next available person or machine, but to a *specific* person or machine. With this principle, employees can determine, for example, that there is a capacity problem at a particular workstation and then analyze ways to resolve it.

The first three principles define the system in detail by specifying how employees do work, interact with each other, and design work flows. These specifications actually are "hypotheses" about the way the system should work. For example, if something goes wrong at a workstation enough times, the hypothesis about the methods the employee uses to do work is rejected. The fourth principle, then, is that any improvement to the system must be made in accordance with the scientific method, under the guidance of a teacher, at the lowest possible organizational level. The scientific method involves clearly stating a verifiable hypothesis of the form, "If we make the following specific changes, we expect to achieve this specific outcome." The hypothesis must then be tested under a variety of conditions. Working with a teacher, who is often the employees' supervisor, is a key to becoming a learning organization. Employees learn the scientific method and eventually become teachers of others. Finally, making improvements at the lowest level of the organization means that the employees who are actually doing the work are actively involved in making improvements.

These four principles are deceptively simple; however, they are difficult to replicate. Nonetheless, those organizations that have successfully implemented them have enjoyed the benefits of a lean system that adapts to change.

Source: Spear, Steven and H. Kent Bowen. "Decoding the DNA of the Toyota Production System." *Harvard Business Review* (September–October 1999), pp. 97–106.

lean systems Operations systems that are designed to create efficient processes by taking a total systems perspective.

THE CONCEPT OF **lean systems** embodies much of what we have already covered in this text. It focuses on operations strategy, processes, technology, quality, capacity, layout, supply chains, inventory, and resource planning. Lean systems "put it all together" to create efficient processes. They are known by many different names, including *zero inventory, synchronous manufacturing, stockless production* (Hewlett-Packard), *material as needed* (Harley-Davidson), and *continuous flow manufacturing* (IBM), each with their own operational differences. In this chapter, however, we will focus on the most popular system that incorporates the generic elements of lean systems—the just-in-time (JIT) system. The **just-in-time (JIT) philosophy** is simple but powerful—*eliminate waste* by cutting unnecessary inventory and removing nonvalue-added activities in operations. The goals are to produce goods and services as needed and to continuously improve the value-added benefits of operations. A **JIT system** is the organization of resources, information flows, and decision rules that can enable an organization to realize the benefits of the JIT philosophy. Often a crisis (such as being faced with going out of business or closing a plant) galvanizes management and labor to work together to change traditional operating practices. Converting from traditional manufacturing to a just-in-time system brings up not only inventory control issues but also process management and scheduling issues. In this chapter, we identify the characteristics of lean systems as embodied in JIT systems, discuss how they can be used for continuous improvement of operations, and indicate how manufacturing and service operations utilize such systems. We also address the strategic implications of lean systems and some of the implementation issues that companies face.

just-in-time (JIT) philosophy The belief that waste can be eliminated by cutting unnecessary inventory and removing nonvalue-added activities in operations.

JIT system The organization of resources, information flows, and decision rules that enable an organization to realize the benefits of a JIT philosophy.

CHARACTERISTICS OF LEAN SYSTEMS: JUST-IN-TIME OPERATIONS

The just-in-time system, a primary example of lean systems, focuses on reducing inefficiency and unproductive time in processes to improve continuously the process and the quality of the products or services they produce. Employee involvement and the reduction of nonvalue-added activities are essential to JIT operations. In this section, we discuss the following characteristics of JIT systems: pull method of material flow, consistently high quality, small lot sizes, uniform workstation loads, standardized components and work methods, close supplier ties, flexible workforce, line flows, automated production, and preventive maintenance.

PULL METHOD OF MATERIALS FLOW

Just-in-time systems utilize the pull method of materials flow. However, another popular method is the push method. To differentiate between these two systems, let's first consider the production system for a Quarter Pounder at a McDonald's restaurant. There are two workstations. The burger maker is the person responsible for producing this burger: Burger patties must be fried; buns must be toasted and then dressed with ketchup, pickles, mayonnaise, lettuce, and cheese; and the patties must be inserted into buns and put on a tray. The final assembler takes the tray, wraps the burgers in paper, and restocks the inventory. Inventories must be kept low because any burgers left unsold after seven minutes must be destroyed.

The flow of materials is from the burger maker to the final assembler to the customer. One way to manage this flow is by using the **push method,** in which the production of the item begins in advance of customer needs. With this method, management schedules the receipt of all raw materials (e.g., meat, buns, and condiments) and authorizes the start of production, all in advance of Quarter Pounder needs. The burger maker starts production of 24 burgers (the capacity of the griddle) and, when

push method A method in which the production of the item begins in advance of customer needs.

Fast-food workers using the pull system to serve their customers at a McDonald's store in Taipei, Taiwan. The burger maker and assembler are behind the racks, which are readily available to the workers at the sales counter.

they are completed, pushes them along to the final assembler's station, where they might have to wait until the final assembler is ready for them. The packaged burgers then wait on a warming tray until a customer purchases one.

pull method A method in which customer demand activates production of the item.

The other way to manage the flow among the burger maker, the final assembler, and the customer is to use the **pull method,** in which customer demand activates production of the item. With the pull method, as customers purchase burgers, the final assembler checks the inventory level of burgers and, when they are almost depleted, orders six more. The burger maker produces the six burgers and gives the tray to the final assembler, who completes the assembly and places the burgers in the inventory for sale. The pull method is better for the production of burgers: The two workers can coordinate the two workstations to keep inventory low, important because of the 7-minute time limit. The production of burgers is a highly repetitive process, setup times and process times are low, and the flow of materials is well defined. There is no need to produce to anticipated needs more than a few minutes ahead.

Under what circumstances can a just-in-time system be used effectively?

Firms that tend to have highly repetitive manufacturing processes and well-defined material flows use just-in-time systems because the pull method allows closer control of inventory and production at the workstations. Other firms, such as those producing a large variety of products in low volumes with low repeatability in the production process, tend to use a push method such as MRP. In this case, a customer order is promised for delivery on some future date. Production is started at the first workstation and pushed ahead to the next one. Inventory can accumulate at each workstation because workstations are responsible for producing many other orders and may be busy at any particular time.

CONSISTENTLY HIGH QUALITY

Just-in-time systems seek to eliminate scrap and rework in order to achieve a uniform flow of materials. Efficient JIT operations require conformance to product or service specifications and implementation of the behavioral and statistical methods of total quality management (TQM) (see Chapter 5, "Quality"). JIT systems control quality at the source, with workers acting as their own quality inspectors.

Management must realize the enormous responsibility this method places on the workers and must prepare them properly, as one GM division quickly learned. When Buick City began using JIT in 1985, management authorized its workers to stop the production line by pulling a cord if quality problems arose at their stations—a practice the Japanese call *andon*. GM also eliminated production-line inspectors and cut the number of supervisors by half. Stopping the line, however, is a costly action that brings a problem to everyone's attention. The workers were not prepared for that responsibility; productivity and quality took a nose-dive. The paint on Le Sabres was not shiny enough. The seams were not straight. The top of the dashboard had an unintended wave. Management, labor, and engineering formed a team to correct the problems. Work methods were changed, and the *andon* system was modified to include a yellow warning cord so that workers could call for help without stopping the line.

SMALL LOT SIZES

Rather than building up a cushion of inventory, users of JIT systems maintain inventory with lot sizes that are as small as possible. Small lot sizes have three benefits. First, small lot sizes reduce *cycle* inventory, the inventory in excess of the safety stock carried between orders (see Chapter 10, "Inventory Management"). The average cycle inventory equals one-half the lot size: As the lot size gets smaller, so does cycle inventory. Reducing cycle inventory reduces the time and space involved in manufacturing and holding inventory. Figure 13.1 shows the effect on cycle inventory of reducing the lot size from 100 to 50 for a uniform demand of 10 units per hour: Cycle inventory is cut in half.

Second, small lot sizes help cut lead times. A decline in lead time in turn cuts pipeline (WIP) inventory because the total processing time at each workstation is greater for large lots than for small lots. Also, a large lot often has to wait longer to be processed at the next workstation while that workstation finishes working on another large lot. In addition, if any defective items are discovered, large lots cause longer delays because the entire lot must be inspected to find all the items that need rework.

Finally, small lots help achieve a uniform operating system workload. Large lots consume large chunks of processing time on workstations and, therefore, complicate

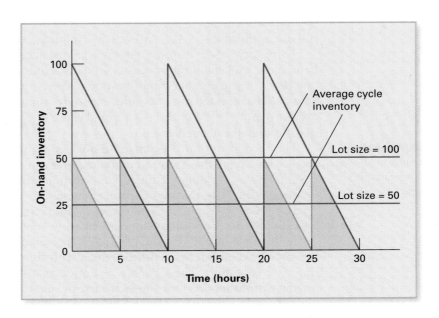

FIGURE 13.1

Implications of Small and Large Lot Sizes for Cycle Inventory

scheduling. Small lots can be juggled more effectively, enabling schedulers to utilize capacities more efficiently. In addition, small lots allow workstations to accommodate mixed-model production (more than one item) by reducing waiting-line times for production. We return to this point when we discuss uniform workstation loads.

Although small lot sizes are beneficial to operations, they have the disadvantage of increased setup frequency. In operations where the setup times are normally low, as in the McDonald's example, small lots are feasible. However, in fabrication operations with sizable setup times, increasing the frequency of setups may result in wasting employee and equipment time. These operations must reduce setup times to realize the benefits of small-lot production.

Achieving low setup times often requires close cooperation among engineering, management, and labor. For example, changing dies on large presses to form automobile parts from sheet metal can take three to four hours. At Honda's Marysville, Ohio, plant—where four stamping lines stamp all the exterior and major interior body panels for Accord production—teams worked on ways to reduce the changeover time for the massive dies. As a result, a complete change of dies for a giant 2,400-ton press now takes less than eight minutes. The goal of **single-digit setup** means having setup times of less than 10 minutes. Some techniques to reduce setup times include using conveyors for die storage, moving large dies with cranes, simplifying dies, enacting machine controls, using microcomputers to automatically feed and position work, and preparing for changeovers while the current job is being processed.

single-digit setup The goal of having a setup time of less than 10 minutes.

UNIFORM WORKSTATION LOADS

The JIT system works best if the daily load on individual workstations is relatively uniform. Uniform loads can be achieved by assembling the same type and number of units each day, thus creating a uniform daily demand at all workstations. Capacity planning, which recognizes capacity constraints at critical workstations, and line balancing are used to develop the monthly master production schedule. For example, at Toyota the aggregate production plan may call for 4,500 vehicles per week for the next month. That requires two full shifts, five days per week, producing 900 vehicles each day, or 450 per shift. Three models are produced: Camry (C), Avalon (A), and Sienna (S). Suppose that Toyota needs 200 Camrys, 150 Avalons, and 100 Siennas per shift to satisfy market demand. To produce 450 units in one shift of 480 minutes, the line must roll out a vehicle every 480/450 = 1.067 minutes.

Three ways of devising a master production schedule for the vehicles are of interest here. First, with big-lot production, all daily requirements of a model are produced in one batch before another model is started. The sequence of 200 C's, 150 A's, and 100 S's would be repeated once per shift. Not only would these big lots increase the average cycle inventory level but they also would cause lumpy requirements on all the workstations feeding the assembly line.

The second option uses **mixed-model assembly,** producing a mix of models in smaller lots. Note that the production requirements are in the ratio of 4 C's to 3 A's to 2 S's, found by dividing the model's production requirements by the greatest common divisor, or 50. Thus, the Toyota planner could develop a production cycle consisting of 9 units: 4 C's, 3 A's, and 2 S's. The cycle would repeat in 9(1.067) = 9.60 minutes, for a total of 50 times per shift (480 min/9.60 min = 50).

mixed-model assembly A type of assembly that produces a mix of models in smaller lots.

A sequence of C–S–C–A–C–A–C–S–A, repeated 50 times per shift, would achieve the same total output as the other options. This third option is feasible only if the setup times are very short. The sequence generates a steady rate of component requirements for the various models and allows the use of small lot sizes at the feeder workstations. Consequently, the capacity requirements at those stations are greatly smoothed. These requirements can be compared to actual capacities during the planning phase, and modifications to the production cycle, production requirements, or capacities can be made as necessary.

STANDARDIZED COMPONENTS AND WORK METHODS

The standardization of components, called *part commonality* or *modularity,* increases repeatability. For example, a firm producing 10 products from 1,000 different components could redesign its products so that they consist of only 100 different components with larger daily requirements. Because the requirements per component increase, so does repeatability; that is, each worker performs a standardized task or work method more often each day. Productivity tends to increase because, with increased repetition, workers learn to do the task more efficiently. Standardization of components and work methods aids in achieving the high-productivity, low-inventory objectives of JIT systems.

CLOSE SUPPLIER TIES

Because JIT systems operate with very low levels of inventory, close relationships with suppliers are necessary. Stock shipments must be frequent, have short lead times, arrive on schedule, and be of high quality. A contract might require a supplier to deliver goods to a factory as often as several times per day. Purchasing managers focus on three areas: reducing the number of suppliers, using local suppliers, and improving supplier relations.

Typically, one of the first actions undertaken when a JIT system is implemented is to pare the number of suppliers. Xerox, for example, reduced the number of its suppliers from 5,000 to just 300. This approach puts a lot of pressure on these suppliers to deliver high-quality components on time. To compensate, JIT users extend their contracts with these suppliers and give them firm advance-order information. In addition, they include their suppliers in the early phases of product design to avoid problems after production has begun. They also work with their suppliers' vendors, trying to achieve JIT inventory flows throughout the entire supply chain.

Manufacturers using JIT systems generally utilize local suppliers. For instance, when GM located its Saturn complex in Tennessee, many suppliers clustered nearby. Harley-Davidson reduced the number of its suppliers and gave preference to those close to its plants—for example, three-fourths of the suppliers for the Milwaukee engine plant are located within a 175-mile radius. Geographic proximity means that the company can reduce the need for safety stocks. Companies that have no suppliers close by must rely on a finely tuned supplier delivery system. For example, New United Motor Manufacturing, Incorporated (NUMMI), the joint venture between GM and Toyota in California, has suppliers in Indiana, Ohio, and Michigan. Through a carefully coordinated system involving trains and piggyback truck trailers, suppliers deliver enough parts for exactly one day's production each day.

Users of JIT systems also find that a cooperative orientation with suppliers is essential (see Chapter 8, "Supply-Chain Management"). The JIT philosophy is to look for ways to improve efficiency and reduce inventories throughout the supply chain. Close cooperation between companies and their suppliers can be a win–win situation for everyone. Better communication of component requirements, for example, enables more efficient inventory planning and delivery scheduling by suppliers, thereby improving supplier profit margins. Customers can then negotiate lower component prices. Suppliers also should be included in the design of new products so that inefficient component designs can be avoided before production begins. Close supplier relations cannot be established and maintained if companies view their suppliers as adversaries whenever contracts are negotiated. Rather, they should consider suppliers to be partners in a venture wherein both parties have an interest in maintaining a long-term, profitable relationship.

FLEXIBLE WORKFORCE

Workers in flexible workforces can be trained to perform more than one job. When the skill levels required to perform most tasks are low—at a McDonald's restaurant, for instance—a high degree of flexibility in the workforce can be achieved with little training. In situations requiring higher skill levels, shifting workers to other jobs may require extensive, costly training. Flexibility can be very beneficial: Workers can be shifted among workstations to help relieve bottlenecks as they arise without resorting to inventory buffers—an important aspect of the uniform flow of JIT systems. Also, they can step in and do the job for those on vacation or out sick. Although assigning workers to tasks they do not usually perform may reduce efficiency, some rotation relieves boredom and refreshes workers.

LINE FLOWS

Line flows can reduce the frequency of setups. If volumes of specific products are large enough, groups of machines and workers can be organized into a product layout (see Chapter 7, "Location and Layout") to eliminate setups entirely. If volume is insufficient to keep a line of similar products busy, *group technology* can be used to design small production lines that manufacture, in volume, families of components with common attributes. Changeovers from a component in one product family to the next component in the same family are minimal.

   Another tactic used to reduce or eliminate setups is the one-worker, multiple-machines (OWMM) approach, which essentially is a one-person line. One worker operates several machines, with each machine advancing the process a step at a time. Because the same product is made repeatedly, setups are eliminated. For example, in a McDonald's restaurant, the person preparing fish sandwiches uses the OWMM approach. When the signal is given to produce more fish sandwiches, the employee puts the fish patties into the fish fryer and sets the timer. Then while the fish are frying, he puts the buns into the steamer. When the buns are finished, he puts them on a tray and dresses them with condiments. When the fish patties are ready, he inserts them into the buns. He then places the completed sandwiches on the shelf for the final assembler to package for the customer. The cycle is repeated throughout the day.

AUTOMATED PRODUCTION

Automation plays a big role in JIT systems and is a key to low-cost operations. Money freed up because of JIT inventory reductions or other efficiencies can be invested in automation to reduce costs. The benefits, of course, are greater profits, greater market share (because prices can be cut), or both. Automation should be planned carefully, however. Many managers believe that if some automation is good, more is better. That is not always the case. When GM initiated Buick City, for example, it installed 250 robots, some with vision systems for mounting windshields. Unfortunately, the robots skipped black cars because they could not "see" them. New software eventually solved the problem; however, GM management found that humans could do some jobs better than robots and replaced 30 robots with humans.

PREVENTIVE MAINTENANCE

Because JIT emphasizes finely tuned flows of materials and little buffer inventory between workstations, unplanned machine downtime can be disruptive. Preventive maintenance can reduce the frequency and duration of machine downtime. After performing routine maintenance activities, the technician can test other parts that might need to be replaced. Replacement during regularly scheduled maintenance periods is easier and quicker than dealing with machine failures during production. Maintenance is done on a schedule that balances the cost of the preventive maintenance program against the risks and costs of machine failure.

Another tactic is to make workers responsible for routinely maintaining their own equipment and develop employee pride in keeping their machines in top condition. This tactic, however, typically is limited to general housekeeping chores, minor lubrication, and adjustments. Maintenance of high-tech machines needs trained specialists. Doing even simple maintenance tasks goes a long way toward improving machine performance, though.

CONTINUOUS IMPROVEMENT

How can lean systems facilitate continuous improvement?

By spotlighting areas that need improvement, lean systems lead to continuous improvement in quality and productivity. For example, Figure 13.2 characterizes the philosophy behind continuous improvement with lean systems. In manufacturing, the water surface represents product and component inventory levels. In services, the water surface represents service system capacity, such as staff levels. The rocks represent problems encountered in manufacturing or service delivery. When the water surface is high enough, the boat passes over the rocks because the high level of inventory or capacity covers up problems. As inventory shrinks, rocks are exposed. Ultimately, the boat will hit a rock if the water surface falls far enough. Through lean systems, workers, supervisors, engineers, and analysts apply methods for continuous improvement to demolish the exposed rock (see Chapter 2, "Process Management" and Chapter 5, "Quality").

FIGURE 13.2

Continuous Improvement with Lean Systems

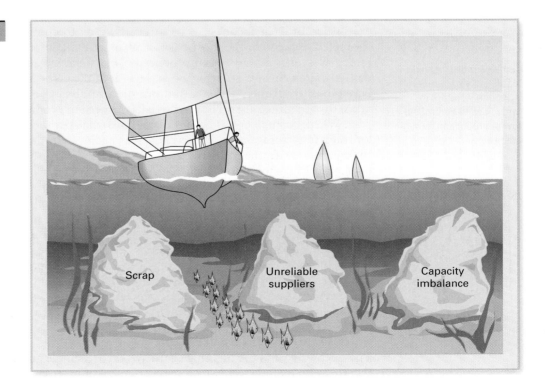

Scrap

Unreliable suppliers

Capacity imbalance

The coordination required for the pull system of material flows in lean systems identifies problems in time for corrective action to be taken.

In manufacturing, eliminating the problem of too much scrap might require improving work methods, employee quality training, and supplier quality. The desire to eliminate capacity imbalances might focus attention on the master production schedule and workforce flexibility. Reducing unreliable deliveries calls for cooperating better with suppliers or replacing suppliers. Maintaining low inventories, periodically stressing the system to identify problems, and focusing on the elements of the lean system lie at the heart of continuous improvement. For example, the Kawasaki plant in Nebraska periodically cuts safety stocks almost to zero. Problems are exposed, recorded, and later assigned as improvement projects. After the improvements have been made, inventories are permanently cut to the new level. The Japanese have used this trial-and-error process to develop more efficient manufacturing operations.

Service operations that are integral to both manufacturing and service organizations, including scheduling, billing, order taking, accounting, and financial tasks, also can be improved with lean systems. As in manufacturing, continuous improvement means that employees and managers continue to seek ways to improve operations. However, the mechanics of highlighting the areas needing improvement are different. In service operations, a common approach used by managers to place stress on the system is to reduce the number of employees doing a particular operation or series of operations until the process begins to slow or come to a halt. The problems can be identified, and ways for overcoming them can be explored. We return to the use of lean systems in services later.

THE KANBAN SYSTEM

How is the flow of materials in a factory controlled in a JIT system?

kanban A word meaning "card" or "visible record" in Japanese; refers to cards used to control the flow of production through a factory.

One of the most publicized aspects of lean systems, and the Toyota Production System in particular, is the kanban system developed by Toyota. **Kanban,** meaning "card" or "visible record" in Japanese, refers to cards used to control the flow of production through a factory. In the most basic kanban system, a card is attached to each container of items that have been produced. The container holds a given percent of the daily requirements for an item. When the user of the parts empties a container, the card is removed from the container and put on a receiving post. The empty container is taken to the storage area. The card signals the need to produce another container of the part. When a container has been refilled, the card is put on the container, which is then returned to a storage area. The cycle begins again when the user of the parts retrieves the container with the card attached.

Figure 13.3 shows how a single-card kanban system works when a fabrication cell feeds two assembly lines. As an assembly line needs more parts, the kanban card for those parts is taken to the receiving post and a full container of parts is removed from the storage area. The receiving post accumulates cards for both assembly lines and sequences the production of replenishment parts. In this example, the fabrication cell will produce product 2 before it produces product 1. The cell consists of three different operations, but operation 2 has two workstations. Once production has been initiated in the cell, the product begins on operation 1, but could be routed to either of the workstations performing operation 2, depending on the workload at the time. Finally, the product is processed on operation 3 before being taken to the storage area.

GENERAL OPERATING RULES

The operating rules for the single-card system are simple and are designed to facilitate the flow of materials while maintaining control of inventory levels.

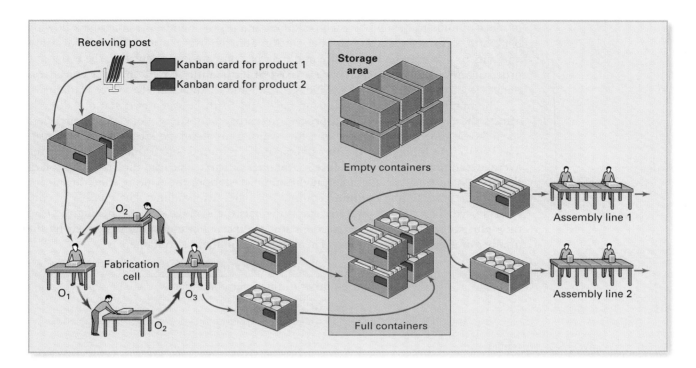

FIGURE 13.3

Single-Card Kanban System

1. Each container must have a card.

2. The assembly line always withdraws materials from the fabrication cell. The fabrication cell never pushes parts to the assembly line because, sooner or later, parts will be supplied that are not yet needed for production.

3. Containers of parts must never be removed from a storage area without a kanban first being posted on the receiving post.

4. The containers should always contain the same number of good parts. The use of nonstandard containers or irregularly filled containers disrupts the production flow of the assembly line.

5. Only nondefective parts should be passed along to the assembly line to make the best use of materials and workers' time.

6. Total production should not exceed the total amount authorized on the kanbans in the system.

Toyota uses a two-card system, based on a withdrawal card and a production-order card, to control withdrawal quantities more closely. The withdrawal card specifies the item and the quantity the user of the item should withdraw from the producer of the item, as well as the stocking locations for both the user and the producer. The production-order card specifies the item and the production quantity to be produced, the materials required and where to find them, and where to store the finished item. Materials cannot be withdrawn without a withdrawal card, and production cannot begin without a production-order card. The cards are attached to containers when production commences.

DETERMINING THE NUMBER OF CONTAINERS

The number of authorized containers in the Toyota Production System determines the amount of authorized inventory. Management must make two determinations: (1) the number of units to be held by each container and (2) the number of containers flowing back and forth between the supplier station and the user station. The first decision amounts to determining the lot size and may be compared to calculating the economic order quantity (EOQ) or specifying a fixed order quantity based on other considerations (see Chapter 10, "Inventory Management" and Chapter 12, "Resource Planning").

The number of containers flowing back and forth between two stations directly affects the quantities of work-in-process inventory and safety stock. The containers spend some time in production, in a line waiting, in a storage location, or in transit. The key to determining the number of containers required is to estimate accurately the average lead time needed to produce a container of parts. The lead time is a function of the processing time per container at the supplier station, the waiting time during the production process, and the time required for materials handling. The number of containers needed to support the user station equals the average demand during the lead time plus some safety stock to account for unexpected circumstances, divided by the number of units in one container. Therefore, the number of containers is

$$k = \frac{\text{Average demand during lead time } plus \text{ safety stock}}{\text{Number of units per container}}$$

$$= \frac{d(\overline{w} + \overline{p})(1 + \alpha)}{c}$$

where

k = number of containers for a part

d = expected daily demand for the part, in units

$\overline{w}$ = average waiting time during the production process plus materials handling time per container, in fractions of a day

$\overline{p}$ = average processing time per container, in fractions of a day

c = quantity in a standard container of the part

α = a policy variable that reflects the efficiency of the workstations producing and using the part (Toyota uses a value of no more than 10 percent)

**TUTOR
13.1**

The number of containers must, of course, be an integer. Rounding k up provides more inventory than desired, whereas rounding k down provides less.

The kanban system allows management to fine-tune the flow of materials in the system in a straightforward way. For example, removing cards from the system reduces the number of authorized containers of the part, thus reducing the inventory of the part.

The container quantity, c, and the efficiency factor, α, are variables that management can use to control inventory. Adjusting c changes the lot sizes, and adjusting α changes the amount of safety stock. The kanban system actually is a special form of the base-stock system (see Chapter 10, "Inventory Management"). In this case, the stocking level is $d(\overline{w} + \overline{p})(1 + \alpha)$, and the order quantity is fixed at c units. Each time a container of parts is removed from the base stock, authorization is given to replace it. See the Solved Problem for a detailed example of how to apply the equation for the number of containers in a kanban system.

OTHER KANBAN SIGNALS

Cards are not the only way to signal the need for more production of a part. Other less formal methods are possible, including container and containerless systems.

CONTAINER SYSTEM. Sometimes the container itself can be used as a signal device: An empty container signals the need to fill it. Unisys took this approach for low-value items. The amount of inventory of the part is adjusted by adding or removing containers. This system works well when the container is specially designed for a part and no other parts could accidentally be put in it. Such is the case when the container is actually a pallet or fixture used to position the part during precision processing.

CONTAINERLESS SYSTEM. Systems requiring no containers have been devised. In assembly-line operations, operators having their own workbench areas put completed units on painted squares, one unit per square. Each painted square represents a container, and the number of painted squares on each operator's bench is calculated to balance the line flow. When the subsequent user removes a unit from one of the producer's squares, the empty square signals the need to produce another unit.

McDonald's uses a containerless system. A command from the manager or the final assembler starts production, or the number of hamburgers in the ramp itself signals the need. Either way, the customer dictates production.

JIT II

The JIT II concept was conceived and implemented by the Bose Corporation, producer of high-quality professional sound systems and speaker systems. In a JIT II system, the supplier is brought into the plant to be an active member of the purchasing office of the customer. The *in-plant representative* is on site full-time at the supplier's expense and is empowered to plan and schedule the replenishment of materials from the supplier. This is an example of vendor-managed inventories (see Chapter 8, "Supply-Chain Management"). Typically, the representative's duties include

- ❐ issuing purchase orders to his or her own firm on behalf of Bose
- ❐ working on design ideas to help save costs and improve manufacturing processes
- ❐ managing production schedules for suppliers, materials contractors, and other subcontractors

The in-plant representative replaces the buyer, the salesperson, and sometimes the materials planner in a typical JIT arrangement. Thus, JIT II fosters extremely close interaction with suppliers. Bose started the system in 1987, and by 1993, there were 12 in-plant representatives billing about 25 percent of the total purchasing budget. Although more representatives will be added, the qualifications for a supplier to be included in the program are stringent.

In general, JIT II offers the following benefits to the customer:

- ❐ Liberated from administrative tasks, the purchasing staff is able to work on improving efficiencies in other areas of procurement.
- ❐ Communication and purchase order placement are improved dramatically.
- ❐ The cost of materials is reduced immediately, and the savings are ongoing.
- ❐ Preferred suppliers are brought into the product design process earlier.
- ❐ A natural foundation is provided for electronic data interchange (EDI), effective paperwork, and administrative savings.

In general, JIT II offers the following benefits to the supplier:

- ❐ It eliminates sales effort.
- ❐ Communication and purchase order placement are improved dramatically.
- ❐ The volume of business rises at the start of the program and continues to grow as new products are introduced.

❐ An evergreen contract is provided, with no end date and no rebidding.

❐ The supplier can communicate with and sell directly to engineering.

❐ Invoicing and payment administration are efficient.

Several large corporations have implemented JIT II in their supply chains. IBM and Intel have more than 50 on-site JIT II suppliers. AT&T, Honeywell, Roadway Express, Ingersoll-Rand, and Westinghouse also use the system. JIT II is an advance over other just-in-time systems because it provides the organizational structure needed to improve supplier coordination by integrating the logistics, production, and purchasing processes.

LEAN SYSTEMS IN SERVICES

How can lean systems be used in a service environment?

Lean systems and the just-in-time philosophy also can be applied to the production of services. We have already discussed some of the elements of the JIT system used in a McDonald's restaurant. In general, service environments may benefit from lean systems such as JIT if their operations are repetitive, have reasonably high volumes, and deal with tangible items such as sandwiches, mail, checks, or bills. In other words, the services must involve "manufacturing-like" operations. Other services involving a high degree of customization, such as haircutting, can also make use of JIT systems but to a lesser degree—basically utilizing elements of the just-in-time philosophy in their operations.

 The focus of JIT systems is on improving the process; therefore, some of the JIT concepts useful for manufacturers are also useful for service providers. These concepts include the following:

❐ *Consistently High Quality.*   Benchmarking, service design, and quality function deployment can be used successfully in service operations. Service employees can be taught the value of providing defect-free services.

❐ *Uniform Facility Loads.*   Reservation systems and differential pricing are two ways in which service providers can level the loads on their facilities.

❐ *Standardized Work Methods.*   In highly repetitive service operations, great efficiencies can be gained by analyzing work methods and standardizing improvements for all employees to use. For example, UPS consistently monitors work methods and revises them as necessary to improve service.

❐ *Close Supplier Ties.*   Volume services such as fast-food restaurants and mass merchandisers such as Wal-Mart and Kmart require close supplier contacts to ensure frequent, short lead time and high-quality shipments of supplies.

❐ *Flexible Workforce.*   The more customized the service, the greater is the need for a multiskilled workforce. For example, stereo component repair shops require broadly trained personnel who can identify a wide variety of problems and then repair the defective unit. The employees at a sectional center post office have more narrowly defined jobs because of the repetitive nature of the tasks they must perform, and thus they do not have to acquire many alternative skills.

❐ *Automation.*   Automation can play a big role in providing just-in-time services. For example, banks offer ATMs that provide various bank services on demand 24 hours a day.

❐ *Preventive Maintenance.*   Services that are highly dependent on machinery can make good use of routine preventive maintenance. For example, entertainment services such as Walt Disney World must have dependable people-moving apparatus to accommodate large volumes of customers.

❏ *Pull Method of Material Flows.*   Service operations where tangible items are processed, such as fast-food restaurants, can utilize the pull method.

❏ *Line Flows.*   Managers of service operations can organize their employees and equipment to provide uniform flows through the system and eliminate wasted employee time. Banks use this strategy in their check-processing operations, as does UPS in its parcel-sorting process.

STRATEGIC IMPLICATIONS OF LEAN SYSTEMS

When corporate strategy centers on dramatic improvements in inventory turnover and labor productivity, a just-in-time philosophy can be the solution. For example, lean systems such as just-in-time form an integral part of corporate strategies emphasizing time-based competition because they focus on cutting cycle times, improving inventory turnover, and increasing labor productivity. In this section, we consider competitive priorities and product or service flows, as well as the operational benefits of lean systems as represented by JIT.

COMPETITIVE PRIORITIES

Low cost and consistent quality are the priorities emphasized most often in JIT systems. Superior features and volume flexibility are emphasized less often. The ability to provide product or service variety depends on the degree of flexibility designed into the production system. Such is the case with firms using an assemble-to-order strategy. For example, mixed-model automobile assembly lines allow variety in output in terms of color, options, and even body style. JIT systems such as the Toyota Production System work well in this environment. Production to customized, individual orders, however, usually is not attempted with a JIT system. The erratic demand and last-minute rush jobs of customized orders in make-to-order or customized service environments do not link well with a system designed to produce at a constant daily rate utilizing low inventory or capacity buffers.

FLOWS

A JIT system involves line flows to achieve high-volume, low-cost production of products or services. Workers and machines are organized around product or service flows and arranged to conform to the sequence of work operations. With line flows, a unit of work finished at one station goes almost immediately to the next station, thereby reducing lead time and inventory. Process repetition makes opportunities for methods improvement more visible. Line flows support the make-to-stock, standardized services, and assemble-to-order strategies (see Chapter 1, "Competing with Operations").

OPERATIONAL BENEFITS

Just-in-time systems have many operational benefits. They

❏ reduce space requirements

❏ reduce inventory investment in purchased parts, raw materials, work in process, and finished goods

❏ reduce lead times

❏ increase the productivity of direct-labor employees, indirect-support employees, and clerical staff

❏ increase equipment utilization

❏ reduce paperwork and require only simple planning systems

❑ set valid priorities for scheduling

❑ encourage participation by the workforce

❑ increase product or service quality

One goal is to drive setup times so low that production of one end unit or part becomes economical. Although this goal is rarely achieved, the focus still is on small-lot production. In addition, constant attention is given to removing nonvalue-added activities in processes. The result is less need for storage space, inventory investment, or capacity. Smaller lot sizes and smoothed flows of materials help reduce lead times, increase employee productivity, and improve equipment utilization.

A primary operational benefit is the simplicity of the system. For example, in manufacturing, product mix or volume changes planned by the MPS can be accomplished by adjusting the number of kanbans in the system. The priority of each production order is reflected in the sequence of the kanbans on the post. Production orders for parts that are running low are placed before those for parts that have more supply.

Just-in-time systems also involve a considerable amount of employee participation through small-group interaction sessions, which have resulted in improvements in many aspects of operations, not the least of which is product or service quality. Overall, the advantages of JIT systems have caused many managers to reevaluate their own systems and consider adapting operations to the JIT philosophy.

IMPLEMENTATION ISSUES

What can be done to make employees more receptive to the changes associated with just-in-time systems?

The benefits of lean systems seem to be outstanding, yet problems can arise even after a lean system has long been operational. In this section, we address some of the issues managers should be aware of when implementing a lean system such as JIT.

ORGANIZATIONAL CONSIDERATIONS

Implementing a JIT system requires management to consider issues of worker stress, cooperation and trust among workers and management, and reward systems and labor classifications.

HUMAN COSTS OF JIT SYSTEMS. Just-in-time systems can be coupled with statistical process control (SPC) to reduce variations in outputs. However, this combination requires a high degree of regimentation and sometimes causes stress in the workforce. In a JIT system, workers must meet specified cycle times, and, with SPC, they must follow prescribed problem-solving methods. Such systems might make workers feel pushed and stressed, causing productivity losses or quality reductions. In addition, workers might feel that they have lost some autonomy because of the close linkages in materials flows between stations with little or no safety stocks. Managers can mitigate some of these effects by allowing slack in the system through the judicious use of safety stock inventories or capacity slack and by emphasizing materials flows instead of worker pace. Managers also can promote the use of work teams and allow them to determine their task assignments or rotations within the team's domain of responsibility.

COOPERATION AND TRUST. In a JIT system workers and first-line supervisors must take on responsibilities formerly assigned to middle managers and support staff. Activities such as scheduling, expediting, and improving productivity become part of the duties of lower-level personnel. Consequently, organizational relationships must be reoriented to build close cooperation and mutual trust between the workforce and management.

Such cooperation and trust may be difficult to achieve, particularly in light of the typical adversarial positions taken by labor and management in the past.

REWARD SYSTEMS AND LABOR CLASSIFICATIONS. In some instances, the reward system must be revamped when a JIT system is implemented. At General Motors, for example, a plan to reduce stock at one plant ran into trouble because the production superintendent refused to cut back production of unneeded parts; his salary was based on his plant's production volume.

The realignment of reward systems is not the only hurdle. Labor contracts traditionally have reduced management's flexibility in reassigning workers as the need arises. A typical automobile plant in the United States has several unions and dozens of labor classifications. To gain more flexibility, management in some cases has obtained union concessions by granting other types of benefits. In other cases, management has relocated plants to take advantage of nonunion or foreign labor. In contrast, at Toyota management deals with only one company union, and there are only eight different labor classifications in a typical plant.

PROCESS CONSIDERATIONS

Firms using JIT systems typically have some dominant work flows. To take advantage of JIT practices, firms might have to change their existing layouts. Certain workstations might have to be moved closer together, and cells of machines devoted to particular families of components may have to be established. A survey of 68 firms using JIT systems indicated that the single most important factor in successful implementation is changing product flows and layout to a cellular design (Billesbach, 1991). However, rearranging a plant to conform to JIT practices can be costly. For example, whereas many plants now receive raw materials and purchased parts by rail, to facilitate smaller, more frequent JIT shipments, truck deliveries would be preferable. Loading docks might have to be reconstructed or expanded and certain operations relocated to accommodate the change in transportation mode and quantities of arriving materials.

INVENTORY AND SCHEDULING

Firms need to have stable master production schedules, short setups, and frequent, reliable supplies of materials and components to achieve the full potential of the JIT concept.

MPS STABILITY. Daily production schedules in high-volume, make-to-stock environments must be stable for extended periods. At Toyota, the master production schedule is stated in fractions of days over a three-month period and is revised only once a month. The first month of the schedule is frozen to avoid disruptive changes in the daily production schedule for each workstation; that is, the workstations execute the same work schedule each day of the month. At the beginning of each month, kanbans are reissued for the new daily production rate. Stable schedules are needed so that production lines can be balanced and new assignments found for employees who otherwise would be underutilized. Just-in-time systems used in high-volume, make-to-stock environments cannot respond quickly to scheduling changes because little slack inventory or capacity is available to absorb these changes.

SETUPS. If the inventory advantages of a JIT system are to be realized, small lot sizes must be used. However, because small lots require a large number of setups, companies must significantly reduce setup times. Some companies have not been able to achieve short setup times and, therefore, have to use large-lot production, negating some of the advantages of JIT practices. Also, JIT systems are vulnerable to lengthy changeovers to new products because the low levels of finished goods inventory will be insufficient to

MANAGERIAL **PRACTICE**

Implementing Lean Manufacturing Principles at Cessna

Cessna Aircraft (www.cessna.com) is a leading manufacturer of business jets, utility planes, and single-engine piston-powered personal aircraft. Almost half of all the general aviation planes shipped in 1999 were Cessnas. The planes range in price from $150,000 for a single-engine piston-powered aircraft to over $17 million for a business jet. However, 10 years ago, the company decided to abandon the production of single-engine piston-powered planes because of the liability the company incurred for just about any accident involving a Cessna, regardless of the circumstances. After legislation in 1994 limited the liability of aircraft manufacturers, Cessna decided to get back into the manufacture of small planes by building a new plant in Independence, Kansas. It was an opportunity to incorporate a new lean manufacturing system to a product line that had not changed much over the years, with the exception of the avionics in the cockpit and a new, efficient engine, which was outsourced. To do so, however, Cessna had to learn how to go from a craftwork mentality, which is what they had when they last produced small aircraft, to a modern manufacturing mentality that involves a whole new way of doing things.

Cessna adopted three lean manufacturing practices in its new plant. First, management committed to the team concept (see Chapter 2, "Process Management" and Chapter 5, "Quality"). Teamwork fosters workforce flexibility because team members learn the duties of other team members and can shift across assembly lines as needed. However, because of a shortage of technically qualified employees, Cessna had to hire employees short on sheet metal skills but willing to work as a team and to assume responsibility. Productivity initially suffered, but retired assembly-line workers were recalled to serve as mentors to teach the new employees the skills and confidence they needed to do their jobs. It has taken four years to bring the teams to the point of learning about conflict resolution, problem solving, and flexibility.

Second, Cessna initiated vendor-managed inventories with several of its suppliers. For example, two Honeywell field engineers who also help with problems after installation maintain a 30-day avionics inventory worth $30 million on-site. In addition, a warehouse nearby was opened to house the inventories of several suppliers. The warehouse operations are being integrated with the plant schedule so that inventory will be delivered daily to the production line. Suppliers initially balked at the idea, but eventually saw its advantages.

Single-engine Cessna airplanes roll off the assembly line at Independence, Kansas. Three versions of single-engine planes are built at the southeast Kansas plant, using the concepts of lean manufacturing systems.

Finally, Cessna has incorporated manufacturing cells and group technology in their manufacturing process and has moved away from a batch process approach that supported a make-to-stock strategy. In the past, Cessna had a network of dealers who took what was sent to them, maintained large inventories to support the dealers, and had to give incentives to get rid of excess inventories. Today, Cessna assembles to order. This change in manufacturing strategy required a change in the manufacturing process as well as a change in the way Cessna does business with its dealers (see Chapter 1, "Competing with Operations" and Chapter 2, "Process Management").

Cessna has made the transition from craftwork to modern manufacturing, but not without hard work. Although inventory investment has shown improvement, it still takes twice as many hours to build a model 172 than it did in the 1980s. The theoretical capacity of the plant is 2,000 planes a year, but the annual target four years after the start of operations was only 975 planes a year. Much of the slow start-up was due to initiating a brand-new workforce. This experience at Cessna shows that switching to modern manufacturing methods is a long-term commitment.

Source: Siekman, Phillip. "Cessna Tackles Lean Manufacturing." *Fortune* (May 1, 2000), pp. I222 B–I222 Z.

cover demand while the system is down. If changeover times cannot be reduced, large finished goods inventories of the old product must be accumulated to compensate. In the automobile industry, every week that a plant is shut down for new-model changeover costs between $16 million and $20 million in pretax profits.

PURCHASING AND LOGISTICS. If frequent, small shipments of purchased items cannot be arranged with suppliers, large inventory savings for these items cannot be realized. In the United States, such arrangements may prove difficult because of the geographic dispersion of suppliers.

The shipments of raw materials and components must be reliable because of the low inventory levels in JIT systems. A plant can be shut down because of a lack of materials.

The Managerial Practice feature shows that implementing a lean system can take a long time.

LEAN SYSTEMS ACROSS THE ORGANIZATION

The philosophy of lean systems has application throughout the organization. A theme of this text is that organizations create products or services with processes, which cut across functional boundaries to create value for customers—who can be internal or external. Lean systems focus on efficient value creation, which applies to any process in the organization.

To take advantage of lean systems, companies must clearly define the value of their products or services as perceived by their customers (see Chapter 5, "Quality"). Every product or service category must be carefully scrutinized for excessive complexity or unnecessary features and options. The goal should be to deliver products or services that precisely match the customer's needs without waste. Then the company must identify the sequence of activities and the processes involved that are *essential* to the creation of the product or service by drawing flow charts and developing process charts (see Chapter 2, "Process Management"). Activities that are value-added (those tasks that transform the product or service in some measurable way) should be clearly differentiated from those that are nonvalue added (wasted effort that could be eliminated without any impact on the customer).

Once the activities are identified and the flows are charted, the barriers to the flow of value must be eliminated. For example, these barriers can be found in the factory in the form of large batches and excessive inventory; in the product development process in the form of excessive documentation, approvals, and meetings; or in the order-entry process in the form of incomplete product or service information or poorly designed Web pages. These barriers are examples of the rocks in Figure 13.2. Once these rocks are removed, the firm is free to allow its customers to "pull" value, which is the real market demand that becomes the trigger for all activities to follow. Lean systems certainly are important to all processes in the organization.

EQUATION SUMMARY

1. Number of containers:

$$k = \frac{\text{Average demand during lead time } + \text{ Safety stock}}{\text{Number of units per container}}$$

$$= \frac{d(\overline{w} + \overline{p})(1 + \alpha)}{c}$$

CHAPTER HIGHLIGHTS

❑ Lean systems focus on the efficient delivery of products or services. A just-in-time system, a popular lean system, is designed to produce or deliver just the right products or services in just the right quantities just in time to serve subsequent processes or customers.

❑ Some of the key elements of JIT systems are a pull method to manage material flow, consistently high quality, small lot sizes, uniform workstation loads, standardized components and work methods, close supplier ties, flexible workforce, line flow strategy, automated production, preventive maintenance, and continuous improvement.

❑ A single-card JIT system uses a kanban to control production flow. The authorized inventory of a part is a function of the number of authorized cards for that item. The number of cards depends on average demand during manufacturing lead time, the container size, and a policy variable to adjust for unexpected occurrences. Many other methods may be used to signal the need for material replenishment and production.

❑ The JIT II system provides an organizational structure for improved supplier coordination by integrating the logistics, production, and purchasing processes.

❑ Just-in-time concepts can be applied to the production of services. Service organizations that have repetitive operations, maintain reasonably high volume, and deal with some tangible item are most likely to benefit from JIT practices.

❑ For operations competing on the basis of low cost and consistent quality, JIT system advantages include reductions in inventory, space requirements, and paperwork and increases in productivity, employee participation, and quality. JIT systems require fundamental changes in the way *all* of the firm's business functions are performed. Increasing cooperation and trust between management and labor, basing rewards on team rather than individual performance, and replacing adversarial supplier relationships with partnerships are some of the basic cultural changes involved in JIT system implementation.

SOLVED PROBLEM

A company using a kanban system has an inefficient machine group. For example, the daily demand for part L105A is 3,000 units. The average waiting time for a container of parts is 0.8 day. The processing time for a container of L105A is 0.2 day, and a container holds 270 units. Currently, there are 20 containers for this item.

a. What is the value of the policy variable, α?

b. What is the total planned inventory (work in process and finished goods) for item L105A?

c. Suppose that the policy variable, α, were 0. How many containers would be needed now? What is the effect of the policy variable in this example?

SOLUTION

a. We use the equation for the number of containers and then solve for α:

$$k = \frac{d(\overline{w} + \overline{p})(1 + \alpha)}{c}$$

$$= \frac{3,000(0.8 + 0.2)(1 + \alpha)}{270} = 20$$

and

$$(1 + \alpha) = \frac{20(270)}{3,000(0.8 + 0.2)} = 1.8$$

$$\alpha = 1.8 - 1 = 0.8$$

b. With 20 containers in the system and each container holding 270 units, the total planned inventory is 20(270) = 5,400 units.

c. If $\alpha = 0$,

$$k = \frac{3{,}000(0.8 + 0.2)(1 + 0)}{270} = 11.11 \quad \text{or} \quad 12 \text{ containers}$$

The policy variable adjusts the number of containers. In this case, the difference is quite dramatic because $\overline{w} + \overline{p}$ is fairly large and the number of units per container is small relative to daily demand.

CD-ROM RESOURCES

The Student CD-ROM that accompanies this text contains the following resources, which allow you to further practice and apply the concepts presented in this chapter.

- ❏ **OM Explorer Tutor:** OM Explorer contains a tutor program that will help you learn how to apply the equation for determining the number of containers in a kanban system. See the Chapter 13 folder in OM Explorer. See also the exercise requiring the use of this tutor program.

- ❏ **OM Explorer Solver:** OM Explorer has a program that can be used to solve general problems involving the determination of the correct number of containers for a kanban system. See the Lean Systems folder in OM Explorer.

- ❏ **Equation Summary:** All the equations for this chapter can be found in one convenient location.

- ❏ **Discussion Questions:** Two questions will challenge your understanding of the philosophy of lean systems and the human considerations in implementing these systems.

- ❏ **Case: Copper Kettle Catering.** What would you recommend the owners of Copper Kettle Catering do to take advantage of JIT concepts in operating their business?

INTERACTIVE RESOURCES

The Interactive Web site associated with this text (www.prenhall.com/ritzman) contains many tools and activities specifically designed for this chapter. The following items are recommended to enhance your understanding of the material in this chapter.

- ❏ **Internet Activities:** Try out three different links to lean systems topics including lean production, logistic support for JIT, and component modularity.

- ❏ **Internet Tour:** Explore JIT practices at New United Motors Manufacturing, Inc.

PROBLEMS

1. The Harvey motorcycle company produces three models: the Tiger, a sure-footed dirt bike; the LX2000, a nimble cafe racer; and the Golden, a large interstate tourer. This month's master production schedule calls for the production of 54 Goldens, 42 LX2000s, and 30 Tigers per seven-hour shift.

   a. What average cycle time is required for the assembly line to achieve the production quota in seven hours?

   b. If mixed-model scheduling is used, how many of each model will be produced before the production cycle is repeated?

   c. Determine a satisfactory production sequence for the ultimate in small-lot production: one unit.

   d. The design of a new model, the Cheetah, includes features from the Tiger, LX2000, and Golden models. The resulting blended design has an indecisive character and is expected to attract some sales from the other models. Determine a mixed-model schedule resulting in 52 Goldens, 39 LX2000s, 26 Tigers, and 13 Cheetahs per seven-hour shift. Although the total number of motorcycles produced per day will increase only slightly, what problem might be anticipated in implementing this change from the production schedule indicated in part (b)?

2. 💿 **OM Explorer** A fabrication cell at Spradley's Sprockets uses the pull method to supply gears to an assembly line. George Jitson is in charge of the assembly line, which requires 500 gears per day. Containers typically wait 0.20 day in the fabrication cell. Each container holds 20 gears, and one container requires 1.8 days in machine time. Setup times are negligible. If the policy variable for unforeseen contingencies is set at 5 percent, how many containers should Jitson authorize for the gear replenishment system?

3. 💿 **OM Explorer** An assembly line requires two components: gadjits and widjits. Gadjits are produced by center 1 and widjits by center 2. Each unit of the end item, called a jit-together, requires 3 gadjits and 2 widjits, as shown in Figure 13.4. The daily production quota on the assembly line is 800 jit-togethers.

The container for gadjits holds 80 units. The policy variable for center 1 is set at 0.09. The average waiting time for a container of gadjits is 0.09 day, and 0.06 day is needed to produce a container. The container for widjits holds 50 units, and the policy variable for center 2 is 0.08. The aver-

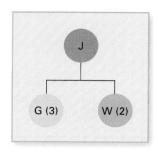

FIGURE 13.4

age waiting time per container of widgits is 0.14 day, and the time required to process a container is 0.20 day.

a. How many containers are needed for gadjits?

b. How many containers are needed for widjits?

4. 💿 **OM Explorer** The master schedule at Mazda calls for 1,200 Mazdas to be produced during each of 22 production days in January and 900 Mazdas to be produced during each of 20 production days in February. Mazda uses a kanban system to communicate with Gesundheit, a nearby supplier of tires. Mazda purchases four tires per vehicle from Gesundheit. The safety stock policy variable, α, is 0.15. The container (a delivery truck) size is 200 tires. The average waiting time plus materials handling time is 0.16 day per container. Assembly lines are rebalanced at the beginning of each month. The average processing time per container in January is 0.10 day. February processing time will average 0.125 day per container. How many containers should be authorized for January? How many for February?

SELECTED REFERENCES

Beckett, W. K., and K. Dang. "Synchronous Manufacturing, New Methods, New Mind Set." *Journal of Business Strategy,* vol. 12 (1992), pp. 53–56.

Billesbach, Thomas J. "A Study of the Implementation of Just-in-Time in the United States." *Production and Inventory Management Journal* (Third Quarter 1991), pp. 1–4.

Golhar, D. Y., and C. L. Stam. "The Just-in-Time Philosophy: A Literature Review." *International Journal of Production Research,* vol. 29 (1991), pp. 657–676.

Hall, Robert W. "The Americanization of the Toyota System." *Target,* vol. 15, no. 1 (First Quarter 1999), pp. 52–54.

Hall, R. W. *Driving the Productivity Machine.* Falls Church, VA: The American Production and Inventory Control Society, 1981.

Karmarkar, U. "Getting Control of Just-in-Time." *Harvard Business Review* (September–October 1989), pp. 123–131.

Klein, J. A. "The Human Costs of Manufacturing Reform." *Harvard Business Review* (March–April 1989), pp. 60–66.

Mascitelli, Ron. "Lean Thinking: It's About Efficient Value Creation." *Target,* vol. 16, no. 2 (Second Quarter 2000), pp. 22–26.

McClenahen, John S. "So Long, Salespeople, and Good-bye, Buyers—JIT II Is Here." *Industry Week* (February 18, 1991), pp. 48–65.

Millstein, Mitchell. "How to Make Your MRP System Flow." *APICS—The Performance Advantage* (July 2000), pp. 47–49.

Syberg, Keith. "Best Practices (BP) Program: Honda of America Manufacturing." *Target,* vol. 15, no. 2 (Second Quarter 1999), pp. 46–48.

Appendix: Normal Distribution

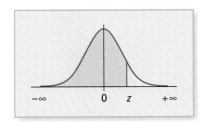

	.00	.01	.02	.03	.04	.05	.06	.07	.08	.09
.0	.5000	.5040	.5080	.5120	.5160	.5199	.5239	.5279	.5319	.5359
.1	.5398	.5438	.5478	.5517	.5557	.5596	.5636	.5675	.5714	.5753
.2	.5793	.5832	.5871	.5910	.5948	.5987	.6026	.6064	.6103	.6141
.3	.6179	.6217	.6255	.6293	.6331	.6368	.6406	.6443	.6480	.6517
.4	.6554	.6591	.6628	.6664	.6700	.6736	.6772	.6808	.6844	.6879
.5	.6915	.6950	.6985	.7019	.7054	.7088	.7123	.7157	.7190	.7224
.6	.7257	.7291	.7324	.7357	.7389	.7422	.7454	.7486	.7517	.7549
.7	.7580	.7611	.7642	.7673	.7704	.7734	.7764	.7794	.7823	.7852
.8	.7881	.7910	.7939	.7967	.7995	.8023	.8051	.8078	.8106	.8133
.9	.8159	.8186	.8212	.8238	.8264	.8289	.8315	.8340	.8365	.8389
1.0	.8413	.8438	.8461	.8485	.8508	.8531	.8554	.8577	.8599	.8621
1.1	.8643	.8665	.8686	.8708	.8729	.8749	.8770	.8790	.8810	.8830
1.2	.8849	.8869	.8888	.8907	.8925	.8944	.8962	.8980	.8997	.9015
1.3	.9032	.9049	.9066	.9082	.9099	.9115	.9131	.9147	.9162	.9177
1.4	.9192	.9207	.9222	.9236	.9251	.9265	.9279	.9292	.9306	.9319
1.5	.9332	.9345	.9357	.9370	.9382	.9394	.9406	.9418	.9429	.9441
1.6	.9452	.9463	.9474	.9484	.9495	.9505	.9515	.9525	.9535	.9545
1.7	.9554	.9564	.9573	.9582	.9591	.9599	.9608	.9616	.9625	.9633
1.8	.9641	.9649	.9656	.9664	.9671	.9678	.9686	.9693	.9699	.9706
1.9	.9713	.9719	.9726	.9732	.9738	.9744	.9750	.9756	.9761	.9767
2.0	.9772	.9778	.9783	.9788	.9793	.9798	.9803	.9808	.9812	.9817
2.1	.9821	.9826	.9830	.9834	.9838	.9842	.9846	.9850	.9854	.9857
2.2	.9861	.9864	.9868	.9871	.9875	.9878	.9881	.9884	.9887	.9890
2.3	.9893	.9896	.9898	.9901	.9904	.9906	.9909	.9911	.9913	.9916
2.4	.9918	.9920	.9922	.9925	.9927	.9929	.9931	.9932	.9934	.9936
2.5	.9938	.9940	.9941	.9943	.9945	.9946	.9948	.9949	.9951	.9952
2.6	.9953	.9955	.9956	.9957	.9959	.9960	.9961	.9962	.9963	.9964
2.7	.9965	.9966	.9967	.9968	.9969	.9970	.9971	.9972	.9973	.9974
2.8	.9974	.9975	.9976	.9977	.9977	.9978	.9979	.9979	.9980	.9981
2.9	.9981	.9982	.9982	.9983	.9984	.9984	.9985	.9985	.9986	.9986
3.0	.9987	.9987	.9987	.9988	.9988	.9989	.9989	.9989	.9990	.9990
3.1	.9990	.9991	.9991	.9991	.9992	.9992	.9992	.9992	.9993	.9993
3.2	.9993	.9993	.9994	.9994	.9994	.9994	.9994	.9995	.9995	.9995
3.3	.9995	.9995	.9995	.9996	.9996	.9996	.9996	.9996	.9996	.9997
3.4	.9997	.9997	.9997	.9997	.9997	.9997	.9997	.9997	.9997	.9998

Name Index

Note: Any page number preceded by a letter means that the topic is located on the CD-ROM.

Subject Index

Note: Any page number preceded by a letter means that the topic is located on the CD-ROM.

Photo Credits

Mechanisms of MICROBIAL DISEASE

Second Edition

Mechanisms of

MICROBIAL DISEASE

Second Edition

Moselio Schaechter, Ph.D.
Distinguished Professor and Chairman
Department of Molecular Biology and Microbiology
Tufts University School of Medicine
Boston Massachusetts

Gerald Medoff, M.D.
Professor
Departments of Medicine and Microbiology
and Immunology
Director, Infectious Diseases Division
Washington University School of Medicine
St. Louis, Missouri

Barry I. Eisenstein, M.D.
Vice President
Lilly Research Laboratories
Eli Lilly and Company
Indianapolis, Indiana
Formerly Professor and Chairman
Department of Microbiology and Immunology
Professor of Internal Medicine
University of Michigan Medical School
Ann Arbor, Michigan

Williams & Wilkins

BALTIMORE • PHILADELPHIA • HONG KONG
LONDON • MUNICH • SYDNEY • TOKYO

A WAVERLY COMPANY

Editor: Timothy S. Satterfield
Managing Editor: Linda Napora
Copy Editor: Shelley Potler
Designer: Wilma E. Rosenberger
Illustration Planner: Wayne Hubbel
Production Coordinator: Charles E. Zeller

Copyright © 1993
Williams & Wilkins
428 East Preston Street
Balitmore, Maryland 21202, USA

Accurate indications, adverse reactions, and dosage schedules for drugs are provided in this book, but it is possible that they may change. The reader is urged to review the package information data of the manufacturers of the medications mentioned.

Printed in the United States of Ameria

First Edition 1989

Library of Congress Cataloging in Publication Data

Mechanisms of microbial disease / [edited by] Moselio Schaechter,
  Gerald Medoff, Barry I. Eisenstein. — 2nd ed.
       p.   cm.
     Includes index.
     ISBN 0-683-07606-X
     1. Bacterial diseases—Pathogenesis. 2. Communicable disesases-
  -Pathogenesis. I. Schaechter, Moselio. II. Medoff, Gerald, 1936-
     III. Eisenstein, Barry I.
     [DNLM: 1. Bacteria—pathogenicity. 2. Communicable Diseases-
  -microbiology. 3. Communicable Diseases—physiopathology.
     4. Fungi—pathogenicity. 5. Viruses—pathogenicity. QW 700 M4856]
  QR201.B34M43   1993
  616.9—ac20
  DNLM/DLC
  for Library of Congress   91-47523
                                                                  CIP

                                                              94 95 96
                                                    2 3 4 5 6 7 8 9 10

*To Judith, Joyce, and
the memory of Barbara*

Preface

The first edition of *Mechanisms of Microbial Disease* was well received by faculty members and especially by students. Particularly well liked has been our *leitmotif*, the notion of presenting the material in a pathobiological framework in the context of clinical cases. This format seems to lend itself to an active form of studying and to be easily adaptable to problem-based learning.

The Second Edition retains this basic philosophy. We have heeded comments about the need for greater coverage of the field. Thus, we have interspersed more immunological, molecular, and genetic material throughout the book, and there is a new chapter on microbial genetics. We have added chapters on viruses, including the introductory aspects of virology, and there is now a chapter on AIDS.

In Section II, Infectious Agents, most of the chapters on bacterial and viral agents contain a new feature that we call "Paradigm." Here we discuss certain general principles that are best illustrated with the agents described in that chapter, but which can be applied to others as well. In this fashion, we avoid overloading the introductory chapters of the book and introduce current material in the context of specific pathogens.

Medical sciences, with one major exception, deal with a single species, *Homo sapiens*. The exception is the science of infectious diseases, which involves hundreds of bacteria, viruses, fungi, and protozoa. This poses a special problem to students and teachers of this subject alike.

Obviously, the impact of microbial disease cannot be overstated. We live with the constant menace of these diseases, most mild or treatable, but invariably made more threatening when our defense mechanisms are weakened. We must cope with organisms that have developed resistance to antimicrobial drugs. In addition, we become aware of new or newly recognized diseases: AIDS, Legionnaires' disease, Lyme disease, and others. Many diseases are on the wane, some, like smallpox, are less prevalent due to human intervention, whereas others occur less frequently for unknown reasons. Altogether, there is a staggering number of facts about microbial agents and the diseases they cause. What are we, beginners or veteran students, to do?

Traditionally, the teaching of this subject has been based too much on the memorization of facts (the "bug parade"), frequently with little distinction of what is important. We propose that there is a better approach, based on the use of two principles:

- Material about microbial agents and how the host responds to them is presented solely for the purpose of understanding the mechanism of infectious diseases. Aspects of microorganisms that are not important in the causation of disease are left for other books.
- Focusing on the common features of all host-parasite relationships facilitates learning and recall. Necessary facts can then be organized on a predictable conceptual framework.

Our presentation is derived directly from relevant biological and medical phenomena. For this reason, we have made extensive use of clinical case presentations. This approach helps introduce both biological and clinical realism and, more important, suggests which questions need to be discussed. The cases presented have, for the most part, a favorable clinical outcome; this is generally realistic because more people survive episodes of infection than die of them.

This textbook is intended for use in courses on medical microbiology and infectious diseases for medical students and other health professionals, graduate students, and advanced undergraduates. Students using this book should have some familiarity with basic aspects of molecular and cellular biology; we have tried to keep the medical and technical jargon to a minimum. As taught in medical schools, this topic is often divided between two courses: one on microbiology and another on infectious diseases (frequently embedded within a pathophysiology course). Our intent is to bridge the contents of these two courses by first discussing the major infectious agents as biological models (Sections I and II), and then presenting ways in which the major systems of the body are affected by infectious diseases (Section III). Because the purpose of this book is to develop a conceptual framework, it highlights certain infectious agents and diseases and does not attempt to present the material in exhaustive fashion. It is not intended as a reference manual; the depth of coverage is left purposefully uneven.

Following the chapters on each group of infectious agents (bacteria, viruses, fungi, and animal parasites), there are review charts. Filling in the blank spaces in these review charts outlines the scope of the material and this organized information will be helpful in preparing for examinations. Only the most common agents of human infectious diseases are listed, with reference to relevant chapters in this book. This Second Edition also includes sections with brief answers to the "Self-assessment Questions" and completed versions of the "Review Charts."

If our goals in preparing this work are achieved, we will have conveyed mechanisms of microbial disease as well as the concepts that can be called upon with future developments in this exciting and rapidly changing field.

Moselio Schaechter
Gerald Medoff
Barry I. Eisenstein

Acknowledgments

We sincerely thank the following persons for their generous help with the work involved in this edition: Elliott Androphy, Gail Cassell, Jenifer Coburn, John Coffin, Dean Dawson, Vic DiRita, David Friedman, George Healy, Ralph Isberg, Albert Kapikian, Carol Kumamoto, Michael Malamy, Fred Neidhardt, Thalia Nicas, Susannah Rankin, Eric Rubin, Anne Skvorak, Linc Sonenshein, Gary J. Weil, Andrew Wright, and David Wyler. Special thanks go to Cary Engleberg, Kay Holmes, Rod Nairn, and Richard Olds. Their extensive revisions in the areas of their expertise were carried out with caring insight, and singular understanding.

We are grateful to Susan Nelson-DiCunzolo for her conscientious and imaginative support in various phases of manuscript preparation. Not only did she take care of innumerable problems, but in many cases, anticipated and corrected them before they could escalate. We thank our copy editor, Shelley Potler, and our production coordinator, Charles Zeller, for their careful and constructive work. As with the previous edition, we thank Tim Satterfield and Linda Napora for their thoughtful editorial and personal support. We are indebted to them and others at Williams & Wilkins for their understanding and trust.

Most of the illustrations are the work of a gifted artist, Christo Popoff, whose efforts are gratefully acknowledged. We also thank René Gallegos for help in computer graphics.

Contributors

George M. Baer, M.D.
Director, Laboratories Baer
Colonia Condesa, Mexico
Formerly with Department of Health and Human Services
Centers for Disease Control
Atlanta, Georgia

Michael Barza, M.D.
Professor
Department of Medicine
Tufts University School of Medicine
Associate Chief, Division of Geographic Medicine and Infectious Disease
New England Medical Center
Boston, Massachusetts

John M. Coffin, Ph.D.
Professor
Department of Molecular Biology and Microbiology
Tufts University School of Medicine
Boston, Massachusetts

David T. Durack, D.Phil. (Oxon), M.B.
Chief, Division of Infectious Diseases
Duke University Medical Center
Durham, North Carolina

Barry I. Eisenstein, M.D.
Vice President
Lilly Research Laboratories
Eli Lilly and Company
Indianapolis, Indiana
Formerly Professor and Chairman
Department of Microbiology and Immunology
Professor of Internal Medicine
University of Michigan Medical School
Ann Arbor, Michigan

N. Cary Engleberg, M.D.
Associate Professor
Departments of Internal Medicine and Microbiology and Immunology
University of Michigan Medical School
Ann Arbor, Michigan

Bernard N. Fields, M.D.
Adele Lehman Professor and Chairman
Department of Microbiology and Molecular Genetics
Harvard Medical School
Boston, Massachusetts

Janet R. Gilsdorf, M.D.
Director, Pediatric Infectious Diseases
Associate Professor of Pediatrics
University of Michigan Medical Center
Ann Arbor, Michigan

Sherwood L. Gorbach, M.D.
Professor of Community Health and Medicine
Department of Community Health
Nutrition Infection Unit
Tufts University School of Medicine
Boston, Massachusetts

Penelope J. Hitchcock, D.V.M., M.S.
Acting Branch Chief
Sexually Transmitted Diseases Branch
National Institutes of Health
National Institute of Allergy and Infectious Disease
Bethesda, Maryland

William R. Jacobs, Jr., M.D.
Assistant Professor
Department of Microbiology and Immunology
Albert Einstein College of Medicine
Bronx, New York

Adolf W. Karchmer, M.D.
Chief, Division of Infectious Diseases
New England Deaconess Hospital
Boston, Massachusetts

Gary Ketner, M.D.
Associate Professor
Department of Immunology and Infectious Diseases
The Johns Hopkins University
School of Public Health
Baltimore, Maryland

Gerald T. Keusch, M.D.
Professor
Department of Medicine
Tufts University School of Medicine
Chief, Division of Geographic Medicine and Infectious Diseases
New England Medical Center
Boston, Massachusetts

George S. Kobayashi, Ph.D.
Professor
Department of Microbiology and Immunology and
Department of Internal Medicine
Washington University School of Medicine
St. Louis, Missouri

Donald J. Krogstad, M.D.
Henderson Professor and Chair
Department of Tropical Medicine
Tulane University
School of Public Health and Tropical Medicine
New Orleans, Louisiana

Zell A. McGee, M.D.

Professor of Medicine and Pathology
Head, Center for Infectious Diseases, Diagnostic Microbiology, and Immunology
University of Utah School of Medicine
Salt Lake City, Utah

Gerald Medoff, M.D.

Professor
Departments of Medicine and Microbiology and Immunology
Director, Infectious Diseases Division
Washington University School of Medicine
St. Louis, Missouri

Cody Meissner, M.D.

Chief, Division of Infectious Disease
New England Medicine Center
Associate Professor
Department of Pediatrics
Tufts University School of Medicine
Boston, Massachusetts

Richard W. Moyer, Ph.D.

Professor and Chairman
Department of Immunology and Medical Microbiology
College of Medicine, University of Florida
Gainesville, Florida

Andrew Plaut, M.D.

Professor
Department of Medicine
Tufts University School of Medicine and New England Medical Center
Boston, Massachusetts

William G. Powderly, M.D.

Assistant Professor
Department of Medicine
Infectious Diseases Division
Washington University School of Medicine
Staff Physician
Veterans Affairs Medical Center
St. Louis, Missouri

Edward N. Robinson, Jr., M.D.

Clinical Associate Professor of Medicine
University of North Carolina
The Moses H. Cone Memorial Hospital
Internal Medicine Teaching Program
Greensboro, North Carolina

Moselio Schaechter, Ph.D.

Distinguished Professor and Chairman
Department of Molecular Biology and Microbiology
Tufts University School of Medicine
Boston, Massachusetts

David Schlessinger, Ph.D.
Professor
Department of Molecular Microbiology
Washington University School of Medicine
St. Louis, Missouri

Arnold L. Smith, M.D.
Professor of Pediatrics
Adjunct Professor of Microbiology
University of Washington School of Medicine
Chief, Division of Infectious Diseases
Children's Medical Center
Seattle, Washington

David R. Snydman, M.D.
Director, Clinical Microbiology
New England Medical Center
Professor
Departments of Medicine and Pathology
Tufts University School of Medicine
Boston, Massachusetts

John K. Spitznagel, M.D.
Professor and Former Chairman
Department of Microbiology and Immunology
Emory University School of Medicine
Atlanta, Georgia

Allen C. Steere, M.D.
Chief, Division of Rheumatology
Department of Medicine
New England Medical Center
Boston, Massachusetts

Gregory A. Storch, M.D.
Associate Professor
Departments of Pediatrics and Medicine
Washington University School of Medicine
St. Louis, Missouri

Stephen E. Straus, M.D.
Chief, Laboratory of Clinical Investigation
National Institute of Allergy and Infectious Diseases
National Institutes of Health
Bethesda, Maryland

Francis P. Tally, M.D.
Executive Director
Infectious Disease and Molecular Biology
Lederle Laboratories
Pearl River, New York

Donald M. Thea, M.D.
Assistant Professor
Division of Geographic Medicine and Infectious Diseases
Department of Medicine
Tufts University School of Medicine and New England Medical Center
Boston, Massachusetts

Debbie S. Toder, M.D.
Assistant Professor of Pediatrics and Microbiology and Immunology
Department of Pediatrics
University of Rochester Medical Center
Rochester, New York

David H. Walker, M.D.
Professor and Chairman
Department of Pathology
University of Texas Medical Branch
Galveston, Texas

Ellen Whitnack, M.D.
Associate Professor of Medicine
University of Tennessee, Memphis
Clincial Investigator
VA Medical Center
Memphis, Tennessee

Marion L. Woods II, M.D., M.P.H.
Assistant Professor of Medicine
Division of Infectious Diseases
Department of Medicine
University of Utah
Salt Lake City, Utah

Victor L. Yu, M.D.
Professor of Medicine
University of Pittsburgh
Chief, Infectious Disease Section
Veteran Affairs
Pittsburgh, Pennsylvania

H. Kirk Ziegler, Ph.D.
Associate Professor
Department of Microbiology and Immunology
Emory University School of Medicine
Atlanta, Georgia

Contents

Section III. Pathophysiology of Infectious Diseases ∎

Section I
Principles

Establishment of Infectious Diseases

1

Moselio Schaechter and Barry I. Eisenstein

As a student and as a physician you are going to face a large number of facts about infectious agents and the diseases they cause. How can you learn this much material? Given the magnitude of the task, trying to deal with all the bits of information singly and in isolation would be difficult and unproductive.

Fortunately, it is possible to develop a conceptual framework on which to hang the multitude of facts, based on the features that characterize all forms of parasitism. These features fall into two generalizations:

1. The following events take place in all infectious diseases:
   Encounter: The agent meets the host.
   Entry: The agent enters the host.
   Spread: The agent spreads from the site of entry.
   Multiplication: The agent multiplies in the host.
   Damage: The agent, the host response, or both cause tissue damage.
   Outcome: The agent or the host wins out, or they learn to coexist.

2. All these steps require the breaching of host defenses. What distinguishes one parasite from another is the manner in which each elicits and combats these host defenses.

ENCOUNTER

Most of us first encounter microorganisms at birth. Microbiologically speaking, we lead a sterile existence while in our mother's womb. This is true for two reasons: First, the unborn is well shielded from the microorganisms in the exterior environment by the fetal membranes. Second, the mother is not a likely source of microorganisms for the unborn child. The mother's blood carries infectious agents only sporadically and in small numbers. In addition, the placenta is a formidable obstacle to the passage of microorganisms into the fetus. Still, such passage is possible and some diseases are acquired in just this way. Examples of these so-called congenital infections are **rubella** (German measles), **syphilis**, or **cytomegalovirus** (CMV).

First Encounters

The first encounter with environmental microorganisms usually takes place at birth. During parturition, the newborn comes in contact with microorganisms present in the mother's vaginal canal and on her skin. Thus, from the very beginning, the newborn faces the challenge of living in the intimate company of a bewildering number of microorganisms. The mother, however, does not send the newborn into the world totally unprotected. Through her circulation she endows the fetus with a vast repertoire of specific antibodies. Some immunological inheritance is further provided by the mother's milk (colostrum), which also contains maternal antibodies. Sooner or later, however, these acquired defenses wane and the child must cope on his or her own. The microbial challenge is renewed time and again because all of us come in contact with new organisms for the rest of our lives. Most of these organisms rapidly disappear from the body, whereas others are adroit colonizers and will become part of the normal flora for extended times. A few will cause disease.

Endogenous vs. Exogenous Encounters

Microbial diseases may be contracted in two general ways: exogenously and endogenously.

EXOGENOUSLY ACQUIRED DISEASES

Exogenously acquired diseases are those that result from the encounter with agents in the environment. Thus, we "catch" a cold from others, or we get sick with typhoid fever from eating or drinking contaminated food or water. Disease-causing agents can be acquired from the outside in various ways: food, water, air, objects, insect bites, or other humans or animals with whom we share our environment. Many agents are readily transmitted among human beings through the exchange of bodily fluids; for instance, by sneezing, touching, or sexual intercourse. The way we encounter the disease agent often suggests a mode of prevention (Table 1.1). Note also that prevention has been successful for many of the serious epidemics, at least in the developed countries of the world. With the exception of vaccination, most preventive measures involve better sanitation and raising the standard of living, rather than employing medical procedures.

ENDOGENOUSLY ACQUIRED DISEASES

Endogenously acquired diseases are those that result from encounters with agents in or on the body. Members of the microbial flora that are normally present on our skin or mucous membranes may cause disease, usually when they penetrate into deeper tissues. Thus, a cut may lead to pus caused by the staphylococci that inhabit the healthy skin. Here the encounter with the agent took place long before the disease,

Table 1.1. Examples of Encounters and Disease Prevention

Type of Contact	Example	Type of Agent	Source	Strategy for Prevention	Preventive Aim
Inhalation	Common cold	Virus	Aerosol from infected persons	None	Difficult to avoid contact
	Coccidiodomycosis	Fungus	Soil	None	Difficult to avoid contact
Ingestion	Typhoid fever	Bacterium	Water, food	Sanitation	Lower infecting dose
	Salmonella food poisoning	Bacterium	Food	Sanitation	Lower infecting dose
Sexual contact	Gonorrhea	Bacterium	Person	Social behavior	Avoid contact
Wound	Surgical infections	Bacteria	Normal flora surroundings	Aseptic techniques	Avoid contact
Insect bite	Malaria	Protozoan	Mosquito	Insect control	Eliminate vector

namely, at the time of colonization of the skin by the staphylococci. A distinction must be made between colonization and infectious disease. Colonization denotes the presence of microorganisms in a site of the body, and does not necessarily imply that this leads to tissue damage and signs and symptoms of disease. It does suggest, however, that the microorganisms have invaded that site of the body and can multiply there.

NORMAL FLORA

The difference between endogenous and exogenous infections is sometimes quite sharp, as shown by the preceding examples. However, in many other instances, the demarcation becomes less clear because it may be difficult to define precisely what constitutes the normal flora (see Chapter 2). For example, some people harbor certain strains of virulent streptococci in their throats for a considerable time but only rarely come down with strep throat. Now, before any symptoms arise, we may ask, "Was the streptococcus a member of the normal flora?" The answer is yes, if by "normal flora" we mean organisms in or on our body that are not in the process of causing disease. The answer is no if we consider that this kind of streptococcus is not found in the throats of about 95% of all healthy people and that when it is present, it frequently causes disease. There is no easy way out of this ambiguity, and the terms must be used operationally. Obviously, if we cannot define precisely what the normal flora is, we cannot always distinguish between endogenous and exogenous infections.

Another reason why the distinction is so vague is that exposure to highly virulent agents does not always lead to disease. For example, even at the height of the deadly black plague and typhus epidemics, only about one half of the population became sick, although most people were likely to have encountered the disease agent.

Thus, the encounter of humans and microbes is quite varied. Each bacterium, virus, fungus, or animal parasite has its quirks. For that matter, each human being displays an idiosyncratic pattern of responses. Even within one individual the pattern usually changes with age, nutritional state, and many other factors.

ENTRY

Much of what we normally think as being inside of the body is topologically connected with the outside (Fig. 1.1). For instance, the surfaces of the lumen of the intestine, the alveoli of the lung, the bile canaliculi, and the tubules of the kidney are in direct connection with the exterior. In fact, almost all of the organs contained within the thorax and abdomen have this topological characteristic. In principle, a crawling insect could go from the mouth to the anus without penetrating any mucous membrane, although it would have to go through several sphincters and valves. In reality, these "external" sites of the body have powerful mechanisms that keep out invading microorganisms. With the exception of much of the digestive tract and the lower reaches of the genitourinary system, these sites are normally sterile.

Entry, then, means either the ingress of microorganisms into body cavities that are contiguous with the outside, or the **penetration** into deeper tissue after crossing an epithelial barrier. We will discuss both aspects of entry in some detail.

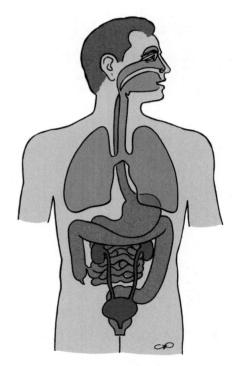

Figure 1.1. The regions of the body in direct contact with the exterior. Note that they include the outer aspect of the digestive, respiratory, and urogenital systems. These systems account for most of the organs of the thorax and abdomen. The main systems that do not have such direct connections are the musculoskeletal, nervous, circulatory, and endocrine systems. Not included in the drawing is the peritoneal cavity, which, in women, is connected to the outside via the Fallopian tubes.

Ingress: Entry Without Crossing Epithelial Barriers

Obviously, microorganisms get into the intestine by being swallowed and into the lung by being inhaled. There is not a comparable term for the process that allows ingress into the urinary tract or the genital system, which can can also become populated by external microorganisms. Microorganisms can cause serious diseases without getting deep into the tissue. Examples of serious infectious diseases that occur without bacterial penetration through epithelial surfaces are cholera, whooping cough, and infections of the urinary bladder.

INHALATION

To enter the respiratory system, microorganisms face a series of aerodynamic and hydrodynamic obstacles. Microorganisms are inhaled in the **aerosol droplets** or **dust particles** contained in the air we breathe. The air column is not uniform but is buffeted by complex anatomic structures (nasal turbinates, oropharynx, larynx). Accordingly, the surgical removal of the larynx (with its nooks and crannies) predisposes to diseases of the lower respiratory tract. Those microorganisms that arrive in the lower reaches of the respiratory tree face the powerful upward sweeping action of the ciliary epithelium. As expected, persons in whom this is impaired (e.g., heavy smokers) are more likely to get sick with pneumonia. The colonization of these sites requires that the microorganisms be able to stick to the epithelial surface. Once again, such organisms may cause disease without penetrating the epithelial barrier.

INGESTION

When contaminated food or water is ingested, microorganisms face a powerful host defense, **the acid in the stomach**. The stomach is a chemical disinfection chamber where many microorganisms are destroyed. Its effectiveness of microbial killing is not always the same since it is determined by the length of time microorganisms spend in the stomach, which depends on the kind and amount of the food eaten. Even under conditions of greatest destruction, some bacteria and yeasts escape alive, although their original number may have been reduced one million-fold or more. This may seem like a lot of bacterial killing, but be aware that some diseases, such as bacillary dysentery, can be acquired from just a few hundred organisms.

Bacteria, fungi, parasites, and viruses that escape this barrier enter the duodenum. Here they meet the enzymes of the pancreatic juice, the bile salts, and the strong sweeping force of **peristalsis**. Not unexpectedly, very few get a foothold at this site or anywhere else in the upper reaches of the small intestine. Toward the ileum, the situation is more favorable to bacterial life, but even here the few organisms that gain a foothold must avoid being washed away. Indeed, bacteria found in this region have special mechanisms that allow them to adhere to the epithelial cells of the intestinal mucosa. As will be discussed in Chapter 2, several surface components of these bacteria serve as **adhesins**. The main adhesins are the hair-like pili and the surface polysaccharides. As mentioned already, bacteria at this site may cause disease **without penetrating through the mucosal epithelium**. Cholera, and its milder relative, **travelers' diarrhea**, are the manifestations of the local production of powerful toxins in the intestine that affect the epithelial cells. The bacteria that produce these toxins need not enter the host cells at all.

Penetration: Entry into Tissues After Crossing Epithelial Barriers

Penetration into tissues takes many forms. Some microorganisms can pass directly through epithelia, especially mucous membranes that consist of a single cell layer. To penetrate the skin, which is tough and multilayered, most infecting agents must be carried across by insect bites or must await breaks in the skin. On the other hand, certain worms can burrow unaided through the skin and invade the host. Hookworms, for example, are parasites that may be acquired by walking barefoot on contaminated soil.

To penetrate into mucosal epithelial cells, many agents first interact with specific receptors on the surface of the host cell. This phenomenon has been studied intensively with viruses, some of which have a complex mechanism for attachment and internalization. For instance, influenza viruses have surface components that bind to receptors on the surface of sensitive host cells. Binding is soon followed by the uptake of the virus particles by the cells. In the case of bacteria, these two functions, attachment and internalization, are also being studied intensively. For example, it has been possible recently to clone bacterial genes that confer to *Escherichia coli*, which are normally noninvasive, the ability to enter cells into strains.

Microorganisms may also be actively carried into tissue by white cells or by macrophages that lie on the outside of the body. There are, for instance, macrophages that reside in the alveoli of the lungs and are known as dust cells, which can pick up infectious agents by phagocytosis. Most of the time they carry the agents upward on the ciliary epithelium, but occasionally these macrophages can reenter the body and carry their load of microorganisms into deeper locations. Such a mechanism of cell-mediated entry may function at other mucous membranes as well. It is thought, for example, that acquired immunodeficiency syndrome (AIDS) may be sexually transmitted by the penetration of virus-laden macrophages from semen.

INSECT BITES

Insect bites may lead to the penetration of viruses (viral encephalitis or yellow fever), bacteria (plague, typhus), protozoa (malaria, sleeping sickness), or worms (river blindness, elephantiasis). In the case of protozoa and higher animal parasites, residence in the insect is part of complex life cycles. The life stage of the parasite in the insect is often quite different from that found in the person. Insects also spread diseases by carrying microorganisms on their surfaces and contaminating foodstuff or the skin. A particularly unsavory example is that of the so-called reduviid bug, which defecates at the same time it bites. Parasites contained in the insect's feces are then introduced by scratching the bite area. A serious protozoal infection, Chagas' disease, is transmitted in this manner.

CUTS AND WOUNDS

Penetration from cuts and wounds is a common occurrence that is often unnoticed because it does not usually lead to symptoms of disease. For example, brushing one's teeth or vigorously defecating causes minute abrasions of epithelial membranes. Bacteria can then penetrate in small numbers in the blood, but they are rapidly removed by the filtering mechanisms of the reticuloendothelial system. However, if internal tissues are damaged or if the defense mechanisms are disrupted, circulating bacteria may gain a foothold and cause serious diseases. An example is **subacute bacterial endocarditis**, a disease that was devastating before the availability of antibiotics. This infection was usually caused by oral streptococci that became implanted on heart valves that had been damaged by a previous disease, usually rheumatic fever.

ORGAN TRANSPLANTS AND BLOOD TRANSFUSION

There is yet another way for organisms to penetrate into deeper tissue, namely, as the unfortunate consequence of organ transplants or blood transfusions. For instance, transplants of corneas have been known to result in the infection of recipients with a virus that causes a slow degenerative disease of the central nervous system (**Creutzfeldt-Jakob disease**). Kidney transplants sometimes result in infections by an agent called cytomegalovirus (CMV), perhaps because the virus resided in the transplanted kidney. A transplanted organ is not necessarily the source of infection since the immune response of transplant recipients must be suppressed to avoid graft rejection. In such a patient, an endogenous virus may now be able to multiply.

Of the infectious agents that may be acquired via blood transfusions, none causes greater concern than the virus of AIDS. However, many others, such as hepatitis B virus can also be transmitted in this manner. Screening of blood in blood banks has become an imperative.

Inoculum Size

The likelihood that organisms from the flora of the skin or mucous membranes might cause disease depends on many factors. Among them is the size of the inoculum, meaning that a few organisms are unlikely to result in an infection; **it usually takes many infecting agents to overcome the local defenses.** An example is what happens when people take baths in contaminated hot tubs. At times the water can become a veritable culture broth with as many as 100 million bacteria (*Pseudomonas*) per milliliter. In such numbers, bacteria that are normally harmless can overcome the normal defenses of the skin and cause skin infection all over the body. Clearly, what a surgeon tries to achieve in prepping an area before making an incision is to **reduce the number of bacteria** that may invade a surgical wound. Infections are almost inevitable if large numbers of microorganisms are deposited in deeper tissues, either from dirty skin or from contamination by soil or other microbial-rich material. This requires a great deal of attention in the treatment of patients with open wounds, even in the modern era of powerful antimicrobial drugs.

SPREAD

The term "spread" also has two shades of meaning. It suggests direct, lateral propagation of organisms from the original site of entry to contiguous tissues, but it can also refer to dissemination to distant sites. Either way, microorganisms spread and multiply only if they overcome host defenses. It should be kept in mind that spread sometimes precedes and sometimes follows microbial multiplication in the body. For instance, the parasite that causes malaria enters the body through a mosquito bite and is distributed throughout the bloodstream before it has a chance to increase in numbers. On the other hand, staphylococci that infect a cut must multiply locally before spreading to distant sites.

The role of host defenses in impeding the spread of microorganisms requires a fair understanding of the immune response and of the innate defense mechanisms. They are presented in detail in Chapters 6 and 7 and are a central theme of this book. For now, it is important to keep in mind the dynamic nature of host-parasite interactions; for every defense mechanism in existence, microbes develop strategies to try to overcome it. The host, in turn, adapts to such new challenges and this elicits yet different responses from the agents. This intricate counterpoint is played out, sometimes over extended periods of time, until one of three things happens: (a) the host wins out; (b) the parasite overcomes the host; or (c) they learn to live with one another in an uneasy truce.

Anatomical Factors

The pattern of spread of microorganisms from a given site is often dictated by anatomical considerations, so that a knowledge of human anatomy often helps us understand infectious diseases. Consider a localized infection, a bacterial abscess of the lung, as an example. The abscess may burst open and allow the organisms to escape into the bronchial tree or, if pointed outward, to the pleural cavity. **Spread in one or the other direction will have different consequences**—in the first case, it may lead to a generalized pneumonia; in the second, it may lead to pleurisy. Another example is the infection from the middle ear, a condition more common in children than in adults. This age difference is explained, in part, by developmental changes that take place in the Eustachian tubes with growth. These conduits are nearly horizontal in children and become more steeply inclined with age. For this and other reasons, the Eustachian tubes of children do not drain as well as those of adults. Note how knowledge of human anatomy helps us understand a disease process.

Spread of microorganisms is greatly influenced by **fluid dynamics**. Thus, infected fluids in the interior of the body tend to flow along fascial planes. For example, infection of one site of the meninges will usually result in generalized meningitis, since there are no barriers to impede the spread of the infected cerebrospinal fluid. The same is true for the pleura, the pericardium, and the synovial cavities. Of course, the most extensive liquid system of the body, the blood, is replete with defense mechanisms. All the liquids of the body (blood, lymph, cerebrospinal fluid (CSF), synovial fluid, urine, tears, etc.) contain different antimicrobial defense factors that, if overcome, result in disease.

Active Participation by Microorganisms

Infectious agents are not always silent partners in the process of spreading. Some contribute to it by actively moving. Worms wiggle, amoebae crawl, many bacteria swim. Some of these movements appear random, others are probably in response to chemotactic signals. Spreading can also be facilitated by chemical rather than mechanical action. For instance, streptococci manufacture a variety of extracellular hydrolases that let them break out of the walling-in force of the inflammatory response. They make a protease that breaks up fibrin, a hyaluronidase that hydrolyzes hyaluronic acid of connective tissue, and a deoxyribonuclease that reduces the viscosity of pus caused by the release of DNA from lysed white cells. Other bacteria make elastases, collagenases, or other powerful proteases. Such organisms can break through some of the natural surface barriers or can penetrate through thick viscous pus that would otherwise impede their spread. At a more superficial site, fungi that cause athlete's foot make keratin-hydrolyzing enzymes that help them spread through the horny layers of the skin. These factors confer clear selective advantages on the microorganisms that produce them.

MULTIPLICATION

Rarely do infectious agents cause disease without first multiplying within the body. The number of microorganisms we inhale or ingest (the size of the inoculum) is usually too small to produce symptoms directly. Infectious agents must grow before their presence is felt (Fig. 1.2). Of course, the ingestion of bacterial toxins such as those of botulism or staphylococcal food poisoning leads to disease directly, but these conditions are intoxications, not infections.

In most cases, symptoms manifest some time after the organisms have entered the body. This **incubation period** reflects the time needed for the infectious agents to overcome early defenses and to grow to a certain population size. The subject of the host defenses against microbial multiplication is a lengthy and varied one. Later in this chapter we will bring up some of their less obvious manifestations. Not infrequently, defense mechanisms go overboard and contribute to tissue damage in infections.

Microbial Nutrition

As microbial nutrition goes, the body would seem to be a rich medium. Body fluids such as plasma contain sugars, vitamins, minerals, and other substances can be used for growth by bacteria, fungi, and animal parasites. Still, if fresh plasma in a test tube is inoculated with a

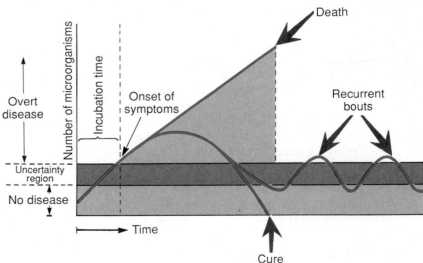

Figure 1.2.   Microbial multiplication and clinical manifestations of disease. The number of microorganisms present in a patient must exceed a given threshold to cause disease. If the number is below this threshold, no signs and symptoms of disease will be apparent. In some cases, the numbers will oscillate above and below the threshold, resulting in recurrent bouts of disease. Note that this is an idealized schematic drawing. In reality, the threshold of overt disease is not fixed but varies with the physiological state of the host.

culture of bacteria, the bacterial growth is sparse. The major reason is the inhibitory effect of antimicrobial substances such as lysozyme and constituents of the complement system.

Plasma and many other body fluids contain very little free iron since this metal is combined with extremely avid iron-binding proteins. This point, which has been studied in detail, appears to be significant in limiting the growth of bacteria in the body. Bacteria need iron for the synthesis of their cytochromes and other enzymes. In fact, the body sequesters iron to defend itself against bacteria. When a sufficient number of organisms enters the body, iron-binding proteins are poured into plasma and tissue fluids. In other words, the body tries to limit further the availability of free iron by sequestering an ever greater amount of it.

The spectrum of nutritional requirements of microorganisms associated with the body reflects their ecological habits. For instance, many of the bacteria **that grow mainly in the human body**, such as staphylococci or certain streptococci, require several amino acids and vitamins. Organisms that are found both in the body but also in soil or water are usually much less picky and can fulfill their organic requirements with simple carbon compounds. Examples are *E. coli* and many *Pseudomonas*, which can grow in laboratory "minimal media."

Physical Factors

The physical environment of the body selects for microorganisms that grow within certain ranges of temperature, osmotic pressure, and pH. Organisms that are almost always found in association with their host tend to have a narrow temperature optimum. Organisms that are also found in the environment, such as *Pseudomonas*, also grow well at lower temperatures. Poliovirus, being a virus, can only replicate just a few degrees over normal human body temperature. Fever, then, may be a defense mechanism that may serve to limit the disease. (Do you want to think again before prescribing two aspirins and asking the patient to call you in the morning?) Fungi that cause athletes's foot do not grow well at temperatures above around 30°C and are found only on the cooler body surfaces. It follows that, in most circumstances, these fungi cannot cause internal diseases. As with nutritional requirements, the breadth of the temperature range for growth is often dictated by the organism's habits.

DAMAGE

There are nearly as many kinds of damage as there are infectious diseases. The type and intensity of the damage depend on the tissues and organs affected; therefore, it is difficult to make generalizations. Damage in infectious processes may be loosely categorized as due to (*a*) mechanical causes, (*b*) cell death, (*c*) pharmacological alterations of metabolism, and (*d*) vehement host responses. These manifestations are interrelated, and several are usually seen at one time.

Mechanical Causes

If infectious agents are large enough and are present in sufficient numbers, they may obstruct vital passages. Such a mechanical obstruction occurs, although rarely, in children with an overload of worms in their intestine. A heavy infestation with the large roundworm, *Ascaris* (15–35 cm long and about 0.5 cm thick) may result in the occlusion of the intestinal lumen. A single worm may also migrate into the common bile duct and obstruct the passage of bile.

More often, mechanical obstruction results not from the infectious agents alone but from the **inflammatory response of the host elicited by their presence**. An example is the disease **elephantiasis**, an enormous swelling of limbs or the scrotum caused by small worms, the filariae, becoming lodged in lymphatics. Their presence sets off a tissue reaction that occludes the vessels, causing swelling and hypertrophy.

Almost any duct or tube-like organ, thick or thin, may be **obstructed by infections**, sometimes with life-threatening consequences. Some examples are the inflammation of the epiglottis, which may impede the passage of air; the spread of inflammation from the middle ear to the meninges, which can result in hydrocephalus (a dilatation of the cerebral ventricles due to obstruction of the flow of cerebrospinal fluid [CSF]); infection of the prostate, which may obstruct the flow of urine from the bladder; and an inflammatory reaction to the eggs of a liver fluke, which may result in severe disturbances of portal circulation.

Cell Death

The effect of cell death depends on (a) which cells are involved, (b) how many are infected, and (c) how fast the infection proceeds. If the cells belong to an essential organ, such as the heart or the brain, the outcome is likely to be serious and could even be fatal. For example, myocarditis, the infection of the heart muscle, is sometimes a fulminating disease when it is caused by an agent called Coxsackievirus. On the other hand, myocarditis is usually a chronic condition when the infecting organism is a less virulent parasite, as with the trypanosome of Chagas' disease. Coxsackievirus is also thought to kill the insulin-producing cells of the islets of the pancreas and may be one of the causes of infantile diabetes.

Sometimes the effects of cell death are easily seen. For instance, in patients with **gas gangrene**, lysis of red blood cells and the outpouring of hemoglobin may result in a reddish or burgundy appearance of serum and urine. **Rocky Mountain spotted fever** derives its name from the **skin rash** produced by blood spilled when endothelial cells of small vessels are killed by infecting rickettsiae. In both examples, the **cells break open and liberate the infectious agents into the bloodstream**.

Some bacteria kill cells by poisoning them with toxins. Sometimes toxins function in the immediate surroundings of the bacteria that produce them. For example, the bacteria that cause **dysentery** kill nearby epithelial cells of the intestinal mucosa. Other bacteria produce toxins that act at great distances. An example is **diphtheria**, where bacteria in the throat produce a toxin that affects the heart and the nervous system. Toxins produced by bacteria are among the most powerful cell poisons known and work at extraordinarily low concentrations. It has been estimated that a single molecule of diphtheria toxin is sufficient to kill a sensitive cell. Considerable knowledge has been gathered about how these toxins work and will be presented in the chapters on individual organisms and in Chapter 7.

Pharmacological Alterations of Metabolism

Certain infectious diseases do not involve the direct killing of cells at all. Among these are some of the most severe ones, such as **tetanus**, **botulism**, or **cholera**. They are caused by bacterial toxins that alter important aspects of metabolism in ways that resemble the action of hormones or other pharmacological effectors. **Tetanus toxin works on motor cells**, leading to a spastic paralysis. **Botulism toxin interferes with the release of acetylcholine at cholinergic synapses and neuromuscular junctions**, resulting in a flaccid paralysis. Cholera toxin increases the level of cyclic adenosine monophosphate (cAMP) in intestinal cells, which leads to a massive diarrhea because of loss of water and electrolytes. In all of these cases, the affected cells remain intact.

Damage Due to Host Responses

Almost always, the symptoms of infectious diseases are not produced by the microorganisms alone but also by the response of the host to their presence. Hardly ever is the host response so finely tuned that it does just what is desired of it. Its overemphatic expression may well help the host survive in the long run, but it contributes greatly to the immediate signs and symptoms. There are two manifestations of this, damage due to inflammation and damage from the immune response.

INFLAMMATION

Pus. The most familiar example of inflammation is **pus**, which consists of a mixture of dead and live white blood cells, bacteria, and exudate. Pus results from the **rapid migration of neutrophils** to a site where bacteria are present. Neutrophils are called up by chemotactic substances produced by the bacteria themselves as well as by tissue and serum components. When neutrophils die, they release powerful hydrolases from their lysosomal granules. These enzymes **damage surrounding tissues, extending the lesion to adjacent areas**.

Abscesses. When pus is walled off, the lesion is called an abscess. An example is a boil, the familiar furuncle that most people have experienced on their skin. It is caused by the stoppage of a sebaceous gland, which gives staphylococci normally present on the skin an initial opportunity for sheltered growth. Organisms do, however, advertise their presence by producing chemotaxins, and neutrophils arrive at the scene to join battle. It should be noted than the anatomical location of this battlefield is all important. An abscess in the skin may be painful, but one in the brain could be fatal. Pus may be damaging locally, but this is a small price to pay for containing the infection. Patients with genetic defects in neutrophil function suffer from severe recurrent infections. Despite antibiotic treatment, many such patients do not survive into adolescence.

Prostaglandins. The presence of bacteria in tissues also elicits a generalized reaction known as the acute phase response. Bacteria set off the outpouring of a powerful protein called interleukin-1 (IL-1), which acts on the fever centers to raise body temperature. IL-1 stimulates the synthesis of substances called prostaglandins, which work on the thermoregulatory center of the brain. Prostaglandins are also responsible for the feeling of malaise, that ill-defined but well-known sensation of "feeling sick" that besets us when we have the common cold. Aspirin and acetaminophen interfere with the production of prostaglandins, thereby reducing fever and malaise.

Endotoxin. With many common bacteria, the so-called Gram-negative bacteria, the acute phase response is elicited by a major component of their surface, a lipopolysaccharide known as endotoxin. In small amounts, endotoxin elicits fever and mobilizes certain defense mechanisms. In large amounts, it results in shock and intravascular coagulation. Thus, the body response to the presence of these bacteria depends on the amount of endotoxin present.

Immune Response

The immune response is complex and has multiple manifestations. There are many ways in which it may go awry and cause damage. Immune responses are usually classified as "humoral," related to circulating antibodies, and "cellular," elicited by special cells of the immune system. Both may cause damage.

HUMORAL IMMUNITY

Infecting agents elicit the formation of specific antibodies. In the circulation and in tissues, antibodies combine with the infecting agents or with some of their soluble products. These antigen-antibody complexes evoke an inflammatory response. How do they do this? The answer requires knowledge of a complex set of serum proteins, the **complement system**. In the presence of antigen-antibody complexes, these proteins become activated by a series of proteolytic reactions, the so-called **classical pathway** of activation. Complement can also be activated by the presence of microorganisms alone, resulting in the **alternative pathway**. The products of these proteolytic cleavages are pharmacologically active. Some work on platelets and white cells to produce substances that increase vascular permeability and vasodilation. The result is edema, the outpouring of fluids into tissues. Other complement factors act on white blood cells, some as chemotaxins, and others to make bacteria more easily phagocytized. The result of these activities is, on the one hand, the mobilization of powerful defenses against invading microorganisms, and, on the other hand, inflammation.

Antigen-antibody complexes sometimes are deposited on the membrane of the glomeruli of the kidneys, resulting in impairment of kidney function, a condition called glomerulonephritis. This condition is seen as the aftermath of certain streptococcal and viral infections. Similar effects also take place in blood vessels, leading to visible skin rashes.

CELLULAR IMMUNITY

A different type of response is expressed via special cells of the immune system and is called cell-mediated immunity (CMI). This complex phenomenon leads to the activation and mobilization of macrophages, the powerful phagocytic cells that participate in the later stages of inflammation to clean up debris and remaining microorganisms.

Cell-mediated immunity is associated with chronic inflammation, the histological changes that limit the spread of infections but also cause lesions in tissues. These damaging activities are characteristic of chronic infections, often caused by intracellular microorganisms and viruses. An example is chronic tuberculosis, where the main damage to tissue is due to cell-mediated immunity. It is elicited by the tubercle bacilli, which have the ability to persist in cells for a long time. As the result, pathological changes associated with cell-mediated immunity lead to the production of **tubercles** or **granulomas**, and eventually, to destruction of tissue cells.

It is worth repeating that although the immune responses may cause tissue damage, in most instances, the price is well worth it. The point is illustrated in people who have genetic or acquired defects in their immune system. Unfortunately, such people are no longer a medical rarity. The advent and spread of AIDS has placed hundreds of thousands of persons in this category. The result is that these patients are ravaged and later killed by microorganisms that cause little or no disease in healthy persons. In the immunocompetent person, for example, active tuberculosis causes much damage but **if this leads to death, it is usually only after many years.** In the immunocompromised patient, the disease can become rampant in a much shorter period.

OUTCOME

There is nothing simple about infectious diseases, be they mild or life threatening. A large number of properties of the invading agent and of the host leads to an intricate and ever-changing interplay. It is not always possible to figure out the relative role of the known properties, not to mention those that still await discovery. To complicate matters, humans are beset by a huge number of possible invaders. New ones emerge, apparently under our very eyes, to be added to the long list.

Therefore, the student of medical microbiology faces a demanding challenge. The fascination of the topic may not suffice to overcome the problems in studying so much detail. We suggest that a student is helped by resorting to a conceptual framework such as the one used in this chapter, based on the fact that all host-parasite interactions have steps in common. As we indicate at the beginning of this chapter, parasites and host must encounter, the parasite must enter the host, spread and multiply, and eventually cause damage. All these steps require the breaching of host defenses. If these facts are kept in mind, the myriads of facts will fall into place logically. May you thereby be able to enjoy one of the liveliest and most important subjects in all of biology and medicine!

SUGGESTED READING

Mims CA. The pathogenesis of infectious diseases, 3rd ed. New York: Academic Press, 1987.

McNeill WH. Plagues and peoples. Garden City, NY: Anchor Books, 1976.

Taussig MJ. Processes in pathology and microbiology, 2nd ed. Boston: Blackwell Science Publications, 1984.

Normal Microbial Flora

2

Barry I. Eisenstein and Moselio Schaechter

The human body normally contains thousands of species of bacteria and a smaller number of viruses, fungi, and protozoa. The great majority are commensals, meaning that they eat alongside us without causing harm. We do not carry all of them all of the time, but their number at any instant is still formidable. At any one time, each of us possesses an individualized spectrum of species and strains. In the words of the Romans, *suum quique*, to each his own.

The object of all living organisms, microbes included, is to grow, to prosper, and to reproduce. The most successful microbe is the one that can rapidly and efficiently become two microbes. Note that in thinking about the nature of success among these organisms, "pathogenicity" or "virulence" need not be mentioned. In fact, the most virulent pathogens, those that kill their hosts, may be the least well adapted for survival. After all, why would a guest paying no rent want to set fire to his or her home? So before exploring the world of pathogens (the "misfits"), it is instructive first to consider our normal guests who behave so well. Keep in mind, though, that even the most domesticated among them can cause trouble if given a chance.

WHAT IS NORMAL FLORA?

We define as members of the normal flora those microorganisms that are frequently found on or within the body of healthy persons (Fig. 2.1). Some of these organisms are found in association with the body of humans or animals only; others can also live freely in the environment.

The line of demarcation of what constitutes the normal flora is often not clear. Consider, for instance, the meningococcus or the pneumococcus; both are true pathogens capable of causing meningitis, pneumonia, or septicemia. Either one is found in the throat of about 10% of healthy people; thus, they can be counted as members of the normal flora in these individuals but not in 90% of the population. In any one of us they may come and go as sporadic denizens of our throat. Therefore, such organisms should be called transient members of the normal flora of some individuals. You are correct if you have already surmised that these pathogens do not usually cause trouble even in colonized individuals. What is not obvious is that disease by either of these two organisms does not occur without prior colonization. Thus, colonization is necessary, yet insufficient, for meningococcal or pneumococcal disease. But this is not a universal prerequisite for all infections, many of which develop soon after entry of the infectious agent into the body without the need for a prolonged period of colonization. Examples of this are malaria or the common cold.

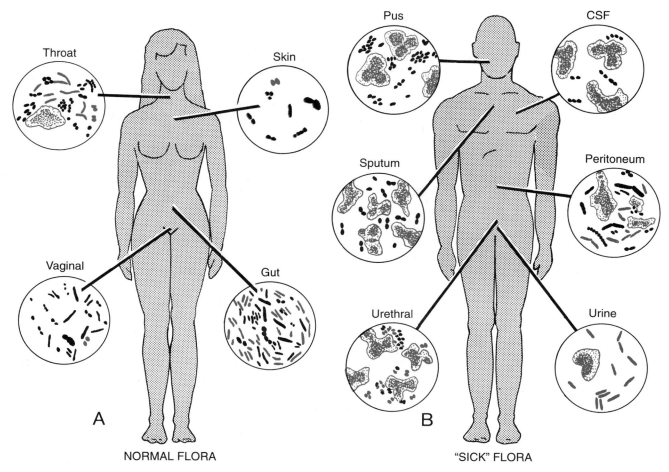

Figure 2.1.   The bacterial flora in health (A) and disease (B). Typical bacteria seen in the microbe-laden sites of the body are shown in schematic fashion. Gram-positive bacteria are shown in *black*; Gram-negative bacteria are shown in *color*.

The problem with many of the definitions in this field is that they are not absolute. The same problems in defining what constitutes the normal microbial flora pertain to terms such as pathogenicity and virulence. As we will see in subsequent chapters, these terms depend not only on properties of the infectious agent, but to a critical extent, on the state of the defenses of the host. Keep in mind, too, that disease often results from the active interaction between microbe and host. Many of the signs and symptoms of infections are actually due to the host's own inflammatory response in an effort to contain the infection. A good analogy: fire-fighters occasionally outdo the destruction due to fire by producing even more water damage to the property being protected.

WHAT PARTS OF THE BODY ARE INVOLVED?

Let us now consider the parts of the body that are colonized by the normal flora. Those that usually contain large amounts of microorganisms are:

Skin—moist areas especially, e.g., groin, between toes;
Respiratory tract—nose and oropharynx;
Digestive tract—mouth and large intestine;

Urinary tract—anterior parts of the urethra; and
Genital system—vagina.

Bacteria and, to lesser extent, fungi and protozoa, **reside and actively proliferate** at these sites. Other parts of the body contain small numbers of microorganisms, most often in transit. These sites include the rest of **the respiratory and digestive tracts, the urinary bladder, and the uterus.** Finding pathogenic microorganisms at these sites is highly suggestive of disease, but it is not proof. At the other extreme are certain tissues and organs that are usually sterile. The presence of microorganisms at these sites is usually considered of diagnostic significance. Included here are **blood, cerebrospinal fluid (CSF), synovial fluid, and deep tissues in general.**

The number of bacteria in sites that contain thriving microbial communities varies over a wide range. In highly protected areas, bacteria are almost as densely packed as is physically possible. For instance, the gingival pockets around teeth contain wall-to-wall bacteria. Normal feces consists of about one-third bacteria by weight. It is worth realizing what this means in terms of the number of organisms. If the average bacterium is about 1 μm^3 in volume, the densest possible packing would result in a mass of 1×10^{12}/ml. Such numbers are actually approached in certain parts of the body. In contrast, sites that are not quite as hospitable, such as skin, mouth, and vagina, may have populations that are more like one to ten million bacteria per milliliter of fluid or per gram of scrapings.

HOW DO MICROORGANISMS PERSIST IN THE BODY?

To colonize the human body, invading microorganisms must be able to resist host mechanisms that could dislodge or kill them, as well as to compete successfully with other microbial species. Picture a bacterial cell entering the mouth and the problems it faces trying to remain at this site. Strong liquid currents would wash it away unless the organism adhered to the surface of the teeth or the mucous membranes. In addition, saliva contains antibacterial compounds, such as enzymes and antibodies, although these substances are not equally damaging to all bacterial species. At sites of the mouth that are not exposed to the flushing action of saliva, such as the crevices of the gums, the organism would find a large resident flora that already occupies likely adherence sites. These resident organisms also produce antimicrobial substances, such as acids derived from their metabolism of sugars, that may be inimical to the invader.

Although massive bacterial colonization of the mouth is normal, only occasionally do these microbes cause trouble there. One example is the dental disease, periodontitis, which results when overgrowth with particular bacterial strains occurs in the gingival crevices and results in disease to the gums. Another example is when the respiratory defenses are lowered (e.g., from a poor cough reflex due to a stroke or from smoking-induced paralysis of the ciliary clearance mechanisms). Under these conditions, "aspiration pneumonia" is more likely to occur. The bacteriological etiology of such pneumonias is highly dependent on which organisms happen to be colonizing the mouth or throat at the time of the aspiration. If the person is unlucky enough to be colonized with a virulent strain of the pneumococcus, then only a small amount of mouth/pharyngeal content suffices to result in a severe pneumonia. In fact, most cases of pneumococcal pneumonia are not associated with obvious aspiration at all, but rather with imperceptible "microaspirations." If the oropharynx is not colonized with such virulent bacteria, a significantly larger amount of aspirated material must reach the lungs to cause disease. Thus, stroke victims or highly inebriated persons, who are prone to significant aspiration, frequently develop smoldering anaerobic pneumonias, reflecting the fact that anaerobic bacteria in the mouth normally outnumber aerobic bacteria by a factor of 100–1000.

An example of the factors involved in colonization can be seen by the study of an adhesive protein called **fibronectin**. This protein coats the mucosal surfaces of epithelial cells and has a strong attachment predilection for the so-called Gram-positive organisms (in Chapter 3 you will find the basis for the division of bacteria into two almost equal groups, the Gram positives and the Gram negatives). Fibronectin is probably important in establishing the nature of the bacterial flora in the mouth and pharynx, as suggested by the following findings. The oropharynx of individuals in poor general health, including many hospitalized patients, becomes deficient in fibronectin. With low levels of this protein, Gram-negative organisms tend to displace Gram positives, in part because the fibronectin-denuded mucosal cells reveal receptors for components of the bacterial surface called pili or fimbriae, which are adhesive organelles found on Gram-negative, but not on Gram-positive, bacteria (see Chapter 3). The high incidence of Gram-negative pneumonia in hospitalized patients can now be explained by these considerations of adherence specificity, compounded by the selective pressure of antimicrobial drugs used in the hospital. (Gram negatives are, generally speaking, more drug resistant than Gram positives.) In fact, aspiration-related Gram-negative pneumonias, along with catheter-associated infections of the urinary tract and bloodstream (which are often Gram-positive bacteria), are the most important causes of hospital-associated (**nosocomial**) infections, at great cost in patient lives and the finances of managing patient care.

The example of the mouth can be extended to the large intestine, the vagina, the perineum, the skin, and other sites that are normally laden with microbes. It follows that colonization by new organisms is an unlikely event and that the successful colonizer must be unusually adept at resisting host and microbial defenses. The colonization of sites that are normally sterile or that carry a sparse load of microorganisms tends to be easier to accomplish due to the lack of microbial competition. Such sites include the small intestine and all the deep tissues not in direct contact with the outside. Not surprisingly, host defenses are typically more intensive at such sites. Not too many microbes survive the alternating acid and alkaline baths of our upper gastrointestinal tracts or the sea of antibodies, complement, and phagocytic cells of our deep tissues. Obviously, in our long history of coexistence and coevolution with the microbial world, our bodies have learned what territory is safe to share and what is off limits. And, we have managed to share this space preferentially with well-behaved guests. Foreign devices, like plastic catheters stuck into arteries and veins, are famous for upsetting the delicate ecological balance between microbes and host tissues.

The attributes of microbes that permit them to colonize the body make a long list and, to a large extent, determine what makes each pathogenic organism distinct. Such attributes will be discussed in detail in the chapters on individual organisms. Table 2.1 lists the classes of microbial properties that allow successful colonization.

Table 2.1. Some Issues in Bacterial Colonization

Anticolonizing Property of the Host	Examples of How Bacteria Overcome It
Sweeping microbes away by liquid currents	Adhering to epithelial cells (e.g. gonococci stick to the mucous membrane of the urethra)
Killing microbes with the host's phagocytes	Avoiding being taken up (e.g., the pneumococcus is surrounded by a slimy capsule that impairs uptake by neutrophils)
	Killing the phagocyte (e.g., certain streptococci produce a toxin that makes holes in the neutrophil membrane)
Starving microbes for lack of needed nutrients	Deriving needed nutrients from host cells (e.g., certain staphylococci lyse red blood cells and use their hemoglobin as a source of iron)

SOME INFECTIOUS AGENTS STRONGLY PREFER CERTAIN SITES IN THE BODY, OTHERS DO NOT

At first glance, it may appear that microorganisms usually cause disease in specific organs only. To some extent, this is true: hepatitis viruses affect the liver, encephalitis and rabies virus affect the brain, the common cold viruses affect the nasal epithelium. Such a list is easier to construct for viruses, which tend to be tissue specific, than for bacteria, which often show a wide range of **tissue tropism**. Some bacteria, such as the cholera bacillus have strong predilections (the small intestine, in this case), whereas others (e.g., the staphylococcus) may infect almost any site of the body. In some cases, tissue tropism can be attributed to tissue-specific cellular properties, such as the presence of specific receptors on the surface of certain cells (e.g., fibronectin, with its affinity for Gram-positive bacteria). In other instances, physical properties, such as the temperature of the organ, may be the determinants of tropism.

The complexities of tissue tropism in bacteria have already been discussed above in relation to colonization of the oropharynx. It can also be illustrated with the example of the gonococcus. This bacterium most often causes infection of the urethra, but the throat, rectum, or the eyes may also be affected. Where the lesion occurs in this disease depends on the site of entry of the organism. Pharyngeal and rectal gonorrhea are the result of nonvaginal intercourse, whereas ophthalmia (eye infection) is due to the infection of the eyes of a neonate as it passes through the birth canal of the infected mother. Thus, it is clear that the gonococcus has no absolute predilection for the mucous membranes of a given organ. How about other types of tissue? Strains of gonococci that survive in circulation show a marked predilection for certain organs, the joints being the foremost example. Thus, gonococcal arthritis is one of the most common complications of gonorrhea. In this case, the reasons for the site predilection at the joints is not known, but it is clear that the gonococcus has strong tropism for certain deep tissues, not only for epithelial membranes.

Tissue tropism often relies on the existence of specific receptors on the surface of certain cells. This is seen most clearly in the case of viruses and may explain why, in general, these agents show such a great degree of tropism. Influenza virus, for example, relies on special glycoproteins found on the surface of respiratory epithelial cells for its attachment. HIV, the virus of AIDS, attaches to protein receptors found selectively on certain lymphocytes and macrophages. Other examples include fibronectin in the oropharynx (discussed previously), and mucosal cells of the urinary tract in individuals with the P blood-group antigen (99% of the population), which binds *Escherichia coli*-carrying P-pilus organelles (see Chapter 3). Much effort, particularly in novel forms of antiviral therapy, is going into discovering ways to neutralize the action of receptors, thereby avoiding infection by the agents that recognize them.

The temperature of an organ sometimes is a determinant of the location of the infectious agent. Thus, the viruses of the common cold are found in the nasal epithelium and not in internal organs because these agents do not grow at the higher temperature inside the body. Likewise, the spirochete of syphilis is sensitive to higher than normal body temperatures, which induced certain physicians of the preantibiotic era to try to cure syphilis by injecting patients with the agent of malaria!

IMPORTANCE OF THE NORMAL FLORA

The normal flora plays an important role in health and disease, as seen by the following examples. The most easily perceptible manifestation of the activities of the normal flora is the production of the various odors associated with epithelial surfaces of the human body. A germ-free human would not need to make use of deodorants.

Common Source of Infection

The normal flora is the source of many opportunistic infections. When commensal organisms find themselves in unaccustomed sites of the body, they may cause disease. For example, anaerobic bacteria, usually of the genus *Bacteroides*, are carried in the intestine of normal persons and may produce abscesses if they penetrate into deeper tissues via traumatic or surgical wounds. Staphylococci from the skin and nose, or streptococci and Gram-negative cocci from the throat and mouth, are also responsible for infections of this sort. In fact, *Staphylococcus epidermidis*, the most prevalent organism on the skin, has a strong predilection for attaching nonspecifically to plastic catheters, which occasionally results in severe bloodstream infections in patients with intravenous catheters. Likewise, *E. coli*, a normal inhabitant of the gastrointestinal tract, is by far the most common cause of urinary tract infection. In general, **physicians see more patients with disease due to the "normal flora" than due to agents acquired from outside the body.**

These facts point out that the definition of virulence is very elusive and that no microorganism is intrinsically benign or pathogenic. **Under the right circumstances, any microorganism that can grow in the body can cause disease.** This statement needs to be qualified: members of the normal flora do not all have the same pathogenic potential. Some cause disease more readily than others because they are endowed with special virulence properties. This is readily seen in peritonitis produced from the release of intestinal bacteria through a break in the gut wall. The resulting infection is usually caused by a few bacterial species only, comprising a small fraction of the total number of species present in the inoculum.

The definition of virulence is not intrinsic to the microorganisms but depends also on the state of immune competence of the host. Members of the normal flora often invade organs and tissues in immune compromised patients. Thus, the yeast *Candida*, a harmless commensal in about one-third of normal people, is a common cause of bloodstream infection in patients undergoing vigorous cancer chemotherapy. *Pneumocystis carinii* is a common inhabitant of the lungs of healthy persons, but can cause a specific kind of pneumonia and becomes one of the principal causes of death in patients with AIDS.

Immune Stimulation

Our repertoire of immunoglobulins reflects, in part, the antigenic stimulation by the normal flora. In general, we do not have high antibody titers to the individual bacteria, viruses, or fungi that inhabit our body. Nonetheless, even in low concentrations, these antibodies serve as a defense mechanism. Here, then, is a clear benefit from our normal flora. Among the antibodies produced in response to bacterial stimulation are those of the IgA class, which are secreted through mucous membranes. While the role of these immunoglobulins is not well understood, it seems reasonable that they are an important first line of defense and that they interfere, possibly on a daily basis, with the colonization of deeper tissues by commensal organisms.

Antibodies elicited by the antigenic challenge of the normal flora sometimes cross-react with normal tissue components. A good example are antibodies against the ABO blood group substances. You may remember that people that belong to the A group have anti-B antibodies and, conversely, B group individuals make anti-A antibodies. People in the O group make both anti-A and anti-B antibodies. You may wonder about the source of antigenic stimulation for these antibodies. On reflection, this is not obvious. Why should one make antibodies against a blood group different than one's own? The reason is not that we come in contact with red blood cells of a different type, since obviously very few of us get blood transfusions, especially with the wrong type blood. The answer to this puzzle is that bacteria from the intestinal flora contain antigens that cross-react with both A and B blood substance. These antigens are a source of antigenic stimulation. We make antibodies against these foreign blood group antigens but not against those of our own group because we are immunologically tolerant to the "self" antigens but not to the "foreign" ones.

This type of cross-reactivity does not usually cause disease. In fact, there is good evidence that cross-reactivity among bacterial antigens can be protective. For example, antibodies raised against various bacteria that normally reside in the bowel have been shown to cross-react with the polysaccharide capsule of meningitis-producing strains of meningococci; the presence of the antibodies is protective against this form of bacterial meningitis. Contrariwise, it is possible for antibodies cross-reactive to microbial antigens to play an insidiously harmful role in health. For instance, the serious disease lupus erythematosus is associated with the production of antibodies against one's own DNA. There is some evidence that the antigens that set off the production of these antibodies are not nucleic acids but may be cross-reacting bacterial lipopolysaccharides.

Keeping Out Invaders

In some sites of the body, the normal flora keeps out pathogens. This happens in several ways. Commensal bacteria have the physical advantage of previous occupancy, especially on epithelial surfaces. Some commensal bacteria produce substances that are inhibitors to newcomers, such as antibiotics or lethal proteins called bacteriocins. It is not surprising, therefore, that colonization by a new species or a new strain is not a frequent event.

This long-known fact became relevant once again in the 1970s in connection with experiments done to assess the safety of new bacterial strains engineered by molecular cloning. The most commonly used organism for this purpose was (and probably still is) a particular strain of *E. coli* called K12. This strain was originally isolated from a person's feces, but has had a long residence in the laboratory. When human volunteers were fed this strain in large numbers, they retained it for only 1 day. The conventional interpretation is that in its sojourn in the laboratory the strain had lost its colonizing capacity. In other words, this strain can no longer outcompete the resident members of the bacterial flora of the gut.

When the normal flora is nearly wiped out with antibiotics, both exogenous and endogenous microorganisms are given the chance to cause disease. For example, the infecting dose of a *Salmonella* strain decreases almost a million-fold after mice are given streptomycin. Patients treated with certain antibiotics that are particularly effective in the gut may suffer from diarrhea, due to the overgrowth of yeasts or staphylococci. With the administration of some drugs, notably clindamycin, a particular organism, *Clostridium difficile*, produces a serious disease called pseudomembranous colitis (see Chapter 21). This organism is a minor member of the normal flora but can grow to a large population density when its neighbors are suppressed.

Role in Human Nutrition and Metabolism?

The normal flora of the intestine plays a role in human nutrition and metabolism, but little is known about the extent of this influence. Why is it so difficult to figure this out? Obviously, humans cannot be made "germ free" at will; most of the information comes from work with animals and its relevance to human nutrition is uncertain. Nonetheless, it is likely that a biomass as huge and metabolically active as that in the large intestine plays a role in the nutritional balance of the host. It is known, for instance, that several intestinal bacteria, like *E. coli* and *Bacteroides* species, synthesize vitamin K, which may be an important source of this vitamin for human beings and animals.

The metabolism of several key compounds involves excretion from the liver into the intestine and their return from there to the liver. This enterohepatic circulatory loop is particularly important for sex steroid hormones and bile salts. These substances are excreted through the bile in conjugated form as glucuronides or sulfates but cannot be reabsorbed in this form. Members of the intestinal bacterial flora make glucuronidases and sulfatases that can deconjugate these compounds. The extent to which these activities are physiologically important is not yet known.

Source of Carcinogens?

The flora of the large intestine may produce carcinogens. The compounds that we ingest are chemically transformed by the varied metabolic activities of the gut flora. Many potential carcinogens are active only after being modified. Some of the known modifications are carried out by enzymes of intestinal bacteria. An example is the artificial sweetener cyclamate that is converted to the active bladder carcinogen cyclohexamine by bacterial sulfatases. The importance of the normal importance of the normal flora in production of carcinogens is difficult to assess, but it is a subject of considerable scrutiny.

HOW DO WE STUDY WHAT NORMAL FLORA DOES?

Much of what we know about the role of the normal flora in nutrition and prevention of disease comes from studying animals reared under sterile conditions, the so-called germ-free animals. Rats and mice resemble humans in many physiological properties but differ in important details. Nonetheless, germ-free animal research has produced interesting information.

Small mammals can be reared in the germ-free condition if they are placed in a sterile chamber after a cesarean birth. Chickens can be hatched from eggs whose shell surface has been sterilized. Usually the germ-free chamber is provided with gloves and ports to allow manipulation and the exchange of food and other material without breaking the sterility barrier. Many species of animals breed under these conditions and large colonies can be established. It is even possible to obtain germ-free rats and mice from commercial suppliers.

In general, rodents thrive under germ-free conditions as long as their diet is supplemented with vitamins. They even gain weight faster than do conventional animals. As expected, their concentration of immunoglobulins is reduced, especially if the diet is chemically defined and does not contain antigenic compounds. One of the more interesting characteristics of germ-free animals is that the histology of their intestines looks quite different from the usual. The most visible difference is in the lamina propria; it has only a few lymphocytes, plasma cells, and macrophages. By contrast, in conventional animals, the same tissue is heavily infiltrated with these cells. This suggests that the "normal" intestine is in a constant state of chronic inflammation!

MEMBERS OF NORMAL FLORA

What types of microorganisms constitute normal flora? The vast majority are bacteria. We also carry viruses, fungi, protozoa, and occasionally, worms, but in the healthy person these are present in smaller numbers than the bacteria. In the early days of microbiology, it was thought that most bacteria of the body were aerobes or facultative anaerobes. For a long time, E. coli was believed to be one of the principal members of the fecal flora. This erroneous conclusion was because most of the members of normal bacteria flora are strict anaerobes and do not grow on media incubated in the ordinary manner in air. Only by using special techniques of anaerobic cultivation has it been realized that in the gingival pocket or in feces, strict anaerobes outnumber the others by 1000 to 1 or more. Bacteria do not have to be located far from the air to find themselves under anaerobic conditions, because oxygen has very low solubility in water. Furthermore, the few molecules of oxygen that diffuse into deeper layers are readily used by host cells or by actively metabolizing aerobes and facultative anaerobes. Thus, anaerobic conditions can be found a fraction of a millimeter below the surface.

Table 2.2 shows the distribution and occurrence of the most prominent bacteria in selected parts of the human body. It should be understood that the organisms mentioned, although the most frequently encountered, represent only a minute fraction of the number of genera and species represented. The total number of taxonomic groups is probably well in the thousands. As an example, in a particularly de-

Table 2.2. Normal Bacterial Flora

| | Examples of Frequent Types | | | | |
| | Gram-positive | | Gram-negative | | Others |
	Cocci	Rods	Cocci	Rods	
Skin	Staphylococci	Corynebacteria *Propionobacterium acnes*	Enteric bacilli (on some sites)		
Oropharynx	α-Hemolytic streptococci Gaffkya	Corynebacteria	*Neisseria*	*Haemophilus* *Bacteroides*	*Mycoplasma* *Spirochetes*
Large intestine	Micrococcus streptococci (enterococci)	Lactobacilli		Enteric bacilli *Clostridia* *Bacteroides* *Pseudomonas*	
Vagina	Streptococci	Lactobacilli		*Bacteroides*	*Mycoplasma*

tailed study, the intestinal flora of a single person alone yielded about 400 distinct species of bacteria.

Newborn babies become colonized very rapidly by a varied microbial flora, especially in their intestine. In animals and probably in humans, there is a time sequence in the appearance of different organisms. The earliest colonizers are *E. coli*, streptococci, and some clostridia. Within 24 hours or so, lactobacilli appear and are followed within a few days by the major anaerobes that characterize the normal intestinal flora.

Little is known of the complex reasons why different species vary in their colonizing capacity and in their ability to compete with others. It seems likely that specific properties of bacteria, such as their pili, allow them to attach and survive in different microenvironments within the intestine. Thus, the microbial flora is different at the base of the intestinal crypts, in the mucus that covers the villi, or in the lumen of the gut. Normally, the intestinal flora of one individual is remarkably constant. This stability suggests that each successful colonizer is equipped with powerful devices to withstand the challenge from newly ingested microorganisms.

CONCLUSIONS

Our knowledge about the role of normal flora in health and disease is derived largely from a few circumstances of uncertain significance: studies with germ-free animals, observation of patients on antibiotics, etc. We are left with the impression that, from the immunological and microbiological point of view, normal flora contributes to the maintenance of health mainly by excluding potential invaders and possibly by long-term immunological stimulation. Nutritionally speaking, the microbial biomass within us plays a role in recycling certain important compounds and probably in supplying vitamin K. The negative side is that members of the normal flora are opportunistic pathogens and may cause disease when present in unaccustomed tissues and organs. We do not have the choice of living in a germ-free environment. In a microbe-laden world, it is reasonable to conclude that normal microbial flora is adapted to do more good than harm.

Self-assessment Questions

1. Name four infections caused by members of the normal flora and the factors that allow them to cause disease.

2. What is the immunological significance of normal flora?

3. How does normal flora ward off colonization by external pathogens?

4. Which portions of the body are usually heavily colonized? Which have a transient microbial flora? Which are usually sterile? What main factors dictate these ecological relationships?

5. Which main groups of bacteria are associated with the heavily colonized parts of the body?

6. What general strategies are available to study the role of normal flora?

ANSWERS TO ALL SELF-ASSESSMENT QUESTIONS CAN BE FOUND BEGINNING ON PAGE 899.

SUGGESTED READING

Rosebury T. Life on man. New York: The Viking Press, 1969. (A delightful popularization.)

Rosebury T. Microorganisms indigenous to man. New York: McGraw-Hill, 1962.

Biology of Infectious Agents

3

*David Schlessinger, Moselio Schaechter,
and Barry I. Eisenstein*

WHAT DO WE WANT TO KNOW ABOUT MICROORGANISMS?

Mainly, we want to know how pathogenic microorganisms harm the host and what we can do about it. This requires more than understanding of how they cause disease. For example, features of bacterial anatomy and metabolism have suggested targets for the successful development of powerful antibiotics. Similarly, unraveling details of viral structures and metabolism has led to the production of protective vaccines and to the beginnings of antiviral therapy.

From the point of view of students of infectious diseases, the life cycle of microorganisms may be critical to understand their capacity to cause disease. For example, establishing the etiology of Legionnaires' disease required an analysis of bacterial survival in the cooling water towers of large hotels. Control of malaria has been based on knowing that a critical density of both the mosquito vector and infected people is required for the spread of the parasite.

PROCARYOTIC AND EUKARYOTIC PATHOGENS

The world of pathogenic microbiology spans the largest cleft in the living world, that between the procaryotes and the eukaryotes. Bacteria belong to the procaryotes, whereas fungi, protozoa, and worms are eukaryotes. Procaryotes lack nuclei and other internal membrane-bound organelles. They do not carry out endocytosis and are incapable of ingesting particles or liquid droplets. Procaryotes differ from eukaryotes in important biochemical details, such as the composition of their ribosomes and lipids (Fig. 3.1). Procaryotes are usually haploid, with a single chromosome and extrachromosomal plasmids; eukaryotes have a diploid phase and many chromosomes.

Differences in organization between procaryotes and eukaryotes have important consequences for the way that they synthesize certain macromolecules. For instance, not having a nuclear membrane allows procaryotes to carry out protein synthesis using chains of messenger RNA that are, themselves, in the act of being synthesized. In other words, translation can be coupled to transcription and begin rapidly on new mRNA chains. In eukaryotes, the two processes cannot be directly linked. Transcripts of heterogeneous nuclear RNA must first be processed in the nucleus before they are transported across the nuclear membrane to the ribosomes in the cytoplasm. Only then can eukaryotic protein synthesis take place.

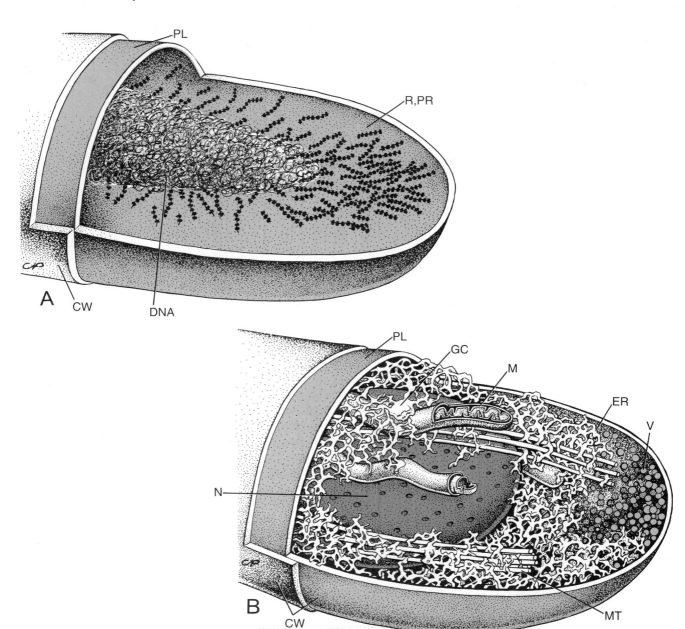

Figure 3.1.   Ultrastructure of typical bacterial and fungal cells. A. Inside the cell wall (*CW*) and membrane or plasmalemma (*PL*), a bacterium is filled with ribosomes (*R*), poly-ribosomes (*PR*), and proteins. DNA fibrils cluster near the center of the cell in a coiled mass. **B.** The cell wall (*CW*) and plasmalemma (*PL*), of a hyphal tip surround the Golgi complex (*GC*), mitochondria (*M*), vacuoles (*V*), endoplasmic reticulum (*ER*), microtubules (*MT*), and nucleus (*N*) characteristic of the eukaryotic cell. The DNA in the nucleus and the ribosomes and proteins of the cytoplasm are not indicated, for clarity.

Table 3.1 shows a comparison of the regulation of gene expression between *Escherichia coli*, the paradigm of a bacterium, and the best known of the lower eukaryotes, a yeast. A review of basic biochemistry and molecular biology may be appropriate to understand this material.

PROBLEMS OF UNICELLULARITY

Free-living organisms face constant challenges in their environ-ment. The demands made on microorganisms fall into three general

Table 3.1. Transcription/Processing of mRNA in Typical Procaryotes and Eukaryotes

	Escherichia coli (Procaryote)	Yeast (Eukaryote)
Gene regulation	Operon-polycistronic mRNA	Single genes; developmental block of genes
Organization of genome	Single gene copies	Single gene copies plus repetitive DNA
Chromosomes	One	Many
Ploidy	Haploid	Haploid/diploid cycle
"Cytoplasmic" DNA	Plasmids	Mitochondria, kinetoplasts
Colinearity of gene/mRNA	Precise sequence	Introns within gene
Level of regulation	Mostly transcriptional	Often post-transcriptional regulation by protein turnover, etc.
Relation of transcription and translation	Coupled	Uncoupled
Processing of mRNA	Rare; some cleavages at double-stranded functional domains	Poly(A) at 3′-end Cap at 5′-end; splicing, sites in mRNA
Stability of mRNA	Unstable	Range of stability; some very stable mRNA
Translation of mRNA		
First amino acid	Formylated methionine	Methionine
Signal for start	Ribosome binding site preceding AUG	Binding to 5′-end, use of first AUG along mRNA
Initiation factors	Three	>Six
Ribosomes	30S + 50S = 70S Characteristic inhibitors	40S + 60S = 80S Characteristic inhibitors

categories: **nutrition**, related to the intermittent availability of food; **occupancy**, related to the need to remain in a certain habitat; **resistance** to damaging agents.

Life of Feast or Famine

Frequently in their existence, microorganisms run out of nutrients. Consider a bacterium like *E. coli* that lives in the large intestine of human beings. Every so often, some 20 times a day on average, the ileocecal valve opens and nutrient-rich contents squirt from the small intestine into the cecum. Here a large bacterial flora rapidly uses the nutrients, soon making the environment fallow. Clearly, the different bacteria normally present at this site have adapted to a life of feast and famine. On the one hand, they are able to utilize nutritional substrates rapidly when they become available, and to compete efficiently with their microbial neighbors. On the other hand, they must be able to adapt to the lack of nutrients during periods of starvation, and must also be poised for action whenever nutrients again become plentiful. Two themes emerge in the evolution of such cells, i.e., **efficiency** and **adaptability**. We will see how these two properties are manifested in bacteria.

Colonization and Occupancy

Not all problems in the microbial world are nutritional. In certain environments, survival depends on being able to remain in a given place and to avoid being swept away by liquid currents. Many species of bacteria ensure their occupancy by developing devices for sticking to surfaces. For instance, bacteria attach to the surface of our teeth by elaborating adhesive polysaccharides. When built up sufficiently, they form dental plaque. Likewise, in our intestine, there is an abundant microbial flora that adheres to the epithelial wall and which is different from the one that is living free in the lumen. Note that the "wall" flora faces different nutritional problems from the "lumen" flora and, consequently, that the selective pressure on these two populations is very different.

Resisting Damaging Agents

Microorganisms often encounter chemical or physical agents that threaten their existence. Not unexpectedly, they have evolved mechanisms that allow them to cope with these life-threatening challenges. Among the better studied are structural devices and physiological responses that protect them (up to a point) from such environmental insults as membrane-damaging chemicals, heat, or DNA-damaging radiation. Microorganisms also use genetic strategies to withstand antibiotics and can develop resistance to these substances in a number of ways (Chapter 5). Attempts by the physician to rid tissues of pathogenic organisms are counteracted by the mechanisms developed by the organisms to thwart these efforts.

SMALL SIZE PROMOTES METABOLIC EFFICIENCY

The microbial world is composed of small entities, generally below the range of what the unaided human eye can see. Consequently, large numbers can be packed in small volumes. Typical bacteria are approximately 1 μm in diameter and, if they were stacked neatly as tiny blocks, 10^{12} would occupy 1 cm^3 and weigh about 1 g. In suspension, the turbidity contributed by such small particles is so minimal that a clear fluid-like urine becomes visibly cloudy only when bacteria exceed about 1–10 million/ml. It will not surprise you that each of us is currently carrying a load of some 10–100 trillion bacteria in our large intestine, surpassing the number of our own eukaryotic cells.

Being small allows high metabolic rates because the surface to volume ratio increases as the size of cells decreases. Ultimately, biochemical reactions are limited by diffusion, and the smaller the cells, the less limiting it is. Consequently, bacteria are in intimate contact with external nutrients and are capable of metabolic rates orders of magnitude higher than those of eukaryotic cells. They can grow extremely fast and some double once every 15 minutes under optimal conditions. One measure of the rapidity of their metabolic flux is that small metabolites (amino acids, sugars, and nucleotides—the building blocks of macromolecules) constitute about 1% of their total dry weight. Some microbial eukaryotes, such as yeasts and other fungi, have comparable efficiency.

The amazing speed with which these small cells convert nutrients into energy and biosynthetic building blocks requires the coordination of metabolic activities. This subject is reviewed below; first for bacteria, then for yeast cells. Features of cell structure and macromolecular synthesis help us understand how individual species of bacteria maximize their chance for survival and suggest how we may intervene therapeutically against pathogenic organisms and anticipate their defenses.

BACTERIA HAVE COMPLEX ENVELOPES AND APPENDAGES

Bacteria are surrounded by a complex set of envelopes and appendages that differ in composition in individual species. Some of these structures are useful in certain environments only and are dispensable under laboratory conditions. These surface components often determine whether an organism can survive in a particular environment and cause disease.

Like all cells, bacteria have an indispensable structure, the cytoplasmic membrane. Most bacteria also form elaborate structures outside the membrane, namely a cell wall and some, an "outer membrane," flagella, pili, and a capsule. These structures can amount to 10–20% of the dry weight of the cell (as in other organisms, the "wet weight" is about ⅔ water). The reason for the extra layers outside the cell membrane becomes clear if one considers the stresses that bacteria must face in natural surroundings. For example, intestinal bacteria like *E. coli* are exposed to bile salts that would dissolve an unprotected cell membrane. Envelope layers and appendages are used by bacteria to adhere to surfaces and also for protection from phagocytes and other defense mechanisms. Virulence is often determined by the presence or absence of these cell-bound constituents.

The surface components of bacteria are what the host senses first during colonization. Consequently, many of the properties of the surface components are relevant both to the establishment of infection and to the response of the host to the organisms. The strongest antibody response to bacterial antigens is usually directed toward surface antigens.

PROTECTION OF THE CYTOPLASMIC MEMBRANE

Bacteria have three principal ways to protect their cytoplasmic membrane from environmental stresses, such as low osmotic pressure or the presence of detergents. These solutions are represented by the **Gram positives**, **Gram negatives**, **acid-fast** (e.g., *Mycobacteria*), and others (e.g., spirochetes). Figure 3.2 illustrates the first two.

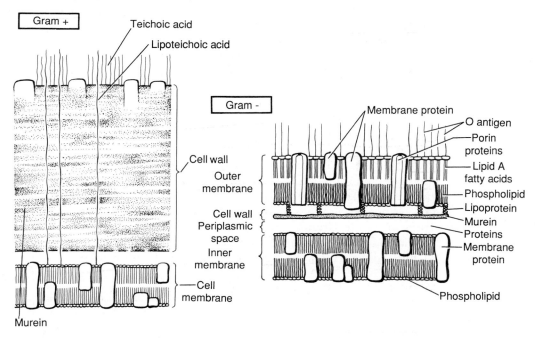

Figure 3.2.   The envelope structure a Gram positive (*left*) and a Gram negative (*right*). Capsules and appendages are not shown, nor are surface proteins like the M protein of streptococci indicated. Note the 20-fold greater amount of peptidoglycan in the Gram positive. The outer membrane of the Gram-negative envelopes shows O antigen polysaccharide molecules covering the outer layer.

The Gram's stain (named after an early Danish microbiologist) divides most bacteria into two groups, nearly equal in number and importance. This staining procedure is central in microbiology and must be learned by every medical student in due course. In brief, it depends on the ability of certain bacteria (the Gram positives) to retain a complex of a purple dye and iodine when challenged with a brief alcohol wash (Table 3.2). Gram negatives do not retain the dye and can later be counterstained with a dye of a different color, usually red. This distinction turns out to be correlated with fundamental differences in the cell envelope of these two classes of bacteria.

Gram-positive Solution

Gram-positive bacteria protect their membrane with a thick **cell wall**. The major constituent of the wall is a complex polymer of sugars and amino acids called **murein** or **peptidoglycan** (Fig. 3.3). Murein is the critical component in maintaining the shape and rigidity of both Gram positives and Gram negatives, but plays a larger role in protecting the cell membrane of Gram positives. It is a polymer unique to bacteria. How does it contribute to the defense of cell integrity? Murein is composed of glycan (sugar) chains that are cross-linked to one another via peptides. The overall structure is similar in all cases, but differs somewhat in chemical details (see, for example, Fig. 3.4). This polymeric fabric is wrapped around the length and width of the bacterium to form a sac of the size and shape of the organism. Depending on the shape of the murein sac, bacteria may have the appearance of **bacilli** (rods), **cocci** (spheres), or **spirilla** (helices). The rigid murein corset allows bacteria to survive in media of lesser osmotic pressure than that of their cytoplasm. In the absence of a rigid corset-like structure to push against, the membrane bursts and the cells lyse. This can be demonstrated experimentally by removing the murein with **lysozyme**, a hydrolytic enzyme present in many human and animal tissues. Treatment with lysozyme causes bacteria to lyse in a low osmotic pressure environment. If lysozyme-treated bacteria are kept in an iso-osmotic medium, they do not lyse but become spherical. Such structures are called **spheroplasts**.

The cell wall of Gram positives is made up of many layers of the sac-like murein, so thick that it impedes the passage of hydrophobic compounds. This is because the sugars and charged amino acids make murein highly polar and surround the cells with a dense hydrophilic layer. Thus, many Gram positives can withstand certain noxious hydrophobic compounds, including the bile salts in the intestine. The feature that makes bacteria Gram positive, the ability to retain the dye-iodine complex, also seems to depend on the characteristic murein structure of the Gram-positive wall.

Gram-positive walls contain other unique polymers, for example, **teichoic acids**, which are chains of ribitol or glycerol linked by phos-

Table 3.2. Gram Stain Procedure	
Gram Stain	Acid-fast Stain
1. Stain with crystal violet (purple)	1. Stain with hot carbol-fuchsin (red)
2. Modify with potassium iodide	
3. Decolorize with alcohol; only Gram positives remain purple	2. Decolorize with acid alcohol; only acid-fast remain red
4. Counterstain with safranin: Gram negatives become pink; Gram positives remain purple	3. Counterstain with methylene blue: acid-fast remain red; others become blue

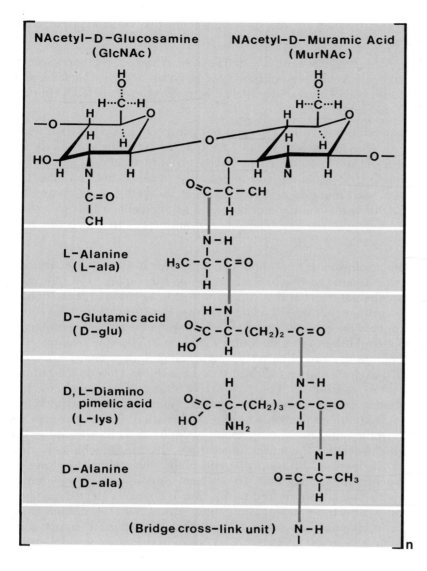

Figure 3.3. Structure of murein. The basic repeating unit of alternating *NAcetyl glucosamine (GlcNac)* and substituted muramic acid (N-acetyl glucosamine connected to an O-lactyl ether and the pentapeptide).

phodiester bonds (Fig. 3.5). Teichoic acids will be discussed in connection with individual groups of bacteria because at least some of them appear to play a role in pathogenesis.

Gram-negative Solution

Gram negatives have adopted a radically different solution to the problem of protection of the cytoplasmic membrane. They make a completely different structure, an **outer membrane**, which is built up outside the murein cell wall (Fig. 3.2). The outer membrane is chemically distinct from the usual biological membranes and has built into it the ability to resist damaging chemicals. It is a bilayered structure, but its outer leaflet contains a unique component in addition to phospholipids. This is a **bacterial lipopolysaccharide or LPS**, a complex molecule not found elsewhere in nature.

Bacterial Lipopolysaccharide

LPS consist of three portions (Fig. 3.6):

- One is a lipid called **lipid A**, and anchors LPS in the outer leaflet of the membrane. Lipid A is an unusual glycolipid composed of disac-

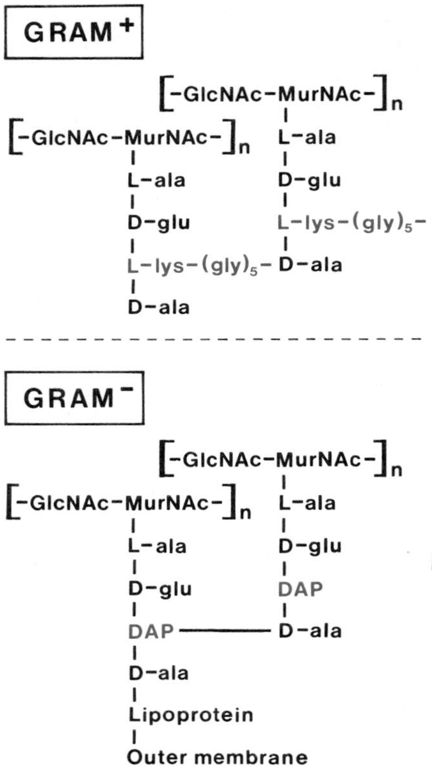

GRAM⁺

GRAM⁻

Figure 3.4. Typical structure of murein in Gram-positive and Gram-negative bacteria. In the Gram positives, peptide chains are cross-linked through a peptide bond between the free amino group of lysine and the terminal carboxyl group of a *D-ala* residue. In the Gram negatives, the cross-link is between diaminopimelic acid (*DAP*) and *D-ala*. Other *D-ala* resides are linked to a lipoprotein that is attached to the outer membrane.

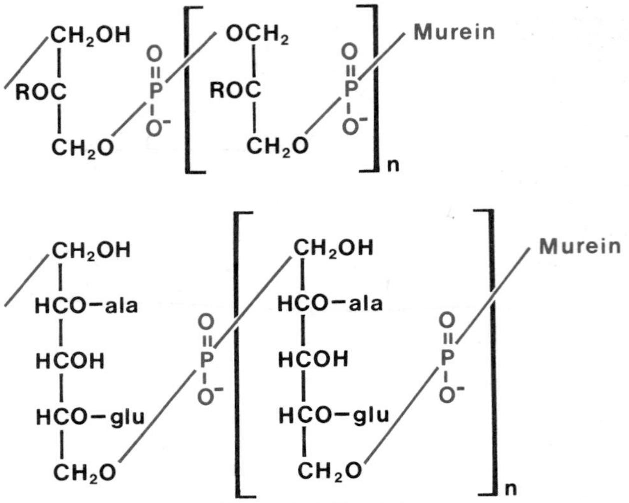

Figure 3.5. Teichoic acid structure. The repeating unit of ribitol and glycerol teichoic acids are shown. The chains in Gram-positive organisms vary in length and amounts.

charides to which are attached short-chain fatty acids and phosphate groups.

- The second component is a short series of sugars, the core, whose structure is relatively constant among Gram-negative bacteria and includes two characteristic sugars, **keto-deoxyoctanate** (*KDO* in Fig. 3.6) and a heptose.

- The third component is a long carbohydrate chain, up to 40 sugars in length, the **O antigen** (Fig. 3.6). The hydrophilic carbohydrate chains of the O antigen cover the bacterial surface and exclude hydrophobic compounds. The importance of the O antigen chains is shown with mutants deficient in their biosynthesis. Mutants that make either no O antigen or merely shortened chains become sensitive to compounds like bile salts and antibiotics to which the wild type is resistant.

Thus, exclusion of hydrophobic compounds in Gram-negative bacteria, as in Gram-positive bacteria, relies on surrounding the cells with hydrophilic polysaccharides, different in structure and organization in the two groups. Because of its lipid nature, the outer membrane could be expected to exclude hydrophilic compounds as well. Seemingly nothing could then cross the outer membrane. Thus, by dealing with the problem of protection of the cytoplasmic membrane, the Gram-negative bacteria appear to have created a new one. How do they transport their nutrients? Are the active transport devices of the cytoplasmic membrane copied in the outer membrane? This would not only be wasteful but probably incompatible with the protective role assigned to the outer membrane. Once again, bacteria have found an interesting solution: the outer membrane has special channels that permit the passive diffusion of hydrophilic compounds like sugars, amino acids, and certain ions. These channels consist of protein molecules with holes, aptly called porins. Porin channels are narrow, just right to permit the entry of compounds up to 600–700 daltons (Fig. 3.2). The channels are small enough that hydrophobic compounds would come in contact with the polar "wall" of the channel and thereby be excluded.

Certain hydrophilic compounds that are sometimes necessary for survival are larger than the exclusion limit of porins. These larger molecules include vitamin B_{12}, sugars larger than trisaccharides, and iron

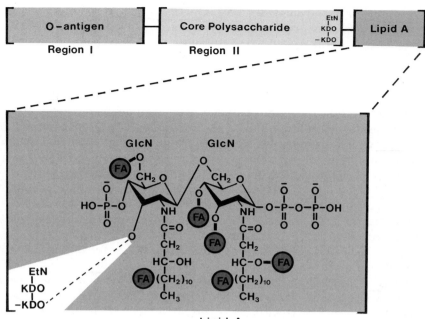

Figure 3.6.   The structure of lipopolysaccharide. In a typical *Salmonella*, *region I* shows a characteristic series of sugars in the polysaccharide. *Region II* also shows some variation, but always ends with ketodeoxyoctanate (*KDO*), L-arabinose, two substituted amino-glucose residues, and an ethanolamine (*EtN*) residue. The molecules of fatty acid (*FA*) attached to the sugars vary with the organism, but are always a major source of the hydrophobicity of the molecule.

in the form of chelates. Such compounds cross the outer membrane by separate, specific permeation mechanisms that utilize proteins especially designed to translocate each of these compounds. Thus, the outer membrane allows the passage of small hydrophilic compounds, excludes hydrophobic compounds, large or small, and allows the entry of some larger hydrophilic molecules by especially dedicated mechanisms.

The dual membrane system of Gram-negative bacteria creates a compartment called the **periplasmic space** or **periplasm** on the outside of the cytoplasmic or inner membrane. This compartment contains the murein layer and a gel-like solution of components that facilitate nutrition. These include degradative enzymes (phosphatases, nucleases, proteases, etc.) that break down large and impermeable molecules to "digestible" size. In addition, the periplasm contains so-called **binding proteins** that help soak up sugars and amino acids from the medium. It also contains enzymes that inactivate antibiotics such penicillins and cephalosporins, the β-lactamases. The Gram-positive bacteria do not have a defined periplasmic compartment and secrete similar enzymes into the medium.

The outer membrane barrier constitutes both an advantage and a disadvantage to Gram-negative bacteria. For example, some bacteriophages use proteins in the outer membrane as attachment sites for infecting their host bacteria. On the other hand, the outer membrane confers considerable resistance to many antibiotics. Broadly speaking, Gram-negative bacteria are more resistant to many antibiotics, especially penicillin.

The peculiarly Gram-negative solution to the problems of protecting the cytoplasmic membrane has unexpected biological consequences. The lipopolysaccharide of the outer membrane is highly reactive in the host. The lipid A component has a large number of biological activities. It elicits fever and activates a series of immunological and biochemical events that lead to the mobilization of host defense mechanisms. In large doses, this compound, also known as **endotoxin**, can cause shock and even death (see Chapter 7 for details). The O antigen portion, as the name denotes, is highly antigenic. O antigens come in many varieties, each defining a species or a subspecies of Gram-negative bacteria.

Acid-fast Solution

A few bacterial types, notably, the tubercle bacillus, have developed yet another solution to the problems of environmental challenge to the cytoplasmic membrane. Their cell walls contain large amounts of waxes, which are complex long-chain hydrocarbons with sugars and other modifying groups. Having such a protective cover, these organisms are impervious to many harsh chemicals, including acids. If a dye is introduced into these cells, for instance, by brief heating, it cannot be removed by dilute hydrochloric acid, as would be the case in all other bacteria. These organisms are, therefore, called acid-fast or acid-resistant (Table 3.2).

The waxy coat is interlaced with murein, polysaccharides, and lipids. It enables the organisms to resist the action of many noxious chemicals as well as killing by white blood cells. All this is at a cost; these organisms grow very slowly, possibly because the rate of uptake of nutrients is limited by their waxy covering. Some, like the human tubercle bacillus, divide once every 24 hours.

MUREIN AND ANTIBIOTICS THAT INHIBIT ITS SYNTHESIS

The uniqueness of bacterial murein makes it a natural target for antibiotics. Drugs that block its formation lead to lysis and death of susceptible bacteria. It is not surprising, therefore, that some of the clinically most effective antibiotics, the **penicillins** and the **cephalosporins**, act by inhibiting murein synthesis. They are among the most unequivocally bactericidal antibiotics and among those least toxic to humans. The critical steps in their mode of action are presented in Figures 3.7 and 3.8.

Murein, like many other polysaccharides, is synthesized from nucleotide-bound building blocks. These monomeric units are composed of uridine diphosphate plus either NAcetyl-glucosamine (GlcNAc) or NAcetyl-muramic acid (an unusual sugar, the 3-O-D lactic acid derivative of G1cNAc). The latter has a peptide chain attached to it (Fig. 3.3). The monomeric units are made in the cytoplasm and transferred from uridine-diphosphate to a **lipid carrier** in the membrane (Fig. 3.7). Disaccharides are then linked to a growing chain of murein. This step is inhibited by the antibiotic **vancomycin**. Regeneration of the lipid carrier is inhibited by another antibiotic, **bacitracin**.

The final reaction in murein synthesis is transpeptidation. The long chains of disaccharides are cross-linked to make a two-dimensional network (Fig. 3.8). The cross-linking reaction consists of forming a peptide bond between D-alanine (D-ala) on one chain and the free N-end of a lysine or a diaminopimelic acid (DAP) on the other chain. The linkage is formed with the **subterminal** D-ala, and the **terminal** D-ala is cleaved away in the process. Thus, the reaction is the exchange of one peptide bond (that between the two D-alanines) with another—a true transpeptidation. **Cycloserine** is an antibiotic that inhibits the ligation of the two D-ala residues and also inhibits the racemase that forms D-ala from L-ala, the common constituent of proteins. The amino acids that make up the peptides vary in different organisms but the D-ala cross-bridge to either lysine or to DAP acid is universal. This reaction is inhibited by most penicillins and cephalosporins.

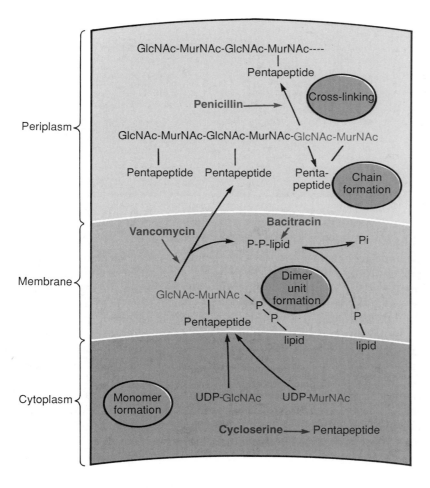

Figure 3.7.   Biosynthesis of murein, indicating the site of action of a number of antibiotics. The successive steps occurring in the cytoplasm, at the cytoplasmic membrane, and outside the membrane (in the periplasm of Gram negatives; in the murein layer of Gram positives) are indicated, along with the points of attack of cycloserine, bacitracin, vancomycin, and penicillin.

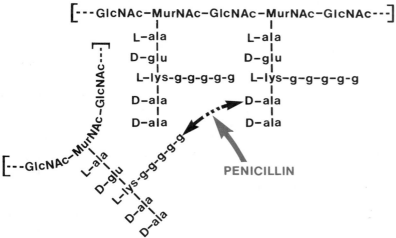

Figure 3.8.   Formation of cross-links in murein, and the point of penicillin action in detail. In this case of a typical Gram-positive murein structure, a cross-link forms between the last glycine residue (*g*) in one chain and the penultimate D-alanine in another chain as indicated by the *double-headed arrow*. At that point, penicillin intervenes.

The reason why penicillin inhibits transpeptidation may lie in its stereochemical similarity with the D-ala-D-ala dimer (Figs. 3.8 and 3.9). In the presence of the drug, the transpeptidase becomes confused; instead of synthesizing an intermediate D-ala-enzyme complex, it makes a lethal penicilloyl-enzyme complex.

Antibiotics that inhibit murein synthesis almost invariably kill bacteria by lysing them. In contrast with lysozyme, these drugs do not affect murein itself, only its synthesis. How then do they cause lysis? Cells treated with these drugs continue to synthesize their cytoplasmic

Figure 3.9. The resemblance of part of the penicillin structure to the backbone of *D-ala-D-ala* is indicated, with the *arrows* at the bonds broken during covalent attachment to the enzyme involved.

Penicillin   D-ala-D-ala

components and increase in mass. The enlarged cytoplasm is not restrained by a properly cross-linked murein sac, with the result that the cell contents extrude and the cells lyse. Cells that are not growing are not lysed by penicillin—they are not increasing in mass. Consider: would it be advisable to administer an antibiotic that inhibits cell growth at the same time that the patient is receiving penicillin?

Penicillins and cephalosporins have an unusual property; they bind covalently to certain proteins of the cytoplasmic membrane, the so-called **penicillin-binding proteins** (PBPs). These drugs are especially reactive because they have a highly strained β-lactam ring that can be readily hydrolyzed. Individual species of bacteria have a characteristic set of PBPs, each with a different affinity for a given penicillin. These proteins are thought to be involved in the cross-linking of murein. At least three types of PBPs have been distinguished; one seems to be especially involved in the generalized cross-linking that occurs at many points in the periphery of the cell. Another may participate in the special cross-linking at the junction (septum) between separating daughter cells. The third appears to function at points where the nascent murein "turns corners" to determine cell shape. The functional distinction among PBPs has been facilitated by a penicillin called **mecillinam** that binds to only one of these proteins (Fig. 3.10). Mecillinam blocks only part of murein cross-linking, and leads to the release of constraints on the cell shape of *E. coli*. This results in the formation of large, unstable spherical cells that slowly lyse. In mutants resistant to mecillinam, this particular PBP is modified and no longer binds β-lactam antibiotics. These mutants remain susceptible to penicillins that bind to other PBPs.

This simple concept, that cells lyse by outgrowing their coats, encounters some difficulties. First, in cultures treated with penicillin, there is usually a small number of "persisters," bacteria that stop growing but do not lyse. Second, for some types of bacteria, penicillin is bacteriostatic, not bactericidal. These bacteria are called "tolerant." How do we explain "persisters" or "tolerant" bacteria? It appears that tolerant organisms are deficient in an **autolysin**, a bacterial enzyme that cleaves murein. Bacteria use such an enzyme to break open some bonds of murein at the septum, which permits the separation of daughter cells during cell division. Normally, the activity of autolysin is tightly controlled. Treatment with penicillin may arouse it to more unrestrained action. The role of autolysin in penicillin-induced lysis is well illustrated with pneumococci, which are extraordinarily susceptible to lysis. Autolysin-defective mutants are found among penicillin-resistant derivatives; these mutants are not lysed even by strong

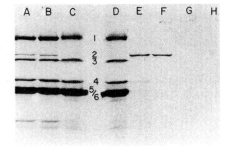

Figure 3.10. Binding of penicillin to membrane proteins (*PBPs*) of wild-type and mecillinam-resistant *E. coli*. Radioactive penicillin binds to a number of proteins. In the resistant mutant, the only protein to which mecillinam binds is missing. I4C-Labeled benzylpenicillin (*A-D*) or mecillinam (*E-H*) were bound to cell envelopes from a wild-type strain and one resistant to mecillinam. The inner membranes were solubilized in detergent and the radioactive proteins separated by gel electrophoresis and detected by autoradiography. Benzylpenicillin binds to six PBPs in wild-type cells (*A-B*) and five in the mutant (*C-D*); mecillinam binds only to one protein in the wild-type cells (*E-F*) and not at all in the mutant cells (*G-H*).

detergents. Thus, bacteria do not burst easily. Rather than a spontaneous explosion, lysis involves active steps of self-destruction.

There are exceptions to the universal use of murein to maintain bacterial cell integrity. The mycoplasmas have no murein and consequently are not rigid and have almost no defined shape. As expected, they are resistant to penicillin. Some, like an agent of pneumonia, *Mycoplasma pneumoniae*, contain sterols in their membrane, an unusual feature among procaryotes. It is puzzling how mycoplasmas cope well without a rigid cell wall. Although these organisms are quite delicate in culture, they are common in the human body and in the environment. There are other exceptions to the ubiquity of mureins, especially among a separate group of bacteria known as the *Archaebacteria*. Thus, there are unorthodox and, as yet, poorly understood means by which some bacteria safeguard their integrity.

CYTOPLASMIC MEMBRANE

The cytoplasmic membrane of bacteria is a busy place. It assumes functions that in eukaryotic cells are distributed among the plasma membrane and intracellular organelles. Most critical is its role in the uptake of substrates from the medium. Bacteria take up mainly small molecular weight compounds and only rarely macromolecules and phosphate esters. These compounds are usually hydrolyzed by enzymes in the periplasm or in the surrounding medium, and the resulting breakdown products, e.g., peptides, oligosaccharides, nucleosides, phosphate, etc. can then be transported across the cytoplasmic membrane.

The cytoplasmic membrane contains specific carrier proteins called **permeases** that facilitate the entry of most metabolites. In some cases, the carrier facilitates the equilibration of a compound inside and outside of the cell (Fig. 3.11). However, in most cases, carrier-mediated transport requires the expenditure of energy. This permits the internal concentration of certain substances to be as much as 10^5 times higher than that in the medium surrounding the cell.

Transport Across the Cytoplasmic Membrane

The three main versions of transport are illustrated in Figure 3.11.

1. Carrier-mediated diffusion. This takes place when a substance is carried across the membrane down a concentration gradient. An example of a compound that is transported this way is glycerol. This mechanism does not concentrate compounds in the inside of the cells relative to the outside environment. Uptake is driven by intracellular utilization of the compound. For instance, the concentration of free glycerol inside cells is lowered by its phosphorylation to glycerol-3-phosphate. More glycerol is then taken up to equilibrate with the outside concentration.

2. Phosphorylation-linked transport. This energy-dependent mechanism is used for the transport of certain sugars. Substances transported in this manner are chemically altered in the process, which is why it is also known as **group translocation**. The example of glucose is shown in Figure 3.11. The sugar binds to a specific carrier in the membrane (e.g., "enzyme 2"). The glucose-enzyme 2 complex interacts with "enzyme 3-phosphate" to yield glucose-6-phosphate, which can then be further metabolized (Fig. 3.11).

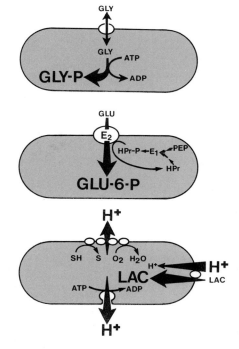

Figure 3.11. Mechanics of transport. Three types of transport in *E. coli* are shown: facilitated diffusion; group translocation; active transport with the lac permease.

3. **Active transport**. In active transport, energy is utilized to drive the accumulation of substrate. A substrate, for instance, the sugar lactose, is concentrated unchanged inside the cell, which makes the transport of additional molecules energetically unfavorable. To drive the transport of lactose, the cells use energy stored in an electrochemical gradient of protons, the **proton-motive force**. This gradient is generated by the extrusion of protons from the cell (Fig. 3.11), resulting from the oxidation of metabolic intermediates like NADH or by hydrolysis of adenosine triphosphate (ATP). Lactose is accumulated intracellularly by coupling its **energetically unfavorable** transport with the **energetically favorable** reentry of protons into the relatively alkaline cytoplasm of the cell. Thus, transport of this type take place via a symport, which requires the simultaneous uptake of molecules, H^+ and sugar.

Each type of transport system involves specific protein molecules. Some of these aid the process by modifying or concentrating substrates in the periplasmic space of Gram negatives. These **binding proteins** are specific for sugars, nucleotides, etc. The periplasmic space also contains nucleosidases, nucleases, peptidases, proteases, and other hydrolytic enzymes. The actual transport process is carried out by membrane-bound carriers called **permeases**, which are involved in the types of transport mentioned above. We do not have a physical picture of how permeases respond to the proton gradient, but we know that they assume different configurations on the inside and outside of the cytoplasmic membrane. Thus, permeases have a high affinity for substrate on the outside and a low affinity on the inside. However they work, they are essential for transport. For example, in the much studied lactose system, cells that lack a functional permease remain impervious to the sugar even when soaked in concentrations approaching syrup!

These various mechanisms of transport are used to different extents by different bacteria. In general, few substrates equilibrate across membranes without the expenditure of energy. Among the energy-requiring mechanisms, "group translocations" are used to a different extent; *E. coli*, for instance, transports a wide variety of sugars in this way, whereas strictly aerobic bacteria use it little. All in all, active transport dominates the repertoire of transport mechanisms in bacteria, especially when nutrients must be concentrated from the medium to support cell growth.

Uptake of Iron

The uptake of iron deserves special mention. Iron is not available in free form in the blood and many tissues because it is bound by proteins like transferrin or ceruloplasmin, yet is essential for the growth of bacteria. Many bacteria that inhabit the human body have developed ingenious mechanisms to obtain the amounts of this element they need for growth. They excrete chelating compounds known as **siderophores** that bind iron with great avidity. Each organism can take up its own particular form of complexed iron; individual complexes are unique enough to be less digestible for other organisms. However, in response to the competition for iron, many bacteria have multiple siderophores and uptake systems, thus trying to gain an edge on the other organisms in the same environment; some can efficiently extract iron from transferrin, an advantage at our own expense.

Other Functions of the Bacterial Membrane

The cytoplasmic membrane of bacteria is also the site where cytochromes are located and oxidative metabolism is carried out. Thus, it performs the role of the mitochondria of eukaryotic cells. Another function of the bacterial membrane is to act like a primitive mitotic apparatus. It is thought that bacterial DNA is attached to the cell membrane, with each newly replicated molecule adhering to the two sides of the septum made during cell division. When the bacterium divides, each half receives one of the daughter chromosomes.

The membrane is also the location of nascent proteins destined either for secretion or for incorporation in the membrane itself. Some bacteria secrete as much as 10% of all of the proteins they make, including toxins and other virulence factors. The nascent peptide chains, containing the hydrophobic "signal sequences" at the N-termini, are translocated from ribosomes across the cytoplasmic membrane by an energy-requiring mechanism. Proteins that are to be secreted are released into the environment while those that become part of the membrane structure are retained within it. Note that in the Gram-negative bacteria there is an added problem, that of transporting proteins to the outer membrane. It is not known exactly how this takes place.

Some bacteria have also an exceptional ability to take up huge DNA molecules. The phenomenon was first demonstrated by genetic transformation of pneumococci and occurs among other bacterial species. Some, like *E. coli*, must be coaxed to take up DNA by the addition of calcium ions. Very little is known about the mechanism of uptake of DNA by bacteria but it appears that, like active transport, it depends on the proton-motive force.

In spite of its versatility and range of activities, the cytoplasmic membrane of bacteria is rarely the site of action of useful antibiotics (see Chapter 3). May this be due to its overall similarity in structure to the membranes of eukaryotic cells?

DNA AND CHROMOSOME MECHANICS

The genome of bacteria consists of a single circular chromosome of double-stranded DNA. For all of its importance, it accounts for only some 2% of the cellular dry weight. The chromosome of *E. coli* has a molecular weight of about 3×10^9 daltons, or about 5 million base pairs. This codes for about 2–3000 genes, over half of which have been identified. The total description of the *E. coli* genome (its DNA sequence) seems only a few years away, making this the genetically best known of all living organisms.

Bacteria must solve a demanding topological problem in organizing their DNA, since it is a long and thin molecule. If stretched out, it would be about 1000 times the length of the cell. If a bacterium were to be magnified to the size of a human being, its DNA would be about a mile long. The DNA is coiled in a central irregular structure called the nucleoid. Its physical state is unknown and somewhat mysterious, because in the test tube, a solution 100 times more dilute is a gel! About all that is known about the physical state of the DNA is that it is twisted into **supercoils** (analogous to twisted telephone coils) and that this condition is indispensable for its organization, its replication, and the transcription of a number of genes. Supercoiling is thought to be achieved by the balance of the action of two topoisomerases. One of these, **DNA gyrase**, introduces supercoils into circular DNA, an action counteracted by a second enzyme, **topoisomerase I**, which relaxes the supercoils by making single-strand nicks.

Like all macromolecular synthesis, DNA replication has three stages: initiation, elongation, and termination. Replication takes place bidirectionally, that is, DNA synthesis starts at a precise place on the chromosome, the **replicative origin**, and proceeds away from it in both directions. The two moving polymerase complexes meet halfway around the chromosome. To replicate, the DNA helix in *E. coli* must unwind and rotate at some 6000 rpm. One wonders how this can take place without entanglement of the tightly coiled nucleoid.

The timing of chromosome replication is a highly regulated process and is coupled to growth and cell division. At a given temperature, the rate of DNA polymerase movement is independent of the growth rate of the cells. In *E. coli*, DNA replication takes 40 minutes, whether the cells are growing slowly or fast. In slowly growing cells, e.g., those dividing once every 100 minutes, one round of synthesis occurs in each division cycle, and no DNA is synthesized during the remaining 60 minutes. In very fast-growing cells (dividing, for example, every 20 minutes), initiation of rounds of replication is adapted to produce new chromosomes as often as the cell divides (Fig. 3.12). Inasmuch as each chromosome requires 40 minutes to be synthesized, replication will initiate again on a strand, long before its own replication has completed. Thus, chromosome replication in bacteria is regulated by how often the process gets started, i.e., by the frequency of initiation of DNA synthesis.

Figure 3.12.   Replication of DNA in slow and fast-growing *E. coli*. Replication begins at a specific site, the origin, and proceeds in both directions toward a terminus. The process takes about 40 minutes at 37°C. In a culture doubling every 20 minutes, this requires that the process initiate every 20 minutes, that is, before the previous round of replication has terminated. In such cultures the DNA is undergoing multifork replication.

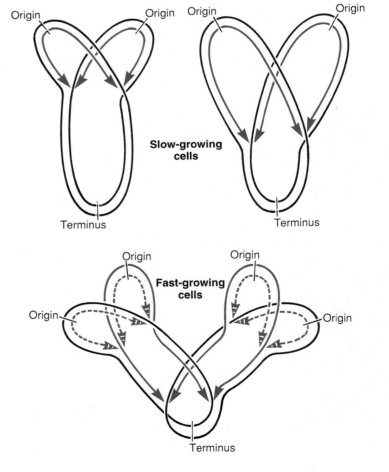

How Do Antibiotics Inhibit DNA Metabolism?

Most inhibitors of DNA replication bind to DNA and are too toxic for clinical use. An interesting exception is **metronidazole**, a drug that is itself inert, but that can be selectively modified to an active form by some bacteria. This compound contains a nitro group that must be **partially** reduced to render the molecule active. Full reduction to the amino state makes the molecule inactive again. Partial reduction is achieved by anaerobic bacteria but only rarely by the cells of the human body or by aerobic bacteria.

Partially reduced metronidazole is incorporated into the DNA of the bacteria. This is an example of lethal synthesis because the metronidazole-containing DNA molecules are unstable. It follows that metronidazole and related drugs are particularly useful against anaerobic bacteria and against amoebas, which also grow anaerobically. These drugs, however, are not ideal. To a small extent, the partial reduction to active agents occurs in normal tissue, leading to possible mutagenesis and, perhaps, to carcinogenesis as well.

Other DNA inhibitors act selectively by binding to specific enzymes. **Nalidixic acid**, for example, inhibits DNA gyrase and is bactericidal. Whether it binds to the counterpart human enzyme in vivo is not known, but it is relatively nontoxic. A whole new class of antibacterial compounds, called the **quinolones**, that interfere with DNA gyrase, are being actively developed by pharmaceutical companies.

GENE EXPRESSION: UNIQUENESS OF PROCARYOTIC RNA POLYMERASE AND RIBOSOMES

The bacterial cytoplasm is composed largely of proteins (about 40% of the dry weight, with about one million molecules per cell) and RNA (up to 35% of the dry weight in rapidly growing cells). Bacterial ribosomes have smaller subunits (30S and 50S vs. 40S and 60S) and smaller RNA molecules than do their eukaryotic counterparts. Bacterial ribosomal RNAs have sedimentation values of 16S and 23S and, combined with 21 and 35 different proteins, respectively, make up the ribosomal subunits. These join together in the 70S ribosomes that move along messenger RNA (mRNA) molecules to synthesize proteins.

The large requirement for proteins makes their synthesis the principal biosynthetic activity of rapidly growing bacteria. A large proportion of a bacterium's energy and metabolic building blocks is devoted to the assembly of the protein-synthesizing machinery, including ribosomes and RNA polymerase. Over a considerable range of growth rates, RNA is made at a rate proportional to the number of RNA polymerase molecules engaged in the process of transcription. Likewise, the rate of protein synthesis is proportional to the cellular concentration of ribosomes. This suggests that the rate of polymerization of single chains of RNA or protein remains constant whether cells are growing rapidly or slowly. Remember that this is also true for DNA replication (see above). Thus, the synthesis of the principal macromolecules of bacteria is regulated by the frequency with which each chain is initiated and not by altering their rate of manufacture of each molecule (the speed of chain elongation).

Cells growing rapidly increase the frequency of initiation of RNA or protein synthesis by an analogous mechanism to that used to generate chromosomes more often than once every 40 minutes. As one RNA polymerase molecule moves away from the start site on the DNA, another can become engaged, so that a single gene can be concurrently transcribed into many RNA molecules. Likewise, a single mRNA can be translated by many ribosomes simultaneously, creating a structure called a polyribosome or polysome.

Antibiotics That Inhibit Transcription and Translation

Antibiotics may act selectively at initiation or elongation of macromolecular synthesis. For example, **rifampin**, a powerful inhibitor of bacterial transcription, acts at the initiation step. How does it recognize this step? This drug binds strongly to molecules of RNA polymerase that are floating freely in the cytoplasm, but much less well to polymerase molecules that are bound to DNA. As a result, a polymerase that is bound to DNA and has initiated RNA synthesis will not be inactivated by rifampin until it completes its round of RNA synthesis and is released from the DNA. Rifampin is clinically useful, particularly in the treatment of tuberculosis and leprosy, in part because it is relatively nontoxic. The reason is that mammalian RNA polymerases do not bind rifampin.

The largest class of clinically useful antibiotics, apart from the β-lactams, consists of those that inhibit protein synthesis. Some of them work by binding to ribosomes, either to the large subunit or to the small subunit (Table 3.3). The reason that bacteria are selectively

Table 3.3. Antibiotics—Mechanisms of Action of Commonly Used Antimicrobial Agents

β-lactams—Murein synthesis inhibitors	
Penicillins and cephalosporins	Interfere with cell wall biosynthesis through interaction with penicillin-binding proteins; autolysis
Polyenes—Inhibitors of membrane function	
Amphotericin B	Bind to sterols in eukaryotic cell membranes, leading to membrane leakiness and, at high levels, lysis
Sulfonamides—Folate antagonists	
Sulfanilamide	Competitive inhibitor of dehydropteroate synthesis; blocks synthesis of tetrahydrofolate, and cell-linked metabolic pathways
Aminoglycosides—Protein-synthesis inhibitors	
Streptomycin	Bind to 30S subunit of bacterial ribosome; cause
Kanamycin	translational misreading and inhibit elongation of pro-
Neomycin	tein chain; kill by blocking initiation of protein synthesis
Gentamicin	
Amikacin	
Tobramycin	
Other protein-synthesis inhibitors	
Chloramphenicol	Bind to ribosome 50S subunit; inhibit protein synthesis
Erythromycin	at chain elongation step
Lincomycin	
Fusidic acid	Blocks protein synthesis by interaction with soluble elongation factor G (the translocation factor)
RNA synthesis inhibitors	
Rifampin	Binds to bacterial RNA polymerase and blocks transcription (synthesis of RNA) at initiation step
DNA synthesis inhibitors	
Nitrofurans	Partially reduced nitro groups give additional products
Metronidazole	on DNA that lead to cidal strand breakage
Nalidixic acid	Interfere with DNA replication by inhibiting the action of
Novobiocin	DNA gyrase
Ciprofloxacin and other quinolones	
Mercury salts, organomercurials	Inhibit protein function by interaction with sulfhydryl groups

targeted is that the ribosome of procaryotes is different from that of eukaryotes. Among these ribosomally active antibiotics are **chloramphenicol**, **lincomycin**, and **erythromycin**, which block the formation of peptide bonds by binding at or near the aminoacyl tRNA binding site on the large ribosomal subunit. After some time, the previously synthesized peptidyl tRNA is released and hydrolyzed. The ribosomal subunits are then released from the mRNA and are free to rejoin other mRNA molecules to start another abortive cycle. This leads to a truncated version of the ribosome cycle (Fig. 3.13). As a result, when these antibiotics are withdrawn, many free ribosomes are present and ready to resume normal protein synthesis. This explains why the action of these drugs is reversible and why these antibiotics are bacteriostatic and not bactericidal. It should be pointed out that this does not necessarily diminish their usefulness. When bacteria are kept in check by bacteriostatic drugs, they are usually cleared from tissues by the body defense mechanisms.

One important group of protein synthesis inhibitors, the **aminoglycosides**, is bactericidal. How they kill bacteria has not yet been satisfactorily explained, but we have some hints. Aminoglycosides, like **streptomycin**, **kanamycin**, and **neomycin**, are taken up by bacteria and bind to the smaller 30S ribosomal subunit. This is their critical site of action, as demonstrated by the finding that a single amino acid change in a mutated 30S ribosomal protein leads to resistance to these drugs. Binding of aminoglycosides has many effects on ribosome function; for instance, the interaction of the 30S and 50S subunits becomes tighter, and the elongation of peptide chains is inhibited. Typical of the action of this group of antibiotics is the accumulation of free ribosomes as aberrant 70S particles and not as 30S and 50S subunits. This coincides with cell death. Accumulating 70S ribosomes result from abortive attempts to initiate protein synthesis and do not function appreciably in protein synthesis. However, they bind to mRNA and, thus, block the function of ribosomes that are still unaffected by the drug. The inhibition of protein synthesis by aminoglycosides is apparently irreversible because, once the drug is taken up, it cannot be removed from the cell. Thus, cells treated with these drugs cannot recover, which is one possible way to explain why the aminoglycosides are bactericidal.

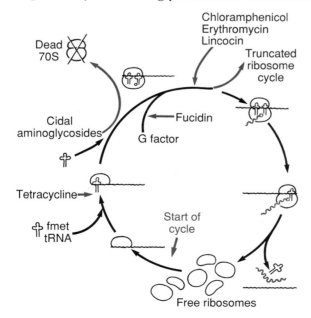

Figure 3.13. Antibiotic blockage of the ribosome cycle. The normal cycle of 30S and 50S subunits in and out of polysomes is recalled, with the assembly of a 70S initiation complex, elongation of the polypeptide chain as the ribosome moves across the mRNA, and release of all components on completion of the polypeptide. Points of blockage by antibiotics are shown. Tetracycline inhibits aminoacyl tRNA binding; cidal aminoglycosides provoke formation of "dead" aberrant initiation complexes; fucidin blocks translocation by elongation factor G; and others block elongation, leading to premature dissociation of the active complex.

CAPSULES, FLAGELLA, AND PILI: HOW BACTERIA COPE IN CERTAIN ENVIRONMENTS

The morphological variety of bacteria is not limited to walls and membranes. Some bacteria, but by no means all, have other exterior structures such as capsules, flagella, and pili. These components are dispensable, that is, they are important for survival under certain circumstances but not under others. The **capsule** is a slimy outer coating made by certain bacteria. Under laboratory conditions, the capsule is not needed and the organisms may grow well without it. Capsules usually consist of high molecular weight polysaccharides that make the bacteria very slippery and difficult for white blood cells to phagocytize. As you will see, pneumococci, meningococci, and other bacteria that are likely to encounter phagocytes during their infective cycle are indeed encapsulated. In the laboratory, colonies of encapsulated bacteria on agar plates are viscous and shiny. Colonies of nonencapsulated organisms are usually smaller and appear dull.

Protruding through the surface layers of many bacteria are two kinds of filaments, **flagella**, and **pili** (also called **fimbriae**) (Fig. 3.14). Flagella are long, helical filaments that endow bacteria with motility. Many successful pathogens are motile, which probably aids their spread in the environment and possibly in the body of the host. Depending on the species, a single bacterial cell may have one flagellum or many flagella (Fig. 3.15). In some, the flagella are located at the ends of the cells (polar) and, in others, they are at random points around the periphery (peritrichous, or "hairy all over"). This distinction is useful in taxonomy and in diagnostic microbiology. Pili are involved in the attachment of bacteria to cells and to other surfaces (see below).

Bacterial Chemotaxis

The movement caused by flagella is used by bacteria for chemotaxis, i.e., movement toward substances that attract and away from those that repel. Considerable research has shown that bacterial chemotaxis is based on the following sophisticated mechanism: flagella spin around from their point of attachment at the cell surface. Each flagellum has a counterclockwise helical pitch and, when there are several on a bacterium, they array themselves in coherent bundles as long as they all rotate counterclockwise. When the flagella are arranged in these bundles, they beat in the same sense and the bacteria swim in a straight line (Fig. 3.16). However, when flagella rotate clockwise, they get in

Figure 3.14. *Escherichia coli* mating. The cell covered with numerous appendages (pili or fimbriae) is a genetic donor connected to a recipient cell (without appendages) by the so-called F-pilus. The F-pilus is a specialized structure (sex pilus) itself controlled by genes on the fertility, or F plasmid. The F-pilus has been labeled by special virus particles that infect donor cells via the F-pilus. The other pili surrounding the cell have no role in conjugation but are required by *E. coli* for colonization and pathogenicity in the intestinal and urinary tracts of humans and animals.

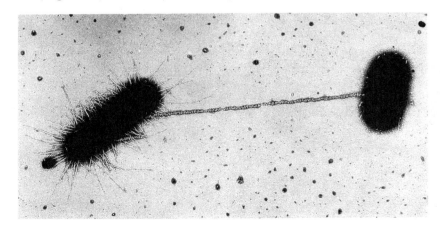

each other's way and cannot form bundles. As a result, the bacteria tumble in random fashion. The two types of motion, swimming and tumbling, account for bacterial chemotaxis. In the absence of attractants or repellents, bacteria alternate indifferently between swimming and tumbling. When an attractant is sensed, swimming lasts longer than tumbling, whereas swimming stops more quickly when a repellent is present. The net result is movement toward attractants and away from repellents. Little is known about the role of chemotaxis in pathogenesis, but it would be surprising if it were not important in some instances in guiding bacteria toward cellular targets or possibly away from white blood cells.

Bacterial Adhesion and Pili (Fimbriae)

Whether by active chemotaxis or more passive mechanisms, microorganisms are attracted to specific tissues. Sometimes this **tissue tropism** results from the selective survival of the organism in a particular environment; for example, the fungi that cause athletes' foot cannot grow at 37°C, which explains why they are found only on the skin and not in the interior of the body. In other cases, tropism involves attachment of surface components of the organisms to specific receptors present on the cells of certain tissues. The bacterial structures most often involved in attachment are the pili. These are filaments shorter than flagella and distributed, often in large numbers, over the surface of some bacteria. Bacteria that can conjugate have, in addition, specialized **sex pili**. These are rather different structures from the "common pili." They are much longer and link the donor (male) and recipient (female) cells during transfer of DNA by conjugation. Sex pili are usually coded for by genes carried on "fertility" plasmids (Chapter 4).

Pili allow bacteria to adhere to the surface of host cells, or, in the case of sex pili, to other bacteria. Virtually all Gram-negative bacteria possess "common pili," which help them adhere to mucosal surfaces throughout the gastrointestinal tract. Individuals under high physical stress, such as those ill enough to be in the hospital, tend to lose the adhesive protein found in the mucosa of the oropharynx, fibronectin, which preferentially binds to Gram-positive bacteria. Under these circumstances of fibronectin depletion, the common pili help the Gram-negative bacteria colonize the mouth and throat much more avidly than normal. Specialized strains of *E. coli* that cause traveler's diarrhea possess an additional type of pilus that allows adherence to cells of the small intestine where the bacteria secrete a toxin that causes the symptoms of the disease. Other strains of *E. coli* that cause urinary tract infection have been found to possess yet another form of pilus ("P-pili") that specialize in adherence to the urinary tract. Likewise, pili are essential for gonococci to infect the epithelial cells of the genitourinary tract, again by facilitating bacterial adherence and colonization.

Pili have other roles in disease. Like capsules, they can be antiphagocytic. They are also highly changeable and permit some organisms to put on a succession of disguises that enables them to outflank the immune system. This has been studied in detail in the gonococcus. Gonococci have a large number of genes that code for variants of the protein, **pilin**, that polymerizes to form pili. Each version of pilin is antigenically distinct and elicits the formation of different antibodies. In the presence of antibodies to one type of pilin, there is rapid selection for variants of gonococci that have switched to the synthesis of another antigenic type of pilin. Thus, they keep one step

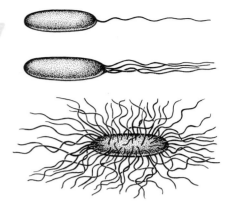

Figure 3.15. Arrangement of flagella in some types of bacteria.

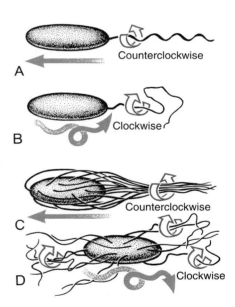

Figure 3.16. Flagellar arrangement and motility. A. A bacterium moving smoothly right to left when its single polar flagellum rotates *counterclockwise*; this is the same direction as the thread of the helix formed by the flagellin molecules in the flagellum. **B.** The same bacterium tumbles generally left to right when the flagellum rotates *clockwise*. **C** and **D.** With a peritrichous bacterium, *counterclockwise* rotation (**C**) produces a coherent bundle of flagella and smooth movement; the tumbling produced by *clockwise* rotation is extreme (**D**).

ahead in this quick-change scenario. Only one (or a few) of the large repertoire of pilin genes is active at any time. The molecular basis for the shift from one pilin to another is that pilin genes contain two types of sequences; one codes for a constant portion of the pilin protein that is not very antigenic, and the second codes for a variable region that is highly antigenic. At intervals, a constant region will recombine with a variable region to form a gene that codes for a complete pilin protein. The result is that many varieties of pilin genes can arise and be expressed, allowing the organisms to survive for long times in the face of the host immune response. It is easy to see why attempts to immunize against gonococci using a particular pilin vaccine have failed so far.

Such specific rearrangements of portions of genes are not unique. A comparable shuffling of constant and variable portions of genes gives rise to the magnificent variety of antibodies made by the body. In microorganisms, analogous mechanisms have been found in yeast, in the bacteria that cause relapsing fever (*Borrelia*) and in the protozoa that cause sleeping sickness (trypanosomes). By a related mechanism, organisms that cause food poisoning and other illnesses, the *Salmonella*, undergo rapid changes between expression and nonexpression of genes that code for the protein of flagella. This change in flagellar synthesis is called **phase variation** and is based on the control of a gene for flagellar protein. The gene can be inverted on the chromosome and can only be read in one of the two orientations.

NUTRITION AND ENERGY METABOLISM

Bacteria survive and grow in a large variety of habitats. Whatever their habitat, all bacteria must synthesize cellular constituents in a coordinated manner to grow. The required building blocks must either be provided at suitable levels in the medium or be synthesized in proper amounts by the organisms themselves. With regard to their nutritional requirements, bacteria can be divided into two large groups. In one are the photosynthetic or chemosynthetic bacteria that subsist on CO_2 and minerals, using either light or chemical energy. The other includes all of the organisms that need preformed organic components. All pathogenic microorganisms fall in the second group, but within it, they have many gradations of nutritional needs. Some, like *E. coli*, are satisfied with glucose and some inorganic material (Table 3.4). Other pathogenic bacteria, like their human host, are unable to make one or more essential metabolites—vitamins, amino acids, purines, pyrimidines, etc.—which must be supplied as growth factors.

Bacteria also have a wide range of responses to oxygen. At the extremes are the **strict aerobes**, which must have oxygen to grow. An example is the tubercle bacillus, which thrives in the portions of the body that are better oxygenated, like the lungs. At the other extreme are the **strict or obligate anaerobes**, bacteria that cannot grow in the presence

Table 3.4. Glucose Minimal Medium

	Per Liter	Main Source of
Na_2HPO_4	6.0 g	P, buffering power, osmotic strength
KH_2PO_4	3.0 g	P, buffering power, osmotic strength
NH_4Cl	1.0 g	N
$MgSO_4$	0.012 g	Mg, S
$CaCl_2$	0.011 g	Ca
Glucose	2.0 g	Energy, carbon building blocks

of oxygen, such as the organisms that cause botulism and tetanus. The largest number of bacteria that are medically important can grow whether or not oxygen is present. They are called **facultative anaerobes**, and include *E. coli* and other intestinal bacteria.

These differences in the response to oxygen mirror the way bacteria oxidize substrates to obtain energy. Strict aerobes carry out **respiration** only, the process in which the final electron acceptor in a series of coupled oxidation-reductions is molecular oxygen. Strict anaerobes carry out **fermentation**, where the final hydrogen acceptor is an organic molecule. Examples of organic electron acceptors are pyruvate, which is reduced to lactate in the lactic acid fermentation, or acetyl-CoA, which is reduced to alcohol in ethanol fermentation. Facultative anaerobes are capable of either form of metabolism, depending on whether oxygen is present or absent. Thus, they will respire in its presence and ferment in its absence.

Respiration yields more energy per molecule of substrate oxidized. Therefore, fermentative organisms must turn over more substrate to obtain the same amount of energy. The industrial microbiologist takes advantage of this for the purpose of maximizing either the yield of cell mass or the amount of metabolic products formed. Under what conditions of oxygenation, would you grow yeast in a fermentation tank if the intended product were (*a*) yeast cake, or (*b*) alcohol?

We have mentioned that *E. coli* can use glucose as its sole organic source. It can also utilize other compounds, like lactose, fructose, or one of several amino acids. The list includes some 30 known substances, but this is not particularly impressive compared to species of *Pseudomonas*, which can grow on any of several hundred organic compounds. No wonder such nearly omnivorous *Pseudomonas* have been used by genetic engineers to construct strains for use in the degradation of environmental pollutants. And no wonder *Pseudomonas* species are omnipresent in the water supply and the soil where they can take advantage of a great variety of substrates.

Although these bacteria can manage on meager solutions of glucose and a few salts, they do not disdain richer fare. When *E. coli* is given a mixture of amino acids, sugars, vitamins, etc., it will use the compounds provided rather than making them endogenously. The result is sparing of energy and biosynthetic potential, and faster growth. In the laboratory, it is possible to culture bacteria in media that are truly spartan, the so-called **minimal media**, which are water solutions of glucose, ammonia, phosphate, sulfate, and other minerals (Table 3.4). Conversely, they can be grown in a rich medium, a **nutrient broth** that contains meat extract and soluble partial hydrolysates of complex proteins. Add agar to these solutions and you have the corresponding solid media.

Some bacteria can grow only in complex media and have nutritional requirements that rival or exceed those of humans. The organisms are said to be **nutritionally fastidious**. This is characteristic of highly parasitic species that are found in close association with the rich environment of the human body. Examples of these organisms are the staphylococci or the streptococci that can grow only if provided with a long list of compounds. As expected, bacteria that can get by with only a few nutrients, *E. coli* or *Pseudomonas*, are found also in less enriched habitats, like bodies of water. The ecology of an organism usually gives good hints of its nutritional requirements.

Certain bacteria cannot grow in artificial media at all and only replicate inside host cells. These bacteria, like *Chlamydia*, are known as obligate intracellular parasites. Other bacteria, such as *Treponema pallidum* (the causative agent of syphilis) or *Mycobacterium leprae* (leprosy) should be able to grow on laboratory media because they grow extracellularly in the host. However, microbiologists have not been able to figure out how to get them to do it.

GROWING AND RESTING STATES

When bacteria find themselves in a suitable environment, they grow and eventually divide. The time it takes for a bacterium to become two is called the **generation time** or **doubling time**. For example, *E. coli* requires about 20 minutes to double in rich nutrient broth and 1–2 hours in minimal medium at 37°C. Growth will go on until the population reaches a certain density when the nutrients in the environment become exhausted or toxic metabolites accumulate. Until this occurs, the bacteria grow in an unhindered manner and are physiologically all alike. This condition is called **balanced growth**, since all cell constituents will increase proportionally over the same period of time. Such a steady state does not exist for long in nature because the environment usually undergoes rapid changes.

Measurement of Bacterial Growth and a Few Definitions

How is bacterial growth measured? The most direct way is to take samples at different times and count the number of bacteria under a microscope using a hemocytometer chamber. This tedious procedure has been superseded by electronic particle analyzers that detect bacteria as little semiconductors in an electric field. Either of these procedures measures the number of bacteria as physical particles. In other words, they give the body count, with no discrimination between living and dead bacteria. This is known as the **total count**. The total count can also be conveniently estimated by measuring a property proportional to the number of bacteria present, for instance, the turbidity of a liquid culture.

Often, it is important to determine the number of **living** or **viable** bacteria. This number is determined by a **colony count**, which is carried out by placing an appropriate dilution on solid growth medium. Since colonies arise from living bacteria, the number of colonies multiplied by the dilution factor is the number of **colony forming units** or **CFUs** originally present. Note that if bacteria grow in clumps, like staphylococci, or chains, like streptococci, the number of CFUs is an underestimate of the total number of living bacteria present.

Law of Growth

Balanced growth can be described mathematically as follows. Let N be the number of bacteria and t the time, then

$$dN/dt = Nk$$

where k is the **growth rate constant**. By integration, we obtain the growth law:

$$N_t = N_o e^{kt}$$

where N_t is the number of bacteria at time t and N_o is the initial number of bacteria at time = 0. This describes a geometric progression that holds for many natural phenomena. In situations that lead to cell death (for instance, sterilizing heat or antiseptic chemicals), the decrease in viable bacteria is described by the same equation, but with a negative constant. The same equation also describes the decay with time of a radioactive isotope or the kinetics of degradation of unstable mRNA molecules in cells.

Growth in the Real World

If balanced growth went unchecked, a single bacterium dividing twice an hour would produce a mass as large as that of the earth in just 2 days. Instead, when bacteria grow to a certain density, they either exhaust required nutrients or they accumulate toxic levels of metabolites (Fig. 3.17). They may run out of the carbon source, a required inorganic compound, or essential amino acids or vitamins. For aerobic bacteria, crowding leads to the exhaustion of oxygen since it is poorly soluble in water. Toxic metabolites may be hydrogen peroxide for some anaerobes that lack catalase, or acids formed by fermentation, which results in a pH too low to be compatible with growth. Which of these factors actually slows down growth first depends on the strain of bacteria and on the composition of the culture medium. For example, in a well-buffered medium, *E. coli* may exhaust nutrients before the pH drops, while the converse may be true in poorly buffered media. The stage of the culture where growth stops is known as the **stationary phase**.

The explosiveness of exponential growth means that even a small number of bacteria may initiate an infection. An example of unhampered growth that leads to dangerous illness is acute bacterial meningitis in a child. Bacteria that cause this disease, like the meningococcus, grow so rapidly in the patient that the physician may have to intervene immediately to avoid a fatal outcome. On the other hand, not all pathogens grow fast. For example, tubercle bacilli divide every 24 hours or so even under optimal conditions. The disease they cause is chronic and takes considerable time to be manifested.

In the tissues of the body, bacteria are often stressed by nutritional limitations or by the damaging action of the defense mechanisms. Consequently, bacterial populations in the body are rarely fully viable. To permit them to adapt to such conditions, bacteria do not cease all metabolic activities when they stop growing. Instead, they may cease net growth but continue some synthetic activities that permit them to make specific constituents needed for adaptation. To use a laboratory example, when *E. coli* cultures exhaust glucose they continue to carry out a low level of protein synthesis, sufficient to adapt to the utilization of other nutrients, such as other sugars that may be present. Energy and building blocks are supplied by turnover of cell material that is not

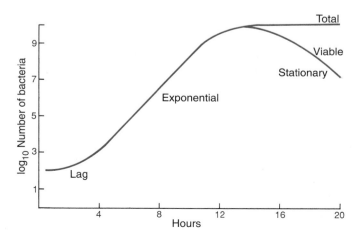

Figure 3.17. The growth of a bacterial culture. Bacteria in the inoculum sometime resumes growth slowly (lag phase, hours 0–5). They then enter the exponential phase of growth (hours 5–10). When foodstuff is exhausted or toxic material accumulates, they enter the stationary phase (hours 10 onward). During the stationary phase, bacterial cultures sometimes lose their viability, as reflected in the viable count, often without losing cell integrity (maintaining a constant total count).

needed in the stationary phase. A major source of amino acids are ribosomes and pre-existing proteins that are present in excess under these conditions. Their breakdown products can also be oxidized to supply energy. This process of feeding on itself allows adaptability and postpones death, which might otherwise occur by random degradative events in the absence of synthetic activities.

Bacteria are exposed to countless kinds of injury and have developed special adaptive mechanisms to cope with many of them. For example, damage to the DNA of *E. coli* by ultraviolet light activates a set of genes that code for proteins capable of repairing this damage. This is known as the **SOS response**. Other protective responses are turned on when bacteria are starved for the source of carbon, nitrogen, or phosphorus; when the temperature is raised abruptly; or when anaerobic cultures are suddenly exposed to oxygen. In each case, the rapidity of adaptation is a tribute to the powers of bacterial adaptation.

Even when they are not growing, bacteria can still cause damage to their host. In the first place, nongrowing bacteria are still immunogenic and can elicit immune responses with both beneficial and detrimental results. In the second place, production of toxins often starts or accelerates when bacteria enter the stationary phase. In some cases, we can fathom the reason for this timing because toxin production provides certain bacteria with nutrients. For example, some streptococci make enzymes that lyse red blood cells and proteases that degrade hemoglobin. The organisms are thus supplied with amino acids plus a source of iron. Why do these organisms make their hemolysins mainly in the stationary phase? Clearly, as long as they are growing, they must already be supplied with enough iron and needed amino acids. Why should they then expend energy to make hemolysins?

Cessation of growth of some bacteria initiates **sporulation**. This results in the production of metabolically inert spores that are extraordinarily resistant to chemical and physical insults. During sporulation, the "mother cell" is eventually lysed. The cytoplasmic contents that are released sometimes contain large amounts of toxins. This happens in tetanus, gas gangrene, and other diseases caused by sporulating bacteria.

The relationship between microbial growth and pathogenesis is far from simple but should be kept in mind when attempting to understand the etiology and course of infections.

Mechanisms of Adaptation

Both over short periods and throughout evolutionary times, bacteria are selected for their efficient and economical ways of coping with the environment. Inefficient strains are rapidly lost in competition with others that use their resources more effectively. Metabolic efficiency is characterized by parsimony, that is, bacteria tend not to make compounds they cannot use at the time. There are important exceptions to this statement, but, by and large, it illustrates the economy and efficiency of the bacterial way of life.

We know a great deal about the mechanisms bacteria use to adapt to changing environmental conditions. As more information is gathered, it becomes evident that there is a large number of mechanisms operating specifically under given circumstances. To use a specific example, take a culture of *E. coli* growing in a minimal medium and add to it an excess of the amino acid leucine. Within seconds, the endogenous synthesis of leucine will be stopped and the cells will utilize the exogenously supplied leucine exclusively. From the point of view of the economy of the bacteria, this is desirable, as it saves the metabolic energy expended for biosynthesis of leucine. The same phenomenon occurs if other amino acids, purines, pyrimidines, or other metabolites were added.

Regulation of Enzyme Activity

How did the bacteria switch off the synthesis of leucine? When the enzymes of the metabolic pathway dedicated to the synthesis of leucine were studied, it was found that the first enzyme in the pathway is inhibited by leucine, and will not function in its presence. This inhibition is due to **allosteric** properties of the enzyme, that is, its ability to change conformation by the binding of an effector, in this case, leucine. Why was the first enzyme and not the others in the pathway affected? The reason is economic, because by stopping the flow of substrates at the very beginning of the pathway there is no waste of unusable metabolites. This effect is known as **feedback** or **end-product inhibition**.

Regulation of Enzyme Synthesis

Feedback inhibition suffices to stop the synthesis of leucine in the leucine-fed culture. If this were all, the organisms would still synthesize the biosynthetic enzymes for leucine, at a cost of considerable energy. This is wasteful and would place the organisms at a selective disadvantage vis-à-vis more efficient ones. To avoid such an unnecessary expenditure, the cell rapidly turns off the synthesis of the enzymes of the leucine biosynthetic pathway. How is this done? It is a characteristic of procaryotic cells that the enzymes involved in a metabolic pathway are often strung together in a multigenic segment of DNA called an **operon**. Transcription of all of the genes of an operon into mRNA can be turned on or off together by throwing a single regulatory switch. One end of the operon where transcription starts, there a series of regulatory sequences that do not code for amino acids but are recognized by the regulatory mechanisms. One of these sequences is the **promoter** site, where RNA polymerase binds to initiate the synthesis of mRNA. We will discuss two such mechanisms of **regulation of gene expression** used to switch operons on and off.

The operons involved in the biosynthesis of amino acids, such as leucine, are usually regulated by a mechanism called **attenuation**. This is how it works, still taking leucine as an example. A small stretch of mRNA is synthesized from the beginning of the coding sequence of the leucine operon, regardless of the presence or absence of leucine. The RNA polymerase now encounters a region called the **attenuator**, where, in the presence of leucine, transcription is terminated. This achieves the desired effect of not making the unneeded biosynthetic enzymes. In the absence of leucine, when the biosynthetic enzymes become essential, the secondary structure of the nascent mRNA at the attenuator region is altered in such a way that transcription, and therefore translation, can proceed. Details of how this works are shown in Figure 3.18.

Another mechanism for turning on or off the synthesis of enzymes is found in the case of many enzymes involved in the utilization of sugars. Taking the utilization of lactose as an example, if this sugar were the sole carbon source, the bacteria must make the enzyme

Figure 3.18. Regulation of enzyme synthesis by attenuation. Transcription stops when a termination stem and loop structure involving sequences *C* and *D* is formed. The *left side* of the drawing show how the absence of leucine causes ribosomes to stop at sequence *A* and to prevent the formation of the *CD* stem and loop structure. This allows RNA polymerase (not shown) to continue transcription past this region. On the *right side*, when leucine is present, ribosomes continue to sequence *B*, allowing the formation of the *CD* termination stem and loop structure. In this case, RNA polymerase cannot proceed and transcription stops.

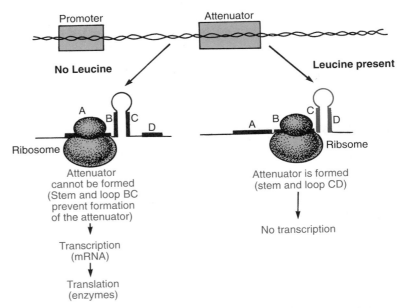

β-galactosidase, which is necessary to convert lactose into glucose and galactose. In the absence of lactose, as in the case of a culture growing solely on glucose, the synthesis of β-galactosidase is unnecessary and wasteful. This is how the synthesis of the enzyme is regulated (Fig. 3.19). At the beginning of the operon, just past the promoter, there is a regulatory sequence known as the **operator**, where a protein called the repressor binds. With the repressor binds to the operator, transcription cannot begin. In the presence of lactose, the repressor undergoes a conformational change to render it incapable of binding to the operator. Note that the lactose repressor is an allosteric protein, capable of undergoing conformational changes under the influence of an effector. The result is that when lactose is added to a culture, the repressor becomes inactive and cannot bind to the operator, thus allowing the synthesis of β-galactosidase to proceed. β-Galactosidase is an example of an **inducible enzyme**, one made on demand, as contrasted with a **constitutive enzyme**, one that must be made at all times, such as RNA polymerase. In the case of β-galactosidase, lactose (or, more precisely, one of its metabolites) is known as the **inducer**.

Overview of Regulation

Regulation of gene expression by attenuation, repression, or other mechanisms results in the relatively rapid switching of gene expression on and off. The reason is that, in bacteria, mRNA molecules are relatively short lived and undergo rapid turnover. Thus, after the synthesis of an enzyme is stopped, the amount of residual enzyme produced will be very small. In addition, what enzyme is left may be subject to feedback inhibition and little of its product will be made. Note that all forms of regulation come at energy cost. Thus, feedback inhibition requires that the protein be more complex than just what is needed for catalytic activity. Regulation of enzyme synthesis by attenuation depends on the synthesis of a stretch of mRNA that will not be used if the enzymes of the operon are not made. Using a repressor to regulate an operon likewise requires the constitutive synthesis of protein repressor molecules. The energy cost of making regulatory devices is weighted against the greater disadvantage that cells would have in not being able to switch on and off major biosynthetic pathways. Thus, free-living

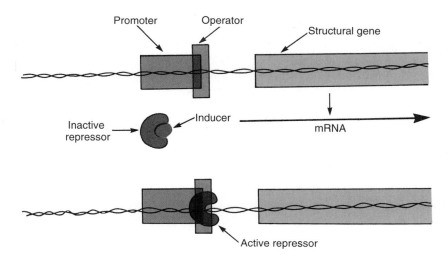

Promoter   Operator

Structural gene

Inactive repressor → Inducer

mRNA

Active repressor

Figure 3.19. The Operon model: regulation of β-galactosidase synthesis by repression and derepression. The repressor protein for the genes encoding enzymes for lactose utilization exists in two states, active, when the sugar inducer is absent, and inactive, when the inducer is present. The *top* of the figure shows that when the inducer (*in color*) is present, the *inactive repressor* cannot bind to the operator region of the operon. Without a bound repressor, transcription can proceed and the enzyme β-galactosidase is formed. In the absence of lactose, the repressor is in the active form and binds to the operator, thus preventing transcription from taking place.

cells such as bacteria must balance their powers of efficiency and adaptability.

The theme of efficiency and adaptability to environmental changes recurs throughout this book, especially when considering how microorganisms cope with the changes they encounter when entering the body and certain of its tissues and organs.

Self-assessment Questions

1. What distinguishes procaryotes from eukaryotes? Compare a typical bacterium with a typical eukaryotic cell.

2. Discuss the physiological and structural consequences of bacteria being small.

3. What are the structural features of a "typical" bacterium? What distinguished Gram positives from Gram negatives?

4. Describe the outer membrane of Gram negatives and discuss its role in bacterial ecology and virulence.

5. How does penicillin work?

6. What are the principal mechanisms used by bacteria to take up substrates?

7. Discuss DNA replication in *E. coli*.

8. Is it clear to you why some protein-synthesis-inhibiting antibiotics are bacteriostatic? Discuss why some others are bactericidal.

9. Discuss the role of bacterial flagella and pili in growth and pathogenesis.

10. What are the main ways in which bacteria derive their energy? What is the relation between this and how they cope with oxygen?

11. Discuss the law of bacterial growth and some of its consequences in the real world.

12. Discuss the difference between regulation by feedback inhibition and by control of gene expression.

13. Give two examples of regulation of enzyme synthesis in bacteria.

14. What happens when bacteria are exposed to potentially lethal challenges, such as high temperatures?

SUGGESTED READING

Neidhardt FC, Ingraham JL, Schaechter M. Physiology of the bacterial cell. Sunderland, MA: Sinauer Assoc, 1990.

Neidhardt FC, et al. *Escherichia coli* and *Salmonella typhimurium.* Washington, DC: American Society of Microbiology, 2 vols. 1987. (This is an encyclopedic treatise on the structure, function, and heredity of these organisms.)

Genetics of Bacteria

4

Moselio Schaechter and Barry I. Eisenstein

In this chapter, we will use an example from the literature to illustrate how genetic methods can be used to study questions of pathogenesis. The example we have chosen is from an investigation in the establishment of disease by a pathogenic organism. The purpose of this research was to study the mechanism of penetration into host cells of a bacterium called *Yersinia pseudotuberculosis*, a relative of the plague bacillus that causes severe diarrhea. This investigation illustrates some issues of central importance to bacterial genetics and how they can be approached experimentally. We also present the basic concepts of bacterial genetics in a more conventional way, with definitions of major concepts in this field. **Definitions are found at the end of this chapter and should be used in the order and to the extent that suits each reader.**

An early step in the disease caused by *Y. pseudotuberculosis* is the penetration of the organisms into the cells lining the small intestine. The ability to penetrate into host cells is not common to all pathogenic bacteria and represents a distinct **virulence factor** (see "**Virulence Factor**"). The basic assumption in this investigation was that *Y. pseudotuberculosis* possesses a gene or genes that encode proteins involved in the penetration of animal cells. To establish the existence of such genes and how they work, the investigators, Isberg, Falkow and their collaborators (see Suggested Reading), cloned portions of the *Y. pseudotuberculosis* genome into strains of *Escherichia coli* **incapable of penetrating host cells**. They isolated *E. coli* clones that became capable of entering mammalian cells in culture and then found that these new strains contain a single gene involved in penetration. This gene encodes a *Yersinia* protein located in the outer membrane of the bacterium called **invasin** (Inv). The gene for invasin is now known as *inv* and strains carrying it are designated *inv*+ (or, phenotypically, Inv+). By convention, genes and gene products have a basic three-letter designation. The abbreviations for the gene products (proteins) or the phenotype of a cell are capitalized in plain text (as in Inv) whereas those of the genes themselves are italicized (as in *inv*).

Unfolding the steps in this investigation is an interesting story concerning both molecular genetics and bacterial pathogenesis. In this chapter, we will consider this story in some detail. For didactic reasons, some of the experiments described are not precisely those carried out, nor were they necessarily performed in the order presented. Basically, though, the investigation consisted of several steps that are outlined in Figure 4.1. The steps were as follows:

1. As a first step in cloning the gene or genes of *Y. pseudotuberculosis* involved in invasion, the DNA of this organism was **isolated** and **cut** into a large number of fragments.

Figure 4.1. The general scheme of the study of invasin.

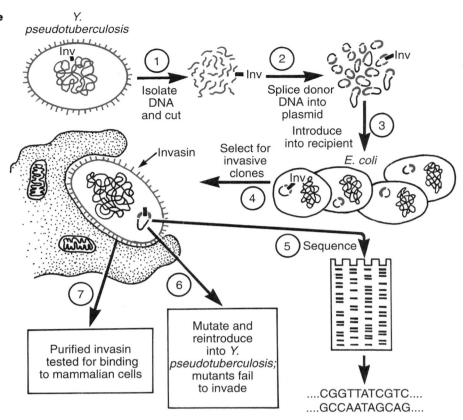

2. Fragments were individually **spliced** into plasmids that were used as a carrier. Enough plasmids containing spliced *Y. pseudotuberculosis* DNA were generated to ensure that, overall, the whole genome of that organism was included.

3. The collection of spliced plasmids was introduced by **genetic transformation** into *E. coli*. Conditions were used so that each transformed *E. coli* was likely to contain a plasmid carrying a different *Y. pseudotuberculosis* DNA fragment.

4. Clones of *E. coli* carrying the hypothetical *inv* gene or genes were selected by their ability to **penetrate** into animal cells. The finding of such clones indicated the existence of an invasion (*inv*) gene.

5. Penetrating clones of *E. coli* were found to contain a **new protein** that was called invasin. The DNA sequence of the *inv* gene was determined and found to correspond to the amino acid sequence of invasin.

6. The *inv* gene was **mutated** to an inactive form and **reintroduced** into the donor *Y. pseudotuberculosis*. These strains could not penetrate animal cells, which established that invasin functions not only in the artificial *E. coli* construct, but actually plays a role in the invasiveness of its natural host, *Y. pseudotuberculosis*.

7. Purified invasin protein was shown to **bind** to mammalian cells, proving, in combination with the genetic results, that this protein suffices for the attachment of bacteria.

MOLECULAR CLONING

The general strategy for cloning a gene consists of **cutting** the DNA of the donor organism into fragments, one of which contains the desired sequence, and to **introduce the mixture** of fragments into a suitable recipient organism. Only few of the recipient cells will contain the gene in question, and these must be isolated by taking advantage of some property that allows them to be selected. A key aspect of this strategy and, indeed, one of the most powerful aspects of microbial genetics, is the **ability to select rare events**. To use a simple example, one can place 100 million sensitive bacteria or more on the surface of an agar plate containing an antibiotic and have a few colonies (clones) of drug-resistant mutants grow out after incubation. Thus, one can study, with ease, events that happen with a probability of 1×10^{-8} or even less. It is gratifying that this figure is of the same order of magnitude as the size of a needle divided into that of a medium-sized haystack!

In this study, the first step in cloning the gene or genes for bacterial invasiveness was to isolate DNA from the donor *Y. pseudotuberculosis* and cut it into thousands of different fragments (**Step 1**). For reasons to be discussed later, it is convenient to incorporate such fragments into a larger DNA carrier molecule or "**cloning vector.**" To facilitate this, the DNA of *Y. pseudotuberculosis* was cut in a way that allows fragments to be readily spliced into a carrier plasmid. DNA was cut with an appropriate restriction enzyme known by its abbreviation, Sau 3A (see **Restriction enzymes**). This particular enzyme recognizes a specific four-base sequence in DNA (G·A·T·C) and cleaves the DNA molecules whenever it encounters this sequence. The cleavage is asymmetric in that the site of cutting on one strand is a few bases away from that on the other strand. This results in fragments with frayed ends (Fig. 4.2). When such restriction fragments are placed in the right conditions of ionic strength and temperature, the frayed ends will join (**anneal**) by forming hydrogen bonds between their complementary purine and pyrimidine bases (Fig. 4.2).

In the present study, a new plasmid was constructed by annealing the Sau 3A restriction fragments of *Y. pseudotuberculosis*-DNA with an *E. coli* plasmid (**Step 2**). The loosely joined molecules were then covalently linked using the enzyme DNA ligase (Fig. 4.3). Note that a large number of different molecules will result from this annealing and ligation, most of them irrelevant to this study. From this complex mixture, how did the authors find the molecules that contain the gene(s) for invasion? Notice that if the chromosome of the donor *Y. pseudotuberculosis* was cut into more than 1000 fragments, the chances of finding the desired clone are less than 1×10^{-3}. In this study, the investigators sought out the desired plasmids by introducing the ligated mixture into recipient *E. coli* cells and selecting those that were capable of invasion (**Step 3**).

Let us now consider why it was advisable to splice the donor DNA into a plasmid vector. If the donor DNA is to cause a stable change in a recipient bacterium, it must be replicated. An entering DNA molecule that could not replicate would be lost from the population, without further genetic consequences (Fig. 4.4). Intracellular DNA replication requires that the DNA molecule possess a **replicative origin**, a sequence recognized by specific protein initiation factors that allow the process to start. In bacteria, the chromosome has a single replicative origin (unlike eukaryotic chromosomes that have several origins each). When a bacterial chromosome is cut into fragments, most of them are unlikely to contain the origin, and therefore, will not be able to carry out independent replication. One way to ensure that DNA fragments will replicate is, therefore, to **splice** them into DNA molecules that possess a replicative origin. The small extrachromosomal DNA molecules capable of replicating independently, the **plasmids** (see "**Plasmids**"), are

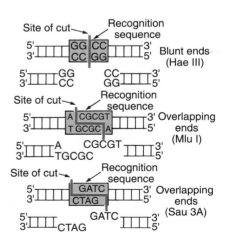

Figure 4.2. Restriction enzymes. The recognition sequence and site of cuts of three restriction enzymes are shown. Restriction enzymes are known by a three-letter abbreviation of their bacterial species of origin (*Hae III = Haemophilus aegypticus; Mlu I = Micrococcus luteus; Sau 3A = Staphylococcus aureus*).

Figure 4.3. Engineering a plasmid for molecular cloning. DNA to be cloned and that of a suitable vector (here shown as a plasmid) are cut with a restriction enzyme that produces overlapping ends with the same sequence (here shown as *GATC*). When the two classes of molecules are mixed, some of them will join (anneal) with one another because of the complementary sequences of their protruding ends. The molecules can now be covalently linked using the enzyme DNA ligase to yield a new plasmid that contains the DNA to be cloned.

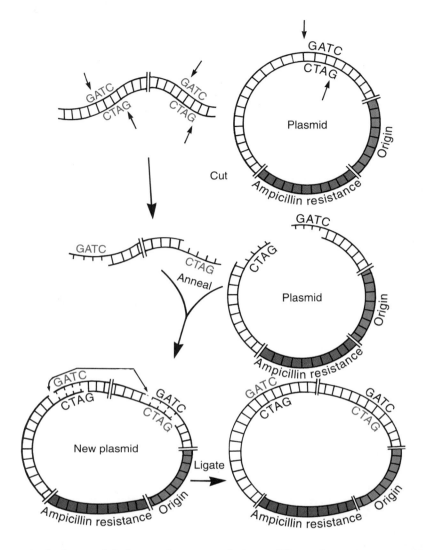

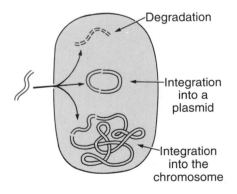

Figure 4.4. Possible fate of DNA introduced into bacteria. Linear DNA is degraded unless it is integrated into a stable replicon, such as a plasmid or the chromosome of the recipient bacterium. If the DNA is in circular form and is capable of replication, it can propagate and become a plasmid. Neither linear nor circular DNA will survive the restriction enzymes of the cell unless they are properly methylated.

particularly useful for such manipulations. Plasmids are commonly used in recombinant DNA experiments as vectors to carry foreign DNA into recipient bacteria.

The entry of plasmid-borne donor DNA into a recipient bacterium still does not ensure that genetic change will take place. Bacteria try to thwart the effects of foreign DNA, which could lead to genetic changes and endanger the integrity of the genome. Most bacteria possess restriction enzymes and other nucleases designed particularly to degrade foreign DNA. To ensure that this did not take place in the experiment under consideration (and that the entering DNA was protected), the chosen recipient *E. coli* strain was a mutant in genes for restriction enzymes, and thus, was impaired in its ability to degrade foreign DNA.

The uptake of purified DNA that results in a genetic change is called **genetic transformation** (see "**Genetic Transformation**"). In *E. coli*, transformation is a relatively rare event and, under special laboratory conditions, only a small proportion of the cells in the population (at most, 1×10^{-3}) can be expected to contain **any** DNA from the donor bacteria. Given that fewer than 1 in 1000 of the cells that were successfully transformed are likely to contain the genes in question, it became important to discard all the bacteria that failed to take up any DNA. Such **stable transformants**, in this case *E. coli* cells containing *Y. pseu-*

dotuberculosis DNA, were selected by a simple strategy. The cloning vector was chosen for having an easily selectable property, e.g., carrying a gene for resistance to an antibiotic, in this case ampicillin. Thus, only the bacteria that acquired the plasmid would grow in an ampicillin-containing agar medium and make individual colonies, whereas the others would not. Ampicillin resistance is a **selectable marker** that allowed the investigators to isolate the recipients that took up donor DNA from the majority that did not.

Note that each ampicillin-resistant clone (in this case, a colony on agar) is likely to contain a different restriction fragment of *Y. pseudotuberculosis*, thus, a different gene or genes from that organism. The collection of such clones is collectively known as a **genomic library** of the donor organism (Fig. 4.5). At this stage, the investigators still have not obtained a pure culture of *E. coli* containing the gene or genes for invasion.

SELECTING THE DESIRED CLONE

How were the clones containing the gene or genes for invasion isolated from the large number that did not? In principle, the wished-for clones could be identified by screening a large number of colonies, that is, by assaying them one at a time for the ability to invade mammalian cells. This brute-force approach could be extraordinarily demanding because, in this case, thousands of colonies would have had to be tested individually. Indeed, such tedious work must be done when there is no adequate selection procedure to pick out the desired clones. Note that selection of drug-resistant clones (as used above) permits testing only of cells that took up DNA from the medium, a 1000-fold saving in effort.

In this study, the ampicillin-resistant cultures were not just screened, but were actually enriched by **selection** of those capable of penetrating animal cells (**Step 4**). Inv$^+$ clones were selected from the Inv$^-$ majority using by the following procedure (Fig. 4.6). The recipient *E. coli* were tested for their ability to invade cultured human cells. Noninvasive bacteria remained outside the cells and were removed by washing with cold buffer. The remaining bacteria were cultured and, to make sure they had not just slipped by the selection step, retested for their ability to invade animal cells. Those passing this test were considered to carry the *inv* gene and to be Inv$^+$. This selection readily permitted the isolation of one bacterium capable of invasion from among thousands that could not. Thus, several Inv$^+$ clones were obtained and used for further study. In a comparison test, *E. coli* carrying the *inv* gene penetrated cells with the same high efficiency as the parental *Y. pseudotuberculosis*, whereas the parent *E. coli* (lacking the *inv* gene) could barely invade cells at all (Table 4.1).

This selection technique did not necessarily differentiate between bacteria that resisted washing because they simply attached to the host cell surface from those that had become truly intracellular. For this reason, the selection procedure was refined to obtain truly invasive bacteria. The investigators did this by taking advantage of the inability of **the bactericidal antibiotic gentamicin to enter mammalian cells.** Gentamicin was added after the bacteria were given a chance to penetrate the host cells; therefore, those that did not penetrate were killed by the antibiotic, whereas the intracellular ones survived the treatment. The ability of Inv$^+$ bacteria to penetrate mammalian cells was later confirmed by looking for intracellular bacteria in thin sections examined under the electron microscope (Fig. 4.7).

Creating a genomic library

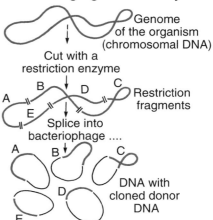

Figure 4.5. Creating a genomic library. The DNA of an organism is cut into restriction fragments (here shown as *A* through *E*), which are annealed to the DNA of a phage. After ligation, these molecules are packaged in vitro into a mature phage that can be used to infect recipient bacteria.

Figure 4.6. Selection for bacteria containing a cloned *inv* gene. The steps in the selection procedure are shown.

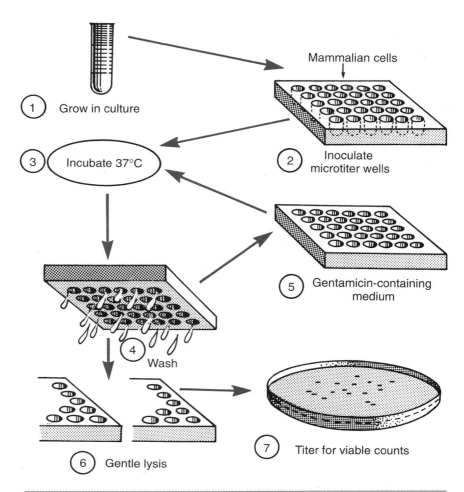

Table 4.1. *inv* Locus Encodes Efficient Binding to HEp-2 Cells		
	% Bound	
Strain	0°C	37°C
Parental *Y. pseudotuberculosis*	40.1	43.3
E. coli + *inv* plasmid	38.3	42.5
E. coli + mutant *inv* plasmid	0.8	1.0

ESTABLISHING THAT THE *inv* GENE ENCODES THE Inv PROTEIN

As soon as Inv⁺ clones of *E. coli* became available, the investigators began to study the invasin protein. Comparing the protein profile of membranes prepared from Inv⁺ and Inv⁻ strains, they found that the Inv⁺ bacteria had an extra component, visible as a new band after polyacrylamide gel electrophoresis (**PAGE**). This protein had a **molecular weight of 103,000 daltons** and, upon further fractionation, was found to be located in the **outer membrane**. Is this the protein that is responsible for penetration of the Inv⁺ strains? The investigators' approach to this question was to try to correlate the biochemical with the genetic findings.

One of the first determinations to be made at this point was to **identify the gene for invasion** in the cloned DNA of Inv⁺ strains. The most direct way to identify a gene for a specific protein is to juxtapose the sequences of the DNA and of the protein. To conclude that a gene en-

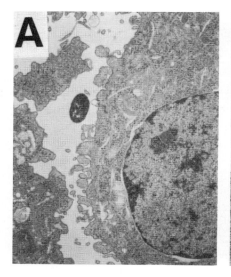 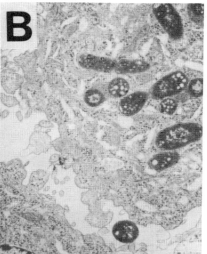

Figure 4.7. Ultrathin sections of mammalian cells incubated with bacterial strains observed under the electron microscope. A. Section of animal cells incubated with *Y. pseudotuberculosis* strain *inv⁻*. Note that the *inv⁻* strain is not found inside the cells and that the rare bacterium found in these sections is not in close opposition to the cell. **B.** Section showing cytoplasm of cell infected with *Y. pseudotuberculosis* strain *inv⁺*.

codes a particular protein, the amino acid sequence of the protein must be shown to **match the sequence** of the corresponding triplet codons on a stretch of DNA according to the rules of the genetic code. In reality, demonstrating the correspondence between the two sequences can be a demanding task. The usual strategy is to carry out this work in steps, the first one being to **estimate the length of the protein and of the gene**. As in the case in this investigation, if a protein can be identified as a specific band in polyacrylamide gel electrophoresis, it is easy to ascertain its **approximate molecular weight**. Likewise, the size of the gene can be determined using genetic techniques, as described below. Thus, even before sequence information becomes available, it is often possible to determine if a protein and a gene correspond in molecular length (**Step 5**).

Eventually, when the sequence of the region of the DNA becomes known, the likely presence of a gene can be established by inspection (Fig. 4.8). A gene may be defined as a DNA sequence spanning a start codon (the one coding for the first amino acid of the protein) and a termination codon, as long as both are in the same translational reading frame (that is, they are separated by trios of bases only). The stretch of DNA defined by the start and stop codons is known as an **open reading frame** (**ORF**).

At an early stage of an investigation, the problem with this approach is that sequencing a long DNA fragment is time consuming. What is done in practice is to narrow down the region containing the gene by first using certain genetic manipulations. A convenient genetic technique used to determine the size of a gene is called **deletion mapping** (Fig. 4.9). This technique depends on the use of **genetic deletions**, that is, artificially shortened versions of the gene. Deletions can be made in vitro by cutting portions of the region at two sites using restriction enzymes. The resulting fragment is discarded and the ends of the remaining DNA are **ligated** together to give a shortened region. Choosing different restriction enzymes allows one to vary the size of the fragment to be excised and to produce a collection of **deletions** of different lengths. When reintroduced into a recipient bacterium, deletions that extend into essential portions of the gene will be inactive. In the pres-

Figure 4.8. An open reading frame that defines a possible gene on a DNA sequence. The promoter recognition site is defined by six base pairs at position −35 and six base pairs at position −10, relative to the start of transcription (position + 1). The termination site is shown as an inverted repeat of eight base pairs followed immediately by four A-T pairs. These sequences are not identical between genes and vary somewhat around preferred "consensus" sequences. The *dots* denote bases that differ from gene to gene. The length of the *double broken lines* between the initiation and the termination signals depends on the length of the gene.

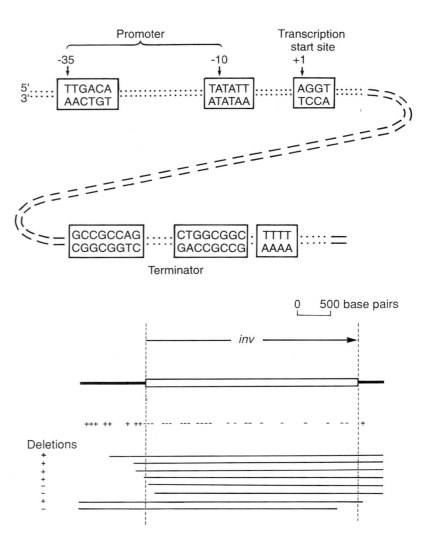

Figure 4.9. Deletion mapping. Physical and genetic map of *inv* region encoded on a plasmid that contains a fragment of *Y. pseudotuberculosis*-chromosomal DNA. Shown is a restriction map of the chromosomal DNA present on this plasmid, the sites of deletion mutations, and the phenotypes of these mutations. (−): deletions that eliminate the ability of *E. coli* strains harboring this plasmid to enter mammalian cells. (+): deletions that have no effect on the entry phenotype. *Open box*: region of DNA encoding *inv* locus, as determined by deletion mutations. *Horizontal lines* correspond to DNA still remaining on the deletion-derived plasmids.

ent study, deletions within the *inv* gene would be expected to render recipient bacteria Inv⁻, whereas deletions lying outside the gene would not (Fig. 4.9). The amount deleted could be determined by sizing the remaining DNA, allowing one to establish the approximate length of the gene. This information allowed the isolation of a region of the chromosome that spanned the gene which, now being of manageable size, could be conveniently sequenced.

When the sequence of the DNA region containing the *inv* gene was inspected, it was seen to contain an open reading frame 2964 bases long. Is this the actual *inv* gene? As mentioned above, the molecular weight of the invasin protein had been determined to be 103,000 daltons. With this number at hand, one can predict what the size of the *inv* gene should be. Taking the average molecular weight of the amino acids of the protein to be approximately 10^4 daltons, invasin should be made up of about 990 amino acids. Given that three DNA nucleotides are required to code for a single amino acid, the gene should be about 990×3, or 2970 bases long, in good agreement with the DNA sequencing data. Thus, these measurements indicated that the *inv* gene corresponded to the invasin protein in length, suggesting that the *inv* gene indeed encodes for this protein. This point was definitively settled when the sequence of this gene and portions the sequence of invasin were juxtaposed; the sequences of codon corresponded precisely to that of the amino acids.

Mutations in the *inv* Gene

So far, the experiments were done with the wild-type (normal) gene for invasin. When introduced into a surrogate organism that normally lacks it (i.e., *E. coli*), the *inv* gene made penetration into mammalian cells possible. However, this does not strictly prove that the *inv* gene is responsible for the invasiveness of the original organism, *Y. pseudotuberculosis*. You may think that this is a pedantic point of contention, but it needs to be investigated for the following reason. The two species involved differ considerably in their genetic makeup (i.e., are not **isogenic**) and it is possible that, in one of them, invasin acts together with some other gene product to facilitate invasion potential. In other words, does invasin work in its natural host, *Y. pseudotuberculosis*, in the same way as in *E. coli*?

To establish this point, the cloned *inv* gene was mutated (see "**Mutants**" and "**Mutation**") and reintroduced into the original *Y. pseudotuberculosis*. Cells containing the mutated gene were indeed impaired in penetration, demonstrating that *inv* itself is necessary for invasion (Table 4.2). The mutagenesis experiment was then carried out.

Mutations had already been created by the insertion of **transposons** at random sites on the *inv*-containing plasmid in *E. coli*. Transposons are movable genetic elements that can insert, often at random sites, in a chromosome or a plasmid (see "**Transposons**"). The insertion of a transposon in a gene extends its length unnaturally and disrupts the target gene. Strains carrying this type of mutation are known as **insertion mutants**. In this study, insertion mutants were made, reintroduced into *Y. pseudotuberculosis*, and substituted for the wild-type *inv* gene on the chromosome (**Step 6**). How did the investigators go about substituting a mutant gene for the wild type? The first step was to reintroduce DNA into *Y. pseudotuberculosis*. The genetic tools that can be used with this organism are not as well developed as with *E. coli*; thus, introducing genetic material by transformation or, as an alternative, by way of a phage (see "**Transduction**") was not an available choice. On the other hand, it was known that DNA could be transferred into *Y. pseudotuberculosis* from *E. coli* by cell-to-cell contact through the process known as conjugation (see "**Conjugation**").

Once the desired mutated *inv*-DNA was introduced into *Y. pseudotuberculosis*, a problem arose because the **resident wild-type *inv* gene** could mask the defect due to the mutation; i.e., if the two forms are both present, the wild type one of the gene might be dominant over the mutant one. The investigators solved this problem by eliminating

---

Table 4.2. Entry-defective Mutants Are Also Defective for Binding Cultured Mammalian Cells

Plasmid containing	Entry Phenotype[a]	% Bound
inv gene	+	39.0
No *inv* gene	−	0.34
Mutant *inv* gene	−	0.54

[a] Entry was measured by allowing bacteria to bind to HEp-2 cells and, after 200 minutes of incubation, treating the cells with the antibiotic gentamicin. This drug cannot penetrate into HEp-2 cells; thus, it kills extracellular but not internalized bacteria. The bacteria that have entered can then be counted by carrying out colony counts ("viable counts") on a suitable agar medium.

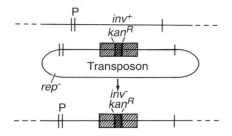

Figure 4.10. Replacing the wild type *inv* ⁺ gene by a mutant *inv* ⁻. A wild type *Y. pseudotuberculosis* was transformed with a plasmid incapable of replication (rep⁻) that carried an *inv* gene inactivated by insertion of a transposon. The transposon also carried a gene for kanamycin resistance (*kanᴿ*). Stable transformants were selected by virtue of their kanamycin resistance. Such strains arose by a double genetic cross between the chromosome and the plasmid at their region of homology, the *inv* gene. These strains will have an Inv⁻ phenotype because the mutant *inv* ⁻ gene substituted for the wild type *inv* ⁺.

the wild-type resident gene and replacing it altogether with the mutated form. How was this done? The plasmid used for transfer had three important properties:

1. The transposon inserted into the *inv* gene carried within it a gene for resistance to the antibiotic kanamycin.

2. The plasmid was engineered to have a defect in a gene required for its replication in *Y. pseudotuberculosis* and would be readily lost in the recipient population. To survive, the defective *inv* gene on the transposon would have to "jump" into the *Y. pseudotuberculosis* chromosome.

3. Integration was possible because the plasmid carried enough *Y. pseudotuberculosis* DNA to permit homologous recombination with the chromosomal DNA (Fig. 4.10).

Recombination events taking place on both sides of the transposon would lead to the excision of the resident *inv*⁺ gene (see "**Recombination**") and its replacement by the mutant form of the gene. The result is a *Y. pseudotuberculosis* strain that only has an inactive *inv* gene in its chromosome and is kanamycin resistant (Fig. 4.10). The phenotype of the new strain is denoted as Inv⁻ Kanᴿ.

The newly constructed Inv⁻ Kanᴿ *Y. pseudotuberculosis* was found to be greatly impaired in its ability to penetrate mammalian cells. The penetration efficiency of the mutant is 0.1% that of its parental Inv⁺ strain. Note that this experiment depended on the construction of **isogenic strains**, that is, bacterial strains that vary only in the gene in question. The comparison of the phenotypic properties of isogenic strains in appropriate animal models of infection is a powerful tool to determine the molecular basis of bacterial pathogenesis.

Consistent with the quantitative measurements were electron microscopic observations of thin sections prepared from these infections. The authors were unable to find internalized bacteria when mammalian cells were incubated with the *Y. pseudotuberculosis* Inv⁻ mutant (Fig. 4.7), in contrast to the large numbers of intracellular bacteria seen with the parental Inv⁺ strain. The rare Inv⁻ bacteria that could be found in these thin sections were always outside the mammalian cells.

How Many Genes Code for Invasiveness?

The results of the DNA sequencing and protein measurement experiments presented strongly suggest that *inv* is a single gene. In support of this notion, the authors further stated: "We found that all the insertion mutations located within the *inv* locus fell into a **single complementation group**." This means that to determine if invasiveness may be encoded by more than one gene, these workers carried out a **complementation test**. A complementation test consists of introducing two **separate mutations** into the same bacterium. In this study, one of the mutations was located on the chromosome, the other on a plasmid. Under these circumstances, if the *inv* activity were to be carried by two genes encoding for two individual proteins, say **A** and **B**, the **A** gene of one mutant would make normal **B** product and vice versa. In this case, a complete set of **A** and **B** proteins would be made, the two mutations would complement each other, and the bacterium would have the invasive phenotype. On the other hand, if the activity were determined by one gene only, complementation could not occur. Indeed, when the investigators carried out complementation tests with several pairs of *inv*⁻

mutants, they never found restoration of invasiveness, which strongly suggests that this activity is encoded by a single gene and mediated by a single gene product.

How Do We Know That the Protein Encoded by the *inv* Gene Is Directly Responsible for Invasion?

Although the genetic approach is very powerful, it does not by itself support the irrefutable conclusion that the protein product of the *inv* gene is directly responsible for the invasion phenotype. There is still the possibility that the *inv* gene acts indirectly, both in *Y. pseudotuberculosis* and *E. coli*. Further experiments with purified invasin showed that this protein acts directly on the first event needed for penetration into mammalian cells, namely, binding to their surface. Mammalian cells in suspension were found to bind to purified invasin immobilized on a cellulose surface and not to other bacterial proteins (**Step 7**). Thus, the protein itself must be the direct mediator of the adherence of the bacteria to the surface of mammalian cells.

Further studies revealed that penetration of *Y. pseudotuberculosis* into host cells is more complicated than first imagined. It was found, for instance, that the synthesis of invasin depends on the temperature of cultivation of the organism. At body temperature, relatively little invasin is synthesized, whereas the bacteria grown at 25°C make a great deal of this protein. This finding suggests that invasin is made by bacteria in the environment (food, water) and that this protein is particularly relevant to the first event in the disease in humans, the penetration of the bacteria into intestinal cells. Once inside the body, invasin synthesis is stopped by the high temperature, and entry into other cells may be dictated by other proteins not detected in this investigation. Subsequent studies from several laboratories showed that such proteins could indeed be demonstrated. The authors suggest that invasin, by being extremely active in penetration, may inadvertently promote phagocytosis of the bacteria and their possible destruction. Thus, it may be to the organism's advantage to use the powerful invasin system at first, but then to rely on more subtle means to penetrate additional host cells. This is not the first instance where a sophisticated biological system of regulation has been found to operate in the various steps in the establishment of an infectious disease.

The experiments with *Y. pseudotuberculosis* demonstrate how the combined use of genetics, biochemistry, and cell biology help us to understand better the mechanisms of microbial pathogenesis. In situations where the prime virulence factor is a toxin (as will be discussed in subsequent chapters), the biochemical approach is often the most direct means to determine the mechanism of pathogenesis. But, in dealing with more complex microbial-host interactions, the genetic approach provides the first means to dissect the many factors involved so that they can be meaningfully analyzed.

SUGGESTED READING

Isberg RR. Mammalian cell adhesion functions and cellular penetration of enteropathogenic *Yersinia* species. Molec Microbiol 1989;3:1449–1493.

Isberg RR, Leong JM. Cultured mammalian cells attach to the invasin protein of *Yersinia pseudotuberculosis*. Proc Natl Acad Sci USA 1988;85: 6682–6686.

Isberg RR, Voorhis DL, Falkow S. Identification of invasin: a protein that allows enteric bacteria to penetrate cultured mammalian cells. Cell 1987;50: 769–778.

Definitions

Virulence factor. This term, in the strictest sense, refers to substances produced by a microorganism that, in pure form, can harm the host. The classic examples of virulence factors are bacterial toxins, discussed in Chapter 9. More recently, workers in the field have started to use the term to mean any component of the microbe that is required for, or that potentiates, its ability to cause disease. By this looser definition, even a substance that, when purified, is nontoxic to host tissue could still be a virulence factor if its absence would make the microbe significantly less capable of causing disease (less virulent). Excluded from the definition are any genes (and gene products) that are essential for normal growth of the microbe. Thus, a factor required by a bacterium for growth on laboratory medium is not considered to be a virulence factor, whereas a factor that potentiates the ability of the bacterium to invade the human bloodstream is. The classic virulence factors, the toxins, were traditionally studied biochemically; detailed structural-activity relationships were evaluated to determine precisely the "active site" of the toxin molecule and how it worked. Evaluation of the broader category of virulence factors is now being approached primarily genetically. The hallmark of these studies is the comparison of isogenic strains in the appropriate model of infection. Isogenic strains consist of a wild-type parent and a derivative that is identical genetically except for a single mutation. Models of infection range anywhere from a full-blown experimental animal that develops a typical illness, to tissue or cell cultures that can be invaded, adhered to, propagated upon, or evaded (in terms of phagocytic or other host defense cells).

Virulence, or the ability to cause an infectious disease, is always multifactorial, since the infectious disease process is invariably complex. At each stage of the process, different virulence factors are needed by pathogenic microorganisms to cause disease. Major investigative goals presently are to determine:

- What are the virulence factors involved in the infection of interest?

- On a biochemical and physiological level, how are these factors involved in the establishment of the disease?

- Given that the microenvironment varies at each of these steps, how does the parasite regulate the requisite factors? In particular, are there special environmental signals that are interpreted by the microbe to turn on or off a whole set of genes? How is this signal transduced?

Each infectious agent has its own way of performing many of these functions. Nevertheless, it is now being recognized that many microbes share similar approaches to similar problems. In the ensuing chapters, these sorts of general points will be made into **paradigms**. Each microorganism has at least one interesting property that teaches us things about the cellular and molecular pathogenesis of many different microbes.

Restriction enzymes. These nucleases are "magic scissors" that cut both strands of the DNA at specific sequences, producing pieces of different length. The length of a fragment depends on the distance between two recognition sequences. If one of the sequences of an individual is mutated, the cut will not be made at that sequence and the fragment generated will be longer. Since a single base change can eliminate a site or create a new one for a particular enzyme, specific fragments generated by a given restriction enzyme may be of different lengths, reflecting differences between individuals in a population. This **restriction fragment length polymorphism (RFLP)** is used to identify individual humans, for example, in forensic medicine.

Several hundred restriction enzymes with different specificities are currently available. The sequence recognized by a given restriction enzyme may be four, five, or more bases long. The number of cuts made in a piece of DNA depends on the frequency of occurrence of such sequence; thus, enzymes that recognize the more abundant shorter sequences make more cuts than those that recognize longer sequences. For example, an enzyme that recognizes a four-base sequence will cut on the average once every 256 nucleotides ($1/4^4$), whereas one that recognizes a six-base sequence cuts on the average once every 4096 nucleotides ($1/4^6$). By choosing the appropriate enzyme, the DNA of an organism can be divided into a larger or smaller number of **restriction fragments**. Many restriction enzymes make staggered cuts on each of the DNA strands, thus leaving overlapping ends at the site of the cut, whereas others cut precisely across the double strand, giving blunt ends (Fig. 4.2).

Restriction enzymes are not merely laboratory tools but also serve to protect the species that makes them from foreign DNA. How do restriction enzymes recognize that DNA is foreign and not the bacterium's own? Besides making a specific restriction enzyme, each species is also capable of modifying the corresponding DNA sequence by **methylation**. The bacterium's methylated DNA is resistant to the restriction enzyme whereas the foreign, unmethylated DNA will be cleaved. Such systems protect cells, for example, from killing by DNA viruses.

Genetic transformation (and other means of genetic transfer). Transformation consists of the exchange of genetic material among bacteria by way of naked DNA. Some bacteria take up DNA spontaneously from the medium and incorporate it into their genome. Such strains are said to be **competent**. Bacteria are not necessarily competent at all times and competence may be an inducible property. Pneumococci, for instance, become competent when their culture reaches the stationary phase of growth. At that time, some of them secrete a protein called **competence factor** that induces their neighbors to become competent. Competence factor acts to expose DNA-binding proteins on the cell surface.

Other species do not have an innate mechanism for DNA uptake but may be coaxed to incorporate DNA by changing their surface properties. In the case of *E. coli*, increasing the ionic strength of the medium and raising the temperature changes membrane permeability properties and allows this normally recalcitrant species to take up DNA. This is an example of artificially induced competence and is used extensively in genetic engineering experiments.

How do competent bacteria ensure that DNA from other species does not become incorporated into their genome? There are several mechanisms to recognize "self" from "nonself," other than the restriction enzyme systems. Some of these systems operate intracellularly; others operate before the DNA enters the cell. Certain bacterial species, such as the pneumococci, are indiscriminate in their uptake of DNA. Once bound to the surface, the DNA is cut by nucleases into small fragments (six to eight kilobases). One of the strands of the DNA is now degraded and the other is taken up. The intracellular strand will undergo recombination with the genome of the recipient only if it has nearly the same sequence of bases; that is, if it is homologous. Heterologous DNA, on the other hand, is rapidly degraded with no genetic consequence.

Other bacterial species, such as *Haemophilus influenzae*, are more discriminating and take up DNA from the same or related species only. How does this species recognize homologous DNA? On its membrane, *Haemophilus* carries a protein that binds specifically to an 11-base pair sequence that is frequently found in *Haemophilus* DNA but that is rare in other species. Note that a given 11 base pair sequence occurs at random once in 4^{11} (or about 5 million bases). A typical bacterial chromosome is 3–5 million base pairs in length. Thus, the fact that this "password" is common in *Haemophilus* is an unusual property of this organism. In *Haemophilus*, as in many other Gram negatives, DNA is taken up as a double strand, but only one strand participates in recombination with the host genome.

Transformation is not the only way to introduce foreign genes (Fig. 4.11). DNA can be introduced by way of a **bacteriophage** or **phage** (see "**Bacteriophages**"). This procedure, the transfer of genes by way of a phage, is known as **transduction** (see "**Transduction**"). The third major way that foreign DNA is taken up by a host, **conjugation**, involves cell-to-cell contact. The choice of technique used to introduce DNA depends on the recipient bacteria and on details of the experimental strategy.

Figure 4.11. Modes to introduce DNA into bacteria. A. Transformation, using naked DNA. **B.** Transduction, using phages. **C.** Conjugation, by cell-to-cell contact.

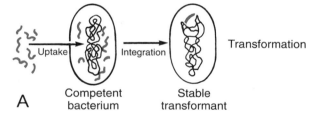

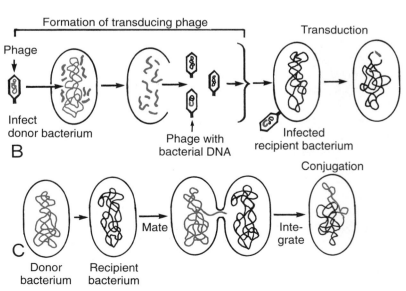

Plasmids.   Plasmids are autonomously replicating (extrachromosomal) double-stranded DNA molecules. They are a dispensable addition to the genetic material of most bacteria but often encode properties that are required for survival in certain environments. The most medically relevant plasmid-encoded properties are antibiotic resistance and virulence factors, including toxin production. Plasmids come in many varieties, differing in size, types of genes they possess, and ability to transfer among bacteria. They range in size from those that carry some 100 genes to those that have only about five genes. Like the bacterial chromosome, plasmids regulate their own replication. Thus, each constitutes an independent replicating entity known as a **replicon**, which possesses its own **origin of replication** and regulatory proteins.

The number of plasmids per cell depends on how closely their replication is linked to that of the chromosome. In some cases, the connection is tight and the number of plasmids (**copy number**) is small, sometimes just one or two per cell. This type of control is characteristic of large plasmids. Small plasmids tend to be present in high numbers, sometimes as many as 50–100 copies per cell. Such plasmids are useful in genetic engineering work where the product of a particular gene needs to be expressed in large amounts.

Some plasmids mediate their own transfer between bacteria of the same or different species. These are known as **conjugative plasmids** (see "Conjugation"). The F factor involved in *E. coli* conjugation is the best studied example. Such plasmids carry genes encoding products, such as the sex pilus, that are involved in the cell-to-cell contact. Many antibiotic-resistance plasmids, known as R plasmids, are also conjugative. Those that, in addition, are promiscuous in their ability to replicate in different hosts are the most likely to spread drug resistance among unrelated bacterial species. Such plasmids have contributed to the dramatic increase in antimicrobial resistance.

Bacteriophages.   Bacteriophages or **phages** are viruses that infect bacteria (Fig. 4.12). Like all viruses, they are composed of either DNA or RNA (never both) surrounded by a protein shell, the **capsid**. Some bacteriophages have a tail structure and tail fibers that are involved in attachment to the host bacteria. The nucleic acid may be double stranded or single stranded. In some phages, the capsid is surrounded by a lipid-containing layer that probably plays a role in their attachment to host cell membranes. Other phages contain proteins and other non-nucleic acid constituents within their capsids. In size and shape, phages range from the very small (containing about six genes) to the large and complex (with more than 100 genes). Details of the biology of viruses are described in Chapter 30.

Phages are of two general types, virulent and temperate (Fig. 4.13). In each case, the life cycle begins by attachment to the host cells by way of attachment proteins that recognize specific receptors on the host cells. Like all viruses, phages lose their structural integrity during their replication. Their capsid and nucleic acid separate, usually just after attachment to the host bacteria. In typical cases, the nucleic acid is injected into the host cells and the capsid remains on the outside. In **virulent phages**, viral nucleic acid replicates soon after it enters, to yield tens, hundreds, or even thousands of copies. Independently, the capsid proteins are synthesized and, together with the viral nucleic acid and other constituents, as-

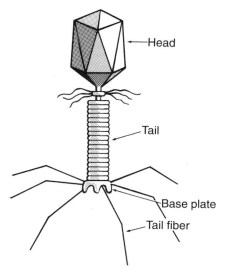

Figure 4.12.   Structure of phage T4. T4 is a phage that infects *E. coli* and is representative of a family of large and complex viruses.

Figure 4.13. Lysogenic and lytic pathways of phage development. After adsorption of the phage to the host bacteria and penetration of the phage DNA, one of two events are possible, depending on environmental conditions. The *lysogenic pathway* leads to the stable integration of the phage genome into that of the host. The *lytic pathway* leads to phage multiplication and the eventual release of new phage particles.

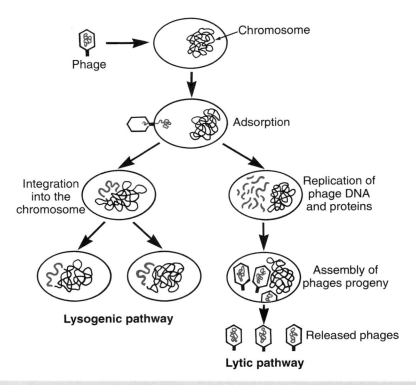

semble to make the complete virus particle, called a **virion**. Phage virions are released by lysis of the host cell or by extrusion though the membrane. This sequence of events is known as the **lytic cycle**, because the host bacterium is eventually destroyed.

Depending on environmental conditions, **temperate** phages may go through a lytic cycle, as described for virulent phage, or an alternative one called **lysogeny**. In the lysogenic life cycle, phage genes are repressed and the viral nucleic acid, instead of replicating, is integrated into the host genome. Such phages always contain double-stranded DNA and not RNA. Integration is a special type of genetic recombination, which results in the linear extension of the host genome. The bacterial chromosome becomes elongated by the amount of viral genome incorporated. The integrated phage genome is known as the **prophage**; host cells carrying a prophage are called **lysogens** and the condition of being integrated is known as **lysogeny**. With some *E. coli* phages, such as **Mu (μ)**, the prophage integrates at many sites on the chromosome. With other phages, such as **lambda (λ)**, integration takes place at specific sites on the *E. coli* chromosome only. In some situations, the lysogenic phage carries one or more genes that profoundly affect the virulence of the host bacterium. One classic case is with phage β of *Corynebacterium diphtheriae*, the causative agent of diphtheria. Diphtheria toxin (see Chapter 9 for details) is encoded by the phage; only lysogenic bacteria, therefore, are capable of producing the disease, diphtheria.

How do we know that a bacterium is lysogenic, that is, that it contains a prophage? It is often possible to reverse the lysogenic state, that is, to have the prophage become derepressed and enter a lytic cycle. This event happens spontaneously, albeit rarely, or can be **induced** to higher frequency by ultraviolet light or chemical mutagens. When the prophage DNA excises from the chromosome, it may carry with it some of the previously adjacent bacterial genes. The viruses that result can bring these genes from their cell of origin to another cell (see "**Transduction**").

Transduction. Transduction is the introduction of genetic material into bacteria by way of the phage infection apparatus (Fig. 4.12). Transducing phages are usually temperate phages that arise when prophages are induced and, in the process of excision from the chromosome, pick up some of the adjacent genes. Such imperfect cutting is rare and, if carried to extremes, results in phage particles that cannot replicate. Such defective phages retain the ability to infect a new host once and to introduce bacterial or other genes into it. This type of **specialized transduction** is limited to the genes that were adjacent to the prophage on the chromosome. If the prophage is of the lambda type and integrates at specific sites only, transduction will be limited to the genes to the right and the left of this site. Mu-type phages, which integrate at many sites, will pick up almost any small group of physically contiguous genes and transduce them to a new host.

During the assembly process of some phages (whether temperate or virulent), the capsid may not be filled with viral DNA, but may pick up any DNA near it. Fragments of chromosomal DNA from the host can thus be packaged into capsids, making particles that are totally defective in reproduction but that can still attach to new host cells and inject their DNA. The particles so produced are called **pseudovirions**, and the transfer of their DNA is called **generalized transduction**. Pseudovirions can also be created artificially by carrying out the viral assembly reaction in vitro using the components of the capsid and any DNA molecules, including those that are produced by cloning techniques. Thus, pseudovirions can be a useful DNA delivery system for genetic engineering.

Transposable elements. Transposable elements ("hopping genes") are DNA segments that can insert themselves into a DNA molecule as well as excise from it. Thus, these elements can transfer from one chromosomal location to another, from a chromosome to a plasmid, or vice versa. The two steps, integration and excision, are carried out by different mechanisms. There are two varieties of transposable elements: insertion sequences that have the minimal genetic information for transposition; and transposons that carry extra genes in addition to those required for transposition.

1. **Insertion sequences (IS elements)** are relatively small DNA pieces, about one to two kilobases long, with two characteristic properties. First, they have specific sequences at both their ends that are **inverted repeats** of one another (Fig. 4.14). Second, these sequences are recognized by enzymes encoded

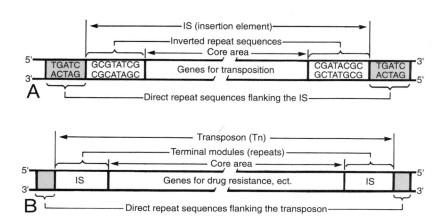

Figure 4.14. Insertion sequences and transposons. A. Insertion sequence (*IS element*). **B.** Transposon (*Tn*).

within the IS elements that carry out integration into a target site.

2. **Transposons (Tn)** are more complex DNA molecules capable of insertion into a genome. The integration of a transposon or an insertion sequence within a gene disrupts the gene and constitutes an **insertion mutation**. Transposons integrate by several distinct mechanisms, some resembling the one used by IS elements.

The characteristic of transposons is that they can carry extraneous genes (Fig. 4.14). These genes may be of clinical interest, such as those for antibiotic resistance. Certain plasmids, e.g., the widely distributed R plasmids, carry one or more drug-resistance transposons. It is the ability of these determinants to hop from one plasmid to another that provides bacteria with tremendous flexibility in developing resistance to the hostile environment such as a hospital, which is usually inundated with antibiotics. Because of selective pressure, R plasmids may acquire ever more transposons with new drug-resistance genes. Since many of these R plasmids are conjugative, the spread of **multiple drug resistance** can occur between different types of bacteria with the use of only one antibiotic in the environment. Under such conditions, although only one resistance marker is being selected, the other resistance markers are carried from one bacterial strain to another as fellow travelers.

Linkage. In the case of bacteria, which usually possess only one chromosome, the word linkage denotes the degree to which two genes are located close to one another (how closely linked they are). The degree of linkage can be measured by the frequency of recombinations that takes place between the two genes; that is, the closer they are, the less the chance of recombination between them. There is not a direct correspondence between the frequency of recombination and the physical length of DNA, as would be expected if recombination were to take place uniformly along the chromosome. The reason for this discrepancy is that there are hot spots on the chromosome where recombination is more frequent and that distort the linear relationship between linkage and physical distance.

Genetic measurements of linkage may some day become superfluous, when the DNA sequence of an organism becomes completely known. However, with the exception of *E. coli* and a few small viruses, whose DNA has been totally or nearly totally sequenced, this remains a goal for the future. A large-scale project is underway to sequence the human genome, but, in view of the large size of the human DNA, fulfilling this goal will require many years.

Mutants. Mutants are organisms that differ genetically from the **wild type**, the kind found most abundantly in nature. For a mutant to be useful for experimental study, it must differ not only in its **genotype** (its DNA sequence), but also in a demonstrable property, its **phenotype**. Spontaneous mutations are rare, generally occurring **for a given gene** once in 10^6–10^9 cell divisions. This frequency can be increased many-fold by mutagenesis.

By studying the consequences of mutations in important genes, such as the toxin gene of a virulent organism, geneticists can assess the function of the gene product (the toxin). In addition, mutations can be used as **markers** to carry out genetic manipulations. Markers are useful if they are easy to select; for example, those that impart antibiotic resistance or the ability to grow on a given substrate, e.g., lactose. When the positions of such markers on the chromosome are known, genetic crosses can be used to determine the positions of other genes.

It is easy to see how mutants in dispensable functions may be obtained and studied. How can we study mutations in functions that are essential under all growth conditions, since, by definition, they will be lethal? This can be done using **conditional mutants**, where the mutation is expressed under one condition but not another. For example, a mutation in RNA polymerase may be expressed at high temperature, e.g., 40°C, but not at 30°C. A culture can be maintained and grown at the lower (**permissive**) temperature but its defect is manifested at the higher (**nonpermissive**) temperature.

Mutation.   Mutations are changes in the coding sequence of genes (whereas mutants are the organisms that carry a mutation). Mutations arise by a variety of alterations in the DNA. Some of these changes are relatively small, such as single-base substitutions. Others involve a greater amount of DNA, either by deletion, insertion, or inversion of more than one base pair. Mutations occurs spontaneously at characteristic rates, usually once in 10^6–10^9 bacterial divisions. Mutation is often the result of errors during DNA replication. Normally such errors are corrected during the process of synthesis itself, but a few escape. The rate of mutagenesis can be increased 1 thousand- to 1 million-fold by the addition of mutagenic agents.

Many chemical and physical agents are mutagenic; many are even normally present in the environment. Some, such as chemical analogs of the DNA bases, result in the replacement of one base by another (e.g., guanine for adenine). Base substitutions may not have an effect on the encoded protein because there is redundancy in the genetic code (i.e., 64 possible codons encode only 22 amino acids plus three "stop" codons). On the other hand, a single base change may create a **missense mutation**, where one amino acid in a protein is substituted for another. Such a change does not always affect the function of the encoded protein, but when it does, the defect in the protein may result in a **mutant phenotype**. If the mutation results in the change from an amino acid-specifying codon to a stop codon (e.g., UAA), such a **nonsense mutation** will result in a truncated protein. Ionizing radiation and certain alkylating agents lead to the deletions of one or more bases. A single base deletion results in a **frameshift mutation**, where the triplet code is read in a different frame, producing a totally different sequence of amino acids in a peptide. Larger deletions may also result in a frame shift (if they involve bases in numbers other than 3 or its multiples), but in every case, lead to the formation of incomplete, often inactive proteins. Insertion mutations can be produced by the integration of transposable elements such as transposons or insertion sequences (see "**Transposable Elements**") into a gene. Insertions may likewise inactivate proteins because they introduce an unnatural string of amino acids into a protein. Both deletions and insertions can be detected by biochemical means, such as using restriction enzymes. Knowing the location and length of deletions or insertions can be used in genetic mapping to delineate the length and position of a gene.

Conjugation.   Conjugation in bacteria consists of cell-to-cell contact resulting in the unidirectional transfer of genetic material from

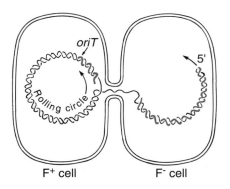

F⁺ cell   F⁻ cell

Figure 4.15. Transfer of F plasmid from an F⁺ to an F⁻ cell. A single DNA strand generated by replication is transferred from the donor to the recipient cell. The complementary strand is then synthesized in the recipient to reconstitute the complete F plasmid.

a donor to a recipient cell (Fig. 4.15). Bacteria themselves are not genetically endowed to carry out conjugation. To be able to mate, they must carry **conjugative plasmids** that possess the genes necessary for this process to occur. For instance, the F plasmid of *E. coli*, (see "**Plasmids**") codes for several conjugative functions, including a **sex pilus**, a specialized structure that differs from the common pili in functioning as a conjugal bridge between donor and recipient bacteria. The process of transfer of the DNA is complex and conjugation requires the products of some 20 plasmid genes. Transfer takes place by a special form of replication of the F plasmid in the donor cell as shown in Figure 4.15.

In general, conjugative plasmids cause transfer of their own DNA only. However, if a conjugative plasmid becomes integrated into the chromosome, it will transfer not only itself but also the chromosomal genes that are located "downstream" from it. In principle, the entire chromosome could be transferred to a recipient cell during conjugation. Transfer of the DNA is a linear process and is relatively slow, taking more than 2 hours for the passage of the entire chromosome. The mating bridge between the two cells is fragile and seldom persists that long. Thus, in most cases, the only portion of the donor DNA to transfer is that proximal to the origin of transfer. The closer a gene is to the origin, the sooner it will be transferred. The timing of transfer, therefore, is related to the position of the gene on the chromosome and this fact has been used, by a series of interrupted coitus experiments, to map the *E. coli* genome.

Recombination.   When a DNA fragment enters a bacterial cell, it may become incorporated into the chromosome by recombination. There are two types of recombination, known as homologous and site-specific.

Homologous recombination takes place when the entering DNA has substantial similarity with sequences on the chromosome. Sequence homology must be sufficient to allow the first step in recombination, namely, **pairing** of the two regions. The paired molecules then undergo a reaction known as a **crossover** between them. If two crossovers take place along the same chromosome, the entering DNA replaces the resident sequences (Fig. 4.10).

Site-specific recombination does not require extensive sequence homology among the recombining molecules. Specific enzymes different from those working on homologous recombination are required for this reaction. Each of these **integrases** recognizes a specific sequence as a site for recombination. Examples of site-specific recombination are the integration of the genomes of temperate phages (see "**Bacteriophages**") or of transposable elements (see "**Transposable Elements**").

Biological Basis for Antibacterial Action

5

David Schlessinger

Killing microorganisms is relatively simple as long as it does not have to be done selectively. They can be killed by heat, radiation, strong acids, etc. To target them specifically, without damaging host cells and tissues, is much more difficult. According to the formulation originally made by Paul Ehrlich in 1906, what we want is a "specific chemotherapy." We are indebted to the microorganisms themselves for producing many chemotherapeutic agents, the antibacterial antibiotics. We discussed how antibiotics act in Chapter 3. Here we will discuss the biological basis for the usefulness of these drugs, including how bacteria defend themselves against them. This chapter focuses mainly on antibacterial drugs. **Antiviral drugs are discussed in Chapter 43; antifungal drugs are discussed in Chapter 45; antiprotozoal drugs are in Chapters 50 and 51, and antihelmithic drugs are in Chapters 52 and 53.**

WHERE DID ANTIBIOTICS COME FROM AND WHEN?

Organisms in the environment—soil, water, or areas of the human body—attempt to gain an advantage over others by secreting specific chemicals. Some do it directly by excreting antibiotics. Others carry this out in more subtle ways. In Chapter 3, we mentioned that microorganisms secrete iron-chelating compounds and are capable of reabsorbing their own iron-bearing product. In this manner, the iron concentration is reduced to a level that does not permit the growth of other organisms that do not have this iron-scavenging capacity. Thus, in complex environments, competition for nutrients combines with the action of antibiotic substances to produce a balanced microbial ecology.

In the last 30 years, we have taken advantage of this natural warfare for our own purposes. We borrow antibiotics from one organism to combat others. This has resulted in a medical revolution of immense proportions. Figure 5.1 shows the increase in human longevity since the introduction of antibiotic therapy. Since we all take for granted the use of antibiotics, it is hard to recapture the early impact of modern chemotherapy. You might ask older family members how they feared the loss of a loved one from pneumonia or postoperative infections; or talk to older physicians about how powerless they were when treating children with meningococcal meningitis or subacute bacterial endocarditis. There is a price to pay for our therapeutic progress. The selective pressure exerted by antibiotics on bacteria is so great that, within

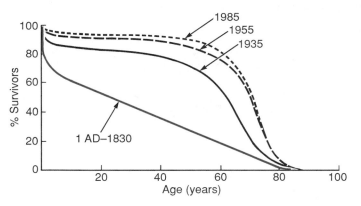

Figure 5.1. Survival of human populations as a function of age. Average life expectancy (50% level) remained at 25 years until 1830. Between then and 1935, the impact of sanitation, public health, and immunization extended the life expectancy. Antibiotics (along with nutrition and health education) added an average of another 8 years. Note that more recent medical breakthroughs have not extended average life expectancy very much.

one human generation, they have responded most vigorously by becoming resistant, often to several antibiotics.

The first important antimicrobial agents were not antibiotics but synthetically made **antimetabolites**. Ehrlich's seminal work derived from his own findings that dyes used in histochemistry became bound to cell-specific receptors. "Why then," he asked, "should not such dyes be made to be toxic for specific organisms?" Ehrlich's intuition was validated by workers in the mammoth German chemical industry, who systematically synthesized thousands of compounds and tested them for biological effects. In 1934, Domagk found that one of these, Prontosil, cured a fatal streptococcal infection in mice. It was then shown that Prontosil was inactive on pure cultures of bacteria in vitro but was hydrolyzed in vivo to the active drug, **sulfanilamide**. Cures with this first of the sulfa drugs were soon reported. These findings gave impetus to the efforts to purify penicillin, a true antibiotic that had been detected as the product of a mold by Fleming in 1928. The new era had arrived; the search for new antimetabolites and antibiotics has continued uninterrupted ever since.

WHAT IS THE BASIS FOR SELECTIVE ANTIMICROBIAL ACTION?

Example of Sulfonamides

Early on, it was found that extracts from yeast contain a substance that antagonizes the action of sulfonamides. When purified, this proved to be para-aminobenzoic acid (PAB; Fig. 5.2), a component of folic acid. Sulfanilamide was, therefore, the first structural analog of a natural metabolite, the first **antimetabolite**. The similarity in the structure of the two compounds is obvious in this case. Following this lead, hundreds of thousands of antimetabolites have been tested for possible therapeutic value. In the sulfa class alone, thousands of derivatives with small and large modifications have been studied; about 25 of them are still in use.

The competition between sulfonamide and PAB regarding their action on bacteria is illustrated in Figure 5.3; when more drug is added, proportionally more PAB is required to counteract its action. This type of antagonism is called **competitive inhibition**. The mechanism of action of sulfanilamide was clarified when the function of PAB became better known. Since PAB was found to be a constituent of folic acid (Fig. 5.2), it was inferred that sulfa drugs inhibit the synthesis of this vitamin, and thereby, of the coenzymes that contain it. The main coenzyme is tetrahydroformyl folic acid, which functions in the reactions that add one carbon unit to synthesize nucleosides and certain amino

Precursor

H₂N—⬡—COOH
PAB

H₂N—⬡—SO₂NH₂
SULFANILAMIDE

Dihydropteroic acid

⬡—C−N—⬡—COOH

Folic acid

AGCT
Amino acids

Precursors

DHFA

THFA

Trimethoprim
Amethopterin
Methotrexate
Pyrimethamine

Figure 5.2. Inhibition of folic acid synthesis (by sulfa) and its function (by other antibacterial drugs). The addition of sulfanilamide instead of para-amino benzoic acid to dihydroxypteroic acid inhibits the synthesis of folic acid. In addition, the resulting analog functions as a "lethal product."

acids (Fig. 5.2). So, it was reasoned that (*a*) folic acid should suppress the action of sulfa drugs, and that (*b*) if bacteria were given enough folic acid to satisfy their growth requirement, no amount of an inhibitor of folic acid synthesis could suppress their growth. Unlike the case of **PAB**, antagonism of sulfas by folic acid is **noncompetitive**. This expectation was confirmed (Fig. 5.3).

There is a reason why the effectiveness of sulfa drugs is surprising. Cells of our body require *preformed* folic acid; this explains why they are unaffected by sulfonamides, which inhibit the *synthesis* of this compound, not its utilization. On the other hand, the folic acid we require must be present in the circulation and in tissues. Why then can't bacteria use it, and escape sulfonamide action? The reason seems to be that many bacteria that make folic acid lack a system for the uptake of preformed folic acid and cannot benefit from its presence in the environment. Thus, they must make their own folic acid, which makes them susceptible to sulfa drugs. Folic acid everywhere, and not a molecule to save them!

WHAT LIMITS THE EFFICACY OF ANTIMICROBIAL DRUGS?

The mechanism of action of a drug is only one of the properties that determines its potential usefulness. You will learn of many others, e.g., pharmacodynamics, cost, likelihood of patient compliance. Here we will consider briefly three kinds of limitations on the efficacy of antimicrobial drugs that are related directly to their mode of action: the speed with which the drugs work, the sensitivity of the microbial target, and the side effects on the host.

1. The practical efficacy of drugs sometimes depends on how fast they stop bacteria in their tracks. The case of sulfanilamide is instructive. When the drug is given to a culture of susceptible bacteria, they keep growing for about two to four generations before their growth is inhibited (Fig. 5.4). The reason for this delay is that each bacterium contains enough preformed folic acid to meet the demand of up to 16 daughter cells. Only after that many cells are formed does the drug become bacteriostatic. Inhibition by sulfonamides, then, is dependent on their continued presence.

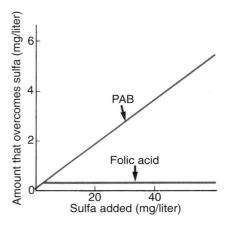

Figure 5.3. *PAB* overcomes *sulfa* addition competitively; *folic acid*, noncompetitively.

Figure 5.4. The effect of bacteriostatic and bactericidal drugs on the growth of bacteria. Note that certain bacteriostatic drugs may not inhibit growth for some time. In the case of sulfa drugs, this is due to time required to use up preformed folic acid in the bacteria.

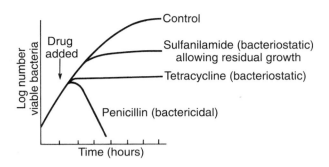

Other things being equal, a **bactericidal** agent, one that kills microorganisms rapidly, is preferable to a bacteriostatic one that inhibits growth reversibly. Organisms that remain alive in the presence of a drug may still be harmful to the host, either by continuing to produce toxins or by becoming resistant to the drug and eventually resuming growth. Nevertheless, even the preference for bactericidal agents depends on the circumstances. For example, an inhibitor of protein synthesis, such as erythromycin, is bacteriostatic but stops the synthesis of protein toxins abruptly. In contrast, penicillin kills bacteria but not immediately; during the lag before the drug exerts its cidal lytic effect, the organisms continue to produce toxins. In experimental infections of mice with an agent of gas gangrene, *Clostridium perfringens*, a static drug protected the animals better than a cidal one. In practical terms, static antibiotics are also generally effective. Ultimately, inhibition of bacterial growth gives the defense mechanisms of the body the chance to get rid of the organisms.

The distinction of static vs. cidal should not be taken as absolute. First, the action of a drug may differ in different organisms. For example, the modified aminoglycoside spectinomycin is static for *Escherichia coli* and cidal for gonococci. Some drugs show odd kinetics of action that make them difficult to classify. For example, rifampin rapidly kills 99% of *E. coli* cells in vitro, but is static for the remaining 1%, perhaps because they are particularly resistant during a phase of their cell cycle. In other cases, a combination of two static drugs may achieve a cidal action. Despite these ambiguities, the criterion of static vs. cidal is generally useful in considering the outcome of drug therapy.

2. The efficacy of antimicrobial drugs depends on the degree of sensitivity of the intended target organisms. Every agent is effective against a defined range or spectrum of organisms. Broad-spectrum antibiotics, effective against a wide range of bacteria might, a priori, be thought to be preferable to drugs with narrow spectra. Several practical considerations, such as cost, argue against the widespread use of broadside antibiotics. These drugs should be reserved for appropriate situations, as in cases when the etiological agent cannot be determined before therapy begins, or for immunocompromised patients who may be subject to simultaneous infection by several agents.

The spectrum of microbial susceptibility depends not only on the organisms but also on the conditions of the infection. For example, aminoglycosides are taken up poorly by bacteria under anaerobic conditions. Thus, these drugs are ineffective against anaerobes. Also, the level of a drug achievable at the site of infection places limits on its usefulness. For example, nitrofurantoin is concentrated in the urine and is effective in many cases of urinary tract infections. On the other hand, the rapid excretion of this drug also means that it does not reach effective levels in tissues or blood.

3. A most important limitation is that antimicrobial drugs may have side effects on the host. In antimicrobial chemotherapy, as in daily life, there is no such thing as a free lunch. One tries to optimize the **therapeutic index**, the ratio between the effective and the toxic dose. It must be kept in mind that the degree of selectivity allowed depends on the plight of the patient. Sulfa drugs, for example, are relatively nontoxic. Other inhibitors of folic acid metabolism, e.g., methotrexate, are very toxic in humans but are used as anticancer agents. Sometimes there is no choice.

Infectious agents that do not penetrate into deep tissues provide special cases in therapy. Topical applications for skin infections are less likely to produce side effects. This permits extensive use of agents, such as the antibacterial drug polymixin and the antifungal antibiotic nystatin, that can harm host cell membranes. This also applies to drugs against intestinal worms, which topologically are also located outside body tissues.

Astute clinical observation sometimes can turn side effects to advantage, sometimes outside the field of antimicrobial pharmacology. Some derivatives of sulfonamides cause blood acidosis, and alkaline urine, and have a diuretic effect. These effects are weak, but they led to the synthesis of an important group of modern diuretics. Similarly, some sulfa drugs produce hypoglycemia, which led to the development of new drugs for the treatment of diabetes.

MANY WAYS IN WHICH ANTIBIOTICS ARE SELECTIVE

In the case of sulfa drugs, selectivity is based on the fact that bacteria, but not humans, have the need to synthesize their own folic acid. Any step in metabolism, unique to microorganisms or not, is a potential target for antimicrobial action. All that is needed is selective toxicity. In the same pathway as that affected by sulfonamides, the drug **trimethoprim** blocks the **function** rather than the **synthesis** of folic acid (Fig. 5.2). It inhibits the enzyme dihydrofolate reductase that catalyzes the reduction of dihydrofolate to tetrahydrofolate. This enzyme is absolutely necessary for human cells as well as for bacteria, but the amount needed to cause 50% enzyme inhibition is 0.005 mM for bacteria, 0.07 mM for protozoa, and 250 mM for mammals. Thus, the drug can be used against bacteria and protozoa without causing harm to humans.

This is an example of efficacy based on the relative insensitivity of the host compared with bacterial targets. In another instance, e.g., tetracycline, the target of both host cells and bacteria is sensitive, but bacteria, unlike mammalian cells, *concentrate* the antibiotic. As a result, tetracycline is effective even against intracellular organisms (e.g., chlamydiae).

The armamentarium of antimicrobials includes drugs that affect the synthesis or function of every class of microbial macromolecules. Extreme selectivity is achieved when the biochemical target is absent in the host cells. The best examples are the penicillins, which affect the biosynthesis of the murein layer of the bacterial cell wall (Chapter 3). No comparable structure exists in mammalian cells, which are totally insensitive to the action of these antibiotics. Nonetheless, even penicillins can have two undesirable side effects. Some individuals cannot take them because they have a strong allergic reaction. Also, administration of ampicillin, one of the most widely used of the penicillins, may lead to the destruction of the normal bacterial flora, particularly of the gut. This sometimes leads to colitis, overgrowth by fungi, and other complications. Thus, even a nearly perfect antibiotic comes with a price tag.

HOW DO PATHOGENS CIRCUMVENT THE ACTION OF ANTIBIOTICS?

The power of antibiotics is so pervasive that, within years of their introduction, resistant organisms may supplant susceptible ones. At what point in the action of antibiotics does resistance come into play? The activity of antimicrobial drugs can be broken into a sequence of three steps. First, the drugs must associate with the bacteria and penetrate their envelope. Second, they must be transported to an intracellular site of action. Third, they must bind to their specific biochemical target. Resistance to drugs may occur at each of these steps. Pathogenic microorganisms act like sophisticated biochemists and have developed a multitude of ways to do this. The clinically relevant mechanisms of resistance include:

- Preventing access to the target site by inhibiting uptake or increasing excretion of the drug;
- Modifying the target site;
- Reducing the physiological importance of the target site;
- Competitively binding the drug;
- Synthesizing an enzyme that inactivates the drug.

All of these mechanisms have been recognized in clinical pathogens, but the most common is the last one. Some of the examples introduced in Chapter 3 are treated more fully below. A more extensive list of mechanisms of antibacterial resistance is shown in Table 5.1.

Table 5.1. Most Common Mechanisms of Resistance to Antibacterial Agents

Agent	Plasmid-borne	Resistance Mechanism
Penicillins and cephalosporins	Yes	Hydrolysis of β-lactam ring by β-lactamase
Chloramphenicol	Yes	Acetylation of hydroxyl groups of chloramphenicol transacetylase; interference with transport into cell
Tetracyclines	Yes	Exit pump pushes drug out of cell
Aminoglycosides (streptomycin, kanamycin, gentamicin, tobramycin, amikacin, etc.)	Yes	Enzymatic modification of drug by R plasmid-encoded enzyme; drug has reduced affinity for ribosome, and transport into cell is reduced
Sulfanilamides	Yes	Sulfanilamide-resistant dihydropteroate synthase
Trimethoprim	Yes	Trimethoprim-resistant dihydrofolate reductase
Erythromycin	Yes	Enzymatic modification (methylation of 23S ribosomal RNA)
Lincomycin	Yes	RNA of susceptible cells converts ribosome to drug resistance (unable to bind inhibitor)
Mercury (merthiolate)	Yes	Enzymatic reduction of mercury salts to metallic state and vaporization
Nalidixic acid, rifampin, ciprofloxacin, etc.	No	Resistance arises by spontaneous mutation of gyrase, nitrofurans, other target enzymes
Methicillin	No	Change in penicillin-binding protein (not in β-lactamase)

β-Lactams and Resistance to Them

In Chapter 3, we summarized the effects of the antibiotics, penicillins and cephalosporins, on cell wall formation and their consequences for bacterial survival. This is a large group of drugs, and for various reasons, their efficacy varies greatly.

In general, these antibiotics contain a β-lactam ring (Fig. 5.5). Particular side chains permit the drugs to penetrate the outer membrane of Gram-negative bacteria and, thus, to extend the list of susceptible organisms. They become "broad-spectrum antibiotics." Other substitutions make these drugs more easily absorbed or more resistant to stomach acid, thus making them effective oral chemotherapeutic agents.

An example of drug development is the transformation of cephalosporin. The original drug is more resistant to inactivating enzymes than penicillin but it is less potent. The addition of new side chains created a so-called second generation of cephalosporins with markedly greater potency, especially against Gram negatives. A third generation with a somewhat different spectrum has been synthesized by replacing the sulfur in the ring nucleus with an oxygen (Fig. 5.5). Cephalosporins in this class have two important advantages. First, they extend the spectrum of activity to organisms like *Pseudomonas* and *Haemophilus influenzae* that were resistant to most of the previous ones. Second, unlike the previous cephalosporins, they penetrate well into the central nervous system. This has made them especially useful in the treatment of Gram-negative meningitis.

The bactericidal action of the β-lactam antibiotics requires the following steps:

1. Association with the bacteria;

2. In Gram negatives, penetration through the outer membrane and the periplasmic space;

3. Interaction with penicillin-binding proteins on the cytoplasmic membrane;

4. Activation of an autolysin that degrades the cell wall murein.

The principal mechanism of resistance to the β-lactams is the elaboration of inactivating enzymes, the β-lactamases. So far, more than 100 β-lactamases have been identified, a small number of which account for most of the clinically encountered resistance. They can be divided into two categories, the penicillinases and the cephalosporinases. There is a fair degree of crossing over: i.e., a cephalosporinase may also inactivate a penicillin and vice versa, but with different efficiency.

In general, Gram-positive bacteria such as the staphylococci produce extracellular β-lactamases. Being secreted into the medium, these enzymes destroy the antibiotic before it comes in contact with the bacterial surface. Gram-positive β-lactamases are often made in large amounts after induction by the corresponding antibiotic. Adding more drug only induces the formation of greater amounts of enzyme and, as a result, resistance cannot usually be overcome even with massive doses. In the Gram negatives, β-lactamases are found in the periplasm or are bound to the inner membrane. They are often constitutive; that is, they are produced at a constant rate that does not increase with the addition of the drugs. In clinical terms, this means

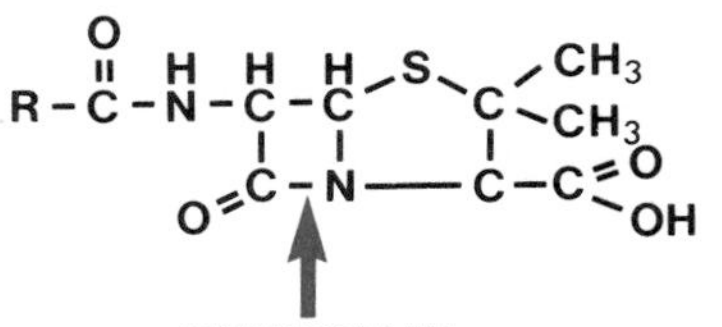

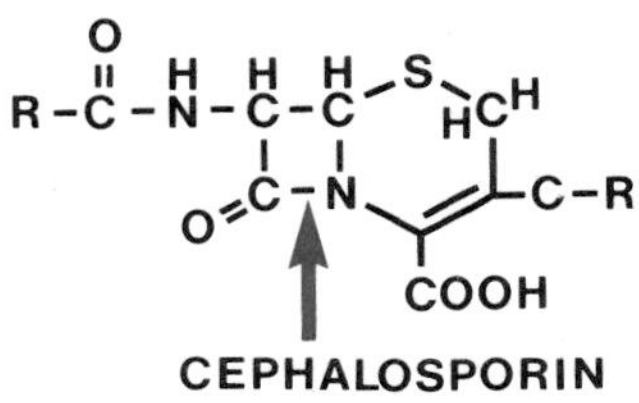

Figure 5.5. Core structure of *penicillins* and *cephalosporins*. The R groups specify the particular antibiotic; *arrows* indicate the bond broken during function and during inactivation by β-lactamases.

that resistance in these organisms can sometimes be overcome with higher doses of antibiotic.

β-Lactamase-dependent resistance to penicillins and cephalosporins is widespread among pathogenic bacteria. It has become so common in staphylococci, both in those acquired in hospitals and in the community, that infecting strains of these organisms must be considered penicillin resistant unless proven otherwise by antibiotic susceptibility tests.

The history of β-lactam resistance among the Gram negatives is different. With few exceptions, like the gonococcus, these organisms are resistant to the first drug of this group, the original penicillin G. However, when challenged with the newer drugs to which they are susceptible, the Gram negatives have been more slow to develop resistance. For example, prior to 1974, *Haemophilus influenzae*, an important pathogen in meningitis and pulmonary infections, was universally susceptible to the penicillin derivative ampicillin. This antibiotic was considered the drug of choice in treatment of *H. influenzae* infections. However in 1975, it became apparent that 10–20% of the isolates of *H. influenzae* elaborate an ampicillin degrading β-lactamase. This enzyme is encoded in a highly promiscuous plasmid, which probably accounts for the rapid spread of ampicillin resistance in this organism.

A similar reversal has occurred with the gonococcus. This organism used to be universally susceptible to penicillin, although higher levels of the drug have been gradually required over the last 30 years. In 1976, highly penicillin-resistant strains were isolated in two widely separated areas of the world. The gene coding for this resistance is carried on a transposon, which hops to other strains of gonococci and to other aerobic Gram negatives. Thus, we can no longer rely on penicillin as the universal agent for the treatment of gonorrhea.

These examples illustrate the role of transferable genetic elements in the spread of β-lactamase resistance. Plasmids and transposons have increased in importance since the early days of the antibiotic era. The first strains that became antibiotic resistant harbored chromosomal genes and only later were they replaced by strains with plasmid-borne resistance. The result is an increase in the spread of resistance to what previously were enclaves safe for antibacterial therapy. Thus, not only is there increased resistance in *H. influenzae* and gonococci, but there are scattered reports of resistance in other previously highly susceptible organisms, such as the pneumococci. If this pattern were to spread further and include other important β-lactam-susceptible pathogens like the meningococci and certain streptococci, it would be a serious blow to our ability to treat some important infectious diseases.

Other mechanisms of resistance to β-lactams have been reported. In a few instances, bacterial resistance has been attributed to poor penetration of the drugs or to mutations in the penicillin-binding proteins. This type of resistance sometimes takes on global proportions in the staphylococci. Some strains of *Staphylococcus aureus* become resistant to most of the known penicillins and cephalosporins, including a rather different one called methicillin. For this reason, these strains have the blanket designation of *methicillin-resistant S. aureus*, or **MRSA**. They are responsible for some of the worst outbreaks of hospital-acquired infection in recent history. These strains can only be treated successfully with another inhibitor of cell wall synthesis, vancomycin, a cyclic glycopeptide antibiotic. However, resistance to vancomycin has been reported. If these strains take hold and become more prevalent, we would revert to a situation equivalent to that of the preantibiotics era.

Finally, certain strains of pneumococci and staphylococci are inhibited rather than killed by certain levels of β-lactams. This results in a form of partial resistance called **tolerance**. In the case of tolerant pneumococci, the drugs are bacteriostatic and not bactericidal because these strains lack high enough levels of the suicidal autolysin. Bacterial tolerance may possibly explain some of the relapses in treating staphylococcal and streptococcal infections. However, compared with drug inactivation by β-lactamases, this accounts only for a small percentage of clinically important resistance.

Antiribosomal Antibiotics: Effectiveness and Resistance

The effectiveness of the second largest class of antibacterial agents, the antiribosomal antibiotics, is based on structural differences between the ribosomes of bacteria and of eukaryotic cells. In higher cells, ribosomes have larger RNA molecules and more protein components. Typical drugs of this group, such as streptomycin or erythromycin, bind to bacterial but not to mammalian ribosomes. The difference is not always absolute and does not completely explain the selective toxicity of all the drugs. In the first place, some antibiotics like tetracycline work in vitro as well on mammalian as on bacterial ribosomes. Second, mammalian cells have bacterial-like ribosomes in their mitochondria, and these are sensitive to many of the drugs of this class. The reason why these drugs are not toxic is thought to be that they cannot pass through the plasma membrane. However, some patients experience damage to their bone marrow after treatment with chloramphenicol. We may speculate that this results from the selective uptake of the drug into the mitochondria of highly oxidative bone marrow stem cells.

Other toxic side effects of these antibiotics cannot be anticipated from their mechanism of action. Examples are chelation of magnesium by tetracyclines with attendant bone and tooth malformation in children, or toxicity of various aminoglycosides for the eighth cranial nerve. Another significant complication is the inhibition of normal bacterial flora, as seen in the diarrhea that results from treatment with some of these drugs.

Tetracycline—Resistance by Drug Excretion

Resistance to the antiribosomal antibiotic can take many forms because these drugs must go through many steps to reach their targets. Tetracycline, for example, must:

1. Bind to the cytoplasmic membrane, which, in the case of Gram negatives, requires passage through the outer membrane and the periplasmic space; and

2. Be transported across the cytoplasmic membrane by an active transport mechanism. This has been shown to have two components, an initial rapid uptake and a second phase of slower uptake.

Resistant strains do not accumulate tetracycline within the cell. The reason is not, as might be expected, failure to take up the drug. Rather, the intracellular concentration is kept low by an exit mechanism that actively **excretes** the drug. Tetracycline resistance has been found in almost all bacteria, including Gram positives and Gram negatives, aerobes, and anaerobes. In addition to this novel mechanism of resistance, *Bacteroides* also possesses a more traditional mechanism leading to the destruction of this drug.

Chloramphenicol—Resistance by Drug Inactivation

Many kinds of bacteria have become resistant to chloramphenicol since its introduction. Recent examples of resistance to this drug have been in outbreaks of bacillary dysentery and typhoid that occurred in Central America and Mexico in the late 1960s and the early 1970s. Since this was considered the drug of choice for these diseases, it was widely administered. Patients did not respond to the treatment and many died.

Bacterial resistance to chloramphenicol is mediated by two mechanisms. First, a bacterial enzyme **acetylates** it to an acetyl or diacetyl ester. The acetylated derivatives are biologically inert because they cannot bind to the ribosomes. The enzyme, **acetyl transferase**, is responsible for the widespread resistance to chloramphenicol in aerobic bacteria, both Gram positives and Gram negatives. The genes coding for this enzyme are also plasmid-borne. The second mechanism for chloramphenicol inactivation has been demonstrated in anaerobic bacteria, which reduce a p-nitro group on the molecule.

Macrolides—Resistance by Target Modification

The macrolide antibiotics, another important group, are represented in clinical medicine by erythromycin, lincomycin, and clindamycin. The target of these drugs can be modified in a particularly interesting way, by **methylation** of 23S ribosomal RNA of susceptible Gram-positive bacteria. This modification makes the 50S ribosomal subunits resistant to the drugs. The **methylase** involved is usually made from a plasmid gene under highly regulated conditions: little enzyme is formed during normal bacterial growth, but it is rapidly synthesized upon the addition of a macrolide.

Aminoglycosides—Resistance by Transport or Drug Inactivation

Perhaps the most complex mechanism of action of all antiribosomal antibiotics is that of the aminoglycosides. They must go through the following steps:

1. Penetration of the outer membrane of Gram negatives;

2. Association with a two-stage active transport system; this is a one way irreversible system, unlike that of tetracycline or most metabolites;

3. Binding to the 30S ribosome subunit to inhibit protein synthesis, primarily at or near the initiation step, and to increase "miscoding" by the ribosomes that still manage to function; coding results in "nonsense proteins."

Two major mechanisms of resistance to aminoglycosides have been recognized in Gram-negative bacteria. The first is the **inactivation of their transport**; this is the mechanism of resistance in anaerobic bacteria. The second uses **inactivating enzymes**, and is the most common mechanism in clinical isolates. Many distinct enzymes that inactivate these drugs have been identified in coliforms, pseudomonads, and staphylococci. Each one can inactivate more than one aminoglycoside, but usually not all of them. Thus, a given strain can become resistant to, say, streptomycin, kanamycin, and tobramycin, but remain fully susceptible to amikacin. Usually, the aminoglycoside inactivating enzymes are encoded by genes carried on plasmids or transposons, and more than one enzyme may be carried by one plasmid.

Selectivity and Limitations of Antifungal Agents

As we move up phylogenetically and consider eukaryotic pathogens, the differences between host and parasite begin to narrow. For example, most of the antibiotics that inhibit fungal ribosomes are active against human ribosomes and therefore useless. Therapeutic agents against fungi, viruses, and animal parasites are often quite toxic. Nevertheless, there are antifungal agents with selective toxicity.

Especially interesting examples are the polyenes (see Chapter 45), which bind more avidly to the ergosterol in the membranes of fungi than to cholesterol in the membranes of higher eukaryotes. The margin of safety is depicted in Figure 5.6, which shows that yeasts are about 200-fold more sensitive to the polyene amphotericin B than are cultured human cells. Amphotericin B is one of the few antifungal compounds that is sufficiently nontoxic to be used systemically. Yet its efficacy is limited; at the higher effective doses, it also damages membranes of kidney cells.

The imidazoles are another group of antifungal agents that have greater specificity for the fungal than for the animal cytochrome P-450 demethylase involved in sterol synthesis. These antifungal agents can be used topically to treat local infections, or systemically to treat invasive disease (see Chapters 45–47).

Griseofulvin, a second potent antifungal agent (Chapter 48), binds tightly to newly formed keratin and is effective against many superficial skin and nail infections. The required levels are nontoxic enough that the drug can be ingested orally for extended periods, although at higher levels, cytotoxicity and carcinogenesis have been demonstrated in animal studies.

IF ONE ANTIBIOTIC IS GOOD, ARE TWO BETTER?

A recurrent and potent argument for counteracting drug resistance in microorganisms can be made for the administration of several antibiotics at once. Mutants resistant to a drug occur with frequencies of 10^{-6} to 10^{-9} per generation. Thus, outgrowth of resistant bacteria can easily take place and be a significant clinical risk. Let us assume that resistance to drug A has a frequency of 10^{-6} per generation. If drug B has a similar frequency of resistant mutants and is given simultaneously, the chance of a single bacterium becoming resistant to both antibiotics is $10^{-6} \times 10^{-6}$, or 10^{-12}, which is vanishingly small.

An excellent example of this concept in practice is the combined therapy with sulfamethoxazole and trimethoprim. Although both drugs act on one-carbon metabolism, their sites of action are different and resistance to one does not influence resistance to the other.

Another example is antifungal therapy by the joint administration of amphotericin B and 5-fluorocytosine. The two act synergistically because 5-fluorocytosine is highly toxic in high doses, but can be used effectively at lower blood levels if the fungal membrane is selectively perturbed to become more permeable (Fig. 5.7).

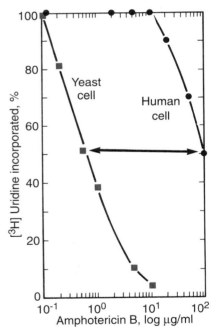

Figure 5.6.   Inhibition of RNA synthesis in yeast (*Saccharomyces cerevisiae*) or cultured human HeLa cells by increasing doses of *amphotericin B*. RNA synthesis was measured by the incorporation of [³H] uridine into acid-insoluble RNA during a 10-minute pulse in replicate samples in the presence of the indicated amounts of antibiotic.

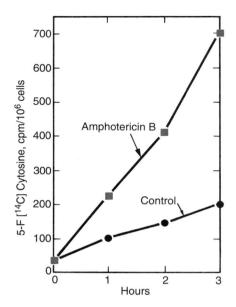

Figure 5.7. The synergistic activity of amphotericin B and 5-fluorocytosine. The uptake of labeled 5-fluorocytosine into growing *Candida albicans* is shown in presence and the absence of 0.2 μg/ml amphotericin B.

The use of drugs in combination is not without problems. In fact, three outcomes are possible:

1. **Synergism**—for example, when penicillin is given along with streptomycin, the penetration of streptomycin is often enhanced.

2. **Antagonism** by one of the two drugs—thus, when chloramphenicol is given along with penicillin, it blocks protein synthesis, preventing the cell growth that is required for penicillin to cause lysis. The result is dominance by the weaker, bacteriostatic drug.

3. **Indifference**—each drug works no better and no worse alone than in combination with the other.

There are further cautions regarding multiple drug administration. Thus, drugs may show **synergism in toxicity**, as well as in antimicrobial action (an example is the heightened damage to the kidney by the joint administration of vancomycin and an aminoglycoside). Finally, in a hospital setting, the main sources of drug resistance are the members of the resident bacterial flora. Therefore, the choice of whether to administer multiple drugs and which ones to pick should be governed by the spectrum of multiple drug resistance of the dominant organisms in that hospital.

ARE SUPERGERMS A THREAT?

Some of the genes that lead to antibiotic resistance are chromosomal and part of the patrimony of the bacterial species. Many of these genes are plasmid-borne and are probably acquired from other bacteria (Table 5.1).

Resistance genes, both chromosomal and on plasmids, predate the use of antibiotics. Such genes have been found in strains frozen away before the introduction of the drugs or in isolates from areas where antibiotics have never been knowingly introduced. The selective pressure of the widespread use of antibiotics has resulted in an increasing frequency of resistant bacteria. In broad terms, the spread of resistance genes increases with the usage of drugs in a particular geographic area or medical center. Multiple resistance genes may accumulate in a given strain by the effective mechanism of gene transposition (see "**Transposons**," Chapter 4). This process could lead to the emergence of "supergerms," microorganisms resistant to a large number of antimicrobial agents. Near-supergerm status has been achieved by occasional isolates that are resistant to 15 or more antibiotics!

Not all species have the potential to become "supergerms." Some species have probably not developed an effective system of DNA transfer. Others have a transfer system that is limited in its capacity to spread multiple drug resistance. For example, staphylococcal plasmids usually do not bear multiple drug-resistance genes. They are usually transferred by phage transduction; this mode of transmission may restrict the size of the DNA that can be transferred. Meningococci, group A streptococci, and the spirochete of syphilis by and large remain as susceptible to penicillin today as they were when the drug was first used.

The threat of accumulating resistance factors is nevertheless quite real. During the 6 years that followed the introduction of penicillin, resistant hospital isolates of *S. aureus* climbed from a very low level to more than 80% of the total. As mentioned above, drug-resistant strains of gonococci, *H. influenzae*, and pneumococci have been found recently. With the successive accumulation of resistance to many penicillinase-resistant penicillins, other agents of greater toxicity, such as vancomycin, have been reluctantly restored to clinical use.

The countermeasures taken against resistant organisms include the continued development of more effective antibiotics (see the example of cephalosporins). Certainly the war between therapy and resistance mechanisms is unlikely to abate, but the battles must continue to be won. The alternative would be to give up what many physicians and historians of science regard as the difference between modern medicine and the Dark Ages.

Self-assessment Questions

1. Prepare yourself to give a short talk to laymen about the history and importance of antibiotics in medicine. What would you emphasize?

2. Describe the mode of action of sulfonamides. What is meant by competitive and noncompetitive inhibition? What is the basis of their selective toxicity?

3. Distinguish between bactericidal and bacteriostatic drugs. Under what conditions is one type preferable to the other?

4. What are the general mechanisms for bacterial resistance to antibiotics? Give examples of each class.

5. Discuss the steps required for β-lactam antibiotics activity. Which steps are commonly modified in resistant mutants?

6. Describe the mode of action of the following protein-synthesis inhibiting antibiotics: tetracycline, chloramphenicol, macrolides, and aminoglycosides. What steps become modified in resistant mutants?

7. Discuss the general mode of action of antifungal drugs.

8. Discuss two reasons for the use of multiple antibiotics to treat a patient. Why is it sometimes undesirable?

SUGGESTED READING

Gale EF, et al. The molecular basis of antibiotic action. New York: John Wiley & Sons, 1981.

Constitutive Defenses of the Body

6

John K. Spitznagel

DEFENSES AGAINST MICROBES

We humans have a unique ability to shape our environment. In good part, our sanitary lifestyle determines the extent of encounter with exogenous microorganisms, including potential pathogens. Our degree of health is influenced by our material wealth and how it determines cleanliness and nutrition. Thus, defenses against infectious diseases begin with the way we affect our environment and one another. The children of the very poor, living in crowded, inadequately ventilated housing, and eating a diet lacking in proteins, are much more likely to contract infectious diseases such as, for example, tuberculosis. The reason is two-fold: poor nutrition diminishes the effectiveness of body defenses, and crowding makes the encounter with tubercle bacilli more frequent. The adults in such families may already have tuberculosis and, in close quarters, become a ready source of contagion. This chain of circumstances, poor nutrition and greater exposure, makes it likely that the child will be infected, contract the disease, and, in time, become a source of further infection. Defenses against these events are clear; they include good nutrition, adequate housing, and treatment of the ill. While these favorable conditions occur readily in an affluent society, they have to be fostered with care and sacrifice in the developing countries of the world.

Our environmental defenses against infectious diseases are only partly medical. Good food in sufficient quantity, uncontaminated water, freedom from insects and rodents—all of these are primary concerns of the sanitary engineer and the social scientist. Some activities, on the other hand, are directly related to medicine, such as immunization, or treatment of human carriers or patients likely to contribute to the spread of disease.

We will leave this subject to the chapter on Epidemiology (Chapter 73). For now, we will continue with the body's own defense mechanisms.

PHYSICAL AND CHEMICAL BARRIERS TO ENTRY

Defenses intensify as microorganisms encounter the skin and the mucous membranes. Throughout life, the body surfaces tolerate a rich and complex flora that is usually harmless, but capable of causing opportunistic infections. In contrast, domains of the body just a few micrometers beneath the epidermis or the mucous membranes are usually free of microorganisms. In this and the next chapter, we will ask how the body maintains this microbial gradient, from microbe-associated surfaces to aseptic inter- and intracellular tissue domains. The question is important because a breakdown of this gradient is usually what infection is about.

Before microorganisms can enter the normally aseptic regions of the body, they must pass through the barriers of the skin, the conjunctivae of the eye, or the mucous membranes of the respiratory, alimentary, or urogenital tracts.

Each barrier has its own protective mechanisms (Table 6.1). For example, the low pH of the stomach effectively kills many bacteria and viruses. Another example is the skin, which is bathed with oils and moisture from the sebaceous and sweat glands. These secretions contain fatty acids that are inhibitory to bacterial growth. The skin further cleans itself of adherent microorganisms by desquamation, as the keratinized squamous cells are steadily sloughed off and replaced with new layers. This formidable barrier is seldom breached except by injuries such as burns, cuts, or wounds. Once across the skin, microorganisms encounter powerful defenses in the underlying soft tissues. However, these do not work at full capacity under all conditions. For instance, abrasions or lacerations impair the local vascular and lymphatic circulation and interfere with soluble and cellular defense mechanisms to render the underlying connective tissue vulnerable. When this occurs, substantially fewer microorganisms are required to cause infection. This effect is seen in chronically debilitated patients who suffer from decubitus ulcers (bed sores), which become contaminated and are constantly infected with normally harmless organisms on the skin. When an injury introduces foreign bodies, such as splinters or particles of

Table 6.1. Constitutive Defenses: Barriers to Infection

Physical		
System or Organ	Cell Type	Clearing Mechanism
Skin	Squamous	Desquamation
Mucous membranes	Columnar nonciliated (e.g., gastrointestinal tract)	Peristalsis
	Columnar ciliated (e.g., trachea)	Mucociliary movement
	Cuboidal ciliated (e.g., nasopharynx)	Tears, saliva, mucus, sweat
	Secretory	Flow of liquids

Chemical		
System or Organ	Source	Substances
Skin	Sweat, sebaceous glands	Organic acids
Mucous membranes	Parietal cells of stomach	Hydrochloric acid, Low pH
	Secretions	Antimicrobial compounds
	Neutrophils	Lysozyme, peroxidase, lactoferrin
Lung	A cells	Pulmonary surfactant
Upper alimentary	Salivary glands	Thiocyanate
	Neutrophils	Myeloperoxidase
		Cationic proteins
		Lactoferrin
		Lysozyme
Small bowel and below	Liver via biliary tree	Bile acids
	Gut flora	Low molecular weight fatty acids

soil, the impairment of the defensive mechanisms is even more profound.

Mucous Membranes

The mucous membranes of the mouth, pharynx, esophagus, and lower urinary tract comprise several layers of epithelial cells, whereas those of the lower respiratory, gastrointestinal, and upper urinary tracts are delicate single layers of epithelial cells, often endowed with specialized functions. Membranes of the alveoli and the intestine are very thin because they serve as exchangers of gases, fluids, and solutes. They are easily traumatized, especially when subjected to high pressures or abrasions. In fact, this happens daily in the colon during defecation and in the mouth during vigorous toothbrushing.

Many mucous membranes are covered by a protective layer of mucus, which provides a mechanical and chemical barrier, yet permits proper function. Mucus is a giant, cross-linked, gel-like structure made up of glycoprotein subunits. It entraps particles and prevents them from reaching the mucous membrane. Mucus is hydrophilic and allows diffusion of many substances produced by the body, including antimicrobial enzymes such as lysozyme and peroxidase. Its rheological properties enable it to bear substantial weight and yet be readily moved by the motion of the cilia of the underlying cells.

Thus, each region of the body surface is endowed with physical and chemical barriers to microbes that otherwise may do harm in deep tissues. These special barriers will be dealt with in more detail in chapters on infections of the systems and regions of the body (Chapters 56–64).

Asepsis of deep tissues depends heavily on complex antimicrobial mechanisms; some of which are constitutive, others are inducible. The constitutive systems are known collectively as the **inflammatory response** and the inducible systems are known as the **immune response**.

CONSTITUTIVE DEFENSES—INTRODUCTION

When a microorganism crosses the protective epidermis of the skin or the epithelia of mucous membranes, it encounters defense mechanisms that are **constitutive** in the sense that they do not require previous contact with the invading microorganisms (Table 6.1). The most powerful of these defenses is not manifested in all tissues at all times but must be called up. It is **inflammation**, or the **inflammatory response**. It is elicited by a complex set of alert signals and pharmacological mediators, some of which are part of an intricate collection of interacting serum proteins called the **complement system**. This system, never completely inactive, is normally in an idling state. Its activity is greatly increased, usually locally, by the presence of microorganisms in tissues. An important consequence of these activities is the recruitment of **phagocytes**, white blood cells that are able to ingest and often kill invading bacteria and other microorganisms (see Fig. 6.6).

Early investigators believed that constitutive mechanisms lacked the potency of the inducible immune response. It was gradually learned that the two responses are interrelated; the inducible response cannot be expressed in the absence of constitutive mediators. It is now clear that these mediators sound the alarm for the inducible response and, in the meantime, they hold the invading microorganisms at bay. The two systems act synergistically to provide a magnificently enhanced defense system. The body then becomes: "A Fortress built by Nature for herself against Infection....," to appropriate what Shakespeare said (in a distinctly different context).

INFLAMMATION

Inflammation is the sum of the changes that occur in tissue as the reaction to injury. At first, it is a purely local happening, manifested by pain, swelling, or both, and a sense of heat and throbbing of the injured part. The inflamed site appears red and shiny, hot and painful to the touch as the result of alterations in local blood vessels and lymphatics. These changes are dynamic and undergo predictable and continued evolution. The tissues may return to normal or they may become scarred. The outcome depends on the extent of damage done by trauma, by the infecting microorganisms, or by the inflammatory response itself. These rapid changes characterize **acute inflammation**. If acute inflammation does not cure the problem, it may change character and become a **chronic inflammation**. Both processes are essential for defense yet both can damage the structure and function of tissues. A more detailed description can be found in pathology textbooks (see also Suggested Reading).

What are the underlying changes in acute inflammation? Briefly, the **blood supply to the affected part increases due to vasodilatation, and capillaries become more permeable**, allowing fluid and large molecules to cross the endothelium. This is important because antibodies and complement components normally tend to remain within the vasculature. Inflammation allows them to enter the tissues. White blood cells, first neutrophils, and later monocytes accumulate on the increasingly sticky endothelium of inflamed capillaries. In greater and greater numbers, white blood cells cross the capillary endothelia by **diapedesis**, migrate into surrounding tissue, and move by chemotaxis toward the injured site (see Fig. 6.2). Thus, redness and increased heat are due to greatly increased blood flow in the area. Swelling is caused by the outpouring of fluid and white blood cells. In mild inflammation, the fluid has a low protein content, as in the contents of a blister. This is known as the **serous exudate**. In severe inflammation, the fluid is known as **fibrinous exudate**, is rich in fibrinogen and other proteins, and eventually clots due to fibrin formation. Pain is caused by the release of chemical mediators (see below) and by the mechanical compression of nerves.

An important consequence of inflammation is that the **pH of inflamed tissues is lowered**. This is due to the production of lactic acid by the inflammatory cells that enter the area. Low pH itself is antimicrobial and results in killing, for instance, of *Escherichia coli*. Moreover, the antimicrobial action of small molecular weight organic acids is enhanced at low pH. Low pH may alter microbial sensitivity to antibiotics and antimicrobial tissue peptides, making them either more resistant or more sensitive. The oxygen tension in inflamed tissue also changes, first increasing when circulation is increased by vasodilation, then decreasing when circulation is impaired by edema, necrosis, or vascular spasm.

Molecular Mediators of Inflammation and the Acute Phase Response

Inflammation due to microorganisms often starts with the activation of complement or of the blood clotting cascade. This sets off the production and release of a number of the **chemical mediators of inflam-**

mation that are responsible for vascular permeability, vasodilation, and pain. The complement and the clotting systems are interactive, since either one can set off the other (see Chapter 62 for details).

Among the best known chemical mediators is **histamine**, which dilates the blood vessels and increases their permeability. It has many other activities that are described in textbooks of pharmacology. Three small peptides called **anaphylatoxins C3a, C4a, and C5a**, produced by activation of the complement system (see Table 6.3), stimulate the release of histamine from mast cells.

Other inflammatory mediators include the so-called **kinins** (Table 6.2), small basic peptides that alter vascular tone, increase permeability, and initiate or potentiate the release of other mediators from leukocytes. The best known one is **bradykinin**, whose potency in increasing vascular permeability rivals that of histamine. Kinins are produced by cleavage of larger proteins, the **kininogens**, by activation of enzymes produced during the clotting cascade or released from granulocytes. These enzymes are known as **kallikreins**. A key compound in these complex interactions is the Hageman factor, which induces the production of the mediators mentioned above after becoming activated during inflammation. One of the compounds that elicits the activation of **Hageman factor** is the endotoxin (lipopolysaccharide) of Gram-negative bacteria (see Chapter 3 for details). Hageman factor also plays an important role in blood coagulation, an important aspect of the tissue changes observed during inflammation.

Another class of mediators acts on the motility and metabolism of white blood cells. They are the **leukotrienes** and the **prostaglandins**. Leukotrienes, prostaglandins, and certain phospholipids also cause the aggregation of blood platelets, an important step in arresting bleeding. Prostaglandins formed in the hypothalamus also act on the thermoregulatory centers of the brain and cause fever. Aspirin and indomethacin prevent the synthesis and the effects of these substances by inhibiting the cyclooxygenase pathway by which they are synthesized. Note than in preventing the synthesis of these compounds, these drugs remove not only an important warning sign that infection may be present but also interfere with an antimicrobial mechanism.

During inflammation, certain proteins are released, chiefly from the liver, and their concentration increases in serum. Collectively, their rise is known as the **acute phase response**. Some of these proteins, for example, the so-called **C-reactive protein, lipopolysaccharide-binding proteins** and **serum amyloid A protein**, increase 1000-fold or more in concentration. Others, such as α_1-**antitrypsin** and **complement factor B**, increase by two- or three-fold. These proteins appear to play different roles in the inflammatory response. For instance, C-reactive protein (so called because it reacts with the C polysaccharide of pneumococci and with antigens of other bacteria, see Chapter 13) may either enhance or attenuate the inflammatory response by activating complement (see below), as do the lipopolysaccharide-binding proteins that bind and inactivate the endotoxin of the outer membrane of Gram negatives. α_1-Antitrypsin inhibits proteases that function in inflammation. Another important class of proteins mobilized during the acute phase response are those, e.g., transferrin, that avidly bind iron and other metals. This reduces the availability of required ions for invading microorganisms and helps inhibit their growth.

Evidence suggests that the acute phase response is invoked primarily by proteins formed by "activated monocytes" (see below). Two members of the family of mediators known as cytokines have been implicated in eliciting this response.

Table 6.2. Some Constitutive Defenses

Ions and Small Molecules	Source	Function
Reduced oxygen species, OH· O$_2^-$, OH·/H$_2$O$_2$	Phagocytes, occasionally bacteria	O$_2$ tension in tissues influences microbial growth; reduced oxygen molecules are antimicrobial
Chloride ion	Body fluids	Cl$^-$ combines with myeloperoxidase and H$_2$O$_2$ to form a potent antimicrobial system
Hydrogen ion	Phagocytes (and other cells)	Antimicrobial in high concentrations
Fatty acids	Metabolites (of phagocytes and other cells)	Most antibacterial at low pH
Platelet-activating factor (an alkylacetyl glycerophosphocholine)	Leukocytes and many other cells	Effects are multiple; causes platelet aggregation and degranulation; activates monocytes but inhibits T-lymphocyte proliferation

Single Protein Systems	Source	Function
Lactoferrin	Neutrophils, other granulocytes	Binds iron, limits bacterial growth
Transferrin	Liver	Binds iron, limits bacterial growth
Interferons	Virus-infected cells of many types	Limit virus multiplication
IL-1	Macrophages	Induces fever and acute phase proteins, some of which are antimicrobial; makes vascular endothelium sticky
Interleukin-6	Phagocytes, endothelial cells	Mediates acute phase response; growth factor for B cells
IL-8	Activated phagocytes and other cells	Chemotactic for neutrophils and monocytes
TNF	Macrophages	Multiple activities: death of certain cells, stimulation of others; wasting
Lysozyme	Neutrophils, macrophages, tears, saliva, urine	Antimicrobial for many bacteria (degrades murein)
Fibronectin	Macrophages, fibroblasts	Opsonin for staphylococci

Complex Protein Systems	Source	Function
Complement cascade	Macrophages, hepatic parenchymal cells	Products increase vascular permeability, cause smooth muscle contractions; chemotactic; opsonize bacteria; Bactericidal
Coagulation system Kinins	Produced by the action of specific proteases (the kallikreins) on certain liver glycoproteins called kininogens	Permeability, vasodilation, increase vascular permeability pain
Fibrinopeptides	Fibrinogen	Chemotactic
Hageman factor	Clotting cascade	Triggers several inflammatory events in the coagulation system

Cytokines

A microbe in host tissues triggers alarm systems that, in Shakespeare's words, "Cry havoc and let slip the dogs of war." If inflammation and collateral tissue damage are the havoc that ensues, the phagocytes and lymphocytes summoned are the dogs of war. Commanding these impressive host responses are the **cytokines**, proteins secreted by the macrophages and lymphocytes themselves. Cytokines are induced by and interact with many systems in distant cells, in adjacent cells, and in the cells that produce them. The number of cytokines is impressive; at least 11 called **interleukins** (IL plus a number) are now described, and several similar proteins known by other names have also been recognized. Cytokines are very much involved in the induction of the immune response as well as in inflammation and so they are dealt with in further detail in Chapter 7 (see Table 7.3).

Several of the cytokines (literally, **cell movers**) are so important to inflammation that they must be mentioned here. **IL-1** is involved in many inflammatory events, including production of fever, induction of adherence proteins on endothelial cells (see section on "adhesion molecules in inflammation"), enhancement of vascular permeability and coagulation, and induction of the respiratory burst in neutrophils and monocytes. In many instances, IL-1 acts by stimulating its target cells to express prostaglandins that, in turn, act on other cells. **Tumor necrosis factor (TNF)** has many activities including the capacity to kill tumor cells, to cause cachexia (wasting) in infection and in cancer, and to cause fever. **IL-6** has multiple effects but one of its most interesting actions is to induce the synthesis of acute phase proteins by the liver. **IL-8** is released by mononuclear phagocytes and endothelial cells in response to IL-1 and TNF and is a powerful chemotaxin and activator of oxygen radical production by neutrophils and macrophages. It contributes to accumulation of pus in inflammation.

We can easily imagine these actions are beneficial to the host and detrimental to the infecting agent if we think of them from the microbe's point of view. As you might suspect, powerful substances like cytokines can and do contribute to local and general tissue damage. Nevertheless, the overall effect of the cytokines is to orchestrate the protective mechanisms of the host. This is testified to by the vulnerability of patients who cannot mount inflammatory responses and who, as a result, rapidly succumb to infection.

COMPLEMENT

Activation of the Classical and Alternative Pathways

You will rapidly become aware that the complement system is extraordinarily complex. It has many components that are known by unfamiliar names (Table 6.3), it mediates a large number of biological effects, and it interacts with other complex systems, such as blood clotting and specific immune responses. The complement system plays an essential role in health and disease, thus some familiarity with it is needed. It will be presented here in abbreviated form. For greater detail, consult an immunology textbook (see Suggested Reading).

The system derives its name from the original belief that it "complements" or "completes" the immune response. Only later was it realized that it plays a crucial role even in the absence of specific antibodies. The complement system is constitutive and, in the immunological sense, nonspecific. Normally, the complement system "ticks over"

Table 6.3. Components of the Complement System[a]

Component	Role in the Complement Cascade
Classical Pathway	
C1q	Binds to Fc region of Ig in Ab-Ag complexes; This binding leads to the activation of C1r
C1r	C1r is cleaved on activation to generate $\overline{C1r}$, a smaller fragment of C1r, which is a serine protease that cleaves C1s
C1s	C1s is cleaved to produce a fragment $\overline{C1s}$, a serine protease; this, in turn, cleaves C4 and C2
C4	Is split by $\overline{C1s}$ into the anaphylatoxin C4a, and the protein C4b that binds to the surface membrane and becomes part of the C3 convertase
C2	Binds to C4b and is cleaved by $\overline{C1s}$ into C2b, which is a serine protease component of the C3/C5 convertase, and C2a that diffuses away
C3 (also part of the alternative pathway)	Cleaved by C2b into the anaphylatoxin C3a, and the protein C3b, which is an opsonin and is also part of the C3/C5 convertases
Alternative Pathway	
Factor B (Bf)	Analogous to C2 in the classical pathway
Factor D (D)	A serine protease that activates factor B by cleaving it
Membrane attack complex (MAC)	
C5	Cleaved by the convertase complex; C5a is an anaphylatoxin, C5b is the anchoring protein for C6
C6	Binds to C5b and this complex becomes the anchor for C7
C7	Binds to the C5b, C6 complex and then C5b, C6, C7 inserts into the membrane and becomes an anchor for C8
C8	Attaches to C5b, C6, C7 and produces a stable membrane-associated complex that can bind C9
C9	Polymerizes at the site of the C5-C8 complex; This completes formation of the fully lytic MAC
Complement receptors	
Complement receptor type 1 (CR1)	Accelerates dissociation of the C3 convertases, enhances phagocytosis of C3b- or C4b-coated microorganisms
Complement receptor type 2 (CR2)	Clearance of complement-containing immune complexes, cell surface receptor for Epstein-Barr virus (EBV)
Complement receptor type 3 (CR3)	Adhesion protein (integrin family), important in phagocytosis of iC3b-coated microorganisms
Complement receptor type 4 (CR4)	Member of the integrin family of proteins, important in phagocytosis of iC3b-coated microorganisms.

[a]The proteins that regulate complement activity are listed separately in Table 6.5.

slowly. It must be **activated** to become a significant part of the defense mechanisms (Fig. 6.1). Once activated, it functions to enhance the antimicrobial defenses in several ways:

- It makes invading microbes susceptible to phagocytosis.

- It lyses some of them directly.

- It produces substances that are chemotactic for white blood cells.

- And, as we have already seen, it promotes the inflammatory response.

The complement system can be activated in one of two ways, which start out separately but eventually converge to make the same end-products. In either case, activation results from proteolytic cleavage of inert larger proteins. Some important steps depend on the function of

Figure 6.1. Activation of complement through the classical and alternative pathways. See text for details.

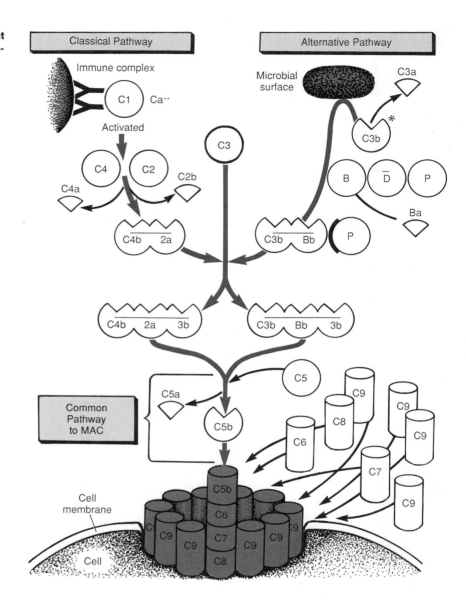

complexes made by binding together several of the cleaved fragments. The two activation pathways are known as **classical** and **alternative** (Fig. 6.1). **The classical pathway is usually set in motion by the presence of antigen-antibody complexes** (Fig. 6.1). It is the most noticeable of the two and was described first, hence its name. The alternative pathway is elicited **independently of antibodies** (Fig. 6.1), often by bacterial surface components, such as lipopolysaccharides.

Nomenclature

The complement system comprises as many as 26 proteins, most of them in serum and a few that are part of cell membranes. The nomenclature of complement components is complicated by their sheer numbers and by the chronology of their discovery. The major components of the classical pathway are designated by the letter C followed by a number, for example, **C3** (see Table 6.3). When the component is cleaved in the process of activation, its pieces receive an additional letter, **a** or **b**. Thus, **C3a** and **C3b** are the products of proteolytic cleavage of C3. The "a" usually designates a small soluble peptide, whereas "b" denotes a larger peptide that may bind to cell surfaces. When cleavage products form an active enzyme, this is indicated by a superscript bar, for example $C\overline{4b2b}$. Components of the alternative pathway are designated by letters, such as **B**, **D**, **P**, except for **C3b**, which is formed by either pathway. Control proteins for the classical pathway are known by a combination of letters and numbers, while those for the alternative pathway are called **H** and **I** (see Table 6.5). What an alphabet soup this is!

Role of Complement in Host Defenses—Overview of the Functions of Complement Proteins

Activation of the complement system is involved in several important aspects of host defenses. Patients genetically unable to manufacture some of the crucial complement components are particularly susceptible to bacterial infections. Hereditary defects in almost all of the complement components (Table 6.4) have been observed. Many of these individuals live healthy lives but, in some cases, life-threatening conditions can result. These patients are also subject to unusual noninfectious disease.

Two activities of complement are specifically directed toward enhancing phagocytosis, which is probably the most effective of the constitutive defenses against microorganisms. They are the recruitment of white cells by chemotactic proteins (such as C5a, Fig. 6.2), and the facilitation of phagocytosis by proteins called **opsonins** (Fig. 6.3).

Other components of complement are responsible for the lysis of bacteria, some viruses, and foreign cells. They may even lyse infected tissue cells that appear alien because they contain viral or other foreign proteins in their cell membrane. Lysis is carried out by a so-called **membrane attack complex** that has the ability to insert itself into membranes and to alter their permeability (Fig. 6.1). This activity is partic-

Table 6.4. Hereditary Complement Deficiencies and Their Role in Microbial Pathogenesis

Affected Component	Defective Function	Infectious Disease Associations
Classical Pathway		
C1q, C1r, or C1s	Activation of the classical pathway	Susceptibility to pyogenic infections
C4	Activation of the classical pathway	Susceptibility to pyogenic infections
C2	Activation of the classical pathway	Susceptibility to pyogenic infections
C3	Activation of the classical and alternative pathways Opsonization Phagocytosis	Pyogenic infections, these may be frequent and can be fatal. This deficiency points out the central importance of C3 in handling these microorganisms
Alternative Pathway (Note: no known defect in Factor B)		
D	Activation of the alternative pathway	Susceptibility to pyogenic infections
P	Activation of the alternative pathway	Frequent pyogenic infections; fulminant meningococcemia
Attack complex		
C5, C6, C7, C8, C9	MAC formation and cell lysis	Enhanced susceptibility to disseminated *Neisseria* infections

Figure 6.2. Chemotactic action of C5a diffusing from bacteria toward a postcapillary venule. See text for details.

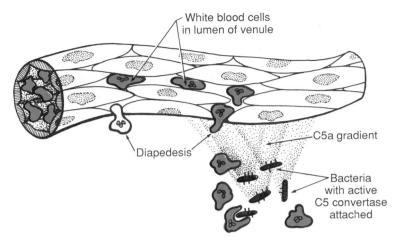

Figure 6.3. Opsonization enhances phagocytosis. This is a schematic representation of *E. coli* opsonized with immunoglobulin (IgG) and complement component C3b. The Fc and C3b ligands on the bacteria attach to the phagocyte through specific receptors. The mechanism of this interaction probably resembles that of a zipper or, perhaps like the fabric called Velcro. Thus, sequential binding leads to the ingestion of the bacteria by the phagocytic membrane, until the vesicle formed is pinched off as a new organelle inside the phagocyte. Meanwhile, degranulation, the fusion of granules with the phagocytic vesicle form a destructive chamber for the bacteria. The secondary granules (*SG*) and the azurophil granules (*AG*), also known as primary granules, fuse their membranes with that of the nascent phagosome, thus making a phagolysosome. Phagocytes tend to be sloppy eaters, so there is some "drooling" and the enzymes and surfactant proteins enter the surrounding fluid, contributing to the tissue changes of inflammation.

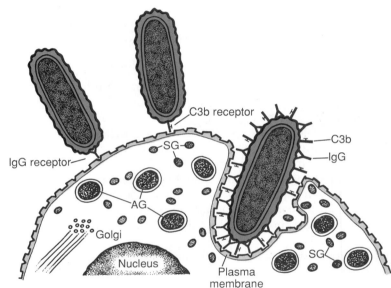

ularly important with bacteria that resist phagocytosis, such as meningococci and gonococci. Indeed, genetic deficiencies of the proteins involved in the formation of the membrane attack complex make individuals prone to infections by these particular organisms (Table 6.4).

Complement activation induces the inflammatory response via the formation of IL-1, TNF, and anaphylatoxins. These activities can be considered beneficial, insofar as the inflammatory response helps fight invading microorganisms. However, they also have negative manifestations that, at times, are quite severe. In persons with hypersensitivity disorders, the inflammatory response causes damage to sensitive tissues, especially by causing leukocytes to secrete their lysosomal enzymes. These diseases include rheumatoid arthritis, serum sickness, and infective endocarditis.

Crucial Step in Complement Activation: Cleavage of C3

The two pathways of complement activation converge at a biochemical step, the **cleavage of component C3** (Fig. 6.1). From then on, the remaining steps are similar. The enzymes responsible for this activity, **C3 convertases**, yield fragments **C3a** and **C3b**. Both of these components are pharmacologically active. C3a is an anaphylatoxin and C3b has several functions: it is an opsonin, and it also binds to platelets to make them release mediators of inflammation. C3b also becomes part of the C3 convertase of the alternative pathway to make more of itself and participates in the further steps of complement activation.

The action of either C3 convertase is potentially dangerous, since it produces mediators of inflammation. It is not surprising, therefore, that the body contains powerful inhibitors of the convertases. This is discussed below (see "Regulation of Complement" below).

C3 Convertase of the Alternative Pathway

How is the alternative pathway activated? C3 is constantly cleaved to generate C3b but most of the C3b fragments formed are inactivated by specific inhibitors. Some C3b fragments survive by binding covalently to the surface of bacteria. This **surface-bound C3b** is protected from inactivation and can participate in subsequent complement reactions. Thus, the **alternative pathway is elicited by the stabilization of C3b**, which may be caused by the presence of bacteria.

C3 Convertase of the Classical Pathway

Activation of complement by the classical pathway usually occurs in the presence of antigen-antibody complexes and, thus, is set off as the result of an induced immunological response. It may, however, be elicited in the absence of antibodies. The classical pathway involves a protein complex called **C1** and two proteins, **C2** and **C4**. C1 is unusual in structure and function; it is composed of three proteins, **C1q**, **C1r**, and **C1s**. C1q is made up six subunits, each shaped like a tulip (Fig. 6.4).

Complement activation by this pathway proceeds as follows: The globular "head" of C1q binds to the Fc portion of antibodies in antigen-antibody complexes. This binding takes place with immunoglobulins **IgG** and **IgM** but not the others. Other substances may bind to C1q in the absence of antibodies, including bacterial glycolipids and polysaccharides and urate crystals. Binding of C1q to antigen-antibody complexes, or to the other substances mentioned, activates C1r to become a protease that carries out the next step in the pathway, the cleavage of C1s. The activated enzyme C1s in turn cleaves C2 and C4 and its fragments C4b2b become the **C3 convertase of the classical pathway**.

The process strongly resembles the formation of the alternative pathway C3 convertase in that C4b, like C3b, binds covalently to nearby membranes. This process is also subject to positive feedback, and the production of this convertase may also be amplified as ever more C4 molecules are converted. Even further amplification takes place when this convertase cleaves C3 molecules to make C3b.

Late Steps in Complement Activation—Membrane Attack Complex (MAC)

Once C3b is formed by either pathway, further steps in complement activation can take place (Fig. 6.1). Both C3 convertases combine with C3b fragments to become **C5 convertases**, which cleave **C5** to produce two important fragments, **C5a** and **C5b**. Like C3a, C5a is an **anaphylatoxin**, but has other activities as well. It is a powerful chemoattractant for phagocytes. The other fragment, C5b, is involved in making the final product of the complement cascade, the membrane attack complex, consisting of C5b, C6, C7, C8, and C9. This is an armor-piercing

Figure 6.4. Electron micrograph of complement component C1q $\times$ 500,000. In this lateral view, six terminal subunits are connected to a central subunit by fibrillar strands.

weapon that can punch holes in bacteria and, in some cases, in tissue cells (Fig. 6.5). Damage to cells and bacteria results from inserting in their membranes the donut-shaped multimers of C9, assembled with the help of the other components. The resulting hole makes cells permeable to ions and sugars. Water enters the cells and raises their pressure, which eventually kills them.

Regulation of Complement Activation

The complement system is programmed to destroy. It must, therefore, be strictly regulated. Fortunately, spontaneous activation in the blood is sharply controlled by several mechanisms. The classical pathway depends on Ag-Ab complexes for activation whereas the alternative pathway C3 convertase is unstable unless deposited on a foreign surface. Activation in body fluids is also prevented by multiple regulatory proteins (Table 6.5). There are both fluid-phase and membrane-bound proteins that inhibit the activities of components of both the classical and alternative pathways (Table 6.5). For example, the formation of the C3 convertase of both pathways is inhibited by **decay accelerating factor (DAF)**. DAF is a membrane glycoprotein, found on many cell types, that binds to C4b, inhibiting the binding of C2, and therefore, the formation of the classical pathway C3 convertase (Fig. 6.1). DAF also binds to C3b generated in the alternative pathway. This prevents the binding of factor B and consequently prevents the assembly of the alternative pathway C3 convertase (Fig. 6.1). There are many other stages at which complement activities are regulated (Table 6.5)

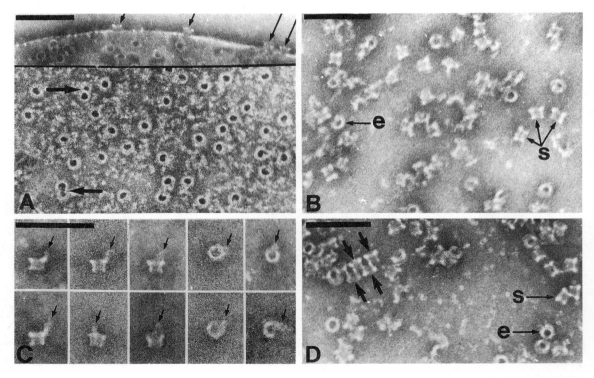

Figure 6.5.   Membrane attack complex (MAC) seen directly under the electron microscope. A. MACs inserted into complement-lysed red blood cell membranes. MACs are shown in their lateral projections. **B.** Isolated MACs in a detergent solution. **C.** MACs showing a small stalk that carried the C5 and C6 determinants. **D.** Oligomers of C9 made by incubation of purified C9 component. Note their resemblance to MACs, except for the absence of the stalk. The *scale bars* indicate 100 nm.

and this careful control underscores the damage that complement components are capable of inflicting on normal cells and tissues.

The importance of these inhibitory proteins is also seen in persons who lack them due to genetic defects. For example, C1 inhibitor deficiency is associated with a seriously debilitating disease, **angioedema**, which can cause death by asphyxiation due to airway obstruction. Deficiency of H protein, or I protein, is associated with **recurrent pyogenic infections**. These conditions arise from faulty regulation, which leads to the imbalance in the concentration of other complement components. Another serious hereditary disease, **paroxysmal nocturnal hemoglobinuria**, is due to defective function of inhibitory proteins on the surface of red blood cells. Each red blood cell binds as many as 1000 molecules of C3b per day. The reason these cells are not lysed is that they have three inhibitory proteins on their surface. These components are integral membrane glycoproteins (DAF; homologous restriction factor, or HRF; and an inhibitor of formation of the membrane attack complex, CD59 or MIRL). In patients with this disease, these proteins do not function because they are not properly inserted in the membrane. The disease manifests itself as bouts of intravascular hemolysis, in part due to complement lysis.

MICROBIAL VIEW OF COMPLEMENT AND OTHER DEFENSES IN SERUM

Serum prepared from fresh blood kills many types of bacteria and other microorganisms. This is due largely to complement and the omnipresent enzyme, lysozyme. Of the two, complement is more important because it kills a wider variety of bacterial species. It also paves the way for lysozyme to degrade many bacteria.

Table 6.5. Proteins That Regulate Complement Activity

Component	Function
Soluble serum proteins	
C1 inhibitor (C1 INH)	Inhibits $\overline{C1r}$ and $\overline{C1s}$ and prevents their participation in the classical pathway
C4 binding	Binds to C4b and enhances the decay of the protein (C4bp), part of the classical pathway C3 convertase
Factor H (H)	Binds to C3b and enhances the decay of the alternative pathway C3 convertase
Factor I (I)	Proteolytically inactivates C4b and C3b
Properdin (P)	Binds to the C3-C5 convertase and stabilizes it
Anaphylatoxin (ANA-IN) inactivator	Proteolytically inactivates the anaphylatoxins, C3a, C4a, and C5a
S-protein (S) (vitronectin)	Inhibits insertion of the MAC into the lipid bilayer by binding to the C5b-7 complex
Integral membrane proteins	
Complement receptor type 1 (CR1)	Accelerates dissociation of both C3 convertases
Membrane cofactor protein (MCP)	Cofactor for factor 1-mediated cleavage of C3b
Decay accelerating factor (DAF)	Accelerates dissociation of both C3 convertases
Membrane inhibitor of reactive lysis (MIRL, CD59)	Prevents MAC formation
Homologous restriction factor (HRF)	Blocks MAC insertion into the surface of cells

Complement kills bacteria by inserting the membrane attack complex. Enveloped viruses are also sensitive to the pore-forming complex. Not surprisingly, sensitive microbes have evolved countermeasures, some of which are discussed in Chapter 68. An interesting example with respect to complement is provided by herpes simplex virus (HSV). One of the glycoproteins of HSV, glycoprotein C, contains a region that has an amino acid sequence similar to that of part of complement receptor Type 1 (CR1). This allows glycoprotein C to bind complement component C3b, thereby interfering with complement mediated neutralization of the virus.

Lysozyme

This enzyme is found in most body secretions and is present in blood in large amounts (4 µg/ml). It specifically cleaves bacterial cell murein at its sugar backbone, as well as chitin of fungi (and invertebrates). Lysozyme is the only enzyme with this activity present in vertebrates. It may well represent an adaptive mechanism that keeps animals from becoming deposits of murein and chitin. This is fortunate because these two compounds activate complement and are, therefore, highly inflammatory.

Lysozyme acts mainly on Gram-positive bacteria, although many species have evolved resistant modifications of their cell wall chemistry. Gram-negative bacteria are resistant because their murein substrate is shielded by their outer membranes. Thus, lysozyme may work synergistically with complement. If the outer membrane of Gram-negatives is disrupted by the membrane attack complex of complement, murein is then available for degradation by lysozyme. Despite the impressive effects of complement and lysozyme, it should be emphasized that many bacteria are resistant to them. This does not diminish the importance of the so-called serum bactericidal activity in destroying invading bacteria. As stated already, complement-deficient patients are particularly prone to bacterial infections. Lysozyme deficiency in humans has not been described, thus it is difficult to assess the real contribution of this enzyme.

LEUKOCYTE CHEMOTAXINS—SOUNDING THE ALARM

We have already seen that a product of complement activation, C5a, is an attractant for neutrophils and monocytes. It is not the only one; chemically distinct chemotaxins are also made by bacteria and by nucleated blood cells. Prominent among them are the leukotrienes, which are lipid products of cell membrane metabolism (see above) and IL-8, a product of monocytes and macrophages.

The chemotaxins made by bacteria have an interesting origin. You may remember that many bacterial proteins "mature" after their synthesis, when a peptide is clipped off from their N-terminus. These peptides begin with N-formyl-methionine, the initiator amino acid in procaryotic protein synthesis (Table 3.2). Eukaryotic cells do not use this device. Remarkably, these cleaved peptides are recognized by the host as strong chemoattractants for phagocytes. They differ in activity depending on their amino acid sequence, but some are remarkably potent. N-formylmethionyl-leucyl-phenylalanine, for example, is active at concentrations of 10^{-11} molar! Thus, living bacteria loudly advertise their presence when they synthesize proteins.

Chemotaxins enhance and direct the motility and, to a limited extent, the oxidative metabolism of phagocytic cells. As we will see later, this is important in the killing of bacteria. Chemotaxins diffuse away from the microorganisms that make them. This creates a concentration gradient in the surrounding tissues. If the tissues are inflamed, neutrophils are already poised for action on the vascular endothelia, which were made sticky by IL-1 produced by activated macrophages. When they sense the chemotaxins, the neutrophils travel along the gradient, cross the endothelial cells, and move in tissues toward the microorganisms. This chemical homing mechanism guides the neutrophils precisely and efficiently to their targets.

OPSONIZATION AND OPSONINS—HOST RESPONSE TO MICROBIAL COUNTERDEFENSES

Bacteria and fungi have evolved effective strategies for escaping phagocytosis (see Chapter 8). Some, for instance, build capsules around themselves that make them too slippery for the phagocytes to ingest. The body defenses, in turn, have mechanisms to cope with these obstacles. Chief among them are the **opsonins**, the substances that enhance the ability of phagocytes to ingest microorganisms (see Fig. 6.3). "Opsonin" is related to the Latin word *opsonium*, which means "relish," an apt term for what makes bacteria more appetizing to phagocytes.

Several substances normally serve as opsonins, among them are antibodies and the C3b component of complement. C3b binds covalently to the surface of bacteria, thus providing a ligand that is recognized by receptors on neutrophils, monocytes, and macrophages. Microorganisms coated with C3b become anchored to the surface of phagocytes, which facilitates their uptake. There are four white blood cell receptors for C3b and its various cleavage products. These receptors are called **CR1**, **CR2**, **CR3**, and **CR4**, for "complement receptor." Children who are deficient in one of them, CR3 (the receptor for iC3b, a cleavage product of C3b), are highly vulnerable to bacterial infections. These children have a syndrome known as **leukocyte adhesion deficiency**.

In a following section, we will discuss how antibodies may also function as opsonins, and how all of these substances alter the metabolism of phagocytes to make them more effective in taking up and killing microorganisms.

PHAGOCYTES: MAIN LINE OF CONSTITUTIVE DEFENSE

Of all the constitutive antimicrobial defenses of the body, the most potent is the cellular response. It consists of the influx of neutrophils, eosinophils, and monocytes into infected tissues. You should be versed in the properties of these cell types (Table 6.6) and may wish to review an immunology or pathology textbook.

Neutrophils

Neutrophils are actively motile phagocytic cells produced in the bone marrow. They differentiate from stem cells over a period of about 2 weeks. During this time, they produce two kinds of microscopically visible granules, first the azurophil, and later the specific granules (Table 6.7). When they mature—in numbers of about 10^{10}/day—they emerge into the peripheral blood and circulate for an average of 6.5 hours. They then disappear into the capillary bed where they

Table 6.6. Constitutive Defenses of the White Blood Cells

Phagocyte	Source	Function
Neutrophil	Bone marrow via stem cells to peripheral blood	Adherence, chemotaxis, diapedesis Phagocytosis Degranulation Antimicrobial action, oxidative and nonoxidative
Eosinophil	Similar to neutrophil	Antiparasitic action, nonoxidative and oxidative
Monocyte	Bone marrow via stem cells Promonocyte to peripheral blood	Adherence, chemotaxis Diapedesis Phagocytosis Antimicrobial actions secretion of cytokines
Macrophage	Monocytes of the peripheral blood	As for monocytes Synthesis of important molecules, including complement components Lysozyme, IL-1, IL-8, tumor necrosis factor and other cytokines, plasminogen activator, other proteases, undefined mediators, and important cell membrane components including MHC class I and II product (see Table 6.7); immunologic functions include but are not limited to antigen processing, antigen presentation, etc.

Table 6.7. Substances Associated with the Azurophil and Specific Granules of Neutrophils

Granule Type	Antimicrobials O₂-Independent	O₂-Dependent	Other
Azurophil (lysosome)	CAP57[a] CAP37 BPI[b] Elastase Cathepsin G Defensins[c] Lysozyme	Myeloperoxidase[d]	
Specific	Lactoferrin Lysozyme	NADPH oxidase[e] cofactors	C5a receptors Bacterial chemotaxin receptors Collagenase Gelatinase Vitamin B₁₂-binding protein

[a]CAP signifies cationic antimicrobial proteins.
[b]Bacterial permeability-inducing protein.
[c]Low molecular weight cationic antimicrobial proteins.
[d]Myeloperoxidase together with Cl and hydrogen peroxide form a potent antimicrobial system.
[e]This enzyme complex forms with fusion of specific granule membranes with the cytoplasmic membrane. The specific granules are believed to contribute the cytochrome component of the complex and the flavoprotein, while the neutrophil cytoplasmic membrane contributes an NADPH oxidase to the complex.

"marginate," that is, they adhere to the endothelium of blood vessels. When summoned by chemotaxins, they become "unglued" and cross the endothelium by diapedesis through the cell junctions, traverse the basement membrane, and enter the extravascular tissue spaces (Fig. 6.2).

As we have seen, neutrophils and monocytes can be enticed into foci of infection by gradients of chemoattractant molecular fragments generated by the complement system of the host and the formylated by-products of microbial protein synthesis. What guarantees these phagocytes will arrive precisely where they are needed?

The way it works is that neutrophils and monocytes, as well as the endothelial cells to which they must adhere, become sticky (see Fig. 6.2). The molecular explanation is simple; it is due to sugar on surface proteins. The glycoproteins involved include three receptor molecules on the endothelial cells and three or so on the phagocytes. Other adhesion molecules are part of the specific inducible immune response (Chapter 7).

The crux of the problem is this: blood cells that originate in the marrow must enter the bloodstream and be able to circulate there without sticking. For its part, the endothelial cells lining the blood vessels must avoid becoming sticky and thus permit the circulation of the blood cells. At the proper time, however, both leukocytes and endothelial cells must become adherent. Transitions from nonadherent to adherent are critical for the leukocytes to leave the circulation and move through the tissues. Clearly leukocytes and endothelial cells are subject to regulatory mechanisms that direct these responses. We have already seen that complement fragments such as C5a and cytokines such as IL-1, TNF, and IL-8 have just such directive and regulatory roles, attracting leukocytes and stimulating endothelial cells, upregulating their stickiness and causing them to produce additional cytokines and prostaglandins.

The importance of the glycoprotein receptors for endothelial cells that are present on neutrophils is illustrated in people with congenital defects in these proteins. Neutrophils of these patients are unable to pass through the vascular endothelium, and, in addition, fail to orient, bind, and ingest particles. These defective neutrophils are unable to form pus. Patients with this condition are said to have congenital leukocyte adhesion deficiency (LAD) and suffer recurrent, often fatal infections. The reason that neutrophils of LAD patients do not pass through endothelia is that their receptors fail to bind to the endothelial cells. The reason for failure to bind to and ingest bacteria is that one of the receptors (called Mac-1) that normally binds the complement opsonin iC3b is defective. It is noteworthy that these molecules are of great interest to the pharmaceutical industry where great efforts are being made to discover drugs with which to control leukocyte adhesion functions.

In a healthy person, this activity is most vigorous in the submucosa of the alimentary tract. The alimentary tract has an enormous microbial population just one cell layer away from the host's aseptic tissues. This abundant flora generates large amounts of chemotaxins, recruiting the bulk of the normally available neutrophils. Thus, the submucosa of the gut is in a constant state of inflammation, which keeps the microbial flora of the lumen in check. Failure of the bone marrow to make neutrophils due to toxic chemicals or radiation, or for any reason at all, results in infections that emanate from the gut.

Monocytes and Macrophages

Slower to arrive at the sites of microbial invasion are the **monocytes**. These circulating members of the mononuclear family eventually settle down in tissues and become known as the resident **tissue macrophages**. While monocytes and macrophages share a common progenitor with the neutrophils, their kinetics of maturation and appearance are substantially different. Unlike the neutrophils, monocytes **continue essential aspects of their differentiation after they leave the bone marrow**. Most important, monocytes and macrophages represent both constitutive and inducible defense mechanisms, a point that will be elaborated further (Chapter 7). Suffice it to mention that these mononuclear cells become involved in cooperative interactions with the cells of the immune system and play a crucial role in **cell-mediated immunity**. In general, monocytes and macrophages come into play slowly, **often days after neutrophils have been active** in combating invading microorganisms. The neutrophils play a role in recruiting mononuclear cells because they release a granule protein (CAP 37) that is a potent specific attractant for monocytes. This delay is seen in patients that become neutropenic from chemicals or radiation. If the neutropenia develops slowly, there is time for monocytes to replace the disappearing neutrophils. The risk of infection is much smaller in these patients than in those with an abrupt onset of neutropenia.

It is important to realize that tissue or resident macrophages exist throughout the body. They have different names and functions, depending on the tissue. Thus, they are called Kupffer cells in the liver, alveolar macrophages in the lungs, osteoclasts in the bone, microglia in the brain, etc. They can and do phagocytize invading microorganisms. Tissue macrophages contribute greatly to the inflammatory response by releasing IL-1, which enhances sticking of neutrophils to the capillary endothelia, and TNF, which activates newly arrived neutrophils. In addition, tissue macrophages release an activator of the acute phase reaction (IL-6) and an attractant for neutrophils (IL-8). These macrophages are replenished by the arrival and differentiation of monocytes from the bone marrow. The most active macrophages arise from monocytes delivered to sites of inflammation.

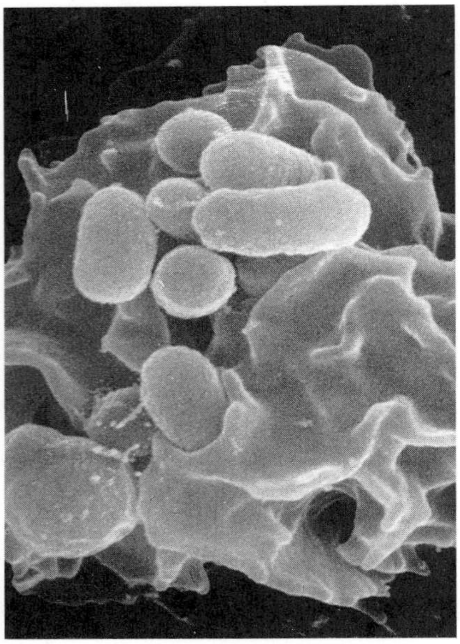

How Do Neutrophils Kill Microorganisms?

Once near their microbial target, neutrophils must do several things to carry out their antimicrobial action. They must attach and ingest the organisms, either spontaneously or with the aid of opsonins, and then kill them (Figs. 6.3, 6.6–6.8, and 7.5).

The granules of the neutrophils may be considered as enlarged lysosomes, packed with large amounts of powerful hydrolytic enzymes and other active substances. They are contained within unit membranes (Figs. 6.7 and 6.8). The **azurophil**, or **primary granules**, contain lysozyme, elastase, a chymotrypsin-like protease, myeloperoxidase, and several cationic proteins that are also powerfully antibacterial (Table 6.7). The **specific**, or **secondary**, granules contain a cytochrome, the iron-binding protein lactoferrin, a protein that binds vitamin B_{12}, and a collagenase.

The membrane of neutrophils contains the receptors for chemotaxins and opsonins. After chemotaxins bind to them, the receptor molecules are internalized and replaced with new ones. What makes chemotaxis so effective is that **neutrophils are unusually motile**. They

Figure 6.6. Phagocytosis of E. coli by a neutrophil. Neutrophils were incubated with E. coli. After 60 seconds, one bacterium is partially engulfed into a phagosome, a cluster of bacteria are attached to the neutrophil surface. Scanning electron micrograph, ×19,000. See Fig. 22.3 for an electron micrograph of phagocytized Legionella.

move by rearranging together their cytoplasmic microfilaments and their microtubules. Actin and myosin in microfilaments are affected by a protein, gelsolin (which invites the comparison of neutrophils with muscle cells.) During chemotaxis, portions of the neutrophils that face upstream in the chemotactic gradient form a structure called a **lamellopodium**, where the cytoplasm is densely packed with microfilaments. The portions of the cell that face downstream in the gradient form a knob-like structure, the **uropod**.

Phagocytosis differs from pinocytosis, in that **particles** rather than just liquids are taken up. Phagocytes enfold bacteria or other particles of suitable size in a pouch-like structure, the **phagosome**, which invaginates, displacing the nucleus and the granules toward the uropod (Figs. 6.6, 6.8, and 7.5). The cytoplasmic granules soon discharge their contents into the phagosome by fusion of their membranes, forming a new structure known as the **phagolysosome**. The phagolysosome quickly pinches off and becomes a separate cytoplasmic organelle. By the time the pinching off is completed, the fusion of the granules is well underway and bacteria can already be seen to be coated with antibacterial proteins. Thus, like poisonous snakes that disable their prey before swallowing it, neutrophils kill bacteria before they completely ingest them.

The bacteria become enfolded into the plasma membrane of the neutrophils by a zipper-like action, with the receptors on the phagocyte surface progressively attaching to the ligands on the bacterial surface (Figs. 6.3 and 6.7). This binding stimulates two mechanisms that lead to killing of bacteria by phagocytes; one is set in motion by a vigorous burst of oxidative metabolism that leads to the production of hydrogen peroxide and other compounds lethal to microorganisms (Figs. 6.7 and 6.8). This is the **oxygen-dependent killing**. Phagocytosis also results in the discharge of toxic compounds from the granules into the phagosome. This is known as **oxygen-independent killing**.

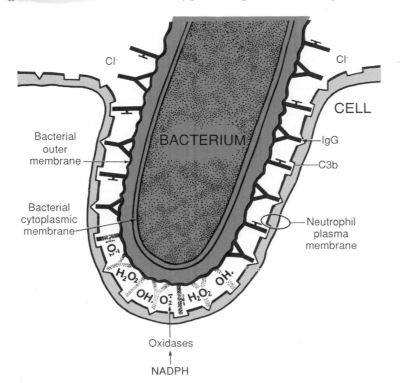

Figure 6.7. NADPH oxidase catalyzes the formation of bactericidal O_2^- and transforms it to H_2O_2. A portion of the phagolysosome showing the relationship between the enzyme (oxidase) that catalyzes oxidation of reduced pyridine nucleotides (NADPH) and reduction of O_2 to O_2^-, H_2O_2 and formation of free hydroxyl radicals that gain access to phagolysosome. The H_2O_2 reacts with myeloperoxidase and chloride ion to form hypochlorous acid. This highly cytotoxic substance is lethal for microorganisms. Curiously, the phagocytic vacuole seems to be able to contain these highly toxic reactions, protecting the phagocyte long enough to accomplish its mission.

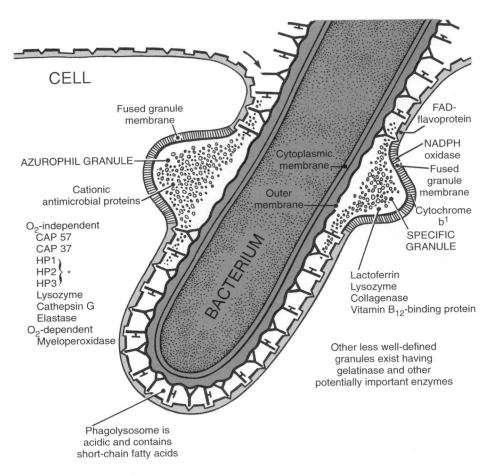

CELL

Fused granule membrane

AZUROPHIL GRANULE

Cationic antimicrobial proteins

O_2-independent
CAP 57
CAP 37
HP1
HP2 } *
HP3
Lysozyme
Cathepsin G
Elastase
O_2-dependent
Myeloperoxidase

Cytoplasmic membrane

Outer membrane

BACTERIUM

FAD-flavoprotein

NADPH oxidase

Fused granule membrane

Cytochrome b¹

SPECIFIC GRANULE

Lactoferrin
Lysozyme
Collagenase
Vitamin B_{12}-binding protein

Other less well-defined granules exist having gelatinase and other potentially important enzymes

Phagolysosome is acidic and contains short-chain fatty acids

* So-called defensins

Figure 6.8. Fusion between the phagosome and the granules. As noted in Figure 6.7, fusion between the membranes of the specific granules and the cytoplasmic membrane completes the enzyme complex that generates reduced oxygen species, including the H_2O_2 that forms antimicrobial compound, with chloride and myeloperoxidase. Fusion of the specific and azurophil granules with the phagosome activates the oxygen-independent antimicrobial mechanisms.

Specific granules seem to fuse first. They deliver several proteins to the phagolysomes; lysozyme will attack the murein of many bacteria and lactoferrin will bind iron tenaciously, denying bacteria this essential metal. Lactoferrin bound to iron also has direct antimicrobial action. The azurophil granules release highly complex mixtures including cationic antimicrobial proteins CAP57, CAP37, and the defensins. Two proteolytic enzymes, cathepsin G and elastase, as well as lysozyme, are also delivered by azurophil granules. Finally, oxygen-independent antimicrobial action is also mediated by hydrogen ion and short-chain fatty acids produced by the glycolytic metabolism of the neutrophil.

OXYGEN-DEPENDENT KILLING

How does oxygen-dependent killing take place? Fusion of the specific granule membranes with the phagosome membrane (which is derived from the plasma membrane) brings together three components: **NADPH oxidase** of the plasma membrane (characterized as an **FAD-flavoprotein cytochrome reductase**) joins a unique cytochrome b in the membrane of specific granules. This complex, in the presence of a quinone, reduces oxygen (O_2) to superoxide anion, O_2^-. The superoxide ion is changed to hydrogen peroxide by the following reaction: $2 O_2^- + H_2O \rightarrow H_2O_2 + O_2$, in a very rapid reaction catalyzed by an enzyme called **superoxide dismutase**.

The importance of these oxidative processes in killing bacteria is illustrated in children with a congenital defect called **chronic granulomatous disease (CGD)**, which results in the failure to make the superoxide anion. These children have a decreased amount of one of the essential components, the cytochrome b. Although their neutrophils can phagocytize normally, they do not efficiently oxidize NADPH and kill via the oxidative pathway. The reason this is a condition of childhood is that it results in such severe infections that patients seldom survive into adulthood, even with the use of antibiotics.

How does the oxidative process kill microorganisms? This is a complex business, involving several different radicals and chemical species. Hydrogen peroxide plays an important role because, with the help of an enzyme called **myeloperoxidase**, it converts chloride ions into the highly toxic hypochlorous ions, the same chemical found in common bleach (Figs. 6.7, 6.8, and Table 6.7). Myeloperoxidase is delivered to the phagolysosome by fusion of the azurophil granules. In some cases, hydrogen peroxide is produced by the bacteria themselves. For instance, pneumococci release a lot of H_2O_2 because they lack the enzyme catalase that can destroy this compound. Thus, pneumococci literally commit suicide inside the phagocytic vacuole. Accordingly, pneumococci are not particularly dangerous to patients with chronic granulomatous disease, whose cells do not make enough hydrogen peroxide.

OXYGEN-INDEPENDENT KILLING

Oxygen-independent killing mechanisms are also triggered by the binding of opsonized bacteria to the plasma membrane of neutrophils (Fig. 6.7 and Table 6.7). Specific granules seem to fuse to phagosomes first and deliver several bactericidal proteins, including **lysozyme** and **lactoferrin**. The azurophil granules discharge **antimicrobial cationic proteins** into phagosomes. Some of these proteins are "amphipathic" (partly hydrophilic and partly hydrophobic) and resemble other cationic surface-active agents. Apparently these proteins disrupt the outer membrane of Gram-negative bacteria and kill them by causing leakage of vital components. Each of these substances has a unique antimicrobial spectrum, but they tend to affect Gram-negative bacteria more than Gram positives. These proteins may account for the survival of some of the children with chronic granulomatous disease.

The oxygen-independent mechanism also accounts for bacterial killing under the highly anaerobic conditions found in deep abscesses. Recently, deficiencies in cationic proteins have been described in patients with chronic skin infections and abscesses. A genetic disease known as the Chediak-Higashi syndrome is due to the premature fusion of neutrophil granules while the cells are still in the bone marrow. Thus, when mature neutrophils of these patients phagocytize bacteria, their granules have already been spent, substantially reducing the killing power of these cells. The granules of cells from these patients also lack certain cationic proteins, especially cathepsin G.

How do various kinds of bacteria differ in their sensitivity to the two bactericidal mechanisms of neutrophils? In general, the organisms found in the gut, such as Gram-negative rods, are readily killed by the oxygen-independent mechanism. Gram-positive bacteria of the kind found on the skin and in the upper respiratory epithelia tend to be resistant to oxygen-independent killing and are killed chiefly by the oxygen-dependent pathway. Does this reflect the abundance of oxygen in the skin and its absence in the gut?

Eosinophils

The eosinophils parallel the neutrophils in lifestyle and function. However, their attention is not directed so much at bacteria as it is to animal parasites. Indeed, the increase of these cells in the circulation, **eosinophilia**, is the hallmark of multicellular parasitic diseases such as schistosomiasis or trichinosis. The reason for this specificity is not known. It has been shown that the cytoplasmic granules of the eosinophils carry large amounts of an enzyme known as eosinophil peroxidase, as well as specific cationic proteins. These compounds have the power to kill certain parasites. Thus, eosinophils have an anti-infectious armamentarium similar to that of neutrophils, but specifically targeted to certain higher parasites.

Killing by Monocytes and Macrophages

Together, monocytes and macrophages serve to mop up what is left at the scene of the battle between microorganisms and neutrophils. They phagocytize the microorganisms and the debris that is left by the neutrophils. Their mechanisms of chemotaxis, phagocytosis, and microbial killing resemble those of the neutrophils. An important point is that these cells, unlike the neutrophils, continue to differentiate after they leave the bone marrow and, under proper stimulation, change into a **state of activation**. Activated macrophages phagocytize more vigorously, take up more oxygen, and secrete a large quantity of hydrolytic enzymes. In general, they are better prepared to kill microorganisms and, appropriately, have been called the "angry" macrophages. **Macrophage activation is elicited by substances made in response to the presence of microorganisms**, like complement fragment C3b or γ-interferon. They may also become activated by a variety of other compounds, such as endotoxin of Gram negatives. Although some bacteria, fungi, and protozoa can grow within unstimulated macrophages, in general they tend to be killed when these cells become activated.

Perhaps the most important property of macrophages is their capacity to participate in the induction of specific immune responses. In this role of living garbage collectors they help rid the body not only of invading microorganisms but also tumor and other foreign cells. They do this by stimulating the development of the lymphocytes involved in the immune response. In turn, they respond to signals from some of these lymphocytes that stimulate differentiation and activation of macrophages. In this way, macrophages and the cells of the induced immune system "talk" to each other. In fact, they carry out an animated conversation that results in a strong interaction between the constitutive and the induced systems of defense.

SUGGESTED READING

Abbas AK, Lichtman AH, Pober JS. Cellular and molecular immunology. Philadelphia: WB Saunders Co., 1991.

Bachner RL. Chronic granulomatous disease of childhood: clinical, pathological, biochemical, molecular, and genetic aspects. Pediatr Pathol 1990;10: 143–153.

Cotran RS, Kumar V, Robbins SL. Pathologic basis of disease, 4th ed. Philadelphia: WB Saunders Co., 1989.

Frank MM. Complement in the pathophysiology of human disease. N Engl J Med 1987;316:1525–1530.

Klein J. Immunology. Oxford: Blackwell Scientific Publications, Inc., 1990.

Muller-Eberhard HJ. Molecular organization and function of the complement system. Ann Rev Biochem 1988;57:312–347.

Paul WE. Fundamental immunology. New York: Raven Press, 1989.

Roitt I, Brostoff J, Male D. Immunology. London: Gower Medical Publishing, 1989.

Rotrosen D, Gallin JI. Disorders of phagocyte function. Ann Rev Immunol 1987;5:127–150.

Spitznagel JK. Antibiotic proteins of human neutrophils. J Clin Invest 1990;86:1381–1386.

Springer TA. Adhesion receptors of the immune system. Nature 1990:346:425–434

Induced Defenses of the Body

7

H. Kirk Ziegler (with the editorial assistance of Roderick Nairn)

INNATE VS. ACQUIRED IMMUNITY

As discussed in the previous chapter, innate immune responses are those that do not depend on prior exposure to the invading agent and, in general, do not increase after exposure to the nonself entity. For the most part, such mechanisms are relatively nonspecific and supply the initial lines of defense against invading pathogens.

In contrast to innate immunity, specific acquired defense reactions are highly selective for the nonself entity and are qualitatively and quantitatively altered by antigenic exposure. The two salient hallmarks are **specificity and memory**.

SPECIFICITY: SELF-NONSELF DISCRIMINATION

Immunological defenses are based on the ability to recognize **self from nonself** and, in that way, maintain the individuality and integrity of the organism. Self may be defined as the tissues, cells, and molecules present as an integral part of the organism, encoded by the genome. Nonself is everything else. The general rule in immune defenses is that the immune system recognizes entities in the nonself world, known as antigens, and responds in a way that eliminates the antigens from the self environment. In people, if the nonself entity is a pathogenic microorganism, the process is directed toward the successful resolution of an infection.

The maintenance of individuality or integrity of an organism is a fundamental need. Immunological defenses are normal biological phenomena common to all living organisms, including microorganisms. Bacteria use nucleases to fight invading DNA that could contaminate their genome, and elaborate toxic substances to conquer their immediate environment; the struggle among microbes is reflected in antibiotics and antibiotic resistance mechanisms. Some parasites use camouflage by coating themselves with host antigens. Viruses ensure their survival by using such tricks as hiding in host DNA. When the survival needs and defenses of microbes conflict with ours, we have the pathology of infectious disease. As Lewis Thomas said, *"Disease usually results from inconclusive negotiations for symbiosis, an overstepping of the line by one side or the other, a biological misinterpretation of the boundaries."* From a microbial point of view, there is little to be gained by causing disease. Pathogenicity is the side effect of the border dispute. In fact, many of the symptoms of infection are caused not by the presence of the microbe, but rather by the immune defense mechanisms invoked. Our arsenal for fighting a microbe is so powerful that, possibly, we are in more danger from ourselves than from the microbe. In the words of Thomas, we live in a war zone in the midst of exploding devices; we are mined.

What is the cost of maintaining individuality via defense reactions? Perhaps we "pay the price" by getting old and dying; one explanation of aging is that tissue degeneration is caused by the protracted battle of self and nonself with the resulting accumulation of damage. The immune system makes occasional mistakes in discriminating self from nonself (autoimmune reactions). Effector molecules activated during border disputes with microbes can damage host cells and tissues. And sacrificing a few cells for the good of the organism, as occurs with the "miniamputations" that take place in the destruction of virus-infected cells, is a sound but ultimately damaging strategy. Thus, the challenge of the immune system is to provide an efficient and powerful means for recognizing the millions of different components of the nonself world and to respond with minimal damage to our own tissues. For this, nature has provided higher animals with highly specific immune defenses that are evoked only when needed. This is called **specific acquired immunity**.

MEMORY: CONCEPT OF IMMUNIZATION

The immune system has the capacity to remember prior exposure to an antigen and the ability to respond more rapidly and to a greater extent on a repeat exposure. This feature of the immune system has been exploited to protect people by immunization. To illustrate the concept of immunization, consider an experimental infection in mice with a microbial pathogen (Fig. 7.1). Groups of immunologically naive (normal) mice are injected with different numbers of organisms and their survival is noted after an appropriate period of time. With 10^4 bacteria, one-half of the animals die, thus defining a so-called **lethal dose 50%** ($LD_{50} = 10^4$). If the same experiment is performed with the animals that have recovered from the first infection (e.g., those animals receiving, for instance, 10^3 organisms), immunity or resistance to the lethal effects of the infection is illustrated by the finding that it now takes 10^7 microbes to kill one-half of the animals. Thus, these animals have acquired enhanced resistance or immunity to the pathogen by prior antigenic exposure, i.e., they remember their previous history. The specificity of this acquired immunity is illustrated by the observation that such animals are no more resistant to an antigenically unrelated pathogen than are normal controls. Thus, the immune system has re-

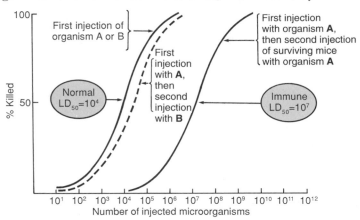

Figure 7.1. Specific Acquired Immunity. In this experiment, groups of animals were injected as indicated with antigenically unrelated pathogenic microorganisms, designated A and B. The percentage of animals killed by the infection is plotted as a function of the number of microorganisms injected into each animal. Note that animals that receive a first injection with microbe A are resistant or immune to secondary challenge with microbe A.

membered the specific prior insult and has successfully adapted to maintain the health of the organism. This capacity is termed **immunological memory**.

Immunity can be broadly classified as either **humoral or cellular**. This distinction is based on the ability to transfer resistance to normal animals or humans using either the serum (humors) or the cells of the immune donor. Specific humoral immunity results from the action of proteins in serum called **antibodies**, while cellular immunity is mediated by antigen specific **T lymphocytes**. Both antibody (the product of B lymphocytes) and T lymphocytes contribute to immunity, but the relative importance of humoral and cellular immunity varies with the type of pathogen and the site of infection. For example, resistance to a toxin is usually predominantly humoral, as antibodies bind to and neutralize the injurious activity of the toxin. Also, antibody binds to antigen, which makes it easier for phagocytic cells to ingest it and to activate the complement systems (Chapter 6). In contrast, pathogens that can multiply within host cells are not accessible to antibody. Immunity to such microbes requires the cooperative efforts of T lymphocytes and macrophages. This reaction is mediated by the **secretion of** soluble factors called **cytokines**, which are released mainly by T cells and macrophages (Chapter 6). Certain cytokines called **macrophage-activating factors** enhance the cytocidal functions of macrophages, allowing them to kill intracellular microbes. Also, cell-mediated immunity can be expressed by the direct action of a subset of T cells termed **cytotoxic T lymphocytes**. These cells recognize antigens on the surface of infected cells. For example, cytotoxic T lymphocytes can lyse virus-infected cells early in the virus-infection cycle, that is, before mass production of virus progeny occurs. Thus, specific acquired immunity is expressed either by direct cell-cell interaction or secretion of antibodies and cytokines.

CLONAL SELECTION—CENTRAL PARADIGM OF IMMUNOLOGY

The specificity and memory of acquired immunity is mediated by **lymphocytes** and their receptors through a process of **clonal selection** (Fig. 7.2). The clonal selection hypothesis suggests that there are millions of different lymphocytes, each with receptors specific for a particular antigen. These lymphocyte surface receptors consist of an **immunoglobulin** on B lymphocytes and a related protein on T lymphocytes called the **T-cell receptor**. When an antigen binds to its specific receptor on a lymphocyte, that particular lymphocyte proliferates and differentiates. This results in the clonal expansion of the lymphocytes of that specificity. Thus, specific immunological memory is due to the predominance of clones of lymphocytes of a particular specificity. In the example described above (Fig. 7.1), the specifically immune mice can handle a larger number of microbes because they now have many more lymphocytes with receptors specific for the microbial antigens.

IMMUNOLOGICAL MEMORY: PRIMARY VS. SECONDARY RESPONSES

When an antigen is encountered for the first time, the immune system makes a **primary immune response** (Fig. 7.2). The subsequent encounters are called **secondary responses**. If one measures the amount of antibody generated in a primary and a secondary response, marked

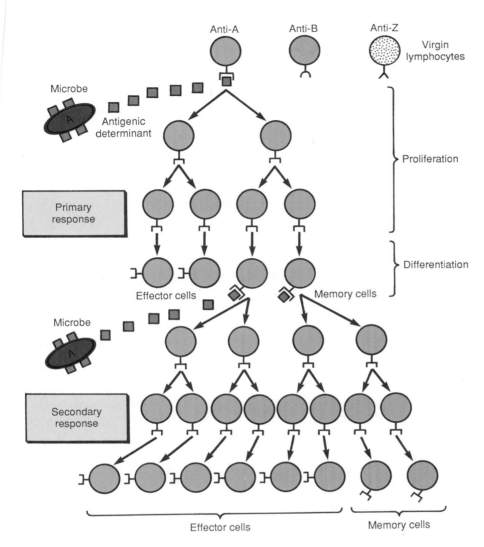

Figure 7.2. Clonal Selection. When an antigen (designated by the *squares*) is introduced into the immune system, the antigen binds to clones of lymphocytes with receptors for that antigen, and this initiates the proliferation and differentiation of the lymphocytes indicated. [Lymphocyte clones reactive with other antigens (e.g., circles and triangles, not shown) are not stimulated.] As such, antigen is said to select certain clones for proliferation. Note that upon secondary contact with the same antigen, a relatively large number of clones (memory cells) can interact with the antigen. This accounts for specific immunological memory. This process occurs with both B and T lymphocytes. For simplicity, the function of antigen-presenting cells and other molecular interactions are not shown.

differences are noted (Fig. 7.3). The secondary response occurs after a shorter lag period; it is of greater intensity and it has a longer duration. In addition, different kinds of immunoglobulins are produced in the secondary response.

The faster and stronger secondary response (also called the **anamnestic or memory response**) results from clonal selection and differentiation that occur during the initial contact with an antigen. The clonal proliferation of lymphocytes is followed by a dual pathway of differentiation of both B- and T-cell lineages. By yet unknown mechanisms, some of the progeny become **effector cells**—cells capable of causing an immediate effect, whereas others become memory cells. In general, effector cells express their function for a finite and usually short period of time. For example, plasma cells are the effector cells of the B-cell

Figure 7.3. Primary and Secondary Immune Responses. The antibody response to antigens *A* and *B* are shown as a function of time after primary and secondary stimulation with antigens as indicated. Note the faster and stronger secondary response to antigen *A*.

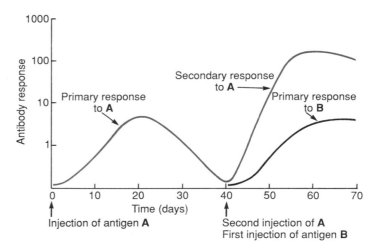

lineage; cytotoxic cells are the effector cells of the cytotoxic T lymphocyte (CTL) lineage. Immunological memory is due to the fact that the memory lymphocytes are long lived and can persist for years. They are capable of rapid differentiation into effector cells when stimulated with antigen. For the B-cell lineage, memory cells are poised to secrete large amounts of antibody rapidly when appropriately activated by secondary contact with antigen.

IMMUNOLOGICAL TOLERANCE

A major question in immunology is: How does the immune system distinguish self from nonself? There are two possibilities. One is that the genes coding for the antigen receptors specific for self-molecules are simply not present in the genome. The other (and correct one) is that the immune system is intrinsically capable of responding to both self and nonself entities but that mechanisms exist to prevent potentially disastrous reactions to self. The existence of **autoimmune diseases** (immune responses to self-components that result in pathology) indicates that at least some self-recognition can occur.

Several experimental observations indicate that the immune system "learns" not to respond to self components early in development. For example, if an antigen is injected into a mouse at birth, a time when the immune system is still immature, it will not respond to that antigen as an adult. A similar phenomenon occurs in genetically different twins who have shared a common circulation before birth. They do not react to the tissue antigens of their partner. Thus, the immune system can learn to tolerate a normally foreign antigen as if it were a self component. The state of antigen-specific immunological unresponsiveness is called **acquired immunological tolerance**. Immunological tolerance may be thought of as "negative immunological memory"; prior exposure to antigen results in a decreased response (rather than a heightened one) to the antigen. Like immunological memory, immunological tolerance is an active response that requires antigenic exposure and is mediated by lymphocytes.

Under special circumstances, and with some difficulty, immunological tolerance can be demonstrated in immunologically mature animals. Induction of tolerance is favored by intravenous injection of soluble protein antigen in either very large or in repeated small amounts. Also, the use of immunosuppressive treatments, such as X-irradiation or certain immunosuppressive drugs, can promote the induction of tolerance. Both T cells and B cells can be "tolerized" experimentally, but T-cell tolerance is easier to achieve and may be more relevant to the natural tolerance to self antigens.

Whenever tolerance to self breaks down, autoimmune disease may result. For example, in **systemic lupus erythematosus (SLE)**, patients produce antibodies to their own nucleic acids; and in **myasthenia gravis**, they produce antibodies to acetylcholine receptors. Both result in severe chronic illnesses. **Multiple sclerosis**, a disease characterized by chronic demyelination of the central nervous system, is thought to result from T-cell reactivity to the myelin-associated self-proteins. The onset of certain autoimmune disorders is often associated with microbial infections, which allows us to speculate that microbial products may somehow alter self components or modulate the processes that normally maintain tolerance to self-components.

The precise mechanisms of immunological tolerance are not known. There are three major possibilities for which experimental evidence exists.

1. Clones of lymphocytes potentially reactive to a particular antigen may be eliminated. For the T-cell lineage, this **clonal deletion** is thought to occur in the thymus during T-cell maturation. In fact, many newly made T cells do not leave the thymus because they represent the "forbidden" self-reactive clones. The well-established importance of thymic education in the development of the T-cell receptor repertoire adds credence to this concept. Clonal deletion has also been observed to occur with B cells, but this process may be less frequent than in T cells.

2. Specific clones may be present but may have received negative signals through their receptor systems and, thus, may be less responsive to antigen. Immature B lymphocytes behave in this manner. This functional inactivation has been termed **clonal anergy**. Functional inactivation of T cells has also been observed when antigen is provided in the absence of a second costimulatory signal from antigen-presenting cells.

3. The response of lymphocyte clones may be actively inhibited by the action of suppressor T cells. However, the precise role of suppressor cells remains controversial.

The issue of tolerance induction is of obvious importance in organ transplantation, inasmuch as the immune response represents a major barrier to graft survival. Also, intelligent intervention in the control of disease caused by too much (autoimmunity and hypersensitivity) or too little (immunodeficiencies and infections) immune reactivity will require a thorough understanding of these regulatory pathways.

In many ways, the immune system is analogous to the nervous system. Both are complex, and both are composed of very large numbers of phenotypically distinct cells. These cells interact in positive and negative ways, and this cellular network is dispersed throughout the body to patrol and to guard its identity. Both systems are involved in pattern recognition. With a keen sense of touch, the immune system has the precise capacity for discrimination. It can distinguish proteins that differ in only one amino acid and can perceive differences between isomers of simple chemicals. Collectively, the cells of the immune system have intelligence and morality in telling the good (self) from the bad (nonself), with a memory that lasts a lifetime. Both systems rely on effective intracellular communication via synaptic transmission of chemical signals. However, unlike the hard wiring of the nervous system, the immune system employs transient mobile interconnections among cells with a dynamic and renewable capacity.

CELLULAR BASIS OF IMMUNE RESPONSES

Lymphocyte Function

To supply strong and appropriate immune defenses, nature has imposed a division of labor among the lymphocytes. **B lymphocytes,** when stimulated by antigens and by the appropriate products of other lymphocytes and macrophages, proliferate and then differentiate into plasma cells whose sole purpose is to synthesize and to secrete antibody molecules. Each of these antibody factories can secrete 2000 molecules/second. These terminally differentiated cells are so committed to synthesis and secretion that they are incapable of further growth, and they die after several days. In general, the specificity of the secreted antibody is identical to the blueprint present on their cell surfaces as the antigen receptor. Thus, B lymphocytes with a given receptor specificity expand clonally to increase their numbers, which then undergo differentiation to plasma cells. Each of these groups of cells is capable of secreting a large number of similar yet functionally specialized antibodies—what a well-designed system for acquiring heightened reactivity to the nonself world!

In contrast to B cells, antigen activation of T lymphocytes does not lead to the production of secreted forms of antigen-receptor molecules. Rather, differentiated T cells express their functions through direct cell-cell interaction and via the secretion of cytokines. There are several functionally distinct subsets of T cells. **Helper T cells** help other cells perform optimally; they help B cells make antibody, T cells become cytotoxic, and macrophages kill microbes. **Cytotoxic T cells** recognize and destroy cells infected with microbial pathogens such as viruses. **Suppressor T cells** downregulate the activity of B cells and other T cells. Thus, the functional diversity of T lymphocytes is expressed by separate subsets of cells.

Lymphocytes are all morphologically similar, but can be identified by surface markers (Table 7.1). These markers are also known as **differentiation antigens** since they appear at certain stages of lymphocyte differentiation. Mature human T cells express the characteristic proteins called CD3. Helper T cells bear the CD4 protein. Cytotoxic T lymphocytes (CTLs) and suppressor T cells express the CD8 marker. In peripheral blood, about 45% of the lymphocytes are CD4 positive (CD4+) and 30% are CD8 positive (CD8+). (The rest are null cells [more later] and B cells.) These markers can be used for diagnostic purposes. Patients with AIDS, for example, have low numbers of CD4+ cells, which indicates an immunodeficiency.

Table 7.1. Human T-lymphocyte Markers

Surface Marker		Cellular Distribution
T Designation	Cluster Designation	
T_3	CD3	Mature T cells
T_4	CD4	Helper/inducer T cells
T_8	CD8	Cytotoxic/supressor cells

Lymphocyte Development

Lymphocytes are found in the blood, lymphoid tissues, the lymph, and in smaller numbers in tissues throughout the body, especially at sites of inflammation. The total number of lymphocytes in man is large (about 2×10^{12}) and the total mass of the immune system is comparable to that of the liver or the brain. Like other blood cells, lymphocytes are derived from the pluripotent hemopoietic stems cells in the fetal liver and the bone marrow of adults. Lymphocyte development occurs by two major pathways corresponding to the two major subsets, B and T lymphocytes (Fig. 7.4).

By one pathway, the progeny of stem cells migrates from the bone marrow and enters the **thymus**. In this **central or primary lymphoid organ**, the development of thymus-derived (T) lymphocytes takes place. Here they "learn" to express receptors for antigens and to select appropriate specificities. This "thymic education" process is beginning to be better understood. Molecules produced by thymic epithelial cells and macrophages play important roles in both **positive** and **negative selection** of thymocytes bearing appropriate receptors. During development in the thymus, there is an ordered expression of surface markers such as CD11, CD6, CD4, and CD8. As T cells leave the thymus, they express either CD4 or CD8 and then begin to express CD3. At this point, these T cells are functionally mature. Upon exiting the thymus, the lymphocytes travel to the **secondary or peripheral lymphoid organs**, where responses to foreign antigen occur and mature lymphocyte function is expressed. The peripheral lymphoid organs include the spleen, lymph nodes, and gut-associated lymphoid tissue (Peyer's patches, appendix, tonsils, and adenoids).

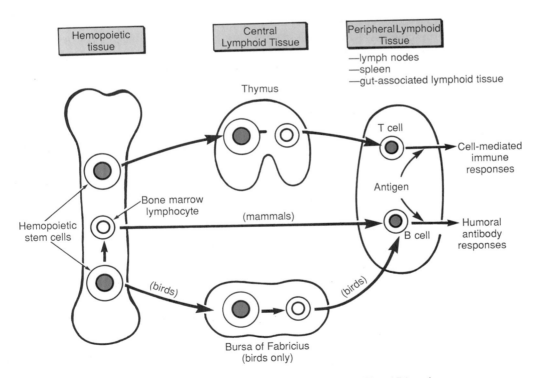

Figure 7.4.   Lymphocyte Development. The development of functional T and B lymphocytes occurs in primary lymphoid organs and the response to antigen takes place in peripheral lymphoid tissue. B and T lymphocytes have different pathways of development.

The other major lymphocyte population, the B cells, are so named because, in birds, their development is dependent upon maturation in a central lymphoid organ termed the bursa (B) of Fabricius. Mammals have no bursa of Fabricius; so B-cell development probably occurs in the hemopoietic tissue or in secondary lymphoid organs.

While lymphocyte development is dynamic and continues throughout the life of mammals, the importance of primary lymphoid organs is most easily demonstrable in young animals. For example, removal of the thymus at birth prevents the development of T cells and results in severely impaired immune responses in the adult. However, if the thymus is removed from adult animals, little if any deficit in immune responsiveness occurs. This is because lymphocytes are relatively long lived, and possibly, because other sites of lymphocyte development take over in adults.

The separate developmental pathways of B and T lymphocytes in humans was first illustrated in naturally occurring abnormalities. Genetically caused immunodeficiencies, such as one called **DiGeorge syndrome**, result in a selective decrease of T lymphocytes, while patients with **X-linked agammaglobulinemia** (Bruton's disease) have normal T-cell function but cannot make antibodies.

Lymphocyte Circulation

Lymphocytes patrol the body from their home bases in the lymphoid organs. A great majority of T cells, and some B cells, continuously recirculate between the blood and lymph. They leave the bloodstream by traversing specialized endothelial cells in venules and enter the tissues. Molecules known as **homing receptors** are present on the lymphocyte surface. These receptors recognize other molecules known as **vascular addressins** on endothelial venules and this interaction facilitates lymphocyte homing to particular tissues. Other molecules of the **integrin family** (such as leukocyte function associated antigen-1, LFA-1) are involved in nonorgan-specific binding to endothelial venules. After passing through the tissues and cruising for intimate contact with antigens, these lymphocytes travel via the fluid flow and accumulate in lymphatic vessels that connect to a series of downstream lymph nodes. From there, they enter progressively larger lymphatic vessels and eventually complete their round trip by passing back into the blood via the thoracic duct. This recirculation promotes the contact of lymphocytes with antigens and ensures that information about a localized antigenic insult is dispersed throughout the body. Thus, systemic immunity is produced.

The pattern of lymphatic circulation and the structure of the lymph nodes both play important roles in immune responsiveness. Consider a microbe that has penetrated the defenses of the skin and is present in the extracellular fluid in the tissues. Through the inflammatory response, the microbe will be swept by the fluid flow into the blind-end afferent lymphatics present in almost all tissues (notable exceptions include the central nervous system, placenta). The lymph is deposited into a meshwork of lymphoid cells that have the efficient ability to bind and to ingest the microbe. These cells are collectively referred to as the **reticuloendothelial system** (RES), which includes macrophages and comparable cells with different names, depending on their characteristics and anatomical locations. These sticky cells are arranged in a filter-like array interspersed with lymphocytes and are the site where the antigen is trapped. The immune system has the invading microbe right where it wants it, bound by cells capable of "processing" and "presenting" the antigen (Fig. 7.5) and surrounded by the lymphocytes poised to engage it with specific receptors ("Go ahead, make my day!"). As a consequence of the filtering action of the lymph node, the lymph exiting the node via the efferent lymphatic vessel and ultimately emptying into the blood is microbe-free, in other words, sterile. The antigen trapped in the lymph node then initiates the immune response.

Cellular Cooperation And Lymphocyte Activation

Most immune responses require intimate cellular cooperation among the lymphocytes, macrophages, and other accessory cells. These cells "talk" to each other by direct cell-cell interactions and by secreting cytokines, as illustrated in Figure 7.7. Electron micrographs of lymphocyte-macrophage interactions are shown in Figure 7.6.

To differentiate into antibody-secreting cells, B lymphocytes must interact with T lymphocytes and be stimulated by their cytokines. The probable steps involved are:

1. Binding of antigens to B cells via their immunoglobulin receptors;

2. Processing and "presentation" of the antigen to T cells; this involves the proteolysis of protein antigens in lysosomes and/or endocytic vesicles, and the transfer of resulting antigen fragments to the B-cell surface, where they can be recognized by receptors on T cells (see Fig. 7.5);

3. Direct delivery of T-cell derived cytokines to B cells by cell-to-cell contact; this combination of signals drives the proliferation of B cells and their differentiation into plasma cells. Thus, by presenting antigens on their surface, B cells get efficient help from T cells.

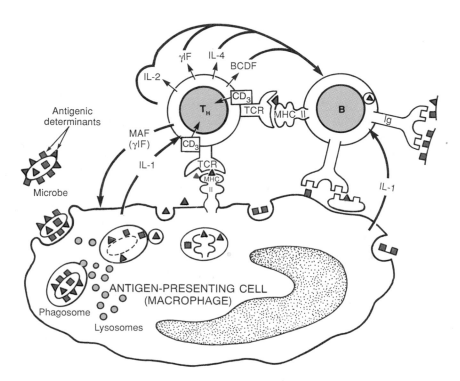

Figure 7.5. Cellular Interactions. The processing, presentation, and recognition of antigen by lymphocytes is illustrated. Note that both macrophages and B cells express class II MHC gene products and can present antigen to helper T cells. Activated helper T cells (T$_H$) produce a shower of cytokines that have powerful and diverse effects on the cells of the immune system. Following these events, intense lymphocyte proliferation and differentiation take place.

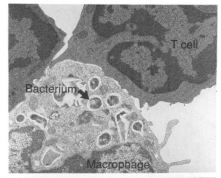

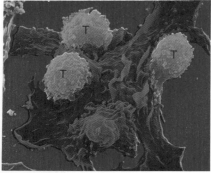

Figure 7.6. Electron Micrographs of T Cell-Macrophage Interactions. In these photographs, T cells are recognizing bacterial antigens on the surface of macrophages. Transmission electron microscopy is used in the *top* illustration and scanning electron microscopy is used in the *bottom* illustration. Note the bacteria present in the phagosomes of macrophages (*top*) and the extensive membrane-membrane interaction between T cells and macrophages. This interaction is antigen specific (i.e., mediated by the T-cell receptor) and requires the expression of class II MHC gene products by the macrophage. See Figure 7.5 for schematic view of molecular interactions. (Photographs by Ziegler, Cotran, and Unanue.)

Macrophages also contribute to lymphocyte activation by elaborating interleukin-1 (IL-1) and by processing and presenting antigens to T cells. The resulting activated T lymphocytes communicate with B cells and macrophages via the release of a variety of cytokines. These include growth factors such as **interleukin-2** (IL-2) and **interleukin-4** (IL-4).

All of this activity in the secondary lymphoid organs alters the lymphocyte traffic patterns and structure of the lymph node. After antigen trapping, there is an initial period (about 24 hours) of decreased flow of lymphocytes from the node followed by an increased flow. Vessels dilate, blood flow increases, and lymphocytes proliferate. These events cause the nodes to become enlarged; hence, the classic "swollen glands." Lymphocytes specific for the antigen in question appear to localize at the site of the immune response, the nodes where the antigen is trapped.

ANTIGENS

Any organic macromolecule can potentially act as an antigen. In descending order of antigenicity, proteins, polysaccharides, lipids, and nucleic acids all have been shown to be antigenic under the correct circumstances. The portions of an antigen that combine with the antigen-binding site of lymphocyte receptors are called **antigenic determinants or epitopes**. The size of an antigenic determinant may be 10 amino acids or 5–6 sugar molecules. Since most antigens are large molecules, they can have many epitopes and, thus, can stimulate many different lymphocyte clones. Such a response is said to be **polyclonal**. When one is dealing with the response of a single clone of cells—a situation achievable only under special circumstances—the response is called monoclonal. Antigens are classified according to the relative thymus dependency of the antibody response. While all B-cell responses are enhanced by the action of helper T cells, certain antigens can elicit antibody production without T cells. Such antigens, referred to as **T-cell-independent antigens**, have many repeats of an epitope, and/or have the ability to cause B cells to proliferate. Many of these antigens are associated with bacterial cell envelopes; lipopolysaccharide from Gram-negative bacteria and pneumococcal capsular polysaccharide are two examples. This direct elicitation of antibody may play an important role in the rapid response to bacterial invasion.

Antigenicity is the capacity of a molecule to interact with an immune recognition molecule such as an antibody. **Immunogenicity** is the capacity of a molecule to elicit an immune response. This is an operational definition and depends on many factors. In general, large molecules with multiple antigenic determinants are better antigens than small molecular weight substances. Very small compounds, called **haptens**, can elicit an immune response but only when coupled to a larger molecule called a **carrier**. Examples of haptens are simple sugars, certain drugs (e.g, penicillin), and chemical side chains such as dinitrophenyl groups, which are used experimentally. Also relevant are the **dose** of antigen, the **route** of immunization, and the presence of **adjuvants**, agents that enhance the immune response. From a microbiological view, live microorganisms are generally better antigens and make better vaccines than dead ones. Most relevant to immunogenicity is the degree of difference between the antigen molecule and any analogous structure present as self. In general, the greater degree of phylogenetic difference between self and nonself, the greater the immune response.

IMMUNOGLOBULINS

Structure and Function

The term antibody is usually used for immunoglobulins that have specific antigen-binding capacity. Immunoglobulins play two roles and exist in two structurally different forms; one as **membrane receptors on resting B lymphocytes** and the other as **major secretory products of fully differentiated plasma cells.** Antibody can bind antigen and then mediate several other activities or functions in the interaction with other cells and molecules of the immune system .

Antibody molecules fall into several different yet related classes. Consider the secreted immunoglobulin of the G class (IgG) as the prototypical structure (Fig. 7.7). It is a Y-shaped protein with identical antigen-binding sites at the tip of each arm. With these two binding sites, it is called **bivalent**. The proteolytic enzyme papain cuts the antibody molecule into functionally distinct Fc and Fab fragments. The cleaved arms of the Y represent fragments with antigen-binding ability and are called Fab fragments. The tail of the Y is called the Fc because it is the fragment that is easily crystallizable. **The Fc portion directs important functions of antibody other than antigen binding. These effector** functions include complement activation and interaction with specific Fc receptors (Chapter 6). Different classes of antibody molecules may have identical antigen-binding sites but different Fc parts, therefore, supplying different functions.

The multiple binding sites of an antibody molecule give it the ability to cross-link soluble antigen molecules into a large lattice, provided the antigen has three or more antigenic determinants. When this complex of antigens and antibodies reaches a certain size, it comes out of solution. This is called **immunoprecipitation**. Antigen-binding and cross-linking reactions are aided by the flexibility of the parts of the molecule where the arms meet the tail, the so-called **hinge region**. Within a lattice of bound antigens and antibodies, there is a multiple display of the Fc parts. They can then work cooperatively in a multivalent fashion that enhances their binding avidity to cells with Fc receptors and to the C1 component of complement. Immunoglobulin G (IgG) consists of four polypeptide chains, two identical **light (L) chains**

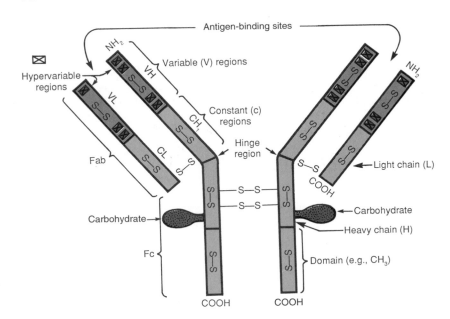

Figure 7.7. Structure of IgG. Immunoglobulin of the IgG class is composed of two heavy and two light chains. Note that portions of the amino terminal regions of both heavy and light chains form the antigen-combining sites. The Fc part is formed by the heavy chains alone.

(each about 220 amino acids) and two identical **heavy** (**H**) chains (each about 440 amino acids). The chains are held together both by covalent interchain disulfide bonds and noncovalent interactions. Each antigen-binding site is formed by a portion of both a heavy chain and a light chain. The Fc part is composed of the carboxy-terminal halves of the two heavy chains.

Both heavy and light chains are made up of repeating segments or domains that fold independently to form compact functional units. Each domain, about 110 amino acids long, has one intrachain disulfide bond and a characteristic three-dimensional structure called the **immunoglobulin fold**. Each domain is a sandwich of three and four antiparallel polypeptide strands in a β-sheet configuration.

In mammals, there are five major immunoglobulin classes or isotypes. The classes of antibody differ in structure and function, as summarized in Table 7.2. Classes are based on differences in the heavy chains. The isotypes are called **IgM, IgD, IgG, IgE, and IgA**, with their respective heavy chains designated by Greek letters, μ, δ, γ, ε, and α. There are two different types of light chains, λ and κ. The heavy chains determine the unique biological activity of the different isotypes. A single antibody molecule has only one type of heavy chain; it can have **either** two κ or two λ light chains but never one of each. This ensures that both antigen-binding sites are identical.

IgG

IgG is the major class in the blood. It is produced in greater amounts in the secondary response than in the primary response. IgG can activate complement, bind to "professional" phagocytes via its Fc part, participate in **antibody-dependent cell-mediated cytotoxicity** (**ADCC**) with killer (**K**) cells (see null cells below), and cross the placenta to supply some protection to neonates. In humans, there are four major sub-

Table 7.2. Human Immunoglobulins

Isotype	Structure	Concentration in Serum, mg/m;	No. of Heavy Chain Domains	Distinguishing Feature or Functions
IgM	B cell	1.5	5	First in development and response
IgD	B cell	0.03	5	B-cell receptor
IgG		12.5	4	Opsonin, ADCC
IgE	Mast cell or basophil	0.00005	5	Allergic response
IgA	SC	0.05 3.5	4	In secretions (GALT)

classes of IgG: IgG1, IgG2, IgG3, and IgG4. These differ in their ability to activate complement (IgG4 does not) and to bind to macrophage Fc receptors (IgG1 and IgG3 do).

IgM

IgM is the major product in the primary immune response and is the predominant antibody produced in response to thymus-independent antigens. Secretory IgM consists of five copies of the basic four-chain unit (2 L + 2 H chains) and, therefore, has 10 antigen-binding sites. This multivalency promotes its ability to cross-link, while its multiple Fc parts make it a very efficient activator of complement. IgM also contains an extra protein called J (joining) chain that aids in the polymerization process within plasma cells. The large size of IgM (about 970,000 daltons) confines it to the blood and it is not found in substantial quantities in tissues.

Membrane IgM is an important antigen receptor on B cells. It is an integral membrane protein, anchored by a hydrophobic carboxy terminus. Unlike secreted IgM, but resembling IgG, membrane IgM is a four-chain structure with two antigen-binding sites. Its heavy chain is the first to be produced during B-cell development. It may be important as a receptor of "tolerogenic" signals that lead to clonal anergy and immunological tolerance. Membrane IgM may be constitutively expressed on both resting and memory B cells. Plasma cells do not express a membrane form of immunoglobulin.

IgD

IgD is another membrane immunoglobulin predominantly found on resting B cells. Human IgD is also a four-chain molecule like IgG, but with a very long hinge region. Its very low concentration in the blood may be explained by its sensitivity to proteolysis at the hinge region and the rarity of IgD-secreting plasma cells. Its only function may be as a membrane receptor for antigen. During B-cell ontogeny, IgD is expressed after IgM. The appearance of IgD renders the B cell functionally mature, thus it can no longer be easily "tolerized" upon contact with antigen.

IgA

IgA is present in seromucous secretions such as milk, tears, saliva, perspiration, and secretions of the lung and gut. Small amounts are also found in the blood. In secretions, IgA molecules consist of two copies of IgG-like molecules covalently attached via disulfide bonds with an intervening J chain. They are also associated with another protein called **secretory component**, which is synthesized by epithelial cells. The secretory component is a portion of an integral membrane protein known as the **poly Ig receptor** that plays a key role in the transport of IgA across the epithelial cells into the lumen. Secretory component, which is attached to secreted IgA, also acts as a stabilizer and protector against the proteolytic activity present in secretions. IgA is synthesized at a very high rate in the lymphoid tissue of the gut, especially the Peyer's patches. The body produces amounts of IgA equal to or greater than those of any other immunoglobulin class. IgA can neither activate complement nor bind well to Fc receptors, but it may play an important role in preventing the attachment and subsequent invasion of pathogenic microbes, a kind of strategic defense initiative at the external surface.

IgE

IgE is the antibody class that occurs in serum at the lowest concentration. IgE is responsible for the clinical manifestations of allergies such as hay fever, asthma, and hives. Its Fc region specifically binds to very high-affinity receptors present on the surfaces of mast cells and basophils. Cell-bound IgE then serves as a receptor for antigen. The cross-linking of these receptors by antigen causes the release of a variety of biologically active agents. One such agent, histamine, causes smooth muscle contraction and increases in vascular permeability. These effects may have some protective function by enhancing the influx of cells, antibodies, and complement into the site of inflammation. IgE is also important in the response to parasitic infection (principally by worms) as it is often greatly elevated in the serum of patients with these diseases. IgE participates in antibody-dependent cell-mediated killing of parasites by macrophages and eosinophils, cells that possess low-affinity Fc receptors specific for IgE. Is the price for allergy worth paying because IgE defends us against parasites?

Membrane and Secreted Immunoglobulins

With the possible exception of IgD, all immunoglobulins exist in two versions: a **membrane form** and a **secreted form**. The membrane form has an extra carboxy-terminal portion on the heavy chain that anchors it to the membrane and perhaps plays a role in signal transduction. For example, memory B cells that are "ready" to secrete IgG contain a membrane form of IgG. Upon activation by antigen, the switch from a membrane form to a secreted form occurs via an alteration of mRNA mediated by differential RNA processing.

Structural Basis of Antigen-binding Specificity

Each class of antibodies includes millions of different molecules, each with unique antigen-binding specificity and amino acid sequence. This diversity provides the variety of functions of each isotype, and the multitude of specific antigen-binding sites required for a sophisticated mobile defense system. All of this presents formidable genetic problems. Their solution involves some very special mechanisms of gene expression. For example, immunoglobulins turned out to be the first known exception to the "one gene, one polypeptide" rule.

Each light chain and each heavy chain consist of two major regions, **variable** and **constant** regions. These were originally identified by comparing the amino acid sequences of different immunoglobulin molecules. As the names imply, the sequences in the constant regions are similar, whereas the variable region sequences differ considerably from antibody to antibody. These comparisons were made possible by the fact that patients with B-cell tumors called myelomas make large amounts of a given immunoglobulin molecule. The immunoglobulin that accumulates in the blood of each patient is called a **myeloma protein**. The urine of these patients often contains free immunoglobulin light chains called **Bence Jones proteins**.

For light chains, the carboxy-terminal halves of chains of the same type (κ or λ) have the same sequence, while the amino-terminal parts are different. For heavy chains, a variable region of similar size (about 110 amino acids) is present at the amino terminus, while the rest of the molecule is rather constant. Within the variable regions, differences are clustered into three regions of the light chains and four regions of the heavy chains. These regions, each about 4–12 amino acids long, are known as **hypervariable regions**. From x-ray diffraction studies, it is now clear that the variable regions of the light and heavy chains are so folded that the hypervariable regions form an antigen-binding pocket that can accommodate antigenic determinants that are the size of about five to six sugars or about 10 amino acids. Thus, the amino-terminal variable parts of the light and heavy chains form the antigen-binding site. Their amino acid differences provide the structural basis for the diversity of antigen-binding function.

The interaction of antigen with antibody is a reversible bimolecular reaction. Unlike enzyme-substrate reactions, neither of the reactants is permanently altered. The binding of antigen to the antigen-combining site is mediated by the sum of many noncovalent forces such as hydrophobic and hydrogen bonds, van der Waals forces, and ionic interactions. Since these forces are effective at short distances, a tight fit takes place when the surfaces are complementary, that is, if the size and shape of the antigen fits to the combining site on the antibody. The goodness of the fit is referred to as **affinity**. It can be determined experimentally by quantitating the affinity constant of the antigen-antibody interaction. **Avidity** of the antigen-antibody interaction is the total binding strength of all of the sites together; the multivalency of IgM, for example, increases the avidity.

Antibody Specificity and Quantitation

Specificity is defined as the ability of antibodies produced in response to an antigen to react with that antigen and not with others. Antibodies can be incredibly specific. They can discriminate atomic differences between simple chemicals and single amino acid substitutions in proteins. There are exceptions, and specificity may be imperfect, leading to cross-reactions. For example, antibody raised to antigen X may cross-react with antigen Y. This is due to the presence of a similar molecular configuration on the two antigens.

Specificity can be improved and cross-reactions can be minimized by the use of **monoclonal antibodies**. By an elegant procedure illustrated in Figure 7.8, cells can be generated that secrete homogeneous antibody molecules with a single kind of binding site. An antibody-forming B cell is fused with a myeloma cell resulting in a hybrid cell (called a hybridoma) with the combined properties of both fusion partners, the ability to secrete specific antibody, and the capacity for rapid and sustained growth. The use of special culture media that permit the growth of only the hybrid cells, coupled with methods for isolation of the progeny of individual hybridomas results in the propagation of monoclonal antibody-producing cells. This procedure has revolutionized biology and medicine by making unlimited quantities of homogeneous antibodies available for a variety of applications. The methods for detecting antibody and antigens are numerous. Some rely on the ability of antibody to precipitate antigen that can be visualized or quantitated—these include quantitative immunoprecipitation, immuno-double diffusion or the Ouchterlony test, single radial immunodiffusion (SRID) or the Mancini test, immunoelectrophoresis (IEP), etc. Other tests rely on antigen-antibody interactions that are detected by coupling antibody or antigen with a radioactive tracer (radioimmunoassay or RIA), an enzyme (enzyme-linked immunosorbent assay or ELISA), or a fluorescent compound (immunofluorescence or fluorescence immunoassays or FIA). These tests are described in Chapter 55.

Figure 7.8. Production of Monoclonal Antibodies. Sequential steps in the procedure used to generate monoclonal antibodies is illustrated.

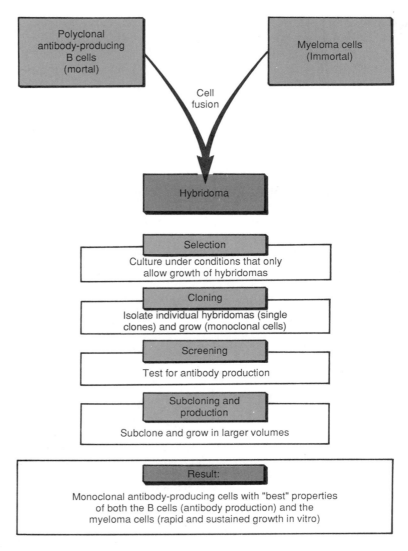

Still other assays make use of the ability of antibody to cross-link and agglutinate antigen-bearing cells (e.g, antibodies to red cells can be detected by hemagglutination) or activate complement when bound to antigen (complement fixation test).

Evolution of the Immunoglobulin Supergene Family

As previously discussed, the heavy and light chains are made of homologous domains and each domain has a characteristic three-dimensional structure called the **immunoglobulin fold**. The homology among the domains suggests that the immunoglobulin chains arose in evolution by a series of gene duplications of the basic 110-amino acid unit. It is now clear that the immunoglobulin fold is a fundamental structural unit that defines a whole family of homologous proteins, called **the immunoglobulin supergene family** (Fig. 7.9). Members of the family include immunoglobulin, the T-cell receptor, molecules of the major histocompatibility complex (**MHC**), and other lymphocyte surface proteins such as CD4, and CD8. Recent counts show that there are more than 20 members of the family expressed by cells of the immune system and the nervous system. New members of the family will undoubtedly continue to be detected.

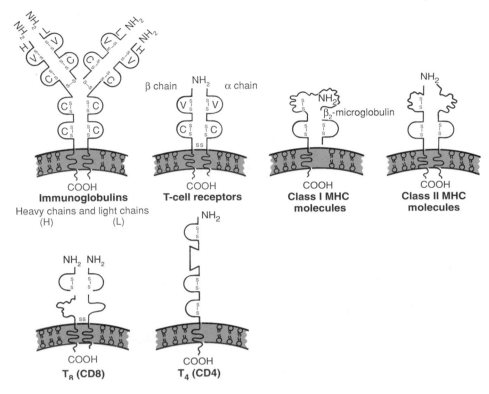

Figure 7.9.   The Immunoglobulin Supergene Family. Schematic diagrams of some of the members of the immunoglobulin supergene family are shown. Immunoglobulin, β_2-microglobulin, and class I MHC have been studied by x-ray diffraction and the three-dimensional structure is known. Other structures are predicted from the amino acid sequence inferred from the nucleotide sequences of cloned genes. Homology units (or domains) are depicted by intrachain disulfide-bonded loops. These loops represent globular domains each with the polypeptide chain folded into a β-pleated sheet configuration. Irregular loops represent imperfect folding into such a configuration. (See *Immunology Today* 1987;8:298 for more details.)

It is possible that the supergene family evolved to supply a common function to the family members. It is clear that the functions of the domains of immunoglobulin heavy and light chains are to interact, to stabilize the immunoglobulin molecule, and to form the antigen-binding site. Similarly, the family may have evolved to mediate cell-to-cell interactions via significant binding affinity between family members, as discussed below.

Generation of Diversity (GOD)

One major challenge to the immune system is to provide millions, perhaps billions of antibodies specific for almost any antigenic determinant. The issue at hand is how to do this without requiring an unreasonably large amount of genetic material.

Immunoglobulins are produced from three groups of similar genes on separate chromosomes, corresponding to the κ light, λ light, and heavy chains, respectively. Each pool contains many variable region genes (and subdivisions of variable gene segments), located at a distance upstream of the constant region genes. During B-cell development, variable genes are **translocated** to a position closer to a particular constant gene. By this arrangement, the chains (composed of variable and constant regions) can be transcribed and translated.

The first translocation that occurs in B-cell development brings a particular variable region gene segment into proximity of the μ-constant gene, and thus, leads to the expression of heavy chains for IgM. Other translocations occur during this differentiation, so that a particular variable gene is connected more closely to other heavy chain constant genes, allowing the expression of other isotypes of antibody (Fig. 7.10). This phenomenon is called **class switching**. These events occur by a process known as **site-specific recombination**, which depends on specific recombination sequences flanking each gene segment. These translocations account for the fact that different classes of antibody may have the same antigen-binding specificity.

Variable region genes are actually made up of two or three separate variable **gene segments**. A segment is defined as a contiguous stretch of DNA that is ultimately translated into a portion of the mature polypeptide. Two segments code for the variable region of each light chain; they are called V for variable and J for joining segments. Three segments are involved for heavy chains: V, D (diversity), and J segments (see Figs. 7.10 and 7.11). During assembly of a complete variable region gene, these segments are brought into proximity to permit transcription. Because there are several different V, J, and D segments, many unique combinations can be created by somatic recombination, thereby increasing antibody diversity. For example, in the mouse, variable heavy-chain genes are made up of about 200 V segments, 10 D segments, and 4 J segments. Random combination could produce 8000 ($200 \times 10 \times 4 = 8000$) unique variable heavy chains. Similarly, if the 200 or so variable light-chain κ gene segments were to recombine with the 4 J segments, about 800 unique variable genes would be gener-

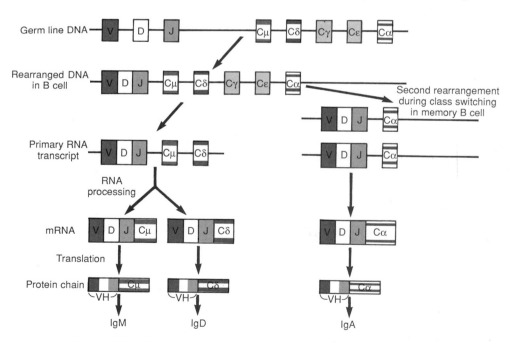

Figure 7.10.   Organization and Expression of Immunoglobulin Heavy-Chain Genes. The gene rearrangements that occur during B-cell development and the response to antigen are depicted. DNA segments that encode for individual portions of the mature protein are carried separately in the *germ line DNA*. These gene segments must rearrange as indicated for expression to occur. The joining of a given variable gene to different constant region genes permits the production of different isotypes (classes) of antibody with identical antigen-binding characteristics. The genes are not drawn to scale and many details are omitted.

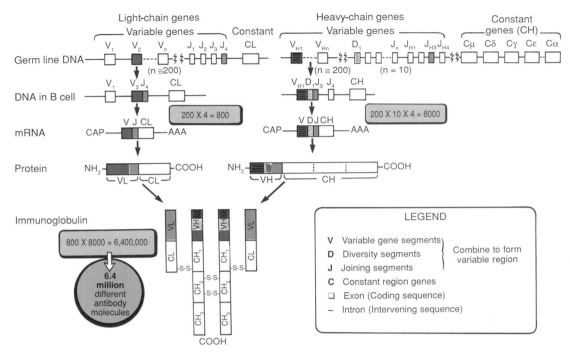

Figure 7.11. Generation of Diversity. This illustration depicts the mechanism by which a large number of unique immunoglobulin molecules is created. The number of unique variable regions and antigen-combining sites created at each step is calculated. For example, with heavy chains, the 200 *V* segments can combine with any of the 10 *D* segments and 4 *J* segments to create 8000 different variable regions. The number of *V*, *D*, and *J* segments present are, in some cases, minimal estimates and the actual numbers of segments vary among different species. A similar mechanism occurs for the generation of diversity in T-cell receptors (not shown).

ated. Also, because the antigen-binding site is generated by both heavy and light chains, the random association of **H** and **L** chains could yield about 6.4 million (8000 × 800 = 6400000) different antibody molecules. (This process is like creating a large number of different meals in a Chinese restaurant by choosing one from column **A**, one from column **B**, and so on; see figure 7.11.)

Additional diversity can be created by the inaccuracy during the cutting and joining of the V, D, and J segments, known as **junctional diversity**. Also, point mutations in and around the V region genes can occur. This is called **somatic mutation**. These mechanisms probably increase antibody diversity by a factor of 10–100. Somatic mutation may play an important role in antibody production during secondary responses to antigen. Such mutations may serve as a mechanism to "fine tune" the affinity of a particular antibody. Additionally, somatic mutations may reflect the immune system's attempt to "anticipate" changes in antigens. For example, the genes of an invading microorganism are subject to mutations that can potentially change antigens to a form unrecognizable by a particular antibody and, thus, evade the immune response. The antibody genes may also "play this game" and "gamble" that somatic mutations in variable genes produce changes in the binding site that complement changes in the antigen, thus permitting successful recognition and destruction of the invader.

Thus, somatic recombination of segments, junctional diversity, somatic mutation, and combinatorial joining of light and heavy chains, all act to increase antibody diversity for a total of possibly 10^8 different antibody molecules. This huge repertoire is apparently sufficient to deal with the antigenic universe. But, this is only half of the story. The other arm of immune defense, the T lymphocytes, can likely generate, by similar mechanisms, a repertoire of 10 million or more antigen-binding molecules.

T LYMPHOCYTES AND CELL-MEDIATED IMMUNITY

Cell-mediated immune reactions are those mediated by the thymus-derived T lymphocytes. Like B lymphocytes and the antibody responses, T lymphocytes can specifically recognize and react to highly diverse structures. Both types of lymphocytes respond to antigen and mediate memory responses by clonal selection. However, T-cell antigen recognition and function differ from B cells in several important aspects. **First,** there are several functionally distinct categories of T cells—cytotoxic cells, inducer or helper cells, and suppressor cells. **Second,** T cells recognize antigen when it is associated with proteins of the major histocompatibility complex (MHC, see below). More will be said about MHC-encoded proteins later in this chapter. In general, cytotoxic T cells "see" antigen in association with "class I MHC" molecules, whereas helper T cells recognize a molecular configuration formed by the physical association of processed antigen with "class II MHC" molecules. **Third,** the developmental pathways are different; T cells depend on the thymus for important differentiation and selection events. **Fourth,** a number of lymphocyte accessory molecules, important for T-cell activation, are not expressed by B cells. Fifth, the receptor for antigen used by T cells is related to immunoglobulin, but is structurally and genetically distinct. In general, the T-cell receptor is not designed to be a secretory product like antibody.

T-Cell Receptor Complex

T cells recognize and respond to antigen by using integral membrane glycoproteins called the **T-cell receptors** (TCR). There are two types of TCR. The most completely characterized receptor is a disulfide-linked heterodimer of two polypeptide chains, designated α and β, each having a molecular weight of about 40–50 kilodaltons. The other receptor has two similar chains designated γ and δ. Each chain contains N-terminal variable regions unique to particular clones of T cells and carboxy-terminal constant regions shared among T cells. This basic structure has been identified on both helper T cells and cytotoxic T cells. The receptor(s) for antigen on suppressor T cells has not been identified.

The T-cell receptor has a domain structure homologous to immunoglobulin, which would place it in the Ig supergene family (Fig. 7.9). Like immunoglobulin, T-cell receptors are constructed by somatic recombination of genes carried separately in the genome. For example, α-chain genes include a single constant region, about 50 J segments, and about 75 V segments. Upstream of the β constant region genes there are about 12 J segments, 2 D segments, and about 25 V segments. With both chains, junctional diversity increases the repertoire, but somatic mutation does not appear to play a role in increasing diversity. Like diversity created with the construction of an immunoglobulin gene, many different unique α, β, γ, and δ chains can be constructed by the random combinations of V, J, and D segments. By combinatorial associations of different chains, a very large repertoire of T-cell receptors can be potentially generated. Interestingly enough, there appears to be much greater junctional diversity in TCR genes than in Ig genes and the repertoire of TCRs may be even greater than for antibodies. It is certainly comparable to the range of antibody diversity and big enough to deal with the antigenic universe.

How does the triggering of these receptors translate into the expression of function? We know that other membrane proteins of T cells are involved in as yet poorly understood but well established accessory roles. One of these is designated the **CD3 complex**. This is a group of five major proteins noncovalently linked to the T-cell receptor. The CD3 complex must be present for proper T-cell function but does not bind directly to antigen. It appears to be involved in transmitting signals to the cell interior that result in cell activation.

Functional T-Cell Subpopulations

T lymphocytes are divided into three main functional groups—cytotoxic T cells, helper or inducer T cells, and suppressor T cells. The latter two are also known as regulatory T cells since they modulate the activity of other cells.

CYTOTOXIC T CELLS

Cytotoxic T lymphocytes can specifically recognize and destroy antigen-bearing cells. They defend us against certain viral diseases (and possibly bacterial diseases caused by intracellular pathogens) by reacting with antigens expressed on the surface of infected cells. Prevention of viral replication results from their ability to recognize very low levels of antigen and to kill such target cells before production of virus progeny. Intimate effector cell-target cell interaction is required for killing. This cellular adhesion is aided in an undefined way by **lymphocyte function-associated** molecules such as **LFA-1**. Following binding to the target cell, the CD8 molecule and the CD3 complex are involved in expression of lytic function.

The mechanism of killing is not certain, but the most attractive hypothesis is termed the **granule exocytosis model**. Evidence exists that the T cell secretes a protein termed **granule cytolysin or perforin** from intracellular granules onto the target cell membrane. This protein then assembles into amphipathic channel-forming structures—which are analogous to the membrane attack complex of complement—that cause permeability changes in the target cell and eventual osmotic lysis. **Cytotoxic T lymphocytes** may also induce a nuclease activity in the target cell so that both cellular and viral DNA is destroyed. It is clear that the effector T cell is not damaged in this process and can kill multiple target cells.

HELPER T CELLS

Helper or inducer T lymphocytes are essential for optimal proliferation and differentiation of B cells and cytotoxic T-cell precursors. They are also important for increasing the ability of macrophages to ingest and to destroy microbial pathogens and to kill tumor cells. They display characteristic surface markers including CD3 and CD4. CD3 is involved in signal transduction and CD4 acts by stabilizing cellular interactions by binding to portions of the class II MHC molecules present on B cells and macrophages.

When activated, T-helper cells release a variety of cytokines. These include several interleukins (IL), such as IL-2, that stimulate lymphocytes, and macrophage activating factors (MAF) such as γ-interferon.

The properties of some cytokines are summarized in Table 7.3. There are too many cytokines to list completely here. For example, at the last count, there are 12 interleukins.

Because of this secretory function, many if not all of the activities of helper T cells can be duplicated by the appropriate mix of active cytokines. However, the most efficient delivery of helper T-cell-derived cytokines to B cells and macrophages is accomplished by the direct physical interaction between the cells. This occurs when antigen is presented by B cells so that helper T cells interact with it on the B cell's surface. Likewise, macrophage activation via helper T-cell-derived γ-interferon is aided by macrophage-mediated antigen presentation.

SUPPRESSOR T CELLS

Suppressor T cells downregulate the response of B cells or other T cells to antigens. They remain the most enigmatic regulatory T cell. One thing that is clear is that they regulate responses in an antigen-specific manner. They certainly do not use the same receptor for antigen employed by T-helper or T-cytotoxic cells. Suppression can be mediated by soluble factors from suppressor T cells. The current confusion about suppressor T cells will only be mitigated when their antigen receptors are identified and characterized, and the mechanisms involved in their postulated roles in cellular interactions are elucidated.

Null Cells Or "Third Population Cells"

In addition to B and T lymphocytes there are yet other functionally important cells that lack the classical surface markers and functions of T cells, B cells, and macrophages. As the name implies, these cells lack the readily detectable markers and functions of macrophages, B cells, and T lymphocytes. While their lineage remains unclear, they are generally considered to be lymphocyte-like. This group includes two types

Table 7.3. Cytokines

Name	Major Cellular Source	Major Activities
Interleukin-1 (IL-1)	Macrophages, others	Co-stimulation of various cells (e.g., T cells), increases body temperature
Interleukin-2 (IL-2)	T cells	Causes proliferation of activated T and B cells
Interleukin-4 (IL-4)	T cells (CD4+)	Promotes B- and T-cell growth, promotes IgE class switching
γ-interferon	T cells, NK cells	Activates macrophages, promotes MHC expression and B-cell differentiation
Tumor necrosis factor (TNF)	Macrophages	Causes death of certain cells, promotes growth and differentiation, causes wasting
Lymphotoxin	T cells	Similar to TNF, activation of neutrophils and endothelial cells
Colony-stimulating factor (CSF)	T cells, macrophages, and others	Growth and differentiation of hematopoietic cells

of cells, **natural killer (NK)** cells and the **killer (K)** cells responsible for **antibody-dependent cell mediated cytotoxicity** (ADCC). NK cells can efficiently kill certain types of tumor- and virus-infected cells with some selectivity, but not with the precise specificity displayed by cytotoxic T lymphocytes. While NK cells do not require the thymus for development, some evidence indicates that they may be lineally related to T cells. NK cells have prominent cytoplasmic granules and have been called **large granular lymphocytes (LGL)**. These granules contain a protein with several names such as granule cytolysin, perforin, or NK cell cytotoxic factor. Granule exocytosis, as described for the cytotoxic T cell is the likely mechanism of killing by NK and K cells.

K cells express high-affinity Fc receptors that are employed to recognize and destroy antibody coated cells. IgG is the predominant class responsible for directing the specificity of cytotoxic activity. These cells can kill certain bacteria and mammalian cells. K cells and NK cells are either the same population of cells or part of largely overlapping subsets. The activity of both NK and K cells is increased in response to cytokines such as γ-interferon and they can proliferate in response to IL-2. NK cells themselves can also produce cytokines such as γ-interferon, IL-1, and IL-2.

NK and K cells just do not fit into the standard cellular categories. Perhaps they are "all purpose" cells with some of the properties of both lymphocytes and macrophages.

Macrophages

A discussion of cell-mediated immunity would not be complete without discussion of the mononuclear phagocyte or macrophage. Macrophages develop from myeloid stem cells in the bone marrow. There, as promonocytes, they are capable of intense proliferation (driven by colony stimulating factor, CSF-1). These cells then enter the blood, where they are called **monocytes**. After several days in the blood, they seed various tissues where they are considered mature macrophages. They have several names and specialized functions depending on their anatomical location. For example, in the lung they are called alveolar macrophages; in the brain, microglial cells; in the liver, Kupffer cells; and in the skin, Langerhans cells. (Some believe that Langerhans cells are distinct from macrophages in that they lack the ability for rapid phagocytosis.)

In general, mature macrophages have a limited capacity for proliferation. Thus, the increase in number of monocytes in the blood (monocytosis) or at inflammatory sites is not due to local proliferation but rather to greater influx from the bone marrow. Macrophages are readily distinguished from lymphocytes by function, morphology, and surface markers. Unlike lymphocytes, macrophages have horseshoe-shaped nuclei, prominent cytoplasmic granules, and the ability to ingest particles and to adhere to surfaces. While macrophages play crucial roles in constitutive defense reactions, as described in Chapter 6, their most important roles may be related to their symbiotic relationship with lymphocytes. Macrophages help lymphocytes by processing and presenting antigen and by elaborating molecules such as IL-1. Conversely, lymphocytes help macrophages through the elaboration of cytokines.

One such group of cytokines is known as **macrophage-activating factors (MAF)**, the most well defined of which is γ-interferon. This cytokine augments a variety of macrophage functions, such as antigen presentation, phagocytic functions involving complement component C3b and antibody fragment Fc, and destruction of intracellular microbial pathogens and extracellular tumor cells.

Macrophages probably have several mechanisms for expression of cytocidal function. In addition to those discussed in Chapter 6, activated macrophages secrete **tumor necrosis factor (TNF)**. TNF has several biological activities, including tumor killing and antiviral effects. Macrophages also release other antiviral substances, **α/β interferons**. The expression of macrophage-mediated cytotoxicity is dramatically modulated by a number of bacterial products such as lipopolysaccharide (LPS) from Gram-negative bacteria (Chapters 3 and 9). **LPS** dramatically increases macrophage cytolytic activity and other defensive activities.

The growth and differentiation of macrophages from bone marrow-derived stem cells is mediated by the **colony-stimulating factors**, working in synergy with cytokines. Other T-cell-derived cytokines are thought to be important for the accumulation of macrophages at certain inflammatory sites; macrophages are attracted to the sites of elaboration by **macrophage chemotactic factor(s) (MCF)** and prevented from leaving by **migration inhibitory factor(s) (MIF)**. Both MIF and MAF are molecularly heterogeneous and require further definition.

Antigen-Presenting and Dendritic Cells

Cells with the ability to present antigens to lymphocytes are functionally classified as **antigen-presenting cells**. They include macrophages, B cells, and dendritic cells, all of which appear to have several required functions.

- Antigen binding;

- Antigen processing;

- Expression of class II MHC gene products (see below);

- Elaboration of IL-1.

Dendritic cells get their name from their long slender processes and irregularly shaped nuclei. They are effective antigen-presenting cells and are thought to be important in cooperative interactions with lymphocytes. They are found in small numbers in lymphoid tissue, and their lineage is unclear. They have little or no phagocytic activity and carry neither B- nor T-cell receptors. They do have Fc receptors, C3 receptors, and express class II MHC proteins. (There are at least four kinds of these cells, with somewhat different locations and functional properties: lymphoid, follicular, interdigitating dendritic cells, and Langerhans cells.)

The various cells involved in immune responses are shown in Table 7.4. **In summary**, the relationships among lymphocytes and their products is so intricate and interdependent that it is difficult to speak of an individual cell without reference to other members of the partnership. Like the nervous system, it is difficult to appreciate the function of an individual neuron without understanding the collective activities of networks of functioning cells and molecules. Thus, a major challenge for the future is to define the rate-limiting steps of the various cellular and molecular interactions and to understand the regulation of immune physiology.

Table 7.4. Cells of the Immune System

Cell	Surface Components	Function
T lymphocytes	T_3	Involved in cell-mediated immunity
Helper T cells (T_H)	T_4 ⎫ ⎬ T-cell receptor complex: α, β dimer associated with T_3	Recognizes antigen with class II MHC; promotes differentiation of B cells and cytotoxic T cells; activates macrophages
Cytotoxic T cells (CTL)	T_8 ⎭	Recognizes antigen with class I MHC; kills antigen-expressing cells
γ/δ T cells	Probably all T_4 and T_8 negative	Respond to commonly encountered microbial antigens perhaps at epithelial boundaries; MHC restriction and function unknown
Suppressor T cells	T_8 Receptor for antigen unknown	Downregulates the activities of others lymphocytes
B lymphocytes	Surface immunoglobulin, Fc receptors, class II MHC	Recognizes antigen directly; differentiates into antibody-producing plasma cells, antigen presentation
Large granular lymphocytes (LGL) K cells	Fc receptor	Kills antibody-coated cells (ADCC)
NK cells	Receptor for target "antigen" unknown	Kills cells with some selectivity
Macrophages	Fc receptor, C3 receptor; some have class II MHC; can bind to wide variety of substance via surface "receptors"	Antigen presentation; phagocytosis killing of microbes and tumor cells; secretion of IL-1
Dendritic cells	Fc receptor, C3 receptor, class II MHC	Antigen presentation
Mast cells (tissues) and basophils (blood)	High-affinity receptors for IgE	Allergic responses; histamine release
Neutrophils	Fc receptor, C3 receptor, C5 receptor and FMLP receptor	Phagocytosis and killing of bacteria, yeast, and fungi
Eosinophils		Phagocytosis and elimination of parasites

MAJOR HISTOCOMPATIBILITY COMPLEX (MHC)

The MHC consists of proteins originally discovered as being responsible for the rejection of tissue or organ grafts. Only later did it became clear that they perform a far more crucial role, that of helping T cells recognize foreign antigens. The MHC has played several tricks on immunologists. One trick was that they made us focus first on issues concerning graft rejection and tissue transplantation among members of a species. While such strong transplantation antigens are indeed encoded by the MHC (thus the name), the importance of hindering organ transplantation makes no immediate sense for survival value and for the normal protective immune responses against pathogenic microbes.

Another trick that immunologists are still struggling with is the association of disease susceptibility with certain alleles of MHC genes. For example, it remains a mystery why people with a particular MHC allele (HLA-B27) are at a 300-fold greater risk of developing the degenerative disease ankylosing spondylitis. There are ideas, of course! One of the most popular is that a surface antigen of the microbe associated with ankylosing spondylitis, *Klebsiella*, mimics the host HLA-B27 molecule, and therefore, the host is unresponsive to the microbe. Other ongoing tricks of the MHC include the control of mating behavior (sex) by the MHC. Mating is disfavored among mice with similar MHC genes and this may serve to increase genetic polymorphism. Interestingly, mice can smell minor differences (three amino acids) in the MHC expressed by other mice—strange, but true.

Straight Dope On MHC

Unless we are being tricked again, we now believe that the main role of the MHC is in **mediating cell-to-cell communication**. MHC-encoded cell-surface proteins "hold" foreign antigens in the "proper" configuration for recognition by T cells and serve to "guide" the appropriate subpopulation of T cells to the appropriate antigen-expressing surface. Thus, **T cells recognize foreign antigens in association with self-MHC molecules**.

Chemistry and Cellular Location of MHC

There are two structurally and functionally different classes of MHC molecules, conveniently termed class I and class II. As summarized in Table 7.5, these classes differ in genetic loci, chain structure, cell distribution, and function with different T-cell subsets. In general, **class I molecules direct the activity of cytotoxic T lymphocytes. Class II guide the function of helper T cells**.

Mature class I molecules are composed of two subunits, a single 345-amino acid polypeptide encoded by the MHC and a smaller protein called β_2-**microglobulin**. The class I chains are integral membrane proteins. The three-dimensional structure of a human class I MHC molecule has been determined. MHC molecules are members of the immunoglobulin supergene family. β_2-microglobulin is also homologous to immunoglobulin constant regions. Class II molecules (also called Ia molecules or Ia antigens) are structured from two noncovalently linked glycoproteins, an α-chain (MW about 33,000 Da) and a β-chain (MW about 28,000 Da). Each chain is a transmembrane protein with two external domains, again homologous to immunoglobulin (another family member; see Fig. 7.9).

Table 7.5. Properties of Class I and Class II MHC Proteins

	Class I	Class II
Genetic loci	HLA-A, HLA-B, HLA-C	HLA-D (DP,DQ,DR)
Chain structure	45,000 mol wt glycoprotein + β_2-microglobulin	α-chain (33,000 mol wt) β-chain (28,000 mol wt)
Cell distribution	Almost all nucleated somatic cells	B cells, some macrophages dendritic cells, thymus epithelial cells, and activated T cells
Functions in presenting antigen to	Cytotoxic T cells (CD8+ cells)	Helper T cells (CD4+ cells)

Class I gene products are expressed on almost all nucleated somatic cells. Up to 1% of total membrane proteins are class I molecules. In contrast, class II molecules normally display a more restricted cell distribution. All B cells and some macrophages, dendritic cells, thymus epithelial cell, and activated T cells express class II molecules. Many cell types (including epithelial, endodermal, and parenchymal cells) can express class II under certain abnormal clinical situations such as graft rejection and autoimmune diseases.

The cellular distribution of class I and class II molecules is thought to reflect differences in their function. Cytotoxic T cells patrol the tissues "looking for" abnormal cells such as potentially dangerous cancer cells or virus-infected cells. The advantage of recognizing both class I and foreign antigen is that the cytotoxic T cell can focus its function on the source of the potential trouble. This cellular surveillance by cytotoxic T cells requires the global expression of class I molecules. In contrast, the more restricted expression of class II molecules directs the function of helper T cells to those cells requiring the help, i.e., B cells and macrophages. Thus, during evolution, T-helper cells "learned" to recognize antigens associated with B cells and macrophages, while cytotoxic T cells "learn" to pay attention to all somatic cells expressing suspicious structures—alterations of self.

MHC Genetics

Class I molecules are encoded in humans by gene loci called HLA-A, HLA-B, and HLA-C. Class II proteins are encoded by genes in the HLA-D region, subdivided into the HLA-D region and include the DP, DQ, and DR subregions. Each subregion can encode for one or more polypeptide chains.

The MHC is the most polymorphic group of genes known in higher vertebrates. Within a species, there is a very large number of different alleles (alternate forms of the same gene). For example, hundreds of different class I glycoproteins can be expressed by a species as a whole. However, the diversity of MHC proteins is different than that of antibody molecules. MHC genes do not undergo somatic rearrangements like immunoglobulin and T-cell receptor genes. Each of us can make millions of different antibody molecules, but we inherit only a single MHC allele at each locus from each parent. Thus, MHC polymorphism must have to do with survival of the species, not of the individual.

Immune response genes (Ir genes) are the class II MHC genes that control responses of helper T cells (similar control of cytotoxic T lymphocytes by class I MHC genes also occurs). Certain MHC alleles are associated with low responsiveness, while others determine high responsiveness to a particular antigenic determinant. These effects are antigen specific, such that a given individual or group of inbred animals can be a low responder to antigen X but a high responder to antigen Y. While high responsiveness is dominant, under certain circumstances a cross between two allelic dissimilar low responders can give a high responder. This results from the creation of a unique class II molecule by combinatorial association of an α chain from one parent with a β chain from the other (or vice versa).

What Do MHC Molecules Do?

MHC molecules can physically interact with antigen. This binding is required for effective immune responses and likely serves as the basis for immune response gene control. Class II molecules from high responders can bind processed antigen, while low-responder class II molecules cannot bind the antigenic determinant in question.

Exogenous protein antigens are endocytosed by antigen-presenting cells, such as macrophages, and then degraded by proteolysis in acidic lysosomal/endosomal compartments. Peptide epitopes derived from this degradation are then bound to nascent **class II MHC molecules** and transported via the Golgi apparatus to the cell surface. When the protein antigen is endogenous to the antigen-presenting cell (such as a viral protein), then **MHC class I molecules** bind the antigenic peptides derived from processing of the endogenous antigen. This interaction between foreign peptide and MHC class I probably occurs in the endoplasmic reticulum and, then, the peptide-MHC complex is transported to the cell surface.

Some bacterial antigens, for example, the staphylococcal enterotoxins, bind outside the peptide binding groove of the MHC class II molecules and are recognized by large numbers of T cells. Since the frequency of enterotoxin-sensitive T cells is much higher than for regular antigens, these enterotoxins have been called **superantigens**. Because of the large number of activated T cells after exposure to enterotoxins, there are complications such as shock and fever that can lead eventually to death.

The interaction among the T-cell receptor, the MHC molecules, and the foreign processed antigen may be thought of as a ternary complex in which each component of the complex interacts with the other two proteins (see Fig. 7.12). The sum of the separate affinities creates a trimolecular interaction of high avidity. The interactive ability of the T-cell receptor and the MHC, both members of the immunoglobulin supergene family, may be due to the common three-dimensional structure. Just as the domains of heavy and light chains of immunoglobulin interact to stabilize structure and to form a binding site for antigen, MHC molecules and the T-cell receptor interact to form a binding site for processed antigen. Similarly, the familial structure of accessory molecules such as CD4 and CD8 may contribute to cell-to-cell interaction through associations with class II and class I MHC molecules, respectively. Family members like to stick together (see Fig. 7.9).

Additionally, the T-cell receptor may be conceptualized as specific for any "new" molecular configurations created by the binding of foreign antigen to the MHC protein. As such, T cells recognize "alterations of self." Armed with this concept, the obsession of T cells with foreign MHC molecules (as in the powerful transplantation reactions) can be understood. An individual T-cell clone can react with both foreign antigen in the context of self MHC molecules and with certain foreign MHC molecules alone. As such, the T cell is "seeing" nonself in two forms—an allelic form of self, the foreign MHC, and an "altered self" caused by the bound antigenic determinant. Thus, self MHC + antigen X "looks like" nonself MHC. Because of this molecular mimicry and the fact that microbial antigens make for a huge number of antigenic experiences, the strong response to foreign MHC molecules, as with transplantation reactions, is likely due to the many clones of T cells that react with microbial antigens in the context of self-MHC molecules. This "unfortunate" cross-reaction makes transplantation of organs impossible without careful matching the MHC of the donor and recipient and/or using immunosuppressive treatments. Similar considerations may also explain why increased risk of certain autoimmune diseases is associated with certain MHC alleles. Since tolerance to self-

Figure 7.12. The Interaction of the T-cell Receptor, Processed Peptide Antigen, and Class II MHC molecule. MHC molecules bind antigenic peptides in a selective manner. The MHC molecule has a peptide-binding groove composed of polymorphic residues in two helices over a floor of conserved residues in a β-pleated sheet. The processed antigenic peptide of between 8 and 20 amino acids in length fits into the groove like a "hot dog in a bun." Residues of T-cell receptor interact with the antigenic peptide and with the MHC molecule.

antigens is controlled by the MHC (just like responses to foreign antigens) it is possible that cross-reactions between microbial antigens and self-antigens occur with certain combinations of self MHC and foreign antigen experience. As such, the defensive reaction to microbes may result in the side effect of autoimmune disease (see below).

Since the MHC controls immune responsiveness, does MHC polymorphism have survival value? Consider an epidemic within a species caused by highly pathogenic microorganism that is weakly immunogenic. This hypothetical microbe may have antigenic determinants that bind poorly to most kinds of MHC molecules. In this "Andromeda Strain" scenario, MHC polymorphism may increase the chances that at least certain members of the species would have the "right" MHC molecules (high responders) and make a protective response to the pathogen. At least some members of a species would survive.

In summary, the MHC is crucial to the understanding of T-cell specificity and function. Our current understanding of these molecules is that they bind antigenic determinants and guide the activities of T-cell subsets. MHC molecules can transport antigenic determinants from the inside of the antigen-presenting cell, where processing occurs, to the cell surface, where recognition can occur (see Fig. 7.5). MHC molecules may also protect portions of antigens from complete degradation. Additional roles for the MHC may be as unambiguous markers for self so that the critical process of tolerance to self tissue can be maintained. The MHC may even be a "leftover" recognition system from the days when we were swimming about in primordial ooze trying to reject the dissimilar and bind to the similar. Their possible role as cell interaction molecules in developmental processes has also not been overlooked. Clearly, all of the answers about these crucial molecules are not in. Are we being tricked again? Let's hope not.

REGULATION OF THE IMMUNE RESPONSE (IMMUNOREGULATION)

The immune response to foreign antigen must be regulated. Otherwise, once it were initiated, our body would fill up with lymphocytes and antibody. There are five major ways by which the immune response is downregulated. These involve: the limited life span of effector cells; antigen removal; antibody feedback; suppressor cells; and the idiotypic network.

1. The immune response is self-limiting in that the functional life span of effector cells is short. For example, plasma cells can live only a few days.

2. Since continuous production of effector cells requires antigen, another way to downregulate the response is to remove the antigen. This is, in fact, the primary goal of the protective immune responses. The elicited antibody combines with antigen and the resulting immune complexes are more rapidly removed by the garbage collectors of the body, the cells of the reticuloendothelial system. For example, proteins are rendered nonantigenic by complete digestion to amino acids in the lysosomes of macrophages. Such antigen degradation is more efficiently performed by the activated macrophages.

3. Another fundamental mechanism is feedback regulation by antibody. Soluble antibody can cover antigenic determinants and

prevent binding to B-cell receptors. Also, the Fc parts of the antigen-bound antibody can cross-link Fc receptors on the B cell and thereby send an "off signal" for B-cell proliferation and differentiation.

4. Suppressor cells regulate immune responses via complex regulatory cell circuits. Suppressor T cells are generated in response to increased numbers of helper T cells. Thus, helper T cells activate suppressor T cells that can, in turn, downregulate the helper T cells. This feedback pathway allows the activity of both cells to be self-regulating. The action of suppressor cells may be mediated by soluble suppressor factors that are molecularly heterogeneous. However, the exact nature of these molecules has not been established and remains controversial.

5. The fifth and most intriguing way that the immune response is regulated involves the so-called **idiotypic network** as proposed by Niels Jerne. He proposed that the antigen-combining sites of the lymphocyte's antigen receptors are themselves antigenic. He called the antigens associated with the combining sites **idiotypic determinants** (also called **idiotopes**). Because an individual idiotope is present in very small concentrations in the body, immunological tolerance to self idiotopes is not established. Thus, immune responses can be generated to self idiotypic determinants. Antibodies raised against these determinants can prevent the binding of antigen to the antibody. Consequently, antigen can block the interaction of the anti-idiotypic antibody with idiotypic determinants on the target antibody. These facts suggested to Jerne the network theory (see Fig. 7.13).

The network theory is based on two functions of the antibody molecules; its traditional role in binding antigen and **its ability to be an antigen.** When animals are immunized with antigen X, the concentration of anti-X antibody is greatly increased. This increase in anti-X antibody is then perceived by the immune system, and antibody reactive to the idiotypic determinants of anti-X antibody is generated. The anti-idiotypic antibody can then elicit the production of another wave of antibody. Thus, antigen X stimulates anti-X antibody (Ab_1) that stimulate anti-(anti-X antibody) antibody (Ab_2) that stimulates anti-[anti-(anti-X antibody) antibody] antibody (Ab_3), and so on. Each response wave, however, is dampened by regulatory mechanisms.

The network theory gives the immune system the ability to regulate itself using only itself. Idiotypic determinants may be thought of as the "internal images" of the external antigens. In other words, antibody against an antigen-binding site "looks like" the antigen. Because some antibodies are made even in the absence of foreign antigen, a vast number of immune responses are always going on. These internal reflections, a web of opposing immune responses, are in a dynamic equilibrium (a kind of immunological "muscle tone"). What we perceive as an immune response when foreign antigen is introduced is simply the perturbation of the pre-existing network and the establishment of a new position of equilibrium.

Anti-idiotypic antibody can regulate immune responses in both positive and negative ways. Anti-idiotypic antibody can be used instead of antigen to immunize animals; its potential utility as vaccines has been well demonstrated in mice and rats. Inhibition, rather than activation, is noted when the anti-idiotypic antibody is of a class that can bind

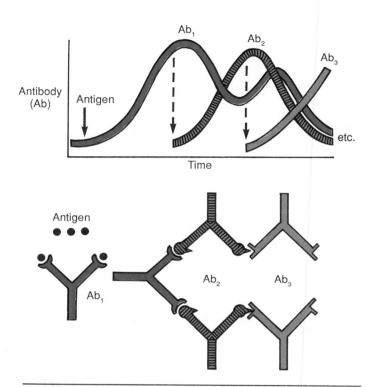

Ab₁ directed against antigenic determinant (epitope)
Ab₂ directed against idiotypic determinant (idiotope) of Ab₁
Ab₃ directed against idiotope of Ab₂

Figure 7.13.   The Idiotypic Network. The amount of antibody produced is plotted as a function of time after injection of foreign antigen. When antibody-1 (Ab₁, directed against the epitope of the antigen) reaches a high concentration, it is sensed by the immune system and antibody-2 (Ab₂) is made against the idiotope (or variable region) of Ab₁. A similar reaction then occurs with Ab₃ and so forth.

complement and Fc receptors. In this case, it is likely that the anti-idiotypic antibody suppresses responses by elimination of the clones of lymphocytes that express the idiotypic determinant.

Using the ability of anti-idiotypic antibody to mimic antigen, it is also possible to generate antibody to a cell constituent that is difficult to purify. For example, it is possible to make antibodies to a hormone receptor (e.g., the acetylcholine receptor) without ever using the receptor as antigen. Because both hormone receptor and the antihormone antibody can bind to the hormone, antibody raised against the antihormone antibody can bind the hormone receptor. These observations illustrate the useful tricks that can be used to identify structures by knowing only their biological activity.

It is all a matter of molecular complementarity. *"Nature (the idiotypic network), she shows us only surfaces, but she's a million fathoms (receptors) deep,"* said Ralph Waldo Emerson.

IMMUNOPATHOLOGY

Immunopathology refers to disease caused by inappropriate immune responses. Immune responses that fail to distinguish self from nonself may result in **autoimmune diseases**. Responses that are exaggerated or inappropriate for protective function are called **hypersensitivity reactions**; and defects in defense reactions manifested by recurring infections are known as **immunodeficiency diseases**. Thus, immune responses that are misdirected, too strong, or too weak can result in pathology.

Autoimmune Diseases

Autoimmune reactions are those directed against the body's own tissues, cells, or molecules. These occur when the regulatory events involved in immunological tolerance are subverted or otherwise malfunction. Self-antigens or autoantigens, the targets of autoimmune reactions, may be intracellular components, receptors, cell membrane components, extracellular components, plasma proteins, or hormones. Depending on the autoantigen, the disease may be organ specific (e.g., Graves' disease with the primary site in the thyroid gland) or nonorgan specific (e.g., systemic lupus erythematosus with symptoms affecting many systems). Both antibody and T-cell responses to self-antigens may cause disease.

Tissue damage by the immune response may be caused by the sharing of antigenic determinants between host and parasite. Given the biological relationships of hosts and parasites, it is not surprising that microorganisms and vertebrates sometimes share antigenic determinants. However, it is not known how such determinants elicit immune response, since they should be recognized by the body as "self" and tolerance to such antigens should be established.

Autoimmune reactions have been implicated in two puzzling disorders that follow infections by certain streptococci. Rheumatic fever and glomerulonephritis are uncommon but severe sequels of otherwise mundane "strep throats." We know that antigens in the cell walls of the infecting streptococci cross-react with components of heart muscle or kidney glomeruli and that antibodies reactive with self tissues are present in such patients. However, the precise role of autoimmune reactions in these diseases is still unclear.

Because immunological tolerance to self-components hidden from the immune system cannot be established, immune responses to self-antigens occur when such sequestered antigens are released or abnormally expressed. Tissue and cellular damage may result in the release of antigenic intracellular molecules. The resulting immune reactions may cause continued cellular trauma, the further release of sequestered antigens, and perpetuation of the inflammatory process. Self-components present in organs such as the central nervous system (which lack conventional lymphatics, and thus, frequent contact with lymphocytes) may elicit strong immune responses in an unusual context. For example, in experimental animals, injection of self-CNS tissue mixed with an adjuvant may cause a demyelinating encephalitis that resembles the human disease multiple sclerosis. It is also thought that the abnormal expression of class II MHC gene products on cells other than the antigen-presenting B cells and macrophages may permit effective local immune reactions to self-antigens on these cells.

Autoimmune disease may also result from alterations of self-components by environmental agents. For example, there is a class of autoimmune hemolytic anemias that are known to be drug induced. The drug may bind to red cells and permit immune responses to the drug-associated self-components. Conceivably, alterations of self-components by interactions with microbial products may also contribute to autoimmune reactions. Additionally, there are many microbial agents that are able to activate lymphocytes polyclonally and, thus, possibly bypass the normal regulatory pathways that maintain tolerance to self.

Finally, it is important to note that self-reactivity may occur in the absence of pathology. The idiotypic network, for example, is a web of responses to self-idiotopes. Also, the association of a particular disease with autoimmune reactions does not necessarily imply a direct cause and effect relationship. An autoreaction may be secondary to the pathological changes caused by another mechanism.

Hypersensitivity Reactions

The term hypersensitivity is used for immune responses that occur in an exaggerated or inappropriate manner. These reactions are also called **allergic reactions** and the antigens involved are called **allergens**. None of the many clinical manifestations of hypersensitivity are pleasant.

As the name implies, hypersensitivity reactions occur in individuals who have been previously sensitized to the antigen; they are secondary responses. They have been classified by Gell and Coombs into four major types according to the speed of the reaction and the nature of the immunological reactions involved. While they are grouped separately, in reality they rarely, if ever, occur in complete isolation from each other. Nonetheless, they are useful conceptual frameworks for review of immune reactions (Fig. 7.14). Types I, II, and III are all antibody-mediated. Type IV is cell-mediated.

TYPE I OR IMMEDIATE HYPERSENSITIVITY

These occur within minutes of exposure to antigen. The cross-linking of mast cell-bound IgE by the allergen triggers the release of vasoactive amines that produce inflammation. It is not known why some antigens elicit IgE production and cause such responses. While it is not entirely clear why only certain individuals suffer from these reactions, genetic control by class II MHC genes plays a significant role. Examples include allergic asthma, hay fever, urticaria, and anaphylactic reactions to insect venom.

TYPE II OR CYTOTOXIC HYPERSENSITIVITY

Antibody binding to cell-surface antigens is followed by antibody-dependent cell-mediated cytotoxicity by K cells, or complement-mediated lysis. Examples of type II diseases include transfusion reactions, hemolytic disease of the newborn, and certain drug allergies resulting in hemolytic anemia. Tissues can also be damaged by cytotoxic T lymphocytes but these will be discussed below as a form of cell-mediated hypersensitivity.

TYPE III OR IMMUNE COMPLEX-MEDIATED HYPERSENSITIVITY

This kind of immunopathological damage is caused by the activation of complement by immune complexes (via the classical pathway) and the mobilization of white blood cells, especially neutrophils. Antigens may be soluble or associated with small particles like viruses. The antigen-antibody complex activates the complement pathway and the resulting complement fragments (C3a, C5a; see Chapter 6) causes an inflammatory response. The resulting vascular permeability changes and

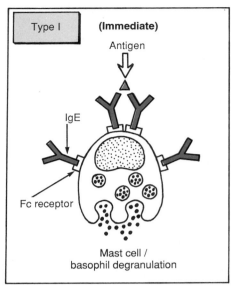

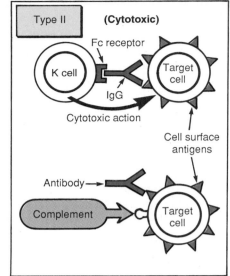

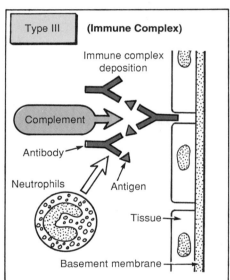

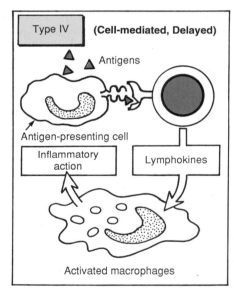

Figure 7.14. Hypersensitivity Reactions. Hypersensitivity reactions are secondary responses to antigen that occur in an exaggerated or inappropriate form. These have been classified by Gell and Coombs into four major types. Types I, II, and III are antibody-mediated while type IV is cell-mediated. Serious pathology can result from these reactions.

influx of neutrophils (and later macrophages) elicits symptoms like fever, skin rash, and arthritis. Thus, the deposition of antigen-antibody complexes in certain tissues can elicit inflammatory reactions that result in damage and disruption of normal organ function. The site of deposition of immune complexes dictates the pathology observed. Why complexes show affinity for particular tissues (kidney, joints, etc.) is not clear, but certain hemodynamic factors as well as the size of the immune complexes are thought to be critical. A relatively high or persistent antigen load characterizes these conditions. Hypersensitivity reactions may result from persistent infection with certain bacteria (streptococcal infections), viruses (hepatitis B), parasites (the *Plasmodium* agents of malaria), or worms (filariae, the agents of elephantiasis).

Examples of type III reactions include glomerulonephritis, alveolitis, and certain autoimmune diseases.

TYPE IV—CELL-MEDIATED REACTION OR DELAYED TYPE HYPERSENSITIVITY (DTH)

This is so named because symptoms appear at least 24–48 hours after antigen exposure. It is caused by the activation of T cells, the release of cytokines, and the subsequent influx of macrophages to the site. Allergic contact dermatitis (e.g., poison ivy) and the skin test for exposure to tubercle bacilli, called the tuberculin test, are examples of DTH reactions.

Cell-mediated hypersensitivity is often characteristic of infections by intracellular slow-growing pathogens, typified by the tubercle bacilli and fungi by *Histoplasma capsulatum*, the agent of histoplasmosis. Circulating antibodies here play a minor role because the organisms are shielded from them in their intracellular location. Chronic inflammations are usually manifestations of cell-mediated immune reactions. The activation of T cells, the release of cytokines, and the subsequent influx of macrophages to the site of antigen may result in a lesion called the **granuloma**. This is a densely packed collection of macrophages that fuse to produce characteristic giant cells, surrounded by epithelioid cells and lymphocytes. This is usually a slow progressing but nonetheless active lesion, in that the host attempts to contain the infection but the microorganisms continue to grow intracellularly at slow rates. Whether the lesion progresses or resolves depends on many factors, principally, on the rate of release of antigens from the organism.

A prototype of this kind of immunological industry is the disease leprosy. It is caused by an organism called *Mycobacterium leprae*, a relative of the tubercles bacillus. These organisms survive inside monocytes, probably by virtue of possessing a thick layer of wax (see Chapters 3 and 23). In one form of the disease, lepromatous leprosy, the organisms elicit the production of granulomas that damage sensory nerves. This results in anesthesia of fingers or whole limbs. Because the patient has little feeling in the affected areas, these become subject to repeated trauma and secondary infection by bacteria. This cycle of injury and repair leads to some of the deformities characteristic of untreated cases of the disease.

While CD4-expressing T cells are most noted for their release of cytokines and elicitation of DTH reactions, CD8-bearing T cells can also release cytokines and participate in cell-mediated immunity. The mouse analogues of CD8+ cells have been shown to play a protective role in cutaneous leishmaniasis (Leishmania are protozoan parasites) and in immunity to certain intracellular bacteria. Whether these effects are due to cytokine elaboration or by the direct cytotoxic effector function of such cells is unclear.

The tissue-damaging effect of cytotoxic T lymphocytes has been noted in the immunopathology of persistent viral infection. Infection of mice with lymphocytic choriomeningitis virus (LCMV) is a good example. LCMV is an arenavirus that is relatively noncytopathic. When injected into neonatal mice, a persistent infection is produced and the mice, even as adults, remain healthy. In contrast, the injection of adult mice with the virus causes a rapid death from meningochoroidoencephalitis. However, death is prevented in adult mice by immunosuppression with x-irradiation, thymectomy, or pharmacological means.

Thus, it is the immune response to the virus (cytotoxic T lymphocytes) rather than the virus itself that causes death. Neonatal mice are not killed by the virus because they are immunoincompetent and presumably develop tolerance to viral antigens as in the process of tolerance to self-antigens. Similar mechanisms may be involved in the chronic infection of humans with measles virus, which can cause a severe degenerative disease and death due to subacute sclerosing panencephalitis (SSPE). It is believed that the immunopathology associated with a variety of persistent virus infections may be due, at least in part, to the action of cytotoxic T lymphocytes and other immunological mechanisms (see Chapters 30 and 33).

It is clear that persistent immune responses by both antibody and T lymphocytes may have severe immunopathological results.

Immunodeficiencies

Perhaps the most serious forms of pathology involving the immune system result from the loss of immune function. Immunodeficiency diseases may be acquired or congenital. Congenital immunodeficiencies are tragic "experiments of nature" that have proven to be important tools for defining the differentiation pathways of lymphocytes described above. Of the acquired immunodeficiencies, the most worrisome example is, of course, the acquired immunodeficiency syndrome or AIDS. In AIDS, the virus binds to the CD4 protein of helper T cells and destroys them. The reduction in the number of CD4+ helper cells produces a profound immunosuppression that leads to severe infections with commensal and normally avirulent microorganisms. *Pneumocystis carinii* pneumonia, herpes simplex infections, candidiasis, and disseminated Kaposi's sarcoma are some of the more common manifestation of AIDS. (See Chapter 37 for further discussion of AIDS and its opportunistic diseases.) Thus, the AIDS virus has developed an ingenious and nefarious strategy for survival, infection and destruction of the very cells that could help fight back. AIDS patients succumb not to HIV infection itself, but rather to overwhelming opportunistic infections. A better understanding of the immune system and of the invading AIDS virus offers hope for the future.

SUMMARY

Our immune system faces three major challenges in maintaining our health:

1. How to distinguish an apparently infinite array of foreign antigens and ensure that a specific response in made even when antigen is present in small concentrations;

2. How to ensure that the response is appropriate to the foreign agent so that the foreign agent is eliminated; and

3. How to avoid responding to self-antigens and damaging self. The immune system meets these challenges with specific acquired immune responses. Such responses have been described as a "microcosm of evolution operating on somatic cells."

The first challenge is met by generating millions of different antigen receptors. These receptors are distributed among millions of different lymphocyte clones. The diversity created by genetic recombination and mutation are not unlike the mechanisms that generated diversity during evolution of various species. A kind of "survival of the fittest" process operates with lymphocytes in that those lymphocytes "fit" for protective defense reactions are encouraged to "survive." Lymphocytes respond to antigens in the individual's environment and are stimulated to proliferate and differentiate into long-lived memory cells by a process of clonal selection. The symbiotic relationships among lymphocytes and macrophages ensures that efficient responses are made to even small amounts of antigen.

The second problem of how to ensure that the response is appropriate to the invading foreign agent is solved, at least in part, by the division of labor among the lymphocytes, and may be mediated by the guiding function of the MHC glycoproteins. B cells make various classes of antibody and cell-mediated responses are mediated by separate subclasses of T lymphocytes. MHC molecules channel antigens into pathways for recognition by either helper or cytotoxic T cells. Also, the various antibody isotypes may help to ensure that appropriate responses are made in the proper places and sequences. The amplification of constitutive defense reactions by products of the specific acquired immune responses, (e.g., opsonization with antibody and macrophage activation by cytokines) makes for efficient elimination of the foreign agent.

The third challenge of preventing damage to self is met by a precise discrimination between self and nonself through the processes of immunological tolerance and immunoregulation. During development, lymphocytes with receptors specific for self-components are downregulated, and, perhaps akin to evolutionary pressures, T lymphocytes reactive to self are eliminated in the thymus. Responses to foreign agents must also be delicately controlled by feedback mechanisms to prevent damage to our tissues. When this immunoregulation is imprecise, we have autoimmune disease and hypersensitivity reactions with disastrous consequences to our health.

Thus, the double-edged sword of immune defense is delicately balanced to fight the foreign and to protect the self by remarkable abilities for specific recognition and precise regulation.

CODA—INTEGRATION OF DEFENSE MECHANISMS

As previously discussed (Chapter 6 and this chapter), higher animals have a multitude of means to discriminate self from nonself and to maintain the integrity and health of the individual. Nature has provided a system with many layers of defensive fail-safe mechanisms. The advantages of this should be obvious. Failure at any one level can often be compensated by success at another. These "layered" defense reactions differ in terms of speed, specificity, and strength, but they are interactive and cooperative.

More primitive defense reactions, such as the toxins and enzymes of procaryotic organisms or the phagocytic cells of invertebrates, were not discarded during the development of the more sophisticated specific acquired immune responses of mammals. Instead, the new mechanisms of defense were layered on top of the older ones; and, most importantly, the specific induced defenses evolved to interact bidirectionally with the more primitive innate or constitutive defense reactions, so that both types of reactions would work best in concert. To prevent infectious disease, humans may avoid contact with microbes, prevent their entry (keep them on the epithelial side), or destroy them if they breach the defensive barriers. We will review briefly the defense reactions against a microbe once it has gained entry. Multiple defense reactions will be emphasized.

Gauntlet of the Body's Defenses

Consider a microbe running the gauntlet of immune defenses in a human being. There are three phases in these defenses. In the first stage, the microbe is sensed by the host as foreign and innate defense reactions are expressed. In the second stage, the foreign entity is processed by cells and the specific immune response is initiated. In the third phase, the innate defense reactions interact with the induced defense reactions, resulting in the efficient elimination of the invading microbe. The importance of each of these stages in host defense varies with the invading organisms and their principal pathogenic mechanisms.

STAGE 1. INNATE (CONSTITUTIVE) SENSING

Important reactions in the first or "sensing" stage involve the functions of complement, interleukins, interferons, phagocytes, killer cells, and other elements of the inflammatory response. Through random collisions and ill-defined attachment mechanisms, phagocytes have the intrinsic ability to ingest and to destroy microbes. These are amplified by activation of complement and by white blood cell chemotaxis. Important events include the recruitment of phagocytes, especially the faster neutrophils, in response to microbial products such as the bacterial chemotaxin formyl-met-leu-phe (Chapter 6). If the alternative pathway of complement is activated, the movement of phagocytes toward the microbe is aided by C5a. Complement activation may also generate the opsonin C3b that promotes phagocytosis of the microbe as well as the membrane attack complex, which can directly lyse certain bacteria and viruses.

The concerted action of these cells and molecules may result in death and digestion of microbes. If a microbe fails to negotiate this first level of the gauntlet, no further action is required by the immune system. In fact, specific lymphocyte responses are not even elicited. However, if destruction is incomplete, the short-lived neutrophils begin to disintegrate and the later-arriving macrophages must come into play. Macrophages play important roles as garbage collectors and domestic engineers, as they arrive to digest debris and remaining microbes. Macrophages also play perhaps an even more important role as liaison between phagocytes and lymphocytes in initiating the next stage of immune defense.

STAGE 2. SPECIFIC IMMUNE RESPONSES

The second stage of defense is the generation of specific immune responses (this stage is also called the afferent immune response). Macrophages process microbial antigens and express them on their cell surface in association with class II MHC gene products. In this form, antigens may be recognized by helper or inducer T lymphocytes (CD4+). Virus-infected cells that have escaped innate defenses express viral antigens on the surface in association with class I MHC gene products. These antigen-MHC complexes are recognizable by the precursors of cytotoxic T lymphocytes (CD8+). Still other microbial antigens may be relatively intact and may be able to interact directly with the receptors on B lymphocytes.

The engagement of antigen-specific receptors and the subsequent cellular and molecular interactions lead to proliferation and differentiation of lymphocytes. This process of clonal selection and memory cell production accounts for specific acquired immunity. Effector cells (e.g., plasma cells and cytotoxic T cells) are also generated in this process. Such cells and/or their products may then mediate several important functions in the third and final stage of immune defenses; the specific, amplified, efferent phase.

STAGE 3. SPECIFIC AND AMPLIFIED EFFERENT PHASE

The third stage involves the concerted action and cooperation of both innate and specific acquired immune responses. In this stage, the host uses every means available to eliminate the invader; this is the ultimate and bloodiest battle in the war. Thus, this stage is not just a simple addition or layering of the specific induced defenses over the innate defenses, but also the synergistic effect of both. For example, antibody helps activate complement more efficiently via the classical pathway. In turn, complement activation makes for more efficient killing of microbes and accelerates chemotaxis and opsonization by phagocytes. Antibodies neutralize toxins that impair the function of leukocytes and prevent the invasion of new microbes. Antibodies also enhance and direct the function of the large granular lymphocytes (NK cells and the K cells) to perform ADCC, antibody-dependent cell-mediated cytotoxicity.

In this stage, functions and products of T lymphocytes also play key roles in amplifying innate defense reactions. Notably, macrophage-activating factors elaborated by T cells dramatically improve the phagocytic killing mechanisms. For example, cytokines increase the expression of macrophage Fc receptors, which, in turn, promotes the function of antibody as an opsonin. Macrophage activation by T-lymphocyte cytokines is especially important in the elimination of intracellular pathogens that have managed to escape initial destruction and live inside macrophages. Cytokines released by T cells (e.g., γ-interferon) also increase the expression of MHC molecules on macrophages and other cells and, thus, augment antigen presentation.

These are just a few of the examples by which products of induced defenses interact with innate defense mechanisms during the elimination of invading microbes. If this array of cooperative defenses were not impressive enough, there is an even more intelligent strategy for defense. Even after the successful resolution of the infection, the immune system quietly waits, anticipating the next encounter with the microbe. Immunological memory ensures that the next response to the microbe will be even stronger and faster and more interactive with innate defense reactions.

SUGGESTED READING

Abbas AK, Lichtman AH, Pober JS. Cellular and molecular immunology. Philadelphia: WB Saunders Co, 1991.
Klein J. Immunology. Oxford: Blackwell Scientific Publications, 1990.
Paul WE. Fundamental immunology, 2nd ed. New York: Raven Press, 1989.
Roitt IM, Brostoff J, Male DK. Immunology, 2nd ed. London: Gower Medical Publishing, 1989.

Microbial Subversion of Host Defenses

8

Andrew Plaut

When a microorganism causes an infection, it creates a hostile environment for itself. The host responds by mobilizing defenses that impair the organism's growth and threaten its existence. In most cases the host prevails, but the existence of infectious diseases demonstrates that this is not always true and that microorganisms can thwart or evade the host defenses. The microbial countermeasures involved can be thought of as virulence factors, even though they do not contribute directly to tissue damage. Generally speaking, each species of infectious agents develops an individual spectrum of survival strategies. For every successful infection by a microorganism, we must ask: **How does it survive in its particular location of the body?** We know some of the answers, but by no means do we know all.

Host defenses do not operate in isolation but are interrelated. The strategies that microorganisms use to subvert them are correspondingly complex and difficult to classify. We will divide these strategies into those directed against constitutive defenses—**complement and phagocytosis**—and against induced defenses—**humoral and cellular immunity**. Microorganisms invading a host that has not encountered them previously will meet these defenses in this order.

Many microbial countermeasures are known from in vitro experimental situations and it is not always possible to determine if they also operate in human disease. This is a subject of intensive research that has clear therapeutic and prophylactic implications.

DEFENDING AGAINST COMPLEMENT

The most effective way to protect against the antimicrobial components of complement is to prevent their activation. Bacteria do this in several ways (Table 8.1). One is by **masking** surface components that activate by the alternative pathway. For example, the cell wall murein of *Staphylococcus aureus* is a good complement activator, but is overlaid by a capsule that prevents this activity. Group B streptococci and strains of *Escherichia coli* that possess capsules rich in sialic acid also inhibit activation by the alternative pathway.

Meningococci have another mechanism to avoid activation of complement. When these organisms enter the blood, they become **coated with circulating IgA antibodies**, a class of immunoglobulins that does not activate the complement cascade. Furthermore, this binding prevents other kinds of antibodies (capable of setting off complement activation by the classical pathway) from reaching the surface of the organisms. Although this seemingly protective role of IgA sounds su-

Table 8.1. Some Microbial Anticomplement Strategies

1. Mask activating substances
   Coating with capsule (e.g., staphylococci)
   Coating with IgA antibodies (e.g., meningococci)
2. Appropriate inhibitor of activation to their surface
   Binding component H by *E. coli*, group B streptococci
   Binding decay accelerating factors by schistosome
   Mimicking component C4bp by vaccinia virus
3. Cover up target of membrane attack complex (e.g., *E. coli*, salmonellae)
4. Inactivate complement chemotaxin C5a (e.g., *P. aeruginosa*)

perficially like host stupidity, it more likely reveals our ignorance of the role of the IgA class of immunoglobulins.

Some Gram-negative bacteria, such as *Salmonella* or *E. coli*, resist the action of complement by yet another mechanism. They do not prevent formation of the complement membrane attack complex, but rather, **hinder access to its target**, the bacterial outer membrane. "Smooth" strains, which have a long O antigen polysaccharide chain, do not allow access of the membrane attack complex to their cell surface, whereas "rough" mutants, which have little or no O antigen, are readily killed by it. This correlates well with pathogenicity, inasmuch as smooth strains tend to be virulent while rough strains are not.

There is a price to pay for having capsules and other protective surface structures; most of them are highly antigenic and, in time, elicit the production of anticapsular antibodies that enable the activation of complement by the classical pathway. Notice that these organisms defend themselves better against the more immediate host defense, activation of complement by the alternative pathway, than against later events, the formation of antibodies.

Certain viruses have also evolved defensive systems against complement. For example, herpes simplex virus has an envelope glycoprotein that binds the complement component C3b, thus inhibiting the activation by the alternative pathway. Vaccinia virus-infected cells secrete a viral encoded protein that shares amino acid homology with C4bp, a complement control protein that binds to the C4b fragment. By mimicking the action of the host C4bp, the virus limits activation by the classical pathway and causes the accelerated decay of C3 convertase. Mutants of vaccinia virus that lack the protein produced smaller, more rapidly healing skin lesions in experimental animals. Thus, this virus uses part of its genome to encode for proteins required not for replication, but rather to interfere with normal host defensive mechanism.

A parasite called *Schistosoma mansoni*, the cause of schistosomiasis, is subject to immune attack by the complement system starting at approximately the time it moves from the skin to the blood. It is known that older parasites (about 2 days old) are less active in activating complement by the alternative pathway than the infective larval stages that originally penetrate the skin. How do the older parasites, about to enter the bloodstream, avoid the potentially injurious activation of complement? To understand this, we must recall how host cells normally in contact with plasma avoid activating complement. Normal cells bear proteins called **decay accelerating factors** (DAF) that reduce complement activation by inhibiting C3 deposition onto membranes. Experiments with schistosomes have shown that they incorporate host DAF proteins into their membranes. Thus, appropriating the host's DAF is a way by which parasites prevent the activation of complement in the blood by the same mechanism used by host cells.

SUBVERTING PHAGOCYTOSIS

The very large number of ways microorganisms avoid being killed by phagocytes highlights the central role of phagocytosis in the evolution of parasitism and infection. The host attempts to overcome these microbial countermeasures, and these efforts are answered by yet other microbial tactics. A point must be made at the outset: being taken up by a cell is not necessarily a bad thing from the microbe's point of view. A powerful counterdefensive strategy is for microorganisms to grow within nonphagocytic host cells where they are shielded from antibodies or certain antimicrobial drugs.

Here we will discuss a few examples of strategies used by microorganisms to withstand the killing power of phagocytic cells. Various aspects of phagocytosis are affected, from the arrival of the phagocytes at the scene to the killing powers of phagocytic cells (Table 8.2).

Inhibiting Phagocyte Recruitment

We have already seen that some microorganisms avoid the activation of complement; in so doing, they prevent the secondary release of che-

Table 8.2. Microbial Strategies to Evade Phagocyte Function[a]

Antiphagocyte Activity	Mechanism	Examples
Avoiding being phagocytized		
Diversion (to nonproductive use)	Activate complement C5a	Streptococci
	Leucoaggregation	Gram-negative enterics
	Pulmonary sequestration	
"Playing hard to get"	Slimy capsule on organisms	Pneumococci, meningococci, *Haemophilus influenzae, Bacteroides fragilis,* many others
	M protein	Group A streptococci
	Pili	Gonococci
Humiliation	Release of adenylate cyclase leading to high cAMP levels; all phagocyte functions depressed	*Bordetella pertussis* (toxin)
Paralysis	Make cells unresponsive to chemotactic factors	*Capnocytophaga*
	Induce inhibitors of migration	Tubercle bacilli
	Inactivate chemotaxins (C5a)	Leprosy bacilli
After being phagocytized		
Murder	Membrane lysis	Streptococci (streptolysin O)
		Pseudomonas (exotoxin A)
		Staphylococcus aureus (α-toxin)
Indifference (resist lysosomal enzymes)	?	*Salmonella typhimurium*
		Mycobacteria sp.
		Leishmania sp.
Disablement (inhibit phagosome-lysosome fusion)	?	Tubercle bacilli
	?	*Toxoplasma*
Disablement (inhibit oxidative killing)	Inhibit respiratory burst	Virulent salmonellae
		Legionella pneumophila
	Catalase breaks down H_2O_2	*Listeria monocytogenes*
		Staphylococcus aureus
Escape (from from phagosome into cytoplasm)	Phospholipase?	Rickettsiae
	?	Influenza viruses

[a]Modified from a table by Mark Klempner.

motaxins for neutrophils, thus reducing the chance of encountering these cells. Other organisms directly inhibit neutrophil motility and chemotaxis, which are essential elements for a successful phagocytic response. An example is the agent of whooping cough, *Bordetella pertussis*, which produces a toxin that increases the neutrophil level of cyclic AMP (Chapter 20). This leads to paralysis instead of chemotaxis of these cells that are highly motile toward bacteria. Another pertussis toxin impairs the migration of monocytes.

Microbial Killing of Phagocytes

Many pathogenic bacteria produce exotoxins called **leukocidins** that kill neutrophils and macrophages. These soluble products work at a distance and, thus, may protect bacteria before the phagocytes come near them. In many cases, however, microbes kill after they are ingested, which means that the phagocyte commits suicide by carrying out phagocytosis. Examples of leukocidins are discussed in detail in the chapter on bacterial toxins (Chapter 9). For now, you should know that typical leukocidin-producers are highly invasive bacteria, such as *Pseudomonas*, staphylococci, group A streptococci, and the clostridia that cause gas gangrene.

Escaping Ingestion

The pre-eminent microbial counterdefense to phagocytosis is its capsule. One of the more captivating visual experiences in microbiology is to watch a preparation of live neutrophils and encapsulated pneumococci under the microscope. Every time a neutrophil attempts to embrace a pneumococcus, the slimy bacterium squeezes away with what looks like total indifference. Repeated attempts are no more successful; eventually it becomes difficult not to share the frustration of the neutrophil.

The picture changes when a small amount of specific antiserum is added. Now the neutrophils have no trouble engulfing the opsonized pneumococci. Thus, anticapsular antibodies provide protective immunity against infection by encapsulated bacteria. However, bacteria have evolved measures to counter opsonization either by complement components or by specific antibodies. Any mechanism that inhibits activation of complement (see above), or synthesis or activity of antibodies (see below) will reduce the probability of opsonization.

Staphylococci, streptococci, and probably other bacteria have evolved a mechanism to reduce opsonization even when antibodies are present; they make a surface component, **protein A**, that binds to IgG molecules by the "wrong" end, the Fc portion. These antibodies cannot act as opsonins because they cannot bind to the Fc receptors on phagocytic cells, not to mention that their Fab region is "waving in the breeze." It is not known to what extent this antiphagocytic mechanism plays a role in actual infections.

How Microorganisms Survive Inside Phagocytes

Microorganisms have many ways to survive once they are taken up by host cells. These include entry into the cytoplasm (a privileged site), inhibiting fusion of lysosomes with the phagosomes, and resisting the oxidative or nonoxidative killing mechanisms of white blood cells. These mechanisms are discussed in detail below.

Escaping Into the Cytoplasm

The trypanosomes of Chagas disease or the rickettsiae of Rocky Mountain spotted fever cross the membrane of the phagocytic vesicle, the **phagosome**, and enter into the cytoplasm itself. Inasmuch as lysosomes do not release their contents in the cytoplasm, the microorganisms are now protected from lysosomal enzymes. It is not known with certainty how the organisms exit the phagosome, although rickettsiae possess a surface-bound phospholipase that may be responsible for weakening the phagosomal membrane.

Inhibiting the Fusion of Lysosomes with Phagosomes

When lysosomes fuse with phagosomes, they release powerful microbicidal enzymes (Chapter 6). Inhibiting this fusion is a clear benefit to intraphagosomal microorganisms. Several examples of this mode of resistance are the bacteria that cause tuberculosis, psittacosis, or Legionnaires' disease. How do they do it? In the case of the tubercle bacilli, this inhibition seems to be induced by complex glycolipids of the organisms called the sulfatides, although this point is still under study. Clearly, inhibition of fusion must be due to a modification of the membrane of the phagosome. The microorganisms must contribute to this modification using compounds that they secrete or that are present on their surface.

Resisting Lysosomal Enzymes

Some microorganisms are innately resistant to the lysosomal enzymes and survive in the so-called phago-lysosome, the vesicle formed by fusion of the lysosomes with the phagosomes. Examples are protozoa called *Leishmania*, which cause several severe tropical diseases. Resistance of leishmanias to lysosomal enzymes may be due to resistant cell surfaces and, in addition, to the excretion of enzyme inhibitors. Note that the pH of the phago-lysosome may be as low as 4, which means that leishmanias can thrive in what one might regard as an extreme environment.

Inhibiting the Phagocytes' Oxidative Pathway

There are several ways in which microorganisms do this. The bacillus of Legionnaires' disease inhibits the hexose-monophosphate shunt and oxygen consumption in neutrophils, thus reducing the respiratory burst used by these cells for killing engulfed microorganisms. Staphylococci produce a powerful catalase that breaks down the hydrogen peroxide necessary for oxidative killing.

Effect of Antibodies

Antibodies against the attacking organisms sometimes help dismantle these survival mechanisms. For instance, rickettsiae that are coated with antibodies lose their capacity to pass through the phagosome membrane; lysosomes will eventually fuse with the phagosomes, leading to the destruction of these organisms. Note that in these cases antibodies do not inhibit entry of the microorganisms into cells but, rather, they interfere with subsequent specific steps.

SUBVERTING THE IMMUNE RESPONSES

Immunosuppression

Some infections result in suppression of the immune responses. What is the outcome of the direct assault on the immunologic apparatus of the host by an invading organism? The host becomes susceptible to other agents and the threat to survival is heightened. Patients may suffer from several infections, which expands considerably the complexities of their clinical problem.

The ability of infectious agents to cause immunodeficiency has reached its known limit with AIDS. Immunodeficiency in this disease is especially profound because the AIDS virus (**HIV, human immunodeficiency virus**) infects the T_4 (inducer-helper) subset of lymphocytes (see Chapter 6). The process of infection is intimately associated with the immunological role of these cells. Depletion of T_4 cells leads to collapse of the immune system, which topples like a roman arch whose keystone is removed. The result is lymphopenia (reduction in circulating lymphocytes), impaired delayed hypersensitivity, defective responses of T cells to antigens, and reduction in the numbers of T cells that are cytotoxic for tumor cells and virus-infected cells. Even B-cell function becomes disordered, with reduced production of specific immunoglobulins and the increased, chaotic production of nonspecific immunoglobulins; paradoxically, AIDS patients may have an abnormally high level of circulating immunoglobulins. All of these events lead to the opportunistic infections and tumors that make AIDS a uniformly lethal illness. If evasion of immunity is a biological imperative for HIV, the process clearly reaches grim levels of excess.

The extensive regulatory interactions of the immunocompetent cells may go awry when even minor changes are introduced into the network. For some 85 years, long before AIDS, it has been known that measles is immunosuppressive. There is good evidence, for example, that tuberculosis is more common after widespread measles outbreaks. Since then, immunosuppression has been found to follow other viral infections as well, e.g., hepatitis B and influenza. These viruses function more subtly than HIV, impairing the function of lymphoid cells without causing major structural changes. T lymphocytes infected with measles virus in vitro do not die but they lose certain functions, e.g., the capacity to mount a delayed hypersensitivity reaction (Chapter 7). B cells infected with measles virus stop synthesizing and releasing immunoglobulins. The effect is intrinsic to B cells and is not secondary to the action of the virus on T cells or macrophages.

In some cases, immune suppression is the result of inhibition of the synthesis of lymphokines. Recent experiments with leishmanias, the protozoa that cause leishmaniasis, showed that when these organisms are growing in macrophages, they suppress the production of interleukin-1. This is significant because interleukin-1 is a critical product of infected macrophages and initiates a series of immunological and inflammatory events that leads to the eradication of the infection (Chapter 6). These findings may explain an old observation, that successful infection in so-called visceral leishmaniasis is associated with T-cell unresponsiveness. This parasite seems to go one step further in arranging for immune evasion by suppressing the capacity of macrophages to make the class 1 and 2 products of the major histocompatibility complex (MHC), an event that has the potential for marked suppression of cell-mediated immunity.

Infection of lymphocytes is not necessarily an immune suppressive tactic of the microbe. A large number of microorganisms infect the lymphoreticular tissues but do not cause global disturbances to host immunity. For example, the bacteria that cause typhoid fever or brucellosis live in lymph nodes for long periods of time without inducing noticeable immune suppression.

Masquerading by Changing Antigenic Coats

Certain bacteria, viruses, and protozoa are unusually adept at frustrating immune recognition by changing their surface antigens. The classical cases are trypanosomes, gonococci, the agents of relapsing fever, HIV, and influenza viruses. (See the paradigm, Chapter 14.)

Case of the Trypanosomes

One of the best studied examples of antigenic variation is seen with the protozoan that causes sleeping sickness, *Trypanosoma brucei*. The organism affects humans and domestic animals and infects the blood and interstitial fluids. Thus, trypanosomes are exposed to circulating antibodies. Trypanosomes are covered with a thick protein coat called **variable surface glycoprotein**, which undergoes periodic antigenic changes during the infection. These parasites have several hundred genes that encode for different antigens but they express only one at at time (Chapters 49 and 50). When antibodies against one type are made, the number of parasites in the blood of an infected host drops, but they are soon replaced by a new antigenic type. There can be many successive waves of antigenically different parasites in a single host. Thus, protective immunity does not function well against this master of disguise.

GONOCOCCUS AND ITS ADHESIN

Like the trypanosome (a eukaryotic cell), some bacteria can also switch their surface antigens. A good example is the gonococcus, which undergoes periodic changes in **pilin**, the protein that makes up its pili, the apparent means of attachment of host cells. Details of how this occurs are discussed in Chapters 3 and 14. In addition to changes in the antigenicity of pilin, the major outer membrane proteins of gonococci also undergo antigenic variation. Thus, the surface of these organisms displays a highly variable antigenic profile to the host immune system.

INFLUENZA AND ANTIGENIC VARIATION AMONG INFLUENZA VIRUSES

The tendency of influenza to reappear in a population on a regular basis is due, in part, to the great ability of influenza viruses to undergo antigenic variation. This is the major obstacle to the development of a truly effective vaccine against this disease. Minor changes are called **antigenic drift** and occur every 2 or 3 years. Major antigenic changes, called **antigenic shifts**, take place every 10 years or so. These changes involve two surface proteins, a **hemagglutinin** that serves to bind to cell-surface receptors, and a **neuraminidase** that changes these receptors. How these proteins are involved in attachment and penetration of the virus is discussed in Chapter 35.

Proteolysis of Antibodies

A number of bacteria—gonococci, meningococci, *Haemophilus influenzae*—and some dental pathogenic streptococci make extracellular proteases that specifically inactivate secretory IgA. They cleave it at the hinge region to yield complete but relatively ineffective fragments. IgA is the major immunoglobulin isotype on human mucosal surfaces and consists of subclasses 1 and 2. The relative importance of these subclasses is not known, but only subclass 1 is cleaved by these proteases. IgA1 proteases from different bacteria are all highly specific for this substrate but they have biochemical and genetic differences that suggest that this property has evolved independently. The proteases are present in active form in tissues and fluids infected by the bacteria that produce them. Nonpathogenic relatives of these organisms are protease negative. Notice that this suggests, although it does not prove, a role for IgA proteases in pathogenesis.

In some instances, it is known that when an organism cleaves IgA, it keeps the Fab fragment attached. This makes the antigens unavailable for binding by intact antibody molecules. This phenomenon has been called fabulation (after "Fab") and may serve to protect organisms from antibodies. Fabulation may be more widely used by pathogens than is currently known.

Viral Latency

The more chronic an infection, the more lasting must be the mechanisms for microbial evasion of host defenses. This is well illustrated in herpes infection. To limit access from circulating defenses, Herpesvirus does not usually enter the extracellular fluid but passes from cell to cell via cytoplasmic bridges. Also, even intracellular herpes viruses have a major mechanism for evading attack, i.e., **latency**, whereby they reside within nerve cells but do not proliferate (Chapter 40). In these circumstances, viruses are not affected by antibodies, cell-mediated immunity, or interferon. They can then survive for long periods of time in the presence of well-developed host defense mechanisms. Later, often when the host defenses have subsided, the viruses may reactivate to cause disease and perhaps even cancer. *"He who fights and runs away may live to fight another day."*

SUGGESTED READING

Cox FEG. How parasites evade the immune response. Immunology Today 1984;5:29.

Haywood AM. Patterns of persistent viral infections. N Engl J Med 1986;315:939–948.

Johnston RB Jr. Recurrent bacterial infections in children. N Engl J Med 1984;310:1237–1243.

Parsons M, Nelson RG, Agabedian N. Antigenic variation in African trypanosomes: DNA rearrangements program immune evasion. Immunology Today 1984;5:43–50.

Seifert HS, So M. Genetic mechanisms of bacterial antigenic variation. Microbiol Rev 1988;52:327–336.

Bacterial Toxins

9

David Schlessinger and Moselio Schaechter

DEFINITIONS

Toxins, like antibiotics, are biological weapons. The analogy is somewhat macabre because antibiotics affect microbes, whereas toxins are directed at us. Bacterial toxins are soluble substances that alter the normal metabolism of host cells with deleterious effects on the host. They are the salient feature of some bacterial diseases and are responsible for their main signs and symptoms. Understanding how they work helps us understand the pathophysiology of many infectious diseases and, in some instances, reveals to us important facts about normal processes. We understand a few toxins in detail and, for the rest, must await the result of further work. Individual toxins will be treated in detail in the chapters on specific bacterial pathogens. Here we will discuss the basic concept of how bacterial toxins function to cause damage in the host. Traditionally, toxins are associated with bacterial diseases, but this probably reflects our ignorance. It seems quite possible that toxins play important roles in diseases caused by fungi, protozoa, and worms.

A clear distinction is made between **exotoxins** and **endotoxins**. Exotoxins are proteins produced by bacteria that are usually secreted into the surrounding medium, but are sometimes bound to the bacterial surface and released upon lysis. In contrast, endotoxins are the lipopolysaccharides of the outer membrane of Gram-negative bacteria and act as toxins under special circumstances only.

Bacterial exotoxins vary in their specificity; some act on certain cell types only, whereas others can affect a wide range of cells and tissues. Some bacteria make a single toxin, others are known to produce ten or more (Table 9.1 gives some examples). Some bacteria, like the pneumococci, make no known toxins and probably cause disease by mechanisms that do not require them. For each pathogen that makes a toxin, we would ideally like to know whether the toxin is important in the process of infection. To find out we may ask:

- Does the toxin in purified form produce damage? (in experimental animals or cells in culture, of course)
- Is virulence quantitatively correlated with toxin production?
- Can a specific antibody (antitoxin) prevent or alleviate the manifestations of the disease?
- If toxin production is impaired by a mutation in the pathogen, is the disease process affected?

In cases where a toxin is shown to be important, we want to know how it works:

- What is its mechanism of action?
- Why is it specific for certain cells or tissues?

Table 9.1. Major Toxinogenic Organisms

Toxin	Effects	Mechanism
Bacillus anthracis		
Protective antigen	Required for other toxins	"B" components
Edema factor	Edema	Internal adenylate cyclase; calmodulin dependent
Lethal factor	Pulmonary edema	Kills certain cells (All three factors together give vascular, permeability, neurotoxicity)
Bordetella pertussis		
Adenylate cyclase	Inhibits, kills white cells	Adenylate cyclase; can be calmodulin independent
Pertussis toxin	Many hormonal effects	ADP-ribosylation of G-binding protein
Tracheal cytotoxin (others)	Kills cilia bearing cells	?
Campylobacter jejuni		
Enterotoxin	Diarrhea	Cholera-like
Clostridium botulinum		
Botulinum toxin	Neurotoxin	Blocks neuromuscular junctions presynaptical flaccid paralysis
Clostridium difficile		
Enterotoxin	Hemorrhagic diarrhea	Acts at membranes
Cytotoxin	Cytoplasmic; cells lose filaments	
Clostridia		
α-toxin	Necrosis in gas gangrene; cytolytic, lethal	Phospholipase C
β-toxin	Necrotic enteritis	?
Enterotoxin (others)	Food poisoning; diarrhea	Cytoxin; damages membranes
Clostridium tetani		
Tetanus toxin	Spastic paralysis	Inhibits GABA and glycine release from nerve terminals at inhibitor synapsis
Corynebacterium diphtheriae		
Diphtheria toxin	Kills cells	ADP-ribosylates elongation factor 2
Escherichia coli (and often other enterics)		
Heat-labile enterotoxins	Diarrhea	Identical to cholera toxin
Cytotoxin	Hemorrhagic colitis	Like *Shigella* toxin
Legionella pneumophila		
Cytotoxin	Lyses cells	?
Listeria monocytogenes		
Listeriolysin	Membrane damage	Like streptolysin O
Pseudomonas aeruginosa		
Exotoxin A (others)	Kills cells	Like diphtheria toxin
Shigella dysenteriae		
Shigella toxin	Kills cells	Inactivates 60S ribosomes
Staphylococcus aureus		
α-toxin	Hemolytic, leukocytic, paralysis of smooth muscle	Lytic pores in membranes
β-toxin	Cytolytic	Sphingomyelinase
δ-lysin	Cytolytic	Detergent-like action
Enterotoxins	Food poisoning (emesis, diarrhea)	Superantigens
Toxic shock syndrome toxin(s)	Fever, headache, arthalgia, neutropenia, rash	Mediated through IL-1 induction
Exfoliating (others)	Sloughing of skin ("scalded skin syndrome")	?
Streptococcus pneumoniae		
Pneumolysin	Cytolysin	Similar to streptolysin O
Streptococcus pyogenes		
Streptolysin O	Cytolysin	Cholesterol target
Erythrogenic toxin (others)	Fever, neutropenia, rash of scarlet fever	Mediated through IL-1
Vibrio cholerae		
Cholera toxin (others)	Diarrhea	Hormone-independent activation of adenyl cyclase
Yersinia enterocolitica		
Heat-stable enterotoxin	Diarrhea	Like *E. coli*

● Does the pathogen make other toxins? Do they interact with one another?

These questions have been answered in detail only in the few cases where modern research methodology has been fully exploited. The answers come easiest when the action of a single toxin accounts for the symptoms of the disease. This is the case in cholera, diphtheria, tetanus, and botulism. By contrast, many pathogenic bacteria, such as staphylococci and streptococci, make several toxins. In such multifactorial situations, the importance of individual toxins is difficult to assess.

PRODUCTION OF TOXINS

Toxins share with antibiotics an ambivalent position in the life of the organisms that produce them. On one hand, they are dispensable, not necessarily required for growth; on the other hand, they may be essential for survival and spread of the bacteria under certain conditions.

In agreement with the dispensability of toxins, the genes that encode them are frequently carried by DNA elements that are themselves dispensable, i.e., plasmids and temperate bacteriophages. Examples of phage-coded genes are those for the toxins of diphtheria, botulism, and scarlet fever. Plasmids carry genes for the toxins with which *Escherichia coli* causes diarrhea and certain staphylococci cause "scalded skin syndrome." The location of these genes on mobile DNA molecules ensures that the ability to produce toxin may rapidly spread to nontoxigenic bacteria. Conversely, the property may also be lost from the bacteria by "curing" the cells of plasmids or prophages. In experimental studies, this provides a simple way of making nontoxigenic bacteria that are otherwise identical to the toxin-producing ones.

Some toxins are produced continuously by growing bacteria, others are synthesized when the cells enter the stationary phase. Note that this is often true for antibiotics and other "secondary metabolites," which are also made as growth stops or slows down. In some instances, there is some teleological sense to this. For example, certain toxins help bacteria obtain nutrients that have become scarce. High levels of diphtheria toxin are produced only when the diphtheria bacilli run out of iron. Since there is very little free iron in normal tissues, may this be a way for the organisms to obtain it from the cells killed by the toxin?

Sporulating bacteria sometimes release toxins during spore formation. In this process, the bacterial cells in which the spores are formed eventually lyse, which leads to the liberation of cytoplasmic proteins including toxins that may have accumulated. Examples are toxins made by the organisms that cause botulism, gas gangrene, or tetanus, all members of the genus *Clostridium*. In a heterogeneous environment, like a contaminated wound, some organisms are growing while others are sporulating. This means that the toxins will be produced continuously during the course of the infection.

MECHANISM OF ACTION

Some toxins **act locally** to help bacteria stay alive by killing nearby white blood cells. Others help the organisms spread in host tissues by degrading the proteins of the connective tissue matrix. Still other toxins **disseminate** far from the site where they are synthesized. This is the case for diphtheria toxin, which is manufactured in the throat but acts on remote organs, including the heart and the brain. Note that neither the mechanism nor the site of action of a toxin can be predicted. Nor is it always possible to understand the benefit to the bacteria of making toxins, especially those that act at a distance. This only reflects our ignorance, for it must be true that toxins help bacteria grow and survive.

Bacterial toxins work at extraordinarily low levels and include the strongest poisons known. One gram of tetanus, botulinum, or shigella toxins is enough to kill about 10 million people. One hundred-fold more is required for the action of diphtheria toxin, and one thousand-fold more for others (for example, pseudomonas A toxin).

Toxins cause damage in various ways (Table 9.1); some lyse host cells, others stop cell growth, and still others exaggerate normal physiological mechanisms. By depressing or augmenting particular functions, toxins may kill a person without directly damaging any cells. For example, tetanus toxin paralyzes the body without affecting the integrity of the target neurons. Cholera toxin turns up a normal secretory process, using a normal regulatory mechanism of the epithelial cells of the intestine. This results in the huge loss of water characteristic of cholera. No abnormal lesions result—the toxin acts by causing hyperactivity of a normal process.

Toxins That Help Bacteria Spread in Tissues

Certain toxins contribute to disease without targeting any particular type of cells. These include degradative enzymes that function as spreading factors by facilitating the dispersal of infecting organisms. For example, some streptococci secrete a hyaluronidase that breaks down hyaluronic acid, the ground substance of connective tissue. The organisms also secrete a DNAase, which thins out pus made viscous by the DNA released from dead white blood cells. A streptococcal protease, streptokinase, cleaves a precursor of plasminogen activator to an active form. This converts plasminogen to plasmin, the serum protease that, in turn, attacks fibrin clots. Streptokinase can thus eliminate fibrin barriers that may be in the way of invading streptococci.

Similar roles have been suggested for the collagenases and elastases produced by other organisms. Such "meat tenderizers" are unregulated forms of enzymes that also exist in the uninfected host, but whose activity is normally under control.

Toxins That Lyse Cells

A large and common class of toxins kills host cells by destroying their membranes. They usually act (a) as lipases or (b) by inserting themselves in the membrane to form pores.

An example of a lipase toxin is the lecithinase formed by the clostridia of gas gangrene. This enzyme lyses cells indiscriminately because its main substrate, phosphatidylcholine (lecithin), is ubiquitous in mammalian membranes. Several toxins of this sort are known as hemolysins because they are usually measured by their ability to lyse red blood cells. This does not mean, however, that they only affect these cells. White blood cells are often targets for these toxins. Thus, organisms eliminate potential host defenses and, at the same time, create a necrotic, nutritionally rich anaerobic milieu in which they thrive.

The other class of membrane-damaging toxins are those that insert themselves in membranes to make protein pores. These channels make the membranes more permeable, water pours into the cytoplasm, and the cells begin to swell. When this process continues beyond a certain point, the cells burst. Even at toxin concentrations too low to cause lysis, cellular functions may be severely damaged by slight perturbations of permeability that may cause leakage of potassium ions needed for protein synthesis and cell viability. Thus, low levels of this kind of toxin effectively inhibit the function of the phagocytes, the first line of host defense. Note that these toxins are not enzymes but act to form nonselective channels for water and ions, "ionophores," much like certain antibiotics.

The pattern of ion leakage and of subsequent damage is similar for many toxins. These nonenzymatic toxins work by a mechanism similar to that of the membrane attack complex of complement (see Chapter 6). The pores formed by this complex contain aggregates of unfolded C9 and other components in a doughnut-like array that is unusually resistant to proteases and detergents. Such a fortified structure is seen with many toxins that make pores. This general resistance very likely contributes to the stability of the toxin at the cell surface.

α-Toxin of Staphylococci

An example of a toxin that works in this manner is the α-toxin of *Staphylococcus aureus*. It is an example of a **homogeneous pore former**; i.e., each pore has the same number of protein molecules. Here a protein with molecular weight of 34,000 daltons forms hexamers with an external diameter of 8.5–10.0 nm and an internal channel 2–3 nm across, more than sufficient to allow free passage of most metabolites. (See Fig. 6.5 for similar-looking channels produced by the membrane attack complex of complement.)

Among the specific consequences of the action of this toxin are the aggregation of platelets and narrowing of small blood vessels, leading to tissue necrosis. α-Toxin, as well as the C9 component of complement, becomes denatured by contact with low-density serum lipoprotein. This effect has suggested that a "nonimmune" neutralization may occur in vivo.

Streptococcal Streptolysin O

The pore-forming toxins of the other major class are **heterogeneous**, that is, they form pores of various sizes and with different numbers of monomer molecules. The prototype of this class is **streptolysin O**, one of the toxins produced by certain streptococci. Streptolysin O ("O" for "oxygen labile") binds to cholesterol in the cell membrane. The free toxin may be inactivated by cholesterol, but once it is incorporated in the membrane, it becomes impervious to it. The toxin consists of monomers, 89,000 daltons in weight, that, together with cholesterol, forms large curved rods. The diameter of the resulting channels is up to 30 nm. The aggregates are large enough to be easily visible in the electron microscope and the pores are easily demonstrable in both the inner and outer leaflets of the membrane.

For unknown reasons, streptolysin O lyses red blood cells but not neutrophils or macrophages. Still, these white blood cells are killed by low levels of this toxin because it acts preferentially on the membranes of lysosomes, releasing their hydrolytic enzymes. This results in damage to the cytoplasmic contents and leads to cell death. In addition, the lysosomal enzymes released from killed neutrophils damage the surrounding tissue. Pores made by toxins need not be large or well defined. A toxin made by *E. coli* binds to the membrane as monomers, yet allows the free passage of ions. Apparently, "minipores" can be very effective.

What happens to pore proteins? At low concentrations, they can be repaired. Since neutrophils can shed membrane-associated components of complement, they probably throw off toxin-mediated channels as well. In general, however, toxin-formed pores resist proteolytic attack and tend to survive for a long time.

TOXINS THAT BLOCK PROTEIN SYNTHESIS

In contrast to the toxins that act on the surface of cells, which are highly variable in structure and mode of action, those that act inside cells show a number of similarities (Fig. 9.1). (*a*) Most have two portions; one involved in binding to the cell membrane, the other responsible for the toxic activity. In some toxins, these two activities are carried by a single polypeptide chain; in others, by two different chains. These chains are called **A** for "active" and **B** for "binding" and these toxins are known as **A-B toxins**. (*b*) Binding to the membrane may be followed by receptor-mediated endocytosis and internalization of the toxin, although some investigators propose as an alternative the direct passage through a pore. (*c*) The A moiety is often still latent after uptake. It may be activated by proteolytic cleavage and reduction of disulfide bridges. For example, diphtheria, cholera, tetanus, and *Shigella* toxins are all synthesized as inactive precursors that must be activated to become toxic. (*d*) Finally, many of these toxins have a common mode of action; they catalyze the transfer of the adenosine diphosphate (**ADP**) group from the coenzyme NAD to target proteins. These **ADP-ribosyltransferases** are exemplified by diphtheria toxin, cholera toxin, and exotoxin A of *Pseudomonas aeruginosa*.

Diphtheria Toxin

Diphtheria toxin, one of the best studied of all bacterial toxins, is a single polypeptide chain with A and B portions. The receptor for the B portion is found on the membrane of all the cells of susceptible species. When the toxin binds to this receptor, the molecule is cleaved at a protease sensitive site between the A and B portions, which remain covalently associated by disulfide linkage. The entire receptor-toxin complex then enters the cell by receptor-mediated endocytosis, just like hormones and certain viruses. Once the toxin enters the cell, reduction of the disulfide bond separates the A and B portions. The acidic conditions prevailing within endosomal vesicles promote insertion of the B chain into the endosomal membrane. Somehow, this facilitates passage of fragment A into the cytosol. Thus, both endocytosis (passage across the cell membrane) and membrane translocation (out of the vesicles into the cytoplasm) are required for fragment A to reach the cytoplasm and begin its toxic action.

The A fragment is resistant to denaturation and is long lived inside cells. This accounts, in part, for its potency; a single molecule can kill a cell. Killing takes place by a specific mechanism of protein modification, **ADP-ribosylation**. Many toxins are capable of this reaction, but diphtheria and pseudomonas A exotoxins have a specific target, the **elongation factor 2**, or **EF-2**, a factor in eucaryotic protein synthesis that catalyzes the hydrolysis of guanosine triphosphate (GTP) required for the movement of ribosomes on mRNA. The reaction is

$$EF\text{-}2 + NAD^+ \rightarrow ADPR\text{---}EF\text{-}2 + H^+$$

where ADPR is adenosine diphosphate ribose.

EF-2 is the only known substrate for diphtheria and pseudomonas exotoxin A toxins. The reason for the specificity is that EF-2 contains a

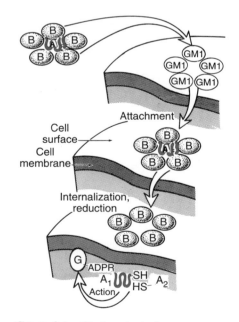

Figure 9.1. Cholera toxin becomes active. The *B* ("binding") component is thought to become incorporated in the membrane by binding to a ganglioside receptor (*GM1*) and the *A* ("active") component enters the cell.

rare modification in one of its histidine residues and this is the site recognized by these toxins for ADP-ribosylation. Mutant cells in which this histidine cannot be modified become resistant to the toxins. The addition of ADP-ribose inactivates EF-2 and kills cells by an irreversible block of protein synthesis.

Pharmacological Toxins

Here we will discuss toxins that function by elevating or depressing normal cell functions but that do not result in death of their target cells.

TOXINS THAT ELEVATE CYCLIC AMP—CHOLERA TOXIN

Among the toxins that do not damage cells, an important class works by raising the concentration of cyclic AMP (cAMP). Phagocytic cells are often an important target because an excess of cAMP inhibits chemotaxis and phagocytosis, thus reducing the cells' power to kill microorganisms. The level of cAMP may be increased in several ways. Some pathogens pour out cAMP directly, others secrete an adenyl cyclase to make more cAMP from ATP, and still others make a toxin that alters the activity of the adenylate cyclase of host cells.

One of the best studied of the toxins that modifies the host's adenylate cyclase is cholera toxin. The target tissue for this toxin is the epithelium of the small intestine. The toxin has separate A and B subunits; the B component has specific affinity for the intestinal epithelial mucosa. As with diphtheria toxin, the A subunit ADP-ribosylates a target protein that, here again, is a GTPase. In this case, the target protein is part of a complex that makes cAMP. When the GTPase is modified by the toxin, the synthesis of cAMP becomes unregulated and is made in large amounts. By an incompletely understood process, this provokes loss of fluids and copious diarrhea characteristic of cholera.

Both the structure of cholera toxin and its mechanism of action are known in detail (Fig. 9.1). The binding component consists of five B subunits that form a doughnut structure visible in the electron microscope. A single enzymatic A subunit sits partly on and partly within the hole of the doughnut. The A subunit is synthesized as a single chain that is cleaved after secretion into two pieces, A_1 and A_2, which are held together by disulfide bridges. The whole toxin (one A_1, one A_2, five B subunits) binds to five ganglioside receptors on the the surface of intestinal epithelial cells. The A_1-A_2 portion now enters the cell and is cleaved into the A_1 and A_2 pieces, perhaps by reduction of the disulfide bridges. The A_1 fragment is enzymatically active and can now act on its target protein.

To understand how cholera toxin elevates the cAMP level, let us examine how the synthesis of this compound is regulated normally, an intricate business. The adenylate cyclase complex, which includes two proteins known as G protein and the cyclase itself, is membrane bound in the intestinal cells (Fig. 9.2). The key to the working of the cyclase complex is that G protein is a GTP-binding protein that has two conformational states. When it binds GTP, it stimulates adenylate cyclase to make cAMP; whereas when it binds GDP, it is inactive in this respect. This effect is normally of short duration, because G protein is also a GTPase that cleaves GTP to GDP. The activity of adenyl cyclase is thus determined by the balance of binding and hydrolysis of GTP by G protein.

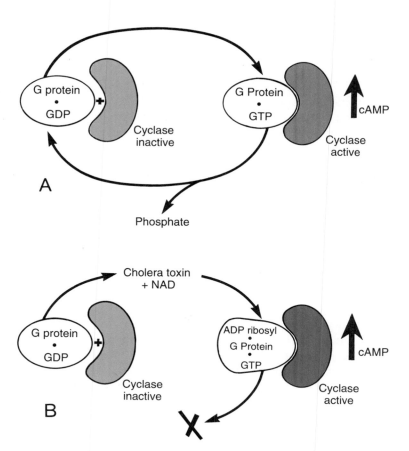

Figure 9.2. The action of cholera toxin. G, R, and cyclase all interact with the membrane. **A.** G protein binds *GTP*, stimulated by the complex of R protein and its cognate hormone. With GTP bound, G protein activates adenyl cyclase. **B.** *Cholera toxin* ribosylates G protein, which now cannot hydrolyze GTP and remains in the stimulatory GTP-bound form to keep adenyl cyclase making *cAMP*.

How does cholera toxin act to increase the level of cAMP? Cholera toxin promotes the "active" state of G protein. Cholera toxin works by ADP-ribosylating G protein at one of its arginine residues. **G protein is now locked in the conformation that stimulates adenylate cyclase.** The interminable synthesis of cAMP provokes the movement of massive quantities of fluid across the intestinal membrane and into the lumen of the gut.

Activation of adenylate cyclase by ADP-ribosylation is a strategy adopted by a number of other diarrhea-producing enterotoxins, like the labile toxin or LT enterotoxin of *E. coli*. Other toxins, like one produced by *Bordetella pertussis*, the agent of whooping cough, raise cAMP in leukocytes. This results in impairment of motility of leukocytes and of their ability to migrate toward invading bacteria.

Toxins That Block Nerve Function

Among the most lethal toxins known are those of tetanus and botulism (Table 9.1). They are produced by members of the anaerobic spore-forming genus, *Clostridium*. Both of these toxins act on the nervous system, tetanus toxin to produce irreversible muscle contraction, botulinum toxin to block muscle contraction.

Tetanus and botulinum toxins, like diphtheria toxin, consist of single polypeptide chains (molecular weight about 150,000 daltons) that contain putative A and B regions. Binding is to ganglioside receptors which, in this case, are specific to nervous tissue. These toxins are also activated by proteolysis and disulfide reduction, and they function intracellularly. Their potency suggests that they may well act enzymatically, in a manner analogous to diphtheria toxin, but this is speculative at present.

Tetanus Toxin

Tetanus bacilli rarely move from their location in wounds, and their toxin acts at a distance, on the central nervous system. Tetanus is one of the best examples of a disease that results from the action of a single toxin. Once bound to cell membranes, tetanus toxin is internalized, probably by receptor-mediated endocytosis, and flows via retrograde transport through axonal processes to the spinal cord. There the toxin interferes with synaptic transmission by preferentially inhibiting the **release of inhibitory neurotransmitters** such as glycine from inhibitory interneurons. The excitatory and inhibitory effects of motor neurons become increasingly unbalanced, causing rigid muscle contraction. Thus, while the physiological basis of action is understood, its biochemical basis remains unknown. It is not known why it is especially active on the inhibitory synapses.

BOTULINUM TOXIN

Unlike tetanus toxin, botulinum toxin is seldom produced in wounds but is made in contaminated food kept under anaerobic conditions, e.g., improperly sterilized canned beans or sausages. The disease is, therefore, a true intoxication, and does not require the presence of the organisms at all. Botulinum toxin is not destroyed by proteases of the digestive tract, apparently because it is protected by complexing with other proteins. In fact, intestinal proteases activate the toxin, which is a single polypeptide chain with A and B portions.

In contrast to tetanus toxin, botulinum toxin affects peripheral nerve endings. Once across the gut lining, it is carried in the blood to neuromuscular junctions. There it may bind to gangliosides at motor nerve endplates, where it is taken up. The subsequent events are not known, but they result in a **presynaptic block of the release of acetylcholine**. The interruption of nerve stimulation causes an irreversible relaxation of muscles, leading to respiratory arrest.

IMMUNE PROTECTION AGAINST TOXINS

Since toxins are foreign proteins and are antigenic, immune protection of the host is an optimistic possibility. For some disease, like tetanus, the clinical disease itself does not confer immunity to subsequent infections, probably because the toxin is produced in amounts too small to be an effective immunogen. On the other hand, vaccination and treatment with antitoxins has been used successfully in tetanus and other diseases. Of course, active immunization cannot be carried out by injecting the toxins themselves. Fortunately, many toxins can be modified chemically to retain their immunogenicity while losing their toxicity. Such toxoids are commonly used for the prevention of *diph*-theria and *te*tanus (as part of the widely used *DPT* shots). Initial doses in the first months of an infant's life are effective, and boosters every 10 years are sufficient to maintain immunity. As may be anticipated, infection by the organisms can still occur in individuals immune only to the toxin, but serious disease does not ensue.

Active disease in a nonimmune individual may be combated by the administration of antitoxin. However, once toxins are bound to the cells, antitoxins are usually ineffective because the toxins are rapidly internalized and become unavailable to the antibody molecules.

Therefore, treatment with antitoxins must be very rapid to be useful. Another serious drawback of this "passive immunization" is that the antitoxin is sometimes produced in horses or other animals. As a result, antitoxin administration can lead to serum sickness, an immune reaction against foreign proteins.

Recombinant DNA technology may refine some of the vaccination procedures and it may be possible to immunize using tailor-made fragments of the toxin. The B fragments seem to be particularly promising candidates because antibodies prevent binding of a toxin that block the initial steps of toxin action. In the absence of A fragment, the B fragments are innocuous and could be administered with little risk.

Not all toxin-mediated diseases respond to vaccination. In particular, vaccines against cholera administered systemically have been of limited value. Protection here requires the intestinal secretion of IgA antibodies against the toxin (to prevent its action) and against the bacterial adhesins (to prevent their colonization). Vaccines administered by injection give poor or short-lived protection, in part because they do not induce the formation of effective amounts of IgA antibodies. Alternatives are being exploited, based on knowledge of how the toxin works. In one case, a preparation of B subunits is administered orally along with killed cholera bacilli. This procedure produces a secretory IgA response and seems to protect quite well. Another possibility that has been considered is the administration of "protective colonizers," mutants that can only make the B subunit of the toxin but that may colonize by virtue of their adhesins.

Bacterial toxins are being used in attempts to make them useful delivery systems for drugs, for example, coupling a specific antibody to an A subunit of a toxin. The antibody would then seek out the specific cell, and the toxin fragment would kill it. The results of these attempts have thus far been equivocal and have often been colored by side reactions. Nonetheless, the idea of turning toxins to advantage remains appealing.

ENDOTOXIN: SOMETIMES A TOXIN, USUALLY AN IMMUNOSTIMULANT

Endotoxin is the lipopolysaccharide (LPS) of the outer membrane of Gram-negative bacteria. It plays an important role in the diseases caused by these organisms. In small amounts, endotoxin elicits a series of **alarm reactions**—fever, activation of complement by the alternative pathway, activation of macrophages, and stimulation of B lymphocytes. In large amounts, it produces shock and even death. The term endotoxin is misleading on two counts. It is not "endo" (internal), and only in large amount is it a toxin. Endotoxin is full of surprises and complications. To quote Lewis Thomas:

"The most spectacular examples of host governance of disease mechanisms are the array of responses elicited in various animals by the lipopolysaccharide endotoxins of Gram-negative bacteria. Here the microbial toxin does not even seem to be, in itself, toxic. Although the material has powerful effects on various cell and tissue, including polymorphonuclear leukocytes, platelets, lymphocytes, macrophages, arteriolar smooth muscle, and on complement and the coagulation mechanism, all of these effects represent perfectly normal responses, things done every day in the course of normal living. What makes it a disaster is that they are turned on all at once by the host, as though in response to an alarm signal, and the outcome is widespread tissue destruction, as in the generalized Shwartzman reaction, or outright failure of the circulation of blood, as in endotoxin shock."

Endotoxin and exotoxins are different in most important ways. Endotoxin is not a protein, like the exotoxins, but rather a complex molecule with some exotic chemical constituents not found elsewhere in nature. Most exotoxins have a single mode of action. Endotoxin, on the other hand, induces many and different pharmacological and immunological changes at low and at high concentrations. Our knowledge of endotoxin is still fragmentary and, at times, its study stirs up considerable controversy. Welcome, then, to the immunopharmacologists' Explorers' Club.

CHEMISTRY OF ENDOTOXIN

The complex chemistry of endotoxin does not, as yet, cast a light on how it works. As discussed in Chapter 3, bacterial lipopolysaccharide is composed of three parts; a glycophospholipid, called **lipid A**, a **core** of sugars, ethanolamine and phosphate, and the **O antigen**, a long side chain of species-specific, often unusual sugars (Fig. 3.6). Of these parts of the molecule, the active one is the lipid A while the others serve as carriers. Lipid A alone is water insoluble (because it is hydrophobic) and inert, but its activity is restored when complexed even with artificial large molecular weight carriers, like proteins. The structure of lipid A is unusual (Fig. 3.6). It contains uniquely short fatty acids (12, 14, and 16 carbons in length), some with hydroxyl groups.

MAJOR EFFECTS OF ENDOTOXIN

In low and high amounts, endotoxin does two major things in the body (Fig. 9.3). At the low range of concentrations it sets off a series of **alarm reactions** and at high range it induces **shock**. The extent to which these complex events overlap depends not only on the amount

Figure 9.3. The action of endotoxin at low and high concentrations. See text for details.

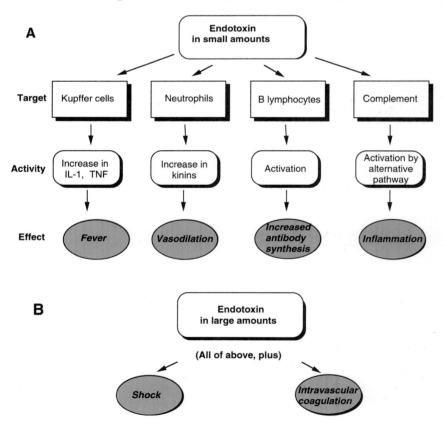

of endotoxin, but also on the route of injection and the previous exposure of the host to this substance.

Four types of cells are the **primary target cells** for endotoxin: the mononuclear phagocytes (peripheral blood monocytes, macrophages of the spleen, bone marrow, lung alveoli, peritoneal cavity, Kupffer cells), neutrophils, platelets, and B lymphocytes. These cells probably have specific endotoxin receptors, although at present this is still an unsettled question.

Alarm Reactions to Endotoxin

FEVER

Endotoxin acts as a **pyrogen**, i.e., causes fever, when Gram-negative bacteria accumulate in tissue in sufficient amounts to come in contact with the circulation. In the words of Lewis Thomas elsewhere in his essay, endotoxin becomes propaganda, information that bacteria are present. Fever is elicited by extremely small amounts of endotoxin. About 100 ng (0.1 µg) injected intravenously in an adult human volunteer produce a measurable **pyrogenic response**, or fever. Note that this amount comes from about ten million enteric bacteria, not a particularly large amount of microbial mass. The normal intestinal flora contains perhaps one million times more bacteria than that. If all the endotoxin in the bowel were to enter the bloodstream and if fever followed an absurdly linear response, we would have a temperature of about one million degrees! Obviously, the amount of endotoxin that spills over from the gut into the portal circulation is probably quite small. Nonetheless, this amount of endotoxin serves in healthy people as constant low level stimulation of the immune response without pathological manifestations. Low titers of antibodies to endotoxin are found in most healthy persons.

Fever is produced by endotoxin inducing the release of a protein known as **endogenous pyrogen** from mononuclear phagocytes. The best known of these proteins are **interleukin-1** and **tumor necrosis factor**, which set off a complex series of events known as the **acute phase response** (Chapter 6). Gram-positive bacteria also induce fever but, lacking endotoxin, they elicit it through their cell wall components, which also causes the release of interleukin-1 and tumor necrosis factor.

ACTIVATION OF COMPLEMENT

Endotoxin activates complement directly by the alternative pathway (see Chapter 6). At low endotoxin concentrations, the events most likely to be of consequence to the bacteria are the production of the membrane attack complex, plus phagocyte chemotaxis and opsonization. Neutrophils are called up, especially by C5a, and, because of the opsonizing effect of C3b, become available for phagocytosis. Complement activation also leads to the production of anaphylatoxins (C3a, C5a), which lead to increased capillary permeability and release of lysosomal enzymes from neutrophils (degranulation). Together, these effects produce an inflammatory response.

ACTIVATION OF MACROPHAGES

Endotoxin activates macrophages; that is, it stimulates them to increase their production of lysosomal enzymes, to speed up their rate of phagocytosis, and to secrete some of their hydrolases into the medium. Once activated, macrophages become supreme scavengers and are able to handle larger numbers of invading microorganisms. Their exuberance extends itself to killing certain cancer cells, partly by direct attachment and partly by releasing proteins such as tumor necrosis factor. The ability of endotoxin, via macrophages, to limit the growth of certain tumors has been recognized for some time and is the subject of continued investigation. Endotoxin derivatives belong to a class of potential anticancer agents known as **biological response modifiers** that are being evaluated for use in clinical work.

STIMULATION OF B LYMPHOCYTES

By inducing the release of interleukin-1, endotoxin induces B lymphocytes (but not T lymphocytes) to divide. B lymphocytes mature into antibody-producing cells, thus adding to resistance to infection by increasing the level of antibodies. In this capacity, endotoxin is an **immunological adjuvant**.

Effects of High Amounts of Endotoxin—Shock

The full panoply of the activities of endotoxin is displayed when it is administered in large amounts. This is seen, fortunately rarely, in a condition known as **bacterial sepsis**, when the body is overwhelmed, often by Gram-negative bacteria like *E. coli*, *Pseudomonas aeruginosa*, or meningococci (see Chapters 14, 19, and 62). The result is a frequently lethal condition known as **endotoxic shock**, which is manifested by a serious drop in blood pressure, **hypotension**, and by **disseminated intravascular coagulation**.

Hypotension is due to a complex series of reactions elicited by endotoxin. It has recently been proposed that the key mediators in endotoxin-induced hypotension are tumor necrosis factor and interleukin-1. Thus, the extent of hypotension is considerably reduced by the administration of antisera against tumor necrosis factor or interleukin-1 prior to the injection of endotoxin. An earlier view is that decreased resistance of peripheral vessels is due to a build up of vasoactive amines (histamine and kinins). Considerable work is being carried out to clarify the situation and to understand the molecular basis for endotoxin shock.

Disseminated intravascular coagulation (DIC) is the name given to the deposition of thrombi in small vessels, with consequent damage to the areas deprived of blood supply. The effect is most severe in the kidneys, where it leads to cortical necrosis. Other organs also affected are the brain, the lungs, and the adrenals. In some cases of meningococcal infection, adrenal insufficiency due to infarction leads to rapid death, a condition known as the **Waterhouse-Friderichsen** syndrome. Endotoxin contributes to coagulation of blood in three ways: (*a*) it activates blood factor XII (the so-called Hageman factor), to set off the intrinsic clotting cascade; (*b*) it causes platelets to release the contents of their granules, which are involved in clotting; (*c*) it makes neutrophils give off basic proteins that are known to stabilize fibrin clots.

SUMMARY

Endotoxin is the visiting card of Gram-negative bacteria. When it is noticed, the body sets off a series of alarm reactions that rapidly help it fend off the invaders. These include the mobilization of neutrophils, the activation of macrophages, and the stimulation of B lymphocytes. In large amounts, endotoxin becomes deserving of its name and induces shock and widespread coagulation. This suggests that we have evolved successful defense mechanisms against Gram-negative bacteria but have not developed ways of regulating them in every instance.

Self-assessment Questions

1. Discuss how certain toxins lyse host cells.

2. How do toxins that have an A-B structure work?

3. Which group of toxins has no obvious B portion?

4. What is the basis for believing that diphtheria toxin is the critical feature of the disease?

5. How does cholera toxin act?

6. Contrast the mode of action of tetanus toxin to botulinum toxin.

7. What are the ideal properties of a toxoid to be used for vaccination?

8. What are the main differences between exotoxins and endotoxins?

9. Contrast the local to the systemic activities of low amounts of endotoxin.

10. Discuss the effects of high amounts of endotoxin.

SUGGESTED READING

Bhakdi S, Tranum-Jensen J. Damage to mammalian cells by proteins that form transmembrane pores. Rev Physiol Biochem Pharmacol 1987;107: 147–223.

Lewis T. The medusa and the snail. New York: The Viking Press, 1979.

Middlebrook JL, Dorland RB. Bacterial toxins: cellular mechanisms of action. Microbiol Rev 1984;48:199–221.

Stephen J, Pietrowski RA. Bacterial toxins. Aspects of microbiology 2. Washington, DC: Am Soc Microbiol, 1984, 104 pp.

Taussig MJ. Processes in pathology and microbiology. Oxford: Blackwell Scientific Publications, 1984, 914 pp.

Section II
Infectious Agents

Bacteria
Viruses
Fungi
Animal Parasites

Introduction to Pathogenic Bacteria

10

Moselio Schaechter

Thousands of species of bacteria, both commensal and pathogenic, are found in association with the human body. You will need to know only the principal ones, but even they make a long list. Before venturing into the thicket of bacterial taxonomy, you may consider a few guideposts. It is useful, for instance, to learn the names of the organisms in relation to where they fit in the microbial scheme of things. For example, it is helpful to know that staphylococci and streptococci both belong to a group called the **Gram-positive cocci**, that *Escherichia coli* is classified among the **Gram-negative enteric bacteria**, that the tubercle bacillus belongs to the **acid-fast bacteria**, and so forth. This chapter is intended as a study aid. We recommend that you not try to assimilate all this material at once but that you refer to this chapter later when studying individual types of bacteria.

We will use a practical scheme to divide the main pathogenic bacteria rather than ones used in the science of bacterial taxonomy (Fig. 10.1). In broad terms, medically interesting bacteria belong to one of two large categories:

- The "typical" bacteria, rods and spheres without many morphological embellishments. These "garden variety" bacteria include both Gram positives and Gram negatives, rods and cocci.

- Those that do not fall in this group.

Like all other forms of life, bacteria are named by their genus, as in *Escherichia*, and species, as in *coli*. Conventionally, after its first use in a text, the genus name is shortened to the first letter, e.g., *E. coli*. Many bacteria also have common names, usually related to the main disease that they cause, e.g., the "cholera bacillus," the "tubercle bacillus." Occasionally, it may be useful to figure out the derivation of genus and species names. Many of them attempt to honor famous microbiologists (e.g., *Escherichia* is named after Dr. Escherich, *Salmonella* after Dr. Salmon and not after the fish), but some are descriptive. To take examples from other areas of Microbiology, "retrovirus" refers to viruses that replicate using reverse transcriptase, "pyogenes" (as in *Streptococcus pyogenes*) indicates that it causes pus, and "nana" (dwarf) means that *Hymenolepis nana* is the "dwarf tapeworm."

A confusing aspect of bacterial taxonomy is that there is usually considerable variety within a species. Thus, a *Staphylococcus aureus* isolated from one patient may be distinctly virulent, whereas another one may not be. We refer to these isolates as **strains**. The point is well illustrated with *E. coli*; this designation includes the common strain of mo-

Figure 10.1. The major groups of medically important bacteria. This illustration is a practical representation of the principal groups of pathogenic bacteria. It is meant to be a study aid, and not a taxonomic or phylogenetic tree.

lecular biology, known as K12, as well as less benevolent ones that cause infection of the kidney, the intestine, or the meninges. All are *E. coli*, but each is of a different strain.

"TYPICAL" BACTERIA

Please recall that the Gram stain property reflects fundamental differences among bacteria. These differences are mainly in their permeability properties and surface components. The chief differences are the presence of an outer membrane in the Gram negatives and of a thick murein layer in the Gram positives (Chapter 2). These organisms can also be divided into rods and cocci, giving us four boxes in which to place them (Fig. 10.2).

Keep in mind that Gram positives differ more from Gram negatives than cocci do from rods. For instance, the streptococci, which are Gram positive, are closely related to certain Gram-positive rods, the lactobacilli, but quite distant from Gram-negative cocci such as the gonococci.

In the laboratory, the Gram stain makes the positives look dark violet, the negatives red (see Chapter 2 for details). If you have never done a Gram stain or if you have forgotten how, it is carried out by first treating a smear with a stain called crystal violet, which is taken up by most bacteria. Second, after washing with water, the slide is exposed to a solution of iodine. This modifies the violet dye to make a dye-iodine complex. Third, the preparation is treated with alcohol or acetone for a brief time, a few seconds. At this point, Gram positives retain the violet dye and Gram negatives are decolorized. This step must be carried out with care because too short a treatment will result in underdecolorization and all of the stained bacteria will remain violet. Overdecolorization, on the other hand, will remove the dye from Gram positives. With experience, this step can be done just right. To be able to see the now colorless Gram negatives, the fourth step is to counterstain them with a red dye.

The four groups in Figure 10.2 are fairly evenly represented in the normal flora of the bacteria-rich milieu of the body, the mouth, the pharynx, and the large intestine. This is not true for the major pathogenic organisms. The Gram-positive cocci and the Gram-negative rods are the most common agents of infections, followed by the Gram-negative cocci, and, last, the Gram-positive rods.

Gram-positive Cocci

STREPTOCOCCI

These bacteria grow in chains of round cells—like strings of pearls—and constitute a large and diverse group. They are subdivided according to the changes they produce when grown on agar containing blood. Thus, β-hemolytic streptococci (or "beta strep"), which cause most streptococcal infections, lyse the red blood cell, causing an area of clearing around the colonies. The α-hemolytic streptococci produce a different change, a greening of the hemoglobin. Other streptococci do not change the blood at all. Many streptococci are nonpathogenic and are found in the environment as well as in the normal human intestine. Some are associated with dairy products and contribute to the manufacture of cheese.

Streptococci do not carry out respiration but only fermentation. This is characteristic of anaerobic bacteria, and indeed, some streptococci are strict anaerobes. Most of the pathogenic species grow in air, which makes them **oxygen-tolerant anaerobes**. Colonies of streptococci are usually small on agar. Streptococci make a lot of extracellular proteins, some of which are virulence factors involved in spreading the organisms through tissues and damaging host cells.

The main pathogens in this genus are the β-hemolytic strains. These are further subclassified into groups by the presence of different so-called C antigens, which are cell wall polysaccharides. Of all the groups (A through R), the most important ones in human disease are those of group A. They cause "strep throat," infections of soft tissues elsewhere, and other serious infections. These infections may be followed by important complications, like rheumatic fever or glomerulonephritis. The full taxonomic name of these organisms is *Streptococcus pyogenes*, but you will hear them referred to as "group A strep."

STAPHYLOCOCCI

There are three main species; thus, this group is not as diverse as the streptococci. They are called *S. aureus*, *S. epidermidis*, and *S. saprophyticus*. Staphylococci have no specific arrangement under the microscope but look like arrays of buckshot or bunches of grapes ("staphylo" comes from the Greek word for grapes). They are more robust than streptococci and withstand many chemical and physical

Gram-positive cocci	Gram-positive rods
Gram-negative cocci	Gram-negative rods

Figure 10.2. The "Big Four" "typical" bacteria.

agents and are hard to eradicate from the human environment. They make larger colonies on agar and are aerobes.

Staphylococci are found on many sites of the body, especially on the skin. They are the most likely organisms to cause pus in wounds and may produce serious infections in deep tissues, such as osteomyelitis (infection of the bone marrow), endocarditis (infection of the heart valves), etc. Like the streptococci, they also secrete a large number of extracellular enzymes and toxins. One of these, **coagulase**, clots plasma and is useful in classification since only the more pathogenic species, *S. aureus*, makes this enzyme.

Gram-negative Cocci

These include several genera of medical importance, but the most important one is the *Neisseria*. This genus includes many organisms found in the normal mouth and pharynx and two important pathogens, the **gonococcus** and the **meningococcus**. Like all Gram negatives, they possess an outer membrane that contains endotoxin (lipopolysaccharide). The gonococcus obviously causes gonorrhea, and the meningococcus causes meningitis and a severe septicemia.

Gram-positive Rods

Abundant in the environment, this group includes bacteria that only infrequently cause diseases, at least in the developed regions of the world. One, diphtheria, was a deadly disease in children until vaccination nearly eradicated it. The agent of diphtheria is called *Corynebacterium diphtheriae* and has many relatives called **diphtheroids**. These are common inhabitants of the skin and mucous membranes and can cause opportunistic infections. (Note that "diphtheria" has two 'h's.)

In the human environment, the most common organisms in this group are the **spore-forming rods**. Microscopically, they are the largest of the "typical" bacteria, five to ten times the volume of an average *E. coli*, about 1 μm^3. They are divided into two genera: the **aerobic Bacillus**, whose only important pathogen is *B. anthracis*, which causes anthrax, and the **strict anaerobes**, members of the genus *Clostridium*. Clostridia are medically important because they include species like *C. botulinum*, which causes botulism, *C. tetani*, the agent of tetanus, and several that produce gas gangrene (most often, *C. perfringens*). Symptoms of these diseases are caused by powerful exotoxins. Among the most commonly encountered clostridial diseases is pseudomembranous colitis, caused by *C. difficile*.

Another important pathogen among the Gram-positive rods is *Listeria monocytogenes*, which occasionally causes serious infections in infants and in adults who are immune compromised.

Gram-negative Rods

ENTERIC BACTERIA

The Gram-negative rods are a large group of bacteria and include many important pathogens. Here the **enteric bacteria** stand out. Their paradigm is *E. coli*, the "typical" bacterium par excellence. The enteric bacteria (or family *Enterobacteriaceae*) comprise many genera, including the *Salmonella* of typhoid fever and food poisoning and the *Shigella* of bacillary dysentery. The enteric bacteria have in common the ability to grow readily on laboratory media, to make middle-sized colonies (usually less than 1 mm across), not to make spores, or have special cell arrangements. Many, but not all, are motile. They are divided among those that ferment lactose (*E. coli* and others), and those that do not (*Salmonella*, *Shigella*). Although many pathogens are nonlactose fermenters, this is not a firm rule and has many exceptions both ways. Included in the enterics are also the organisms that cause plague and certain intestinal infections (*Yersinia*).

Among their more distant cousins are Gram-negative rods that differ in metabolism and somewhat in morphology. These include the genus *Pseudomonas* and the cholera bacillus, *Vibrio cholerae*. A close relative of *Vibrio* is *Campylobacter jejuni*, a common agents of infectious diarrhea, and an organism implicated in gastritis and gastric ulcers, *Helicobacteri pylori*. Pseudomonads, as the members of the *Pseudomonas* are sometimes called, are often found in waters—rivers, lakes, swimming pools, tap water—frequent sources of human infection.

"FASTIDIOUS SMALL GRAM-NEGATIVE RODS"

Besides the organisms mentioned above, the Gram-negative rods include an important and heterogeneous group of genera. They can be lumped, somewhat arbitrarily, into a group that may be awkwardly described as the "fastidious, small, Gram-negative rods" because they have complex nutritional requirements and tend to be smaller than, for example, *E. coli*. Included in this group are the following genera: *Haemophilus* (pneumonia and meningitis), *Bordetella* (whooping cough), *Brucella* (brucellosis), *Francisella* (tularemia), and others. *Legionella*, the agent of Legionnaires' disease is also a small Gram-negative rod, but varies considerably from the others in its habitat (soil, water) and chemical composition.

STRICTLY ANAEROBIC GRAM-NEGATIVE RODS

Finally, an important group of Gram-negative rods is distinguished by its strict anaerobic way of life. Clinically, the most noteworthy of these organisms belongs to the genus *Bacteroides*. They are extremely common in the human body, often the most frequent members of the intestinal flora. They are also found in the gingival pockets that surround the teeth. Normally not bothersome, members of this genus may cause serious diseases when deposited in deep tissues. They are associated, for example, with peritonitis, the abdominal infection that results from the outpouring of intestinal content into the peritoneum. These organisms usually do not cause disease alone but are found in association with other bacteria to cause mixed or polymicrobial infections. Obviously, they will not grow if incubated aerobically and require special anaerobic techniques for their growth and detection.

"NOT SO TYPICAL" BACTERIA

This taxonomic hodgepodge includes organisms that have their own special characteristics with regard to shape, size, or staining properties. They do not have much in common, other than being of medical importance. Each group, then, stands alone.

Acid-fast Bacteria

This group is almost synonymous with the genus *Mycobacterium*, which includes the **tubercle bacillus**, *M. tuberculosis*, and the **leprosy bacillus**, *M. leprae*. Acid-fastness refers to the fact that these organisms are nearly impervious to many chemicals and must be stained by a special procedure (Chapter 2). They are surrounded by a waxy envelope that can only be penetrated by dyes if the bacteria are heated or treated with detergents. For them, the Gram stain is irrelevant because they do not take up regular dyes.

The special staining procedure used is called the **Ziehl-Neelsen technique**. Its most frequently used modification consists of treating smears with a solution of a red dye (fuchsin) that contains detergents. After washing, the smear is treated with a solution of 3% hydrochloric acid that removes the dye from all bacteria except the acid-fast ones. The preparation is then exposed to a blue dye, which "counterstains" other bacteria, white blood cells, etc. Tubercle or leprosy bacilli, the "red bugs," are clearly visible against the blue background.

Several species of mycobacteria found living free in the environment may cause opportunistic infections, especially in immune compromised patients. These environmental species are sometimes called **atypical acid-fast bacilli**. Among the most commonly encountered of these are members of a complex known as *Mycobacterium avium-intracellulare*. Mycobacteria grow slowly and are quite resistant to chemical agents but not to heat.

The name of this genus contains the root word for fungus (myco-). The reason is that these organisms sometimes form branches that vaguely suggest the fungi. Even more akin to fungi in morphology are relatives of the mycobacteria, the *Actinomycetes*. These organisms take up the Gram stain and are Gram positive. Some are also weakly acid-fast. They make true branches and long filaments with complex structures, which places them among the most highly differentiated of the procaryotes. There are two pathogenic genera, *Nocardia*, which are aerobic, and *Actinomyces*, which are strict anaerobes. They cause certain forms of pneumonia and soft-tissue infections. A generally non-pathogenic genus, *Streptomyces*, includes organisms that make important antibiotics (streptomycin, tetracycline, etc.)

Spirochetes

These bacteria are helical, in the shape of a spring (not a screw). They include the agent of syphilis, *Treponema pallidum*, whose species name ("pale") refers to the fact that these organisms are so thin that they do not take up enough dye to be readily seen under the microscope. Unstained, they can be seen with a phase contrast or a darkfield microscope. The spirochetes of syphilis have the distinction of not being readily cultivated in the laboratory.

Other spirochetes include the genus *Leptospira*, which causes a disease called icterohemorrhagic fever, and *Borrelia recurrentis*, the agent of relapsing fever. Lyme disease (called after the town in Connecticut) is also caused by a spirochete, *Borrelia burgdorferi* and is one of the most important spirochetoses in the Eastern and Western United States. All of the organisms of this group stand out because of their distinct helical morphology.

Chlamydiae

These are small strict intracellular little bacteria that cannot be grown in artificial media. They are among the smallest cellular forms of life but have a fairly complex life cycle. They possess a different morphological form when they are growing inside cells or when they are in transit between them. *Chlamydia trachomatis* is the most common cause of sexually transmitted diseases (chlamydial urethritis) and other more unusual infections. *C. pneumoniae* is an agent of pneumonia in young adults. These organisms set up housekeeping in phagocytic vesicles of their host cells and obtain their energy from them.

Rickettsiae

These are also small, intracellular bacteria that cause epidemic typhus, Rocky Mountain spotted fever, and other diseases. Each species is transmitted by the bite of a differ kind of arthropod (lice, fleas, ticks, etc.), with the exception of *Coxiella burnetii*, the agent of Q fever, which may also be acquired by inhalation. Rickettsiae are small, rod-shaped bacteria without distinctive stages in their growth cycle.

Mycoplasma

Perhaps most evolutionarily distant from all other bacteria, these are organisms that lack a rigid cell wall. They are quite plastic in structure, grow slowly on laboratory media, and have special nutritional requirements. The most unique of these is the need for sterols, which are not required by any other group of bacteria. Mycoplasma lack murein and, consequently, are resistant to penicillin and other cell wall antibiotics. The oldest known human pathogenic mycoplasma is *Mycoplasma pneumoniae*, which causes a form of pneumonia. Others, e.g., *Ureaplasma urealyticum* have been implicated in different diseases.

Mycoplasma resemble wall-less forms that can be produced in the laboratory, the so called L-forms. Regular bacteria take on the same amorphous appearance as the mycoplasma when their cell wall is removed with lysozyme or when murein synthesis is inhibited with penicillin. This usually leads to cell lysis, but if they are placed in a hypertonic medium, they can be grown as colonies that resemble those of the mycoplasma. However, the similarity is only superficial. L-forms can usually revert to the regular bacterial form when they are removed from lysozyme or penicillin. Mycoplasma, on the other hand, do not. Mycoplasma also differ from all other bacteria in terms of the degree of relatedness as measured by DNA hybridization.

New Concepts Regarding Microbial Flora

There are many examples of microorganisms that can be seen under the microscope but that cannot be cultured. Some have been suspected of causing important diseases, but the point has been difficult to establish without pure cultures. New technologies have allowed us to make some progress in this area. For example, an organism that is visible-but-not-culturable is seen in tissues of patients with a disease known as cat-stratch fever and is suspected of being the causative agent. The DNA of this organism has been isolated from tissues and amplified by a technique called the polymerase chain reaction (PCR, see Chapter 55). Hybridization studies with this DNA revealed that the organism may be related to the rickettsiae. In time, information obtained by these and other methods may help establish the etiological role of this organism.

Cloning techniques have been useful in studies of well known but nonculturable bacteria, such as the treponeme of syphilis or the mycobacterium of leprosy. The genes of these agents have been introduced into surrogate organisms, such as *E. coli* and many of the protein gene products have been studied, especially with regard to their immunological properties.

More and more possible agents of disease are being recognized and studied because of the ecological disturbance introduced by the HIV virus of AIDS and other agents of immunosuppression. Bacteria, viruses, fungi, protozoa, and worms, which were previously unknown or known to be present only in animals or in the environment, have now joined the list of potential or known human pathogens (Chapter 66). The combination of new technologies and the changes in the human immune condition will undoubtedly lead to the finding of many more agents of infectious diseases. At the same time, with progress in sanitation and vaccination, many of the classic infectious pathogens are waning in importance. The list of important pathogens is a forever changing one.

Despite all these changes, many things remain the same. Over the hundred years or so that microorganisms have been studied in the laboratory, they have exhibited remarkable genetic constancy. For instance, the staphylococci or streptococci of today fit their original descriptions from the end of the last century. Likewise, a microbiologist from Koch's laboratory would have no problem correctly identifying a modern strain of *E. coli* or tubercle bacilli. On the other hand, important changes have occurred practically before our eyes. Virtually all of the pathogenic bacteria have become significantly more resistant to every new antibiotic that has been introduced in the last five decades. For example, pathogenic staphylococci are now almost universally resistant to penicillin, although in the 1950s, when the drug came into general use, their ancestors were sensitive to it.

In many of the following chapters on individual infectious agents you will find sections called Paradigms. These sections highlight points of general relevance to other agents as well.

Staphylococci: Abscesses and Other Diseases

Francis P. Tally

11

Staphylococci (**Gram-positive cocci**) are among the most common of the **pyogenic** or pus-producing bacteria. They produce local abscesses almost any place in the body, from the skin (pimples) to the bone marrow (osteomyelitis). Occasionally, they cause more specific diseases like endocarditis.

Staphylococci produce a large number of toxins and enzymes that act locally, mainly to help them withstand phagocytosis by neutrophils. They are among the most resistant of the pathogenic bacteria and are hard to eliminate from the human environment. Thus, they are responsible for many hospital-acquired infections. Special strains also produce toxins that cause different types of disease; namely, food poisoning, toxic shock syndrome (TSS), and a disease, mainly of children, called scalded skin syndrome.

CASE

Mr. S., a 45-year-old pastry chef, cut his left forearm with a knife during the course of his work. Over the next week, he noticed swelling, redness, and warmth at the site. He thought it was just a reaction to the cut, but after 4 more days, he developed fever with shaking chills and came to the emergency room with severe low back pain. On physical examination, he had a fever of 39.4°C, his left forearm was swollen with an area of central softness, indicating an abscess. He had tenderness to pressure over his lower spine.

The laboratory reported that Mr. S. had a high white cell count. A Gram's stain of pus aspirated from the forearm showed Gram-positive cocci in clusters (Fig. 11.1). Staphylococcus aureus was cultured from the pus. Blood cultures were positive for the same organism. X-rays of the lumbar spine showed erosion of the third lumbar vertebra, suggesting the infection called osteomyelitis (Fig. 11.2). The organism was resistant to penicillin but sensitive to oxacillin, which was used to treat Mr. S. with good results.

The day after Mr. S. was admitted to the hospital, the local public health department was notified that eight persons who had patronized his restaurant had developed severe vomiting and diarrhea 4–6 hours after eating there. Cultures of cream pies remaining in the refrigerator were positive for S. aureus. A preformed staphylococcal toxin called enterotoxin B was detected in the cream pies. The organisms from the contaminated food belonged to the same phage type (see below) as the ones isolated from the patient's abscess and blood, and were, therefore, likely to be the same.

Figure 11.1. Gram stain of *S. aureus* in pus.

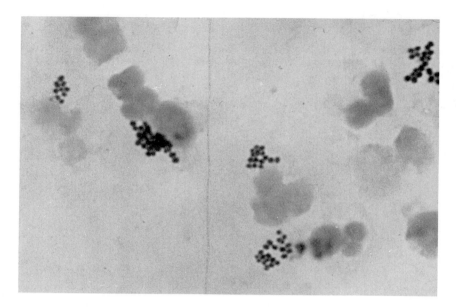

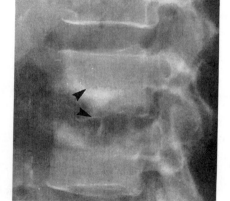

Figure 11.2.   X-ray of vertebrae showing infection of the intervertebral disk space. Compare the sharp edge of the normal vertebral plates (above and below) with the ragged eroded edges of the involved vertebral plates (*arrows*).

A number of questions arise:

1. What was the source of the organisms that infected Mr. S.?

2. What contributed to the development of the abscess in the skin?

3. How did *S. aureus* invade his bloodstream?

4. How did *S. aureus* cause infection in the bone?

5. What caused the food poisoning in the patrons of Mr. S.'s restaurant?

6. What are the properties of *S. aureus* that allow it to cause such different types of disease?

The case of Mr. S. illustrates several features typical of staphylococcal infections. The initial lesion was mild and localized. It resulted in a boil, which is the most common manifestation of staphylococcal disease. Most of the time this is self-terminating, although in this case it progressed to involve the bloodstream and eventually led to a metastatic involvement of a vertebra. Mr. S. was relatively fortunate because the infection of the vertebra, while highly worrisome, is not immediately life threatening. Had it occurred in his heart or in his brain, Mr. S. would have been at immediate and serious risk.

S. aureus **causes more frequent and more varied diseases than perhaps any other human pathogen.** Some of these diseases are unrelated with regard to their symptoms and epidemiology. Our case includes infection of the skin, an **abscess** in deep tissue, and **food poisoning**, which is far from the end of the list (Table 11.1). Among the more specialized staphylococcal diseases are the **TSS**, triggered by the use of highly absorbent menstrual tampons, and a serious condition of children called **scalded skin syndrome.**

ORGANISM

S. aureus is a large Gram-positive coccus that grows in clusters. It is one of the hardiest of the nonspore-forming bacteria and can survive for long periods on dry inanimate objects. It is also relatively resistant to heat. For these reasons, it is hard to eliminate once it is introduced in the human environment.

Table 11.1. Diseases Caused By Staphylococci

Skin and soft-tissue infections
  Furuncles, carbuncles
  Wound infections (traumatic, surgical)
  Cellulitis
  Impetigo (also caused by streptococci)

Bacteremia (frequently with metastatic abscesses)

Endocarditis

Central nervous system infections
  Brain abscess
  Meningitis—rare
  Epidural abscess

Pulmonary infections
  Embolic
  Aspiration

Musculoskeletal
  Osteomyelitis
  Arthritis

Genitourinary tract
  Renal carbuncle
  Lower urinary tract infection

Unrelated diseases caused by toxins
  Toxic shock syndrome (TSS)
  Scalded skin syndrome
  Food poisoning (gastroenteritis)

The genus *Staphylococcus* includes several species (Table 11.2). The most common one is *S. epidermidis*, which is found on the skin of many people and only occasionally causes disease. *S. aureus* is less common but generally more pathogenic. The species name ("golden") refers to the fact that, on agar, its colonies are pigmented with a bronze color, while other species make white colonies. A third species, *S. saprophyticus*, is unique in that it apparently causes urinary tract infections only. The genus *Staphylococcus* contains other species of occasional medical importance, which are described in standard microbiological texts. The three species mentioned suffice for our purposes. It is relatively easy to identify this genus in the laboratory. All of its members make large, creamy colonies on nutrient agar and, in a Gram stain, they look like clusters of grapes. *S. aureus* is best distinguished from other species of the genus using the the **coagulase test**. Coagulase, an enzyme that clots plasma, is made by *S. aureus* but not by the others.

Within a species of staphylococci, **individual strains** can be identified by differences in resistance to different antibiotics, or, more commonly, by a procedure called **phage typing**. This is carried out by determining the sensitivity of a strain to a number of standard bacteriophages. Its usefulness in epidemiology can be seen in our case report; finding the same pattern of phage sensitivity in the isolates from Mr. S.'s abscess and from the contaminated cream pies served to establish their epidemiological link.

ENCOUNTER

Staphylococci share their environment with that of human beings. They live on people and survive on inanimate surfaces with which they have contact, such as bedding, clothing, door knobs, etc., the so-called "fomites." Humans are the major reservoir for *S. aureus*. The organisms frequently colonize the external nares and are found in about 30% of normal individuals. They can also be found transiently on the skin, in

Table 11.2. Properties of Various Species of Staphylococci

Species	Frequency of Disease	Coagulase	Color of colonies	Mannitol Fermentation	Novobiocin Resistance
S. aureus	Common	+	Bronze	+	−
S. epidermidis	Common	−	White	−	−
S. saprophyticus	Occasional	−	White	−	+
Others—Different responses by individual species					

the oropharynx, and in feces. Staphylococci are well equipped to colonize the skin because they grow at high salt and lipid concentrations.

The ability of S. *aureus* to colonize the skin and mucosal surfaces has been associated with a bacterial cell-surface protein that binds to **fibronectin**, an extracellular matrix protein. A fibronectin-binding protein (**FNBP**) has been identified on the surface of S. *aureus*. FNBP is an important virulence factor in S. *aureus* invasion of deeper tissues by allowing attachment to exposed fibronectin in wounds.

Staphylococci spread from person to person, usually via hand contact. They can also spread by aerosols produced by patients with pneumonia. Babies are colonized shortly after birth, a present from people in their immediate surroundings. Some will become carriers for prolonged periods of time while others will harbor the organisms only intermittently. For unknown reasons, people in certain occupations, including physicians, nurses, and other hospital workers, are more prone to colonization. Also, certain patient groups, including diabetic patients, those patients on hemodialysis, and chronic intravenous drug abusers, have a higher carriage rate than the general population.

ENTRY

Staphylococci and most other bacteria do not usually penetrate into deep tissue unless the skin or the mucous membranes are damaged or are actually cut. This may come about by burns, accidental wounds, lacerations, insect bites, surgical intervention, or associated skin diseases. In the case of Mr. S., the organisms penetrated via a cut. If present in very large numbers, some bacteria are able to enter spontaneously and cause disease. This happens with staphylococci in cases of poor hygiene or prolonged moisture of the skin, which permit their growth in large numbers. Skin infections can also be caused by immersion into pools that contain large numbers of *Pseudomonas* (Chapter 19). It is not known if these infections are really due to spontaneous penetration or if the organisms enter through unseen cuts and abrasions.

SPREAD AND MULTIPLICATION

Once they have entered tissues, survival of staphylococci depends on several factors: the number of entering organisms; the site involved; the speed with which the body mounts an inflammatory response; and the immunological history of the person. When the inoculum is small and the host is immunologically competent, infections by these and other organisms are usually aborted. Nonetheless, staphylococci possess a particularly complex but effective pathogenic strategy, and even healthy persons find it difficult to combat S. *aureus*. Luckily, the area of inflammation most often remains localized and the organisms are contained.

DAMAGE

Local staphylococcal infections lead to the formation of a collection of pus called an **abscess**. Abscesses in the skin are called boils, or, in medical parlance, furuncles. Multiple interconnected abscesses are called carbuncles. Alternatively, staphylococci may spread in the subcutaneous or submucosal tissue and cause a diffuse inflammation called **cellulitis**. In most cases, these infections are caused by S. aureus and not by the other staphylococcal species.

The development of an abscess is a complex process that involves both bacterial and host factors (Fig. 11.3). The early events are characteristic of an **acute inflammatory reaction,** with the rapid and extensive participation of neutrophils. Chemotactic factors, derived both from bacteria and complement, are made in large amounts. A proportion of the bacteria not only survive this onslaught but are even capable of killing and lysing many of the neutrophils that have ingested them. This results in the outpouring of large amounts of lysosomal enzymes, which damage surrounding tissue.

The inflammatory area rapidly gets surrounded by a thick-walled fibrin capsule. The center of the abscess is usually necrotic and consists of the debris of dead neutrophils, dead and live bacteria, and edematous fluid. This, then, is an abscess: a well-defined area containing pus. From the point of view of the host, it represents a containment of invading organisms in one site. But there is an associated cost, i.e., abscesses may cause serious symptoms if they are located in vital parts of the body.

From this picture, it becomes apparent that staphylococcal infection represents a titanic struggle between the white blood cells and the invading organisms (Fig. 11.3). Many of the virulence factors of S. aureus are designed either to avoid their phagocytosis or to allow their survival in the phagocytes once taken up. These virulence factors will be discussed in detail below. Despite their impressive strategy, S. aureus does not always win, and neutrophils usually gain the upper hand. The importance of neutrophils in this fight is highlighted in children with a hereditary defect in phagocyte function called **chronic granulomatous disease** (Chapter 66). This is a fatal disease characterized by frequent and serious infections with S. aureus. Neutrophils of

Figure 11.3. Virulence properties of S. aureus in pus and abscess formation.

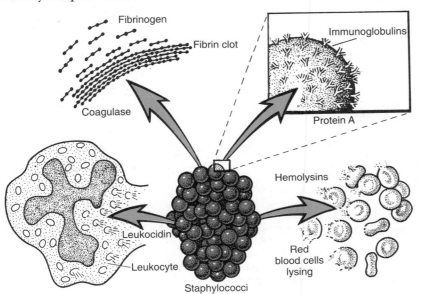

these patients are defective in their ability to make sufficient hydrogen peroxide to set off the oxidative killing pathway. In these children, the balance between staphylococci and phagocytes is clearly shifted toward the microorganisms.

The interaction between staphylococci and neutrophils is an example of how complex the struggle between them can be. The organisms produce an unusually large number of relevant substances: soluble enzymes, toxins, and constituents of the cell envelopes (Table 11.3). This formidable list invites speculation; why has it been necessary for these successful organisms to develop such a varied strategy? With other organisms, a capsule suffices to resist phagocytosis. Perhaps different factors predominate in different loci of the infection. The staphylococcal situation is not easy to analyze, and much remains to be learned. Molecular methods including gene transfer, gene cloning, and protein characterization, discussed in Chapter 4, have been developed in *S. aureus* to study the virulence factors of this versatile pathogen. The role of many of the virulence factors of this organism remains confused. It appears that these factors do not impart virulence singly, but that they act in concert with other factors to permit the pathogen to cause disease via tissue destruction and, thus, avoidance of host defenses.

What are the main factors that are thought to allow survival vis-à-vis the neutrophils? To begin with, the cell surface; *S. aureus* organisms are sometimes surrounded by **a capsule** that prevents phagocytosis, but probably not to the extent seen with pneumococci or meningococci. **The cell wall murein** of *S. aureus* activates complement by the alternate pathway, thus contributing to the inflammatory response. Note that in this regard staphylococcal murein resembles the endotoxin of Gram negatives. Another important **wall constituent** is **teichoic acid** (a polymer of ribitol and glycerophosphates, Chapter 3), which also appears to be involved in complement activation and, possibly, in the adherence of these organisms to mucosal cells.

A fourth wall component, **protein A**, has a most unexpected property; it binds nonspecifically to the Fc terminus of immunoglobulin G of almost all subclasses (Fig. 11.3). This incapacitates these molecules in their function as antibodies since their business end, the Fab portion, is now dangling away from the surface of the organisms. This interferes with opsonization by reducing the amount of Fc residues available for opsonization. Although the protein A-Fc combination is nonspecific, it acts like an antigen-antibody complex in that it activates complement through the classical pathway.

In addition to these components, *S. aureus* secretes several enzymes and toxins that are almost certainly directed toward the struggle with phagocytes (Fig. 11.3). **Leukocidin** makes pores in the membrane of neutrophils and is probably responsible for their killing. **Catalase** con-

Table 11.3. Soluble Virulence Factors of *Staphylococcus aureus*

Leukocidin—damages white blood cells
Catalase—probably reduces killing by phagocytes
Coagulase—causes plasma to clot
Hemolysins—lyses red blood cells and others (five kinds known)
Hyaluronidase—may help spread by destroying connective tissue ground substance
β-lactamase—inactivates penicillins
Exfoliatin—causes sloughing of skin in scalded skin syndrome
Toxic shock toxin—involved in toxic shock syndrome
Enterotoxins—cause food poisoning (seven kinds known)

verts hydrogen peroxide to water and may help counteract the neutrophil's ability to kill via the production of oxygen-free radicals. **Coagulase** converts fibrinogen to fibrin and probably helps prevent the phagocytosis of the organisms because white cells penetrate fibrin clots poorly.

As if this weaponry were insufficient, *S. aureus* elaborates other enzymes that probably participate in its pathogenesis. Among them are several **hemolysins** (α through ε) that may contribute to the availability of iron for the organisms by lysing red blood cells. Many strains make a **hyaluronidase** that hydrolyzes the matrix of connective tissue and perhaps facilitates the spread along tissue planes. Clearer is the role of β-lactamase, a powerful enzyme that hydrolyzes the classical penicillins. It is found in about 90% of *S. aureus* strains and is responsible for the infamous penicillin resistance of this organism. The gene for this enzyme is carried on plasmids that can be readily transferred, probably accounting for the rapid spread of penicillin resistance among the staphylococci.

In the case of Mr. S., the organisms escaped from the abscess in the skin and found themselves in the bloodstream. This is not the usual outcome since most local staphylococcal diseases are self-limiting and do not result in metastatic infections. In healthy individuals, the organisms that escape from the local abscess are usually destroyed by the clearance mechanisms of the blood and the lymph. In the case of Mr. S., there was no reason to think that his defenses were impaired, although this could have been true temporarily. On the other hand, the "shower" of organisms from the skin lesion could have been so great that it overwhelmed the capacity of the body to destroy them. When staphylococci become implanted in deep tissues they colonize best those areas that have been traumatized by previous diseases or by surgical intervention. Otherwise, the choice of the site seems random and is probably dictated by the clearing capacity of the organ and the amount of blood flowing through it. The main sites of metastatic abscesses are the highly vascularized organs: bones, lungs, and kidneys. Immunocompromised patients frequently have multiple staphylococcal metastases, which can lead to serious and often fatal diseases.

Once implanted in deep tissue and able to survive, staphylococci elicit an inflammatory reaction similar to that of skin abscess. In the words of Pasteur, "Osteomyelitis is a boil of the bone marrow" (Chapter 61). The consequences of abscess formation in deep sites depend on their location. Nowhere is it more devastating than in the heart or the brain. On the other hand, if the function of the organ is not directly compromised, staphylococcal abscesses can endure for considerable time and produce relatively mild symptoms. At times, these tax the diagnostic acumen of the physician.

Paradigm: The Multifactorial Nature of Pathogenesis

Staphylococci are classic representatives of a group referred to as "pyogenic," or pus-producing bacteria. How do the pyogenic bacteria cause disease? Despite significant progress in the understanding of bacterial pathogenesis at the cellular and molecular level, there is not yet a complete answer to this question. The major reason is that the pathogenesis of pyogenic infections is clearly **complex** and **multifactorial**.

Like many other pyogenic bacteria, staphylococci elicit inflammation by secreting leukocyte **chemotaxins** plus a large number of **toxins** and **enzymes** that enhance the response. Some of these proteins, such as leukocidin, kill neutrophils, or, as catalase, inhibit their antibacterial activities. Others factors, e.g., coagulase, are involved in extracellular changes that favor abscess formation. Many of these bacterial products have been purified and their activities have been characterized, but the precise role that each plays in the actual infectious process is difficult to assess. What is needed is an approach that integrates the whole infectious process while at the same time focusing attention to the activity of a single factor. The best way to do this is to construct a **mutation** in a gene that encodes a factor of interest, then to compare the mutant carrying this mutation with its **isogenic** parent in some appropriate experimental model of disease. This comparison should allow the determination of what effect the loss of the particular factor plays in the disease. The process could then be repeated for each of the potential virulence factors.

How does one determine on which virulence factor to focus? Without initial biochemical evidence that a particular bacterial product is a toxin (which would make it an obvious choice), the investigator is often at a loss in trying to figure out what property of the bacterium has a given role in pathogenesis. As a first step in the process of making sense of multifactorial pathogenesis, the investigator often seeks an **epidemiological correlation** between a large number of bacterial strains associated with a particular infection and a bacterial trait. In the case of *Staphylococcus*, it has long been known that strains isolated from severe lesions tend to be from the species *aureus*, which can be distinguished from other staphylococcal species by virtue of secreting **coagulase**, an enzyme that clots plasma. The fact that **coagulase-positive** staphylococci are, epidemiologically speaking, more virulent suggests that coagulase is an important factor in the pathogenesis of staphylococcal infections, but it does not prove it. At this stage of the investigation, there is **correlation** without direct evidence of **causation**. Moreover, still remaining would be questions about the role of other possible virulence factors of *S. aureus*.

These issues were addressed by constructing isogenic strains of *S. aureus* that contained mutations in various putative virulence genes (i.e., genes for traits that were epidemiologically correlated with virulence). These strains were tested in a mouse mastitis model, in which the organisms were injected into the mammary glands. The resulting histopathological changes were reproducible and could be readily recorded. The result obtained was that coagulase-negative mutants were less virulent than the wild type. It was shown, moreover, that mutants defective in a **hemolysin** had comparably lower virulence, suggesting that this factor is at least as important as coagulase in causing disease. Furthermore, double mutants, defective in both factors, had markedly lower virulence than either single mutant, suggesting that both factors are needed and that they do not cause disease in the same manner (i.e., their effects are additive or even synergistic). Other factors, namely, protein A on the surface of the organisms, did not appear to be important in causing the short-term mastitis. This is not the end of the story, though. There is now some doubt about the role of coagulase because, in contrast to these studies with animal models of infection, a newer study has recently shown that coagulase-negative mutants are no less virulent than the wild type! Obviously, there is a problem with one or both of these studies; or, perhaps both are right, but they are looking at slightly different questions. After all, an animal model does not replicate human disease precisely. Alternatively, the genetics may not be quite right, since these organisms are harder to work with genetically than, say, *Escherichia coli*. Once genetic manipulation is perfected in the staphylococci, much more will be learned about the many traits that make *S. aureus* such a powerful pathogen.

OTHER SPECIES OF STAPHYLOCOCCI

S. epidermidis, the common inhabitant of the normal skin, rarely causes disease. However, infections with *S. epidermidis* are found with increasing frequency in patients with implanted artificial devices like prosthetic joints or intravenous catheters. When defense mechanisms are impaired, they can cause serious infections, such as septicemia and endocarditis. A potential virulence factor of these organisms is a slime layer that has been found in upward of 80% of disease-causing isolates. It is thought that this slime layer allows the organisms to stick to the surface of plastics used in various devices.

S. saprophyticus may be the most highly specialized of the staphylococci in terms of pathogenicity because it is almost entirely associated with urinary tract infections. The reason for this is not yet known, but it seems likely that this organism has unique binding properties to the epithelium of the urethra or of the bladder.

STAPHYLOCOCCAL TOXIN DISEASES

In contrast with these classical complicated infections, three staphylococcal toxin-related diseases are relatively straightforward. The symptoms of each of these diseases are caused by a different toxin. The first is called **scalded skin syndrome** and is a life-threatening disease, mainly of children, that results in extensive sloughing of the skin. A toxin, known as **exfoliatin**, causes these symptoms in laboratory animals. Its role has been clearly established because the administration of specific antitoxin prevents the skin lesions in humans or mice.

A second disease caused by a toxin, **TSS**, is characterized by fever, skin rash, hypotension, and the dysfunction of several essential systems. The disease is associated with the use of highly absorbent menstrual tampons, which apparently foster the growth of the organisms. TSS is not limited to a vaginal portal of entry. It can follow surgical procedures where tissue becomes infected or other staphylococcal skin infections, and can occur in men as well as in women. The toxin involved cannot be studied as readily as exfoliatin because it does not cause all of the symptoms of the disease in laboratory animals. It does cause fever by the same mechanism as the endotoxin of enteric bacteria, namely, by stimulating the formation of interleukin-1 (IL-1), the endogenous pyrogen. It can be clearly implicated in staphylococcal toxic shock because it has been found in all strains isolated from patients with this disease and only rarely in other isolates.

Finally, there is a group of staphylococcal **enterotoxins** that, even in the absence of the organism, is a major cause of **food poisoning**, as in our case report. The staphylococcal enterotoxins cause intensive intestinal peristalsis, apparently by working directly on the vomit center of the brain. They are very heat stable and are not necessarily destroyed by cooking. These toxins mimic the disease when administered to laboratory animals. Note that the same strain of S. aureus can cause several of the diseases mentioned. In the case described here, a single strain was responsible for Mr. S.'s bone and soft tissue infection as well as for food poisoning in the unfortunate people who ate the pastries prepared by him.

DIAGNOSIS

Recognizing staphylococcal infections is not usually a difficult diagnostic problem. They are among the most frequent infections seen both in the community and in the hospital. However, they must be quickly recognized so that appropriate therapy can be initiated.

A localized abscess in a seriously ill patient should be aspirated and the contents should be examined by the Gram stain and by culture.

Clusters of large Gram-positive cocci point to staphylococcal infection. The patient's blood should also be cultured to determine if the organisms have invaded the bloodstream. A common problem with blood cultures is to distinguish between *S. aureus* and *S. epidermidis*, since the latter is a common contaminant and is considered pathogenic only under special circumstances. The coagulase test serves to separate these two species.

THERAPY

A staphylococcal abscess like the ones seen in Mr. S. should be drained and an appropriate antibiotic should be administered. The early and widespread arrival of penicillin-resistant strains in the 1960s caused grave therapeutic problems and sent a shock wave through the medical community. It seems entirely in character that the earliest organism to accommodate to these powerful drugs should have been the adaptable *Staphylococcus*.

The human response was to develop penicillins and cephalosporins that are resistant to β-lactamase, the hydrolytic enzyme responsible for penicillin resistance. In most cases, antibiotic resistance is coded for by genes carried on plasmids, which probably accounts for the rapid spread of resistant organisms. There appears to be a race between the synthetic chemists and the organisms, because no sooner are new drugs introduced than reports of staphylococcal resistance begin to appear. More recently, there has been a disturbing increase in numbers of infections caused by staphylococci resistant to the newer β-lactamase-resistant penicillins and cephalosporins. Both *S. aureus* and *S. epidermidis* fall within this group and infections by these organisms require treatment with vancomycin.

Methicillin resistance in *S. aureus* is mediated by the production of a novel penicillin-binding protein (PBP 2a) that is able to maintain cell wall integrity during growth and cell division when the usual enzymes are inhibited by β-lactam antibiotics. The protein is encoded by a chromosomal gene called mecA. mecA has also been found in coagulase-negative staphylococci and is responsible for the worldwide spread of methicillin-resistant staphylococci. In the US, 15% of nosocomial *S. aureus* are methicillin resistant while 75% of *S. epidermidis* are resistant. Production of PBP 2a by mecA varies considerably and is known to be controlled by at least three genetic systems. The enzyme is induced by the presence of β-lactam antibiotics, the exact control mechanisms are not known.

Other classes of antibiotics (e.g., aminoglycosides, macrolides) may be useful second-line agents in the treatment of certain kinds of staphylococcal infections (particularly in penicillin-allergic patients), although some strains are resistant to them as well. The choice of drugs should be based on the antibiotic sensitivity of the infecting strain and the special characteristics of the patient. Therapy should also be sufficiently prolonged to ensure elimination of the organisms.

Over the years, vaccines have been developed for the treatment of recurrent, recalcitrant staphylococcal infections and to prevent the carrier state. Success has been limited, probably because circulating antibodies play a relatively minor role in these infections.

CONCLUSION

Staphylococci are potent pathogens, widely found in the human environment, and are able to cause a number of infections. They are hardy organisms that can survive under adverse conditions. They possess a large number of virulence determinants that allow them to cause serious diseases by different mechanisms. The most common diseases caused by these versatile pathogens are pyogenic infections, sometimes leading to the formation of abscesses in deep tissues. They can also cause distinct disease entities by making specific toxins.

Staphylococci have learned to adapt to new environments by acquiring antimicrobial resistance and even new virulence factors, as witnessed recently by the emergence of a new disease, TSS. These organisms have been around for a long time and will probably employ new mechanisms to cause serious diseases. It behooves the physician to respect them and to be aware of their presence.

Self-assessment Questions

1. What general types of diseases are due to staphylococci? Which are the most frequent and serious?

2. What are the structural, physiological, and ecological characteristics of the staphylococci? Which are the main types?

3. Regarding different staphylococcal diseases, how do we encounter these organisms?

4. How do staphylococci enter deep tissues? How do they set up residence? How do they cause disease? Why is this question particularly difficult for some staphylococcal infections but not for others?

5. How does the body respond to different staphylococcal infections?

6. What are the therapeutic problems encountered in different staphylococcal infections? How has this changed through recent history?

SUGGESTED READING

Chesney PJ, Bergdoll MS, Davis JP, Vergeront JM. The disease spectrum, epidemiology, and etiology of toxic shock syndrome. Ann Rev Microbiol 1984;38:315.

Easmon CSF, Adlam C. Staphylococci and staphylococcal infections. New York: Academic Press, 1984.

Jacoby GA, Archer GL. New mechanisms of bacterial resistance to antimicrobial agents. N Engl J Med 1991;321:601–612.

Radetsky P. The rise and (maybe not the) fall of toxic shock syndrome. Science 1985;85:72.

Sheagren JN. *Staphylococcus aureus*: the persistent pathogen. Part 1. N Engl J Med 1988;310:1386.

Sheagren JN. *Staphylococcus aureus*: the persistent pathogen. Part 2. N Engl J Med 1984;310:1437.

Streptococci 12

Ellen Whitnack

The streptococci are a heterogeneous group of bacteria comprising a number of species that colonize and infect humans and animals. In humans, they cause diseases ranging from the familiar "strep throat" to neonatal meningitis to brain abscess to endocarditis to gangrene. Members of this diverse group of organisms share several features: Grampositive staining; growth in chains resembling short strings of beads; and fermentative (anaerobic) metabolism, although most are oxygen tolerant and grow readily in air.

Streptococci are classified in three different ways, each of which has some clinical relevance.

Hemolysis pattern: When grown (as is customary) on blood agar, which is red and nearly opaque, streptococcal colonies may be surrounded by a zone of partial hemolysis with a **greenish discoloration** of the hemoglobin (α-hemolysis) or a clear zone of **complete hemolysis** (β-hemolysis). γ-"Hemolytic" streptococci are actually **nonhemolytic** and have no surrounding zone.

Lancefield group: Streptococci may be grouped serologically according to the major cell-wall carbohydrate antigens. Groups are lettered A through T; some streptococci are nongroupable.

Species: Like other bacteria, streptococci are speciated according to their metabolic reactions in various culture media. There are several dozen species.

These classifications are independent of one another, in that a given species may encompass more than one group or hemolysis pattern and vice versa. The result is a fearful muddle, but fortunately for clinical purposes, the classification can be considerably simplified. We will use a scheme shown in Figure 12.1, which is a slightly condensed version of one actually used in many hospital laboratories. The pneumococcus (*Streptococcus pneumoniae*) is so important that it is covered in a separate chapter (Chapter 13). In this chapter, we will discuss the remaining groups. Pride of place belongs to the group A streptococcus, which, since its discovery about a century ago by Pasteur, has caused the greatest variety of diseases, killed the most patients, and stimulated the most research of any streptococcus.

GROUP A STREPTOCOCCI

Case 1

M., a 6-year old boy, came home from school tired and cranky. By suppertime, he was hot and flushed and was complaining of a sore throat; he refused to eat, and vomited once. His mother took him to an evening clinic, where his tempera-

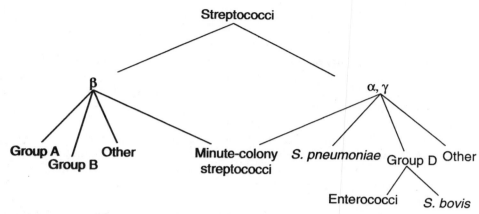

Figure 12.1.   A classification of streptococci. β-Hemolytic streptococci are sometimes called simply "hemolytic streptococci." α- And γ-hemolytic strep are lumped because most species or groups on this side of the diagram exhibit both patterns. Often such organisms are called "viridans" (green) streptococci after the greenish color seen in a hemolysis.

ture was noted to be 39.4°C. The doctor found that M. had a red throat with grayish-white exudate on both tonsils, and his cervical lymph nodes were enlarged and tender. A throat swab was taken for a rapid enzyme immunoassay test to detect streptococcal group A antigen; it was positive. The doctor prescribed a shot of a long-acting penicillin preparation. Within 2 days, M. felt fine.

Case 2

The year was 1846, the place, the Allgemeines Krankenhaus in Vienna. Frau M., a 31-year-old woman, had been delivered of her fourth child on the previous day after 36 hours of labor. She had lost quite a bit of blood and had been pale, weak, and restless all afternoon. Early in the evening she suddenly had a shaking chill, followed by a high fever. The lochia (postpartum uterine discharge) became thin and malodorous. By midnight, Frau M. was delirious, with a weak, thready pulse; by morning, she was dead. Hers was the sixth such case on Division A that week.

The following questions arise:

1. Is "strep throat" a trivial disease?

2. Why did M.'s physician use long-acting instead of regular penicillin?

3. Were M.'s sore throat and Frau M.'s death caused by the same kind of streptococci?

4. How do people "catch" streptococci? Are they part of the normal bacterial flora?

5. M.'s throat showed purulent inflammation. Is pus typical of streptococcal diseases? Do streptococci cause pus by the same mechanisms as, say, the staphylococci?

Diseases Caused by Group A Streptococci

Most group A streptococci belong to the species *S. pyogenes*, and for practical purposes, "group A strep" and "*S. pyogenes*" are synonyms. This organism has caused human disease since antiquity, but seems to have reached its peak of virulence in the 19th century, when it was a real scourge; indeed, until the middle of the present century, serious streptococcal diseases were common and much feared. **Strep throat** and **scarlet fever** (strep throat with a red skin rash) were dreaded for their frequent complications: peritonsillar abscess ("quinsy"), otitis, mastoiditis, and occasionally, septicemia and meningitis. As recently as the 1930s, group A streptococci were the most common cause of sepsis, accounting for perhaps two-thirds of the cases. **Streptococcal pharyngitis** (M.'s problem) was not infrequently followed by **acute rheumatic fever**, an inflammatory disease affecting principally the heart and joints that could produce permanent damage to the heart valves, with lifelong disability and early death from embolic stroke, bacterial endocarditis, and heart failure. There were once entire wards—indeed, entire hospitals—devoted to the care of children with acute rheumatic fever. Group A streptococcal **pneumonia** was noted for its aggressiveness and its tendency to produce large empyemas (collections of purulent fluid in the pleural cavity). **Impetigo**, itself a trivial skin infection, could be followed by **acute glomerulonephritis**; this problem could also occur after a strep throat.

Streptococcal infections of the soft tissues were often fatal; **erysipelas**, an infection of the skin and subcutaneous tissues, swept through Civil War encampments "like a scythe" (in the words of the historian James McPherson). Streptococcal **necrotizing fasciitis** and **myositis** could complicate any wound, civilian or military, with lethal results unless the infected tissue could be excised or amputated. Today's older surgeons have vivid memories of "hospital gangrene" (streptococcal necrotizing fasciitis complicating surgical wounds). Even now, battle casualties are treated with prophylactic penicillin.

Finally, the group A streptococcus was the most common cause of Frau M.'s affliction, **puerperal fever** (postpartum endomyometritis and septicemia, also known as childbed fever). It was this organism (although he did not know it at the time) that Ignaz Semmelweis was combating when, suspecting contagion via material carried on the hands of physicians who had performed autopsies, he required doctors attending parturient women at the Allgemeines Krankenhaus to disinfect their hands with chloride of lime before examining the patients. The death rate fell from 9.92% in 1847 to 1.27% 2 years later, earning Semmelweis a permanent place in the medical pantheon (although not in his own lifetime).

Simple strep throat and impetigo are still common infections, but the incidence of serious streptococcal infections, as well as rheumatic fever, has been decreasing since World War II and probably earlier, at least in developed countries. One cannot simply attribute this to penicillin treatment, because the incidence of severe infections—prior to treatment—has been decreasing, as has the incidence of rheumatic fever following untreated strep throats. Rather, the nature of the organism seems to have changed. Perhaps improved living standards (better hygiene, less crowding), along with the widespread use of penicillin, have interfered with the rapid person-to-person transmission of the organism. In any event, as of the mid-1980s, serious streptococcal disease seemed to be nearly extinct.

However, in 1985, an outbreak of **rheumatic fever** occurred in Salt Lake City—nothing like the "old days," but dramatic nevertheless: 18.1 cases per 100,000 children per year, an eight-fold increase over the previous 15-year average. Since then, outbreaks have occurred in several other locations, particularly in the Ohio valley, and an increased incidence of acute rheumatic fever over baseline levels has been reported nationwide. At the same time, case reports of serious streptococcal infections have accumulated, including **severe septic ill-**

nesses that have killed up to one-third of their victims—including healthy young people—despite penicillin treatment. These illnesses include a **"toxic strep syndrome"** reminiscent of staphylococcal toxic shock syndrome (TSS—see Chapter 11), with hypotension, renal failure, and a desquamating red rash. The resurgence of serious streptococcal disease has stimulated a renewed interest in the group A streptococcus, together with some apprehension at the return of an old enemy.

Encounter

Group A streptococci live on human skin and mucous membranes; pharyngeal carriage rates among school-aged children in the winter months may be as high as 20%. The organism spreads from person to person, asymptomatically for the most part, probably by infected droplets, perhaps by hand-to-hand-to-mouth contact. Food-borne outbreaks of streptococcal pharyngitis occur occasionally when food handled by a carrier is allowed to stand at room temperature. In the case of skin and soft-tissue infections, additional modes of transmission by fomites such as towels, by shed skin scales (as might occur in an operating room), and by direct skin-to-skin contact seem likely.

Entry

The first step in the establishment of a streptococcal infection, as for all epithelial infections, is the adherence of the bacteria to the epithelial cells, so that the organisms can multiply without getting swept away by fluid secretions. A leading candidate for the streptococcal **adhesin** involved in pharyngeal colonization is **lipoteichoic acid (LTA)**. Teichoic acid and LTA are constituents of the cell envelope of many Grampositive bacteria (Chapter 3). The LTA of group A streptococci is a polymer of about 25 **glycerolphosphate** subunits with a **lipid** (palmitate) attached at the end. Streptococci with abundant LTA on their surface are generally sticky, but they also interact specifically with **fibronectin**, a host protein that coats the epithelial cells of the oropharynx. The interaction is mediated by the lipid moiety. One would not expect a hydrophobic structure of any size to protrude from a cell surface, and it is thought that the LTA may be forced into this "inside-out" orientation by complexing its polyglycerol phosphate backbone to a surface protein called **M protein** (see Fig. 12.2).

Spread

The spread of group A streptococci in tissues seems to depend on how the infection is acquired. Streptococcal **infections of the skin or mucous membranes usually remain well localized**. Impetigo, at worst, becomes an inflamed ulcer called **ecthyma**. Pharyngeal infections may be locally very severe, with necrosis and abscess formation in and about the tonsils and, occasionally, with seeding of the bloodstream; however, spread to adjacent tissues is uncommon. When it does occur, the result is usually **facial erysipelas**; the path taken by the streptococci between the pharynx and the facial skin is not known. Streptococci can infect other epithelia of the upper respiratory tract, such as the sinus and the middle ear, where again they may be locally invasive, as in mastoiditis.

In contrast, streptococci infecting deeper tissues (as in a wound) may spread very rapidly. The reason may be that they secrete digestive

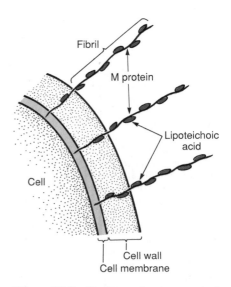

Figure 12.2. Surface structures of S. pyogenes. Extruding from the cell membrane are fibrils of M protein "decorated" with molecules of LTA (*lipoteichoic acid*).

enzymes including proteases, hyaluronidase, DNAase, and streptokinase. **Streptokinase** binds to host **plasminogen** to form complexes that catalyze the conversion of plasminogen to **plasmin**, which, in turn, **degrades fibrin** and a number of other proteins. (A very similar enzyme from a group C species is used to promote the dissolution of clots, especially in the coronary arteries of patients with heart attacks.) These enzymes together allow the streptococcus to break down almost any large molecule in its path, permitting rapid spread through tissues. Indeed, pus from streptococcal infections is characteristically thin and runny because the large molecules responsible for the viscosity of pus—principally DNA and fibrin—have been degraded. It is not clear why deeper infections (erysipelas, fasciitis) are characterized by rapid and extensive local spread while epithelial infections (impetigo, pharyngitis) are not.

Multiplication

To multiply in tissues, streptococci must avoid phagocytosis. Resistance to phagocytosis is the best understood virulence mechanism of the group A streptococcus. Three surface molecules are responsible: **M protein**, which is a rod-shaped molecule that projects from the surface of the bacterial cell as a layer of fuzz; **hyaluronic acid**, which forms a mucoid capsule; and, possibly, a recently discovered **C5a peptidase**, which inactivates a potent phagocyte chemotaxin made during complement activation (see Chapter 6).

M PROTEIN

M protein (Fig. 12.3) is the most important antiphagocytic factor of *S. pyogenes* and is the central theme in streptococcal pathogenesis. This protein is required for virulence; organisms lacking M protein are readily opsonized by complement via the alternate pathway. Organisms bearing M protein bind fibrinogen, fibrin, and their degradation products to form a dense coating on the organism's surface, blocking complement deposition (Fig. 12.4). The fibrinogen molecules bind to the outer halves of the M protein molecules, near the tips. Even in the absence of fibrinogen and its derivatives, M protein-bearing streptococci are poorly opsonized by the alternate pathway. As with other particles that fail to activate this pathway, C3 convertase that happens to form on the surface is rapidly disrupted by the complement control protein factor H, retarding the further deposition of opsonic complement (see Chapter 8).

Fortunately for the host, there is a way around these antiopsonic defenses; the tips of the M protein molecules project past the fibrinogen coat, so that **antibody to M protein** can opsonize the organism. Antibody to M protein is the only antistreptococcal antibody that can opsonize group A streptococci, and, once acquired, it protects the host against infection. Unfortunately for us, there are approximately **80 different M proteins (serotypes)**, and protective immunity is strictly type specific, so repeated strep infections with different serotypes are possible. The carboxy halves of the molecule are highly conserved from one serotype to another, but the amino terminal halves vary, especially at the tips, accounting for the numerous serotypes. Since this is the half that binds opsonic antibody, this **antigenic or serotypic variation** provides a means for the organism to maintain itself in the human population; as ever more individuals become immune to a particular M protein, new variants appear. How do different serotypes arise? M pro-

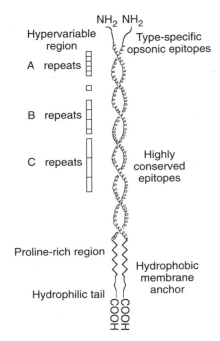

Figure 12.3. Group A streptococcal M protein. M protein molecules are typically about 500 residues long. They are anchored in the cell membrane by a hydrophobic sequence near the carboxy terminus; they then traverse the cell wall via a sequence rich in glycine and proline, and finally, emerge to project from the cell wall as fibrils. The fibrils are mostly α-helical, and contain two or three blocks of repeating amino acid sequences. There is a seven-residue periodicity in the placement of hydrophobic amino acids that favors a coiled-coil conformation, so that each fibril actually consists of two α-helical M molecules wound about each other. The amino-terminal halves of the M protein, despite their structural heterogeneity, retain the ability to bind fibrinogen, which protects the organism from nonspecific opsonization by the alternative pathway of complement.

tein molecules contain blocks of amino acid sequence repeats, typically about 40 residues long, that result from gene duplication. These blocks are similar, but due to mutations, not identical. DNA encoding a given block may recombine with that encoding a slightly different block to result in recombinant strands with base sequences that differ from either parent. Thus, new epitopes can arise by recombination at a rate exceeding the usual random mutation rates.

HYALURONIC ACID CAPSULE

This is the second antiphagocytic structure on the streptococcal surface. It makes the organism generally slippery and interferes with the attachment of phagocytes. Paradoxically, the organisms secrete a hyaluronidase that destroys this capsule in the course of tissue infections. The capsule also interferes with attachment to epithelial cells in vitro, yet these organisms can attach quite efficiently. Does the organism shut off capsule production—or turn on hyaluronidase production—when it is in contact with epithelial surfaces? Streptococci recovered during outbreaks of acute rheumatic fever are generally very heavily encapsulated. Hyaluronic acid is, at most, only very weakly immunogenic, being a "self" antigen. What, then, is its role in the pathogenesis of that disease? Is its synthesis co-regulated with that of a rheumatogenic antigen? These questions are as yet unanswered.

C5a PEPTIDASE

The third antiphagocytic molecule is **C5a peptidase**, which cleaves six amino acids from the carboxy terminus of **C5a**, the principal **chemotactic factor** generated by the complement cascade. The cleaved molecule is inactive. In a mouse model of intraperitoneal infection, mutant streptococci lacking C5a peptidase attracted phagocytes more rapidly than did wild-type organisms. Death rates, however, were the same. It is still possible that C5a peptidase functions together with the virulence factors in the highly multifactorial pathogenesis of streptococcal infection.

Damage

Streptococci characteristically evoke an intense inflammatory response in tissues. The organisms elaborate many substances that can damage mammalian cells or activate phagocytes and lymphocytes, but their exact role in vivo is not well worked out, for at least two reasons: (*a*) **isogenic mutants** are only just now becoming available, and (*b*) there are no good animal models for infections by these organisms. Here we will mention two toxin groups, the **streptolysins** and the **pyrogenic exotoxins**. **Streptolysins S and O** are the toxins responsible for the hemolysis seen on blood agar. They can **lyse virtually any type of cell**, not just the erythrocyte. Streptococci bearing streptolysin S on their surface kill the phagocytes that have ingested them, but not before the phagocytes kill the streptococci. The importance of these toxins in disease pathogenesis is uncertain because they are readily inactivated by phospholipids and other substances found in serum; hemolysis, for instance, is not a feature of streptococcal infection. Still, no other substances have emerged as more likely agents in the tissue necrosis seen in some infections.

The three streptococcal **pyrogenic exotoxins (SPEs) A, B, and C** belong to a larger family of pyrogenic toxins that includes the staphylo-

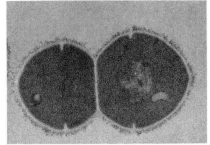
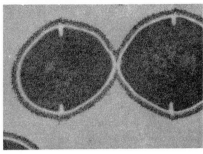

Figure 12.4. Group A streptococci. On the *top* are organisms as they appear after growth in broth culture. Note the fuzzy layer on the surface, which is made of M protein and LTA. The hyaluronate capsule is in a dehydrated and collapsed state because of the fixation process, and cannot be seen. On the *bottom* are the same streptococci after brief immersion in plasma. Note the dense appearance of the fuzzy layer, which is produced by fibrinogen bound to the M protein. In this young culture, the chains are two or three bacterial cells long. Cross-walls are beginning to form in preparation for the next cell division.

coccal enterotoxins and staphylococcal TSS toxin (see Chapter 11). These proteins are structurally diverse but there is some sequence homology among them. The streptococcal toxins have also been called **"erythrogenic toxins"** because they are responsible for the red rash of scarlet fever. Pyrogenic exotoxins have a number of biological properties in common. They are **T-cell mitogens** (or, more accurately, **superantigens**; see below), and they enhance delayed hypersensitivity reactions and suppress antibody responses. SPEs potentiate the biological effects of Gram-negative endotoxin, and, like endotoxin, stimulate monocytes to release **tumor necrosis factor** and **interleukin-1**, the principal mediators of septic shock (see Chapter 6). The reappearance of severe shock-inducing streptococcal infections has been epidemiologically associated with the reappearance of **SPE A** in streptococcal isolates, much as in former days, when severe scarlet fever was mostly due to streptococci that elaborated SPE A. In a recent study, eight of ten strains isolated from severe infections accompanied by shock produced SPE A. Why SPE A should have almost disappeared only to return years later is a mystery.

Acute Rheumatic Fever

Severe, life-threatening streptococcal infections may be increasing in incidence, but they are still not everyday affairs. Far more common is simple strep throat, which, in most cases, would get better without any treatment. Strep throat is unique, however, in that it is the only infection that may be followed by **acute rheumatic fever** (ARF), which can be an extremely serious disease. Acute rheumatic fever is a **"nonsuppurative sequel"** of group A streptococcal pharyngitis, as opposed to suppurative complications such as peritonsillar abscess. It is manifested in most patients by **polyarthritis**, **carditis**, or both. Other manifestations seen occasionally include a neurological disorder called Sydenham's chorea (St. Vitus' dance), subcutaneous nodules, and a rash called erythema marginatum. All of these manifestations eventually resolve, except for carditis.

In the worst cases, patients with acute rheumatic carditis die of **intractable heart failure** in the midst of the acute attack. More commonly, they survive and recover; but in some patients (generally those with the more severe symptoms during the acute attack), cardiac damage progresses insidiously to severe **valvular scarring**, with both narrowing of the orifice (**stenosis**) and inability to close properly, resulting in back-flow (**regurgitation**). This creates a new series of complications; some directly from impaired heart function, others from **bacterial endocarditis**, resulting from the seeding of the damaged valves by bacteria that find their way into the bloodstream (see Chapter 67).

SOME KEY OBSERVATIONS

- Only group A streptococci cause acute rheumatic fever, and the pharynx is the only site of infection that is ever followed by acute rheumatic fever. Some group A serotypes are "rheumatogenic"; others are not.

- The streptococcal infection must evoke an immune response in the host. Carriage of the organism without an immune response, or symptomatic infection without an immune response (as sometimes occurs when patients are treated promptly, and even, on occasion, in untreated cases), does not result in rheumatic fever.

- Acute rheumatic fever can be completely prevented by treating the pharyngitis with penicillin. Treatment can be delayed for as much as a week and still be effective, but it must continue until all organisms are eradicated. In fact, **the main reason to give penicillin to anyone with a sore throat is to prevent acute rheumatic fever.**

- Rheumatic fever can occur after asymptomatic infection; indeed, one-third or more of acute rheumatic fever patients cannot recall a sore throat. How, then, do we know that these patients had a strep infection? Infection is indicated by their high titers of antibodies to various streptococcal antigens.

- Acute rheumatic fever itself does not respond to penicillin, nor is there convincing evidence of streptococcal cells, living, dead, or fragmented, in affected tissues.

- Once a person has had an attack of acute rheumatic fever, he or she remains highly susceptible to recurrences following subsequent strep throats, each of which may cause further heart damage. These patients must take prophylactic antibiotics well into adulthood, if not for life.

- There is no known innate resistance to strep throat, but no more than 10% of people are susceptible to rheumatic fever.

PATHOGENESIS OF ACUTE RHEUMATIC FEVER

Acute rheumatic fever is caused by only group A streptococci (some of them), and only in the pharynx, and only in humans (some of them) —no wonder the pathogenesis of this disease has baffled five generations of investigators. The leading hypothesis for some years has been that acute rheumatic fever is an **autoimmune disease** evoked by the streptococcal infection. Streptococci possess a number of antigens that cross-react, that is, **share epitopes**, with human tissues, notably heart muscle and valvular connective tissue. Some of these epitopes are an integral part of the M protein molecule. Antibodies to certain purified M proteins react with myosin, phosphorylase, and several other unidentified proteins in heart tissue, as well as with proteins in brain and synovium. Furthermore, **autoantibodies** are found in the blood of persons with rheumatic fever. This may sound like strong circumstantial evidence for humoral autoimmune disease, but, in fact, these antibodies are not likely to be the explanation for acute rheumatic fever. For one thing, autoantibodies are also found in persons who have had uncomplicated pharyngitis, although in lower titer. Another argument against a role for autoantibodies is that the latent period between pharyngitis and acute rheumatic fever is just as long in recurrent attacks as in initial attacks.

Current research on the pathogenesis of acute rheumatic fever is focused on the hypothesis that **cellular autoimmunity**, rather than humoral autoimmunity, is the pathogenetic mechanism, and that streptococcal antigens evoke "**cross-reactive T cells.**" For example, various streptococcal preparations, including fragments of M protein containing the heart cross-reactive epitopes, stimulate the production of cytotoxic T cells active against cultured cardiac myocytes. The pyrogenic exotoxins are another area of interest. These molecules are "**superantigens**"; like ordinary antigens, they stimulate T-cell proliferation in the context of class II major histocompatibility complex (MHC) molecules on antigen-presenting cells (Chapter 7), but they interact with conserved regions of the V domain of the T-cell receptor rather than with the hypervariable regions, so that polyclonal activation results, i.e., the formation of large numbers of antibody molecules with different specificities. Recent data suggest that certain regions of M protein, too, have this property. This phenomenon could conceivably account for the breaking of tolerance to self-antigens and the induction of autoimmunity. Work in these areas is still in an early stage of development, but in the absence of an animal model, studies such as these are the most promising avenue toward unraveling the pathogenesis of acute rheumatic fever.

Acute Glomerulonephritis

Acute glomerulonephritis (AGN) is the other nonsuppurative sequel of streptococcal infection. Acute glomerulonephritis is caused by only a few serotypes (M types) and probably only certain strains within those serotypes. This disease differs from acute rheumatic fever in several key ways. Unlike acute rheumatic fever, it may follow either pharyngitis or impetigo. In some outbreaks, the attack rate is as high as 40%, suggesting that susceptibility is common, if not universal. Recurrent attacks are rare, probably because the number of nephritogenic strains is so limited. AGN is not reliably prevented by penicillin treatment.

Acute glomerulonephritis results in hypoalbuminemia (because of a glomerular protein leak) and salt retention. Patients look pale, with puffy eyes and swollen hands and feet. Their urine contains abnormal quantities of protein, leukocytes, and erythrocytes; so many that the urine may have a "smoky" or "rusty" appearance. The severity of AGN ranges from asymptomatic (detected only by urinalysis) to acute renal shutdown, but most patients do well.

The pathogenesis of acute glomerulonephritis would seem to involve an inflammatory response evoked by immune complexes because lumpy deposits of immunoglobulin G (IgG) and complement (C3) are found on the epithelial side of the basement membrane, and complement levels in the blood are depressed. The nature of the antigens involved is not known. Autoimmunity is a possibility, in that cross-reactions have been described between streptococcal antigens and glomerular tissue. Alternatively, streptococcal antigens could be deposited in the glomeruli, either before or after complexing with antibody. Currently, there is considerable interest in a protein, "endostreptosin," found in the cytoplasm and cell membrane of nephritogenic streptococci. This protein has been found beneath the glomerular basement membrane in kidney biopsy specimens early in the course of AGN and may turn out to be the culprit antigen.

Paradigm: Molecular Mimicry

In this chapter, we encounter two diseases, acute poststreptococcal glomerulonephritis and acute rheumatic fever, that are ultimately caused by a pathogenic microbe (the group A streptococcus) but that occur **after** the infection has subsided. These are only two of many such diseases, most of which involve **inflammation** of one sort or another. The inflammatory component and the latent period between infection and disease (typically several days to a few weeks), create the suspicion of an immune pathogenesis.

How do these diseases come about? Broadly speaking, there are four adverse things that a microorganism can do to its host:

- Destroy cells, either by invading them or by secreting lethal cytotoxins;
- Cause cells to malfunction, by parasitizing them or intoxicating them;
- Evoke a nonspecific inflammatory response;
- Evoke a specific immune response.

For instance, a microbe might invoke an inflammatory response resulting in destruction of microbial cells. This results in the release of toxic cell constituents that damage certain host cells, creating a "neoantigen" or revealing a "cryptoantigen" that evokes the production of antibodies. Such antibodies combine with the antigens to form **fixed** and **circulating immune complexes**; the former promote further inflammation at the **site of infection**, whereas the latter evoke inflammatory responses at the **site of deposition**; or perhaps the microbe has among its thousands of epitopes a few that are also present in host molecules (**"molecular mimicry"**). If the host is somehow seduced into amplifying the normally quiescent response to these "self"-epitopes, an autoimmune disease could result. Clearly, sorting out the pathogenetic mechanism of a particular disease is a complex and challenging task. In particular, two problems bedevil the search for an immune pathogenesis in postinfectious diseases: (a) **identifying the antigens** (microbial, host, or both) against which the immune response is directed; and (b) **distinguishing autoimmune responses** that **cause** cell damage from those that merely **result** from it, and are not pathogenetic in themselves.

There is a group of diseases termed "the seronegative (i.e., rheumatoid factor-negative) spondylarthropathies" (SNSAs) that includes the **"reactive arthritis"** that follows gastrointestinal (GI) and genitourinary infections due to a variety of bacteria (*Chlamydia, Shigella, Yersinia, Salmonella,* and *Campylobacter*). Some patients with reactive arthritis have urethritis and conjunctivitis as well (Reiter's syndrome). **Ankylosing spondylitis** (AS), i.e., spinal arthritis resulting in fusion, is another disease in the SNSA family; it, too, is sometimes associated with gastrointestinal or genitourinary inflammation (e.g., Crohn's disease, chronic prostatitis). Antigens of several enteric and urogenital pathogens have been found in the (sterile) joint fluid of some patients with reactive arthritis, suggesting that the arthritis could be simply an inflammatory response to bacterial antigens in situ. However, most patients with these diseases have the HLA-B27 MHC haplotype. (See Chapter 7 for a discussion of MHC.) Thus, approximately 90% of Caucasian AS patients have the HLA-B27 allele. Approximately 80% of patients with Reiter's disease have this HLA allele also.

How is HLA-B27 involved in these diseases? We do not know yet. Investigators determined that HLA-B27 shares structural features with a bacterial protein. This finding, coupled with reports that antibodies specific for certain bacteria, such as *Klebsiella pneumoniae* will also bind specifically to cells expressing HLA-B27, suggests that an immune response mounted during certain bacterial infections could result in the production of antibodies that cross-react with self, causing cell and tissue damage and, hence, disease. This is the "molecular mimicry" hypothesis.

There are problems with this hypothesis in connection with AS, not the least of which is that HLA-B27 is expressed on all cells; therefore, an antiself humoral response would not be expected to produce a disease restricted to the synovial joints of the spine as is found in AS. However, there is a way to reconcile these facts. Benjamin and Parham in their "arthritogenic peptide" model suggest that AS is the result of a T-cell-mediated immune response to a **peptide-HLA-B27 combination**. The tissue specificity of the disease is explained by hypothesizing that the peptide is normally found in synovial joints only. Thus, the explanation for the apparent autoimmune nature of AS would be that certain pathogens contain proteins that are **processed by antigen-presenting cells** to give peptides similar to joint tissue-specific self peptides that normally bind to HLA-B27. Infections would then stimulate the normally very low levels of T cells capable of recognizing this HLA-B27-peptide combination and a cytotoxic T-lymphocyte-mediated response. This response would be enhanced by further peptide released from damaged cells in joint tissues, ultimately resulting in the disease state we know as AS.

It is also likely that certain **chronic inflammatory diseases that do not follow any particular infection** are, nonetheless, the result of immune responses to microbial antigens. Numerous pathogens have been proposed as possible causes of such diseases as rheumatoid arthritis, systemic lupus erythematosus, and juvenile chronic arthritis (and, in fact, a subset of juvenile arthritis patients has turned out to have Lyme disease; see Chapter 25). Currently, there is much interest in molecular mimicry between bacterial and human **heat-shock proteins** (HSPs) as a stimulus to autoimmune reactions. HSPs are so called because their expression is stimulated by heating the cells and other forms of stress. Homologies have been discovered between human mitochondrial HSPs and those of a variety of bacteria. In a recent study, T cells from patients with juvenile chronic arthritis proliferated in response to human HSP60 and to bacterial HSP, especially cells harvested from affected joints. Perhaps bacterial HSPs evoke an immune response that is perpetuated by the human protein.

The preceding discussion owes much to the review of the immune basis of autoimmune diseases by Sinha, Lopez and McDevitt in *Science* (1990;248: 1380–1388) and the hypotheses concerning the role of B27 in AS developed by Benjamin and Parham in *Immunology Today* (1990;11:137–142).

Diagnosis and Treatment of Group A Streptococcal Infections

The diagnosis of group A streptococcal infections other than pharyngitis is straightforward. Impetigo and erysipelas can be diagnosed by sight; **impetigo** is a cluster of small vesicles on a pink base that break down to honey-colored crusts, and **erysipelas** is a raised, fiery red patch of skin with a sharply demarcated, rapidly advancing margin. Severe infections such as **fasciitis** and **sepsis** can be diagnosed by cultures of pus and blood. In such serious diseases, antibiotics active against streptococci should be started immediately, without waiting for the cultures to grow.

Pharyngitis, on the other hand, presents problems. There is no reliable way to tell strep throat from **viral pharyngitis** by physical examination, so the definitive diagnosis requires **throat culture**. The results take 2 or 3 days to come back; therefore, the patient must either have a (possibly unnecessary) shot of penicillin or return for a second visit. When the results do come back, a positive culture has only a 50% chance of representing a true infection because of the high rate of asymptomatic carriage. What is currently done (as in M.'s case) is to perform a test for the group A carbohydrate antigen in the office, which can be accomplished in less than an hour using a commercial kit. These kits use antigroup A carbohydrate antibodies in **latex agglutination tests** or **enzyme immunoassays**. Like cultures, these tests suffer from the carriage vs. infection problem, but at least the results are available before the patient goes home. The rapid tests are not as sensitive as a throat culture, so a negative must be confirmed by culture.

Standard treatment for pharyngitis is a **single injection** of a slowly absorbed penicillin (benzathine penicillin), which produces detectable blood levels of penicillin for 3–4 weeks. **Oral penicillin** can be used, but is less reliable because the patients tend to stop taking it as soon as they feel better, which is not **sufficient therapy** to eradicate the organism and to prevent rheumatic fever. Like diagnosis, treatment has its knotty issues. Penicillin is not 100% effective; should the patient be retested in 10–14 days to make sure that the streptococci have been eradicated? If the organisms are still around, do they represent persistent, dangerous infection or merely a harmless post-treatment carrier state? (Postinfection carriage is seen in many types of epithelial infections.) How should a treatment failure be retreated, given that penicillin did not work the first time? Discussion of such issues is beyond the scope of this text, but be aware that strep throat is not a simple problem, and that hundreds of millions of dollars—and some lives—hang on the answers to these questions.

The diagnosis of acute rheumatic fever depends on evidence of a **preceding streptococcal infection**. This is best obtained by serological tests, of which three are in common use: antistreptolysin O; anti-DNAase B; and a commercial latex agglutination test (Streptozyme) made with a mixture of streptococcal antigens. The antistreptolysin O and anti-DNAase B test are preferred for the diagnosis of acute rheumatic fever.

Prevention of Streptococcal Infections

The only way to prevent streptococcal infection is to take antibiotics, usually penicillin, unless the patient is allergic to it. Preventive therapy is prescribed for household contacts of acute rheumatic fever patients; for closed populations (e.g., military recruits) to control and to prevent outbreaks; and for persons who have had rheumatic fever, to prevent recurrences. The last group must take penicillin continuously, usually in the form of monthly injections of benzathine penicillin.

Clearly, a streptococcal **vaccine** would be desirable. Recall that type-specific anti-M antibody opsonizes streptococci of that serotype and protects against infection. A vaccine could, therefore, consist of purified M proteins of the prevalent serotypes. However, the vaccine must exclude epitopes that cross-react with human tissues. Development of such a vaccine is laborious but technically feasible, and is, in fact, in progress. A second approach is to find an immunogen that protects against multiple serotypes, perhaps by evoking antibodies that block adherence to epithelial cells or that block the binding of fibrinogen. Such a vaccine would have to act at the mucosal level. Studies of this type are also underway, but they are at a very early stage.

GROUP B STREPTOCOCCI

Most human group B streptococci inhabit the **lower GI** and **female genital tracts** and belong to the species S. *agalactiae*. Vaginal colonization is found in 20% or more of healthy women. This figure includes **pregnant women**, who pass the organism along to their babies during birth. Other organisms transmitted this way include *Chlamydia trachomatis* and herpes simplex virus (see Chapter 68). If the mother, and therefore, the baby, happen to lack protective antibody, the streptococci can invade the mucosae and, in some cases, enter the bloodstream. In the past 20 years, group B streptococci have emerged as the leading cause of **neonatal sepsis** and **meningitis** (the two generally go together). Neonatal group B sepsis is a devastating disease: 10–20% of the babies die, and one-third to one-half of the survivors have permanent brain damage. Group B streptococci also cause cellulitis and blood-borne infections such as arthritis and meningitis in adults, particularly elderly patients, diabetic patients, alcoholic patients, and, on occasion, parturient women.

Unlike the hyaluronate capsule of group A streptococci, the **polysaccharide capsules** of group B streptococci are not host constituents and are, therefore, immunogenic. One serotype, III, accounts for over one-half of neonatal group B streptococcal infections. Anticapsular antibodies opsonize the organisms and protect against invasive disease. The best way to prevent neonatal disease ought to be to immunize the mother during pregnancy with capsular polysaccharides; her IgG antibodies would cross the placenta and protect the baby. Unfortunately, capsular polysaccharides are not as immunogenic as one would wish and only about 60% of adults respond to type III polysaccharide. Vaccines employing polysaccharide-protein conjugates analogous to *Haemophilus influenzae* vaccines (Chapter 15) show promise and are currently under development.

OTHER PATHOGENIC STREPTOCOCCI

Other Large-colony Streptococci

The remaining human isolates of β-hemolytic streptococci that make large colonies on agar belong, for the most part, to groups C and G. These organisms are very similar to group A and have been termed "pyogenes-like," but are recovered much less frequently. Like group A, they may be isolated from the normal human pharynx, vagina, GI tract, and skin. Both have M protein, and group C has a hyaluronic acid capsule. Both groups bind fibrinogen, secrete many of the same extracellular enzymes as group A strep, and cause similar types of infections including pharyngitis, cellulitis, and blood-borne infections. Both groups have been implicated in acute glomerulonephritis, but neither has been known to cause rheumatic fever.

Minute-colony Streptococci

Minute-colony streptococci (the colonies are about pinhead size) are part of the normal flora of the mucous membranes, particularly of the oropharynx. The taxonomy of this group is confusing; suffice it to say that a recent proposal places them all in one species, *anginosus* (the name *milleri* is also frequently encountered). These organisms may have any of the three hemolytic patterns and belong to some of the same serological groups as large-colony streptococci. The distinction is important, because minute-colony streptococci are quite different from the "regular" kind. They are microaerophilic or anaerobic, and are most noted for causing skin, lung, brain, orofacial, and intra-abdominal abscesses, usually in mixed infections with other organisms.

Group D Streptococci

Group D streptococci are, for the most part, α- (green) or γ- (non) hemolytic. They are divided into two groups, **enterococci** and **nonenterococci**. The enterococci have recently been assigned to their own genus, *Enterococcus*. As the name implies, they are normal flora of the intestinal tract, as well as the genitourinary tract. If a prize were ever awarded for being "the world's toughest pathogenic bacteria," enterococci would probably win it. These organisms can grow in salt concentrations seven-fold higher than normal tissue fluids, and can grow in detergents, including 60% bile. Unlike most other streptococci, they are merely inhibited, not killed, by penicillin and are resistant to cephalosporins. One of the few effective modes of therapy takes advantage of **antibiotic synergism**; penicillin alone only arrests their growth, and aminoglycosides, such as gentamicin, are without effect except at very high concentrations, but the combination kills the organism. It is thought that the penicillin disrupts the cell wall sufficiently to allow the aminoglycoside to enter the cell and kill it. Unfortunately, some enterococci are becoming resistant to aminoglycosides even in the presence of penicillin, leaving the clinician with no way to kill them. In the 1990s, this may prove to be a serious problem in treating infections in which bactericidal therapy is required for cure, such as for endocarditis (see Chapter 62).

Fortunately, these organisms are of low virulence. Usually they are recovered from mixed infections in which they seem to be "along for the ride" with other, more virulent organisms such as Gram-negative bacilli and anaerobes. Enterococci are being recovered from hospitalized patients ever more frequently, probably because of the widespread use of cephalosporins, which suppress the competing flora. Bedsores, wounds, and intra-abdominal infections are particularly apt to yield enterococci. Most infections due solely to enterococci are urinary tract infections. Occasionally, however, enterococci cause much more serious disease, particularly endocarditis, which occurs in drug addicts and in the elderly.

The **nonenterococcal** species most commonly causing human disease is S. bovis. This organism does not grow in high salt concentrations, and most strains are killed by penicillin. S. bovis inhabits the GI tract. There is a strong association between bacteremia due to this organism and colonic lesions, particularly tumors. Patients with otherwise unexplained S. bovis bacteremia are thoroughly investigated for colonic carcinoma.

Viridans Streptococci

Viridans ("greening") streptococci other than those already mentioned are not further identified in most clinical laboratories, which report them simply as "α- (or γ-) hemolytic Streptococcus spp. (species)" or some such designation. They comprise a number of species inhabiting the normal oropharynx, where they make up 30–60% of the bacterial flora. They are of generally **low virulence**, but are the most common cause of subacute **bacterial endocarditis** affecting abnormal heart valves (see Chapter 62). Part of the reason is surely simple opportunity; they frequently seed the bloodstream during tooth-brushing, chewing, and the like. The ability of viridans species to cause endocarditis has been correlated with the production of sticky **dextrans**, which may facilitate adherence to the platelet-fibrin thrombi that form on damaged valve surfaces. Dextran production is not present in all endocarditis-associated strains, however, and there are undoubtedly other adherence mechanisms.

The viridans streptococci also include the pathogens responsible for one of the most common infectious diseases, which of all the minor infections probably exacts the greatest financial toll on the average person: **dental caries**. The pathogens in question are the *"mutans"* group of streptococci, consisting of S. mutans and several closely related species. These organisms have surface proteins that bind to salivary glycoproteins deposited on teeth (the pellicle). They thrive on dietary sucrose, which they metabolize into sticky glucan polymers both inside the cell and on the surface. This process involves the expression of a number of surface proteins, including glucosyltransferases involved in glucan synthesis. In some strains, these proteins can mediate attachment of the organisms to the pellicle. (An aside: the notion of specific adherence of bacteria as the first step in pathogenesis, encountered repeatedly in this book, was first developed by researchers studying dental caries.) Sticky masses of bacteria build up on the tooth surface to form **plaque**. *S. mutans* is only one of approximately 200 species that have been found in plaque, but in an environment well supplied with sucrose, it can amount to 50% or more of the bacteria present. Cavity formation results when the *S. mutans* (and also lactobacilli) ferment sugars to lactic acid, which demineralizes the tooth enamel. Many bacteria carry out lactic acid fermentation; the unique feature of *S. mutans* and lactobacilli is that they remain metabolically active in a low pH environment, so that the process is perpetuated.

Antibody to several of the adhesive surface proteins has been shown to protect against tooth decay in experimental situations, raising the possibility of a **vaccine against dental caries**. Unfortunately, some of these proteins elicit autoantibodies in experimental animals, including rheumatoid factors and heart-reactive antibodies. Vaccine development will, therefore, depend on the same type of sophisticated molecular dissection that is being used to develop a group A streptococcal vaccine.

Self-assessment Questions

1. What morphological and physiological properties distinguish the genus *Streptococcus*? What are the main groups within this genus?

2. What factors contribute to spread in streptococcal lesions?

3. Discuss the role of M protein in streptococcal pathogenesis.

4. What are the main diseases caused by streptococci? How can they be grouped by: (*a*) symptoms; (*b*) types of streptococci?

5. Discuss the immunological aftermath of suppurative streptococcal infections.

6. What are the problems in the microbiological diagnosis of streptococcal infections?

SUGGESTED READINGS

Cone LA, Woodard DR, Schlievert PM, Tomory GS. Clinical and bacteriologic observations of a toxic shock-like syndrome due to *Streptococcus pyogenes*. N Engl J Med 1987;317:146–149.

Schwartz B, Facklam RR, Breimen RF. Changing epidemiology of group A streptococcal infection in the USA. Lancet 1990;336:1167–1171.

Stollerman GH. Rheumatogenic streptococci and the return of rheumatic fever. Adv Intern Med 1990;35:1–25.

Pneumococcus and Bacterial Pneumonia

13

Gregory A. Storch

The pneumococcus is the most frequent causative agent of acute bacterial pneumonia and one of the classic bacterial pathogens. It yields to antibiotic therapy but remains a serious medical problem, especially in certain risk groups.

The pneumococcus, *Streptococcus pneumoniae*, is a Gram-positive coccus that belongs to the group of α-hemolytic streptococci. Its outstanding characteristic is an ample polysaccharide capsule that shields it from phagocytosis and that is highly antigenic. The capsule is the main virulence factor of the organism, which does not make important exotoxins but causes disease by eliciting a powerful inflammatory reaction.

CASE

Mr. P., a 58-year-old salesman who is a heavy smoker and an alcoholic, noted that he had nasal congestion and a low grade fever. Two days later he abruptly developed a shaking chill, cough, and severe pain on the right side of his chest that got worse with breathing. The cough was productive of rust-colored sputum. When he was seen in the emergency room, he appeared acutely ill and had a temperature of 104° F. His respiratory rate was relatively rapid at 40/minute. His breathing was shallow, with little movement of the right side of the thorax. This pattern of breathing, in which one side of the chest is held immobile by pain, is knows as "splinting."

The laboratory reported that his white blood cell count was 23,000/μl, indicative of leukocytosis (an increase in the number of circulating white blood cells) and with 23% "band" forms, indicative of rapid leukocyte synthesis and mobilization. A chest x-ray revealed consolidation of the right upper lobe (Fig. 13.1). A Gram stain of the sputum showed many neutrophils and lancet-shaped Gram-positive diplococci (Fig. 13.2). Blood was obtained for culture and treatment was begun with penicillin. Both the blood cultures and sputum cultures were positive for the pneumococcus, S. pneumoniae. Two days later, Mr. P. was much improved, and, after 8 more days on penicillin, he recovered completely.

Mr. P.'s case illustrates many of the classical manifestations of pneumococcal pneumonia: abrupt onset of severe symptoms, ill appearance of the patient, rust-colored sputum, homogeneous involvement of an entire lobe of the lung, leukocytosis, and rapid response to penicillin. **Bacteremia**, the presence of bacteria in the bloodstream, can be demonstrated in about 25% of the cases and is indicative of more severe illness. This is a dramatic illness, serious enough to threaten the life of an affected patient who may have been well only a few days earlier. It was one of most important causes of death in the preantibiotic era. Today,

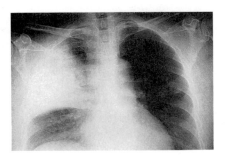

Figure 13.1. Chest x-ray reveals homogeneous consolidation involving the right upper lobe. The air spaces of the lobe have become filled with liquid.

thanks to penicillin and other antibiotics active against the pneumococcus, it is less often fatal. Nevertheless, it remains the most common form of bacterial pneumonia and may still be extremely serious. Even now, about 5% of all patients die from it, with fatality rates much higher in elderly or debilitated patients and those with bacteremia, even when they are treated with an appropriate antibiotic.

Many aspects of pneumococcal pneumonia have been carefully studied and merit attention. Perhaps the central motif is that the pneumococcus appears to cause disease in an existential way. As far as is known, its presence alone elicits an acute inflammation that accounts for the major symptoms. It produces no powerful exotoxins. Certain other respiratory pathogens, especially *Haemophilus influenzae* type b and *Klebsiella pneumoniae*, also have a thick polysaccharide capsule and do not produce exotoxins. However, the pneumococcus differs from these Gram-negative bacteria in that it does not contain endotoxin.

PNEUMOCOCCI

The pneumococcus is classified in the genus *Streptococcus*, based on its morphology and purely fermentative energy metabolism. Like other "aerobic" streptococci, the pneumococcus is anomalous in being able to grow in air, a somewhat unusual feature of strictly fermentative bacteria. The placement of *S. pneumoniae* among the streptococci is supported by the high degree of DNA homology among these organisms.

Pneumococci are Gram positive and commonly grow in pairs (diplococci), but may form short chains. They are surrounded by an ample **polysaccharide capsule** that imparts a mucoid or "smooth" appearance to colonies on agar. You may recall that the ability of an extract from smooth strains to transform "rough," unencapsulated strains to smooth ones led to the discovery that DNA is the carrier of genetic information by Avery, McCarty, and MacLeod in 1944.

When a suspension of killed pneumococci is injected into a rabbit, the most prominent antibodies made are ones directed against the capsular polysaccharide. When early workers tested antipneumococcal antisera against different strains of pneumococci, they found a strong reaction with the strains used to produce the antiserum and only weak or no reaction with many other strains. This allowed them to determine that there are some 84 different **serotypes**, each reacting with its specific typing serum. The basis for these antigenic differences lies in the chemical structure of the capsular polysaccharide of each serotype. Because the capsule prevents phagocytosis, nonencapsulated strains rarely, if ever, cause disease and are rarely found in nature. Antibodies to the capsule play a major role in protection against subsequent infections by pneumococci of the same serotype.

The capsule is not the only pneumococcal component of immunological interest. Also important is the so called **C-substance**, a choline containing teichoic acid that is part of the cell wall. The serum of most people contains a **nonantibody** β-globulin, called **C-reactive protein** because it reacts with the C-substance. When these two components react with one another, the resulting complex activates the complement cascade, leading to the release of inflammatory mediators as well as opsonizing the organisms to enhance phagocytosis. C-reactive protein levels are increased in the sera of patients with many inflammatory diseases, not just pneumococcal infection and,

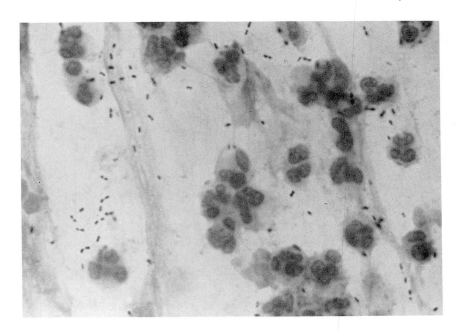

Figure 13.2. Gram stain of sputum revealing many neutrophils and "lancet-shaped" Gram-positive diplococci.

thus, are referred to as **acute phase reactant** (Chapter 7). These characteristics have led to the speculation that C-reactive protein is a primitive, undifferentiated host defense mechanism against infection. The fact that all strains of pneumococci have the same C-substance has led to attempts to use this single component in a vaccine that would elicit protection against all serotypes. Unfortunately, this has not proved successful to date.

ENCOUNTER

Pneumococcal pneumonia is the major form of **bacterial pneumonia** acquired in the community (as opposed to being hospital-acquired, see Chapter 71). It is estimated that there are about 500,000 cases of this disease per year in the U.S. The incidence is higher in certain subgroups, including children younger than 5 years, adults older than 40 years, blacks, and native Americans. The reason for this distribution is not known; but poverty and a debilitated state of health are **risk factors. Certain diseases also predispose** to pneumococcal infections, including sickle cell anemia, Hodgkin's disease, multiple myeloma, HIV infection, and the absence of the spleen for any reason. **Alcoholism** is also an important risk factor. Pneumococcal infections are also distinctly seasonal, with the highest incidence in the winter and early spring. Most cases are sporadic, but outbreaks take place, particularly in residential institutions, army barracks, and work camps, where people are housed under crowded conditions.

The **reservoir** of S. pneumoniae is thought to be humans who harbor the organism, rather than animals or the inanimate environment. **Transmission** occurs directly from person to person. In this light, it might seem surprising that if the physician had asked Mr. P. whether he had been exposed recently to another person with pneumonia, the answer would probably have been no. The reason is that most people who harbor pneumococci experience no symptoms at all.

Colonization by pneumococci typically occurs in the **nasopharynx.** The outcome may be (*a*) clearance of the organisms, (*b*) asymptomatic persistence for several months (the carrier state), or (*c*) progression to

Table 13.1. Likelihood of Colonization with *S. pneumoniae*

Group	Percentage with *S. pneumoniae* Colonization
Preschool children	38–45
Elementary school children	29–35
Junior high school children	9–25
Adults with children at home	18–29
Adults without children at home	6

disease. The outcome of colonization is determined by the intrinsic virulence of the colonizing strain and the efficiency of host defense mechanisms. It turns out that some serotypes of *S. pneumoniae* are more virulent than others. Some cause severe disease, whereas others are commonly isolated from the nasopharynx of asymptomatic persons. The interval between colonization and the onset of disease is variable (and ordinarily undefinable in clinical practice), but there is some evidence that disease is most likely to occur shortly after colonization.

Several aspects of colonization with *S. pneumoniae* have been elucidated by longitudinal studies in which nasopharyngeal cultures were obtained at regular intervals from healthy individuals. Pneumococci were recovered in as many as **two-thirds of normal preschool children**. In general, colonization is less common in adults, although contact with children increases its frequency. The results of one study that illustrates these findings are shown in Table 13.1. One individual may become colonized many times, usually with different serotypes. The extent to which colonization stimulates the immune response is not known. In one study, 50% of colonized children but only a few adults had antibodies to their homologous strain. It has been suggested that secretory IgA antibodies are important in determining whether or not colonization takes place after exposure.

Transmission from a sick person, or more commonly, from an asymptomatic carrier, is via **droplets** of respiratory secretions that remain air-borne over a distance of a few feet. Infecting organisms may also be carried on hands contaminated with secretions. Transmission occurs readily within families and in closed institutions. Because there are many more healthy carriers than sick people, most of the links in the chain of transmission from person to person are invisible. This contrasts with a disease such as measles, which is also transmitted from person to person but where asymptomatic colonization does not take place, so that each link in the chain is evident.

Paradigm: Bacterial Capsule as Defense Against Opsonization and Phagocytosis

The pneumococcus shares the property of possessing an antiphagocytic capsule with a number of other extracellular pathogenic bacteria. Important examples of encapsulated bacteria are *H. influenzae* type b and *Neisseria meningitidis* (the meningococcus), which, together with the pneumococcus, are the most frequent causes of bacterial meningitis. Nonencapsulated pneumococci are readily opsonized and phagocytosed; consequently, they are avirulent. It takes over ten thousand nonencapsulated pneumococci that have been injected into the peritoneal cavity to kill a mouse, but only about ten encapsulated bacteria. This represents a thousand-fold difference in virulence!

Compared with nonencapsulated bacteria, encapsulated pneumococci are not well recognized by the first line of humoral defense in the body, the alternative pathway of the complement system, which would normally serve to opsonize (i.e., make more tasty) the bacterial particles for subsequent phagocytosis. Lacking prior opsonization, the bacteria are virtually ignored by the neutrophils, the host's front line of defense in the bloodstream. Adding to the antidefensive nature of the capsule is the fact that its constituent polysaccharide, which is hydrophilic relative to the surface of the phagocytic cell, is particularly resistant to phagocytosis anyway.

If the capsule provides the pneumococcus with "stealth-like" capability, how is the host ever able to come to grips with this formidable opponent? In the initial encounter, some binding of complement components does occur, so that the bacteria are, at least partially, opsonized. This degree of opsonization is inadequate to potentiate intravascular phagocytosis (or, in the case of the mouse peritoneal model, intraperitoneal phagocytosis), but it is sufficient to permit clearance by the macrophages of the spleen, the body's premier particle filter. This assumes, of course, that the quantity of bacteria in the circulation is not too great, as sometimes occurs in severe, neglected pneumococcal pneumonia. Individuals who do not have a spleen for any cause (congenital, sickle cell anemia, post-traumatic or therapeutic splenectomy, and others), are at grave risk of succumbing to overwhelming sepsis with these encapsulated bacteria, even with a small initial inoculum. For this reason many asplenic patients are treated with life-long, low-dose penicillin to abort any incipient pneumococcal bacteremia.

Once the initial encounter with an encapsulated bacterium has been successfully turned back, the host, within several weeks, develops anticapsular antibodies that are protective against future encounters with that strain. Anticapsular antibodies are more efficient than the alternative complement pathway at opsonizing encapsulated bacteria. Even asplenic patients who have anticapsular antibodies are relatively well protected against bacteremia with that strain. For this reason, it makes particularly good sense to immunize these patients with pneumococcal vaccine, which contains a mixture of the most common serotypes of pneumococcal capsule.

ENTRY

Most of the time, infections of the lung are **prevented** by elaborate mechanisms, including the tortuous pathway that air and inhaled particles must follow to reach the lungs, the epiglottis that protects the airway from aspiration, the cough reflex, the presence of a layer of sticky mucus that is continuously swept upward by the cilia of the respiratory epithelium, and alveolar macrophages. These mechanisms are ordinarily highly effective in preventing progression from colonization to infection. However, a number of factors can interfere with them, including loss of consciousness, cigarette smoking, alcohol consumption, viral infections, or excess fluid in the lungs.

How do these considerations relate to the case of Mr. P.? The source of the infecting organisms was certainly another individual who may have been entirely healthy. It is possible that Mr. P. had the misfortune to acquire one of the more virulent pneumococcal serotypes. His smoking and alcohol consumption may have depressed his defense mechanisms by weakening his cough reflex and decreasing the activity of alveolar macrophages.

SPREAD, MULTIPLICATION, AND DAMAGE

Pneumococci have a particular **predilection for the human respiratory tract**, but we do not know the reasons for this marked tropism. Besides the **lung**, they are also a major cause of infection at **other sites in the respiratory tract**, including the paranasal sinuses and the middle ear. In addition, they are one of the three most common causes of bacterial meningitis, along with *H. influenzae* type b and the meningococcus. Finally, pneumococci may cause infection at other sites, such as the heart valves, the conjunctivae, the joints, or the peritoneal cavity.

Much of what is known now about the pathogenesis of pneumococcal pneumonia derives from studies carried out in the 1940s by W. Barry Wood and his colleagues. They produced pneumonia by injecting pneumococci suspended in mucin into the bronchi of anesthetized mice. Animals were sacrificed at various times and histological sections of the lungs were examined. Four zones of the pneumonic process were identified (Fig. 13.3). In the original study, all four zones were found simultaneously in different regions of the lung, with the first one located at the expanding edge of the involved area. Thus, it makes sense to think that the four zones correspond to **four stages of the inflammatory process**.

In the **first stage**, the lung alveoli become filled with serous fluid containing many organisms but few inflammatory cells. In some unknown manner, pneumococci in the alveoli stimulate the outpouring of fluid, which serves as a culture medium for the rapid multiplication of the organisms. The alveolar fluid also provides a rapid means of spread of the infection, both into adjacent alveoli through the pores of Kohn and to nearby areas of the lung via the bronchioles. Note that the outpouring of fluid could have less severe consequences in many other organs. In the lungs, it represents a threat to the basic function of that organ, namely gas exchange.

In the **second stage, early consolidation**, the alveoli are infiltrated by neutrophils and red blood cells. Strong **chemotactic signals**, produced by the pneumococci and by the alternative pathway of **complement**, lead to the recruitment of large numbers of neutrophils. The stage is now set for the classic struggle between bacteria and phagocytes. On the one hand, pneumococci resist being taken up by virtue of their capsule; on the other hand, if they are ingested by the neutrophils, they are rapidly killed. Clearly, the extent of successful phagocy-

Figure 13.3. Four zones or stages of lung involvement in pneumococcal pneumonia. Pneumonia was induced in rats by intrabronchial installation of live pneumococci suspended in mucin. **A.** Alveoli filled with clear exudate (×430, original magnification). **B.** Early consolidation. Organisms are plentiful, some engulfed by neutrophils (×430, original magnification). **C.** Late consolidation. A closely packed cellular infiltrate is present and phagocytosis of organisms has occurred (×530, original magnification). **D.** Resolution found at center of lesion. Macrophages are present, and the exudate is beginning to clear (×430, original magnification).

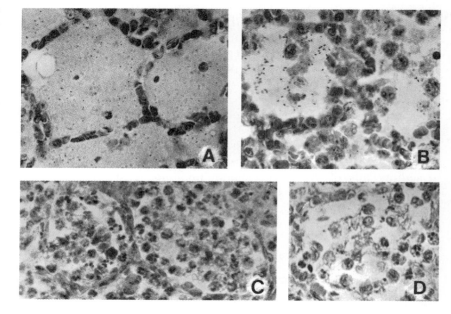

tosis determines the outcome of the infection. Fortunately, there are mechanisms that make even the heavily encapsulated pneumococci more "digestible" to the neutrophils. If the patient has had previous contact with pneumococci of the invading serotype, he or she will have developed type-specific antibodies that interact with complement to **opsonize** the organisms and facilitate their uptake. If the individual lacks specific immunity, the organisms may be opsonized by complement components, activated by the alternative pathway, and possibly, by the interaction of pneumococcal C-substance with C-reactive protein of the serum. Binding of complement components differs among pneumococcal serotypes, which may explain, in part, why some are more virulent than others.

In the case of our patient, Mr. P., neutrophils failed to contain the pneumococci early on, and the infection progressed to adjacent areas until a whole lobe of his left lung became involved. What accounted for his fever and ill appearance? We do not really know, because while the lung involvement was serious the resulting impairment of gas exchange cannot really explain why the patient is so sick in this disease. It is likely that the systemic manifestations are due either directly to pneumococcal components in the circulation, or to products of the inflammatory response induced by the bacteria.

The **third stage** of pneumococcal pneumonia is called **late consolidation**. Here, the alveoli are packed with victorious neutrophils and only a few remaining pneumococci. On a gross level, the affected areas of the lungs are heavy and resemble the liver in appearance, a state that early pathologists called **hepatization**. In the **fourth and final stage, resolution**, neutrophils are replaced by scavenging macrophages, which clear the debris resulting from the inflammatory process. One of the remarkable aspects of pneumococcal pneumonia is that, in most cases, the architecture of the lung is eventually restored to its normal condition. This is very different from what takes place in many other forms of pneumonia, where recovery is accompanied by necrosis, with normal lung tissue being replaced by fibrous scar tissue during recovery.

Pneumococcal pneumonia may lead to both local and distant complications. The most common local complication is pleural effusion, the outpouring of fluid in the pleura, present in about one-quarter of all cases. Usually, the pleural fluid is a sterile exudate, stimulated by the adjacent inflammation. However, in about 1% of cases, pneumococci can be isolated from this site. Infection of the pleural space is called **empyema**, a condition that must be treated by drainage of the infected fluid and administration of appropriate antibiotics.

Distant complications of pneumococcal pneumonia result from spread of the organisms **via the bloodstream**. In the early stages of pneumonia, the organisms may enter the lymphatics draining the infected area of the lungs, pass into the thoracic duct, and from there into the bloodstream. Pneumococcemia can be documented by positive blood cultures in about 25% of the cases, but probably occurs much more often, at least transiently. When bacteremia is present, the organisms may cause infection at secondary sites, such as the meninges, heart valves, joints, or peritoneal cavity. Had Mr. P. not responded quickly to penicillin therapy, the physician caring for him would have been on guard for such complications.

Host defenses against pneumococcal bacteremia depend largely on the **reticuloendothelial system** to remove circulating bacteria from the bloodstream. **Humoral factors**, including antibodies, complement, and perhaps, C-reactive protein, assist macrophages in the spleen, liver, and lymph nodes in carrying out their filtering function. The critical role of the **spleen** is demonstrated by the overwhelming bacteremia that sometimes strikes individuals whose spleen has been removed surgically, or whose splenic function is compromised by another disease such as sickle cell anemia. In these people, bacteremia caused by pneumococci or occasionally by other encapsulated bacteria, such as *H. influenzae*, may be so fulminant that death occurs within hours of the first symptoms.

DIAGNOSIS

Pneumococcal pneumonia can often be suspected on **clinical grounds**. Even though the astute physician may be able to make an educated guess, laboratory confirmation is essential. The first step is to do a **Gram stain of a specimen of sputum**. If it contains neutrophils and more than 10 lancet-shaped Gram-positive diplococci per oil immersion field, the diagnosis of pneumococcal pneumonia is likely. In the case of Mr. P., the results of the Gram stain of sputum confirmed the clinical suspicion and justified the use of penicillin as initial therapy.

In Mr. P.'s case, final identification was made by **culturing** the sputum. The culture was performed by streaking the specimen on **blood agar and chocolate agar** (so-called because of its appearance, due to its content of boiled blood). Pneumococcal colonies are surrounded by an area of α-hemolysis, familiar to those who have seen it. Inasmuch as most streptococci normally present in the body are also α-hemolytic, pneumococci must be differentiated by other properties, like their lancet shape and their sensitivity to a compound called **optochin**. Because the pneumococcus is a fastidious organism with exacting growth requirements, it is not always cultured from sputum of patients with pneumococcal pneumonia. Thus, a negative sputum culture does not rule out pneumococcal pneumonia.

Unfortunately, the interpretation of a positive sputum culture is not always straightforward. It may indicate the cause of the patient's pneumonia, but it may also be the result of contamination of the sputum specimen as it passes through the mouth of a colonized individual. This is an instance where a laboratory finding must be interpreted with an eye toward the clinical context. In contrast, **growth of S. pneumoniae from Mr. P.'s blood** could be considered definitive proof of the etiology of the disease. In recent years, there has been interest in the use of specific antisera to detect the capsular antigen directly in sputum, blood, or urine, thus obviating the need for culture. Unfortunately, these techniques tend to be positive in no more than 50% of the cases of pneumococcal pneumonia. To sum this up, laboratory confirmation is not achieved even now in a substantial proportion of cases of pneumococcal pneumonia.

PREVENTION AND TREATMENT

Penicillin revolutionized the treatment of pneumococcal pneumonia. Before its advent, treatment of this disease consisted of the administration of specific immune horse serum. This was associated with complications, especially serum sickness, but it did reduce the mortality rate. The effectiveness of penicillin became evident from its first use in the 1940s, and it rapidly supplanted serum therapy. Other antibiotics, such as erythromycin, are available for patients who are allergic to penicillin.

Despite the dramatic effectiveness of penicillin, the **mortality rate** in pneumococcal pneumonia remains unacceptably high. There are two reasons for this. First, pneumococcal infections sometimes progress very rapidly and patients are already near death when they seek medical attention. Second, some patients are debilitated by other diseases and succumb from the combined effects of the two conditions. Drug resistance is another problem in the therapy of pneumococcal infections. For many years, penicillin resistance was virtually unknown in the pneumococcus. However, in 1977, an outbreak in South Africa was caused by strains with a high level of resistance to penicillin and other antibiotics. This has not yet been a problem in the United States, although an increasing number of isolates have a low or an intermediate level of penicillin resistance. Fortunately, most infections by these strains yield to high levels of the drug. This is not the case in pneumococcal meningitis, where incomplete penetration of penicillin into the central nervous system may make it impossible to achieve therapeutic levels.

What about a **vaccine**? It would be useful, especially for the members of the population who are at risk. Of course, the antigenic diversity of the pneumococcus is a significant barrier to developing a vaccine based on the polysaccharide capsular antigens. Nonetheless, most cases of pneumococcal pneumonia are caused by 12–18 serotypes. Accordingly, a vaccine based on these types was approved for use in 1977. It is recommended for the elderly and those with diseases that predispose to pneumococcal infections. Unfortunately, patients with Hodgkin's disease or multiple myeloma, who are especially at risk, often do not respond to the vaccine in terms of a good antibody response. Likewise, young children, in whom pneumococcal infections are also important, also respond poorly to polysaccharide vaccines in general, including this one (see Chapter 15 for a discussion of vaccination of children against *H. influenzae*). For these reasons, the vaccine has yet to have a dramatic impact on the overall morbidity and mortality caused by this organism. Perhaps when its use becomes more widespread or a more effective vaccine is developed, vaccination may affect the prevalence and severity of pneumococcal infections.

CONCLUSIONS

Pneumococcal pneumonia has evolved from one of the major infectious causes of death to a fairly frequent disease that usually yields to treatment. Certain risk factors can be clearly identified, but it remains obscure why some seemingly healthy people become affected. Pneumococci are frequent colonizers and it is not obvious what makes them cause disease in some individuals but not others.

Pneumococcal pneumonia begins locally as an acute inflammation that involves mainly the alveoli and spreads laterally to adjacent areas. It exemplifies the classical stages of inflammation—exudate formation, influx of neutrophils, and resolution via macrophages. The local pathological manifestations do not explain the high fever and other systemic signs of the disease.

The main virulence factor and principal antigen of pneumococci is a capsular polysaccharide. It has many antigenic varieties that subdivide this species into distinct serotypes. A "polyvalent" vaccine composed of the most common serotypes is currently available.

Self-assessment Questions

1. Discuss the epidemiological features of pneumococcal pneumonia.

2. What properties of pneumococci are thought to be relevant to their pathogenesis? Given that the pneumococcus can be transformed with DNA, what experiment would you suggest that may help elucidate them?

3. Describe the histopathological events in pneumococcal pneumonia.

4. What would be your main concerns in treating an elderly patient with this disease? What about the patient without a spleen?

5. Discuss the complications in the diagnosis of pneumococcal infections of different organs.

SUGGESTED READING

Austrian R. Random gleanings from a life with the pneumococcus. J Infect Dis 1975;131:474–484.

Breimen RF, Spika JS, Navarro JJ, Darby CP. Pneumococcal bacteremia in Charleston Country, South Carolina. Arch Int Med 1990;150:1401–1405.

Rein MF, Gwaltney JM Jr, O'Brien WM, Jennings RH, Mandell GL. Accuracy of Gram's stain in identifying pneumococci in sputum. JAMA 1978;239: 2671–2673.

Sims RV, Steinmann WC, McConville JH, King LR, Zwick WC, Schwartz JS. The clinical effectiveness of pneumococcal vaccine in the elderly. Ann Int Med 1988;108:653–657.

Neisseriae: Gonococcus and Meningococcus

Penelope J. Hitchcock, Edward N. Robinson, Jr. and Zell A. McGee

The Gram-negative cocci, in contrast with the great variety of pathogenic Gram-negative bacilli, comprise only one genus of organisms that frequently cause disease. This genus, *Neisseria*, has two important species that are pathogenic for humans, *N. gonorrhoeae*, the agent of gonorrhea, and *N. meningitidis*, a major cause of septicemia and meningitis. The gonococcus attaches to the mucosal epithelia of the male urethra or female cervix where it elicits a brisk inflammatory response. Ascent of the organism into the female upper reproductive tract results in infection and inflammation of the uterus and fallopian tubes, also called pelvic inflammatory disease (PID). This condition may result in tubal scarring, which can lead to ectopic pregnancy (development of the embryo in the fallopian tube rather than the uterus) or infertility. In men, ascent of the organism into the upper reproductive tract is less frequent, but may cause epididymitis. Certain strains of gonococci can invade the bloodstream and can cause skin lesions or arthritis.

Meningococci are surrounded by a large capsule that endows them with a great ability to withstand defense mechanisms in the circulation and may grow to high numbers in the blood. Meningococci shed large amounts of outer membrane material as membrane blebs that contain lipopolysaccharide (endotoxin). This lipopolysaccharide/endotoxin induces the production and release into the bloodstream of potent biological mediators, such as tumor necrosis factor (TNF), that elicit the systemic signs of meningococcemia, disseminated intravascular coagulation, and shock. Meningococci also have a predilection for entering the central nervous system (CNS) and causing that most dreaded complication, bacterial meningitis.

CASE

Ms. J., an 18-year-old black woman, woke up in the morning to find that her left knee was hot, swollen, and very painful. She could not walk to work and a friend offered her a ride to the clinic. While she was waiting and filling out a questionnaire, she realized that her right hand was stiff and it was hard to hold the pen tightly. She also remembered a burning sensation when she urinated.

A history taken by a medical student revealed that Ms. J. had three male sexual partners during the last month, one of whom was new. Ms. J. had never

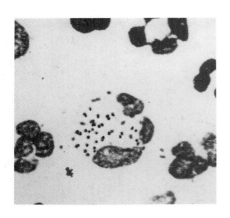

Figure 14.1. Gram stain of urethral pus. Note the neutrophil with gonococci on its surface.

had a swollen joint before; however, she had a history of sexually transmitted diseases, including the "clap" (gonorrhea) and syphilis. Physical examination revealed a tender knee joint which yielded purulent synovial fluid on aspiration. The fluid had 80,000 leukocytes/mm³. She had a cervical discharge that, on Gram staining, showed Gram-negative cocci in association with neutrophils (Fig. 14.1). On culture, the discharge was positive for gonococci, whereas the synovial fluid and blood were negative.

Ms. J. was offered an HIV test, which she declined to take. After a course of treatment with ceftriaxone, a third-generation cephalosporin, she appeared to be free of infection based on the disappearance of symptoms and negative cultures.

We can ask the following questions:

1. From whom did Ms. J. acquire the organisms?

2. What are the chances that the organisms causing the urethral discharge also caused the arthritis?

3. How did the bacteria get to the joints?

4. Would the proper use of condoms have prevented these infections?

5. Did you expect the joint fluid to be culture negative?

6. Is Ms. J.'s risk of becoming HIV-positive altered because of his gonococcal infection?

The gonococcus (*Neisseria gonorrhoeae*) usually causes an uncomplicated, localized cervicitis and urethritis. In addition, it may cause PID and disseminated gonococcal infection (DGI) (Table 14.1). About two million new cases of gonorrhea are reported every year in the U.S. Of the infectious diseases that must legally be reported to the U.S. Public Health Service, gonococcal infections surpass in frequency all other bacterial or viral infections. Note, however, that the more frequent bacterial sexually transmitted disease, chlamydial infection, is not reportable at present. Gonococcal infections and their complications are responsible for $1 billion in annual medical costs in the U.S. alone.

NEISSERIAE

The gonococcus and the meningococcus belong to the genus *Neisseria*, the main group of Gram-negative cocci associated with human disease. This genus includes a number of nonpathogenic members that are often found in the bodies of healthy people, especially in the nasopharynx. One of these, recently renamed *Branhamella catarrhalis*, is emerging as an important cause of upper respiratory tract infections, especially in immunocompromised patients. The neisseriae are aerobes and require complex media but can grow anaerobically. They have typical Gram-negative cell envelopes containing endotoxin. The neisseriae are fragile and do not survive for long outside of their human host. Virtually the only source of infection for Ms. J. is another infected person (and not a toilet seat).

On initial culture from patients, *Neisseria* grows best in an atmosphere with increased CO_2 (typically provided by a "candle jar," which is a canister that uses a burning candle to convert O_2 to CO_2) and on a complex medium containing boiled blood, iron, and vitamins ("chocolate agar").

There are substantial, albeit poorly understood, differences in the pathogenic potential of **different strains** of gonococci. Based on the

Table 14.1. Gonococcal Infections: Sites and Types

A. Lower tract infections
1. Cervicitis
2. Urethritis (male and female)
3. Abscess formation in glands adjacent to the vagina, e.g., Skene's duct or Bartholin's glands

B. Upper tract infections
1. Endometritis (uterine infection)
2. Epididymitis
3. Pelvic inflammatory disease (PID) (infection of the fallopian tube [salpingitis], the ovary, or adnexal tissues)

C. Other (nonreproductive tract) localized sites
1. Proctitis (rectal gonorrhea)
2. Pharyngitis
3. Ophthalmia neonatorum (bilateral conjunctivitis in infants born of mothers infected with gonococci)
4. Extension of the infection to areas contiguous with the pelvis causing peritonitis or perihepatitis (Fitz-Hugh and Curtis syndrome)

D. Disseminated gonococcal infection (DGI)
1. Dermatitis-arthritis-tenosynovitis syndrome: fever, polyarthritis, and tenosynovitis (infection or inflammation of joints and/or tendon sheaths) together with dermatitis (vesicles or pustules on a hemorrhagic base) caused either by immune complexes or by whole gonococci
2. Monoarticular septic arthritis (one infected joint)
3. Rarely, endocarditis (infection involves heart valves) or meningitis (infection of the central nervous system)

characteristics of the bacterial outer membrane, a given strain may have a propensity to cause uncomplicated cervicitis or urethritis, or complicated conditions, PID, or DGI. Host factors (e.g., complement function) are thought to be important in the severity and clinical presentation of the disease. Likewise, different strains of meningococci vary in their pathogenic potential, which is associated with the presence or absence of certain outer membrane proteins.

ENCOUNTER AND ENTRY

Gonococci are obligate human pathogens. They do not spontaneously infect other animals, nor will they cause disease in any convenient experimental animal; nor do they reside free in the environment. It follows that humans must serve as the reservoir for these organisms. Both men and women may carry gonococci without demonstrating symptoms but the prevalence of asymptomatic carriers is greater among women. Asymptomatic carriers of either sex represent a major problem in the control of gonorrhea because, if not symptomatic, they are unlikely to be diagnosed or to receive treatment. Note that in conjunction with its insidious disease profile, the gonococcus has evolved to maximize its transmissibility. For this reason, it is important to culture and to treat the known contacts of a patient with this disease.

Once gonococci are introduced into the vagina or the urethral mucosa of either gender, they seek columnar epithelial cells of the distal urethra or cervix where they attach to the surface of the cells and multiply. Several surface structures of the organisms allow them to anchor to the urethral or vaginal epithelial cells. Gonococci possess pili (Fig. 14.2) and other surface proteins that are presumed to mediate attachment to host cells. Both pili and the surface proteins are regulated by sophisticated genetic mechanisms that enable the bacteria to control the presence or absence of these components (a phenomenon called **phase variation**, see "Paradigm" below) or to control their com-

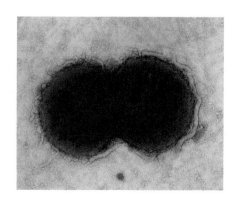

Figure 14.2. Transmission electron micrograph of *Neisseria gonorrhoeae*. Note the presence of pili, long thin strands of protein, emanating from the surface of the organisms.

position (**antigenic variation**). Pili and surface proteins are immunodominant, that is, they are "seen" by the immune system, but their changeability makes them ineffective targets. It is not surprising that antibodies to these components are not protective against gonococcal infection.

Gonococci may or may not be taken up by neutrophils, depending upon the type of outer membrane proteins they possess—some of the outer membrane proteins are called colony opacity-associated proteins or "Opa proteins." Organisms that lack these proteins are not engulfed by neutrophils. Gonococci lacking these Opa proteins are commonly associated with PID, DGI, and arthritis.

Paradigm: Immunological Consequences of Antigenic and Phase Variations

Being human parasites of long standing, gonococci are a paradigm of organisms that have evolved a sophisticated relationship with their host. They have managed to avoid, subvert, or ignore the immunodominant host response. The strategies that gonococci have evolved include:

- Antigenic variation—qualitative surface changes;

- Phase variation—turning on or off surface components;

- Production of IgA1 protease, an enzyme that inactivates the major type of antibody produced at mucosal surfaces;

- Occupation of intracellular environments—to avoid killing by serum and white blood cells.

The development of protective immunity is also complicated by the presence of other infections. Coinfection with more than one STD pathogen will alter natural barriers in the environment of the reproductive tract, and may lower the infectious dose of the next pathogen.

In the quest for a gonococcal vaccine, a great deal of effort has been devoted to understanding the molecular mechanisms of gonococcal phase and antigenic variation. At least three outer membrane molecules undergo phase variation, antigenic variation, or both—pili, opacity-related proteins (Opa proteins), and lipopolysaccharide (LPS) (endotoxin). The gonococcus is not alone in this capability. A number of other bacteria perform the same sleight of hand, as do viruses (e.g., influenza virus) and protozoa (e.g., trypanosomes). Examples of other bacteria capable of antigenic changes include *Salmonella typhimurium* and *Borrelia recurrentis*. The species name of the latter organism reminds us of the recurrent nature of the fever it causes, where each bout of fever is due to the emergence of a new antigenic type, and defeverescence (decreased fever) is associated with production of antibodies against the new antigenic type.

We know several ways by which genetic rearrangements produce changes in the antigenic structure of a bacterial surface molecule. The two best studied mechanisms are called **phase variation**, which consists of turning the synthesis of an antigenic component on or off, and **antigenic variation**, where a particular antigen is synthesized from among a large repertoire of antigenic types.

Phase variation is best illustrated with *Salmonella*, which relies on a molecular mechanism that is quite distinct from that at work in the gonococcus. In *Salmonella*, there are two different flagella types that a given strain can make, but only one of them is ever expressed at a given time. The genetic basis for going back and forth between the two types, A and B, depends upon a switching mechanism on the DNA and an elegant coupling of their expression. The region of the DNA where the switching occurs is a stretch of about 1000 base pairs that contains the transcriptional promoter for the A type. A specialized recombination enzyme can **flip-flop** this region by recognizing inverted repeated DNA sequences at both ends (Fig. 14.3). When the DNA is facing one way, the type A promoter is active, but, facing the other way, the promoter points away from the structural gene for the A type that cannot now not be transcribed. You can now see how the gene for type A is turned on and off, but how does the gene for type B get turned off? Why is transcription of the two genes mutually exclusive? The answer is that the two genes are coupled by virtue of the fact that the promoter for A not only transcribes the A gene, but it also transcribes a **repressor** gene for the type B gene! Thus, when type A is turned on, the repressor for type B is made and type B is not synthesized. When the promoter for type A faces the other way, neither it nor the type B repressor are made, thus type B flagella can now be expressed.

Antigenic variation of gonococcal pili results from a different molecular mechanism. In the gonococcal chromosome, there are one or sometimes two copies of complete pilin genes (pilin is the structural protein of pili). In addition, there are at least six to eight silent copies of the gene (silent copies lack upstream regulatory signals). By DNA recombination that depends on the sequence homology of these genes, a silent copy of the gene is moved into the site of the complete copy. The previously silent gene can now use the regulatory signals and can be transcribed into a functional mRNA, which is then translated into an antigenically distinct pilus (Fig. 14.3). Because constant reshuffling and point mutation of these various genetic elements is possible, **the number of pilus antigens that the gonococcus can make is enormous**. It is a more powerful method for antigenic diversity than phase variation. It is also reminiscent of the way antibodies are made in higher life forms.

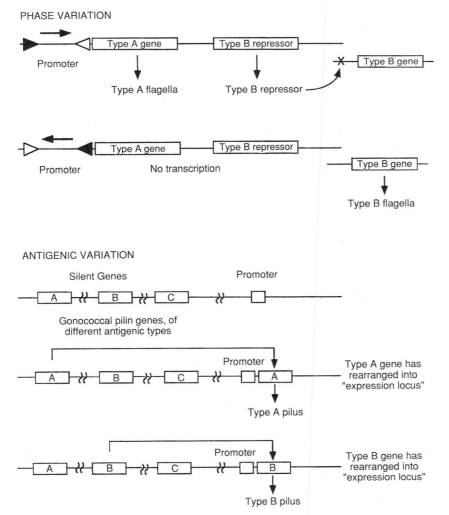

PHASE VARIATION

Type A gene — Type B repressor — Type B gene

Promoter

Type A flagella — Type B repressor — Type B gene

Promoter — No transcription — Type A gene — Type B repressor — Type B gene

Type B flagella

ANTIGENIC VARIATION

Silent Genes — Promoter

A — B — C

Gonococcal pilin genes, of different antigenic types

A — B — C — Promoter — A

Type A gene has rearranged into "expression locus"

Type A pilus

A — B — C — Promoter — B

Type B gene has rearranged into "expression locus"

Type B pilus

Figure 14.3. **Phase variation in *Salmonella* and antigenic variation in the gonococcus.**

SPREAD AND MULTIPLICATION

After colonizing the mucosal cell surface, gonococci multiply rapidly, and are shed in large numbers into the genital secretions of infected men and women. Gonococci do not have flagella and are not motile. How they spread up into the urethra or through the cervix is not known for certain, although they may be aided by urethral or uterine contractions or perhaps by attaching to sperm that serve as convenient transport vehicles.

Mucosal secretions contain two major types of immunoglobulins, IgA1 and IgA2. Gonococci produce an extracellular protease that specifically cleaves IgA1 in the hinge region. This property is shared with some other bacteria that also inhabit mucosal epithelia, such as *Haemophilus influenzae* and certain streptococci. How this protease influences pathogenicity is not known. Speculations include the possibility that it may help the organisms escape phagocytosis by removing the Fc end of the immunoglobulin from gonococcus-bound IgA molecules. Because the Fc region is the portion recognized by phagocytes, the organisms are less prone to be taken up by white blood cells.

What we know about invasion of epithelial cells by gonococci is assumed from studies with in vitro organ culture of human fallopian tubes. Two types of cells comprise the epithelial mucosal surface of human fallopian tubes—ciliated cells and nonciliated cells. The nonciliated cells have finger-like processes, called microvilli, on their luminal surface. When gonococci are incubated with fallopian tube sections, a number of events changes occur:

- **Attachment**—gonococci attach to the nonciliated cells.

- **Ciliary stasis**—motility of the ciliated cells slows and ultimately ceases. Ciliary activity is thought to be important not only in transporting the egg from the ovary to the uterus but, as in the respiratory tree, in providing a flushing mechanism for clearing bacteria from the mucosal surface.

- **Ciliated cells**—they die and are selectively sloughed from the epithelial surface (Fig. 14.4). This step does not require intact organisms and can be elicited by gonococcal LPS or murein fragments (parts of the cell wall).

- **Internalization**—the microvilli of nonciliated cells, acting as pseudopodia, engulf the bacteria. Gonococci are then internalized by these "nonprofessional" phagocytes by a process known as parasite-directed endocytosis.

- **Intracellular replication**—the organisms are transported to the interior of the cell within phagocytic vacuoles. These vacuoles coalesce to form larger vacuoles, within which the gonococci multiply. Inside the nonciliated cells, gonococci are sheltered from antibodies, professional phagocytes, and antibiotics that do not enter human cells well.
Intracellular traffic—the gonococci are transported to the base of the nonciliated cells where the bacteria-laden vacuoles fuse with the basement membrane.

- **Exocytosis**—the phagocytic vacuoles discharge their gonococci into the subepithelial connective tissue. It is from here, we presume, that the organisms either cause local inflammation or they enter blood vessels to cause disseminated disease.

Figure 14.4. Scanning electron micrograph of human fallopian tube tissue 20 hours after infection with *Neisseria gonorrhoeae.* Note that gonococci attach almost exclusively to the surface of nonciliated cells. The damage occurs to the ciliated cells. Ciliated cells sloughed from the surface of the mucosa at the *left* and at the *center*, whereas intact ciliated cells are seen at the *top* and *right* of the photomicrograph.

Survival Of Gonococci In The Bloodstream

Normal human serum has the capability to kill circulating organisms of many Gram-negative species, including *N. gonorrhoeae*. (In contrast, Gram-positive bacteria are resistant to the bactericidal action of serum.) This natural protective effect depends upon complement activation and IgG and IgM antibodies. In the case of the gonococcus, the targets for antibodies are the **lipopolysaccharide (LPS)**, the major outer membrane protein called **protein I**, and other proteins exposed on the surface of the organisms. Thus, for gonococci to survive in the bloodstream, they must be able to evade this defense mechanism.

Strains of gonococci that are usually associated with disseminated infections are serum resistant by virtue of having different surface constituents than their serum-sensitive counterparts. Some serum-resistant gonococcal strains are altered in their LPS by the addition of a **sialic acid** molecule on the short, core carbohydrate chain. Because sialic acid is a surface component of red blood cells, it is believed that this modification camouflages the organisms and protects them from the antibodies responsible for serum killing. Serum-resistant strains are more sensitive to penicillin and have specific nutritional requirements. It is not clear whether these properties have anything directly to do with the ability of the organisms to disseminate, or whether these properties are closely linked genetically.

Host factors also affect the outcome of gonococcal infections. For example, individuals deficient in the terminal components of the complement cascade (the membrane attack complex) are predisposed to recurrent systemic neisserial infections, with both gonococci and meningococci.

The manifestations of disseminated gonococcal infection include **pustular skin lesions** with a surrounding red areola, inflammation of the tendons and joints (**tenosynovitis**), and/or frank infections of the joints (**suppurative arthritis**). More times than not, despite appropriate attempts at cultivation, blood, joint fluid, or skin lesion cultures are sterile. There are several plausible explanations for this phenomenon.

First, gonococci may be present but in numbers too low to be detectable in culture. Second, the nutritional requirements of these organisms may be extraordinary and it may not be possible to isolate them using normal culture conditions. Third, in cases of tenosynovitis, fragments of cell wall murein (murein) or perhaps immune complexes consisting of gonococcal antigens and host antibodies, rather than viable gonococci, may deposit in synovial tissue and cause local inflammation. The latter possibility is supported by experiments in rats that showed that purified gonococcal murein, when injected into joints, induces arthritis. If this were to apply to humans, active joint infection need not be present at the site of intense inflammation.

DAMAGE

Gonococci do not secrete exotoxins, thus, the damage that they produce is most likely caused by LPS and host (endogenous) substances. In addition to death of ciliated cells, demonstrated in the fallopian tube model, nonciliated epithelial cells containing gonococci may lyse, releasing cellular tissue factors that mediate inflammation. The inflammatory response in the male urethra is probably responsible for local symptoms such as pain on urination (dysuria) and a urethral discharge of pus. It is noteworthy that these symptoms do not distinguish gonococcal urethritis from that caused by other genital pathogens, like the chlamydiae (Chapter 26). However, the urethral discharge in gonorrhea tends to be more copious, thick, and greenish yellow, and the reported pain is more intense. Women with gonococcal cervicitis are more often asymptomatic compared with men with urethritis.

OUTCOME OF GONOCOCCAL INFECTION

What is the outcome of gonorrhea? Data from the preantibiotic era suggest that symptoms of urethral infection in males usually subside in several weeks without treatment. However, repeated infections, if untreated, may lead to **scarring and stricture of the urethra**. Such sequelae of gonococcal infection are now relatively unusual, inasmuch as most males seek medical attention once urethritis becomes apparent. Symptoms of **cervicitis** include cervical discharge (reported as vaginal discharge), bleeding, and pain. Paradoxically, local urogenital infections are asymptomatic in approximately 30% of women and, many times, are heralded by the complications of the infection. **Chronic fallopian tube inflammation** can lead to scarring and stricture, resulting in such long-term sequelae as **chronic pelvic pain, ectopic pregnancy, recurrent PIDs** by chlamydiae and other organisms, and **infertility**. For reasons unknown, disseminated gonococcal infections occur predominantly in women. Gonococcal **arthritis** is the most common type of joint infection in sexually active adults.

The outcome of gonococcal infection depends not only on the gender of the patient but also on the timeliness of medical attention. Prompt treatment decreases the risk of ascending or disseminated infection and the resulting sequelae.

MENINGOCOCCAL INFECTION

Gonococci and meningococci are taxonomic cousins; the two organisms share about 80% of their DNA base sequences as measured by DNA hybridization, and both possess similar LPS endotoxins. Both organisms can colonize mucous membranes without causing symptoms.

(It is estimated that, in endemic areas, up to 10% of the population may be meningococcal carriers.) Both gonococci and meningococci can cause purulent infections. Nevertheless, they usually cause a contrasting spectrum of diseases. Gonococci most often produce a localized inflammation; even when the gonococci spread to the bloodstream, the infection is rarely lethal, whereas meningococcal infection of the bloodstream is a systemic and life-threatening disease. Why do these two species cause such different illnesses? It is probably significant that the meningococcus is **heavily encapsulated** and possesses a **hemolysin**, factors that may play a role in the pathogenicity of this organism.

There are occasional epidemics of meningococcal meningitis, but the more usual outcome of exposure to the organism is colonization of the nasopharynx with no local symptoms or systemic consequences. The reason why some people develop disease and others do not is not easy to fathom because, based on organ cultures of nasal epithelium, the mechanism of penetration through mucous membranes appears to be similar for the meningococcus in the nasopharynx and the gonococcus in the fallopian tube. What is known, though, is that patients susceptible to meningococcal meningitis are deficient in **anticapsular antibodies** that are bactericidal to the organism. Individuals with capsule-specific antibodies, presumably produced in response to past colonization, resist the ability of the meningococcus to invade the bloodstream. These observations were instrumental in developing the currently used protective vaccines that are made of purified capsular material.

Once in the bloodstream, the meningococcus multiplies extremely quickly, reaching blood titers that are among the highest known for any bacteria. It is possible, for example, to observe the organisms directly on a smear of the buffy coat, the layer containing the white cells when whole blood is centrifuged, something that is seldom seen with other bacterial septicemias.

The entry of meningococci into the bloodstream can lead to a devastating disease, **purpura fulminans** caused by **DIC** with skin manifestations (**petechiae** and **ecchymoses**), **meningitis**, **shock**, and **death**. DIC is accompanied by shock, fever, and other responses to endotoxin mediated by tumor necrosis factor and interleukin-1. Thus, these systemic signs are the direct consequence of the ability of the meningococcus to survive and multiply in the bloodstream. As mentioned above, meningococcal disease is effectively prevented by vaccination using capsular polysaccharide. The exception of note is disease caused by group B meningococci. In these strains, the capsule of group B strains contains a polymer of sialic acid that is not immunogenic and does not elicit protective antibodies.

By contrast, when gonococci reach the bloodstream of most individuals, they are usually killed by host defense mechanisms. Even the serum resistant strains do not grow appreciably in the circulation, although they may survive long enough to reach other organs. Although gonococcal meningitis and endocarditis have been reported on rare occasion, gonococcal bacteremia is seldom fatal.

DIAGNOSIS

Finding neutrophils containing Gram-negative diplococci in cervical or urethral secretions is generally presumptive evidence of gonococcal infection. It is another very good reason why medical students should learn how to perform and interpret Gram stains. Positive microscopic findings justify beginning antibiotic therapy before the results of cultures are known.

As the social implications of gonorrhea can be as serious as the medical consequences, the physician must confirm the clinical findings by culturing or using genetic probes. It is also important that quality control efforts monitor how the laboratory goes about identifying these organisms. Misidentifying nonpathogenic neisseriae for N. gonorrhoeae can damage personal relationships and lead to law suits. There are three reasons to culture: (a) to be completely certain of the identity of the infecting microorganism, (b) to identify infection in asymptomatic individuals, and (c) to deal with public health and legal ramifications. Another important reason for culture, i.e., to rule out antibiotic resistance, is not presently an issue in these infections because there have been no reports of resistance to the current drug of choice for gonococcal infections, the broad-spectrum antibiotic, ceftriaxone.

Gonococci grow on several kinds of media that allow presumptive identification within a day. The most commonly used medium is called "chocolate agar" because it contains heated blood and has the appearance of milk chocolate. Special varieties of this medium are known by such names as "Thayer-Martin medium" and "Martin-Lewis medium"; each contains different antibiotics to inhibit other bacterial species and yeasts. Specimens taken from the cervix, urethra, and other sites that contain bacteria should always be cultured on chocolate agar with antibiotics (e.g., Thayer-Martin or Martin-Lewis medium) to inhibit the normal flora. It is noteworthy that an occasional strain of gonococci is sensitive to the antibiotics used in the Thayer-Martin medium. It is for this reason that fluids that are normally sterile (e.g., cerebrospinal fluid, blood, synovial fluid) should be cultured on chocolate agar without antibiotics to allow better recovery of these antibiotic-sensitive gonococcal strains.

All members of the genus *Neisseria* and related genera possess an oxidative enzyme that makes the colonies turn purple when flooded with a so-called "oxidase reagent." If a Gram-negative diplococcus is **oxidase positive**, it is a member of *Neisseria* or a close relative. To distinguish *N. gonorrhoeae* from the other species of this genus, the microbiological laboratory determines the pattern of fermentation of various sugars. Unlike other neisseriae, gonococci utilize glucose but not maltose or sucrose and meningococci utilize both glucose and maltose.

TREATMENT

A relatively high proportion of gonococci now bear a plasmid that encodes a β-lactamase, an enzyme that destroys penicillins. Gonococci bearing the resistance plasmids are capable of causing serious locally invasive diseases such as PID as well as disseminated gonococcal infections. As a consequence of this widespread penicillin resistance, the recommended initial therapy of gonorrhea is no longer penicillin, but a β-lactamase-resistant cephalosporin, ceftriaxone.

PREVENTION

Despite effective antimicrobials and active public health measures, over two million cases of gonococcal infections occur annually in the U.S. Prevention efforts must be based on a multipronged approach that includes:

- Early diagnosis and treatment;
- Partner notification;
- Behavioral interventions including condom use and decreasing the number of sexual partners;
- Vaccine development and utilization.

Attempts at vaccine development have been complicated because gonococci, as solely human pathogens, have a long-standing and sophisticated relationship with their host. These organisms have managed to survive the host's immune response, as discussed in the paradigm section. Several of the strategies employed by gonococci are antigenic variation, phase variation, and the occupation of protective intracellular environments. Also, the gonococcus presents some of its most variable antigens (pili, Opa) as immunodominant targets for the host. This provides superb camouflage for the pathogen because these antigens are not protective (i.e., making antibodies against them does not protect the host). For this reason, pili, being highly variable among strains, are not viewed as good vaccine candidates.

CONCLUSIONS

The mode of transmission as well as the biological properties of gonococci combine to give them a unique set of characteristics. Gonococci, by virtue of possessing strong adhesins, are well adapted for their usual portal of entry, the genital tract of humans. They have the ability to traverse epithelial cells and either to cause local inflammation or to disseminate to other parts of the body. Meningococci have an outstanding ability to survive in the bloodstream and to cause systemic infections that often have disastrous consequences.

Gonococci and meningococci are found only in human beings, some of whom act as asymptomatic carriers. In principle, effective vaccines should prevent new infections or control and prevent disease. It is hoped that such vaccines will become available soon.

Self-assessment Questions

1. What are the microbiological distinguishing features of the gonococci? How do they differ from meningococci?

2. Starting with an infected male partner, discuss the events that lead to gonococcal pelvic inflammatory disease.

3. What are three approaches to prevent gonorrhea?

4. Why is it difficult to make an effective vaccine against the gonococcus?

5. Discuss the serious clinical consequences of gonorrhea.

SUGGESTED READING

Britigan BE, Cohen MS, Sparling PF. Gonococcal infection: a model of molecular pathogenesis. N Engl J Med 1985;312:1683–1694.
Faruki H, Kohmescher RN, McKinney WP, Sparling PF. A community-based outbreak of infection with penicillin-resistant *Neisseria gonorrhoeae* not producing penicillinase (chromosomally mediated resistance). N Engl J Med 1985;313:607–611.

Figueroa JE, Densen P. Infectious diseases associated with complement deficiencies. Clin Microbiol Rev 1991;4:359–395.

Gibbs C, Haas R, Meyer TF. Structural and functional modulation of gonococcal surface proteins. Microbiol Pathol 1988;4:393–399.

Holmes KK, et al. Sexually transmitted diseases. New York: McGraw-Hill, 1990.

McGee ZA, Pavia AT. Is the concept, "agents of sexually transmitted disease" still valid? J. Sex Transm Dis 1991;18:69–71.

Stephens DS. Gonococcal and meningococcal pathogenesis as defined by human cell, cell culture, and organ culture assays. Clin Microbiol Rev 1989;2 (Suppl):S104–S111.

Haemophilus influenzae: An Important Cause of Meningitis

15

Arnold L. Smith

Haemophilus influenzae, a nutritionally fastidious small Gram-negative rod, causes pneumonia in persons of all ages and meningitis in young children. The reason for the occurrence of meningitis in young children may be immunological; the principal antigen of this bacterium is a capsular polysaccharide that is processed by a T-cell-independent route, one that is not yet developed in children less than 18 months old. Recent vaccines have made this antigen T-dependent by coupling it to various proteins. These "conjugate vaccines" evoke an antibody response even in newborns.

H. influenzae is not known to produce soluble toxins, but does have endotoxin. It is usually surrounded by a thick carbohydrate capsule, which allows it to escape phagocytosis and travel to the central nervous system.

CASE

M., a 9-month-old baby, awoke from his afternoon nap fussy and slightly irritable. His mother thought he had a low grade fever and gave him some liquids and acetaminophen to reduce his fever. She reported he was fussy throughout the next night, but seemed less feverish in the morning. However, he felt warm around noon, refused lunch, vomited, and could not be consoled. His temperature was 103.2°F and he became difficult to arouse. He was then taken to a pediatrician, who interviewed the mother, examined the infant, and performed a lumbar puncture.

A Gram stain of the cerebrospinal fluid (CSF) showed white cells and many pleomorphic Gram-negative rods (Fig. 15.1). A sample of CSF was mixed on a slide with specific antisera against the serological types of the capsular antigen of H. influenzae. The antisera are absorbed on the surface of latex particles that agglutinate (through lattice formation) in the presence of antigen (Chapter 55). This permitted the immediate diagnosis of meningitis due to H. influenzae *type b*. The diagnosis was later confirmed when the organism grew in culture.

M.'s parents had many questions:

1. What are M.'s chances of recovery?

2. Are there complications of the disease?

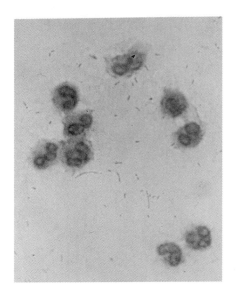

Figure 15.1. Gram stain of *H. influenzae* in purulent CSF.

3. What is the treatment?

4. Could M.'s sister, 3-year-old Ann, acquire the disease?

To answer these questions you should know something about:

1. How is the disease acquired and how do the organisms get into the central nervous system?

2. How does *H. influenzae* cause disease?

3. What complications may arise?

4. What is the epidemiology of this infection?

5. What immune mechanisms might prevent this infection?

6. What treatment and preventive measures are available?

Bacterial meningitis is a serious disease, primarily of infants and children. It may be caused by a variety of organisms (Table 15.1), with *H. influenzae* heading the list. The fatality rate has not changed substantially since the introduction of antibiotics and is currently around 5%. More importantly, meningitis may cause permanent neurological deficits, but early treatment minimizes the duration and severity of the infection and decreases the likelihood of sequelae. Meningitis imposes a diagnostic imperative on the physician and diagnosis must be achieved with great dispatch.

H. influenzae causes infections of the upper and lower respiratory tract in persons of all ages, particularly in those with underlying lung disease. However, meningitis due to these organisms is confined to a narrow age group, usually between 6 and 60 months of age.

INTRODUCTION TO THE AGENT

Haemophilus are small Gram-negative facultative anaerobic rods with complex nutritional requirements. Their name means "blood-loving" and was given because members of the genus need either one or both of two compounds found in blood, the so-called **X and V factors**. X factor is hematin and V factor is NAD or a similar compound. Heating blood to make chocolate agar releases these compounds, as well as other nutrients, which allow *Haemophilus* species to grow. *H. influenzae* requires protoporphyrin IX, iron and any pyridine nucleotide for aerobic growth.

Table 15.1. Etiology of Bacterial Meningitis

Age	Underlying Disease	Bacterial Pathogen	
		Most Common	Other
Birth–2 months	None	Streptococcus agalactiae (group B)	E. coli Listeria monocytogenes
2 months–60 months	None	H. influenzae	N. meningitidis S. pneumoniae
>60 months	None	S. pneumoniae	N. meningitidis[a]
Any age	Cranial surgery	S. aureus	S. epidermidis
Any age	Immunosuppression from cancer chemotherapy	Streptococci	E. coli P. aeruginosa Klebsiellae

[a]Occurs in epidemics.

The most important human pathogen in the genus *Haemophilus* is *H. influenzae*, known colloquially (in English-speaking countries) as "H. flu." It got its species name in a great influenza pandemic of the World War I. It was first thought to cause the disease, and it took over a dozen years to figure out that influenza is caused by the influenza virus and that H. flu is a common secondary invader.

Many strains of these organisms are surrounded by a carbohydrate capsule that is antiphagocytic. The capsular material comes in six antigenic types that can be distinguished readily by their reaction with specific antibodies. Note that the detection of specific capsular antigen permitted a nearly instantaneous diagnosis in M.'s case. His organism was type b, which accounts for nearly all cases of H. flu meningitis. This capsule is made up of polymers of the pentoses **ribose** and **ribitol**, linked through **phosphodiester** bonds. Some other strains of H. flu that cause disease, notably middle ear infections, bronchitis, and pneumonia in adults are nonencapsulated.

Several components of H. flu are thought to be important in facilitating invasive disease. Strains created in the laboratory lacking these components are less virulent in certain animal models. The primary virulence factor appears to be the **capsule**; strains lacking this surface structure are unable to cause bacteremia, even when inoculated intravenously. **Pili, lipopolysaccharide** (LPS, endotoxin), and certain **outer membrane proteins** (such as those facilitating iron acquisition) are necessary for a given strain to be fully virulent. Pili and LPS are subject to antigenic variation and environmental modulation. However, at present, the role these processes play in pathogenesis is not clear.

ENCOUNTER

H. flu is an organism totally adapted to humans and not naturally found elsewhere. It is frequently recovered from the nasopharynx of almost anyone except newborn infants. By 3 months of age, virtually all children carry the organism. However, there is a significant difference between these normal commensal strains and those isolated from patients with meningitis. The usual commensal strains are seldom encapsulated whereas the ones cultured from spinal fluid invariably are. The meaning of these observations is not clear. Are there two totally separate kinds of H. flu? Or may noncapsulated strains become pathogenic by acquiring a capsule via induction of latent capsule genes or genetic change? The first possibility, that H. flu consists of at least two distinct strains, appears more likely because typeable and nonencapsulated H. flu show considerable genetic distance, as judged by differences in the electrophoretic mobility of certain "housekeeping" enzymes.

In experimental studies with infant mice, the introduction of *H. influenzae* type b into the nose is all that was necessary for systemic infection to occur. In the same studies, it was found that the organisms were readily transmitted to other infant animals in close contact. In humans, there is a similar type of secondary transmission that is also age dependent. About 4% of children less than 5 years of age in close contact with an H. flu patient develop the disease. Thus, M.'s sister Ann is at significant risk.

ENTRY, SPREAD, AND MULTIPLICATION

H. flu are deposited on the respiratory epithelium of the upper airway (probably the nose) as small droplets. The organism has several mechanisms for overcoming mucociliary clearance; pili and another surface adhesin attach the bacterium to the nasal mucosa. Replication at that site produces colonization. Most *H. influenzae* appear to have the capacity to **invade** respiratory epithelium. If the invading strain can make a capsule, it will evade phagocytosis and enter the bloodstream through the lymphatics. In the submucosa, both the capsulated and nonencapsulated strains evoke an **inflammatory response**. In the lower respiratory tract (where the epithelium is damaged by air pollutants), this results in **bronchitis**. In the upper respiratory tract, invasion of the nasal mucosa elicits a slight rhinorrhea.

In some children, the bacterium invades the tissues of the larynx: the epiglottis, the arytenoid folds, and posterior wall of the hypopharynx. **Cellulitis** of these structures results in acute inflammation, accompanied by intense edema. This swelling may close the airway and produces death. The disease is called **epiglottitis**, and is invariably due to H. flu type b that has also invaded the bloodstream. Once an airway is established, the infection and inflammation quickly resolve with antibiotic administration.

H. flu **meningitis** results from the invasion of the bloodstream in young infants (Fig. 15.2). The organisms survive in the blood as long as circulating antibodies are not present in effective amounts. The titer of bactericidal antibodies correlates well with immunity. Anticapsular antibodies are strong opsonins and permit the organisms to be taken up and killed by fixed phagocytes.

Figure 15.2. The pathogenesis of *H. influenzae* meningitis.

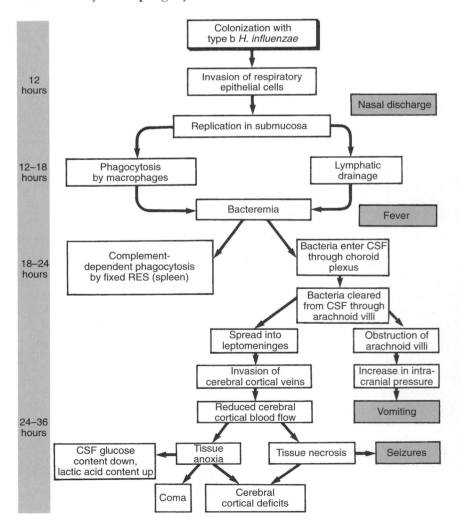

Paradigm: Age-related Antibody Response

We can now attempt to explain the unusual age dependence of H. flu meningitis. In a classic microbiological study, Fothergill and Wright showed in 1933 that, as antibody levels to the organisms fall, disease incidence rises (Fig. 15.3). Children between the ages of 3 and 24 months are naturally deficient in antibodies directed against the type b capsule. Some children do not have these antibodies until they are 5 years old; they remain susceptible to H. flu meningitis until that age. The greater the ability of the blood to kill H. flu, the fewer the cases of the disease.

The change with age has been explained as follows. Children are born with maternal antibodies and are protected as long as these antibodies are present; hence the low incidence of cases before a few months of age. Much later, after the age of 2 years, antibody titers rise and the disease becomes less frequent. The puzzling aspect of the curve is, why don't younger children make antibodies if they are colonized with the organisms earlier in life? The answer is twofold. Early colonization is usually by nonencapsulated strains; thus, the young children may not actually have encountered the capsular antigens. In addition and more puzzling is the fact that immunity against capsular antigen type b does not arise before 2 or 3 years of age. The reason for this immunological unresponsiveness is probably due to the chemical nature of the polyribophosphate antigen. Polysaccharide antigens like this are not processed via T cells but are T-cell independent. The ability to generate this immune response is not yet developed in infants, who rely on T-cell antigen processing (see Chapter 44 for a discussion of immunization strategies in infants).

Age-dependent antibody formation is found with other common respiratory pathogens. Anticapsular antibodies to pneumococci and meningococci are present at birth, passively from the maternal circulation, then decline. "Natural" acquisition with increasing age varies dramatically with each capsular type, even within a species: anti-type III polysaccharide of the pneumococcus regularly appears by 6 months of age, while anti-type XIII is present only in one-half of 36-month-old infants. A similar situation exists with the meningococcus. All three of these capsulated bacteria are common pathogens in infants and children. It is not known what antigen (or antigens) induce this "natural" immunity. Many commensal bacteria, and even certain foods, have epitopes that are cross-reactive with anti-type b capsule antibodies.

An important fact to remember is that anticapsular antibodies protect against H. flu b disease by opsonization, with tissue macrophages clearing the bacteria from the bloodstream. In older children or young adults who lack a spleen, the susceptibility to sepsis due to H. flu (and the pneumococcus) persists. Thus, these individuals are at risk even if they are likely to have anticapsular antibody.

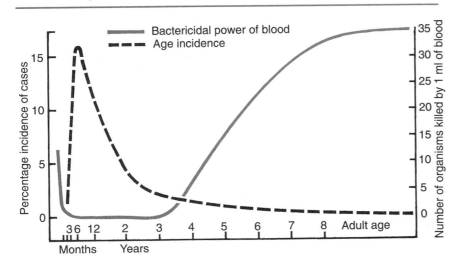

Figure 15.3. Relation of age to the incidence of *H. influenzae* meningitis and the bactericidal titers in blood of the population.

Once in the blood, how do the organisms reach the meninges? From studies with laboratory animals, we know that the route of delivery is the cerebral arteries. The very first histological lesion in the brain is an acute inflammation of the choroid plexi. Note that this is the most logical site to cross the blood-brain barrier since it is the site of manufacture of the CSF and is highly vascularized. However, other organisms that cause bacteremias do not have such marked tropism for the meninges. The marked predilection of H. flu for these tissues has not been explained.

Local damage in the plexal capillaries allows H. flu to enter the CSF. Since the choroid plexi are located in the lateral cerebral ventricles, the organisms enter this compartment first and are then carried into the cisterna magna and over the convexities of the brain. The CSF becomes enriched with inflammatory exudate and is a good place for H. flu to multiply. Blockage of CSF outflow through the arachnoid villi by the inflammation causes the intracranial pressure to increase. This produces the early symptoms of meningitis—vomiting, lethargy, depressed cortical function. It accounts for the rapidity of the symptoms in the disease, as seen in M.'s case.

DAMAGE

H. flu makes no known exotoxins. Its endotoxin is probably responsible for fever, intravascular coagulation, and, perhaps, other systemic manifestations. H. flu causes damage by evoking an inflammatory response. Phagocytosis results in bacterial degradation that releases endotoxin and possibly other compounds with a direct effect on tissues. In addition, the organism makes an extracellular protease that is specific for human secretory immunoglobulin, IgA. H. flu shares this property with other bacteria that inhabit mucous membranes, such as the gonococci and certain streptococci (see Chapters 8 and 14). The role of this protease can only be surmised at present, but it may work to inhibit phagocytosis by removing the Fc fragments (which are pointing away from the organisms but are recognized by receptors on phagocytic cells).

Cerebral cortical dysfunction occurs via impairment of both the circulation and of the flow of CSF. The meninges support part of the vasculature of the brain; cerebral arteries and veins run through this connective tissue to nourish the outer gray matter. Inflammation of the meninges may extend through the wall of the cerebral veins, which then become partially or completely thrombosed. Decreased blood flow leads to various forms of cerebral dysfunction, depending on the site of the cortex that is affected. Inflammation around the arachnoid villi in the dura mater blocks the flow of CSF. Pressure in the subarachnoid space then increases, leading to a rise in intracranial pressure.

This picture is similar in meningitis caused by the meningococcus and the pneumococcus. However, the consequences are different. Meningococcal meningitis, adequately treated, usually resolves without sequelae and patients commonly recover without any further signs. H. flu meningitis, on the other hand, leads to further neurological damage in about one of ten infants, even with optimal therapy. This damage includes blindness, deafness, or obstructive hydrocephalus. Mental retardation is also common, manifested primarily in poor reading and language skills. One explanation for this difference is the magnitude of the inflammation of the subarachnoid space. It is least with meningococci, moderate with H. flu, and intense with pneumococci.

About one-third of the survivors of pneumococcal meningitis have severe neurological sequelae.

DIAGNOSIS

In the case of M., we have already seen how examination of the CSF can yield rapid and accurate diagnosis. When the number of bacteria present is small, direct microscopic examination may not be revealing, and cultures must be performed. *Haemophilus* colonies are small but appear within 24 hours on chocolate agar. Three of the common meningeal pathogens can be differentiated in the bacteriological laboratory using the information in Table 15.2.

Other tests on the CSF seek to document the extent of the inflammation and its effects on brain metabolism. These tests include counting the number and type of leukocytes and determining the protein and glucose content. Inflamed capillaries leak proteins into the CSF, increasing the concentration. Decreased glucose content in the CSF is indicative of meningitis because of the decrease in cerebrocortical blood flow. Under conditions of partial anoxia, glucose is predominantly metabolized via anaerobic glycolysis. Since this is an inefficient mode of energy production relative to respiration, more glucose must be utilized than is delivered to the brain. Thus, the CSF glucose concentration falls. As the glucose concentration decreases, the concentration of lactic acid increases, lowering the pH and leading to other metabolic consequences.

TREATMENT AND PREVENTION

For antibacterial agents to be effective in bacterial meningitis, they must be able to enter the CSF and be bactericidal. The reason why bacteriostatic drugs usually do not do well is that the infection takes place in a virtually closed system. Here, even nongrowing bacteria may cause significant damage. Several classes of antibiotics are bactericidal for *H. influenzae*—semisynthetic penicillins, cephalosporins, chloramphenicol, and even aminoglycosides; this is not a hardy organism. The choice of antibiotic depends on the susceptibility of the *H. influenzae* b, and its potential to penetrate into the CSF when standard doses are administered intravenously. In 1991, one-third of all H. flu isolated in the U.S. from the CSF produced β-lactamase, whereas less than 2% produced chloramphenicol acetyltransferase. Most physicians administer a third-generation cephalosporin (e.g., ceftriaxone or cefotaxime) as these agents are not hydrolyzed by the H. flu β-lactamase and reach CSF concentrations that greatly exceed the minimum required for bactericidal activity. Chloramphenicol is administered in some hospitals, but serum concentrations and the blood cells must be monitored for toxicity. Recent clinical trials indicate that short courses of corticoste-

Table 15.2. Bacteriological Identification of Common Meningeal Pathogens

Organism	Commonly Used Media (Agar)	Colonial Morphology	Gram Stain Morphology, Reaction/Cell Shape
H. influenzae	Chocolate	Iridescent gray, smooth	Negative, pleomorphic
S. pneumoniae	Blood, chocolate	Gray-white, smooth mucoid	Positive, lancet shaped
N. meningitidis	Chocolate	Small, bluish gray	Negative, diplococci

roids administered along with antibiotics early in the disease may be beneficial in reducing the incidence of sequelae of meningitis. It is presumed that steroids exert this effect by decreasing the inflammatory response to infection in the brain.

A **vaccine** against H. flu is very much needed. The greatest preventive challenge with this organism is to protect the children who are at highest risk of getting meningitis from this organism. Note, however, the paradox—the children who are in greatest danger belong to an age group that is immunologically unresponsive to type b capsular antigen. The H. flu b capsule, a large polymer of ribose, ribitol, and phosphate, has been covalently coupled to a variety of protein toxoids commonly administered to young children (Table 15.3). In one instance, a haptenic fragment of the polysaccharide has been coupled to a mutated diphtheria toxin; the same effect as linking it with a toxoid. Two preparations of these conjugate vaccines are protective in young infants in recent studies. These vaccines are likely to markedly decrease the incidence of H. flu meningitis.

The antibiotic rifampin can be used as a **chemoprophylactic** for children who have been in contact with patients. Ann, the sister of the sick infant, could well benefit from the administration of this drug. However, this type of prevention should be used in a limited way because of adverse side effects and the rapid emergence of drug resistance among the organisms.

CONCLUSION

H. influenzae is a typical human pathogen that causes respiratory infections as well as a serious form of acute meningitis. This disease seeks out individuals who do not have anticapsular antibodies in their blood; namely, young children who are immunologically unresponsive to the principal virulence factor, the capsular carbohydrate.

These organisms cause damage mainly by eliciting an inflammatory response. When this takes place in the meninges, the consequence is a very severe disease. In an unacceptably large proportion of children,

Table 15.3. Characteristics of *H. influenzae* B Conjugate Vaccines

Vaccine[a]	Polysaccharide	Carrier Protein	Target Population	
			Immunogenic	Protective
PRP-T	Native	Tetanus toxoid	+	?
Oligo-CRM	20 sugar oligosaccharide	CRM[197] hapten	+	+
PRP-D	Selected by size	Diphtheria toxoid	±	−
PRP-OMP	Native	Outer membrane proteins of meningococcus	+	+

Advantages of Conjugate Vaccines over PRP[a] Alone Vaccine

Conjugate vaccines (compared to PRP alone vaccine):
  Induce protective antibody in infants 3 months of age and older
  Promote T-cell-dependent antibody response
  Produce higher levels of antibody
  Lead to higher proportion of IgM antibodies
  Can respond to a booster dose of vaccine
  Are effective in preventing serious *H. influenzae* type b disease in infants and
    children as young as 3 months of age

[a]PRP, polyribophosphate; T, tetanus toxoid; CRM197, a missense mutation in diphtheria toxin yielding a nontoxic but immunogenic molecule; D, diphtheria toxoid; OMP, a preparation containing several outer membrane proteins from the group B meningococcus.

this leads to mental retardation. Among the outstanding problems in the understanding and control of these organisms are:

1. How are the pathogenic varieties acquired?

2. Why do they have a marked tropism for the meninges?

3. How do they elicit a strong inflammation?

Self-assessment Questions

1. What are the microbiological characteristics of *H. influenzae*?

2. Explain the age distribution of *H. influenzae* meningitis.

3. What problems are in the way of making an effective vaccine against this disease?

4. What virulence factors of *H. influenzae* can you name?

5. How do you suppose *H. influenzae* enters the CNS?

6. Contrast meningitis caused by *H. influenzae* to that caused by meningococci.

SUGGESTED READING

Sell SH, Wright PF, eds. *Haemophilus influenzae*—epidemiology, immunology and prevention of disease. New York: Elsevier, 1982.

Sande MA, Smith AL, Root RK. Bacterial meningitis. New York: Churchill Livingstone, 1985.

Bacteroides and Abscesses

16

Francis P. Tally

Spillage of microbe-laden materials, such as the contents of the intestine or of the oropharynx, into deep tissues often results in infections due to a mixture of bacteria. Examples are peritonitis caused by a ruptured appendix, or a pulmonary abscess due to aspiration of oropharyngeal bacteria. From such sites it is usually possible to isolate many different combinations of infecting bacteria. These infections represent the opposite pole from the "one germ—one disease" concept; that is, they are polymicrobial rather than monomicrobial.

The bacteria involved include strict anaerobes and facultative anaerobes (such as Enterobacteriaceae), probably interacting in complex metabolic ways. This chapter will focus on one of the most frequently involved genera, the *Bacteroides*. These strictly anaerobic Gram-negative rods are common members of the normal oral and gut flora. However, the main pathogen of the genus, *B. fragilis*, has special pathogenic attributes. One of these properties is probably its antiphagocytic capsule, but others still remain to be elucidated.

HISTORICAL VIGNETTE

The famous magician Houdini died of peritonitis. Houdini was known for his astounding feats of escape while enchained and enclosed in containers submerged in water. He possessed amazing physical strength, and, as a point of outside interest, could control many muscles, including, it is said, some that are normally not under voluntary control. His fame was the cause of his demise. Houdini received an unexpected blow to his abdomen from a bystander intent on testing his legendary muscular powers. This resulted in the rupture of the magician's large intestine and his death a few days later.

Had Houdini lived today and been in the hands of a competent physician who would have treated him with antibiotics, he would have had a good chance of surviving. Let us contrast what happened to Houdini to a more recent case of a related problem, a perforated appendix.

CASE

Ms. A., an 18-year-old college freshman, was admitted to the hospital with diffuse abdominal pain, diarrhea, and nausea without vomiting. Her pain was localized to the right side of the abdomen. Physical examination revealed tenderness in the lower quadrant of her abdomen, principally over McBurney's point. She was given a cephalosporin antibiotic and taken to the operating room where her ruptured appendix was removed. Cultures of the peritoneal cavity in the neighborhood of the appendix grew a mixture of bacteria, typical of those found in stool. On the second day after the operation, her temperature spiked to 38.6°C. Blood cultures obtained preoperatively grew E. coli.

Ms. A. improved postoperatively and completed a 7-day course of the cephalosporin. Because she had no further symptoms and her blood cultures were negative, the antibiotic was stopped. However, 36 hours later, her temperature was 38.8°C and she felt diffuse pain over the site of the appendectomy. A CAT scan of her abdomen revealed a retroperitoneal abscess. Cultures obtained after drainage of the abscess grew B. fragilis. *She was again treated with antibiotics (this time a mixture of gentamicin and clindamycin to cover, respectively, the Gram-negative aerobes and the anaerobes) for 8 more days and had an uneventful recovery.*

Several questions are raised by Ms. A.'s case:

1. How did the two episodes of her disease differ with regard to pathogenesis and to the kind of bacteria involved?

2. How did anaerobic bacteria survive in oxygenated tissue? Why did they survive the first course of antibiotic treatment?

3. How do the organisms involved, specifically *B. fragilis*, cause damage?

4. Was Ms. A. treated properly?

No other place in the body is more prone to becoming contaminated by a large number of endogenous bacteria than the peritoneal cavity. The resulting intra-abdominal sepsis illustrates dramatically what happens when microorganisms are introduced in large numbers into the wrong place. The spillage of a few milliliters of intestinal content in the peritoneal cavity delivers many billions of bacteria to a customarily sterile site. Left untreated, peritonitis is often fatal, as in the case of Houdini. Indeed, in the preantibiotic era, perforation of the colon was a medical catastrophe. Nowadays the mortality rate is lower but still significant, between 1% and 5%, and the diagnosis and management of these cases is far from simple. The physician who is not aware of the proper choice of antibiotics and the need for supportive therapy may well lose a patient to this disease.

Two points should be emphasized. In the first place, intra-abdominal infections typically result in **biphasic diseases**, as in the case of Ms. A. They start with an acute inflammation and progress to the formation of localized abscesses. Second, of the hundreds of species contained in the colonic inoculum, a few are most commonly isolated from abscesses. *B. fragilis* is found in the majority of cases and is the single most important of the anaerobic bacteria associated with abscess formation. It is seldom found alone and is typically co-cultured with a variety of other bacteria.

The largest number of intra-abdominal infections are caused by the rupture of infected appendices or intestinal diverticula, the abnormal outpouchings of the colon. In the U.S., it has been estimated that there are over 250,000 cases of appendicitis and some 350,000 cases of diverticulitis. Of these infections, about 15% perforate and result in peritonitis and many produce abscesses as a late complication. The prevalence of diverticula increases with aging and so does diverticulitis as the cause of intra-abdominal infection.

INTRODUCTION TO THE *BACTEROIDES* AND OTHER STRICTLY ANAEROBIC BACTERIA

Bacteroides are obligate anaerobic, Gram-negative rods, present in large amounts in the large intestine of humans and other vertebrates. They number 10^{11} or more per gram of feces, and are the dominant organisms along with anaerobic streptococci. The *Bacteroides* group comprises many species (Table 16.1), of which *B. fragilis* and *B. thetaiotamicron* are the most prominent pathogens. Among *Bacteroides*, *B. fragilis* is a minor component, usually present in concentrations of 10^8 or 10^9 per gram of feces. The reasons why this species becomes dominant in deep tissue infections will be discussed below. Other members of the genus that are implicated in human infections include *B. melaninogenicus*, so called because it produces black-pigmented colonies on blood-containing agar. This organism is often found in the oral cavity as a member of the gingival flora and has been implicated in periodontal disease. Although this organism is also found in other sites, it is most commonly associated with infections of oral origin, including aspiration pneumonia (Chapter 56) and rather serious infections following human bites. Other *Bacteroides* are associated with infections of the peritoneal cavity that originate from the vagina. Table 16.1 includes the major strictly anaerobic bacteria of clinical significance, except the clostridia, which are described in Chapter 21.

Bacteroides are not killed by short exposure to oxygen, although they clearly do not grow in its presence. *B. fragilis* is among the most oxygen-resistant members of the genus. This is because it contains **superoxide dismutase**, which detoxifies oxygen radicals, and catalase, which breaks down hydrogen peroxide. The *Bacteroides* obtain energy by fermentation of carbohydrates. They can use complex polysaccharides such as the mucins present in the colon, which may be why they are present in such large numbers in feces.

The outer membrane of *B. fragilis* contains a **lipopolysaccharide** different from that of the typical endotoxins of the Enterobacteriaceae in that it is not toxic. This characteristic is not typical of this group of organisms. For example, the lipopolysaccharide of *Fusobacterium necrophorum*, another common oral Gram-negative strict anaerobe, is distinctly endotoxic. An outer polysaccharide **capsule** protects *B. fragilis* from phagocytosis and is involved in some unknown manner in attachment to mesothelial cells and in abscess formation. These organisms produce many periplasmic enzymes, such as **lipases,**

Table 16.1. Major Clinically Significant Nonspore-forming Anaerobic Bacteria

Group	Genus	Typical Species	Typical Disease
Gram-negative rods			
	Bacteroides (*fragilis* group)	fragilis, thetaiotamicron	Intra-abdominal infections
	Bacteroides (pigmented group)	melaninogenicus, gingivalis	Oral, dental, pleuropulmonary infections
	Bacteroides	bivius	Pelvic infections
	Fusobacterium	nucleatum, necrophorum	Oral, dental, pleuropulmonary infections
Gram-positive rods			
	Actinomyces	israelii	Actinomycosis (lumpy jaw)
	Propionobacterium	acnes	Infections of prosthetic devices
Gram-positive cocci			
	Peptostreptococcus	magnus, asaccharolyticus, anaerobius	Intra-abdominal, soft tissue, bone and joint infections

proteases, and a **neuraminidase**. Their role in pathogenesis is suggestive but has not been well documented as yet. Most likely, *B. fragilis* has multiple virulence factors, as seen in the staphylococci, streptococci, pseudomonads, and other multifactorial pathogens.

ENTRY, SPREAD, AND MULTIPLICATION

Breaching of the colon wall can be result from blunt trauma, a ruptured bowel, a penetrating wound, or from abdominal surgery. In the case of Houdini, a sudden impact caused the colon literally to explode. In Ms. A.'s case, obstruction of outflow from the appendix led to inflammation and eventually to its perforation. Whatever the mechanism, the number of organisms contaminating the peritoneal cavity is enormous. Despite this, phagocytes can be mobilized rapidly in huge amounts to the infected site and, up to a point, dispose of large numbers of bacteria. The minimal infecting dose that results in disease in humans is possibly quite high, perhaps several milliliters of intestinal content, as judged from experiments with laboratory animals.

Organisms that enter the peritoneal cavity find themselves first in a liquid phase that could, in principle, lead to their dissemination throughout the cavity. However, the omentum and the loops of the small intestine drape themselves around areas of inflammation and serve to contain the infection. This takes time, but the abscesses that eventually develop are usually well localized. Lymphatic drainage and the effect of gravity also influence the location of abscesses. These are the likely reasons why Ms. A.'s abscess was found at a retroperitoneal site even though the original bacterial spill took place by her appendix.

Given the diversity of the bacterial inoculum, a large number of factors must be involved in determining which species become dominant in the infection. Many intestinal bacteria can grow in the peritoneal fluid, which is not particularly antibacterial. The first line of defense is most likely the mobilization of phagocytic cells, which happens rapidly. Thus, bacteria that eventually survive and grow must be quite resistant to phagocytosis. In fact, many are encapsulated. This may well be one major reason for the predominance of *B. fragilis*, since it is among the members of the genus *Bacteroides* with the largest capsule.

At the moment when the colon contents are spilled, the peritoneal cavity is well oxygenated and highly oxygen-sensitive anaerobes are killed. The first organisms that become numerically dominant are facultative anaerobes, especially *Escherichia coli*. However, many of the less oxygen-sensitive strict anaerobes survive and can be isolated both from the fluid and from the surface of mesothelial cells. Eventually, the site of infection will become increasingly anaerobic, in part because facultative anaerobes metabolize what oxygen is present and, in part, because the site becomes increasingly avascular. The surviving strict anaerobes can then take over. That synergy between various microorganisms required for abscess formation is clearly demonstrated in studies with animals. The inoculation of single species of intestinal bacteria seldom leads to infection, while infection with a mixture of facultative and strict anaerobes produces acute inflammation and abscess formation.

In peritoneal abscesses, the dominant *B. fragilis* is often accompanied not only by facultative anaerobes but also by other strict anaerobes, such as members of the genus *Clostridium* or anaerobic streptococci (*Peptococcus*, *Peptostreptococcus*).

DAMAGE

If the peritoneal defenses are unable to eradicate spilled intestinal contents, an abscess will usually develop. The areas of inflammation become walled-in and surrounded by a thick, fibrous collagen-containing capsule. Inside are live and dead white blood cells, bacteria, and cell debris. In general terms, these abscesses resemble those caused by the staphylococci (Chapter 11).

Intra-abdominal abscesses extract a high toll from the host because they can extend to nearby sites, with resultant necrosis of adjacent tissue. In addition, they are reservoirs from which the organisms may enter the bloodstream. The resulting bacteremia may produce septic shock or cause metastatic infections at distant sites. The reasons for shock are not known, but may not be due to the LPS of these organisms, since it is nontoxic. Vigorous intervention with antibiotics helped Ms. A. overcome her bacteremia.

OTHER *BACTEROIDES* INFECTIONS

In addition to *B. fragilis*, other species of this genus are also found in abscesses of the female genital tract, usually due to contamination with the vaginal flora. Here the infecting organisms ascend through the cervix, the uterus, and fallopian tubes to reach the neighborhood of the ovaries. The resulting infection is known as **pelvic inflammatory disease (PID)**. Predisposing causes are scarring of the fallopian tubes due to previous infections by chlamydiae or gonococci (see Chapter 14), which impairs the downward action of the cilia of epithelial cells in the fallopian tubes. Tubo-ovarian abscesses, which occasionally complicate PID, often lead to infertility. The most common agent of this disease is not *B. fragilis*, but *B. bivius*, a common inhabitant of the human vagina.

DIAGNOSIS

Proper chemotherapy of mixed bacterial infections requires the determination of the bacterial species involved and of their antibiotic sensitivity. Specialized techniques are required for growing members of the genus *Bacteroides* and other anaerobes. In general, these call for limiting the exposure of the specimen to oxygen because even oxygen-tolerant strains may eventually be killed. Clinical specimens must be protected from the air using special collecting devices and transported to the laboratory without delay. The most convenient way to handle and to culture clinical specimens is by the use of an incubator in the form of a glove box, a device where the atmosphere can be made anaerobic by flushing with a mixture of inert gases (Fig. 16.1). This equipment is specialized and costly and not all hospital laboratories are equipped with it. It is possible, however, to carry out anaerobic microbiological work with smaller but less convenient glass jars.

TREATMENT

Localized purulent infections, such as abscesses, usually require dual therapy; namely, drainage of the contents and administration of antibiotics. Additionally, the anatomical defect that allows spillage from the intestine must be repaired. Thus, a combined medical and surgical approach is often necessary in cases of intra-abdominal infections.

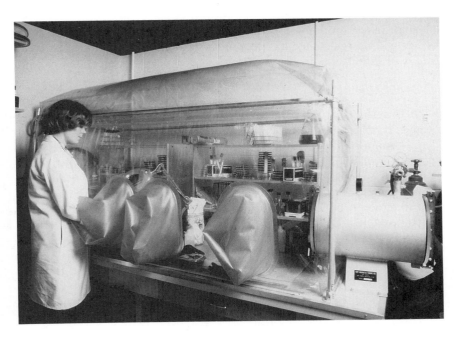

Figure 16.1. An anaerobic glove box used for the culture of strictly anaerobic bacteria. Such a device is used for large-scale work and for experimentation. Note the port on *right*, which is used to introduce and remove material from the chamber, has two doors (not visible), and can be independently flushed free of oxygen.

Table 16.2. Antimicrobial Therapy of Experimental Peritonitis[a]

Treatment Regimen	Acute Mortality (%)	Abscess Formation in Survivors (%)
Untreated	37	100
Gentamicin alone	4	98
Clindamycin alone	35	5
Gentamicin and clindamycin	7	6

[a]A gelatin capsule containing fresh rat feces was placed in the peritoneal cavity of normal rats. The drugs were administered at the same time.

In the past, antibacterial therapy was difficult because *B. fragilis* is resistant to many common antibiotics. Fortunately, several agents have excellent activity against this organism (imipenem, clindamycin, metronidazole, carbopenems, and β-lactamase inhibitors combined with extended spectrum penicillins). It must be kept in mind, however, that the target in these infections is seldom a single bacterial species but a mixed flora with different sensitivities. For this reason, a combination of antibiotics or an antibiotic effective against both aerobes and anaerobes is usually given. The need for using more than one drug or a drug with a broad spectrum of activity is seen in a study with experimental animals described in Table 16.2. It is apparent that both mortality and abscess formation are significantly reduced only when the combination of antibiotics is used. Gentamicin presumably reduces mortality due to the the aerobe (*E. coli*), and clindamycin prevents abscess formation by *B. fragilis*. In the case of Ms. A., it is likely that the cephalosporin first administered was effective against *E. coli* but not against *B. fragilis*. Her second treatment recognized the need for an appropriate choice and she also received clindamycin, an effective drug against this organism.

Bacteroides cells possess sophisticated genetic systems to transfer genes for drug resistance. Plasmids and transposons can be transferred between *B. fragilis* and *E. coli*; although genes from *B. fragilis* are not efficiently expressed in *E. coli* and vice versa, this transfer may be important in the epidemiology of drug resistance. From a practical point of view, drug resistance has become a significant problem in the treatment of infections by *B. fragilis*.

CONCLUSION

B. fragilis is a versatile pathogen that colonizes the human large bowel. It possesses special virulence characteristics because it emerges from a numerically inferior position in the normal intestinal flora to become a dominant pathogen in normally sterile tissue. Left for future work is the elucidation of the role of the virulence factors. Among the many questions that may be asked: Is the capsule alone sufficient to resist phagocytosis? Do the various enzymes secreted by the organisms participate in damage? How do they do it? What is the role of the capsule? Two facts bode well for our ability to obtain answers to at least some of these questions. One is the development of a genetic system that allows the manipulation of the corresponding genes and the construction of suitable mutants. The other is the existence of relevant animal models for experimental abscess formation by this organism. Thus, genetically well-characterized mutants can be tested for their virulence.

Although the diseases caused by *B. fragilis* can be cured, the organisms still present challenges to therapy and, above all, to prevention. Unfortunately, there is presently no way to prevent these infections.

Self-assessment Questions

1. What are the major medical problems caused by *B. fragilis*? How serious are they? Why was *Bacteroides* not implicated in many of these conditions until recently?

2. What are *Bacteroides*? Describe their major structural, physiological, and ecological properties.

3. What do we know about the pathophysiology of *B. fragilis* infections? (Clue: not much)

4. What are the special therapeutic and diagnostic problems of these infections?

SUGGESTED READING

Finegold SM. Anaerobic bacteria in human disease. New York: Academic Press, 1977.

Gorbach SL, Bartlett JG. Anaerobic infections. N Engl J Med 1974;290:1177–1184; 290:1237–1354; 290:1289–1294.

Tally FP, Ho JL. Management of patients with intraabdominal infection due to colonic perforation. In: Current clinical topics in infectious diseases. New York: McGraw-Hill, 1987.

Enteric Bacteria: "Secretory" (Watery) Diarrhea

17

Gerald T. Keusch

Diarrhea is experienced by all of us at some time in life. It is usually little more than a bothersome watery stool. However, in developing countries, it is one of the leading causes of infant mortality, killing over 5 million children every year. In addition, it contributes greatly to malnutrition and to retarded physical and mental development. For these reasons, diarrhea has been singled out for a determined control effort by the World Health Organization.

Diarrhea lies at one end of the spectrum of intestinal infections and consists of **loss of electrolytes and fluids**, sometimes in enormous amounts. The extreme example of this problem is cholera; "traveler's diarrhea" is a milder form in adults. At the other end of the spectrum are bloody diarrhea and dysentery, diseases caused when certain organisms **invade the intestinal mucosa**, which leads to inflammation and local tissue damage. These latter infections will be discussed in Chapter 18.

Secretory diarrhea occurs when the causative organisms are able to **colonize** the digestive tract. In every case, these agents must overcome multiple host defenses in either the small or the large intestine. The pathogens may also produce powerful **toxins** acting on the gut, called **enterotoxins**. A large variety of different bacteria are involved, conveniently known as "enteric pathogens."

CASES

Mr. D., a 33-year-old blood group O, fully immunized, rather nervous accountant who is taking H_2 blockers for ulcer disease, his 29-year-old healthy wife, and their 10-month-old baby returned from a 2-week trip to a South American country. The next morning, Mr. D. passed a semisolid stool, followed quickly by a large watery bowel movement. Within an hour he passed another large watery stool, now of an opaque gray-white color. He vomited several times and became slightly sweaty. When this movement was followed by another large watery stool a short time later, Mr. D. called his physician who advised him to go to the University Hospital and report to the emergency room. There he was afebrile but observed to have a rapid heart rate with a somewhat feeble pulse and mildly decreased blood pressure. Mr. D. complained of muscle cramps and dizziness. There were no abnormalities in the rest of the physical examination and laboratory results showed only findings consistent with dehydration.

Mr. D. was given 2 liters of fluid intravenously and then placed on oral rehydration solution (ORS). Culture grew Vibrio cholerae, *strain 01 E1 Tor, the same as a concurrent epidemic strain in Latin America. Stool volumes progressively diminished over 48 hours and the patient was discharged in his usual state of good health.*

Two weeks later, the D. infant stopped feeding, and soon thereafter developed diarrhea and his temperature rose to 38°C. The child was noted to be passing watery brown stools, and was brought to the pediatrician. The baby was mildly to moderately dehydrated, with an estimated fluid loss of around 7% of body weight, and the physician admitted him to the hospital. Microscopic examination of the stool revealed neither leukocytes nor red blood cells. Over the next 2 days, baby D. was rehydrated by the oral administration of a commercially available sugar-salt solution. His fever soon abated and his appetite returned although the diarrhea persisted. The initial report of stool cultures was "normal fecal flora"; however, 2 days later, the laboratory identified a so-called 0111:H4 strain of enteropathogenic Escherichia coli. Baby D. was discharged after 4 days, markedly improved but with continuing mild diarrhea that lasted for a few more days. The baby had lost 1 lb in weight, but he returned to his normal growth pattern by the following month.

The following questions suggest themselves:

1. Are all enteric bacteria capable of causing disease or are some more frequently pathogenic than others?

2. Where do the organisms come from?

3. What are the main types of intestinal diseases due to enteric bacteria? Why do the organisms cause different intensity of symptoms in individual people?

4. What virulence factors are involved in colonization? What factors are involved in causing symptoms?

5. What is the proper therapy for different kinds of diseases of the intestinal tract?

6. Can these diseases be prevented?

The two males in the D. family developed two different secretory diarrheal diseases—one, caused by *V. cholerae*, was clearly related to travel. Watery diarrheas result from the encounter with certain bacteria, viruses, or protozoa normally absent from the person's usual environment. The most common bacterial offenders in the U.S. are certain strains of *E. coli* present in food or water contaminated with human or, possibly, with animal feces. These strains may circulate in the local population, but the majority (especially adults) will usually remain asymptomatic, undoubtedly due to the immunity afforded by previous exposure. Other common causes of watery diarrhea in the U.S. are a diverse group of viruses (such as rotavirus, coronavirus, calicivirus) or protozoa (*Giardia, Cryptosporidium*).

Pathogenic bacteria can be readily isolated from about one-third of these patients' stools, and whereas some may have *V. cholerae* or other important pathogens, the predominant isolate is *E. coli*; this is indistinguishable by routine laboratory studies from strains isolated from healthy individuals. As many as 40% of the younger patients will be suffering from **rotaviruses** (see Chapter 36) and many are infected with **protozoa** such as *Giardia* or *Cryptosporidium* (see Chapter 51).

The scope of diarrheal disease is vast; the day that baby D. was admitted to the hospital, more than 200 patients arrived at the Treatment Centre of the International Center for Diarrhoeal Disease Research in Dhaka, Bangladesh. This scene is repeated every day of the year in that city. All of these individuals have diarrhea, most are under 10 years of age, and about one in ten will be admitted to the hospital wards because they are losing body fluids at such a tremendous rate that unless treated, they will develop life-threatening dehydration within 24 hours. Some are already in shock because of fluid losses greater than 10% of their usual body weight and they will die unless replacement fluids are administered right away. Most, dehydrated to a degree similar to baby D., will be given oral rehydrating solutions, and instead of being admitted to the hospital, will be sent home because of limited bed capacity. Some of these babies may later worsen and die.

Cholera is the paradigm of a secretory diarrhea. It has been endemic in the Indian subcontinent for centuries, but since the early 19th century, has periodically spread in pandemic fashion throughout the world. In the 1850s, a thousand patients a day were dying of cholera in London, New York, and Philadelphia. In the 1970s, virtually nobody died when cholera reached Europe during the present (7th) recorded pandemic. Endemic cholera, however, has long since disappeared from the developed world, with the exception of a small endemic focus along the Gulf Coast of the U.S. In contrast, it has now become endemic in Africa and will no doubt now be endemic, for decades at least, in Latin America. In such endemic regions, the disease is primarily a childhood disease affecting those who are less than 10 years old inasmuch as immunity develops with exposure over time, providing protection to most but not to all adults. During epidemic spread in previously cholera-free areas, all age groups are susceptible. This is typical of the age pattern of endemic vs. epidemic infections.

INTRODUCTION TO THE AGENTS

Most of the bacteria that cause diarrheal disease belong to a large family of Gram-negative rods, the **Enterobacteriaceae**, and some belong to the **Vibrionaceae**. The Enterobacteriaceae include members of the normal flora of the colon as well as some that are more commonly pathogenic. In spite of their name, the group also includes organisms that cause disease in other systems of the body, especially the urinary and respiratory tracts, as well as sepsis and meningitis. Enterobacteriaceae, commonly known as "enterics," comprise a large number of species that are differentiated on the bases of serological and metabolic details (Table 17.1). The family Vibrionaceae includes many nonpathogenic vibrios but also includes the major cause of cholera, V. cholerae. In the family history presented, the father developed proven cholera, no doubt contracted in South America, while the infant had diarrhea due to an enteropathogenic (**EPEC**) E. coli serotype, which may have been acquired as readily in the U.S. as in Latin America.

E. coli is the most abundant facultative anaerobe in normal human feces, commonly present in concentrations of 10^7–10^8/g. In the colon, strict anaerobes (e.g., Bacteroides) outnumber facultative anaerobes by 100-fold or more. Most fecal E. coli isolates seldom cause disease; some human strains have been cultivated in the laboratory for so long that they have lost the ability to colonize humans. These include the famous K12 strain that occupies center stage in molecular biology and has the distinction of being the best known of all cellular forms of life.

Unfortunately, when it comes to predicting the disease caused by species of enteric bacteria, things are not so simple. If E. coli or the other species of enterics were each the cause of a single type of diarrheal disease, the diagnosis could be made just by noting the characteristics of the illness. However, **different strains of** E. coli **can cause a**

Table 17.1. Main Genera of Pathogenic Enterobacteriaceae and Vibrionaceae

Genus	Main Reservoirs[a]	Principal Diseases
Escherichia	Colon of vertebrates	Diarrhea, dysentery, urinary tract infections, meningitis in children
Shigella	?	Dysentery
Salmonella	GI system of animals, humans	Diarrhea, septicemia, enteric fevers (including typhoid fever), focal infections
Proteus	? Colon of vertebrates, ? water, ? soil	Urinary tract infections
Klebsiella, Enterobacter, Serratia, Citrobacter	? Colon of vertebrates, water, sewage	Pneumonia, septicemia, compromised patients
Others		
Yersinia	Rodents, pigs, water	Plague, dysentery, lymphadenitis
Campylobacter	GI system of animals, water	Diarrhea, septicemia

[a]? denotes uncertainty

spectrum of clinical diseases. To make matters worse, there is a great deal of overlap among species as well, and different organisms may cause seemingly similar clinical illnesses. Thus, watery diarrhea due to *E. coli* resembles that seen in mild cases of cholera; other strains of *E. coli* cause a febrile dysentery not unlike that due to *Shigella*, the classic agents of bacillary dysentery, whereas certain species of *Shigella* often cause watery diarrhea like that of *E. coli*.

All strains of *E. coli* share the basic taxonomic features of the species, even though they may have different virulence factors. Unless these factors are looked for, the routine clinical microbiological laboratory will not distinguish among pathogenic, or between pathogenic and nonpathogenic *E. coli*. Indeed, for the D. family infant, the laboratory sought and found just one kind of diarrhea-causing *E. coli*, enteropathogenic *E. coli*, or **EPEC** (see below). In the clinical laboratory, while one *E. coli* may resemble another, the clinician and the epidemiologist know that this is far from being the case and patients know this even more intimately!

How then can one tell these strains apart? One classical way is to determine their antigenic differences. There are about 170 different serological types of **O antigens**. In addition, the motile strains have different kinds of **H antigens**, the flagellar protein. Some strains of *E. coli* also have a capsular polysaccharide called **K antigens**. The various assortments of these antigens help subclassify a strain of *E. coli*. Similar serologic typing is especially useful for the *Salmonella*, which comprise approximately 2000 serotypes. The practical significance of these serological differences is shown in Table 17.2. However, serological specificity does not necessarily predict virulence and, in the future, diagnosis will be based on identification of virulence genes or gene products in an isolate, using DNA probes, PCR, and other methods (Chapter 55).

ENCOUNTER

Some enteric pathogens are **well adapted to the external environment** and only incidentally cause disease. The best example is the cholera bacillus, which lives in brackish rivers and tidal estuaries, including

Table 17.2. Examples of Serotypes of Pathogenic *E. coli*

	Symptoms	Epidemiology	Typical serotypes[a]	Number of serotypes
Enteropathogenic (EPEC)	"Traveler's" diarrhea	Infants primarily	O26:H111	Many
Enterotoxigenic (ETEC)	Watery diarrhea	Worldwide; all ages; food- and water-borne	O6:H⁻	A few more
Enteroinvasive (EIEC)	Bloody diarrhea and dysentery		O29:H⁻	Many more
Enterohemorrhagic (EHEC)	Bloody diarrhea and dysentery	? Zoonosis	O157:H7	No or few others

[a]The letter O refers to "somatic" antigens, part of the bacterial lipopolysaccharide, and their numbers to different antigenic serotypes. The letter H refers to "flagellar" antigens, and the numbers to different antigenic serotypes. H antigens are missing in nonmotile strains.

the Gulf of Mexico along the Texas and Louisiana borders. The cholera organism is a human pathogen and does not naturally infect animals. However, its normal habitat is brackish (somewhat salty) coastal waters, and it can be characterized as a moderately halophilic (salt-loving) marine organism. From this habitat, it may infect humans or get into the food and water chain and then be transmitted to other humans. In the U.S., transmission is primarily associated with eating raw or partially cooked shellfish harvested from Gulf coastal waters. These fish may be shipped to other areas of the U.S., resulting in distant outbreaks.

Many enteric pathogens are **host adapted** and are found mainly in association with the body of humans and/or of certain animals. Strict animal host-adapted strains may be incapable of causing human disease. The route for transmission of enteric pathogens is from feces to mouth; however, many intermediaries can intervene. These have been characterized as the 7 "F's": feces, food, fluids, fingers, flies, fomites (inanimate objects), and fornication.

Enteric pathogens vary considerably with regard to their host specificity. Some infect a limited number of host species, whereas others have a broad host range. Some strains of *E. coli* are quite human specific; most of the infections they cause are by organisms derived from other humans. In contrast, many strains of *Salmonella* colonize or infect animals as well and are transmitted as **zoonoses** from animals to people (see Chapter 69).

When the number of organisms needed to cause infection is small, for example, less than 10,000, they may be acquired by contact with contaminated objects, for it is surprising how many times individuals, especially children, put fingers, toys, or other inanimate objects in the mouth during ordinary daily activities. Flies may transmit virulent organisms by picking them up on their feet or proboscis and depositing them on foodstuff. Here the organisms may multiply further.

The number of organisms required to cause disease is probably better known for enteric bacteria than for most other organisms. Experimental human infections have been induced in volunteers who agreed to drink buffered solutions containing a known number of living bacteria. Such studies showed that a few hundred *Shigella dysenteriae* are sufficient to cause disease in many volunteers. In contrast, 1000–10,000 *Shigella flexneri* and over 100 million enterotoxigenic *E. coli* are required to cause the same attack rate. A direct consequence of a small infective dose is that, under the same conditions, *Shigella* are generally transmitted from person to person, because small inocula are readily passed by fingers or objects after contact with stool or soiled diapers. It is more difficult to transfer directly the large required amount of *E. coli*. It would take about a (visible) pea-sized lump of feces! It is much more likely that large numbers of organisms enter by the ingestion of contaminated food or water where the organisms have already multiplied.

Despite the high standards of modern hygiene, we are nonetheless in constant touch with enteric bacteria. Our earth can be described as a globe coated with a veneer of feces, the difference between one place and another being the thickness of the veneer. This means that each day we all ingest feces to a greater or lesser extent, depending on our age (which determines behavior) and the state of environmental sanitation. Because potential pathogens are so common, we might ask why do not we get diarrhea every day? The answer to this question requires an understanding of the mechanisms of pathogenesis of these diseases and host defenses, both specific and nonspecific.

ENTRY

Having arrived at the mouth, microorganisms face a long and perilous journey along the alimentary canal to their final destiny. The gastrointestinal tract is an open tube lined with differentiated epithelial cells that keep bacteria outside the body and deliver them to the exterior through the anus. The journey is perilous, because the microorganisms face host defenses designed to kill them or to propel them back to the outside world. They are subjected to wide variation in pH, from less than 1 in the stomach to 9 or higher near the ampulla of Vater, where the bicarbonate-buffered pancreatic juice enters the lumen of the gut. Moving into the small intestine, they will be swimming in the 9 or so liters of fluid that enter the gut each day, partly from food and drink but primarily from endogenous secretions. They will be smothered in mucus, rolled up in sticky polysaccharide balls, and kneaded and squeezed and swept distally toward the anus by peristaltic motions of the bowel unless they find a way to hold on. During the journey, they will be accosted by soluble proteins such as lysozyme, proteases, and lipases, as well as bile salts, secretory immunoglobulins of the IgA class, and phagocytic and lymphoid cells. Where they pause on their journey in the large intestine, they meet the populous normal flora that resists implantation by new species; in part by previous occupancy of adhesion sites on the gut wall, and in part by producing inhibitory substances.

The efficiency of these host defenses is the reason why the infectious dose of most noninvasive enteric pathogens is high and disease is not the norm. Certain conditions, however, may provide an advantage to the pathogen. For example, when they arrive in the stomach mixed with food, the organisms are protected from stomach acid, and their infectious dose is lowered considerably. In some patients, gastric acidity and secretory capacity are seriously diminished. Whether this is due to intrinsic disease (pernicious anemia), infections such as by *Helicobacter pylori* (gastritis), prior surgery (gastric resection, diversions, or transections of the vagus), or antiulcer drugs that inhibit gastric acid secretion, such patients are at risk of infection with bacteria that are acid sensitive, like the cholera bacillus and *Salmonella*, which are ordinarily devastated by exposure to gastric acid.

For a very good reason (the sensitivity of the cholera vibrio to acid), individuals who are hypochlorhydric for any reason, including prior ulcer surgery or therapeutic use of H_2 blockers, are at increased risk. Mr. D. was also an ulcer patient receiving H_2 blockers to cut down on gastric acid secretion. Therefore, he was an easier prey for cholera, and both of these risk factors may have contributed to his illness. A large inoculum of organisms is usually required to overcome gastric acid, and this is why person to person contact is not usually involved in transmission of cholera.

SPREAD AND MULTIPLICATION

The cholera vibrio infecting Mr. D. colonized the proximal small bowel. The EPEC infecting baby D. colonized the mid-distal small intestine. Neither will invade the mucosa. They both recognize preferred hosts and tissues by means of surface **adhesins** specific for receptors on the intestinal brush border membranes. This allows them to attach to the intestinal epithelium and avoid being swept away. At the level of the jejunum and ileum they have little competition because the resident flora is scant or nonexistent. For uncertain reasons, blood group O persons such as Mr. D. are excessively susceptible to cholera.

Adherence is not a simple feat because the surface of both microbe and host is negatively charged and should be mutually repulsive. However, the surface charges are not evenly distributed in either, and patches of greater or lesser negativity permit electrostatic attractions, aided by weaker attractive forces, such as hydrogen bonding, Van der Waals forces, and hydrophobic interactions. If such contact were via long, thin appendages, the attachment would be stronger than by the apposition of large, flat surfaces. This is indeed what nature has chosen to do. Adhesins (or colonization factors) are frequently found on **pili**— long, thin structures that fulfill the above criteria. Adherence is generally via sugar-binding proteins and carbohydrates present in glycoproteins or glycolipids on one or the other interacting cell, much like other specific receptor-ligand binding events. (See Chapter 3 and "Paradigm.")

Paradigm: Adherence and Colonization

In all of the enteric bacteria studied to date, the ability of the organism to colonize the mucosal surface of the gastrointestinal tract has been shown to depend upon the ability of the microorganism to **adhere** to defined parts of the mucosal surface. This bacterial adherence is most typically due to a specific interaction between molecules on the bacterial surface (the **"adhesin"**) and molecules on the host surface (the **"receptor"**). Among the enteric bacteria, the most important and ubiquitous adhesins are the organelles known as **pili** (or fimbriae) (see Chapters 2 and 3). Virtually all Gram-negative bacteria possess "common pili," proteinaceous rods that help them stick to mucosal surfaces throughout the gastrointestinal tract. These common pili have a special affinity for mannose-containing molecules in mucosal membranes; mannose-containing lipids and mannose-containing proteins are the receptors that permit bacterial adherence.

Specialized strains of *E. coli* that cause traveler's diarrhea possess an **additional type of pilus** that enhances adherence to cells of the small intestine, where the bacteria secrete a toxin that causes the symptoms of the disease. The close adherence of the bacteria to the mucosal surface not only promotes colonization, it also potentiates the action of the toxin, perhaps by allowing its efficient deposition on the mucosal toxin receptors.

A particularly interesting form of adhesion is seen in certain strains of *E. coli* that cause urinary tract infection. These strains possess yet another form of pilus, the so-called "P-pili", which are specific for adherence to the urinary tract. They are called P-pili because the **receptor** is a complex galactose-containing molecule that is also part of the P blood group antigen. Only 1% of the population is P antigen-negative and, since these people contain no P-pilus receptor, they are not susceptible to colonization by P-pilus-carrying strains of *E. coli*. These individuals do not suffer from urinary tract infections mediated by the usual route (i.e., mucosal colonization followed by ascending invasion of the bacteria into the bladder). The urinary tract of these individuals can become infected only when the normal route is bypassed, for example, by the use of an indwelling urinary catheter.

Bacterial adherence is critical in a number of infectious diseases other than those due to enteric bacteria. Virtually any infection involving a mucosal surface requires an adhesin-receptor interaction. For example, pili are essential for gonococci to infect the epithelial cells of the genitourinary tract, again by facilitating bacterial adherence and colonization. Streptococci adhere to the mucous membranes of the pharynx by virtue of the interaction between streptococcal lipoteichoic acid (the adhesin) and mucosal fibronectin (the receptor). Patients who lose the normal mucosal fibronectin, because of severe physical stress, become colonized in their upper respiratory tracts with Gram-negative bacteria, such as *E. coli*, *Klebsiella*, and *Pseudomonas*, rather than the normal Gram-positive flora. These bacteria are then in a strategic location to cause Gram-negative pneumonia during episodes of microaspiration, which often occurs in intubated, semiconscious individuals. These infections are the bane of severely ill hospitalized patients.

DAMAGE

The diarrhea of Mr. D. was due to the action of an exotoxin, cholera toxin, that acts on the epithelial cells of the small intestine. Once past the stomach, the organism is able to use its colonization factors, such as a **pilus** (known as **TcpA**, or **toxin co-regulated pilus**) to establish itself in the proximal small bowel. There, it can elaborate soluble virulence factors such as a hemagglutinin-protease to lyse intestinal mucus (to get closer to the epithelial cell surface) and, perhaps, to assist attachment. Another soluble factor released is cholera toxin, which is the prototype of a family of similar proteins able to (*a*) bind to a ganglioside (which allows toxin to bind to cells) and (*b*) function as **ADP-ribosylating enzymes**. The enzymes covalently transfer the ADP-ribosyl moiety from nicotine adenine dinucleotide (NAD) to acceptors; in the case of cholera toxin, the acceptor is the GTP-binding Gs regulatory component of **adenylate cyclase**. As described in Chapter 9, ADP-ribosylation of Gs locks the cyclase catalytic unit into the "on" position so that ATP is continuously converted to 3'–5' cyclic adenosine monophosphate (**cAMP**). This molecule is a classic intracellular "second message" in biological cell control systems; increased levels of cAMP in the small bowel cells turn off sodium absorption by villous cells and increase chloride secretion by crypt cells. The net result is increased NaCl in the gut lumen, which holds on to water by osmotic forces, and leads to excretion of the unabsorbed isotonic fluid as diarrheal stool. In the case of cholera, the volume is so prodigious that the patient is rapidly dehydrated, may go into shock, and, if not quickly treated, may die. Given access to isotonic replacement fluids, no one should die of cholera. Mortality rates in epidemic situations exceeding 1% are evidence of lack of public health resources and/or inappropriate case management by inexperienced clinical personnel.

It is undoubtedly important that the genes for cholera toxin and the TcpA pilus are **coordinately regulated**. This means that both are turned on at the same time, suggesting a common activation mechanism, so that their products can be used together by the organism in causing illness. An increasing number of genes involved in virulence have been shown to be controlled by master switches, often called **global regulatory elements** (see "Paradigm" in Chapter 20), responsive to environmental signals such as temperature, calcium, iron, or other factors. Through these signals, pathogens determine that they are in a host and switch on the virulence genes they need to survive. In this way, they do not waste energy and substrates making products they do not require outside of the host. The switching is extremely rapid once the signal is perceived.

Certain *E. coli* also produce one or both of two **enterotoxins** called **LT** and **ST** because one is heat labile and the other is heat stable. Both act by changing the net fluid transport in the gut from absorption to secretion. LT is structurally similar to cholera toxin and activates the adenylate cyclase-cyclic GMP system (Chapter 9). Thus, enterotoxigenic *E. coli* (ETEC) diarrhea resembles cholera in the mode of action of one of its toxins; however, cholera is usually a much more serious disease because it leads to the secretion of much greater amounts of liquid. In neither disease is the intestinal mucosa visibly damaged; the watery stool does not contain white or red blood cells; no inflammatory process occurs in the gut wall. Gut cells activated by LT or cholera toxin remain in that state until death; ST effects on guanylate cyclase are turned off if the toxin is washed away from the cell. Similar toxins are described in a number of other pathogens of the gut including *Salmonella*, *Campylobacter*, *Yersinia*, and *Aeromonas*.

Baby D. was infected with an EPEC strain, one of a small group of specific serotypes of *E. coli* originally recognized because they cause outbreaks of diarrhea in the newborn nursery and could be identified by their O and H antigens. For many years, EPEC serotypes were found in more asymptomatic than symptomatic individuals and their role as pathogens was questioned, especially when nursery epidemics seemed to disappear. Were these earlier outbreaks really due to EPEC or were they due to an unrecognized virus or another organism?

Today, there is no doubt about the pathogenic potential of EPEC serotypes. Although the role of serogroup antigens in pathogenesis is not direct, these still serve as markers for virulent strains that possess other genes that control disease-causing properties (Table 17.3). These genes include *eaf*-encoding EPEC adherence factor, a surface protein mediating the ability of the organism to adhere to target epithelial cells by a characteristic "localized" pattern on limited regions of the plasma membrane like a microcolony. A second recently described gene is *eae*, encoding the *E. coli* attaching and effacing factor, which permits tight adherence of the organism and leads to cytoskeletal rearrangements that damage microvilli forming a broad, flat pedestal ("effacement") beneath the attached microorganism. This damage to the absorptive surface significantly contributes to the diarrhea fluids, although there may be additional factors as well.

While there are probes for these genes, and their action can be detected in tissue culture, neither assay system is used today for specific

Table 17.3. Virulence Determinants in Pig Strains of *E. coli*

Strains with Plasmid-borne Genes for	Colonization of Jejunum	Animals with Diarrhea
None	No	0
K88 pili alone	Yes	3/11 tested (mild)
Enterotoxin alone	No	0
Both K88 pili and enterotoxin	Yes	12/16 tested

diagnosis, and clinical laboratories still do what they have been doing for over four decades, i.e., look for the EPEC serotypes and report these.

OTHER INFECTIONS CAUSED BY *VIBRIOS* AND *E. COLI*

The most common causes of clinical diarrhea are one serogroup of *V. cholerae*, namely 01. There are other non-01 pathogenic *V. cholerae*-causing diarrhea often called NAG or nonagglutinable vibrios because they do not agglutinate in anti-01 sera. They will, of course, agglutinate in antibody specific for their serogroup. Another distinctive marine species, *V. parahemolyticus*, causes a bloody diarrhea and is associated with ingestion of sushi or raw shellfish, especially in Japan. Other *Vibrio* species, such as *V. vulnificus* or *alginolyticus*, are often acquired through an injury or a break in the skin.

EPEC and ETEC strains of *E. coli* represent just the earliest described diarrhea-causing *E. coli* species (Table 17.4). The repertoire is already large and consists of a veritable alphabet soup of pathogenic groups: EPEC, ETEC, EIEC, EHEC, EAggEC, and possibly more awaiting in the wings. Each is associated with identifiable genetic traits and characteristic epidemiology, and causes distinctive conditions. EIEC and EHEC are discussed in the next chapter. EAggEC autoagglutinate (aggregate) in tissue culture and are associated with early (in children who are less than 6 months of age) diarrhea, often persisting for weeks with marked nutritional consequences.

At the other end of the spectrum from ETEC are the **enteroinvasive** *E. coli* or **EIEC** strains. They cause dysentery, resemble the classical agents of this disease the *Shigella*, and are discussed in Chapter 18.

This is not the end of the list of diseases caused by *E. coli*. For example, these organisms are the most common cause of **urinary tract infections** (Chapter 59). Many of the *E. coli* strains that cause pyelonephritis possess pili that bind to a glycolipid constituent of kidney tissue. This explains, in part, the tropism of these organisms. Other strains, which possess a capsular polysaccharide called K1 antigen, are invasive in young infants and cause **bacteremia** and systemic diseases, such as **meningitis** (Chapter 58). In every case, specific virulence factors are critical in determining the nature of the resulting disease. Many of these are known; others are being investigated. Still others remain to be discovered.

Table 17.4. Gram-negative Rods That Cause Diarrhea And Dysentery

	Diarrhea	Dysentery	
		Ileitis	Colitis
Enterobacteriaceae			
E. coli ETEC	+		
E. coli EIEC			+
E. coli EHEC			+
E. coli EPEC		+	
Shigella			+
Salmonella (not *typhi*)	+		
Salmonella typhi		+	
Yersinia enterocolitica			+
Vibrionaceae and other			
Vibrio cholerae	+		
Campylobacter jejuni	+		
Other vibrios	+		

DIAGNOSIS

Mr. D. was diagnosed as having a case of cholera because his physician both knew about the ongoing epidemic in the country Mr. D. visited and alerted the laboratory so that special media, not routinely employed, could be used. On the usual media, the sugar fermentation patterns of the organism cause it to resemble commensals and it will not be picked for further diagnostic studies. On the special media, however, the distinctive *V. cholerae* colonies could be easily identified, and this was confirmed at the Centers for Disease Control in Atlanta, Georgia, and shown to be genetically identical to the epidemic strain and not the Gulf Coast endemic strain. By these means, the epidemiology of this case was demonstrated to be that of an imported case that constitutes no threat to the local population because it was not related to contaminated seafood able to cause a common source outbreak.

Let us consider how the stool from baby D. was handled. In addition to the use of cholera-selective media (because of the father's diagnosis), it was inoculated into various media designed for both **selection** and **differentiation** of possible pathogens. Just by incubating culture in air, the numerically dominant strict anaerobes were not allowed to grow. The media were chosen to permit the growth of enteric bacteria and not others. Media of this sort contain dyes (e.g., eosin and methylene blue, as in the so-called EMB agar) or bile salts, which inhibit growth of Gram positives. These media are not especially rich and do not allow the growth of the fastidious Gram negatives.

All of the pathogenic strains of *E. coli* described look alike, both on agar plates and under the microscope. Most enteric Gram-negative rods are also similar under the microscope and on nutrient agar. They are further classified on the basis of biochemical and nutritional properties, such as differences in the sugars they ferment. Some of the classical intestinal pathogens, like *Salmonella* and *Shigella*, do not ferment lactose, and for this reason, this sugar is usually included in the medium, together with a colored pH indicator. Lactose-fermenting colonies turn a distinctive color due to the production of acid. The lactose negatives are picked for further determinative work. But other pathogens cannot be selected by this method and must be sought by other techniques.

With the help of this ingenious array of differential and selective media, it is usually simple to isolate *E. coli* even from samples that contain many different bacteria. These media and other special tests permit the laboratory to narrow down the identification to the main groups of Enterobacteriaceae (Table 17.1). Classifying *E. coli* into serological subgroups is not a task that most clinical laboratories are prepared to carry out, and serotype is only associated with and not the cause of virulence. Indeed, the only serological reagents currently available commercially are antisera directed against EPEC strains.

THERAPY AND PROPHYLAXIS

The therapeutic needs in the case of the D. family are to restore fluid losses, to correct metabolic imbalances, and to improve their physiological function. Luckily, "secretory" diarrheas are usually self-limiting and terminate without specific antibiotics, as long as the patient can be kept well hydrated and prevented from going into shock. Mr. D. required intravenous fluids at first. Baby D. did well with just an oral salt-sugar solution designed to enhance a physiological transport system for glucose in conjunction with sodium.

This simple form of therapy, if universally applied, could save the lives of millions of children every year throughout the developing world. Unfortunately, it not easy to ensure that such a simple solution becomes available in every country and household. Considerable experience has taught us that there are practical problems in making sure the salt and sugar solution is made correctly, and that adequate amounts are given at the right time. Much effort is now being devoted to determining how to teach this methodology. The problem has not been solved.

Considerable efforts have been devoted to vaccine development. The challenge has been two-fold: (a) to identify and prepare protective antigens; and (b) to find a way to present the antigen in a way that leads to a local immune response in the intestine. So far, partial success has been achieved with live oral vaccines with attenuated or genetically engineered strains. It is important to note that no vaccines for enteric pathogens have become available for routine use. Molecular techniques are being used to develop a new generation of vaccines, which should result in significant progress in the near future and may allow the use of purified nonviable antigen preparations.

CONCLUSIONS

Diarrhea is not only the trivial bother that besets all of us occasionally. It is a major cause of infant death in the developing world. Symptomatic treatment by fluid replacement requires widespread educational effort.

In every instance, local defenses of the gastrointestinal tract must be overcome for disease to occur. The efficacy of these defense mechanisms is best demonstrated by the fact that, in developed countries, we seldom succumb to intestinal infections, despite the fact that the gut is a tube open to the exterior. Disease is seen when the load of pathogens in the environment and their opportunity for transmittal are high, and when predisposing causes like malnutrition, which impair host defenses, are present as well.

Self-assessment Questions

1. What are the main defenses of each segment of the gastrointestinal tract against microorganisms?

2. Which are the main types of bacteria that cause intestinal infections? What distinguishes them in the laboratory?

3. Explain the main virulence factors of each group of intestinal pathogens.

4. How many types of disease do different strains of *E. coli* produce?

5. How would drugs effective against bacterial diarrhea and dysentery differ?

6. What issues should be considered in the prevention of intestinal bacterial infections?

SUGGESTED READING

Archer DL, Young FE. Contemporary issues: diseases with a food vector. Clin Microbiol Rev 1988;1:377–398

Ciba Foundation Symposium. Microbial toxin and diarrhoeal diseases. London: Pitman, 1985;no. 112.

Eisenstein BI, Jones GW The spectrum of infections and pathogenic mechanisms of *Escherichia coli*. Adv Intern Med 1988;33:231–252.

Karmali MA. Infection by verocytotoxin-producing *Escherichia coli*. Clin Microbiol Rev 1989;2:15–38.

Levine MM, Xu JG, Kaper JB, Lior H, Prado V, Tall B, Nataro J, Karch H, Wachsmuth K. A DNA probe to identify enterohemorrhagic *Escherichia coli* of 0157:H7 and other serotypes that cause hemorrhagic colitis and hemolytic uremic syndrome. J Infect Dis 1987;156:175–182.

Middlebrook JL, Dorland RB. Bacterial toxins: cellular mechanisms of action. Microbiol Rev 1984;48:199–221.

Vial PA, Robins-Browne R, Lior H, Prado V, Kaper JB, Nataro JP, Maneval D, Elsayed A, Levine MM. Characterization of enteroadherent-aggregative *Escherichia coli*, a putative agent of diarrheal disease. J Infect Dis 1988;158:70–79.

Invasive and Tissue-damaging Enteric Bacterial Pathogens: Bloody Diarrhea and Dysentery

18

Gerald T. Keusch and Donald M. Thea

INTRODUCTION TO THE AGENTS

Bacteria producing watery diarrheal disease are described in the previous chapter. Those organisms colonize the proximal or distal small bowel and induce the accumulation of fluid in the bowel lumen either by affecting the biochemistry of electrolyte transport or by altering the structure of the microvillus membrane where ion transport occurs. This chapter concerns another group of pathogens that cause **structural damage to the intestine**, most commonly the large bowel although the distal portion of the small bowel may be affected too. These organisms either invade or otherwise damage the mucosa, leading to **bloody diarrhea** or **dysentery**. The latter is a clinical syndrome distinguished by the **frequent passage of stools** (often more than 30/day), typically of **small volume with gross blood and pus**, and with certain symptoms such as **cramps** and **pain** caused by straining to pass stool (which is known as "tenesmus").

The reduction in mortality caused by watery ("secretory") diarrheas caused by the extensive use of oral rehydration therapy has highlighted the continuing mortality due to invasive and inflammatory diarrheas, especially in developing countries. These serious, sometimes life-threatening infections frequently require the use of antibiotics; thus, drug resistance is often an additional concern. The need for antibiotics is especially problematic in developing countries where effective new drugs are either not available or too expensive for most patients to afford. To make matters worse, clinical services in these regions are often not able to manage the associated systemic complications optimally.

This chapter will focus on *Shigella*, the prototypic invasive enteric pathogen. *Salmonella* will also receive attention because, although it also invades the gut mucosa, its clinical manifestations differ. We will also consider enterohemorrhagic *E. coli* that does not invade but still produces a bloody diarrhea. The discussion of *Salmonella* includes *S. typhi*, the agent of typhoid fever because, like the nontyphoidal salmonellae, it is acquired by the oral route, enters the host by invading across the intestinal mucosa, and often causes intestinal symptoms as part of the clinical presentation. Nonetheless, typhoid is a unique syndrome, probably best characterized as a systemic infection of mononuclear phagocytes, caused primarily (but not exclusively) by *S. typhi*. It illustrates how changes in properties from one member of a genus to another can lead to dramatic differences in the clinical manifestations they cause.

CASE 1. *SHIGELLA* DYSENTERY

Infant V., a 22-month-old female living in a low income area in a Texas city near the Mexican border became febrile, lost her appetite, and developed watery diarrhea. By the next day, there was less diarrhea, but her parents noticed mucus and a bloody tinge of the stool. The number of stools and the bloody characteristics increased and the baby began to vomit. The parents became worried and brought the child to a hospital emergency room, where her temperature was found to be 40°C. Shortly after arrival, she had a generalized seizure. Physical examination revealed a sick-appearing, somnolent infant with mild dehydration and hyperactive bowel sounds. Laboratory results showed leukocytosis and a mild decrease in serum sodium and glucose. The child was given fluids and an antibiotic. Several days later, Shigella flexneri grew from the stool culture. No further seizures occurred, and over the next few days, the dysentery subsided. The child had lost 2 lb in weight, however, and did not catch up to her growth curve until a month later.

CASE 2. TYPHOID FEVER

Ms. J., a Southeast Asian exchange student, returned home for a 3-month visit. Near the end of her visit, she cared for her aunt who had had high fevers and some diarrhea. Three weeks later, when back in the United States, Ms. J. had a shaking chill and fever to 38.5°C, with headache, myalgia, and anorexia. Fever continued and progressively increased over the next several days. When seen at the Student Health Service, she appeared ill and confused. The abdomen was diffusely tender, and the liver and spleen were enlarged, although there was no evident jaundice. In spite of the high fever, the pulse was relatively low at 90, and the white blood cell count was only 3000 with a moderate monocytosis.

The initial blood cultures grew S. typhi. Therapy with trimethoprim-sulfamethoxazole was initiated and continued for a total of 14 days. The fever gradually abated over the next 5 days, and the patient made an uneventful recovery. However, 6 weeks later, all of her symptoms recurred, including a maximum daily fever of 38.5°C. S. typhi was again isolated from blood culture, and it was still sensitive to trimethoprim-sulfamethoxazole. She was treated again for 2 weeks with the same drug with a rapid response. There were no further recurrences.

CASE 3. *E. COLI* ENTEROHEMORRHAGIC DISEASE

Mr. R., an 85-year-old resident of a nursing home, was awakened by the onset of severe abdominal cramps, primarily in the right lower quadrant of the abdomen. Later in the morning, watery diarrhea occurring every 15–30 minutes developed, initially with small amounts of visible blood. Later in the day, bright red stools with what seemed to be pure blood appeared. He was nauseated but not vomiting. When seen the next morning by the physician on call, there was no fever, and the clinical examination of the abdomen was unremarkable except for increased bowel sounds.

Because of an elevated white blood cell count, Mr. R. was hospitalized. Frankly bloody stools continued, and a barium enema was performed, revealing only edema of the ascending and transverse colon with areas of spasm.

Routine stool cultures were negative for Salmonella, Shigella, Campylobacter *and* Yersinia; *however, sorbitol-nonfermenting* E. coli *was recovered and putatively identified as serotype O157:H7, later confirmed by the State Public Health Laboratories. The patient was treated with intravenous fluids and an antibiotic and gradually recovered over the next 7 days. By the time he was discharged back to the nursing home, his stool was negative for the* E. coli *isolate.*

The following questions arise:

1. What is the source of these pathogens and how are they transmitted?

2. How do they avoid host defenses and enter the host?

3. What are the mechanisms resulting in bloody diarrhea and dysentery?

4. What is the impact of fluid therapy? What is the impact of antibiotics?

5. Why does typhoid fever sometimes relapse?

6. What are the most effective control measures?

7. Are any of these patients likely to become carriers?

To answer these questions you need to have an understanding of the epidemiology and pathobiology of invasive or tissue-damaging pathogens, and, in addition, comprehend the special features of *S. typhi* that permit it to cause a systemic disease with continuous bacteremia and fever.

The classic causes of the **dysentery syndrome** are bacteria of the genus *Shigella* and the protozoan *Entamoeba histolytica* (Chapter 51). These are old diseases, and epidemics of dysentery, probably due to *Shigella*, are clearly described in the Old Testament and in Thucidydes's histories of the Greek wars. However, it is only in the past two decades that clear concepts of the pathobiology of these have been developed.

In general, most of the organisms causing dysentery invade intestinal epithelial cells and damage the intestine. This leads to a leukocyte inflammatory response in the lamina propria, with destruction of epithelial cells, release of inflammatory mediators, and, most probably, vascular abnormalities, including endothelial cell damage that results in extravasation of blood.

Although 30,000–40,000 cases of salmonellosis are reported in the United States each year (probably greatly underestimating the actual number of infections, which are probably in the 1–2 million range), there are only a few hundred cases of typhoid fever, most of which are imported from endemic regions abroad. This is a good estimate of actual cases and represents a clear-cut change from the description of typhoid fever at the turn of the 20th century as recorded in Chapter 1 of Osler's 1897 textbook of medicine. At that time, an estimated half million cases occurred each year in the United States, with approximately 40,000 deaths annually.

An alternative to the dysentery syndrome is **bloody diarrhea**, which is characterized by a greater volume of stools and the presence of visible blood (Table 18.1). It is associated with invasion of the gut mucosa by, for example, nontyphoidal salmonellae, *Campylobacter*, and *Yersinia*. Certain serotypes of *E. coli*, such as O157:H7, O26:H11, and

Table 18.1. Definitions of Intestinal Infections

Secretory or watery diarrhea
    Stools: copious, watery, no blood, no pus
    Tissue invasion: absent
    Site: small intestine
    Examples: *V. cholerae, E. coli* ETEC strains

Dysentery
    Stools: scant volume, pus, blood
    Tissue invasion: present
    Site: large intestine
    Examples: shigellae, *Entamoeba histolytica*

Bloody watery diarrhea
    Stools: copious, watery, blood, pus (sometimes)
    Tissue invasion: present
    Site: small intestine
    Examples: salmonellae, *Campylobacter, Yersinia*

Hemorrhagic colitis
    Stools: copious, watery, blood, no pus
    Tissue invasion: absent
    Site: large intestine
    Examples: *E. coli* EHEC strains

others, **do not invade** gut cells but still damage the colonic mucosa to cause bloody diarrhea. This disease is known as **hemorrhagic colitis**; consequently, these strains have been grouped together as **enterohemorrhagic** *E. coli* or **EHEC**.

SHIGELLAE

The genus consists of four species, which are serologically grouped on the basis of the carbohydrate somatic antigens of their lipopolysaccharide (LPS). These include the prototype species *S. dysenteriae* (group A), *S. flexneri* (group B), *S. boydii* (group C), and *S. sonnei* (group D). There are multiple serotypes with serogroups A, B, and C, and multiple colicin types of *S. sonnei*. This order also roughly corresponds to their virulence, with *S. dysenteriae* type 1 (which is now encountered primarily in developing countries) causing the most serious illness and *S. sonnei* (the predominant isolate in the U.S. and industrialized countries in general) causing the mildest illness. Since all of these organisms share many virulence properties, including basic mechanisms of cell invasion and intracellular spread, other reasons must exist for the observed clinical differences.

It is interesting to note that there have been major changes in the prevalence of the different *Shigella* species over the past century. After *S. dysenteriae* type 1 was described in the late 1890s by Kiyoshi Shiga (in whose honor the genus is named) during the course of a severe epidemic of lethal dysentery in Japan, the species virtually disappeared from the globe after World War I. In its place, *S. flexneri* emerged as the dominant pathogen internationally, and the result was fewer epidemics and a broader spectrum of illness, ranging from the very severe to the mild. After World War II, *S. flexneri* was replaced by *S. sonnei* in the developed countries, accompanied by a dramatic reduction in frequency of dysentery or grossly bloody diarrhea. In contrast, *S. flexneri* remained the major isolate in developing nations, and severe clinical disease continued to be a problem. In 1969, dysentery mortality increased sharply in Guatemala with the reappearance of epidemic *Shigella dysenteriae* type 1. After the Latin America outbreak, this species appeared a few years later in Africa and Asia and has now become endemic in these regions.

Recently, a resurgence of severe *S. flexneri* infection has occurred in the U.S., mostly among young adult males and apparently related to homosexual practices. Persistent and recurrent shigellosis has been a problem in AIDS patients. During this time, *S. boydii* has remained largely confined to the Indian subcontinent, where it causes a disease spectrum intermediate between *S. flexneri* and *S. sonnei*. While it would be important to understand why and how such major global shifts in organism prevalence occur, the reasons remain obscure.

ENCOUNTER

Shigellae are highly host-adapted bacteria that cause natural infections in humans and only occasionally in other higher primates. In contrast to the watery diarrhea-causing organisms described in the previous chapter, the inoculum needed for *Shigella* infection is very small, ranging from just a few hundred to a few thousand organisms. This makes it easy to transmit infection from person to person. Direct contact spread is the most common route, but this does not exclude transmission through food or water contaminated with feces. Sexually transmitted *S. flexneri*, noted above, is a newly described direct route for infection among homosexual males engaging in anal sex. Whereas this mechanism may explain the observed increase in *S. flexneri* isolates among young adult males in the U.S., it does not explain why this species and not the more prevalent *S. sonnei* has been selected out for transmission in this way.

Shigellae appear to resist the killing effect of acid in vitro and especially in vivo (there is also no apparent increase in susceptibility in patients with **low gastric acidity**, a condition termed **hypochlorhydria**. Recently, it has been shown that acid resistance in *Shigella* is expressed only as growth of the organisms slows down. Transposon insertions that reverse acid resistance map to the **katF** gene, which controls production of a novel RNA polymerase sigma factor. The katF protein is involved in regulating other genes that may be important in the overall stress response of bacteria. A current hypothesis suggests that *Shigella*, being in the growth phase when excreted in the stool, is poised to upregulate **katF** when they encounter adverse conditions such as low temperature, dryness, UV light, or restricted nutrient supply. When this happens, the proteins needed for acid resistance are among those turned on. Since this happens in the environment, the survivors are able to resist gastric acid when they are once again ingested by a human. Their ability to resist acid and reach the small bowel certainly contributes to their success as pathogens.

ENTRY, SPREAD, AND MULTIPLICATION

Once past the stomach, the organisms encounter the normally bacteria-free, slightly alkaline small bowel. The source of the watery diarrhea in shigellosis has remained controversial. It is not disputed that *Shigella* invade human colonic epithelial cells, multiply within them, and spread from cell to cell. This leads to focal mucosal ulcers through which erythrocytes and white blood cells exude to produce the typical dysenteric stool.

Invasion of, and survival within, gut cells is a complex process that involves multiple genes present on both a large 120–140 MDal plasmid and on the chromosome (Fig. 18.1). *Shigella* invasion is, therefore, a model that should allow better understanding of the invasive properties of other enteric bacteria. Although no specific adhesin has been described, some adherence mechanism seems likely to account for the ability of the nonmotile *Shigella* organisms to approach the mucosal surface prior to cell invasion. Several plasmid-encoded outer membrane proteins (called **invasion plasmid antigens, ipas**) are required for invasion. Subsequently, ingested organisms are taken up into vesicles by the normally nonphagocytic mucosal epithelial cells in a manner akin to phagocytosis. This process requires major reorganization of actin and cytoskeletal elements, just as occurs in phagocytosis.

To cause clinical disease, the organism must also rapidly escape from the vesicle to the cytoplasm. This is assisted or mediated by a membrane lytic protein originally called a **hemolysin**. Hemolysis is a convenient assay to study this class of proteins, as it uses readily available erythrocytes and a simple technique. But in this case, as in many other situations, hemolysis does not occur in vivo and concentration on the "hemolysin" function may divert attention from the real function of the molecule. For the shigellae, this function is to release the organism into the cytoplasm of the invaded epithelial cell. Once there, the organisms multiply and migrate by an as yet uncertain mechanism along polymerized actin fibrils to reach the plasma membrane. They can then invade

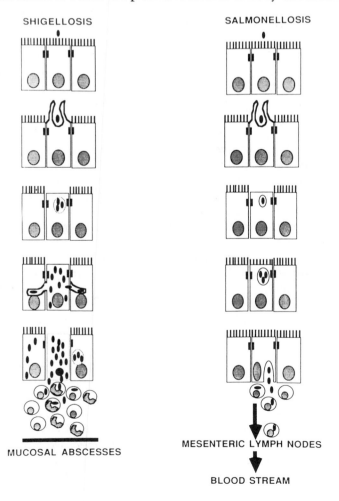

Figure 18.1. Invasion strategies of *Shigella* compared with *Salmonella* in the intestinal epithelium.

SHIGELLOSIS

SALMONELLOSIS

MUCOSAL ABSCESSES

MESENTERIC LYMPH NODES

BLOOD STREAM

adjacent cells, which soon die and are sloughed off, creating focal **ulcers** and an **inflammatory response in the lamina propria**. These latter features are the two most characteristic histological lesions associated with *Shigella* infection. In spite of the mucosal changes, however, bacteremia is uncommon, except for *S. dysenteriae* type 1 infection, which is highly resistant to serum bactericidal activity. In patients with this disease, bacteremia rates as high as 8–10% are reported, especially in poorly nourished infants in the third world. This is, no doubt, promoted by defects in host defenses associated with malnutrition; for example, depressed complement activity, which predisposes to bacteremia.

DAMAGE

There are at least two mechanisms by which *Shigella* damages intestinal epithelial cells. First, the **invasion process** per se is associated with structural alterations of the cytoskeleton in each epithelial cell, leading to focal mucosal damage. Any mutation that impairs the capacity of these organisms to invade renders them avirulent. Second, the capability of the shigellae to produce **cytotoxins** leads to the death of epithelial cells including human colonic mucosal cells. The most potent and best characterized of these cytotoxins is called Shiga toxin and is produced by *S. dysenteriae* type 1. Of the four *Shigella* species, this one alone carries the gene for Shiga toxin. The nature and relatedness of cytotoxins made by the other species is not known. Shiga toxin is a highly specific enzyme that reversibly inactivates the mammalian 60S ribosomal subunit, resulting in irreversible cessation of protein synthesis. Experiments in monkeys have shown that *S. dysenteriae* type 1 with deletions in the Shiga toxin gene can still cause disease, but cause much less damage to the mucosa that the wild type bacterium. This is compelling evidence that both invasion and toxin production play an important role in pathogenesis, and may explain why the highly toxigenic *S. dysenteriae* type 1 is the most virulent of all *Shigella* species and why it causes the most severe clinical illness.

It is curious that *S. sonnei* is as invasive as *S. dysenteriae* type 1 and uses the same mechanisms to accomplish this, but only rarely causes the dysentery syndrome; most commonly, it leads to a self-limited watery diarrhea. The basis for these differences is not understood. A simple distinguishing characteristic of this diarrhea, which separates it from the mild *E. coli* or rotavirus diarrhea that it resembles, is the presence of large numbers of leukocytes in stool, readily visible by light microscopy of stool. Whereas these cells are evidence of an inflammatory response in the gut, this is either not severe or widespread enough to cause bloody diarrhea or dysentery with *S. sonnei*. This lends credence to the proposition that the absence of the gene for Shiga toxin explains why the illness is so mild compared to *S. dysenteriae*.

DIAGNOSIS

You now know that *Shigella* causes a spectrum of clinical illness ranging from mild watery diarrhea to severe dysentery, depending, in part, on the infecting species. Because the mild diarrhea resembles that of other pathogens, and the presence of leukocytes in diarrheal stool is a simple indicator of an invasive pathogen, examination of a fecal sample for leukocytes provides immediately useful diagnostic information. In the same way, clinical presentation with bloody diarrhea or the dysentery syndrome is another direct clue to the presence of a tissue-damaging invasive pathogen. In some parts of the world, up to 50% of patients with bloody diarrhea or dysentery are culture positive for *Shigella*.

Specific diagnosis of shigellosis, is, unfortunately, entirely dependent on the laboratory demonstration of the organism. Isolation rates depend first on rapid processing of the stool sample, either streaking directly onto isolation agar or, in field studies, into a **transport medium** (known as Cary-Blair or buffered glycerol saline) to hold for later streaking. This is the most crucial step, for although it is not very difficult to identify *Shigella*, the organism readily dies in acid stool unless quickly processed. These media have been designed to detect the lactose-negative phenotype characteristic of *Shigella* to permit the picking of colonies for study. A rapid presumptive diagnosis can be made by suspending suspicious colonies and carrying out agglutination reactions with antisera to group antigens of *Shigella*. Additional information is provided by testing for sugar fermentation patterns, which allow genus and species identification.

Now that genes characteristic of *Shigella* have been cloned and sequenced, it has become possible to identify the organism more rapidly by looking for specific genes. The methods use DNA probes complementary for *Shigella* genes, or amplification methods such as PCR to detect *Shigella*-specific sequences (Chapter 55). These methods can ultimately be applied to stool samples, or to food or water, for quick diagnosis and to trace transmission routes. They are likely to come into increasing and widespread use in the U.S. in the next decade, but, because of cost and facilities, are less likely to be introduced in developing countries where the severe disease is found.

THERAPY AND PROPHYLAXIS

Shigellosis is only rarely a significantly dehydrating illness. Thus, it is rare to need intravenous fluids to treat this infection, and oral fluids usually suffice to correct the moderate degree of dehydration and electrolyte abnormality encountered. In the more severe cases, almost always associated with high fever and/or dysentery, the use of antibiotics to which the organism is susceptible is known to reduce the duration of illness and the period of infectivity to others. Reducing the infective period is particularly important because the small inoculum needed for infection with *Shigella* frequently results in transmission to other household members.

Proper choice of antibiotics is complicated by the apparent ease with which the organisms acquire antibiotic resistance; it is not pure chance that transferrable antibiotic resistance was discovered first in *Shigella*. The problem is greatest in developing countries where multiresistant *S. dysenteriae* type 1 is most commonly found, and where cost and availability of the newest antimicrobials are limiting factors. In such situations, clinicians have made use of nalidixic acid, the first member of the quinolone class of drugs. In spite of its potential to cause cartilage damage in children, this drug has been successfully employed during the past 10 years for the treatment of epidemic *S. dysenteriae* type 1 infection, with no obvious evidence of any adverse effect. However, prospective systemic toxicity follow-up studies have not been performed. The most reliably effective drugs at present are the 4-fluoroquinolones. Their use in the U.S. is limited by the Food and Drug Administration to individuals over the age of 17 because of the persistent concern that joint damage may be provoked in the young.

There is no licensed effective vaccine for shigellosis, but many candidates are under study, using molecules discovered in the past decade as candidates for vaccine antigens. These are being altered and packaged in different ways; for example, by gene deletions, gene alterations, and gene transfers to avirulent strains. The goal is to produce living attenuated vaccines that can be administered by mouth and immunize the gut itself. There is also renewed interest in the possibility of using nonliving antigens for the same purpose, and various gene fusions and chemically conjugated vaccine antigens are being made and tested in experimental systems. Ultimately, however, these vaccines must be tested in humans, since no animal model truly mimics human shigellosis.

NONTYPHOIDAL *SALMONELLA* AND TYPHOID FEVER—INTRODUCTION TO THE AGENTS

The genus *Salmonella* is named in honor of Daniel Salmon, who was Director of the Bureau of Animal Industry when the prototype organism, *S. choleraesuis*, was isolated by Theobald Smith from swine suffering from cholera-like diarrhea. This is a vast genus, comprising well over 2000 distinguishable strains (and still counting, as new isolates continue to be identified). Despite this diversity, there are just three species, *S. choleraesuis* (containing the one organism), *S. typhi* (consisting of just the typhoid bacillus), and *S. enteritidis* (which includes all of the rest) (Table 18.2).

Salmonellae are distinguished from one another by their expression of multiple different somatic (O), flagellar (H), and capsular (K) antigens, and by their differing patterns of biochemical reactivity. Individual isolates simultaneously express more than one O and H antigen, and it is the pattern of the combination of these antigens that is employed in the serological classification of the rather huge species *S. enteritidis*. Both *S. choleraesuis* and *S. typhi* are highly **host adapted** to pigs and humans, respectively; however, both can cause human infection. *S. enteritidis* includes serotypes adapted either to humans or animals, as well as nonhost-adapted organisms. The **nonhost-adapted strains**, which can infect many species, are the most common causes of *Salmonella* diarrhea, although only a small fraction of the total number of different *S. enteritidis* strains are recovered from infected humans.

The individual strains of *S. enteritidis* are serotypes and their common name often refers to the location where the organism was first isolated, for example *S. enteritidis* serotype *newport* (usually abbreviated *S. newport*) or *S. enteritidis* serotype *dar-es-salaam* (*S. dar-es-salaam*). Some are named for the animals with which they are primarily associated, e.g., *S. gallinarum* (chickens) or *S. typhimurium* (causing typhoid-like disease in mice), and some are named after people involved in their isolation (e.g., *S. schottmuelleri*).

Table 18.2. Species of *Salmonella*

Name	Number of serotypes	Usual Hosts	Antigens
Salmonella typhi	1	Humans	O, H, Vi
Salmonella choleraesuis	1	Animals	Many different O, H
Salmonella enteritidis	About 2000	Animals, humans	Many different O, H

There are a few characteristic clinical syndromes associated with the genus *Salmonella*. These include **typhoid fever** (caused by mainly by *S. typhi*), **focal infection of vascular endothelium** (*S. choleraesuis*) or particular organ systems (*S. typhimurium*), for example, **osteomyelitis** in sickle cell disease patients, and **diarrhea** (due to many *S. enteritidis* serotypes).

ENCOUNTER

In contrast with the shigellae, the salmonellae have a clear predilection for hypochlorhydric subjects, i.e., individuals with low or absent stomach acidity. The relatively large inoculum required to infect human volunteers with normal gastric acid secretion who are given bicarbonate to neutralize the acid (more than a million organisms) is increased by 10- to 100-fold in the absence of bicarbonate. Typhoid fever is ultimately always traceable to a human carrier (such as Typhoid Mary), although the routes of transmission to the patient may be convoluted and involve contaminated water or food as vehicles. This may be contrasted with the diarrhea-causing salmonellae, which are most often nonhost-adapted and frequently transmitted as a zoonosis through the food chain. It is interesting that, because of its strictly limited human host range, *S. typhi*, but not the nonadapted organism *S. typhimurium* (which causes a typhoid-like disease in mice), is a potential target for eradication. However, *S. typhimurium* is the most common *Salmonella* isolate in the U.S.

ENTRY

In contrast to the shigellae, which use the epithelial cell as the environment to multiply intracellularly, salmonellae including *S. typhi* are taken up by the gut epithelial cells, transit to the basal membrane without multiplying, and are released into the lamina propria (Fig. 18.2). For the salmonellae, then, the gut epithelial cell is not their habitat for growth and multiplication so much as a barrier to be crossed, and, in the initial passage, the gut cell is apparently not harmed.

SPREAD AND MULTIPLICATION

As nontyphoidal salmonellae penetrate the mucosa to reach the lamina propria, they often enter the **bloodstream** and may be recovered in blood cultures early in the course of the disease. They normally do not cause sustained bacteremia because they are rapidly taken up by the phagocytic cell system and effectively killed. Exceptions to this rule, which appear to spread systemically much more often than the other serotypes of the species, often causing focal systemic infections are *S. typhimurium* and, possibly, a serotype of *S. enteritidis*. **Clinical conditions that significantly impair functioning of the mononuclear phagocyte system** enhance susceptibility to *Salmonella* bacteremia. For example, patients with sickle cell anemia, in whom chronic hemolysis may lead to functional impairment of the phagocytic system, have a ten-fold higher incidence of invasive salmonellosis. A marked increase in incidence and severity of infection is observed as well in immunosuppressing diseases, particularly AIDS, but also in leukemia or lymphoma patients, and in chronic granulomatous disease.

The **diarrhea-causing** *Salmonella* multiply in the lamina propria, where they induce fluid secretion by as yet uncertain mechanisms. Various investigators have presented evidence that these organisms

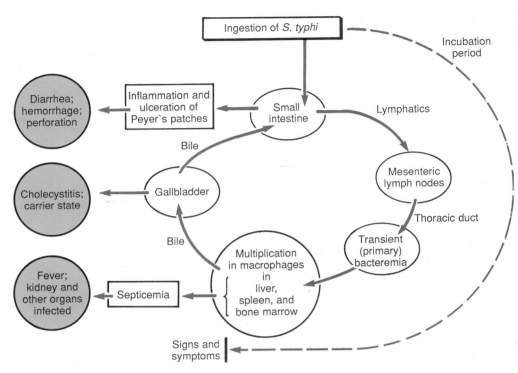

Figure 18.2.   Pathogenesis of typhoid fever.

produce a cholera toxin-like molecule, induce cAMP, prostaglandins, or other inflammatory mediators that may alter electrolyte and fluid transport across the mucosa, or make toxins inhibiting protein synthesis, and thus superficially resembling Shiga toxin. The evidence is not yet conclusive. However, as these organisms are not specifically adapted to survive within the intracellular environment of the phagocytic vesicle, they are cleared by phagocytosis and the diarrhea is, therefore, self-limited.

In the case of the **typhoid bacilli**, passage into the small bowel is followed by invasion across the mucosa and the rapid sequestration of organisms within the mononuclear cells in regional lymph nodes. An initial bacteremia carries them to the liver and spleen. This systemic spread is clinically silent and brief, as the bacteria are cleared from the circulation. A period of multiplication in macrophages of liver, spleen, and mesenteric lymph nodes follows, representing the asymptomatic incubation period of typhoid fever in humans.

In contrast to the nontyphoidal salmonellae, **typhoid bacilli are not killed and they steadily multiply within macrophages**. When the number of intracellular organisms reaches a threshold, they are released to the bloodstream, initiating a period of continuous bacteremia. This event signals the start of clinical illness, manifested by daily high fevers of 39–40°C continuing for 4–8 weeks in untreated cases. In addition, the bacteremia leads to invasion of the gallbladder, kidney, and reinvasion of the gut mucosa, especially at the Peyer's patches. Thus, the organism can be isolated not only from blood, but also from stool and urine at this stage. Uptake of organisms by monocyte/macrophages in bone marrow makes this site a useful source of culture material when other sites are negative, as it may actually enrich for the organism and facilitate isolation.

It is interesting that, in mice at least, a gene has been identified that confers the ability to more rapidly eradicate intracellular *S.*

typhimurium or *S. enteritidis*, the murine models for typhoid-like disease. This gene, *ity*, is closely linked (and may be identical) to a gene modulating host response to two other facultative intracellular pathogens, the protozoan *Leishmania*, and the attenuated mycobacterium BCG, the vaccine strain for tuberculosis. Recent studies have shown this locus is also linked to the genes for the interleukin-1 receptor and for susceptibility to type 1 diabetes in the nonobese diabetic (NOD) mouse.

DAMAGE

We have already mentioned that nontyphoidal *Salmonella* can induce an inflammatory response in the gut mucosa. The specific role of invasion gene products and toxins is not yet well defined. Some of the damage caused in gut mucosa is clearly due to the inflammatory response itself, which is elicited in the lamina propria.

In the case of the typhoid bacilli, invasion of the gallbladder may be temporary or may result in the long-term colonization that characterizes the typhoid carrier state, especially in the presence of gall stones. In some cases, an acute necrotizing cholecystitis may result. *S. typhi* survives well in gall stones, and it can be recovered from the center of a cut open stone; viable organisms may be obtained after submersion of the stone into bactericidal concentrations of antibiotics. This is a source of prolonged carriage and a means for the convalescent host to continue to excrete the organism in the stool. While one classic teaching is that the secondary (prolonged) bacteremia is the mechanism for secondary gut invasion, it is possible that bacteria reaching the gut lumen via the bile may localize to and penetrate M cells, causing strong inflammatory responses. Invasion of the kidney has been associated with glomerulonephritis. Secondary reinvasion of the gut leads to a more common event, severe bleeding and/or perforation, attributable to the marked inflammatory response induced in the Peyer's patches. The clinical prognosis is much worse when these events occur.

The various species of *Salmonella* differ with regard to their ability to adhere to endovascular surfaces and cause endocarditis or endothelial infection. Despite its predilection for entering the bloodstream and the continuous bacteremia it causes, *S. typhi* only rarely adheres to vascular epithelia and is a very uncommon cause of endocarditis. In contrast, *S. choleraesuis* and *S. enteritidis* adhere well to these surfaces and lead to endothelial infections that are tenacious and difficult to treat, often necessitating valve replacement.

DIAGNOSIS

Salmonellosis is generally diagnosed by the microbiology laboratory through the use of selective media for isolation and a combination of biochemical, serological, and physical parameters for the specific identification. Salmonellae are nonlactose fermenters, and the same media used for shigellae serve to pick out suspicious colonies. These are inoculated onto differential media such as triple sugar iron agar (TSI), which allows the technician to confirm the lactose-negative phenotype rapidly and the ability of the isolate to ferment glucose anaerobically. These characteristics are like shigellae, however, it may be possible to detect motility and H_2S in the TSI tube, which are clues to the correct identification. Sugar fermentations and other biochemical properties, and serological identification of various somatic O and flagellar H antigens allow the general classification of the isolate to the proper genus. Most clinical laboratories will then determine the major O-serogroup antigen (A-E for human pathogens) and stop at that stage of presumptive identification; they are not prepared to carry the process to the bioserotype level because they lack the multiple typing sera required, as well as the time or funds to do it. Serological identification is most useful for epidemiological purposes, and the Centers for Disease Control or various State Public Health Laboratories may serve as reference labs.

Typhoid fever is not recognized in the asymptomatic incubation period. The specific diagnosis is usually made by blood culture, and these usually become positive early in the course of clinical illness (Fig. 18.3). *S. typhi* is not difficult to identify in blood culture because it is likely to be the only organism present. When isolated from the stool, it is necessary to use selective media, usually containing bile salts to inhibit the growth of the normal Gram-positive and Gram-negative fecal flora. Gram-negative bacilli have some resistance to bile salts, but not to high concentrations, since bile salts are reabsorbed in the ileum and are reduced in concentration in the stool. In contrast, *S. typhi* survives in bile itself within the gallbladder, and resists high concentrations of bile salts. Colonies of *S. typhi* are initially recognized by their lactose-negative phenotype on isolation media and the production of small amounts of H_2S, which results in a trace of a black reaction product in TSI agar. The suspicion is supported by serogrouping to identify the major somatic O antigen. *S. typhi* is in group D and is also positive for the capsular Vi antigen.

A serological diagnosis of typhoid can also be made based on O and H antibody titers. A rising titer or a single very high O antigen titer is suggestive. The Vi antigen also elicits an antibody response; however, a few other organisms also produce the same antigen and detection of anti-Vi antibody is not conclusive for *S. typhi*. These tests are all simple agglutination assays in which killed organisms are mixed with patient sera. If antibodies are present, they cross-link organisms, resulting in the formation of bacterial clumps visible to the naked eye. The highest dilution of serum that results in agglutination is the antibody titer.

THERAPY AND PROPHYLAXIS

In the past, the recommendation was not to treat *Salmonella* diarrhea with antibiotics, because no diminution in disease duration could be demonstrated; instead, a prolongation in the stool carriage was observed. This is no longer the case with the introduction of new fluoroquinolones, which both eradicate the organism and decrease the period of illness. These drugs are not currently approved for use in children under the age of 17 years, because of the potential danger of cartilage damage that has been observed in animal toxicity studies. The treatment of diarrhea due to salmonellae in young children is, thus, a problem.

Systemic *Salmonella* infections do require antimicrobial therapy, and a number of drugs may be used, depending on antibiotic resistance patterns. These include β-lactams such as ampicillin, amoxicillin, or the combination of one of these drugs with a β-lactamase inhibitor such as clavulanic acid or sulbactam (e.g., Augmentin, Unasyn), a third-generation cephalosporin, the combination of trimethoprim and sulfamethoxazole (Bactrim, Septra), or one of the new 4-fluoroquinolones.

Prophylaxis at the present time is restricted to behavioral measures, such as avoidance of potentially contaminated food or water by travel-

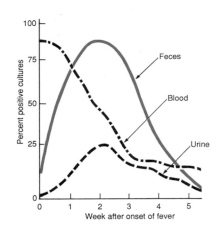

Figure 18.3. The isolation of typhoid bacilli from various sources in the course of untreated typhoid fever. The late rise in positive stool cultures is because of secondary invasion of the gut by organisms from the gallbladder.

ers to developing countries. This is especially important in an individual with diminished gastric acid secretory capacity, either because of disease or drugs, for example H_2 blockers for ulcer therapy. Vaccines do not exist, although considerable work is currently underway to develop attenuated strains for immunization and for use as vaccine vectors to carry and to deliver exogenous foreign antigens to the hosts immune system.

The typhoid bacilli have been almost invariably susceptible to chloramphenicol since its introduction nearly 5 decades ago, and it has remained the therapeutic gold standard for this infection. Resistant strains have emerged from time to time, but these are not sustained in the environment, and except for a clonal epidemic, is an unlikely (but always possible) event. Ampicillin and trimethoprim-sulfamethoxazole have been almost as effective clinically, but resistance is more common. At the present time, the new fluoroquinolones are uniformly active, and there are many choices available to the clinician, including some third-generation cephalosporins. It is interesting that, since the introduction of effective antimicrobial therapy for typhoid, infections are rapidly brought under control and mortality is decreased. However, the relapse rate has significantly increased. This may be because early therapy aborts immune responses necessary for preventing relapse while treatment fails to eradicate every intracellular organism in the course of therapy. If there is no effective cell-mediated immunity, these survivors may multiply to the point where bacteremia and symptoms occur again.

Progress in typhoid vaccine development has occurred in the past few years. A live oral attenuated strain, containing a mutated galactose epimerase, is able to penetrate the mucosal M cells but not survive, because the enzyme defect results in the accumulation of galactose that is ultimately toxic. Thus, natural immunity can develop while the organism self-destructs. In addition, purified Vi polysaccharide vaccine induces protection in older children and adults with a single injection. Each of these vaccines has an efficacy of 60–80% in various studies.

Typhoid carriers are a public health concern because they often are asymptomatic shedders; they not only carry the organism but constantly spread them via their feces. Treatment of typhoid carriers has been difficult, but also represented a social imperative. Since there was no successful treatment in her day, Typhoid Mary was jailed. Today the recommended course of action is prolonged antibiotic therapy (a new 4-fluoroquinolone may be the most effective form), with removal of gallstones if these are present as well, or cholecystectomy.

ENTEROHEMORRHAGIC *E. COLI*—INTRODUCTION TO THE AGENT

The enterohemorrhagic *E. coli* comprise a limited number of *E. coli* serotypes that can cause a characteristic nonfebrile bloody diarrhea known as hemorrhagic colitis. The most common of these serotypes in the U.S. is O157:H7, but others, particularly O26, are found with greater frequency elsewhere in the world. EHEC have two special characteristics of pathogenic importance. First, they produce high levels of one or both of two related cytotoxins resembling Shiga toxin in both structure and function, exerting the same enzymatic action and binding specificity. These toxins are, therefore, called Shiga-like toxins (SLT I or II) (they are often called Verotoxins in Canada and Europe). Second, they possess a gene highly homologous to the EPEC attaching

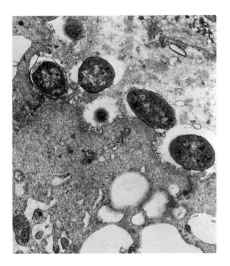

Figure 18.4. Electron micrograph of colon from monkey infected with O157:H7 strain isolated from a human with hemorrhagic colitis. This animal developed bloody diarrhea. Note the attaching bacteria and the altered epithelial cell membrane beneath them showing the classical "cup" and "pedestal" formation associated with EHEC and EPEC expressing the *eae* gene (original magnification, 28,526 ×).

and effacing *eae* gene, which functions in an analogous manner in EHEC (Fig. 18.4). It is the combination of eae and SLT production that presumably damages the gut mucosa and results in the clinical manifestations of hemorrhagic colitis.

ENCOUNTER

E. coli O157:H7, the predominant EHEC strain in the U.S., causes both outbreaks and sporadic disease. It may be transmitted primarily as a zoonosis from animals to humans. The organism is commonly isolated from cattle and several outbreaks have been traced to undercooked hamburgers. It was first reported to be a human pathogen only in 1983 and relatively little is known about its behavior in nature. For example, the infectious dose, the clinical importance of diminished gastric acid production, and the mechanism for transmission of sporadic EHEC infection remain poorly understood.

ENTRY AND MULTIPLICATION

Once past the stomach, EHEC colonize the terminal regions of the bowel where they remain confined to the surface of the gut mucosa and do not invade systemically. Within the colon, the organisms attach to epithelial cells and multiply locally. The disease is usually self-limiting but the mechanisms for control of infection are not defined.

DAMAGE

Wherever **EHEC** attach to the colon they cause structural damage to the surface epithelial cell membrane beneath the attached organisms. This is due to the effects of the *eae* gene, which induces dramatic rearrangements of actin and cytoskeletal elements leading to the so-called "attaching and effacing" lesion of the brush border. In addition, EHEC produce SLT cytotoxins that promote inflammation of the colonic mucosa, resulting in focal purulent exudates and bleeding. Systemic manifestations associated with **EHEC** (**hemolytic-uremic syndrome, HUS,** or **thrombotic thrombocytopenic purpura, TTP**), are believed to be related to systemic absorption of SLT, possibly in combination with endotoxin. These syndromes represent the clinical response to endothelial damage of glomeruli and the central nervous system. In vitro the SLT toxins are cytotoxic for endothelial cells in primary or long-term culture, although how this results in later physiological effects is not yet understood. Beyond this, the virulence characteristics of EHEC are still under study. The availability of isogenic strains differing in one characteristic only, and the use of animal models of local and distant pathology will permit an analysis of the microbial factors causing these tissue-damaging manifestations.

DIAGNOSIS

The syndrome of hemorrhagic colitis is sufficiently characteristic that it can be recognized by good clinicians and the stool cultured for O157:H7 straight away. Cultures taken early in the illness are much more likely to be positive than those obtained after a few days. The screening method capitalizes on a property relatively unique to serotype O157:H7; namely, the inability of O157 but not other EHEC serotypes to ferment sorbitol, in contrast to over 99% of stool *E. coli* that are sorbitol positive. Nonfermenting colonies are selected from growth on sorbitol-MacConkey agar as putative EHEC; these can be confirmed as O157 with a commercial latex agglutination test, which appears to be both highly sensitive and specific. Unfortunately, even this is not necessarily sufficient for laboratory diagnosis since other organisms, for example, *E. hermannii* (present in foods such as raw milk and beef), can be sorbitol negative and also agglutinate in serotype O157 antisera. *E. hermannii* can be distinguished from O157 by cellobiose fermentation, and it would be particularly important to test for this property in isolates from food.

Sporadic illness due to EHEC is not as readily diagnosed. These episodes are not necessarily associated with bloody diarrhea, and if use of sorbitol-MacConkey agar is restricted to classical cases, prevalence of O157:H7 will be underestimated. Gene probes are available for SLT I and II, and will identify these organisms, although probe methodology is not routine in clinical laboratories as of yet. Because toxin genes in EHEC are carried by temperate phage, they can be induced by the drug mitomycin C. SLT production in colonies grown on mitomycin C-containing agar is markedly enhanced, permitting detection of the toxin by means of a monoclonal antibody followed by a second antibody-alkaline phosphatase complex and substrate. Toxin-producing colonies turn blue and are readily distinguished from the non-toxin producers.

THERAPY AND PROPHYLAXIS

Treatment for EHEC infections has not been established. There is some controversy at this time because a few investigators have suggested that antibiotic therapy may increase the likelihood of hemolytic-uremic syndrome (HUS). There is no proof for this hypothesis, nor is there a plausible reason why this should be so. Patients developing HUS may be clinically worse and more likely to be treated with antibiotics so that an apparent association between antibiotic use and HUS is observed. Fluid therapy is relatively simple because large volume losses associated with dehydration are not the typical picture of EHEC. The major challenge is to treat the complications of EHEC, such as HUS, for which supportive measures, including dialysis if needed for renal failure, are indicated. Recovery is usually complete, although significant sequelae will occur in some individuals, including chronic renal failure leading to transplantation.

CONCLUSIONS

Of the bacterial pathogens that damage the intestinal mucosa and lead to bloody and/or inflammatory enteritis, most are invasive into intestinal tissue, such as *Shigella, Salmonella, Yersinia,* and *Campylobacter* and lead to damage of tissue by the inflammatory response they elicit or by making cytotoxins that alter gut epithelial cells. The enterohemorrhagic *E. coli* (EHEC) are exceptions. While not invasive, EHEC can alter cytoskeletal elements of the brush border by means of the eae gene product and affect the viability of epithelial cells via production of cytotoxins (SLT I and II).

Pathogenesis is much better understood today. For example, multiple genes have been identified in controlling the complex process of invasion by *Shigella,* the leading cause of dysentery, although it is uncertain why certain *Shigella* species (*S. sonnei,* for example) primarily cause an inflammatory watery diarrhea that is indistinguishable from the disease caused by nontyphoidal salmonellae. At the same time, *Salmonella* can, on occasion, lead to frankly bloody diarrhea or dysentery. The noninvasive EHEC typically cause nonfebrile grossly bloody diarrhea with cramps, often described as passing liquid blood and known as hemorrhagic colitis. The differences in clinical manifestations can be ascribed to the specific virulence factors these organisms express.

Salmonella typhi is a highly human adapted organism that enters the host via a fecal-oral route and is invasive across the intestinal mucosa. However, unlike nontyphoidal salmonellae, it results in typhoid fever and not diarrhea. Typhoid is a fundamentally different infection in which the organism behaves as a classical facultative intracellular pathogen of the mononuclear phagocytes, within which they survive. Both microbial and host genes have been identified that affect this interaction, although the basic pathogenic mechanisms are not well understood.

Self-assessment Questions

1. Describe the steps in pathogenesis of shigellosis. Relate these to the clinical events of dysentery.

2. Describe the characteristics of enterohemorrhagic *E. coli* and the nature of the disease they cause.

3. Describe the properties of typhoid bacilli that help explain the complex cycle of typhoid fever.

4. Given the route of transmission of *Shigella*, *Salmonella*, and the enterohemorrhagic *E. coli*, what precautions can be taken to lessen the risk of infection with these organisms?

5. Which, if any, of these infections represents a problem in AIDS patients?

SUGGESTED READING

Acheson DWK, Donohue-Rolfe A, Keusch GT. The family of shiga and shiga like toxins. In: Alouf JE, Freer JH, Eds. Sourcebook of bacterial protein toxins. New York: Academic Press, 1991.

Bennish, ML, Wojtyniak, BJ. Mortality from shigellosis: community and hospital data. Rev Infect Dis 1991;13 (suppl 4):245–251.

Bryant HE, Athar MA, Pai CH. Risk factors for *Escherichia coli* O157:H7 infection in an urban community. J Infect Dis 1989;160:858–864.

Cleary TG, Lopez EL. The Shiga-like toxin-producing *Escherichia coli* and hemolytic uremic syndrome. Pediatr Infect Dis J 1989;8:720–724.

Hale TL. Genetic basis of virulence in *Shigella* species. Microbiol Rev 1991;55:206–224.

Jerse AE, Gicquelais KG, Kaper JB. Plasmid and chromosomal elements involved in the pathogenesis of attaching and effacing *Escherichia coli*. Infect Immunol 1991;59:3869–3875.

Pseudomonas aeruginosa: Ubiquitous Pathogen

19

Debbie S. Toder

Pseudomonads are common inhabitants of soil and water, and contact with healthy humans is widespread but usually insignificant. However, these organisms are important opportunistic pathogens that cause a variety of infections in immunocompromised patients, such as burn victims, cancer patients, and children with cystic fibrosis. Pseudomonads are flexible in their nutritional requirements and are capable of using a wide variety of carbon and nitrogen sources to grow in diverse environments.

Because of this adaptability and their intrinsic and acquired resistance to many common antibiotics, pseudomonads find the hospital environment accommodating. Equipment that requires a wet, body-temperature environment, such as dialysis tubing and respiratory therapy equipment, is particularly susceptible to contamination. In the hospital, *Pseudomonas aeruginosa* can be cultured from handwashing sinks, hand creams, and even certain cleaning solutions. Whereas few healthy humans are colonized with *P. aeruginosa*, admission to the hospital increases the carriage rate.

CASE 1

R. is a 4-year-old Caucasian boy on maintenance chemotherapy for acute lymphocytic leukemia (now in remission). He was brought by his parents to the emergency room because he had had fevers as high as 41°C over the preceding 24 hours. In the emergency room, he was alert but ill-appearing and preferred to sit on his mother's lap. He was pale, his breath and pulse were rapid, and he was in mild respiratory distress with clear lung fields. Despite his fever, his extremities were cool and clammy. Because he had required many intravenous medications, a central venous catheter had been surgically implanted. The site where this entered the skin was intact and dry without any redness.

Blood analysis showed that he had a white blood count of 300/mm³ (about 10% of normal). A third-generation cephalosporin (ceftazidime) and an aminoglycoside (tobramycin) were started intravenously. Within the next hours, R.'s status deteriorated with worsening respiratory distress, requiring intubation and mechanical ventilation, and circulatory failure requiring fluid therapy and drugs to increase his blood pressure. The tentative diagnosis of **shock** *probably due to* **sepsis** *(bacterial infection of the bloodstream) was made.*

The initial blood cultures were positive for P. aeruginosa, *but those obtained during fevers the second and third days of hospitalization were nega-*

281

tive. R. gradually improved and was able to be weaned from drugs used to increase his blood pressure and ventilatory support. His next course of cancer chemotherapy was delayed because his blood counts remained low, but these did improve and this therapy was continued.

The following questions arise:

- What was the main predisposing factor?
- Where did the organism come from? How did it gain entry into the bloodstream?
- What caused the symptoms of the infection?
- What other sites could become infected in such a patient?

The child in this case was at risk for infection by virtue of impaired host defenses caused by his malignancy and its treatment. While it did not play a role in this instance, an **indwelling catheter**, most commonly in the bladder or a vein, or an **endotracheal tube**, increases risk by serving as a portal for infection.

As in this case, *P. aeruginosa* generally causes disease in humans only where there is **local or systemic breach of the immune system** (Table 19.1). Local lesions are often seen in people with corneal abrasions, burns, and surgical wounds. *P. aeruginosa* also causes osteomyelitis following puncture wound (typically with a nail) of the foot. *P. aeruginosa* infects chronic cutaneous ulcers in persons with impaired local circulation, such as diabetics. Once the organism has gained entry into a patient, **dissemination** through the bloodstream and **sepsis** are possible. Patients with severe defects in immunity, such as those induced by malignancies, diabetes, chemotherapeutic or other immunosuppressive agents, are at greatest risk from systemic pseudomonal infections. Infections in these patients are most often caused by those bacteria with which they are colonized. Therefore, acquisition of *P. aeruginosa* and other Gram negatives in the hospital is an important problem.

Table 19.1. Relationship Between Selected Predisposing Factors and Varieties of *Pseudomonas* Infections

Predisposing Factor	Type of Infection
I. Local breach of the immune system	
Cystic fibrosis	Pneumonia, chronic recurrent
Trauma	Osteomyelitis
I.V. drug abuse	Endocarditis, septic arthritis, osteomyelitis
Neurosurgical operations	Meningitis
Surgical operations	Pneumonia
Tracheostomy	Pneumonia
Intravenous lines	Cellulitis, suppurative thrombophlebitis
Corneal injury	Panophthalmitis
Kidney stones	Urinary tract infection
Catheterization	Urinary tract colonization and urinary tract infection
II. Systemic	
Neutropenia	Septicemia, pneumonia, abscesses
Diabetes	Malignant otitis externa
Premature infants and neonates	Septicemia, meningitis, enteritis
III. Both systemic and local	
Burns	Burn wound infection, septicemia

CASE 2

The parents of Z., a 2-year-old girl with a chronic cough, became alarmed because her cough worsened over a week's time and they noticed that her color started to "become poor" with coughing. Her parents are now unable to remember when she was last cough-free and describe that she sometimes spits out yellow-green mucus after forceful coughing, most often on arising in the morning.

On examination, Z. was an alert but pasty and pale-looking child showing increased respiratory effort and rapid breathing. On inspiration, crackles were heard throughout the lung fields. Her extremities showed moderate clubbing with mild cyanosis. A chest x-ray (Fig. 19.1) showed increased (abnormal) interstitial and peribronchial markings. By gagging the child with a sterile swab, a specimen of the green mucus was obtained and sent for Gram stain and culture.

Based on the history, physical examination, and x-ray, the physicians caring for the child suspected that Z. had cystic fibrosis. Intravenous ceftazidime and tobramycin were administered while awaiting the results of a chloride sweat test (diagnostic of cystic fibrosis) and sputum culture. The sputum Gram stain showed many Gram-negative bacilli. In culture, these were initially described as nonlactose fermenting Gram-negative rods and then identified as P. aeruginosa. Z. gradually improved and, after 2 weeks of therapy, her x-ray (Fig. 19.2) showed improvement.

The following questions could be asked:

- How does *Pseudomonas* infection differ between the two cases?

- Do the same strains of *Pseudomonas* infect patients with cystic fibrosis and others?

- What was the route of entry of the organism in this case?

- Do antibiotics help in such a case?

This case illustrates an early episode in the course of *Pseudomonas* infection in cystic fibrosis. Bronchopulmonary *Pseudomonas* infection in this disease is characterized by exacerbations and remissions, although the organism is probably never completely eradicated. Despite this, antipseudomonal antibiotic therapy leads to a decrease in the number of organisms in the sputum and improved pulmonary function. Interestingly, antibiotics with little in vitro antipseudomonal activity often appear to improve the clinical status of patients with cystic fibrosis. It may be that these antibiotics down-regulate the production of

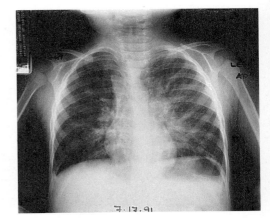

Figure 19.1. Interstitial and peribronchial markings seen pretreatment.

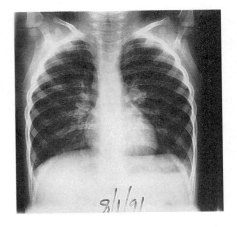

Figure 19.2. Same patient as shown in Figure 19.1, after 2 weeks of intravenously administered ceftazidime and tobramycin.

virulence factors by *Pseudomonas* in the cystic fibrosis lung. In vitro, subinhibitory concentrations of antibiotics have been shown to have this effect. The behavior and appearance of *P. aeruginosa* is different in the cystic fibrosis lung than in other infections; mucoid strains are associated almost exclusively with this disease. The polysaccharide responsible for the mucoid phenotype does not, by itself, cause tissue destruction, but it may enable the organisms to evade host defenses and persist in the lung.

Pseudomonas infection in cystic fibrosis is unique because of its exceptionally chronic course; affected individuals may become infected in childhood and despite continued infection live, with current therapy, into the fourth or fifth decade of life. Although the infection is never cleared and lung function progressively declines, *Pseudomonas* sepsis virtually never occurs in cystic fibrosis.

PSEUDOMONADS

The members of the genus *Pseudomonas*, colloquially called the **pseudomonads**, belong to a large group of aerobic nonfermenting, actively motile Gram-negative rods. About one-third of clinical isolates are pigmented, producing characteristic green or blue-green colonies colored by the water-soluble pigment, **pyocyanin**. Colonies on agar plates have a characteristic fruity or grape-like odor, which is sometimes noticed near wounds or other sites that are heavily colonized with these organisms.

The medically most important species of this genus is *P. aeruginosa*, but others may cause disease infrequently. *P. aeruginosa* makes a large number of cellular and secreted molecules that participate in its pathogenesis (Table 19.2). As discussed in relation to Case 2, some strains associated with cystic fibrosis make a polysaccharide **capsule** consisting of a compound called **alginate** that makes colonies mucoid.

Pseudomonads are rapidly growing, robust organisms that can persist in marginal environments. Consequently, they are difficult to eradicate from contaminated areas, e.g., hospital rooms, clinics, operating rooms, and medical equipment such as respiratory support devices. They may even survive in some antiseptic solutions used to disinfect instruments and endoscopes.

These organisms do not carry out fermentations, obtaining their energy from the oxidation of sugars. Nevertheless, many strains can grow anaerobically using nitrate as a terminal electron acceptor. Pseudomonads have minimal nutritional requirements, needing only acetate and ammonia as sources of carbon and nitrogen. These simple needs are met by a large number of organic compounds, so they grow well on simple media, including nutrient agar and the media used for enteric bacteria. Being nearly omnivorous makes them popular candidates for industrial and environmental uses, such as cleaning up toxic wastes. The first patent awarded for a genetically engineered bacterium was for a pseudomonad designed to clean up petroleum spills by its ability to oxidize hydrocarbons.

Most pseudomonads (except *P. mallei*) are motile, with one or several polar flagella. In this, they differ from *Escherichia coli* and other enterobacteriaceae, which have flagella all around the cell. In fact, pseudomonads are taxonomically quite distant from the enterobacteriaceae. Most pseudomonads produce indophenol oxidase, an enzyme that renders them positive in the oxidase test frequently used in diag-

Table 19.2. Virulence Factors of *P. aeruginosa*

Product	Location	Mechanism of Action	Possible Contribution to Virulence
Pili	Polar	Adherence	Colonization
Lipopolysaccharide	Outer membrane	Lipid A is biologically active portion	Stimulates release of vasoactive peptides, activates clotting; fibrinolytic complement systems
Flagellum	Polar	Motility	Dissemination
Exotoxin A	Secreted	ADP-ribosylation of EF-2	Tissue damage
Exoenzyme S	Secreted	ADP-ribosylation of several proteins (not EF-2)	Tissue damage
Elastase	Secreted	Cleavage of elastin, collagen, immunoglobulins, complement components, etc.	Tissue damage
Alkaline protease	Secreted	Proteolysis	Tissue damage
Phospholipase C (heat-labile hemolysin)	Secreted	Hydrolysis of phospholipids, especially those in eukaryotic membranes	Tissue damage obtaining inorganic phosphate
Heat-stable phospholipase	Secreted	Hydrolysis of phospholipids, especially those in eukaryotic membranes	Tissue damage obtaining inorganic phosphate

Table 19.3. Antibiotic Resistance of *P. aeruginosa*

Antibiotic Class (Examples)	Mechanism of Action	Types of Resistance
β-lactams antipseudomonal penicillins, e.g., ticarcillin; cephalosporins, e.g., ceftazidine	Inhibit completion of cell-wall cross-linking	Plasmid-encoded β-lactamase; chromosomal β-lactamase; decreased affinity of penicillin-binding proteins; ? altered porins
Aminoglycosides e.g., tobramycin, gentamicin	Inhibit protein synthesis at the 30S ribosomal unit	Aminoglycoside-modifying enzymes; altered ribosome structure; decreased uptake of aminoglycoside
Quinolones e.g., ciprofloxacin	Inhibit DNA gyrase	Mutations in DNA gyrase; alterations of outer membrane proteins

nostic microbiology. They share this characteristic with the neisseriae; few other clinically important bacteria are oxidase positive.

Pseudomonads are resistant to many commonly used antibiotics, including first- and second-generation penicillins and cephalosporins, tetracyclines, chloramphenicol, and vancomycin (Table 19.3). The aminoglycosides, fluoroquinolones, and some newer β-lactams are usually effective. Because the resistance pattern among *Pseudomonas* strains varies from hospital to hospital and changes from year to year, the proper choice of antibiotics must be based upon continuous surveillance of drug sensitivity.

ENCOUNTER AND ENTRY

Because *P. aeruginosa* lives in the water and soil, it can be found on vegetables and living plants as well as in water taps, drains, and other wet surfaces. The organisms may be ingested from such sources. Splashed water from a contaminated sink or droplets suctioned from a colonized endotracheal tube may spread the organisms. If present in large enough numbers, pseudomonads may enter the skin, possibly through insignificant abrasions. This happens when people take baths in contaminated hot tubs, which may result in infections involving the hair follicles (**folliculitis**) that are all over the body. The favorable conditions of temperature in hot tubs allow for spectacular blooms of *Pseudomonas* that reach up to 100 million organisms per ml!

P. aeruginosa **does not adhere to normal intact epithelium.** In vitro, pili act as an adhesins to buccal and tracheal epithelial cells but the receptor molecules on epithelial cells have not been identified. Some investigators have suggested that, in the lung, **mucin** may be the site of adherence. Animal models of adherence that involve injury of epithelium before exposure to the organisms have proven informative. Influenza virus, endotracheal intubation, and treatment with chemicals have been used to damage airway epithelium. Piliated strains adhered better to damaged tracheal epithelium than did otherwise identical nonpiliated strains. These models are attractive because they take into account the clinical observation that *Pseudomonas* infections occur when the immune system—local or systemic—is breached. Similar approaches have been taken to investigate burn wound infections and corneal infections. Infection of the cornea occurs when there has been some abrasion or injury (often associated with contact lenses).

Appropriate animal models have been developed to study the pathogenesis of some of these human infections such as corneal and burn wound infections. Developing an animal model of the chronic, persistent lung infection seen in cystic fibrosis is more difficult and illustrates the importance of adherence and persistence. When *Pseudomonas* are instilled intratracheally in an animal, the organisms are either cleared or the animal dies of acute pneumonia. To overcome this problem, the organisms are embedded in agar beads before instillation. Histological changes resembling those seen in cystic fibrosis lung infection now occur. Unfortunately, the artificial introduction of the organisms does not allow one to elucidate aspects of encounter or entry. The creation of a transgenic animal with the ion transport defect of cystic fibrosis will most likely be the key to investigation of these early aspects of *Pseudomonas* infection in cystic fibrosis.

SPREAD AND MULTIPLICATION

Pseudomonads are typical extracellular pathogens. Their growth in tissue depends largely upon their ability to resist ingestion by neutrophils. Many strains possess an antiphagocytic polysaccharide slime layer and make cytolytic exotoxins. Nonetheless, the low frequency of pseudomonad infections in healthy persons shows that the phagocytes usually have the upper hand. Patients, like the individual in Case 1, with reduced numbers of circulating neutrophils, are at high risk.

What determines whether colonization, local infection, or systemic infection occurs after contact with *Pseudomonas*? The use of isogenic strains of *Pseudomonas* in animal models allows one to study the role of a given gene product. Animals are infected with strains differing only in one gene, allowing pathogenic differences to be attributed to the product of this gene. In a burned mouse model, strains deficient in a number of extracellular products (**toxin A, elastase or exoenzyme S,** Table 19.2) persist in the wound but do not disseminate. Strains lacking **flagella** are also less virulent than wild-type strains. Tissue damage by toxins and proteases may facilitate flagella-mediated mobility and invasion.

Pseudomonas employ several strategies to obtain scarce nutrients during their infection. Obtaining **iron** is vital and difficult; virtually all of the iron in human serum is tightly bound to transferrin. *Pseudomonas* produce iron-binding compounds or **siderophores,** which compete with transferrin for iron. Interestingly, in a retrospective study, leukemic patients who became bacteremic with *P. aeruginosa* have more decreased total iron-binding capacity than a group of patients who became colonized but not infected. Iron limitation increases the production of two extracellular products of *P. aeruginosa*, elastase and exotoxin A. In turn, these proteins may damage tissue or create conditions (e.g., lower pH) that make iron more accessible to the organisms. When another necessary nutrient, **phosphate**, is limited, *P. aeruginosa* increases production of phospholipase C. This enzyme hydrolyzes phospholipids from host cell membranes to release phosphate in an available form.

To survive in the host, *Pseudomonas* must not only obtain nutrition but must also be able to evade host defenses. In the bloodstream, the organisms do not usually survive and are only cause sepsis in immunocompromised patients, such as Case 1. **Neutrophils** are clearly involved in curbing the proliferation of the organisms, as seen by the increased incidence of *Pseudomonas* sepsis in persons with severe neutropenia.

In cystic fibrosis (Case 2), the organisms find themselves in an environment that is deficient in normal defenses. In cystic fibrosis, ion transport across the respiratory epithelium is abnormal due to a defect in **CFTR**, the cystic fibrosis transmembrane regulator protein. Presumably due to dehydration of respiratory secretions, these patients have thick tenacious secretions and impairment of the mucociliary system, which normally rids the lungs of inhaled particles and bacteria. Phagocytes function normally in cystic fibrosis and there are high levels of antibodies to pseudomonal antigens in most chronically infected patients. There is evidence, however, that these antibodies may be defective in their function, specifically in their ability to opsonize *Pseudomonas*. The mucoid **exopolysaccharide** or **alginate** produced by *Pseudomonas* in chronic infection of the cystic fibrosis lung may shield the organism from the immune system. Strains that produce alginate produce less protease and toxins than do nonmucoid cells. Such mucoid strains also grow more slowly. These apparent disadvantages and the high energy cost to the cell of producing alginate must be offset by improved survival in the cystic fibrosis lung. *Pseudomonas* also attacks components of the immune system; elastase cleaves complement and immunoglobulins, and alkaline protease inhibits the activities of γ-interferon.

DAMAGE

Like other Gram negatives, *Pseudomonas* can cause hypotension and shock, as in Case 1; most likely because their cell walls contain **lipopolysaccharide**, also known as endotoxin (see Chapter 9). The organisms also elaborate a wide variety of exotoxins that can cause local inflammation, tissue destruction, and abscess formation (Table 19.2). As discussed above, local tissue damage may be necessary for acquisition of nutrients by the organisms; in this case, damage allows the organism to persist. Damage may also be necessary for dissemination; as mentioned before, strains lacking exotoxins or elastase persist locally in burn wounds but fail to disseminate.

Epidemiological and animal studies demonstrate the importance of various virulence factors (Table 19.2). The mechanism of action of some of these factors is fully known; for most, it is not. **Exotoxin A** is a toxin of the group that inactivates host target proteins by modifying them through the addition of an **adenosine-ribose-diphosphate** moiety of nicotinamide, a process known as **ADP-ribosylation** (Chapter 9).

The *Pseudomonas* exotoxin A resembles diphtheria toxin in that the target protein is a factor involved in host cell protein synthesis, **elongation factor 2**, or **EF-2**. In vivo, this activity contributes to morbidity and mortality, as demonstrated by EF-2 depletion in the liver of infected mice.

Other compounds, such as **elastase**, have multiple biological activities; determining which of these are most important in vivo has proven difficult. Elastase cleaves not only elastin but also collagen, complement components, and immunoglobulins. In addition to damaging tissues directly by these activities, elastase may increase susceptibility to tissue damage by neutrophil elastase because it cleaves α_1-proteinase inhibitor and other proteinase inhibitors. Recently a second protease has been shown to cleave elastin.

The outcome of *Pseudomonas* infection depends upon the nature and severity of the infection, the state of host defenses, and the promptness and efficacy of treatment. A high-grade bacteremia in a neutropenic patient carries a 50–70% mortality rate. *Pseudomonas* endocarditis likewise carries a high mortality, up to 50%.

DIAGNOSIS, PREVENTION, AND TREATMENT

P. aeruginosa is easily cultured and identified by the clinical microbiology laboratory. Knowledge of prevailing patterns of susceptibility and resistance in a given hospital allows for empiric therapy while awaiting culture and sensitivity results. Because this bacterium is known for its ability to develop antibiotic resistance (Table 19.3) even during a single course of therapy, two antibiotics are usually used in combination. The ability to develop and acquire antibiotic resistance contributes to the success of *Pseudomonas* in the hospital environment as does the resistance of the organism to many commonly used disinfecting agents. Attention to infection control measures may allow prevention of some *Pseudomonas* nosocomial infections.

CONCLUSIONS

P. aeruginosa is a paradigm of an opportunistic environmental pathogen. It is abundant in our environment, causing diseases mainly in patients who have impaired body defenses. Occasionally, it overcomes the defenses of healthy persons, but this is likely only if the inoculum size is very large. Prevention and treatment of *Pseudomonas* infection in patients debilitated by major underlying diseases is an important goal in modern medicine.

Self-assessment Questions

1. Describe the microbiological characteristics of the pseudomonads.

2. What are the main clinical syndromes caused by *P. aeruginosa*?

3. What types of patients are most often infected?

4. Describe some of the virulence factors of these organisms?

5. List some of the therapeutic problems encountered in pseudomonad infections.

SUGGESTED READING

Nicas TI, Iglewski BH. The contribution of exoproducts to virulence of *Pseudomonas aeruginosa*. Can J Microbiol 1985;31:387–392.

Prince A. Antibiotic resistance of *Pseudomonas* species. J Pediatr 1986;108: 830–834.

Teres D, Schweers P, Bushnell LS, et al. Sources of *Pseudomonas aeruginosa* infection in a respiratory/surgical intensive-therapy unit. Lancet 1973;1: 415–417.

Thomassen MJ, Demko CA, Doershuk CF. Cystic fibrosis: a review of pulmonary infection and interventions. Pediatr Pulmonol 1987.

Bordetella pertussis and Whooping Cough

20

Arnold L. Smith

The agent of whooping cough, *Bordetella pertussis*, is found on epithelial cells of the bronchioles of patients. These Gram-negative rods make powerful toxins that penetrate tissues, kill cells, immobilize the ciliary elevator, and cause the accumulation of thick mucus in the airway. The characteristic "whooping" cough may be due to sensitization of cough receptors in the trachea by a toxin and to the patient's effort to expectorate the mucus. Killed whole organisms, added to diphtheria and tetanus toxoids, yield the "DPT vaccine" given to infants. The pertussis component of the vaccine is responsible for some of its rare side effects.

CASE

Eight weeks after her birth, P. was taken to her family doctor for a checkup and her first baby shot. The immunization was postponed for a month because she had a slight cold and a runny nose. This may have been acquired from one of her three siblings or her grandfather who lived with the family, all of whom had had colds recently. Subsequently, P. began sneezing and coughing. It seemed that any loud noise would bring on a coughing spell. P.'s mother became concerned when P. turned blue after a series of coughing spells that ended with vomiting. Later, during an examination of the infant by a physician, P. had a series of "barky" coughs, after which she vomited and could not catch her breath. Her mother was told that P. had whooping cough and needed to be hospitalized.

The laboratory report showed an elevated white blood cell count in her blood, chiefly due to a large increase in the number of lymphocytes. A nasopharyngeal specimen contained B. pertussis *by fluorescent antibody detection, the causative agent of whooping cough.*

P.'s mother wanted to know the following:

- How dangerous is whooping cough?
- Why was the physician sure of the diagnosis?
- Where did P. catch the "bug?"
- Will antibiotics make her better?
- When can she get her baby shots?

If you had to answer these questions, you would have to know something about

- The epidemiology of *B. pertussis;*

- How the infection causes disease;
- The pros and cons of vaccination; and
- How whooping cough is diagnosed.

Whooping cough, or pertussis, is a severe childhood disease that has been nearly eradicated due to vaccination. Baby shots contain killed *B. pertussis*, the "P" in DPT, which is very effective in preventing the disease. In recent years, the number of infants who have not received the vaccine has increased. The result is that the number of cases of whooping cough in the U.S. has risen sharply in recent years. In 1981, the childhood incidence of whooping cough was 0.5/100,000 population. This increased three-fold to 1.5/100,000 children by 1985.

Whooping cough is an important disease for three reasons:

- It is highly communicable among susceptible infants less than 1 year of age.
- It is life threatening in infants with underlying cardiac or pulmonary disease.
- It can lead to neurological sequelae.

The local manifestations of whooping cough are those of bronchitis, with accumulation of mucus, inflammatory cells, bacteria, and dead epithelial cells in the airway. The mucociliary elevator is impaired by damage to the ciliary epithelial cells and the cough is more easily triggered due to sensitization of cough receptors. A result is the violent cough that gives the disease its name. In addition, patients with whooping cough have systemic manifestations, such as low-grade fever, malaise, and lymphocytosis. Feeding may precipitate a coughing attack in infants precluding adequate oral intake; this can lead to dehydration.

BORDETELLA

Bordetella are small, Gram-negative, strictly aerobic rods that belong to the group of nutritionally fastidious organisms that includes the genus *Haemophilus*. *Bordetella* are grown in complex media containing blood, which fulfill their nutritional requirements, plus other additives to neutralize fatty acids and other inhibitory compounds. *Bordetella* are also very sensitive to chemical and physical agents in the environment and do not survive outside the body for appreciable periods of time.

B. pertussis has specific adhesins that permit them to attach to epithelial cells of the respiratory tract. They also manufacture exotoxins that penetrate into host cells and ultimately produce the signs and symptoms of the disease. As with other Gram negatives, *B. pertussis* possesses endotoxin, which is probably responsible for the fever and perhaps for some of the other signs of the disease as well (Table 20.1).

ENCOUNTER

These delicate bacteria are thought to be exclusively human pathogens because they neither survive in the environment nor are known to infect other animal species. Their reservoir is not really known because they are rarely recovered from the nasopharynx of healthy persons. The failure to recover *B. pertussis* may be due to their ability to enter respiratory epithelial cells of carriers. The turnover of epithelial cells

Table 20.1. Major Toxins and Virulence Factors of *B. pertussis*

Name	Chemical Nature	Site of Action	Biochemical Activities	Physiological Effects
Pertussis toxin	Protein	Local and systemic	ADP-ribosylates protein	Impairs neutrophil chemotaxis, phagocytosis, and bactericidal activity; encephalopathy; lymphocytosis; hypoglycemia
Adenylate cyclase	Protein	Local	Converts ATP to cAMP	Histamine sensitization mimics pertussis toxin activity on neutrophils; increases capillary permeability leading to edema
Tracheal cytotoxin	Murein	Local	?	Kills ciliated respiratory epithelial cells; adjuvant
Endotoxin	Lipopolysaccharide	Systemic	?	Fever; adjuvant
Pili (fimbriae)	Protein	Local	?	Facilitating adherence to respiratory epithelium
Filamentous hemagglutinin	Protein	Local	?	Binds bacteria to cilia
Hemolysin	?	Local	?	Cytotoxic for respiratory epithelium

would then make the sequestered bacteria available for transmission. The organisms are exceptionally contagious and may affect upward of 90% of the members of a nonimmune family that becomes exposed.

Not all people will recognize that they have been infected because the classical symptoms of whooping cough are dependent on the state of immunity. Young infants have whooping, paroxysmal cough with vomiting and respiratory distress. In people older than 15 years, the disease may be indistiguishable from a mild "viral" upper respiratory tract disease without cough. This milder manifestation of *B. pertussis* disease may be attributed to host resistance due to immunization or previous infection. It becomes important, then, for the physician who is treating a baby like P. to take a complete history of all family members and to alert them to the possibility that they may contract whooping cough. It should be pointed out that the epidemiology of this disease is not always clear because vaccination records for childhood diseases are often poorly kept.

ENTRY

B. pertussis enter the trachea and bronchi by inhalation. The organisms attach to the cilia of epithelial cells of the large airways and are seldom found anywhere else (Figs. 20.1 and 20.2). Whooping cough is entirely a superficial infection, which means that the organisms do not invade tissue; other important bacterial diseases with this characteristic include diphtheria and cholera. *B. pertussis* shows a strong tissue tropism for the ciliated epithelium of the respiratory tract. The reason for this phenomenon is not clearly understood, but it may be due to the specific interaction between *pertussis* adhesins (which are as yet poorly characterized) and receptors on the cells of this tissue. The cell receptors to which *B. pertussis* bind are probably glycoproteins. Table 20.2 describes an experiment that suggests that the ligand on the bacteria is a protein (trypsin sensitive) and that the receptors on the cells contain carbohydrate (binding can be prevented by competition with added carbohydrates or by oxidation with periodate).

SPREAD AND MULTIPLICATION

The first stages of whooping cough result in a mild inflammatory response in the submucosa, which is manifested clinically by infrequent

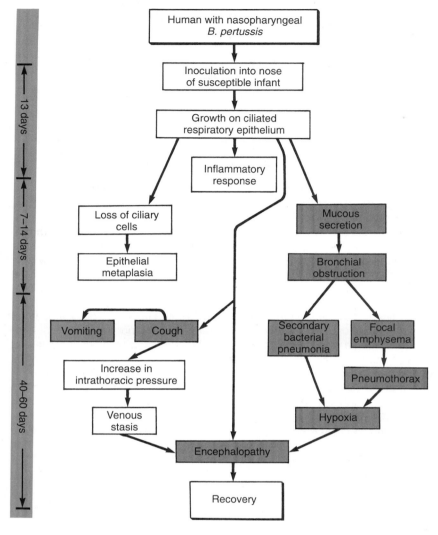

Figure 20.1. Pathogenesis of *B. pertussis*.

coughing, a runny nose, and a low grade fever. Administration of the vaccine at this stage is not indicated. At this so-called catarrhal stage, the organisms multiply rapidly and spread to contiguous areas. Within a few days, there are masses of bacteria entrapped in the cilia and thick mucus (Fig. 20.2). The epithelium remains intact, but the submucosa beneath it becomes increasingly inflamed and the peribronchial lymph nodes enlarged. Reactive hyperplasia in the lymph nodes indicates that bacterial products are transported to those sites from their superficial origin in the bronchial lumen. Destruction of respiratory epithelial cells, which also evokes subepithelial inflammation, may also occur in prolonged infections.

Approximately 3 weeks after entry of the organisms, the cough becomes intense and uncontrollable. At the end of a series of coughs, there is a forced inspiration, the "whoop." Severe disease, which can be fatal, is primarily due to asynchronous coughing resulting in disturbed cardiopulmonary physiology. This cough persists with varying severity for another 2 months. It results from attempts by the body to clear the airways of the large amount of material that accumulates on the epithelium when the "mucociliary elevator" is impaired (Chapter 45) and more sensitive cough receptors. Fatal disease is not advantageous to the bacterium and *B. pertussis* utilizes several strategies to survive and be transmitted from person to person.

Figure 20.2. *B. pertussis* adhering to dilated respiratory epithelial cells seen in the scanning electron microscope. Note the clump of bacteria attached to the partially extruded epithelial cell (*arrow*).

Table 20.2. Effect of Pretreatment of Bacteria or Ciliated Cells on Cell Binding of B. pertussis

Treatment	Of Bacteria	Of Cells
Trypsin	Decrease	No effect
Antibodies to B. pertussis adhesins	Decrease	No effect
Specific carbohydrates	No effect	Decrease adherence
Periodate	No effect	Decrease adherence

Paradigm: Global Regulation of Virulence— How does *B. pertussis* know what environment it is in?

B. pertussis can be regularly isolated during the catarrhal phase of whooping cough, but the frequency of recovering it progressively decreases with time, often as symptoms increase. Moreover, *B. pertussis* isolated early is often different from that isolated later in the disease. The early isolates have a distinctive colonial morphology, produce a variety of toxins (adenylate cyclase, pertussis toxin, dermonecrotic toxin, and hemolysin) and possess surface components that are thought to aid in establishing infection (pili, filamentous hemagglutinin, capsule, and several unique outer membrane proteins). Possession of these virulence factors permits the organisms to infect another susceptible human. Thus, *B. pertussis* alternates between two different states, virulent and avirulent. The virulent *B. pertussis* rapidly become avirulent if grown at 25° (close to the temperature of the external nares), rather than 37° (the internal body temperature). Return of avirulent *B. pertussis* to the virulent state readily occur when grown at 37°C. In addition, the concentration of magnesium and nicotinic acid also modulate the virulence state. How does the organism switch between these two environmentally determined states?

The switch between avirulent and virulent is under the control of a **central regulatory gene**. When the bacterium senses the lower temperature (25°C), the expression of 20 or more genes is terminated. The synthesis of toxins and other virulence factors is discontinued and certain surface antigens are no longer expressed. In the avirulent state, the organisms persist in the anterior nares because they do not elicit a strong host response and do not express virulence-associated antigens to which the host has produced antibodies. This strategy favors prolonged carriage and spread to another susceptible person.

For *B. pertussis* to modulate its virulence in response to environmental stimuli, it must be able to sense changes in the environment. In common with other bacterial systems, *B. pertussis* has a mechanism for **signal transduction**, that is, for converting an environmental signal (e.g., changes in temperature or in concentration of magnesium or nicotinic acid) into the expression of certain genes. Signal transduction is a general phenomenon that requires two activities, often carried out by two separate proteins (Fig. 20.3). The two components are:

- the **sensor/transmitter** protein that is affected by the environmental changes to become an active **protein kinase**; in the active state, the kinase is capable of phosphorylating the second component,

- the **response regulator** protein, which regulates expression of specific genes.

The sensor/transmitters are transmembrane proteins that, in Gram negatives, project from the surface of the cytoplasmic membrane into the periplasmic space. When the external, or sensor portion of the sensor/transmitter detects changes in the environment in the periplasmic space, its cytoplasmic portion transmits the signal to a response regulator that regulates gene expression. Signal transduction consists of phosphorylating the re-

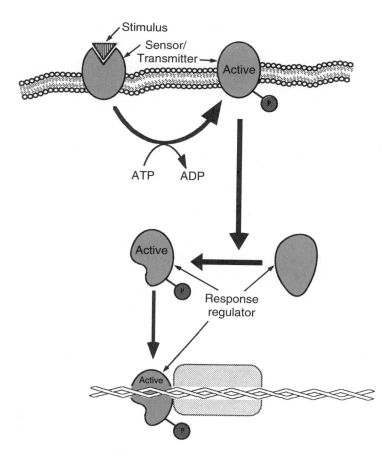

Figure 20.3.   The two-component regulatory system for signal transduction. The sensor/transmitter is activated by a signal to become an active protein kinase capable of phosphorylating a response regulator. In the phosphorylated form, the regulator protein acts on DNA to either allow or to prevent the expression of a specific set of genes.

sponse regulator, which can act either as a repressor or an activator (depending on the target operon).

In the case of *B. pertussis*, the response regulatory protein, when phosphorylated at 37°, becomes an activator of transcription of a set of virulence genes. In contrast, at 25°, the sensor/transmitter protein is inactive, the response regulator is not phosphorylated, and the virulence genes are not transcribed (Fig. 20.3).

This kind of **global regulation** of virulence by environmental signals operates in several other pathogens. Thus, *Vibrio cholerae* and *Corynebacterium diphtheriae* have two-component regulatory systems. Portions of the transmitter and receiver molecules are conserved among different genera of bacteria. In *Salmonella*, *Shigella*, and *Yersinia*, virulence genes are also regulated by the temperature via a similar two-component regulatory system.

DAMAGE

B. pertussis has an impressive array of virulence factors (Table 20.1). One of its most important, *pertussis* toxin, resembles cholera toxin in affecting **cyclic AMP** metabolism. It is also an **A-B toxin**, consisting of an A (active) subunit and a B (binding) subunit (Chapter 9). The toxin attaches to host cells via the B subunit, allowing the A fragment to enter and act in the cytoplasm. Like cholera toxin, diphtheria toxin, and *Pseudomonas* exotoxin A, *pertussis* toxin is also an **ADP-ribosyltransferase**; it splits the nicotinamide portion from NAD and attaches the remaining ADP-ribose (adenosine-diphosphoriboside) to the host cell proteins (Chapter 9). One of the most striking physiological changes in whooping cough, the peripheral lymphocytosis, is due to *pertussis* toxin. As with cholera toxin, one of the host cell proteins targets for ADP-ribosylation is a G-protein involved in the regulation of adenylate cyclase. ADP-ribosylation of this enzyme results in an increase in cyclic AMP, which inhibits several functions of neutrophils, such as chemotaxis and the oxidative burst. In its preoccupation to make a lot of cyclic AMP, *B. pertussis* also secretes an **extracellular adenylate cyclase** that can enter the host cells and increase their content of cyclic AMP.

Local damage is probably caused by a **tracheal cytotoxin**, which kills ciliated cells specifically and leads their extrusion from the epithelium. Curiously, this exotoxin is not a protein, but consists of a portion of the cell wall murein (Fig. 20.4). Its biochemical origin is not known, but it may originate from murein biosynthesis or processing. A similar compound is made by gonococci (Chapter 14) and acts in an analogous fashion by killing ciliated epithelial cells in the fallopian tubes. It is likely that tracheal cytotoxin is not the only one involved in local damage, but that other substances elaborated by these organisms also contribute to it. *B. pertussis* also produces a hemolysin that can inflict cytotoxicity on nucleated human cells. Thus, there are many mechanisms by which the organism can inflict local damage.

Given the nature of the local damage, is it likely that antibodies will have a significant effect on the cause of the disease? Pre-existing antibodies produced by previous infections or by vaccination prevent the disease, especially if they are of the IgA type. However, once the disease is established, antibodies may play a lesser role. When the exotoxins have entered their target cells, they become impervious to antibodies.

DIAGNOSIS

Whooping cough is an uncommon disease in countries where the DPT vaccine is widely used. For this reason, neither clinicians nor the laboratory are always alert to this particular diagnosis. This is true even though the clinical symptoms are usually quite distinctive. It is important to remember that laboratory diagnosis of *B. pertussis* is difficult because the organisms are in decreasing numbers when the symptoms are increasing. Thus, as a clinician, you will find that *B. pertussis* can be cultured only from a small number of patients.

Specimens for culture must be taken with care to minimize potential contamination from commensals in the throat. A small swab is placed in the posterior wall of the pharynx and the patient allowed to cough. The swab is often treated with a drop of penicillin solution to kill other normally occurring bacteria that are sensitive to penicillin (to which *B.*

Figure 20.4. Portion of cell wall murein that corresponds to the structure of tracheal cytotoxin. *GlcNac* = N-acetylglucosamine; *MurNac* = N-acetylmuramic acid; *meso-DAP* = meso-diaminopimelic acid; *ala* = alanine; *glu* = glutamic acid.

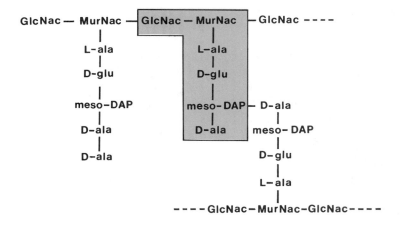

pertussis is resistant). The swab is then applied to the surface of a plate containing a medium called Bordet-Gengou, which is incubated for 2–3 days. Positive identification of the organisms may then be carried out using specific antisera.

PREVENTION AND TREATMENT

The vaccine against *pertussis* consists of a killed suspension of *B. pertussis* cells mixed with purified diphtheria and tetanus toxoid proteins. Such a suspension contains significant amounts of the various *pertussis* toxins; some less than others because not all the toxins are released equally from the bacterial cells. Pili are also carried along in the preparation.

The side effects associated with the use of DPT vaccine have been attributed largely to the *pertussis* component and not to the other two. The vaccine can produce three types of complications:

- Fever, malaise, and pain at the site of the injection are seen in about 20% of the infants inoculated. This is commonly seen with vaccines prepared from whole bacteria that contain murein, Gram-negative lipopolysaccharide (LPS), and other substances that elicit an inflammatory response.

- Convulsions occur in about one in 2000 children vaccinated. This may not represent the true incidence because a small number of children, about one in 30,000, suffer from spontaneous convulsions called idiopathic seizures and some children will have seizures with fever due to any course.

- More serious central nervous reactions occur rarely, at an estimated rate of one in every 110,000 children vaccinated. What would the number of these complications be in similar populations that do not receive the vaccine? Such a comparable population does not presently exist in countries where the vaccine is widely used.

In assessing the risks of using the DPT vaccine, one must weigh the potential for severe complication against the undisputed benefits of the vaccine in nearly eradicating whooping cough. Many epidemiologists are convinced that vaccination should be widespread. In fact, all states in the U.S. have laws requiring children to be immunized against *pertussis*. Vaccination is required prior to enrollment in school or, in some areas, in day care centers. In special cases, most states allow exemptions for certain medical reasons. For example, the vaccine should not be given to children with minor illnesses or those receiving antihistamines or certain other types of medication. The vaccine is usually administered by three injections over a period of 2 months. If the first of these gives an adverse reaction, the treatment should be discontinued.

Meanwhile, considerable effort is being expended to make the vaccine risk-free. If specific protective immunogen could be identified, whole bacterial cells would not have to be used. Presumably, some of the side effects are due to bacterial constituents other than those required to stimulate a protective response. These "impurities" would be left out of a more purified vaccine preparation. It may turn out, however, that purified *pertussis* toxin is, itself, responsible for some of the side effects of the vaccine. In addition, this protein is an immunological adjuvant and it may contribute to the immunogenicity of the other components of the DPT vaccine. Thus, *pertussis* vaccination is not a simple matter.

CONCLUSIONS

Until a safer vaccine becomes available, whooping cough will continue to be a serious medical concern. In the meanwhile, there is much to be learned from the specific aspects of the pathogenesis of the causative agent. *B. pertussis* is a superficial pathogen, rarely penetrating into deep tissues. It produces a series of powerful toxins, most of which function to counteract the defense mechanisms of the lower respiratory tract.

Self-assessment Questions

1. Discuss the aspects of whooping cough that can be directly attributed to the location of the organisms in the body.

2. How does *B. pertussis* cause systemic symptoms, given its superficial location?

3. Describe the activity of the main toxins of *B. pertussis*.

4. Discuss the pros and cons of the *pertussis* component of the DPT vaccine.

5. Whooping cough is unlikely to be completely eradicated from the planet. Why?

SUGGESTED READING

Goldman WE. *Bordetella pertussis* tracheal cytotoxin: damage to the epithelium. In: Leive L, ed. Microbiology—1986. Washington, DC: American Society of Microbiology, 1986:70–74.

Hewlett EL, Weiss AA. Conclusions. In: Leive L, ed. Microbiology—1986. Washington, DC: American Society of Microbiology, 1986:79.

Hewlett EL, Weiss AA. *Pertussis* toxin: mechanisms of action, biological effects, and roles in clinical pertussis. In: Leive L, ed. Microbiology—1986. Washington, DC: American Society of Microbiology, 1986:75–78.

Miller JF, Mekalanos JJ, Falkow S. Coordinate regulation and sensory transduction in the control of bacterial virulence. Science 1989;243:916–922.

Pittman, M. The concept of pertussis as a toxin mediated disease. Pediatr Infect Dis 1984;3:467–486.

Tuomanen E. Adherence of *Bordetella pertussis* to human cilia: implications for disease prevention and therapy. In: Leive L, ed. Microbiology—1986. Washington, DC: American Society of Microbiology, 1986;59–64.

Weiss AA, Hewlett EL. Virulence factors of *Bordetella pertussis*. Ann Rev Microbiol 1986;40:661–686.

Clostridia   21

Sherwood L. Gorbach

Clostridia are strict Gram-positive rods responsible for several unrelated diseases with different clinical manifestations. These include **pseudomembranous colitis** (an inflammatory disease of the colon), **botulism, tetanus,** soft tissue infections including muscle invasion (**gas gangrene** and **cellulitis**—an infection of subcutaneous connective tissue), and **food poisoning**. Many of the clostridial diseases are serious and life threatening. All are caused by **exotoxins** secreted by the clostridia. In the case of botulism, the disease is acquired by eating toxin-contaminated food; the clinical symptoms are produced by the toxin without colonization and invasion by the organism.

CASE

An 81-year-old man was hospitalized with a history of 38.5° fevers for the preceding 5 days. Because of confusion and inability to care for himself, he had been a resident of a local nursing home for 3 years. However, he had been able to dress himself and move about the wards until a week before his hospital admission, when he complained of weakness and could not get out of bed. Except for a urinary tract infection 4 weeks previously, for which he was treated with a 10-day course of ampicillin, he had experienced no recent illness.

On physical examination, he was resting comfortably in bed but appeared confused and rather unhappy about the change in his surroundings. He was unable to give a history and could not answer questions about his current condition. His temperature was 39°; the other vital signs were normal. Except for mild dehydration, there were no localized physical findings. Abdominal examination was unremarkable.

As the house staff and attending physician pondered the diagnostic possibilities at the bedside the next morning, their deliberations were interrupted by the staff nurse, who informed the group that the patient had passed two loose bowel movements during the night. Indeed, the attending physician's olfaction, perhaps heightened by the new information, now recognized the occurrence of another such event, no doubt triggered by deep palpation of the patient's abdomen.

A stool specimen was sent to the laboratory, which within 24 hours yielded a positive test for the toxin of Clostridium difficile. Specific treatment for antibiotic-associated diarrhea caused by C. difficile was begun with oral vancomycin. The patient became afebrile within 36 hours, and he was able to return to his nursing home without further laboratory investigations within 72 hours.

Questions that are raised:

1. Why is the history of previous treatment with ampicillin germane to the diagnosis?

2. What is the significance of the nursing home in this condition?

3. What is the role of the spores of *C. difficile* in the disease process?

C. difficile is an anaerobic, Gram-positive, spore-forming rod first identified in 1935. As the name implies, it has fastidious growth requirements. Although isolated occasionally in blood cultures and in wounds, it went unrecognized as a cause of diarrheal disease until 1977, when it was identified as the organism responsible for a severe ulcerating disease of the large bowel known as **pseudomembranous colitis (PMC)**. Since then, the organism has been linked to a spectrum of intestinal disorders **associated with antibiotic treatment**, ranging from an asymptomatic carrier state, to mild or moderate diarrhea, to fulminating, life-threatening PMC.

The organism is harbored in the large intestine of humans, where it tends to remain in a dormant state in low numbers. It can also be found in environmental sources, particularly in hospitals. Under adverse conditions, the organism reverts to its highly resistant spore form. The spores can be cultured from the floor, bedpan, and toilet in a hospital room occupied by a patient with *C. difficile* in the feces, as well as from the hands and clothing of medical and nursing personnel. The mode of transmission is via the spore form, which is extremely difficult to eradicate from the environment. *C. difficile* is currently the **major cause of diarrhea acquired in a hospital**. In nursing homes, where patients tend to stay for prolonged periods, 20–30% of the residents are colonized asymptomatically with *C. difficile*.

A remarkable feature of *C. difficile* diarrhea is its association with antimicrobial drugs. Most symptomatic patients have received an antimicrobial agent at some time in the recent past. Virtually all antimicrobial drugs have been implicated; however, the most common are cephalosporins, ampicillin, and clindamycin. (This order reflects the frequency of use of the drugs in clinical practice; actually, clindamycin is associated with a higher incidence of disease per exposure to the drug.)

The risk associated with use of a particular antimicrobial drug is not necessarily related to its in vitro activity against *C. difficile*. Ampicillin, for example, is active in vitro against all strains of the organism, whereas clindamycin is active against only two-thirds of strains, yet clindamycin is associated with higher risk. This apparent paradox is related to the relative resistance of the spore form of *C. difficile* to almost all antimicrobial drugs. The sequence of events in antibiotic-associated *C. difficile* diarrhea begins with suppression of normal flora by the antimicrobial drug, with persistence of the spore form of *C. difficile*. Clindamycin has the ability to suppress anaerobic bacteria in the flora, which represents the major component, and this may explain the higher risk of its use. *C. difficile* is either present already in the flora or is acquired from the hospital environment during antibiotic treatment. The antibiotic, which represents a hostile influence, forces the organism into its spore state. At some time during or after antibiotic administration, the spores germinate and the vegetative form of *C. difficile* grows in large numbers, producing its toxins. When toxin production achieves a critical level in the large bowel, diarrhea begins.

Like other toxin-related gastrointestinal infections (notably, diarrhea caused by *Vibrio cholerae* and toxigenic *Escherichia coli*), bacterial invasion of the bowel wall is not found in *C. difficile* diarrhea. Instead, the organism elaborates its toxins in the intestinal lumen, and the toxins cause damage to the cellular lining of the bowel wall. The major toxins are designated **A** and **B**. **Toxin A** causes both fluid production and damage to the mucosa of the large bowel, and it is responsible for the clinical disease. **Toxin B** is a cytotoxin that causes abnormalities in tissue-culture systems; this property is used to advantage in the standard laboratory test to diagnose the disease by detecting toxin in the feces.

CLOSTRIDIUM

The genus *Clostridium* is composed of Gram-positive, spore-forming anaerobic rods that live in soil and in the intestine of animals (Fig. 21.1). Production of protein toxins by at least 14 of these clostridial species is associated with a range of diseases, including botulism, tetanus, gas gangrene, food poisoning, diarrhea, and pseudomembranous colitis. The toxins responsible for botulism and tetanus are **neurotoxins**, whereas those causing gas gangrene and intestinal infections are **cytotoxins**; that is, they cause direct damage to cells. In the case of botulism, the entire disease is caused by preformed toxin in contaminated food; thus, the **organism itself need not be present** in the victim. In tetanus and pseudomembranous colitis (PMC), the organisms are ensconced in the host, either in a wound in the case of tetanus, or in the bowel lumen in PMC. However, the organism itself does not invade the tissues, it merely produces toxins that cause the disease. Gas gangrene has the dual virulence factors of toxin production and tissue invasiveness by the organism. Clostridia can also produce suppurative wounds and tissue abscesses in which the organism acts as a simple invader, without systemic signs of toxin production (Table 21.1).

Besides the 30 clostridial species encountered in human infections, there are another 50 or more species found in the environment, particularly in soil and in animal wastes. Clostridia are metabolically highly active and many strains have important industrial uses: clostridial fermentation of crude substrates produces useful chemicals such as alcohols and acetone, and some species are used in the production of fermented foods and cheese. The clostridia used for these purposes, like most members of the genus, are not ordinarily pathogenic.

BOTULISM—ENCOUNTER

Clostridium botulinum, like other clostridia, forms spores to survive in its usual habitat of soil and marine sediment. The spores contaminate meats, vegetables, and fish. Because the spores are relatively heat resistant, they survive during food processing and canning when the temperatures are not high enough to kill them. Under the anaerobic conditions of canned foods, the spores germinate and release potent toxins. Proteolytic enzymes produced by some strains of the organism cause spoilage of the food, but in many cases, the food has a normal appearance and taste. Even an experimental nibble of such food can contain enough toxin to cause lethal disease.

DAMAGE

C. botulinum produces eight immunologically distinct neurotoxins (types A, B, C_α, C_β, D, E, F, and G). Human cases are associated mostly with types A and B, and occasionally with type E, which is formed in fish products. As the interest in home canning and prepared foods has increased, there has been a concomitant increase in the cases of food-

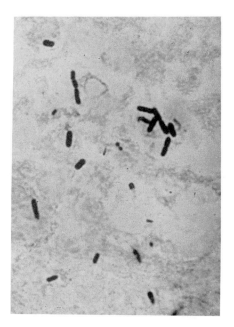

Figure 21.1.   Gram stain of *C. perfringens* **in exudate from gas gangrene.** Note absence of neutrophils.

Table 21.1. Major Clostridial Diseases

	Toxin Production	Tissue Invasiveness
Botulism		
Botulinum food poisoning	+	−
Infant botulism	+	−
Wound botulism	+	±
Tetanus	+	±
Pseudomembranous colitis	+	±
Gas gangrene	+	+
Suppurative wounds and abscess	−	+

borne botulism. Among the most potent poisons known, botulinum toxins are proteins of 150 kilodaltons that can be crystallized to a white powder of unknown taste. One microgram is sufficient to kill a large family, and 0.25 kg could kill all the people on earth.

Botulism is an intoxication caused by the ingestion of a preformed neurotoxin, which prevents the release of the neurotransmitter **acetylcholine**, thereby interfering with neurotransmission at **peripheral cholinergic synapses**. The clinical disease, which is manifest within 12–36 hours after ingestion, is a flaccid paralysis of muscle. **Cranial nerves** are affected first, particularly those involving the eyes, producing diplopia (double vision) and blurred vision. Difficulty with swallowing is an early sign. **A descending paralysis** ensues, involving weakness of striated muscle groups, especially in the neck and extremities, with subsequent involvement of respiratory muscles. The toxin does not act by directly killing cells nor does it produce systemic signs of fever or sepsis. Patients generally succumb to paralysis and respiratory failure.

Infant botulism is a rare form of paralytic disease occurring in infants between 3 and 20 weeks of age. It produces a generalized hypotonic ("floppy") state. The infant's cry becomes feeble and the suck reflex is weak. In this disease, *C. botulinum* colonizes the **large intestine**, where it produces toxin. Infant botulism differs from the classic botulinum food poisoning in the following ways: the toxin is not found in food but rather it is produced in the infant's intestinal tract; the condition has a slow onset, probably because the toxin is absorbed more slowly from the large intestine; and the disease has a favorable outcome in the majority of cases, without specific treatment.

Wound botulism is another rare form of the disease in which a traumatic wound is contaminated by spores of *C. botulinum*. Toxins are produced at the wound site; they are absorbed into the tissues and cause a severe neurological disease similar to that of food-borne botulism.

TREATMENT AND PREVENTION

Specific antitoxin is available for types A, B, and E intoxication. The trivalent antitoxin should be administered as soon as possible to bind any circulating toxin. Because this antitoxin is raised in horses, there is a high incidence of hypersensitivity reactions associated with its use. The most important aspect of treatment is supportive care, which is necessary to maintain respirations and other vital functions. Patients should be given parenteral nutrition. The illness may last for many weeks, and individual muscles may be paralyzed for months or even permanently. With good supportive care, the mortality from botulism is currently 25%.

Botulism can be prevented by proper canning methods. Although the spores are heat resistant, the toxins are heat labile, and terminal heating of contaminated food can avoid the disease. As a result of improvements in the canning industry, outbreaks associated with commercial foods are quite rare, and most cases of botulism now are associated with home canning.

TETANUS

Tetanus is a tragic disease, not only because of its severity, but because it can be completely prevented by appropriate immunization. Indeed, prevention of tetanus by active immunization has been one of the triumphs of modern bacteriology. Experience with tetanus in the two World Wars of this century demonstrated beyond doubt the benefits of the tetanus toxoid vaccine. Universal immunization of the American forces in World War II virtually eliminated this disease as a complication of traumatic injuries in soldiers. In developing countries where immunization is not widely practiced, tetanus remains a serious public health problem.

ENCOUNTER, ENTRY, SPREAD, AND MULTIPLICATION

C. tetani is ubiquitous in the gastrointestinal tract of humans and animals and in soil samples. Because of their resistance to environmental conditions, the tetanus spores contaminate the wounds of trauma victims.

Most cases of tetanus are associated with a traumatic wound. Tissue necrosis, anoxia, and other bacterial contaminants in the wound provide a permissive environment for germination of tetanus spores and elaboration of toxin. **Neonatal tetanus** results from contamination of the umbilical cord at the time of delivery, either through unsanitary procedures or local customs of wrapping the cord in dung or mud.

DAMAGE

The major toxin, known as **tetanospasmin**, which accounts for all symptoms of tetanus, is a 150-kilodalton protein molecule composed of a heavy chain and a light chain held together by a disulfide bridge. Like other A-B two-chain toxins, the individual heavy and light chains are nontoxic. The complete toxin attaches to peripheral nerves in the region of the wound, where it is transmitted to **cranial nerve nuclei** either through intraspinal transmission among involved motor neurons or via bloodstream delivery of toxin to other neuromuscular junctions. The major action of tetanus toxin is **inhibition of transmitter release and normal inhibitory input**, thereby causing the lower motor neuron to increase resting tone, producing the characteristic **reflex spasms**. Several types of transmitters are blocked, including GABA (γ-aminobutyric acid). Clinically, the disease presents as a **spastic paralysis**. Generalized tetanus, responsible for about 80% of cases, usually begins with trismus or "lockjaw," which is caused by tetanic spasm of the masseter muscles, preventing opening of the mouth. The disease typically descends, initially involving the neck and back muscles, progressing to produce board-like rigidity of the abdominal musculature, eventually causing stiffness of the extremities. Individual muscle groups go into spasm, leading to a generalized spasm that is characterized by a toxic seizure, adduction of the arms, arching of the neck and back, extension of the legs and clenching of the fists (Fig. 21.2). Death

Figure 21.2. Advanced tetanus may lead to opisthotonos, the bending backwards of the body caused by spastic paralysis of the strong extensors of the back. This classical illustration of a British soldier wounded in 1809 in the Napoleonic Wars, portrays this condition, as well as "sardonic smile" and lockjaw, caused by spasms of facial muscles.

usually results from respiratory failure caused by paralysis of chest muscles.

TREATMENT AND PREVENTION

The treatment of tetanus is mainly a physiological exercise in preventing complications. Antitoxin should be given at the earliest possible moment, but it is often a futile gesture inasmuch as any toxin that has been elaborated is already fixed to the nerve cells in an irreversible state. Antibiotic treatment, particularly penicillin G, is directed at the organism because it may continue to produce toxin in the wound. In addition, surgical debridement should be undertaken of the involved wound to eliminate the environmental niche of the organism.

Prevention of tetanus is achieved through **immunization**. Active immunization should be carried out in all infants and children and in pregnant women who have not been previously immunized. The antigen is **tetanus toxoid**, a form of the toxin that has been inactivated in formalin but retains its antigenicity. It forms the "T" of the DPT vaccine given to infants and children. Passive immunization in the form of human globulin is administered to people with a "tetanus-prone wound." Because the disease itself does not cause sufficient antibody production for subsequent protection, it is necessary to immunize tetanus patients with the toxoid as well. This is because the amount of toxin present in the diseased patient is too small to be immunogenic. It is a tribute to the enormous potency of tetanus toxin that such a small amount is still sufficient to produce severe symptoms.

GAS GANGRENE AND OTHER CLOSTRIDIAL TISSUE INFECTIONS

Traumatic wounds are commonly contaminated with clostridial spores that are widespread in soil. As distinguished from tetanus and botulism, in which the organisms have little or no invasive properties, the clostridia in wound infections cause local damage in addition to systemic effects. The major pathogen of wound infections, *C. perfringens*, elaborates a variety of toxins that act both locally and systemically. The more common form of clostridial wound infections is a localized cellulitis that can usually be cured with surgical management and antibiotics. More severe trauma can be associated with gas **gangrene**, a necrotizing, gas-forming process of muscle associated with systemic signs of shock.

ENCOUNTER, ENTRY, SPREAD, AND MULTIPLICATION

C. perfringens and a variety of other organisms are found in soil and in the intestinal tract of many animals. In wartime, 20–30% of wounds are contaminated by these organisms. The physiological state of the wound site is critical to allowing the organism to germinate and to produce its toxins. The proper conditions are a low oxidation-reduction potential (anaerobic conditions), compromised blood supply, calcium ions, and the availability of various peptides and amino acids, all characteristic of damaged tissue.

DAMAGE

C. perfringens elaborates 12 toxins, but the α-toxin, a **lecithinase** that damages cell membranes, is the major, and perhaps only, toxin responsible for gas gangrene. The muscle is destroyed (**myonecrosis**) so it no longer reacts to stimuli. It grows black and gangrenous. Abundant gas is produced by the organism, resulting in **crepitance**, which can be palpated as small gas bubbles under the skin. Systemically, the patient develops fever, sweating, low blood pressure, and decreased urinary output. The patient generally succumbs to shock and renal failure within a few days of onset.

TREATMENT AND PREVENTION

Treatment of gas gangrene involves surgical removal of the involved muscle, which may necessitate extensive resection and even amputation of the affected limb. Antibiotics such as penicillin are administered to control the wound infection, but they are ineffective without adequate surgical debridement and drainage. Antitoxin, which is produced in horses, has had a negligible effect in this disease, and it is not recommended for treatment. Oxygen administered under high pressure (hyperbaric) is used in centers with appropriate chambers. Hyperbaric oxygen inhibits production of the α-toxin and suppresses growth of the organism in tissue. Milder forms of clostridial wound infection, without evidence of myonecrosis or systemic effects, can be managed with more conservative surgical intervention and appropriate antibiotics.

Prevention of gas gangrene and other clostridial wound infections involves prompt and appropriate attention to traumatic injuries. Under war conditions, front-line hospitals and evacuation facilities have ameliorated the damage caused by gunshot and shrapnel. Trauma units, now available in most American cities, have reduced the incidence of clostridial soft tissue infections by prompt attention to injured wounds.

CONCLUSIONS

The major pathogenic species of clostridia have a broad spectrum of colonization and invasiveness. In botulinal food poisoning, the organisms do not invade the body at all; in tetanus, they barely set up household in tissues; and in clostridial gangrene, they have considerable invasive capacity.

The toxins of tetanus and botulism both act on the nervous system and both are extraordinarily potent. They differ, however, in the way that they enter the body and in the details of their mode of action. These toxins cause serious disease without killing their target cells, whereas those involved in wound infection and pseudomembranous colitis are generally cytolitic.

Self-assessment Questions

1. Discuss the properties of clostridia that help explain their ecology.

2. What elicits pseudomembranous colitis? Which people are at risk from this disease?

3. Why is ingesting botulinum toxin more dangerous than ingesting tetanus toxin? Why is infant botulism usually a mild disease?

4. Contrast the mode of action of tetanus and botulinum toxins on the nervous system.

5. We are usually immunized against tetanus early in life. Why don't we get immunized against the other clostridial infections?

SUGGESTED READING

Finegold SM. Aerobic bacteria in human disease. New York: Academic Press, 1977.

Gorbach SL. *Clostridium perfringens* and other clostridia. In: Gorbach SL, Bartlett JG, Blacklow NR. Infectious diseases. Philadelphia: WB Saunders, 1992:1587–1596.

Gorbach SL. Gas gangrene and other clostridial skin and soft tissue infections. In: Gorbach SL, Bartlett JG, Blacklow NR. Infectious Diseases. Philadelphia: WB Saunders, 1992:764–770.

Hart GB, Lamb RC, Strauss MB. Gas gangrene. J Trauma 1983;23:991.

Smith LD, Williams BL: The pathogenic anaerobic bacteria, ed. 3. Springfield, IL: Charles C Thomas, 1984.

Legionella: Parasite of Cells

22

N. Cary Engleberg

The legionellae are aerobic Gram-negative bacilli that are parasites of unicellular organisms in nature and opportunistic invaders of phagocytic cells in humans. These bacteria are found in a variety of natural aquatic habitats and, all too often, are inhabitants of manmade water distribution systems. They are fastidious organisms, and their isolation from water or from infected tissues requires specially formulated culture media. The mechanism of transmission from contaminated environmental sources to humans is uncertain; however, when these microorganisms are deposited in the air spaces of the lungs, legionellae may produce a severe form of pneumonia called Legionnaires' disease. Because this infection is often associated with contaminated water systems, large institutional outbreaks of Legionnaires' disease may occur (e.g., in hospitals and hotels).

CASE

Mrs. R., a 57-year-old female, was admitted to the hospital with high fever and altered mental status. Eight days earlier, she had developed a "flu-like" illness with fever, anorexia, malaise, headache, and muscle aches. She later developed a cough that became progressively worse but was productive of only scanty, clear sputum. Five days before admission, she saw a local physician who ordered a chest x-ray. The x-ray showed a small left upper lobe infiltrate, consistent with pneumonia. She was treated with oral cephalexin (a first-generation cephalosporin antibiotic). Her fever and chills increased steadily, and she became confused and lethargic. Mrs. R.'s past medical history was unremarkable, but she had smoked 1 pack of cigarettes a day for 40 years.

On admission, her temperature was 104°F, her heart rate was 88 beats/minute, and she was cyanotic. The white cell count was 13,700/mm³, the serum sodium was 132 mEq/L, and the patient was severely hypoxic with an arterial PO$_2$ of 51 mm Hg (on oxygen therapy). Gram stain of sputum showed numerous polymorphonuclear leukocytes (PMNs) but no bacteria. Chest x-ray showed extension of her left upper lobe infiltrate and a new right middle lobe infiltrate.

The patient was intubated and placed on mechanical ventilation in the intensive care unit (ICU). She was placed on broad-spectrum antibiotics, including high-dose erythromycin. Shortly after admission, her blood pressure dropped precipitously, and she required vasopressive agents. After a stormy ICU course, the patient began to improve slowly, and eventually recovered. Respiratory secretions, obtained by aspiration through the endotracheal tube, were negative for Legionella pneumophila *by the direct fluorescent antibody (DFA) test, but a culture of the specimen grew the organism after 3 days of incubation.*

The case of Mrs. R. raises several questions:

- How did Mrs. R. acquire *L. pneumophila*, and why wasn't anyone in her family or workplace also infected?

- Why was the diagnosis of Legionnaires' disease so difficult to make in this case?

- Why did Mrs. R.'s pneumonia worsen during treatment with an antibiotic that can efficiently kill *L. pneumophila* growing in the laboratory?

HISTORICAL ASPECTS

Legionella was unknown as a bacterial species until 1976, when a highly publicized outbreak of Legionnaires' disease occurred among attendees at an American Legion convention in Philadelphia. In all, 182 attendees became ill, and 29 died. For an uncomfortable period after the convention, the cause of the epidemic remained obscure. Eventually, researchers from the Centers for Disease Control discovered the bacterial pathogen by inoculating lung tissue from patients into the peritoneal cavity of guinea pigs. They discovered that the agent could be passed to egg yolks and eventually to supplemented artificial media. Soon after the bacterium (*L. pneumophila*) was isolated, culture and serological methods were developed to facilitate the clinical diagnosis of Legionnaires' disease, and *Legionella* spp. were recognized as a significant cause of pneumonia in many parts of the world.

FAMILY LEGIONELLACEAE

L. pneumophila will not grow on routine bacteriological media. Instead, a special medium has been composed to meet the peculiar nutritional needs of this organism. The bacterium requires high levels of the amino acid, cysteine, as well as supplements of inorganic iron for optimal growth. In addition, the concentration of sodium must be kept low, and activated charcoal must be added to absorb inhibitory substances in the media.

Once microbiologists learned how to grow *L. pneumophila* in the laboratory, related organisms were isolated from human and environmental sources. Thirty separate species have been identified within the genus *Legionella*, and they comprise the only genus in the family Legionellaceae. DNA-DNA hybridization studies indicate that the Legionellaceae have no close relatives among known bacteria.

In nature, the Legionellaceae are found in ponds, lakes, and hot springs, where they may feed on organic matter generated by photosynthetic algae and other plant life. Like other bacteria in these environments, they are fed upon by protozoans. However, legionellae may actually profit from ingestion by protozoans and, instead of being killed and digested like other bacteria, they may grow to large numbers inside these unicellular organisms.

ENCOUNTER

The source of the 1976 Philadelphia outbreak was never identified, but investigations of numerous later outbreaks established a link between the occurrence of Legionnaires' disease and the colonization of plumbing systems with *L. pneumophila*. In hospitals or hotels where epidemics have occurred, the *L. pneumophila* strain isolated from respiratory cultures of patients may also be found in tap water, in swabs taken from faucets or shower heads, or in sediment from hot water tanks. In some respects, *Legionella* is particularly well-adapted to these environments. The bacterium grows at temperatures up to 46°C and tolerates much higher temperatures, and it is relatively chlorine resistant compared with enteric bacteria. On the other hand, given the strict nutritional requirements of this organism, it is not surprising to find it in association with other microorganisms, such as protozoans or bacteria, which are commonly found in water systems and which may provide essential nutrients to support the growth of *Legionella*.

Legionnaires' disease is nearly always a primary pulmonary infection and is never transmitted from person to person. Instead, humans acquire the infection from an environmental source, usually a water distribution system colonized with the microorganism (Fig. 22.1). In the laboratory, it is possible to generate water aerosols of *L. pneumophila* that will infect guinea pigs and produce an illness that mimics Legionnaires' disease. Similar aerosols containing *L. pneumophila* can be produced by forceful showers, humidifiers, fountains, respiratory therapy equipment, or evaporative cooling towers associated with central air conditioning systems. Whether aerosols of this kind play a major role in the transmission of the infection to humans (i.e., by the air-borne route) is still uncertain. A plausible alternative suggestion is that infection may result from microaspiration of bacteria from the oropharynx or mouth into the lower pulmonary airways, during or after the ingestion of contaminated water or ice. The circumstances of Mrs. R.'s exposure are unknown, but if water was the likely source, she may have acquired the infection at home, at work, or at any place where running water is available.

In outbreak situations, only a minority of exposed individuals actually become infected. In these uncontrolled situations, the risk of infection depends not only on the size and amount of the inhaled inoculum, but also on the susceptibility of individual host. Although not much is known about the infectious inoculum that leads to *L. pneumophila* outbreaks, several host factors are known to predispose individuals to infection. These include cigarette smoking, advanced age, chronic pulmonary disease, and immunosuppression (e.g., transplant patients, patients on corticosteroid therapy). Mrs. R. may have been particularly susceptible to infection because of her significant smoking history. Although we do not know the source of her infection, it is possible that other less susceptible individuals were exposed to the same source as Mrs. R. but did not become infected.

Figure 22.1. *Legionella* may colonize sections of pipe such as this one, which is lined with scale (inorganic crust) and detritus (organic matter and bacteria).

ENTRY, SPREAD, AND MULTIPLICATION

In the air spaces of the lung, *Legionella* are ingested by resident alveolar macrophages. These phagocytic cells, which are normally regarded as a front line of defense against invaders, fail to kill or even to inhibit the growth of *L. pneumophila* in the lung. In laboratory experiments that model this process, *L. pneumophila* actually grows faster in cultures with human macrophages than in artificial media. Moreover, there are several lines of evidence to suggest that phagocytosis and intracellular growth are essential events in the pathogenesis of Legionnaires' disease. In human disease, histological sections of infected lung tissue show that most bacteria are inside cells. In experimental animal infections, *L. pneumophila* washed from the lungs during the early stages of infection are nearly all cell associated. In fact, the susceptibility of a given animal species to infection can be predicted by the capacity of macrophages from that species to support the growth of *L. pneumophila*. For example, *L. pneumophila* grows rapidly in guinea pig macrophages in vitro, and guinea pigs are exquisitely sensitive to infection; whereas the bacteria cannot grow in mouse macrophages nor can they infect mice. Finally, mutants of *L. pneumophila* that have either a partly or a completely impaired capacity to infect macrophages are comparably impaired in their capacity to cause disease in susceptible animals.

Paradigm—Intracellular Parasitism

To grow in phagocytic cells, pathogens must be able to out-maneuver their host. They must evade the antimicrobial defenses with which these cells are armed, and they must satisfy their nutritional requirements by competing successfully with the host cell for essential intracellular nutrients. To meet these necessities, bacterial and eukaryotic pathogens follow one of the three intracellular lifestyles depicted in Figure 22.2. As the figure suggests, phylogenetically unrelated organisms may have a common strategy for intracellular survival and growth. The precise mechanisms and virulence factors that mediate these events in different species are usually very different and have evolved independently.

The ability to survive phagosome-lysosome fusion may involve adaptation of the pathogen's surface or of its metabolism or both. Gram-negative enteric organisms with smooth lipopolysaccharide, such as salmonellae, are less susceptible to killing by lysosomal contents than are rough mutants that lack the long polysaccharide chains on their surface. Similarly, mycobacteria may be protected by the relatively waxy nature of their surfaces. The leishmaniae are adapted to the hostile environment of the acidified phagosome by possession of metabolic enzymes that function well at the very low pH.

For organisms that multiply in the host cell cytoplasm, escape from the phagosome is an essential part of their survival. *Listeria monocytogenes*, a Gram-positive bacillus that causes septicemia and meningitis, is a case in point. After ingestion, *Listeria* secretes a hemolysin that is necessary for the dissolution of the phagosomal membrane. Once the bacterium is free in the cytoplasm, it divides and initiates a process of direct spread to adjacent host cells. Mutant *Listeria* that cannot produce this hemolysin cannot escape the phagosome; they neither grow nor survive in the host cell.

Figure 22.2. Three lifestyles of intracellular pathogens.

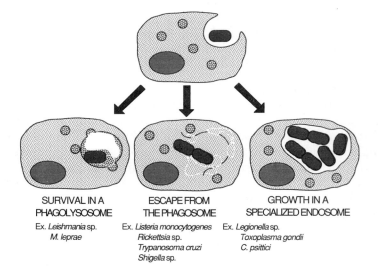

SURVIVAL IN A PHAGOLYSOSOME	ESCAPE FROM THE PHAGOSOME	GROWTH IN A SPECIALIZED ENDOSOME
Ex. *Leishmania* sp. *M. leprae*	Ex. *Listeria monocytogenes* *Rickettsia* sp. *Trypanosoma cruzi* *Shigella* sp.	Ex. *Legionella* sp. *Toxoplasma gondii* *C. psittici*

The legionellae and several other unrelated pathogens remain within a membrane-bound endosome after ingestion. These organisms owe their survival to inadequate responses of both the oxidative and the nonoxidative intracellular killing mechanisms of phagocytes. Typically, the respiratory burst and the resulting production of microbicidal oxygen derivatives is blunted or absent. Likewise, the acidification of the phagosome and the fusion of the phagosome with lysosomes, thereby exposing the ingested organism to toxic lysosomal contents, does not occur.

Regardless of the mechanism involved, intracellular parasitism has consequences in clinical medicine. Intracellular organisms are less accessible both to the host immune response and to antimicrobial agents. Recovery from infection may require a cell-mediated immune response that will inhibit or kill intracellular organisms. Such a response generally takes longer to mount than an antibody response. As a result, therapy of these infections is generally of longer duration, and relapses, presumably resulting from the re-emergence of surviving intracellular organisms, are more common than with most extracellular infections. In selecting optimal antimicrobial therapy, the capacity of drugs to penetrate infected host cells must be considered. Antibiotics that penetrate poorly into host cells are generally less useful in treating these infections.

L. pneumophila are ingested spontaneously by phagocytic cells; the molecular mechanism that triggers phagocytosis is unknown. However, in the presence of serum, the bacteria fix complement to their surface. They are resistant to the lytic effects of complement, and the presence of surface-bound C′3 enhances uptake by phagocytic cells by several orders of magnitude. Uptake mediated solely by host cell complement receptors is associated with less stimulation of intracellular antimicrobial activities, and it is possible that this mode of uptake largely accounts for the survival of *L. pneumophila* after ingestion.

After ingestion, the normal acidification of the phagosome and fusion with lysosomes is inhibited (Fig. 22.3). Instead, the phagosome associates first with other intracellular membranes (e.g., mitochondrial, nuclear) and then later becomes studded with ribosomes. Similar events have been observed with other intracellular pathogens that follow a similar intracellular life cycle. Within the specialized endosome,

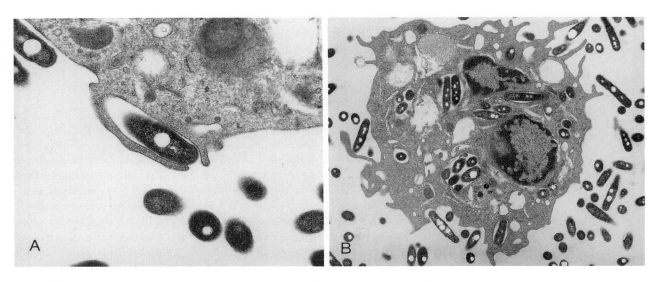

Figure 22.3. Electron micrographs. **A.** Uptake of *L. pneumophila* by a macrophage. **B.** *L. pneumophila* begin to multiply within membrane-bound phagosomes within the host macrophage.

bacterial multiplication proceeds until the host cell is literally packed with bacteria. Eventually, the cell dies and ruptures, releasing bacterial progeny that can reinitiate the cycle in other cells.

DAMAGE

Macrophages infected with *L. pneumophila* release cytokines that may contribute to the influx of blood monocytes and neutrophils into the air spaces of the lung. As nodular areas of infection enlarge, they become visible as infiltrates on the chest x-ray. These areas typically evolve into microabscesses and may coalesce to form cavities. The bronchi and bronchioles are not affected. During florid infection, *L. pneumophila* can be isolated from the blood or from a variety of organ tissues.

Much of the local damage produced by the infection is attributable to the vigor of the host inflammatory response. There is some debate about the role of bacterial products. *L. pneumophila* possesses a lipo-polysaccharide that is weakly endotoxic, and it produces an extracellular protease that has cytolytic and hemolytic activity. There is conflicting evidence about the potential role of the protease. Although the purified protease can damage the lungs of experimental animals, protease-deficient mutants of *L. pneumophila* are as virulent as wild-type strains.

Illness in humans usually begins with "flu-like" complaints, as in the case of Mrs. R. Virtually all patients with Legionnaires' disease have fever, and they typically develop clinical features of pneumonia—cough, shortness of breath, and possibly chest pain. Patients rarely have the grossly purulent (thick yellow or green) sputum associated with bacterial bronchopneumonias. Watery diarrhea is present in 25–50% of patients with Legionnaires' disease, and nausea, vomiting or abdominal pain may also be present. Blood oxygen levels may be low and may contribute to mental status changes, as seen in Mrs. R.'s case. Typically, blood counts show only moderate elevation of total leukocytes, without a preponderance of neutrophils. In many patients, the serum sodium concentration is below normal when they are first seen, and in severe cases, other laboratory tests may suggest dysfunction of the kidneys or liver. None of these clinical features is sufficiently specific to establish the diagnosis of Legionnaires' disease, inasmuch as any of them can occur in association with other pneumonias.

IMMUNITY

Experience with animal infections suggests that specific antibodies may play a role in containing *L. pneumophila* infection but that recovery requires a cell-mediated immune response. Antibodies produced during infection may bind to the bacterial surface and enhance their uptake of the bacteria by neutrophils. Although *L. pneumophila* are not efficiently killed by neutrophils, they cannot grow in these cells.

In contrast to the humoral response, the cellular immune response limits the growth of *L. pneumophila* in macrophages. By cellular immune processes described in Chapter 7, *Legionella*-immune lymphocytes proliferate and accumulate in areas of bacterial growth. There, further contact with *Legionella* antigen, in the context of Class II histocompatibility molecules, induces the local release of lymphokines. One of the most important of these lymphokines, γ-interferon, is known to suppress the growth of *L. pneumophila* in macrophages by inducing these cells to limit the availability of iron to the intracellular bacteria. Limiting this essential nutrient and eliminating the intracellular niche as a site for multiplication may be the critical function of the immune system in controlling *L. pneumophila* infection.

DIAGNOSIS

The laboratory diagnosis of Legionnaires' disease may be difficult. The bacteria are not present in large numbers in the sputum, and they stain poorly. The Gram stain usually suggests an "atypical" pneumonia, showing abundant PMNs and the absence of bacteria. In this clinical setting, several rapid diagnostic techniques are available that may help make a prompt diagnosis of Legionnaires' disease. They include examination of sputum by direct fluorescent antibody staining (DFA) or by DNA probe, or detection of *L. pneumophila* serogroup 1 antigen in the urine by an enzyme immunoassay. Although these tests may be useful in guiding the initial therapy of the patient, none of these methods is sufficiently sensitive or specific to be relied upon as the sole method of diagnosis. Culture is the most specific way to diagnose the infection, although 3–5 days of incubation may be required before *Legionella* colonies can be identified. In addition, cultures of sputum may be negative in 30–50% of patients who have *Legionella* infection diagnosed by other criteria. Culture is more sensitive when specimens are taken directly from the lower respiratory tract or when specimens are treated to limit the growth of normal flora.

Because the laboratory diagnosis of Legionnaires' disease is imperfect and occasionally untimely, it is sometimes necessary to treat patients for this potentially fatal disease on suspicion. As a case in point, Mrs. R. was recognized as having a severe, atypical pneumonia that progressed in spite of treatment with an oral cephalosporin antibiotic. In the absence of an alternative etiological diagnosis, she was treated with an antibiotic regimen that is known to be effective in Legionnaires' disease, pending the results of culture for *L. pneumophila*. This clinical decision may have saved her life.

TREATMENT AND PREVENTION

Legionellae grown in culture are sensitive to most antibiotics. However, successful antibiotic therapy requires drugs that can penetrate into infected cells, such as erythromycin and tetracycline. As in Mrs. R.'s case, it is not unusual for patients actually to become worse while on treatment with a penicillin or cephalosporin antibiotic because these antibiotics penetrate into eukaryotic cells poorly.

Prevention of Legionnaires' disease is presently practiced at an institutional level. In hospitals, hotels, and other large buildings where cases have occurred, water systems are checked regularly for legionellae. When found, the systems are flushed and decontaminated by hyperchlorination, ultraviolet irradiation, or superheating of the water to 60°C.

Protective immunity has been induced in guinea pigs by injection of various bacterial protein fractions or by inhalation of a live, mutant strain of *L. pneumophila* that cannot grow intracellularly. Immunization of humans, particularly those with one of the high-risk conditions mentioned above, may be possible in the foreseeable future.

OTHER LEGIONELLAE AND *LEGIONELLA*-ASSOCIATED DISEASES

In addition to *L. pneumophila*, several other species of *Legionella* have been found to cause human disease. In general, these are also water-related infections, and they produce clinical features comparable to Legionnaires' disease. Prominent among these species is *L. micdadei*, which was known as the Pittsburgh Pneumonia Agent before its relationship to *L. pneumophila* was established.

Certain legionellae have also been associated with an illness called Pontiac fever. The illness was first recognized during a 1968 outbreak at the county health department building in Pontiac, Michigan. In this outbreak, 95% of the departmental employees became ill with fever, muscle aches, headache, and dizziness that resolved spontaneously in 2–5 days. The cause of this flu-like illness was not identified at the time, but serum samples from patients and lung tissue from guinea pigs exposed to the building air were kept frozen for future reference. After the identification of *L. pneumophila* 9 years later, the frozen specimens were retested. The Pontiac patients were found to have had a rise in specific *Legionella* antibodies, and the guinea pig lungs yielded growth of *L. pneumophila* in culture.

Like Legionnaires' disease, Pontiac fever is an air-borne disease; but there the similarity ends. Unlike Legionnaires' disease, Pontiac fever typically affects a high proportion of exposed individuals, and it affects healthy, as well as high-risk, individuals. It does not produce pneumonia and is never fatal. It may not be an infection at all, but rather a manifestation of hypersensitivity. How the same bacteria can produce such different clinical syndromes is still a mystery.

CONCLUSION

The legionellae produce an air-borne infection of the lungs that results in a life-threatening pneumonia. Infection depends upon the capacity of the bacterium to grow within phagocytic cells of the host. Treatment and immune mechanisms are beneficial insofar as they can affect the bacteria that occupy this intracellular niche.

Self-assessment Questions

1. Discuss the ecological characteristics of *L. pneumophila* and their relation to the epidemiology of legionellosis.

2. Why does legionellosis tend to manifest itself in outbreaks?

3. Contrast pneumonia due to *Legionella* with that due to pneumococci (Chapter 13).

4. Why don't all of us come down with legionellosis, given the widespread occurrence of the organisms?

5. What other pathogenic bacteria are acquired from the water supply routes other than ingestion?

SUGGESTED READING

Cianciotto NP, Eisenstein BI, Engleberg NC, Shuman H. Genetics and molecular pathogenesis of *Legionella pneumophila*, an intracellular parasite of macrophages. Molec Biol Med 1989;6:409–424.

Fraser DW, Tsai TR, Orenstein W, et al. Legionnaires' disease: description of an epidemic of pneumonia. N Engl J Med 1977;297:1189–1197.

Horwitz MA. The immunobiology of *Legionella pneumophila*. In: Moulder JW, ed. Intracellular parasitism. Boca Raton, FL: CRC Press, 1989:141–156.

Mandell GL, Douglas Jr RG, Bennett JE. Principles and practice of infectious disease, ed. 3. New York: John Wiley & Sons, 1990:1764–1782.

Muder RR, Yu VL, Woo AH. Mode of transmission of *Legionella pneumophila*; a critical review. Arch Intern Med 1986;146:1607–1612.

Winn WC Jr. Legionnaires' disease: historical perspective. Clin Microbiol Rev 1988;1:60–81.

Mycobacteria: Tuberculosis and Leprosy

23

John K. Spitznagel and William R. Jacobs, Jr.

"The captain of all the men of death that came against him to take him away, was the Consumption, for it was that that brought him down to his grave."
John Bunyan (1628–1688)

Tuberculosis conjures up the image of a contagious, chronic, severe disease of the lungs that is often fatal. Actually, that is only one of the manifestations of infection by tubercle bacilli. Tuberculosis is not a single disease but a condition that varies in severity depending on the history of previous exposure to the organisms. The infection of a previously unexposed person is usually mild and self-limiting. In rare instances, it can proceed directly to a severe generalized disease. Much more often though, the infected person heals and never manifests full-blown tuberculosis.

A few individuals come down with a secondary disease, often many years after the primary exposure. They become ill because the bacteria that caused the primary disease persist in the body by escaping host defense mechanisms. The secondary illness more often fits the classical description of tuberculosis. Many of the symptoms of this form of the disease are not caused by the tubercle bacilli themselves, but result from immunological hypersensitivity reactions of the host to products of the bacteria. If uncontrolled, these can be destructive to tissues.

Thus, tuberculosis is a complex of microbiological and immunological events that escapes simple definition. It serves as a paradigm of chronic infectious diseases, most of which share with it the persistence of the agent in the body and the prominent role of the host responses in the manifestations of the disease.

CASE

Ms. C., a 24-year-old African-American schoolteacher and housewife, had recently lost more than 10% of her weight, had night sweats, and felt feverish. She had a cough that produced greenish sputum flecked with blood. Her physician suspected that she might be suffering from pulmonary tuberculosis and administered a tuberculin skin test. Forty-eight hours later, Ms. C. showed a strong positive skin reaction, with thickening of the skin and redness at the injection site. The physician referred her to the local health department, where the diagnosis of tuberculosis was confirmed by a chest x-ray (Fig. 23.1) and the presence of "acid-fast bacilli" in a stained smear of her sputum. A careful history revealed that between the ages of 10 and 12 years, she had lived with an aunt, now deceased, who was said to have had tuberculosis. Given the symptoms, the tuberculin test, plus the radiological and laboratory findings, Ms. C. undoubtedly suffered from tuberculosis.

Ms. C. became worried about her health and wondered about her ability to continue working in school. She and her husband had planned to have a baby soon, but she thought that "pregnancy and new babies do not mix well with tuberculosis." Her physician reassured her that she stood a good chance of being cured. Effective antibiotics could be taken by mouth, although she had to take them for many months. Once treatment was initiated, she could resume her teaching and, in time, plan a pregnancy.

Relevant questions are:

1. How could Ms. C. have contracted tuberculosis in today's world? Did she get it from her aunt?

2. Did she later develop clinical signs and symptoms from this possible early contact with tubercle bacilli?

3. Why did it take so long Ms. C. to show signs of an active tubercular infection?

4. What pathobiological events account for her current signs and symptoms? Why did she have fevers, weight loss, cough, bloody sputum, a "positive" skin reaction, and an abnormal chest x-ray?

5. What is the chance that Ms. C. may pass the disease to her husband? Her students? Others?

Tuberculosis or "consumption" (as it used to be called) has been one of the great afflictions of mankind. It has, however, yielded dramatically to improvement in the living standard and is generally responsive to chemotherapy. However, today, tuberculosis still ranks as a major infectious cause of death in the world. The World Health Organization estimates that there are over 10 million new cases of tuberculosis and 3 million deaths resulting from tuberculosis each year.

Tuberculosis is rising at alarming rates in the United States, coincident with the increase in **AIDS** cases. For over a century, there was a steady decline in the number of cases of this disease in the U.S. and other industrialized countries. The numbers of cases of tuberculosis rose by 3% to 6% from 1986–1990, which may not sound too great. However, the increase is much larger than that in the large cities of the U.S. (Fig. 23.2) and is extraordinarily high in minority populations (Fig. 23.3).

In the last century, tuberculosis was a puzzling topic of myths; it was even referred to as the "consumptive passion." The disease was thought to afflict sensitive, passionate people, and to endow them with a pale, languid look that was celebrated in literature and opera (e.g., Shelley's "*The Sensitive Plant*," Verdi's "*La Traviata*," Puccini's "*La Boheme*"). It was not until the end of the last century, when the cause of the disease was elucidated by Robert Koch, that the myth dispelled.

MYCOBACTERIA

Tubercle bacilli belong to a distinctive genus of bacteria, *Mycobacterium*. This genus includes several species that are closely related (Table 23.1). Species other than *M. tuberculosis* were first called "atypical mycobacteria" because they only partially resembled the tubercle

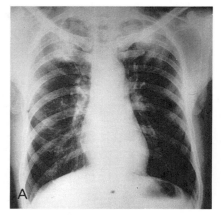

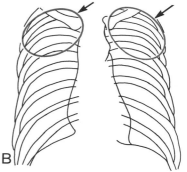

Figure 23.1. Pulmonary tuberculosis. Chest radiograph of young adult with recent cough and loss of weight showing bilateral upper lobe shadowing. The x-ray is of a different person from the one described in the text, but the abnormalities are comparable to those seen in the x-rays of that patient. The areas most affected are *circled* in the drawing.

Figure 23.2. Rates of tuberculosis by state, in the United States in 1989.

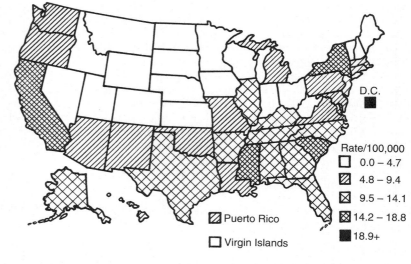

Rate/100,000
☐ 0.0 – 4.7
▨ 4.8 – 9.4
⊠ 9.5 – 14.1
▩ 14.2 – 18.8
■ 18.9+

▨ Puerto Rico
☐ Virgin Islands

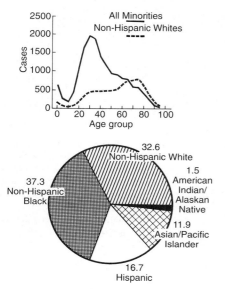

Figure 23.3. The incidence of tuberculosis by age and ethnicity in the United States in 1989.

bacillus; they are now known to cause a variety of diseases. Also included in this genus is the agent of leprosy, *M. leprae*. Several mycobacteria are harmless organisms, some of which live on the human body without causing disease (e.g., the smegma bacillus), or in the environment, especially the soil. The genus is distinguishable because of two characteristics: acid-fastness and slow growth.

Acid-Fastness—Mycobacterial Hallmark

Mycobacteria belong to a small group of bacteria that have the unusual ability to retain dyes when treated with acid solutions. The reason for this acid-fastness is that mycobacteria are surrounded by unique chemical components, namely waxes. Mycobacterial waxes are long-chain hydrocarbons (incidentally, one of the leading researchers in this field is an ex-petroleum chemist!) The main wax is called **mycolic acid**, and is a β-hydroxy fatty acid linked covalently to the cell wall murein. The waxes of mycobacteria are also important in pathogenesis, as will be discussed later.

As may be expected, the waxy barrier makes a big difference in the permeability properties of these organisms. Common stains do not penetrate the wax layer; for instance, mycobacteria do not take up the dyes used in the Gram stain and, therefore, cannot be labeled Gram positive or Gram negative. It is possible, however, to stain them using special techniques. One is to melt the wax temporarily by heating a smear of the bacteria while it is covered with a saturated solution of a basic dye, such as fuchsin. Alternatively, one can add a detergent to the stain. The stained smear is then treated with 3% hydrochloric acid in ethanol, which decolorizes nearly all organisms except for the mycobacteria. The smear is then counterstained with a blue dye to provide a contrasting background.

Resistance of mycobacteria to chemical and physical agents helps them survive both in the body and in the exterior environment. Thus, they are unusually resistant to killing by phagocytes. Since they are also highly **resistant to germicides**, preparations used to disinfect surfaces must be tested by the manufacturer for their power to kill mycobacteria (mycobactericidal disinfectants usually contain iodine or strong detergents). Mycobacteria are also highly **resistant to drying**, which contributes to their potential for transmission. The wax coating

Table 23.1. Characteristics of Mycobacteria of Major Clinical Importance[a]

Species	Reservoir	Virulence for Humans	Main Disease Caused	Case-to-Case Transmission	In Vitro Growth Rate	Optimum Growth Temperature (°C)
M. tuberculosis	Human	+++	Tuberculosis	Yes	S	37
M. bovis	Animals	+++	Tuberculosis	Rare	S	37
Bacillus Calmette-Guerin (BCG)	Artificial culture	±	Local lesion	Very Rare	S	37
M. kansasii	Environmental	+	Tuberculosis-like	No	S	37
M. scrofulaceum	Environmental	+	Lymphadenitis	No	S	37
M. avium-intracellulare	Environmental birds	+	Tuberculosis-like	No	S	37
M. fortuitum	Environmental	±	Skin abscesses	No	F	37
M. marinum	Water, fish	±	Skin granuloma	No	S	30
M. ulcerans	Probably environmental; tropical	+	Severe skin ulceration	No	S	30
M. leprae	Human	+++	Leprosy	Yes	None	Not Applicable

[a]This table omits many essentially saprophytic mycobacteria. S = slow. F = fast.

does not, however, help them withstand heat. For instance, they are killed during pasteurization of milk (e.g., heating to 60°C for 30 minutes).

Slow Growth

Mycobacteria grow very slowly. Their generation time is measured in hours, not minutes; it is not uncommon for pathogenic members of the genus to require 24 hours to double in laboratory media. Some mycobacteria glow faster than that, but still considerably more slowly than common bacteria. It is possible that slow growth results from inability to transport nutrients rapidly across the wax layer. Slow growth causes delays in diagnosis by culture; laboratory cultures of clinical material are incubated for up to 8 weeks! (To avoid drying up of the culture medium, the laboratory uses tightly capped test tubes rather than Petri dishes.) On agar, colonies of mycobacteria look like irregular waxy lumps, and are usually quite raised over the agar surface. Touching colonies with an inoculating needle will show that they stick to the medium, are hard to pick up, and cannot be easily dispersed in a drop of water to make a smear.

Not all mycobacteria can be grown in artificial media. The leprosy bacillus has so far resisted cultivation outside the body of humans or a few animals. The inability to grow these bacteria under routine laboratory conditions continues to impede leprosy research. Much effort is being expended to develop rapid diagnostic methods for both the tubercle and leprosy bacilli, making use of DNA probes and nucleic acid amplification (see Chapter 55).

ENCOUNTER AND ENTRY

It is likely that Ms. C. contracted tuberculosis by breathing aerosols or dust particles containing tubercle bacilli. Most likely, bacteria-laden droplets were produced by her aunt's frequent coughing bouts. In fact, air-borne transmission of tuberculosis is an efficient means to spread the disease for a least two reasons:

• If untreated, the disease can lead to the formation of open pulmonary lesions that contain large numbers of bacteria. Coughing spreads the organisms from such lesions into the environment.

- Because tubercle bacilli are highly resistant to drying, they are capable of surviving for a long time in the air and house dust. This is important because, most often, tubercle bacilli enter into the lung in bacteria-containing so-called droplet nuclei, the products of dried aerosols. Such particles are effective infectious material because they stay suspended in the air for a long time; not becoming trapped in the mucosal blanket, they can gain access to the alveoli.

These two characteristics account for the epidemiology of tuberculosis: it is widespread in crowded areas, primarily among young children who are exposed repeatedly to the organisms.

The inoculum size of tubercle bacilli required to cause infections is usually high. There is a direct relationship between the number of bacilli in a patient's sputum and the likelihood that exposed family members will contract the disease. The location of the organisms in the body depends largely on the site of entry. For example, infection of the lungs (which is most prevalent in countries such as the U.S.) results from inhalation of the bacteria. Infection of the intestine or the tonsils is usually due to ingestion of the organisms, because tubercle bacilli may be acquired by drinking unpasteurized milk from infected cows. Cattle suffer from a disease similar to human tuberculosis, but caused by bovine strains of mycobacteria, *M. bovis*.

SPREAD, MULTIPLICATION, DAMAGE

Tubercle bacilli do not produce exotoxins or endotoxin. The severe manifestations of tuberculosis are linked to host reactions to the organisms; damage is caused by uncontrolled, progressive, chronic inflammation, and by organisms living with macrophages. It follows that infection has different manifestations in a "virgin" host than in a person who has been infected previously. Tuberculosis manifests itself in two major forms:

- **Primary tuberculosis** is the disease of persons who are infected for the first time. It is usually mild and often asymptomatic. Occasionally, however, the primary disease progresses directly to cause systemic diseases, such as tuberculous meningitis, miliary tuberculosis, or both (see below). In these cases, the immune reaction fails to develop.

- **Secondary tuberculosis** is usually due to the **reactivation** of dormant organisms within the body. This is the distinctive presentation of tuberculosis, a chronic disease associated with extensive tissue damage, often progressing to death if untreated.

Primary Tuberculosis

After Ms. C. inhaled tubercle bacilli as a child, she might have developed flu-like symptoms of lower respiratory infection (or she may not have had any symptoms at all). She probably developed an acute localized inflammation that was soon followed by a more chronic inflammatory response.

Primary tuberculosis is characterized by a sequence of pathobiological steps (Fig. 23.4). Tubercle bacilli are ingested by resident macrophages of the pulmonary alveoli (Fig. 23.5). Here the organisms multiply, first within these cells and later, within nonresident macrophages that collect in the area. Loaded with mycobacteria, newly arrived cells migrate through the lymphatics to the hylar lymph nodes,

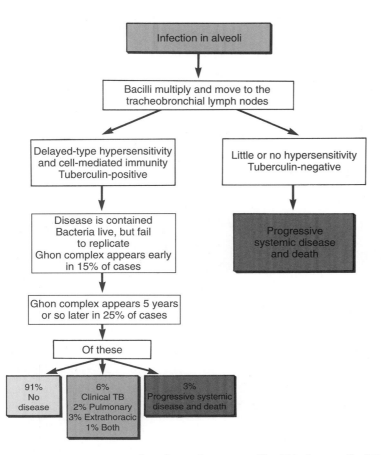

Figure 23.4. The history of untreated tuberculosis.

where an immune response develops, dominated by T-helper cells (Fig. 23.6). Inflammation will now be present in several places—at the original site of infection, along lymphatic channels, and in the regional lymph nodes. This sequence of events takes about 30 days. Despite their slow growth, the mycobacteria will have multiplied substantially by this time and be found in large numbers.

At this stage of the infection, the tuberculin skin test usually becomes positive and a chest x-ray reveals growing patches of density in the lung. The immune defenses now manage to curb the proliferation of the organisms and retard their local spread, while macrophages, activated by T cells, begin to kill the organisms or to slow down their growth. A certain number of tubercle bacilli will already have disseminated throughout the body (Fig. 23.6). In the tissues, especially in the hylar lymph nodes, the organisms are contained in **tubercles**, small **granulomas** consisting of epithelioid cells, giant cells, and lymphocytes. (Granuloma formation is partly caused by one of the waxes of the organisms known as **cord factor**, because it is responsible for growth of the organisms in rope-like arrangements. Note: Injection of cord factor results in granulomas indistinguishable from those caused by tubercle bacilli.) With time, the centers of the tubercles become necrotic and advance to form acellular masses of cheesy debris, termed **caseous material**. The combination of a single lesion in the lung, often just under the pleura, and caseation in the bronchial lymph nodes is called the **Ghon complex**.

Primary tuberculosis may take two courses (Fig. 23.4). In people who are otherwise healthy, the lesions heal spontaneously and become fibrotic or calcified. These lesions usually persist for a lifetime and can be seen years later in chest x-rays as radiopaque nodules. In immuno-

Figure 23.5. Tubercle bacilli enter through the respiratory tract.

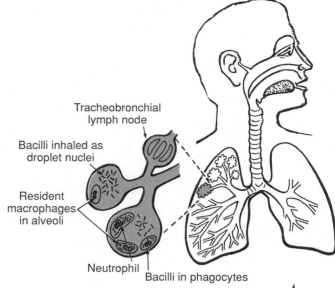

Tracheobronchial lymph node

Bacilli inhaled as droplet nuclei

Resident macrophages in alveoli

Neutrophil

Bacilli in phagocytes

Figure 23.6. Tubercle bacilli multiply in phagocytes and spread to lymph nodes and the circulation.

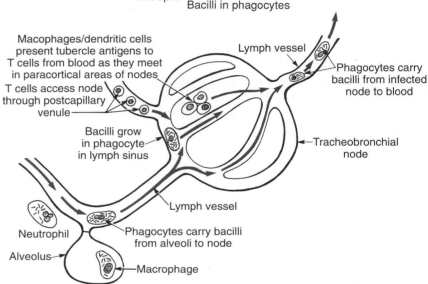

Macophages/dendritic cells present tubercle antigens to T cells from blood as they meet in paracortical areas of nodes

T cells access node through postcapillary venule

Bacilli grow in phagocyte in lymph sinus

Lymph vessel

Phagocytes carry bacilli from infected node to blood

Tracheobronchial node

Lymph vessel

Neutrophil

Alveolus

Phagocytes carry bacilli from alveoli to node

Macrophage

compromised persons, the organisms may invade the bloodstream. The organisms can then localize and cause disease in almost any organ of the body. This can lead to a potentially fatal generalized infection known as **disseminated miliary tuberculosis**. In this case, tubercles are visible in many organs, including the liver, spleen, kidneys, brain, and meninges. The name "miliary" is derived from the resemblance of the tubercles to grains of millet (bird seed).

How does primary tuberculosis come to a halt? Clearly, the original cellular response fails to curb the multiplication of the organisms. However, with time, **cellular immunity** to the organisms develops. Macrophages that become activated by lymphokines produced by T lymphocytes can now inhibit the intracellular growth of the tubercle bacilli. (A review of the complex topic of cell-mediated immunity might be helpful at this time—see Chapter 7.) As might be expected from the intracellular location of the organisms, **humoral immunity** does not play a major role in the immune response to tuberculosis. Antibodies appear in the circulation but do not seem to play an effective defensive role, nor are they useful as a diagnostic tool.

Although activated macrophages usually kill intracellular bacteria, they cannot always destroy the exceptionally hardy tubercle bacilli. Intracellular organisms may, however, be kept in check for long periods of time. An uneasy equilibrium is reached; some macrophages kill the organisms, others are themselves killed and release their bacterial contents, still others are in a state of balance and contain within them dormant bacteria for a long period of time. Immunological processing of those bacteria that are killed leads to continued antigenic stimulation.

The involvement of macrophages has its price. Two substances produced by these cells, interleukin-1 and tumor necrosis factor (Chapter 6), are known to contribute to the symptoms of the disease. Among its various activities, **interleukin-1** acts as the mediator of the fever experienced by patients with tuberculosis. **Tumor necrosis factor**, or **cachectin**, interferes with lipid metabolism and leads to severe weight loss.

DELAYED-TYPE HYPERSENSITIVITY AND THE TUBERCULIN REACTION

Immunological reactivity to tuberculosis can be demonstrated by the **tuberculin skin test**. The test is carried out by injecting proteins made by tubercle bacilli, known as **tuberculin**. (The material commonly used is not an isolated protein molecule, but a mixture known as **PPD**, which stands for "purified protein derivative.") A positive reaction indicates cellular immunity to tubercle bacilli and is indicated by reddening and thickening of the skin 2–3 days later. This **delayed-type hypersensitivity reaction** reflects the local events that take place in the infected tissue. Depending on the site of the reaction, delayed-type hypersensitivity may account for diverse manifestations, e.g., pleurisy with effusion (the sometimes massive accumulation of exudate in the pleural cavities), or the sudden inflammation of the meninges in **tuberculous meningitis**. Surprisingly few tubercle bacilli are present in the pleural fluid or in the cerebrospinal fluid during these infections, but they are able to cause a severe inflammation as the result of a local tuberculin reaction. Likewise, the number of inflammatory cells is also very small. Aspects of the pathogenesis of tuberculosis are depicted in Figure 23.4.

Tubercle bacilli not only elicit cell-mediated immunity but also raise the general level of immunological responsiveness. This **adjuvant** effect is used experimentally to increase immunostimulation to other antigens. A mixture of killed tubercle bacilli, mineral oil, and a surfactant is known as **Freund's adjuvant**. Its active component is a fragment of the organisms' murein, a **muramyl dipeptide** or **MDP**.

Secondary Tuberculosis

Years after acquiring primary tuberculosis, some people (such as Ms. C.) develop the chronic, necrotic, progressive symptoms that characterize tuberculosis (Fig. 23.4). The flare-up can sometimes be blamed on impairment of immune function; clearly, any compromise of the T-cell-macrophage immune system may render a person abnormally vulnerable to **reactivation** of mycobacteria that have been carried in the body in latent form. Of course, **reinfection** with externally acquired tubercle bacilli could lead to the same manifestations. Certain infections, such as measles, are known to depress transiently the cell-mediated immune responses, including the tuberculin reaction, and are known to predispose patients to reactivation tuberculosis. It is likely that other common agents have similar effects but are less clinically evident. Patients receiving corticosteroids for inflammatory diseases, undergoing cancer chemotherapy, or suffering from AIDS may become afflicted with tuberculosis. In other cases, the precipitating cause of reactivation of the disease is not known.

Subtle depression of the immune system due to hormonal or other causes may go undetected. Ms. C. did not suffer from malnutrition, which has also been shown to elicit reactivation disease. A contributing factor in her case may be that dark-skinned persons are more susceptible to the disease (Fig. 23.3). The existence of genetic factors is inferred from the high incidence of clinical disease in persons with a specific histocompatibility type, HLA-Bev15. The reason that the disease becomes active in older people may possibly be due to a poorly understood loss of immune competence that occurs with aging.

The most common location of secondary tuberculosis is the apex of the lungs. This may be due to the greater level of oxygenation at this site, which gives the highly aerobic tubercle bacilli an edge in growth. Lesions slowly become necrotic, caseate, and eventually merge into larger lesions. With time, the caseous lesions liquefy and discharge their contents into bronchi. This event has several serious consequences. It results in a well-aerated cavity where the organisms can actively proliferate. The discharge of caseous material also distributes the organisms to other sites in the lung, which can lead to a rapidly progressing disease known as "galloping consumption." In addition, the bacteria-laden contents of caseous lesions are coughed up and become a source of environmental contamination. Because inflammation of the surface of the bronchi causes increased mucus secretion and stimulation of the cough reflex, patients cough up sputum. Destruction of tissues results in bloody sputa. In advanced tuberculosis, blood vessels may become exposed to the cavities produced by necrosis and patients may die of hemorrhage if these vessels rupture.

What accounted for the various symptoms of Ms. C.? Her fever, weight loss, and night sweats may have been due to the release of interleukin-1 and tumor necrosis factor from the many macrophages involved. Her sputum probably included mucus from inflamed bronchi and material from caseous lesions. Bronchial inflammation may have been caused by a local tuberculin reaction, due to the tuberculoprotein in the caseous material. At this time, she became infectious and able to transmit tuberculosis to others.

RANGE OF MANIFESTATIONS OF TUBERCULOSIS

Tuberculosis is insidious. Most people are unaware of their initial encounter with the organisms. As few as 5–9% of all infected persons experience clinical evidence of the disease within 5 years of infection (Fig. 23.4). This group includes those unfortunate patients who do not develop sufficient cellular immunity in time to contain the organisms and who develop miliary tuberculosis. This rampant infection is very different from secondary reactivation tuberculosis (although it is sometimes manifested in patients with this condition as well).

Secondary tuberculosis usually becomes noticeable 1 or 2 years after the primary disease, probably because it takes that long to develop full-blown delayed-type hypersensitivity. Although it is most commonly localized in the lung, secondary infection may affect the genitourinary or gastrointestinal tracts, the testicles, the fallopian tubes, the ovaries, or the skin (in other words, almost any organ). Tuberculosis of bone is especially debilitating when it involves the spine, which may collapse as the result of tissue destruction, resulting in life-long disability. It is clear that **the course of the disease is unpredictable on anatomical grounds alone because the organisms have the ability to colonize practically any site of the body.**

In view of the damage caused in tuberculosis by the immune responses of the host, one may well ask which is worse: the severe cell-mediated immune response to the disease and its resulting damage, or no immune response to tuberculosis at all. Without cellular immunity and delayed hypersensitivity there would be no development of caseation necrosis. However, the tubercle bacilli would not be held in check and would proliferate unimpeded. The result could be, for example, miliary tuberculosis, a disease that can kill much more rapidly than chronic pulmonary tuberculosis. Thus, the immune response serves to contain the disease, even if it eventually causes a great deal of damage. In fact, the body relies on three defensive strategies. One involves the antimicrobial action of activated macrophages. The second consists of walling off and containing the lesion by fibrosis and calcification. The third, which may be called "self-debridement," consists of attempts by the body to expel the caseous material through the bronchiotracheal tree or other ducts. The upshot is that defense mechanisms allow a large proportion of patients with tuberculosis to curb progression of the disease for life. Some, because of evident immune compromise or for undefined idiosyncratic features of their immune system, fail to deal with the organisms. They develop clinical disease and many die of tuberculosis.

DIAGNOSIS

Tuberculin Skin Test

The tuberculin skin test is the most widely used tool to diagnose tuberculosis. It only detects delayed hypersensitivity, however, and does not indicate the presence of active disease. The tuberculin test is usually performed by injecting a small amount of PPD, a mixture of proteins from tubercle bacilli, into the skin of the forearm. A positive test is indicated by reddening and thickening of the skin 48–72 hours after injection. The most important criterion for a positive test is the thickening and hardening (induration) of the skin at the site of injection. This is due to infiltration of the area by mononuclear phagocytes and T cells.

This test is especially useful in populations, such as those in the U.S., where tuberculosis has become rare, where less than 1% of children and young adults in such groups now give a positive test. On the other hand, the test is much less useful in regions where a high proportion of the population is tuberculin positive or has received the BCG vaccine (see below). A positive test in the wake of an earlier negative one indicates recent exposure to tubercle bacilli, which constitutes a call for therapeutic intervention (see below). Medical personnel are definitely at risk, especially when exposed to infectious patients. This is why medical students should be tested at intervals for tuberculin reactivity.

There are certain caveats to remember regarding this test. Patients who are immunocompromised (e.g., patients with AIDS) may fail to give a positive reaction. Such people are said to be **anergic** or **unresponsive.** A control test is usually carried out to determine if the person being tested is generally anergic. This is done by injecting small amounts of antigens from the yeast, *Candida*, an organism so ubiquitous that most people have developed delayed hypersensitivity to it before reaching adulthood. A positive tuberculin test result may also be caused by cross-reactive immunity to mycobacteria other than the tubercle bacillus. Thus, a person infected with **atypical mycobacteria** may give a positive tuberculin test. This is important to recognize, inasmuch as mycobacteria of this group are often resistant to antitubercular drugs.

Microscopic and Cultural Diagnostic Tests

A rapid diagnostic approach includes a careful history, direct examination of sputum or exudates, a tuberculin test, and a chest x-ray (Fig. 23.1). Although direct examination is a simple, easily learned procedure, it requires guidance because tubercle bacilli are sometimes so slender that they may escape casual examination. Fortunately, they stand out because they are the only red objects in a smear stained by the most common procedure, the Ziehl-Neelsen method. Direct examination of sputum is especially important because the infectiousness of a patient is dependent on the presence of "red bugs," tubercle bacilli, in the sputum. **Because of its usefulness, every medical student should know how to carry out an acid-fast stain.** In the future, more sensitive methods of rapid diagnosis may become generally available. Such methods are particularly useful in the diagnosis of tubercular meningitis, and include the detection of a tubercle bacillus-specific antigen and a lipid, tuberculostearic acid, in the cerebrospinal fluid.

The only rigorous diagnostic method is the cultivation of the organisms. The problem is that is usually takes 2–8 weeks before a positive culture can be read with assurance. This time may be shorted by coupling culturing with the polymerase chain reaction (PCR, Chapter 55). Despite this, culturing may be crucial when microscopic examination is negative. Sputa from patients with active tuberculosis may have too few organisms to be detected microscopically, but may still give rise to a positive culture. Finally, if there is growth of tubercle bacilli, it is important to test them for antibiotic sensitivity.

What other conditions resemble tuberculosis? Table 23.1 shows that they are numerous. The main ones are those caused by the atypical mycobacteria, the most common of which are *M. avium-intracellulare* and *M. kansasii*. Disease caused by these organisms tends to be less severe and more indolent, but it can also lead to disability and even death. Both are important complications in AIDS patients. Other diseases that must be included in the differential diagnosis are those caused by actinomycetes, *Nocardia*, and systemic fungi (see Chapter 38).

TREATMENT

We now have excellent therapeutic resources against tuberculosis; they include several highly effective drugs that can be administered by mouth to ambulatory patients, such as **rifampin, isoniazid** (INH), pyrazinamide, and **ethambutol** (Table 23.1). These drugs are relatively inexpensive (by the standards of affluent countries) and work well if taken for 9 months. Treatment quickly renders the patient noncontagious, so that quarantine is no longer required. Because instituting therapy is an urgent matter, it is advisable to start it before the results of cultures are obtained, as long as the clinical findings (history, examination, x-ray), a positive smear, and a positive tuberculin test suggest the disease.

Thirty years of clinical investigation have uncovered the importance of **multiple drug therapy**. The reason is that tubercle bacilli readily become resistant to antimycobacterial drugs. Chromosomal mutations yield levels of resistance up to 1000-fold greater than the wild type, and arise in one of every 10^6 to 10^7 bacteria. A tuberculous cavity may contain as many as 10^{11} bacteria. Not surprisingly, drug-resistant mutants appear more frequently in patients with multiplying tubercle bacilli. Unfortunately, drug-resistant organisms arise frequently in certain underdeveloped countries, where up to 60% of the isolates of *M. tuberculosis* are resistant to one of the major antitubercular drugs. The solution is clear—give at least two drugs. The chance that one organism will become resistant to two drugs simultaneously is infinitesimally small (Chapter 5). However, this simple measure can be too costly in economically poor countries. The economic impasse can be illustrated by the following; in some countries, it takes the total economic output of one worker to support the drug therapy of just one patient with tuberculosis.

Another reason for multiple drug therapy of tuberculosis is that some of the agents used act **synergistically**. For example, INH acts on intracellular mycobacteria, while rifampin works both on intra- and extracellular organisms, including slow-growing strains. Administered together, these drugs are much more effective than either one given alone. Another drug, pyrazinamide, is also used for chemotherapy. A newly introduced derivative of rifampin, rifabutin, appears to be effective against rifampin-resistant tubercle bacilli. This drug also shows promise for the treatment of infections by the *M. avium-intracellulare* complex.

Owing to the chronic, variable nature of tuberculosis, it has taken many years to ascertain the most appropriate term for antituberculosis treatment. In general, it is now believed that 6–9 months is adequate for pulmonary disease. Extrapulmonary tuberculosis may require longer-term therapy. A current regime includes INH and rifampin given concurrently for 6 months and pyrazinamide during the first 2 months.

AIDS AND MYCOBACTERIAL INFECTIONS

Tuberculosis is again becoming a major problem due to the epidemic of AIDS. In the U.S., the increase in AIDS cases is the likely reason for the reversal of the long downward trend in cases of tuberculosis. Of the many infections associated with AIDS, tuberculosis stands out because it spreads easily by the respiratory route. It is both preventable and treatable. You should be aware that not only is the person infected with HIV more susceptible to the tubercle bacillus, but the person carrying latent *M. tuberculosis* is much more likely to reactivate the organisms and develop the clinical symptoms of tuberculosis after becoming infected with HIV.

The incidence of tuberculosis among AIDS patients is 500 times that of the general population. The problem for the clinician is complicated by the differences in incidence of AIDS and tuberculosis in different groups. For example, between 1985 and 1989, the reported cases of tuberculosis in the 25- to 44-year-old age group, those with the highest incidence of AIDS, increased by 37% among African-Americans, 43% among Hispanics, and 11% among Caucasians. The distinction between HIV infection and AIDS is also important because the incidence and severity of tuberculosis correlates with the major immunological manifestation of AIDS, the loss of CD_4 or helper T cells (Chapter 7).

AIDS patients with tuberculosis are more likely to develop extrapulmonary disease, involving the lymph nodes, the bone marrow, the genitourinary tract, and the central nervous system. Most of these patients have positive blood cultures for tubercle bacilli. In other words, patients with AIDS react like the small group of people in Figure 23.5 who develop rapidly advancing or miliary tuberculosis soon after primary infection. The likely reason for these manifestations is the depletion of CD_4 T cells which, with the associate loss of macrophage function, leads to the impairment of cell-mediated immunity.

Because tuberculosis in HIV-infected people and AIDS patients is communicable and fatal, it becomes very important to diagnose and to treat it. In addition to the tools used to diagnose tuberculosis in the immunocompetent patient, the use of blood cultures becomes central in these cases. The tuberculin skin test, which may become negative due to anergy in AIDS patients, is still useful in HIV-infected persons who have not progressed to AIDS. These patients respond to a similar treatment as other tuberculosis patients. Because sputum containing the organisms can be readily sterilized, these patients do not need to be isolated from others.

An alarming recent occurrence is the appearance of *M. tuberculosis* organisms resistant to all of the usual therapeutic agents. Infections due to these organisms have occurred in patients with AIDS and even in normal hosts. We may be faced with returning full circle to dealing with these infections in the same way that we did before medical therapy—opening of the sanitarium and isolation of these patients.

In addition to tuberculosis, AIDS patients, because of their diminished cell-mediated immunity, suffer from a variety of other opportunistic infections (Chapter 67). A particularly serious one is due to *M. avium-intracellulare*, and other "atypical mycobacteria." Before the AIDS epidemic, *M. avium* was rarely described as a cause of pneumonia, and disseminated infections with this organism were virtually unheard of. *M. avium* is often found in water and soil and is harmless to most immunocompetent individuals. It is becoming a greater problem in AIDS patients, particularly late in the course of HIV infection. Today, almost 8% of AIDS patients have disseminated *M. avium* infections, up from 5% just 2 years ago. Systematic infections of *M. avium* normally involve many organs where the organisms multiply to as many as 10^{10} acid-fast bacilli per gram of tissue. *M. avium* infections are more difficult to treat than those caused by *M. tuberculosis* infections, because *M. avium* is more resistant to most antibiotics. Successful chemotherapy normally requires four or five drugs in combination. Recent promising additions to drug therapy are the fluoroquinoline derivatives, such as ciprofloxacin, and the newer macrolides, such as clarithromycin; these classes of drugs offer new hope to this difficult-to-treat infection. However, much more basic research is needed to understand the pathogenesis of *M. avium* infections and to understand their innate resistance to the antituberculosis antibiotics.

PREVENTION

The history of tuberculosis strongly suggests that it can be effectively controlled by sanitary measures and improved standards of living. For now, in disadvantaged parts of the world, we must rely on other measures. One problem is that we have **no effective vaccine made from killed organisms.** The immunology of tuberculosis tells us why; by and large, killed vaccines produce circulating antibodies, which are of limited importance in this disease. To elicit a cell-mediated immune response, antigens must be present for long periods. This is best accomplished with vaccines that contain live organisms, which can persist in the body for long times.

There is such a live mycobacterial vaccine, know as **BCG**, or "Bacille Calmette-Guerin," after its French discoverers. It consists of a bovine strain of tubercle bacilli that lost its virulence after prolonged cultivation in vitro. It appears to be a reliably avirulent mutant and has given no signs of reverting to a virulent form. It is now considered useful in parts of the world where tuberculosis is endemic and where other preventive measures are not generally available. The safe and efficient properties of the BCG vaccine make it a good candidate as a carrier for antigens of other organisms. Genes for such antigens are being cloned into the BCG agent in efforts to make a "multivaccine" to protect against a number of infectious diseases. These developments are discussed in Chapter 44.

BCG vaccine has a drawback because it causes the recipient to "convert" to tuberculin positive (in fact, this is a criterion for successful immunization). BCG vaccination thus eliminates a valuable clinical indicator, inasmuch as conversion to tuberculin positivity is an early warning of infection. To preserve tuberculin conversion as a clinical indicator of new cases, BCG is not used in the U.S. or other countries with low incidence of tuberculosis. It has become standard practice to administer INH to personnel at risk or to selected persons who have converted to a positive tuberculin reaction. Such treatment is called **chemoprophylaxis.** The rationale for using only one drug is that such individuals carry significantly fewer than the 10^7 organisms needed for a good chance of drug resistance to develop.

Because tuberculosis is communicable, and not everyone with the disease is aware that he or she can infect others, it is a dangerous public health hazard. It is estimated that there are 10–15 million asymptomatic infected persons in the U.S. today. Greater than 90% of the current cases of tuberculosis are believed to come from this group. Consequently, Ms. C. and her contacts should be followed. Because her husband had a positive tuberculin test and a negative chest x-ray, he was placed on a prophylactic treatment with INH. The students who came in contact with Ms. C. were tuberculin tested. Two pupils in her class were tuberculin positive and were also started on INH prophylactically. The rest of the class remained tuberculin negative, and were retested several months later. For details of chemotherapy and chemoprophylaxis, you may wish to consult a clinical text.

CONCLUSION

Tuberculosis is one of the best studied examples of a human disease caused by facultative intracellular pathogens. An essential point to remember about tuberculosis is that the major lesions of the established disease are due to the hypersensitivity developed from previous exposure to the organism. They are different on the first and on subsequent encounters.

The tubercle bacillus, because of its unusual waxy envelope, grows slowly and is a highly successful parasite, usually sparing the life of its victim for many years. By eventually damaging the lungs, it ensures its spread from the body into the environment and increases its chances of infecting other people. The availability of modern antitubercular drugs places control of the disease within reach. Achieving this goal requires sanitation measures coupled with screening, detection, and prophylactic chemotherapy. Where economical and political reasons make it difficult to mount such an effort, vaccination with BCG can help reduce the burden of this disease.

LEPROSY

Leprosy shares some of its pathobiological features with tuberculosis but differs in its clinical manifestations. The contrast in the social response to the two diseases could not be greater or more paradoxical. Because lesions found in leprosy are far more visible, the victims of this disease were long shunned with great vehemence, even though these individuals are much less infectious than patients with tuberculosis! Tuberculosis, the more "sociably acceptable" of the two diseases, is actually far more contagious. Leprosy is rare in the U.S. today, but is still of worldwide importance. There are an estimated 2 million patients, mainly in tropical Third World countries, where the disease causes economic loss and human misery.

Leprosy is caused by *M. leprae*, which has been studied less extensively than the tubercle bacillus because it cannot be cultivated in vitro. This organism was one of the first found to be associated with a human disease. G.A. Hansen discovered *M. leprae* in lesions of leprosy patients in 1873 and, hence, leprosy is often called **Hansen's disease.** The first successful propagation of the leprosy bacillus in the laboratory did not occur until 1960, when it was discovered that *M. leprae* could grow in the footpads of mice. Even then, the yields of the organisms are low. In 1970, it was found that *M. leprae* causes a systemic infection in the nine-banded armadillo, where it grows to more than 10^{10} bacilli per gram of infected tissue. This finding revolutionized leprosy research because, for the first time, sufficient quantities of the organisms were available for basic research on the proteins, nucleic acids, lipids, and carbohydrates of *M. leprae*. Today, many genes encoding important antigens of this organism have been cloned and expressed in *Escherichia coli*, providing novel reagents for the analysis of the host response in this disease. The ability to grow *M. leprae* in animals has accelerated studies on drug sensitivity; before this, studies depended largely on clinical impressions. Animal experimentation has established the importance of several drugs (dapsone, rifampin, clofazamine). As with tuberculosis, it is important to use two drugs together to avoid selection of drug-resistant mutants.

Leprosy bacilli grow best at low temperatures. Accordingly, they appear to multiply most rapidly in the skin and in the appendages of human hosts. There are two polar forms of leprosy, **lepromatous** and **tuberculoid.** Intermediate forms occur as well (Table 23.2). **Lepromatous leprosy** causes loss of eyebrows, and thickened and enlarged nares, ears, and cheeks, resulting in a lion-like appearance (leonine facies). Both skin and nerves may be involved. With time, the loss of local sensation leads to inadvertent lesions in the face and extremities. These may become secondarily infected, eventually resulting in bone resorption, disfigurement, and mutilating lesions. Lepromatous leprosy is associated with diminished delayed hypersensitivity to **lepromin,** which is a preparation of antigens of the leprosy bacilli extracted

Table 23.2. The Spectrum of Leprosy

Type of Leprosy	Tuberculoid	Borderline	Lepromatoid
Acid-fast bacilli	None —————————————→		Many in tissue
Cell-mediated immunity to *M. leprae*	High —————————→ Low to none —————→		
Antibodies titer to *M. leprae*	Low titer —————————————→ High		
	or none		
Nerve damage	High ———→ Low —————————————→		

from human lepromatous tissue. This lack of a response is characterized by the immune suppression specific to *M. leprae* cells and, thus, is a virulence factor characteristic of these organisms (see "Paradigm").

Tuberculoid leprosy often appears with red blotchy lesions with anesthetic areas on the face, trunk, and extremities. It causes palpable thickening in peripheral nerves because the bacilli grow in the nerve sheaths. Patients with these symptoms are usually sensitive to lepromin. In contrast to the lepromatous form, patients with tuberculoid leprosy have an active cell-mediated immune response to *M. leprae*. It is difficult to find any acid-fast bacilli in a tuberculoid lesion.

Thus, lepromatous leprosy is the malignant form of the disease; it is analogous to systemic progressive (miliary) tuberculosis, where the organisms grow profusely. In both of these instances, the cell-mediated immune response is weak. It is not clear why cell-mediated immunity is decreased in leprosy patients; the suspicion lingers that the infecting organisms themselves play a role in this immunosuppression. There is recent evidence that persons belonging to the histocompatibility haplotype HLA-DR3 are more susceptible to tuberculoid leprosy, and those in the HLA-MT1 class are more susceptible to lepromatous leprosy. The degree to which cell-mediated immunity is impaired determines the extent of the lepromatous manifestations. Whereas full-blown cases of lepromatous leprosy show no reactivity to lepromin, borderline cases show some.

Tuberculoid leprosy is analogous to secondary tuberculosis in that this form of leprosy provokes vigorous cell-mediated immunity and exaggerated allergic responses. To further the analogy, lesions in lepromatous leprosy are filled with leprosy bacilli, whereas the organisms are hard to find in the tissues in tuberculoid leprosy. The prognosis with tuberculoid leprosy tends to be better than with lepromatous leprosy. In some cases, tuberculoid leprosy is a self-limiting disease; it may, however, progress to the lepromatous form.

Paradigm: Modulating the Cellular Immune Response

How do intracellular pathogens evade the host cellular immune responses? Pathogens that live inside host cells are not affected by antibodies but are killed by a cellular immune response. Do such pathogens have the ability to suppress cell-mediated responses directed specifically against them? *M. leprae*, the causative agent of leprosy, appears to be one example of a bacterial pathogen that does.

M. leprae, like *M. tuberculosis* and *M. avium-intracellulare*, survives and multiplies within macrophages. These mycobacteria have an arsenal of defenses that they use to escape killing by professional killing cells. For instance, phenolic glycolipid, a surface lipid of *M. leprae*, has been implicated as a defense against oxidative killing by macrophages. *M. tuberculosis* has long been thought to have specific mechanisms that inhibit phagosome-lysosome fusions. It is likely that the slow growth of *M. leprae*, a hallmark characteristic of this pathogen, also contributes to its survival within the host.

However, macrophages are not alone in their fight against intracellular pathogens. To have the maximal killing potential, macrophages must be activated. Activation of macrophages is mediated by cytokines that are produced by specific T cells. In some forms of leprosy, it appears as if *M. leprae* has the ability **to reduce or to suppress the number of specific T cells** produced by the host that would activate the macrophages in which *M. leprae* was growing. Without being stimulated by these T cells, the macrophages are incapable of killing the intracellular mycobacteria. Thus, by modulating the T-cell population within a host, a pathogen enhances its own survival.

Leprosy is a uniquely clear example of a disease whose spectrum of clinical presentations correlates with the presence or absence of specific T-cell responses. At one end of the spectrum is tuberculoid leprosy, a form of leprosy in which patients possess active *M. leprae*-specific T cells that can activate *M. leprae*-infected macrophages. In this form of leprosy, nerve damage is thought to be mediated by these T-cell responses. Lepromatous leprosy, in contrast to tuberculoid leprosy, is at the other end of the spectrum and is characterized by the total absence of *M. leprae*-specific T-cell activity that would stimulate macrophages. It appears that *M. leprae* has the ability to elicit the production of a set of regulatory T cells, namely **T-suppressor cells**, that inhibit the proliferation of T cells, which, in turn, activate *M. leprae*-infected macrophages. The ability to modulate T-cell responses via the induction of T-suppressor cells is also shared by the parasitic agents of leishmaniasis and schistosomiasis.

The epidemiology of leprosy is not well understood. Clearly, it is a communicable disease. It appears that infected persons must live in close contact with potential victims for long periods to transmit the disease. Victims of lepromatous leprosy tend to shed bacilli from their nasal septa. This is undoubtedly one source of contagion; it is not known if there are others.

The prognosis of leprosy patients has dramatically improved with the introduction of effective drugs, such as dapsone, rifampin, and clofazamine. Paradoxically, some of these drugs cause such effective destruction of the organisms that the antigens released cause a distressing inflammation called erythema nodosum leprosum. With appropriate treatment, however, patients can be cured with a few residual effects. Unfortunately, drug resistance is a serious problem for some patients with leprosy. Because of this, efforts are being made to develop a vaccine using antigens produced from cloned *M. leprae* genes or armadillo-derived *M. leprae*. Recent evidence suggests that BCG vaccination can protect against *M. leprae* infection and major trials are under way comparing the efficacy of BCG alone with BCG mixed with armadillo-derived, heat killed *M. leprae* preparations. In addition, it may now be possible to introduce selected antigens into BCG to make effective recombinant vaccines.

Self-assessment Questions

1. Which characteristics of the mycobacteria are attributable to their waxy coat?

2. What must be accomplished to carry out a successful acid-fast stain?

3. Which properties of mycobacteria contribute to their encounter with humans?

4. Which property of tubercle bacilli is most likely to account for tissue damage in primary tuberculosis in tuberculin-positive individuals? What accounts for the tissue damage?

5. Cell-mediated immunity in tuberculosis is responsible for tissue damage. On balance, is this type of immune response good or bad for the host?

6. What are the differences and similarities in the immune response to leprosy and tuberculosis?

7. What steps are usually taken in the microbiological diagnosis of tuberculosis? What problems are encountered with each step? Why are serological techniques not usually employed?

SUGGESTED READING

Anonymous. Mycobacterioses and the acquired immunodeficiency syndrome. Joint position paper of the American Thoracic Society and the Centers for Disease Control. Am Rev Respir Dis 1987;136:492–496.

Barnes PF, et al. Tuberculosis in patients with human immunodeficiencies. N Engl J Med 1991;324:1644–1649.

Bloom BR. Learning from leprosy: a perspective on immunology and the Third World. J Immunol 1986;137:1–10.

Dannenberg AM. Pathogenesis of tuberculosis. In: Fishman AP, ed. Pulmonary diseases and disorders. New York: McGraw-Hill, 1980:1264–1281.

Horsburgh Jr CR. *Mycobacterium avium* complex infection in the acquired immunodeficiency syndrome. N Engl J Med 1991;324:1332–1338.

Rook GA. Progress in the immunology of mycobacterioses. Clin Exp Immunol 1987;69:1–9.

Stover CK, et al. New use of BCG for recombinant vaccines. Nature 1991;351:456–460.

Syphilis: Disease with a History

24

*Edward N. Robinson, Jr., Penelope J. Hitchcock,
and Zell A. McGee*

Syphilis is one of the classical sexually transmitted diseases. It has often occupied central stage in the history of medicine and is resurging as an important infection after waning in recent years. It remains a puzzling and mystifying disease, characterized by several stages with dramatically different clinical presentations. The first two stages (primary and secondary) manifest themselves as acute and subacute disease, whereas tertiary syphilis is a chronic disease of many years' duration. The agent may be transmitted from an infected mother to her fetus and may cause congenital syphilis.

The agent of syphilis is a spirochete, *Treponema pallidum*, which cannot be cultured in artificial media. It does not produce toxins and little is known about its pathogenic attributes or the reasons why it escapes the immune system. Fortunately, *T. pallidum* remains very sensitive to penicillin, which is why the disease is easily treatable today.

CASE

Mr. B., a 24-year-old homosexual man, came to the clinic with fever, swollen lymph nodes, and spotty discolorations of his skin, including the palms of his hands and the soles of his feet. He had recently noted a penny-sized gray, translucent lesion on the inner aspect of his lower lip. The physician recognized the "macular rash" on the palms and the soles and the lesion on his lip as characteristic of secondary syphilis. Mr. B. reported that he engages in oral sex and also in anal-receptive intercourse.

A scraping of Mr. B.'s lip lesion was examined under a dark-field microscope; it revealed the presence of large numbers of corkscrew-shaped spirochetes. The laboratory reported "positive serology," which indicated the presence of the characteristic serum antibodies associated with syphilis. These laboratory findings confirmed the diagnosis of secondary syphilis. Mr. B. was treated with a course of penicillin, and his lesions and his symptoms abated. He was considered cured even though his "serology" remained positive for several years.

HISTORY OF SYPHILIS—"FOR ONE SMALL PLEASURE I SUFFER A THOUSAND MISFORTUNES"

The pathway of the global spread of syphilis is a controversial subject that is not likely to be resolved. One view is that Christopher Columbus brought the organism back to Spain from the New World. The first documented outbreaks of syphilis occurred in Europe shortly after Columbus' return, but this point is not evidence of the American origin of the disease.

The spread of syphilis through Europe was rapid and, for the first few decades, it was accompanied by a very high mortality rate. In 1494, King Charles VIII of France invaded Italy with an army of mercenaries from many countries, including Spain. Because little actual fighting took place, at first, much of the campaign was spent consorting with female camp followers. The attacking forces were devastated and the mercenaries dispersed to their home countries carrying syphilis to all of Europe. What the defending army was unable to accomplish, syphilis did. Understandably, nobody wanted to claim syphilis as their own:

"The Italians called it the Spanish or the French disease; the French called it the Italian or Neapolitan disease; the English called it the French disease; the Russians called it the Polish disease. And . . . . the first Spaniards who recognized the disease called it the disease of Espaniola, which meant, at that time, the disease of Haiti."

Fracastorius' poem, *Syphilis Sive Morbus Gallicus*, published in 1530, assigned to the "venereal pox" a nonpolitical name, that of the shepherd Syphilos. Ambroise Paré, in 1575, referred to it as "Lues Venerea," the lover's plague. During the 16th and 17th centuries, many clinical manifestations of syphilis were observed and catalogued. One of the most puzzling aspects of the disease is that within a few years of its emergence, it ceased to be a rapid killer and acquired the complex clinical manifestations by which we know it now (Fig. 24.1). The change in the organism's virulence, from high to moderate, is supportive of the notion that the most successful pathogens do not kill their host. In fact, the less severe the symptoms, the less likely the pathogen will be eliminated. The epitome of this principle is the organism that is asymptomatic—the host is neither diagnosed nor treated. The main selective force in nature is the ability to reproduce and not the ability to cause disease. *T. pallidum* is particularly successful as a human parasite because, among others, it possesses the following traits—spread by sexual transmission, efficient transmission from one adult to another (horizontal transmission), long infectious period, transmission from mother to child (vertical transmission), long persistence in the host, and usually, lethality only after decades of infection.

As a general rule, sexually transmitted diseases do not "travel alone." Thus, for early physicians, it was difficult to separate the manifestations of one disease (gonorrhea) from another (syphilis) because one person might be infected with both at the same time. Many of the physicians who studied these diseases thought that they were separate entities. Unfortunately, John Hunter confused the issue for six decades. In 1767, Hunter, in a courageous but ill-conceived experiment, placed onto his skin pus taken from the urethra of a man with gonorrhea. A chancre ensued. Undoubtedly, Hunter had taken pus from a man that was coinfected with both *Neisseria gonorrhoeae* and *Treponema pallidum*. It was not until 60 years later that Philippe Ricord correctly distinguished the two diseases, one from the other. It was Ricord who recognized the stages of syphilis (primary, secondary, and tertiary).

One of the medical profession's most ignoble episodes began in the 1930s. Syphilis research of a kind that is now widely considered reprehensible was carried out in 1932 in Macon County, Georgia (the so-

Figure 24.1. In previous years, syphilis stirred the imagination to extremes of gloom and hysteria. This French illustration ascribes to syphilis a degree of mortality that has not been seen since the advent of serological testing and penicillin therapy in this century.

called "Tuskegee experiment") and continued for decades thereafter. Under the auspices of the U.S. Public Health Service, physicians withheld treatment from several hundred black men infected with syphilis. In an attempt to document the natural course of the disease, a progression well known from previous medical studies, doctors allowed these men to develop the cardiac and neurological impairments that are the hallmark of tertiary syphilis. Penicillin was available and known to be effective against syphilis during part of the trial.

How Has Syphilis Changed in Recent Decades?

Between 1947 and 1965, there was a dramatic decline in the cases of syphilis reported in the U.S. However, since then, the incidence of primary and secondary syphilis has risen again from about 6000 new cases in 1956 to about 50,000 in 1990. Although primary syphilis rates were higher among men than women, the epidemic of the disease in women was accompanied by a parallel increase in rates of congenital syphilis.

Historically, homosexual males were a significant reservoir of syphilis in the U.S. Rectal intercourse results in the localization of the syphilitic chancre, the primary lesion, in the rectal mucosa. Because this location is hidden from sight and chancres are usually painless, the rectal chancre is often overlooked by both patient and physician. With changing behavior dictated by the fear of AIDS, e.g., reduced number of sexual partners and increased use of condoms, the incidence of syphilis among homosexual males has decreased dramatically. Currently, the syphilis epidemic is focused in regions of the South and Northeast. Infection is spreading among heterosexuals, those of low socioeconomic status, blacks, and users of drugs, especially crack cocaine.

TREPONEMES

The agent of syphilis is a **spirochete**, a group of bacteria with a highly characteristic appearance. Spirochetes are helical, slender, relatively long cells (Fig. 24.2). Spirochetes are widespread in nature; only a few cause disease in humans and animals. The principal human spirochetoses are syphilis, **Lyme disease** (Chapter 25), **relapsing fever** (caused by members of the genus *Borrelia*), and **leptospirosis** (due to *Leptospira*). The treponeme of syphilis has some close relatives that cause other diseases (e.g., yaws, pinta, bejel), found mostly in tropical countries .

T. pallidum is so thin (0.1–0.2 μm) that it cannot be seen by standard microscopic techniques. It can be visualized by special stains (silver impregnation or immunofluorescence) or with special lighting (dark-field microscopy). When observed in a freshly prepared wet mount using a dark-field microscope, it exhibits a characteristic corkscrew-like movement and flexion. The organisms resemble Gram-negative bacteria in having an outer membrane, which, although lipid rich, does not contain classical lipopolysaccharide. Unlike the flagella of other bacteria, which protrude freely into the medium, those of spirochetes are contained within the periplasm.

The amount of information regarding the mechanisms by which *T. pallidum* causes disease has been limited both by the inability to cultivate the organisms serially in artificial media and by the lack of a suitable animal model. In artificial media, these bacteria can be kept alive for only short periods of time—for a few divisions at the most. To by-

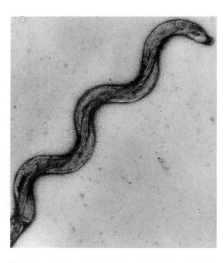

Figure 24.2. Electron photomicrograph of *T. pallidum*, negatively stained. Note at the dark end of the organism, the insertion points of the periplasmic flagella (rope-like contractile structures), which enable the organisms to engage in their typical corkscrew-like motility.

pass these constraints, efforts have focused on producing and characterizing specific proteins of *T. pallidum* using genes cloned into *E. coli* vectors.

ENCOUNTER, ENTRY, SPREAD, AND MULTIPLICATION

T. pallidum is very sensitive to drying, disinfectants, and heat (as low as 42°C). Therefore, they are unlikely to be acquired by means other than by personal contact. Neither the toilet seat nor the hot tub can be blamed. The two major routes of transmission are sexual and transplacental. Sexual exposure to a person with an active chancre carries a high probability of acquiring syphilis.

The organisms enter a susceptible host through the mucous membranes or the minute abrasions in the skin surface that occur during sexual intercourse. Once in the subepithelial tissues, the organisms replicate locally in an extracellular location (Fig. 24.3). In culture, they adhere to cells by their tapered ends and probably stick to cells in tissue by the same means. Not all of them stick, and many are soon carried through lymphatic channels to the systemic circulation. Thus, even if the initial manifestation of the disease consists of an isolated skin lesion, syphilis is a systemic disease almost from the outset.

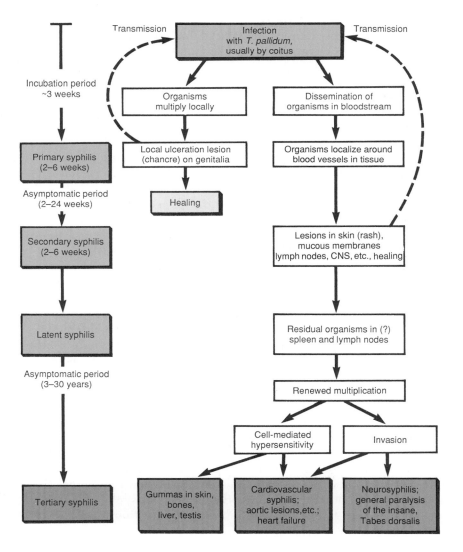

Figure 24.3. The pathogenesis of syphilis.

Treponemes can cross the placental barrier from the bloodstream of an infected mother and cause disease in the fetus. It is not known how the organisms cross this barrier. Chapter 68 has a general discussion of this issue.

DAMAGE

Initially, neutrophils migrate to the area of inoculation, and are later replaced by lymphocytes and macrophages. The result of the battle between the locally replicating treponemes and the cellular defenses of the host is the lesion of **primary syphilis**, a painless ulcer—the **syphilitic chancre** (Fig. 24.4). The time between the initial introduction of the organisms and the appearance of the ulcer depends on the size of the inoculum. The more treponemes enter, the earlier the chancre appears. This lesion heals spontaneously in 2–6 weeks, but by this time the spirochetes have spread through the bloodstream and may be causing lesions in other parts of the body. It is these diverse lesions that comprise the cluster of findings that characterize "secondary syphilis" such as that manifested in Mr. B.

The syphilitic chancre and other genital ulcer diseases are associated with increased risk of human immunodeficiency virus (HIV) transmission. Patients who have genital ulcers are estimated to have a three- to five-fold increase risk of acquiring HIV infection. Furthermore, recent studies have demonstrated that HIV can be isolated from genital ulcers, which increases the likelihood of transmitting the virus. The possible role of the chancre in facilitating the transmission of AIDS underscores the importance of recognizing and promptly treating primary syphilis.

Three to six weeks after the ulcer heals, the secondary form of the disease occurs in about 50% of the cases. **Secondary syphilis** is the systemic spread of the infection, and is the manifestation of replication of the treponemes in the lymph nodes, the liver, joints, muscles, skin, and mucous membranes distant from the site of the primary chancre. The signs and symptoms of secondary syphilis may be so varied, and involve such different tissues and organs, that the disease has been called "the great imitator." The rash and other manifestations of secondary syphilis resolve in the course of weeks to months, but recur within 1 year or so in about one-fourth of affected individuals (Fig. 24.3).

This biphasic course of the disease is puzzling for various reasons. Why does the primary chancre heal? (We do not even understand how spirochetes kill so many epidermal cells to create a chancre.) Why do the defense mechanisms that are so successful in resolving the primary chancre not function as well systemically during secondary syphilis? How does the organism survive in the body for long periods of time? Where are the organisms located—intracellularly or extracellularly? What is the role of the specific immune response to the organism in the disease process? Or, when penicillin therapy of syphilis results in fever and sometimes shock (the so-called Jarisch-Herxheimer reaction), the clinical events strongly suggest the release of interleukin-1 (IL-1, which causes fever), and the release of tumor necrosis factor/cachectin (TNF, which causes shock—see Chapters 6 and 7). If this hypothesis is correct, which molecules do the spirochetes release to stimulate the production of these potent cytokines? We do not have answers to these questions or to others regarding other aspects of syphilis. It remains one of the more fascinating and puzzling of infectious diseases.

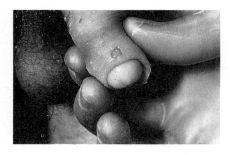

Figure 24.4. Chancre of the penis. This is the first manifestation of syphilis in some patients. The lesion was painless and, on dark-field examination, had many motile, "corkscrewing" spirochetes present, thus confirming the diagnosis of syphilis. Note that the hand of the examiner is appropriately gloved!

The mechanisms whereby treponemes evade host defenses over a period of years are not well understood. Recently, it has been demonstrated that the proteins in the outer layer of the bacterium are not exposed to the surface. In other words, antibodies specific for these proteins cannot bind the organism's surface. It is not known whether the proteins are obscured by some sort of undefined "coat," such as a capsule, or whether they protrude from the surface only part of the time.

The mystery deepens with the resolution of the secondary phase. In about one-third of individuals, the organisms disappear and the person is spontaneously cured. In the remaining two-thirds, the treponemes remain latent for years without causing signs or symptoms (Fig. 24.3). In about one-half of this group, the manifestations of **tertiary syphilis** eventually develop, sometimes years or even decades after the primary infection.

In adults, tertiary syphilis is responsible for a majority of the morbidity and mortality associated with the disease. Fortunately, tertiary syphilis is very uncommon in the U.S., where routine serological screening identifies most cases before this stage can develop. The hallmark of tertiary syphilis is the destruction of tissue from a response to the presence of treponemal antigens. The clinical-pathological manifestations are those of **vasculitis** and **chronic inflammation**. Soft masses, the gummas, composed of few treponemes and inflammatory cells, are lesions that commonly destroy bone and soft tissue ("late benign syphilis"), but may involve vital organs, such as the liver as well. In cardiovascular syphilis, vasculitis involves the nutrient arteries supplying the thoracic aorta. Destruction of the elastic tissue in the aorta media leads to dilatation of the wall and to aortic valve insufficiency, or to the formation of aortic aneurysms with resultant rupture of the aorta. The central nervous system may also be involved, either by direct invasion of the parenchyma by treponemes or by brain infarction caused by vasculitis.

The clinical findings of neurosyphilis can be subtle. The severity of the manifestations depends on the location of the lesions. Involvement of the dorsal columns of the spinal cord results in loss of position sensation, a classic condition known as **tabes dorsalis**. It is often manifested as ataxic gait; in turn, this usually results in trauma to the knee and ankle joints, which results in bone overgrowth, and misalignment of the knee, or occasionally the ankle, the so-called "Charcot's joint." There may also be cutaneous sensory loss over the lower chest, inner aspects of the arms, and lower legs. A generalized involvement of the brain leads to impaired motor function (**paresis**) as well as to gradual loss of higher integrative functions and personality changes. This clinical picture is known as **general paralysis of the insane**. A physical sign of neurosyphilis is the Argyll-Robertson pupil—the pupil fails to react to light but accommodates when an object is moved from far to near the eye. If left untreated, neurosyphilis may ultimately lead to death of the patient.

The lesions of tertiary syphilis usually contain few or no treponemes. What then causes lesions in the tissues? Researchers have demonstrated that the immune system likely plays a deleterious role in the development of the syphilitic lesions. Is it an exaggerated hypersensitivity? Or, could it be a cross-reaction between treponemal and tissue antigens, in other words, an autoimmune response? Once again, the answer is not known. However, cross-reactive antibodies are elicited and are the basis for the most widely utilized tool to detect the disease, the serological test for syphilis.

Congenital Syphilis

Despite the availability of serological tests that can detect latent forms of syphilis, despite the availability of inexpensive and safe antibiotics, and despite the (welcome) persistent antibiotic sensitivity of the causative organisms, about 2000–3000 babies were born with congenital syphilis in the U.S. in 1990. But this number under-represents the problem; the majority of infected fetuses likely die in utero. Among those who make it to term, the manifestations are varied, ranging from life-threatening organ damage to silent infections. They can also include congenital malformations that are immediately apparent as well as developmental abnormalities that become manifest only as the child gets older. These congenital anomalies include premature birth, intra-uterine growth retardation, and multiple organ failure (e.g., central nervous system infection, pneumonia, enlargement of the liver and spleen). The most common manifestations of syphilis become evident at about 2 years of age and include facial and tooth deformities (the so-called Hutchinson's incisors and "mulberry" molars). Other less common findings include deafness, arthritis, and "saber shins." Congenital syphilis is especially tragic because it is completely preventable by penicillin therapy of women found to be have a positive serological test for syphilis early in pregnancy . . . if they get prenatal care.

DIAGNOSIS

Before this century, physicians relied on the clinical manifestations of the disease to make a diagnosis of syphilis. Therefore, only those with obvious skin or mucosal lesions were considered to have syphilis and, thus, received therapy. Patients having asymptomatic or latent syphilis were undiagnosed and, therefore, untreated. In 1906, Wassermann, Neisser, and Bruck reported that visible flocculation occurred when extracts of livers of infants who had died of congenital syphilis were mixed with sera of syphilitic adults. It later developed that the same reaction took place with extracts from normal livers or other tissues. In other words, the sera of patients with syphilis have antibodies that react with normal human tissue. The tissue component turned out to be a lipid present in the membranes of mitochondria, called **cardiolipin**. Why patients with syphilis form these curious antibodies is not known. As a matter of fact, these antibodies are produced in patients with other diseases as well; biological "false-positive" tests for syphilis occur in patients with hemolytic anemia, systemic lupus erythematosus, leprosy, narcotics abuse, and aging.

The original test of Wassermann and colleagues led to the development of more rapid and reproducible tests. There are several variations known by their eponyms (e.g., the **V**enereal **D**iseases **R**eference **L**aboratory test, **VDRL**, or the **R**apid **P**lasma **R**eagin, **RPR**). They are cheap and easy to perform, which makes them suitable for the initial screening of large numbers of serum samples, as in premarital "blood tests." However, their relative lack of specificity makes it necessary to test all positive samples by more specific but more technically demanding and more expensive tests directed against treponemal antigens. Two such treponeme specific tests are called the Fluorescent Treponemal Antibody test (**FTA**) and the **T. p**allidum **I**mmobilization (**TPI**) test. The

FTA uses indirect immunofluorescence. Patient serum is mixed with a film of *T. pallidum* and allowed to react. Antitreponemal antibodies are detected by adding fluorescent rabbit or goat antibodies against human γ-globulin. These antibodies react with bound human antibodies and make the treponemes visible under a fluorescence microscope. Another specific test is the TPI and relies on the inhibition of treponemal motility by specific antibodies in a patient's serum. These tests require specialized reagents and equipment, and are usually offered by reference laboratories.

TREATMENT—"ONE NIGHT WITH VENUS, THE REST OF LIFE WITH MERCURY"

Two major advances in the diagnosis and management of syphilis have occurred during the 20th century—the development of serological tests for diagnosing syphilis and the use of penicillin for treating the disease. Fortunately for Mr. B. and for the rest of the world, the organisms are still exquisitely sensitive to penicillin.

Before penicillin, treatment depended on an arsenic-containing compound synthesized by Ehrlich early in this century (it was the first effective synthetic chemotherapeutic agent). It was called "606," in recognition of 605 previous failures in that laboratory. Before the introduction of penicillin, therapy consisted of the tedious, expensive, and dangerous administration of arsenic and mercury or bismuth for a minimum of 2 months and as long as 2 or 3 years. An alternative therapy was the induction of fever, based on the heat sensitivity of *T. pallidum*. Fever was induced by the intravenous injection of killed typhoid bacilli (and their endotoxin), or, in an extreme burst of therapeutic zeal, fever was induced by deliberately giving a patient malaria (quinine was available to treat the malaria)! Currently, the treatment of latent syphilis relies on the continued sensitivity of *T. pallidum* to penicillin and on the body's ability to maintain effective blood levels of the drug (intramuscular benzathine penicillin, "bicillin") for long periods of time. Treatment failures with benzathine penicillin have been observed in neurosyphilis and in HIV-infected patients with syphilis. The likely reason is the inability of the oil-based penicillin to pass the blood-brain barrier to achieve an effective concentration. Aqueous penicillin G, administered repeatedly in high doses intravenously, is probably effective in cases of neurosyphilis.

CONCLUSIONS

During the second half of the 1980s, the largest single-year increase in infectious syphilis in more than a quarter of a century was reported in the U.S. During this period, a concomitant increase in congenital syphilis was observed. In addition, genital ulcer diseases, such as syphilis, increase the risk of HIV transmission.

Several factors are fueling the syphilis epidemic: use of crack cocaine; a decline in socioeconomic and educational levels among groups at risk; and limited access to health care, due, in part, to the overburdening of health care facilities by the AIDS epidemic.

Among all the STDs, syphilis should be one of the easiest to control for the following reasons:

- The cases are clustered—most of this increase is occurring in a low-income minority, heterosexuals and their children.

● Good diagnostic tests are available—these are not expensive and give accurate, fairly rapid results.

● Treatment is available—in single doses, an inexpensive antibiotic, penicillin, is effective for primary and secondary syphilis. Furthermore, antibiotic resistance is not a problem.

The solutions, therefore, involve social, behavioral, and biomedical research efforts. Our inability to prevent and to control syphilis speaks to our shortcomings in biomedical research as well as in societal program and service delivery. To paraphrase Winston Churchill's comment on Russia, syphilis is "a riddle wrapped in a mystery inside an enigma." Whether we will be able to deal effectively with this enigma remains to be seen.

Self-assessment Questions

1. What is the likely role of antitreponemal antibodies in each of the three stages of syphilis?

2. How would you explain the resolution of primary syphilis and the emergence of the secondary stage?

3. In what ways does tertiary syphilis appear to be an autoimmune disease?

4. During which stage of syphilis is a patient most contagious?

5. What would it take to make syphilis disappear from the face of the earth?

6. If you were involved in syphilis research, what problems would you tackle?

SUGGESTED READING

Benedek TG. The "Tuskegee study" of syphilis: analysis of moral versus methodologic aspects. J Chron Dis 1978;31:35–50.

Dennie CC. A history of syphilis. Springfield, IL: Charles C Thomas, 1962.

Fichtner RR, Sevgi O, Aral SO, et al. Syphilis in the United States: 1967–1979. Sex Transm Dis 1983;10:77–80.

Inglefinger FJ. The unethical in medical ethics. Ann Int Med 1975;83: 264–269.

Perine PL, Handsfield HH, Holmes KK, Blount JH. Epidemiology of the sexually transmitted diseases. Ann Rev Public Health 1985;6:85–106.

Pussey WA. The history and epidemiology of syphilis. Springfield, IL: Charles C Thomas, 1933.

Rathburn KC. Congenital syphilis. Sex Transm Dis 1983;10:93–99.

Stamm WE, Handsfield HH, Rompalo AM, Ashley RL, Roberts PL, Corey L. The association between genital ulcer disease and acquisition of HIV infection in homosexual men. JAMA 1988;260:1429–1433.

Lyme Disease

25

Allen C. Steere

Lyme disease or Lyme borreliosis is a recently recognized illness caused by the tick-borne spirochete, *Borrelia burgdorferi*. Prior to the recognition of this disease, *Borrelia* species were only known to cause an illness called relapsing fever. Although it differs from syphilis in the mode of transmission, Lyme disease resembles syphilis in its multisystem involvement, occurrence in stages, and mimicry of other diseases.

As with syphilis, Lyme disease usually begins with localized infection of the skin manifested by a characteristic expanding skin lesion called erythema migrans that occurs at the site of the tick bite (Stage 1). Within several days to weeks, the spirochete may spread to other sites (Stage 2), particularly other skin sites, the nervous system, joints, the heart, or the eyes. Symptoms are typically intermittent and changing at this time in the illness. After months to years, sometimes following long periods of latent infection, the spirochete may cause chronic infection (Stage 3), most commonly of the joints, the nervous system, or the skin.

CASE

Mr. T., a 27-year-old male resident of Connecticut, developed joint and muscle pains and an expanding erythematous skin lesion on the leg during July. Three days later, he experienced severe headache, neck stiffness, photophobia, and mild thought disturbances. Soon thereafter, multiple secondary annular skin lesions appeared and then a right-sided facial palsy. He was found to have a high titer of IgM antibodies against B. burgdorferi, *but the IgG response to the spirochete was negative. These symptoms resolved or improved within several weeks.*

One month later, he had severe neuritic pain on the skin of his abdomen within the distribution of the T8 through T11 dermatomes. This was followed by intermittent arthralgias, which occurred in one joint at a time for several days followed by longer pain-free periods. During the second year of illness, he had the sudden onset of severe swelling of one knee and then the other. The joint fluid had numerous white cells, and his antibody response to B. burgdorferi *was high for IgG and low for IgM. His immunogenetic profile showed that he had the HLA-DR4 and HLA-DR2 specificities. The knees remained continually swollen for about 1 year, but then resolved.*

Seven years after disease onset, he began to notice forgetfulness, lethargy, somnolence, and hearing impairment in the left ear. He still had a markedly elevated IgG antibody titer to B. burgdorferi *but no detectable IgM antibody. Spinal fluid analysis showed elevated total protein and evidence of antibody to the spirochete. He was treated with intravenous ceftriaxone for 30 days. His memory deficit and fatigue improved within the following several months.*

HISTORY OF LYME DISEASE

Lyme disease was described as a distinct entity in 1977 because of geographic clustering of children in Lyme, Connecticut thought to have juvenile rheumatoid arthritis. The rural setting of the case clusters and the identification of erythema migrans as a feature of the illness suggested that the disorder was transmitted by an arthropod. It soon became apparent that Lyme disease was a multisystem illness that affected primarily the skin, the nervous system, the heart, and joints. Epidemiological studies of patients with erythema migrans implicated certain *Ixodes* ticks as vectors of the disease. Further epidemiological features of this disease are described in Chapter 73.

In addition to providing clues about the cause of the disease, erythema migrans linked Lyme disease in the U.S. with certain syndromes in Europe. Early in this century, several European investigators described the characteristic expanding skin lesion, which they attributed to *Ixodes* tick bites. Many years later, it was recognized that erythema migrans could be followed by a chronic skin disease, which had already been described as a separate entity. In the 1940s, a neurological syndrome (called Bannwarth's syndrome, meningopolyneuritis, or meningoradiculitis) was described in Europe. This syndrome is sometimes preceded by an erythema.

These various syndromes were brought together conclusively in 1982, when the causative agent, a previously unrecognized spirochete now called *B. burgdorferi*, was isolated from *Ixodes dammini* ticks. The spirochete was then recovered from patients with Lyme disease in the U.S., and from those with erythema migrans, Bannwarth's syndrome, or acrodermatitis in Europe. The patients' immune responses were linked conclusively with this organism. Although there are regional variations, the basic outlines of the disease are similar worldwide, and its most common name is Lyme disease or Lyme borreliosis.

Whereas the various clinical manifestations of syphilis were brought together as a single entity in the 19th century, the many manifestations of Lyme disease were not recognized as being part of a single entity until the 1980s. In both diseases, the causative spirochete may survive for years and, after long periods of latency, may cause slowly progressive disease, particularly of the nervous system; in both diseases, the mechanisms of spirochetal attachment and survival and the ways in which the organism damages host tissues are incompletely understood.

Why has Lyme disease become a recent major concern in certain parts of the world? The most obvious reason is the recent recognition of the disease, which had escaped definition in the past. However, Lyme disease is now spreading in the northeastern U.S., where it causes focal epidemics. This is thought to be due to a large increase in the number of deer and the deer tick, *Ixodes dammini*, which transmits this infection in the northeastern and midwestern U.S. At the same time, rural areas where deer and deer tick live have become increasingly populated with susceptible suburbanites who have not been previously exposed to the spirochete.

BORRELIA

Borrelia species, along with the leptospira and treponemes, belong to the **spirochetes**. Like all spirochetes, the **flagella** of *Borrelia* are encased with an **outer membrane** that is only loosely associated with the underlying structures. *Borrelia* are longer and more loosely coiled than the other spirochetes. Their outer membrane is unique in that the genes encoding it are located on plasmids. This arrangement may be advantageous to the organism in making antigenic changes in these proteins. The *Borrelia* species are fastidious and grow best at 33°C in a complex liquid medium (called Barbour-Stoenner-Kelly medium).

Of the *Borrelia* species, *B. burgdorferi* is the longest (20–30 µm) and narrowest (0.2–0.3 µm) (Fig. 25.1), and it has fewer flagella (7–11). All isolates of *B. burgdorferi* examined to date have had four to nine extrachromosomal plasmids. These include the typical super-coiled variety, but also an unusual type of linear plasmid that has not been found in other procaryotic organisms. One of these small linear plasmids (49 kb) codes for the two major outer-surface proteins of the spirochete, A and B. These outer-membrane proteins may undergo antigenic variation during the course of the disease, but this variation seems to be minor as compared with that of relapsing fever *Borrelia*.

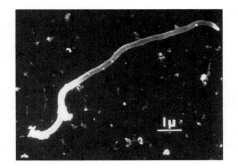

Figure 25.1. Scanning electron micrograph of *Borrelia burgdorferi*.

ENCOUNTER, ENTRY, SPREAD, AND MULTIPLICATION

The Lyme disease spirochete is transmitted by certain ticks of the *Ixodes ricinus* complex that normally feed on mice and deer. The deer provide the nearly ideal "Club Med Cruise" environment for the adult activities of dining, meeting, and mating, with an opportunity for travel included. In humans, after the spirochete is injected by the tick, it may spread locally in the skin or it may disseminate via the lymph or blood to practically any site. As shown in an in vitro assay, virulent strains of *B. burgdorferi* are able to resist elimination by peripheral blood mononuclear cells, macrophages, and neutrophils, whereas avirulent strains are not. Thus, the spirochete apparently expresses a virulence factor that helps it avoid the first line in the host defense system against infection.

In vitro studies have also demonstrated that *B. burgdorferi* may adhere to many different cells from invertebrate and vertebrate sources, including tick and human. However, evidence for tissue tropism comes from **adherence to glycolipids**. The organism adheres more to **galacto-cerebroside**, which is located on the surface of oligodendroglia in the brain, than to other structurally related glycolipids.

In cell cultures, *B. burgdorferi* seems to cross a cell monolayer primarily at **intercellular junctions** although it can perhaps penetrate through the cytoplasm of a cell. Antibody to the outer-surface proteins A and B may reduce attachment of the spirochete to cells. In a rat model, permeability changes in the blood-brain barrier can be shown beginning 12 hours after inoculation of *B. burgdorferi*, and the organism may be cultured from the spinal fluid within 24 hours. Although the organism certainly has its preferred niches, such as the nervous system or joints, it is not yet known how it is able to sequester itself in these sites, in some instances for years. One possibility is that it is able to live intracellularly in certain cells, but there is, as yet, no evidence for this hypothesis.

DAMAGE

Local spread of *B. burgdorferi* in the skin results in a distinct skin lesion, **erythema migrans** (Stage 1, Table 25.1). **Disseminated infection** (Stage 2) is often associated with characteristic symptoms in the skin, the nervous system, and musculoskeletal sites, including secondary annular skin lesions, excruciating headache, mild neck stiffness, and mi-

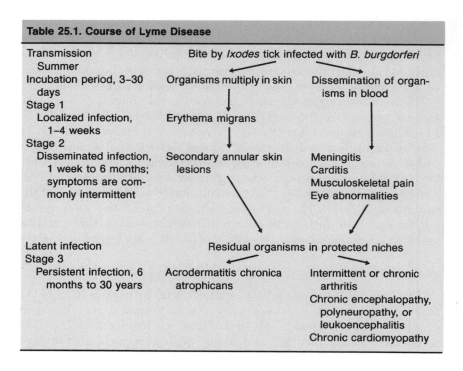

Table 25.1. Course of Lyme Disease

Transmission Summer	Bite by *Ixodes* tick infected with *B. burgdorferi*	

Incubation period, 3–30
  days
	Organisms multiply in skin	Dissemination of organ-
		  isms in blood

Stage 1		
Localized infection, 1–4 weeks	Erythema migrans	
Stage 2		

Disseminated infection,
    1 week to 6 months;
    symptoms are com-
    monly intermittent
	Secondary annular skin
	  lesions
		Meningitis
		Carditis
		Musculoskeletal pain
		Eye abnormalities

Latent infection	Residual organisms in protected niches	
Stage 3		

Persistent infection, 6
    months to 30 years
	Acrodermatitis chronica
	  atrophicans
		Intermittent or chronic
		  arthritis
		Chronic encephalopathy,
		  polyneuropathy, or
		  leukoencephalitis
		Chronic cardiomyopathy

gratory pain in joints, bursae, tendons, muscle, or bone. The spirochete has been seen in or recovered from most of these tissue sites during this stage of the illness.

B. burgdorferi is not known to produce direct damage to these tissues or to elaborate toxins. Rather, it seems to damage tissue because it may persist in these sites and may elicit an immune response that causes "bystander" injury to the host. Histologically, all affected tissues show an infiltration of lymphocytes and plentiful plasma cells. Plasma-cell precursors are large and may resemble immunoblasts or Reed-Sternberg cells. Some degree of **vascular damage**, including mild vasculitis or occlusion, may be seen in multiple sites, suggesting that the spirochete or immune complexes were present in and around blood vessels.

Within several weeks, patients' mononuclear cells begin to have heightened responsiveness to *B. burgdorferi* antigens and mitogens, less suppressor cell activity than normal, and decreased natural killer cell activity. The specific IgM response to the spirochete peaks between the third and sixth week and is often associated with evidence of polyclonal activation of B cells, including elevated total serum IgM levels, circulating immune complexes, and cryoglobulins. The specific IgG response then develops gradually to an increasing array of spirochetal polypeptides. For reasons that are not understood, the immune response to outer-surface proteins A and B typically does not occur, if at all, until the second year of illness.

Months after disease onset, patients in the U.S. usually begin to have brief attacks of **arthritis**, especially in the knee. Although the pattern varies, episodes of arthritis often become longer during the second and third years of illness, and in a small percentage of patients, chronic arthritis begins during this period (Stage 3, Table 25.1). The synovial lesion in these patients looks like that of the other chronic inflammatory arthritides, including rheumatoid arthritis. As with a number of other rheumatic diseases, chronic Lyme arthritis appears to have an **immunogenetic basis** inasmuch as the majority of the patients have the HLA-

DR4 or HLA-DR2 specificities. The arthritis in these patients typically does not respond to antibiotic therapy. Thus, in genetically susceptible people, *B. burgdorferi* appears to trigger an immune response with features of autoimmune reactions. Such reactions may continue for some time after the organisms have been killed, possibly because of cross-reactive antigens.

Chronic neurological involvement, affecting either the peripheral or the central nervous system, may also occur in Lyme borreliosis, sometimes following years of latent infection. The most common form of **chronic central nervous system involvement** affects memory, mood, or sleep, sometimes with subtle language disturbance. Because Lyme encephalopathy generally responds to antibiotic therapy, the pathological process is presumed to be a mild, multifocal, and generalized infection of the brain that leads to little destruction of neurons. In addition to encephalopathy, many patients have **peripheral sensory symptoms** such as tingling sensations or pain. Biopsies in these patients show predominantly axonal injury with perivascular infiltration of lymphocytes and plasmacytes around epineural vessels. Less commonly, patients may have a multiple sclerosis-like picture, the significance of which is tantalizing but not yet known.

The best example of prolonged latency followed by persistent infection in Lyme borreliosis is a late skin lesion known as **acrodermatitis chronica atrophicans**, which has been observed primarily in Europe. This skin lesion usually begins insidiously with bluish-red discoloration and swollen skin on an extremity. The lesion's inflammatory phase may persist for many years or for decades, and it gradually leads to atrophy of the skin. *B. burgdorferi* has been cultured from such lesions as much as 10 years after their onset.

DIAGNOSIS

Because culture and direct visualization of *B. burgdorferi* from patients' specimens are difficult, serological testing is currently the most practical laboratory aid in diagnosis. As with syphilis, the specific immune response in Lyme disease may be delayed, and patients with Stage 1 infection are often seronegative. After the first several weeks of infection, particularly if the spirochete disseminates, most patients become seropositive. As with other serological tests, false-positive and false-negative results may occur. Immunoblotting ("Western blots," see Chapters 37 and 55) is a helpful technique in sorting out false-positive results, and may aid in the identification of patients with minimal antibody responses early or late in the illness. In a small percentage of patients, antibiotic therapy early in the illness seems to abort the specific humoral immune response, but a few spirochetes may survive in sequestered sites. These patients may still have a cellular immune response to the spirochete, shown by proliferative assay, even though antibody to the organism cannot be demonstrated. Under development are exquisitely sensitive tests based on nucleic acid amplification, using the polymerase chain reaction.

TREATMENT

The treatment of Lyme disease is guided by the stage and manifestation of the disease. For early Lyme disease, oral doxycycline or amoxicillin is generally effective therapy. In contrast with *T. pallidum*, *B. burgdorferi* is only moderately sensitive to penicillin, and consequently, this drug is used less frequently. The duration of therapy is guided by the clinical response. For patients with arthritis, 30-day courses of doxycycline or amoxicillin are often curative. Intravenous therapy is generally necessary for patients with objective neurological involvement, and the third-generation cephalosporin drugs (e.g., ceftriaxone or cefotaxime) are used most often for this purpose. Intravenous antibiotic therapy is also standard for patients with high-degree atrioventricular block or cardiomegaly. The appropriate treatment for asymptomatic infection or for Lyme disease during pregnancy remains in question. No vaccine is yet available.

COMPARISON OF SPIROCHETOSES

In addition to Lyme disease and syphilis, the spirochetoses that affect humans in the U.S. include **leptospirosis** and another borreliosis, **relapsing fever** (Table 25.2). Except for syphilis, these are zoonotic diseases that only incidentally affect humans when they are bitten by ticks (as in relapsing fever), or come in contact with infected animal urine (as in leptospirosis). The initial phases of these spirochetal infections have many similarities, including symptoms such as fever, headache, myalgias, meningitis, photophobia, malaise, or fatigue (see Chapter 24 on syphilis). However, each of these diseases also has unique clinical features. As suggested by the name, relapsing fever is associated with intermittent episodes of high fever that are thought to be due to antigenic variations in the major outer membrane of that spirochete. Leptospirosis has a predilection for the kidney.

Both Lyme disease and syphilis have certain features in common (Chapter 24); both may occur in stages over a period of years, and typically cause neurological abnormalities late in the illness, although with different neurological syndromes. Relapsing fever and leptospirosis, on the other hand, differ in having unique clinical features.

Except for relapsing fever, where the agent may be seen in the blood, diagnosis of the spirochetoses is generally by recognition of a characteristic clinical picture. Serological tests are used to confirm the diagnosis. The spirochetes are generally susceptible to a large number of antibiotics.

Table 25.2. Main Features of the Spirochetoses

Name of Disease	Causative Agent	Mode of Transmission	Unique Clinical Aspects
Lyme disease	*Borrelia burgdorferi*	Ticks of the *Ixodes ricinus* complex	Erythema migrans, recurrent arthritis
Relapsing fever	*Borrelia recurrentis, B. hermsii,* others	Human body louse Ticks (*Ornithodorus*)	Recurrent high fever
Syphilis	*Treponema pallidum*	Sexual contact	Chancre, tabes dorsalis, aortitis
Leptospirosis	*Leptospira* sp.	Contact (urine) with infected animals	Jaundice, renal involvement

Self-assessment Questions

1. How does *Borrelia burgdorferi* differ from "ordinary" bacteria? How does it differ from *Treponema pallidum*?

2. Prepare a short talk on the epidemiology of Lyme disease for presentation to concerned parents in your community.

3. In what ways does Lyme disease resemble syphilis?

4. Which features of each of the three stages of Lyme borreliosis is typical of this illness?

5. Why does Lyme disease have some of the attributes of an autoimmune disease?

SUGGESTED READING

Barbour AG, Hayes SF. Biology of *Borrelia* species. Microbiol Rev 1986;50:381–400.

Steere AC. Lyme disease. N Engl J Med 1989;321:586–596.

Steere AC. Lyme disease. In: Wilson JD, Braunwald E, Isselbacher KJ, Petersdorf RG, Martin JB, Fauci AS, Root RK, eds. Harrison's principles of internal medicine, 12th ed., New York: McGraw-Hill, 1991:547–548.

Chlamydiae—Genital and Respiratory Pathogens

26

Marion L. Woods, II, Edward N. Robinson, Jr., Zell A. McGee, and Penelope J. Hitchcock

Chlamydiae are the most frequent bacterial cause of sexually transmitted disease, which typically manifests as cervicitis and urethritis. Chlamydial cervicitis can lead to a number of pathological conditions in the fallopian tubes, ovaries, and peritoneal cavity, collectively referred to as pelvic inflammatory disease (PID). PID, in turn, can progress to tubal scarring and to severe consequences, infertility, ectopic pregnancy, and chronic pelvic pain. Chlamydiae also cause infections of the eye and other organs; *Chlamydia trachomatis* is the leading cause of preventable blindness worldwide. *C. psittaci* is a frequent pathogen of birds and domestic animals and can cause a pneumonia, psittacosis, in humans. The most recently identified pathogen in this genus, *C. pneumoniae*, is another important cause of human pneumonia.

All chlamydiae are **strict intracellular bacteria** and cannot be grown on cell-free media. Their life cycle includes two stages, the reticulate body, which is the replicative and metabolically active form, and the elementary body, which is the transit form from one host cell to another.

CASE

A 23-year-old male, Mr. C., saw a physician with the complaint of a purulent discharge from his penis. The diagnosis of gonorrhea was made (see Chapter 14) and he was given ceftriaxone (a cephalosporin) by intramuscular injection. He improved initially, but over the previous 3 days he noticed a milder but persistent urethral discharge and pain on urination. Worried that he might not have been cured, he went to a Sexually Transmitted Diseases Clinic for evaluation. He reported having had no sexual intercourse since his last visit. His latest sexual partner, Ms. G., accompanied him to the clinic, although she had no complaints of pain, vaginal irritation, or discharge.

On physical examination, Mr. C. had a small amount of clear urethral discharge. Ms. G. was found to have a greenish discharge emanating from her cervical os. Her cervix was inflamed and bled easily when a swab was used to remove adherent secretions. Gram stains of the secretions from both Mr. C. and Ms. G. revealed numerous neutrophils but no evidence of Gram-negative diplococci, which, if present, would indicate persistence of the gonococci.

Mr. C. was told that he had "postgonococcal urethritis," a condition that may be caused by C. trachomatis. *This diagnosis was confirmed by finding the organisms in a smear of the pus treated with fluorescent antibodies. The incubation time of infections with chlamydiae is generally longer than with gonococci. The ceftriaxone therapy may have eradicated the gonococci in Mr. C., but did not rid him of chlamydiae, probably because chlamydiae are intracellular and neither penicillins nor cephalosporins penetrate human cells adequately. Therefore, Mr. C. may have experienced the overlapping manifestations of two infectious agents acquired simultaneously. Ms. G. was told that she had "mucopurulent cervicitis," the female counterpart of gonococcal and chlamydial urethritis.*

The original treatment that was given to Mr. C. did not follow the current recommendations of the U.S. Public Health Service, which take into account that about 45% of the cases of gonorrhea have coexisting chlamydial infections. The recommended treatment of uncomplicated gonorrhea is the administration of both a cephalosporin for the gonococcus and a tetracycline for the chlamydiae. At the clinic, both patients were treated with tetracycline and were strongly advised to return after finishing therapy to ensure that they had no evidence of either the gonococcal or the chlamydial disease.

Mr. C. did not return to the clinic for a check-up, but Ms. G. did. Upon examination, a cervical discharge was noted. Marked tenderness of the left adnexa was elicited both by direct palpation and by moving the cervix back and forth. This finding strongly suggested the presence of salpingitis, inflammation of the fallopian tubes. A cervical swab was taken and placed into transport medium for chlamydial culture. Ms. G. reported that she had not been feeling ill but had remembered the doctor's advice about coming in for a check-up. When she showed the doctor her bottle of pills, there were ten left— her explanation for the leftovers was that "she may have missed a few doses."

Questions that arise include:

1. What are chlamydiae and what diseases do they cause?

2. How frequent are these infections?

3. How do chlamydiae cause disease?

4. How are these infections diagnosed? How are they differentiated from gonorrhea?

5. What is the best treatment and prophylaxis?

6. What are the chances that Ms. G. will have another episode of PID?

7. Is it likely that she will have permanent or serious damage from this disease?

DISEASES CAUSED BY CHLAMYDIAE

Chlamydiae are small bacteria that can only grow inside of host cells and cause many different diseases (Table 26.1). At least three species cause disease in humans, *C. trachomatis*, *C. psittaci*, and *C. pneumo-*

Table 26.1. Human Syndromes Caused by *Chlamydia* species

Serotype	Syndrome
A, B, C,	Trachoma
D through K	Mucopurulent cervicitis; nongonococcal urethritis, epididymitis, proctitis, PID, including endometritis, salpingitis, and perihepatitis; neonatal inclusion conjunctivitis, and infant pneumonia
L1, L2, L3	Lymphogranuloma venereum
C. pneumoniae	Pneumonia and upper respiratory disease
C. psittaci	Psittacosis or ornithosis; systemic "flu-like" disease

niae. C. trachomatis, the agent involved in the cases described above, is the more diversified of the three species in humans; it causes diseases, acute and chronic, of the mucous membranes of the eye, the lungs, the genital tract, and other organs. *C. trachomatis* can be subdivided into several strains, called biovars (Table 26.1), each associated with a different spectrum of diseases. One of the most serious of these diseases is **trachoma**, an infection of the **eye** that can readily lead to blindness if untreated. It is common in the Middle East and in other arid parts of the world, and it is still the leading cause of blindness in some developing countries.

Genital infections are usually caused by another group of biovars, although "ocular strains" can also cause genital infections. *C. trachomatis* infections are the most common of the bacterial sexually transmitted diseases in the U.S., with approximately 4 million cases a year. Genital chlamydial infection is usually manifested as a **mild cervicitis** or **urethritis**, often with little pain and minimal exudate. The mildness of the symptoms may explain why the disease often goes unrecognized. Because many people go undiagnosed and untreated, it is likely that the number of people who carry the organism in this country is much higher than the above figure suggests, and that the vast majority of carriers do not realize it.

Chlamydial infection has only recently been recognized as a cause of urethritis. Until recently, if a man had urethritis, a smear of the pus would be Gram stained and examined. If Gram-negative diplococci were seen, the diagnosis of gonorrhea was made; if negative, the diagnosis was "nongonococcal urethritis" and the cause of the disease was not usually determined.

The most important aspect of this infection occurs in women. As with gonococcal infections, chlamydial cervicitis can lead to ascending infections of the upper genital tract, subsequent tubal scarring, and PID. Complications such as ectopic pregnancy, infertility, or recurrent PID are the cause of significant morbidity, mortality, and health care costs (Chapter 14).

Certain biovars of *C. trachomatis* cause especially severe genital tract infections; these strains are more invasive and usually cause a disease, **lymphogranuloma venereum** (LGV), that results in abscesses of lymph nodes. **Psittacosis** or **ornithosis**, a form of pneumonia, is the major disease caused by another species of chlamydia, *C. psittaci*, which can be acquired from birds, sheep, and other animals. *C. pneumoniae* is a frequent cause of upper and lower **respiratory tract disease** of humans. Respiratory infections caused by *C. pneumoniae* are quite common. Serological studies performed in seven different areas of the world indicate that 40–60% of individuals have been infected with *C. pneumoniae* by the time they reach adulthood.

Chlamydiae

Because of their morphology and DNA composition, chlamydiae are procaryotes (Fig. 26.1). Their procaryotic nature is underscored by the fact that they are sensitive to typical antibacterial antibiotics such as the penicillins, the cephalosporins, erythromycin, and tetracycline. Chlamydiae have two membranes, a cytoplasmic membrane and a double-layered outer membrane, in the fashion of Gram-negative bacteria. A cell wall murein layer has not been demonstrated, despite the presence of penicillin-binding proteins known to play a role in murein synthesis. These proteins are probably responsible for the sensitivity

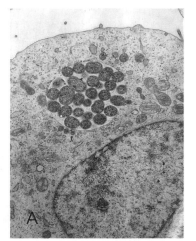
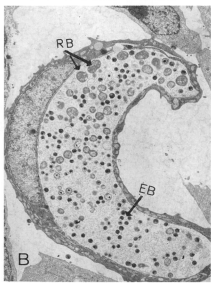

Figure 26.1. A. Metabolically active and dividing reticulate bodies of *C. trachomatis* contained in a phagosomal vesicle. **B.** Late, mature *C. trachomatis* inclusion containing both reticulate bodies (*RB*) and elementary bodies (*EB*).

of this organism to penicillin under laboratory conditions. However, penicillins and cephalosporins are not useful in treating chlamydial infections because those antibiotics do not penetrate well into human cells where the chlamydiae reside.

The chlamydial genome is very small, about 15% the size of that of *Escherichia coli*, and encodes for no more than 500 proteins. Chlamydiae are strict intracellular parasites and the reason they cannot multiply outside host cells may be because they cannot generate their own energy or adenosine triphosphate (ATP). They do not have oxidative enzymes such as flavoproteins or cytochromes, and rely on their host cells for energy-rich compounds such as ATP. Other factors, as yet unknown, must contribute to the chlamydiae's dependency on host cells, because these organisms, although they cannot multiply extracellularly, are capable of synthesizing proteins in vitro when provided with ATP and amino acids. Intracellularly, chlamydiae synthesize their own macromolecules as part of their developmental cycle.

ENTRY, MULTIPLICATION, AND SPREAD

In the course of human infection, chlamydiae enter epithelial cells very quickly. Because these cells are nonprofessional phagocytes, the chlamydiae provide the impetus for their own uptake, a process called **parasite-directed endocytosis**. Chlamydiae are taken up within phagosomes (membrane-bound vacuoles) like most intracellular parasites (Figs. 26.1–26.3). Once inside the phagosomes, chlamydiae grow into microscopic colonies (known as intracytoplasmic inclusions) that eventually can occupy more than half of the cell's volume. Chlamydiae avoid the microbicidal enzymes of the lysosomes by inhibiting the fusion of these organelles with the phagosomes. If chlamydiae are coated with specific antibodies before ingestion, phagolysosomal fusion is not inhibited; instead, lysosomes pour their enzymatic contents into the phagosomes, and the organisms are killed. This suggests that some surface component of the chlamydiae (which can be masked or inactivated by host antibodies) prevents the fusion.

For a small procaryote, the life cycle of a *Chlamydia* is unusually rich in events. The infectious form of the organisms, those that are transferred from cell to cell and from host to host, are small, tight spheres called **elementary bodies** (Fig. 26.1). Once these enter the host cells, they differentiate, become larger and metabolically active, and multiply by binary fission. These replicative forms of chlamydiae are called **reticulate bodies**, from their mesh-like appearance in stained preparations. Reticulate bodies are very fragile and must redifferentiate into elementary bodies (the infectious form of the organism) before exiting the cell.

This unusual life cycle can be understood if the following is kept in mind. Reticulate bodies do not survive well outside cells and quickly lose their infectivity. Elementary bodies, on the other hand, can withstand all sorts of damaging conditions and, therefore, have been likened to bacterial spores. The analogy is appropriate because, like in spores, the outer membrane of elementary bodies is a tough layer of proteins that are **highly cross-linked** by disulfide bridges. The reversibility of these linkages is probably crucial to the transformation from elementary bodies to reticulate bodies when the chlamydiae enter host cells. If the chlamydia-containing phagosomes are treated with reducing agents, the disulfide bridges of the envelope proteins are broken, converting the organisms to forms with the appearance of reticulate bod-

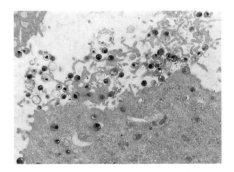

Figure 26.2.   The infectious process is initiated by absorption of the chlamydiae to microvilli of columnar epithelial cells. The elementary bodies appear to travel down the microvilli to the base where they enter via specialized coated pits.

Figure 26.3. The life cycle of chlamy-diae.

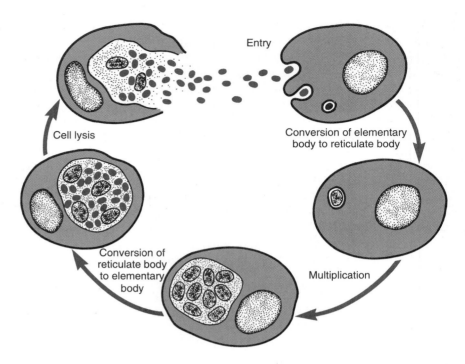

ies. It is not known if this is the mechanism that takes places naturally, but it seems plausible because of the reducing conditions found inside of cells. The reverse process, the conversion of reticulate bodies into elementary bodies, could, in principle, be caused by the oxidative conditions that arise late in infection, which would cause the disulfide bonds to be re-formed; however, limitation of nutrients may also be a stimulus for this conversion. The point to keep in mind is that these organisms have a dimorphic life cycle; that is, they have one morphological form, the reticulate body, for reproduction and another one, the elementary body, for extracellular survival and transit to new host cells.

DAMAGE

How do chlamydiae damage their host cells? In *C. trachomatis* infection, host cells seem to tolerate a large load of chlamydiae before damage becomes apparent. After ingestion by host cells, the organisms multiply rapidly and quickly reach large numbers. In cell culture, cells lyse within 36–72 hours releasing a large number of elementary bodies that invade adjacent cells. The genital lesions of chlamydial disease are the result of acute and chronic inflammation. The symptoms described by Mr. C. can probably be ascribed to the acute stages of this process. The infection elicits inflammatory cytokines, which appear to initiate and facilitate an inflammatory reaction and scarring. Neutrophils are the first cells on the scene. In chronic chlamydial infection, the tissues are infiltrated by macrophages and lymphocytes.

When the disease is located in the male urethra, symptoms are usually self-limiting. However, symptoms of infection can recur after asymptomatic periods. It is difficult to determine whether the recurrence of symptoms is caused by a persistent latent infection or by reinfection. The former suggests that humoral and cellular immunity may be insufficient to combat these organisms in their intracellular location. The location of the organisms during the silent periods, if the organisms persist, is not known.

Blindness of patients with trachoma is the result of inflammation of the conjunctiva followed by vascularization and scarring of the cornea. Eventually, the cornea is so infiltrated by blood vessels and scar tissue that it becomes opaque. The inflammation of the tissues in the region interferes with the flow of tears, which is an important defense mechanism against many bacteria. A common complication is secondary infection by other bacteria. Together, these processes lead to blindness.

Recently, important advances have been made in our understanding of the mechanisms of chlamydia-induced scarring. In an animal model of trachoma, chronic exposure to a chlamydial surface protein, called the heat shock protein, induces intense inflammation. Heat shock proteins are a family of stress-induced proteins that protect the integrity of DNA during different types of environmental stress (including heat). Heat shock proteins are produced by all living organisms, although their sequence varies from species to species. In other words, heat shock proteins from humans, mice, bacteria, and algae are similar but have demonstrable differences.

In the animal model of trachoma, chlamydiae cause an initial eye infection that can be self-limiting or can be eradicated with antibiotics. If the chlamydial heat shock protein is subsequently inoculated into the eye, an inflammation results that can lead to blindness. Examination of the conjunctiva of the animals showed that large numbers of lymphocytes and macrophages had infiltrated the tissues. High titers of antibodies to the heat shock protein were also demonstrated in the animals.

Researchers have looked for an antibody response to heat shock protein in patients with ocular scarring caused by trachoma and with tubal scarring following chlamydial PID. In both cases, high antibody titers to heat shock protein correlated with scarring disease. These antibodies react with the portion of the heat shock protein that is unique to chlamydiae, suggesting that the antibodies were induced by the organisms. Currently, investigators believe that heat shock protein-induced inflammation is fundamental to the process of scarring following chlamydial infections. Thus, as in gonococcal infections, the host's own response to the infection produces tissue damage; the host response is the disease.

DIAGNOSIS

Genital chlamydial infections must be differentiated from gonorrhea and other purulent infections because the drugs of choice are different for each disease. Because chlamydiae cannot grow outside of host cells, culturing the organisms from clinical specimens is expensive and time-consuming. A number of chlamydial antigen detection tests have been developed, including direct microscopic demonstration of the organisms in exudates, by means of the **fluorescence antibody** technique. This technique is a rapid method of diagnosing chlamydial infections, but has been replaced in some laboratories by the detection of *Chlamydia*-specific DNA sequences.

TREATMENT

Two aspects of the life cycle of chlamydiae have a direct impact on how chlamydial infections of the genital tract are treated. As mentioned above, because the organisms are only active intracellularly, antibiotics must penetrate the host cells if they are to find their targets.

Table 26.2. Who Should Receive Antichlamydial Therapy?

Patients with any of the diseases listed in Table 26.1
Patients with gonorrhea
All of their sexual partners
Neonates born to women with untreated chlamydial infections

Only extended therapy with antimicrobial agents that penetrate host cells can result in the eradication of these organisms. Among the effective drugs are tetracyclines, erythromycin, other macrolides, and sulfonamides.

The second aspect of the chlamydial lifestyle relevant to therapy is that chlamydial infections are commonly silent. Individuals shown to be infected with chlamydiae or their sexual contacts can be sources of infection and should be treated. The recommended list of those who should receive antibiotics against chlamydiae is presented in Table 26.2.

Historically, noncompliance by the patient has proven to be a major problem in effectively treating chlamydial infection. Many antimicrobials must be taken two to four times each day for 7–10 days. Once symptoms decrease in severity or, more commonly, in the absence of symptoms, patients often fail to complete the regimen. Antibiotic resistance has not been a problem; however, nontreatment or incomplete treatment may be a contributing factor in ascending infection in women. In fact, animal models have demonstrated that infectious chlamydiae can be found in the uterus and fallopian tubes as early as 1 week following cervical infection. For this reason, PID prevention is absolutely dependent on prevention of cervical infection and early diagnosis and effective treatment. Newer antibiotics that allow single-dose therapy of chlamydial genital infections have been licensed but are expensive compared to older drugs.

INFECTION OF NEONATES

Like most other pathogens of the reproductive tract, chlamydiae can be transmitted from the mother to the baby during passage through the birth canal. *Chlamydia* infection in the baby may present as conjunctivitis or pneumonia. In many infants, undiagnosed, untreated pneumonia will result in chronic respiratory disease.

CONCLUSIONS

Because of the minimal symptoms but severe scarring that they usually provoke, chlamydiae are very important agents of disease; i.e., infection may lead to significant complications. Chlamydiae have an intriguing two-stage life cycle that helps them evade effective host responses to infection. The details of their metabolic dependence on host cells, the way in which they inhibit the fusion of lysosomes with phagosomes, or how they differentiate into the infectious elementary bodies are unknown. Important advances in our understanding of the above factors and of the molecular mechanisms that lead to scarring will likely facilitate targeted approaches to treatment, diagnosis, and vaccine development.

Self-assessment Questions

1. How do reticulate bodies differ from elementary bodies? What is the biochemical difference in the outer membrane that occurs?

2. What is known about the energy requirements for intracellular multiplication of these organisms? How do they survive in macrophages?

3. Why are asymptomatic genital infections by chlamydiae a public health problem? What are the possible complications for women?

4. Awareness of sexually transmitted chlamydial infections alters the therapeutic strategy for all sexually transmitted diseases. Why? How does it alter it?

5. What aspect of "chlamydiology" would you select for further study?

SUGGESTED READING

Grayston JT, Campbell LA, Kuo C-C, Mordhorst CH, Saikku P, Thom DH, Wang S-P. A new respiratory tract pathogen: *Chlamydia pneumoniae* strain TWAR. J Infect Dis 1990;161:618–625.

McGee ZA, Gorby GL, Updike WS. The use of neutrophils, macrophages and organ cultures to assess the penetration of human cells by antimicrobials. Prog Drug Res 1989;33:84–92.

McGee ZA, Gorby GL, Wyrick PB, Hodinka R, Hoffman LH. Parasite-directed endocytosis. Rev Infect Dis 1988;10:S311–S316.

Moulder JW. Comparative biology of intracellular parasitism. Microbiol Rev 1985;49:298–337.

Rocky Mountain Spotted Fever and Other Rickettsioses

27

David H. Walker

Rickettsiae comprise a large collection of bacteria that can only grow inside eukaryotic cells. Together with the chlamydiae, the rickettsiae are the principal medically important **obligate intracellular bacteria**. The other defining characteristic of these organisms is their epidemiology. Most rickettsioses are zoonoses, infections that are transmitted from animals to humans, mainly through arthropod vectors (ticks, mites, fleas, lice, and chiggers).

The most important rickettsiosis in the U.S., **Rocky Mountain spotted fever**, is a serious, life-threatening disease. In common with many other species of rickettsiae, the causative agent invades vascular endothelial cells, causing generalized vascular damage. Another important disease is Q fever, often seen as a pneumonia. A number of other rickettsioses have played an important role at other times in history and some appear to emerge anew in **AIDS** patients.

CASE

L., a 9-year-old girl, was taken to her pediatrician on May 31, 2 days after the onset of fever, severe headache, and muscle pains. The next day she developed nausea, vomiting, and abdominal pain, and was admitted to the hospital for observation for possible appendicitis. On the second hospital day, an erythematous rash consisting of 2- to 4-mm macules (areas of discoloration) appeared on her wrists and ankles. Within 24 hours of its onset, the rash involved the arms, legs, and trunk and many of the lesions had become maculopapular (discolored and raised) with petechiae (dark red caused by bleeding in the skin). A serological test for Rocky Mountain spotted fever and cultures of the blood, cerebrospinal fluid (CSF), and urine were negative. L. became stuporous and had edema in her face and extremities.

Treatment with intravenous doxycycline was begun for the suspected diagnosis of Rocky Mountain spotted fever. Within 72 hours, L. was alert and afebrile. She was sent home after 4 days in the hospital with instructions to take oral doxycycline for 3 more days. By the time of discharge from the hospital, the rash had faded remarkably.

L. lived in a mobile home on the outskirts of Burlington, North Carolina and played after school in the nearby high grass and weeds. Her mother had removed several ticks from her body nearly every day during the month of May before she became sick. When L. returned to her pediatrician at the end of June, she was completely recovered. A serum sample was collected and sent along with one collected during the acute hospitalization to the state public health laboratory in Raleigh. A dramatic rise in titer of antibody to Rickettsia rickettsii *was detected in the convalescent sample.*

Ponder the following questions:

- What caused the rash, stupor, and gastrointestinal symptoms?

- Why was the serological test for Rocky Mountain spotted fever negative in the hospital?

- Assuming that rickettsiae were circulating in the blood, why were the blood cultures negative?

- How did a girl from an eastern state get Rocky Mountain spotted fever?

Paradigm—Vectors and Reservoirs

Most rickettsial diseases are classic zoonoses, diseases that are transmitted to humans from their usual ecological niche in other animals. In the zoonoses, regardless of the pathogen, the animals constitute the **reservoir**, from which the agents are transmitted either directly or via an arthropod **vector**. Direct spread to humans occurs in a variety of ways—some are **air-borne** (e.g., Q fever, psittacosis, and pulmonary anthrax); some are **water-borne** (e.g., giardiasis and leptospirosis); some are **food-borne** (e.g., trichinosis, bovine tuberculosis, and brucellosis); or some are transmitted **via animal bites** (e.g., rabies). Transmission via vectors involves flying insects such as mosquitoes (malaria) and flies (leishmaniasis), or nonflying arthropods such as fleas (plague), lice (epidemic typhus), or ticks (Lyme disease). The zoonoses are discussed in detail in Chapter 69.

In some cases, zoonotic agents have a complex life cycle, involving differentiation into morphologically different forms in the reservoir, vector, and host. Many of these agents are relatively sensitive to environmental factors and, during transmission from reservoir to human host, are protected by being inside a living vector.

The control of zoonoses presents special problems not always shared by other infectious diseases. The animal reservoir can rarely be treated or eliminated as a source of transmission. In some cases, eradication of vectors can be attempted, as with mosquitoes that transmit malaria. For the spotted fevers and scrub typhus, eradication of the vectors is more difficult because ticks, mites, or chiggers live in grassy and scrub areas. These rickettsiae are maintained in nature by **transovarian transmission**, i.e., passage of the rickettsiae from one generation to the next through infected ova. In this case, the life cycle of the agents does not require infection of human beings, who then become "dead-end hosts" and are not significantly involved in transmission of the organisms.

When control of reservoirs or vectors is impractical, vaccination is sometimes helpful, as in the case of yellow fever and some other viral zoonoses. Antimicrobial treatment only helps the individual patient; rickettsiae, for example, persist in nature in infected arthropods where they are not exposed to antibiotics. Vigilance for zoonoses presents special problems and often requires the collaboration of physicians and field biologists.

RICKETTSIOSES

Characteristics of the rickettsioses are shown in Table 27.1. The classic rickettsiosis, **epidemic typhus**, has been one of the most important infectious diseases in terms of its devastating effects on humanity. This disease has determined the outcome of most European wars be-

Table 27.1. Etiology and Epidemiology of the Principal Rickettsioses

Rickettsial	Disease Agent	Reservoir in Nature	Transmission	Geographic Distribution
R. rickettsii	Rocky Mountain spotted fever	Ticks (transovarian transmission)	Tick bite	North and South America
R. conorii	Boutonneuse fever	Ticks (transovarian transmission)	Tick bite	Southern Europe, Africa, and Asia
R. prowazekii	Epidemic typhus	Humans, flying squirrels	Louse feces	Potentially worldwide
	Recrudescent typhus	Humans	None	Potentially worldwide
R. typhi	Murine typhus	Fleas and rats	Flea feces	Worldwide, especially tropics and subtropics
R. tsutsugamushi	Scrub typhus	Chiggers (transovarian transmission)	Chigger bite	Asia, Oceania, and North Australia
Ehrlichia chaffeensis	Human ehrlichiosis	Unknown	Tick bite	North America
C. burnetii	Q fever	Cattle, sheep, goats, other livestock, cats,	Aerosol from infected birth products and ticks	Worldwide
Rochalimaea quintana	Trench fever	Humans	Louse feces	Europe (World War I) and North America
Rochalimaea-related bacterium	Bacillary angiomatosis	Cats	Unknown	Presumably worldwide

tween 1500 and 1900. During and immediately after World War I and the Russian Revolution, 30 million persons suffered from epidemic typhus, and 3 million of them died. The human body louse transmits *R. prowazekii* by depositing its feces on the skin. The discovery of effective insecticides permitted delousing to interrupt transmission of epidemic typhus.

The most common rickettsiosis in the U.S. is **Rocky Mountain spotted fever**. It affects approximately 600 people annually, especially in the eastern and southern states rather than in the Rocky Mountains, where it was first described. This can be an extremely serious disease, with a mortality rate of about 20% if untreated. Because it responds well to certain antibiotics, especially in the early stages, a speedy diagnosis is essential. The typhus group and spotted fever group of diseases are characterized by disseminated vascular infection. Injury in the lungs, central nervous system (CNS), and other systemic microcirculation may cause neurological signs, seizures, coma, acute respiratory failure, shock, and acute renal failure.

Q fever is significantly different from the typhus and spotted fever infections in having an acute form, manifested mainly as a pneumonia, and a chronic form, where the heart is usually affected. The causative agent, *Coxiella burnetii* grows in the macrophages in the lung, liver, bone marrow, and spleen, where it stimulates granuloma formation. In one rickettsiosis (ehrlichiosis), the organisms grow in white blood cells.

RICKETTSIAE

Rickettsiae are small bacteria that resemble Gram-negative rods by virtue of having an outer membrane and a thin murein layer (Fig. 27.1). However, they are not readily stainable by the Gram method. As measured by **DNA homology**, the evolutionary family tree of bacteria reveals that spotted fever and typhus rickettsiae are relatively closely related to *Ehrlichia* and *Rochalimaea*. In contrast, *C. burnetii* is more closely related to *Legionella* and only distantly related to the other rickettsiae. Spotted fever and typhus rickettsiae have lipopolysaccharides that are antigenically distinct for each group.

Figure 27.1. Electron micrograph of a thin section of a human endothelial cell infected with *R. rickettsii*, the etiological agent of Rocky Mountain spotted fever. The rickettsiae are the dark, rod-shaped bacteria in the nucleus, about the same size as mitochondria and smaller than most other bacteria. These rickettsiae have invaded the nucleus. Although usually *R. rickettsii* organisms occupy the cytoplasm and few enter the nucleus, their presence in this location is characteristic of spotted fever rickettsiae and would be most unusual for other rickettsiae, *Mycobacteria*, *Salmonella*, *Legionella*, etc.

Rickettsiae are highly adapted to the intracellular niche, where they propagate by binary fission with a generation time of 8–10 hours. Rickettsiae thrive in the high potassium environment of the eukaryotic cytosol and have specific membrane transport systems for acquiring ATP, amino acids, and other metabolites from the host cell. Unlike chlamydiae, rickettsiae are not strict energy parasites, as they are also able to synthesize at least some of their required ATP. Far from being degenerate life-forms, rickettsiae are capable of independent metabolism (e.g., trichloroacetic acid [TCA] cycle and electron transport system) and use their own biosynthetic machinery to make proteins and other complex components. However, they cannot be cultivated on artificial medium and, in the laboratory, they must be grown in animals, embryonated eggs, or cell cultures.

ENCOUNTER AND ENTRY

The rickettsiae of Rocky Mountain spotted fever are transmitted from tick to tick by the transovarian route usually causing little harm to this host. Note that the ticks involved (*Dermacentor* species) are different from the *Ixodes* that transmit Lyme disease (Chapter 25). Many wild animals are bitten by *Dermacentor* ticks; they become transiently infected and represent a transient reservoir of the rickettsiae. Thus, this disease cannot be eradicated by public health measures. Risk of transmission can be eluded by the use of tick repellents and protective clothing (although lovers of the outdoors may find this annoying). Individuals may prevent this illness by removing ticks from the skin before the bacteria are inoculated, usually between 6 and 24 hours after attachment. The 1985 distribution of cases of the disease in the U.S. is shown in Figure 27.2.

SPREAD, MULTIPLICATION, AND DAMAGE

Rocky Mountain spotted fever begins an average of 1 week after an infected adult tick inoculates *R. rickettsii* into the skin while taking a blood meal. The rickettsiae spread throughout the body via the bloodstream. Upon encountering vascular endothelial cells, rickettsiae attach to the cell membrane and enter by inducing these cells to engulf them (Fig. 27.3 and Table 27.2). Once inside the cells, rickettsiae rap-

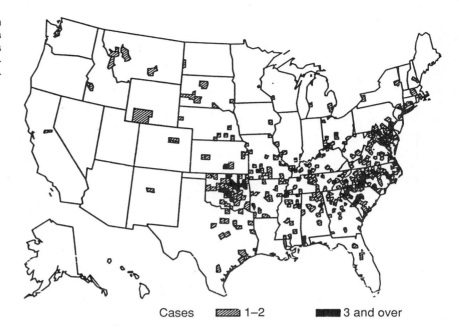

Figure 27.2. Cases of Rocky Mountain spotted fever reported in 1985 by counties in the U.S. Even though the disease was first recognized in the Rocky Mountain region, most cases now occur in the southeastern and south central states.

Cases ▨ 1–2   ▮ 3 and over

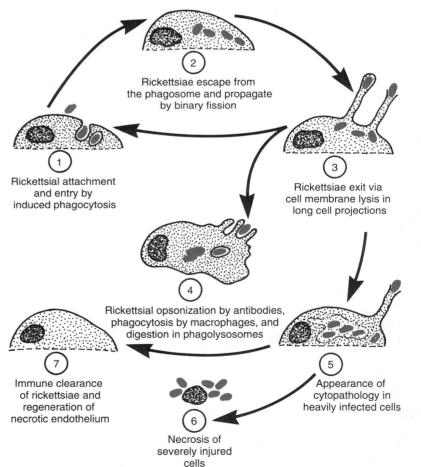

Figure 27.3. Sequence of rickettsia-host cell interactions in Rocky Mountain spotted fever.

idly escape from the phagosome into the cytosol, presumably by lysis of the phagosomal membrane by a phospholipase.

Ensconced in the cytosol, the agent of Rocky Mountain spotted fever, *R. rickettsii* multiplies and spreads to other endothelial cells by release through the cell membrane from the end of long cellular projections. Injury to the host cell correlates with the quantity of bacteria accumulated intracellularly. The subcellular target of injury appears to be the cell membrane; however, the mechanism of damage to this structure is not known, but may be due to the action of phospholipase, protease, or free radical-induced membrane lipid peroxidation.

The effects of the damage to foci of contiguous endothelial cells are visible in the skin where dilation of the blood vessels produces the early pink rash. Later, leakage of fluid through the infected endothelium results in cutaneous edema, and leakage of red blood cells results in hemorrhagic spots, from which the name of the disease is derived (Fig. 27.4). Within the blood vessels of the brain, lung, heart, liver, and other visceral organs, these same events occur and lead to encephalitis, pneumonitis, cardiac arrhythmia, nausea, vomiting, and abdominal pain.

Even before the introduction of effective antimicrobial treatment, 75% of patients with Rocky Mountain spotted fever survived. Clearance of intracellular rickettsiae from the endothelium is achieved by the concerted effects of the immune system with important contributions of cell-mediated immunity, particularly T lymphocytes and their cytokines, such as γ-interferon and tumor necrosis factor. A fatal outcome is more likely to occur in males, older individuals, alcohol abusers, and glucose-6-phosphate dehydrogenase-deficient patients.

A number of similar diseases are caused by antigenically related organisms. The geographic distribution of these diseases coincides with that of infected **ticks** (e.g., in Southern Europe, Africa, and Asia— boutonneuse fever and Israel spotted fever; in Australia—Queensland tick typhus; in northern Asia—another tick typhus) or **mites** (in North America and Asia—rickettsialpox). A substantial number of people become infected while traveling in southern Europe or Africa, where their activities expose them to ticks. Upon returning home to North America or northern Europe, they seek medical attention for what is recognized by the astute physician as boutonneuse fever. The prevalence of antibodies to spotted fever group rickettsiae among healthy subjects in the affected countries suggests that many infections are not diagnosed.

TYPHUS GROUP FEVERS

The classic epidemic disease, typhus fever, is spread among humans by the body louse and is associated with high mortality and dramatic epidemics. In the U.S., the human disease is not seen except for cases of **recrudescent typhus**, which is due to reactivation of the agent, *R.*

Table 27.2. Cellular and Subcellular Locations of Rickettsiae

Rickettsial Genus	Host Target Cell	Cellular Location
Rickettsia	Endothelium	Cytosol
Coxiella	Macrophages	Phagolysosome
Ehrlichia	Leukocytes	Cytoplasmic phagosomal vacuole
Rochalimaea	None	Extracellular

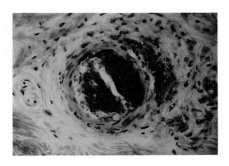

Figure 27.4. Severe injury to the arterial endothelium and media resulted in red blood cell extravasation and a thrombus plugging the vascular lesion.

prowazekii, that has lain latent in the body for years or even decades after recovery from epidemic typhus, or zoonotic typhus from flying squirrels. Recrudescent typhus (Brill-Zinsser disease) was described in the late 1800s in New York City among immigrants from eastern Europe, where epidemics of typhus were notorious. It is presumed that epidemics of typhus can be ignited from a patient with recrudescent typhus and body lice, which spread the infection to other persons. Absence of epidemic typhus in developed countries today is an effect of the socioeconomic conditions and low prevalence of human body lice. When war, natural disasters, and famine occur, epidemic typhus has often followed. This is a disease of crowding, poverty, and "lousy" sanitary conditions. It is foolish to believe that epidemic typhus could never return.

The reservoir of the epidemic typhus rickettsiae is not only human beings but also flying squirrels and their fleas and lice. The infection has been transmitted from this source to humans in the eastern U.S. Could an epidemic of typhus arise from one of these cases? Possibly.

A more prevalent and widely dispersed rickettsiosis is **murine typhus**. This endemic disease is caused by *R. typhi*, which is transmitted in a natural cycle between rats and rat fleas. Humans become infected by the deposition of infected flea feces on their skin. Murine typhus occurs throughout the tropics and subtropics and was an important problem in the southern U.S. until the development of insecticides and intense efforts at rat control.

SCRUB TYPHUS

Scrub typhus is a vivid example of a disease of major importance in parts of the world distant from the everyday lives of Americans and Europeans. Our attention was rudely required when we were thrown into contact with the ecological conditions that occurred during World War II in the South Pacific, Burma, and China, and during the Vietnam War. *R. tsutsugamushi* infected 18,000 soldiers in World War II and was one of the major causes of undiagnosed febrile illness among soldiers in Vietnam. The indigenous populations of endemic areas in many countries of Asia are continuously exposed to the risk of this infection. In a study in rural Malaysia, scrub typhus was the most frequent reason for febrile hospitalization.

There are several factors that exacerbate the problem of scrub typhus. The organisms exist as a mosaic of different antigenic types, and immunity to one strain wanes over a period of a few years and to other strains after a few months. Subsequently, the patient becomes fully susceptible to reinfection. To make matters worse, clinical diagnosis is difficult because rash and eschar, considered the textbook hallmarks of the disease, are absent in the majority of cases. In many endemic areas, medical care is suboptimal, and laboratory diagnosis is virtually nonexistent. Scrub typhus is a neglected disease that, from time to time, rivets the attention of missionaries, the military, medical examination committees, and medical students who enjoy trying to pronounce *tsutsugamushi*.

OTHER RICKETTSIOSES

Q fever was named for query, referring to its unknown etiology at the time of the description of the disease. The etiological agent, *C. burnetii*, stands apart from other rickettsiae, and the disease differs from other rickettsioses in its clinical manifestations, pathological lesions, and epidemiology. Extracellularly, the organisms are much more **resistant** than the other rickettsiae to the many deleterious effects of the environment. Resistance may be due to formation of a **spore-like** structure that has been observed by electron microscopy. Consequently, this agent does not require the protection afforded by a living vector but may also be transmitted via aerosols. Q fever is distinctly zoonotic, and the main reservoirs are infected sheep and other animals. The organisms are present in large amounts in the placenta and fetal membranes and are spread in copious numbers during birthing of ewes. The disease is most often seen among sheep farmers, veterinarians, and workers in laboratories that use sheep for experimentation.

The kind of disease produced by various strains of *C. burnetii* (e.g., acute pneumonia or chronic endocarditis) has been correlated with specific markers in the organisms, namely lipopolysaccharide type and plasmid DNA sequence. Acute infection may be asymptomatic or associated with nonspecific influenza-like febrile illness, atypical pneumonia, or granulomatous hepatitis. Chronic infection is usually diagnosed in patients with a long course, cardiac valvular infection, and negative routine blood cultures for bacteria. The pathogenic mechanisms appear to be largely immunopathological with T-lymphocyte-mediated granulomas in self-limited disease and an immune complex-mediated component in some cases of chronic illness.

Previously unrecognized infectious diseases continue to be described; **human ehrlichiosis** is among the newest to be discovered. Most cases are clinically similar to Rocky Mountain spotted fever and are characterized by fever, headache, tick-bite, and often, severe multisystem involvement, but with a lower incidence of rash. The spectrum of severity is quite broad ranging from asymptomatic to fatal. The *Ehrlichia* invade monocytes, macrophages, lymphocytes, and neutrophils often causing a reduction in numbers of circulating leukocytes, as well as low platelet counts. More than 200 cases of human ehrlichiosis have been documented since the first recognized case in 1986.

During World War I, a disease that differed from epidemic typhus but was also transmitted by body lice was recognized on both the eastern and western fronts. The infection is known as **trench fever** because of its prevalence in the conditions along the front lines. *Rochalimaea quintana*, (named after the Brazilian microbiologist da Rocha-Lima and the typical 5-day febrile course) should have been removed from the obligate intracellular family Rickettsiaceae when it was successfully cultivated on blood agar. However, tradition was vindicated by the molecular genetic demonstration that *R. quintana* is related at the level of DNA homology to typhus rickettsiae.

The subject of trench fever might have been generally ignored but for the surprising discovery that **bacillary angiomatosis** and **bacillary peliosis**, pseudoneoplastic vascular lesions of the skin and viscera of AIDS patients, contain organisms that are close relatives of *R. quintana*. This agent has not been cultivated and its identity has been established only by amplifying its DNA by the polymerase chain reaction and using the product for DNA sequencing. This organism represents a new entity, albeit one with an historic relative.

DIAGNOSIS

The difficulty in the clinical diagnosis of rickettsioses is usually underestimated, particularly at the time the patient first visits a physician and treatment is most effective. During the first 3 days of illness, only

3% of patients with Rocky Mountain spotted fever have the classic triad of fever, rash, and history of tick-bite. In contrast to most infectious diseases, in rickettsiosis the clinical microbiology laboratory is seldom helpful in establishing a diagnosis in the acute stage of the illness. Very few laboratories attempt to isolate rickettsiae because of the technical requirements for inoculation of antibiotic-free cell culture, animals, or embryonated hen's eggs at the right stage of development. In addition, the handling of these agents is notoriously hazardous.

For these reasons, the diagnosis of most rickettsioses requires considerable diagnostic acumen by physicians. Laboratory confirmation of rickettsioses is usually achieved in the convalescent stage by demonstrating a four-fold or greater rise in the titer of antibodies to specific rickettsial antigens. The only rickettsial disease that can be expected to have diagnostic levels of antibodies at the time the patient seeks medical attention is chronic Q fever. The serological methods that are usually employed are indirect fluorescent antibody assay, latex agglutination, and complement fixation (see Chapter 55), and newer ones are under development. An archaic test that should be relegated to books on the history of medicine is the Weil-Felix test. This test relies on the agglutination of certain strains of the enteric bacterium, *Proteus vulgaris*, which shares cross-reactive antigens with certain rickettsiae. The results of the Weil-Felix test are nonspecific and insensitive, yet many hospitals persist in using it despite the availability of better methods.

For all of its archaic aspect, it is worth recounting how the Weil-Felix test was put to a humanitarian use by two Polish physicians in World War II; they were aware that the occupying Germans did not send people suspected of having epidemic typhus to labor camps. Ingeniously, these doctors inoculated the people of several villages with an innocuous vaccine consisting of killed *P. vulgaris*. The high Weil-Felix titer of the serum of these people was taken by the German medical staff to indicate that these villages were hotbeds of epidemic typhus and the inhabitants were spared, thanks to the microbiological acumen of the two physicians.

TREATMENT

Rickettsial diseases generally respond well to antimicrobial agents that enter host cells and are active in the intracellular environment. Most of these diseases respond to oral or intravenous therapy with doxycycline, tetracycline, or chloramphenicol, each of which has its particular advantages and disadvantages under particular circumstances. Fluoroquinolone antimicrobial drugs are becoming established as effective treatment for some rickettsioses. Penicillins, aminoglycosides, and other antimicrobials do not affect the course of rickettsial diseases. Sulfa drugs actually seem to exacerbate the spotted fevers and typhus fevers.

CONCLUSIONS

Rickettsial infections are not very common in the U.S. but some of them can be life threatening. They must be diagnosed promptly, and antibiotic therapy must be instituted with due speed. The most devastating disease caused by these organisms, epidemic typhus, has receded in importance due to louse control.

Rickettsiae are delicate organisms (except that of Q fever) but are well adapted to intracellular life and to passage from reservoir to host via arthropods. Their localization in blood vessels causes vascular injury with increased permeability and hemorrhages, sometimes with severe consequences.

Self-assessment Questions

1. What epidemiological features are shared by all rickettsioses but not necessarily by Q fever?

2. Describe three characteristics of rickettsiae that set them apart from other groups of bacteria.

3. What are the characteristics of the pathogenesis of Rocky Mountain spotted fever?

4. How could one study pathogenic properties of rickettsiae even though they cannot be grown in cell-free media?

SUGGESTED READING

Hechemy KE, Paretsky D, Walker DH, Mallavia LP. Rickettsiology: current issues and perspectives. Ann NY Acad Sci 1990;590.

Marrie TJ. Q fever. Vol I. Boca Raton, FL: CRC Press, 1990.

Walker DH. Biology of rickettsial diseases. Vols I and II. Boca Raton, FL: CRC Press, 1988.

Walker DH. Rocky Mountain spotted fever: a disease in need of microbiological concern. Clin Microbiol Rev 1989;2:227–240.

Winkler HH. Rickettsia species (as organisms). Ann Rev Microbiol 1990;44:131–153.

Zinsser H. Rats, lice and history. Boston: Little, Brown, 1935; Bantam edition.

Mycoplasma: Curiosity and Pathogen

28

Gregory A. Storch

The mycoplasmata belong to a highly distinct group of bacteria that lack a cell wall and require sterols for growth. Most of the species associated with the human body are innocuous, but one is a common cause of pneumonia, while others cause infections in the genitourinary tract of adults and in the respiratory tract and central nervous system (CNS) of newborn infants. The organisms are sensitive to certain broad-spectrum antibiotics that inhibit functions other than cell wall synthesis.

CASE

M., a 7-year-old girl who previously had been in good health developed fever, headache, and a dry cough. Her 12-year-old brother had had similar symptoms 2 weeks earlier. Over the next 2 days, her temperature increased and the cough worsened, becoming productive of small amounts of clear sputum. Her physician noted that she appeared slightly pale, had a temperature of 39.3°C and a respiratory rate of 40/minute. Scattered rales (abnormal respiratory sounds) were heard through the stethoscope over the right posterior lung.

Her white blood cell count was in the normal range, 8600/µl, with a normal differential (the ratio between the various cell types). She was slightly anemic (hematocrit of 29%) and had an increased number of reticulocytes. A Gram stain of her sputum revealed only rare neutrophils and no bacteria. Her chest x-ray showed an infiltrate of the left midlung field (Fig. 28.1). A special test to detect so-called cold hemagglutinins was positive. This finding and the clinical picture allowed the tentative diagnosis of primary atypical pneumonia caused by Mycoplasma pneumoniae. *M. was treated with erythromycin and made an uneventful recovery.*

Questions that arise from this case include:

- How did M. acquire the organism?

- What are the distinguishing features of the *Mycoplasma*?

- What is known about the pathogenic properties of these organisms?

- How could a definitive diagnosis be made?

- What can M.'s family do to avoid spreading the organisms to other family members?

M. pneumoniae is a common cause of pneumonia in children and young adults. As in M.'s case, the illness usually has a less abrupt onset and is milder than pneumococcal pneumonia. Occasional cases may be quite severe, especially in individuals with sickle cell disease. Headache and cough are prominent clinical features. Before the etiology of this disease became known, it was referred to as "primary atypical pneumonia," to distinguish it from "typical" cases of lobar pneumonia (usually caused by pneumococci). Clinicians knew that patients with typical pneumonia responded to penicillin, while those with atypical pneumonia did not.

MYCOPLASMA

The mycoplasmata have a number of unusual features:

- They are the **smallest** organisms capable of growth on cell-free media. They are classified with the bacteria because, in general, they have the structure and composition of procaryotes.

- They are unique among the bacteria in that they **lack a rigid cell** wall (no murein) and can assume a variety of shapes. This characteristic has important implications for antibiotic therapy, because many commonly used antibiotics (especially the β-lactams) act by inhibiting cell wall murein synthesis, and thus are ineffective against mycoplasmata.

- Their cell membrane contains **sterols** that, with some exceptions, must be supplied in the medium to support their growth.

- Mycoplasmata are **common in nature** and capable of living in **unusual environments**, such as high temperature springs and the acid outflows of mining wastes.

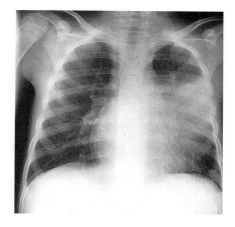

Figure 28.1. Chest x-ray reveals an infiltrate in the left midlung field.

Only three species are known to cause human disease (Table 28.1). They are *M. pneumoniae*, a common cause of respiratory disease, and two organisms that account for some cases of infections of the genitourinary tract, *M. hominis*, and *Ureaplasma urealyticum*. The last two organisms can also be isolated from many newborns, especially from the respiratory tract and the CNS. Other species are commonly found as part of the normal human flora but have not been linked to disease. On the other hand, different species cause a number of severe diseases in domestic animals.

Mycoplasmata can be readily cultivated in the laboratory, although most species require special media that contain sterols. *M. pneumoniae* grows slowly, and several weeks may be required for colonies to become evident. The colonies are much smaller than those of the com-

Table 28.1. Common Mycoplasmata and Diseases They Cause

Organism	Disease	Site
M. pneumoniae	Primary atypical pneumonia	Respiratory tract
M. hominis	Pelvic inflammatory disease, other	Genitourinary tract
U. urealyticum	Urethritis	Genitourinary tract
M. genitalium	?Urethritis	Genitourinary tract
M. fermentans	??HIV cofactor	?
M. salivarium, M. orale	None	Mouth, oropharynx
Others (less common)	None	Genitourinary tract, oropharynx

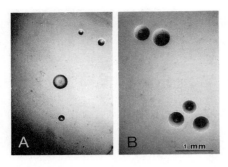

Figure 28.2. Colonies of *M. pneumoniae*. Note their small size and "fried egg" appearance, especially in B.

mon bacteria and have a dense center that gives them a fried egg appearance (Fig. 28.2). *M. hominis* can be grown on the blood agar plates used in all clinical microbiology laboratories. However, this organism is probably often undetected because it make very small colonies that may not be noted unless the culture plate is examined under a dissecting microscope.

ENCOUNTER AND ENTRY

Infected humans constitute the only known **reservoir** of *M. pneumoniae*. Patients become ill following exposure to the respiratory secretions of persons harboring the organism. In contrast to the pneumococcus, prolonged asymptomatic colonization with *M. pneumoniae* is uncommon. In most cases, the source of the infection is not recognized because most *Mycoplasma* infections are mild. *M. pneumoniae* infections are **moderately contagious** and spread within household or residential institutions is sometimes observed. In these situations, an interval between cases of 2–3 weeks is sometimes discerned.

Mycoplasma infection begins with the **binding** of *Mycoplasma* organisms to the respiratory epithelium. Microscopic studies of *M. pneumoniae* have revealed a specialized terminal attachment structure. A special protein is found in this structure and is thought to mediate attachment of the organisms to a receptor on the respiratory epithelium. Monoclonal antibodies to this protein inhibit the attachment of *M. pneumoniae*.

SPREAD AND MULTIPLICATION, DAMAGE

The pathogenesis of *M. pneumoniae* infection differs markedly from that of the other forms of pneumonia, such as that caused by the pneumococcus or *Legionella pneumophila*, because it is largely **limited to the respiratory mucosa** that lines the airways. There is no evidence of involvement of the lung alveoli. An infiltrate of mononuclear cells is present, surrounding infected bronchi and bronchioles. The pattern of involvement is that of a **bronchopneumonia** rather than a lobar process.

In experimentally infected tracheal organ cultures, the organisms are seen lined up along the mucosa, oriented with the terminal attachment structure in contact with the epithelium (Fig. 28.3). *Mycoplasma* infection is not highly destructive of tissue, but **ciliary function is impaired** in cells with *Mycoplasma* bound to their exterior. This is thought to result from local elaboration of **tissue-toxic substances**, probably including hydrogen peroxide. The main cells in the inflammatory response elicited by *M. pneumoniae* are **lymphocytes**, with very few neutrophils. Some immune compromised patients with *Mycoplasma* infection do not have visible pulmonary infiltrates, which suggests that the immune response may play a role in causing the manifestations of disease.

The clinical manifestations of *M. pneumoniae* infections are generally limited to the respiratory tract but other organs are occasionally involved. M., the patient described above, had a mild **hemolytic anemia**, which was caused by an antibody stimulated by mycoplasma. This is an **IgM** antibody that binds to red blood cells and at reduced temperatures, causes them to agglutinate (stick together). These antibodies are called **cold hemagglutinins**, and are detectable in about 50% of severe *Mycoplasma* infections. Only a small minority of these patients actually experience clinically significant hemolysis. We do not know the reason why *M. pneumoniae* infection stimulates the production of cold agglutinins.

Unusual complications of *M. pneumoniae* infections include **encephalitis** and other CNS complications. Some patients develop a **rash** known as erythema multiforme. The pathogenic mechanisms that account for these complications are not yet known. Mycoplasmata have also been implicated in the pathogenesis of **AIDS**, a subject that is being vigorously investigated.

DIAGNOSIS

Culturing *Mycoplasma* takes a week or more and requires special media and experienced personnel. Consequently, the diagnosis of *Mycoplasma* pneumonia is usually suspected from **clinical features** and confirmed by **serological tests**. This has the undesirable feature that the diagnosis cannot be made until convalescent phase serum becomes available, long after therapeutic decisions about the patient must be made. Thus, *M. pneumoniae* is an attractive target for the development of rapid diagnostic tests that do not involve culture, such as immunoassays to detect *Mycoplasma* antigens, or nucleic acid hybridization to detect specific mycoplasmal nucleic acids.

In contrast to pneumococcal pneumonia, sputum production is scanty and the sputum is nonpurulent. The peripheral blood usually does not show the leukocytosis and marked increase in young forms characteristic of pneumococcal infection. The chest x-ray in *Mycoplasma* pneumonia is highly variable, but most commonly reveals a patchy infiltrate suggestive of bronchopneumonia .

Cold hemagglutinins can be rapidly demonstrated at the bedside; blood drawn from the patient into a tube containing an anticoagulant will look clumpy when placed in an ice bucket. The clumps disappear when the tube is warmed up again.

GENITAL MYCOPLASMATA

In epidemiology and pathogenesis, the infections caused by the genital mycoplasmata, *U. urealyticum* and *M. hominis*, differ considerably from infection by *M. pneumoniae*. These organisms are common residents of the genitourinary tract, especially of sexually active people. They are almost certainly transmitted through sexual contact and are also commonly transmitted vertically, from mother to newborn infant during pregnancy and at the time of birth. Not surprisingly, most of the diseases caused by these organisms affect the genitourinary tract of newborns. *U. urealyticum* is clearly established as the cause of urethritis and *M. hominis* as that of pelvic inflammatory disease (Chapter 65). Both organisms can cause chorioamnionitis (inflammation of the fetal membranes) and postpartum fever. Spontaneous abortion and premature delivery have been linked to these organisms, although this association has not been definitively proven. Several provocative studies have demonstrated an association between *U. urealyticum* and chronic lung disease in very low birth weight premature infants. Both organisms have also been isolated from the spinal fluid of newborn infants. This association is confusing because some of these infants have evidence of CNS inflammation, but others do not. It is possible that, at least in some cases, mycoplasmata are innocent bystanders in the CNS, whereas in other cases, they are responsible for disease.

Figure 28.3. Transmission electron photomicrograph of a hamster tracheal ring infected with *M. pneumoniae*. Note the orientation of the *Mycoplasma* via their specialized tip-like organelle that permits close association with the respiratory epithelium (×50,000, original magnification). *M*, Mycoplasma; *m*, microvillus, and *c*, cilia.

PREVENTION AND TREATMENT

No vaccine is currently available to prevent *Mycoplasma* infections. Treatment with erythromycin or tetracycline is effective, although it should be remembered that *M. hominis* is uniformly resistant to erythromycin.

CONCLUSIONS

Mycoplasmata call attention to themselves because they lack a cell wall, many require sterols, and they make characteristic small colonies on agar. These organisms show a marked tropism for mucous membranes and produce characteristic clinical manifestations.

A mycoplasma, *M. pneumoniae*, is unequivocally responsible for a common form of pneumonia in humans. Other mycoplasmata are commonly found in the genitourinary tract of adults and in the respiratory tract and the CNS of newborn infants. In these settings, the presence of these organisms is not uniformly associated with disease. Our state of knowledge about the mycoplasmata and their role in disease is still in flux. The possible role of a *Mycoplasma* as a cofactor in causing **AIDS** is also under investigation. The association of mycoplasmata with a wide variety of clinical symptoms in animals suggests that the full extent of their role in human disease may not yet be fully appreciated.

Self-assessment Questions

1. What distinguishes the *Mycoplasma* from other bacteria?

2. Discuss the pathophysiology of *Mycoplasma* pneumonia.

3. Compare the epidemiology of pneumonia due to *Mycoplasma* with that due to pneumococci or *Legionella*.

4. Why do you think it has been difficult to establish definitely the role of *Mycoplasma* in certain diseases?

SUGGESTED READING

Cassell CH, Cole BC. Mycoplasmas as agents of human disease. N Engl J Med 1981;304:80–89.

Cassell GH, Wautes KB, Crouse DT. Perinatal *Mycoplasma* infections. Clin Perinatol 1991;18

Foy HM, Kenny GE, Conney MK, Allan ID. Long-term epidemiology of infections with *Mycoplasma pneumoniae*. J Infect Dis 1979;139:681–687.

Levin S. The atypical pneumonia syndrome. JAMA 1984;251:945–948.

Murrays HW, Masur H, Senterfit LB, Roberts RB. The protean manifestations of *Mycoplasma pneumoniae* infection in adults. Am J Med 1975;58:279–282.

Strategies to Combat Bacterial Infections

29

Francis P. Tally

Over the last 1 or 2 centuries, health and longevity of people living in developed countries have taken a quantum jump forward. Disease is the exception and premature death is relatively uncommon. Two interrelated factors have contributed to this—improvement in nutrition and control of infectious diseases. The greatest initial strides in reducing the incidence of infectious disease were due to preventive measures, largely purification of the water supply and control of human wastes and disease vectors. Later on, in the last 100 years, these measures were joined by medical intervention—vaccination and antimicrobial therapy. Preventive measures, not therapy, have played the greatest role in the control of infectious diseases.

This chapter deals with use of antibacterial drugs for prevention therapy of infectious diseases. The emphasis here is on bacteria, but the same principles apply to all other infectious agents. **Antiviral strategies are described in Chapter 43. The subject of antibacterial and antiviral vaccination is treated in detail in Chapter 44.**

THERAPY

Despite the great advances in preventive medicine in the last century, until recently little could be done to treat patients with infectious diseases. The medical literature up to about 1930 is full of vivid descriptions of gruesome infections by streptococci, staphylococci, and clostridia. The dawning of the age of antimicrobial therapy, with the introduction of the sulfonamides in the 1930s, allowed physicians finally to cure many of these fatal infections. Here is a description of the first time penicillin was used clinically:

"The time had now come to find a suitable patient for the first test of the therapeutic power of penicillin in man. . . . In the septic ward at the Radcliffe Infirmary (Oxford, England) there was an unfortunate policeman aged 43 who had a sore on his lip 4 months previously, from which he developed a combined staphylococcal and streptococcal septicæmia. He had multiple abscesses on his face and orbits: he also had osteomyelitis of his right humerus with discharging sinuses, and abscesses in his lungs. He was in great pain and was desperately ill. There was all to gain for him in a trial of penicillin and nothing to lose. Penicillin treatment was started on 12 February 1941, with 200 mg (10,000 units) intravenously initially and then 300 mg every three hours. . . Four days later there was striking improvement, and after 5 days the patient was vastly better, afebrile and eating well, and there was obvious resolution of the abscesses on his face and scalp and in his right orbit."

Unfortunately, this first clinical trial of penicillin terminated abruptly because the total supply of the drug was exhausted by the 5-day course of treatment, despite efforts to recover the drug from the patient's urine. The patient died 4 weeks later.

Although the experiment ended tragically, it served to demonstrate the efficacy and superiority of the new therapy over any that was available until that time. In time, it has become increasingly more difficult to prove the superiority of new antibiotics over those already in use. In assessing new drugs, pharmaceutical companies must carry out complex and expensive trials that include laboratory work, experimental animals, and lengthy clinical studies. The practicing physician may often find it difficult to evaluate such intricate studies.

The selection of an appropriate drug from those presently available is also not a simple matter. For example, the β-lactam imipenem may be thought to be a true "wonder drug," because it has the widest antibacterial spectrum of any antibiotic presently available and is resistant to inactivating β-lactamases. However, there are specific infections for which a simple penicillin (which may have neither of these desirable properties) is preferable. For example, because of its broad spectrum, imipenem may wipe out other members of the normal bacterial flora, and lead to colonization by resistant species. In addition, imipenem is far more expensive. Thus, pharmacokinetic properties of the drugs, their cost, and many other properties also enter as considerations. The selection of an appropriate drug involves the following criteria:

- Which pathogens are causing the infection? If we cannot determine their identity in a timely manner, what are the likely possibilities?

- What antibiotics are they susceptible to?

- Will the drug penetrate to the site of infection and will it work under the conditions at that site?

- What is the toxicity of the drug to the patient?

- What are the consequences of multiple antibiotic therapy?

- What is the effect of the drug on the microbial ecology? Will its use contribute to the emergence of broadly based antibiotic resistance, and thus pose a threat to the patient being treated and to other infected patients in the community?

- Are other host factors relevant to the proposed therapy?

Note that, in many cases, the proper conclusion may be that the patient should not to be treated with antimicrobial drugs at all because the benefit of such treatment is not likely to outweigh its drawbacks.

Infecting Organisms

The proper choice of an antimicrobial drug depends on the identification of the infecting organisms. Consider, for example, patients with recurrent urinary tract infection. Often the infection is caused by *Escherichia coli*, but it may be due to group D streptococci, to *Pseudomonas aeruginosa*, or to one of the other enterobacteriaceae, such as *Klebsiella*, *Enterobacter*, or *Serratia*. These organisms have differing susceptibilities, and the determination of their antimicrobial susceptibility is mandatory.

Note that, in many cases, the physician treating recurrent urinary tract infections can usually wait for the result of laboratory cultures and drug susceptibility testing. This may take 2 or more days. However, when the symptoms of the disease are severe, treatment may have to be instituted with only a presumption as to the nature of the causative agents. In such cases, "shotgun" antimicrobial therapy should be broad enough to cover all the likely pathogens and require several drugs. To do this, physicians must take into account factors pertinent to the individual patient and to the local environment, especially recent experience with similar cases and the antibiotic susceptibility pattern in their hospital or community. Empirical therapy may also have to be started when an adequate sample of infected material for direct analysis or culture cannot be obtained.

The drawbacks of "shotgun" antibiotic therapy are:

- Failure to "cover" the pathogen;

- Synergistic toxicity of multiple drugs;

- Possible antagonism between drugs;

- Increased likelihood of superinfection by resistant bacteria or fungi;

- Increased cost.

Obviously, these disadvantages are minimized when the identity of the infecting agent can be determined. In general, the more rapid the diagnosis, the sooner proper therapy can be instituted. Much effort is being expended on the development of rapid diagnostic methods, but most still require 1 or several days (for details, see Chapter 55).

Antibiotic Susceptibility

Within broad limits, bacteria fall into large groups with regards to antibiotic susceptibility. Gram-positive bacteria, possibly because they lack an outer membrane (Chapter 3), are more permeable to many of the classical antibiotics and are generally more susceptible than Gram negatives. For example, streptococci and pneumococci are usually about 1000-fold more susceptible to penicillin G than *E. coli*. However, the exceptions are too numerous to make these generalizations very useful. Much depends on the presence of antibiotic-resistant strains in a particular environment. Nationwide and local monitoring of resistant strains is helpful in providing general guidelines, but basically each individual isolate should be tested for susceptibility.

The importance of microbial drug resistance is illustrated by the catastrophic outbreaks of chloramphenicol resistance that occurred in Mexico in the late 1960s and early 1970s with *Shigella* dysentery and later with *Salmonella* infection. In the initial epidemics, it was not recognized that the reason patients failed to respond to chloramphenicol was that the bacteria had become resistant. Rather, it was thought that the disease was caused by a protozoan parasite. A similar scenario occurred 2 years later in outbreaks of typhoid fever, with *Salmonella typhi* that was also chloramphenicol resistant. It is estimated that more than 30,000 people died in each of these outbreaks because they were treated with chloramphenicol alone. **It is extremely important that drug resistance be monitored on a nationwide and local basis, and that the information be made readily available to medical personnel.**

The simplest and most widely used assay for microbial susceptibility is to place a disk containing the antibiotic on an agar plate inoculated with the organisms. As the antibiotic diffuses into the agar, it inhibits bacterial growth up to the limit of the effective concentration (Fig.

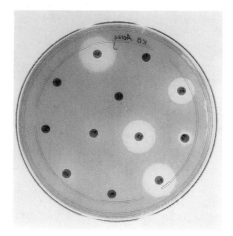

Figure 29.1. The disk-diffusion method for determining antibiotic susceptibility. Bacteria were uniformly seeded on the surface of a nutrient agar plate, and filter paper disks containing different antibiotics were placed at intervals over the surface. After incubation, susceptibility to some of the antibiotics is indicated by clear areas around the disks. The diameter of the clear area depends on the extent of diffusion of the drug throughout the agar. Resistance to other antibiotics is indicated by growth (turbidity) up to the edge of the disks.

29.1). This **disk-diffusion method** is not, however, a quantitative technique, because many factors influence the diffusion of the drug. Quantitative techniques use of dilutions of the drug in liquid media and provide an estimate of the **minimum inhibitory concentration (MIC)**.

STATIC VERSUS CIDAL DRUGS

The **minimum inhibitory concentration (MIC)** tells us the **bacteriostatic** concentration of a drug but not the **bactericidal** one. The two are not usually the same; most agents that are bactericidal are bacteriostatic at lower concentrations. The **minimum bactericidal concentration** or **MBC** is determined by subculturing the tubes that have no visible growth into antibiotic-free media (which allows replication of bacteria whose growth had been inhibited but which are still alive.) This is a time-consuming technique with some technical problems. It may, however, yield important information because bactericidal and bacteriostatic drugs are not always equally effective. For example, in patients with endocarditis and meningitis, the outcome with bactericidal drugs is frequently more satisfactory. Bactericidal drugs tend to be superior in immunocompromised patients, especially in those who are neutropenic.

MULTIPLE DRUG THERAPY

The use of combinations of antibiotics (usually two drugs) has evoked comments of "reckless poly-pharmacy," but is clearly needed in a number of clinical situations. As discussed in Chapter 5, when drugs are combined, there are three main possible results:

- **Synergism**, where the two in combination work better than one. An example is the use of trimethoprim and sulfamethoxazole for *E. coli* and *Shigella* enteric infections. The two drugs work on folate metabolism, but inhibit different steps (Chapter 5). Synergistic action may also be indirect, for example, by one drug preventing the inactivation of another, as in the case of inhibition of β-lactamases by clavulanic acid.

- **Antagonism**, an undesirable effect that may lead to treatment failure. An example is the combination of penicillin and any of a number of protein-synthesis inhibitors (chloramphenicol, tetracycline) for the treatment of pneumococcal meningitis. The fatality rate among patients treated with the drug combination has been shown to be significantly higher than with penicillin alone. For reasons unknown, antagonism that can be readily demonstrated between two drugs in vitro often fails to be manifested with the same pair of drugs in clinical situations.

- **Indifference**, in which case each drug acts independently of the other.

There are various indications for combined therapy, e.g.:

- To prevent the emergence of resistant organisms, e.g., in tuberculosis, where this has proven particularly effective;

- To treat polymicrobial infections such as intra-abdominal abscesses, where each organism may be susceptible to different drugs;

- As initial empiric therapy to "cover" multiple potential pathogens.

In other instances, the reason for multiple therapy may be more subtle. For instance, the use of several drugs may allow a lower dosage of each one, which may avoid problems of toxicity. It may also necessary to achieve drug synergy for the treatment of severe, particularly recalcitrant infections, such as endocarditis or bacteremia in a granulocytopenic patient.

Local Factors and Pharmacokinetics

In the early steps of many infections, tissue inflammation changes the environment in which an antibiotic is to work. If the infection is not controlled, cell death and tissue necrosis change conditions even further. In an abscess caused by staphylococci or a mixed anaerobic-aerobic flora, the environment will become anaerobic and the pH may drop to as low as 5.5. Antibiotics must be selected for their ability to function under these conditions. As shown in Table 29.1, the function of aminoglycosides is diminished at low pH or in the presence of a high concentration of divalent cation

The pharmacokinetic factors that should be considered in the choice of drugs include (a) absorption, (b) distribution in tissues, and (c) excretion. The **absorption** profile of a drug dictates its route of administration. The most convenient route is usually by mouth, and is used with highly absorbable antibiotics such as the quinolones or chloramphenicol. Many antibiotics, such as vancomycin, the aminoglycosides and newer β-lactams, are not absorbed via the gastrointestinal tract and must be given by parenteral injection. A major exception to this rule is the use of nonabsorbable antibiotics to treat infections limited to the gastrointestinal tract, for example, oral vancomycin to treat *Clostridium difficile*-induced diarrhea or colitis. Also, drugs cannot be given orally if the patient is vomiting or in shock because absorption becomes unreliable.

Distribution of drugs takes place via the circulation and is followed by entry into tissues by passive diffusion. The diffusion and polarity properties of antibiotics are relevant here, as they are with all drugs. Some antibiotics bind to plasma proteins, which has a good and a bad side. On the one hand, this limits the amount of unbound drug that is available for diffusion; on the other hand, the drug remains available for a much longer time.

The **barriers that must be crossed by the drug** are a vital consideration. Drugs that cross the blood-brain barrier most readily are nonpolar at neutral pH. This is critically important because of the seriousness of infections of the central nervous system (CNS). Note, however, that the permeability properties of the blood-brain barrier may become modified during infection. Two other organs with impor-

Table 29.1. Physicochemical Conditions That Affect the Activity of Antimicrobial Agents

	Decrease	Increase
Low pH	Aminoglycosides Some β-lactams	Tetracycline Chloramphenicol (porin changes) Erythromycin
Low redox potential	Aminoglycosides	Metronidazole
High divalent cation Concentration	Aminoglycosides Tetracycline (Ca^{++})	

tant barriers are the eye and the prostate, and infections at each of these sites require careful selection of drugs. Infections of the interior of the eye may require direct injection of drugs into the tissue. Similar considerations regarding the placental barrier are discussed in Chapter 68. Some drugs can efficiently penetrate into host cells, a property that may be important in the treatment of intracellular infections, such as those caused by *Chlamydia* or *Legionella*. Erythromycin and rifampin are examples of drugs that have these property.

Lastly, consideration must be given to the speed of **excretion** of the drug. Most drugs are excreted by the kidney. Certain drugs (e.g., chloramphenicol, erythromycin, lincomycin) are excreted by the liver via the biliary tree. Some of the newer cephalosporins are excreted via both liver and kidneys. This pattern of excretion can be used to advantage in infections of the urinary tract or the biliary tree. However, the status of renal or hepatic function must be taken into account because an effective drug level may only be reached if the excretion mechanisms are working properly.

Antibiotic Toxicity

Antibiotics, like all drugs, have toxic side effects. Toxicity is sometimes so severe as to limit the general usefulness of some of them. For example, chloramphenicol is associated with cases of fatal aplastic anemia, and is used only in life-threatening infections, such as meningitis with ampicillin-resistant *Haemophilus influenzae*. As with all drugs, antibiotic toxicity is generally dose dependent, although unexpected idiosyncratic reactions may occur. The main types of toxic manifestations discussed below represent an overview of the subject. Practicing physicians need more detailed information and must constantly update it.

ALLERGY

Antimicrobial agents may be recognized as foreign substances by the immune system, resulting in sensitization of some individuals. The most common antibacterial drugs associated with severe allergic reactions are the penicillins, cephalosporins, and sulfonamides. A likely reason why penicillins lead this list is that they readily bind to proteins and function as haptens to elicit IgE antibody responses. The most severe reactions result in immediate hypersensitive responses—hives, angioneurotic edema, and anaphylactic shock. These complications may be fatal. Mild to fairly severe allergic reactions range from rash, urticaria (hives), lymphadenopathy, asthma, and fever. In some cases, fever may confuse the clinical picture because it may be attributed to the infection and not to the drug. Previous history of drug sensitivity often dictates the choice of other agents. If a history of allergy is questionable, the patient may be skin tested with the drug in question.

OTHER SYSTEMIC REACTIONS

All major organs of the body may be affected by toxicity from antibiotics. The most frequent reactions involve the **gastrointestinal tract**, ranging in extremes from mild distaste to perforation of the colon. The most common reactions are gastrointestinal distress and diarrhea, which often require that the drug be discontinued. These manifestations are often due to a direct stimulatory effect of the drugs on the sympathetic nervous system. However, diarrhea may be due to changes in the intestinal flora, which can be more troublesome. This form of toxicity usually occurs late in the course of treatment and may be manifested only after treatment is stopped. About one-third of the cases of antibiotic-associated diarrhea are due to the overgrowth of *C. difficile* (Chapter 21). The spectrum of diseases caused by this organism ranges from a trivial and self-limiting diarrhea to a severe and life-threatening pseudomembranous colitis.

The **liver** is the major site of drug metabolism and is frequently affected. Many drugs induce mild alterations of function of the hepatic parenchyma, usually manifested by an increase in the serum level of certain transaminases. Some drugs affect biliary excretion. Most of these manifestations are mild and reversible, although cases of liver failure have been reported in pregnant women treated with tetracycline.

The **kidney** is also a frequent site of adverse reactions, resulting in decreased renal function. These are caused by three general mechanisms:

1. Immunological damage to the glomeruli, blocking filtration;

2. Damage to the tubules;

3. Obstruction of the collecting system by crystals of the drug.

This is an important problem because many drugs are excreted via the urinary tract. Unrecognized decrease in renal function may result not only in ineffective levels in the urine but also in toxic serum levels of the drug. The aminoglycosides are the most important class of drugs that cause these side effects. They also cause eighth cranial nerve toxicity (deafness and imbalance). The frequency of these toxic reactions is so high that it requires frequent monitoring of renal function and of the blood levels of the drug.

Other organs that are sometimes affected by antimicrobial agents include the skin, which may be affected by allergic reactions or, more seriously, by exfoliative dermatitis and a disease known as the Stevens-Johnson syndrome that leads to the formation of bullae, large vesicles on the skin, and inflammation of the eyes and mucous membranes. The **hemopoietic system** may also be adversely affected, leading to decreased production of red and white blood cells in the bone marrow. Furthermore, peripheral red and white blood cells may become immunologically sensitized, resulting in their hemolysis or sequestration by fixed macrophages. Also affected at times are the circulatory system, the CNS, the musculoskeletal system, and the respiratory tract. Most of these manifestations are specific to individual drugs. The information about them is made available to physicians in reference manuals published periodically, which should be consulted before prescribing medication.

INTERACTIONS WITH NONANTIMICROBIAL DRUGS

Antimicrobial drugs sometimes interact with other medications that a patient may be taking. The drugs may interact directly or by affecting an enzyme that influences their pharmacology. The drugs most commonly affected are anticoagulants and anticonvulsants. An example follows:

A 67-year-old woman with recurrent thrombophlebitis and pulmonary embolism (blood clots in the lung) had been asymptomatic on an oral anticoagulant (warfarin) that maintained her clotting or prothrombin time at 24 seconds, twice the normal value). She had been recently found to have pulmonary tuberculosis and was placed on isoniazid and rifampin. Several days later, she required hospitalization for recurrence of her thrombophlebitis (inflammation of the veins of the leg). Laboratory evaluation revealed that her prothrombin time was only 2 seconds above normal, despite taking the same amount of warfarin. Her physician then learned that rifampin induces the liver to make a warfarin-inactivating enzyme. Rifampin was stopped and the patient was treated with intravenous heparin to raise her clotting time.

This is an example of the numerous interactions that occurs among drugs. The potential consequences may be catastrophic for the patient, particularly if the therapy affected is life saving, as in the example above. Imagine the problem if the patient had required anticoagulation therapy to prevent clotting on an artificial heart valve. The converse effect, prolongation of clotting time, may also occur with sulfonamides and metronidazole and lead to massive gastrointestinal bleeding. The severity of such complications cannot be overestimated and the message must never be lost on the practitioner.

PROPHYLACTIC USE OF ANTIMICROBIAL DRUGS

Soon after the introduction of effective antibacterial agents in the 1930s, it became clear that they could be used not only to treat infections but to prevent them as well. This is a complex and controversial subject because the use of antibiotics to prevent infections carries risks as well as benefits. Antimicrobial drugs may be used prophylactically for two purposes:

- To prevent the acquisition of exogenous pathogens; an example is the administration of antibiotics to persons who are exposed to patients with menigococcal infections. The meningococcus spreads rapidly among susceptible individuals but antibiotics such as rifampin can usually forestall its clinical manifestations. Likewise, the antituberculous drug, isoniazid, is given to persons who are at high risk of acquiring tuberculosis, such as the children living in the same quarters as a patient with pulmonary tuberculosis (Chapter 23).

- To prevent commensal organisms from spreading from their usual residence to normally sterile sites of the body; the use of antibiotics to prevent postoperative infections in certain high-risk surgical procedures also falls in this category. An example is the administration of antibiotics to patients with with damaged heart valves who are, therefore, at risk of acquiring endocarditis. The drugs are used here to prevent bacteremia and infection of damaged heart valves when such patients undergo dental or major or minor surgical procedures (see Chapter 63).

The risks involved in antibiotic prophylaxis must be clearly understood. They include: allergy or other toxic reactions to the drugs, selection of resistant mutants, and masking or delaying the diagnosis of infections. The following criteria should be fulfilled for the prophylactic use of antibiotics:

- A surgical or medical intervention should carry a significant risk of microbial contamination. This usually occurs when the surgeon crosses a tissue plane that contains a luxuriant microbial flora, such as the colon or the oral cavity. Here the incidence of infection is unacceptably high and the administration of prophylactic antibiotics is necessary. Antibiotic prophylaxis should also be used when the risk of infection is low but its outcome is potentially disastrous; for instance, in surgery for the implantation of heart valve or hip prostheses. It is not indicated when the risk is low and the outcome is trivial, such as in a hernia operation.

- The antibiotics used prophylactically should be directed against the most likely pathogens. Previous studies should suggest which infectious agents are likely to be involved and the drugs to which they are probably susceptible. In operations involving the colon, antibiotics should cover the prime pathogens in fecal material. When surgery crosses the oral mucosa, prophylactic antibiotics with a narrow spectrum are indicated because most of the bacteria in the oral cavity are susceptible to penicillin.

- A suitable concentration of the drug must be achievable at the right time in the relevant tissues. Studies in experimental animals (which have also been confirmed in randomized human studies) have shown that prophylactic antibiotics were of no value if given after surgery was completed. However, they were effective if given just before surgery. It makes sense that a drug should be present in the body when the wound is likely to get contaminated; once the wound is closed, it rapidly becomes impermeable to exogenous bacteria.

- Antimicrobial drugs should be used for a short time to minimize the emergence of drug resistance. Indications for the prophylactic use of antibiotics are expanding with the occurrence of new diseases, new drugs, and new therapeutic methods.

SUGGESTED READING

American Medical Association. Drug evaluation, 6th ed. Chicago: American Medical Association, 1986.

Handbook of antimicrobial therapy. The Medical Letter. Published yearly.

Moellering RC. Principles of anti-infective therapy. In: Mandel GL, Douglas RG, Bennett JE, eds. Principles and practice of infectious diseases, 3rd ed. New York: John Wiley & Sons, 1990.

Reese RR, Betts RF. A practical approach to infectious diseases, 3rd ed. Boston: Little, Brown & Co., 1991:764–1007.

Sande MA, Mandel GL. Antimicrobial agents. General considerations. In: Pharmacological basis of therapeutics, 8th ed. Gilman AG, Goodman LS, Rall TW, Murray F, eds. New York: Macmillan, 1991.

Review of the Main Pathogenic Bacteria

These charts are intended to review the general features of the main human pathogenic bacteria. Included are the organisms of greatest medical relevance.

Many of the bacteria that cause relatively uncommon diseases were not included. Complete this chart as a method of reviewing this subject matter.

Organism	Gram Reaction, Morphology, Other Distinguishing Traits	Common Habitat and Mode of Encounter	Main Pathogenic Mechanism(s)	Typical Disease(s)	Relevant Chapters
Staphylococcus aureus					6, 11, 60, 61, 72
Staphylococcus epidermidis					11, 66
Group A streptococci					12, 60, 63
Other β-hemolytic streptococci					12, 68
α-Hemolytic streptococci					12, 63
Pneumococcus (S. pneumoniae)					13, 56
Meningococcus (Neisseria meningitidis)					14, 58
Gonococcus (N. gonorrhoeae)					14, 65
Haemophilus influenzae					15, 64
Bacteroides sp.					16, 60
Escherichia coli					17, 57, 59, 68, 72
Shigella sp.					18, 57
Klebsiella pneumoniae					17, 56, 66
Proteus sp.					17, 59
Vibrio cholerae					17, 57
Salmonella sp.					18, 57

Organism	Gram Reaction, Morphology, Other Distinguishing Traits	Common Habitat and Mode of Encounter	Main Pathogenic Mechanism(s)	Typical Disease(s)	Relevant Chapters
Pseudomonas aeruginosa					19, 62, 66
Bordetella pertussis					20
Other enterics (Enterobacter, Citrobacter, Serratia, Campylobacter, Yersinia)					17, 57
Helicobacter pylori					17, 57
Clostridium difficile					21
C. botulinum					21
C. tetani					21
C. perfringens and others					21, 72
Legionella pneumophila					22
Mycobacterium tuberculosis and others					28, 67
M. leprae					28
Treponema pallidum					24, 65
Borrelia burgdorferi					25, 77
Chlamydia trachomatis					26, 65
Rickettsia sp.					27
Mycoplasma sp.					28, 56

The following charts refer to pathogenic characteristics of bacteria. Complete these charts as a method of reviewing this subject matter.

Capsulated Bacteria of Medical Importance

Genus and Species			
1.		6.	
2.		7.	
3.		8.	
4.		9.	
5.			

Medically Important Strict Anaerobes

Genus and Species			
1.		6.	
2.		7.	
3.		8.	
4.		9.	
5.		10.	

Typically Pyogenic (pus-producing) Bacteria

Genus and Species			
1.		4.	
2.		5.	
3.		6.	

Major Bacterial Toxins

Genus and Species			
1.		4.	
2.		5.	
3.		6.	

Biology of Viruses

30

Bernard N. Fields

The fundamental difference between viruses and all other infectious agents is in their mechanism of reproduction. Unlike cellular forms of life, viruses do not just divide in half. Virus replication is carried out by the host cell machinery synthesizing multiple copies of the viral genome and viral proteins. These viral constituents assemble spontaneously within the host cell to form progeny virus particles. Viruses have no means to produce energy and contain a few enzymes at most. Thus, viruses are totally dependent on host cells; they are **obligate intracellular parasites**. Viruses are important pathogens of virtually all forms of life, including humans and other animals, plants, fungi, and bacteria. Because they are relatively amenable to study, viruses play a key role as models in molecular biology. A description of viruses that affect bacteria, the **bacteriophages**, can be found in Chapter 4.

Viruses are small, although the largest ones (e.g., the smallpox virus) are just visible with the light microscope and fall within the lower range of size of bacteria (e.g., the mycoplasmas or chlamydiae). Viruses vary in volume over a 1000-fold range and in structure from relatively simple to very complex (Fig. 30.1). The nucleic acid of a virus is either DNA or RNA, **never both**.

STRUCTURE AND CLASSIFICATION OF VIRUSES

A virus particle is known as a **virion** and contains a **core** of either DNA or RNA surrounded by a protein shell. The smallest viral genomes encode three or four proteins; the larger genomes encode more than 50 structural proteins and enzymes. The number of proteins encoded may be greater than predicted from the size of its nucleic acid because of the economic arrangement of some viral genomes; thus, the same stretch of nucleic acid may contain multiple open reading frames and/or overlapping regions that can be transcribed into several distinct mRNAs. The nucleotide sequence of part or all of the genomes of many viruses has been determined.

The viral nucleic acid is surrounded by a **capsid**, a single- or double-protein shell. Together, the nucleic acid and the capsid are referred to as the **nucleocapsid**. Capsids are composed of smaller repetitive subunits (**capsomers**) arranged in symmetric patterns. The repeating subunits of viral proteins self-assemble into mature virions.

Capsomers are arranged in two fundamental patterns of capsid structural symmetry, **icosahedral** and **helical**. Viruses with icosahedral symmetry contain a defined number of structural subunits (20 triangular faces and 12 vertices), whereas this number is not specified in viruses with helical symmetry. Viruses with icosahedral symmetry generally follow simple principles of geometric organization (Fig.

Figure 30.1. Examples of viral morphology.

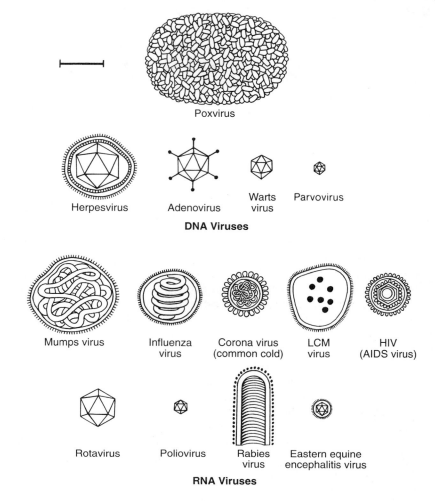

Poxvirus

Herpesvirus   Adenovirus   Warts virus   Parvovirus

DNA Viruses

Mumps virus   Influenza virus   Corona virus (common cold)   LCM virus   HIV (AIDS virus)

Rotavirus   Poliovirus   Rabies virus   Eastern equine encephalitis virus

RNA Viruses

30.2). In these viruses, the nucleic acid is usually in a condensed form and is geometrically independent of the surrounding capsid structure. Retroviruses such as HIV, the virus that causes AIDS, have a mixed symmetry, icosahedral in the capsid, and helical in the nucleic acid core. Some of the largest viruses, such as that of smallpox, have more complex structural patterns.

Human viruses with helical symmetry invariably have RNA genomes. A general feature of these viruses is that the protein subunits of the capsid are bound in a regular, periodic fashion along the RNA. This close interaction is in sharp contrast to the loose interactions in viruses with icosahedral symmetry and imposes further constraints for viral assembly.

Many viruses possess an **envelope** that surrounds the nucleocapsid (Fig. 30.2). The viral envelope is composed of virus-specific proteins plus lipids and carbohydrates derived from host cell membranes. Different viruses utilize different types of host cell membranes for budding, e.g., the nuclear membrane, endoplasmic reticulum, Golgi apparatus, or cytoplasmic membrane. The host cell components are added during final stages of assembly as the virus buds through one of these membranes. In some cases, the virus-specific envelope proteins include a **matrix protein** (**M protein**) that lines the inner side of the envelope and is in contact with the nucleocapsid (Fig. 30.3). Virus-specific glycoproteins may protrude from the outer surface of the envelope forming structures known as **spikes**. Certain viruses contain

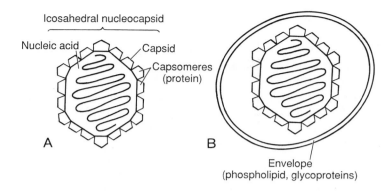

Icosahedral nucleocapsid

Nucleic acid

Capsid

Capsomeres (protein)

A

B

Envelope
(phospholipid, glycoproteins)

Figure 30.2. Basic viral forms. *A.* Icosahedral, nonenveloped; *B.* icosahedral, enveloped; *C.* helical, nonenveloped; *D.* helical, enveloped.

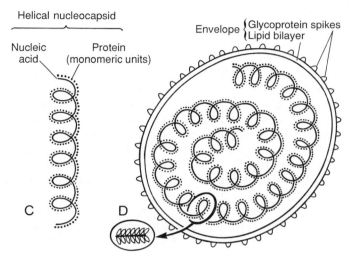

Helical nucleocapsid

Nucleic acid

Protein (monomeric units)

Envelope { Glycoprotein spikes
Lipid bilayer

C

D

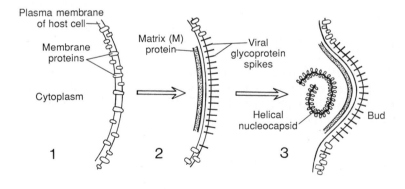

Plasma membrane of host cell

Membrane proteins

Cytoplasm

Matrix (M) protein

Viral glycoprotein spikes

Helical nucleocapsid

Bud

1

2

3

Figure 30.3. Viral budding through the cytoplasmic membrane.

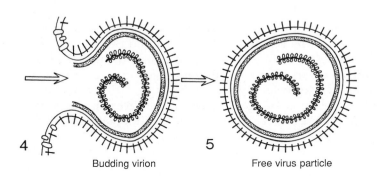

4

Budding virion

5

Free virus particle

surface glycoproteins that agglutinate red blood cells (**hemagglutinins**) by binding to receptors on the red cell surface.

Many viruses possess **virion-associated enzymatic activities**, depending on the strategy used for replication of their nucleic acid. The viral enzyme that make virus-specific mRNA, which is required for the synthesis of all viral proteins, may be an RNA-dependent RNA polymerase (**RNA transcriptases**) or a DNA-dependent RNA polymerase. Retroviruses contain an RNA-dependent DNA polymerase known as **reverse transcriptase**. Some viruses have mRNA processing enzymes such as "capping enzymes" that modify viral mRNAs at their 5′ end by adding a methylguanosine cap, or enzymes that polyadenylate the 3′ end of viral mRNA. Additional virally encoded enzymes include protein kinases, nucleoside triphosphate phosphatases, endonucleases, and RNAses. Certain viruses, such as that of influenza, have enzymes on their surface (e.g., neuraminidase) that are involved in the attachment to host cells.

The principal viruses that cause disease in humans belong to about a dozen different genera comprising hundreds of species. Each species often contains a number of individual strains that differ in virulence and antigenic properties (serotypes). Viruses are classified using a combination of genetic, physicochemical, and biological factors. These include the type and structure of the viral nucleic acid (single- or double-stranded RNA or DNA), the nature of virion ultrastructure (including size, type of capsid symmetry, and the presence or absence of an envelope), as well as their strategy for genome replication (Table 30.1 and Fig. 30.4). In many instances, electron-micrographic studies provide sufficient information to identify both the family and the genus to which a virus belongs. Subdivisions within these major taxonomic groups are usually based on immunological, cytopathological, pathogenetic, or epidemiological features. The present-day classification of viruses will probably be revised as increased knowledge of their nucleic acid sequences will permit reassessment of the degree of their genetic relatedness.

REPLICATION

The steps in viral replication include infection of a susceptible cell, reproduction of the nucleic acid and proteins, and assembly and release of infectious progeny. The diversity among viruses in terms of structure and type of genomic material is reflected in a large number of replicative strategies.

Attachment and Penetration

The first stage of viral infection of target cells begins with adsorption of the virus particles and ends when the first infectious progeny virus are formed. This stage is called the **eclipse period**, because during this period there is a dramatic drop in the amount of infectious virus that can be recovered from disrupted cells.

The first step in the attachment of viruses to host cells is **adsorption**, an initially reversible step resulting from random collisions between virions and target cells. Approximately 1 in 10^3–10^4 of such collisions leads to tighter binding. Attachment requires appropriate ionic and pH conditions but is largely temperature independent and does not require energy. The next step involves the specific binding of viral proteins to receptors on the cell surface. The virion structure that mediates cell attachment has been identified for a number of viruses.

Table 30.1. Classification of Viruses

Family	Example	Nucleic Acid Polarity or Structure[a]	Genome Size, Kilobases or Kilobase Pairs	Envelope	Capsid Symmetry
RNA Viruses					
Single-stranded					
Picornaviridae	Poliovirus	(+)	7.2–8.4	No	I
Togaviridae	Rubella virus	(+)	12	Yes	I
Flaviviridae	Yellow fever virus	(+)	10	Yes	I
Coronaviridae	Coronaviruses	(+)	16–21	Yes	H
Rhabdoviridae	Rabies virus	(−)	13–16	Yes	H
Paramyxoviridae	Measles virus	(−)	16–20	Yes	H
Orthomyxoviridae	Influenza viruses	(−) 8 segments[b]	14	Yes	H
Bunyaviridae	California encephalitis virus	Three circular (−) segments	13–21	Yes	H
Arenaviridae	Lymphocytic choriomeningitis virus	Two circular (−)	10–14	Yes	H
Retroviridae	HIV	Two identical molecules (+)	3–9	Yes	I-capsid H-nucleocapsid (probable)
Double-stranded					
Reoviridae	Rotaviruses	10–12 segments[c]	16–27	No	I
DNA Viruses					
Single-stranded					
Parvoviridae	Human parvovirus B-19	ss (+) or (−)	5	No	I
Mixed strandedness					
Hepadnaviridae	Hepatitis B	ds with ss portions	3	Yes	Unk
Double-stranded					
Papovaviridae	JC virus	Circular	8	No	I
Adenoviridae	Human adenoviruses		36–38	No	I
Herpesviridae	Herpes simplex virus		120–220	Yes	I
Poxviridae	Vaccinia	Covalently closed ends	130–280	Yes	Complex

[a]NOTE: (+) message sense; (−) anti-message sense; I = icosahedral; H = helical; Unk = unknown.
[b]Influenza C = 7 segments
[c]Reovirus, orbivirus =10 segments; rotavirus = 11 segments; Colorado tick fever = 12 segments.

For enveloped viruses, the viral attachment protein is typically one of the spikes inserted on the outer surface of the viral envelope, such as the hemagglutinin of influenza viruses. Some enveloped viruses, such as the herpesviruses and vaccinia, have more than one type of cell attachment protein. In nonenveloped viruses, surface peptides often function as the viral attachment proteins.

The nature of the cellular receptors for animal viruses has been determined in only a few specific cases. Even when the specific receptor is still unknown, it has been possible to identify "families" or classes of cellular receptors using competition binding studies. Viruses of the same species, but different serotypes, may compete for the same receptors of the same class (e.g., poliovirus serotypes 1, 2, 3) or different classes (e.g., human rhinovirus 2 and 14). Viruses from different families may also compete for the same class of receptor. Binding studies suggest that there are generally 10^4–10^6 viral binding sites (receptors) per cell.

Once adsorption has occurred, the entire virion or a substructure containing the viral genome and virion polymerases must be translocated across the plasma membrane of the cell. The rate of penetration depends on the nature of the virus, the type of cells being infected, and environmental factors such as temperature. Some

Figure 30.4. The main groups of human viruses. This is a practical representation and does not represent phylogenetic relationships.

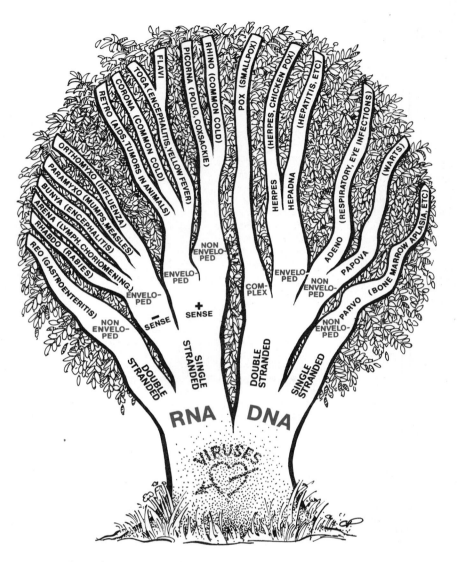

nonenveloped viruses such as poliovirus undergo a process of receptor-mediated endocytosis (**viropexis**) and appear in the cytoplasm within endocytic vesicles (endosomes). Other nonenveloped viruses are thought to be capable of crossing the plasma membrane directly and appear free in the cytoplasm without entering endocytic vesicles.

Enveloped viruses utilize at least two strategies for penetration. The first is exemplified by Semliki Forest virus. This virus binds to specific cell-surface receptors that then aggregate at distinct sites on the plasma membrane (**coated pits**) and are internalized by receptor-mediated endocytosis. The virions subsequently appear inside clathrin-coated vesicles within the cell cytoplasm (Fig. 30.5). The viral envelope then fuses with the endosomal membrane to cause the release of the viral nucleocapsid into the cytoplasm. A second mechanism for penetration of enveloped viruses occurs with paramyxoviruses (e.g., Sendai virus), where the viral envelope fuses directly with the cell plasma membrane and the viral nucleocapsid is discharged free into the cytoplasm.

The next step in viral replication is **uncoating**, the process of removing or disaggregating part or all of the viral capsid to make the viral genome accessible to the transcription and translation machinery. In many cases, penetration and uncoating are part of a single process.

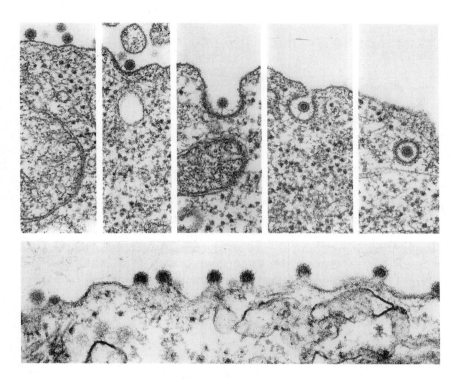

Figure 30.5. Penetration and release of an enveloped virus (Semliki Forest virus). The *top five* thin sections show stages in adherence of the virus to clathrin-coated pits and the gradual invagination of the membrane carrying the virus into the interior within a clathrin-coated endosome. The *bottom section* shows the release of the virus by budding from the membrane.

Certain viruses undergo an alteration in capsid structure leading to a loss of an internal protein as they are translocated across the plasma membrane. Structural alterations associated with loss of this protein may facilitate entry of the viral nucleic acid into the cytoplasm.

Nonenveloped viruses may induce fusion of lysosomes with the endosome and have their capsids removed by lysosomal enzymes. In the case of certain reoviruses, endosomal proteases sequentially remove the outer capsid proteins to produce a "subviral particle." In the process, the viral transcriptase becomes activated. Uncoating of poxviruses, such as vaccinia, takes place in two steps: first, the degradation of the outer protein coat by endosomal enzymes, followed by the degradation of the remaining nucleocapsid, liberating the viral DNA.

Macromolecular Synthesis

The first step in the synthesis of all viral macromolecules requires the translation of viral messenger RNA (mRNA) into virus-specific proteins. How is viral mRNA made? Viruses that contain double-stranded DNA can synthesize mRNA by the same process as the cell, using a DNA-dependent RNA polymerase. RNA viruses, however, must make their mRNA from RNA, which involves a different mechanism. A number of strategies have evolved to synthesize viral mRNA by transcription of viral genomes as well as for the translation of this mRNA into protein (Fig. 30.6). These variations are described in detail in chapters on individual virus groups (Chapters 31–42).

SINGLE-STRANDED POSITIVE POLARITY RNA VIRUSES

The simplest strategy is for the nucleic acid of the virion to function directly as mRNA. Examples of viruses that use this approach are the picornaviruses (e.g., poliovirus) and togaviruses (e.g., Eastern equine encephalitis virus), which contain single-stranded RNA of the same sequence complementarity as mRNA. By convention, the genome of such viruses is said to have **positive** (+) strand polarity. Upon entry in

Figure 30.6. The basic viral strategies for making messenger RNA.

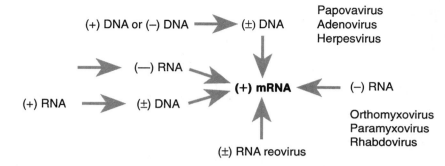

the host cell, the mRNA is translated to produce the various viral proteins. In the case of certain viruses, such as poliovirus, cellular ribosomes bind to the mRNA to form large polyribosomes that produce a single large polyprotein. This large precursor molecule is then cleaved in a series of proteolytic steps to produce the proteins of the core and the capsid. Note that this unusual arrangement results in the synthesis of equimolar amounts of each viral protein.

In these viruses, how is the viral RNA synthesized? Here, a **virally encoded RNA polymerase**, known as **transcriptase**, synthesizes a complementary (−) **strand RNA** using the genomic RNA as template. In turn, the newly synthesized RNA serves as template for the synthesis of more genomic (+) strand RNA. The new genomic RNAs may serve either as mRNAs or as precursor RNAs for progeny virions.

SINGLE-STRANDED NEGATIVE POLARITY RNA VIRUSES

RNA viruses whose genome consists of (−) single-stranded RNA must use a different strategy to make mRNA. Here the genome is replicated via a (+) single-stranded RNA intermediate, which then serves as a template to synthesize more (−) single-stranded genomic RNA. Mammalian cells do not possess enzymes that use RNA as templates for making RNA. Viruses that use this strategy must, therefore, contain an RNA transcriptase in their virion, which is introduced into the host cells during infection.

Some (−) single-stranded RNA viruses (e.g., influenza viruses) have **segmented genomes** consisting of more than one RNA molecule. RNA replication results in a unique mRNA for each viral protein rather than a single large polycistronic mRNA molecule. The presence of multiple mRNAs allows each to be regulated independently, thus allowing for the production of different amounts of individual virally encoded proteins. Other viruses have evolved a particularly economic way of using a given amount of genetic information; a single region of genomic RNA may have multiple reading frames, each of which is transcribed into unique mRNAs, which, in turn, are translated into distinct proteins.

DOUBLE-STRANDED RNA VIRUSES

Like with DNA, the information contained in double-stranded RNA must first be copied into a (+) single strand of RNA to act as mRNA. Because of its double-strandedness, the virion RNA cannot function directly as mRNA (even though it contains a [+] strand). Viruses with double-stranded RNA genomes, such as the reoviruses, contain a virally encoded RNA-transcriptase that transcribes (+) single-stranded RNAs from the (−) strands of the viral genome. The double-stranded RNA genome is always found in segments, each of which results in a unique mRNA.

RNA VIRUSES THAT REPLICATE VIA A DNA INTERMEDIATE

The retroviruses (such as **HIV**) contain (+) single-stranded RNA but utilize the unique replicative strategy of using a DNA intermediate. Viral (+) single-stranded RNA serves as a template for a virion RNA-dependent DNA polymerase (**reverse transcriptase**). The DNA is then integrated into chromosomal DNA in the host cell nucleus where it may reside for a long time. In this regard, integrated retroviruses resemble the prophages of lysogenic bacteriophages. Transcription of the integrated viral DNA, just like the chromosomal DNA, is carried out by the host cell RNA polymerases.

DNA VIRUSES

In general, DNA-containing viruses make mRNA using strategies similar to those of eukaryotic cells. In cells infected with papovaviruses (e.g., wart viruses), adenoviruses, and herpesviruses, transcription of viral DNA into mRNA occurs in the nucleus of the host cell and depends on host cell enzymes. In the case of papovaviruses (e.g., an oncogenic monkey virus called SV40), the initial proteins produced after infection are the **T antigens** (**tumor antigens**). Because they are the first viral proteins to be synthesized, T antigens are called **early proteins**. Some of the T antigens enhance DNA replication by binding near the site of initiation of DNA replication. Subsequently, mRNAs encoding the capsid polypeptides (**late proteins**) are transcribed. In SV40 virus, the early mRNAs are all derived from only one of the two viral DNA strands (referred to as the **E** or **Early** strand), and the late mRNAs from the other (the **L** or **Late** strand). Adenoviruses also have early and late genes, but they are intermixed along both strands of the viral DNA rather than on separate strands.

The individual mRNAs for both early and late proteins often correspond to sequences of viral DNA (**exons**) separated by spacer sequences, the **introns**. The products of transcription are RNA molecules whose sequence is the same as that of the DNA. These immature mRNA molecules are then extensively cut and spliced, which removes the intervening introns. In many cases, mRNAs are synthesized from overlapping regions of the viral DNA. This type of redundancy reduces the amount of viral DNA needed to encode a certain number of viral proteins and is another example of genetic economy among the viruses.

Poxviruses are the most structurally intricate of the animal viruses, and their replicative cycle is correspondingly complex (see Chapter 42 for details). All of the initial steps of transcription and translation occur in the host cell cytoplasm; hence, these viruses cannot use the host RNA polymerases, which are localized in the nucleus. Consequently, poxviruses carry their own DNA-dependent RNA polymerase to initiate transcription. One of the virus-encoded early proteins is responsible for a second stage of uncoating that is necessary to make the viral DNA fully accessible for transcription and replication. Replication, transcription, and later viral assembly all occur in virus-initiated "factories" within the host cell cytoplasm. Early proteins include a number of enzymes (e.g., a DNA polymerase and a thymidine kinase), as well as some structural proteins. As infection proceeds, DNA replication begins, the synthesis of the early nonstructural proteins ceases, and the synthesis of late proteins takes place. Many of the late proteins are structural proteins but others include enzymes and proteins that appear to play a role in viral assembly.

Assembly of Progeny Virions and Release from the Host Cell

Once replication of the viral genome and synthesis of the viral proteins have been completed, intact virions can be assembled and released from the host cells. Assembly of the nonenveloped viruses and the nucleocapsid of enveloped viruses often proceed in a crystallization-like fashion, which depends on the self-assembly of viral capsomers. Once the capsid is formed, it is filled with the genomic nucleic acid of the virus to make a viable virion (Fig. 30.7).

In most cases, nonenveloped virions are released when the cell lyses. Events leading to cell disruption include inhibition of the synthesis of host cell macromolecules and lipids, disorganization of the host cell cytoskeleton, and alteration of host cell membrane structure. Membrane disruption may result in increased cell permeability and the release of proteolytic enzymes from lysosomes. The failure to replenish energy-rich substrate molecules inhibits the function of ion transport pumps and disturbs transport of essential nutrients and cellular waste products.

Enveloped viruses are typically released from infected cells by budding. This process may or may not be lethal to the cell. In all cases, virus-specified proteins are inserted into host cell membranes in a fashion that restructures the membrane by displacing some of its normal protein components. Viral capsids may then bind to virus-specified matrix proteins that line the cytoplasmic side of these altered patches

Figure 30.7. Adenovirus replication in cell culture.

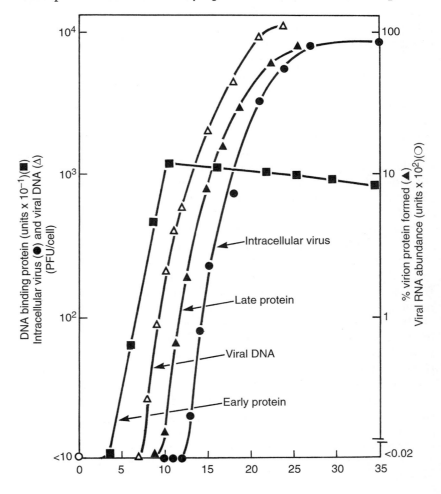

of membrane (Fig. 30.3). In the case of the smallest enveloped viruses, the togaviruses, the capsids bind directly to intracytoplasmic domains of viral proteins inserted in the host cell membrane, rather than to matrix proteins.

Defective Viruses, Virioids, and Prions

Certain viruses cause disease even though they cannot replicate autonomously. To replicate, such **defective viruses** (e.g., the delta hepatitis virus) require coinfection with a "helper" virus. Infection with the delta virus is dependent on a coincident infection with hepatitis B virus (**HBV**) and does not occur in its absence. Coinfection with HBV and the delta virus frequently results in fulminant hepatitis, apparently by allowing the derepression and increased multiplication of HBV. Conversely, the defective adeno-associated human parvoviruses do not appear to alter significantly the disease produced by the helper adenovirus alone. Defective viruses can only be detected by searching for their antigens, using specific nucleic acid probes, or inducing their replication by the presence of helper viruses.

Recent years have seen the discovery of new classes of infectious agents, **virioids** and **prions**. These are the smallest known agents of disease. Virioids cause disease in plants and consist of naked, covalently closed circles of single-stranded RNA, less than 300–400 nucleotides in length. In spite of this very small size, virioids replicate without the help of viruses. How they replicate and cause disease remains unknown.

Prions are thought to differ from both viruses and virioids in that they may consist of proteins and not nucleic acids. Theoretically, the prion proteins are encoded by cellular genes and function as regulatory signals. There is evidence to suggest that the neurodegenerative diseases, Creutzfeld-Jakob disease and kuru, may be caused by prions. These diseases, as well as the so-called slow virus diseases (Chapter 33), remind us to be ready for further surprises.

PATHOBIOLOGY OF VIRAL DISEASES

The signs and symptoms of disease are the culmination of a series of interactions between the virus and the host. After encountering the host, a virus must be able to enter it, undergo a period of primary replication, and then spread to its final target tissue. Once a virus reaches its target organs, it must then infect and successfully replicate in a susceptible population of host cells.

When a cell is infected by a virus there are three possible consequences (Fig. 30.8).

1. In a **lytic infection**, the virus undergoes multiple rounds of replication. This results in the death of the host cell, which has acted as a factory for virus production. The number of viral particles produced in a single cell in a lytic infection vary from a few with some viruses to thousands with others. Examples of lytic infections are those caused by polio or influenza viruses.

2. At the opposite end of the spectrum is a **latent infection**, which does not result in the immediate production of progeny virus. Latent infections are usually caused by DNA viruses or retroviruses, and are a property of DNA persistence either as an extrachromosomal element (as with some herpesviruses), or integrated into the

Figure 30.8. The three types of viral infections.

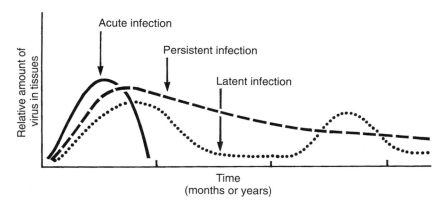

host cell (as with the retroviruses). During cell growth, the genome of the virus is replicated along with the chromosomes of the host cell. An example of latent infection is that produced by herpes simplex virus type 1, which upon **reactivation** of the virus, results in fever blisters and zoster. In the cases of a retrovirus, latent infections may result in **transformation** of the cell, a cancerous state.

3. **A persistent infection** differs from a lytic and a latent infection in that virus particles continue to be shed after the period of acute illness has passed. It is marked by a slow release of virus particles without death of the host cell and any other overt injury. This kind of infection is usually associated with RNA viruses. The amount of virus produced is usually lower than in lytic infections and the viruses are often altered ("mutated") from the original ones. Persistent infections are associated with a defective host immunity that is too weak to rid the body of the infection. Often, persistent infections do not result in overt disease. Hepatitis B virus causes a persistent infection in the liver that may lead to chronic hepatitis and even liver cancer.

Encounter and Entry

Transmission of a virus from an infected host to a susceptible individual may take many forms. Human-to-human transmission occurs from an acutely ill individual, from a chronic carrier, or from mother to fetus. Transmission may be via the environment or by direct contact, such as sexual contact (as in AIDS). Environmental spread may involve fecal-oral contamination (as in the diarrhea caused by rotaviruses), aerosols (as in chickenpox), or direct inoculation via infected needles or blood products (as in hepatitis B). Animal-to-human transmission usually takes place via the bite of the diseased animal itself (as in rabies) or via the bite of an insect vector (as in viral encephalitis).

For most viruses it is not known how many particles are required to initiate a respiratory infection. For influenza A, adenovirus, or coxsackie A21 virus, as few as 10 particles may suffice. In other cases, the number is likely to be considerably larger.

RESPIRATORY ROUTE

Respiratory infection takes place by means of aerosol droplets, nasal secretions, or saliva. Respiratory aerosolization usually occurs via coughing or sneezing. A sneeze may generate up to 2 million aerosol particles and a cough up to 90,000. The fate of these particles depends both on ambient environmental conditions (e.g., humidity, wind currents) and particle size. Small particles remain air-borne longer and may escape the filtering action of the nose, which traps particles larger than 6 μm in diameter. The number of viral particles aerosolized sometimes varies even for different strains of the same virus. Aerosolization is not the only possible route of respiratory transmission. Epstein-Barr virus (**EBV**) is typically spread by saliva during kissing. A critical pathway of spread for rhinoviruses that cause the common cold, is, surprisingly, not via aerosols but from hands to eyes, nose, or mouth—a cycle that can be interrupted by hand washing.

Entry via the respiratory route requires that the virus overcome a formidable series of host defenses. In the lung, immunological defenses include secretory IgA, natural killer (**NK**) cells, and macrophages. Nonspecific glycoprotein viral inhibitors are present in tracheobronchial mucus. Ciliated respiratory epithelial cells continually move mucus away from the lower respiratory tract.

GASTROINTESTINAL ROUTE

Gastrointestinal transmission occurs when viruses that are shed in feces contaminate food or water that are then ingested by a susceptible individual ("fecal-oral spread"). Stool-tainted hands, resulting from poor personal hygiene, provide another vehicle of spread for enteric viruses. The high incidence of enteric virus infections in infant day care centers and institutions for the mentally impaired reflects the difficulty of maintaining hygiene in these settings.

Gastrointestinal transmission is limited to those viruses that can withstand the conditions found in this system. The harsh acidic environment of the stomach inactivates acid-labile viruses such as rhinoviruses. Bile salts, present in the lumen of the small intestine, can destroy the lipid envelope of many viruses and may account for the fact that entry via the gastrointestinal route is limited largely to nonenveloped viruses. Proteolytic enzymes and secretory IgA also contribute to host antiviral defenses in the gastrointestinal tract. Certain proteolysis-resistant viral capsid proteins allow some viruses to withstand digestion in the gut.

For some enteric viruses, passage across the mucosal barrier of the gut is mediated by a specific population of cells overlying Peyer's patches known as **microfold (M)** cells. These cells, and perhaps their analogs in bronchial lymphoid tissue, appear to facilitate transport of some viruses, including reoviruses and possibly enteroviruses, across the small intestine.

TRANSCUTANEOUS ROUTE

The stratum corneum of the skin provides both a physical and a biological barrier against the entry of viruses. Some viruses overcome the skin barrier by direct inoculation via insect or animal bites or via mechanical devices such as needles.

In viral diseases where the vector is an insect or an infected animal, the disease cycle may be quite complex. In dengue fever, there is a continuing cycle between humans and infected mosquitoes. Dengue viruses multiply in the gut of a mosquito, spread to its salivary glands, and are injected into a human during the mosquito's blood meal. The infected person develops a high-titer level of viruses in the bloodstream (**viremia**), which is sufficient to allow the viruses to be picked up by an uninfected mosquito during biting. In other arthropod-borne virus infections, the human being is a "dead-end host" because the degree of viremia in infected individuals is insufficient to transmit the infection to a new group of insect vectors. Examples of this type of cycle are found in the togaviruses, such as various equine encephalitis viruses. The normal animal reservoirs for these *ar*thropod-*bo*rne viruses (**arbo**viruses) include small birds and mammals. Horses, like humans, are usually a dead-end host, although in Venezuelan equine encephalitis, horses may be a reservoir of virus.

Some arbovirus infections do not require a viremic vertebrate intermediate host. The virus is passed in transovarian fashion to the progeny of an infected tick or mosquito or by sexual transmission between male and female mosquitoes. Transovarian transmission may allow survival of arthropod viruses through the winter months.

Iatrogenic (physician- or hospital-related) inoculation sometimes allows the entry of a large number of viruses. Hepatitis B virus (HBV), cytomegalovirus (CMV), and human immunodeficiency virus (HIV) may all be present in contaminated blood products used for transfusion. Infected corneal transplants, instruments used in neurosurgical procedures, and pituitary tissues used to prepare growth hormone have been implicated as causes of the Creutzfeldt-Jakob disease. Iatrogenic inoculation may be purposeful and benevolent, as in the case of parenteral vaccination using live attenuated virus (e.g., the measles or Sabin polio vaccines).

SEXUAL ROUTE

Sexual transmission with entry across the genitourinary or rectal mucosa is important for herpes simplex virus type 2 (HSV-2), cytomegalovirus (CMV), hepatitis B virus, and HIV. In many cases, the virus spreads to other organs of the body but, in some, e.g., HSV-2, lesions are often found near the site of entry.

ENDOGENOUS AND EXOGENOUS VIRUSES

Most viral diseases result from exposure to **exogenous** virus. However, in some cases, disease results from the reactivation of an **endogenous** virus, which has been latent within specific host cells. Examples of infections caused by reactivated endogenous viruses include shingles (herpes zoster), progressive multifocal leukoencephalopathy (caused by JC or BK papovaviruses), recurrent labial and genital herpes (herpes simplex), and some types of cytomegalovirus infections.

In the majority of cases, transmission of viral illnesses occurs between members of a susceptible host population (**horizontal spread**). **Vertical spread** of infection occurs when the fetus becomes infected in utero through virus carried in the germ cell line, virus infecting the placenta, or virus in the maternal birth canal. Rubella virus, cytomegalovirus, herpes simplex virus, varicella-zoster virus, and hepatitis B virus can all produce vertically transmitted congenital infections.

Multiplication and Spread

For some viruses, the processes of entry, primary replication, and tissue tropism all occur at the same anatomic site. Examples of this type of viral infection include the upper and lower respiratory infections caused by the rhinoviruses, ortho- and paramyxoviruses; the enteritis caused by rotaviruses; and the dermatological lesions induced by human papillomavirus (warts). In other cases, a virus enters at one site and, to produce disease, must subsequently spread to a distant area, such as the central nervous system (CNS). In such cases, it is useful to distinguish between primary viral multiplication near the entry site and secondary multiplication at the eventual target organ or tissue (Fig. 30.9). Enteroviruses enter via the gastrointestinal tract and spread to the CNS to produce meningitis, encephalitis, and/or poliomyelitis. Measles virus and varicella virus enter the body through the respiratory tract but then spread to produce skin disease (exanthem) and, often, generalized organ involvement. Neural, hematogenous, and lymphatic pathways are all utilized by viruses to spread to target tissues.

A great deal of viral replication may occur before any signs or symptoms of clinical illness are detectable. This **incubation period** varies from a few days (influenza), to weeks (measles, varicella), to months (rabies, hepatitis), to years (slow viruses). Viral infection does not always lead to overt clinical disease. The percentage of those infected who develop overt disease ranges from 100% (rabies, measles) to 0 (**BK, JC** papovaviruses). In many cases, symptomatic disease is less common in children than in adults (e.g., **EBV** mononucleosis, paralytic poliomyelitis, hepatitis A virus infection).

NEURAL SPREAD

Examples of agents that spread via nerves include the rabies virus, herpes simplex virus, chickenpox (varicella-zoster) virus, and the scrapie agent of sheep. The herpes simplex virus apparently enters the nerves via receptors located primarily near synaptic endings rather than on the nerve cell body. Rabies virus accumulates at the motor endplate of the neuromuscular junction (**NMJ**) and may utilize the acetylcholine receptor (**AChR**) or a closely related structure to enter the distal axons of motor neurons. Rabies virus also infects muscle and spreads via motor and sensory nerves to the spinal cord.

The kinetics of neural spread for rabies, herpes simplex, and polio strongly suggest that the agents utilize intraneuronal mechanisms involved in fast axonal transport. The scrapie agent of sheep appears to spread slowly along neural pathways and may be an example of movement via slow axonal transport. Infection of Schwann cells may provide

Figure 30.9. Systemic vs. localized virus infection.

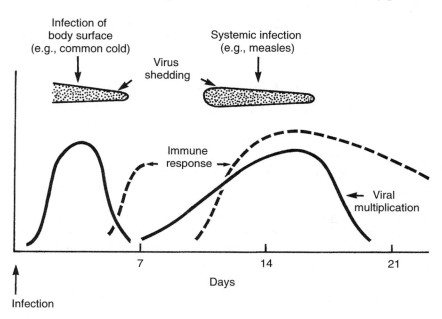

another "neural" pathway to the CNS. Neural spread is important not only for entry into the CNS but also for spread within the CNS and from the CNS to the periphery (as in herpetic infections).

The olfactory pathway represents a special category of neural spread. The rod processes of olfactory receptor cells lie exposed in the olfactory mucosa and are the only place in the body where the nervous system is in direct contact with the environment. Under experimental conditions, intranasal or aerosol inoculations of rabies virus, herpes simplex virus, poliovirus, and some togaviruses lead to CNS infection via the olfactory route. This route may provide a pathway to the CNS in humans for rabies and, possibly, other viruses in circumstances where high titer aerosols are present, such as in caves occupied by large numbers of rabid bats or in accidental laboratory-acquired infections. The olfactory route of spread might explain the localization of herpes simplex virus in the orbitofrontal and medial temporal cortex in cases of herpes simplex encephalitis.

HEMATOGENOUS SPREAD

Hematogenous spread is an important mechanism for many viruses. A period of primary replication usually precedes the initial viremia and may be asymptomatic or result in prodromal symptoms. For enteric viruses, primary replication occurs in Peyer's patches and peritonsillar lymphatic tissue. For respiratory viruses, primary replication takes place in epithelial or alveolar cells; for many enteroviruses and togaviruses, in skeletal muscle. In some cases, virus travels via lymphatics from the site of initial multiplication to regional lymph nodes before entering the bloodstream. The initial (primary) viremia often disseminates the virus to tissues such as the spleen and liver where continued multiplication in parenchymal cells leads to an amplified secondary viremia. Growth in endothelial cells may help sustain the viremic phase in some togavirus infections. Sustained secondary amplification of the viremia is required if a virus is to overcome clearance by reticuloendothelial cells.

Blood-borne virus particles may travel free or in association with cellular elements. Hepatitis B virus, picornaviruses, and togaviruses all travel free within plasma; Colorado tick fever virus and Rift valley fever virus are associated with red blood cells; Epstein-Barr virus, cytomegalovirus, rubella, and human immunodeficiency virus are lymphocyte- or monocyte-associated diseases.

MULTIPLE PATHWAYS FOR SPREAD

In some cases, viruses use different pathways of spread at different stages in the infectious cycle. Varicella-zoster virus disseminates to the skin by the hematogenous route to produce "chickenpox," then spreads centripetally along nerves from the skin to neurons in the dorsal root ganglion where it remains latent. Reactivation results in centrifugal spread of virus down sensory nerves to their skin dermatome and the production of "shingles" (zoster). Neural spread of virus presumably accounts for recurrent episodes of oral and genital infection caused by the herpes simplex virus. Poliovirus represents an example of a virus capable of spreading by both hematogenous and neural routes. The hematogenous route is generally accepted as the primary pathway to the CNS, although the virus may spread to the CNS via autonomic nerves in the gut. Axonal transport may play a role in the spread of poliovirus within the CNS.

HOST FACTORS IN DEFENSE AND DAMAGE

A large number of constitutive and induced host defenses are involved in viral infections. The age and genetic background of the host have important implications for the outcome of certain viral infections. Newborns, for example, are particularly susceptible to severe disseminated herpes simplex virus infections. In contrast, many of the exanthematous illnesses, poliovirus infection, and Epstein-Barr virus infection are typically more severe in older individuals than in children. In mice, specific genes help determine susceptibility to certain viral infections, acting through effects on the immune system, interferon production, or viral receptors. Inadequate host nutritional status may increase susceptibility to infections such as measles, perhaps by depressing cell-mediated immunity. This accounts for the high mortality associated with measles in some developing countries. The host may also influence viral infections in other ways that are still poorly understood. Stress may trigger recurrent fever blisters (herpes labialis). Strenuous exercise may have an adverse effect on the course of polio.

The most important induced defense mechanism against viral infections is usually cell-mediated immunity. Patients with defective cell immunity but normal antibody-forming capacity often recover poorly from viral infections. Conversely, patients who lack antibodies but have normal cell-mediated immunity responses do not ordinarily suffer abnormally from viral diseases. Phagocytosis by neutrophils does not play as important a role in viral as in bacterial infections. Macrophages, on the other hand, are often involved in viral containment as well as in the spread of viruses in the body.

Antibody Response

Most viruses are good antigens for stimulating the immune response because they contain a large number of foreign proteins, each of which may contain multiple antigenic sites. In addition, although the amount of viral antigenic material may initially be quite small, it becomes amplified during viral replication. However, antibodies do not usually play a primary role in terminating acute viral infections but are very important in preventing reinfection. In some cases, antibodies may themselves be implicated in the pathogenesis of disease (e.g., in dengue fever).

The immunogenicity of viruses depends on the nature of the virus itself and on a variety of host factors. The slow virus agents (prions?) that are responsible for neurological degenerative diseases such as kuru and Creutzfeldt-Jakob disease do not appear to provoke any detectable immune response in the host, probably due to their neural habitat. The route of viral infection may also play a role in immunity. In experimental influenza infections, intravenous inoculation is more immunogenic than intraperitoneal inoculation, which, in turn, exceeds the subcutaneous route.

In cases where antibodies protect the host by destroying the infectivity of virus, they are referred to as **neutralizing antibodies**. These antibodies usually are directed against epitopes present on viral proteins that are located on the surface of the virus particle. The binding of neutralizing antibodies to virus is generally a reversible reaction. Viral infectivity may be reduced because neutralizing antibodies may inhibit various steps of the replication cycle such as attachment, penetration, or uncoating of virus. In addition, such antibodies may produce aggregation of virions, accelerate viral degradation in vesicles, or enhance viral opsonization and subsequent phagocytosis. In the case of poliovirus, neutralizing antibody binding appears to induce a conformational rearrangement of the viral outer capsid, which blocks viral uncoating but not attachment.

Complement

Viruses can trigger the activation of both the alternative and classic pathways of complement in the absence of an antibody response. Activated complement components (e.g., C3b) may act as opsonins to enhance phagocytosis of viruses (Chapter 6). Activation of the alternative complement pathway, in combination with antibody, may produce lysis of enveloped viruses or virus-infected cells. Although the complement system plays a role in the protection against viral infection in animals, human complement deficiency states are not typically associated with an increase in the frequency or severity of viral illnesses. Thus, this system is not likely to play as big a role in defending against viral as against bacterial infections.

Cell-mediated Immunity

Cell-mediated immunity is ordinarily a major factor in both the termination of viral infections and the pathogenesis of these diseases. Because of the viral intracellular habitat, infected cells are susceptible to the action of lymphocytes that recognize viral antigens on their surface (Chapter 6). Virus-infected cells can be lysed by several types of lymphoid cells through both the antibody-independent and the antibody-dependent pathways.

Independent of antibody, cytotoxicity by **natural killer** cells (NK) provides one of the earliest host defenses against viral infection (peak activity at 2–3 days) and precedes the appearance of antibody (7 days), cytotoxic T lymphocytes (CTL), and delayed type hypersensitivity (DTH). NK cells are large granular lymphocytes that bind to infected cells and then secrete cytotoxic molecules contained in azurophilic granular vesicles (Chapter 6). These cells do not represent a specific virus-induced defense mechanism although they are activated nonspecifically by interferons (see below).

Antibodies participate in the lysis of infected cells via antibody-dependent cell-mediated cytotoxicity (**ADCC**, Chapter 7). In ADCC reactions, virus-specific antibody bound to antigens on the surface of infected cells interacts with receptors for the Fc portion of IgG on the surface of specialized lymphocytoid cells, NK cells. Binding of IgG to the Fc receptor activates the NK cells and results in target cell killing. Macrophages, lymphocytes, and neutrophils also have Fc receptors and may also participate in ADCC.

Cytotoxic T lymphocytes (CTLs) constitute a specific virus-induced defense mechanism because they must be activated by antigen presented by macrophages or other antigen-presenting cells. Lysis of infected cells mediated by CTLs is typically restricted to class I histocompatibility antigens, although examples of class II-restricted CTLs have been described (Chapter 7). In contrast to neutralizing antibodies that typically recognize epitopes on intact viral surface proteins, CTLs recognize protein fragments derived from both the viral surface and internal proteins. The pathways by which these peptides are processed, appear on the surface of infected cells, and interact with MHC antigens are subjects of active investigation.

Virus-induced Immunopathology

Immunological injury results from cell lysis elicited by one or more of the mechanisms described above. Such damage is seen in those children who were immunized with inactivated measles virus vaccine and who develop severe disease when later infected with the same virus. The role of cell-mediated immunity is dramatically illustrated in mice infected with the virus that causes lymphochoriomeningitis. When this virus is inoculated intracerebrally, normal mice die within about a week. However, mice whose cell-mediated immunity has been suppressed by irradiation survive even though virus multiplication is unaffected.

Virus-induced immunopathology may also result from antibody production. Viruses may combine with virus-specific antibodies to form circulating immune complexes to cause a variety of lesions. Immune complexes become trapped in basement membranes at a variety of sites including the skin, the kidney, the choroid plexus, and the walls of blood vessels. Accumulation of immune complexes results in tissue injury by attracting and activating a variety of inflammatory mediators. In addition, virus stimulation of B lymphocytes may induce cross-reacting antibodies to normal host structures that contain antigenic regions similar to those of the virus (**molecular mimicry**).

Interferons

In addition to the usual humoral and cellular defense mechanisms, viral infections elicit an inducible defense mechanism, the **interferons**. These are proteins encoded by the host cells whose synthesis is induced by viruses and other agents. Interferons inhibit viral replication indirectly by inducing the synthesis of cellular proteins that minimize viral replication. The discovery and practical applications of interferons are discussed in the chapter on Antiviral Strategies (Chapter 43).

There are three main kinds of interferons (Table 43.2), called α, β and γ. Leukocytes produce more than a dozen ("leukocyte") interferons that share about 70% amino acid sequence homology. β-("Fibroblast") Interferon is produced by fibroblasts and epithelial cells and has 30% homology to α-interferons. Immune or γ-interferon is usually induced by the activation of T cells by specific antigens, but can also be induced by other compounds, including bacterial endotoxin.

Interferons are induced by both active and inactivated viruses, by double-stranded RNA, and by a number of other compounds. The amount of interferon produced varies with different viruses. All interferons act at extremely low concentrations and are generally most active in cells of the species in which they are induced ("species specific"), presumably because of variation in the nature of the interferon receptor. Interferon production appears to involve a derepression of cellular genes induced by the presence of viral nucleic acid in the host cell cytoplasm. This results in the rapid production of mRNAs for interferon and subsequent interferon synthesis.

Newly produced interferon is released into extracellular fluid and then binds to a specific receptor on adjacent cells. Consequently, interferon tends to act locally rather than systemically. Binding of interferon to a receptor leads to a complex series of events. A protein kinase is synthesized that phosphorylates a protein-synthesis initiation factor. In the phosphorylated form, this factor cannot participate in the formation of the protein-initiation complex, thus leading to inhibition of viral protein synthesis. In addition, an induced 2, 5-oligoisoadenylate synthetase produces 2, 5-oligoadenylates, which, in turn, activate a cellular endonuclease (RNase L) that degrades viral mRNA. Interferons also increase the activity of NK cells, CTLs, and cells involved in ADCC reactions. The relative importance of each of these activities in creating the interferon-induced antiviral state is not established.

DIAGNOSIS OF VIRAL DISEASES

A reasonably accurate diagnosis of some viral illnesses, such as measles, can be made on clinical grounds alone. In other cases, the best that can be done clinically is to identify the group of viruses that are the likely pathogens. More definitive diagnosis is often necessary because some of the available antiviral agents have an activity that is limited to certain types of viruses only. Definitive diagnosis requires the isolation of the virus in animals or in tissue culture, identification of the virus or detection of virus-specific antigens or viral nucleic acids in tissues or body fluids, or demonstration of specific serological responses. Appropriate specimens must be obtained for diagnostic studies during a suitable phase of the illness. Specimens must be rapidly transported and adequate clinical information must be provided to the diagnostic laboratories.

Isolation of virus from clinical specimens is done in cell cultures, embryonated eggs, and animals such as suckling mice. Cell culture techniques involve the use of primary cultures of cells prepared from organs of freshly killed animals (e.g., monkey kidney cells); of human diploid cell lines; and continuous (heterodiploid) cell lines such as HeLa, HEp-2, BHK-21, and vero. Some viruses grow better on certain cell lines than others. Inoculation into the amniotic cavity or the allantoic cavity of embryonated chicken eggs is useful for the isolation of influenza virus. Intraperitoneal and intracerebral inoculation into neonatal mice may be necessary for isolation of coxsackie A viruses and may help in the isolation of many arboviruses, rabies virus, arenaviruses, and orbiviruses. Adult mice or guinea pigs are used to isolate lymphocytic choriomeningitis (LCM) virus. Identification of the agent responsible for slow virus diseases such as kuru and Creutzfeldt-Jakob disease may require intracerebral inoculation of higher primates, such as chimpanzees.

Once cell cultures have been inoculated, the specimens are examined for distinctive patterns of **cytopathic effect** (CPE). Viruses such as that of herpes simplex and many enteroviruses produce early CPE, whereas CPE due to cytomegalovirus (CMV), rubella, and some adenoviruses may take weeks. Cultured cells are examined for cell lysis and vacuolization. The presence of syncytia suggests herpes simplex virus (HSV), respiratory syncytial virus, measles, or mumps virus. Cytomegaly is seen with HSV, varicella-zoster virus (VZV), and CMV.

Immunocytochemical staining of cell cultures to detect viral antigens using fluorescein or enzyme-conjugated specific antiviral antibodies may aid in the detection and identification of many viruses. Ortho- and paramyxoviruses (influenza, parainfluenza, measles, mumps) may be detected by the ability of infected cultures to adsorb certain red blood cells (**hemadsorption**).

Identification of virus particles or antigens in tissue specimens provides another important method of viral diagnosis. Skin scrapings from the base of vesicles help identify HSV or VZV. Similar techniques may help identify CMV-infected cells in urine sediment or measles-infected cells in scrapings from characteristic spots in the mouth (Koplik spots). In some cases, examination of specimens by electron microscopy (EM) is of diagnostic value, but only when viruses are present in high concentrations. Using special techniques as few as 10^4 particles per milliliter may be detected. The use of specific antisera to aggregate virus in prepared stool specimens facilitates EM detection of rotaviruses, hepatitis A virus, and the Norwalk agent. EM examination of brain biopsy specimens may allow identification of herpes simplex encephalitis and slow viruses.

A four-fold or greater increase in the antibody titer to a specific viral agent in a patient's acute and convalescent (3–4 weeks later) sera is usually considered diagnostic of acute infection. A single serum specimen is only occasionally useful in viral diagnosis. A number of different types of antibodies including neutralizing, complement-fixing, and hemagglutination-inhibiting antibodies are routinely assayed (see Chapter 55 for details on these techniques). The time course of these antibody responses and their sensitivity and specificity differ greatly.

Restriction enzyme analysis of the genomes of DNA viruses (e.g., herpes simplex virus, cytomegalovirus) and oligonucleotide fingerprinting of ribonuclease T, cleaved genomes of RNA viruses (e.g., influenza, dengue fever, enteroviruses) are valuable in epidemiological studies and in establishing the origin of certain types of viral isolates. In situ hybridization and the polymerase chain reaction technique (or other nucleic acid-amplification methods) may enable the detection of even single copies of virus genomes in tissue samples or cells from body fluids. Some of these extremely sensitive methods are becoming commercially available and may help revolutionize rapid viral diagnosis.

Treatment and prevention of viral diseases are discussed in further detail in Chapters 43 ("Antiviral Strategies") and 44 ("Vaccination Strategies") and in the chapters on the individual viruses.

Self-assessment Questions

1. Why are viruses not considered to be cellular forms of life?

2. How do viruses with icosahedral and helical symmetry differ in the connection between their nucleic acid and capsid?

3. Draw from memory a sketch of a typical nonenveloped and enveloped virus.

4. Why is the nucleic acid of (−) strand RNA viruses noninfectious?

5. Name three ways in which the mRNA of animal viruses resembles that of eukaryotic cells.

6. Why are the DNA-containing poxviruses not able to use the DNA replicative machinery of the cell?

7. Name two strategies used by viruses to make extra use of the information in the genome.

8. Define lytic, latent, and persistent viral infections.

9. Name three ways used by viruses to spread in the nervous system.

10. Viruses spread through the blood in three different ways. Name them.

11. How do antibodies contribute to immunopathology in viral diseases?

12. Why are live attenuated viral vaccines usually more effective than killed vaccines? Give two general reasons.

13. How does the activity of NK cells differ from that of CTL cells in viral infections?

14. Discuss how interferons differ from antibodies in their origin, specificity, and mode of action in viral infections.

15. Name four methods by which viruses may be detected in clinical specimens.

SUGGESTED READING

Fields BN, Knipe DM, eds. Fundamental virology. New York: Raven, 1991.
White DO, Fenner F. Medical virology, 3rd ed. New York: Academic Press, 1986.

Picornaviruses: Polio, Other Enteroviruses, and the Rhinoviruses

31

Cody Meissner and Gregory A. Storch

The **picornaviruses** (*pico* = small, *rna* = RNA-containing) are a family of small RNA viruses consisting of two major groups: (*a*) the **enteroviruses**, which include poliovirus and other pathogens, and (*b*) the **rhinoviruses**, which are among the most common agents of the common cold. The **hepatitis A virus** is a member of a separate group of picornaviruses. In this chapter, the enteroviruses and the rhinoviruses will be treated separately.

POLIOMYELITIS

Poliomyelitis is no longer a common disease in the U.S., although it continues to be important in some developing countries. Paradoxically, its dreaded consequences, paralysis and death, are more common in unvaccinated individuals living in countries with a high standard of sanitation. Polio serves as a good model for understanding the epidemiology and pathogenesis of viral infections because of the tropism exhibited by the virus, the well-understood and comparatively simple replication cycle of poliovirus, and the relative ease with which it can be studied in the laboratory. Furthermore, several related viruses (other enteroviruses) continue to cause important diseases in the U.S.

CASE—AN OUTBREAK OF POLIOMYELITIS

In October, 1972, 11 of 130 students attending a private school in Greenwich, Connecticut came down with paralytic poliomyelitis. Three weeks elapsed between the first and the last case. Nine of the 11 cases were boys who were 12–17 years of age, and all were members either of the football or the soccer team. The clinical history of these patients was similar; they reported "flu-like" symptoms—fever up to 39°C, sore throat, and muscle pains. These lasted 1–3 days. Two to three days afterward, they complained of stiff neck, increased muscle pain, and fever up to 41°C. This was followed by flaccid paralysis of the legs that varied in intensity from relatively minor to totally incapacitating. During the first 3 weeks of October, 17 other students were seen at the school infirmary with nonspecific complaints that suggested an acute viral syndrome.

Poliomyelitis was diagnosed by serological studies based on a rising titer of antibodies to type 1 poliovirus, but not types 2 and 3. The diagnosis was confirmed by the isolation of type 1 virus from the feces and throat washings of patients with paralytic disease. More than 50% of the students of the school had received no oral polio vaccine because of religious convictions. A small number of day students at the school lived at home, where they interacted with friends from surrounding towns in activities that included swimming classes at the local YMCA. Paralytic disease did not occur among nonmembers of the school. An immunization survey of the public schools revealed that more than 95% of the students had been vaccinated.

Several questions are raised by this outbreak:

1. Where did the virus come from and how did it spread among the students?

2. What caused the illness among the 17 students who complained of nonspecific signs and symptoms?

3. Why did the disease not spread to all the students or to the community outside of the school?

4. How does poliovirus cause paralysis and the other symptoms of the disease?

5. What could have been done to halt further spread of polio in the school?

Poliomyelitis is an ancient disease and has been one of the most dreaded since prebiblical times. An Egyptian stone slab from about 1350 B.C. shows a young priest with the typical withered leg of a polio survivor (Fig. 31.1). In the prevaccine era of the early 1950s, there were about 21,000 paralytic cases a year in the U.S. The figure is now less than 30 cases a year—a striking testimony to the efficacy of the polio vaccine. The dramatic virtual elimination of this disease from this country and much of Europe is one of the spectacular triumphs of medical research.

The history of poliomyelitis has seen major changes in disease incidence and age distribution. Before the 1900s, most infections occurred in infants. Few developed paralytic disease because, in infants, the virus is not as neurotropic and is more likely to confine its replication to the alimentary tract. Poor standards of sanitation and crowding facilitated transmission of virus, particularly among children in the first year of life. Infection, symptomatic or not, confers lifelong immunity and, if widespread, prevents large outbreaks from taking place in older persons.

Around the turn of the century, the situation changed when improved living conditions limited circulation of the virus. As unexposed children without immunity grew older, they entered an increasingly larger pool of susceptible individuals. Introduction of poliovirus into this community resulted in more frequent infections later in life, and resulted in devastating epidemics of paralytic disease. This is because older persons are more likely to develop paralytic disease when infected by poliovirus. In a sense, polio became a disease of affluent societies. This, then, is an example of changes in severity of a disease due to changes in the host rather than in the infectious agent. Underdeveloped countries of the world continue to experience the endemic pattern of poliovirus infection early in life, even today.

Figure 31.1. An early case of paralytic polio? This Egyptian stele depicting the typical paralysis of a polio victim dates from the 18th dynasty (1580–1350 B.C.)

ENTEROVIRUSES

Polioviruses belong to a heterogeneous group of viruses called the **enteroviruses**, which derive their name from their natural habitat that is the gastrointestinal tract. There are **six major groups** of enteroviruses. The most notorious member of this group is, in fact, poliovirus, and more is known about its molecular biology and mechanism of pathogenesis than the other enteroviruses. Polioviruses are divided into three antigenic types. Most epidemics are caused by type 1. Other enteroviruses include *Coxsackievirus*, first isolated during a polio outbreak in Coxsackie, New York, and *Echovirus* (enteric cytopathic human orphan virus), so called because initially they could not be linked to any human disease, having been isolated from feces of individuals who had no symptoms. This distinction has been dropped for newly discovered enteroviruses and they are now simply assigned a number, e.g., enterovirus 70.

Hepatitis A was originally classified as enterovirus type 72 because of similarities to other enteroviruses. As more information has been acquired about this virus regarding differences in nucleotide sequences, poor growth in cell culture, and resistance to conditions that inactivate other picornaviruses, it has become clear that hepatitis A should be classified in a separate genus.

Enteroviruses belong to the **picornavirus** family (pico = small, rna = RNA-containing, Fig. 31.2). The family contains a second genus, the *Rhinovirus*, which are the most frequent isolates from patients with the common cold. Differences in the two genera of picornaviruses help explain why they cause disease in certain sites of the body. Enteroviruses are more resistant to gastric acidity (stable at pH 3.0) and to bile. Rhinoviruses replicate best at 33°C, a temperature found in the nose, while enteroviruses prefer the core body temperature, 37°C. Also, rhinoviruses are acid labile and are readily inactivated by gastric secretions. This may help explain why rhinoviruses seldom cause pneumonia and enteroviruses are an infrequent cause of the common cold.

ENCOUNTER AND ENTRY

Enteroviruses are secreted in large amounts in **stool**. In the outbreak at the school in Connecticut, the likely source of contamination was a single individual, who shed high titers of virus from his or her gastrointestinal tract. A summer or early fall outbreak is typical of countries in temperate climates, whereas, in the tropics, the diseases caused by these agents are endemic and occur throughout the year. The major portal of entry is the mouth, and primarily from person to person via the oral-fecal route.

SPREAD AND REPLICATION

Soon after ingestion, enteroviruses **replicate in the lymphoid tissue of the pharynx and the intestine.** They may then spread throughout

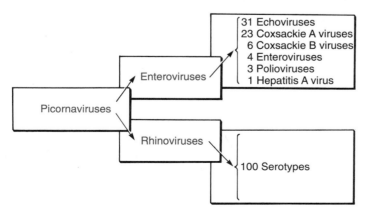

Figure 31.2. The Picornavirus family includes the genera *Rhinovirus* and *Enterovirus* with many different clinically important species.

the body via the **bloodstream** (Fig. 31.3). In most cases, the infection does not proceed further; enteroviruses are either contained in the Peyer's patches of the small intestine or are kept in check soon after the onset of the viremia. With poliovirus, the distinction between infection and disease is particularly important.

When **viremia** persists, distant sites become seeded as the viruses localize in their target organs. Their tropism is due to the presence of specific receptors on the membranes of target cells. All three types of poliovirus share similar receptors because saturation of binding sites with, say, an excess of type 1 virus blocks the binding of types 2 or 3. Binding of coxsackie or other enteroviruses remains unaffected, indicating different binding sites for these related viruses.

Replication of poliovirus is better understood than that of the other enteroviruses, in part because they reproduce rapidly and yield high titers in cell culture. Polioviruses are a prototype of **positive-strand viruses**, meaning that their genomic RNA can act directly as messenger RNA (mRNA). The first step in their replication cycle is uncoating, which, oddly enough, begins while the viruses are still extracellular. Once they are taken up, uncoating is completed and their genomic RNA is released into the cytoplasm, where replication and assembly take place. Poliovirus RNA is single-stranded and, as is typical of eukaryotic mRNAs, has a poly (A) tract at the 3′ end on the genome. A viral protein called VPg is attached to the 5′ end. This protein is not essential for infectivity, but may be involved in packaging the genome in the virion and in priming poliovirus RNA synthesis.

Synthesis of poliovirus proteins has been studied extensively and has revealed several unexpected facts. A single long polypeptide, a **polyprotein**, is synthesized in the cytoplasm using the host cells' protein synthesizing apparatus. A series of post-translational cleavage reactions cuts the polyprotein into four structural proteins and about seven nonstructural proteins (Fig. 31.4). After this processing, the structural proteins can assemble to make the capsid. We do not know why

Figure 31.3. The pathogenesis of poliovirus infection.

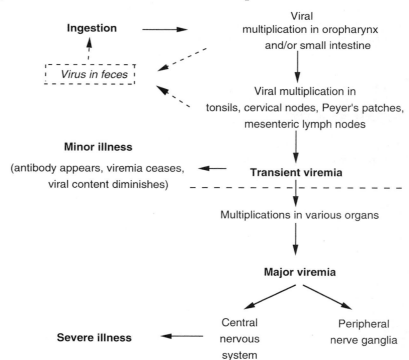

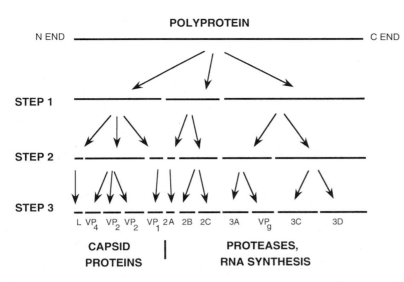

Figure 31.4. The synthesis of poliovirus polyprotein and its subsequent cleavage into structural proteins and virus encoded enzymes.

poliovirus has evolved to translate its messenger into a polyprotein, but this mechanism allows each protein to be made in equal amounts. Several of these proteins are **proteases** involved in the stepwise cleavage of the polyprotein, one is an **RNA-dependent RNA polymerase**, and the others are **structural constituents of the virions**.

The **RNA-dependent RNA polymerase** responsible for poliovirus RNA replication is an unusual enzyme not found in eukaryotic cells (whose RNA is made from DNA templates) and is accordingly encoded by the viral genome. The enzyme makes complementary negative strands of RNA, which, in turn, serve as templates for additional positive-strand copies of the genome. As the structural viral proteins accumulate, increasing amounts of viral RNA are encapsidated into mature virions. The viral particles are then released as the host cell is destroyed.

Under optimal conditions of cell culture, roughly 1000 infectious virus particles are released per cell. A complete cycle of replication, from viral attachment to the release of progeny virus, is completed within about 10 hours, which is unusually rapid for animal viruses. Other enteroviruses follow a similar scheme of replication.

DAMAGE

Poliovirus is a typically **lytic** virus and its replication is accompanied by destruction of infected host cells. Enterovirus infections typically have 2- to 5-day incubation periods. The viruses may continue to replicate in the intestine and be shed in the stool for weeks or months after all symptoms are gone. In the school outbreak, virus continued to circulate and to infect new students for some time. This explains the onset of symptoms in different students over a 3-week period.

Polioviruses spread from the gastrointestinal tract to the central nervous system, where they replicate in the neurons of the gray matter of both brain and spinal cord. Virus travels via the bloodstream, although spread along neural pathways is also possible. The characteristic flaccid paralysis of limb muscles occurs when anterior horn cells of the spinal cord are destroyed. A most severe form of disease is **bulbar poliomyelitis**, the paralysis of the respiratory muscles resulting from involvement of the medulla oblongata. It is this type of polio that led to the development of "iron lungs," cumbersome predecessors of modern respirators that made patients inhale and exhale by external changes in pressure. The mortality rate in paralytic cases of poliomyelitis is 2–3%.

Why is infection by enteroviruses, and poliovirus in particular, often so **mild** or **asymptomatic**? Apparently, many factors are at work. They include the size of the viral inoculum, the concentration of viruses in the blood, the virulence of individual virus strains, and the presence of circulating antibodies. The same virus may cause different illnesses in different individuals. In the school outbreak described above, there was a spectrum of disease caused by one strain of poliovirus. Among the **host factors** involved, physical exertion and trauma correlate with increased risk of paralysis. This may explain, in part, the observation that 9 of the 11 students affected were actively participating in football and soccer. Another predisposing factor for bulbar poliomyelitis is tonsillectomy, perhaps due to lower titers of antipolio antibodies in the nasal secretions of immunized persons. Circulating antibodies may play an important role in controlling infections due to enteroviruses, as seen in patients with agammaglobulinemias, who have difficulty in resolving infections by echovirus.

DISEASES CAUSED BY OTHER ENTEROVIRUSES

The most frequent diseases caused by enteroviruses in the U.S. are due to **coxsackievirus** (Table 31.1). They cause a large number of illnesses, differing somewhat between those caused by group A and group B. Both cause so-called **aseptic meningitis**, a term used for nonbacterial meningitis. In addition, group A viruses cause **herpangina**, a fever of sudden onset with vesicles or ulcers on the tonsils and palate. Group B viruses also infect other organs, particularly the heart. In general, echoviruses produce similar diseases (Table 31.1).

Most of these infections are not sufficiently unique to allow a specific diagnosis on clinical grounds alone. For example, the skin rash (exanthem) due to coxsackievirus and echovirus are indistinguishable. One important exception is **hand, foot, and mouth disease**, a readily identifiable febrile illness that produces blisters in the palate, hands, and feet. It is usually caused by a specific type of coxsackievirus, type A16.

During the viremic phase, these enteroviruses infect any of several organs and do not exhibit the same tropism for cells of the CNS as poliovirus. Infected newborns are at particular risk of severe disease, unless they have acquired enough protective antibodies from their mother. Their own immune system may be insufficiently developed to curtail an enterovirus infection. Neonates may acquire coxsackievirus or echovirus by transplacental passage of the virus near term, from

Table 31.1. Major Enterovirus Diseases

Disease	Polio	Coxsackievirus Type A	Coxsackievirus Type B	Echovirus	Enterovirus
Asymptomatic infection	+	+	+	+	+
Viral meningitis	+	+	+	+	+
Paralytic disease	+	+	+	+	−
Febrile exanthems (rash)	−	+	+	+	+
Acute respiratory disease	−	+	+	+	+
Myopericarditis	−	+	+	+	−
Orchitis	−	−	+	+	−

contact with maternal fecal material during birth, or from conventional person-to-person passage.

DIAGNOSIS AND THERAPY

Because diseases caused by enteroviruses are seldom sufficiently characteristic to enable a diagnosis on purely clinical grounds, it may be helpful to take into account certain epidemiological features. A person who becomes ill with symptoms of viral meningitis in the summer or early fall during a community-wide outbreak of coxsackievirus is likely to be a victim of that agent.

During endemic months, when enteroviruses circulate in a community, they can be readily isolated from throat washings or fecal specimens from symptomatic as well as asymptomatic persons. In this setting, recovery of an enterovirus from the throat or feces of an ill person does not prove that the symptoms are due to an enterovirus, as many asymptomatic people have enteroviruses in their stool. Definitive proof requires isolation of the virus from the involved site, such as cerebrospinal or pericardial fluids. Serological tests are not practical here because related enteroviruses do not share common antigens.

At present, there is no therapy for infections by enteroviruses, with the possible exception of the administration of γ-globulin to immune-compromised patients suffering from severe echovirus or coxsackie-virus infections.

PREVENTION

A disease caused by an agent whose only reservoir is human beings is a candidate not only for control but for elimination. The best example is smallpox, which appears to have been erased from the face of the earth, except for stocks of the virus maintained for research purposes. Polio may be a candidate for this sort of medical success. The issues surrounding polio vaccination merit close examination. Vigorous efforts to develop an effective polio vaccine go hand in hand with seminal developments in virology, mainly the use of cell cultures to study viral multiplication. The **killed Salk vaccine** was introduced in 1955 and led to a precipitous decline in the incidence of both paralytic and nonparalytic disease (Fig. 31.5). In 1961, the **oral live attenuated Sabin vac-**

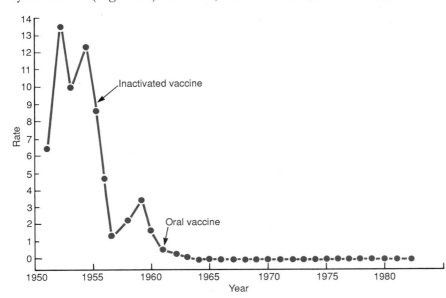

Figure 31.5. The incidence of paralytic poliomyelitis in the U.S. 1977–1982. Reported cases per 100,000 population.

cine was introduced in this country and it soon replaced the Salk vaccine. Considerable controversy surrounded the introduction of a live vaccine after the killed vaccine had already demonstrated its effectiveness. A comparison of the two vaccines is shown in Table 31.2.

The original arguments continue to form the basis for the use of the live vaccine (Fig. 31.6). Antibody production by the killed vaccine is not always long lasting and is slow to develop. Repeated booster shots are necessary. Perhaps most important, the immune response elicited by the live, attenuated vaccine closely resembles that brought about by natural poliovirus infection. The reason is that the live, attenuated vaccine is administered orally, resulting in an active infection in the intestine and stimulating the local formation of secretory antibodies. In contrast, the killed vaccine is administered by injection and produces immunity in the circulation but not in the intestine (Fig. 31.6). Thus, a recipient of the killed vaccine while protected from symptomatic disease, could still propagate and spread the virus.

Because immunization rates in this country never approach 100%, the live vaccine would reduce the number of individuals who may act as reservoirs for poliovirus. **Contacts** of individuals given the live, attenuated vaccine may be asymptomatically infected, regardless of their immunization status. In most instances, this contact produces a booster response in already immunized individuals. In the infrequent setting where the **vaccine strain spreads to nonimmunized persons**, the community may benefit from the increased number of immune individuals. However, spread of live virus by this means is not without harm; at least half of the few cases of paralytic poliomyelitis in the U.S. today are thought to be due to the virus used in the live vaccine. During replication in the gut of vaccine recipients, the vaccine strain may very rarely back mutate to a less attenuated, more virulent strain before it is passed on to contacts. At least some of the individuals who develop vaccine-associated disease are immune deficient. It should be emphasized, however, that the **risk of developing polio from the vaccine strain is extraordinarily small**, about one case of paralytic polio per 2.6 million doses distributed. Also, at times, the live vaccine has

Table 31.2. The Poliovirus Vaccines	
Advantages	Disadvantages
1. Inactivated vaccine (Salk) Cannot undergo genetic mutation to increased virulence	a. Fails to elicit gut immunity b. Requires parenteral administration c. Expensive d. Some lots have inadequate antigenic potency e. Confers immunity only after four boosters f. Stringent control of production required to ensure inactivation
2. Live, attenuated vaccine (Sabin) a. Relatively inexpensive and easily administered b. Induces both systemic and local immunity c. Maintains potency without refrigeration d. Prepared in human cells eliminating risk of latent viruses found in monkey kidney cells e. Induces herd immunity	a. Can mutate to more virulent strain b. Less reliable in tropical climates

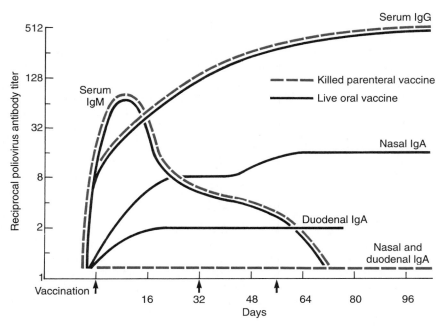

Figure 31.6. The antibody response to the live and killed poliovirus vaccine. The levels of serum IgG, as well as nasal and duodenal IgA are compared as a function of time after vaccination.

been found to contain contaminating viruses from the monkey cells used for cultivation.

The live vaccine should not be used in certain circumstances. Generally, immunocompromised individuals should not receive a live vaccine, including the Sabin vaccine. In some underdeveloped countries, the live, attenuated vaccine has not resulted in an acceptable antibody response. One reason for vaccine failure seems to be interference from other enteroviruses already replicating in the intestine. For this reason, the live vaccine is given to children in five doses, which ought to minimize the likelihood of other enterovirus replicating at the time of vaccination.

ERADICATION OF POLIOMYELITIS

The introduction of the inactivated polio vaccine in 1955 and the live attenuated vaccine in 1961 have had a dramatic impact worldwide on the morbidity and mortality of poliomyelitis. Because of the success of the immunization program in many countries, attempts have been initiated to eradicate the disease from geographic regions where it remains endemic. These efforts have been largely unsuccessful in certain countries, largely because of lack of resources.

CONCLUSIONS

Enteroviruses commonly cause infections in human beings. They are readily communicable but only rarely do they cause severe disease. Illnesses caused by enteroviruses may be highly tissue specific (poliovirus) or they can affect many organs (coxsackievirus and echovirus infections). These diseases are often difficult to distinguish clinically, and their presumptive diagnosis is often based on the epidemiological picture. The success in eradicating polio with vaccination is providential, inasmuch as there is no other known way to control this disease.

HUMAN RHINOVIRUSES AND THE COMMON COLD

The human rhinovirus remains the agent most closely linked to the **common cold**. Along with the enteroviruses (poliovirus, Coxsackie A and B viruses, echoviruses, and hepatitis A virus), the rhinoviruses comprise the Picornaviridae family. Unlike other respiratory viruses such as influenza, parainfluenza, or respiratory syncytial virus, rhinoviruses have no lipid envelope surrounding the viral nucleocapsid. As is also true for the enteroviruses, antigenic diversity is a striking characteristic of the rhinoviruses, with nearly 100 serotypes recognized to date. (Any two rhinovirus isolates are considered to be of different serotypes if their infectivity is not neutralized by the same antiserum.) Although there is some cross-reactivity among different serotypes, the extent of **antigenic diversity** has caused pessimism about the prospects for a rhinovirus vaccine.

CASE OF THE COMMON COLD

Ms. C., a 28-year-old woman realized she was getting a cold when she noticed a scratchy feeling in the throat, sneezing, nasal discharge, low-grade fever, and malaise. The symptoms worsened, reaching a peak after 48 hours. Within several days, her nasal discharge thickened and was slightly yellowish, and then subsided over the next several days. All of her other symptoms resolved completely within about 7 days of onset. She thought that she acquired the illness from her 7-year-old child, who had had similar symptoms a few days earlier.

ENCOUNTER

Rhinovirus infections are very common. The average person experiences approximately one such infection per year, and school-age children and those in contact with them may experience many more. These infections occur most commonly in the fall and spring. Multiple serotypes circulate simultaneously but, over time, different serotypes predominate.

Infected humans, particularly children, are the only known reservoir for these viruses. The mode of transmission has been the subject of intense experimental study. One series of experiments demonstrated that transmission may occur if individuals touch their nose or eyes after their hands became contaminated with rhinovirus (either from contaminated nasal secretions or environmental objects). In recent experiments, susceptible volunteers played poker with persons who had symptomatic rhinovirus infection, and became infected even if they were restrained from touching their face (Fig. 31.7). This suggests that rhinovirus infection may be transmitted by aerosols, as well as by direct inoculation. The effective production and dispersal of aerosol droplets during a sneeze is shown in Figure 31.8.

ENTRY, SPREAD, AND MULTIPLICATION

In experimental studies, even a **small inoculum** of rhinovirus suffices to initiate an infection. The first step in infection is the binding of the virus to specific **receptors** on respiratory epithelial cells. Recently, workers in this field were surprised to find that most of the diverse rhinovirus serotypes all bind to the same receptor. The remaining serotypes bind to a second receptor. The major group receptor was found to be a well-known molecule designated ICAM-1 (intercellular adhesion molecule-1). ICAM-1 is a member of the immunoglobulin supergene family and is known to play an important role in cell adhesion processes in the immune response. Thus, the human rhinoviruses join a small but possibly growing number of viruses whose receptors are molecules with known cellular functions. Other examples are rabies

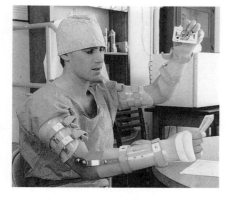

Figure 31.7. Participant in an experiment designed to study the mode of transmission of rhinoviruses. The arm braces worn by the subject allowed normal poker playing but prevented the wearer from touching any part of his head or face.

Figure 31.8. Droplet dispersal following a sneeze by a patient with a cold; note strings of mucus.

virus and the acetylcholine receptor (Chapter 34), HIV and the CD_4 molecule (Chapter 37), and the Epstein-Barr virus and the receptor for complement component C3 (Chapter 40).

An interesting notion concerning the interaction between rhinovirus and its receptor is that expression of ICAM-1 on the cell surface is increased by certain inflammatory mediators that may be relevant in rhinovirus infection, suggesting that rhinovirus-induced inflammation may facilitate the entry of the virus into nearby uninfected cells and, thus, spread the infection.

Detailed structural studies of rhinoviruses have revealed that the part of the virus that binds to the cellular receptor is located within a cleft or "canyon" on the surface of the virion. Neutralizing antibodies are thought to prevent infection by binding to the virions at sites near the canyon, making it impossible for the binding site on the virus to come in contact with the cellular receptor. The detailed molecular scheme of rhinovirus replication within the infected cell is similar to that described for poliovirus.

Rhinoviruses are thought to spread in respiratory epithelium by local extension. In experimental colds, the posterior nasopharynx is the site of the most intense infection. Neither viremia nor infection at sites outside of the respiratory tract is known to occur in these infections.

DAMAGE

The nose of a patient with a cold becomes engorged with blood (hyperemic) and edematous. The thin nasal discharge contains large amounts of serum proteins. As the cold progresses, the discharge becomes mucopurulent and contains many cells, especially neutrophils. Respiratory epithelial cells are also present, some of which contain rhinovirus antigens, indicating that they are infected by the virus. If a biopsy of the mucosa were to be performed early in the course of a cold, it would reveal edema of subepithelial connective tissue with relatively small numbers of inflammatory cells. In contrast to some other viral respiratory infections, particularly influenza, only minimal histopathological changes would be observed, even in areas where viral antigens are present.

How does rhinovirus infection produce its characteristic disease manifestations? In general, **there is a correlation between the severity of the cold and the amount of rhinovirus that can be recovered.** Large amounts of virus are found without tissue destruction, however, indicating that disease manifestations must be produced by mechanisms other than viral-induced cytopathology. Further support for this notion comes from finding that **nasal secretions of persons with a cold contain large amounts of the vasoactive substance bradykinin.** In addition, it is thought that direct stimulation of nerve endings in the nasal mucosa produces some of the manifestations of the cold.

Despite the discomfort resulting from the events occurring in the nose, most rhinovirus infections are mild and have few other consequences. The most common complications are sinusitis, otitis media, and exacerbation of chronic bronchitis or asthma. Rarely, more severe infections with probable lower respiratory tract involvement may occur, especially in compromised hosts such as premature infants with chronic lung disease. Sinusitis or otitis media complicating a cold is usually due to bacterial infections that develop because the normal draining of the sinuses or the middle ear is blocked.

PREVENTION AND TREATMENT

Some degree of **immunity** to rhinovirus infection does develop. Infected people generate immunity effective against viruses of the same serotype. This immunity may be due, at least in part, to antibodies found in nasal secretions. It is reasonable to speculate that antirhinovirus antibody, particularly of the **IgA class,** might exert a protective effect by blocking the binding of the virus to the cell receptor.

A **vaccine** to prevent the common cold does not yet appear feasible, not only because of the serological diversity of these viruses, but also because they account for no more than 50% of colds. Nevertheless, several novel approaches to prophylaxis are currently being explored. One is the use of recombinant α-interferon administered by nasal spray. In recent studies, this was effective in preventing colds if used just after the first cold occurred in a family. An earlier approach of using interferon nasal sprays throughout the cold season was not successful because the nasal symptoms produced by long-term interferon administration were as bothersome as those of a cold (Chapter 43). Other chemotherapeutic agents are also under study. New approaches of this kind may finally lead to progress in controlling the widely experienced miseries of the common cold.

Self-assessment Questions

1. Discuss the changes in severity and incidence of polio in the U.S. in the last 100 years.

2. What diseases do the enteroviruses cause? What are their common clinical features?

3. Discuss the replication cycle of poliovirus.

4. What are the problems associated with vaccination against polio?

5. Discuss how the eradication of smallpox may help us eradicate polio.

6. Describe features of the attachment of rhinoviruses to human cells.

7. Describe the pathogenesis of rhinovirus infection.

SUGGESTED READING

Evans AL. Viral infections of humans, 2nd ed. New York: Plenum Medical Book Co., 1982:182–251.

Feigen RD, Cherry JD. Textbook of pediatric infectious diseases. Philadelphia: WB Saunders, 1981:1316–1365.

International symposium on poliomyelitis control. Rev Infect Dis 1984;6: (Suppl 2).

Arthropod-borne Viruses

32

Cody Meissner

The arthropod-borne viruses (**arboviruses**) are a varied group of agents that cause a wide range of illnesses, from the mild influenza-like infections to encephalitis or hemorrhagic fevers. These diseases are more prevalent in the tropics than in the temperate regions of the world because they follow the distribution of the mosquitoes and flies involved in their transmission. The principal diseases in this group are dengue, yellow fever, and a large number of encephalitides. For some of these diseases, prevention is possible by vaccination, but effective therapeutic measures are not available.

CASE

In the summer before he was to enter medical school, Mr. R. was content to spend the month of July sunning himself on the beaches of Maryland. The weather was particularly hot and wet. His favorite spot was a pond in a wooded area where he could watch the horses of a nearby farm. One afternoon, he suddenly became lethargic and fatigued and went home to bed. That evening he was awakened for supper by his father but felt confused and was not hungry. By 10 p.m., he had a fever of 40.7°C and refused to answer questions. Four hours later, his father had difficulty arousing him and brought him to the emergency room of a local hospital. Several hours after admission, he became unresponsive to simple commands. He gradually deteriorated, with periods of increasing stupor and paralysis of his limbs. He lapsed into coma 2 weeks after admission and died 2 weeks after that.

Sera obtained from Mr. R. showed a rise in antibody titer against EEE virus from less than 1:10 to 1:80. At autopsy, examination of his brain showed disseminated small foci of necrosis in both the gray matter and the white matter. EEE virus was isolated from brain tissue by intracerebral inoculation of suckling mice at the state laboratory. Thus, the diagnosis of EEE virus could be made unequivocally on the grounds of the laboratory data and the clinical manifestations.

Questions that arose include:

1. Where and how did Mr. R. acquire the virus?

2. How frequent is this disease and when is it most common?

3. What other viruses cause similar diseases?

4. What measures could Mr. R. have taken to prevent the disease?

Eastern equine encephalitis (EEE) is an often fatal but fortunately rare disease. Between 1955 and 1985 there were a total of 178 cases in this country. The virus causing EEE is found among marsh birds that live in the fresh water swamps of the Atlantic and Gulf states and in regions around the Great Lakes. The reason this disease is rare in people is that the mosquitoes that transmit this disease among marsh herons and egrets do not usually bite humans. Only when people-biting mosquitoes become involved are humans at risk. The likelihood that a person infected with this virus manifests clinical disease ranges from about 1 in 4 in children to as low as 1 in 50 in adults. The fatality rate among those that manifest symptoms is very high, 50–80%. In children, mental retardation occurs in as many as half the survivors.

ARBOVIRUSES

Arboviruses are a large group of viruses that share two characteristics: (a) transmission by arthropod vectors and (b) an RNA genome (Table 32.1). More than 100 different members are known to infect humans. Many cause **encephalitis** while others produce **yellow fever**, **hemorrhagic fever**, or **dengue fever**, diseases characterized by internal hemorrhages, severe pains of joints and muscles, and skin rashes. Arboviruses are sometimes named after the disease they cause but often after the place where they have been found (Semliki Forest, Rift Valley fever, Colorado tick fever, Venezuelan equine encephalitis, O'nyong nyong, etc.). They are diseases of wild and domesticated animals, with humans only accidentally infected. The vectors include mosquitoes, ticks, and flies. Some diseases that are not transmitted by an arthropod vector are caused by viruses that are biochemically similar to members of this group. For example, the virus that causes rubella belongs to the same group as EEE virus, although it is transmitted directly from person to person.

Table 32.1. Important Human Arboviruses

Genus and Example	Main Disease Manifestations	Primary Vector	Major Geographic Distribution
Togaviridae Family			
Alphavirus			
Eastern equine encephalitis	Encephalitis	Mosquito	Eastern U.S., Caribbean
Western equine encephalitis	Encephalitis	Mosquito	Western U.S., Canada, Mexico, Brazil
Venezuelan equine encephalitis	Encephalitis	Mosquito	Central and South America, Texas, Florida
Many others	Fevers, encephalitis	Mosquito	Africa, Asia, Central and South America
Flaviviridae Family			
Flavivirus			
St. Louis encephalitis	Encephalitis	Mosquito	North America
Japanese B encephalitis	Encephalitis	Mosquito	Japan, East Asia
Dengue	Fevers, hemorrhages (sometimes)	Mosquito	All tropics
Yellow fever	Hemorrhagic fever	Mosquito	Africa, Central and South America
Many others	Encephalitis	Mosquito, tick	Worldwide
Bunyaviridae Family			
Bunyavirus			
California	Encephalitis	Mosquito	North America
Rift valley	Fever	Mosquito	Africa
Others	Fevers	Mosquito, flies	Worldwide
Reoviridae Family			
Orbivirus			
Colorado tick fever	Fever	Tick	North America

The members of two main families of arboviruses (Togaviridae and Flaviviridae) have enveloped virions that contain a **single-stranded positive-sense RNA genome**. The RNA serves as messenger RNA and is transcribed directly into large proteins. These are cleaved after synthesis to make both regulatory proteins and the structural proteins of the virion. Members of another important family (Bunyaviridae) contain a **single-stranded negative-sense genome** and carry an RNA transcriptase in their virion. The envelope contains surface glycoprotein spikes that it acquires as they bud through the cytoplasmic membrane. The lipid-containing envelope appears to be essential for viral integrity because treatment with detergents or lipid solvents inactivates these viruses. Many enveloped viruses are also sensitive to drying, suggesting that transmission by arthropods may be a way to protect these agents from detrimental environmental factors.

ENCOUNTER

The natural life cycle for the viruses that cause EEE and other encephalitides is from bird to bird, via the bite of mosquitoes (Fig. 32.1). It is not known if the virus survives the winter in cold climates or if it is reintroduced each year by migrating birds. As the name implies, horses acquire EEE, but they seldom if ever play a role in the development of human infection. The virus is present in the horses' blood for so short a time that it is unlikely the horse would be bitten by a mosquito during the viremic phase. Horses, like humans, do not participate in the normal life cycle of the virus, but they are important **sentinel** animals, alerting that the virus has escaped its normal biological boundaries and is a threat to humans.

A certain period of time must pass before a mosquito that has acquired the virus can transmit it. Mosquitoes do not become sick with the virus, and once infected, can spread it for the rest of their lives (one season). The normal vertebrate hosts of the virus (birds) are also relatively unaffected, thus permitting a stable life cycle. The frequency of encounter is dictated by the proximity to humans of both the animal reservoir and the insect vector.

ENTRY, SPREAD, AND MULTIPLICATION

EEE virus gains access to humans via the bite of an infected mosquito. Virus-containing saliva is introduced into the capillary bed as the mosquito's proboscis penetrates the skin and endothelial cells of the capillary wall. The virus localizes in the vascular endothelium and the lymphatic cells of the reticuloendothelial system, where replication occurs. **A primary viremia** is induced as the virus is liberated from these infected cells. This period is of short duration, and about the time when Mr. R.'s symptoms first appeared, the virus had probably already been cleared from his blood.

DAMAGE

In many instances, infection by EEE and related viruses does not progress past the stage of replication in the vascular endothelium. If viremia does occur in a patient without a protective antibody titer, the virus may localize elsewhere, primarily in the central nervous system. The clinical manifestations seen in Mr. R's case are consistent with damage to various parts of the brain, as subsequently confirmed at autopsy.

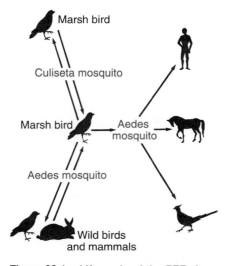

Figure 32.1. Life cycle of the EEE virus. The complete cycle takes place between wild birds by the bite of *Culiseta* mosquitoes and between wild birds and wild mammals via *Aedes* mosquitoes. One-way spread to humans, horses, and pheasants takes place by the bite of *Aedes* mosquitoes.

It is not known how EEE virus crosses the blood-brain barrier, or why this happens in only some of the infected persons. Damage to brain and cerebellar tissue appears to be due largely to vascular involvement. Small hemorrhages are seen throughout these organs, with little preferred localization. Neurons are severely affected and many die, leading to extensive necrosis.

DISEASES CAUSED BY OTHER ARBOVIRUSES

In the U.S., other encephalitides closely related to EEE are seen, called **St. Louis encephalitis (SLE)** and **western equine encephalitis (WEE)**. Of these, SLE is the most common, having caused about 5000 cases between 1955 and 1985. Occasionally SLE occurs in epidemics, including one in 1975 that resulted in some 1800 cases. Fortunately, it is a milder disease than EEE. **Japanese encephalitis** was relatively common in Japan, but its spread has been stemmed by the use of a killed virus vaccine administered to pigs and children.

The arbovirus disease of greatest historical importance is **yellow fever**. It has caused fearsome and extensive epidemics in Africa and the Americas. Despite the presence of suitable vectors and hosts, yellow fever has never taken hold in Asia. The devastating impact of yellow fever on the U.S. Army in Cuba during the Spanish-American war led Walter Reed to his classic investigation into the etiology of the disease. His success in identifying a filtrable agent as the cause of yellow fever was the first proof that viruses cause human disease. Control of the disease is achieved by vaccination and by control of the vector, the mosquito *Aedes aegypti*.

Yellow fever continues to be a serious disease in much of western Africa and the Americas, where the mosquito has not been eradicated. An epidemic in central Nigeria in 1986 caused nearly 5000 deaths in the first 3 weeks of the outbreak. African monkeys, which remain asymptomatic after infection, are the reservoir in parts of Africa. In contrast, the virus may cause devastating epidemics in monkeys of Central and South America. As a consequence, outbreaks of yellow fever in monkeys are continually moving from one region of that continent to another.

Dengue fever is another arbovirus disease transmitted by the same mosquitoes. It is the most prevalent human disease caused by arboviruses and is found in tropical and subtropical regions of much of the world. Fortunately, it does not cause significant mortality. Clinical manifestations include sudden onset of fever, headache, pain behind the eye, and lumbosacral pain, often followed by a generalized rash. The incubation period may last up to 7 days, and North American travelers to endemic areas may become sick several days after returning home. This disease differs from other arbovirus infections in that it is not a zoonosis but is transmitted by mosquitoes directly from person to person.

DIAGNOSIS

Diagnosis of diseases caused by any arbovirus on clinical grounds alone is difficult, because of the paucity of specific findings on physical examination. Proof of the etiology requires either isolation of the virus or demonstration of a rise in antibody titer during the illness. Both were accomplished in the case of Mr. R. The virus of EEE cannot usually be isolated from the blood of an infected person because the viremic phase is brief. Isolation of the virus from tissues such as brain should be attempted only in laboratories with appropriate containment facilities because of the danger of infection to laboratory workers.

The serological tests performed on Mr. R.'s serum sought specific antibodies against the virus using a **complement fixation** assay (Chapter 55). This is one of the oldest serological tests, dating from the early part of the century. As a test for syphilis, it was known as the Wassermann test.

THERAPY AND PROPHYLAXIS

Lack of specific therapy for these diseases increases the emphasis on their prevention. In endemic regions, community surveillance programs should be established to follow the density of vectors (i.e., mosquitoes) during the appropriate season of the year. At appropriate times, personal protection against mosquitoes should be emphasized (e.g., the use of repellents and bed nets). In part of the U.S., the appearance of even a single case of viral encephalitis often causes great concern in the population and among public health workers. Widespread aerial spraying of insecticides is sometimes carried out, not without causing considerable controversy. Because arboviruses cannot spread from infected patients directly, person-to-person contact is not a concern.

Vaccines against many of the arboviruses that cause encephalitides are either available or under development. Vaccination is an important consideration for travelers to areas where yellow fever is endemic. A live attenuated vaccine induces good immunity for at least 10 years.

Self-assessment Questions

1. What are the main disease types caused by the arboviruses?

2. How does the mode of transmission of arboviruses affect their geographic distribution and weather pattern?

3. How do positive-strand viruses differ from negative-strand viruses?

4. What is the relationship among humans, horses, and birds with regard to the epidemiology of arbovirus encephalitides?

5. Why is it important in the U.S. to notice if horses suffer from viral encephalitis during the summer months?

SUGGESTED READING

Hayes EB, Gubler DJ. Dengue and dengue hemorrhagic fever. Pediatr Infect Dis J 1992:11:311–317.

Monath TP. Flaviviruses. In: Fields BN, Knipe DM, eds. Virology, 2nd ed. New York: Raven Press, 1990:763–814.

Peters CJ, Dalrymple JM. Alphaviruses. In: Fields BN, Knipe DM, eds. Virology, 2nd ed. New York: Raven Press, 1990:713–761.

Whitley RJ. Viral encephalitis. N Engl J Med 1990;323:242–250.

Paramyxoviruses: Measles, Mumps, Slow Viruses, and the Respiratory Syncytial Virus

33

Stephen E. Straus and Gregory A. Storch

The family of viruses known as Paramyxoviridae (Table 33.1) includes several medically important pathogens that possess particular affinities for infecting and damaging respiratory tract and central nervous system tissue. For example, the genus *Paramyxovirus* within this family consists of the mumps and parainfluenza viruses. Prior to development of live attenuated mumps vaccine recommended for infants at age 15 months, mumps was recognized as a common cause of epidemics of glandular inflammation (salivary, pancreas, testes) and associated meningoencephalitis. The current lack of an effective vaccine for the parainfluenza viruses leaves those viruses as major causes of childhood croup (laryngotracheitis) that appear in epidemic waves each fall.

This chapter focuses primarily on members of two other genera of the Paramyxoviridae family, the measles virus and the respiratory syncytial virus (RSV). RSV is the major cause of serious respiratory infection in young infants. It has been chosen for detailed description as an example of an important viral pathogen that has eluded serious attempts to develop an effective vaccine. Before getting into the reasons for that, we begin with a more optimistic story, that of measles.

CASE

Ms. M., an aspiring journalist, took ill just before crucial college midterm examinations. She had looked forward to a relaxed spring break after these examinations, but now her ability to take them seems in doubt. She feels miserable, has fever, a runny nose, cough, a blotchy rash, and is told by the health service physician that she might have measles. "That's absurd," she thinks, "Only little kids get measles and I think I had it as a child."

Her rash appeared first on the neck and head, then spread to the trunk and extremities during the next few days. At first, the rash was composed of discrete, reddish lesions that blanched on pressure. They then quickly merged together and became increasingly brownish.

If you were the university health service physician, it would be your responsibility to make a definitive diagnosis, despite Ms. M.'s protesta-

Table 33.1. Classification of Paramyxoviruses

Family	
Paramyxoviridae	
Genus	
Pneumovirus	Respiratory syncytial virus
Paramyxovirus	Mumps virus, parainfluenza virus
Morbillivirus	Measles, canine distemper virus

tions, and to take several steps to ensure that if it were measles, she would not contribute to the further spread of the illness on campus. What must you know?

1. Given the current rarity of the disease in the U.S., is it reasonable to consider measles as a probable diagnosis?

2. What information can be gleaned from the medical history of the patient, her physical findings, and laboratory tests to confirm or rule out the diagnosis of measles?

3. Could Ms. M. have had measles previously and now have it again?

4. What other illnesses are associated with rashes, and could any of them be Ms. M.'s problem?

5. What complications might Ms. M. or others experience from this illness?

6. How can transmission of measles to others be prevented?

These and other issues are addressed in this chapter.

History and Epidemiology of Measles

The history of measles is one of the most interesting, colorful, and generally underappreciated of all of the infectious diseases. Except for plague, cholera, typhus, and smallpox, measles has perhaps had the greatest impact on people, on the successes or failures of their explorations, their colonization attempts, their military campaigns, and their ability to survive to old age. Curiously, among the general public, these facts are little known. The availability of an effective vaccine has so reduced the incidence of measles in developed nations that we have been quick to forget that it is among the most spectacularly contagious of human infections, one that is still a major killer of children in underdeveloped countries.

Measles is an ancient disease. A Moslem physician of the 10th century, Rhazes, is credited with its first recorded accounts. Numerous epidemics swept across Europe through the Middle Ages and the Reformation period. Measles accompanied European explorers and immigrants to isolated new lands where the indigenous populations were susceptible to the disease. Among the most dramatic and informative effects of measles in totally susceptible populations was that of the 1851 epidemic in the Faroe Islands neighboring Greenland. Within 6 weeks, all but five of the 4000 inhabitants of the affected region contracted measles! Similar epidemics were responsible for decimating the Hawaiians and other isolated native populations upon their first contact with infected Europeans.

The study of measles made a natural progression from the field to the laboratory. In a model of early scientific investigation, Home demonstrated in the mid-18th century that measles could be transmitted by exposure to blood of infected individuals. These findings were confirmed in 1905 and extended several years later through studies of experimental transmission to monkeys. In 1954, Enders and Peebles reported successful growth of measles virus in cultured cells. This paved the way for studies of the molecular biology of measles virus and for the important development of an effective, live, attenuated measles virus vaccine.

MEASLES VIRUS (AGENT)

The disease is caused by the measles virus, a *Morbillivirus* of the paramyxovirus family (Table 33.1). The members of this virus family are pleomorphic, meaning that they have a variety of different shapes. The viral genome, composed of RNA, is contained within a helical nucleocapsid that is surrounded by a lipid bilayer envelope (Fig. 33.1). The surface is studded with glycoproteins that project from the envelope surface.

Measles virus has a single-stranded, nonsegmented RNA genome with negative sense (Fig. 33.2). Individual mRNAs, transcribed from the parental RNA, are translated into measles proteins. Important measles virus envelope proteins include hemagglutinins, whereas those in the related mumps viruses have both hemagglutinin and neuraminidase activity (Fig. 33.1). These proteins are named after easily identified biological properties and are more fully described in the chapter on influenza virus (Chapter 35).

Measles virus possesses an additional protein known as the **F** (for "fusion") **protein**, which endows the virus with the ability to **cause membranes to fuse together.** Presumably, the F protein participates in fusion of the infecting virus to the cell membrane. Secondarily, its expression on the surface of infected cells during viral replication causes fusion of adjacent cells. This results in one classic hallmark of measles virus infection, namely, the formation of **giant cells**, or syncytia (Fig. 33.3). (Discussion of a related RSV protein follows in the sections emphasizing that virus.) Measles virus also contains an **M** (for "matrix") **protein** on the inner surface of the viral envelope. This protein is said to participate in the proper envelopment of assembling nucleocapsids and to be required for spread of infectious progeny virions to adjacent cells. Other internal proteins, a large protein (**L**) and the polymerase (**P**) are believed to participate in transcription and genome replication. Measles replication is manifested not only by formation of syncytia, but also by the appearance of eosinophilic inclusions in the cytoplasm and the nucleus. These inclusions are aggregates of proteins that take up the eosin (red) stain commonly used in staining tissue slices.

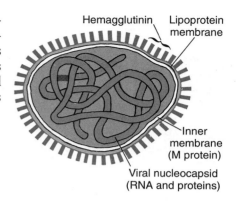

Figure 33.1.   Schematic diagram of measles virus.

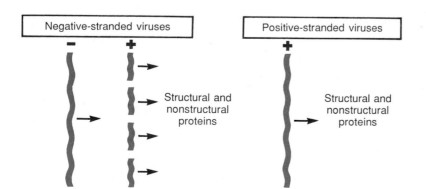

Figure 33.2.   Transcription and translation of proteins by negative-stranded and positive-stranded RNA viruses.

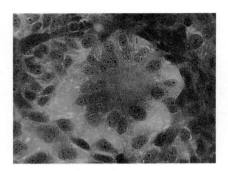

Figure 33.3. Giant cell (syncytium) formation in measles pneumonia.

ENCOUNTER

What do you need to know to consider further if Ms. M. has measles or to discount that possibility? First, did she ever have measles or has she been vaccinated? Before vaccination programs were initiated in this country, measles occurred primarily in 5- to 6-year-old children, and Ms. M. may have been too young to remember her early childhood diseases. A parent or an older sibling might recall; a simple phone call could be of help with her history. Because even these histories commonly prove unreliable, it would be more useful to obtain evidence of proper childhood vaccination, a fact widely solicited today by university health services from newly accepted applicants. Second, we would want to ask whether Ms. M. has recently been in contact with anyone who has this disease; however, patients are not usually aware of measles exposure until a cluster of cases is recognized.

The infection is extremely contagious, maximally so during the 2- to 3-day period prior to the appearance of the rash. Experiments done with virus-containing aerosols have shown that the disease can be acquired through inhalation. Therefore, Ms. M.'s exposure may have involved a seemingly innocuous encounter in an elevator, a bus, or anywhere. For instructive purposes, let us assume that other cases of measles have recently been recognized among individuals at Ms. M.'s university.

SPREAD AND MULTIPLICATION

Measles virus is inhaled during exposure to individuals with measles. It is believed that the virus replicates in respiratory epithelial cells and, about 3 days later, spreads through the bloodstream to infect distant body sites, including the lung and lymphoid tissues of the tonsils, lymph nodes, gastrointestinal tract, and spleen. After a few more days, a second, larger wave of virus is released from these sites into the bloodstream, producing maximal symptoms and skin involvement. Infections, like measles, that involve multiple replicative cycles and spread from the site of inoculation to local and then to distant sites typically have incubation periods of at least 10–14 days. Infections that manifest themselves at or near the site of inoculation (e.g., herpes simplex and influenza) and do not disseminate characteristically have short incubation periods (2–7 days).

DAMAGE

Most of the pathology associated with measles infection can be attributed directly to viral invasion and **cytopathic destruction of tissues** (Fig. 33.4). It seems likely, however, that some of the features of the disease are attributable to damage inflicted by the host immune responses to the virus. Measles causes the classic viral **enanthem** (lesions on mucous membranes) in the mouth called **Koplik's spots**, as well as a diffuse **exanthem** (external lesions), the typical measles rash. Biopsies of measles lesions show viral antigens and particles in the tissues, but the most prominent finding is an intense inflammatory response with edema and mononuclear infiltration. Immunodeficient children occasionally fail to develop a rash during measles infections, which suggests that the inflammatory response may be a major cause of tissue damage in the mucocutaneous lesions.

Both the humoral and the cellular immune responses modulate the outcome of acute measles infection. Administration of measles-specific

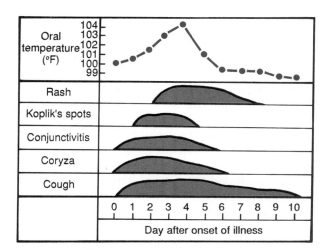

Figure 33.4. Signs and symptoms of measles infection.

globulin to susceptible individuals shortly after exposure to the virus will ameliorate the infection. The cellular immune response, however, is probably the major determinant of protection against severe measles infection and reinfection. Patients with agammaglobulinemia tolerate measles well, whereas those with congenital or acquired cellular immune deficits, such as those associated with acute leukemia, are prone to severe or fatal infection. Virus replication and spread are intense and unbridled, leading to fulminant pneumonia, respiratory failure, and death.

Measles infection itself stresses and further decreases cellular immunity. During measles infections, patients are at an increased risk of reactivating herpes simplex infections and tuberculosis, and transiently losing their delayed hypersensitivity response to tuberculin and to other antigens.

How Does the Host Respond to Measles?

Acute measles virus infection is nearly always symptomatic and is inevitably accompanied by immune responses in immunocompetent people. IgM antibodies circulate within 1 week of development of the rash and persist for several weeks or months. IgG antibodies can be detected in serum shortly after the IgM antibodies; they peak within a few weeks and gradually decline, although they persist for life. Secretory IgA antibodies are detectable in nasal secretions. A measles-specific lymphocyte-mediated immune response can be demonstrated in acute infection. So can interferon, whose levels wane rapidly with convalescence. The cellular immunity persists for life; thus, Ms. M. probably had neither the vaccine nor the disease in childhood.

DIAGNOSIS

With a known exposure, and certainly with the classic "measly" or **morbilliform** appearance (Fig. 33.5), a tentative diagnosis of measles can be made on clinical grounds with some confidence. There are, however, more precise means of establishing the diagnosis, and it is appropriate to employ such tests whenever the appearance or the history is in doubt.

The definitive diagnostic tool is virus isolation. The virus can be recovered from nasopharyngeal secretions, blood, or urine any time after the onset of symptoms and until the second or third day of rash. The procedure is expensive and not routinely available, so that most physicians appropriately resort to serodiagnostic studies.

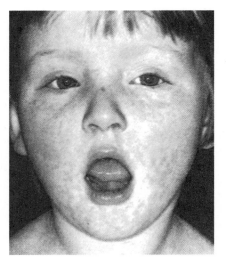

Figure 33.5. A child with measles, showing classic rash, runny nose, and conjunctivitis.

Serum collected very early in the course of the infection (the acute phase) already contains measurable IgM antibodies to measles antigens but little or no IgG antibody to the virus. The rapid evolution of an immune response to viral proteins results in a rise in antimeasles IgG level, so that the quantity of such antibodies would be greater 2–4 weeks after the onset of the illness. By then, most measles infections have resolved. Several serological methods are applicable, but the most widely used tests involve hemagglutination inhibition or an enzyme immunoassay (ELISA test, see Chapter 55). Recently, tests for measles IgG antibodies have become available and can be used to diagnose measles from a single blood sample obtained early in the illness.

As the health service physician, you can confirm Ms. M.'s diagnosis by collecting serum to test for measles IgM antibodies. Alternatively, you could store serum during her first visit to your office and ask her to return about 2 weeks later to have another serum specimen drawn. At that time, you would submit both specimens for testing. A typical confirmatory result might be an eight-fold rise in HAI titer, from 1:8 to 1:64, between the samples. These numbers mean the following: in the first sample there was already a sufficient quantity of measles antibody to be detectable in the assay when the serum was diluted eight times, but not more; in the convalescent serum specimen, there was so much more measles antibody that it could still be detected in serum that had been diluted 64-fold.

Complications

As implied above, immunologically competent individuals experience few complications, although the course of measles infection tends to be more severe in adults than in children and, even in children, measles is not benign. The infection itself is prostrating. The most common complications involve superinfections of the middle ear and the lung, primarily with pneumococci, staphylococci, or meningococci. Injury to respiratory tract tissues may render a patient more susceptible to bacterial superinfection. Pneumonia is the major reason for hospitalization in measles cases. It can be especially severe if the pneumonia is caused by the virus itself (giant cell pneumonitis) rather than by superinfecting bacteria.

About 1 in 1000 children with measles experience neurological complications. In general, these symptoms appear several days after resolution of the rash and consist of fever, headache, irritability, confusion, and seizures. Most patients survive this meningoencephalitis, but permanent sequelae include deafness, mental retardation, and seizure disorders.

Death from measles, which is rare in developed countries, stems largely from pulmonary and central nervous system complications. In developing nations, measles remains a major killer, felling tens of thousands of infants each year and making measles a major priority of international health programs. There are several reasons for the remarkable prevalence of measles in children of the Third World. First, even though there is an effective vaccination for the single strain of measles virus that circulates, unchanged from year to year around the world, vaccination is expensive and beyond the meager public health resources of many countries. Second, because the vaccine is a live one, it is stable only when stored in the cold, necessitating a "cold chain"— the endless link of refrigerated containers for shipment and storage— until it reaches the ultimate consumer. This, too, is a barrier to use in developing nations. Third, modern diagnostic and therapeutic tools are often not available to limit evolving complications. Finally, and most importantly, the infants of these regions frequently lack the immunological resources to combat the measles virus and other complicating pathogens. Malnutrition impairs cellular immune defenses (Chapter 74) and poor hygiene favors bacterial superinfection of the skin and respiratory tract (Chapter 71).

PREVENTION

Assuming that our patient, Ms. M., has measles, she may already have exposed others to her virus, at school or elsewhere. Is it possible to break the cycle of the infection in her community? Yes. We noted above that immune serum globulin can modify measles infection. This is appropriate for exposed individuals who are at risk of complicated infection, which includes infants who are less than 1 year old and especially includes children with leukemia or other disorders associated with substantial cellular immune impairment.

Of greater value, however, is the measles vaccine. A number of different ones have been developed. The first one, a killed virus vaccine, provided limited protection and only modified the disease associated with subsequent exposure to measles virus. The resulting **atypical measles syndrome** has many clinical features that differ from those of classic measles. Atypical measles occurs in young adults and adolescents and is difficult to diagnose because the exanthem has a highly variable appearance and pleuropulmonary complications are frequent.

Antibodies that neutralize virus infectivity are required to limit the spread of measles virus to uninfected cells. Many antibodies can also be induced by viral proteins but fail to inactivate the virus. The killed measles vaccine induces little antibody to the F (fusion) protein but high levels of antibody to the hemagglutinin. Inasmuch as antibody to the F protein is required to prevent cell-to-cell spread of measles virus, the killed vaccine provided only partial protection against infection.

A live attenuated virus vaccine is well tolerated and confers durable immunity. Measles vaccine is usually administered together with those against mumps and rubella, all consisting of attenuated live viruses (see Chapter 44). Currently, the recommendation is that it be given at 15 months of age. The reason for this choice is interesting. Virtually all maternal antibody to measles vaccine is likely to have disappeared from the child's circulation by 1 year of age. Only a small proportion of the children of that age have sufficient residual antibody to prevent the vaccine virus from growing enough to elicit an adequate immune response. Unfortunately, 1-year-olds do not mount strong enough immune responses to measles vaccine, so the age of 15 months was chosen because responses are often much better by then. The problem with delaying vaccination until 15 months is that it leaves most of the infants at risk for measles from the time that their maternally derived protection has waned until they are vaccinated. When epidemics occur, the age of vaccination is dropped to 6 months, with a second dose given at 15 months.

Measles vaccination is very successful and is a model for effective prevention of important common viral infections (Fig. 33.6). Current epidemics in the U.S. and developed countries result from suboptimal vaccination of the population. The Centers for Disease Control have urged universal vaccination, and most states have now mandated that a child must be vaccinated before being accepted into primary school.

Figure 33.6.   Reported cases of measles in the U.S., 1950–1990, showing the profound decline in measles incidence since the introduction of the vaccine, and the recent resurgence of the disease.

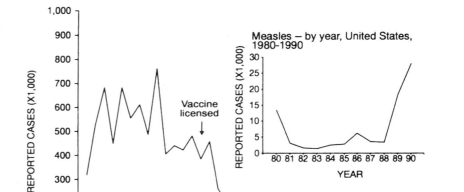

MEASLES (rubeola) — By year, United States, 1950–1990

The eradication of measles infection may be within our reach and has been championed by public health authorities in many countries; however, recent years have seen upsurges in measles incidence. The occurrence of outbreaks in high school- and college-age individuals probably reflects the combined effects of inadequate immunization (for example, immunization at too young an age), lack of immunization, and the occasional vaccine failure. These considerations led to the recommendation that all individuals born after 1956 should have two doses of the measles vaccine. The year 1956 was chosen as a cutoff because it has been found that most individuals born before that year are immune as the result of natural measles infection. An even more challenging problem is the continued occurrence of measles in preschool-age children in the inner city. These outbreaks will be ended by renewed efforts at vaccine delivery to disadvantaged populations with suboptimal access to an adequate health care delivery system.

As the university health service physician, your responsibilities extend well beyond diagnosing and caring for Ms. M. You are obliged to report her infection to state health authorities who track measles outbreaks. More importantly, you would need to see that all possible efforts are made to institute a campus-wide search to identify Ms. M.'s potential contacts and others who may be susceptible to measles. If evidence of pre-existing immunity cannot be obtained, vaccination is required.

SUBACUTE SCLEROSING PANENCEPHALITIS AND THE SLOW VIRUS INFECTIONS

A process known as a **slow virus infection** consists of the gradual appearance of disease months or years after a virus enters the body. It is to be distinguished from chronic viral infections such as that associated with hepatitis B virus (see Chapter 41) in which the disease progresses steadily after exposure. It is also different from recurrent viral infections like zoster (see Chapter 40), in which the virus can remain dormant for decades before reactivating.

A slow virus infection is unrecognized and undetectable for a long time, until it produces a slowly progressive disorder, one that is characteristically fatal. The best studied slow virus infections of man involve central nervous system degeneration and include **Kuru, Creutzfeldt-Jakob disease (CJD)** and **subacute sclerosing panencephalitis (SSPE)**. Kuru and CJD are caused by "unconventional agents," meaning that their exact nature is undefined.

SSPE is caused by a kind of measles virus, and is the best understood of the slow virus infections. Although rare, SSPE has captured the attention of the scientific and medical communities. It is a slowly progressive, unrelenting and untreatable, degenerative, neurological disorder that is characterized by scarring and demyelination of many areas of the brain. Death usually occurs within 2 years of onset. The incidence of SSPE is diminished in parallel with the decrease in measles cases that followed the introduction of the measles vaccine (Fig. 33.6).

SSPE occurs several years after the initial measles infection and is less likely to occur in individuals who received live measles vaccine. The remarkable aspect of the pathogenesis of SSPE is its association with an **altered measles virus**. How or why the alteration occurs in the virus is unknown but, presumably, it results from a spontaneous mutation. Using special techniques, the virus can be recovered from the brains of some affected patients, but its pattern of replication in brain, cultured cells, or experimental animals is altered. It appears that the measles M protein, normally involved in virus assembly, is not expressed normally; thus, the release of infectious progeny virus is impaired.

RESPIRATORY SYNCYTIAL VIRUS (RSV)

A cousin of the measles virus, RSV infection is well known to all physicians who care for young children. Its most characteristic clinical manifestation, bronchiolitis, the inflammation of the terminal bronchioles. Because of its extensive morbidity and significant mortality (approximately 4500 deaths per year in the U.S.), RSV infection is a major candidate for vaccine development. Efforts to make an effective human vaccine have all failed so far.

CASE

A 4-month-old infant boy developed a nasal discharge, low-grade fever, and was fussy. The next day, the parents called the pediatrician because he was having difficulty breathing. On examination, he had an obvious nasal discharge and was breathing 60 times per minute with mild nasal flaring and rib retractions. Auscultation of the lungs revealed scattered rales (crackles) and wheezes. A chest x-ray revealed hyperexpansion and patchy infiltrates in the lungs. The baby was admitted to the hospital, where treatment consisted of oxygen, humidified air delivered via a mist tent, fluids, and suctioning of secretions. He began to improve after 48 hours and was discharged home, where the symptoms gradually resolved over the next 7 days. A fluorescent antibody stain of nasal secretions performed on the day of admission was positive for respiratory syncytial virus antigen, and 3 days later, a culture was reported as positive for that virus.

RSV (AGENT)

RSV also has a single-stranded, nonsegmented RNA genome that is of negative sense. The entire genome has been cloned and sequenced.

Ten genes and their corresponding proteins have been identified. Unlike measles virus (or the influenza or parainfluenza viruses), no hemagglutinin activity has been identified. Two virally specified surface glycoproteins are prominent. One of them, the large glycoprotein, or G, is responsible for the initial binding of the virus to the host cell; the other, the fusion protein, or F, permits fusion of the viral envelope with the host cell membrane, leading to entry of the virus. The F protein also induces fusion of membranes of the infected cells. RSV gets its name resulting from the formation of syncytia, or multinucleated masses of fused cells.

In comparison to the rhinoviruses or the influenza viruses, isolates of RSV display less antigenic heterogeneity; however, recent studies have defined two distinct groups, A and B, as well as subgroups within each group. Both groups A and B circulate concurrently and have been detected in many locations throughout the world. The relationship of this antigenic diversity to the immunology or pathogenesis of RSV infection is not yet known, although recent evidence suggests that, of the two groups, infections caused by the group A viruses may be more severe.

ENCOUNTER AND ENTRY

The epidemiology of RSV infection has been extensively studied. The virus has been found in every part of the world where it has been sought. In temperate areas, it causes a highly seasonal disease, with epidemics every winter and essentially disease-free summers. Infection occurs in early childhood almost universally. Most infections lead to symptomatic illness, but no more than 1% are severe enough to require hospitalization. The mortality rate for hospitalized cases is less than 5%, but is higher in patients at risk, especially those with congenital heart disease, bronchopulmonary dysplasia related to prematurity, neuromuscular disease, or immune deficiency.

The only known source of RSV is infected humans who shed the virus in nasal secretions. As in the case of the rhinoviruses, transmission is thought to occur when secretions containing virus contaminate the hands of individuals. Small-particle air-borne transmission plays, at most, a minor role in transmission. In a classical experiment, volunteers in close physical contact with RSV-infected infants were more readily infected than those who remained 6 feet away (Table 33.2).

SPREAD, MULTIPLICATION, AND DAMAGE

Infection proceeds downward along the respiratory mucosa starting from the initial site of inoculation. Cell-to-cell transmission of virus may be important in this process. It is possible that aspiration of virus-contaminated secretions accelerates the process. There is no clinically significant spread to distant sites.

Table 33.2. Transmission of Respiratory Syncytial Virus

Volunteers	Cuddlers[a]	Touchers[b]	Sitters[c]
Exposed	7	10	14
Infected	5	4	0
Incubation time	4 days	5.5 days	

[a]Close contact with infected infant
[b]Self inoculation after touching surfaces contaminated with infants' secretions
[c]Sitting over 6 feet from infected infant

Severe RSV infection results in one of two somewhat overlapping clinical syndromes: (*a*) bronchiolitis and (*b*) pneumonia. The child with bronchiolitis has difficulty breathing and there is functional evidence of obstruction of the airways that resembles asthma. Breathing is very noisy, with wheezing. As illustrated in the case history, the chest x-ray reveals hyperexpansion of the lungs, resulting from trapped air; it may also show streaky infiltrates, usually in both lungs. In the child with pneumonia, pulmonary infiltrates are more prominent. Wheezing and hyperexpansion may also occur, but less prominently than in bronchiolitis. In either syndrome, the airways are inflamed and edematous.

Tissue sections from fatal cases show necrosis of the epithelial cells that line the small bronchioles. There is also infiltration of lymphocytes among the mucosal epithelial cells and evidence of increased mucous secretion. The underlying elastic and muscle fibers are not affected. In cases of pneumonia, alveolar involvement consisting of swelling of the alveolar lining cells and interstitial inflammation accompanies bronchiolar involvement.

Bronchiolitis can be distinguished from asthma because bronchiolitis usually occurs in infants 2–8 months of age in whom bronchial smooth muscle is incompletely developed. Thus, smooth muscle contraction may be less important in bronchiolitis than in asthma. If an individual bronchiole is completely obstructed, the portion of the lung ventilated by it may collapse. If obstruction is incomplete, a ball-valve effect may occur, leading to hyperexpansion of the distal lung. The entire process is associated with mismatches in ventilation and perfusion of the lung, and results in decreased oxygenation, along with the increased work of breathing.

In most cases, the infection is self-limited, and recovery begins after several days; however, in the severe cases that occur in children compromised by other diseases, there may be respiratory failure, and the child may die unless mechanical ventilation is provided. There is considerable concern that severe bronchiolitis in infancy may be associated with chronic lung disease in later life. Infants with bronchiolitis are more likely to have episodes of wheezing as they grow older, but any relationship between bronchiolitis in infancy and chronic lung disease in adulthood remains conjectural.

Doubts have been raised about the role of the immune system in protecting against RSV infections. First, most individuals experience multiple infections with RSV, indicating that immunity is incomplete. Second, infants are often infected at a time when they still have serum-neutralizing antibody from their mothers. Despite these negative findings, there is now evidence that the immune system provides protection. Most importantly, children with both congenital and acquired immune deficiencies suffer prolonged and severe RSV infection. Infants with high levels of serum antibody against RSV are less likely to develop lower respiratory tract involvement than infants with lower levels. Finally, in experimental animals, the administration of monoclonal antibodies to RSV glycoproteins or inoculation with vaccinia virus genetically engineered to express these antigens prevents lower respiratory tract involvement (although not usually nasal infection).

Do immune mechanisms contribute to the clinical manifestations of RSV infection? This is hinted by its resemblance to asthma, a process that involves the immune-mediated release of bronchoconstricting inflammatory mediators. Increased levels of histamine and IgE antibody directed against RSV have been found in nasal secretions from children with RSV bronchiolitis. Another hint that the immune system might contribute to RSV disease derives from an experience in the 1960s with an experimental killed RSV vaccine. Children given this vaccine not only were unprotected against RSV infection, but actually developed more severe disease following natural exposure to RSV! It is now known that the killed vaccine elicited only a partial antibody response against the virus, much the same as described above for early measles vaccines. The responses were sufficient to permit immune-mediated damage to tissues once exposure to the infection had occurred, but not sufficient to limit virus growth and spread.

PREVENTION AND TREATMENT

Because RSV infection is so prevalent and accounts for considerable morbidity, this virus is an important candidate for vaccine development. For a number of years there was understandably little activity in this area, for fear of repeating the experience with the earlier vaccine. Recently, interest in an RSV vaccine has been renewed, and promising results have been reported by cloning DNA copies of the viral genes. By using individual genes cloned into vaccinia virus vectors (Chapter 42), it has been possible to show that the immune response associated with either the F or G glycoprotein can protect small mammals, such as the mouse and the cotton rat, against RSV challenge. The immune response to F tends to be broad, whereas that to G tends to be specific for the RSV group (A or B) used to induce the immune response. Ongoing work is evaluating the use of vaccines composed of the F and/or G glycoproteins that have been produced by cloning RSV genes into expression vectors. One approach of particular interest has been to produce a chimerical protein composed of the extracellular domains of both F and G.

In the area of treatment, a new era began recently with the introduction of the antiviral drug ribavirin to treat severe RSV infection (Chapter 43). This drug is given by aerosol and is generally reserved for very severe RSV infections occurring in infants whose condition is already compromised, especially by chronic lung disease resulting from immaturity or from congenital heart disease.

Self-assessment Questions

1. What peculiar effects do measles and RSV have on tissue cells?

2. Describe the replication cycle of measles virus.

3. Discuss the role of the immune responses to Paramyxoviridae.

4. What problems are associated with vaccination against measles and RSV?

5. How could we eradicate measles from the face of the earth?

SUGGESTED READING

Hall WR, Hall CB. Atypical measles in adolescents: evaluation of clinical and pulmonary function. Ann Intern Med 1979;90:882–886.

Katz SL, Krugman S, Quinn TC. International symposium on measles immunization. J infect Dis 1983;5:389–625.

McIntosh K, Chanock RM. Respiratory syncytial virus. In: Fields BN, Knipe DM, et al. Virology, 2nd ed. New York: Raven Press, 1990:1045–1072.

Morgan EM, Rapp F. Measles virus and its associated diseases. Bacteriol Rev 1977;41:636–666.

Norby E, Oxman MN. Measles virus. In: Fields BN, Knipe DM, et al. Virology, 2nd ed. New York: Raven Press, 1990:1013–1044.

Rabies

34

George M. Baer

Rabies is a disease that has instilled terror in human society. The reasons are that, with rare exceptions, all of the people who are bitten by a rabid animal and who develop symptoms, die, and that many of the symptoms of rabies in patients are visible and frightening. In developed countries, the disease in dogs has been controlled with canine vaccines, and, consequently, human rabies cases have become very rare. Surveillance in these countries is still important, because the rabies virus is still commonly found in a variety of wild animals (including foxes, skunks, raccoons, and insectivorous bats). A limited number of countries are free of the disease, mainly islands such as England, Australia, Japan, Taiwan, and most of the small Caribbean islands. The disease is still common in many developing countries, where canine rabies persists and thousands of people are vaccinated for exposure to potentially rabid animals, mainly dogs.

This chapter will discuss the distribution of rabies in various parts of the world and the animal species involved, as well as the excretion of virus in those animals, the diagnosis of the disease, and treatment of persons exposed (including the crucial question: to treat or not to treat).

CASE 1

As Mr. V., a 38-year-old dock hand, was walking home in suburban Seattle, Washington, he was suddenly attacked by an average size brown dog, which bit him on the right calf, and only let go when hit repeatedly with a lunch box. The dog then ran away. Mrs. V. cleaned her husband's many puncture wounds when he got home. Both Mr. and Mrs. V. were concerned about rabies and called their state health department. They were told that there had been no rabies in dogs in Washington in decades, and only two cases of rabies in any terrestrial animal; only bats had been reported rabid in the last decade. The couple was told not to worry about rabies in the dog.

Mr. V. asked his family doctor the following questions:

1. Should he have been treated for rabies exposure?

2. If he had been bitten by a bat that then flew away would the treatment have been different?

3. Did he consult the proper advisors in seeking rabies treatment recommendations?

CASE 2

Mr. R., a 22-year-old phlebotomist, was bitten on the right index finger by a bat while at a cavern in Mercedes, Texas. He did not obtain medical care for the bite in spite of being urged to do so by his friends. Forty-eight days later, he complained of weakness in his right hand and presented at an emergency room; based on a history of a puncture wound with a catfish fin earlier in the week, he was treated with antibiotic and tetanus toxoid.

Several days later, Mr. R. was admitted to the intensive care unit of a hospital with a preliminary diagnosis of encephalitis or tetanus because of intermittent episodes of rigidity, breath holding, hallucinations, and difficulty in swallowing. He was intubated because he had uncontrollable oral secretions. At that time, Mr. R.'s supervisor from work reported to the hospital authorities the history of bat bite; serum, cerebrospinal fluid (CSF), and skin samples were taken for laboratory work-up; all of the specimens were negative for rabies antigens. Despite supportive therapy, Mr. R.'s condition deteriorated and he died 4 days later after an increase in severity of his earlier symptoms, followed by coma and respiratory failure.

Postmortem samples of brain tissue were positive for rabies by the fluorescent antibody test. The rabies variant isolated was identified serologically as identical to those found in Mexican freetail bats. Because of numerous possible contacts he had had with people—family, friends, co-workers, and medical personnel—while sick (and immediately before), rabies postexposure prophylaxis was begun for 67 of 105 possible contacts.

The following questions arose:

1. Is this a "typical" case of rabies in the U.S.?

2. What treatment would Mr. R. have received had he gone to the hospital when he was bitten?

3. What would have been the chances of success if Mr. R. had been treated for rabies?

4. How many cases of human rabies have there been in the U.S. in the last decade?

5. How many persons are immunized in the U.S. each year?

6. Are many people usually exposed to human rabies cases?

7. Were Mr. R.'s symptoms typical of human rabies cases?

HISTORY OF RABIES

One would expect that a disease transmitted by the bite of many kinds of animals would have been recognized in antiquity, and that is so: in the Eshnunna Code of the third millennium B.C. it is written:

"If a dog is mad and the authorities have brought the fact to the knowledge of its owner; if he does not keep it in, and it bites a man and causes his death, then the owner shall pay . . .40 shekels of silver. If it bites a slave and causes his death he shall pay 15 shekels of silver."

Definite evidence that saliva was infective came in the early 19th century when a German scientist (Zinke) painted saliva from a rabid dog on wounds of a dachshund's leg, and caused the disease. The role of the central nervous system in rabies was demonstrated by Pasteur in 1881 when he injected rabbits intracerebrally (rather than intramuscularly) with a suspension of brain taken from a rabid cow and reproduced the disease. Pasteur produced the first rabies vaccines by passing infectious material (he did not know it was a virus) through repeated passages in the spinal cords of rabbits. The spinal cords were partially inactivated by drying over potash for various periods of time. He first vaccinated with cords dried for 14 days, then gradually used cords treated less and less, until the last injection employed fully virulent cord suspensions.

The early studies on vaccine efficacy were done in dogs, but the results from those studies led to the triumphant use of a spinal cord ("Pasteur") vaccine in humans in July, 1885. Over the next few decades, there were many changes in vaccine preparation, including inactivation of virus by chemical means (phenol) and dilution of the vaccine rather than "aging" of cords. Rabies vaccines today are mostly inactivated products, and are either produced in tissue culture (in developed countries) or in young adult sheep or suckling mice (in some developing countries). The earlier type of vaccines prepared with nervous system tissue result in postvaccinal demyelination and tissue destruction in 3–4% of vaccinated individuals. The use of these vaccines should be discouraged.

RABIES VIRUS

Viruses of the *Lyssavirus* genus of the Rhabdoviridae family of RNA viruses are known to infect dozens of mammalian species, including humans. The reason for this unusually broad host range is not known. The viruses are **bullet-shaped** (approximately 180 nm in length by 75 nm in width, which is fairly large for a virus, Fig. 34.1). The rabies virus contains an external **glycoprotein** (G) coat, located immediately outside a peripheral **matrix (M) protein**. The infectious component of the virus is the helical **ribonucleoprotein (RNP)** core, an unsegmented single-stranded RNA tightly encased in the major **N protein**. The genome of this virus is of negative polarity, thus the virion contains an RNA-dependent viral **RNA transcriptase**. The replication cycle of this virus takes place entirely in the cytoplasm of infected cells and results in the formation of numerous viral particles. Masses of nucleocapsids accumulate in the cytoplasm to form inclusions called **Negri bodies** that can be seen in stained preparations or by immunofluorescence (Fig. 34.2).

Resistance to rabies infection has long been correlated with the presence of neutralizing antibody, and the relationship between those antibodies and protection has been well established in a variety of animal species. With very few exceptions, suitably potent vaccines prepared from any of the lyssaviruses protect against the strains of virus found in nature; exceptions are Mokola and Lagos bat viruses, both found, to date, only in Africa.

ENCOUNTER

From 1980–1990 there were 13 human rabies deaths in the U.S., of which nine were imported, with the remaining four due to exposures to wild animals or to unidentified animals. In 1989, there were nearly 5000 cases of animal rabies, of which nearly 90% were in wild animals; of the affected domestic animals, 160 were dogs and 212 were cats. Although most rabies cases in the U.S. are obviously found in wild animals, most people are vaccinated for exposure to dogs and cats that are either rabid or that have escaped in areas of endemic rabies and cannot be located.

Rabies epidemiology varies greatly from country to country. In almost all of Africa, Asia, and Latin America rabies has been and continues to be a disease of dogs, accounting for over 90% of human treatments and 90% of human rabies deaths. Where canine rabies persists, human rabies remains common and millions of persons are vaccinated for exposures to rabid animals, mostly dogs. For instance, an estimated 25,000–50,000 people die of rabies in India every year.

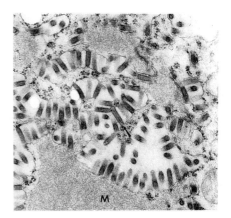

Figure 34.1. Neuron of a dog inoculated with rabies virus. An ultrathin section of a cell showing randomly spaced viral matrices (*M*) and virions (*arrow*) budding from the endoplasmic reticulum membranes; original magnification, ×62,560.

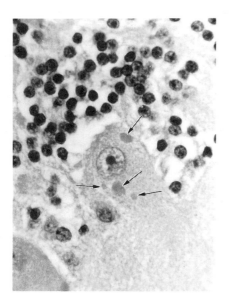

Figure 34.2. Negri bodies in a neuron of a rabid dog. Hematoxylin-eosin; original magnification, ×560.

In much of the developed world, however, rabies in dogs has been controlled and the disease primarily affects a variety of wild animals and the animals they bite. In western Europe, for instance, the red fox is the primary transmitter of rabies, and most cases are found in that species; in the U.S. and Canada, rabies is carried by skunks, raccoons, foxes, and insectivorous bats. It is crucial to know the exact location of rabid animals within each state through state health departments or federal health agencies because this information will assist in deciding whether to recommend treatment for persons bitten by animals. If a given species has not been reported to be rabid in an area (e.g., terrestrial animals in the Pacific Northwest), there is usually no need to treat persons exposed to those animals in that area. If a person is bitten by a bat, however, that is a different matter because rabid bats have been found in those states. Some animal species are almost never diagnosed as rabid, including rodents (mice, rats, hamsters) and lagomorphs (rabbits and hares).

Approximately 20,000 persons are vaccinated against rabies in the U.S. each year. Only a small number of persons who are vaccinated are known to have actually been bitten by a rabid animal.

The bite of a rabid animal does not necessarily result in rabies. Contrary to popular beliefs, humans are surprisingly refractory to the rabies virus. The incidence of disease after the bite of a known rabid dog is about 15%, although this figure goes up considerably with severe bites on the face and head.

The problems of encounter with the rabies virus are very different from those in other virus diseases, inasmuch as the location and time of possible virus entry (by bite) are known. Questions that are particular to rabies include:

- Did a bite or break of the skin really occur?
- Has rabies been reported in the state or region where the bite occurred?
- Was the biting animal rabid—is it available for laboratory diagnosis or did it escape?
- Is the species known commonly to carry the virus?
- Is the biting animal a dog or cat that can be observed? (If so, the period of presymptomatic virus transmission is known to be a maximum of 10 days; if a person has been bitten by a dog 11 days before it gets sick, no treatment is needed).

SPREAD AND MULTIPLICATION

After rabies viruses enter the body by bite, there is a variable incubation period lasting 1–2 months but rarely years. The length of this period depends on the size of the viral inoculum and the length of the neural path from the wound to the brain. Thus, severe bites on face and head tend to result in a shorter incubation period.

Studies in experimental animals have shown that, during the incubation period, the virus remains at or close to the bite. It is not known exactly where the virus resides during that period nor what stimulates it to advance to the peripheral and central nervous system by this route. When the virus eventually reaches the peripheral nerves, it quickly advances to the spinal ganglia, spinal cord, and brain. The virus moves passively within the axoplasm of peripheral nerves to the central nervous system.

The possible role of the neuromuscular junction in virus pathogenesis has been studied, as well as the role of the acetylcholine receptor. From the brain, the virus often returns to the periphery using the same axoplasmic route as used for centripetal movement. A favored peripheral site is the highly innervated submaxillary salivary glands, but the virus is found in many other tissues. In approximately 25% of dogs, the virus never reaches these glands or any exit route. The levels of virus in the salivary gland tissue of rabid animals may be 1000 or more times the level found in the brain, suggesting that the virus replicates at this site as well. The location in the salivary glands helps explain the transmission of virus from one animal to another.

Paradigm: What Determines How a Virus Spreads In The Body?

To produce systemic illness, a virus must spread from its site of entry and primary replication to distant target tissues. This aspect of viral pathogenesis is well exemplified by neurotropic viruses that enter the body through a number of different portals (e.g., respiratory, gastrointestinal, or venereal) and then spread to reach the central nervous system (CNS). The two principal pathways of spread to the CNS are through the bloodstream and through the nerves. Most neurotropic viruses (e.g., arboviruses, enteroviruses, measles virus, and mumps virus) reach the CNS by **hematogenous spread**. Others (e.g., rabies virus and herpes simplex virus) reach the CNS by neural spread. Almost nothing is known about the viral genes and proteins or the cellular mechanisms responsible for determining which pathway will be used by viruses to spread within the infected host. Below, we present one of the outstanding examples of the few investigations that have been carried out to resolve these questions.

In an attempt to determine which viral genes are involved in the mode of spread, a study has been carried out with reoviruses that, in the laboratory, cause infections of the CNS of newborn mice. Reovirus type 3 infects neurons and produces a lethal necrotizing **encephalitis** after intracerebral inoculation. Type 1, on the other hand, infects ependymal cells and produces hydrocephalus. This suggests that type 3 is transported via nerves to the CNS and within it, whereas type 1 utilizes a non-neural pathway.

To investigate if reovirus types 1 and 3 use different pathways of spread to the CNS, investigators (Tyler KL, McPhee DL, Fields BN. Distinct pathways of viral spread in the host determined by reovirus S1 gene segment. Science 1986;233:770–774) took advantage of the fact that the motor and sensory neurons innervating the hindlimb and forelimb footpads are located in different regions of the spinal cord. If type 3 spreads via nerves, it should appear preferentially in the region of the spinal cord containing the neurons innervating the skin and musculature at the site of viral inoculation. If type 1 spreads through the bloodstream, it should appear in all regions of the spinal cord in equivalent amounts and with similar kinetics. When type 3 and type 1 were injected into the forelimb and hindlimb footpads of neonatal mice, type 3 appeared first, and in much higher titer, in the region of the spinal cord innervating the injected limb. In contrast, type 1, after either hindlimb or forelimb inoculation, appeared at essentially the same time and in equivalent titer in all regions of the spinal cord. These results support the hypothesis that type 3 spreads through nerves and type 1 spreads via the bloodstream to reach the CNS.

To confirm these results, the spread of types 1 and 3 from the hindlimb to the spinal cord was studied after section of the sciatic nerve. Since the sciatic nerve is the principal neural pathway from the hindlimb to the spinal cord, its section should completely prevent spread of virus from the hindlimb through nerves but should not affect its capacity to spread through bloodstream. As predicted, sciatic nerve section completely inhibited spread of type 3 to the spinal cord but had no significant effect on the spread of type 1.

Genetic analysis allows the conclusion that a single viral-encoded protein is responsible for determining the pattern of spread of reoviruses. Passive immunization of mice with antibodies directed against the type 3 protein, but not against the type 1 protein, inhibits the neural spread of type 3. It is not yet known how this protein determines the tropism of the two types of reoviruses for neurons and ependymal cells, respectively. It is likely that a combined genetic, biochemical study of animal model systems will help understand the mode of spread of viruses in the body.

DAMAGE

There is surprisingly limited histopathological change in the CNS of animals or humans dying of rabies. Neurons of infected animals and humans contain typical intracytoplasmic inclusions, the **Negri bodies**. These inclusions are highly pathognomonic, that is, indicative of the specific disease, and in the case of rabies may be the only such sign. In some cases, there may, in addition, be limited perivascular cuffing and limited neuronal necrosis. These limited changes are in striking contrast to the marked symptoms seen in human rabies.

Symptoms usually start with difficulty in swallowing and increased muscle tone. **Hydrophobia**, the contractions of the muscles involved in swallowing, is sometimes elicited by the mere sight of liquid. Eventually, patients develop signs of extensive damage to the CNS, progress to **coma**, and die. Rabies virus can be detected in and isolated from almost all tissues in the body.

DIAGNOSIS

Until 1960, rabies diagnosis in suspect animals was limited to the detection of **Negri bodies** in Ammon's horn and cerebellum (the inclusions are found in approximately 75% of positive cases), and **inoculation into mice** of specimens from brains without Negri bodies. This resulted in the immediate diagnosis of part of the positive cases but a delayed diagnosis of the rest, usually a period of 2–4 weeks until the inoculated mice either died of rabies or survived.

In 1960, the **fluorescent antibody** technique was introduced whereby brain impressions are stained with a fluorescein-tagged antibody. This technique is used throughout the developed world. Diagnosis can also be made in persons with encephalitis by fluorescent staining of skin biopsies of the nape of the neck where many hair follicles are found (the infected nerve network around hair follicles fluoresces) during the early encephalitic period. This has become the diagnostic procedure of choice early in the disease. Neutralizing antibodies are found in the serum and CSF later in infection, usually 8–10 days after the encephalitic symptoms appear.

PREVENTION

Vaccination of Animals

It should not be forgotten that rabies is a **zoonosis**, a disease transmitted to humans by animals. To that end, the best protection against the disease can be achieved by the elimination of the disease in dogs (and cats) by **vaccinating** those animals and creating a barrier to animal-to-animal transmission (either dog-to-dog or wild animal-to-dog) or by vaccinating wild animals (vaccines have already been developed for foxes and raccoons). Vaccination of wild animals has been done successfully on a mass scale with air drops of baited oral vaccine.

Postexposure Treatment of Humans

Once the decision to treat has been made, human treatment consists of three steps: (a) **local wound treatment**, (b) passive administration of **antibody** (antiserum or immunoglobulin), and (c) **vaccination**. Superficial wounds can be washed with soap and water; deep wounds should be flushed and swabbed with Quaternary ammonium compounds or other viricidal substances. The passive antibody administered in developed countries is **human rabies immune globulin (HRIG)** collected from immunized persons and administered as soon as possible after rabies exposure; one-half infiltrated at the bite site and one-half administered intramuscularly.

Vaccination with modern tissue culture vaccines consists of a series of five doses, all administered intramuscularly in the deltoid region, 1 ml each, over a 4-week period. The most common vaccines are prepared with several kinds of human or monkey cells in culture from which the virus is purified. Two vaccines are licensed in the U.S., human diploid vaccine and rhesus diploid vaccine. All individuals given such a treatment have developed the expected level of antibodies. When the combination of globulin and vaccine has been properly applied in a timely fashion, **no treatment failures have been noted**. Only rare complications have been seen after such treatment. It is interesting that chloroquine, a drug used for antimalarial prophylaxis, inhibits or suppresses antibody development in vaccine recipients. This fact must be taken into account when administering pre-exposure rabies vaccine in areas where malarial prophylaxis may be in use.

CONCLUSIONS

You now know that the decision not to vaccinate Mr. V. was based on sound epidemiological principles, specifically the absence of reported rabies cases in the main species affected in other parts of the region (raccoons and skunks, in this case). In the case of Mr. R., on the other hand, we noted that treatment was not administered, with disastrous consequences. The main point in rabies control, it must be remembered, is control of the disease in the animals that bite people. Because the prime offender is the dog, canine vaccination is essential in rabies zones.

Self-assessment Questions

1. How does the epidemiology of rabies vary between developed and developing countries?

2. What are the issues that should be considered in treating a person who has been bitten by an animal whose health status is unknown?

3. What are the general features of the rabies virus?

4. What should be the strategy in treating a person bitten by a rabid animal?

SUGGESTED READING

Expert Committee on Rabies, 8th Report, World Health Organization, Geneva, Switzerland, 1988.

Fishbein D. Human rabies. In: Baer GM, ed. The natural history of rabies. Boca Raton, FL: CRC Press, 1991.

Rabies Prevention—United States, 1991. Recommendations of the Advisory Committee on Immunization Practices (ACIP). Centers for Disease Control, U.S. Public Health Service. Immunization Practices, U.S. Public Health Service, 1991.

Influenza and Its Virus

35

Stephen E. Straus

Influenza (the "flu") ranks among the major epidemic diseases in developed countries. On several occasions in our history it has spread throughout the world, causing **pandemics**. In healthy adults, it is a relatively mild disease; however, it contributes significantly to the mortality of the elderly and of persons with underlying respiratory and cardiac problems. The main reason why influenza has not been eradicated is that the viruses have the ability to change their main antigens, **hemagglutinin** and **neuraminidase**. Thus, previous exposure or vaccination does not ensure immunity against newly emerging strains of the virus. Up-to-date vaccines, containing different combinations of antigens, are administered during epidemics to persons at risk. Several drugs are effective in the treatment of this disease.

Influenza viruses are enveloped and belong to the **Orthomyxovirus** group. Their **RNA genome is divided into eight segments of negative polarity**. It is not known how these segments are assembled in the progeny virions to ensure that each viral particle contains a complete copy of the genome.

CASE

When Ms. I., a healthy 40-year-old school teacher, was told by her doctor that she probably had influenza, she realized that she has never forgotten the early winter of 1957. It seemed as if everyone in her entire family had developed the flu. With all of the coughing, chills, and aches, it was hard to get any sleep. Everyone had to take turns getting out of bed to get aspirin or fluids for the ones who were the weakest. Schools were closed for several days during the outbreak because so many teachers and students had become ill. The most upsetting recollection, though, was the death of her grandfather. He was a smoker and had a little heart trouble, but basically he was quite sound. Then he developed the flu. His illness began as it did in the rest of the family, although he coughed and spit a bit more. One night, his fever increased and he started to get very short of breath. He was rushed to the hospital but died in 2 days despite antibiotics and oxygen.

Now the news reports indicate that a new strain of flu has gotten a foothold in the U.S., this one apparently from the Far East. Ms. I. is apprehensive about the possible effects of this new Asian flu, and particularly, that her aging parents, who live downstairs from her, may be vulnerable. Ms. I. has a runny nose, mild sore throat, and cough, not much different from many colds she has had over the years, but the amount of fever, muscle aches, and fatigue were bad enough for her to consult the family's doctor. He did not carry out laboratory tests but based a tentative diagnosis on the clinical picture and on a bulletin he received from the State Board of Health about the presence of a new strain of influenza virus in the area. If Ms. I. had a typical course, he predicts that she will feel sick for 4–7 days, but the fatigue and dry cough may last for days or even weeks thereafter. Because Ms. I. visits so often with her parents, they are advised to come in to get a flu shot and a several week-supply of amantadine pills.

This chapter will explain why the 1957 influenza epidemic was so severe. Ms. I. is probably also asking several other questions, including:

1. How do new influenza strains arise?
2. Why are people susceptible to repeated influenza infections?
3. What makes some strains of influenza more dangerous than others?
4. Why do her parents need a flu shot when they have had one before?
5. What will the amantadine do for her parents and why shouldn't she get it also?

Beyond the classic presentation of influenza, such as that in Ms. I.'s case, lies an entire spectrum of pulmonary complications that are more likely to develop in certain settings; i.e., during pregnancy, in the elderly, and in any individual with congenital or acquired cardiopulmonary diseases. A few such individuals are at risk for the development of either primary influenza pneumonia, a devastating virus infection of the lung parenchyma, or more typically, secondary bacterial pneumonia.

Influenza has many imitators. Similar, but less severe illnesses caused by other viruses are all commonly called the "flu." Gastrointestinal symptoms such as cramping, nausea, vomiting, and diarrhea are not common features of influenza (except in children), and the term "intestinal flu" is a total misnomer.

HISTORY OF INFLUENZA

Epidemics of brief illness with fever, cough, and severe weakness were described by Hippocrates in the 5th century B.C. and reported repeatedly throughout the Middle Ages. Since 1173, over 300 outbreaks of influenza-like illness have been recorded at an average interval of 2.4 years. The development of intercontinental travel and commerce made possible the first known **pandemic** (global epidemic) of influenza, which occurred in 1580 and originated in Asia, spreading to Europe, and later to the Americas. Twenty-two pandemics of influenza illness have been recorded since the early 18th century; the most dramatic of these was the Great Spanish influenza pandemic of 1918–1919 in which over 20 million people died worldwide.

Influenza is an Italian word indicating the medical belief that the illness resulted from the "influence" of atmospheric factors. An infectious etiology for influenza was not seriously espoused until the end of the last century when a bacillus, now known as *Haemophilus influenzae*, was recovered from the sputum of patients with this syndrome. The viral etiology of influenza was finally proven in 1933, when the contagious component in patient secretions was shown to pass through porcelain filters fine enough to exclude bacteria. The virus was first grown in the laboratory in 1940 (in fertilized chicken eggs) and, by 1950, the three serological types of influenza known to infect people were recognized.

INFLUENZA VIRUSES

Influenza viruses belong to the family **Orthomyxoviridae** and include three types, A, B, and C that were originally defined serologically. Infection with one serotype affords no protection against the other types. Over the years of study, important structural, epidemiological, and clinical differences among the three types were defined, as summarized in Table 35.1.

Influenza A viruses are among the best studied of human RNA viruses. The entire amino acid sequence and the three-dimensional structure of some of their proteins are known, as are the sequences of all the RNA segments of representative strains of each viral serotype. The influenza A virus genome consists, surprisingly, of **eight discrete segments** of single-stranded **RNA of negative polarity** indicating that they must be transcribed into translatable messages.

Influenza viruses are enveloped (Figs. 35.1 and 35.2). The viral envelope is covered with **spikes**, or **peplomers**, which, in the cases of influenza A and B strains, are made up of two different proteins, the **hemagglutinin** and the **neuraminidase**. Influenza C viruses have a single protein with both hemagglutinin and neuraminidase activity. Each of the influenza serotypes can be further subdivided into strains on the basis of subtle yet important differences, i.e., the makeup of their viral surface antigens. Matrix proteins line the inner aspects of the viral envelope while other internal proteins, polymerases and the nucleoproteins, are associated with the viral RNA.

How Do These Viruses Replicate?

Many biochemical and molecular aspects of the replication cycle of the influenza virus have been elucidated. They illustrate important aspects of virus-host cell interaction and will be presented in some detail. Influenza infection starts with binding of the viral **hemagglutinin** to N-acetylneuraminic acid components of various cell surface **glycoproteins** or **glycolipids**. After binding to these receptors, the viruses are engulfed in phagosomes, where they become uncoated. The acidic milieu of the lysosomes (which fuse with the phagosomes) alters the conformation of the viral hemagglutinin, uncovering peptide sequences that stimulate **fusion of membranes**. The result is that the **viral membrane fuses with the phagolysosomal membrane**, releasing the nucleocapsid into the cytoplasm. The next events, further uncoating the virus and transporting the viral RNAs to the nucleus for replication, are not well understood.

Replication of influenza viruses is set in motion within an hour after infection and begins with **RNA transcription** that uses the infecting RNA genome as the direct template. This cannot be carried out by any known host cell enzymes and requires a **viral RNA-dependent RNA**

Table 35.1. Comparison of Influenza, A, B, and C Viruses			
	A	B	C
Severity of illness	++++	++	+
Animal reservoir	Yes	No	No
Spread in humans	Pandemic	Epidemic	Sporadic
Antigenic changes	Shift, drift	Drift	Drift
No. of RNA segments	8	8	7
No. of surface glycoproteins	2	2	1

Figure 35.1. The structure of influenza virus detailing its surface proteins and segmented genome.

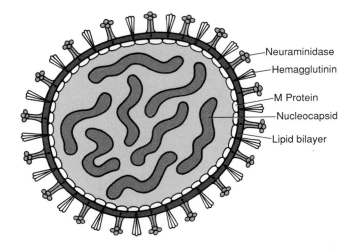

Neuraminidase
Hemagglutinin
M Protein
Nucleocapsid
Lipid bilayer

Figure 35.2. Assembly of influenza virus at the cell surface and subsequent release.

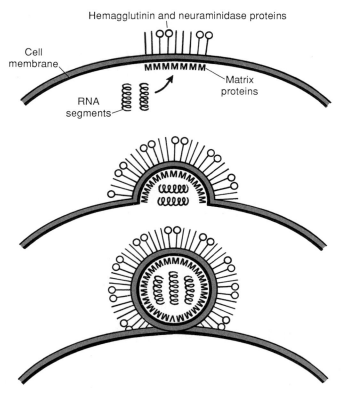

Hemagglutinin and neuraminidase proteins

Cell membrane

MMMMMMM

Matrix proteins

RNA segments

polymerase activity provided by components of the infecting viral core (polymerase proteins PB1 and PB2). The transcripts made are of positive polarity and serve as **messengers** for protein synthesis. Each mRNA transcript is longer than the parental negative strands because after transcription its 5′ end is **"capped"** by the addition of methylated nucleotides and its 3′ end is **polyadenylated**.

Some of the details of the post-transcriptional **modification** of influenza mRNAs have been elucidated. Unlike the situation with most RNA viruses, replication of the influenza virus takes place in the **nucleus**. This is necessary because the influenza virus, unlike many other negative-stranded RNA viruses, lacks capping and methylating enzyme activities. In a remarkable and unique feat of **molecular parasitism**, influenza viruses evolved the means to "steal" the methylated caps plus 10–13 of the first nucleotides from the 5′ ends of cellular mRNAs that had been previously synthesized and modified in the nucleus.

Ultimately 10 transcripts are synthesized from the eight genomic RNAs and **translated** in the cytoplasm into seven structural and three nonstructural proteins (Table 35.2). How are the special **RNA molecules destined for packaging into progeny virions made?** Apparently, two viral proteins (polymerase, PA, and the nucleoprotein, NP) facilitate the transcription of a special set of RNAs, identical in length to the infecting strands. These **full-length positive strands are neither capped nor polyadenylated** and, therefore, cannot direct protein synthesis. Instead, they are copied directly, again, to yield RNAs of negative polarity that are suitable for incorporation into new virus particles.

INFLUENZA VIRUS HEMAGGLUTININ AND NEURAMINIDASE

The **hemagglutinin** and **neuraminidase** of these viruses are two of the best studied of all viral proteins, and seem to be the most important **determinants of influenza virulence.** They migrate to the cell membrane to assemble in patches on the outer surface of the cell membrane, displacing cellular membrane proteins that usually reside there (Fig. 35.2). Their complete amino acid sequence is known and their three-dimensional conformation has been determined by x-ray crystallography. Each of the 400 or so hemagglutinin spikes of a virion is composed of three identical polypeptides. Each spike has a **hydrophobic** end, which is embedded in the lipid envelope, and a **hydrophilic** end, which projects outward. The hemagglutinin attaches to the cell **receptor**, and antibodies directed against it neutralize virus infectivity. Some of the hemagglutinin sequence is highly conserved among diverse strains of each viral type, but specific regions vary greatly, allowing serological discrimination between virus types. These antigenic differences between hemagglutinin determine the extent of cross-reactive immunity, and therefore, the severity of disease in partially immune hosts.

The other peplomer, the **neuraminidase** protein, looks like a square-topped, mushroom-like projection from the cell surface. Each peplomer is comprised of four identical peptides with a **hydrophobic** foot embedded in the viral envelope, and a stalk with a **hydrophilic** head that projects outward. As with the hemagglutinin, variable domains of the neuraminidase are important for serotyping and immune recognition. The neuraminidase is important for **releasing** the virus from the infected cell by **removing receptors** for the hemagglutinin on the cell surface. Antibodies to neuraminidase decrease the efficiency of virus spread both in culture and in tissues. Operationally, neuraminidase is

Table 35.2. Influenza Virus RNA Segments and Their Protein Products

RNA Segment	Protein	Function and Location in Virion
1	Polymerase-B2	RNA synthesis; core protein
2	Polymerase-B1	RNA synthesis; core protein
3	Polymerase-A	RNA synthesis; core protein
4	Hemagglutinin	Attachment to cell surface
5	Nucleoprotein	RNA synthesis; core receptor
6	Neuraminidase	Release of virus from cell envelope
7	Matrix-1, matrix-2	Virus maturation? envelope
8	Nonstructural-1, nonstructural-2	RNA synthesis? nonstructural

assayed by addition of red blood cells to an influenza virus suspension. The red cells agglutinate but then elute spontaneously at 37°. Disaggregation is due to the neuraminidase, which cleaves the bonds that form between the viral hemagglutinin and the N-acetylneuraminic acid on the red cell surface.

A third envelope-associated protein, the **matrix protein**, attaches to the inner aspect of the viral membrane, perhaps recognizing the presence of transmembrane viral polypeptides. It might be considered a **"scaffolding"** protein on which viral nucleocapsids are constructed. As new copies of the viral genome are synthesized, they assemble together with the polymerase proteins and nucleoprotein at the inner cell membrane sites coated with the matrix protein. The virus gradually takes shape by the evagination of the altered cell membrane around the developing viral core. Ultimately, a new particle **buds off** from the cell surface.

How Do Influenza Viruses Get Assembled?

The assembly of infectious viruses that have multiple genome segments is a remarkable process. At least **one copy of each of the different RNA segments must be packaged for the virion to be infectious.** How a complete set of RNAs is selected is not known, but several possibilities can be imagined. If it were an entirely random process in which the assembling nucleocapsid were to entrap the first eight RNA segments that come along, the proportion that becomes infectious would be very small. It has been estimated that this proportion is about 10% of the total particles, so this model cannot be correct. How, then, is it done? If all of the segments were linked to each other by proteins, they could be replicated together and then drawn into an assembling nucleocapsid like links of sausage. No evidence for such a nucleoprotein complex has been found. The hypothesis that is currently favored suggests that the influenza virus is so flexible in construction that it can package more than eight RNA segments. Some of the larger virions may contain 15 segments or more. The probability of including a complete complement of gene segments into an assembling particle, thus, becomes much greater.

Antigenic Variation Among the Influenza Viruses. To understand intelligently the features of influenza epidemiology, one must understand a molecular feature of this virus that has been alluded to previously, namely, its remarkable capacity for **antigenic change.** Whereas strains of many other viruses remain nearly identical year after year, influenza virus strains vary—sometimes slightly and sometimes enormously—from one year to the next. Variety is the way of life among these viruses.

Changes actually occur in several of the viral proteins, but the most easily assayed ones take place in the two outer envelope proteins, **hemagglutinin** and **neuraminidase**. The strains of virus involved in any given outbreak are identified by the serological properties of the two proteins. Slight variations in either protein are said to represent **antigenic drift**. A major change in the neuraminidase or hemagglutinin is termed **antigenic shift**.

Antigenic drift takes place in nature by changes in **small, discrete, and highly variable domains** of the proteins, presumably through random point mutations in the nucleic acid and selection of strains that escape neutralization by the antibodies of the host. Major **antigenic shifts** are believed to result from an entirely different process, involving the **exchange of genes from different virus strains.** To understand this process, it is useful to recall that influenza virus contains a multi-segmented genome. If a cell is infected simultaneously with two or more different influenza viruses, the RNA segments from each parental strain become shuffled and are dealt out to the progeny in random order. Each developing virus particle encapsidates some segments from both parental strains (Fig. 35.3). This process of **genetic reassortment** occurs with very high frequency. Successful reassortants in nature are ones that escape neutralization in the serum of hosts that had previously been infected with antigenically similar viruses.

These mechanisms would be of no epidemiological relevance unless people are likely to become infected with different influenza strains. What evidence is there that these processes occur in nature? What is the origin of the different connecting strains? First, we know that **human influenza A strains are similar to animal influenza strains.** In the laboratory, human and animal strains reassort readily to generate hybrid progeny. Second, **human influenza A strains have been recovered from animals** in the field. The influenza virus strain associated with the great 1918–1919 Spanish pandemic apparently became adapted to infect **swine,** because pigs were later found to be infected with viruses related to the 1918 human strains. Third, strains recovered from wild ducks and horses are antigenically similar to strains later recovered during human epidemics. Thus, it is believed that **animals provide a reservoir** from which new genetic variants of human influenza virus can be drawn. The largest and most extensive animal reservoir is in birds.

To understand this better, imagine a cell that is **coinfected** with a human and an avian influenza A virus. The hybrid that arises may contain the avian hemagglutinin and neuraminidase genes but the remainder of the genes may be of the human virus type. Such a hybrid virus has no problem replicating efficiently in human cells. If humans had never been exposed to the avian hemagglutinin and neuraminidase antigens, such a hybrid virus would not be recognized by the immune system and could spread rapidly in the population. The possible result might be an epidemic, possibly a pandemic.

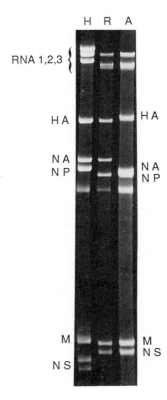

Figure 35.3. Genetic reassortment of influenza viral RNA segments. In this study, human (*H*) and avian (*A*) strains of influenza virus were used together to infect cells in culture. A recombinant (*R*) strain of progeny virus was derived. Each individual segment makes a separate band in gel electrophoresis. The recombinant strain contains some human and some avian RNA segments.

Paradigm: Viral Evolution

Viral evolution depends on the same forces that determine evolution in cellular organisms, namely, **genetic variability** and **selection.** What characterizes evolution among the viruses is the high degree of their variability, which is particularly marked among the ones with an RNA genome. RNA viruses are especially variable because of the intrinsically greater **instability** of RNA molecules, the relatively low **fidelity** of the enzymes that replicate RNA (including reverse transcriptase), and the **segmented genomes** of certain of them. Notice that arrangement into segmented genomes allows the segments to be rapidly reassorted among the progeny viruses, which is reminiscent of the reassortment of chromosomes in higher cells. Contrast this with unimolecular genomes, which undergo genetic change either by mutation or genetic recombination, which are intrinsically more infrequent. The high frequency with which new serotypes of influenza viruses arise almost every year can be explained by their segmented genome.

It is not possible to sort out the importance of each of the myriad of factors operating on viral selection, but, among the more obvious ones, we can count the production of interferons, antibodies, and cellular immunity, both in the circulation and in tissues. Because of the importance of antibodies in neutralizing viruses and in impeding their growth, it can be expected that the greatest variability will be seen in the **antigens recognized by antibodies.** In fact, the most evident viral antigens, such as those in the envelope of the enveloped viruses, tend to be more strain specific than the proteins of the capsomere or those contained within the capsid.

Other selective forces may be attributed to the **special environment** of certain viruses. Take, for example, the rhinoviruses of the common cold or the influenza viruses, both of which reside on the respiratory epithelium and are highly variable, even for RNA viruses. In their usual environment, these viruses become exposed to **IgA antibodies**, which make reversible complexes with their antigens, and are less apt to neutralize the viral infectivity. Because these antibodies only partially impair viral growth, they allow a large population of virions to accumulate, thus increasing the probability that mutations will arise. Among the mutants, some may be even less sensitive to mucosal antibodies and will be, therefore, selected. Viruses found in the bloodstream, on the other hand, are effectively neutralized by circulatory IgG and will not replicate in sufficient numbers for mutants to accumulate. These expectations are generally borne out because RNA viruses found in the circulation, such as measles and mumps, show considerably less antigenic variation than the influenza viruses.

Besides viral mutations that result in resistance to the immune response, those that impart resistance to antiviral chemotherapeutic agents are also of clinical interest. The prevalence of **drug-resistant mutants** is becoming an increasingly serious problem with the greater use of certain antiviral drugs. For example, drug-resistant herpes simplex viruses frequently arise after prolonged therapy with acyclovir.

Also clinically important are **attenuated mutants**, which have decreased virulence but can multiply in the host. Certain of these mutants may be sufficiently stable and antigenically reactive to be used in live vaccines, for example, in the polio or yellow fever vaccines. The stability of these attenuated viruses and their lack of reversion to virulence is probably due to the fact that they differ from the virulent parents by many bases in their nucleic acids.

ENCOUNTER

With these molecular features as a background, it is possible to comprehend the complex pattern of influenza infection over the ages. Over a **century** ago, it was recognized that **some epidemics of the disease are associated with higher than usual mortality from cardiopulmonary disease.** This allows the tracking and recognition of types of influenza that are epidemic from year to year. The Centers for Disease Control tabulate the total cardiopulmonary mortality for each week in each region of the U.S. Almost every winter, the expected mortality increases. **When deaths in a region of the country exceed the expected level by a certain amount, an influenza epidemic is suspected** in that region (Fig. 35.4). More precise characterization and proof of the onset of an epidemic are then based on the recovery and antigenic typing of virus strains at sentinel clinics in the region.

Through these surveillance mechanisms, we have learned that influenza infection occurs in the U.S. on an annual basis, beginning typically in the fall and generally terminating in the late winter. In most years, the influenza outbreaks are mild and sporadic, but every few years more severe epidemics develop. Pandemics (causing disease worldwide) appear less frequently; in this century they arose in 1918, 1957, and 1968.

Thus, influenza may be **endemic** (present but causing relatively few cases), **epidemic** (affecting many people in one area), or **pandemic.** Why does this illness have three different patterns? The answer lies in

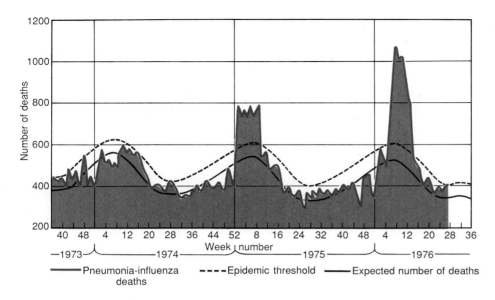

Figure 35.4.   The rate of death from respiratory disease in the U.S. from 1973–1976. A higher than expected rate of respiratory deaths indicates the occurrence of influenza epidemics.

the distribution of immunity in the population. Individuals who have been infected in the past with a specific strain of influenza virus become immune to that strain. If the same strain were to be reintroduced the next year, it would cause disease mainly among those who missed the earlier outbreak. For that year, influenza would be endemic. When antigenic drift occurs in the circulating influenza strains, the differences are sufficient to permit epidemics, because illness occurs even among those who developed some immunity from earlier infections. Major antigenic shifts, however, lead to pandemics. Because nearly the whole population is susceptible, many are likely to be infected.

The strains that cause illness each year are identified by the serological properties of their neuraminidase and hemagglutinin. A uniform classification scheme has been adopted internationally for these antigens. New influenza strains are named by their type, city or country of first isolation, strain, year of recovery, and hemagglutinin and neuraminidase subtypes. An example is the A/Victoria/3/75/H3N2. Thirteen different hemagglutinin (Hl-H13) and nine different neuraminidase subtypes (Nl-N9) have been recognized in viruses recovered from humans, swine, horses, and birds. Table 35.3 lists the influenza A virus strains associated with the most serious pandemics in this century. The influenza pandemic of 1957 led to the demise of Ms. I.'s grandfather because this virus was antigenically quite different from the earlier H1N1 virus.

Table 35.4 shows how minor and major antigenic changes can be measured and how these findings are reflected in the virulence of a circulating influenza A strain. In this example, stored sera collected from a large group of individuals in 1968 and 1972 were tested for their levels of antibodies directed against influenza A hemagglutinin. Prior immunity existing in 1972 to new H3 strains limited the spread and impact of the virus but an epidemic still occurred among those with partial immunity and those (particularly children) who missed the 1968 pandemic.

Table 35.3. Major Antigenic Shifts in Influenza A Strain in Recent Years

Year	Strain Designation[a]	Common Name
1947	H1N1	Spanish
1957	H2N2	Asian
1968	H3N2	Hong Kong
1976	H1N1 (swine)	Swine
1977	H1N1	USSR

[a]H, hemagglutinin; N, neuraminidase.

Table 35.4. Antigenic Drift in Influenza A Strain[a]

Year Sera Collected	Mean Hemagglutination Inhibition Antibody Titer to		
	H2	H3[68]	H3[72]
1968	1:100	<1:10	<1:10
1972	1:100	1:80	1:30

[a]Each serum was tested against three influenza A virus strains; a strain containing an H2 type of hemagglutinin similar to that associated with the prior 1957 pandemic, the H3-containing strain associated with the 1968 pandemic, and the similar but slightly different H3-containing strain associated with the 1972 epidemic.

ENTRY

Influenza can be transmitted to the nasopharynx of susceptible individuals by **inhalation** of large-particle aerosols, but the major vehicle for transmission is **small-particle aerosols** liberated during sneezes or coughs. Experimental observations suggest that small droplets are capable of reaching the terminal bronchioles and alveoli. If they contain a single infectious dose of virus, this may be sufficient to induce disease. It is possible that the virus may also be transmitted from hand to nose after touching virus-bearing objects. In general, young children are the most efficient transmitters of the infection, spreading it among their friends and to their families. Thus, in 1957, our patient, Ms. I., may have been the index case for influenza in her family, having brought it home from school; in an ironic way, she now suffers from influenza that she acquired from her own pupils.

SPREAD, MULTIPLICATION, AND DAMAGE

Influenza viruses infect primarily upper and lower respiratory tract epithelial cells. Viral multiplication leads to lysis of these cells and to the release of viral antigens and destructive cellular enzymes. The host responds with an influx of **macrophages** and **lymphocytes**, followed by an outpouring of **humoral mediators of inflammation**, including interferon. This response helps clear superinfecting bacteria and fungi, inhibit virus replication, and destroy vitally infected epithelia cells. Release of **interleukin-1** from macrophages results in fever, while **interferon** probably causes the diffuse muscular aches and fatigue that is characteristic of influenza (which is one of the reasons for the limited therapeutic use of interferon). The inflammatory mediators provoke **vasodilation** and **edema**. In the nose, this results in stuffiness and rhinorrhea. In the tracheobronchial tree, the irritation caused by the debris and the host responses stimulates mucus production. The remaining undamaged ciliated epithelium and the cough reflexes help propel the mucus and debris upward. In areas where extensive destruction of epithelium has occurred superinfecting bacteria, especially virulent encapsulated ones, can gain a foothold, leading to secondary bacterial bronchitis or pneumonia.

The role of **cellular immune responses** in influenza is not known. Patients with cellular immune impairment are not at substantially increased risk for influenza infections. The **humoral responses** to the viral outer envelope proteins seem more important. The example in Table 35.4 shows that the presence of **neutralizing antibody** to hemagglutinin will protect against or limit infection. Antibody to the neuraminidase seems to modify the spread of virus through the respiratory tract and can prevent illness. Thus, in an individual with partial immunity to neuraminidase, the disease may be restricted to the upper respiratory tract.

The **bacterial superinfection** that complicates influenza infection is confined, typically to a single pulmonary lobe and involves pneumococci, staphylococci, or *H. influenzae*; hence, the incorrect attribution of the cause of this disease a century ago to *H. influenzae*. These pneumonias present as recurrent fever and progressive purulent cough in an individual whose initial symptoms of influenza appeared to be on the wane. Bacterial pneumonia and cardiac failure account for most of the increase in mortality associated with influenza each year. The demise in 1957 of Ms. I.'s grandfather was probably due to bacterial superinfection. The cumulative effects of a lifetime of insults to the respiratory tract from pollution, smoking, and prior infections gradually degrade one's ability to counter the growth of bacteria in influenza-damaged airways.

Influenza is also a major cause of disease in children. It is an important cause of **croup**. Infection in the upper respiratory tract results in an inflammatory response and local swelling sufficient to obstruct the Eustachian tubes and the openings of the facial sinuses. Stasis of fluid proximal to the obstruction provides fertile ground for bacterial growth. Thus, otitis and sinusitis are common complications of influenza, especially in children.

Rare but serious complications of influenza that are less frequent than bacterial pneumonia include primary influenza **pneumonia** and **Reye syndrome**. The former is a rare process in which extensive viral and later bacterial destruction of small airways and alveoli occur. Clinically, this is suspected when fulminant multilobar pneumonia and hypoxia are observed.

Reye syndrome is a poorly understood illness of children recently infected with influenza or varicella. There is progressive metabolic **encephalopathy** and, frequently, death. Neither the pathogenesis nor the role of aspirin use as a risk factor for Reye syndrome are understood.

DIAGNOSIS

The clinical manifestations of influenza virus infection readily suggest the diagnosis. When flu is widespread throughout a community in the winter months, the diagnosis is likely to be correct. Definitive laboratory diagnoses are usually made for purposes of research or for epidemiological surveillance. The virus can readily be **grown** from nasopharyngeal swabs or washes by inoculation into cell cultures. Virus replication is detected by a simple assay for the expression of the **viral hemagglutinin**. Guinea pig red blood cells are added to the cultures and adhere to the surface of cells in which the virus is replicating.

A variety of **serological techniques** are available for diagnosing past influenza A infection. **Hemagglutination inhibition** (as used in Table 35.4) and neutralization are most often utilized. Their major value is in defining the serological character of new virus strains and for seroepidemiological surveillance.

PREVENTION AND TREATMENT

The major treatments for influenza infections are the time-proven ones involving hydration, rest, and antipyretics, especially acetaminophen rather than aspirin (to decrease the likelihood of the aspirin-associated postinfluenza Reye syndrome). For most people, these conservative measures are adequate. On the other hand, influenza A is the first virus for which successful systemic antiviral chemotherapy was developed. In the early 1960s, it was recognized that **amantadine** (Fig. 43.2), a compound now more widely utilized for the treatment of Parkinsonism, effectively diminishes the duration and severity of influenza A infection. It is most effective when given prophylactically, before an individual is exposed to the virus, leading to a 70–80% reduction in the development of symptoms. Amantadine is, therefore, used for prophylaxis of influenza for the weeks the infection seems to be in the local community for elderly institutionalized individuals and patients with cardiopulmonary compromise.

The precise mechanism by which amantadine exerts its antiviral effect is not known. The drug has been shown to interfere with early replicative events, including uncoating of the virions. A related compound, **rimantadine**, appears equally effective and has improved pharmacokinetics, so that there is a lower incidence of the mild confusion and discomfort that attend amantadine use, particularly in the elderly individual. Unfortunately, both agents are active only against the influenza A strains of virus.

A different class of agent, represented by the nucleoside analog **ribavirin** (Fig. 43.2), is active against both influenza A and B viruses. In early trials of ribavirin in which the agent was inhaled as a fine-particle aerosol, there was evidence of rapid clearance of virus and resolution of symptoms. The complexity of aerosol administration of ribavirin and modest benefits has limited its use to compassionate treatment of rare hospitalized patients with suspected primary influenza pneumonia.

In reality, none of the medications for influenza is used widely enough to affect our public health. However, the control of influenza is a major international effort. Under the auspices of the World Health Organization, **sentinel clinics** monitor and track the emergence and spread of influenza in both animals and man. When this becomes evident in a country, local public health authorities announce cautionary warnings that the elderly or chronically impaired patients should avoid contact with individuals with upper respiratory infections.

The most powerful thrust of the influenza control program focuses on **vaccination**. The current vaccines contain viral **hemagglutinin** and **neuraminidase** proteins from killed virus. These vaccines reduce the incidence and morbidity of influenza by about 75%. The major problem with these vaccines is that they do not provide permanent immunity to the disease. The fault is not with the vaccines themselves, which provide relatively durable immunity, but with the antigenic variations of the virus. Authorities in the U.S. convene each year to review data on worldwide influenza patterns and to attempt to predict the **strains** that are likely to emerge in the coming season. There is then a frantic effort to prepare adequate vaccine for those strains in time for the onset of the next influenza season. The vaccine formula is altered yearly, and vaccination must be performed annually to afford maximal protection.

Unfortunately, the experts can guess wrong regarding the strains of virus that will circulate in the coming seasons, but this is not the major problem with influenza vaccination. Most Americans, including those who would benefit the most, are not vaccinated. Many are either apathetic or fear federally sponsored vaccine programs. Some of the recent fear stems from the apparent increase in cases of Guillian-Barré syndrome, a rare neurological complication of vaccination, in the year following nationwide use of the swine influenza vaccine in the mid-1970s. The fear that the vaccine was responsible for this serious neurological problem still discourages some individuals from obtaining the appropriate vaccination.

Newer classes of vaccines are being studied. More effective than the killed virus vaccines are live, attenuated, cold-adapted vaccines, which can be rapidly prepared for each season. Vaccine virus growth is largely limited to the cooler parts of the upper respiratory tract of the recipient yet still induce potent cell-mediated as well as humoral immune responses. Thus, they are likely to induce greater and more durable immunity than the current influenza vaccines. Further field trials are necessary before these new vaccines are approved.

CONCLUSION

We can now answer all of Ms. I.'s concerns about influenza. Although her seronegative children might experience severe influenza, it is unlikely that Ms. I. will come down with this illness at this time since substantially altered strains enter the community only infrequently. These new strains develop by mutation and genetic reassortment. It is the antigenic differences in these strains that permit them to infect individuals who have had prior influenza infection. Because Ms. I.'s parents are elderly, they should seek medical consultation for annual vaccination, and, if the influenza season has already begun, possibly receive amantadine prophylaxis along with vaccination. If any of the family members become infected, amantadine treatment should be considered on a case by case basis.

Self-assessment Questions

1. Describe the structure of influenza viruses and their replication cycle. What is peculiar about them?

2. Why do influenza epidemics recur? What causes influenza pandemics?

3. What role do hemagglutinin and neuraminidase play in the pathogenesis of influenza?

4. Compare antigenic drifts and shifts in influenza with antigenic variation in the pili of the gonococcus (Chapter 4) and with the generation of immunological diversity (Chapter 7).

5. Discuss the immune response in influenza.

6. How would you counsel elderly patients about the need for influenza vaccination?

SUGGESTED READING

Crosby AW, Jr. Epidemic and peace, 1918. Westport, CT: Greenwood Press, 1976.

Dolin R, Reichman RC, Madore HP, et al. A controlled trial of amantadine and rimantadine in the prophylaxis of influenza A infection. N Engl J Med 1982; 307:580–584.

Kilbourne ED, ed. The influenza viruses and influenza. New York: Academic Press, 1975.

Louria DB, Blumenfeld HL, Ellis JT, Kilbourne ED, Rogers DE. Studies on influenza in the pandemic of 1957–1958. II. Pulmonary complications of influenza. J Clin Invest 1959;38:213–265.

Palese P, Young JF. Variation of influenza A, B, and C viruses. Science 1982;215:1468–1474.

Rotaviruses and Other Viral Agents of Gastroenteritis

36

Cody Meissner

On a worldwide basis, 4–10 million children die each year from the complications of infectious gastroenteritis. In the U.S., while fewer than 500 children per year die from infectious diarrhea, more than 200,000 children under 5 years of age are hospitalized because of diarrhea-induced dehydration. Before the 1970s, the etiological agents for diarrhea that could be diagnosed were bacteria or protozoa and, even though viruses were often suspected, most cases of viral gastroenteritis went undiagnosed. In 1972, the **Norwalk agent** was first identified by electron microscopic examination of stool specimens when a convalescent serum specimen was mixed with an acute stool specimen and clumped particles of virus were observed. This agent is now recognized as the **most common cause of clusters of viral diarrhea in adults**. In 1978, **rotavirus** was identified by electron microscopic examination of stool specimens. This agent is now known to be the **most commonly recognized agent of gastroenteritis in children**. At least three additional viral agents are recognized as important causes of diarrhea: (*a*) **enteric adenoviruses**, (*b*) **caliciviruses**, and (*c*) **astroviruses** (Table 36.1). Viral agents were slow to be recognized as causes of gastroenteritis primarily because they do not grow well in cell culture. It was only as the technique of electron microscopy was applied to stool

Table 36.1. Viral Causes of Gastroenteritis in Humans

Type	Genome	Medical Significance
Rotavirus		
Group A	ds-segmented RNA	Major cause of diarrhea in children 6–24 months
Group B, C (atypical rotaviruses)	ds-segmented RNA	Rare in U.S.
Norwalk virus	RNA	Major cause of diarrhea epidemics in adults
Small, round structured viruses (SRSV)		
Enteric adenovirus	ds, linear DNA	Second to rotavirus as cause of diarrhea in children, less important in adults
Calicivirus	RNA	Infects adults and children
Astrovirus	(+)ssRNA	Infects mainly children and elderly

specimens as a diagnostic tool that these agents were recognized. It is likely that additional viral agents will be identified as causes of gastroenteritis as 40–50% of diarrhea cases are still of uncertain etiology.

CASE

M.A., a 7-month-old living in Washington, D.C., was recently switched from breast feeding to bottle feeding. Usually a satisfied and happy child, on March 29 she became irritable, began to vomit, and had a low-grade fever. Mild upper respiratory symptoms also developed, with cough, nasal discharge, and pharyngitis. The gastrointestinal (GI) symptoms persisted for 2 days and she was brought to the pediatrician who made the diagnosis of **rotavirus gastroenteritis** *by detecting viral antigen in the stool with an ELISA (enzyme-linked immunosorbent assay, see Chapter 55). Oral rehydration solution was given at home and M.A. made an uneventful recovery by the sixth day.*

The following questions arise:

1. How did M.A. acquire the virus?

2. Is there any significance to the fact that this is springtime?

3. Will she ever have the same disease?

4. Why did the pediatrician suspect this etiological agent?

ENCOUNTER

The peak incidence of rotavirus infection in the U.S. occurs between 6 months and 2 years of age. **Most individuals have experienced infection** and are immune to severe disease due to rotavirus by 4 years of age. Seropositive older children or adults who are re-exposed to a high inoculum of virus or who become immunocompromised may experience mild illness. Parents of young children experiencing a primary rotavirus infection may develop mild symptoms. Certain individuals known to be at increased risk of complications of dehydration due to viral gastroenteritis include malnourished children and adults, particularly in developing countries, and the elderly, who may experience waning immunity with age.

Rotavirus-induced disease has a **seasonal distribution** in the U.S., peaking in the winter and becoming rare in the warmer months. In tropical countries, endemic rotavirus infection occurs throughout the year. Recent studies have shown that rotaviruses cause a unique annual epidemic that moves sequentially from west to east. The epidemic first peaks in October and November in Mexico and the Southwestern states, progressing across the country during winter months and peaking in the Northeast and the Canadian Maritime Provinces in March and April (Fig. 36.1). Other viruses, such as influenza virus and respiratory syncytial virus, also have a characteristic seasonal appearance but this predictable wave of spread is unique to rotavirus. It has been suggested that weather conditions, such as low temperature and low relative humidity, facilitate viral survival on fomites, thereby enhancing transmission. However, the epidemic begins in the warm climate of Mexico but peak activity occurs simultaneously in northern and southern cities with different temperatures and levels of humidity. Therefore, this theory does not fully explain this unusual form of spread.

As with other viral illnesses, it is well recognized that some children will develop rotavirus gastroenteritis without having had contact with

Figure 36.1.   Peaks of rotavirus activity in North America between 1984 and 1988. The months with the highest activity are capitalized.

symptomatic individuals. Acquisition may result from encounter with an individual who is asymptomatically shedding virus. Such asymptomatic excretion of rotavirus is well recognized to occur for up to 1 week before the onset of diarrhea and for days following resolution of symptoms. Other children may shed rotavirus and never experience symptoms.

ENTRY

Endemic rotavirus disease is caused primarily by person-to-person transmission. The principal means of transmission is by the **fecal-oral route**. Rotavirus is excreted in stool in high levels that reach 10^9 infectious particles/ml stool. **Transmission of as few as 10 infectious particles can result in infection.** Outbreaks due to contamination of a municipal water supply and to food-borne transmission have been reported but appear to be rare. There has been speculation that rotavirus may spread by the **respiratory route** via infectious aerosol. This possibility is based on well described epidemics in which fecal-oral transmission cannot be documented and on the observation that respiratory symptoms may precede the development of gastroenteritis by a day or two. Most outbreaks of viral gastroenteritis due to the Norwalk agent can be traced to contamination of a common source, such as shellfish or contamination of municipal or well water.

SPREAD AND MULTIPLICATION

Rotaviruses are among the very few human viruses with a **double-stranded RNA genome**, which resembles double-stranded DNA in structure. Another distinguishing property (shared by the orthomyxoviruses) is that the genome of rotaviruses is **segmented**. The morphological appearance of rotavirus particles in the electron microscope is a wheel with short spokes and an outer rim (*rota* means wheel in Latin) (Fig. 36.2). The particle possesses an icosahedral structure with an inner and an outer capsid. Infectivity requires an intact outer membrane that is necessary for **acid stability**, a critical characteristic for microorganisms whose portal of entry is the gastrointestinal tract. Two outer capsid proteins, a hemagglutinin (VP4) and a glycoprotein (VP7), induce formation of neutralizing antibodies.

The capsid contains 11 segments of double-stranded RNA as well as a viral **RNA-dependent RNA polymerase (transcriptase)** for transcription of individual RNA segments into mRNA. This enzyme is absent in animal cells and must be introduced from the virion during infection. By the use of in vitro translation and by analysis of viruses that have undergone genomic reassortment, the gene product (structural and nonstructural proteins) of each of the 11 segments has been defined.

Rotavirus replication requires **protease** treatment for most viral strains to become infective. The proteolytic activity cleaves an outer capsid protein, enhancing viral penetration into cells. Viral replication then proceeds in the cytoplasm with the formation of both positive- and negative-strand RNA (Fig. 36.3). **Positive-strand RNA** functions as mRNA and associates with **negative-strand RNA** to form double-strand segments. Particles form in the cytoplasm and mature by budding through the endoplasmic reticulum when surface proteins are acquired. Mature viral particles are released into the extracellular environment with lysis of the infected cell.

Six groups of rotaviruses have been identified based on antigenic characteristics (A through F). **Group A rotaviruses** share a common antigen and are the only rotaviruses recognized to cause frequent infections in the U.S. **Group B rotaviruses** are best known as a cause of diarrhea in swine, but have caused outbreaks in adults and children in China. The other groups are either infrequent or their role in human disease is not clear.

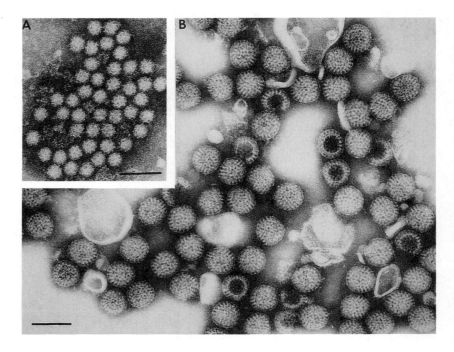

Figure 36.2. Electron micrograph of negatively stained viral particles. *A*, Norwalk virus; *B*, rotavirus.

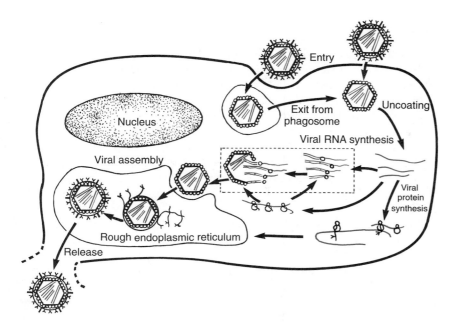

Figure 36.3. The rotavirus replication cycle.

DAMAGE

Rotaviruses produce a spectrum of disease ranging from asymptomatic infection to mild diarrhea, to severe diarrhea with potentially fatal dehydration. Severe **gastroenteritis** generally occurs in children between 6 and 24 months, as in the case of M.A. Rotavirus infections typically have a 2-day incubation period with vomiting often preceding the onset of gastroenteritis by 2 or 3 days. **Watery diarrhea** may last 3–8 days in infants who become symptomatic. **Fever** and **abdominal** cramps are common. Red blood cells or leukocytes are generally not found in the stool of patients with rotavirus gastroenteritis.

Morphological changes have been identified on biopsies of the mucosa of the proximal small intestine of infants and children experiencing rotavirus gastroenteritis; these include shortening and atrophy of the villi, denuded villi, and mononuclear cell infiltration of the lamina propria.

In infants who are less than 6 months of age, rotavirus infection is less common, except for premature neonates who may acquire the infection during outbreaks in neonatal units. Normal, term infants often remain asymptomatic even while shedding rotavirus in the stool, for reasons that are not well understood. It may be that maternal antibody transferred during the third trimester protects term infants, and that premature infants are born before they can acquire maternal antirotavirus antibody. In children who are more than 6 months of age, rotavirus is a major nosocomial pathogen.

Adults generally experience a mild or even asymptomatic infection due to rotavirus. This is because **long-term immunity** generally follows a primary infection. Symptoms become apparent when the inoculum size is large enough to overcome pre-existing immunity. In some instances, rotaviruses may be a cause of travelers' diarrhea in children and adults, although it is less common than other pathogens in this setting.

Chronic diarrhea and prolonged shedding has been associated with rotavirus infection in children with **T-cell immunodeficiencies**. Patients undergoing immunosuppression for bone marrow transplantation are also recognized to be at increased risk.

DIAGNOSIS

Because most of the viral agents that cause gastroenteritis grow poorly in cell culture, assays that detect viral antigen in stool specimen have become the most widely used method of diagnosis. **Antigen detection assays**, as used in M.A.'s case, are widely available for rotavirus and adenovirus detection. For other viral causes of gastroenteritis, the electron microscope can be used to study an individual stool specimen, looking for a characteristic viral morphology. However, a relatively high viral titer must be present in the stool specimen for the virus to be seen by this method. Immune electron microscopy increases the sensitivity by adding virus-specific antibody that aggregates viral particles in the field.

Serology is generally not a useful means of diagnosis. Most persons experiencing a viral gastroenteritis will undergo a four-fold or greater rise in antibody titer between an acute and convalescent specimen drawn 2–3 weeks apart. However, satisfactory assays are not widely available. To screen for antibodies to a specific agent, a sufficient supply of viral antigen must be available. Because most intestinal viruses cannot be easily propagated, plentiful antigen is not available, making serological screening useful in a research setting only.

THERAPY AND PREVENTION

At present, there are no established therapies for the management of viral gastroenteritis. Adherence to universal precautions for **infection control**, such as handwashing and barrier methods (gloves, gowns) are important for minimizing disease spread. Patient care is directed at supportive measures with particular attention focused on the **prevention of dehydration** by the use of intravenous hydration or oral rehydration therapy.

Several potential new approaches to prevention and therapy of viral gastroenteritis are being considered. Since mucosal surfaces may contain only small concentrations of secretory IgA antibodies, **oral administration of** γ-globulin preparations containing increased titers of antibody against enteric viruses might be useful to increase antiviral activity. A second approach involves the use of **protease inhibitors**. Rotaviruses require proteolytic activity to cleave surface proteins before efficient cell penetrations can occur. Other enteric viruses may require a similar activity. By preventing such cleavage with a protease inhibitor, it may be possible to attenuate an infection. Numerous questions need to be considered such as the impact of protease activity on digestion. A third approach involves **oral immunization** with a live, attenuated rotavirus vaccine. Two important concerns about a vaccine relate (*a*) to the ability of high-risk neonates to mount an effective immune response against a vaccine strain and (*b*) to ensure that an attenuated virus cannot cause disease in susceptible contacts.

OTHER ENTERIC VIRUSES

While rotaviruses are the most widely recognized cause of viral enteric infections, other agents are clearly important. The **Norwalk virus** is the prototype of a group referred to as Norwalk-like viruses or **small, round structured viruses** (SRSV) (Fig. 36.2). Members of this group are named after the geographic area where an outbreak was described (e.g., Hawaii agent, Montgomery County agent). While these viruses cause sporadic, endemic disease, they usually come to attention through the development of **explosive outbreaks**. They are transmitted by contaminated food or water, or person-to-person contact. **Adenoviruses** are best known as a cause of upper respiratory tract disease (Chapter 38). However, two fastidious serotypes (numbers 40 and 41) in particular are now recognized to cause diarrhea, especially in children who are less than 2 years of age. Outbreaks due to **caliciviruses** have been described mainly in institutions. Based on the prevalence of specific antibodies, most individuals have been infected with these viruses by 12 years of age. **Astroviruses** are another group of incompletely understood viruses that cause enteric disease, primarily in children.

SUGGESTED READING

Dolin R, Treanor JJ, Madore HP. Novel agents of viral enteritis in humans. J Infect Dis 1987;155:365–376.

Ward RL, Bernstein DI, Young EC, Sherwood JR, Knowlton DR, Schiff GM. Human rotavirus studies in volunteers: determination of infectious dose and serological response to infection. J Infect Dis 1986;154:871–880.

Yolken RH, Maldonado Y, Rinney J, Vonderfecht S. Epidemiology and potential methods for prevention of neonatal intestinal viral infections. Rev Infect Dis 1990;12 (Suppl 4):S421–S427.

Human Retroviruses: AIDS and Other Diseases

37

Cody Meissner and John M. Coffin

It is difficult to overestimate AIDS. C. Everett Koop, the former Surgeon General of the United States, wrote:

"AIDS is a life-threatening disease and a major public issue. Its impact on our society is and will continue to be devastating. By the end of 1991, an estimated 270,000 cases of AIDS will have occurred, with 179,000 deaths within the decade since the disease was first recognized. In the year 1991, an estimated 145,000 patients with AIDS will need health and support services at a total cost of between $8 and $16 billion."

Two attributes make AIDS unique among infectious diseases: (*a*) it is uniformly fatal and (*b*) most of its devastating symptoms are not caused directly by the causative agent. With suppression of the host's immune response by the AIDS virus (or human immunodeficiency virus, HIV), opportunistic organisms are free to cause disease. Most symptoms seen in an AIDS patient result from secondary infections.

AIDS first appeared in the U.S. in 1978 and the syndrome was described in 1981 among gay men with multiple sexual partners. There is evidence that unrecognized cases may have occurred earlier. By late 1981, the disease was reported in heterosexual intravenous drug abusers. The first cases among individuals with hemophilia receiving transfusions of human factor VIII were described in 1982. Soon, transmission of the presumed infectious agent to heterosexual partners of infected intravenous drug abusers and bisexual men was documented.

The clinical manifestations of AIDS are described in detail in Chapter 67.

CASE

Baby boy G. was born by cesarean section after a 36-week gestation to a 19-year-old prostitute with terminal AIDS. The mother had developed a second episode of Pneumocystis carinii *pneumonia 2 weeks prior to delivery. Despite intensive therapy including intubation and mechanical ventilation, the mother died 2 hours following delivery because of respiratory failure.*

IgG antibodies to HIV were detected in the infant both by an ELISA test and by western blot analysis (see under "Diagnosis"). The infant received no blood or blood products. By 4 months of age, he experienced poor weight gain, extensive thrush (oral candidiasis), diffuse lymphadenopathy (enlargement of lymph nodes), and persistent diarrhea. He developed a rapidly pro-

gressive pneumonia and died of Pneumocystis *pneumonia.* Cytomegalovirus *was cultured from lung tissue obtained at autopsy.*

The diagnosis of AIDS in this infant was based on his birth from a known HIV-infected mother and on the absence of findings to suggest another cause for the neonatal immunodeficient state. The infant's positive HIV serology (i.e., antibodies to HIV), however, may have been due to maternal antibodies transmitted transplacentally. Passively acquired maternal antibodies to HIV may persist until 15 months of age; thus, positive serology in young children alone does not mean that they are infected with the virus. Since the child was born by cesarean section, had no contact with his mother after delivery, and had received no blood products, it is most likely that his infection was acquired by transplacental passage in utero.

HISTORY OF RETROVIRUSES

Understanding the role of retroviruses as the etiological agents of AIDS requires a historical detour through the puzzling connection between viruses and cancer. It includes a challenge to a traditional tenet of molecular biology that genetic information flows from DNA through RNA intermediates to protein. In the late 1960s, an unusual class of viruses was recognized to carry genetic information in molecules of RNA. While RNA-containing viruses were not a novelty, these viruses were unique because they contained the formerly unrecognized enzyme, **reverse transcriptase**. This enzyme uses RNA as a template and reverses the conventional flow of genetic information by synthesizing a copy of complementary DNA that ultimately integrates into the genome of the host cell. This DNA, called the **provirus**, serves as an intermediate stage in the replicative cycle.

Some of these viruses (now called **retroviruses** in recognition of their reverse or "retro" mode of replication) are capable of causing tumors. A virus of this type was first isolated in 1911, when Peyton Rous reported that tumors in chickens could be caused by a virus readily transmissible by filtered extracts (later known as **RSV**, for Rous Sarcoma Virus). Since then, hundreds of retroviruses have been isolated from many groups of vertebrates. In the early 1960s, a cancer-inducing cat virus was discovered, now called the **feline leukemia virus**. This virus proved to be important in understanding the biology of retroviruses for two reasons. First, it induces an immunodeficiency in cats similar to the one later observed in AIDS patients. Second, feline leukemia virus is transmitted among cats in a household setting, providing a valuable model for epidemiological analysis of retrovirus infection.

Until the late 1960s, there was considerable skepticism that a virus could mediate the transmission of cancer. Because cancer appeared to be a genetic alteration, it was difficult to conceive how an RNA-containing virus could interact with the DNA of the host cell to produce oncogenic changes. The discovery of reverse transcriptase suggested a mechanism for the induction of permanent genetic change.

ISOLATION AND CHARACTERIZATION OF HUMAN RETROVIRUSES

Since 1980, two groups of **retroviruses capable of causing disease in humans** have been isolated and characterized (Table 37.1). For several years before 1980, there had been suspicion that retroviruses might be agents of human disease, but the point could not be proved because these viruses did not grow in cultured cells. Several advances in cell

Table 37.1. Pathogenic Human Retroviruses

HTLV Group	
HTLV-I	Causative agent of certain cutaneous T-cell lymphomas; implicated in HTLV-I myelopathy (also called tropical spastic papaparesis)
HTLV-II	Not conclusively linked to a specific disease; found in cases of hairy T-cell leukemia
Lentiviruses	
HIV-1	Causative agent of AIDS
HIV-2	Related to, but distinct from HIV-1; described as a cause of AIDS, particularly in West Africa

culture technology overcame this obstacle. One of the most important was the discovery of **T-cell growth factor** (or interleukin-2, IL-2), which stimulates the growth of T lymphocytes in vitro. These lymphocytes could then be used for the isolation of human T-cell lymphotropic viruses. The first, **HTLV-I**, was isolated from the cells of two patients with adult T-cell lymphoma. Subsequent HTLV-I isolates from other leukemia patients were shown to be closely related, as determined by serology and nucleic acid hybridization. Epidemiological studies suggested a causal relationship between infection by HTLV-I and the development of lymphoma in a few percent of infected individuals as many as 40 years later. A similar virus, **HTLV-II**, was later isolated from a patient with hairy cell leukemia but its role in human disease is less clear at the present time.

The malignant diseases caused by HTLV-I, adult cell leukemia and lymphoma, are uniformly fatal, but are relatively rare (even in infected individuals) and have been limited to certain specific populations. More recently, HTLV-I infection has been associated with certain progressive spinal cord diseases, such as tropical spastic paraparesis and HTLV-I-associated myelopathy. HTLV-I has been implicated in these diseases because of the presence of specific antibodies and the isolation of the virus from the cerebrospinal fluid (CSF) and serum of such patients.

HTLV-I attracted considerable attention, both because it was the first known human retrovirus and because of the novel features of its biology. Although extremely uncommon in the U.S. at the present time, there is concern about the spread of this virus through the blood supply, and routine screening of donated blood for evidence of infection by this virus is being instituted. Fortuitously, studies of this virus provided the technology needed for the isolation of the **AIDS** agent several years later. Thus, AIDS was shown to be caused by a retrovirus within 3 years after the first description of the disease in 1981. When first isolated, this virus had several names, but it is now known as **human immunodeficiency virus (HIV)**. The remainder of this chapter will focus on this virus.

Paradigm: New Epidemics of Infectious Diseases

How do new epidemics of infectious diseases arise? In some cases, such as influenza, the virus is already present in the human or animal population and undergoes antigenic rearrangement to produce new, more virulent strains. In other instances, the agent is present as a relatively innocuous commensal in animals and, by a genetic change, becomes virulent for humans.

In the case of the AIDS epidemic, there is considerable genetic evidence that viruses related to HIV have existed in nonhuman primate populations for a long time. There are two possibilities to explain the emergence of the AIDS epidemic in humans. One is that the nonhuman primate viruses have mutated to a more virulent form; the other is that virulent strains were there all along. In either case, the important variables are changes in human behavior that have facilitated the spread of the virus among people. It is possible that sporadic cases of AIDS existed among people in contact with infected monkeys or apes, but that the virus did not spread much beyond the affected individuals. What set off the AIDS epidemic may have been the increase in transmission of HIV between people brought forth by the urbanization of certain regions of Africa, changes in sexual habits, and the contamination of intravenous needles used by consumers of drugs.

What do we know about the abating of severe epidemics of infectious diseases? The AIDS epidemic of today has a vivid historical parallel. At the end of the 15th century, an apparently new disease, **syphilis**, swept through Europe in epidemic proportions. For the first 60 years of its history, this was a very different illness from that we now know. Instead of progressing (if untreated) to the chronic manifestations of the tertiary stage, 15th and 16th century syphilis was an acute disease with high mortality. We do not know what caused the abrupt change in the pathological picture of syphilis, but we can speculate. For any disease that is spread directly among people, an agent that causes an acute killing disease results in the elimination of infected contacts, with **great reduction in its transmissibility**. Eventually, such a strain will be supplanted by a milder one that causes a chronic illness and, thus, has a greater chance of being transmitted to a new host. This may, in fact, have happened for HIV or HIV-like viruses in monkeys and apes. AIDS in humans, on the other hand, is unlikely to result in such a balanced situation because an HIV-carrying person can be the source of transmission of the virus over a long period of time. Thus, the biological basis for the abatement of the AIDS epidemic is not at all obvious. Interrupting the AIDS epidemic cannot depend on evolutionary changes in either the host or in the virus but will require effective antiviral vaccination or chemotherapy.

RETROVIRUSES

Retroviruses have a small, spherical virion surrounded by a lipid envelope (Fig. 37.1). The genome contains two identical RNA molecules

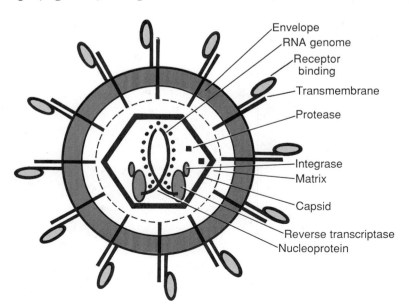

Envelope
RNA genome
Receptor binding
Transmembrane
Protease
Integrase
Matrix
Capsid
Reverse transcriptase
Nucleoprotein

Figure 37.1. Retrovirus structure. A schematic drawing showing the virion proteins and other structures.

linked in a dimeric structure. These molecules resemble eukaryotic mRNA because they contain a **cap structure** at the 5' end and **poly A sequence** at the 3' end. Three viral genes are necessary for the replication of retroviruses. The *gag* gene codes for three or four core proteins. The *pol* gene codes for **reverse transcriptase** or **DNA polymerase**, the enzyme responsible for replication of the genome, as well as for **integrase**, the enzyme necessary for integration of viral DNA into the host cell genome. The *env* gene codes for the two **envelope glycoproteins**. Noncoding sequences include terminally redundant regions and unique regions near the ends of the genome. Reverse transcriptase (RNA-dependent DNA polymerases) molecules are associated with the genome and are carried within the virion.

In addition to the genes common to all retroviruses, *gag*, *pol*, and *env*, the HIV genome contains at least six other genes (see below). These encode functions that seem to be important in regulating the complex replication cycle of this virus, which may exist in a latent state in the infected cell and then undergo rapid replication at the appropriate time.

Virus Life Cycle

The replication cycle of HIV (Figs. 37.2 and 37.3) includes the following steps:

- **Binding.** Once in close proximity to a helper T-lymphocyte, HIV recognizes and binds to the CD_4 receptor molecule via its envelope glycoprotein. Antibodies to either the viral envelope protein or the cell receptor block this interaction and prevent infection. The presence on the cell surface of the CD_4 molecule, which plays an important role in immunological function (Chapter 7), determines the primary target cells for infection.

- **Fusion.** Another step in the replicative cycle is fusion of the virus envelope with the cell membrane. As the result, the virion loses its integrity and characteristic morphology. The virus core, including genomic RNA and reverse transcriptase molecules, is released into the cytoplasm.

- **Synthesis of DNA.** Reverse transcriptase now synthesizes a complementary DNA molecule corresponding to the viral RNA genome. The enzyme then synthesizes the second DNA strand (complementary to the first), generating a double-stranded DNA molecule. In

Figure 37.2. Electron micrographs showing successive stages in the assembly and budding of the human retroviruses HTLV-I (top row) and HIV (bottom row). Note the difference in structure of the core in the two types of mature virions (c).

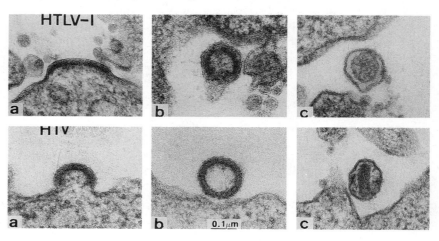

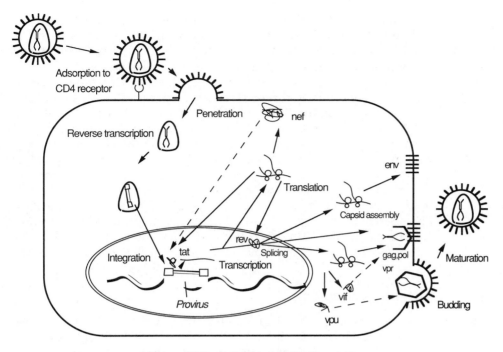

Figure 37.3.   Retrovirus replication cycle.

the process of making the DNA, portions of ends of the genomic RNA are copied twice, leading to a structure at each end of the DNA called the **long terminal repeat** or **LTR**.

- **Integration**. The double-stranded DNA molecule is transported to the nucleus and integrated into host cell chromosomes. A virus-coded enzyme, called **integrase**, is responsible for this reaction, which involves joining the ends of each **LTR** to cut cellular DNA. The retrovirus integration process resembles the mechanism of motion of some transposable elements of bacteria (Chapter 4). In the integrated state, viral genetic material is called the **provirus**. The provirus behaves like a cellular gene in that it is passed to daughter cells at division and contains signals that control its transcription into RNA.

- **Synthesis of progeny virus**. In the "productive phase," viral DNA is transcribed into messenger RNA by host cell RNA polymerase. Signals that direct the cell's RNA synthetic machinery are found in the **LTR** and resemble signals used by the cell for making its own RNAs. After transcription, some of these viral RNA molecules are used as messengers for the synthesis of viral proteins. Others become incorporated as genomes into progeny viral particles. Assembly takes place at the cell surface as the structural proteins assembly with genomes and acquire their envelope by passage through the cytoplasmic membrane (Figs. 37.2 and 37.3). Morphological changes in the virion after budding are caused by cleavage of the protein precursors.

- **Latency and trans-activation**. The replication cycle described so far is common in outline to all retroviruses. HIV and related viruses are unusual in several ways: (*a*) Infection also involves a **latent** phase in which infected cells contain a provirus but do not express viral RNA or proteins. (*b*) Expression of viral macromolecules is subject to regulation by viral gene products that operate as soluble elements (in "trans"). This phenomenon is known as **trans-activation**. At least two HIV genes (called **tat** and **rev**, see Fig. 37.4) function as **trans-activating** factors, which greatly increase the expression of viral RNAs and proteins. *tat* causes a greater level of RNA to be made by RNA polymerase, and *rev* affects the way that the RNAs are processed and translated into protein C. Their proviruses contain signals that can turn on expression when HIV-infected cells are stimulated by antigen or infected by some other viruses (such as a herpesvirus). These features appear to be related in an important way: after infection of lymphocytes and integration of the provirus, the infection process may be halted, to be reinitiated much later in an explosive way by unknown stimuli. The outcome is a high level of trans-activation, resulting in a burst of virus production and rapid death of the cell. The need for secondary stimuli to complete the replication cycle may account for the unpredictable timing of the disease.

Antigenic Variation

A unique characteristic of infection by HIV is that the immune response of the host is unable to curtail completely viral replication (although it may be important in suppressing it during the latent phase of the disease). This is a paradox, because for most other viral infections, the presence of antibody indicates immunity, protection from infection, and a favorable prognosis. How is HIV able to survive despite the host's immune response? Two mechanisms may be at work here. Latently infected cells that do not express surface antigens may not be detectable by the immune response, and the virus may be able to mask or change its antigenic specificity.

Which HIV gene products are important in directing the immune response of the host? HIV genes that code for internal viral proteins (*gag* and *pol*) show relative stability from one isolate to the next, but the *env* gene displays frequent mutations that lead to variations of its product, the surface glycoprotein. Antibodies to *gag* and *pol* proteins are found in infected individuals, but do not seem to be important. Antibodies to the envelope proteins, on the other hand, can neutralize the virus. HIV envelope glycoproteins have two unusual features. First, they are extensively coated with polysaccharide side-chains that, because they are added by host enzymes, are antigenically invisible to the host. Second, they contain **hypervariable regions** that permit the virus to present new antigenic configurations to the host. In contrast, the segments of the surface glycoprotein that are involved in the interaction of cellular receptors must be genetically conserved. Conserved

Figure 37.4. Genetic organization of human retroviruses. The *top line* in each case shows the provirus with control sequences shown as *boxes* at the ends. The *lower boxes* indicate the location of the viral genes, with *dotted lines* showing genes whose function is uncertain. Note that both of these viruses have genes in addition to those that code for virion proteins (*gag*, *pol*, and *env*).

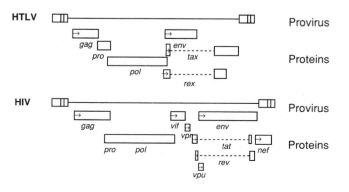

segments may then be hidden and protected from neutralizing antibodies by the hypervariable regions. HIV can constantly vary its surface antigenic composition, which may allow it to avoid inactivation. If this turns out to be an important mechanism, HIV would resemble influenza viruses and trypanosomes of sleeping sickness in that it withstands the immune response by changing major surface antigens. Such a mechanism would hinder the development of an effective vaccine containing the surface glycoprotein.

Recently, a new retrovirus has been isolated from patients with AIDS and who live in West Africa. This new isolate, called **HIV-II,** has an envelope glycoprotein that is more closely related to a monkey virus (simian immunodeficiency virus, SIV) than to HIV. Epidemiological features of this virus, such as its routes of transmission, are not yet known. Major sequence differences exist between the two HIV types. Antibodies against the surface glycoprotein of HIV type I only partially cross-react with HIV type II. Antibodies directed against core proteins of HIV-I and HIV-II show some cross-reactivity. Thus, AIDS may be caused by one or more distinct but related viruses.

ENCOUNTER

The distribution of HIV infection in the population is consistent with an agent that is extremely labile in a free state and that cannot readily enter through intact body surfaces. In this respect, it is similar to (but less contagious than) hepatitis B virus, which has a similar epidemiological pattern in the United States. HIV has been detected in a number of body fluids including peripheral blood, semen, cervical secretions, breast milk, urine, CSF, saliva, and tears. It is unlikely that the last four represent an important means of transmission. With few exceptions, HIV transmission in the U.S. occurs at the present time by one of three routes: sexual contact, intravenous drug abuse, and vertical passage from infected mothers to offsprings. At present, heterosexual transmission and congenital transmission from infected mother to child are becoming more important in the spread of AIDS in the U.S. The incidence of AIDS in various risk groups is shown in Table 37.2.

In 1991, homosexual and bisexual men accounted for approximately 70% of AIDS cases in the U.S. (including 8% who are also intravenous drug abusers). The most prominent risk factors for acquisition of infec-

Table 37.2. Incidence (per Million Population) of AIDS and Relative Risk by Racial and Ethnic Groups, Age, and Transmission Categories, 1981–1987[a]

Category	White	Black	Hispanic	Other
Adult men	380.8 (1.0)	1068.1 (2.8)[b]	1036.3 (2.7)[b]	141.0 (0.4)[b]
Adult women	12.2 (1.0)	161.1 (13.2)[b]	104.6 (8.6)[b]	11.1 (0.9)
Homosexual men	298.6 (1.0)	413.8 (1.4)[b]	513.9 (1.7)[b]	94.7 (0.3)[b]
Bisexual men	46.8 (1.0)	177.7 (3.8)[b]	126.3 (2.7)[b]	24.9 (0.9)[b]
Heterosexual intravenous drug abusers	10.1 (1.0)	201.2 (19.9)[b]	195.1 (19.3)[b]	4.2 (0.3)[b]
Hemophilia	2.6 (1.0)	1.4 (0.6)[b]	2.7 (1.0)	1.7 (0.7)
Transfusion	5.1 (1.0)	7.5 (1.5)	6.5 (1.3)	5.0 (1.0)
Pediatric (all causes)	3.8 (1.0)	46.3 (12.1)[b]	26.1 (6.8)[b]	3.2 (0.8)

[a]Relative risk shown in parentheses; relative to incidence in whites
[b]Relative risk significantly different from 1.0 ($P < 0.05$).

tion are a high number of sexual partners and participation in sexual practices that increase the risk of transmission due to damage of the anorectal mucosa (mainly receptive anal intercourse, which allows the virus to enter the bloodstream through tears in the rectal mucosa or through direct infection of the epithelial cells of the rectum).

As the AIDS epidemic has continued, intravenous drug abusers represent the second largest group with HIV infection in the U.S., about 15–20% of total cases. Importantly, this group acts as a bridge for the spread of HIV infection to nonhomosexual contacts. Seventy-five percent of AIDS transmission due to heterosexual activity involves at least one partner who uses intravenous drugs. Transmission among drug abusers occurs because of sharing contaminated needles and syringes that contain a residue of blood (including infected white blood cells) from previous users. Seropositivity among drug abusers correlates with frequency of injection, needle sharing, and demographic factors. Major urban areas of the U.S., including New York City, Newark, and surrounding areas and Miami, contain a high proportion of members of this group.

HIV transmission by blood transfusion has been exceedingly rare since March 1985, although more than 12,000 individuals may have been infected by this route before that time. Hemophiliacs have long been identified as a group at risk for blood-borne viruses, such as hepatitis B and non-A non-B. This is because they receive preparations of factor VIII and factor IX obtained from plasma pooled from thousands of donors. Currently, 75–90% of frequent adult recipients of factor VIII are positive for antibodies to HIV. As of July 1989, 5% of the 20,000 hemophiliacs in the U.S. have developed AIDS. The most rapid period of seroconversion among hemophiliacs occurred between 1982 and 1984. At the present time, factor VIII concentrates are unlikely to contain HIV because blood donors are screened for HIV antibodies and because plasma products are treated with heat or chemicals to inactivate contaminating viruses. AIDS is now the most common cause of death among hemophiliacs.

Heterosexual transmission of HIV has been implicated in approximately 5% of reported cases. There is concern that this mode of transmission may increase more rapidly in the U.S. because it is already the most common one in most other countries. The proportion of cases of AIDS acquired by individuals who have no known risk factor other than heterosexual contact with HIV-infected persons increased from 1.1% in 1982 to 2.3% in 1986. Most of these individuals reported sexual contact with either intravenous drug abusers or bisexual males. Transmission rates to long-term heterosexual partners of AIDS patients vary widely, from less than 10% to 70%. The low transmission rate seen in spouses of HIV-positive hemophiliacs suggests that, in many instances, the virus is not easily transmitted even over a period of several years. In other instances, transmission may occur after one or two sexual contacts only. Possible explanations for this disparity include genetic factors influencing susceptibility, increased virulence of certain strains of HIV, and variable communicability in different stages of the infection. Of the persons who acquire HIV by heterosexual contacts, 17% are male and 83% are female. Thus, transmission occurs more readily from infected males to female contacts than vice versa, but it does take place in both directions. Vaginal transmission from females to males may occur less frequently due to unfavorable factors for HIV survival in the vagina, and because such transmission may require penile ulcerations or damage to the male urethral mucosa.

Heterosexual transfer of HIV is more common in certain countries. For example, the overall ratio of male to female AIDS cases in Zaire is approximately 1:1 as opposed to 13:1 in the U.S. One study showed that heterosexual African males with AIDS had a markedly higher number of sexual partners than matched controls without AIDS. Other possible factors include lowered resistance due to coexistent sexually transmitted diseases. Regardless of differences in rates of transmission in the various groups, the prevention of major heterosexual epidemics must focus on all young, sexually active individuals. In some areas of Africa, AIDS is now the leading cause of death among adult males.

Congenital transmission, as in the case of baby G., is the most important route of transmission of pediatric AIDS. As of April 1991, there were 2900 cases of AIDS in children under 13 years of age in the U.S. This represents 2% of the total AIDS cases in the U.S. More than 90% of all new pediatric cases are acquired by birth from an HIV-seropositive mother. Approximately 50% of children with AIDS are born to mothers who are intravenous drug abusers. In some urban areas, this can amount to very large numbers. In New York City, for example, one in 20 newborns has antibodies to HIV. Approximately 30% of these children are infected with HIV. Intrauterine transmission appears to be the principal mode of infection, although there is evidence for infection during the birth process as well as for postnatal acquisition from breast milk.

HIV transmission among health care workers is an area of particular concern. Extensive studies have confirmed that HIV transmission in a medical setting is exceedingly rare. The risk of infection following accidental sticking with needles used to draw blood from HIV-infected patients is less than 0.5%. The risk from exposure of mucous membranes or contamination of apparently intact skin is considerably less. With the general adoption of "universal precautions," which assume that blood or other fluids from all patients are potentially infectious, HIV spread to health care workers should remain an unusual event. The spread of HIV from health care workers to patients is also rare, but a few cases have been reported. At this writing, recommendations for dealing with this important issue are still pending.

It is important to emphasize that spread of HIV among nonsexual household contacts is exceedingly rare. More than 12 studies involving over 700 family members or boarding school contacts of AIDS patients failed to detect a single instance of transmission.

Arthropod vectors have been proposed as a route of transmission, but there is no evidence for this whatever. If arthropods, such as mosquitoes or ticks, were important, children in Third World countries would be frequently infected, as they are often victims of bites. In fact, the occurrence of AIDS in children outside recognized risk groups is highly unusual, making this an unlikely mechanism of transmission.

ENTRY, SPREAD, AND MULTIPLICATION

The mechanism by which HIV establishes an infection in the host is poorly understood because of the variable course of the disease and the scarcity of infected cells, especially during the long latent phase of infection. Most likely, HIV enters the host contained within infected cells, e.g., macrophages, lymphocytes, or spermatozoa, although infection with free virus also occurs. Such cells are deposited in tissues and enter the body either through microabrasions on the surface of mucous membranes or through penetration of intact skin with a needle.

While HIV can infect an expanding list of cell types, two major groups of cells in the body serve as preferred targets for infection by HIV—helper T lymphocytes and monocytes. On their surface, both of these cells contain the specific CD_4 (or T4) protein, which serves as the receptor necessary for virus entry. Most of our knowledge of HIV replication comes from studies using cells derived from human T-cell tumors, which can be grown in the laboratory.

DAMAGE

Our knowledge of the molecular events that modulate lymphocyte damage in HIV-infected patients is still rudimentary. However, on the basis of known abnormalities of humoral and cellular immunity, it is possible to outline a sequence of events that follows HIV infection.

HIV preferentially infects **helper T cells**, i.e., lymphocytes that express the CD_4 surface antigen. This protein defines this subset of T cells and serves as the receptor for attachment of HIV. Many of these cells are killed by replication of the virus. Even cells that survive can participate in killing, because such cells express viral envelope protein molecules and, in turn, can bind to CD_4 receptors on other cells. The result is cell-to-cell aggregation and eventual fusion, resulting in the formation of large multinucleated syncytia (Figs. 33.3 and 37.5).

Damage to and depletion of helper T cells during HIV replication results in a characteristic change in the ratio of helper/suppressor-cytotoxic cells. Depletion of helper T cells results in a reduction in total circulating lymphocytes (lymphopenia) and a relative increase in the number of suppressor-cytotoxic lymphocytes.

In addition to quantitative T-cell deficits, HIV induces functional T-cell abnormalities. Normally, these cells modulate the function of other cells in the immune system, including B cells, monocytes, and natural killer cells. These interactions require the function of the CD_4 protein (see Chapter 7). Infection with HIV results in loss of the CD_4 receptor from the cell surface and can, thus, derange these functions even if the infected cells survive.

An important unresolved question is how HIV replication results in dysfunction and death of infected helper T lymphocytes, a small percentage of which are infected. Various mechanisms that interfere with cell metabolism have been proposed. For example, does the formation of large syncytia of T lymphocytes sequester a sufficient number to explain their depletion? Is there a toxic protein made by HIV but not by other retroviruses? Does unintegrated HIV DNA build up, with possible disruption of cellular biosynthetic activities? Do the infected lymphocytes undergo premature differentiation and senility? Do T-helper cells become inactivated by loss of CD_4 from the cell surface? All of these phenomena can be observed in cell cultures but their importance in natural infections is not clear.

Recently, the specific CD_4 marker characteristic of helper T lymphocytes has been found in membranes of other cell types, including circulating monocytes and macrophages, natural killer cells, certain B lymphocytes, and neuronal cells. These cells may also become infected and damaged by viral replication or, in addition, may serve as a reservoir for virus latency. Defects in killing secondary invading microorganisms may be attributes of HIV infection of macrophages and monocytes, as well as by the loss of helper T cells. Furthermore, macrophage-related cells called Langerhans cells, which form part of

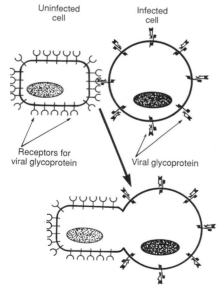

Figure 37.5. Mechanism of HIV-mediated cell fusion.

epithelial surfaces, have been found to be highly sensitive to HIV and may be an important entry point for sexually transmitted infection.

Even though many patients with AIDS have elevated immunoglobulin levels in their serum, their ability to produce antibodies against specific antigens may be impaired. For example, children with HIV infections cannot make antibodies against the specific capsular polysaccharide antigens of the pneumococcus and *Haemophilus influenzae* type b. This defect may be due to direct impairment of B lymphocytes as well as to the loss of helper T lymphocytes.

Some Clinical Consequences

AIDS represents the terminal stage of infection by HIV. Clinical syndromes vary with different stages of infection.

Initial HIV infection (Group I) may be associated with a mononucleosis-like syndrome approximately a few weeks following exposure. This may include fever, a skin rash, muscle aches, lymphadenopathy, and meningitis. In the vast majority of patients, detectable levels of viral antigens are present in the blood, inducing antibody production by the host. Seroconversion (the development of detectable antibodies to HIV) occurs a few weeks to months after the initial infection. With the increase in antibody titer comes the virtual disappearance of virus, indicating that the initial immune response effectively eliminates the vast majority of virus and infected cells, but a small surviving population remains. The infected individual often becomes asymptomatic as viral antigens either disappear or are present at low levels. HIV antibodies can still be detected in serum and viral replication continues at a low level.

Why HIV replication is kept under control during this asymptomatic period remains one of the main questions to be left unanswered about AIDS. There seems not to be a true latent state (as with Herpes viruses) inasmuch as very small amounts of replicating virus can be found at all stages. At any one time, however, there may be latently infected cells that contain viral DNA but do not make virus proteins and are not seen by the immune system. In culture, some infected monocytes will not begin to make virus until activated to differentiation into macrophages. Thus, repeated activation of the immune system during the asymptomatic phase may contribute to enhanced virus replication and progression of the disease.

Once infected, an individual may become completely asymptomatic (Group II) or develop persistent generalized lymphadenopathy (Group III). Lymphadenopathy may persist or resolve before progressing over months to years to pre-AIDS conditions characterized by diarrhea, oral candidiasis, weight loss, and fever.

Patients will progress to develop AIDS (Group IV) with opportunistic infections, Kaposi's sarcoma, and/or B cell lymphomas (Table 37.3). In the cases described above, both mother and child eventually died of *Pneumocystis carinii* pneumonia. For information on *P. carinii*, see Chapter 50, and for details on infections of the compromised patient, see Chapter 66. The majority of adult AIDS patients also develop neurological symptoms. This may be due to a secondary infection by opportunistic organisms such as the protozoan *Toxoplasma gondii* or the fungus *Cryptococcus neoformans*, or to the development of malignancies of the central nervous system (CNS). HIV may invade the CNS directly and replicate in neurons. Presumably, the virus is carried to the

Table 37.3. Secondary Infections Found in HIV-infected Patients with Immunodeficiency

Protozoan and helminthic infection
    Intestinal infection with *Cryptosporidium* or *Isospora* causing chronic diarrhea
    Strongyloidiasis disseminated beyond the GI tract
    Toxoplasmosis disseminated beyond the liver, spleen, or lymph nodes
Fungal infections
    Pneumocystis carinii[a] pneumonia
    Candida esophagitis
    Pulmonary candidiasis
    Cryptococcosis of the CNS
    Disseminated histoplasmosis
Bacterial infections
    Disseminated infection with *Mycobacterium avium* complex
Viral infections
    Disseminated cytomegalovirus infection
    Herpes simplex virus infection, either disseminated, or of the lungs, GI tract
    Progressive multifocal leukoencephalopathy

[a]Taxonomy uncertain

CNS by circulating monocytes. It is not known if damage to brain cells is due to the release of toxic substances from the monocytes or to direct damage to neurons by replicating virus.

The most important single factor in the development of AIDS in HIV-infected individuals is time. Most, if not all HIV-infected individuals will ultimately develop AIDS. Several factors affect survival rates, including age, gender, type of initial diagnosis, and immune status. For example, patients who develop Kaposi's sarcoma have significantly longer survival than patients who present with certain opportunistic infections, perhaps because the former are diagnosed at an earlier stage of altered cellular immunity. Overall, the 5-year survival rate of patients with AIDS ranges from 3–15%. These figures indicate not only the seriousness of HIV infection, but also the magnitude of the health problem in years to come. Even if no one became infected with HIV from now on, the incidence of the disease will continue to increase into the next century. It is not known if the probability of progression to AIDS is increased by "cofactors" (e.g., diseases often seen in some of the risk groups, such as hepatitis, cytomegalovirus, herpes infections) or by genetic determinants. Before the availability of AZT (azidothymidine, zidovudine), the median survival time among AIDS patients was about 12 months. Recent studies have shown that this figure is about doubled among patients who receive antiretroviral and other antimicrobial therapy.

DIAGNOSIS

Before the viral etiological agent was identified, diagnosis of AIDS was based solely on clinical findings. The presence of specific opportunistic infections or certain tumors such as Kaposi's sarcoma in high-risk groups was necessary before the disease could be suspected. Patients in the early stages of infection could not be identified. In September, 1992 the Centers for Disease Control issued revised criteria for a **case definition of AIDS** based on the presence or absence of laboratory evidence of HIV infection (Table 37.4). Evidence of infection is generally based on the presence of antibodies to HIV. The presence of virus in blood or tissues can be documented by growth of the virus in cell culture or by molecular methods, but these techniques have not

Table 37.4. Selected Features of the Case Definition for AIDS[a]

If laboratory evidence regarding HIV Infection is not available, several conditions serve as indicators, including specified manifestations of infections by any of the following: *Candida* (fungus) *Cryptococcus* (fungus), *Cryptosporidium* (protozoan), cytomegalovirus, herpes simplex virus, *Mycobacterium avium* complex (bacteria), *Pneumocystis carinii* (fungus?), *Toxoplasma* (protozoan); other indicators are specified manifestations of Kaposi's sarcoma, brain lymphoma, leukoencephalopathy, and several others

If laboratory evidence for HIV infection is present, any of the above diseases indicates a diagnosis of AIDS; to this list are added here specified manifestations of the following: infections by *Isospora* (protozoan), *Coccidioides* (fungus), *Histoplasma* (fungus), *Salmonella* (bacterium), plus other lymphomas, encephalopathy, and HIV-wasting disease; some of these conditions serve as indicators even if diagnosed presumptively (i.e., without waiting for definitive tests)

If there is laboratory evidence against HIV infection, under some conditions, the diagnosis of AIDS cannot be ruled out for surveillance purposes; these conditions are met when the patient is immunodeficient for other causes that cannot be ruled out and has an indicator disease

[a]1987 Revision by the Centers for Disease Control.

been standardized and are not widely available. Remember also that, in the early stages, viremia is rare and only a small percentage of lymphocytes are infected so that such cells may be hard to find. Therefore, laboratory evidence is generally based on serological work.

Serological tests for HIV infection detect and characterize specific anti-HIV antibodies in serum. The ability to grow HIV in culture made such tests possible. It is now clear that close to 100% of HIV-infected individuals have measurable antibodies in their serum. The exceptions are a small group of individuals either in the earliest stages of the disease (before seroconversion) or in the terminal ones (when their B cells are unable to synthesize antibodies). On very rare occasions, certain individuals may "serorevert" (lose detectable antibodies while still carrying the virus). Antibodies may not be detected in an HIV-infected person due to technical problems (false negatives). It is important to remember, therefore, that, in a very limited number of instances, the absence of antibodies does not completely rule out an HIV infection. The persistence of detectable antibodies to HIV is generally accepted as an indication of infection and the ability to transmit the virus.

Initial tests for HIV serology generally are performed by an ELISA test (enzyme-linked immunosorbent assay). This test is carried out by adding a sample of the patient's serum to small plastic cups to which HIV antigen is bound (kits for such assays are commercially available). If antibodies are present, they will complex with HIV antigen. After washing away unreacted components, antihuman immunoglobulin antiserum linked to a readily assayable enzyme, such as a peroxidase, is added. Anti-HIV antibodies in the clinical sample can then be detected by adding a chromogenic enzyme substrate; a positive test is indicated by a suitable color change (see Chapter 55 for details). The test is usually repeated with positive samples and the results are confirmed by immunofluorescence or "Western blot" analysis. The Western blot detects antibodies against individual viral polypeptides that have been separated by electrophoresis and transferred ("blotted") onto a thin membrane filter. (See Chapter 55 for a full discussion of Western blots, ELISAs, and diagnostic principles in HIV infections.)

The ELISA test has a false-positive rate of around 0.4%. With confirmatory Western blot tests, the joint false-positive rate approaches a remarkable 0.005%. However, even these low numbers become worrisome when a population with low prevalence of HIV infection is tested. Thus, it has been estimated that, among non-high-risk female blood donors in the U.S. (whose rate of HIV infection is approximately 1 in 10,000), the likelihood that infection is actually present in a woman with a confirmed positive test is only around 70%. In such a low-risk population, the use of the test raises difficult moral and legal issues.

The predictive value of an AIDS test must be carefully weighed in deciding whether low-risk individuals should be tested. The impact of a positive test result on a person's state of mind, social interactions, marriage, insurance eligibility, and employment opportunities is enormous. How many false positives is our society willing to accept to identify a relatively small number of infected individuals? On the other hand, the beneficial effects of initiating anti-HIV therapy before the onset of AIDS clearly justifies testing of individuals at risk for HIV infection.

PREVENTION

Control of the spread of AIDS has proved to be difficult because a vaccine is not yet available. Control of spread of this disease requires a change in the lifestyle of many individuals. Education appears to be the most important means of reducing the spread of AIDS at the present time. The most important measures include curtailing high-risk practices, such as multiple sexual contacts for both the homosexual and heterosexual population; the use of condoms; awareness of the danger of anal intercourse; and the use of uncontaminated needles for intravenous drug abusers. Evidence that education has an impact on sexual practices comes from experience in the gay community in San Francisco, where transmission of other sexually transmitted diseases, especially gonorrhea, is markedly reduced. While it is not yet known if this has also led to the desired diminution in AIDS cases, it has reduced the spread of HIV in this community.

What problems are encountered in designing an AIDS vaccine? The ability of HIV to change its antigenicity will probably complicate conventional approaches to vaccine development. Antigenic peptides prepared by genetic engineering techniques are currently in the early stages of testing. It should be emphasized that, so far, there is only a limited understanding of the nature of the immune response to HIV infection. Antibody titers in infected individuals are low compared to other viral infections, but the almost complete eradication of the initial viremia suggest that the immune response may be quite effective in controlling the infection for many years and raises hope that a similar immune response induced in uninfected individuals may be sufficient to ward off a primary infection.

It is not known whether a vaccine-induced immune response would confer protection against primary HIV infection. A problem with an HIV vaccine is that the virus is probably transmitted from person to person mainly within infected cells (lymphocytes or macrophages) and, therefore, may not be accessible to the immune system. HIV may be transmitted directly from cell to cell, without going through an extracellular phase. The ability of HIV to induce cell fusion may also reduce the importance of extracellular antibodies. Protection may then require a more complex immune response, probably of the cell-mediated type. Lastly, HIV exists in a number of states within a cell; in the latent state, infected cells harbor virus without expressing viral antigens.

A novel approach to immunization offers some cause for optimism. Patients already infected with HIV were immunized with a cloned HIV envelope protein (gp160). More than one-half of these patients showed an increase in both humoral and cellular immunity to this surface antigen. What is unusual about this result is that it showed enhancement of an already existing immune response. If this approach is shown to be clinically useful, postinfection immunization of this sort may have a role in other chronic viral infections as well. There are, however, a number of problems associated with HIV vaccine development, and testing of an HIV vaccine presents special problems. The chimpanzee is the only animal known to be susceptible to HIV infection (although the infection seems not to progress to AIDS). Vaccine candidates currently being tested include killed whole virus, purified envelope protein, peptides from envelope proteins, and vaccinia virus genetically engineered to produce HIV proteins after infection. The best model system may be a closely related virus (known as simian immunodeficiency virus) found in some monkey species and capable of causing AIDS in other species. In this model, there is good evidence that an inactivated virus vaccine confers an immune response adequate to protect against challenge with the same virus. This gives grounds for optimism that an effective human vaccine can be developed. Even when a potential HIV vaccine has been developed, human clinical trials will be difficult to accomplish. Here are some of the problems:

- Volunteers will have the stigma of becoming HIV-antibody positive;

- What criteria should be established for the volunteers' sexual preference?

- How will we determine if a response is protective?

To provide a statistically significant answer (in view of the low incidence of infection in the population), a huge number of people will have to be vaccinated. The ability of HIV to establish a latent infection will also complicate vaccine trials. If a vaccinated person becomes infected but remains asymptomatic, is that a vaccine failure or a vaccine success? How long should such a person be followed before results can be meaningfully interpreted? None of these questions has easy answers.

THERAPY

There has been some progress in the development of antiretroviral therapy. The life cycle of retroviruses is intimately connected with the replication of mammalian cells, so that only a limited number of metabolic reactions can be singled out for targets of specific chemotherapy. Reverse transcriptase is an attractive target because inhibition of this enzyme should have no effect on the host cell. Many anti-HIV agents now being investigated inhibit this uniquely viral function. **Azidothymidine** (AZT), the only drug presently licensed for treatment of HIV infection, inhibits this enzyme. Initial studies indicate that AZT administration over periods of up to 18 months decreases the frequency of opportunistic infections in selected AIDS patients. In addition, some AZT-treated patients show an increase in the number of helper T cells and an improvement in cell-mediated immunity. Treatment of HIV-positive but asymptomatic individuals has shown effectiveness in slowing down progression to AIDS. Unfortunately, AZT cannot be taken indefinitely due to toxic side effects. Also, AZT-resistant mutants of HIV can be isolated from treated individuals although the clinical impact of this resistance is not yet clear. Nonetheless, this first-generation compound demonstrates that effective drug therapy can be developed.

AZT was the first of a number of dideoxynucleosides to be tested in clinical trials. Each of the drugs inhibits reverse transcriptase after first being phosphorylated intracellularly. Inhibition takes place by one of two mechanisms, i.e., by competing for substrates required for the synthesis of proviral DNA, or by premature termination of growing strand of DNA into which the drug has been incorporated. Mammalian DNA polymerases are more resistant than the viral reverse transcriptase to these drugs. Several new drugs are undergoing clinical trials and one, dideoxyinosine (DDI or didanosine), has been approved for clinical use.

Additional improvement in the condition of many AIDS patients has been achieved by therapy directed at opportunistic infections—most notably, aerosolized pentamidine for the treatment of *P. carinii* infection (see Chapter 67).

CONCLUSIONS

AIDS is a uniquely devastating disease; it kills all of those who exhibit symptoms. It is a chronic illness, often becoming manifested years after the virus is acquired and after the individual has had the opportunity to transmit it. Based on estimates of infected individuals, a threefold increase in the number of cases has been projected between 1987 and 1991 (Fig. 37.6). By inactivating a central cellular component of the immune system, the helper T lymphocyte, HIV produces severe impairment of both humoral and cellular immunity. The disease is lethal because defense against opportunistic pathogens are gone. Diseases that were practically unseen before AIDS (e.g., encephalitis due to *T. gondii*), or under reasonable control (e.g., mycobacterial infections), have become common and highly dangerous among AIDS patients (Chapter 67).

AIDS runs counter to the tenet that a successful parasite does not cause lethal injury to its host, suggesting that HIV may be a relative newcomer among human infectious agents. The disease appeared suddenly in the U.S. and its etiology was established with remarkable

Figure 37.6. Quarterly incidence of AIDS in the U.S. The number of cases per quarter is projected to 1991 based on a statistical extrapolation.

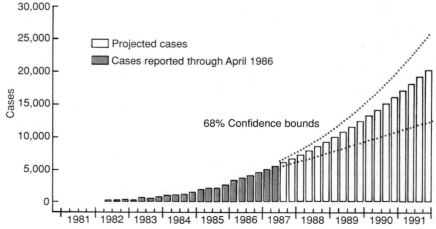

speed. We have acquired a great deal of knowledge about HIV and other retroviruses but we are still unable to explain many of the features of the disease. We do not understand how helper lymphocytes are killed or impaired, or why the infection of a small proportion of them has such devastating effects. Lack of this knowledge hinders the design of drugs and vaccines. The virus is particularly elusive to immunotherapeutic approaches because of variability in surface antigens and other features of its structure and lifestyle.

Prolonging life among those that have acquired the virus presents a major medical problem. In the absence of an effective vaccine or treatment, prevention of HIV transmission among uninfected members of the population depends on public education.

Self-assessment Questions

1. Discuss the structure and mode of replication of retroviruses.

2. How does HIV differ from the other known retroviruses?

3. Imagine having to address a community group regarding AIDS. What would you say about its history, transmissibility in the community, prospects for prevention, and therapy?

4. What important aspects of HIV infection have yet to be elucidated? How could understanding their mechanism help prevent or treat AIDS?

5. What problems are associated with designing an effective AIDS vaccine?

6. If you were asked, what specific areas of research and education on AIDS would you target for the award of research funds?

7. What is your guess about the status of AIDS 10 years from now...20 years from now?

SUGGESTED READING

Coffin J. Genetic variation in AIDS viruses. Cell 1986;46:1–4.

Curran JW, et al. The epidemiology of HIV infection and AIDS in the United States. Science 1987;239:610–616.

Friedland GH, Klein RS. N Engl J Med 1987;317:1125–1135.

Gallo RC. The first human retrovirus. Scientif Am 1986;88–98.

Greene WC. The molecular biology of human immunodeficiency virus type I infection. N Engl J Med 1991;324:308–317.

Moore RD, et al. Zidovudine and the natural history of the acquired immunodeficiency syndrome. N Engl J Med 1991;324:1412–1416.

Yarchoan R, et al. Clinical pharmacology of zidovudine and related dideoxynucleotides. N Engl J Med 1989; 321:726–738.

Adenoviruses 38

Gary Ketner

Adenoviruses are among the most common viruses found in healthy people and are often isolated from the tonsils, adenoids, and stool. They frequently cause acute respiratory diseases that range in severity from one that resembles the common cold to a serious pneumonia. Adenoviruses are also responsible for conjunctivitis and diarrhea. These viruses belong to a large number of individual serotypes that are associated with the different disease manifestations. The presence of adenoviruses in the tissues of healthy persons is due to persistent infections, with shedding of the viruses over periods of months or years.

Adenoviruses have a double-stranded DNA genome, are nonenveloped, and possess icosahedral symmetry. They reproduce in the nucleus of host cells and are released as the result of cell lysis. The replication cycle of adenoviruses has been extensively studied and serves as a paradigm for the replication of all DNA viruses (Table 38.1).

OUTBREAK

Over a period of 3 months, 83 patients who had visited an ophthalmologist office in Erie, Pa. came down with redness of the eyes, eyelid swelling with discharge, photophobia, and change in vision. Only two of these patients had fever or diarrhea. The patients ranged in age from 18–89 years and all had come to the office between 3 and 29 days before the onset of symptoms. Eventually, all of the patients recovered spontaneously. No further outbreaks were reported after a number of measures were taken, including reducing the use of procedures that required instruments.

Epidemiologists from the Centers for Disease Control in Atlanta, GA studied this outbreak of epidemic keratoconjunctivitis and documented the presence of adenovirus serotype 37 in 20 of the 22 patients from whom specimens were obtained. The procedures used were immunofluorescence microscopy of eye specimens and culture in cultured human kidney cells. The virus was also isolated in the office from instruments used to measure visual acuity, from the work surfaces, in eye drops, and from the air conditioning filter. Neither the ophthalmologist nor members of the staff tested positive for the virus or for specific antibodies.

Most **individual** outbreaks of adenovirus infections consist of mild infections of the respiratory and digestive systems. They resemble those caused by other agents and usually remain undiagnosed. Much of our knowledge of adenovirus infection stems from **outbreaks** such as the one described. Outbreaks leading to eye infections by this virus have been repeatedly reported, indicating that transmission from a contaminated environment (instruments, surfaces, etc.) readily occurs. Other outbreaks of eye infections (**"pink eye"**) can be caused by using contaminated swimming pools. The most serious outbreaks of adenoviral infections are seen among military recruits who come down with a

Table 38.1. Association of Adenovirus Infections with Specific Serotypes

Diseases	Common Adenovirus Serotypes
Respiratory infections	1,2,5,6
Pharyngoconjunctivitis	3,7,14
Acute respiratory disease (ARD) or recruits	4,7
Gastrointestinal infection	40,41
Associated with celiac disease	12
Conjunctivitis	2,3,5,7,8,19,21
Epidemic keratoconjunctivitis	8,19,37

serious form of acute pneumonia. Crowding conditions and physical stress appear to contribute to the occurrence of such outbreaks.

For all of their sporadic importance, adenoviruses are common human commensals and relatively mild human pathogens. Their pathogenic mechanisms are not well known, however, a great deal is known about their structure and mode of replication. **Emphasis in this chapter is on basic aspects of the replicative strategy of adenoviruses, which serves as a well-developed example of replication among the large DNA viruses.**

ADENOVIRUSES

Adenoviral Particle

Adenovirus virions are **nonenveloped icosahedral** particles (Fig. 38.1). The shell of the virion is made up of two kinds of capsomeres, **hexons** with six neighbors and **pentons at the vertices of the icosahedron with five neighbors**. The pentons have projecting knobbed **fibers** that give these virions a characteristic "sputnik" appearance. Inside the virion, the viral DNA is associated with several basic proteins in a structure called the core. The predominant component of the viral core is an arginine-rich basic protein that presumably aids in the spatial organization of the viral DNA and neutralizes the negative charges of the DNA. This protein serves to package the adenoviral DNA in a manner analogous to that of histones in the compaction of cellular chromatin.

The genome of the human adenoviruses is a **linear double-stranded DNA** molecule and its sequence has been determined for one serotype. The adenoviral genome has two unusual structural features. First, it is **terminally redundant**; approximately 100 base pairs are repeated in an inverted orientation at each end of the genome. Second, each strand of the genome is covalently attached at its 5′ end to a protein molecule (the **terminal protein; TP**). Both the terminal redundancy and the terminal protein play key roles roles in the replication of adenovirus DNA.

Adenovirus genes with related functions tend to be clustered on the genome and expressed from a common promoter. This arrangement, which is more characteristic of procaryotes than eukaryotes, is also found among other DNA viruses, such as the papovaviruses. This arrangement provides an economical mechanism for coordinating expression of genes whose functions are required at similar times during the infection. Examples of clustered adenoviral genes with related functions are those whose products (a) interact with the host immune system, (b) participate in post-transcriptional events in gene expression, (c) are essential for viral DNA replication, and (d) are compo-

Figure 38.1.   The adenovirus particle. A. Three-dimensional image of the adenovirus capsid reconstructed by computer from cryoelectron micrographs. **B.** Schematic view of the adenovirus particle with the names of individual capsid proteins indicated.

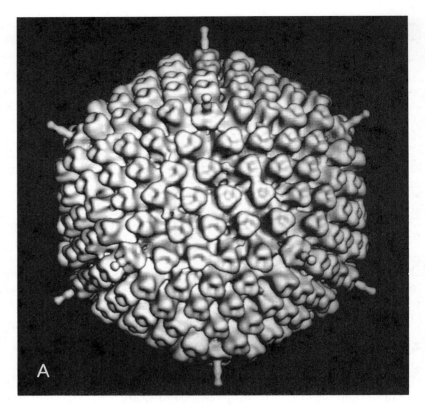

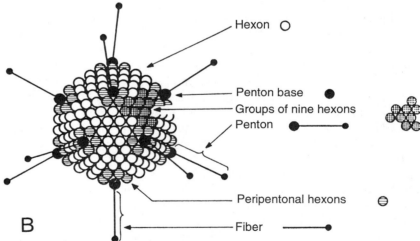

nents of the virions or involved in its assembly. The physical arrangement of these regions is well conserved even among adenoviruses that affect different host species.

Adenoviral Replicative Cycle

ATTACHMENT AND PENETRATION

Adenoviruses attach to **receptors** on the cell surface via their fiber protein. Many cell types possess about 10^5 copies of these surface receptors. The normal function of the receptor (when the virus is not present) is not known. Following attachment, the virus-receptor complex migrates to **clathrin-coated pits**, which form **endosomes** that carry the virus particles into the cell. The pH of the endosome falls, inducing the virions to shed their penton capsomeres and attached fibers. A conformational change in the virions causes endosome rupture and releases the partially disassembled virions into the cytoplasm. The nucleoprotein complex then enters the nucleus, leaving behind most of the rest of its capsid proteins. The core proteins are replaced with cellular histones to form a **chromatin-like complex** and the stage is set for viral gene expression.

ADENOVIRUS GENE EXPRESSION

Most DNA viruses display **temporal regulation** of gene expression. That is, viral gene expression takes place in two or more fairly distinct **phases**, each characterized by the synthesis of a specific set of viral proteins. It is a reasonable supposition that the temporal regulation of gene expression contributes to the efficiency of the viral life cycle. Many of the common properties of viral regulatory systems are clearly consistent with this notion. For example, in most cases, the proteins required for viral DNA replication are synthesized before the proteins that make up the virus particle. This assures the accumulation of a large pool of viral DNA **before** the packaging of viral DNA into capsids begins, and permits DNA replication and capsid gene expression to proceed at high rates even while encapsidation removed DNA from the expression and replication pool.

Temporal regulation is accomplished by a cascade of events; each phase of gene expression depends on the expression of specific genes in the previous phase. This mechanism is also employed by other large DNA viruses, including papovaviruses, herpesviruses, and many bacteriophages. In the case of the adenoviruses, gene expression occurs in three phases termed pre-early, early, and late (Fig. 38.2). In the **pre-early** phase of adenoviral gene expression, a small portion of the genome (about 4%) is expressed, with the production of two regulatory proteins. One of these proteins induces the **early phase**, which is characterized by expression of a new set of viral genes, the **early genes**. These genes are necessary for viral DNA replication and for expression

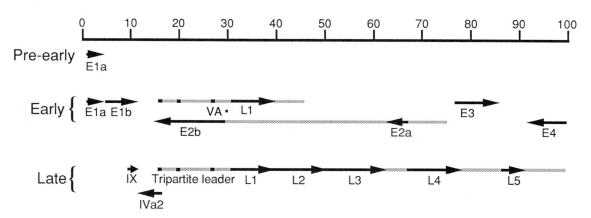

Figure 38.2.   Temporal regulation of the adenovirus transcription. The portions of the adenoviral genome transcribed during the *pre-early*, *early*, and *late* phases of viral infection are indicated by *arrows* under a scale that shows their position on the viral DNA molecule. The regions denoted by *solid lines* encode mRNAs that appear in the cytoplasm; the regions indicated by *stippled lines* are transcribed, but those RNA sequences are removed by splicing events from the RNA molecules that enter the cytoplasm. The early regions are numbered *E1a-E4;* the late regions are *L1-L5.*

of the remaining viral genes. Early gene products permit entry into the **late phase** of gene expression, which is characterized by the abundant expression of the **late genes** that encode the components of the virus particle and proteins necessary for particle assembly.

Most of these regulatory events in adenovirus gene expression occur at the **transcriptional** or **post-transcriptional** steps in cytoplasmic mRNA production. These events take place in the following order:

1. During the **pre-early** phase, only the portion of the genome called **E1a** is transcribed. Expression of E1a genes depends on host enzymes, as expected from the fact that no viral proteins have yet been synthesized. The E1a transcript is spliced (as are essentially all adenoviral mRNAs) to yield two stable cytoplasmic E1a mRNAs, and two proteins are produced. One of these proteins is a **transcriptional activator**, whose presence in the infected cell induces transcription from five viral promoters that remain silent during the pre-early phase. This protein appears to stimulate transcription indirectly, by increasing the activity of endogenous host cell transcriptional factors.

2. The E1a-dependent activation of the five viral early promoters marks the beginning of the **early** phase of gene expression. During this phase, the newly activated viral promoters direct the transcription of early region genes. The RNA transcripts are then spliced to give the individual mRNAs. Protein products of at least six early genes participate in events necessary for progression to the late phase of gene expression; three encode the viral proteins necessary for viral DNA replication and three are required for post-transcriptional events during the late phase.

3. Under the influence of three of the early proteins, viral DNA replication begins. Coincident with onset of viral DNA synthesis is the transition from early-phase to **late**-phase patterns of gene expression. The most dramatic events of this transition affect RNA synthesis from the so-called **major late promoter**. Transcription from this promoter soon greatly increases, until it makes up the majority of new RNA synthesized in the infected cell. This transcript is a very large RNA molecule that is then spliced into most of the late viral mRNAs.

Why is viral DNA replication a prerequisite for late gene expression? We do not really know, although some evidence suggests that the physical act of replication is, in some way, necessary for an individual DNA molecule to serve as a template for late gene expression. Two proteins that appear to be involved in the transport of late mRNAs to the cytoplasm are also required for efficient late gene expression.

As the expression of the viral late genes increases during the early-late transition, the **expression of cellular genes decreases**. Adenoviral infection interferes with host gene expression in two ways. First, the accumulation of cellular mRNAs in the cytoplasm is prevented. Because the rate of synthesis of host RNAs is not reduced in virus-infected cells, it has been suggested that adenovirus specifically **inhibits the transport** of host messages from the nucleus to the cytoplasm. Second, a virally encoded protein appears to inhibit the utilization of existing host mRNAs in the cytoplasm. The consequence of these two actions is that the synthesis of host proteins is greatly reduced.

DNA REPLICATION

DNA-containing animal viruses rely to different extents on host cell proteins for the replication of their genomes. The papovaviruses (Chapter 39) only make a single viral protein that redirects host replication enzymes to replicate the viral genome, whereas herpesviruses (Chapter 40) encode a large number of viral enzymes involved in DNA replication. The adenoviruses fall between these extremes, employing both virally encoded and host proteins in replication.

Replication is initiated within inverted repeated sequences at one or the other end of the adenoviral DNA molecule (see Fig. 38.3). Because of their presence, the two ends have identical sequences and initiation of DNA replication can take place at either end with about equal frequency. After initiation, DNA synthesis proceeds along the template DNA by copying one parental strand and displacing the other (Fig. 38.3). The completion of the synthesis of the first daughter strand produces a duplex molecule consisting of one parental strand and one daughter strand, plus a displaced parental single strand. DNA synthesis is then initiated at the end of the displaced single strand, which serves as the template for the synthesis of the other daughter strand. The synthesis of viral DNA differs from that of host DNA in two respects. First, a single DNA strand is copied at each viral replication fork, while in host cell replication, both strands are copied concurrently. Second, the synthesis of all new viral DNA is continuous; that is, it occurs by the uninterrupted elongation of the growing chain across the entire genome. In host cell DNA replication, one strand at each replication fork is produced continuously, but the other is synthesized discontinuously, as short pieces (Okazaki fragments) that must be joined to produce the finished strand. From a cellular viewpoint, a major difference between viral and cell DNA replication is in the overall timing of the process. Host chromosomes replicate by a well-regulated process that occurs once in a division cycle; viral replication, on the other hand, is uncoordinated and takes place continuously over a period of time.

Adenovirus DNA replication can be carried out in vitro in a system composed of purified proteins, which has led to a fairly detailed biochemical understanding of the events in viral DNA replication. Six proteins are required for optimal viral DNA replication in vitro (and, presumably, in vivo). Three of these are virally encoded—a **DNA polymerase, a DNA-binding protein (DBP)**, and the **preterminal protein (pTP)**, which is the precursor of the terminal protein found in virions. All three of these proteins are products of the transcription of early genes. The remaining three replication proteins are cellular products. Two are DNA-binding proteins that normally function in the transcription of cellular genes in uninfected cells; the third is a topoisomerase.

The most likely sequence of events during initiation involves the **binding of the host factors** to three adjacent blocks of nucleotides in the terminal repeats. The host proteins probably **unwind** the end of the molecule, exposing single-stranded DNA that serves as the template for the actual initiation event. This event is the formation of a phosphodiester linkage between deoxycytosine monophosphate (dCMP, the first residue at the 5′ end of the new DNA strand) and a serine residue in the pTP molecule. In this fashion, **pTP serves as the primer** for adenoviral DNA replication (Fig. 38.3). Protein priming of DNA replication is most unusual; in most systems, primers for DNA replication are short RNA molecules.

Figure 38.3. Adenovirus DNA replication. A. Electron micrograph of a replicating adenovirus DNA molecule. **B.** Schematic representation of the events in adenovirus replication. The molecule shown in **A** is of the type diagrammed in the *second line* of **B**, a duplex with one single-stranded branch. **C.** Details of the initiation of adenovirus DNA replication showing the priming of DNA synthesis by the preterminal protein (labeled *80K*).

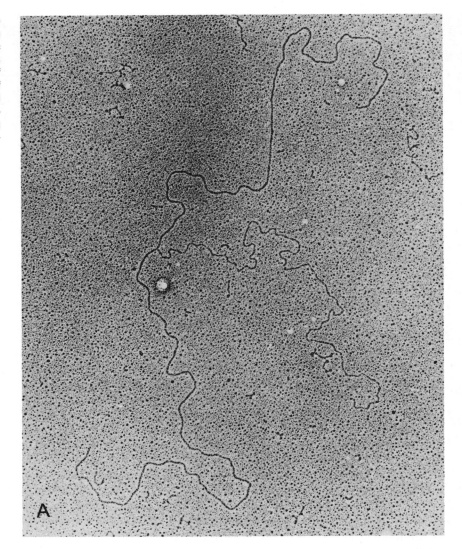

A

After formation of the initial pTP-dCMP linkage, elongation of the new daughter strand proceeds conventionally, by the sequential addition of nucleotides by the viral DNA polymerase to the 3′-OH group of the pTP-bound growing chain. Host proteins do not seem to be necessary for the elongation reaction. As DNA is packaged, proteolytic processing cleaves the pTP molecule bound to each DNA strand to generate the form found in mature virions.

VIRION ASSEMBLY

Particle assembly begins when sufficient amounts of capsid proteins have accumulated. The first step is the assembly in the cytoplasm of free polypeptide chains into hexon and penton capsomeres. Pentons are assembled spontaneously, but hexon assembly requires the participation of a protein that does not appear in the mature particle. Such proteins that assist in assembly but that do not appear in virions are common and are referred to as **scaffold proteins**. Hexons, as well as several minor virion components, are next assembled into an intermediate structure that is later filled with DNA. It is not clear how the DNA enters this empty shell, although it has been suggested that it may pass through one of the open vertices. Perhaps surprisingly, the viral core

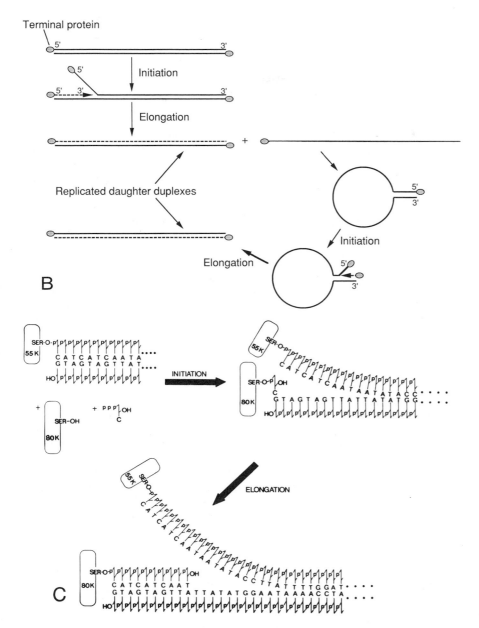

proteins are added to the particles **after** the DNA enters. Finally, the pentons become associated with the capsid, and a series of proteolytic events converts precursor proteins incorporated into the virion into the mature forms. After assembly, adenovirus particles remain associated with the dying cell and are slowly released as the cells autolyse or are destroyed by the immune system.

Paradigm: DNA Virus Replication

The study of DNA viruses can teach us a great deal about the workings of the normal cells. DNA viruses share with their host a general strategy of nucleic acid replication. With some exceptions (e.g., the large poxviruses), viral DNA is synthesized in the nucleus and viral proteins in the cytoplasm. Unlike the (−) strand RNA viruses, DNA viruses do not have to bring into the cell their own nucleic acid replication machinery but can use host enzymes for replication. This process does, however, vary in its details among different virus families, which possess a large number of individual strategies. Some of these viruses redirect the host machinery with a single viral encoded protein (papovaviruses); others make extensive replicating machinery of their own (herpesviruses).

Sharing replication strategies of DNA viruses and the host chromosome has other consequences. The DNA precursor deoxynucleotides are present in the cell in much smaller concentrations than the RNA precursor ribonucleotides. To replicate at a vigorous rate, DNA viruses increase the availability of their precursors by activating the enzymes involved in their biosynthesis. This requirement results in a coupling between DNA virus replication and host DNA metabolism through the action of virally encoded factors that alter the normal control of the host cell cycle. This coupling does not have a counterpart in the replication of RNA viruses.

The various components of the DNA viruses are synthesized according to elaborate regulatory plans and then assembled to make new virions. The genes of some of these viruses are arranged in clusters, which allows common mechanisms of regulation and the coordinate synthesis of groups of proteins. Virally encoded proteins are made in a sequential cascade of pre-early, early, middle, and late protein synthesis (depending on the virus). Early proteins are made using host protein factors, but the subsequent ones require products of the previous steps. Early and middle proteins are usually involved in starting DNA replication whereas late proteins are the structural constituents of the virions.

Adenoviruses are a particularly useful example of DNA viruses because they have been investigated in detail at the biochemical and genetic levels.

INTERACTIONS WITH HOST DEFENSE SYSTEMS

Adenoviruses carry several genes whose functions seem to be in aborting host antiviral defenses. The main immunological defense against viral infection, **cell-mediated immunity**, acts by destroying infected cells. **Cytotoxic T lymphocytes (CTLs)** recognize infected cells by virtue of receptors specific for complexes of **viral antigens bound to a host protein** found on the surface of almost all cells, the **major histocompatibility complex type I (MHC I) antigen.** Cells that do not possess MHC I molecules on their surface do not become targets for destruction by CTLs. Adenoviruses protect themselves from the cell-mediated immune response via two separate mechanisms that interfere with MHC I expression. The first of these is mediated by an early viral protein that **blocks the production of MHC I mRNA** in infected cells. The second effect of adenovirus infection on MHC I expression is mediated by a glycoprotein that **prevents the transport** of newly synthesized MHC I protein molecules to the cell surface. In an animal model system (cotton rats), infections of the lung with viral mutants that do not express these viral proteins induce a much more striking pulmonary infiltration of neutrophils, suggesting that this protein in fact influences the course of disease in vivo.

Tumor necrosis factor (TNF), a host protein produced by monocytes exposed to viruses, lyses many types of virally infected cells. However, adenovirus-infected cells are resistant to TNF. Once again, a viral protein is required for the induction of this resistance.

A third line of defense against viral infection is the antiviral state that can be induced in cells by α and β interferons. Among other effects, the interferons can prevent protein synthesis in virus-infected cells by initiating a chain of events that culminates in the inactivation of the cell's translation apparatus. Adenoviruses break the chain, and prevent the inhibition of protein synthesis through the action of two small

RNA molecules (VA RNAs) encoded by viral genes. One of the host proteins (DAI) critical in the inhibition of protein synthesis by interferon is converted to its active form by double-stranded RNA (dsRNA). dsRNA is produced in the course of infection by most viruses, including adenoviruses. The VA RNAs fold into partially double-stranded structures and bind to DAI, preventing its activation by authentic dsRNA.

Oncogenicity

Adenovirus type 12 was the first DNA-containing virus shown to be able to cause cancer in animals. This discovery sparked a massive search for evidence that adenoviruses (and other DNA animal viruses) were etiological agents of human cancer, and an equally massive effort to determine the mechanism of tumorigenesis by DNA animal viruses. No convincing association between adenoviruses and cancer was revealed by these studies, but they have contributed considerably to knowledge of the molecular basis of tumorigenesis.

All adenovirus serotypes tested induce permanent morphological changes in cultured cells that resemble those that occur during natural carcinogenesis. This process is referred to as transformation. Transformation by adenoviruses requires the products of two viral genes. The role of one of these seems to be to "immortalize" cells, i.e., confer on them the ability to grow indefinitely in culture. The second confers the fully transformed phenotype on immortalized cells. Both of these genes are always found integrated into the genome of cells transformed by adenoviruses and are sufficient for transformation if introduced into cells as recombinant DNA molecules. The adenovirus-transforming gene products are thought to act by interaction with cellular antioncogene products (see Chapter 39).

Adenovirus Infections in Humans

Adenovirus infections are widespread in human populations, accounting for between 5% and 10% of all viral infections. Most of these infections occur in childhood; 75% occur before the age of 14 years, and over half occur before the age of 5 years. Most adenoviral infections affect either the **respiratory tract** or the **gastrointestinal tract**, in about equal numbers. Most patients with adenoviral respiratory diseases recover, although some mortality has been associated with pneumonia.

The usual symptoms of adenoviral respiratory infections resemble those of the common cold, including nasal congestion, inflammation of the upper respiratory tract, and cough. Systemic symptoms such as chills, headache, muscle aches, and fever are common, and conjunctivitis sometimes accompanies the other symptoms (**pharyngoconjunctival fever**). In severe cases, pneumonia can develop. Different serotypes are associated with respiratory disease and pharyngoconjunctival fever. Serotypes 1, 2, 5, and 6 are endemic in most populations and 80% of all young adults have neutralizing antibodies to these types. Other serotypes (4 and 7) are associated with outbreaks of a fairly severe febrile respiratory infection (**acute respiratory disease; ARD**) that affects primarily military recruits during basic training. As many as 80% of some groups of recruits are affected, with one-fourth to one-half of them requiring hospitalization. Crowded conditions and fatigue presumably favor the spread of the disease and increase its severity. College freshmen, who are of similar age, do not, however, appear to suffer from ARD. A live virus vaccine is given as an enteric-coated capsule to newly inducted military personnel.

Adenoviruses are also an important cause of acute gastrointestinal disease in children, and may be responsible for up to 15% of juvenile intestinal infections. Many serotypes of adenoviruses are present, not only in the stool of patients, but in normal stools as well, in contrast with a number of serotypes that are associated solely with disease. Another adenovirus serotype, Ad12, has been implicated in the development of celiac disease. The mechanism in this case appears to depend upon protein sequence homology between an Ad12 early protein and A-gliadin, a component of the cereal grains that activate the disease. It has been suggested that exposure to Ad12 induces an antibody response to A-gliadin, which predisposes to celiac disease.

Less common than respiratory and gastrointestinal disease are adenovirus-induced conjunctivitis without other symptoms. Mild "swimming pool conjunctivitis" is probably most often due to adenoviral infection, as is the more serious, highly contagious **epidemic keratoconjunctivitis** (EKC).

Latent adenovirus infections are very common; adenoviruses can be recovered from as many as 80% of the tonsils or adenoids removed from children. The mechanism of persistence in these cases is not known. It has been reported that viral DNA can persist in tonsillar tissue free of infectious virus, but it is also possible that persistence may be due to a low-level active infection confined to lymphoid tissue by a neutralizing antibody. Early gene products that interact with the host's immune mechanisms may also play a role in persistence.

Adenoviruses can be recovered from immunocompromised individuals, and have been implicated in mortality in several cases. Recently, numerous isolations from patients with immunodeficiency due to HIV infection have been reported, and infection has been associated in some cases with mortality.

Self-assessment Questions

1. Draw a sketch of the organization of an adenovirus virion and point out the function of the major components.

2. What are the stages in the expression of adenovirus genes? Why is there such a series of steps?

3. In what ways does adenovirus DNA replication differ from that of host DNA?

4. How do adenoviruses inhibit protein synthesis of infected cells?

5. How do adenoviruses interfere with the action of interferon?

6. Describe briefly the main diseases caused by adenoviruses. Which tend to occur in outbreaks?

Warts and Other Transforming Viruses

39

Stephen E. Straus

Warts result from persistent infections by a group of small DNA viruses. These tumor-like growths of the skin and mucous membranes are sometimes associated with true malignancies. Some of the distant relatives of these viruses, polyoma and SV40, produce tumors in animals and are among the best studied models of viral oncogenesis.

CASE

As a healthy 24-year-old man with only one steady sexual partner for the past 3 years, W. cannot figure out how or why he managed to get genital warts. Some months ago, he had noticed two small bumps on the side of his penis, but he thought to ignore them with the hope that they would go away by themselves. They did not. The dermatologist whom he had consulted seemed to know right away what they were. No tests were advised, just a laser to burn them away. But, the news that they could come back, are transmissible, and are associated with cancer seemed a bit too much news for one afternoon.

In this chapter, we will address the issues about wart viruses that are raised by W.'s case. Because wart viruses cannot be grown in the laboratory, much of our present understanding of these viruses reflects the burgeoning application of recombinant DNA technology to problems in medical microbiology and infectious diseases. Importantly, the papillomaviruses are the best examples we have of DNA viruses with the potential to cause human cancers.

Few diseases are fraught with as many folk notions about the cause, transmission, and treatment as are warts. They have been endowed with magic and mystery, probably because they may persist for many months or years and then disappear. It was finally shown in our times that warts are caused by viruses (Fig. 39.1). In 1894, an investigator demonstrated their contagious nature by inoculating himself with material from his brother's warts. The viral etiology was established by demonstrating that extracts of warts were still infectious after passing them through bacteria-retaining filters. Warts are caused by many different types of papillomaviruses.

PAPILLOMAVIRUSES

Papillomaviruses are a large group of DNA viruses that include pathogens of humans, mice, monkeys, cattle, birds, fish, and other animals. They belong to a family known as the papovaviruses, an acronym for the most famous members of the group: the **pa**pilloma viruses, the

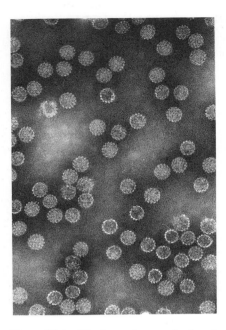

Figure 39.1.   Electron micrograph of purified wart viruses.

polyoma viruses, and the *vacuolating* viruses, notably simian virus SV40. Papillomaviruses differ sufficiently from the other papovaviruses to be placed in a separate genus within the family (Table 39.1).

Papillomaviruses cannot as yet be cultured in vitro, but small quantities of the viruses can be purified from lesions. It is difficult to classify them by the usual serological typing methods, which require large amounts of virus; however, their DNA can be cloned and used in hybridization tests to determine degrees of homology, a process known as genotyping. Viruses that have between 50% and 100% homology under stringent conditions are considered to be related subtypes. Greater differences place them in different types. Minor differences within types can be detected by restriction endonuclease analysis. At the time of writing, there are over 60 human papillomavirus types, divided into several subtypes (Table 39.2). It is likely that this number will increase with further studies.

Much of what we know about the structure and replication of wart viruses comes from analogy with the better studied mouse polyoma and monkey SV40 viruses. All of these papovaviruses consist of nonenveloped particles made up of 72 identical capsomeres in an icosahedral array. The amount of DNA of these viruses is not large and it can code for only a few proteins.

ENCOUNTER AND ENTRY

Human papillomaviruses are acquired by direct contact with lesions of infected people or with virus-containing material in the environment. They are quite stable and may be transferred via scales of exfoliated skin. Any type of direct contact promotes spread of the viruses. In this regard, a major mode of transmission is by sexual contact. These viruses are not highly contagious and epidemics are rare, even within a family. The site of entry, as well as virus type involved, determines the location of the lesions. The normal skin is relatively resistant to entry, and infection takes place more readily when the virus comes in contact with mucous membranes or with traumatized skin. Thus, the most frequent sites of lesions are the commonly injured skin surfaces, such as the fingers, hands, soles, knees, elbows, the penis, vulva and cervix and, much more infrequently, the oropharynx and the larynx. Warts of the soles of the feet, for instance, can result from abrasion on the concrete surfaces of swimming pools. Frequent warts in the hands and fingers of butchers are due to the inoculation of virus into cuts they sustain at these sites. Transmission from mother to child is believed to

Table 39.1. Biological Features of Various Papovaviruses

	Papillomaviruses	Polyomaviruses
Human viruses	Human papillomavirus types 1 - ~60	Human BK virus, human JC virus, human AS virus
Animal viruses	Shope rabbit papillomavirus, bovine papillomavirus, many others	Mouse polyomavirus, simian vacuolating virus 40, and others
Target tissues	Skin, mucous membranes	Brain, kidneys, other organs
Strands transcribed	One	Both
Transforming ability	Yes	Yes
Genome in transformed cells	Usually not integrated	Usually integrated

Table 39.2. Lesions Associated with Human Papillomavirus (HPV) Types

Plantar warts	HPV-1, 4
Common warts	HPV-2
Flat juvenile warts	HPV-3
Anogenital warts[a]	HPV-6
Common warts in meat handlers	HPV-7
Flat warts	HPV-10
Laryngeal and anogenital warts	HPV-11
Macular lesions in EV[b]	HPV-5, -8, -9, -12, -14, -15, -17, -19 to -29
Focal epithelial hyperplasia	HPV-13
Bowenoid papulosis; cervical carcinoma	HPV-16
Cervical carcinoma	HPV-18
Cervical dysplasia	HPV-31
Laryngeal carcinoma	HPV-30
Not described	HPV-32 to 63

[a]Condyloma acuminata.
[b]EV, epidermodysplasia verruciformis, associated with malignant degeneration.

occur during delivery by direct contact of the newborn with the virus in the cervical or vaginal area.

Recent surveys of patients attending the National Health Service clinics in Great Britain have documented that anogenital warts occur in epidemic proportions. Through the 1970s and 1980s, their incidence has risen faster than that of genital herpes. Warts are now the single most common sexually transmitted infection that leads people to seek medical attention in that country. Less complete figures indicate similar trends in the U.S., where genital warts vie with chlamydial infections for first place among the sexually transmitted diseases.

Many people become infected with wart viruses during their lifetime without exhibiting symptoms. This has been demonstrated in two ways. The first is by finding antibody against papillomaviruses in serum. The second, and more compelling, evidence of frequent asymptomatic infection derives from polymerase chain reaction studies of cervical-vaginal cells of healthy women (see Chapter 55 for details). This ultrasensitive method amplifies DNA segments to the point that papillomavirus sequences have been detected in up to 40% of women. The reason why some develop warts or other symptoms is not known, although deficiencies in the immune system can lead to diseases by these viruses—some of them quite serious.

MULTIPLICATION AND SPREAD

The replication of human wart viruses is inferred in part from the better studied polyoma and SV40 viruses. This family of agents produces two types of infections, a lytic one that leads to formation of progeny viruses, and a persistent one that may lead to oncogenic transformation of the host cells. The beginning steps are the same in both cases. After binding to cell receptors, the virions traverse the cytoplasm intact and are uncoated in the nucleus. Here, they replicate, following a well-timed series of events. Early (or pre-DNA synthesis) messenger RNAs are transcribed from about one-half of the genome. These mRNAs exit the nucleus and are translated into early virus proteins in the cytoplasm.

If the infection follows the lytic course, DNA begins to replicate, using one of the early proteins. Replication is not a haphazard process, but begins in a defined region of the genome and proceeds bidirectionally for about 180° around the circle, when the two completed progeny molecules separate. This mode of replication resembles that of the chromosomes of bacteria to a greater extent than it does that of most DNA viruses. DNA replication is accompanied by transcription of the late mRNAs that encode the major viral proteins. These proteins are transported back to the nucleus, where they assemble with the newly replicated DNA to form progeny virions.

Papovaviruses are extremely efficient in their use of genetic material. They are known to be marvels of economy and squeeze the maximum assistance from their host cells. For example, papovaviruses use cellular histones for their "chromosomes" and cell enzymes for replication and transcription. For these reasons, they are valuable models for studies of mammalian cell function. In addition, they make especially efficient use of the information in their own genome. They use several stratagems to read one stretch of DNA in various ways to produce several different proteins. One strategy is to splice a single mRNA molecule in different ways. Another strategy for deriving more information from a DNA sequence is to read the same stretch of DNA in more than one different "frame." In these viruses, such shifts in frame are programmed and result in the synthesis of three different readable mRNAs from the same stretch of DNA. This allows the virus to make more than one protein from the same stretch of DNA.

Because they cannot be grown, what we know of the biology of papillomaviruses comes from studies of their cloned DNA sequences and warts themselves. Apparently, they use slightly different replication strategies from what polyoma and SV40 do. Wart virus DNA is larger and contains information for a few more proteins. All types of human wart viruses, even those that share little DNA homology, have a similar genetic organization.

The papillomaviruses establish a lytic or productive infection only in the keratinized cells of the superficial epithelium. They lie dormant in the deeper epithelial layers of the skin. As these infected cells differentiate and are displaced outward toward the skin surface, the virus can complete its replication cycle. These viruses can persist for many years in the deeper layers of the epidermis. At times, these persistent viruses may lead to oncogenic transformation of their host cells.

How do papovaviruses transform cells? Apparently, transformation occurs when these viruses infect cells incapable of supporting the lytic cycle. With some papovaviruses, these cells are from a different animal species than the one that the virus infects naturally. The papillomaviruses seem to transform cells of their natural host, but do so only in cells whose stages of differentiation preclude a full replicative cycle. Thus, transformation with all papovaviruses appears to result from an abortive growth cycle. Neither replication nor translation of late viral proteins is required. The maintenance of the transformed state, however, does require the continued expression of early viral genes.

The precise mechanism of tumor induction by wart viruses is still murky but is being studied vigorously. The process is undoubtedly complex, being dependent on interactions between virus gene products and selected host cell proteins. The likelihood that transformation occurs seems also to be aided by other factors like herpesviruses, chemical and physical carcinogens, and the host immune system. Even to the degree that this process is understood, it stands as one of the clearest models of human oncogenesis.

Well, what do we know about it? Among the eight or nine genes encoded by papillomaviruses, two of them that are expressed early in the viral replicative cycle, E6 and E7, are required for transformation. The E6 gene appears to possess a regulatory role, perhaps influencing the expression of E7 or other viral or cellular genes. The E7 product appears to be a true transforming agent, an "oncoprotein" as it were. It is closely related to similar proteins that account for transformation by other papovaviruses and adenoviruses. This class of proteins can complex with a normal cellular protein known as p105-RB. The name reflects its size (105 kD) and its association with the human cancer, retinoblastoma. The lack of this protein is associated with the development of the ocular tumor and, thus, the protein is considered to be a natural suppressor of cell proliferation. By complexing with p105-RB, viral oncoproteins may be able to keep the cell from exerting full checks and balances on its inherent potential to proliferate. There must, however, be additional steps involved in control of cell division, which provide other opportunities for cofactors to add to the cumulative risk of a cell escaping regulated growth.

Paradigm: Viral Oncogenesis

Viruses are known to be involved in the production of a few types of cancer in humans, but the theory that viruses cause all tumors curries little favor at present. Most of the viruses that cause tumors in humans or animals have DNA genomes. Only one family of RNA viruses, the retroviruses, is known to be oncogenic. Note, however, that these viruses have a mixed DNA-RNA strategy and are incorporated into the genome of host cells during part of their replication cycle.

The best known human oncogenic viruses belong to the **papillomavirus** (causing, in addition to warts, cervical and other carcinomas) and the **herpesvirus** (e.g., the Epstein-Barr virus associated with Burkitt's lymphoma and nasopharyngeal carcinoma), and the **hepatitis B** virus (associated with primary hepatocellular carcinoma). In addition, certain human viruses cause tumors in animals and may be involved in the production of human cancers as well. These include members of the adenovirus and certain other papovaviruses.

In the laboratory, oncogenic viruses are readily studied by their ability to cause **transformation** of cultured animal cells. Transformed cells may be easily recognized by their altered morphology and nutritional growth requirements. In addition, these cells often become **immortalized**, that is, they do not undergo the senescence and death characteristic of normal diploid cells in culture. In many cases, transformed cells are **malignant**, i.e., they cause tumors when injected into animals.

Perhaps the most important result to arise from the study of transformed cells has been that they usually **do not contain infective virus**. The presence of viral DNA, RNA, and certain antigens can still be detected in these cells, suggesting that the viral genome may have become integrated into host chromosomes in a manner reminiscent of lysogeny in bacteria. **Integration** and **covalent binding** of viral sequences into host chromosomes has been demonstrated with Epstein-Barr virus, hepatitis B virus, and papovaviruses. Human papillomaviruses, on the other hand, may integrate but also persist in the nucleus in a free, **plasmid-like** state, and replicate in synchrony with the chromosomes.

The study of oncogenic viruses has been highly productive and has led to the identification of genes that initiate the cancer process, the **oncogenes**. Some 30 of these genes are known. Oncogenes encoded by the **retroviruses** have sequence homology with normal cellular genes called **proto-oncogenes**, whose products are involved in regulation of normal growth and differentiation, such as specific cell growth factors or their receptors. Oncogenes of the *src* family encode tyrosine protein kinases that regulate key cellular processes; those of the *ras* family encode GTP-binding proteins involved in signal transduction; and others (called *jun, fos, myc*) are activators of transcription by binding to the so-called enhancer sequences located upstream of certain genes. Oncogenes encoded by **DNA viruses** are not known to be related to normal host cell regulatory proteins. They stimulate growth of the cells by activating the machinery for DNA replication.

DAMAGE

Papillomaviruses are thought to infect the cells of the basal layer of the skin and replicate in concert with them. As these cells mature and migrate toward the skin surface, viral replication begins. In the outer skin layers, the infection becomes manifest and is characterized by proliferation and thickening of the basal cell layer and vacuolization of the cytoplasm. These changes lead to the appearance of a wart. Thus, the lesion is not caused by cell destruction, but by cell proliferation.

Warts look different at different sites and are likely to be caused by different sets of virus genotypes. Unfortunately, there is no routine clinical method for determining the virus type associated with a given lesion. This can only be done in a research setting, by biopsying the tissue and by doing nucleic acid hybridization with specific probes.

Physicians have no trouble recognizing the common warts of the hands; they are elevated, firm, fleshy lesions with a sharp border (Fig. 39.2). They range in size between 1 and 10 mm or more in diameter. Proliferation of separate dermal papillae within a lesion results in a coarse, cauliflower-like appearance. On the soles of the feet, warts tend to be more deeply embedded and more keratotic than those on the hands. Warts of the hands and feet are believed to have long incubation times, between 6 and 18 months.

Elsewhere, on the face, knees, or arms, warts tend to be flat and harder to recognize. They are more likely to occur in larger numbers and to be clustered (Fig. 39.3). Anogenital warts (condylomata acuminata) may be either flat or elevated. One or several cauliflower-like lesions may surround the anus, the labia, or the shaft of the penis (Fig. 39.4). Warts of the uterine cervix are usually flat and tend to be missed during casual speculum examinations. Cervical warts have an incubation time of only 2–6 months after sexual contact, perhaps because they do not involve a long maturation process of host cells, as is the case in the skin. They are of special concern, however, because morer than 80% of all cervical carcinomas, local or invasive, contain papillomavirus DNA, especially that of types 16 and 18.

Warts of the larynx occur in preschool-age children and in sexually active adults and can lead to progressive impairment of laryngeal function unless treated. Hoarseness is the usual complaint, but respiratory distress and secondary bacterial pneumonias occur in children and signify the presence of obstructing lesions in the bronchial tree as well. The virus types associated with these lesions, as well as those of the oropharynx, are the same as those that cause anogenital warts, an observation that, as indicated above, suggests perinatal transmission. Oral-genital transmission is also possible, as seen by the greater incidence of these types of warts in gay men.

How does the host respond to infection by these viruses? Both humoral and cellular immunity probably participate, but their respective roles have not been fully elucidated. Type-specific antibodies to external virion antigens of these viruses can be detected in patients' sera.

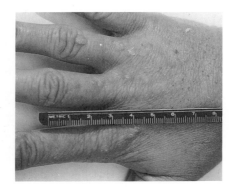

Figure 39.2.   Common warts.

Figure 39.3.   Multiple flat warts on knee.

The infection is primarily controlled by cell-mediated immunity. People who are deficient in their cellular immunity (transplant recipients, patients with AIDS or lymphoma) are more likely to have multiple chronic warts.

A rare but aggressive form of papillomavirus infection occurs in persons with an autosomally inherited defect in cellular immunity. The condition is called EV or epidermodysplasia verruciformis, a term that means "warty looking changes of the epidermis." It is manifested by hundreds or thousands of flat warts. In 30% of these cases, the disease progresses to squamous cell carcinoma of the skin.

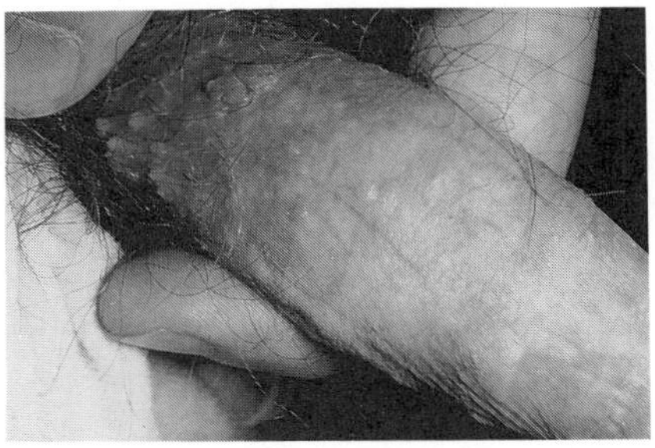

Figure 39.4.   Penile warts.

PAPILLOMAVIRUSES AND CANCER

Papillomaviruses cause warts, which are benign tumors, but progressive damage to cellular regulatory machinery eventually leads some of these warts to assume the characteristics of true malignancies, i.e., the ability to grow, to invade, and to spread. At least 80% of cases of cancer of the cervix are associated with wart viruses. Certain virus types are more likely to initiate dysplastic than frankly neoplastic changes. Even the virus types associated with malignancy cause benign lesions more frequently than malignant ones. The progression from benign to dysplastic to malignant disease is a slow process that can take decades. It is believed that a consequence of the current epidemic of genital warts among sexually active adolescents and young adults may be a dramatic increase in the incidence of cervical cancer in the first decades of the 21st century. There is mounting evidence that, in addition to genital cancers, a number of other human squamous cell tumors, such as some squamous cell carcinomas of the oropharynx, larynx, bronchi, and anus, are associated with wart viruses. In the absence of specific probes for all possible viruses that may be involved, we cannot know the total spectrum of neoplastic disorders associated with papillomaviruses.

TREATMENT

About 50% of common warts regress spontaneously within 1–2 years. Treatment of warts is often considered for cosmetic reasons, but more substantial reasons for desiring therapy include the control of pain, bleeding, impairment of laryngeal function, or the concern of sexual transmission (as in W.'s case). Unfortunately, there are no specific treatments. Nearly all modes of treatment are ablative, like surgical excision, destruction with laser beams, dry ice, or liquid nitrogen, or by the application of strong corrosive or cytotoxic chemicals. These and other approaches have been used with variable long-term success. In a case like W.'s, the treatment may have to be repeated many times.

In view of the high rate with which warts recur after ablative treatment, attention has turned to biological approaches, but most of these have not been successful. The best hope at present is the administration of interferon into the lesions themselves or systemically. α-Interferon causes significant but transient remission in patients with EV, genital, or laryngeal warts.

An important theoretical factor that limits the potential of some forms of therapy is that the viruses often persist in apparently normal tissue adjacent to the warts. Ablation of the lesion may remove one focus of infection, but can leave a residual inoculum nearby that may later result in local recurrence.

PREVENTION

There is no way to prevent becoming infected with wart viruses other than by avoiding contact with the infected surfaces of other people. This is not a practical suggestion, especially due to the extraordinary measures that would have to be taken to prevent the relatively small number of cases of serious disease caused by these viruses. Our case study patient, W., should use condoms, at least until his lesions have disappeared. Condoms may prevent transmission of the virus to or from the penile shaft. Laryngeal warts in the neonate may be avoided if an infected woman is aggressively treated prior to delivery. Some have suggested cesarean sections for pregnant women with genital warts. Unfortunately, genital warts are very common, so that this would lead to a large increase in these operations to protect very few children. The risks of surgery, in most instances, certainly outweigh the benefits.

Considering the strong association of genital warts with cervical cancer, one very important measure is the regular examination of the cervix, Papanicolaou testing, and visual inspection of the cervix (colposcopy). "Painting" the cervix or other suspected mucosal lesions with 3% acetic acid whitens them, making them easier to visualize. Biopsies of suspicious lesions can then be done to detect precancerous changes in time to permit effective treatment.

CONCLUSIONS

Warts are caused by a large number of related DNA viruses (the papillomaviruses) that cause a wide variety of clinical manifestations ranging from the simple, common warts to more serious, proliferative lesions. Fortunately, the benign manifestations are, by far, the most common. Wart viruses have been associated with a number of cancers, especially of the cervix. These viruses are transmitted by direct contact between persons, especially by the sexual route. Effective means of prevention and treatment are not yet available.

Self-assessment Questions

1. Describe the basic properties of wart viruses.

2. Contrast the replication cycle of papillomaviruses in warts with that in virus-associated cancers.

3. Why are warts more than a bothersome clinical problem?

4. Discuss the problems in the treatment of warts.

5. Why are warts difficult to prevent?

SUGGESTED READING

Bunney MH. Viral warts: their biology and treatment. New York: Oxford University Press, 1982;5–9.

Centers for Disease Control. Condyloma acuminatum —United States 1966–1981. Morbid Mortal Wkly Rep 1983;32:306–308.

Editorial. Genital warts, human papillomaviruses, and cervical cancer. Lancet 1985;11:1045–1046.

Eron LJ, Tucker S, et al. Interferon therapy for condylomata acuminata. N Engl J Med 1986;315:1059–1064.

Gissman L, Wolnick L, Ikenberg H, et al. Human papillomavirus type 6 and 11 DNA sequences in genital and laryngeal papillomas and some cervical cancers. Proc Natl Acad Sci USA 1983;80:560–563.

Margolis S. Therapy for condyloma acuminatum: a review. Rev Infect Dis 1982;4:(Suppl) S829–836.

Herpes Simplex Virus and Its Relatives

40

Stephen E. Straus

The term "herpesvirus" refers to several human and animal viruses, the most widely known of which are the herpes simplex viruses, the causative agents of fever blisters and a genital infection. Other herpesviruses also cause important diseases, including infectious mononucleosis, cytomegalovirus infection, and chickenpox. These viruses persist for life in cells of the host, producing a latent infection that can be reactivated at intervals.

CASE

Mr. H., a 26-year-old graduate student, returned home from his first real vacation in years. A lot of rest, fresh air, and a new love. But now, several days after his last sexual contact, he notices painful, itchy sores are developing on the shaft of his penis. He had engaged in oral sex as well and, among his other symptoms, is a sore throat. During a difficult telephone call, his new girlfriend admits to past episodes of genital herpes. Could this be herpes, he wonders? He has heard a lot about herpes infections and known there are several types and that some recur. These are some of the things you need to know to help Mr. H. with his many questions.

- Many microbial agents can cause genital lesions.

- Two types of herpes simplex viruses can cause genital lesions.

- These viruses are both fundamentally similar to and yet different from other herpesviruses.

- Herpes infections are unique in their ability to recur many times.

- Treatment is still limited, and we do not know how to prevent the infections.

These and other aspects of herpesvirus infections will be covered in this chapter.

Despite recent public awareness, herpesviruses are not new causes of human disease. Oral infections similar to what we recognize as being associated with herpes simplex were well described in ancient Greek medical texts. Herpes is probably what Shakespeare had in mind in Romeo and Juliet (Act I, scene iv):

O'er ladies' lips, who straight on kisses dream Which oft the angry Mab with blisters plagues

Today we know that most humans become infected with herpes viruses during their lifetime. The herpesviruses that cause common oral and genital infections are called herpes simplex viruses. They are the best understood of all herpesviruses and are the major focus of this chapter, but there are other herpesviruses. In fact, there are dozens of different ones capable of infecting just about every animal from oysters to humans, causing a varied repertoire of diseases. Two herpes simplex virus (**HSV**) types cause common infections of the skin and mucous membranes, with **HSV 1** being acquired predominantly through the oral route and **HSV 2** through the genital route. The **varicella zoster virus** causes chickenpox and shingles. **Cytomegalovirus** causes hepatitis, pneumonia, and serious congenital infections. The **Epstein-Barr virus** is best known as a cause of infectious mononucleosis, but is also thought to be involved in certain human cancers. A sixth herpesvirus, called the **human herpesvirus type 6**, was discovered in 1986 but little is known of the spectrum of disease it may provoke. **Human herpesvirus type 7** was identified in 1990. As yet, no disease has been linked to it.

Herpesviruses are among the most frequent and constant viral companions of human beings. It is not surprising that they are also among the most interesting.

HERPESVIRUSES

Herpesviruses are relatively large, complex viruses with a double-stranded DNA molecule that is able to code for 50–80 proteins (Fig. 40.1 and Table 40.1). These viruses replicate and assemble in the nuclei of cells; they then bud through and become enveloped in portions of the nuclear and cytoplasmic membranes. One cannot readily distinguish between different herpesviruses by electron microscopy—they all look very much alike (Fig. 40.2). They may be distinguished, however, by serological and DNA hybridization tests. Most herpesviruses are relatively unrelated, however, in terms of their antigens or DNA homology. The exceptions are the two herpes simplex viruses, types 1 and 2, which are quite similar to each other. Antibodies raised to proteins of type 1 react with many of the proteins of type 2 virus but proteins that are totally unique to each type have been identified recently. The DNA of one herpes simplex type hybridizes to DNA of the other type with about one-half of the avidity that it hybridizes to itself. The issue of the relatedness of herpes simplex viruses 1 and 2 is not merely academic. The two viruses cause nearly identical diseases, but the rea-

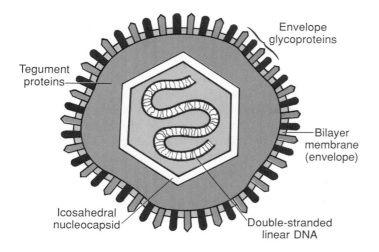

Figure 40.1. Schematic drawing of a herpesvirus.

Table 40.1. Human Herpesviruses
Herpes simplex virus 1 (HSV 1)
Herpes simplex virus 2 (HSV 2)
Varicella zoster virus (VZV)
Cytomegalovirus (CMV)
Epstein-Barr virus (EBV)
Human herpesvirus type 6 (HHV6)
Human herpesvirus type 7 (HHV7)

Figure 40.2. Electron micrograph of a herpesvirus.

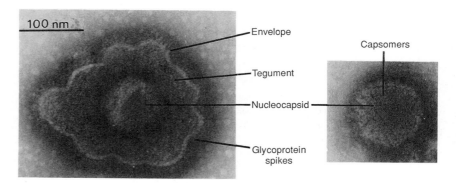

son for their different but overlapping clinical manifestations is still a mystery, despite our knowledge of much of their genetic make-up.

The genomes of the five well-defined human herpesviruses have a unique organization; they are long, double-stranded linear molecules with several repeated and inverted sequences (Fig. 40.3). The DNA can be conveniently considered as having two stretches of unique sequence, one long (**unique long sequence, U_L**) and one that is much shorter (**unique short sequence, U_S**). **Each of these is bracketed by short, identical DNA repeats. For example, at the left-hand end of the herpes simplex U_L is short terminal repeat. An exact copy of this sequence is repeated backwards at the right-hand end of the U_L segment. A perusal of Figure 40.3 is recommended. To complicate things further, in some herpesviruses, each major segment (U_L or U_S) and its terminal repeats can be rearranged** in the DNA either in the forward or the backward direction (Fig. 40.4). In herpes simplex, the various arrangements of the major segments result in four isomeric forms of the genome. All of the sequences are present, whatever the isomeric form of each herpesvirus. We have no idea why this has evolved, but the rearrangements of the DNA during viral replication may provide greater opportunity for the introduction of mutations and evolution of the genome.

ENCOUNTER

Infection with one or more herpesviruses probably occurs sooner or later in every human. Herpes simplex virus type 1 is often spread by kissing or exchange of saliva very early in life. Most children acquire the virus, but if they have avoided doing so, then they have another opportunity to do so when they become sexually active, either through oral-oral or oral-genital contact. *Two-thirds to three-fourths of adults possess antibodies to herpes simplex virus type 1, indicating prior infection.* Herpes type 2 is also spread by oral-oral and oral-genital contact, but is primarily spread by genital-genital contact. It is uncommon before adolescence, but the prevalence of infection rises rapidly with

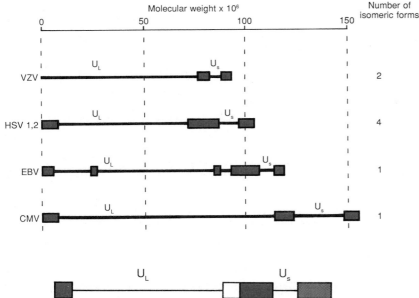

Figure 40.3. The size and organization of herpesvirus genomes. The five human herpesviruses are compared by size in megadaltons, organization of the long unique (U$_L$), short unique (U$_S$), and repeat sequences, and the number of isomeric forms of the genome.

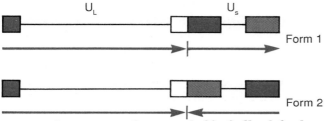

Figure 40.4. Formation of isomers of the herpesvirus DNA. Herpesvirus DNAs can exist in multiple isomeric forms in which the long and/or short genome segments can invert. In this example, two isomeric forms are produced by inversion of the short segment. This type of molecular rearrangement is characteristic of varicella zoster virus (VZV) DNA. Herpes simplex virus DNAs also can independently invert the long segment permitting four possible molecular forms.

sexual activity. *About one-sixth to one-half of all adults have experienced infection with this virus,* depending on the nature and number of sexual encounters.

Most infections with herpes simplex viruses are asymptomatic. Perhaps only one-third of the individuals who harbor the virus recognize symptoms from it. Clinically evident infection with herpes type 2 is increasing, however. Rough estimates suggest about a 10-fold increase from about 1965 to 1985.

ENTRY

Herpesviruses are very fragile and susceptible to drying and inactivation by heat, mild detergent, and solvents. This susceptibility is imposed by their membrane envelope. Because the viruses do not survive well on environmental surfaces, infection with the herpes viruses requires **direct inoculation** of virus into areas where they can replicate. Herpesviruses can infect humans by a variety of different routes (Table 40.2). Mucous membranes of the mouth, eye, genitals, respiratory tract, and anus are the sites most readily infected by herpes simplex viruses. The first line of defense we mount against herpes simplex is our skin, which, under normal conditions, is not readily penetrated or infected by these viruses. It is likely that the thick, horny keratin layer of the superficial epidermis prevents access of these viruses to their receptors. The mucous membranes do not represent such a formidable barrier, and hence, are more readily infected. Thus, our patient, Mr. H., probably acquired genital herpes during sexual contact with the infected tissues of his girl friend.

Cytomegalovirus and Epstein-Barr virus can be transmitted by infected leukocytes during transfusion with blood products, or through saliva and, probably, semen as well. It is believed that saliva is the most common vehicle for transmitting Epstein-Barr virus, which is why the

Table 40.2. Transmission of Human Herpesviruses

Virus	Means of Transmission	Portal of Entry	Initial Target Cells
HSV 1	Direct contact	Mucous membranes, skin	Epithelial
HSV 2	Direct contact	Mucous membranes, skin	Epithelial
VZV	Inhalation, direct contact	Respiratory tract, ?mucous membranes	Epithelial
CMV	Saliva, blood ? urine, ? semen	Bloodstream, mucus membranes	Neutrophil, monocyte, others
EBV	Saliva, blood	Mucous membranes, bloodstream	B lymphocyte, salivary glands

major disease associated with this virus, **infectious mononucleosis,** is occasionally called the **"kissing disease."** Inhalation of viruses borne in aerosols seems to be the way most individuals contract chickenpox (varicella). However, direct inoculation is possible here too. Thus, the mucous membranes provide the primary line of defense against several of the herpesviruses. Direct inoculation or ingestion of virus-bearing materials would first challenge either mucosal or circulating defenses, as the case may be. Nothing is known of the means by which human herpesviruses 6 and 7 are transmitted, but they are acquired early in childhood, so exchange of saliva or contact with some other nongenital mucous membrane surface must be involved.

MULTIPLICATION AND SPREAD

The replication of herpesviruses is complex, but it resembles that of other large DNA viruses (Fig. 40.5). **A lytic** or **productive cycle** of infection begins with the **attachment** of virus particles to susceptible cells. The virions interact with specific receptors via glycoproteins that project from the viral envelope. As with most viruses, we do not know much about these receptors nor why they have evolved at all. In the case of the Epstein-Barr virus, they are present predominantly on B lymphocytes, where they also serve as receptors for complement proteins. The receptor for herpes simplex virus type 1 was recently found also to bind a fibroblast growth factor.

Following binding of the virus to the cell surface, the viral core is **released** and **transported** to the cell nucleus where virus-specific synthetic processes are orchestrated. As with all other viruses, the herpes simplex virus genes are transcribed and translated into proteins in an orderly program, leading ultimately to the production of new progeny virions.

Initially, only five herpes simplex virus **immediate-early genes** are transcribed with the assistance of an activating protein carried in the virion **tegument,** the space between the core and the envelope. In turn, some of these five genes activate expression of about another dozen **early genes** whose protein products are needed to replicate the viral DNA. Following DNA synthesis, about another five dozen genes are turned on. These **late genes** encode proteins that assemble and comprise the progeny virions. Included among the late proteins are glycoproteins that are inserted into the cell's nuclear and cytoplasmic membranes. As the new viral cores are constructed, they bud through the nuclear and cytoplasmic membranes, becoming enveloped in the process. In so doing, some of the glycoproteins are captured, ending up on the outer surface of the virion.

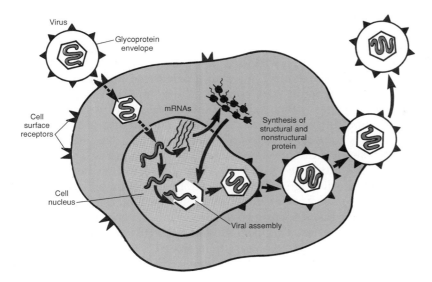

Figure 40.5. Productive infection of a cell by a herpesvirus. The virions are not drawn to scale. In reality, they are much smaller in proportion to the cell.

Unlike many other viruses, newly formed herpesvirus particles are **not efficiently released** into the extracellular space. Rather, as they **bud** out of the cell, they immediately attach to and penetrate into adjacent cells. This process of cell-to-cell spread has several important implications for the pathogenesis of disease associated with each herpesvirus and the host responses to infection by them. Diseases induced by herpes simplex virus, for example, involve local spread and progression of lesions. These are not systemic illnesses. Infection at multiple distant sites is rare with herpes simplex and probably requires the circulation of infected cells rather than of free virus. Chickenpox, cytomegalovirus, and Epstein-Barr viruses induce multisystem diseases—a feature that may be due, in part, to their ability to infect and to be transported in circulating leukocytes.

How Do Host Defenses Limit the Severity of Infection?

The immune response to herpes infections is multifaceted and incompletely understood. Host defenses are adequate to limit the duration and severity of infection and, in some people, are capable of preventing symptomatic recurrences. Within several days of the onset of a herpesvirus infection, antibodies to some of the viral proteins appear in the circulation. However, these antibodies develop too late to modify the infection and have no role in its recurrence. In fact, persons who fail to make antibodies, the agammaglobulinemics, have no special problems with herpesviruses. The likely reason is that these viruses spread from cell to cell and provide little opportunity for antibodies to come in contact with them. **The only phase in the cycle of herpesvirus infection when there is infectious extracellular virus is during the initial encounter.** At that time, antibodies can prevent infection. For this reason, **antisera** to herpesviruses are administered **prophylactically** to persons who are at risk of severe infection (see below under "Prevention"). Overall, **cellular immune** mechanisms are the more important determinants of the severity of the infection and of the likelihood of recurrence.

Certain lymphocytes can **lyse** cells in which herpesviruses are replicating. They do so by detecting the "foreign" viral antigens (mostly glycoproteins) that are displayed on the surfaces of the infected cells. Between infections, the herpesviruses remain hidden from immune recognition and establish a latent infection. The herpes simplex viruses, for example, persist in cells of **neural ganglia**. Somehow, neurons seem to avoid immune recognition and killing by lymphocytes, possibly because part of each neuron is protected by the blood-brain barrier and most of each axon is sheathed in myelin layers. Whatever the reason, the viruses here dwell in a stable **privileged reservoir**.

The ability to mount an adequate cellular immune response to herpesviruses changes with age. The relevant immune effector cells gradually mature during the first month of an infant's life. Until this maturation is complete, herpes infections may be devastating. Neonatal herpes simplex infection is often fatal. By 1 month of age, however, the infant tolerates the virus well. Some herpesviruses became problematic at the other age extreme as well. Reactivation of varicella virus to give the so-called zoster infection occurs with increasing frequency as the patient ages, perhaps providing an indication of the senescence of immune responses. The likelihood of having zoster disease is about 10 times greater at age 80 years than at age 8 years.

There is no better proof of the primacy of lymphocyte-mediated responses in the control of herpesvirus infections than the experience of severely compromised patients. About two-thirds of all bone-marrow transplant recipients experience reactivation herpes simplex infections within the first month after transplantation. Some of these may be quite severe and destructive. Similarly, leukemic children and **AIDS** patients experience frequent and prolonged herpes simplex virus infections.

Do **interferons** play a role in these diseases? These proteins are found in the blood of some patients who are infected systemically with herpesviruses, and they can be detected in the fluid of herpes simplex-induced blisters. Interferons are released both from virally infected epithelial cells and from defending lymphocytes, but their role in the spontaneous limitation of herpesvirus infections in humans is not known. However, large doses of interferon preparations can ameliorate serious varicella zoster, and cytomegalovirus infection, indicating that these proteins have defensive value.

Paradigm: Viral Latency

Viruses are a diverse and successful group of pathogens because they are genetically flexible in evolving strategies that ensure their propagation and spread. One successful strategy involves latency—the long-term presence of the virus within the host in a nonreplicating form.

Latency is different from other forms of virus persistence, namely, chronic infection and malignant cell transformation. Some agents, such as the measles virus, cause a rare chronic infection called SSPE, characterized by ongoing virus replication with incremental but inevitable damage to the host (see Chapter 33). Other viruses are transforming agents (see Chapter 39 on warts) that irrevocably alter cells and ultimately damage their hosts.

Latency is a feature of several infections, such as those caused by adenoviruses, but is best understood for herpesviruses. Each herpesvirus has its particular approach to latency, differing from that of others in terms of the type of cell in which it persists, and which few of its genes are expressed during latency.

One of the most interesting aspects of latency is what it teaches us about immune control of microbial agents. Latency is feasible because the process renders the virus virtually invisible to host immune mechanisms. But latency would not lead to the perpetuation of a virus if it were merely a "dead end" state. There must be means for reactivating the virus from time to time. On those occasions, the virus challenges the immune defenses. If these are adequate, the infection is curtailed, although the latent reservoir remains. If defenses are reduced because of senescence of the immune system with age, immunosuppressive treatment, or some other reason for immunodeficiency to arise, the virus can replicate and spread.

Latency provides an endless source of viruses that can probe immune defenses repeatedly and relentlessly until they are breached. This is guerrilla warfare, not the pitched battlefield on which poxviruses, influenza viruses, and many other agents make their stand. In medicine, as in history, we recognize this to be a viable strategy for all but the most aggressive and well-armed enemy.

DAMAGE

Herpes simplex viruses can be destructive. Epithelial cells in which the virions replicate are ultimately lysed. Under the microscope, changes can be observed in such productively infected cells; their nuclei become **enlarged** and **distorted** by viral cores and aggregates of nucleoproteins (Fig. 40.8). Gradually, the nuclear membrane dissolves and the cell swells and ruptures, but not before virus **spreads** to infect contiguous cells. Thus, a major component of the symptoms and signs of herpes simplex virus infection is the **destruction** of superficial **epithelial cells** in skin and mucous membranes. The spreading viruses quickly affect **regional nerve cells** as well, and some of the symptoms of herpes infections may result from damage to these nerves or from the inflammation that surrounds them. The symptoms include itching, tingling, burning, and pain. The host defenses mounted to limit the infection may also contribute to the severity of symptoms and lesions. **Degranulation** of leukocytes and release of **mediators** in response to local viral infection augment the tissue swelling and inflammation.

Herpes Simplex Virus Infections

Now to return to your patient, Mr. H. Because immune responses take time to evolve, it can be predicted that healing of all his lesions will require 2–3 weeks in a primary infection. Although the outward manifestations of infection disappear completely, Mr. H. will still carry the virus in the **sacral ganglia**, and he may have **recurrent sores** in the genital area an average of three to four times per year for many years (Table 40.3). Because antibody- and cellular-mediated immune responses are elicited during the primary infection, these later recurrences are typically briefer and milder, lasting an average of 7–10 days in all. The immune responses, however, are not adequate to prevent recurrent infection in all individuals.

This describes a typical genital herpes infection in an **adult**. Herpes simplex virus may induce somewhat different conditions depending upon the body site, age, and general host immune capacity (Table 40.4). Herpes simplex viruses may infect nearly any area of the skin. A common site of infection, particularly in health care workers, is the fin-

---

Table 40.3. Stages in Herpes Simplex Infection

Acute mucocutaneous infection
Spread to local sensory nerve endings
Establishment and maintenance of neuronal latency
Reactivation of virus and distal spread
Recurrent cutaneous infection

Table 40.4. Infections Associated with Herpes Simplex Viruses

Infection	Predominant Virus Type	Frequency	Age Group	Usual Outcome	Recurrence
Ocular herpes	1	Common	All	Resolution, visual impairment	Yes
Oral herpes	1>2	Very common	All	Resolution	Yes
Genital herpes	2>1	Common	Adolescents, adults	Resolution	Yes
Neonatal herpes	2>1	Very rare	0-4 weeks impairment	Developmental	No
Meningoencephalitis	2	Uncommon	Adolescents, adults	Resolution	No
Encephalitis	1	Very rare	All	Severe neurological impairment, death	No
Disseminated herpes	1>2	Rare	All	Resolution or death	No

gertip; infection is acquired by touching active herpetic lesions in patients. These infections, known as **herpetic whitlows**, can be exceedingly painful because there is little room in the fingertip for swelling of inflamed tissues.

Herpes can infect the conjunctiva and cornea of the eye, a condition known as **herpetic keratoconjunctivitis**. This infection causes inflammation and swelling in the superficial tissues of the anterior eye, with potential scarring and loss of vision.

As mentioned before, herpes can cause severe and life-threatening infections. Like the newborn, patients with lymphomas, leukemias, or AIDS have inadequate cellular immune defenses. In these individuals, the infection can spread widely across the skin and to vital viscera, especially the lungs, esophagus, liver, and brain. A rare form of herpes simplex virus disease involves reactivation of virus, presumably from the trigeminal ganglion, and its ascent into the brain, rather than the usual descent to the mouth. Encephalitis ensues, characterized by an unusually progressive and destructive inflammation of a unilateral and focal nature. This condition is usually deadly if untreated.

WHY DO HERPES INFECTIONS RECUR?

Perhaps the most remarkable aspect of infection with any herpesvirus is the ability of the virus to **persist** in humans for life. The reason for this persistence is that the virus can initiate a **latent** type of infectious cycle in selected cells, one which is distinct from the productive type just reviewed. In the case of herpes simplex, the virus spreads to infect nerve endings early in the course of the initial mucocutaneous infection (Table 40.3). As hosts for herpes simplex virus, nerve cells are very different from epithelial cells. Rather than permitting a full replicative cycle culminating in the release of progeny virions, most infected neurons develop an **abortive** or **latent** infection. The process is not well defined, but it appears that only **one gene** is expressed, a gene whose role may be to facilitate virus reactivation when the "time is right," whatever that means at the cellular and molecular level. Viral DNA is not synthesized in latency, nor are progeny virions produced. The viral DNA remains **stably associated** with the neuronal nucleus. It is not known whether it is physically **integrated** into the chromosomes or remains a separate **plasmid-like element**, replicating rarely if at all in these nondividing cells.

Similar types of latent infections occur with each of the other human herpesviruses. Varicella zoster viruses also reside in **sensory nerve ganglia**, while cytomegaloviruses reside in **neutrophils** and **monocytes**. The Epstein-Barr viruses are harbored in **B lymphocytes** and **salivary gland cells**. This latent infection **persists for life**. Autopsy studies reveal that nearly all individuals who have been infected with herpes simplex virus harbor the viral DNA in selected nerve ganglia. The **trigeminal (V) ganglia** are the most commonly affected sites (Fig. 40.6), followed by certain **sacral root ganglia**. The trigeminal nerves serve the ocular and oral nerves and the sacral root serves the genital regions, all of which are the sites of most common herpes simplex infection. Under certain circumstances, such as when there are breaks in the skin or open wounds, herpes simplex can penetrate and infect any body site. The virus will establish a latent infection in the sensory nerves serving any such area.

Occasionally, latency is interrupted. Certain factors trigger the **reactivation** of latent herpes simplex virus and produce symptoms. These stimuli include sunburn, systemic infections, immune impairment, emotional stress, and menstruation. We do not know how these seemingly unrelated factors induce viral reactivation. Reactivated herpes simplex viruses **travel down the axonal processes** and bud off from the nerve endings to spread to and infect contiguous mucocutaneous epithelial cells. If the amount of newly replicated virus is small, symptoms are less likely to develop. As you may know personally, symptomatic recurrences of fever blisters are common.

The ability of herpes simplex to establish a lifelong latent infection and to undergo episodic reactivation is one of the most fundamental facts that must be imparted to your patient. He must know that he is likely to experience repeated episodes of genital herpes, each of which renders him potentially contagious.

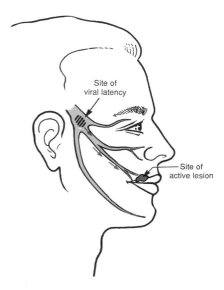

Figure 40.6. The sites of active and latent facial herpes simplex infections.

INFECTIONS CAUSED BY OTHER HERPESVIRUSES

Each of the other herpesviruses causes important and unique clinical syndromes that will be reviewed briefly (Table 40.5). Varicella zoster virus, as the name implies, is associated with only two diseases, **chickenpox** (varicella) and **shingles** (zoster). Chickenpox is a familiar, annoying disease of childhood that results in the appearance of vesicles in the skin. It can be serious in immunodeficient patients. By adult age, 80–90% of all Americans experience chickenpox. The infection is

Table 40.5. Infections Associated with Other Herpesviruses

Virus	Syndrome	Frequency	Age Group	Tissues Involved	Usual Outcome
Cytomegalovirus	Congenital infection	Common	Newborn	Brain, eye, liver, spleen, others	Developmental problems, death
	Mononucleosis	Common	Adolescents, adults	Lymph nodes, liver	Resolution
	Hepatitis	Uncommon	Adolescents, adults	Liver	Resolution
	Pneumonia	Common in immunosuppressed patients	All	Lung	Death
	Retinitis	Common in immunosuppressed patients	All	Eye	Blindness
Epstein-Barr virus	Mononucleosis	Very common	All	Lymph nodes, liver, spleen	Resolution
	Lymphomas	Very rare	All	Lymph nodes, liver, spleen, brain	Death
Varicella zoster	Chickenpox	Very common	All	Skin, others uncommon	Resolution, rarely death
	Shingles (zoster)	Common	Older adults	Skin, nerves, others very uncommon	Resolution, chronic pain, rarely death

rarely asymptomatic. Shingles is caused by the reactivation of latent varicella virus in less than 10% of infected people. It generally involves a rash similar to that of varicella, but it is painful and restricted to the skin area served by a single sensory nerve root in which the virus had lain dormant. The risk of this disease rises sharply with age. In the compromised host, zoster infection can disseminate to cause severe infections.

Most **cytomegalovirus** infections result in few if any symptoms. However, there is a series of well-defined syndromes associated with this virus in individuals of different ages and risk category. About 1% of infections occur in utero, due to **transplacental transmission** of virus from a mother experiencing primary or reactivation cytomegalovirus infection. The newborn may suffer from hemolytic anemias, thrombocytopenia, hepatitis, splenomegaly, rash, and developmental disorders. Infection is common in early childhood, particularly in day care settings. In the population as a whole, about 60% have been infected by 40 years of age.

Severe visceral (lung, eye, brain, liver, colon, etc.) infections with **cytomegalovirus** also occur in transplant recipients, leukemia and lymphoma patients, and AIDS patients. Adolescents and young adults with cytomegalovirus infection develop hepatitis or a mononucleosis-like illness with fever, sore throat, enlarged lymph nodes, and an increase in the number of circulating lymphocytes, some of which have an atypical appearance. These disorders are particularly prevalent in young gay men, nearly all of whom eventually acquire the virus.

Epstein-Barr virus is also very common. Nearly all children in developing nations are infected before the age of 5 years. In industrialized countries, the infection is delayed, occurring in only one-half of people by college age, but in over 90% by age 40 years. Epstein-Barr virus infection in early childhood tends to be mild or asymptomatic. However, if the first exposure to Epstein-Barr virus is delayed until adolescence or early adult age, the expression of the infection is dramatically different and **infectious mononucleosis** often ensues. This syndrome is similar to that caused by cytomegalovirus, with sore throat, fever, and swollen glands. **Atypical lymphocytes** (reactive T cells) circulate in high number, as do "**heterophile**" antibodies, which, as the name implies, have broad reactivities and are not specific for Epstein-Barr virus antigens. The appearance of heterophile antibodies reflects the general (**polyclonal**) stimulation of B lymphocytes to start synthesizing immunoglobulin of diverse specificity, including antibodies to the red blood cells of several different animals. These serve as the basis for simple and rapid diagnostic tests involving hemagglutination.

Both of the recently discovered human **herpesvirus types 6 and 7** infect T lymphocytes. Nothing is known of disease associated with herpes 7. In turn, little is known about herpes 6, but it may be associated with lymphoproliferative disorders. It is proven to cause a common, mild, rash-producing infection of early childhood known as **roseola**, or **exanthem subitum**.

As a group, the herpesviruses have many features in common. They are ubiquitous, generally cause mild diseases that may recur, and are especially problematic for patients with cellular immune deficiencies.

HERPESVIRUSES AND CANCER

Earlier, we reviewed two major types of infection with herpesviruses, namely, productive and latent infection. In vitro, most herpesviruses may also initiate an additional and important type of infectious cycle known as a **transforming infection**. Herpesviruses (especially the Epstein-Barr virus) transform cells in culture, causing them to take on features of malignant tissues. The cells are morphologically altered, become "immortalized," and have different nutritional requirements. It is not really known if this type of infectious cycle actually takes place in humans and leads to malignant disease. Herpesviruses, or at least their proteins or genes, have been found in human cancer cells, but we are not certain whether they include cancer themselves, participate in cancer induction, or are merely not-so-innocent bystanders. Cytomegalovirus is found in many cases of **Kaposi's sarcoma**. Herpes simplex type 2 infection has been linked to **cervical carcinoma**, but it is clear that papillomaviruses and perhaps other factors as well are more important in the pathogenesis of this cancer. The Epstein-Barr virus has been found in the cancerous cells in **nasopharyngeal carcinoma, Burkitt's lymphoma**, and in other **B-cell lymphomas**. Burkitt's lymphoma is a common tumor of children in central Africa. In fact, the nearly universal association of African Burkitt's lymphoma with the Epstein-Barr virus is the strongest reason for believing that a human cancer may be caused by a herpesvirus.

DIAGNOSIS

The astute clinician who understands the biology and pathophysiology of herpes simplex virus infection will have little difficulty in diagnosing herpes. In the case of Mr. H., the history and physical examination were all that was required to suggest herpes. To establish the diagnosis, one must demonstrate the presence of virus or its components in active lesions. Scrapings of lesions like Mr. H.'s can be examined microscopically for multinucleated giant cells whose nuclei contain **eosinophilic inclusions** (Fig. 40.7), the hallmark of herpes replication in tissues. Scrapings may also be stained with specific fluorescein-labeled antisera that will bind to viral proteins and fluoresce when examined with a microscope with an ultraviolet light source.

The definitive diagnostic tool is **virus isolation** in cell culture (Fig. 40.8). Herpes simplex virus grows well in a wide variety of fibroblastic and epithelial cell lines from animals or humans. Replicating viruses induce the type of deformity and cell destruction described earlier. The appearance of these cytopathic changes characteristic of herpes simplex allows definitive diagnosis.

PREVENTION

Herpesviruses are ubiquitous, and it is not practical to avoid contact with all individuals with herpes infections. It is appropriate, however, to avoid sexual contact during active genital herpes infections. Unfortunately, safe and effective vaccines have not been developed for herpes simplex viruses. Even if an effective vaccine were available, it would probably not help those with existing infection. It is unlikely that a vaccine could induce a better immune response than a natural infection, which does not suffice to prevent recurrence.

Other herpesvirus infections can be prevented in selected situations. Severe chickenpox in immunodeficient children may be partially prevented by administration of specific **human immune globulin** promptly after exposure. A live, attenuated **varicella vaccine** has proven effective and may be approved soon for use in normal and im-

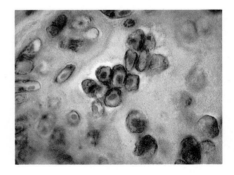

Figure 40.7. Photomicrograph of a biopsy of a skin lesion from a patient with herpes simplex infection. Numerous multinucleated cells containing eosinophilic intranuclear inclusions are apparent.

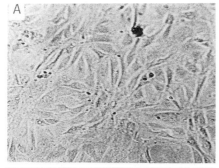

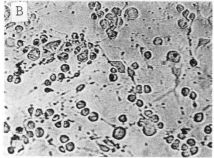

Figure 40.8. Human diploid fibroblasts before (A) and 48 hr after (B) inoculation with herpes simplex virus type 2.

munologically impaired (leukemic) children. For it to be safe and sufficiently effective in leukemics, however, the vaccine must be administered at times when there are reasonable numbers of circulating lymphocytes, such as after a course of chemotherapy has been completed. Live, attenuated vaccines for cytomegalovirus are being studied and may prove useful for certain high-risk individuals.

TREATMENT

Antiviral therapy is still a primitive science. The first glimmers of hope, however, have been in the treatment of herpes simplex virus infections. Nucleoside analogs (see Chapter 43) have been developed that are preferentially utilized by viral synthetic pathways. The most useful antiviral drug to be studied extensively in man is **acyclovir**.

Mr. H. should be given acyclovir because treatment significantly decreases the duration and severity of first episodes of genital herpes. Acyclovir, however, is not a cure because it does not prevent entry of virus into nerve ganglia nor does it remove virus once there. Therefore, patients treated with acyclovir remain susceptible to later recurrences. Long-term treatment with acyclovir pills will suppress most recurrences, and this regimen would be useful for Mr. H. if his recurrences were very frequent.

Severe varicella zoster infections in the immunocompromised host may be ameliorated by intravenous acyclovir or **vidarabine**, another nucleoside analog with antiherpes activity. Treatment of Epstein-Barr virus infections has not been widely explored, but the available agents are not likely to be potent enough to affect these diseases significantly. Two drugs, **ganciclovir** and **foscarnet** afford effective treatments for sight-threatening cytomegalovirus infections in patients with **AIDS**. Unfortunately, these drugs are too toxic for use in milder infections by cytomegalovirus. Now that successful antiviral treatment has became routine so too has the emergence of drug-resistant viruses. For more on this subject, see Chapter 43. Resistance is currently a concern only in selected patients with severe immune deficiencies.

CONCLUSIONS

Mr. H. has genital herpes, one of the common sexually transmitted diseases, most often caused by herpesvirus type 2. His symptoms may become ameliorated with acyclovir but recurrence of the disease at a later time is likely. His sexual partners should avoid contact with sites of active infection.

Herpesviruses display a wide range of biological and medical manifestations. They illustrate an important correlation between the life cycle of the viruses and the clinical manifestations of the diseases they cause. This is a fertile area for the study of viral pathogenesis and oncological transformation.

Self-assessment Questions

1. What are the main types of herpesviruses?

2. Describe the reproductive cycle of a typical herpesvirus, including the latency stage.

3. What is the role of the host defenses in herpesvirus infections? Are there generalizations that apply to most of these infections?

4. What are the main problems in therapy of herpes simplex?

5. If you became involved in work on prevention of herpes simplex infections, how would you go about it?

6. How would you counsel a young person suffering from genital herpes?

SUGGESTED READING

Hirsch MS, Schooley RT. Treatment of herpesvirus infections. N Engl J Med 1983;309:963–970, 1034–1039.

Klein RJ. The pathogenesis of acute, latent and recurrent herpes simplex infections. Arch Virol 1982;72:143–168.

Mandell GL, Douglas RG, Jr, Bennett JE. Principles and practice of infectious disease, ed. 2. New York: John Wiley & Sons, 1985:1282–1341.

Nahmias AJ, Dowdle WR, Schinazi RF. The human herpesvirus: an interdisciplinary perspective. New York: Elsevier Press, 1981.

Weller TH. Varicella and herpes zoster. Changing concepts of the natural history, control, and importance of a not-so-benign virus. N Engl J Med 1983;309:1362–1434.

Viral Hepatitis

Stephen E. Straus

Viral infections of the liver are serious diseases caused by **several unrelated viruses**. They usually have an acute phase that is sometimes followed by a chronic debilitating condition. Chronic infection with at least two of these viruses is associated with an increase in liver cancer. These diseases resemble each other clinically and can only be differentiated with the aid of laboratory tests. They differ in their mode of spread; some are acquired by ingestion of contaminated food and water, while others acquired by sexual contact, injection with contaminated needles, or via blood transfusions. All of the viruses that cause hepatitis are difficult to study in the laboratory; the degree to which they are understood derives largely from the power of new molecular techniques. Hepatitis B virus, as the most clinically important of these viruses, is the emphasis of this chapter. Of particular interest to virologists is that the virus replicates by a unique molecular mechanism.

CASE

Mr. P., a 23-year-old grocery clerk, came to the emergency service of the City Hospital because of jaundice. For several days, he had felt increasingly weak, nauseated, and feverish. He felt pain in the right side of his abdomen and his joints. He had no appetite. Mr. P. thought that he had picked up a bad case of the "stomach flu" until, while shaving, he noted that his eyes were yellow. He reported that he had experimented with a variety of oral and injectable drugs, but denied being addicted. He had a stable job, and a girlfriend with whom he was sexually active.

*The Emergency Room physician suspected that Mr. P. had hepatitis B virus infection, and that he may have acquired it from contaminated needles. The laboratory reported elevation of several indicators of liver injury; namely, serum aminotransferases, bilirubin, and alkaline phosphatase. Antibodies to hepatitis A and C viruses were absent, but an antigen associated with hepatitis B, called HB_sAg, was detected in his serum. These findings confirmed the diagnosis of **acute hepatitis B virus infection**.*

The following questions suggest themselves:

1. What were the key elements in the diagnosis of Mr. P.'s disease?

2. Why did the physician suspect that he acquired the disease from contaminated needles?

3. What caused Mr. P.'s symptoms?

4. What is his prognosis? What treatment could be instituted?

5. Can Mr. P. transmit the disease to others? What counsel can he be given to avoid further transmission?

VIRAL HEPATITIDES

The disease known as epidemic jaundice has been recognized since ancient times and large outbreaks have been observed, particularly during wars and other conditions of deprivation. Not until the middle of this century was it appreciated that the viral hepatitides have multiple causes and that they are distinct from two other forms of "infectious jaundice"; namely, yellow fever and leptospirosis. The disease that follows the injection of blood and blood products has a long incubation period, while that associated with ingestion of contaminated food or water has a shorter incubation period. The first became known as **serum hepatitis**; the second was known as **infectious hepatitis**. Today, these are called **type B** and **type A hepatitis**, respectively.

The distinction between types A and B hepatitis depended on several findings. In a series of elegant studies involving institutionalized retarded individuals, it was shown that there must be more than one etiological agent. The same person could be sequentially infected with different viruses inasmuch as they do not induce cross-protection. In the 1960s to early 1970s, tests for both hepatitis A and B viruses became available, permitting an accurate distinction between the two diseases.

In the late 1970s, Italian scientists described a previously unrecognized antigen in the liver of some individuals with type B hepatitis. Further work found that the antigen belongs to a separate agent, the **"delta" (Δ)** or **"hepatitis D"** virus. This is a distinct virus that only infects patients who are also actively infected with hepatitis B virus.

With the detection of hepatitis A and B viruses, it became apparent that many hepatitis cases could not be ascribed to these viruses and, therefore, were likely to have other etiologies. Those diseases initially became known as **non-A, non-B hepatitis** because there was no serological evidence of recent infection with hepatitis A or B in these cases. Two patterns of non-A, non-B disease emerged upon careful scrutiny. The first is associated with blood transfusions and the use of contaminated needles. The second is a form of hepatitis that appears in waterborne epidemics, primarily in Third World countries. In the late 1980s, the causes of each of these forms of non-A, non-B hepatitis, termed **hepatitis C** virus and **hepatitis E** virus, respectively, were elucidated by direct cloning and amplification of nucleic acids in patients' specimens.

Many other viruses are capable of producing liver inflammation and jaundice (including yellow fever virus, lassa virus, herpes simplex virus, varicella zoster virus, adenoviruses, Epstein-Barr virus, and cytomegalovirus). However, many of these cause other diseases as well, whereas the liver is the primary target organ for the current alphabetic repertoire of hepatitis viruses A through E.

HEPATITIS B VIRUS

The five viruses that infect the liver as their primary target (Table 41.1) differ in structure and replicative strategy. Each exhibits a particular epidemiological profile and mode of transmission (Tables 41.2 and 41.3). We will describe and emphasize the hepatitis B virus and then compare it with the other hepatitis viruses.

Hepatitis B virus belongs to a family of **enveloped DNA viruses**, the Hepadnavirus (Fig. 41.1). Related viruses in this group cause chronic hepatitis, cirrhosis, and liver cancer in ground squirrels, woodchucks,

Table 41.1. Properties of Human Hepatitis Viruses

Agent	Size(nM)	Nucleic Acid Composition	Virus Family
Hepatitis A	27	Single-stranded linear RNA	Picornaviridae
Hepatitis B	42	Nicked, circular, mostly double-stranded DNA	Hepadna-viridae
Hepatitis C	?	RNA	? Flaviviridae
Hepatitis D	37	Single-stranded RNA	?
Hepatitis E	27	RNA	?

Table 41.2. Epidemiology and Transmission of Hepatitis Viruses

	A	B	C	D	E
Epidemiological patterns					
Epidemic	Yes	No	Yes	Yes	Yes
Sporadic	Yes	Yes	Yes	Yes	Yes
Transmission					
Fecal/oral	Yes	No	No	No	Yes
Sexual	Yes	Yes	Probable	Probable	?
Vertical[a]	No	Yes	Probable	Yes	?
Parenteral	Rare	Yes	Yes	Yes	?

[a]Includes transmission in utero and perinatally.

Table 41.3. Clinical Comparison of Diseases Associated with Hepatitis Viruses

	A	B	C	D	E
Incubation period (day)	15–40	60–180	60–120	?	21–42
Asymptomatic infection	Usual	Common	Common	?	?
Chronicity	No	Yes (10%)	Yes (30–60%)	Yes	No
Long-term sequelae	No	Cirrhosis, hepatocellular carcinoma	Cirrhosis, hepatocellular carcinoma	Exacerbation of chronic HBV infection	No

and ducks. Hepatitis B virus contains several proteins useful in diagnosis:

- An envelope protein called **hepatitis B surface antigen** (HB$_s$Ag) or "Australia" antigen;

- The **core antigen** (HB$_c$Ag);

- The **e antigen** (HB$_e$Ag); and

- A viral **DNA polymerase.**

HB$_s$Ag circulates freely in the blood in long linear or small circular aggregates of 22 nm in diameter, or as part of the virions, the so-called "Dane particles" (Fig. 41.2). The blood of infected patients contains enormous numbers of the HB$_s$Ag aggregates, as many as 10^{13} particles per ml. The aggregates vastly outnumber the complete virions in the circulation. Complete virions only attain titers of 10^5–10^7/ml of serum, but they are what makes blood infectious.

HB$_s$Ag is made up of three antigens in various combinations, comprising a number of subtypes that do not appear to differ in virulence or chronicity. They are, however, useful for epidemiological studies of the spread of a strain of virus in a community. Serological analysis of

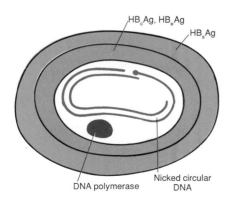

Figure 41.1. Structure of the hepatitis B virus.

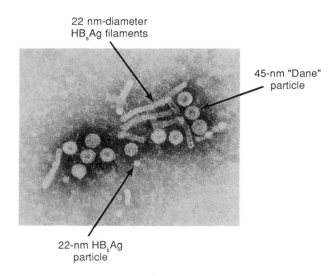

22 nm-diameter
HB_sAg filaments

45-nm "Dane"
particle

22-nm HB_sAg
particle

Figure 41.2. Electron micrograph of 22-nm small, spherical aggregates of hepatitis B surface antigen (HB_sAg) particles, 22-nm wide filamentous aggregates of the antigen, and 42- to 45-nm hepatitis B virus ("Dane") particles.

other cases of hepatitis B among our patient's contacts could link them to Mr. P's.

The viruses of the Hepadnavirus family are unique in genome structure. They have **circular DNA** genomes, about 3200 base pairs in length, consisting of **one strand that is nicked and another that is incomplete** (Fig. 41.1). The incomplete strand is only 1700–2800 bases long. From in vitro studies, it appears that the endogenous DNA polymerase synthesizes the missing stretch during replication. The evolutionary value of this unique genome structure is unknown, but it has obviously not impaired this virus' ability to establish a secure ecological niche for itself. Aspects of the biology of hepatitis B virus are difficult to study because the virus cannot be grown reliably in cultured cells.

OTHER HEPATITIS VIRUSES

The other hepatitis viruses differ considerably from the hepatitis B virus. **Hepatitis A virus** is a **picornavirus**, the family of small RNA viruses (Picornaviridae) related to the Coxsackie viruses and polioviruses (Chapter 31). Progress in studying this virus was also hampered for many years by its limited host range. This virus infects only humans and a few other higher primates. Hepatitis A virus replicates in cultured marmoset liver cells; the process is inefficient, but adequate to yield viral antigen for incorporation into vaccines that are undergoing clinical study.

Hepatitis A virus is a **positive-stranded RNA virus** since its genome RNA serves directly to encode proteins as messenger RNA. The replication of hepatitis A virus is not well understood, but it appears to involve a strategy similar to that employed by other picornaviruses. Replication of hepatitis A takes place in the cytoplasm and involves a double-stranded RNA intermediate.

The data available from sequencing molecularly cloned **hepatitis C virus** RNA suggests that it is related to the **flaviviruses**, a large genus of agents with single-stranded, positive-sense RNA genomes. Members of the genus are best known for being **arthropod-borne** viruses, hence the term arboviruses. One of the most famous and interesting flaviviruses, the **yellow fever virus**, is also known to cause hepatitis.

The **hepatitis D virus** has a remarkable replicative strategy, at least for human viruses. It is a **small, defective RNA virus that can replicate** only in the presence of hepatitis B virus. The RNA genome has long stretches of self-complementary sequences that allow base pairing within the strand. The resulting partially double-stranded structure is unique among known human viruses, and resembles the genome of plant pathogens known as **viroids**. Viroids are "naked viruses" that lack the protein coat; the hepatitis D virus, on the other hand, is not naked RNA, but "borrows" the surface antigen of hepatitis B virus for its own coat. Thus, hepatitis D virus may be considered to be a "parasite's parasite." The remarkable dependence of hepatitis D virus on another virus has a precedent among human viruses; the so-called adeno-associated parvovirus is also defective and replicates only in cells coinfected with adenoviruses.

The **hepatitis E virus** is still not well characterized. Electron microscopic studies identified aggregates of 27-nm (diameter), virus-like particles in the stool of patients. This finding and the sequence for RNA cloned molecularly from patient bile showed that hepatitis E virus is related to other common, nonenveloped RNA viruses, such as the picornaviruses and Norwalk virus.

ENTRY

There are four routes by which hepatitis viruses can be transmitted from human to human (Table 41.2). Transmission of hepatitis B virus takes place largely by exchange of **virus-containing blood and blood products.** It is most likely that Mr. P. acquired hepatitis from a contaminated needle that had been previously used by another actively infected drug user. Nonparenteral transmission also occurs; semen, saliva, and vaginal secretions have been shown to contain hepatitis B virus, so that sexual transmission is common. Thus, it is also possible that Mr. P. contracted hepatitis from his girlfriend, or that he might transmit the infection to her. The inoculation of hepatitis B virus-containing fluids into open wounds or direct injection into the bloodstream are the most efficient means of spreading the infection. In areas where hepatitis B is endemic, such as parts of Africa and Asia, it is also possible that some cases are transmitted by arthropods.

In developed nations, antibodies to hepatitis B virus are found in about 5% of all adults. The highest prevalence is among intravenous drug abusers and promiscuous homosexual men, over 80% of whom are seropositive. Antibodies to this virus are commonly found in developing nations. Among African and East Asian nations, about 50% or more of all people are antibody positive, and 5–15% are chronically infected. Thus, there is an enormous reservoir for this virus. **At least one-quarter billion humans are potentially infectious at any time.**

A major problem with hepatitis B virus infection is transmission to the neonate. In Taiwan, for example, one-third of infants born to HB_sAg-positive mothers become infected. Transmission apparently does not occur in utero, but during delivery or through contact with the mother's blood, milk, or minor skin wounds.

MULTIPLICATION AND SPREAD

The target of hepatitis B virus is the **hepatocyte**. Although recent findings suggest that hepatitis B virus can replicate in pancreatic and bone marrow cells, nearly all that is known about this virus and its infectious processes comes from studies of hepatocytes. As with some other viruses, hepatitis B virus can initiate a number of different types of infection. **Acute productive infection** leads to synthesis of viral

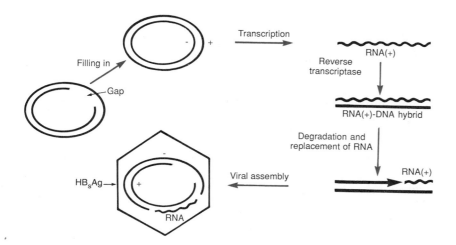

Figure 41.3. Proposed mechanism of hepatitis B virus DNA replication.

DNA. HB$_c$Ag can be detected in the nucleus and HB$_s$Ag can be detected in the cytoplasm, and infected virions are subsequently released into the circulation. Studies of hepatitis B replication are limited to infected liver tissues because the virus has not yet been grown in cultured cells. The restricted tropism of the virus seems to be due to the existence of specific receptor sites for HB$_s$Ag in the liver and few, if any, in other tissues.

Hepatitis B virus replicates in a unique way among DNA viruses (Fig. 41.3). It is the only known human DNA virus that replicates via an RNA intermediate. Its sequence is:

$$\text{partly dsDNA} \rightarrow \text{dsDNA} \rightarrow \text{ssRNA} \rightarrow \text{ssDNA} \rightarrow \text{partly dsDNA.}$$
$$\quad\quad\quad\quad\quad \text{step 1} \quad\quad \text{step 2} \quad\quad \text{step 3} \quad\quad \text{step 4}$$

The virion contains a single-stranded DNA molecule and only part of its complementary strand. The **first step** in replication consists in **filling in the incomplete strand** of the infecting DNA molecule (step 1). This is carried out by the polymerase contained in the virion. The completed molecule then serves as a template for the synthesis of a **full-length RNA intermediate of positive polarity** (step 2). The viral polymerase, which possesses **reverse transcriptase** activity, then synthesizes a **complementary negative DNA** copy on the RNA strand (step 3). The RNA strand is now degraded and the DNA is used to make its **complementary strand** (step 4).

The reason for this convoluted replicative strategy is not known, but it may be related to the fact that, at some point during acute hepatitis B virus infection of hepatocytes, the viral genome **integrates** into the host cell chromosome. Liver specimens from patients or experimental animals with chronic hepatitis B virus infection, especially those which have undergone cancerous transformation, contain one or more copies of the viral DNA integrated in seemingly random fashion into the host cell DNA.

Paradigm: Virus Tropism

Hepatitis viruses are excellent examples of convergent evolution among pathogenic agents. Despite major differences in structure and biology, all five known hepatitis viruses share a remarkably specific tropism. But, by whatever route they gain entry to the body, they "set up shop" in liver cells only. Hepatitis viruses are so dependent on these cells for their growth that we know of no other cell type that supports their replication, despite decades of efforts in the laboratory.

Hepatitis viruses grow only in the liver of primates, those of human, chimpanzee, and in some cases, marmoset, and no other. Even so, cell lines established from biopsies of primate livers only exceptionally support the replication of these viruses.

There are other examples of specific virus tropism, e.g., among encephalitis viruses, gastroenteritis agents, or respiratory viruses. In some cases, these viruses can grow elsewhere in the body, but the damage they inflict is limited to selected organ systems.

In some instances, tropism is determined by the portal of entry. Viruses that penetrate through breaks in the skin, are inhaled, or are ingested may cause infection at the site of entry. Tropism may also reflect the distribution of virus-specific receptors. Thus, HIV infects CD_4-positive cells; EBV infects CR_2-positive cells. Another powerful factor that determines virus tropism is the regulatory and biochemical machinery of the cells themselves. The virus may be able to infect a cell but not to complete its replicative cycle at certain sites. Neurons, for example, do not divide and have little need to sustain the nucleotide pools required for virus replication. Certain cells apparently lack DNA-binding proteins and other factors needed to activate transcription. Such types of host cell limitations may sometimes be overcome by coinfecting agents. For example, adeno-associated viruses grow only in cells that are coinfected with adenoviruses or herpes simplex viruses. Hepatitis D virus grows only in the presence of hepatitis B.

Generally speaking, we do not know what determines the tropism of hepatitis viruses. But there is an important message in this story, that, when decoded, will give us vast new insights about how to control and to prevent virus infections.

DAMAGE

Replication of hepatitis B virus in the liver results in hepatocyte injury and the release of progeny virions into the bloodstream. Cell injury is not due to cytopathic properties of the virus itself but is apparently caused by the **activation of cytotoxic immune mechanisms**. Hepatitis B virus replicates prolifically but inefficiently. Trillions of particles can be detected in the serum, but only a very small fraction of the particles are complete virions rather than HB_sAg envelope aggregates (Fig. 41.2).

In addition to the productive replication process that characterizes the acute infection, hepatitis B virus may also cause a lifelong, **chronic infection of the liver**. In about 10% of cases, the virus or HB_sAg alone circulates in the bloodstream for more than 6 months after the acute infection. Some chronic infections can resolve spontaneously over a period of years. Recurrent hepatitis B virus infection has been documented in patients receiving immunosuppressive treatments, indicating that even when clinically resolved, a reservoir of virus persists. Chronic hepatitis B virus infection most often leads to a **persistent hepatitis**, with mild periportal inflammation. Alternatively, it may result in a **chronic active hepatitis** with more widespread inflammation and necrosis. Chronic active hepatitis leads to **cirrhosis** and **hepatocellular carcinoma**. In Taiwan, the risk of developing primary hepatocellular carcinoma is over 200 times greater in HB_sAg carriers than in noncarriers. It is not known if hepatitis B virus causes the cancer, if the inflammatory process of the chronic infection promotes the cancerous change, or if there are local predisposing causes.

It is interesting that, in patients who develop hepatocellular carcinoma, the virus has integrated into the host genome.

OTHER HEPATITIDES

Hepatitis A

Hepatitis A infections are acquired mainly through **ingestion** of fecally contaminated food and water. It is presumed that, as with other picornaviruses, they are absorbed through the intestine and gain access to the liver directly through the portal circulation. This is its only known site of hepatitis A replication and the place where virus particles are released into the bloodstream and, possibly, also into the bile. This would explain why feces are so infectious. A brief viremic phase occurs during the incubation period and may account for the few documented blood-borne cases of hepatitis A.

The likelihood of experiencing hepatitis A infection and the age of occurrence are highly dependent upon socioeconomic factors. In countries with primitive sanitary facilities, nearly all of the people become infected before age 10 years. In the developed nations, early acquisition of infection is only common in poorer segments of the population. An increased risk of hepatitis A is associated with homosexuality because of oral-anal sex, and with institutionalization because of fecal contamination of the environment.

In terms of the damage inflicted by these other viruses, the hepatitis A virus is more cytopathic than is hepatitis B virus. However, the extent of acute hepatic injury in hepatitis A infection is usually more limited than that seen in hepatitis B. Presumably, this difference results from the greater amount of immune damage in type B hepatitis.

Hepatitis C

In developed nations, most cases of non-A, non-B hepatitis are acquired from transfused blood; these are nearly all associated with acute hepatitis C virus infection. Until 1990, about 5% of all individuals who received blood transfusions developed hepatitis C virus infection; at that time, antibody screening tests became available and all donated blood in the U.S. was subjected to those tests. Between one-third and two-thirds of those patients who received pre-1990 blood transfusions went on to develop chronic hepatitis and viremia.

Hepatitis D

The epidemiology of hepatitis D infection is changing rapidly. First recognized in Southern Europe in the early 1970s, it has been associated with epidemics of unusually severe hepatitis B infections throughout the world and is becoming **increasingly prevalent** in Northern Europe and in North America. At present, 20–30% of all HB_sAg-positive intravenous drug abusers in the U.S. are also infected with it. For this reason, Mr. P. is at risk of acquiring both of the hepatitis B and D viruses by sharing needles with other infected drug abusers.

As mentioned above, the hepatitis D virus only replicates in liver cells in which hepatitis B virus is also actively replicating. **Coinfection** of the liver with hepatitis B and D may lead to **more serious** acute or chronic infection than with hepatitis B virus alone. There are no data to indicate whether coinfection with hepatitis D affects the risk of hepatocellular carcinoma.

Hepatitis E

Throughout the world, most cases of non-A, non-B hepatitis are not associated with exposure to blood or blood products. In fact, about two-thirds of cases of epidemic and sporadic non-A, non-B hepatitis in India, Pakistan, and the Soviet Union appear to caused by **water-borne** viruses, and have a relatively short incubation period. Some of these have proven to be caused by hepatitis E virus.

MANIFESTATIONS AND DIAGNOSIS OF HEPATITIS

Most infections with hepatitis viruses throughout the world are **asymptomatic**, particularly in children (see Table 41.3). These infections differ mainly in their epidemiology. Thus, Mr. P. was suspected of having hepatitis B because he was an intravenous drug user. Otherwise, the clinical features of all acute viral hepatitides are so similar that an accurate diagnosis cannot be made on clinical grounds alone (Fig. 41.4). Apparent infection is often milder and briefer with hepatitis A than with hepatitis B (Fig. 41.5). Fulminant or fatal hepatitis A infection is rare.

Mr. P.'s symptoms and jaundice can be expected to resolve in 2–3 weeks, but fatigue may persist for weeks or months. Mild to moderate elevation of the serum level of certain enzymes released from damaged liver cells can continue from months to years for patients who do not clear the virus. These enzymes include serum alanine and aspartate aminotransferases and alkaline phosphatase.

The diagnosis of hepatitis B infection depends on finding **components of virus** or **specific antibodies** in the blood (Table 41.4). Assays that detect the presence of either circulating HB_sAg, HB_eAg, and DNA polymerase, or antibodies against these antigens, are widely available. This extensive diagnostic armamentarium is usually not required but it permits a detailed determination of the stages of hepatitis B. For example, if HB_sAg, but not HB_eAg, is detected chronically in Mr. P.'s serum, we expect a mild, inapparent, nonprogressive infection that is relatively noncontagious. Were HB_eAg and polymerase to persist in his circulation (reflecting release into the circulation of complete infectious particles), Mr. P. would be relatively more contagious (Fig. 41.6 and Table 41.4).

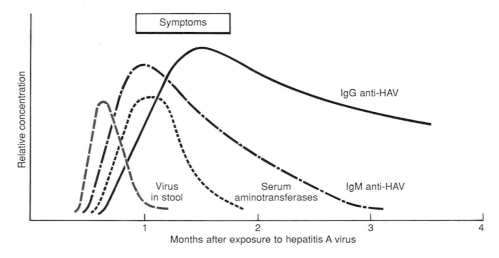

Figure 41.4.   Typical course of acute hepatitis A virus (HAV) infection.

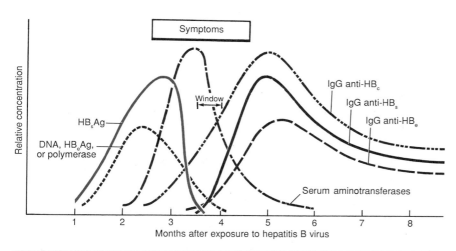

Figure 41.5. Typical course of acute hepatitis B virus infection. Note the "window" of time in which HB$_s$Ag is no longer found, but IgG anti-HB$_s$ has not yet developed in detectable levels.

Table 41.4. Interpretation of Serologic Assays for Hepatitis B Virus (HBV)

HB$_s$Ag	HB$_e$AG	Anti-HB$_c$	Anti-HB$_e$	Anti-HB$_s$	Interpretation
Neg	Neg	Neg	Neg	Neg	No evidence of present or past HBV infection
Pos	Neg	Neg	Neg	Neg	Incubation period of HBV
Pos	Pos	Pos	Neg	Neg	Early in acute infection with HBV or chronic HBV infection with high infectivity
Pos	Neg	Pos	Pos	Neg	Later in acute infection, or chronic HBV infection with lower infectivity

Hepatitis A virus is shed in the stool late in the incubation period of the infection and persists briefly after the onset of symptoms (Fig. 41.4). There are, however, no convenient assays for hepatitis A virus in the stool or blood. For this reason, the laboratory resorts to the detection of IgM or IgG antibodies to this virus. These antibodies are already present at the onset of symptoms.

Hepatitis C virus infection is also indistinguishable clinically from type A or type B hepatitis. Typically, the patient has constitutional symptoms and jaundice for 2–3 weeks, but 30–60% of all cases suffer from a mild, chronic infection that spontaneously goes through periods of exacerbation with corresponding fluctuations in the serum aminotransferase levels. Hepatitis C virus is present at low levels acutely and chronically in the bloodstream. The chronically infected patients not only risk transmitting the disease but are also subject to progressive hepatocellular damage with evolution of cirrhosis and hepatocellular carcinoma over many decades.

Acute hepatitis D infection is recognized by the presence of Δ antigen in the liver and of hepatitis B antigens in the circulation, and subsequently by emergence of antibodies to Δ antigen (Fig. 41.7). In individuals with mixed chronic infections with hepatitis B and D, high titers of IgM and IgG antibodies to the Δ agent persist.

HOW CAN HEPATITIS BE PREVENTED?

Although α-interferon has some effect on the course of chronic hepatitis, there is **no clearly effective treatment** for acute viral hepatitis;

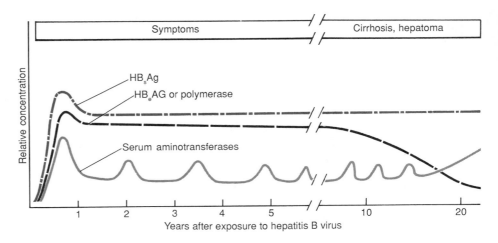

Figure 41.6. **Typical course of chronic hepatitis B virus infection.** After years of undulating symptoms and aminotransferase levels, the circulating Dane particle activity, as reflected in levels of viral DNA, HB_eAg or polymerase may fall or even disappear but cirrhosis and, ultimately, hepatoma may still evolve.

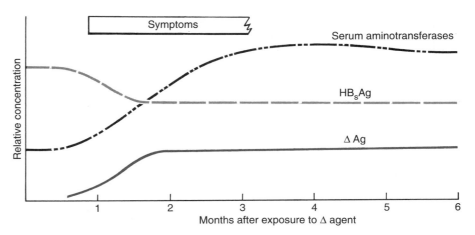

Figure 41.7. **Course of chronic hepatitis B infection exacerbated by infection with the hepatitis D or Δ (delta) agent.** The aminotransferases may rise and the liver histology may shift from that of a chronic persistent to chronic active hepatitis.

thus, preventive measures are of paramount importance. An experimental vaccine for hepatitis A virus has been developed from virus grown in marmoset cell cultures. However, because this virus generally causes low morbidity and mortality, it is unclear if such a vaccine would be utilized widely. Currently, the best preventive strategy against hepatitis A is adequate sanitation and sewage treatment. Those exposed may be treated with immune serum globulin. It has been known for several decades that **globulin administration**, when given as soon as possible, either prevents or reduces the severity of these infections. Immune globulin is also recommended for passive immunization of persons at risk of hepatitis B, namely, intravenous drug users, such as Mr. P., and sexual contacts, such as his girlfriend.

A safe, effective, and widely available **vaccine for hepatitis B** contains surface antigen purified from the pooled sera of chronically infected donors. A newer form of the hepatitis B vaccine contains hepatitis B surface antigen that has been produced in a recombinant yeast vector containing the cloned viral gene. This was the first recombinant DNA-generated vaccine to be used in people.

No vaccines are available for hepatitis C or E, or for hepatitis D (although vaccination for hepatitis B should protect against hepatitis D infection), and the efficacy of immune serum globulin for these infections is unproven.

Any individual who recalls an episode of hepatitis or proves positive for prior infection with hepatitis B or C is ineligible to donate blood. Because Mr. P. has hepatitis B, an agent proven to circulate chronically and to be transmissible by blood products, this admonition must be made known to him. Cases of transfusion-associated hepatitis have been reduced significantly by the use of volunteer donor blood and by universal screening of blood donors for HB$_s$Ag and antibodies to hepatitis C.

CONCLUSIONS

Regarding the case of hepatitis in Mr. P., the key to his diagnosis included his history of intravenous drug use, apparent icterus, elevated aminotransferases, and detection of hepatitis B surface antigen in his serum. The role of contaminated needles was suspected because careful studies have proven that the small amount of blood conveyed when needles are shared is adequate to transmit hepatitis B. Mr. P.'s icterus and other symptoms resulted directly from damage to his liver inflicted by the infection and the immune responses to it. Other than counseling regarding drug use and risk of transmitting hepatitis through needles and unprotected intercourse, there is no treatment available or recommended for Mr. P.

The complex of diseases called viral hepatitis is caused by a number of viruses (A-E) that differ greatly in replicative strategies and epidemiology. There is considerable overlap in the clinical manifestations of the diseases caused by the various agents. Their time course ranges from acute to chronic, and their severity from asymptomatic to chronic debilitating and even life threatening. Hepatitis B tends to cause greater liver damage, probably because this infection activates cytotoxic immune mechanisms. Hepatitis A virus produces greater direct damage to liver cells but the overall extent of injury to the liver is often more limited in this disease than in hepatitis B. Hepatitis C is clinically indistinguishable from hepatitis A or B, but most frequently results in chronic infections.

The various viral hepatitides differ significantly in their mode of acquisition. Hepatitis A is usually acquired by the ingestion of fecally contaminated food; hepatitis B is conveyed by the intravenous or sexual routes, and may be transmitted to neonates during the birth process. Hepatitis C virus is acquired by blood transfusions while hepatitis E is conveyed by contaminated water. Like the hepatitis B virus, the D virus is often inoculated into drug abusers via contaminated needles and syringes. The only effective vaccine available is against hepatitis B.

Self-assessment Questions

1. How do the acute viral hepatitides differ epidemiologically?

2. Discuss the replication cycle of hepatitis B virus. In what ways is this unusual? Why is this hard to study? Can you think of ways to facilitate such investigations?

3. How do hepatitis A and hepatitis B differ in the way they cause tissue damage?

4. Discuss the problems associated with the differential diagnosis of the viral hepatitides.

5. What are the distinguishing features of hepatitis C virus . . . of D virus?

6. Discuss the prophylactic measures available for the viral hepatitides.

SUGGESTED READING

Hollinger FB, Lemon SM, Margolis H, eds. Proceedings of the 1990 international symposium on viral hepatitis and liver disease: contemporary issues and future prospects. Baltimore: Williams & Wilkins, 1991.

Hoofnagle JH, Di Bisceglie AM. Antiviral therapy of viral hepatitis. In: Galasso GJ, Whitley RJ, Meigan TC, eds. Antiviral agents and viral diseases of man. New York: Raven Press Limited, 1990:415–459.

Zuckerman AJ, ed. Viral hepatitis and liver disease. New York: Alan R. Liss, Inc., 1988.

Poxviruses

42

Richard W. Moyer

The poxviruses serve to illustrate two clinically relevant points. First, smallpox is the only known disease to have been eradicated from the earth by mankind and is an example of what the dedicated efforts of human beings can achieve. Second, with the eradication of smallpox, it could be thought that there is little, if any, justification for further study of these viruses, since the smallpox virus no longer exists in the wild and poses no danger to human populations. Paradoxically, close relatives of the smallpox virus have emerged as prime candidates for the construction of live recombinant viral vaccines and offer the hope of protection against a wide variety of other diseases.

CASE

To illustrate a case of smallpox, we must go back to before 1977 (the year the last case was reported), to a developing country where the disease was endemic. A., a 21-year-old living in a small town in Somalia, arose in the morning feeling dreadful. He had a high fever, backache, and a splitting headache. He ate a little breakfast but vomited shortly after finishing it. He wondered if his condition had anything to do with a visit about 10 days ago to his seriously ill cousin, who died shortly thereafter. He steadily deteriorated; his throat became sore and he had a rash with discrete raised lesions. His parents, recognized the all too familiar early symptoms of smallpox and, alarmed, took him to the local hospital.

They were shocked by the condition of the other patients whose room he would soon share. Some were covered with pustules ("pocks"), some of which oozed fluid and emitted a peculiar foul odor. Many had nostrils and lips glued together from the discharge. The pus from burst vesicles soaked through the bedsheets and formed thick yellowish scabs and crusts on the skin. When the pulse of these patients was taken, their skin remained attached to the fingers of the medical personnel. Very few could speak, their tongues being swollen and misshapen, and many had trouble breathing. Swallowing was difficult and so painful that many patients refused nourishment and, in spite of agonizing thirst, refused all fluids. Wails and groans filled the room. Some patients lay there dull and unresponsive, and no longer shook off the persistent flies that lit on their purulent eyelids and swarmed over the inflamed areas of the skin. A. knew that a similar fate awaited him and that there was a good possibility he would follow his cousin to an early death.

HISTORY AND ERADICATION OF SMALLPOX

Smallpox or variola is an ancient disease of humanity. Social and political behavior were profoundly influenced by this disease, which was widespread throughout the world. Two centuries ago, this disease was endemic in parts of Europe and North America. Everyone was at risk, and only those who had had the disease and survived could be counted on to live to a reasonable age. The more severe form of the disease,

variola major, had a mortality rate of 25%, but a milder form, **variola minor** or alastrim resulted in a 1% case fatality rate. Smallpox (so called to differentiate it from the "large pox," or syphilis) was known to all, for its clinical signs were both horrible and characteristic. Survivors were generally scarred for life, regenerating human reminders that new cases were possible at any time. Since the early 1800s, smallpox could be controlled by vaccination, a procedure popularized by the English physician Edward Jenner, who remembered from his youth that cowgirls who had contracted cowpox did not contract smallpox. The virus of cowpox causes a mild disease in people, but induces an immune response sufficiently cross-reactive to prevent the multiplication of the related variola virus. By the beginning of this century, antismallpox vaccination became mandatory in the developed countries in the world. Because the disease has been eradicated, vaccination is no longer practiced. Students can still see for themselves how widespread this procedure was because of the characteristic vaccination scar visible on the arm or thigh of nearly anyone over 30 years of age.

Worldwide smallpox eradication was achieved by a vaccination campaign carried out by the World Health Organization. The vaccine used consists of a virus different from the original cowpox virus used by Jenner. This virus, now called the **vaccinia virus**, has an uncertain origin and may well be an attenuated smallpox virus. The vaccine is administered by puncturing the skin and allowing the virus to enter and to multiply locally. The vaccine virus is very stable, allowing the vaccine to be distributed to distant areas around the world that lack refrigeration. In rare cases, the vaccine virus causes complications, some of them serious in nature.

The smallpox vaccination campaign led, literally, to tracking down every last remaining case of smallpox and vaccinating all the contacts. The last known case of the disease was reported in Somalia in 1977. Since then, two laboratory workers in England died from accidental exposure to the virus. The stock of smallpox virus is now kept under conditions of high security in only a few laboratories in the world.

Smallpox eradication represents as much a triumph of universal motivation, transcending political and social ideology, as a medical and scientific achievement. The key features of the global eradication are summarized in Table 42.1. This history has been superbly documented in a book published by the World Health Organization entitled "Smallpox and its Eradication" (Fenner et al. Geneva: WHO, 1988).

POXVIRUSES

With smallpox eradicated, why should we worry about how this virus replicates? One reason is that the smallpox virus belong to a unique group of viruses that tell us a great deal about replication strategies in general. In addition, the vaccinia virus is being used for the production of new live vaccines to be used in the control of many other infectious diseases.

The **poxviruses** are a large group of related agents responsible for a variety of diseases in humans, animals and insects, of which smallpox, or variola, is the most notorious (Table 42.2). These are the **largest of the animal viruses**, overlapping in size with the smaller bacteria (chlamydiae and mycoplasmas), and are barely visible under the light microscope. Poxviruses are "brick-like" structures with two membrane layers surrounding a nucleoprotein DNA core. The 200-kilobase double-stranded viral DNA is the **largest genome** among animal vi-

Table 42.1. Factors Involved in the Eradication of Smallpox

1. The disease is severe and clearly worthy of eradication.
2. Smallpox is strictly a human disease with no known animal or inanimate reservoirs. The outcome for an infected individual was either death or permanent recovery. Subclinical or persistent infections were virtually unknown. Individuals who recover are permanently immune.
3. Accurate diagnosis is relatively easy even by partially trained personnel; clinical features were distinctive and easy to recognize. The scarring of infected individuals leaves a record of the disease.
4. The disease spreads rather slowly. Generally it takes 2–3 weeks between generation of cases.
5. All strains of variola virus are indistinguishable antigenically. There was only one worldwide serotype.
6. The virus is relatively resistant to inactivation by physical and chemical agents. This facilitated the development of freeze-dried vaccine, essential for use in hot, rural, undeveloped countries with unreliable refrigeration facilities. Inexpensive vaccination can be carried out by unskilled medical personnel.
7. The worldwide unification of people of various political persuasions was focused toward the common goal.

Table 42.2. Some of the Principal Poxviruses That Affect Humans

Name	Characteristics
Variola (smallpox)	Causes smallpox in humans
Vaccinia (cowpox)	Causes cowpox and a self-limiting occupational disease in humans
Miller's nodules virus (paravaccinia)	Causes vesicular lesions different from those of cowpox; the lesions do not become pustular
Monkeypox	Causes a zoonotic disease indistinguishable from smallpox
Tanapox virus	Causes epidemics of a febrile illness with one or two pock-like lesions; may be related to that of monkeypox
Molluscum contagiosum virus	Causes an uncommon skin proliferative disease, mainly in children
Contagious pustular dermatitis virus (ORF)	Sheep disease that causes a rare occupational disease in humans, usually consisting of a single lesion on a finger

ruses and is capable of encoding approximately 200 proteins. When visualized in cross-section under electron microscope, the core is a concave structure delineated by two oval structures referred to as lateral bodies, whose function is unknown.

The DNA of these viruses has a special structural feature; the two strands are covalently joined at the ends to form **telomeric** structures, like those found at the ends of eukaryotic chromosomes. This property explains the ability of the DNA to reanneal rapidly or "snap-back" upon denaturation, as complete separation of the strands is prevented because they are physically joined.

A second unique feature of these viruses is that they are the **only known DNA viruses that replicate and develop totally within the cytoplasm.** An overview of their replication strategy is shown in Figure 42.1. The uncoating of the virions takes place in **two stages**, befitting their double-membrane structure. Upon entry into a susceptible cell, an **initial uncoating** by host enzymes releases a transcriptionally active viral core. This core is responsible for the synthesis of **early mRNAs** that are translated into proteins responsible for more extensive breakdown of the core. The **final uncoating** liberates the DNA and allows it to serve as a template both for replication and for the expression of additional genes, including those for structural proteins. DNA replica-

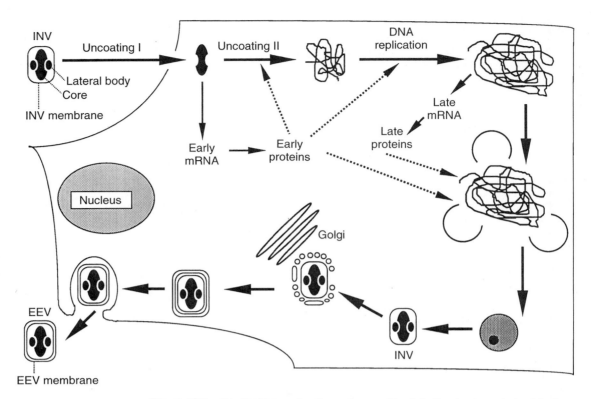

Figure 42.1. Replication cycle of poxviruses. The infection is characterized by two stages of uncoating. The first is mediated by the cell; the second is mediated by viral encoded products. Viral DNA replication begins about 2–5 hours after infection. Morphogenesis begins at about 4 hours and the cycle is complete at 12–24 hours after infection. The ratio of intracellular naked virus (*INV*) to that of extracellular enveloped virus (*EEV*) is quite variable and dependent on both the virus strain and the host cell.

tion results in the formation of unique, large, dense, DNA-containing inclusion bodies referred to as **virosomes** or viral **"factories."** Following DNA replication, the complex process of virion assembly begins, resulting in the formation of infectious, so-called **intracellular naked virus (INV)** not normally released from infected cells. Additional maturation mediated by the Golgi apparatus leads to envelopment of **INV** within the second membrane, and exit from the cell to form infectious **extracellular enveloped virus (EEV). EEV** is thought to be involved in cell-to-cell spread of the viruses. The virus and some intermediates in the assembly process are shown in Figure 42.2.

A consequence of replication in the cytoplasm is that these viruses cannot depend on the host machinery, which is located in the nucleus, but must encode many if not all the enzymes necessary for replication and transcription of their genes. Indeed, poxvirus DNA replication can take place in enucleated host cells. The cytoplasmic location requires that virus-encoded enzymes necessary for the transcription of prereplicative (early) viral genes be packaged within the virions. Without such enzymes, there would be no obvious way to initiate viral gene expression upon infection. Because transcriptional enzymes are present within the virion, permeabilization of purified virions leads to the synthesis of completely functional translatable mRNAs in the presence of appropriate substrates. Note that, for viruses, the poxviruses carry an impressive array of macromolecular biosyntheses. They do require some host proteins (the large subunit of RNA polymerase II has been suggested), but the main biosynthetic components they lack are the ribosomes. Does the complexity of poxviruses suggest that a virus could evolve into a cellular form of life? Perhaps, but this cannot be the sole origin of cellular life because this path could not be taken without earlier cells serving as the host for the virus.

POXVIRUS PATHOGENESIS

Smallpox is acquired from inhalation. The virus first multiplies near this portal of entry, in the epithelial cells of the upper respiratory tract. The virus then spreads via the **bloodstream** to many internal tissues and organs, where it undergoes extensive multiplication. Large amounts of virus then re-enter the bloodstream, generating a **second viremia** that leads to focal infections of the skin, kidneys, lungs, intestines, and other organs including, occasionally, the brain. As with many other systemic viral infections, **the symptoms of disease only become noticeable after the virus has spread in the body and is present in high titers**. Localization in the skin is followed by multiplication in the epithelial cells leading eventually to the characteristic skin eruption. Beginning as a rash, the lesions progress to the pus-filled pustules by the second week from onset of symptoms. This purulent reaction is not due to secondary bacterial infection because the contents of the lesions are usually sterile.

The severity of the symptoms in advanced cases of smallpox may be attributed, in part, to toxic properties of the virus itself, which multiplies rapidly and accumulates in large numbers. A cell-mediated immune reaction also appears to play an important role in the disease because rabbits rendered immunodeficient do not form pustules although viral multiplication is not inhibited.

POXVIRUSES AS LIVE VIRAL VACCINES

Almost at the same time that smallpox was certified by the World Health Organization as being eradicated, the potential of using relatives of the variola virus (vaccinia, and members of other poxvirus genera) as candidates for recombinant live viral vaccines against other pathogens was appreciated. The reasoning behind the idea is straightforward. In the smallpox eradication program, vaccinia virus was employed as an effective live vaccine immunogen to generate long-term protective immunity against smallpox. Many data were collected during the smallpox eradication program regarding both the efficacy and the probability of complications caused by this virus in human populations. It was reasoned that it should be possible to employ the tools of modern molecular biology to splice foreign gene or genes within the relatively innocuous vaccinia virus genome. If such a virus were then used to "vaccinate" an individual, one should expect not only long-term immunity against smallpox but against other diseases as well.

A generic example of the construction of recombinant live vaccines is shown in Figure 42.3. It is possible to consider using a single recombinant poxvirus containing a variety of antigens to immunize against a number of pathogens. The technology also allows constructing vaccines for domestic animals with the potential of not only improving the human food chain but possibly eliminating the animal reservoirs of zoonoses that are difficult to control. The application of these vaccines to animal populations has another attractive dimension because these viruses are sufficiently stable to be incorporated into oral baits, suggesting that their use might be extended to wild animal populations. At present, many potential vaccine constructions based on the principles outlined here are being developed and tested.

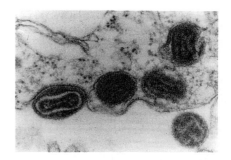

Figure 42.2. Electron micrograph showing vaccinia virions in various stages of assembly and release from the cell.

Figure 42.3. Method for construction of live, poxvirus-recombinant vaccines expressing foreign antigens. A DNA fragment from the poxvirus, encoding a nonessential gene (e.g., thymidine kinase or *TK*) is cloned into a bacterial plasmid. Within the coding region of that gene, a poxvirus transcription regulatory signal (promoter) is spliced next to a cloning site that can be manipulated easily. DNA containing the coding region of the foreign gene is then inserted "downstream" and adjacent to the poxvirus promoter. Coinfection of a susceptible host cell with wild-type vaccinia virus and the plasmid containing the foreign gene flanked by the two segments of the interrupted viral gene leads to "gene replacement" of the wild-type gene in the virus by the foreign gene. This replacement takes place via homologous recombination between the two "arms" of the disrupted gene of the plasmid and the wild-type gene of the virus. If the viral gene chosen for the insertion of the viral gene is thymidine kinase, insertion of the foreign gene leads to conversion of the virus to the thymidine kinase-negative phenotype.

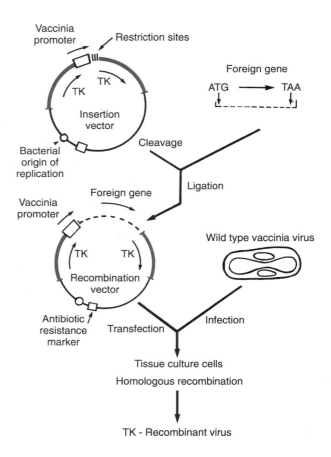

Self-assessment Questions

1. Human populations are no longer immunized against smallpox. What risks do you think this may involve?

2. Are there potential dangers in using recombinant poxvirus vaccines as general immunogens in humans and/or animals?

3. Assuming that the appropriate vaccinia-based recombinant vaccines are available, would you suggest that **AIDS** sufferers be vaccinated against opportunistic infections using recombinant live poxvirus-based vaccines?

4. What are the reasons that poxvirus-based recombinant vaccines are particularly attractive for use in developing countries?

5. Based on the lessons of the smallpox eradication program, what other diseases, based on biological considerations, might be plausibly targeted for worldwide eradication?

SUGGESTED READING

Buller RML, Palumbo GJ. Poxvirus pathogenesis. Microbiol Rev 1991; 55:80–122.

Fenner F, Henderson DA, Arita I, Jezek Z, Ladnyi ID. Smallpox and its eradication. Geneva, Switzerland: World Health Organization, 1988:1460 pp.

Fenner F, Wittek R, Dumbell KR. The orthopoxviruses. New York: Academic Press, 1989:432 pp.

Moyer RW, Turner PC, eds. Poxviruses. Current topics in microbiology and immunology. New York: Springer-Verlag, 1990:163, 211 pp.

Strategies to Combat Viral Infections

43

Stephen E. Straus

"There is always some little thing that is too big for us."
Don Marquis (in *Archy and Mehitabel*)

The key to successful prevention and therapy of viral diseases is antiviral specificity. The methods employed must impair the ability of a virus to replicate and to spread while doing little to the host cells themselves. This chapter deals with some strategies for combating viral infections in people that have shown promise. The emphasis is on antiviral drugs, with some initial discussion of immunoglobulins and interferons as ways of passively augmenting immune responses. **Vaccines are historically the most effective and important means of controlling viral infections; vaccines are reviewed elsewhere in the context of specific infections and, in a general way, in Chapter 44.**

Over the past 50 years, the achievements with drugs effective against bacteria, and to a lesser extent, against fungi and animal parasites, led to the optimistic assumption that similar chemotherapeutic strategies could be successfully exploited for viruses as well. A key question is, do the facts meet these expectations?

Antiviral drugs have been sought since the early days of eukaryotic cell virology. Thousands of compounds have been randomly screened against viruses in many taxonomic groups. Many substances were found to inhibit virus replication, but mostly because they were toxic to the host cells themselves. It became increasingly clear that virus growth is inextricably tied to host cell processes. The emerging science of animal virology revealed only few points at which one could safely sever the Gordian knots that link viruses and their hosts. Skepticism replaced optimism about the likelihood of obtaining safe and effective antiviral agents.

During the past decade, enthusiasm has been restored. This has resulted from the sophisticated elucidation of biochemical targets at which viral replication may be impaired, and more directly, from clear demonstrations that some drugs are safe and effective, at least for a few viruses.

This chapter addresses a variety of strategies by which virus replication can be inhibited, and summarizes a series of successful applications to human viral disease.

PHYSICAL AND CHEMICAL APPROACHES

The most obvious approach to treating viral infections is to block the infectivity of the offending agent. This is easy to do in the laboratory because many viruses are fragile and easily disrupted. A temperature of 50°C, mild detergent, solvents, chelating agents, and numerous other chemical and physical processes all destroy viral infectivity. This results in disinfection, but obviously not in therapeutic options. Nevertheless, such measures can be useful to prevent acquisition of infection. Studies have proven that, for instance, transmission of the viruses of the common cold by direct contact can be diminished by washing hands or by using iodine-impregnated facial tissues.

IMMUNOGLOBULINS

Immunological approaches to blocking viral infectivity are more practical and some are appropriate and effective in humans. **Specific antisera** can be raised in animals that, when mixed with viruses, will neutralize viral infectivity. Immune globulins pooled from human sera are commercially available for prophylaxis and therapeutic management of several infections (Table 43.1).

There are, however, both real and theoretical limitations to the use of immune globulins for managing human viral diseases. **First**, many **sera are not readily available** in large amounts nor do they have adequate antiviral antibody titers. The development of human monoclonal antibody technology provides a way to circumvent this limitation. **Second, sera may be contaminated** with viruses or other infectious agents. The methods by which the serum immunoglobulins are purified and stabilized kill many known agents, but unknown or nonconventional viruses may resist the process. A classic example of this type of problem occurred during World War II. Several thousand soldiers in the U.S. Army developed infectious hepatitis after receiving a yellow fever vaccine that had been stabilized by the addition of contaminated human serum. **Third**, the successful prophylactic use of these sera depends on **early recognition** of exposure. Later in the incubation period of virus infections sera are of no practical value. Chickenpox represents a practical situation in which the timing of immunoglobulin prophylaxis is critical. Human immunoglobulin pooled from patients recovering from

Table 43.1. Use of Human Immune Serum Globulins for Postexposure Prophylaxis of Virus Infections

Infection	Preparation	Indication
Measles	Pooled human globulin	Susceptible immunodeficient patients
Poliovirus	Pooled human globulin	Susceptibles
Varicella	Varicella zoster human immune globulin	Susceptible immunodeficient pregnant patients
Rabies	Rabies human immune globulin	All cases
Smallpox	Vaccinia human immune globulin	Susceptibles
Hepatitis A virus	Pooled human globulin	All susceptibles
Hepatitis B virus	Pooled human globulin	All susceptibles, high-risk susceptibles
	Hepatitis B human immune globulin	
Cytomegalovirus[a]	CMV human immune globulin	Susceptible transplant patients
Vaccinia	Vaccinia human immune globulin	Progressive infection
Echoviruses	Pooled human globulin	Chronic myositis or meningoencephalitis
Arenaviruses	Lassa human immune plasma	Lassa fever
	Junin human immune plasma	Argentinean hemorrhagic fever
	Machupo human immune plasma	Bolivian hemorrhagic fever
Hantaan virus	Hantaan human immune plasma	Korean hemorrhagic fever
Respiratory syncytial virus	Pooled human globulin	Bronchiolitis, pneumonia

[a]Experimental

zoster (shingles) infection is effective in preventing severe varicella (chickenpox). A series of clinical studies have proved that the antisera can prevent infection reliably only if they are administered within the first 3–4 days after exposure.

Other imaginative immunoglobulin-based approaches to management of viral infections are being developed. Theoretically, monoclonal antibodies directed at the cellular receptor for a virus could sterically hinder virus binding. Unfortunately, the nature of the receptor is not known for many viruses, making it impossible to produce the desired monoclonal antibodies since this requires screening a large number of hybridoma cells with a suitable antigen. Without the antigen, this methodology cannot be used. On the other hand, an immediately applicable case is that of HIV, where the cellular receptor is known to be the CD_4 antigen, for which monoclonal antibodies already exist. Treatment with anti-CD_4 antibody is now undergoing clinical testing to determine its ability to prevent the growth and spread of the AIDS retrovirus.

Conventional immunoprophylactic and immunotherapeutic interventions all require an extracellular phase of virus infection. Indeed, most viral infections are initiated by extracellular attachment of free virus. Once the infection is established, however, the therapeutic effects of immunoglobulins are limited to those viruses that freely traverse the extracellular space to infect neighboring or distant cells. The enteroviruses are clear examples (Chapter 31). Immunoglobulins provide effective therapy for some enterovirus infections, such as the serious but rare form of enteroviral encephalitis that develops in patients with agammaglobulinemia. In contrast, infections with herpesviruses, which typically spread directly from cell to cell, cannot be ameliorated by specific immunoglobulins.

A particular limitation of immunoglobulin is its ability to achieve adequate concentration at **mucosal surfaces**. A creative means of bypassing this problem is to deliver the immunoglobulin as an aerosol for pulmonary infections, such as the bronchiolitis and pneumonia associated with respiratory syncytial virus. Studies in experimentally infected cotton rats showed that equivalent results could be achieved in treatment of respiratory syncytial virus infection with large quantities of parenteral immunoglobulin or very small quantities of globulin delivered by aerosol. Recent trials in infants are similarly encouraging.

INHIBITION OF VIRUS REPLICATION

Antiviral Drugs

For most viral infections, exposure cannot be determined soon enough to permit effective immunoprophylaxis. Thus, a more practical and flexible approach is treatment of infected individuals with substances that inhibit the viruses at a specific point in the viral replicative cycle. A review of the relevant discussion of viral replication in Chapter 30 would be appropriate at this point.

Every step and every biochemical reaction involved in virus replication is conceivably a target for intervention. Inhibition of processes that depend on cellular metabolic pools, energy sources, and enzymes, however, is likely to result in unacceptable cell toxicity. It is easy to see why no "penicillin" has yet been discovered for viruses. Fortunately, some steps in virus replication differ sufficiently from the cellular ones; for instance, they can be inhibited with little or no impact on the host cell. Examples of such specific processes include penetration or uncoating of the virus, synthesis of viral enzymes necessary for viral nucleic acid synthesis, translation, modification, or assembly of viral proteins, and release of the virus from the cell. Figure 43.1 shows the steps in an idealized virus growth cycle where various agents have been found to act.

There are two points to be aware of in considering the current state of antiviral drug development. **First**, most compounds available have very **narrow spectra of activity**. Very few useful substances inhibit more than one class of viruses. **The reason for this may lie in the enormous diversity of viral structures and replicative strategies.** In contrast, it is not surprising that antibacterial drugs can have broad activity spectra. Excepting for differences in the cell envelopes, most bacteria utilize much the same replicative strategies, often different from those of eukaryotic cells. Thus, bacteria have many potential targets in common with one another.

Second, few substances that impair **virus uncoating or penetration** are available. Even worse, we have no substances that safely **inhibit virus assembly**. These early and late phases of the viral replicative processes are most dependent on the proper association of viral structural elements with cellular ones rather than on de novo synthetic events. To date, nearly all of the potentially useful antiviral substances inhibit nucleic acid synthesis. The following is a survey of some of the major compounds being investigated or in clinical use for viral infections.

INTERFERON

Interferons were the first and still are among the most extensively studied of antiviral substances. They are not synthetic drugs, but rather, they are proteins made by the body itself. The discovery of interferon by Isaacs and Lindenmann in 1957 involved a brilliant and fortuitous observation, somewhat analogous to Fleming's recognition of penicillin in moldy cultures. Isaacs was interested in studying **viral in-**

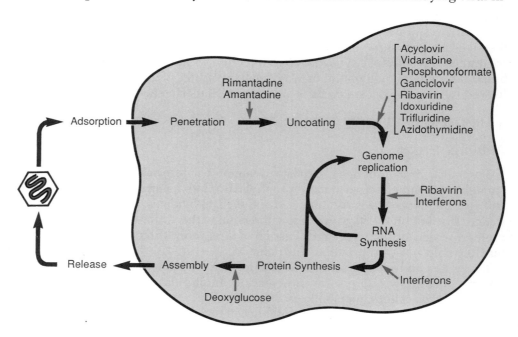

Figure 43.1.   Schematic life cycle of viruses showing the steps at which replication can be inhibited by various drugs. The *pink* area shows the intracellular space.

terference, a phenomenon still poorly understood in which infection renders a cell resistant to subsequent infection with a different virus. This property of virus-infected cells allowed, for example, the first laboratory detection of rubella virus; although this virus does not produce visible damage to cells in culture, it does render them refractory to secondary infection with other viruses that can produce cytopathic damage.

In studying viral interference, Isaacs and Lindenmann noted that resistance to viral infection could be transferred to uninfected cultures by the addition of media from infected cell cultures. The cell-free factors that mediated the transferable resistance to virus infection were found to be proteins, which they termed interferons. Two properties of interferons were quickly appreciated and led to the hope that, at last, broad-spectrum antiviral therapy may become available. **First,** interferons released from cells in response to infection by one virus provide resistance to infection by many other viruses; thus, **interferons are not virus specific. Second,** the proteins are present in extremely small amounts, indicating that they are **very potent molecules.** It was reasoned that if interferons could be purified in sufficient quantities, they would be potent therapeutic agents with a broad spectrum of activity. As natural substances, it seemed likely that they would be relatively nontoxic—although one might wonder why large amounts are not mobilized spontaneously during infections!

Today we know that earlier assumptions were largely naive and only partially correct. Large amounts of interferons can now be generated by sophisticated purification methods or by recombinant DNA technology, and their mechanisms of action, biological properties, and therapeutic potencies are finally being adequately defined. It is now known that there are **three classes** of interferons, including nearly two dozen different proteins (Table 43.2). Antiviral activity varies with each type and class of interferon. In cell culture, interferons exert their antiviral effects by inducing cells to synthesize a number of enzymes that regulate transcription and translation of viral proteins. Both in animals and humans, the impact of treatment with interferons is more complex than in cell cultures because these compounds not only inhibit viral replication but also modulate host immune responses to the infection.

Clinical trials have shown that interferons, despite their natural origin, are inherently **toxic** and cause fatigue, fever, and myalgias, and occasionally, bone marrow suppression and neurological problems. In fact, the recipients of interferons complain so frequently of **flu-like symptoms** that it can be reasonably argued that many of the constitutional complaints that attend common viral infections may result from host responses mediated by interferon.

Interferon treatment ameliorates severe varicella or zoster infections in immune-compromised hosts, delays cytomegalovirus infections in transplant recipients, and prevents reactivation of herpes

Table 43.2. Human Interferons

Current Name	Produced by	Typical Inducers
IFNα	Leukocytes	Viruses
IFNβ	Fibroblasts	Viruses
IFNγ	T cells	Antigens
		Mitogens

simplex in patients undergoing trigeminal nerve root decompression, but none of these actions is so impressive as to make interferon into the desired classic of theory.

As indicated in Chapter 41, the hepatitis B and C viruses exhibit a strong proclivity for producing chronic infections and progressive destruction of the liver. Studies in the mid-1970s showed that injections of leukocyte interferon leads to transient reductions in levels of circulating B virus. Validation of these findings of infection was not feasible, however, until the availability of essentially unlimited quantities of a recombinant human α-interferon. Up to one-third of all patients with chronic hepatitis B virus infection show reductions in virus levels in the blood and liver damage that is sustained following completion of treatment with recombinant α-interferon. With the discovery in 1989 of hepatitis C virus came the opportunity to examine similar evidence of improvement of hepatitis. Recombinant α-interferon proved even more beneficial for that setting. It is now licensed for prolonged treatment of both chronic hepatitis B virus and hepatitis C virus infections.

Why do interferons not show more dramatic clinical activity for many other viruses? Inadequate dosage cannot explain their limitations because circulating levels of the newer recombinant interferon preparations can exceed those observed in untreated infections. Here are some possible reasons why interferons may not be the hoped-for wonder drugs. First, the production of different interferons may vary in response to different viruses. In a given infection, the antiviral activity achieved may depend on the relative amount of each interferon expressed at a particular site. This may not be precisely duplicated by exogenous administration. Second, interferons exhibit their most potent activity against a number of RNA viruses that do not cause serious human disease.

Even with these limitations it should be recognized that interferons play other therapeutic roles, with some effectiveness against certain animal parasites and particular types of cancer. Among other viral infections, preliminary data suggest that interferon speeds the resolution of certain papillomavirus infections (see Chapter 39). Several trials of topical and systemic interferon are under way for a number of these infections. Studies have already led to licensing of recombinant α-interferon for intralesional treatment of refractory anogenital warts.

AMANTADINE

Amantadine (l-adamantanamine hydrochloride) and its analog, rimantadine (a-methyl-adamantanamine hydrochloride) are primary symmetrical amines (Fig. 43.2 and Table 43.3) whose chemical structures give no clues as to the basis for their antiviral activities. They resemble nothing else known to exist in biological systems. Both compounds are potent inhibitors of the replication of **influenza A virus**. Their precise mechanisms of action are still being debated. Some data indicate that these compounds block the primary transcription of viral messages. More compelling data suggest that the site of action is earlier and results in the inhibition of viral uncoating. Amantadine has been found to be selectively concentrated in lysosomes and, at high concentrations, raises intralysosomal pH. This may impair the lysosome-mediated activation of influenza hemagglutinin that is required for penetration of the viral nucleocapsid into the cytoplasm and its subsequent uncoating. However, the drug is more effective at lower

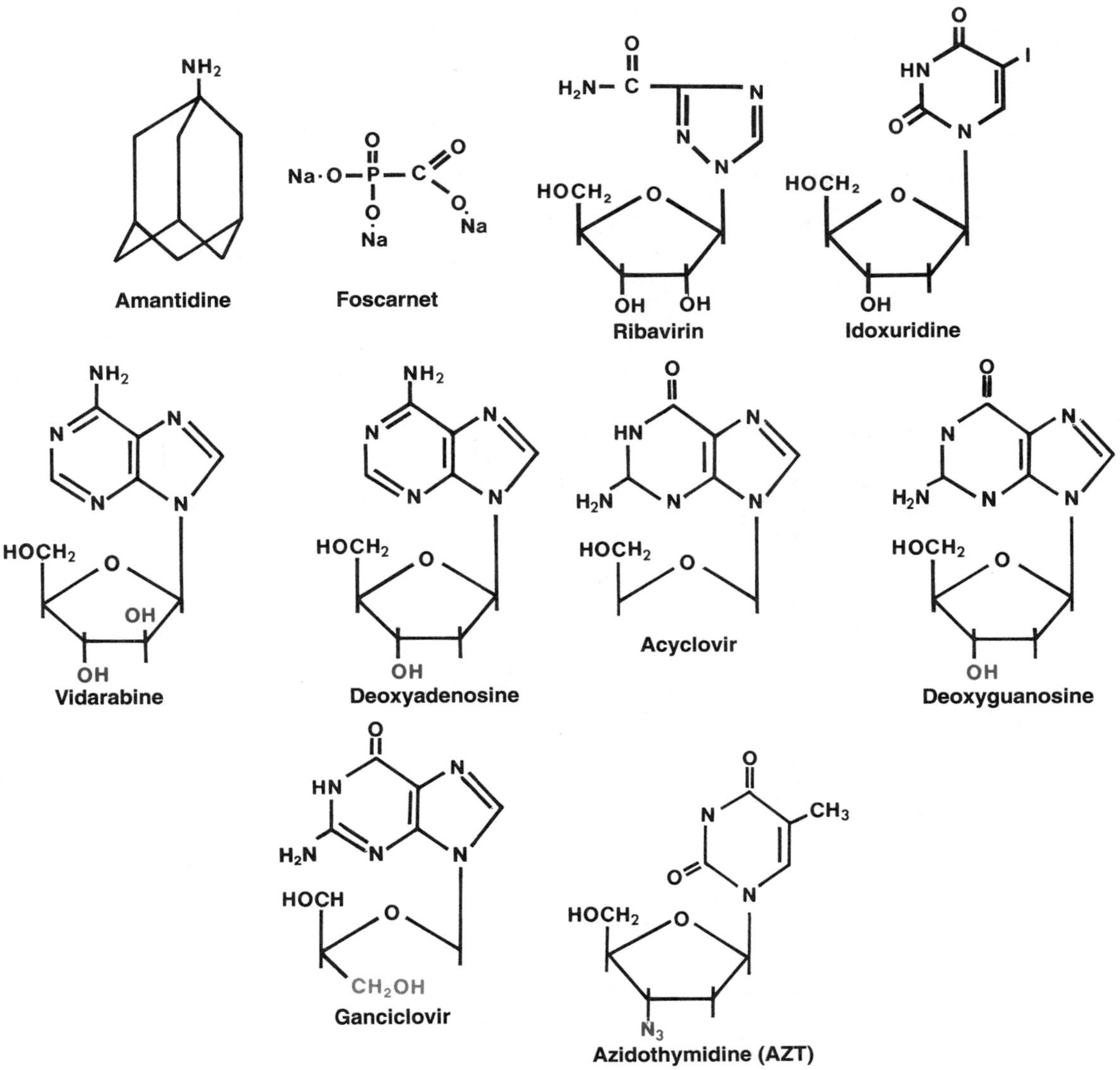

Figure 43.2. Structures of clinically useful antiviral chemotherapeutic agents.

concentrations than those required to raise the intralysosomal pH. Thus, its mode of action remains obscure.

The anti-influenzal activity of amantadine was first reported in 1961 but enthusiasm for its clinical activity was low. The compound was nearly abandoned but for the fortuitous observation that it is extremely beneficial for controlling the disordered motor activity in Parkinsonism. This may be only a therapeutic coincidence and does not necessarily suggest an association between Parkinsonism and viral infections.

Controlled studies of laboratory-induced or naturally occurring influenza A infections demonstrated that amantadine and rimantadine exert significant prophylactic and therapeutic effects. Optimum use of these drugs is when the encounter with influenza A can be predicted, such as during epidemics. When treatment is initiated before exposure to the virus, these drugs prevent clinical disease in over three-fourths of cases. For patients whose treatment is begun shortly after the first signs of influenza A infection become apparent, the reduction in severity of symptoms is about 50%.

Table 43.3. Some Clinically Useful Antiviral Drugs

Drug	Route	Clinical Indications	Side Effects
Amantadine	Oral	Prevention and treatment of influenza A infections	Insomnia, confusion
Ribavirin	Aerosol	Treatment of respiratory syncytial virus pneumonia	
Idoxuridine	Ophthalmic ointment	Herpes simplex keratoconjunctivitis	
Vidarabine	Intravenous	Life-threatening herpes simplex infections in neonate	Vomiting, seizures, coma, bone marrow suppression
Acyclovir	Topical ointment	Primary genital herpes, mucocutaneous herpes simplex infections in compromised host	
	Oral	Treatment and suppression of primary and recurrent genital herpes, mucocutaneous herpes simplex infections in compromised host, zoster in normal or compromised host	Mild nausea
	Intravenous	Life-threatening herpes simplex infections in neonates, compromised host, or with encephalitis, varicella, or zoster in compromised host	Renal failure, seizures, coma
Ganciclovir	Intravenous	Treatment and suppression of sight or life-threatening cytomegalovirus infections in AIDS and some transplant recipients	Marked bone marrow suppression
Foscarnet	Intravenous	Treatment of acyclovir-resistant herpes simplex and varicella zoster infections in compromised host, treatment and suppression of cytomegalovirus retinitis in AIDS	Renal failure, coma
Zidovudine	Oral	Treatment and suppression of human immunodeficiency virus disease	Bone marrow suppression
Dideoxyinosine	Oral	Treatment and suppression of human immunodeficiency virus disease refractory to zidovudine	Peripheral neuropathy, pancreatitis

Both amantadine and rimantadine are well tolerated at the therapeutic dose level. About 3–5% of amantadine recipients (but very few rimantadine recipients) report mild central nervous system reactions, including jitteriness, insomnia, and difficulty in concentrating. Recent work has shown both agents to be fundamentally similar in therapeutic and toxic potential, but rimantadine achieves lower peak blood levels.

Amantadine is recommended for the **prophylaxis** of individuals who are at increased risk of severe infection during suspected influenza A epidemics. These include the elderly and patients with chronic cardiopulmonary disease. It is also recommended that treatment be initiated in these groups at the first sign of influenza. Even taking into account the limited therapeutic value of amantadine and rimantadine, the medical community has been slow to use them widely for influenza.

RIBAVIRIN

This purine nucleoside analog (*l*-D-ribofuranosyl-1,2,4-triazole-3-carboxamide) is a relatively **broad-spectrum** antiviral agent (Fig. 43.2 and Table 43.3) meaning that, in cell culture, it inhibits some DNA viruses, including herpes simplex, and many RNA viruses, including influenza A and B, respiratory syncytial virus, parainfluenza virus, measles virus, and several arenaviruses. The mechanism of action of this drug is also controversial. Because it is an analog of **guanosine**, its phosphorylated form may inhibit the synthesis of guanosine-5′-monophosphate, upon which DNA and RNA synthesis depend. As a more circumscribed mechanism, ribavirin has been found to impair **capping** of virus-specific messenger RNA (the addition of especially methylated guanine nucleotides to the 5′ end of RNA molecules).

Ribavirin is readily available in many developing countries for the oral treatment of human virus infections despite the lack of adequate data to recommend its use. Anecdotal reports suggested that, for example, ribavirin might be effective as an oral treatment in both influenza A and influenza B infections; but unfortunately, controlled studies showed some hematological toxicity and no clear efficacy.

A novel method of administering the drug avoids its systemic toxicity and yet enhances its antiviral activity. It involves delivery of the drug directly and in high concentrations to the critical site of influenza infection, namely, the lung. Inhalation of an aerosol of ribavirin was shown to limit significantly the severity and duration of influenza A and B infection. Recent studies have proven the efficacy of this delivery system for infection with respiratory syncytial virus, which is associated with severe bronchiolitis and pneumonia in infants.

A remarkable property of ribavirin is its activity against several highly virulent arenaviruses associated with hemorrhagic fever syndromes. In monkeys infected with these agents, intravenous and oral ribavirin have proven useful. Recently, an open trial of oral ribavirin in Western Africa showed that it reduces the mortality rate from the dreaded Lassa fever.

IDOXURIDINE

In the late 1950s, a large effort was undertaken to synthesize and screen nucleoside analogs for use in cancer treatment. By-products of the program were novel compounds that were also tested for antiviral activity. Idoxuridine (5-iodo-2′-deoxyuridine) is one agent that emerged from that program and that demonstrates in vitro activity against herpes simplex virus at nontoxic concentrations (Fig. 43.2 and Table 43.3). By the early 1960s, topical application of this compound had been shown to speed the resolution of **corneal herpes**. Thus, idoxuridine became the first antiviral drug to be widely used. There was great temptation to extend its indications to other herpes simplex infections.

It soon became apparent that casual and uncontrolled trials can lead to inappropriately optimistic conclusions. For example, when idoxuridine was tried for life-threatening infections, such as herpes simplex encephalitis, early anecdotes were optimistic. In controlled trials, it was found that the drug-treated patients did no better, and possibly worse, than the placebo recipients. Idoxuridine is simply too toxic for systemic use. This study proved the necessity for placebo-controlled trials for evaluation of antiviral drugs.

Early studies with topical idoxuridine also documented that the efficacy of treatment of cutaneous herpes is limited by the ability of a drug to penetrate the skin. Dissolution of idoxuridine in a vehicle such as dimethyl sulfoxide allowed better skin penetration and improved its activity in animal models, but in human studies, the agent was still too weak to be of significant benefit.

VIDARABINE

Arabinosyl adenine (vidarabine, ara-A, 9-D-arabinofuranosyladenine) is less active against herpesviruses than idoxuridine in vitro (Fig. 43.2 and Table 43.3). However, it is much **less cytotoxic** than idoxuridine and has what is known as a significantly greater **therapeutic ratio**, meaning that the ratio between the toxic concentration of the drug to that which inhibits virus replication is much greater than 1. For idoxuridine, the ratio is about 2; for vidarabine, the ratio is about 40. Thus, effective doses of vidarabine can be given systemically with modest toxicity.

Large, well-designed controlled clinical trials have found that topical vidarabine is too weak to ameliorate oral or genital herpes infections in otherwise normal persons. Intravenously, however, vidarabine was proven to decrease the mortality of herpes simplex encephalitis and neonatal herpes simplex infections, and to lessen the morbidity of severe varicella and zoster infections in immunocompromised children and adults. These observations proved that serious human viral infections are amenable to specific therapeutic intervention. The pessimism regarding prospects for antiviral drug development began to wane.

ACYCLOVIR

Acyclovir (acycloguanosine, 9-[2-hydroxyethoxymethyl] guanine) has already supplanted vidarabine for treatment of several human herpesvirus infections (Fig. 43.2 and Table 43.3). It is the first agent approved for clinical use that resulted from a rational and directed search for antiviral compounds. This strategy is being increasingly exploited. Once we know that a compound has some activity, it can be further modified and its derivatives tested for increased activity and better pharmacological properties such as stability, solubility, or gastrointestinal absorption.

The mechanism of action of acyclovir has been well studied. Like idoxuridine and vidarabine, acyclovir is an **inhibitor of DNA polymerase**. When its activity against the cellular and viral polymerases is compared, acyclovir exhibits a therapeutic ratio that substantially exceeds that of either of the older drugs, namely, about 1000. The reason is interesting; for acyclovir to inhibit DNA polymerase, it must be phosphorylated in vitro by **thymidine kinase** (Fig. 43.3). It turns out that the herpes simplex virus encodes a thymidine kinase that has the unique property of phosphorylating acyclovir far better than does the cells' own kinase. The resulting monophosphate is then further phosphorylated by cellular enzymes to generate **acyclovir triphosphate**. This moiety inhibits the DNA polymerases of some herpesviruses because its incorporation into nascent strands of DNA blocks further replication. Viral DNA polymerase is unable to attach bases beyond the point of addition of acyclovir because the drug lacks the 3′ carbon of the sugar ring at which phosphodiester bonds link nucleosides together.

How do these biochemical mechanisms translate into acyclovir's in vitro potency for each herpesvirus? Herpes simplex virus types 1 and 2 are effectively inhibited with submicromolar concentrations of acyclovir (Table 43.4). Epstein-Barr virus and varicella zoster virus are less sensitive to the drug, whereas cytomegalovirus is not well inhibited. Why? We have only a partial answer to explain why the herpesvi-

Figure 43.3. Phosphorylation of acyclovir by thymidine kinase.

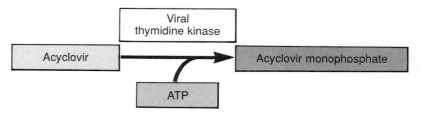

Table 43.4. Typical Concentrations of Acyclovir Required for 50% Inhibition of Herpesvirus Replication in Cell Culture

Virus	µg/ml
Herpes simplex 1	0.1
Herpes simplex 2	0.3
Varicella zoster virus	3
Epstein-Barr virus	3
Cytomegalovirus	>40

ruses vary in their sensitivity to this compound. We know that the polymerase of each virus differs in the degree to which it substitutes acyclovir triphosphate for the natural substrate guanosine triphosphate. Cytomegalovirus does not encode its own thymidine kinase and inhibitory concentrations of acyclovir triphosphate cannot be generated in cytomegalovirus-infected cells.

The clinical response to acyclovir therapy of patients has closely paralleled these in vitro results. The most significant benefits accrue in patients with herpes simplex virus infections. Clinical responses to acyclovir therapy are also seen in patients with varicella and zoster infections. Acyclovir has not reproducibly helped in alleviating cytomegalovirus infections.

The greatest benefit from acyclovir comes from treatment of prolonged or severe mucocutaneous herpes simplex virus infections. These include the first infections of normal patients or any infection of immunodeficient hosts. Topical, oral, and intravenous formulations of acyclovir speed the clearing of virus, hasten the resolution of symptoms, and shorten the time for the lesions to heal (Fig. 43.4). Herpes infections in normal patients, which are inherently milder, are not helped by topical acyclovir treatment; these infections do not warrant intravenous therapy. A modest reduction in the severity of the milder forms of herpes infections can be achieved with prompt administration of oral acyclovir.

Acyclovir does not prevent or terminate latency of herpesviruses. In other words, the infection is as likely to recur whether or not acyclovir treatment is instituted promptly. Nevertheless, there is an effective way of circumventing this limitation. Long-term treatment with oral acyclovir suppresses most expected herpetic recurrences (Fig. 43.5). However, the suppressive effect of the drug is limited to the period of treatment. Even after years of continuous treatment, recurrences may develop promptly after its termination. This leads to an unusual dilemma for practitioners—acyclovir, like nearly all drugs, is not free of toxic effects after long-term administration. An additional source of concern is that the virus may develop resistance to the drug. Thus, one needs to exercise restraint and judgment in selecting young patients for long-term, noncurative treatment for such a nonprogressive disorder.

GANCICLOVIR

The most serious gap in acyclovir's antiviral spectrum is its lack of activity against cytomegalovirus. A major cause of morbidity and mortality in transplant recipients and AIDS patients, cytomegalovirus has long been a major target for antiviral chemotherapy. The drugs mentioned above, alone or in various combinations, all fall short of ameliorating cytomegalovirus disease.

Figure 43.4.   Comparison of intravenous acyclovir and placebo treatment on the duration of virus shedding (*A*) and time to healing (*B*) in normal patients with first episode of genital herpes.

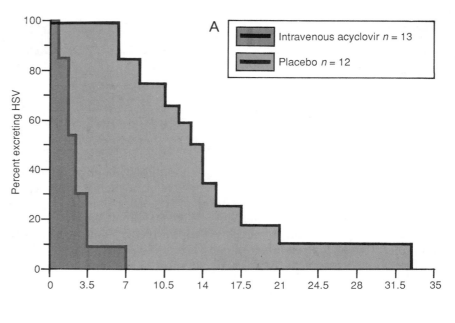

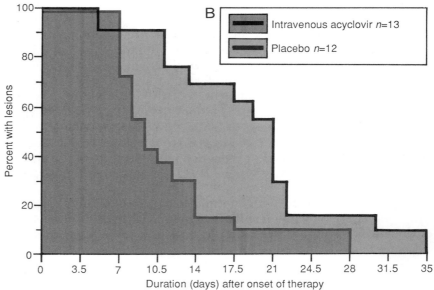

In studying modifications of the acycloguanosine (acyclovir) molecule, one compound, ganciclovir (9-[1,3-dihydroxy-2-propoxymethyl] guanine) was found to have greatly improved activity against cytomegalovirus (Fig. 43.2 and Table 43.3). Its mechanism of action is similar to that of acyclovir, with preferential phosphorylation by viral kinases and inhibition of the viral DNA polymerase. The fact that it inhibits cytomegalovirus replication has led some to speculate that this virus may possess a still uncharacterized nucleotide kinase or, more likely, that infection stimulates the cellular kinases. It is more toxic than acyclovir, very possibly because cellular polymerases can utilize ganciclovir triphosphate better than acyclovir triphosphate. Furthermore, its free 3' position permits chain elongation beyond the points of its incorporation, thus making the compound a potential mutagen.

Ganciclovir proved to be the first agent to reduce the amount of cytomegalovirus that can be recovered from an infected patient. Cymegalovirus-induced retinitis in AIDS patients is stabilized by

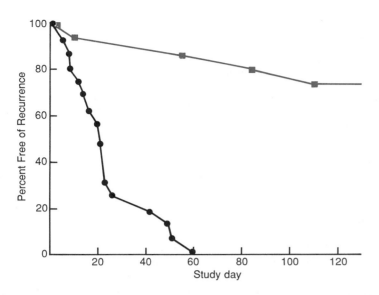

Figure 43.5. Patients with frequently recurring genital herpes were treated chronically with placebo (*black*) or acyclovir capsules (*colored*). The likelihood of remaining free of recurrence is shown by study day.

ganciclovir, but reactivation and progressive infection are seen in many patients once the treatment is stopped. Thus, essentially life-long suppressive therapy is required. The acyclovir has had less salutary effects in those bone marrow transplant recipients who rapidly develop fatal cytomegalovirus pneumonia. Even when the drug is used, the basic course of the infection remains unremitting and nearly always fatal. However, expectant treatment of transplant recipients at high risk of cytomegalovirus pneumonia is very effective.

ZIDOVUDINE (AZIDOTHYMIDINE, AZT)

The strategies that led to the development of effective antiherpes agents are now being widely exploited. The synthesis of nucleoside analogs that can inhibit RNA and DNA polymerases, as well as other known viral enzymes, should, by the end of this century, lead to drugs with many additional therapeutic indications. Nowhere is the need more urgent than for agents that inhibit reverse transcriptases or other retrovirus-specific enzymes. Screening compounds for their ability to inhibit the growth of AIDS viruses has identified several likely candidates for clinical testing. Some of these have already proven too toxic but a few other candidates are hopeful.

Particularly promising is **zidovudine** (Fig. 43.2 and Table 43.3). It inhibits HIV virus replication at concentrations of 0.1–0.5 µg/ml, readily achieved via oral or parenteral routes but below the cytotoxic level. Zidovudine has proven to benefit patients with AIDS and opportunistic infections or with AIDS-related complex (ARC). Treatment improves the immune status, weight, and feeling of well-being, and prevents new opportunistic infections. Most important, zidovudine-treated patients live longer, and when used in asymptomatic patients with only slightly reduced CD_4 counts, the drug slows the relentless progression to ARC and AIDS. Unfortunately, this drug is toxic for the bone marrow, and its use over months and years necessitates repeated blood transfusions. Once the value of zidovudine was established, close examination of dosing led to the realization that lower doses are still effective. Nevertheless, worldwide efforts are being made to identify alternative treatment regimens with this and other drugs. Among the alternative drugs being considered are other nucleoside analogs, such as dideoxyinosine and dideoxycytidine. Other retroviral targets such as the viral protease and transactivating protein are being evaluated for additional, novel means of treating and suppressing AIDS.

DRUG RESISTANCE

The early days of antibacterial chemotherapy were marked by blissful naiveté about the impact of drug resistance. Those who study antiviral compounds are now forearmed with this knowledge and are careful to screen virus isolates from treated patients for evidence of drug resistance. Not surprisingly, resistant mutants can be readily prepared in the laboratory by growing viruses at subinhibitory drug concentrations. Resistant strains have been recovered from patients as well. In the normal host, resistance has not proven to be especially troublesome. There may be two major reasons for this:

- Most viral infections resolve spontaneously as a result of the successful efforts of the cellular immune defenses. The goal of antiviral therapy in such instances is to **speed resolution**. Emergence of drug resistance may lead to delay in virus clearing, but in general, the resistant viruses would present a problem mainly for individuals with impaired immune defenses.

- Development of drug resistance may lead to a **reduction of the inherent virulence** of some viruses. Herpes simplex strains become resistant to acyclovir predominantly because of mutations in the gene for thymidine kinase. Thymidine kinase deficiency, however, renders strains less virulent in animals and is less likely to establish latent neural infection. In fact, patients with strains resistant to acyclovir do not suffer severe infections. Moreover, recurrences are associated with reactivation of the original drug-sensitive strains that remained unaltered in the nerve ganglia.

Unfortunately, antiviral resistance is emerging as a problem in severely immunocompromised patients. The best studied examples are acyclovir-resistant herpes simplex, zoster, and cytomegalovirus infections in AIDS patients. A new drug with a completely distinct mechanism of action is the current answer to the treatment of these difficult, resistant infections. Foscarnet, sodium phosphonoformate (Table 43.3), is a direct inhibitor of herpesvirus DNA polymerases. Although it is not potent enough as a topical drug to benefit normal patients with genital herpes, it is adequate as an intravenous treatment of resistant herpes and zoster and as an alternate treatment for cytomegalovirus retinitis.

SUGGESTED READING

Dolin R. Antiviral chemotherapy and chemoprophylaxis. Science 1985;227: 1296–1303.

Galasso G J, et al., eds. Antiviral agents and viral diseases of man. New York: Raven Press, 1984.

Vaccines and Antisera in the Prevention and Treatment of Infection

44

Sherwood L. Gorbach

The dramatic decrease in the incidence of classic infectious diseases since the middle of the 19th century is due largely to two factors, improved sanitation and development of vaccines. The availability of potable water supplies and sewage disposal, along with improvements in housing, have made major impacts on the diseases transmitted by food and water and those associated with close living quarters, e.g., typhoid fever, cholera, tuberculosis, typhus, and plague. Immunization with vaccines has led to the eradication of smallpox and improvements in polio, measles, rubella (German measles), diphtheria, pertussis, and tetanus. Despite these advances, classic infections still cause havoc in the developing countries because of inadequate sanitation or the unavailability of vaccines. These represent failures of economics and politics rather than deficiencies in scientific knowledge or public health awareness.

Yet infectious diseases continue to cause serious morbidity and mortality, even in industrialized countries. Vaccines have not been developed for many pathogens and there are difficulties in instituting public health control measures, for example, for sexually transmitted diseases. Included in the group of unconquered infections are most viral diseases, particularly those in the respiratory and gastrointestinal tracts, sexually transmitted diseases (syphilis, gonorrhea, and chlamydia), and AIDS. While rejoicing in the triumphs over many classic infectious diseases, we should not be complacent about the tremendous tasks ahead in dealing with those insidious microbes that continue to attack us in our food and drink, in the air we breathe, and even in our love.

APPROACHES TO IMMUNIZATION

Several immunization strategies are available to prevent or to treat infectious diseases; the choice depends on the type of microorganism, the age of the host, and the time frame of contact between the host and the pathogen (Table 44.1). **Active immunization** with vaccines or toxoids leads to prolonged immunity and is generally preferred over **passive immunization** (administering immune globulins) for prevention of infection. The list of vaccines licensed in the U.S. is shown in Table 44.2. Vaccination alone may not ensure protection from disease. As a rule, antibody production with a live vaccine takes at least 1–3 weeks

Table 44.1. Immunization Agents for Preventing or Treating Infectious Diseases

Active immunization: the induction of antibody and other immune mechanisms to prevent infectious diseases

Vaccine—An immunizing agent derived from microorganisms (or parasites), consisting either of:

Live, attenuated microorganisms (Sabin polio vaccine, measles vaccine)

Live, not attenuated microorganisms (adenovirus vaccine, given by the oral/GI route to induce immunity in the respiratory tract)

Killed microorganisms or fractions

Killed whole agents (Salk polio vaccine)

Extracts of microorganisms, such as soluble capsular polysaccharide (pneumococcal vaccine) or immunologically active fractions (Hepatitis B vaccine)

Toxoid: an inactivated bacterial toxin that has lost its damaging ("toxic") properties but is able to induce protective antibody; diphtheria and tetanus toxins are adsorbed with aluminum salts to produce their respective toxoids

Passive immunization: administration of exogenously produced antibodies to provide temporary treatment or prevention of infectious diseases

Immune globulin: a mixture of antibodies produced by fractionating large pools of blood plasma

Specific immune globulin: Antibody produced by fractionating donor blood pools selected for high antibody titer to a specific microorganism

Table 44.2. Vaccines Licensed for Use in Humans in the U.S.

	Live	Killed	Fractions
Viral	Adenovirus Measles Mumps Polio (Sabin) Rubella Yellow Fever	Influenza (whole virus) Polio (Salk) Rabies (human diploid)	Hepatitis B (inactivated surface antigen) Influenza ("split" vaccine)
Bacterial	BCG (tuberculosis) Typhoid (oral)	Cholera Pertussis Plague Typhoid	Diphtheria (toxoid) *Haemophilus* B polysaccharide (PRP-polyribosylribitol phosphate) Meningococcal (polysaccharide) Pneumococcal (polysaccharide-23 valent) Tetanus (toxoid)

to develop; with a killed vaccine or toxoid, it can take several weeks, often requiring two or three doses at 3-week intervals. Because most infectious diseases have a short incubation period, usually less than 2 weeks, it is often a futile gesture to use active immunization for postexposure control. If available, passive immunization with specific globulins or antitoxins should then be used after contact (Table 44.3). Certain diseases have a long incubation period (hepatitis B, 6–24 weeks) or a variable incubation period (rabies, tetanus); combined active and passive immunization are used for postexposure control in these settings.

LIVE VS. KILLED VACCINES

Vaccines are made with either live, attenuated microorganisms, killed microorganisms, or microbial extracts (Table 44.1). There are advantages and disadvantages to using a live or killed vaccine, although only with the polio and typhoid vaccines is a choice available between

Table 44.3. Specific Immune Globulins and Antitoxins

Human Immune Globulins
  Hepatitis B
  Pertussis
  Rabies
  Tetanus (antitoxin)
  Vaccinia
  Varicella zoster

Equine Antitoxins
  Botulism (types A, B, E)
  Diphtheria

the two types (Table 44.2). Killed vaccines have been used traditionally because they are easier to manufacture and pose no risk of vaccine-associated infection. The pros and cons of the two types of polio vaccines are discussed in detail in Chapter 31 and are listed in Table 31.2.

A favored approach in vaccine development at the present time is an attempt to define the active virulence factor(s) in the pathogen. A vaccine can then be manufactured by using extracts of the critical virulence factor, e.g., the capsular polysaccharides of the pneumococcus vaccine, the surface antigen of the hepatitis B vaccine, and the "split" influenza vaccine that contains the hemagglutinin and neuraminidase antigens. But immunity to a killed vaccine is not as effective or long lasting as immunity to a live, attenuated vaccine, which more closely mimics the natural disease. However, attenuation of the virulent pathogen to a tame vaccine strain can be technically difficult. Even when successful, there is a small but finite danger that the vaccine strain will revert to a pathogen in a susceptible host. Vaccine-associated poliomyelitis, for example, occurs approximately 1 per 1–3 million doses of live polio vaccine.

TYPE OF IMMUNE RESPONSE

Immunizing agents can produce immunity through B-cell proliferation leading to antibody production, with or without the help of T-cells. Pneumococcal polysaccharide induces B-cell type-specific protective antibody (Chapter 13). Similarly, the polysaccharide of *Haemophilus influenzae* type b induces B-cell production of antibody without a contribution of T-helper cells (Chapter 15). These **T-cell-independent antigens** are characterized by low antibody titers, particularly in children who are less than 18 months of age. Thus, a conventional *H. influenzae* polysaccharide vaccine does not provide protection for the young age group (3–18 months) in which infection with this organism is most deadly. By **conjugation** (covalent linkage) of the *Haemophilus* polysaccharide, known as **polyribosylribitol phosphate** (PRP), with a protein antigen, such as diphtheria protein or the outer membrane protein from *Neisseria*, *Haemophilus* vaccines have been developed that produce a T-cell-dependent antibody response (Chapter 15 and Table 15.3). In contrast to the PRP-only vaccines used in the past, the conjugate vaccines are able to induce antibody in infants at 3 months of age, with higher levels of serum antibody, and a higher proportion in the immunoglobulin M (IgM) class (Table 15.3). In addition, there is a strong booster response with revaccination. Field trials with the new conjugate vaccines have demonstrated significant protection of infants against serious infections caused by *H. influenzae* type b, particularly meningitis.

Certain pathogenic microorganisms use mucosal surfaces either for replication and/or penetration. Respiratory, gastrointestinal, and vaginal mucous membranes are the sites of attack. Secretory IgA antibodies produced at the mucosal surface offer protection against organisms such as polio, rubella, influenza, gonorrhea, and cholera. The optimal strategy against these pathogens would be a vaccine that induces secretory immunity at the critical site. Only a few such vaccines have been developed, but they are notably effective, e.g., polio, adenovirus, and the oral typhoid vaccine. Other mucosal invaders have eluded the developers of vaccines.

The live adenovirus vaccine represents a novel approach to vaccination. In this case, the live vaccine virus strains are not attenuated, but they are administered by the oral route (via ingestion of an enteric-coated tablet) that results in an asymptomatic infection with subsequent immunity. Ingested virus does not reach the respiratory tract, but produces an intestinal infection that stimulates a systemic immune response against subsequent adenovirus-induced respiratory infections.

AGE OF IMMUNIZATION

Newborns receive a supply of serum IgG antibody from their mothers, which gives them substantial protection for 3–6 months against those diseases to which the mother was immune. Maternal milk also contains secretory antibodies that provide some protection against intestinal and respiratory tract infections. The infant's antibody-producing capacity develops slowly during the first year of life. Although immunization is not yet fully efficient, it is desirable to start it at 2 months of age because certain diseases are not only common but particularly severe in this age group (e.g., whooping cough, *H. influenzae* meningitis). As with infants, the **elderly** have a reduced capacity for antibody response to vaccines. For this group, a larger dose of influenza vaccine is needed to achieve adequate protection. Pneumococcal infections are particularly severe in the elderly, and they should be protected by the pneumococcal polyvalent (23 types) polysaccharide vaccine.

DURATION OF IMMUNITY

As a rule, **live vaccines give longer, even lifelong, immunity,** whereas vaccines made of killed organisms, extracts or toxoid have shorter term immunity lasting months to years. However, the immunity to live, attenuated vaccines may also wane, leaving the host susceptible to natural disease that can occur later in life and with atypical features.

The best example of faltering immunity with a live virus vaccine is the story of measles vaccination. Before 1956, when initial trials of measles vaccines were undertaken, virtually every adult in the U.S. had contact with measles, as indicated by the high prevalence of serum antibody to this virus (Chapter 33). The immunization campaign in the 1960s and 1970s reduced the cases of measles to less than 1% of the previous numbers. In recent years, however, dramatic increases in measles have occurred, principally in two age groups, preschool children, where the disease has been traditionally most common, and in older children and young adults. The reason for cases in the preschool group is that vaccination rates in certain parts of the U.S. are low. In older children and young adults, most of whom have been vaccinated appropriately, the presentation of an atypical form of measles is related to failure of vaccination to hold its immunity. As a result of these trends, the current recommendations for vaccination against measles include two doses, the first one given at 15 months of age (vaccine efficacy in younger children under 11 months of age is low), and the second dose at entrance to middle school (11–12 years of age). Whether this schedule will produce lifelong immunity can only be resolved by future observations.

SELECTION OF ANTIGENS

Infective agents possess tens, hundreds, and even thousands of antigens. Such diversity is reflected in their number of genes, which can vary from as few as six in polyoma virus to many thousand in protozoa such as malaria. The principal immune response that establishes protection in the host is usually related to a small number of antigens, often located on the **surface** of the microorganism. In some instances, a vaccine can protect against all strains of the organism, as with the hepatitis B vaccine, which is composed of surface antigen. In other situations, such as the pneumococcus, protective antibody is developed against a specific capsular polysaccharide, of which more than 80 distinct types have been discovered. Immunity to one polysaccharide type does not convey immunity to any other type. For this reason, the pneumococcal vaccine is composed of 23 different polysaccharides, comprising the most common types causing disease. In the case of rhinovirus infections, the most frequent cause of the common cold, at least 100 types are known and it has proven impractical to develop a vaccine that confers protection to enough of these antigenic types. Influenza virus vaccines are changed each year to deal with the different antigens of the influenza A and B virus strains in circulation. Minor antigenic "drifts" occur annually in both influenza A and B virus strains, whereas major antigenic changes, known as antigenic "shifts," occur about every 10 years. Vaccines must be modified to accommodate both antigenic drifts and shifts (Chapter 35).

IMMUNIZATION OF SPECIAL POPULATIONS

Individuals with underlying illnesses are at high risk of infections for which efficient immunizing agents are available (Table 44.4). Such individuals should receive active immunization, even though they may mount a less complete immune response and have reduced benefits of such intervention. Patients with sickle cell disease may develop a fatal pneumococcal infection, which presents with astounding rapidity and leads to death by septicemia and disseminated intravascular coagulation (DIC). The pneumococcal vaccine, while not fully effective in these patients, nevertheless provides some protection. Similarly, persons who are either born without a spleen or who have had their spleen removed surgically are also at high risk to develop overwhelming infections with encapsulated organisms such as pneumococci, and should receive the vaccine.

Other special groups that should be targeted for vaccination are the elderly, for influenza and pneumococcal vaccines; children with leukemia who have been exposed to chickenpox; health care workers, who may have exposure to hepatitis B and rubella; and travelers, depending on local health conditions at their destination.

Live, attenuated vaccines should be avoided in immunocompromised hosts because the organism may be sufficiently pathogenic to cause progressive disease in such individuals. The only exception,

Table 44.4. Immunization in Special Populations

Population	Immunization	Comment
Sickle cell disease; splenectomized patient	Pneumococcal vaccine	Pneumococcal infection is often fatal
Elderly	Influenza and pneumococcal vaccines	
Children with leukemia	Varicella zoster immune globulin (postexposure)	Chickenpox causes severe, often fatal disease in leukemics
Health care workers	Hepatitis B vaccine	
	Rubella vaccine	In nonimmune women
Travelers	Immune globulin	For Hepatitis A
	Yellow fever, plague, typhoid, meningococcal vaccines	Depends on local conditions
Pregnancy	Tetanus toxoid	Particularly in developing countries to prevent neonatal tetanus

based on experience, is the recommended use of the live measles, mumps, and rubella (MMR) vaccine in HIV-positive children to avoid the potentially severe effects of the natural diseases, particularly measles.

DPT (DIPHTHERIA, PERTUSSIS, TETANUS) VACCINE

DPT vaccine is the oldest and most successful combination vaccine used in childhood. It consists of a combination of two toxoids (**diphtheria** and **tetanus**) and a killed, whole-cell vaccine (**pertussis**). Administration of the vaccine is legally mandated for all children in the U.S. The preferred schedule is initial vaccination at 2 months of age, followed by three injections up to 15 months of age. A booster is given at entry to primary school. Thereafter, a booster of tetanus toxoid (full dose) and diphtheria toxoid (reduced dose) is given every 10 years. A booster dose of pertussis vaccine is not recommended after school age because the disease is less common and less severe in older children and adults. To emphasize further the efficacy of these vaccines, two of these classic infections are reviewed below. The third, tetanus, is covered in Chapter 21.

Diphtheria

Before widespread introduction to immunization, diphtheria was a major and, in some areas, the leading cause of death in young children. Epidemics of diphtheria in colonial America killed up to one-third of the children in a community. The organism is spread mainly by airborne respiratory droplets. Occasionally, direct contact with persons with diphtheria of the skin is responsible for epidemic spread. Communicability is fostered by close living quarters, especially in the fall and winter months.

Widespread vaccination in childhood has had an extraordinary effect on the occurrence of this disease in the U.S.; hundreds of thousands of cases were reported annually in the 1920s, compared to only five cases per year at the present time. While immunized and partially immunized persons can develop diphtheria, the disease occurs more frequently and is more lethal in unvaccinated individuals.

The clinical picture of diphtheria consists of local infection of the nasopharynx, which can lead to obstruction of the airway, and the later complications associated with elaboration of toxin. While *Corynebacterium diphtheriae* does not invade the mucosal surface, it does produce a thick, mucoid, gray membrane that coats the entire oral cavity, extending upward into the nasal passages, and downward to the respiratory tract and even into the bronchial tree. Obstruction of the airway can lead to death in the early phases of the disease. Most of the serious complications, however, are associated with the exotoxin (Chapter 9). Although all cells of the body are sensitive to the toxin, the major clinical effects are seen in the heart and nervous system. Up to 25% of patients with diphtheria experience cardiac complications, consisting initially of irregular heart beat and progressing to myocarditis and congestive heart failure. The effects on the cardiac conduction system are severe, and many patients have permanent arrhythmias and abnormal electrocardiograms. Neuropathy is also extremely common, especially in patients with severe diphtheria. The initial manifestations are local paralysis of the palate and swallowing mechanisms, followed by cranial nerve abnormalities and peripheral neuritis.

Antibiotic therapy is used to kill the organism at the local site of infection, but it has no effect on the liberated toxin nor on the obstructive problems in the respiratory tract. Diphtheria antitoxin is an immune serum produced in horses. It can neutralize circulating toxin, but does not bind to toxin that has entered the cell. Hence, it should be given early and only on a single occasion because antibiotic therapy will curtail further toxin production. Horse serum may cause serum sickness, a serious complication of passive immunization with diphtheria antitoxin. Supportive care for maintaining respiratory status and treating heart failure are essential components of successful treatment.

Active immunization with toxoid, as part of the DPT vaccine, has virtually eliminated diphtheria as a public health problem in the U.S. Outbreaks still occur sporadically, and the cases are invariably in members of minority groups who have low rates of DPT immunization. Because of waning immunity, a booster shot is recommended every 10 years for adults.

Pertussis

Whooping cough is not a single toxin disease, as is tetanus and diphtheria. *B. pertussis* produces an array of proteins, toxins, and biologically active substances, many of which play a role in the complex evolution of the clinical disease (Chapter 20). The organism initially attaches, but does not penetrate, the ciliated respiratory epithelial cells. The various toxins are released, which cause local damage to the mucosa and suppress mobilization of mucous, leading to accumulation of thick secretions. The pertussis toxin also produces the systemic signs and complications.

Worldwide, more than 50 million cases of whooping cough are reported annually, accompanied by over half a million deaths. Most of these cases occur in developing countries, although relaxation of immunization schedules in certain developed countries has led to epidemics in recent years. The disease is remarkably contagious, with attack rates as high as 90% among susceptibles. Nearly half of reported cases occur in children under 1 year of age, and the infants also experience the highest mortality. Inexplicably, females are infected more often than males. In older children and adults, in whom the disease has occurred with increased frequency in recent years due to waning immunity following vaccination, or lack of primary vaccination altogether, pertussis may cause a mild illness with a prolonged, hacking cough.

Antibiotic treatment of whooping cough is only marginally effective, and the mainstay of therapy is control of serious side effects. Because of the high incidence of complications, and the considerable mortality seen in infants, prevention by vaccine is clearly preferred to relying on treatment.

Pertussis vaccine is a killed suspension of the whole organism. Vaccine efficacy is approximately 80%, and this immunity lasts for at least 3 years. In communities in which the vaccine is widely employed, pertussis has become a rare disease in childhood. Conversely, when pertussis vaccination was allowed to decline as a result of concerns about vaccine safety, as in England and Japan during the 1970s, there were sharp epidemics of pertussis, which required reinstitution of a vaccine program.

Adverse reactions are common after DPT vaccination, and they are related mostly to the pertussis component. More than 60% of recipients experience reactions at the injection site and fever. About 1 in 2000 recipients have seizures, related to the fever rather than to the vaccine itself. Serious neurological reactions leading to permanent brain damage or death have been ascribed to pertussis vaccine. Concerns about these reactions lead to relaxation of vaccine requirements, which, in turn, produced epidemics of pertussis in areas in which the disease had been rare. An expert committee of the American Academy of Pediatrics recently has concluded that **"pertussis vaccine has not been proven to be a cause of brain damage."** While cases of vaccine-related brain damage may in fact occur, the overwhelming evidence at the present time is that such serious neurological events are extremely rare and should not stand in the way of universal vaccination for whooping cough.

USE OF BCG AND VACCINIA VIRUS AS RECOMBINANT VACCINE VECTORS

Recent technological developments have enabled the introduction of recombinant DNA into mycobacteria, such as BCG (Chapter 23), and into the vaccinia virus (Chapter 42). The feasibility of introducing foreign genes makes it possible to consider developing these agents into **recombinant multiple vaccine** vehicles. A multivaccine could be made by cloning and expressing a gene encoding a foreign antigen from another pathogen into BCG or vaccinia virus. The hope is that when the live BCG or vaccinia virus expressing the foreign antigen is administered to an animal or human, protective immune responses would be elicited not only to these agents but also to the pathogenic agent from which the antigen was cloned.

BCG has numerous attractive advantages as a vaccine vector. First, BCG itself is a very safe vaccine. Since 1948, BCG has been administered to over 2 billion people and the number of side effects is minimal. Second, BCG is the only live vaccine other than oral polio that can be administered soon after birth. The ability to administer a vaccine early in life could increase the number of children that receive it and, also, allow for development of novel vaccines that could be effective early in life, such as against measles. Third, BCG is a potent adjuvant and has the ability to immunize humans from 5–50 years. Fourth, since BCG lives within macrophages, it provides the possibility of generating T-cell-mediated immunity to the cloned foreign antigen. A drawback of BCG is that it will only "take" if the person has no immunity to tuberculosis. BCG will not establish itself in people who have been colonized by *M. tuberculosis* or some other cross-reacting mycobacteria. For this reason, BCG can only be given once and much thought will have to go into the formulation of a BCG-recombinant vaccine to be given on a wide scale. Similar considerations apply to a recombinant vaccinia virus multivaccine (Chapter 42).

SUGGESTED READING

Immunization Practices Advisory Committee. General recommendations on immunization. Morbid Mortal Wkly Rep (CDC) 1989;38:223.

Klein JO. Immunization of children and adults. In Gorbach SL, Bartlett JG, Blacklow N, eds. Infectious diseases. Philadelphia: WB Saunders, 1992.

Plotkin SA, Mortimer EA Jr., eds. Vaccines. Philadelphia: WB Saunders, 1988.

Review of the Main Pathogenic Viruses

This chart is intended to review the main human viruses. Included are the agents of greatest medical relevance.

Many of the viruses that cause relatively uncommon diseases are not included. This chart may be completed to review material you have covered under this topic.

Virus	Group or Family	Nucleic Acid, Cellular Site of Replication State if Enveloped	Other Important Attributes	Disease(s) and Systems Involved	Relevant Chapter(s)
Poliovirus					31
Coxsackie and other enteroviruses					31
Rhinoviruses					31
Arbovirus encephalitis					32
Rubella					32, 49
Measles					33
Respiratory syncytial virus					33
Rabies					34
Influenza					35
Rotavirus					36
HIV					37
Adenovirus					38
Papillomavirus					39
Herpes simplex					40

Virus	Group or Family	Nucleic Acid, Cellular Site of Replication State if Enveloped	Other Important Attributes	Disease(s) and Systems Involved	Relevant Chapter(s)
Epstein-Barr virus (EBV) cytomegalovirus (CMV), varicella-zoster					40
Hepatitis A					31, 41
Hepatitis B					31
Smallpox					42

Introduction to the Fungi and the Mycoses

George S. Kobayashi and Gerald Medoff

WHAT ARE THE PATHOGENIC FUNGI?

In most people's minds, fungi conjure up the image of mildew and old shoes, moldy bread, or skin infections with graphic names like "athlete's foot" or "jock itch." In fact, fungi have a major influence on the health and livelihood of people throughout the world. They cause a wide spectrum of clinical disease, from simple cosmetic problems to potentially lethal systemic infections. They play an important role in degrading organic waste material in nature but are also economically destructive and cause widespread damage to food and fabrics. Fungi are used commercially in many fermentations, and produce steroid hormone derivatives and antibiotics, such as penicillin.

Fungi are **eukaryotes**, with a defined nucleus enclosed by a nuclear membrane, a cell membrane that contains lipids, glycoproteins, and sterols, mitochondria, Golgi apparatus, ribosomes bound to endoplasmic reticulum, and a cytoskeleton with microtubules, microfilaments, and intermediate filaments (Chapter 3). Of course, this description applies to animal cells as well, a fact that constitutes a major problem in dealing with fungal infections. The infecting organisms are so similar to their host cells, that it is difficult to devise therapeutic strategies specific for the parasite and nontoxic to the host.

Shapes and Structures

Pathogenic fungi have two forms—**filamentous**, the molds, and **unicellular**, the yeasts. Molds grow as microscopic, branching, thread-like filaments. These are called **hyphae** and are collectively referred to as the **mycelium**. A mycelium is what you see when you look at the white mat on moldy fruit. The hyphae are either septate (divided by partitions) or coenocytic (multinucleate without cross walls), a feature that is used in laboratory diagnosis (Fig. 45.1). On agar, hyphae grow outward from the point of inoculation by extension of the tips of filaments and then branch repeatedly.

Yeasts are single cells, ovoid or spherical, with a rigid cell wall and the same cellular complexity as the hyphae. Most yeasts divide by budding and a few by binary fission like bacteria (Fig. 45.2). On agar, they form colonies that are similar to those of bacteria but usually become considerably larger. Some also produce a polysaccharide capsule, an important characteristic of the yeast that causes the disease cryptococcosis, *Cryptococcus neoformans*.

Dimorphism and Growth

Many important pathogenic fungi have two growth forms and can exist either as molds or as yeasts. For example, the agent of histoplasmosis, *Histoplasma capsulatum* grows as yeast in some conditions and as mycelium in others (Fig. 45.3). This phenomenon is called **dimorphism**. In the laboratory, the transition between these two phases can be reversibly induced by changes in temperature, with the yeast phase being more typical of human body temperature.

The yeast-mycelium or mycelium-yeast shift is frequently associated with a change from a free-living organism to a parasite. With most fungi that cause systemic infections, e.g., the agents of histoplasmosis and blastomycosis, the parasitic form is the yeast while the mold form is found in the environment (soil). In a few unusual instances, such as with *Candida*, this rule is reversed and the mycelial form is the one found in tissues.

Not all pathogenic fungi are dimorphic and undergo morphological changes when they infect a host. Aspergilli, among the most common molds in the environment, are always filamentous, whereas *C. neoformans* is always a yeast. Certain yeasts, particularly species of *Candida*, carry out a modified form of budding in which newly budded cells remain attached and become elongated like links of sausages. These aggregates are called **pseudohyphae** or, in the aggregate, **pseudomycelium** (Fig. 45.4).

Most of the molecular biology and genetics of fungi has been studied using the common baker's or brewer's yeast, *Saccharomyces cerevisiae*; and to a lesser extent, the molds *Aspergillus nidulans* and *Neurospora crassa*. Less is known about pathogenic fungi, although active studies are being carried out on their virulence factors and dimorphic transitions. In the laboratory, most fungi are grown in media similar to those used for bacteria, though usually at a lower pH. All fungi are basically aerobic, but baker's yeast can grow for short periods without oxygen. In general, fungi prefer 25–30°C, *although some of the organisms that cause deep mycoses grow well at 37°C and one thermophilic pathogen, Aspergillus fumigatus, grows well up to 50°C.*

Fungi belong to a separate kingdom, the *Eumycota*, and are classified on the basis of their mode of sexual and asexual reproduction, morphology, life cycle and to some extent, physiology. Until recently, the mode of sexual reproduction of most human fungal pathogens was not known. For this reason, they were dumped into a catch-all category, the *Fungi imperfecti*. Since the 1960s, the sexual reproductive states have been found for an increasing number of skin pathogenic fungi. Although the rules of nomenclature give preference to names of the perfect or sexual state (if known), the longer-established and more familiar names of the imperfect state are still used. Thus, the diagnostic

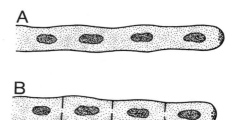

Figure 45.1. Somatic hyphae. A. apical portion of nonseptate (coenocytic) hypha; the protoplasm is continuous and multinucleated. **B.** Apical portion of septate hyphae; protoplasm is interrupted by cross walls.

Figure 45.2. Vegetative reproduction of yeast. A. Cell reproducing by budding (blastospores formation). **B.** Cell reproducing by fission (cross-wall formation).

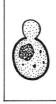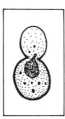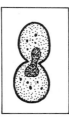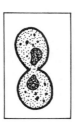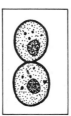

6   5   4   3   2   1

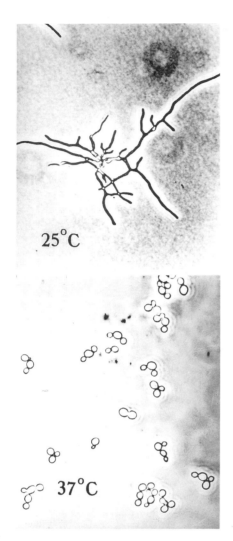

Figure 45.3. Temperature-induced morphogenesis in *Histoplasma capsulatum*. Cultures grow in the mycelial phase at 25°C and as yeasts at 37°C.

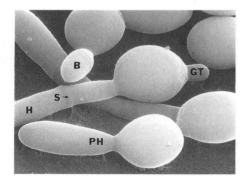

Figure 45.4. Electron photomicrograph of *Candida albicans*. The following cellular morphological characters are illustrated: pseudohypha (*PH*); hypha (*H*) with septum (*S*); germ-tube (*GT*); blastospore (*B*).

laboratory will report the isolation of *C. neoformans* or *H. capsulatum* rather than the less familiar names of the sexual states.

MYCOSES

Fungal infections can be classified by areas of the body that are primarily affected.

- **Superficial mycoses** are infections limited to the outermost layers of skin and hair. In general, they are mild infections with minimal or no inflammatory response. They are mainly cosmetic problems that are mild, readily diagnosed, and respond well to therapy. There are four infections in this group, two of which involve hairs of the scalp (black and white piedra), and two involve the glabrous skin (tinea nigra and tinea versicolor).

- Slightly deeper in the epidermis are found the sites of the **cutaneous mycoses**, like athlete's foot or ringworm. The fungi that cause these conditions are called the **dermatophytes**. The diseases they cause may be acute or chronic, depending on the etiological agent and immunological status of the patient. In general, they are more difficult to treat than the superficial fungal infections. The etiological agents belong to three genera, *Microsporum*, *Trichophyton*, and *Epidermophyton*. The clinical diseases are called the tineas and are described according to the area of the body involved (e.g., tinea capitis involves the head, tinea pedis involves the feet, tinea corporis involves the body, etc.)

- The **subcutaneous mycoses** are a distinctive group of fungal disease that involve the dermis and the subcutaneous tissue. They are caused by fungi that are commonly isolated from the environment and produce disease only under unusual circumstances. Many of these infections mimic those caused by bacteria. With two exceptions (**lymphangitic sporotrichosis** and **chromoblastomycosis**), the subcutaneous mycoses do not respond well to antifungal chemotherapy. Excision of the lesion or amputation are the only ways these diseases can be managed. Examples are subcutaneous phycomycosis, eumycotic mycetoma, phaeophyphomycosis, chromoblastomycosis, and lymphangitic sporotrichosis.

- **Systemic mycoses** are infections with invasion of the internal organs of the body. It is convenient to differentiate between the systemic mycoses caused by **primary pathogens**, such as *H. capsulatum* or *C. immitis*, which can cause disease in healthy individuals, and those caused by **opportunistic fungi**, such as *C. albicans*, which have only marginal pathogenicity and generally require a debilitated host for progressive infection to take place. In the primary systemic mycoses, most healthy people affected usually have mild signs or subclinical manifestations. In contrast, opportunistic fungal infections in the debilitated host almost always produce significant disease.

ENCOUNTER

With a handful of important exceptions, fungi implicated in human diseases are free-living in nature. Most mycoses are acquired as a result of accidental encounters by inhalation or traumatic implantation from an exogenous source. *H. capsulatum* is found in soil contaminated by the excreta of bats, chickens, and starlings. *C. neoformans* is associated with pigeon roosts and soils contaminated by pigeon droppings.

Some of these fungi have distinct geographic preferences. Thus, *C. immitis* is found in the bioclimatic area known as the Lower Sonoran life zone of the southwestern U.S. and similar geographic sites in Central and South America. This region has arid or semiarid climates, hot summers, few winter freezes, and alkaline soils. *C. immitis* has been found only in the New World (North, Central, and South America). On this note, paracoccidioidomycosis, a disease caused by *Paracoccidioides brasiliensis* is geographically limited to South and Central America. *Blastomyces dermatitidis*, once thought to exist only in the North American continent, has been found to have endemic foci in Africa. *Sporothrix schenckii* has been isolated frequently from rose and barberry thorns and decaying vegetation.

In contrast to these environmental habitats, many of us carry *C. albicans* in the mouth, gastrointestinal tract, and other mucous membrane linings as part of our normal flora. *Pityrosporum ovale* are yeasts found on the healthy human skin, particularly in the upper trunk, face, and scalp, the areas that are rich in sebaceous glands, which make lipids used by these organisms. Finally, dermatophytes that cause ringworm and athlete's foot are occasionally found on the skin and scalp of individuals in the absence of symptoms; they are thought to represent transient colonization or a carrier state.

ENTRY

The level of innate immunity in most humans is high because fungal infections are usually mild and self-limiting. The intact skin or mucosal surfaces are the primary barriers to infection. Desiccation, epithelial cell turnover, fatty acids, and the low pH of the skin are believed to be important factors in host resistance. Also, the bacterial flora of the skin and mucous membranes compete with fungi and hinder their unrestricted growth. Alterations in the balance of the normal flora by use of antibiotics or changes in nutrition allow fungi like *C. albicans* to proliferate and increase the likelihood of entry and infection. Violation of the natural barriers by trauma or foreign bodies allows entry of fungi into sterile areas of the body. As in all infections, the outcome is determined by the virulence of the infecting organism, the size of the inoculum, and the adequacy of the host defenses.

SPREAD AND MULTIPLICATION

Within tissues, fungi are restrained by a variety of nonspecific mechanisms. Using *C. albicans* as an example, the fungistatic effect of serum has been shown to be due, in part, to transferrins, the human iron-binding proteins that deprive microbes of the iron they need for making respiratory enzymes. Serum also contains β-globulins, which cause a nonimmunological clumping of *Candida* and facilitate their elimination by inflammatory cells.

Tissue reaction to the presence of fungi varies with the species, the site of proliferation, and the duration of infection. Some mycoses are characterized by a low-grade inflammatory response, which does not eliminate the fungi. Fungal cells can sometimes persist within macrophages or giant cells without being killed. For example, yeast cells of *H. capsulatum* can proliferate within the cytoplasm of macrophages and neutrophils and spread to other organs of the body within those cells (Fig. 45.5). Why they are able to survive within macrophages is not known, but recent work suggests that they may be resistant to lysosomal enzymes. Most of the time, however, nonspecific inflammatory

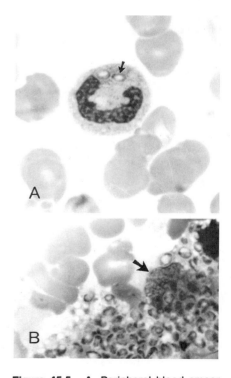

Figure 45.5. A. Peripheral blood smear showing neutrophil with phagocytized yeast cells (*arrow*) of *Histoplasma capsulatum*. **B.** Bone marrow aspirate showing histiocytes (*arrows*) filled with phagocytized yeast cells of *H. capsulatum*.

reactions are critically important in eliminating fungi. Phagocytosis by neutrophils is the primary mechanism that prevents the establishment of fungal infections, and is usually the most effective. Consistent with this, the frequency and virulence of disseminated *Candida* and *Aspergillus* infections is greater in patients with low numbers of neutrophils or with disorders of neutrophil functions, such as chronic granulomatous disease or myeloperoxidase deficiency. In the case of *Candida*, phagocytized yeast cells are killed intracellularly by both the oxygen-dependent and -independent mechanisms.

In some cases, phagocytosis fails. For example, *C. neoformans* causes meningitis in people with normal phagocytic function. Just as with the encapsulated bacteria, these organisms escape phagocytosis because they are surrounded by a thick viscous capsule.

Fungi that are too big to be ingested can, nevertheless, be killed by immunological mechanisms. Fungal cells and their extracellular products are highly antigenic and evoke both cellular and humoral responses. There is evidence that antibodies play a role in the elimination of fungi from the body. Along with complement, antibodies participate in the extracellular killing of *A. fumigatus* and pseudohyphae of *C. albicans* by lymphocytes and phagocytic cells (Fig. 45.6). Instead of "ingesting" and "digesting" the fungi, phagocytic cells appear to secrete lethal lysosomal enzymes.

Resistance to fungal disease is due mainly to cellular or T-lymphocyte-mediated immunity. This can be inferred from animal experiments and from the clinical observation that patients with depressed cellular immunity are especially prone to invasive and serious systemic fungal disease. For example, patients with **AIDS** commonly have mucocutaneous candidiasis and serious systemic infections with *C. neoformans*. As can be expected, patients with **AIDS** who live in endemic areas have an increased propensity to acquire or to activate the fungi that cause disseminated histoplasmosis or coccidioidomycosis.

DAMAGE

As far as is known, fungi that cause invasive disease do not secrete toxins that harm the host. Tissue damage most probably results from direct **invasion** with displacement, **destruction** of vital structures, and toxic effects of the **inflammatory response**. Fungi may also grow as masses of cells (fungus balls) that can occlude bronchi in the lung or tubules or even ureters in kidneys, leading to obstruction of outflow of biological fluids (sputum, urine) and secondary infection and tissue damage. *Aspergillus* or *Mucor* species have the propensity to grow in the walls of arteries or veins, leading to occlusion and ischemic tissue necrosis. Mats of fungi are formed as vegetations on heart valves in fungal endocarditis. Pieces can break off and travel through the blood to any organ in the body and cause arterial occlusion with resultant tissue necrosis.

DIAGNOSIS

Fungal infections are diagnosed in the laboratory by direct **microscopy**, **culture**, and **serology**. Morphological characteristics of the organisms are valuable in the identification of all fungi, both in tissues and in culture. These are particularly useful in the diagnosis of serious systemic infections. Among the distinctive characteristics are the spherules of *C. immitis* in tissue (Fig. 45.7), the typical large budding yeasts of *B. dermatitidis* in pus (Fig. 45.8), the coenocytic hyphae of

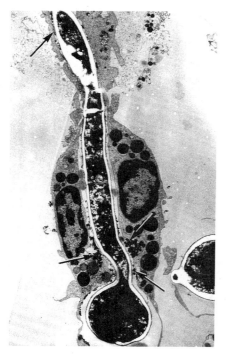

Figure 45.6. Electron photomicrograph of phagocytic cell ingesting a hypha of *Candida albicans*.

mucormycosis (Fig. 45.9), or the encapsulated yeast cells of *C. neofor-mans* in cerebrospinal fluid or brain tissue (Fig. 47.3). Their detection provides an immediate and reliable diagnosis in systemic infections. For opportunistic pathogens such as *Mucor*, *Candida*, and *Aspergillus*, microscopic examination of clinical specimens is particularly useful because culture alone may not be helpful (inasmuch as these organisms are in the environment and can be part of the normal flora of the body). Here, histological evidence of infection in tissue is usually the single most valuable diagnostic procedure, although a negative finding does not rule out infection.

Pathogenic fungi may also be recovered from infected tissues using **culture** procedures. When the organism isolated is a primary pathogen, such as *H. capsulatum*, the diagnosis is unequivocal. Isolation of opportunistic organisms like *Candida* from superficial locations may have little clinical significance because it could represent colonization, but culturing them from blood is always significant.

Culturing clinical specimens does not always result in growth of the organism. This is often true with invasive *Aspergillus* infections, which yield positive blood cultures in less than 10% of cases. We do not know why. Perhaps only a small portion of the mycelium is actively growing and capable of producing a positive culture, or possibly, a large inoculum of these fungi is required for growth in vitro.

Fungi grow slowly and there is often considerable delay between the time the specimen is obtained and a positive culture. Relying on the results of the cultures may, therefore, cause a significant delay in starting therapy. Despite these limitations, cultures should always be done because "when they work, they work well."

Detection of **antibodies** specific for fungal antigens is sometimes helpful in diagnosis, particularly for the deep-seated mycoses. Many serological and skin tests are available, but the results provide only presumptive evidence for infection and must be interpreted in light of clinical findings. It is particularly difficult to interpret the significance of positive skin tests to *H. capsulatum* in parts of the world where the disease is endemic. Almost everyone living in these areas has been exposed to this fungus and has developed a positive skin test indicative of delayed-type hypersensitivity. The tests are further limited in usefulness because the antigens available are not specific enough. False-positive tests may also be due to symptomless colonization, previous subclinical infections, or anamnestic response due to previous skin tests. Delayed or false-negative responses, particularly in the immunosuppressed host, may also be a problem.

Recently, procedures for detecting circulating fungal antigens in body fluids have been developed. The most successful one detects soluble capsular polysaccharides of *C. neoformans* in cerebrospinal fluid. It is highly specific and sensitive. Similar tests for other fungi are not available now but may well be developed.

TREATMENT

It is extremely important to realize that not all fungal infections require treatment. As stated previously, humans have a high innate resistance to most of these agents. Most infections with *H. capsulatum* or *C. immitis* are subclinical, self-limiting, and do not result in disease. Some candidal infections respond to supportive measures, such as improving the nutritional status of the host or eliminating predisposing factors, e.g., intravenous lines, catheters, and the administration of broad-

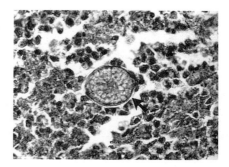

Figure 45.7. Surgical specimen of lung showing mature spherule of *Coccidioides immitis*-containing endospores.

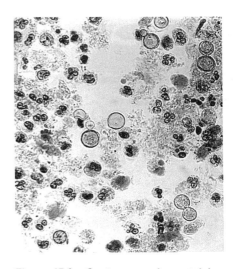

Figure 45.8. Sputum sample containing budding yeast cells of *Blastomyces dermatitidis*.

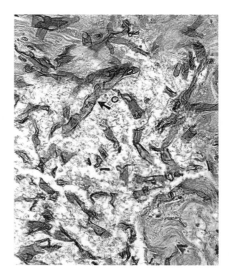

Figure 45.9. Section of lung showing ribbon-like nonseptate hyphae (*arrows*) characteristic of agents such as *Mucor* spp. that cause zygomycosis.

Table 45.1. Antifungal Antibiotics

Class	Compounds	Mechanism	Uses
Polyene	Amphotericin B Nystatin	Binds to sterols causing perturbations in cell membrane	Systemic disease; topical disease
Azole	Clotrimazole Miconazole Ketoconazole Fluconazole Itraconazole	Inhibits ergosterol biosynthesis	Topical disease; systemic disease
Pyrimidine	5-fluorocytosine (5FC)	Inhibits DNA and RNA synthesis	Systemic disease
Grisans	Griseofulvin	Inhibits microtubule assembly	Topical disease

spectrum antibiotics. Management of these fungal infections is much easier when these causes are recognized and corrected.

Most antifungal agents in common use affect fungi more than host cells, but not by much (Chapter 5). Toxicity is a real problem in the treatment of these diseases. In addition, many antifungal compounds have limited therapeutic value because of problems with solubility, stability, and absorption. Compared to antibacterial agents, the number of effective antifungal agents is quite small (Chapter 5). With the increase in frequency of fungal infections, the search for additional effective agents has expanded.

Most useful antifungal antibiotics fall into one of two categories—those that affect fungal cell membranes, and those that are taken up by the cell and interrupt cellular processes (Chapter 5). Table 45.1 lists some of the useful antifungal agents and their most likely mechanisms of action.

SUGGESTED READING

Chandler FW, Kaplan W, Ajello L. Histopathology of mycotic infections. Chicago: Year Book, 1980.

McGinnis MR. Current topics in medical mycology, vols. 1 and 2. New York: Springer Verlag, 1985, 1988.

Medoff G, Brajtburg J, Kobayashi GS, Bolard J. Antifungal agents useful in therapy of systemic fungal infections. Ann Rev Pharmacol 1983;23:303–330.

Reiss E. Molecular immunology of mycotic and antinomycotic infections. New York: Elsevier, 1986.

Rippon JW. Medical mycology: the pathogenic fungi and pathogenic actinomycetes, 3rd ed. Philadelphia: WB Saunders, 1988.

Systemic Mycoses Caused by Primary Pathogens

46

Gerald Medoff and George S. Kobayashi

CASES—AN OUTBREAK

Thirty-five members of several families from the Midwest camped on a farm in northwestern Tennessee for 2 weeks. In return for the use of the site, they helped the farmer clean out an old barn on the property. The barn had not been used for about 20 years and had become a gathering place for starlings. The walls and ground were caked with bird droppings and, inasmuch as the weather had been quite dry, considerable dust was stirred up when the ground was raked and the walls washed. The cleaning took several hours. Everyone then went home.

Over the next 6–12 days, 18 members of the group got sick with chills, fever, cough, and headache (Table 46.1). Several had substernal discomfort and others had painful red bumps on the front of their legs below the knee. Two patients had severe joint pains that shifted from the knees to the ankles and wrists.

In about 2 weeks, 14 of the campers got well without treatment. Several of these patients had seen their physician and had had chest x-rays. They showed infiltrates that disappeared after several weeks. Repeat chest x-rays on these patients 1 year later showed calcified hilar lymph nodes and calcified nodules in the periphery of the lungs (Fig. 46.1). Over the next year, one of these patients developed shortness of breath and progressive swelling of the lower extremities and the face. More x-rays showed a mass in his mediastinum, which compressed several bronchi. A venogram showed compression of the superior and inferior vena cava as well. Four of the other campers developed progressive histoplasmosis.

This is a description of a typical outbreak of histoplasmosis. Analysis of the case histories (Table 46.1) will reveal the most important points of the pathophysiology of the disease.

ENCOUNTER

The outbreak occurred in the state of Tennessee, which is in the so-called **"histo belt,"** a geographic area in the southeastern portion of the U.S. bordering the Mississippi and Ohio river valleys. The outbreak described is typical because cases often occur in clusters after a common exposure. The endemic zone extends through many of the tropical countries of the world. A clinically distinct form of histoplasmosis occurs in Africa (caused by a variety known as *Histoplasma capsulatum* var. *duboisii*) and is characterized by involvement of subcutaneous tis-

Table 46.1. Outcome of Infection with *H. capsulatum* in 35 Patients

Number of Patients	Clinical Course	Physical Findings	Chest X-rays	Laboratory Results
17	Asymptomatic	None	Lung infiltrates or mild increase in lymph node size, calcifications	Positive antibody reaction to antigens of *H. capsulatum;* positive skin tests with histoplasmin
18	Symptoms	Enlarged lymph nodes, rales on auscultation, skin lesions	Patchy infiltrates, enlarged hilar lymph nodes, calcified lymph nodes with calcified granulomas in the lung	Most developed positive antibody tests; most developed positive skin tests with histoplasmin antigen; cultures of sputum of the 14 patients were positive for *H. capsulatum*

sue, the skin, and bones, with little or no evidence of pulmonary disease.

H. capsulatum is a **soil organism** whose growth is enhanced by bird or bat excreta. Common sources of infection are old barns used as roosting sites by starlings, grackles, or chickens. Bat-roosting sites, such as trees or caves, are also important sources of the organism, particularly in the tropics. In the outbreak described, the dry weather, coupled with the vigorous activities of the group, led to the aerosolization of spores and fragments of hyphae. These were inhaled, and their small size allowed them to evade the anatomic defense mechanisms of the respiratory tract and reach the alveoli of the lung (Chapter 56).

ENTRY

The events following entry of *H. capsulatum* into the alveoli are unknown, but based on the physiology of the organism and the relevant factors in host defense, we can construct the following scheme: when spores or mycelial fragments of *H. capsulatum* are exposed to human body temperatures of 37°C, they transform into the yeast phase. Experiments with animals indicate that this transformation is required for pathogenicity. Also, only yeast cells are seen in tissues of infected hosts. The virulence of different strains of *H. capsulatum* is related to their level of tolerance to the elevated temperature; low levels of virulence and tolerance to elevated temperatures are associated with a delayed transformation to the yeast phase and slower growth of the yeast.

SPREAD AND MULTIPLICATION

In tissue, yeast cells of *H. capsulatum* are found **within macrophages** only. However, phagocytosis does not always lead to killing, and the intracellular habitat paradoxically results in protection of the fungus from other defenses of the host. What determines whether or not the macrophages will kill the yeast phase? Here again, we lack information but the following factors are probably important:

- If the **inoculum** of organisms is very large, macrophages are simply overwhelmed by the sheer number of organisms they ingest.

- Macrophages have to be **activated** to kill the fungi efficiently. Activation of macrophages, which occurs rapidly in a host sensitized by previous infection, would limit the infection.

- After ingestion, the organisms avoid being killed, perhaps by preventing the oxygen burst, or phagosome-lysosome fusion, or by resisting or neutralizing the degradative effects of lysosomes.

The outcome of the initial interaction between the host cells and the fungi is either death of the organisms or inhibition of their multiplication and spread to local lymphatics and from there to other organs. After 1–2 weeks, cellular immunity is stimulated and host reticuloendothelial cells become more efficient in limiting growth and multiplication of the fungus. The infection is thus curtailed and eventually resolves. Yeast cells may remain viable within **calcified lesions** for years and may be a source for reactivation of infection when immunity wanes. This sequence of events is the same as in tuberculosis, and, in fact, the granulomas formed in response to *H. capsulatum* are very similar to those seen in tuberculosis (and, for that matter, all primary systemic mycoses).

Seventeen of the people exposed to *H. capsulatum* in the barn were asymptomatic. Perhaps they only inhaled a small number of organisms or had been sensitized by prior infection to deal efficiently with renewed exposure. About 80–90% of adults who have lived in the "histo belt" have positive skin tests to antigens of *H. capsulatum*, evidence of their cellular immunity.

DAMAGE

Fourteen of the people experienced a self-limited disease that disappeared, presumably as cellular immunity developed. These people were left with the scars of the disease, seen on chest x-rays as calcified granulomas (Fig. 46.1). It is not known why calcifications occur, but macrophages in granulomas make a factor that elevates calcium levels in the blood. All of these people had elevated antibody titers to fungal antigens. One person in this group developed a particularly intense immune response, which resulted in a proliferative tissue reaction (**mediastinal granulomatosis**). Eventually, the advanced fibrosis impinged on vital structures in the chest (sclerosing mediastinitis). This process was not due to active infection but to the immune response gone awry. This is a rare complication of infection with *H. capsulatum*, and can only be treated surgically by removing the fibrotic tissue.

Each of the four people who developed progressive disease after the initial infection illustrates the failure of an important component of host defenses to limit infection:

- Patient A had severe chronic obstructive pulmonary disease and emphysema. Because of the anatomic abnormalities and scarring in his lung, he could not clear the infection. An effective systemic response and the use of potent antifungal therapy limited the infection to the lung. Increasing damage to the lung by continued infection and local spread resulted in further destruction and a relentless downhill course until he died from pulmonary insufficiency 5 years after the onset of infection.

- In patient B, there was continued disease in the lungs and, ultimately, dissemination of the infection to other organs. Failure to limit and to contain the infection may have been due to a particularly large inoculum inhaled at the time of exposure or to some subtle or transient defect in host defenses. In disseminated histoplasmosis, T-cell function is defective but it is not known whether this is the cause or the result of the disease. One of the manifestations of the disease is ulcerations of the oral mucosa. It is not unusual to find mucosal lesions as the sole sign of disease. We do not understand why *H. capsulatum* has this unusual tropism for mucous membranes. It is not

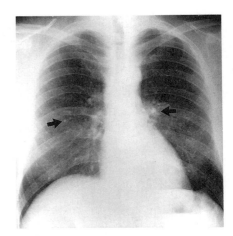

Figure 46.1.   Chest x-ray showing calcifications of the lung and mediastinal lymph nodes consistent with healed histoplasmosis.

Table 46.2. Systemic Mycoses Caused by Primary Pathogens

Disease	Etiological Agent	Epidemiology	Clinical Disease	Histopathology	Therapy
Histoplasmosis	*H. capsulatum:* dimorphic; mycelial in the environment; in tissue, a budding yeast usually found within phagocytes	Endemic in the U.S. in the Ohio and Mississippi River Valleys; also worldwide; Soil organism whose growth is enhanced in locations contaminated by bird or bat excreta	About 90% of all primary cases are not clinically significant; In the endemic area, many individuals have x-ray signs consistent with past disease (i.e., calcification) but cannot give a history of relevant infections; they will require treatment; here there may be underlying conditions that makes these individuals prone to progressive disease	Yeasts are found in histiocytes; there are epithelioid granulomas	Ketoconazole is the drug of choice; amphotericin B is used in treatment of failures or rapidly progressive disease
Blastomycosis	*Blastomyces dermatitidis:* dimorphic; in tissue, a yeast with buds attached to parent cell by broad base usually found in microabscesses	Isolated cases occur all over North America	Pulmonary infection with chronic skin and bone disease; other forms are urogenital disseminated disease involving multiple organs; like the fungi causing the other primary systemic infections, the organism is inhaled and invades via the lungs; however, in disseminated disease, the lung fields are frequently clear and free of disease	Large budding yeasts with broad bases are characteristic and seen in microabcesses and granulomas	Same drugs as in histoplasmosis
Coccidioidomycosis	*Coccidioides immitis:* dimorphic; in tissues, the organism develops into a sporangium ("spherule") 10–70 µm in diameter, filled with endospores	Southwestern U.S. and parts of Central and South America; epidemics may be associated with dust storms	Approximately 60% of these infections are asymptomatic; 40% are symptomatic with the spectrum of disease ranging from mild influenza-like complaints to frank pneumonia and spread to other areas of the body, including the CNS; dark-skinned patients (African-Americans and Orientals) appear to be more prone to develop progressive disseminated disease	Pyogenic, granulomatous, and mixed cellular reactions are present; spherules and endospores are seen	Ketoconazole is effective in nonmeningeal disease; parental amphotericin B and direct instillation of the drug into the CNS is required to treat meningitis; oral fluconazole may be effective in CNS disease
Paracoccidioidomycosis	*Paracoccidioides brasiliensis:* dimorphic; in tissues, a yeast with several budding cells attached to its surface	Most countries of South America and parts of Central America; the infection is strikingly more common in males than in females	Pulmonary disease is often inapparent, as in blastomycosis; ulcerative granulomas of buccal, nasal, and occasionally the gastrointestinal mucosa indicate dissemination	Very similar to that seen in blastomycosis	Ketoconazole is the therapeutic agent of choice; amphotericin B is used in treatment failures

unique to this disease, but does help in the diagnosis. The fungus also spreads to many other organs, including the bone marrow and the adrenal glands, where it causes insufficiency of adrenal function (Addison's disease), a complication also seen in disseminated tuberculosis. This patient was treated with ketoconazole and did well. In general, when disseminated disease is diagnosed early in an otherwise apparently normal host, the prognosis is good.

● Patient C suffered an acute overwhelming pulmonary infection, probably because she had been previously sensitized and, on this occasion, may have inhaled a very large inoculum. The damage to her lungs probably resulted from direct tissue damage by the fungi and from the inflammatory reaction made more severe by the previous sensitization. This patient was critically ill because her pulmonary function was severely compromised. After treatment with amphotericin B, the patient improved and the pulmonary infiltrates cleared rapidly.

● Patient D had AIDS. Because he lacked a normal T-cell response, he succumbed to an overwhelming infection, which spread to every organ. He was unresponsive to intensive therapy with amphotericin B. This underlines the importance of the cooperation between host defenses and chemotherapy for a successful outcome. Disseminated histoplasmosis occurs in patients with AIDS either as the result of newly acquired infection or by reactivation of old disease. Like the tubercle bacillus, *H. capsulatum* may persist in a dormant state in cells of the reticuloendothelial system for many years after primary infection and may reactivate when host resistance becomes severely impaired.

OTHER SYSTEMIC MYCOSES

The pathophysiology and clinical manifestations of histoplasmosis are very similar to those of the other primary systemic mycoses listed in Table 46.2 and all can be categorized along with tuberculosis as granulomatous infections.

SUGGESTED READING

Bradsher DA. Blastomycosis. Inf Dis Clin North Am 1988;2:877–898.
Stevens DA. Coccidioidomycosis, a text. New York: Plenum Medical Book Co., 1983.
Wheat JL. Histoplasmosis. Inf Dis Clin North Am 1988;2:841–860.

Systemic Mycoses Caused by Opportunistic Fungi

47

Gerald Medoff and George S. Kobayashi

The more pathogenic the infecting microorganism, the less host susceptibility it needs to cause disease. The fungi we describe here are not very pathogenic, and to cause disease, need help, usually in the form of decreased host resistance. Understanding the underlying host defects in opportunistic fungal infections may allow us to reverse or to lessen the predisposing factors. If we cannot accomplish this, the prognosis is worse.

Patients at high risk are those with malignancies, organ or bone transplants, **AIDS**, burns, operations, trauma, or illnesses that require long-term use of intravenous or intra-arterial catheters. Also at risk are patients who have received broad-spectrum antibacterial therapy and whose normal intestinal bacterial flora has markedly decreased. In such cases, fungi like *Candida albicans* proliferate unchecked and can replace the bacteria of the normal flora.

On the basis of clinical experience, a decrease in the number of functioning neutrophils is the most important host defect that affects the response to fungal infection. These infections are hard enough to treat in a normal host, but cure is almost impossible when there are few functioning white cells. Premature babies and the elderly also tend to do poorly when infected with fungi. Why do you think this is the case?

The weakly pathogenic fungi that cause opportunistic systemic mycoses are nearly ubiquitous. They may be part of our flora or they may be inhaled or ingested from the environment.

CASE OF ENDOGENOUS INFECTION

A 19-year-old woman, Ms. J., was involved in a bicycle accident and sustained severe cervical spinal cord trauma resulting in quadriplegia. She required an indwelling urinary catheter, which led to multiple urinary tract infections. These were treated with a variety of broad-spectrum antibiotics. She has also had several episodes of Candida *infections of her mouth, perineal area, and vagina.*

At the time of the present admission to the hospital, there was again evidence of urinary tract infection manifested by cloudy urine and fever. On the 10th hospital day, urography revealed a large left kidney with delayed function and poor urine concentration.

Microscopic examination of sediment obtained by centrifuging urine samples and specimens of tissue obtained surgically showed budding yeast cells, pseudohyphae, and hyphal elements; this permitted a rapid presumptive di-

agnosis of Candida *infection. Further laboratory tests identified the organism as* C. albicans. *Blood cultures taken after a febrile episode grew the same organism.*

*   C. albicans is the most frequent species that causes this type of infection, although infection may also be due to other species. Careful examination of the retina with an ophthalmoscope revealed a "fluffy" cottony growth due to the organism. Ms. J.'s heart valve became infected and she developed a heart murmur. In addition, she developed weakness on the right side of her face.*

Candida are carried in the posterior pharynx and the bowel of many healthy individuals. In the case of Ms. J., there was overgrowth of this organism because the normal flora was suppressed by the multiple courses of antibiotics. This yeast then contaminated the bladder and the infection spread into the urinary system. *Candida* appears to have a particular tropism for the kidney. From the kidney, the yeast probably spread through the blood to the several different organs described above. This spread was probably due to an organism-laden clot that traveled to her brain from her infected heart valve. Disseminated candidiasis often follows such a series of devastating events. Systemic infection is usually preceded by other superficial infections, like those involving the mouth, the pharynx, the esophagus, or other parts of the gastrointestinal tract or the vagina.

All forms of systemic *Candida* infections are potentially life threatening and require therapy. Consideration should always be given to the primary predisposing factors, and these should be minimized or reversed. In the case of Ms. J., the catheter and intravenous lines were probably infected at the time of the candidemia and had to be changed. Carefully monitored doses of amphotericin B and 5-fluorocytosine were used. Had the response not been adequate, Ms. J.'s infected heart valve would have had to be removed and replaced by a prosthesis.

This is an example of an opportunistic infection resulting from anatomic defects in the host. The white blood count and the immune responses were normal, yet successful management with antifungal drugs required repair of the anatomic defects. The prognosis is guarded.

CASE OF EXOGENOUS INFECTION

*   Mr. S., a 25-year-old man was hospitalized for treatment of acute lymphocytic leukemia. The initial diagnosis was made 20 months earlier when he complained of general malaise and weakness. At the time, his white blood cell count was greater than 100,000/mm³ with 93% lymphocytes and lymphoblasts, all values much greater than normal. A bone marrow aspiration established the diagnosis of leukemia. He was treated with anticancer drugs, which produced a complete remission.*

*   One year later, he had a relapse of leukemia. He was treated with large doses of the anticancer agents cyclophosphamide and cytarabine, which resulted in leukopenia and thrombocytopenia. A chest x-ray showed nodular lesions in both lungs. Blood cultures were negative. Microscopic examination of sputum specimens and a skin biopsy of a purpuric lesion revealed septate branching hyphae 7–10 μm in diameter and several hundred μm in length (Fig. 47.1). Cultures resulted in colonies of a white mold that quickly developed a smoky gray color. This, and the shape and arrangement of the asexual spores identified the organism as* Aspergillus fumigatus.

*   Serological tests yielded an antibody titer of 1:4 to* Aspergillus *antigens, which is not conclusive. Nevertheless, based on the clinical findings and the microscopic and culture results, a diagnosis of invasive aspergillosis was made. Therapy with amphotericin B was immediately initiated on Mr. S. Often, treatment for fungal infections in this kind of host has to start on the*

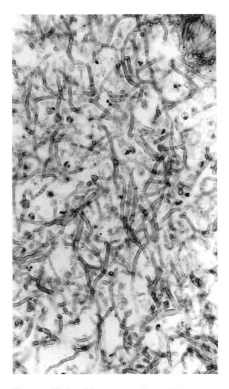

Figure 47.1. Tissue section of lung infected with *Aspergillus fumigatus.* Septate hyphae and dichotomous branching are characteristic features of organisms belonging to this group of fungi.

basis of clinical suspicion because diagnosis by culture of blood or other body fluids is inconclusive.

Aspergilli are a group of molds so ubiquitous that they may easily be cultured from the air, soil, or moldy vegetation. The major pathogenic species is *A. fumigatus*, but others may also cause disease. They are not part of the normal flora of humans and do not grow in normal tissue. They cause invasive disease only in profoundly immunocompromised subjects, particularly those with neutropenia, like **Mr. S.** The initial site of invasion is usually the lung or the paranasal sinuses, and this was probably the case in this patient. The lesions seen in x-rays include focal consolidation, lobar pneumonia, and lung cavities that contain "fungus balls" of the mold (Fig. 47.2). Patients with such invasive infections also have intracerebral abscesses, necrotic ulcers of skin, and lesions of bone, liver, and the breast.

Aspergillus may also cause noninfectious disease, such as allergy or asthma, following either inhalation and growth of the fungus in the bronchial tree (**allergic bronchopulmonary aspergillosis**). Aspergilli also elaborate toxic metabolic products, the aflatoxins, which are hepatotoxic or carcinogenic, although their role in cancers of humans has not been established.

OTHER MYCOSES CAUSED BY OPPORTUNISTIC FUNGI

Severely immunocompromised hosts suffer from a large number of other opportunistic systemic fungal infections as well. The etiology of the most frequent ones are listed in Table 47.1. The so-called zygomycoses have two principal clinical presentations. The **rhinocerebral form** is unique to diabetics, particularly those with diabetic ketoacidosis. These patients often have sinus infections, periorbital cellulitis (infection of the connective tissue around the eye), and tissue necrosis that may extend to the central nervous system. It is not known why dia-

Figure 47.2.   A chest x-ray of primary *Aspergillus pneumonia* with "fungus balls."

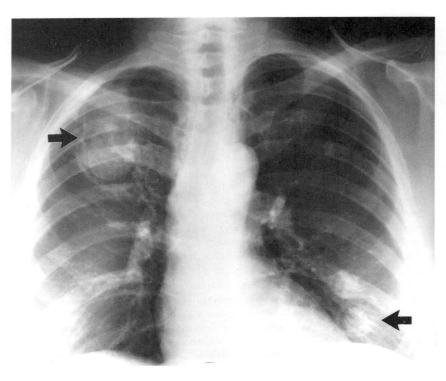

Table 47.1. Mycoses Caused by Opportunistic Fungi

Disease	Fungus	Predisposing Factors	Involvement	Therapy
Cryptococcosis	*Cryptococcus neoformans*	Immunosuppression, none	Lung, most prominent in CNS, kidney, bone	Amphoteracin B + 5-FC, fluconazole
Candidiasis	*Candida albicans* and other species	Immunosuppression, broad-spectrum antibiotics, foreign bodies	Mucosal areas, GI tract, blood, kidney, other organs	Amphotericin B + 5-FC, fluconazole
Aspergillosis	*Aspergillus fumigatus* and other species	Immunosuppression	Lungs, other organs	Amphotericin B
Zygomycosis	Serveral genera and species of *Phycomyces*	Diabetes, burn, immunosuppression	Blood vessels, eye, CNS, nose, sinuses, lungs	Amphotericin B
Other	Many other genera and species (each one infrequent)	Immunosuppression, trauma, or not known	Lungs, CNS, soft tissue, joints, eye, disseminated infection	Amphotericin B, miconazole

betes predisposes to this infection, but it has been postulated, on the basis of laboratory data, that the acidotic state of the diabetic patient stimulates growth of this fungus.

The second type, **disseminated zygomycosis**, has a clinical presentation almost identical to that of disseminated aspergillosis. In contrast to the hyphae of *Aspergillus* and *Candida*, the fungal elements seen in pathological specimens of zygomycosis are nonseptate, branch irregularly, and produce bizarre balloon-shaped cells.

Cryptococcosis is usually listed among the opportunistic fungal infection, although it also occurs in normal persons. In recent years, cryptococcal infection, particularly meningitis, has occurred most prominently in patients with **AIDS** (see Chapter 67). In fact, 90% of patients with cryptococcal meningitis in the U.S. have **AIDS** and it is estimated that this form of meningitis will eventually develop in 5–10% of all **AIDS** patients.

The etiological agent is an encapsulated yeast, *Cryptococcus neoformans*, which is found in the excreta of birds, particularly pigeons. The organism is also found on rotted fruits and vegetables. The organism is inhaled into the lungs where it can cause pneumonia. However, the most frequent clinical presentation is meningitis. There is no explanation for the striking tropism of this organism for the central nervous system. Brain abscesses caused by *C. neoformans* have a particularly interesting feature; they (usually) elicit little or no tissue response (Fig. 47.3). Thus, damage is caused by displacement and pressure on brain tissue rather than by inflammation. The mechanism is also not known, but may have something to do with the properties of the capsule.

The diagnosis of cryptococcal meningitis is made by examining samples of cerebrospinal fluid for budding yeast cells with capsules outlined by India Ink particles (Fig. 47.4). A serological test can detect soluble capsular polysaccharide in the cerebrospinal fluid of over 90% of patients with this disease. Both microscopic and serological tests can be performed right after lumbar puncture and the diagnosis may be made before obtaining results from a culture, which takes several days. This allows early therapy with a combination of amphotericin B and 5-fluorocytosine. More recently, fluconazole has also been used successfully.

Prognosis depends on the overall clinical status of the patient. A good prognostic sign is a falling antigen titer followed by the detection of circulating antibodies to the cryptococcal polysaccharide. If there is

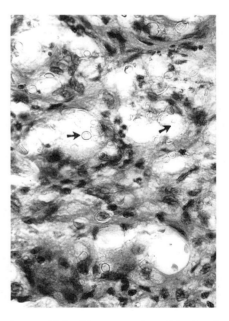

Figure 47.3. Tissue section of brain of patient with cryptococcosis. Note yeast cells (*arrows*) typical of *Cryptococcus neoformans* within spaces occupied by capsular material and general absence of cellular response.

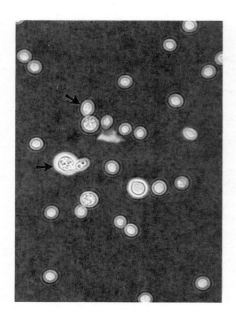

Figure 47.4.   India ink preparation of spinal fluid containing encapsulated yeast cells of *Cryptococcus neoformans.*

no underlying disease, 80–90% of patients respond to therapy. If patients are severely immunocompromised, less than 50% will survive. Patients with AIDS respond to therapy but will relapse after treatment is stopped. For this reason, lifelong antifungal therapy is required to suppress the infection.

SUGGESTED READING

Levitz SM. Aspergillosis. Inf Dis Clin North Am 1988;3:1–18.

Macher AM, DeVinatea ML, Tuur M, Anzritt P. AIDS and the mycoses. Inf Dis Clin North Am 1988;2:827–840.

Odds FC. *Candida* and candidiosis, 2nd ed. Philadelphia: WB Saunders Co., 1988.

Subcutaneous, Cutaneous, and Superficial Mycoses

48

Gerald Medoff and George S. Kobayashi

SUBCUTANEOUS MYCOSES

A distinctive group of fungal diseases involve the subcutaneous tissue, the dermis, and the epidermis. These subcutaneous infections originate in the deeper tissue layers and eventually extend out through the dermis and the epidermis. Spread through the bloodstream is unusual but the lymphatics may be involved as far as the draining lymph nodes. Most of these mycoses, along with other "jungle rots," are confined to tropical climates. Sporotrichosis is the only relatively common infection in temperate climates.

Subcutaneous infections are called mycoses of implantation because the organisms enter the skin via thorns or splinters. Consequently, sporotrichosis is considered to be an occupational risk for gardeners, florists, and plant hobbyists. In addition to involving the subcutaneous tissue, the diseases of this group have several other features in common.

- Encounter: the etiological agents are ubiquitous and usually found in soil or decaying vegetation.

- Entry: the patient can usually give a history of trauma preceding appearance of lesions. As a result, the infections occur on the parts of the body that are most prone to be traumatized, e.g., feet, legs, hands, buttocks.

- Spread: these infections are slow in onset and lesions evolve over many months. This persistence may be due to the noninvasive properties of this group of organisms and may be fostered by tissue damage and foreign material in the wounds. Malnutrition, which is common in the populations most frequently infected, may also be a factor.

- Diagnosis: some of these organisms are commonly encountered in the laboratory, and single isolations must, therefore, be confirmed by repeated cultures. The presence of fungi with a characteristic morphology in tissue specimens is helpful in diagnosis.

- Treatment: with few exceptions (sporotrichosis, chromoblastomycosis), the subcutaneous mycoses are difficult to treat and often require surgical intervention. The reason for the lack of response to drug therapy is unknown. Possibly, the organisms are only marginally sensitive to antifungal agents, but more likely, the chronic inflammatory reaction makes these fungi inaccessible both to drugs and to host defense mechanisms.

Subcutaneous sporotrichosis responds to potassium iodide, which is puzzling inasmuch as this compound has no in vitro effect against the fungus. The reason for its therapeutic effect is not known, although some think that it may affect the host response to infection. It is interesting that only the subcutaneous form of sporotrichosis responds well to this compound.

Several bacterial infections, such as those caused by *Staphylococcus*, *Nocardia*, or *Actinomyces* or by atypical mycobacteria, may mimic clinical and pathological manifestations of the subcutaneous fungal infections. Because most of these can be treated with antibacterial antibiotics, it is extremely important to determine the etiology of the infection. This is most effectively done by surgical biopsy. In the case of sporotrichosis, culture is more useful than histology, because the yeast-like organisms are difficult to find on histopathological examination. Table 48.1 summarizes the important features of the principal subcutaneous mycoses.

CUTANEOUS MYCOSES OR DERMATOMYCOSES

The dermatomycoses of humans include a wide spectrum of infections of the skin and its appendages (hair and nails) by fungi known as dermatophytes. In the asexual state, these fungi are classified in the genera *Microsporum*, *Trichophyton*, and *Epidermophyton* on the basis of sporulation patterns and morphological features of development.

Table 48.1. Fungi—Subcutaneous Mycoses

Disease	Etiological Agent(s)	Clinical Disease	Therapy
Sporotrichosis	*Sporothrix schenckii*	Lymphocutaneous sporotrichosis is the disease most commonly associated with this fungus; the organism gains access to the deep layers of skin by traumatic implantation; a small hard painless nodule appears at the site of injury and it enlarges into a fluctuant mass that eventually breaks down and ulcerates; as the primary lesion enlarges, several other nodules begin to develop along lymphatics that drain that site; they also become fluctuant and ulcerate; the infection rarely extends beyond regional lymphatics	Saturated solution of potassium iodide given orally is the drug of choice; amphotericin B is used for diseases involving the lung and other organs
Chromoblastomycosis	*Fonsecaea pedrosoi*; many species	Most common form—warty, vegetative lesions that look like a cauliflower	Surgical excision and cryosurgery; 5-fluorocytosine has been used successfully, but response depends on the organism
Others, e.g., rhinosporidiosis, lobomycosis, etc.	Many species	Many manifestations—deep subcutaneous masses, wart-like lesions, polyps, etc.	Surgical excision, antifungal drugs

Some species are found worldwide, others are geographically restricted to certain parts of the world. These patterns are becoming disrupted by the increasing mobility of the world's population.

CASES

Two adult teaching volunteers in a school for mentally handicapped children were seen by their physicians because each had developed well-demarcated, scaly, itchy lesions on their skin (Fig. 481). Clinical history revealed that these lesions had developed over a period of several weeks since they started their work. Both were childless and had no contact with domestic or wild animals. Microscopic examination of skin scales taken from the lesions showed the presence of fungal elements (Fig. 48.2) and cultures grew Trichophyton tonsurans.

An epidemiological inquiry and clinical survey of seven students in the school revealed that two had patchy hair loss (alopecia). One of these had typical ringworm of the scalp and the other had highly inflammatory lesions associated with ringworm called kerion (Fig. 48.3). The five other students appeared asymptomatic except for mild dandruff. Cultures of scalp scrapings of two of these were positive for T. tonsurans.

The parents of the children were notified of these findings and asked to have their family physician examine the siblings of each student. The brother of one of the asymptomatic students who had a positive culture for T. tonsurans was found to have ringworm of the scalp. All of the children and the two adults were treated with griseofulvin and all responded well.

This example of an outbreak of dermatophytosis illustrates several points:

● In occupations where adults come into close contact with children, such as nursing and teaching of the handicapped, it is not uncommon to find ringworm of the body in adults during outbreaks of ringworm of the scalp in the children, both caused by the same organism.

● The clinical manifestations of these infections are variable. Of the five students who had what appeared to be dandruff, two grew the fungus from the scalp. The two others had hair loss and distinct clinical diseases, regular ringworm and kerion.

● Ringworm of the scalp is a frequent problem in the pediatric population. At puberty, it spontaneously ceases to be a problem, treated or untreated. In the adult population, ringworm of the scalp is rare. The patient usually has close association with infected children or animals that have clinical disease.

ENCOUNTER

Different species of dermatophytes have different ecological niches. Some species are most frequently isolated from the soil and are called geophilic. Other species, found most often in association with domestic and wild animals, are called zoophilic. A third group, the anthropophilic ones, are found almost exclusively in association with humans and their habitat.

It is important to identify the species to determine the possible source of infection. Identification even has some prognostic value. The anthropophilic dermatophytes tend to cause chronic infections and may be difficult to treat. The zoophilic and geophilic ones tend to cause inflammatory lesions that may heal spontaneously.

Dermatophytes are not members of the normal skin flora. Although they are occasionally found in people's toe clefts, these fungi almost al-

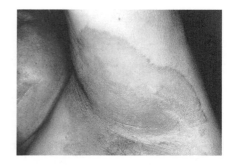

Figure 48.1. Clinical appearance of tinea corporis. Note the well-demarcated border of the lesions, which suggest that a worm or larva is at the margin, hence the terms ringworm or "tinea" (worm) to describe the lesions.

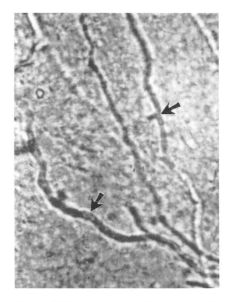

Figure 48.2. Specimen taken from skin of patient with tinea corporis, treated with 10% potassium hydroxide. A positive preparation is indicated by presence of hyphae (*arrows*).

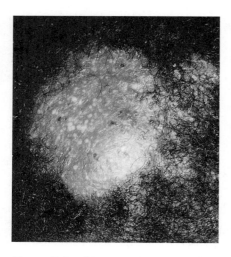

Figure 48.3.   Clinical photograph of tinea capitis showing the inflammatory lesion called "kerion."

ways cause some minor pathology once they become established. The disease caused by these fungi is called **ringworm** or **tinea**. The term tinea comes from Latin (worm) and refers to the serpentine lesions that characterize these infections and that look as if a worm is burrowing at the margin. This term is used in conjunction with the part of the body that is affected to describe the disease, e.g., **tinea capitis** (head), **tinea pedis** (feet), **tinea corporis** (body), **tinea cruris** (crotch). Other terms often are used by the layman to describe these diseases, such as athlete's foot, jock itch, jungle rot, etc.

ENTRY

Experimental studies on dermatophyte infections have been useful for understanding their clinical manifestations. Volunteers who immersed their feet in water teeming with viable spores of the causative fungi did not get athlete's foot unless the skin was first traumatized. Continuous moist conditions were also important, and infections took place when the skin was occluded with nonporous materials. This increases hydration and temperature of the skin and interferes with the natural barrier function of the superficial layer, the stratum corneum. Such conditions are caused by wearing nonporous shoes or covering the skin with occlusive bandages.

SPREAD AND MULTIPLICATION

A classical ringworm lesion is characterized by the presence of fungal mycelium in the stratum corneum. Growth of the fungus sometimes result in minimal clinical signs of infection. In active disease there is an inflammatory reaction in the underlying epidermis and dermis. There is often scaling, indicating increased epidermal turnover. Toe nails and finger nails as well as hair follicles and hair shaft may be invaded. The fungi particularly prefer keratinized tissues and do not invade living cells or the incompletely keratinized zone of the hair bulb. Although keratinases have been found in some dermatophytes, their role in the disease is unknown.

DAMAGE

The clinical features of this disease are all related to the inflammation of the epidermis, the dermis, and the hair follicles. What sets this off is an immunologically mediated reaction to the fungal antigens that diffuse from the infected epidermis. You could call this a biological contact dermatitis. The extent of the inflammatory response and cellular infiltration correlate well with the degree of delayed hypersensitivity of the skin to extracts of the dermatophyte ("trichophytin"). The term kerion is used to describe the highly inflammatory pustular form of infection in the scalp and beard areas. The pus results from secondary bacterial infections.

The ring-shaped characteristic of dermatophyte lesions is the result of the organism growing outwardly in a centrifugal pattern. The area of the lesion that would yield viable fungal elements is at the inflamed margin. The central area generally has few or no viable fungi, and the healing tissue is refractory to infection. This pattern simulates the centrifugal growth of "fairy ring" mushrooms in a grassy field.

Systemic infections by dermatophytes are extremely rare, no matter how impaired the host. The most likely reasons are inability of dermatophytes to grow at body temperature and the presence of nonspecific serum factors (e.g., transferrin).

Environmental and cultural habits associated with types of clothing and shoes contribute to the incidence of dermatophytosis. Studies on institutionalized populations and families show that close and crowded living conditions are important in spreading the infections. Immunological factors also contribute to their incidence and there is evidence that natural cell-mediated resistance to these infections is important.

The prevalence of dermatophytes and the incidence of disease are both difficult to determine since these diseases do not have to be reported to the U.S. Public Health Service. Fragmentary surveys from epidemiological studies and case reports indicate that these are among the most common of human diseases. They are among the most common skin disorders in children under the age of 12 years and the second most common in older populations.

Different age groups manifest these diseases at different anatomic sites. In the pediatric population, the most prevalent problem is ringworm of the scalp, which is most common in the 5-to 10-year olds. At puberty, this ceases to be a problem. On the other hand, athlete's foot, which is rarely a disease in childhood, gradually becomes the predominant infection and remains so throughout life. The reason for this shift is not well understood, but may be due to changes in the composition of sebum that occur at puberty, particularly in the even-numbered saturated fatty acids that have natural fungistatic activity. The fact that humans are generally shod is perhaps the major factor that leads to the high incidence of athlete's foot in adults.

In the U.S., there is a disproportionate incidence of ringworm of the scalp in black children. We do not know why. Natives of India have higher incidence of this disease than resident Europeans. Studies from the Vietnam war revealed that athlete's foot in U.S. servicemen was mainly caused by *Trichophyton mentagraphytes*, whereas the native Vietnamese were more susceptible to *T. rubrum*.

The incidence of dermatophytosis is higher in males than in females, with ratios of 3:1 for ringworm of the scalp and 6:1 for athlete's foot. Tinea cruris (jock itch) is also common in males and rare in females. Infection of the nails of the hands is more common in females, but nails of the feet are more often involved in males.

DIAGNOSIS

When examined microscopically in scrapings of the skin surface in infected areas, dermatophytes all look alike. In culture, however, dermatophyte colonies have complex morphological characteristics that distinguish genus and species. Under the microscope, they differ in the morphology of specialized large multicelled spores, the macroconidia.

TREATMENT

The dermatophytoses may be treated topically or systemically. Systemic treatment is necessary when hair or nails are infected because locally applied fungicides do not penetrate the tissue matrix where the fungus resides.

There are various local applications, creams, ointments, lotions, or paints that, when used regularly for 3 weeks or more, will clear many of the localized ringworm infections. Controlled trials have not demonstrated a clear leader among antiringworm drugs. In most cases, regular application is more important than the choice of agent.

Two antiringworm agents are given systemically of by oral administration; they are the antibiotic griseofulvin and the imidazole derivative ketoconazole.

SUPERFICIAL MYCOSES

Many of us harbor fungi on our skin and hairs without signs of disease. At times, these fungal members of our normal flora cause very superficial infections that go no deeper than the stratum corneum. They are frequently mild, do not stimulate an inflammatory response, and may go unnoticed. These conditions are often seen in warm and moist climates, but one, tinea versicolor, is frequently found in the temperate areas. Superficial mycoses are usually easy to treat with topical keratolytic agents.

Review of the Medically Important Fungi

This chart may be completed to review material covered under this topic.

	Name of Disease or Fungus	Epidemiology	Main Symptoms
Systemic "true pathogens" 1.			
2.			
3.			
Systemic opportunistic 1.			
2.			
3.			
Subcutaneous 1.			
2.			
Superficial 1.			
2.			

Introduction to Parasitology

49

Donald J. Krogstad

In developed countries, parasitology suggests the strange and exotic—"worms, wheezes, and weird diseases." **Parasitic diseases** occur most frequently in developing countries but parasitic infections, often without clinical symptoms, are common even in developed countries and are being recognized with increasing frequency (Table 49.1). In North America and Europe, parasitic diseases are particularly prevalent among immunosuppressed patients.

Several parasitic diseases of humans are zoonoses—caused by agents that also infect other mammals, birds, or reptiles (see Chapter 69 and Paradigm, Chapter 27). In some instances, the parasites require both humans and animals to complete their life cycle. For example, the developmental cycle of the beef tapeworm requires that both humans and cattle become infected. In other instances, parasites of animals infect humans, but cannot complete their biological development. An example is the blood fluke (schistosome) of birds, which causes "swimmer's itch." This parasite cannot complete its developmental stages in people; humans represent "dead-end hosts."

As with other infectious agents, here too we must distinguish between infection and disease. For example, a large proportion of the adults in the U.S. have been infected with the protozoa *Toxoplasma gondii*, as shown by the prevalence of antitoxoplasma antibodies. However, few people become ill from this infection. Similarly, people with small numbers of intestinal worms are typically asymptomatic. This is well demonstrated in the case of hookworms, which produce anemia by ingesting blood from vessels in the intestinal wall. Each worm causes the loss of a small amount of blood (0.03–0.15 ml/day); thus, the severity of the disease is related to the number of worms present.

Table 49.1. Estimated Worldwide Prevalence of Parasitic Infections

Toxoplasmosis	1–2 billion
Ascariasis	1 billion
Hookworm disease	800–900 million
Amebiasis	200–400 million
Schistosomiasis	200–300 million
Malaria	200–300 million
Filariasis	250 million
Giardiasis	200 million
Pinworm infection	60–100 million
Strongyloidiasis	50–80 million
Guinea worm infection	20–40 million
Trypanosomiasis	15–20 million
Leishmaniasis	1–2 million

In contrast to the acute illnesses caused by many bacteria or viruses, parasitic diseases are usually more chronic and are rarely lethal over a short period of time, even if untreated. There are, however, important exceptions, such as malaria caused by *Plasmodium falciparum*, which may be rapidly fatal in normal nonimmune persons. Other usually "mild" parasitic infections may cause disseminated disease and death in immunocompromised patients (e.g., toxoplasmosis).

Definitions

Protozoa. Protozoa are one-celled eukaryotes. Protozoan parasites of medical interest include the agents of amebiasis, giardiasis, malaria, cryptosporidiosis, leishmaniasis, and trypanosomiasis. Within the human host, some protozoa are intracellular (malaria parasites live within red cells; leishmania live within macrophages), whereas others are extracellular (amoebae and giardia reside in the gastrointestinal tract; pneumocystis—which may be a fungus—is found free in the alveolus of the lung).

Protozoa that infect the blood and deep tissues are often intracellular and unable to withstand the external environment. Consequently, their life cycle does not usually include free environmental stages, and they are typically transmitted from one host to another by the bites of arthropods. For example, the plasmodia that cause malaria are transmitted by mosquitoes. Extracellular intestinal protozoa, on the other hand, are transmitted most often by the fecal-oral route. These parasites typically have an active, or **trophozoite** form that carries out vegetative growth and replication, and a dormant **cyst** form that is resistant to drying and to acid in the stomach, thus allowing them to survive the transition between one host and another.

Helminths. Helminths, or worms, are multicellular animals (metazoa), considerably larger than the protozoa. Indeed, a human intestinal roundworm (*Ascaris lumbricoides*) bears a resemblance to an earthworm. Many different helminths such as tapeworms, hookworms, pinworms, whipworms, and others cause human disease. Because of their large size, helminths are extracellular. They are sometimes found within tissues in a resting form called a **cyst**.

Most helminths infect the intestinal tract, but several important ones infect the internal organs and a few cause disease both in the intestine and in the deep tissues. Many helminths have complex life cycles that involve environmental or animal reservoirs. They may be transmitted by insect bites, by oral ingestion, or via the penetration of unbroken skin.

Vectors. Vectors are living transmitters of disease. A well-known example is the female *Anopheles* mosquito, which transmits malaria. Other important vectors and the diseases they transmit include tsetse flies—sleeping sickness, black flies—river blindness, kissing bugs—Chagas' disease, and ticks — babesiosis. Most vectors are **arthropods**, such as mosquitoes, flies, and mites. Arthropods may transmit not only parasites but also bacteria (e.g., the agents of Lyme disease or Rocky Mountain spotted fever) and viruses (e.g., encephalitis viruses).

Reservoirs. Reservoirs are the sources of parasites in the environment. Reservoirs of parasitic infections may be other animals (pigs for trichinosis and pork tapeworm, cattle for beef tapeworm), in the environment (contaminated soil for roundworms and hookworms), or other humans (malarial plasmodia, amoebae).

ENTRY

A striking aspect of animal parasites is the number of ways they have evolved to enter the host. The most common modes of entry are by oral ingestion or penetration through the skin. Transmission of parasitic disease is often due to contamination of food or water, or to inadequate control of human wastes. This generalization is most applicable to diseases transmitted by the fecal-oral route or by larval penetration of the skin. Arthropod-borne disease transmission is dependent on inadequate sanitation to provide stagnant water for vector breeding; this mode of transmission may be extraordinarily effective. For instance, malaria may be acquired by a single bite of an infected female mosquito during a stop at an airport in an endemic area.

SPREAD AND MULTIPLICATION

Although some parasitic diseases may be acquired by the ingestion or inoculation of only a few eggs or cysts, a sizable inoculum is often required. The size of the effective inoculum has been determined for a few parasites by experimental infections in human volunteers and animals, usually in conjunction with careful quantitative epidemiological studies. For example, large inocula are needed to produce amebiasis in humans. In some instances, such as ascariasis, the larger the inoculum, the more severe the disease.

Species and Tissue Tropisms

The life cycle of a parasite is based on species and tissue **tropisms**, which determine the organs and tissues of the host in which it can survive. Unfortunately, little is known about the basis of this important aspect of parasitism. For example, it is not known why the larvae of *Strongyloides* invade the bowel wall, whereas those of hookworms remain in the intestinal lumen. Nor is it known why the pork tapeworm can cause cysticercosis (a deep tissue infection) in humans, whereas the beef tapeworm cannot. Studies indicate that tropisms may depend on specific receptors found on certain cell types but not on others. Thus, Duffy factor on the red blood cell surface is essential for the entry of one type of malaria parasite (*Plasmodium vivax*) into the red blood cell. For this reason, people who lack Duffy factor (black Africans) are resistant to *P. vivax* infection.

Temperature may also play an important role in the ability of parasites to infect and to cause disease. For example, *Leishmania donovani* replicates well at 37°C and causes visceral leishmaniasis or kala-azar, a disease of the bone marrow, liver, and spleen. In contrast, *L. tropica* grows well at 25–30°C but poorly at 37°C, and causes an infection of the skin. Temperature changes alone induce specific stage transitions in the life cycle of many parasites. For instance, leishmanias synthesize heat-shock proteins when they are transferred from the cooler insect into the warmer human body (from about 25°C to 37°C). This process appears to play an essential role in the transformation of the parasite from the insect stage to the human stage (it is analogous to the mycelium-to-yeast transformation in dimorphic fungi).

DAMAGE AND HOST RESPONSE

As with other infectious agents, the manifestations of parasitic disease are due not only to activities of the parasite, but also to host responses. This is almost invariably true for the animal parasites that lodge in deep tissue, where they elicit an inflammatory response. **Chronic inflammation** is the hallmark of diseases such as schistosomiasis or lymphatic filariasis. Sometimes the inflammatory response may persist after the parasite dies, as in trichinosis, or is exacerbated by the death of the parasite, as in cysticercosis.

Parasites, like other microorganisms, stimulate the immune response and elicit both antibody production and cell-mediated immunity. They are, however, adept at circumventing these defense mechanisms. For instance, adult schistosomes (blood flukes) coat themselves with host plasma proteins and are, thus, not recognized as foreign. As a result, they are able to live within the circulatory system for decades without immune-mediated destruction. Trypanosomes avoid immune-mediated elimination by changing their predominant surface antigens. Intracellular parasites are often protected by their location and by special devices that they have evolved. For example, leishmanias, which live in the phagolysosomes of macrophages, secrete a superoxide dismutase that presumably protects them from killing by the phagocytes' superoxide production.

In worm infections, eosinophils appear in large numbers in the blood, probably in response to the parasites' surface glycoproteins and polysaccharides. **Eosinophilia** is often accompanied by increased production of IgE. Together, eosinophils and IgE appear to play a role in killing multicellular parasites. These responses are also useful in diagnosis, because they are typical of metazoan infections; they are not seen in protozoan infections.

Certain parasites cause the death of host tissue cells directly. Among the better studied examples is the amoeba, *Entamoeba histolytica*, whose virulent strains destroy cells in culture. The process begins with the adherence of the amoebae to the mammalian cells, mediated by lectins on the organisms and specific receptors on the surface of the cells. However, little is known of the subsequent steps that lead to cell death. Nonpathogenic amoebae do not destroy mammalian cells in vitro.

Clinical Complications

The most important complications of many parasitic diseases occur years later. For instance, persons with schistosomiasis typically have chronic infection and bleeding from either the gastrointestinal (GI) tract (*S. mansoni*) or the urinary tract (*S. haematobium*). Years later, persons with heavy infections may develop chronic complications, such as portal hypertension and esophageal varices (*S. mansoni*) or obstruction or cancer of the urinary tract (*S. haematobium*). Important clinical complications may also occur at sites distant from the original infection. Thus, infections due to the pork tapeworm (*Taenia solium*) are asymptomatic when the adult parasite remains in the intestine. Late complications result if the larval forms of the parasite hatch from the egg, cross the intestine to enter the bloodstream, and encyst in deeper tissues. This form of the parasite is called a **cysticercus**. These cysts are small (0.5–1.5 cm) and produce no major difficulties when they lodge in skeletal muscle. However, when they lodge in the central nervous system, they may produce hydrocephalus by blocking the flow of cerebrospinal fluid, or seizures by acting as a mass lesion in the brain.

Similarly, Chagas' disease (American trypanosomiasis), produces a relatively trivial skin lesion at the time of the initial infection. This may lead to a rapidly progressive acute infection in young children or, many years later, to chronic infection in older persons. In patients with chronic infection, nerve damage may lead to failure of intestinal motility from massive distention of the esophagus or colon, or to heart block from damage to the cardiac conduction system. Fortunately, the majority of infected persons do not develop these complications. There are no clearly defined risk factors that identify persons most likely to develop these late complications.

UNDERSTANDING THE LIFE CYCLE OF PARASITES MAY HELP IN DIAGNOSIS

The life cycles of parasites often suggest useful clues for diagnosis (Fig. 49.1). For instance, in the life cycle of hookworms, the adult female lives in the lumen of the human bowel. This predicts that she will release eggs into the stool, which is indeed the case. As a result, the examination of stool for eggs is an effective and sensitive means of diagnosing hookworm infection. In contrast, stool examination is of little diagnostic value for *Strongyloides* infection, in which the female invades the bowel wall, and lays her eggs there rather than in the intestinal lumen. Because few, if any, *Strongyloides* eggs are released into the intestinal lumen, they are rarely seen on stool examination.

Figure 49.1. Idealized (model) parasite life cycle. The human stages of the life cycle are in the *top half* of these and subsequent diagrams. The extrahuman stages (in animate or inanimate reservoirs) are in the *lower half*. As the parasite matures (progressing clockwise through the extrahuman stages), it reaches the infective stage, invades the human host, matures, replicates, and ultimately completes the life cycle by producing infective forms that are taken up by a vector or released into the environment.

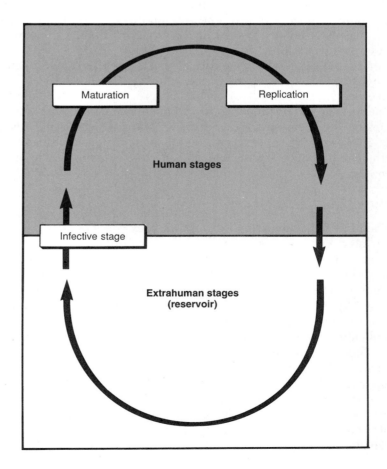

ENVIRONMENTAL CONSTRAINTS ON PARASITIC DISEASES

Understanding the life cycle often explains why a given parasitic disease is found in one area but not in another (Table 49.2). For example, the transmission of schistosomiasis depends on the intermediate snail host, which is not present in the North America or Europe. Viable eggs released from infected persons will not produce forms infective for humans if they cannot find a suitable snail host in which to mature. Thus, schistosomiasis is not endemic in the U.S. and will not be unless an intermediate snail host becomes established, no matter how many people with the disease enter the U.S. In contrast, *Anopheles* mosquitoes capable of transmitting malaria are found in the U.S. Therefore, recent immigrants or travelers who acquired malaria in endemic areas may infect the indigenous mosquito pool. Transmission of malaria by this mechanism took place in the U.S. after World War II, the Korean war, and the Vietnam war. For this reason, ongoing malaria surveillance is particularly important when large numbers of people from malaria-endemic areas enter the U.S. and settle in parts of the country where substantial numbers of anopheline mosquitoes are present.

Table 49.2. Geographic Context of Parasitic Infection

Indigenous to the U.S. Mainland	Imported
Intestinal Helminths	
Ascaris lumbricoides (roundworm)	*Ancylostoma braziliensis* (hookworm)
Enterobius vermicularis (pinworm)	*Schistosoma mansoni* (schistosomiasis)
Trichuris trichiura (whipworm)	*Schistosoma hematobium*
Strongyloides stercoralis (threadworm)	*Schistosoma japonicum*
Necator americanus (hookworm)	
Taenia saginata (beef tapeworm)	
Taenia solium (pork tapeworm)	
Diphyllobothrium latum (fish tapeworm)	
Hymenolepis nana (dwarf tapeworm)	
Toxocara canis, cati (visceral larva migrans)	
Trichinella spiralis (trichina)	
Echinococcus	
Echinococcus granulosus	*Echinococcus multilocularis*
Filarias	
Dirofilaria immitis (canine filariasis)	*Wuchereria bancrofti*
	Brugia malayi
	Onchocerca volvulus
	Loa loa
	Dracunculus medinensis
Flukes	
	Paragonimus westermani (lung fluke)
	Clonorchis sinensis (liver fluke)
Protozoa	
Entamoeba histolytica (amebiasis)	*Plasmodium vivax, falciparum, ovale, malariae*
Giardia lamblia (giardiasis)	
Toxoplasma gondii (toxoplasmosis)	*Leishmania donovani, tropica*
Babesia microti (babesiosis)	*Balantidium coli* (balantidiasis)
Pneumocystis carinii (pneumocystosis)	*Trypanosoma cruzi* (Chagas' disease)
Trichomonas vaginalis (trichomoniasis)	*Trypanosoma brucei* (African sleeping sickness)
Naegleria fowleri (meningoencephalitis)	
Cryptosporidium (cryptosporidiosis)	

STRATEGIES TO COMBAT PARASITIC INFECTIONS

The life cycles of parasites provide important clues for the control of transmission (Fig. 49.2 and Table 49.3). For example, the infectious larvae of hookworms mature in human excrement and then penetrate human skin on contact. Therefore, **sanitation** and wearing of shoes are effective in reducing the incidence of hookworm infection. This disease was prevalent in the southern U.S. until these preventive measures were instituted on a large scale by the Rockefeller Commission in the 1930s. Sanitation is effective in preventing many parasitic infections—ascariasis, strongyloidiasis, hookworm infection, pinworm infection, beef and pork tapeworm infection, schistosomiasis, amebiasis, giardiasis, and cryptosporidiosis. An understanding of the parasite's life cycle is also helpful in the choice of antiparasitic drugs. For example, different drugs are necessary for the intestinal and tissue stages of the pork tapeworm (*Taenia solium*); one drug, niclosamide, is effective against teniasis (intestinal infection), whereas another, praziquantel, is used to treat the tissue stage of *T. solium* infection (cysticercosis).

Antiparasite strategies fall into three general categories: (*a*) drugs for chemoprophylaxis or treatment, (*b*) immunization, and (*c*) control measures in the field. Eradication programs have generally proven effective only when more than one of these strategies has been used simultaneously.

Drugs

CHEMOPROPHYLAXIS

The requirements for a drug to be acceptable for chemoprophylaxis in healthy persons are substantially more stringent than those for use in the treatment of ill people. Minor side effects that are tolerable for short periods of time in sick persons (e.g., headache, nausea, or other GI disturbances) are unacceptable for indefinite periods of time in persons who are well.

An example of successful chemoprophylaxis has been the use of chloroquine to prevent malaria. This drug produces plasma levels that suppress infection by all the agents of malaria, except drug-resistant strains of *Plasmodium falciparum*. Chloroquine taken once a week produces effective blood levels for about 1 week because it has a plasma half-life greater than 4 days. The main disadvantage of this drug is that some strains of *P. falciparum* have become resistant to it. Pneumonia due to *Pneumocystis carinii* is another infection that may be prevented by drugs. Chemoprophylaxis with the antifolate combination trimethoprim-sulfamethoxazole or with aerosolized pentamidine sharply reduces the risk of this infection among persons with **AIDS**.

TREATMENT

Treatment is generally an inefficient means of disease control because often there is a long delay between infection and clinical presentation (10–20 years or longer for schistosomiasis). If treatment is to be effective in reducing the transmission of a parasite, it must be given early, when the patients are first infectious. However, many patients are asymptomatic when they are infectious and are no longer infectious by the time they show symptoms (as in cysticercosis).

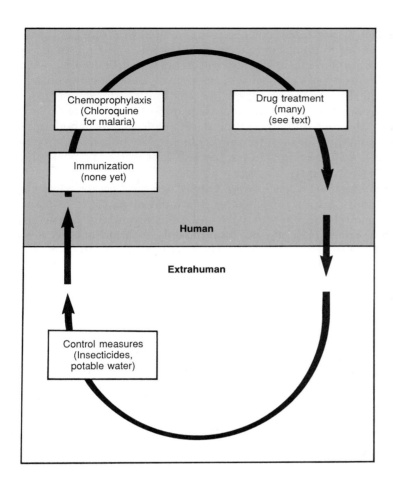

Figure 49.2.   Points of potential intervention in the parasite life cycle. Control measures interfere with the replication or the survival of the extrahuman stages of the parasite. They reduce the incidence of infection by reducing the number of infective stages to which humans are exposed. Immunization (vaccination) prevents symptomatic infection by inhibiting or killing the parasite as it enters (or replicates within) the human host. Chemoprophylaxis is used to inhibit parasite replication to prevent symptomatic infection. Neither immunization nor chemoprophylaxis prevents the initial entry of the parasite. Drug treatment is used to prevent death or severe morbidity in persons with established infections.

Table 49.3. Modes of Spread of Some Parasitic Diseases

Human to Human	Animal to Human
Fecal-oral spread	
Cryptosporidiosis	Cryptosporidiosis
Amebiasis	Toxoplasmosis
Giardiasis	Visceral larva migrans
Strongyloidiasis[a]	Echinococcosis
Ascariasis[b]	
Trichuris infection[b]	
Fecal-cutaneous contact, without ingestion	
Strongyloidiasis	Creeping eruption (dog or cat hookworm)
Hookworm infection	
Vector-borne	
Lymphatic filariasis	Trypanosomiasis (sleeping sickness,
Onchocerciasis	Chagas' disease)
Malaria	Leishmaniasis
Leishmaniasis	
Inadequate cooking	
	Beef tapeworm (*Taenia saginata*)
	Pork tapeworm (*Taenia solium*)
	Fish tapeworm (*Diphyllobothrium latum*)
	Toxoplasmosis (*Toxoplasma gondii*)

[a]Usually transmitted by fecal-cutaneous contact but may also be transmitted by the fecal-oral route.
[b]May require a period of time outside the human host in order to be infectious.

Many of the treatment regimens for parasitic disease are used to prevent the systemic complications of chronic infection (such as portal hypertension in schistosomiasis or seizures in cysticercosis), which are often caused by host reactions. In contrast, many local manifestations (such as the passage of eggs in the stool in schistosomiasis or of proglottids or eggs in the intestinal stage of tapeworm infection) are relatively tolerable. Other treatment regimens are designed to relieve acute complications—intravenous glucose for coma due to hypoglycemia in *P. falciparum* malaria or steroids for severe inflammation of the heart or brain in trichinosis.

In the last 5–10 years, several new drugs have appeared that constitute significant advances in the treatment of parasitic diseases; i.e., praziquantel for cysticercosis and schistosomiasis, ivermectin for onchocerciasis (Chapter 53), and possibly, α-difluoromethylornithine (DFMO) for African trypanosomiasis (Chapter 50). In each case, the previously available drugs were toxic and often ineffective. Before praziquantel, there was no medical treatment for cysticercosis (the tissue invasive form of pork tapeworm infection).

Immunity and Immunization

MAJOR PROBLEM—EVASION OF THE HOST IMMUNE RESPONSE

Many important parasites survive and produce disease because they are able to evade the host immune response. It is easy to see here that vaccines would not be helpful. Schistosomes masquerade as "self" by covering themselves with host antigens. Because of this protection, circulating antibodies (produced spontaneously or by vaccination) may not bind to their corresponding antigens and may, thus, be ineffective against these parasites. Trypanosomes evade the host immune response using another strategy, by altering their surface antigens (see Chapter 50 and Paradigm, Chapter 14). When the host develops an effective immune response to one antigen, clones of trypanosomes emerge that express different antigens on their surface, leading to continued high-grade parasitemia. An effective vaccine against all of these antigenic types seems extremely unlikely.

STAGE-SPECIFIC ANTIGENS AND ANTIGENIC VARIATION— FURTHER PROBLEMS IN DESIGNING VACCINES

A parasite typically has different proteins or polysaccharides on its surface at different stages of its life cycle. Many of these components are antigenic, imparting different immunological characteristics to each stage of the parasite life cycle. For example, the form of the malaria parasite that is injected into humans by the mosquito is antigenically distinct from the form that infects red blood cells. Consequently, a person immunized with the insect form (the sporozoite) is susceptible to infection by the red blood cell stage of the parasite (the merozoite). Thus, an effective malaria vaccine will likely need to contain major antigens derived from several different stages of the parasite's life cycle.

The development of effective vaccines requires a thorough understanding of the immune response to parasitic infection. For instance, certain epitopes on the surface proteins of malarial parasites are repeated sequences capable of stimulating the greatest production of antibodies. Only in the last few years has it been realized that other epitopes of this protein may play an important role in cell-mediated immunity. Efforts to develop vaccines are under way for several important parasitic diseases other than malaria, namely, schistosomiasis, onchocerciasis, lymphatic filariasis, and toxoplasmosis.

Control Measures

Effective control measures are potentially available for all parasitic diseases. The most effective measures are related to the mode of transmission and to the parasite's life cycle (Fig. 49.2). For example, mosquitoes that transmit malaria often bite at night, when people are sleeping. Many of these mosquitoes rest under the eaves of houses, thus insecticides such as DDT may reduce malaria transmission substantially when sprayed under the eaves. Unfortunately, this strategy is limited because some mosquitoes have developed resistance to DDT and because some bite outside the house during the day.

In areas such as North America and Europe, transmission of parasitic disease is often low because sanitation interrupts the parasite's life cycle. However, even simple methods of interrupting transmission are beyond the means of many developing countries. Potable water, for example, is unavailable or too expensive in many parts of the world. During the dry season, the transmission of infection by the water-borne and fecal-oral routes increases in these regions because the small amounts of water available are used for both washing and drinking. Thus, control measures are often more difficult to implement in the developing countries where the major parasitic diseases are endemic.

CONCLUSIONS

The most striking difference between parasites and other infectious agents is the variety of host vectors and stages in their life cycles. Although at first bewildering, these life cycles provide important clues to understanding the parasitic diseases and help in their diagnosis, as well as in the development of public health strategies. In most cases, we still do not know the biological basis for the ability of different stages of parasites to invade different hosts and different types of tissues.

Parasitic diseases are more prevalent in areas with inadequate sanitation, but are also important in regions with apparently high sanitary standards, such as Europe and North America. This is frequently due to the susceptibility of immunocompromised patients to these infections which, like toxoplasmosis and pneumocystis, are quite prevalent but subclinical in individuals with normal immune function. In immunocompromised patients, parasites escape their normal constraints and may multiply to high and dangerous numbers.

SUGGESTED READING

Brown HW, Neva FA. Basic clinical parasitology, 5th ed. Norwalk, CT: Appleton-Century-Croft, 1983.

Cohen S, Warren KS. Immunology of parasitic infections, 2nd ed. London and Boston: Blackwell, 1986.

Desowitz RS. New Guinea tapeworms and Jewish grandmothers: tales of parasites and people. Norton, 1981.

Englund PT, Sher A, eds. The biology of parasitism: a molecular and immunological approach. New York: Alan R. Liss, 1988.

Kean BH, Mott KE, Russel AJ. Tropical medicine and parasitology: classical investigations. Ithaca, NY: Cornell Univ. Press, 1978.

Rose ME, McLaren JD, eds. Pathophysiological responses to parasites. London: British Society for Parasitology, 1986.

Trager W. Living together: the biology of animal parasitism. New York: Plenum Press, 1986.

Warren KS, Mahmoud AAF. Tropical and geographic medicine. New York: McGraw-Hill, 1984.

Wyler DJ. Modern parasite biology. New York: WH Freeman & Co., 1990.

Blood and Tissue Protozoa

50

Donald J. Krogstad

Protozoa that produce bloodstream infection typically cause anemia by destroying red blood cells (malaria and babesia). Protozoa that infect tissues may cause significant damage to the eyes, the brain, or the heart (toxoplasmosis), to the brain (African sleeping sickness), or to the heart and the gastrointestinal tract (Chagas' disease). The major blood and tissue protozoa are presented in Table 50.1.

PARASITES OF RED BLOOD CELLS

Malaria

Malaria is the most important of all protozoan diseases and is said to have caused "the greatest harm to the greatest number" of all infectious diseases. It occurs in many tropical and semitropical regions of the world (Table 49.1), with approximately 200–300 million cases annually. An estimated 2–3 million people die of malaria each year, especially malnourished African children. The reservoir of malaria is the infected human; transmission is via the bite of infected female anopheline mosquitoes.

CASE

Mr. M. is a 54-year-old businessman from Liverpool who traveled to East Africa (Kenya and Tanzania) on a business trip, and then went on a photographic safari. After 1 week in Nairobi, he took a 10-day trip through the wildlife preserves of Serengeti and Ngorogoro, with a final visit to Mombasa on the Indian Ocean. During his flight home, 9 days after leaving the game parks, he developed a flu-like syndrome with headache, muscle aches, and a temperature of 38°C. After his return home, he saw a physician who diagnosed influenza (which can also cause headache, muscle aches, and fever). He had returned to England in February during an outbreak of influenza A.

Mr. M. was given acetaminophen, which initially reduced his fever and muscle aches. However, he felt worse the next day; he suddenly developed an intense chill that lasted for about 30 minutes and was followed by a fever to 40.2°C of 6 hours' duration. When the fever abated, Mr. M. became drenched in sweat, and felt exhausted and drained. These symptoms continued to worsen and he was brought to the hospital unconscious 2 days later. On examination, he had edema of the lungs. He showed no signs of endocarditis and a lumbar puncture was negative for bacterial meningitis.

*The attending physician, drawing on his experience while serving in the armed services abroad, recognized that the clinical manifestations of Mr. M. were typical of a **malarial paroxysm**. The recent history of travel to endemic areas helped sharpen the physician's suspicion of the disease, and the diagno-*

597

Table 50.1. Comparison of Major Blood and Tissue Protozoa

Organism	Reservoir	Mode of Transmission	Clinical Manifestations
Blood Protozoa			
Plasmodia (malaria)	Infected humans	Vector-borne by the female *Anopheles* mosquito	Fever and chills with red cell lysis
Babesia (babesiosis)	Rodents—voles, deer, mice	Vector-borne by the hard-bodied *Ixodes* tick	Fever and chills with red cell lysis
Tissue Protozoa			
Toxoplasma gondii (toxoplasmosis)	Sheep, pigs, cattle, cats	Food-borne by the ingestion of inadequately cooked beef or lamb Fecal-oral by the ingestion of infectious oocysts in cat feces	Intrauterine (congenital) infection may produce severe retardation Mononucleosis-like illness most common Infection of the brain (encephalitis) or heart (myocarditis) in severely immunocompromised patients
Leishmania (leishmaniasis)	Infected humans, dogs, jackals, foxes, rats, ground squirrels, gerbils	Vector-borne by infected *Phlebotomus* sandflies	Trivial or mild (self-healing) skin lesions Disfiguring mucocutaneous lesions Systemic illness with involvement of liver, spleen, and bone marrow
Pneumocystis carinii[a] (pneumocystosis)	Probably in infected humans and animals	Probably air-borne for initial infection Disease typically represents activation of previously quiescent infection with natural or iatrogenic immunosuppression	Pneumonia
Trypanosoma cruzi (Chagas' disease, American trypanosomiasis)	Wildlife and domestic animals (zoonosis)	Vector-borne by reduviid bugs followed by rubbing infected feces in the bite wound	GI tract dysfunction from autonomic nerve damage (megacolon, megaesophagus) Cardiac dysfunction from damage to the conducting system (right bundle branch block)
Trypanosoma brucei gambiense, or *rhodesiense* (African trypanosomiasis, sleeping sickness)	Infected humans Wildlife and cattle	Vector-borne by the tsetse fly	Systemic illness with fever, headache, muscle, and joint pains Progresses to CNS involvement with altered speech, gait, and reflexes (encephalitis)

[a] Recent evidence suggests that this organism may be a fungus.

sis was confirmed when a Giemsa-stained smear of the patient's blood revealed large numbers of parasites within red blood cells. They were identified as Plasmodium falciparum by their characteristic ring shape. His hematocrit (packed red cell volume) was 18% (normal is 40–45%). Urinalysis revealed extensive hemolysis; his serum creatinine (a measure of renal function) was 5.4 mg/100 ml (normal is 1 mg or less per 100 ml).

Treatment was begun with intravenous quinidine, which is effective against P. falciparum strains resistant to the more commonly used antimalarial, chloroquine. Mr. M. was also given intravenous glucose as a precaution against hypoglycemia (which may produce coma in patients with severe P. falciparum malaria). Hypoglycemia may result both from consumption of glucose by large numbers of parasites and from the direct release of insulin from the pancreas produced by quinidine or quinine. For his pulmonary edema, Mr. M. required artificial ventilation with a respirator. He was given multiple trans-

fusions for his anemia and was put on a dialysis machine because of his kidney failure. He recovered and was discharged after spending 10 days in the intensive care unit.

ENCOUNTER AND ENTRY

Malaria may be transmitted to humans by the mosquito vector 9–17 days after a female *Anopheles* mosquito ingests blood from a person infected with human species of *Plasmodium*. Infected persons typically develop symptoms of malaria 8–30 days later. Most cases of malaria in Europe and North America represent infections imported in persons who have traveled to endemic areas (**imported malaria**). However, mosquitoes that can serve as vectors exist in the U.S. (*Anopheles*). When these mosquitoes bite travelers infected with plasmodia, malaria may be introduced into the U.S., i.e., it may be transmitted to persons who have never traveled abroad. Introductions of malaria have occurred with the return of large numbers of infected veterans after several wars and more recently near San Diego, California, in association with infected Mexican migrant workers. Malaria may also be transmitted by blood transfusion or by the sharing of needles among intravenous drug users (**induced malaria**).

SPREAD AND MULTIPLICATION

The life cycle of the malaria parasite is complex and rich in morphological detail (Fig. 50.1). In brief, the organisms are injected under the skin by infected mosquitoes as **sporozoites**. They travel through the blood and enter liver cells. After 8–14 days in the liver, they mature and are released once again into the bloodstream, in a form that can invade red blood cells (**merozoites**). After 2 or 3 days, the infected red blood cells burst, liberating a new generation of infective merozoites that infect previously unparasitized red blood cells. This part of the life cycle consists of asexual reproduction in the red blood cell. In the blood, some of the plasmodia may also develop into sexual blood stages (**gametocytes**), which may be taken up by mosquitoes to carry out their sexual reproductive cycle. The parasites undergo further changes in the mosquito before once again becoming infective sporozoites. In each of these stages, the plasmodial cells are distinguishable morphologically (Fig. 50.1).

Human malaria is caused by four species of plasmodia that vary in their innate virulence. A major reason for this difference is that the various plasmodial species prefer red blood cells of different ages: *P. falciparum* **invades erythrocytes of all ages**, producing the highest parasitemias and the greatest risk of mortality; *P. vivax* prefers reticulocytes and young RBCs; *P. malariae* prefers older ones. Both *P. vivax* and *P. malariae* infect only 1–2% or less of RBCs, and thus, produce less severe disease. The fourth species, *P. ovale* is virtually identical to *P. vivax* clinically and morphologically .

The intracellular location of the malaria parasite within the red blood cell has two important consequences:

- Red blood cells infected with *P. falciparum* develop special knobs on their surface as the result of parasite-induced changes in the RBC membrane. These knobs facilitate the adherence of infected RBCs to the endothelium of the venules and capillaries, and explain the localization of *P. falciparum*-infected cells in the deep vascular bed.

Figure 50.1. Malaria life cycle. Sporozoites released from the salivary gland of the female *Anopheles* mosquito are injected under the skin when the mosquito bites a human (*1*). They then travel through the bloodstream and enter the liver (*2*). Within liver cells, the parasites mature to **tissue schizonts** (*4*). They are then released into the bloodstream as **merozoites** (*5*) and produce symptomatic infection as they invade and destroy red blood cells (*RBCs*). However, some parasites remain dormant in the liver as **hypnozoites** (*2, dashed lines from 1–3*). These parasites (in *P. vivax, P. ovale*) cause relapsing malaria. Once within the bloodstream, merozoites (*5*) invade RBCs (*6*), and mature to the **ring** (*7, 8*), **trophozoite** (*9*), and **schizont** (*10*) asexual stages. Schizonts lyse their host RBCs as they complete their maturation and release the next generation of merozoites (*11*), which invades previously uninfected RBCs.

Within RBCs, some parasites differentiate to sexual forms (male and female **gametocytes**, *12*). When these are taken up by a female *Anopheles* mosquito, the male gametocyte loses its flagellum to produce **male gametes**, which fertilize the **female gamete** (*13*) to produce a **zygote** (*14*). The zygote invades the gut of the mosquito (*15*) and develops into an **oocyst** (*16*). Mature oocysts produce **sporozoites**, which migrate to the salivary gland of the mosquito (*1*) and repeat the cycle. The *dashed line* between *12* and *13* indicates that absence of the mosquito vector precludes natural transmission via this cycle. Note that infection by the injection of infected blood bypasses this constraint and permits transmission of malaria among intravenous drug addicts and to persons who receive blood transfusions from infected donors.

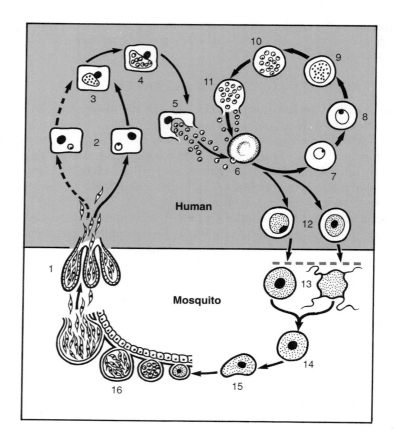

- The presence of the plasmodium makes red blood cells less deformable. Because the spleen recognizes and removes older (less deformable) red blood cells from the circulation, it also recognizes parasitized erythrocytes as less deformable, and plays an active role in removing them from the circulation. Not surprisingly, splenectomized people have higher degrees of parasitemia and more severe infections.

DAMAGE

The main manifestations of malaria are fever, chills, and anemia. The typical malarial paroxysm (as in Mr. M.'s case) coincides with the simultaneous lysis of many red blood cells and the release of large numbers of merozoites. It is not clear what causes these manifestations or how synchronous parasite development is maintained in vivo. Although malaria could cause the release of a pyrogen, such a substance has not been demonstrated. Most likely, fever results from macrophage release of tumor necrosis factor and/or interleukin-1 than can be accounted for by the degree of parasitemia. Thus, uninfected red blood cells may also be destroyed prematurely. Recent studies have suggested that tumor necrosis factor (cachectin) released by host cells in malaria may be responsible for complications, such as edema of the lungs and shock (as seen in the case of Mr. M.; see also Chapter 62 on sepsis).

The in vivo cycle of parasite replication can be quite synchronous and may produce a regular fever pattern—every 2 days with *P. vivax* or *P. ovale*, every 3 days with *P. malariae*. In contrast, the fever pattern is often irregular with *P. falciparum*, especially in nonimmune patients. Other frequent clinical presentations include an influenza-like syndrome (fever, muscle aches, and malaise) and gastroenteritis (nausea, diarrhea, vomiting). Patients with these signs and symptoms are frequently misdiagnosed, especially if the physician is not acquainted with malaria or fails to obtain a history of recent travel.

Human Genetics and Malaria

Genetic polymorphism of several human genes affects the entry, multiplication, and survival of malarial parasites, and is important in determining the outcome of the infection. For example, parasite invasion of RBCs depends on specific surface molecules on the RBC. For *P. falciparum* and *P. vivax*, these are glycophorin A and the Duffy blood group antigen, respectively. The variable susceptibility of American blacks to *P. vivax* infection is consistent with the distribution of Duffy antigen. African blacks are Duffy-negative and, thus, are resistant to *P. vivax* infection.

Because falciparum malaria is such a devastating disease, it is likely that it has been a powerful selective force in human evolution. Many epidemiological studies have shown that **sickle cell hemoglobin (HbS)** is common in areas of Africa with a high incidence of *P. falciparum*. Malaria is seldom found in carriers of the sickle cell trait, which suggests that this genetic determinant imparts a selective advantage to people living in areas where the parasite is common. Furthermore, in vitro studies have shown that, at oxygen tensions similar to those in tissue, the parasites grow poorly in red blood cells with sickle cell hemoglobin, or HbS (Fig. 50.2). Thus, the black African population trades off the risk of a fatal disease, sickle cell anemia in the homozygous, for the protection of a larger group of the population, the heterozygous HbS carriers. This is an example of a balanced genetic polymorphism.

How does the sickle cell trait protect from malaria? *P. falciparum*-infected RBCs adhere to the walls of blood vessels via knobs that form as the parasites mature. This adherence to the peripheral microcirculation sequesters the parasitized RBCs in an area of reduced oxygen tension, which facilitates sickling, potassium loss, and the killing of the parasites.

Other genetic abnormalities that restrict the growth of malarial parasites within RBCs are glucose-6-phosphate dehydrogenase deficiency

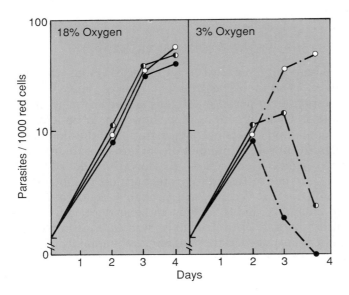

Figure 50.2. Effect of hypoxia on parasite growth in sickle hemoglobin red blood cells. In 18% oxygen, *P. falciparum* grows as well in sickle hemoglobin (*SS*) red blood cells (*filled circles*) as in either heterozygous (*SA*) red cells (*half-filled circles*) or normal (*AA*) RBCs (*open circles*) in 18% oxygen (*left panel*). In contrast, in 3% oxygen, *P. falciparum* parasites grow much less well in SS cells than in SS or SA cells (*right panel*).

(G6PD) and thalassemia. In the case of G6PD, it is thought that the reduced ability of the RBCs to produce NADPH via the pentose phosphate shunt results in an oxidative stress that inhibits parasite growth.

DIAGNOSIS

The laboratory diagnosis of malaria is made by microscopic examination of a Giemsa-stained smear of peripheral blood using the oil immersion objective (Table 50.2). Wright's stain, which is used more often in the clinical hematology laboratory, stains the parasites less well. If the degree of parasitemia is low, a "thick smear" may be used to increase sensitivity. Because RBCs are lysed in the preparation of thick smears, this procedure provides no information about the effect of the parasite on the size of the RBCs or about the intracellular location of the parasite within the RBCs (central or peripheral). These morphological characteristics help a trained technologist differentiate among the species of plasmodia.

For practical purposes, the infecting species in acutely ill patients is either *P. falciparum* or *P. vivax*. This is because *P. malariae* most often causes subacute or chronic infections (*P. malariae* may produce acute infections in nonimmune people) and *P. ovale* malaria is clinically so similar to *P. vivax* malaria that the distinction is usually insignificant. The morphological characteristics of the parasite allow one to distinguish *P. vivax* from *P. falciparum*. *P. vivax* causes infected RBCs to enlarge progressively as the parasite matures and produces eosinophilic "stippling" in the RBCs (SchüSchuffer's dots). Neither red cell enlargement nor Schiffner's dots occur with *P. falciparum*. This distinction is important because *P. falciparum* infection poses a greater risk of death and is the only human malaria species that may be chloroquine resistant.

Serological testing is of little value for the diagnosis of malaria in the acutely ill patient. This is because patients do not develop species-specific antibodies to the parasites for 3–5 weeks but treatment must begin within 1–2 days of the onset of symptoms. Recent work has shown that hybridization with DNA probes may be useful in the diagnosis of malaria (Chapter 55). The sensitivity of this technique is similar to that of the thick blood smear. However, the procedure presently requires the use of radioactive isotopes and is, therefore, not practical in the field in many developing countries.

PREVENTION AND TREATMENT

Natural immunity to malaria is imperfect. Persons who have lived in malarious areas all their lives and who have evidence of humoral and cellular responses to parasite antigens are nevertheless infected on a regular basis. Their infections tend, however, to be less severe than those of nonimmune persons, suggesting that the immune response plays a significant role. A number of workers have shown that antibodies directed against sporozoites, the form introduced by the insect (Fig. 50.1), are not sufficient to protect against the infection. For this reason, an effective vaccine will probably need to stimulate cell-mediated immunity, and to include antigens derived from the various stages of the parasite. Unfortunately, studies of cell-mediated immunity are not as advanced as those of humoral immunity. The future will tell if such a vaccine is possible.

Chloroquine is the single most widely used drug for antimalarial chemoprophylaxis and treatment. It is effective against all strains of

Table 50.2. Morphological Diagnosis of Malaria

	P. falciparum	P. vivax
Reliable criteria		
Only rings on the peripheral smear	Yes	No
Enlargement of parasitized red blood cells	No	Yes
Schüffner's dots	No	Yes
Banana-shaped gametocytes	Yes[a]	No
Less reliable criteria		
Peripheral location of parasite within the red blood cell	Typical	Rare
Multiply infected red cells	Frequent	Rare

[a]Characteristic *P. falciparum* gametocytes may first appear days to a week after the patient first becomes ill and seeks medical attention.

Plasmodium, except for resistant strains of *P. falciparum*. Such strains are now present in parts of Southeast Asia, South America, and Africa and complicate the prophylaxis and treatment of malaria. Thus, Mr. M. might well have acquired *P. falciparum* infection in East Africa even if he had been on chloroquine chemoprophylaxis. In contrast, he would have been protected in Haiti, where there is no chloroquine resistance. Updates on the prevalence of chloroquine-resistant *P. falciparum* and recommendations for antimalarial prophylaxis are published annually by the Centers for Disease Control and the World Health Organization.

Chloroquine is the only antimalarial considered to be safe in pregnancy. The chloroquine doses used for antimalarial chemoprophylaxis (5 mg base/kg/week) do not damage the retina, which is a risk when taking this drug at higher doses (5–10 mg base/kg/day) for the treatment of rheumatoid arthritis and other rheumatoid diseases.

Patients infected with chloroquine-resistant *P. falciparum* can be treated with other agents, such as mefloquine, quinine, quinidine, or Fansidar. Because quinine and Fansidar are potentially toxic, they are used more often for treatment than for chemoprophylaxis. Fansidar, for example, may produce generalized skin reactions with loss of epithelial integrity. Because persons with these complications are at significant risk of death from fluid and electrolyte loss and from infections, the indications for Fansidar in the chemoprophylaxis of malaria have been restricted. Amodiaquine, an analog of chloroquine, is effective in vitro and in vivo against many moderately chloroquine-resistant *P. falciparum*. However, recent studies indicate that this drug causes agranulocytosis and severe hepatitis. Therefore, it is not recommended for antimalarial chemoprophylaxis.

Chloroquine is not effective against the liver (hypnozoite) stages of *P. vivax* or *P. ovale*. Primaquine is effective against these stages and is used to prevent late relapses from maturation of the hypnozoite (to the tissue schizont stage and the subsequent release of infectious merozoites). However, primaquine is more toxic than chloroquine. It causes hemolysis in patients with G6PD deficiency, as well as nausea, vomiting, and diarrhea in patients with normal levels of the enzyme. Primaquine is not indicated for either *P. falciparum* or *P. malariae* infections because these parasites do not produce a dormant (hypnozoite) stage in the liver.

Mosquito control with insecticides and drainage of breeding sites has been the mainstay of malaria control in many countries, and has resulted in a dramatic decline in the incidence of the disease. Unfortunately, these measures are expensive and do not always work because mosquitoes may become resistant to some of the insecticides used. In endemic areas, individuals should protect themselves with mosquito netting, house screening, and insect repellants. The best hope for controlling malaria is the development of improved antimalarials and/or an effective vaccine.

Babesiosis

Like the plasmodia of malaria, *Babesia* are intraerythrocytic parasites and also produce illness by destroying the red blood cells they infect. Babesiosis, unlike malaria, is endemic in the U.S., especially in the East Coast (notably on Shelter Island, Nantucket, and Martha's Vineyard). *Babesia microti*, the usual cause of human babesiosis in the U.S., is rarely fatal. *B. bovis* and *B. argentina*, which have been reported more frequently from Europe, are fatal more often.

CLINICAL AND PARASITOLOGICAL FEATURES

Patients with babesiosis typically have a mild illness with fever, chills, sweats, muscle aches, and fatigue; the illness is difficult to diagnose. As in malaria, splenectomized patients are at **risk** of more severe disease. In persons with an intact spleen, the percentage of infected RBCs is usually 0.2% or less; it can rise to over 10% in splenectomized patients. In fact, the disease was first detected by postmortem studies of splenectomized patients. As in malaria, the spleen is thought to remove the less deformable babesia-infected RBCs from the circulation.

The life cycle of *Babesia* is shown in Figure 50.3. The natural reservoirs are small rodents such as field mice. The vector is the same tick that transmits Lyme disease and both infections may occasionally be transmitted at the same time. Humans are infected accidentally in endemic areas and are not thought to contribute to the maintenance of the parasite's life cycle. The epidemiology of the disease is restricted by the presence of a suitable tick vector and wildlife reservoir, and by human contact with them.

The laboratory diagnosis of babesiosis requires finding the parasites in Giemsa-stained blood films using the oil immersion objective. They are seen as small rings, often in tetrads. These are the only forms found in peripheral blood and may be missed easily when the parasitemia is low. Their ring shape makes them easy to confuse with a similar form of *P. falciparum*. The distinction between the two is important because *Babesia* infections are treated with different chemotherapeutic agents than malaria. Clindamycin plus quinine is used for babesiosis, versus a variety of drugs for malaria (see above).

Antibodies to *Babesia* can be detected in most infected persons. However, they often appear too late (3–4 weeks after the onset of infection) to be helpful in the diagnosis and treatment of acute babesiosis.

TISSUE PROTOZOA

Toxoplasmosis

Infection with the agent of toxoplasmosis, *Toxoplasma gondii*, is very common in humans; 35–40% of the adults in the U.S. have been infected by this organism as judged by the prevalence of antitoxoplasma antibodies. However, fewer than 1% are ever diagnosed as having toxoplasmosis. In the few persons with signs and symptoms of active infec-

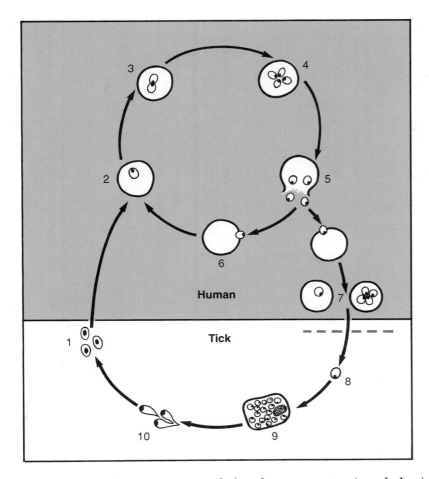

Figure 50.3. Babesia life cycle. Infectious merozoites are injected under the skin by the hard bodied tick (*Ixodes*) vector (*1*. They invade RBCs directly (*2*). There is no intermediate liver stage in babesiosis as there is in malaria. Once within the RBCs, parasites replicate asexually by binary fission (*3*). Babesia characteristically form tetrads (*4*), lyse their host RBCs as they mature (*5*), and complete the cycle when parasitized RBCs are ingested by the tick vector (*6*). The *line* between *7* and *8* indicates that natural transmission does not occur in areas without the hard-bodied tick.

tion, the clinical presentation of the disease varies (see below). Toxoplasmosis is particularly damaging for immunocompromised patients, such as those with **AIDS**, and for the developing fetus. *T. gondii* can cause three distinct syndromes:

- A "mononucleosis"-like syndrome in which tests for the common viral agents of mononucleosis—Epstein-Barr virus and cytomegalovirus—are negative;

- A congenital infection that may have severe consequences if acquired in the first trimester of pregnancy; a clinical case description and a discussion of the effects of *T. gondii* on the developing fetus are presented in Chapter 53.

- Infections in immunocompromised hosts (especially those with **AIDS**), often involving the brain or the heart.

ENCOUNTER

People acquire *Toxoplasma* infection by eating inadequately cooked meat or by ingesting food contaminated with infected cat feces. The more common of the two modes of transmission appears to be via the ingestion of inadequately cooked meat (lamb, mutton, or possibly beef) that contains the parasite's **tissue cyst** (produced by asexual reproduction, see Fig. 50.4). Less frequently, humans become infected by accidentally ingesting minute amounts of cat feces containing fertile cysts called **oocysts**. The frequency with which this occurs is in dispute and

Figure 50.4.   *Toxoplasma* life cycle. Humans and other mammals become infected with *Toxoplasma* by ingesting inadequately cooked meat containing tissue cysts or by ingesting infectious oocysts excreted in the feces of infected cats (*1*). Once in the human host, the oocysts mature to **tachyzoites** (*2*), enter the bloodstream and disseminate throughout the body (*3*). After the initial acute infection, most people mount a successful immune response that eliminates the active infectious (tachyzoite) form of the parasite and leaves only tissue cysts with dormant organisms (*4*). A similar progression is observed within the cat (steps 1–4), where the parasite also invades intestinal epithelial cells (*6*), but, in addition, establishes a sexual cycle (*8, 9*), which results in the formation (*10*) and release (*11*) of infectious oocysts. The *solid line* below step 4 in the *upper half* of the diagram indicates that human tissue infection is a dead end. Unless there is animal consumption of human remains or cannibalism, human tissue cysts disintegrate after the death of the host.

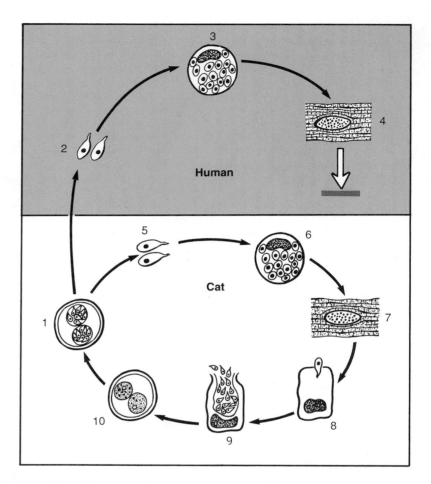

is difficult to determine because a minority of *Toxoplasma*-infected cats excrete oocysts in their stools and because we do not know how frequently humans ingest cat feces. The evidence that cats are important in the transmission of *Toxoplasma* to humans comes from the observation that toxoplasmosis is absent from areas that do not have cats, such as isolated Pacific atolls. Once cats are introduced, humans become infected. In addition, one outbreak of *Toxoplasma* infection in Georgia was traced to *Toxoplasma*-infected cats in a stable frequented by the affected patients. Cats are necessary to complete the life cycle of the parasite because they harbor the sexual cycle of the organisms and produce environmentally resistant infective cysts in their stool.

After ingestion, the parasites are released from tissue cysts (oocysts) in the small intestine and penetrate the gut wall. They invade the bloodstream and disseminate throughout the body, including the brain and the heart. Over the first 4–6 weeks, normal hosts mount an immune response that controls the infection; it leads to the formation of dormant tissue cysts in different parts of the body and to resistance to reinfection. Unless the person becomes immunosuppressed at some time in the future, the infection remains inactive.

PATHOGENESIS, DIAGNOSIS, AND TREATMENT

In the active phase of infection, *Toxoplasma* are found within macrophages and can be observed with the high dry or oil immersion objectives. They survive intracellularly, in part by preventing acidification of phagosomes and/or their fusion with lysosomes. However, when macrophages become activated, they are able to kill these parasites. In the absence of an adequate immune response, *Toxoplasma* causes local inflammation that may result in severe necrosis and tissue damage. AIDS patients, if untreated, may die of *Toxoplasma* infection of the brain.

In the immunologically competent host, the diagnosis of acute toxoplasmosis can be made by a rising antibody titer, especially of IgM antibodies. However, this measurement is often insensitive in the immunocompromised patient, who may be unable to produce a diagnostic rise in antibody titer. *Toxoplasma* tissue cysts may be recognized by their characteristic appearance in Giemsa-stained biopsy material. The trophozoites associated with acute infection may be difficult to detect morphologically; brain biopsy material should be stained with fluorescent or peroxidase-labeled antitoxoplasma antibodies to increase the sensitivity of detection.

Most otherwise healthy persons do not need treatment for this infection. In congenital infections, it is often too late to begin treatment. For this reason many physicians screen women for antitoxoplasma antibody at the time of marriage. Women with pre-existing antibodies (before pregnancy) have virtually no risk of producing a congenitally infected child. With this screening strategy, one can concentrate on the women who sero-convert, offering them counseling, therapeutic abortion (if early in pregnancy), or treatment with experimental drugs, such as spiramycin. The risk of severe complications in the fetus is greatest for women who sero-convert in the first trimester of pregnancy. The frequency of congenital infection is greatest in the third trimester, but most of the children infected late in gestation have no detectable disease at the time of birth. Unfortunately, a variety of developmental problems are evident among these initially "asymptomatic" children later in childhood. If the diagnosis is made in time, immunocompromised patients may benefit from treatment with chemotherapeutic drugs (such as pyrimethamine plus sulfadoxine, or trimethoprim plus sulfamethoxazole).

Pneumocystis Infection

As with *Toxoplasma*, *Pneumocystis* infection is common, but overt disease is rare among normal persons. The widespread distribution of this organism is demonstrated by the proportion of people over the age of 4 years who have antibodies to it, over 70% in the U.S. In fact, *Pneumocystis* qualifies as a member of the normal human flora. In contrast to *Toxoplasma*, this organism typically causes only one disease—pneumonia. It has become the hallmark of the AIDS patient, for whom it is highly virulent (Chapter 67). It also causes serious disease among malnourished children and other immunosuppressed persons, and may produce disease at other sites (spleen, bone marrow).

CASE

Ms. F., a 45-year-old woman, had been generally healthy before admission to the hospital. In the preceding 4 months, her weight had decreased from 58 to 47 kg and she reported night sweats and fatigue. Her history included the usual childhood diseases, two uneventful pregnancies, and two blood transfusions in Haiti 3 years ago, which she received for injuries sustained during an automobile accident.

On admission, she had a fever of 38.4°C, nonproductive cough, bilateral pulmonary infiltrates on chest film, and mild hypoxia. On the basis of her history of blood transfusion in Haiti, she was tested for HIV antibodies and found positive. An open lung biopsy revealed Pneumocystis carinii. *She was treated with antibacterial chemotherapeutic agents that have proven effective against this protozoan, trimethoprim-sulfamethoxazole. However, her white blood count fell with this treatment and she was switched to pentamidine. Over the next 10 days, her white blood cell count rose and she recovered from the illness despite some renal insufficiency due to the pentamidine. She was discharged after 20 days in the hospital.*

PATHOGENESIS, DIAGNOSIS, AND TREATMENT

The full life cycle of this organism is not known. Until recently, it was classified as an animal parasite; new studies of its ribosomal RNA homologies indicate that it is probably a fungus. The organism is found frequently on careful examination of sections of lungs of people who have died from other causes. The epidemiological evidence for person-to-person or animal-to-human transmission is confusing and controversial. Active *P. carinii* infection may be elicited by giving steroids to normal rats, suggesting that they normally carry these organisms. It is not clear why *Pneumocystis* produces only pneumonia (perhaps it requires an increased oxygen tension). Rarely *Pneumocystis* organisms are seen at other sites, such as the spleen.

The diagnosis of *P. carinii* infection usually requires demonstration of the organism in open lung or transbronchial biopsies or bronchoalveolar lavage fluid using the high dry objective (Fig. 50.5). The organisms are seldom seen in sputum, except in patients with **AIDS**. Rapid microscopic staining techniques must be used because of the need for timely diagnosis. Serological tests are of limited value because a diagnostic rise in antibody titer often takes 2–3 weeks after the onset of symptoms and may not occur in severely immunocompromised patients. With an acutely ill patient, one cannot wait weeks to obtain a second specimen before beginning treatment. Also, a baseline earlier serum sample is often not available. Antigen detection tests are being developed but are not yet sufficiently sensitive or specific.

The two treatment regimens used in the case of **Ms. F.** are thought to be equally effective. Chemoprophylaxis with trimethoprim-sulfamethoxazole is useful for children who are at high risk, such as those with acute lymphocytic leukemia. According to a recent study, these drugs are also effective for chemoprophylaxis in patients with **AIDS**. Chronic use of these drugs may, however, be complicated by their potential bone marrow toxicity (leading to decreased counts of white and red blood cells and platelets). Other regimens under study include the use of trimetrexate or dapsone, or pentamidine that is aerosolized (rather than administered parenterally) to reduce its toxicity.

Figure 50.5. *Pneumocystis carinii. Left.* Pneumocystis carinii is usually identified by the staining of cysts with Gomori methenamine silver nitrate (as in this figure). The cysts contain dark bodies that, in some instances, as in the two upper organisms, may look like parentheses. The cyst wall often appears folded. *Right.* This figure is of a Giemsa-stained preparation showing *P. carinii* trophozoites, but not cysts. The large clump of cells is typical of that seen in AIDS patients. Giemsa does not stain the cysts, but these are recognized as round, clear areas. The *inset* a shows *P. carinii* cyst in which nuclei of the intracystic organism are arranged in clockface fashion.

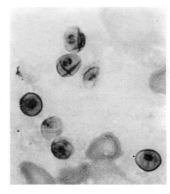
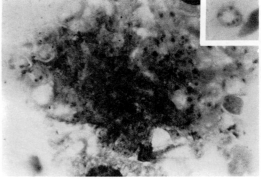

LEISHMANIASIS

Leishmania species produce a spectrum of clinical syndromes, from superficial ulcers to serious lesions of the liver, spleen, and bone marrow, accompanied by systemic signs, such as fever, weight loss, and anemia. Several species are pathogenic for humans. The reason for the great diversity in clinical disease is not well understood, but is due, in part, to the temperature preferences of the different species. Superficial lesions are produced by *Leishmania* species that grow better at lower temperatures (25–30°C) whereas those that invade the viscera grow better at 37°C.

CASE

Mr. Q., a 26-year-old graduate student in anthropology returned from a 6 month expedition to Peru with a nonhealing 2 × 5 cm lesion on his right shin. He reported that almost everyone in his group of 15 had similar lesions but that his was one of the few that had not healed. A smear of a biopsy from the edge of the lesion stained with Giemsa revealed Leishmania-containing macrophages. Mr. Q. was given the antiprotozoal drug pentostam for 4 weeks. The lesion began to heal slowly and he was cured ultimately after treatment.

Leishmania and their Transmission

Leishmania are small protozoa that belong to the **flagellates** because they possess a prominent flagellum during part of their life cycle. In the cytoplasm, the flagellum is connected to an organelle called the kinetoplast that, like mitochondria, has its own **DNA**.

Leishmania are transmitted by the bite of sandflies—small, short-lived insects that feed on many mammals. The phlebotomine sandflies that transmit leishmaniasis are generally found in tropical or subtropical parts of the world, which explains why this disease is rare in North America and Europe. However, phlebotomine sandflies are occasionally found in more temperate regions, and indigenous cases have been reported in the U.S. Like malaria, leishmaniasis is seen mainly among travelers returning from tropical countries. Reservoirs of *Leishmania* include rodents, dogs, other animals, and infected humans.

PATHOGENESIS, DIAGNOSIS, AND TREATMENT

There are several species of *Leishmania*, each of which has different tissue tropisms and clinical manifestations. The diseases they cause include **localized skin ulcer** such as "chiclero disease" (after the harvesters of chewing gum, "chicle"), **mucocutaneous lesions** ("espundia"), **disseminated cutaneous leishmaniasis**, and **disseminated visceral leishmaniasis** ("kala azar"). Mr. Q. had a form of cutaneous leishmaniasis that usually heals poorly and requires treatment.

The life cycle of *Leishmania* is shown in Figure 50.6. These parasites are well adapted to the human host. After internalization by macrophages into phagosomes, they differentiate into a form (**amastigote**) that elicits little production of hydrogen peroxide by macrophages. Thus, they rapidly become better able to survive in phagocytes. They also form their own superoxide dismutase, which protects them from superoxide made by macrophages during their oxidative burst. Finally, the uptake of nutrients, such as glucose and proline by amastigotes, is actually dependent on the acidic pH of the phagosome.

Leishmaniasis is best diagnosed by histological examination of biopsy material using the high dry objective. However, this does not per-

Figure 50.6. *Leishmania* **life cycle.** The flagellated (**promastigote**) insect form of the parasite (*1*) is injected under the skin by the sandfly (*Phlebotomus*) vector (*2*). Once within the human host, the parasite transforms to a nonflagellated (**amastigote**) form that is better prepared to evade the host immune response (it stimulates less release of H_2O_2 from mononuclear cells than the promastigote and produces its own superoxide dismutase). The parasite then invades reticuloendothelial cells (*3*), replicates (*4*), lyses those cells (*5*), and repeats the same sequence in other reticuloendothelial cells (*6*).

In endemic areas, the cycle is completed when previously uninfected sandflies acquire infectious leishmanial amastigotes by biting infected humans (*7*). The amastigotes then transform to flagellated promastigotes (*8*) and replicate in the sandfly GI tract (*9*). Infective promastigotes are injected under the skin of another human when the parasitized sandfly takes a blood meal (*1* and *2*). The *dashed line* between *6* and *7* indicates that transmission is blocked at this point in nonendemic areas such as the U.S. because the sandfly (*Phlebotomus*) vector is not present.

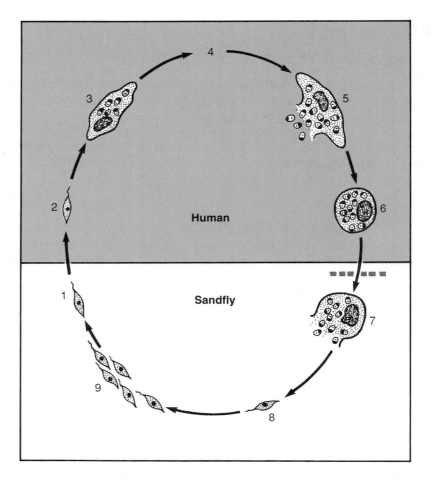

mit one to distinguish among the different species which, although they produce different clinical pictures, look alike under the microscope. *Leishmania* species can be distinguished by culture or by analyzing patterns of isoenzymes or of DNA restriction endonuclease fragments. A recently developed DNA hybridization technique allows one to distinguish parasite species in biopsy material without the need for culture. The increased sensitivity of this method takes advantage of repetitive DNA sequences (minicircles) in the kinetoplast.

A variety of drugs are used to treat leishmaniasis, especially for the invasive forms of the disease. Antimony-containing compounds are modestly successful. However, disease of deep organs, such as the bone marrow, may produce fatal anemia and granulocytopenia, despite treatment.

American Trypanosomiasis—Chagas' Disease

Chagas' disease is caused by *Trypanosoma cruzi*. Infection with *T. cruzi* is common throughout Latin America. Overt disease is much less common, however, and the factors responsible for this difference are poorly understood.

CASE

Señor R., a 58-year-old Brazilian businessman, was admitted to a hospital in Sao Paolo for the evaluation of chronic constipation. Radiological examination of his gastrointestinal (GI) tract revealed a large dilated colon (megacolon) and a somewhat less dilated esophagus (megaesophagus). A blood sample revealed antibodies to T. cruzi. *Because no drugs are effective after the onset of complications, Señor R. was not given antiparasitic treatment.*

PATHOGENESIS, DIAGNOSIS, AND TREATMENT

The life cycle of *T. cruzi* is shown in Figure 50.7. In the endemic areas of South and Central America, most persons are infected by *T. cruzi* in childhood. The soft tissue and lymph node swelling around the eye produced by the bite of an infected reduviid bug (Romaña's sign) is so characteristic that it is virtually diagnostic. Although some persons develop serious (even fatal) illness, most develop a relatively mild disease, recover spontaneously, and remain asymptomatic. A small proportion of the people infected with *T. cruzi* develop complications 10–20 years later. The complications of Chagas' disease result from damage to nerves in the GI tract (megaesophagus, megacolon) or to conducting tissue in the heart (right bundle branch block). Infected reduviid bugs are present in the southern U.S. and are presumably responsible for the sporadic cases of Chagas' disease observed among lifelong residents of Florida, Louisiana, Mississippi, or California.

It is not clear why infection with *T. cruzi* produces autonomic nerve damage in the GI tract (leading to megaesophagus or megacolon) or why it damages the cardiac conduction system. Usually, few organisms and a number of lymphocytes are seen in damaged tissue. Fibrosis is the hallmark of the pathology. Consequently, several investigators have postulated that autoimmune mechanisms may play a significant role in the pathogenesis of these complications.

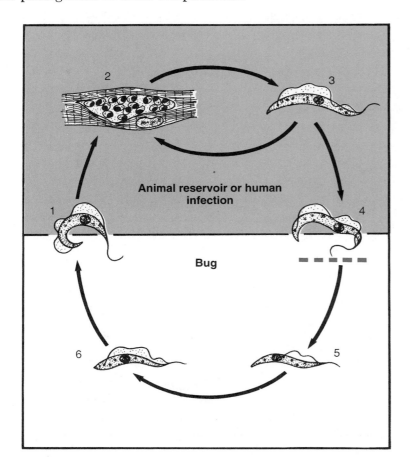

Figure 50.7.   Chagas' Disease (American Trypanosomiasis). The reduviid bug vector deposits feces containing infectious **trypomastigotes** on the skin (*1*). People rub the itching bite wound, allowing the parasites to enter the bloodstream. In the human host, the trypomastigote transforms to an **amastigote** (analogous to the leishmanial amastigote) as it invades tissue such as muscle (*2*). Cells containing large numbers of amastigotes often rupture, liberating large numbers of trypomastigotes (*3*), which invade other host cells (*arrow* from *3* back to *2*), or may be taken up by the vector to complete the cycle.

In the vector (*5*), the parasite replicates as an **epimastigote** and produces additional infectious trypomastigotes (*1*). The *dashed line below 4* indicates that natural transmission does not occur in areas without the reduviid bug vector. Although reduviid bugs are present in the Southern U.S., indigenous cases are rare.

The diagnosis of early infection is usually based on the appearance of the patient. Organisms may often be found in the blood if it is cultured in an appropriate medium or detected by the infection of reduviid bugs that have purposely been allowed to feed upon the patient. Antibodies appear within several weeks. Antibody titers usually remain positive for years. The diagnosis of chronic infection with complications is based on a positive antibody titer or history of exposure plus a known complication (such as megaesophagus, megacolon, or a cardiac conduction defect).

Patients with early acute Chagas' disease may respond to treatment with an experimental drug (benzimidazole, nitrofurazone). However, no treatment is known to be effective for patients with late complications. This may be because the critical damage has already taken place and is no longer reversible.

African Trypanosomiasis—Sleeping Sickness

Sleeping sickness is caused by *Trypanosoma brucei* (Fig. 50.8). The infection is transmitted by the bite of infected tsetse flies in Africa. A remarkable feature of the parasite is its ability to change its predominant surface antigen repeatedly as the host develops immunity to the previous surface antigen. *T. brucei* and its vectors differ in several biological characteristics from *T. cruzi*, and the vectors of Chagas' disease. For example, *T. brucei* resides in the salivary glands of tsetse flies, and is transmitted directly by bites. *T. cruzi*, on the other hand, grows in the intestine of reduviid bugs, and is transmitted when feces deposited by the biting insect are introduced into the bite by scratching.

Figure 50.8. Sleeping sickness (African trypanosomiasis). The tsetse fly vector inoculates infectious **trypomastigotes** under the skin (*1*) when it bites humans or other mammals. Once inside the new host (*2*), the parasite replicates in the bloodstream by binary fission as a trypomastigote (*3*). Unlike *Leishmania* and the trypanosome that causes Chagas' disease, the trypanosomes that cause African sleeping sickness do not have promastigote or amastigote forms. The rate of movement of trypomastigotes from the bloodstream and lymph nodes to the CNS determines when the illness changes from a systemic (hemolymphatic) infection to an encephalitis. Circulating trypomastigotes (*4*) taken up anew by tsetse flies complete the cycle.

Within the tsetse fly, the parasites replicate in the GI tract and transform to epimastigotes (*5*). The *line below 4* indicates that natural transmission does not occur in countries such as the U.S. where the tsetse fly vector is not present.

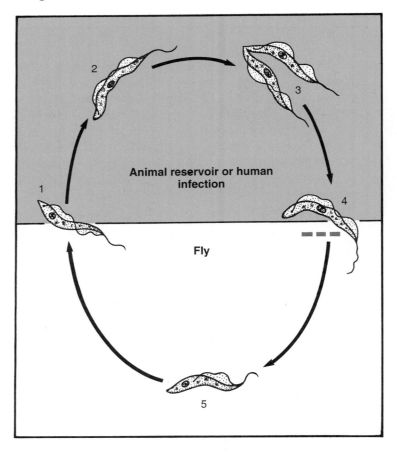

CASE

The patient, Mr. S., was a 32-year-old student from Kenya living in Canada. He had fevers to 38°C and swollen lymph nodes at the back of his neck (occipital adenopathy or Winterbottom's sign) for 8 months. Two weeks ago, he developed a severe headache, stiff neck, and an aversion to light (photophobia). Trypanosomes were seen on Giemsa-stained specimens of blood and cerebrospinal fluid under the oil immersion objective. Mr. S. was treated with two drugs—suramin for hemolymphatic infection, and an arsenical (tryparsamide) for CNS infection. He recovered after 4 weeks of treatment.

PATHOGENESIS, DIAGNOSIS, AND TREATMENT

The spread of African trypanosomiasis is restricted by the distribution of its tsetse fly vector (*Glossina*) and of the animal reservoirs. In East Africa, the main reservoirs are wild game animals (such as impalas); in West Africa, the principal reservoirs are infected humans and domestic animals, such as cattle. Several weeks to months after the initial infection, patients develop a systemic illness with fever, swollen lymph nodes, and trypanosomes in the bloodstream. After several months (the East African form) or years (the West African form), the parasite crosses into the CNS and infects the brain and spinal fluid.

During months or years of chronic bloodstream infection, patients undergo bouts of parasitemia (Fig. 50.9). During each bout, the parasite changes its dominant surface antigen (a glycoprotein), thus avoiding immune destruction by the host. The genetic basis for this variation has been studied in some detail. The genome of these parasites contains hundreds or thousands of genes for antigenically different surface glycoproteins, although only one is expressed at a time. Transcription of these genes is by a special mechanism—it requires that the gene be copied and that this copy be transposed into a special site in the genome, a "reading station." At their original site, these genes remain silent. The transposed gene is the one that is expressed.

Several drugs, including pentamidine and suramin, have some usefulness during the systemic stage of this infection. However, treatment is much more difficult after the infection has crossed into the CNS because toxic drugs, such as arsenicals, are required. Recent studies suggest that α-difluoromethyl ornithine (DFMO) may be effective for cases with CNS involvement. If this is the case, DFMO will substantially reduce the morbidity of treatment.

Free-living Amebae

A number of protozoa, principally *Naegleria*, *Acathamoeba*, and *Hartmanella*, have no known animal reservoir but produce serious systemic diseases, such as meningoencephalitis (inflammation of the meninges and the brain). These organisms may also cause infection of the eye, especially among persons wearing contact lenses.

CASE

The patient was a 6-year-old girl living in Virginia. Three days ago, in the month of August, she swam in a nearby lake. Although she was well previously, within 2 days she developed a severe headache, neck stiffness, and eye pain on exposure to light (photophobia). A lumbar puncture revealed 300 mononucleated cells per mm³ and a few neutrophils. Many of these cells were actively motile in a wet mount, suggesting that they were not leukocytes but

Figure 50.9. Periodic fluctuation in the number of *Trypanosoma brucei* in the blood of a patient with African trypanosomiasis.

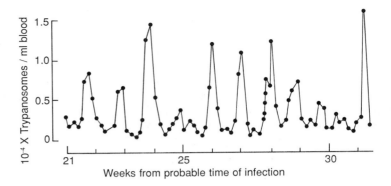

amebae. Despite treatment with antimicrobial drugs, the patient died 3 days later. Several other children who swam in the same lake also had headaches and mild neck stiffness, but recovered spontaneously.

PATHOGENESIS, DIAGNOSIS, AND TREATMENT

There are two types of amebic meningoencephalitis: (*a*) A usually fatal disease caused by *Naegleria fowleri*, as in this case, which typically occurs in young, previously healthy people, and is associated with extensive exposure to fresh water lakes that harbor these amebae; and (*b*) a disease caused by *Acanthamoeba* or *Hartmanella*, which is typically seen in older patients who are immunocompromised (such as those with lymphoma or diabetes). Both types of disease, once they become clinically apparent, tend to progress despite treatment. Although there are reports of recovery using multiple drugs (amphotericin B, miconazole, and rifampin), these regimens have not proven to be reproducibly effective.

In the meningoencephalitis caused by *Naegleria*, the parasite is thought to enter the CNS via the cribriform plate along the olfactory nerve tracts. Trauma or increased pressure, as may occur when diving into water, are believed to facilitate the entry of the organisms into the CNS. *Acanthamoeba* or *Hartmanella* are thought to spread to the CNS via the bloodstream. This is because patients with this disease often are found to have foci of infection at distant sites, such as the lung on postmortem examination.

Infection of the cornea (keratitis) is produced by some of these free-living amebae, and is an increasingly important (often undiagnosed) cause of visual loss among contact lens wearers or persons with other ocular trauma. It is important to recognize this infection (by morphological examination of Giemsa-stained material using the high dry or oil immersion objectives), because treatment with topical or systemic imidazoles may save the patient's sight. These parasites may gain access to the eye from contaminated fluids used to clean contact lenses.

SUGGESTED READING

MALARIA

Cranston HA, Boylan CW, Sutera SP, et al. *Plasmodium falciparum* abolishes physiologic red cell deformability. Science 1984;223:400–403.

Ferreira A, Schofield L, Enea V, et al. Inhibition of development of exoerythrocytic forms of malaria parasites by γ-interferon. Science 1986;232:881–884.

Friedman MJ. Erythrocytic mechanism of sickle cell resistance to malaria. Proc Natl Acad Sci USA 1978;75:1994–1997.

Hoffman SL, Nussenzweig V, Sadoff JC, Nussenzweig RS. Progress toward malaria preerythrocytic vaccines. Science 1991;252:520–522.

Hoffman SL, Oster CN, Plowe CV, et al. Naturally acquired antibodies to sporozoites do not prevent malaria: vaccine development implications. Science 1987;237:639–642.

Krogstad DJ, Gluzman IY, Kyle DE, et al. Efflux of chloroquine from *Plasmodium falciparum*: mechanism of chloroquine resistance. Science 1987;238:1283–1285.

Krogstad DJ, Schlessinger PH. Acid vesicle function, intracellular pathogens and the action of chloroquine against *Plasmodium falciparum*. N Engl J Med 1987;317:542–549.

Miller LH, Howard RJ, Carter R, Good MF, Nussenzweig V, Nussenzweig RS. Research towards malaria vaccines. Science 1986;234:1249–1256.

BABESIOSIS

Ruebush TK II, Juranek DD, Chisholm ES, et al. Human babesiosis on Nantucket Island: evidence for self-limited and subliminal infections. N Engl J Med 1977;297:825–827.

TOXOPLASMOSIS

Daffos F, Forester F, Capella-Pavlovsky M, Thulliez P, Aufrant C, Valenti D, Cox WL. Prenatal management of 746 pregnancies at risk for congenital toxoplasmosis. N Engl J Med 1988;318:271–275.

Remington JS, Klein JO, eds. Infectious diseases of the fetus and newborn, 2nd ed. Philadelphia: WB Saunders, 1983.

Shepp DH, Hackman RC, Conley FK, et al. *Toxoplasma gondii* reactivation identified by detection of parasitemia in culture. Ann Intern Med 1985;103:218–221.

PNEUMOCYSTIS

Hughes WT, Rivera GK, Schell MJ, et al. Successful intermittent chromoprophylaxis for *Pneumocystis carinii* pneumonitis. N Engl J Med 1987;316:1627–1632.

Walzer PD, Perl DD, Krogstad DJ, et al. *Pneumocystis carinii* pneumonia in the United States: epidemiologic, diagnostic and clinical features. Ann Intern Med 1974;80:83–93.

LEISHMANIASIS

Chang KP, Bray RS, eds. Leishmaniasis. Amsterdam: Elsevier, 1985.

Zilberstein D, Dwyer DM. Proton motive force-driven active transport of D-glucose and L-proline in the protozoan parasite *Leishmania donovanis*. Proc Natl Acad Sci USA 1988;83:1716–1720.

TRYPANOSOMIASIS

Englund PT, Hayduk SL, Marini JC. The molecular biology of trypanosomes. Annu Rev Biochem 1982;51:695–726.

Hudson L, ed. The biology of trypanosomes. New York and Berlin: Springer-Verlag, 1985.

Intestinal and Vaginal Protozoa

51

Donald J. Krogstad

Between 5% and 10% of all people in the developing countries of the world harbor the pathogenic ameba *Entamoeba histolytica* in their stool. In the U.S., the figure is less than 1%. *Cryptosporidium* and *Giardia* are more frequent in the U.S., but their prevalence varies considerably among different regions. Other protozoa also live in the lumen of organs besides the intestine. The main one is *Trichomonas vaginalis*, a common agent of vaginitis. It is usually transmitted sexually.

AMEBIASIS

The agent of amebiasis is *E. histolytica*. As its species name indicates, it may cause lysis of host tissue, especially in the colon. The lesions start as small ulcerations of the intestinal epithelium and spread laterally when they encounter the deeper layers of the colon, eventually producing flask-shaped ulcers. The organisms may also spread through the bloodstream to produce abscesses in the liver, the brain, and other organs. Despite their pathogenic potential, these organisms cause few or no symptoms in the majority of persons infected.

CASE

The patient, Mr. A., is a 26-year-old who was discharged from the U.S. Army 2 years previously. He spent 3 of his 6 military years abroad, including tours of duty in Korea, Panama, and Germany. During the last 2 years he developed intermittent diarrhea, with blood and mucus visible in the stool. Sigmoidoscopy (endoscopic examination of the colon) and an x-ray study of the intestine after a barium enema revealed pseudopolyps, consistent with inflammatory bowel disease. He was diagnosed as having ulcerative colitis, an inflammatory bowel disease of unknown cause, and was treated with steroids for that condition.

At the time of admission to the hospital, 4 months after beginning steroid therapy, Mr. A. reported the loss of about 11 kg of weight (down to 67 kg) and a recent increase in bloody stools and abdominal pain. He had no fever (probably because he was medicated with a large amount of steroids). Examination of his stool under the microscope showed many white and red blood cells but no amebae. However, a serological test for E. histolytica *antibodies in serum (indirect hemagglutination) revealed a titer of 1:2000, which is high. A CT scan showed abscesses in the liver, lungs, and brain.*

He had a stormy hospital stay with several episodes of bacteremia (secondary to disruption of the intestinal mucosa by the parasites) but recovered ultimately after the steroids were tapered and he was treated with the antiamebic agent, metronidazole.

Table 51.1. Comparison of Major Intestinal Protozoa

Organism	Reservoir	Mode of Transmission	Clinical Manifestations
Entamoeba histolytica (amebiasis)	Infected humans	Fecal-oral transmission by the ingestion of feces containing infectious cysts	Bloody diarrhea (dysentery) Distant abscesses (especially liver) Asymptomatic intestinal infection
Giardia lamblia (giardiasis)	Infected humans, and other mammals	Fecal-oral transmission by the ingestion of feces containing infectious cysts	Watery diarrhea, may also cause steatorrhea and malabsorption Asymptomatic intestinal infection
Cryptosporidium (cryptosporidiosis)	Infected humans, and a wide variety of other animal hosts (zoonosis)	Fecal-oral transmission by the ingestion of feces containing infectious cysts	Watery diarrhea

ENCOUNTER

E. histolytica is transmitted from person to person via the fecal-oral route. It has a simple life cycle, with two forms—the actively growing, vegetative **trophozoite** and the dormant but highly resistant **cyst** (Fig. 51.1). The critical factors responsible for the transition between trophozoites and cysts are not understood. The transmission of *Entamoeba* and *Giardia* has a paradoxical aspect; i.e., patients with diarrhea pose a minor threat of transmission because they excrete the actively growing trophozoites, which are labile—they are easily destroyed by drying in the environment or acid in the stomach. On the other hand, asymptomatic carriers excrete the tough cyst form of the parasite; they represent a greater danger of transmission because the cysts are resistant to drying and to gastric acid. This paradox illustrates the biological principle that successful parasites generally do not harm the host. When amebae are in balance with their host, they are excreted as cysts, which ensures the survival of the species.

Because the parasite is infectious in the cyst stage and does not require a period of differentiation in the environment, transmission of amebiasis is not restricted to warm climates. In fact, *E. histolytica* may be transmitted in temperate and even polar regions. All that is necessary for transmission is that the feces of a carrier contaminate food or water. Sexual transmission (anal-oral or oral-genital) is also important, particularly among homosexual men.

PATHOGENESIS OF AMEBIASIS

E. histolytica is frequently found within the human colon in persons without symptoms of disease. To damage tissues, the amebae must adhere to specific receptors on host cells. The fact that this attachment is inhibited by intestinal mucus suggests that disruption of the mucus layer may be a critical event in the pathogenesis of amebiasis. Damage to host cells requires intimate cell-to-cell contact and takes place in three distinct steps—receptor-mediated attachment to the mammalian target cell, contact-dependent killing, and ingestion of the killed host cell by the ameba. Although certain strains of *E. histolytica* produce an enterotoxin, it is not yet clear whether enterotoxin production correlates with virulence.

White blood cells do not control amebic infection in the nonimmune host: pathogenic strains of amebae actually kill neutrophils and nonac-

Figure 51.1. *Entamoeba histolytica* **life cycle.** Humans acquire amebic infection by oral ingestion of the cyst form of the parasite (*1*). Viable cysts may be ingested from the external environment (where they remain stable and infectious for prolonged periods after excretion), from the stool of other infected persons, or from the stools of the patients themselves (the *arrow* from *7* to *2*). In the upper GI tract, the parasite excysts after passing through the stomach (*2*), replicates asexually by binary fission (*3*), and transforms to the potentially pathogenic trophozoite form (*4*) that is typically found in the large intestine. Trophozoites die rapidly when they are shed into the external environment (*5*) (*solid line below 5* on the diagram). When conditions in the GI tract are unfavorable, trophozoites transform into cysts (*6* and *7*) that can remain dormant for long periods of time in the host and the environment.

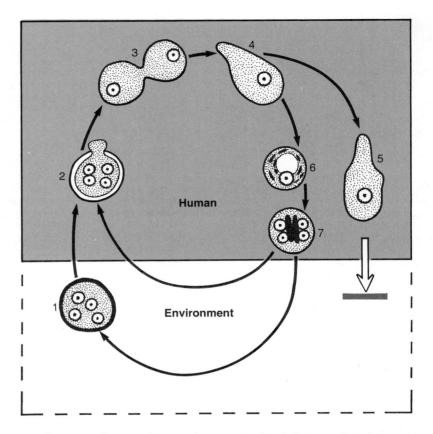

tivated macrophages. (Note the reversal of the usual "phagocyte-ingests-invader" theme.) The situation is different in the immune hosts in whom the most important line of defense appears to be cell-mediated immunity. This is suggested by finding that amebae can be killed in vitro by activated macrophages. Also, persons given steroids (which suppress cell-mediated immunity) tend to have disseminated infection despite high titers of antibodies, as was the case with Mr. A. Thus, circulating antibodies may not play a critical role in protection against amebic infection.

DIAGNOSIS

The identification of *E. histolytica* in stools by microscopic examination is one of the most challenging diagnostic procedures in microbiology. The reason is that nonpathogenic amebae or even white blood cells in stool can be mistaken for amebae, resulting in false-positive laboratory reports. Reliable results require examination by an experienced technologist using a high dry or oil immersion objectives. False-negative results are due frequently to the insensitivity of microscopic examination or to interfering substances, like the barium given for x-rays. Thus, although a positive stool is helpful in diagnosis, a negative result does not prove that amebiasis is absent. For this reason, serological diagnosis is often attempted and is of considerable value. Serology is positive in over 80% of people with invasion of the intestinal mucosa and in over 96–100% of persons with systemic (metastatic) disease. In the U.S., 1% or less of the general population has antibodies to *E. histolytica*. Among asymptomatic carriers, the prevalence is approximately 10–15%. This is an instance in which circulating antibodies are of little protective value but are a good marker for the disease.

TREATMENT

The drug of choice for active amebic infection is metronidazole, the same antimicrobial used to treat infections caused by anaerobic bacteria. Pathogenic amebae carry out anaerobic metabolism and are able to reduce metronidazole partly and convert it into the active form in the same manner as *Bacteroides* (see Chapters 2 and 16). This drug is particularly suitable for infections of the nervous system because it crosses the blood-brain barrier well. Carriers with cysts in their stool and no evidence of active disease are treated with drugs such as diiodohydroxyquin or entamide furoate.

GIARDIASIS

The agent of giardiasis is an intestinal protozoan called *Giardia lamblia*, which is distributed all over the world. In the U.S., it is found in areas of poor sanitation or in day care centers, where there is frequent opportunity for fecal-oral transmission. *Giardia* typically produces a mild but annoying diarrheal disease, often localized to the duodenum and jejunum.

CASE

Ms. R. is a 36-year-old woman with an unremarkable medical history. Two months previous to seeing her physician, she visited Colorado for 10 days of backpacking. One week after her return, she developed diarrhea with three to

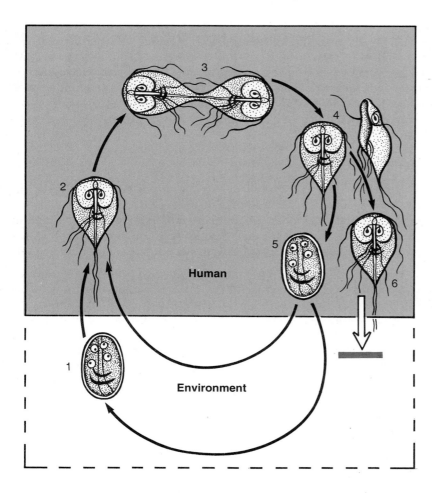

Figure 51.2. *Giardia lamblia* life cycle. Humans acquire giardiasis by ingesting the cyst form of the parasite (*1*). As in amebiasis, the parasite excysts and transforms to a trophozoite in the upper GI tract (*2*), where it replicates asexually by binary fission (*3*). Trophozoites cause disease by attaching to the epithelium of the small intestine via a ventral sucking disk (*4*). As indicated by the *solid line* and *open arrow below 6*, trophozoites are not infectious for others because they are readily killed by drying in the external environment. As in amebiasis, humans acquire infection by ingesting cysts from the external environment (*1*), from the stools of other patients, or from their own stool (*arrow from 5 to 2*).

five watery stools per day. These contained no pus or blood. She did not report fever or chills. She had a stool examination and was told that it was positive for G. lamblia. *She was treated with an antiparasitic drug, atabrine, and improved markedly over a 7-day period. Since then, her symptoms have recurred and the organisms have again been found in her stool.*

CLINICAL ASPECTS

As with *E. histolytica,* giardiasis is acquired by ingestion of the cyst form of the parasite (Fig. 51.2). The acid in the stomach not only does not kill the cysts, but actually prepares them for change into the vegetative trophozoite form in the duodenum. *Giardia* trophozoites attach to the epithelium of the duodenum and jejunum using a ventral sucking disk. The vegetative forms have the characteristic appearance of a face adorned with mustache-like flagella visible under the high dry objective (Fig. 51.2). Cysts of *Giardia* are highly resistant in the environment and are found increasingly in ostensibly "pure" mountain streams contaminated by the feces of infected animals or humans. Giardiasis has been known as the "hiker's disease, but is also common in urban environments with poor sanitation, e.g., day care centers. Like pathogenic amebae, these organisms may be transmitted in cold as well as in warm climates. Giardiasis is also an important infection among homosexual males.

Signs of malnutrition due to malabsorption may occur as a result of extensive infection, which may literally cover the mucosal surface of the small intestine (Fig. 51.3). Unlike *E. histolytica, Giardia* is not invasive and does not produce bloody diarrhea or metastatic infection. Giardiasis is treated with atabrine, a drug previously used in malaria. As with Ms. R., relapses occur frequently. Although these relapses usually respond to retreatment, potential sources of reinfection (such as contaminated water and food, and infected sexual partners) must be considered. Metronidazole and a furan-type drug (furazolidone) have also been used. Hikers and campers may prevent unpleasant episodes of diarrhea by boiling their drinking water or treating it with iodine or chlorine.

CRYPTOSPORIDIOSIS

Cryptosporidiosis is a zoonosis, an animal disease that affects humans only accidentally. It was first discovered as a cause of diarrhea among veterinary students and animal handlers who acquired it from calves they were treating for diarrhea. It is now clear that cryptosporidiosis is an important diarrheal disease in both developed and developing countries.

CASE

Mr. H. received a renal transplant 2 years ago. He was well until 6 weeks ago, although he had taken immunosuppressive drugs to prevent graft rejection. Six weeks ago, he began to have watery stools three to eight times a day. He reported no fever, nor did he see blood or pus in the stools. A microscopic examination of his stool (with the oil immersion objective) using an acid-fast stain revealed the presence of cryptosporidia (these organisms have the property, unusual among protozoa, of being acid-fast).

CLINICAL ASPECTS

Cryptosporidium resembles *Toxoplasma* in that infectious oocyst forms are produced in the intestine and spread to other animals. How-

Figure 51.3. Scanning electron micrograph of *Giardia lamblia*. Top. Scanning electron micrograph of *G. lamblia* adhering to the GI epithelium via its ventral sucking disk. Patients with giardiasis may have a significant reduction in the amount of absorptive surface available because of the large number of adhering parasites. **Bottom.** Upon detaching from the intestinal epithelium, the organisms often leave a clear impression on the microvillous surface (*upper circles*).

ever, unlike *Toxoplasma*, cryptosporidia do not invade the intestinal epithelial cells, nor do they disseminate to produce systemic infection. They carry out their whole life cycle among the microvilli of the small intestine (Fig. 51.4). In immunocompetent people, the life cycle takes place only once or twice; it results in a single episode of diarrhea that usually lasts than 2 weeks or less. In the immunocompromised patient, the life cycle of the organism is repeated many times and is associated with persistent watery diarrhea.

Cryptosporidiosis is often acquired in rural areas because of greater contact with animals. However, it may also spread from person to person in crowded urban environments such as day care centers. It is now recognized as a frequent cause of diarrhea in Great Britain and the U.S. It is particularly important among patients with AIDS or AIDS-related syndromes.

TRICHOMONIASIS

Trichomonas vaginalis is an extremely common inhabitant of the vagina—found in 15% or more of women, where it occasionally causes vaginitis. Less common and less pathogenic are species of *Trichomonas* found in the GI tract (*T. hominis*) or the mouth (*T. tenax*).

CLINICAL ASPECTS

T. vaginalis infection is transmitted by sexual intercourse. However, the parasite cannot replicate in the acid environment of the normal va-

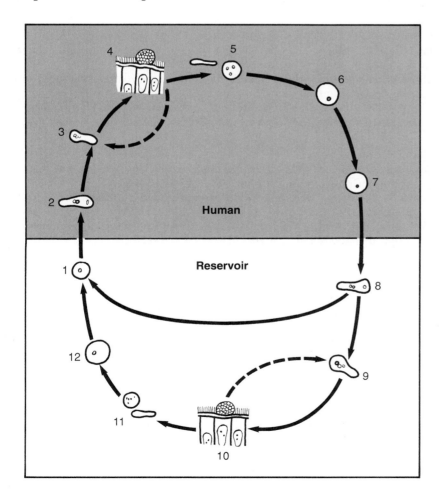

Figure 51.4. *Cryptosporidium* **life cycle.** Humans acquire infection by ingesting infectious oocysts (*1*), which were excreted by themselves (*4, 5*), by other infected humans, or by animal hosts such as calves, birds, or reptiles (*8, 9, 10, 11, 12*). Once inside the human host (*2*), the parasite attaches to the epithelial surface of the GI tract and replicates (*3*), producing additional infectious oocysts (*4*). Unlike *Toxoplasma* (another coccidian parasite), cryptosporidia do not invade GI epithelial cells or disseminate through the bloodstream. In the immunologically normal host, cryptosporidia undergo only one cycle of asexual reproduction and produce a self-limited diarrhea. In the immunocompromised host, cryptosporidia undergo multiple cycles of asexual replication (*5*) and may produce watery diarrhea that continues indefinitely.

gina (pH 4.9). The vaginitis observed in infected woman is typically associated with a frothy creamy discharge. Symptomatic *T. vaginalis* infection is uncommon among men, although most partners of symptomatic woman become infected. On occasion, men develop symptomatic *T. vaginalis* infection of the urethra, epididymis, or prostate. Rarely penile ulcers are observed in infected men.

TREATMENT

Single-dose metronidazole treatment is recommended by most investigators. Alternatives include timidazole (another nitromidazole that has been used extensively in Europe), when it is approved by the U.S. Food and Drug Administration. In pregnant woman (in whom there is particular concern about the potential carcinogenic effects of the nitromidazoles), douching with vinegar may suppress symptomatic infection by lowering vaginal pH. Male sexual partners must be treated too, to prevent "ping-pong" relapse, a common feature of sexually transmitted diseases.

SUGGESTED READING

AMEBIASIS

Allason-Jones E, Mindel A, Sargeaunt P, Williams P. *Entamoeba histolytica* as a common intestinal parasite in homosexual men. N Engl J Med 1986; 315:353–356.

Martinez-Palomo A, ed. Amebiasis. Amsterdam: Elsevier, 1986.

Ravdin JI, ed. Amebiasis: human infection by *Entamoeba histolytica*. New York: Wiley, 1988.

GIARDIASIS

Erlandsen SL, Meyer EA, eds. *Giardia* and giardiasis: biology, pathogenesis and epidemiology. New York: Plenum, 1984.

Gillin FD, Reiner DS, Gault MJ, et al. Encystation and expression of cyst antigens by *Giardia lamblia* in vitro. Science 1987;235:1040–1043.

Lev B, Ward H, Keusch GT, Pereira ME. Lectin activation in *Giardia lamblia* by host protease: a novel host-parasite interaction. Science 1986;232: 71–73.

CRYPTOSPORIDIOSIS

Jokipii L, Jokipii AM. Timing of symptoms and oocyst excretion in human cryptosporidiosis. N Engl J Med 1986;315:1643–1647.

Soave R, Armstrong D. *Cryptosporidium* and cryptosporidiosis. Rev Inf Dis 1986;8:1012–1023.

Wolfson JS, Richter JM, Waldron MA, et al. Cryptosporidiosis in immunocompetent patents. N Engl J Med 1984;312:1278–1282.

Intestinal Helminths

52

Donald J. Krogstad

The helminths or worms are multicellular animals. They include many free-living harmless species but also some pathogenic ones that infect a high proportion of all people on earth (Table 52.1). Helminthic diseases are sometimes mistakenly thought to be a problem peculiar to the tropics. In fact, people in the temperate zone (especially if immunocompromised) may become seriously afflicted by these diseases.

Helminths are the largest parasites that affect humans, ranging in size from 10-yard-long tapeworms down to pinworms, which are barely visible with the naked eye. Many are able to carry out their life cycle within the human body, but others have complex life cycles that include insect vectors and animal reservoirs. Helminths fall into three large groups, **roundworms** (*Nematodes*), **tapeworms** (*Cestodes*), and **flukes** (*Trematodes*), generally distinguishable by their shape. They will be discussed briefly below; specialized parasitology textbooks should be consulted for details.

As we move from the world of unicellular microbes into that of multicellular animals, we must retain some of the main themes of host-parasite interaction. Thus, the most important factors that determine the severity of helminthic infections are the **number of worms** and the **immune state of the patient.** Normal people can tolerate a sizable number of worms, especially in the intestine, with few if any clinical symptoms. Most frequently, worms are kept in check, and the infection does not progress significantly. However, in the immunocompromised patient (whether suffering from malnutrition, therapeutic immunosuppression, or a disease such as AIDS), helminthic infections may well cause serious illness. Helminths produce disease by a variety of pathogenic mechanisms, the main ones being mechanical (including ob-

Table 52.1. Pathophysiological Mechanisms in Helminthic Diseases

Mechanism	Example
Mechanical obstruction or mass effect	
Intestinal obstruction	*Ascaris* "worm ball"
Lymphatic obstruction	Lymphatic filariasis (elephantiasis)
Displacement of normal tissue	Echinococcosis ("hydatid disease")
	Cysticercosis
Facilitating bacterial invasion into normally sterile spaces	
	Strongyloidiasis
Production of anemia (nutritional)	
Due to sucking blood	Hookworms
Due to vitamin B_{12} depletion	Fish tapeworm
Chronic inflammation	
	Schistosomiasis
	Onchocerciasis

struction), tissue invasion, chronic inflammation, and nutritional (loss of blood or of vitamin B_{12}) (Table 52.1). The type of clinical manifestation produced usually depends on the organ or tissue where the damage occurs.

From the point of view of human disease, helminths can be divided into the **intestinal helminths** (this chapter) and the **blood and tissue helminths** (Chapter 53). Intestinal helminths tend to cause chronic infections that may contribute to the malnutrition of their host (Table 52.1). If present in large numbers, they may also occlude the intestinal lumen. Intestinal helminths can be divided into the roundworms, which enter the body by passage through the skin as well as through the mouth, and the tapeworms, which are acquired solely through the mouth.

INTESTINAL ROUNDWORMS USUALLY ACQUIRED BY PASSAGE THROUGH THE SKIN

The most important examples of this group of human roundworms are *Strongyloides* and hookworms (Table 52.2).

Strongyloidiasis

We will use strongyloidiasis as a paradigm of intestinal parasitic disease. This disease is prevalent in tropical areas of the globe but may also be found elsewhere. If the infecting worms are present in large numbers, they may cause intestinal malfunction. They may perforate the intestinal wall, resulting in serious bacterial septicemias. In addition, they may reinfect the same host, especially if immunocompromised, to produce a lethal systemic disease.

CASE

S., 3-year-old girl living in in a Caribbean island, appeared malnourished (her height and weight placed her below the third percentile for her age), but

Table 52.2. Main Intestinal Helminths

Example	Reservoir	Clinical Manifestations
Acquired by passage through the skin		
Roundworms		
Strongyloides stercoralis	Infected humans	GI manifestations that may mimic peptic ulcer or gallbladder disease; disseminated infection ("hyperinfection syndrome")
Hookworms	Infected humans	Iron-deficiency anemia from chronic GI blood loss
N. americanus		
A. duodenale		
Acquired by ingestion		
Roundworms		
Ascaris lumbricoides	Infected humans	Often asymptomatic except for passage of 25- to 30-cm worms; may produce GI or biliary obstruction, or peritonitis from intestinal perforation
Pinworm	Infected humans, especially	Itching of the perianal or genital region
Enterobius vermicularis	children	
Whipworm	Infected humans	Often asymptomatic; damage to intestinal mucosa, malnutrition and anemia if severe
Trichuris trichiura		
Tapeworms		
Taenia solium	Pigs	Intestinal infection (teniasis) is typically asymptomatic; for cysticercosis, see Table 53.1
T. saginata	Cattle	Intestinal infection (teniasis) is typically asymptomatic
Diphyllobothrium latuum	Fish	Intestinal infection is typically asymptomatic, but may lead to vitamin B_{12} deficiency

had otherwise been well. Two weeks before admission, she developed abdominal pain and diarrhea, which became bloody 1 week later. When she was admitted to the hospital, her abdomen was rigid on palpation (consistent with peritonitis). Stool examination revealed larvae of Strongyloides stercoralis, *although they were originally misidentified as those of hookworms. S. was taken to the operating room and found to have multiple perforations of the small and large intestine, with diffuse peritonitis. Despite antibiotic treatment for her bacteremia (secondary to peritonitis), she died 3 days after surgery.*

ENCOUNTER AND ENTRY

The life cycle of *Strongyloides* does not require an external soil phase. (Fig. 52.1). In areas of poor sanitation, this worm is transmitted via human feces, regardless of climate. Thus, strongyloidiasis outbreaks have been reported from institutions for the mentally retarded in temperate zones, from Eskimo settlements north of the Arctic circle, and from the tropics.

Strongyloides penetrate human skin as **filariform larvae** (perhaps best remembered by thinking of them as "filing" their way through the skin). Thus, transmission of these parasites does not require the ingestion of contaminated feces; transmission is typically fecal-cutaneous, not fecal-oral. People become infected with *Strongyloides* by contact with infected human stool or with soil that has been contaminated by human stool containing filariform larvae. After they penetrate the skin, filariform larvae enter the bloodstream and lymphatics and become trapped in the lungs. Here they break through the alveolar wall into the alveolar lumen, are coughed up, and then are swallowed into the GI tract where they continue their life cycle. (Fig. 52.1), primarily in the duodenum and jejunum.

PATHOBIOLOGY

Many people infected with *Strongyloides* carry a small number of the worms in the intestine and few exhibit clinical manifestations. Like other intestinal roundworms, *Strongyloides* has three opportunities to cause damage during its life cycle:

- While passing through the skin—*Strongyloides* does not usually cause damage at this step, but other worms (e.g., hookworms) may produce itching and a rash, neither of which tend to be severe.

- During passage through the lungs—*Strongyloides* may elicit a transient response characterized by cough, wheezing, and fever.

- In the intestine—although *Strongyloides* infection is usually asymptomatic, it may cause pain, vomiting, and diarrhea when the number of worms becomes large.

Invasion of the Bowel Wall and Replication in the Human Host

Unlike the other intestinal roundworms, female *Strongyloides* have the unusual ability to invade the bowel wall to lay their eggs. This may cause severe disease because rhabditiform larvae hatching from these eggs can cross the intestinal wall into the peritoneum, causing intestinal perforations that permit intestinal bacteria to follow and to produce peritonitis. As a result, strongyloidiasis may produce acute clinical syndromes (such as the peritonitis in the case described), or may mimic more chronic abdominal problems such as peptic ulcer or

Figure 52.1. The general *Strongyloides* and human hookworm life cycle. The invasive filariform larvae of these parasites penetrate unbroken human skin (*1*). Once inside the host, *Strongyloides* and human hookworm larvae migrate through the subcutaneous tissues to the bloodstream (*2*), enter the lung by crossing into the alveoli (*3*), travel up the trachea, and are coughed up and swallowed into the GI tract (*4*). In contrast to *Strongyloides* and hookworm, the filariform larvae that cause creeping eruption (the larvae of dog or cat hookworms) are unable to enter the bloodstream and migrate to the lung. Instead, they wander through the subcutaneous tissues causing cutaneous larva migrans. The *solid line* and *open arrow* (*above* and to the *left* of *1*) indicate that the larvae of this parasite are unable to complete their normal life cycle in a human host.

The larvae of *Strongyloides* and hookworm mature (*5*) within the upper GI tract. As shown on the *right side* of the diagram, female hookworm larvae remain within the lumen of the GI tract, releasing their eggs into the stool (*6*), which then pass into the environment (*9*). Because the female *Strongyloides* larvae enter the bowel wall, their eggs do not appear in the stool (*left side* of *6*) and only the larvae (*7*) are normally found in the stool. On occasion, these larvae mature to the filariform stage in the GI tract (*8*) to produce endogenous reinfection (autoinfection). Because hookworm larvae require maturation in the environment to become infectious (*bottom half* of the diagram), autoinfection cannot occur in this disease.

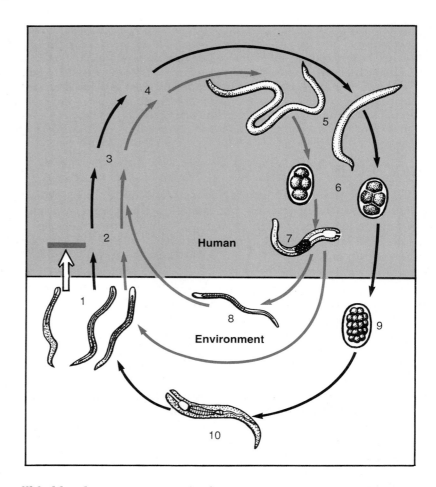

gallbladder disease. Because the female *Strongyloides* lay their eggs in the bowel wall instead of the intestinal lumen, the larvae may hatch and mature while still in the body. Thus, they are often infectious within the intestinal mucosa or by the time they reach the anal or perirectal area. Reinfection may then occur from larval invasion of the perianal skin even if the patient has not been exposed to new external sources of infection. *Strongyloides* reinfection produces a characteristic snakelike (serpiginous) urticarial rash ("larva currens"), which is typically located near the anus. As in the case of S., the process of **endogenous reinfection** may produce a fatal **hyperinfection syndrome**.

Immunosuppression and Strongyloidiasis

Patients immunosuppressed by malnutrition (as was S.) or by drugs have a much greater risk of dissemination and of the hyperinfection syndrome. In fact, in the tropics, strongyloidiasis is a major cause of death in kidney transplant recipients. Presumably, these patients can control the infection before transplantation, but become unable to do so when their cell-mediated immunity is compromised by the immunosuppressive drugs used to avoid rejection of the transplanted kidney.

Because the hyperinfection syndrome is often seen in patients with impaired cell-mediated immunity, it seems likely that this kind of immunity is the critical factor in the control of strongyloidiasis. The relative role of mononuclear cells and eosinophils has not been elucidated, nor is it known if these worms coat themselves with host proteins.

Strongyloides infections may become chronic and produce symptoms for decades. Persistent infections lasting over 35–40 years have been described among former prisoners of war (from World War II). These persons often have chronic syndromes that are misdiagnosed as peptic ulcer or gallbladder disease and fail to respond to medical or surgical treatments for those conditions. Patients in whom autoinfection has been controlled may develop urticarial skin lesions from the migration of larvae at the surface of the skin.

DIAGNOSIS AND TREATMENT

Strongyloidiasis is often difficult to diagnose because the worms lay their eggs in the bowel wall and the eggs are rarely found in the stool. In addition, *Strongyloides* larvae are easily confused with hookworm larvae (as in our case). Both are readily detected with low power (100×) magnification. Because stool examination is insensitive and potentially confusing, serology can be useful in the evaluation of problem patients. Unfortunately, serology is limited by the fact that a positive antibody titer does not distinguish between past and present infection.

Patients with strongyloidiasis typically have a marked eosinophilia (10–20% of white blood cells, over 10,000–20,000 eosinophils per μl of blood). However, if eosinophilia is not reported in a severely ill patient, it does not exclude the disease. Factors that may limit the magnitude of the eosinophilia in persons with the hyperinfection syndrome include both the basic T-cell defect(s) predisposing to the syndrome and the outpouring of neutrophils resulting from secondary bacterial infection, which may obscure the eosinophilia (note the difference between determining the **percentage** of eosinophils among all white blood cells and their **absolute number** per microliter). Patients thought to have strongyloidiasis should be studied first by stool examination. Even if three or more stool examinations reveal no larvae, examination of the duodenal contents or duodenal biopsy may be positive.

Thiabendazole has been the drug of choice for strongyloidiasis although it may produces vomiting and has other side effects. Thiabenzadole is thought to act by binding to β-tubulin of the parasite. Recent studies suggest that ivermectin may also be effective.

OTHER INTESTINAL HELMINTHS THAT PENETRATE SKIN—HOOKWORMS

Hookworm disease is caused by two species of roundworms— *Necator americanus* and *Ancylostoma duodenale*. Human hookworms carry out the same general life cycle as *Strongyloides*, but differ from it in several ways:

- After being shed in the stool, hookworm eggs require a period of maturation in a warm environment to produce infective filariform larvae (unlike *Strongyloides*). Consequently, **hookworm infection is restricted to warm climates.** Transmission of hookworm infection requires contamination of the soil with untreated human feces and subsequent exposure of unprotected human skin to the infected feces. Hookworm infection may be prevented by sanitation (using indoor or outdoor toilets or treating feces used for fertilizer), or by wearing shoes. Hookworm infection was common in the Southern U.S. until the early part of this century.

● Hookworms cannot complete their life cycle in the human host (unlike *Strongyloides*). Thus, hookworm infection cannot produce a hyperinfection syndrome.

● Unlike *Strongyloides*, hookworms do not invade the bowel wall and, thus, do not produce severe bacterial superinfections.

● Hookworms produce chronic anemia by hanging on to the intestinal mucosa with their teeth, secreting an anticoagulant, and sucking the patient's blood. This results in a slow steady blood loss (0.03 ml per worm per day for *Necator americanus*; 0.15 ml for *Ancylostoma duodenale*). Hookworms affect some 800–900 million people throughout the globe; it has been estimated that the total loss of human blood to these little vampires is at least 1 million liters daily. The severity of the anemia is proportional to the worm burden. Severe infections in children may produce chronic anemia that may lead to developmental retardation.

● As they penetrate the skin at the time of initial infection, hookworm larvae may also cause local manifestations; namely, itching and irritation ("ground itch"). People may also become infected with the cat and dog hookworms; this condition is known as **creeping eruption** (or cutaneous larva migrans). Unlike *Strongyloides* or human hookworm, the filariform larvae of dog or cat hookworms cannot make their way from the skin into the circulation. As a result, the filariform larvae crawl randomly in the skin and die after several days to a week.

DIAGNOSIS AND TREATMENT

The adult female hookworm releases 10,000–20,000 eggs per day into the bowel lumen, which makes it easy to diagnose significant hookworm infections by stool examination using low power (100×) magnification. In fact, it is possible to estimate the number of worms present and the average daily blood loss by quantitating the number of eggs in the stool.

Mebendazole, pyrantel pamoate, and several other drugs can be effectively used to treat hookworm infection. Mebendazole, like thiabendazole, binds to the β-tubulin of the parasite. Emergency treatment is not required because hookworms produce chronic, but not acute or invasive disease. Patients with hookworm disease may require dietary supplementation with iron and folic acid to produce sufficient numbers of red blood cells to correct their anemia.

INTESTINAL HELMINTHS ACQUIRED BY INGESTION

Another large group of intestinal helminths are acquired by ingestion rather than by penetration throughout the skin. Helminths in this group belong to widely separate taxonomic groups, roundworms (the human and animal *Ascaris*, pinworms, and whipworms) and tapeworms. These parasites infect large numbers of people and cause infections that range from asymptomatic to very severe.

Ascariasis

Ascaris is one of the largest of the human parasites, up to 30 cm in length, and one of the most frequently encountered worldwide. It affects perhaps one-quarter of the human population, including a substantial number of people in the Southern U.S. A few *Ascaris* are generally well tolerated, but a large worm load may cause serious illness.

CASE

A 4-year-old boy who lived in the Southern U.S. had been well until 3 weeks previously, although he had always been small for his age (height and weight at the 10th percentile). His parents reported that he passed "earthworms" with his stool. For the last 2–3 weeks, he had had vague abdominal pain with nausea. He had been unable to eat, his abdomen was distended, and he had no bowel movements for 5 days. X-rays of his abdomen were consistent with intestinal obstruction. Stool examination revealed large numbers of Ascaris eggs. He was given mebendazole and placed on intravenous fluids. One day after beginning treatment, he passed large numbers of Ascaris. Three days later, his abdomen was no longer distended, he was able to eat and drink, and had a normal bowel movement.

ENCOUNTER AND PATHOBIOLOGY

After excretion in the stool, *Ascaris* eggs require several weeks in a warm environment to mature to the infective stage (Fig. 52.2). For this reason, ascariasis, like hookworm disease, is restricted to warm climates and to areas where the soil is contaminated by untreated human feces. Unlike hookworms and *Strongyloides*, *Ascaris* larvae cannot penetrate the skin and are acquired exclusively via the fecal-oral route. The eggs must be ingested to complete the cycle. Generally speaking,

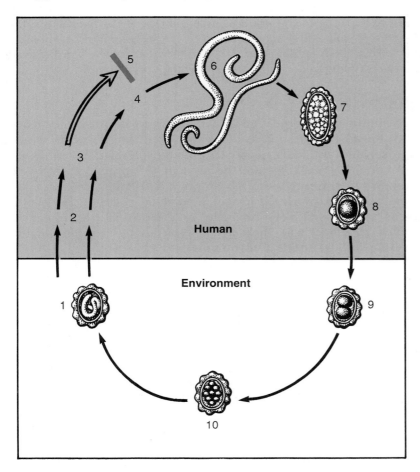

Figure 52.2. *Ascaris* life cycle. *Ascaris lumbricoides* (human roundworm) and dog or cat roundworm (visceral larva migrans). Humans acquire these infections by ingesting embryonated roundworm eggs from the environment (*1*). After ingestion, the parasites hatch in the upper intestine (*2*), cross the bowel wall (*3*), and enter the bloodstream. The human *Ascaris* (*innermost* set of *arrows* in the *top half* of the diagram) enters the lung by crossing into the alveolus (*4*), travels up the trachea, is swallowed and re-enters the GI tract to develop to a mature adult (*6*). The *open arrow* and *solid line* on the diagram indicate that neither dog or cat *Ascaris* are able to enter the lung from the bloodstream. As a result, these parasites wander aimlessly through deep tissues and are unable to return to the GI tract (*5*). Thus, stool examinations are negative in patients with visceral larva migrans and positive in patients with human *Ascaris* infection (*7*).

In the environment, fertilized *Ascaris* eggs (*8*) germinate and divide (*9, 10*) and produce embryonated eggs that are infectious on oral ingestion. This process takes several weeks and requires a warm moist climate. In visceral larva migrans, the infectious eggs are shed by infected dogs or cats, rather than by humans.

the other phases of the *Ascaris* life cycle inside the human host resemble those of hookworms. Once ingested, the larvae hatch in the small intestine, penetrate the mucosa and submucosa, and enter venules or lymphatics. They travel to the lung, and migrate up the trachea to the pharynx, where they are swallowed and regain access to the gastrointestinal tract. The worms mature in the intestinal lumen and the females release their eggs into the stool.

Large numbers of larvae (from a large number of ingested eggs) may produce pneumonia as they cross from the bloodstream into the lungs. This reaction may be particularly severe if the patient has been sensitized by previous *Ascaris* infection. Later, if adult worms are present in large numbers in the intestine, they may form a large mass (worm ball) and produce intestinal obstruction, as in the case presented. On occasion, individual worms may produce biliary obstruction (by migrating up the bile duct and occluding it) or peritonitis (by perforating the intestinal wall). Moderate intestinal worm burdens, on the other hand, may be totally asymptomatic.

Humans may also be infected by ingesting dog or cat *Ascaris*, also by fecal-oral transmission. The resulting infection is known as **visceral larva migrans**. These worms (like the animal hookworms that cause creeping eruption) are unable to complete their cycle in humans, who are dead-end hosts. The abortive nature of human infection by parasites of other primary hosts (dog or cat *Ascaris*—visceral larva migrans; dog or cat hookworms—creeping eruption) is a vivid reminder of the specificity of host-parasite interactions. After leaving the intestine, dog or cat *Ascaris* wander randomly through the tissues rather than crossing the lung to the trachea. Enlargement of the liver and spleen (hepatosplenomegaly) may result from the inflammatory response to the worms. Eosinophilia is usually marked because the worms invade the deep tissues.

DIAGNOSIS AND TREATMENT

Ascariasis is diagnosed readily by stool examination using low-power (100×) magnification, inasmuch as each adult female worm releases approximately 200,000 eggs per day into the intestinal lumen. As with hookworm, one can estimate the number of worms present by the numbers of eggs in the stool.

Mebendazole, pyrantel pamoate, piperazine, and a number of other agents treat *Ascaris* infection of the gastrointestinal tract effectively. Medical treatment with these agents typically relieves intestinal obstruction without surgical intervention.

Pinworm

Pinworm infection is common in both temperate and tropical regions, affecting at least 200 million people. It is most prevalent among small children, who typically infect their siblings and parents, and among institutionalized persons. Pinworms seldom produce serious disease, but may cause considerable discomfort. A typical case would be that of a healthy 3-year-old girl who is brought to the pediatrician because she has developed what the mother thinks to be "unacceptable behavior," i.e., she frequently scratches herself in the anal and vaginal areas.

Pinworms do not require an extrinsic incubation period, thus the infection is transmitted readily in any area with fecal-oral contamination (Fig. 52.3). The eggs resist drying and may be transmitted to other

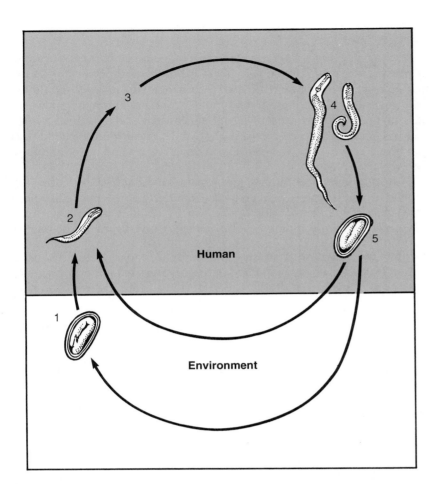

Figure 52.3. Pinworm life cycle—*Entero-bius vermicularis.* Humans acquire pinworm infection by the ingestion of embryonated eggs (*1*). After ingestion, these eggs hatch in the small intestine (*2*), mature to adults in the large intestine (*3, 4*) and produce eggs (*5*). Because the gravid female lays her eggs in the perianal area, the eggs may be shed into the environment (*lower half* of diagram) or inadvertently ingested by the patient or their close contacts when fingers which scratched the perianal area are licked or used to prepare food.

members of the household from bed clothes or dust. After oral ingestion, the eggs hatch in the duodenum and jejunum. After maturation and fertilization, the larvae mature in the ileum and large intestine. Gravid females migrate out of the rectum to the perianal skin to lay eggs. Perianal itching (the most typical presentation) results from the deposition of eggs by the gravid female in that area and may be caused by dermal sensitivity to parasite antigens. Scratching facilitates the spread of the infection because infective eggs may be picked up and spread to the same person or to others. Other moist areas, such as the vagina, may also be affected. On occasion, the parasite may be found in the lumen of the appendix, although this is rarely thought to produce appendicitis.

DIAGNOSIS AND TREATMENT

Pinworm infection is easy to diagnose using a microscope slide covered with cellophane tape (adhesive side out) or its commercially prepared paddle version. The buttocks are gently separated and the slide (or paddle) is placed between them before the patient arises in the morning. Pinworm eggs are large enough to be identified under the microscope using low-power (100×) magnification.

A number of anthelminthics, including mebendazole, pyrantel pamoate, and other drugs, treat pinworm infection effectively. The major concern is to assure that the entire family is treated (including relatives who live with or visit the infected child, babysitters, and other children at the daycare center), because one untreated person may reinfect others.

Intestinal Tapeworms

As the name suggests, tapeworms are long and ribbon-like, made up of rectangular segments in a chain. An individual tapeworm is an animal colony; each segment (known as a **proglottid**) is a self-contained unit capable of reproduction, metabolism, and food uptake (tapeworms have no gut). Tapeworms attach to the intestinal wall by a head (**scolex**) that has sucking disks or grooves (Fig. 52.3). In their intermediate animal host, these worms penetrate into deep tissues and develop into infective larval forms.

The most common human tapeworms are acquired by eating uncooked or inadequately cooked beef (*Taenia saginata*), pork (*Taenia solium*), fish (*Diphyllobothrium latum*), or by contact with rodent feces (*Hymenolepis nana*). Some tapeworms cause two types of disease:

- **Intestinal infection (teniasis)**, caused by the pork, beef, fish, or rodent tapeworms—the clinical picture of intestinal infection is generally mild, and is essentially the same for all four tapeworms.

- **Deep tissue infection**, produced by the pork tapeworm (**cysticercosis**) or the carnivore tapeworm (**echinococcosis**, or **hydatid disease**).

These two types of diseases are very different and must be distinguished. Unfortunately, confusion is possible because one tapeworm (pork tapeworm) may produce both teniasis and deep tissue infection in the same patient.

CASE

The wife of a high-ranking government official accompanied her husband on a trip to the Near East. During a diplomatic reception, they were served steak tartare (raw beef), a traditional dish in that region. Three months later, she noticed thin white rectangular segments in her stool (approximately 1 × 2 × 0.2 cm.). She experienced nausea, apparently brought about by seeing the worms in her stool. Laboratory studies revealed that the segments were proglottids of Taenia saginata. *Her stool also contained eggs of this worm.*

She was reassured by her physician, who told her that this infection is unlikely to have clinical consequences in a healthy person. On the other hand, he could understand her revulsion at seeing the worm segments in her stool and visualizing the rest of the worm inside her. The physician prescribed niclosamide, which led to the elimination of the rest of the tapeworm.

ENCOUNTER

The life cycle of beef tapeworm requires both humans and cattle (Fig. 52.4). Cattle become infected by ingesting human feces containing the parasite's eggs; humans become infected by eating beef that contains larvae (cysticerci). The eggs hatch in the intestine of cattle and enter their bloodstream to lodge in peripheral tissues, where they develop into cysticerci (Chapter 53). Beef tapeworm infection can only exist in areas where infected humans defecate near cattle. These areas, however, are found in most of countries of the world.

All human intestinal tapeworm infections correlate with gastronomic preferences; they are found mainly among people who consume their meat undercooked or raw (as in the case described). This is not the only factor involved, because transmission clearly depends on a

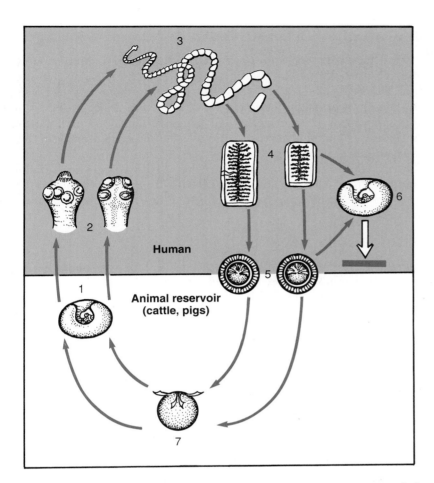

Figure 52.4. Intestinal tapeworm life cycle—*Taenia solium* (pork tapeworm) and *Taenia saginata* (beef tapeworm). Humans acquire these infections by ingesting the tissue stage of the parasite (cysticercus) in inadequately cooked meat (*1*). The parasite then hatches in the intestine (*2*) and matures to an intestinal tapeworm 10 meters or more in length (*3*). The pork tapeworm (*outside* of diagram) has a crown of spines on its head and also has fewer pairs of lateral uterine branches in its proglottids (segments) than the beef tapeworm (*4*). The eggs of these two parasites (*5*) are identical morphologically. As shown in the diagram, only the pork tapeworm (*Taenia solium*) produces human cysticercosis (*6*). When human feces containing viable eggs are ingested by either pigs or cattle, the eggs hatch (*7*) and produce the tissue (cysticercal) stage of the infection in those animals (*1*) to complete the cycle.

lack of sanitation. These diseases are common in many parts of the world, but are infrequent in Western Europe and the U.S., with the exception of fish tapeworms, which may have a resurgence thanks to the increased consumption of sushi (raw fish á la Japonais). Cooking effectively destroys the larvae, but cooks have been known to become infected by tasting raw food during preparation; fish tapeworm infection is said to be an occupational hazard of Jewish or Scandinavian grandmothers making "gefilte fish" or "lutefisk."

PATHOBIOLOGY

The infectious tissue larvae from the intermediate host (beef, pork, fish) hatch in the human small intestine and mature into adult tapeworms. The worms may live in the human intestine for several decades and attain lengths of up to 10 meters, which has given rise to the popular but mistaken notion that they increase a person's appetite by consuming a significant amount of their food intake.

Most patients are asymptomatic, but some have nausea, diarrhea, and weight loss. The infection is usually noted only because of the presence of proglottids in the stool. In the case of fish tapeworm infection, almost half the cases have low levels of vitamin B_{12}, leading to serious so-called megaloblastic anemia. This deficiency appears to be due to competition between the host and the parasite for this vitamin in the diet. Note that the intestinal disease caused by tapeworm is very different from that in the tissues (Chapter 53).

DIAGNOSIS AND TREATMENT

Most tapeworm infections are readily diagnosed by stool examination. The proglottids are macroscopic and can be seen by the naked eye. The eggs are large enough (31–43 μm in diameter) to be seen using low-power magnification (100 ×). Although the eggs of pork and beef tapeworms are identical, their proglottids may be distinguished by the experienced observer (those of *T. solium* have uteri with fewer pairs of lateral branches).

Most patients (more than 90%) are cured with a single dose of niclosamide. Those who are not cured often had nausea or vomiting with their first treatment, and typically respond to a second treatment with the drug.

SUGGESTED READING

Ettling J. The germ of laziness: Rockefeller philanthropy and public health in the new South. Cambridge: Harvard University Press, 1981.

Freedman DO, Zierdt WS, Lujan A, Nutman TB. The efficacy of ivermectin in the chemotherapy of gastrointestinal helminthiasis in humans. J Infect Dis 1989;159:1151–1153.

Genta RM, Weesner R, Douce RW, Huitger-O'Connor T, Walzer PD. Strongyloidiasis in U.S. veterans of the Vietnam and other wars. JAMA 1987; 258:49–52.

Maxwell C, Hussain R, Nutman TB, Poindexter RW, Little MD, Schad GA, Ottesen EA. The clinical and immunological responses of normal human volunteers to low dose hookworm (*Necator americanus*) infection. Am J Trop Med Hyg 1987;37:126–134.

Neva FA. Biology and immunology of human strongyloidiasis. J Infect Dis 1986;153:397–406.

Phillis JA, Harrold AJ, Whiteman GV, et al. Pulmonary infiltrates, asthma and eosinophilia due to *Ascaris suum* infestation in man. N Engl J Med 1972;286:965–970. (An account of a fraternity stunt in which unsuspecting students were given pig ascaris.)

Tissue and Blood Helminths

53

Donald J. Krogstad

Helminths cause a variety of diseases by establishing residence in deep tissues. As with the intestinal helminths, some are acquired by ingestion and others by penetration through the skin—either by direct entry of the parasites or by insect bites. The diseases they produce almost invariably involve chronic inflammation, and thus, are due, in part, to the host immune response to the parasite. As with the intestinal helminths, when the worm burden is low, infections are almost always asymptomatic. Because many worms are long lived in humans, a large number may gradually accumulate as the consequence of repeated encounters. When present in large numbers in sensitive target organs, helminths may produce severe disease and even death. Helminths that cause deep tissue infections include members of all three groups—roundworms, tapeworms, and flukes (Table 53.1).

TISSUE HELMINTHS ACQUIRED BY INGESTION

The main helminths in this group are the roundworm *Trichinella* and the tapeworms that invade deep tissues.

Trichinosis

Trichinosis is caused by the presence of *Trichinella spiralis* larvae in the heart, skeletal muscle, brain, or gastrointestinal (GI) tract. Most infected people are asymptomatic and are not seriously ill. Paradoxically, trichinosis is more common in the U.S. than in a number of developing countries. This is because many other countries are more careful to ensure that pigs are not fed uncooked garbage contaminated with viable *Trichinella* larvae. Fortunately, there are only a few hundred clinically significant cases in the U.S. each year.

CASE

A 45-year-old immigrant from Laos who was living in California had been well until 3 days after celebrating with relatives at a feast that featured a highly seasoned but undercooked pork dish. Two days after the celebration, he developed diarrhea and abdominal pain. Two days later, he developed severe muscle pain, swelling around the eyes, and headache. Physical examination revealed "splinter" hemorrhages in his fingernails. Laboratory studies demonstrated a marked eosinophilia (12,000/μl). Biopsies of his tender muscles and of the splinter hemorrhages revealed Trichinella *larvae.*

635

Table 53.1. Main Tissue and Blood Helminths

Examples	Reservoir	Mode of Transmission	Clinical Manifestations
Acquired by ingestion			
Tapeworms			
Hydatid disease: *Echino-coccus granulosus*	Sheep, cattle, horses	Fecal-oral (eggs)	Tissue-displacing and invasive lesions, most common in liver but seen in lung, CNS, and elsewhere
Cysticercosis: *Taenia solium* (cysticerci)	Pigs	Food-borne	Tissue-displacing lesions most critical in CNS
Roundworms	Dogs	Fecal-oral (eggs)	Systemic illness with malaise,
Visceral larva migrans: *Toxocara canis* *T. catis*	Cats		eosinophilia, often enlarged liver and spleen
Trichinosis: *Trichinella spiralis*	Pigs (also bears) (larvae)	Food-borne	Mild infection produces malaise, mild diarrhea, and periorbital edema; severe infection may be life threatening with CNS and heart involvement
Guinea worm: *Dracunculus medinensis*	Infected humans (larvae)	Water-borne-oral	Malaise, fever, other systemic symptoms when the adult worm emerges 1 year after initial infection
Flukes			
Lung fluke: *Paragonimus westermani*	Animals, humans? (metacercariae in crabs)	Food-borne	Cysts rupture in lung, leading to secondary bacterial infection, chronic bronchitis, and a tuberculosis-like picture
Liver fluke: *Chlonorchis sinensis*	Fish, animals, humans	Food-borne (metacercariae in fresh-water fish)	Often asymptomatic; if worm load is high, can lead to biliary stones, chronic inflammation, liver cancer
Acquired by passage through the skin			
Blood flukes Schistosomes: *S. mansoni,* *S. haematobium,* *S. japonicum*	Infected humans	Water-cutaneous (cercariae)	Symptoms vary with the intensity of infection, from asymptomatic to hematuria and bladder cancer (*S. haematobium*), and blood in stool and portal hypertension (*S. mansoni* and *S. japonicum*)
Roundworms			
Cutaneous larva migrans (dog, cat hookworms)	Dogs, cats	Fecal-cutaneous (filariform larvae)	Superficial skin lesions progressing at a rate of ≤ 2 cm/day
Filaria			
Lymphatic filariasis *Wuchereria bancrofti,* *Brugia malayi*	Infected humans (larvae)	Mosquito bite	Vary from asymptomatic to massive enlargement of the legs, scrotum, and breasts with recurrent filarial fevers
River blindness: *Onchocerca volvulus*	Infected humans (larvae)	Blackfly bite	Multiple subcutaneous nodules; blindness from reaction to microfilariae crossing the eye

ENCOUNTER AND PATHOBIOLOGY

The life cycle of *Trichinella* is illustrated in Figure 53.1. After the ingestion of meat containing viable encysted *Trichinella* (usually in undercooked pork), the infective larvae hatch and mature in the small intestine of pigs or humans. The adult worms release larvae that cross the mucosa to enter the intestinal lymphatics and the bloodstream (producing diarrhea and pain in the process). These larvae are then carried to all parts of the body via the bloodstream. The larvae encyst in striated and cardiac muscle fibers, and produce a marked initial inflammatory response. The cysts usually calcify, although the worms may remain viable for up to 30 years. The cycle is completed when meat containing viable larvae is eaten.

In recent years, the incidence of trichinosis has diminished, as judged by the prevalence of *Trichinella* cysts at autopsy. The figure has decreased from 16% to less than 1% over the last 30–40 years, partly because of legislation prohibiting the use of uncooked garbage for feeding pigs, and partly because of increased public awareness about the danger of eating undercooked pork. *Trichinella* is also found in other animals, such as wild pigs and bears, including polar bears, and has caused several outbreaks among hunters and in Eskimo communities.

The manifestations of this disease correlate with the load of worms in tissues, and range from asymptomatic to fatal. Several studies suggest that larger inocula (ingestion of many viable larvae) result in more severe disease with a shorter incubation period (2–3 days vs. 10 days or

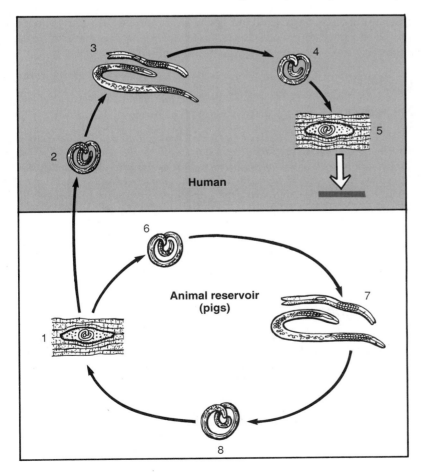

Figure 53.1. *Trichinella* **life cycle—** *Trichinella spiralis.* Humans acquire trichinosis by the ingestion of undercooked pork containing viable encysted *Trichinella* larvae (*1*). After ingestion, these larvae hatch in the intestine (*2*), mature to adults (*3*), and release larvae that invade the intestinal wall and enter the bloodstream (*4*), encysting in striated or cardiac muscle (*5*). As indicated by the *open arrow* and *solid line below 5* on the diagram, human infection is normally a dead end in terms of the natural transmission of trichinosis. Similar phenomena are observed in the pig reservoir, and in bears, which may also harbor *Trichinella* larvae (*6–8* on the *lower half* of the diagram).

more). Patients with 1000–5000 larvae per gram of tissue may die from involvement of the heart or central nervous system. Studies in experimental animals suggest that cell-mediated immunity is important in the control of *Trichinella* infection. For instance, the marked eosinophilia seen with repeated infection requires intact cell-mediated immunity (previously sensitized T cells).

DIAGNOSIS AND TREATMENT

Rises in antibody titer are diagnostic. However, they typically occur 3–4 weeks or more after the initial infection and are thus useless for the management of severely ill patients (in whom the incubation period may be as short as 2–3 days). In severely ill patients (as in the case presented), muscle biopsy often reveals *Trichinella* larvae under low-power (100×) magnification and permits a definitive diagnosis long before serological testing.

Both steroids and thiabendazole have been used in severely ill patients (with myocarditis and/or encephalitis). However, no drugs have been shown to be effective in controlled clinical trials. Although thiabendazole and mebendazole have been used for their antihelminthic activity, they also have anti-inflammatory activity and may produce symptomatic improvement by that mechanism.

Tissue Forms of Tapeworm Infection

The larvae (cysticerci) of a few species of tapeworms infect deep tissues of humans and cause diseases that may have severe manifestations. Their life cycle is illustrated in Figure 53.2. Illness caused by the tissue form of the pork tapeworm is known as cysticercosis; that due to tapeworms of carnivores is known as echinococcosis.

CASES

Cysticercosis

A 33-year-old nurse had been a Peace Corps volunteer in Thailand 10 years earlier. After her return, she found proglottids of the pork tapeworm Taenia solium *in her stool. Two years previously (8 years after her return), she noticed multiple subcutaneous nodules across her chest and on her arms. She now had headaches and two generalized seizures and was brought to the Emergency Room. A CT scan of her brain revealed 42 lesions consistent with cysticerci. Her headaches worsened during treatment with praziquantel. However, with steroids to reduce brain swelling and antiepileptic drugs to control her seizures, she was able to complete the praziquantel treatment. She was withdrawn from the antiepileptics 1 year later and has had no additional seizures.*

Echinococcosis

A 39-year-old Navajo woman was examined for abdominal pain. Two years previously, she had first noticed a sensation of fullness in the right upper quadrant of her abdomen. Since that time, this sensation has increased and there is now an obvious swelling (8 × 10 cm) in the area of the liver. Stool examination revealed no tapeworm eggs. A CT scan of the liver demonstrated a large (12-cm diameter) encapsulated lesion consistent with tapeworm cysts. Serological testing revealed antibodies against Echinococcus. *Because of the size of the liver lesion, the mass was removed surgically, using liquid nitrogen to freeze the mass and prevent spillage of its contents into the peritoneum.*

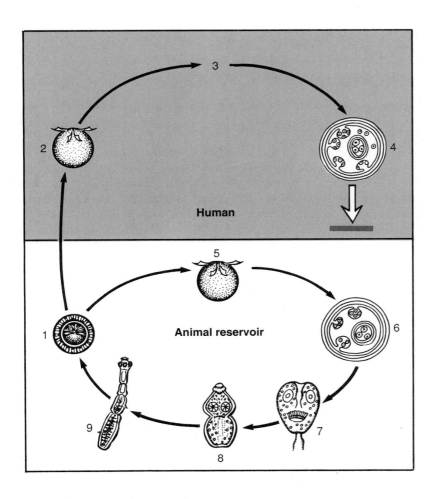

Figure 53.2. Echinococcal life cycle. This tapeworm has a tissue stage, but not a tapeworm stage in humans. Humans acquire the infection by ingesting eggs in the feces of infected carnivores (*1*), such as dogs or wolves. After ingestion, the eggs hatch in the intestine (*2*) and the larvae cross from the GI tract to the tissues (*3*), where they develop into cysts containing daughter cysts (*4*). As indicated by the *open arrow* and *solid line below 4*, this is a dead-end infection in humans.

In the extrahuman carnivore reservoirs, echinococcal tapeworm infection is acquired by ingesting the contaminated remains of herbivores infected with the tissue cyst stage of the parasite. Herbivores acquire the tissue cyst stage by ingesting eggs in the stool of infected carnivores (*1*). These eggs are identical morphologically to those produced by *Taenia solium* and *T. saginata*. After ingestion by an herbivore, the eggs hatch, cross the GI tract, and produce tissue cysts like those seen in humans (especially in the liver, *6*). When ingested by carnivores, they also produce scolices (*7*), which mature (*8*) to tapeworms (*9*) that release infective eggs in the stool(*1*) to complete the cycle.

ENCOUNTER

Echinococcus infections are acquired by ingesting infective eggs, rather than tissue cysticerci. The usual source of *Echinococcus granulosus* is the stool of dogs or other carnivores (wolves, coyotes). Thus, transmission is by the fecal-oral route, not by eating contaminated meat. The infectious forms of the parasite hatch in the small intestine but do not reside there. Rather, they penetrate the intestinal wall and form cysticerci in many organs.

Echinococcosis or hydatid disease is found in most areas of the world, including the U.S. The cycle is maintained between sheep and sheep dogs in the southwestern U.S. Native Americans who keep sheep in that region are often victims of the disease. There is also a "sylvatic" cycle in the northern U.S. and Alaska, with wolves as the carnivores, and elk and other large game as the herbivores. *E. multilocularis* is an analogous parasite for which foxes and cats are the carnivore hosts and mice and voles are the herbivores.

Human cysticercosis is believed to be acquired by ingesting *T. solium* eggs (from feces containing infective eggs). However, some workers believe that cysticercosis may also result endogenously from teniasis (intestinal infection by the tapeworm form of the parasite). The life cycle of *T. solium* requires that pigs become infected by ingesting the eggs of this parasite and that humans eat inadequately cooked pork (this is analogous to the beef tapeworm life cycle). These conditions exist in many areas of the developing world. In Mexico, as many as 10–

15% of persons hospitalized for neurological problems have evidence of CNS cysticercosis at autopsy.

PATHOBIOLOGY

The sequence of events in echinococcosis and in cysticercosis is generally similar. The parasites lodge under the skin or within internal organs, such as the brain or liver, and develop a cyst wall surrounded by a fibrous capsule of host origin. In echinococcosis, the cysts enlarge over time to form daughter cysts (each of which has an embryonic tapeworm). Echinococcal cysts in the liver usually produce few symptoms until they reach 8–10 cm or more in diameter. They then may leak or rupture, and pose a significant risk of death from anaphylaxis.

On the other hand, in cysticercosis, the cyst remains constant in size at 1–2 cm, until it dies, when its effect on the surrounding host tissue may increase due to the host's inflammatory response. Peripheral cysticerci outside the CNS are usually asymptomatic. However, within the CNS, even small cysticerci may cause cerebral dysfunction, including seizures and blindness. This is a good example of the correlation between the location and the severity of a disease. Cysticerci may cause symptoms when the parasites die and displacement of normal tissue is magnified by the host's inflammatory response. This typically occurs 5–10 years after infection, but may occur as much as 50 years later.

DIAGNOSIS AND TREATMENT

Because cysticerci may be present in patients without evidence of intestinal infection, *T. solium* cysticercosis is usually diagnosed by its deep tissue manifestations (including lesions visible by CT scan or by "soft" x-ray technique in the long axes of skeletal muscles). A positive serological test for antibodies to *T. solium* is helpful, especially among persons who live in Europe, the U.S., or other areas of low incidence. This test is typically negative in persons with intestinal *T. solium* infection only.

Praziquantel is effective in the treatment of cysticercosis and is thought to act as a calcium agonist. It kills the organism and decreases the size of the lesions because the fluid-filled cyst collapses and most of the parasite is ultimately resorbed by the host. However, CNS symptoms may transiently worsen during treatment because of the inflammatory response to dying cysticerci. As indicated in the case presentation, the concomitant use of steroids typically alleviates the headaches and seizures that may be caused by this treatment. Treatment is an inefficient means of disease control because of the delay between intestinal infection (when patients are asymptomatic, although their stool is infectious for pigs) and clinical presentation (when their stool is no longer infectious for pigs). If treatment is to be effective in reducing transmission of the parasites, it must be given early, when the patients are infectious. Before praziquantel, there was no medical treatment for cysticercosis. At best, individual cystericerci at critical locations, such as the aqueduct of Sylvius in the brain, could be excised surgically.

No drugs have been shown to be safe and effective for echinococcosis. Although mebendazole has been used, most reports are anecdotal and the drug has been associated with several sudden (otherwise unexplained) deaths. Surgical removal can cure the infection although there is risk of spillage and dissemination of the infection. A number of special techniques have been tried in an effort to prevent spillage or to kill organisms that are released during surgery (instillation of formalin or silver nitrate, cryosurgery with liquid nitrogen).

TISSUE HELMINTHS THAT PENETRATE THROUGH THE SKIN

This group includes worms that can cross the skin directly, the **schistosomes** (blood flukes), and those that penetrate via insect bites, the **filariae** (roundworms).

Schistosomiasis

Schistosomiasis is an important and frequent disease in tropical regions. It is estimated that about 200–300 million people are affected worldwide. Schistosomiasis produces a variety of clinical syndromes, depending on the anatomic location of the adult worms and the eggs that they release. There are three main pathogenic species with different geographic distributions, found largely in warm climates—*Schistosoma haematobium*, *S. mansoni*, and *S. japonicum*. Their distribution depends on the presence of the snail intermediate host. The schistosomal life cycle is illustrated in Figure 53.3.

CASES

Case 1—Intestinal Schistosomiasis

A 48-year-old woman from Egypt had noticed for many years that her stool was dark. During the last year, she also has had two episodes of vomiting blood. Examination of her esophagus and stomach with a fiberoptic gastroscope revealed dilated veins in the esophagus which were oozing large amounts of blood. Because viable eggs of S. mansoni *were still being excreted in her stool, she was treated with praziquantel.*

Case 2—Schistosomiasis of the Bladder

A 38-year-old European man had worked in West Africa for 10 years on a rice-growing irrigation scheme. During the past year, he noticed blood in his urine. Examination of his urine showed the presence of S. hematobium *eggs. At cystoscopy, his bladder had a cobblestone pattern, consistent with the granulomatous changes seen in schistosomiasis. Typical eggs were seen in the bladder biopsies taken during cystoscopy. He was treated with a single dose of praziquantel (40 mg/kg).*

ENCOUNTER AND PATHOBIOLOGY

The life cycle of schistosomes requires development in certain species of fresh water snails, which are their intermediate hosts. The infective stage of the parasite emerges from the snails and swims in water until it finds a suitable host. Because these snails are not present in the U.S., schistosomiasis cannot be transmitted in the U.S., despite the migration of infected persons from Africa and the Middle East. Suitable snails are present in parts of the Caribbean.

The infective forms released from the snails are called **cercariae**. They are capable of burrowing through the skin of people standing, swimming, or walking through infected water, as in rice paddies (Case 2). In the body, the cercariae lose their tails and change into forms called **schistosomulae**, which can enter the bloodstream. The parasites then pass through the pulmonary circulation to the portal venous system, where they mature. After several weeks, pairs of male and female

Figure 53.3. Schistosomal life cycle. Humans acquire schistosomiasis by the exposure of unprotected skin to water containing infectious cercariae (*1*). The cercariae penetrate unbroken skin (*2*), lose their tails, and become schistosomulae (*3*). They then travel throughout the bloodstream, cross the lungs (*4*), and mature (*5*) in the venous system of the liver to adult worms (*6*). After a period of 6–8 weeks, pairs of adult worms travel to the venous plexuses of the bladder (*S. haematobium*), the large intestine (*S. mansoni*), or the small intestine (*S. japonicum*), where they remain for decades releasing their characteristic eggs (*left to right* for *S. hematobium, S. mansoni,* and *S. japonicum* at *7*).

Eggs released into fresh water hatch to miracidia (*8*), which invade the snail intermediate host where they mature to sporocysts (*9*). They then release cercariae (*1*) to complete the cycle.

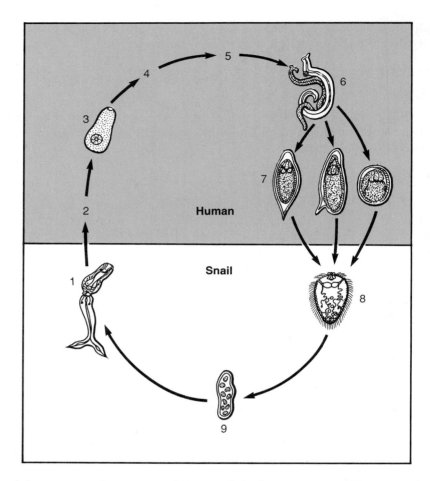

adults move to the venous plexuses of the large intestine (*S. mansoni*), small intestine (*S. japonicum*), or bladder (*S. hematobium*). The mating worms remain locked together, copulating in the venous system for 10 years or more. The eggs they release may be excreted via the stool (*S. mansoni, S. japonicum*) or the urine (*S. hematobium*). The life cycle is completed when the eggs are released into fresh water, where they hatch and penetrate the appropriate snail intermediate host.

S. mansoni and *S. japonicum* adult worms reside in the venous plexuses of the intestine. There they release eggs that travel to the intestine and the liver. The host immune response to the eggs produces the pathological changes of schistosomiasis, such as periportal fibrosis in the liver, which may lead to portal hypertension and, thus, to dilated collateral veins in the esophagus (esophageal varices, as in Case 1). *S. hematobium* adults live in the venous plexus of the urinary bladder and produce blood in the urine (hematuria), granulomatous inflammatory changes in the bladder, and bladder carcinoma. Changes in the bladder and ureters (ureterovesical obstruction) produced by the host immune response to these schistosomes may cause secondary bacterial infections of the bladder, leading occasionally to Gram-negative septicemia.

The pathological changes in schistosomiasis are due primarily to the host's inflammatory immune response to the eggs. As in other helminthic infections that invade the tissues, eosinophilia and elevated IgE levels are common among infected persons. Recent data suggest that IgE antibodies against the adult worm may protect against reinfection. Because adult worms are not recognized as foreign, they may live in the bloodstream for decades. Two important anomalous host-parasite interactions are central to the pathogenesis of schistosomiasis:

- One is the profound fibrotic reaction to schistosome eggs that is probably mediated by cytokines, and produces the important pathology of the disease and its long-term complications. The reasons for this excessive immune response are not clear, but include reactivity of the regulatory (T_4) subsets of T lymphocytes to schistosome egg antigen.

- Another is the lack of an effective immune response to male and female adult worms, which reside in the vascular system for decades without being eliminated by the host. Studies have shown that adult worms have adsorbed host proteins (including serum albumin and HLA antigens) on their surface. These findings suggest that the parasite disguises itself with these host proteins to evade the host's immune response.

Cercariae often produce itching as they penetrate the skin. The cercariae of nonhuman schistosomes (of birds and fish) also cause itching as they penetrate the skin (swimmers' itch, clam diggers' itch), but do not enter the bloodstream or mature within the human body.

DIAGNOSIS AND TREATMENT

Most schistosome infections are diagnosed readily by microscopic examination of stool (S. mansoni, S. japonicum) or urine (S. hematobium) or by biopsy of a rectal valve (S. mansoni). Schistosome eggs (150 × 60 µm) are large enough to be identified easily under the microscope with low-power (100×) magnification. Unfortunately, it can be difficult to find schistosome eggs in the stool or urine of patients who are chronically infected and at risk of developing long-term complications. In such patients, serological testing for antischistosome antibodies may be of value. However, a positive serological test does not distinguish between recent vs. old or light vs. severe infections. Serological testing is most useful in people who have had single, defined exposures in endemic areas. It is of little use for lifelong residents of endemic areas, inasmuch as most are seropositive but may or may not experience complications.

Praziquantel is the treatment of choice for schistosomiasis. Oxamniquine is an alternative for S. mansoni and may also be given as a single oral dose. Both of these drugs have permitted oral mass treatment programs, which were impossible with the prolonged intravenous protocols necessary with the antimonial drugs used previously. Antischistosome antimonials were often toxic. They produced hepatitis, myalgias, fever, and frequently failed to eradicate the adult worms.

FILARIASIS

The main filarial infections in humans are **lymphatic filariasis (elephantiasis)** and **onchocerciasis (river blindness)**. The adult filarial worms live in the lymphatics in lymphatic filariasis and in subcutaneous tissue in onchocerciasis. Their offspring, known as **microfilariae**, travel through the subcutaneous tissue or circulate in the blood. Lymphatic filariasis affects some 200 million people in tropical regions, especially in Asia. This disease leads to tissue swelling, some of elephantine proportions (hence, the name elephantiasis). Some 50 million persons in Africa, Asia, and tropical Latin America have onchocerciasis; about 10% of them will become blind from the disease and some 30% will have visual impairments. There are West African villages where most people become blind from this disease by the time they reach adulthood. None of these diseases are endemic in the U.S. The life cycle of filariae is illustrated in Figure 53.4.

CASES

Elephantiasis

A 48-year-old native of a Philippine island lived in a village where many men and women had elephantiasis. He first noticed swelling of his right leg when he was 20 years old. Since that time, he has had intermittent fevers to 38.5–39.0°C associated with red streaks from his groin to the foot on both legs. Both feet and his scrotum are now chronically swollen. Typical microfilariae consistent with Wuchereria bancrofti were seen in a Giemsa-stained blood smear taken at 2 AM. His recurrent episodes of lymphangitis were treated with an antimicrobial effective against streptococci. The antifilarial drug diethylcarbamazine was given, but discontinued when it produced shock and hypotension.

Onchocerciasis

A 32-year-old man from Nigeria was seen for an evaluation in a hospital of a nearby town. His village was situated near a rapidly running stream where the men fish and hunt. Like many of his neighbors, he began to lose vision in his late 20s. Three nodules (2 × 3 × 2 cm) are present on his trunk. Skin snips reveal microfilariae of Onchocerca volvulus. He was treated with a single oral dose of ivermectin.

ENCOUNTER AND PATHOBIOLOGY

Infective filarial larvae are injected into the skin by biting insects. The distribution of the diseases is limited primarily by that of their vectors and of infected persons. Onchocerciasis, which is transmitted by Simulium black flies is not found in the U.S., where it would not be possible to transmit the disease (because these black flies are not present), even if infected persons were found in large numbers. In contrast, lymphatic filariasis is transmitted by species of mosquitoes that are present in the U.S. This disease is not endemic in the U.S. because there is no reservoir of infected persons.

The typical manifestations of lymphatic filariasis are low-grade fever and inflammation of lymphatics and lymph nodes. With repeated episodes, the lymphatics become occluded and fluids leak into tissues, and produce severe swelling. As the disease progresses, patients with adult worms frequently experience repeated episodes of acute inflammation. The lower limbs and the scrotum may become swollen to gigantic size. The diurnal cycle observed in lymphatic filariasis facilitates transmission because the microfilariae are more prevalent in the bloodstream at night, when mosquitoes bite more frequently. Onchocerciasis is manifested by subcutaneous nodules, primarily on the head and neck in Central America, on the trunk and pelvis in Africa. Nodule formation is not as serious as the inflammatory response that may cause blindness and dermatitis.

The inflammatory response is directed against the microfilariae in onchocerciasis and against the adult worms in lymphatic filariasis. Adult filarial worms are tolerated for years in the lymphatics and the subcutaneous tissues (like adult schistosomes). The mechanisms re-

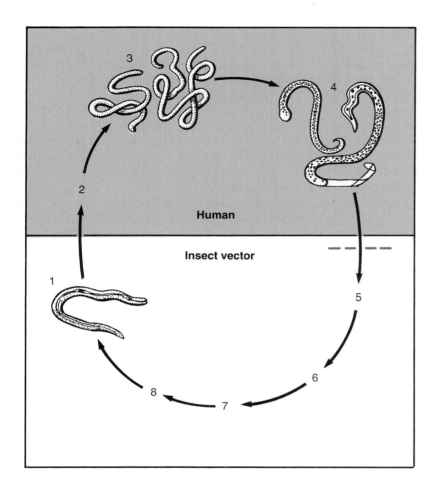

Figure 53.4. Filarial life cycle—onchocerciasis, lymphatic filariasis. Humans acquire infection with the filariae that cause onchocerciasis or elephantiasis by the bite of blackflies or mosquitoes respectively. After third-stage larvae (*1*) are injected under the skin by the vector, the larvae mature (*2*) to adult worms (*3*) that release microfilariae in the subcutaneous tissue (onchocerciasis) or in lymphatics (lymphatic filariasis) (*4*).

Microfilariae ingested by the insect vector during feeding mature through a series of stages (*5–8*) to infectious third-stage larvae (*1*) within approximately 2 weeks. The *line above 5* on the diagram indicates that natural transmission of onchocercasis does not occur in countries such as the U.S. because the blackflies necessary to complete the life cycle are not present. Although the mosquitoes that transmit lymphatic filariasis are present in the U.S., transmission does not occur because there is no reservoir of infected humans.

sponsible for this immunological unresponsiveness are not well understood, but include increased activity of specific subsets (T_8) of suppressor T cells.

DIAGNOSIS AND TREATMENT

Infections that release microfilariae into the bloodstream (lymphatic filariasis) may be diagnosed by examining smears of peripheral blood. The microfilariae may be scarce and difficult to find. The sensitivity of the method can be increased by lysing red blood cells with a detergent and using a filter to trap the remaining white cells and microfilariae, and by sampling the blood at night for microfilariae with nocturnal periodicity (*W. bancrofti*). Filarial infections that release microfilariae into the skin are diagnosed by examining a skin snip. In all of these specimens, microfilariae are identified with Giemsa stain under the high dry or oil immersion objectives. Recent studies suggest that antigen detection using antifilarial antibodies may be a more sensitive and convenient method.

The treatment available for lymphatic filariasis is unsatisfactory. The drugs diethylcarbamazine and ivermectin reduce the number of circulating microfilariae but do not eliminate the adult worms. Diethylcarbamazine, in particular, may produce severe systemic reactions (as in Case 1). These reactions may be caused by the sudden release of large amounts of antigen, allowing the formation of damaging antigen-antibody complexes (type **III** hypersensitivity reaction, Chapter 5). Diethylcarbamazine treatment may exacerbate the pathology of onchocerciasis, and should not be used for onchocerciasis. Several drugs (e.g., suramin) have been used to kill the adult worms but are rarely employed because of their toxicity. In onchocerciasis, recent studies indicate that a single oral dose of ivermectin reduces microfilarial counts in the skin for up to 6 months with relatively few side effects. These studies suggest that ivermectin is likely to become the drug of choice for the treatment of onchocerciasis. Surgical resection of subcutaneous nodules in onchocerciasis removes the source of microfilariae and may, thus, decrease the risk blindness. However, it is impossible to be sure that all nodules have been removed because they are often in deep tissue and are not palpable.

Prevention of these diseases relies mainly on vector control. Unfortunately, the flies that transmit onchocerciasis breed in clean, fast-running streams and rivers. Although they can be controlled readily with insecticides, effective spraying may be difficult in these areas.

SUGGESTED READING

Trichinella
Campbell WC. *Trichinella* and trichinosis. New York: Plenum Press, 1983.

Tapeworms
Palacios E, Rodriguez CJ, Taveras JM. Cysticercosis of the central nervous system. Springfield, IL: Charles C Thomas, 1983.

Smith JD, Thompson RCA. The Biology of *Echinococcus* and hydatid disease. London, Boston: Allen and Unwin, 1986.

Sotelo J, Escobedo F, Rodriguez-Carbajal J, Torres B, Rubio-Donnadieu F. Therapy of parenchymal brain cysticercosis with praziquantel. Am J Trop Med Hyg 1984;38:380–385.

Schistosomes
Brindley PJ, Sher A. The chemotherapeutic effect of praziquantel against *Schistosoma mansoni* is dependent on host antibody response. J Immunol 1987;139:215–220.

Brindley PJ, Strand M, Norden AP, Sher A. Role of host antibody in the chemotherapeutic action against *Schistosoma mansoni*: identification of target antigens. Molec Biochem Parasitol 1989;34:99–108.

Capron A, Dessaaint JP, Caprom M, Ouma JH, Butterworth AE. Immunity to schistosomes: progress towards a vaccine. Science 1987;238:1065–1072.

Hagan P, Blumenthal UJ, Dunn D, Simpson AJG, Wilkins HA. Human IgE, IgG4, and resistance to reinfection with *Schistosoma hematobium*. Nature 1991;349:243–245.

MacInnis AJ, ed. Upjohn-UCLA symposium on molecular paradigms for eradicating helminthic parasites. New York: Liss, 1987.

Filariasis
Cupp EW, Bernardo MJ, Kiszewski AE, Collins RC, Taylor HR, Aziz MA, Greene BM. The effects of ivermectin on transmission of *Onchocerca volvulus*. Science 1986;259:740–742.

Evered D, Clark S, ed. Symposium on filariasis. Ciba Foundation Symp. 127. New York:Wiley, 1987.

Kumarasawami V, Ottesen EA, Vijayasekaran V, Devi U, Swaminathan M, Aziz MA, Savina GR, Prabhakar R, Tripathy SP. Ivermectin for the treatment of *Wuchereria bancrofti* filariasis: efficacy and adverse reactions. JAMA 1988;259:3150–3153.

Lai RB, Ottesen EA. Enhanced diagnostic specificity in human filariasis by IgG4 antibody assessment. J Infect Dis 1988;158:1034–1037.

Lobos E, Weiss N, Karam M, Taylor HR, Ottesen EA, Nutman TB. An immunogenic *Onchocerca volvulus* antigen: a specific and early marker of infection. Science 1991;251:1603–1605.

Ectoparasites (Scabies and Lice)

54

Edward N. Robinson, Jr. and Zell A. McGee

Scabies is caused by mites; "crabs" are caused by lice. These and other ectoparasites live in the skin and do not enter the deep tissues (Table 54.1). Most of us are also bitten, at least on occasion, by mosquitoes, flies, fleas, ticks, and chiggers, who do this chiefly for the purpose of sucking our blood. When these arthropods reside on our skin for long periods of time, it is called an infestation. Scabies and pediculosis (crabs) are treatable common infestations. Because the mode of transmission of scabies is not only sexual, other close (nonsexual) contacts should also be treated.

CASE

Mr. S., a 25-year-old man, had been plagued for several weeks by an intensely pruritic (itchy) rash consisting of reddened bumps (papules) located in his groin and on his elbows and hands. He had not slept well for 2 days because of constant itching and scratching. The severity of the itching was evidenced by the excoriations (scratch marks) on his skin and by the blood on his bedclothes from scratching each night. He lived with his wife and two children who had no such symptoms, and a dog with the mange.

LIFE CYCLE

What is scabies? It is a disease caused by *Sarcoptes scabiei*, a 400-μm long mite with no distinct head, two pairs of front legs or suckers, and two pairs of hind bristles. Scabies mites look rather like catcher's mitts with legs. In the realm of parasites, sarcoptes are true travelers; they can move up to an inch per minute and can travel from the neck to the wrist in a few hours. Once on the surface of an unsuspecting human, they speed to those areas of the body where they like to live—the hands (especially finger webs and the sides of fingers), parts of the wrists, elbows, axillae, breasts, and around the umbilicus, groin, and buttock. Scabies are rarely found on the skin above the neck.

Scabies mites do not survive long on inanimate objects (fomites). They are readily killed at elevated temperatures (10 minutes at 50°C) and are paralyzed by cool temperatures (16°C). The natural reservoir of *S. scabiei* is the human skin.

Scabies mites burrow into the superficial layers of skin at 0.5–5.0 mm/day (Fig. 54.1). Their life span is 30 days. Each mite spends its existence burrowing, ingesting, munching on skin, and, occasionally, coming to the surface to search for a mate. After mating, the female lays two to three eggs per day within the burrow (Fig. 54.2).

Table 54.1. Some Ectoparasites of Humans		
Type of Ectoparasite	Genus Name	Infestation
Mites	*Sarcoptes*	Scabies
Lice	*Pediculus*	Body or head lice
	Phthirus	Pubic lice (crabs)
Maggots	*Dermatobia*	Botfly myiasis (maggot infestation)

OTHER ECTOPARASITES

Other *Sarcoptes* mites are among the etiological agents of dog mange (itching and hair loss) and may be transmitted from dogs to humans. However, dog scabies do not find humans very palatable and this infestation is limited both in location (arms and legs of the dog owner) and time.

Scabies may be differentiated on clinical and morphological grounds from the other common cause of genital infestation, *Phthirus pubis*, also known as pubic lice or "crabs" (Table 54.1). Pubic lice are surface dwellers and do not burrow into the skin. They possess three pairs of legs containing hook-like claws with which they hang onto hair shafts. The adults feed by anchoring their mouths to the skin, stabbing an opening, pouring saliva into the wound to prevent clotting, and sucking blood. The female pubic louse glues her eggs ("nits") to the base of hair shafts. Most eggs are found within 5 mm of the base of the hair because the eggs hatch within 5–10 days and the hair shaft grows at a millimeter or less per day. The eggs are cemented on the hair and will not slide along the hair shaft like dandruff. Frequently when small "scabs" are removed from an infested groin and examined under the light microscope, they will get up and walk away, i.e., they are adult lice.

ENCOUNTER

For many years, it was thought that scabies was only found in the unwashed and poor and was predominantly transmitted through "social adventures" such as sexual promiscuity. However, the misconception that scabetic infestation is only a disease of misfits and the unfortunate was eliminated in a delightfully written paper by John H. Stokes (JAMA 1936;106:674). He wrote:

"Scabies is a disease of herding, promiscuity and travel, of family, school and vacation life. A plague of armies, tenements and slums. It may with equal force invade a pedigreed school, Camp Wawa Wawa or the baronial castle on the hill. An ever present differential consideration, wholly without social boundaries, the possible explanation of the itches of the tycoon, the socialite and the university professor equally with the mechanic's daughter on relief."

Indeed, Napoleon Bonaparte may have struck his famous pose while scratching at periumbilical scabies. Roughly 5–30% of any population may be found to be harboring scabies mites depending on the culture, extent of crowding, and state of hygiene. During the first part of this century, scabies pandemics occurred in 30-year cycles and were attributed partially to the waning of herd immunity. However, these cycles coincided with two World Wars that impacted drastically on crowding, and on cleanliness. The absence of a pandemic during the last two decades has been attributed to the lack of World War, rather than any appreciable change in herd immunity toward scabies.

Figure 54.1.   Scabetic burrow in the stratum corneum of the skin, partially opened by sectioning parallel to the skin surface. At the *extreme right* is a mite egg. In the *middle* is a larval mite with the front half hidden under the ledge.

Scabies have become labeled as sexually transmitted even though the majority of scabetic infestations are not transmitted from groin to groin. Infestations are transmitted more readily by close physical contact (e.g., by holding hands or sleeping in the same bed with an infested partner) than by brief sexual encounters. The majority of scabetic infestations are introduced into households by friends or relatives. School children who hold hands are excellent vectors for spreading scabies from one household to another.

PATHOBIOLOGY

Two host defenses limit the number of scabetic mites on any individual—the immune response and hygiene. As the mites burrow through the uppermost layers of skin, they leave trails of feces and eggs in their wake (Fig. 54.1). This detritus consists of foreign proteins and antigens to which the host eventually responds with hypersensitivity. It may take weeks or months before an immune response is mounted. However, once hypersensitivity is established, intense inflammation ensues in the areas of infestation. Indeed, the serpiginous (snake-like) tracts or burrows of the mite are frequently outlined by inflammation. This inflammation causes the itching of scabies. The scabies mites themselves are not felt. The inflammation reduces, but does not eliminate scabies mites from the host. Once an inflammatory response occurs, the scabies mites tend to move elsewhere on the body, as if the inflamed area were no longer habitable or palatable.

The second aspect of host defense is mechanical debridement and hygiene. The act of scratching removes skin containing eggs and tunneling mites. Mites wandering on the surface of the skin are washed away during bathing.

The importance of host responses in controlling scabies is illustrated by a rare entity known as "Norwegian scabies." This occurs in individuals who do not itch or cannot scratch. These people are usually not able to mount a hypersensitivity response because of nutritional deficiencies, cancer, AIDS, or steroids, or may have diseases that block the ability to perceive the pain of inflammation (leprosy, spinal cord injuries, or tabes dorsalis/neurosyphilis). In these individuals, the scabies mites reproduce unopposed. Such debilitated persons may harbor 3 million mites in their thickly crusted skin. Because people with Norwegian scabies are typically unaware of their infestation, it is generally discovered only when people who have come in contact with them develop symptomatic scabies.

Currently, Norwegian scabies is simply called "crusted scabies." Knowing that it occurs in immunocompromised patients, it was not surprising when the report of this condition in conjunction with AIDS appeared. The reason why scabies presents differently in immunocompromised patients is not entirely clear. In the absence of an immune reaction, there may be less itching and less dislodging of the mites by scratching; or the immune system may be less effective in eliminating mites, assuming that is one of its functions. Regardless of the reason, scabies can be added to the growing list of diseases that present in a different manner clinically in patients with an immunocompromising condition such as AIDS.

Both typical and crusted scabies, by breaching an important protective barrier, the skin, predispose to skin infections and even to subsequent life-threatening bloodstream infection with potentially pathogenic skin bacteria such as staphylococci and Group A streptococci.

Figure 54.2. Scanning electron micrograph of a scabies mite and two eggs within a burrow in a patient's skin. The two bright structures beneath the mite are eggs collapsed by drying in preparation of the specimen.

Thus, it is important to consider and to test for scabies in the presence of telltale symptoms and signs.

DIAGNOSIS

Several historical clues should raise the suspicion of scabies. Few other dermatological conditions produce nocturnal itching that result in bloody sheets and pajamas. Few other dermatological conditions spread to sexual partners or to other members of a household or an institution.

Once suspicion is aroused, the finding of scabetic burrows or the actual mites in the skin is diagnostic. Burrows can frequently be hard to see with the unaided eye. Shining a light tangentially to the skin and using a hand-held magnifying glass may help visualize burrows that are otherwise hard to see. Alternatively, liquid tetracycline may be placed on the surface of involved skin and allowed to seep into the burrow. When ultraviolet light is shined on the lesion, tetracycline fluoresces and outlines the burrow. Similar results can be obtained using blue or black ink. A word of caution: when wiping the affected area with alcohol to remove the excess tetracycline or ink, it is best to warn the patient that alcohol on an excoriated scabetic papule may be quite uncomfortable.

TREATMENT

Several effective creams and lotions kill scabies mites as well as pubic lice. Each of the creams must be applied to the entire body from the neck down with special attention to the areas preferred by the parasite. Clothes and bed linens should be washed in the hot cycle of a washing machine (there is no need to boil them). Furniture can generally be considered safe. All members of the household, whether symptomatic or not, should receive similar treatment to eradicate the infestation from the household.

The most important point to stress with any individual being treated with scabicides is that the itching and rash result from the immune response to the detritus of the scabies mites—alive or dead. Resistance of the mites to scabicides has not been documented. Thus, even though all mites are killed with one or two applications of the scabicide, the patient still has intense itching due to the presence of dead but antigenic mites. These symptoms may persist for weeks until residual scabetic antigens are shed with the skin. The natural tendency of most patients is to assume that they are still infested because they are still itching. This leads to the repetitive application of creams and lotions. The scabicides prescribed most frequently will cause dry skin when used repeatedly. Dry skin itches, and a vicious cycle is established.

There are a few readily identifiable causes for failure of scabicides to remove the infestations:

- Inappropriate application of the lotion (were there areas of skin that were missed?);

- Reinfestation (were all members of the household and sexual partners treated?);

- Reemergence of scabies from ova that were not killed during a single application of lotion.

Given this wealth of information regarding *Sarcoptes scabiei*, how do we counsel Mr. S.? The fact that he had scabies may or may not be related to any extramarital misadventures on his part. Scabies is transmitted socially and, only occasionally, sexually. The most likely persons to introduce scabies into any household are generally children who acquire it at school.

Mr. S may be the only one who has symptoms, but the chances are that several members of his household are infested. Therefore, each member of the household should receive therapy to interrupt incubating (asymptomatic) scabies and to prevent reinfestations. It is unlikely that the dog was the source of Mr. S.'s problems. If its mange is due to canine scabies, the dog can be treated with a chlordane dip.

SUGGESTED READING

Friedman R. The story of scabies. New York: Froben Press, 1947.

Inserra DW, Bickley LK. Crusted scabies in acquired immunodeficiency syndrome. Int J Dermatol 1990;29:287–289.

Orkin M, ed. Scabies and pediculosis. Philadelphia: JB Lippincott, 1977.

Review of the Main Pathogenic Animal Parasites

These charts are intended to help you review the main animal parasites only. Included are the parasites of greatest medical relevance.

Many of the animal parasites that cause relatively uncommon diseases are not included. These charts may be completed to review the material covered under this topic.

PROTOZOA

	Reservoir	Mode of Transmission	Location in Body	Disease and Main Attributes	Chapter(s)
Blood					50, 62
Malaria (Plasmodium vivax, malariae, falciparum)					50
Babesia					50
Deep tissue					50, 62
Toxoplasma					50, 68
Pneumocystis					50, 66
Leishmania					50
Trypanosomes (Sleeping sickness and Chagas' disease)					50
Intestinal					51
Entamoeba histolytica					51
Giardia lamblia					51
Cryptosporidium					51

HELMINTHS (WORMS)

(Try to *recognize* Latin names. You need not memorize them)

	Reservoir	Mode of Transmission	Location in Body	Disease and Main Attributes	Chapter(s)
Intestinal					51
Tapeworms (*Taenia*, several)					52
Hookworms (*Ancylostoma, Necator*)					52
Ascaris (*A. lumbricoides*) (+visceral larva migrans)					52
Pinworms (*Enterobius vermicularis*)					52
Whipworms (*Trichuris trichiura*)					52
Blood and deep tissue					50, 62
Cysticercus (*Taenia solium*) and Echinococcus					53
Trichina (*Trichinella spiralis*)					53
Schistosomes (*S. haematobium*), *S. mansoni*, *S. japonicum*)					53
Filaria (*Wuchereria, Brugia, Onchocerca*)					53

Section III
Pathophysiology of Infectious Diseases

Diagnostic Principles

55

N. Cary Engleberg

The role of the clinical microbiology laboratory is to determine whether potential pathogens are present in tissues, body fluids, or secretions of patients, and if present, to identify them. This service is indispensable to the modern clinician, because information about the pathogen's identity is of critical importance in predicting the course of the infection and in guiding the selection of appropriate therapy. This information can be generated in any of four possible ways:

- Cultivation and identification of microorganisms from patient samples;
- Microscopic examination of patient samples;
- Measurement of a pathogen-specific immune response in the patient;
- Detection of pathogen-specific macromolecules in patient samples.

The extent and reliability of the information that the laboratory can provide varies depending on the nature of the pathogen. Some pathogens (e.g., *Staphylococcus aureus*) are easily detected, cultivated, identified, and characterized; others (e.g., *Toxoplasma gondii*) require extraordinary measures merely to detect their presence. However, the capabilities of the modern clinical microbiology laboratory are expanding and improving rapidly, thanks to the technological revolution in molecular biology. New diagnostic procedures are being introduced into clinical practice at an ever-increasing pace. Critical-minded clinicians need to understand the principles underlying both the new and the old methods to make an informed assessment of their value and reliability and to use them wisely.

CASES

Patient 1

A 28-year-old male was admitted to the hospital with fever and weight loss. Because of his history of intravenous heroin use, the patient had been tested for human immunodeficiency virus (HIV) infection 4 years earlier; he was found to have positive enzyme-linked immunosorbent assay (ELISA) and Western blot tests. Six months earlier, he had had an episode of acute fever, cough, and shortness of breath; bronchial washings obtained through a bronchoscope revealed Pneumocystis carinii *cysts upon microscopic examination. The patient was treated successfully for that infection and did well subsequently on antiretroviral therapy. However, 2 months before the current hospital admission, he began losing weight, and 3 weeks before admission, he began having drenching night sweats, chills, and periodic temperature elevations to 103°F.*

Laboratory evaluation revealed a significant anemia and mildly elevated liver enzymes. The chest x-ray was negative. Three blood cultures were obtained to rule out endocarditis and were eventually reported to be negative. Over the next 10 days, the patient continued to have symptoms and lost another 2 lb. A bone marrow aspirate was obtained and showed a few acid-fast bacilli. The patient was started on isoniazid, rifampin, pyrazinamide, and ethambutol for possible tuberculosis (TB). In spite of this treatment, his symptoms continued. Four weeks into therapy, the mycobacterial culture of the marrow aspirate was reported to have grown Mycobacterium avium-intracellulare (or MAI). All of the anti-TB drugs were stopped and the patient was begun on four different drugs for MAI (amikacin, rifampin, ethambutol, and ciprofloxacin). Some improvement was subsequently noted.

Patient 2

A 58-year-old woman was told after she donated blood that she had tested positive for the "AIDS virus" using a screening blood test, the ELISA. The test was repeated, and again was positive a second time. The patient could not understand how she could have become infected with the virus; she had been sexually inactive since the death of her husband 12 years earlier, and she had never used intravenous drugs or had a blood transfusion. A Western blot using the same blood sample was sent to a reference laboratory, but was reported as "indeterminate." The patient was quite unnerved by these results and insisted on more definitive testing to determine whether or not she had been exposed to the virus. To satisfy this request, her blood was tested for the p24 antigen of HIV and for HIV nucleic acids using the polymerase chain reaction. Both tests were negative.

These cases illustrate the use of various diagnostic techniques in the evaluation of two very different clinical situations. In this chapter, the methodological basis of the tests used in these cases will be discussed. In addition, the reader may wish to consider the following specific questions:

1. Could the diagnosis of of MAI have been made earlier in Patient 1 so as to avoid 4 weeks of unnecessary therapy for tuberculosis?

2. Can Patient 2 feel confident that she has not been infected with HIV? And if so, why was her ELISA positive?

ASSESSING THE PERFORMANCE OF LABORATORY TESTS

When a microbiological test correctly predicts the presence of a pathogen, the result is referred to as a **true-positive**. Similarly, a negative test obtained in the absence of the pathogen is a **true-negative**. Inaccuracies occur either because the laboratory test is negative in the presence of the pathogen (**false-negative**) or positive in the absence of the pathogen (**false-positives**).

The terms defined in Figure 55.1 are commonly used to describe the performance and value of all diagnostic tests. These terms are defined mathematically in the figure, but they can also be remembered in more operational terms. For example, in measuring the ability of a particular test to identify a pathogenic microorganism in a patient specimen, the **sensitivity** of the test is the likelihood that it will be positive when the pathogen is present. The **specificity** of the test measures the likelihood that it will be negative if the pathogen is not present.

In clinical practice, diagnostic tests with 100% sensitivity and 100% specificity do not exist. However, the clinician can make use of poten-

TEST RESULTS

	Positive	Negative
Organism present	True-positives	False-negatives
Organism absent	False-positives	True-negatives

$$\text{Sensitivity} = \frac{\text{True-positives}}{\text{True-positives} + \text{false-negatives}} \times 100\%$$

$$\text{Specificity} = \frac{\text{True-negatives}}{\text{True-negatives} + \text{false-positives}} \times 100\%$$

Figure 55.1. Definitions of terms used in evaluating diagnostic tests.

tially inaccurate tests by knowing how they perform and by using a combination of tests that may yield a high level of diagnostic certainty. A test that is very sensitive, but not particularly specific, may be very useful in screening for the presence of an infection. As an example, the RPR or VDRL tests are commonly used to screen patients for syphilis, even though several other infectious and noninfectious conditions can cause these tests to be falsely positive. However, nearly all patients who have syphilis have positive RPR or VDRL tests after the primary (chancre) stage. Therefore, one can "rule out" the diagnosis of syphilis if the result is negative. If the RPR or VDRL is positive, then a second, confirmatory test must be employed to determine whether syphilis is actually present or not. In contrast to a screening test, a test used to "rule in" a suspected diagnosis must be highly specific; it need not be very sensitive. The case of Patient 2 illustrates a similar sequence of testing. In this case, the screening test for HIV (the ELISA) was falsely positive. The specific confirmatory test, the cumbersome and more costly Western blot assay, was "indeterminate," and less conventional methods (to be discussed later in this chapter) were used in an attempt to clarify the patient's uncertain serological status.

The case of Patient 2 also illustrates another important point. The predictive value of a diagnostic test is influenced by the frequency of the infection in the population being tested. If the specificity of the HIV-ELISA is 99.8%, it will register a false-positive result in one of every 500 negative individuals tested. If the prevalence of infection in a given population is less than 1 in 500, then there will be more false-positive tests than true-positive tests, and the positive predictive value will be poor. Although HIV infection is not rare in the general population, it is extremely rare among elderly women with no apparent risk factors, and a positive result in such a patient is most likely to be a false-positive response. In contrast, in populations with a high prevalence, e.g., among intravenous drug users like Patient 1, there will be a higher proportion of true-positive tests. Although the same test was used to assay serum from both Patients 1 and 2, a positive result in Patient 1 is more predictive of HIV infection than in Patient 2. The lesson is that **the interpretation of a laboratory result depends not only on the technical accuracy of the method use, but also on the prevalence of the disease or infection in the population to which the patient belongs.**

DIAGNOSIS OF INFECTIONS BY CULTURE

Culturing is usually the most specific method for establishing the presence of a particular pathogen in a patient sample, although in many situations, it may not be sensitive or clinically practical. Culture of helminthic and protozoal pathogens is virtually never performed for diagnostic purposes, but it is a routine for most bacterial and fungal infections. Because chlamydiae and viruses are obligate intracellular pathogens, they can be propagated and identified only in appropriate tissue cultures. Some microorganisms cannot be cultured in clinical microbiology laboratories (e.g., hepatitis viruses, *Treponema pallidum*, *M. leprae*, *P. carinii*), either because the necessary conditions for their cultivation in vitro are not yet known or because the available culture systems are inefficient and impractical. Cultivation of certain other pathogens, such as rickettsiae and certain systemic fungi, is shunned by most clinical laboratories because of the hazards involved in handling these microorganisms.

General Principles

As a rule, the choice of culture methods and media is tailored to the nature and source of the specimen and the question that the culture is meant to address. For example, when a specimen of pus from an abdominal abscess is cultured, the implied question is, what microorganism(s) is(are) present in the abscess? The assumption is that any organisms present are causative and that chemotherapy directed against them will be beneficial. To answer the question, the sample is cultured on a variety of agar-based media and in broth medium, under both aerobic and anaerobic conditions. In this situation, the culture strategy is to recover **any and all microorganisms** that might inhabit such an abscess.

In contrast to this open-ended approach, some cultures are performed primarily to determine whether a particular pathogen is present or not. An example is the throat culture for *Streptococcus pyogenes* in cases of exudative pharyngitis, because *S. pyogenes* is the only culturable bacterial agent for which treatment is indicated. For this purpose, throat swab specimens are inoculated only onto nutrient sheep's blood agar plates, which support the growth of streptococci and permit the identification of the characteristic β-hemolysis of *S. pyogenes*. Incidentally, β-hemolysis is a sensitive criterion for screening the bacterial isolates, although it is not specific for *S. pyogenes*, and culture confirmation requires additional testing.

Special culture media and handling are required in certain situations. *Haemophilus influenzae* and the pathogenic *Neisseria* grow only on "chocolate" agar (made from boiled blood, not chocolate), *Legionella pneumophila* grows only on a specially supplemented, charcoal-containing medium (see Chapter 22), and mycobacteria grow only on specially composed media after several weeks of incubation. *Campylobacter* sp. require specific incubation temperatures, atmosphere composition, and media for successful cultivation from stool. Isolation of *Bacteroides*, clostridia, or other obligate anaerobes requires that collection, transport, and culture of the specimen be performed without undue exposure to air.

Cultures from nonsterile body sites present yet another problem, namely, the inhibition or obscuring of the pathogen's growth by an abundant normal flora. In these situations, selective media may be needed. Thayer-Martin is an example of a selective medium; it is chocolate agar containing antibiotics that inhibit the growth of members of the normal flora in the genitourinary tract, but not the growth of *N. gonorrhoeae*. Selective and semiselective media are also used to cultivate enteric pathogens from stool specimens or respiratory pathogens from sputum. One disadvantage of selective media is that they may inhibit the growth of some strains of the pathogen of interest. Therefore, selective media should be used only for specimens that are likely to contain contaminating normal flora.

Like all other diagnostic methods, culture results require interpretation by an informed physician. In some situations (e.g., meningitis, urinary tract infection), a negative culture is quite reassuring that the etiology of the patient's problem is not a bacterial or fungal infection. In other situations (e.g., community-acquired pneumonia, inflammatory diarrhea), the sensitivity of culture diagnosis is relatively poor. For example, a negative culture for *S. pneumoniae* does not rule out this agent as the cause of a bacterial pneumonia, because the sensitivity of sputum culture for this fastidious pathogen is usually about 50%.

When cultures are positive, their true meaning must also be considered. One must always question whether the isolate is the actual cause of the patient's illness. In cultures from nonsterile body sites, the question is whether the isolate represents normal flora (colonization) or an etiological agent (infection). In cultures from normally sterile body sites, the question is whether the isolate represents a contaminant or an etiological agent. Contamination may occur when patient samples are obtained with imperfect sterile technique. Typically, specimens obtained by needle puncture become contaminated with normal skin flora (e.g., *Staphylococcus epidermidis*, diphtheroids, streptococci). Because these bacteria may occasionally cause true infections, the physician must consider the clinical circumstances of the individual patient to judge whether the isolate is a contaminant or not. In many cases, it is necessary to reisolate the same organism from repeated cultures to be convinced of its significance. As another example, almost all voided urine collections have some degree of contamination; true infection is associated with a certain concentration of bacteria in the specimen. But a urine sample that is left sitting for hours will soon be grossly contaminated as the microorganisms start growing in the specimen.

Blood Culture

The simplest, time-worn method for blood culture involves the direct inoculation of a blood sample into nutrient broth, followed by incubation at 37°C and periodic checks for turbidity as an indicator of microbial growth. Microorganisms from broth cultures are eventually transferred to agar plates, or **subcultured**, to permit species identification. In recent years, newer methods have gained popularity for their increased sensitivity and rapidity. In one method, the **lysis-centrifugation technique**, blood is collected directly into a tube containing a solution that lyses blood cells. The unlysed, dense material, which includes any microorganisms, is pelleted by centrifugation to the bottom of the tube where it can be removed and inoculated directly onto an appropriate agar-based medium. In addition to its increased sensitivity for some pathogens, this technique has the advantage of bypassing the usual subculture step, inasmuch as the isolates grow primarily as colonies on agar plates. Other modern systems are entirely automated; growth in the inoculated blood culture bottles is monitored by assaying a by-product of microbial growth (e.g., CO_2). In **radiometric culture systems**, the medium includes a soluble nutrient, such as a fatty acid, that has been labeled with a radioisotope, such as carbon-14. At intervals after incubation, the cultures are sampled automatically by needle puncture through a rubber diaphragm at the top of the each bottle. Culture samples are then analyzed to determine whether a significant proportion of the radioisotope has been converted to an insoluble form, by incorporation into growing microorganisms. By this sensitive technique, growth of organisms is detected long before visible turbidity develops.

Culture Identification

Once a significant microorganism has been isolated in culture, it must be identified. Classically, this is done by determining phenotypic properties, such as motility, utilization of various nutrient substrates in culture, or production of various enzymes, hemolysins, or detectable by-products of metabolism. Because regrowth is required for many of these tests, definitive identification typically requires another day of culture.

Microorganisms in culture are sometimes identified more rapidly using antibody-based techniques that will discussed in more detail in the next section. Viruses are frequently identified in culture by their binding of specific antiviral antibodies, or by the ability of a specific antiserum to neutralize them when inoculated into fresh tissue culture. Another more recent development in culture identification involves the use of nucleic acid probes. These methods will be discussed fully in the final section of this chapter.

Antimicrobial Sensitivity Testing

Perhaps the most important advantage of culture diagnosis over other methods is that the isolate is available to be tested for susceptibility to antimicrobial agents, often the most important piece of therapeutically related information to be obtained. The reader is referred to Chapter 29 for a discussion of antibiotic sensitivity testing of bacteria. Fungal and viral pathogens can also be tested for drug susceptibility, but these tests are beyond the capabilities of most clinical microbiology laboratories.

DIAGNOSIS OF INFECTIONS BY MICROSCOPY

Some pathogens can be accurately identified by direct microscopic examination, because they possess characteristic morphological features, movement, or staining properties. In certain infections, microscopic diagnosis is highly sensitive and specific. It is also a rapid technique that permits the physician to initiate treatment without having to wait for the results of a culture.

Nearly all helminthic and most protozoal infections are routinely diagnosed by microscopy. Many fungal pathogens also have characteristic morphological features. Notably, *Cryptococcus neoformans* meningitis is diagnosed most rapidly by finding encapsulated yeast in the spinal fluid. By staining the fluid background with India ink or nigrosin, the transparent capsule of the yeast is visualized (see Fig. 47.4). In contrast, most bacteria are morphologically too simple to permit microscopic identification; however, there are a few exceptions. The diagnosis of syphilis can easily be made by visualizing the spirochetes in fresh scrapings of primary or secondary lesions, by their characteristic form and bending motions. Although viruses cannot be seen using light microscopy, virus-induced changes in host cell morphology may be diagnostic. Examples include the multinucleated giant cells seen in scrapings from herpes simplex or varicella zoster virus lesions (the "Tzanck smear") and the specific intracellular inclusion bodies seen in tissues that are actively infected with cytomegalovirus.

Stains

Although a species identification is rarely possible, bacterial pathogens may be visualized and assigned to morphological and functional groups using special stains. The basic principles of the **Gram stain** and the **acid-fast stains** were described in Chapter 3. The Gram stain is both rapid and simple to perform and can be carried out on virtually any body fluid or tissue. It may yield clinically useful information of three kinds. First, the stain may simply confirm the presence of bacteria in a normally sterile body fluid (e.g., cerebrospinal fluid [CSF], pleural fluid, urine). Second, the staining properties and morphology of the organisms in a sample or culture direct further efforts at species identification and the empiric selection of antibiotics for the patient. Third, in certain clinical specimens, the observation of some morphological types is virtually diagnostic. For example, the presence of Gram-negative diplococci in the leukocytes of urethral pus is highly suggestive of *N. gonorrhoeae*. The same morphological type seen in samples of CSF is nearly always *N. meningitidis*.

The Gram stains are much less useful when samples are obtained from nonsterile body sites, owing to the presence of normal flora. Considerable experience and skill is required to interpret Gram stains of coughed sputum specimens, because they are typically contaminated with oropharyngeal bacteria that are indistinguishable from respiratory pathogens. In contrast, acid-fast bacteria (i.e., mycobacteria) are not normally found in the respiratory tract, and a coughed sputum harboring them suggests pulmonary tuberculosis. In general, acid-fast bacteria in smears of sputum or normally sterile tissues are assumed to be *M. tuberculosis* until proven otherwise. This was the basis for the presumptive treatment of Patient 1, although his acid-fast organism was cultured and eventually identified as an atypical mycobacterium.

A variety of other stains are used to visualize pathogens that are otherwise transparent. Among the most commonly used stains are the **Giemsa stain** for systemic protozoal infections (e.g., malaria), iodine stains for intestinal helminths, and silver stains for systemic fungal pathogens. In Case 1, a special stain was used to visualize *P. carinii* in a sample of bronchial fluid.

Antibody-based Identification

The accuracy of microscopic identification of bacterial and viral pathogens is enhanced when specific antibodies are used in conjunction with direct microscopy. A classic example is the identification of *S. pneumoniae* by the addition of anticapsular antiserum to a wet preparation of bacteria on a slide (i.e., the "Quellung reaction"). Visible swelling of the capsule in the presence of antiserum identifies the organism as the pneumococcus. More modern approaches to antibody-directed diagnosis involve the attachment (or conjugation) of a detectable substance to the antibody molecules so that the microscopist can actually see where the antibodies bind. As an example, for the **direct fluorescent antibody (DFA) test** for Legionnaires' disease,

Legionella antibodies are conjugated with the fluorescent compound, fluorescein isothiocyanate. The patient's specimen is fixed to a slide and then treated with the conjugated antibodies. After washing, the slide is examined using a fluorescence microscope, and bacteria that glow with a bright yellow color when illuminated with ultraviolet light can be assumed to be *Legionella* that have bound the fluorescein-conjugated *Legionella* antibodies. The same DFA technique can be used to identify any pathogen to which specific antibodies can be produced.

Clearly, the specificity of antibody-based identification of pathogens depends on the specificity of the antibodies used. Animal antiserum is polyclonal, a complex mixture of antibodies that bind to a variety of different domains on a variety of different antigenic molecules (Fig. 55.2). When polyclonal antiserum is used in a diagnostic test, therefore, there is a high likelihood that unwanted cross-reactions with other microorganisms will occur. The original *Legionella* DFA test employs rabbit antiserum, and false-positive tests due to the presence of cross-reacting, non-*Legionella* bacteria in patient samples occasionally occur. The specificity of this test is enhanced when monospecific or monoclonal antibodies are used, as suggested in Figure 55.2. The principles illustrated in this figure apply to all antibody-based methods of diagnosis, including the serological antigen detection tests described in the next few sections of this chapter.

Figure 55.2. The specificity of three types of immunoglobulin preparations. Antibodies raised to react with bacterium A may cross-react with bacterium B. Polyclonal antiserum is cross-reactive because these bacteria have protein antigens in common. In this case, monospecific antiserum raised against a single antigen of bacterium A is also cross-reactive, because one of the antibody-binding sites on this antigen is shared by an antigen of bacterium B. However, a monoclonal antibody defines a binding site (epitope) on this antigen that is unique to bacterium A and has no cross-reactivity.

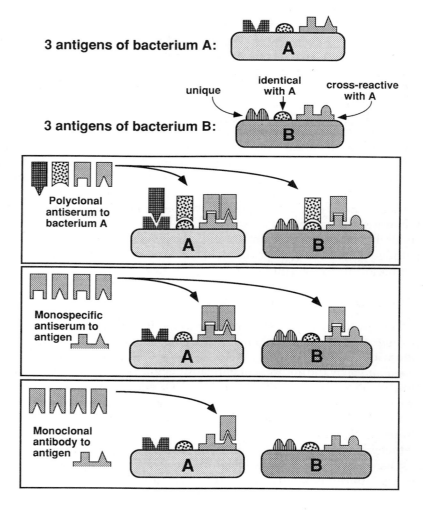

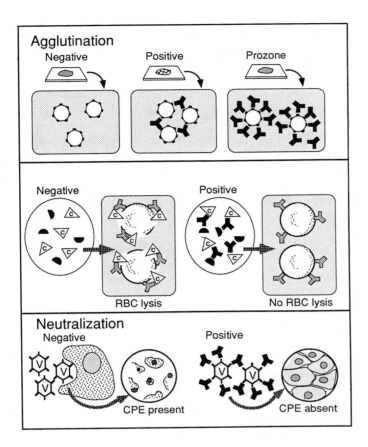

Figure 55.3. **Functional methods for detection of specific antibodies. Agglutination:** When specific antibodies (Y-shaped structures) are present in the patient's serum, they bind to the particle coated with microbial antigen (*black semicircles*). The bivalent antibody forms bridges between particles and causes visible clumping. When there is much more antibody than antigen in the mixture, a false-negative result, or prozone phenomenon, may occur. Paradoxically, a serum sample that is negative because of a prozone, becomes positive when it is diluted. **Complement fixation:** Patient serum is incubated with antigen and complement (the numerous individual complement components are contained in each *triangle*). Sheep RBCs coated with anti-RBC antibodies (*gray Y-shaped structures*) are then added. If specific antibodies are absent in the serum, complement is free to be "fixed" by the anti-RBC antibodies, and the RBCs are lysed by the complement attack complex. If specific antibodies are present in they serum, they will have bound to antigen during the first incubation step and affixed all available complement, so that none is available to lyse antibody coated RBCs in the second step of the test. **Neutralization:** In the absence of specific neutralizing antibody, virus added to tissue culture results in infection and cytopathic effect (CPE). When specific antibodies are present, they block viral structures critical for binding and uptake into host cells; no infection or CPE is observed.

MEASUREMENT OF THE ANTIBODY RESPONSE TO INFECTION

Serological tests measure the patient's humoral response to an infection. Because human serum contains antibodies with a wide range of specificities, these tests are designed to measure only those antibodies that are directed at specific microbial antigens. Older serological methods measure these specific antibodies by detecting their function in the presence of antigen. For example, the addition of patient serum to a sample of killed organisms may result in visible **agglutination** (clumping), if agglutinating antibodies are present. In more specific agglutination tests, purified microbial antigens are used to coat inert particles, such as a latex beads (**latex agglutination**) or red blood cells (**hemagglutination**). The **complement fixation test** measures the ability of patient serum to trigger the complement cascade in the presence of antigen, and **neutralizing antibody tests** measure the capacity of serum to inhibit growth in culture (Fig. 55.3). Neutralization assays are rarely used clinically, but are used frequently in research to assess protective immunity to viral infections. In all of these tests, the amount of specific antibody present in the patient's serum is quantified by testing dilutions of the serum. The highest dilution of the patient's serum that still has the measured function, or **endpoint** (i.e., agglutination, complement fixation, or neutralization) is the positive **titer** for that assay.

Later generations of serological tests do not depend on specific antibody function, but measure the presence of specific antibodies directly. Most of these tests are **solid-phase assays**, that is, they use either the pathogen or antigens from the pathogen, fixed to a solid support, such as a slide, the sides of a test tube, or an inert bead (Fig. 55.4). In the direct assays, patient serum is added to this system, and specific antibodies are bound and immobilized to the fixed antigen. All other antibodies and serum components remain in solution and can thus be washed away. The presence of the bound specific antibody is typically detected by adding a labeled antibody directed against human immunoglobulin molecules. These anti-(human)-immunoglobulin antibodies are raised in animals by immunization with human antibodies. A popular format for these tests is the ELISA. In ELISAs, the "second antibody" is conjugated to an enzyme, such as peroxidase or alkaline phosphatase, that will catalyze the production of visibly colored compounds from colorless precursors. An alternative method, the **indirect fluorescent antibody (IFA)** test, utilizes a second antibody labeled with fluorescein, and the fixed antigen is usually an intact microorganism. In a positive test, the fixed microorganisms glow when illuminated with ultraviolet light. In both of these direct assays, the anti-immunoglobulin may also be made specific for IgG or IgM, so that the test recognizes only antibodies of a certain class.

Figure 55.4. Direct and competitive ELISA serology for the detection of specific antibodies in patient serum.

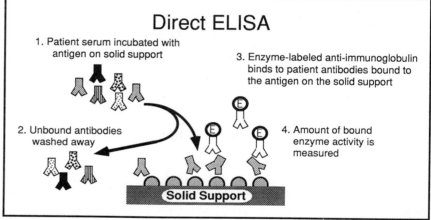

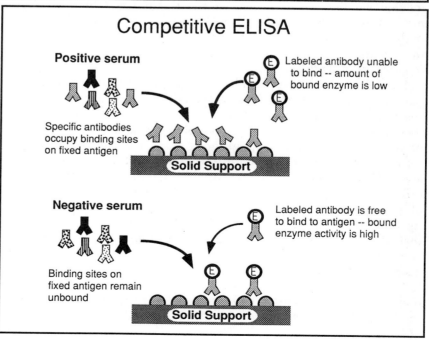

In **competitive assays**, the labeled, "second" antibody is directed at the antigen, rather than at human immunoglobulin. In these tests, the assay measures the capacity of the patient serum to compete for binding with the antigen. Therefore, the intensity of the signal from the bound label **decreases** with increasing amounts of amounts of specific antibody in the patient serum.

The specificity of a serological test is determined by the antigen used to capture the antibody in the direct test formats or by the reactivity of the labeled antibody or antisera used in the competitive assays. A "Western blot," used in Case 2, is one of the most specific serological methods available. In this test, the antigenic molecules from a pathogen are first separated according to their size using electrophoresis. The whole series of antigens is then "blotted" onto a solid support and then incubated with the patient's serum (Fig. 55.5). It is then possible to determine whether the patient's antibodies are directed against pathogen-specific or cross-reactive antigens. This additional level of analysis allows the discrimination of specific and nonspecific reactions. Western blotting has become a mainstay for confirming the serological diagnosis of HIV infection (Fig. 37.6).

Serological tests for particular infectious diseases may be both sensitive and specific, but their utility in clinical management is often limited. Because these tests depend upon the immune response to infection, they have limited utility in the early diagnosis of acute infections, before the patient develops specific antibodies. Serology is typically more useful in determining whether infection with a particular pathogen has occurred at any time in the past, such as in establishing the presence of infection with HIV in Cases 1 and 2. The physician must decide whether the positive serology is due to the patient's current illness or to an infection months or years earlier. There are two ways to make this determination. One way is to measure the patient's specific antibody titer at two points in time, usually several weeks apart

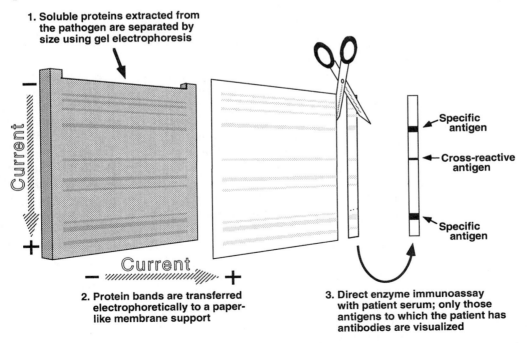

1. Soluble proteins extracted from the pathogen are separated by size using gel electrophoresis

Current

Current

2. Protein bands are transferred electrophoretically to a paper-like membrane support

3. Direct enzyme immunoassay with patient serum; only those antigens to which the patient has antibodies are visualized

Specific antigen

Cross-reactive antigen

Specific antigen

Figure 55.5.   Western blot. By determining which antigens ("bands") the patient serum reacts with, it is possible to determine whether the reactivity is due to specific or cross-reactive antibodies.

(**acute and convalescent titers**). If a significant increase in the amount of antibody occurs, this indicates a recent or ongoing infection with the pathogen. Another way to diagnose a recent infection serologically is to measure specific IgM antibodies against the pathogen. In the course of most infections, specific IgM antibodies appear first and tend to disappear a few weeks or months after onset.

DIAGNOSIS OF INFECTION BY DETECTING MICROBIAL MACROMOLECULES

In the investigation of a crime, a detective may look for traces left by the perpetrator in the hope these clues will lead to the discovery or positive identification of the criminal. The investigator may look for footprints, telltale fibers from clothing, or dust for fingerprints. Similarly, the microbial culprit associated with an infection can often be identified by recognizing its products or parts, provided that these "parts" are as specific for the pathogen as fingerprints are for an individual criminal. In microbiology, these identifications are made either by detecting an antigen(s) or a nucleic acid sequence that is specific for a particular pathogen. Interestingly, criminologists may also use these laboratory methods when traces of blood or body fluids are the available clues for analysis.

Detection tests have inherent disadvantages and advantages compared with standard culture diagnosis. Among the disadvantages are the imperfect specificity, the inability to study further the infecting pathogen (e.g., for antimicrobial sensitivity, strain typing), and the need to perform separate tests for each suspected pathogen. Advantages include the capacity to diagnose the infection within hours rather than days and greater sensitivity in certain settings (e.g., the potential to detect the presence of a pathogen after treatment with antimicrobials has rendered the culture negative).

Detection of Microbial Antigens

Antigen detection tests are like serological tests in reverse; instead of using the microbial antigen to capture antibodies from patient serum, specific antibodies are used to capture microbial antigens from a patient sample. In most of these assays, the "capture" antibody is bound to a solid support. Some antigens, such as capsular polysaccharides, consist of repetitive sequences of sugars. Because each molecule can bind antibody at multiple sites, it is possible to detect these polyvalent antigens in a simple agglutination assay (Fig. 55.6). Several widely performed tests use antibody-coated latex beads (**latex agglutination tests**) to detect capsular material from meningococcus, *S. pneumoniae*, *H. influenzae*, *C. neoformans*, and others. These tests may be performed, as a panel, on CSF samples to make an early diagnosis of meningitis.

For many other antigens, the presence of the captured molecule is detected using a second antibody (e.g., in the "sandwich ELISA"; Fig. 55.7). In this test, the sample is incubated with the antibody-coated solid support, and then all of the unbound material in the sample is washed away. An enzyme-labeled second antibody, which is also directed against the microbial antigen, is then added (forming a sandwich of the antigen between two layers of antibody). The amount of second antibody that is retained by the solid support is proportional to the amount of antigen that is bound. One of the numerous clinical as-

Antigen Detection by Particle Agglutination

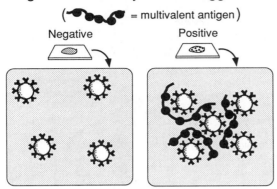

(![multivalent antigen symbol] = multivalent antigen)

Negative   Positive

Figure 55.6. Detection of a polyvalent antigen by particle agglutination. Particles are coated with specific antibodies. If a multivalent antigen is present in the patient sample, bridges forms between the particles, causing clumping. As with antibody detection by agglutination, false-negative prozones may occur if there is an overabundance of antigen (see Fig. 55.3). In these cases, dilution of sample will give a positive reaction.

says that exploit this format is the HIV p24 antigen test used in the case of Patient 2. This is a sensitive test for the presence of HIV virions in the blood, but like other antigen capture assays, it may be falsely negative if the patient's serum contains high titers of specific antibodies (i.e., anti-p24) that may complex with the antigen and prevent its capture.

Another common antigen detection format is the radioimmunoassay (**RIA**) (Fig. 55.7). This test is a competitive assay in which measured amounts of radiolabeled antigen compete with antigen in the sample for binding to a fixed amount of specific antibody. RIAs may be performed as solid-phase assays (i.e., with antibody coating a solid support) and as liquid phase assays, in which antigen-antibody complexes are precipitated from solution before radiometry.

Nucleic Acid-Based Diagnosis of Infection

The double helix of DNA is composed of two separate strands held together by hydrogen bonding between complementary bases (adenine to thymine, guanine to cytosine). Because they are bound by relatively weak hydrogen bonds, the two strands of DNA can be separated into single strands by heating. When the temperature is once again lowered, random molecular interactions will eventually bring the complementary strands together, and they will connect (or **hybridize**), reforming double-stranded DNA. Hybridization will occur only when the two strands are a genuine complementary pair. A short, single-stranded DNA sequence (or **probe**) can be chosen so that it will hybridize **only** to a perfect complementary **"target" sequence**. This interaction is the basis for diagnostic DNA probe tests, and the potential precision of this interaction accounts for the high degree of specificity of these tests.

Because nucleic acid sequences encode all of the structural and functional elements of a microorganism, it is always possible to find unique probes from among the sequences that encode structures or functions unique to a particular group of organisms. Also, probe tests are not limited to DNA:DNA hybridization; stable DNA:RNA and RNA:RNA hybrids also occur. In fact, a popular target sequence for diagnostic tests is ribosomal RNA (rRNA), because these sequences differ among species, and because most nonviral pathogens contain thousands of identical copies of rRNA (but only one copy of most other genes). In theory, this natural duplication would make any assay to detect rRNA thousands of times more sensitive.

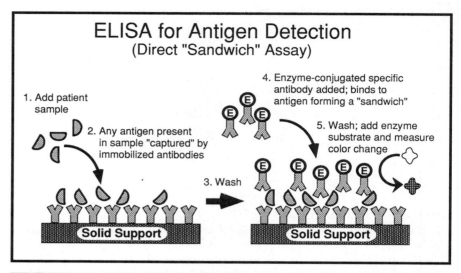

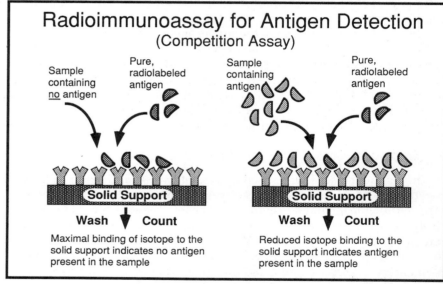

Figure 55.7. Detection of a microbial antigen by "sandwich ELISA" and radioimmunoassay (RIA). ELISA: "capture antibody" bound to a solid support binds antigen from the patient sample while other nonspecific contents of the sample are washed away. The presence of the captured antigen is detected using a second, specific antibody conjugated to an enzyme. In the last step of the procedure, the activity of the enzyme bound to the solid support is measured using a color-producing substrate; color production signals the presence of the antigen, which is sandwiched between the two antibodies. **RIA:** The patient sample is combined with a measured, tiny amount of purified, radiolabeled antigen in the presence of a specific antibody. If the patient sample contains no antigen, then all of the labeled antigen will complex with the antibody, and all of the radioactivity will be bound in immune complexes. If the patient sample contains antigen, it will compete with the labeled antigen for binding to the available antibody, and there will be less radioactivity associated with immune complexes. RIAs may be done in solution (with immune complexes precipitated and counted) or in solid-phase assays (with specific antibody bound to a solid support).

The elements of diagnostic probe tests are similar, even though the formats may differ (Fig. 55.8). The single-stranded probe DNA is labeled with a radioisotope, an enzyme, or any variety of other detectable labels. The patient's sample must be treated so that any microorganisms are disrupted, and DNA and RNA is released and denatured (i.e., converted to single strands). After the labeled probe and sample are coincubated, the assay measures the amount of probe that hybridizes to nucleic acids in the sample. For most assays, bound and unbound probe are separated before measurement of the label. This is accomplished by attachment to a solid support, in a manner analogous to the separation steps in serological and antigen detection tests. In **filter hybridization** and **in situ hybridization** tests, the target sequences are denatured and fixed to a solid support before the probe is added, so that unbound probe can simply be washed off (Fig. 55.8). In **solution hybridization**, the probe:target hybrid is bound selectively to a solid support after hybridization.

Patient samples must contain several thousand target organisms to elicit a positive probe test using any of the methods diagrammed in Figure 55.8. Therefore, the infections that are best suited for direct diagnosis by these techniques are mucosal infections with pathogens that are difficult to grow in culture or to identify by other means. Among these are sexually transmitted diseases (e.g., *Chlamydia*), respiratory infections (e.g., *Mycoplasma* and *Legionella*), various enteric infections, and some viral infections.

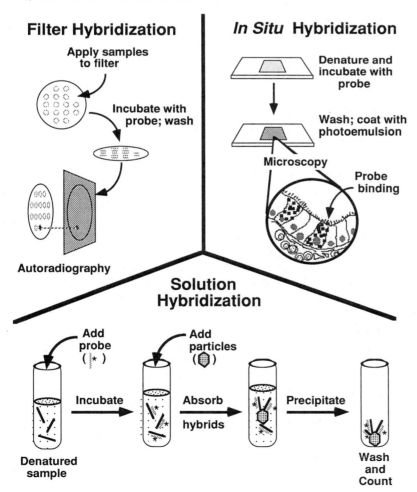

Figure 55.8. Nucleic acid probes—the basic formats. For simplicity, each assay format is depicted using a radiolabeled probe; nonisotopic methods of probe detection are also available for these tests. In filter hybridization assays, DNA samples are denatured and spotted in rows onto a membrane. After incubation with the probe, positive samples are detected by the presence of a signal associated with a given spot by autoradiography. In situ hybridization involves release and denaturation of DNA from intact tissue specimens, usually fixed to a microscopic slide. After incubation with the probe, the slide is overlaid with a photographic emulsion that creates opaque, microscopic grains at sites of radioactive emissions. The anatomical structures to which the probe has hybridized can then be visualized by microscopy. In solution hybridization, the probe and the denatured patient sample are incubated together in solution. After hybridization, the double-stranded hybrids are precipitated from solution and separated from any unbound probe DNA. If the target sequence was present in the sample, then radioactive counts, representing hybridized probe, are detected in the precipitated fraction.

Some probe tests, although not sufficiently sensitive for testing clinical samples directly, may be useful for early identification of pathogens in culture. For example, some viruses can be detected in tissue culture using DNA probes well before any cytopathic effects are noticed by microscopy. (DFA and other antigen detection techniques may also be used for this purpose.) Cultures of *Mycobacteria* require 4–6 weeks of incubation before colonies are visible, and then several more days for species identification. Early testing of incubating cultures with DNA probes for *M. tuberculosis* and *M. avium-intracellulare* might have significantly hastened the correct diagnosis and treatment in the case of Patient 1.

Nucleic Acid Amplification

An essential function of all genomic DNA and RNA is its capacity to be reproduced efficiently and accurately. Nucleic acid amplification methods, such as the **polymerase chain reaction** (or **PCR**), exploit this natural function selectively so that specific sequences of interest are reproduced in large amounts. To design a PCR test, a specific sequence of microbial nucleic acid must be known. Two short DNA probes (or "primers") are then synthesized so that they will hybridize to opposite strands of the target DNA sequence (Fig. 55.9). In the assay, three components are added to the DNA extracted from the patient's specimen—the primers, deoxyribonucleotides (dNTPs), and heat-stable DNA polymerase. The reactants are subjected to repetitive cycles of temperature change that result in denaturation of DNA (heating), hybridization with the primers (cooling), and DNA synthesis. In first cycle of the reaction, the DNA delineated by the two primers is duplicated, each strand acting as a template for synthesis of a second, complementary strand beginning with the bound primer. With the synthesis of each new strand of DNA, there is also the generation of a new primer-binding site. Consequently, each new strand also becomes a new template for subsequent rounds of primer-initiated synthesis. With every cycle, the number of copies of the DNA segment between the primers (and therefore, templates for further synthesis) doubles. That is, a "chain reaction" occurs and results in geometrically increasing amounts of the target DNA. In this respect, PCR is analogous to the biological process of DNA replication and fission that occurs in populations of dividing cells; however, in PCR, the exponential synthesis is limited to the DNA segment bounded by the two synthetic primers.

The great strength of PCR is its sensitivity. Theoretically, the chain reaction can be initiated by a single copy of the target sequence. But this exquisite sensitivity is also the major pitfall of the procedure as a clinical diagnostic tool. There is a serious potential for cross-contamination ("microcontamination") in laboratories that process numerous, similar samples every day. The prevention of false-positive PCR results is a matter of great concern, because there may be no equally sensitive, alternative method to verify a positive PCR result. At the very least, all positives should be retested until the technology becomes more reliable as a diagnostic tool.

PCR and other methods of nucleic acid amplification are presently being used to detect infectious agents that elude more conventional methods of diagnosis. For many infectious diseases, PCR may be the only method that is sufficiently sensitive to detect a particular pathogen in routine clinical specimens. The case of Patient 2 illustrates a clinical situation in which a negative PCR test was used to support the

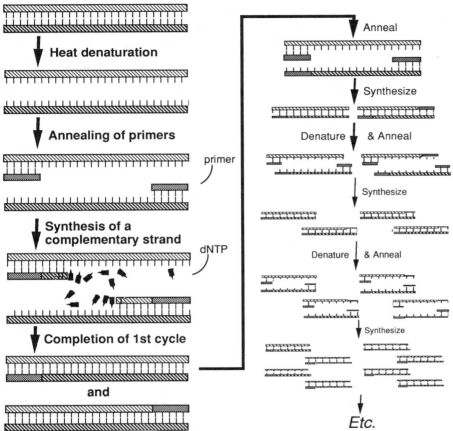

Figure 55.9. Nucleic acid amplification—the polymerase chain reaction. In this assay, the DNA in the patient sample is mixed with specific primers, deoxynucleotide triphosphates (dNTPs), and a thermostable DNA polymerase enzyme (see text). The reaction involves three steps that are repeated in sequence: (*1*) Heat denaturation, which permits complementary strands of the target DNA separate; (*2*) annealing, as the primers hybridize to opposite strands of the targeted sequence when the temperature is lowered; (*3*) synthesis, as the polymerase incorporates the dNTPS into a new complementary strand of DNA, in a sequential and unidirectional manner, beginning at each hybridized primer. Note that synthesis from either primer generates a new site to which the opposite primer can hybridize in the next cycle. Each time this cycle is repeated, the number of double-stranded target DNA sequences available to bind the two primers doubles. One target DNA molecule subjected to 30 repetitions of the PCR would result in 2^{30} copies of the target sequence. The products of the reaction are detected by gel electrophoresis or by a gene probe specific for the sequences between the two primers.

conclusion that the screening serology for HIV was falsely positive. What would Patient 2 have been told if the PCR result had been positive? Can you see why microcontamination is such a major issue?

CONCLUSION

There are many different ways to establish the presence of a pathogenic microorganism in an ill patient. All methods have the potential for inaccuracy, either in failing to detect a pathogen or an immune response when present or in inappropriately signaling their presence when the pathogen or the immune response are absent. Some tests are more sensitive or more specific than others, and these measures of performance will determine how and when they are used. But even when a test is accurate in analyzing a given sample, the simple presence of a microorganism in the specimen or of antibodies against a pathogen in patient serum is not always indicative of active infection, nor does it necessarily establish the cause of illness. For these reasons, there is always a need for interpretation with any microbiological test, regardless of its technical performance characteristics. In the final analysis, there is no substitute for the interpretive skills of the clinician in placing microbiological test results into the context of an individual patient's illness.

Respiratory System 56

Gregory A. Storch

The respiratory tract is the most common site for infection by pathogenic microorganisms. Perhaps because they occur so often and are usually mild, respiratory infections are frequently taken for granted. In fact, they represent an immense disease burden on our society and, thus, have a major economic impact. Upper respiratory infections (**URIs**) account for more visits to physicians than any other diagnosis. It has been estimated that, in the U.S., influenza-like illnesses are responsible for more than 400 million days of restricted activity each year. In addition, some respiratory infections have severe consequences, especially in individuals compromised by other diseases. Pneumonia, the most severe form of respiratory infection, is frequently life threatening and still accounts for a large number of deaths in the U.S. population.

That the respiratory tract becomes infected frequently is not surprising when we consider that it is in direct contact with the environment and is continuously exposed to microorganisms suspended in the air we breathe. Some are highly virulent and may infect a normal person even in small numbers; but most do not cause infection unless other factors interfere with host defenses. The warm, moist environment of the respiratory tract seems an ideal place for the growth of microorganisms. One of the questions that this chapter will address is why these frequent infections are not even more frequent.

Infection may be localized at any level of the respiratory tract, and the location is a major determinant of the clinical manifestations. The clinical syndromes associated with infection at different locations are shown in Figure 56.1. Infections of the conjunctivae, the middle ear, and the paranasal sinuses are included because these areas are continuous with the respiratory tract and are lined by respiratory epithelium. Several important diseases of this system are discussed in other chapters (pneumococcal pneumonia, Chapter 13; whooping cough, Chapter 20; pulmonary tuberculosis, Chapter 23; chlamydial pneumonitis, Chapter 26; *Mycoplasma* pneumonia, Chapter 28; rhinoviruses, Chapter 31; respiratory syncytial virus, Chapter 33; influenza, Chapter 35; infections of the sinuses and middle ear, Chapter 64).

The clinical manifestations of respiratory tract infection also depend on the causative agent. Thus, viruses are particularly important in the upper respiratory tract and account for most cases of pharyngitis. Bacteria are the most important causes of otitis media, sinusitis, pharyngitis, epiglottitis, bronchitis, and pneumonia. Fungi and protozoa rarely cause serious respiratory tract infection in normal individuals, but are important causes of pneumonia in the immune compromised host. Some of the common pathogens that produce infection at different locations in this system are listed in Table 56.1. Their relative contribution to respiratory tract disease is shown in Figure 56.2.

Figure 56.1. Clinical syndromes associated with infection at different locations within the respiratory tract.

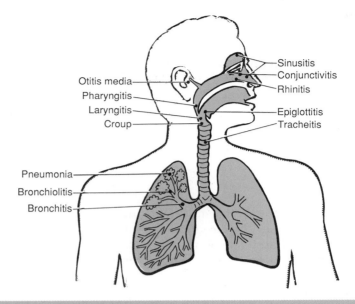

Table 56.1. Pathogens Producing Disease at Different Levels of the Respiratory Tract

Location	Common Pathogens
Nasopharynx	Rhinovirus, *Coronavirus,* other respiratory viruses, *Staphylococcus aureus*
Oropharynx	Group A streptococcus (*Streptococcus pyogenes*), *Corynebacterium diphtheriae,* Epstein-Barr virus, adenovirus, enteroviruses
Conjunctiva	*S. pneumoniae, Haemophilus influenzae, Neisseria gonorrhoeae, Chlamydia trachomatis,* adenovirus
Middle ear and paranasal sinuses	*Streptococcus pneumoniae, H. influenzae, Moraxella catarrhalis, Group A streptococcus* *Branhamella* *S. pyogenes*
Epiglottitis	*Haemophilus influenzae*
Larynx-trachea	Parainfluenza viruses, *S. aureus*
Bronchi	*S. pneumoniae, H. influenzae, Mycoplasma pneumoniae,* influenza viruses, measles virus
Bronchioles	Respiratory syncytial virus
Lungs	See Table 56.5

%
1. 38.5 Rhinoviruses
2. 16.9 Parainfluenza viruses
3. 13.3 Group A β-hemolytic streptococci
4. 11.9 Influenza viruses
5. 05.9 Respiratory syncytial virus
6. 04.7 *Mycoplasma* & other
7. 04.5 Adenoviruses
8. 04.3 Enteroviruses

Figure 56.2. Relative contribution of viruses, *Mycoplasma,* and group A streptococci to total respiratory infection in Tecumseh, Michigan.

Although the casual observer may think that there is a constant background of respiratory tract infections in the population, close observation coupled with laboratory studies reveal that there are large and small epidemics due to specific agents. The results of careful viral surveillance carried out in Houston, Texas over a period of several years are shown in Figure 56.3.

Some microorganisms have a strong predilection for certain sites in the respiratory tract, either because of specific tropism or selective survival. The reason that the common cold occurs in the nose and not further down the respiratory tract is that the cold viruses grow best at 33°C—a temperature found in the nose and not in the lungs.

This chapter divides the respiratory system into three major anatomic regions:

- Nose and throat;

- Airways;

- Lungs.

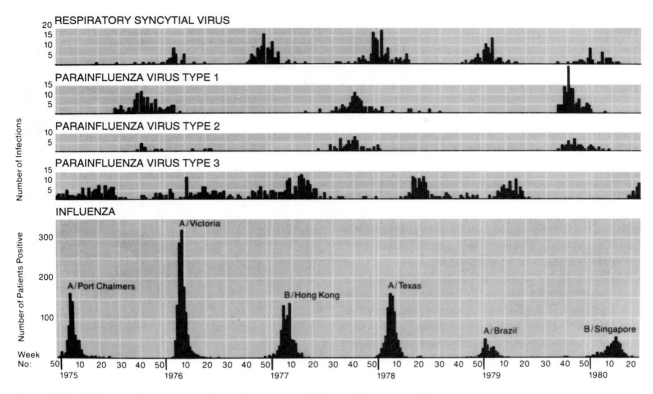

Figure 56.3.   Patterns of occurrence of, respiratory syncytial, parainfluenza, and influenza virus infections in Houston, Texas.

INFECTIONS OF THE NOSE AND THROAT

Case of Pharyngitis

F., a 5-year-old child who was in good general health, was brought to the pediatrician because of fever, irritability, and a sore throat that began 1 day earlier. On examination, he had a 102°F temperature and his conjunctivae and oropharynx were erythematous; his tonsils were enlarged and coated with a patchy white exudate and his anterior cervical lymph nodes were enlarged and tender. The rest of the examination was unremarkable. A throat culture was negative for group A streptococcus. The symptoms worsened slightly over the next day and then resolved without treatment over a 5-day period.

Although the posterior nasopharynx merges with the oropharynx, there are important differences between infections of the nose and throat. Some are illustrated in the above cases. Most infections of the nasopharynx are caused by viruses and give rise to the signs and symptoms that are known collectively as the **common cold** (Fig. 56.4 and see Fig. 31.7). Approximately 40–50% of colds are caused by the **rhinovirus** group (as discussed in detail in Chapter 31). **Coronaviruses** are the next most common group of agents, accounting for approximately 10% of colds. The remainder are caused by a variety of respiratory viruses listed in Table 56.2. Although the patient with a cold may experience a scratchy feeling in the throat, nasal symptoms are usually more prominent. Bacterial infection of the nose occurs occasionally, but this is not a common clinical problem.

Infection of the oropharynx, **pharyngitis**, is associated with discomfort in the throat, especially during swallowing. Sometimes, nasal symptoms are also present. Viruses and bacteria are the most common

Figure 56.4. Droplet dispersal following a sneeze by a patient with a cold; note strings of mucus.

Table 56.2. Causes of the Common Cold

Agent	Relative Importance
Rhinovirus	++++
Coronavirus	++
Parainfluenza virus	+[a]
Respiratory syncytial virus	+[a]
Influenza virus	+
Adenovirus	+
Other viruses	++
Unknown	++++

[a]++ or more in children.

etiological agents (Table 56.3). It is difficult to differentiate between viral and **bacterial** pharyngitis on the basis of clinical findings; in practice, the distinction is made by performing a throat culture or a rapid diagnostic test to detect group A streptococci, which is, by far, the most important bacterial cause of pharyngitis. Other streptococci account for a small proportion of cases, as do gonococci in sexually active individuals. In the past, oropharyngeal diphtheria caused an important form of pharyngitis, but this disease is rarely seen in the U.S. today. Among the viruses, the adenovirus group is particularly prominent and may be suspected if conjunctivitis is also present (pharyngoconjunctival fever). In adolescents and young adults, Epstein-Barr virus is a common cause of pharyngitis, which is one of the manifestations of infectious mononucleosis. The enteroviruses, especially the group A coxsackie viruses, sometimes produce small vesicles on the mucous membrane of the throat. This clinical picture is known as **herpangina**.

INFECTIONS OF THE EPIGLOTTIS

Case of Epiglottitis

A 3-year-old girl was put to bed with a low-grade temperature. In the middle of the night she awoke and her parents found that her fever was higher and that she had trouble breathing. The family pediatrician told the parents to take the child immediately to the local hospital. On examination, the child was sitting upright and drooling. A presumptive diagnosis of epiglottitis was made and the child taken to the operating room, where an endotracheal tube was inserted. An x-ray of the lateral neck was taken en route to the operating room. and revealed swelling of the epiglottis (Fig. 56.5). When her throat was examined as she was being intubated, her epiglottis was seen to be very red

Table 56.3. Causes of Pharyngitis

Agent	Relative Importance
Streptococcus pyogenes (Group A β-hemolytic)	++++
Rhinovirus	++
Adenovirus	++
Coronavirus	++
Epstein-Barr virus	++
Herpes simplex virus	+
Parainfluenza virus	+
Influenza virus	+
Coxsackie virus	+
Mixed anaerobic bacteria	+
Neisseria gonorrhoeae	+
Corynebacterium diphtheriae	+
C. hemolyticum	+
Mycoplasma pneumoniae	+
Francisella tularensis	+
Unknown	++++

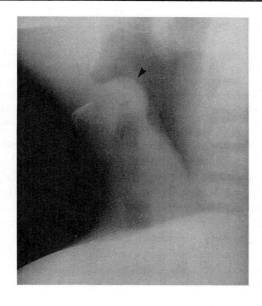

Figure 56.5.   X-ray of the neck, taken in a lateral projection, reveals marked swelling of the epiglottis (*arrow*).

and swollen. She was treated with antibiotics effective against Haemophilus influenzae *type b. The next day, the laboratory reported that blood and epiglottis cultures grew* H. influenzae. *She responded promptly to treatment and made a complete recovery.*

Acute epiglottitis is probably the most serious form of URI. This distinct clinical syndrome can be rapidly fatal because the airway may become completely obstructed from swelling of the epiglottis and surrounding structures. Acute epiglottitis occurs most often in young children, with the cause almost invariably *H. influenzae* type b (see Chapter 15). It is fortunately relatively uncommon, encountered less than once a year in a busy pediatric practice; but the practitioner must always be vigilant because early recognition of acute epiglottitis is extremely important to prevent airway obstruction.

Pathobiology of Epiglottitis

This disease probably becomes established by direct extension of infection from the nasopharynx. Bacteremia is almost always present and is secondary to infection of the epiglottitis. We do not know what determines who among the many individuals colonized with *H. influenzae* type b develops this disease. Nor do we understand the marked tropism of this organism for the epiglottis nor why other bacteria or viruses rarely cause epiglottitis.

Epiglottitis is an acute inflammation, with edema and infiltration with neutrophils. Microabscesses containing *H. influenzae* type b may be present. Metastatic complications are less common in epiglottitis than in *H. influenzae* meningitis, possibly because patients with epiglottitis seek medical attention earlier in the course of their illness. Fortunately, epiglottitis responds readily to treatment with antibiotics, and the outcome is good provided early recognition allows the airway to be protected, as illustrated in this case.

INFECTIONS OF THE LARYNX AND TRACHEA

Case of Croup

A 19-month-old boy developed a runny nose, hoarseness, cough, and a low-grade temperature. His pediatrician diagnosed a viral URI and prescribed no specific treatment. That night, the child suffered from a barking cough. His breathing was forced and noisy, especially with inspiration. Alarmed, the parents called the pediatrician, who told them that the child undoubtedly had croup. He advised them to take the child in the bathroom steamed up by running the hot water in the shower, and to call back 15 minutes later if the respiratory difficulty worsened. In fact, it subsided and the child fell back to sleep. A similar but milder episode occurred the next night. Over the next few days, all of the symptoms gradually resolved.

Infection of the larynx and upper airway in young children is often associated with the clinical syndrome of **croup**, as in this case. Croup (the obstruction of the upper airway) has a characteristically sudden onset, barking cough, difficulty with respiration, and often sudden resolution. Almost all cases are caused by viruses, especially the **parainfluenza viruses**. Infection with parainfluenza virus types 1 to 3 is very common in young children, and repeated infections may occur. Rarely, bacteria—particularly *Staphylococcus aureus*, cause clinical findings similar to those of viral croup. Typically, mild upper respiratory symptoms such as nasal discharge and dry cough are present 1–3 days before the signs of airway obstruction become evident. In most cases, the illness is self-limited and resolves after 3–7 days.

In adults, the major clinical manifestation of infections of the larynx is hoarseness. Most acute laryngeal infection in adults is caused by respiratory viruses. Although these infections may be annoying, they are generally mild and self-limited. Other less common causes of laryngeal infection include tubercle bacilli and yeast such as *Candida albicans*, especially in immune compromised patients.

Pathobiology of Croup

Infection begins at or near the site of original inoculation in the upper airway and spreads downward by direct extension. Viremia and spread to sites outside of the airway have no known clinical consequences. The upper airway obstruction characteristic of croup results from swelling of the tracheal mucous membrane. Because the tracheal wall has nonexpandable rings of cartilage, swelling of the mucous membrane results in narrowing of the tracheal lumen, which worsens during inspiration, resulting in inspiratory stridor. Histamine and IgE antibody specific for parainfluenza virus have been detected in naso-pharyngeal secretions of children with croup, suggesting that immuno-logical mechanisms involving inflammatory mediators may be involved in pathogenesis.

Some children experience recurrent episodes of croup, suggesting that they may have a predisposition to airway hyperreactivity, although the basis for this remains unknown. Most children admitted to the hospital with croup have greater reduction in the oxygen content of their blood than can be explained by the degree of obstruction to airflow. This suggests that the lungs as well as the airways may be involved in the infectious process. No specific drug treatment for parainfluenza virus infection is available at this time, and management consists of providing oxygen and support of the airway if needed.

INFECTIONS OF THE LARGE BRONCHI

Case of Influenza

A 28-year-old physician developed symptoms of cough, myalgias (aches and pains in the muscles), headache made worse by the coughing, substernal chest pain, and high fever. She suspected influenza because an outbreak was in progress and she had recently taken care of several patients with similar symptoms. During the next 3 days, she felt awful and was bedridden because of weakness and a persistent temperature of 103°F. The symptoms gradually resolved over the next few days without specific treatment, and after 7–10 days, she was able to resume her usual activities. A viral throat culture she took on the first day of illness confirmed the diagnosis of viral influenza.

Many different organisms cause infections of the large bronchi. Among viruses, the prototype is influenza, illustrated here and more fully discussed in Chapter 30. Bronchitis is also caused by other viruses, mycoplasmata, chlamydiae, pneumococci, and *H. influenzae.*

INFECTIONS OF THE BRONCHIOLES

Respiratory Syncytial Virus (RSV)

RSV is often described as the most dangerous cause of respiratory infection in young children. In addition to bronchiolitis, it also causes pneumonia and URI. Like the influenza and parainfluenza viruses, RSV is a member of the negative-stranded RNA paramyxovirus family. It is enveloped, with two virally specified glycoproteins as part of the structure. One of them, the **large glycoprotein**, or **G**, is responsible for the initial binding of the virus to the host cell; the other, the **fusion protein**, or **F**, permits fusion of the viral envelope with the host cell membrane, leading to entry of the virus (Table 56.4). The F protein also induces the fusion of the membranes of infected cells. RSV gets its name from the resulting formation of **syncytia** or multinucleated

Table 56.4. Transmission of Respiratory Syncytial Virus

Volunteers	Cuddlers[a]	Touchers[b]	Sitters[c]
Exposed	7	10	14
Infected	5	4	0
Incubation time	4 days	5.5 days	

[a]Close contact with infected infant.
[b]Self-inoculation after touching surfaces contaminated with infant's secretions.
[c]Sitting over 6 ft from infected infant.

masses of fused cells (see Fig. 36.3 for a similar syncytium produced by measles virus). RSVs are divided into two groups, each of which is further divided into subtypes. The clinical and epidemiological significance of these differences is still unknown. RSV and its associated clinical syndromes are discussed in Chapter 33.

INFECTIONS OF THE LUNGS

Pneumonia, infection of the lung parenchyma, may be caused by many different pathogens, sometimes with distinctive clinical manifestations. Thus, pneumonia is not one disease but many different ones that share a common anatomic location. Pneumonias can be classified in various ways. We will use a clinical and epidemiological classification (Table 56.5), based on the perspective of the clinician encountering patients with pneumonia. This classification is important because it can form the basis for managing the patient's illness even before a specific etiology has been proven.

In this classification, the first important distinction is between **acute pneumonia** (fairly sudden onset with progression of symptoms over a very few days), and **subacute and chronic pneumonia**. Among the acute pneumonias, a second very important distinction is made between **cases acquired in the community and cases acquired by patients in hospitals** (when hospitalized for conditions other than pneumonia). These cases are referred to as **hospital-acquired or nosocomial infections**, and are classified separately because the responsible pathogens

Table 56.5. Classification of Pneumonia Syndromes	
I. Acute	
Community-acquired	
1. Person-to-person transmission	*Streptococcus pneumoniae, Mycoplasma pneumoniae Hemophilus influenzae, Staphylococcus aureus S. pyogenes, Klebsiella pneumoniae, Neisseria meningitidis, Branhamella catarrhalis, Chlamydia pneumoniae* (?), Influenza virus
2. Animal or environmental exposure	*Legionella pneumophila, Francisella tularensis, Coxiella burnetii, Chlamydia psittaci, Yersinia pestis* (plague), *Bacillus anthracis* (anthrax), *Pseudomonas pseudomallei* (melioidosis), *Pasteurella multocida* (pasteurellosis)
3. Pneumonia in the infant and young child	*C. trachomatis*, respiratory syncytial virus and other respiratory viruses, *S. aureus*, Group B streptococci, cytomegalovirus, *Ureaplasma urealyticum* (?), *Pneumocystis carinii* (?) *S. pneumoniae, H. influenzae* type b.
B. Nosocomial pneumonia	*Enterobacteriaceae, P. aeruginosa, Acinetobacter calcoaceticus, S. aureus*
II. Subacute or Chronic	
A. Pulmonary tuberculosis	*Mycobacterium tuberculosis*
B. Fungal	*Histoplasma capsulatum, Blastomyces dermatitidis, Coccidioides immitis, Cryptococcus neoformans*
C. Aspiration of pneumonia and lung abscess	Mixed anaerobic and aerobic bacterial organisms
III. Pneumonia in the immunocompromised patient	*P. carinii*, cytomegalovirus, atypical mycobacteria, *Nocardia, Aspergillus, Phycomycetes, Candida*

are frequently different from those that produce pneumonia in non-hospitalized individuals.

Most of the common forms of acute community-acquired pneumonia are caused by pathogens that are **transmitted from person to person** (for example, pneumococci). A second group, encountered less frequently under ordinary circumstances, includes pneumonias caused by **pathogens that have an animal or environmental reservoir**. In many cases, the diagnosis of pneumonias of this group is difficult unless the physician seeks out the circumstances of exposures (for example, exposure to a parrot leading to psittacosis). **Pneumonias in infants and young children** are placed in a third group because they have a distinctive etiological spectrum.

In contrast to patients with acute pneumonia are those with lung infections that have been present for weeks or months. Several forms of subacute and chronic pneumonias can be distinguished. They are tuberculosis, fungal pneumonia, and anaerobic lung abscesses. It is important to realize that this classification is based on the common clinical patterns of disease, but that exceptions occur. For example, occasional patients with tuberculosis, histoplasmosis, or lung abscesses may experience acute, rapidly progressing disease.

Case 1—Community-acquired Pneumonia

P., an 8-month-old Native American boy who had been previously in good health, was brought to a physician because of fever and rapid breathing. On examination, he was noted to look acutely ill, to have a temperature of 104.4°F, and a respiratory rate of 70/minute. A chest x-ray revealed consolidation of the right middle and lower lobes (Fig. 56.6). His white cell count was 26,000/µl, which is markedly elevated over the normal. Because sputum samples cannot usually be obtained from young children, a rapid latex agglutination test for H. influenzae *type b antigen was performed on the boy's*

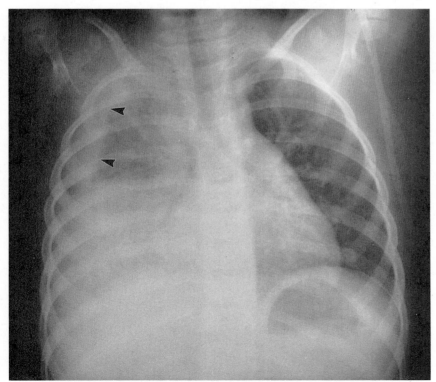

Figure 56.6. Chest x-ray of patient with *Haemophilus influenzae* type b pneumonia reveals consolidation of the middle and lower lobes. A plural effusion is also present (*arrows*).

urine. *The result was positive, suggesting that this organism was responsible for the pneumonia. (Antigen detection tests such as latex agglutination are convenient because they give rapid answers. They are especially useful when the patient has been treated with antibiotics, rendering cultures negative. In this case, antigen was still detectable). P. was treated with antibiotics effective against that organism and recovered uneventfully. Blood cultures drawn before antibiotics were given were positive for* H. influenzae *type b.*

Case 2—Pneumonia in a Chronic Alcoholic

Mr. L., a 52-year-old man with severe chronic alcoholism, was brought to an emergency room by a policeman who had found him lying on a street. Physical examination revealed a lethargic, disheveled, middle-aged man with a temperature of 102.0°F and a respiratory rate of 36/minute. During respiration, the left side of the chest moved much less than the right side (splinting). On auscultation, there was evidence of consolidation of the upper lobe of the left lung. A sample of bloody sputum was obtained by tracheal suction, and a Gram stain revealed many neutrophils and Gram-negative rods. A chest x-ray confirmed the consolidation of the left lower lobe (Fig. 56.7).

Mr. L. was treated with broad-spectrum antibiotics. The sputum culture was reported to have a heavy growth of Klebsiella pneumoniae, *one of the Enterobacteriaceae. Mr. L.'s hospital course was stormy and he required mechanical ventilation for 4 days. Eventually he recovered and was discharged to a chronic care hospital after 3 weeks.*

Comments

What are the complaints of the patients and the findings on examination that lead physicians to make the diagnosis of pneumonia? Most patients with the disease have fever and feel sick. Many also present

Figure 56.7.   Pneumonia caused by *Klebsiella pneumoniae*. Chest x-ray reveals extensive consolidation of the left lower lobe. Cavity formation is apparent within the involved area (*arrow*).

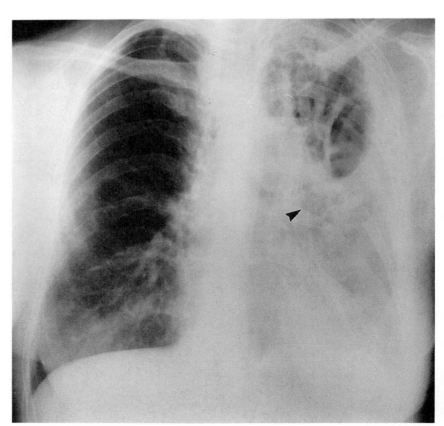

with clues, often very obvious, that point to the chest as the location of disease. Some clues are chest pain, frequently "pleuritic" (exacerbated by respiratory motion), and a cough that may or may not be productive of sputum. Those with extensive involvement of the lungs may have shortness of breath, rapid respiration, and poor color, even cyanosis. If breathing is painful, expansion of the chest may be limited (splinting). Auscultation may reveal "rales," which are usually indicative of alveolar disease. The most important diagnostic finding of all is a chest x-ray. Pneumonia is usually visible as a shadow or "infiltrate," the pattern of which may be a clue to the identity of the pathogen causing pneumonia. Skilled interpretation is important, because other processes, tumors, pulmonary edema, or pulmonary hemorrhage, may produce radiographic changes very similar to those of pneumonia.

In general, the most common forms of acute community-acquired pneumonias are those caused by the pneumococcus and *Mycoplasma pneumoniae*, described in Chapters 13 and 28, respectively. A newly recognized organism, *Chlamydia pneumoniae*, may also be an important cause of community-acquired pneumonia. The clinical features of P., the 8-month-old baby (his ill appearance, high temperature, elevated white blood cell count, and chest x-ray), all would lead the physician to suspect an acute bacterial pneumonia. These manifestations are characteristic of pneumococcal pneumonia, which is common in all age groups (see Fig. 13.1 for a chest x-ray of a case of pneumococcal pneumonia). However, the astute physician may be tipped off to *Haemophilus* as the etiology in this case by the age and ethnic background of the child. *H. influenzae* type b accounts for a high proportion of serious systemic bacterial infections in children in the first year of life. Although it affects children in all socioeconomic groups, the incidence is higher in nonwhites and is particularly high among Native Americans and Alaskan Eskimos. It is important to recognize this etiological agent, first because of its tendency to cause meningitis and other forms of invasive infection and second, because it is frequently resistant to antibiotics that may be used to treat pneumococcal pneumonia.

A particular aspect of acute pneumonia occurring in children under 2 years of age is that they are more often caused by viruses than by bacteria. Illness caused by RSV, influenza, and parainfluenza viruses or adenoviruses tends to be milder, and spontaneous recovery is the rule unless the child is compromised in some other way. This is a unique situation, because viruses are infrequent causes of community-acquired pneumonia in other age groups. Influenza virus may cause pneumonia in adults, but mostly due to bacterial superinfection. Children who develop pneumonia in the first few months of life are often infected with organisms acquired from the mother, including chlamydiae and cytomegalovirus.

Case 2 illustrates another form of acute community-acquired pneumonia, that caused by aerobic Gram-negative bacilli. The factors that place such an individual at risk for this disease, chronic alcoholism and exposure, also predispose him to pneumonia caused by the pneumococcus, *Legionella pneumophila*, and anaerobic bacteria (aspiration pneumonia). The clinical features of this case, including the involvement of the right upper lobe, bulging at an interlobar fissure (indicative of the expansive nature of the inflammatory process), and bloody sputum, are characteristic of pneumonia due to *K. pneumoniae*. However, these characteristics are not unique, and similar illness may be caused by many other bacteria. Laboratory testing is required to make the specific etiological diagnosis. In current medical practice, most cases of pneumonia caused by members of the Enterobacteriaceae occur in hospital patients or residents of nursing homes.

ENCOUNTER

Encounter with the agents that cause pneumonia takes place in different ways:

- **Colonization-infection**, where the causative organism is transmitted from person to person usually without environmental reservoirs. Transmission is typically air-borne over short distances, or by contaminated secretions or fomites. In the case of some pathogens such as the pneumococcus, *H. influenzae*, and *Staphylococcus aureus*, most individuals who encounter the organism become colonized, but only a few develop disease, directly, or after a variable period of colonization.

- Pneumonias may be caused by organisms **associated with the environment or with animals**. Most of these are transmitted by the air-borne route, although some have insect vectors. Organisms that follow this pattern are shown in Table 56.6. An example is Legionnaires' disease, discussed in detail in Chapter 22.

- **Aspiration pneumonias** are usually caused by entry into the lungs of the normal microbial contents of the upper respiratory tract. Typical cases lead to lung abscess and other anaerobic lung infections. The causative agents are part of the normal oral flora, which may cause disease when translocated in large numbers to an abnormal location.

ENTRY AND SPREAD

Pathogens may reach the lungs by one of five routes: (*a*) direct inhalation, (*b*) aspiration of upper airway contents, (*c*) spread along the mucous membrane surface, (*d*) hematogenous spread, and rarely, (*e*) direct penetration. Of these, inhalation and aspiration are the most common.

Inhalation and Aspiration

Obviously, the respiratory tract is exposed to potential pathogens suspended in the inhaled air. Less obvious is that it is also exposed to potential pathogens by aspiration of oropharyngeal contents. Studies with radioactive tracers have shown that in normal individuals, aspiration is not uncommon during deep sleep. In addition, intoxication or unconsciousness may cause an individual to aspirate large amounts of oropharyngeal material or even material from the stomach and upper

Table 56.6. Pneumonia Resulting from Unusual Exposure		
Disease	Causative Organism	Source
Psittacosis (parrot fever)	*Chlamydia psittaci*	Infected birds
Q fever	*Coxiella burnetii*	Infected animals
Histoplasmosis	*Histoplasma capsulatum*	Infected soil, bats
Coccidioidomycosis	*Coccidioides immitis*	Soil
Cryptococcosis	*Cryptococcus neoformans*	Soil, pigeons
Plague	*Yersinia pestis*	Infected animals, insect vectors
Melioidiosis	*Pseudomonas pseudomallei*	Soil
Tularemia	*Francisella tularensis*	Infected animals, ticks

small intestine (see Chapter 57 on Gastrointestinal Infections). Defenses that protect against aspiration include the epiglottis, which physically protects the airway; the laryngeal spasm reflex, which also prevents material from entering it; and the cough reflex, which expels material from the airway. Aspiration of oropharyngeal contents is the most important mode of entry for organisms that exhibit the colonization-infection pattern.

Direct Spread

Respiratory viruses such as influenza and respiratory syncytial virus initiate infection in the upper airway and spread to the lower respiratory tract by spreading directly along the respiratory epithelium, a route possibly facilitated by aspiration.

In **hematogenous spread**, the lung is a secondary site of infection. This mechanism is unusual but clearly implicated in cases of staphylococcal pneumonia in intravenous drug abusers. In many of these cases, the tricuspid heart valve is infected, and pulmonary infection results when infectious material from the valve embolizes to the lungs. Hematogenous spread has also been implicated in some cases of pneumonia caused by *E. coli* and other Gram-negative rods.

Defense Mechanisms Of The Lungs

The defense of the lungs (Fig. 56.8) begins in the nose, where specialized hairs, known as vibrissae, filter out large particles suspended in inhaled air. Large particles (more than 10 µm in diameter) tend to

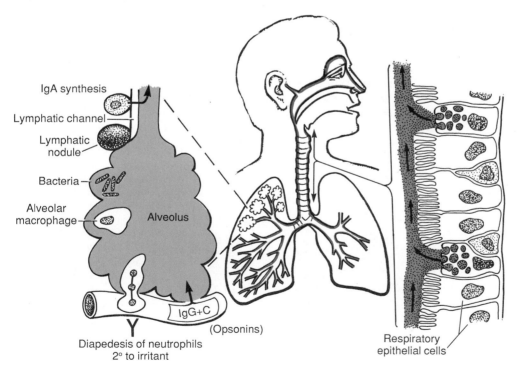

Figure 56.8. The defense mechanisms of the respiratory tract. Aerodynamic factors include the presence of vibrissae in the nasal passage and abrupt changes in the direction of flow of the air column. The epiglottis and cough reflex prevent introduction of particulate matter into the lower airway. The ciliated respiratory epithelium propels the overlying mucus layer (*red*) upward toward the mouth. In the alveoli, macrophages, humoral factors (including immunoglobulins and complement), and neutrophils (when inflammation is present) all assist in preventing or clearing infection.

settle at points of abrupt changes in direction of airflow, such as the posterior nasopharynx. Smaller particles, less than 3 μm in diameter, are likely to elude these barriers and reach the terminal bronchioles and alveoli. The importance of the upper airway structures in defending the lungs is illustrated in patients in whom these structures are bypassed. Endotracheal tubes used in anesthesia and mechanical ventilation provide a conduit from the outside environment to the lower airway; patients with these tubes in place are **markedly** predisposed to pneumonia.

The respiratory epithelium itself has specialized defenses against infection. The tight junctions between cells prevent direct penetration. Epithelial cells from the nose to the terminal bronchioles are covered with cilia that beat coordinately. Overlying them is a covering of mucus containing antimicrobial compounds such as lysozyme, lactoferrin, and secretory IgA antibodies. Each ciliated cell has approximately 200 cilia, which beat at speeds up to 500 times per minute, serving to move the overlying mucus layer upward toward the larynx at a rate as high as 4–6 mm/minute. The cilia and mucus are called the mucociliary escalator. Certain patients with impaired ciliary function have frequent respiratory infections. An example is a condition known as Kartagener's syndrome, in which patients have structurally and functionally altered cilia (these patients also exhibit the dramatic condition called dextrocardia, or right-sided heart). Ciliary function may also be impaired by viral or *Mycoplasma* infections and is at risk of damage by smoking (Fig. 56.9).

The final lung defenses are found in the alveoli—IgA antibodies, complement components, possibly surfactant itself, and most important, the alveolar macrophages. These phagocytic cells function as active scavengers, ingesting and killing invading pathogens. When they cannot contain infection by themselves, they are helped by other phagocytic cells that do not normally reside in the lungs, especially neutrophils. Encapsulated bacteria can effectively evade phagocytosis, while others not only survive but can multiply within phagocytic cells. Thus, tubercle bacilli, *Histoplasma capsulatum* and *Legionella* find a haven within macrophages, resist killing, and multiply in large numbers. If macrophages become activated through nonspecific or specific im-

Figure 56.9. Electron micrograph of nasal epithelium from a healthy child (A) and a child with adenovirus infection (B). The nasal epithelium in **A** is characteristic of the pseudostratified ciliated columnar epithelium lining the large conducting airways. Normal ciliated cells are seen on either side of a mucous cell that is filled and distended with secretory material. **B** shows the altered ultrastructure and loss of ciliated cells that may accompany viral infection.

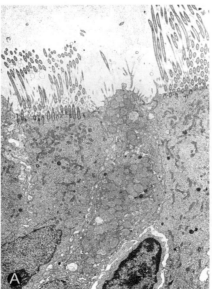
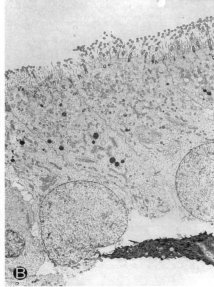

mune mechanisms, they can limit the multiplication of such intracellular invaders.

In the case of viral infection, the cells invaded are often not normally phagocytic and lack obvious means to kill the invader. Histopathological studies of the lungs (or other affected tissues) of patients with viral infection show infiltration by large numbers of lymphocytes and plasma cells, suggesting that viral infection stimulates the recruitment of lymphoid cells rather than neutrophils. These lymphocytes contribute to host defense by antibody production and by attacking infected cells via cytotoxic T-lymphocytes, natural killer cells, and antibody-dependent cell-mediated cytotoxicity.

DAMAGE

The deleterious effects of pneumonia on the host fall into two categories:

- Systemic effects that result from infection any place in the body, including fever, shock (particularly with Gram-negative bacilli), and wasting (for example, in chronic tuberculosis);

- Interference with the ability of the lungs to carry out air exchange; this may result from marked thickening of the membrane that separates erythrocytes from inspired air in the alveoli. In bronchopneumonia, difficulty in gas exchange probably results from regional mismatches in the ventilation and perfusion of the lungs.

There are marked differences in the amount of permanent lung damage in the various types of pneumonia. It is remarkable that, in severe pneumococcal pneumonia, the lung often heals completely without any scar formation (Fig. 13.4). The reason is that although there is an exuberant inflammatory response within the alveoli, there is no necrosis of the underlying lung skeleton that could provoke scar formation and permanent loss of functional lung tissue. In contrast, lung infections caused by Gram-negative rods and anaerobic bacteria frequently result in permanent lung tissue destruction. The fibrotic healing of a necrotizing pneumonia is referred to as **healing by organization**.

The specific manifestations of pneumonia vary widely and fall into several patterns. The commonly used terminology is confusing because it derives, in part, from gross pathology, microscopic histopathology, and chest x-ray. Adding to the confusion is the custom of using terms differently in different settings. Nevertheless, these terms are in widespread use and we will attempt to define them.

- **Lobar pneumonia** refers to a homogeneous involvement of a distinct region of the lung. Most of the involvement is within the alveoli, and the bronchioles and the interstitium are relatively spared. The infection spreads between alveoli until it is contained by the anatomic barriers that separate one segment from another. Thus, an entire segment or even an entire lobe becomes involved (Figs. 13.1, 56.10). The most frequent agents of lobar pneumonia in adults are the pneumococcus, *H. influenzae*, and *Legionella*.

- In **bronchopneumonia**, the pathological process originates in the small airways and extends to nearby areas of the lung. The process is much more patchy than lobar pneumonia, often occurring in more than one area of the lung and not confined by the anatomic barriers

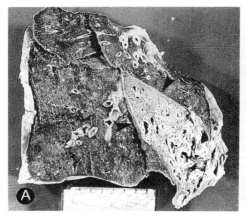
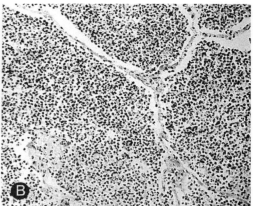

Figure 56.10. Lobar pneumonia. A is an autopsy specimen in which homogeneous consolidation of the right middle lobe is evident (*arrow*). **B** is a microscopic view showing lung alveoli filled with an infiltrate of inflammatory cells including both neutrophils and mononuclear cells. Note the lack of involvement of the interstitium.

(Fig. 56.11). Typical causes of bronchopneumonia include *M. pneumoniae* and respiratory viruses.

- **Interstitial pneumonia** refers to involvement of the lung interstitium. When viral infections such as influenza involve the lung, they tend to produce an interstitial pneumonia (Fig. 56.12). One of the most common causes is cytomegalovirus, which usually infects patients with severe suppression of the immune system. *P. carinii* pneumonia in **AIDS** patients falls in this category.

  - A fourth pattern of involvement is the **lung abscess**. Here, one or more areas of lung parenchyma are replaced by cavities filled with debris generated by the infectious process. Many bacteria and fungi are capable of producing lung abscesses, but currently, a large proportion of cases are caused by anaerobic bacteria.

Infections may spread from the lung beyond the respiratory tract; for example, into the pleural space, creating a condition called **empyema**. More rarely, the process may extend to involve mediastinal structures such as the pericardium. Microorganisms may spread outside of the chest via the lymphatic drainage of the lung, reaching the bloodstream via the thoracic duct. Brain abscess, pyogenic arthritis, and endocarditis are all unusual but well-known complications of bacterial pneumonia.

Some Examples Of Other Pneumonias

ASPIRATION PNEUMONIAS

Case 3—Aspiration Pneumonia Leading To A Lung Abscess

Mr. A., a 46-year-old man with a poorly controlled seizure disorder, was brought to a physician because of cough, fever, and weight loss occurring over a 2-week period. A physical examination revealed an ill-appearing male with a temperature of 101°F and a foul-smelling breath. He had "amphoric" breath sounds (resembling those produced by blowing across the mouth of a bottle), suggestive of a lung cavity. A chest x-ray showed a large cavity in the left midlung with extensive surrounding inflammation (Fig. 56.13). He was admitted to the hospital and treated with high-dose intravenous penicillin. He began to feel better almost immediately and his fever disappeared over the course of a week. After 3 months on oral penicillin, he was judged to be cured.

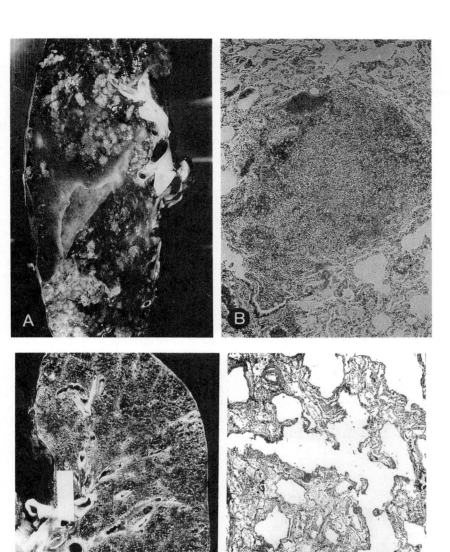

Figure 56.11. Bronchopneumonia. A is an autopsy specimen showing multiple areas of bronchopneumonia. Each area represents inflammation centered around an airway. **B** is a microscopic view showing an area of inflammation in a region distal to a respiratory bronchiole.

Figure 56.12. Interstitial pneumonia. A is an autopsy specimen showing diffuse interstitial involvement of the lung from a patient who died with influenza pneumonia. Characteristic features are the uniform panlobar involvement with no predictable relationship to microscopic air passages and the accentuation of air spaces. **B** is a microscopic view of the same lung revealing involvement of both the interstitium and the alveoli. A uniformly dilated alveolar duct is present lined in areas by hyaline membrane, which would appear eosinophilic and refractile when viewed microscopically. The interstitium is widened and sparsely infiltrated by mononuclear cells.

Lung abscesses such as those of Mr. A. (Case 3) are usually a consequence of gross aspiration of oropharyngeal or gastric contents. The resulting infection has a number of distinguishing features:

- The clinical course tends to be less acute than that of most other forms of bacterial pneumonia. Mr. A may have been ill for several weeks or even months before seeking medical attention.

- The typical lung abscess represents a polymicrobial infection with multiple species of bacteria. The bacteria most commonly involved are anaerobes and microaerophilic organisms from the normal flora of the mouth. Lung abscesses can also result from infection with other organisms that can also destroy lung tissue, including *S. aureus*, *K. pneumoniae*, mycobacteria, and others.

Although the definitive diagnosis is usually made on the basis of the chest x-ray, there may be clues that may lead the astute physician to

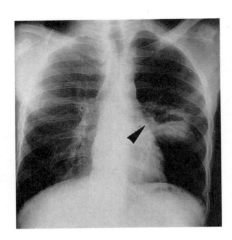

Figure 56.13.   Lung abscess. X-ray showing a cavitary lesion (*arrow*) with surrounding infiltrate.

suspect a lung abscess. Cough, malaise, and fever of several weeks' duration, sometimes accompanied by unexplained weight loss, should make the physician think of subacute processes in the chest, both infectious and noninfectious. Risk factors, if present, are an important clue pointing toward lung abscess. Finally, as in the case of Mr. A., the patient's breath and sputum may have a putrid odor that is highly suggestive of anaerobic infection. In some cases, this odor is so strong that the diagnosis can be suspected as soon as the physician enters the patient's room.

Lung abscesses typically occur following the aspiration of a larger quantity of oropharyngeal contents than can be disposed by the normal defense mechanisms of the lung. Thus, the disease occurs most often in individuals who are prone to aspirate. The most important risk factor is alteration of consciousness for any reason, including anesthesia, sedation, intoxication, drug overdose, injuries, and seizures. Lung abscess may also be caused by fragments of teeth aspirated during dental procedures.

In some cases of severe aspiration, gastric contents may enter the lungs. Probably because of their low pH and proteolytic enzymes, gastric contents induce an intense chemical pneumonitis that is not, in itself, an infection; but secondary infection of the injured lung may occur.

If not treated promptly, lung abscess may spread to involve the pleural space, resulting in empyema. An unusual distant complication of lung abscess is brain abscess, resulting from spread of the infection via the bloodstream. It is notable that infections at distant sites other than the brain are extremely infrequent as a complication of lung abscesses.

PNEUMONIAS IN IMMUNE COMPROMISED PATIENTS

Pneumonia is a common occurrence in immune compromised individuals, including those who undergo cancer chemotherapy, those with AIDS, and those with congenital immunodeficiencies (Chapters 66 and 67). Most cases are caused by opportunistic pathogens that rarely cause infections in normal individuals. Examples include *P. carinii*, the fungus *Aspergillus fumigatus*, and the virus cytomegalovirus. Many of these infections can be diagnosed only by carrying out invasive procedures such as bronchoscopy or lung biopsy. Some patients, especially those with more severe forms of immunodeficiency, may be infected with more than one pathogen at a time. At the extreme, patients with AIDS are not uncommonly infected simultaneously with *P. carinii*, cytomegalovirus, and others.

PNEUMONIAS RESULTING FROM UNUSUAL EXPOSURES

A number of pneumonias not commonly encountered in day-to-day practice result from agents found in animals or in the environment (Table 56.6). These infections occur when peoples' activities bring them into contact with these organisms. For example, *C. psittaci* is a common cause of disease in birds, and **psittacosis** or **parrot fever** may be acquired by inhalation (Chapter 26). This illness is unlikely to be diagnosed correctly unless the physician obtains the history of contact with birds.

Another example is **Q fever**, caused by the rickettsia *Coxiella burnetii* and usually acquired from sheep, goats, and cattle. The organism is stable in the environment, and infection can occur after exposure to contaminated material from infected animals. Here too, the diagnosis is difficult unless the physician elicits the history of exposure to animals or their environment. Several fungal infections also affect the lungs (Chapter 46), e.g., **histoplasmosis**, especially in the Mississippi and Ohio river valleys, particularly where the soil has been enriched by bird droppings; **coccidioidomycosis** in the deserts of the southwestern U.S.; and **cryptococcosis**, in areas frequented by pigeons. The latter is frequently but not exclusively found in individuals who are immunocompromised.

DIAGNOSIS

There is considerable overlap in the clinical manifestations of pneumonia but the astute physician may be able to use some refined clinical and epidemiological indicators to arrive at a specific diagnosis. For instance, pneumococcal pneumonia may occur at any age, but has a predilection for the very young and the elderly. It usually has a rapid onset and an acute course. *H. influenzae* is suspected in children less than 4 years old and in adults with chronic lung disease. Lobar involvement is less common with staphylococci than with pneumococci, and progression is even more rapid. Patients with staphylococcal pneumonia are more likely to belong to several risk groups, such as debilitated nursing home residents, individuals who have recently had influenza, intravenous drug users, or children under 1 year of age. Patients with cystic fibrosis may also suffer from staphylococcal pneumonia, although in these cases, pneumonia is most frequently caused by *Pseudomonas aeruginosa*. Pneumonia caused by *K. pneumoniae* occurs in hospital or nursing home residents, but is also seen in the community, usually in debilitated individuals. Because *K. pneumonia* is also a necrotizing process, the sputum is often bloody, resembling currant jelly.

A markedly elevated neutrophil count is generally indicative of bacterial infection, especially when accompanied by an increased proportion of immature cells. The examination of sputum is often quite revealing. For example, thick yellow or greenish sputum is suggestive of bacterial infection. The presence of squamous epithelial cells in large numbers indicates contamination by oropharyngeal contents, and a culture of such a specimen may yield misleading information. Large numbers of neutrophils indicate bacterial infection—although their absence does not rule it out, especially if the patient is neutropenic. Finding a predominant organism in the Gram stain may point toward the etiological agent. Thus, lancet-shaped Gram-positive diplococci suggest pneumococci, large round Gram-positive cocci in clusters, staphylococci, small pleomorphic Gram-negative rods, *H. influenzae*, and larger and thicker Gram-negative rods, enterics such as *K. pneumoniae*. Unfortunately, the microscopic examination of sputum has limitations—some patients cannot produce sputum, and the agents of Legionnaires' disease and *Mycoplasma* pneumonia are not visible by routine microscopy.

Sputum culture has other limitations. First, mycobacteria, *Mycoplasma*, and viruses require specialized culture methods. Second, many of the bacteria that frequently cause pneumonia are also common colonizers of the upper airway, so that culturing these organisms is not proof that they are causing illness. This particular problem may be circumvented, although with difficulty, by bypassing the contaminated upper airways and obtaining the specimen directly from the site of infection in the lower airways. This can be done in several ways. One is transtracheal aspiration, a procedure in which a large-bore needle is inserted through the cricoid membrane of the trachea and is used to aspirate secretions. This technique is not widely used because of its potential complications. A second method, used only occasionally, is transthoracic needle aspiration, usually under fluoroscopic or computed tomographic guidance. The most widely employed method for obtaining a specimen from the lower airways is by bronchoscopy, or passage of an endoscope into the bronchial tree. This allows visualization of the airway as well as aspiration of material for specimens. In actual practice, bronchoscopy is usually reserved for immunocompromised patients and those whose illness is especially severe.

TREATMENT

The importance of making a specific etiological diagnosis in pneumonia is that treatment differs markedly depending on the causative agent. For example, penicillin is highly effective for pneumococcal pneumonia but would be ineffective in most cases of *Mycoplasma*, staphylococcal, or *Haemophilus* pneumonia. It would certainly not be effective for tuberculosis or histoplasmosis.

The tremendous diversity of potential etiologies makes it impractical to discuss the coverage for all possible agents. What should be remembered is that careful consideration of clinical and epidemiological factors often allows the physician to institute a rational and effective plan while efforts are under way to establish a specific microbiological diagnosis.

SUGGESTED READING

Brain JD, Proctor DF, Reid LM, eds. Respiratory defense mechanisms. New York and Basel: Marcel Dekker, Inc., 1977.

Denny FW, Clyde WA, Jr. Acute lower respiratory infections in non-hospitalized children. J Pediatr 1986:108:635.

Dick EC, Jennings LC, Mink KA, Wartgow CD, Inhorn SL. Aerosol transmission of rhinovirus colds. J Infect Dis 1987;156:442–448.

Green GM. In defense of the lung. Am Rev Respir Dis 1970;102s:691–705.

Huxley EJ, Viroslav J, Gray WR, Pierce AK. Pharyngeal aspiration in normal adults and patients with depressed consciousness. Am J Med 1978;64: 564–568.

Pennington JE, ed. Respiratory infections: diagnosis and management. New York: Raven Press, 1983.

Sande MA, Hudson LD, Root RK, eds. Respiratory infections. New York, Edinburgh, London, Melbourne: Churchill Livingstone, 1986.

Digestive System

57

Donald M. Thea and Gerald T. Keusch

The digestive system is a microbiologist's paradise. In health or disease, it is a microbial garden of unsurpassed variety and complexity. It varies in degrees of colonization from the "buggiest" parts of the body, at both ends, to the nearly sterile environment of the small intestine and accessory glands (Fig. 57.1). The pathway through the alimentary tract is studded with different ecosystems occupied by site-specific microbial populations. The normal stomach is an effective sterilization chamber that limits the entry of microorganisms to the small bowel and beyond, thus providing nonspecific protection against many enteric pathogens.

A community of perhaps 400 distinct species of bacteria, fungi, and protozoa form the resident flora of the normal gastrointestinal (GI) tract. Bacteria in the colon are present at approximately one-tenth of their theoretical density limit ($\geq 10^{12}$/g) and, amazingly, produce no intestinal dysfunction. On the contrary, they form a symbiotic relationship with the host (Chapter 2). This is achieved with remarkable stability and constancy of the microbial population. While we furnish it with room and board, it provides a number of essential services for us. Among these are accessory digestive functions such as converting unabsorbable carbohydrates to absorbable organic acids, supplying essential vitamin K, and aiding in the reabsorption and conservation of estrogens and androgens excreted in the bile. The mere presence of the normal organisms helps us resist colonization by invading pathogens.

The frequency of infections of the digestive system varies from the most prevalent human infectious disease, dental caries, to fairly common diarrheas and food poisoning, to unusual opportunistic infections of immune compromised patients. Worldwide, diarrheal diseases are a far greater cause of morbidity and mortality than are the more familiar diseases of the industrialized nations (heart disease, cancer, and strokes). Unfortunately, infants and small children are disproportionately affected, especially in the parts of the world that have poor sanitation and nutrition. Despite a significant decline in the mortality associated with diarrheal disease in the U.S., it remains among the most common complaint of people seen in general medical practice. Along with middle ear infections, it is the bane of day care centers and is messier.

Infections of this system range in severity from asymptomatic or silent infections (e.g., polio) through mild diarrhea (e.g., most rotavirus infections) to life-threatening loss of fluid and electrolytes (e.g., cholera) or severe mucosal ulceration complicated by intestinal perforation (e.g., bacillary dysentery). Likewise, the nature and clinical manifestations of these infections are variable. This is not surprising when one

Figure 57.1. The GI tract and typical numbers of bacteria at the main sites.

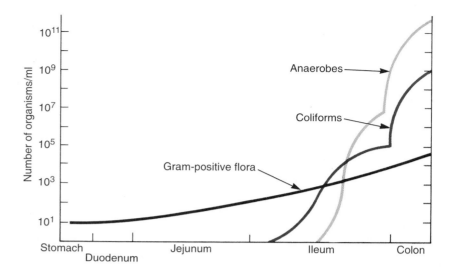

considers the striking local differentiation along the alimentary tract and in the associated hepatobiliary tree and pancreas (Fig. 57.2).

ENTRY

Each portion of the alimentary tract has special anatomic, physiological, and biochemical barriers to infection (Fig. 57.2). The most general impediment to infective agents is an unbroken mucosal epithelium covering all parts of this system. Its importance is illustrated when people receive ionizing radiation or cytotoxic cancer chemotherapy, which interferes with the normal replacement of sloughed epithelial cells. Some of the earliest manifestations of damage are nausea, vomiting, and mucositis, superficial ulcerations of the mucosa of the entire GI tract. Members of the normal flora can now reach deep tissues and may even disseminate through the bloodstream to other organs.

Some defense mechanisms, such as **mucus formation** and **gut motility**, hinder the adherence of microorganisms to the epithelial wall. In the intestine, the mucus layer functions as a mechanical obstacle to protect the epithelium; it also coats bacteria, which makes it easier to pass them along by peristalsis. **Glycocalyx**, the glycoprotein and polysaccharide layer that covers the surface of cells is many "bacterial body lengths" in depth and has "decoy" binding sites that entrap certain invading organisms. **Bile** plays an important role in selecting which bacteria and viruses are able to colonize the intestines. As expected, both organisms of the normal flora and common intestinal pathogens are resistant to the detergent action of bile salts. Most enteric viruses, polio or hepatitis A for example, lack a lipid-containing envelope that could make them sensitive to bile. Certain bacteria, e.g., the typhoid bacilli, are so highly bile resistant that they can even grow in the gallbladder.

A number of cellular and soluble factors have less well-understood defensive functions. For instance, there is evidence that secretory IgA immunoglobulins and the protein lactoferrin in mother's milk help prevent colonization of the infant by certain bacteria. While it is likely that IgA has a similar function in adults, it has been difficult to prove its role as a host defense mechanism. The intestinal tract is also the final stopping point for white blood cells, especially neutrophils. It is not known if exit of these cells into the lumen of the gut plays a role in controlling pathogens or in maintaining the balance with the normal flora.

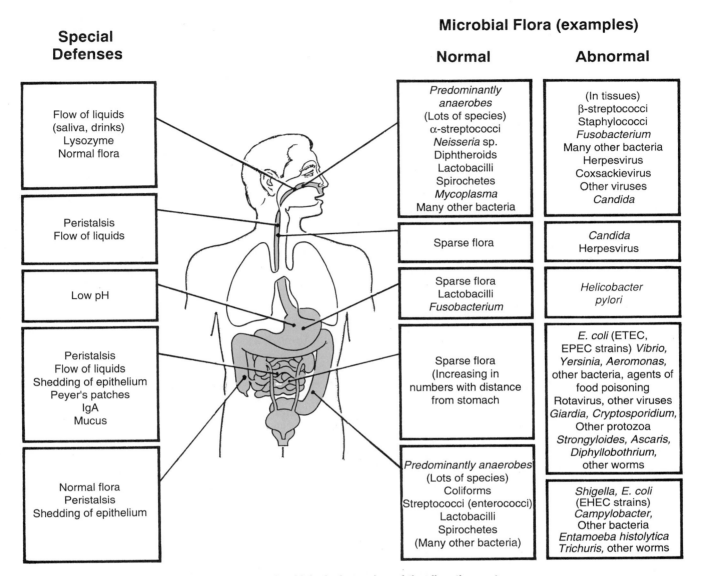

Figure 57.2.   A microbiological overview of the digestive system.

Could this be a reason why the gut is so often the source of systemic infections in granulocytopenic patients?

ESTABLISHMENT OF INFECTIOUS DISEASE IN THE DIGESTIVE SYSTEM

Under what conditions do infectious agents overcome these defense mechanisms? Several circumstances predispose to the establishment of infectious disease in the alimentary tract either by pathogens or by members of the normal flora:

● **Anatomic alterations.** Obstructions to the flow of liquids remove one of the most powerful defensive mechanisms of this system. Thus, stones in the gallbladder that impede the flow of bile predispose the biliary tree to infections. The presence of large diverticuli (intestinal outpunches) or the surgical formation of intestinal "blind loops" create sites with reduced flow of intestinal contents, leading to bacterial overgrowth and metabolic derangements.

- **Changes in stomach acidity.** Alteration of the acid barrier of the stomach by disease, surgery, or drugs increases the survival of pathogens across this organ and may lead to bacterial infection downstream.

- **Alterations in the normal flora.** In the regions of the digestive tract that are most heavily colonized—the mouth and the colon—changes in the density or composition of the flora may permit pathogens to become established. The most frequent cause of such an alteration is the use of broad-spectrum antibiotics.

- **Encounter with specific pathogenic agents.** Certain bacteria, viruses, protozoa, and helminths cause disease even in the absence of predisposing factors. Note that at each site, pathogens must be able to resist the specific local defenses. In general, they all resist stomach acid and have certain virulence factors (e.g., pili for adhesion, toxin production). However, microorganisms face different survival problems in the mouth, the small intestine, or the colon and possess different specific attributes.

DAMAGE

The signs and symptoms of infections related to the digestive system are produced in several general ways:

- **Pharmacological action.** Some bacteria produce toxins that alter normal intestinal function without causing lasting damage to their target cells. Typical examples are the enterotoxins made by *Vibrio cholerae* or by some strains of *Escherichia coli*, which provoke copious watery diarrhea. Because the small bowel is primarily responsible for absorbing most of the 9–10 liters of fluid that pass through the gut each day, small reductions in its absorptive capacity result in arrival of large amounts of fluid to the colon, overwhelming its relatively modest absorptive capacity. "Overflow" diarrhea results; it may rapidly lead to profound dehydration and electrolyte loss, as seen in cholera.

- **Local inflammation.** Any site of the alimentary tract may become inflamed as the consequence of microbial invasion. In many instances, the invasion is limited to the epithelial layer but may spread to contiguous tissue and beyond. The mouth is often affected, usually in the gums, by infections caused by bacteria that normally reside in the gingival pocket (periodontitis). In the intestine, infections causing inflammation can result in dysentery.

- **Deep tissue invasion.** This takes place because certain organisms have the ability to spread to adjacent tissues and to enter the blood or lymph. Examples are the worm *Strongyloides* or the protozoan *Entamoeba*, which are capable of burrowing through the intestinal wall, or *Salmonella*, which penetrate the lymphatics and may eventually reach the bloodstream. Interestingly, *Strongyloides* itself is often colonized by gut bacteria; as a result, invasion with this worm can result in polymicrobial septicemia.

- **Perforation.** When the mucosal epithelia are perforated, the normal flora spills into sterile areas and invades deep tissue, often with serious consequences. Thus, rupture of an inflamed appendix may lead to peritonitis, and to traumatic perforation of the esophagus to mediastinitis.

The variety of infectious diseases of this system is daunting. Your task will be simplified by keeping in mind the pathophysiological steps involved in establishing an infectious disease. Because they differ greatly in their clinical manifestations, we divide this chapter into infectious diseases of the principal sites of infection—the mouth, stomach, biliary tree, and intestines.

MOUTH

Virtually all of the pathogens of the alimentary tract enter through the mouth. It is the portal that allows microorganisms to enter the body aboard food, fluids, or fingers. What are the specific defenses of the mouth?

- The nonpathogenic resident flora, including bacteria (Table 57.1), fungi (e.g., *Candida*), and protozoa (e.g., the ameba *Entamoeba gingivalis*); these organisms resist the establishment of newcomers both by the occupancy of suitable sites and by the production of acids and other metabolic inhibitors.

- The mechanical action of saliva and the tongue; we produce more than a liter of saliva per day that, with assistance from the tongue, mechanically dislodges and flushes microorganisms from mucosal surfaces. Should salivary flow be reduced, as with dehydration or during fasting, the bacterial content of saliva increases markedly.

- Antimicrobial constituents of saliva, notably lysozyme and secreted antibodies; as mentioned above, secretory IgA selectively inhibits the adherence of certain bacteria to mucosal cells. Lysozyme is effective mainly against Gram-positive bacteria.

Several properties allow bacteria to evade these host defenses. Some are able to stick to teeth or mucosal surfaces. Attachment to teeth is not direct, but rather to a coating of sticky macromolecules, mainly proteins, the **dental pellicle**. The bacteria themselves produce polysaccharides that help in adherence. For example, *Streptococcus mutans* transforms sucrose into polysaccharides (dextrans and levans), which are particularly sticky. They are layered on the pellicle to form a matrix that allows further adherence of other organisms. The result is

Table 57.1. Composition of the Intestinal Flora of Adult Humans

Bacterial Species	Bacterial Concentration (ml or g)			
	Stomach	Jejunum	Ileum	Colon
Total viable count	$0-10^3$	$0-10^5$	10^2-10^7	$10^{10}-10^{12}$
Aerobes or facultative anaerobes				
Enterobacteria	$0-10^2$	$0-10^3$	10^2-10^7	10^4-10^{10}
Streptococci	$0-10^2$	$0-10^4$	10^2-10^6	10^5-10^{10}
Staphylococci	$0-10^2$	$0-10^3$	10^2-10^5	10^4-10^9
Lactobacilli	$0-10^3$	$0-10^4$	10^2-10^5	10^4-10^{10}
Fungi	$0-10^2$	$0-10^2$	10^2-10^4	10^4-10^6
Anaerobes				
Bacteroides	Rare	$0-10^3$	10^3-10^7	$10^{10}-10^{12}$
Bifidobacteria	Rare	$0-10^4$	10^3-10^9	10^8-10^{12}
Streptococci	Rare	$0-10^3$	10^2-10^6	$10^{10}-10^{12}$
Clostridia	Rare	Rare	10^2-10^6	10^6-10^{11}
Eubacteria	Rare	Rare	Rare	10^9-10^{12}

dental plaque, one of the densest collections of bacteria in the body—and perhaps the first human microbial flora to be seen under a microscope by van Leeuwenhoek in the 17th century. Microbial metabolism in plaque transforms dietary sugar into acids, mainly lactic acid, that are responsible for **dental caries** (cavities). Other bacteria, especially strict anaerobes, reside in the gingival crevices between the tooth and gum, where they evade the washing effects of the saliva and of normal tooth brushing.

The bacteria of the indigenous oral flora are not highly virulent, but when there is a break in the mucosal barrier, such as with advanced **gingivitis (periodontal disease)**, they may invade surrounding healthy tissue. This is also the likely portal of entry of α-hemolytic streptococci that cause subacute bacterial endocarditis in patients with rheumatic heart disease. A synergistic cooperation between several different types of bacteria, both aerobic and strictly anaerobic, leads to a severe and rapidly advancing mixed infection of the soft tissues about the oral cavity. **Ludwig's angina**, a polymicrobial infection of the sublingual and submandibular spaces that arises from a tooth (often the second and third mandibular molars), is a cellulitis—an infection of submucosal or subcutaneous connective tissue—that may, at times, progress rapidly, compromise the airway, and threaten the patient with asphyxiation.

CASE OF THRUSH

*C., a 7-month-old girl, was treated by her pediatrician for a middle ear infection. She was given a 7-day course of a penicillin, amoxicillin, which cleared the infection within 4 days. Antibiotics were continued, but on the 6th day of therapy, the mother noticed that the child was irritable and feeding poorly. During a follow-up visit at the clinic, her pediatrician noted several creamy white, curd-like patches on the tongue and buccal mucosa. When scraped, they were clearly painful and left a raw, bleeding surface. Microscopic examination showed yeast and filamentous elements typical of fungi. This permitted the diagnosis of **thrush**, or **oral candidiasis**. Antibiotics were stopped, a topical antifungal solution was administered, and the patches disappeared within 2 days.*

PATHOBIOLOGY

The white patches adherent to the oral mucosa consisted of **pseudomembranes** made up of the yeast *Candida*, mixed with desquamated epithelial cells, leukocytes, oral bacteria, necrotic tissue, and food debris. *Candida albicans* and related species are yeasts found in the environment that establish themselves in the alimentary tract early in life (Chapter 47). The adult vagina is commonly colonized with these organisms, and they may be acquired by the baby during delivery. Small numbers of *Candida* live harmlessly in the alimentary tract until the balance between indigenous bacterial flora and host defenses is upset. In the case of C., this occurred with the administration of antibiotics, which killed many of the normal oral bacteria and allowed the *Candida* to proliferate.

Candida exploits changes in the normal host flora, breaks in the mucous membrane, decreased number or function of neutrophils, or defects in complement, humoral, or cellular immunity. Predisposing conditions for oral and other forms of candidiasis include endocrine disturbances, malnutrition, malignancy, immunosuppressive drugs or infections, genetic abnormalities of the immune system, and HIV infection. Normal individuals are also frequently affected. *Candida* vaginitis is commonly encountered in postpubertal women who are taking broad-spectrum antibiotics, often because of urinary tract infections. The prolonged use of inhaled steroids for asthmatics may also predispose to candidal overgrowth in the mouth. In the more pronounced forms of immunodeficiency, the organism may disseminate through the bloodstream and infect virtually any organ system.

Candida may also invade the esophagus, an organ little prone to infection. Candidal esophagitis is seen in patients with specific T-cell abnormalities, such as chronic mucocutaneous candidiasis or AIDS. The differential diagnosis of esophagitis in immune compromised patients includes infection by herpes simplex type 1 virus (HSV). This is the second most common infection of the esophagus and has clinical manifestations similar to those caused by *Candida*.

DIAGNOSIS

Thrush is characteristic in appearance and the diagnosis can usually be made on inspection. It is confirmed by examination of scraped material under a microscope and detection of characteristic pseudohyphae. Culture is not necessary and often misleading, because *Candida* is a commensal and can be cultured from the mouths of many normal people.

PREVENTION AND TREATMENT

Because candidal colonization of the GI tract is frequent, prevention and treatment consist primarily of correcting predisposing factors and avoiding the unnecessary use of antibiotics. Candidiasis of the mouth is usually superficial and responds to the topical application of antifungal agents such as nystatin. If the infection reaches deeper than the mucosa, it may be necessary to use a systemic antifungal agent, such as intravenous amphotericin B.

STOMACH

Until recently, the stomach has received little attention as a locus of infections of the alimentary tract. It was not considered to be infected often, although it was always appreciated that it plays an important role in protecting the gut further downstream by its secretion of acid. The vast majority of oral or food-borne bacteria, washed with saliva into the stomach, are destroyed under these conditions.

In some individuals, the stomach is indeed sterile, and in most others, the concentration of bacteria is very low, generally less than 10^3 bacteria/ml. Among the bacteria that are found in the stomach, the predominant ones are Gram positives, e.g., *Streptococcus*, *Staphylococcus*, *Lactobacillus*, and *Peptostreptococcus*. In the normal stomach, there are very few enteric Gram-negative rods, *Bacteroides*, or *Clostridium*—organisms typically associated with the lower GI tract.

It is now believed that gastric infections nevertheless occur and much more commonly than was previously thought. A newly identified bacterial species, *Helicobacter pylori* is associated with and may be involved in the production of gastritis and, perhaps, peptic ulcers. It has yet to be determined conclusively whether this is a true pathogen or merely a commensal organism on a previously altered mucosa. However, suggestive evidence is mounting; it has been isolated from the gastric mucosa of 95% of patients with peptic ulcer disease and virtually all of those with active chronic gastritis. This organism is rarely found in healthy people. A volunteer inoculated with *H. pylori* developed gastritis, which cleared after being given antibiotics. Will gastric ulcers enter the ranks of infectious diseases?

Some bacteria, including pathogens, if introduced into the stomach with food, will survive and enter the small intestine alive. This depends largely on the buffering effects of food, especially in patients who do not produce normal amounts of gastric hydrochloric acid because of disease, partial or total gastrectomy, drug therapy (e.g., H_2-blockers), or antacid consumption. The infective dose of cholera bacilli or salmonellae in human volunteers, for example, was 10 thousand-fold lower when the organisms were administered together with 2 g of sodium bicarbonate.

When gastric acidity is chronically decreased, a condition known as **achlorhydria**, the stomach usually becomes colonized by enteric Gram-negative rods. This could have two important consequences:

1. Increase in the number of enteric bacteria in the small bowel, which contributes to the development of a disease called the bacterial overgrowth syndrome (see below);

2. Regurgitation of the abnormal gastric flora, which becomes a source of nosocomial (hospital-acquired) aspiration pneumonia (Chapter 56).

BILIARY TREE AND THE LIVER

Infections of the gallbladder (**cholecystitis**) are a frequent complication of obstruction to the flow of bile due, for example, to gallstones. The clinical presentation is often sudden and dramatic. The hallmark is pain, which may build to a crescendo and then subside, only to recur soon. This pattern is called **biliary colic**. Nausea and vomiting are usual accompaniments and may be intractable. The majority of cases have shaking chills, high spiking fever, and jaundice caused by obstruction of the duct. These manifestations may become more severe if the obstruction also involves the common bile duct. In these cases, the infection and inflammation may ascend to the intrahepatic bile ducts, a condition known as **ascending cholangitis**.

The ascending spread of a bacterial infection to the liver parenchyma may result in abscess formation. Given the large amount of blood filtered by the liver, seeding may also occur in cases of bacteremia. Among the bacteria that cause liver infections are those derived from the bowel, which are carried to the liver by the portal system. Primary bacterial infections of the liver parenchyma itself are not common, perhaps contravened by the enormous defensive capacity of the Kupffer cells. Bacteria that infect the liver tend to be intracellular pathogens that survive life in macrophages to cause granulomatous infections. Examples are the agents of typhoid fever, Q fever, brucellosis, and tuberculosis. In most instances, the lesions characteristic of these diseases are not found primarily in the liver.

Infectious diseases of the liver will not be discussed in detail here. The most important ones are due to hepatitis viruses (Chapter 41). The liver is also the site of parasitic infections such as amebiasis (Chapter 51), schistosomiasis (Chapter 53), leishmaniasis (Chapter 50), and others. An important, although clinically silent part of the life cycle of the malarial parasites takes place here.

CASE

Ms. F., an obese 48-year-old mother of eight with a vague history of intermittent "stomach problems," awoke with moderate midepigastric pain. Approximately 2 hours before going to bed, she had eaten a large meal of fried chicken and vegetables. The pain soon shifted to her right upper quadrant and was occasionally felt in the area of the right scapula. She vomited several times and then improved but had residual pain for several days with numerous similar but less intense attacks. By the 6th day, she felt sick again and developed jaundice and a shaking chill. In the emergency room, she was in obvious pain and had a temperature of 40° C. Her skin was slightly yellowish. There was marked tenderness to palpation of the right upper quadrant of her abdomen. An 8-cm tubular mass was felt under the margin of the right ribs. Her white blood cell count was elevated (14,000/μl), suggesting a bacterial infection. Her liver function tests were abnormal—in particular, serum bilirubin and alkaline phosphatase were elevated—suggesting biliary obstruction.

Blood was drawn for culturing and antibiotic therapy was begun. An ultrasound examination showed that her gallbladder was markedly distended and contained several stones. Other tests showed that the gallbladder was not emptying properly. The diagnosis of acute cholecystitis was made. Within 36 hours of admission, the pain improved and the fever resolved. The blood cultures grew E. coli. The patient was scheduled for surgery to remove the affected gallbladder and stones.

PATHOBIOLOGY

Both infections of the gallbladder (**cholecystitis**) and of the bile duct (**cholangitis**) are secondary consequences of obstruction. Usually, the process begins not with infection but with obstruction and distention. Under these conditions, bile constituents become concentrated, which may initiate a cycle of inflammation and damage in the gallbladder wall. The disease may not progress, but the process increases the probability that infection may develop. It is common to obtain from patients with these diseases a history of recurrent attacks of biliary colic, resulting from obstruction of the biliary outlet. It is possible that Ms. F.'s vague "stomach problems" of the past were episodes of mild biliary colic caused by transient and/or partial obstructions of the duct by her gallstones. In time, her gallbladder became infected and the character of her illness changed.

Once bacterial infection becomes established, tissue damage may be accelerated by the resulting inflammatory response. Healing is unlikely to occur without relief of the obstruction, spontaneous or surgical, and specific antimicrobial therapy.

A particularly rapid and severe form of gallbladder infection is seen in patients with compromised arterial blood supply to the gallbladder wall, such as diabetics or the elderly. If the infecting organisms invade the gallbladder wall, they may produce a condition called **emphysematous cholecystitis**. It is distinguished by rapid clinical onset, extensive gangrene, presence of gas in the gallbladder wall (when caused by gas-forming species, such as *Clostridia*), and high mortality. Surgical removal of the gallbladder (cholecystectomy) is indicated because of the frequent occurrence of gangrene, high risk of perforation and extensive peritonitis.

The typical clinical presentation of cholangitis is similar to cholecystitis, as in Ms. F.'s case, but is more consistently accompanied by fever, chills, jaundice, and pain with ascent into the liver. The most common obstructing causes are stones, strictures, and neoplasms. Considerable pressure within the duct seems to be a prerequisite for infection. Experiments in dogs have shown that the normal common ductal pressure of 70 mm H_2O must be raised to 250 mm H_2O before *E. coli* injected into the bloodstream produces infection in the gallbladder. It is not known why the resulting distention facilitates bacterial invasion of the duct wall, but microscopic tears or ischemic damage are obvious possibilities.

Organisms that infect the gallbladder and bile duct are usually derived from the GI tract, *E. coli* being the single most frequent one. Approximately 40% of these infections are caused by a mixed facultative and strictly anaerobic flora. They ascend from the duodenum, which normally contains few microorganisms but becomes colonized where there is bacterial overgrowth in the stomach (achlorhydria) or the small bowel (blind loops, diverticula, obstruction).

Typhoid bacilli have an unusual predilection for the gallbladder (Chapter 18). These organisms may persist for long times within or on the surface of the gallstones. They produce little or no inflammation, and the person may not be aware of being a carrier. All carriers, cognizant or not, shed bacteria into the environment and may infect other people.

DIAGNOSIS

When the clinical presentation of cholecystitis is typical, as in the example of Ms. F., a tentative diagnosis of cholecystitis can be made on clinical grounds. Unfortunately, this disease is especially prone to misdiagnosis, because it often presents itself in a less typical form. Probably the most helpful test is an imaging technique that can reliably visualize obstruction or distention in the biliary system, such as ultrasound or radionuclide scanning. Direct culture of the infected bile is rarely performed, because of the difficulty in obtaining a specimen. Instead, microbiological diagnosis depends on growing bacteria from the blood.

PREVENTION AND TREATMENT

Treatment should be individualized for each patient, but antibiotics should be started fast, without waiting for the blood culture results, if symptoms of the disease are severe. The drugs should be chosen for their activity against the usual intestinal facultative anaerobic flora and strict anaerobes, and should, of course, be started after blood cultures have been drawn. In any case, to effect a definitive cure, the underlying obstruction must be relieved. This may occur spontaneously or require surgery. The timing and need for surgery to remove stones and an inflamed gallbladder is controversial. There are sound arguments for both early and late cholecystectomy, although there is no disagreement on the need for surgery when there is threat of impending perforation or of emphysematous cholecystitis.

SMALL AND LARGE INTESTINE

We will now discuss diseases that illustrate the diversity of infectious problems of the gut, based on host factors and on virulence attributes of the organisms. Examples of other classic infections of the intestines caused by bacteria are discussed in Chapters 17 and 18, and by animal parasites in Chapters 51 and 52.

BACTERIAL OVERGROWTH SYNDROME

The anatomy and physiology of our alimentary tract ensure that we have first crack at the food we eat (Fig. 57.3). Thanks to the sterilizing power of the stomach and the defenses of the small intestine, we absorb most of our nutrients without microbial competition. The human intestinal contents, rich in unabsorbed sugars, fats, and other nutrients, do not normally come in contact with large numbers of bacteria.

The presence of a large microbial biomass in the absorptive small intestine leads to competition for certain vitamins and malabsorption of fats. It produces a disease known as **bacterial overgrowth syndrome**. The study of bacterial overgrowth in the small intestine has helped us understand the normal relationship of the gut flora to gut function.

CASE

Two years before the current illness, Mr. O., a 65-year-old man, had an operation for removal of a tumor that obstructed his stomach outlet. The surgeon removed part of the stomach and duodenum and connected the remainder of the stomach with the jejunum (gastrojejunostomy), bypassing the unresected duodenum. He subsequently developed chronic diarrhea and his weight dropped from 63 kg to 44 kg. His nutritional history indicated that his food intake was adequate and could not account for the weight loss. The diarrhea had recently become bulky, smelly, and greasy. He felt fatigued, was short of breath on exertion, and had numbness and tingling in the hands and feet. On examination, he was extremely thin and appeared ill with a pale complexion.

Laboratory tests showed a severe anemia with large red blood cells ("megaloblastic" anemia) and leukopenia with many hypersegmented neutrophils. The serum level of vitamin A and its precursor, carotene, was depressed and that of vitamin B_{12} was undetectable, although intrinsic factor was present in his gastric juice. Several tests of GI function revealed malabsorption. He was diagnosed as suffering from bacterial overgrowth syndrome. (Although not done in this case, intubation of the small bowel might well have revealed about 10^9 B. fragilis and 10^6 E. coli per ml of bowel content). Fat-soluble vitamins and vitamin B_{12} were replaced and Mr. O. was placed on a course of tetracycline. The diarrhea resolved and the tests of absorptive function improved. He continued on antibiotic therapy and, over the next 2 months, he returned to his normal weight and felt entirely well.

PATHOBIOLOGY

Prior surgery left this patient with a loop of small bowel removed from the main flow of intestinal contents. The result of this "blind loop" was stasis of the contents without the normal and continuous flushing action of the intestinal segment. The resulting bacterial proliferation led to impaired absorption of fats and fat-soluble vitamins (see below).

Bacterial overgrowth in the small intestine may also arise from a number of abnormalities that produce blind loops, other than surgical procedures or diverticuli. Motor abnormalities may severely depress peristalsis (diabetic neuropathy, scleroderma, gastric atony), or gastric achlorhydria may permit large bacterial inocula to reach the proximal small bowel. Under these conditions, bacterial overgrowth occurs very rapidly, another testimony to the sterilizing power of the stomach and the small intestine. As stagnation progresses, the small number of bacteria normally present increases dramatically. Careful anaerobic sampling of the small intestine in these conditions has revealed counts as

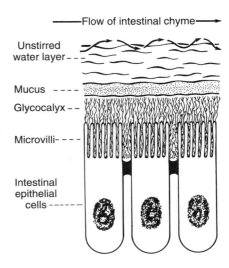

Figure 57.3. Schematic representation of host barriers faced by intestinal pathogens.

high as 10^{10} bacteria/ml, levels comparable to those in the colon. By far, the most numerous bacteria and those most likely to be responsible for the physiological derangement are strict anaerobes, mainly *Bacteroides*.

Bacterial overgrowth in the small intestine may have the following effects:

● Increased fecal fat, **steatorrhea**; this is due primarily to malabsorption of fat as consequence of depletion of the bile acid pool. Why this depletion? Because bile acids such as cholic acid are normally conjugated with glycine or taurine in the liver, secreted in the bile, and reabsorbed in the terminal ileum in the conjugated form. Bacterial overgrowth can deconjugate these compounds, making them unavailable for reabsorption, which leads to a deficiency of bile salts needed to form fat micelles for absorption in the proximal gut.

● **Deficiency of vitamin B_{12}**; normally, vitamin B_{12} (or cobalamin) is complexed with intrinsic factor from the stomach and absorbed in this form from the terminal ileum. With bacterial overgrowth, it is utilized by bacteria, making it unavailable for uptake by the host. With prolonged B_{12} malabsorption (longer than 1 year), endogenous stores are depleted, and cellular systems with a high rate of turnover and DNA synthesis (bone marrow, central nervous system, gut epithelium) are severely impaired. The result are megaloblastic anemia and structural gut abnormalities. The epithelial villi are shortened due to decreased turnover and atrophy of enterocytes, decreasing the absorptive area. Thus, bacterial overgrowth sets off a cascade of malabsorptive events. Vitamin B_{12} is also required for myelin synthesis, and its deficiency results in degeneration of the spinal cord, producing a classical neurological syndrome.

● **Diarrhea**, the excess of fecal water and electrolyte excretion; this is not seen in all patients with this condition, but usually results from the degradation of unabsorbed carbohydrates in the colon by the normal flora, resulting in an increased concentration of osmotically active solutes. Diarrhea then results from this osmotic load because water will move across the mucosa into the lumen. Deconjugated bile salts can also affect the absorptive function of the colon, and unabsorbed bile salts in the colon can cause clinically manifest diarrhea.

● **Malabsorption of vitamins A and D**; malabsorption of fat-soluble vitamins, particularly A and D, causes severe visual disturbance (night blindness) and softening of the bones (osteomalacia). Interestingly, vitamin K deficiency does not usually occur. The reduced absorption of this other fat-soluble vitamin is offset by the markedly increased vitamin production by the plentiful bacteria—ordinarily, our main source of vitamin K.

DIAGNOSIS AND TREATMENT

This condition is usually diagnosed when malabsorption and nutritional deficiencies are present together with predisposing anatomic or physiological conditions, such as intestinal blind loops. Treatment requires correction of the surgical or medical predisposing condition in conjunction with careful nutritional repletion and, most importantly, broad-spectrum antibiotic therapy. This condition has a tendency to relapse and repeated courses of therapy may be necessary.

DIARRHEA AND DYSENTERY

Diarrhea is a final common pathway of intestinal responses to many inciting agents. It is caused by some infections but is also seen in a large number of noninfectious conditions. Diarrhea is an increase in the daily amount of stool water, although a patient usually refers as much to the frequency of movement as to their consistency. It may be caused by different mechanisms and manifest itself in different forms. Dysentery is a more circumscribed term used for inflammatory disorders, mainly of the colon, ordinarily not accompanied by large increases in stool volume. Diarrhea can be considered an adaptive mechanism, developed by the body to rid itself of noxious material (or by the microorganisms to ensure their transfer from one host to another!) There is an obvious if teleological analogy with vomiting, which is used to rid the stomach of noxious material. In the "old days," both events were elicited enthusiastically in households by giving children either tincture of ipecac or castor oil for any of a number of reasons. It used to be a cruel part of growing up, and still is in much of the world.

The cases presented here illustrate distinctive ecological features of the pathogens or of their interactions with the host.

CASE 1—*Vibrio cholerae*

Approximately 2 days after returning from Mardi Gras in New Orleans, Mr. V., a 24-year-old student who was the runner up in the raw oyster eating contest, abruptly started to vomit. Within hours, he was restricted to the bathroom with voluminous and nearly continuous but painless watery diarrhea. Soon thereafter, he became lightheaded, with a rapid pulse and a feeling of marked lethargy and weakness. Later that evening, his roommate brought him to the emergency room, where he was found to be afebrile but profoundly dehydrated, with severely altered levels of serum electrolytes.

In the hospital, it was noticed that his stool was not very fecal and had the appearance of "rice water" (so called because of the numerous flecks of mucus in a slightly yellow fluid), without blood or bile. Microscopic examination revealed no white blood cells. Curiously, the stool had a sweetish smell, very different from that of normal. Intravenous rehydration was administered initially and then switched to an oral rehydration solution. The physician requested that the laboratory look for V. cholerae and stool was cultured on a special medium called TCBS agar. A stool culture became positive for V. cholerae on the second hospital day and he was diagnosed as suffering from cholera. Stool volume had diminished somewhat by this time but because it was still brisk, he was given tetracycline for 2 days. By the end of the fourth hospital day, he was discharged with all symptoms and abnormalities resolved.

CASE 2—*Shigella sonnei*

*T., a 4-year-old boy attending a community day care center, became irritable and developed watery diarrhea. His mother noted a low-grade fever and put him to bed. About 24 hours later he was worse, with a fever of 40.0°C and complained of abdominal pain, mostly in the left lower quadrant. His diarrhea decreased in volume but increased in frequency and was obviously painful. Because his stool contained blood, mucus, and pus, his mother brought T. to the pediatrician, who noted that the child was mildly dehydrated and had many white blood cells when his stool was examined microscopically. T. was the fifth child with similar complaints from the same day care center seen by the pediatrician in the past 2 days. S. sonnei was cultured from the stool of each of them, permitting the diagnosis of an outbreak of **bacillary dysentery**.*

Inasmuch as these isolates were all resistant to ampicillin, T. was given tri-methoprim and sulfamethoxazole for 5 days. All symptoms resolved 4 days later.

CASE 3—ROTAVIRUS

*M.A., a 7-month-old girl, was recently switched from breast to bottle feeding. Usually a satisfied and happy child, she became irritable, began to vomit, and had a low-grade fever. Mild upper respiratory symptoms also developed, with cough, nasal discharge, and pharyngitis. The GI symptoms persisted for 2 days and she was brought to the pediatrician who made the diagnosis of **rotavirus gastroenteritis** by detecting viral antigen in the stool with an ELISA (enzyme-linked immunosorbent assay). Oral rehydration solution was given at home and M.A. made an uneventful recovery by the sixth day.*

CASE 4—*Yersinia enterocolitica*

Mr. C. took his family to Southern Sweden to visit his parents who were dairy farmers outside Malmö. S., 5 years old, and I., 12 years old, enjoyed helping care for the numerous domestic animals on the farm. They were also fond of eating home-cured meat and drinking fresh raw milk. Between 7 and 10 days of arrival, all members of the C. family became ill. S. developed watery, mucoid diarrhea with occasional flecks of blood, low-grade fever, and diffuse abdominal pain, all of which resolved spontaneously after 4 days. I.'s episode began similarly, but worsened after 3 days, when her pain localized to the right lower quadrant, associated with high fever and leukocytosis. At the hospital where she was brought, I.'s signs and symptoms suggested appendicitis. On surgery, her appendix was found to be normal; however, the terminal ileum was inflamed, with many enlarged mesenteric lymph nodes.

Stool cultures done on admission were specially cultured at 25°C and grew Y. enterocolitica. By that time, I. had made a nearly complete recovery. Mr. C., like S., developed an acute mucoid diarrhea, abdominal pain, and fever that remitted by the fourth day. Three weeks later, he developed painful swelling of several joints and a painful raised rash over his shins (erythema nodosum). In spite of lack of symptoms of ongoing gastrointestinal disease, his stool tested positive for Yersinia and he was treated with trimethoprim-sulfamethoxazole. The rash and arthritis slowly resolved but returned several months later and then spontaneously remitted for good.

As these cases illustrate, the gut reacts to infecting organisms in a number of ways: (*a*) diarrhea, characterized by increased fluid and electrolyte loss in the stool, and (*b*) dysentery, a bloody and often purulent enteric discharge accompanied by pain, fever, and cramps. These diseases are also distinguished by their anatomic site. Diarrhea is usually a disease of the small bowel and dysentery of the large bowel. They are generally caused by different agents, but some (e.g., *Shigella*) may cause either diarrhea or dysentery. The same organism may cause distinct clinical manifestations in people that differ only in age (e.g., *Y. enterocolitica*).

ENCOUNTER

The list of intestinal pathogens keeps expanding as well-known organisms appear in unexpected frequency and in new settings, and as new ones are recognized (Figs. 57.4 and 57.5, Table 57.2). In previous chapters, we discussed some of the more common agents of intestinal infections (Chapter 17, Secretory Diarrhea; Chapter 18, Invasive enteric bacteria; Chapter 51, amebiasis; Chapter 49; and Chapter 52, Intestinal worms; food poisoning is discussed in Chapter 72). To this list

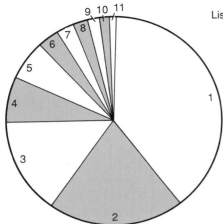

List by frequency in travelers to USA:

1. *E. coli* (ETEC strains)
2. *Shigella*
3. Rotavirus
4. *Yersinia, Vibrio*
5. Norwalk virus
6. *Salmonella*
7. *Campylobacter*
8. *Cryptosporidium*
9. *Giardia*
10. *E. histolytica*
11. *Strongyloides*

Figure 57.4. Distribution of agents of diarrhea in travelers to the U.S.

List by frequency in residents in USA:

1. Rotavirus
2. Norwalk virus
3. *E. coli* (ETEC strains)
4. *Giardia*
5. *Campylobacter*
6. *Yersinia, Vibrio*
7. *Cryptosporidium*
8. *Salmonella*
9. *Shigella*
10. *E. histolytica*
11. *Strongyloides*

Figure 57.5. Distribution of agents of diarrhea in residents of the U.S.

Table 57.2. Some Etiological Agents of Diarrhea

Organism	Source
Escherichia coli	Human feces-contaminated foods
Salmonella	Contaminated foods, especially poultry products
Shigella	Fecal-oral
Campylobacter	Farm animals, contaminated food (e.g., raw eggs)
Yersinia enterocolitica	Animal products
Vibrio cholerae	Water and shellfish
Vibrio parahemolyticus	Seafood (e.g., sardines, shellfish)
Bacillus cereus	Contaminated foods (e.g., recooked rice)
Clostridium perfringens	Contaminated foods (e.g., reheated meat)
Entamoeba histolytica	Human feces-contaminated foods and water
Giardia lamblia	Human feces-contaminated foods and water
Cryptosporidium	Fecal-oral and water

we should add a few more. *Campylobacter jejuni,* formerly thought to be a rare cause of diarrhea, is now known to be one of the most common intestinal pathogens throughout the world. Within the last several years, *Aeromonas hydrophila* and *Pleisomonas* sp. have become established as important agents of water-borne or shellfish-associated outbreaks. Likewise, the protozoan *Cryptosporidium* (Chapter 51) has emerged as one of the most common agents of childhood diarrhea here and abroad, whereas it was formerly thought to affect mainly animals (and, occasionally, animal handlers or severely immunocompromised people). Another protozoan, *Enterocytozoon bienensi*, has been found to be the cause of diarrhea in some AIDS patients. Diarrhea may be caused in large numbers of patients either by new viruses in normal hosts (calicivirus, astrovirus, enteric adenovirus), or by well-known viruses in immunocompromised patients (cytomegalovirus, herpes simplex virus). As the list of enteric pathogens lengthens and we begin to understand how they produce disease, the practical challenge of diagnosis and treatment increases.

The cases described illustrate some points of microbial ecology and how people encounter certain microorganisms. *V. cholerae* is normally found in brackish tidal waters. In the U.S., it is endemic in the Gulf of Mexico near New Orleans and in the Pacific Ocean near Southern California. Shellfish can concentrate bacteria present in the water. Mr. V., the cholera patient, was no doubt infected by eating an enormous helping of oysters. He may have been susceptible due to achlorohydria (which was not evaluated) or he may have ingested an unfortunately high concentration of the organisms along with his plate of bivalves. Transmission across state lines occurs with shipment of shellfish, primarily Gulf crabs.

Unlike the cholera bacilli, which are environmental organisms, *Shigella* is found only in close association with humans. It takes relatively few organisms to cause shigellosis (also known as bacillary dysentery); this is one reason why the disease readily spreads between persons in close contact. The outbreak in a day care center is typical of transmission between individuals sharing close quarters and often encountering fecal material. Thus, in the U.S., it is seen most frequently where hygiene breaks down, as in day care centers or mental institutions. *Y. enterocolitica* has yet another ecological characteristic—it is often zoonotic (acquired from infected animals, see Chapter 69) and may be transmitted by drinking raw milk.

Diarrhea affecting infants who are 6 to about 24 months old is most likely of viral etiology, with rotavirus by far the most common. In temperate regions, this is seasonal and produces "winter vomiting disease"; in tropical zones, it occurs all year around. Adults may be silent carriers and introduce the virus into the family. In areas of the world where malnutrition is prevalent, severe diarrhea is associated with measles, which is highly contagious and kills large numbers of infants. The use of the measles vaccine in these populations may reduce the incidence of this life-threatening diarrhea. A distinct group of enteric infections is seen in male homosexuals. The special conditions of anal intercourse permit the distal bowel to become infected by pathogens typically associated with sexually transmitted diseases. Proctocolitis due to *Neisseria gonorrhoeae*, *Chlamydia trachomatis*, herpes simplex virus, or *Treponema pallidum* has been recognized as the Gay Bowel Syndrome. The modifications of sexual practices among homosexual men initiated by the AIDS epidemic have diminished the frequency of these infections. More usual enteric pathogens, such as *Campylobacter*, *Shigella*, and *Entamoeba histolytica*, may be transmitted sexually on occasion via analingus.

DAMAGE

With certain exceptions and overlaps, enteric infections can be distinguished by their anatomic location (Table 57.3) or the ability of the causative agents to invade tissues or produce a toxin or both. For this reason, we will consider the small and large intestine separately.

Table 57.3. Clinical Features of Diarrheal Disease

	Small Bowel	Large Bowel
Pathogens	*V. cholerae* *E. coli* (LT/ST strains) Rotavirus Norwalk agent (virus) *G. lamblia* *Cryptosporidium*	*Shigella* *E. coli* (EIEC, or invasive) *Campylobacter* *Entamoeba histolytica*
Location of pain	Midabdomen	Lower abdomen, rectum
Volume of stool	Large	Small
Type of stool	Watery	Mucoid
Blood in stool	Rare	Common
WBCs in stool	Rare	Common (except in amebiasis)
Proctoscopy	Normal	Mucosal ulcers; hemorrhagic friable mucosa

SMALL INTESTINE

The mechanisms involved in diarrhea arising in the small intestine differ according to the type of pathogenic agent:

- Viruses that cause death of intestinal epithelial cells; the main agents are the rotaviruses (Case 3), the so-called Norwalk agent, and enteroviruses. These viruses cause diarrhea by destroying enterocytes at the villi and not affecting those in the crypts. Normally, the villus cells absorb electrolyte from the gut lumen whereas crypt cells secrete chloride ions. Destroying the villus cells leads to decreased fluid absorption, which results in net secretion of fluid into the lumen. In addition, the microvillar membrane of the villus cells has a rich supply of disaccharidases. When the membrane is destroyed, disaccharides are not broken down or absorbed but pass into the colon where they are metabolized by the bacterial flora to osmotically more active compounds. Thus, fluid is drawn into the lumen, which worsens the diarrhea and is partly responsible for a postenteritic syndrome seen in children in whom mild diarrhea persists for considerable time after the infection is resolved.

- Toxigenic bacteria that colonize in the intestine, e.g., *V. cholerae*, and toxigenic *E. coli*; diarrhea is secondary to their production of toxins that may cause the accumulation of cyclic nucleotides (cAMP, cGTP), which, in turn, stimulate net chloride secretion, and/or inhibit sodium uptake resulting in fluid loss. These mechanisms are discussed in detail in Chapter 9.

- Protozoa, *Giardia* and *Cryptosporidium*, which infect the small bowel (Chapter 51); it is not yet known if a toxin is involved, nor how these organisms colonize or invade the gut epithelium.

- Bacteria that cause true food poisoning; this form of diarrhea occurs when toxigenic bacteria (e.g., *S. aureus*, *B. cereus*) are allowed to proliferate in food some time before it is eaten. This results in the accumulation of toxins that are ingested along with the food. Because bacterial multiplication in the body is not necessary, the effects are often felt within a few hours after the tainted meal is eaten. Examples are discussed in Chapter 72.

Clearly, not all infections of the small intestine produce a secretory diarrhea. Some organisms such as *C. jejuni* or *Y. enterocolitica* (as illustrated by the C. family in Case 4) may infect the terminal ileum, producing a watery, sometimes bloody stool. The varied presentations of illness in the C. family also illustrates the age-related differences in disease caused by the same organism. *Y. enterocolitica* is somewhat unique in this respect. Little is known about the reasons for this. It infects primarily the terminal ileum and colon in all patients, but in infants who are less than 5 years of age, it manifests itself as watery diarrhea. In older children, like S., diarrhea may be minimal or absent and the mesenteric adenitis may mimic an acute appendicitis. Many of the adults get arthritis within weeks after the onset of diarrhea. This is probably an immunological phenomenon, as organisms are not found in the joint fluid. Interestingly, those affected by arthritis often possess the histocompatibility antigen HLA-B27.

LARGE INTESTINE

Bacterial pathogens that affect the large intestine tend to produce epithelial damage, mucosal inflammation, and dysentery. The major large bowel invasive pathogens causing dysentery are *Shigella, Salmonella, Campylobacter, Yersinia*, certain strains of *E. coli*, and *Entameba*. Because inflammation is prominent and is usually located in the distal large bowel, pain often worsens with bowel movements (**tenesmus**). The mucosa is easily damaged and looks ulcerated when examined by proctoscopy (**Fig. 57.6**). The fecal effluent may initially be watery and substantial, but, later, it decreases in volume and soon consists of blood, mucus, and pus (see Fig. 17.1). White blood cells are typically scarce in amebic dysentery because they are lysed by the amebic trophozoites present in the lesions. Certain bacteria (*Campylobacter, Salmonella*, and *Yersinia*) produce an inflammatory illness in the terminal ileum with occasional extension to the colon resulting in dysentery. A different disease is caused by *C. difficile* and its toxins, usually arising after administration of antibiotics that wipe out or alter the other resident flora. It is manifested by an adherent pseudomembrane with considerable mucosal inflammation and damage but without tissue invasion (Chapter 21).

Serious complications arise occasionally from infection of the colon by invasive organisms. Shigellosis may be associated with severe malnutrition, leading to a protein deficiency syndrome in children known as kwashiorkor (see Fig. 61.5). Shigellosis sometimes results in rectal prolapse or in a frequently fatal distention of the colon known as toxic megacolon, with a complete cessation of colonic peristalsis. Systemic complications may also occur, leading to clinical manifestations known as the hemolytic uremic syndrome, leukemoid reactions with very high white blood cell counts, encephalopathy, and others. Amebiasis may lead to intestinal perforation or obstruction, or the organisms may spread to produce abscesses in other organs, especially in the liver.

GUT-ASSOCIATED LYMPH TISSUE

A third type of enteric infection is exemplified by typhoid fever (Chapter 18) and is occasionally seen with *Yersinia* species and *Campylobacter fetus*. It is characterized by invasion of the gut-associated lymph tissue of the small bowel. From there, the organisms disseminate to the liver and to the bloodstream (**enteric fever**) or regional

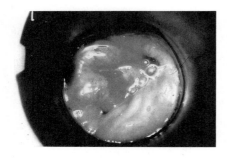

Figure 57.6. Proctoscopic view of the rectum of a patient with Shigella dysentery. The inflamed bloody mucosa and the excessive mucus secretions are readily seen.

lymph system (**mesenteric adenitis**). Diarrhea may be absent or transient, and if fecal leukocytes are present, they tend to be mononuclear, attesting to the chronic nature of these infections. I. of the C. family in Case 4 suffered from this type of disease.

SURGICAL COMPLICATIONS OF INTESTINAL INFECTIONS

Perforation of the wall of either the small or the large intestine may be caused by trauma or by intestinal infections. Either way, it results in spillage of intestinal contents into the normally sterile peritoneal cavity. Infections may lead to perforation in one of two ways: (*a*) direct damage to the gut wall by the inflammatory response (edema and cellular infiltration), or (*b*) bursting due to increase in pressure due to altered peristalsis or inflammatory obstruction. The severity of the resulting peritonitis is generally related to the volume of the inoculum, its pattern of spread in the abdomen, and the ability of the omentum to wall off the abscess. A small amount of fecal contents may be handled by the defenses in the peritoneum, but a large inoculum can easily overwhelm them. These infections tend to be severe, and if untreated are often life threatening. They are caused by a mixture of strict anaerobes and facultative anaerobic bacteria and represent a classical therapeutic challenge. Pathogenic mechanisms are discussed in Chapter 16.

DIAGNOSIS

Most of the patients with acute diarrhea have a mild and self-limited course and never seek medical attention. It is not practical to search for enteric pathogens in all patients with diarrhea. Nor, in a large proportion of cases, is it warranted to do more than to give replenishing fluids and electrolytes, by mouth and not intravenously, unless the patient is in hypovolemic shock. A careful history of the symptoms is the most important part of the investigation and often narrows the diagnostic possibilities. The clues that suggest a form of disease requiring specific therapy (e.g., antimicrobial drugs) include fever, tenesmus, persistent or severe abdominal pain, weight loss, blood in the stool, recent travel, antibiotic use or raw seafood meals, male homosexual practices, or prolonged duration of symptoms.

Culturing of stool samples for "enteric pathogens," which is often and reflexively requested by many physicians, is primarily intended to isolate species of *Salmonella* and *Shigella*. Isolation or identification of the other enteric pathogens requires special culture techniques, evaluation of serotype, or tests for toxin production (Chapter 55). Animal parasites, protozoa, or helminths may require special concentration or staining procedures. Therefore, it is important to narrow the list of possible organisms that are sought and to inform the laboratory to avoid overburdening it with mountains of stool. Note how this can be of help, if laboratory personnel know that you suspect *Y. enterocolitica*, they would incubate cultures at 25°C; at this temperature, the organisms are motile and readily distinguishable from other similar pathogens. Because of the newly recognized high prevalence of *C. jejuni*, it is appropriate to request that this organism be especially looked for, especially in cases with fever and tenesmus, or if leukocytes are present in the stool. In this instance, the laboratory would use special selective media and an incubation temperature higher than 37°C. *V. cholerae* was isolated from Mr. V.'s stool because the laboratory had been alerted to this possibility and used a nonroutine selective medium, TCBS agar.

If nonbloody diarrhea persists or remains unexplained, a sample of upper small bowel contents may be examined for *G. lamblia* or *S. stercoralis* by use of a string that has been swallowed, allowed to pass into the duodenum, and then retrieved. *Cryptosporidium* infection is diagnosed in stool or in biopsy specimens because these organisms are acid-fast, an unusual feature among protozoa.

It should be remembered that the clinical value of a particular test is determined by whether or not the results will meaningfully affect the management of the patient. Sometimes the information is used not for treatment of the individual patient, but to determine if special isolation measures are warranted. Thus, the presence of rotavirus in M.A.'s stool (Case 3) did not materially change the treatment plan. Antibacterial antibiotics were not indicated anyway, and rehydration would have been administered in any event. However, the positive ELISA test for rotaviruses suggested that if she were hospitalized or near to other susceptible infants, she would have to be isolated from them.

TREATMENT

Most acute infectious diarrheas are mild, self-limited, and best treated with oral fluid replacement and continued feeding. When to resort to specific antimicrobial or more aggressive intravenous replacement therapy is determined by the severity or duration of diarrhea or the presence of shock or dysenteric symptoms. In general, infections caused by toxigenic and invasive *E. coli*, *V. cholerae*, and *Shigella* are improved with antibiotics. The disadvantage is that these organisms may develop drug resistance. Also, antibiotic treatment (except for the use of new fluoroquinolones) may not alter the course and may increase the risk of developing a carrier state, with the potential of increased spread of the infection, as with *Salmonella*. Other specific antimicrobials are prescribed for helminths, *G. lamblia*, *E. histolytica*, or gonococcal proctitis.

Antidiarrheal agents may reduce the frequency of stools but there is no evidence to suggest that these drugs shorten the course of the illness. In fact, by increasing gut transit time, antimotility agents may impair the clearance of the original pathogen and, thus, prolong the infection and, very possibly, enhance the risk of invasiveness and septicemia. In addition, anticholinergics or opiates may produce the life-threatening condition of intestinal stasis known as the toxic megalocolon, especially in children and those with inflammatory diarrhea.

An important medical breakthrough has been the development of oral rehydration therapy for mild to moderate diarrhea. Following the discovery that sodium and glucose transport are coupled in the small intestine, it was observed that the oral administration of glucose with essential electrolytes dramatically accelerates absorption of sodium, with water following passively (i.e., without the expenditure of energy) to maintain osmolality. Moderate dehydration associated with cholera or other small bowel diarrheas should now be corrected with oral replacement. Even in severe dehydration, which requires rapid intravenous fluids to correct or prevent shock, oral rehydration may later be used alone for maintenance of adequate hydration. The impact of this simple concept on worldwide mortality from dehydration cannot be overstated, especially in the poorest corners of the globe where the problem is prevalent and severe. In these areas, the use of intravenous therapy is too expensive and trained personnel are too scarce to provide it to more than a small proportion of patients. Technically uneducated people can be trained to mix the proper ingredients (sometime using bottle caps as measuring devices) or to dissolve prepackaged mixtures. The recipe for oral rehydration is remarkably simple.

To one liter of water add:

½ teaspoon salt (3 g)
¼ teaspoon bicarbonate (1.5 g)
¼ teaspoon KCl (1.5 g)
4 tablespoons sugar (20 g)

SUGGESTED READING

ESOPHAGITIS

Goff JS. Infectious causes of esophagitis. Ann Rev Med 1988; 39:163–169.
Odds FC. *Candida* infections: an overview. CRC Crit Rev Microbiol 1987; 15:1–5.

GASTRITIS

Graham DY, Klein PD. *Campylobacter pyloridis*: the past, the present, and speculations about the future. Am J Gastroenterol 1987;82:283–286.
Waghorn DJ. *Campylobacter pyloridis*: a new organism to explain an old problem? Postgrad Med J 1987;63:533–537.

BACTERIAL OVERGROWTH SYNDROME

Marthias JR, Clench MH. Review: pathophysiology of diarrhea caused by bacterial overgrowth of the small intestine. Am J Med Sci 1985;289:243–248.
Sherman P, Lichtman S. Small bowel bacterial overgrowth syndrome. Dig Dis 1987;5:157–171.

INTESTINAL INFECTIONS

Bacterial diarrhea. In: Clin Gastroenterol 1986;15:21–37.
Cantley JR. Infectious diarrhea: pathogenesis and risk factors. J Med 1985; 78:165–244.
Formal SB, Hale TL, Sansonetti P. Invasive enteric pathogens. Rev Infect Dis 1983;5 (Suppl 14):S702–S707.
Infectious diarrhea. Which culprit? Which strategy? Postgrad Med 1983; 73:175–182.
Levine MM. Antimicrobial therapy in infectious diarrhea. Rev Infect Dis 1986;(Suppl 2):S207–S216.
Nelson JD. Epidemiology of diarrheal diseases in the United States. Am J Med 1985;78 (Suppl 6B):91–97.
Quin TC, Bender BS, Bartlett JG. Antimicrobial therapy for infectious diarrhea. Disease-A-Month 1986;32:165–244.

Central Nervous System   58

Arnold L. Smith

Infections of the central nervous system (CNS) are relatively infrequent but tend to have extremely serious consequences. Untreated bacterial meningitis, for example, is fatal in over 70% of cases. Antibiotics have reduced mortality in these diseases to less than 10%, but this is still unacceptably high. In addition, some CNS infections in childhood leave serious neurological sequelae that impair mental development and produce sensory deficits.

From a microbiological point of view, the brain and the spinal cord have distinctive attributes—at the same time they are well protected and highly vulnerable. Thus, the CNS is anatomically protected by bones and membranes that shield it from the exterior. However, in a limited space, the effects of infections tend to be magnified; even minor swelling and inflammation cause significant damage. This is especially true in view of the essential functions of the CNS. These two sides of the coin are also apparent on the physiological level; the blood-brain barrier inhibits passage of microorganisms and toxic substances into the brain and cerebrospinal fluid (CSF). Yet the same barrier impedes the passage of humoral and cellular defensive elements from the blood. It also hinders the passage of many antimicrobial drugs, sometimes narrowing the therapeutic options.

To understand the pathogenesis and outcome of infections in this distinctive part of the body, you will need to recollect general aspects of neuroanatomy and neurophysiology. The brain and spinal cord are suspended in the CSF and are surrounded by three layers of meninges, i.e., the pia mater and arachnoid, which constitute the leptomeninges, and the dura mater or pachymeninges (Fig. 58.1). Infections of the CNS can be grouped by their anatomic location into infection of the brain parenchyma, **encephalitis**; infection of the meninges, **meningitis**; and infection of spinal cord tissue, **myelitis**. This anatomic separation of CNS infections is somewhat artificial, because all of these areas are connected and may be infected at the same time. In many cases, therefore, it is correct to speak of meningoencephalitis or even meningomyeloencephalitis.

Infections of the CNS may be caused by bacteria, viruses, fungi, or animal parasites that are either encountered in the environment or are members of the normal flora on body surfaces. In almost all CNS infections, the causative agents were previously introduced into peripheral tissues of the host and made their way to the CNS either **via the systemic circulation** or **via neural pathways**. For instance, pathogens may have colonized the respiratory epithelium, penetrated it, and then entered the circulation (e.g., the meningococcus), or entered the bloodstream via the bite of an arthropod (e.g., Eastern equine encephalitis virus), of a dog (e.g., rabies virus), or through the placenta (e.g., rubella virus). A third way that

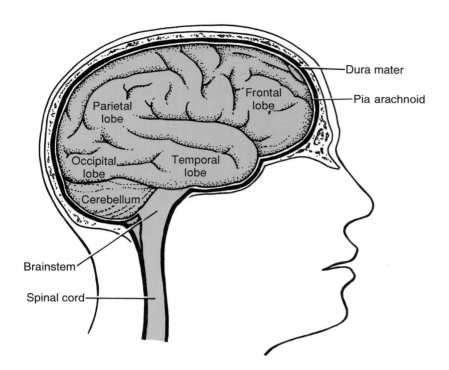

Figure 58.1. Gross anatomy of the cranium. The brain is within closed space, surrounded by the meninges (dura mater and pia arachnoid) in close approximation to mucosal surface containing commensal flora (the nasopharynx).

microorganisms may enter the CNS is **by direct inoculation**, usually associated with trauma. In certain infections, the organisms are lodged within the CNS in a latent state and then manifest active disease some time in the future (e.g., tuberculosis or polyomaviruses). The main types of infections and the most common etiologies are listed in Table 58.1.

ENCOUNTER

Infections of the CNS are caused by a small percentage of the pathogens that infect humans. Thus, these organisms must possess special characteristics that permit them to localize in the CNS. The most frequent agents and the types of disease they cause tend to fall into distinct categories—certain bacteria (pneumococci, *Haemophilus influenzae*, meningococci) classically caused meningitis but rarely caused infections of brain parenchyma, whereas others (staphylococci, anaerobic streptococci) cause brain abscesses but seldom cause meningitis. Some viruses cause encephalitis (herpes simplex); others cause meningitis (enteroviruses).

Once inside the CNS, viruses sometimes localize in specific regions. Certain viruses show an extreme tropism for certain neural cell types, e.g., polio for the motor neurons of the spinal cord and medulla, and mumps virus for the cells of the ependyma of the fetus. The basis for such tropism is probably the distribution of viral receptors on specific cells. Some clues regarding this point come from experiments with reoviruses (see Chapter 8 for a detailed study). Depending on their type of surface hemagglutinin, reoviruses cause different kinds of severe infections of the CNS when injected into laboratory animals. Two types of hemagglutinin differ in their ability to bind to receptors on distinct neural cells. Viruses with Type 1 hemagglutinin bind to ependymal cells, replicate, and cause inflammation at that site. Damage to the ependymal cells leads to occlusion of the ventricular aqueduct and to hydrocephalus (i.e., dilation of the ventricular system due to obstruction of CSF flow). In contrast, Type 3 viruses bind to neurons and cause

Table 58.1. Type of Infection and Frequent Causative Agents

1. Acute meningitis
   Bacteria
      N. meningitidis
      H. influenzae, type b
      S. pneumoniae
      Group B streptococci
      E. coli
   Viruses
      Mumps virus
      Enteroviruses
2. Chronic meningitis
      M. tuberculosis
      C. neoformans
      Other fungi
3. Acute encephalitis
      Viruses
      Arboviruses
      Herpesviruses
      Enteroviruses
      Mumps virus
4. Acute abscesses
   Bacteria
      Staphylococci
      Mixed anaerobe/aerobe flora
      Group A or D streptococci
5. Chronic abscesses
   Bacteria
      M. tuberculosis
   Fungi
      C. neoformans
   Animal parasites
      Cysticercus (*Taenia*)

a fatal encephalitis (without ependymal cell infection). Thus, the anatomic location of these viruses depends, at least in part, on the specificity of their surface proteins for host cell receptors. This, in turn, determines the type of disease produced.

Localization is also believed to be favored by differences in blood flow. Does this explain why polio virus commonly infects the anterior horn cells of the spinal cord on the side of the dominant hand? Right-handed people are indeed more often affected on their right side.

Bacteria that cause CNS infections tend to differ in patients of different ages. Thus, in the newborn, bacterial meningitis is most commonly caused by *Escherichia coli* and group B β-hemolytic *Streptococcus agalactiae*. Both are encapsulated strains. Over one-half of the *E. coli* strains have a capsule made up of **K1 antigen**, suggesting that neuropathogenic strains have been specially selected from the plethora of antigenically distinct *E. coli* strains. In contrast to other *E. coli* capsular antigens, K1 is a polysaccharide **rich in sialic acid**. So are capsular polysaccharides of group B streptococci. Why sialic acid? Apparently, polysaccharides containing this compound aid in bacterial adherence (and growth) on the meninges. K1 antigen also has antiphagocytic properties and inhibits the alternative pathway of complement activation.

WHO, WHERE, AND WHEN

The foremost epidemiological features of infections of the CNS are age, geographic location, and the time of the year. For example, encephalitis in infants is more likely to be due to enteroviruses, because enteroviruses are spread by the fecal-oral route and children are more prone to come in contact with contaminated feces (Chapter 35). In adults, encephalitis is more likely to be due to arboviruses (Table 58.2). Spread of arboviruses by arthropods also has seasonal variations, which follow the life cycle of the vectors (Chapter 55). Overall, the most common viral encephalitis in adults is caused by herpes simplex virus, and it does not have a specific seasonal distribution. The geographic distribution of some of these viruses is well illustrated by the name given to the diseases caused by arboviruses (Eastern, Western, Japanese encephalitis, etc.) This is sometimes misleading because St. Louis encephalitis, for example, was first studied in that city, but is the arbovirus disease most commonly encountered throughout the U.S.

In addition to acute encephalitis, where the symptoms coincide with viral invasion of the CNS, there is also postinfectious encephalitis, and "slow virus" CNS infection. Postinfectious encephalitis appears to come about by two mechanisms—the virus persistently infects cells of the CNS in a latent state, or an autoimmune reaction to sequestered CNS-specific antigens. In certain types of postinfectious encephalitides, both mechanisms appear operative. Chronic progressive, uniformly fatal, CNS infections are caused by a group of viruses that are called "slow viruses." These agents are named after the disease they produce, because the clinical description of the disease preceded the recognition of a viral etiology. Thus, Creutzfeldt-Jakob disease (CJD virus) and Kuru are human examples of slow virus infections; there are may similar diseases in animals (e.g., scrapie). Patients who develop an illness characterized by primary immune deficiency (i.e., Hodgkin's disease), or who become immune deficient secondary to anticancer chemotherapy, can develop a progressive multifocal leukoencephalopathy (PML). This disease (PML), is caused by activation of a polyomavirus called JCV. Most individuals acquire JCV early in childhood, have self-limited disease, but the virus becomes latent within the CNS. Immune suppression then permits renewed viral replication and progressive disease.

ENTRY

Hematogenous Route

Most cases of CNS infection are caused by entry of the organisms from the circulation (Fig. 58.2). The precise mechanism that permits

Table 58.2. Viruses Causing Encephalitis

Virus	Geographic Location	Major Age Group	Predominant Season	Notable Feature
Herpes simplex	All	All	None	Focal symptoms
St. Louis encephalitis	All	Older adults	Summer-fall	Most cases mild
Eastern equine encephalitis	East coast and Texas	Children	Summer-fall	Disabling sequelae
Western equine encephalitis	West of Mississippi	Infants to children	Summer-fall	
California equine encephalitis	East of Mississippi	Older children	Summer-fall	
Enteroviruses	All	Infants to children	Summer	Severity inverse to age
Rabies	All	All	All	Animal bite
Varicella	All	Children	Winter	Rare
HIV	All	Adults	All	Dementia in AIDS patients

Figure 58.2. Pathways of entry of agents that cause CNS infections. In blood-borne infections, agents from the respiratory tract, gut, or vascular epithelium enter via the choroid plexi. Inside the CNS, they spread either by contiguity or through extracellular spaces. Some neurotropic viruses reach the brain via peripheral nerves or via the olfactory nerve endings.

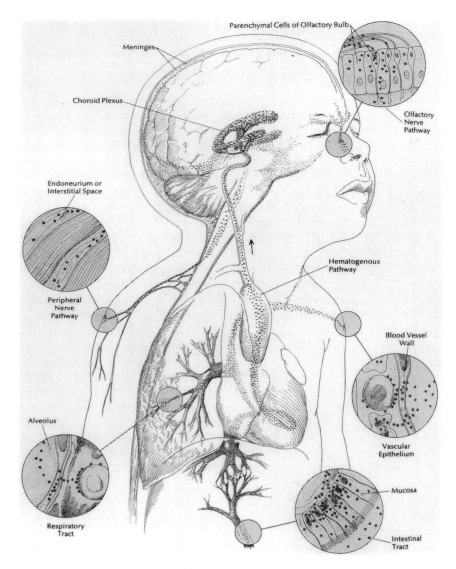

them to penetrate the blood-brain barrier is not known. It is presumed that the choroid plexi, the site of the greatest formation of the CSF, provide the most common site of entry. These are highly vascular structures, and inflammation of the blood side may result in the spillage of microorganisms into the CNS side. The likelihood of CNS infection is generally correlated with the microbial load of the blood (Chapter 15 on *H. influenzae*).

Neural Route

Most neurotropic viruses also reach the CNS by the circulation, but a few utilize special neural pathways (Fig. 58.2). The best known case of neural transmission is rabies, where the virus travels to the anterior horns of the spinal cord via peripheral nerves. Rabies virus enters the axon of a peripheral nerve and travels to neuronal perikaryon in retrograde fashion, presumably on a microtubular filament. Another well-known example of neural transmission is herpes simplex, where the virus ascends via the trigeminal nerve root (Chapter 31). As mentioned above, experimental studies with reoviruses showed that the choice of the hematogenous or the neural route depends on genetic differences in the viral hemagglutinin (Chapter 8).

We should also mention the speculative but intriguing notion that viruses and other infectious agents may penetrate the body via the olfactory nerve endings, which are the only elements of the nervous system in direct contact with the exterior. Experimental studies suggest that herpes viruses may reach the brain by this route. The ameba *Naegleria*, which causes a rare but lethal meningoencephalitis, is also thought to penetrate the CNS by trauma to the cribriform plate, as might happen when a person dives into water containing these amebae.

SPREAD AND MULTIPLICATION

Once a pathogen has reached the CNS, it finds itself in a relatively sequestered compartment that does not have as ready a recourse to defense mechanisms as most other regions of the body. For example, complement levels are very low in the CSF, apparently due to poor penetration from the blood, and also because the CSF contains a substance that partially inactivates complement. Therefore, lysis or phagocytosis of bacteria do not readily occur in the brain, the meninges, and the CSF. However, the CNS is not as immunologically restricted as was once supposed. It possesses an intrinsic immunological surveillance mechanism in the microglia. Microglia have many surface markers identical to peripheral blood monocytes, suggesting that the latter migrate to the brain to evolve into microglia. In addition, it is now believed that the CNS has a lymph-like system consisting of the Virchow-Robin spaces (the perivascular sheaths surrounding the blood vessels as they enter the brain). These spaces contain macrophages and lymphocytes, and are thought to be the site where these cells enter into the CSF. Does the existence of these mechanisms suggest that infections of the CNS are more frequent than is believed, but are often kept in check by host defenses?

DAMAGE

Tissue dysfunction in CNS infections is caused in a variety of ways. Death of host cells may be due directly to the action of bacterial toxins, to lytic cycles of viral replication, or as the result of intracellular growth of bacteria and fungi. In most infections, however, cell death and tissue destruction result from the host's own inflammatory response. The multiplication and spread of microorganisms in the CNS elicits an inflammatory response similar to, but generally less intense, than that seen in other areas of the body. Characteristic of inflammation of the CNS are infiltration of microglia and proliferation of astrocytes. As in other parts of the body, the inflammatory response of the CNS has a humoral and a cellular component. The humoral component develops first and consists of edema caused by increased capillary permeability. Neutrophils and macrophages infiltrate the area, phagocytizing microorganisms as well as dead cells. Neutrophils often lyse in the process, releasing enzymes that digest cells and tissue material in the immediate area.

Swelling of the brain due to inflammation within the closed cranial vault (cerebral edema) may, by itself, produce cerebral cortical symptoms from decreased capillary perfusion. More severe forms of cerebral edema can cause herniation of the temporal lobe through the falx, or of the brainstem into the foramen magnum, producing severe brain damage or death. Thus, neurological symptoms during infection of the CNS may be due to **focal tissue lesions**, which produce specific functional deficits, or due to cerebral edema that leads to **global loss of higher cerebral cortical function**.

The functional characteristics of the CNS often help diagnose specific kinds of infections and identify the areas involved. For example, psychosis, impairment of memory, and seizures suggest herpes simplex encephalitis (because of the preferred involvement of the temporal lobe); stiffness of the neck without impairment of cerebral function is characteristic of viral meningitis; flaccid paralysis of the lower extremities suggests polio virus infection of the motor neurons of the spinal cord. Figure 58.3 depicts focal symptoms produced by certain CNS infections.

The following case histories and discussion describe characteristic infections of the CNS and how they are diagnosed. They include cases of meningitis, acute encephalitis, postinfectious or late encephalitis, and brain abscess.

MENINGITIS

The majority of cases of meningitis can be classified in simple ways:

● Clinical presentation: acute, subacute, or chronic;

● By etiology: bacterial, fungal, or viral;

● By epidemiology: sporadic or epidemic.

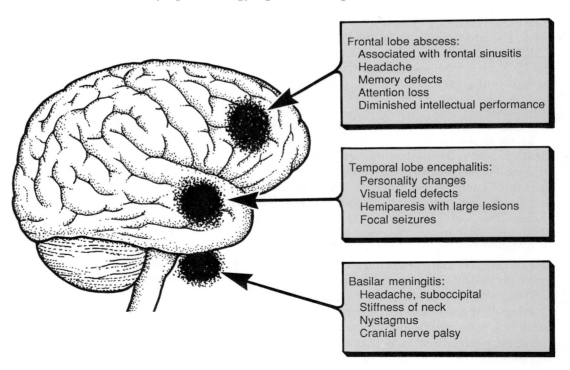

Frontal lobe abscess:
   Associated with frontal sinusitis
   Headache
   Memory defects
   Attention loss
   Diminished intellectual performance

Temporal lobe encephalitis:
   Personality changes
   Visual field defects
   Hemiparesis with large lesions
   Focal seizures

Basilar meningitis:
   Headache, suboccipital
   Stiffness of neck
   Nystagmus
   Cranial nerve palsy

Figure 58.3.   Anatomic basis of localization of symptoms in CNS infections. Focal involvement of cerebral cortex produces specific signs and symptoms depending on the primary function of that part of the brain. In contrast, pyogenic meningitis produces global cerebral cortical dysfunction due to diffuse cerebral edema.

Acute meningitis is often caused by bacteria, chiefly *E. coli* and group B streptococci in young infants, meningococci, *H. influenzae*, and pneumococci in children, and pneumococci in adults (see Table 15.2). Overall, *H. influenzae* is the most common cause of meningitis, even though it infects mainly children between the ages of 6 and 60 months (Chapter 15). Subacute or chronic meningitis tends to be caused by fungi (mainly *Cryptococcus*) or by tubercle bacilli (all organisms that cause chronic inflammatory, granulomatous tissue reactions). Below we discuss an outbreak of meningococcal meningitis, an event that is known to occur when young adults are placed together.

Case—Outbreak of Acute Meningitis

One week after arriving at the Army recruit campe at Fort Ord (California), Pvt. T.A. had become the first of three cases of meningitis. He had a precipitous onset of fever and headache and, within hours, felt a pain in his neck when he moved his head. On lumbar puncture, his pressure was slightly elevated, 220 mm H$_2$O (the normal range is 70–200 mm H$_2$O). A smear of the CSF revealed small Gram-negative coccobacilli and numerous leukocytes (Fig. 58.4). A culture grew the meningococcus, Neisseria meningitidis. Two weeks after intravenous administration of penicillin G, he nearly completely recovered, when Pvt. F.H. developed the same symptoms and was admitted to the hospital. When Pvt. B.W. was diagnosed the next morning with the same illness, the remaining soldiers in the camp became alarmed. Their fears calmed when the medical corps personnel explained that this meningococcal meningitis "epidemic" would be stopped by the prophylactic administration of antibiotics to all.

*At about the same time, Pvt. V.L. was assigned to Fort Leonard Wood (Missouri). When he arrived there, he had a fever, slight headache, and some nausea. The next day, when putting on his boots, he noticed that his neck was stiff. When he went to the infirmary, he immediately had a lumbar puncture: the CSF pressure was 90 mm H$_2$O, nearly in the normal range, and the fluid contained 76 neutrophils/μl, 80 mg/dl of protein (an elevated value—see Table 58.3), and 66 mg/dl of glucose, in the normal range. He was observed in the hospital for 3 days and was discharged with a diagnosis of **aseptic meningitis** when his CSF proved to be sterile and his symptoms resolved.*

Why did meningococcal meningitis, the illness of Pvt. B.W., produce alarm and called for preventive measures, whereas aseptic meningitis,

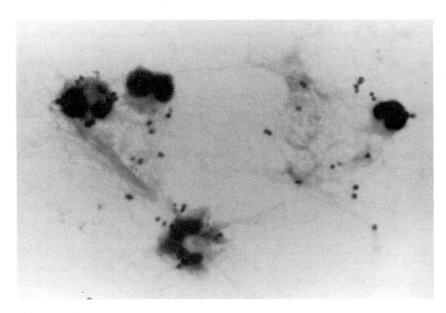

Figure 58.4. Gram stain of CSF from a patient with meningococcal meningitis. Gram-negative coccobacilli and neutrophils are evident.

that of Pvt. V.L., was just observed? How does the pathobiology of these diseases differ and how can they be differentiated?

Encounter and Entry

Meningococci are acquired by inhalation of aerosol droplets from asymptomatic human carriers. It is likely that, in the outbreak at Fort Ord, most of the recruits were exposed to the organisms from another individual, since meningococci are found in the oropharynx of about 10% of healthy people. This frequent degree of colonization does not, however, always correlate directly with outbreaks, because individual strains of meningococci vary considerably in virulence. The reason why so many people become colonized but only a few get sick is not truly known. The best hint comes from observation that susceptible individuals lack antibodies against the meningococcal capsular antigen, whereas those who become carriers have such protective antibodies. There is also a striking association between congenital deficiency in the late components of the complement cascade and neisserial infection, with either meningococci or gonococci. These findings suggest that the immunological repertoire of an individual plays a role in determining who does and who does not manifest the disease.

Spread, Multiplication, and Damage

Meningococcal meningitis may be a distinct clinical event, as in the cases of the soldiers at Fort Ord, but it may also follow an overwhelming septicemia caused by these organisms. In such cases, the symptoms of meningitis only add to an already grave clinical picture; the presence of organisms in the blood in large numbers causes severe nonneural manifestations, such as shock and intravascular coagulation. These signs are due to the high blood content of Gram-negative endotoxin. In such cases, it is proper to speak of **meningococcal septicemia**, rather than meningococcal meningitis.

The clinical manifestations of acute meningitis, caused by meningococci, *H. influenzae*, or other bacteria, are fever, a stiff neck (nuchal rigidity), headache, and occasionally other focal CNS dysfunctions. These symptoms are due to the inflammatory response to meningeal invasion. Pus in the subarachnoid spaces may spread over the brain, the cerebellum, and the spinal cord. It tends to be particularly thick in pneumococcal and *Haemophilus* infections, which leads to blockage of various foramina and to an increased CSF pressure, resulting in headache and nausea. In meningococcal meningitis, the CSF pressure is usually only slightly elevated. The extent of inflammation varies considerably, with the intrinsic virulence of the strains and the immune state of the patient. Severe signs and symptoms of meningeal irritation, "meningismus," include involuntary extension of the neck and back to keep the dura from being stretched at the point where spinal nerves exit the spinal foramina. Additional symptoms, such as altered vision, may be caused by compression of the nerves that emanate from the base of the brain. Spasm or thrombosis of blood vessels may lead to small or large strokes.

In general, meningitis leaves fewer traces when caused by meningococci than by the other bacteria. *H. influenzae* meningitis is often followed by mental retardation and/or deafness. Some of these deficits are cortical, presumably due to decrease in cerebral cortical blood flow during the acute stages of the disease.

Diagnosis

An acute infection of the CNS presents a diagnostic problem of grave urgency. Saving the life of a child with meningococcal meningitis sometimes requires instituting proper therapy within minutes. Fortunately, examination of a Gram stain of the CSF obtained by lumbar puncture may rapidly give a presumptive diagnosis. Examination of the CSF is absolutely necessary when acute meningitis is suspected. Table 58.3 shows the pattern of inflammation in the CSF in various CNS infections.

The elements of inflammatory response in the CSF may also be helpful in determining whether the infection is likely to be bacterial or viral and even in suggesting specific infectious agents. A large number of neutrophils points to a bacterial infection, whereas the predominance of lymphocytes suggest a viral etiology. Recall that the symptoms of Pvt. B.W. were almost identical to Pvt. V.L.; the nature of their illnesses was discerned by CSF examination. Gram stain examination of the spinal fluid should be a routine procedure because it reveals infecting bacteria in about 50% of the cases of meningitis.

Culture of CSF is the means of definitively establishing the etiology and is useful for making a specific choice of antibiotics (Table 15.2). More rapid tests are based on identification of unique microbial constituents in the CSF. Most of these tests are based on detecting a specific antigen, such as a bacterial or fungal capsular polysaccharides. Future methods may test for specific genes rather than their antigenic products.

Prevention and Treatment

Vaccination against meningococci is limited to high-risk groups, such as military recruits. Currently, U.S. military personnel receive a meningococcal vaccine when they arrive in a recruit camp. The vaccine contains capsular polysaccharides of Type A and C meningococci, the most common types to cause meningococcal epidemics, plus two rare types. An effective vaccine against Type B meningococci, which cause the majority of cases of meningococcal meningitis in the U.S., is not available. However, even if it were available, it would probably not be used because most of these cases are sporadic and do not occur often enough to warrant widespread vaccination. Chemoprophylaxis with rifampin or minocycline will eradicate nasopharyngeal carriage in 90% of the recipients.

To treat bacterial meningitis effectively, antibiotics to which the bacteria is susceptible must penetrate the CSF in an active form. β-Lactams are usually administered for the common forms of bacterial meningitis. These drugs are highly polar and enter the CSF poorly by

Table 58.3. Usual Composition of the Cerebrospinal Fluid in Various Infections

	None	Acute Bacterial Meningitis	Fungal and Viral Meningitis	Herpes Encephalitis	Brain Abscess
Leukocytes (no./µl)	0–6	>1000	100–500	10–1000	10–500
% Neutrophils	0	>50	<10	<50	<50
Red blood cells (no./µl)	0–2	0–10	0–2	10–500	10–100
Glucose (mg/dl)[a]	40–80	<30	≤40	>30	>40
Protein (mg/dl)	20–50	>100	50–100	>75	50–100

[a]Diagnostic values are best interpreted as the ratio of glucose levels in the blood to those in the CSF.

diffusion through the blood-brain and blood-CSF barriers. The average drug concentration in CSF normally achieved is 15% that of serum. However, β-lactams also enter the CSF through capillary leaks that are enhanced by inflammation, and these drugs, thus, may reach therapeutic levels in patients with meningitis. It has been estimated that for the drugs to be effective, it is necessary to achieve a CSF concentration that is 8–10 times that of the minimal bactericidal concentration (MBC) measured in the laboratory. The reason for this is not really known.

New β-lactams, such as cefotaxime and ceftriaxone, are very potent and produce CSF concentrations that exceed the MBC by 20-fold or more. As the inflammation resolves, the β-lactam concentration decreases, but is still adequate to sterilize the CSF. Other antibiotics such as chloramphenicol and tetracycline are lipophilic and diffuse readily across blood-brain and blood-CSF barriers. They achieve effective CSF concentrations independent of the presence or magnitude of the meningeal inflammation and are active against *H. influenzae* and meningococci. Chloramphenicol, however, may produce serious toxic side effects and its serum levels should be monitored (a practice that may be prohibitive in economically disadvantaged countries). Tetracycline may cause permanent discoloration of the teeth, mitigating its administration to young children.

An important aspect of the treatment of meningitis is to control the increased intracranial pressure. Cerebral edema may further decrease the already diminished cerebral blood flow and depress oxidative glucose metabolism. Death may ensue from compression of the brain stem into the foramen magnum (i.e., herniation). Supportive measures must ensure that the patient is adequately oxygenated and that blood glucose is in the normal range. Recently, corticosteroids have been shown to decrease morbidity in certain kinds of bacterial meningitis. Rapid therapy is of utmost importance. Antibiotics should be administered intravenously very early and in high enough doses to achieve adequate CNS concentrations. Bacterial meningitis is a true medical emergency.

VIRAL MENINGITIS

Viremia gives viruses the opportunity to invade the CNS and cause so-called **aseptic meningitis**. This traditional term only means that the CSF is sterile on routine culture. The term is also used for infections by other agents that do not grow on the usual bacteriological media (e.g., fungi, leptospira, *Treponema pallidum*). Aseptic meningitis may also be caused by noninfectious etiologies such as certain cancers or cerebral collagen-vascular disease. In viral meningitis, the brain is usually involved as well, and the illness, therefore, should be described as a meningoencephalitis. However, the meningeal signs (stiff neck and headache) are more prominent than those of cerebral involvement.

Viral meningitis can be distinguished from bacterial meningitis because it produces a milder disease, a low to moderate inflammatory reaction in the CSF, consisting primarily of lymphocytes. Pvt. V.L. had the clinical disease and CSF findings typical of viral and not fungal meningitis (chiefly, a large number of leukocytes and normal glucose level, see Table 58.3). For this reason, antibiotics were not administered and he was only observed in the hospital. His improvement without antibacterial or antifungal treatment points further to a viral etiology. If Pvt. V.L. had not improved, another cause for his symptoms and the presence of leukocytes in the CSF would have had to be found.

Viral meningitis can be proved by isolation of a virus from the CSF. However, this is seldom accomplished in enough time to aid in treatment. Isolating a virus known to cause aseptic meningitis from the throat or stool of a patient with appropriate symptoms suggests, but does not prove it is the etiology of aseptic meningitis.

In infants less than 1 year of age, it is frequently difficult to distinguish bacterial and aseptic meningitis. The newborn has a limited repertoire of responses, and the relative immaturity of its reticuloendothelial system may not permit an adult-type inflammatory response. The presence of bacterial polysaccharide in the CSF helps make this distinction. However, the absence of bacterial antigens does not eliminate the diagnosis of pyogenic meningitis. As a result, most infants with the symptoms of acute meningitis and an increase of leukocytes in the CSF are treated with antibiotics.

CHRONIC MENINGITIS

Case

Ms. L., a 32-year-old woman, immigrated to the U.S. 1 year ago from the Solomon Islands, together with her husband and three children. Four weeks later, her oldest child came home from day care with chickenpox. Two weeks later, she and the rest of the family also developed the disease. As her rash faded, she developed a headache and again had fever. Over the next week, she lost her appetite and vomited a few times. These symptoms persisted for an additional week and she became apathetic. When she became stuporous 4 days later, she was taken to a hospital.

The diagnosis of varicella (chickenpox) encephalitis was considered, but the fact that her chickenpox began a month ago made this unlikely because invasion by this virus would have occurred earlier, during active disease. On physical examination, she was deaf in her right ear and had paralysis of the right side of her face. A chest radiograph showed a right upper lobe pneumonia. A technetium-99 brain scan showed increased uptake at the base of her brain, and a cranial CT indicated increased intracranial pressure. On lumbar puncture, the CSF pressure was 310 mm H_2O (highly elevated) and the fluid contained 350 leukocytes/μl, of which 87% were lymphocytes, and a protein concentration of 68 mg/dl (elevated). A Gram stain and an acid-fast stain did not show any organisms, but the CSF contained a lipid typical of tubercle bacilli, tuberculostearic acid, which allowed the diagnosis of tuberculous meningitis (see Chapter 22 for other procedures). Subsequently, Mycobacterium tuberculosis grew from her CSF, and was found to be susceptible to streptomycin, rifampin, and isoniazid. Ms. L. was treated with these agents for 6 weeks and was then discharged, to continue on oral rifampin and isoniazid for an additional 9 months (see Chapter 22 for a discussion of this therapeutic regimen).

Pathobiology

Ms. L. came from a geographic region where pulmonary tuberculosis is endemic. During primary infection, tubercle bacilli were deposited in many organs (including the brain), where they become contained with granulomas. Ms. L.'s chickenpox suppressed her cell-mediated immunity, and the tubercle bacilli were now able to multiply and cause inflammation. In the brain, granulomas located near the ventricles spilled tubercle bacilli into the CSF. The organisms then spread throughout the subarachnoid space, and, for reasons as yet unknown, became most prevalent in the basilar cisterns. As cell-mediated immunity returned, it elicited an intense delayed hypersensitivity-type reaction to the organisms. Granulomas formed around cranial nerves caused their dysfunction. In Ms. L.'s case, the nerves affected were cranial VII and VIII (as indicated by deafness and paralysis of the side of the face, respectively). Inflammation of the meninges compromised her cerebral blood flow, leading to the stupor (which could have progressed to coma). In Ms. L.'s case, the CSF findings and indolent course were consistent with chronic meningitis and both fungi and *M. tuberculosis* had to be considered. The presence of a tubercular lipid (tuberculostearic acid) in the CSF made the diagnosis of tuberculous meningitis likely, and it was confirmed by the isolation from the CSF of *M. tuberculosis*.

ENCEPHALITIS

Acute encephalitis is almost invariably caused by a virus, with herpes simplex the most frequent in the U.S., followed by the togaviruses (encephalitis viruses). These viruses are listed in Table 58.2 and described in detail in Chapters 31 and 55. They cause extremely serious illnesses which, if untreated, have mortality rates of 75% or greater. Fortunately, herpes simplex encephalitis can be treated if diagnosed early.

Herpes Simplex Encephalitis

Ms. H., a 19-year-old woman living in the inner city, was brought to the emergency room by her mother because she was "acting funny." Her mother reported that, on arising, she thought "there were devils in the room," and she nearly destroyed her bedroom trying to escape them. On her way to the hospital, Ms. H. hallucinated intermittently, telling her mother that she was smelling roses. In the prior 3 days, she had some mild nausea and vomiting. In the emergency room, her urine was found to contain "angel dust" (phencyclidine) and she was admitted to the psychiatric ward. There she was noted to have a low-grade fever and received a phenothiazine tranquilizer (haloperidol). After 2 days, she had a generalized seizure and then became comatose.

Because convulsions are not associated with phencyclidine intoxication and are not a side effect of phenothiazines, there was a good likelihood that Ms. H. had a CNS infection. Her fever and seizures made this suspicion more probable. CSF obtained by lumbar puncture contained 280 erythrocytes and 350 mononuclear leukocytes/μl. The glucose content was in the normal range (48 mg/dl) and the protein concentration elevated (126 mg/dl; see Table 58.3 for normal values). A technetium-99 scan showed increased uptake in the left temporal lobe, indicating involvement of brain tissue (see under "Diagnosis"). In light of her recent neurological history, these findings prompted a biopsy of the temporal lobe, a preferred site for herpes simplex. A tissue sample was sectioned and, upon examination by immunofluorescent microscopy, indicated the presence of herpes simplex antigen. Herpes virus grew in cell cultures inoculated with the biopsy material. Ms. H. was treated with acyclovir for 2 weeks, which halted the progression of her neurological symptoms, but she had many residual signs of neurological impairment, which needed extensive rehabilitation therapy.

Pathobiology

Herpes simplex encephalitis is not a frequent disease, although it is the most common of the severe encephalitides. It usually follows the chronic latent infection characteristic of this virus. Genital herpes may also produce infection of the lower spinal cord and meninges, but this is rare. It is not known why, in some individuals, the virus travels centripetally (up the nerve) from the trigeminal ganglia, instead of following the more usual centrifugal route. Fibers emerging from the trigeminal ganglia innervate the dura of the middle and anterior fossae and the meningeal arteries of the area. Herpes simplex viruses may use this route to spread to the meninges and meningeal arteries and, from there, to the meningeal nerves and the contiguous cortex. This postulated pattern may explain the frequent localization of herpes virus in the temporal and frontal lobes.

The characteristic manifestations of viral encephalitis are cerebral dysfunction (e.g., abnormal behavior, altered consciousness, and seizures). Fever, nausea, and vomiting are also common, possibly due to increased intracranial pressure. Thus, Ms. H. had many of the typical signs and symptoms of the disease. Many of the manifestations of herpes simplex encephalitis are due to necrosis of neurons, especially of the temporal and frontal lobes. This is accompanied by inflammation, with infiltration of mononuclear cells from the perivascular sheaths (Virchow-Robin spaces). Her sites of involvement included the portion of the temporal lobe responsible for the sense of smell; hence her olfactory hallucination (smelling roses). The lesions are usually on one side only, probably because the viruses ascended from one of the trigeminal ganglia only.

Diagnosis

Patients are suspected of having herpetic encephalitis if they have fever and focal cerebral cortical lesions, particularly in the frontal and temporal lobes. Diagnostic tests are necessary to document the clinical impression that there is inflammation (i.e., CSF pleocytosis—the increase in the number of cells in the CSF) and focal involvement of cerebral tissue. A radioactive brain scan with technetium is the most sensitive test to indicate brain tissue involvement. Technetium-99, an artificial radioactive element, is injected in the blood covalently bound to serum albumin. Leaking from cerebral capillaries is detected by ^{99}Tc spilling into tissues. If the area of brain that is destroyed by HSV is large enough, damage may sometimes be detected by cranial CT examination.

The only conclusive way to diagnose herpetic encephalitis is by a brain biopsy, as was done with Ms. H. However, in patients with a history and physical findings of herpes encephalitis, acyclovir (a relatively nontoxic drug) is usually administered without further studies. The value of a brain biopsy is demonstrated by the fact that in approximately one-fourth of adults suspected of having herpes encephalitis, pathological examination of biopsy material revealed other diseases, e.g., cancer, bleeding, fungal infections, which require other forms of treatment.

Brain tissue obtained on biopsy is examined by conventional microscopy and is tested for herpes-specific antigens. This is currently done using fluorescent conjugated monoclonal or polyclonal antisera directed against an HSV glycoprotein. Culturing HSV from brain tissue provides unequivocal evidence of encephalitis, but takes more time. Since HSV spreads by contiguous cell-to-cell contact (Chapter 31), it can rarely be cultured from the CSF.

Many clinical conditions mimic herpetic encephalitis, particularly in adults. These include enterovirus or arbovirus encephalitis, cerebral collagen vascular disease, tumors, and even cryptococcal meningitis. A brain biopsy may sound like a dangerous invasive procedure. In skilled hands, it carries relatively little risk.

Treatment

As stated above, in patients with encephalitis, it is essential to determine if the disease is due to herpes simplex, because the morbidity and mortality of this disease can be decreased by drug treatment. Two antiviral agents, acyclovir and arabinosyl adenine, are available for the treatment of herpes encephalitis (Chapter 37). In a randomized chemotherapy trial, carried out chiefly with adult herpetic encephalitis patients, the mortality rate and the sequelae were reduced with acyclovir treatment (in one study, the overall mortality rate was reduced from 70% to 20%). With either agent, the outcome is related to the severity of disease at the time antiviral chemotherapy is begun, thus, the urgency to begin treatment. As with the bacterial meningitides, supportive care must not be neglected. Sequelae are due to destruction of cerebral gray matter. Such lesions in the temporal or frontal lobes may result in personality changes, whereas involvement of the white matter may lead to significant paralysis.

LATE ENCEPHALITIS

Inflammation of brain substance can occur some time after the initial invasion of the CNS. This can be due to an autoimmune reaction, continued unrestricted viral replication, or reactivation of latent virus.

Case

T. was 13 months old when he was placed in a large day care center in Philadelphia. After 1 month of daily attendance (approximately 6 hours each day), he developed a fever of 101° F, cough, watery eyes, and runny nose. Each day, his maximum temperature was slightly higher, but on the third day of illness, he developed a rash. It began as small (3–4 mm diameter) red macules on the face and neck. Within hours it had begum to spread down over the chest, became bright red, and became palpable. T. was taken to this physician who, after examining him, told the mother he had measles. Over the next few days, his rash became more extensive, but his fever and respiratory symptoms lessened. T. was well until 8 years of age, when he began having problems in school. His teachers first felt it was behavioral, but over a period of a few months noted that his ability in math (a subject he loved) seemed to be regressing. T.'s parents took him to a neurologist who, on additional questioning, found that T.'s skill in baseball had also been slipping; he appeared more awkward and was stumbling often. The neurologists performed a lumbar puncture and obtained an electroencephalogram. Several weeks later, without any perceptible change in T.'s clinical condition, the neurologist told the family that T.'s illness was due to the measles virus. The disease was called subacute sclerosing panencephalitis (SSPE) and was ultimately fatal.

T.'s parents were devastated and doubtful. How could the physician be sure this was due to measles? Why did T. develop the illness? Could it have been prevented? Is there a treatment now?

Pathobiology

T. suffered a rare complication of measles virus infection. At the time of the initial infection, the virus invaded virtually all organs in the body. In the overwhelming majority of patients, the virus replication and spread is terminated by host immunity. In rare patients with unrecognized deficiency in cell-mediated immunity, there is progressive encephalitis with seizures and motor deficits appearing after 1 week of disease. This illness is due to unrestricted viral replication and spread. This illness is distinguished from "postinfectious" encephalitis. In this form of measles-associated encephalitis, the patient begins recovering from measles but precipitously develops obtundation or coma, coincident with the reappearance of fever. This complication is relatively common, affecting 1 in every 1000 children with measles. It is one of the major rationales for measles vaccination. Why didn't T. receive the measles vaccine? A modified measles virus, along with mumps and rubella, is given to children at 15 months of age. Before that time, most children still have maternal antibody (received in utero) preventing an effective immune response. Thus, T. was too young to have received the measles vaccine, when he was exposed.

T.'s symptoms were typical of SSPE, mental deterioration followed by loss of motor skills. The physician made the diagnosis of SSPE by obtaining a characteristic pattern on the electroencephalogram, and by finding increased concentrations of antibodies to measles virus-specific proteins in the CSF. Often, patients with SSPE will have very high serum antibody titers, but measles virus replication in the brain evokes local production of antibodies. This results in the CSF concentration of specific antibodies exceeding that in serum. SSPE is an extremely rare complication of measles, occurring in only 1 of 100,000 cases of measles.

It is not clear how the measles virus manages to become latent. Virus is present in neurons and glial cells, but it appears in genes that encode for membrane antigens are silenced, so that the organism is sequestered from the host immune response. Latency appears to be due also to selective inhibition (or mutation) of viral genome expression. One measles virus-specific protein, termed M-protein, is involved in the budding of mature virus from the cell. Failure to be assembled into mature virus would favor retention of the virus in the cell. Because cells of the CNS do not turn over (as does liver, for example), the virus can remain latent for a long period of time. Slow replication of the defective virus leads to slow progression of CNS symptoms in SSPE. Unfortunately, there is no specific treatment for SSPE. In addition to measles, rubella and the polyomaviruses can cause latent infection of the CNS, i.e., reactivation at a time distant from the acute infection can produce encephalitis.

ABSCESSES

Brain abscesses typically follow two diseases—congenital heart disease and chronic parameningeal infections. In a patient with endocarditis, a septic embolus from the heart may rarely cause a brain abscess.

Case

Ms. T., a 29-year-old housewife, complained of earache. She had had many such episodes since childhood, especially of the left ear, but this one was associated with a headache that made her nauseated. She vomited once. After 4 days of these symptoms, she was driven to the hospital because she had developed a large "blind spot" in her right field of vision. At the hospital, it was noted that she had a low-grade fever of 38.1°C. A CT scan of the head revealed a 4 × 3 cm mass in her left occipital lobe, consistent with an abscess (Fig. 58.5).

A neurosurgeon performed a needle aspiration of the abscess under CT guidance. A smear of the aspirate revealed Gram-positive cocci, and the material grew Staphylococcus aureus when cultured. Ms. T. was treated with intravenous nafcillin (to cover S. aureus) and metronidazole (to cover anaerobic bacteria) for 4 weeks, during which period serial CT examinations

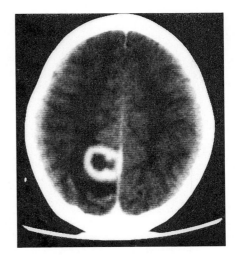

Figure 58.5. Computerized tomogram of the cranium of a patient with an abscess in left occipital lobe. The liquefied (necrotic) material in the abscess center appears dark. The white rim surround the abscess is its wall, which is visualized because of its vascularization and contiguous vasodilation. All of the intracranial vasculature is visualized because γ-ray absorbing material was infused intravenously at the time the radiograph was obtained.

showed the abscess to be shrinking. She recovered completely, with the exception of a remaining small blind spot in the right visual field.

Pathobiology

The case of Ms. T. may well have started with a chronic infection of the middle ear or mastoid. Her history points to that—particularly because of the long-term earache. Chronic infections of the middle ear, the mastoid, or the sinuses often involve the bony structures that surround them, plus their vasculature. Veins that bridge the temporal bone and the cerebral cortex may become infected (septic thrombophlebitis), leading to a decrease in local blood supply and providing a reservoir of bacteria.

Abscesses may appear at many locations of the brain and the subdural or epidural meningeal spaces. Infarction of cerebral cortex during meningitis produces a subdural abscess that is poorly localized; this is called **subdural empyema.** If an empyema is not completely drained, it will slowly resolve, as will an abscess in other parts of the body. In contrast with intracerebral abscesses, those located on the outside of the dura mater (**epidural abscesses**) are invariably related to contiguous infection of bone, sometimes secondary to infection of the paranasal sinuses or mastoids.

Decrease in the blood supply to an area of the brain leads to a condition called **encephalomalacia,** the softening of the brain tissue that accompanies cell death. Bacteria that are transiently found in the circulation may lodge themselves in these softened and necrotic areas and cause abscess formation. Children with cyanotic congenital heart disease have multiple areas of encephalomalacia throughout their brain and many suffer from brain abscesses. In Ms. T.'s case, septic phlebitis of veins that pass from the temporal bone to the cortex not only produced encephalomalacia, but also supplied the bacteria that caused the abscess. Abscesses may also be a complication of meningitis, if cerebral vasculitis is severe enough to produce infarction of brain substance. This usually occurs in the watershed areas, on the margin between adjacent vascular territories where the vasculature least overlaps.

The symptoms caused by brain abscesses are due to increased intracranial pressure and to destruction of tissue at specific locations. When the frontal lobe is involved, there is diminished intellectual performance, memory deficits, drowsiness, and perhaps some memory loss (Fig. 58.3). Temporal lobe involvement results in visual field defects and, occasionally, in difficulty in speaking. In some patients, mastoiditis leads to cerebellar abscesses, resulting in incoordination, ataxia, and falling toward the affected side.

Acute abscesses in the CNS are frequently caused by a mixed bacterial flora consisting of strict and facultative anaerobes. They represent the mixture of bacteria found in the mouth, or in a parameningeal focus such as an infected middle ear, mastoid, or sinus. Staphylococci can also infect brain tissue if delivered to that location in a septic embolus from an infected heart valve.

Chronic abscesses may be located in either the meninges or the brain tissue. The most common causative agents are tubercle bacilli, *Cryptococcus*, and other fungi. Chronic abscesses are invariably due to metastatic spread from foci elsewhere, but, sometimes, the CNS manifestations may be the first indication of the presence of the organisms. These abscesses usually follow a course of remission and relapse. They are often associated with a loss of cell-mediated immunity, when the causative agents are no longer kept in check at the primary focus.

Brain abscesses may also develop from head injuries that allow the direct penetration of microorganisms. Some fractures of the temporal bone are said never to heal completely, and thus, become a chronic portal of entry for bacteria from the middle ear and the mastoid. Invasion of the CNS may follow neurosurgical or orthopaedic procedures of the brain or the spinal column. Brain abscesses that result from trauma or surgical procedures are usually due to *S. aureus* or Gram-negative bacilli.

Diagnosis

Diagnosis of brain abscess is aided by several imaging techniques. A brain scan with technetium-99 will show an area of increased radioactivity in the wall of the abscess (where the capillaries are inflamed and leaking) and an avascular central portion (the abscess cavity). This area often looks like a "donut" on the scan (Fig. 58.5). Cranial CT may also demonstrate the same structures—a fluid avascular abscess cavity and a overly vascularized (hyperemic) rim surrounding the cavity. Lumbar puncture is inadvisable in an individual suspected of having a brain abscess, as the increased intracranial pressure may cause brainstem herniation with lumbar decompression.

Aspiration of the abscess cavity yields material for cytological analysis, Gram stain, and culture. Anaerobes are common in brain abscess and the aspirate should immediately be cultured anaerobically. Often a smear will show the presence of lots of Gram-positive cocci, Gram-positive rods, and perhaps a few Gram-negative rods, yet only *S. aureus* will grow in culture. In such a case, the bacteria that failed to grow can be assumed to be oxygen-sensitive anaerobes.

Treatment

Like abscesses elsewhere, brain abscesses must usually be drained to effect resolution. In addition, aspiration of the contents of an abscess helps lower the increased intracranial pressure and improves the patient's condition. Focal symptoms due to tissue destruction will not be improved, but the lesion can be contained from further increase in size by the administration of antibiotics.

Antibiotic therapy is not always effective in the treatment of brain abscesses. Inflammation of the meninges is usually too slight to enhance penetration of antibiotics into the CSF. In addition, most antibiotics function poorly in an abscess. Ideally, an antibiotic should be chosen based on the susceptibility of organisms isolated from the abscess cavity, but aspiration of material for culture and susceptibility testing is not always practical. Usually a β-lactam and a lipophilic antibiotic active against anaerobes are administered together.

CONCLUSIONS

The anatomic and physiological protective mechanisms of the CNS effectively limit access of microorganisms. On the other hand, if infective agents succeed in penetrating the tissues of the system, the same mechanisms tend to exacerbate the symptoms of disease.

The most frequent infections of the CNS are caused by relatively few agents. Typically, the organisms tend to cause specific disease manifestations; encephalitis is almost exclusively caused by viruses, acute meningitis by bacteria, chronic meningitis by tubercle bacilli and the cryptococcus. Bacterial abscesses, in contrast, are frequently caused by a mixture of bacteria derived from the normal flora of the mouth and oropharynx.

Infections of the CNS are often very severe and life threatening. Many require immediate action, based on acute clinical assessment and, when available, rapid diagnostic tests. The most important diagnostic procedure is the examination of the CSF for microorganisms, white blood cells, and the determination of the concentration of glucose and protein. Fortunately, there are drugs that are effective for many of even the most dangerous conditions, such as herpetic encephalitis.

SUGGESTED READING

Notkins AL, Oldstone MBA, eds. Concepts in viral pathogenesis. New York: Springer Verlag, 1984.

Rosenblum ML, Hoff JT, Norman D, Edwards MS, Berg BO. Nonoperative treatment of brain abscesses in selected high-risk patients. J Neurosurg 1980;52:217–225.

Sequiera LW, Carrasco LH, Curry A, et al. Detection of herpes-simplex virus genome in brain tissue. Lancet 1979;2:609–612.

Weiner LP, Fleming JO. Viral infections of the nervous system. J Neurosurg 1984;61:207–244.

Whitley RJ, Alford CA, Hirsch MS, et al. (The NIAID Collaborative Antiviral Study Group). Vidabirine versus acyclovir therapy in herpes simplex encephalitis. N Engl J Med 1986;314:144–149.

Urinary Tract

59

Michael Barza

From the distal urethra to the calyces of the kidney, the urinary tract is lined with a sheet of epithelium that is continuous with that of the skin. Thus, the epithelial surface is a potential pathway for entry of microorganisms from the outside world. Most urinary tract infections (UTIs) arise by the ascent of bacteria following colonization of the periurethral area by fecal organisms (especially *Escherichia coli*). Hematogenous infection of the kidney is much rarer. The main defenses against UTIs are the flow of urine and the sloughing of epithelial cells to which bacteria may be attached. Immune defenses (humoral or cellular) play little role here.

In view of the ready access of bacteria to the urinary tract, it is not surprising that **UTIs** are second in incidence only to infections of the respiratory tract. They rank first among the **bacterial** diseases of adults that come to the attention of physicians. The majority of patients are women, presumably because the female urethra is much shorter than the male urethra. An antibacterial effect of prostatic secretions may also offer some protection to the male. Thus, **bacteriuria** (the presence of bacteria in the urine), whether symptomatic or asymptomatic, is generally more common in women than in men at all ages (Fig. 59.1). As many as 20% of all women have an episode of urinary tract infection by the age of 30 years. There are an estimated 3 million office visits for this complaint each year in the U.S. alone. **Recurrent episodes** of UTIs afflict about one in ten women at some time in their life.

All portions of the urinary tract may be affected, but the most common UTIs are infections of the bladder (**cystitis**) and the kidney (**pyelonephritis**). Infection of the urethra alone, or **urethritis**, is discussed with the sexually transmitted diseases (see Chapter 65). Prostatic infection is usually considered as separate from UTI, although chronic bacterial prostatitis may lead to recurrent UTI. **Renal abscesses** may occur as a result of ascending UTI or of bacteremia, and pyelonephritis may also result from bacteremia, without other involvement of the urinary tract. As in other infectious diseases, the physician usually suspects UTI on the basis of characteristic symptoms and signs and confirms the diagnosis by means of culture.

CASE OF BACTERIAL PYELONEPHRITIS IN AN INFANT

D., a 3-month-old boy was gaining weight very slowly. On examination, the only other clinical or laboratory abnormality was the finding of 3 × 10⁵ E. coli per ml of urine. D. was treated with intravenous ampicillin for 1 week and began to gain weight more rapidly. However, after 6 weeks, it was again noted that he was not gaining weight and had E. coli bacteriuria. Over the next 2 months, the laboratory reported comparable bacterial counts with the same organism on two more occasions. Radiological studies showed that D. had re-

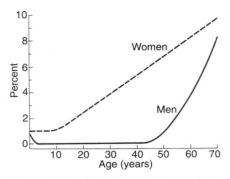

Figure 59.1. Prevalence of bacteriuria according to age and sex.

flux of urine from the bladder into the ureter and scarring of the pelvis of the left kidney. No obstruction was seen. A tentative diagnosis of **bacterial pyelonephritis** was made. Treatment was given with intravenous ampicillin followed by oral ampicillin for 6 weeks in an attempt to eradicate the infection. This regimen was successful and D. had no further problems with UTI.

CASE OF RECURRENT CYSTITIS

Ms. C., a 23-year-old woman had five attacks of acute **cystitis** (painful urination, increased frequency and urgency) in the year since her marriage. The diagnosis was based on the clinical picture and the laboratory finding of bacteriuria. Three attacks were caused by E. coli, one by Staphylococcus saprophyticus, and one by Proteus mirabilis. Urinary colony counts in the various episodes ranged from 10^2 to $10^6/ml$. Each attack responded either to trimethoprim-sulfamethoxazole or to ampicillin given for 1 week. Recurrences were noted at 1-week to 3-month intervals after stopping therapy. Treated with long-term antibiotic prophylaxis, she did well and had no further recurrences.

CASE OF PYELONEPHRITIS AND BACTEREMIA

Mr. P., a 65-year-old man, was admitted to the hospital with acute urinary tract obstruction due to prostatic hypertrophy. He was confused, had a temperature of 40.1°C, and his blood pressure was lower than normal. Cultures of his urine and blood yielded Proteus vulgaris. A urinary catheter was placed to relieve the obstruction. He was diagnosed as suffering from bacterial pyelonephritis with secondary bacteremia. After treatment with antibiotics, he underwent cystoscopy and resection of his hypertrophied prostate gland without further significant problems.

PATHOBIOLOGY OF UTI

As in other sites, host-parasite interactions in the urinary tract include the entry of microorganisms, their spread and multiplication, and the damage they cause (Fig. 59.2). But, in the urinary tract, **mechanical factors**, especially those that obstruct the normal flow of urine, play a particularly important role in disease. Cellular and humoral immunity are not as important in the defense against UTIs as the normal flow of urine and other anatomic factors.

ENTRY

Access of infectious agents into the urinary tract is nearly always by **ascent from the urethra**. Blood-borne infections are a relatively infrequent source and are apt to result in renal abscesses rather than in ordinary UTI. Renal abscess following bacteremia probably results from the lodging of blood-borne organisms in the glomeruli. Most ascending UTIs are caused by enteric or skin bacteria, as in the three cases presented, followed in frequency by chlamydiae, the fungus *Candida albicans*, and, rarely by viruses, protozoa, or worms. The fecal bacteria, the most frequent cause of UTI, are not a random sample but are a **selected subset of the intestinal flora**. Strict anaerobic species of bacteria rarely cause UTI. Over 80% of acute UTI in patients without anatomic abnormalities (**uncomplicated UTI**) are caused by strains of *E. coli* that possess certain virulence factors. Other members of the enteric bacilli and the group B and D streptococci are also prominent (Table 59.1). Some infections, especially in women, are caused by *S. saprophyticus* or by *C. albicans*. The reason for the prominence of these species can be par-

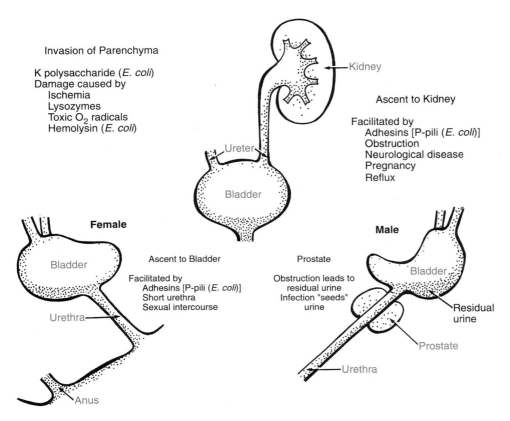

Figure 59.2. Pathogenesis of urinary tract infections.

Table 59.1. Causative Agents of Urinary Tract Infection			
Uncomplicated	%	Complicated[a] or Nosocomial	%
	80%		
Escherichia coli	20%	Escherichia coli	
Proteus mirabilis		Klebsiella	
Other Enterobacteriaceae		Other Enterobacteriaceae	80%
Staphylococcus saprophyticus		Pseudomonas aeruginosa	
	20%		
Streptococci (enterococci and group B streptococci)		Serratia	
Chlamydiae			

[a]Patients with structural or neurological abnormalities of the urinary tract

tially surmised; adhesion to epithelial cells appears to be the most important single determinant of pathogenicity.

Some prospective studies in women with recurrent UTIs, such as Ms. C., indicate that, shortly before the onset of bladder infections, an increasing number of fecal bacteria colonize the epithelium of the vagina and around the urinary meatus. When the number of bacteria becomes large enough, the organisms may enter the urethra and the bladder and overwhelm the normal defense mechanisms. However, large numbers of bacteria alone may not be enough to cause UTI; mechanical and other factors may contribute to causing infection. We shall consider how host and bacterial factors play a role in the entry phase of UTI.

Host Factors

The much greater prevalence of UTI among women than men has been attributed to the fact that invading microorganisms have a shorter trip to travel through the female urethra to reach the bladder. Once bacteria have colonized the introitus, their entry into the urinary bladder is facilitated by mechanical factors including sexual intercourse, the use of a contraceptive diaphragm, or the presence of a Foley catheter. The prevalence of bacteriuria in women rises sharply with sexual activity; celibate women have a smaller frequency of bacteriuria than sexually active women. Sexual intercourse contributes to UTI, perhaps by "massaging" bacteria upward into the bladder, hence the term "honeymoon cystitis." Knowledge of these issues may allow the physician to help the patient who is suffering from recurrent UTI. Voiding after intercourse protects against the development of infection. Contraceptive diaphragms make it more difficult to empty the bladder completely and the presence of residual urine in the bladder fosters bacteremia. Likewise, neurological disease affecting the bladder muscles impairs emptying of the bladder and also appears to contribute to UTI. Women who are particularly prone to recurrent UTI have been found to possess a greater than normal density of **bacterial receptors on their uroepithelial cells**. In other words, their epithelial cells are particularly "sticky" for bacteria. Individuals with certain blood group antigens are more prone than others to develop recurrent UTI. The hypothesis is that these individuals lack substances on their epithelial cells that obscure receptors for *E. coli*.

Men are less prone to get UTI, possibly because of their longer urethra and the presence of antimicrobial substances in the prostatic fluid. An increased frequency of UTI in older men correlates with the onset of prostatic hypertrophy, which leads to obstruction to voiding. Occasionally, the prostate gland itself may become infected and serve as a nidus from which bacteria may emerge periodically to cause relapsing infections. Mr. P.'s enlarged prostate was removed and could not contribute further to infection.

UTI in patients with structural abnormalities of the urinary tract, including stones, obstructions, or catheters, are known as **"complicated UTI."** These infections, especially those associated with urinary catheters, are often caused by species of Gram-negative organisms such as *Klebsiella*, *Enterobacter*, *Acinetobacter*, *Serratia* sp. or *Pseudomonas aeruginosa*, which are relatively resistant to antibiotics (Table 59.1). These species are often selected by antimicrobial agents given for the treatment of other infections, particularly in hospitalized patients. The administration of antimicrobial agents to prevent UTI in patients with urinary catheters has little effect except to foster infection by resistant organisms. Patients with urinary stones often have infection caused by urea-splitting microorganisms, especially *Proteus* sp., which raise the pH of the urine and lead to the formation of "struvite" calculi. Complicated UTI is also important medically because of the high likelihood of **spread** to the kidney (pyelonephritis) and the bloodstream (sepsis), as discussed below.

Bacterial Factors

Of the bacterial factors predisposing to UTI, the best studied one is the ability of organisms to stick to the mucosa of the urinary tract. Adhesion to epithelial cells ensures that bacteria are not readily washed out by the flow of urine. Many causative agents of UTI have strong adhesins, usually in the form of pili (sometimes called fimbriae, see Chapter 3). These protein appendages help overcome the repulsive forces between the surface of bacterial and epithelial cells, both types of cells being hydrophobic and negatively charged. In *E. coli*, the so-called **P pili** appear to play a role in the establishment of infection both in the bladder and in the kidney. These pili stick specifically to galactose-containing receptors on epithelial cells; the receptors are contained in the P group blood antigen, which is present in 99% of the population. In one study of women with recurrent UTI, P pili were present in 29% of random fecal isolates of *E. coli*, in 65% of isolates from patients with cystitis, and in 100% of isolates from patients with pyelonephritis.

Spread to the Kidney

The most serious consequence of bladder infection is the ascent of microorganisms to the kidneys to produce pyelonephritis. Any factor that contributes to the retrograde flow of urine may contribute to the establishment of pyelonephritis. The more common examples of such predisposing factors include:

- **Reflux of urine** from the bladder into the ureters; this is a frequent problem in children and is caused by incomplete closing of the ureterovesical valves. It can lead to regurgitation of contaminated urine from the bladder into the ureter and the calyces. Reflux is frequently corrected spontaneously as the child grows. This abnormality may have been a contributory cause for the pyelonephritis in the case of baby D.

- **Other physiological malfunctions; neurological disorders** lead to poor emptying of the bladder. The hormonal and anatomic effects of pregnancy cause dilatation and decreased peristalsis of the ureters. Diabetic patients are also prone to pyelonephritis for reasons that are not fully understood.

- **Urethral catheters**; these present at least two risk factors for cystitis and pyelonephritis—they serve as a conduit along which bacteria can spread, and as a nidus for persistent infection. Most patients who acquire UTI in the hospital become infected as the result of instrumentation of the urinary tract, especially from the use of an indwelling catheter. Scrupulous adherence to good technique, such as maintaining closed drainage and placing the collection bag below the level of the bladder, is helpful but cannot fully prevent these infections. The prevalence of bacteriuria in patients **increases by about 5% for each day the catheter is in place**. In these patients, many of the infecting strains do not have the usual adhesins; they are able to ascend along the catheter without having to adhere to the mucosa.

- **Urinary tract stones**; once colonized by bacteria, stones serve as a nidus for relapsing infections of the bladder and of the kidney. Bacteria may also contribute to the formation of such "infection stones." Species of *Proteus* split urea to form ammonium hydroxide, which raises the pH of the urine and facilitates the formation of "struvite" calculi (consisting of ammonium magnesium phosphate, which becomes increasingly insoluble as the pH rises).

DAMAGE

Bacteria do not generally invade the mucosa of the lower urinary tract. The symptoms of cystitis and urethritis are caused mainly by superficial irritation. By contrast, bacteria that reach the parenchyma of the kidney (i.e., the upper urinary tract) produce the systemic manifestations of fever, chills, and leukocytosis, which, together with the localized symptoms of flank pain, are the hallmarks of pyelonephritis. Pyelonephritis is often accompanied by bacteremia, but need not be to produce the systemic manifestations. It has been suggested that hyperosmolarity in the renal pelvis diminishes the function of neutrophils and, thereby, facilitates invasion of the kidneys, but this is in dispute. Antibody is produced as the result of tissue invasion but probably plays little role in host defenses.

Strains of *E. coli* that possess certain capsular polysaccharides appear to be particularly invasive, perhaps because these polysaccharides inhibit phagocytosis. For reasons that are not clear, hemolysin production by some *E. coli* strains also appears to contribute to renal damage; and, of course, the endotoxin of Gram negatives may also contribute to inflammation and damage of the renal parenchyma (see Chapter 62). Mention has already been made of the association of *Proteus* and stone formation. Stones are particularly bad for the urinary tract in that they often cause obstruction, which, by itself, can significantly damage the kidney. Obstruction with infection is particularly dangerous because it leads to life-threatening sepsis and rapid kidney destruction.

BACTERIURIA AND COLONY COUNTS—DIAGNOSTIC PROBLEM

As was mentioned earlier in this chapter, laboratory confirmation of the diagnosis of UTI depends upon culture of the urine, but the interpretation of such cultures is made difficult because voided urine usually contains contaminating bacteria from the urethral meatus. Normal precautions of cleansing the external genitalia and collecting a "clean-catch" midstream specimen reduce the degree of contamination but do not totally prevent the problem. Urine collected by needle aspiration of the bladder or by urethral catheterization contains fewer contaminants than voided urine (Table 59.2), but these procedures are not practical. Certain species that are common members of the skin flora, including coagulase-negative staphylococci and diphtheroids, are more likely to be contaminants than are enteric Gram-negative bacilli, but this is not a reliable means to distinguish between true bacteriuria and contaminated urine. Repeated cultures may be obtained to determine the reproducibility of the findings but this is costly and time-consuming.

Table 59.2. Definitions of "Significant Bacteriuria" in Selected Groups of Patients

Population	"Significant Bacteriuria"
Asymptomatic bacteriuria	$\geq 10^5$ cfu/ml
Acute pyelonephritis	$\geq 10^5$ cfu/ml
Women with acute dysuria	$\geq 10^2$ cfu/ml in women with abnormal pyuria (best shown for coliforms; not clear if same criteria applicable for staphylococci
Patients with indwelling urinary catheters	$\geq 10^2$ cfu/ml

For practical purposes, the distinction between **significant bacteriuria** and contamination of the urine is based on the enumeration of the number of bacteria in the urine. This approach relies on the experimental observation that there are usually more bacteria present in the urine of patients with "true bacteriuria" than in the urine of patients in whom the microorganisms are present only as contaminants. The following guidelines have been developed that apply mainly to the Gram-negative bacteria. In the asymptomatic patient, a level of 10^5 colonies per ml of urine or greater is considered indicative of infection (Fig. 59.3, Table 59.2). Among patients **with symptoms of cystitis**, even 10^2 colonies per ml is considered significant. The reason for the difference in threshold is that, in the asymptomatic patient, there is a greater likelihood that low counts represent contamination rather than true bacteriuria.

The reasons why some patients with cystitis have high and others have low bacterial counts in the urine are not known. Indeed, the same patient may have high counts on one occasion and low ones on another, as was the case with Ms. C., the patient described above. Of course, urine must be cultured as soon as possible after it has been obtained to avoid bacterial growth in vitro, which would produce spuriously high counts.

As shown in Figure 59.1 and Table 59.2, asymptomatic bacteriuria is infrequent in both sexes at birth. The incidence of all UTIs begins to rise in young women as they reach the sexually active years. By contrast, the frequency remains low in men until they reach the age when hypertrophy of the prostate becomes common (Fig. 59.1 and Table 59.2).

MAIN UTIs

Most patients come to medical attention for UTIs because they have symptoms. In young children, such as baby D., the symptoms may not call particular attention to the urinary tract. In adults, the symptoms of UTI are usually related to the lower portion of the urinary tract (**cystitis**) or to the upper one (**pyelonephritis**).

Cystitis

Patients with cystitis, like Ms. C., have dysuria (painful urination), urgency (the need to urinate without delay), and increased frequency

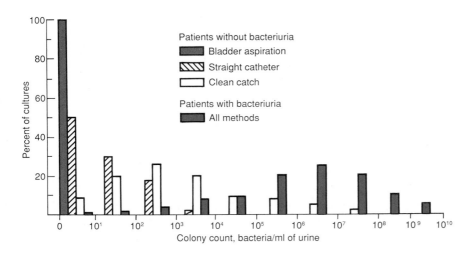

Figure 59.3. Colony counts for women with and without bacteriuria. Results are similar for men except that colony counts from those without bacteriuria are lower using the clean-catch technique for urine collection.

of urination. These symptoms result from irritation of the mucosa of the lower urinary tract as a result of the infection.

Vaginitis may produce symptoms that are somewhat similar to those produced by UTI. Vaginitis may result from infection with *Trichomonas* or *C. albicans*. "Nonspecific vaginitis" appears to be the result of complex interactions among various anaerobic bacteria, including the newly recognized *Mobiluncus* sp., and possibly *Gardnerella vaginalis*. Although patients with vaginitis may experience pain on urination, the discomfort is perceived as external and there is usually no urgency or frequency of urination (in contrast to the symptoms of UTI).

In about 10–20% of patients with cystitis, the infection is caused by chlamydiae, which are missed by the usual bacteriological culture techniques. Most patients with cystitis have an increased number of white cells in their urine, **abnormal pyuria**. Most of those with cystitis and abnormal pyuria respond to treatment with antibacterial drugs, whether their urinary bacteria counts are low (less than 10^2 colonies/ml) or high (more than 10^5 colonies/ml). However, about 30% of patients with cystitis and low bacterial counts **do not have abnormal pyuria**; these patients do not respond to antibiotics, and the etiology of their disease remains unknown.

Urethritis

Most of the infections that cause purulent urethritis **without cystitis** are sexually transmitted. Urethritis may be gonococcal or nongonococcal. Most cases of nongonococcal urethritis are thought to be caused by strains of *C. trachomatis*, certain mycoplasmas (e.g., *Ureaplasma urealyticum*) or combinations of these species, but there is disagreement on this subject. Furthermore, in some cases, the causative agent of urethritis is simply not known. For some details, see Chapters 14 (Gonococcus) and 26 (Chlamydiae).

Pyelonephritis

In contrast to cystitis, pyelonephritis is an invasive infection that leads to fever, flank pain, and tenderness; there is usually peripheral leukocytosis. These signs were seen in the case of Mr. P. The urine of patients with pyelonephritis often contains microscopic **white blood cell casts**, elongated structures composed of cells that were tightly packed in the tubules and excreted in a proteinaceous matrix. Their presence indicates involvement of the renal tubules. Some patients with pyelonephritis, like Mr. P., develop bacteremia, which may lead to shock and death. Renal abscesses are also occasional complications of bacterial pyelonephritis.

Problem in Distinguishing Upper From Lower UTI

Clearly, upper and lower UTIs differ in their potential to cause serious disease. As we shall see, they also have different implications for therapy, in that treatment of pyelonephritis is usually more intensive and carried out for a longer time than treatment of lower UTI. Unfortunately, it is not always easy to distinguish between these infections. Upper UTI are often accompanied by fever and flank pain. These symptoms strongly suggest involvement of the kidney. However, 30–

50% of women with symptoms of cystitis alone have bacteria in the upper urinary tract even though they have no symptoms of kidney involvement. They may be suffering from a mild, subclinical pyelonephritis. Radiological studies sometimes help in pointing to upper UTI but are costly and not highly sensitive; and they also involve some risk.

Presently, the most accurate way to determine the site of involvement in UTI is to catheterize the ureters and to obtain a sample directly. To try to avoid this costly and somewhat risky procedure, a test has been developed based on the assumption that invasion of the kidney leads to the production of specific antibodies that will coat the bacteria in the urine. It is known as the **antibody-coated bacteriuria test**. Coating by antibodies can be seen in a smear of urine sediment stained with fluorescein-labeled antihuman γ-globulin antibody. Unfortunately, thus far, the test has proven to be falsely negative in as many as 40% of patients with pyelonephritis and falsely positive in as many as 15% of patients without pyelonephritis. Men with bacterial prostatitis, for example, often have a positive reaction because this is a tissue invasive infection.

On practical grounds, the distinction between upper and lower UTI may have to be made empirically, based on the response to the administration of of antibiotics (see below). In the absence of symptoms pointing to renal involvement or of factors predisposing to renal involvement, physicians will often treat patients for cystitis alone. Relapse of the infection may be the first clue to renal involvement, and may lead to more intensive treatment.

Recurrent Infections: Relapse vs. Reinfection

Among the most significant problems in the management of patients with UTI is the tendency of the infection to recur. Ms. C. exemplifies the situation. Recurrence may be either a **relapse**, i.e., the recrudescence of the original infection, or, more commonly, **reinfection**, the occurrence of a new infection. Relapse is caused by the same strain of organism that caused the original infection and often occurs shortly after cessation of treatment. This suggests that the causative agent has persisted in the urinary tract or nearby—possibly because of an anatomic problem such as an obstruction or a stone. By contrast, reinfection may be caused by the original organism or by a different one, and can occur at any time after treatment is stopped. It does not suggest an anatomic abnormality. Ms. C. suffered from reinfections, as shown by the fact that the offending organism was different in each attack.

"Complicated" UTI and Nosocomial Infections

UTI occurring in patients with a structurally normal urinary tract are called **uncomplicated UTI**. Infections in patients with anatomic abnormalities, stones, or indwelling catheters are called **complicated UTI**. The latter have a tendency to relapse unless the predisposing factors can be removed. In the case of Mr. P., resection of the prostate and removal of the catheter contributed to his cure. Nosocomial UTIs, i.e., UTIs acquired in the hospital, are usually the consequence of instrumentation, mainly catheterization of the bladder. The selective action of antibiotics commonly used in hospitalized patients tends to favor infection by species of bacteria that are relatively resistant to antibiotics.

TREATMENT AND PREVENTION

The basic tenets in the treatment and prevention of UTI follow the concepts of the pathogenesis of these infections (Table 59.3). The choice of antibacterial drugs should include the following considerations:

1. Is the infecting agent susceptible to the drug or drugs?

2. Can an effective drug concentration be achieved at the site of infection?

3. What is the likely effect of therapy on the recurrence of infection?

It is not generally necessary to do a **follow-up urine culture** in patients with UTI whose symptoms resolve with treatment unless the patient belongs to one of the risk groups in which asymptomatic bacteriuria merits treatment (see below).

Asymptomatic Bacteriuria

Asymptomatic bacteriuria is common, especially in older patients. In the past, it was thought that asymptomatic bacteriuria was an important contributor to chronic nephritis, to renal failure and hypertension, and even to premature death. Although the issue remains somewhat controversial, it is now believed that asymptomatic bacteriuria generally does not have significant consequences and need not be treated in most patients. Indeed, in the elderly, debilitated patients in whom it is commonly detected, it is difficult to eradicate the infection and recurrence after treatment is usual.

Table 59.3. Principles of Treatment of Urinary Tract Infection

Type of Infection	Treatment	Rationale
Cystitis	Single-dose Rx or short course (e.g., 3 days)	Effective for bacterial cystitis; will not be effective in patients with early pyelonephritis, chlamydial cystitis or infection caused by resistant bacteria, which will be detected by follow-up culture or by relapse of symptoms
Acute urethral syndrome with "abnormal pyuria"	Single-dose Rx, if no response, 10 days of doxycycline or TMP-SMX	Coliforms or staphylococci respond to many agents, chlamydia (found in 20%) should respond to doxycycline or possibly TMP-SMX; patients without abnormal pyuria don't respond to antibacterial drugs
Pyelonephritis	At least 2 weeks (some say 4–8 weeks) of full doses IV or by mouth; tend to prefer bactericidal drug, but one based on susceptibility tests	Not many data re importance of bactericidal vs. bacteriostatic drug or optimal duration of Rx, but with shorter courses, the relapse rate is high (e.g., 10–50% relapse after 7–14 days of treatment)
Asymptomatic bacteriuria	Mainly indicated for pregnant women, young children, or patients about to undergo instrumentation of the urinary tract	25–40% of pregnant women with asymptomatic bacteriuria develop pyelonephritis if not treated
Recurrent infection Multiple reinfection	Individual attack usually responds well to short-course treatment	Main issue is of prophylaxis: continuous or postintercourse
Relapse	Long-term treatment (e.g., 4–8 weeks)	Usually suggests tissue invasion or structural abnormality and usually merits IVP or other evaluation

There are three main groups in whom asymptomatic bacteriuria should be treated. One is **pregnant women** because, without treatment, 25–40% of them will develop pyelonephritis with possible adverse consequences for the pregnancy. The second group is **preschool children** because reflux from the bladder to the ureters may lead to ascent of the infection into the kidneys with resultant renal scarring. The third group is patients with **structurally abnormal urinary tracts** and those who are about to undergo **instrumentation** of the urinary tract, because there is a high risk of the development of ascending UTI. Asymptomatic bacteriuria is several times as frequent in diabetic women as in nondiabetic women, for unknown reasons. It is not clear if these patients should be treated.

CYSTITIS

This is the most common type of UTI encountered by the physician. Most of the cases are caused by organisms that are relatively susceptible to antibacterial antibiotics. A single large dose of a drug suffices to eradicate most uncomplicated infections, presumably because of the high concentration of the drug in the urine and the lack of tissue invasion by the bacteria. Slightly higher cure rates are obtained if the treatment is given for 3 days. It does not matter if the antibacterial agent is bacteriostatic or bactericidal. Short-course treatment has the advantage of lower drug cost, lower rate of side effects, and lesser chance of selection of resistant strains. (This practice is not always followed. Ms. C. was treated with several week-long courses of drug therapy.)

The most common choice is trimethoprim-sulfamethoxazole (Bactrim, Septra), which is effective against the usual Gram-negative pathogens; it is inexpensive, and generally well tolerated. Ampicillin (or amoxicillin) works less well for reasons that are not clear. For infection caused by resistant organisms, a quinolone is a good choice or possibly amoxicillin with the β-lactamase inhibitor, clavulanic acid (Augmentin) or an oral cephalosporin. For patients with suspected chlamydial infection, doxycycline or another tetracycline should be used. About 80–90% of patients with uncomplicated cystitis can be cured with a 3-day course of therapy. Patients in whom there is a failure of treatment of cystitis should be suspected of having occult (subclinical) pyelonephritis or prostatitis and should be retreated but for a longer period.

Pyelonephritis, Prostatitis, Renal Abscess

These patients should be treated for longer periods of time than those with simple cystitis, i.e., 2 weeks or more. Longer treatment than for cystitis makes sense because these infections involve deeper tissues, from which it may be difficult to eradicate the bacteria. For uncomplicated pyelonephritis, 2 weeks of treatment is as effective as 6 weeks. Physicians tend to prefer bactericidal over bacteriostatic drugs for the treatment of pyelonephritis, but this preference is not based on the results of controlled clinical studies. Patients with pyelonephritis are usually treated in the hospital, often with drugs given intravenously. Empiric therapy that is reliably effective against Gram-negative bacteria should be used initially (e.g., a broad-spectrum β-lactam, an aminoglycoside, or a quinolone). Upon availability of antimicrobial susceptibility tests for the recovered etiological agent, therapy may be changed to a more narrow-spectrum, less expensive, less toxic drug, such as trimethoprim-sulfamethoxazole. Once the patient's condition improves, the oral route may be used. In men with suspected prostatitis, prolonged treatment with an appropriate drug likely to penetrate the prostate is advisable, e.g., trimethoprim-sulfamethoxazole, doxycycline, or a quinolone. Most renal abscesses can be cured by antibiotic treatment alone, but some require a drainage procedure. Pyogenic perinephric abscesses usually require drainage.

Nosocomial UTI

UTI acquired in the hospital is often caused by bacteria that are resistant to orally administered antibiotics, and requires treatment with a broad-spectrum β-lactam or an aminoglycoside. Prophylactic administration of antibiotics in the catheterized patient is not recommended, because the result is usually simply to postpone the infection by a day or so and to select resistant bacteria. The usual indication to start treatment is the development of fever. Treatment in such patients will usually keep the infection under control but will not eradicate it. Eradication usually requires removal of the foreign body (e.g., the catheter).

RECURRENT INFECTIONS

The greatest challenge in treating patients with UTI is not usually the management of the initial infection but the problem of recurrence. We have already emphasized the importance of distinguishing between relapse and reinfection, because the management of these two types of recurrences is different.

In patients with frequent reinfections, the major goal should be to interrupt the cycle of colonization of the introitus and infection of the bladder. Good success is achieved with drugs such as trimethoprim-sulfamethoxazole or some quinolones, which reach high concentrations not only in the urine but also in vaginal secretions. Special studies to search for anatomic abnormalities, by x-rays or ultrasound, for example, are not usually called for because the likelihood of finding abnormalities is very low. However, such studies may be indicated in very young patients or in those with unusual frequency of recurrence.

Relapse of infection, by contrast, signals either a structural abnormality (stone, obstruction, bladder dysfunction) or invasion of deep tissues (pyelonephritis, renal abscess, bacterial prostatitis) and merits not only long-term treatment with antibiotics but also urological studies and radiographic studies (e.g., intravenous pyelogram) to detect the abnormality.

CONCLUSIONS

The lining of the urinary tract is open to the exterior of the body, and, not surprisingly, often becomes colonized by fecal bacteria. Organisms successful at colonizing tend to be the ones capable of adhering to the epithelial cells and not readily washed away by the urine.

The defense mechanisms of this system of the body are different from those that operate at many other sites. Here, neither white cells nor antibodies occupy center stage. Rather, the major role is played by mechanical factors, especially the normal flow of urine. Accordingly, interruptions in these defenses predispose persons to colonization and infection. A particularly important feature of these infections is that they recur unless the underlying predisposing factor is found and the condition is corrected. An optimal approach to treatment and prevention must take these facts into account.

SUGGESTED READING

Brumfitt W, Gargan RA, Hamilton-Miller JMT. Periurethral enterobacterial carriage preceding urinary infection. Lancet 1987;1:924–926.

Johnson JR, Stamm WE. Urinary tract infections in women: diagnosis and treatment. Ann Intern Med 1989;111:906–917.

Kamaroff AL. Acute dysuria in women. N Engl J Med 1984;310:368–375.

Scheinfeld J, Schaeffer AJ, Cordon-Cardo C, Rogatko A, Fair WR. Association of the Lewis blood-group phenotype with recurrent urinary tract infections in women. N Engl J Med 1989;320:773–777.

Schoolnik GK. How *Escherichia coli* infects the urinary tract. N Engl J Med 1989;320:804–805.

Stark RP, Maki DG. Bacteriuria in the catheterized patient. What quantitative level is relevant? N Engl J Med 1984;311:560–564.

Strom BL, Colins M, West SL, Kreisberg J, Weller S. Sexual activity, contraceptive use, and other risk factors for symptomatic and asymptomatic bacteriuria. Ann Intern Med 1987;107:816–823.

Zhanel GC, Harding GKM, Guay DRP. Asymptomatic bacteriuria. Which patients should be treated? Arch Intern Med 1990;150:1389–1396.

Skin and Soft Tissue 60

Francis P. Tally

Inflamed hangnails, infected cuts, and athlete's foot happen to us so frequently that we scarcely take notice. These mild and usually inconsequential conditions represent one extreme of the infections of the skin. The other extreme includes less frequent but potentially serious diseases, such as herpes zoster, candidiasis, or bacterial cellulitis. Infections of the skin may be caused by viruses, fungi, or bacteria. In addition, many diseases that affect other organs have cutaneous manifestations. Visible skin lesions may be the telltale sign of systemic infections by viruses (e.g., smallpox, measles, chickenpox), fungi (e.g., cryptococcosis, blastomycosis), or bacteria (e.g., syphilis, tuberculosis, scarlet fever, meningococcemia).

Primary infections of the skin and systemic infections with cutaneous manifestations are discussed throughout this book in the context of specific agents (for the main ones, see Chapter 11, staphylococci; Chapter 12, streptococci; Chapter 19, *Pseudomonas*; Chapter 39, warts; Chapter 33, measles; and Chapter 48, fungi). This chapter will be limited to bacterial skin infections, emphasizing those that reveal important pathobiological concepts. These infections frequently involve the "soft tissues" underlying the skin, subcutaneous fat, and superficial fasciae, which are also included in this discussion.

An understanding of the pathogenesis of skin and soft tissue infections requires knowledge of the anatomy and physiology of this part of the body. The skin is divided into three distinct layers, the epidermis, dermis, and fat layer. The **epidermis** is a thin, self-renewing epidermal sheet that covers the body. Over most of the body, it is about the thickness of two of the sheets of this book (0.1 mm) and is devoid of vessels and nerves. The basal cells of the epidermis, the **keratinocytes**, divide, differentiate, and eventually slough. As they rise from the basal layer to the surface, they become more stratified and produce a cornified layer of dead cells, the **stratum corneum**. This outermost epidermal layer consists of dead keratinocytes rich in the tough fibrous protein keratin and stuck together by intercellular neutral lipids. The stratum corneum is the major physical barrier that prevents environmental chemicals and microorganisms from entering the body. In addition to the keratinocytes, the epidermis contains minor cell types, the **Langerhans cells** and the pigment-containing **melanocytes**. Langerhans cells are fixed tissue macrophages, a distal outpost of the immune system that serves to process antigens that breach the stratum corneum.

So-called **skin appendages**, including hairs, oil (sebaceous) glands, and sweat glands, originate from the basal layer of the epidermis. They invaginate into the dermis and exit to the surface through the epidermis. Bacteria may bypass the stratum corneum by traversing these conduits.

The **dermis** is several millimeters thick and is separated from the epidermis by a basement membrane. The fibrous proteins **collagen** and **elastin** are embedded in a glycoprotein matrix and constitute the strong supportive dermal structure. Through it courses a rich plexus of blood vessels and lymphatics. Interruption of dermal blood flow predisposes to infection by restricting access of humoral and cellular defenses against invaders and by compromising the nutrition of the epidermal barrier.

Subcutaneous fat, the third layer of the skin, consists predominantly of lipid cells that play not only an aesthetic role, but are also effective as heat insulators, shock absorbers, and depots of caloric reserves. Below this layer is a **superficial fascia** that separates the skin from muscles. As described below, any or all these layers of "soft tissue" may be involved in a given infectious process.

ENCOUNTER

The skin is sterile only at birth. It is soon colonized by a flora that includes both anaerobic and aerobic bacteria, ranging from 10^2–10^4 CFU (colony forming units)/cm^2 of surface. Many factors affect the distribution, composition, and density of this flora, few of which are understood. They include not only the environmental climate, which differs throughout the world, but also the microclimates of the body. The "tropical swamps" of the axilla and the groin are markedly different from the "deserts" of the back.

The two properties that make the skin hostile to bacterial growth are **exfoliation** and **dryness**. The constant sloughing of the stratum corneum dislodges many of the bacteria that adhere to its surface. The importance of dryness can be seen when occlusive dressings are applied; within 2 or 3 days, bacterial counts may increase from 10^2 to over 10^7 CFU/cm^2. Accordingly, bacterial counts are much higher in the moist areas than in drier regions. Other factors that contribute to limiting bacterial growth are low pH, low temperature, and chemical composition. The skin has a pH of approximately 5.5, the result of hydrolysis of sebum lipids by the skin bacteria themselves. Growth of some microorganisms is further hindered by the skin's low temperature, with an average of about 33°C. Parts of the skin are also frequently salty due to the evaporation of sweat, which selects for salt-resistant species, such as *Staphylococcus epidermidis*. Some organisms are also inhibited by the lipid content of the skin surface.

The bacterial flora of the skin, like that of mucous membranes, also helps protect the host from invasion by pathogens and skin infections are more likely to occur when it is wiped out. The mechanisms involved are not known but may include saturation of binding sites, competition for nutrients, and production of bacteriocins and other inhibitory chemicals.

Members of the resident flora are of low virulence and rarely cause significant infections. Included are **resident bacteria**, capable of multiplication on the skin and regularly present, and **transient bacteria**, which survive on the skin for a time but cannot develop permanent residency. Members of the transient flora are deposited on the skin either from mucous membrane "fallout" or from the environment. Evidence is accumulating that specific adhesins are required for some bacteria to adhere to the skin before they are able to colonize it.

The dry and exposed areas of the skin are normally colonized with Gram-positive bacteria (including *S. epidermidis*, micrococci, anaerobic Gram-positive cocci, and both anaerobic and aerobic diphtheroids.) *Proprionibacterium acnes*, a Gram-positive rod, thrives in the sebaceous areas. Facultative and anaerobic Gram-negative rods more often colonize the axilla and groin regions and other moist areas, such as the web of the toes. For some unknown reason, in bedridden patients with serious medical illnesses, there is increased colonization of Gram-negative bacilli on the skin.

The most important organisms of the transient flora are the common pathogens of cutaneous infections, *S. aureus* and *Streptococcus pyogenes*. These organisms are found more often on exposed skin than on areas normally protected by clothing. *S. aureus* is found commonly on the face and upper body rather than on the trunk and legs, probably because the reservoir for this organism is the upper respiratory tract. Table 60.1 lists some of the important pathogens that transiently colonize the skin and the infections they cause.

ENTRY, SPREAD, AND MULTIPLICATION

Infectious agents enter the skin and its underlying soft tissues in many different ways:

- **From the outside,** via cuts, wounds, insect bites, skin disease, or other breaks in the integrity of the stratum corneum;

- **From within,** from underlying tissue or carried by blood or lymph.

Table 60.1. Members of the Skin Flora and the Infections They Cause

Resident Flora
  Propionibacterium acnes
  Staphylococcus epidermidis—infection around foreign bodies (prosthetic devices, etc.)
  Micrococci
  Anaerobic Gram-positive cocci
  Aerobic Gram-negative bacilli (low numbers)
  Pityrosporum ovale (a yeast)
Transient Flora
  Bacteria
    Frequent:
    Staphylococcus aureus—abscesses, toxic shock, and bacteremia
    Streptococcus pyogenes—cellulitis, lymphangitis

    Infrequent:
    Haemophilus influenzae—cellulitis
    Clostridia—gangrene
    Francisella tularensis—tularemia
    Bacillus anthracis—anthrax
    Pseudomonas aeruginosa—hot tub infection
    Pseudomonas cepacia—foot infection ("foot rot")
    Mycobacterium marinum—"fish tank cellulitis"
  Fungi
    Candida albicans—diaper rash, chronic paronychia
    Dermatophytes—tinea infections (ringworm)
  Viruses
    Frequent:
    Herpes simplex I and II—perioral—"cold sore"; genital infection
    Papilloma—warts

    Infrequent:
    Molluscum contagiosum—wart-like lesions

Once microorganisms have penetrated the skin, they may spread locally and invade the lymphatics or the bloodstream. As a result, infections that are originally confined to the skin and soft tissues may ultimately cause complications in other areas of the body. An example of staphylococcal osteomyelitis following a skin abscess is discussed in Chapter 11.

In some bacteria, spreading is associated with specific virulence factors; an example is **hyaluronidase** (also called **spreading factor**), an extracellular enzyme made both by *S. pyogenes* and *S. aureus* (Chapter 11). Other enzymes, such as hemolysins, lipases, collagenase, and elastases are elaborated by cutaneous pathogens and probably play a role in pathogenesis (see Chapter 9). **In general,** *S. aureus* **infections tend to localize, i.e., form abscesses, whereas** *S. pyogenes* **infections spread more extensively through tissues.**

What is the role of cellular and humoral immunity in the skin? Neutrophils are attracted to the infected area by chemoattractants elaborated by the bacteria, by tissue macrophages, and by activation of complement via the alternative pathway. A local antimicrobial effort is mounted by the epidermal macrophages, the Langerhans cells, through the elaboration of cytokines. Patients with acquired and congenital immunodeficiencies have an increased frequency of certain skin infections, e.g., *Candida*, which suggests that cellular immunity is important in skin defenses. When microorganisms breach the stratum corneum and begin to multiply, the host's traditional defenses are mobilized to the skin as elsewhere. When the defenses are defective, infections of the skin become frequent events.

DAMAGE

Cellular damage to the skin and soft tissues may be mediated by toxins, degradative enzymes, and the induction of the host cellular responses that destroy tissues. The kind of infection caused by the invasion of microorganisms in the skin depends on the level of penetration and on the host response. Infections of skin and soft tissue may be divided into three classes:

- Exogenous infections that result from direct invasion from the external environment;
- Endogenous infections due to invasion from an internal source, such as the blood or an infected organ;
- Toxin-induced skin diseases, caused by toxins produced at a distant site.

EXOGENOUS INFECTIONS

There is controversy about whether potent pathogens are able to penetrate the normal skin directly, when present in high concentrations, or whether they enter via imperceptible microscopic lesions. When there are no noticeable mechanical interruptions, it takes a high numbers of potent pathogens to produce exogenous skin and soft tissue infection; experimental studies have shown that colonization of the skin by more than 10^6 *S. aureus*/cm^2 of skin is required to cause skin lesions. Normally, bacteria grow to such high densities only under special circumstances, such as when the skin gets very dirty or is kept moist for prolonged periods of time. Once the skin barrier is broken from trauma or surgery, infection may be caused by as few as 10–100 *S. aureus*/cm². A number of conditions predispose one to skin invasion:

- **Excessive moisture** may result from the use of occlusive dressings or from wet diapers in babies. Obese people accumulate moisture in their intertriginous folds. **Immersion infection** is seen in people who spend much time in wet or swampy areas and cannot allow their footwear to dry out, such as troops during training or combat. Moisture induces skin maceration and a breakdown of the stratum corneum. It is estimated that, among U.S. foot soldiers in Vietnam, disability was more often due to skin infections than to combat-associated wounds. Staphylococci and streptococci are frequently responsible, but water-borne Gram-negative bacteria may also be involved. The modern era has heralded a new type of immersion infection, that acquired by bathing in hot tubs containing high numbers of *P. aeruginosa* (Chapter 19).

Trauma is the most common factor leading to skin and soft tissue infection. It may be mild, as in a torn hangnail or cracks in the skin due to athlete's foot. Major forms of trauma that place the patient at risk include surgery ("organized trauma"), gunshot wounds, crush injuries (automobile accidents), or burns, with large areas of skin denuded and left open. Infections in surgical wounds are a major cause of morbidity in postoperative patients. Infections are also the primary cause of mortality in burn victims, once their acute problems of fluid balance are controlled.

Many procedures used in the hospital breach the skin, the most common being the use of **percutaneous** ("through the skin") **catheters**. The list of such devices has grown enormously: it includes central venous lines, peritoneal dialysis catheters, tubes to drain body cavities, temporary pacemaker lines, chemotherapy infusion lines, and parenteral nutrition lines. Indeed, the most common reason for premature removal of these catheters is bacterial infection. Another type of skin infection in hospitalized patients are the cutaneous lesions that develop secondary to pressure injury—the so-called bed sores. Constant pressure leads to skin necrosis and frequently to secondary infection.

Any condition that compromises the blood supply predisposes the skin to invasion by causing barrier breakdown and limiting defenses. This may occur following peripheral vascular disease, as in diabetic patients, elderly patients, or patients with vasculitis. In the diabetic patient, compromise of the vascular supply is often accompanied by peripheral sensory neuropathy; these patients are sometimes not aware of traumatic damage to their skin. Secondary infections may also follow certain noninfectious skin diseases known as atopic dermatitis or pemphigus vulgaris.

The skin responds to invading microorganisms in a limited number of ways, which fall into three general categories:

- **Spreading infections**, called **impetigo** when confined to the epidermis, **erysipelas** when involving the dermal lymphatics, and cellulitis when the major focus is the subcutaneous fat layer;

- **Abscess formation**, known as folliculitis, boils (furuncles), and carbuncles;

- **Necrotizing infections**, including fasciitis and gas gangrene (myonecrosis).

• The organisms commonly implicated are listed in Table 60.2. Cellulitis is illustrated in the following case.

STREPTOCOCCAL CELLULITIS

Case

*A 27-year-old emergency medical technician was seen for a slight infection around the nail of his left index finger (medically called **paronychia**). The lesion was drained and a culture of the pus grew a group A β-hemolytic streptococcus (S. pyogenes). The patient was not given antimicrobial agents because the physician believed that drainage was sufficient. Five days later, the patient complained of fever and severe pain in the forearm, which had become swollen and reddish (erythematous). His temperature was 40.2°C and he was sweaty and hot. A patchy rash extended from the left upper arm to the shoulder. Lymph nodes in the axilla were enlarged and tender. The patient was admitted to the hospital with a diagnosis of **streptococcal cellulitis**. He was treated successfully with high doses of penicillin. Blood cultures drawn before starting chemotherapy also yielded group A S. pyogenes.*

Comments

Cellulitis refers to an acute inflammatory process that involves subcutaneous tissue, characterized by areas of redness, induration, heat, and tenderness. The borders usually blend with the surrounding tissues, which distinguishes it from erysipelas where the lesions are frequently sharply demarcated. Cellulitis may spread very rapidly and is often accompanied by lymphangitis and inflammation of the draining lymph nodes. Over 90% of cases are due to *S. aureus* and group A streptococci and the rest to a variety of bacteria. In children, *Haemophilus influenzae* type b is an important cause of cellulitis, and may be characterized by a blue tint of the overlying erythema (such a case is described in Chapter 64). Cellulitis associated with cat or dog bites or scratches is often due to *Pasteurella multocida* (see Chapter 69). This organism is a normal inhabitant of the oral flora of many domestic and wild animals. When injected into the skin through a bite or scratches, it causes a rapidly spreading and painful cellulitis.

The pathological processes in cellulitis develop rapidly and may progress within 24–48 hours from a minor injury to severe septicemia. Characteristically, the tissues contain few organisms, but have a marked inflammatory response, probably caused by the toxins and inflammation-provoking compounds elaborated by the invading bacteria. The ability of group A streptococci to spread through the tissues is aided by hyaluronidase and other spreading factors mentioned above.

Table 60.2. Some Frequent Exogenous Infections of the Skin and Soft Tissues

Disease	Organisms
Folliculitis	Staphylococci, *Pseudomonas*
Abscesses	Staphylococci
Impetigo	Streptococci, staphylococci
Erysipelas	Streptococci
Lymphangitis	Streptococci
Cellulitis	Streptococci, staphylococci, *H. influenzae* (in children)
Synergistic cellulitis	Streptococci, enteric bacteria, anaerobes
Fasciitis	Streptococci, enteric bacteria, anaerobes

Impetigo is a characteristic infection of the epidermis, manifested by intraepidermal vesicles filled with exudate, which eventually result in a weeping and crusting lesion (Fig. 60.1). It is caused either by group A streptococci or staphylococci and is a disease of children, seen mainly in exposed areas of the body during warm and moist weather. It is not usually associated with systemic signs or symptoms.

Erysipelas is a more serious disease, characterized by tender superficial erythematous and edematous lesions. The infection spreads primarily in the superficial lymphatics of the dermis Figure 60.2. The rash is usually confluent but is sharply demarcated from the surrounding normal skin, and extends very rapidly. It is seen most frequently in adults with edema of the extremities and often occurs on the face. By far, the most common organisms that cause erysipelas are group A streptococci. Infection of the deep lymphatics, or **lymphangitis**, is also caused by group A streptococci. Erysipelas used to be one of the most serious complications of surgery and puerperal sepsis (postpartum infection, see Chapter 12), and had a high mortality rate. Its severity and incidence have markedly decreased over the last few decades. The decline can be explained only partially by the widespread use of penicillin to treat streptococcal infections.

SKIN ABSCESSES

Case

A 37-year-old roofer came to the emergency room with a painful swelling on the left side of his neck and fever (Fig. 60.3). He had previously been healthy except for occasional boils. Three days before, he noted a minor irri-

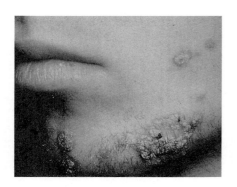

Figure 60.1.   A case of impetigo, showing a superficial crusting infection of the face.

Figure 60.2.   A case of erysipelas due to *S. pyogenes* in a patient with a pre-existing skin disease (psoriasis).

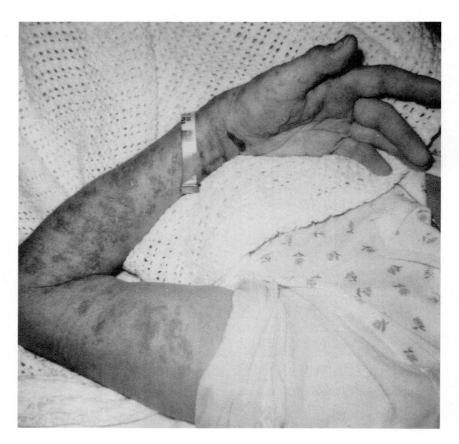

tation around some whiskers. The lesion progressed to the size of a walnut, which prevented him from buttoning his shirt. Physical examination revealed a febrile (temperature 38.8°C) healthy man in mild distress. On his left anterior cervical area at the beard line there was a 2 × 3 cm mass with a soft center, surrounded by a rash. Needle aspiration of the mass yielded about 1 ml of pus which, under the microscope, showed large Gram-positive cocci in clusters and many neutrophils. A culture grew S. aureus. The abscess was incised and drained, and he was successfully treated with antibiotics.

Comments

Cutaneous abscesses usually begin as superficial infections in and around hair follicles, called **folliculitis**. This is a pustular eruption usually associated with *S. aureus*. In the follicle, bacteria are somewhat sequestered from defense mechanisms and are capable of forming microabscesses. If not controlled, these abscesses enlarge to become **furuncles**, better known as **common boils**. If a number of boils cluster together to form a large multifocal infection, the lesion is called a **carbuncle**. Furuncles may be a recurring and frustrating problem in patients, especially young ones, who are chronic nasal carriers of virulent *S. aureus*. Although these lesions are confined to the skin, they may be a source of bacteremia and complications, as in the case of osteomyelitis described in Chapter 11.

The pathological processes that lead to abscess formation involve a massive influx of neutrophils and walling-off of the infected site. This is deposition of fibrin (fostered by staphylococcal coagulase), and by stimulation of fibroblasts to produce a fibrous capsule. The results is a well-organized infection, containing necrotic white blood cells and huge numbers of bacteria—i.e., pus. The pathological steps that lead to abscess formation include tissue destruction by the invading organisms and by the massive release of lysosomal enzymes from lysing neutrophils, and deposition of fibrin (Chapter 11). The unique physicochemical characteristics of abscesses are discussed in the chapter on antimicrobial strategies (Chapter 29). Therapy of an abscess is usually two-pronged; removal of pus by incision and drainage, and when warranted, treatment with antimicrobial agents.

NECROTIZING INFECTIONS

Case

A slightly feverish 57-year-old diabetic woman came to the emergency room after 2 days of pain in her right foot. When her pain started, she had noticed tenderness and serous (watery) discharge between her third and fourth toes. She had been bothered recently by an ulcer on the sole of her foot, apparently caused by constant scraping against her shoe. On physical examination, she appeared ill and had a temperature of 39.8°C. Her whole right foot was swollen with patchy erythema, cyanosis, and signs of necrosis. There was crusting and oozing around her third and fourth toe (Fig. 60.4).

Cultures of the exudate and the blood were taken and the patient was started on antibiotics. After 24 hours, she showed no clinical improvement and the infection continued to move up her leg. She was taken to the operating room, and multiple incisions revealed necrotic fasciitis extending to the upper thigh. As much necrotic tissue as possible was removed. Cultures from the wound grew out the anaerobic Gram-negative rod Bacteroides fragilis, and an enteric bacterium, Enterobacter. Her blood cultures were negative. She slowly recovered and underwent a second operation for closure of her wound.

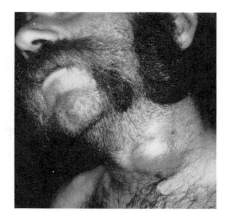

Figure 60.3. Skin abscess in the neck developing from an infected hair follicle of the beard.

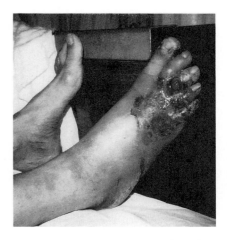

Figure 60.4. Necrotizing cellulitis of the foot due to a mixed anaerobic-aerobic infection. The patient was diabetic and the infection arose from an ulcer on the sole of the foot.

Comments

This is a case of **synergistic necrotizing fasciitis**, probably started by the entry of bacteria through the ulcer on the sole of her foot. Diabetics frequently suffer from poor skin circulation and lack of local sensation, which may have been the reason for the development of the ulcer. The infection spread rapidly along the superficial fascia that separates subcutaneous fat and muscle. The vessels and nerves that supply the skin course this fascia, and their destruction leads to the patchy necrosis and cutaneous anesthesia that characterizes such a rapidly spreading and dangerous infection.

Tissue necrosis occurs to some extent in most infections but the term **necrotizing infections** (or **gangrenous infections**) is reserved for those where extensive necrosis is the outstanding characteristic. Gas from bacterial metabolism is sometimes found in these lesions (Chapter 21). Necrotizing infections of the skin are often caused by S. *pyogenes*, or as in this case, by the synergistic combination of enteric Gram-negative rods and strict anaerobes, such as *Bacteroides* or clostridia (Chapter 16). If a necrotizing infection is suspected, the diagnosis should be confirmed by inspection of the fascia on surgical exploration. This disease must be distinguished from the more severe clostridial gas gangrene or myonecrosis, which involves the muscle (Chapter 21). Antibiotic treatment of necrotizing fasciitis rarely works, probably because of the compromised blood supply; extensive surgical debridement is mandatory.

INVASION FROM WITHIN

The skin may become infected by microorganisms that spread from another infected site, either by direct extension from an underlying focus or via the bloodstream. Such secondary infections occur in both immunocompetent and immunosuppressed hosts but with different degrees of incidence and severity. Some of the types of skin infections that occur from within are listed in Table 60.3. Systemic infections are manifested in a variety of ways:

- **Abscesses**—these may result from intravascular infections such as endocarditis, particularly when due to S. *aureus*.

- **Necrosis**—this manifestation is seen in chronic meningococcemia or in overwhelming meningococcal septicemia, where there may be large areas of confluent necrosis of the skin called **purpura fulminans**, the skin manifestation of disseminated intravascular coagulation (Fig. 60.5). Milder forms of necrosis are also seen, for example, in disseminated gonorrhea. In the immunocompromised host, there is a unique skin lesion called **ecthyma gangrenosum**, usually seen with P. *aeruginosa* septicemia. A case of this disease is presented below.

- Many infections are accompanied by **rashes** or exanthems. These are seen in a large variety of infections, caused by rickettsiae, other bacteria, and viruses. They are subdivided as hemorrhagic rashes, often accompanied by necrosis (as in meningococcemia, Fig. 60.5) and macular (spotted) rashes (as in typhoid fever or Rocky Mountain spotted fever). Rashes are prominent in several viral infections, such as measles and rubella, and are known as the **viral exanthems** (Chapter 33 and Table 60.4).

Table 60.3. Examples of Sources of Endogenous Skin Infections

A. Direct Extension
1. Osteomyelitis—draining sinus
2. Septic arthritis—draining sinus
3. Lymphadenitis
   a. Tuberculosis
   b. Atypical mycobacteriosis
   c. Streptococcal or staphylococcal infection
4. Oral infection—dental sepsis
   a. Actinomycosis (lumpy jaw)
   b. Mixed cellulitis
5. Intra-abdominal—necrotizing infection
6. Herpes simplex
7. Zoster varicella
B. Hematogenous Spread
1. Bacteremia
   Meningococcus
   Staphylococcus
   Pseudomonas
2. Endocarditis
3. Fungemia—*Candida*
4. Viremia—varicella, measles
5. Recurrent viral infections
   Herpes simplex
   Zoster
6. Rickettsioses
   Rocky Mountain spotted fever
   Epidemic or endemic typhus

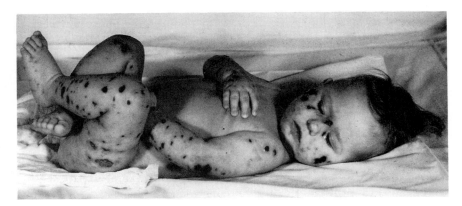

Figure 60.5.   Hemorrhagic purpura due to disseminated intravascular coagulation in a child with meningococcal septicemia.

Table 60.4. Some Viral Diseases with Cutaneous Manifestations

Disease	Etiological Agent	Principal Cutaneous Manifestation
Herpes simplex	Herpes simplex virus	"Cold sore" on lip Vesicles in genital area
Herpes zoster	Varicella virus	Shingles—vesicles over specific dermotome(s)
Chickenpox (varicella)	Varicella virus	Vesicles, becoming purulent, then dry, crusted lesions
Measles	Measles virus	Maculopapular rash
German measles	Rubella virus	Maculopapular rash
Smallpox (eradicated)	Smallpox virus	Uniform pustular vesicles

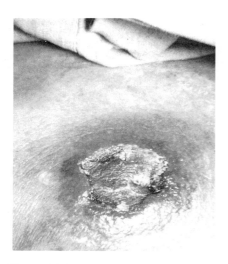

Figure 60.6.   Ecthyma gangrenosum, a necrotic skin lesion due to *P. aeruginosa*.

• A large number of cutaneous lesions are themselves **noninfectious** but are secondary to septicemia or other systemic infections. They include hemorrhages, petechiae, and special manifestations of subacute bacterial endocarditis called Osler nodes and Janeway spots (Chapter 63). They are due to vasculitis, probably caused by deposition of immune complexes.

PSEUDOMONAS ECTHYMA GANGRENOSUM

Case

A 52-year-old man underwent chemotherapy with cytotoxic agents for an aggressive lymphoma. As the result of the chemotherapy, his white blood cell count fell to fewer than 100 cells per microliter of blood. The patient suddenly developed shaking chills and fever, and complained of pain over his left shoulder. Examination of the area showed an erythematous round area with a central vesicle (Fig. 60.6). Because of the suspicion of Gram-negative bacteremia, the patient was started on broad-spectrum antimicrobial agents. Within a matter of a few hours, the lesion on the left shoulder developed a necrotic center with surrounding erythema, a lesion known as **ecthyma gangrenosum**. A biopsy of the lesion showed that it contained an infarcted blood vessel teeming with bacteria. Cultures of the biopsy material and the blood grew P. aeruginosa. The patient responded to the antimicrobial chemotherapy with resolution of fever and clearing of the skin lesions.

Comments

This case exemplifies a specific skin lesion resulting from seeding of the skin with *P. aeruginosa*. One of the characteristics of endogenous infection with this organism is arteritis resulting in infarction of the skin from vascular insufficiency. This organism grows in the infarcted area and causes necrosis by the production of exotoxin A and other toxins (see Chapter 19). Biopsy of the necrotic area revealed no neutrophil infiltrate because of the patient's granulocytopenia. Instead there was infarction of blood vessels by bacterial emboli, with destruction of the arterial wall and bacterial invasion of the surrounding tissues.

This characteristic lesion usually is diagnostic of Gram-negative bacteremia, with *P. aeruginosa* the most common organism encountered. Other Gram-negative rods may also be involved, e.g., *Klebsiella* and *Serratia*; occasionally, *S. aureus* also causes these manifestations. It is imperative that the physician treat early—before bacteriological confirmation—because the mortality rate in untreated granulocytopenic patients with Gram-negative bacteremia is 50% within 24 hours.

CUTANEOUS RESPONSES TO BACTERIAL TOXINS

The skin responds to toxins elaborated during infections that take place at a distant site. An example is seen in scarlet fever, a pharyngitis caused by certain strains of group A streptococci that elaborate an exotoxin called **erythrogenic factor**. This toxin spreads through the bloodstream and is responsible for the red rash, "strawberry tongue" and desquamation of the skin of the extremities. Scarlet fever used to be a serious disease of childhood; the marked decrease in its severity over the last century has defied explanation.

Staphylococci cause two specific toxin-induced skin diseases—**scalded skin syndrome** and **toxic shock syndrome**. Staphylococcal scalded skin syndrome, a disease of infants, is due to the action of a toxin, **exfoliatin**, that separates the epidermis by destroying the intracellular connections (desmosomes). The result resembles skin scalded with hot water. The other staphylococcal toxin skin disease, toxic shock syndrome, is presented below.

TOXIC SHOCK SYNDROME

Case

A 24-year-old man had an operation to repair an inguinal hernia. Five days later, he developed shaking chills and a rash that started on his trunk and rapidly spread to the head and extremities. He became progressively sicker over the next 48 hours, developing a sore throat, headache, myalgias (muscle pains), vomiting, diarrhea, and postural dizziness (dizzy when upright, suggesting low blood pressure). On physical examination, he had a diffuse rash with some blanching on pressure. His eyes were inflamed with conjuctivitis, and he had an erythematous pharynx and a "strawberry" tongue. His inguinal wound was draining a brown odorless material.

Laboratory examination revealed a high white blood cell count and elevated high serum creatinine (5.7 mg/dl), indicating acute renal failure. A Gram stain of the material from the wound showed Gram-positive cocci in clusters, and grew S. aureus. The organism tested positive for the toxic shock syndrome toxin. The patient ultimately showed desquamation of his hands and trunk (Fig. 60.7). He was placed on antibiotics and eventually recovered.

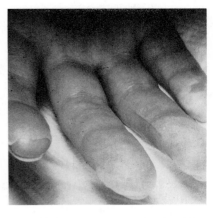

Figure 60.7.   Desquamation of the skin of the hand in a patient with staphylococcal toxic shock.

Comments

This case is a typical clinical presentation of toxic shock syndrome (TSS). The disease is due to an exotoxin produced by *S. aureus* strains that cause minor infections, such as small surgical wounds. This syndrome was first described in children in the early 1970s. It became widely known in the early 1980s when young menstruating women using "super tampons" developed this impressive syndrome; if untreated, TSS can be fatal. The tampons used facilitated the colonization of the vagina with *S. aureus*; the toxin was then absorbed to act systemically. Today tampon-associated TSS is rare; more commonly, it occurs after an infection, as illustrated in this case.

CONCLUSIONS

The skin and its underlying soft tissues protect the body from hostile influences in the environment. To penetrate these barrier, infectious agents are most often helped by traumatic breaks, the bite of insects, or other skin diseases. Microorganisms may also lodge in the skin and soft tissues as the result of hematogenous or lymphatic dissemination. The resulting diseases are extraordinarily varied and are caused by a wide variety of mechanisms. Thus, the hallmark of infectious diseases of the skin and soft tissues is variety in the clinical presentation.

The skin also acts as a diagnostic window for a multitude of diseases. The clinician can acquire a wealth of critical information by careful examination of the skin.

SUGGESTED READING

Noble WC. Microbiology of the human skin, 2nd ed. London: Lloyd-Luke, 1981.

Noble WC. Microbial skin disease: its epidemiology. London: Edward Arnold, 1981.

Swartz M. Skin and soft tissue infections. In: Mandel GL, Douglas RG, Bennett JE, eds. Principles and practice of infectious diseases, 2nd ed. New York: John Wiley & Sons, 1985.

Weinberg A, Swartz M. In: Fitzpatrick, et al. Dermatology and general medicine textbook. New York: McGraw-Hill, 1979:1415–1472.

Bone, Joints, and Muscles

61

Gerald Medoff

BONE INFECTIONS

Infections of bone, or osteomyelitis, may result from blood-borne infections (hematogenous) or from the direct introduction of microorganisms from external (environmental) or contiguous sources (soft tissues or joints). A special type of the latter category is the infection of the bones of the feet that occurs in patients with diabetes. The pathophysiology of the diseases, the types of infecting agents, and the kinds of treatments and prognoses are frequently different. For this reason, they will be discussed separately.

Case of Hematogenous Osteomyelitis

O., a 15-year-old boy received an injury to the lower part of his right thigh in a high school football game. The pain was so intense that he had to leave the game. The pain then subsided for several hours but returned that night and he developed chills followed by a fever to 103°F. A physician who saw him the next day noted that the lower right thigh was hot, swollen, and tender. The knee joint was normal with full range of motion. The patient had a temperature of 101°F. The physician noted several small boils on the neck and chest of the patient. Some were scarred and crusted and the patient admitted squeezing them in the past 2 days. X-rays of the right femur showed soft tissue swelling without any abnormalities of the bone.

O. has acute hematogenous osteomyelitis and the most likely infecting organism is Staphylococcus aureus. *This diagnosis becomes even more plausible when the pathophysiology of the infection is understood.*

Which features of the history and physical examination of the patient point to this diagnosis?

- The trauma to the leg suffered in the football game damaged the distal femur and probably resulted in rupture of small blood vessels and formation of hematoma or blood clot in the bone. The disruption in the normal anatomical barriers made the bone more susceptible to infection.

- Manipulation of the boils by the patient probably resulted in bacteremia, with *S. aureus* a likely infecting organism. Blood-borne *S. aureus* could have then seeded the traumatized bone and caused the infection.

- The history of chills and fever, as well as pain and inflammation over the area of trauma, indicate that an infection is in progress. The normal x-ray does not rule out osteomyelitis because it may take several weeks for the characteristic changes in the bone to appear (periosteal proliferation or elevation, loss of bone cortex, bone lysis, etc.). Why do you think this is so? Most likely, it is because about 50% of bone must be destroyed before bone lysis can be detected on x-ray. A radionuclide bone scan would be more likely to be positive early in the disease because it measures inflammation, although not infallibly.

Pathophysiology of Acute Hematogenous Osteomyelitis

Bone has a high rate of synthesis and resorption, two processes that depend on a rich vascular supply. Many blood-borne infections, therefore, involve actively growing sites; this explains why hematogenous osteomyelitis occurs mostly in children and adolescents, at a time of life when long bones are growing rapidly. The most frequent sites are the growing ends (metaphysis, Fig. 61.1A) of long bones because this is the site of growth and of most rapid turnover. This is particularly true when this part of the bone has suffered severe trauma with disruption of blood vessels and hematoma formation.

The anatomy of the vascular supply of the metaphysis also predisposes this area to infection. The capillaries from the nutrient arteries of bone make sharp loops close to the growth plate and then expand to large sinusoidal vessels that connect with the venous network of the medullary cavity. The sudden increase in diameter of these vessels slows blood flow and results in sludging of red blood cells (Fig. 61.1B). This is a fertile area for the growth of bacteria because microclots form spontaneously in areas of slow blood flow. Clots retain bacteria and allow them to proliferate shielded from neutrophils. The result is inflammation, small areas of bone necrosis, and an acid pH, all of which cause more tissue destruction and more bacterial growth. The endothelial cells in the capillary loop and sinusoids in the bone lack phagocytic properties, which also predisposes these areas to infection.

What Should the Physician Have Done?

The physician should have realized that the local pain and the systemic signs of infection (chills and fever) were indicative of a serious disease, acute osteomyelitis, which calls for admission to the hospital; blood cultures should have been obtained and the patient should have been started on antibiotics. Because about 90% of the patients with

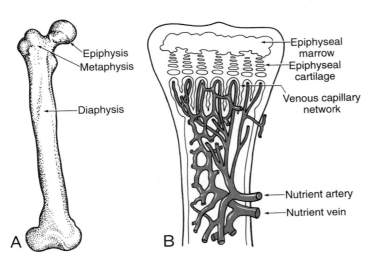

Figure 61.1. **A.** Femur showing epiphysis, metaphysis, and diaphysis. **B.** Schematic representation of the vascular supply of a long bone.

this clinical presentation are infected with *S. aureus*, a penicillinase-resistant penicillin or a cephalosporin should have been used empirically. If the patient had specific predisposing conditions, other bacterial etiologies would have been more likely (e.g., *Salmonella* infection in patients with sickle cell disease or *Pseudomonas aeruginosa* in drug users). In this case, aspiration or biopsy of bones for culture would be indicated to make identification of the organism more certain.

Treatment of osteomyelitis requires a high daily dose of antibiotic continued for 4–6 weeks. High doses are necessary to penetrate bone tissue, but we can only conjecture as to why treatment must be continued for a prolonged period of time. The areas of bone necrosis that result from the infection are likely to shield the bacteria from body defenses. These areas have to be resorbed, which is a slow process. Meanwhile, antibiotics may help keep the bacteria in check and prevent them from spreading to adjacent areas.

If appropriate treatment is started early in the course of the infection, before very much bone necrosis occurs, patients respond quickly and cure can be achieved in greater than 90% of cases. If fever and pain continue for 24–48 hours after treatment is started, surgical drainage may be indicated. Blood cultures will be positive in about one-third of cases, which may obviate the necessity of surgery to determine the infectious agent.

Although *S. aureus* is the most frequent infecting organism in hematogenous osteomyelitis, other organisms can also cause the disease. It is apparent from the clinical setting that these organisms may be involved in the infection. Table 61.1 lists other infecting organisms and the clinical situations that suggest them.

Course of The Untreated Disease

Unfortunately, the diagnosis was missed in our patient. O. was given an oral antibiotic by his physician and sent home. He was not seen again by a physician for another 2 weeks when he returned to the emergency room because of continued fever and pain in his leg. A repeat x-ray of O.'s leg showed definite osteomyelitis (Fig. 61.2) and he was admitted to the hospital and started on intravenous treatment with a cephalosporin. Unfortunately, his disease had progressed into the subacute and chronic phase of osteomyelitis. By now, the compromised blood supply resulted in small avascular pieces of bone or **sequestra**. The blood supply was disrupted by the pressure caused by inflammation. The chance of medical cure had significantly lessened because of

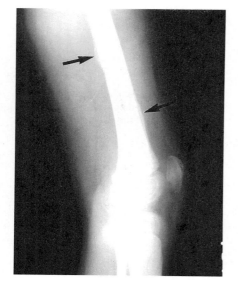

Figure 61.2. X-ray showing changes in osteomyelitis showing sclerosis and periosteal changes.

Table 61.1. Some Predisposing Causes and Etiological Organisms Leading to Osteomyelitis

Predisposing Causes	Etiological Organisms
Infancy	Group B Streptococcus
Childhood	*Haemophilus influenzae*
Sickle cell disease	*Salmonella* sp.
Immunosuppression	Opportunistic fungi, *Nocardia*, *Pseudomonas*
Residing in an endemic area	*C. immitis, H. capsulatum*
Trauma to the jaw	*Actinomyces israelii*
Animal exposure	*Brucella* sp.
Pulmonary tuberculosis	*M. tuberculosis*

the delay in diagnosis. Over the next few years, the patient had a slowly progressive infection with several acute flare-ups each year. Over the next 10 years, he spent many days in the hospital and had multiple surgical procedures to drain pus and cut away infected dead bone (Fig. 61.3). He suffered several fractures because of the weakened bone and finally, at the age of 25 years, he had to have his leg amputated because it was feared that the infection would spread into his hip joint and pelvis. Thus, an infection that should have been easily treated with antibiotics was converted into a more complex disease (chronic osteomyelitis) that required vigorous medical and surgical intervention, culminating in amputation of the leg to preserve the patient's life.

Hematogenous Osteomyelitis At Different Ages

INFANTS

The clinical presentation of hematogenous osteomyelitis depends a great deal on the age of the patient. This is due to the changing characteristics of the bone in different age groups. In the infant, the bone is soft and the periosteum is loosely attached to the cortex. Infection can, therefore, spread and rupture through the thin cortical bone into the subperiosteal space. Subperiosteal abscesses are common in this age group and lead to a tremendous stimulation of periosteal bone formation at this inappropriate site, as periosteal cells transform into osteoblasts. This new bone formation is disorganized and produces a weakened bone called an **involucrum** (Fig. 61.4) Osteomyelitis in the infant can be a terrible disease because, early in life, the capillaries of the metaphysis extend into the epiphyseal growth plate. The infection can then spread by this route into the epiphysis and can seriously affect growth of the bone. In addition, the infection can also rupture into the joint space and cause infectious arthritis. Consequently, osteomyelitis in the infant can result in a severe destructive process with marked deformity of bone and abnormalities of growth that will affect the patient for the rest of his or her life (Fig. 61.5).

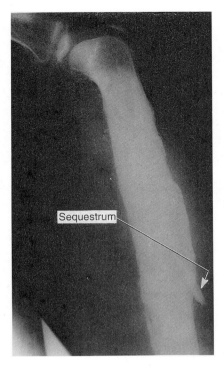

Figure 61.3. X-ray showing changes in more advanced osteomyelitis with extensive bone lesions. *Sequestrum*, an area of bone necrosis, is indicated by the *arrow*.

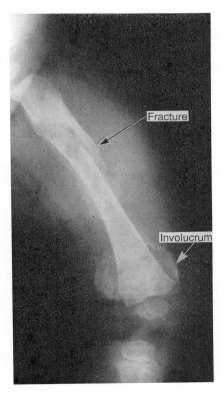

Figure 61.4. *Involucrum* secondary to extensive periosteal reaction and fracture due to weakened infected bone.

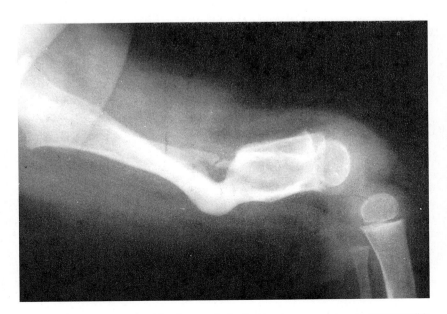

Figure 61.5. Deformity resulting from pathological fracture secondary to osteomyelitis.

CHILDREN

Between the age of 1 year and puberty, infection is generally contained in the metaphysis because the bone is more calcified and there are no vessels connecting the metaphysis and the epiphysis. Also, the periosteum is more tightly adhered to the cortex in this age group, so that rupture of infection into the subperiosteal space and formation of involucrum is less likely. Thus, the purulent infectious process will probably be contained in bone, but this has other consequences. Within the bone, pressure builds and results in occlusion of arterioles and clot formation in the capillaries.

Necrosis of bone is the end result of this process—the necrotic sequestrum (see Fig. 61.3). Such an area is no longer in contact with the vasculature and acts as a foreign body on which organisms can proliferate out of reach of host defenses and antibiotics. Ultimately, the sequestrum must be resorbed (by the body) or removed surgically if the infection is to be cured. With increasing age, this complication is even more likely because the bone is more calcified and the periosteum even more attached to bone. This is what happened to O.

ADULTS

Hematogenous osteomyelitis also occurs in adults, in whom the most commonly involved bones are the vertebrae of the spine. The reason for the preferential involvement is unknown; it may relate to the degenerative changes and vascular proliferation in the disk space between the vertebrae that normally occur with age. The infection almost always begins in the disk space and then spreads to the two contiguous vertebrae. Abnormalities of the disk space with erosion of the vertebral plates on x-ray is always infectious and not a malignancy. This is one of the most reliable rules in radiology (see Fig. 11.2).

Staphylococcus aureus is still the most frequent infecting organism, but in vertebral osteomyelitis there is a high frequency of Gram-negative bacterial infection. There are probably several reasons for this. First, Gram-negative bacteremia resulting from sources in the bowel, gallbladder, and urinary tract is more frequent in the population over the age of 60 years. Second, the pelvic veins flow into the paravertebral plexus (Batson's plexus), and infection of bone may occur from drainage of infected pelvic organs (like the bladder and kidneys), which empty their blood into the complex ramifications and anastomoses of this venous system.

Diagnostic Approaches

Because of the variety of the etiological agents, cultures and a determination of antibiotic sensitivity are imperative. If blood cultures are negative, tissue biopsies must be obtained for this purpose. Aspiration or needle biopsy of the disk space can be done with guidance from x-rays or a CAT scan. Most of these infections respond to medical therapy, but the neurological status of the patient has to be carefully followed inasmuch as the infection may spread from the vertebral body into the subdural or subarachnoid space through the rich venous and arterial plexus of the paravertebral circulation (Fig. 61.6). Sensory or motor changes imply spread of the infection into the epidural space and may necessitate surgical drainage to prevent permanent damage to

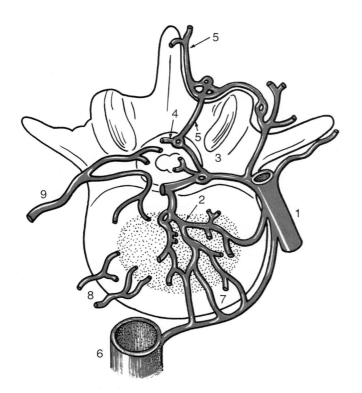

Figure 61.6. Vascular supply of a vertebral body showing the connections of the rich venous and arterial plexus of the paravertebral circulation. *1*, Ascending lumbar vein, *2*, intraosseous vertebral venous plexus; *3*, intervertebral vein; *4*; transverse internal vertebral venous plexus; *5*, posterior external venous plexus; *6*, inferior vena cava; *7*, anterior external vertebral venous plexus; *8*, nutrient branches from the segmental artery; *9*, spinal artery and its branches.

the nerves of the spinal cord. Thus, proper management of these cases requires a good understanding of anatomy, neurology, and pathophysiology.

Osteomyelitis Secondary to External or Contiguous Foci of Infection

Bone infection may also result from the direct introduction of microorganisms from an external or contiguous sources. Penetrating trauma is an obvious example of this type of infection. Another type is postoperative infection, particularly when surgery involves placement of a foreign body like a prosthesis or fixation device, such as is done to stabilize a hip fracture (Fig. 61.7). This is often a difficult problem to treat both because the bone has been traumatized and the foreign body can act as an avascular sanctuary for the persistence of bacteria. The problem of whether or not to remove the fixation device or prosthesis is a particularly complex one. On the one hand, the device is necessary for appropriate fixation of the bone (it has been put there for a good reason, i.e., to stabilize a fracture); on the other hand, its presence may prevent the elimination of bacteria. These decisions require close interactions between surgeons and internists to determine if and when removal is appropriate.

Although *S. aureus* is still the number one infecting organism in this type of osteomyelitis, others are also common. Frequently, the type of pathogen reflects the circumstances of the trauma and the area of the body involved. Contamination of the wound with soil often leads to infection by Gram-negative bacteria. Postoperative infections are frequently due to *S. aureus*. A wound may become contaminated with bacteria that are part of the fecal flora, particularly in an incontinent patient with a hip fracture.

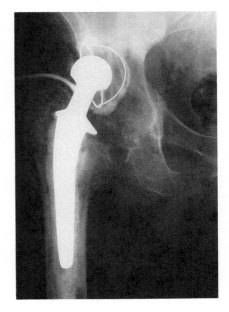

Figure 61.7. Osteomyelitis in bone with a prosthetic fixation device.

Osteomyelitis in Diabetic Patients

A special category of osteomyelitis is that which occurs in diabetic patients because of the vascular insufficiency and nerve damage characteristic of diabetes. Skin and soft tissue ulcerations on the feet of such patients may penetrate into the bone (Fig. 60.6). These infections are usually caused by a mixed bacterial flora, with the actual species reflecting the area of involvement. *S. aureus*, *Streptococcus* species, Gram-negative bacteria, and anaerobic bacteria are all commonly involved. These infections are particularly hard to treat because the organisms grow in necrotic bone with poor vascular supply. Here, again, therapy involves the use of antibiotics effective against the specific organisms, plus careful surgical debridement. Because of the poor vascular supply to the bone in diabetics, phagocytic cells and antibiotics penetrate poorly into the infected area and therapy is often unsuccessful. Unfortunately, amputation is frequently the end result of what started as a trivial soft tissue infection of the foot. This is why prevention, by paying attention to foot care, is vital to the survival of a patient with diabetes. This point cannot be stressed too much.

INFECTION OF JOINTS

A swollen, red hot, painful joint in a patient with fever raises questions similar to those osteomyelitis. First, is this an infection? Noninfectious inflammatory joint disease secondary to trauma, gout, pseudogout, or rheumatoid arthritis can also present in this manner. Second, if there is infection, how did it get there? As in osteomyelitis, infection can be seeded from a bacteremic focus, it can be introduced directly into the joint by trauma, by a medical of surgical procedure, or can extend into the joint space from the bone. Third, what is the infecting organism? All three of these questions can usually be answered by obtaining a complete history, doing a careful physical examination and analyzing fluid obtained by aspiration of the joint. Confirmatory evidence is provided by finding that the joint fluid contains inflammatory white cells and other abnormalities that indicate infection.

Synovial fluid consists of water, electrolytes, and other low molecular weight substances filtered from plasma, as well as components synthesized and secreted by synovial cells. Serum proteins are present in normal synovial fluid, but in lower concentrations than in plasma. The absence of fibrinogen explains why normal synovial fluid does not clot. The inflammatory reaction in synovial fluid is due to the interaction of serum proteins, phagocytic host cells, and microorganisms.

It is important to recognize that diagnosis of one joint disease does not preclude a second. Therefore, a joint deformed by arthritis can become infected with bacteria, particularly if that joint has recently been operated on or if steroids have been injected into it. The key to understanding the disease process is to obtain joint fluid for analysis and culture.

Infections of the joints can be caused by bacteria, viruses, and fungi. One can differentiate among these possibilities by the clinical presentation of the patient and by the results of laboratory tests on the joint fluid. In general, bacterial infections are more common than the other types of infections and produce a higher number of white blood cells in the joint fluid, with a predominance of neutrophils. The frequency with which specific bacterial agents cause septic arthritis varies with age. Once again, *S. aureus* is the most common overall cause and affects all age groups. *Haemophilus influenzae* type b is most frequent in infants between the ages of 6 months and 3 years. The *Gonococcus* is the leading cause in sexually active adults and accounts for 30–50% of hospital admissions for suppurative arthritis in adults under 30 years of age.

The etiological organism causing septic arthritis can be identified by Gram stain and culture of joint fluid. Even if the Gram stain is negative, antibiotic treatment should be started immediately after joint fluid and blood are obtained for culture to prevent continued infection and destruction of the structures in the joint. Table 61.2 lists the relative frequency of infecting organism and the clinical situations in which they are most likely to occur. Certain organisms, like the *Gonococcus, S. aureus,* and several spirochetes have an unusual tropism for the joints. The reason for this is unknown.

In addition to appropriate antibiotic therapy given parenterally and in high doses, the infected synovial fluid should be drained. This can be done by repeated aspirations or by open surgical drainage. One resorts to the latter when the former fails. Open drainage is always done in septic arthritis of the hip joint. This is required to prevent necrosis of the head of the femur that results because the blood supply to this part of the bone is too tenuous. Once again, a review of anatomy helps understand infectious process.

INFECTIONS OF MUSCLE (MYOSITIS)

All of us have experienced the muscle aches and stiffness (myalgia) that occur commonly when we have a viral illness ("the flu"). In fact, these myalgias are prominent features of a variety of infections such as viral illness, rickettsial infection, and even osteomyelitis and bacterial endocarditis. Fever is often accompanied by muscle pains or myalgias. It is rare that the infecting organisms are directly involved in myalgias. Most often, this muscle involvement is indirect, probably due to the accelerated catabolism of skeletal muscle, part of the so-called acute phase response that accompanies sepsis and trauma. This catabolism is probably mediated by several products of macrophages (monokines) including interleukin-1 and tumor necrosis factor. The systemic symptoms resulting from these macrophage products are mediated by the increased synthesis of prostaglandin E_2, which, in turn, activates muscle proteases. The same substances lead to the production of fever in the hypothalamus. All of this explains why inhibitors of prostaglandin

Table 61.2. Most Frequent Causes of Bacterial Arthritis by Age

Organism	Neonates	Children 2 months-2 years	3–10 years	Adults
Staphylococcus aureus	10–25%	1–10%	10–25%	25–75%
Streptococcus species (group A, viridans, microaerophilic, anaerobic *S. pneumoniae*	1–10%	10–25%	10–25%	10–25%
Group B streptococci	10–25%	Rare	Rare	1–10%
Haemophilus influenzae, type b	Rare	25–75%	1–10%	Rare
Neisseria	Rare	1–10%	10–25%	10–25%[a]
Gram-negative bacilli	10–25%	1–10%	1–10%	1–10%
Anaerobes	Rare	Rare	Rare	Rare
Other	1–10%	Rare	1–10%	Rare

[a]Generally adults less than 30 years of age.

synthesis, like aspirin, make us feel better, and help resolve both fever and muscle aches.

Specific Muscle Infections

Specific infections of skeletal muscle are uncommon. When they occur, they may be due to a wide range of organisms including bacteria, fungi, viruses, and parasitic agents. Muscles may be invaded either from contiguous sites of infection, or by hematogenous spread from a distant focus. The kinds of infection and their frequency depend on the host, geographic area, or eating habits, of the patient.

Several of the clinical presentations are so distinctive that they readily suggest the etiological agent. For example, the presence of gas in muscle makes one think of gas gangrene secondary to *Clostridium perfringens*. Generalized muscle pain and peripheral eosinophilia in a patient who has eaten undercooked pork should raise the possibility of trichinosis.

Table 61.3 lists several of the more common causes of infectious myositis and their specific clinical presentations. Therapy of nonspecific myalgia is usually symptomatic. When a specific etiological agent is identified, therapy should be directed at this agent. Prompt drainage of abscesses and extensive surgical debridement may be necessary if necrotic tissue is present.

Table 61.3. Pathogenesis of Muscle Infections

Pathogenesis	Clinical Presentation	Principal Specific Etiologies
Localized and spread from a contiguous site	Gas gangrene	*Clostridium perfringens*; occasionally other clostridial species
	Synergistic myositis or gangrene	Mixed infections; anaerobic bacteria and enteric bacteria
	Muscle abscesses	*Staphylococcus aureus*, Group A, hemolytic streptococcus, Gram-negative bacteria
	Miscellaneous	*Mycobacterium, Nocardia, Actinomyces*, fungi
Hematogenous spread	Bacterial	Group A, B hemolytic streptococcus, *S. aureus,* Gram-negative bacteria
	Fungal	*Candida, Aspergillus, H. capsulatum, C. immitis*
	Mycobacterial	Typical and atypical mycobacteria, *Trichinella*
	Parasitic	*Dracunculus medinensis,* malaria, filariasis, etc.
	Viral	Influenza, echovirus, coxsackie, Epstein-Barr virus

SUGGESTED READING

Smith JW. Infectious arthritis. In: Mandell G, Douglas G, Bennett JE, eds. Principles and practice of infectious diseases, 3rd ed. New York: John Wiley and Sons, 1990:911.

Swartz MN. Myositis. In: Mandell G, Douglas G, Bennett JE, eds. Principles and practice of infectious diseases, 3rd ed. New York: John Wiley and Sons, 1990:812.

Waldvogel FA, Medoff G, Swartz MN. Osteomyelitis: a review of clinical features, therapeutic considerations and unusual aspects (parts 1, 2, and 3). N Engl J Med 1970;282:198, 282:260, and 282:316.

Waldvogel FA, Vesey H. Osteomyelitis: the past decade. N Engl J Med 1980;303:360.

Sepsis 62

Ellen Whitnack

Sepsis is roughly equivalent to what is known in the world at large as "blood-poisoning." Before refining our notions of it, let us consider two cases that might be called "sepsis, old and new."

CASE 1

G.L., a 48-year-old farmer, cut his thumb 1 day while installing the spreaders on his combine. The next morning, the thumb was sore and the skin surrounding the cut was red, but Mr. L., who needed to get his soybeans in before the rain started, resumed combining until well after dark. By the time he got back to the house, the thumb was swollen and throbbing, with some yellowish-white material oozing out. Mr. L. noticed two red streaks going up the inside of his forearm. He was just thinking that he'd better get his thumb looked at when suddenly he had a shaking chill and felt queasy. His wife drove him 17 miles to the county hospital. By the time they got there, Mr. L.'s temperature had reached 39.7°C. He was flushed and ill-appearing, with a pulse of 125 and a blood pressure of 100/60, compared to his usual of 145/85. Blood cultures were drawn, and Mr. L. was started on intravenous fluids and antibiotics. By morning, he was somewhat better; by the following day, he was a new man, and his subsequent recovery and wound-healing were uneventful. The blood cultures, which turned positive on the third day, grew *Staphylococcus aureus*.

CASE 2

L.J., a 59-year-old woman with cervical carcinoma, underwent extensive pelvic surgery to remove the tumor, including removal of all pelvic organs, removal of a segment of ileum to construct a new bladder, and a colostomy. At first, she seemed to be recovering well. During the evening of the third postoperative day, the nurse on the evening shift noticed that Mrs. J.'s respiratory rate, which had been 16–18/minute, was 26. Mrs. J. said she felt reasonably OK, not short of breath or in much pain, and her temperature was actually subnormal—36.2°C. The next morning on rounds, Mrs. J. had some fever, 38.3°C, but she continued to feel fairly well, her wound showed no sign of infection, and her abdomen was no more tender than expected. That afternoon, however, Mrs. J. was clearly in trouble. She was flushed, anxious, and restless; her blood pressure was down from 135/75 to 105/58, and her temperature was 39.2°C. Blood cultures were drawn, antibiotics were started, and intravenous fluids were infused rapidly, which brought the blood pressure up. Thereafter, Mrs. J. got worse. By morning, she was short of breath and had excess fluid throughout her lungs. Fluids were cut back; now a vasopressor was required to maintain the blood pressure. This required monitoring in the intensive care unit. To better assess her hemodynamic status, the superior vena cava and one pulmonary artery were catheterized (the latter via the jugular vein, right atrium, and right ventricle). Mrs. J. had a cardiac output nearly double the normal for a resting adult of her size, but her systemic vascular resistance was extremely low, accounting for her low blood pressure despite the high *cardiac output. Over the next 24 hours, Mrs. J. continued to do poorly, and her urine output dropped nearly to zero. The surgeon decided that re-exploration was warranted because of persistent sepsis in the face of broad-spectrum antimicrobial therapy. At surgery, the suture line attaching the ileum to the colon was found to be partially disrupted, with leakage of bowel contents, intense inflammation of the mesentery, and early abscess formation. Appropriate repairs were made and drains were inserted. Thereafter, Mrs. J. recovered slowly but completely. The blood cultures remained sterile.*

WHAT IS SEPSIS?

"Sepsis" is an ancient Greek word meaning, roughly, "putrefaction." For most of medical history "septic" referred to an inflammatory process yielding foul-smelling pus, such as a septic wound or a septic abortion. The pus had to be malodorous to be considered pathological; the white, odorless pus so commonly encountered in wounds was considered a good thing—"good and laudable pus"—and essential for proper healing. All that changed with the microbiological discoveries of Pasteur and Lister. The term septic for a local infection is still used, but the requirement for a foul odor has long since been dropped with the recognition that any pus usually represents infection, which is not good for wound-healing. To be sure, if a wound must be infected, better that leukocytes should be there to fight the invaders—hence, the pus; but better yet if the wound does not get infected in the first place.

Microbiological discoveries in the last century also provided an explanation of why patients with septic wounds sometimes got so sick; the microbes spread, first to the lymphatics (hence the red streaks on Mr. L.'s arm) and then to the bloodstream, producing "septic blood"—**septicemia**—and "pyemia"—pus in the blood, or as we now call it, leukocytosis. Was the patient sick because of the effects of the microbes (or, as it was thought, microbial toxins) on the blood itself, or did the blood serve to carry the toxins to the tissues? This was a matter of considerable debate; what was clear was that a local process had become systemic.

Early on, it was recognized that viable bacteria could be present in the blood—**bacteremia**—without much in the way of illness. On the other hand, if a severe systemic illness was present, bacteremia could generally be found; thus, septicemic patients were bacteremic by definition. What, then, is **sepsis**? Until quite recently, sepsis and septicemia were essentially synonyms, and still are in many texts. However, in the past 20 years or so, ideas about the nature of septicemia/sepsis have evolved, in two ways.

First, sepsis has come to be as much a **physiological** as a clinical or microbiological term. ("Clinical" means "as determined at the bedside by signs and symptoms," as opposed to laboratory tests and invasive procedures.) The widespread use of hemodynamic monitoring in intensive care units has shown that patients with clinical sepsis—fever or hypothermia, tachycardia, subnormal blood pressure, and subnormal urine output—characteristically have an **increased cardiac output** and a greatly **decreased peripheral vascular resistance**, as in Mrs. J.'s case. Patients with these "septic hemodynamics" are **not necessarily bacteremic**; indeed, they need not have a bacterial infection at all. Sepsis has resulted from infections with fungi (especially *Candida*), parasites (falciparum malaria), and even viruses (adenovirus). In bacterial sepsis, which is by far the commonest kind, 20–50% of the patients do not have bacteremia.

Second, we have come to realize that the sepsis syndrome results from the **release of cytokines** from host cells (macrophages) stimulated by microbial substances. It is the host's own molecules, not the microbe's, that are the proximate cause of sepsis, although, in certain special cases (e.g., clostridial α-toxin), bacterial toxins may contribute to the pathogenesis of the illness by a direct toxicity. Sepsis is, therefore, **the final common path of host response** to a variety of microbial molecules.

For these reasons, septicemia in the old sense of bacteremia plus severe systemic illness is on its way to obsolescence, being replaced with sepsis or "the sepsis syndrome." We will think of sepsis as a **severe systemic illness marked by characteristic hemodynamic derangements and organ malfunction, brought about by the interaction of certain microbial products with host reticuloendothelial cells.**

Sepsis leaves no organ or system untouched. In protracted cases of sepsis such as those complicating abdominal surgery, one organ after another may fail—a situation called, appropriately enough, the **multiorgan failure syndrome (MOFS).**

Brain: septic patients commonly are confused, delirious, stuporous, or comatose.

Heart: myocardial contractility is depressed in sepsis. The heart compensates by dilating and beating faster, and cardiac output is characteristically increased, but in advanced cases, compensatory mechanisms fail and cardiac output drops to low levels.

Vasculature: despite the high cardiac output, blood pressure falls because of massive peripheral vasodilatation. The combination of very low blood pressure (in adults, often defined as less than 90 mm Hg systolic) and high cardiac output has been termed **"warm shock"** because the patient has warm or even flushed skin, in contrast to other common forms of shock. One might wonder what is wrong with having a low blood pressure so long as the cardiac output is high; the justification for the term "shock" is that despite the high cardiac output, there is evidence of inadequate perfusion of selected vascular beds, particularly in the kidney, liver, and gut, and evidence of oxygen starvation of tissues in the form of lactic acidosis (see below). Warm shock is also sometimes called "early shock," but this is a misnomer, in that the hyperdynamic phase of septic shock is really the main event, not a preliminary phase. Late in the course of sepsis, as cardiac output falls, peripheral vasodilatation is replaced by vasoconstriction. The skin becomes pale and cold, the hands and feet are bluish purple, and the patient expires in **"cold shock"** similar to that seen after a massive heart attack or hemorrhage.

Clotting system: endothelial damage can lead to extensive microvascular thrombosis, or **disseminated intravascular coagulation (DIC).** DIC consumes platelets and clotting factors, leaving the patient with a bleeding tendency, so that there may be thrombosis and bleeding at the same time. Activation of the fibrinolytic system counteracts the thrombosis, but adds to the coagulopathy because some fibrin degradation products inhibit clotting.

Lung: in sepsis, the **capillaries are generally leaky**; in the lung, capillary endothelial damage may be enhanced by activated neutrophils that adhere to the pulmonary endothelium in large numbers. Fluid exudes into the interstitium and alveolar spaces, the lung becomes soggy and stiff, and adequate gas exchange is impossible, a state of affairs known as the **adult respiratory distress syndrome (ARDS)**. Oxygen must be pumped into the patient's lungs under pressure.

Kidney: acute renal failure due to **acute tubular necrosis** occurs.

Liver: stasis of bile, focal necrosis, and **jaundice** are common.

Gastrointestinal tract: hemorrhagic necrosis of the mucosa occurs, probably, at least in part, because of ischemia. Loss of mucosal integrity can lead to massive **hemorrhage**.

Endocrine and metabolic effects: sepsis is a **catabolic state**, with massive proteolysis, lipolysis, and glycogenolysis. Stress hormones (cortisol, catecholamines, glucagon) circulate in high levels. Oxygen metabolism is deranged; an abnormally high fraction of the oxygen sent to the tissues is returned to the heart unused, either because some vascular beds are not perfused or because some cells are too sick (metabolically speaking) to use the oxygen delivered to them. Either way, in the absence of a functioning Krebs cycle, glycolysis proceeds at a high rate and the pyruvic acid so formed is reduced to lactic acid, resulting in **lactic acidosis**.

ENCOUNTER

Most cases of sepsis result from infections with endogenous bacterial flora. Before midcentury, the group A streptococcus (Chapter 12) was the leading cause of sepsis, with *Staphylococcus aureus* (Chapter 11) coming in second. Most cases due to these Gram-positive cocci resulted from wounds, puerperal fever, and abortions. Other infections leading to sepsis included pyelonephritis (**urosepsis**), generally caused by enteric Gram-negative bacilli such as *Escherichia coli*, and intra-abdominal infections such as appendicitis with rupture, generally caused by mixtures of enterics and anaerobes such as *Bacteroides fragilis*. *Neisseria meningitidis* occasionally caused fulminant sepsis in healthy people with no more predisposition than, perhaps, a viral upper respiratory tract infection (see Chapter 56).

All of these infections still exist, particularly staphylococcal sepsis and urosepsis, and streptococcal sepsis, rare in recent years, may be making a comeback (see Chapter 12). However, the years since World War II have seen an expanding population of chronically ill, debilitated, immunocompromised, and (therefore) hospitalized people, to the point that the majority of cases of sepsis now arise in hospitalized patients—**nosocomial sepsis**. Hospitalized patients—and the various lines and tubes that penetrate their skin and body orifices—tend to become colonized with a special population of hospital microbes brought to them on the (inadequately washed) hands of personnel. In the 1950s, the leading cause of nosocomial sepsis was "hospital staph," but since then, probably because of the use of antibiotics, the major cause of sepsis has been an ever more antibiotic-resistant population of enteric Gram-negative bacilli and nonfermenters such as *Pseudomonas aeruginosa* (Chapter 19). **"Gram-negative sepsis"** (meaning, of course, Gram-negative bacterial sepsis) is now the commonest type of sepsis overall.

ENTRY, SPREAD, AND MULTIPLICATION

Most cases of sepsis start with a localized infection of some sort, including not only tissue infections but infected foreign bodies such as intravenous catheters (**"line sepsis"**). Sepsis can also occur when damage to an epithelial surface that is normally heavily colonized (for example, the colonic mucosa) permits the passage of bacteria or bacterial products into the circulation, or when defects in clearance mechanisms allow otherwise insignificant bacterial growth to get out of hand. For sepsis to occur, three things seem to be necessary:

- **A large population of infecting or colonizing microorganisms;** this, in turn, implies some combination of a large inoculum, defects in the host's containment and clearance mechanisms, and strong microbial resistance to host defenses.

- **The presence of bacterial products capable of stimulating the release of host cytokines;** many microbes can cause sepsis, but some rarely do; for example, enterococci (Chapter 12) seem to be rather bland, nontoxic organisms that cause bacteremia frequently, but sepsis rarely.

- **The widespread dissemination of these microbial products to the host's reticuloendothelial system;** bacteremia is obviously a convenient way to achieve this, but microbial products can also be disseminated from a localized source, particularly in the gastrointestinal tract or the peritoneal cavity, as happened in Mrs. J.'s case.

WHAT DEFECTS IN HOST DEFENSE PARTICULARLY PREDISPOSE TO SEPSIS?

Although *N. meningitidis* causes sepsis in healthy people, and some cases of staphylococcal sepsis arise for no apparent reason, the vast majority of cases occur in patients with defects in host defenses, for example:

- **Disruption or penetration of anatomical barriers**—wounds, intravascular catheters, and contaminated intravenous drugs and medications are obvious examples. Others include ischemic necrosis (as in the gut) and tumors. Cytotoxic chemotherapy damages rapidly dividing cells including intestinal epithelium.

- **Devitalized tissue**—necrotic tissue has no blood supply and, therefore, no phagocytes, complement, or antibody to protect it. It is also a rich culture medium.

- **Granulocytopenia and defective granulocyte function**—neutrophils are the first line of defense against many bacteria as well as fungal hyphae and pseudohyphae. Granulocytopenia, as occurs, for instance, during chemotherapy with agents toxic to the bone marrow, predisposes to infections from bacteria and such fungi as *Candida*. Some of the increased susceptibility to sepsis seen in neonates ("sepsis neonatorum") and in patients with diabetes and cirrhosis may be due to defective neutrophil chemotaxis or killing (see Chapter 66).

- **Complement defects**—hereditary defects in various complement components are associated with bacteremia and sepsis. Defects in "late" components (C5-C9) create a particular susceptibility to neisserial infections (Chapter 6). Some clinicians check a complement level on any patient presenting with bacteremia, sepsis, or meningitis due to *N. meningitidis*.

- **Immune defects**—loss of opsonic and bactericidal antibody (humoral defects) and loss of the ability to activate macrophages in response to specific antigenic stimuli (cellular defects) predispose to sepsis. Aside from patients with obvious immune system disease or granulocytopenia, most patients known to be predisposed to bacterial infections and sepsis, including elderly persons and patients with chronic renal disease, hepatic disease, diabetes, alcoholism, or malnutrition, have subtle immune defects of one sort or another. Elderly patients, for example, have progressive depletion of competent CD_4 lymphocytes. However, the specific defects have not been well defined in all cases.

- **Splenic malfunction or absence**—without the spleen, clearance of encapsulated bacteria from the blood is impaired. Persons who lack a functioning spleen (for example, sickle-cell patients) are susceptible to fulminant sepsis due to bacteria such as *S. pneumoniae, Haemophilus influenzae,* and *N. meningitidis.* Such persons are immunized against these bacteria (to the extent possible, see Chapter 66) and warned not to take flu-like illnesses lightly. Some take antibiotics on a long-term basis for prophylaxis.

DAMAGE

We have alluded to "microbial molecules" that interact with host macrophages to initiate the train of events eventuating in the sepsis syndrome. These substances have not been identified with certainty, with one outstanding exception; endotoxin or **lipopolysaccharide (LPS)**, specifically its lipid A moiety, which is the main component of the outer leaflet of the outer membrane of the Gram-negative bacterial cell (Chapter 3). In animals, LPS administration elicits many features of experimental sepsis; in man, LPS (in small doses!) causes fever, chills, rapid breathing, and a mild version of the cardiovascular alterations seen in sepsis—decreased myocardial contractility, increased cardiac output, decreased systemic vascular resistance, and hypotension.

Although the mechanism by which LPS produces its many effects has not been determined in all cases, it looks as if LPS is not directly responsible for any of them. LPS is nontoxic (except at unrealistically high doses) in a strain of mice called C3H/HeJ unless the mice first receive a transplant of normal marrow. These mice, it turns out, have a mutant gene encoding a defective protein (? a component of the signal transduction pathway) required for the response of macrophages to stimulation by LPS. The transplanted marrow supplies normal, responsive macrophages. Thus, it would seem to be the macrophage, not the microbe, that actually causes the sepsis syndrome.

How does the macrophage do it? The principal mediator of the effects of LPS is a cytokine secreted by macrophages called **tumor necrosis factor α (TNF)** or **cachectin.** (The former name comes from the antitumor effects of the protein, the latter from its ability to produce wasting in animal models of certain chronic parasitic infections. Like many cytokine names, neither term conveys the breadth or depth of the protein's physiological role.) TNF, like LPS, can induce a sepsis-like state in experimental animals, and is the only host mediator known to do this when administered in isolation. TNF stimulates the macrophages to produce interleukin-1b (IL-1). TNF and IL-1 have the largest number of target genes of any known natural substances. They act synergistically on macrophages (in a sort of positive feedback loop) and on other cells, particularly neutrophils and endothelial cells, to alter their surfaces by expressing certain membrane proteins and to produce a variety of additional mediators. In fact, **once sepsis is underway, the endothelial cell may be the key cell, both as target and effector.**

Elucidating the secondary effects of TNF and IL-1 has become a very complex field of investigation as the list of mediators gets ever longer, and it is not always clear whether a given mediator produces its effects directly or through additional mediators. Some of the mediators of sepsis, and their pathological effects, are shown in Table 62.1.

WHY DOES THE BODY SELF-DESTRUCT?

We normally think of the body as self-protective, and expect that its response to insult will be in the direction of damage control and repair. In sepsis, however, the host seems bent on self-destruction. Why is this? Have the microbes tricked the host into a maladaptive response? Or is the sepsis syndrome, however deadly, a protective mechanism, such that the host would die even faster without it? What **good** are TNF, IL-1 and all the rest in the acute response to an infecting organism?

Recall the CH3/HeJ mouse, which does not respond to LPS. These mice are killed by a much **lower** inoculum of Gram-negative bacilli than are normal mice, and are **protected** by pretreatment with TNF and IL-1. Or consider a mouse model of infection with *Listeria monocytogenes*, in which anti-TNF antibody exacerbates the disease; or a model of granuloma formation in mycobacterial infection, in which anti-TNF prevents killing of the mycobacteria by the granulomas. Observations such as these suggest that TNF is part of a legitimate system of host defense. In sepsis, the host is fighting infection with every weapon at its command, but the deployment is so massive that the toll from friendly fire precludes victory.

DIAGNOSIS AND TREATMENT OF SEPSIS

The signs of sepsis may be obvious, as in Mr. L.'s case, or subtle, as in Mrs. J.'s. Delay in diagnosis is particularly likely when there is no fever.

Table 62.1. Putative Mediators of Sepsis

Mediator	Physiological Effects
Tumor necrosis factor	Mimics sepsis syndrome; margination of neutrophils is particularly striking after TNF administration
Interleukin-1	Fever, increased adhesiveness of endothelial cells and leukocytes, endothelial procoagulant activity
Interleukins-2, -4, -6, -8	Hypotension, capillary leak, decreased myocardial contractility, synthesis of "acute-phase" proteins (e.g., fibrinogen) by the liver, leukocyte chemotaxis
Hageman factor (factor XII), tissue factor, factor X	Coagulation, fibrinolysis
Complement cascade	Neutrophil chemotaxis, neutrophil aggregation, capillary leak
Endorphins	Hypotension
Leukotrienes and thromboxane	Platelet aggregation, neutrophil adhesion, capillary leak, decreased myocardial contractility
Prostaglandins (especially E_2 and I_2)	Hypotension, neutrophil adhesion to endothelium, fever, muscle aches, muscle proteolysis
Bradykinin (via factor XII and kallikrein)	Hypotension, capillary leak
Serotonin	Pulmonary hypertension, capillary leak
Histamine	Hypotension, capillary leak
Platelet activating factor (PAF) (currently a hot research topic)	Hypotension, capillary leak, platelet aggregation, leukocyte activation, decreased myocardial contractility
Phagocyte products—lysosomal proteins, oxygen free radicals	Endothelial cell damage, capillary leak
Myocardial depressant factor (can be passively transferred)	Decreased myocardial contractility
Endothelin-1	Vasoconstriction, especially in the kidney
Endothelial relaxing factor (? nitric oxide)—another hot research topic	Hypotension

Easily overlooked or misinterpreted signs of early sepsis include decreased (rather than increased) temperature, increased respiratory rate, increased heart rate, nausea, and mental confusion. The initial fall in blood pressure may not be very striking. Changes in the results of routine laboratory studies are likewise nonspecific and include either leukocytosis or leukopenia and a fall in the level of serum bicarbonate, reflecting the development of lactic acidosis.

In most patients with sepsis, the blood cultures will be positive, although the bacteria may take a few days to grow. In some critically ill patients, the diagnosis of sepsis becomes apparent when the central catheters are placed, revealing the characteristic hemodynamic changes. Very few acute illnesses other than sepsis produce a rise in cardiac output and a fall in systemic vascular resistance.

The mainstays of therapy of sepsis are **maximization of oxygen delivery** to the tissues, **drainage** of pus and **debridement** of devitalized tissue, and, of course, **antibiotics**. Sepsis is, as mentioned, a state of oxygen starvation. An abnormally low fraction of oxygen is extracted from the arterial blood, but if more oxygen is supplied, more will be extracted—the more, the better. Measures to maximize oxygen delivery include: (a) high oxygen content of the air supplied to the patient; (b) use of a ventilator to keep the airways under pressure throughout the respiratory cycle; (c) intravenous fluids to maintain the blood volume; (d) transfusions, if needed, to increase the hemoglobin content of the blood (but not too much; red cells increase the viscosity of the blood, with deleterious effects on microcirculatory flow); and (e) adrenergic drugs to maintain tissue perfusion pressure, increase myocardial contractility, and correct the maldistribution of the circulation. Debridement of devitalized tissue and drainage of pus are essential, as illustrated by Mrs. J., who did not get better, despite antibiotics, until her abscess was drained.

An interesting issue is whether antibiotics might actually be temporarily deleterious even as they control the infection. After all, if antibiotics kill bacteria, they will cause the release of toxic bacterial components such as endotoxin. A transient deleterious effect of antibiotic therapy has, in fact, been demonstrated in two clinical situations—bacterial meningitis, which is essentially sepsis within the central nervous system (see Chapter 58), and massive bacteremia in immunocompromised, granulocytopenic patients. In ordinary cases of sepsis, a deleterious effect of antibiotics is not obvious to the clinician and, in any case, there is nothing for it; the infection must be controlled or the patient will die. Even with the best treatment, the mortality of sepsis that has reached the organ failure stage is $\geq 50\%$.

For some years, investigators have pursued the idea that interference with bacterial or host mediators might be beneficial in the treatment of sepsis. Various antagonists and blocking agents have been tried in experimental models. A discouraging feature of many of these experiments is that the measures succeed, but only if used at or before the time of bacterial challenge; for example, corticosteroids, which block TNF mRNA translation, protect against sepsis if given ahead of time, but are of no value in clinical situations, because a shotgun blast of TNF has already been released by the macrophages by the time sepsis is diagnosed. However, two recent studies have shown decreased mortality in patients with Gram-negative sepsis treated with monoclonal antibodies against lipid A. At the time of this writing, a therapeutic trial of a monoclonal antibody against TNF is in progress in centers across the U.S. The day may come when patients with sepsis are routinely given a cocktail of anticytokine antibodies, soluble receptors to act as decoys for mediators, receptor blocking agents, and inhibitors of mediator synthesis to tide them over while the antibiotics do their work. The trick will be to reduce the deleterious effects of host mediators without neutralizing their ability to perform essential defensive functions.

SUGGESTED READING

Beutler B. The explosion of septic shock. Curr Opinion Infect Dis 1991; 13:623–627.

Bone RC. The pathophysiology of sepsis. Ann Intern Med 1991;115:457–469

Dinarello CA. The proinflammatory cytokines interleukin-1 and tumor necrosis factor and the treatment of the septic shock syndrome. J Infect Dis 1991;163;1177–1184.

Tracey KJ, Fong Y, Hesse DG, Manogue KR, Lee AT, Kuo GC, Lowry SF, Cerami A: Anti-cachectin/TNF monoclonal antibodies prevent septic shock during lethal bacteraemia. Nature 1987;330:662–664.

Ziegler EJ (and 14 others). Treatment of gram-negative bacteremia and septic shock with HA-1A human monoclonal antibody against endotoxin—a randomized, double-blind, placebo-controlled trial. N Engl J Med 1991;324: 429–436.

Intravascular Infection

63

Adolf W. Karchmer

A great variety of microorganisms gain entry to the intravascular space and are passively carried throughout the circulatory system, either suspended in the plasma or within various cellular components of blood. Usually, entry into the circulatory tree is a chance event of short duration. Sometimes, it represents a brief phase of an infection that is centered primarily in another organ system. However, for some bacteria and protozoa, the primary site of infection is within the vascular system, i.e., the cellular components of blood or the structural elements of the circulatory system. For example, *Plasmodium* species (the causes of malaria), *Babesia microti* (the cause of babesiosis), and *Bartonella bacilliformis* (the agent of Oroya fever) produce disease as a consequence of invading or adhering to erythrocytes. Occasionally, microorganisms infect the endothelial surface of a specific component of the cardiovascular system. These intravascular infections are called **endarteritis** when involving an artery, **endocarditis** when affecting an endothelial site in the heart, and **phlebitis** if localized in the lumen of a vein.

Infective phlebitis occurs mainly by direct spread from an adjacent focus of infection or when intravascular foreign bodies that have been implanted in veins become infected. **Infective endarteritis** arises in an analogous manner and, on rare occasions, when congenital arterial deficits (coarctation of the aorta) or diseased arterial endothelium (atherosclerotic plaques) become infected during transient bacteremia. **Infective endocarditis**, with the exception of episodes that arise as a consequence of cardiac surgery or intracardiac instrumentation, results from seeding of endothelial sites by microorganisms that are transiently present in the circulatory tree. Most vascular endothelial infections are caused by bacteria and, on rare occasions, by fungi. Infective endocarditis is the prototype of the spontaneously occurring intravascular endothelial infections and will be the focus of this chapter. The term "endocarditis" will refer here to "infectious endocarditis."

CASE

Mrs. A.D., a 75-year-old woman with a history of a systolic ejection heart murmur and mild aortic stenosis, hypertension, and diabetes was admitted to the hospital because of 6 weeks of intermittent fevers, malaise, weakness, and loss of appetite. The day before admission, she noted her temperature to be 41.2°C and discovered that she was 14 lb below her usual weight.

On examination, Mrs. D. was pale. Her temperature was 38.1°C, heart rate 100, and blood pressure 150/90 mm Hg. Three small hemorrhages were noted on the right palpebral conjunctiva. The fundi were normal. She was edentulous. On cardiac examination, a grade III/VI systolic ejection heart murmur was heard at the base of the heart suggesting aortic stenosis and a grade I/VI, brief, high-pitched decrescendo diastolic murmur was heard at the left sternal border indicating aortic insufficiency as well. The spleen could not be palpated.

Her laboratory tests revealed a hematocrit of 27% (normal is greater than 36%), a normal leukocyte count, a sedimentation rate of 92 mm/hour (normal is less than 15 mm/hour), a creatinine level of 1.9 mg/dl (normal is less than 1.3 mg/dl) and a urine analysis that showed 25–30 red blood cells/high power field but no white blood cells or casts. Six blood cultures obtained over 48 hours were all positive for Streptococcus bovis.

Penicillin, 3 million units intravenously every 4 hours, was begun as treatment for subacute bacterial endocarditis. On the sixth hospital day, the patient was found unresponsive, with a dilated left pupil. An emergency cranial CAT scan revealed a large left parietal hematoma. The patient died on the eighth hospital day.

Autopsy confirmed vegetations on the aortic valve at the closure line. The valve was bicuspid and thickened. A Gram stain of the vegetation confirmed the presence of Gram-positive cocci. Small embolic infarcts were noted in the myocardium and in a slightly enlarged spleen. There were changes of focal glomerulonephritis and several small infarcts in both kidneys. A massive subarachnoid and left parietal intracerebral hemorrhage from an apparent leaking aneurysm (a mycotic aneurysm or sac-like dilatation, which results from growth of bacteria in the vessel wall) was noted.

DEFINITION AND CLASSIFICATION OF ENDOCARDITIS

Infective endocarditis is the disease caused by infection of the endothelial surface of the heart. Usually, the infection is localized on one of the cardiac valves but it may also occur on one of the cordae tendineae or on areas of the atrial or ventricular wall. Infective endocarditis has been **classified** according to the **tempo of the clinical illness**, the **microbiological cause**, and the **clinical setting or site** of infection. During the preantibiotic era, when endocarditis was universally fatal, disease was classified by time from onset of symptoms until death. Acute endocarditis was characterized by hectic fever, marked toxicity, and death in days to 6 weeks. Subacute endocarditis was a more indolent disease; it was manifest by less striking temperatures, gradual wasting, and death in 6 weeks to 3 months. Chronic endocarditis was an even more indolent disease and symptoms smoldered for more than 3 months. Acute endocarditis was commonly caused by invasive extracellular pyogenic bacteria such as *S. aureus, Streptococcus pneumoniae, S. pyogenes* (Group A streptococci), and *Neisseria gonorrhoeae.* In contrast, subacute and chronic endocarditis were typically caused by less virulent nonpyogenic bacteria, including α-hemolytic streptococci (so called viridans streptococci), enterococci, and fastidious Gramnegative coccobacilli (primarily *Haemophilus aphrophilus, Cardiobacterium hominis,* and *Actinobacillus actinomycetemcomitans*). Subacute and chronic endocarditis occurred in patients with pre-existing valvular heart disease. Acute endocarditis was not restricted to patients with valvular dysfunction but commonly affected patients without underlying valvular disease.

This classification based on duration of symptoms before death is no longer appropriate because therapy alters the course of the infection. **The terms acute and subacute continue to be used, however, to describe the course of disease before the initiation of treatment.** Patients presenting with a markedly febrile, toxic course lasting only days to several weeks are said to have **acute endocarditis**, whereas those with lower fevers, an illness marked by anorexia, weakness, and weight loss, and who have been symptomatic for several weeks are considered to have **subacute endocarditis**. The tendency nowadays is to avoid such classifications in favor of brief descriptions that include the microbiological cause, the type and site of the infected valve, and predisposing event. Thus, "α-hemolytic streptococcal native valve endocarditis," "*S. aureus* tricuspid valve endocarditis in an intravenous drug abuser," or "*S. epidermidis* prosthetic aortic valve endocarditis," provide a more precise diagnosis and specific implications regarding therapy and prognosis.

EPIDEMIOLOGY

In a careful study of carried out in Olmstead County, Minnesota between 1950 and 1981, the frequency of infective endocarditis was 3.8 cases/100,000 person-years. In the United Kingdom, in 1977 through 1984, the attack rate for endocarditis was estimated to be 1.5–2.5/ 100,000 person-years. Endocarditis accounts for approximately one of each 1000 admissions to large general hospitals. The median age of patients with endocarditis has increased steadily since the preantibiotic era; in the 1920s, the median age was less than 30 years, whereas currently more than 50% of cases occur in persons over 50 years of age.

The importance of structural heart disease as the substrate for endocarditis has also changed. Thus, **acute rheumatic fever** has become a less common predisposing factor for endocarditis, along with its reduced incidence in developed countries. **Congenital cardiac defects** (especially bicuspid aortic valves, ventricular septal defects, tetralogy of Fallot, and patent ductus arteriosus), **degenerative valvular disease** (calcific valvular disease), and **mitral valve prolapse** with mitral regurgitation have become more prominent predisposing causes for endocarditis. In recent reports, about 20% of endocarditis patients were found to have infection on a prolapsing regurgitant mitral valve. **Prosthetic heart valves** have become an important site for the establishment of endocarditis.

Endocarditis affects older and older people, for the following reasons:

- People with congenital heart disease live longer.

- Prosthetic valves to correct valve dysfunction are implanted more frequently in this age group.

- The age of the general population and, therefore, those with degenerative valve disease has increased.

- Rheumatic heart disease (a disease with onset at a younger age) has decreased in prevalence.

- Genitourinary tract infections and manipulations, colonic pathology (benign polyps and malignancy), and nosocomial bacteremias are more common in the elderly.

Conversely, the current epidemic of intravenous drug abuse has raised the incidence of endocarditis among younger persons. However, here the pattern is different. Endocarditis associated with rheumatic, congenital, and degenerative valvular disease is primarily an aortic or mitral valve infection. In intravenous drug abusers, it affects not only previously normal left heart valves, but in one-half of the cases, a normal tricuspid valve. Between 15% and 30% of patients with endocarditis who do not abuse drugs are not known to have a prior valvular abnormality.

ENCOUNTER

Endocarditis is caused by many different microorganisms, but the most prevalent are **streptococci**, **enterococci**, and **staphylococci** (Table 63.1). Specific organisms have a predilection for the type of valve that is infected (native vs. prosthetic) and the event or site causing the endocarditis-inciting bacteremia (dental source, intravenous drug abuse, nosocomial infection).

The organisms that cause native valve endocarditis tend to differ in acute and subacute infections. In **acute endocarditis**, *S. aureus* accounts for 60% of cases, the rest being caused by pneumococci, streptococci, and aerobic Gram-negative bacilli. In contrast, in **subacute endocarditis**, α-hemolytic and nonhemolytic streptococci cause 60% of infection, with enterococci, coagulase-negative staphylococci, and fastidious Gram-negative rods causing the rest. Among the streptococci causing the subacute illness, *S. mitior, S. bovis, S. sanguis,* and *S. mutans* predominate and account for 70% of the isolates.

The organisms that cause infection among **intravenous drug users** vary depending upon whether infection involves the **tricuspid valve** (or occasionally the pulmonic valve) or the **valves of the left heart**. In these patients, *S. aureus* causes 75% of right-sided endocarditis, whereas a broader range of organisms cause left-sided infection (*S. aureus*, 25%; streptococci, 15%; enterococci, 25%; Gram-negative bacilli, 8%; and fungi, 10%.)

The microbiology of **prosthetic valve** endocarditis depends on the time after surgery when infection becomes symptomatic. During the **initial year** after valve placement, many infections are **nosocomial** and often the result of perioperative wound contamination. Paralleling other nosocomial infections, staphylococci cause 65% of cases during this first year, with Gram-negative rods, corynebacteria, and fungi

Table 63.1. Microbiology of Infective Endocarditis (Percent incidence)

Organism	Native Valve Endocarditis	Intravenous Drug Abuse	Prosthetic Value Endocarditis	
			Onset in First Year Following Surgery	Onset More Than a Year Following Surgery
Streptococci				
Viridans, α-hemolytic, nonhemolytic	35	8	5	25
S. bovis	10	<5	<5	<5
Other	<5	<1	<1	<1
Enterococci	10	8	<5	10
Staphylococci				
S. aureus	30	50	10	15
Coagulase negative	5	<5	55	20
Gram-negative aerobic rods	<5	8	5	<5
Fastidious Gram-negative coccobacilli[a]	5	<1	<1	8
Fungi	<5	5	5	<1
Miscellaneous	<5	<5	10[b]	<5
Polymicrobial	<1	5	<5	<1
Culture negative	5	5	8	5

[a]Includes *Haemophilus* sp., *Actinobacillus actinomycetemcomitans, Cardiobacterium hominis, Eikenella,* and *Kingella*
[b]Includes *Corynebacterium* sp.

each accounting for 5%. Prosthetic valve endocarditis with symptoms beginning **more than a year** after valve surgery is community acquired and the consequence of transient bacteremias similar to those that give rise to native valve endocarditis. Accordingly, these infections are caused by streptococci, *S. aureus*, enterococci, and fastidious Gram-negative coccobacilli. Coagulase-negative staphylococci remain an important cause of these infections. In the first year patients, 80% of these coagulase-negative staphylococci are β-lactam antibiotic-resistant *S. epidermidis*, whereas patients that become infected later, have other, often β-lactam sensitive, staphylococcal species. This suggests that, in late-onset cases of staphylococcal prosthetic endocarditis, the infection is probably acquired as a consequence of transient bacteremia.

ENTRY AND COLONIZATION

Transient bacteremia is a common event (Chapter 62). It occurs when heavily colonized mucosal surfaces are traumatized and even spontaneously when mucosal surfaces are diseased (Table 63.2). For example, spontaneous bacteremia was documented in 10% of patients with severe gingival disease who were studied before a dental procedure. In spite of the frequency of bacteremia and the broad spectrum of organisms that gain entry into the circulatory system, endocarditis remains a relatively rare occurrence. A small group of bacteria, the majority of which are not considered notably virulent, cause the majority of cases. Also puzzling is that these infections are confined primarily to the aortic and mitral valves and are not seen in the broad expanse of the rest of the vascular endothelial surface. What factors operate to produce this uniform pattern?

Table 63.2. Frequency of Transient Bacteremia in Selected Settings

Type of Event	Percentage of Patients with Bacteremia	Common Organisms Recovered
Oral cavity		
Dental extractions	30–80	Streptococci, diphtheroids, *S. epidermidis*
Tooth rocking	85	
Chewing paraffin	50	
Gingival surgery	30–85	
Airway	38	Streptococci, *Haemophilus* spp., diphtheroids
Tonsillectomy		
Bronchoscopy (rigid scope)	15	Streptococci, *S. epidermidis*, aerobic Gram-negative rods
Gastrointestinal tract		
Upper gastrointestinal endoscopy	8–12	Streptococci, *S. epidermidis*, diphtheroids, *Neisseria*
Colonoscopy	2–10	Aerobic Gram-negative rods, streptococci, *Bacteroides*
Urinary tract		
Urethral dilation	20–36	Aerobic Gram-negative rods, diphtheroids, streptococci
Cystoscopy	17	
Transurethral prostatic resection	10–45	
Genital tract		
Parturition	0–5	Aerobic Gram-negative rods, streptococci
Intrauterine device insertion/removal	0	

Normal vascular endothelium is resistant to bacterial infection. This can be inferred from the relative infrequency of endocarditis involving normal heart valves as well as from the difficulty of inducing endocarditis in laboratory animals. Microscopic examination of the traumatized valve in experimental animal models reveals that intravenously injected bacteria initially adhere to aggregates of platelets and fibrin, the so-called **nonbacterial thrombotic vegetations**. Whether platelet-fibrin vegetations are a prerequisite for the development of endocarditis in humans is not known, but several lines of evidence suggest that these lesions play a prominent role. In autopsies, nonbacterial thrombotic vegetations (so-called marantic endocarditis), although infrequent, are found on the atrial side of the mitral valve or the ventricular side of the aortic valve along the line of the valve closure. This is the exact valve site most frequently involved in infective endocarditis.

Infective endocarditis is commonly associated with cardiac abnormalities that allow blood to flow from a very high-pressure area through a narrowing into a low pressure reservoir. This hydrodynamic condition is present in ventricular septal defect and mitral and aortic regurgitation. This flow pattern results in a **Venturi effect** in which a low-pressure area is formed immediately downstream and laterally to the narrowed orifice. This pattern, combined with turbulent flow, allows platelet-fibrin aggregates to form on the low-pressure side of regurgitant aortic or mitral valves and ventricular septal defects. Additionally, high-velocity jet streams of blood flowing through these regurgitant valves and septal defects cause areas of endothelial injury on the wall of the left atrium, the right ventricle, or the chordae tendineae-anterior mitral valve leaflet. In turn, platelet-fibrin thrombi form at the sites of endothelial injury and serve as a nidus for infective endocarditis (Fig. 63.1). Of interest, cardiac lesions that result in low-pressure gradients (ostium secundum atrial septal defect) or low-flow and reduced turbulence (chronic congestive heart failure) are rarely the setting of infective endocarditis.

To cause disease, organisms must not only enter the circulation but must also be able to **survive host defenses** and **adhere to the vegetations**. As noted, a broad array of bacteria gain entry to the circulation yet only a limited number of organisms are common causes of endocarditis. Those organisms are resistant to complement-mediated serum bactericidal activity In the rabbit model of endocarditis, strains of *Escherichia coli*, *Serratia marcescens*, and *Pseudomonas aeruginosa* that are resistant to the bactericidal activity of serum reliably produce endocarditis when injected intravenously, whereas strains susceptible to serum killing do not.

Organisms that cause endocarditis have the ability to **adhere** to the vegetation or valve. Organisms that are frequent causes of endocarditis have been found to be more adherent to aortic valve endothelium than those that rarely cause the disease. A number of extracellular and cell surface properties promote the adherence of selected bacteria to platelet-fibrin vegetations. *S. mutans*, *S. sanguis*, *S. bovis*, the streptococci commonly implicated as causes of endocarditis, produce extracellular **dextran** that mediates vigorous adherence to platelet-fibrin aggregates on aortic valve endothelium. This adherence is reduced by eliminating extracellular dextran and is restored when this polymer is replaced. The ability of *S. sanguis* to produce endocarditis is directly proportional to the amount of dextran produced. Finally, streptococci more commonly associated with endocarditis are almost always

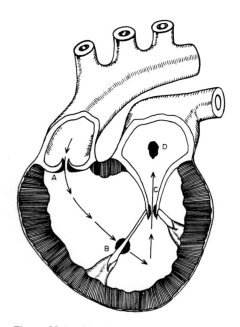

Figure 63.1. The location of endocarditic vegetations in relation to high velocity regurgitant blood flow. The *arrows* indicate the high-velocity stream of blood. As a result of regurgitant flow through the orifice of the incompetent aortic valve, lesions form on the ventricular surface of the valve (*A*), or on the chordae tendineae of the anterior mitral leaflet (*B*). Regurgitant flow across the incompetent mitral valve into the low-pressure left atrium allows a vegetation to form on the atrial surface of the mitral valve (*C*) or at the site of jet stream impact on the atrial wall (*D*).

dextran-producing organisms, whereas those less frequently associated with this disease are not.

The mechanism of adherence of endocarditis-causing strains is more complex than by dextran alone. As noted, dextran negative organisms, such as enterococci and *S. aureus*, are frequent causes of the disease. Here, cell wall lipoteichoic acid promotes adherence to platelet-fibrin aggregates. Endocarditis-producing organisms bind more vigorously to **fibronectin** than do organisms rarely implicated in the disease, suggesting a role for this host protein in mediating microbial adherence to cardiac valves. Fibronectin is present on the surface of nonbacterial thrombotic vegetations but not on intact endothelial surfaces (Chapter 12). *S. aureus*, for example, has well-characterized fibronectin receptors. Fibrinogen, which binds to normal endothelial cells, plus additional plasma factors, mediates adherence of *S. aureus* to normal endothelial cells in the absence of platelet-fibrin thrombi. This effect, which occurs through the *S. aureus*-fibrinogen receptor (clumping factor) and is not related to fibronectin, may promote attachment of *S. aureus* to intact valvular endothelium as is postulated to occur in some cases of acute endocarditis in patients without prior cardiac disease.

Vegetation formation and bacterial growth feed upon one another. When a vegetation is colonized by bacteria, it tends to grow by continued deposition of platelets and fibrin. Viridans streptococci promote platelet aggregation and stimulate valve endothelial and stromal cells to express a tissue factor (tissue thromboplastin) that stimulates continued fibrin deposition and thus growth of the vegetation. Coagulase-positive staphylococci probably stimulate the formation of vegetation both by the release of tissue thromboplastin and by the local activation of coagulation. In turn, the vegetation allows increased bacterial proliferation, leading to dense populations of organisms (10^8–10^9 bacteria/g of tissue). Several factors are known to contribute to this mutual interaction. Aortic and mitral valve vegetations are relatively devoid of phagocytic cells, permitting bacterial proliferation to proceed unimpaired by host defenses. On the other hand, experimental data suggest that phagocytic cells limit infection at extracardiac, intravascular sites and on the tricuspid valve (perhaps a factor why bacteremic infection of these sites is infrequent). When animals with experimental endocarditis are treated with anticoagulation or fibrinolytic therapy, the size of vegetation is reduced, illustrating the pivotal role of continued local thrombosis in vegetation growth.

SPREAD AND DAMAGE

The vegetation is the cardinal pathological feature of infective endocarditis (Fig. 63.2). Classically, vegetations occur along the line of valve closure on the low-pressure surface of the regurgitant valve or septal defect, or at the site of a jet stream lesion. Vegetations may vary in size from a few millimeters to a centimeter or larger and may be single or multiple. They may be friable and fragment to form emboli. Microscopically, vegetations are a mass of fibrin, platelets, and clumps of bacteria; neutrophils are rare. Microorganisms deep in vegetations are often metabolically inactive whereas the more superficial ones are actively proliferating. The broad array of symptoms and signs associated with endocarditis (Table 63. 3) arise through four mechanisms:

- Persistent bacteremia;

Figure 63.2.   Vegetation on a heart valve from a patient with bacterial endocarditis.

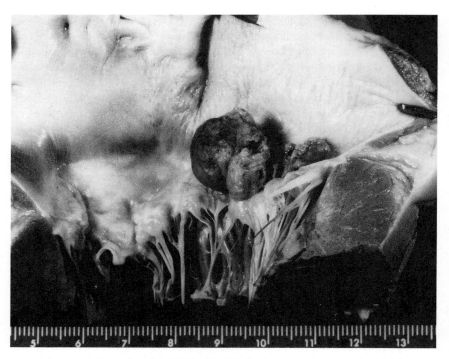

Table 63.3. Symptoms and Signs Associated with Infective Endocarditis

Symptom	Frequency (%)	Sign	Frequency (%)
Fever	90	Fever	90
Weakness	50	Murmur	85
Sweats	30	Embolic event	35
Anorexia	50	Peripheral manifestations	
Weight loss	60	Osler's nodes	10
Malaise	60	Petechiae	25
Myalgia-arthralgia	15	Janeway lesion	5–10
Back pain	10	Retinal lesion	<5
Confusion	10	Stroke	20
		Splenomegaly	25–50
		Septic complications	20

- Tissue destruction by infecting organisms;

- Fragmentation of vegetations into the circulation causing peripheral emboli;

- Stimulation of antibodies that combines with bacterial antigens to form circulating immune complexes.

Organisms proliferating near the surface of the vegetation are continuously shed into the blood. Although the concentration of organisms in the blood varies over time, infective endocarditis is characterized by a continuous bacteremia. The bacteremia undoubtedly mediates the release of various cytokines, resulting in the constitutional symptoms associated with endocarditis, e.g., fever, sweats, fatigue, anorexia, weight loss.

Damage of tissues in endocarditis may occur at the intracardiac site of infection or at a remote site that has been infected during bacteremia. **Intracardiac damage** most commonly involves distortion and destruction of valve leaflets, rupture of a chordae tendineae, or in the case of infected prosthetic valves, dehiscence from the annulus. The resulting valvular destruction may precipitate congestive heart failure. Infection may also extend beyond the valve leaflet into the annulus to cause a perivalvular abscess. Clinical clues to invasive infection, especially that complicating aortic valve endocarditis, include fever persisting in the face of appropriate antimicrobial therapy, new electrocardiographic conduction changes (a consequence of the anatomic proximity of the atrioventricular conduction system, the bundle of His, and the bundle branches to the mitral and aortic annulus), and pericarditis (a consequence of extension of infection into the pericardial space). Vegetations, valve function, hemodynamic status, and perivalvular-myocardial abscess are now demonstrable by transthoracic or transesophageal echocardiography. Whereas intracardiac complications occur with all causes of endocarditis, they are more common when infection is caused by virulent pyogenic bacteria. These complications are a major cause of endocarditis related mortality. Nevertheless, they are often amenable to surgical correction.

Infection of remote sites often complicates endocarditis caused by pyogenic bacteria. Included among such infections are septic arthritis, osteomyelitis, splenic or kidney abscess, and meningeal or parenchymal brain abscesses. Infection in the vasa vasorum of larger arteries of patients with subacute endocarditis and arteritis beginning at the site of arterial occlusion from septic emboli in patients with *S. aureus* endocarditis give rise to **mycotic aneurysms**. These lesions, which can occur in any artery, are usually asymptomatic until they rupture (see case presentation).

Among the most common and widely recognized clinical features of infective endocarditis are **peripheral emboli**. Emboli are recognized clinically in 25–35% of patients and are found at autopsy in 45–65% of patients with this disease. They may cause arterial occlusion, infarction, and secondary complications in virtually any organ. Clinically, they are most notable as the cause of embolic stroke, acute myocardial infarction, and abdominal, flank, and back pain resulting from intestinal, splenic, and renal infarction, respectively. In tricuspid valve endocarditis caused by *S. aureus*, which commonly occurs among intravenous drug abusers, septic pulmonary artery emboli with secondary pneumonia, lung abscess, or pyopneumothorax are a prominent component of the clinical picture.

Circulating **immune complexes**, containing antigen from the causative organisms, are detectable in the majority of patients; the concentration of the complexes has been correlated with prolonged duration of the disease, occurrence of extracardiac manifestation, and reduced serum complement concentrations. Tissue injury mediated by deposition of circulating immune complexes has been described in the skin, choroid plexus, spleen, and synovium. Clinical findings such as Osler's nodes, petechiae, vasculitic purpura, and arthralgia have been attributed to the deposition of immune complexes in skin, arterial wall, and synovium. An alternative to the role of immune complex in causing these lesions are septic emboli.

Glomerulonephritis is the best documented immune-mediated complication of endocarditis (see Chapter 12 for a consideration of the role of streptococci). Focal embolic glomerulonephritis, a lesion with few clinical consequences, and diffuse proliferative glomerulonephritis, that results in an active urine sediment and is commonly associated with decreased creatinine clearance, are recognized as part of a continuum of immune renal injury. In patients with prolonged episodes of subacute streptococcal endocarditis, circulating immune complexes formed intravascularly during antibody excess deposit in a subendothelial location in the glomerulus. Immunofluorescent studies demonstrate IgG and early complement components on the glomerular basement membrane in a lumpy-bumpy distribution (Fig. 63.3). Although in earlier reports glomerulonephritis was found commonly at autopsy of patients dying with untreated subacute endocarditis, the frequency among contemporary endocarditis patients is not known. It is probably not infrequent, generally mild (primarily focal) and remits with effective therapy of the infection. Acute staphylococcal endocarditis causes an immune-mediated glomerulonephritis as a consequence of staphylococcal antigen deposition at the glomerular basement membrane and subsequent activation of the alternate complement pathway. This lesion may be found in more than 25% of patients with *S. aureus* endocarditis of less than 2 weeks' duration.

Figure 63.3.   Immune complex glomerulonephritis. A. Glomerulus stained with PAS (450 ×). A membranoproliferative pattern is present with expansion of the mesangium, hypercellularity, cells in the capillary lumen (*single arrow*), and a double-contoured basement membrane characteristic of subendothelial immune complex deposition (*double arrow*). **B.** Electron micrograph of a glomerular tuft revealing electron dense immune complex deposits in the mesangium (*single arrow*) and subendothelial capillary space (*double arrow*). The basement membrane splits to surround the subendothelial deposits giving rise to the double-contoured appearance noted in **A.** These deposits will be stained by fluorescent tagged antihuman IgG in a lumpy-bumpy distribution. *Mes* = mesangium; *Ep* = epithelial cell; *US* = urinary (Bowman's) space.

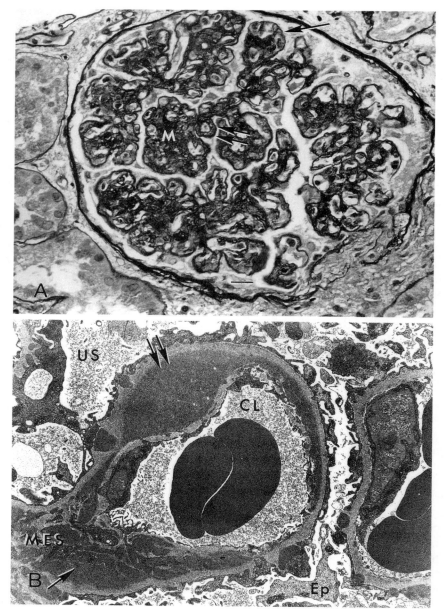

DIAGNOSIS

The diagnosis of endocarditis is suggested by the clinical picture and is clinically confirmed by documenting persistent bacteremia, i.e., multiple positive blood cultures for the same organisms over 24–48 hours. Likewise, blood cultures positive for the organisms that commonly cause endocarditis should cause one to consider this diagnosis carefully, even in the absence of other clinical findings. Without prior antibiotic therapy, at least 95% of patients with endocarditis will have positive blood cultures and, in almost all of these patients, one of the initial two cultures will be positive. Depending upon the susceptibility of the organism, administration of antibiotics during the preceding 2 weeks may markedly reduce the frequency of positive blood cultures. Therefore, to avoid false-negative blood cultures, **cultures should be obtained before antibiotics are given**. Transthoracic echocardiography, followed by transesophageal echocardiography if necessary, is a highly sensitive and specific approach to the identification of vegetations on valves and intracardiac complications. Although this approach is not suitable for screening patients with little clinical evidence of endocarditis, it can aid in making the diagnosis by identifying typical vegetations in patients where the disease is highly suspected. Other laboratory tests that are frequently abnormal in patients with endocarditis, e.g., hematocrit, sedimentation rate, urine analysis, circulating immune complex concentration, rheumatoid factor, are not helpful in making a specific diagnosis.

TREATMENT

Effective treatment for endocarditis requires that the causative agent be identified and its antimicrobial susceptibility be determined. This information allows the design of an effective antimicrobial regimen. Because host defenses are not very impressive at the vegetation, bactericidal antibiotics or combinations of antibiotics are required for optimal therapy. Antibiotics are administered parenterally to achieve high serum concentrations, necessary to penetrate into the depths of relatively avascular vegetations. The reduced metabolic state of organisms deep in vegetations may render these cells difficult to eradicate and supports the prolonged antibiotic courses advocated for most patients with infective endocarditis. Fungi and drug-resistant Gram-negative rods are difficult to eradicate with antibiotic therapy. Surgery to excise these infected valves may allow eradication of these infections. Additionally, the survival of patients with intracardiac complications, such as valve dysfunction causing congestive heart failure or perivalvular abscess, has been greatly enhanced by surgery to debride sites of infection, restore anatomic defects, and replace a dysfunctional valve with a prosthesis.

PROPHYLAXIS

The value of prophylactic antibiotics to prevent endocarditis in patients at risk is uncertain because no carefully controlled studies have been performed. Nevertheless, animal studies and clinical observations that most patients with α-hemolytic streptococcal endocarditis who had previous dental work had not received antibiotics support the use of antibiotic prophylaxis. Patients at risk typically include those with heart valve lesions who are undergoing procedures that may lead to bacteremia with organisms that are the most common causes of endocarditis. Therefore, it is recommended that patients with known rheumatic heart disease or heart valve malformations from other causes be given penicillin just before, and for a short time after, such procedures as cleaning and extraction of teeth. An aminoglycoside should be added to the penicillin before invasive maneuvers in the gastrointestinal or genitourinary tracts to prevent infection by the *Enterococcus*. Prophylactic use of antibiotics is particularly important in patients who have a prosthetic heart valve. Bacterial endocarditis in such patients has such a bad prognosis that attempts to prevent it are mandatory.

SUGGESTED READING

Bach BA. Immunologic manifestations. In: Sande MA, Kaye D, Root RK, eds. Endocarditis, contemporary issues in infectious diseases. New York: Churchill Livingstone, 1984;33–58.

Bayer AS, Theofilopoulos AN. Immunopathogenetic aspects of infective endocarditis. Chest 1990;97:204–212.

Freedman LR. The pathogenesis of infective endocarditis. J Antimicrob Chemother 1987;20(Suppl A):1–6.

Hutter AM, Moellering RC. Assessment of the patient with suspected endocarditis. JAMA 1976;235:1603–1605.

Scheld WM. Pathogenesis and pathophysiology of infective endocarditis. In: Sande MA, Kaye D, Root RK, eds. Endocarditis, contemporary issues in infectious diseases. New York: Churchill Livingstone, 1984;1–32.

Scheld WM, Sande MA. Endocarditis and intravascular infections. In: Mandell GL, Douglas RG Jr., Bennett JE, eds. Principles and practice of infectious diseases, 3rd ed. New York: Churchill Livingstone, 1990;670–706.

Weinstein L, Schlesinger JJ. Pathoanatomic, pathophysiologic and clinical correlations in endocarditis. N Engl J Med 1974;291:832–837, 1122–1126.

Head and Neck

64

Arnold L. Smith

Infections of the head and neck occur most commonly when organisms reach the soft tissue and interstitial spaces of this area by extension from contiguous mucosal surfaces. Less commonly, they may be seeded from the bloodstream. Regardless of the route by which the infectious agents reach the tissue, manifestations of head and neck infections come to medical attention because of signs and symptoms of **inflammation**. Infections of these parts of the body result in cellulitis, lymphadenitis, or abscesses of soft tissues. The resulting swelling may be readily recognized, for example, when it causes facial cellulitis, or when it affects a physiological function (such as swallowing).

ENCOUNTER AND ENTRY

The **air-filled cavities** of the head (sinuses, mastoids, middle ear) are lined with respiratory epithelium (Fig. 64.1). Infections of these spaces result when their normal drainage route becomes blocked. With blockage, the ciliated respiratory epithelium, which normally functions to remove bacteria by entrapping them in mucus and propelling the mucus out, can no longer function. Once aerobic bacteria have reached their maximum growth, oxygen in the blocked cavity is depleted and anaerobes can grow. High densities of bacteria release fragments of cell envelopes (such as lipopolysaccharide or murein subunits), which elicit an inflammatory response, leading to swelling and more blockage. The inflammation produces the symptoms of such infections.

Frequently, when the infection involves soft tissue or lymph nodes, a **previous infection** due to viruses or group A streptococci served to disrupt the integrity of the epithelial surface. Histological examination of respiratory mucosa during acute viral infections shows loss of ciliated epithelial cells and thinning of the mucosal layer. Extension of this process results in physical loss of continuity of the epithelium, allowing bacteria to enter the underlying soft tissue and produce cellulitis or to overwhelm the defenses in the lymph nodes and produce lymphadenitis.

In **sinusitis**, the ostia may become blocked because of a viral upper respiratory infection, or more commonly, by allergy, both of which produce edema. In the **middle ear**, eustachian tube dysfunction may occur congenitally (as in infants with cleft palate who lack the muscle to open the medial orifice of the eustachian tube), as a result of a viral upper respiratory tract infection, or caused by allergy. Because the cavity of the middle ear is contiguous with the mastoid ear cells, every individual with acute otitis media also has mastoiditis, which is an acute inflammatory reaction in the mastoid ear cells.

Figure 64.1. Superior view of the face sectioned through the level of the ethmoid sinus.

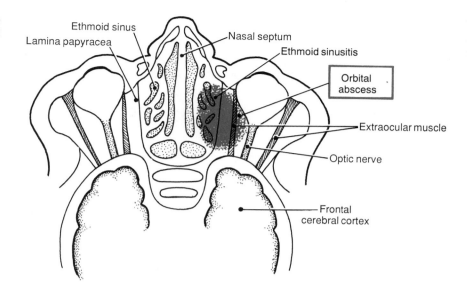

The most common bacterial infections of the head and neck are listed in Table 64.1. The bacteria that cause infections of the head and neck are those commonly isolated from the surface of the upper respiratory tract, i.e., *Streptococcus pneumoniae*, *Haemophilus influenzae*, *Staphylococcus aureus*, *S. pyogenes*, and anaerobic bacteria. Four clinical cases are discussed below.

CASE 1. OTITIS MEDIA

E., a 14-month-old girl, came down with the same "cold" that her sister had had for the past 3 days. She then stopped taking her bottle, became irritable, and developed a temperature of 39.8° C. She continued to feed poorly and had a low-grade fever and irritability, which prompted her mother to take her to a physician. In the doctor's office, the nurse used a tympanometer to measure the mobility of E.'s ear drum (see below), and told the mother that E. had an ear infection. On further examination, the physician agreed, and prescribed the antibiotic amoxicillin.

E.'s mother had many questions:

- Should E.'s sister be brought in and checked for an ear infection?

- Is an ear infection contagious?

- How does a machine (the tympanometer) diagnose an ear infection?

- Should a culture be obtained before antibiotics are prescribed?

- How can the doctor be sure that amoxicillin is the right antibiotic for E.?

- Are there complications of ear infections?

Otitis media is one of the most common infections seen by family physicians and pediatricians. The majority of the cases occur in children between 6 and 36 months of age, the average child having two episodes per year during the first 3 years of life. Why are children especially sensitive to this type of infection? A likely predisposing cause is that the eustachian tubes are distended in infancy. Supine feeding (the bottle at bedtime) permits reflux of pharyngeal contents

Table 64.1. Infections of the Head and Neck

Infections of air-filled cavities
    Otitis media
    Sinusitis
    Mastoiditis
Infections of structures contiguous to air-filled cavities
    Orbital cellulitis or abscess
    Cavernous sinus thrombosis or thrombophlebitis
    Lateral sinus thrombosis or thrombophlebitis
    Cervical adenitis
Infections of soft tissues
    Conjunctivitis
    Fascial cellulitis
    Abscess of canine fossa
    Lymphadenitis
    Parapharyngeal abscess
        Paratonsillar
        Pteromaxillary
        Lateral neck
    Thyroiditis
Infections of embryonic remnants
    Branchial cleft cellulitis or abscess
        Thyroglossal duct cellulitis or abscess

into the lumen of the eustachian tubes, leading to inflammation and occlusion. Dysfunction of the eustachian tubes is also facilitated by upper respiratory infections of the abundant lymphoid tissue around the medial orifice, such as those caused by respiratory syncytial virus, influenza A or B, or adenovirus. Members of the normal upper respiratory flora (pneumococci, *H. influenzae*, and, occasionally, *S. aureus*, *Branhamella catarrhalis*, and group A streptococci) become entrapped in the middle ear and proliferate. An antecedent viral infection may also predispose to bacterial replication in the middle ear by direct damage to the respiratory epithelium.

The consequences of inflammation of the middle ear are consonant with the anatomy of this region. Early in the course of the infection, submucosal edema and hemorrhage lead to the outpouring of exudate into the lumen. A fluid-filled lumen makes the tympanic membrane relatively immobile and impairs hearing. Mobility can be measured by pneumatic otoscopy (changing the air pressure on the ear drum while looking at it), or by tympanometry (a technique that measures the ability of the ear drum to reflect sound at various air pressures). In the normal ventilated ear, tension on the tympanic membrane varies with the pressure exerted on it. With fluid in the middle ear, the tympanic membrane cannot stretch with changes in pressure, and the acoustic impedance (or compliance) does not change.

Frequently in otitis media, the epithelium of the middle ear undergoes marked histological changes—mucus-secreting cells increase in numbers and even form glands. Mucin is secreted into the middle ear, possibly in an effort to entrap and "wash-out" bacteria and inflammatory debris. These changes are elicited by bacterial cell wall material and secreted toxins. The usual exit route for fluids, the eustachian tube, may become occluded. Drainage of the fluid either by using drugs that restore eustachian tube function, or by direct drainage through a tube inserted through the ear drum, permits the metaplastic epithelium to return to normal and the middle ear to become ventilated.

The middle ear may become infected with any of the bacteria present in the upper respiratory tract. As with upper respiratory tract infections (e.g., sinusitis), the primary pathogens are pneumococci and *H. influenzae* (80% of the total). Antibiotics, alone or in combination, active against these two species have proven effective in the treatment of otitis media. Thus, empiric antibiotic administration directed against the most common pathogens is justifiable in this disease. It is not necessary to aspirate the middle ear fluid (a painful procedure) for culture and susceptibility testing.

Although most ear infections treated with antibiotics resolve without complications, chronic and recurrent episodes of otitis media may lead to sequelae such as brain abscess or meningeal epidural abscess. Usually the patient has had a perforated ear drum. In such cases, the pathogens include not only members of the upper respiratory flora, but occasionally enteric Gram-negative bacilli that gain access to the middle ear through the perforated ear drum.

CASE 2. CELLULITIS IN THE ORBIT OF THE EYE

B., a 14-year-old girl, has had intermittent problems with allergies, manifested primarily as a runny nose, watery eyes, and episodes of fullness in the front part of her face and nose. One morning, she developed fever, headache, cough, and had a foul taste in her mouth. She interpreted this as another one of her allergies and took an antihistamine pill and some antipyretics. However, the next morning, she awoke with a severe headache, felt terribly ill, and could not open her left eye. Her pediatrician noted marked redness and swelling around her eye and a slight exudate from the eyelids. When she retracted her eyelids she found that B.'s left eye was slightly deviated down and laterally. She recommended that B. should immediately see an ear, nose, and throat physician as she probably had a serious illness, orbital cellulitis.

B. and her family wondered what was going on.

- What is orbital cellulitis?

- Why should she see an ENT physician if her problem was with her eye?

- Was this not just another one of her allergies?

- What about getting antibiotics?

B.'s orbital cellulitis—inflammation of the submucosal connective tissue of the eye socket—is a complication of acute sinusitis. The anterior and lateral border of the ethmoid sinuses form the medial and superior border of the orbit. The orbit is then separated from the ethmoid sinus by the lamina papyracea, which is literally a paper-thin piece of bone. Infection in the ethmoid sinus may break through this thin piece of bone and enter the orbit. If the infection is localized, it becomes an intraorbital but extraocular abscess (Fig. 64.1).

The physician quickly recognized the disease, because of the region of the orbit that was affected (superior and medial) and the displacement of the eye down and out. Had she measured it, she would have found that the eyeball was exophthalmic, i.e., it protruded out of the orbit. This may often not be appreciated without a measuring device. Exophthalmus is due to the edema in the orbit, literally making the cavity smaller and forcing the eye out. As might be expected, other signs of orbital cellulitis include limitation of the movement of the eye as the muscles become edematous and stretched. In addition, stretching of the optic nerve may decrease visual acuity, a very serious complication, and lead to blindness.

Because the source of orbital cellulitis is the sinus, the treatment of choice is surgical drainage. This will decompress the orbit and allow the eyeball to return to its normal place. Treatment of this infection should also include the administration of antibiotics. As with other infections of the head and neck, bacteria isolated from the infected sites represent the oral pharyngeal flora. In the more virulent infections, such as the one experienced by B., there is a higher probability that *S. aureus* will be isolated. Here, the antibiotics to be administered should be active against *S. aureus* as well as members of the upper respiratory tract flora.

CASE 3. FACIAL CELLULITIS

R., a 14-month-old baby boy, was not sleeping through the night and seemed hungry all of the time. His mother started supplementing his food with a bottle of milk containing cereal. One afternoon, when he awoke from his nap, his mother noted that he was fussy, had a low-grade temperature, and had a slight swelling of his cheek. She thought he might have bumped it with the bottle as he frequently did when feeding himself in the crib. That evening when she put him to bed, he seemed a little improved but still irritable and his cheek was somewhat swollen and had a slightly purplish hue. His temperature seemed increased, but other than that, he seemed well. The next morning, his mother thought that he was worse. She took his temperature and found that it was 41.6°C. She took him to the family doctor who told her that R. would need hospitalization for antibiotic treatment of facial cellulitis.

His mother had many questions:

- Was this cellulitis different from the kind that she had on her head following work in the garden?

- Why did R. need to be hospitalized to receive antibiotics for cellulitis?

- How did the bacteria get into R.'s cheek?

- Will the antibiotics cure R.?

Facial cellulitis in infants is almost exclusively an infection caused by *H. influenzae* type b. The pathogenesis is not entirely clear, but it is probable that minor facial trauma allows blood to seep into the soft tissues. When transient *H. influenzae* bacteremia occurs, the organisms seed and grow in the traumatized subcutaneous tissue using the extravasated red blood cells as a source of nutrition (the organism is not called "haemo-philus" [blood-loving] for nothing: it requires, among other cofactors, heme for growth). Because the soft tissue was seeded via the bloodstream, the infant is at risk for other infectious complications of *H. influenzae* bacteremia (such as meningitis, septic arthritis, and osteomyelitis) and requires hospitalization for vigorous treatment and careful observation.

H. influenzae does not make cell-damaging exotoxins, thus the inflammation in tissues is minimal. Often, as in R.'s case, the distinction between a slight bruise on the face and cellulitis is difficult to make. The telling clue is that the swelling seems out of proportion to the magnitude of the facial trauma, and that the infant has a high fever. One of the reasons R.'s physician suspected that the etiological agent was *H. influenzae* was the typical purplish (not reddish) hue of the inflamed region. The reason for this special coloration is not known, but it is characteristic.

H. influenzae cellulitis resolves with the administration of appropriate antibiotics. Because secondary diseases due to *H. influenzae* are serious, the usual treatment is to administer antibiotics intravenously until the cellulitis has resolved.

CASE 4. PARAPHARYNGEAL ABSCESS

Before going to bed one evening, Ms. J., a 19-year-old college student, noticed a "scratchy throat" with slight pain. Over the next 4 days, she had an increasingly sore throat and her right ear began to ache. She thought she had a fever and took aspirin. On the morning of the sixth day of her illness, Ms. J. found that she could barely open her mouth to eat breakfast. When she did get food in, it was difficult for her to swallow. Her roommate noted that her voice was of lower pitch and decreased in volume, as though she had something hot in her mouth. She went to the infirmary, where the physician, after looking in her mouth, told her that hospitalization was necessary for additional tests, and possibly for surgery.

Ms. J. had several questions:

- How could surgery help a sore throat?

- Don't sore throats go away by themselves?

- Does her roommate have to worry about catching this illness?

Ms. J. had symptoms that are typical of a **parapharyngeal abscess**. In her case, the most likely diagnosis was that of a **peritonsillar abscess**. This was evident by examination of the mouth. Tonsils lie between the two palatal pillars, with their superior poles overlying a portion of the superior pharyngeal constrictor muscle and their medial portion, the medial pterygoid muscle. These are two of the four muscles that function to open the mouth. Inflammation behind the tonsil adjacent to these muscles causes their dysfunction. Trismus, the inability to open one's mouth, is caused by dysfunction of the medial pterygoid, while the inability to initiate swallowing is due to dysfunction of the superior pharyngeal constrictor. Failure to elevate the palate results from edema in that area; this leads to a muffled, "hot potato" voice, even though the tongue is unaffected. Ms. J. could swallow, as there was no mechanical obstruction to a bolus of food entering her esophagus, but inflammation of the superior constrictor made it hard to initiate the process (Fig. 64.2). When one looks in the mouth of patients with peritonsillar abscess, the tonsil appears medially and downward displaced and, on palpation, may feel as though it is floating. This is caused by the pus pushing it from behind.

Bacteria that cause this illness are, as in most head and neck infections, those commonly found in the oral pharynx. Most of these organisms commonly are commensals, but **group A streptococci** are responsible for approximately one-half of the cases of peritonsillar abscess. The infection seems first to cause a cellulitis of the peritonsillar tissues, followed by local necrosis. The aerobic and anaerobic flora of the oral pharyngeal epithelium then gain access to the necrotic tissue in the interstitial space.

The primary therapy is surgical drainage. Antibiotic therapy of choice for this disease should include a drug (such as penicillin G) active against common mouth anaerobes and aerobes but also effective against *S. aureus*. In most cases, the choice is a semisynthetic penicillin that is resistant to β-lactamase.

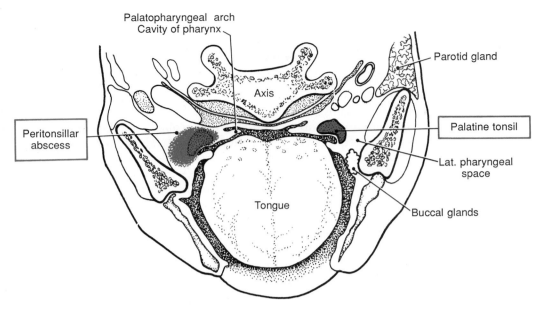

Figure 64.2. Cross-section of the oropharynx through the tonsils.

CASE 5. CONJUNCTIVITIS

J. was an active 9-year-old boy who returned from summer camp in good health. The next day he awoke with swelling of his right eye and the sensation that he had "something stuck" in his eye. His left eye felt fine. His mother took him to a physician when she noted that the inside of both his upper and lower eyelid looked "bloody" and tears from that eye were blood-tinged. The examining physician noted a tender, palpable lymph node just in front of the right ear and a mild runny nose. In spite of J. now having blurred vision with the right eye, the physician placed a patch over the eye and told the mother it was a "virus" and all would be well in 5 days.

The mother questioned the physician's wisdom and asked several questions:

- Why is the other eye not involved if it is a virus?
- Didn't the bloody tears indicate something in the eye?
- Could she and J.'s father develop the eye infection?
- Shouldn't antibiotics be prescribed for an eye infection?

Conjunctivitis is an extremely common infection in children and young adults. Conjunctivitis can be caused by viruses, bacteria, or obligate intracellular organisms such as chlamydiae. Conjunctivitis should be distinguished from more serious conditions such as **keratitis** or **iritis**. A distinguishing feature is that, in keratitis, in addition to diffuse inflammation of the eye, gritty irritation, and excessive lacrimation, there is impaired vision, eye pain, and photophobia. When conjunctivitis occurs alone, it is most commonly caused by *H. influenzae* (42%), adenovirus (22%), and *S. pneumoniae* (12%); a minority, approximately 3%, will be caused by pneumococci.

The only clinically distinguishing features between adenoviral disease and bacterial conjunctivitis is that the former tend to have upper respiratory symptoms (up to one-half in some studies), hyperplasia of lymphoid follicles beneath the conjunctiva, and hyperemia of the palpebral conjunctiva as well as conjunctival hemorrhages on the globe. In addition, "hemorrhagic" conjunctivitis is almost exclusively adenovirus disease. Adenoviral conjunctivitis may also be accompanied by a diffuse superficial keratitis in which there is subepithelial corneal infiltrates in three-quarters of the patients. This causes transient blurring of the vision. Adenoviral keratoconjunctivitis is more commonly associated with preauricular lymphadenopathy. Thus, on history and physical examination alone, the physician has a high likelihood of making the correct diagnosis.

Organisms are introduced into the eye probably by the contact with hands of contacts. Rarely, the agent can be introduced into the eye by respiratory droplets. Serious infections of the anterior portion of the eye are due to herpes simplex virus (HSV), *Pseudomonas aeruginosa*, and, in undeveloped nations, *Chlamydia trachomatis*. Herpes simplex (and varicella zoster) cause vesicular lesions on the eyelid in addition to the usual symptoms of conjunctivitis. There is no other distinguishing feature between HSV conjunctivitis and adenoviral conjunctivitis. The significance of herpes simplex conjunctivitis is that severe keratitis develops in 50% of all ocular herpes infections; it is the most common cause of severe corneal ulceration in children in the U.S. Moreover, herpes simplex keratitis is second only to trauma in causing acquired blindness in children. Because of the serious nature of herpetic keratoconjunctivitis and its high likelihood of its recurrence, these patients should be cared for by an ophthalmologist. Varicella zoster conjunctivitis occurs in approximately 4% of all the children with chickenpox. Because the virus is delivered to the skin via the vascular compartment, vesicles present on the lateral aspect of the tip of the nose invariably predict involvement of the eye; vesicles at this location reflect the involvement of nasociliary branch of the first division of the trigeminal nerve, thus, subsequent involvement of the anterior structures of the eye are inevitable.

Symptomatic treatment of adenoviral conjunctivitis consists of removing exudate, if it is matted, with a saline-moist cotton and patching to relieve pain. There are no currently available chemotherapeutic agents active against adenovirus. In patients with suspected bacterial conjunctivitis, the administration of an antibiotic ointment (polymyxin and bacitracin) four times a day increases a rate of resolution greater than that seen with placebo alone. Other acceptable ophthalmic preparations contain tetracycline, gentamicin, or erythromycin.

Herpetic infections of the eye are treated with idoxuridine, trifluorothymidine, vidarabine, and acyclovir. Available data suggest that the overwhelming majority of herpetic corneal ulcers treated with trifluorothymidine resolve within 2 weeks. Ideal administration of topical antiviral agents to the eye requires that they be administered every 1–2 hours.

Within 3 days, J.'s signs and symptoms were absent. The physician removed his eye patch and no further treatment was administered. If the physician's initial diagnosis had been erroneous, a reasonable approach would be to re-examine, seeking evidence of herpes simplex, and to have administered antibiotic ointment if there was no herpes, but exudate was still present.

CASE 6. CERVICAL LYMPHADENITIS

M. is an 18-year-old Caucasian woman who had lived in Minneapolis all of her life. She and her family were in good health, proud of the fact that no family members had ever been hospitalized. Six weeks after arriving at the University of Wisconsin, she experienced a mild sore throat and a low grade temperature (100°F orally). On going to bed that night, she noted a small, slightly tender lump beneath the angle of her jaw. Upon awakening in the morning, the lump was the size of a walnut, more tender, and she felt feverish although her temperature was not higher. At the Student Health Service, a physician told M. that she would need a throat culture and some blood tests before she could prescribe treatment.

The physician told M. that she had cervical adenitis and that a throat culture was needed to determine if group A streptococci were the likely etiological agents. The blood test was a complete blood count with differential and a screening for heterophile antibody.

Upon hearing this report, M.'s parents had many questions:

- Is this a life-threatening illness?

- Is this cancer?

- Why did she need blood tests?

- Could the physician prescribe antibiotics?

Cervical adenitis, inflammation of the lymph nodes in the neck, may be due to many infectious agents. Because these lymph nodes receive drainage from the mouth, gums, posterior pharynx, as well as the face, cheek, and nose, it is conceivable that many infectious agents can produce swelling and tenderness of lymph nodes. Depending upon the nature of the infectious agent in the lymph node, the influx of cells causing the swelling is either polymorphonuclear leukocytes or histiocytes and lymphocytes. Table 64.2 records agents that can cause cervi-

Table 64.2. Agents of Lymphadenitis

Agent	Generalized Lymphadenopathy	Isolated Cervical Disease	Suppuration
Bacterial			
Streptococcus pyogenes, group A	+	+	+
Staphylococcus aureus	0	+	+
Atypical mycobacteria	0	+	+
Corynebacteria diphtheriae	0	+	0
Mycobacterium tuberculosis	+	+	+
Brucella sp.	+	0	0
Francisella tularensis	0	+	+
Strict anaerobes	0	+	0
Yersinia pestis	0	+	+
Cat-scratch agent (*Rochalimaea*)	0	+	+
Pseudomonas pseudomallei	0	+	+
Viral			
Measles	+	0	0
Rubella	+	0	0
EBV	+	0	0
Adenovirus (groups 3 and 7)	0	+	0
Herpes simplex	0	+	0
Cytomegalovirus	+	0	0
Mumps	0	0	0
HIV	+	0	0
Fungal			
Histoplasma capsulatum	+	0	0
Coccidioides immitis	+	+	0
Aspergillus sp.	0	+	0
Parasitic			
Toxoplasma gondii	+	0	0
Trypanosoma brucei	+	0	0

cal adenitis. There are some generalizations possible. In general, bacterial infections cause disease that is isolated to one cervical lymph node and make the center lymph node necrose (i.e., cause suppuration). In contrast, viral infections of the cervical lymph nodes are rarely localized exclusively to one region, such as the neck; lymph nodes that are readily detected by palpation in other parts of the body are also swollen. In addition, only bacterial infections of the lymph nodes produce suppuration.

The physician's approach to the patient with cervical adenitis relies heavily on the epidemiological considerations. From an inspection of Table 64.2, it is clear that numerous agents might be the cause of the disease. Infections of certain agents only occur in certain parts of the world (i.e., trypanosomiasis in tropical countries and *Pseudomonas pseudomallei* in southeast Asia). Other important information consists of recent contact with animals (important for the diagnosis of tularemia, plague, and cat scratch disease) and immunization status, which is important in determining if the patient has measles, rubella, or mumps.

In this individual, a common cause of cervical adenitis, tuberculosis, can be excluded. Tuberculosis of the cervical lymph glands occurs in individuals with pulmonary tuberculosis who inoculate the mouth through coughing. Rarely, it is acquired through the ingestion of milk contaminated with *Mycobacterium tuberculosis*. In the continental U.S., the overwhelming majority of *M. tuberculosis* infections (other than those in HIV-infected individuals) occurs in individuals recently emigrated to this country and in native Americans. Thus, *M. tuberculosis* is unlikely on epidemiological grounds. Moreover, the rapidity of onset of the swelling is also against this being a tuberculous infection.

The major etiological agents that need to be considered in M.'s case are *S. pyogenes* (the group A streptococcus), *S. aureus*, and Epstein-Barr virus (EBV) infection. In individuals with Epstein-Barr virus infection, there is usually sore throat, fever, and swelling in the neck. In addition, approximately one-half of the patients have headache, severe loss of appetite, malaise, muscle aches (with one-fifth having muscle aches and chills). As might be expected, the virus does not have a propensity to be inoculated into one side of the pharynx; thus, most cervical adenitis due to EBV infection is bilateral.

The test ordered by the physician was a heterophile antibody titer. This antibody is present in 90% of the cases. It may not be present at the time of initial symptoms so the physician would be prudent to repeat these tests 2 weeks later if the antibody is initially absent. Most bacterial cervical adenitis presents with symptoms much like M.'s—unilateral swelling of a single lymph node with minimal upper respiratory or constitutional complaints. The most common bacterial etiology is group A streptococcus or *S. aureus*. Finding the group A streptococcus in the pharynx would add strength to the diagnosis. Needle aspiration of the lymph node (with or without suppuration) is the only ultimate means of assuring the diagnosis. Thus, the prudent physician would administer an antibiotic active against both bacteria. The importance of finding group A streptococci in the throat is that treatment would have to be continued for at least 10 days to assure eradication of the *Streptococcus* and to prevent sequelae.

SUGGESTED READING

Brook I. Microbiology of retropharyngeal abscesses in children. Am J Dis Child 1987;141:202.

Henderson FW, Collier AM, Sanyal MA, Watkins JM, Fairlough DL, Clyde WL, Denny FW. A longitudinal study of respiratory viruses and bacteria in the etiology of acute otitis media with effusion. N Engl J Med 1982; 306:1377.

Meyerhoff WL, Giebink GS. Pathology and microbiology of otitis media. Laryngoscope 1982;92:273.

Peter G, Smith AL. Group A streptococcal infections of the skin and pharynx. N Engl J Med 1977;297:311, 365.

Schlossberg D. Infections of the head and neck. New York: Springer Verlag, 1987.

Siegel JD. Eye infections encountered by the pediatrician. Pediatr Infect Dis 1986;5:741.

Sexually Transmitted Diseases

65

Penelope J. Hitchcock

For review of the individual agents of sexually transmitted diseases, see Chapter 14 (gonococci), Chapter 24 (syphilis), Chapter 26 (chlamydiae), Chapter 37 (HIV), Chapter 39 (warts), Chapter 40 (herpes), and Chapter 54 (scabies).

Sexually transmitted diseases (**STDs**) are a broad but relatively well-defined group of infectious diseases, generally with acute manifestations that often progress to a chronic clinical picture. STDs rank among the most important of all infectious diseases in view of the physical, psychological, and economic damage they cause to human beings.

The agents of STDs are highly varied (Table 65.1); they include representatives of such different groups as the pyogenic cocci (gonococci), spirochetes (*Treponema pallidum* of syphilis), fastidious Gram-negative rods (*Haemophilus ducreyi* of chancroid), strict intracellular bacteria (chlamydiae), viruses (herpes, human papilloma [warts] viruses, and HIV), protozoa (*Trichomonas*), and arthropods (scabies, pubic lice). There are other agents of STDs but these are encountered less frequently in developed countries.

ENCOUNTER AND ENTRY

Most of the agents of STDs enter the body at local sites, through the mucosal or squamous epithelial layers of the vagina, cervix, urethra, rectum, or oral pharynx. HIV is transmitted primarily by sexual contact, although improperly processed blood products or hypodermic needles are also a source of infection.

It is possible to make a few other generalizations regarding the STDs and their agents. Nearly all of the agents of STDs are **relatively sensitive** to chemical and physical factors and are practically never found free in the environment. Animal reservoirs are also unknown for most of these agents; thus, the **asymptomatic human carrier** is the most frequent reservoir. This limited distribution of the agents alone makes these diseases theoretical candidates for eradication, but formidable medical, social, and political obstacles lie in the way of achieving it.

SPREAD AND MULTIPLICATION

All agents of STDs have a great capacity to resist the host's nonspecific defense mechanisms and are infectious, i.e., are able to attach to and enter tissue with relative ease. The fact that chronic manifestations of STDs are relatively frequent is an indication that the agents often cause asymptomatic disease and are not easily eliminated by specific

Table 65.1. Sexually Transmitted Diseases and Their Agents

Disease	Agent
Chlamydial infection	*Chlamydia trachomatis* (all biovars but L)
Gonorrhea	*Neisseria gonorrhoeae*
Genital herpes	Herpes simplex virus type II and type I
Warts, anogenital cancer	Human papillomavirus
Trichomoniasis	*Trichomonas vaginalis*
AIDS	HIV
Chancroid	*Haemophilus ducreyi*
Syphilis	*Treponema pallidum*
Lymphogranuloma venereum (LVG)	*Chlamydia trachomatis* (L biovars)
Granuloma inguinale	*Calymmatobacterium granulomatis*
Candidiasis	*Candida albicans*
Bacterial vaginosis	*Gardnerella vaginalis*

immune responses. The strategies employed to withstand antimicrobial defenses are varied and should be reviewed by reading the chapters on specific agents

DAMAGE

The acute manifestations of the most frequent STDs fall into three groups: (*a*) **mucopurulent cervicitis** and **urethritis**, as in gonorrhea and chlamydial infection; (*b*) **genital ulcer disease**, as in syphilis, chancroid, and genital herpes; (*c*) **genital warts**, caused by human papillomavirus.

With the exception of **HIV**, the agents of STDs tend to cause primary lesions at or near the site of entry. It is not uncommon for these lesions to be so indolent as to go unnoticed or to be located at an anatomical site as to be invisible. As a consequence, diagnosis and treatment are often delayed, enabling the transmission and progression of the disease to continue.

The most serious consequences of STDs relate to progression to chronic infections. These include:

- **Pelvic inflammatory disease** (**PID**), an ascending infection of the uterus and fallopian tubes caused by gonococci and chlamydia;

- **Anogenital cancer**, including **cervical cancer**, caused by some human papillomavirus types;

- Secondary and tertiary **syphilis**;

- **Recurrent herpes** infection.

Many of these chronic infections cause additional adverse sequelae, including:

- Fallopian tube scarring resulting in **infertility** and **ectopic pregnancy**;

- **Congenital diseases** such as in syphilis, herpes, papillomatosis, and chlamydial infection;

- **Increased risk of acquiring HIV**, due to genital ulcers (found in syphilis, chancroid, and herpes) or altered genital mucosa (found in gonorrhea and chlamydial infection);

- **Adverse outcomes of pregnancy** including premature termination, fetal wastage, low birth weight, and premature rupture of membranes.

MAGNITUDE OF THE PROBLEM

During the last half of this century, there has been a dramatic increase in STDs worldwide. In the last 25 years, several new STDs have been recognized worldwide and dramatic increases have been documented in most STDs in the U.S. Adolescents and minority populations have been disproportionately affected. This year, more than 9 million cases of STDs, including HIV infection, will occur; 63% of them will be in people who are less than 24 years of age.

Annually, approximately 2 million new cases of gonorrhea occur in the U.S., at an enormous physical, emotional, and social cost (Table 65.2). Gonorrhea alone costs an estimated $1 billion each year. Of these cases, 25% are in teenagers. In addition, gonococcal antibiotic resistance has been on the rise in the last decade. The public is becoming aware of the large increase in chlamydial infections, with an annual incidence in the U.S. of about 4 million cases.

Table 65.2. Dimensions of the STD Problem

Gonorrhea—*Neisseria gonorrhoeae*	Chlamydial Infection—*Chlamydia trachomatis*	Pelvic Inflammatory Disease (PID)	Syphilis—*Treponema pallidum*	Genital Herpes—Herpes Simplex Virus (HSV) I and II	Chancroid—*Haemophilus ducreyi*	Genital Warts—Human Papillomavirus (HPV)	AIDS—Human Immunodeficiency Virus (HIV)
Approximately 2 million new cases annually Overall slight decrease in incidence, but increases in Black teenage boys; 25% of cases in teenagers Rates more than 30 times higher in Blacks than in Caucasians Four new types of antibiotic resistance emerged in the last decade; almost 10% of isolates now resistant compared with approximatedly 0.1% in 1980 Estimated annual cost almost $1 billion	Most common bacterial STD; approximately 4 million cases annually Incidence increasing Control complicated by frequency of asymptomatic disease, cost, and technical difficulty of diagnostic tests, lack of single dose therapy, and failure to institute routine partner notification Comprehensive annual cost estimated at more than $2.8 billion	Approximately 1 million cases each year, due to untreated or inadequately treated gonococcal and chlamydial infections Responsible for 15–30% of infertility and 50% of tubal pregnancies (both of which are increasing) Comprehensive annual costs estimated to exceed $4.2 billion	In 1990, over 52,000 primary and secondary cases were reported Infectious syphilis at highest level in over 40 years Increases concentrated in Black men and women; rates over 50 times higher than in Caucasians Increases in women echoed by a five-fold increase in congenital cases since 1983	Approximately 30 million Americans infected; 500,000 new cases annually First visits to physicians for genital HSV increased seven-fold between 1966 and 1989 Annual costs roughly $68 million	In 1990, there were 2653 reported cases Increased more than 500% during 1980s; sharp decline in 1990	Estimated 24–40 million people infected Approximately ½–1 million new cases annually First visits to physicians for genital warts increased seven-fold between 1966 and 1987; now declining	Approximately 180,000 AIDS cases in first 10 years of epidemic; 1–1.5 million persons HIV infected 56,000–71,000 new AIDS cases expected in 1991 Increase in AIDS cases now greater in women than men AIDs projected to be among top five causes of death in women 15–44 years of age by end of 1991

STDs that cause genital ulcer disease have kept pace with this increase. In some areas, such as New York City, where the problem is particularly acute, the incidence of congenital syphilis increased more than 600% between 1986 and 1988. Cases of congenital infection are again expected to have more than doubled in a single year between 1988 and 1989. Between 1980 and 1987, the annual incidence of chancroid increased more than 500% due to multiple outbreaks across the U.S. Approximately 30 million Americans are afflicted with genital herpes (HSV).

Recently, anogenital cancer has been demonstrated to be causally associated with human papillomavirus (HPV). In the U.S., it is estimated that as many as 24 million people are infected with HPV, a virus that is extremely difficult to detect and eradicate.

POPULATION DYNAMICS

Efforts at prevention and control of STDs require an understanding of the factors that are responsible for their spread and progression. Although STDs share a common mode of transmission, each one of them presents unique challenges to diagnosis, therapy, and prevention. A large number of biological and social forces are involved in the dynamics of STD transmission. To make sense of this multitude of variables, it is convenient to separate them according to a model proposed by May and Anderson, which states that **the rate of movement of an STD through the population depends on:** (*a*) **the transmissibility of the infectious agent;** (*b*) **the rate of new partner acquisition as well as the partners' sexual history, and** (*c*) **the duration of infectiousness.** Each one of the variables in this model is affected by biological, behavioral, and social risk factors.

Transmissibility of the Agent (or Infectivity Rate)

The infectivity rate is defined as the **risk of acquiring infection during a single contact with an infected partner.** For each STD, the rate varies with behavioral factors and with the biological properties of the host and the agents (Table 65.3). Each pathogen has unique pathophysiological parameters that affect the infectivity rate. For example, the number of organisms necessary to establish infection, the infec-

Table 65.3. Factors Involved in the Transmission of STDs

Transmission or Complication Rate	Rate and Nature of Partner Exchange	Duration of Infectiousness or Active Infections	Sociocultural Context
Sexual practices[a]	Number of partners/time[a]	Infecting organism	Socioeconomic status[a]
Age of coital debut[a]	Type of partner (e.g., membership in core)[a]	Host response	Residence[a]
Age		Health care behavior[a]	Educational status[a]
Genetic susceptibility	Age	routine STD screening	Religion[a]
Gender	Age of coital debut[a]	early diagnosis and therapy	Race
Contraceptive method[a]	Gender	of symptoms	Ethnicity (see Text)
Alcohol use (see text)[a]		compliance with therapy	Marital status[a]
Drug use (intravenous and other)[a]		compliance with partner notification	Sexual preference[a]
Smoking (see text)[a]		Vaccine use	
Prior/coexisting STDs		Douching and other intravaginal preparations	
Intravaginal and intra-anal preparations (including douching)[a]			
Circumcision status (see text)[a]			

[a]Behavioral factor.

tious dose, varies both with the agent and with individual host factors. In each case, gender, genetic susceptibility, age of exposure, coinfection with other infectious organisms, and immunological status must be considered. A pathogen such as HIV, which possesses specific surface molecules for attachment to host cell receptors that are found primarily on rectal epithelial cells as well as on lymphocytes. Sexual behavior would be an important factor here since infected people who practice anal intercourse might transmit the infection more frequently than those than those who practice vaginal intercourse.

Behavioral factors, including drug and alcohol use, contraceptive practices, circumcision, douching, and specific sexual practices, impact on the infectivity rate. A number of studies have focused on risk-taking behavior among adolescents. The data suggest that aggregate risk-taking may be a characteristic of a subset of adolescents. For example, smoking, alcohol, and other substance abuse, having high numbers of sexual partners, and excessive automobile speeding are high-risk behaviors that are highly coassociated. Geographical analysis of HIV seroprevalence and the presence of tribal taboos against the practice of circumcision has revealed a high positive correlation in Africa. Additional studies are in progress to determine the cause-and-effect relationship between intact foreskin and increased transmission of HIV. Such transmission could be facilitated by the poor hygiene often associated with the lack of circumcision, the associated increased prevalence of genital ulcer diseases (e.g., chancroid, syphilis, herpes), or both.

Rate of New Partner Acquisition

The rate of new partner acquisition is the **number of new partners an individual has over a specified period of time**. This parameter depends on the probability that any given partner may be infected. The greater the number of partners, the greater is the chance that one of them is infected. Surveys indicate that most people have only a few sexual partners over their lifetime and that propagation of STD epidemics is actually attributable to a small number of individuals with a large number of sexual partners, referred to as the core. Thus, the number of sexual partners an individual has, determines membership in the core. Sexual activity among core members **sustains** the disease, sexual activity outside the core **spreads** the disease.

Common characteristics of STD core members include individuals living in an urban environment, of low socioeconomic status, between 15 and 30 years old, often of an ethnic minority group, and participating in illicit drug use and prostitution. The size of the core may differ with each pathogen and is influenced both by the infectivity rate and the duration of the infection. It is important to note that asymptomatic infections, such as those due to chlamydiae or HIV, are usually not confined to a core.

In considering the degree of risk involved in a sexual encounter, each person must take into account the probability that the partner is a core member; this, of course, requires being able to identify a core member. This is often very difficult to determine because identification depends on such variables as the length of the relationship before sexual activity, the circumstances under which the partners met, and the ability to obtain risk-related information from the partner before sexual activity.

Duration of Infectivity

The duration of infectivity is the **length of time that an individual is capable of transmitting the infection**. Included in this factor are biological characteristics of both the pathogen and the host. Some pathogens (for example, chlamydiae) commonly cause asymptomatic disease; carriers of chlamydiae do not know they are infected and do not seek treatment. Thus, they remain able to transmit the disease. The carrier state may involve partial immunity, in which case the number of infectious organisms may be so low that the person is asymptomatic but still infectious. Antimicrobial sensitivity is also an important factor in duration of infectivity; if an agent is drug resistant, treatment will fail and the infective period will be increased.

Factors that impact on the duration of infectivity include access to and use of health care as well as attitudes and behaviors of health care providers. Access to health care is affected by the location of the clinic, the speed with which care can be obtained, and the cost of the services. The likelihood that an individual will seek care is influenced by such factors as the stigma associated with using an STD facility, knowledge of the existence of the facility, and the perception of the quality of services provided.

Other factors that influence the duration of infectivity include the existence of effective screening programs (dependent on accurate, sensitive, easy to use, and inexpensive diagnostic tests), partner notification (which is essential in preventing "ping-pong" transmission even if one partner is treated), and effective treatment protocols (the fewer the doses, the more likely compliance will occur; the ideal is a single effective dose given at the time of diagnosis). Duration of infectivity also depends on access to programs designed to influence behavior (such as the use of condoms) and the availability of vaccines (as well as their effectiveness, distribution, acceptance, and administration).

Finally, all variables that influence the spread of infection are influenced by the sociocultural context in which the infection occurs. This context is time dependent, and influenced by historical and current political, economic, and biotechnological forces. The characteristics of a population define what is considered normal and acceptable. Ultimately, all of the factors dictate individual and institutional beliefs, values, intentions, and behaviors that affect the transmissibility of STDs (Table 65.3). An example of how race and ethnicity are different with respect to risk markers is as follows. Among different ethnic groups of African Americans, anthropological data suggest that gender-power relationships, which significantly influence STD rates, vary systematically by region of residence. This variability appears to reflect the country of origin and the patrilineal or matrilineal social heritage for distinct African-American groups. For example, preliminary data suggest that black women descendent from patrilineal societies have higher rates of STDs than those descendent from matrilineal societies.

GROUPS AT RISK

The multiple, long-term, devastating consequences of STDs affect women and infants disproportionately (Table 65.4). STDs are especially prevalent among the young. In the U.S., 63% of all STD cases occur in persons less than 25 years old. There is reason to worry that these problems of the young may get worse because sexual activity

Table 65.4. STD Complications

10–40% of women with untreated chlamydial and/or gonococcal cervicitis develop PID

Approximately 17–25% of women with PID become infertile

Risk of potentially fatal tubal pregnancy increases six- to ten-fold after PID; tubal pregnancy is the leading cause of maternal death in Black women in the U.S.

Several biotypes of HPV are associated with cervical cancer, which kills almost 5000 American women yearly and is the second most common cause of cancer deaths in women worldwide

STDs cause spontaneous abortion, stillbirth, premature delivery, low birth weight, and permanently disabling infant infections

among teenagers is increasing and adolescents often reject precautions, in part due to a perception of invulnerability. Biological factors also compound these behavioral risk factors. Thus, features of the cervical anatomy of adolescents (primarily cervical ectopy) increase the likelihood of chlamydial or gonococcal infection. Hormone changes in puberty alter the vaginal flora and natural mucus barriers to infection, and immunological naiveté facilitates the acquisition and progression of STDs.

The current STD epidemic in the U.S. disproportionately affects minority groups. Both the incidence of STDs and long-term sequelae are consistently higher among non-Caucasians. During the second half of this century, syphilis increased enormously among low-income, inner city heterosexuals and their children. In the 1980s, the incidence of gonorrhea decreased in Caucasians of both sexes and increased in Blacks. A recent survey showed that Black males were approximately three times more likely than Caucasians to be seropositive to herpes simplex virus type 2 (HSV-2). The difference between females was six-fold.

Although non-Caucasian women comprise 17% of the total female population of the U.S., they represent a disproportionate share (33%) of consultations for pelvic inflammatory disease (PID). In addition, ectopic pregnancy was 1.5 times more common among minority females than among Caucasians. Furthermore, minority teenagers with ectopic pregnancies were almost six times more likely to die as their Caucasian counterparts.

PELVIC INFLAMMATORY DISEASE

Pelvic inflammatory disease (**PID**), or **female upper reproductive tract infection**, is an ascending infection of the uterus, fallopian tubes, ovaries, and adjacent peritoneal linings. PID frequently results in severe, irreversible sequelae such as infertility, ectopic pregnancy, and chronic pelvic pain. A case of postchlamydial PID is described in Chapter 14.

PID is the most serious and most costly common consequence of STDs affecting women. It is estimated that, in the U.S., 10–15% of women of reproductive age have had at least one episode of PID, and that annually between 750,000 and 1,000,000 new cases are added to this figure. The highest annual incidence is in sexually active females who have approximately a one in eight chance of developing PID.

Pathobiology

The events that lead to PID are not well understood. It is likely that almost all cases involve the ascending spread of infection from the lower to the upper genital tract. A proportion of cases progresses to develop chronic sequelae.

Most cases of PID are caused by the sexually transmitted organisms *Neisseria gonorrhoeae* or *Chlamydia trachomatis*, and follow cervicitis and urethritis. Other "endogenous" organisms that have been implicated in the etiology of PID include *M. hominis, M. genitalium, Ureaplasma urealyticum*, and numerous aerobic and anaerobic bacteria. These bacteria are referred to as endogenous because they are often isolated from the lower tract in the absence of any disease. Little is known about the pathogenesis of these infections. In many cases, a primary episode of gonococcal and chlamydial PID is followed by subsequent episodes of PID caused by the endogenous organisms. The pathogenesis of gonococcal and chlamydial PID, as well as their clinical manifestations, probably represent nonspecific inflammatory responses to invasion that result in tissue damage, as well as the specific immune responses to gonococci or chlamydiae.

Several **anatomical factors** appear to be important in the pathogenesis of gonococcal or chlamydial PID:

- The **cervix**—gonococcal or chlamydial cervical infection may damage the endocervical canal, break down the mucus plug in the endocervix, and allow ascent of these pathogens, as well as endogenous vaginal organisms.

- Increase in the size of the **zone of ectopy** (extension of the columnar epithelium on to the ectocervix) may result in increased susceptibility to infection by these organisms because these cells are preferential sites of attachment and invasion. Age-related changes in the zone of ectopy, cervical mucus, or host defense mechanisms may play a role in determining whether lower genital tract infections linger, spread to the endometrium and fallopian tubes, or are resolved.

Other host defenses are probably useful in preventing centripetal spread of organisms. These include: (*a*) tubal ciliary movement (unidirectional toward the uterus); (*b*) flow of mucus in the tubal lumen (toward the uterus); (*c*) myometrial contractions during menses (resulting in sloughing of the endometrium).

Several hormonal factors appear to be important in the pathogenesis of PID. **Oral contraceptives** may increase risk of cervical chlamydial infection. Experimentally, both estrogen and progesterone are reported to facilitate the growth and survival of chlamydial infection; however, oral contraceptives decrease the penetrability of the cervical mucus, thus interfering with ascent of infection. Oral contraceptives also increase the size of the zone of cervical ectopy that is the site of attachment for chlamydiae and gonococci. Most cases of gonococcal PID occur within 7 days of **onset of menses**; hormonal changes during the menstrual cycle may lead to changes in the cervical mucus plug, permitting passage of organisms, particularly when estrogen levels are high and progesterone levels are relatively low. The reflux of infected blood during menstrual uterine contractions may also provide a route of entry into the fallopian tubes.

GONOCOCCAL PID

The ability to cause PID is not equally distributed among all strains of gonococci. Strains with a **major outer membrane** protein called IB are much more likely to cause PID. The pathophysiological changes that occur are derived from studies on the interaction of gonococci with fallopian tube explants (Chapter 14). In the presence of the organisms, motility of ciliated epithelial cells slows and ultimately ceases. Ciliated cells are selectively sloughed from the epithelial surface, apparently due to the toxic action of lipopolysaccharide (LPS) or murein fragments. Gonococci attach to nonciliated epithelial cells via pili and outer membrane protein II, and induce phagocytosis. The organisms replicate within phagosomal vesicles and move to the basal portion of the cells and exit into the subepithelium to cause inflammation.

The inflammatory response to gonococcal infection is mediated by a number of soluble factors. Damage to ciliated cells may be caused, in part, by **tumor necrosis factor** (TNF), which is released from fallopian tube explants after incubation with viable gonococci or purified LPS. PID causing strains of gonococci elicit the formation of **complement component C5a**, a chemoattractant for neutrophils. Experimental evidence suggests gonococci in the upper tract may be protected by a coating of ineffective antibodies and complement.

CHLAMYDIAL PID

The steps in infection include attachment of the organisms to cells, probably via specific receptor-ligand interactions, but these have not yet been confirmed. The chlamydial major outer membrane protein appears to be involved in these interactions. The organisms actively induce uptake by a process called **parasite-mediated endocytosis**. Phagolysosomal fusion does not occur probably due to the function of ill-defined surface components of the **elementary bodies** (the infectious form of the organism). The *Chlamydia*-containing phagosomes, referred to as **inclusions**, are visible in histological preparations. Within the phagosomes, elementary bodies differentiate into **reticulate bodies** (the metabolic form of the organism). The life cycle of these organisms is described in detail in Chapter 26.

Not all elementary bodies within an inclusion differentiate, a point of possible clinical significance for the following reason. It is not known if the remaining elementary bodies are infective, but is is likely that they are resistant to bacteriostatic antibiotics such as tetracycline; thus, they may represent a dormant form that could be responsible for treatment failure and recurrences. Ultimately, the reticulate bodies reorganize into new elementary bodies and, in time, are released from the host cell to infect adjacent cells.

Chlamydial infections have a greater mononuclear response that those caused by gonococci, but neutrophils are also seen, mainly in the early phases of the inflammatory response. The chronic sequelae of chlamydial disease may be due to cell-mediated immunity. A surface protein of the organisms, known as the 57 kDal heat shock protein may be the target antigen of a delayed hypersensitivity reaction. In epidemiological studies, high titers of antibodies against this protein have been shown to be prognosticators of tubal scarring, a long-term sequelae of PID.

Coinfections by Gonococci and Chlamydiae

The high prevalence of gonococcal and chlamydial coinfection has prompted recommendations that patients with either infection be treated for both (see "Treatment"). Experimentally, simultaneous gonococcal infection facilitates chlamydial replication in cervical epithelia by about 100-fold. It has been proposed that parasite-mediated endocytosis by nonciliated epithelial cells alters host surface structure, and that the first pathogen may facilitate engulfment of the second one.

Bacterial Vaginosis and PID

Bacterial vaginosis (BV) is an asymptomatic or mildly symptomatic disequilibrium with suppression of lactobacilli (especially species that produce hydrogen peroxide), with an increase in a variety of species including *Gardnerella vaginalis*, anaerobic streptococci, *Bacteroides* species, and genital mycoplasmas. The result is an asymptomatic or mildly symptomatic infection. Whether BV predisposes women to polymicrobial PID remains speculative. To date, no host factor has been identified that increases susceptibility to PID, with the possible exception of the use of intrauterine devices (IUDs). It seems likely that IUDs increase the risk of BV by hindering the mechanisms that eliminate bacteria from the upper female genital tract. Recently, BV has been shown to increase the risk for premature rupture of membranes and premature delivery.

Risk factors for PID

The role of sexual behavior in the development of PID and its sequelae is not well understood. However, multiple sexual partners, young age at first sexual intercourse, high frequency of sexual intercourse, douching, and high rate of acquiring new sexual partners within the 30 days before developing PID appear to be risk factors. Both high-risk sexual behaviors and prevalence of STDs are more frequent in adolescents and young adults; thus, these groups have a higher incidence of PID. Several biological risk factors also change with age, namely lower titers of protective antibody, larger zones of cervical ectopy that may facilitate attachment of pathogens, and easier penetrability of the cervical mucus plug, facilitating pathogen ascent. The difference in the incidence of PID among ethnic groups is smaller than that of lower genital tract infections. This observation contradicts the assumption that race is a marker for poor health-care behaviors. Low socioeconomic status is probably a better marker for high-risk sexual and poor health behaviors that result in the greater prevalence of STDs and PID in the population.

Contraceptive practices also influence the occurrence of PID. The use of an IUD increases the risk of this complication, primarily in the first several months after insertion. In contrast to IUDs, combined estrogen/progesterone oral contraceptive pills and barrier methods are slightly protective against PID. Barrier contraceptive methods should, therefore, be recommended over IUDs, particularly to young, nulliparous women who are sexually active with more than one partner. It has been repeatedly shown that vaginal douching is also associated with PID.

PID results in infertility and ectopic pregnancy, but its exact frequency is unknown. Estimates have ranged from 15–30% of all active PID cases. In addition, an estimated 50% of ectopic pregnancies are caused by previous PID. Ectopic pregnancy is the principal cause of pregnancy-related mortality among Black women in the U.S.

HIV AND STDs

The AIDS pandemic has focused attention on STDs for several reasons (Table 65.5). The relationships between HIV infection and

Table 65.5. STDs and AIDS
Most STDs increase the risk of HIV transmission at least three- to five-fold
HIV infection makes it more difficult to treat several other STDs (e.g., syphilis and chancroid)
STDs and HIV infection can greatly amplify each other, so STD control is critical to HIV prevention
HIV infection probably potentiates the progression of HPV infection to anogenital (primarily cervical) cancer

other STDs are unique, complex, and intriguing. They explain, in part, the global spread of the HIV epidemic, and may well provide insights into the pathogenesis of all sexually transmitted infections. Furthermore, these relationships have compelling implications for efforts to control HIV.

The two obvious relationships between HIV infection and other STDs are: (a) increased transmission of HIV due to other STDs; (b) alteration in the history, diagnosis, or response to therapy of other STDs due to HIV infection.

The risk of HIV transmission is increased three- to five-fold in the presence of both the genital ulcer diseases and nonulcerative STDs such as gonorrhea and chlamydial infection. HPV infection and anogenital warts do not appear to facilitate HIV transmission, perhaps because they do not usually cause breaks in the skin or mucous membranes.

As with other infections, the compromised immune system of AIDS patients results in particularly serious manifestations of other STDs. The available information is not conclusive, but there are data to suggest that HIV prolongs the duration of genital ulcer disease, resulting in more persistent lesions, more frequent recurrences, and more common treatment failures. In addition, these patients often have atypical presentations, resulting in misdiagnosis. Although not definitive, the infectiousness and prevalence of genital ulcer disease may be increased by HIV infection.

HIV infection appears to affect systemic manifestations of STDs. Systemic complications, such as PID or disseminated gonococcal infection, seem to be accelerated in AIDS patients. HIV infection probably increases progression of HPV-associated neoplasia. AIDS patients also have an altered course of regarding the diagnosis, treatment, and progression of syphilis.

In the past, the potential significance of the bidirectional interplay between HIV infection and other STDs has not been fully appreciated. If HIV coinfection prolongs infectivity of certain STDs, and if the same STDs facilitate transmission of HIV, the two infections should greatly amplify one another. The increases in HIV and STD incidence may well contribute to the rapid spread of HIV in some heterosexual populations and may represent "epidemiological synergy" between diseases that are linked by a common mode of transmission.

How Is the Transmission of HIV Enhanced by Other STDs?

It is likely that the inflammatory changes that accompany STDs facilitate HIV entry by altering the barrier function of the genital mucosal epithelium and recruit inflammatory cells into the genital tract. In fact, HIV has been isolated directly from genital ulcers in both men and women. It is recognized that intercourse during menses increases risk of HIV transmission; therefore, it is likely that mucosal irritation, friability, and bleeding may shorten the route to target cells and impair the function of natural defenses. These defenses normally include an intact mucus layer and tight junctions between epithelial cells.

Other factors are likely to play a role in facilitating the transmission of HIV (Table 65.5). It is well known that HIV enters lymphocytes and macrophages. STD-induced inflammation increases the number of these cells, thus, increasing the number of target cells for HIV invasion. The result may well reduce the HIV infectious dose.

The interrelationship between AIDS and other STDs may also involve an interplay at the systemic level of the immune response. Several STD pathogens activate T lymphocytes, which may lead to increased susceptibility to HIV infection and possibly to HIV replication.

Molecular interactions may also contribute to the pathogenesis of HIV infection and other STDs. For example, HSV may potentiate HIV infection by stimulating the expression of surface receptors needed for HIV attachment. Conversely, HIV gene products have been shown to be potent intracellular transactivating factors. It may be that these factors enhance the growth of herpesvirus and human papillomavirus.

PREVENTION AND CONTROL

Prevention and control of sexually transmitted diseases is a multifaceted problem. Depending upon the circumstances, the objective may be prevention of infection, transmission, disease, or disease progression. These can be achieved through a number of approaches, such as effective vaccines, interruption of transmission, progression through behavioral interventions, and curative medical interventions. The necessary tools include information about the prevalence of known high-risk behaviors and corresponding effective behavioral interventions, safe, efficacious vaccines, diagnostic tests, effective therapeutics, an efficient network of health care facilities and trained, effective health care professionals.

In an ideal world, we would have safe, efficacious vaccines that were universally implemented, and an acceptable, infallible barrier method for STD prophylaxis would be available. This method could be used without partner cooperation or knowledge, i.e., controlled by either a male or a female. Furthermore, we would have fail-safe diagnostic tests as well as screening tests that were used regularly with all sexually active people. STDs and sexual behavior would be completely destigmatized and dealt with in a value-neutral fashion. Partner-notification would be conducted in this socially acceptable atmosphere and, therefore, would be more effective. In addition, we would have reliable prognostic indicators for disease resolution or progression, not to mention the availability of single-dose curative therapies effective in both and acute and chronic stages for each bacterial, viral, and parasitic STD. The health care system would be efficient, adequately funded, oriented toward disease prevention, pleasant, and accessible. Health care providers would be expertly trained medically, psychologically, and socially to prevent as well as to treat STDs. Oh, and all of these tools would be inexpensive, i.e., less than $1 cost to patient.

In reality, almost all of these tools are still in the realm of fantasy. We have no vaccines for STDs except for hepatitis B, and that vaccine is embarrassingly underutilized. For some STDs, medical therapy is either unavailable (e.g., viral diseases) or problematic (e.g., antimicrobial resistance), and the bad news goes on. Given that we are interested in preferentially facilitating practical goals, how would we order our priorities for technological advances?

Development and use of inexpensive, simple, rapid diagnostic tests that are appropriate for resource-limited settings, such as inner cities (where the majority of STDs occur), is a fundamental component of STD prevention and control. Such tests are particularly important for diagnosis of STDs in women. In resource-limited settings, clinical algorithms based on recognition of symptoms and signs of STDs have been useful for diagnosis and treatment of urethritis and genital ulcer disease in men, but are far less useful for diagnosis of STDs in women. The special requirements of resource-limited settings force us to conclude that useful diagnostics tests should be: (a) inexpensive— provider cost less than $1.00 (U.S.) per patient; (b) simple—no equipment and minimal training required; (c) rapid—results available before the patient leaves the clinic; (d) performed on convenient specimens—simple to collect, socioculturally acceptable, no separation or preparation needed; (e) able to utilize stable reagents— long shelf-life, no refrigeration required; (f) packaged simply—functional, low cost; and (g) appropriately sensitive and specific—dependent, in part, on the potential morbidity and cost for undetected infection, and the cost of the resulting treatment. Examples of diagnostic tests with the appropriate format are the occult fecal blood card and the urine glucose dipstick. No such STD test presently exists. In the future, public health-conscious physicians will need to emphasize this medical need so that rapid, simple, inexpensive tests are preferentially developed over those that are fancier, but also prohibitively expensive for this population.

The second order on the wish list is for safe and effective, single-dose therapies. Noncompliance is a formidable problem where treatment regimens involve multiple-dose therapy for prolonged periods, especially when treatment exceeds the duration of symptoms. Again, these should be inexpensive, have a long shelf-life, have minimal side effects, and be safe for use during pregnancy. Theoretically, this approach should decrease the likelihood of antibiotic resistance. An example of such an advance is the recent development of azithromycin (an erythromycin-like macrolide antibiotic), which is a single-dose treatment for chlamydial infection.

The role of the health care provider is an integral part of an STD prevention and control program. Currently, many medical school curricula lack focused STD training. Ideally, an integrated approach, including basic biomedical, clinical, epidemiological, and behavioral training would be most effective.

The good news is that although each STD presents unique diagnostic, therapeutic, and prevention challenges, all STDs (by definition) share a common mode of transmission. Interruption of transmission and progression may be accomplished most effectively through behavioral approaches. Important areas for intervention include sexual and contraceptive practices, patterns of partner selection and change, substance use, health care utilization, and health care provider attitudes.

Although much research is needed to identify both target behaviors and effective interventions for heterogeneous populations, our current understanding has allowed us to move forward while awaiting results from ongoing and future studies. Behavioral interventions based on decreasing partner numbers, use of barrier methods and, in some populations, delay of onset of sexual activity are being implemented. Interestingly, the role of the health care provider is critical, as in the case of vaccines where the single most important determinant of vaccine use is physician recommendation. Early studies indicate health care providers appear to be a critical component of an effective information delivery system—especially for adolescents.

As mentioned earlier, target populations include adolescents and all groups comprised of individuals who have multiple partners (i.e., greater than 10 per lifetime). Use of commercial television of social-marketing campaigns (e.g., condom advertisement) may be effective. However, given the limited impact of public service announcements, positive treatment of STD risk issues in sexually explicit television programs and movies may be the most effective and cost-effective way to influence and sustain behavior change as evidenced by "campaigns" to increase seat belt usage and to decrease cigarette smoking.

In summary, the STD epidemic is a complex, multifaceted problem that mandates multifaceted approaches for prevention and control. Vaccines, diagnostics, therapeutics, health care delivery systems, and behavioral interventions will each play an important part in achieving these interrelated goals.

SUGGESTED READING

Hitchcock PJ, Wasserheit JN, Harris JR, Holmes KK. Sexually transmitted diseases in the AIDS era: development of STD diagnostics for resource-limited settings in a global priority. Sex Transm Dis 1991;18:133–135.

Holmes KK, Mardh P-A, Sparling PF, et al., eds. Sexually transmitted diseases. New York: McGraw Hill, 1990.

NIAID Expert Committee on Pelvic Inflammatory Disease. Pelvic inflammatory disease: research directions in the 1990s. Sex Transm Dis 1991; 18:46–64.

Wasserheit JN. Epidemiological synergy: inter-relationships between HIV infection and other STDs. In: Chen L, Segal S, Sepulveda J, eds. AIDS and reproductive health. New York: Plenum Press, 1992.

Infections of the Compromised Patient

66

William G. Powderly

A person is considered to be compromised when suffering either from the disruption of specific defenses of a particular organ or system, or from systemic abnormalities of humoral or cellular immunity. In most cases, it is possible to predict the general type of infection such a patient is likely to acquire, depending on which component of the defense mechanisms is disturbed. However, when the immune deficiency is general and profound, the patient may acquire any of a number of widely differing infections. Several of these may even occur at the same time.

We have the opportunity to learn a great deal about the workings of the normal defense mechanisms by studying what happens when they become impaired. Ultimately, our knowledge of the relative importance of humoral and cellular immunity is derived from observing patients with immunodeficiencies. Thus, we note that persons with agammaglobulinemia are especially susceptible to extracellular bacteria that cause acute inflammation, whereas those with defects in cell-mediated immunity fall prey more readily to viruses, fungi, mycobacteria, and other intracellular agents of chronic diseases. The practical need to understand the risk factors associated with defects in defenses against invading microorganisms cannot be overestimated. Opportunistic infections have assumed immense importance in modern medicine, primarily because many of the major technological advances in therapeutics have been accompanied by iatrogenic disruption of body defense mechanisms.

In most instances, infections of compromised patients are caused by agents that are commonly known to be pathogenic. However, especially severe forms of immune compromise open the door for infections by organisms that are normally not considered to be virulent, including many that are common in the normal flora and the environment. Unexpected extremes have been reached in scattered cases of infections of heart valves and other vital tissues by mushrooms (in their mycelial form) and colorless algae! Note how this underscores that the definition of virulence must include not only obvious pathogenic properties of the microorganism but also the range of susceptibility of the patient.

This chapter will recapitulate the consequence of risk factors mentioned throughout this book. Here we will present them according to the type of abnormality or defect in specific mechanisms.

CASE

A 17-year-old girl, who came to the hospital with fever and bruising, was eventually found to suffer from acute myelogenous leukemia. Remission of the leukemia was achieved with chemotherapy, and allogeneic (nontwin) bone marrow transplantation was attempted in the hope of curing her leukemia. Five days after the transplantation, she had no detectable circulating white blood cells and 2 days thereafter, she became febrile. Blood cultures taken at this time were positive for Escherichia coli. She responded well to antibiotics, and defervesced rapidly.

Eight days later, she again became febrile, and blood cultures were positive for Candida albicans. Although she was placed on antifungals, she remained febrile for 4 days but rapidly defervesced upon removal of a venous catheter (that had been implanted in her subclavian vein for intravenous drug administration). At this time (19 days post-transplantation), white blood cells started to appear in her circulation, indicating that the transplanted marrow had successfully engrafted and was starting to function.

Thirty-one days after her transplantation, she became short of breath, and chest x-ray showed a diffuse pneumonia. Examination of a tissue sample obtained at lung biopsy revealed the presence of Pneumocystis carinii. Treatment with trimethoprim/sulfamethoxazole was started and she responded slowly to therapy. She was discharged from hospital 2 months after her transplantation, but 10 days later, she developed a painful cutaneous herpes zoster infection. She remained well for the next 3 months, although she had developed mild chronic graft-versus-host disease. She returned again to hospital 5 months after her transplantation, with a complaint of fever and shortness of breath. Physical examination and chest x-ray revealed a lobar pneumonia, and both blood and sputum cultures grew Streptococcus pneumoniae. She responded well to penicillin therapy and remained well thereafter.

Patients who have undergone bone marrow transplantation provide an extreme example of the profound disturbances of normal body defenses that predispose to infection. For example, disruption of anatomic barriers by radiation and chemotherapy, causing skin and mucosal ulcerations, provides sites of entry for invasive organisms. Severe neutropenia is characteristic of the immediate post-transplant period, and although granulocyte recovery begins in the third week after transplantation, qualitative defects remain for some time. Cellular immune function, which now depends on donor macrophages and T cells, remains abnormal for several months. It is also compromised by the use of immunosuppressive therapy to treat graft-versus-host disease. Although IgG and IgM levels may return to normal after 4–5 months, B-cell function remains disturbed and antibody levels to specific organisms, such as pneumococci, may remain depressed for years.

With the example of this clinical case in mind, we will review the disturbances in specific body defense mechanisms and their consequences.

ABNORMALITIES OF LOCAL DEFENSE

We are protected from microbial invasion by the mechanical and biochemical barrier provided by skin and mucous membranes and by the presence of a normal commensal flora. Disruption of local mechanical barriers may occur as a consequence of instrumentation (e.g., intravenous or urinary catheterization), surgery, drugs, or burns. Under these circumstances, the infecting organisms are usually members of the commensal flora resident at the site. Thus, breaching the skin with intravenous catheters may introduce *Staphylococcus epidermidis* into the bloodstream, with subsequent septicemia (Chapter 62).

The consequences of immunological or biochemical impairment at the level of the integuments are less well understood. For example, we do not know with certainty if secreted IgA immunoglobulins or lysozyme contributes to resistance to infection. We suspect, however, that people with IgA deficiency are more prone to sinusitis, pneumonia, or specific gastrointestinal infections (e.g., giardiasis). Persons with genetic defects in lysozyme have not yet been found.

Burns provide an extreme example of the critical role of the intact integument on resistance to infection. The necrotic skin tissue is an excellent culture medium for bacteria, thus increasing the size of the inoculum. In addition, the thermal injury itself leads to a poorly understood suppression of white blood cell function. It is not surprising then that skin and subcutaneous tissue infections and septicemias with *S. aureus* or *P. aeruginosa* are major challenges in the management of patients with severe burns.

The normal bacterial flora may be disrupted in numbers and kinds of organisms as the result of antibiotic treatment, which may result in superinfection by organisms resistant to the drug. This happens particularly often in the intestine, sometimes as the result of antibiotic "prepping" of patients for abdominal surgery. Pseudomembranous colitis due to *Clostridium difficile* is a complication of such therapy (Chapter 21).

Some tissues possess additional local defense mechanisms. A good example is the lungs, where the combination of mucous production by goblet cells and ciliary activity of the respiratory epithelial cells serves to trap microbes and carry them out of the lungs. Disruption of this disposal system predisposes to pneumonia (Chapter 56). An extreme example of this occurs in **cystic fibrosis**, a chronic condition of genetic origin characterized by the production of abnormally thick mucus. These patients suffer from recurrent pneumonia, and are often colonized by the opportunistic bacterium *P. aeruginosa*. Most patients are unable to clear this organism from the respiratory tract and may die from respiratory failure after repeated episodes of pneumonia.

DISTURBANCE IN PHAGOCYTIC NUMBERS AND FUNCTION

Once the first line of defense is breached, neutrophils assume a critical role in checking the spread of invasive disease. Defects in neutrophil activity, either qualitative or quantitative, predispose patients to infection with certain bacteria and fungi (Table 66.1). These defects may involve: (*a*) a decreased number of phagocytic cells; (*b*) impairment of their chemotactic response; and, (*c*) lowering of their ability to kill microorganisms.

Granulocytopenia (a decrease in the number of circulating neutrophils) clearly predisposes to infection. Myelosuppressive cancer chemotherapy is the most common cause of granulocytopenia in hospitals. Neutropenia also occurs in bone marrow failure due to aplasia, autoimmune disease, hematological malignancy, or tumor invading the bone marrow. Serious infections, usually accompanied by bacteremia, are a frequent and often life-threatening problem in these hosts. The most important correlation is between the number of circulating neutrophils

Table 66.1. Common Causes of Compromise and their Consequences

Impaired Function	Common Infecting Organisms	Sites Commonly Affected
Barrier		
Integument	Pyogenic cocci, enteric bacteria	Skin, subcutaneous connective tissue
Normal microbial flora	Pyogenic cocci, enteric bacteria, *Clostridium difficile, Candida albicans*	Skin, intestine
Phagocyte functions		
Chemotaxis	*Staphylococcus aureus*, enteric bacteria	Skin, respiratory tract
Neutropenia	*S. aureus*, enteric bacteria	Skin, respiratory tract
Microbial killing	*S. aureus, Aspergillus*	Skin, visceral abscesses
Humoral functions		
Hypogammaglobulinemia	Pyogenic bacteria	Any site
IgA deficiency	Pyogenic bacteria	Respiratory tract
Lack of spleen	Pneumococcus, *H. influenzae*	Septicemia
Complement deficiency:		
C1q, C2, or C3	Pyogenic bacteria	Bacteremia, meningitis
C5, C6, C7, C8, or C9	*Neisseria*	Meningitis, arthritis
Cell-mediated immunity	Viruses, fungi, protozoa, intracellular bacteria	Any site

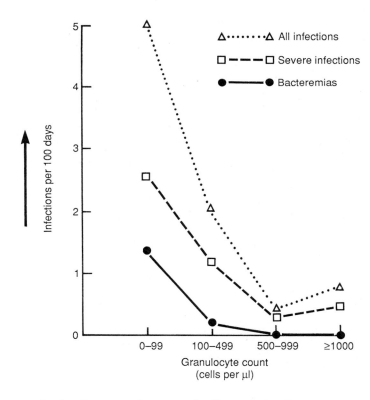

Figure 66.1. Relationship between the incidence of infection and the absolute neutrophil count in patients with acute nonlymphocyte leukemia. The incidence of infection rises as the neutrophil count decreases.

and the risk of infection. The rate of infection clearly increases as the number of neutrophils decreases (Fig. 66.1). Disturbances of the integrity of the skin and gastrointestinal tract, often the result of chemotherapy or radiation therapy, are also important in the pathogenesis of these infections. The organisms responsible are usually derived from the patient's own flora, particularly that of the bowel. Gram-negative enteric bacilli and staphylococci are the most common bacterial pathogens. Prolonged antibacterial therapy predisposes to colonization by fungi, *Candida* and *Aspergillus* being important causes of fungal sepsis and mortality in this population.

Chemotactic dysfunction of phagocytes is uncommon and is usually congenital in origin. Defective neutrophil chemotaxis may result from inadequate signaling of the neutrophil, from abnormalities of neutrophil receptors for chemoattractants, or from disorders in cell locomotion. *S. aureus* is the most important pathogen in these patients, who are usually seen with recurrent cutaneous or deep abscesses.

Most often, abnormalities in microbial killing power are inherited. Of the many disorders that have been described, the most common is **chronic granulomatous disease**, a condition in which neutrophils fail to mount a respiratory burst during phagocytosis. The reason for this deficiency is that the enzyme NADPH oxidase is defective, and hydrogen peroxide is not formed. Patients with this disorder are at risk of infection with catalase-positive organisms, especially *S. aureus*. A Gram-negative rod, *Serratia marcescens*, also causes infections in these patients, as do fungi (especially *Aspergillus*). These organisms are relatively resistant to the nonoxidative killing mechanisms of neutrophils. On the other hand, bacteria such as pneumococci and other streptococci that make their own hydrogen peroxide but have no catalase, are likely to be killed by the defective neutrophils. The reason is that these neutrophils still contain myeloperoxidase. This enzyme can utilize hydrogen peroxide made by bacterial metabolism to produce lethal radicals (Chapter 6). In effect, these bacteria commit suicide.

ABNORMALITIES IN HUMORAL IMMUNITY

Immunoglobulin deficiency may be congenital (e.g., Bruton's X-linked agammaglobulinemia) or acquired (e.g., common variable immunodeficiency). Acquired hypogammaglobulinemia may also arise as a consequence of conditions that lead to protein loss (nephrotic syndrome, intestinal lymphangiectasia), cancers of cells that make immunoglobulins (multiple myeloma, chronic lymphocytic leukemia), or burns. Defective B-lymphocyte function also occurs as a consequence of bone marrow transplantation, as noted in the case above. The predominant infectious disease problem in these patients is recurrent upper and lower respiratory tract infection due to encapsulated bacteria, reflecting the important role of antibodies in opsonization of encapsulated bacteria.

Complement deficiencies are rare and are also characterized by predisposition to infection with encapsulated bacteria (see Table 6.4). *Neisseria* are a special problem for patients with deficiencies of any of the late complement components (C6, C7, C8, or C9), because complement-mediated lysis is required to kill these organisms. Many bacteria infect patients with defects earlier in the complement cascade. Most clinically significant complement deficiencies are congenitally acquired.

The spleen is intimately concerned with adequate performance of the humoral arm of the immune system, both as a source of complement- and antibody-producing B cells, and as the organ primarily responsible for the removal of opsonized microbes from the bloodstream. Defects in spleen function may be a consequence of splenectomy or of diseases such as sickle cell anemia. In these situations, patients are at risk of infection with encapsulated bacteria, e.g., pneumococci and *Haemophilus*. These bacterial infections may be fulminant in patients with splenic deficiency. Bacteremia and septic shock often result, and mortality is high unless appropriate therapy is introduced rapidly.

DISORDERS OF CELL-MEDIATED IMMUNITY

Defects in the function or number of macrophages and T lymphocytes lead to an increased risk of infection with bacteria that survive intracellularly, as well as with viruses, fungi, and protozoa (Table 66.1).

Patients with defective cell-mediated immunity may be divided into two groups, depending on whether their defect is congenital or acquired. Primary disorders of cell-mediated immunity are usually diagnosed in childhood and are lethal, with death usually arising from opportunistic infections before adulthood.

Acquired defects in cell-mediated immunity are seen in an increasingly large population of patients treated in hospitals. The enormous success in transplant surgery is a consequence of the development of drugs (such as cyclosporin) that suppress the graft-versus-host response and prevent rejection of the transplant. These immunosuppressive drugs also interfere with normal cell-mediated immunity, and all of these patients are at increased risk of opportunistic infection. Some immunosuppressive drugs, especially corticosteroids, are also used to treat a variety of inflammatory diseases. Cell-mediated immunity is also disordered in patients with lymphoma.

The most profound example of defective cell-mediated immunity occurs in acquired immunodeficiency syndrome (AIDS, Chapter 67). Here, depletion of CD_4+-helper T cells due to HIV infection leads almost inevitably to death from uncontrolled opportunistic infection or malignancy. Patients have profound disturbances of cell-mediated immunity, especially that mediated by cytotoxic lymphocytes and macrophages and develop infections with eukaryotic agents (e.g., *P. carinii*), viruses (e.g., cytomegalovirus), and intracellular bacteria (e.g., mycobacteria).

MANAGEMENT OF INFECTION IN COMPROMISED HOSTS: GENERAL CONSIDERATIONS

As with all infections, treatment in the compromised host should be directed against the specific infecting organism. However, defective host response heightens the risk of severe infection, and there may be an urgent need to begin treatment presumptively, based on the most likely etiological possibilities. Knowing the type of immune defect, the likely resident microbial flora, the site and clinical features of the infection, and some epidemiological features often makes it possible to predict the likely infecting organism. For example, in granulocytopenic patients, broad-spectrum antibiotics with activity against both Gram-positive bacteria and Enterobacteriaceae and other Gram-negative bacteria should be given at the first sign of infection, such as fever. Patients with decreased spleen function should be treated with drugs active against pneumococci and *H. influenzae*. A diffuse pneumonia involving most of the lung in a patient with AIDS is most likely due to *P. carinii*. However, this is not always the case, and it is often necessary to identify specifically the causative organism so that appropriate treatment may be started or toxic therapy avoided. Specimens should be obtained before starting therapy, and there should be coordination between the clinician and the microbiology laboratory to assure the recovery and identification of opportunistic pathogens. Unless warned, the microbiological laboratory may consider *S. epidermidis* a contaminant from the skin and not report it.

It is particularly important to attempt to reverse the immune defect; whenever practical, iatrogenic causes should be eliminated. Catheters should be removed, or at least changed; immunosuppressive drugs should be discontinued whenever possible. In some transplant recipients, it may even be necessary to allow the transplant to be rejected by suspending immunosuppressive therapy to permit an adequate host response to infection. In other cases, replacement therapy is of benefit. Passive administration of immunoglobulins decreases the incidence of infection in patients with hypogammaglobulinemia. Granulocyte transfusions may benefit some granulocytopenic patients with refractory Gram-negative bacterial infections.

Preventive measure are also important in caring for these patients. Simple procedures such as care with use and insertion of catheters, careful handwashing, and appropriate isolation techniques may reduce the incidence of opportunistic infection acquired in hospitals. Some vaccines (e.g., against influenza virus or pneumococci) may be of benefit. It is essential to remember that live vaccines should be given with caution to immunocompromised hosts because even attenuated viruses may cause severe disease in these patients. Prophylactic antibiotics are rarely of benefit; major exceptions are the use of penicillin to prevent pneumococcal infections in children with sickle cell disease, and the use of trimethoprim/sulfamethoxazole or pentamidine to prevent *Pneumocystis* pneumonia in patients with severe defects in cell-mediated immunity (see Chapter 67 on AIDS).

SUGGESTED READING

Ho M, Dummer JS. Risk factors and approaches to infections in transplant recipients. In: Principles and practice of infectious diseases, 3rd ed. Mandell G, Douglas R, Bennet J, eds. New York: Churchill Livingstone, 1991: 2284–2291.

Rotrosen D, Fallin JI. Evaluation of the patient with suspected immunodeficiency. In: Principles and practice of infectious diseases, 3rd ed. Mandell G, Douglas R, Bennet J, eds. New York: Churchill Livingstone, 1991: 139–147.

Rubin RH, Young LS. Clinical approach to infection in the compromised host, 2nd ed. New York: Plenum Publishing, 1988.

Schimpff SC. Infections in the compromised host—an overview. In: Principles and practice of infectious diseases, 3rd ed. Mandell G, Douglas R, Bennet J, eds. New York: Churchill Livingstone, 1991:2258–2265.

Acquired Immunodeficiency Syndrome

67

William G. Powderly

It is estimated that by 1990 between 1.5 and 2.5 million persons in the U.S. have been infected with human immunodeficiency virus (HIV), the causative agent of the acquired immunodeficiency syndrome (AIDS). The World Heath Organization estimates that as many as 10 million persons have been infected worldwide. By 1990, over 100,000 people had died of AIDS in the U.S. alone. Unless curative therapy is developed, most of remaining infected individuals will develop AIDS and ultimately die from its consequences. In the interim, the infected individuals will infect others.

The impact of this disease cannot be overemphasized. By 1990, AIDS was second only to accidents as the leading cause of death in the U.S. among men 20–45 years of age. Its importance is rapidly rising among women. In some parts of Africa, this is the leading cause of death among young adults.

AIDS is a constellation of clinical illnesses, primarily opportunistic infections and malignancies (Table 67.1), that are the consequence of the destruction of the immune system by HIV. For any infected person, AIDS is the final manifestation of an infection that started many years previously. HIV infection is continuous and relentless in its progression. The progressive nature of the infection has been well characterized and there are several ways of classifying its stages (Table 67.2). This chapter will describe the course of a typical HIV infection in terms of these progressive stages. The virology of HIV is discussed in detail in Chapter 37.

EARLY ACUTE HIV INFECTION

J.P., a 26-year-old married bisexual man, who works as a hospital phlebotomist, is seen in his physician's office complaining of a 1-week history of fever, swollen lymph node, and headache. He states that he had unprotected sexual contact with a new male partner 3 weeks previously. On examination, he has a red, inflamed pharynx, enlarged cervical lymph nodes, and a red splotchy rash all over his body.

J.'s complaints and manifestations are nonspecific and extremely common. His presentation is typical of many viral infections, included that caused by HIV and the Epstein-Barr virus (see Chapter 40). The possibility of HIV infection should particularly be kept in mind if the patient is a member of a high-risk group, i.e., homosexual or bisexual

Table 67.1. AIDS defining illnesses*

Multiple or recurrent bacterial infections (2 in a 2-year period) affecting a child less than 13 years of age. These include septicemia, pneumonia, meningitis, bone or joint infection, or internal abscess caused by *Hemophilus influenzae, Streptococcus,* or other pyogenic bacteria.
Candidiasis of the esophagus, trachea, bronchi or lungs.
Disseminated coccidioidomycosis.
Extrapulmonary cryptococcosis.
Chronic cryptosporidiosis, with diarrhea for >1 month.
Cytomegalovirus infection.
Mucocutaneous Herpes virus infection persisting for more than 1 month.
HIV encephalopathy.
Disseminated histoplasmosis.
Isosporiasis, with diarrhea for >1 month
Kaposi's sarcoma.
Primary lymphoma of the brain.
Non-Hodgkin's lymphoma of B cell or unknown phenotype, including Burkitt's lymphoma, small noncleaved lymphoma, and immunoblastic lymphoma.
Lymphoid interstitial pneumonia affecting a child <13 years.
Disseminated mycobacterial infection (not *M. tuberculosis*).
Tuberculosis (pulmonary or extrapulmonary).
Pneumocystis carinii infection.
Progressive multifocal leucoencephalopathy.
Recurrent *Salmonella* infection.
Toxoplasmosis of the brain.
Invasive cervical cancer.
Recurrent pneumonia (more than one episode in 1 year).

*Any of these diseases indicates a diagnosis of AIDS, in the presence of laboratory evidence of HIV infection.

Table 67.2. CDC Classification of HIV Infection

| | Clinical Categories | | |
CD4 lumphocyte count	Asymptomatic or acute infection	Symptomatic, non-AIDS[+]	AIDS-indicating illness*
>500/mm^3	A1	B1	C1
200–499/mm^3	A2	B2	C2
<200/mm^3	A3	B3	C3

[+]Includes patients with conditions such as oral candidiasis, cervical dysplasia, oral hairy leukoplakia, fever or diarrhea, recurrent or multidermatomal herpes zoster, listeriosis, peripheral neuropathy.
*See Table 1.

WALTER REED STAGING CLASSIFICATION FOR HIV DISEASE

Stage 1:	CD$_4$ lymphocyte count >400 cells/mm^3, normal delayed type hypersensitivity (DTH).
Stage 2:	Stage 1 plus chronic lymphadenopathy.
Stage 3:	CD$_4$ lymphocyte count <400 cells/mm^3, normal delayed type hypersensitivity (DTH).
Stage 4:	CD$_4$ lymphocyte count <400 cells/mm^3, partial anergy.
Stage 5:	CD$_4$ lymphocyte count <400 cells/mm^3, complete anergy or candidiasis.
Stage 6:	CD$_4$ lymphocyte count <400 cells/mm^3, opportunistic infection.

men, intravenous drug users, or their sexual partners. This patient has a number of risk factors for HIV infection—he is bisexual, he recently had sex with a new partner who could have been infected, and he is a hospital phlebotomist.

Could J. have an HIV infection? Acute illness occurs in 50–90% of persons 2–4 weeks after infection by HIV. In the majority of such cases, the only symptoms are mild fever and sore throat. A small subgroup may have fever, myalgias, lethargy, pharyngitis, arthralgias, lymphadenopathy, and a maculopapular rash of the trunk. Some patients have aseptic meningitis, and the headache that J. complained of may have been caused by mild meningeal irritation. The illness typically lasts 3–14 days and complete recovery is the rule, even in patients with neurological complications.

Can HIV be diagnosed at this stage? Because of the early onset of HIV infection, antibody to HIV is usually not detectable initially, but level of the **core (p24) antigen** is often extremely high. Follow-up serological testing is needed to make a diagnosis. There is no specific therapy for acute HIV disease. Therefore, although HIV testing should be offered to patients at this stage, it will be negative and will be used primarily to establish a baseline.

DIAGNOSTIC TESTS FOR HIV

After counseling about the implications and possible outcome of HIV testing, J. had an HIV test, which was negative. He returned for follow-up 6 weeks later. His symptoms have resolved completely and he feels well. Serological testing at this time revealed a positive enzyme-linked immunosorbent assay (ELISA) and Western blot, signifying antibodies specific to HIV.

How accurate are the tests for HIV? Can we be sure J. is infected? A definitive diagnosis of infection could be achieved by culturing the virus, but this is difficult to perform in early infection. HIV infection is generally diagnosed by detecting circulating antibodies to the virus. Unlike most antibody tests, in which the presence of specific antibodies signifies past infection with the agent in question, **a positive HIV antibody test signifies current infection.** Any individual who has HIV antibodies must be assumed to have active infection that can be transmitted to others. It is extremely important, therefore, that such individuals be counseled on the issues involved in transmission so that further spread can be minimized.

Specific anti-HIV antibodies generally appear 6–12 weeks after infection. However, studies using the polymerase chain reaction (Chapter 55) to test for specific HIV DNA have shown that, very rarely, some infected individuals do not develop antibodies for several months or years after exposure. These unusual individuals will have a **false-negative** serological test for HIV. In addition, some patients in the terminal phases of AIDS have negative serological tests (presumably because of severe B-cell dysfunction). However, patients with advanced disease can usually be identified by other than serological means.

The most common method used for testing for HIV antibodies is **ELISA.** This test is performed by adding a sample of the patient's serum to small wells in which HIV antigens are bound. If antibodies are present, they will complex with the antigen. Anti-immunoglobulin antibody linked to an identifier enzyme is then added to bind to the complex. Although this test is highly sensitive (more than 99%), it is not completely specific and **false-positive** results occur. When screening a large population (such as the adults in the U.S.), even a false-positive rate of less than 0.01% means that many individuals who are not infected will be misidentified. Such persons could face potential discrimination in insurance, employment, and housing. The incidence of false-positives, no matter how low, is a strong argument against indiscriminate testing without obtaining the permission of the patient.

For these reasons, ELISA-positive results should be verified with a more specific test. In most laboratories, this test is a **Western blot** (Fig. 37.5). This test detects antibodies to specific viral polypeptides. The Western blot is an extremely sensitive and specific way to test for HIV antibodies; however, it is too time-consuming and expensive to be used for primary screening purposes.

Rarely, some people exhibit nonspecific cross-reactivity in serological HIV tests and may be difficult to distinguish from patients with early HIV infection. The true pattern can usually be determined by repeating the Western blot after 3–4 months. By then, a person with true infection will usually have developed new antibodies to different epitopes (which show up in the Western blot), whereas those with nonspecific reactivity will have the same pattern as before. Waiting to repeat HIV tests can be a very difficult time for patients, who will need counseling and support to help them understand the limitations of technology.

Other assays to determine the presence of HIV infection are available, but are not always useful. The p24 antigen is the viral core protein, produced by the **gag** gene and its presence denotes active viral replication. However, this antigen is not detectable in the serum of all patients and this test is not useful diagnostically. HIV can be cultured from lymphocytes of most infected individuals but this test is technically difficult and is rarely used outside of research settings. The polymerase chain reaction (PCR) is another technique, currently limited to research laboratories, but may eventually be useful in cases where antibody detection is unhelpful (e.g., in infants born to infected mothers) or difficult to interpret (like indeterminate Western blots).

ENCOUNTER AND ENTRY

J. has clearly **seroconverted** (from negative to positive) and so, is infected with HIV. How did he get his infection? HIV is transmitted primarily by direct inoculation of infected blood or body fluids into the host. Thus, the epidemiology of HIV mirrors that of viruses spread by such means, e.g., hepatitis B and C. Most cases of HIV infections are acquired sexually and practices that are potentially associated with trauma, such as receptive anal intercourse, facilitate the spread of the virus. Other sexually transmitted diseases, especially chancroid, are associated with an increased risk of HIV transmission, possibly because the epithelial barrier is breached by the genital ulcers. In the U.S. and other western countries, HIV initially infected mainly homosexual men and was wrongly perceived as a disease of that community. However, in other parts of the world, sexual transmission of HIV is predominantly heterosexual. In the U.S., there has been a steady rise in the number of cases of HIV infection acquired by heterosexual contact. There is some evidence that women may be more easily infected than men, but transmission clearly occurs in both directions.

Contact with infected blood or blood products is another important form of transmission of HIV. Initially, this was recognized because of the occurrence of AIDS cases among people with **hemophilia** who had been given infected factor VIII and factor IX, or who had received HIV-infected blood transfusions. This mode of spread has considerably diminished since blood donors were tested and plasma was treated to inactivate the virus. However, this mode of transmission has not been eliminated completely, because of the "window period" in early infection, when HIV-infected blood donors have not yet developed antibodies. Blood-borne spread of HIV remains a considerable problem among intravenous drug users who share needles and syringes. Individuals who exchange sex for drugs may then infect their predominantly heterosexual sexual partners. Infected women may infect their children in utero and between 15% and 30% of these infants will be infected with the virus. The reason why all such children are not infected is unknown, although it may be related, in part, to maternal immune responses to HIV. Transmission may also occur during the birth process and via breast milk.

HIV is also a worrisome occupational problem for **health care workers**. Exposure to HIV-infected blood, predominantly by needle-stick injuries, is now a significant hazard for health care workers. The risk of infection after such exposure is low; it is estimated that 1 in 300 such exposures will lead to infection and very few cases of AIDS have been documented to have occurred because of occupational injury. Transmission in the opposite direction (i.e., from infected health care worker to patient) has also been documented in at least one occasion, in the case of an infected dentist. The adoption of universal precautions (assuming all blood or other fluids are potentially infected) is extremely important to prevent this kind of transmission.

We can see, therefore, that J. could have been infected in a number of ways. He is a bisexual man with a recent new sexual partner and he is also a phlebotomist who may have had exposure to infected blood. Statistically, it is most likely that he acquired HIV from sexual contact.

When should people be tested for HIV infection? Persons with HIV disease seek medical attention at different stages of the disease. Many patients with early HIV infection do not seek medical attention and do not know they are infected until they develop AIDS itself. However, most patients are seen by a physician before they have developed AIDS. Many seek to be tested for HIV, not because of symptoms, but because they perceive that some aspect of their lifestyle may put them at risk. Others seek out a physician with complaints that are not obviously due to HIV disease, and the diagnosis is made when their physician counsels them to have HIV testing performed.

CONSEQUENCES OF BEING HIV POSITIVE

J. returned to his physician's office 2 weeks later to get the results of his antibody tests. When told he is HIV-positive, he became very anxious and asked, "Does this mean I have AIDS?"

Learning that he or she is HIV positive is an extremely difficult time for a patient. There is much anxiety about the possibility of AIDS and there is worry about transmission of the disease to close family members. Counseling patients is, therefore, extremely important at this point. Patients should be reminded how the disease is spread and educated fully of their duty to protect other people, especially their sexual contacts. Infected persons should be informed that abstinence from sexual intercourse is the only sure way of avoiding transmission. Sexual practices that do not involve contact with semen or vaginal secretions are considered safe. Condom use is essential if patients are going to continue to have sexual intercourse. In contrast to their sexual partners, patients should be reassured that casual contact with others does not pose a risk. This also applies to infected children.

In addition to informing his male and female sexual partners that he is HIV positive and taking precautions not to infect them, J. needs to consider his occupation. If his hospital duties include the performance of invasive procedures, he should think about transferring to another position.

Will J. get AIDS? Probably yes, because a positive HIV test indicates the risk of progressing to AIDS. The probability of this happening can be estimated by determining the degree of immunodeficiency. The most helpful measurement is the level of T-lymphocyte subsets. Because the **CD$_4$ (T$_4$ or helper-inducer) lymphocytes** are a specific target of HIV, measurement of the number of these cells in the circulation indicates the degree of immune impairment, thus the risk of developing AIDS. The normal T$_4$ count in adults ranges from 800–2000 cells/mm^3. An increased loss of these cells over time is the usual pattern of progressive HIV infection (Fig. 67.1). However, by itself, the T$_4$ lymphocyte count is not an absolute indicator of the probability of developing AIDS. There are many asymptomatic HIV-infected persons with T$_4$ counts of less than 200 cells/mm^3, but in general, the lower the T$_4$ count, the greater the risk of developing AIDS soon. The **rate** of decline of T$_4$ cells over time may also give important prognostic clues.

There are other markers of disease activity such as serum levels of p24 antigen and β$_2$-microglobulin. The p24 antigen is the viral core protein and its presence indicates viral replication and suggests a poor prognosis. β$_2$-microglobulin is a protein whose serum levels correlate to some degree with lymphocyte activation. High levels of this protein in asymptomatic patients have been associated with a greater probability of progression to AIDS. These tests are largely used in research settings.

Symptoms or clinical illnesses that suggest immunodeficiency also help identify patients who are likely to progress more rapidly to AIDS. Consequently, a careful history should be taken regarding fever, night sweats, unintentional weight loss, or unexplained diarrhea. The presence of *Candida* infection in the mouth (thrush) also indicates a poor prognosis. In spite of these prognostic markers, **we cannot tell precisely how quickly any particular patient will progress to develop AIDS.** The mechanisms controlling the rate of progression are not well understood. There has been some suggestion that cofactors, such as other infectious agents like *Mycoplasma incognitus* and HTLV-1 infection, may be important determinants of progression.

Because most HIV-infected individuals develop progressive immunodeficiency, they should be assessed for occult infections that may become problems later. Tuberculin skin testing and chest x-ray should be performed, because reactivation tuberculosis is extremely common in HIV-infected persons. Those who test positive should be treated

Figure 67.1. The natural history of HIV disease.

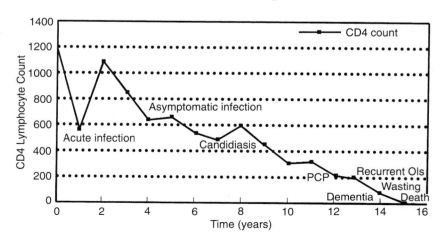

prophylactically with isoniazid. Patients with positive serology for syphilis require intensive antitreponemal therapy, particularly if there is any suspicion of neurosyphilis. Baseline cytomegalovirus (CMV) and *Toxoplasma* antibody testing identifies persons at risk for reactivation disease by these agents. HIV-positive individuals are also candidates for vaccination against pneumococcal disease and annual immunization against influenza. Because patients are also at risk for hepatitis B, they should be tested for this virus, and those who are negative should be offered vaccination against it.

PROGRESSION TO AIDS

J.'s CD_4 lymphocyte count is measured and found to be 750 cells /mm³. He is otherwise completely well.

At this point, J. can be advised that he has no evidence of significant immune impairment. He should be told to return to his physician every 6 months, so his CD_4 lymphocyte count can be measured. Recent studies have shown that specific antiretroviral drug treatment should be started when the CD_4 cell count is less than 500 cells/mm³, even if the patient is asymptomatic because such treatment delays the onset of AIDS. It is important, therefore, that the CD_4 cell count be monitored regularly.

Unfortunately, J. did not keep his scheduled appointments. Four years later, he returned to his physician's office complaining of a blistering rash on his left shoulder and upper torso. On further questioning, he also complained of sore throat and white spots in his mouth. Examination showed oral thrush, enlarged nontender cervical, axillary and inguinal lymph nodes, and a vesicular (blistering) rash in a dermatomal distribution consistent with shingles. At this time, his CD_4 lymphocyte count was 280 cells/mm³.

Acute HIV infection is followed by a latent period during which infected individuals are asymptomatic and appear healthy. The duration of this period is variable and ranges from 18 months to over 15 years. The median time is approximately 10 years. Although we refer to this period as asymptomatic, in fact, many patients have complaints that are not obviously linked to HIV infection or to the associated immunodeficiency. For example, HIV-infected persons are particularly prone to the development of skin complaints. The reason is unknown, but infection of the epidermal Langerhans cells may be a contributory factor. Many patients complain of excessively dry skin and pruritus, seborrheic dermatitis with eczema, folliculitis, and psoriasis. A new onset of severe psoriasis, eczema, or folliculitis in a previously healthy adult should raise the possibility of HIV infection. Furthermore, reactivation of herpes zoster (shingles), as occurred with J., may also be a sentinel of HIV infection. Patients are also prone to recurrent herpes simplex infection, molluscum contagiosum, and drug eruptions. In addition, a type of skin cancer, **cutaneous Kaposi's sarcoma**, may be the first manifestation of AIDS. It is characterized by blue-violet palpable, nonpruritic, painless lesions.

Patients in this stage may also present with localized or generalized lymphatic enlargement, as J. did. Painless generalized lymphadenopathy is a common manifestation of HIV disease, but has no prognostic significance. On the other hand, localized adenopathy or changes in already enlarged nodes may be early signs of infection or malignancy and should be investigated.

Recurrent mucocutaneous candidiasis (vaginal or oral in women, oral in men) and extensive oral aphthous ulcerations (canker sores) are common early manifestations of HIV infection and identify patients at greater risk of developing AIDS. Hairy leukoplakia (plaques of thickened mucosa on the tongue and elsewhere in the mouth) maybe caused by Epstein-Barr virus and also occurs early in HIV disease.

Abnormal laboratory findings may also be found early in HIV disease. Many infected individuals have isolated hematologic cytopenias, usually anemia, lymphopenia, or thrombocytopenia. Abnormalities in liver function tests are also common usually due to previous or concurrent viral hepatitis.

The progressive loss of CD_4 lymphocytes and the oral *Candida* infection suggest that J.'s cell-mediated immunity has significantly diminished since his physician last saw him. J. does not yet have AIDS. However, he can be classified as having **AIDS-related complex or ARC**. Although patients with ARC may not develop AIDS for several years, ARC is a poor prognostic sign and is an indication for starting specific antiretroviral treatment. What should J.'s physician do?

TREATMENT OF AIDS-RELATED COMPLEX AND EARLY AIDS

J. should start specific antiretroviral treatment and prophylactic therapy to prevent *Pneumocystis carinii* infection. Studies of the antiviral agent, azidothymidine (zidovudine), have shown that it can delay the onset of AIDS when given to patients with CD_4 cell counts of less than 500 cells/mm³. This drug, the first one approved for the treatment of HIV infection, is an inhibitor of reverse transcriptase. It slows the progression of AIDS, is associated with temporary increases of CD_4 cell counts, and may decrease the frequency of opportunistic infections.

Pneumocystis pneumonia is a preventable disease. Prospective studies of HIV-positive patients have shown that at least one-third of patients with CD_4 lymphocyte counts less than 200 cells/mm³ will develop *Pneumocystis* pneumonia within 3 years. The risk is considerably greater if the patients are also symptomatic (i.e., have fever, night sweats, weight loss, or oral candidiasis). The risk of this infection may be substantially reduced with prophylactic therapy using trimethoprim-sulfamethoxazole or aerosolized pentamidine. *Pneumocystis* pneumonia is less clearly correlated with CD_4 lymphocyte counts in children. HIV-infected infants with CD_4 cell counts less than 1500 cells/mm³ should be considered as candidates for prophylaxis.

CLINICAL MANIFESTATIONS OF AIDS

J.'s physician prescribed zidovudine and trimethoprim-sulfamethoxazole tablets. Ten days later, J. stopped the trimethoprim-sulfamethoxazole because

Table 67.3. AIDS-related Complex (ARC)
Unexplained weight loss (10% of body weight in 6 months)
Fevers ± night sweats persisting for 1 month
Unexplained diarrhea persisting for 30 days
Recurrent oral candidiasis
Multidermatomal herpes zoster
Oral hairy leukoplakia
Chronic debilitating fatigue

of an itchy rash, but did not inform his doctor. Six months later, he turned up at a local emergency room complaining of a 6-day history of gradually worsening dry cough and shortness of breath. His temperature was 40°C and his chest x-ray showed a diffuse bilateral interstitial pneumonia. Examination of fluid from bronchoalveolar lavage revealed Pneumocystis carinii.

J. now has AIDS. The signs and symptoms of *Pneumocystis* pneumonia place him in that category, but any of a number of other opportunistic infections, singly or in groups, would have led to the same diagnosis. Table 67.1 indicates the major infections associated with AIDS, most of which are due to **intracellular agents that are usually controlled by cell-mediated immunity**. These infections are often the result of endogenous reactivation of previously acquired organisms, rather than newly acquired infection.

Most AIDS-related infections do not occur until the CD_4 count falls below 200 cells/mm³. Kaposi's sarcoma is the major exception to this rule because its occurrence seems to be independent of the underlying T-cell depletion. Infections in AIDS patients are characterized by a high density of organisms and disseminated disease, as well as infections with multiple different organisms. A further general principle is that these infections are rarely cured. Control of disease consequently requires prolonged acute therapy as well as long-term use of antimicrobial agents to prevent relapses.

Lung Infections

Pneumonia caused by *Pneumocystis* is the most frequent opportunistic infection associated with AIDS and occurs in between 25% and 60% of all patients. The typical symptoms are fever, cough, and shortness of breath. Although this infection most typically affects the lung, it may involve other sites, especially the liver, lymph nodes, and choroid. Although treatable, *Pneumocystis* pneumonia is associated with a mortality of 10–20% from irreversible respiratory failure.

An opportunistic infection such as *Pneumocystis* pneumonia does not mean that patients will automatically develop multiple medical problems and soon die. The use of specific antiretroviral therapy, such as zidovudine, and anti-*Pneumocystis* drugs has led to an improvement in the quality and length of life for AIDS patients. Many of them will be able to live and work normally for some time. Nevertheless, there is no specific curative therapy, and the progressive decline in immunity will continue; progressive deterioration with repeated episodes of infection is the normal pattern for patients with advanced HIV disease.

Gastrointestinal Infections

After the episode of pneumonia, J. made a complete recovery and was able to return to work. He took zidovudine and aerosolized pentamidine as Pneumocystis *prophylaxis. J. had no problems for about a year, when he saw his physician and complained of difficulty in swallowing and diarrhea. His diarrhea was intermittent, but could be as bad as 20 bouts of loose watery stools per day. On examining his mouth, there were multiple white plaques on his palate and tongue.*

Gastrointestinal problems are common in patients with AIDS. Infection of the mouth and pharynx with *Candida* is almost universal in patients with profound immunodeficiency, but is usually manageable. A substantial number of patients go on to develop esophageal candidiasis, which may cause pain and difficulty on swallowing, leading to considerable weight loss. Esophageal infection may also be caused by the herpes viruses, herpes simplex and cytomegalovirus (CMV), although they more typically involve other sites. Herpes simplex causes recurrent skin infections, especially perirectally, that can become resistant to therapy. CMV typically causes disseminated disease with viremia. Involvement of the colon may lead to severe abdominal pain and diarrhea. CMV infection of the eye presents as blurred vision and may progress to blindness.

Diarrhea is an extremely common problem in patients with advanced AIDS and may be very severe, difficult to diagnose, and to treat. It may be caused by a large number of agents, such as:

- CMV and other viruses;

- Enteric Gram-negative bacteria such as *Salmonella* and *Shigella* (with accompanying bacteremia);

- Mycobacterial infection (especially the *Mycobacterium-avium* complex (MAC)) that affect the small bowel and colon and cause malabsorption and diarrhea;

- Intestinal parasites such as *Giardia*, *Isospora*, and *Cryptosporidium*.

Malignancies such as Kaposi's sarcoma or lymphoma involving the stomach or colon may also cause gastrointestinal symptoms. Furthermore, HIV itself may infect the cells of the gastrointestinal tract and cause an enteropathy, with diarrhea.

To investigate J.'s intestinal distress, it will be necessary to culture his stool and to examine it microscopically for parasites. If this does not give an answer, it may be necessary to perform more invasive tests.

Mycobacterial and Fungal Infections

J. was found to have esophageal candidiasis and Salmonella *infection, and was treated with resolution of his symptoms. Two months later, he was admitted to hospital with a high fever, cough, and shortness of breath. His x-ray showed a lobar pneumonia, sputum cultures grew* Streptococcus pneumoniae. *He responded very rapidly to penicillin treatment.*

Although *Pneumocystis* is a frequent cause of pneumonia in AIDS patients, other causes must be considered, such as pneumococci, *Haemophilus influenzae*, and enteric Gram-negative rods. Tuberculosis is another important cause of pneumonia in AIDS, and it may disseminate widely to cause lymphadenitis, hepatitis, or meningitis.

Although most opportunistic infections occur at a time of severe immunodeficiency, tuberculosis is an exception and may occur earlier, when the immune function of AIDS patients is only mildly impaired (i.e., in the "asymptomatic" phase). Consequently, HIV infection should be considered in the event of pulmonary tuberculosis in previously healthy young adults or adolescents. Infected patients can easily spread tuberculosis to household and other close contacts. Indeed, the rise in incidence of tuberculosis in the U.S. that began in the late 1980s can be attributed to a large extent to the spread of tuberculosis among HIV-infected persons and their close contacts.

Disseminated infection with the *Mycobacterium-avium* complex, is also common in AIDS. Although this organism may cause pneumonia, it more typically causes disseminated disease and particularly infects the lymph-reticular organs and the gastrointestinal tract. Typically, patients develop fever, night sweats, weight loss, and enlarged livers and spleens. Some also develop diarrhea. Very similar symptoms are seen in patients with disseminated fungal infection, such as histoplasmosis, which is common in patients from the midwestern U.S. and Latin America. Disseminated coccidioidomycosis is found in patients from the southwestern U.S.

Infections of the Nervous System

After the episode of pneumonia, J. returned to work. Four months later, he developed high fever and a new headache. He went to his doctor's office and although his examination was normal, his doctor recommended a spinal tap. This showed a normal cell count, normal glucose and protein, but an India ink smear of cerebrospinal fluid showed it to be packed with Cryptococcus neoformans. *J. responded well to antifungal treatment.*

Opportunistic infections may also cause neurological problems in AIDS patients. Fever and headache are the most common presentations of infection with the fungus, *Cryptococcus neoformans*, which typically causes meningitis. J.'s case illustrates one of the major problems of treating such infections in a patient with AIDS. His spinal fluid is teeming with fungi, yet because of his immune defect, he is unable to mount a very effective inflammatory response (thus his normal cell count, glucose, and protein).

Other opportunistic infections can affect the brain. Reactivation of infection with the parasite, *Toxoplasma gondii*, typically causes a brain abscess. Such patients may present with headache, confusion, or seizures. Infection with another virus, the JC papovavirus, causes a progressive and fatal encephalopathy. CMV causes retinitis, and occasionally encephalitis.

Infections by HIV Itself

J. became increasingly concerned about his weight loss. In fact, when his records were reviewed, his weight loss over the previous year was impressive—90 lb, although he currently felt he was eating fairly well. He also noted fevers and night sweats as an increasing problem and was having intermittent bouts of severe diarrhea.

What J. is experiencing is progressive AIDS. HIV itself can directly affect many organs of the body, such as the intestine and the kidney. HIV nephropathy is manifested by proteinuria, the nephrotic syndrome, and kidney failure, and may respond to antiretroviral therapy. Myopathy and myositis both occur and may be related to HIV infection or to the effects of drug therapy. A cardiomyopathy also occurs. One of the most distressing features of late AIDS is a wasting syndrome that is characterized by profound weight loss with concomitant loss of muscle mass. This usually portends an early demise.

Oncological Manifestations in Advanced AIDS

Later, J. returned to his physician having noted the development of several purple-red skin lesions on his legs and trunk. These are biopsied and Kaposi's sarcoma is diagnosed.

It is important to realize that the illnesses we associate with AIDS are changing in frequency and importance. As physicians have become more adept in dealing with infections such as *Pneumocystis* pneumonia, other infections (e.g., due to mycobacteria and CMV) have assumed greater importance. So too, have the neurological manifestations of HIV (see below) and malignancies. As patients live longer with profound immunodeficiency, malignancies are seen more frequently. The two most common ones are Kaposi's sarcoma and lymphoma.

There is epidemiological evidence to suggest that Kaposi's sarcoma may be associated with an as yet unidentified infectious agent. It is most commonly seen in male homosexuals with HIV disease. Its occurrence is independent of the underlying immunodepletion, although it behaves more aggressively and is more difficult to treat as the CD_4 lymphocyte count falls. In its mildest form, it may merely cause localized skin disease, without significant morbidity. Severe cases of Kaposi's sarcoma show wide dissemination, involving the lymph nodes, gastrointestinal tract, and lungs, and may be fatal.

Both Hodgkin's disease and non-Hodgkin's lymphoma occur more frequently in HIV-infected patients, with the latter becoming an increasingly important problem. Involvement of the central nervous system is extremely common and is usually associated with very poor prognosis. Epstein-Barr virus has been identified by in situ hybridization in many cases of CNS lymphoma, suggesting a possible role for this virus in the pathogenesis of this tumor.

Neurological Manifestations in Advanced AIDS

J. missed his next two doctor's appointments, and the next time he came to the office he was accompanied by his parents who noticed that he had become more forgetful and withdrawn. They informed the physician that J. was fired from his job because he was constantly late and could not concentrate on tasks. When his physician examined him, he appeared inattentive and, although he knew who and where he was, he had problems remembering simple commands. The physician ordered a CT scan of his head, which showed profound brain atrophy.

Although we have seen that opportunistic infections and lymphomas can involve the nervous system, by far the most common neurological problems are caused by HIV itself. HIV is a lentivirus and, like many other in this group, is neurotropic. Infection of the nervous system occurs very early in the disease, probably soon after exposure. The presence of HIV in the nervous system has been documented by viral culture of brain tissue, in situ hybridization demonstrating viral DNA sequences, and electron micrographic identification of retroviral particles. Within the CNS, the virus resides predominantly in macrophages and cells derived from macrophages.

Manifestations of nervous system involvement may occur at any stage of HIV disease. Acute primary infection may be complicated by aseptic meningitis, encephalitis, myelitis, or inflammatory neuropathies like the Guillain-Barré syndrome. Later in the disease, patients may have peripheral neuropathies, both motor and sensory, or spinal cord syndromes, resembling subacute combined degeneration of the cord. By far the most common form of neurological disease however is HIV-associated encephalopathy, which ultimately will lead to progressive dementia, as in the case of J. In its earliest form, this may consist of generalized mental slowing, difficulty concentrating, and forgetfulness, all of which must be differentiated from the depression that often accompanies HIV infection. In the later stages, patients have profound deficits in cognitive, motor, and sensory functions, and may be totally unable to care for themselves. Computed tomographic (CT) scans of the brain often show considerable atrophy (Fig. 67.2). Severe dementia is almost inevitably fatal.

OUTCOME

Two weeks later, J.'s parents called the physician to tell him that J. died at home that day.

J.'s outcome is typical of the usual course of HIV infection and it appears that most, if not all, HIV-infected individuals will proceed to an inevitable end. Although HIV disease is, as yet, incurable and fatal, its pace shows considerable individual variation. With improved antiretroviral therapy, better survival from opportunistic infection and use of prophylactic antimicrobial therapy, HIV infection is becoming a chronic disease.

GENETIC AND DEVELOPMENTAL PREDISPOSITION TO AIDS

Would this course have differed if the patient had been a woman? Probably not, although some of the indicator diseases may have been different. As mentioned earlier, recurrent vaginal candidiasis is a common and troublesome complaint in HIV-infected women. In addition, there is increasing evidence that human papilloma virus infection may behave more aggressively in women with HIV infection. Consequently, cancer of the uterine cervix may emerge as an important complication.

We do not know if AIDS behaves differently in various ethnic groups. Because most drug therapeutic studies have been done mainly with Caucasian males, we are not certain that treatment is as effective in women or in other ethnic groups. It should be noted that there no indications that drug treatment is ineffective or harmful; thus, no person should be left untreated because they belong to a particular racial group or gender.

HIV infection in children follows a similar course, with progressive immunodeficiency, recurrent opportunistic infections, and neurological involvement. However, the pace of the disease is much more rapid in infants. Transmission is usually vertical (i.e., acquired from the mother) and between 13% and 40% of babies born to HIV-infected mothers will acquire HIV infection. The median time to progression to AIDS for these children is only 2 years and, consequently, their life expectancy is extremely short. In addition to their opportunistic infections, most infants fail to thrive (i.e., have an abnormal growth rate) and many have developmental delays secondary to HIV brain infection. Recurrent bacterial infections (otitis, pneumonia) are common (and related to B-cell dysfunction). However, as with adults, antiretroviral treatment and prophylactic therapy for infection do improve the quality and quantity of life.

MANAGEMENT OF HIV-INFECTED PATIENTS

Management of the HIV-infected patient involves a long-term commitment from all physicians and other members of the health team not only to medical care but also to support and to educate the patient and the family. Patients need to be alerted about symptoms that require prompt medical attention, such as changes in fever pat-

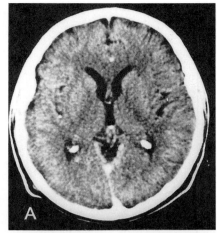
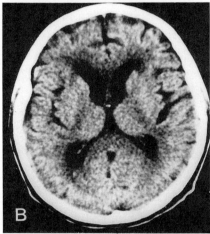

Figure 67.2. Computed tomography of the brain in a patient with AIDS. A. Normal CT scan. **B.** Scan from the same patient 4 months later when he presented with mental slowing and confusion. Note the profound loss of brain substance and consequent enlargement of the fluid-filled ventricles.

terns, or new onsets of cough or headache. Physicians must be prepared to deal with the many complaints that develop, and distinguish those that herald important complications. Patients must be educated about the modes of transmission so that new cases can be prevented. In addition, the members of the health team need to help the patient cope with the changing social dimensions of his disease. Confidentiality and maintenance of employment and insurance benefits are prime concerns. Most patients with AIDS wish to be treated as much as possible at home, with family and friends, all of whom need support and education.

Starting antiretroviral therapy early in the disease (in asymptomatic patients with less than 500 CD_4 lymphocytes/mm³) has been shown to delay the progression of disease. Most antivirals developed to date, such as **azidothymidine**, or **AZT** (zidovudine) and **dideoxyinosine** (didanosine), act by inhibition of reverse transcriptase, the retroviral specific DNA polymerase (see Chapter 37). However, other steps in viral replication, such as viral adherence to target cells and release from infected cells, are potential targets for antiviral agents and candidate therapies based on these strategies are in trial. Cellular enzymes involved in viral synthesis such as proteases, glycosidases, and myristylases are also being considered as possible targets for inhibitors. It is likely that, in a manner analogous to the therapy of tuberculosis, future chemotherapy for HIV will involve combinations of agents acting at different sites to achieve synergism and delay the emergence of resistant viruses.

By far, the best approach to AIDS is prevention. Development of an effective vaccine would eliminate the future threat of this disease. However, the development of an HIV vaccine has been hampered by many problems. One is our incomplete understanding of the host immune response to the virus; although many individuals develop neutralizing antibodies to HIV, their role in vivo is unclear. Thus, circulating antibodies effectively clear the bloodstream of infectious virus yet fail to prevent the progression of HIV infections. In addition, HIV shows great variability in its major antigens (Chapter 37). Finally, the testing of HIV vaccines for protective efficacy will require putting people at risk of infection and, thus, raises major ethical concerns. Even after vaccines are developed and applied, it may be decades before the problem goes away.

Until vaccines are developed, education to reduce transmission of HIV remains the only effective way of tackling its spread. Controversial though it may be, the most effective approach to AIDS prevention is education and the use of measures to reduce sexual spread (such as condoms) and intravenous drug use.

In conclusion, AIDS is a devastating disease that will continue to have a profound effect on society. Scientifically, it has enhanced our understanding of the human immune system. The practice of medicine has been irrevocably changed with the recognition of this new incurable disease. In western societies, the crisis has forced us to face issues such as the economics and inequity of health care delivery, and discrimination in employment and insurance. Despite our recognition of these problems, the sobering truth is that mortality will continue to increase and the devastation due to this virus will continue for the foreseeable future. AIDS will decimate communities in the developing world that lack the resources to treat infected individuals or to prevent further transmission. Little relief is in sight.

SUGGESTED READING

Chaisson RE, Volberding PA. Clinical manifestations of HIV infection. In: Mandell G, Douglas R, Bennett R, eds. Principles and practice of infectious diseases, 3rd ed. New York: Churchill Livingstone, 1990:1059–1092.

De Vita VT, Hellman S, Rosenberg SA, eds. AIDS. Etiology, diagnosis, treatment and prevention, 2nd ed. Philadelphia: JB Lippincott, 1988.

Leoung G, Mills J, eds. Opportunistic infections in patients with the acquired immunodeficiency syndrome. New York: Marcel Dekker, 1989.

Sande MA, Volberding PA, eds. The medical management of AIDS, 2nd ed. Orlando: WB Saunders, 1990.

Congenital and Neonatal Infections

68

Janet R. Gilsdorf

During prenatal life and the first 4 weeks after birth, fetuses and newborn babies are susceptible to a variety of infections that are unique to this period of life. Congenital (also called intrauterine or prenatal) infections are those that occur during fetal life, and are the result of maternal infection that has been transmitted to the fetus. Neonatal infections (those occurring during the first 4 weeks after birth) are generally acquired by the baby from microbial agents present in the environment. Both congenital and neonatal infections are characterized by microorganisms and clinical presentations that are uncommon in older children or adults. Agents such as *Toxoplasma gondii*, cytomegalovirus (CMV), and rubella virus may cause infections that are devastating to the developing fetus, but are relatively minor or asymptomatic in neonates or older infants. Conversely, agents such as *Escherichia coli* and herpes simplex virus cause overwhelming and often fatal infections in neonates, but do not usually infect fetuses, probably because these organisms do not cross the placental barrier.

SPECIAL IMMUNOLOGICAL PROBLEMS OF THE FETUS AND THE PREGNANT MOTHER

The development of the mammalian fetus poses an immunological paradox; the immune systems of the mother and her developing fetus must be modulated to avoid mutual rejection. The fetus is antigenically distinct from its mother, but suppression of certain aspects of the maternal immune system during pregnancy, and the limited number of transplant antigens expressed by the fetal unit (fetus and placenta) act in harmony to prevent maternal rejection of the fetus. In addition, the fetal immune system is not fully mature, thus preventing "graft-versus-host" type of rejection of maternal tissues by the fetus.

The humoral immune responses of the fetus are detectable as early as 2 months of gestation but do not "ripen" until about 2 years of age. "Fetal immunodeficiency" is due to many factors, including the inability of fetal and neonatal mononuclear cells to produce macrophage-activating factors. In the absence of cytokines (such as γ-interferon), neither a cytotoxic proliferative response nor an immune response can be mounted effectively. The fetal immune defect is in the production of cytokines (which act as intercellular signals), and, partially, in the cellular antimicrobial machinery itself. Placental or neonatal macrophages permit the intracellular replication of certain microorganisms (such as *T. gondii*), whereas macrophages from adults kill them. In the mother, cytokines are present in the placental circulation but are not transported to the fetus, where they might activate the immune response of her "graft," i.e., the baby.

The fetus is protected from infection by several special defense mechanisms including the fetal membranes, which shelter it from external microorganisms and the placenta, which protects the fetus from many maternal microorganisms. The mother further protects her fetus with an endowment of considerable quantities of immunoglobulins, largely of the IgG class. At term, the fetal concentration of IgG antibodies may be greater than that of the mother, as the placenta actively transports these molecules into the fetal circulation by a mechanism of receptor-mediated endocytosis. Conversely, a baby born several months prematurely may not have received a full complement of maternal antibodies, which contributes to the increased risk of infection of such babies. IgM does not cross the placenta but may be synthesized by an infant in response to an infection. Maternal IgG is slowly metabolized by the newborn infant; some maternal antibodies, such as those against bacterial polysaccharides, are undetectable in the infant's serum 2–4 months after birth whereas other antibodies, such as those against measles and HIV, may persist for as long as 12–15 months. In addition, breast milk contains IgA antibodies that appear to protect nursing infants against certain gastrointestinal pathogens.

PRENATALLY ACQUIRED INFECTIONS

Case

Baby L. was born at 37 weeks' gestation, following an uneventful pregnancy to a 28-year-old healthy mother. His two siblings had been born with no difficulties and are healthy at ages 2 and 4 years. On physical examination about 30 minutes postdelivery, the the baby was found to weigh 3 kg (3rd percentile for a term baby) and to have a head circumference of 38 cm (well below the 3rd percentile for a term baby). He was somewhat pale and had numerous purplish spots that were nonblanching on his trunk, back, face, and all four extremities. His vital signs were stable and his cardiopulmonary examination was unremarkable. Abdominal examination revealed enlarged liver and spleen. The urine from this baby grew CMV on viral culture, thus establishing the diagnosis of congenital CMV infection.

The parents had many questions about their son and his illness. The physician reassured them that they had not done anything that was conducive to the child's illness. On the other hand, no explanation could be given for the fact that this child was sick and the two previous ones normal. The answer to the parent's question: "How could our baby get an infection before he was even born?" requires an understanding of the establishment of intrauterine infections.

Comment

This baby presents clinical signs and symptoms typical of prenatal infections, including signs of poor intrauterine growth and evidence of multisystem disease (including microcephaly, a rash compatible with thrombocytopenia, and hepatosplenomegaly). Notably, the symptoms of this infection were present at the time of birth. Also characteristic of many intrauterine infections is the fact that the mother was asymptomatic during her pregnancy.

Microbial Agents

A variety of microbial agents can infect the human fetus, including bacteria, viruses, and parasites (Table 68.1). The bacterial agents that

Table 68.1 Infectious Agents Causing Congenital Intrauterine Disease

	Persistent Postnatal Infection	Teratogenic	Trimester of Greatest Impact on Fetus		
			1st	2nd	3rd
Bacteria					
Treponema pallidum	+	−	−	+	+
Mycobacterium tuberculosis	−	−	−	+	
Viruses					
Cytomegalovirus	+	+		?	
Rubella	+	+	++	+	−
Varicella zoster	+	+	+	−	+
Parvovirus B19	−	−	+	+	−
Herpes simplex	+	−	+	+	+
?HIV	+	?		?	
Protozoa					
Toxoplasma gondii	+	−	+	+	−

actively infect fetuses are the spirochete of syphilis, _Treponema pallidum_, and _Mycobacterium tuberculosis_. A number of viruses may infect human fetuses, and those with the highest morbidity and mortality to the fetus are rubella virus and CMV. Varicella virus, parvovirus, and possibly, human immunodeficiency virus (HIV) also occasionally infect the fetus but result in different clinical pictures from the classical intrauterine infection as described in the case. One parasite, _T. gondii_, is also an important intrauterine pathogen.

Although many other infectious agents not directly infect the fetus, maternal illness may indirectly affect the outcome of pregnancy. For example, maternal Gram-negative bacterial infections (typhoid fever, septicemia, or urinary tract infection), malaria, or measles may result in abortion, stillbirth, or premature delivery because of hypoxia, high fever, or other metabolic abnormalities in the mother.

ENTRY AND ENCOUNTER

During pregnancy, mothers may become infected with agents that invade the blood and, thus, possibly infect the fetus. For example, pregnant women may acquire syphilis, herpes simplex virus, or CMV by sexual transmission. Mothers may also be infected by person-to-person or air-borne transmission of _M. tuberculosis_, varicella, rubella, and CMV. Fomites in the environment may harbor microbial agents that may infect a pregnant mother; e.g., toxoplasmosis cysts are present in the feces of cats and in raw meat.

Entry of microorganisms into a fetus takes place in one of two ways: (_a_) through amniotic leaks that allow direct access of organisms from the vaginal tract—such leaks develop rarely and only late in pregnancy; (_b_) from the mother's blood—organisms using this route encounter a variety of host defense factors in the placenta, including the villous trophoblasts, tissue macrophages, and locally produced immune factors such as antibodies or lymphokines. When infection of the placenta occurs, it may or may not progress to fetal infection (Fig. 68.1), depending on the infecting agent and the integrity of the placental defenses.

Timing of the maternal infection is an important determinant of fetal infection and outcome. For unknown reasons, _T. pallidum_ and _M._

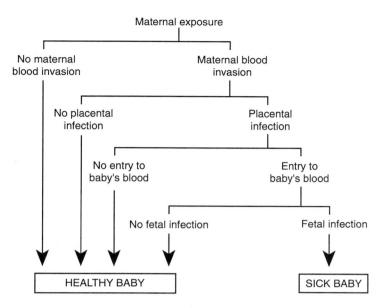

tuberculosis appear incapable of traversing the placental barrier before about 26 weeks of pregnancy. On the other hand, *T. gondii*, CMV, rubella virus, and parvovirus can infect the fetus during the first trimester, when the impact on fetal development is greatest. Infection late in pregnancy with these organisms has usually no adverse effects on the baby. Varicella zoster infection may, on rare occasions, have teratogenic effects, but only if the mother is infected during the first or early second trimester. However, when maternal varicella infections occur within 5 days of delivery, the baby is at high risk of serious, overwhelming infection because the virus will readily cross the placenta and the baby will be born before protective maternal antibodies are made. In this circumstance, the newborn is treated with antivaricella zoster immune globulin to try to prevent severe infection.

DAMAGE

Three types of effects on the growing and developing fetus may result from intrauterine infection.

- One is the interference with normal organogenesis, which may result in structural abnormalities in tissues and organs. Thus, congenital rubella may result in cataracts and pigmentary defects of the retina, patent ductus arteriosus, pulmonary artery stenosis, pulmonary valvular stenosis of the heart, or sensorineural deafness. The types and extent of teratogenic effects on the fetus are highly dependent on the time during gestation of maternal infection. Specific fetal tissues, such as the eyes and heart, are most susceptible to viral damage during very discrete periods of organogenesis in the first half of pregnancy.

- The second effect on the developing fetus results from the inflammatory reaction in response to tissue infection. For example, congenital CMV or toxoplasmosis infections result in cerebritis, which subsequently may lead to cerebral atrophy and intracranial calcifications.

- The third effect relates to placental insufficiency due to placental infection. Inflammation and fibrosis associated with placental infection may compromise normal growth and development of the baby, leading to low birth weight, premature birth, or fetal death.

Although the damage to fetal cells and organs occurs prenatally at the time of the infection, the effects of the damage may not become clinically apparent until several months after birth. For example, deafness or mental retardation as a result of congenital rubella or CMV infection will not be manifested clinically until children have reached an age in which language and other cognitive skills can be evaluated. In addition, certain tissue damage continues after birth in some congenital infections (such as rubella, CMV, and untreated syphilis) as the microbes continue to replicate even after delivery.

DIAGNOSIS

Exposure of a mother to a potentially damaging infectious agent during pregnancy warrants attempts to document firmly the presence of an infection, because this information may be important in deciding for or against termination of the pregnancy. During pregnancy, detection of either IgM antibodies specific for the microbial agent or a changing titer of specific IgG antibodies in the mother's serum may be helpful in diagnosing congenital toxoplasmosis, CMV, congenital rubella, or syphilis.

In an ill neonate, such as the one presented in the case history, an attempt should be made to identify the presence of an infecting agent in various tissue specimens or body fluids. Urine, buffy coat, or cerebral spinal fluid specimens should be cultured for the presence of CMV, and nasopharyngeal specimens, urine, buffy coat and cerebral spinal fluid should be cultured for the presence of rubella virus. Techniques for culturing *Toxoplasma* and *T. pallidum* are not available in routine diagnostic laboratories. Dark-field examination of material from the base of an oral or skin lesion may reveal the presence of *T. pallidum*, and an immunoassay may identify CMV or *T. pallidum* antigens in tissue specimens.

Because culture techniques either are not available or require a number of days before an agent is isolated, the diagnosis of congenital infection may rely on evidence of the immune response in the baby. Because IgG antibodies are readily passed through, and sometimes concentrated by, the placenta, finding such antibodies in the baby is not, by itself, diagnostic of intrauterine infection. Maternal IgG antibodies cannot be distinguished from those that would be produced by a congenitally infected newborn. Maternal IgM antibodies, on the other hand, do not readily cross the placenta; thus, the presence of CMV, rubella virus, or *Toxoplasma* specific IgM antibodies in a baby strongly suggests that the baby has been infected and is generating his own immune response.

The interpretation of serological data in newborns may be complicated by maternal-fetal blood transfusion, or by suppressing the fetal production of antibodies by the infectious process itself. A useful way to diagnose congenital infections retrospectively using serology is to monitor the antibody titer in the baby over several months. Because the half-life of maternal IgG is approximately 20 days, most of the maternal IgG will have been degraded after several months, and any IgG detectable in the baby is most likely to be of infant origin. Thus, in the congenitally infected baby, IgG antibodies will remain or increase in titer over time, whereas in an uninfected baby, specific antibodies of maternal origin will eventually disappear.

TREATMENT

The availability and success of treatment for congenitally acquired infections varies with the infectious agent. Penicillin G is very effective in treating congenital syphilis. If syphilis is detected before delivery, penicillin given to the mother will be readily delivered through the placenta to the fetus and the infection will be adequately treated. Infants infected with *Toxoplasma* have been successfully treated with combination of pyrimethimine and sulfadiazine, although the optimal dosage and duration of therapy remain uncertain. Presently, no treatment is available for congenital rubella or CMV. The recent development of new antiviral agents with apparent improved efficacy against CMV in immunocompromised individuals suggests that, in the future, effective antimicrobial agents against CMV may become available.

PREVENTION

Prevention of congenital infections depends on assuring excellent health of the mother. Appropriate immunization during childhood (or postpartum in nonimmune mothers) will protect a mother and her baby against rubella. Similarly, immunization of individuals living in endemic areas against *M. tuberculosis* with BCG vaccine may protect some mothers and babies against tuberculosis. Routine prenatal examination will reveal syphilis or tuberculosis in infected mothers, and adequate treatment of the mother will prevent ongoing infection in her baby. Good hygiene practices that include appropriate handwashing may protect susceptible pregnant mothers from primary toxoplasmosis infection after exposure to cat feces containing *T. gondii* cysts or from primary CMV infection after exposure to young children (who frequently excrete CMV). Adequate cooking of meat will prevent ingestion of *Toxoplasma* cysts.

PERINATALLY ACQUIRED INFECTION

Case

C.C. is a 14-day-old baby brought to the emergency room with a 24-hour history of fever to 38.9°C, poor feeding, lethargy, and irritability. The baby was born at term to a 22 year-old mother following an uneventful pregnancy. C.C. was discharged home with his mother 24 hours after delivery and has reportedly been doing well at home until the previous day, when the mother had to wake the baby for feeding. The baby then nursed only weakly and only for a short period of time.

Work-up in the emergency room revealed a high peripheral white blood cell count (24,000/mm³ with 68% segmented, 20% bands, and 12% lymphocytes). Examination of the cerebrospinal fluid revealed the presence of 230 white blood cells, 90% of which were neutrophils, suggestive of an acute bacterial infection. The cerebrospinal fluid had an elevated protein content (83 g/dl), and a low glucose concentration (20 mg/dl with a concomitant serum glucose of 80 mg/dl—see Chapter 58 for a detailed explanation of these findings), also in keeping with a bacterial infection. A Gram stain of the cerebrospinal fluid showed Gram-positive cocci in chains, and the culture grew group B β-hemolytic streptococci (Streptococcus agalactiae). The baby was given penicillin G and gentamicin as initial therapy. After a rocky hospital course characterized by apneic spells, seizures, and, later, poor feeding, the baby was sent home following a 21-day course of antibiotic therapy. At age 8 months, he was delayed in achieving appropriate developmental milestones.

This baby was apparently healthy and normal at birth and developed acute symptoms suggestive of infection at age of 2 weeks. Thus, the infection was most likely acquired after birth rather than before it. The presence of an inflammatory reaction in the cerebrospinal fluid suggests that this baby is suffering from bacterial meningitis, which is one of the more frequent kinds of severe perinatally acquired infections.

Comment

Unlike many other animal species, human infants at birth are incomplete in many aspects of their development, and possess an immature immune system. The newborn is supplied by the mother with antibodies from the circulation and with protective factors in breast milk. Breast milk contains IgA type antibodies, white blood cells, and lysozyme. The growth of Gram-negative enteric bacteria in the intestinal tract is suppressed in breast-fed babies, possibly by the growth of Gram-positive lactobacilli and perhaps by presence of the iron-sequestering protein, lactoferrin. Epidemiological studies in India, for example, have shown that low birth weight babies fed breast milk developed fewer infections than those who were formula fed.

Although neonates have maternal antibodies, they are obviously not protected against organisms to which their mothers have not generated an immune response. In addition, their humoral immune system is immature; for example, they are unable to generate antibodies against certain types of antigens, particularly polysaccharides. Also, their cellular immune system is suppressed as evidenced by decreased natural killed (NK) cytotoxicity and antibody-dependent cell-mediated cytotoxicity (ADCC), and their phagocytic cells show decreased function. Thus, otherwise normal healthy neonates are, to some extent, immunocompromised (Table 68.2). The risk of infection is even greater in premature babies because their immune systems are more immature and their care sometimes requires procedures that invade the skin and mucous membrane barriers, such as intravenous lines, chest tubes, endotracheal tubes, etc.

This is a difficult period in life and the risks to the neonate are great indeed. Without proper attention to sanitary measures such as good handwashing, bathing with clean water, and sterile milk, the rate of infant mortality can be prodigious. The expectation that most babies will survive the first few years of life is of recent origin even in developed countries, and has yet to be realized in many of the developing ones.

Microbial Agent

The most common types of bacteria that cause perinatally acquired infections are present in the maternal vaginal tract and include *E. coli*, group B β-hemolytic streptococci, *Listeria monocytogenes*, and *Haemophilus influenzae*. Other bacteria that are present in the baby's postnatal environment may also cause neonatal infection, and include other Gram-negative enteric bacilli, *S. aureus*, *M. tuberculosis*, or coagulase-negative staphylococci.

Several viruses are unique in their predilection for neonates. Herpes simplex virus, most commonly type 2, can cause serious multiorgan system infection that may clinically resemble acute bacterial sepsis. Perinatal transmission of varicella zoster virus or enteroviruses may also result in overwhelming infection with multiorgan failure. Human immunodeficiency virus (HIV) may be transmitted perinatally, although infected babies are usually asymptomatic during the neonatal period. Hepatitis B virus is frequently transmitted perinatally from a carrier mother to her baby. However, neonates infected with hepatitis

B virus are generally asymptomatic and when symptoms do develop, they occur following the usual 2- to 3-month incubation period.

Fungal infections with *Candida albicans* as well as with other *Candida* species play an increasingly important role in infections of sick, hospitalized neonates, especially prematurely born babies. Parasites are not an important cause of neonatally acquired infections in the U.S., as neonates are seldom exposed to the environmental conditions required for transmission. *Chlamydia trachomatis* and *Neisseria gonorrhoeae* may infect the respiratory (including ocular) mucous membranes during birth, and may cause neonatal conjunctivitis.

Although the baby described in the case was infected with group B streptococci, his clinical presentation was identical to that of babies with meningitis caused by other bacterial pathogens.

ENTRY AND ENCOUNTER

Babies come in contact with the agents causing perinatal infections in various ways. The bacterial agents causing neonatal sepsis, such as *E. coli*, group B streptococci, *Listeria monocytogenes*, and *Haemophilus influenzae* all normally colonize the maternal vaginal tract. During vaginal delivery, the skin and mucous membranes of the infant are exposed to these bacteria. Within the first 24–48 hours after birth, babies become colonized with these organisms, particularly on their nasopharynx, skin, and around the umbilical stump. Colonization of the neonatal gastrointestinal tract occurs more slowly. Babies may also be exposed at the time of delivery to blood-borne agents that do not readily cross the placenta. This seems to be the most common mechanism of perinatal acquisition of hepatitis B virus and HIV.

A variety of environmental hazards also promotes the invasion of the human neonates by bacteria and fungi (Table 68.2). During labor, many infants are monitored for evidence of fetal distress by the application of monitoring devices to the fetal scalp as it presents in the vaginal tract. This procedure may allow access of skin organisms to the baby's blood. In addition, after the umbilical cord is severed, the healing stump provides a potential route for bacterial invasion. Many prematurely born newborns require intensive medical support such as intratracheal intubation with artificial ventilation, alimentation, and antibiotic therapy through intravenous lines, and a variety of other therapeutic or diagnostic procedures that are invasive to the otherwise protective barriers of the skin and mucous membranes.

DAMAGE

The effect of perinatally acquired infections on the neonate is extremely variable and depends on the type of organism, the organ or organ systems infected, and the degree of relative immunosuppression of the baby. However, the early clinical manifestations of infections in neonates are nonspecific, and include poor feeding, lethargy, or irri-

Table 68.2. Factors that Place Newborn Infants at Increased Risk of Infection

Primary (inherent)
1. Immature host defenses
2. Naive, inexperienced immune system

Secondary (environmental)
1. Hospital environment exposes them to drug-resistant pathogenic organisms
2. Medical intervention invades protective barriers of skin and mucous membranes

tability. The outcome often depends on the speed with which antimicrobial and supportive therapy are initiated. For example, without appropriate antibiotic therapy, bacterial sepsis or meningitis can proceed to severe neonatal illness or death within 12–24 hours. Even with timely, appropriate antibiotic therapy, the mortality of neonatal sepsis is between 25% and 40%, and significant neurological sequelae are seen in 20–50% of survivors of neonatal meningitis.

The extent of involvement and the morbidity of perinatally acquired infections varies greatly from baby to baby. Herpes simplex infection may involve a single organ such as the skin, with cutaneous vesicles being the only sign of infection, or it may be a serious multiorgan systemic infection involving the liver, central nervous system, lungs, and skin, ultimately resulting in severe brain damage or death. In contrast, hepatitis B is generally asymptomatic in the neonates but neonates infected with hepatitis B virus are at extremely high risk (more than 90%) of becoming chronic carriers of hepatitis B and, as young adults, are at risk for hepatic cirrhosis or hepatocellular carcinoma.

DIAGNOSIS

Diagnosis of a perinatally acquired infection depends on the recognition of suggestive signs and symptoms. Fever, poor feeding, lethargy, or irritability may be the only presenting sign and symptom of neonatal septicemia and/or meningitis, and may be very subtle. Thus, the possibility of perinatal infection needs to be considered in neonates exhibiting even these nonspecific symptoms. Other, more specific symptoms, such as conjunctivitis or skin rash, may suggest a more focal infectious process.

Diagnosis is firmly established by the isolation of an etiological agent from potentially infected body sites. However, the causative agents may not always be detected by culturing, either because of antimicrobial therapy given before collection of specimens or because specimens likely to reveal the organism cannot easily be obtained (such as lung, liver, or brain biopsy specimens). Detection of viral or bacterial antigens in serum, urine, or cerebrospinal fluid in these situations may reveal the causative agent. Antigen detection is routinely available for group B streptococci, *E. coli* K1 (which cross-reacts with the group B capsule of *Neisseria meningitidis*), HIV, and hepatitis B virus. In situations such as neonatal herpes simplex infections, for which viral culture is usually difficult or nonrewarding and antigen detection probes are not readily available, the diagnosis may be supported by detection of an immune response in the baby, either by evidence of antigen-specific IgM antibodies or a rise in antigen-specific IgG antibody.

TREATMENT

Successful treatment of perinatally infected babies depends on the type of microbial agent, on the availability of the specific antimicrobial therapy, and on the rapidity with which appropriate therapy is instituted. A variety of very effective and relatively safe antimicrobial agents are available for the treatment of neonatal septicemia due to *E. coli*, *H. influenzae*, group B streptococci, and *L. monocytogenes*. In addition, antifungal agents are quite effective in treating fungal infections. The antiviral agent acyclovir has been shown to be effective in treating neonates with herpes simplex virus infections. In general, the efficacy of treatment and the outcome are improved with early initiation of treatment. The dosing levels and dosing intervals of drugs differ in neonates from those in older children or adults because neonates have decreased renal and hepatic elimination of most drugs and increased volumes of distribution of many drugs.

PREVENTION

Because prematurely born infants are at greater risk of perinatal infection than full-term neonates, prevention of premature delivery prevents a significant number of neonatal infections. Prematurely born babies require sometimes prolonged hospital care and invasive medical interventions; therefore, strict attention to infection control practices in the care of ill neonates (e.g., handwashing and equipment decontamination) also decreases the risk of neonatal infection.

SUGGESTED READING

McCracken GH Jr, Freij BJ. Infectious diseases of the fetus and newborn. In: Feigin RD, Cherry , eds. Textbook of pediatric infectious diseases. Philadelphia: WB Saunders, 1987.

Remington JS, Klein JD, eds. Infectious diseases of the fetus and newborn infant. Philadelphia: WB Saunders, 1990.

Zoonoses 69

Victor L. Yu

Diseases that are transmitted from animals to humans are called **zoonoses** or **zoonotic diseases**. They are difficult to control because the existence of an animal reservoir makes it hard to eliminate them. Consider, for example, the problems involved in controlling rodents in the deserts of the southwestern U.S. that are infected with the plague, or large herds of wildebeest that carry sleeping sickness in Central Africa. Animal-related diseases have caused untold damage to people in the past, and continue to be of enormous concern, especially in tropical areas of the world.

Zoonoses are defined as those infectious diseases that are naturally transmitted between vertebrate animals and humans. The word is derived from the Greek, "zoon," meaning animal, and "nosos," meaning disease. The persons at greatest risk of acquiring zoonoses are, of course, those who work in close proximity to animals, such as farmers, veterinarians, slaughterhouse workers, and animal researchers. The most common sources of zoonotic diseases are domestic animals, namely pets and farm animals. Over 100 million cats and dogs are kept as pets in the U.S., and over 30 human diseases can be acquired from them, although each is rare.

With the international movement of animals, importation of zoonotic diseases from one geographic locale to another takes place with increasing frequency. For example, Marburg virus disease was first documented in laboratory workers in Germany after they had contact with monkeys imported from Africa for use in vaccine research.

Adaptation to a host is basic to the survival of many microorganisms. Prolonged interaction between the host and individual microbial species results in a balanced relationship that allows both to survive. In some cases of zoonoses, the pathogenic organism is part of the commensal flora of the animal (for example, organisms associated with animal bites). In most cases, the animals involved show no apparent disease despite carriage of the organism (for example, histoplasmosis in birds). In diseases associated with arthropod vectors, abnormal physiology or behavior by the arthropod is rarely demonstrable despite carriage of an infecting organism. On the other hand, if the organism invades previously unexposed animal or human populations, infections may be extraordinarily destructive because evolutionary host defenses have not had sufficient time to develop. If, in addition, the social situation and ignorance of the presence of the microorganism leads to a situation in which transmission of the organism is unimpeded, explosive epidemics can ensue. Outbreaks of plague and histoplasmosis are examples.

Many organisms have become adapted to specific hosts. For example, individual species of *Brucella*, the etiological agent of brucellosis, prefer different mammalian hosts; *Brucella melitensis* infects sheep and goats, *B. abortus* infects cattle, *B. suis* infects pigs, *B. canis* infects dogs, and *B. rangiferi tarandi* infects reindeer.

ENCOUNTER

Transmission of zoonotic agents from animals to humans has two scenarios: (*a*) people are "**dead-end hosts,**" accidental intruders in an animal-to-animal chain and cannot transmit the agent further; (*b*) **people may transmit** an agent acquired from animals to other people and/or animals.

In the second scenario, the organisms go from animals to humans and from them to other humans or even to other animals. The route of transmission may change in the process. For instance, plague bacilli enter the human body via flea bites, multiply, and may then go from person to person by inhalation of droplets produced by the cough of patients. Similarly, the virus of Korean hemorrhagic fever may be acquired by eating food contaminated with the excreta of rodents, but can then spread by the respiratory route. In salmonellosis, the organisms enter humans by the ingestion of contaminated animal products and can then spread via the fecal-oral route to other people.

The **pathogenesis of zoonotic diseases** in the animal reservoir often helps one understand the nuances of their transmission to humans. The most successful organisms are those that cause an indolent, low-grade disease in the animal, but which are easily spread. They present great problems to the control of zoonotic diseases. An example is leptospirosis, a chronic, often asymptomatic infection of rats and domestic animals, especially dogs. The organisms multiply in the kidney tubules and are excreted in the urine. The disease can then be acquired by people who come in contact with contaminated urine, e.g., by swimming in an irrigation ditch. Similarly, cows infected with tuberculosis can shed the tubercle bacilli in their milk without undue signs of disease. In all of these cases, the animals have become shedders, because the agents have the ability to persist for long periods of time. Persistence is sometimes due to localization of the organisms at sheltered sites. Such sites are the kidney tubules in the case of *Leptospira* or the mammary glands for *Brucella*.

ENTRY

The zoonoses illustrate the diverse ways that microorganisms gain access to the human host, in this case, from animal reservoirs. The basic modes of entry are **penetration of the skin, inhalation, and ingestion.** Few microorganisms can penetrate the skin or mucous membrane directly, nor can they all traverse the distance between hosts. But evolutionary innovations have overcome these physical and biological barriers. Many organisms use an intermediary **vector** that can serve both the function of delivery and entry. For example, a tsetse fly that carries the trypanosomes of sleeping sickness bridges the distance between infected cattle and people, introducing the organisms when it bites.

In zoonoses transmitted by **arthropod vectors**, the microorganisms may undergo developmental changes within the vectors. Particularly elaborate examples are seen in the protozoa of malaria or sleeping sickness. In other zoonoses, developmental changes take place within a vertebrate host, as in the case of tapeworms and other metazoan parasites. Finally, organisms involved in yet other zoonoses carry out developmental changes in the external environment, such as soil, bodies of water, food, or plants. For example, hookworm eggs hatch in soil and the larvae simply wait for a mammalian host.

The diversity of modes of transmission is well illustrated with a group of related diseases, the viral hemorrhagic fevers. These illnesses are found in tropical climates and have similar clinical manifestations; they include Lassa fever, Marburg virus disease, and Crimean-Congo hemorrhagic fever. In all three of these diseases, the infection can be transmitted from person to person by direct contact. What is intriguing is how these viruses reach the human host from their animal reservoir. The Lassa virus is frequently present in mice and is transmitted to humans by ingestion of foodstuff contaminated with their urine. The Marburg virus is transmitted from monkeys to humans by direct contact. Finally, the Crimean-Congo hemorrhagic fever virus is transmitted from domestic animals to humans via tick bites.

Penetration Through the Skin

The epidermis of the skin may be breached in a number of ways to permit entry of microorganisms. One obvious mechanism is direct entry through minute **abrasions** or open **wounds** (Table 69.1). The organisms themselves may facilitate penetration of the skin. For instance, the fungi that cause athlete's foot produce an enzyme that hydrolyzes

Table 69.1. Direct Skin Penetration

Disease	Organism Name	Group	Animal	Alternative Portals
Bacteria				
Anthrax spore former	Bacillus anthracis (herbivores)	Gram-positive aerobic bacteria	Domestic mammals	Inhalation, ingestion
Brucellosis	Brucella melitensis B. abortus B. suis B. canis	Gram-negative rods	Goats, sheep Cattle Swine Dogs	Inhalation, ingestion
Erysipeloid	Erysipelothrix rhusiopathiae	Gram-positive rods	Swine, poultry, fish	
Leptospirosis	Leptospira interrogans	Spirochete	Rodents, foxes, domestic animals	Ingestion
Melioidosis	Pseudomonas pseudomallei	Gram-negative rods	Rodents	Ingestion
Glanders	Pseudomonas mallei	Gram-negative rods	Equines, domestic mammals	Inhalation
Tularemia	Francisella tularensis	Gram-negative rods	Rabbits, rodents	Inhalation, ingestion, arthropod vector
Viruses				
Foot and mouth disease	Aphthovirus	Picornavirus family	Cattle	
Orf (contagious ecthyma)	Parapox virus	Poxvirus family	Sheep, goats	
Vesicular stomatitis	Vesicular stomatitis	Rhabdovirus family	Cattle, horses	
Parasite				
Cutaneous larva migrans (creeping eruption)	Ancylostoma caninum (dog hookworm) Ancylostoma braziliense (dog and cat hookworm)	Nematode Nematode		Dogs, cats, carnivores
Fungi				
Dermatophytes	Zoophilic trichophytons, microsporums	Fungi	Dogs, cats, cattle	
Miscellaneous				
Cat scratch fever	Rochalimaea	Gram-negative rods	Cats, dogs suspected	Animal bite

the keratin of the stratum corneum, whereas hookworms have "teeth" that allow them to chew their way through the epidermis. Microorganisms may also gain entry via arthropod vectors by sting or bite (Table 69.2). Finally, animals themselves may neatly solve the problem of entry by biting the victim (Table 69.3).

The anatomic sites that are usually penetrated by infectious agents are not only those that come in contact with the organisms, but also those that are more likely to experience abrasions or wounds. Thus, exposed extremities tend to be sites of infection in erysipeloid, anthrax, and cat scratch fever.

ARTHROPOD VECTORS

This fascinating mode of transmission is the most complex because it requires living intermediaries. Some function as "flying syringes"

Table 69.2. Arthropod Vectors

Disease	Vector	Organism	Microbial Group	Animal Reservoir	Alternative Portals
Bacteria					
Lyme disease	Tick	*Borrelia burgdorferi*	Spirochete	Rodents, deer	
Plague—bubonic	Flea	*Yersinia pestis*	Gram-negative rods	Urban rats, rodents	Skin penetration
Relapsing fever	Tick	*Borrelia* species	Spirochete	Rodent, wild mammals	
Tularemia	Tick, biting flies	*Francisella tularensis*	Gram-negative rods	Rodents, wild mammals, birds	Inhalation, ingestion, skin penetration
Rocky Mountain Spotted fever	Tick	*Rickettsia rickettsii*	Rickettsia	Wild rodents, dogs	
Scrub typhus	Mite (chigger)	*Rickettsia tsutsugamushi*	Rickettsia	Wild rodents, rats	
Murine typhus	Flea	*Rickettsia typhi*	Rickettsia	Rats	
Rickettsialpox	Mite	*Rickettsia akari*	Rickettsia	Mice	
Ehrlichiosis	Ticks	*Ehrlichia canis*	Ehrlichia	Canines, especially dogs	
Viruses					
Yellow Fever	Mosquito	Flavivirus	Togavirus family	Primates	
Encephalitis Eastern equine Western equine Venezuelan equine	Mosquito	Alphavirus	Togavirus family	Birds, horses	
St. Louis	Mosquito	Flavivirus	Togavirus family	Birds	
California	Mosquito	Bunyavirus	Bunyavirus family	Mammals, wild rodents	
Rift Valley fever	Mosquito	Bunyavirus	Bunyavirus family	Sheep, goats, cattle	
Crimean-Congo hemorrhagic fever	Tick	Bunyavirus	Bunyavirus family	Domestic mammals, rodents	
Colorado tick fever	Tick	Orbivirus	Reovirus family	Rodents	
Protozoa					
Babesiosis	Tick	*Babesia* species		Domestic and wild animals	
Leishmaniasis (Kala-azar, cutaneous Leishmaniasis)	Sandfly	*Leishmania* species		Dogs, foxes, rodents, wild mammals	
American trypanosomiasis	Reduviid bug (kissing bug)	*Trypanosoma cruzi*		Dogs, cats, opossums, armadillos, wild mammals	
African-sleeping sickness	Tsetse fly	*Trypanosoma* species		Reptiles, cattle, wild animals	

Table 69.3. Animal Bite

Disease	Organism Name	Group	Animal	Alternative Portal
Bacteria				
Pasteurellosis	*Pasteurella multocida*	Gram neg rod	Dogs, cats, birds, and wild mammals	Skin penetration
Rat bite fever	*Spirillum minor*	Spirilla	Rats, mice, cats	Skin penetration, ingestion
	Streptobacillus moniliformis	Gram-negative rods	Rats, rodents, turkeys	
"DF-2"	*Capnocytophaga canimorsus*	Gram-negative rods	Dogs	
Viruses				
Rabies	Rabies virus	Rhabdovirus	Domestic mammals, skunks, foxes, opossums, bats, cattle	
Herpes B encephalomyelitis	Herpesvirus simiae (Monkey Pox virus)	Herpes virus	Monkeys	
Fungi				
Blastomycosis	*Blastomyces dermatitidis*	Dimorphic fungi	Dogs	

(mosquitoes or biting flies), whereas others jump (fleas), or crawl (ticks or mites) (see Table 69.2). Transmission by arthropod vectors can be either mechanical or biological. In mechanical transmission, the vector simply transports the transmission. Biting flies, for instance, often serve as mechanical vectors. After feeding on an infected animal, the insect digests the blood meal and contaminates its mouth and feces. When it moves to a human, microorganisms can be transmitted with the next bite. In an even more passive way, insects may transmit diseases without biting, just by contaminating foodstuff with organisms they carry on their legs. *Salmonella* may be transported in this manner by house flies that picked them up from feces of diseased animals.

In biological transmission, part of the developmental cycle of the microorganism must take place within an arthropod vector. This is most often seen with protozoa. For instance, in American trypanosomiasis (Chagas disease), the organisms multiply and pass through developmental stages within reduviid bugs. After these vectors suck blood from the infected animals, the ingested trypanosomes multiply in the gut and transform into flagellar forms. The insect feces are infective. They enter the human host when the insect's feces are deposited at the site of the bite during feeding; the trypanosomes gain access when the host rubs them into the skin while scratching the insect bite.

ANIMAL BITES

Animal bites introduce two kinds of flora into deep tissue; the flora that is present on the skin of the recipient, and, more often, that which is found in the mouth and teeth of the biting animal. Table 69.3 lists the more common pathogens that are transmitted by bites.

The most common pathogen associated with animal bites, especially by cats, is a bacterium, *Pasteurella multocida*, which can cause skin and soft tissue infections at the site of inoculation, and can also cause disseminated infections following invasion into the bloodstream. A condition known as rat-bite fever can be caused by one of two organisms, a Gram-negative called *Streptobacillus moniliformis* or a spirillum, *Spirillum minor*. Both organisms are members of the oropharyngeal flora of rats.

Viral diseases that can be transmitted through animal bites include rabies and a herpes virus of monkeys. The latter is usually transmitted by the bites of monkeys in a zoo or a laboratory. Both of these viruses are present in the saliva of the biting animal and both are neurotropic. They migrate to the central nervous system and cause paralysis, encephalitis, and even respiratory arrest.

Inhalation

Zoonotic microorganisms may be inhaled in two ways: (a) from infected droplets aerosolized from the respiratory tract of animals, as in the case of bovine tuberculosis; or (b) from an inanimate reservoir, generally soil, that had been contaminated with excreta or carcasses of infected animals. Examples are anthrax or Q fever, which are caused by spore-forming organisms that are resistant in the environment. As can logically be expected, the primary clinical manifestation of zoonoses acquired by inhalation is pneumonia (Table 69.4). Disseminated infections occur after invasion of the bloodstream.

Ingestion

Most zoonoses that are acquired by ingestion are caused by bacteria or by animal parasites (Table 69.5). The bacterial diseases are acquired by ingestion of the organisms directly, usually in contaminated foodstuffs. Salmonellosis has emerged as one of the most prevalent zoonotic diseases in the U.S. The reservoir for *Salmonella* includes poultry, eggs, and dairy products. The addition of antibiotics to animal feed has been postulated to increase the virulence and infectivity of the organism in humans.

Animal parasites are usually ingested as ova or cysts. In some cases, these must be activated in the human host as part of the developmental cycle of the parasite. In others, a cyst may contain viable organisms.

CLINICAL MANIFESTATIONS IN HUMAN HOSTS

The clinical manifestations of zoonotic infections generally depend on the **portal of entry**. If the route is inhalation, the primary disease is

Table 69.4. Inhalation

Disease	Organism Name	Group	Animal Reservoir	Inhalant	Alternative Portals
Bacteria					
Anthrax (Woolsorter's disease)	*Bacillus anthracis*	Gram-positive aerobic spore-forming rods	Goats, sheep	Spores from wool, animal hides	Skin penetration
Tuberculosis	*Mycobacterium tuberculosis*	Acid-fast bacillus	Domestic mammals	Contaminated respiratory secretions	
Q fever	*Coxiella burnetii*	Rickettsia	Domestic animals	Soil, fomites, contaminated with animal excretions	
Ornithoses (psittacosis)	*Chlamydia psittaci*	Chlamydia	Parrots, turkeys, birds	Dried excreta from infected birds	
Fungi					
Histoplasmosis	*Histoplasma capsulatum*		Birds, bats	Microconidia from contaminated soil	
Viruses					
Lymphocytic choriomeningitis	Lymphocytic choriomeningitis virus	Arenavirus family	Mice, hamsters, rodents	Infected aerosols	Skin penetration, animal bite

Table 69.5. Ingestion

Disease	Organism Name	Group	Animal	Ingestant (Contaminated Foodstuff)	Alternative Portals
Bacteria					
Brucellosis	*Brucella melitensis* *B. abortus*	Gram-negative rods	Goats, cattle	Dairy products	Skin penetration
Campylobacter infection	*Campylobacter jejuni*	Gram-negative rods	Domestic mammals, fowl	Milk, water, meat, poultry	
Listeriosis	*Listeria monocytogenes*	Gram-positive rods	Domestic mammals, rodents, birds	Vegetables, water, cheese	Skin penetration
Salmonellosis	*Salmonella* species (not typhi)	Gram-negative rods	Fowl, domestic mammals, turtles	Milk, eggs, meat, poultry, shellfish	
Tuberculosis	*Mycobacterium bovis*	Acid-fast bacillus	Cattle	Milk	Inhalation
Virus					
Lassa fever	Arenavirus family		Mouse	Contaminated food	Inhalation
Protozoa					
Giardiasis	*Giardia lamblia*		Wild animals	Cyst in water	
Cryptosporidiosis	*Cryptosporidium*		Calves	Oocyst	
Toxoplasmosis	*Toxoplasma gondii*		Cat	Oocyst from cat feces; tissue cyst from uncooked meat	
Helminths					
Tapeworms	*Taenia saginata*	Cestode	Cattle	Larva (cysticercus) in undercooked beef	
	Taenia solium	Cestode	Pigs	Larva (cysticercus) in undercooked pork; ova in soil	
	Diphyllobothrium latum	Cestode	Fish	Larva in raw fish	
	Echinococcus	Cestode	Dogs, sheep, reindeer, caribou, wolves	Ova	
Anisakiasis	*Anisakis*	Nematode	Marine fish	Larva in undercooked fish	
Trichinosis	*Trichinella spiralis*	Nematode	Pigs, domestic mammals, wild mammals, rodents	Larval cysts	
Visceral larva migrans	*Toxocara canis* (roundworm of dogs)	Nematode	Dog	Ova in soil	

usually pneumonia. If the organisms penetrate the skin, the primary manifestations are cellulitis near the site of entry, often followed by regional lymphadenitis (plague, tularemia, anthrax). The organisms may then disseminate to other tissue via the bloodstream. Ingestion of the organisms leads to early gastrointestinal symptoms and later systemic symptoms following dissemination through the bloodstream. For parasites, the clinical manifestations depend on the target organ favored by the released organism. In cysticercosis, central nervous system dysfunction results from encystment of the larvae in the brain; in trichinosis, myalgias result from the encystment of the larvae in skeletal muscles; in echinococcosis, abdominal pains result from enlarging cysts in the liver; in giardiasis, diarrhea and malabsorption result from invasion of the small intestine by trophozoites; in Lyme disease, neurologic, cardiac, and arthritic symptoms arise from spirochetal invasion of the central nervous system, the heart, and the joints.

All of these points are well illustrated in tularemia, inasmuch as the causative bacillus, *Francisella tularensis*, may enter humans via **multi-**

ple portals. When it penetrates the skin via minute abrasions, a papule develops at the site of entry and later ulcerates. This is followed by regional lymphadenopathy and fever (ulceroglandular form). The organisms can accidentally be inoculated into the skin or the conjunctiva during the skinning of an infected carcass, resulting in symptoms of conjunctivitis and cervical lymphadenopathy (oculoglandular form). The bacteria can also be inhaled as a result of a laboratory accident or via dust contaminated with excretions from infected rodents. The disease is then characterized by pharyngitis, pneumonia, fever, and muscle aches (pneumonic form). The organisms may be transmitted by bites of ticks or flies, resulting in systemic manifestations at various sites. If the portal of entry into the human host differs from that of the animal, the clinical manifestations will differ correspondingly. For example, ornithosis in birds results in diarrhea and systemic signs for the bird because the *Chlamydia* enter via the gastrointestinal tract. In humans, the same organisms cause pneumonia and cough because they usually enter via the respiratory route.

Finally, it should be noted that when an organism has remained in close contact with the host for many generations, clinical symptoms tend to be latent or subacute. For example, lassitude is a cardinal symptom in many parasitic infections.

CONTROL

The control of zoonoses must be approached in a multidisciplinary manner because of the issues regarding the animal reservoir and the mode of transmission of the agents. The measures that must be taken range across human and veterinary medicine, sanitary engineering, and, in some instances, entomology and wildlife zoology. Some appropriate interventions include eradication of the infected animal reservoir (slaughter of infected domestic or wild animals), protection of the animals before they can become infected (improved sanitary practices, vaccination, antibiotics), killing the organisms before they can come in contact with humans (pasteurization of milk, cooking of food), or, for zoonoses that depend on arthropod vectors, the eradication of flies, mosquitoes, etc. (insecticide application, sanitation). Experience has taught us that single approaches do not work as well as an integrated attack on several sanitary and medical fronts.

CASE

"Dr. Rieux felt his anxiety increasing after every visit. That evening a neighbor of his old patient in the suburbs started vomiting, pressing his hand to his groin, and running a high fever accompanied by delirium. The lymph nodes were much bigger. One of them was beginning to suppurate, and presently split open like an overripe fruit. Obviously, the abscesses had to be lanced. Two crisscross strokes, and the lymph nodes disgorged a mixture of blood and pus. His limbs stretched out as far as he could manage, the sick man went on bleeding. Dark patches appeared on the legs and stomach; sometimes a lymph node would stop suppurating, then suddenly swell again. Usually the sick man died, in a stench of corruption.

The local press, so lavish of news about the rats, now had nothing to say. For rats died in the streets; men in their homes. And newspapers are concerned only with the street. So long as each individual doctor had come across only two or three cases, no one had thought of taking any action. But it was merely a matter of adding up the figure, and once this had been done, the total was startling. In a very few days, the number of cases had risen by leaps and bounds, and it had become evident to all observers of this strange malady that a real epidemic had set in. Dr. Castel, one of Rieux's colleagues and a much older man than he, came to see him.

"Naturally," he said to Rieux, "you know what it is."

"I am waiting for the post-mortems."

"Well, I know. And I don't need any post-mortems. I was in China for a good part of my career, and I saw some cases in Paris some twenty years ago. Only no one dared to call them by their name on that occasion. The usual taboo, of course; the public mustn't be alarmed, for that wouldn't do at all. And then, as one of my colleagues said, 'It's unthinkable. Everyone knows it's ceased to appear in western Europe.' Yes, everyone knew that—except the dead men. Come now, Rieux, you know as well as I do what it is."

Rieux pondered. He was looking out of the window of his surgery, at the tall cliff that closed the half-circle of the bay on the far horizon. Though blue, the sky had a dull sheen that was softening as the light declined.

"Yes, Castel," he replied. "It's hardly credible. But everything points to it being the plague."

The following questions may be asked of this narration:

- Why were "limbs stretched out" in the patient described? What were the dark patches?

- What is the meaning of the massive die-off of rats?

- How did this "strange malady" spread so quickly?

Historical Perspective

No infectious disease has caused more havoc to more people in the world than the plague. The first described pandemic occurred in the 6th century A.D. and killed an estimated 100 million people in its 50-year rampage. The second major pandemic, the Black Death, originated in Asia in the 14th century and spread to the Near East and Europe. In Europe alone, one-fourth of the population died of the disease. The third pandemic originated in Burma in the 1890s, spread to Chinese seaports, and from there to other continents, including North America, via rat-infested ships. This pandemic led to the establishment of the organism in wild rodents of many countries. Sporadic cases arise from this reservoir. About 25 confirmed cases are reported each year in the U.S., mainly in the western desert regions.

Agent of Plague

The plague is caused by a Gram-negative rod of the family Enterobacteriaceae called *Yersinia pestis*. Special stains bring out a bipolar appearance of the organism that makes it look like a safety pin.

ENCOUNTER

The disease is mainly transmitted by fleas from rodent to rodent and then to people (Fig. 69.1). Any of 1500 species of fleas may transmit the agent, but the oriental rat flea is the classic vector in human epidemics.

The plague has been detected in every continent except Australia. Most cases now occur in Southeast Asia. In the 1960s, outbreaks in South Vietnam took place as a result of disruption caused by the war, which led to increased contact between people and an abundant rat population. In the U.S., there has been a modest increase in the number of cases reported in the past several decades.

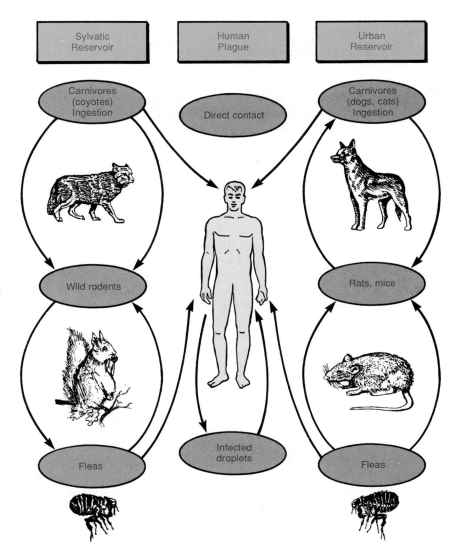

Figure 69.1. **Plague is perpetuated in rodent reservoirs and spread to humans via three cycles. 1 (left).** Sylvatic cycle among wild rodents via transmission by fleas. Other mammals including skunks and coyotes may also acquire the organism by ingestion of infected animals. **2 (right).** Urban cycle that is transmitted by the rat flea among urban rat populations. **3 (center).** Human plague can be transmitted by contact with infected animal tissue, bite of the fleas, or by infected aerosols from other humans.

Rodents are relatively resistant to *Y. pestis* and become the reservoir of the organisms between epidemics. Field mice, rats, hares and rabbits, as well as cats and dogs, are potential hosts for infected fleas. In the western U.S., prairie dogs and squirrels have become important reservoirs as well. Infected fleas can survive a year or more without access to a mammalian host, and can then infect rodents that enter abandoned burrows.

Humans can become infected from this natural reservoir by the bite of infected fleas or, rarely, by lice and ticks. Plague can also be acquired by direct contact with dead or infected animals or with soil from contaminated burrows. Dogs and cats may transmit the disease via infected saliva or by the transfer of infected fleas. Human populations in or near "enzootic" regions, where the reservoir animals become sick sporadically, are at particular risk when epidemics have been associated with "epizootics," or episodes of high mortality among rats. Fleas, deprived of their normal host by the massive rat die-offs, seek human beings in their stead. Explosive epidemics of primary plague pneumonia can also result from direct respiratory transmission of *Y. pestis* via aerosol droplets.

ENTRY

Y. pestis enters the body either by the bite of fleas or, less commonly, by inhalation. The organisms make a coagulase that works together with an enzyme in the intestinal tract of some of the fleas to clot the ingested blood. The resulting fibrin-bacterial matrix blocks the lumen of the intestinal tract. As a result, the flea cannot feed, becomes hungry, and, thus, makes repeated and intensive attempts to feed. This increases the chances for transmission, especially because the flea regurgitates the organism into the bite wound.

SPREAD, MULTIPLICATION, AND DAMAGE

Once inside human tissue, *Y. pestis* survives phagocytosis and multiplies within macrophages. During this time, the organisms produce a capsule that allows them to resist further phagocytosis. The organisms multiply explosively and spread to regional lymph nodes via the lymphatics. These nodes become enlarged by the inflammatory response, edema, and hemorrhagic necrosis, leading to characteristic lesions, the "buboes," which give the disease the name bubonic plague. The organisms manufacture several virulence factors, including fibrinolytic enzymes, a coagulase, exotoxins, and the Gram-negative endotoxin.

Bacterial invasion followed by inflammation takes place throughout the body, especially in the liver and spleen. Disseminated intravascular coagulation can produce thrombi in the capillaries of the kidneys, adrenal glands, skin, and lungs. "Black death" refers to the diffuse hemorrhagic changes in the skin plus the cyanosis caused by pneumonia. Symptoms may begin as early as 2 days after exposure and usually begin with fever, headache, generalized aches, and malaise. Patients with enlarging inguinal buboes characteristically flex or extend their extremities in an attempt to immobilize the lesions and lessen the pain. The extreme tenderness appears early and is a diagnostic feature of the plague. The disease also has two other main manifestations, **septicemic plague** and **pneumonic plague**, both of which have high mortality.

PREVENTION

The plague can be prevented by controlling fleas with insecticides and rodents by extermination, and by improving sanitation by garbage disposal. Antibiotic therapy is quite effective, which makes quarantine of patients and their contacts less important today. Ships from ports known to be infected with the disease may be quarantined and their cargo fumigated. Circular shields placed around each hawser at the dock prevent rats from leaving and entering the ship.

SUGGESTED READING

Acha PN, Szyfres B. Zoonoses and communicable diseases common to man and animals, 2nd ed. Washington, DC: Pan American Health Organization, WHO, 1989.

Butler T. Plague and other *Yersinia* infections. New York: Plenum Press, 1983.

Last JM, ed. Maxcy-Rosenau public health and preventive medicine, 11th ed. New York: Appleton-Century-Crofts, 1980.

Steele JH, ed. CRC handbook series in zoonoses. Boca Raton: CRC Press, 1979–1982.

Fever of Unknown Origin

70

David T. Durack

Fever is a universal and oft-repeated experience for humankind. The phenomenon of raised body temperature is so familiar that everyone appreciates something of its significance. Most episodes of fever are trivial or transient, while some signify the presence of serious disease. This chapter discusses an important and diagnostically troublesome subgroup of fevers that persist for weeks without immediate explanation. This condition is termed **fever of unknown origin (FUO)**.

PATHOPHYSIOLOGY OF FEVER

Body temperature depends upon the balance between heat gained and heat lost. The main sources of heat are intermediary metabolism and, in warm climates, radiation, convection, and conduction from the environment. Heat is lost to the environment by radiation, convection, and evaporation of sweat; some heat is lost in expired air. In homeothermic animals, normal body temperature is controlled within a narrow range by the thermoregulatory center, located in the brain in the preoptic hypothalamus, near the floor of the third ventricle. In healthy humans sleeping normal hours, diurnal variation results in lower temperatures between midnight and midmorning, and in higher temperatures in the late afternoon and evening.

External stimuli, such as pathogenic microorganisms, cause fever by a complex sequence of events. Microbes or their products act as **exogenous pyrogens**, which stimulate macrophages to release **endogenous pyrogen** into the bloodstream. This substance is **interleukin-1 (IL-1)**, which mediates fever as well as many other important biological responses (Chapters 6, 7, 9, and 62). IL-1 is the final common pathophysiological pathway by which diverse stimuli cause fever. IL-1 circulates to the thermoregulatory center and "resets the thermostat" to a higher setting. (This step, mediated by the synthesis of certain prostaglandins, may be interrupted by aspirin and other prostaglandin inhibitors.) The thermoregulatory center then stimulates vasomotor responses that **conserve** heat by constriction of blood vessels in the skin, and by shivering, which **produces** heat from rapid, uncontrolled muscular contractions called rigors. Conversely, the body can rid itself of heat by radiation through vasodilation of peripheral blood vessels and evaporation of sweat. Cyclic diurnal temperature variations still may be present in the feverish patient after the thermoregulatory center has reset, but the pattern is often exaggerated or distorted.

DEFINITION OF FUO

Clinically significant fever may be defined as an oral temperature above 37.6°C (100.4°F) or a rectal temperature above 38.0°C (101°F). Because fever is such a common symptom, often with a trivial or easily diagnosed cause, a practical definition of FUO is needed. In the past, FUO was defined as **continuous or intermittent fever of at least 38.0°C (100.4°F) for at least 3 weeks, which remained undiagnosed after at least 1 week of investigation in hospital.** The most important of these criteria is the requirement for duration of 3 weeks or more; this eliminates most common, self-limited infections and transient postoperative fevers. Today, the requirement for 1 week of in-hospital investigation is no longer strictly necessary for the definition of FUO, because so many important diagnostic tests can now be performed on outpatients.

CASE

Mr. J., a 45-year-old married Caucasian male who owned a filling station, developed persistent daily fevers to 39.9°C with heavy sweats. After 2 months, he had lost 7 kg in weight despite reasonably good appetite. He felt rather weak, but continued to work. He had not traveled outside his home state of Virginia, and his family history was unremarkable except for pulmonary tuberculosis in an uncle 35 years ago. On examination, the patient had a temperature of 39.1°C but otherwise looked well. Chest x-ray was normal except for a small calcified hilar lymph node. There was a soft heart murmur but no signs of heart disease. Blood counts showed a mild anemia. The erythrocyte sedimentation rate (rate of settling of red blood cells) was raised to 30 mm/hour (normal is less than 15 mm/hour). Such an increase is a nonspecific indication that an inflammatory process may be present. Urinalysis showed 30 red blood cells and 20 white blood cells per high-power field (both values abnormal); renal function was normal, and urine culture showed no significant growth after 2 days. He had not responded to three courses of different oral antibiotics prescribed by his local doctor for possible urinary tract infection.

Mr. J. was admitted to the hospital for further investigations. A skin test showed delayed hypersensitivity reactions to mumps, Candida, and tuberculin antigens. Six blood cultures were negative. Microscopic examination of a bone marrow aspirate was unrevealing and its culture was negative after 1 week. A liver biopsy was normal, also with negative culture. Repeat urinalysis again showed some red and white blood cells, but urine culture was again negative after 2 days. X-ray of the kidneys by intravenous pyelogram showed mild irregularity and dilatation of the collecting system. The patient continued to have intermittent high fevers associated with heavy sweats while in the hospital.

The following questions are suggested by this case:

- What are the most likely diagnoses?

- What is the best sequence of investigations to establish a diagnosis?

- Why is Mr. J. losing weight?

- Is the disease likely to be fatal if untreated?

Mr. J. had a fever of unknown origin. A hidden disease process caused some of his macrophages to release IL-1 intermittently into the bloodstream. His body's homeostatic mechanisms responded by increased heat production and heat conservation, raising body temperature to an abnormally high level dictated by the thermoregulatory center. While his body temperature was rising, Mr. J. looked pale, felt cold, and experienced chills and rigors. When the temperature fell again, either naturally or due to antipyretic treatment with a drug like aspirin, Mr. J. experienced drenching sweats.

Several factors could contribute to weight loss, which often is prominent in patients with FUO. Poor appetite, nausea, and vomiting may lead to various degrees of starvation. Fluid and electrolytes may be lost via sweating, vomiting, and diarrhea. Fever may accelerate protein catabolism. Very important to these processes is the synthesis of **tumor necrosis factor**, also called **cachectin**, by macrophages, especially in response to chronic infections (Chapter 4). This important biological response modifier inhibits lipoprotein lipase and leads to severe protein catabolism. It is probably the leading reason for the weight loss in Mr. J., the patient described above.

CAUSES OF FUO

The list of illnesses that can cause FUO is long. Nevertheless, patients with FUO can generally be classified into these few general categories—infections, neoplasms, rheumatic, and collagen vascular diseases, and miscellaneous other diagnoses (Table 70.1). Except in some specialized hospitals, the largest category is infections (30–35% of total). A small but important subgroup frustrates all investigative efforts, remaining undiagnosed. In the case above, the leading diagnostic categories seemed to be a hidden chronic infection or malignancy. The diagnosis of collagen-vascular diseases is unlikely due to absence of

Table 70.1. Main Diagnostic Categories and Selected Examples of Underlying Diseases

Main Diagnostic Categories	Selected Examples	Approximate Frequency
Infection	Abdominal abscesses Tuberculosis, infective endocarditis Rheumatic fever Urinary tract infections Brucellosis, salmonellosis, tularemia, Q fever, etc.	30%
Neoplasms	Lymphomas, e.g., Hodgkin's disease Carcinomas, primary or metastatic, etc.	30%
Collagen-vascular diseases	Vasculitides: temporal arteritis, giant cell arteritis, Wegener's granulomatosis, polyarteritis nodosa Systemic lupus erythematosus Rheumatic fever Rheumatoid and juvenile rheumatoid arthritis	15%
Miscellaneous	Pulmonary emboli Drug fever Sarcoidosis Atrial myxoma Familial Mediterranean fever Hepatitis: granulomatous; chronic infectious; active; alcoholic Inflammatory bowel disease Cyclic neutropenia Subacute thyroiditis Whipple's disease Factitious fever Habitual hyperthermia Other	15%
Undiagnosed		10%

joint, muscle, or skin involvement. The slow tempo of disease, extending over more than 2 months, also makes acute bacterial infections unlikely.

Important factors in considering possible causes of FUO in an individual patient include age, geography, exposure history, and underlying disease. For example, a child is less likely to have a malignancy than an adult is. An FUO in a patient from Southeast Asia is likely to have a different cause than one in the U.S. and certain animal exposures (dogs, sheep, etc.) raise interesting possibilities about etiologies. Finally, a patient with AIDS or leukemia is likely to have a different etiology than a patient without an underlying disease.

APPROACHES TO DIAGNOSIS AND MANAGEMENT OF FUO

A patient with FUO presents a fascinating and often frustrating diagnostic puzzle. Optimal investigation and management requires thoroughness, patience, and persistence. Myriad diagnostic tests are available. Rational selection of appropriate tests must be based on clinical findings or abnormalities found as initial laboratory tests (Table 70.2). For reasons of efficiency and economy, the investigation of a patient with FUO should progress in an orderly fashion through several sequential stages (Table 70.3). The speed with which these diagnostic steps are taken is determined by the tempo of the disease process.

Patients with evidence of rapid progression should be admitted to a hospital for accelerated diagnostic testing. If, on the other hand, fever has been present for weeks without serious weight loss, weakness, or other complications, investigations may begin in the outpatient clinic. The diagnostic sequence progresses to the next stage only when the present stage fails to yield the answer. In many cases, Stage 3 and especially Stage 4 are not reached, because a diagnosis was already made in an earlier stage.

Despite the increasing sophistication of diagnostic tests, the proportion of cases of FUO that remain undiagnosed—approximately 10%—has changed little over the past two decades. However, newer diagnostic tests (such as computerized tomography) have reduced the frequency with which, in the absence of a diagnosis, exploratory laparotomy (surgical opening of the abdominal wall) and/or a therapeutic trial must be performed.

The problems in diagnosing FUO are well illustrated by the case of Mr. J. The first stage of his evaluation revealed nonspecific findings—fever, weight loss, mild anemia, some red blood cells, and leukocytes in his urine. Although these did not yield a diagnosis, they established that he had an active, chronic disease that was affecting his whole body. The presence of objective laboratory abnormalities such as anemia and increased erythrocyte sedimentation rate excluded a purely psychiatric cause of weight loss, such as depression.

The second stage of Mr. J.'s work-up (in the hospital) again did not yield a diagnosis, but provided further useful information. His positive skin tests showed that (*a*) he was capable of mounting a normal cell-mediated immune response to ubiquitous antigens such as mumps and *Candida*, and (*b*) that he had encountered tuberculosis in the past. This latter observation fits with the history of tuberculosis in his uncle many years ago, and with the calcified lymph node seen in his chest x-ray. Could tuberculosis be the cause of his FUO? If so, it must be localized outside the lung because the chest x-ray did not reveal active pulmo-

Table 70.2. Examples of Clinical and Laboratory Findings that May Present in FUO, Related to Leading Etiological Possibilities

	Differential Diagnosis	Useful Investigations
Lymphadenopathy	Cytomegalovirus, Epstein-Barr virus	Antibody titers
	Malignancies, especially lymphomas	Biopsies, computerized tomography
	Lymphogranuloma venereum	Biopsy, antibody
	Toxoplasmosis, tularemia	Antibody, biopsy
	Cat-scratch fever	Biopsy, special stains
Pneumonitis	Cytomegalovirus	Lung biopsy, serology
	Tularemia, psittacosis, Q fever	Serology
	Fungal infection	Biopsy, serology
Heart murmur	Rheumatic fever	Echocardiogram, antibody titers
	Infective endocarditis	Blood cultures, echocardiogram
	Atrial myxoma	Echocardiogram
Anemia	Infective endocarditis	Blood cultures
	Tuberculosis	Delayed hypersensitivity skin test; biopsies; cultures
	Malignancy	Biopsies of involved tissues
	Preleukemia	Bone marrow biopsy
Lymphocytosis	Tuberculosis	Skin tests; culture; staining
	Infectious mononucleosis	Epstein-Barr virus antibody titers
	Cytomegalovirus infection	Cytomegalovirus antibody titers, culture
Neutropenia	Systemic lupus erythematosus	Antinuclear antibody; anti-DNA
	Tuberculosis	Skin tests; culture; stains
	Lymphoma	Biopsy involved tissues
	Cyclic neutropenia	Repeat white blood cell count and differential three times/week for 1 month
Monocytosis	Tuberculosis	Skin tests: culture; stains
	Brucellosis	*Brucella* titers
	Hodgkin's disease	Biopsy involved tissues
	Inflammatory bowel disease	Barium studies; endoscopy with biopsies
Elevated erythrocyte sedimentation	Infective endocarditis	Blood cultures
	Temporal arteritis	Biopsy temporal arteries
	Acute rheumatic fever	Antistreptolysin O; throat culture; joint aspiration
	Still's disease	Clinical diagnosis
	Lymphoma	Biopsy involved tissues
	Subacute thyroiditis	Antithyroglobulin antibodies
Hypercalcemia	Parathyroid adenoma	Endocrine consult
	Hypernephroma	Urinalysis; IV pyelogram
	Sarcoidosis	Chest radiograph; angiotensin-converting enzyme
Elevated alkaline phosphatase	Liver disease, obstructive or infiltrative, including infection or malignancy	Liver-spleen scan; liver biopsy for malignancy
	Hypernephroma	Intravenous pyelogram
	Subacute thyroiditis	Antithyroglobulin antibody titer
	Subacute osteomyelitis	Bone scan
	Still's disease	Clinical diagnosis
	Temporal arteritis	Biopsy
Low serum complement	Infective endocarditis	Blood culture
	Collagen-vascular diseases	Serological studies
Rheumatoid factor	Infective endocarditis	Repeat titers, blood cultures
	Old age	Repeat titers
	Collagen-vascular disease	Serological studies

nary tuberculosis. The leukocytes present in Mr. J.'s urine could be due to renal tuberculosis, a diagnosis that would also explain his abnormal urogram.

The third stage of the investigation provided further important positive and negative findings. Histological examination of the bone marrow and liver biopsies showed no evidence of an occult malignancy, such as Hodgkin's lymphoma. An echocardiogram revealed no vegetations on the heart valves; this, together with negative blood cultures, made infective endocarditis unlikely.

Table 70.3. Four Sequential Stages in the Diagnosis and Management of FUO

Stage 1	Complete history, including travel, immunization, exposure
	Detailed physical examination
	Screening tests: blood count, sedimentation rate, urinalysis and urine culture, chest x-ray, blood cultures
Stage 2	Review history, checking for omissions
	Repeat detailed physical examination
	Specific diagnostic tests: delayed hypersensitivity skin tests, urine culture for tuberculosis or CMV, serological tests for infection and collagen-vascular diseases; echocardiogram; diagnostic imaging: upper and lower GI barium studies; intravenous urogram; lung scan, bone scan, CT scan, lymphangiogram; magnetic resonance imaging
Stage 3	Invasive tests: Bone marrow biopsy and culture, liver biopsy and culture, biopsy of abnormal tissues, endoscopy with biopsies, temporal artery biopsy, open lung biopsy, exploratory laparotomy
Stage 4	Therapeutic trials: Prostaglandin inhibitors: aspirin, indomethacin; corticosteroid therapy: prednisone, dexamethasone; antituberculous therapy: isoniazid plus ethambutol; antibacterial therapy: ampicillin plus gentamicin.

At this point, a presumptive diagnosis was made of renal tuberculosis. Mr. J. was treated empirically with isoniazid and rifampin. At follow-up 6 weeks later, his fever had resolved and he felt well, although he still had a few leukocytes in his urine. The microbiological laboratory reported at this time that his urine culture had grown an acid-fast organism, presumably *Mycobacterium tuberculosis*. Final identification of the organism, and thus confirmation of the diagnosis, followed 2 weeks later. Mr. J. completed 18 months of treatment with INH and rifampin, during which he felt well and had no further fevers.

SUGGESTED READING

Aduan RP, Fauci AS, Dale DC, et al. Prolonged fever of unknown origin. Clin Res 1978;26:558A.

Dinarello CA, Wolff SM. Fever of unknown origin. In: Mandell GL, Douglas RG Jr, Bennett JE, eds. Principles and practice of infectious diseases, 2nd ed. New York: John Wiley and Sons, 1985:339.

Larson EB, Featherstone HJ, Pedersdorf RG. Fever of undetermined origin: diagnosis and follow up of 105 cases, 1970–1980. Medicine 1982;61:269.

Murphy PA. Temperature regulation and the pathogenesis of fever. In: Mandell GL, Douglas RG Jr, Bennett JE, eds. Principles and practice of infectious diseases, 2nd ed. New York: John Wiley and Sons, 1985:334.

Wolff SM, Fauci AS, Dale DC. Unusual etiologies of fever and their evaluation. Ann Rev Med 1975;26:277.

Nosocomial and Iatrogenic Infections

71

David R. Snydman

OVERVIEW

Approximately 5% of all patients develop an infection during their stay in the hospital. These hospital-acquired conditions are known as **nosocomial** infections. An infection that is the result of intervention by a physician, in or out of a hospital, is known as **iatrogenic**. Nosocomial infections often result in prolongation of hospital stay and are extraordinarily costly in terms of morbidity and even mortality. It is estimated that about 5 billion dollars are spent each year for the management of hospital-acquired infections in the U.S.

A number of factors related to hospitalization predispose patients to the risk of a hospital-acquired infection. The most important ones are those that violate the host's own defenses. Invasive procedures, often seemingly benign, produce **new portals of entry** for microorganisms from the patient's own flora or from the environment. Examples are the use of devices such as endotracheal tubes, mechanical ventilators, intravenous or intra-arterial catheters, and surgical procedures in general.

Broadly speaking, the incidence of nosocomial infections is related to the severity of the underlying disease—i.e., patients who have a high likelihood of dying during their hospitalization also run a higher risk of developing nosocomial infections. In contrast, patients who are admitted with less severe disease have a lesser chance of acquiring infections in the hospital. This underscores the need for improved management of the severely compromised patient. Unfortunately, it is estimated that only about one-third to one-half of all nosocomial infections are preventable under the most favorable conditions.

AGENTS OF NOSOCOMIAL AND IATROGENIC INFECTIONS

Generally speaking, the organisms that cause nosocomial and iatrogenic infections are similar to those found elsewhere in the community. The most common causative agents are usually not especially pathogenic. In fact, sometimes they are even less pathogenic than those that cause disease outside of the hospital, which illustrates the greater sensitivity of the hospitalized patient to infections.

A salient example is the emergence of *Serratia marcescens* as a hospital-acquired pathogen. This bacterium was thought to be so benign that it was used in the 1950s to trace the movement of air in a subway system, or to determine the movement of bacteria into the urethra through the catheter-meatal interface. This "nonpathogen" has became the source of significant nosocomial infections, although it rarely causes disease outside the hospital.

Like many pathogens associated with nosocomial infections, *Serratia* has acquired significant antibiotic resistance. Gram-negative bacterial strains that possess plasmid-mediated, multiple antibiotic resistance are commonly encountered in nosocomial infections. Plasmid transfer occurs among different strains of the same species and even among different genera. **Transfer of antibiotic resistance** has been demonstrated in the urine of patients with Foley catheters and on their skin. Presumably, transfer of antibiotic resistance takes place in the gastrointestinal tract as well. Antibiotic-resistant pathogens have become so common that we regularly encounter methicillin-resistant *Staphylococcus aureus*, and aminoglycoside-resistant Gram-negative bacteria in nosocomial infections. Examples of nosocomial pathogens are seen in Table 71.1. The list of pathogens that can cause nosocomial infections encompasses the agents of practically all infections. Given inadequate levels of hygiene, such as are found in many developing countries, polio, measles, tetanus, and tuberculosis can all be common nosocomial problems.

ENCOUNTER

A hospital is a microenvironment where organisms can be transferred in a variety of ways from one individual to another, or from the hospital staff to the patients (Fig. 71.1). Transmission between individuals may be direct, by hand contact, or indirect, by inhalation, ingestion, or puncture through the integument. Examples are infections due to methicillin-resistant staphylococci, which spread directly between patients or via hospital personnel. Tubercle bacilli are transmitted through aerosolization and inhalation. Viral agents, such as those of varicella or influenza, may be spread through the air to susceptible immunocompromised individuals. Blood used for transfusions may be contaminated with hepatitis viruses A, B, and C, or HIV. Food handlers may contaminate food eaten by patients, and physicians and nurses may introduce microorganisms into deeper tissues during operations or while dressing surgical or other wounds. Unusual epidemics can

Table 71.1. Common Hospital-acquired Infections and Frequently Associated Organisms

Type of Infection	Most Common Organism
Surgical wounds	*Staphylococcus aureus*
	Escherichia coli
	Streptococcus faecalis
Pneumonia	*Klebsiella pneumoniae*
	Pseudomonas aeruginosa
	Staphylococcus aureus
	Enterobacter sp.
	Escherichia coli
Intravenous catheter	*Staphylococcus epidermidis*
	Staphylococcus aureus
	Streptococcus faecalis
	Candida sp.
Urinary catheter	*Escherichia coli*
	Streptococcus faecalis
	Pseudomonas aeruginosa
	Klebsiella sp.

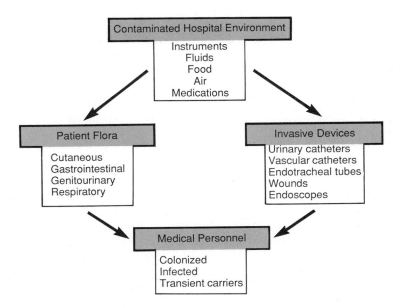

Figure 71.1. Sources of hospital-acquired infections.

sometimes be traced to **specific** carriers among members of the hospital staff. For example, well-documented epidemics caused by group A streptococci have been attributed to carriers who had contact with patients in the operating room. In one epidemic, the organisms were located in the carrier's vagina, from where they were presumably aerosolized through normal body movements.

Microorganisms that spread to patients may be **endemic** to the hospital environment. Notable examples include the fungi that cause aspergillosis, which may be present as more or less visible mildew on moist room walls or construction panels. Infections by exogenous organisms may also be acquired from improperly sterilized surgical instruments and even contaminated disinfectant solutions! Fortunately, these are rare events in a proper hospital setting.

Patients acquire nosocomial infections as the result of breaks in their own defenses and from their inability to combat infection. These breaks usually occur as the result of **invasive diagnostic or therapeutic interventions** that physicians perform on their patients. For these reasons, the most common nosocomial infections affect the urinary tract, because catheterization of the bladder is frequently used with bedridden patients. The commonly used Foley catheter bypasses the normal mucosal barriers and facilitates the entry of organisms that colonize the skin or the urinary introitus. The next most frequent type of infection is that of surgical wounds, followed by respiratory tract infections, each of which involves invasive procedures.

ENTRY

Skin Penetration

The skin barrier is breached by the use of intravenous catheters or devices used to measure intravascular pressure. The longer they stay in place, the higher the risk of both local infection and bacteremia. This underscores the need for vigilance in the care of patients with indwelling devices. In national surveys in the U.S., the rate of nosocomial bacteremia has almost doubled in the decade of the 1980s, and that due to *Staphylococcus epidermidis*, tripled. In the writer's institution,

1 in 100 patients develops hospital-acquired bacteremia, half of which are due to the implantation of intravascular devices.

Another example of the role of the normal skin in protecting from microbial invasion is that of burn victims. Frequently, patients who have extensive second or third degree burns will become colonized with bacteria, especially *Pseudomonas aeruginosa*. Necrotizing lesions at the site of skin damage are accompanied by sepsis, the major cause of death in burn victims.

Inhalation

The most common cause of nosocomial pneumonia is the use of an **endotracheal tube**. This bypasses the normal epithelial defenses and allows the entry of organisms via aerosols. In the early 1960s, when mechanical ventilation of the lungs was being developed, it was recognized that epidemics of Gram-negative pneumonia occurred because nebulized mists contained bacteria-laden aerosols. An understanding of the problem brought about changes in design, which have virtually eliminated the ventilator as a source of hospital-acquired pneumonia. Patients with endotracheal tubes still develop pneumonia, but now the offending organisms tend to come from the patient's stomach or intestine and colonize the nasopharynx. From here, they may become aspirated into the lungs. Other examples of nosocomial infections acquired by inhalation can be seen in hospital epidemics of influenza and varicella, which are particularly troubling for immunocompromised patients.

Ingestion

Epidemics of nosocomial infection sometimes result from the ingestion of pathogenic bacteria. The organisms are often those associated with community-acquired infections, like *Salmonella*, hepatitis **A** virus, and rotavirus, the latter being most frequent among neonates or infants. Epidemics of salmonellosis in hospitals usually result from eating foods contaminated during preparation. They have also resulted from the use of contaminated animal products used for diagnostic purposes, such as carmine dye.

Inanimate Environment

The complexity of a hospital environment provides innumerable opportunities for the encounter of patients with microorganisms. Some of these are specific for these environments and not usually found elsewhere. An example is the use of **contaminated intravenous solutions**, which have caused many epidemics. Contamination rarely takes place at the point of manufacture; more commonly, it occurs during the **handling of bottles and infusion lines**.

Instruments and dressings improperly sterilized before surgery also provide a possible source of infection. A whole technology has developed around the problems of determining if autoclaves and sterilizing ovens perform their expected task. Thus, it is customary to insert a vial containing bacterial spores with the material to be autoclaved, and to determine spore viability afterward. Deviance from established procedures may well result in improper sterilization and in contamination of surgical or other wounds.

MODEL INFECTIONS

Case 1—Urinary Tract Infection

Mr. H., a 67-year-old gentleman, underwent a transurethral prostectomy for cancer of the prostate. Because of concern for postoperative bleeding from straining during urination, he had a Foley catheter placed into the bladder. Three days later, Mr. H. developed a urinary tract infection with low-grade fever, some pain, and pyuria. Quantitative urine counts yielded 3×10^5 colonies of Escherichia coli *per ml of urine. The organisms were resistant to all tested antibiotics except for the aminoglycosides. Within 2 days, Mr. H. developed bacteremia with hypotension and shock. Physicians were eventually able to control the bacteremia with gentamicin therapy. Fortunately, Mr. H. recovered completely and was discharged.*

How did Mr. H. acquire this infection? This is a classic case of a nosocomial infection of the urinary tract. The use of Foley catheters for more than 1 or 2 days often results in contamination of the bladder, especially by fecal coliforms. Nowadays catheters are usually provided with an expandable collection bag for the urine, thus making this a closed system. Nonetheless, the risk of bacteriuria is cumulative and still occurs at a rate between 5% and 8%/day. The risk of bacteriuria is related to the skill of the person inserting the catheter, the sex and age of the patient, and the duration of catheterization.

Case 2—Nosocomial Wound Infection

Ms. Z., an 82-year-old lady with rheumatic heart disease, underwent a mitral valve replacement along with surgery for a coronary artery bypass graft. Her postoperative course was complicated by bleeding in the mediastinum, which required more surgery. She did well after these operations and was discharged after 12 days. Three weeks later, Ms. Z. noticed some purulent drainage along the wound site on her chest. She continued to have pain but did not complain about it to her family, assuming that the pain was related to her healing process. When she returned to see the surgeon 1 month later, she reported her pain and low-grade fever. The surgeon noted that there was considerable drainage at the wound site. Probing the wound, he noticed a lot of pus.

Ms. Z. was hospitalized again for radical debridement (cleaning) of her chest wound. Cultures of the pus yielded S. epidermidis. *She was treated intravenously with vancomycin for 6 weeks and her wound was debrided with removal of the wires in her sternum. At the end of this period, she required a plastic surgical procedure and a muscle flap to close the wound. After 2 more months of hospitalization, she was discharged and continued her convalescence at home.*

This case illustrates the problem of surgical wound infections and the serious impact they can have on the patient's recovery. Wound infections of the mediastinum complicate between 1% and 5% of open heart surgery. If the infection reaches deep portions of the chest, its effect can be extremely serious. Patients frequently require multiple surgical interventions with removal of devitalized bone, cartilage, and other tissue.

Surgical wound infections are the most costly of all nosocomial infections. Some are clearly preventable. They are frequently due to *S. aureus,* but the example used here illustrates that *S. epidermidis,* a normal skin commensal, may also be a significant pathogen. In the case of Ms. Z., the source of the infection was probably her own skin flora. As with other infections, the establishment depends on the size of the inoculum, the pathogenic potential of the invading organisms, and the state of the host defenses. All of these factors should be taken into account before planning surgical treatment. In cases where infection would be devastating, as in artificial hip implants, surgeons may go to great lengths, such as using laminar air flow systems and prophylactic antibiotics.

Case 3—Primary Bacteremia

Fifty-nine-year-old Mr. S. was hospitalized with acute myocardial infarction. His disease was so severe that he required a catheter to measure his cardiac pressure and output. Unfortunately, the catheter was left in place for several more days than was probably necessary. Six days after his infarction, Mr. S. developed fever, leukocytosis, and inflammation at the site of insertion of the catheter. Four blood cultures all revealed the presence of S. aureus. He was treated with intravenous antibiotics; however, a new cardiac murmur was noted 7 days into therapy. An echocardiogram revealed the development of a tricuspid valve vegetation. Mr. S. required 4 weeks of antibiotic therapy for his hospital-acquired, catheter-related endocarditis.

This case illustrates an example of primary bacteremia, which is defined as bacteremia that cannot be ascribed to another focus of infection. Primary bacteremia is frequently either the result of a contaminated intravenous line or associated with granulocytopenia in the immunosuppressed leukemic patient.

There are many different areas, from the bottle to the intravenous catheter, where contamination may occur during the course of intravenous therapy. The risk of intravenous catheter-related infection is generally influenced by the type of catheter and the duration of catheterization. Patients who have large-bore catheters that require surgical insertion have the highest risk. If the catheter is left in place for 48 hours or longer, there is a 2–3% risk of bacteremia. In the example cited, the patient developed endocarditis, a rare but recognized complication. The usual pathogens tend to be *S. aureus, S. epidermidis,* a variety of Gram-negative rods, or *Candida* (Table 71.1).

There have also been nationwide outbreaks of intravenous fluid-related infection due to contamination of intravenous bottles at manufacture. The pathogens that have been involved in these situations have usually been relatively nonpathogenic species of *Enterobacter.* These organisms are able to grow in sugar water solutions at room temperature.

Another example of primary bacteremia is generally seen in leukemia or lymphoma patients who are granulocytopenic as a result of cancer chemotherapy. Patients will frequently become bacteremic, primarily from an intestinal focus. The usual pathogens in this setting are Gram-negative rods, which may originate from the patient's endogenous flora or may be exogenously acquired in the hospital.

Case 4—Nosocomial Pneumonia

Ms. J. was hospitalized for therapy of acute leukemia. Over a 3-week period, her blood cell count remained low as a result of her chemotherapy. At the end of this period, she developed a pulmonary infiltrate and sinusitis. She was treated with broad-spectrum antibiotics but failed to respond. Her lung involvement progressed and she was subjected to an open lung biopsy. A species of Aspergillus (A. fumigatus) was cultured from this material. She was started on amphotericin B but become progressively more ill and died within a week.

Nosocomial aspergillosis, while not common, has recently been seen more often among immunosuppressed patients. A number of reported epidemics have been linked to hospital construction and contamination of air conditioning systems. Large numbers of fungal spores in the air lead to nasal or bronchial colonization. Immunosuppression and the resultant granulocytopenia, along with broad-spectrum antibacterial antibiotics, help the organism become established in the airways.

This is an example of a relatively uncommon form of acquisition of organisms that cause nosocomial pneumonia. More often, patients aspirate stomach or nasopharyngeal contents as the result of their debilitation. Infections acquired in this manner are frequently due to a mixed aerobic-anaerobic bacterial flora. Unfortunately, nosocomial pneumonia is the least preventable of all hospital-acquired infections and is associated with the highest mortality rate.

Case 5—Nosocomial Blood-borne Disease

Dr. T. developed a needlestick injury while recapping a needle from a patient who abused intravenous drugs. About 2 months later, Dr. T. developed arthralgias, fatigue, malaise, and became jaundiced. He slowly recovered but lost 3 months of work. He was diagnosed as having hepatitis B.

For decades, hepatitis B has been recognized as a nosocomial hazard for both health workers and patients. Needlestick transmission has been a recognized hazard, with rates of transmission approaching 25%. Blood transfusions constituted a major threat to patients before the early 1970s. Fortunately, realizing the risk of transmission of hepatitis B virus and using HBsAg screening has markedly reduced the blood-borne transmission of this virus.

Foremost among the ways of preventing needlestick injuries is the common sense avoidance of recapping needles, which accounts for 30% of these injuries. Hepatitis B can be prevented by vaccination, which should be given to all health workers. However, needlestick transmission of hepatitis C and HIV can still occur, and, for the unaware, hepatitis B still poses a problem.

CONTROL

Control of nosocomial infections requires awareness by all health care professionals. **Handwashing** between patient contacts is a simple but much neglected procedure. It can decrease transmission of microorganisms between hospital staff and patients. The use of **aseptic techniques** during surgical and other invasive procedures, as stressed in surgical training, significantly prevents these infections.

Hospitals have instituted **infection control committees**, whose responsibility is to oversee all aspects of infection control within the institution. They supervise surveillance of hospital-acquired infections, establish policies and procedures to prevent such infections, and have the power to intervene when necessary in investigations of epidemics or other problems. Most hospitals have specific personnel, **infection control practitioners**, who are assigned these tasks and function as the "eyes and ears" of the committee. These individuals are responsible for tracing epidemics, monitoring the infection rate, and determining the level of isolation of patients. But, there is still a good deal to be learned. Of course, intense efforts are invested in trying to prevent infections in the increasing number of immunocompromised hosts and in working out effective means to prevent nosocomial pneumonias.

SUGGESTED READING

Altemeir WA, Burke JF, Pruitt BA, Saudusky WR, eds. Manual of control of infection in surgical patients, 2nd ed. Philadelphia: JB Lippincott, 1984.

Bennett JV. In: Brachman PS, ed. Hospital infections, 2nd ed. Boston: Little, Brown, 1986.

Dixon RE, ed. Nosocomial infections. Stoneham, MA: Yorke Medical Books, 1981.

Wenzel RP, ed. Prevention and control of nosocomial infections. Baltimore: Williams & Wilkins, 1987.

Wenzel RP, ed. CRC handbook of hospital acquired infections. Boca Raton: CRC Press, 1981.

Food-borne Diseases

72

David R. Snydman

Food-borne infections are a significant public health problem. In the U.S., they are a major cause of morbidity, although an infrequent cause of mortality. Between 1983 and 1987, there were 909 outbreaks reported to the Centers for Disease Control from virtually all 50 states. The number of ill people reported to the health authorities in these outbreaks totaled more than 50,000 with 134 deaths. Surveillance suggests that the true scope of infection related to food probably is 10–100 times more frequent.

A food-borne disease **outbreak** is defined by two criteria: (*a*) two or more persons experiencing a similar illness, usually gastrointestinal, after ingestion of the same food; and (*b*) epidemiological analysis implicating food as the source of the illness. There are certain exceptions to this definition. For example, one case of botulism constitutes an outbreak for the purposes of epidemiological investigation and control.

The most common diseases in the U.S. acquired by ingestion of contaminated food are those usually called **food poisoning**. They are defined as diseases caused by the consumption of food contaminated with bacteria, bacterial toxins, parasites, viruses, and chemicals. Bacteria cause approximately two-thirds of the food-borne outbreaks in the U.S. for which an etiology can be determined. However, it should be noted that only in 44% of such outbreaks is the etiology confirmed.

This chapter will deal with **infectious diarrheas from food poisoning** in general, and, more specifically, with its three main types:

- **Intoxications** due to toxin preformed in the food; in these cases, the organism no longer has to be alive. Examples of causative bacteria are *Staphylococcus aureus*, *Clostridium botulinum*, and *Bacillus cereus*.

- **Intoxications due to toxins manufactured in the body**, after live organisms such as *Vibrio cholerae* or *Clostridium perfringens* are ingested;

- **Intestinal invasive diseases**, such as gastroenteritis due to invasive organisms, e.g., *Salmonella* and *Campylobacter*.

The distinction between food poisoning caused by toxin-producing organisms and by invasive pathogens is important clinically and epidemiologically. In general, **diseases due to toxin-forming organisms** such as *S. aureus* have a short incubation period and are characterized by upper gastrointestinal complaints, such as nausea and vomiting. Diarrhea is less frequent, and constitutional symptoms, e.g., fever and chills, are uncommon. In contrast, **food poisonings from more invasive organisms**, such as *Salmonella*, usually have a longer incubation period and are characterized by fever, chills, and lower gastrointestinal complaints. Diarrhea, often bloody or containing pus or mucus, is more prominent than nausea or vomiting.

Therefore, we generally categorize food poisoning by whether intoxication or invasion is most prominent. There is some overlap in this classification scheme, because organisms like *Shigella* or *Salmonella* may have invasive properties as well as being able to produce toxin.

Let us turn to outbreaks and cases in the U.S. (Table 72.1). The most frequently recognized agents of bacterial food poisoning are generally limited to a dozen organisms (Table 72.2). *Salmonella* outbreaks pre-

Table 72.1. Confirmed Food-borne Disease Outbreaks, Cases and Deaths, United States, 1983–1987

Etiology	Cases	Outbreaks	Deaths
Bacterial			
Salmonella	31,245	342	39
Shigella	9971	44	2
S. aureus	3181	47	0
C. perfringens	2743	24	2
Campylobacter	727	28	1
E. coli	640	7	4
B. cereus	261	13	0
C. botulinum	212	73	8
V. parahaemolyticus	11	3	0
V. cholerae	3	2	0
Other	259	3	74
Subtotal	50,283	599	130
Viral			
Norwalk virus	1164	10	0
Hepatitis A	1067	29	1
Other viral	558	2	1
Subtotal	2790	41	2
Parasitic			
Trichinella	162	33	1
Giardia	41	3	0
Subtotal	203	36	1
Chemical	1244	232	2
Total	54,540	909	134

Table 72.2. Some Characteristics of Bacterial Food Poisoning

Organism	Mechanism	Incubation Period	Vehicles	Features
S. aureus	Heat-stable toxin	1–6 hours	Ham, pastry, baked goods	Vomiting
B. cereus	Heat-stable toxin	1–6 hours	Fried rice	Vomiting
	Heat-labile toxin	8–24 hours	Cream sauce	Diarrhea
Salmonella	Invasion	16–48 hours	Chicken, beef, eggs, milk	Fever, diarrhea
Campylobacter	Invasion	16–48 hours	Chicken, beef, milk	Fever, diarrhea
V. parahemolyticus	Invasion (toxin?)	16–72 hours	Shellfish	Fever, diarrhea
Y. enterocolitica	Invasion (toxin?)	16–72 hours	Milk, tofu	Diarrhea
E. coli	Toxin	16–72 hours	Salads	Diarrhea
	0157:H7 (vero toxin)	16–48 hours	Beef	Fever, diarrhea
C. perfringens	Toxin	8–12 hours	beef, poultry, gravy	Diarrhea

dominate among the confirmed outbreaks and constitute over half of the reported cases of food-borne illness. This is due, in part, to the ease of recognition and to the awareness of physicians and the public. Shigellas are the next most frequent cause of food-borne outbreaks, associated with 20% of reported cases. *S. aureus* and *C. perfringens* are the next most frequent, associated with 5–6% of reported cases. *Campylobacter*, hepatitis A and Norwalk viruses, and other pathogens cause illness less frequently. Parasites and chemical agents acquired from food are rarer.

It is important to note that etiological patterns vary throughout the world. They depend on many factors, such as food preferences, awareness by physicians and the public, and laboratory capabilities. For example, in the U.S., food poisoning by *Salmonella* and *Shigella* represent about 70% of the outbreaks. In contrast, *C. perfringens* is implicated in over 90% of the recognized food-borne illness in England and Wales. Japan has yet different etiological patterns, with *Vibrio parahaemolyticus* gastroenteritis representing over 50% of the reported outbreaks. For travelers from the U.S. to countries such as Mexico, the most common cause of diarrhea ("turista") is an enterotoxigenic *Escherichia coli.*

INTOXICATIONS

Case 1—*Staphylococcus aureus*

As the aircraft cruised at 35,000 feet, the cabin attendants passed out a lunch meal that included ham sandwiches. Two hours later, two-thirds of the passengers aboard the 747 jet plane developed nausea and vomiting. Diarrhea occurred in about one-third of those affected. The waiting lines for the facilities trailed down the aisle. As a result of such epidemics, rules for serving the cockpit crew different meals went into effect (without increasing the number of toilets).

What was the cause of the outbreak?
How could one meal have affected such a large number of individuals?

In the epidemic described, about two-thirds of the passengers were served ham sliced by a chef who had a pustular lesion on his hand. *S. aureus* was isolated from the lesion along with the identical strain from the ham. The passengers had ingested food contaminated with one of the many *S. aureus* toxins.

ENCOUNTER

Staphylococcal food-borne outbreaks are characterized by explosive onset 1–6 hours after consuming contaminated food. Attack rates are usually quite high because very small quantities of staphylococcal enterotoxin can cause illness. In outbreaks involving single families and uniform doses of enterotoxin, virtually 100% of individuals are affected. **The staphylococcal enterotoxin is resistant to heat** and is still present in food after cooking, even though the causative organism has been killed.

Outbreaks from staphylococci may occur at any time of the year, but most are reported during the warm weather months. Staphylococci are carried by so many people that food preparation in almost any setting may be involved. Most outbreaks are reported from large gatherings, i.e., schools, group picnics, clubs, and restaurants. Many different foods have been implicated: ham, canned beef, pork, or any salted meat, and cream-filled cakes or pastries such as cream puffs. Potato and macaroni salads are occasionally involved. Foods that have a high content of salt (ham) or sugar (custard) selectively favor the growth of staphylococci.

Foods that are involved in outbreaks have usually been cut, sliced, grated, mixed, or ground by workers who are carriers of enterotoxin-producing strains of staphylococci. Even though animal carcasses may be contaminated before processing, competitive growth from other members of the flora usually limits the staphylococci. Therefore, the primary mechanism of transmission is from the food handler to the food product. Most commonly, the contaminated food has been allowed to sit at room temperature for some time before preparation or cooking, thus allowing the toxin to be produced in significant quantities.

CLINICAL FEATURES

The symptoms of staphylococcal food poisoning are primarily profuse vomiting, nausea, and abdominal cramps, often followed by diarrhea. In severe cases, blood may be observed in the vomitus or stool. Rarely, hypotension and marked prostration may occur, but recovery is usually complete in 24–48 hours.

DIAGNOSIS

Staphylococcal food poisoning should be considered in anyone with severe vomiting, nausea, cramps and some diarrhea. A history of ingesting meats of high salt or sugar content may be helpful. Usually the best epidemiological clue, especially if a number of individuals are ill, is the short incubation period (1–6 hours). Of the bacterial food-borne diseases, only *B. cereus* has similar symptoms, with a short incubation period and a marked vomiting syndrome. Because the *B. cereus* vomiting syndrome is closely allied with rice, the epidemiological distinction can usually be easily made.

The diagnosis can be confirmed by culturing the incriminated food, the skin or nose of the food handler, or occasionally, the vomitus or stools of affected individuals. The recovered *S. aureus* may be phage-typed to prove identity between isolated strains (see Chapter 11). Detection of staphylococcal enterotoxin will be the ultimate means of making the diagnosis once an appropriate test becomes generally available.

Case 2—*Clostridium perfringens*

> A group of college dormitory residents sat down for a turkey feast around 6 o'clock one evening. They consumed turkey, giblets, gravy, and "all the fixins." Around 2:00 in the morning, the first of many awoke with severe intestinal cramps and watery diarrhea. Most of the students in the group became ill with similar symptoms around 6:00 in the morning. Several required hospitalization in the college infirmary. Fortunately, the wave of diarrhea resolved within 24 hours.

What is the likely agent of this disease?
What is the pathophysiology of this type of diarrhea?
How could such an outbreak be prevented?

ENCOUNTER

The lengthy time of onset of symptoms, the clinical manifestations, and the fact that most of the persons present at the meal got sick point to *Clostridium perfringens* as a likely cause of the outbreak. *C. perfrin-*

gens food poisoning is the fourth most common cause of food-borne disease in the U.S. Because this diagnosis is often difficult to establish, we must assume that these reports represent a small fraction of the actual cases that occur.

Epidemics of *C. perfringens* are usually characterized by high attack rates, affecting a large proportion of individuals. The incubation period in most outbreaks varies between 8 and 14 hours (median of 12 hours), but can be as long as 72 hours. For reasons that are not clear, more cases of *C. perfringens* food poisoning are reported in the fall and winter months. The nadir of reported cases is in the summer, in marked contrasts to outbreaks of *Salmonella* and staphylococcal food poisoning. It may be that the kinds of food usually implicated, such as stews, are eaten less frequently in the summer.

Outbreaks due to this organism are most frequently reported from institutions or large gatherings. The latter is probably a reporting artefact, inasmuch as, frequently, only such groups recognize the illness as food poisoning. In the late 1940s, it was discovered that *C. perfringens* caused outbreaks of severe and often lethal intestinal disease labeled **enteritis necroticans** that affected people in Germany and New Guinea (where it is termed "pig-bel," see below).

PATHOPHYSIOLOGY

This form of food poisoning often takes place when poultry, meat,or fish is precooked and then reheated before serving. Spores of the organisms resist the first heating and then germinate in the food. The second heating must be inadequate to kill them; therefore, they are ingested either as spores or as vegetative cells. In the intestine, the organisms begin to sporulate, forming the toxin.

Diarrhea is caused by a heat-labile protein enterotoxin with a molecular weight of approximately 34,000 daltons. The clostridial toxin differs from cholera toxin in the several respects; its activity is maximal in the ileum and minimal in the duodenum, just opposite to that of cholera toxin. Clostridial enterotoxin inhibits glucose transport, damages the intestinal epithelium, and causes protein loss into the intestinal lumen; no such effects are observed with cholera toxin. Recently, *C. perfringens* enterotoxin has been detected in the stools of affected individuals. Enterotoxin activity disappears quickly from stool but can be measured in serum.

Immunity in this disease is not well understood. In one study, 65% of Americans and 84% of Brazilians had antienterotoxin activity in serum. The significance of this finding is unknown at present; in none of the outbreaks studied to date was blood available that had been drawn before an outbreak, which would have permitted a correlation between antienterotoxin immunity and the disease. In animal studies, enterotoxin antiserum blocks the action of the toxin on ligated rabbit loops. It is not known, however, if the presence of antibody in serum has any effect on toxin activity in the intestine.

CLINICAL FEATURES

C. perfringens food poisoning is generally characterized by watery diarrhea and severe crampy abdominal pain, usually without vomiting, beginning 8–24 hours after the incriminated meal. Fever, chills, headache, or other signs of infection usually are not present.

The illness is of short duration, 24 hours or less. Rare fatalities have been recorded in debilitated or hospitalized patients who are victims of clostridial food poisoning.

ENTERITIS NECROTICANS

Enteritis necroticans ("pig-bel") is a very different illness characterized by high attack rates in children in New Guinea, coupled with a high mortality. Outbreaks of the disease have been clearly related to the consumption of pig in large native feasts. Improperly cooked pork is consumed in large quantities over 3–4 days.

This is a severe necrotizing disease of the small intestine. After a 24-hour incubation period, illness ensues with intense abdominal pain, bloody diarrhea, vomiting, and shock. The mortality rate is about 40%, usually due to intestinal perforation. The disease is caused by a toxin known as β-toxin, a 35-kilodalton protein that is unusually sensitive to proteases and is, thus, rapidly inactivated by the intestinal enzyme trypsin. The disease usually affects people who eat large, high-protein meals which overwhelm their intestinal trypsin.

DIAGNOSIS

The diagnosis of *C. perfringens* food poisoning should be considered in any diarrheal illness characterized by abdominal pain and moderate to severe diarrhea, unaccompanied by fever and chills. Usually many individuals are involved in the outbreak; the suspect food is beef or chicken that has been stewed, roasted, or boiled earlier, and then allowed to sit without proper refrigeration. The incubation period is 8–14 hours; occasional outbreaks have incubation periods as short as 5–6 or as long as 22 hours.

A form of food poisoning due to *Bacillus cereus* may have similar symptoms, and can only be ruled out by bacteriological study. Enterotoxigenic *E. coli* may also produce these symptoms, although low-grade fever is often present. *Vibrio cholerae* produces more profuse diarrhea, which helps differentiate it from clostridial intoxication. *Salmonella* or *Campylobacter* infections are usually accompanied by fever, a longer incubation period, and more marked systemic signs.

Because *C. perfringens* may be isolated from normal stools, it is helpful to utilize an established serotyping schema to distinguish between about 20 different serotypes. In an outbreak, the same serotype of *C. perfringens* should be recovered from all cases and from the food they ate. If food specimens are not available, the diagnosis may be made by isolating organisms of the same serotype from the stool of most ill individuals but not from that of suitable controls. In the absence of either of these findings, culturing 10^5 or more organisms per gram of food is highly suggestive.

Case 3—*Bacillus cereus*

CASE—OUTBREAK

Six medical students returned to class after a lunch break in Chinatown. Lunch consisted of hot and sour soup, spring rolls, fried rice, and three other Chinese entrées. Two hours later, while listening to Prof. S. expound on the hazards of mushroom poisoning, four of the six felt the urge to vomit and had to excuse themselves from class.

The following questions arose:

Which food is most likely to have contributed to this early onset form of food poisoning?

How could food become so generally contaminated?

ENCOUNTER

B. cereus has been increasingly recognized as a significant cause of food poisoning since about 1970. One percent or less of all outbreaks in the U.S. are caused by this organism. Data from other countries are still generally sparse.

The incubation period for the outbreaks of emetic illness is usually 2–3 hours, whereas that for the diarrheal outbreaks is 6–14 hours. The clear-cut association between this vomiting syndrome and fried rice deserves emphasis. Most outbreaks of syndrome in the U.S. and in Great Britain implicate this dish as the vehicle. The diarrheal illness, however, has been caused by a variety of vehicles including boiled beef, sausage, chicken soup, vanilla sauce, and puddings.

B. cereus is found in about 25% of foodstuff sampled, including cream, pudding, meat, spices, dry potatoes, dry milk, spaghetti sauces, and rice. Contamination of food products generally occurs before they are cooked. The organisms will grow if the food is maintained at 30°C to 50°C during preparation. Spores survive extreme temperatures and, when allowed to cool relatively slowly, will germinate and multiply. There is no evidence that human carriage of the organism or other means of contamination play a role in transmission.

Contamination of rice by *B. cereus* is attributed to the practice common in Oriental restaurants of allowing large portions of boiled rice to drain unrefrigerated to avoid clumping. The flash frying in the final preparation of certain rice dishes (e.g., fried rice) does not raise the temperature sufficiently to destroy the preformed heat-stable toxin.

PATHOPHYSIOLOGY

Several extracellular toxins produced by strains of *B. cereus* may contribute to their virulence, including an enterotoxin that causes fluid accumulation in the rabbit intestine and stimulates the adenyl cyclase-cyclic AMP system in intestinal epithelial cells (Chapter 9).

A second presumptive toxin has been isolated from a strain of *B. cereus* implicated in an outbreak of vomiting-type illness. Cell-free culture filtrates from this strain do not produce fluid accumulation in rabbit intestine, do not stimulate the adenyl cyclase-cyclic AMP system, and only produce vomiting when fed to rhesus monkeys. This "vomiting toxin" is heat stable.

CLINICAL FEATURES

Food poisoning due to *B. cereus* has two main clinical manifestations, diarrheal and emetic. The diarrheal, long incubation form of the illness is characterized by diarrhea (96%), abdominal cramps (75%), and vomiting (23%). Fever is uncommon. The duration of disease ranges from 20–36 hours, with a median of 24 hours.

The emetic form of the illness has as predominant symptoms vomiting (100%) and abdominal cramps (100%). Diarrhea is only present in one-third of affected individuals. The duration of this illness ranges from 8–10 hours with a median of 9 hours. In both types of illness, the disease is usually mild and self-limited.

The vomiting syndrome must be differentiated from *S. aureus* food poisoning. As stated above, the association with fried rice is epidemiologically useful in differentiating the two organisms.

FOOD POISONING DUE TO INVASIVE ORGANISMS

Case 4—*Salmonella* gastroenteritis

> *Forty-eight hours after eating poorly cooked chicken, Mr. T. developed fever, shaking chills, abdominal cramps and blood tinged diarrhea. The illness lasted several days, and fever and diarrhea gradually abated. Mr. T. is a 65-year-old individual with a silent abdominal arterial aneurysm. Unbeknown to him or to his physician, the organisms causing his febrile diarrheic episode seeded the bloodstream and invaded the aneurysm. Ten days after the initial episode, Mr. T. developed more fever and chills, and his aneurysm expanded. Blood cultures were positive for* Salmonella typhimurium. *Surgery and antibiotics were required. Fortunately, Mr. T. survived.*

This case underscores the invasive potential of several bacteria associated with food poisoning. A number of organisms are associated with invasiveness; particularly common agents are *Salmonella* and *Campylobacter*. More uncommon bacterial causes are *Vibrio parahaemolyticus*, *Yersinia enterocolitica*, and a specific strain of *E. coli*. Invasiveness is generally associated with the presence of neutrophils in stool and systemic signs like fever, chills, myalgias, and headache. These organisms are discussed in Chapters 17 and 18.

Other Invasive Agents of Food Poisoning

Vibrio parahaemolyticus

The organism, like *Vibrio cholera*, is often associated with contaminated shellfish. The organism tends to behave as one of the "invasive" pathogens, rather than as a toxin-producing one, such as *V. cholera*.

Yersinia enterocolitica

Y. enterocolitica is a Gram-negative rod that has recently been implicated as a cause of food poisoning. Contaminated milk has been one well-documented source. Infection due to this organism generally resembles the invasive variety although a heat-stable enterotoxin has been described. Tissue invasion, frequently mimicking acute appendicitis, is very common with this infection. At surgery, the appendix of such patients may be spared but the mesenteric lymph nodes surrounding the appendix will be markedly inflamed.

Escherichia coli

Although *E. coli* is part of the host's normal flora, there are some toxigenic and enteropathogenic strains that are associated with food poisoning. Toxigenic *E. coli* occurs in about 50% of travelers' diarrhea (Chapter 17). These organisms are ingested by travelers through contaminated salads, raw fruits, and vegetables. This syndrome is usually associated with watery diarrhea. Fever is less common. The organisms make both a heat-labile and heat-stable enterotoxin.

There is also a syndrome of bloody diarrhea, generally without fever caused by a "vero toxin"-producing strain of *E. coli* (serotype O157:H7). The mechanism of action of this toxin appears to be identical to that of *Shigella*, the agent of bacillary dysentery. A rare consequence of this illness in children is the hemolytic uremia syndrome (Chapter 18), which can lead to severe damage to the kidney and hemolytic anemia. The agent has been epidemiologically connected to poorly cooked hamburger.

"ARIZONA"

The organism called "Arizona" is a motile Gram-negative rod closely related to *Salmonella*. It has been implicated in outbreaks of gastroenteritis and enteric fever. Various vehicles have included eggs or poultry as the contaminated products. Because of the similarities to *Salmonella*, contaminated animal products should be considered the usual vehicle.

The syndromes of "Arizona" infection are also very similar to salmonellosis. Gastroenteritis, enteric fever, bacteremia, or localized infection have been described. The incubation period is similar to *Salmonella*. Usually, symptoms develop 24–48 hours after ingestion of contaminated food. Fever, headache, nausea, vomiting, abdominal pain, and watery diarrhea may occur, as well as marked prostration. Symptoms may persist for several days. Therapy and prevention are also similar to those employed for salmonellosis.

Listeria monocytogenes

This organism is becoming increasingly recognized as a food-borne pathogen. *Listeria monocytogenes* is a Gram-positive, motile rod that is relatively heat resistant; it withstands pasteurization of milk. *Listeria* is widely distributed in nature, found in the intestinal tract of various animals and man, as well as in sewage, soil, and water.

The syndromes usually associated with listeriosis include meningitis, bacteremia, or focal metastatic disease. Frequently, gastrointestinal symptoms such as diarrhea precede the bacteremic disease. The organism has a propensity to affect adults who are either immunosuppressed or pregnant. The evidence that *Listeria* is related to food-borne illness is accumulating from investigations of several recent epidemics. Contaminated cole slaw, raw and pasteurized milk have been implicated as vehicles for epidemic listeriosis. The source of sporadic *Listeria* infection is less well understood.

CONTROL AND PREVENTION

The common theme that ties all food-borne illnesses together is the improper handling of food before its consumption. In a study of factors responsible for food-borne outbreaks in the U.S. over a 15-year period, it was shown that inadequate refrigeration is the single most frequent factor (Table 72.3). Usually, other factors are also associated with a

Table 72.3. Factors That Contributed to Food-borne Disease Outbreaks in the United States from 1961–1976

Factor	Percentage Implicated[a]
Inadequate refrigeration	47
Food prepared too far in advance of service	21
Infected person with poor personal hygiene	21
Inadequate cooking	16
Inadequate holding temperature	16
Inadequate reheating	12
Contaminated raw ingredient	11
Cross-contamination	7
Dirty equipment	7

[a]Percentage values total more than 100% because more than one factor may contribute to food-borne outbreak.

specific outbreak, such as advanced preparation of food without adequate storage, or improper reheating. To a lesser degree, contaminated equipment, cross-contamination, and poor personal hygiene of food preparation personnel may contribute to outbreaks. The ubiquity of *Salmonella*, *Campylobacter*, *B. cereus*, and *C. perfringens* makes it mandatory that food be cooked properly and stored at low temperature. It becomes obvious that control is based on inhibiting bacterial growth, preventing contamination after preparation, and killing potential pathogens with cooking. In general, foods should be heated to internal temperatures of 165°F, but lower temperatures for longer periods of time is also effective. (Would you like to think twice before ordering "steak tartare, sushi, or other uncooked or undercooked meat or fish?). Once cooked or processed, foods must be held at temperatures of 40°F or below.

Although these control measures are standard, many places where food preparation takes place do not abide by them. It is through diligent efforts of public health officials that reported outbreaks are investigated and food preparation techniques corrected. Therefore, recognition and reporting of food-borne illness becomes essential in the control of the problem. Education of the public, nurses, physicians, and eating establishment personnel is crucial to the control of food-borne illness. Carriage of most of the organisms considered in this chapter is not a problem, with the exception of staphylococci. Inasmuch as staphylococcal carriage is necessary for the development of this illness, food handlers must be educated to watch for boils and pustules.

TREATMENT

Because these illnesses are generally self-limited and, for the most part, toxin-mediated, antibiotics play no major role either in therapy or prophylaxis. Fluid replacement is a major consideration in all of these illnesses. Occasionally, with more invasive pathogens such as *Salmonella*, *Shigella*, *Listeria*, or *Campylobacter*, antibiotic therapy may be necessary.

SUGGESTED READING

Centers for Disease Control. Foodborne disease outbreaks. Annual summary.

Dack GM, ed. Food poisoning. Chicago: The University of Chicago Press, 1956.

Fleming DE, Cochi SL, MacDonald KL, et al. Pasteurized milk as a vehicle of infection in an outbreak of listeriosis. N Engl J Med 1985;312:404–407.

Lowenstein MS. Epidemiology of *Clostridium perfringens* food poisoning. N Engl J Med 1972;286:1026–1028.

Reimann H, Bryan FL, eds. Foodborne infections and intoxications, 2nd ed. New York: Academic Press, 1979.

Terranova W, Blake PA. *Bacillus cereus* food poisoning. N Engl J Med 1978;289:143–144.

Principles of Epidemiology

73

David R. Snydman

Epidemiology is the study of the determinants of disease in a population. It deals with both infectious and noninfectious etiologies. When infectious agents are involved, the aim is to understand their mode of transmission and what predisposes a population to a particular agent. The practical purpose of epidemiology is to control the **spread** of disease in a population, **either by limiting microbial transmission or by altering the susceptibility of a population.** Commonly used measures include removing the source of the agent, controlling its transmission, and immunizing the population.

This chapter will consider epidemiological concepts and methods through the examination of an epidemiological "case," the investigation of a new disease. This will be followed by the consideration of general epidemiological issues.

EPIDEMIOLOGICAL "CASE"

In October, 1975, the Department of Health of Connecticut received separate calls from two mothers living on rural roads in the towns of Lyme and Old Lyme. They reported that several children in their households and the neighborhood had what appeared to be arthritis. They had voiced their concern to local physicians and were not deterred by being told that arthritis is "not infectious."

Given the unusual nature of these reports, the epidemiologists considered the following questions:

Were these cases related?
Were there other similar cases?
Was this an infectious form of arthritis?
What forms of arthritis are infectious?

After discussing the cases with the parents and local physicians, the epidemiologists decided that this situation deserved looking into. What steps did they take and what principles did they apply to their study?

EPIDEMIOLOGICAL METHODOLOGY

The Connecticut epidemiologists undertook what is known as an **epidemic investigation**, the study of the extent, characteristics, mode of transmission, and etiology of a cluster of cases. It is perhaps the most self-evident of the methods used in epidemiology, but by no means the only one. Others, including **case-control studies, cohort studies,** and **epidemiological interventions**, are discussed below.

An **epidemic investigation** is undertaken when there is an **increase in the number of cases of a disease over what is considered to be the norm or standard**. In the Connecticut study, it was necessary to determine first if indeed this was an epidemic. The determination of an epidemic depends solely on the background incidence of the disease in the population and not on an absolute cut-off point. For example, before the advent of the polio vaccine in the 1950s, there were about 50,000 cases of the disease in the U.S. annually. After the vaccine came into widespread use, the number of case dropped dramatically to about 10 per year. Therefore, one or two cases of polio might be considered to be an epidemic!

In addition to epidemics, there are endemic and pandemic diseases. An **endemic infectious disease** is one that is consistently found in the population, such as dental caries, gonorrhea, or athlete's foot. **A pandemic** is a worldwide epidemic; examples are the current AIDS pandemic, or the Spanish flu pandemic of 1918–1919.

Case Definition

The investigators of the cases of Connecticut arthritis began by asking whether other individuals had the same disease. They first had to establish a set of clinical criteria known as the **case definition**. After all, many people have arthritis. From the mothers, physicians, and school nurses in the area, they obtained a list of other individuals who may have had the same symptoms. After examining the patients and taking careful histories they included, as fitting the case definition, those with the following clinical picture: (*a*) a sudden onset of swelling and pain in a knee or other large joint lasting a week to several months; (*b*) those affected had had several attacks that recurred several times at intervals of a few months; (*c*) nearly one-half of those affected also had fever and fatigue.

Time, Place, and Personal Characteristics of Patients

Armed with a usable case definition, the investigators found other cases in Old Lyme and two adjacent towns. The best source of additional cases were the two determined mothers who had made the original phone calls. Between current and past episodes, the investigators collected 51 cases that conformed to the case definition. They could now proceed to determine what epidemiologists call the time, place, and personal characteristics of these cases. The **time characteristics** include the **time of onset** of the disease and its **duration**. As shown in Figure 73.1, many of the Connecticut cases clustered in the summer and early fall. The duration of each bout of the disease varied from a week to a few months, and 69% of the cases had recurrences of the symptoms. Not knowing at this time the etiology of the disease, they could not determine another important time characteristic, namely the **incubation period**, or the interval from exposure to the first onset of symptoms.

Place characteristics are primarily the site of residence and the area in which the affected cases lived. For occupation-related illnesses, this can also include the place of work. The cases were concentrated in

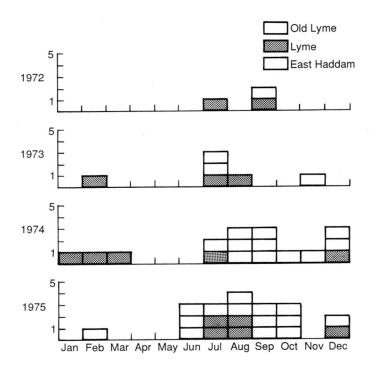

three adjacent towns on the eastern side of the Connecticut River. Most of the patients lived in wooded areas near streams and lakes. **Personal characteristics** include the age and sex of the patients and any possible genetic predisposition to the disease. Of the 51 cases, 39 were children, nearly evenly divided between the sexes. There was no discernible familial pattern. The epidemiologists now listed the cases by the time of onset and constructed what is called an **epidemic curve.** They gave this outbreak the name "Lyme arthritis," later modified to **Lyme disease,** its current eponym.

The epidemiologists now posed other questions. Was the outbreak a surveillance artifact based on the fact that many questions about arthritis were being asked by outsiders? The simplest way to assess this was to go elsewhere and to ask the same questions. The answer, from surveying towns across the Connecticut River, was that increased interest did not result in an increase in the number of cases of arthritis reported. The team then asked: was this an infectious disease? The most common arthritic conditions of childhood, such as juvenile rheumatoid arthritis, are collagen vascular problems and not known to be infectious. Nonetheless, the clustering of cases, the fact that most of them began in the summer or early fall, and that they were most frequently located in wooded areas along lakes or streams suggested an arthropod transmitted disease, possibly viral. If so, would it be a new one?

Is Lyme Disease Communicable?

Many infectious diseases are **communicable,** e.g., measles, polio, or tuberculosis. Others, such as a ruptured appendix, urinary tract infections, or osteomyelitis, are not. Was Lyme disease communicable, or did it merely affect especially susceptible individuals? To answer this question, the investigators attempted to trace contacts, but even in families with multiple affected members, the onset of illness had usually taken place in different years. They tried to identify a common exposure, but none could be found. However, there was an intriguing clue. About one-quarter of the patients had reported that the symptoms of arthritis were preceded by an unusual skin rash. The rash had started as a red spot that spread to form a 6-inch ring. What was the connection? An astute dermatology consultant remembered that similar manifestations had been described in 1910 in Sweden and attributed to tick bites. This rash went by the impressive name of "erythema chronicum migrans."

The investigators undertook a **case control study**, matching of the cases with a similar group of control or unaffected persons. After matching for age, sex, and any other relevant factors, the epidemiologists looked for any differences between the two groups that may give clues as to possible risk factors. They found one—those affected were more likely to live in a household with pets. One consequence is that they were more likely to come in contact with the ticks that dogs and cats pick up in the woods of that region. In a roundabout way, this clue became more credible when they remembered a suggestive clinical finding.

So far, the connection between the rash and Lyme disease depended on **retrospective evidence**. To make the connection stronger, it became appropriate to ask if patients with the signs of erythema chronicum migrans progress to develop Lyme disease? The team set up a **prospective study**, looking for patients with the rash and observing them for some time. Indeed, of 32 new cases of erythema chronicum migrans, 19 progressed to show the signs and symptoms of Lyme disease. The "tick connection" became even more plausible after a thorough entomological survey. Insects and ticks were collected from Lyme and surroundings, with the finding that adult ticks were 16 times more abundant on the east side of the Connecticut River than on the west side. This corresponded roughly to the proportion of incidence of cases of Lyme disease in the two areas. In addition, many more tick bites were reported by the arthritis patients than by their neighbors without the disease. Thus, the tick-rash-arthritis connection seemed more and more plausible. We will see that the final proof of this scheme awaited the discovery of the etiological agent and the direct demonstration of its transmission via ticks.

At the same time, a **surveillance network** had been set up in Connecticut and part of the adjacent states to gather information about other cases. A careful study revealed that, contrary to the earliest reports, the disease was more frequent in adults than in children. It was easier to recognize arthritis as an unusual occurrence in children. Many arthritis patients had serious manifestations, such as neurological dysfunction and myocarditis. Thus, the disease turned out to be considerably more complex than described by the original case definition. This illustrates an important epidemiological point. An early case definition is, of necessity, tentative, and may be modified when the full spectrum of the disease becomes known. As an example of a complex case definition, see the one developed for AIDS (Table 37.4).

Search for the Etiological Agent

So far, the investigators could conclude with assurance that Lyme disease was an infection, most likely transmitted by ticks. It appeared to be a new clinical entity. However, until this time, the search for the etiological agent had proved unproductive. Despite many attempts, no laboratory had succeeded in isolating a virus, which, at the time, seemed to be a good candidate for being the agent of the disease. On the other hand, the investigators collected anecdotal evidence that tetracycline, erythromycin, or penicillin were clinically effective. With time, more physicians reported on the beneficial effect of antibiotics, making a bacterial etiology more likely. At about this time, entomologists and microbiologists at the Rocky Mountain Public Health Laboratory in Montana, who were experts on tick-borne diseases, examined ticks sent from the affected area and found that the gut of many specimens contained unusual spirochetes. Were these the agents of Lyme disease?

Using a culture medium that supports the growth of tick- or louse-borne spirochetes, the microbiologists succeeded in growing a newly recognized spirochete. Soon thereafter, they isolated the spirochete from human cases and the immune responses of patients were linked to this organism. The spirochete was classified among the *Borrelia*, a group that includes the agent of another tick-borne disease also found in the U.S., recurrent fever. The agent of Lyme disease was given the name *B. burgdorferi*, in honor of the entomologist who discovered the organism in the ticks.

With a simple diagnostic test at hand, investigators in many parts of the world could carry out serological surveys or **serosurveys**, that is, they determined the proportion of persons with antibodies to *B. burgdorferi*. In general, serosurveys allow recognition of a wide range of clinical manifestations, from asymptomatic cases to full-blown disease. This is important because, in most infectious diseases, there are many more asymptomatic than clinically overt cases. Using these techniques, Lyme disease has been diagnosed in other parts of the U.S., especially on the East and West Coasts, as well as in Canada, Europe, Asia, and Australia. It is considered a serious disease, especially because of its important and chronic neurological manifestations.

The original puzzle of "Lyme arthritis" had now been solved. A few years after the original phone calls, a new disease was described, its agent and mode of transmission were identified, and preventive and therapeutic measures had been instituted. Note that it took the joint effort of epidemiologists, clinicians, entomologists, microbiologists, and alert and determined members of the public.

VARIETY OF THE ROUTES OF TRANSMISSION

Humans As Reservoirs

We now turn from a specific example to a more general consideration of epidemiological principles. The first is the mode of transmission (Table 73.1). **Transmission from human to human** may take place from parent to offspring or between mature individuals. **Vertical transmission** refers to the passage of an agent from an infected mother to her fetus or infant. The most intimate mode is via the **transplacental route**. Examples of such congenitally acquired diseases are syphilis, and rubella. Newborns may also pick up chlamydiae, gonococci, cytomegalovirus, or hepatitis B virus during passage through the birth canal. Other organisms may be transmitted via mother's milk.

Horizontal transmission may be between individuals in close proximity or living far away, and includes intimate modes, such as sexual intercourse, or more casual ones, such as touching another person, breathing of aerosols, etc. The actual path of an organism from one person to another depends on the way the agent exits the body of the

Table 73.1. Examples of Modes of Transmission

Modes of Transmission	Example	Factor	Route of Entry
Direct contact			
Respiratory aerosol	Influenza	Crowding?	Lung
	Tuberculosis	Household	Lung
Nasal secretions	Respiratory syncytial virus	Household, nosocomial	Upper respiratory tract
Droplets	Meningococcus	Crowding	Nasopharynx
Skin	Streptococcus (impetigo)	Crowding	Skin
Semen	AIDS	Sexual contact	Mucous membrane
Transplacental	Hepatitis B	Carrier	Mother
Indirect contact			
Blood	Hepatitis B	Transfusion, needlestick	Blood
	AIDS	Transfusion	Blood
Stool	Hepatitis A	Ingestion	GI tract
Animal	*Salmonella*	Ingestion	GI tract
Inanimate	*Legionella*	Water contamination	Respiratory tract
Arthropod vector			
Tick	Lyme disease	Bite	Skin, blood
Mosquito	Malaria	Bite	Blood

donor. Thus, bacteria or viruses that infect the respiratory tract are often expelled as aerosols during coughing and even talking, and may be inhaled by bystanders. If the organism is resistant to drying, as is the case with the tubercle bacillus, the danger of inhalation may persist for a long time. Intestinal pathogens often cause diarrhea, which increases their distribution in the environment and, under conditions of poor sanitation, results in contaminated drinking water and foodstuffs.

Some diseases are acquired by breaching the skin or mucous membranes by trauma, an insect bite, blood transfusions, or contaminated hypodermic needles. Agents that are transmitted in this fashion include the AIDS or hepatitis B viruses. Many of the agents that are transmitted by insect vectors have different life cycles in the vector and in the host. Note that some of these organisms may be transmitted by more than one of these routes. Thus, HIV infection may be passed transplacentally, by sexual intercourse, or by the use of needles.

Nonhuman Reservoirs

Other diseases are acquired from **nonhuman reservoirs**. These include the **zoonoses** (Chapter 69), where the reservoir is an animal. Transmission from the animal may be direct, as in the bite from a rabid dog, or via insect vectors, as in the plague or the viral encephalitides. Lyme disease is also a zoonosis in which the natural reservoir are mammals such as deer that share the same ticks with humans.

For other diseases, the **reservoir is the inanimate environment** and the organisms live freely in nature. For example, the clostridia of gas gangrene are commonly found in soils. However, humans or animals may contribute to the frequency with which the agents are found in nature. Thus, cholera bacilli grow naturally in warm estuaries, probably on the surface of shellfish. However, contamination from human feces may help the organisms become established in a previously uninfected area.

Incubation Periods And Communicability

The length of the incubation period differs considerably among infectious diseases, from a few hours to months and years (Table 73.2). It

Table 73.2. Examples of Incubation Periods

Disease	Range of Period
Staphylococcal food poisoning	1–6 hours
Clostridial food poisoning	12–24 hours
Hepatitis A	14–42 days
Hepatitis B	30–180 days
Gonorrhea	2–9 days
Salmonellosis	0.5–3 days
Epstein-Barr virus infection	21–49 days
Mycoplasma pneumoniae infection	8–21 days
Varicella	10–21 days
AIDS	5 years or more
Leprosy	7 months to 5 years

is influenced by many factors. For example, a large infective dose may shorten it and a small one may lengthen it. To the epidemiologists, the incubation period is particularly important because, **during this time, some diseases may be transmitted from asymptomatic patients.** Control of transmission may, therefore, have to rely on special surveillance methods that include infected but asymptomatic persons. The periods of incubation and of communicability are not always the same. For example, the incubation period in hepatitis A most commonly lasts for 3–4 weeks. However, individuals can communicate the virus only for 1 or 2 weeks before the onset of the disease.

The period of communicability may extend itself long after the disease symptoms abate, as in the case of chronic carriers. For example, hepatitis B carriers can usually transmit the virus for the length of time they carry it. In many of the preceding chapters, the carrier state has been discussed at some length (see Chapter 14 for discussion of the gonococcus; Chapter 18 for *Salmonella typhi*; Chapter 26 for chlamydiae; Chapter 37 for HIV; Chapter 40 for herpesviruses; and Chapter 41 for hepatitis viruses).

Individual Susceptibility

Human beings differ in their predisposition to infectious diseases. We have all encountered individuals who seem more prone to respiratory or intestinal infections than the majority. For many of these persons, we do not know the reason for this variability. They may have subtle deficiencies in certain of their defense mechanisms. When these deficiencies become severe and the risks are more evident, the cause is often easier to ascertain. Chapter 66 discusses the consequences of the major kinds of innate and acquired immune deficiencies.

The epidemiologist must be aware of the different susceptibility of members of the population. Age, sex, nutritional status, previous exposure, and immune competence all contribute to a greater or to a lesser susceptibility to a particular infectious disease. Thus, children and older persons are frequently more susceptible to bacterial pneumonia or intestinal infections. The incidence of the carrier state of hepatitis B is greater in males than in females. It is also more frequent among individuals with Down syndrome or those receiving hemodialysis.

Genetic factors are also known to play a role, although for the most part, the data are inconclusive. The importance of these factors is often difficult to unravel from a myriad of socioeconomic factors, such as those that contribute to the state of health and nutrition. Nonetheless, the role of genetic factors has been well established in certain diseases.

It was shown, for example, that among identical twins living apart, if one contracted tuberculosis, the other had a much greater chance than average of getting the disease. Nonidentical twins did not show this pattern. One of the most intensively studied genetic effects is the decreased susceptibility to malaria of persons with the sickle cell trait (Chapter 50). It is also well established that non-Caucasians are more prone to the disseminated form of coccidioidomycosis than Caucasians.

PRACTICAL ASPECTS OF EPIDEMIOLOGY

In a civilized society, epidemiology is everyone's business. The practicing physician and all members of the health team must be aware of the public health implications of a given patient's infectious disease. To safeguard both the public interest and the rights of privacy of patients, a considerable body of local and national laws has been developed in most countries of the world. For instance, in the U.S., certain communicable diseases are **notifiable**, that is, physicians are obliged to report them to the U.S. Public Health Service. The information collected is published in a readily available pamphlet, the **Morbidity and Mortality Weekly Reports**, or **MMWR**, which lists all routine information and calls attention to unusual occurrences. In addition, each state has its own surveillance mechanism and reporting requirements for the study of communicable diseases within its borders. Each has a **State Board of Health** and a **Reference Laboratory** equipped to carry out special diagnostic tests that are often outside the scope of hospital laboratories.

CONCLUSIONS

Epidemiology may appear to be a remote discipline, practiced mainly by public health officials. In fact, it pervades all forms of medical practice and furnishes important clues for the diagnosis of infectious diseases. Thus, inquiry into time and place characteristics should be part of the usual process of taking a clinical history. Epidemiological information may reveal how people encounter disease agents, and can help reduce exposure and spread of infectious diseases.

SUGGESTED READING

Esdaile JM, Feinstein AR. Lyme disease: a medical detective story. 1985 Medical and Health Annual. Encyclopedia Britannica: 267–271.

Rothman JK. Modern epidemiology. Boston: Little, Brown, 1986.

Sackett DL, Haynes RB, Tugwell P. Clinical epidemiology. A basic science for clinical medicine. Boston: Little, Brown, 1985.

Steere AC, Malawista SE, Snydman DR, et al. Lyme arthritis. An epidemic of oligoarticular arthritis in children and adults in three Connecticut communities. Arthrit Rheum 1977;20:7–17.

Nutrition and Infection

74

Gerald T. Keusch

Malnutrition remains the most prevalent cause of acquired immunodeficiency in the world, leading to significant morbidity and mortality from infection. Malnutrition, impaired host defenses, and infection interact cyclically to produce progressive worsening of the host, resulting in death unless corrected (Fig. 74.1).

The initial manifestation of malnutrition is often an infection, typically manifested by loss of appetite (anorexia) and fever. Even with a mild cold, people are usually satisfied with a cup of tea and a slice of toast and may become nauseated at the sight of normally mouthwatering food; therefore, food intake usually drops off. At the same time, fever imposes greater demands for energy, because, on average, energy-consuming enzymatic reactions speed up by 13% per degree rise in temperature. In patients with severe septicemia, the resting metabolic rate rises as much as 35–40% above normal.

Greater energy demands during infections are accompanied by marked changes in host metabolism, regardless of the causative organism. The purpose of these changes appears to be preparing the host to survive the infection by consuming its own body stores of energy and protein, as if in anticipation of the decrease in food intake. As the host tissues are utilized, the individual loses weight and is literally consumed in the process. These dramatic changes have been recognized since antiquity and are the reason why tuberculosis, for example, is popularly called consumption in several languages. Tuberculosis is a good example of a chronic infectious disease that causes wasting, although it is not necessary that the process be chronic. Acute infections also cause detectable catabolism of host tissue. Small losses may be induced even by attenuated live virus vaccines.

ENERGY METABOLISM

With decreased food intake and increased caloric demands, how does the host face the shortfall in energy? **Glucose oxidation rate** increases, even though the patient experiences hyperglycemia (typical of fasting) and a delayed glucose disappearance curve (as in diabetes). The readily available endogenous sources of glucose are the carbohydrate stores (e.g., liver glycogen), which suffice for some 24 hours only, and fat, a large store that may not be as efficiently used in infection as it is during starvation. The only other **large energy stores** are the **body proteins**, which can be converted into energy by proteolysis, deamination of amino acids, and conversion of carbon skeletons into glucose. **Gluconeogenesis**, as this process is called, increases in the liver of infected patients, utilizing alanine and other substrates. Amino acids are lost because of deamination, which leads to loss of nitrogen in the

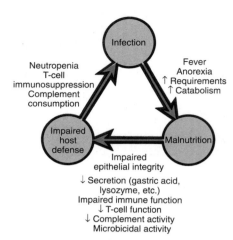

Figure 74.1. The triangle of interaction between malnutrition, infection, and host defenses. Malnutrition may be initiated by primary or secondary dietary deficiency (e.g., malabsorptive states), or by metabolic effects of infection. The consequences of this are impairment in host defenses, which, in turn, lead to an increased burden of infection and further malnutrition.

urine, and oxidation of their carbon skeleton, resulting in CO_2 excretion via the lungs. These adaptations are facilitated by elevated levels of insulin, glucagon, growth hormone, and corticosteroids, all of which are seen in the infected host.

PROTEIN METABOLISM

Gluconeogenesis is not the only process fed by proteolysis of host tissue. **New protein synthesis** also increases dramatically in the liver, using amino acids released from muscle. Some of the new proteins synthesized are components of the host defense response (see Chapter 6); examples are **C3** and **complement factor B** (used in the alternative pathway of activation). Some of the proteins made in large amounts during infection are found in very low concentrations in the normal host. These include **C-reactive protein** and **serum amyloid A**, which may play immunoregulatory functions. Still other proteins serve as transport or carrier proteins, such as haptoglobulin or the copper-binding protein, **ceruloplasmin**, or function as enzyme inhibitors, such as α_1-**antitrypsin** or α_1-**antichymotrypsin**. At the same time, there is a reduction in the rate of synthesis of the hepatic export proteins, **albumin** and **transferrin**, regulated at the transcriptional level. The concentration of these proteins in serum drops to very low levels, inversely proportional to the severity of the stimulus, and may be predictive of the outcome of the infection.

Alterations in plasma proteins induced by inflammation are put to use in the diagnostic laboratory. For example, the increases in fibrinogen levels due to the acute phase response causes the stacking of red blood cells as in a pile of coins ("rouleaux" formation), resulting in their more rapid sedimentation. An elevated "sed rate" is a simple and general marker of inflammation.

LIPID METABOLISM

In some infections (typically, Gram-negative bacterial septicemia), serum becomes milky due to an impressive **increase in the concentration of triglycerides**. This is due to an increase in hepatic fatty acid synthesis induced by the cytokines tumor necrosis factor (**TNF**), interleukin-1 (**IL-1**), and IL-6. In addition, the ability to store fats is inhibited, contributing to the excessive levels of lipids in serum. Although there are plenty of lipids around, they cannot be effectively used for energy production via oxidation of ketones. This is due, in part, to a so-called "pseudodiabetic" hormonal imbalance in the patient with bacterial septicemia. However, elevated levels of **VLDL** (very low-density lipoproteins) may help detoxify lipopolysaccharide endotoxin and some viruses, and thus, may be a protective mechanism.

MINERAL METABOLISM

A characteristic change in patients with severe acute infections is a drop in the serum level of **iron** and **zinc**, and an increase in that of **copper**. These changes are due to alterations in level of proteins that bind these cations. The increase in copper results from the increased production of the copper-binding plasma protein, **ceruloplasmin**. The decrease in iron is due primarily to increase in the synthesis of **apoferritin**, another acute phase protein that binds iron and prevents its release from labile intracellular pools. Conversion of this storage iron to **hemosiderin**, a nonreutilizable form of iron that is unavailable for hematopoiesis, ultimately results in the anemia of chronic infections. The decrease in the zinc level results from the synthesis of **metallothionin**, an intracellular zinc-binding protein.

What is the effect of changes in the levels of these serum cations? Reduction in serum iron may have a protective effect by reducing the amount available for the growth of pathogens, at least for those that lack efficient iron uptake mechanisms (see Chapter 3). The decrease of zinc in serum is accompanied by its increase in lymphoid cells where it may also contribute to their proliferative ability in response to antigenic stimulation, because key enzymes in this process are zinc-containing metalloenzymes, for example, thymidine kinase. Ceruloplasmin oxidizes ferrous iron, increasing the availability of this cation for hematopoiesis, partly compensating for the lack of iron.

MECHANISMS OF METABOLIC CHANGES

Many of the metabolic alterations that accompany infections can be attributed to the action of at least three cytokines, **IL-1, IL-6,** and **TNF** (or cachectin). These physiologically reactive proteins are made by activated macrophages in response to a variety of stimuli, such as the presence of endotoxin or the act of phagocytosis. IL-1 was first known as "endogenous pyrogen," a leukocyte product that acts on the hypothalamic temperature regulation centers to produce fever (Chapters 6 and 70). It was later discovered that IL-1 mediates other responses, including the shift of zinc and iron from serum to tissues and the activation of T lymphocytes. IL-1 induces IL-6 synthesis and acts synergistically with TNF.

IL-1 has a wide range of activities that affect host metabolism and the immune response (Fig. 74.2). Acting at the crossroads of metabolic and immunological responses to infection, IL-1 is critically important in the survival of the host under stress. When injected into experimental subjects, it reproduces the major metabolic changes associated with infection described above. IL-1 appears to act by activating the expression of selected genes to produce the proteins of the acute phase response, which are characteristic of the infected state (Chapter 6). It increases production of prostaglandin E_2, which serves as a second messenger at tissue and cellular levels. Some of these activities are due to the ability of IL-1 to increase production of IL-6.

TNF or cachectin shares a number of biological properties with IL-1 and is an inducer of IL-1 (Fig. 74.2). It rapidly produces anorexia and weight loss when given to experimental animals. It produces severe depletion of the fat stores, inhibiting the production of lipoprotein lipase and lipid anabolic enzymes. TNF, like IL-1, also causes fever, increases phagocytic activity of neutrophils, upregulates the expression of genes in the liver for acute phase proteins, and downregulates albumin and transferrin (Chapter 6). In high doses, TNF causes a lethal shock syndrome, which is prevented by the administration of anti-TNF antibodies. Thus, like IL-1, TNF probably plays a role in the pathogenesis of septic shock. It is interesting that the production of both of these cytokines is downregulated at the transcriptional and translational level by glucocorticoids, which may exert a protective effect in the septic shock patient.

CONSEQUENCES OF METABOLIC CHANGES

The loss of protein and energy reserves that occurs during the febrile period of infections leaves the patient at an ebb of nutrient re-

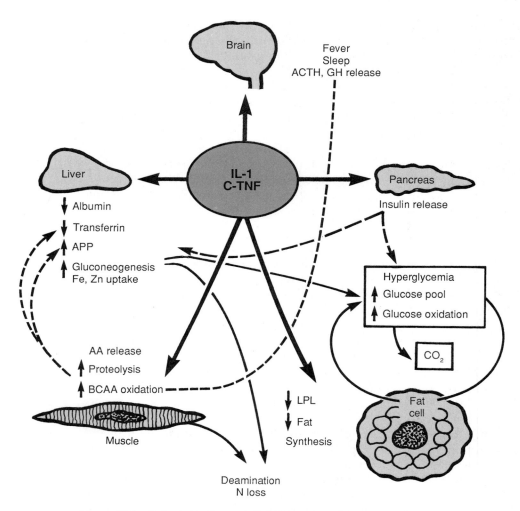

Figure 74.2.   Schematic diagram of the tissue targets for interleukin-1 (IL-1) and/or tumor necrosis factor (TNF) in the metabolic response to infection.

serves. During convalescence, these must be restored. As a rule, replenishment takes about four times longer than loss. Thus, for 1 week of illness, about 1 month is required to replenish the patient, assuming that adequate nutrients are available. Stress-related malnutrition of this sort is not uncommon in the U.S. and other industrialized countries, but is generally not an insurmountable problem. Acute infection-related malnutrition can be reversed by resuming normal diet, and, if necessary, in severely ill hospitalized patients, by enteral or parenteral nutritional rehabilitation. In developing countries, however, the available diet may be inadequate to allow repletion to occur in timely fashion, if at all. The high prevalence of infections in the young means that new diseases may ensue before the patient is nutritionally restored, adding new losses to the deficit left over from the previous episode. Repeated infections result in cumulative losses that lead to severe states of malnutrition.

In children, dietary intake is used not only for normal tissue maintenance and turnover, but for net growth as well. The stress of infection results in cessation of growth and in weight loss. In affluent societies, such growth faltering is quickly erased by rapid catch-up during convalescence. Growth rates may jump by as much as seven times normal during this period. In countries with inadequate diets and frequent infections, the host may never catch up, and this is the reason why adults may be short in stature (except, of course, in certain genetically short-statured populations, such as the Pygmies). Body size may not matter, but infant mortality does. To combat the excessive mortality in children in developing countries, organizations such as UNICEF and the World Health Organization are attempting to promote child survival by reducing the incidence and impact of childhood infections and by improving infant nutrition and encouraging breast feeding.

EFFECT OF MALNUTRITION ON THE IMMUNE SYSTEM

"We are what we eat" is as true for the immune system as it is for the rest of the body. In the past two decades, the impact of malnutrition on the immune system has been demonstrated both in clinical and experimental studies. Most human malnutrition develops in populations that eat inadequate and monotonous diets lacking several nutrients, including energy sources, proteins, minerals, and vitamins. Only rarely are single nutritional deficiencies observed. This mosaic of deficiency diseases is commonly called **protein-energy malnutrition** (PEM). It usually includes deficiencies in iron, zinc, other trace minerals, vitamin A, and often, water- and fat-soluble vitamins.

PEM has a profound impact on certain host defense systems. Most consistent is the **inhibition of cell-mediated immunity** due primarily to a lack of mature functionally differentiated T lymphocytes (Fig. 74.3). The total number of lymphocytes may be normal, but the proportion of mature T cells is decreased and that of null cells is increased. Thus, functions that depend on mature T cells, such as proliferative responses to mitogens, are likely to be diminished. A manifestation of this deficit is a depressed response in PEM patients to skin test antigens that elicit a delayed hypersensitivity reaction, such as tuberculin. The defect in mature T lymphocytes is probably located in the thymus, which fails to induce differentiation of committed T cells (see Chapter 7 for details). It is not yet known with certainty what the mechanism is, but there are suggestions that it may be due to a lack of **thymic hormones** that induce maturation of T lymphocytes. Defects in cell-

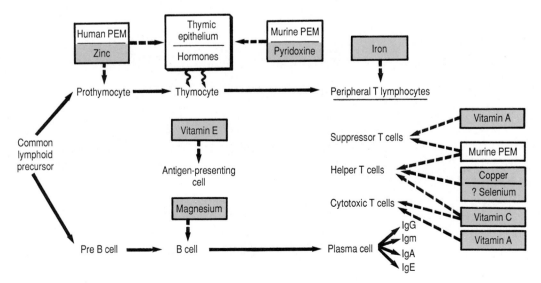

Figure 74.3.   Localization of the specific effects of nutrients on the immunological network.

mediated immunity are the likely reason for the susceptibility of **PEM** patients to intracellular infections such as tuberculosis and to progressive viral diseases such as measles.

Although B cells and immunoglobulin levels are normal in **PEM** patients, they show a **diminished production of certain antibodies**. Many antigens depend on T cells to help initiate the B-cell response. Similarly, the switch from IgM to IgG production is T-cell dependent; a defect in this event may be reflected in the persistence of low-affinity IgM antibodies. In malnourished patients, **some vaccines do not elicit a good antibody response** (e.g., typhoid O antigen, live polio vaccines), whereas other do (e.g., tetanus toxoid, live smallpox vaccine). Thus, **the nutritional state of a population must be taken into account when embarking on an immunization campaign** because protective antibody responses may not occur. Another abnormality in antibody response associated with malnutrition is the **depression in the secretory IgA** at mucosal surfaces.

In PEM patients, the **complement system is generally depressed**. Both classical and alternative activation pathways are affected, especially the latter (Fig. 74.4). All complement components are reduced

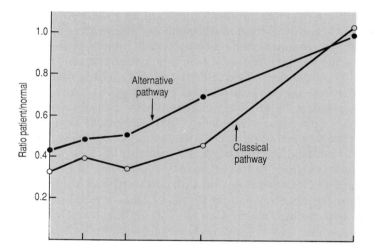

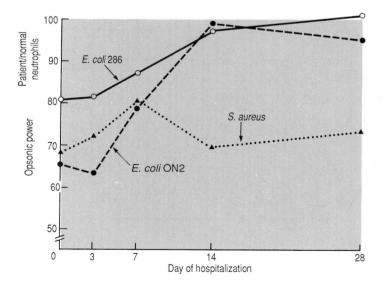

Figure 74.4. Complement and opsonic activity of serum from Guatemalan children with acute protein-energy malnutrition measured over 28 days of nutritional rehabilitation. The *upper panel* shows the level of complement activity via the classical pathway (*open circles*) and via the alternative pathway (*closed circles*). The *lower panel* shows levels of opsonization of *E. coli* via the classical pathway (*open circles*) and the alternative pathway (*closed circles*). Opsonization of *S. aureus* by antibody (not by complement factors) is also shown (*closed triangles*).

These results indicate that the alternative pathway appears to be less affected by malnutrition than the classical pathway. Of the two, the classical pathway is more active in that it leads to a higher degree of opsonization. Note that opsonization of *S. aureus* by immunoglobulins is unaffected by the nutritional status.

in plasma concentration, especially C3 and factor B. This depression may be due to more than one mechanism, including not only reduced synthesis but also greater consumption of complement components during the response to infection. Complement deficiency may condition the host to Gram-negative bacterial infections (Chapter 6).

Phagocytosis and intracellular killing of microorganisms are close to normal in cells of PEM patients studied in vitro. However, there may be functional abnormalities in vivo because of deficits in the accessory humoral factors required for a normal phagocytic response, including complement and immunoglobulin opsonins.

CLINICAL CONSEQUENCES OF ACQUIRED IMMUNE DEFECTS IN PEM

An important principle in infectious diseases is that the success in combating infection depends on the speed and the magnitude with which the host mobilizes defense mechanisms. Small defects in individual components may be unimportant alone, but together can lead to a sluggish response, which may make the difference between asymptomatic infection and severe illness. Generally speaking, the extent to which malnutrition causes disruption of host defenses is related to its intensity. In severe cases, children display a spectrum of clinical manifestations known as **kwashiorkor** (Fig. 74.5).

The clinician should be aware of the patient's nutritional status, whether in developing or in nutritionally affluent countries. For example, elective surgical patients should be screened for their cell-mediated immune status. When malnutrition is found, steps should be taken to correct the problem by appropriate nutritional rehabilitation. This will result in lower morbidity and mortality.

The effects of poor and adequate nutrition in early development are illustrated by a case below that illustrates the multifaceted manifestations of malnutrition on childhood infections.

CASE

J. was born in the highlands of a South American country of native Indian parents. Pregnancy, which was unsupervised, and birth, which was attended by a traditional midwife, were uneventful. J.'s birth was at full term and her weight, 2540 g, was close to the village mean (which is at the 10th percentile of the figures provided for the U.S. by NCHS, the National Center for Health Statistics, Fig. 74.6). The baby took breast milk shortly after birth and had no problem feeding for the first 4 months, when weaning began.

A sample of cord blood had been obtained as part of a prospective research project. Analysis showed an elevated IgM and a low IgA level, consistent with intrauterine antigenic stimulation of the fetus, suggesting prenatal infection (see Chapter 68 for details).

J. developed conjunctivitis at 3 weeks, a urinary tract infection at 5 weeks, and diarrhea lasting 10 days at age 2 months. Weight gain followed the village mean for 2 months and was parallel to the NCHS mean. Thereafter, infectious episodes, including diarrhea, acute respiratory illness, and skin infections, occurred with greater frequency and were associated with periods of deceleration in growth or actual weight loss (Fig. 74.6). At age 11 1/2 months, J. developed bloody diarrhea, fever, and, in a few days, swelling around the eyes, abdomen, and the feet. She was brought to the hospital where acute dysentery and kwashiorkor were diagnosed. Antibiotics and an infusion of glucose were begun. J.'s temperature diminished over the next few days, but the edema increased, anorexia persisted, and she became increas-

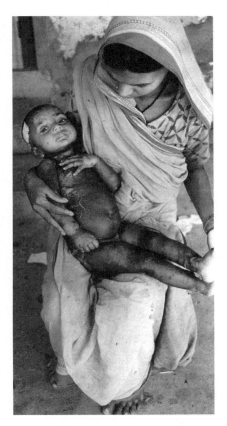

Figure 74.5. A young Bangladeshi child with acute kwashiorkor (a syndrome due to severe chronic protein deficiency) following *Shigella* dysentery. His belly is bloated and the lower extremities edematous, masking a significant loss of lean body mass. Also typical are the scaling black "pellagroid" rash and the apathetic appearance.

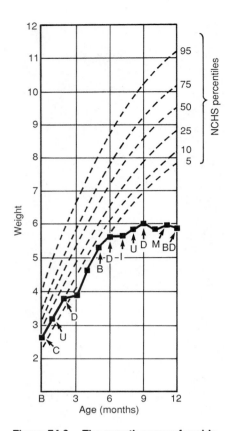

Figure 74.6.   The growth curves for girls, indicating the National Center for Health Statistics percentile standards for the reference population (United States). Baby J.'s progress is shown by the *closed squares.* Symbols: *C* = conjunctivitis; *U* = upper respiratory tract infection; *B* = bronchitis; *I* = impetigo; *M* = measles; *D* = watery diarrhea; *BD* = bloody diarrhea.

ingly lethargic. On the seventh day after admission, she became hypothermic, hypotensive, and unresponsive. Her appearance was similar to that of the child shown in Figure 74.5. Had cultures been taken, it is most likely that Shigella flexneri *would have been found in J.'s stool and* Escherichia coli *in her blood. She died later that evening, on the day of her first birthday.*

Comments

Baby J.'s defenses faced formidable microbial challenges from the first moment of her life. She was soon caught in a downward spiral, with a series of infections contributing to her state of malnutrition. J.'s condition was exacerbated by lack of an adequate diet after weaning, and she suffered from **PEM**. Her clinical course could not be improved by access to appropriate medical care, especially antibiotics and symptomatic care. Most of the metabolic and immunological events characteristic of malnutrition contributed to the weakening of her defenses.

It seems fitting to end this book with the hope that preventable conditions such as J.'s will become more and more exceptional rather than all too common events in human history.

SUGGESTED READING

Beisel WR. Metabolic effects of infection. Prog Food Nutr Sci 1984;8: 43–75.

Dinarello C. Interleukin-1 and interleukin-1 antagonism. Blood 1991;77: 1627–1652.

Grunfeld C, Palladino MA Jr. Tumor necrosis factor: immunological, antitumor, metabolic and cardiovascular activities. Adv Intl Med 1990; 35: 45–71.

Keusch GT, Scrimshaw NS. Selective primary health care: strategies for control of disease in the developing world. XXIII. Control of infection to reduce the prevalence of infantile and childhood malnutrition. Rev Infect Dis 1986;8:273–287.

Keusch GT, Wilson CS, Waksal SD. Nutrition, host defenses, and the lymphoid system. In: Gallin JI, Fauci AS, eds. Advances in host defenses, vol. 2. New York: Raven Press, 1983.

Answers to Self-assessment Questions

Section I

Chapter 2/ Normal Microbial Flora

1. Aspiration pneumonia due to the entry of diverse members of the oral flora into lungs, facilitated by defective ciliary action or factors that increase aspiration (e.g., sedation, drugs, etc.). Peritonitis by entry of members of the fecal flora into the peritoneal cavity via a ruptured appendix or a traumatic break in the intestinal wall. Cystitis caused by fecal *Escherichia coli* due to stasis in the urine flow (e.g., catheterization). Subacute bacteria endocarditis due to oral α-hemolytic streptococci due to their introduction into the circulation of a patient with heart valve disease. *Pneumocystis carinii* pneumonia in AIDS patients due to impaired immune responses. Many other examples could be cited.

2. Normal flora, especially of the gut, is a constant source of low-level antigenic stimulation. The resulting antibodies and cell-mediated immunity are probably involved in defense against certain infections. Some of the antibodies may cross-react with heterologous cell constituents, such as red blood cells of a different ABO type. It is conceivable that some of these antibodies may be involved in autoimmune reactions.

3. The resident flora wards off external pathogens by prior colonization of available sites and by forming metabolites (such as acids, H_2S) that are inimical to invaders. The immune response against members of the normal flora may have cross-reactivity against possible pathogens.

4. The most colonized parts of the body are the mouth and the large intestine, followed by the vagina and the skin. Transiently, microorganisms may be found in the rest of the digestive and respiratory systems. More rarely, the lower urinary tract may be colonized by small numbers of microorganisms. The deep tissues are normally sterile.

5. The main groups are Gram-positive cocci and Gram-negative rods, mainly strict anaerobes.

6. The effects of the normal flora may be observed by comparing germ-free and conventional animals as well as humans whose flora has been disturbed by antimicrobial therapy or surgical interventions.

Chapter 3/ Biology of Infectious Agents

1. Procaryotes lack internal membrane-bound organelles; they do not have a distinct mitotic apparatus and are not capable of endocytosis. With some exceptions, procaryotes have a murein cell wall. Procaryotic ribosomes are smaller than those of eukaryotes

and differ in sensitivity to antibiotics. Lacking a nuclear membrane, transcription and translation may be directly coupled in procaryotes.

2. Smallness makes for faster diffusion of substrates and metabolites. The distance between structural parts makes it possible to connect them directly, as with the transcriptional and translational machineries.

3. Gram positives have a thick murein layer lacking lipopolysaccharide (endotoxin); Gram negatives have a thin one with a distinct outer membrane containing lipopolysaccharide. Gram negatives have pili (fimbriae); Gram positives generally do not.

4. The outer membrane of Gram negatives serves to protect the inner membrane from hydrophobic toxic compounds by virtue of its lipopolysaccharide outer leaflet. To make passage of substrates possible, this membrane has pores formed by proteins called porins. These pores have a molecular size exclusion of 600–700 daltons. Transport mechanisms for specific larger compounds such as iron chelates also exist. Lipopolysaccharide functions as endotoxin, which causes fever, and in large doses, shock.

5. Penicillin works by covalently binding to penicillin-binding proteins involved in the synthesis of cell wall murein. Other biosynthetic processes are not inhibited; thus, the cells "outgrow their coats" and, via the activity of autolysins, burst in hypotonic media.

6. Facilitated diffusion, group translocations, and active transport (via permeases) are the principal mechanisms.

7. DNA replication starts at the replicative origin and proceeds bidirectionally until the replication machinery reaches the terminus. In growing bacteria, the rate of replication is nearly independent of the growth rate. To accommodate for growth that is faster than the rate of replication, bacteria initiate new rounds of replication before the previous ones have finished.

8. Inhibition of protein synthesis does not necessarily cause death because ribosomes may just be released prematurely from mRNA but remain available for future use. Bactericidal protein-inhibiting antibiotics bind to ribosomes and render them inactive even after removal of the drug.

9. Bacterial flagella are organs of propulsion and serve in chemotaxis toward attractants such as nutrients and away from toxic repellents. Pili (fimbriae) participate in the adherence of bacteria to surfaces such as those of animal cells, thus facilitating colonization.

10. Bacteria obtain energy by fermentation, using an organic electron receptor, or respiration, using an inorganic electron receptor, usually oxygen. Fermentation is usually carried out in the absence of oxygen; thus, fermentative bacteria may be obligate or facultative anaerobes. Facultative anaerobes and obligate aerobes require oxygen (or other inorganic electron acceptors such as nitrate or sulfate) to respire. Oxygen is generally toxic to obligate anaerobes.

11. The law of bacterial growth states that the number of cells is a direct function of the number of cells present and an exponential function of a rate constant. In the real world, this condition obtains only for short periods of time, when neither nutrients nor toxic metabolites are limiting.

12. Feedback inhibition results in diminution of enzyme activity but not in the amount of enzyme. Control of gene expression results in

reduction in the synthesis of gene products, e.g., enzymes, but not in the activity of the formed enzyme.

13. Repression of enzyme synthesis via a repressor, attenuation via early termination of mRNA synthesis are two examples.

14. Bacteria respond to lethal challenges by exhibiting global responses that involve activation and inhibition of selected genes. In some cases, the genes involved are transcribed by special σ factors of RNA polymerase.

Chapter 5/ Biological Basis for Antibacterials

1. Mention the sudden availability of such substances after World War II, the concept of selective toxicity, examples of specific metabolic targets. Give examples of diseases that can be effectively treated. Discuss the general concept of drug resistance, its importance in medicine, and why antibiotics should be used prudently (e.g., not against insensitive agents and with a view toward resistance).

2. Sulfonamides compete with para-aminobenzoic acid for the synthesis of folic acid, needed for the synthesis of purines, thymine, thiamine, and other metabolites. Bacteria must make their own folic acid and cannot take it up from the medium. Animal cells can take up preformed folic acid, therefore, are not affected by these drugs.

3. Bactericidal drugs kill bacteria; bacteriostatic ones inhibit their growth. Bactericidal drugs are needed to rid the body of persistent bacteria that cannot be readily cleared by body defenses. This is especially true in bacterial endocarditis and meningitis, or in any infection when the leukocyte count is very low (as after cancer chemotherapy). On the other hand, some bactericidal drugs may take longer to act than bacteriostatic ones, allowing for the accumulation of toxins.

4. Acquired resistance occurs with: (a) inactivation of the drug by hydrolysis (e.g., β-lactamases) or chemical modification (e.g., acetylases); (b) replacement of a sensitive enzyme by a resistant one (e.g., sulfonamide-resistant enzymes in folic acid synthesis); (c) decreased binding affinity for ribosomes (e.g., aminoglycosides); (d) decrease transport into cells (e.g., aminoglycosides); and (e) increased exit from cell (e.g., tetracyclines). Natural resistance occurs from: (a) low accessibility to the target (e.g., Gram-negative bacteria and penicillin), and (b) absence of a target (e.g., mycoplasmata, which lack murein, and penicillin).

5. Association with bacteria, penetration into periplasm in Gram negatives, interaction with penicillin-binding proteins, and activation of an autolysin are the steps involved in β-lactam antibiotics. The most common resistance mechanism affect the first step by hydrolysis of the drugs by β-lactamases.

6. Tetracycline binds to bacteria and is transported into cytoplasm where it inhibits the formation of initiation complex in protein synthesis; resistance is by an increased exit from the cells. Chloramphenicol and macrolides (lincomycin, erythromycin) inhibit the chain elongation step; resistance to chloramphenicol is by acetylation of the drug, to macrolides by modification of ribosome or rRNA. Aminoglycosides cause translational misreading and inhibit elongation of protein chains; resistance is by enzymatic modification of drugs.

7. Antifungal agents generally work by inhibiting the synthesis of fungal cell sterols (ergosterol), which are different from animal cell sterols (cholesterol).

8. Two drugs decrease the chance of a mutant resistant to both arising. (This is particularly important with infections characterized by a large number of infecting bacteria, such as tuberculosis.) A separate advantage of two drugs is that, together, they may cover a wider spectrum of sensitive bacteria. (This is particularly useful in life-threatening infections.) Use of multiple antibiotics may be undesirable because of possible antagonism, additive (or synergistic) toxicity, and the emergence of drug resistance among the bacteria and drug sensitization among the patients.

Chapter 9/ Bacterial Toxins

1. Toxins lyse host cells by destroying membranes via the hydrolysis of compounds such as lecithin (e.g., clostridial lecithinases) or by inserting into membranes to make pores (e.g., staphylococcal α-toxin—a homogeneous pore former, and streptococcal streptolysin O—a heterogeneous pore former).

2. The B portion binds to receptors on the surface of target cells, allowing the A portion (active) to enter and cause damage. In some toxins, the A and B portion are part of the same molecule (e.g., diphtheria toxin), in others they are two separate entities (e.g., cholera toxin).

3. Toxins that work as extracellular hydrolases need not penetrate cells to act (e.g., hyaluronidase, streptokinase). Also, any cytolytic toxins that need not enter cells to cause damage need not possess a B portion.

4. Antitoxins to purified toxin protect against the disease in humans and experimental animals. Nontoxigenic mutants do not cause disease in experimental animals. All isolates from patients with the disease are toxigenic.

5. Cholera toxin acts by ADP-ribosylating G protein, which, in this form, cannot hydrolyze GTP. This modified G protein is locked in a conformation that keeps stimulating adenylate cyclase to make cAMP.

6. Tetanus toxin works on the central nervous system to inhibit the release of inhibitory neurotransmitters, causing neuromuscular excitation. Botulinum toxin works on peripheral nerves causing a presynaptic block in the release of acetylcholine, which results in muscle relaxation.

7. A toxoid should be highly immunogenic and minimally toxic. It should lead to the formation of effective antitoxins. Other practical features include stability, reasonable solubility, and ease of preparation.

8. Exotoxins are secreted proteins; endotoxins are cell membrane lipopolysaccharides. Exotoxins have a limited repertoire of individual activities; endotoxins act on a variety of cells and the complement system. Exotoxins are usually more potent.

9. In low amounts, endotoxins cause local inflammation via activation of macrophages and complement. Systemically, endotoxin in low amounts causes fever.

10. In high amounts, endotoxins cause shock via the increase in interleukin-1 and tumor necrosis factor, plus disseminated intravascular coagulation by activating the clotting mechanisms.

Section II—Bacteria

Chapter 11—Staphylococci: Abscesses and Other Diseases

1. Abscesses and other pyogenic infections of almost any tissue or organ, staphylococcal food poisoning, toxic shock syndrome, and

scalded skin syndrome are the most frequent staphylococcal diseases.

2. Staphylococci are Gram-positive cocci that make sizable colonies on regular agar media, form grape cluster-like cellular arrangements, and secrete extracellular proteins, some of which are virulence factors. Many staphylococci are salt-resistant, one reason why they can (and do) reside on the skin. The main types are the coagulase-positive S. aureus (the most common pathogenic staph), S. epidermidis (an opportunistic pathogen that colonizes surfaces, such as those of prosthetic devices and plastic catheters), S. saprophyticus, and other opportunistic pathogens.

3. Staphylococci that cause abscesses and other pyogenic infections, scalded skin syndrome, and toxic shock may be acquired either from the environment or may be members of the flora of the patient. Staphylococci that cause food poisoning are ingested with contaminated food.

4. Staphylococci generally enter deep tissues through trauma-induced openings but subtler ways of penetration cannot be discounted. Once inside, they ward off the action of phagocytes by producing a cytotoxin (α-toxin), a catalase that impedes oxidative killing by neutrophils, and coagulase that renders the organisms less accessible. The presence of protein A hinders the opsonic activity of antibodies. The pathogenesis of staphylococcal pyogenic infections is extraordinarily multifactorial and it becomes difficult to dissect the role of the major virulence factors. Other staphylococcal diseases (toxic shock syndrome, scalded skin syndrome, food poisoning) can be attributed to be action of a single toxin.

5. Pyogenic infections elicit inflammatory responses. Toxic shock toxin induces the formation of a number of cytokines. The body responds to staphylococcal enterotoxin in the gastrointestinal tract by trying to eliminate the organism via diarrhea. Not much is known about scalded skin syndrome.

6. Pyogenic infections require drainage and the administration of antibiotics. The abscesses formed impede the penetration and activity of many antibiotics, as well as the normal host defenses. Penicillin resistance became a hallmark of staphylococci only after the widespread use of antibiotics became established. Scalded skin and toxic shock syndromes require systemic physiological support.

Chapter 12/ Streptococci

1. Streptococci make chains by always dividing along the same plane and remaining attached after cell division. They carry out fermentative metabolism only. Some are strict anaerobes, others indifferent to oxygen. They are divided by the type of hemolysis (α, β, γ). β-Hemolytic streptococci can be further divided into groups (A, B, etc.) according to the serology of their C carbohydrate.

2. Streptococci are helped in their spread by making extracellular hydrolases such as hyaluronidase, streptokinase (a fibrinolysin), and DNAase.

3. M proteins (of which there are some 80 serological types) are strongly antiphagocytic. In some individuals, a cross-reactive autoimmune response may be elicited by the M protein.

4. The main diseases are pyogenic infections and postsuppurative glomerulonephritis and rheumatic fever (due to group A, β-hemolytic streptococci) and subacute bacterial endocarditis (by α-hemolytic streptococci).

5. Postsuppurative rheumatic fever is thought to result either from cross-reactivity between myocardial and streptococcal components

(i.e., M protein) or from the production of a streptococcal cardio-toxin. Postsuppurative glomerulonephritis has several theories, including cross-reactivity, deposition of streptococcal antigens in the glomeruli followed by an in situ reaction with circulating antibodies, deposition of circulating immune complexes, and nephrotoxic action of streptococcal toxins.

6. Diagnostic problems include differentiating potential pathogens from harmless commensals in the throat. Material from postsuppurative sequelae does not usually carry the organisms and the diagnosis is usually not made on a bacteriological basis.

Chapter 13/ Pneumococcus and Bacterial Pneumonia

1. Pneumococcal pneumonia is usually community-acquired. The reservoir is human beings, with the organism typically colonizing the nasopharynx of a small proportion of normal individuals who stay healthy. Illness rarely occurs without predisposing factors, including aspiration (due to poor cough reflex or lowered consciousness), debilitation, sickle cell anemia, various tumors, lack of spleen. The disease is seen most often in the winter and spring. Cases are usually sporadic but outbreaks may occur under crowded conditions.

2. The capsule of the Pneumococcus is thought to be its main virulence factor as it impedes phagocytosis. A comparison of encapsulated and unencapsulated isogenic strains (identical except in the capsule) has shed light on this issue. A comparison of other traits between isogenic capsulated strains may uncover other virulence factors.

3. (a) Inflammation begins with an outpouring of clear fluid into the alveoli. (b) Early consolidation brings in neutrophils and red blood cells. (c) Late consolidation leads to the solidification of the tissue ("hepatization") with a greater number of neutrophils. (d) In resolution, neutrophils are replaced by macrophages.

4. The disease may progress very rapidly in elderly patients; thus, early and vigorous intervention is called for. Individuals without spleens are predisposed to a severe septicemic form of the disease, which occurs because of the inadequate ability to clear the organism from the bloodstream. These individuals are often treated prophylactically with monthly injections of long-acting penicillin (or daily oral erythromycin in those with allergy to penicillin).

5. Sputum from the respiratory tree may contain Gram-positive cocci that resemble pneumococci under the microscope. Positive sputum cultures may be due to contamination of the material with commensal pneumococci from the oropharynx. Positive blood or cerebrospinal fluid cultures (because they are obtained from normally sterile regions) are generally diagnostic.

Chapter 14/ Neisseriae: Gonococcus and Meningococcus

1. Gonococci are Gram-negative, oxidase-positive diplococci. Meningococci look the same but are usually more heavily encapsulated. Meningococci are more likely to cause serious systemic disease.

2. When a male partner infects the female, the organisms cause urethritis by adherence to epithelial cells via pili, extracellular multiplication, spread up the genital tract, penetration into nonciliated cells, passage to the base of these cells, and extrusion into the submucosal tissue causing an inflammatory response. If the infection reaches the fallopian tubes, the resulting inflammation will cause scarring and impair ciliary function of the epithelial cells.

This allows other organisms from the vagina to reach the peritoneal cavity and cause inflammation in the abdominal pelvis.

3. Early diagnosis and treatment, partner notification, behavioral interventions (use of condom, decreasing number of sexual partners), and vaccination with a vaccine, when an effective one becomes available.

4. The main problem is the antigenic variation in one of the main antigenic components, the pilin protein of pili. In addition, to be effective, a vaccine must elicit secretory immunity.

5. Gonorrhea may lead to salpingitis and ectopic pregnancy, pelvic inflammatory response, scarring of the urethra in males, arthritis, and other systemic infections. It is a major cause of female infertility.

Chapter 15/ *Haemophilus influenzae*: Important Cause of Meningitis

1. *H. influenzae* are small Gram-negative rods; they are facultative anaerobes with complex nutritional requirements. Some strains have a capsule. Strains with type b capsules are the most common pathogens. Type b capsules consist of polymers of ribose and ribitol phosphate.

2. Very young children carry maternal antibodies but are not able to make their own until 2–3 years of age (because the T-cell-independent antibody response takes longer to develop); they are usually colonized by noncapsulated strains; thus, they do not elicit protective antibodies.

3. A vaccine made up of the capsular antigens would not be effective in the young children who cannot make antibodies against them. A protein-conjugated vaccine is currently in use.

4. Some virulence factors include: capsule (in some), endotoxin, IgA protease (probably).

5. A plausible notion is that the organisms are caught in the highly vascularized choroid plexi and cause a local inflammation that impairs the blood-brain barrier. Another notion is that the organisms may be carried into the CNS via macrophages.

6. Meningococcal meningitis usually resolve without CNS sequelae, perhaps because of the mild degree of inflammation in the subarachnoid space. This inflammation is stronger in *H. influenzae* meningitis, which leads to frequent CNS sequelae.

Chapter 16/ *Bacteroides* and Abscesses

1. *B. fragilis* causes abscesses in the peritoneal cavity, the lungs, and other sites. Untreated, such conditions may be life-threatening. Infections by anaerobes were often not recognized because anaerobic cultures were not generally carried out.

2. *Bacteroides* are Gram-negative strictly anaerobic rods found in large amounts in the vertebrate gut and mouth. These organisms are fermentative and resist oxygen although they cannot grow in its presence.

3. *B. fragilis* is among the most oxygen-tolerant of the human strict anaerobes, probably because it makes both superoxide dismutase and catalase. It makes a capsule that protects it from phagocytosis and may be involved in attachment to cell surfaces. Neuraminidase and other hydrolytic enzymes may play a role in pathogenesis.

4. Abscesses caused by anaerobes and mixed flora organisms are often not accessible to drugs and require drainage. Many anaerobes are resistant to common antibiotics and treatment requires special

drugs. Bacteriological diagnosis requires specialized anaerobic techniques.

Chapter 17/ Enteric Bacteria: "Secretory" (Watery) Diarrhea

1. Through the digestive system there is flow of liquids that may propel microorganism along, unless these stick to surfaces or reside in crevices. IgA antibodies are secreted throughout most of the digestive tract. In the mouth, lysozyme of saliva is active against certain bacteria. The stomach has low pH and pepsin, the small intestine has the pancreatic enzymes plus bile salts, the large intestine has a metabolically active resident flora.

2. *Salmonella, Shigella*, certain strains of *E. coli, Campylobacter, Yersinia*, and *Vibrio cholerae* cause intestinal infections. They can be distinguished on the basis of biochemical reactions and their serological differences.

3. Most enteropathogenic bacteria have adhesins that permit them to bind to the surface of gut cells. All of the Gram-negative ones have endotoxins. Enterotoxins are produced by certain strains of *E. coli, S. aureus, C. perfringens*, and *V. cholerae*. Invasiveness properties of *Shigella* are associated with the production of cytocidal toxins. *Yersinia* has recently been found to possess a protein, invasin, that allows it to enter epithelial cells.

4. Different strains of *E. coli* cause the following diseases: in the intestine, enterotoxigenic or watery diarrhea from the colon, enteropathogenic or watery diarrhea from the ileum, enteroinvasive or dysentery disease, enterohemorrhagic or hemorrhagic colitis. In the urinary tract, *E. coli* causes cystitis, pyelonephritis, prostatitis. In young infants, *E. coli* strains may cause septicemia and meningitis.

5. Treatment of watery bacterial diarrhea should be aimed at fluid replacement and physiological support and, if necessary, at eliminating the causative agents. Treatment of dysentery should be aimed at eliminating the causative agent.

6. Immunization is not likely to work unless secretory IgA antibodies are formed. Vigorous prophylactic antimicrobial therapy might eliminate the normal flora and give opportunistic organisms the chance to colonize.

Chapter 18/ Invasive and Tissue-damaging Enteric Bacterial Pathogens: Bloody Diarrhea and Dysentery

1. The steps are: ingestion; spread from small intestine to mesenteric lymph nodes; primary bacteremia; multiplication in macrophages, especially in liver; septicemia (fever); spread to gallbladder; reinfection of small intestine (inflammation, ulceration of Peyer's patches leading to diarrhea, hemorrhage, perforation).

2. The systemic manifestations of typhoid are fever, enlarged liver and spleen, and CNS involvement. Local manifestations are inflammation of the small intestine with diarrhea, hemorrhage, and possible perforation. An important distinction between typhoid fever and *Salmonella* gastroenteritis (which is due to nontyphoidal strains of *Salmonella*) is that typhoid fever is rarely associated with diarrhea (in fact, constipation in the early phases is frequent).

3. Typhoid bacilli, as a minimum, must be able to resist the acid in the stomach, invade the small intestine, survive within macrophages, withstand the action of bile, cause local inflammation.

4. Within the body, the organisms' resistance to bile contributes to the carrier state. Ability to reside in macrophages may also be involved.

Outside of the body, the ability to survive in water and food is present.

5. *Salmonella* gastroenteritis is not strictly speaking a form of food poisoning because it requires the multiplication of the organisms in the intestine (which takes time) and is not due to a preformed toxin (unlike, for example, staphylococcal gastroenteritis, which typically occurs within hours).

6. Food should be well cooked and not placed in contact with surfaces and utensils previously used to prepare the food when raw.

Chapter 19/ *Pseudomonas aeruginosa*

1. Pseudomonads are Gram-negative aerobic rods with polar flagella. They can utilize a wide variety of substrates, which is why certain specialized strains are being tried for the clean up of oil spills and toxic wastes. Their hardiness makes them ubiquitous inhabitants of sinks, faucets, and other water supplies.

2. *P. aeruginosa* causes infections of the lung in cystic fibrosis and in intubated patients on respirators; infections on the skin in burn victims; septicemia in immunodeficient patients, sometimes with necrotic lesions in the skin; endocarditis in intravenous drug addicts; local or system infections after surgery or trauma; urinary tract infections in persons with urine stasis due to kidney stones or catheterization.

3. Some virulence factors are: exotoxin A, cell necrosis by ADP-ribosylation of elongation factor 2 of protein synthesis; elastase, by breakdown of elastin; phospholipase C by breakdown of cell membranes; endotoxin.

4. Patients with *Pseudomonas* infections are often immunodeficient and require vigorous antimicrobial therapy. However, the organisms are relatively drug resistant. Problems may be encountered with access of drugs, as in cystic fibrosis and burns patients.

Chapter 20/ *Bordetella pertussis* and Whooping Cough

1. Local effects are inflammation due to pertussis toxin, which inactivates phagocytic action, and to tracheal cytotoxin; cough due to accumulation of mucus; hypoxia due to bronchial obstruction and secondary bacterial pneumonia. Systemic manifestations are low-grade fever, possibly due to endotoxin; heightened sensitivity to histamine and serotonin, due to increase in cAMP by the bacterial adenylate cyclase; encephalopathy, probably due to pertussis toxin.

2. Systemic manifestations are due to the formation of exotoxins, such as exotoxin A and adenylate cyclase, that may act at a distance. Hypoxia may result in systemic manifestations.

3. Pertussis toxin ADP-ribosylates adenylate cyclase to increase its activity and increase the production of cAMP. Bacterial adenylate cyclase itself raises the cAMP concentration. Tracheal cytotoxin kills ciliated respiratory epithelial cells by an unknown mechanism. Endotoxin works primarily by increasing the production of interleukin-1 and tissue necrosis factor.

4. The pro is that the vaccine is highly effective in preventing whooping cough. The cons are that the vaccine may cause fever and local pain in about 1 of 5 children, convulsions in a small number (about 1 in 2000 children), serious brain complication in very few (fewer than 1 in 100,000 children). The incidence of serious complications is probably less than that of whooping cough, which is a serious and potentially life-threatening disease, although the precise odds are not known.

5. It is difficult to eradicate a disease caused by a frequent member of the normal flora where the carrier state is not likely to be affected greatly by vaccination or the administration of drugs.

Chapter 21/ Clostridia

1. Spore formation explains the ability of clostridia to survive at high temperature, e.g., in certain prepared foods. These organisms make powerful hydrolytic enzymes (some of which are exotoxins) that help explain why they are often involved in the decomposition of dead animals and plants, which, by itself, may account for the common finding of clostridia in soils. The fact that these organisms are strict anaerobes does not help explain their location because they are often found in well oxygenated substrates such as top layers of soils.

2. Pseudomembranous colitis is due to the overgrowth of *Clostridium difficile* as the result of vigorous therapy with antibiotics that affect most members of the normal bacterial flora. Patients at risk are obviously those who receive this class of antibiotics for whatever reason.

3. Botulinum toxin is resistant to acid in the stomach, whereas tetanus toxin is not. In fact, botulinum toxin is activated in the stomach. In addition, tetanus toxin is not absorbed by the small intestine, while botulinum toxin is. The reason that infant botulism is usually a mild disease is probably because, in that condition, the organisms are found in the large intestine where the toxin is absorbed more poorly than from the small intestine.

4. Tetanus toxin works on the CNS to inhibit the release of inhibitory neurotransmitters, causing neuromuscular excitation. Botulinum toxin works on peripheral nerves causing a presynaptic block in the release of acetylcholine, which results in muscle relaxation.

5. Immunization against *C. difficile* is unlikely to work because the organism resides in the large intestine, where antibodies are not apt to be effective. In addition to this reason, immunization against botulism and clostridial gas gangrene is an ineffective measure because these diseases are not widespread and the toxins belong to an inconveniently large number of antigenic types.

Chapter 22/ *Legionella*: Parasite of Cells

1. *Legionella* survive in bodies of water and grow in association with protozoa found in such habitats. This aquatic habitat leads to the presence of the organisms in water supplies. In addition, the organisms are relatively resistant to high temperatures and are sometimes found in hot water tanks. From such locations, the organisms may be acquired by inhalation of aerosols of contaminated water.

2. Outbreaks of legionellosis are probably due to the contamination of water supplies used by many people, such as guests of hotels.

3. *Legionella* pneumonia is an interstitial infection of the submucosal tissue of the alveoli of the lung and the organisms replicate within alveolar macrophages. Pneumococcal pneumonia is more of a superficial infection of the alveolar lumen, the organisms do not replicate intracellularly.

4. The inoculum of *Legionella pneumophila* normally encountered can be handled adequately by most healthy individuals. The establishment of the disease often requires some degree of immune compromise, thereby allowing intracellular replication of the microorganisms. Activation of macrophages leads to inhibition of intracellular replication.

5. The main ones are the pseudomonads, which may be acquired by inhalation or by penetration through the skin.

Chapter 23/ Mycobacteria: Tuberculosis and Leprosy

1. The organisms are acid-fast because the waxy coat affects the penetration of many compounds. Consequently, mycobacteria grow slowly. Also, these organisms are resistant to drying but sensitive to heating. Finally, the waxy coat probably protects the organisms from the usually lethal phagocytic enzymes, thereby allowing the bacteria to reside and grow within macrophages.

2. The waxy coat of mycobacteria must be loosened temporarily to allow dyes to penetrate. This must be a reversible reaction, otherwise the organisms would remain permeable and sensitive to the subsequent treatment with dilute acids.

3. By causing pulmonary infections and, eventually, the coughing up of the bacteria-laden content of caseous lesions, mycobacteria become abundant in the human environment. The bacteria are spread by aerosolization. Resistance to drying allows them to remain in the environment, e.g., dust, for long periods of time.

4. The ability of the organisms to withstand life inside macrophages and, thus, to cause a cell-mediated immunity. Tissue damage is attributable to granuloma formation, delayed type hypersensitivity and formation of interleukin-1 and tumor necrosis factor.

5. In those who develop disease, tissue damage is due to the cell-mediated immunity, which, if progressive, may be responsible for death in chronic tuberculosis. However, the majority of infected individuals, as determined by a positive response to tuberculin, never get ill with tuberculosis. Presumably, cell-mediated immunity is walling off the infection locally with minimal collateral damage to the host. Moreover, in the absence of the cell-mediated immunity response (as in some patients with AIDS), tubercle bacilli may grow rapidly and cause progressive systemic disease and rapid death.

6. The hallmark of both diseases is cell-mediated immunity. In its presence, tuberculoid leprosy resembles secondary tuberculosis in fundamental ways, although different organs and tissues are usually affected. The absence of cell-mediated immunity leads to lepromatous leprosy, which resembles systemic progressive tuberculosis but is a proportionately more frequent outcome.

7. The first step is usually the microscopic examination of smears of clinical material stained by the acid-fast method or immunofluorescent dyes. This technique may fail because of inexperience by the operator or because the concentration of bacteria is too low. Culturing clinical material requires long incubations (sometimes 3 weeks or more) because the organisms grow slowly. Serological techniques may reveal the presence of antibodies or cell-mediated immunity, neither of which indicates active disease. Newer genetically based techniques (e.g., the polymerase chain reaction or other DNA amplification methods), if commercially developed, may allow rapid diagnosis.

Chapter 24/ Syphilis

1. In primary syphilis, antibodies are not likely to be formed in sufficient titer until nearly the end of this phase. Antibodies may contribute to resolution of secondary syphilitic lesions. In tertiary syphilis, antibodies are unlikely to play a large role because the organisms are not found in many of the lesions. However, antibodies may prevent the multiplication and further spread of the organisms.

2. There is no simple answer to this phenomenon. Healing of local lesions is probably due to local reactions that contain the organisms at the site but do not prevent their systemic spread.

3. Suggestions for autoimmunity in tertiary syphilis are the absence of organisms from many of the lesions and the Wasserman-type serological test, which is based on the presence of antibodies against a normal tissue component, cardiolipin. Positive Wasserman serology is seen in other diseases, such as lupus erythematosus, which are strongly suspected of being autoimmune diseases.

4. It depends on the nature of the contact. A patient with primary syphilis is highly contagious because of open sores in genital areas. However, the skin and mucosal lesions of secondary syphilis are teeming with organisms and contact with these lesions may lead to spread of the disease.

5. The organisms are apparently only found in humans. They are still sensitive to drugs such as penicillin. The simultaneous injection of repeated doses of penicillin to every human may well lower the human load of treponemes. However, in some of the lesions of tertiary syphilis (gummas), the organisms are still present and may not be accessible by drugs. Thus, a public health surveillance of all known patients with syphilis and their contacts would be required.

6. There are many answers, such as: try to grow the organisms in culture, clone their genes, and study possible virulence factors and antigens; try to set up an animal model that allows the detailed analysis of immunological events during the three stages of the disease.

Chapter 25/ Lyme Disease

1. *B. burgdorferi* is a thin, helical shaped rod with bundles of flagella contained within its outer membrane. Unlike *T. pallidum*, it can be cultivated in artificial media and is arthropod borne.

2. Emphasize the reservoirs (small rodents, deer), the need for vigilance and protection from various form of ticks, the geographic distribution (both coasts of U.S., some midwestern states), early symptoms (skin, joints), the seriousness of systemic and neurological manifestations, and available chemotherapy. You may want to mention the history of the disease and how the mothers of infected children helped in its elucidation (Chapter 73).

3. Both have analogous three stages, neurological manifestations late in disease, respond to antibiotics.

4. Primary—erythema migrans. Secondary—neuritic pain of skin, arthralgias. Tertiary—impairment in certain cortical functions (forgetfulness, lethargy, fatigue, hearing impairment).

5. The majority of the patients have the HLA-DR4 or HLA-DR2 specificities. The arthritis in these patients typically does not respond to antibiotic therapy. Such reactions may continue for some time after the organisms have been killed, possibly because of cross-reactive antigens.

Chapter 26/ Chlamydiae: Genital and Respiratory Pathogens

1. Replicating chlamydiae (reticulate bodies) are larger than transit forms (elementary bodies), are metabolically active, and are much more sensitive to manipulation and environmental influences. The likely biochemical basis for the change between the two forms is that elementary bodies are surrounded by structural proteins rich in disulfide bridges. Under reducing conditions, as obtained when inside phagosomes, these bridges are broken, unraveling the sur-

face proteins and allowing the reticulate bodies to metabolize, to grow, and to divide.

2. Chlamydiae are thought to be strict intracellular parasites because they do not have the machinery for energy metabolism, they are "energy parasites." Chlamydiae probably survive inside macrophages by inhibiting the fusion of lysosomes with phagosomes.

3. Genital infections by chlamydiae are a public health problem mainly by virtue of their ability to cause secondary infections, such as those that lead to salpingitis, and to subsequent ectopic pregnancy and pelvic inflammatory disease.

4. The organisms are intracellular; thus, drugs must be chosen with regard to their ability to penetrate host cells. Therapy should be instituted even with mild or asymptomatic cases to prevent sequelae by these infections.

Chapter 27/ Rocky Mountain Spotted Fever and Other Rickettsiae

1. Most rickettsioses are arthropod-borne; Q fever may be acquired by inhalation.

2. On the one hand, rickettsiae are capable of at least some energy metabolism, which sets them aside from the chlamydiae. On the other hand, with the exception of the organism of trench fever, they are strict intracellular parasites and are not known to grow outside cells.

3. Rocky Mountain spotted fever is a vasculitis due to the localization of the organisms in endothelia of small vessels. Cell damage, possibly caused by the growth of the organisms or by cell-mediated immunity, leads to localized hemorrhages. These are seen as the skin rashes characteristic of the disease.

4. One way to study rickettsiae is to grow them in animal cells in culture. Rickettsiae may be isolated from cell constituents and some of their in vitro properties studied. In addition, rickettsial genes may be cloned into suitable host bacteria or other cells.

Chapter 28/ *Mycoplasma*: Curiosity and Pathogen

1. *Mycoplasma* do not have rigid cell wall; therefore, they are sensitive to altered osmolarity of their environment. Some, but not all of them, require sterols for growth. They have the smallest known genomes of free-living cellular organisms.

2. Humans are the only known reservoir of *Mycoplasma pneumoniae*. The organism is acquired by inhalation and causes disease without prolonged colonization. *M. pneumoniae* bind to epithelial cells of the lower respiratory tree but not of the alveoli. The organisms impair ciliary function by the formation of toxic compounds, possibly hydrogen peroxide. The immune response appears to contribute to symptoms in this infection.

3. *Mycoplasma* pneumonia is an infection of the mucosa of the airways, not of the alveoli. It is a bronchopneumonia, not a lobar pneumonia, as with pneumococci, not an interstitial pneumonia, as in legionellosis.

4. *Mycoplasma* are not detected on regular bacteriological media and require specialized techniques for growth in the laboratory.

Section II. Viruses

Chapter 30/ Biology of Viruses

1. They do not maintain their physical integrity during replication but their nucleic acid is separated from the capsid.

2. The nucleic acid and capsid proteins of icosahedral viruses are

loosely connected, whereas those of helical viruses are tightly connected and must "fit" properly in order to assemble correctly.

3. See Figure 30.2.

4. The nucleic acid of host cells does not have enzymes that can replicate negative-strand (−) RNA.

5. It is subject to splicing, contains a 5′ methylguanosine cap, and a 3′ polyadenylate chain.

6. Poxviruses replicate in the cytoplasm, where the DNA-synthesizing enzymes are not found.

7. Frame-shift of the same region of nucleic acid, giving different coding sequences and coding for overlapping genes.

8. Lytic infections lead to cell death. Latent infection are when the virus replicates alongside the host cell. Persistent infections occur when the virus continues to replicate faster than the host cell but does not cause appreciable clinical manifestations.

9. Viruses spread via the nerves (neural), the blood (hematogenous), and by the olfactory route (through the cribriform plate).

10. In the blood, viruses spread free, associated with monocytes and lymphocytes, or with red blood cells.

11. Antibodies contribute by forming immune complexes and by stimulating the host to make antibodies against some of its own component (molecular mimicry).

12. Attenuated live vaccines may induce both local and systemic immunity. The virus may persist in the body and caused renewed antigenic stimulation. The virus may spread within the population, thus "vaccinating" nonvaccinated individuals.

13. NK cells appear before CTLs and are not virus specific.

14. Interferons are not made by antibody-producing cells, but by fibroblasts, lymphocytes, and macrophages. They are not specific but may affect a large number of virus infections. They inhibit viral replication by promoting degradation of viral mRNA and thus the synthesis of viral proteins.

15. Viruses are detected by viral cultivation in cell culture or in animals, immunofluorescence, morphological detection of viral particles or inclusion bodies, detection of virus-specific nucleic acid sequences, detection of specific antibodies.

Chapter 31/ Picornaviruses: Polio, Enteroviruses, and the Rhinoviruses

1. Polio used to be a nearly endemic disease in the very young, in whom CNS manifestations were not as severe or frequent as in adolescents. With sanitation, early contact was less frequent, the disease more often caused paralytic manifestations.

2. See Table 31.1—all of these viruses may cause asymptomatic infection and meningitis.

3. Poliovirus is a positive-strand virus and its genomic RNA acts as mRNA. The first step in the replication cycle is uncoating. Replication and assembly take place in the cytoplasm. A viral protein called VPg is attached to the 5′ end. A single polyprotein is synthesized in the cytoplasm using the host protein synthesizing apparatus. Post-translational cleavage reactions cuts the polyprotein into structural and nonstructural proteins. Nonstructural proteins are proteases involved in polyprotein cleavage and one is an RNA-dependent RNA polymerase. The structural proteins assemble to make the capsid.

4. See Table 31.2.

5. It suggests that a disease that is not known to be transmitted except between humans could be eradicated. The experience with smallpox vaccination and follow-up of known cases suggests strategies that may be successful with polio as well.

6. Rhinoviruses bind to specific receptors on respiratory epithelial cells. Most of the serotypes bind to the same receptor, others to a second receptor. The major group receptor are the intercellular adhesion molecule-1 (ICAM-1), a member of the immunoglobulin supergene family known to play a role in cell adhesion in the immune response.

7. There is a correlation between the severity of the cold and the amount of rhinovirus that can be recovered. Large amounts of virus are found without tissue destruction. Nasal secretions of persons with a cold contain large amounts of the vasoactive substance bradykinin. Direct stimulation of nerve endings in the nasal mucosa produces some of the manifestations of the cold.

Chapter 32/ Arthropod-borne Viruses

1. Arboviruses cause viral encephalitides, hemorrhagic fevers, yellow fever, and dengue fever.

2. Because they are arthropod-borne, transmission depends on the presence of vectors in a region and how these are affected by the weather.

3. Positive-strand virus RNA functions as the m-RNA for the production of virus-encoded proteins. Negative-strand virus RNA must first be transcribed, but animal cells do not have enzymes with such an activity; thus, a virion-associated enzyme must enter infected cells.

4. The natural life cycle for the viruses that cause encephalitides is from bird to bird, via the bite of mosquitoes. Horses acquire the virus, but they seldom play a role in human infection. The equine viremic phase is so short that it is unlikely a horse would be bitten by a mosquito during that time. Mosquitoes do not become sick with the virus and, once infected, can spread it for the rest of their lives (one season). The normal hosts of the virus (birds) are also relatively unaffected, thus permitting a stable life cycle. The frequency of encounter is dictated by the proximity of humans to the animal reservoir and the insect vector.

5. Horses are important sentinel animals, alerting that the virus has escaped its normal biological boundaries and is a threat to humans.

Chapter 33/ Paramyxoviruses: Measles, Mumps, Slow Viruses, and the Respiratory Syncytial Virus

1. They cause extensive fusion of infected host cells (syncytia formation).

2. The single-stranded, nonsegmented RNA genome with negative sense is transcribed into individual mRNAs, which are translated into measles proteins. This virus replicates in the nucleus—which is unusual for RNA viruses.

3. Both the humoral and the cellular immune responses modulate the outcome of measles. Measles-specific globulin given shortly after exposure to the virus ameliorates the infection, but cellular immunity is probably the major determinant of protection. Agammaglobulinemic patients tolerate measles well, but those with congenital or acquired cellular immune deficits get severe or fatal infection. Measles infection itself decreases cellular immunity and measles patients are at an increased risk of reactivating herpes simplex

infections and tuberculosis. They transiently lose delayed hyper-sensitivity to tuberculin and other antigens.

4. The current recommendation is that the live attenuated virus vaccine be given at 15 months of age because nearly all maternal antibody to measles is gone by that age. However, delaying vaccination leaves infants at risk for measles between the time that the maternally derived protection has waned until they are vaccinated.

5. By vaccination with the attenuated virus vaccine of all children after 15 month of age and surveillance for new cases that would require intensive vaccination in that region. For the vaccine to "take" effectively, widespread immunodeficiency among children in certain developing countries should be addressed, partly by improving nutrition.

Chapter 34/ Rabies

1. In developed countries, the disease in dogs has been controlled with canine vaccines, and human rabies cases have become very rare. Surveillance in these countries is still important, because the rabies virus is still commonly found in wild animals. In many developing countries, canine rabies persists and thousands of people are vaccinated for exposure to potentially rabid animals.

2. Did a bite or break of the skin really occur? Has rabies been reported in region where the bite occurred? Was the biting animal rabid—is it available for laboratory diagnosis or did it escape? Is the species known commonly to carry the virus? Can the biting animal be observed?

3. Members of the Rhabdoviridae family of RNA viruses, known to infect many mammals, including humans. Virions are shaped like a bullet, contain an external glycoprotein coat located outside a peripheral matrix protein, have a helical ribonucleoprotein core, and an unsegmented single-stranded RNA. The genome is of negative polarity; thus, the virion contains an RNA-dependent viral RNA transcriptase. The replication cycle of this virus takes place entirely in the cytoplasm of infected cells and results in the formation of numerous viral particles. Masses of nucleocapsids accumulate in the cytoplasm to form Negri bodies.

4. Human treatment consists of three steps: local wound treatment, passive administration of antibody (antiserum or immunoglobulin), and vaccination.

Chapter 35/ Influenza and Its Virus

1. See Figure 35.1. Replication steps, after attachment and penetration: Uncoating, nucleocapsid to nucleus. Viral replicase make mRNA from viral (−) strand. "Stealing" 5′ cap and 3′ polyA chains. M-RNA ← cytoplasm to make viral proteins. Viral (−) strands made in nucleus from (+) strands (segments). Viral segments assemble on cytoplasm; membrane at sites of insertion of envelope proteins; bud out of infected cell; a peculiarity is the segmented genome.

2. Antigenic variation (shifts and drifts) in animal reservoirs cause epidemics. Pandemics are caused by antigenic shifts.

3. They are involved in attachment of virions to host cells, antigenic variation. *HA* is involved in phagolysosomal fusion, *NA* in virion release from the cell.

4. They all use a "cassette" mechanism, whereby silent genes are rearranged on the genome to be placed under the control of an active promoter.

5. The humoral responses to the viral outer envelope proteins seem to be most important. Neutralizing antibody to hemagglutinin protects against or limits infection. Antibody to the neuraminidase seems to modify the spread of virus through the respiratory tract and can prevent illness.

6. Influenza may be a serious disease in the elderly. The vaccine reduce the incidence and morbidity of influenza by about 75% and its benefit/risk ratio increases in the elderly.

Chapter 37/ Human Retroviruses: AIDS and Other Diseases

1. Small spherical virion surrounded by a lipid envelope; genome contains two identical RNA molecules resembling eukaryotic mRNA with a 5′ cap structure and a 3′ poly A sequence. The replication cycle includes binding to the CD_4 receptor molecule via the envelope glycoprotein; fusion of the envelope with the cell membrane. Genomic RNA is released into the cytoplasm, including reverse transcriptase. Synthesis of DNA by reverse transcriptase, generating a double-stranded DNA molecule. Integration into host cell chromosomes via integrase, by joining the ends of each LTR to cut cellular DNA. Synthesis of progeny virus by transcribing viral DNA into messenger RNA by host cell RNA polymerase. Assembly at the cell surface and release without cell lysis.

2. See Table 37.1.

3. There are many ways to approach this question and you should choose the one that you are comfortable with.

4. There are many points that could be considered. Examples are that we do not understand how helper lymphocytes are killed or impaired, or why the infection of a small proportion of them has such devastating effects.

5. The antigenic variation of HIV is a problem. Are antibodies against any viral antigen likely to protect? How about for cell-mediated immunity? Vaccine testing faces very difficult ethical and practical issues.

6 and 7. See the answer for question 3.

Chapter 38/ Adenoviruses

1. See Figure 38.1.

2. Adenoviral gene expression takes place in three phases termed pre-early, early, and late; each phase is characterized by the synthesis of a specific set of viral proteins. The proteins required for viral DNA replication are synthesized before the proteins that make up the virus particle. This assures the accumulation of a large pool of viral DNA before the packaging of viral DNA into capsids begins.

3. A single DNA strand is copied at each viral replication fork, while in host cell replication, both strands are copied concurrently. The synthesis of all new viral DNA is continuous, whereas in host cells one strand is produced continuously, but the other is synthesized discontinuously, as short pieces that must be joined to produce the finished strand. Host chromosome replication occurs once in a division cycle; viral replication is uncoordinated and takes place continuously over a period of time.

4. First, the accumulation of cellular mRNAs in the cytoplasm is prevented, probably by inhibiting the transport of host messages from the nucleus to the cytoplasm. Second, a virally encoded protein appears to inhibit the utilization of existing host mRNAs in the cytoplasm.

5. Adenoviruses prevent the inhibition of protein synthesis via two small RNA molecules (VA RNAs) encoded by viral genes. One of the host proteins (DAI) critical in the inhibition of protein synthesis by interferon is converted to its active form by double-stranded RNA (dsRNA). dsRNA is produced in the course of infection by adenoviruses. The VA RNAs fold into partially double-stranded structures and bind to DAI, preventing its activation by authentic dsRNA.

6. Respiratory infections, pharyngoconjunctivitis, acute respiratory disease, gastrointestinal infection, conjunctivitis, epidemic kerato-conjunctivitis are caused by adenoviruses.

Chapter 39/Warts

1. Nonenveloped DNA viruses; circular, double-stranded genomes; transmission by direct inoculation; replication in skin and mucous membranes; long-term latent carriage in epithelial cells; transformation and cancer formation.

2. In warts, the viruses complete their full growth cycle. Progeny are shed from the lesion surface. In associated cancers, replication is restricted. Only a couple of genes are expressed, which lead to cell transformation.

3. Warts are painful, unsightly, chronic, transmissible, can damage the larynx and airways, and can slowly lead to skin or genitourinary malignancies.

4. There are no antiviral drugs that specifically interfere with wart virus replication, largely because these viruses are completely dependent on host cell machinery. The virus persists in a latent form for years and can "wait out" any treatment interval.

5. Only a small percentage of infected people have recognizable symptoms; they spread infection unwittingly. Major wart proteins have not yet been cloned or tested as vaccine candidates.

Chapter 40/ Herpes Simplex and Its Relatives

1. Herpesviruses include neurotropic herpes viruses: HSV1, HSV2, VZV; and lymphotropic herpes viruses: EBV, HHV6, HHV7, (CMV).

2. Binding and uncoating cascade of gene expression—immediate, early, late; DNA replication; assembly in nucleus; maturation and spread by budding from nuclear and cytoplasmic membranes; destruction of cell; latency in proper host cell occurs with expression of 1 (HSV1 or 2) to 10 (EBV) of the many viral genes.

3. Antibodies are effective at preventing primary infection, otherwise cellular immunity is important. Impaired cellular immunity leads to severe or frequent primary or recurrent infections.

4. Initiating treatment quickly enough to completely abort the infection is impossible. Drugs have no effect on the latent state of viruses. The virus may reactivate at a later date, regardless of the nature or duration of treatment.

5. Define risk groups. Identify behaviors that lead to spread of infection and educate with respect to these. Characterize immunogenic proteins. Develop animal models of infections and test vaccines.

6. Counsel with compassion. Educate patients regarding true (rather than mythical) risks and means of preventing spread. Employ acyclovir when appropriate.

Chapter 41/ Viral Hepatitis

1. See Table 41.2.

2. Hepatitis B virus is the only known human DNA virus that replicates via an RNA intermediate. Its sequence is partly dsDNA → dsDNA → ssRNA → ssDNA. Hepatitis B virus is the only known human DNA virus that replicates via an RNA intermediate. The virus has not yet been grown in cultured cells and studies are limited to infected liver tissues. Developing a better way of growing the virus would help in its study.

3. Hepatitis A virus is more cytopathic than is hepatitis B virus, which causes damage mainly via the immune response. However, the extent of acute hepatic injury in hepatitis A infection is usually more limited than in hepatitis B.

4. These diseases are difficult to distinguish on clinical grounds alone and require laboratory work, mainly serology.

5. Hepatitis C virus has a single-stranded positive-sense RNA genome and is related to the flaviviruses. Hepatitis C infection is often acquired by transfusion. The hepatitis D virus is a small, defective RNA virus that can replicate only in the presence of hepatitis B virus. This virus "borrows" the surface antigen of hepatitis B virus for its own coat (a "parasite's parasite").

6. The best preventive strategy against hepatitis A is adequate sanitation and sewage treatment. Those exposed may be treated as soon as possible with immune serum globulin. Immune globulin is also recommended for passive immunization of persons at risk of hepatitis B, e.g., intravenous drug users. Vaccines for hepatitis B consist of surface antigen purified from sera of infected donors or are produced by cloning viral genes into yeast. No vaccines are available for hepatitis C, D, or E, although vaccination for hepatitis B should protect against hepatitis D infection.

Chapter 42/ Poxviruses

1. There are several small but finite possibilities—the virus may still exist in nature, possibly in unknown animal of human reservoirs; or a related animal virus may mutate or recombine to resemble human smallpox virus.

2. Any live vaccine may theoretically be able to revert to virulence. In practice, deletions of virulence genes should ensure that this is a highly unlikely event.

3. It depends on the level of immunodeficiency of the patient. In an advanced state, the vaccine is not likely to lead to an immune response. Also, any live virus, even if attenuated, may cause a serious infection in such patients.

4. The vaccine is relatively cheap, stable at room temperature, and easy to administer with scarce resources.

5. All diseases that have only human reservoirs and that can be controlled by vaccination. Examples are syphilis, gonorrhea, measles, and, possibly, AIDS.

Review of the Main Pathogenic Bacteria

Organism	Gram Reaction, Morphology, Other Distinguishing Traits	Common Habitat and Mode of Encounter	Main Pathogenic Mechanism(s)	Typical Disease(s)	Relevant Chapters
Staphylococcus aureus	Positive, cocci in grape-like arrays	Nose, skin (carriers), breaks through skin and mucous membranes, ingestion of toxin-containing food	Acute inflammation and abscess formation involving many extracellular toxins (coagulase, leukocidin, catalase, toxic shock toxin, enterotoxins) and cell surface components (capsule, murein, teichoic acid, protein A)	Pyogenic infections and abscesses of many organs (e.g., subcutaneous tissue, bone marrow, endocardium), septicemia, toxic shock, food poisoning	6, 11, 60, 61, 72
Staphylococcus epidermidis	Positive, cocci in grape-like arrays	Skin, intestine (normal flora), breaks in skin and mucous membranes	Adherence and colonization of prostheses, intravenous devices via a slime layer	Infections of implanted devices, compromised patients	11, 66
Group A streptococci	Positive, cocci in chains, β-hemolytic	Throat (carriers), breaks through skin and mucous membranes	Inflammation due to surface components (M protein, lipoteichoic acids, hyaluronic acid, C5a peptidase, murein), extracellular enzymes (hemolysin, streptokinase, pyrogenic exotoxins); postsuppurative sequelae due to as yet uncertain factors	Skin diseases (e.g., erysipelas, impetigo), tonsillitis, scarlet fever, septicemia, rheumatic fever, glomerulonephritis	12, 60, 63
Other β-hemolytic streptococci	Positive (some normal flora), cocci in chains	Large intestine, vagina	Inflammation involving capsular polysaccharides	Neonatal septicemia and meningitis	12, 68
α-Hemolytic streptococci	Positive (normal flora), cocci in chains	Throat, intestine, G.U. tract	Colonization of damaged heart valves due to adhesion of organisms transiently in blood	Bacterial endocarditis, rarely others	12, 63
Pneumococcus (*S. pneumoniae*)	Positive, diplococci, α-hemolytic	Throat (carriers), inhalation, hand contact	Inflammation facilitated by resistance to phagocytosis (capsule)	Pneumonia, empyema, meningitis, endocarditis, etc.	13, 56
Meningococcus (*Neisseria meningitidis*)	Gram negative, diplococci	Throat (carriers), inhalation, hand contact	Inflammation facilitated by resistance to phagocytosis (capsule), endotoxin	Septicemia, meningitis	14, 58
Gonococcus (*N. gonorrheae*)	Gram negative, diplococci	Genital tract (carriers, some asymptomatic), contact with secretions.	Inflammation due to endotoxin, pili and surface protein adhesins, IgA1 protease	Urethritis, salpingitis, pelvic inflammatory disease	14, 65
Haemophilus influenzae	Gram negative, small rods, nutritionally fastidious	Throat (carriers), inhalation, hand contact	Inflammation facilitated by resistance to phagocytosis (capsule), endotoxin, IgA1 protease, pili, outer membrane protein	Meningitis (infants, 3 months to 2 years) with sequelae, respiratory infections, cellulitis	15, 64

Organism	Gram Reaction, Morphology, Other Distinguishing Traits	Common Habitat and Mode of Encounter	Main Pathogenic Mechanism(s)	Typical Disease(s)	Relevant Chapters
Bacteroides sp.	Gram negative, rods, anaerobes	Intestine, vagina (normal flora)	Inflammation of sensitive sites after entry of organisms from intestinal, oral flora	Abscesses (e.g., in peritoneum, lungs) often as part of mixed flora	16, 60
Escherichia coli	Gram negative, rods, many strains differing in pathogenic mechanisms (ETEC, EPEC, EHEC, etc.)	Fecally contaminated bodies of water, foods, personal contact, ingestion	Various forms of diarrhea, dysentery, due to enterotoxins, endotoxin, Shiga-like toxins, adhesins; some of these factors are also involved in deep tissue infections	Secretory diarrhea (tourist disease), cystitis, septicemia, meningitis	17, 57, 59, 68, 72
Shigella sp.	Gram negative, rods, several species differing in pathogenicity	Fecally contaminated foods, personal contact, ingestion (small inoculum suffices)	Inflammation due to invasion of small intestine mucosa helped by Shiga toxin, adhesins	Dysentery (inflammatory disease)	18, 57
Klebsiella pneumoniae	Gram negative, rods, heavily encapsulated	Usually, inhalation of oral contents	Inflammation facilitated by resistance to phagocytosis (capsule), perhaps endotoxin	Pneumonia, other inflammations in compromised patients	17, 56, 66
Proteus sp.	Gram negative, rods, urea splitters (grow at high pH)	Probably fecal contamination from same individual	Inflammation, usually of urinary tract	Urinary tract inflammatory disease; associated with urinary calculi formation	17, 59
Vibrio cholerae	Gram negative, curved rods	Bodies of water, ingestion	Massive watery diarrhea due to cholera toxin (ADP-ribosylating) adhesins	Cholera (intense watery diarrhea)	17, 57
Salmonella sp.	Gram negative, rods, species differing in pathogenicity (incl. *S. typhi*)	Fecally contaminated foods, personal contact, some strains zoonotic, ingestion	Able to multiply in macrophages due to largely unknown factors, diarrhea probably due to toxins	Typhoid and related fevers, gastroenteritis, septicemia	18, 57
Pseudomonas aeruginosa	Gram negative, rods, oxidative metabolism only	Water, soils, foods, inhalation, ingestion, penetration through breaks in epithelia	Toxins (toxin A [ADP-ribosylating] elastase, exotoxin S, endotoxin), adhesins, alginate in cystic fibrosis	Pyogenic infection in burn patients, diabetics; lung infection in cystic fibrosis	19, 62, 66
Bordetella pertussis	Gram negative, small rods, nutritionally fastidious	Throat (carriers), inhalation, hand contact	Pertussis toxin (ADP-ribosylating), adenylate cyclase, tracheal cytotoxin, adhesins	Whooping cough	20
Other enterics (*Enterobacter Citrobacter Serratia, Campylobacter, Yersinia*	Gram negative, rods	Usually fecal contamination, some derived from rodents	Virulence factors not well known, but probably include endotoxins	Various forms of diarrheas, dysenteries; some cause systemic disease and local inflammations	17, 57
Helicobacter pylori	Gram negative, rods	Frequently found in stomach	Inflammation due to uncharacterized factors	Gastritis, perhaps gastric ulcers	17, 57
Clostridium difficile	Gram positive, spore-forming rods, anaerobes	Intestine (normal flora?)	Toxins	Pseudomembranous colitis	21

Organism	Gram Reaction, Morphology, Other Distinguishing Traits	Common Habitat and Mode of Encounter	Main Pathogenic Mechanism(s)	Typical Disease(s)	Relevant Chapters
C. botulinum	Gram positive, spore-forming rods, anaerobes	Soil, contaminated food, intestine; ingestion of preformed toxin (adult botulism)	Botulinum toxin	Botulism (flaccid paralysis), infant and wound botulism	21
C. tetani	Gram positive, spore-forming rods, anaerobes	Soil, contaminated food, intestine; punctures of skin, wounds	Tetanus toxin	Tetanus (spastic paralysis)	21
C. perfringens and others	Gram positive, spore-forming rods, anaerobes	Soil, contaminated food, intestine; wound contamination, ingestion	Lecithinase, other hydrolytic enzymes	Myonecrosis, gas gangrene, food poisoning	21, 72
Legionella pneumophila	Gram negative, small rods, nutritionally fastidious	Water (air conditioning cooling systems, building water supply); inhalation, ingestion	Induces cellular response by as yet uncertain mechanisms	Pneumonia, systemic infections	22
Mycobacterium tuberculosis and others	Acid-fast (non-Gram stainable), thin rods, slow growing	Human environment and secretions (*M. tuberculosis*), soil, waters (*M. avium-intracellulare* et al.)	Chronic inflammation due to bacterial persistence in macrophages, release of cytokines, adjuvant effect	Primary and secondary tuberculosis, *M. avium-intracellulare* etc., typically infect AIDS patients	28, 67
M. leprae	Acid fast (non-Gram stainable), thin rods, slow growing	Human environment and secretions	Chronic inflammation due to bacterial persistence in macrophages, release of cytokines	Tuberculoid and lepromatous leprosy	28
Treponema pallidum	Non-Gram stainable, thin, helical rods, motile, not cultivable	Infected persons, acquired by intimate contact with human secretions	Chancre in first stage, acute inflammation in second, chronic inflammation and perhaps autoimmune-like sequelae in third; virulence factors not know	Syphilis	24, 65
Borrelia burgdorferi	Non-Gram stainable, thin, helical rods	Wild animal reservoir, transmitted to humans via tick bite	Three stages of infection, vaguely reminiscent of syphilis; virulence factors not known, but some preference for attachment to brain gangliosides	Lyme disease	25, 77
Chlamydia trachomatis	Non-Gram stainable, small organism in two forms (elementary {EB} and reticulate bodies {RBI}), strict intracellular parasite, not culturable extracellulary	Humans, direct contacts with genital and other secretions containing EB	Inflammation due to host cell destruction caused by intracellular growth of RB	Genital infection with possible PID, lymphogranuloma, pneumonia, neonatal conjunctivitis	26, 65
Rickettsia sp.	Non-Gram stainable, small intracellular rods, strict intracellular parasite, not culturable extracellularly	Animal reservoirs, insect vectors, possibly human carriers in epidemic typhus	Damage to vascular endothelia due to multiplication of the organisms; leakage of fluid, leading to damage of vital organ function	Rocky Mt. spotted fever, various types of typhus, Q fever	27

Organism	Gram Reaction, Morphology, Other Distinguishing Traits	Common Habitat and Mode of Encounter	Main Pathogenic Mechanism(s)	Typical Disease(s)	Relevant Chapters
Mycoplasma sp.	Small, non-Gram stainable, lacking cell wall, some needing sterols for growth	Human carriers, animals, environment	Damage to respiratory epithelium, loss of ciliary function; perhaps due to organism's metabolites, including hydrogen peroxide	Bronchopneumonia, expecially in young adults; genital and intrauterine infections	28, 56

Capsulated Bacteria of Medical Importance

Genus and Species

1.	Pneumococcus	6.	*Staphylococcus aureus* (some strains)
2.	Meningococcus	7.	*Escherichia coli* (some strains)
3.	*Haemophilus influenzae*	8.	Gonococcus (some strains)
4.	*Klebsiella pneumoniae*	9.	*Bacteroides fragilis* (some strains)
5.	*Streptococcus pyogenes* (some strains)		

Medically Important Strict Anaerobes

Genus and Species

1.	*Clostridium difficile*	6.	*Bacteroides fragilis*
2.	*C. botulinum*	7.	Several other *Bacteroides*
3.	*C. tetani*	8.	*Actinomyces bovis*
4.	*C. perfringens*	9.	Some streptococci
5.	Several other clostridia	10.	Other members of the normal flora

Typically Pyogenic (pus-producing) Bacteria

Genus and Species

1.	*Staphylococcus aureus*	4.	Gonococcus
2.	*S. epidermidis*	5.	*Pseudomonas aeruginosa*
3.	*Streptococcus pyogenes*	6.	Pneumococcus

Major Bacterial Toxins (see Table 9.1, p. 163)

Review of the Main Pathogenic Viruses

This chart is intended to review the main human viruses. Included are the agents of greatest medical relevance.

Many of the viruses that cause relatively uncommon diseases are not included. This chart may be completed to review material you have covered under this topic.

Virus	Group or Family	Nucleic Acid, Cellular Site of Replication, State if Enveloped	Other Important Attributes	Disease(s) and Systems Involved	Relevant Chapter(s)
Poliovirus	Picornaviruses	RNA (+ strand), cytoplasm	Makes polyprotein; lyses host cells; travels from intestine to anterior horn of spinal cord, medulla	Poliomyelitis; CNS, GI	31
Coxsackie and other enteroviruses	Picornaviruses	RNA (+ strand), cytoplasm	Infants are at particular risk	Meningitis, herpangina, exanthems	31
Rhinoviruses	Picornaviruses	RNA (+ strand), cytoplasm	Many serotypes	Common cold	31
Arbovirus encephalitis	Togaviruses, Flaviviruses, Bunyaviruses	RNA (+ strand), (Bunyavirus, (−) strand), cytoplasm, enveloped	Many kinds, arthropod-borne, often animal reservoirs; vascular damage in CNS	Eastern, Western equine, St. Louis, Japanese B, other encephalitis	32
Rubella	Togaviruses	RNA (+ strand), cytoplasm, enveloped	Causes exanthems	Rubella	32, 49
Measles	Paramyxoviruses	RNA (+ strand), nucleus, enveloped	Damage due to host response; causes cell fusion Depresses cellular immunity	Measles and its complications Subacute sclerosing panencephalitis by related viruses	33
Respiratory syncytial virus	Paramyxoviruses	RNA (+ strand), cytoplasm, enveloped	Syncytia formation due to cell fusion	Bronchiolitis in children	33
Rabies	Rhabdoviruses	RNA (− strand), cytoplasm, enveloped	Spreads by neural path, first up, then down axons	Rabies	34
Influenza	Orthomyxoviruses	RNA (− strand), segmented genome, nucleus, enveloped	Antigenic variation (shifts and drifts) in hemagglutinin and neuraminidase; human and animal reservoirs	Influenza and its complications	35
Rotavirus	Reoviruses	RNA, double-stranded, segments, cytoplasm, enveloped	Seasonal occurrence of disease	Most common agent of gastroenteritis, especially in children	36

Virus	Group or Family	Nucleic Acid, Cellular Site of Replication State if Enveloped	Other Important Attributes	Disease(s) and Systems Involved	Relevant Chapter(s)
HIV	Retroviruses	RNA (+ strand), two identical copies, nucleus, enveloped	Must integrate into host genome via reserve transcriptase for replication, antigenic	AIDS	37
Adenovirus	Adenoviruses	DNA, double-stranded (terminally redundant), nucleus	Many antigenic types, oncogenic; gene expression during replication is temporally regulated	Gastroenteritis, acute respiratory disease, conjunctivitis	38
Papillomavirus	Papovaviruses	DNA, double-stranded, circular, nucleus	Many antigenic types, some more oncogenic; some are sexually transmitted	Warts, cervical carcinoma	39
Herpes simplex	Herpesviruses	DNA, double-stranded, nucleus, enveloped	Persistent infections; capable of latency; not often extracellular	Fever blisters (genital and nongenital), ocular, CNS infection	40
Epstein-Barr virus (EBV) cytomegalovirus (CMV), varicella-zoster	Herpesviruses	DNA, double-stranded, nucleus, enveloped	Similar replication cycle as in herpes simplex; capable of cell transformation (especially EBV)	Infectious mononucleosis, CMV infection and chickenpox	40
Hepatitis A	Picornaviruses	RNA (+) strand, cytoplasm, enveloped	Usually food- or water-borne	Hepatitis	31, 41
Hepatitis B	Hepadnaviruses	DNA, double-stranded with single-stranded portions, nucleus, enveloped	Replicates via an RNA intermediate; transmitted sexually, congenitally, or parenterally	Hepatitis	31
Smallpox	Poxviruses	DNA, double-stranded, nucleus, enveloped	Disease has been eradicated via vaccination Viruses of this type may be useful for recombinant vaccines	Smallpox	42

Review of the Medically Important Fungi See Tables 46.2, p. 572; 47.1, p. 577; 48.1, p. 580.

Review of the Main Pathogenic Animal Parasites See Tables 50.1, p. 598; 51.1, p. 617; 52.2, p. 624; 53.1, p. 636.

Figure and Table Credits

Figures

Figure 3.1. From Kobayashi GS, et al. In: Szaniszlo PJ, ed. Fungal dysmorphism. New York, Plenum Publications, 1985. *E. coli* lysate courtesy of O.L. Miller, Jr. and B. Hamkalo.

Figure 3.2. Modified from DiRienzo JM, et al. The outer membrane proteins of Gram-negative bacteria: Biosynthesis, assembly, and function. Ann Rev Biochem 1978;47: 481.

Figure 3.9. From Blumberg P, Strominger JL. Interaction of penicillin with the bacterial cell wall: penicillin-binding proteins and penicillin-sensitive enzymes. Bacterial Rev 1974:38:291–335.

Figure 3.10. From Spratt B. Distinct penicillin binding proteins involved in the division, elongation and shape of *Escherichia coli* K12. Proc Natl Acad Sci USA 1975; 72:2999.

Figure 3.11. From Kaback HR. Ion gradient coupled transport. From Andreoli TE, Hoffman JS, Sanastil DD, et al. Physiology of membrane disorders. New York: Plenum Publications, 1986:387–407.

Figure 3.14. Electron micrograph courtesy of Drs. C.C. Brinton and J. Carnham.

Figure 3.16. Adapted from Boyd RF, Hoerl BG. Basic medical microbiology. Boston: Little, Brown, 1986.

Figure 4.12. From Wilson G, Dick HM. In: Topley and Wilson's Principles of bacteriology, virology, and immunity, 7th ed. Baltimore: Williams & Wilkins, 1983.

Figure 4.14. From Neihardt FC, et al. Physiology of the bacterial cell. Sunderland, MA: Sinauer Associates, Inc., 1990.

Figure 4.15. From Neihardt, et al. Physiology of the bacterial cell. Sunderland, MA: Sinauer Associates, Inc., 1990.

Figure 5.1. Adapted from Strehler BL. Implications of aging research for society. Fed Proc 1975;34:6.

Figure 5.2. Adapted from Gale EF, et al. The molecular basis of antibiotic action, ed. 2. New York: J. Wiley & Sons, 1981.

Figure 5.6. From Kwan CN, et al. Potentiation of the antifungal effects of antibiotics by amphotericin B. Antimicrob Agents Chemother 1972;2:61.

Figure 5.7. From Medoff G, et al. Potentiation of rifampicin and 5-fluorocytosine and antifungal antibiotics by amphotericin B. Proc Natl Acad Sci USA 1972;69:196.

Figure 6.4. From Knobel HR, Villinger W, Isliker H. Chemical analysis and electron microscopy studies of human C1q prepared by different methods. Eur J Immunol 1975;5:78–82.

Figure 6.5. From Bhakdi S, Tranum-Jensen J. Mechanism of complement cytolysis and the concept of channel-forming proteins. Phil Trans Roy Soc London B 1984;306: 311.

Figure 6.6. From MacRae EK, Pzyzwansky KB, Cooney MH, Spitznagel IK. Scanning electron microscopic observations of early stages of phagocytosis of *E. coli* by human neutrophils. Cell Tiss Res 1980;209: 65–70.

Figure 7.6. Courtesy of K. Ziegler, R. Cotran, and E. Unanue.

Figure 13.1. Courtesy of Dr. Stuart S. Sagel.

Figure 13.2. From Schering Slide Library, Schering Corp., Kenilworth, NJ, copyright owner. All rights reserved.

Figure 13.3. From Wood WB, Jr. Studies on the cellular immunology of acute bacterial infections. Harvey Lectures 1951–1952; 47:72–98.

Figure 14.1. From Schering Slide Library, Schering Corp., Kenilworth, NJ, copyright owner. All rights reserved.

Figure 14.4. From McGee Z, et al. Pathogenic mechanisms of *Neisseria gonorrheae*: observation on damage to human fallopian tubes in organ culture by gonococci of colony type 1 or type 4. J Infect Dis 1981: 143:413–422.

Figure 15.1. From Schering Slide Library, Schering Corp., Kenilworth, NJ, copyright owner. All rights reserved.

Figure 15.3. From Fothergill LD, Wright JJ. Influenzal meningitis: the relation of age, incidence to the bactericidal power of blood against the causal organism. J Immunol 1933;24:273–284.

Figure 16.1. Courtesy of Coy Laboratories, Ann Arbor, MI.

Figure 18.2. From Taussig MJ. Processes in pathology and microbiology, 2nd ed. Oxford, UK: Blackwell Scientific Publications, 1984.

Figure 20.2. From Muse KE, et al. Scanning electron microscopuc study of hamster tracheal organ cultures infected with *Bordetella pertussis*. J Infect Dis 1977; 136:771–777.

Figure 20.4. Courtesy of Dr. W.E. Goldman.

Figure 21.1. From Schering Slide Library, Schering Corp., Kenilworth, NJ, copyright owner. All rights reserved.

Figure 22.3. From Elliot JA, Winn WC, Jr. Treatment of alveolar macrophages with cytochalasin D inhibits uptake and subsequent growth of *Legionella pneumophila*. Infect Immunol 1986;51:33.

Figure 23.2. 1989 Tuberculosis Statistics in the United States, Centers for Disease Control, Atlanta, GA.

Figure 23.3. 1989 Tuberculosis Statistics in the United States, Centers for Disease Control, Atlanta, GA.

Figure 23.4. Adapted from Myers JA. The natural history of tuberculosis in the human body. JAMA 1965;194:1086.

Figure 24.2. Courtesy of Dr. E. M. Walker, Department of Microbiology and Immunology, UCLA School of Medicine, Los Angeles, CA.

Figure 24.3. From Taussig MJ. Processes in pathology and microbiology, 2nd ed. Oxford, UK: Blackwell Scientific Publications, 1984.

Figure 26.1. Courtesy of Drs. L. Hodinka and P.R. Wyrick.

Figure 26.2. Courtesy of Drs. R.L. Hodinka and P.R. Wyrick.

Figure 27.1. Courtesy of Dr. D.J. Silverman, School of Medicine, University of Maryland, Baltimore, MD.

Figure 27.2. Data from the Centers for Disease Control. Rocky Mountain spotted fever—United States, 1985. MMWR 1986; 35:247–249.

Figure 27.4. Courtesy of Dr. Gustav Dammin, Harvard Medical School, Cambridge, MA.

Figure 28.1. Courtesy of Dr. Gary Shackleford.

Figure 28.2. Courtesy of W.A. Clyde, Jr.

Figure 28.3. From Hu PC, et al. Surface parasitism by *Mycoplasma pneumoniae* of respiratory epithelium. J Exp Med 1977; 145:1328.

Figure 29.1. Courtesy of Dr. D.J. Krogstad.

Figure 30.1. From White DO, Fenner F. Medical virology, 3rd ed. New York: Academic Press, 1986.

Figure 30.2. From Taussig MJ. Processes in pathology and microbiology, 2nd ed. Oxford, UK: Blackwell Scientific Publications, 1984.

Figure 30.3. From Taussig MJ. Processes in pathology and microbiology, 2nd ed. Oxford, UK: Blackwell Scientific Publications, 1984.

Figure 30.7. Modified from Wold S, et al. In: Nayak DP, ed. Molecular biology of animal viruses. vol. 2. New York: Marcel Dekker, Inc., 1978.

Figure 30.9. From Mims CA. The pathogenesis of infectious disease, 3rd ed. New York: Academic Press, 1987.

Figure 31.1. From Lyons AS, Petracelli RJ. Medicine: an illustrated history. New York: Harry M. Abrams, 1978.

Figure 31.5. Data from Centers for Disease Control, Atlanta, GA.

Figure 31.7. From Dick EC, Jennings LC, Mink KA, Wartgow CD, Inhorn SL. Aerosol transmission of rhinovirus colds. J Infect Dis 1987;156:442–448.

Figure 31.8. From Jennison. Aerobiology 1947;17:106.

Figure 33.1. Modified from Morgan EM, Rapp F. Measles virus and its associated diseases. Bacteriol Rev 1977;41:636–666.

Figure 33.3. From Morgan EM, Rapp F. Measles virus and its associated diseases. Bacteriol Rev 1977;41:636–666.

Figure 33.4. From Krugman, S, Katz S. Infectious diseases of children. St. Louis: CV Mosby, 1981:145.

Figure 33.5. From Emond RTD. Color atlas of infectious diseases. London: Wolfe Medical Publications, 1987.

Figure 34.1. Courtesy of Dr. Makonnen Fekadu, Centers for Disease Control, Atlanta, GA.

Figure 34.2. Courtesy of Dr. Makonnen Fekadu, Centers for Disease Control, Atlanta, GA.

Figure 36.1. Modified from LeBaron CW, Lew J, Glass RI, et al. Annual retrovirus epidemic patterns in North America: results of a 5-year retrospective survey of 88 centers in Canada, Mexico, and the United States. JAMA 1990;264:984.

Figure 36.2. Courtesy of A. Kapikian.

Figure 36.3. Modified from Fields BN, et al., eds. Virology. New York: Raven Press, 1990.

Figure 37.2. Courtesy of Dr. M. Gonda.

Figure 38.1. *A* from Burnett R.M. Cell 1991;67:145–154. *B* from Philipson and Pettersson. Advances in tumor virus research. vol 18. New York: Academic Press.

Figure 38.3. From Kelly TJ, Jr. Adenovirus DNA replication. In: Ginsberg HS, ed. The adenoviruses. New York: Plenum Publishing, 1984:278, 298.

Figure 39.1. Courtesy of Dr. K.V. Shah.

Figure 40.8. From Hsiung GD, Mayo DR, Lucia HL, Landry ML. Genital herpes: pathogenesis and chemotherapy in a guinea pig model. Rev Infect Dis 1984; 6:33–50.

Figure 41.2. Courtesy of Dr. John Jerin.

Figure 43.4. From Corey L, et al. Intravenous acyclovir for the treatment of primary genital herpes. Ann Intern Med 1983;98: 914–921.

Figure 43.5. From Straus S, et al. Suppression of recurrent genital herpes with oral acyclovir. Trans Assoc Am Phys 1984;97; 278–283.

Figure 45.4. From Cole GT, Nozawa Y. Dimorphism. In: Cole GT, Kendrick B, eds. Biology of conidial fungi. New York: Academic Press, 1981.

Figure 45.5. Courtesy of Laurel Krewson.

Figure 45.6. Courtesy of Dr. R. D. Diamond.

Figure 45.8. Courtesy of Dr. B. H. Cooper.

Figure 50.2. From Friedman MJ. Erythrocytic mechanism of sickle cell resistance to malaria. Proc Natl Acad Sci USA 1978;75: 1994.

Figure 50.5. Courtesy of Drs. M.S. Bartlett and J.W. Smith, Indiana University School of Medicine.

Figure 50.9. Redrawn from Ross R, Thompson D. Proc Roy Soc London, series B 1910;82:411–415.

Figure 51.3. Courtesy of Dr. Stanley L. Erlandsen, Washington University School of Medicine, St. Louis, MO.

Figure 54.1. From Shelley WB, Shelley ED. Scanning electron microscopy of the scabies burrow and its contents, with special reference to the *Sarcoptes scabiei* egg. J Acad Dermatol 1983;9:673–679.

Figure 54.2. From Shelley WB, Shelley ED. Itch mite on the way to work. JAMA 1983;249:1353.

Figure 56.2. Data from Monto AS, Ullman BM. JAMA 1974;227:164–169.

Figure 56.3. Data from Glezen WP, et al. N Engl J Med 1973;288:498–505. Reprinted with permission from Virology, The Upjohn Co., 1983.

Figure 56.4. From Dick EC, Jennings LC, Mink KA, Wartgow CD, Inhorn SL. Aerosol transmission of rhinovirus colds. J Infect Dis 1987;156:442–448.

Figure 56.5. From Jennison. Aerobiology 1947;17:106.

Figure 56.6. Courtesy of Dr. G. Shackleford.

Figure 56.7. Courtesy of Dr. G. Shackleford.

Figure 56.8. Courtesy of Dr. S.S. Sagel.

Figure 56.11. Courtesy of Dr. C. Kuhn.

Figure 56.12. Courtesy of Dr. C. Kuhn.

Figure 56.13. Courtesy of Dr. C. Kuhn.

Figure 56.14. Courtesy of Dr. S.S. Sagel.

Figure 57.3. From Cawley JR. Infectious

diarrhea. Am J Med 1985;78 (Suppl 6B): 65–71.

Figure 58.2. From Menkes JH. Viral neurological infections in children. Hosp Pract 1977;12:100–109.

Figure 58.4. Courtesy of Dr. E.J. Bottone, Mount Sinai Hospital, New York.

Figure 59.1. Redrawn from Fass RJ, et al. Urinary tract infection. Practical aspects of diagnosis and treatment. JAMA 1973;225: 1509–1513.

Figure 59.2. Redrawn from Fass RJ, et al. Urinary tract infection. Practical aspects of diagnosis and treatment. JAMA 1973;225: 1509–1513.

Figure 59.3. Redrawn from Fass RJ, et al. Urinary tract infection. Practical aspects of diagnosis and treatment. JAMA 1973;225: 1509–1513.

Figure 61.6. Adapted from Medoff G. Osteomyelitis: a review of clinical features, therapeutic considerations, and unusual aspects. N Engl J Med 1970;282:260–266.

Figure 63.1. Adapted from Rodbard S. Blood velocity and endocarditis. Circulation 1963;27:18–28.

Figure 66.1. From Joshi J, Schimpff S. Infections in the compromised host. In: Mandell G, Douglas G, Bennett JE, eds. Principles and practice of infectious diseases. New York: John Wiley & Sons, 1985:697.

Figure 74.1. From Keusch GT, Farthing MJG. Nutrition and infection. Ann Rev Nutr 1986;6:131–154.

Figure 74.3. From Keusch GT, et al. Nutrition, host defense and the lymphoid system. In: Gallin JI, Fauci AS, eds. Advances in host defense mechanism. vol. 2. New York: Raven Press, 1983.

Figure 74.4. From Keusch GT, et al. Impairment of hemolytic complement activation by both the classical and alternative pathways in serum from patients with kwashiorkor. J Pediatr 1984;105:434–435.

Tables

Table 6.4. Adapted from Klein J. Immunology, Table 8.6, Oxford, UK: Blackwell Scientific, 1990; and Abbas AK, Lichtman AH, Pober JS. Cell and molecular immunology, Table 13.5, Philadelphia: WB Saunders, 1991.

Table 6.5. Adapted from Abbas AK, Lichtman AH, Pober JS. Cell and molecular immunology, Table 13.5, Philadelphia: WB Saunders, 1991.

Table 13.1. Adapted from Hendley JO, Sande MA, Stewart PM, et al. Spread of *Streptococcus pneumoniae* in families. I. Carriage rates and distribution of types. J Infect Dis 1975;13:55–61.

Table 30.1. Murphy FA. In: Fields BN, Knipe DM, eds. Fundamental virology. New York: Raven Press, 1991; Tyler KL,

Fields BN. In: Lannette EH, et al., eds. Laboratory diagnosis of infectious diseases, vol. 2. New York: Springer-Verlag, 1988.
Table 35.1. Adapted from unpublished material of B. Murphy.
Table 35.4. Adapted from unpublished material of B. Murphy.
Table 37.2. Adapted from Curran JW, Jaffe HW, Hardy AM, et al. Epidemiology of HIV infection and AIDS in the United States. Science 1988;239:610.
Table 37.3. From Lifson AR, Curran JW.

Epidemiology of AIDS: current trends and prevention. In: Gottlieb MS, et al., eds. Current Topics in AIDS. New York: John Wiley & Sons, 1987.
Table 56.4. Data from Hall CB, Douglas RW. J Pediatr 1981;99:100.
Table 57.1. From Keusch GT, Gorbach SL. Ecology of the gastrointestinal tract. In: Berkse, et al., eds. Gastroenterology, ed. 4. Philadelphia: WB Saunders, 1985.
Table 57.3. Adapted from Gorbach SL. Infectious diarrhea. In: Sleisenger WH, Ford-

tran SS, eds. Gastrointestinal disease. Pathophysiology, diagnosis, and management. Philadelphia: WB Saunders, 1983:956.
Table 66.1. Adapted from Johnston RB. Recurrent bacterial infections in children. N Engl J Med 1984;310:1237–1243. Reprinted by permission of the *New England Journal of Medicine.*
Table 67.1. Revision of the CDC surveillance definition for the acquired immunodeficiency syndrome. MMWR 1987;Suppl 1S.

Index

Page numbers in *italics* denote figures; those followed by *t* denote tables.

Mucosal surface
  immune globulin concentration at, 539
  vaccine activity at, 554
Mucous membrane, as barrier to microbial
    entry, 91–92, 91t
Mucus, protective function, 92, 696
Multi-organ failure syndrome, 772–773
Multiple drug therapy, in tuberculosis, 327
Multiple myeloma, pneumococcal
    pneumonia in, 215
Multiple sclerosis, autoantibodies in, 119
Multiplication, of microorganisms, 10–11, 10
    (see also under specific
    microorganism)
Mumps disease, lymphadenitis in, 799t
Mumps virus, 425
  morphology, 386
Muramyl dipeptide, in Freund's adjuvant,
    323
Murein
  absence, 39
  antibiotic effects on, 36–38, 37–38
  Bordetella pertussis, 296, 296
  gonococcal, 230
  Gram-negative bacteria, 31
  Gram-positive bacteria, 31, 32, 33
  lysozyme action on, 104
  protective mechanism, 32
  staphylococcal, 192
  structure, 33, 33–34
  synthesis, 36–37, 37
Murine typhus, 360t, 364
  arthropod vectors, 851t
Muscle(s)
  abscess, 768, 768t
  gangrenous (see Gas gangrene)
  infections, 767–768, 768t
  spasm, in tetanus, 303–304, 303
Mutants
  conditional, 75
  definition, 74–75
Mutation
  definition, 75
  frameshift, 75
  in virulence factor study, 194
  insertion, 65, 74–85
  invasiveness gene, 65–66, 65t, 66
  missense, 75
  nonsense, 75
  poliovirus, 414
  somatic, in immunoglobulin production,
    133
  spontaneous, 75
  streptococci, 202–203
  viruses, 452
Myalgia, 767
myc oncogenes, 500
Mycelium, fungal, 562
Mycobacteria
  acid-fastness, 318–319
  atypical, 317–318, 319t
    lymphadenitis in, 799t
    tuberculin test reaction and, 326
  culture, 319
  encounter with, 319–320
  entry, 319–320
  growth rate, 319, 319t

nonpathogenic, 318
  species, 317–318, 319t
  staining, 318
  survival mechanisms, 318–319
Mycobacterial infections (see also Leprosy;
    Tuberculosis)
  in HIV infection, 325–326
Mycobacterium avium-intracellulare, 184
  antibiotic resistance, 328
  characteristics, 319t
  identification, 672
  infections, 326–327
    in HIV infection, 327–328, 832–833
Mycobacterium bovis
  characteristics, 319t
  entry, 854t
Mycobacterium fortuitum, characteristics,
    319t
Mycobacterium kansasii
  characteristics, 319t
  infections, 326
Mycobacterium leprae, 183–184, 330–332,
    331t
  characteristics, 319t
  granuloma formation from, 149
Mycobacterium marinum, characteristics,
    319t
Mycobacterium scrofulaceum,
    characteristics, 319t
Mycobacterium tuberculosis, 183–184 (see
    also Tuberculosis)
  antibiotic resistance, 327–328
  characteristics, 319t
  culture, 326
  damage from, 320–323, 321–322
  encounter with, 319–320
  entry, 319–320
  identification, 672
  killed, in Freund's adjuvant, 323
  microscopic identification, 663
  multiplication, 320–323, 321–322
  phagocytosis, 320–321, 321–322
  reactivation, 323–324
  spread, 320–323, 321–322
Mycobacterium tuberculosis infections (see
    also Tuberculosis)
  meningitis, 323, 727–728
Mycobacterium ulcerans, characteristics,
    319t
Mycolic acid, 318
Mycoplasma fermentans, 369t
Mycoplasma genitalium infections, 369t
  pelvic inflammatory disease, 809
Mycoplasma hominis
  characteristics, 369
  culture, 370
Mycoplasma hominis infections, 369t
  genital, 371
  pelvic inflammatory disease, 809
Mycoplasma incognitus, in HIV infection,
    828
Mycoplasma orale, 369t
Mycoplasma pneumoniae, 185
  characteristics, 369–370, 370
  culture, 369–370, 370
  damage from, 370–371, 371
  encounter with, 370

entry, 370 multiplication, 370–371, 371
  spread, 370–371, 371
Mycoplasma pneumoniae infections, 369t
  case study, 368, 369
  diagnosis, 371
  incubation period, 889t
  pathogenesis, 370–371, 371
  pneumonia, 685
  prevention, 372
Mycoplasma salivarium, 369t
Mycoplasmata, 185, 368–372
  characteristics, 369–370, 369t, 370
  culture, 369
  damage from, 370–371
  distribution in nature, 369
  encounter with, 370
  entry, 370
  genital, 371
  in normal microbial flora, 25t
  in vaginitis, 811
  multiplication, 370–371
  murein absence in, 39
  spread, 370–371, 371
Mycoses (see Fungal infections)
Mycotic aneurysm, in endocarditis, 787
Myelitis, definition, 716
Myeloma protein, 128
Myeloperoxidase, in phagocytosis, 109, 111,
    820
Myocardial depressant factor, in sepsis, 776t
Myocarditis, cell death in, 12
Myonecrosis, in gas gangrene, 305
Myopericarditis, in enteroviral infections,
    412t
Myositis, 767–768, 768t
  streptococcal, 200

N protein, rabies virus, 439
NADPH oxidase, in phagocytosis, 109, 110,
    820
Naegleria, central nervous system entry, 721
Naegleria fowleri, 613–614
Nalidixic acid
  in shigellosis, 271
  mechanism of action, 43, 44t
  resistance to, mechanism, 82t
Nasopharynx
  carcinoma, Epstein-Barr virus and, 515
  infections, causative agents, 676t
Natural killer cells
  function, 137, 139t
  in viral infections, 402
  surface components, 139t
Necator americanus, 627–628 (see also
    Hookworms and hookworm
    infections)
  reservoirs, 624t
Neck infections (see Head and neck
    infections)
Necrosis
  bone, in osteomyelitis, 764
  sepsis and, 774
Necrotizing fasciitis, streptococcal, 2
Necrotizing infections, 752, 755–756
    (see also Gas gangrene)
Needlestick injury, disease transm
    827, 871